EUROPE
and
THE WORLD

From the Renaissance to the Second World War

EUROPE
and
THE WORLD

From the Renaissance to the Second World War

Sailendra Nath Sen MA, PhD, DLitt
Former Professor of History
University of Calcutta

New Central Book Agency (P) Ltd

Co-Published by

Bijay Publications
E-mail : bijaypublications@gmail.com

Exclusively Distributed by

Bijay Pustak Bhandar (P) Ltd
90/6A M. G. Road, Bhawani Dutta Lane, Kolkata-700007
✆ : (033) 4605-7856, 8777898576, 8274916104
E-mail : bijaypustakbhandar@gmail.com

NCBA

REGD OFFICE
8/1 Chintamoni Das Lane, Kolkata 700 009, India
email: ncbakolkata@gmail.com

OVERSEAS
NCBA (UK) Ltd, 149 Park Avenue North, Northampton, NN3 2HY, UK
email: ncbauk@yahoo.com

CORPORATE OFFICE
501A/1 Right Side [Upper Ground Floor]
Govind Puri, Kalkaji, New Delhi 110 019
email: delhincba@gmail.com

BIJAY PUBLICATIONS
90/6A M. G. Road, Bhawani Dutta Lane, Kolkata-7
E-mail : bijaypublications@gmail.com

BIJAY PUSTAK BHANDAR (P) LTD
90/6A M. G. Road, Bhawani Dutta Lane, Kolkata-7
E-mail : bijaypustakbhandar@gmail.com

EUROPE AND THE WORLD • S N Sen

First Published: 1998
First Central Edition: May 2013
Reprinted: 2015, 2016, 2025

PUBLISHER • PRINTER
New Central Book Agency (P) Ltd
8/1 Chintamoni Das Lane, Kolkata 700 009

TYPESETTERS
New Central Book Agency (P) Ltd
8/1 Chintamoni Das Lane, Kolkata 700 009

Allied Print Systems
197-B Muktaram Babu Street, Kolkata 700 007

CO-PUBLISHED BY
Bijay Publications
90/6A M G Road, Bhawani Dutta Lane, Kolkata 700007

PROOF CHECKING
Subas Maitra, Rina Basak

PROJECT TEAM
Pradip Biswas, Prodip Baidya, Somenath Ganguly and Prabhat Jas

ISBN: 978 81 7381 744 1

Price ₹ 895.00

To

My Teacher

PROFESSOR R P PATWARDHAN, MA (Oxon), IES

(1892-1980)

To

My Teacher

PROFESSOR R P PATWARDHAN, MA (Oxon), IES

(1892-1980)

To

My Teacher

PROFESSOR R P PATWARDHAN, MA (Oxon), IES

(1892-1980)

CONTENTS

Preface to the First Central Edition **ix-x**
Preface to the First Edition **xi-xii**

ADVENT OF MODERN AGE

1. Geographical Discoveries 3-6
2. Decline of Feudalism—Rise of Capitalism 7-10
3. Renaissance in Europe 11-20
4. The Reformation 21-31
5. The New Absolute Monarchies—Emergence of the National State 32-36
6. Commercial Revolution in Western Europe—Mercantilism 37-39
7. Growth of Parliamentary Institution in England 40-44
8. The Thirty Years' War—Its Significance in European History 45-50
9. Ascendancy of France 51-58
10. The Emergence of a Scientific View of the World—The Age of Enlightenment 59-69
11. The American Revolution—Its Significance 70-78

EUROPE IN FERMENT

12. Introduction 81-87
13. The French Revolution 88-128
14. The Industrial Revolution 129-138
15. Restoration and Reaction 139-148
16. France (1815-70) 149-171
17. Austria-Hungary (1815-1867) 172-185
18. Growth of the German Empire (1815-1871) 186-205
19. Unification of Italy 206-217
20. Reaction and Reform in Russia 218-228
21. The Eastern Question—Part I 229-246
22. The Making of Modern England 247-261
23. Capitalism and Socialism 262-280
24. The Imperial Expansion 281-295
25. The Third French Republic 296-315
26. The German Empire (1871-1914) 316-345
27. Austria-Hungary (1867-1945) 346-359
28. The Eastern Question—Part II 360-369
29. The First World War 370-395

30. Reparation, Inter-Allied Debts 396-412
31. The League of Nations 413-418
32. Great Britain (1868-1945) 419-436
33. Reform and Revolution in Russia 437-461
34. Rise of Fascism in Europe: Italy 462-471
35. Germany: Drift Towards War 472-495
36. The Second World War 496-516
37. Minor European Countries 517-552

EMERGENCE OF NON-EUROPEAN COUNTRIES

38. Emergence of the United States of America 555-568
39. Crisis and Confidence in the United States of America (1867-1945) 569-590
40. The Latin America 591-612
41. Asian Giants—China and Japan 613-653
42. Arab Nationalism: The Middle East 654-671
43. India and South-East Asia 672-697

THE TEXTURE OF EUROPEAN CULTURE

44. Social Transformation 701-713
45. Economic Change 714-731
46. Education 732-740
47. Religion 741-752
48. Progress in Science and Technology 753-777
49. Literature 778-800
50. Music 801-804
51. Art and Architecture 805-819
52. Epilogue 820-822

BIBLIOGRAPHY 823-848

INDEX 849-913

Preface to the First Central Edition

From my excursions to different libraries in India and abroad, I found it difficult to pick up a single volume which comprehends World History from 1500 to 1945 embodying all the facets of political, diplomatic, social, economic and cultural strands. Political history can be understood better if the texture of culture is woven around it for better appreciation of the forces of change that envelop a country's onward march to progress. Though the space allotted to intellectual history in the book may not be sufficient for unfolding the drama of World History for about 450 years, I have made an humble attempt to delineate the main strands of cultural forces operating in the period that may kindle yearning for more knowledge to younger generations. In the fast-changing world of computer, laptop, internet, television and telecommunication, students of history hardly find sufficient time for serious study of comprehending World History in several volumes. If an attempt is made to harness various facts of history in a single volume by incorporating fresh authentic materials based on efforts of generations of scholars, the attempt would indeed be rewarding.

I have tried to explain historical facts in their own sequence without any pre-conceived notion making the bald narrative as interesting as possible and leaving the readers to draw inference in their own fashion. I cannot resist the temptation of quoting the prophetic words of H.A.L. Fisher who wrote in his magnum opus **A History of Europe** in January 1936: 'Men wiser and more learned than I have discerned in history a plot, a rhythm, a predestined pattern. These harmonies are concealed from me. I can see only one emergency following upon another as wave follows upon wave, only one great fact with respect to which, since it is unique, there can be no generalisations, only one safe rule for the historian: that he should recognise in the development of human destinies the play of the contingent and the unforeseen.'

The period so teeming with momentous events and fraught with far-reaching consequences like the geographical discoveries, Renaissance and Reformation in Europe, emergence of the nation state, Mercantilism, the Thirty Years' War, Ascendancy of France, Enlightenment, the French Revolution, the Industrial Revolution have been focussed in the light of recent researches embodied in learned monographs. Other events overshadowing the previous ones like the French Revolutions of 1830 and 1848, multi-racial problems of Austria-Hungary, Crimean War, Unification of Italy and Germany, realignment of forces resulting in the Triple Alliance and Triple Entente, the spoliation of Afro-Asian Countries, the sabre-rattling of Austria and Germany in 1914, the Russian Revolution of 1917, the dictated Peace of Versailles, the imposing and infructuous facade of the League of Nations unable to control aggressions of—the Axis powers—Germany, Italy and Japan and the drift towards the Second World War, are so exhaustive in their presentation that may tax the patience of the reader. Along with the plethora of material concerning the European countries, the historian feels baffled by the emerging forces of the New World, the Latin American and the Afro-Asian countries fretting with impatience for the attainment of independence! While the main thrust is on major European and non-European countries, I have not neglected the lesser important powers like the Scandinavian countries, Belgium, Holland, Poland, Greece, Turkey, Spain, Portugal, and Switzerland. History is a continuous process—sometimes deflected and shaped by towering personalities like Napoleon,

Metternich, Mazzini, Cavour, Sun Yat Sen, Mussolini, Hitler, Churchill, Karl Marx, Abraham Lincoln, and Roosevelt. I have not neglected their role in contemporary politics. The period from 1500-1945 is not an age of conflict, it is a formative period in world cultural accomplishment in different branches of humanities, science and technology, art and architecture, literature and music. I have found exhilrating joy in being able to get a glimpse of all these enduring fruits of human civilisation.

I wish to reiterate that the book contains little that is original. I have tried to weave the tangled skein of momentous events with new findings explored with painstaking care by modern generations of scholars. My labour will be amply rewarded if the students and readers find this account of events of some use, if not of sheer delight.

SAILENDRA NATH SEN

Saraswati Puja
15 February 2013
Kolkata

PREFACE TO THE FIRST EDITION

From my excursions to different libraries in India and abroad, I found it difficult to pick up a single volume which comprehends the history of Europe and the World from 1789 to 1945 embodying all the facets of political, diplomatic, social, economic and cultural strands. Political history can be understood better if the texture of culture is studied simultaneously for better appreciation of the forces of change that envelop a country's onward march to progress. Though the space allotted to intellectual history in the book may not be sufficient for unfolding the drama of World History for five hundred years, yet I have made an humble attempt to delineate the main cultural forces operating in the period that may kindle yearning for more knowledge to younger generations. In the fast-changing world of computer and space age, television and telecommunication, men find it difficult to find sufficient time for serious study usually consigning the studies of World History in several volumes to oblivion. If an attempt can be made to harness various facts of history in a single volume by incorporating authentic materials based on efforts of generations of scholars, it is likely to be appreciated by students and general readers alike.

I have tried to explain historical facts in their own sequence without any pre-conceived notion making the bald narrative as interesting as possible and leaving the readers to draw inference in their own fashion. I cannot resist the temptation of quoting the prophetic words of H.A.L. Fisher who wrote in his *magnum opus A History of Europe* in January 1936: 'Men wiser and more learned than I have discerned in history a plot, a rhythm, a predestined pattern. These harmonies are concealed from me. I can see only one emergency following upon another as wave follows upon wave, only one great fact with respect to which, since it is unique, there can be no generalisations, only one safe rule for the historian: that he should recognise in the development of human destinies the play of the contingent and the unforeseen.'

The period so teeming with momentous events and fraught with far-reaching consequences like the, French Revolution, the Industrial Revolution, Revolutions of 1830 and 1848, multi-racial problems of Austria-Hungary, Crimean War, Unification of Italy and Germany, realignment of forces resulting in Triple Alliance and Triple Entente, the spoliation of Afro-Asian countries, the sabre-rattling of Austria and Germany in 1914, the Russian Revolution of 1917, the dictated peace of Versailles, the imposing and infructuous facade of the League of Nations unable to control aggressions of Germany, Italy and Japan and the drift towards the Second World War, are so exhaustive that may entail the devotion and toil of lifelong study of any historian. Along with the plethora of material concerning the European countries, the historian feels baffled by the emerging forces of the New World, the Latin American and the Afro-Asian countries fretting with impatience for the attainment of independence. While the main thrust is on major European and non-European countries, I have not neglected the lesser important powers like Norway, Sweden, Denmark, Belgium, Holland, Finland, Poland, Greece, Turkey, Spain, Portugal, and Switzerland. History is a continues process—sometimes deflected and shaped by towering personalities like Napoleon, Metternich, Mazzini, Cavour, Sun Yat Sen, Mussolini, Hitler, Churchill, Karl Marx, Abraham Lincoln, and Roosevelt. I have not neglected their role in contemporary politics. The period is not an age of conflict, it is a period of creative accomplishment in different branches of science and technology, art and architecture, literature and music. I have found exhilarating joy in catching a glimpse of all these enduring fruits of human civilisation.

The book has been devised chiefly for the use of University students in Europe and elsewhere and rests on my experience of teaching for several decades in undergraduate and postgraduate classes. I am aware of the imperfections of so ambitious an undertaking but my labour will be amply repaid if the students and readers find this account of events of some use, if not of sheer delight. The study of Europe and the World is so absorbing and fascinating that it may provoke in mankind a desire to live in peace and harmony chastened by horrors of war and leavened by the hues of cultural vibgyor.

SAILENDRA NATH SEN

1998
Kolkata

ADVENT OF MODERN AGE

CHAPTER 1

GEOGRAPHICAL DISCOVERIES

In the hundred years from the mid-fifteenth to the mid-sixteenth century, a combination of circumstances stimulated men to seek new routes. *Firstly*, toward the end of the fourteenth century, the vast empire of the Mongols was breaking up exposing the western merchants to the hazards of uncertainty. *Secondly*, the growing power of the Ottoman Turks, who were hostile to the Christians, blocked the outlets to the Mediterranean from the East. For Prince Henry the exploration of the West African coast and the Atlantic islands acted as an impetus for his strategy of the encirclement of Islam. However, apart from religion, the founding of colonies was due to empire builders who were more guided by political and mercantile interests.[1] *Thirdly*, new nations on the Atlantic shores of Europe were now ready to seek overseas trade.

Henry the Navigator, Prince of Portugal, began the first great enterprise of the Age of Discovery—the search for a sea route by South to Cathay. His curiosity was unbounded. Moreover, he was interested in new navigational aids and better ship design. He is rightly regarded as the initiator of the great age of discovery and the European thrust towards world dominion. In addition, he hoped that by sailing south and then east along the coast of Africa, Arab power in North Africa could be attacked from the rear. The promotion of profitable trade was another motive. He wanted to divert the Guinea trade in gold and ivory from its routes across North Africa and to channel it *via* the sea route to Portugal.

Throughout the fifteenth century a series of expeditions were sent to explore the coast of Africa. In 1445 the Portuguese Navigator Dinis Dias reached the mouth of the Senegal. In 1455 and 1456 Alvise Ca' da Mosto made voyages to Gambia and the Cape Verde Islands. Prince Henry died in 1460 after a career that had brought the colonization of Madeira Islands and the Azores.[2] Henry's captain, Diogo Cao, discovered the Congo River in 1482. King John II sought to establish two routes: the first, a land and sea route through Egypt and Ethiopia to the Red Sea and the Indian Ocean and the second, a sea route around the southern shores of Africa. In 1487, a Portuguese emissary, Pero da Cavilha, successfully followed the first route. In the same year, another Portuguese navigator, Bartholomew Diaz, rounded the Cape of Storms and reached South Africa. On the return voyage, he sighted the Cape and set up a pillar upon it to mark its discovery.

A Genoese sea captain, **Christopher Columbus,** asked **King John II of Portugal** to sponsor him on a voyage to the west. King John turned him down and it was Queen Isabella of Castille who finally subsidized Columbus' four westward voyages in search of 'the Indies' between 1492 to 1502. In 1497 a Portuguese captain, Vasco da Gama, sailed in command of a fleet and reached Calicut on India's west coast. Another Portuguese fleet set out in 1500 under the command of Pedro Alvarez Cabral. It resulted in the establishment of a factory at Cochin after which he discovered Brazil. Soon trading posts,

1. The Europeans went overseas in increasing numbers for reasons of trade of conquest and increasingly of religion. For many, it provided the first meeting with people of different races.
2. In 1479, the Treaty of Alcacovas was concluded between Portugal and Spain. By the Treaty, the Portuguese monopoly of the trade and settlement of the West African coast and the possession of all the known Atlantic lands except the Canaries Islands were confirmed.

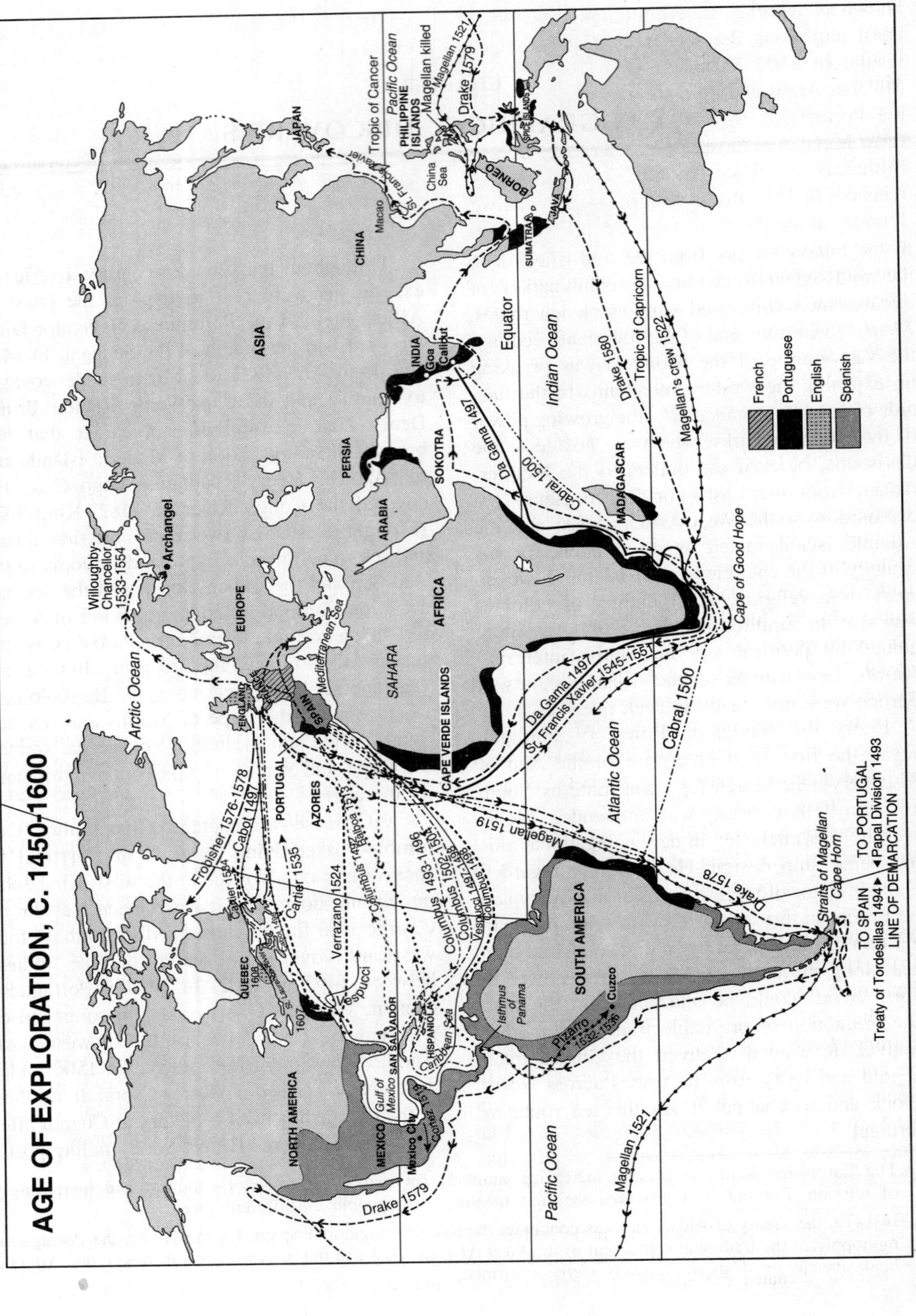

AGE OF EXPLORATION, C. 1450-1600
French
Portuguese
English
Spanish
NORTH AMERICA
SOUTH AMERICA
EUROPE
ASIA
AFRICA
SAHARA
ARABIA
PERSIA
INDIA
CHINA
JAPAN
MEXICO
Mexico City
QUEBEC 1608
ENGLAND
FRANCE
SPAIN
PORTUGAL
AZORES
CAPE VERDE ISLANDS
MADAGASCAR
SOKOTRA
SUMATRA
JAVA
BORNEO
PHILIPPINE ISLANDS
SPICE ISLANDS
Macao
Goa
Calicut
Archangel
Cuzco
SAN SALVADOR
HISPANIOLA
Gulf of Mexico
Caribbean Sea
Isthmus of Panama
Straits of Magellan
Cape Horn
Cape of Good Hope
Mediterranean Sea
China Sea
Arctic Ocean
Atlantic Ocean
Pacific Ocean
Indian Ocean
Equator
Tropic of Cancer
Tropic of Capricorn
Willoughby Chancellor 1533-1554
Frobisher 1576-1578
Cabot 1497
Cartier 1534
Cartier 1535
Verrazano 1524
Vespucci
Balboa 1513
Columbus 1492
Columbus 1493-1496
Columbus 1502-1504
Columbus 1498
Vespucci 1497-1498
Cortez 1519
Pizarro 1532-1536
Magellan 1519
Magellan 1521
Magellan killed
Magellan's crew 1522
Drake 1578
Drake 1579
Drake 1580
Da Gama 1497
Cabral 1500
St. Francis Xavier 1545-1551
St. Francis Xavier
TO SPAIN
TO PORTUGAL
Treaty of Tordesillas 1494
Papal Division 1493
LINE OF DEMARCATION

known as factories, were built along the African coast and along the shores of the Indian peninsula. In 1502 Vasco da Gama defeated the Malabar Arabs and bombarded Calicut. In 1511 the Portuguese established a base at Malacca (now Melaka, Malayasia); in 1511 and 1512, the Moluccas or Spice Islands, and Java were reached. In 1557 the trading post of Macau was founded at the mouth of the Canton River. Thus, the Portuguese, not the Turks, destroyed the commercial supremacy of the Italian cities. The Portuguese reached the height of their power in the sixteenth century. They controlled the Arab trade routes from Hormuz and Socotra and, with a firm foothold at Goa and minor islands, they controlled the trade of the West coast of India. But Portugal had overreached itself. It was, therefore, the Dutch, the English, and the French who in the long run, reaped the harvest of Portuguese enterprise.

Fortituous circumstances led Christopher Columbus to his famous discovering voyage under the Spanish flag. Columbus was a brilliant sailor who, by his glowing resolution, pursued his dream tenaciously. Crossing the Atlantic, he struck Watling Island, one of the Bahamas, on October 12, 1492 and named it San Salvador. With the help of the local Indians, the ships reached Cuba and then Haiti. A second voyage in 1493 and 1494 further explored the islands of the "Indies". On his third voyage in 1498 Columbus discovered Trinidad, entered the Gulf of Paria, on the Coast of which is now Venezuela, and annexed for Spain 'a very great continent'. On a fourth voyage from 1502 to 1504, he explored the coast of Central America from Hondurus to Darien on the Isthmus of Panama.[3]

The great navigator was suspended from his command and sent back to Spain in chains to be confronted by the disgruntled investors. In Spain, the country of his adoption, he died on 20 May 1506, a disgraced man, but he left an imperishable fame by the discovery of America. The forces of European expansion with their slaving and search for gold, had tantalizing effect on him and were at that time quite beyond his control. However, he succeeded. Columbus' towering stature as a seaman and navigator, the sheer power of his religious convictions, his personal magnetism, his courage, his endurance, his determination and, above all, his achievements as an explorer, should continue to be recognised.

Christopher Columbus

The fever of exploration gripped others. In England, Bristol was the port best placed to nurture adventurous seamen. In the latter part of the 15th century John Cabot, with his wife and three sons, came to Bristol from Genoa. With one small ship, he set out in May 1497. From Newfoundland, Cabot explored southward. From his second voyage in 1498 he did not return. But his voyages in high latitudes represented almost as great a navigational feat as those of Columbus. Sebastian Cabot, son of John, gained a great reputation as a promoter of Atlantic exploration. In 1499 Amerigo Vespucci, an Italian merchant, together with the Spanish explorer Alonso de Ojeda, explored the north coast of South America. His graphic description of the lands became popular and Waldseemuller, on his map of 1507, gave the name America to the southern part of

3. In his four voyages Columbus discovered the numerous islands of the West Indies, Trinidad, the long stretch of mainland coast of Honduras and Costa Rica. However, his constant importunities for financial succour alienated the Spanish monarchs and they refused to send him on any more exploration.

the continent. In 1513 a stowaway, Vasco Nunez de Balbao, walked across the isthmus of Panama and sighted the Pacific.

The voyage of the Portuguese navigator Ferdinand Magellan, from 1519 to 1521 was interesting. Familiar with the long sea route to Asia—eastward from Europe via the Cape of Good Hope—he was convinced that there must be an easier sea route westward. In August 1519 five Spanish ships sailed under his command first to the Cape Verde Islands and thence to Brazil. Standing offshore, they then sailed southward along the east coast of South America. Magellan's ships sailed south along the coast of Patagonia. *Finally*, on October 21, 1520, Magellan found a strait leading westward. It was a miracle that three of the five ships got through its 325 mile length. After 38 days, they sailed out into the open ocean. The ocean seemed calm; Magellan consequently named it the Pacific.

The Pacific, however, proved to be of vast extent. For 14 weeks the little ships sailed on a north westerly course without encountering land. Short of food and water, the sailors were totally exhausted. At last, on March 6, 1521, they landed at the island of Guam. Ten days later they reached the Philippines, where Magellan was killed in a local quarrel. The survivors, in two ships, sailed on to the Moluccas. One ship attempted but failed to return across the Pacific. The remaining ship 'Vittoria', laden with spices, under the command of the Spanish navigator Juan Sebastian de Elcano, sailed alone across the Indian Ocean, rounded the Cape of Good Hope, and arrived at Seville on September 9, 1522, with a crew of 21 survivors of the 239 Europeans who had set sail three years earlier.

The Spaniards did not hestitate to apply their military might. They settled in Cuba in 1511 and used it as a base for further campaigns. In 1519-20 Hernando Cortez seized the Aztec empire in Mexico. In the 1520s and 1530s permanent settlements were established in Costa Rica, Hondurus, Guatemela and New Granada (Colombia and Venezuela). Pizaro seized the empire of the Incas in Peru after 1532.

The first circumnavigation marked the close of the Age of Discovery. It proved beyond doubt that the earth was round, that the Pacific and the Atlantic were separate oceans, and that the Americas lay between them. Magellan and his men had demonstrated that Columbus had discovered a New World and not the route to China and that Columbus' Indies—the West Indies were separated from the East Indies by a vast ocean.

The centuries that elapsed since the Age of Discovery saw the end of dreams of easy routes to the East by the north, the discovery of Australasia and Antartica, and the identification of the major features of the continental interiors.

'Intercourse with America had a profound impact on European culture. A gulf began to open between those countries which had ready access to the New world and those which did not.' Karl Marx and Friedrich Engles in the **Communist Manifesto** (1848) propounded that the discovery of America and the rounding of the Cape gave opportunities to the rising bourgeoise. The East Indian and Chinese markets, the colonization of America, trade with the colonies, boosted commerce, nevigation and industry. Walter Prescot Webb regarded Europe as a metropolis and America as its great frontier.

CHAPTER 2

DECLINE OF FEUDALISM—RISE OF CAPITALISM

Decline of Feudalism

The feudal system was in its essence a means of providing protection through a kind of relationship established between various military chiefs or lords. In an agricultural society it was necessary that the peasants should receive protection to enable them to till the land they occupied. As the occupancy of the land was due to favour of some lord, it was the latter who was ready, in his own interest, to accord them protection. While for this occupancy—which included protection—the peasants paid by certain services such as working for a fixed number of days on the lord's estate. At first peasants were serfs, and thus bound to the land which they held. Moreover, tenure of the land was often hereditary, not subject to confiscation. The relations between lord and serf were not purely economic. During the heyday of feudalism, the lords exercised police and judicial rights over his serfs. This politico-economic unit was known as the "manor". In course of time serfdom declined. Later on, the obligation to work for the lord was often commuted into payments in money or kind.

The other side of feudalism was concerned with the relations of several lords with one another. A manor or a group of manors usually constituted what was known as a 'fief', a tract of land held by one lord as vassal of another, to whom, in return, he owed certain customary services, such as the obligation to fight for him; it was also understood that this overlord owed his vassal special protection. This contractual relationship between lord and vassal might be extended in an ascending scale until we reach the apex of the pyramid, which is usually the king. Primarily the relationship was military. However, there were other obligations which the feudal vassal owed his lord; he was required occasionally to pay him a sum of money. The ties between each lord and his several vassals were based on contract. The jurisdiction of the king himself was limited to the peasants on his domains and the vassals who owed him services.

The feudal system which is usually identified with Europe was a fortunate phenomenon in the mediaeval society. The services which the king received from his vassals enabled the former to form the modern state at the expense of feudalism. The feudal system became general throughout Europe, though in most of Italy it early disappeared.

The classic age of feudalism was usually from the tenth to the thirteenth centuries. There were two feudal ages the first from the ninth to the mid-eleventh centuries, where small-scale arrangements prevailed between war-lords and peasants and a second feudal age from the mid-eleventh to the mid-thirteenth century which saw the growth of hereditary nobility.

With the rise of a money economy in Europe, the basic feudal relationship began to dissolve. The nobles accelerated the process of leasing their own lands to peasants and commuting customary peasant services to fixed money payments. In this way, aristocratic incomes were protected against deflation so long as peasants could manage the stipulated payments. The peasantry continued to attain legal status from land-bound serfs to free tenant farmers until by 1500, serfdom had almost disappeared from Western Europe. In general, the peasant lost much of his servile status by commuting his manorial obligations of labour services into cash. There changes had begun in the high Middle Ages and were completed by 1500.

In Eastern Europe the peasant's lot was worse than in the west. The late mediaeval landed nobility of both Eastern and Western Europe, guarded its privileges against peasantry and monarchy. For a time, in both east and west, this nobility tried to reverse the trend towards stronger royal government. With the exception of Russia, eastern monarchies made no real progress against their nobles, but by the later fifteenth century, western monarchies were beginning to curb the independence of the landed aristocracy. The new Tudor monarchy tended to favour the mercantile class, but in Spain and France the nobility was rewarded for its political submissiveness.

During the eleventh and twelfth centuries the feudal system spread from France into England, Germany and the Crusader states of the Holy Land. At the same time, kings and dukes were resorting to the hiring of mercenaries for warfare and civil servants for the administration of their realms. As the twelfth century progressed, the feudal vassal was often asked to pay a tax in lieu of his personal service in the feudal army. With the income from this tax, called **scutage,** a monarch could hire professional warriors who were better trained and better disciplined. The feudal aristocracy retained its lands and much of its power, and even continued to produce warriors. But the knights of the new age expected to be paid. They no longer served at their own expense in return for their fiefs. Once the paying of taxes had replaced personal service as the vassal's primary obligation, feudalism had lost its soul.

It was through the strong arm of the king that feudalism gave way. If the king had a domain, he had at least the nucleus of territorial power. The French kings, being atop the feudal pyramid, had also a domain of their own. It was a rare stroke of fortune that for eleven generations there was always a son to succeed. In France, Spain and England the royal power grew and became the matrix of the modern state.

In France, the kings from the twelfth century seized every opportunity of extending and consolidating their power. The king used every occasion for stretching his prerogative. Sometimes, as a result of negotiation, his laws were accepted on the domains of these nobles; sometimes he usurped the right of sending his officials to collect the feudal **aide** directly from their tenants. The extension of the royal domain gave the king a greater power than of his vassals. As early as the eleventh century the crown had begun the practice of hiring mercenary troops to augment its power. Thus the royal power had emerged as a new element of order, a stabilizing force in the social system.

In its long struggle with feudalism the crown got valuable assistance from a vigorous middle class, who were its natural allies in checking the violence of the nobles. In France many towns were granted new charters directly by the king. In Spain the towns received every encouragement to resist the nobles. It was through the alliance of king and burghers that the power of the Spanish grandees was eventually broken. In Spain of the twelfth century representatives of the towns participated in the feudal assembly, the Cortes. In the fourteenth century occurred the first meeting of the estates-general in France where the representatives of the towns sat beside the landed feudal classes. It was from such bodies that the crown solicited money. Thus the money power contributed to enhance the royal power. Naturally it was from the middle class, paid by money instead of by lands that the king recruited the bulk of the personnel of his administration.

The expanding needs of the royal treasury accounted for much of the attack on vested interests. Philip the Fair did not scruple to invade clerical immunities from taxation. To the nobles he allowed the privilege of commuting their military service if they wished. Though such taxes were by custom extraordinary, they had the effect of weakening feudalism. The military dependence of the crown upon its vassals was fast becoming obsolete by the employment of mercenaries. Thus, the crown by its superior military power was able to buttress its power and gradually extend it. The invention of gunpowder gave the crown a decided advantage over the traditional weapons of feudalism as well as a means of destroying its stronghold.

According to some historians the breakdown of feudalism was due to the commercial expansion which introduced money economy. The growth of trade and money dealings caused labour services to be commuted to money rent. According to Henry Pirenne it was the revival of long distance trade from the twelfth century onwards destroyed the sufficient manorial economy of feudal Europe. Moreover, in parts of Europe, the need for labour services declined owing to the fragmentation of holdings. According to Bloch the decline of labour services and of serfdom in France was due to the decline of demesne lands as the lords preferred to stay in towns. The fragmentation of land lessened the need of labour services which were replaced by cash rents and hired labour.

The demographic crisis, i.e., depopulation caused by war, famine and diseases led to changes in the agrarian social structure. The depopulation affected the supply of labour and led to the rise of urban wages. The economic crisis imposed heavy burdens on the peasants which led them to seek fortunes elsewhere. According to Hilton the main factor in the decline of feudalism in Western Europe was the constant struggle of the small producers to emancipate themselves from the bonds of feudal exploitation.

Rise of Capitalism

In the twelfth and thirteenth centuries western Europe passed to a money economy. The use of money vastly simplified exchange. It enabled the landlord to exact money instead of produce from his serfs. Moreover, the use of money was expedient for facilitating exchange, as was the conveyance of large sums of money was fraught with danger. Thus, quite early, bills of exchange came into use, first in Italy, then in other countries. Incidentally, these instruments of credit lightened the burden on the small stock of money in circulation and led naturally to a great expansion of business. Perhaps they involved a degree of mutual confidence which lies at the basis of credit. Much less of this virtue, however, was present in money-lending, as evidenced by the excessive interest rates charged. At first, in the hands of the Jews, money-lending became so profitable that Italians came to engage in it. The later Crusades were financed by this means. From the money-lender developed the banker. Apart from the lending of money, the mediaeval banker was initially a mere custodian of funds left in his care for safe-keeping, for which service the depositor paid a certain sum. Then he bacame a sort of clearing house for the transfer of money from one of his depositors to another in the event of one of them incurring a debt to another. Finally, the banker loaned out some of his deposits at interest, and by the close of the thirteenth century large sums of money were invested in the promotion of trade. The Florentines reaped immense fortunes in banking. As early as the thirteenth century the banking houses of Florence had agents far and wide; they collected the revenues of the Pope, financed the English wool trade and frequently lent to needy monarchs on condition of certain concession. The profitable use of money as capital was an important stage in Europe's economic development.

The development of a money economy led to the rise of capitalism. The bill of exchange had obviated the need of shipping large sums of money. In the later Middle Ages, bills payable to order or at a stated time and promissory notes also came into use. It was capitalism, operating in such forms, that opened out the limited horizon of the towns and gave them a wider market. Such a movement was, of course, only gradual. Sometimes it was a lord, or even a monastery that used its surplus revenues from land to serve as capital. Probably shipping had been the first field of enterprise promoted by the use of capital. Commerce in the Middle Ages being more highly developed than industry, commercial capital dominated industry.

Despite its obvious advantages, it was not without some difficulties that capitalism had made its way. The risks involved were great, though commercial insurance based on regular payment of premiums was in existence at the beginning of the fourteenth century. In a society that was just becoming initiated into the mysteries of a money economy the temptation to be dishonest was almost irresistible. While kings debased the currency, there was much cheating among money-changers. Moreover, speculation followed naturally in the wake of capitalism and the eventual establishment of bourses afforded easy opportunities for gambling. Yet those bourses themselves marked an important step forward. To dabble in securities that represented goods, instead of handling the goods themselves, simplified the technique of commerce. Thus the development of capitalism was a stabilizing influence in the economic world, while, at the same time, it led to greater fluidity of wealth.

The great influx of gold and silver from America more than trebled the world's supply. There was now more money in circulation and consequently more persons anxious to put it to profitable use. Hence the increased importance of banking. The most striking example of a credit institution was the bourse or stock exchange of Antwerp where large stores of capital were accumulated and loaned out. When Antwerp declined as a result of Religious Wars, the centre of the financial world shifted to Amsterdam, the Dutch having become the greatest capitalists of Europe by the end of the seventeenth century. In 1608 the Bank of Amsterdam had been founded—a place where money could be deposited and a clearing house of exchange, but a reservoir of capital which might be invested in profitable undertakings, such as one of the chartered companies. Banking was becoming more and more a corporate, less and less an individual or family affair. In 1694, the Bank of England had been founded, the original purpose of which was to issue paper money on the strength of the government's credit. Thanks also to increase of capital, interest rates were lowered, and, owing to greater volume of business, prices became more stable.

CHAPTER 3

RENAISSANCE IN EUROPE

Renaissance means rebirth. Its usage in the fourteenth and fifteenth centuries derives from Italian scholars who believed that the centuries following the Fall of Rome had been dominated by the barbarians. By way of contrast, their own age marked a revival of classical learning and art. By 1435 Matteo Palmieri, a patriotic Florentine, was thanking God for having been 'born in this new age, so full of hope and promise.' In 1860 the German-Swiss historian Jacob Burckhardt popularised this view in a famous book The **Civilisation of the Renaissance in Italy**. He believed that the Renaissance was a "golden age" of beauty and individualism when aesthetic considerations dominated the minds of men. Burckhard's followers, arguing that the Renaissance produced a new civilisation—no longer mediaeval but recognisably modern—have influenced the later historical writing.

The term Renaissance, however, is not easy to define. One American historian complained, 'Ever since the Renaissance invented itself some six hundred years ago, there has been no agreement as to what it is." The Renaissance did not merely refer to the growing interest in classical art and learning. Nor did it involve a total rejection of medieval values or the conscious abandonment of Christian belief. The term Renaissance or 'Rebirth' was used in the sense of 'spiritual rebirth' or 'resurrection from the dead.' In its broader aspect, the movement signified a gradual evolution through which society passed in the fourteenth and fifteenth centuries, causing men to burst the fetters with which medievalism had hedged them in. Its fundamental spirit was that of inquiry. It emphasised the fact that civilisation was not static but a moving panorama which opened up wide vista of knowledge. It partly comprised the discovery of a new world, the cultivation of learning, the founding of new sciences, the flowering of art, and an essentially critical spirit.

While the spirit of the Renaissance took many forms, it was expressed earliest by the intellectual movement called Humanism. Humanism was initiated by secular men of letters rather than by the scholar-clerics. Humanism began and achieved fruition first in Italy. The fall of Constantinople in 1453 provided Humanism with a major boost, for many eastern scholars fled to Italy.

Humanism had several significant features. *Firstly*, it encompassed human nature in all its manifestations; *Secondly*, it stressed the universatility of truth found in all philosophical and theological schools, a system known as syncretism. *Thirdly*, it emphasised the dignity of man. In place of the medieval ideal of a life of penance, the Humanists looked to the struggle of creation and the attempt to exert mastery over nature. *Finally*, Humanism looked forward to rebirth of a lost human spirit and wisdom. In this endeavour, the Humanists assisted in the consolidation of a new spiritual and intellectual outlook and in the development of a new body of knowledge. The effect of Humanism was to free men from the shackles of religious orthodoxy, to inspire free enquiry and criticism, and to engender a belief in the possibilities of human thought. "Renaissance humanism affirmed the autonomy of man and his freedom in the spheres of cultural creation, science and art. Herein lay its truth, for it was essential that the creative force of humanity should surmount the obstacles and prohibitions that medieval Christianity put in its way.'

The Italian humanists heralded a revival of learning in conscious opposition to scholasticism. Classical humanism became a movement which grew among many educated laymen. They were not enamoured of the medieval monastic ideal nor the abstract philosophical doctrines of the scholastics. Medieval scholars had also used the classics widely, but they had subordinated them to theology and scholastic philosophy. Humanists—whose manuscript collections were extensive—approached the classical learning with a different purpose.

The first to give classical studies a new turn was Petrarch (Petrarca), (1304-1374), a Florentine poet and scholar. He reestablished moral philosophy as a secular study and insisted on the value of literature—especially classical Latin literature—as a means of self-improvement. In classical literature, especially in Cicero's writings, he found his model of literary style and moral philosophy. Noting that Cicero had been an active statesman, Petrarch turned his attention to "Civic humanism". Here he made a lasting contribution, for Cicero taught that the primary task of man is action in, and service to, the community.

Petrarch conceived of religion as moral philosophy rather than knowledge of doctrine. He involved himself in conflict with traditional ascetic life by the exaltation of ideal womanhood. The tensions generated by this conflict found expression in his **soul's secret**, an imaginary exchange of letters with St. Augustine. Petrarch agreed with the great theologian on many points but insisted on living in one world at a time. 'There is a certain justification of my way of life', he writes to Augustine :

> It may be only glory that we seek here, but I persuade myself that so long as we remain here, that is right. Another glory awaits us in heaven and he who reaches there will not wish even to think of earthly fame. So this is the natural order, that among mortals the care of things mortal should come first; to the transitory will then succeed the eternal; from the first to the second is the natural progression.

More than anything else, Petrarch praised civic activity. His successors, inflamed by his enthusiasm for classical studies, gave increasing emphasis to Augustine's "earthly city" as against his "heavenly" one.

It was Boccaccio who transmitted Cicero's civic humanism to Florence, where they found their fullest development between 1375 and 1450. At the beginning of the 15th century, when Milan was threatening to overrun Florence, the humanist Chancellor Coluccio Salutati (1331-1406) had rallied the Florentines by reminding them that their city was 'the daughter of Rome.' Salutati's pupil, Leonardo Bruni (1370-1444) who also served as Chancellor, took up this line in his panegyrics of Florence. According to Bruni, the roots of Florentine liberty went very deep as the Etruscans had founded free cities in Tuscancy even before the rise of Rome. There equality was recognised for all citizens and individual excellence was rewarded. This close relation between freedom and achievement, argued Bruni, explained Florence's superiority in culture as well as in politics. Florence was the home of Italy's greatest poets, the pioneer in both vernacular and Latin Literature, and the seat of the Greek revival. A constellation of illustrious men—Michelangelo, Donatello, Filippo Lippi, Boticelli and to those great artists must be added Machiavelli the publicist, Guicciardini the historian, Leonardo da Vinci and Lorenzo, made Florence the artistic and intellectual Capital of Europe. As the first home of the Renaissance, Florence can fairly lay claim to the be 'mother of modern Europe'.

Bruni's version of Florentine superiority inspired the latter to hold out against Milanese agression. However, this 'civic humanism' represented the ideal rather than the reality of the 15th century communal history. While republican humanism was running its course, classical scholarship matured in method. Boccaccio contributed to a deeper knowledge by compiling biographies of famous men and women, and a genealogy of the gods. Scholars collected manuscripts of classical Latin and Greek authors. Humanist scholars promoted Greek and Latin in their ancient styles and a respect for original sources. Lorenzo Valla (1405-57), rhetorician and philologist, was pioneer of scientific historical criticism. His bold treatise criticising the authenticity of the Donation of Constantine opened a new epoch in European scholarship. He pointed out that if the Empire of the Western world had really been surrendered to the Pope, the gift would have been manifest by the evidence of papal coins. He observed that the original text had never been produced. It is a remarkable evidence of the toleration which prevailed in Italy that despite this vitriolic attack upon the privileges of the Papacy, Valla became the secretary of Pope Nicholas V. Historical consciousness was a real revolution of the Renaissance.

Italian humanists differed from traditional theologians and scholastics. Most of them totally ignored mataphysics and formal theology. Instead, they were concerned with practical questions of human relationship. Language was basic because it was the means of social communication. To the humanists religion was a part of nature, therefore, they did not break formally with the Church. Italian humanists made their greatest impact as educators. They contributed heavily to the development of both science and law. Their emphasis on mathematics and their recovery of classical texts from antiquity helped the scientific revolution that culminated in the seventeenth century. The emphasis on classical language got a fillip. As late as the nineteenth and even the twentieth century, classical education was the hallmark of Western countries.

The Church, the princes, and the aristocracy were the principal patrons of Italian humanism. As republics declined, civic humanism waned. In Florence Cosimo de Medici founded a formal school of philosophy—the Platonic Academy—headed successively by Marsilio Ficino and Pico della Mirandola. Both championed free will and dignity of man, but also exalted the contemplated life above the active.

In Florence popular preacher Savonarola (1452-98) became the leading figure behind an attempt to restore Florentine republicanism when the Medici were driven out by an invading army in 1494. For four years his sermons steered the Florentine republic. His puritanism and his attacks on Pope Alexander VI made him many enemies. In 1497 he was excommunicated by the Pope and in the following year was executed. After a short interlude, the Medici regained control over the city.

From Italy, humanism spread to other parts of Europe. In fact, intellectual ferment was noticeable from an early date in northern Europe. But here humanism had many different facets. In general, it was less aesthetic than Italian humanism. Philology and the classics were more subordinated to religion and metaphysics. In Spain, philological and linguistic studies spread rapidly during the reign of Ferdinand and Isabella, but they were strictly subordinated to theology. This brand of humanism culminated in the career of Cardinal Ximenes, Queen Isabella's confessor, head of the Spanish Inquisition. Ximenes was responsible for the founding and reform of several universities, notably Alcaba. Xiemenes' crowning philological achievement was a polyglot Bible. The Scriptures were presented in different languages. Other Spanish humanists—such as Juan Luis—Vives (1492-1540)—proved more receptive to the advanced doctrines of Erasmus of Rotterdam.

France, the hearth of medieval scholasticism, responded more creatively to Italian humanism. The royal court of Francis I patronized the 'new learning'. The ferment sought a fusion of traditionalism, religious mysticism and classical forms. Prominent among them were Lefebvre d' Etaples, Guillaume Briconnet, bishop of Meaux and Guillaume Bude—all flourished around the turn of the sixteenth century. They devoted their energies to religion based on the Scriptures. They devalued the sacraments and exalted conduct as the essence of Christianity. In adages like 'salvation by faith alone', they seemed to anticipate a Protestant theme. Alongside this strain of French thought ran the secular naturalism of Francois Rabelais, physician and humanist. His **Gargantua** and **Pantagruel** pilloried scholasticism and proposed an ideal 'monastic system' in which universal learning and will power would set all the rules.

The German humanists were primarily interested in religious reform. The most accomplished German humanist was Johann Reuchlin (1455-1522), a jurist and professor who mastered not only Greek and Latin but also Herbrew literature.

England also drew inspiration from the late Italian Renaissance. The most famous was Thomas More (1478-1535), a lawyer who served

Henry VIII. More published a mocking satire on contemporary England, **Utopia,** which showed that non-Christian people could create a near-perfect society. In this and other writings, More exhibited a warm sympathy for the lower classes, and a concept of limited government. Caught up by the religious controversies of the Reformation, he became an anti-Protestant polemicist. Wavering between loyalty to Henry VIII as head of the English Church and loalty to the Roman Church, More chose the latter. He became a martyr and was canonised in the twentieth century.

Overshadowing the reputations of contemporary humanists, emerged the cosmopolitan 'Prince of the humanists'—Erasmus of Rotterdam (1467-1536). He was a student of theology at the University of Paris and a nomadic scholar. Attracted by the works of Lorenzo Valla, he rejected contemporary scholasticism and spent the remainder of his life outside cloister walls. In his visit to England in 1500, he became deeply acquainted with Thomas More and John Colet, who encouraged him to follow a career of religious scholarship. Returning to the Continent, he began a prolific publishing career, editing the early Church Fathers and a Greek edition of the New Testament. His writings covered a wide field ranging from the classics, works of satirical criticism, personal letters and paraphrases from the New Testament. Erasmus' classical scholarship could never be an end in itself. Among Erasmus' publications were the **Adages**, a selection of classical quotations, and the **Colloquies**, a reader much used in schools.

In his writings on the theological subjects, Erasmus decried rituals, doctrines and external observances in favour of a Christian ethic defined by the letters of Paul and the Sermon on the Mount. He worked to reform Christianity. His 'social gospel' involved a drastic social transformation. Erasmus became known to posterity primarily as a satirical critic who tried to take an independent course through the confessional wrangles of the early Reformation. Best known of his writings has been **The Praise of Folly**, a tract in which Folly, a laconic woman, twists the foibles of society, clergy, businessmen and scholars. The book ran into 43 editions in his lifetime. His satire and humour were intolerable to both doctrinal Protestants and traditionalist Catholics. He did more than anyone else to marry the new humanism with Catholic tradition. 'He was a priest with a strong streak of anti-clericalism; a scholar with a deep loathing of pedantry; a royal and imperial pensioner who lacerated kings and princes; a true Protestant against the abuses of the Church who took no part in the Reformation; a devoted humanist and a devoted Christian.'

During the late Renaissance four concepts of the state were formulated : the Roman Law or absolutist conception; the divine-right theory; the humanistic idealism of Erasmus; and the political realism of Machiavelli. Roman Law in its absolutist form was revived in 1100 by Irnerirus of Bologna. It attracted townsmen because it recognised absolute property rights, and contractual obligations basic to capitalist society. There took place absolute state of the late Renaissance as the Roman Law principle 'The will of Prince has the force of law' supported the growing authoritarianism of Renaissance rulers.

The doctrine of the divine right of kings received its impetus from the Roman-law absolutism; kings were accountable to God alone; resistance to them was a cardinal sin. Erasmian humanists had a fundamental reservation about Roman lawyers. For Thomas More and Erasmus, the king was neither the possessor of the kingdom nor above the law. In his **Institution of a Christian Prince**, Erasmus advocated that the prince's first duty was to care for the commonweal of his subjects. He ought to tax the luxuries rather than the necessities of life. The influence of Erasmus was profound in republican towns, the Low countries, and in England.

The most significant approach to politics during the Renaissance was the realism of Machiavelli and Guicciardini. Nicolo Machiavelli (1469-1527) became the most famous political theorist. Born into a prominent Florentine family, he entered public service in 1498. After serving as secretary of the secret committee for public affairs, in the Chancery, he served as a diplomatic agent to France, Germany, Switzerland and various parts of Italy.

Apart from his **Art of War** which advocated the restoration of citizen's army, his most significant political works were **The Prince** and **The Discourses on the First Ten Books of Titus Livy.** His writings reflected secular humanism, but he included topics like conspiracies, assassinations and the use of terror. With instructive examples drawn from the lessons of history, he was of opinion that men could foresee events and prevent future errors. He was considered as the first empiricist in modern political science.

Best known as the author of **The Prince** (1513), a short treatise on how to acquire power, create a state, and keep it. **Machiavelli** argued that success in politics had its own rules. This shocked his readers so much that they coined his name into synonyms for the Devil and for crafty and unscrupulous tactics. Machiavelli began with the axiom that people are immoderate in their ambitions and likely to oppress each other whenever free to do so. To get them to limit their selfishness and act for the common good should be the primordial task of government. This was the central problem of politics, made acute for Machiavelli by the twin disasters of his time, the decline of free government in the city-states and the invasion of Italy by French, German, and Spanish armies. In **The Prince,** he advocated his emergency solution : Italy needed a new leader fired with the ideal of unifying the people and driving out the barbarians. Whatever its author may have intended, **The Prince** offered a rationale for power politics in a world of competing states. In his scheme of things, force was decisive in human affairs.

Machiavelli was influenced by humanist culture in many ways, including his reverence for classical antiquity and his concern with politics. The "new path" in politics that he announced in **The Prince** was an effort to provide a guide for political action based on the lessons of history. In his passionate republicanism he showed himself to be the heir of the great humanists of a century earlier. Machiavelli was best remembered for his cynical aphorisms: 'The nearer people are to the Church of Rome', he wrote, 'the more irreligious they are.' 'A prince who desires to maintain his position must learn to be good or not as needs may require.' 'War should be the only study of a prince. He should look upon peace only as a breathing space which gives him the means to execute military plans.'

Machiavelli

It was in art that the spirit of the Renaissance reached its acme. Art came to be seen as a branch of knowledge capable of providing man with images of God and his creations as well as with insights into man's position in the universe. In the hands of men like Leonardo da Vinci it was even a science, a means for exploring nature. Art was to be based on the observation of the visible world and practiced according to mathematical principles of balance, harmony and perspective. In the works of painters like Masaccio, the brothers Lorenzetti, Fra Angelico, Botticelli, Perugion, Piero della Francesca, Raphael and Titian; sculptors such as Pisano, Donatello, Verrocchio, Ghiberti, and Michelangelo; and architects such as Alberti, Brunelleschi, Palladio, Michelozzo and Filarte, the dignity of man found expression in the arts.

In Italy the Renaissance proper was preceded by intellectual upsurge in the late 13th and early 14th centuries, which drew inspiration from Franciscan radicalism. St. Francis had not favoured scholasticism of the prevailing Christian Theology and harped on the beauties and spiritual value of nature. His example was emulated by the Italian artists and poets. The work of the most famous artist of the proto-Renaissance period, Giotto (1276-1337), reveals a new pictorial style that depends on clear, simple structure rather than on the flat, linear decorativeness of his predecessors. The great poet Dante lived at about the same time as Giotto and his poetry shows a similar concern with inward experience and variations of human nature. Although his **Divine Comedy** belongs to the Middle Ages, its subjective spirit and power of expression look forward to the Renaissance. "The originality of the **Divine Comedy** does not consist in its apocalyptic character but in its genius, in the beauty of its language, the technique of its metre, the depth of its thought, the range and glow of its imagination." Petrach and Boccaccio also belong to this proto-Renaissance period. Unfortunately, the terrible plague of 1348 and subsequent civil wars overshadowed both the revival of humanistic studies and the growing interest in individualism and naturalism. The spirit of the Renaissance was to appear again in the 15th century.

In 1401 a competition was held at Florence to award the commission for bronze doors to be placed on the baptistery of San Giovanni. Lorenzo Ghiberti, Fillippo Brunelleschi and Donatello left for Rome, where they immersed themselves in the study of ancient architecture and sculpture. They returned to Florence with enriched knowledge and the rationalised art of the ancient world was reborn.

The work of Brunelleschi, architect and sculptor, is illustrative. He was the first to work out mathematical laws of linear perspective and to emulate classical styles of building. Commissioned to remodel Florence, he introduced round columns, rounded arches, pilasters and domes. Another architect, Leon Ballista Alberti (1405-71), developed a more initiative classicism and desired to make architecture a mathematical science of balance and proportion. Donatello, who excelled in creating balance, between scientific realism and classical models, cast a David designed to stand alone in a garden. In another feat of symmetry and balance, Donatello cast at Padua one of the first equestrian statues. In this work, the movements of the horse and the rider are in perfect harmony. Other sculptors, such as Verrocchio, equalled or surpassed Donatello in specific projects, but Donatello came closer than any other to achieving perfection.

As an art, painting was slow to respond to classical stimulation. But Masaccio—who died in 1428 at the age of 27—introduced mathematical laws of perspective. He was realistic without being Gothic. His figures exist in three-dimensional space, so that the viewer feels able to touch them. In the expressions of the two lifelike nudes, **Adam** and **Eve**, he portrayed the pathos of man's expulsion from the Garden of Eden. Before Masaccio, Florence had been the fountainhead of Renaissance sculpture. Now it became the centre of painting's 'rebirth'.

High Renaissance art, which flourished for about 35 years, from the early 1490s to 1527, revolved around three towering personalities—**Leonardo da** Vinci (1452-1519), **Michelangelo** (1475-1564), and **Raphael** (1483-1520). Each of the three embodied an important aspect of the period. Leonardo was the ultimate Renaissance man, a solitary genius to whom no branch of study was foreign. Michelangelo emanated creative power, conceiving vast projects that drew inspiration from the human body. Raphael created works that perfectly expressed the classical spirit—harmonious, beautiful and serene.

Leonardo da Vinci

Realism in painting made the canvas a transparent windowpane with nature on the other side. "That picture is most praiseworthy", wrote

Leonardo da Vinci, "which most clearly resembles the thing to be imitated." No paintings better conformed to this dictum than his own. He noted hitherto unobserved colour and line aberrations in ocular perception and combined these with the use of light and shade to secure a better illustration of perspective. He tempered his realism with a classical sense of decorum, selecting elements of ideal beauty from his environment. His fame rests on a few completed works. Among them are the "Mona Lisa", "The Virgin of the Rocks" and "The Last Supper."

Michelangelo

During the second half of the fifteenth century artists began to draw inspiration from classical literature than from contemporary life. The realistic imitations of da Vinci and Alberti gave way to Greeco-Roman gods, heroes, battles and myths painted by such artists as Mantegna and Piero de Cosimo. Other painters—such as Botticelli—were influenced by the philosophy of Neoplatonism. His **Allegory of Spring** and **Birth of Venus** depict hierarchies of spirits, types of soul and forms of love. Artists of the High Renaissance no longer considered themselves recorders of external nature; rather, they were creative geniuses inspired by divine spirit.

Compared to the youthful realism of the previous century, High Renaissance art emphasized grandeur, perfection of form and self-assurance. Artists were often encouraged by the patronage of monarchs in Rome and northern Italy. By 1500 the major artists were highly rewarded individuals of great prestige and affluence who travelled from one court to another. The most ambitious patron of the High Renaissance was Pope Julius II, who called Bramante, Raphael, Michelangelo and others to Rome.

Donato Bramante (1444-1514) came to Rome in 1499, when he was 55. Bramante was a student of Roman architecture who brought principles of mathematics and physics to bear on his work. His first Roman masterpiece, the Tempietto (1502) at S. Pietro in Montorio, is a centralised dome structure that recalls classical temple architecture. Pope Julius II (1503-13) chose Bramante to be papal architect, and together they devised a plan to replace the fourth century old St. Peter's with a new church of stupendous size. The project was not completed, however, until long after Bramante's death.

Raphael's greatest work "The School of Athens' (1508-11) was painted in the Vatican.

Raphael

In this large fresco Raphael brought together representatives of the Aristotelian and Platonic schools of thought. Instead of the densely packed turbulent surface of Michelangelo's surface, Raphael placed his groups of conversing philosophers and artists in a vast court with vaults receding into the distance. Raphael was initially influenced by Leonardo, and he incorporated the pyramidal composition and beautifully modelled faces of "The Virgin of the Rocks" into many of his paintings of the Madonna.

Michelangelo's early sculptures, such as the 'Pieta' and 'The David', reveal a breathtaking ability in the service of greater expressive power. The Pope set him to work from 1508 to 1512 on frescoes of the Sistine Chapel and later on the plans of St. Peter's. Ideal beauty was to be found in the nude human form which he used in his depictions of creation and of man's early Biblical hisory. He included no crucification or judgement scenes until Pope Paul III pressed him into doing a wall on the chapel entitled the **Last Judgement.** Michelangelo was primarily a sculptor rather than a painter or architect. His most classical work was **David,** a relaxed and serene but powerful giant who could kill his Biblical opponent without miraculous intervention. In sculpture, as in painting, Michelangelo relied on his own subjective standards and produced art for art's sake.

In quality of works and in grandeur of restrained style the High Renaissance far surpassed the early Italian Renaissance. It was no longer primarily a Florentine or exclusively Italian phenomenon. Venice rivalled Rome as a centre of High Renaissance art. There a school of painters appeared whose members relied more on colour and oil-painted texture than on light and shade. This school was carried to its great heights by Titian (1488-1576) whose work are too varied to be classified. He helped introduce a new phase of Italian art—**Mannerism,** the imitation of individual masters and the distortion of classical techniques.

The Early Renaissance of fifteenth century was followed by the High Renaissance in the mid-sixteenth century. The great innovative figures included Paolo Uccello (1397-1475), conqueror of perspective, Andrea Mantegna (1431-1506), master of realistic action, and Sandro Botticelli (1446-1510), the magical blender of landscape and human form. Innovative in form and colour were the daring canvases of Antonio Allegri, of the Venetians Tiziano Vercelli (Titian, 1477-1576) and Jacopo Robusti or of the Cretan Domenico Theotocopuli, who found his way to Toledo. The art of northern Europe, first prominent in Burgundy, developed strongly and independently. The German School formed around Albrecht Durer (1471-1528), Lucas Cranach of Nuremberg (1472-1533), the landscapist Albrecht Altdorfer of Regensburg (1480-1538) and the portraitist Hans Holbein of Augsburg (1497-1543). Finally, one has to take account of powerful and original artists including the extraordinary Wit Stwosz (1447-1533), who worked in Germany and Poland, the fantastic Dutchman Hieronymus Bosch with his visions of Hell or the Flemist painter Pieter Bruegel the Elder (1525-69).

In its naturalism Renaissance art was partly an outgrowth of Gothic art. Medieval artists had used allegorical symbols, not seeking to imitate nature. Gothic painters and scuptors began to portray individuals rather than types. In northern France of the thirteenth century they began to master the techniques of realistic detail. At the Burgundian court, the Low country sculptor Claus Sluter achieved fleshlike verisimilitude with painted stone. The Van Eyck brothers, especially Jan (c. 1370-1440) painted almost photographic altar pieces with oil paint. Although they achieved marked realism, northern Gothic artists, like the architects of Gothic cathedrals, multiplied picturesque details without achieving consistency of form; nor did they master the portrayal of natural space. Gothic realism became universal during the Renaissance. It was the preeminent art form of the era, especially in northern Europe. In Italy, the plastic arts were dominated by Gothic realism until the fifteenth century.

Renaissance literature was characterised by an explosion of the vernacular languages. The work of the humanists gave way in the sixteenth century to the launch of full-blown national literatures. This was established in French by the poems of the **Pleiade**, in Portuguese by Luix de Camoens (1524-80), in Spanish by Miguel Cervantes (1547-1616), in Dutch by Anna Bijns (1494-1575) and Joost Van den Vondel, in Polish by Jan Kochanowski (1530-84), in English by the Elizabethan poets and dramatists Spenser, Marlowe and Shakespeare. In Italian, where the tradition was deep-rooted, it was consolidated by Ludovico Ariosto (1474-1533) and Torquato Tasso (1544-95).

Not all Europe's linguistic communities produced a corpus of serious literature. Especially Germany, Russia, and the Balkans lagged behind as they were still preoccupied with religious pursuits. Apart from Luther, German literature produced few giants. Between the satirical **Narrenschiff** or 'Ship of Fools' (1494) of Sebastian Brant (1457-1521) and the novel **Simplicissimus** (1669) of Christofels von Gremmelshausen (c. 1625-76), there was little particular published beyond religious tracts. In Central Europe, literature continued to be written in the international language of Latin. After Dante and Petrach, the chief exponents of neo-Latin poetry included the German Conrad Pickel, alias 'Celtes' (1459-1508), the first poet laureate of the Holy Roman Empire, Ianus Pannonius (1434-72), the Hungarian, the Italians Fracastorious (1483-1553) and Alciati (1492-1550), and the Poles Dantiscus (1485-1548) and Ianicius (1516-43).

The Renaissance had given fillip to the older movement of Church Reform. Humanists and reformers both fretted against orthodox clerical attitudes. Moreover, by encouraging the critical study of the New Testament, both led the rising generation to dream about the lost virtues of primitive Christianity. In this connection, it may be said in the metaphorical language that 'Erasmus laid the egg and Luther hatched it'.

Renaissance Science and Technology

According to medieval scientists, matter was composed of four elements—earth, air, water and fire. The cosmos was a series of concentric spheres in motion, the further ones carrying the stars around in their daily courses. At the centre was the globe of Earth, static. The Earth had three landmasses—Europe, Asia and Africa. Human beings were composed of four humours—black and yellow bile, blood and phlegm—and the body's health was determined by the relative proportions of each. The cosmos was alive with a universal consciousness with which people could interact in various ways and the heavenly bodies were generally believed to influence human character and events.

These views shaped the way educated people experienced and interpreted phenomena. But people who did not read or write books had belief in magic, spells, spirits, and witchcraft. The Church preferred that Christians seek their wellbeing through faith, the sacraments. Most clergy, however, shared the common beliefs in occult forces and lent their authority to them. The collaboration of formal doctrine and popular belief had some of its most terrible consequences during the Renaissance, such as pogroms against Jews, and witchhunts.

Among the formally educated, traditional science was transformed by the mathematical conceptions of Copernicus, Harvey, Kepler, Galileo and Newton. The twentieth century historian of science, Thomas Kuhn, hailed these contributions as major innovations in science. Humanist scholars provided both originals and translations of ancient Greek scientific works which enriched knowledge in physics, astronomy, medicine, botany, and other disciplines. Thus, the revival of ancient science brought heliocentric astronomy to the fore. Renaissance philosophers, most notably Jacopo Zabarella, analyzed and formulated the rules of the deductive and inductive methods by which scientists worked.

In mathematics the Renaissance made great contributions to the rise of modern science. Humanists included arithmetic and geometry in the liberal arts curriculum; artists furthered the geometrization of space in their work on perspective. The interest in algebra in the Renaissance universities was 'creating a kind of fever'. It produced some mathematical theorists of the first rank, including Niccolo Tertaglia and Girolamo Cardano. Renaissance scholars made a significant contribution to mathematics by translating and publishing, in 1544, some unknown works of Archimedes.

In the realm of technology, the image of the Renaissance was the manipulator of the hidden forces of nature. Engineers and technicians of the 15th and 16th centuries achieved remarkable results. Warfare was one of the changes that stimulated new theoretical questions. With the spread of the use of artillery, questions about the motion of bodies in space became more insistent. The manufacture of guns, pistols and cannons also stimulated metallurgy and fortification; town planning and reforms in the standards of measurement were related to the problems of geometry. The Renaissance preoccupation with alchemy, the parent of Chemistry, was stimulated by the shortage of precious metals.

The most important technological advance of all had little to do with nature. This was the development of printing about the mid-15th century in Germany. Johannes Guttenberg is usually called its inventor, but many people were associated with it. Block printing on wood came to the west from China between 1250 and 1350, papermaking came from China by way of the Arabs to Spain, whereas the Flemish technique of oil painting was the origin of the printers' ink. Three men—Gutenberg and his contemporaries Johann Fust and Peter Schoffer took the final steps of casting metal types and locking it into a wooden press. The invention spread like wildfire, reaching Italy by 1467, Hungary and Poland in the 1470s, and Scandinavia by 1483. By 1500 the presses of Europe had produced some six million books.

In short, the development of printing amounted to a communication revolution and transformed, the conditions of life. The communication revolution enhanced human opportunities for enlightenment and created undreamed-of possibilities. During the Reformation "... The New homogeneity of the printed page seemed to inspire a subliminal faith in the validity of the printed Bible as bypassing the traditional oral authority of the Church. It was as if print, uniform and repeatable commodity that it was, had the power of creating a new hypnotic superstition of the book as independent of and uncontaminated by human agency." "Print in turning the vernaculars into mass media, or closed systems, created the uniform, centralizing forces of modern nationalism."

CHAPTER 4

THE REFORMATION

While the Church's intellectual ascendancy was shattered by the Renaissance, this movement left her religious domination unimpaired. Even the sceptics did not break outwardly with the Church. Yet the Renaissance paved the way for the Reformation. The object of the religious movement called the "Reformation" was to heal certain abuses and to reform the structure of religious life. That movement, by involving a secession from the Universal Church, is also called the Protestant Revolt. But its effects were far-reaching and of such significance that it was rather a revolution—a religious revolution allowing the individual liberty to follow in religion the dictates of his heart.

The religious revival at the end of the fifteenth century was caused by revulsion at the decadence of the clergy. Despite the declared intention of calling a General Council every ten years, the Church had not called one since 1430. The canonization of a long line of saints—from St. Vincent Ferrer and St. Bernardine of Siena to St. Casimir of Poland (1458-84)—could not detract from the lack of religious fervour as a whole. In the very nature of things Churchmen did nto live in the same environment that surrounded Jesus and the Twelve. The Church was an institution which became rich through the pious bequests of the faithful. The pious abhorred Innocent VIII (1484-92), who performed marriage ceremonies for his own illegitimate children in the Vatican, and Alexander VI who was found to be depraved. The Renaissance Popes had fallen into the vices prevalent in Italian society. The dignity of the Church suffered when the Popes had been forced to leave the Eternal city for virtual exile in Avignon in France. The sight of two or three Popes wrangling for the mantle of St. Peter was even more painful. The Church was also, at the same time, torn with a strife which left it divided against itself. It was in the fourteenth century that the Renaissance came to weaken men's faith in its omniscience. Though the moral tone of the Chruch had greatly improved after the return from Avignon, the conduct of the Popes themselves was enough to be deprecated. Many devoted Chruchmen demanded "reformation in head and numbers" which had been a solemn issue at the Councils of the fifteenth century. Thus William of Ockham (c. 1394) spoke up as a reformer within the Franciscan order. He wished to return this religious order to the ideal of poverty, which it had generally relinquished. He maintained that Pope John XXII was heretical. When the Church was in danger of heresy, lay people must come to its rescue. This meant reform.

The Church's traditions had become the objects of assault. In England, John Wycliffe questioned the Papal power and the hold of the medieval church. Wycliffe also directed his attention toward reform of the Church. His instrument was the moral law of the Bible. In 1380, he helped to make it available to rulers and ruled alike. In Bohemia, Jan Hus, who became Rector of the University of Prague, began to criticize the luxury-minded clergy. He argued that the Pope had no right to use the temporal sword. Hus's fulminations against the Chruch led to his death by burning at the Council of Constance in 1415.

Alongside the moral revulsion there appeared a further sign of stirring in the late medieval church. In Italy, Lorenzo Valla (1407-57) exposed a number of forgeries that had given the Papacy many of its powers and much of its domain. In Germany, Johannes Reuchlin (1455-1522)

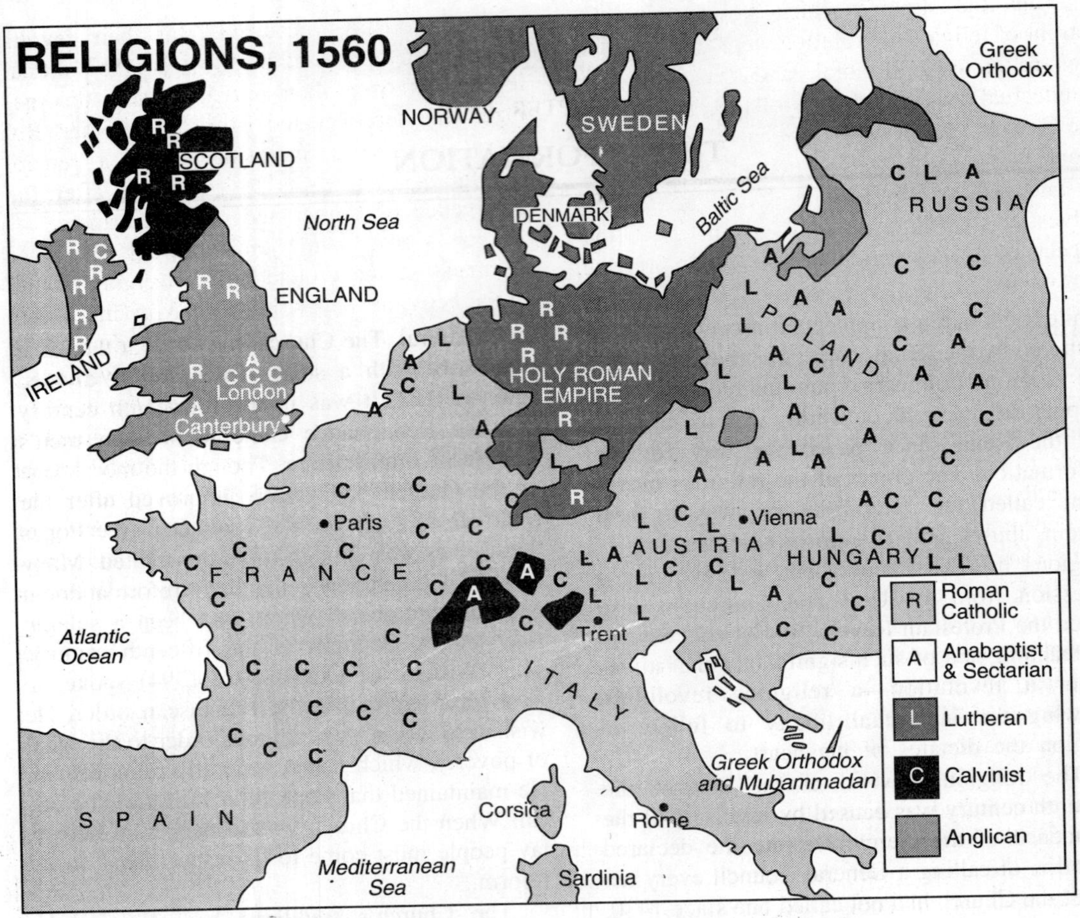

Religion in Europe (1560)

studied Greek and Hebrew and questioned the traditional claims of the church. In Holland, Desiderius Erasmus (c. 1466-1536), used his erudition and his satiric pen to question the practices of the church.

The distaste for Papacy increased at a time of rising nationalist spirits. The Popes, who had long meddled in the politics of Germany, France and England, faced setbacks when the monarchies in each country acquired new power. The sovereigns found a need to assert this power against the Papacy.

Another factor that disturbed a complacent late medieval church was a flowering of mysticism in the spirit of Heister Eckehart (d. 1327) or Johann Tauler (1361). These people gained adherence by claiming to have a direct access to God, ignoring many of the Church's rites and practices.

While the Reformers attacked people in high places, they also regarded Catholicism as being in need of reform. Devotion to Virgin Mary had come to look superstitious to them. Such practices such as pilgrims visiting shrines seemed to perpetuate a kind of paganism under a Christian veneer. The pestilences and plagues of the fourteenth century had bred an inordinate fear of death which led the Church to exploit ordinary people by offering salvation for sale. By the turn of the sixteenth century much of Europe was ripe for reforms that Catholicism could neither contain nor ignore.

Thus the streams which flowed into the torrent of religious revolution were various. One was religious and, moral, and the other was intellectual striking at some of the doctrines of the Chruch. Another was political. None of them alone was capable of producing a torrent. But in one way or another they converged themselves irresistibly to the end—all in fact, being aspects of the Renaissance converged to produce a revolution.

Lutheran Revolt—German Reformation

The Protestant Reformation triumphed first in Germany for several reasons. *Firstly*, Germany consisted of small states whose princes were too weak to mitigate the abuses of the Church. Secondly, some true priests who still exercised an enormous authority among the pious Germans criticised the Chruch's abuses.

The Church exercised enormous power under the Holy Roman Empire. Not only did the Papacy draw far more revenues from it than the Emperor, but certain clerical states—chiefly the electorates of Mainz, Cologne as well as numerous principalities of bishops and abbots—interfered too much in public affairs. Though some local princes had restricted the authority of the Church, the lack of an effective central government in the empire left the Church stronger.

Germans at all social levels resented the power of the Church. The great princes tried to fetter it and to prevent revenues from flowing to Rome. Guildsmen and merchants resented the tax exemptions of the Church. The peasants resented the paying of tithes and the ecclesiastical support of the nobility which was oppressing them. Economic hardships hit Germany hard around 1500. Business enterprises suffered owing to the shifting of trade and industry to the Atlantic seaboard. Economic misery affected the majority of the Germans, except the Church and the upper echelons of society. Social discontent and resentment of the Church reinforced each other.

Meanwhile, popular leaders began to organise revolts against the Church and the princes demanding an end to financial corruption, nepotism and indirect taxation on items of consumption and commerce. In the southern countries, peasant uprisings occurred. But their revolts failed as the oppressed had no access to political lever, Moreover, their uprisings were disorganized and disconnected from one another. But there appeared an incipient fear of a general rovolution which was to culminate after the emergence of Luther and early reformers.

For a short time the different levels of German discontent found their converging ground in the activities and writings of **Martin Luther** (1483-1546) in Saxony and Ulrich Zwingli in Zurich. Born of a middle class family, Luther was reared in an atmosphere of Catholic piety. Educated in urban schools, he obtained a bachelor's and master's degree in liberal arts at Erfurt University. Urged by his parents, he enrolled in the law school at the University of Erfurt in 1505, although he would have preferred to devote himself to religion. Within a

Martin Luther

few months, however, fearing that his sins would prevent his salvation, he joined an Augustine cloister at Erfurt in 1505.

Between 1505 and 1517 Luther devoted his time in cleansing himself of sin through fastings and prayer. While preparing his lectures on the Bible for the new University of Wittenberg, he found the solution to his torment in one of St. Paul's letters to the Romans. Man could become righteous only by confessing his innate sinfulness, throwing himself on God's mercy, and accepting His Grace. Salvation was not to be found in pious acts but by faith alone. On his own, man remained essentially depraved. Luther found this 'doctrine of faith' not in the Papacy or tradition of the Church but in the scriptures.

The spark which lighted the conflagration was the affair of the Indulgences in 1517. An easy way by which the Papacy raised money was by granting an 'Indulgence', a cancellation of some of the punishment imposed by divine justice upon the sinner, after his guilt had been pardoned through the priestly absolution. A common means of escaping such temporal punishments was that of giving a sum of money for a sacred end. A plenary indulgence signified "the removal of the entire punishment due to sin so that no expiation in purgatory was necessary" and it could be obtained either for oneself or for one of the departed. To the masses it seemed a cheap way of getting out of future agonies.

This arrangement proved to be a popular way of raising money because it was voluntary and could provoke no resentment. By this means crusades, cathedrals, hospitals and even bridges were financed. At first the Indulgence applied only to penalties imposed by the Church on earth. Then it was extended to penalties imposed by God in purgatory. In Luther's day, immediate release from purgatory was being offered, and the remission not only of penalties but even of sins was assured. Thus the Indulgence enroached upon the sacrament of penance.

The nadir of the Church's reputation reached during the papacies of Alexander VI (1492-1503) and Julius II (1503-13). Alexander's passions were for gold, women and the careers of his bastard children. Julius gratified 'an innate love of war and conquest' in 1508, when he was planning to pay for his wars and for St. Peter's through the sale in Germany of 'Indulgences', Rome was visited by Martin Luther. Luther was shocked to find the depravity of the Pope. 'Even depravity', wrote Ranke, 'may have its perfection'.

Luther's fury was heightened by the appearance in Germany of a friar, Johann Tetzel, who was selling Indulgences. Tetzel had been banished from the territory of the Elector of Saxony, who had no desire to see his subjects pouring large sums into Papal coffers. A contemporary wrote :

> It is incredible what this ignorant and impudent friar gave out. He said that if they contributed readily and bought grace and indulgence, all the hills of St. Annaburg would become pure massive silver, that so soon as the coin rang in the chest, the soul for whom the money was paid would go straightway to heaven.

It was this effrontery which provoked Luther on October 31, 1517, All Saints' Eve, to take the fateful step of nailing a sheet of 95 Theses or arguments upon the door of the castle Church of Wittenberg. Most of these propositions were not revolutionary. But he challenged authority of the Pope over purgatory and that he could not transfer the "surplus" of good works accumulated by past saints to the "credits" of present sinnners through his Indulgences.

By this time Luther had reached the fundamental conviction which inspired him to chart his future course of action. Prayer and fasting brought him no solace, nor lightened the burden of sin. On the one hand he saw the utter wickedness of man, on the other the resplendent goodness of god. Where could he find a bridge across the dark chasm? Faith was the bridge. Faith, the condition of grace, Grace, the reward of Faith, were all that mattered in the mundanic world. It was a graft from the tree of his master, St. Augustine.

Luther had written his 95 Theses in Latin but within two weeks they were translated into German and widely circulated. What might normally have been a 'squabble among monks' now became a celebrated public issue. By 1520 Luther had become a firebrand. He had denied the divine origin of the Papacy and praised John Hus, who had been condemned as a heretic just over a century earlier. In June 1520, Pope Leo X finally issued the bull **Exsurge Domine** excommunicating Luther and his associates.

By the end of 1520 Luther had completed his break with Rome and appealed directly to the public in a series of tracts. His **Address to the Christian Nobility of the German Nation** was directed to the princes, calling on them to reform the Church. This appeal to the civil power to reform the Church was a return to the earlier practice of the Middle Ages when Emperors had deposed and replaced unworthy Popes. The Christian ruler, being himself a priest, could reform the Church in externals, as the Church might excommunicate him in spirituals.

Another tract, **The Babylonian Captivity,** dealt with the sacraments. Luther reduced the number of the sacraments from seven to two. The seven were baptism, the Eucharist or mass, penance, confirmation, ordination, marriage, and extreme unction. Luther defined a sacrament as rite instituted by Christ himself. By this token only baptism and the Eucharist were strictly sacraments and penance only as confession. By the third tract, **On the Freedom of a Christian**, directed to Leo X, Luther completed and made irreparable his breach with Rome. In it Luther developed more fully his concept of the efficacy of faith and God's grace. He observed to the Pope :

> For your see which is called the Roman curia, which neither you nor any man can deny to be more corrupt than Babylon and Sodom, I have indeed shown my detestation, and have been indignant that the Christian people should be deluded under your name and under cover of the Roman Church; and so I have resisted and will continue to resist so long as the spirit of faith lives in me.

In December 1520 Luther publicly burned the Papal Bull—thus exposing himself to death at the stake. However, he was saved from the fate by Elector Frederick of Saxony. Although Frederick himself never broke with the Church, he suggested to the newly elected Holy Roman Emperor, Charles V, that Luther's case be heard at the imperial diet, which was to meet at Worms in April 1521. Since this was a secular tribunal the attempt was made to prove that he was not simply a heretic but also a rebel whose views were more subversive of the civil than of the ecclesiastical order. Luther was brought before the Diet and given an opportunity to repudiate his books. But he replied:

> Unless I am convicted by Scripture and plain reason—I do not accept the authority of Popes and councils, for they have contradicted each other—my conscience is captive to the World of God. I cannot and I will not recant anything for to go against conscience is neither right nor safe. God help me. Amen.

After that he was spirited away by the Saxon Elector's men and hidden in the Wartburg castle. In this place of exile Luther set about translating the New Testament into German. Luther's German Bible not only served as a spiritual guide but also transformed the German vernacular into a literary language. He also continued to pen influential tracts. In one powerful piece he appealed to monks and nuns to leave their cloisters. Luther's revolt was characterized by considerable personal courage, but for its success it depended on the simultaneous revolt of the German princes.

Luther had attributed German misery solely to clerical greed and obscurantism. But fellow pamphleteers such as Martin Bucer anticipated reorganisation of society based on divine justice and Scriptural text. An influential anonymous tract urged the peasants to coerce authorities into accepting reform without overt revolution. In Saxony, Thomas Muntzer preached revolution against princes. After 1521 the slogans of the major reformers penetrated the lower classes. Often led by former monks, urban masses attacked the existing order. In widespread areas peasants began to withhold tithes, dues and services. After a poor harvest in 1524, the condition of the peasant of south-western Germany was rife with discontent. Their hostility was known in German history as the Great Peasants' War. Most of these revolts were inspired by a common programme of reform—**The Twelve Articles of the German Peasantry**, which swept northward. The Articles, written in the form of a contract, asserted that society and politics should rest on scripture. The rebels sought to enforce these contracts by witholding dues, tithes and services from the authorities.

Luther's defiance of the Church might have provoked the peasants' rebellion. But he had no sympathy for the Twelve Articles of the Peasants. When rebel bands infested north as far Thuringia, Luther published his appeal Against the Murderous and Thieving Hordes of Peasants, defending the social order and the princes' rights. After a merciless slaughter of about 10,000 peasants, the revolt collapsed. Many rebels returned to Roman Catholicism. Others either resigned themselves to their lot or joined the Anabaptist movement that swept across Germany from Switzerland.

After the Peasant's Revolt several German princes like Philip of Hesse, Elector John of Saxony, and Casimir of Brandenburg had become converts to Lutheranism. Several imperial cities also adopted Lutheranism or modifications of it. The Diet of Speyer (1526) resolved to leave each prince free until a general council should be called to interpret the Edict of Worms.

Philip of Hesse seized this opportunity to confiscate all church property and to instal Lutheran clergymen. His example was soon followed in Saxony, Brandenburg, Prussia, Denmark, Sweden, Wurtemberg and other principalities. Everywhere the chief beneficiaries were the privileged orders of town and the country and the "Christian magistracy"—usually a prince or a king. The clergy relied on him to root out all remnants of Roman Catholicism as well as the new heresies, especially Anabaptism. The reformers emphasised that their work was purely spiritual. Most of the changes were confined to doctrine and liturgy: the number of sacraments was reduced to two—baptism and liturgy of the Lord's Supper : monasticism was suppressed.

For a generation these changes took place without imperial intervention, for the Emperor was too preoccupied to fight the Turks and France at the same time. But in 1529, after his victory over France, Charles could attend to the Lutheran problem. A decree issued at the second Diet of Speyer in 1529 forbade all religious innovations. The Lutheran princes and 14 imperial cities protested formally, but in vain.

Strengthened by the defeat of the Turks at Vienna, Charles V, in 1530, attended the Diet of Augsburg in person. Failing to effect a compromise between the Lutherans and the Catholics, Charles ordered a return to the traditional faith. Led by Philip of Hesse, the Lutheran Princes organised the League of Smalkald for defence against a Catholic League and the Emperor. Hostilities were postponed as Charles was too preoccupied with the Turks and the French to fight the Lutherans. During the next few years, however, the Lutheran princes fought the Emperor's forces, gaining military support from France in return for the transfer of three imperial archbishoprics in the western Rhineland to France. Their victory was sealed in September 1555 by the Peace of Augsberg.

The settlement formally recognised the right of each German prince to choose the Lutheran or Roman Catholic faith and to impose it on his subjects. The principle involved was **Cuius regio eius religio**—the religion of the ruler must be that of the realm. Dissenters would not be tolerated. Germany was now equally divided between Lutheran and Catholic States, and the Reformation there was over.

Meanwhile Lutheranism had spread to other parts of Northern and Central Europe. It was able to exist as the faith of a minority in Poland, Bohemia and Hungary. But the Kingdoms of Norway—Denmark and Sweden—Finland, and the Baltic States set up national Lutheran Churches. Thus, in much of Europe, Lutheranism either was established as an act of state or was tolerated as a minority religion.

Meanwhile, the Reformation movement within Germany diversified almost immediately and other reform movements arose independently of Luther. In 1518, in Switzerland, Huldrych Zwingli (1484-1531), correspondent of Erasmus, and 'people's priest' at Zurich, challenged the Roman church. Like Luther, he denounced Indulgences and he shared Luther's concept of justification by faith. He rejected the authority of the bishops and he taught that the Eucharist was no more than a symbolic ceremony. He was killed at Cappel in 1531, carrying the Protestant banner in a war against the five Catholic cantons that had split the Swiss Confederation. He launched an important Protestant trend and claimed the democratic right of the local congregations to control their own affairs.

In 1521, the Anabatists, the most radical sect of the time, made their appearance in Saxony. They claimed that all people needed to be rebaptized since they repudiated the Roman Church's authority. They also challenged established political authority, seeking to found an ideal Christian republic based on evangelical principles. Although they lived in different parts of Europe and differed on certain issues, the Anabatists shared three basic principles : (1) the

Church is a voluntary association; (2) Church and state should be separate; (3) religious liberty should prevail. This programme threatened all the existing churches—both Protestant and Catholic. The Anabaptists were Christendom's first fundamentalists. By the mid-sixteenth century the Catholic and Protestant authorities had executed tens of thousands of Anabaptists in north-western and Central Europe. They recovered under Menno Simons (1496-1561) and survived as the progenitors of numerous seventeenth century sects including the Baptists, the Unitarians and the Quakers.

Role of Calvin

Another form of Protestantism was Calvinism, named for **John Calvin** (1509-64), a Frenchman

John Calvin

educated in humanist and legal studies. Until his mid-twenties Calvin thought of himself as primarily a man of letters. Then he experienced a metamorphosis which goaded him into a seeker of knowledge of God and his law through the Bible. He fled to France in 1534 and later took up his residence in the French-speaking Swiss city of Geneva in 1536. It was during this period that he published his most important work—the **Institutes of the Christian Religion**.

The **Institutes** was the most authoritative statement of Protestant theology to come out of the Reformation. Here was a emphatic demonstration of how man should live in close communion with his Creator. The main goal of the true Christian was to know God. According to Calvin, God predestined some men to eternal life and others to eternal damnation. Yet he was a merciful Saviour as well as a stern Father. In Calvin's system all aspects of life were subordinated to the absolute standard of Scriptural revelation. All morality should serve the advancement of the Kingdom of God on earth.

In ethical matters, Calvin established a new code which made his followers easily recognisable. A good Calvinist was to abhor all forms of pleasure and frivolity—dancing, songs, drinking, gaming, flirtation, bright clothes, even vivacious gestures. His life was to be marked by sobriety, self-restraint, hard work and, above all, godliness. Although Calvin did not impose celibacy, he tried to establish a universal monastic standard. Thus all laymen were to take the sacrament weekly and submit themselves to daily sermons. Legislation of morals was equally stringent in Lutheran and Anglican Church, but Calvin and his followers enforced their laws with particular zeal by threatening excommunication.

Unlike the Anglican and Lutheran Churches, the Calvinist Church was not subservient to secular authority. Calvinism adopted a system of synods representing the clergy and elders. Through them the state was to serve as the handmaiden of the Church. Instead of introducing a separation of Church and state, Calvin sought to reassert the authority of the clergy over the social and political order.

Excepting for a period of three years (1538-41), Calvin lived in Geneva from 1536 to his death in 1564. Here he framed a new type of theocratic state which exercised an influence over the 'reformed' churches throughout the world. He welcomed conditions under which pastors and laymen alike would be subjected to a rigorous control. So a supreme council, part lay, part clerical was set up in Geneva to enforce a code of penalties on laxities of private life and belief. It was a inquisitorial government which was a source of much cruelty and suffering. In Geneva it led to the burning of Servetus, the Unitarian, with the concurrence of Calvin himself.

It was part of Calvin's greatness that he was not only the central figure in a wide European movement, he made of it the high school of reformed religion. Calvin had created a doctrine and a programme of church discipline with a great potential appeal. In 1559 he founded an academy in Geneva for the instruction and training of ministers. Hundreds of Protestant leaders from other countries studied there and then brought his teachings back to their native lands.

"Of all the forms assumed by the Protestant Reformation, Calvinism has been the most far-reaching in its scope and the most profound in its influence." In Western Europe it often appealed to the rising urban bourgeoisie, and in France to the nobility. In Eastern Europe, it appealed both to the landed gentry and to the magnates. In England, Calvinism began to make an impact after the death of Henry VIII in 1548. It exercised such an influence over the Thirty-nine Articles (1571) which constitute the declared creed of the National Church, that Queen Elizabeth was excommunicated as a Calvinist. Afterwards and during the period of the Long Parliament, Calvinism became a predominant force in English politics. With the Restoration it receded into the background. In 1560 John Knox (1513-72), who had studied in Geneva, Persuaded the Scottish Parliament to accept a modified version of Calvinism, a form known as Presbyterianism.

In France the Calvinists were known as Hugenots. They spread rapidly in the south and west and in the urban population of all provinces. They formed the backbone of the Bourbon party during the Wars of Religion. In Germany, Calvinism was long opposed both by Lutherans and Catholics. It received its major support from the Elector-Palatine Frederick III and from the conversion of Hohenzollerns of Brandenburg. In the Netherlands, the rise of Calvinism provided a basic factor in the split between the Catholic provinces to the west and the united Provinces to the east. In Poland, Lithuania, Bohemia and Hungary, Calvinism appealed to a cross-section of the landed gentry.

Reformation In England

The Reformation in England was political rather than religious, a quarrel between the king and the Pope. The dispute had its root in the assumption that the king was competent to provide an heir to the throne. The issue that sparked it was King Henry VIII's desire to divorce his wife, Catherine of Aragon. She had given Henry a daughter, the princess Mary, but no son. Henry expected Papal compliance for setting aside Catherine. Indeed, it had been twice recently done within the circle of his own family. His brother-in-law Suffolk had repudiated a wife, his sister Margaret had repudiated a husband, and both had married again under a dispensation from the compliant Pope Clement VII. Having fallen in love with Anne Boleyn, and being determined to make this young beauty his lawful wife, Henry tried to force Papal compliance. The divorce would have been granted had Catherine not been the aunt of Charles V, who was not prepared to see her cast aside in favour of another wife.

In 1532, Henry allowed himself to be convinced by his able adviser, Thomas Cromwell, that the divorce did not need the sanction of the Pope and that Parliament could settle the matter. Between 1532 and 1534 Parliament, guided by Cromwell, passed a series of Acts that created the independent Church of England. The Act of Supremacy, 1534, made the king the supreme head of the Church. Sir Thomas More and Bishop Fisher, the two greatest figure in the last age of Catholic England, went to the block rather than swear the oath. The new Archbishop of Canterbury, Thomas Cranmer, used his power to declare Henry's first marriage void and to marry him publicly to the pregnant Anne Boleyn. The major changes under Henry were the suppression of the monasteries, the introduction of the Bible in the vernacular in the churches, and permission to the clergy to marry, though this was later revoked.

On his accession to the throne in 1547, young Edward VI was hailed by Cranmer and other Protestants as England's Josiah. Protestantism advanced rapidly during his reign through the systematic reformation of doctrine, worship and discipline. England became a legally Protestant (Anglican) country under Henry VIII's successors. Archbishop Cranmer produced his **Book of Common Prayer** and revised the doctrine and ceremonies of the Church of England along the lines of the Continental Reformed churches.

Protestantism received a temporary setback during the reign of Mary (1553-58), Henry and Catherine's Catholic daughter. Many, including Cranmer, died as martyrs to the Protestant cause. Others fled to the European continent. Leading clergymen in exile published material justifying rebellion against an idolatrous ruler. Many saw in Geneva, a haven for English exiles, a working model of a disciplied Church. Exiles produced two large volumes of incalculable consequence for English religious thought. John Fox's **Acts and Monuments,** popularly known as the **The Book of Martyrs**, and the Geneva Bible were the most popular books in England for many years.

Elizabeth I, beginning her rule in 1558 could rule England only as a Protestant, since she was an illegitimate child in Catholic eyes. Two Statutes promulgated in her first year—the Act of Supremacy, stating that the Queen was the 'Supreme governor' of the Church of England, and the Act of Uniformity, ensuring that English worship should follow **The Book of Common Prayer**—defined the nature of the English religious establishment. In 1563 she approved as the prescribed faith the Thirty-nine Articles, which were deliberately vague so as to satisfy as many people as possible. A sizable minority of English Catholics, as well as the Irish, resisted the forced imposition of the Anglican Church on them and clung to their Catholicism. Before the end of Elizabeth's reign, the English Puritans also began to challenge Anglicanism.

The effects of Protestantism were manifest in every sphere of European life. By highlighting the efficacy of Bible-reading, it made a major impact on education. In the economic sphere it made a major contribution to the rise of capitalism. In politics it proved a major bone of contention—both between states and between rival groupings within states. By dividing the Catholic world in two, it goaded the Roman Church to Reform which it had repeatedly postponed. Above all, it shattered the ideal of a united Christendom. Until the 1530s, Christendom had been split into two halves—Orthodox and Catholic. Now it was split into three; Orthodox, Catholic and Protestant.

The Counter-Reformation

The Counter-Reformation given its name by Protestant historians, was born to oppose the Protestant Reformation. In the campaign against Protestantism, called the Counter-Reformation, the Jesuits, the Inquisition and the Hapsburg rulers of Spain and Austria tried to win Protestants and Catholic Dissidents to the Roman faith.

The pontificate of Paul III (1534-49) saw the urgency of change. He revitalised the Sacred College, commissioned inquiry into Church reform, patronised the Jesuits, and launched the Council of Trent. Until the 1530s the Sacred College of Cardinals, which elected the Popes, became the Vatican's power-house for change. The Church had always gained strength whenever new monastic orders were founded. During the first half of the sixteenth century a number of new religious orders in Italy and Spain helped revive Catholic piety and charitable activities. But the most influential was the 'Society of Jesus' the 'shock troops of the Counter-Reformation', founded by a disabled Spanish soldier, Ignatius of Loyola (1491-1556). In 1523 he set out on a pilgrimage via Rome and Venice to Jerusalem. He abjured his family, lived on bread and water, and by a rigorous course of prayer subjected himself to communion with the Divine. He hungered for knowledge and eventually came to Paris, the Queen of Universities, where he studied for seven years. There he conceived the idea of an enterprise of holy Chivalry to be carried out by a company of devoted souls.

With six of his followers, Loyola founded the Society of Jesuits—popularly known as the Jesuits. In 1540 the Pope made the Jesuits an order and the members took the vows of poverty, chastity and obedience to the Papacy. The Jesuits championed a personal and emotional religion along with the rigours of methodical prayer. They were commissioned soldiers of God to propagate His doctrine by public preaching, acts of charity, and especially public education. The new order expanded rapidly all over the world—from Mexico to Japan. One of the original founders, Francis Xavier (1506-52), is credited with hundreds of thousands of converts in India, China, Malaya and Japan.

The aims of Loyola were as practical as they were visionary. It was the duty of the Jesuit to preach, to hear confession, to educate. The Jesuits convinced the sinner that he had not really sinned at all unless he had fully intended to do so. The Jesuits championed a personal and emotional religion, combining the rigours of methodical prayer with a vivid and dramatic style of Church art. Finally, the Jesuits played a key role in reaffirming official Catholic theology at the Council of Trent.

The Council, summoned by Pope Paul III, met intermittently from 1545 until 1563. Its work completed the reform within the Roman Catholic Church and became the rockbed of Catholicism. The Council of Trent reaffirmed the official doctrine: man's nature is tainted by original sin; God offers his grace to everyone. The core of Catholicism is redemption through Christ: each man can earn this gift of grace through love of God, demonstrated in faith and good works. Each man chooses to accept God's grace or reject it of his own free will. The Church alone is his guide in interpreting Christ's teachings, which include the Holy Scriptures. It alone administers the seven sacraments, clarified at Trent, which are the visible symbols of God's grace. All Catholics are compelled to accept this doctrine on pain of excommunication.

The main reform of the Council of Trent was directed against the abuses of the clergy. To raise the educational standard of the Parish priests, the Council required every diocese to have a seminary to train them. It strengthened the authority of the bishops, forbade them to hold more than one benefice, and required them to reside in their dioceses. Disciplinary reforms attacked the corruption of the clergy. There was an attempt to regulate the training of candidates for the priesthood; measures were taken against luxurious living on the part of the clergy, the appointment of relatives to church office, and the absence of the bishops from their dioceses.

The Council assigned the following tasks to the Holy See : (1) publication of an Index of books Catholics would be forbidden to read (2) compilation of a Cathechism for the use of parish priests, (3) revision of the breviary, (4) revision of the missal.

The next two Popes completed the reform within the Church and then took up the work of the Counter-Reformation in earnest. The "Holy Office" of the General Roman Inquisition, founded in 1542, tried a number of suspected heretics. Spain's territorial conquests in Italy extended Jesuit influence and led to the repression of controversial Italian thought. Elsewhere, Spain introduced its own Inquisition into most of its far-flung possessions. The Spanish Inquisition was to become the chief instrument of Philip II's anti-Protestant crusade.

Critics of the Council of Trent highlighted its neglect of practical ethics, its failure to give Catholics a moral code comparable to that of the Protestants. An English Catholic wrote: 'It impressed on the Church the stamp of an intolerant age, and perpetuated the spirit of an austere immorality.' The Protestant historian Ranke stressed the paradox of a Council which had intended to regulate the Papacy. Instead, by oaths of loyalty, detailed regulations and punishments, the Catholic hierarchy was made subservient to the pope. 'Discipline was restored, but all the faculties of directing it were centred in Rome.'

The religious ethos promoted by the Counter-Reformation emphasised the discipline and collective life of the faithful. It reflected the authority of enforcement given to the hierarchy and insisted on regular confession as a sign of submission. It was supported by a variety of communal practices—pilgrimages, ceremonies and processions and the tapestry of accompanying art, architecture and music. Unlike the Protestant preachers, who stressed individual conscience and probity, all too often the Catholic clergy was urged to render to blind obedience.

The impact of the Counter-Reformation was felt throughout Europe. Traditional support for the Church was strongest in Italy and Spain. The Spanish Netherlands were turned into a hotbed of Catholic militancy. Yet an important reaction against the prevailing zeal followed. Cornelius Jansen (1585-1638), Bishop of Ypres and critic of the Jesuits, in his work **Augustinus** (1640) attacked the theological nuances and superficial morality of his day. Though he never wavered in his loyalty to Rome, several of his propositions on the issue of Divine Grace approached the Protestant standpoint.

Switzerland was rent by the hostility of the Catholic and the Protestant cantons. But a pro-Roman Catholic 'Ultramontane' Party grew who committed the most atrocious deed by massacaring 20,000 Huguenots on 23 August 1572. In the seventeenth century, Jansenism offered a middle way. The Kingdom of England was targeted for reconversion. Ireland was confirmed in its Catholicism. In Austria, the Counter-Reformation became inextricably woven with the ruling dynasty and its politics. A special brand of Catholicism, called 'Confessional Absolutism' emerged. The Jesuits exercised considerable influence over education in Vienna and Prague. Western Hungary, Slovakia, Croatia, Silesia, Bohemia—all belonged to this same sphere.

In Germany an uneasy rapproachement between Catholics and Protestants took place in 1555 at the Peace of Augsburg. Each prince was to decide on the religion of his subjects. Germany was turned into a religious patchwork where, however, the Catholic princes held the upper hand. In the world of growing religious intolerance, Poland-Lithuania could rightly boast of its role as Europe's haven of toleration. With its varied population, it contained a mosaic of the Catholic, Orthodox, Judaic and Muslim faiths. In 1573 the Polish Parliament passed a statute of permanent and universal toleration. Under Sigismund III Vasa (1587-1632), a votary of the Jesuits, the Ultramontane Party reasserted the Catholic supremacy. But progress was slow.

Elsewhere in Eastern Europe the Counter-Reformation exercised great influence. The Vatican under Gregory XIII (1572-85) cast its influence not only over Sweden and Poland but even Russia. By the end of the seventeenth century the Jesuits had made Poland one of the most Catholic countries in Europe.

All over Europe religious frenzy affected the progress of the arts. Protestantism questioned the very propriety of artistic endeavour. The plastic arts often covered secular subjects. In some countries, such as Holland or Scotland, hymn-singing became the core of the music. In the Catholic countries, all branches of the arts exhibited sumptuous and theatrical displays of the Church's glory, and power. This trend is known as 'Baroque'. Baroque painting was dominated by Michelangelo, Caravaggio (1573-1610), by the Flamish Paul Rubens (1577-1640) and by the Spaniard Diego Velasquez (1599-1660).

Religious fervour dominated the wars of the sixteenth and seventeenth centuries. Protestant fears of Catholic domination surfaced in Germany in 1531-48 which ended with the Peace of Augsburg; in the French Wars of Religion, 1562-98; in the Swedish Civil War, 1592-1604, in the Thirty Years' War, 1618-48. Catholic fears of Protestant domination inspired many episodes such as the Pilgrimage of Grace (1536) in England, Irish resistance to Cromwell, Polish resistance to the Swedes in 1655-60. In the east, the protracted campaigns between Russians and Poles—1578-82, 1610-19, 1632-34, 1654-67—assumed the colour of a Holy war between Catholics and Orthodox. 'Senseless bloodletting in the name of religion inevitably sparked off a reaction in the minds of intelligent people. The Wars of Religion offered fertile soil for the fragile seeds of reason and science'.

CHAPTER 5

THE NEW ABSOLUTE MONARCHIES—EMERGENCE OF THE NATIONAL STATE

The Nation-State and 'nationalism' are terms frequently applied to the sixteenth century. They were invented by the historians in the nineteenth century looking for the origins of the nation-states of their own day. They properly conveyed the strong sense of sovereignty which both monarch and subjects assumed, as the unity of the Middle Ages disintegrated.

Il Principe (The Prince), written by Niccolo Machiavelli (1469-1527) in 1513, served as the bedrock for all such rulers who wished to assume unfettered power. Machiavelli, historian, dramatist and Florentine diplomat, wrote his book in the hope that it would inspire a prince to fulfil Dante's dream of a unified Italy. With its universal appeal, it highlighted the art of **Machtpolitik** or untrammelled power politics. At one level, Machiavellianism caused derision. Concepts such as 'honourable frauds' became notorious. However, if **The Prince** is read in conjuction with the **Discourses** on Livy, Machiavelli may be judged as an advocate of limited government, of the rule of law and of liberty. His cynical view on frailties of human nature provides the basic ground on which constitutional structures have to be built. Some of his cynical aphorisms are best remembered: 'The nearer people are to the Church of Rome, the more irreligious they are.' 'A Prince who desires to maintain his position must learn to be good or not as needs may require.' 'War should be the only study of a prince. He should look upon peace only as a breathing space which gives him the means to execute military plans.'

In the fifteenth century, changes in the structure of European polity, coupled with a new intellectual temper, suggested that the Middle Age had ended and a new era had begun. The Papacy, the symbol of the spiritual unity of Christendom, lost much of its halo in the Great Western Schism and became vitiated with the lay ideals prevailing in the Italian peninsula. In the sixteenth century, the Protestant Reformation reacted against the corruption of the Holy See, and the Roman Catholic Church responded by a revival of piety known as the Counter Reformation. While the forces generated by the Protestant movement were gathering strength, the narrow horizons of the old world were widened by the expansion of Europe to America and the East.

In western Europe, nation-states emerged under the aegis of strong monarchical governments. Centralised bureaucracy came to replace medieval government. Secular values prevailed in politics and the concept of a balance of power came to dominate international relations. Diplomacy and warfare were conducted by new methods. Permanent embassies were accredited between sovereigns and standing armies of professional and mercenary soldiers replaced the feudal army. At the same time, scientific discoveries shook faith in the traditional cosmology. The systems of Aristotle and Ptolemy were undermined by Copernicus, Galileo, and Kepler.

The strengthening of royal power in some quarters did not herald the advent of absolutism. In France, the restraints on the king were so great that scholars doubted whether under Francis I the French government was more consultative or less decentralised. In England, after the advent of Tudor monarchy, it was Parliament which asserted itself under the subsequent rule of the Stuarts. In the Holy Roman Empire, the Imperial Diet asserted against the Emperor. In Poland-Lithuania, republicanism triumpled over monarchy.

Of the two most famous political treatises of the period, the **De la Republique** (1577) of Jean Bodin favoured constitutional monarchy, while the **Leviathan** (1650) of Thomas Hobbes made use of contract theory to favour absolutism. Hobbes maintained that kings held unlimited rights because their subjects had voluntarily surrendered their own rights. Monarchy for the modern state was a regrettable necessity.

Every state has a constitution which defines the relationships between the rulers and the ruled. Beginning in the late fifteenth century the kings of France, England, and Spain tried to change the constitutions of their kingdoms in order to increase their powers. These 'New Monarchs' created new agencies of strong central government. Their progress was aided by a desire among their subjects for a strong leader capable of containing the disorders and insecurities of the fourteenth and fifteenth centuries. The king thus acquired the aura of a hero. But in most places there was strong resistance to the change from the medieval to the modern form of monarchy.

Spain

The development of modern Spanish monarchy began with Ferdinand of Aragon (1479-1516) and his wife, Isabella of Castile (1474-1504). As in France and England, the monarchs in Spain wrested power from the nobles and strengthened the royal government. Ferdinand and Isabella rallied the church and the common people to the crown by playing on their hatred for Jews and Moors. In 1480 Ferdinand and Isabella established the Inquisition to investigate the Christian orthodoxy or converted Jews. They forced the Jews to leave Spain in 1492 and expelled the Muslims ten years later. They continued to use the Inquisition to rally support and soon it became the most effective institution the Spanish monarchy had for strengthening its own power.

'For a few fabulous decades Spain was to be the greatest power on earth and all but the master of Europe'. Under Philip II (1556-98) it stood at the pinnacle of political and cultural power, until undermined by the hostility of France and England, and by the revolt of the Netherlands. Under Philip's successors Philip III (1598-1621), Philip IV (1621-65) and the imbecile Charles II (1665-1700), it never recovered from a decadent dynasty and for its entanglement in the Thirty Years' War. Philip II, a tireless monarch, tried to enforce a spiritual and administrative uniformity against various odds. In 1580 he seized his mother's vast Portuguese inheritance. He relentlessly pursued the dream of 'one monarch, one empire, one sword.' In the process, he goaded his imprisoned son to death; he drove the persecuted Moriscos of Granada to rebel in 1568-9, the Dutch to rebel in 1572, and Aragon in 1561-2. He was considered by his adversaries, like William the Silent, simply 'a murderer and a liar.' He remained completely impervious to the sensitivities of others. Absolute master of Church in Spain, he sought to eliminate the Church's enemies across Europe. He intervened against the Huguenots in France. But fortune did not favour him. By the 1590s a general crisis enveloped him. The Great Armada of 1588 had been dashed by storms. The Dutch stubbornly resisted. Plague swept the Spanish cities. Burdened by taxes and hit by agricultural failures, the countryside was beginning to depopulate. There was misery amidst splendour and sense of disillusionment. After Philip's death, the Spanish Habsburg's sought in vain to restore their fallen fortunes.

France, too, entered a period of renewed vigour and splendour. Less encumbered by distant colonies, and geographically more compact, she was a worthy rival for the Habsburgs. Francis I (1515-1547), an ambitious and capable ruler, was the first of the New Monarchs in France. He negotiated with Pope Leo X the Concordat of Bologna and gained a large degree of control over the Catholic Church in France. He won the gratitude of the merchant class by not overburdening them with taxes. Francis was careful to show respect for the privileges of the various provinces and social classes. While retaining their loyalty he gained an increasing proportion of his revenue from the sale of offices and from one-tenth of the Church's income to which he was entitled. Francis patronised the arts and built a sumptuous Renaissance Court at Fontainebleau, about 40 miles south-west of Paris. This new court, the symbol of a powerful monarchy, attracted a new class of royal servants to whom Francis sold or gave offices, honours and privileges. He gained his own ascendancy by keeping the different privileged classes in constant rivalry and making them dependent on him.

In his attempt to break imperial encirclement, Francis I did not hesitate to seek allies. He eventually recruited Henry VIII of England to his side. He laid ignominious plans with the Protestant princes of Germany. In 1536, in the famous capitulations, he made common cause with the infidel Suleiman the Magnificent. In the shifting changes of Italy he was supported both by the Popes and the Republic of Venice. The result was four more wars.

Having lost its foothold on the Continent, England turned its energies into the affairs of its immediate neighbours and into overseas venture. The British Isles—consisting of England, Wales, and Ireland—lacked national cohesion. But under the Tudors it exhibited great vigour. Notwithstanding the religious conflicts of the age, Henry VIII (1509-48) and his three children Edward VI (1548-53), Mary I (1553-58) and Elizabeth I (1558-1601) created the Church of England, the lasting symbiosis of Monarchy and Parliament and the Royal Navy.

Like his contemporary Francis, Henry VIII strengthened the monarchy considerably. The Tudor Dynasty consistently sought the support of the lesser gentry and middle classes. In this new tradition, Henry enabled the new peers to enrich themselves with the lands of the dissolved monasteries. Most of the country gentry served as the king's justices of the peace, as the local administrators of all decrees of the central government, and as its tax collectors. The merchants did not challenge the political power of the gentry and the crown as long as they were given freedom in commerce. Under Henry VIII, middle-class lawyers like Thomas Cromwell rose to the highest ranks in the royal goverment.

With the support of the new peers, the gentry and the middle classes, Henry asserted the complete sovereignty of the state. England already had the most uniform and centralised judicial system in Europe; Henry's ministers now transformed the Court of the Star Chamber into a major instrument for strengthening royal power. Henry had to share his sovereignty with Parliament, since it alone could change the law of the land and grant new taxes. However, Henry and, later, Elizabeth I, managed to get Parliament to do his bidding.

Sweden's fortunes were tied to the Vasas, in the search for supremacy in the Baltic. In 1527, at the Diet of Vasteras, Gustavus created a church much to his liking. He retained the Catholic rite; but by transferring the landed wealth of the Church to his followers, he created a strong base for a powerful monarchy. His second son John III (1568-92) married the Polish princess and his grandson, Sigismund Vasa (1592-1604), was elected King of Poland. Sigismund was the last hope of Sweden's fading Catholic party and, by the Civil War which engulfed his reign the majority of the nobles identified national independence with Protestantism. Sigismund was deposed in favour of his uncle, Charles IX (1604-11), parent of the Protestant line.

The Young Gustavus Adolphus (1611-32) pursued an energetic foreign policy. Possessed of an immense talent, a navy and a native army, he recovered Kalmar from Denmark in 1613, intervened in Muscovy's affairs in 1614-17, attacked Poland-Lithuania in 1617-29, taking Riga (1621) and besieging Danzig (1626-29). In 1628, with French support, he made his sensational entry into Germany. Under Queen Christina (1632-54), Sweden attained its summit of power with the conquest of Holland. Her cousin Charles X (1654-60) tried to preempt the ambitious policy of Moscow by intervening in Poland-Lithuania. His untimely death led to the comprehensive settlement of the Treaty of Oliva (1660) which ended the Vasa feud and confirmed the independence of Prussia. 'Sweden never gained control of the Baltic... For half a century she played a disproportionate part in European affairs—the terror of the north, the military wonder of the age, the most active of the Protestant power'.

Poland-Lihuania was another country which experienced its 'Golden Age' during the sixteenth and early seventeenth centuries. The two countries merged their separate institutions by the Union of Lublin. Thereafter the Polish nobility and the Roman Catholic faith dominated the orthodox lands of Lithuania and held the frontiers against Muscovy, the Cossacks, and the Tartars. Under Zygmunt I (1506-48) and Zygmunt-August (1548-72), it enjoyed strong links with Italy. Cracow hosted one of the most vibrant of Renaissance courts. The 'Republic' or 'Commonwealth' which came into being at the Union of Lublin (1569) was an early form of Ausgleich between Polish and Lithuanian interests. The Kingdom of Poland accepted the Grand Duchy of Lithuania as an equal partner. In the eighty years which separated the Union of Lublin from the general crisis of 1648, the 'Republic' fared better than its neighbours. The cities, especially Danzig, prospered and the Counter-Reformation did not cause open strife. The monarchy retained its general authority. Though the first elected king Henry Valois (1574-5) was an unmitigated disaster, the next vigorous Stefan Batory (1576-86) commanded respect. His war against Ivan the Terrible in 1578-82 paid rich dividend: possession of Livonia. The third King, Sigismund Vasa (1587-1632) a suffered many vicissitudes.

Turkey and Eastern Europe

A contemporary who rivalled the power and prestige of Francis I and Charles V was the ruler of the Ottoman Empire, Sultan Suleiman I the Magnificent (1520-66). With their infantry corps (the Janissaries), their artillery and their cavalry, the Ottomans were the foremost military power in Europe. A counterpoise was provided by the rise of the powerful military order of the Safavids in Persia. Suleiman overran Iraq and even challenged Portuguese dominion of the Indian Ocean from his bases in Suez and Basra. The Crimean Tartars acknowledged his supremacy as did the Corsair powers of Algiers, Tunis and Tripoli. His armies conquered Hungary in 1526 and threatened Vienna in 1529. With the expansion of his authority along the North African coast and the Adriatic littoral, it seemed as if the Mediterranean, like the Black Sea and the Aegean, might become an Ottoman lake.

Turkish rule was an unlimited despotism, suffering from none of the financial and constitutional weaknesses of the western states. With its disciplined standing army, the Ottoman Empire feared no internal threat except during the periods of disputed succession. Sometimes the Sultan was to content himself with the overlordship of frontier provinces. Moldavia and Walachia were for a time held in this fashion and Transylvania accepted Suleiman as its master in return for support against Ferdinand of Austria.

Despite the expeditions of Charles V against Algiers and Tunis, and the vigorous resistance of Venice and Genoa in the war of 1537-40, the Ottomans retained the initiative in the Mediterranean. Even after Spain, the Papacy, Venice and Genoa had crushed the Turkish army in 1571 in the Battle of Lepanto, the Ottomans took Cyprus and recovered Tunis. North Africa remained an outpost of Islam, but the Ottoman Empire did not again threaten Europe by land and sea until in the date 17th century.

In the 16th century eastern Europe displayed the opposite tendency to the advance of princely absolutism in the west. Here the landowning class achieved a political independence that weakened the power of the monarchy. The towns entered a period of decline and the propertied class reduced their peasantry to servitude. In Poland and Bohemia the peasants were reduced to serfdom in 1493 and 1497, respectively, and in Hungary the last peasant rights were suppressed after the rising of 1514. The gentry controlled Polish in the Sejm (parliament) and when the first Vasa king, Sigismund III, tried to reassert the authority of the Crown in 1587, the opportunity had passed.

Farther to the east, the grand principality of Moscow emerged as a new and powerful despotism. Muscovy became the heir to Kiev during the reign of Ivan III the Great in the second half of the fifteenth century. By his marriage with the Byzantine princess Sofia, Ivan also laid claim to the traditions of Constantinople. His capture of Novogord and repudiation of Tatar overlordship began a movement of Muscovite expansion which was continued by the seizure of Smolensk by his son Basil III and by the campaigns of his grandson Ivan IV the Terrible (1533-84). The latter destroyed the Khanates of Kazan and Astrakhan and reached the Baltic by his conquest of Livonia. He was the first to use the title of Tsar, and his arbitrary exercise of power was more ruthless than that of the Ottoman Sultan. By establishing the **Oprichnina**, the forerunner of subsequent Russian security agencies, he was able to unleash a reign of unrestrained terror. By appointing the first Patriarch of Moscow, he completed the separate and dependent nature of the Russian Orthodox Church, henceforth severed from all outside influences. After his death Muscovy was engulfed in the vortex of troubles, when Polish, Swedish and Cossack armies devastated the land. The accession of the Romanov dynasty in 1613 heralded a period of gradual recovery. Except for occasional embassies, Muscovy remained isolated from the west. Despite its relationship with Greek civilisation, it knew nothing of the Renaissance. It was equally untouched by Reformation and Counter-Reformation, the consequences by which convulsed western Europe in the late sixteenth century.

CHAPTER 6

COMMERCIAL REVOLUTION IN WESTERN EUROPE—MERCANTILISM

Mercantilism—economic theory and practice common in Europe from the 16th to the 18th century—promoted governmental regulation of a nation's economy for the purpose of augmenting state power at the expense of rival national powers. It was the economic counterpart of political absolutism. Its 17th century publicists—Thomas Mun in England, Jean-Baptiste Colbert in France, and Antonio Serra in Italy—never used the term themselves. It was given currency by the Scottish economist Adam Smith in his **Wealth of Nations** (1776). The mercantile theory held that colonies exist for the economic benefit of the mother country and are useless unless they help to achieve profit. The mother nation should draw raw materials from its possessions and sell them finished goods, with the balance favouring the European country. This trade should be monopolistic, with foreign intruders barred.

The motives of pushing national interests beyond the portals of Europe were various—political, religious and economic. The political motives were interwined with the economic. In so far as national governments sought opportunities of enrichment in order to augment their power in Europe, the inspiration was political. Such was certainly the object of Spain. Religious motives actuated the Spanish and Portuguese courts. While the Spaniards hoped to bring the true faith to the heathen, the Portuguese were eager to destroy the Mahommedans whom they encountered. Later on, the hope of freedom from persecution led certain elements to seek asylum across the seas. However, the Huguenots sought the refuge of English colonies, as the colonies of their own country were barred to them. But the predominant motive force of all the imperialist powers was economic. Most of the European countries sent exploring expeditions in all directions in order to get direct control of the treasures of the East, especially spices. When a new world was opened up, the quest of gold and silver gripped the Europeans. Then the various resources of the newly discovered lands such as tea, coffee, sugar, tobacco, furs, as well as raw materials for manufacture such as cotton and wool became the objects of attention. The mercantile system gave added stimulus to the planting of colonies. Governments were interested not only because the traffic enriched their subjects but also because they saw in it new openings for taxation. The movement also received additional stimulus because it enabled the countries to gratify their taste for new or cheaper luxuries. In any case, the opening up of new fields accelerated trade and governments are always susceptible to the lure of easy money. Risk of capital at first was an affair of governments; but the risk was soon to be shifted to the private agencies, the chartered companies.

In trading with distant countries the English merchants had learned that it was necessary to bind themselves into a company for the purpose of distributing the risk and for providing adequate means of protecting their stations. The genesis of the so-called Merchant Adventurers dated from the early fifteenth century. It received a charter from the crown with a monopoly of trade and a common fund for joint expenses. The idea of a monopoly dated as far back as the Emperor Frederick II in the twelfth century and the efforts of the guilds had always been in the direction of engrossing the local market. In the case of the Merchant Adventurers and other "regulated" companies, any member was free to carry on his trade as an independent merchant. Parallel, however, with the regulated company, ran the joint-stock company—which traded as a corporate body and whose members owned a part of the common stock and shared all profits or losses. The most glaring examples of this type were the English East India Company, founded in 1600, the Dutch East India Company, founded in 1602, and the French East India Company, in 1664.

Despite some marginal differences between the different charters, nearly all had certain features in common. They were given a monopoly as against other merchants; they were empowered to acquire land, establish trading posts, and to make laws. By implication they might make treaties with native princes or wage wars. As a matter of fact, they exercised sovereign rights in the name of the government to which they belonged. Unlike the Spanish and Portuguese merchants, most of the chartered companies enjoyed very large initiative. Some of the continental companies, especially the French, were heavily subsidised by the government. However, there was little difficulty in obtaining capital either through the selling of shares or by raising loans.

While for most countries the chartered company was the favourite method of trade and commerce with the East, the role of the companies in transactions with the West proved less enduring. Whereas the countries in the East, characterized by a dense population, were not adapted to colonisation, most of the North America—sparsely populated—afforded admirable opportunities for settlement. As settlers in the English colonies began to increase, they resented the control of a Board of Directors whose headquarters were in London. Having failed to protect the monopoly granted to the Companies the Crown finally took the step of revoking their charters altogether.

The growing importance of the chartered company, especially the joint-stock company, was keenly felt owing to the tremendous opportunities presented by the opening of new stores of wealth. Another means of meeting this abundance of wealth was known as 'Mercantilism'. As an economic conception it included, first of all, the notion of national self-sufficiency, and such an idea was explained by the emergence of the modern state itself. The practice of state intervention to regulate trade and commerce had been a very early phenomenon. But mercantilism developed into something more aggressive than this idea of economic self-defence. It denoted commercial aggression deliberately waged at the expenses of one's neighbours. The keenness of the competition for the trade in the East and the inflow of gold and silver from the West opened up a vast prospect. It came to be generally believed that the accumulated stock of bullion was the index of a nation's wealth. Therefore, it became the policy of all governments to prevent all exportation of the precious metals, and to attract as much of it to their own dominions. This latter object was to be obtained by securing a 'favourable balance of trade.' This quest of self-dependence and to outbid a commercial rival were a logical culmination to the process of political consolidation and territorial aggrandizement that formed the keynote of seventeenth century. Mercantilism was inherent in the spirit of the age.

The colonies played an important part in the system. They were required to supply the mother country with things that would dispense her from buying elsewhere and, above all, to send her the raw materials that were needed for manufactures. The colony was, of course, not to be permitted to manufacture anything that might jeopardise the industries of the mother country. Thus a cardinal feature of mercantilism was that the resources of the colonies were exclusively reserved for the mother country. Metropolis and colonies were together to form one economic unit.

Besides the attainment of economic independence, mercantilism strove for supremacy in commercial competition. This involved four things : the establishment of protective tariffs, designed not only to protect home industries but to discourage the importation of foreign goods; the artificial stimulation of industry by government subsidies and other privileges; the maintenance of high standards of quality for manufactured goods; and the securing of commercial treaties.

The goal of all this endeavour was to force the foreigner to buy more than he sold. By the Methuen Treaty with Portugal in 1703, Great Britain secured a monopoly of the Portuguese market for her goods. Yet with the passage of time, the mercantilists—especially in England—gave much less weight to the purely monetary aspects of their doctrines. The unfavourable balance of trade of England with France was offset by the influx of Huguenots refugees who brought their wealth and technical skill to England. As capitalism developed, the investments possessed by one people in the country of another tended to bridge the gulf between the exports and imports. In any case, governmental regulation was designed to foster the native industries and to outbid the foreign competitors.

Despite the main features of mercantilism, there were some subtle difference in scope or application. English mercantilist policy paid great attention to shipping. The Navigation Acts restricting the importation of goods, except in English ships, was one of the most rigorous applications of the mercantile system. In England, where the guilds were defunct, government control of industry was inevitably more direct, whereas, in France, where the guilds formed a conveniant economic unit and where the crown built up large industries itself, government control was pervasive. One may note that Dutch tariffs were normally low, for the simple reason that Holland required the free flow of imports from all quarters. Mercantilism had a general character and certain objects but its application varied according to conditions. In a sense, Prussia was the most mercantilist country in the world since agriculture was brought within its orbit.

Mercantilism was something of a planned economy and put the nation's prosperity above the interest of the individual. The business element cared nothing else but profit. But government control was very rigid during the time of Elizabeth and James I. But whatever its practical features, mercantilism, as it was applied, often defeated its own ends. Raw materials from abroad were sometimes debarred when certain industries needed them. The English Navigation Acts often prevented the much desired cargoes which the merchants needed. The first, passed by Cromwell's government in 1651, attempted chiefly to exclude the Dutch from England's carrying trade: goods imported from Africa, Asia or America could be brought only in English ships. After the royal Restoration in 1660, Parliament renewed and strengthened the Cromwellian measure. Mercantilism also took little account of the fact that trade itself was broadly international and that an unfavourable balance with one country might be made up by a favourable balance with another. Moreover, the system led frequently to commercial war, which, in turn, led sometimes to actual war. When James I, in the interest of the dyers, stopped the exportation of English cloth until it had first been dyed and finished, the Dutch closed their ports to English cloths, and England was finally forced to recede. In France, Colbert debarred the English goods by imposing high tarriffs. During most of the eighteenth century, England similarly treated France which contributed to strained relations. It is also fairly evident that industry fostered by government—as in France—created a spirit of dependence and inevitably discouraged enterprise.

Later, mercantilism was severely criticised. Advocates of laissez-faire argued that there was really no difference between domestic and foreign trade and that all trade was beneficial—both to the trader and the public. They denied the idea that a nation could grow rich only at the expense of another and argued that trade was, in reality, a two-way affair. Faith in mercantilism waned during the 18th century, because of the influence of French physiocrats, who advocated the rule of nature, whereby trade and industry would be left to follow a natural course.

CHAPTER 7

GROWTH OF PARLIAMENTARY INSTITUTION IN ENGLAND

After emerging from Feudalism into the form of a modern state, England was able to dispense with the rule of an autocratic monarch. The predominant issue in the crucial period of English history was whether the constitutional liberties of the English people were entrenched to withstand the arbitrariness of the monarchy. It may be nöted that England was particulary fortunate in her geography. She enjoyed a greater security than continental states like France or Prussia, and after the loss of Calais in 1558 she remained more or less pacific without challenging the military power of her continental rivals. A greater concentration on domestic affairs had the effect of developing in England a more vigorous national sentiment than anywhere else in Europe. Underlying this sentiment was the Englishman's stubborn insistence on managing his own affairs—a national quality that was perhaps ingrained in his character. To appreciate the force of this historic individualism we should hark back to the growth of the constitution. It was a slow but gradual growth, rather the product of struggle and trial than of the propounding of abstract theories.

The English constitution is a compound of certain usages and rules of procedure, together known as the common law, certain characteristics, customs, parliamentary statutes and judicial interpretations. The Common Law is judge-made law in contradistinction to statutes, that is, Acts passed by parliament. Originally, a body of usages "common" to the realm, it grew by decision and by record, not by enactment. Part of the constitution is written, but much of it is not. Even in its crude beginnings, it received a certain respect from kings and nobles alike. Local self-government, which had been a legacy of the Anglo-Saxon period, was fostered and developed under the Normans; and it was by virtue of the common law that the individual was protected in many of his rights.

During the thirteenth century the English central administration continued to increase in scope. Royal authority over lands and law, which had been advanced so promisingly under Henry II (1154-1189), reached its climax in Edward I's reign. The central government was now issuing statutes binding on all Englishmen and the common law was administered by a powerful system of fixed and itinerant royal courts. Full administrative records were being maintained and the simple Exchequer of Henry I's (1100-1135) day had evolved into a highly efficient machine.

England, like other medieval kingdoms, was a feudal monarchy dominated by the lord-king and his aristocratic vassals. Since the traditional feudal relationships of lord and vassal was a relationship of mutual rights and obligations, a monarchy arising out of such a system tended to be limited rather than absolute. King John (1199-1216) was taxing his subjects as they had never been taxed before. The baronial reaction of 1215 was both a protest against John and an effort to reverse the trend towards royal authoritarianism. On June 15, 1215, the rebellious barons met John at Runnymede on the Thames. The King was presented with a document known as the Articles of the Barons, on the basis of which Magna Carta was drawn up. It was a document hallowed in history and has been interpreted as the fountainhead of English constitutional monarchy. It was remarkable in many ways as it sought to provide protection for all freemen. It was an attempt to provide guarantees against arbitrary disregard of feudal rights. The celebrated Clause 39 promised judgement by peers or by the law of the land to all freemen. The barons, however, were not attempting to dismantle royal government, but, rather, they tried to ensure that the king was beneath rather than above the law. In striving to make King John a good feudal lord, the barons in 1215 were moving, perhaps unconsciously, towards constitutional monarchy.

The chief constitutional problem in the years following the Magna Carta was the question how an unwilling king might be forced to stay within the bounds of law. Magna Carta itself relied on a committee of 25 barons who were empowered—should the king violate the charter—to call upon the English people "to distrain and distress him in every possible way."

During the minority of John's nine-year old son, Henry III (1216-72), the administration was supervised by a baronial council. Ever since its beginning, the English monarchy had customarily arrived at important decisions of policy with the advice of a royal council of nobles, prelates and officials. In Anglo-Saxon times, this council was called the Witenagemot; after 1066 it was known as the **Curia Regis**. Traditionally, royal councils were of two types. Ordinary royal business was conducted in a small council consisting of the King's household officials and some barons. But in moments of crisis, the Kings supplemented the small council by summoning the important noblemen and churchmen of the realm to meet as a great council. It was this great baronial council that eventually evolved into Parliament.

A key factor in the evolution from Great Council to Parliament was the trend in the thirteenth century toward including representatives of the country gentry and the townsmen along with the great barons and prelates. This development resulted from the royal policy of summoning the great council for the purpose of obtaining approval for some uncustomary tax.

The baronial opposition to Henry III arose from the fact that he summoned the great council for the ostensible purpose of obtaining their consent to new taxes. They might have been propelled by the idea 'No taxation without consultation.' They responded to Henry's fiscal demands with increasing reluctance, until matters came to a crisis in 1258. In order to obtain desperately the financial succour, King Henry submitted to a set of baronial limitations on royal power known as the Provisions of Oxford.

These Provisions forced the king to govern according to good custom and in consultation with his magnates. The Great Council was to be summoned at least three times a year and was to include, along with its usual membership, 12 men 'elected' by the 'community', i.e. chosen by the barons. These 12 were empowered to speak for the magnates in the Great Council. The Provisions of Oxford also established a Council of Fifteen, chiefly baronial in composition, which shared with the king control over the royal administration. The Council was given authority over the exchequer and was empowered to appoint the Chancellor and other high officers of state.

The Provisions of Oxford turned out to be unworkable because of baronial factionalism. Henry resumed exclusive control over his government and resorted to arbitrary policies that led the barons into open rebellion. The barons, led by Simon de Montford, defeated the royal army at Lewes in 1264 and captured Henry himself. For the next 15 months, Simon ruled England in the King's name, sharing authority with two baronial colleagues and a committee of magnates similar to that of the Provisions of Oxford. The rule of Simon de Montfort and his Committee was augmented periodically by meetings of the great council—commonly called "Parliaments". In 1265 the monarchy rallied under the leadership of Henry's talented son, Edward. A baronial army was defeated at Evesham and Simon's rebellion faltered and died.

Earlier in 1265 Simon de Montfort had summoned a great council—a parliament—which included for the first time all three of the classes that were to characterise the parliaments of the later Middle Ages. Edward I (1272-1307) fostered the concept of the community of the realm and the practice of calling representative knights of the shire and burgesses from the towns to Parliament. Representatives were needed to give consent to taxation, as well as to enhance communication between the king and his subjects. The process of petitioning the King and his council in Parliament was greatly encouraged. Historians have argued much about the nature of Edward's Parliament. Some see Edward as responding to the dictates of Roman Law, while others interpret the development of Parliament in terms of the practical solution of financial and political problems. Historians used to refer to the 1295 assembly as the Model Parliament because it contained all the elements later associated with the word 'Parliament'. The writ to the sheriffs asking them to call knights and burgesses did, however, reach a final form in 1295. They were to be summoned "with full and sufficient authority on behalf of themselves and the community... to do whatever shall be ordained by common counsel." Representatives of the lower clergy were also summoned. This Parliament was fully representative of local communities and of the whole community of the realm.

In the reign of Edward I, parliament may be said to have acquired an established position, for the king was made to understand that all new taxes were depended on a previous grant from parliament. Generally speaking, the House of Lords was, prior to the seventeenth century, the more important body, though it was customary from as early as 1407 for grants of money to be first made in the Commons and then passed in the Lords. There were also grievances that the crown was expected to redress; and it became customary for parliaments to attach conditions to the granting of supplies. Sometimes also, as in the reign of Edward III (1327-77), parliament granted money for a specific purpose, such as war with Scotland, thus heralding the system of legislative appropriations. Henry IV's (1399-1413) relations with Parliament were uneasy. The main problem was, of course, money. His needs were great, threatened as he was by rebellion in England and war in France. A central issue was Parliament's demand, that the king take back all royal land that had been granted and leased out since 1366. The King could hardly adopt a measure that would cause much upheaval. Arguments in 1406 were so protracted that the Parliament met for 159 days, becoming the longest Parliament of the mediaeval period. On several occasions, the Commons insisted on taxes being spent in the way that they wished, primarily on the defense of the realm.

However, in the matter of sharing the legislative power with the king, Parliament's progress was not so rapid. At first, Parliament merely presented petitions to the crown, which the latter might or might not accede. Since it met only at the royal summons, it was easy for a king to forget his promise. By the middle of the fifteenth century parliament was found enacting many statutes itself, though the royal sanction was necessary to complete the operation. However, little progress was made in the exercise of control over the initiative of the crown. A body known as the Privy Council (an offshoot of the former Great Council) constituted the King's body of advisers, and some of them served as his minister. During the reign of Edward III the commons devised the means known as "impeachment" for getting rid of an unpopular minister. The commons placed its charges before the lords and if the offender was found guilty, his removal was assured. But direct participation of the legislature in governmental policy was yet to come.

Meanwhile, the Common Law extended its protection to the individual subject. In England, theoretically, a person indicted for crime could not be kept in prison indefinitely without a trial. Moreover, any officer of the crown who violated the rights of the individual was liable to be sued before a jury. Thus, in the words of the famous English jurist, Sir John Fortescue, "The King of England cannot alter nor change the laws of the realm according to his pleasure." England had drifted to a different direction from other countries governed by Roman law, according to which the king's pleasure had the force of law. However, Parliament was not the sole repository of the legislative power. Kings had a practice of issuing proclamations which often curtailed the liberty of a subject. Sometimes, the Crown suspended the operation of law by the application of the so-called dispensing power which foreshadowed trouble for the house of Stuarts in the seventeenth century.

In spite of the growth of Parliament, some of the sovereigns of the House of Tudor (there were five sovereigns : Henry VII (1485-1509). Henry VIII (1509-47), Edward VI (1547-53) Mary I (1553-8) and Elizabeth (1558-1603) did govern "according to their pleasure." The Wars of the Roses had something to do with this curious revival of the royal power. Further, the century of civil war which Englishmen had had to endure made them willing to accept a strong monarchy for the sake of their economic interests. The same feeling became evident during the struggles that ensued with the Papacy and Spain. The Tudors did not give the impression of wanting to set up absolute monarchy and they were eager to win the sympathies of their subjects. Before the period closed there were unmistakable signs that Parliament had begun to outgrow the royal tutelage. Thanks to England's constitutional traditions the monarchy was limited in theory, whatever it was in practice. The crown could contest the theory at its own peril. Such was the lesson to be learned by the house of Stuart.

During the Stuart period, there was no longer felt that need of unity in the face of peril, which had kept Englishmen loyal to Elizabeth. The personality of some of the Stuarts invited troubles. James expounded the doctrine of the divine right of Kings and such pronouncements were looked upon as a declaration of war against the Englishman's liberties. As Trevelyan has said, James knew Scotland, but not England, and Charles I knew neither.

The most important reason for the coming struggle between the Crown and the Parliament was the failure of the latter to comprehend the financial needs of the Crown. The struggle between Crown and Parliament was generally over money, though it also involved a defence of Parliament's privileges against attack. Parliament was parsimonious in granting money to James, and there was much wrangling over the nature of the royal prerogative. Under Charles I the struggle became acute. He dissolved the first Parliament because he refused to tolerate criticism of his government. The second fared no better since it refused to grant any money until an unpopular minister was removed. After a bitter experience with his third Parliament, Charles I resolved to get along without this recalcitrant body. In the intervals during which no Parliament met (and none at all met from 1629 to 1640) the king used different expedients for raising money by questionable means. Thrice on different grounds he imprisoned certain members of the House of Commons, onè of whom eventually died in the Tower. Every time parliament had met, it had reiterated its privileges. In the famous Petition of Right (1628) it extorted the royal sanction to a condemnation of arbitrary imprisonment and punishment by martial law. And so the see-saw struggle for political supremacy between the Crown and Parliament went on. On some occasions the House of Commons exceeded its own rights as once it refused to adjourn at the royal command. But more often it was the king who stretched his prerogative. Charles I, for his part, was something of an autocrat who did not brook any opposition. He dismissed his third Parliament with the warning that if it would not give him money he would raise it himself.

It became obvious to the king of England that unless he could pack the House of Commons, he could not hope to become absolute without an army. In 1640 the Scots invaded England. Charles I was forced to accept a humiliating treaty whereby he paid for the upkeep of the Scottish army and agreed to call another Parliament. This Parliament, known as the 'Long Parliament' brought about a constitutional revolution. Charles I was forced to assent to an act that authorised Parliament to meet once every three years whether or not summoned by the Crown (the Triennial Act). He was also made to abolish such unpopular prerogative courts as High Commission and Star Chamber and to eliminate all feudal revenues. His two closest ministers, Strafford and Archbishop Laud, were impeached. A parliamentary statute was passed demanding Strafford's execution, and the king assented to it. Despite all his concessions, a majority of the members of the House of Commons did not trust Charles I with control of the army. The situation came to a head in October 1641 when there was a revolt. Parliament voted by a narrow majority to assume command of the militia, an act that precipitated civil war.

The Crown was loyally supported by most of the nobility. The Parliamentary forces had the advantage of superior resources. Moreover, the rebels produced a man of organizing ability, Oliver Cromwell, whose 'New Model Army' was a potent weapon to vanquish the King's forces and make Charles I a prisoner. Negotiations with the King infuriated the army because it believed that Parliament would compromise its ideals. On December 6, 1648, army troops, under the direction of Colonel Thomas Pride, purged the House of Commons. 45 members were arrested and 186 were kept away. A rump of about 75 active members were left to do the army's bidding. On January 30, 1649, Charles I was beheaded.

A sort of republic was set up, known as the Commonwealth. But as it rested on the army, of which Cromwell was still head, it was actually a military dictatorship. Cromwell died in 1658 leaving his son Richard as his designated successor. But he proved unequal to the emergency. Control over the army fell to General George Monk who reestablished the Long Parlaiment of 1640. Under his direction the Crown was restored to Charles II. In May 1660, Charles II, eldest son of the late King, assumed his duties and by 1661 the constitution had recovered its normal character. Both king and Parliament had to rehearse the rules of cohabitation.

The moral strength of Parliament, compared to its position under the Tudors, had certainly been enhanced as it had made, as well as unmade a king. Politically, the Restoration had achieved a kind of balance between Crown and Parliament. The king could still veto legislation or dissolve Parliament when he chose, but it was Parliament that initiated legislation.

The most irreconciliable issue between king and Parliament was religion. Charles II had Catholic sympathies and a French Catholic queen. His brother and heir-apparent—James, Duke of York, was an open Catholic. In the last four years of his reign, Charles II met no parliament. Charles II died suddently in 1685 and was succeeded by his brother James. He was determined to make the Catholic faith the exclusive religion in his kingdom. In 1687, by virtue of the dispensing power, he suspended the penal laws against both Catholics and Dissenters. These actions opened old sores, but Englishmen would have put up with him if he had had no male heir. In 1688, the queen, however, bore a son, James, heir to the throne. Threatened with an eventual Roman Catholic succession, prominent nobles invited William of Orange (grandson of James I) and his wife Mary, to the throne. In December 1688, James fled to France; and the idea of absolute monarchy was forever shattered. No wonder the English have called it their 'Glorious Revolution.'

The significance of the Revolution of 1688 lay in the fact that it placed sovereignty into the hands of Parliament. The new Parliament that met acclaimed William and Mary as sovereigns but only after they had formally accepted a declaration of rights. With some additions, the declaration was converted into a statute. By the so-called Bill of Rights (1689) all the various abuses—like suspending or dispensing with the laws—were denounced and it was held that without parliamentary consent a standing army was illegal. It has been observed: "The Bill of Rights decided in favour of the people and against the king all the principal questions which had been contested throughout the Stuart period." The doctrine of 'absolute despotic power' as the jurist Blackstone adumbrated had been transferred from the monarch to the elected Parliament. In theory it authorises Parliament the power to rule with all the trappings of authoriatinism that was previously enjoyed by the Kings. An additional safeguard that the king should not rule without parliament was afforded by the Mutiny Act (1690) which made the army dependent upon legislative grant voted for one year's duration. Later, by the Act of Settlement, the judges were made removable only upon the request of both houses—a measure which freed the bench from royal control. The Toleration Act (1689) permitted all forms of Protestant worship; Unitarians were explicitly excluded, as were Catholics and Jews.

CHAPTER 8

THE THIRTY YEARS' WAR— ITS SIGNIFICANCE IN EUROPEAN HISTORY

The Thirty Years' War (1618-48) arose out of a religious revolt in Bohemia, but spread like a prairie fire until most European states were involved in the struggle. 'Almost all', wrote one distinguished historian, 'were actuated by fear rather than by lust of conquest or passion of faith. They wanted peace and they fought for thirty years to be sure of it. They did not learn then, and have not learned since, that war only breeds war.'

On May 23, 1618, a delegation of Czech nobles entered the Hradcany Castle in Prague and threw the Habsburg governors from the window into a castle ditch. They were protesting against recent attack on Protestant churches, against Archduke Ferdinand's assumption of the Bohemian throne without an election, and against his alleged violation of the Royal Charter of Toleration. In May 1619 the rebel army even laid siege to Ferdinand in Vienna. Within weeks, however, they were forced to withdraw because a major Spanish army, partly financed by the Pope, invaded Bohemia.

The appearance of Spanish troops and Papal gold in eastern Europe reawakened the fears of the Protestant rulers of the Empire. To Protestant observers the logic of Spanish intervention seemed aggressive rather than defensive. It was also feared that if the Protestant cause was neglected and, by consequence, suppressed, the Protestant princes adjoining Bohemia were to bear the burden of the victorious army. The same argument carried weight with the director of the Protestant Union, Frederick V of the Palatinate, parts of whose territories adjoined Bohemia. So, when, in the summer of 1619, the Bohemians deposed Ferdinand and offered the Crown to Frederick, he was favourably disposed.

Frederick accepted the Bohemian crown and in so doing rekindled the worst fears of the German Catholics. The Catholic League was recreated, and in December 1619 its leaders authorized the levy of an army of 25,000 men to be used as Maximilian of Bavaria thought fit. At the same time, Philip III and Archduke Albert each promised to send a new army into Germany to assist Ferdinand who had succeeded the late Mathais as the Holy Roman Emperor. The crisis was now apparent and as the Palatinate diplomate court Albert Salms warned his master:

> If it is true that the Bohemians are about to depose Ferdinand and elect another King, let everyone prepare at once for a war lasting twenty, thirty or forty wars. The Spaniards and the House of Austria will deploy all their worldly goods to recover Bohemia.

The Triumph of the Catholics, 1619-29

Frederick V entered Prague and was crowned King in October 1619, but the Catholic net was already closing around him. The axis linking Vienna with Munich, Brussels and Madrid enjoyed widespread support: subsidies came from Rome and Genoa, while Tuscany and Poland sent troops. States favourable to Frederick's cause were persuaded to remain neutral. Spanish diplomacy kept England out of the war, while French efforts persuaded the Protestant Union to remain aloof. The Dutch Republic also did nothing. In the summer of 1620 a Spanish army was able to cross from the Netherlands and occupy the Rhine Palatinate. Meanwhile, the armies of the Emperor and the League, reinforced with Spanish and Italian contingents, invaded the rebel heartland. On November 8, 1620, in the first significant battle of the war, at the White Mountain outside

Prague, Frederick's forces were routed. The unfortunate prince fled northward.

This was total victory and it might have remained the last word but for events in the Low Countries. The Dutch, fearing a concerted attack by both Spanish and Austrian Habsburgs, decided to provide an asylum for the defeated Frederick and to supply diplomatic and military assistance to his cause. In 1622, and again in 1623, armies were raised for Frederick with Dutch money, but they were defeated. The shattered armies retreated towards the Netherlands, drawing the Catholic forces behind them.

The Emperor's political position, however, weakened considerably in the course of 1623. Although his armies won impressive victories in the field, they were able to do so thanks to massive financial and military support from the Catholic League, controlled by Maximilian of Bavaria. Ferdinand II, thanks to Spanish and Papal subsidies, maintained some 15,000 men himself, but the League provided him with perhaps 50,000. Thus Maximilian's armies had, in effect, won Ferdinand's victories. Now that all common enemies had been defeated, Maximilian sought his reward: the lands and electoral title of the outlawed Frederick of the Palatinate. Don Balthasar de Zuniga, chief minister of Ferdinand's major ally, Spain, warned that the consequences of acceding to this demand could be serious. But in October 1622 he died. So in January 1623 the Emperor felt able to proceed with the investiture of Maximilian as Elector Palatine.

Zuniga, however, had been right, the electoral transfer provoked an enormous outcry, for it was clearly unconstitutional. The Golden Bull of 1356, which was universally regarded as the fundamental law of the empire, ordained that the electorate should remain in the Palatine house in perpetuity. The transfer of 1623 thus undermined a cornerstone of the constitution. Inside Germany, a pamphlet war against Maximilian and Ferdinand began; outside, sympathy for Frederick at last created that international body of support for his cause which had previously been lacking. The Dutch and the Palatine exiles engineered an alliance involving France, England, Savoy, Sweden and Denmark that was dedicated to the restoration of Frederick to his forfeited lands and titles (The Hague Alliance, December 9, 1624). Its leader was Christian IV of Denmark (1588-1648), one of the richest rulers in Christendom. He invaded the empire in June 1625 under cover of defending the Protestant cause.

The Protestant diplomatic campaign had not gone unnoticed. Maximilian's field commander, Count Tilly, requested the emperor to send reinforcements. Ferdinand obliged: in the spring of 1625 he authorised Albrecth von Wallenstein, military governor of Prague, to raise an imperial army and to meet the Danish threat. The Danes were routed at the Battle of Lutter (August 26, 1626). The joint armies of Tilly and Wallenstein then conquered the Danish mainland itself. Christian made peace in 1629, promising never again to intervene in the empire.

After the victories, important new policies were initiated by Ferdinand which aimed at exalting the Catholic religion and his own authority. In the Habsburg provinces there was widespread confiscation of land and a new also of loyal landowners like Wallenstein—was established. At the same time freedom of worship for Protestants was restricted or abolished. Fortified by his success in the Habsburg lands, he decided to implement new policies in the empire. First, disloyal rulers were replaced (the Palatinate went to Maximilian, Mecklenburg to Wallens-tein). Next, serious steps were taken to reclaim Church lands that had fallen into Protestant hands. On March 28, 1629, an Edict of Restitution was issued which declared unilaterally that all Church lands secularised since 1552 must be returned at once, that Calvinism was an illegal creed in the empire, and that ecclesistical princes had the same right as secular ones to insist that their subjects should be of the same religion as their ruler. The last cause was clearly contrary to the terms of the Peace of Augsburg, which Protestants regarded as a central pillar of the organisation. However, the imperial edict was enforced by the armies of Wallenstein and Tilly.

The Crisis of the War, 1629-1635

If Maximilian of Bavaria desired the title of Elector as his reward for supporting Ferdinand,

Spain required imperial support for its war against the Dutch. Spain began to think of creating a Baltic navy, with imperial assistance, which would cleanse the inland sea of Dutch shipping. But the plan aborted, for the imperial army failed in 1628 to conquer the port of Stralsund, selected as the base for the new fleet. Now with Denmark defeated, Madrid again pleaded for the loan of an imperial army, and this time the request was granted. In the end, however, the troops did not march to the Netherlands : instead they went to Italy. Lacking the resources to withstand the forces of Spain alone, Italy appealed to France for support. Louis XIII (1610-43) and Cardinal Richelieu (Chief Minister 1624-42) were, however, engaged in a desperate war against the Calvinist subjects. It was only after the defeat of the rebels that the French troops could enter Italy. It was to meet this threat that the Emperor was asked by Philip IV of Spain (1621-65) to send his troops to Italy rather than to the Netherlands. The Dutch Republic was saved from a immediate danger and the Emperor's hold on Germany was weakened.

The Swedish phase, 1628-35, began when Gustavus Adolf (1611-32) sent a contingent to hold Stralsund with the intention of preserving the security of the Baltic. In 1630, fortified by the Treaty of Barwalde with France, he proceeded to restore Protestant fortunes with vigour. In 1631 he failed to relieve Magdeburg, but at Breitenfeld, just outside Leipzig in Saxony, Gustavus was victorious in September 1631. The main Catholic field army was destroyed, and the Swedish Protestant host overran most of Central Germany and Bohemia in the winter of 1631-2. The next summer they occupied Bavaria. Although Gustav died in the battle of Lutzen on November 16, 1632, his forces were again victorious and his cause was directed with equal skill by his chief adviser, Axel Oxenstierna. The Protestant cause faltered until revived once more by the League of Heilbronn. In 1634 Wallenstein opened negotiations, only to be placed under the ban of the Empire and assassinated. After the decisive defeat of the Swedish in the field of Nordlingen, the Emperor made peace with the Lutheran princes at Prague on May 30, 1635. The Edict of Restitution was revoked. The Protestant signatories obtained a guarantee for their form of worship and was allowed to retain for a half century the lands and revenues which they had taken from the Roman Church.

The European War in Germany, 1635-45

The partial settlement of the issue behind the war led many in Germany to look forward to a general peace. Certainly the exhaustion of many areas of the empire was a powerful incentive to end the war. While visiting Germany in 1636, the English physician William Harvey (discoverer of the circulation of blood) wrote:

> The necessity they have here is of making peace on any condition, where there is no more means of making war and scarce of subsistence... This warfare in Germany... threatens, in the end, anarchy and confusion.

Attempts were made to convert the Peace of Prague into a general settlement. In 1636-37, at a meeting of the Electors held at Regensburg in 1636-37, Ferdinand II agreed to pardon any prince who submitted to him and promised to negotiate with foreign powers the terms of peace. But the Emperor's death immediately after the meeting ended this initiative. Then, in 1640, the new Emperor, Ferdinand III (1637-57) made attempts to solve the outstanding German problems of the amnesty question and the restitution of church lands. The attempts at peace were not acceptable to France and Sweden, yet no lasting settlement could be made without them.

At this juncture, the war entered a new and wholly secular phase, losing the religious character and gaining the character of the struggle for the ascendancy between the Bourbons and the Habsburgs in France. There was little indeed of the religious spirit in a struggle in which Catholic France and Protestant Sweden were allied with the Protestant Dutch Republic against Lutheran Germany, Catholic Austria and Catholic Spain. There was little of religion, but there was an intolerable amount of horror which savage mercenary troops could inflict upon a helpless population.

But how could the peace objectives be accomplished? The Heilbronn League did not long survive the Battle of Nordlingen and the Peace of Prague and so it became necessary to find an alternative source of support. For a period of eighteen years (1624-42), the political genius of Richelieu, the Prime Minister of Louis XIII, dominated the European scene. He pursued with unwearied zeal for the greatness of France which involved the unmaking of Germany and the downfall of Spain. In 1635, in the wake of Nordlingen, France signed an offensive and defensive alliance with the Dutch Republic (February 8), with Sweden (April 28), and with Savoy (July 11). France mediated a twenty—year truce between Sweden and Poland (September 12). Finally, on May 19, 1635, France declared war on Spain.

The aims of France were very different from those of Sweden and its German allies. France wished to defeat Spain, its rival for more than a century, and its early campaigns in Germany were intended more to prevent Ferdinand from sending aid to his Spanish cousins. Indeed, France only declared war on Ferdinand in March 1636. Sweden avoided a firm commitment to France, leaving the way clear for a separate peace. The war, however, did not go in favour of the allies. French Swedish forces, operating separately, totally failed to reverse the verdict of Nordlingen. Despite the French gains in Alsace and in the middle of the Rhine, and the Swedish victory, the Habsburgs were not subdued. Thus, in 1641, Oxenstierna abandoned his attempt to maintain independence and threw in his lot with France. By the terms of the Treaty of Hamburg (March 15, 1641), the two sides promised not to make a separate peace. Instead joint negotiations with the Emperor and the German princes began. While the talks proceeded, the war was to continue.

The Treaty of Hamburg had at last created a coalition capable of destroying the power both of Ferdinand III and of Maximilian of Bavaria. On the whole, France attacked Bavaria, and Sweden fought the Emperor. On November 2, 1642 the Habsburg's army was routed in Saxony at the Second Battle of Breitenfeld and the Emperor was saved from further defeat by the outbreak of war between Denmark and Sweden (May 1643-August 1645). Yet, even before Denmark's final surrender, the Swedes were back in Bohemia, and at Jankov (March 6, 1645) they totally destroyed another imperial army. The Emperor and his family fled to Graz, while the Swedes advanced to the Danube and threatened Vienna. In the French campaign against Bavaria, Maximilian's forces were decisively defeated at Allerheim (August 3, 1645).

Jankov and Allerheim were two decisive battles of the war, because they destroyed the possibility of the Catholics obtaining a favourable peace settlement. In September 1645 the Elector of Saxony made a separate peace with Sweden and withdrew from the war. Meanwhile, at the peace conference in session in Westphalia, the imperial delegation began to make concessions.

Making Peace, 1645-48

194 European rulers, great and small, were represented at the Congress of Westphalia. Talks went on constantly from the spring of 1643 until the autumn of 1648. The purely German problems were resolved first. In 1645 and 1646, with the aid of French and Swedish mediation, the territorial rulers were granted a large degree of sovereignty, a general amnesty was issued to all German princes, an eighth electorate was created, the Edict of Restitution was finally abandoned, and Calvinism within the Empire was granted official toleration. It succeeded in securing the acceptance of a formula that recognised as Protestant all church lands in secular hands by January 1, 1624, and granted freedom of worship to religious minorities. The Augsburg Settlement of 1555 was, thus, entirely overthrown, and it was agreed that any change to the new formula must be achieved only through the "amicable composition" of the Catholic and Protestant blocs, not by a simple majority.

The Amicable Composition principle was finally accepted by all parties in 1648, thus solving the last German problem. But this did not lead to immediate peace which owed not a little to the difficulty of satisfying the foreign powers involved. Apart from France and Sweden, representatives from the Dutch Republic, Spain and many other non-German participants in the war were present, each of them eager to secure the best settlement they could. The war in the Netherlands was ended on January 30, 1648, when Philip IV of Spain signed a peace that recognised the Dutch Republic as independent. The French government, led by Cardinal Mazarin, was bitterly opposed to this settlement, since it left Spain free to deploy all its forces in the Low Countries against France; as a consequence, France devoted all its efforts to perpetuating the war in Germany. Although Mazarin had already signed a preleminary agreement with the Emperor in September 1646, which ceded parts of Alsace and Lorraine to France, in 1647-48 he started a new campaign in Germany in order to secure more. On May 17, 1648, another Bavarian army was destroyed near Nordlingen, and Maximilian's lands were occupied by the French.

Mazarin's move was thwarted by two developments. On the one hand, the pressure of war created tensions in France that in June 1648 erupted into the revolt known as the Fronde. On the other hand, Sweden made a separate peace with the Emperor. She was offered half of Pomerania, most of Mecklenburg and Bremen and Verdun; she was to receive a seat in the Imperial Diet. With so many tangible gains, and with Germany so prostrated, it was time to wriggle out of the war, even without France; peace was thus signed on August 6.

Without Sweden, Mazarin realised that France needed to make peace at the earliest opportunity. He, therefore, settled with the Emperor on easy terms. France gained only the transfer of a bundle of rights and territories in Alsace and Lorraine and little else. However, Mazarin could derive satisfaction from the fact that the Emperor was firmly excluded from the Empire and was under oath to provide no further aid to Spain.

Importance of the Peace of Westphalia

Some historians have sought to minimise the achievements of the Thirty Years' War and the peace that ended it. The British historian, C.V. Wedgwood, for example, stated categorically:

> The war solved no problem. Its effect, both immediate and indirect, were either negative or disastrous. It is the outstanding example in European history of meaningless conflict.

It is true that the struggle between France and Spain continued with unabated bitterness until 1659 and that within a decade of the Westphalian Settlement, Sweden was at war with Poland (1655-60), Russia (1656-58) and Denmark (1657-8). Even within the empire, there were disputes, Lorraine remained a theatre of war until the Duke signed a final peace with France in 1661. But to expect a single conflict in early modern times to have solved all of Europe's problems is anachronistic. It is wrong to judge the Congress of Westphalia by the standard of the Congress of Vienna (1815). However, the peace conference that ended the Thirty Years' War settled a number of crucial issues.

It was the beginning of a new order in Europe, and Sweden, for all her military power, was forced to respect it. For more than a century, the settlement of 1648 was widely regarded as the principal guarantee of peace and order in Central Europe. In 1761 Rousseau wrote in praise of the 'balance of power' in Europe which, he believed, was anchored in the constitution of the Holy Roman Empire:

> Despite its imperfections, this Imperial Constitution will certainly, while it lasts, maintain the balance in Europe. No prince need fear lest another dethrone him. The Peace of Westphalia may well remain the foundation of our political system for ever.

A wide difference separates the Germany of Frederick Barbarossa from the weak federation of some three hundred and fifty states which emerged from the Westphalian Congress. Then the Emperor exercised a real though irregular authority in Germany. Now his power, though confirmed in Austria, Bohemia and Hungary, was a shadow among the Germans. As late as 1866, the French statesman Thiers claimed that 'Germany should continue to be composed of independent states connected only by a slender federative thread.' That was the principle proclaimed by all Europe at the Congress of Westphalia. It is indeed the balance of power with its fulcrum in Germany, created by the Thirty Years' War and prolonged by the Peace of Westphalia, was a major achievement. Out of the distractions of Germany and the prostration of Spain there emerged the French military ambition of which Louis XIV and Napoleon took full advantage. In the lands of the Austrian Habsburgs, there were now no powerful estates and no Protestant worship. The Habsburg Monarchy, now under the authority of King-emperor, had became a powerful state in its own right.

One great result of the Peace of Westphalia was the secularisation of politics. After 1625, the role of religious issues in European politics steadily receded. This was perhaps the greatest achievement of the war, for it thus eliminate the major destablising influence in European politics. Religiously, the war had ended in a compromise. The right of the prince to choose his religion was confirmed by the Peace of Westphalia. The Pope Innocent X was offended by the concessions made to France and to the Protestants. In 1650 he denounced the Treaty as 'null, void, invalid, iniquitous, unjust, damnable, reprobate, inane, and devoid of meaning for all time.' His hopes for a united Christendom had been dashed for ever. 'After Westphalia, people who could no longer bear to talk of 'Christendom' began to talk instead of "Europe". 'But the chief result of the Thirty Years' War from the political standpoint was the final dissolution of Christendom, conceived as a moral unit. Henceforth there would be national states which acknowledged no allegiance to the Pope. From now on the peace of Europe must rest on what has been called a sovereign state system.

The Thirty Years' War and the Peace of Westphalia also set a new course for international relations. Out of the deliberations of the diplomats there emerged two basic notions: (1) individual sovereign states were the central forces of political life; and (2) relations between sovereign states were subject to mutually accepted rules. By 1648 national states and national cultures were emerging in Western Europe. The nation-state was to become the typical framework within which modern society developed.

CHAPTER 9

ASCENDANCY OF FRANCE

The welding together of the disjointed France of the Valois regime into a strong and compact state was the work of the Bourbon monarchy. The achievement may be ascribed to Henry IV (1589-1610), the first of the Bourbon kings, and to Richelieu, with some finishing touches to the structure by Mazarin and Louis XIV. This process of development is of considerable importance as it explains the ascendancy of France in the seventeenth century as a beacon light to civilisation.

The country had tottered on the brink of disintegration for three decades. The country was impoverished; industry was at a standstill; much of the land was untilled and the country was burdened with financial bankruptcy. The king had little power to enforce respect. Most of the nobility were in league with the foreign enemy and some parts of country were occupied by the Spanish invaders. To cap all, the religious question still remained unsolved. It was generally recognised that only a strong personality could guarantee the unity of the country. Henry was signally qualified to undertake this formidable task as he was an astute politician and was firm enough to inspire confidence.

Henry IV's policy embraced two features—political and economic. On the political side he accomplished three things. *Firstly,* he won over the disaffected nobility by offering them honours and positions. *Secondly,* Henry made peace with Spain, and removed the foreign invader from the soil of France. *Finally,* he issued the Edict of Nantes (April 13, 1598). Though the official religion was to remain Catholic, Henry IV granted concessions to the Calvinists (Huguenots). They were guaranteed freedom of conscience and the right to practice their religion in certain prescribed areas of the country. Huguenots were made eligible to hold the same offices as Roman Catholics. Although the problem of religion was not finally settled by the Edict of Nantes, Henry did succeed in effecting an extended truce during which he could apply himself to the task of restoring the royal position. The religious settlement was essentially a compromise, an act of political expediency.

The crying need of the monarchy was to improve the economic health of the country. Henry was fortunate in this connection to have the services of Duke de Sully as superintendent of finances. Dishonest officials were dismissed and replaced by upright men. Sully then imposed honesty in the collection of the taxes and economy in the expenditure of the revenue. He embarked upon a series of provincial tours, enforcing the repayment of royal debts, thereby increasing the King's revenue. He promoted agriculture by draining marshes, constructing a canal between the Loire and the Seine, and improving the public highways. He gave direct encouragement to industry, especially the manufacture of luxuries. To facilitate industrial revival, he adopted the mercantilist theory of a protective tariff, thus securing a favourable balance of trade and helping France to enjoy a virtual monopoly of the trade in articles of luxury. He also provided the first real statements of government finances in many year. Sully was not an original financial thinker. He undertook no sweeping changes, contenting himself with making the existing system work, for example, by shifting the emphasis from direct to indirect taxation. He succeeded in building up both an annual surplus and substantial reserves.

Sully, however, favoured a much more cautious domestic policy overall than did his sovereign. He disliked merchants and manufacturers and opposed many of the King's economic ventures. Henry IV believed in direct state intervention and took steps to fix wages and to prohibit strikes of workers. In domestic policy, Henry gave increasing power to Sully at the expense of the rest of his council, while in the provinces the responsibilities of the intendant were widened to include the supervision of potentially dissident groups. Henry also took initiative in making commercial treaties with Spain and England, thereby increasing the volume of French trade. He also promoted commerce by such measures as the development of a merchant marine, and encouraged the colonisation of the lands in North America which led to the founding of Louisburg and Quebec—the beginning of the French empire in the New World.

Henry also directed his attention in rehabilitating France's position among the nations. After his agreement with Spain in 1598, Henry turned his attention to the frontier in the east, where the Duke of Savoy held some districts. It seemed that Savoy's possession of Saluzzo—seized from France during the anarchy of the religious wars—might offer the possibility of an adjustment. After futile negotiations Henry brought the Duke to terms by force. By the Treaty of Lyons (1601) coveted districts were ceded to France while Savoy retained Saluzzo. Convinced of the menance of Habsburg power on three sides, Henry tried to embarrass them by indirect means such as sending subsidies to the Dutch in their struggle with Spain and entering into close relations with various Italian States. Henry made an alliance with the Calvinist Union in Germany and set in readiness three armies to march against Austria and Spain. But his life was cut short when he was stabbed to death in the streets of Paris on May 14, 1610.

Despite his tragic end, Henry's reign of seventeen years had resulted in giving his country a new lease of life. In a very real sense, Henry IV was the creator of Bourbon policy.

Henry's reign was followed by the regency of his widow, Marie de Medicis, who ruled on behalf of their young son, Louis XIII (1610-43). Once more the security of the country seemed to be threatened by the factious elements. The work of Henry IV seemed likely to be undone. The country, however, was rescued by probably the greatest minister of the whole Bourbon dynasty, Cardinal de Richelieu. 'If Henry IV was the architect of the Bourbon France, Richelieu was the master-mason.' It was Richelieu who made the King absolute in fact as well as in theory and made the kingdom the most influential in Europe.

Richelieu first came to the attention of the government in 1614, when he was chosen to present the final address of the clergy at the meeting of the Estates General. His eloquence on this occasion won him the notice of Marie de Medicis, who later appointed him her secretary. By 1616 Richelieu was Secretary of State for war and foreign affairs. His career, however, received a check in the following year when a palace revolution overthrew the regency of the Queen Mother. Richelieu followed the Queen Mother into retirement. But in 1619 he recovered his power by reconciling Louis XIII to his mother. After the death in 1621 of Louis's favourite, Charles d' Albert, Duke de Luynes, Richelieu regained effective power. He became a Cardinal in 1622 and in April 1624 gained access to Louis XIII's council. On the disgrace in 1624 of the superintendent of finance, Charles de la Vieuville, he became Louis's principal minister—a position where he remained till the end of his days. Not possessing good health or much energy, Louis XIII allowed the minister to shape the Bourbon policy.

'Richelieu is one of those characters who by force of personality etch themselves in clear, bold strokes on the canvas of history.' He was the embodiment of intellect and will. He was indefatigable in the pursuit of his object and had a clear vision of the primal needs of France. His first objective was to crush a number of revolts of the nobles, the first of which involved the king's younger brother and heir, Gaston de France, Duke d' Orleans. Louis acted ruthlessly, and one of the conspirators, Henri de Talleyrand, was executed in 1626. Then, in 1630, when the King's life was despaired of, the Queen Mother prepared to move against Richelieu. The king, however, recovered and chose to support Richelieu against the wishes of his mother and wife.

In the course of strengthening royal absolutions, Richelieu also came into conflict with the Huguenots. He believed that their right under the Edict of Nantes to maintain armed fortresses impaired the King's position. Protestant rebellions in 1625 and 1627 convinced the Cardinal of the need for a direct confrontation. The major Huguenot citadel of Lal Rochelle was attacked by royal troops in 1627 and, despite the English attempts to assist the Protestants, fell in the following year. Another royal army marched into Langeudoc, where the Huguenot forces were concentrated, and quickly overcame them. The Peace of Alais (1629) left the Huguenots free to enjoy religious and civil liberties, but abolished those special guarantees which had impaired the unity of France. Little more would be heard of them until Louis XIV decided to repeal Henry IV's Edict of Nantes. By sending officials known as Intendants—chosen from the middle classes—to various parts throughout France, Richelieu kept the nobles under a systematic surveillance.

Richelieu's activities were all-embracing. He encouraged commerce and promoted the manufacture of tapestry, glass, silk, linen and woollen cloth. He gave privileges to companies that established colonies in America, Africa and the West Indies. To protect trading and colonial interests, he created a navy which by 1642 had 63 oceangoing vessels.

Richelieu's determination to make France the greatest power in Europe was based on strategic comprehension. His first aim was the security of France, which he hoped to achieve through the occupation of key points on the country's forntiers lying along imperial and Spanish territories. He thus involved France in the War of the Mantuan Succession (1628-31) in northern Italy. Through diplomatic means he worked for the dismissal of Wallenstein, the brilliant general fighting on the side of the Emperor Ferdinand II, whose forces were threatening to destroy the Protestant princes of Germany in the Thirty Years' War. To undermine the power of the Habsburgs, he prolonged this conflict, negotiating with the United Provinces, with Gustav II Adolf of Sweden, with whom he concluded the subsidy Treaty of Barwalde in 1631, agreeing to pay the Swedish king one million livres per year to continue the war; with Gustav's successor, Count Oxenstierna; and with Bernhard, Duke of Saxe-Weimar. Eventually, in 1635, Richelieu committed France to direct conflict with the Habsburgs. Before his death, he had savoured the triumph of having French arms in the Spanish Netherlands, Lorraine, Alsace and Rousillon.

Richelieu's career was something of a contradictory aspect. He undoubtedly followed in the footsteps of Henry IV and Sully in overcoming the threat of anarchy and disorder that was the legacy of the late 16th century. Indeed, his contemporary reputation was one of extreme ruthlessness and arbitrariness in the application of power. Yet he was never more than the king's subservient creature. Richelieu was no innovators: he devised neither new administrative procedures nor novel methods of taxation to secure the king's authority. Indeed, the power of the great financiers grew with the govern-ment's need for additional war revenue. Richelieu's unique contribution lay in the unstinted devotion he gave to the task of elevating royal authority at home and abroad. 'He worked with a single mind for the greatness of France—as that phrase has been understood by a long line of French statesmen by Mazarin and Louis XIV by Danton and Napoleon, by Delcasse and Clemenceau, by Poincare or his pupil Tordieu.' Richelieu died in 1642, and Louis XIII died the following year. France was once again ruled by a regent, the Queen Mother, Anne of Austria. But the task of governing the country fell increasingly into the hands of another cardinal, Jules Mazarin.

Restricted in the exercise of her power by a council, Anne took the step of persuading the Parliament of Paris to give her plenary power. It is questionable whether the Parliament had this right. Meanwhile Anne took as her counsellor Cardinal Mazarin who was now to govern France. A gifted diplomatist and a typical Italian of his day, he was at the same time a person of tortous methods and dubious personal honesty. The government's financial difficulties were once more at the root of the trouble. In the first few years of the regency a variety of expedients were tried to raise additional revenue for the war with Spain. Mazarin's methods were unscrupulous and exasperating. An explosion, long brewing, took place in Paris. Curiously enough, it was the middle class from whom the attack proceeded. The Parliament now demanded rather peremptorily a share in the government. Anne rejected its demands and arrested its president. Barricades were then raised in the city and a rebellion seemed imminent. But the danger came from unexpected quarter. Taking advantage of the Regency's embarrassments, a large section of the nobility joined the fray. They hoped to regain the power which Richelieu had taken from them. 'It was feudalism's last stand against the absolute monarchy.' Fortunately for France, the feudal nobles had little capacity for such a struggle. "The Fronde" as the rebellion was called because of its essential frivolity, was a failure, partly because of divisions among the nobles, partly because Turenne's defection, and partly because the Regent and Mazarin were ready to exploit the weakness of their enemies. When Mazarin fled into exile, the ostensible object of the revolt had apparently slackened. Actually, when the government had gained the upper hand, Mazarin returned, and his position was unassailable.

After the Frondes, Mazarin continued to play a decisive role in government as chief adviser to the young king. His diplomatic skill was demonstrated when he formed the League of the Rhine in 1658. By this, he held the Emperor in check, and, by an alliance with England, he was able at last to bring Spain to her knees. The result was a triumph for Bourbon policy. By the Peace of Westphalia, signed with the Emperor in 1648, France had acquired most of Alsace, the Emperor's recognition to Metz, Toul and Verdun and the retention of certain strategic areas which gave her an advantage in any future conflict with the Habsburgs. By the Treaty of the Pyrennes negotiated with Spain in 1659, France gained Roussillon and Cerdagne in the South and Artois and number of border towns in the north; and the Rhine became France's forntier in the east, while in the south the Pyrennes now formed an unbroken wall. Only in his effort to get Nice and Savoy did Mazarin fail to achieve his objective. Mazarin died in 1661. The young king had attained his majority, and on Mazarin's death took the reins of power in his own hand.

The Age of Louis XIV (1643-1715)

The reign of Louis XIV was the culmination of greatness of France. 'He was the embodiment of the purest monarchy, the most perfect form of absolutism; the architect and inspiration of a model and uniform system of government; the moving spirit of economic and colonial enterprise, the dictator of artistic end intellectual taste, the "Most Christian King" of a Catholic nation that brooked no religious deviation, the doyen of European diplomacy, the commander of the Continents's most formidable armies'.[1] For a time France became a beacon light to all Europe as she was the most civilised country of Europe. Her kingdom was well administered, her public service the most efficient, her armies and navies the best equipped, her manufactures the best, and her court the most artistic. He buttressed his authority with the divine-right doctrines and proclaimed it across Europe by force of arms.

The monarchy reached its acme of efficiency under Louis XIV. His inner council consisted of only three or four members and excluding the King's relatives. Members of this council were known as ministers. The first of these great men were Michel Le Tellier, Hugues de Lionne, and Nicolas Fouquet; but the latter was disgraced within a year and by 1665 his place had been taken by Mazarin's former secretary, Jean-Baptiste Colbert. Le Tellier had been Secretary of State for military affairs under Mazarin's regime and his greatest contribution under Louis was to reorganise the army, reaching formidable proportion of 400,000 men in times of war. The success of Le Tellier and of his son Louvois, who succeeded him, explained the phenomenal dominance of French arms during Louis's reign. Lionne, the expert in foreign affairs, had been the chief negotiator at the Peace of the Pyrennes. All important matters of state were reviewed at the High Council.

Colbert, however, remains the best-known of these intimate counsellors. Of the 17 ministers constituting the High Council, 5 were members

1. Norman Davies : Europe (1996), PP. 615-16.

of the Colbert family. In 1664 Colbert was appointed superintendent of the King's buildings; in 1665, controller general of finances; in 1669, secretary of state for the navy. His capacity for work and his grasp of details were remarkable; but he was not an original thinker. His chief contribution to the King's finances was to make the machinery more efficient, instead of introducing any innovation. Colbert's first achievement was to present the king with a monthly statement of the financial situation. Within ten years of taking office, Colbert, mainly by tightening up the collection of tax and by rationalising the gathering of indirect taxes, succeeded in producing a surplus revenue. He turned a large part of central and northern France into a free-trade area and gave the responsibility for collecting all indirect taxes there to a new syndicate of tax farmers called the Farmers-General. Under Colbert, the total sum levied from indirect taxation rose from 36 million livres to 62 million.

Colbert's interest chiefly concerned industrial production. Adopting the mercantilist doctrines, Colbert sought to direct the economic life of the country as rigidly as possible. France must be self-sufficient and must be in a position to outclass her business rivals. Mercantilism was applied to a fuller extent than before. It was determined what establishments should produce and how they should produce. There must be no wasteful competition within. Colbert stimulated agriculture by increasing and bettering the means of communications. While, on the one hand, he restricted imports by high tarrifs, on the other hand he stimulated production by royal subsidies and by importing skilled workers. He fostered the manufacture of luxuries which had the motive of giving other monarchs an appetite for these things, thus opening up for France a lucrative foreign market. By all such methods Colbert intended that more money should flow into the kingdom than flow out. It was due in great part to him that the quality of French manufactured goods was superior, in general, to that found elsewhere.

The cultural facade of French empire reached the highest form of development. Under the patronage of Richelieu, literature had flourished. The French language, purified in vocabulary, acquired great precision. The school of French literature, known as Classicism, reached its height in the tragedies of Racine, the comedies of Moliere, and the fables of La Fontaine, as well as in the works of other great writers. Such writers showed unusual literary charm as well as craftsmanship. The literary outburst during this period owed largely to the patronage of the king. All the arts received due attention. Music received the special attention of the king. Architecture and sculpture were fostered for adornment. It was Colbert's organising gifts that brought into being a service of academies, one of painting, one of music, one of architecture. The Academy of France, which concerned itself with letters, of whom Boileau was the leading luminary, developed and conserved the best literary standards of the age. The weaving of tapestries (the famous house of Gobelins was established in 1667), the collecting of paintings and all manner of curios, advanced the development of the arts. Thus arts and letters reached highest point of development in Louis' reign.

Louis XIV's patronage centred on Versailles, the great palace that played an important part in the political life of seventeenth century France. There Andre Le Notre designed the formal gardens, Jules-Hardouin-Mansart added the long familiar garden facade, and Charles Le Brun decorated the Gallery of Mirrors with great magnificence. There the composer Jean-Baptists Lully devised and directed a number of musical entertainments. Thus the palace of Versailles was the stage on which the great king practised his chosen art. The nobles who made up this court gave royalty its proper setting. Louis' emblem was the rising sun; and to be warmed by its rays was the summit of social ambition.

However, Louis too often was blinded by his self-conceit and vanity. His attitude in religion sufficiently illustrates this trait. Inspired by the belief that his subjects should adhere to the King's religion, Louis authorized against the Huguenots a campaign of intrigue and persecution which finally culminated in the revocation of the Edict of Nantes (1685). "One King, one law, one faith" was the adage which Louis fulfilled literally. The royalty, so carefully systematised and so artistically embellished, could not really experiment in science, art or letters. This intellectual output followed conventional lines. This was the inherent weakness of a regime that dazzled its age, but which over-exalted authority as the basis of the modern state.

With the steady growth of the realm there emerged a bureaucracy subject to a greater or less extent to his direct control, but functioning in general as responsible officials. It may be mentioned that all office holders were nominess of the Crown and removable by the Crown. But in general, the king allowed the machinery of state to function without interference.

The pivot of the governmental machinery was the king's council. It met for somewhat less vital matters under a variety of guises. The Council for Dispatches or the Council for the Interior had particular responsibility for home affairs, including the activities of the intendants; the Royal Council for Finances supervised important matters affecting financial aspects of the king's domain lands. These two councils, like the High Council, were presided over by the king in person. But the Royal Council also met under three titles to deal with judicial and administrative matters. The Privy Council judged disputes between individuals or bodies and dispensed the King's final judgements. The State Council for Finance expedited financial matters of secondary importance, while the Financial Arbitration Court was an administrative tribunal settling important disputes between the state and individuals or corporations.

The group composing the High Council contributed a great deal to the basic pattern of administration, particularly in military, fiscal, naval, and commercial activities. Most of the ministers came from the same well-knit group of royal servants. All these counsellors reflected the attitude of the king himself. They favoured a protectionist, paternalist policy in the organisation of industry, the administration of the colonies, or the building up of the navy.

Louis relied chiefly on his provincial intendents to carry out the decisions reached in the High Council. Like the ministers at the centre, they depended upon the king for their security of tenure. In the provinces they could exercise powers of police, raise military forces, regulate industrial, commercial and agricultural affairs, enforce censorship, assign and collect taxes and wield considerable judicial authority in civil and criminal affairs. With no local roots, these agents of the central government created considerable friction and hostility.

It was the task of the King's Council to make the necessary laws. Then, to become valid, it required the king's sanction. After the royal sanction had been given, the Council's project became a law. It is clear that the king might, if he chose, refuse to sanction a projected law, in other words, might exercise a veto.

Under a regime in which all power was derived from the Crown, the old feudal assemblies, the notables, the estates general, and the provincial estates, had no logical place. Henry IV had convoked an assembly of notables in 1596. The notables met rarely during the early Bourbon period. The estates general met once during the period. It was called in 1614 by the regent, Marie de' Medici, under pressure from the nobility. Fortunately for the crown, the preponderance of office holders in the third estate and constant quarrels between the different orders prevented a united front, and the assemblage was dissolved without impairing the royal power.

Louis's Religious Policy

Like most of his contemporaries, Louis believed that toleration had no virtue. Consequently, especially after 1676, Louis intensified the persecution of Protestants. Finally, in 1685, the Edict of Nantes was revoked in order that Louis could claim that he had succeeded in extirpating Protestantism from his realm. The revocation of the Edict of Nantes angered Protestant Europe. The same zeal for uniformity made Louis attack the Jansenists. Louis was disturbed when he felt that these zealous Catholics had taken up an unorthodox position that threatened the unity of the state. Louis sought the support of the Pope for formal condemnation of the creed. Finally, in 1713, the famous Bull was promulgated.

Like many of his predecessors, including Francis I and Henry IV, Louis had leaned heavily upon the traditional Gallican doctrine. According to that doctrine, the French king possessed the right of temporal and spiritual authority—that is, the right to nominate new bishops and to administer and draw the revenue from the bishoprics while they remained vacant. In 1673 Louis extended this right to the whole of the French kingdom despite papal opposition. Eventually, in 1682, the Gallican Articles were published as a law of the French state, asserting that the king was in no way subject to the Pope in temporal matters and reaffirming the indepen-denc of the French church from Rome. The mutual animosity of King and Pope only ended in 1693, when, following William of Orange's successful attempt to secure the English throne, Louis agreed to suspend the edict of 1682; but it was a suspension only, not a recantation.

Thus, in religious matters, in his dealings with the nobility and the Parlement and in his manner of governing the country, Louis appeared to be a modern dictator rather than a 17th century king. However, the comparison is most misleading; neither in theoretical nor in practical terms could Louis XIV be thought of as all-powerful. First of all the legitimacy of his position under the law made him the interpreter of the law and the fount of justice in the kingdom, not a capricious autocrat. Similarly, his kingship bestowed upon him a quasi-spiritual role which obliged him to govern justly in accordance with the laws of god and Christian morality. He was also bound by the need to take counsel. Next, there was the essentially federal nature of the country with its collection of such peripheral provinces as Brittany, Normandy and Provence, all retaining their own Estates and customs.

Perhaps most of all the king was limited by financial stringency. Louis often tried to persuade the cities and the provincial Estates to raise their contributions and the clergy to increase the size of their "free gift'. He also created more offices and annuities. But these were mere palliatives, and the king was forced on two occasions to introduce novel measures. In 1695, he levied a capitation, or head tax, applicable to all French laymen; and in 1710 requiring the clergy and the privileged classes a tenth to be paid to the state from all incomes. It was impossible to be a despot while financial resources were so precarious.

Foreign Affairs

From the beginning of his reign, Louis pursued a vigorous foreign policy. Imbued with the medieval fiction of universal dominion, he twice tried by bribing the Electors to get himself chosen Holy Roman Emperor. It was Spain, the occupant of the Netherlands, whose weakness readily tempted attack. Making an unprovoked aggression, he began war with Spain in 1667, and his armies invaded the Netherlands and Franche Comte. As Spain had no longer any power of resistance, there was nothing to check French aggression. Holland, however, became alarmed at the conquest of the Netherlands, fearing the loss of a buffer state. When she induced England and Sweden to join her, Louis decided to fall back upon his diplomatic skill in 1668. By pushing back the boundary of the Netherlands, Louis acquired several fortresses on the frontier. Meanwhile, by adroit means, he broke up the Triple Alliance and isolated Holland. Then, in the Dutch War that followed shortly afterward (1672-78), Louis intended to warn the Dutch that France was a serious commercial competitor and to force the Dutch to give him a free hand in the Spanish Netherlands. He learned from the war that he could never hope to incorporate a large part of the Netherlands into France against Dutch opposition. At the Treaty of Ryswick in 1697 the Dutch gained the right to keep a series of Dutch barrier fortresses within the southern Netherlands as a check against French aggression. It was Louis's seizure of these fortresses in 1701 that precipitated the War of the Spanish Succession (1701-14).

The king of Spain, Charles II, was an imbecile and childless and when he died in 1700 it was found that in his will Louis' grandson, Philip of Anjou, had been designated his heir. Louis accepted the proffered crown in the name of his grandson and the rest of Europe prepared to resist this new aggression. Moreover, the old question of the balance of power was also involved, since France might now enjoy the privilege of trading with the Spanish colonies, a privilege which the English and the Dutch had long been enjoying. For England, moreover, the revival of the old danger of a strong power in possession of the Netherlands was enough to provoke. The Grand Alliance had been formed, including England, Holland, Austria and, later Brandenburg. After the failure of the French advance on Vienna, France was thrown back on the defensive. Apart from losing her grip over Italy, she was forced to give up the Netherlands as well, thanks to the brilliant generalship of the Duke of Marlborough. However, with the fall of Marlborough and the war party in Great Britain, as well as quarrels among the Allies, the War came to an end by the Utrecht Settlement in 1713. Philip retained the throne of Spain with the stipulation that the two crowns should never be united, and he was forced to cede the Netherlands to Austria. The Dutch got fortified barrier and Britain secured important gains in America, as well as the stronghold of Gibraltar, guarding the entrance to the Mediterranean.

It cannot be denied that Louis was arrogant and that his arrogance aroused fear and resentment in his neighbours. Equally, he was intolerant, like most of his contemporaries, and feared by Protestant powers as the leader of a vengeful Counter-Reformation. Louis frightened Europe with his quest for **la gloire,** by which he meant the favourable verdict of history on his contribution to French security. That contemporary interpretation, still accepted three centuries later, does less than justice to Louis's shrewd appreciation of political realities and of France's long-term interests.

CHAPTER 10

THE EMERGENCE OF A SCIENTIFIC VIEW OF THE WORLD—THE AGE OF ENLIGHTENMENT

By breaking with the prevalent Western intellectual traditions, science emerged as a revolutionary force. This break did not come suddenly. The study of nature had been cultivated for centuries. Fourteenth-century Schoolmen in England and France had already questioned Aristotle's explanation of motion. During the Italian Renaissance the University of Padua had become the centre for Aristolelian scientists seeking natural causes for natural phenomenon. Meanwhile literary humanists immersed themselves with Greek and Hellenistic scientific works, including parts of the writings of Euclid and Archimedes. In 1543 the publication of Archimedes' theories contributed largely to the revival of science.

The Greeks had produced Archimedes and other scientists, yet only in the seventeenth century did the method of Archimedes gradually replace that of Aristotle as the accepted source of knowledge about the natural world. The scientific method displaced philosophy: where philosophy sought knowledge through speculation and logic, science seeks it through experimentally controlled theories.

The discoveries in astronomy illustrate how slowly early modern science progressed. Traditions prevailing in 1500 emanated from Aristotle and Ptolemy, who asserted that a stationary earth occupied the centre of the Universe. According to them stars, sun, planets and the moon were held in circular orbits around the earth. The source of motion was an alleged "prime mover", identified with the Christian god. As Copernicus learned, any effort to reformulate this cosmology was difficult and was dangerous as well.

As a precursor of modern science Pole **Nicolaus Copernicus** (1473-1543) is more significant for having invented a mathematical planetary system than for having postulated a moving earth and a stationary sun. He opened a new vista, which was to explain the movement of bodies in the heavens and on earth in terms of mathematically expressed natural laws. Copernicus held firmly to the notion that heavenly motion was circular.

Nicolaus Copernicus

Vindication for Copernicus's sun-centred hypothesis awaited the observations by Tycho Brahe (1546-1601), the improvement of his theory by Johannes Kepler (1571-1630), the invention of the telescope, and the later achievements of Isaac Newton (1642-1727). The Danish astronomer Tycho Brahe proposed a mathematical theory of the solar sysem that still put the earth at its centre. Inspired by scientific zeal and fortified by Brahe's observations, Kepler worked out a series of laws describing planetary motion. He discovered that the planets' paths were elliptical, and this discovery constitutes his first law of planetary motion. The data of Mars's orbit, observed night after night, forced Kepler to admit that its path traced out an ellipse with the sun at one focus. Because planets speed up as they approach the sun and slow down as they move farther away in their elliptical orbits, a mathematical relationship to describe that fact had to be discovered, from whence Kepler's second law emerges—a line from the sun to the planet sweeps out equal areas of the ellipse in equal times. Finally, he showed in his third law that the distances of the planets from the sun and their orbital speed are mathematically related. While these laws laid the foundations for Newton's astronomy, their importance to Kepler was that they proved the underlying mathematical harmony of the universe.

The Italian **Galileo Galilei** (1564-1642) was the first modern scientist to support mathematical theories about the physical world with observations and experiments. A mathematical genius, Galileo began his career in physics and mechanics in opposition to Aristotelian teachings. By mathematical description and analysis he worked out laws of ballistic trajectories, pendulum movements, and uniform acceleration.

Galileo Galilei

Gelileo's greatest achievement was in the mathematical analysis of motion. Through numerous experiments and mathematical calculations, he discovered the principle of inertia. Here he refuted Aristotle, whose theory of motion had already been under attack for 200 years. According to Aristotle, the purpose of a moving body was to seek a resting place, and it required a continuously acting force to remain in motion. To Galileo, a body in motion along a straight line would not only go on moving indefinitely without any continuously acting force, it would also require some other force to stop it. From this single discovery Galileo was able to build up the whole theory of mechanics. This great achievement showed a rapid evolution in thought requiring clarity of definition, a systematic elaboration of mathematical expression, the rethinking of the nature of motion.

Galileo carried his astronomy much further, however, with a new instrument—the telescope. Through this instrument he detected sunspots, saw the four satellites of Jupiter, followed the phases of Venus, studied the mountains and valleys on the surface of the moon, and noted that the Milky Way was a dense cluster of stars. All these observations were new. In 1610 he published the **Message of the Stars,** which demonstrated that the same laws applied both to the earth and to the heavens.

Galileo's fame spread, but he aroused intense opposition in the Universities and Churches. Scholars steeped in Aristotelian framework rejected his conclusions and even refused to look through his telescope. By 1616 a board of enquiry appointed by the Roman Inquisition had enjoined him to make only hypothetical statements concerning cosmology. Even so, in 1632 he published in Italian for a lay audience the **Dialogue on the Two Principal Systems of the Universe, the Ptolemaic and the Copernican.** While he had support within the Church, clearly Galileo's criterion for scientific truth was not the authority of the Church. For defying its authority, he was summoned before the Inquisition in 1632, forced to retract his conclusions, and put under house arrest. Protestant authorities denounced Galileo. Apart from Galileo's spectacular achievements, he initiated the broad lines of inquiry that were left to a new generation to follow up.

Neither Galileo nor Kepler saw that the same mechanical laws might apply on earth and in the heavens. Descartes suggested that a Universal Mathematics was needed to describe the Universal laws of motion. But not until Newton combined mathematics with new experiments was the synthesis of Galileo's early mechanics and Kepler's celestial mechanics fully achieved.

Descartes and Newton

The Frenchman Rene Descartes (1596-1650) was the Aristotle of the new science and the new philosophy. Like Aristotle, he was a philosopher first. Like Aristotle, he established foolproof methods of acquiring knowledge. Descartes made significant contributions to the science of physics and was one of the world's great mathematicians.

Descartes not only provided an explanation of the behaviour of matter in motion, he also thought it explained everything in the natural world. He provided the explanation by defining matter and motion to include everything else. In other words, it is extension. Motion is the displacement of matter. Descartes said: "Give me motion and extension, and I will construct a world." The world Descartes constructed consisted entirely of particles of matter clashing one another in fixed mechanical patterns.

Descartes made a famous philosophical assumption the autonomy of the human mind. Wanting to know reality as it really was, he began to doubt and finally rejected all the traditional sources of knowledge. There was only one thing that he could not throw out: the fact of his doubting. Here was the basic certainty: 'I think, therefore, I exist' **(Cogito ergo sum)**. From this premise he could advance with full confidence in the knowledge that his thinking would reveal.

Although Descartes was too optimistic in hoping that the mind could duplicate the mechanics of the Universe in the abstract symbols of universal mathematics, his most permanent contribution to modern science was his method of abstract model-building. Descartes also invented an important mathematical tool—analytical geometry. He tried to improve the traditional geometry of his day. He eliminated the visual aspects of geometrical figures by expressing lines and curves in numerical symbols and their relations in equations. In addition, he introduced the idea of movement, which was lacking in Greek geometry. He determined the position of a point on a graph by its distance from the sides of the graph and thus invented the plotting of a curve. In doing so, Descartes cordinated the geometrical idea of representation with the algebraic idea of two variables in an equation having an indefinite number of simultaneous values.

By the late seventeenth century, a number of thinkers had advanced man's knowledge of

Isaac Newton

astronomy, physics and mathematics considerably. The Englishman, Sir **Isaac Newton** (1642-1727) brought all this knowledge together into a grand synthesis. He established the developing physical sciences at a new level where they remained till the nineteenth century. He made optics a branch of physics by demonstrating that the theory of light and the theory of matter complemented each other. He gave the principles of dynamics their explicit form and formulated general laws of motion from which Galileo's principle of inertia and Kepler's laws of planetary motion followed as necessary consequences. For example, he showed that the Moon's motion, given its distance from the Earth, conformed to the same law as that of freely falling bodies at the Earth's surface. In this way he advanced the idea of a universal gravitational force. The gravitational force emanating from the sun is sufficient to keep the planets in their orbits, while such a force emanating from a planet keeps its satellites in their orbits.

Like most great scientists, Newton had to invent new techniques for solving problems that the old ones could not handle. The most pressing problem was the mathematical analysis of continuous changes. To carry through his mathematical deductions, Newton invented infinitesimal calculus. With this tool he was able to calculate the infinitesimal decrease in the force of gravity at increasing distances from the Earth.

Newton shared Descartes' philosophy of nature as a mechanistic order. He tied this order together with the principle of gravity. His most famous book was **The Mathematical Principles of Natural Philosophy**—usually referred to simply as the **Principia,** first published in 1678. In this book he developed a theory that accounted for all matter in motion as if it were regulated by gravity. This explanation worked better than Descartes' notion of impact.

Scientific Societies

The Roman **Academia dei Lincei,** to which Galileo belonged, sponsored his reports on sunspots in 1613. That society disappeared in 1657 and was replaced by the **Accademie del Ciments** (Academy of Experiments), which flourished in Florence from 1657 to 1667. More important societies under official sponsorhip flourished in France and England. The French **Academie des Sciences**, founded in 1666, received financial support from the French Crown. In 1662 Charles II of England chartered, but did not subsidise, the **Royal Society of London for the Promotion of Natural Knowledge**. These societies, through publication of monographs and journals, disseminated detailed reports of their work to foreign scholars. **The Academic del Ciments** repeated and extended Galileo's experiments, employed the barometer invented by Torricelli, studied vacuums, computed the velocity of sound and engaged in studies of the digestive processes of animals. The French society succeeded in computing the approximate speed of light, measured the length of a degree of latitude, and applied the telescope to angular measurement in surveying. The Royal Society of London reached a high level of prestige as Isaac Newton and his contemporaries completed the mathematical synthesis of astronomy and physics.

Newton wrote: "We are to admit, no more causes of natural things than such as are both true and sufficient to explain their appearances." This statement formed the core of scientific methodology. But scientific spokesmen were not unanimous in defining scientific methodology. The English philosopher, Francis Bacon, saw it primarily as empiricism, the use of inductive logic to give meaning to direct observations. But Descartes emphasised the necessity of first having a set of hypotheses, even a completely new metaphysics, before empirical testing could take place.

Between the extremes of Bacon's empiricism and Descartes' rationalism stood experimentalism, an approach that represented scientific methodology at its best. Setting up a hypothesis of how nature might behave and planning an experiment to test it, is a rational process. Galileo, Boyle, and Newton were great exponents of experimentalism.

THE ENLIGHTENMENT

The Englightenment was both a movement and a state of mind. The term represents a phase in the intellectual history of Europe in which influential literarti outlined specific targets for criticism and proposals for action. The real significance of the Enlightenment lies in its combination of principle and pragmatism. Cosequently, it engenders controversy about its character and achievements. Most modern interpreters incline to accept the view that the Enlightenment originated in France, given the number of luminaries that flourished in the country. The term Englightenment was used and cherished by those who believed in the power of mind to liberate and improve. Bernard de Fontenelle, populariser of the scientific discoveries that contributed to the climate of optimism, wrote in 1702 anticipating "a century which will become more enlightened day by day, so that all previous centuries will be lost in darkness by comparison." In Immanuel Kant's view the essential characteristic of the Enlightenment was emancipation from superstition and ignorance.

The perceptions and propaganda of the philosophers have led historians to locate the Age of Reason between the two revolutions—the English of 1688 and the French of 1789—but in conception it should be traced to the humanism of the Renaissance. It was formed by the complementary methods of the Scientific Revolution.

The Enlightenment, according to Kant, was the period in the development of civilisation when 'Mankind grew out of its self-encumbered minority'. The philosophy of the Enlightenment was primarily concerned with epistemology—that is the theory of knowledge. Three Britons—John Locke (1632-1704), Bishop George Berkeley (1685-1753) and David Hume (1711-1736)—opened the quintessential thought of the age of Enlightenment. As empiricists, they all accepted that the scientific method of observation and deduction should be applied to human affairs.

The genesis of Enlightenment was not to be found everywhere. In the seventeenth century it was only found in three places—Poland-Lithuania, Switzerland, England. But they existed above all in the Netherlands—the home of intellectual refugees from Rene Descartes to Spinoza, Shafetsbury, Le Clerc and Bayle. Leyden, Amsterdam and the Hague were the main laboratories of the Enlightenment. Although Frenchmen were forefront in the beginning. France itself did not become the nursery of activity until the mid-eighteenth century.

The preeminence of the French language enabled Frenchmen of the seventeenth century to lay the foundations of cultural ascendancy. The notion of a realm of philosophy superior to sectarian concerns facilitated the transmission of ideas. "I flatter myself" wrote Denis Diderot to the Scottish philosopher David Hume, "that I am, like you, citizen of the great city of the world." "A philosopher," wrote Edward Gibbon, "may consider Europe as a great republic, whose various inhabitants have attained almost the same level of politeness and cultivation." This lofty pronouncement by the author of **The Decline and Fall of the Roman Empire** (1766-88) recalls the common source: the knowledge of classical literature.

The scholars of the Enlightenment recognised a joint inheritance, Christian as well as classical. They felt an affinity with the classical world and admired the achievements of the Greeks, who discovered the reasoning mind, as well as that of the Romans, who adopted Hellenic culture and laid the foundations of church and civil law.

Voltaire specified the "four happy ages"—the centuries of Pericles and Plato, of Cicero and Caesar, of the Medicean Renaissance, and of Louis XIV. The contrast is with "the ages of belief", which were wretched and backward. Writers of the Enlightenment constantly resort to images of relapse and revival. Typically, Jean d' Alembart wrote in the **Preliminary Discourse to the Encyclopadia** of a revival of letters and return to reason.

Role of Science and Mathematics

"The new philosophy puts all in doubt" wrote the poet John Donne. Early seventeenth century poetry and drama portrayed confusion and dismay about the world, God and man. The critical essays of the 16th century French philosopher Michael de Montaigne, musing on human folly and fanaticism, continued to be popular long after his time. Unsettling scientific views were gaining ground. As the new astronomy of Copernicus and Galileo was accepted, the traditional religious beliefs and the old scheme of nature was shaken. In this process, mathematics occupied the central position. It was in the words of Descartes "the general science which should explain all that can be known about quantity and measure, considered independently of any application to a particular subject". When Fontenelle wrote about Descartes "Sometimes one man gives the tone to a whole century" it was not merely of his mathematics that he was thinking. It was the system and the philosophy that Descartes derived from the application of mathematical reasoning to the mysteries of the world. The method expounded in his **Discourse on Method** (1637) was one of doubt : all was uncertain until established by reasoning from self-evident propositions.

A different track had been pursued by Francis Bacon, the great English lawyer, whose influence proved as great as that of Descartes. He called for a new science, to be based on collaborative experiment with a systematic recording of results.

General laws could be established with enough data produced by research and then by inductive reasoning. "Knowledge is power", Bacon said with the conviction that went with a vision of mankind gaining mastery over nature.

While Descartes maintained his hold on French opinion, across the Channel Isaac Newton, a prodigious mathematician, was mounting a crucial challenge. Newton did not break completely with Descartes, and remained faithful to the latter's fundamental idea of the universe as a machine. But Newton's machine operated according to a series of laws, the essence of which was the principle of gravitation— it was everywhere present. If Newton was unique in his contribution to the climate of the Enlightenment, it is because his new system offered certainties in a world of doubts. The belief spread that Newton had explained foreover how the universe worked. In Newton's opinion man, guided by reason, could explain all natural phenomena that was no longer mysterious.

Gradually, however, Newton's work won recognition. Newton's physics was justified by its successful application in different fields. The return of Halley's Comet was accurately predicted. In classical theory, reason was presumed to be common to all human beings and its laws immutable. If Newton was important in contributing to the climate of Enlightenment, it is because his new system offered certainties in a world of doubts. Newton's contemporary, Leibniz, influenced his age by concluding that since God contrived the universal harmony this world must be the best of all possible worlds. He also proposed legal reforms and laboured for the reunification of the Roman Catholic and Lutheran churches.

The Influence of Locke

The writing of John Locke reveals the range of interests that an educated man might pursue and its value: discrimination, shrewdness and originality. The journal of Locke's travel in France (1675-79) is a telling introduction to the world of the Enlightenment. Locke spent the years from 1683 in Holland, where he took refuge from high royalism. During this time Locke wrote the **Essay on Toleration** (1689). Locke popularised the idea that the people had a sovereign power and that the prince was merely a delegate. His **Second Treatise of Civil Government** (1690) offered a theoretical justification for a contractual view of monarchy on the basis of a revocable agreement between ruler and ruled. It was, however, his writings about education, toleration, and morality that were most influential among the philosophers. Locke was the first to treat philosophy as purely critical enquiry. Voltaire admired what Locke called his "historical plain method." The avowed object of his **Essay Concerning Human Understanding** (1690) was "to inquire into the original, certainty, and extent of human knowledge together with the grounds and degrees of belief, opinion and assent." For Locke the mind derives the materials of reason and knowledge from experience. Unlike Descartes' view that men could have innate ideas, in Locke's system knowledge consists of ideas imprinted on the mind through observation of external objects.

Though he suggested that souls were born without the idea of God, Locke did not reject Christianity. Voltaire presented Locke as the advocate of rational faith. In the debate over moral values, Locke provided a new argument for toleration. If Locke was the most influential philosopher, the most prolific writer was Pierre Bayle, whom Voltaire called "the first of the skeptical philosophers." Bayle's **Historical Dictionary** (1697) exposed the fallacies and deceits of the past. "The grounds of doubting are themselves doubtful; we must therefore doubt whether we ought to doubt." Bayle points to the importance of the Dutch Republic in the 17th century. It was urban, centring on Amsterdam, pervaded by a scientific spirit, and characterised by a rich artistic life created by painters. The spirit of Enlightenment is epitomised in the university of Leiden which attracted students from throughout Europe by its excellence in medicine and law and its freedom from ecclesiastical authority.

Order, purity and clarity had dominated traditional theology as represented by its great master, Jacques Benigne Bousset. His **Politique tiree** and **Discours sur I'hestoire** offered a world view and a history based on the Old Testament. Bousset believed in the unity of knowledge as so many branches of Christian faith. His compelling logic and magisterial writing had a strong influence. Bousset had encouraged Richard Simon when he set out to refute Protestantism through historical study of the Bible. Simon's works were banned in 1678, but Dutch printers ensured their circulation. No censorship could prevent the development of the historical method which was making a place for itself in the comprehensive search for truth.

The philosophers assumed that knowledge of nature would make men virtuous. Their programme of progress also called for sweeping humanitarian reforms. Following in the footsteps of the Quakers, they attacked slavery, torture, arbitrary imprisonment, cruel punishments and the inferior status of women. Many also attacked war and militarism, As a means of preventing warfare they relied upon enlightened self-interest, working through a balance of power.

Rational criticism of the existing regime in France had begun during the reign of Louis XIV, but it first obtained wide currency with Montesquieu. During the aristocratic resurgence following the death of Louis XIV, Baron de Montesquieu (1689-1755) opened an era with the **Persian Letters** (1721). In it he had used the supposed correspondence of a Persian visitor to Paris to satirise both the Church and the society. His masterpiece, **The Spirit of Laws**, appeared in 22 editions within 18 months of publication in 1748. Here he tried by inductive methods to go behind the apparent diversity of governmental systems to find a natural law of constitutional and social structure. In the England of his own time he found a political freedom that contrasted with the tyranny of Louis XIV. That freedom, he concluded, was guaranteed by a separation of the executive, legislative and judicial powers. Everywhere he found constitutions conditioned by exigences to which wise legislators were obliged to adjust specific enacments. **The Spirit of the Laws** became a fountainhead of constitutions that embodied the principle of a separation of powers as well as a system of checks and balances of those powers.

Whereas **Montesquieu** represented the enlightened nobility, Jean Francois Marie Arouet—better known as **Voltaire** (1694-1778), was the undisputed Prince of Philosophes. His political education included 11 months in Bastille. Crossing the Channel, Voltaire imbibed English philosophy, literature, science and Deism. Returning for 15 years to the Duchy of Lorraine on the French frontier, he popularised Newton, Locke and the whole English social system. A star of the salons and a confidant of princes—notably Frederick the Great of Prussia—Voltaire finally settled in 1758 at Ferney, on the French-Swiss frontier.

Montesquieu

Voltaire at times played the role of adviser to princes—notably Frederick II—but learned that it was easier to criticise than to change institutions and laws. Like other philosophers living under a regime that denied political opportunity, he was no politician. Nor was he truly a philosopher like Locke, Hume or even Montesquieu. His importance was primarily as an advocate at the bar of public opinion. The case for reform of archaic laws and the war against superstition was presented with passion and authority in his **Philosophical Dictionary. Candide** (1759) shows his elegant command of language. Voltaire displayed a humanitarian rage toward intolerance and inhumanity. In this vein his name is closely related with criticism of organised Christianity. **Ecrasaze I' infame**—"crush the infamous thing", namely intolerance—he wrote. He held the organised church largely responsible for the ignorance, superstition, and fanaticism of the masses. He deplored its role in perverting justice. He had little to put in place of the religion he abused and offered no alternative vision.

Voltaire

David Hume, a Scottish philosopher in revolt against all rationalist systems, questioned all knowledge except individual sensory experience. He attacked self-evident propositions, rational religion based on the assumption of a universal human nature, and rational morality. No man, Hume said, had ever observed "a state of nature", hence assumptions drawn from such an idea could not be verified.

Diderot and the Enclopaedists

The crowning collective achievement of the philosophers was the 17 volume **Encyclopaedia,** published between 1751 and 1780 under the principal editorship of Denis Diderot (1713-1784). It had no less purpose than to "bring together all the knowledge scattered over the face of the earth, to lay its general system before the men with whom we live so that our children will know more, and so that they may at the same time be greater in virtue and in happiness." Its contributors included such celebrities like Montesquieu, Turgot, Rousseau, d' Alembert, Holbach, Voltaire, and, especially, Diderot. The **Encyclopaedia** was much more than a philosophical compilation, it became the outstanding work pupularising the Newtonian revolution and Bacon's ideas of inductive science. The Encyclopaedia was too large, too unwieldy a work to be as effective as Voltaire's tracts. However, as a vehicle for spreading the Enlightenment, it reinforced the activities of the salons, the Masonic lodges, and the increasing number of scientific societies.

The Enclopedists carried faith in empiricism. Diderot explained human conduct entirely in natural terms and occasionally concluded that environment determined it. On a similar basis Claude Helvetius built up a morality based on people's aversion to pain and attraction to pleasure. His political doctrine was Utilitarianism—the greatest good for the greatest number. These ideas were later explained in England by radicals like Jeremy Bentham.

Marquis de Condorcet (1743-94) lived until the early phases of the French Revolution. A mathematician, who had become a popular philosopher, Encyclopedist and activist for anti-slavery and feminism, Condorcet turned his home into a salon, visited by persons like Thomas Paine, Jefferson and Adam Smith. A constitutional monarchist, he helped pen the French Constitution of 1791. He was put in jail and died during the period of the Terror in 1794. During his last days, he penned a celebrated work on progress, **Sketch of the Intellectual Progress of Mankind**. He predicted the spread of the Englightenment and the perfectability of man in a world of equal states and equality of individuals.

Rousseau

Rousseau was the great rebel against eighteenth century civilisation which he thought artifi-cial. For Rousseau all this went against nature, by which he meant man's nature. Rousseau pleaded for civilisation that would allow the emotional side of man's nature to develop in a harmonious way. In the **Discourse on Inequality** (1755) he broadened his criticism to indict the morally corrupting influence of society and rule by and for the rich. According to Rousseau, a moral revolution was the first prerequisite for progress.

Rousseau's greatest longing was to be free for himself which he found impossible. Rousseau devoted his writings to describing the possible ways of reforming civilisation so that other men could be free to be themselves. Rousseau passionately believed that man was born free. It was up to society to help him realise his full capacity for self-determination, through good laws and institutions. This "philosophy of the heart" was a major challenge to the whole civilisation of the Enlightenment. His principal theory, stated in a nutshell, was that man was essentially good, but corrupted by civilisation. He imagined that in some remote age a prince usurped the sovereignty, but that it still properly resided in the community, which might depose the prince if he failed to do his duty. In his **Social Contract** (1762) he says: "The depositories of executive power are not the masters of the people but its officers—The people may establish or remove them as it pleases." Like Locke, Rousseau believed that the people in a 'state of nature' formed a government through a mutual agreement, a social contract. But unlike Locke, Rousseau did not grant even a limited degree of sovereignty.

Rousseau

He laid great stress on what he termed the "general will" which may perhaps be understood as the freedom of the sovereign people operating for the general welfare. A goverment that expresses the general will has the right to force its citizens to obey this law, since people form governments only to guarantee their individual liberty. Another revolutionary idea of Rousseau's was that all men are equal. On this point, too, Rousseau blamed civilisation for destroying the natural equality of men. "It is precisely because the force of things always tend to destroy equally that the force of legislation should always tend to maintain it." Thus the law should force men to be equal as well as free. Critics of Rousseau charged him with favouring the tyranny of the masses, but Rousseau himself did not believe that the sovereignty of the people, that is, democracy, could be achieved in a large state. It could only work in a small city state like Geneva. In fact, when Rousseau later suggested reforms for the constitution of Poland, he recommended the perservation of the elective monarchy, the privileges of the nobles and even serfdom.

Kant

Just as Rousseau's "philosophy of the heart" was to find its fullest expression in nineteenth century romaniticism, Kant's doctrine that the ultimate reality lies in the world of ideas and the spirit launched a second major movement—idealism. In his **Critique of Pure Reason** (1781), **Kant** conducted a series of 'experiments' concerning the 'facts' of human reason. Then he found the laws that tied these facts together.

Kant

According to Kant, we experience the world in terms of certain basic assumptions that already exist in our minds. These assumptions, or categories, exist a priori—that is prior to our experience—and they transcend what is given by experience. It is these a priori alone that dictate the forms by which we know the objects of the natural world. The principle on which these categories—which Kant thought comparable to Newton's laws—depend is the existence of the mind as a living reality, prior to and transcending the senses.

Paralleling his categories of pure reason, Kant's "Categorical Imperative" for morality is an absolute idea. Kant based his view of morality on the assumption that man take full responsibility for respecting the dignity and rights of other men. Like Rousseau, Kant believed that man's natural feelings impelled him toward good will, but Kant emphasised reason as the guide to man's judgement. "Do unto others as you would have them do unto you." This was Kant's "categorical imperative." Kant shared the growing demand of the late eighteenth century for a higher morality and a greater autonomy for the individual personality. In 1784 he proclaimed that "Enlightenment is man's release from his inability to make use of his understanding without direction from another."

The first scientific school of political economy, the Physiocrats, arose in France among the followers of Francois Quesnay (1694-1774), who claimed that they had discovered the laws regulating the flow of money. Apart from supporting governmental regulation of interest rates, the Physiocrats advocated leaving the economy to natural laws of supply and demand and to man's enlightened self-interest (laissez-faire). Government should guarantee the natural rights of property, security and economic liberty. The Physiocrats agreed with many Mercantilists that internal trade barriers were intolerable. They denounced restrictive industrial production codes, guild regulation, protective tariffs, commercial wars. They publicised their new agricultural techniques and accorded the holders full rights over the communal property of peasant villages. They advocated a single tax on the land's net product produced by free labour.

Before the French Revolution, the Physiocrats' influence was small. In 1776, Turgot, Louis XVI's reforming minister of finance, was dismissed for championing their views. In the same year Adam Smith published **An Inquiry concerning the Wealth of Nations.** In this treatise Adam Smith (1723-90) provided that men recognised their true self-interests. But in contrast to the Physiocrats, Smith emphasised trade and labour as principal source of wealth. To government he assigned three tasks : (1) national defense; (2) the administration of justice with the purpose of protecting each member of society against oppression by any other member; and (3) construction and maintenance of essential public utilities. Traditionally, Smith's name has become closely identified with laissez-faire economics. Yet his criticism of certain business practices on moral grounds sets him apart from many later adherents of laissez-faire.

Enlightenment throughout Europe

Enlightenment in other countries consisted of small, isolated groups. In Italy universities like Bologna, Padua and Naples had preserved traditions of scholarship and provided a stimulating base for such original thinkers as Vico and Genovesi. The distinctive feature of the Italian Enlightenment that produced such scientists as Luigi Galvani and Alessandro Volta, was its practical tendency. Its proponents introduced to political philosophy Utilitarianism's slogan "the greatest happiness of the greatest number." The greatest representative of the Italian Enlightenment was Beccaria, whose work included **Of Crimes and Punishments** (1764). In his lifetime it was translated into 22 languages. His pupils included Catherine II of Russia and Jeremy Bentham, the most influential figure in the reform of English law. There was indeed no peculiar feature about his idea of justice. "That bond which is necessary to keep the interest of individuals united, without which men would return to their original state of barbarity" may recall the pessimism of Hobbes. Beccaria condemned torture and capital punishment and stressed the value of equality before the law. Much of the best Enlightened thought comes together in Beccaria's work.

The Enlightenment was a European phenomenon. There was important reforms in late eighteenth century Spain under the benevolent rule of Charles III. Spain was a casebook example of the philosophers' belief that religion stifled freedom of thought. It was a priest, Benits Montenego, who did as much as any man to prepare for the Spanish Enlightenment. Conservatism was, however, well entrenched. "It is an old habit in Spain", wrote the Count de Campomanes, "to condemn everything that is new."

So the accent in Spain was utilitarian as in other countries. Johann Struensee's liberal reforms in Denmark (1771-72) represented justifiable resentment of an oppressive regime. The constitutional changes that followed the first Partition of Poland in 1772 were dictated as much by the need to survive as by the imaginative idealism of King Stanislaw. Reforms in law and government in Catherine the Great's Russia represented the imperative need of the security of the state. In Portugal, Pombal, the rebuilder of post-earthquake Lisbon, was motivated chiefly by the need to restore vitality to the country. Leopold of Tuscany was able to draw on a rich humanist tradition and civic pride.

The Enlightenment's "mighty light which spreads itself over the world", should be related to the growth of the state, the advance of science and the subsequent development of an industrial society. To be challenged to think harder with chance of discovering the truth; to be able to write, speak and worship freely, and to experience equality under the law—were the greatest fruits of the Enlightenment.

CHAPTER 11

THE AMERICAN REVOLUTION—ITS SIGNIFICANCE

The British established thirteen colonies on the east coast of America during the seventeenth century. The most impelling motive was the desire for greater economic opportunity. The first three quarters of the seventeenth century saw a overwhelming number of English settlers in America. But after 1680 England ceased to be the principal source of immigration, as great numbers came from France, Germany, Ireland, Scotland, Switzerland.

Through the 13 colonies were regarded as part of the British Empire, they were free to develop their self-governing institutions. The first step in this direction was the decision in 1619 on the part of the London (Virginia) Company to permit Virginia Colonists representation in the government. From that time onward, it became an accepted principle that the colonists had a right to participate in their own government. In Massachusetts, control of the government passed to elected representatives.

Down to 1763 Great Britain had formulated no consistent policy of empire for her colonial possessions. The guiding principle was that colonies should supply the mother country with raw materials and not compete in manufacturing. But this was not rigidly enforced and the Colonists considered themselves as Commonwealths or states having loose associations with Britain. The distance of a three thousand mile sea between the New World and the mother country encouraged the colonies to defy the authority of the British Parliament.

The Seven Years' War (1756-63) brought about the final expulsion of the French from the North American continent. In the Treaty of Paris of 1763 England took possession of all of Canada, East and West Florida, all territory east of the Mississippi in North America, and St. Vincent, Tobago, and Dominica in the Carribean. The Brisith victory seemed one of the greatest in its history. The British Empire in North America had not only been secured but also greatly expanded. But, in winning the war, Britain had dissolved the empire's most potent material adhesives. Conflicts arose as the interests of the British Empire began to differ from those of the American colonies. And the colonies, now economically more powerful, culturally distinct, ultimately rebelled before submitting to the British plan of empire.

With the acquisition of the vast domain of Canada and the prospect of holding British territories both against the Spaniards to the south and west, the costs of colonial defence continued to increase. The British government decided to tighten up the enforcement of its trade regulations and to make the colonies pay a share of the costs of imperial defence.

The principal parliamentary enactments down to the close of the Seven Years' War had been the various Navigation Acts. These enacted that colonial produce was to be exported only in British ships; some commodities were to be sent to no country but Great Britain; and some were to be shipped to Britain first and thence to other parts of the world. There were also laws restricting the manufacture of certain articles in the colonies.

George Grenville, who became Prime Minister of England in 1763, tried to meet the costs of defence by raising revenue in the colonies. The first measure was the Plantation Act of 1764—usually called the Sugar Act—which imposed a tariff on all sugar or molasses imported by the colonists from foreign coun-

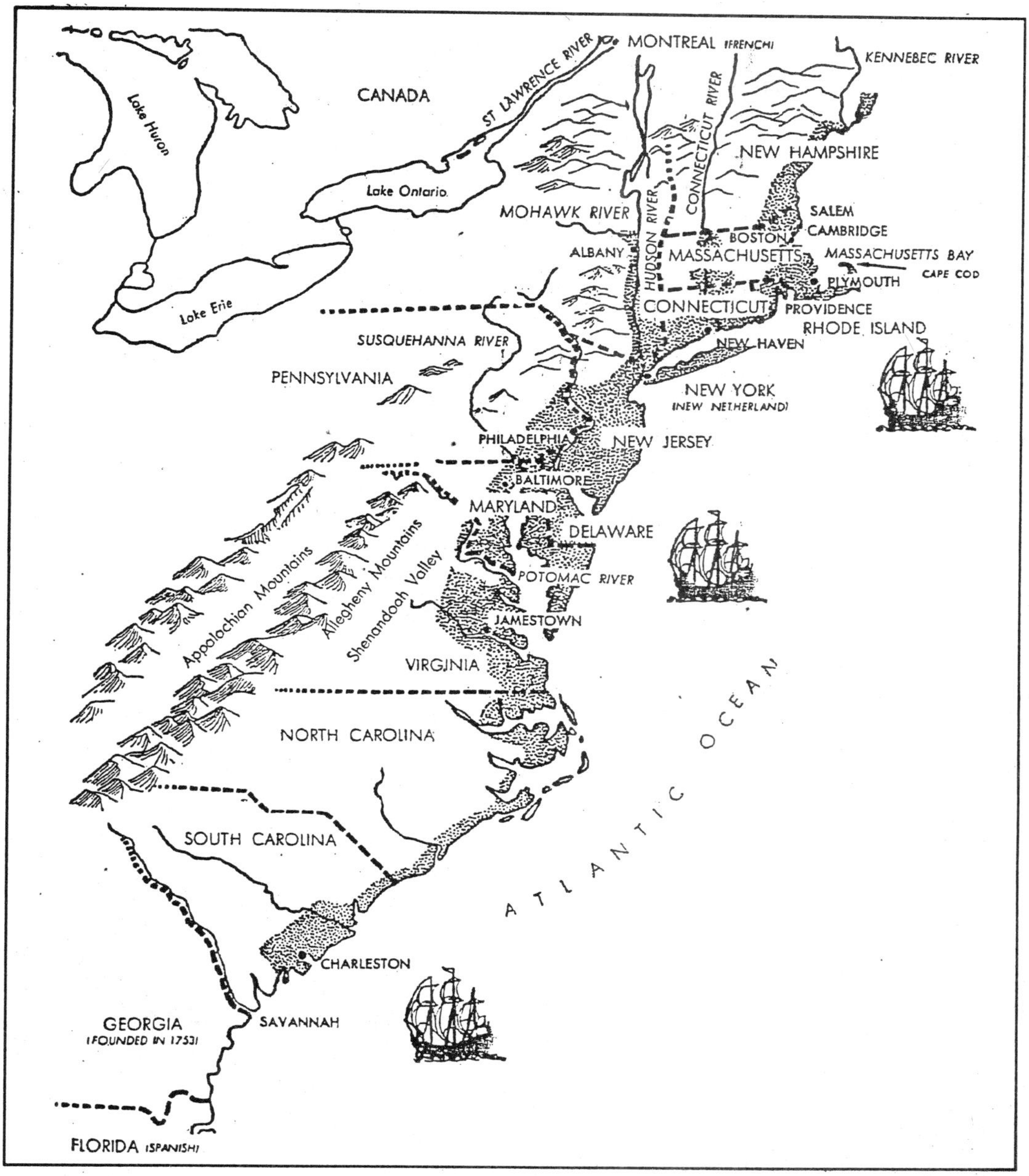

Thirteen British Colonies before American War of Independence

tries. Amended two years later, the Act had the object of raising revenue as its sole purpose. The Sugar Act of 1764 was virtually a reenactment of the old Molasses Act of 1733. The amended Sugar Act put a modest duty on molasses from all sources. The Act also levied duties on wines, silk, coffee, and a number of other luxury articles. To enforce the Act, British warships were stationed along the coast to prevent illegal trading. British tax collectors were empowered to search private houses for smuggled goods.

Another cause of discontent lay in the fact that the export tax on Continental goods shipped to the colonies from Great Britain was raised in 1764 from 2·5 per cent to 5 per cent. Most of the colonists incurred heavy debts to British merchants. At the beginning of the Revolution it was computed that Virginia owed to the British merchants over two million pounds. To repay the debts most provinces issued a good deal of paper money after 1750 and made it legal tender. But the British Parliament stoutly opposed the measure and, in 1764, passed a Currency Act asking the colonies to withdraw paper currency.

Among the economic causes were involved land speculation and the settlement of the West. Needing new land, various colonies claimed the right to an extension as far west as the Mississipi river. By the close of the Seven Years' War there was a great scramble for land in the west. Many of the war veterans had been granted western lands and bounties. One land company after another was being organised. Many great men—Benjamin Franklin, George Washington, Sir William Johnson—were keenly interested in Westward expansion. But fearing that this land hunger would provoke a war with the Indians and to prevent the colonists from spreading too far west, the British Government proclaimed in 1763 that all western territory be reserved for the use of the Indians. Thus at one stroke the British government swept away every western land claim of the 13 colonies. Equally objectionable from the colonial viewpoint was the Billeting Act. Passed early in 1765, it required colonies where royal troops were stationed to provide quarters and certain supplies for their support.

Another ground for dispute lay in the question of imperial defence. Believing that the colonies were incapable of defending themselves it was proposed that they should maintain a force of ten thousand men, part of the cost to be borne by the colonists themselves. In 1765 Lord Grenville passed the famous Stamp Act in the Parliament with little opposition. The Act required that revenue stamps be affixed to all newspapers and legal and other documents. But the Act raised a storm of protest. Soon leading merchants whose every bill of lading would be taxed organised for resistance. Business came to a standstill and trade with the mother country fell off considerably. Organisation like 'Sons of Liberty' came into existence and mob violence broke out in several places. From Massachusetts to South Carolina, the mobs forced the tax collectors to resign their offices and destroyed stamps and other property.

The great significance of the Stamp Act lay in the fact that it forced Americans to formulate a theory of imperial relations. The Virginia Assembly, for example, passed a set of resolutions denouncing taxation without representation as a dangerous innovation and a threat to colonial liberties. Delegates from nine of the colonies met together at New York in October 1765 and denied the right of the British Parliament to tax America. After considerable debate, the Congress at New York adopted a set of resolutions asserting that "no taxes ever have been or can be constitutionally imposed on them, but by their respective legislatures" and that the Stamp Act had a "manifest tendency to subvert the rights and liberties of the Colonists." Plans were adopted to impose an embargo on British goods.

A change of ministry facilitated a change of British policy on taxation. Parliamentary opinion was angered by what it perceived as colonial obduracy, but British merchants were worried about the embargo on British imports. The Marquis of Rockingham, succeeding Grenville, was persuaded to repeal the Stamp Act. The repeal was passed however, on the same day as the Declaratory Act, which declared that Parliament had the power to bind or legislate the colonies "in all cases whatsoever."

The Colonists, jubilant at the repeal of the Stamp Act, were prepared to ignore the Declaratory Act as face-saving window-dressing. John Adams, however, warned that Parliament, armed with this view of its power, would try to tax the colonies again. This happened in 1767 when Charles Townshend, British Chancellor of the Exchequer, passed an Act (Townshend Act) which imposed duties on tea, paper, glass, lead and painters' colours, including beverage. The revenue from the new taxes was to be used to support colonial governors, judges, customs officers and the British army in America. One ominous result was that colonists now began to believe that the British were developing a longterm plan to reduce the colonies to a subservient position.

The colonists were outraged. In Pennsylvania the lawyer and legislator John Dickinson wrote a series of essays which were widely reprinted and exerted a great influence in forming a united colonial opposition. Dickinson agreed that Parliament had supreme power where the whole empire was concerned, but he denied that it had power over internal colonial affairs.

Gradually, however, an united opposition grew. A wide-ranging non-importation policy against British goods was brought into operation. When customs officials sought to collect duties, they were set upon by the populace and roughly handled. The core of the colonial case was that, as British subjects, they were entitled to the same privileges as their fellow subjects in Britain. They could not constitutionally be taxed without their own consent; and because they were unrepresented in the Parliament that voted the taxes, they had not given their consent. James Otis, in two long pamphlets, ceded all sovereign power to Parliament with this proviso. Others, however, began to question whether Parliament did have lawful power to legislate over the colonies.

The British government began to acquire some stability when Lord North became Prime Minister in early 1770. In the same year, in the face of the American policy of nonimportation, the Townshend Tariffs were withdrawn—all except the tax on tea, which was kept for symbolic reasons. Relative calm returned, though it was ruffled on the New England coastline by frequent incidents of defiance of customs officers. One of the most violent clashes occurred in Boston just before the repeal of the Townshend Duties. Threatened by mob violence, a small British detachment opened fire and killed five people, an incident known as the Boston Massacre.

The next step was the formation of a system of committee of correspondence throughout the colonies. Sam Adams of Massachusetts, a born propagandaist and organiser, was the prime mover in this task. The object of the committee was to state the rights and grievances of the colonists and to communicate with other towns on these matters. These committees soon transformed themselves into revolutionary organisations. A Tory writer later testified: 'This was the source of the rebellion. I saw the small seed when it was planted. It was as a grain of mustard. I have watched the plant until it has become as a great tree.'

In 1773 Lord North's administration tried to rescue the East India Company from difficulties that had nothing to do with America. The Tea Act gave the Company, which produced tea in India, a monopoly of distribution in the colonies. Due to the Townshend Tea Tax, the colonists had boycotted the company's trade and, after 1770, a flourishing illegal trade existed. The company decided to sell its tea at a price well under the customary one through its own agents—thus making smuggling unprofitable. Great indignation was aroused in the colonies. It was not only the loss of the tea trade but the principle of monopoly that stung the colonists to action. Boston was not the only port to threaten to reject the tea chests, but its reply was the most dramatic.

On December 16, 1773, a party of Bostonians, led by Sam Adams himself, boarded a British ship and dumped 342 chests of tea into the harbour. "This', said John Adams rapturously "is the most magnificent movement of all. This destruction of the tea is so bold, so daring, so firm, intrepid and flexible, and it must have so important consequences, and so lasting, that I cannot but consider it as an epoch in History." The Boston incident precipitated the crisis. Ignoring the plea of Burke and Chatham, George III and the majority in Parliament passed a series of drastic Acts. In the spring of 1774, Parliament passed a series of measures to bring the insurgent colonies into line. The port of Boston was closed. In the Massachusetts Government Act, Parliament for the first time actually enacted a colonial charter, substituting an appointive Council for the elective one established in 1691 and conferring extensive powers on the Governors and council. A Quartering Act was passed requiring local authorities to find suitable quarters for British soldiers. To make matters worse, Parliament also passed the Quebec Act. The Act extended the boundaries of the province of Quebec, and guaranteed the right of the French inhabitants to enjoy religious freedom. This Act the colonists opposed because it generally threatened to interfere with westward movement and seemed to hem them into the north and northwest by a Roman Catholic dominated absolutist province.

Instead of subduing the colonies, these harsh Acts of parliament galvanised them to a course of action. At the suggestion of the Virginia legislators, colonial representatives were summoned to discuss the united interest of America. On September 5, 1774, the first Continental Congress met at Philadelphia with every colony except Georgia. Its 51 delegates included Washington, Benjamin Franklin, John Adams, John Dickinson and other able men. They addressed to the king and people of Great Britain a Declaration of Rights and Grievances, in which they asserted that the provinces had the power to legislate on their own affairs while conceding Parliamentary regulation of external commerce and imperial affairs. The most important work of the Congress, however, was the formation of the Association which provided for a revival of trade boycott and for a system of inspection committees in every town to supervise nonimportation, nonexportation, and nonconsumption.

With the activities of the Association Committees, a breach widened between the colonists and Britain. A few New England and Virginia delegates were looking forward towards independence. But the prevailling mood was cautious. The King might have effected an alliance with the colonists by timely concessions. George III and Lord North had no intention of making concessions. George III wrote: "The die is now cast, the Colonies must either submit or triumph".

Parliament declared that Massachusetts was in rebellion and decided to suppress the revolt. On April 18, 1775, skirmishes broke out at Lexington and Concord. The news of the battle struck the other colonies like an electric shock. While the alarms of Lexington and Concord were still resounding, the Second Continental Congress met in Philadelphia on May 10, 1775. Vainly did Benjamin Franklin plead for conciliation. The real temper of the Congress was revealed by a stirring declaration of the causes and Necessity of Taking up Arms, the joint product of John Dickinson and Jefferson:

> Our cause is just. Our union is perfect. Our internal resourcs are great, and, if necessary, foreign assistance is undoubtedly attainable. The arms we have been compelled by our enemies to assume, we will employ for the preservation of our liberties, being with one mind resolved to die free men rather than live slaves.

The Congress appointed Colonel George Washington Commander-in-Chief of the American forces.

Yet, despite the military involvement and the appointment of a commander-in-chief, the idea of complete separation from England was still repugnant to many members of the Congress. It was obvious, however, that the colonies could not forever remain half in half out of the empire. However, no compromise came from England. On August 23, 1775, King George issued a proclamation declaring the colonies to be in a state of rebellion. In January 1776, Thomas Paine's fifty-page pamphlet **Common Sense** was published. In vitriolic style, it emphasised the necessity of independence. Paine ridiculed the idea of hereditary monarchy and proclaimed that one honest man was worth more to society "than all the crowned ruffians that ever lived." No pamphlet had ever made such an impact on colonial opinion. The only hope was, however, British concessions. As public opinion hardened in Britain, the hope for reconciliation faded.

Initially there was hesitation in the Congress to take the definitive step of independence. But a strong radical party, based mainly in Philadelphia and its allies in the country, seized power in Pennsylvania in the course of the controversy over independence. Opinion for independence swept the colonies in the spring of 1776. On May 10, 1776, the Continental Congress adopted a resolution of separation from the mother country and assigned a committee to draft a declaration of independence. A committee of five, headed by Thomas Jefferson, drew up a formal Declaration of Independence and proclaimed it on July 4, 1776. It set forth a philosophy of human freedom which became a dynamic force for the succeeding generation.

> That all men are created equal, that they are endowed by their creator with certain inalienable rights, that among these are life, liberty and the pursuit of happiness—that to secure these rights, governments are instituted among men, deriving their just powers from the consent of the governed. That whenever any form of government becomes destructive of these ends, it is the right of the people to alter or to abolish it, and to institute new government, laying its foundation on such principles and organising its powers in such form, as to them shall seem most likely to affect their safety and happiness.

Thomas Jefferson went so far as to argue that frequent revolutions were a good 'medicine' for democracy. 'The tree of liberty', he said, 'must be refreshed from time to time with the blood of patriots and by tyrants.'

The War of Independence

Until early in 1778 the War of Independence, also known as the American Revolution, was a civil war within the British Empire. Later, as France in 1778, Spain in 1779 and the Netherlands in 1780 joined the colonies against Britain, the war became international. From the beginning sea power was vital in determining the course of the war, ultimately enabling the French to help bring about the final British surrender at Yorktown.

The war dragged on for over six years, with fighting in every colony and a dozen pitched battles of importance. The total strength of American forces seldom numbered over 20,000; in 1781 there were only about 29,000 insurgents under arms throughout the country. By contrast, the British army numbered about 42,000. The great majority became efficient soldiers owing to sound training and efficient discipline. In the beginning, the Americans suffered a series of reverses. The first of these was in New York. **Washington** rightly foretold that New York be an early British military objective. The British commander, General Sir William Howe, did not at once press against it. He offered the King's clemency to the rebels if they would stop fighting. His offer was rejected, and 30,000 British soldiers and the British navy opposed Washington's land force of 18,000 men. Defence of New York appeared clearly hopeless, but Washington could not abandon the city without

George Washington

a struggle. However, when Washington's position became untenable, he executed a masterly retreat in small boats from Brooklyn to the Manhattan shore. Howe lost his greatest chance to deal the American cause a crushing blow. For if Washington's army had been captured then, it would have been difficult for the Congress to have raised another.

Washington, though constantly forced back, was able to keep his forces fairly intact until the year's end. Important victories at Trenton and Princeton revived colonial hopes. But once more calamity struck. In September 1777, Howe captured Philadelphia and left Washington to pass an almost despairing winter with his men at Valley Forge. The Americans seemed on the verge of defeat. On the other hand, however, in the fall of 1777, the greatest American victory of the war had been won. The British general, Burgoyne, moved down from Canada, with a force designed to gain control of the Hudson River line and thus isolate New England from the other colonies. He reached the upper Hudson River and was compelled to wait for supplies until the middle of September before he could proceed southward. Meanwhile he sent a raiding force to march across Vermont only to meet stiff resistance. In the meantime, the Americans in the Mohawk Valley prevented the British reinforcements from joining Burgoyne.

The battle on the Vermont line had rallied the population of northern New England, and Burgoyne's delay enabled Washington to dispatch regular troops from the lower Hudson. Burgoyne himself reached the Hudson, but the Americans under General Gates checked him on September 19 and decisively defeated him at Bemis Heights on October 7. Ten days later, Burgoyne surrendered his entire army to the American General Gates at Saratoga. The most significant result of Burgoyne's capitulation was the entry of France into the war. The French had secretly sent financial and material aid since 1776. Now they prepared fleets and armies, although they did not formally declare war until June 1778. In the winter of 1779-80, Louis XVI sent a fine expeditionary force of 6,000 men under General Rochambeau. In addition, French fleets greatly aggravated the difficulties of the British in supplying and reinforcing their armies and British commerce suffered heavily from French and American blockade and from the daring naval operations of John Paul Jones. Britain also suffered from the entry of Spain and Netherlands into the war.

Yet the British forces did not give up the contest without a stubborn struggle. In 1778 they were forced to evacuate Philadelphia and suffered a series of setbacks in the Ohio valley which assured American domination of the north-west. But they continued to press the war in the south. Early in 1780 they captured Charleston, the principal southern seaport, and overran the Carolina country. In the following year they made an effort to conquer Virginia. Cornwallis started to build a base at Yorktown. Learning that the French fleet gained control of the Chesapeake River and of American coastal waters, Washington and Rochambeau moved south to Virginia. By mid-September the Franco-American forces had placed Yorktown under siege, and British rescue efforts proved fruitless. Cornwallis surrendered his army of 8000 on October 19, 1781. With Cornwallis' surrender, the military efforts to halt the Revolution was over. Thereafter, land action in America died out, though the war persisted in other theatres and on the high seas. The last British forces finally left New York on November 25, 1783. Washington then reentered the city in triumph.

It has been pointed out that the British never contrived an overall general strategy for winning the war. In chosing to take minimal risks, the British lost the opportunity to deal potentially mortal blow to the rebellion. There was also a grave lack of understanding and cooperation at crucial moments. Finally, the British relied too much on loyalist support they did not receive. Despite the feeble war efforts, the Americans were also generally to take advantage of their enemy's mistake. The continental Army, moreover, was by no means an inept force. Moreover, Washington, a rock in adversity, learned slowly the art of generalship. The supplies and funds furnished by France from 1776 to 1778 were invaluable, while French military and naval support after 1778 was essential. The outcome, therefore, resulted from a combination of British blunders, American efforts, and French assistance.

Treaty of Paris

Peace negotiations began in earnest in April 1782 and continued through November, when preliminary treaties were signed with the British. These were not to take effect until France concluded peace with Great Britain. In 1783 the Treaty of Paris was signed as final and definitive. By its terms Britain recognised the independence of the United States with generous boundaries, including the Mississippi River on the west. Britain retained Canada but ceded East and West Florida to Spain. Provisions were inserted calling for the payment of American private debts to British citizens, for American access to the Newfoundland fisheries, and for a recommendation by the Continental Congress to the states in favour of fair treatment of the loyalists.

Foundations of the American Republic

As early as May 10, 1776, Congress passed a resolution advising the Colonies to form new governments "such as shall best conduce to the happiness and safety of their constituents." Within a year after the Declaration of Independence, every state but three had drawn up a new constitution.

The problem of financing and organising the war sometimes overlapped with Congress' other major problem, that of defining its relations with the States. The Congress, being only an association of states, had no power to tax individuals. The Articles of Confederation, a plan of government organisation, adopted and put into practice by Congress in 1777, although not ratified by all the States until 1781, gave Congress the right to make requisitions on the States proportionate to their ability to pay.

The Articles of Confederation reflected strong preconceptions of State sovereignty. Article II expressly reserved sovereignty to the States individually, and another article even envisaged the possibility that one State might go to war without the others. Fundamental revisions could be made only with unanimous consent, because the Articles represented a treaty between sovereigns, not the creation of a new nation-state. Other major revisions required the consent of nine States. Yet State sovereignty principles rested on artificial foundations. In fact, the Congress had taken the first step both in recommending that the States form their own governments and in declaring their collective independence. Most important of its domestic responsibilities, by 1787 the Congress had enacted several ordinances establishing procedures for incorporating new territories. The North West Ordinance of 1787 provided for the phased settlement and government of territories in the Ohio Valley, leading to eventual admission as a new State.

The Philadelphia Convention, which met in May 1787, was officially called for by the old Congress to remedy defects in the Articles of Confederation. But the 'Virginia Plan' presented by the Virginia delegates proposed to introduce a new national government in place of the existing confederation. The Constitution, as it emerged after a debate, embodied a strong principle of separation of powers. The chief executive was to be a single figure and was to be elected by an electoral college, meeting in the States. The principal control on the President was the rather remote threat of impeachment. The Virginia Plan's proposal that representation be proportional to population in both Houses was modified by the retention of equal representation for each State in the Senate.

Many expected the legislature to be the most powerful branch of government. But to balance the system, the executive was given a veto, and a judicial system with powers of review was established. It was laid down that the new, federal judiciary would have the power to veto any State laws that conflicted with either the Constitution or with federal statutes.

States were forbidden to pass laws impairing obligations of contract. The Congress was endowned with the basic powers of a modern government. This was a republic. The enlargement of federal power was envisaged when the Congress was given powers to pass legislation 'necessary and proper' for implementing the general purposes of the contribution.

The States retained their civil jurisdiction, but the political centre of gravity shifted to the federal government. The language of the Constitution began in a new style: "We the people of the United States", rather than "We the people of New Hampshire, Massachusettes, etc."

The draft constitution aroused widespread opposition. Anti-Federalists were strong in States such as Virginia, New York and Massachusettes. Anti-Federalists also expressed fears that the new government would fall into the hands of merchants and men of money. Many republicans detected oligarchy in the structure of the Senate, with its six-year-terms. The absence of a bill of rights aroused deep fears of central power. Anti-

Federalists suffered the disadvantage of having no internal coherence or unified purpose. Impassioned arguments were poured forth on both sides. The most sustained pro-Federalist argument, written mainly by Alexander Hamilton, James Madison and John Jay, under the pseudonym of Publius, appeared in the newspapers as **The Federalist**. These essays attacked the feebleness of the confederation and claimed that the new constitution would have advantages for all sectors of society while threatening none. Madison contributed assurances that a multiplicity of interests would counteract each other, preventing the consolidation of power.

The Bill of Rights, steered through the first Congress by Madison's diplomacy, mollified much of the latent opposition. These first 10 amendments, ratified in 1791, adopted into the constitution the basic English Common Law rights. These amendments have guaranteed to citizens of the United States of America—among other rights—freedom of religion, speech, the press, and assembly; a militia instead of standing army, the right to trial by jury; speedy trials by the law of the land, and the prohibition of general warrants.

As a result of the adoption of the Bill of Rights, the wavering States soon came to the support of the Constitution, which was finally adopted on June 21, 1788. The Congress of the Confederation arranged for the first Presidential election, declared the new government would begin on March 4, 1789, and quietly expired. The United States has one of the most effective Constitutions ever devised, a Constitution which, unlike Britain's, is written, but which has expanded flexibly. Gladstone said that "As the British constitution is the most subtle organism which has ever proceeded from progressive history, so the American constitution is the most wonderful work ever struck off at a given time by the brain and purpose of man." Actually it was largely an evolutionary product.

Significance of the Revolution

The American Revolution was a great social upheaval but one that was widely diffused, and different in different regions. The principles of liberty and equality stood in stark contrast with the institution of slavery. One gradual effect of this conflict was the decline of slavery in all the Northern States; another was a spate of manumissions by liberal slave owners in Virginia. Throughout the slave States, the institution of slavery came to be reinforced by a doctrine of racial inferiority. In the 1790s the condition of free blacks deteriorated as States adopted laws restricting their activities.

The War of Independence also dramatised the economic importances of women. Republican ideas spread among women, influencing discussion of women's rights, education, and role in society. Some States modified their inheritance and property laws to permit women to inherit a share of estates and to exercise limited control of property after marriage.

The American Revolution was, in many respects, a manifestation of the Enlightenment in political, civil and ecclesiastical spheres. One of its triumphs was the passage of the Virginia statute for Religious Liberty in 1786. The State would tolerate all religions but give formal favour to none; people were free to follow the dictates of their own religious consciences.

Americans had fought for independence to protect common law rights; they had no programme for legal reform. Gradually, however, some customary practices came to emerge in keeping with republican principles. The outstanding example was the Law of Inheritance. The new States took steps to remove the old rule of primogeniture in favour of equal partition of intestate estates. This conformed both to the egalitarian and the individualist principles preferred by American society. Humanisation of the penal codes, however, occurred gradually in the 19th century.

EUROPE IN FERMENT

CHAPTER 12

INTRODUCTION

In his memoir, Chateaubriand wrote of his age: 'After Napoleon nothing'. Yet this was a period crowded with momentous developments of political upheaval, intellectual ferment, economic growth, scientific progress and literary and artistic vitality. It was, in the words of Victor Hugo: 'a magnificent epoch...the virile age of mankind.'

Before 1789, acquiescence in government was normal, revolution exceptional. But the French Revolution of 1789 unleashed several forces which were to shape European history in the nineteenth century. The Revolution was overtaken by war and emergency methods until Napoleon absorbed power in himself. After the overthrow of Napoleon, constitutional monarchy had been restored in France. It has been observed: 'The role of the Revolution has been immense, but it has remained negative. It destroyed the old regime; it cleared the ground for modern institutions, and on that ground Napoleon erected his edifice of despotism... To the Restoration belongs the honour of having introduced in practice the fundamental principle of modern constitutions: the alliance between liberty and authority. Its work has endured.'

The practice of representative government made little headway before 1848. The period from 1815 to 1848 seems to have formed a golden age of harmony as there was no major conflict between the Great Powers of Europe. After years of war with Napoleon, the Great Powers tried to avoid war by taking recourse to skillful diplomacy. However, the territorial settlement effected at Vienna in 1814-15 did not satisfy all as it violated the principle of national self-determination. The Vienna Settlement denied this right to such peoples as the Belgians, the Germans, the Italians, the Poles, and the Greeks.

The period witnessed the continuous struggle between the conservatism of the ruling classes of the various European states and the liberalism of the educated and professional classes. Liberalism wanted to free the individual from governmental control and to ensure fundamental liberties for all citizens. But the ruling classes of post-Vienna Europe clung tenaciously to conservatism lest any revolutionary upsurge might unsettle the regulated system of government. This inflexible opposition to even moderate proposals of reform led liberals to resort to underground activity and ultimately revolution. To quote Emile Zola, 'If you shut up truth and bury it under the ground, it will but grow, and gather to itself such explosive power that the day it bursts through it will blow up everything in its way.'

Throughout this period there was some kind of insurrection somewhere in Europe, while major outbursts occurred in 1820, 1830 and 1848. The waves of the uprisings were felt in various countries which threatened to jeopardise the peace that was so laboriously built by the reactionary rulers. The most outstanding figure during this period was Metternich of Austria whose doctrine of political immobility was to survive till 1848. The year 1848 seemed to usher in the springtime of the people...'never had a more universal impulse of souls and hearts burst forth from one end of Europe to another.' But the revolutions of 1848 were revolutions largely of intellectuals and 'all that was to result in failure.' Reaction came with devastating effect and Republicanism was doomed to an ephemeral existence.

The most important development of the period was the industrial expansion of several countries, spearheaded by England. The industrial expansion was encouraged by several factors. The first was the increase in Europe population. In the first half of the nineteenth century, there was a forty per cent increase in population which provided the industry a large labour force it needed. At the same time currency reforms, the encouragement of investment by new company and insurance laws made available the capital without which industrial growth would have been impossible. The improved methods of communication like steamboat and railways accelerated the pace of industrial expansion. Finally, the removal of artificial impediments to commercial intercourse like the establishment of Prussian Customs Union and the repeal of the Corn Laws by the British Government in 1846 gave stimulus to industrial growth.

Already, in 1848, Marx and Engels could speak of the 'world market of industries that no longer work up indigenous raw material, but raw material drawn from the remotest zones; industries whose products are consumed, not only at home, but in every quarter of the globe'. In this industrial expansion, England was preeminent. Aided by her natural resources and by her unrivalled naval supremacy, she had by 1850 'triumphantly established herself as the workshop of the world as well as its shipper, trader and banker.' By 1870, the initial changes of the revolution were accomplished.

Industrial Revolution (1760-) brought in its wake unrest of the age. Man became 'the humble servant of these steel giants.' This transformation complicated existing diplomatic relations or created new ones. As industrialism advanced, the old division of society began to break down. The position of the nobles and the clerics was challenged by an emergent bourgeoisie. The distinction between the upper bourgeoisie and lower bourgeoisie or middle class was not yet clear; instead, they were united in their struggle against the older entrenched classes. For this reason, they were supported by the peasants, the artisans and the industrial workers. But strains began to appear very soon between these classes. The revolution of 1848 exposed the hollowness of the alliance between the middle and the lower classes. Belief in political democracy—i.e. equal opportunities to all and socialism or betterment of all—were anathema to middle class liberals.

Rapid advances in material civilisation was due in large measure to contemporary progress in science. Revolutionary work was done by eminent scientists in these years. In mathematics and astronomy, K.F. Gauss of Gottingen and Urbain Leverrier of Paris expanded human awareness of the nature and dimensions of the universe. In physics, Julius Mayer and Hermann Helmholtz of Germany developed the idea of the conservation of energy and laid the foundations of thermodynamics. The first basic work in the practical application of electricity was done by Hans Christian Oersted of Copenhagen and Andra Marie Ampere of Paris. Michael Faraday's formulation of the Theory of Electromagnetic induction was another sensational breakthrough. In chemistry Jons Jakob Berzelius of Stockholm prepared the first fairly accurate table of atomic weights. In plant physiology and soil analysis, Justus Liebig emphasised the use of chemicals in restoring fertility and increasing the production of food. Against the deadly diseases of smallpox, tuberculosis and Asiatic cholera, some advances were made in pathology and diagnostic methods. Some of the notable achievements were the invention of the stethoscope, the discovery of the uses of morphine and the isolation of strychnine and quinine and experimentation with clinical thermometry and anaesthesia. Lister's Germ Theory diminished the incidence of death by blood poisoning. Charles Darwin's theory—of the Origin of the Species with its emphasis upon the survival of the fittest in the continuous struggle for existence—was applied to sociology, politics, economic activity and international diplomacy.

In the face of technical and economic progress, new generations began to run away from romanticism. The novels of Gustave Flaubert and the works of Turgenev, George Eliot and Emile Zola were characterised by new realism. The novels of George Sand and Charles Dickens breathed social criticism and reforming zeal. The works of the Russian novelists Dostoevsky and Tolstoy idealised the rebel with emphasis on the irrational. Among the poets, Tennyson and Heine might obsess themselves with prevailing materialism, but poets like Swinburne, Baudelaire, Verlaine, Mallarme, generally cultivated detachment from contemporary problems.

The deepening materialism and increasing emphasis upon realism led to erosion of religious belief. This was accentuated by the passionate reaction of leading churchmen. The hold of the Roman Catholic Church upon society was threatened by Pope Pius IX's systematic attack upon the intellectual tendencies of the age. The doctrine of papal infallibility seemed to many to be a vain attempt to resist the march of the intellect. Darwin replaced the biblical story of special creation by a Theory of Evolution based upon natural selection. Even the divinity of Christ was questioned anew by Earnest Renan. The conflict between rationalism and religion encouraged Scepticism and Obscurantism. Herzen declared 'universal grief' to be 'the supreme characteristic of our times. A dull weight oppresses the soul of contemporary man; the consciousness of his moral helplessness torments him; the absence of belief in anything whatever causes him to grow old before his time.'

Behind the facade of Industrial Revolution lay the proletariat who lived in misery. The growth of this proletariat led to sharp divisions between the rich and the poor. In Disraeli's famous words in *Sybil,* there emerged 'two nations between whom there is no sympathy; who are as ignorant of other's habits, thoughts and feelings, as if they were dwellers in different zones or inhabitants of different planets.' Appalled at these seamy sides of the new industrialism, some socialists advocated a redistribution of property and communal ownership. Others, more practical, propagated state intervention or the organisation of trade unions.

The *Communist Manifesto* (1848) struck the keynote of the proletariat movement: 'All previous historical movements were movements of minorities, or in the interests of minorities. The proletarian movement is the movement of the immense majority.' Industrialism gave a powerful impetus to democratic ideas. As early as 1833 Tocqueville had noted in his diary:

> The century is primarily democratic. Democracy is like a rising tide; it only recoils to come back with greater force, and soon one sees that for all its fluctuations it is always gaining ground. The immediate future of European society is completely democratic.

Democracy acted in various ways as a levelling agent. Already in 1820 Thierry in France was demanding 'a history of citizens, a history of subjects, a history of the people.' Carlyle in his *French Revolution* foresaw the time when 'History would be attempted on quite other principles; when the court, the senate and the battlefield receding more and more into the background, the temple, the workshop and the Social Hearth will advance more and more into the Foreground.'

The principles of liberalism and nationalism made little headway till 1848. The year heralded a new age and was followed by a period of relative political stability and of great economic prosperity. The only disturbing factor was the Crimean War (1853-1856) which was more than a local war. There appeared in the European stage personalities like Napoleon III, Cavour, Gorchakov, Bismarck whose main interest was to undo the Vienna Settlement. The old European alignments which had previously been defensive now gave way to offensive ones. Within the short space of sixteen years there were five wars in Europe in which the great powers were opposed to one another. The map of Europe was now drastically modified. The 'miracle' of Italian unification was achieved. Still more important was the transformation of Germany into a unified empire which, from its inception, attained the position of hegemony on the continent of Europe. Historians are not oblivious of the tremendous consequences of the development of schools of German thought. As early as 1843 Heine wrote that 'The German revolution will not prove any milder or gentler because it was preceded by the Kantian Critique, the transcendentalism of Fichte, or even by the philosophy of Nature. These doctrines serve to develop revolutionary forces that only wait their time to break forth and to fill the world with terror and awe.'

The American Civil War (1861-1865) occupies in American history the place accorded to the French Revolution in the history of France. It was the first of the modern wars and was momentous in its consequences not only of the United States but also of Europe and the world. 'It unified that nation as it had never been unified before and placed it on the way to become a great world power.' 'The vital issue was not the survival of one nation, more or less, but the survival of a nation committed to the principle that government of the people, by the people, and for the people should not perish from the earth.'

Less spectacular but of equal importance were the political wisdom and flexibility of outlook which enabled the British government to devise a new system of institutional development overseas. The Durham Report of 1839 provided inspiration to establish self-government in the Dominions and gave birth to a new conception of Empire and Commonwealth. Their effects were so profound that by 1870 Australia, New Zealand and the Cape Colony followed the way.

Events in eastern Europe were no less important than those in the West. The invention of the dual monarchy in Austria-Hungary, the emancipation of the serfs in Russia, the weakening of Ottoman Turkish power in Europe and North Africa, the consolidation of expansionist Balkan states in Greece, Serbia and Romania, were pregnant for the future of the world. An era of state-making began in a rudimentary stage in central and eastern Europe. While Cavour and Bismarck struggled to unite Italy and Germany, small Balkan nationalities aspired to attain separate statehood. Finnish, Polish and Bulgarian national aspirations were kindled and Slav peoples stirred under Turkish misrule. The impact of this great upheaval in Europe was felt in Asia. The opening of Japan to Western influences by Commodore Perry in 1854, the establishment of the treaty system in China between 1842 and 1858, and the termination of the East India Company's rule in India in 1858 laid foundations for the process of Westernisation.

In the last quarter of the nineteenth century industry came to predominate in the economics of the United States and most countries in western Europe. New basic industries were introduced particularly in the electrical and chemical. Mechanisation became characteristic of industry in general. The consequence was that between 1870 and 1900 world industrial production increased nearly four times. Aggregate wealth increased with total production. National incomes grew at a faster rate than they had ever been experienced.

There was a considerable increase in the movement of European population. Of the 55 million Europeans who emigrated between 1821 and 1924, a sizable portion went to the United States and half to other areas—to Latin America, Canada, South Africa, Australia and New Zealand. The chief effect of this movement was the opening up of new countries. There was also an expanding demand for European manufactures in these newer lands and the latter playing a large part, as importers as well as exporters, in stimulating the industrialisation of the advanced countries.

Foreign trade became indispensable to most nations between 1870 and 1900. A world market emerged for the first time. World trade expanded by an impressive amount. Despite economic liberalisation and free trade, this was the age of the tariff as well as of an increasingly integrated world economy. While Britain clung to Free Trade, American tariffs were higher than any in Europe. Tariff increases for the protection of industry, beginning with the great German tariff of 1879, stimulated industrialisation as well as protected existing industry.

The consequence of industrialisation and expanding trade was the growth of population. Europe's population increased by over 30 per cent between 1870 and 1900 compared to 11 per cent between 1850 and 1870.

In industrial countries were formed associations of firms like trusts and cartels. In 1886 Nobel established the first international trust, the Dynamite Trust Ltd. Rockefeller, the great individualist, declared that 'the day of combination is here to stay. Individualism has gone, never to return.' Along with the movement towards combination, there began trade unions in different countries. Belgium formally recognised unions in 1866, Austria in 1870, Britain between 1870 and 1876, Spain in 1881, France in 1884, Germany in 1890. The Unions increased their membership.

During this period, the governments undertook the comprehensive regulation of society. There began an unprecedented increase in the powers and functions of government. It began to pay increasing attention to public health, elementary education, the regulation of working conditions and the control of public utilities. Battle was fought against plague, typhus, typhoid, smallpox, cholera, scarlet fever. The average expectation of life increased. Equal attention was paid to the provision of compulsory and free elementary education. Along with advances in public health and education, state control was extended over working conditions. Factory laws were introduced in various countries of Europe between 1870 and 1890. The most important achievement was the introduction of compulsory insurance against accident and sickness for working men. Germany took the lead in this matter and Bismarck's insurance laws of 1883-89 were initiated in various countries of Europe. Government interference in the control of social problems had become so pervasive that it has been said of the British Local Government Bill of 1888 that they had brought 'the entire range of ordinary life, from birth, or even before birth, to burial,... within the ambit of public interest and observation.'

Throughout the nineteenth century which witnessed the American Civil War (1861-65), the Polish insurrection, the Meiji revolution in Japan (1868), the fall of the Empire in France, the restoration of monarchy in Spain and the unification of Germany and Italy, revolutions or political convulsions had been common occurrences. In old monarchical Europe with the exception of the creation of new states in Romania and Bulgaria, and in the New World, except for the downfall of Braganza monarchy in Brazil (1889), the overthrow of Spanish rule in Cuba (1898) and continuance of civil war and *coup d'etat* in smaller Latin American states, there were little changes of political regime.

Within the framework of established regimes there was little constitutional change. In the constitutions of all these countries, none of these parliaments had more than nominal powers against the executive. If liberalism was subsumed in a general conservative trend, it was primarily because the rise of the modern state buttressed the existing forms of government by absorbing more power.

One direct change which the government effected was the democratisation of the suffrage. Although women nowhere got the voting right except in Australia and New Zealand before the twentieth century, universal adult suffrage was achieved in most countries. The initiative was taken by Disraeli and Bismarck from the conviction that an enlarged electorate would be largely conservative. But suffrage was not extended in Portugal, Sweden, Denmark, Austria, Hungary, Romania and some of the German states. In Russia and Turkey, Parliaments did not exist. Most of the states relied on the army and the police and increasing centralisation for the maintenance of stability. The politics of the age was distinguished as much by the growth of authority as by the extension of democracy.

Liberalism suffered when it was taken over by conservative politicians. Liberalism became more doctrinaire and more parochial. Liberal rule ended in Britain in 1885, in Germany in 1878, in Austria and the Netherlands in 1879, in Sweden in 1880, in Belgium in 1884 and in France in 1885. Conservative parties acquired a new lease of life after 1880. Along with it emerged new confessional parties in politics like the Centre party in Germany, the Christian Socialist party in Austria, the clerical parties of Belgium, the Netherlands and Switzerland.

With the exception of five wars involving one or more of the world's leading powers no major war took place till 1914. Beyond Europe, enormous changes were effected without war between the major powers. The operation of the new balance of power between the major European powers sometimes brought crises. Japan declared war against China in 1894, the United States against Spain in 1898. The United States became more cautious in the Far East than in the New World. After the Spanish-American war in the 1900s, the United States, with the seizure of the Philippines and the annexation of Hawaii, emerged as a Pacific power. Until Russia's defeat in the Russo-Japanese war of 1904-05, most problems beyond Europe—except in North America and Latin America—were dominated by European powers.

In the new balance of power, Berlin replaced Vienna and Paris. No power seriously regarded Bismarck's manoeuvres as being dangerous to the system or to peace. The acceptance of the new *status quo* and the common determination to keep the peace after 1871 checked dangerous activity. Beginning with the Austro-German Alliance of 1879, there grew up a network of written undertakings. These alliances were limited to European contingencies. The Anglo-Japanese alliance of 1902 was the beginning of a new phase in international relations.

Whereas international relations after 1815 had rested formally on the 'Concert of Europe' and the 'System of Metternich,' it rested after 1871 upon a balance of power between the major European states and more upon the insatiable ambition of Germany. The system of alliances which Bismarck constructed after 1871 for protecting Germany provoked a counter-system of alliances hinging upon France. As the balance between them prevailed, this proved a deterrent to ignite aggression. But after 1890, when they generated mutual fear of aggression, they brought in its train international crises which culminated in war. These were closely inter-linked with the tensions of the Eastern Question, and with the hectic rivalry of the imperial powers for overseas colonies. A new feature was added when colonial imperialism of the new kind clashed in Asia and Africa. Colonial expansion was more extensive than before and was invoked by a wider circle of powers.

By the 1900s Germany approached a degree of material primacy within Europe which no continental power had possessed since 1815. Beginning in the late 1890s her policy roused the fears and provoked the retaliation of the other powers. In the ensuing struggle, Germany sought the mastery of Europe as no power had sought it for a century.

The first half of the twentieth century was a "period of revolutionary change and crisis" comparable to the "social and intellectual upheaval at the turn of the eleventh and twelfth centuries." Of those forces making for a new kind of world, some characteristics were evident in the beginning of the present century. The 'Dwarfing of Europe' and the power of nationalism outside Europe was foreshadowed by Japan's victory over Russia. It became manifest that the fate of Asia, particularly of China, was not the sole concern of European powers. The creation of the Republic of China by Sun-yat-sen in 1912 foreshadowed the events to come after a few decades. In Europe, the focal point was not the rivalry of the Great Powers or the diplomatic crises of 1905 and 1911; rather they were social, technological, and scientific. The technological and industrial changes affecting everyday life—refrigeration, electricity, the telephone, the motor car—all had their beginnings in the late nineteenth century. The twentieth century opened with two triumphs of invention of momentous consequences: Marconi's transmission of wireless signals across the Atlantic in 1901 and Bright Brothers' first flight of the aeroplane in December 1903.

The twentieth century was the heyday of the scientists whose works had already become evident in the preceding century. Becquerel's discovery of radioactivity in 1896, J. J. Thomson's discovery of the electron in 1897, Rutherford's demonstration in 1911 of atoms emitted in radioactive rays and the theories of Planck (1900) and Einstein (1905, 1916) gave a new dimension to the physics and led to the exploitation of nuclear power. Equally dramatic was the advance of genetics and the discovery of drugs to cure malaria and yellow fever. Lives of millions were transformed by Ehrlich's discovery of salvarsan in 1909 and the development of the sulfa drugs in 1935-38 and penicillin in 1940. The permeative force of science changed the whole aspect and outlook of our civilisation as well our daily lives and our habits of thought.

Into this world erupted the First World War (1914-1918) which brought the United States into Europe as a belligerent. The war followed a century of general peace and of European hegemony. The old structure of European states—the Austrian, German, Ottoman and Czarist empires—disappeared. The dwarfing of Europe had begun as a result of the spirit of rationalism which had become particularly potent in India and the Islamic world. The obvious legacy of the war was the 'great depression' of the early 1930s and the emergence of dictatorships in Germany, Italy, Spain, Portugal and several other countries. Hitler's unlimited ambitions were at least one of the causes of the Second World War (1939-1945).

The new era of world history was marked by the illusion of a return to the old order.

International trade and credit revived, though beset by the war debts and reparations. The League of Nations (1919-1946), though an improvement on the old 'Concert of Europe' (1818-1822), failed to prevent aggression. This was chiefly because it had been granted no effective machinery to enforce its power on the recalcitrant. The United States retreated from open commitment to the European balance of power.

Between the wars imperialism was at its low ebb. The part played by the Dominions in the war gave them new status as independent states., British Commonwealth of Nations was now merely symbolic. In the Middle East the old Turkish Empire dismembered giving way to new states. In Africa, the Caribbean and South East Asia, wind of change was slow to come. The French colonies continued to be administered as permanent dependencies of metropolitan France.

The erosion of European power was actually felt in Japan. While presenting its Twenty-one Demands on China in 1915, Japan had made a claim to dominate China. Japan's invasion of Manchuria in 1931 was a flagrant violation of international law. Behind it lay the rapid growth of population in the East. 'It is no exaggeration to state that the demographic revolution of the half-century between 1890 and 1940 was the basic change marking the transition from one era of history to another.'

The Second World War (1939-1945) was indeed a world war encompassing Europe, Asia, the Atlantic and the Pacific. After the war 'the contours of the contemporary world were clear to see: the dwarfing of Europe, the end of colonial empires, the resurgence of the peoples of Asia and Africa, the predominance of two superpowers—the United States and Russia, the consolidation of revolutionary China (1949), and the move into new realms of scientific discovery, space exploration, technical sophistication, and nuclear weaponry. The violence of the age had brought nemesis to Europe (1949).[1]

1. *The New Cambridge Modern History,* Vol. XII, 2nd edition, P. 9.

CHAPTER 13

THE FRENCH REVOLUTION

The French Revolution: Its Character And Nature

While France in the last quarter of the eighteenth century remained politically the 'France of Louis XIV'—without the Grand Monarch, socially the nation was changing rapidly. But this is not equivalent to saying that the French Revolution was inevitable. 'The Revolution was not a Niagara in the stream of national life, its incidence and situation determined by the presence of a single great fault in the social strata: it was rather the result of the confluence of a host of contributory currents, small and great, flowing together to swell suddenly into a mighty flood.'[1] To understand the way in which the Revolution came about, the hidden and the greater forces, must be studied against the background of broad spectrum of history. Robespierre's analysis of the factors which made the revolution possible merits quotation:

> In states constituted as are nearly all the countries of Europe, there are three powers: the monarchy, the aristocracy, and the people, and the people is powerless. Under such circumstances a revolution can break out only as the result of a gradual process. It begins with the nobles, the clergy, the wealthy, whom the people supports when its interests coincide with theirs in resistance to the dominant power, that of the monarchy. Thus it was that in France the judiciary, the nobles, the clergy, the rich, gave the original impulse to the revolution, the people appeared on the scene only later.[2]

Historians and writers have explained the causes of the French Revolution according to their own prejudices. Edmund Burke, who was a keen observer of the Revolution, was of opinion that the Revolution was not the outcome of a genuine desire for reform, but was the child of the conspiracy of a few literary men and philosophies. The liberal historians like Thiers and Mignet tried to explain it either as a legitimate protest against the tyrannies of the Old Regime or as a social protest of impoverished classes. Jules Michelet, the great historian of the 1940s, saw the Revolution as a spontaneous upsurge of the whole French nation against the despotism and injustice of the Old Regime. For Michelet the people, instead of being a passive instrument in the hands of other classes, 'is the real and living hero of the piece.' Alexis de Tocqueville, agreeing with Mignet and Thiers that the government was despotic and in need of reform, acknowledges the importance of the writings of the Enlightenment in helping to undermine traditional beliefs. Tocqueville argued that the old feudal survivals and aristocratic privileges appeared to be vexatious to the middle classes and peasants who became more conscious of their social importance. The French Revolution was unique in contemporary Europe as what began as a revolt of the nobility later on associated the middle and lower classes in common action against the King and aristocracy. Chateaubriand later wrote that 'the patricians began the revolution and the plebeians completed it.'

Recent historical debate has given a new twist to the genesis of the Revolution. It did not deny the role of the Paris Parliament in blocking the king's reforms and the ideological forces unleashed by the Philosophers. According to some schools the financial crisis following the war of American Independence which hastened

1. *A History of Modern France*, Cobban Alfred, Vol. I, P. 137.
2. Ibid.

the summoning of the Estates General, emanated not from utter bankruptcy but of sheer mismanagement.

Earlier scholars put special emphasis on economic and social problems in accentuating political upheavels. To Marx the French Revolution became the focus of all historical discussions. He was followed by many Marxists and quasi-Marxists. In 1930s C.E. Lbrouse put forth evidence for agragrian crisis in late eighteenth century France that led to acute food shortage and price catastrophe in 1787-89. In the 1950s a long debate followed between the followers of Lefebre and Cobban. However a consensus emerged which highlighted the 'bourgeoisie' interests, Cobban concluded 'the revolution was thiers and for them at least it was a wholly successful revolution.' Another scholar wrote 'the French Revolution constitute the growing point of a long social and economic evolution which made the bourgeoisie the mistress of the world.' But the bourgeois theory was challenged and emphasis was laid on the artisans and are sansculottes.

Social Cause

Though France was the most advanced of all the continental countries, yet socially it had some glaring defects. French society was divided into three hostile groups—the clergy, the nobles and the Third Estate comprising comprehensive category of classes. The clergy or first estate constituted less than two per cent of the population; but the economic power of the Church was considerable. The clergy itself was divided into two classes: higher clergy and lower clergy. The higher clergy—archbishops, bishops and abbots—often enjoyed great wealth. They had large estates and indulged in luxury and vices without caring for their ecclesiastical duties. But the lower clergy profited little by the privileged position of the order. Comprising two-thirds of the order, this group furnished spiritual guidance to the mass of the people. The monastic order was in a state of rapid decay contributing little to moral progress or to the government treasury.

The Second Estate—the nobles—was divided into three sections—country nobles, official nobility and the nobles of the court (courtiers). This irresponsible group was united by the bond of 'privilege'. The country nobles who were in a majority, had small incomes and exacted the utmost farthing from their tenants. Their estates tended to diminish as a result of the laws of inheritance. The official nobility—some four thousand in all—chiefly centered in the Parliament of Paris. Enjoying immense prestige who could fight the monarchy openly they were opposed to the freedom of the press and to all reforms. Much more conspicuous were the courtiers. They were supported by a bankrupt government whose resources they consumed in idle luxury. The classic example of the waste of the national resources was that the royal household numbered four thousand persons.

The Third Estate was a comprehensive category including financiers, merchants, office holders, professionals and the agricultural labourer. Many of them suffered from numerous restrictions on them. The king monopolised salt and other necessary commodities; and manufacturing and trade were minutely regulated by the decrees. But the great bulk of the Third Estate—more than 20 million—was peasants who constituted nine-tenths of the population. The peasant had to pay rent to his feudal lord, tithes to the Church and taxes to the King. It has been estimated that a French peasant could count on less than one-fifth of his income for the use of himself and his family. While one-third of the French peasants owned their land outright, the larger part possessed tiny parcels of land, quite insufficient to feed their families. Arthur Young wrote that in Champagne and Lorraine the division was carried to such a extent that 'a single fruit tree has constituted a farm.'

Agriculture was also backward as the peasant had little capital. Moreover, a prolonged depression was beginning to take its place. After 1778, when France entered the American War, there was a slump resulting in the fall of prices. During these years the net profits of small tenant farmers, peasant proprietors and other sharecroppers tended to fall out of all proportion. Then came the sudden economic catastrophe of 1787-89 which took the form of bad harvests and shortage. The crisis hit the bulk of the peasantry. From agriculture it spread to industry and unemployment reached serious dimension in Paris and the textile centres of Lille, Lyons, Sedan, Rouen and Rheims. 'Thus, peasants and urban craftsmen and workers were drawn together in common hostility to the government, landlords, merchants and speculators; and these, classes entered the Revolution in a context of increasing poverty and hardship rather than of prosperity.'[3]

The middle class or bourgeoisie was the most dynamic element in society as it embraced the intellectuals, the business element and the government officials. They formed a very wide 'middle'. In France in 1789 the bourgeoisie owned between 20 and 30 per cent of all land. Yet the bourgeoisie had their dissatisfaction as too many offices with too little work produced intense frustration. The anti-aristocratic creed of equal political rights and careers open to talents arose from the depressed bourgeoisie, petty lawyers and office-holders, whose aspirations the old order had fostered but had been unable to satisfy. The effects of the French Revolution can best be judged by the words of Mary Wollstonecraft. On 1795, she wrote, the French Society after the Revolution was 'a civilisation founded on reason and morality.'

Intellectual Revolt

There had been growing in Europe, throughout eighteenth century, a revolutionary spirit. This spirit, a spirit of rationalist criticism to the Church, monarchy and nobility, was fostered particularly by the writings of French thinkers and literary men, the philosophers. The French held the foremost place in the world of thought. But this Enlightenment was heralded by the work of such men as Locke, Hume, Gibbon, Robertson in England; Lessing and Kant, Goethe and Schiller in Germany, Benjamin Franklin in America. By 1780s the philosophic tide had reached European intellectuals, but the concrete achievements were not substantial. As Kant declared in 1784, it was the Age of Enlightenment, but not an Enlightened Age.

Though the connection between the Philosopher and the outbreak of the French Revolution in 1789 is somewhat indirect, nevertheless their works played an important role in producing the revolutionary situation. They awakened among the people a critical mind to question the whole foundation of the old order.

Of the earlier rationalists the most famous was Montesquieu (1689-1755). In his earlier work, *The Persian Letters* (1721), a satire on the French society, Montesquieu attacked the privileged class, the corruption of the court and the folly of religious intolerance. His famous book, *The Spirit of the Laws,* which appeared in 1750, had a tremendous success. He was an admirer of the British Constitution as the latter preserved political liberty by the separation of three powers—executive, legislative, and judiciary. The only governments he found acceptable were monarchies and that of Great Britain. Despotism was the worst of all possible governments. Montesquieu emphasised all the restraints that true monarchy ought to observe.

The most revolutionary among the Philosophers was Jean Jacques Rousseau (1712-1778). Napoleon once declared that if Rousseau had never lived there would have been no French Revolution. The influences of his book *Emile* (1762) and *Discourse* on the Arts and Science (1750), were profound. His theory was that man was essentially good, but corrupted by civilisation. 'Man was born free, but everywhere he is in chains.' All government was the outcome of an agreement or contract framed by the people for the promotion of their welfare. Hence all government rests upon the consent of the governed and no ruler can deprive the individual citizen of his natural rights to life, liberty, and property. He declared that sovereign power could not be divided or separated between a number of institutions. Hence he placed sovereignty permanently and inalienably in the hands of the people as a whole. To those dissatisfied with German intellectual life, Rousseau came as a prophet. 'Rousseau,' Goethe observed 'had really touched our sympathies.'

Of the intellectual circle, Voltaire (1694-1778) was the best known and the widest read. An exceedingly prolific writer, his main attack was directed against the Church. His oft-repeated remark was 'Annihilate the infamous thing'

3. Rude George, *Revolutionary Europe*, 1783-1813, P. 74.

(Church). In one of his works, *The Letters on the English* he pointed out that the Church and the nobility in England were not exempt from direct taxation. He was the prince of rationalists and in his scathing attacks on the Church and other pillars of the Old Regime he was something of a crusader.

Dictionaries served useful purpose in standardising and popularising knowledge. Denis Diderot and Jean Le Rond d'Alembert launched in France (1751) the great *Encyclopédie* with the aid of a broad spectrum of experts. Originating in a project merely to translate Chambers' *Cyclopaedia* (1728) into French, this enterprise rapidly grew into an attempt, 17 volumes in all, to summarise the current state of knowledge and 'to transmit it to the men who shall come after us, so that the works of past centuries should not have been works useless for the centuries that shall follow, so that our descendants, becoming better informed, shall become at the same time more virtuous and happier, and so that we do not die without having deserved well of the human race'. The *Encyclopédie* was an attempt to convince the people the value and importance of certain ideas. In this respect the *Encyclopédie* epitomised the sum of 'Enlightened' opinion in the mid-eighteenth century.

Implicit in Enlightenment there developed the principle of utility. The theory of Utility was derived from Locke from his contention that the mainsprings of human action are the pursuit of pleasure. Helvetius (1715-71) expanded this theme and declared in his book on the Mind 1758 that 'customs have always found their source in the real or apparently utility of the public.' In 1764 the Italian Beccaria based the whole Theory of Criminal Law on utilitarian principles. Laws, he declared, in his *On Crimes and Punishment,* ought to be formulated by a 'cool examiner of human nature... and had this only end in view, *the greatest happiness of the greatest number.'* In England, Jeremy Bentham made this principle the keystone of his philosophy of utility. To Helvetius laws were the product of men alone and could be changed by men according to their utility.

Physiocrats or Economists

There was another group known as Physiocrats or Economists that had great influence and an important relation to the work of the Revolution. They were much influenced by the writings of Adam Smith (*The Wealth of Nations,* 1776) who is usually regarded as the greatest protagonist of free trade. David Hume in his *Essays* (1741-42), also pointed out that the true wealth of a country lay in its people and in its industry and not in its stock of precious metals. Protectionism benefitted nobody; therefore all restrictions ware bad. In France, the Physiocrats maintained that the true basis of all wealth was land and agriculture. The sure way to enrich a country was to stimulate its agricultural productivity and to follow the free trade policy. Free trade was to raise the price of goods, higher prices would stimulate productivity, and so, in the long run, there would be economic prosperity. Accordingly, physiocrats advocated the abolition of control on the grain trade and of internal customs barriers. Next to agriculture, trade and manufacturers were secondary activities. The physiocrats—Gournay, Quesnay, Mirabeau, Turgot, Mercier de la Riviere, Dupont de Nemours—were an organised group of propagandists who spread their views from the middle of the eighteenth century. They wrote articles and substantial volumes such as Quesnay's *Theory of Taxation* (1761), Mirabeau's *Friend of Mankind* or Dupont de Nemours' *Physiocracy* (1768). But they also provoked considerable opposition as to decry the importance of commerce and manufactures was in fact to stifle future economic advances.

Weakness of the Monarchy: Financial Crisis

The government of France in the eighteenth century was a highly centralised despotism. After Louis XIV (1643-1715), the monarchy had lost a great deal of vigour and its ability to maintain the loyalty of their subjects. This was due in part to the indolence and personal failings of Louis XV (1715-74) and in part, to the high-handedness of the bureaucracy. Louis XV was never a friend of the *parlements*; he wanted to silence them once and for all. Minister Maupeou dismissed the parliament on 1771. Most of the Frenchmen protested against the policy of the King and the early 1770s saw the beginnings of a crisis of confidence in French public life. 'We are on the verge of a crisis,' wrote Diderot in April 1771, 'which will end in slavery or liberty. If all the *parlements* are dissolved...farewell to every privilege of the various estates constituting a corrective principle which prevents the monarchy from degenerating into despotism.' The *parlements* themselves convinced now of their powerlessness called for a convocation of the representative assembly of the whole nation, the half-forgotten estates-general. The last meeting was called on 1614. Isolated calls of this sort had been heard in times of crisis before, but never had the demand been so consistent or widespread as in 1771.

Louis XVI, on ascending the throne in 1774, was eager to bring about substantial reforms in the administration. Unlike his predecessor he had a high sense of personal responsibility. The old *parlements* were restored. Between 1774 and 1787 they never prevented the government from raising any tax on which it was really determined. Louis XVI's government pursued a two-fold policy. One was to support the American rebels in their conflict with Great Britain. But the war dealt a ruinous blow to the already overburdened finances of the state. The second policy was the avoidance of bankruptcy. Turgot made it the keystone of his programme when he took charge of the finances in 1774. But within two years he had fallen having antagonised everybody by abolishing the *corvee* (a levy on the peasant's time for work on the public highways) and removing restrictions on the wine and grain trades. Louis XVI dismissed him without the opportunity to attempt further reforms. Louis next entrusted the finances to Necker, a vainglorious Swiss banker, He had little sympathy with the way the regime worked. He despised the *parlements* and advocated provincial assemblies. By his ability to raise loans he financed the American war without introducing new taxation. In 1782 he published the *Compte Rendu*—the first public balance sheet of the financial situation of France. But when in the same year he tried to engross overall control of policy, the King dismissed him from office.

Necker's two immediate successors were not capable and had to bear the odium of raising taxes. Finally, in 1783, the King appointed Calonne. Fertile in expedients, the new Controller General began by restoring confidence in the stability of royal finances. By recognising the sacredness of the royal debts and paying the interest on them promptly, he inaugurated an energetic programme of public works. With confidence thus restored, Calonne was able to resume the policy of borrowing. But by August 1786 he found that he had exhausted the market and could borrow no more. Undismayed, Calonne presented the King with a plan for a general land tax to be levied on all classes without distinction, and for the creation of Provincial Assemblies to supervise its collection. To boost production, Calonne proposed other measures—the abolition of internal customs barriers and the freeing of the grain trade from government regulation. Since there was no prospect of persuading the *parlement* to accept such a proposal, he hastily summoned an Assembly of Notables in February 1787. The members of the Assembly of Notables were all nominated by the King and the Assembly itself had not met for 160 years. From the start everything went wrong. The majority opposed the proposals. In vain he appealed to the patriotism of the assemblage. But Lafayette, a Notable, announced that there was only one body competent to undertake reforms and that was the Estates-General.

Calonne fell in April 1787 and was succeeded by Cardinal de Brienne. To everyone's astonishment, Brienne took up his predecessor's plan almost unchanged. But he failed to win the full authority for their enactment that he had hoped for. The Notables resumed their opposition and on 25 May the Notables were dissolved. Brienne now adopted the normal procedure of presenting his edicts for registration by the *parlements*. In 1787 the popularity of the *parlements*—or the sovereign courts, as they were called—were such that they seemed in a position to dictate their will to the King. But these bodies were determined not to sanction proposals that the Notables had felt unable to agree to. The only body with that right, declared the Paris *parlement* in August 1787, was the

Estates-General. But Brienne was equally obdurate. He invoked the king's authority which overrode the *parlement's* objections, promulgated the fiscal decrees and exiled the Paris magistrates. But it was the *parlement* that won the day. The provincial courts, to whom Brienne now turned, rallied to the support of their Paris colleagues. Brienne had no option but to yield and *parlement* was reinstated in September. Arthur Young reported that France was 'on the verge of some great revolution in the government.'

Calling of the Estates-General

Against a background of vague talk about convoking the Estates-General in 1792, the Government offered to abandon the proposed tax reforms in return for the registration of new loans. A special 'royal session' of the *parlement* was held on November 19, 1787, to register the proposals. But the King refused to take a vote and when Duke D'Orleans protested that this was illegal, the King lost his temper, crying 'That makes no difference! It is legal because I wish it.' The duke and two councillors were exiled on the next day.

Public resentment now reached a climax. On January 4, 1788, the *parlement* condemned the arrest and demanded individual liberty as a natural right. On May 3, it published a declaration of the fundamental laws of the Kingdom: that the monarchy was hereditary; that the vote of taxes was a power of the Estates-General; that Frenchmen could not be arrested or detained arbitrarily. The Government concluded that the only way left was to sweep away the opposition of the *parlements.* On May 8, 1788, members of the *parlement* of Paris were exiled and two of them were arrested on the floor of the court. The King obtained registration for six edicts prepared by Lamoignon—the Keeper of the Seals. The *parlements* were not abolished, but they lost the rights of registration and remonstrance which were now transferred to a Plenary Court composed of princes and officers of the Crown.

There was explosion of public fury at this ultimate act of despotism. In the uproar began to be heard the cry of liberty. Many nobles resigned from public positions. The assembly of the clergy refused to vote the government funds. Dauphine, Franche Comte, Provence demanded back their old Provincial Estates. In Rennes, Pau and Grenoble there were violent public demonstrations against the government. In such circumstances, it was inexpedient to float a loan. The ministers of war and navy resigned. Brienne yielded once again. On July 5 he promised to call the Estates-General. On August 8 he suspended the Plenary Court and announced the convocation of the Estates-General on May 1, 1789. On August 24, the Treasury being empty, Brienne tendered his resignation The King recalled Necker, the financial wizard. Lamoignon was dismissed and on September 23 the *parlement* of Paris was reinstated.

On September 25, 1788, the *parlement* announced that the Estates-General should be constituted, as in 1614, in three separate orders—the Clergy, the Nobility and the Third Estate or bourgeois, so that the Clergy and the Nobility would retain the upper hand. To the Third Estate, the forms of 1614 seemed designed to condemn them to perpetual political impotence, always outvoted by the other two orders. The members of the Third Estate, therefore, demanded that three orders were to meet as a single chamber in which each individual should have a vote. Their deputies totalled 621 against 285 for the Nobles and 308 for the Clergy, giving the Third Estate a slight preponderance. Through the 'Committee of 30', the Third Estate launched a campaign in favour of changing the composition of the Estates to the disadvantage of the privileged orders. Pamphlets called for the doubling of the Third Estate's numbers, and for voting by head. Necker, fearing unpopularity, conceded on December 27, 1788, that the Third Estate should have double representation, i.e., they should have as many deputies as the Clergy and Nobility combined. But Necker said nothing about vote by head, without which double representation was meaningless. So as 1789 began there had been a major realignment of forces in France. 'The controversy', remarked a contemporary journalist, 'has completely changed. King, despotism and constitution are now minor questions. The war is between the Third Estate and the other two orders.'

The first four months of 1789 were dominated by elections to the Estates. The elections took place against a background of intense economic hardship following a poor harvest in 1788. By April 1789 it has been estimated that a wage earner in Paris needed 88 per cent of his income to buy bread alone. There were riots in Brittany and Paris. Each electoral assembly drafted a 'notebook of grievances.' In these notebooks, called *cahiers*, were set forth the demands of the French people for redressing their grievances. On matters affecting political and administrative reform, there was a general agreement among the *cahiers* of the three Estates. But the *cahiers* of the Third Estate went much further. They demanded liberty of speech, writing and assembly, freedom from arbitrary arrest and the abolition of age-old privileges of the Clergy and the Nobility. Surprisingly, none of the *cahiers* hinted at the abolition of the monarchy or nobility.

Despite profound disturbance, 900 deputies met at Versailles on May 5, 1789—300 each from the Nobility and the Clergy, 600 from the Third Estate. Neither the King nor Necker provided the leadership expected by the Estates. They offered no programme on which the deputies could act. This was a shocking disappointment, especially to the Third Estate. To the outrage of the Third, it became apparent that the Three Estates were expected to meet and vote separately. Then for five weeks the Third Estate urged members of the Nobility and Clergy to join them in one great assembly. Their determination soon split the Clergy, some of whom crossed over to join the Third Estate on June 15.

On June 17, the Third Estate declared itself the National Assembly of France and provisionally authorised tax collection. They were supported on June 19 by a majority vote of the Clergy. On June 20, the Assembly, finding itself locked out of its hall, repaired to the royal Tennis Court, where it took a solemn oath not to disperse until it had given France a constitution. The 'Tennis Court Oath' was the actual beginning of the French Revolution for in it the representatives of the Third Estate were going against the orders of the King. Unfortunately for the Crown, it chose the wrong course. On June 23, the King held a 'royal session' of the Estates-General in which he announced a programme of reforms. But he coupled it with an order that the Three Estates should remain separate. But it was too late to make the old constitution work. Moreover, the indecisive King took no forceful measure against the revolutionary commoners. Soon these were joined by a number of Clergy and forty-seven liberal Nobles led by Duke d'Orleans. On June 27, the King reluctantly ordered the Three Estates to unite into one body. A contemporary English traveller noted in his diary that 'the whole business now seems over, and the revolution complete.'

But the revolution was far from complete. The court party began at once to move troops at Versailles and Paris to destroy the National Assembly. The Assembly's attitude hardened considerably. On July 7, it set up a constitutional committee and two days later added the word 'Constituent' to its title. The crisis broke on July 11 when the King dismissed Necker and ordered him to leave France immediately. Necker's dismissal now constituted a challenge. Despite his dismal performance at the opening of the Estates, Necker's popularity was undiminished. It came at a time of mounting suspicion of the King's duplicity and at the very moment when the price of bread in Paris reached its highest level of the year. On July 12 Paris exploded at the news. Demonstrators forced the royal garrison to withdraw from Paris. The capital was in the hands of the people. A frantic search for arms began at all the city's strong points. Customs barriers were sacked. The regiment of the French Guards, the capital's permanent garrison, joined the insurgents.

On the morning of July 14 the search for arms and gunpowder led the crowds to an arsenal where they removed 32,000 muskets and then across the city to the Bastille. The old fortress for state prisoners was said to be another arms depot. The Governor of Bastille, De Launay, after a vain effort of resistance, surrendered. The attack on Bastille is best described by Charles Dickens in his 'A Tale of Two Cities': 'with a roar that sounded as if all the breath in France had been shaped into the detested world, the living sea rose, wave on wave, depth on depth, and overflowed the city to that point.' He was murdered in the confusion of the surrender. 'This is a revolt' said Louis on hearing the news. 'Sire', answered Liancourt, 'it is not a revolt, it is a revolution.'

The fall of Bastille, a grim symbol of Bourbon despotism, had far-reaching consequences. As per the leader of the 'whigs," Charles James Fox, (his speech in the British Parliament on 15/7/1789) 'much the greatest event...that ever happened in the world.' The National Assembly was saved and received royal recognition. Matters now proceeded apace. Prominent citizens of Paris now set up a new city council with Bailly as Mayor and Lafayette as commander of the National Guard. On July 17 the King visited Paris in person and expressed his official sanction of what had been done.

The turbulence was far from over. The movement extended to rural France. In many regions, peasants rose and attacked the chateaux of nobles, burned the rolls which recorded the peasants' servitude. In an emotional session on the night of August 4, 1789, the National Assembly destroyed the entire feudal system and put an end to the principle of aristocratic privilege in France. What the nobility and the clergy would not give up in May they surrendered in August in response to the peasant uprising. It was a great step in the legal emancipation of the soil and those who exploited it.

Having finally promulgated its Declaration of the Rights of Man and the Citizen on August 26, the Assembly spent much of September discussing the powers of the King under the future constitution. The King, encouraged by splits between radical and conservative bourgeois deputies, refused his assent to the August decrees and to the Declaration of the Rights. Once more he began to move up troops. To counteract such measures, radical deputies began to organise popular demonstrations. Once more the food crisis lent a particular intensity to popular agitation. During August and September there were constant bread riots in Paris, Versailles and Saint Denis. From mid-September, a leading part in this agitation was played by the women who gave a lead to their menfolk in the great march to Versailles on October 5. They were followed by 30,000 National Guards with Lafayette as their head. Faced with this impressive array, the King had no alternative but to sanction the August decrees and the Declaration of Rights. But these concessions no longer satisfied the insurgents; and the next day, the King and his family were compelled to accompany the marchers back to Paris. Ten days later the National Assembly joined the royal family in Paris.

Work of the National Assembly, June 17, 1789-September 30, 1791

By the end of October 1789 most Frenchmen believed that the Revolution was over. Two royal *coups* had been averted and power transferred to the Nation's representatives, who were now embarking upon the task of devising a constitution. But the body that set itself the task of making a new order of France had, unlike the English parliament, no tradition of continuity. It was the creature of circumstances. Apart from the lack of sound leadership, this body had all the defects of pioneer reformers. The members were inexperienced, and were prone to be so presumptuous that 'every member of the Assembly thought himself capable of everything.'

The first major accomplishment of the National Assembly had been the destruction of the old order in the 'August Days'. Its second was the assertion of the principles on which the new order was to be built—the 'Declaration of the Rights of Man and Citizen'. This Declaration reflected the influence of the natural-law school of philosophy, represented by Locke, Montesquieu and Rousseau. The Declaration was the outcome of hard bargaining between different groups of deputies. Both Mounier and Lafayette, respectively of the Right and Centre, played an important part in its drafting. The Declaration of Rights is remarkable that it neatly balances a statement of universal principles and human rights. The Seventeen Articles of the declaration asserted that men are free and equal, that the people are sovereign, and that *law is an expression of the popular will.* All those liberties of the person, free speech, free assembly, which had been worked out in England and America, were asserted. Equality in the Declaration meant equality before the law and in eligibility for office. According to a French historian, the Declaration was a 'death certificate of the Old Regime'. There were marked similarities to the American Declaration of Independence (1776). The Declaration has been an indisputable factor in the political and social evolution of modern Europe. 'It has found there', says a writer, 'five or six formulae as trenchant as mathematical propositions, true as the truth itself, intoxicating as a vision of the Absolute.' The Declaration prepared a nation for the constitutional changes which were to follow. The greater part of this legislation became incorporated in the Constitution of 1791.

The Assembly then worked out a Constitution which was finally adopted on 14 September 1791. Owing to this part of its work the National Assembly is also known as the Constituent Assembly. France was to be governed by a King and a parliament known as the Legislative Assembly. The Constitution provided a clear separation of powers among executive, legislative and judicial authorities. The King was now described as the 'King of the French'. He was allowed a three-year suspensive veto, but not over constitutional or fiscal legislation. He could declare war and make peace with the consent of the Legislative Assembly and was further empowered to appoint ministers, ambassadors and military officers. But the King had no power to dissolve the Assembly; ministers would be answerable, not to himself but to the Assembly.

The real power was to be entrusted to the Legislative Assembly. It was to consist of a single chamber of 745 members and was to be elected for two years by a system of indirect representation based upon a limited franchise. Annual sessions, freedom from dissolution, the right to initiate legislation, full control over national finance, the power to create or abolish all public offices, the right to enforce the legal responsibility of ministers and a close control over foreign policy endowed the Legislative Assembly with sovereign authority.

The administrative reorganisation of France by the Assembly proved more permanent. There was a sense that this was a unique opportunity to lay the foundations for a better future. 'Let us make haste,' declared the noble deputy Duport, 'while we are still in our political youth, while the fire of liberty still burns within us.' Administration must be decentralised, and controlled by elected representatives. A uniform system was devised based on departments, districts, cantons and communes, which, in its essentials, has survived to the present day. France was divided into 83 departments, 547 districts. 4,732 contons and 44,000 communes, which controlled the collection and assessment of taxes, and exercised sole authority over the troops. The 44,000 Communes 'seemed likely to develop into so many independent republics.' Paris was to have its own municipal council and to be further subdivided into 48 sections armed with powers of election, police, and local justice. The effective decentralisation gave France a new consciousness of national unity.

The judicial system was reorganised similarly. The *parlements* and their subordinate courts disappeared. As in England and America, the judiciary was declared to be independent of the executive. Trial by the jury was introduced, and a start was made of reforming the maze of old laws and customs and replacing it by a uniform code. Justice was made free and equal for all; a network of tribunals was created at municipal, departmental and national level with elective judges. All judges were elected for six-year terms. At the apex were two national tribunals—a Court of Appeals and a High Court.

Financial Measures

The Assembly was called upon to solve the pressing financial difficulty which had compelled the King to summon the Estates-General. Two loans for a hundred and thirteen million livres which were issued on the authority of the Assembly had yielded only twelve million. 'Patriotic offerings' had produced 100 million livres and, again, bankruptcy was at the door. To meet immediate requirements, a land tax was introduced calculated to raise 240 million livres a year. Further taxes were to be levied on personal incomes and movable property, and on commercial and industrial revenues. But these measures were quite insufficient to meet the mounting toll of debt, compensation payment and current expenditure. So exceptional measures had to be found. In November 1789 the Assembly decreed the confiscation of the landed estates held by the Church, and against this property as security it issued paper money called *assignats*. The assignat was a salutary shot in the arm and saved the Assembly from its temporary difficulties. But after 1790 *assignats* suffered steady depreciation and a serious inflation of prices occurred.

Church: Civil Constitution of the Clergy

After confiscating clerical property, the Assembly assumed the right to regulate the Church. The Assembly wanted to give the Church a more efficient and economical organisation, to root out all vestiges of privilege, and to bring the Church in line with political institutions by introducing election of clergy. In February 1790, monasteries and convents were suppressed. In July a 'Civil Constitution of the Clergy' was enacted. This document attempted to redress many of the lower clergy's grievances: they were now assured of decent salaries. The ecclesiastical map was redrawn on more rational lines. The number of bishops was reduced from 139 to 83. Bishops and priests were to be elected by the people and paid by the State. The Catholic Church was, in effect, made a department of the State. The Assembly refused to submit the Civil Constitution, before it became enforced, for the sanction of the Pope.

The Assembly was in a hurry. So, in November 1790, it burned its bridges, declared the Constitution to be in force and required a loyalty oath to the nation from bishops and priests. The result left the Assembly astonished. Only seven out of 160 bishops took the oath, and no more than half of the rest of the clergy. When Pope Pious VI condemned the Civil Constitution, many who had taken the oath withdrew it. France came to have, in effect, two churches—one loyal to the Government, the other to Rome. The Government's clergy were called juring or Patriot Clergy; the rebels were referred to as non-juring or Refractory. The National Assembly retaliated against refractory clergy. Not only did it deprive them their rights as citizen, but deny them their pensions. The position did not improve—non-juring priests constituted a network of potential counter-revolutionaries and continued to disturb the religious life of France. The schism affecting the country lasted till the time of Napoleon (1804-1815).

Estimate of the Work of the Assembly

Although the Declaration tried to be universal, it did not appear to be comprehensive. Economic equality and state obligation to the poor were not mentioned. Property is 'a sacred and inviolable right', and no attempt is made to define or circumscribe it. There is no mention of the rights of assembly and of petitioning. Freedom of opinion is limited by the proviso that it must not disturb public order as established by law. Though the Declaration of Rights had proclaimed the right of all citizens to take part in the making of laws, it had not granted the specific right of suffrage to all citizens, especially those without property. So citizens were divided into 'active' and 'passive', and only the former who paid a direct tax—equivalent to three days' wages—might vote. Even higher qualifications were demanded of those hoping to be elected. The Declaration made no mention of slavery and the slave trade, however free and equal men might theoretically be. The Assembly was forced to admit slavery as economically necessary to all colonies. The declaration, moreover, omitted any Declaration of Duties, an omission not remedied until 1795. In June 1791 the Assembly passed the famous Le Chapelier Law, by which combinations of workers were declared illegal, and the law was not finally repealed until 1884.

In economic policy the Assembly's bourgeois character was evident. Although service dues were abolished, the peasant was obliged to pay an indemnity in order to extinguish certain rights of the manorial lords to their property. A majority of the peasants simply refused to pay any compensation. Still more serious was the over-issuance of the Treaty Bonds, called *assignats,* which shook the national credit and ushered in a new financial crisis. The *assignats* did not pay the national debt or allow the government to meet its expenses. They were not even a successful paper currency. By August 1792, *assignats* were worth 58 per cent of face value; by the end of 1794, 24 per cent, and, by the end of 1796, almost nothing!!

The Civil Constitution of the Clergy alienated the clergy from the Revolution and caused a schism in the Church which profoundly disturbed the religious life of the nation. Another consequence was that, in time, the new Constitutional Church also lost credit, was separated from the State, until the old church was re-established on new foundations by Bonaparte's Concordat of 1801.

The National Assembly failed to establish a stable constitution. The sharp separation of executive and legislature, with the preponderance of power in the hands of the latter made the cooperation between the King and the Assembly impossible. The lack of a strong executive was the main reason for the successful effort of the Paris Commune and the Jacobins to abolish the monarchy and establish a Republic. 'In its fear of reaction the National Assembly ensured a new revolution.'

Nevertheless, with all these shortcomings, a solid core of constructive legislation survived the revolutionary period and was to influence the monarchies and republics of the nineteenth century. Though the immediate gain of the wage-earner was little, tax-exemption and privileges of the nobles had received cruel blow; equality before the law and the 'career open to talents' remained; France retained her administrative and economic unity and the peasants became proprietors of the soil and were freed from tithe and feudal obligations. 'In fact, a great deal of what was permanent in the legislation of the revolutionary years was that contemplated or begun by the Constituent Assembly; and it is no exaggeration to maintain that the legacy that the Revolution left was, in substance, that conceived in the decidedly bourgeois image of the men of 1789.'[4]

Flight to Varennes

Meanwhile certain developments occurred which considerably altered the course of the Revolution. The year 1790 had been a year of comparative social calm. The opening months of 1791 witnessed a revival of agitation. Unemployment was widespread. Popular discontents led to demonstrations against suspected counter-revolutionary elements, such as non-juring priests. The number of *emigres* was increasing and they were seeking foreign support and even beginning to form a counter-revolutionary army. Mirabeau, who was a major supporter of limited monarchy, died prematurely in April 1791. Worst of all, the King was out of sympathy with what was happening. He had been in secret correspondence with rulers of Spain, Sweden and Austria repudiating all concessions made to the Third Estate. On June 20, 1791, the King, accompanied by Marie Antoinette and the royal children, set out at night for the Austrian Netherlands. They nearly reached safely, but were stopped at Varennes and brought back to Paris on June 25. The King was suspended from office but, having given a pledge to accept the pending constitution, he was reinstated.

The episode had an electrifying effect and destroyed many illusions. The majority of the National Assembly was horrified that the main symbol of stability of the Constitution should try to abandon the Revolution. The King's attempted flight confirmed the suspicion that he was a counter-revolutionary in league with non-juring priests, emigres, and reactionary foreign monarchs. There was an outburst of popular republicanism. The political clubs of the capital demanded the King's deposition and the declaration of a republic. A mass demonstration at Champ de Mars in Paris to sign a republican petition was dispersed on July 17, 1791 by Lafayette and the National Guard at a cost of fifty lives. In the aftermath of the 'massacre of the Champ de Mars', hundreds of deputies seceded from the Jacobin Club, and formed a rival association of conservative views, the Feuillant Club. But the Jacobins, among whom Maximilian Robespierre was playing an important role, emerged as the acknowledged leader of the left within the Assembly. And Jacobins, Cordeliers Club and *Sans-culottes* (the small shopkeepers, workshop masters and wage-earners) were united in common opposition to the Constituent Assembly.

Varennes had an international effect. It led to the series of developments culminating in the outbreak of war with Austria and Prussia on April 20, 1792. The Austrian Emperor, Leopold II, Antoinette's brother, issued the Padua Circular on July 5, 1791 inviting European rulers to concert vigorous measures in order to restore 'the liberty and honour' of the French King. This threat, however, was considerably toned down in

4. Rude George, *Revolutionary Europe*, 1783-1815, P. 120.

the Declaration of Pillnitz issued jointly by Austria and Prussia on August 27, 1791. Though there was no suggestion of an immediate armed intervention, the Declaration was a provocation, which both served to unite the counter-revolution both at home and abroad and provided the war party in France a pretext for war.

Elsewhere in Europe, the Revolution evoked a mixed response. Kant, Herder, Wordsworth, Priestley hailed the Revolution with enthusiasm. But those who lamented the confiscation of Church property and the curtailing of royal power became bitter enemies. The most famous critic was the British statesman, Edmund Burke, who published his *Reflections on the Revolution in France* in November 1790. Burke argued that the French experiment was dangerous, irreligious and bound to fail because it proceeded from abstract principles. Burke's *Reflections* opened a great debate on the French Revolution, for he was challenged in 1791 by Thomas Paine.

Legislative Assembly, October 1, 1791-September 20, 1792

On September 30, 1791, the Constitution having been accepted by the King, the Assembly ended its sessions. Elections to the new government took place, and the Legislative Assembly took charge. Elected for a term of two years, it served for less than a year. The Legislative Assembly was composed altogether of inexperienced politicians. The new representatives—745 in number—were divided into several parties. The Constitutionalists called the Feuillants, was perhaps the largest party. They wanted to retain the monarchy with the limitations imposed on the power of the king. The group of radical opinion was called Brissotius, after its leader, Jacques Pierre Brissot, or later, the Girondins—since many of them were from the department of the Gironde. They favoured a republic and preached armed crusade against the crowned heads of Europe. Their main inspiration was the imaginative Madame Roland, who yearned to make of revolutionary France another, more virtuous Rome. The Jacobins were small in number, but the strong support of the Jacobin Club, in which Robespierre, Danton and Marat were all-powerful, made them formidable. It exercised nation-wide influence by organising branch clubs of middle-class radicals all over the country.

Domestic and Foreign Problems

The Legislative Assembly had a multitude of domestic difficulties. The refractory clergy was causing trouble. The religious schism encouraged defiance of the government in other matters; tax collection was difficult. In south of France and in the Vendee, on the west coast, there were clashes between counter-revolutionary peasants and National Guards.

The Legislative Assembly passed a decree requiring all priests to abide by the Civil Constitution of the Clergy. The non-juring clergy, *i.e,* those who refused to accept the Civil Constitution, were to be deprived of their pensions and were to be regarded as traitors. Secondly, it passed another decree ordering all emigrés, including the princes, to return to France by January 1, 1792, or be treated as traitors. The King vetoed these decrees which offended public opinion and increased the suspicion of the people about the sincerity of the King's promises.

Foreign affairs soon became the major concern of the Assembly. From October 1791 on, Brissot preached an armed crusade against France's eastern neighbours, Prussia and Austria, in the course of which the people would rally to the flag of revolution. In December a heated debate took place on the theme between Brissot and Robespierre. Alone of the Jacobin leaders Robespierre opposed Brissot's plan for a war on the grounds that, far from serving the cause of revolution, it would strengthen the hands of its opponents. But Brissot won the day and the main body of the Jacobins and the majority of the deputies to the Legislative Assembly rallied to his view.

In March 1792, Louis appointed a Girondin ministry headed by General Dumouriez and including Roland as Minister of the Interior. It was Dumouriez's belief that the war could be won. Lafayette signalled the Feuillants to support the war. He was convinced that in the event of the French victory the constitutional monarchy would be strengthened. Most surprisingly, the queen and her party began to press for war. If France were victorious, Louis' position would gather strength. If France lost, then her nephew, Francis II of Austria, would restore the King to his absolute powers. After negotiations with Francis II and the German princes had broken down in March, France declared war on Austria on April 20, 1792 and soon faced the combined armies of Austria and Prussia. This was perhaps the most decisive turning-point in the whole French Revolution. Within months, the monarchy would fall and within a year France would be plunged into civil strife.

So the French nation went headlong to war and suffered defeat, humiliation and invasion. Its army was small, disorganised and disaffected. The three columns which invaded the Austrian Netherlands were defeated and routed. Lafayette was forced to retreat and Theobold Dillon was murdered by his own men.

The failure produced an immediate consequence in Paris. Defeat encouraged the well-founded suspicions of treachery of the King. Moreover, economic conditions had deteriorated. The *assignat* had fallen to 63 per cent of its face value and grain riots followed in the provinces. In Paris, the price of sugar had trebled and provision shops were broken into by angry citizens. On June 20, 1792, a Paris mob broke into the royal palace of the Tuileries, forcing the King to wear the cap of liberty and to drink to the health of the nation.

Meanwhile, in early July, the Assembly, ignoring the royal veto, summoned the National Guards to Paris. The Marseilles battalion arrived singing a battle hymn which was soon to become a stirring national anthem. The battle cry became intensified when it transpired a Prussian army under the Duke of Brunswick had crossed the border and was marching on Paris. There was renewed agitation to remove the King and to give power to a patriotic republican executive. The Girondins, still in control of the Legislative Assembly, induced the Assembly on July 11, 1792 to declare the 'Nation in danger'.

On July 14, the King participated in the fall of 'Bastille Day' celebration. On July 15, the Jacobins called for the exile of the King, the election of a new commune and the arrest of Lafayette and all public enemies. By the end of July, 47 of the 48 sections of Paris had declared for the abdication of the king. Popular fears were aroused by the Duke of Brunswick's (commander-in-chief of the Austro-Prussian armies) manifesto of August 1, which threatened Paris with summary vengeance if any harm was done to the royal family. As a measure of self-defence, the Jacobins, militiamen, the Parisian sections and National Guards combined and formed a revolutionary 'Commune' in which Danton was the leading figure. On the night of August 9-10, 1792, the new Commune stormed the Tuileries, massacred the Swiss Guards and forced the royal family to take refuge with the Legislative Assembly. On August 10, a mob descended upon the Assembly and forced that body to vote the suspension of the King. The Legislative Assembly was now shattered when half of its members fled Paris. The royal family was now lodged in a prison known as the Temple. The rump now announced National Convention, the deputies to be elected by universal manhood suffrage. As Lenin was to say many years later, the events of August 10, 1792, revolutionised the Revolution. This was the beginning of the violent phase of the Revolution.

In the six weeks before the Convention met France was governed in effect by the Revolutionary Commune of Paris. In the Commune, Robespierre was all-powerful. 'Watch Committee' of the Commune was apparent in which Marat was the guiding force. The radicalism of the commune was apparent in measures that deported refractory priests, ordered confiscation of emigré property and deprived nobles of all their dues without compensation. In the middle of August 1792, France severed diplomatic relations with the Dutch Republic, Spain, Denmark, Poland, Russia and Italy. Meanwhile the crossing of the French frontier by the Prussian armies under the command of Brunswick on August 19 and Lafayette's desertion to the Austrians intensified the situation The traitorous surrender of the fortress of Longwy on the August 23 and the siege of Verdun, the last fortress on the road to Paris, turned the patriotic frenzy into violent upsurge. The frantic mob broke into the prisons, set up people's tribunals and in five days (September 2-5) executed 1,100 'enemies'. The people had learnt its strength on August 10 and 'no human power,' said Danton, 'could have stopped them.' It was, perhaps, the darkest chapter in the history of the Revolution.

However unsavoury the September massacres were, the event was of some importance. It temporarily destroyed the enemy within. On September 20, 1792, the Legislative Assembly dissolved itself and the Convention met for the first time. On the same day, the French army routed Brunswick's army at Valmy and drove it back across the frontier. Valmy was celebrated by the French as a great triumph. It had saved Paris. French morale soared and the spirit of republicans infused the entire army.

The Convention, September 1792-October 1795

The National Convention, which met on September 21, 1792, replaced the monarchy with a republic. During the next three years the Convention had to perform the delicate task of consolidating the Revolution within France as well as of waging successful foreign war. But it accomplished these tasks by terror, violence, and dictatorship.

The Convention was composed of three main groups. The majority was formed by the great mass of independent deputies, known as the 'Marsh' of Plain. They were not committed to any particular faction. The second group was the so-called Girondins, led by Vergniaud, Brissot, Gensonnet and Guadet. They were now the conservative element who wanted to break the power of the Commune and establish a stable government. Against them were ranged the Jacobins and Mountain, headed by Robespierre, Marat and Danton. Assured of the support of the Commune and mob of Paris, they wished to deprive the Girondins of their supremacy in the Convention.

With Valmy, the tide turned. The Austrians who had besieged Lille were repulsed. Dumouriez won a brilliant victory at Jemappes on the Belgian frontier and within a short time conquered Belgium. Similar success attended French arms in other quarters. One French army conquered a number of places on the Rhine, another occupied Savoy, while a third took Nice. By mid-November 1792 the Convention was in a position to promise 'aid and fraternity to all peoples wishing to recover their liberty.'

Meanwhile, the struggle for power in the Convention was waged over immediate issues. Two questions dominated the early months of the Convention—what to do with the King and what to do about Paris. The Girondins wished to spare the king's life. What worried them most was the new power of the popular movement which they wanted to crush. The Mountain or 'Montaguards' were unequivocal about the king—he should be put on trial, found guilty and executed. After debating the issue of the king's fate for over a month, the Convention voted 361 to 321 for the death penalty. Louis XVI was guillotined on January 21, 1793.

After the King's execution, Britain, Holland and Spain withdrew their ambassadors. Emboldened by victories on all fronts, the Convention declared war on Britain and Holland in February 1793 and on Spain in March. Piedmont, Sardinia and Naples soon joined the coalition against France. The Pope lent moral support and many German states furnished troops. Thus by mid-1793 France found herself at war with almost all the powers of Europe, except Russia.

Military reverses were almost inevitable. The British began to attack French merchantmen which impeded the essential grain shipments from the Baltic and North Africa. 'The entry of Britain into the war introduced an element of single-minded and concerted opposition to the revolutionary cause which had hitherto been wanting.' On March 28, 1793, the French General Dumouriez received a crushing defeat at Neerwinden. He was driven back from the Netherlands and deserted to the enemy. The Girondins, as close associates of Dumouriez, were now exposed.

Meanwhile, the economic situation had deteriorated. The *assignat* had fallen to only half its nominal value in February 1793 and the price of food had soared. On February 25 and 26, 1793, grocer's shops in Paris were invaded by the people. In March, the Paris commune decided to fix the price of bread, by the aid of a subsidy to bakers. To complicate the situation, a bitter peasant revolt—led by nobles and clergy—broke out in March in the Vendee. The movement spread into Brittany.

Against these accumulating dangers, the Convention took firm steps. A Revolutionary Tribunal was set up on March 10 to deal with all those who were accused of hostility to the Government. Vigilance committees were set up everywhere and 'representatives on mission' were sent out from the Convention to centralise authority in the provinces. The death penalty was decreed for armed rebels and a Committee of Public Safety was formed on April 10, to supervise the executive functions of the State. The Committee pushed through the Convention the 'Law of the Maximum', whereby local authorities all over the country were authorised to control the price and supply of bread and flour.

Meanwhile, the Convention became the scene of a desperate struggle for power between the Girondins and the Mountains. An uprising to purge the Assembly of the Girondin leaders was attempted on March 10, 1793 by a small group of extreme revolutionaries known as the Enrages. The attempt proved to be a failure. In May, the Girondins accused the Paris Commune of promoting disorder. They accused Marat of treason and Hebert of inciting to riot. Both were tried and acquitted. On May 30, there were anti-Girondin riots. A great majority of sections formed a Central Revolutionary Committee and directed the revolution of May 31-June 2 with almost military precision. On June 2, the Convention was surrounded by units of the Parisian National Guard. 29 leading Girondins were put under house arrest.

After the purge of the Girondins, half of France rose in revolt against the Convention. Sixty out of France's eightythree departments were beyond the Convention's control. In the south and west the major cities including Lyons, Bordeaux, Marseilles and Toulon went into revolt against the Government. In June 1793, the French armies were defeated in the Rhineland and in Belgium. The defeat of the combination of external and internal enemies which plauged the Republic throughout 1793 demanded unprecedented energies.

The Convention made a bold bid to capture popular support by introducing several reforms. It declared the final abolition of feudal dues without compensation. It approved the principle of revolutionary armies, it promulgated a democratic constitution which it promptly suspended until the return of more tranquil times. In August it issued the decree of the *levee en masse*—an attempt to mobilise every citizen behind the war effort. All this, however, did not satisfy the *Sansculottes* who wanted price controls. On September 4 and 5, in the wake of renewed bread shortages, crowds of working-men invaded the Convention, demanding more bread. On September 29, the Convention passed the law of the *Maximum General,* which fixed the price of not only bread but of a large range of essential goods while raising wages by one-half.

The Reign of Terror, June 1793-July 1794

It was the overwhelming danger both at home and abroad that led to the Reign of Terror. The Terror was an emergency despotism—a 'dictatorship in distress.' It was founded on the theory that only by establishing a despotism could the civil war be ended and unity restored.

The cornerstone of the Terror was the Committee of Public Safety. At first this Committee was charged simply with the management of foreign affairs and of the army, but in the end it practically became omnipotent, effectually governing France throughout the period. Under orders from the Committee were the *deputies on mission,* members of the Convention chosen by twos to go to every department and to every army in the field. Wielding despotic power they were responsible to the Government. Throughout France was established a network of Revolutionary Committees whose primary task was to enforce the law of Suspects which allowed arrest and imprisonment without any proof of guilt. In Paris, a central committee—known as the Committee of General Security—was nominally responsible for all matters relating to police and security.

Such were the principal organs of the terror. By September 1793 the Terror was supposed officially to begin. It was not, at all events, more terrible than the reign of anarchy that preceded it. It was organised terror in contrast to the promiscuous terror of the mob. As Danton said, 'Let us be terrible in order to dispense the people from being terrible.' It is an interesting fact that Danton, Marat and some others had all judged that some sort of dictatorship was a necessary outcome of the Revolution. Even Edmund Burke, a bitter critic of the Revolution, had foretold the ultimate appearance of the dictator.

It is impossible to enumerate the victims of terror. Perhaps 50,000 lives were taken in the provinces during the Terror by order of local tribunals or representatives-on-mission. The Vendean revolt was put down with ruthless severity which resulted in the burning of villages and the massacre of some two thousand people. Further atrocities accompanied the suppression of revolting towns—Lyons, Marseilles, Nantes, Toulon. On October 16, 1793, Marie Antoinette was guillotined. Then followed the execution of Vergniaud, Brissot and other leading Girondins. When Madame Roland was on the way to the scaffold, she observed, 'Liberty, how many crimes are committed in they name.' It is strange that 85 per cent of the victims were neither nobles nor priests and that the majority were of the peasant or working class.

The War

With the suppression of domestic enemies, the Terror took steps to encounter external enemies. Neither materially nor morally was the First Coalition a match for France which the Terror created. Much of this great achievement was due to the organising genius of Carnot, who, in charge of the war department, overhauled every department of the service. On the basis of *levee en masse* (August 1792), which rendered every able-bodied citizen liable for service, thirteen contingents were placed in the field, totalling 750,000 men. Apart from the vigour and resources of the French, the Allies were hampered by a diversity of aims, by mutual jealousies and distracted by a Polish question.

In September 1793 the French scored a victory over the British in the Netherlands, saving Dunkirk for France. In October, General Jourdan, now commander in the Netherlands, defeated the Austrians in the battle of Wattignies. In December, Hoche and Pichegru combined to defeat the Prussians at Landau. In the same month, the British were also driven from Toulon. During the winter the French armies invaded Spain. In June 1794, Jourdan won a resounding victory over the Austrian Duke of Coburg at Fleurus. This was a turning point in the war as it not only forced the Austrians to evacuate Belgium and the Prussians to cease fighting, but also it relieved foreign military pressure on France. In March 1795 (Treaty of Basel) the Prussians made peace, agreeing secretly to cede France the left bank of the Rhine in return for territory in Germany. In January 1795, Pichegru took Amsterdam and in May he completed the conquest of Holland. In June 1795, Spain made peace. Only England and Austria remained in the field against France.

Domestic Achievements

Though the leaders of the Terror governed ruthlessly, they were not blind to the social, economic and administrative problems that plagued the country. The Law of Maximum (September 1793) had given protection to the common man by controlling prices and wages. The right to subsistence, enunciated in the Constitution of 1793, was put to practice by creating jobs in war industry. Social security was provided which granted the aged, ill or disabled small incomes and free housing if needed. Inflation was reversed by issuing republican *assignats* which was declared as the 'money of the poor'.

Economy was rigidly controlled to assure the supply of the army and to ensure the cities against shortages. Under penalties of death, hoarding was prohibited, farmers had to declare the amount of their harvest, and merchants' stocks were subject to inspection. Granaries were established in each district. A national food committee was vested with arbitrary power to seize food and control distribution. Another committee controlled industrial production. The Committee of Public Safety itself regulated exports and imports.

Feudal rights were abolished without any indemnity in June 1793. Some land redistribution was effected by a law which confiscated the property of emigrés. The economic programme of the Terror was capped by the famous Decrees of the Ventose (February-March 1794) which confiscated the property of suspects and its distribution to indigent patriots of the communes. Though the majority considered them socialistic, the middleclass leaders of the time felt that these laws violated the sanctity of private property.

The Terrorists promoted science and technology. Carnot introduced balloons for observation. He also established a 'telegraph' between Paris and Lille—a Semaphore system or 'wig-wig' system that relayed messages along a line of tall towers. The most lasting innovation of the Terror, however, was the metric-decimal system of weights and measures, with gram and metre as the basic units.

The Terrorists made elaborate plans for a complete system of elementary and secondary schools, both tuition free. Elementary education was to be compulsory for all, entry into secondary schools was to be made on the basis of merit. A secondary system of 'central schools' (Colleges) was established, but enrolment was limited and tuition was charged. Some institutions of higher learning planned under the Terror became permanent. The most important are the Ecole Polytechnique (Polytechnic school) and the Ecole Nationale Superieure (Great Normal School or Teachers' College). Others are a school of Oriental languages, a national conservatory of the arts and sciences, and a museum of natural history. In addition, the Terrorists must also be credited with the idea of establishing a National Library (Bibliotheque Nationale) and with the conversion of the palace Louvre into a museum.

The Convention had started the Republican Calendar on September 22, 1792, from which date the years of the Republic were calculated. By decrees of October 5 and November 24, 1793, it approved the Revolutionary Calendar. It called for twelve months of thirty days each, with three ten-day weeks in each month; Sundays were eliminated, as were all Church holidays. The twelve months were named according to the season : Vendemiaire, Brumoire, Frimaire for the autumn; Nivose, Pluviose, Ventose for winter; Germinal, Floreal, Prairial for spring; Messidor, Thermidor, Fructidor for summer.

Fall of Robespierre

Now that the dangers both external and internal were over, the question of bloody repression divided opinions led to a split in the Mountain. Its most radical wing, called the Hebertists, were the followers of Hebert. He, along with Chaumette and Fouche, became leaders of the de-Christianisation movement. They denounced Catholicism as aristocratic, proclaimed the Worship of Reason and finally decreed the closure of all places of worship in Paris. Notre-Dame became the scene of a gigantic 'Festival of Liberty and Reason' on November 10, 1793. The cult of reason affected the provinces and it is estimated that something like 2,400 churches in France fell under its influence.

The Hebertist challenge posed the greatest danger to the Jacobins. It was too much for Robespierre to support this atheism. He believed that a religion which taught a belief in the Supreme Being was necessary to shaping law-abiding citizens. During the winter of 1793-94, Robespierre launched a campaign to discredit the Hebertists. In this he got the support of popular heroes, who had become his opponents, notably Danton and Desmoulins. In March 1794 the Hebertists tried to raise Paris against the Committee of Public Safety. The Hebertists were arrested on March 15 and guillotined on March 24. This equally sealed the fate of Danton and Desmoulins. The charge against them was that they leaned too much towards mercy and conciliation. Robespierre felt himself threatened whilst Danton and his associates lived. On April 5, 1794, Danton, Desmoulins and fifteen others were executed.

While Hebert's execution alienated the rank-and-file Sans-culottes, Danton's death shocked the people and terrified the politicians of the Convention. Meanwhile, for some weeks past, Robespierre and his group had been losing their hold on the Convention. To win popular support, he introduced the 'Cult of the Supreme Being', a new national religion which he hoped would restore public morality. Religion and Terror were to produce the 'Republic of Virtue'. The Convention established the new religion by decree. Festivals were ordered to celebrate the existence of the Almighty and the great days of the Revolution—July 14 (fall of the Bastille), August 10 (the storming of the Tuileries Palace), January 21 (the execution of the king) and May 31 (the fall of the Girondins). On June 8 the festival inaugurating this new religion was carried out.

The Reign of Terror, however, could not cease. In the Convention there was a general fear that Robespierre might eliminate more rivals. This was confirmed when a law was passed—known as the Law of Prairial—on June 10, 1794. The law speeded the process of justice within the Revolutionary Tribunal and deprived the prisoner of any defence. Even the members of the Convention were no longer immune from arrest. From this law sprang the 'Great Terror' which, in Paris, accounted for nearly 1,300 victims.

Robespierre's enemies began to plot his overthrow. Their task was facilitated by two factors. First was the victory of the French over the Austrians at Fleurus on June 24, 1794. So it was whispered that when the crisis was over, there was no justification of the continuation of Terror. Second, on 5 Thermidor (July 23, 1794), Robespierre antagonised the wage-earners by putting a ceiling on wage-earners.

Ignorant of his dwindling support, Robespierre decided to appeal to the Convention. In a long speech in the Convention on July 26, 1794, Robespierre made a general attack on his enemies and pleaded that the Revolution could once more be saved by the removal of a small group of 'impure' men. All feared his vengeance and fear provoked resistance. The Convention declined to allow him the usual courtesy of sending his speech to be printed. On July 27, Robespierre and Saint-Just appeared at the Convention to defend their government. Pandemonium ensued, with members howling for the arrest of the 'Tyrant'. At last it was moved and carried that Robespierre, Saint-Just and his immediate followers should be placed under arrest. On 10 Thermidor Year II (July 28, 1794), Robespierre, Couthon and Saint Just and nineteen of their followers were executed.

The Terror was at an end. There began the 'Thermidorian Reaction'. The Republic lingered on through a series of crises, until Bonaparte's soldiers swept it aside in the *coup d' etat* of 18-19 Brumaire Year VIII (9-10 November 1799).

The Thermidorian Reaction, July 1794-October 1795

The last fourteen months of the Convention are known as the Thermidorian Reaction whose main concern was to dismantle the Terror. The new leaders who emerged in the Convention were Sieyes, Tallion, Freron and Barras. On August 1, 1794, four days after Robespierre's death, the Law of Prairial, defining suspects, was repealed. On August 5, prisoners seized under this law were released. On August 10, the Revolutionary Tribunal was reorganised. It was decided that power should no longer be concentrated in the hands of a few men. On August 24, 16 committees were set up, 12 of them with executive powers; much of the work of the two Committees of Public Safety and General Security was transferred to these committees. In Paris, the Commune was abolished and soon replaced by Commissioners appointed by the Convention.

But if the 'Red Terror' was over, the 'White Terror' of reaction began. The Terror had created many old scores to be settled which reached its height in the following summer. Hundreds of former officials and terrorists were now murdered by Terror gangs calling themselves 'Companies of Jesus' or 'Companies of the Sun.' In the towns, *sanculottes* were harassed by well-dressed *muscadins* or 'gilded youth'. Jacobin clubs were closed. As if to renounce both the de-Christianisation of late 1793, and Robespierre's Cult of the Supreme Being, the Convention declared in September 1794 that the Republic had no established religion.

With the collapse of the Terror, the economic and financial problems of the Republic became acute. The summer of 1794 was dry and the winter of 1794-95 was the coldest in a hundred years. In December 1794, the *Maximum* laws were virtually abolished and free trade in grain was restored. Great distress gripped the populace of Paris. The *assignats* fell rapidly and in May 1795, were worth only seven per cent of their nominal value. There was inflation and prices soared beyond the means of common men. In the provinces, the winter and spring brought near-famine condition.

In Paris, rationed meat was often not available; and the bread ration was quite insufficient even to small consumers.

Such was the background to the great popular insurrections of Germinal and Prairial (April and May 1795). On April 1, 1795 a mob entered the Convention demanding 'Bread and the Constitution of 1793'. But they lacked leaders and the insurrection was easily crushed by Pichegru, in command of the armed forces of Paris. The triumph of the Convention was followed by further reaction against the Jacobins. Prominent terrorists (like Barere, Billand and Collot) were exiled. But as the Convention did nothing to remove the basic cause of these disorders, another popular revolt took place which was most stubborn in its intensity. It lasted four days and opened on May 20, 1795 with invasion of the Assembly by housewives followed by armed battalions. But once more, for lack of leaders and a clear purpose, the rebels were cleared by the National Guardsmen. The insurrection, however, continued in the Faubourg St. Antoine. The City Hall was captured and the convention was surrounded and besieged. But the rebels were bought off with promises and left the field to their opponents. General Menou, with a force of 20,000 men, compelled the Faubourg St. Antoine to surrender. The repression that followed was thorough and ruthless. 14 Deputies of the Mountain were arrested of whom 6 were executed. A Military Commission tried 149 persons, and sentenced 36 to death and 37 to prison. 1,200 were arrested and 1,700 disarmed in a single week. It was an important turning point: it was the end of the popular movement.

With the defeat of the popular revolts, the Convention busied itself to restore France to constitutional life. The democratic constitution of 1793 had to be finally buried and that of 1791 could not be restored. Further safeguards were necessary to guard against a royalist revival in view of the defeat of the French squadron by an English fleet and the landing of 3,600 emigres at Quiberon Bay (June 27, 1795). The Constitution produced by the Convention was designed to limit the voice of the masses. What it produced may fairly be alled a 'bourgeois' constitution. The Constitution lasted until it was overthrown by Napoleon in 1799.

The new Constitution, known as the Constitution of the Year III—was largely inspired by Boissy d' Anglas, champion of the new propertied classes. It opened with the declaration of the duties of the citizen as well as of the rights of man. It established a limited franchise so that those eligible to vote in all France numbered only about 30,000.

The Legislature consisted of two houses—the Council of Elders (Anciens) and the Council of 500 (Cinq Cents). The Elders (250) had to be over forty, the deputies of the 500 over thirty. It was the right of the 500 to initiate all legislation. The Elders could only accept or reject it.

The Executive was to consist of a Directory of Five elected by the Anciens from fifty candidates nominated by the Five Hundred. The Directors were to hold office for five years of whom one was to retire every year. The chairmanship of the Directory was to rotate every three months—a further safeguard against tyranny. The Directors, though appointed by the Councils, could neither sit in them nor initiate their laws. The Directory, however, was given the power to appoint ambassadors and ministers, military officers and members of the administration. Finally, to counteract a royalist upsurge, the Convention laid down that while one-third of both Councils was to retire every year, two-thirds of the deputies to the new legislature must be elected from its own ranks. The aim was to assure continuity and a smooth beginning for constitutional life.

It was this 'regulation of the two-thirds' which added fuel to the fire; for it was manipulated in such a way that the elections could hardly produce any basic change in the character of the Government. The Jacobins, Girondists and even Royalists rose in revolt. On October 5, 1795, 25,000 Parisians, led by Paris Section, Lepeletier, marched on the Convention. The army was again called in, and the commander of the troops who routed the rebels was General Bonaparte. Soon after this, on October 26, 1795, the Convention came to an end. 'By grace of General Bonaparte, the Government of the Directory was free to establish itself; by grace of the same general, the Directory would disappear four years later.'

The Directory, October 1795-November 1799

The period of the Directory proved to be one of confusion and political instability. In part, this was due to the nature of the constitution itself. By providing for annual elections (of one-third of the Councils and one in five of the Directors) it offered a constant invitation to disorder. Moreover, the new rules lacked popular support. By their political expediency and electoral provisions, they had estranged not only royalists and Jacobins, but also the moderate bourgeois. From these weaknesses they never recovered.

The Directors had to grapple the financial problem in the initial stage. The *assignats* were of little value. In April 1796 *mandats* were issued in place of *assignats,* but soon fell to one per cent of their face value. Prices rocketed further. While the new rich displayed their wealth with apparent unconcern, poverty was 'at its lowest depths'.

It was against this background that Babeuf launched his 'Conspiracy of the Equals', the first attempt in history to establish a communist society. He believed that a just regime was impossible so long as the protection of private property continued to dominate politics. In the winter of 1795-96, Babeuf conspired with a group of former Jacobins, clubmen and terrorists to overthrow the Directory by force. On the eve of the insurrection, the leaders of the plot were arrested and the plot came to nothing. A year later Babeuf and some of his principal associates were brought to trial and executed (27/5/1797). The execution of Babeuf made him the last famous martyr of the White Terror. It was Buonarotti—who survived to gain fame during the Revolution of 1830—who kept alive Babeuf's schemes which involved the indoctrination of the people for revolution by secret agents and the infiltration and subversion of the army by the communists.

Foreign Affairs

In foreign affairs, the Directory assumed a greater role. By the beginning of 1796, France's active enemies were Austria, Britain and Sardinia. The Convention had made peace with Holland, Spain and Prussia. Peace had also been made with Portugal, with the German states of Saxony and the two Hesses, with the Italian states of Naples, Parma and the Papacy.

On the last day of 1795 France had signed an armistice with the Austrians on the Rhine front. Using this respite, the Directory planned a decisive frontal attack against Vienna, under the leadership of Moreau and Jourdan. To aid it, another army, put in the charge of General Bonaparte, was to create a diversion against Austrian power in Italy. By the battle of Mondovi, Napoleon defeated the Sardinians and forced them to make an armistice by which they gave up Nice and Savoy to France. Bonaparte's army defeated the Austrians at Lodi on May 10, 1796 and took Milan. By January 1797 he had succeeded in taking the Central Austrian stronghold of Mantua, and in routing a strong Austrian army at the Battle of Rivoli. When Napoleon pressed on to Vienna, the Austrians called for a truce (April 1797).

Peace was delayed for six months. But when Napoleon advanced to the Danube, Austria signed the peace of Campo Formio on October 17, 1797. By this treaty Austria recognised the French annexation of Belgium as well as the creation of a Cisalpine Republic in northern Italy, surrendered the Ionian islands off Greece, but kept Venice and all her territory in Italy and the Adriatic. Under secret treaties, the Austrian Emperor promised to cede to France large districts of the Rhineland, and, in return, was promised part of Bavaria and the ecclesiastical state of Salzburg.

Domestic Affairs

At home the Directory faced its first political crisis with the elections of April 1797. The elections were a royalist triumph. Almost all the one-third new deputies were royalists, and the Elders elected a royalist Director, Barthelemy. On September 4, 1797 (18th Fructidor), the majority of the Directory—called the Trumvirate (Barras, La Revelliere and Reubell)—struck at the royalist majority with help of Bonaparte's lieutenant, Augereau. The Triumvirate expelled the newly elected members from the assemblies and put under arrest Barthelemy and Pichegru, while Carnot escaped. Henceforth the victorious

Directors armed themselves with new powers and relied more on armed force.

The Directors strengthened their position by the *coup d'etat* of 22 Floreal, May 11, 1798, which excluded 106 Deputies from sitting in the Chambers. Having secured its position, the Directory settled down to some useful reforms. Steps were taken to stabilise the currency by withdrawing the discredited paper-money from circulation and declaring a moratorium on all outstanding debts. The system of taxation was overhauled. Following good harvests in 1796-98, the price of grain fell. Yet the government remained at the mercy of contractors and speculators and the budget remained unbalanced. Industry continued to stagnate and foreign trade suffered as a result of war with England.

The Directory could sustain its power by aggressive war. In 1798, Bonaparte had departed on an expedition to Egypt designed to cut off the British from India. After capturing Malta and Alexandria, he marched against Syria. Then followed his reverses which was crowned by the destruction of his fleet by Nelson at Aboukir Bay in the Battle of the Nile (August 1798). By May 1799 he withdrew to Egypt with heavy losses. The campaign produced a Second Coalition against France, which included Turkey and Russia as well as Britain. The war of the Second Coalition proved to be disastrous to France. Her armies were defeated by the Austrian Archduke Charles in Germany and Switzerland and driven from Italy by the Russian general Suvorov. Meanwhile, the Belgian provinces were in revolt.

The Legislative Councils blamed the Directory for French reverses and the elections of April 1799, increased the number of opposition deputies. By the so-called *Coup of Prairial* (June 1799), the Councils deposed one Director and forced the resignation of two others. The new Directors were Sieyes, Barras, Ducos, Moulin and Gohier. Meanwhile, the royalist danger continued. Jacobinism raised its head again and the country was restless. There was further talk of the need to revise the constitution and to provide stable government by strengthening the executive. It was in this atmosphere that Sieyes planned a more decisive *coup d'etat.*

Meanwhile, Napoleon—who knew what was happening in France—made a dash for France. Eluding Nelson's patrols, he reached France in October 1799. He knew his moment had come. Sieyes and his fellow-conspirators, Fouche and Talleyrand, turned to Napoleon, the man of the hour. Sieyes thought that he could handle Napoleon once the *coup* was over. So on 18 Brumaire (November 9, 1799) Bonaparte and his soldiers dismissed the Directors and the legislative councils. A small number of overawed representatives, in collusion with Sieyes, voted for constitutional revision. To carry out this programme, full authority was vested in a provisional consulate of three—Sieyes, Roger-Ducos and Bonaparte. Napoleon, as First Consul, wielded undivided executive authority and the other two Consuls were made little more than rubber stamps. It was the end of the bourgeois Republic and marked a further step towards the establishment of military despotism.

The Consulate, 1799-1804

The executive consisted of three Consuls who were appointed for ten years and were re-eligible. Napoleon, as First Consul, had the right to promulgate laws and full executive authority to appoint and dismiss all officials, civil and military, both in Paris and the provinces. The Second and Third Consuls, Cambaceres and Lebrun, had advisory functions only.

All legislation was framed by the first Consul's nominated Council of State. The Tribunate of a hundred members could pass or reject laws submitted to it by the Government. The Legislative Body, of three hundred numbers, was a dumb assembly, which accepted or rejected, without any power of discussion, laws that had come down from the Tribunate. There was to be a 'Conservative Senate' of sixty members chosen by the Consul. Appointed for life, the Senate was to fill the consular vacancies, appoint the Tribunate and the Legislative Body. It could annul any law which it might consider as violative of the principles of the constitution. Theoretically, universal suffrage was established, but, in practice, popular suffrage was rendered completely ineffective.

The constitution established a system of highly centralised despotism without any checks and balances, All authority came from the First Consul, 'there existed in France no authority that could repair a village bridge, or light the streets of a town, but such as owed its appointment to the central government.' Practically, however, popular sovereignty was gone, Bonaparte was sovereign. He had more extensive powers than Louis XVI had had under the constitution of 1791. He really had the legislative power also. France was still a republic in name, practically, however, it was a monarchy.

Under the existing constitution, Bonaparte enjoyed but a ten-year term as First Consul and he had to share the honour with two colleagues. Such a position could hardly fulfil his ambition. Bonaparte was a masterful opportunist guided by intuition into forces at work. After he had achieved new glories for France by crushing the Second Coalition, Napoleon used a plebiscite in 1802 to force his plans on the government. He became Life Consul, able to nominate most senators, to declare war and make treaties, and to designate his successor.

Foreign Policy of the Consulate

The man who was the ruler of France for the next fifteen years was only thirty years old when he became the First Consul. Born at Ajaccio in Corsica on August 15, 1769, he had received a military education in France and had become a junior artillery officer in the royal army. By 1793 he had been converted to Jacobin ideas, and achieved some distinction in the recapture of Toulon (1793) and the defence of the Convention (1795). In 1796 he was appointed commander-in-chief of Italy where he laid the foundation of his imperishable military fame. His Italian campaign lasted a year from April 1796 to April 1797. He was a military genius and used the new tactics evolved for the mass armies that had been created by the Revolution. With amazing speed and brilliant tactics, Napoleon occupied every fort in northern Italy. When he threatened Vienna, Austria sued for peace. By the Treaty of Campo Formio (October 1797) Austria gave up Belgium to France and abandoned to her the left bank of the Nile. His Egyptian venture to crush the power of England did not prove to be successful and he had to return back to France at an opportune moment. He was a masterful opportunist and seized political power in 1799.

Having set his house in order, Napoleon turned his attention to the foreign enemies of France—Austria, England and Russia. England was difficult to get at. Having sent Moreau to attack the Austrians in Germany, Napoleon himself set out to meet them in Italy. After crossing the Alps, he unexpectedly appeared before the Austrians. In the battle that followed at Marengo the Austrians were routed and Napoleon recovered all Italy at a stroke (1800). In December 1800, Moreau won a decisive victory over the Austrians in Germany at Hohenlinden and threatened Vienna. The Austrian Emperor made peace at Luneville on February 9, 1801. It practically repeated the terms of Campo Formio with a few modifications unfavourable to Austria. Once again Austria recognised the French satellite states—the Cisalpine and Ligurian Republics in northern Italy, the Helvetic Republic in Switzerland, the Batavian Republic of the Dutch, the French occupation of Belgium and the left bank of the Rhine.

After the break-up of the Second Coalition, France remained at war with only one nation, England. Unable to humble England on the sea, Napoleon turned to diplomacy and made use of the grievances of the neutral powers against England. The British ships used to search neutral ships for seizing the enemies goods. Napoleon instigated the Czar of Russia to revive against England the Armed Neutrality, consisting of Russia, Prussia, Sweden and Denmark. The object of this League was to prevent England from searching neutral vessels for French goods. This League, however, was dissolved by the assassination of Czar Paul in March 1801, and by the destruction of the Danish fleet by Nelson at Copenhagen (April 1801).

The English also were successful in Egypt. The British victory at Aboukir, followed by the surrender of the French garrison at Cairo, compelled the French to evacuate Egypt. All these French reverses inclined Napoleon to conclude peace with England. Moreover, the new British Prime Minister, Addington, who succeeded the resolute William Pitt, the Younger, was no longer willing to prosecute the war. Negotiations were opened and the Peace of Amiens was signed (March 27, 1802). England agreed to recognise the French annexation in Europe and to abandon all intervention in continental affairs. England had made war in 1793 to exclude France from Belgium, but she had to make peace in 1802 by accepting her own exclusion from Belgium. The French occupation of Belgium and Holland was to the people of England 'a pistol pointed at the heart of London.' England restored all the French colonies and some of the Dutch and Spanish, retaining only Ceylon and Trinidad. France was to evacuate Egypt. The weakness of the settlement was that England was pledged to a policy of non-intervention in Europe without the compensation of colonial gains. About the Peace of Amiens it was said in England that 'everybody was glad and nobody proud.'

Domestic Reforms

Napoleon's claim to statesmanship rests primarily on the measures of domestic policy. Between 1800 and 1803 Napoleon as First Consul devoted his energy to the internal reorgnisation of France. In this task of reorganisation he brought the same precision and concentration upon essentials which had already distinguished him in war. His domestic reforms are of vital importance in the history not only of France but of Europe as a whole. Using the ablest men regardless of their past loyalties, Napoleon provided the main inspiration to get things done. His overall purpose was a systematic reconstruction of the main legal, financial and administrative institution of France.

One of Napoleon's first acts was to invite back the emigrés and exiles—royalists and republicans alike. Over one lakh emigres received the legal right to return and to recover their estates. Careers were open to talents irrespective of class.

Administration

Napoleon reconstituted the general administration of France. Everything was centralised under his own person. He controlled the law-making process through his Council of State. It was divided into sections for war, marine, finance and legislation. In 1803 the Council was furnished with sixty auditors and after 1804 the number was increased to 120 assigned to ministers. Though under Napoleon the Council of State remained subservient, it developed in due course an *esprit de corps* of its own and became the cornerstone of the French bureaucracy. The ministers were 'political appointees'. Each minister had a council of permanent career bureaucrats. Officials in the local governments were elected. Napoleon appointed prefects of departments, subprefects of districts and mayors of cities. The departmental and district councils, which advised the prefects, were also appointed from Paris. Similar arrangements applied to the officers of police. Napoleon also created a new aristocracy of merit by introducing the 'Order of Legion of Honour.' This satisfied the French love of glory.

A reorganisation of the judiciary was also effected. All judges were appointed. Supervising the system were the Chancellor and Council of State. At the top stood the Court of Cassation. It had civil and criminal jurisdiction but did not decide cases or interpret the laws. Beneath it were the civil and criminal systems which terminated at the lowest level with the justices of peace in the canton. Between were civil courts of first instance, civil appeal courts and criminal courts. In short, Napoleon created the first modern bureaucracy at the cost of local autonomy.

Fiscal and Economic Measures

Napoleon overhauled the financial administration and taxation. In January 1800, Napoleon created the Bank of France, modelled after the Bank of England. Although at first an independent corporation, the Bank of France was entrusted with the management of government loans and tax-collectors' deposits, and, in 1803, it was given the monopoly of issuing bank-notes. The system of collecting taxes was centralised and made more efficiently by Gaudin, in charge of finance. A sinking fund was established—a cash reserve available to guarantee the government's debts. Part of the debt was repudiated and the rest drew regular interest. Metal once more became the general currency. It was a measure of the sound financial policy of the period that between 1799 and 1814, some 75 million francs in gold and silver returned into circulation.

Napoleon imitated the better features of the age of Louis XIV. He inaugurated a vast series of public works. Napoleon continued the protectionist tariff policies of the Directory, which were directed primarily at Britain. Tariff arrangements benefitted France. Everything possible was done to promote industry. Loans were available to industries at low rates, and grants were made to new industries. The Lyons silk industry was revived. Cotton was introduced from the East and was manufactured by means of the spinning jenny. Gas was adopted as an illuminant. There was a growth of 25 per cent in French industry. It may be said that the groundwork for the Industrial Revolution in France was laid during the Napoleonic period. In agriculture and commerce public works benefitted. Napoleon's engineers built or repaired about 50,000 miles of roads. Even remote villages were benefitted.

The Law Codes

The codification of French law was perhaps the most enduring of Napoleon's achievements. 'My real glory,' said Napoleon at St. Helena, 'is not my having won forty battles. What will never be effaced, what will endure for ever, is my civil code.' One of the greatest evils of the ancient regime was the lack of a uniform code of law. The work had begun by Colbert and d'Aguesseau. Although five drafts had been prepared by the revolutionary committees, none of them had been put into execution. Napoleon gave France a common law, laid out simply in seven codes. The first and most important was the Civil Code (1804), called the *Code Napoleon*. This monumental achievement was the work of a commission of jurists; yet all its plans had been supervised by Napoleon himself, who was present at thirty-five out of the eighty-seven sittings devoted to the Civil Code. The Code struck a happy balance between the rival claims of Roman and Customary law.

'The merit of the Civil Code is not that it is exhaustive...but that it fixes the structure of a civilized lay society, based on social equality and religious toleration, on private property and coherent family life.' The Civil Code affected especially the laws of the family, marriage and divorce, the status of women, paternal authority and property. The authority of the father over his wife, his children, and the property of the family was strengthened. Under the new code, wives were subjected to husbands, divorce was made more difficult, and property up to a quarter of the whole could be given away from the family. There was to be equal division of property among all legitimate heirs. The Civil Code guaranteed individual liberty, equality before the law, freedom from arrest without due process as well as the right to choose one's work. It confirmed the abolition of feudalism in all its aspect. The Civil Code—a combination of fruitful innovation and ancient usage—exercises a strong influence throughout Europe. 'Not since the Institutes of Justinian has any compendium of law been so widely copied.'

The other codes are not so important as the Civil Code. The Criminal Code followed in many respects the example of English practice. Though it gave the accused the benefit of an open trial and jury, these advantages were counter-balanced by other provisions, which were less favourable to the protection of the weak and the innocent. For example, the prosecution had more rights than the defence. Further, the judges could order new trials if juries ruled 'illegally'. There was a separate penal code which was brutal. In addition, there were codes of criminal instruction, civil procedure, and for rural and commercial cases.

Religious Policy

An ecclesiastical settlement was no less urgent. Napoleon had a lively sense of the political importance of religion, which was to him 'a social cement, a safety-value'. 'In religion', he once wrote. 'I do not see the mystery of the Incarnation, but the mystery of the social order'; and again 'Society is impossible without inequality, intolerable without a code of morality, and a code of morality unacceptable without religion.' Napoleon's aim was to end the religious strife of the Revolution and find a realistic solution. Taking advantage of the accession in 1800 of a new Pope, Pius VII, Napoleon began negotiations for a Concordat with Papacy. Agreement was reached in July 1801 after a full year of bargaining. Napoleon guaranteed freedom of worship and recognised Roman Catholicism as 'the religion of the great majority of the citizens.' He undertook to pay the salaries of bishops and clergy and won Papal recognition for the confiscation of Church property. The Pope also agreed that all existing bishops would resign and be reinstated by the Pope after nomination by the First Consul. All clergy should take an oath of allegiance to the Government. In April 1802 Napoleon attached to the Concordat two sets of Organic Laws, one of which was a Charter of Protestant liberties, while the other placed the Church more firmly than ever under the control of the secular power. The Organic Laws were not agreed to by the Pope. The Church settlement proved to be ephemeral among his achievements. It might seem that a wiser policy would have been separation of Church and State, but Napoleon was a firm believer in centralisation of power as a principle of statecraft. The intermittent struggle between Church and State which bedevilled French politics for the following century and a half was the inheritance of the Napoleon's Concordat. The Concordat remained in effect until 1905.

Education

The educational reforms of the Consulate reflect Napoleon's attitude towards rigid centralisation. But he also emphasised that the chief purpose of education was to equip youngmen to the service of the state. He eliminated the secondary 'central schools' of the Directory and established forty-five *lycees* or high schools. He allowed municipal colleges and private, mostly Church, schools at the same level. The purpose of the *lycees* was to train future officers and civil servants. There were 6,400 scholarships available, of which 2,400 were reserved for the sons of officers and civil servants and the remaining to the best students of lower schools. The *lycees* were under military discipline and the curriculum included classical languages, rhetoric, morality, logic, mathematics and science. The *lycees* made a poor start, but, by 1813, the education provided was probably the best and the most advanced in Europe.

Napoleon preserved the *Grandes Ecoles* (Great Schools) established by the Convention. The principal ones were the Ecole Polytechnique and Ecole Normale Superieure. The polytechnic trained engineers—civil and military—and the Normal School teachers in Science and Humanities. The great schools still enjoy reputation in France. At the bottom, the primary schools were left to the initiative of the Communes. He preserved the Institut of France, also a creation of the Convention. .After suppressing the department of moral and political sciences by a decree of January 23, 1803, Napoleon reorganised the institut into four: Physical and Mathematical Sciences, French Language and Literature (the Academie Francaise), History and Literature, and Fine Arts. At the head of all came the Imperial University, whose object was to bring the whole educational system of France under the control of the University. Napoleon preserved and expanded the Bibliotheque Nationale (National Library) and provided the Archives Nationales a new home in 1804. The whole structure formed a rigid hierarchy with an imposing bureaucratic apparatus centered in Paris and charged with regulating the educational life of France down to the smallest detail. Napoleon took little interest in women's education. Most girls, he opined, could be educated at home; religion and manners were all they needed to learn.

Thus by his work of reorganisation, Napoleon purged the Revolution of the features which seemed to make for chaos and retained those which might be calculated to render the State a more efficient machine. In that sense, he harnessed the Revolution to the chariot of autocracy. 'I am so much identified with our...monuments, or institutions, all our national acts, that one would not know how to separate me from them,' said Napoleon in 1815. It is true that the Napoleonic genius still pervades France through the Code Napoleon, the judiciary and administration. 'His immediate successor might repudiate his work, they could not undo it, and the Napoleonic state was long to outlive its author and the ends to which he had directed it.'[5]

Napoleon as Emperor

Napoleon's ambition 'knew no bounds. In 1800 a spasmodic effort was made by royalists on the life of Napoleon. Another attempt on Bonapartoe's life was made in 1803 by a group of royalists

5. Cobban Alfred, *A History of Modern France*, 1799-1871, Vol. II, P. 38.

under the Vendean leader, Georges Cadoudal. Cadoudal and other conspirators were arrested and executed. Napoleon widely publicised the Cadoudal conspiracy to create an atmosphere for the final transformation of the First Consul into the Emperor. The name and example of Charlemagne captures the imagination of Napoleon. In 1804, by another popular vote, he was proclaimed 'Emperor of the French', his rule being made hereditary. On December 2, 1804, in the presence of Pope Pious VII. Napoleon placed the crown upon his head. 'I found the crown of France lying on the ground,' Napoleon once said, 'and I picked it up with my sword.'

If the Consulate had brought peace and reform, the Empire involved France in almost continuous war. Even before the Empire was established, France had found herself involved in hostilities (May 1803) with her inveterate enemy, Great Britain. The Peace of Amiens was little more than a truce and constituted no check upon French aggrandisement. As Napoleon himself admitted 'In the existing situation, every treaty of peace means no more to me than a brief armistice.' England, on her part, had also colonial ambitions that could be realised only by war with France. England had accepted France's 'natural frontiers' which, of course, included her occupation of Belgium. But a few months later, Napoleon annexed Piedmont, Parma and Elba, intervened against the Catholic princess of Germany, and imposed a new constitution on Switzerland. He kept French markets closed to the British and forced Spain and the sister republics to do so. Moreover, Napoleon embarked on a new stage of colonial expansion: he had purchased Louisiana from Spain, sent an expedition to San Domingo and even threatened to invade Egypt and India. Not unnaturally, the British refused to give up Malta, as agreed at Amiens, and, encouraged by Russian support, made it the subject of an ultimatum to the French. So war broke out again between England and France in May 1803.

Napoleon began by seizing Hanover, the hereditary German possession of the English. At and end of 1803, Napoleon began to prepare for an invasion of Britain by assembling a great naval armament and a large army at Boulogne. The project, however, did not materialise. But Spain's entry into the war as France's ally at the end of 1804 encouraged him to revive it. While Napoleon turned eastward with his Grand Army in the autumn of 1805, the British Admiral Nelson won the annihilating victory over the combined French and Spanish fleets off Cape Trafalgar, near the Strait of Gibraltar, on October 21, 1805. Nelson lost his life in the battle, but Trafalgar established unquestioned British supremacy on the high seas. Yet the victory of Trafalgar was overshadowed by the triumphs of Napoleon's Grand Army in Germany.

The third coalition against France, which took shape between April and August 1805, consisted of England, Austria, Russia, Sweden and Naples. The Grand Army which Napoleon harnessed was probably the finest fighting force in Europe. On August 24, 1805, he, along with the army, marched for the Rhine. With a tremendous speed, Napoleon brought 190,000 troops across the Rhine and, on October 20, 1805, he surrounded the Austrian General Mack at Ulm and compelled him to surrender with 50,000 men. The Russians withdrew and Napoleon occupied Vienna in November. The Czar Alexander and the Austrian Emperor Francis joined their forces near Austerlitz, to the north of Vienna, in the plain of Moravia. There, on December 2, 1805, Napoleon routed the Austro-Russian force. Austerlitz or the 'Battle of the Three Emperors' was Napoleon's military masterpiece. It was a victory for Napoleon such as Europe had not seen since Duke of Marlborough cut the Franco-Bavarian army in two at Bleinheim (1702).

Czar Alexander escaped and made no attempt to resume hostilities. Emperor Francis II submitted for the third time to the conqueror and signed the Peace of Pressburg (December 27, 1805). By it Austria was excluded from Germany and Italy where she had exercised so great an authority for centuries. The Treaty was in effect a declaration that the Holy Roman Empire existed no longer; in fact it was abolished on August 6, 1806. Austria gave up Venice which was incorporated with the kingdom of Italy and Tyrol, which was incorporated with Bavaria. Her influence in Germany was further reduced by the recognition of her former subject states of Bavaria and Wurtemberg as independent kingdoms.

Austria also ceded Istria and Dalmatia to Napoleon. She retained only the single port of Trieste on the coastline of the Upper Adriatic. The Prussians meanwhile signed an alliance with France and agreed to surrender Neuchatel and Anspach in return for Hanover.

War with Prussia (1806)

Prussia, however, soon found herself involved in hostilities with France. For ten years, since the Peace of Basel in 1795, Prussia had remained neutral in the struggles against Napoleon. In February 1806, Frederick William was forced to close his ports to England. But Prussia had no quarrel with England and the prospect of war embittered relations with Napoleon. In July, the formation of the confederation of the Rhine under Napoleon's protection deprived Prussia of playing the leading role in Germany. But finally when it was whispered that Napoleon, to appease England, was proposing to restore Hanover, the end of Prussian endurance came. In August Prussia mobilised and two months later sent an ultimatum that the French troops should be withdrawn across the Rhine.

The decision came with amazing suddenness. Moreover, it was an ill-timed movement—Russia was not ready, and England, who had entered the alliance, could give no immediate help. The defeat of Prussia was even more swift than that of Austria. On October 14, 1806, the Prussian forces were destroyed in twin battles at Jena and Auerstadt and on October 25, Napoleon entered Berlin in triumph. Frederick William took refuge in Konigsberg while Napoleon prepared to meet the Russians.

War against Russia (1807)

In the winter of 1806-07 the French pursued the Russians, who steadily refused to fight. In February 1807, a bloody and indecisive battle was fought at Eylau. Napoleon lost more than half his men, 35,000 experienced soldiers of the Grand Army. But in June 1807 Napoleon won a victory at Friedland which, as Napoleon observed was 'the worthy sister of Marengo, Austerlitz and Jena.' The Russians were tired of war while Austria was neutral and Britain dilatory. The Treaty of Tilsit was concluded on July 9, 1807 by the two Emperors of Russia and France.

By the Treaty of Tilsit, the two Emperors virtually divided the whole of continental Europe into two spheres of influence—the western to Napoleon and the eastern to Alexander. Russia was given a free hand in dealing with Sweden—and Turkey. Alexander agreed to try to mediate peace between France and Britain, promising, if he failed, to declare war on Britain and to close Russian ports to British commerce. Prussia was treated very roughly and was reduced to a mere torso. She was stripped of her western and Polish territories. A new kingdom of Westphalia was created of which Napoleon made his brother Jerome king. Prussian Poland was taken to form the Grand Duchy of Warsaw which Napoleon gave to the king of Saxony.

The Treaty of Tilsit marked the zenith of Napoleon's power. Central Europe lay at his feet. Prussia became a second-rate power. For his policy of commercial warfare against England, Napoleon had now the cooperation of the Czar. Yet this alliance with Russia proved to be temporary. Moreover, Tilsit led Napoleon into further adventures which ended in disaster. As a matter of fact, Tilsit was the turning-point of his fortune.

The Napoleonic Empire

The Empire of Napoleon in Europe was established as a result of the successive series of brilliant victories. After the Treaty of Tilsit the Napoleonic Empire reached its greatest extent and was firmly consolidated. In building up his Empire, Napoleon was inspired by memories of the universal monarchy of Rome or Charlemagne. He had no desire to satisfy the national aspirations of the people. He, in fact, tried to offer the gains of the Revolution to all Europeans and to establish administrative and judicial systems on French model. He hoped to win the people from their traditional rulers, while making their states more useful to the empire.

The Napoleonic Empire consisted of Belgium, Nice, Savoy, Genoa, Dalmatia and Croatia. Napoleon built up an inner ring of satellite states. These were Holland (with Louis Bonaparte as King), the Confederation of the Rhine (formed in 1806), the Kingdom of Westphalia under Jerome Bonaparte (formed in 1805 with Napoleon as king), the Grand Duchy of Warsaw (formed in 1807—mostly out of Prussia's Polish lands) and Switzerland. Joseph Bonaparte was made king of Naples and Sicily in 1804, and, after 1808, King of Spain. The Confederation of the Rhine was extended in 1807, the Duchy of Warsaw in 1809. Napoleon's allies were Russia, Prussia, Austria, Spain, Denmark, Sweden, Bavaria and Wurtemberg. The Grand Empire reached further additions until 1811 when it covered the whole European mainland, except the Balkans. But by then Napoleon was faced with tough resistance in Spain and Portugal, renewal of the war against Austria and the breakdown of his Continental System.

The chief characteristic of Napoleon's Empire lay in its aim of dominating the whole continent, which he pursued with singular devotion. He also evolved certain techniques of empire. These included—besides the enthronement of his brothers and intermarriages with older ruling houses—the introduction of Code Napoleon and the establishment of a uniform system of administration and justice. Napoleon was aware that what people wanted was efficient administration and general tranquillity, which could be provided through his legal codes and trained administrators. He did so in Belgium, Holland, Italy and Germany. Beyond these areas he had to deal with established regimes—as in Russia and Austria—where he relied not on imperial organisation but on subtle diplomacy. His aim was to prevent any general settlement or pacification of Europe. Whereas, in the West, he aimed at some unity, in the East his concern was to exploit disunity.

The most redeeming feature of the Empire was that Napoleon extended and perpetuated the effects of the French Revolution in France. 'A gust of modernisation blew through Europe in the wake of Napoleonic conquests.' Like any enlightened despot, Napoleon was concerned to centralise and modernise his government and to strengthen his authority. Administrations and judiciaries were remade, feudalism and serfdom were abolished. Equality before the law and of taxation, careers open to talent and freedom of religion became the ideal if not the rule. The Code Napoleon became the simple touchstone, the universal panacea, except in Spain. The Churches were divested of property and direct political power. Free domestic economies were fostered and land ownership widened. There was a concerted effort to promote public welfare, improve public health and promote education, science, arts and literature. Roads, bridges, canals and harbours were built or improved.

The Grand Empire, however, was riddled with contradictions and with the seeds of its own decline. Napoleon, in short, sponsored revolution. This antagonised the European rulers who were destined to strike him down when the opportunity arose. The rising middle classes were dissatisfied by the rigours of the Continental System and by tariff arrangements which subordinated their national economies to those of France. After 1810, with war preparations for the Russian campaign, the benefits of French domination were obscured among all classes by increased taxes and higher conscription quotas. Nevertheless, it should be remembered that if the French Revolution had thrown Europe into the melting pot, Napoleon stirred it about and gave it a shape it was never to lose. Europe could never be the same again, however earnest the attempts of the reactionaries after his fall.

Fall of Napoleon

The three blunders which combined to ruin Napoleon were the Continental System, the Spanish imbroglio, and the Russian invasion.

The Continental System

After Tilsit remained only England as the enemy of France. In 1805 Napoleon had defeated Austria, in 1806 Prussia and in 1807 Russia. As England was still mistress of the seas, Napoleon was compelled to find other means of crippling England. The strength of England, he believed, lay in her export trade, and the nations of Europe formed her chief market. The Continental System was the plan of closing all the ports on the Continent to British trade. This method of crippling Britain through commercial warfare had its genesis partly in the mercantile system which had made war by tariffs a normal feature of the relations between nations. Yet, Napoleon's motive was not wholly military. As the continent possessed few manufacturing industries, Napoleon cherished the hope of getting the whole of this market for French manufactured products.

The use of economic weapons in the struggle for power was not new. Immediately after the declaration of war in 1793, France annulled the hated commercial treaty of 1786. All British goods were excluded from France. As early as 1795 there was a proposal to exclude British trade from the Continent. Napoleon did not have to invent the Continental System. He found an idea already in existence and used it for his own purpose.

Before the inception of this policy, the Pope had been forced as early as 1797 to close his ports to British trade. Since 1799 Napoleon had followed the mercantilist policy of his predecessors in excluding English goods from France and her 'natural frontiers'. Since the renewal of the war with Britain in 1803 British merchandise were prohibited from Otranto in Southern Italy to Hamburg in the North sea.

Napoleon's new policy was declared from Berlin in November 1806. The Berlin Decree declared the British Isles to be in a state of blockade, forbade all commerce with them, and ordered the confiscation and destruction of all English goods found in France or her allies. Britain replied by the orders in Council of November-December 1807 which declared that any port from which British goods were excluded was in a state of blockade and required neutrals trading with the Continent to take out a licence and to pay duty on their cargoes in a British port. Napoleon replied, in turn, by extending the operation of the Continental System. His further Decrees at Fontainebleau and Milan (October-December 1807) threatened all neutral shipping with forfeiture that had touched a British port or had submitted to search by the British navy. Neutral vessels became objects of prey for both the British and the French.

Britain suffered severely from this so-called 'Continental System'. The restrictions on the export of British goods to the Continent caused serious industrial depression. This also led to a rise in the price of gold which had to be exported to pay for imports. Paper currency was much inflated and the price of commodities rose. But, on the whole, the system 'increased rather than diminished the commercial prosperity of England.' Though the European markets were closed to Britain, the rest of the world was open to her. She also found new markets, particularly in Brazil, Spanish America, Near East and in the Baltic. Moreover, it was literally impossible to prevent smuggling. It was principally smuggling that enabled the British to beat the Continental System. The Continental System was 'the most stupendous proof of Napoleon's incapacity as a statesman.' Napoleon's allies, finding their trade stagnating, began to disassociate themselves from the System—in 1809, Turkey, Portugal, Spain and the Spanish colonies; Russia a year later. Even Napoleon's brother, Louis, King of Holland, refused to enforce the blockade as to do so meant the ruin of Holland. Consequently, he was forced to abdicate and Holland was annexed to France (1810). Napoleon also annexed the northern coasts of Germany up to Lubeck, including the fine ports Bremen and Hamburg. In Italy, the Pope proved refractory in enforcing the continental blockade. Thereupon Napoleon annexed part of the Papal States to the so-called Kingdom of Italy. Immediately the Pope excommunicated him. Napoleon, in turn, took the Pope prisoner and kept him such for several years. The Italians resented the debasement of the Papacy, 'one of the historical glories of their country.' 'Among Napoleon's grave errors there was none destined to shake so profoundly the fabric of his power, not in Italy alone, but all over the Catholic world, as this gratuitous affront to the Papal See and to the Roman tradition.'

When the economic crisis of 1811-13 burst on Europe, it was attributed to the Napoleonic system. In France itself, there was widespread unemployment. Napoleon modified his economic legislation and this was the virtual end of the real enforcement of the Continental System. French ships were allowed to trade with England under a neutral flag.

The Spanish War, 1808-14

In the latter part of 1807 Napoleon turned his attention to the Iberian Peninsula in order to bring Portugal within the comprehensive economic system. Once the Continental System was launched in 1806, it became imperative for Napoleon to seal off the whole Iberian Coast from English commerce. He asked Portugal, an old ally of England, to close her ports to British trade. But when she refused to come to terms. Napoleon concluded the secret treaty of Fontainebleau with Spain for the partition of Portugal and her colonies between France and Spain. Soon afterwards, he sent a French army under Junot, which, in conjunction with Spanish troops, occupied Portugal. The royal family of Portugal fled to Brazil under the protection of the English fleet (1807).

Napoleon's design against Portugal was part of his larger scheme for the subjugation of Spain, then ruled by incompetent Bourbon ruler Charles IV. But the real power lay in the hands of the Queen's favourite, Godoy. Spain had taken part with the First Coalition against the French Republic, but had withdrawn in 1795. Since the Peace of Basel in 1795 Spain had been a reluctant ally of France. She had given little money to France and was herself violating the Continental System. To add insult to injury, Godoy had ordered the mobilisation of Spanish troops, an order which, upon the Prussian defeat at Jena, he hastily cancelled. Napoleon determined upon the destruction of another branch of that Bourbon family which had already been driven out of France, Naples and Parma.

Godoy provided a key for opening the Peninsula. He betrayed his country in return for the promise of a Kingdom in Portugal. By the Treaty of Fontainebleau (October 27, 1807), Godoy agreed to allow French troops to cross Spanish territory to attack Portugal. The campaign was successful and allowed Napoleon to introduce considerable bodies of French troops into Spain. Meanwhile, the Spanish Crown Prince Ferdinand, suspecting Godoy of usurping the throne, appealed to Napoleon for help. It was a tempting bait for Napoleon to decide the fate of the Spanish succession. While he considered possible solutions, he sent Murat with an army to Madrid. As Murat advanced, a military revolt broke out in favour of Ferdinand. Charles abdicated the throne in favour of his son Ferdinand, who was acclaimed by the whole country as the man who should free Spain. But Ferdinand repudiated his father's act of abdication and declared that it had been extorted from him by threats. Thereupon Napoleon induced both father and son to come to Bayonne in May, 1808. On May 10, Napoleon coerced both of them to renounce their claims to the throne. He then summoned his own brother Joseph Bonaparte from Naples to assume the vacant throne. Thus, Napoleon was in possession of the whole Peninsula.

Napoleon's policy in Spain was his greatest blunder. He misunderstood the problem with which he had to deal. He was completely unaware of the dogged resistance of the people, proud of their rich heritage and national culture. It saw in Napoleon the invader of national integrity and the despoiler of the crown. Led by Asturias, province after province hurled defiance against the French which was at once 'national in its spontaneity and local in its intensity.' Militarily, it took the form of armed attacks by peasant guerillas, often supported by regular units. Politically, it became organised in a series of insurgent Juntas with their headquarters at Cadiz. Napoleon had no idea of the stupendous task that awaited him. 'If I thought it would cost me 80,000 men, I would not attempt it, but it will not cost more than 12,000' he said. A ghastly miscalculation for it was to cost him half a million men and to end in failure.

In July 1808 Europe was astonished at the unfamiliar news of the surrender of a French army under Dupont at Baylen. Its effects were far-reaching. What Valmy was in the war of the French Revolution against Europe, Baylen was in the war of Europe against Napoleon—the dawn of a new era. Joseph withdrew from Madrid after eleven days' stay. The fortunes of the Spanish patriots were still further advanced by the landing in Portugal of a British force under Sir Arthur Wellesley, a young general who had distinguished himself at the battle of Assaye in India. The Peninsular War had begun.

On landing in Portugal, Wellesley marched upon Lisbon, then held by the French under Junot. The French general attempted an offensive in August 1808 but was defeated at Vimiero. By the Convention of Cintra (August 1808) Junot agreed to withdraw his army to France. Portugal thus became a British base.

The news of Baylen and Vimiero actuated Napoleon to take decisive steps in Spain. He renewed his alliance with Russia by the Convention of Erfurt in order to counteract the hostile design of Austria who had caught the infection of Spanish nationalism. Having thus made his position secure in central Europe, he himself entered Spain in November 1808 at the head of a large army. He scattered the Spanish armies in several engagements, entered Madrid in triumph, and reinstalled his brother Joseph on the throne. He then turned to crush the British troops under Sir John Moore who had marched into northern Spain. Moore's object was to draw off Napoleon from Madrid just to give enough scope for the organisation of the Spanish resistance in the South. Napoleon hurried north from Spain to chase the English army and so Moore began his 'glorious retreat' to Corunna. But Napoleon had to leave for France on January 16, 1809 to deal with the Austrians who were mobilizing for war as well as to crush a conspiracy of Talleyrand, Fouche and his sister Caroline to instal Murat in case he was killed in Spain.

Napoleon was destined never to return to Spain. Meanwhile Wellington was sent out again to Portugal in April 1809, who reorganised the Portuguese army, maintained communications with the guerillas and made only occasional sallies into Spain. Wellington effected a junction with the Spanish army and defeated the French army at Talavera (July 27-28, 1809). The overthrow of Austria at Wagram enabled Napoleon to send his best general Massena with a large army to drive the English from Portugal. Massena took Almeida and invaded Portugal with 70,000 men on September 15, 1810. Wellington fell back and, defeated by the pursuing French at Busaco, was forced to retreat upon Lisbon, where he constructed the famous triple defensive lines of Torres Vedras. Massena found the lines too strong to attack and made a skillful retreat to Cuidad Rodrigo which he reached on April 4, 1811. He lost 25,000 men in this campaign.

Having received reinforcements from England, Wellington besieged Almeida, defeated Massena, who tried to relieve it at Fuentes d'Onoro in early May 1811, and captured Almeida on May 11, 1811. Massena's failure proved a turning point in the Spanish War. It saved Portugal and gave Wellington a base of attack on the lines of the French from Madrid to Bayonne.

In 1812 the French were distracted by the effort of the Russian expedition and so Wellington was in a position to develop an offensive campaign. He captured the fortresses of Ciudad Rodrigo (January 19, 1812) and Badago (April 6, 1812). After defeating the French at Salamanca (July 22, 1812), Wellington entered Madrid. But a temporary concentration of French armies compelled him once more to withdraw into Portugal. The withdrawal of a large force from Spain for Napoleon's Russian campaign including South with the flower of the French army to Germany, enabled Wellington to make a decisive movement in 1813. San Sebastian (August 31, 1813) and Pamplona (October 31, 1813) were captured and Wellington crossed into France, invested Bayonne and defeated the French army at Toulouse (April 10, 1814). But by this time the French cause was already lost for Napoleon had abdicated and the allied armies occupied Paris.

Causes of French Failure

Napoleon had so many calls upon his attention that he could not personally direct all operations in Spain and so could not ensure that unity of action which was essential to success. He left the task mostly to his generals whose jealousies prevented concerted action at many critical junctures.

He underestimated the strength of the Spanish national resistance. Religion and national pride were the chief passions of the Spanish people which goaded them to an obstinate resistance to the French. 'It is a country', said King Joseph, 'like no other; we can find in it neither a spy nor a courier to carry messages.' Spain never succumbed, even in its hour of crisis, to Napoleon. The French Emperor had to learn that 'a whole people is more powerful than disciplined troops.' Moreover, instead of harnessing all his resources into the enterprise, Napoleon hurried away in 1809 before he himself had completed the conquest of Spain. He did not support Massena in 1810; he withdrew Soult in 1812; and in 1813 made futile efforts 'to hold

Spain with armies which, if transferred to Central Europe, might have saved the Empire'.

The physical features of Spain also fought against the French army. This is mountainous and poor, and so it was difficult for the French to secure provision for a large army for any length of time. In between these successive mountain ranges, in the passes and valleys, it was difficult for large French armies to manoeuvre. The physical features afforded great facilities for guerilla warfare, which the Spaniards carried on with utmost persistence and skill, harassed the French armies and, ultimately, enfeebled them.

The help of the British was of utmost importance as the main brunt of formal military operations fell upon them. British military operations were considerably facilitated by the favourable geographical conditions of the Peninsula. 'The British armies had rarely enjoyed upon the Continent a more convenient theatre of war than the territory of Spain and Portugal. The National Rebellion (of Spain) provided them with the benefits of a friendly country, and the command of the sea ensured to them liberty of manoeuvre, continuity of supply, and the certainty of a safe retreat.' The English utilised these advantages to the full.

Thus, the Spanish imbroglio was one of Napoleon's most serious blunders and one of the principal causes of his fall. No wonder Napoleon remarked later, 'It was the Spanish ulcer that ruined me.' Its significance lay in the fact that it was the beginning of a national movement of resistance in other countries, particularly Austria and Prussia. The war proved a festering sore to Napoleon and prevented him from using his available resources in the War of Liberation. If Napoleon had been able to use in Saxony in 1813 the 20,000 soldiers who were serving in Spain he might have gained the victory that he barely missed.

The Austrian War (1809)

The French reverses in Spain may have played some part in the resurgence of Austria, which had remained unreconciled to the humiliation of Austerlitz (December 2, 1805). The Peace of Pressburg had reduced Austria to the position of impotence in Europe. The Spanish rebellion had led something like a patriotic revival in Austria. A flood of patriotic literature called for a war of revenge, while the Archduke Charles and Count Philip von Stadion, the new Chancellor, modernised the army. Negotiations were opened with Prussia and Russia. The war party in Austria was encouraged by Metternich, Austrian ambassador to Paris, who had been told by Talleyrand that the time was ripe for Austria to strike.

Napoleon anticipated the action of Austria by declaring war. The first part of the campaign in Bavaria went easily in favour of the French. The Austrians, though commanded by the Archduke Charles, were swept out of the country with heavy loss in what is known as 'the campaign of five days' (April 18-22, 1809). A rapid thrust brought Napoleon to Vienna on May 13, 1809. But the bulk of the Austrian army was camped on the northern bank of the Danube. Napoleon's effort to cross the Danube resulted in fierce fighting at Aspern and at Essling (May 21-22, 1809), and failed to achieve its purpose. It was his first major defeat and the news of it stirred up a peasant rebellion in Tyrol. Similar movements followed in the centre of Italy. But Napoleon held Vienna and with great circumspection crossed the Danube with an army of 190,000. On July 5, 1809 he met the Austrians at Wagram. It was a complete French victory and an example of his great mastery of tactical skill. But it was costly victory as both sides suffered losses of 20,000 men.

After the battle of Wagram, the Austrians accepted a humiliating peace. Their aged statesman, Thugut, advised surrender. 'Make peace at any price,' he is reported to have said, 'The existence of the Austrian Monarchy is at stake; the dissolution of the French Empire is not far off.' The Austrian Emperor Francis I agreed to the Peace of Vienna which was signed at Schonbrunn on October 14, 1809. Austria surrendered the Illyrian provinces to the French, Salzburg to the Bavarians and Cracow and Lublin to the Grand Duchy of Warsaw. She lost three million and a half of subjects; she had to reduce her army and to pay a considerable war indemnity. But not the least of Napoleon's triumphs was his subsequent marriage with the Emperor's daughter, Marie Louise. Napoleon's motives were to strengthen his north European system and to perpetuate his dynasty. Marriage to a Habsburg princess, might accomplish both—by making Austria a natural ally and by providing a wife who could give him a son. In December 1809 he divorced childless Josephine and in March 1810 married the eighteen year old Marie Louise.

The Russian Invasion (1812)

Napoleon was gradually drawing forward towards that wild Russian adventure which, more than the Peninsular War, brought his downfall. The Franco-Russian alliance at Tilsit rested on no common interests, but on temporary convenience. The friendship between Alexander and Napoleon established at Tilst in 1807 and confirmed at Erfurt in 1808 was resented by the Russian nobility. It had been impaired by the refusal of Napoleon in 1808 to agree to the acquisition of Constantinople by Russia. There were various causes of friction between the two powers.

The Tsarist Government was particularly sensitive to what happened in Poland. The establishment of the Grand Duchy of Warsaw posed a great threat to the security of Russia. The substantial additions made to the Grand Duchy after Austria's defeat in 1809 irritated Alexander. He was annoyed, too, by Napoleon's refusal in 1810 to ratify an agreement not to revive an independent Poland.

Russian refusal to establish matrimonial relation with Napoleon antagonised Napoleon. The French Emperor's Austrian marriage offended the Czar and the coolness which sprang up was heightened by Napoleon's seizure of the Duchy of Oldenburg which belonged to the Czar's brother-in-law.

The ostensible cause of the rupture was the open refusal of Russia in December 1810 to close her ports to neutral ships and, thereby, to English trade. Napoleon was not prepared to tolerate the defection of his Russian ally from the Continental System.

Thus, by the end of 1810, the war between France and Russia seemed inescapable. In 1811 the Czar sought for an alliance with Sweden. Napoleon had antagonised Russia by his seizure of Swedish Pomerania, in punishment for violation of the Continental System. In April 1812, the Crown Prince Bernadotte of Sweden was won over by Czar by the promise that he should be allowed to annex Norway. In May 1812, Turkey granted peace in return for the Russian evacuation of Moldavia and Wallachia. In July 1812, Britain made a treaty with Sweden and Russia and the nucleus of a Fourth Coalition existed. Prussia and Austria, it was known, would join it as soon as the moment was ripe.

Hostilities began in June 1812 after the Czar delivered an ultimatum promising war if the French did not evacuate Prussia and Swedish Pomerania. Napoleon embarked on his Russian campaign almost in the spirit of an adventurer, hoping perhaps, that a decisive victory won upon the borders of the Russian Empire might produce a victorious peace. He was now ambitious enough to add to the role of Charlemagne the renown of Alexander, 'the dream of using Russia as a half-way house between Europe and the East.' In his intoxication of power, Napoleon refused to learn the historical lesson that a bare hundred years earlier, Charles XII had come to grief in undertaking a Russian campaign. 'To embark on so vast an undertaking in the east while Britain remained unconquered in the west was a mistake that Hitler was to repeat 130 years later.' In fact Napoleon later admitted that this had been the greatest mistake of his career.

Napoleon's Grand Army comprised 611,000 men including Prussian and Austrian contingents of 20,000 and 30,000, respectively. There were 100,000 cavalry and a numerous and powerful artillery. He had around him a brilliant staff of officers—Murat, Ney, Eugene Beauharnais and others. Napoleon's forces outnumbered those immediately available to the Czar by almost three to one (611,000 to 210,000). His strategy was simple—to envelop and destroy the enemy as quickly as possible.

On June 24-25, 1812 the Grand Army crossed the Niemen in four main divisions and reached Wilna, the capital of Russian Poland. Despite the friendly disposition of the Russian Poles, Napoleon had lost 55,000 men by sickness or desertion before he reached Wilna. The vast military machine began to crumble away beneath its weight. The Russians adopted the scorched earth policy, luring the enemy further and further into a country which they took pains to devastate. The Russians had studied the Duke of Wellington's methods in Portugal and profited by their study. It was 700 miles from Niemen to Moscow, Napoleon had no intention of going so far, but the strategy of the Russians forced him steadily to proceed. The Czar had announced that he would withdraw into Asia if necessary, rather than sign a peace with the enemy on the sacred soil of Russia. Napoleon hoped for a battle at Smolensk when he reached the place on August 17, 1812. But he succeeded only in getting a rearguard action and a city in flames. But by then—through desertion and exhaustion—only 160,000 of Napoleon's force remained. Instead of remaining at Smolensk (a little over half-way to Moscow), Napoleon pressed on to Moscow hoping that its capture would compel Alexander to submit. 'Every day's march onward from Smolensk cost the French three thousand men.' The Russians, under their new commander, Kutusov, took up a strong position at Borodin on the route to Moscow. In this sanguinary battle of September 7, 1812, the total losses of both sides approached 80,000 men. Neither side secured a decisive victory, but the Russians retreated and the French continued their march.

On September 14, 1812, Napoleon entered Moscow at the head of less than 100,000 men. He found the city deserted and in flames which consumed three-fifths of the city. For a month the Emperor made vain attempts to negotiate peace with the Czar, 300 miles away at St. Petersburg. Winter approached with no sign of Russian surrender, no decision reached and vast areas to control against the savage attacks of Cossack cavalry. Disease and desertions depleted his forces. He could not afford to stay on in Moscow. The defeat of Murat by the Russians on October 18 hastened Napoleon's departure and he left Moscow the next day. Napoleon hoped to return by a route that would afford him provisions. But Kutusov blocked his way at Yaroslavetz and held it against the French attacks. Napoleon was forced back on to the route he had already denuded of resources on his march to Moscow. The great retreat began. Through the November snow the troops trudged, their clothes in rags, without food or shelter, blowing up their ammunition. Discipline broke down, and the troops robbed each other. 'The French host resembled a horde of nomads rather than an army.' The scenes that accompanied this retreat were of unspeakable woe, culminating in the hideous tragedy of the crossing of the Beresina (November 28, 1812), the bridge breaking down under the wild confusion of men fighting to get across. All the while the Cossacks and the Russian soldiers preyed upon their flanks and rears, cutting off stragglers. On December 13, 1813 the French crossed the Niemen and the Russian pursuit stopped. Out of 450,000 who had crossed the river with Napoleon in June, only about 20,000 recrossed in December.

Causes of Napoleon's Failure

The main cause of Napoleon's failure was his strategic mistake in trying to finish in one year a campaign for which two were essential. His worst error was the continuation of his march from Smolensk to Moscow. He might have preserved his army if he had not gone beyoned Smolensk.

Napoleon pronounced that he had been defeated by the Russian winter. But his own bad decisions made his army the victim of the weather. He advanced too far in Russia; he overstretched his supply lines; he delayed too long in Moscow.

In broader context, Napoleon's major mistake was probably in not finishing the Peninsular War first before undertaking the Russian campaign. As it was, he committed himself to a two-front war in 1812. While he marched into Russia, Wellington won startling victories over King Joseph.

The War of Liberation in Germany

The retreat from Moscow gave the signal for the insurrection of the German people against Napoleon's rule which brought in its train defeat, abdication and exile. But even before the Russian disaster, Napoleon had already been aware of the protesting voices of the European peoples themselves. The Napoleonic system, whatever its benefits in times of peace, entailed an increasingly heavy burden in times of war. A constant feature of that system was the obligation of the occupied and vassal countries to pay for the upkeep of French troops as well as their own. A contemporary reported in December 1811:

> There is profound unrest...The example of Spain is being recommended and if war breaks out, every country between the Rhine and the Oder will be the scene of an active insurrection. The underlying cause of these disorders is not only resentment at foreign domination; its deeper causes lie in the ruination of all classes, the crushing burden of taxation, war-levies, the upkeep and quartering of troops, and endless other vexations.

Behind the cause of resentment lay outraged nationalism. For the first time the German peoples were seized with a common passion. It started with the cultural revolution at the turn of the century, when writer like Herder, Tieck, Arndt, Brentano and the Schlegels evoked the legendary glories of the old German Reich. After the catastrophe of Jena, the philosopher Fichte appealed to the German 'Nation' to unite against the despotism of the French.

At first, the patriots looked to Austria. But, after 1807, when two reformers, Stein and Hardenberg, were appointed ministers to Frederick William, Prussia became the symbol of hope of the patriots. Stein abolished serfdom and after the news from Spain, even supported a call for an all-German rising against Napoleon. But Napoleon dismissed him and most of his plans came to nothing. Prussia remained quiescent till Napoleon's discomfiture at Moscow. Stein now became Alexander's adviser. General York, commanding the Prussian contigent in Napoleon's army, signed on his own responsibility the convention of Tauroggen (December 30, 1812) with the Czar, who was resolved to liberate Europe.

The Estates of East Prussia sent resolutions demanding war with France. When at length Frederick William III, urged by Stein and driven by the overwhelming national impulse, determined to join Russia and issued in February 1813 an unprecedented 'Appeal to My People', there was an immediate and spontaneous response. By the Treaty of Kalisch (February 27, 1813), Russia and Prussia made an alliance against France and Alexander promised that Frederick William should receive back all the territory he had lost since 1806. It was also declared that the German princes who refused to fight the French were to be deposed. England, meanwhile, offered subsidies. But Metternich prevaricated preferring to mediate between the two opposing camps while harnessing his resources for any eventuality.

As Austria hesitated, Napoleon decided to make a swift shift of his two other opponents. He had the advantage of numbers: 150,000 against his enemy's 100,000: but he was weak in cavalry and his new recruits were raw and untrained. Planning to capture Leipzig, he won two skirmishes at Lutzen and Bautzen in May 1813. But he could not follow up his victories and his generals were anxious for peace. He had lost more men than the Allies and he feared that Austria would rise in arms against him. So on June 4, 1813 Napoleon made the Armistice of Plestwitz with the Allies. It was to last until July 20, but was extended to August 10.

By the Armistice of Plestwitz the Allies were the gainers. Prussia completed her mobilisation. On June 24, Austria agreed to join the Allies if Napoleon did not accept preliminary terms of peace, which included the dissolution of the Grand Duchy of Warsaw, the return of Illyria to Austria, the restoration of most of Prussia's territory in Germany, and the renunciation of the German annexations of 1810. In an interview with Metternich at Dresden on June 26, Napoleon rejected the terms offering Illyria alone to Austria in return for neutrality. Austria despatched an ultimatum. Napoleon didn't care to reply to it and on August 12, 1813 Austria declared war on France.

The Allies gave overall command to Prince von Schwarzenberg. Operating independently were Bernadotte, the Prussian Field Marshal, Prince Blucher, and the Russian General Bennigsen. Napoleon mustered some 450,000 men in the field—a force slightly inferior to the combined strength of his opponents. But he was handicapped by the divided loyalties of his allies and the lackadaisical programme of his lieutenants. Henceforth, despite his victory—his last victory—over the Austrians at Dresden on August 27, he failed to follow up his success. On all sides news arrived of the defeat of his lieutenants, at Grossbeeren, at Katzbach, at Dennewitz. In September, Napoleon retreated to Leipzig. But within two weeks, the Allies closed in on him again. He chose to fight and for three days (October 16-18, 1813), the great 'Battle of the Nations' raged. Napoleon suffered one of his greatest defeats at the battle of Leipzig, in which he lost 50,000 men and had to fall back to the Rhine. 'Within a little more than a year, two French armies, amounting to nearly a million of men, had perished.'

With the defeat of Leipzig, the whole Napoleonic edifice collapsed. Bavaria and Macklenburg had already seceded to the Allies; the confederation of the Rhine and the Kingdom of Westphalia fell to pieces, the Rhenish provinces were occupied by Prussia and the cities of the Baltic shook off the yoke of Napoleon. The Continental System perished as states opened their ports to Britain. Denmark concluded peace with the Allies, the princes of Germany hastended to make terms for themselves. The Dutch rose in revolt and formed a provisional government under the Prince of Orange; Jerome Bonapate fled, Murat, King of Naples, and his wife Caroline, deserted to the enemy.

Allied sucesses disconcerted Metternich, who became fearful that Russian hegemony would replace French in Germany. Metternich, therefore, persuaded the Allies to offer Napoleon from Frankfurt (November 9, 1813) a peace proposal which included the retention by France of the 'natural frontiers'—of Belgium, Savoy and the Rhenish frontiers—and the renunciation of Spain, Italy and Holland. Napoleon could not bring himself to accept them. By now the armies of the coalition were in Switzerland and on the Rhine, and Wellington had crossed into the Pyrennees.

When the allies invaded France, 'it had entered into the winter of its discontent.' The crying demand was peace. The Senate, called together by Napoleon in December 1813, paid its last homage to Napoleon. But the Legislative Body voted by 223 to 51 an address of unprecedented independence: 'Our ills are at their height. The *patrie* is threatened at all points of the frontier; we are suffering from a destitution unexampled in the whole history of the state. Commerce is destroyed, industry dying...what are the causes of these unutterable miseries? A vexatious administration, excessive taxes, the deplorable methods adopted for their collection, and the even crueller excesses practised for the rectruitment of the armies...A barbarous and endless war swallows up periodically the youth torn from education, agriculture, commerce, and the arts.' This was strong language and Napoleon prorogued the Legislative Body.

On January 1, 1814, Blucher, with 110,000 men, completed his crossing of the Rhine, and Schwarzenberg entered France from Switzerland with 150,000. Behind them, in Germany, were armies totalling another 200,000. In the South, Wellington had invaded France in October 1813. Napoleon, with about 60,000 troops, fought the most brilliant campaigns of his life in early 1814. He struck first in late January at Blucher along the Aube, defeating him at St. Dizier, Brienne, and La Rathiere. On February 1, 1814, Blucher, however, struck back and drove Napoleon from La Rathiere towards Paris.

While the fighting was going on, the Allied on February 7, 1814 offered Napoleon peace at Chatillon on the basis of the frontier of 1791. This involved the surrender of Belgium, Savoy, Nice and the left bank of the Rhine. Napoleon, however, refused the terms and wreaked vengeance on Blucher by defeating him in four successive engagements. This was the most brilliant defensive campaign of his career. He routed Schwarzenberg at Montereau (February 18) and sought to detach Austria from the Allies. Thereupon the four great Allied powers—England, Russia, Prussia and Austria—concluded the Treaty of Chaumont on March 1, 1814. By this the Allies made an alliance for twenty years and pledged themselves not to make separate peace with France and to continue the war with 150,000 apiece until France was reduced within the limits of her ancient frontiers.

The project might have gone awry if France herself had stood firm. The nation at large wanted peace and the civilian population offered no resistance to the advancing allied troops. Hopelessly outnumbered, Napoleon could not prolong the resistance indefinitely and, on March 30, 1814, the Allies entered Paris. Finding that his marshalls (Marmont, Augereau, Nay and Berthier) had deserted him, Napoleon accepted the inevitable and abdicated on April 6. On April 11, the Allies by the Treaty of Fontainebleau, granted him the island of Elba in full sovereignty, with the Duchy of Parma for Marie Louise and a substantial pension for himself and his family. Louis XVIII, brother of the late King, was restored to the throne by the Allies.

The Hundred Days

After Napoleon's departure, the Allies signed a Peace Treaty at Paris (May 1814); France was reduced to her frontiers of 1792—that is, she lost not only Italy and Germany but Belgium and the left bank of the Rhine. France, however, was to be accepted as an equal partner at the congresses to be held to negotiate a general settlement of Europe. After this, the Allies met again at Vienna (September 1814). But the powers failed to reach consensus on the questions of Poland, the Rhineland, Saxony and Italy. But scarcely the diplomats at Vienna involved themselves in the solution of petty jealousies, when the thunderbolt struck. After only ten months Napoleon escaped from Elba, and in March 1815 he landed in the south of France.

Napoleon was aware that the new Government in France had struck no roots and the powers of Europe were engaged in mutual rivalry. The army, too, was disaffected. Henceforth with Napoleon's arrival at Paris (March 20, 1815), the bulk of the army deserted Louis XVIII, who fled. The great majority of the people welcomed Napoleon. But Napoleon's position was extremely critical. On hearing of his return from Elba the powers at the Congress of Vienna patched up their quarrels and declared him an outlaw and branded him 'an Enemy and Disturber of the Tranquillity of the World.' They also renewed their pledges to secure his complete overthrow. They had suffered too much at his hands, and once more geared all their resources to render his collapse inevitable.

Although Napoleon had been able to raise 200,000 soldiers by March, he found that France was strongly opposed to war. Again his marshal's were dubious and he had no allies in Europe, as his brother-in-law Murat, King of Naples, who had risen against the Austrians in Italy, had been routed at Tolentio on May 3, 1815. With a force numbering about 120,000 Napoleon arrived at the Belgian frontier where the Allied forces consisted of two armies, one under Wellington and the other under Blucher. Briefly, Napoleon's plan was that of dividing the enemy and of enveloping the separate parts. On June 15, the French crossed the river Sambre and took Charleroi. Then he defeated Blucher at Ligny, while Marshal Ney with another detachment held Wellington in check at Quartre Bras and prevented him from joining the Prussians. On June 17, Napoleon turned to confront Wellington, leaving Grouchy to prevent the Prussians from coming to help Wellington. Relying on Blucher's promise of help, Wellington resolved to act on the defensive.

Napoleon had to defeat Wellington quickly, then make junction with Grouchy and go after Blucher if the campaign was to be won. On June 18, Napoleon delayed his attack to let the ground suitable for rapid manoeuvres. This delay was of vital importance as it gave the Prussians, whom Grouchy had failed to cut off, more time to join Wellington. For full seven hours Wellington stuck to his ground against the repeated onslaughts of Napoleon. In the afternoon the Prussians under Blucher came up. Caught between the two armies, Napoleon was defeated and the relentless pursuit of the Prussians turned the defeat into a rout. 'Waterloo was the last act of a tragedy, the end of one age and the beginning of another.'

This historic battle was fraught with momentous consequences; but, even if Napoleon had won the day, it is doubtful if he could have carried the victory to its logical conclusion. On June 21 he fled to Paris, abdicated the throne in favour of his son, Napoleon II (the King of Rome). Fearing capture by Blucher's cavalry, he fled on June 29 towards the western coast of France hoping to escape to the United States. Finding it impossible, he surrendered himself on July 15 to Captain Maitland of the *Belleraphon* asking for asylum. 'I have come' he announced, 'like Themistocles to seek the hospitality of the British nation.' Instead of receiving it, however, he was sent to St. Helena, a rocky island in the South Atlantic, which was too far away to enable him to return to France. There, after six years of privation, Napoleon died on May 5, 1821, at the age of fifty-two, leaving an extraordinary legacy to future generations. 'A whole chapter was ended, though like the chapters of all good stories it contained the beginnings of later chapters.'

Causes of Napoleon's Downfall

Napoleon asserted that he was the child of the Revolution But in important points he was opposed to the ideas of the Revolution. In his desire to extend his dominions, he showed himself strongly anti-national, especially in Prussia and Spain. The absolute government which Napoleon established was a negation to the idea of the 'sovereign people'. 'He was the last and greatest of the autocratic legislators who worked in an unfree age.'

By establishing a strong efficient central government Napoleon saved France from anarchy. His foreign policy in the beginning was national and served the best interests of France. But later on, after the Treaty of Tilsit, his foreign policy caused incalculable harm to France. In his determination to humble Britain and his ambitious desire to dominate Europe, he led France to grandiose scheme of conquest which drained the country's resources and paved his ultimate downfall. After Austerlitz none of his wars had the approval of France.

Unlike Richelieu and Louis XIV, Napoleon was not content with the natural frontiers of France. In his desire to dominate other countries, he ruled despotically over the conquered territories. 'War and despotism were inseparable and ingrained parts of his nature.' He dreaded the naval power and commerce of Great Britain. His obsession against England led him to declare in November 1797: 'Our Government must destroy the English monarchy or it must expect itself to be destroyed by these active islanders.' The Continental System was an attempt to unite Europe against Great Britain. 'He wished to subdue Europe by France and Britain by means of Europe.' The Continental System, by which he hoped to ruin the commerce of Britain, proved a failure.

His success emboldened him to further acts of aggression and united Europe against him. He transgressed the limits of practical statesmanship and regarded himself as a modern Charlemagne. Apart from his ambition of making himself master of Europe, he cast his covetous eyes towards the East. 'We are going to make an end of Europe... and become masters of India.'

He was oblivious to the strength of national feeling. The example of the successful national resistance which Spain offered to his aggression was emulated by Russia and Prussia. He lost more than 500,000 men in the Russian campaign, his greatest folly, which gravely impaired his prestige.

Despite the gift of strategic imagination with which he was endowed and his inspiring leadership which led him to repeated victories, he failed to secure effective cooperation among his generals. The issue of war depended less on numbers than on will-power. In his last two campaigns, Napoleon was faced with overwhelming numbers. Almost all Europe was in arms against him. This meant that he had a long line to defend and that he had often to depend upon his generals for important manoeuvres. It is also worthy of note that, owing to the Russian campaign, Napoleon lacked sufficient cavalry to follow up a victory. To cap all, there was the drain of the Peninsular War. A large force had to be deployed on the line of the Pyrennes, and thanks partly to the superior generalship of Wellington, the French were gradually being pushed back into their own territory.

There was a striking contrast to quality of the two opposing armies. Napoleon's army was made up largely of young conscripts, thoroughly inexperienced and not eager to fight; while his Marshals were weary of the war and anxious to enjoy the fruits of honour. Generalship on the side of the Allies was not, it is true, superior, but the armies of the coalition were buoyed up with the spirit of nationalism.

Influence of the French Revolution

The French Revolution heralded the end of the old order of things and saw the beginnings of new institutions. The French Revolution produced such a comprehensive change of programme that the Revolution is rightly regarded as the most important event in the history of modern Europe.

Liberty, Equality, Fraternity—the ideals of the Revolution became the sheet anchor of the French people. The Declaration of the Rights of

Man and the Citizen, proclaimed, in August 1789, freedom of thought and expression, careers open to the talents, equality before the law and the inviolability of the property. Though only a measure of political liberty was allowed by the restored Bourbons and there was no guarantee of the freedom of the press or even of freedom of association, yet a written constitution slowly came into being. The thought of the philosophers, which had so often displayed itself in constitutional experiments, had found a definite anchorage. No longer was monarchy absolute in theory. Strengthened by experiences, the bourgeoisie was to appear at the centre of the stage and bring society nearer to the goal of popular government. The Declaration of the Rights of Man and the Citizen declared property one of the natural rights that was the aim of all political associations to preserve. Perhaps the most candid expression of the principle came from Biossy d' Anglas when he introduced property-owners' charter in the Constitution in 1795:

> We thought to be governed by the best elements among us. The best are the most educated and those most interested in the maintenance of the laws. Now, with very few exceptions you only find such men among those possessing property...A country governed by property-owners belongs to the social order, one governed by those without property is in a state of nature.

But the greatest triumph of the Revolution was the attainment of religious toleration. Here rationalism won a success that was not to be lost. Though the Catholic Church might still enjoy a peculiar prestige, other religious institutions were permitted to remain in the religious life of the nation.

The most striking achievement of the Revolution was in the social field. Privilege was not entirely at an end while the suffrage was restricted, but the old system of privilege had lost most of its stings. Henceforth everyone was equal before the law, and the principle of equality of opportunity was sanctified. Now a commoner could be an army officer and even a poor man a bishop. Primogeniture was abolished; a new law of inheritance gave equal share to younger and elder children. The properties of emigré nobles as well as the dignitaries of the church—bishops, canons, abbots—were confiscated.

Admittedly, the aristocracy had not altogether disappeared. The majority, though bereft of their titles and privileges, had retained their lands even at the height of the terror. The Empire and the Restoration were to bring the nobility an' Indian summer. Thus the aristocracy had been enlarged owning substantial properties and wielding considerable power in the chambers. But it was a new aristocracy chastened by the land-settlement of 1789 and the operation of the Code Napoleon. Outside France, the effect of the Revolution was to give nobilities a new lease of life. Joseph II's fiscal reforms were abandoned, and in Prussia, 1791, saw the promulgation of a long awaited general code of laws which enshrined the rights and privileges of the nobles. 'The nobles,' it declared, 'has an especial right to places of honour in the state.'

One of the greatest gifts of the Revolution to France was uniformity of institutions for all her people. France was at least a political and economic unit, with a common administrative system and a unified body of law. And finally, the emergence of a free, landowning peasantry was a permanent result of the Revolution. 'The bulk of the population consisted of a body of peasant proprietors who are hardworking and thrifty, because out of their own experience they know the value of property, and because they labour for themselves and their families and not for absentee landlords.' Thus, the number of peasant proprietors and their holdings tended to be larger.

But the peasants in other countries did not experience French principles at first hand. In Poland an attempt was made to enlist the support of Polish serfs against the partitioning powers by offering them emancipation. In Russia, the years 1796-98 saw more peasant unrest with 278 outbreaks occurring in 32 provinces. 'All the peasants,' wrote a landlord in 1797, 'have thought that there should be no nobles...This is the self same...spirit of insubordination and independence, which has spread through all Europe.' In Ireland, in 1798, there was a full-scale peasant war. Yet neither in Poland, Ireland nor in Russia did the peasantry derive any benefit from their revolutionary actions.

Though the results of the French Revolution were not enduring in some countries, but in the Low countries, in some of the states along with the Rhine, those of Southern Germany, and the Kingdom of Naples, feudalism gave way to civic equality and religious equality and better system of administration introduced. Even the regeneration of Prussia was undoubtedly the result of the same forces. As an eminent writer puts it: 'No country that had been touched by French influence became ever quite again what it had been before.'

Another great legacy of the French Revolution was the idea of nationalism. This new factor in European politics was destined to act as a potent force in reshaping the boundaries of Europe. The erection of a Kingdom of Italy and the revival of a part of Poland did much respectively for Italian and Polish nationalism; and the German people were animated in their war of liberation. There was a nucleus of intellectuals in almost every country, ready to fight for the principles of democracy and nationalism—all inspired by that movement which had shaken the old Regime. But the arrangement of 1815 put an end to all this force of nationalism.

Democracy was another product of the Revolution. It took deep root in England who was France's most implacable opponent. The English radical movement, enriched by the lessons learned from Revolutionary France, revived in 1807 and contributed its democratic ideas to the reform movements of the nineteenth century, Here the Industrial Revolution played an important part. In other countries, after its defeat in 1795, democracy was slower to revive and it was ruthlessly suppressed as long as the Congress System lasted. It reappeared in France in the Revolution of 1830; and its later development in France and other European countries was a result as much of industrialisation as of the spread of revolutionary ideas.

The French Revolution sent shock waves into the length and breadth of the continent. Apart from these tangible bequests, the French Revolution also left the tradition of popular upsurge and violence which were reenacted throughout Europe in 1848, and in France in 1871. The Spanish liberals of 1820 and 1836—like the French, German and Italian liberals of 1847-48—drew their inspiration from the Declaration of the Rights of Man and the Constitution of 1791. In England, the great popular ferment of 1830 and 1831 was attributed to the French Revolution. Many of the later revolutionaries—Lamartine, Kossuth, Mazzini, Garibaldi—derived their inspiration from the Girondists and Mountains in 1792; and everywhere insurgent nationalism inherited the tricolour of revolutionary France. Babeuf and the Equals, though impotent in France in 1796, found protagonists in the Italian Carbonari and the Russian Decembrists. Babeuf's plan for the communal sharing and ownership of property was, in the 1830s, handed down to the French working men's clubs by his disciple, Buonarotti and has been avidly studied by Socialist leaders from Marx to Lenin.

The French Revolution was hailed by the contemporaries as something unique in the annals of history. Kant predicted in 1798 that the memory of this phenomenon would ever remain in the history of mankind. Some twenty-five years later, Stendhal declared: 'In the two thousand years of recorded world history so sharp a Revolution in customs, ideas and beliefs has perhaps occurred never before.' Even the German nationalist Arndt was constrained to admit in retrospect: 'I should be very ungrateful and also a hyprocrite if I did not avow that we owe an immense amount to that savage and crazy revolution.'

From the beginning the Revolution had a profound impact on Europe's intellectuals. Indeed, it appeared that a new vista of hope was opened. William Wordsworth immortalised that frame of mind in *The Prelude*. Coleridge vividly recalled how 'from the general heart of human mind Hope sprang forth like a full-born Deity.' The young poet Southey and the radicals Thomas Paine and Sir James Mackintosh, ardently embraced the principles of the Revolution.

The Revolution left a deep impress upon the intellectual circles in Germany. Hegel compared that era to a marvellous sunrise. Other leading thinkers of his generation—such as Fichte and Schelling, the aged Kant and the historian Herder—all welcomed the Revolution in no uncertain terms. Arthur O'Connor was not vainglorious when he declared in a speech to the Irish Parliament in May 1795 that 'the whole European mind had undergone a revolution neither confined to this or that country.'

The French Revolution also ushered in the Age of Reason. William Godwin held reason to be an infallible guide to truth. Kant and Hegel, Condorcet and Godwin felt confident that their generation was experiencing the first stages of its establishment on earth.

The greatest fruit of the French Revolution was the idea of equality which spread like wildfire to other European countries and eventually to the four corners of the globe. Like all great human ideals, Paine, in *The Rights of Man, as* early as 1791, advocated a system of taxation which would lead to the redistribution of incomes. It is in the same vein that the Declaration of 1789 asserts that all men have an equal right to well-being and the pursuit of happiness, an idea which the famous French scientist Lavoisier was probably first to proclaim as a political doctrine. Kant went so far as to reject all hereditary privileges and pointed out that the citizen's equality before the law should be regarded as one of man's fundamental rights. Bebeuf and some of his fellow conspirators of 1796 included in their social programme the establishment of 'a true society where there should be neither rich nor poor.' In this way the emphasis gravitated from the monarch to the people or the nation as the source of all sovereignty. Such a tremendous influence the idea of popular sovereignty exercised that Ranke described it as 'the perpetually mobile ferment of the modern world.'

France was pioneer in Europe in granting the Jews full civil rights. On September 28, 1791 Jews were declared equal citizens in France. Thus a process was started for the emancipation of the Jewish people which seemed to have been completed by the Russian Revolution of 1917. Finally, the abolition of slavery owed much to French revolutionary principles.

But if the French Revolution was the high—watermark of enlightened expectations, it also developed a counter-revolution. All over Europe Burke's *Reflections* evoked a response among those who clung to traditional values. Burke was followed by Gentz in Germany and Austria and by Bonald and Joseph de Maistre in France. So, an ideology of counter-revolution grew up which appeared to triumph all along the line in 1815.

But Europe had, in the intervening years, changed beyond the possibility of restoration. Even Metternich's system was impotent to hold back the revolutionary current that broke out again in full fury in 1848. The challenging principles of 1789 and 1793 were certainly not lost sight of. 'The battle for the Rights of Man went on, but it has been fought out under banners and with slogans very different from those of 1789.'

It is generally assumed that French Revolutionary ideas were the necessary precondition for the appearance of nineteenth-century artistic radicalism, also known as the 'avant-garde.'

CHAPTER 14

THE INDUSTRIAL REVOLUTION

The term 'Industrial Revolution' was first used by the French in the eighteenth century. But the term was specifically used for eighteenth century England which underwent a great transformation from predominantly agricultural and commercial pursuits owing to the invention of machines. The dream of Francis Bacon of using the knowledge of nature for human welfare thus became fulfilled in England. In 1826 a Belgian deputy proclaimed that 'All nations have turned their eyes towards industry, the sure and inexhaustible source of wealth; and toward foreign trade which can give immense extension to industry.'

Prelude to Industrialisation

By the end of the eighteenth century, Britain, the Dutch Republic, and France possessed large accumulations of capital. Successful merchants, investors and adventurers multiplied their assets from shipping and colonial plantations. English and Dutch bankers made loan to industrial entrepreneurs. In England, commercial capitalists invested in industrial production during the Napoleonic Wars.

The most outstanding fact of the European history had been the increase in population. This grew from about 100 to 140 millions between 1650 and 1750, to 187 millions by 1800, to 274 millions by 1850. The growth of population cannot be explained by industrialisation. But it is undeniable that there was a significant reduction in mortality during the eighteenth century, and that this was the primary cause of population increase.

The agricultural revolution broke the cycle of endemic famine and diminishing returns from soil exhaustion. Not only was more land cultivated, it was cultivated more efficiently. Various innovations also took place in the history of European agriculture. A recent writer[1] has shown that there were only seven important agricultural inventions in the seventeenth century, eight between 1701 and 1750, thirty between 1751 and 1814, and sixteen between 1815 and 1848.

The agricultural revolution vastly increased food production. This was effected by more intensive cultivation or by importation. New techniques were introduced in northern Italy and the Low countries during the sixteenth and seventeenth centuries; England improved upon them in the eighteenth and nineteenth centuries. New techniques hinged on judicious rotation of crops and the enclosure of land. Enclosure—the consolidation of arable and common lands and their redistribution as compact parcels of private, fenced lands—spread in eighteenth century England. Parliamentary enclosure acts reached their peak between 1791 and 1801.

Although new agriculture and public health were crucial to the transition from agricultural to industrial society, its technical core was the adoption of scientific technology. With few exceptions England prior to the late eighteenth century imitated rather than initiated new technology. But then for a time she took world leadership in inventiveness. She produced a series of inventions that transformed England's methods of production beginning with the cotton textile industry. In 1733, by his invention of the flying shuttle, John Kay doubled the work which the weaver could perform, besides improving its quality. He was followed by James Hargreaves, whose spinning jenny in 1765 multipled eight-

1. G.E. Fussell : *The Farmer Tools*, 1500-1900 (London, 1952).

fold and more the productive power of the weaver. In 1769, Richard Arkwright invented the 'water-frame' which spun cotton thread so firmly that all-cotton cloth could now be made. He was the founder of the English cotton industry. In 1779 Samuel Crompton built a spinning mule. With this machine, stronger and finer thread could be spun than by hand. In 1785, an English clergyman named Edmund Cartwright invented an improved loom—an automatic weaving machine. Hargreaves' Jenny, Arkwright' water-frame, Crompton's Mule and Cartwright's automatic loom brought about an enormous expansion in the cotton trade.

The advent of steam engine in industry opened up a limitless range of opportunity. In 1704, Thomas Newcomer was the first to invent a steam engine which was used for pumping water from the coal-mines. But at deep levels it was useless. James Watt perfected the system. In 1769 he invented the condenser and the rotary motion of the piston. With Mathew Boulton, a rich hardware manufacturer of Birmingham, Watt found it possible to manufacture steam engine. Watt's signal contribution to the Industrial Revolution was the application of steam power to drive machinery.

The increased use of coal and iron was another determining factor of the Industrial Revolution. In the beginning charcoal was used for smelting iron ore. In 1809 coke was used in the place of charcoal which led to much greater use of iron. Humphry Davy's invention of the Saftey Lamp in 1815 ushered an important development in the mining industry. The process of making steel from iron also underwent great improvement. Henry Bessemer announced in 1856 the process (the famous Bessemer Process) by which cast iron could be converted into steel. The Age of Steel had now succeeded the Age of Wood and Stone.

Improved communications were necessary for the exchange of goods. 'Railways, express mails, steamboats, and all possible means of communication are that the educated world seeks', Goethe observed in 1825. In Europe there was a great extension of waterways. Except in England, France and Belgium, canal building in Europe before 1830 was sporadic and nowhere formed part of a national system of transport as in England. The improvement of roads was more widespread. In France and Scotland, the need for roads was partly military; but in England the motives were more economic. Early in the nineteenth century John McAdam, a Scottish engineer, introduced the use of broken stone to make roads better known as 'macadam'.

Apart from better roads and more canals, important development in the techniques of carrying commodities culminated in the locomotive and the steamship. The use of steam engine in locomotive began in 1800. The steam locomotive was first made practical use by a colliery worker, George Stephenson. His first *Rocket* locomotive, tested in 1829, was able to move at the sensational speed of 20 miles per hour. By 1838, Britain had 500 miles of track and 5,000 miles by 1848 and 16,000 miles by 1886. Meanwhile, steam engine was used for maritime communication. Although there was a steamship on the Clyde in 1812 and one on the Seine in 1822, ship development reached its perfection afterwards. It was in 1838 that the first oceanic voyage was made by the steamships—Sirius and the Great Western. Studies of electricity by Faraday and others led to the perfection of telegraphic communication. In 1844 the first telegraph line was established in America.

Causes of Industrial Production in England

Britain was the first country to experience an industrial revolution. There were several causes of this revolution and the reasons for British leadership. In Britain there was comparative freedom from state interference, a large measure of political stability and social mobility, a widespread knowledge of science and technology and greater security for person and property than in Europe. Compared with France, Britain had progressed much farther in the breakdown of economic regulation; compared with Germany, she had the advantages of a national unity and, hence, of an integrated market; compared with Holland, she had coal and iron in abundance.

On the long-term causes of the English industrial revolution there were attributed four factors: the change in economic policy from mercantilism to *laissez faire;* the expansion of

British commerce; the increase in productivity owing to new machines; and the thrift and dedication of early entrepreneurs who made available the capital. In 1816 Frankland Lewis declared in the House of Commons:

> This country was the first manufacturing country state in the world, not because labour was cheaper here than elsewhere, but because our persons and properties were secure—because we had good government—because we possessed some peculiar national advantages—because we had coals in abundance—because we had machinery and mechanical ingenuity...and above all, because we had a vast accumulation of capital, in which no other country could compete with us.

The most important factor was the accumulation of capital in Britain in the second half of the eighteenth century. The pace of economic development quickened when capital was made available at the lower rate of interest. Interest rates fell from 7 or 8 per cent at the beginning of the century to 3 or 4 per cent in 1750. The development of English banking was also remarkable with 52 private banks in London and 400 in the provinces by 1800.

The immediate cause of increasing productivity, however, was undoubtedly technical progress: the use of power-driven machinery; the use of coal and iron; factory production and improved communications. The influence of machines on production was remarkable. 'In my establishment at New Lanark', Robert Owen declared in 1816, 'mechanical powers and operations superintended by about two thousand young persons and adults...now completed as much work as sixty years before would have required the entire working population of Scotland.'

The industrial revolution would not have been possible without the existence of large and accessible markets—at home and abroad. This expansion of markets was made possible, particularly, by reduced prices.

Demographic factor was no less responsible for the Industrial Revolution. An increasing population encouraged the process of the Industrial Revolution. In France there was a long spell of demographic impotence whereas Great Britain enjoyed many advantages; prosperous farms, skilled artisans, plenty of coal-land-iron, commercial entrepreneurs, a burgeoning population and political stability.

With a slowly increasing population, entrepreneurial talent found its main outlet in commerce. The expansion of domestic and international trade after 1740 enabled the economy to yield a rise in real output *per capita*. Between 1782 and 1855 the rate of growth of industrial output varied from 2 to 4 per cent per annum, more than double the rate before 1780, and between 1800 and 1830 real national income *per capita* increased 50 per cent. British trade constituted about 27 per cent of world trade in 1800 and 24 per cent in 1840.

Industrial Revolution owed no less to banking services. In 1832, Nathan Rothschild declared that England was in general 'the Bank for the whole world ... All the transactions in India, in China, in Germany, in the whole world are guided here and settled in this country.' Already in 1800 London was the commercial-financial capital of Europe, providing services of short and long-term credit. Equally significant for the future was the establishment of international banking houses, centred in London. The Rothschilds were among the first to respond to the opportunities afforded by the growth of international finance, having centres at London, Paris, Vienna, Frankfurt and Naples in 1815.

Britain became the workshop of the world from the second half of the eighteenth century. The Napoleonic wars strengthened its grip on the seas and weakened France's access to raw materials. It was not till before 1830 that France began the task of modernisation, and even in 1850 there was little that deserved to be called an industrial revolution. Germany remained almost stationary until 1850. It had to wait until the ZOLLVEREIN. In Italy industrialisation was impeded by political disunity and lack of raw materials.

Rapid Industrialisation in England

Industries in England expanded rapidly after 1830. In 1830 Britain exported cotton goods worth 19 million pounds which rose to 56 million in 1870. Similarly coal and iron production increased sharply. In the metal industries the biggest advance was the conversion of iron into steel. The Bessemer process made steel available for machinery, rail and ships. Then to the Bessemer Process was added the Siemens-Martins 'open hearth' process in the 1860s. In 1878 two Londoners, Thomas and Gilchrist, made it possible to use iron ore by eliminating ruinous phosphorous chemically. The first all-steel bridge was built across the Firth of Forth in 1883-9. From 1888 on steel began to be applied in the building of skyscrapers, while the following year saw the completion of the Eiffel Tower.

From the making of coke for iron smelting, there developed a new industry, for, in producing coke, coal gas is released. In 1812 a gas-lighting company was incorporated in London. In 1832 gas was first used for cooking. By the middle of the nineteenth century many streets were lighted by it.

Rapid advance was made in the field of electricity. The invention of the carbon arc light and improved dynamos made electrical lighting practicable by 1870. The invention of incandescent filament lamp in 1880 by Swan in England and Edison in America founded the electric supply industry. Meanwhile, electricity was employed for the electroplating of metals. A submarine cable to America was successfully laid in 1866 and the telegraph made it possible to get news transmitted and gave a stimulus to newspapers.

Photography was another new industry that arose between 1830 and 1870. It was a Frenchman, Daguerre, who rendered the process practicable. In 1839, he could take pictures in thirty minutes. In 1841 Fox Talbot, developed a quicker process. A decade later the dream of instantaneous photography was realised.

In 1839 the American Charles Goodyear laid the foundation of rubber industry. A Scottish industrial chemist, James Young, discovered in the 1850s how to make naphtha, lubricating oils, paraffin and kerosene by distilling crude oil. The production of petroleum from a two thousand barrels in 1857 rose to five and a half million in 1870. It was in 1885 that Gottlief Daimlar built a road-worthy motor car. Within less than twenty years Western technicians adapted the versatile combustion engine to boats, aeroplanes and land vehicles.

The mechanisation of industries produced professional engineers. There were civil engineers, mechanical engineers, electrical engineers, chemical engineers, marine engineers, sanitary engineers. The engineers were a link between industry and science.

Farming continued to be a source in wealth in Britain. Machinery, applied to agriculture, drastically cut labour costs. Manufacture of fertiliser was begun in England in 1846. The manufacture of synthetic dye in 1856 by an Englishman, William Henry Perkin, marked the beginning of this industry. As the age of chemical and mechanical agriculture advanced, the crops of English landlords rose. In any event, industrialisation greatly increased the amount of capital in England. One estimate is that it rose from 1,500 million pounds sterling in 1750 to 2,500 million in 1833 and to 6,000 million in 1865.

Spread of Industrialisation to the Continent

England was so closely linked with the continent by commercial ties that her impact was felt in other countries as well. Belgium was the first European country to have an industrial revolution. This was due to her favourable location giving access to three great and increasing markets (France, Germany and Britain), navigable rivers supplemented by canals; easily exploited coal land iron ore; a traditional industrial pattern in both textile and metallurgy that provided a skilled labour force; and in Antwerp a great commercial and financial centre. To these advantages were added government patronage of industry, the opening up of the Scheldt, and a long period of 'peace' in a protected market. In 1807 William Cockerill established a large machine shop at Liege. The Cockerill establishment was expanded into an industrial empire and by 1830 it became the largest in Europe. As early as 1834, the Belgian Parliament adopted a plan drawn up by George Stephenson for the construction of a national system of railways. By 1840, Belgium was technologically the most advanced country on the continent—'the one country in Europe', as J. H. Clapham pointed out, 'which kept pace industrially with England'.

France was more slowly industrialised. She had lost both colonies and markets during the long wars. The strength of the guilds, burdensome taxation and a restrictive system of commerce had also hampered industrial development. After 1830, French industries developed behind a wall of tariff which were maintained at high levels till 1860. Especially vitalising for industry was the construction of railways. After 1840, power-driven machinery began to compete with outmoded machinery in the French textile industries. Most of the new factories were concentrated in the north of the country, in Alsace and Lorraine or near Lille, Rouen and Paris. For a brief period before 1870, France became a leading producer of iron, but on the whole the country's industrialisation was slow before 1895.

Germany was originally more backward than France. Although a few factories were built prior to 1830, there was scarcely a beginning of industrialisation after that date. The formation of a customs union (*Zollverein*), including by 1833 most German states, removed many trade barriers. In 1839, with aid from British capital, the first important German railway was built from Dresden to Leipzig. Up to 1830, German economy was predominantly rural. In the quarter-century between 1850 and 1875, German political unification created the largest effective single-market in Europe. By 1875 Germany was producing more coal and iron than Belgium and France; by 1910 it was the greatest industrial producer in Europe and the second trading nation in the world. This phenomenal growth was attributed to the adoption of latest technology, high literacy of the people, her rich resources of iron and coal and an access to the rich ores of Sweden after 1890. As J. M. Keynes observed with little exaggeration: 'The German empire has been built more truly on coal and iron than blood and iron.'

In northern Europe the Baltic, once one of the great centres of European commerce, had declined in importance. The Scandinavian economics were mainly agricultural. British demand for iron and timber gave important incentives to Swedish industrial production. Though Sweden lacked coal and capital, her rich iron deposits, and a highly skilled literate population provided fillip to rapid industrialisation. The resources of Norway were more limited than those of Sweden and there were no signs of real growth by 1830. The prosperity of Denmark lay in the export of food. Denmark controlled the entrance to the Baltic and Copenhagen was an important centre for Baltic trade.

Industrialisation in Russia was uneven. Russian resources were immense but its institutions were primitive. As late as 1900, about 80 per cent of the people derived its income from the soil. The Czarist government threw its full weight behind railway construction after 1857 and behind heavy industry after 1880. At the opening of the twentieth century, Russia was fourth in pig iron production. The period from 1906 to 1914 was one of spectacularly rapid investment and growth.

The United States was abundantly endowed for industrialisation. America's continental resources and her great potential attracted foreign capital. The period from 1807 to 1814 saw some adoption of machinery and factory organisation; tariffs after 1815 helped the textile and iron industries to overcome their difficulties with foreign competitors. But agriculture and commerce remained the chief interest until the civil war; Capital and enterprise found their richest rewards in the unoccupied areas of the west. After 1861 the United States forged ahead rapidly under the umbrella of a government that was responsive to the needs of industry. Loans were made available for great enterprises. Protective tariffs gave industries to grow while taxes were kept low with no large military establishment to support after 1865. The extension of industrialization to the south of the United States, slowly since 1890, increased with rapidity since 1914.

The first of the Asiatic countries to feel the impact of industrialism was India. By 1880 it was felt that the solution of India's economic difficulties was the development of modern industries. The factory system appeared in the 1850s with the building of cotton and jute mills. After a slow growth of cotton textile industry, it began to expand rapidly after 1880. Until 1914 India depended entirely upon imports for her machinery. The First World War (1914-1918) gave a stimulus to the development of iron and steel industry, and also chemical industries, oil and water power.

Industrial development in China was rather slow. Attempts at factory spinning of cotton were made as early as 1860 and were successful after 1880. After China's defeat by Japan, foreign capital was invested in cotton mills, and a large spinning industry grew up in the Shanghai area. But elsewhere there had been little industrialisation, except in Manchuria under Japanese influence.

In Japan the Industrial Revolution began relatively early and developed at a very rapid rate. Though Japan had little in common with the socio-cultural scene of England, we must take into account two circumstances. Japan had a long tradition of importing foreign techniques and culture. For centuries Japan had imitated China and, when China declined, Japan looked towards the West. Moreover, a highly developed system of education in the second half of the eighteenth century enabled Japan to start a new leaf in industrialisation. During 1860s Japan adopted European military science and economy, united the island under the Emperor, and set out to modernise Japan from above. But it was not till after the Sino-Japanese (1894-95) and Russo-Japanese (1904-05) wars did Japan's factory industries develop on any large scale. The First World War caused an enormous expansion of all industries and by 1927 Japan had 49,000 factories.

The process of industrialisation was not the same for all countries. When the Industrial Revolution developed in Germany, Italy, the United States and Japan, things were quite different from those of England in the 1780s. Germany, the United States, Italy and Japan had the advantage of having a model, namely Great Britain. Moreover, between 1780 and 1870, technology had made enormous progress. 'The Industrial Revolution is always essentially the same but the method in which it is accomplished varies according to the different historical conditions.'[2]

Factory System

The Industrial Revolution brought to an end the 'domestic' system of industry. Artisans did their work in their cottages or shops. In the time of the English poet Chaucer (1340-1400) the cutlers of Sheffield lived in cottages to which plots of land were attached. But the Industrial Revolution changed this system. The invention of machines resulted in the building of factories or mills. By the beginning of the nineteenth century there sprang up several hundred factories in England. She had become the 'workshop of the world' by utilising the forces of Nature in the manufacture of goods. 'Nowhere does man exercise such dominion over matter." said Macaulay.

The growth of factories led the people to move from the rural districts to urban areas. Factories were built mostly in the regions of coal and iron. Many new cities—Manchester, Leeds, Birmingham and Sheffield, at one time little towns, became centres of factories. Manchester in 1774 had about 40,000 people; in 1831, about 271,000. The owners of factories were a small class of capitalists, whose object was to exploit the labourer and to amass great fortune. The worker of the factories had to work twelve or fourteen hours a day in sub-human conditions. Women and children were preferred because they were cheaper and easier to manage. Even they were employed in mines. The workers lived in miserable little houses without proper sanitation or ventilation. The pitiable working condition of children and women in the cotton mills and mines could not be imagined by the present generation. Describing the ceaseless toil of the factory workers in Manchester, a doctor observed:

> While the engine runs, the people must work—men, women and children are yoked together with iron and steam...chained fast to the iron machine, which knows no suffering and no weariness.

Small wages, long hours and child labour were not the only things that vitiated the factory system. And, to cap all, hung the fear of unemployment as the new factories produced more goods than could be sold. "It is questionable", wrote John Stuart Mill, "all the mechanised inventions yet made have lightened the day's toil of any human being. They have enabled to greater population to live the same life of drudgery and imprisonment, and an increased

2. Cipolla Carlo M. (Editor): *Fontana Economic History of Europe: The Industrial Revolution*, Vol. 3.

number of manufacturers and others to make large fortunes."

The government was not blind to evils of the factory system. It passed several laws to mitigate the cruelties of the system. The English Chartists thought that if the franchise were extended, their condition would improve; others realised that without permanent organisations—trade union—no radical improvement was possible. In 1824 the government legalised the trade unions. They strove to secure higher wages, small hours of work and better conditions for their members. The Act of 1819 had banned employment of children under 9 years of age and limited the work week for youth between 9 and 18. The Factory Act of 1833 set a landmark in the history of modern factory codes because it provided four inspectors with powers to enforce factory codes. An Act of 1844 introduced the first safety regulations in cotton mills. In 1847 the work day for women and children was reduced to ten hours. Thus the basis for the systematic factory code of 1901 was being built.

Triumph of Economic Liberalism

The way in which the economic life of Europe was developing was explained and defended by British economists of the time, variously known as 'economic liberals' or the 'classical school.' 'Inividualism' was the ideal preached by the defenders of the new order. A group of brilliant writers appeared as defenders of the new industrial order. Their spokesmen were Thomas Robert Malthus, David Ricardo, and John Stuart Mill. Their views were popularised by John Bright and Richard Cobden, leader of the Manchester School. All of them were inspired by Adam Smith, whose *Wealth of Nations*, first published in 1776, became the Bible of the Manchester School. Smith's fundamental thesis was that economic institutions were of natural origin and were subjected to natural laws; therefore they should not be interfered with by human laws.

At the very base of the system of thought was the principle of *laissez-faire* (French, leave things alone). According to its advocates, intervention by the State in the relations between buyer and seller, between employer and employee, was both mischievous. The law of supply and demand fixed the price both of wages and of commodities. The interests of labour and capital, argued the economists, were identical. Any attempt to regulate conditions of labour by legislation would result in the flight of capital. The ideas of classical economists harmonised well with the interests of the manufacturers who dreaded state intervention in economic matters.

Equally significant was the interpretation given by the economists which denigrated the position of labour in industry. In his famous *Essay on the Principle of Population,* Malthus declared that the number of persons tends to grow faster than the food supply. The poor, said Malthus, were the authors of their own poverty. Richardo's theory of 'rent' is determined by population growth. He also enunciated an 'iron law of wages'—wages tend to fall towards the level of bare subsistence. Wages and profits, capital and labour, were in natural conflict with each other. Ricardo favoured capital because he regarded labour as a commodity to be exploited.

By the 1830s economic liberalism became a well-accepted doctrine. Like political liberalism—it stressed freedom—freedom of trade (no tariffs or subsidies), freedom of contract between individuals (no labour unions), freedom from government interference (*laissez-faire),* freedom of competition (no monopolies). Despite growing pessimism of classical economists, the doctrine of economic liberalism won many followers. Industrial capitalists justified the system under which they were growing wealthy. Economic liberalism gained firm foothold in Britain. Between 1800 and 1860, almost all restrictions on private industry and trade were repealed by parliamentary action. By the Cobden Treaty with France in 1860, England had adopted free trade and *laissez-faire* as thoroughly as any nation has ever done.

In France and Germany economic liberalism won some converts. Yet it never triumphed completely. France kept her high tariffs till Napoleon III reduced them to a moderate level by the Cobden Treaty of 1860. The German ZOLLVEREIN tariff of 1834 was a low one. On the whole, continental countries never adopted economic liberalism with as much thoroughness as evinced by Britain.

Effects of Industrial Revolution upon Contemporary Society and Politics

'The Industrial Revolution opened the way to a new world'. With the increase of production in land and industry population grew rapidly. Most of the population growth was centred in cities which assumed importance with the establishment of factories. By 1851 half of England's population had become urban. With the rise of the cities important changes occurred in the structure of the society. The familiar division of landowner and peasant, merchant and artisan continued. But new classes like industrial capitalist and wage-earning proletarians emerged. The Industrial Revolution made capitalists the supreme masters of industry. The wage-earning proletarian was wholly dependent. Along with the fear of unemployment the new proletariat lived in abject poverty. Though in 1925 the workers were permitted to form unions by the Parliament, the latter forbade them to organise strikes. Thus, a new class of bourgeois entrepreneurs arose in oppositon to a class of workers. The former held the reins of government and had great economic power. Everywhere it became self-conscious and formed itself into a political force.

The dismal condition of workers created by industrialisation produced sharp reaction among the thoughtful men. By 1830s opinion gained ground along with Lamartine that 'the proletarian question is one that will cause the most terrible explosion in present-day society, if society and government decline to fathom and resolve it.' An humanitarian factory owner Robert Owen (1771-1858), first improved conditions for his own mills and led agitation for factory legislation and labour organisation. He upheld the view that the capitalist should share a portion of his profits with his employees.

On the continent, criticism of industrialism was more radical than in England. Contemporary with Owen, the French aristocrat St. Simon advocated that the state should assume control of production and distribution. Charles Fourier, another Frenchman, pleaded for a new social organisation based on cooperative communities raising their own food and making their own goods. But a more practical socialist was the Frenchman Louis Blanc who preached that everyone should be remunerated according to his needs. He advocated the right to work and proposed cooperative factories to be guaranteed by the State. Another Frenchman, Proudhon, wanted to abolish private ownership of property and to make credit avaiable to everyone without interest charges.

But the greatest advocates of Socialism were Karl Marx (1818-83) and Friedrich Engels (1820-95). For Marx and Engles history was a struggle between classes. The struggle involved the two classes—the upper middle classes (bourgeoisie) and the proletariat. In *The Communist Manifesto* issued in 1848 Marx made a fervent appeal to the workers of the world to unite, telling them that they had nothing to lose but their chains and the whole world to conquer. He emphasised the international character of labour and taught the working classes that their interests were the same the world over.

England, where the factory system had been worst, was well on the road towards an humanitarian attitude towards social problems. The State began to interfere for the better protection of the working class. 'Social Catholicism'—led by such persons as Ozanam in France and Bishop Ketteler in Germany—combated individualism and selfishness of industrialists and urged state intervention to safeguard the working classes. On the Continent, where industrialisation proceeded at a slower pace, social reforms were inaugurated from the middle of the nineteenth century. Bismarck's State Socialism found general acceptance in Europe. Though new policy of the State hardly realised the ideals of the proletariat, it marked a step forward to meet the claims of that class which had borne the brunt of the Industrial Revolution.

The Industrial Revolutioin brought about a change in the political life of England. The House of Commons was elected on a narrow franchise—an undemocratic system. The old boroughs whose importance had dwindled sent men to the House of Commons while the new industrial towns like Manchester, Sheffield, Birmingham, Leeds, had no representation. A movement for a reform in the House of Commons began.

The First Reform Act was passed in 1832. The Act granted to the industrial bourgeoisie a voice in the Parliament though it did not confer the franchise on the labourers.

As the First Reform Bill did nothing for the proletariat, they presented their petition to Parliament without any effect. From the fact that they called their petition the 'People's Charter', they were termed Chartists. The Chartist programme included universal suffrage, annual parliament, and the secret ballot. Unfortunately for the proletariat, Chartism did not produce a strong leader like William Cobbett. The repeal of the Corn Laws in 1846 greatly reduced the price of food. Duties on grain were reduced and practically abolished at the end of three years. England adopted the principle of Free Trade.

After the failure of the Chartists in 1848, the proletariat had formed trade unions. The trade unionists had found an able friend in John Bright (1811-89) who hated the landed nobility. His agitation led finally to the passing of the Reform Act of 1867. The Act nearly enfranchised all the working men in the towns. In 1884, the franchise was extended to agricultural labourers. In 1901 the British working men organised the Labour Party. By 1928 the enfranchisement of the women was complete.

The influence of Industrial Revolution was felt in British foreign policy. She was anxious to find new markets for her ever-increasing volume of trade as well as to secure raw materials for industries. She found a convenient field in India, where the East India Company deliberately ruined Indian industries with a view to promoting British manufactured articles. The result of the Spanish colonies in America opened the door to British merchants. Lord Palmerstone, who served as British Foreign Minister from 1830 to 1851, encouraged revolution in Germany, Italy and other places with the ulterior object of opening markets for British India.

The Industrial Revolution was a revolution in consumption as well as in production. Machine-made goods were very cheap which stimulated their growing production. Larger production necessitated larger consumption. Luxuries became necessities which led to a higher standard of living for the masses.

The impact of the Industrial Revolution upon politics gave a new dimension to the historical forces. It brought into the political field the capitalists and working-men, the latter struggling to break down the power of aristocracy and absolute monarchy. Democracy became the rallying cry of the new classes.

The Industrial Revolution gave a great impetus to Nationalism. Common economic interests at last gave a solid foundation to the national aspirations of both Germans and Italians. If nationalism was intensified, so was internationalism. The vast international trade that grew up as a result of the Industrial Revolution led the various nations to unite into a common economic life. The established financial groups—such as the Rothschilds, Barings, Laffittes and Hopes—assumed a new preeminence in a world where capital and credit were in great demand. Western Europe was fast becoming one commercial, industrial and financial society.

The Industrial Revolution revolutionised the function of government and politics. Apart from the maintenance of public order and national security, government had to concern itself with the problems of social and economic life. The notion of government and society as mutually interdependent contrary to the old order with the sharp divisions between ruler and subjects, was the most revolutionary notion of modern history. It was the common basis of all the great progressive movements of nineteenth-century Europe.

The Industrial Revolution enabled the European powers to establish economic control over Asia and Africa. Apart from providing raw materials to the European powers, these countries became the scene of international conflict. There were Anglo-French rivalry in Asia and Africa, Anglo-Russian rivalry in Central Asia, Franco-Italian and Franco-German rivalry in Africa. Thus the Industrial Revolution endangered or destroyed the political independence of many countries which became the colonies of the Western powers.

The most striking sequel to industrialisation was the intensification of power rivalries. Uneven economic developments drastically altered the balance of power among those who were technologically advanced. Germany's superior industry as much as its large population was responsible for its emergence as the strongest military power in Europe. As a counterpoise to dominance of Germany, France not only made foreign alliances but also sank investments in Russia and eastern Europe. The United States, hitherto preoccupied on the North American continent, began to penetrate distant areas from the last quarter of the nineteenth century. In the Far East an industrialised Japan defeated China in 1895 and Russia in 1905 and established its hegemony in the region.

As major power rivalries beame tense, military expenditure rose. These developments climaxed in the year 1914. The disciples of Adam Smith, relying on economic laws to produce a harmonious world, had not visualised industrial warfare. The world wars of the twentieth century produced economic disctatorship planned by states bent on aggrandisement. Industrial warfare assume a new dimension when radioactive thermonuclear energy, threatens the continuation of the very society that has produced it.

Industrialisation unleashed the force of migration—first on a local basis, next on a regional basis, and then on an international and intercontinental basis. Unregulated migration brought in its train urban congestion, vagrancy, epidemics, unemployment and abysmal poverty generating organised crime. Benjamin Disreali (1804-81), Prime Minister of England and novelist, wrote in Sybil (1845): 'Two nations between whom there is no intercourse and no sympathy; who are ignorant of each other's habits, thoughts and feelings as if they were inhabitants of different planets'.

In the cultural sphere, education received an impact. Technical education proliferated as industries required technicians and apprentices. Along with it higher scientific education made progress, women's education was launched.

Conclusion

The Industrial Revolution which manifested itself in England spread to other countries. France, Germany and the United States were the countries where the Industrial Revolution reached a few decades afterwards. The Industrial Revolution was a growing process; it did not stop abruptly in the middle of the nineteenth century. Thus the steam engine was followed by the turbine, the gasoline engine and the electric motor. The locomotive was joined by the automobile and the airplane. Human endeavour and scientific discipline enabled the men to establish the telegraph, the telephone, the wireless telegraph, radio, television, laser and space technology. The Industrial Revolution heralded the dawn of a new era—an era marked by man's bold mastery over the forces of nature.

The Industrial Revolution bequeathed as many problems—problems which were many, formidable and pressing. The only event comparable to the Industrial Revolution is the Neolithic Revolution. But the Neolithic Revolution developed in the course of thousands of years. Man had time to adapt gradually. But as a recent writer has observed:

> The Industrial Revolution has invaded the world, turned our very existence upside down and overthrown the structures of all existing human societies in the course of only eight generations. And today it is beginning to press with great urgency new problems of such enormity that the human mind can hardly grasp them—the uncontrolled increase in population, the hydrogen bomb; the pollution of the atmosphere; the destruction of the natural surroundings by industrial waste; the demand for further mass education...the breaking up of the traditional state; the scientific examination of uncontrolled centres of power...Under the weight of these problems the old structures crumble... Everyone has been taken by surprise. It is the story of the 'Sorcerer's Apprentice' which would be funny if it were not tragic[3].

3. Cipolla, Carlo M. (ed.): *Fontana Economic History of Europe: The Industrial Revolution.* Vol. 3, PP. 20-21.

CHAPTER 15

RESTORATION AND REACTION

The battle of Leipzig, October 16-18, 1813, demonstrated the impressive power of the European coalition and drove Napoleon across the Rhine into France. Before the end of the year the French had been confined to territory west of the Rhine. In early February 1814 a conference was convened at the village of Chattilon-sur-Seine where the Allies were determined to confine France to her frontiers of 1792. The conference was held without armistice. Meanwhile Napoleon had been deserted by his last ally Murat and the Allies had overrun a third of France. The Allies presented their terms of peace in a document known as the 'bases de Troyes' on February 17. Napoleon might have ended the war had he been willing to accept the French frontiers of 1792. But a shrunken France was repugnant to Napoleon and he allowed the offer to lapse.

Napoleon's opponents at first failed to agree on war aims, Metternich being particularly distrustful of Russia. The promise of British subsidy and Castlereagh's personal initiative reunited the Allies. At the Treaty of Chaumont, signed on March 9, 1814 the four powers—Britain, Austria, Prussia and Russia—agreed to defend each other against any future attack and undertook to remain in alliance for twenty years. They agreed to restore the Bourbon dynasty to France and proceeded to occupy Paris which fell in March 30, 1814. Napoleon abdicated on April 6, 1814, retiring to the island of Elba.

The Treaty of Paris (May 1814)

The Allies were determined to make a definite arrangement with the defeated enemy, and to reduce the confusion and solve the territorial problems that had been created by the collapse of the Napoleonic empire. The first task was accomplished when the allied powers restored the old dynasty, the House of Bourbons, in the person of Louis XVIII. It was also decided not to saddle France with a punitive peace as it would endanger the restoration of security so ardently desired by the Allies.

The First Peace of Paris was signed with Talleyrand on May 30, 1814. This famous document contained a preamble and thirty-three regular articles with certain additional and secret terms. France lost its territories in Italy, Germany, and the Low countries, and her colonial possessions at Tobago, Santa Lucia, and Isle de France, which were ceded to Britain, and part of San Domingo, given to Spain. France was allowed to retain her frontiers which she had had in January 1792. But she was given certain enclaves, the largest of them being Avignon and its environs, six separate frontier gains including a large one in the Meuse Valley.

The treaty secured French consent to free navigation of the Rhine, independence for Switzerland and the retention of Malta by Britain. Despite pressure exerted by Britain and Prussia on France to pay reparation, the French King was inflexibly opposed to any financial imposition. This determination so impressed the Allies that they abandoned the idea of reparation. They also decided not to insist that France return the art treasures that had been systematically expropriated from the museums and palaces of Europe.

By secret articles, France agreed to abide by the Allied decision in the redistribution of territory to be undertaken at Vienna. It was declared in one of the last paragraphs of the Paris Peace that "all the power engaged on either side in the present war shall, within the space of two months, send plenipotentiaries to Vienna for the purpose of regulating in General Congress, the arrangements which are to complete the provisions of the present Treaty".

The Congress of Vienna

The plenipotentiaries of European powers came to the Austrian capital, Vienna, in September 1814 and busied themselves in negotiations for a period of eight months. The settlement reached at Vienna which was expected to settle all outstanding issues embraced the continent as a whole.

The Congress was in fact an affair of the five major powers—Britain, Austria, Russia, Prussia, and, later on, France. They monopolised the whole business of the conference by retaining control of the territorial questions. To satisfy the susceptibilities of the lesser powers, they were involved in ten special committees like Swiss affairs, Italian affairs, rivers, slave trade and the like. Spain, Portugal and Sweden sat with the Great powers on a Committee of Eight which met frequently.

The Five Great Powers were represented by some of the ablest diplomats of the nineteenth century. Chief among them was Clemens Prince Metternich, the Austrian Foreign Minister, who saw in the ideal of nationalism unleashed by the French Revolution the greatest menace of the era. He was a vainglorious man when he confessed, 'I say to myself twenty times a day how right I am and how wrong the others are. And yet it is so easy to be right.' Nevertheless, Metternich possessed uncommon political gifts as he had become Minister of Foreign Affairs in 1809 at the age of 36 which he continued till 1848. His greatest talent was 'a sensitiveness to the existence of general European interests.' Metternich's interest in reconciling the interests of the powers was shared by the British Foreign Secretary, Viscount Castlereagh. With his distrust of abstract ideas and his preference for flexibility, Castlereagh was the creator of a British style of diplomacy that has continued ever since. It was due to his untiring efforts that the Grand Alliance had been able to survive the conflicting interests of the powers. Now, he wanted to restore the balance of power which would foster security and peace in Europe.

Both Metternich and Castlereagh had more freedom of action than their Russian and Prussian counterparts as the latter had frequently to be swayed by the prejudices of their sovereigns. Thus, Nesselrode, the Russian Foreign Minister, had to satisfy the susceptibilities of his monarch, Tsar Alexander I, an enigmatic personality. The Tsar wavered between the cold mechanics of the balance of power and flights of idealism and religious mysticism. The Prussian delegation was headed by Prince Hardenberg, who was assisted by Wilhelm von Humboldt, the former minister of culture and now ambassador to the court of Vienna. Their efforts to promote Prussian interests were hamstrung by their sovereign, Frederick William III, who often had to play a second fiddle to the Tsar of Russia. Humboldt provided the procedural plans of the Congress and the statistical studies and calculations that served as a basis for the redrawing of the map of Europe.

Another most interesting and clear sighted personality was Talleyrand whose object was to promote and safeguard French interests. He had come to Vienna as the head of the delegation of a defeated power. Having been excluded from the inner meetings of the peace conference, Talleyrand offered leadership to the disgruntled medium sized and small powers. He threatened to withdraw the French delegation from Vienna unless he was included in the 'Big Four'. In early January 1815 France was included in the Four Power arrangement, making it Five, owing to the insistence of Nesselrode and Hardenberg.

The Vienna Settlement: Basic Principles

The territorial settlement made at Vienna was based on three principles: compensation for the victors, legitimacy, and the balance of powers.

Britain, the most persistent enemy of Napoleon and the paymistress of the Allies, took her reward in the form of colonies and naval bases. She occupied Heligoland in the North Sea, Malta and Ionian Islands in the Mediterranean, Cape Colony in South Africa, Ceylon, Isle of France, Demerara, St. Lucia, Tobago and Trinidad. Austria recovered certain Polish lands and Northern Italy, to be henceforth known as the Lombardo-Venetian Kingdom. She also recovered the Illyrian provinces along the eastern coast of the Adriatic—which she had lost in 1809. She also extended westward into the Tyrol and Salzburg, planting herself firmly upon the Alps. These gains, in addition that the restored rulers of Parma, Modena and Tuscany belonged to the Hapsburg family, strengthened Austrian hold on Italy.

The territorial settlement, however, faced a crisis while adjusting claims of Prussia and Russia. Russia retained Finland, which it had conquered from Sweden, Bessarabia, wrested from the Turks and Turkish teritories on the south-east. But when she demanded the Grand Duchy of Warsaw, which had included the Polish districts formerly belonging to Austria and Russia, she encountered opposition from Prussia; the latter was willing to give up their Polish territory if she was given the Kingdom of Saxony, a rich country that lay immediately south of Prussia.

The territorial wranglings were of utmost concern to both Austria and Britain. Both powers were alarmed over Russia's Polish project, which would establish her sway in Central Europe. While if Prussia was allowed to annex Saxony, that would enable the former to establish her predominance in the affairs of Germany, a fact distasteful to Metternich. Both Castlereagh and Metternich were irritated by the defiant and menacing attitude of Russia and Prussia. Relations between the two sets of powers became so embittered that, by the end of December 1814, war loomed large. It was in this critical juncture that Talleyrand proposed that Britain and Austria conclude a secret alliance with France, by which the three powers undertook to resist Prusso-Russian pretensions by force of arms. At first Castlereagh hesitated fearing that such a combination might precipitate war instead of helping to reach an amicable settlement. However, he changed his mind owing to Prussian intransigence with respect to Saxony, and concluded a triple alliance on January 3, 1815 which promised mutual support against an aggressor. Talleyrand reported with great satisfaction to Louis XVIII: 'Now sire, the coalition is dissolved, and for ever. Not only does France no longer stand alone in Europe, but France...is in concert with two of the greatest powers, and three states of the second order.'

As a result of the secret treaty the crisis blew over and a rapprochement followed which pleased everybody except the Prussians. Russia was permitted to take a greater part of the Grand Duchy of Warsaw, while Prussia and Austria retained some of their Polish districts. Prussia was given slightly more than half of Saxony, without Leipzig, in addition to Swedish Pomerania and extensive territory along the Rhine. Prussian statesmen did not like the last arrangement. The Rhinelands were Catholic, friendly to France, and were so detached from the rest of the kingdom that it was necessary to secure special treaty rights for Prusian troops to cross Hanover and Cassel.

One great principle underlying the Vienna Settlement was the restoration, as far as possible, of the boundaries and reigning families of Europe, as they had been before 1789. It was this principle of legitimacy which Talleyrand urged in order to preserve France. In line with this principle, the Bourbons were reinstated in Spain and in the two Sicilies, the House of Organge in Holland, the House of Savoy in Sardinia, the Pope in the Papal states, and a number of German princes in their former possessions. The Swiss Confederation was restored. In the name of legitimacy, Austria recovered Tyrol and most of the territories she had lost.

The principle of legitimacy, however, was not applied consistently. The diplomats refused to restore German States that had ceased to exist as far back as 1803 and they ignored the principle in the case of Italian states. It was Metternich's desire that Italy should simply be a collection of independent states. The doctrine of legitimacy, appealed to for the restoration of dynasties, was ignored in the case of republics.

The third principle which guided the Congress of Vienna was the principle of the balance of powers between the Great Powers so as to discourage unilateral aggression on the part of any of them. This attitude determined the course of action of the Great Powers even if this ncessitated violation of legitimacy. The French, German and Italian questions were settled in accordance with this principle only to establish an enduring peace.

France was reduced to the boundary she possessed before the outbreak of the Revolution. Steps were taken to prevent France from future aggression by surrounding her with a girdle of strong states. Thus Belgium, previously an Austrian province, was joined to Holland as one Kingdom which provided security against France in the north. The Kingdom of Sardinia-Piedmont was strengthened by acquisition of Genoa, thus creating a barrier against French aggression in the south-east.

Germany was left divided into 38 separate states with a Diet legislature under Austrian Presidency. The new Germanic confederation of 38 states was a weak union as there were no federal arrangements and no safeguards of popular liberties.

In Italy, Austria was not only given Lombardy and Venetia but was allowed to extend its influence over the northern duchies of Parma, Modena, Lucca and Tuscany. The purpose was partly to put Austria at par with other powers and partly to place it in a position to prevent French onslaught on Italy. Papal authority was reestablished in Central Italy, and the Kingdom of Sardinia in the north-west recovered the island itself, Piedmont, Savoy and Nice with the addition of Liguria (Genoa).

Among other changes effected in the map of Europe was that Prussia gave Lauenburg to Denmark, Denmark ceded Norway to Sweden, and Sweden, in her turn, surrendered Pomerania to Prussia. The changes were repugnant to the Norwegians and particularly important for Sweden. The settlement provided Switzerland with a loose union of 22 cantons. The powers also promised to guarantee Swiss neutrality.

In addition to territorial arrangements, the treaty also laid down various principles, among them the titles of various German princes, indemnities of one to another, the levy of transit dues on specified roads and navigation rights on international rivers. Britain, which had abolished slave trade in 1807, now sought to suppress it by international agreement. Although many of the powers welcomed the idea, France, Spain and Portugal did not. However, the powers declared that the slave trade was 'repugnant to the principles of humanity and universal morality' and that they agreed in the 'wish of putting an end to a scourge which has so long desolated Africa, degraded Europe, and afflicted humanity.' Portugal accepted abolition north of the equator which, though inadequate, served as a first step toward achieving cherished goal.

Criticism of the Vienna Settlement

The territorial arrangements made at Vienna were destined to endure, with slight modifications, for nearly fifty years. As self-interest predominates in the welter of bargains and agreements, it is futile to discover the operation of any lofty principles. Though the powers championed the doctrine of legitimacy, that is, the principle that princes deprived of their thrones by Napoleon should receive them back again at the hand of collective Europe, the principle was sacrificed in favour of expediency. Republics need not invoke it and even kings were deprived of its benefits. Gustavas IV of Sweden was dethroned and the King of Denmark was forced to acquiesce in the dismemberment of his kingdom.

The principle of nationality was deliberately ignored. The Germans were indignant as they viewed the Germanic confederation a pretentious fraud. 'The German confederation was a mockery of national unity.' A German editor denounced the 'heartless system of statistics' and Blucher compared this Congress to the annual cattle fair. In Italy, Metternich's object was to keep her weak and divided and he succeeded in his object. The Congress of Vienna supported Metternich's contention that Italy was 'a geographical expression.' It was in violation of the principle of nationalism, Austrian domination was established in Italy, that Norway was taken from Denmark and given to Sweden, and Belgium was united with Holland. Gentz, the Secretary of the Congress, wrote after reviewing the work of the Vienna Congress:

> Men had promised themselves an all-embracing reform of the political system of Europe; guarantees for peace; in one word, the return of the Golden Ages. The Congress has resulted in nothing but restoration; agreements between the Great Powers, of little value for the future balance and preservation for the peace of Europe; quite arbitrary alternations in the possessions of less important states... The Protocol of the Congress bears the stamp rather of a temporary agreement than of work destined to last for centuries.

In ignoring the philosophy of the Revolution, the makers of the Vienna Settlement weakened the whole structure they were so laboriously erecting. In 1830 the Belgians rose in revolt and destroyed the edifice of 1815. The arrangements concerning Italy and Germany lasted for half century and underwent profound change thereafter. Among the disaffected were the French who felt hurt by the loss of their natural boundary. The break-up of Poland was in gross violation of the principles of nationality. Thus the Congress of Vienna—which sacrificed the principles of nationality—could not endure long. In the next half-century Europe was destined to witness many wars and revolutions. The Vienna Settlement was made by monarchs and, as such, it ignored the aspirations of the people. "The real charge that may be brought against the monarchs of Vienna is that they ignored the challenge of the French Revolution; that they failed to see that the new forces of democracy and nationality were becoming determining political factors."

The Hundred Days and the Second Peace of Paris (November 1815)

While the Congress of Vienna was coming to a close, the world was startled by the news that Napoleon had escaped from Elba in early March 1815, had landed in France, and had seized the throne. On March 13, the eight signatories of the First Peace of Paris signed a joint statement declaring that Napoleon had placed himself as an outlaw. On March 25, they agreed to a document of nine articles in which they reaffirmed the First Peace of Paris and agreed to mobilise their resources against Napoleon. Thus the coalition was reformed and the result was the crushing defeat of Napoleon on June 18, 1815 in the battle of the Waterloo. The Allies were back in Paris on July 7 and the next day Louis XVIII was reinstalled. Napoleon surrendered and was taken to his desolate destination on St. Helena. The Corsican had only one hundred days of restored power and this was attributed to the policy of moderation toward France in the First Peace of Paris.

The Allies, therefore, adopted a tough policy and finally signed the Second Peace of Paris on November 20, 1815. France was reduced to the frontiers of 1790 and was forced to surrender a number of strategic posts in the north and east. The most important change was the transfer of Saar to Prussia. The terms also provided for the occupation of the France for three to five years by an Allied force, and the payment of an indemnity of 700 million francs.

The Holy Alliance and the Quadruple Alliance

The chief European powers who made territorial settlements at Vienna were determined that they must keep Europe at peace. Two international organisations were ready to do this; the Holy Alliance and the Quadruple Alliance.

The Holy Alliance was born out of the Russian Czar Alexander's romanticism. To the contradictory influences that moulded Alexander's character was added the belief that he was the instrument set apart by the Providence for redeeming the world's problems. But in the pietism of Alexander there was much that was ridiculous and much that was admirable. It was to his 'noble moderation' that France, despite her aggression, owed her existence as a European power of the first rank. In the document which the Tsar laid for signature, the rulers of Prussia, Austria and Russia undertook 'to consider themselves all as members of one and the same Christian nation, the three princes looking on themselves as merely delegated by Providence to govern three branches of One Family, namely Austria, Prussia and Russia, thus confessing that the Christian world, of which they and their people form a part, has in reality no other Sovereign but Him to whom power along really belongs.' Sovereigns were henceforth to conduct their natural relations on 'the sublime truths of the religion of God and Saviour' and of taking as the basis of their external and internal policy the principles of justice, charity and peace. Sovereigns were henceforth to regard each other as brothers and their subjects as their children, whom they were to govern as 'fathers of families.'

The Tsar's appeal to the Christian foundations of European civilisation owed much to his interest in the New Testament and something to the influence of Mme de Krudener, who helped him as a religious mentor.

The Holy Alliance was eventually signed by the European powers on September 26, 1815 except the Prince Regent of England, Pope Pious VII and the Sultan of Turkey. However, the powers signed it, after Metternich had made some amendments in the text: and they did so, more to satisfy the Tsar's religious vanity, than with any seriousness. In his Memoirs, Metternich asserted that the main motive of Austria and Prussia in signing was to 'please the Tsar' which they could do because of the hollowness of the whole scheme.

In its intention the Holy Alliance was neither insincere nor antiliberal; but as political machinery it was useless. Tsar Alexander I vainly tried to 'provide the transparent soul of the Holy Alliance with a body.' Metternich dismissed it a "sonorous nothing" and an "overflow of the pietistic feelings of Emperor Alexnder and the application of Christian principles to politics." Talleyrand called it 'a ludicrous contract' and Castlereagh characterised it as 'a piece of sublime mysticism and nonsense' and likened the document to one of the fulminatins of Cromwell's 'Saints'. Castlereagh warned the British Prime Minister that 'the Emperor's mind is not completely sound.' The Holy Alliance demonstrated the weakness of Christian morality in guiding the destinies of nations and exposed the sinister design of interference of despotic monarchs in the internal governments of smaller nations.

The Holy Alliance was destined to end in failure. But the same could not be said of the Quadruple Alliance signed in Paris on November 20, 1815, after Waterloo. The four Great Powers—Britain, Russia, Austria, and Prussia—undertook to 'guarantee Europe from dangers by which she may be menaced.' The Allies agreed to maintain the Second Treaty of Paris, to prevent the return of Napoleon, and to stand solidly behind the occupation forces. Article VI, in conformity with the spirit of Chaumont, provided:

> In order to consolidate the connections which at the present moment closely unite the four sovereigns, the High Contracting Parties have agreed to renew at fixed intervals, either under their own auspices or by their representative minister, meetings consecrated to great common objects and examination of such measures which shall be judged most salutary for the peace and prosperity of the nations, and for the maintenance of the peace of Europe.

Article VI established the legal basis for the diplomacy by conference and 'marked definitely the ascendancy of the Great Powers' and the principle of the 'European Concert.' Metternich's colleague, Fredrich von Gentz, who had served as Secretary General of the Vienna Congress, envisaged this kind of alliance to build up 'a more complete political structure.' In 1818 France joined the Quadruple Alliance. However, the periodical 'summit' meetings among the Allies bore resemblance of modern day diplomacy and its intention was subject to the same kind of deceptions.

Congress of Aix-la-Chapelle (1818)

The first Congress met at Aix-la-Chapelle in the autumn of 1818. The meeting was convened ostensibly to complete the settlement with France, by making a final adjustment of reparation and by authorising withdrawl of occupation force. France was invited to join a Quintuple Alliance to preserve the peace. Metternich had good reasons to congratulate himself on the success of the first Congress, as it marked the zenith of the system by which the Allied Powers tried to regulate affairs of all continental states. Like the Amphictyonic Council of Greece, the Congress entertained appeals in the most miscellaneous matters. Denmark invoked assistance against Sweden, German princes sought redress for their grievances, the people of Monaco complained against their ruler; and the Congress also dealt with the disputed succession to the Duchy of Baden and the position of Jewish citizens in Prussia and Austria. Like its future progeny, the League of Nations, it was effective in dealing with minor powers but impotent in regard to crucial questions and to great powers. The Congress of Aix-la-Chapelle witnessed, in fact, the first rift in the lute which steadily widened until it engulfed the whole Alliance and shattered it into pieces.

In the first place, the failure to settle the two outstanding questions—the Slave Trade and the Barbary Pirates—showed the inherent weakness of the Congress as no state was prepared to make sacrifices for the common good. In order to suppress the slave trade, Britain suggested that the European States should exercise a mutual right of search, but the proposal was thwarted by jealousy of England's sea power, since none of the countries would tolerate interference with their commercial relations. The Barbary Pirates infested the whole European sea board and Russia was forthright in suggesting an international fleet to be stationed at the Mediterranean to stamp out the evil. Britain was alarmed at the prospect of a Russian navy in the Mediterranean, and the proposal, therefore, fell to the ground.

In Aix-la-Chapelle, the Tsar presented a memorandum in which he sought to clarify the nature of their association. He asserted that the basic object was to maintain the territorial settlements made at Vienna and to guarantee all existing legitimate regimes. Castlereagh did not subscribe to the suggestion of a general guarantee. He made the statement that "the problem of a universal alliance for the peace and happiness of the world has always been one of speculation and hope, but it has never yet been reduced to practice, and if any opinion may be hazarded from its difficulty, it never can."

Congress of Troppau (1820)

The divergence of opinion among the powers persisted when the Congress met at Troppau in 1820. This time Spain provided the bone of contention. A successful military revolution in 1820 forced the King of Spain, Ferdinand VII, to revive the democratic constitution of 1812. Russia wanted allied intervention in Spain to stem the tide of revolution before it engulfed all Europe. Prussia was in favour of the Russian suggestion while Metternich displayed utmost caution. Castlereagh objected and produced the British cabinet's State Paper of May 5, 1820 which rejected collective intervention in the domestic affairs of other states. The Alliance was:

> never intended as a union for the government of the world or for the superintendence of the internal affairs of other States... No country having a representative system of Government could act upon (such a general principle)... We shall be found in our place when actual danger menaces the system of Europe; but this country cannot and will not act upon abstract and speculative principles of precaution. The Alliance which exists had no such purpose in view in its original formation.

France acquiesced and Metternich swallowed it for the sake of isolating Russia.

Tsar Alexander was exasperated but could do nothing against the collective powers. But the situation was playing into his hand in July 1820—there was a military rising in Naples which forced the King to grant a liberal constitution. The Sicilians, in turn, rose against Naples and were ruthlessly put down. In August, a revolt broke out in Portugal as well. To Metternich, if Spain was a nuisance, Naples was a direct threat to Austrian control in Italy. On this ground Castlereagh positively encouraged him to initiate action alone, the motive being to forestall Russian move for collective intervention. But when Russia insisted with French backing on a formal conference of all the Allies to discuss the whole issue of revolutionary problem, Metternich had no other alternative but to acquiesce.

A conference of sovereigns were summoned at Troppau in Octber 1820 to which England sent her ambassador at Vienna as a mere observer. The French position was analogous to that of England. The conference which opened at Troppau on October 23 was a blow to Castlereagh's hopes of preserving the formal unity of the Alliance. When on November 19, 1820, the 'Troppau Protocol' was issued, it was signed by Austria, Russia and Prussia.

The Protocol of Troppau was no more than the extension to all Europe of the Carlsbad Decrees. 'States which have undergone a change of government due to revolution,' so it ran, 'the results of which threaten other States, *ipso facto,* cease to be members of the European Alliance. If owing to such alternations, immediate danger threatens other States, the Powers bind themselves, by peaceful means, or if need be by arms, to bring back the guilty state into the bosom of the Great Alliance.' A second time Castlereagh protested against the attempt 'to reduce to an abstract rule of conduct possible cases of interference in the internal affairs of independent States.' 'The wide sweeping powers claimed for the Allies', he argued, 'conflicted with the Alliance and were an unwarranted assumption of a sovereign Power over the other states of Europe.'

Laibach (1821)

In the adjourned conference at Laibach which met on January 12, 1821, the three powers—Austria, Russia and Prussia—reasserted 'the solidarity of the Allied Powers.' With the French they had some success, but the British observer stuck to the country's policy of non-interference. However, Austrian army intervened in Naples, restored the treacherous King Ferdinand I who revoked the constitution that had been imposed on him. A further suppression of liberalism in Piedmont where a revolution had broken out in March 1821, gave Italy into the hands of Austria.

In the interval between the end of the Laibach Congress and the opening of the Congress of Verone, an insurrection broke out in Greece. Alexander, who considered the Balkan Question as inseparable from Russian politics, was as anxious to take isolated action in Turkey as Metternich had been in Italy, while Metternich was as much determined to prevent him. In the desire to maintain the integrity of Turkey against Russian aggression, Austria was supported by Britain, and thus Metternich succeeded in thwarting Russia's unilaternal action.

Verona (1822)

The fourth and final Congress met at Verona in October 1822. It dealt exclusively with the Spanish Question. Ferdinand VII had been forced to proclaim a constitution, but this did not deter him from invoking foreign help against his own subjects. Tsar Alexander I prosposed collective intervention in Spain on behalf of the King. France advocated intervention either in the name of the Alliance or independently. Arms and supplies were already going to the King and a French *Cordon sanitaire* was already in operation along the frontier.

Meanwhile, Castlereagh had committed suicide on August 12, 1822 and was succeeded by George Canning, whose hosility to congresses was more pronounced than Castlereagh's. The Spanish issue overshadowed all others owing to the failure of a royalist coup in July and the determination of France to assert herself in Spain. On September 27, 1822, Canning declared that 'come what may', England would not be a party to any collective intervention in Spain. However, Russia offered France full support. Austria and Prussia agreed to give France moral support if war broke out between the two.

When the Congress of Verona met, Duke of Wellington emphasised 'a rigid abstinence from any interference in the internal affairs of Spain.' The French Government announced its intention (December 25) to act alone. Canning tried to browbeat France by increasing the fleet and suspending the embargo on arms to Spain and Spanish America. But by March it became clear to France that Britain did not mean war unless the former should attack Portugal or help Spain to recover her colonies. In April 1823 a French force of 100,000 men marched to Madrid and within six months put down the revolution. Ferdinand VII was restored and Spain was in the grip of a savage retaliation. This marked the end of the alliance so far as the Western powers were concerned. Canning did not conceal his gratification. "the issue of Verona (had) split the one and indivisible Alliance in three parts as distinct as the constitution of England, France and Muscovy." "Things are getting back to a wholesome state again." he wrote, "Every nation for itself and God for us all, the time for Aeropageus and the like of that, is gone by."

Having restored absolutism in Spain, the Allies considered restoring to Spain her revolted American Colonies. Britain had made her stand clear in May 1812 and again in July 1817 that no force should be used in any mediation between Spain and her former Colonies. Britain had important trading connections with the former Spanish-American colonies and were not anxious to see Spanish control restored. Having suffered rebuff over the Spanish affairs in Europe, Canning sought revenge in Spanish America where there was the least hope of an *alliance Solidaire.*

Early in October 1823 Canning pressed the French ambassador, Polignac, into disclaiming any French desire for any use of force against the colonies. Canning also suggested that in any settlement between Spain and her revolted American colonies, the United States ought to be consulted. The American Secretary, Adams, was aware of Britain's antipathy to Allied intervention in the affairs of the Spanish colonies.

Canning's attitude was admirably rewarded by President Monroe who announced on December 2, 1823, a far-reaching policy in the Congress. He stated that, since the policy of the Republic was to accept as legitimate all *de facto* governments in Europe and not to interfere in their affairs, so too it would not interefere with existing European colonies or dependencies in America but would not allow any European power to interfere in the affairs of South America. Any attempt, the declaration continued, on the part of the European Powers to extend their system to any portion of the Western hemisphere would be regarded as 'dangerous to our peace and safety' and as 'the manifestation of an unfriendly disposition towards the United States.' Canning welcomed Monroe's message as a death-blow to the European Concert. Canning did not conceal his gratification. 'The Congress was broken in all its limbs before, but the President's speech gives it the *coup de grace.'* He recognised the independence of the Spanish colonies in America, boasting that he 'called a new world into existence to redress the balance of the old.'

St. Petersburg (1824)

During the revolutionary movement of 1820 an uprising took place in Greece. The desperate struggle of the Greeks against the Turks was viewed with sympathy by the powers. Russia was restrained from helping the Greeks by Austrian and British pressure. Tsar Alexander I agreed to renew relations with Turkey for commercial purpose and to remain neutral with regard to Greece without consulting the Allies. He invited them to a conference at St. Petersburg in the spring of 1824 to discuss the Greek question. In January he submitted a secret plan for dividing Greece into three principalities; the Turks would have an annual tribute and garrisons in specified fortresses. To the Allies, the plan was nothing more than ensuring the predominance of Russia while to the Greeks it fell far short of indepencence, which they had craved since 1820. When the plan leaked out in May 1824, it was already dead. Hence, the conference at St. Petersburg withered in June 1824. A second series from February to June 1825 accomplished nothing.

Causes of the Failure of the Concept of Europe

The great powers of Europe which met together to resolve disputes among themselves and to preserve a certain balance of power in the continent met with limited success. The Congress system tried to estabish the principle of general intervention in the internal affairs of different countries, a system which was opposed by England. The key to British policy was principle of non-interference in the affairs of independent states. Both Castlereagh and Canning were advocates of this policy, though the former was anxious to avoid an open rupture with the Allies. His successor, however, had no such qualms and Metternich looked upon him as a 'malevolent meteor hurled by an angry Providence upon Europe.' Nations could not, Canning thought, be governed by universal rules. England was in the 'temperate zone of freedom, not in the Arctic zone of despotism or the torrid zone of democracy.' Canning's letter to the British ambassador at Vienna in 1823 expressed in unmistakable terms the main plank of British foreign policy; "England is under no obligation to interfere, or to assist in interfering, in the internal concerns of independent nation". He added: 'What is the influence we have had in the counsels of the Alliance? We protested at Laibach, we remonstrated at Verona. Our protest was treated as waste-paper; our remonstrances mingled with the air.' Stapleton always declared that Canning had 'a system of policy and that in this consisted both his originality and his greatness. Talleyrand championed Legitimacy, Alexander the Holy Alliance, Metternich acquiesced in the perversion of it into the Neo-Holy Allaince. Alexander and Metternich failed because they sought to restore too much that was old, Canning succeeded because he popularised ideas which were to spread throughout Europe in a generation'.

Most of the powers found ready excuses for intervention: Austria in Naples and Piedmont, France in Spain and Greece, and Russia in Greece and Turkey. The Monroe Doctrine strengthened the British policy of non-intervention and helped to establish the fundamental principle of international relationship. The Concert of Europe was devised to act as a dam against revolution—a policy which met with limited success for a certain period.

Nevertheless, the Congress system was the first serious experiment in international government. At successive Congresses various questions like the arbitration of disputes, the abolition of Slavery, and the navigation of the Danube were considered. It was only when the Concert of Europe became an agency for suppressing the liberties of the people that it earned the bitter attack of England.

The Concert of Europe was an opportunistic alliance of Great Powers and it could not outgrow their narrow reactionary attitudes. 'After 1820 the Congress system became in effect a trade-union of kings for suppressing the liberties of the people.' The smaller powers were naturally opposed to it. The Concert of Europe could not endure long because despotism was not reconcilable with the parliamentary system of government.

CHAPTER 16

FRANCE (1815-1870)

Louis XVIII (1814-24)

The House of Bourbon in the person of Louis XVIII, brother of Louis XVI, had been restored by the Allies after the latter had defeated Napoleon in 1814. It was put back a second time in 1815 after the battle of Waterloo. It has been said that the 'Bourbons came back in the baggage of the Allies'.

The new monarch, Louis XVIII, like Charles II, was determined not to go against the wind of change. He solemnly proclaimed on June 4, 1814, the new constitution, known as the Constitutional Charter, which was to remain in force till the revolution of 1848. According to its provisions full executive authority was vested in the king. He was the supreme head of the State, who had the right to make treaties, to declare war and make peace and to make appointments. Though the legislative power would be shared between the king and the two houses of parliament, the king alone could initiate laws and not even an amendment could be made without his consent. The king was to summon the two Chambers and he might dissolve the Chamber of Deputies. The ministers were responsible to him and not to the two Chambers. Judges were to be nominated by the king.

Parliament was to consist of a Chamber of Peers, nominated by the King for life, and a Chamber of Deputies, elected for a term of five years, but by a restricted body of voters. The suffrage was so limited by age and property qualification that there were less than 100,000 voters out of a population of 2.9 millions and not more than 12,000 were eligible to become Deputies. The two Chambers were on an equal footing in the framing of laws, but the budget had to be voted first by the Chamber of Deputies.

The Constitutional Charter, on the other hand, confirmed the chief political and social victories of the Revolution by proclaiming the equality of all men before the law, freedom of the individual, freedom of thought and expression, freedom of religion. The State recognised all its financial obligations and guaranteed the properties of those who had bought church or emigré properties. It retained the Napoleonic code and maintained Napoleon's administrative system.

The beginning of the new regime was not auspicious. There were four main political groupings in the country; the ultra-Royalists, the Doctrinaires, the Liberals, and the Radicals. The ultra-Royalists, who aimed at the recovery of all ancient noble privileges, regarded the Charter with contempt. In his great novel about Restoration France, *Les Miserables,* Victor Hugo described the hostile attitude of the ultra-Royalists. At the other end of the political spectrum were the Radicals, a confused group of varying views, who had little strength or importance before 1830. While the Doctrinaires were satisfied with the Charter, the Liberals, on the other hand, felt that it was inadequate. As a result of unforeseen events, the Doctrinaires were driven into the arms of the ultras, while the Liberals drifted toward the Radicals.

The first year of Louis XVIII's government after his return was marked by royalist-inspired riots and political murders perpetrated by the ultra-Royalists. Popular reaction had been unleashed in the royalist provinces of the south. The government was criminally negligent in not trying to suppress them. The Chamber of Deputies, called by Louis the *Chambre Introuvable,* was overwhelmingly ultra-Royalist. Under pressure from the *Chambre Introuvable,* the ministry carried repressive measures permitting the imprisonment of suspects without trial and demanding the execution of those who had supported Napoleon during the Hundred Days. As a result, Marshal Ney, Lavalette, Labedoyere were executed. Moved by this blood bath a foreign observer was constrained to observe: 'The French are behaving as if there were no such thing as history or the future.' This wave of 'White Terror' claimed some 200-300 victims at all, not a great number, but it alarmed the Great Powers. Tzar Alexander I and the Duke of Wellington sent warnings to the King 'in the name of the tranquillity of Europe' not to let the reaction go too far. Encouraged by the pressing advice of the Allies, Louis XVIII decided to dissolve the *Chambre Introuvable.*

In September 1816 the King dissolved the Chamber and, in the election which took place, there was a certain swing towards liberalism. In the new Chamber the ministerial party proved to be a majority and the strength of the ultras was much reduced. During the next four years the ministries of Richelieu and Decazes carried out with singular success certain important tasks of reconstruction. The finances were overhauled and French credit was reestablished owing to the skill of two exceptionally able ministers, Baron Louis and Count Corvetto. Furthermore, the prompt payment of heavy war indemnity enabled France not only to be rid of the Allied army of occupation by November 1818, but also restored her to the family of nations. After accomplishing the liberation of the territory, Richelieu resigned his office and Decazes assumed power (29 December 1818). In the meantime the Law Gouvion St. Cyr of 1818 was passed, providing for the reorganisation of the army and laying down the principles—voluntary enlistment, equality of opportunity, and promotion by merit. The army law infuriated the ultras as it destroyed all chances of the nobility securing a monopoly of the best positions. In 1819 a new press law was passed abolishing the censorship and protecting the journalists from the arbitrary action of the government.

The ultras were indignant at the moderation of the King and parliament and did their best to break it down. They got the opportunity of discrediting the monarchy when, on February 13, 1820, Duc de Berry, the King's nephew and heir-presumptive to the throne, was murdered by a fanatic. The royalists, however, put the responsibility on Decazes for inspiring the crime. As Chateaubriand wrote, 'Decazes' foot slipped in the blood and he fell'. The King summoned Richelieu back to head the Government.

The Government now adopted a reactionary policy imposing censorship of the press and assuming supreme power to arrest any person without trial. The government manipulated election procedure in such a way as to give virtual control of the elections (November 1820) in the Chamber of Deputies to the ultra-royalists. When the two Chambers reassembled at the end of 1821 they condemned the government's foreign policy. Richelieu resigned on December 12, 1821, and was succeeded by Villele, a person of extreme royalist persuasion.

The accession of Villele to power marked a triumph of the reaction. He was fertile in expedients, tenacious in his plans, and interested in material welfare. Fresh conspiracies by the Carbonari were foiled and the freedom of the press was severely curtailed. The dominance of the church over education was confirmed by the creation of a Ministry of Church Affairs and Public Instruction. It was Villele who persuaded the hesitant King to intervene in Spain in 1823 which was carried through with complete success. Chateaubriand could boast: 'eight years of peace have not strengthened the legitimate throne as much as have twenty days of war (in Spain)'. The government made political capital out of its advantage. The general election of February 26, and March 6, 1824 returned an immense majority of the ultras while the liberal opposition was reduced from 110 to 19 seats. It was dubbed as 'la chambre retrouvee'. A Septennial Act was passed by which parliament was to sit for seven years.

The King took an unwise decision of dismissing Chateaubriand, who had reached the zenith to support the financial policy of Villele. He was dismissed in the most humiliating way. Chateaubriand at once became head of the counter-opposition and denounced the government in vitriolic terms in the *Journal des debates*: 'An unadventurous administration without glory, full of cunning, greedy for power, a political system out of sympathy with the genius of France and contrary to the spirit of the charter: 'an obscure despotism... corruption raised to the level of system'.

Charles X (1824-30)

Louis XVIII died on September 16, 1824 and was succeeded by his brother Count of Artois as Charles X. The change cut deep: 'Louis XVIII was a moderate of the old Regime and an eighteenth-century freethinker, Charles X was an emigré to the finger-tips and a submissive bigot.' As King he was anxious to do the job well. He quickly announced his adherence to the Charter and relaxed the censorship which Villele had re-established.

Soon afterwards, the reactionary tendencies gained upper hand under the guidance of Villele, who became the undisputed master of the government after Chateaubriand's dismissal. Nearly a billion franc were paid as an indemnity to the nobles for their lands which had been confiscated during the Revolution. The rate of interest on the National Debt was reduced from 5 to 4 per cent, and the economy thus effected enabled the government to indemnify the emigrés for their losses during the Revolution. The small investors suffered from the fall in the rate of interest and the government was accused of having sacrificed the interests of the people to the greed of the emigrés.

At the same time, the government showed undue favour to the Catholic Church. The state budget for the Church was raised to twice than what it was in 1815. Severe laws were passed against those who attacked the Catholic faith. This was followed by other measures relating to the foundation of religious bodies and the admission of Jesuits into France. The University of Paris came under the control of the Archbishop of Paris, having some of its courses suspended by that authority as dangerous to morals. This policy not only alienated the Protestant minority but also others who remained attached to the rationalism of Voltaire.

The Chamber of Peers—the stronghold of Liberalism—began to display signs of resistance. The government suffered two serious parliamentary defeats. In 1826 the attempt to alter the law of succession in favour of the eldest son was defeated. In the following session, in 1827, Villele tried to muzzle the press. Instead of taking recourse to censorship of press, he tried to pass a new law restricting the circulation of newspapers and printed matter in general. The government was obliged to withdraw it in the face of the peers' determined opposition. It was a portent of the future, but the government wilfully shut its eye. In the face of the growing opposition, Villele tried one last stroke. He persuaded the King to appoint 76 new peers to swamp the liberal opposition in the Upper House. At the same time he dissolved the Chamber of Deputies (November 6, 1827) and ordered a general election before it was due, only to take the opposition unawares. It was a gamble and a failure. The elections returned 170 to 180 government supporters, against a majority of large opposition. Villele resigned.

The successor of Villele was Martignac, who attempted to conciliate public opinion by opportune concession. He made changes in administrative personnel and took measures against governmental despotism in revising the electoral lists. The main concessions were made at the expenses of the clergy. The Ministry of Public Instruction was detached from that of Church Affairs; Jesuits were forbidden to teach and University's control over secondary education was reestablished (June 1828). French intervention in favour of Greek independence satisfied the nation's vanity but it did not improve the King's position.

With Martignac, Charles X made a last stab at liberalism. He negotiated secretly with several right-wing royalist factions and thereby fostered opposition against the royalty. A young journalist, Adolph Thiers, remarked: 'We must lock the Bourbons up in the Charter; so hemmed in, they will explode.'

Charles X had neither the wisdom nor the patience of Louis XVIII, which alone would have allowed him to play the part of a constitutional king. In August 1829 Charles X dismissed Martignac and formed a new ministry under Prince Jules de Polignac, a former emigré and a fanatical churchman. Apart from Polignac it included such men as General Bourmont, who had betrayed Napoleon and La Bourdonnaye, who had been active in the White Terror of 1815. Polignac announced his determination 'to reorganise society, to give the clergy their weight in State affairs, to create a powerful aristocracy and to surround it with privileges'. 'There is no such thing as political experience', wrote Wellington, 'with the warning of James II before him, Charles X was setting up a government by priests, through priests, for priests'.

The French people knew that a *coup d' etat* was being prepared. Societies to resist illegal taxation were formed. Agitators, the indefatigable Lafayette, toured the country. The fertile imagination of Frenchmen sought for historical parallel to describe the situation. The talk was now of the Glorious Revolution of 1688, of William of Orange and of the parliamentary monarchy. The Government showed utter bankruptcy in meeting the situation and tried to win some prestige in the field of foreign policy. An army was sent to Algiers and its conquests laid the foundation of the French dominion in North Africa. Paris, however, was not interested in Algiers, but in the nearer controversy between priest and layman, crown and people, which soon drew to a sharp climax.

The clash between cabinet and Chamber came as soon as the new session opened in March 1829. The speech from the throne carried a veiled threat that opposition would be overcome by force. The Chamber replied with an address of no confidence. The King responded by dissolving the Chamber and calling for new elections. This took place in the first week of July 1830. Despite all the efforts of the administration the result gave 274 seats to the opposition against 143 to the ministry. The King could still have saved his throne by changing ministers. In the *National,* Thiers published the formula for constitutional royalty: 'The king reigns and does not govern'.

Charles X did not believe in parliamentary rules. 'Concessions ruined Louis XVI', said he, 'I have either got to mount a horse or a death-cart.' Determined to maintain his prerogative, Charles X invoked Article 14 of the Charter which empowered the King to make any regulations and ordinances necessary for the security of the nation. In the evening of July 25, 1830, the King signed four fateful ordinances brought him by Polignac. In substance, the four ordinances (*a*) completely abolished the freedom of the press, (*b*) dissolved the Chamber just elected: (*c*) modified the electoral law so drastically in favour of the wealthy that only 25,000 electors were to be left in all France, *(d)* ordered a new election to the Chamber under this revised law. These ordinances were unconstitutional, unpopular and intolerable. 'Still another government' said Chateaubriand, 'hurling itself down from the towers of Notre Dame.'

The ordinances aroused Paris, just as Necker's dismissal had in 1789. On July 26, 1830, the Paris journalists published a protest drawn up by Thiers (1797-1877); 'The regime of law is interrupted; that of force has begun. The government has violated the laws; we are dispensed from obeying it.' But the actual revolution was the work neither of the deputies nor of the newspapermen, but of the republican party which, under the leadership of Cavignac, had rallied the students and workingmen. On July 27, the barricades began springing up among the labrynthian lanes in the eastern part of Paris. Against these barricades General Marmont drove his regulars without any success as the soldiers were neither friend nor properly armed for street fighting. On July 28, the insurgents captured Hotel de Ville and the tricolour flag. On the next day, the mob invaded the west, attacked the Louvre and fought with the Swiss guards in the Tuileries. Two of the King's regiments went over to the insurgents. On July 30, the King gave a written promise to dismiss Polignac and revoke the ordinances. But by then it was too late. On August 2, Charles X abdicated in favour of his nine-year old grandson, the Count of Chambord, also known as Duke of Bordeau and fled to England.

The revolutionaries were undecided. Some of them advocated a republic. But others felt that in might invite the intervention of the Great Powers. The liberals, headed by Thiers and Lafeyette, finally decided in favour of Louis Philippe, Duke of Orleans, a member of the Bourbon family. Louis Philippe, in turn, was full of charming promises. He allowed himself to be proclaimed, at first, Lieutenant-General of the

Kingdom. He later on took the title of 'King of the French' instead of 'King of France' and announced 'the Charter shall henceforth be a reality'.

Thus ended ingloriously the restored Bourbon monarchy. But despite its miserable exit the Restoration was no dreary tale of French history. During these fifteen years France had achieved a remarkably rapid national recovery. Until the depression of 1825, she had enjoyed a relative commercial prosperity; her credit had stood high and, from 1819 to 1826, the budget showed a surplus. In the material sphere, Restoration France had much solid achievement to her credit. In literature and arts there had been a remarkable outburst of creative activity. The Romantic movement—of which Chateaubriand and Madame de Stael had been eminent precursors—had received fresh impetus and Hugo, Lamartine, Vigny and Musset had contributed to a literary revival which gathered pace from 1820 onwards. The period also witnessed the foundation of such notable institutions as the Ecole des Chartes (1821), the Ecole des Arts et Manufactures (1828), and the Ecole des Beaux Arts (1830).

However unfortunate the domestic policy of the Restoration France had been, her foreign policy was eminently successful. In the affairs of Spain, Greece and the Eastern Mediterranean, France had played a conspicuous part. She had shared in the spectacular naval victory of Navarino over the Turks in 1827, and her troops had cleared the Morea of Turkish and Egyptian forces in 1828. With the conquest of Algiers in July 1830, France had laid the foundation of a vast French Empire in Africa. As an eminent French historian has aptly put it: 'In their foreign policy, the Bourbons displayed an understanding of French interests.'

Consequences of the July Revolution

The July Revolution was an unexpected affair. It had brought about the end of Charles X and had inaugurated the reign of Louis Philippe. It resulted merely in the transfer of administration from one set of politicians to another. The changes introduced into the constitution were of minor importance. The king was deprived of the power to issue ordinances in emergencies and the right of legislation was given to the Chamber. Press restrictions were abolished. Catholicism ceased to be the established religion. But franchise was not adequately extended.

But the real merit of the Revolution lay in the fact that its significance was negative rather than positive. It resembled the English Revolution of 1688 as—in both cases—no real advance was made in the direction of democracy. But in England and in France the divine right of the nation was substituted for the divine right of Kings. There could be no question that in any struggle between the King and the nation, the latter was bound to prevail. The Revolution of 1830 was the complement of the Revolution of 1789. For the future, the principles of secularism, equality and constitutional liberty rested on firm foundation.

It was an old saying that when France caught cold all Europe sneezed. The effects of the July Revolution were felt in other countries as well. In 1830 Belgium rose in revolt against Holland to which country they had been annexed by the Peace of Vienna. Not only were the two countries separated by history, tradition and conflict, but the Belgians were industrial while the Dutch were agricultural. Thanks to Britain and France, an international conference of 1831 recognised the independence of Belgium. But it was only in 1838 that the Dutch accepted the Treaty of 1831 and recognised Belgian independence. The independence and neutrality of Belgium was guaranteed in 1839 by the Great Powers.

In Germany, especially in Hanover, Saxony, Hesse-Cassel, Bavaria, Baden and Wurtemberg, riots and demonstrations frightened the rulers into granting liberal constitutions. But in Germany liberalism gained a temporary triumph. By 1835 reaction was again triumphant.

In Italy the liberals raised a tricolour flag in the Papal States while outbreaks in Parma and Modena forced their Habsburg rulers to flee to Vienna. But Metternich was quick to suppress the outbreaks by rushing troops into Italy. Despite their immediate failure, the revolutions of 1830 gave birth to the Italian movement for national regeneration.

In November Poland rose in revolt against Russian rule. By the autumn of 1831 the Russians were able to crush the rebellion. Norway, which had been allotted Sweden at Vienna settlement, tried to assert a greater degree of real independence and self-government. By 1830 Prince Bernadotte of Sweden accepted the vitural self-government of Norway. Thus, the political landscape of Europe had changed; the independence of Greece and the development of *Zollverein* in Germany by 1834 were striking illustrations of this changed scenario. Even where rulers had been reinstated by force, as in Italian and German states, their temporary overthrow had reminded Kings everywhere how fragile was their position.

Although Britain did not experience any revolution in 1830, the demand for liberal reform was growing. In 1832 the first Reform Act was passed which increased the number of voters by giving the urban middle class the right to vote. The Reform Act also consolidated the new alignment of political forces in Europe. From the revolutions and other changes of 1830-33, Europe emerged divided into two political regions. In Germany, Italy and Poland the forces of conservatism triumphed over those of liberalism, while in France, Belgium, Switzerland, Portugal, Spain and Britain liberalism triumphed.

July Monarchy and February Revolution of 1848

Louis Philippe was the son of Duke of Orleans called Philippe Egalite who had conspired against Louis XVI and had supported revolutionary ideas—though these did not save him from the guillotine in 1793. Louis Philippe had fought for his country at Valmy and Jemappes and had then gone into exile. This romantic background led him to play the part of a liberal King—a compromise between the Revolution and the monarchy. Fifty-seven years old at the time of his accession, he was admirably fitted to preside over a regime directed by the bourgeoisie.

Louis Philippe's legal title to the throne was very weak. He was invited to ascend the throne by only 219 members of the Chamber of Deputies out of 430, a bare majority. The July Monarchy's precarious hold on the country was admirably summed up by Metternich:

> Louis Philippe finds himself at his accession to the throne in an untenable position. His throne lacks the weight of the plebiscite which was behind all the forms of government from 1792 to 1801; lacks the tremendous support of historical right which was behind the Restoration, lacks the popular force of the republic, the military glory of the empire, the genius and the arm of Napoleon, the Bourbon support of a principle. Its durability will rest solely upon accidents.

It has been aptly remarked: 'There has been no revolution, there has been merely a change in the person of the Head of the State'. Actually Louis Philippe was not democratic as he would never have tolerated in France an English parliamentary system, under which the king reigns but does not govern. He had a policy of his own which was conservative and favoured peace.

The new regime leaned heavily upon a new oligarchy, that of middle classes or bourgeoisie who sought to monopolise power and exercise it in their own interest. They deleted the preamble of the charter of 1814 as it sanctioned the divine right of kings. They weakened the prerogatives of members of the House of Peers and deprived them of their hereditary character. By the law of 1831 the electorate was widened by lowering the age qualification for voters to 25 instead of 30, and the property qualification from 300 francs to 200 and to 100 francs in the case of professional men like lawyers, doctors and professors. Still only about 200,000 people could vote out of a population of thirty-two million and, significantly, the working class was excluded from power. Citizens were eligible to become deputies at the age of 30 instead of 40. The law of double vote was rescinded. Finally, by a law of 1831, the National Guard was so reorganised that service in it was obligatory only for citizens who paid direct taxes. So the middle classes, but not the common people, found themselves enrolled. Censorship was abolished and Catholicism was recognised as the religion of the majority of the Frenchmen.

Thus the French bourgeoisie, having a monopoly of wealth, wielded political power in the Government. The most eloquent spokesman of this class was Francois Guizot (1787-1874), university professor and historian of the English

Revolution. 'The middle class', he said, 'makes public opinion and should govern society. The nobleman is outside that society; he does not know it well enough. The people have not time to think, and express only desires and complaints. The middle class is in a position to be reasonable and liberal'.

As Louis Philippe's rule lacked any popular sanction, it had many enemies from the start—Legitimists, Bonapartists and the Republicans. The Legitimists—also called Carlists—defended the rights of Charles X and his descendants. The Bonapartists recalled the memories of the Napoleonic legend and looked with contempt upon a King whose foreign policy was timid and uninspiring. The Republicans were the most active and dangerous enemies of Louis Philippe and indulged in frequent acts of violence. The society called the *Amis du Peuple* grouped together the most active members in the party. The Republican ideal had a large working-class following and it enjoyed indirect support from many intellectuals; novelists such as George Sand and Eugene Sue; poets, such as Lamartine, historians such as Louis Blanc and Jules Michelet.

Louis Philippe's first government, inaugurated in August 1830, reflected in its composition the diversity of elements which had brought the Revolution. On the one hand there was the so-called Party of Movement, with Lafayette, Laffitte, Dupont de L' Eure and others who held that the event of July were but a prelude to further reform. On the other, there was the party of Resistance whose most prominent members—Casimir Perier and former Doctrinaires such as Guizot and the Duc de Broglie—maintained that the Revolution of 1830 was complete. Louis Philippe thought it prudent to form a new ministry headed by Jacques Laffitte, a banker representing the Party of Movement. But Laffitte, longing for popularity, practised 'government by surrender'. In consequence, Paris witnessed scenes of daily riot. In February 1831, acts of popular violence were directed against the clergy. The foreign policy of the government which gave support to liberal revolution in Belgium, Poland and Italy, was soon discredited.

The Laffitte Government, unable to maintain order, gave way in March 1831 when Louis Philippe turned to the Party of Resistance and installed a ministry under Casimir Perier. He was a man of trememdous will-power and energy, a veritable Prime Minister. Casimir Perier announced as his programme: 'At home, order, without calling on liberty to make any sacrifices; abroad, peace, with no cost to honour.' But Louis Philippe found it difficult to establish the monarchy on a solid foundation. The expectation that the workers entertained that the July Revolution would mean an improvement of their lot was not fulfilled. Disappointment and desperation led to a series of demonstrations of workers in Paris and Lyons. In the silk centre of Lyons wages were low, and there had been experiments in collective bargaining with employers for minimum wage scales. In November 1831 the silk workers broke out into open insurrection when some manufacturers refused to observe the agreements. The government, fearing the spread of revolt, crushed the rising and declared collective bargaining illegal.

Casimir Perier's government did not last much more that a year, for he himself died on May 16, 1832. The Government was heavily at odds with both the Legitimists and the Republicans. In April 1832 a legitimist insurrection seemed possible when the Duchess of Berry, mother of the young Duke of Bordeaux, landed in France and attempted to incite rebellion in the Vendee and elsewhere. She was arrested and imprisoned. But more serious was a republican insurrection in the capital in June 1832. The occasion for it was the funeral of General Lamarque, a very popular republican figure in Parliament. The insurrection set up barricades in part of the capital, and was broken only after two days of bloody fighting.

Accordingly, in October 1832, a new ministry was formed with Marshal Soult as titular head, but Broglie as the real director. The government struck back by passing a series of measures restricting the right of associations and curtailing the freedom of the Press. But it was not to be for long. The *Tribune,* the most aggressive republican paper, which in four years suffered 114 prosecutions, now published a programme for the establishment of a 'social republic'. Hardly had the repressive measures been passed, than new insurrections burst forth in several cities. Particularly important was that in Lyons in April 1834 and an almost simultaneous rising in eastern Paris. The government, largely directed by Thiers, succeeded in suppressing these revolutionary insurrections.

In addition to these sporadic movements, an attempt was made on the life of the King on July 25, 1835 by two republican fanatics, More and Fieschi. Though the King and the princes escaped unhurt, the incident in which eighteen innocent people were killed inspired a revulsion of feeling in favour of the monarch. The government introduced the so-called September Laws of 1835 bringing the press under stricter control and modifying judicial procedure to secure speedy results. Even censorship was reestablished for drawings, caricatures and plays. These laws greatly weakened the July Monrchy. Men felt that individual liberty was an empty word.

The main period of disorders being at an end, Louis Philippe wanted to rule effectively. After the fall of the Broglie Ministry in February 1836, he sought ministerial combinations in which he hoped to keep control himself. In February 1836, Thiers had been called upon to form a ministry. A difference of opinion arose between the King and the minister in a question of foreign policy, and Thiers was forced to resign. The Mole Ministry (September 1836-March 1839) which took his place was known as that of the King's friends. Men began to talk of 'personal rule' and the 'politics of the Court'. The attempt of Mole to form a ministry in the face of a hostile majority in 1837 led to a coalilition of political groups against the 'Ministry of the Court', while in the press voices were raised for 'substitution of parliamentary for personal rule'. On March 8, 1839, Mole, finding himself in a hopeless minority, resigned. Thereupon Marshal Soult became Chief Minister who fell in an attempt to force through the Chambers a large grant to Due de Nemours (Louis' son), and, in May 1840, Thiers reassumed the reins of power. Thiers favoured a more energetic policy, as well as one slightly more democratic in domestic affairs, and Guizot opposed him on both counts. In October 1840 Thiers as Prime Minister was dismissed by the King because he favoured a more ambitious diplomatic programme in the Near East that might precipitate war with England. Guizot then succeeded him to remain Prime Minister until the monarchy collapsed in 1848. Apart from Guizot's own personality, ripened by experience, and the perfect understanding that existed between the King and his minister, the breaking up of the parties in the Chamber contributed to the stability of the government.

Causes of the Revolution of 1848: Tinge of Socialism

The three things combining to overthrow the Orleanist Monarchy were the growing upsurge of socialism, the timid foreign policy, and Guizot's reactionary measures.

The July Monarchy was a government of the bourgeoisie, and of the capitalists. Under the Restoration, but chiefly under Louis Philippe, France was passing from the old industrial system to the new factory system. This transition was in every country painful, giving rise to vexatious labour questions. Thus the Industrial Revolution in France, as in England, had its seamy side—low wages, high prices, wretched housing and unemployment. The number of paupers doubled during the July Monarchy; there was a great increase in violence. One ought to read the classic reports which Heinrich Heine wrote from Paris in 1842:

> Everything is quiet as a winter's night after a new fall of snow. But in the silence you hear continually dripping, dripping, the profits of the Capitalist, as they steadily increase. Sometime there is the smothered sob of poverty, and often too, a scraping sound, like a knife being sharpened.

The disaffection of the workers led many writers to preach new doctrines concerning the organisation of industry and the crucial question of the relations of labour and capital—doctrines henceforth called socialistic. Henri de Saint-Simon (1760-1825) was the first to announce a socialistic scheme for the reorganisation of society in the interest of the most numerous classes. He believed that the State should own the means of production and should organise industry on the principle of 'Labour according to capacity and reward according to service'—a slogan that was to become so popular with later socialism. Saint-

Simon and his followers Bazard and Enfantin advocated that the future peace of society would depend on the success with which relations between the different classes were adjusted. Enfantin wrote:

> Charles X thought that a few soldiers would silence inopportune voices, and the bourgeoisie are almost as blind as he; recent events have helped us to show them up... This is the crux of the whole political problem, that it is no longer a question of priests and noblemen as in '89, or even as in 1829, but one of the people and the bourgeoisie or better off workers and non-workers.

Charles Fourier (1772-1837) attacked the ills of a commercial civilisation which made vice more profitable than virtue. The great sources of evil are cut-throat competition, greed and inhumanity; and the great remedy is association and cooperation. To make work attractive each worker must share in its produce and be guaranteed a sufficient minimum wage. Fourier's ideas were wrapped up in a maze of wild speculation and dogmatic theorising; but the core of his thought that cooperation should replace competition had a wide appeal.

Among the more revolutionary socialists in France, Philippe Buonarroti (1767-1837) preached the necessity of political revolution as a means of winning social reform. More extreme in his views was Auguste Blanqui (1805-81), who called upon the worker to wage relentless war against the bourgeoisie, since there could be no community of interest between the classes. In his emphasis on underground activity, Blanqui was a precursor of those professional revolutionaries considered indispensable for a successful overthrow of bourgeoisie society. He was one of the early anarchists. Anarchist in essence also was the work of Pierre-Joseph Proudhon (1809-65), whose famous book *What is Property?* appeared in 1840, with its bold assertion that property was theft.

The most influential of all the French socialists was Louis Blanc (1811-82) whose *Organisation of Labour*, which appeared in 1839, gave the movement a new direction. Blanc's contention was that competition was ruinous and he wished to replace the competition system of free enterprise with a national economy. He propounded that socialism must be state socialism. The cry was for 'national workshops, where man shall no longer be exploited by man, but the toilers shall share equally the proceeds of their toil.' There was something utopian in his outlook but the public opinion seized on one point only—the right to work. 'We will work and live or we will fight and die' was the watchword of Louis Blanc's followers. Blanc influenced profoundly the French workers and he himself played a prominent role in the revolution of 1848 in France. 'The time for purely political movement in France is past,' wrote Stein in 1842, 'the coming revolution cannot but be a social revolution.'

Meanwhile, France's economic problems were mounting. A bad harvest of 1846 was followed by agricultural distress. An international financial crisis in the same year caused a sharp increase in unemployment. As a consequence, a third of the working population of Paris was being supported by charity in 1847. The government had no machinery for meeting this crisis. In a speech in the Chamber of Deputies in January 1848, de Tocqueville sounded a note of warning that the passions of the working class 'instead of being political, had become social.' 'I believe', he said ominously, 'we are at this moment sleeping on a volcano... In God's name, change the spirit of government; for... that spirit will lead you to the abyss.'

Uninspiring Foreign Policy

During the thirties, Louis Philippe refused to embroil himself with European politics. He was determined at all costs to avoid war. In spite of the sympathy of the French people, he gave no countenance to the insurrection in Poland and Italy. His attempt to exploit the Belgian revolution to the advantage of France failed before the determined attitude of the British Foreign Minister, Palmerston. In the crisis in the Near East in which Mehmet Ali, Pasha of Egypt, declared war against Turkey, France, alone, had sided with the former. France had just conquered Algiers. A close connection between Mehmet Ali and France would probably offer considerable political and commercial advantage in the Mediterranean. Russia and England declared their intention of maintaining the integrity of Turkey. Prussia and

Austria also took up the cause. Thus France alone had befriended Mehmet Ali. Her discomfiture was rendered complete when the Powers met in conference in London in 1840 and made a treaty with Turkey, pledging themselves to force Mehmet Ali to terms. The publication of this treaty stirred the warlike feeling in France. Thiers urged the adoption of bold measures, but the King vigorously opposed such proposals. Thiers resigned and Guizot took his place.

From 1840 Guizot was specially anxious to keep the friendship of British. This had been cemented by the visits of the Queen of England and Prince Consort to France in 1843 and 1848, of Louis Philippe to England in 1844. It was not only a significant epoch in the history of the two countries, but strengthened the position of Louis Philippe at home. But this honeymoon was broken by the sordid affair of the Spanish Marriage. In 1846 Louis Philippe brought it about that the Spanish Queen Isabella should marry Francis, Duke of Cadiz, and her sister Infanta Louisa Duc de Montpensier, Louis Philippe's son. The union between the crowns of France and Spain was never liked by the European powers and especially by England. But the French Government assured the British that the Queen's sister should not marry a French prince until Isabella was married and had had children. But the two marriages were celebrated simultaneously on October 10, 1846 and the Duke of Cadiz was incapable of having children. Palmerston protested in vain the unconstitutional proceeding of the French party. But Guizot's intriguing diplomacy ended in failure; the young queen's husband left the royal palace; his place was taken by the handsome General Serrano of Spanish blood. Moreover, Isabella, filled with just resentment against France, placed the progressive element in power; and English influence once more reigned supreme in Madrid. Thus the *entente cordiale* of France and England collapsed like a pricked bubble. Palmerston declared that he would not speak of the *entente cordiale* 'since it was not only too clearly proved that there was no desire at Paris for either cordiality or *entente*". In France, the foreign policy of the Government was discredited. Thiers rightly interpreted the public opinion when he denounced the dynastic gain as not worth the price of the English alliance which had been paid for it. 'The day on which the King signed the Spanish Marriage,' said Lamartine, 'he signed, I believe, the ultimate, almost certain abdication of his dynasty'.

In 1847, Britain and France were opposed to each other on the question of Swiss federation. Louis Philippe sided with the Roman Catholic and reactionary party, while Palmerston took the part of the liberals, who were Protestant. The Liberal Party was victorious, and France again was found on the losing side.

Domestic Difficulties

On the domestic front, Guizot's policy was one of unyielding conservatism. 'The duty of the government', he declared in 1847, 'is to go slowly, and wisely; to maintain, and to set bounds.' Lamartine, the mouthpiece of the new generation, retorted 'If that were all the genius required of a statesman charged with the direction of affairs, there would be no need of statesman—a post would do as well.' Guizot's great failing was his self-righteousness. He resorted to bribery and corruption to secure the election of loyal deputies, and his shrewd distribution of partonage within the chamber won him the comfortable majorities he desired.

At the end of the year 1846 the various opposition groups demanded the reform of the political institution. At the beginning of the 1847 session Thiers and others put forward a proposal providing for the lowering of the tax-qualification to 100 francs, and the granting of the right to vote to various classes of people. The effect would have been to create about 200,000 new voters. Deputies should be forbidden to be at the same time office-holders, and the number of deputies should be so increased that it would be impossible to corrupt them. Against these proposals, Guizot resolutely set his face.

The opposition determined to have its way. As political meetings were forbidden, they fell back on a method that had been popular in England; the political banquet. Started in Paris in 1847 the banquet campaign spread to the chief provincial towns; Lamartine was the most eloquent speaker as well as Ledru-Rollin, the republican lawyer. The opposition to the government became manifest when the Chambers reassembled in early 1848. Even a section of the conservative voted against the government, whose majority fell to 33. Guizot seemed to be shaken. But the King remained impervious and refused to contemplate any change in the administrative system: 'There will be no reform, I do not wish it. If the Chamber of Deputies votes for it, I have the Chamber of Peers to throw it out. And just supposing the Chamber of Peers votes in favour of it, there remains my veto'.

February Revolution of 1848

Tocqueville later wrote that some 'revolutions are born spontaneously as a sort of chronic disease, suddenly made acute by an unforeseen accident.' The Revolution of 1848 was precisely of this class. Not dismayed by the King's attitude, the opposition arranged a great banquet for February 22, 1848 in Paris. 87 prominent deputies promised to attend. Though the government banned the meeting and the deputies yielded, the populace, however—excited by rumours and counter-rumours—met at the appointed place. Tussle with the police developed into riot. The National Guard was called out, but proved to be against the government. The King, being alarmed, dismissed Guizot and entrusted Mole with the formation of a government. On the evening of February 23, when a mob from Paris attacked the Ministry of Foreign Affairs where Guizot lived, troops fired upon the demonstrators which killed some forty persons.

The news of the massacre swiftly swept through the city. Before night was out, 1,500 barricades had been built in main thoroughfares and across narrow streets. By the morning of February 24, the cry 'Long Live the Republic' rent the air and the revolution assumed a new direction. The troops, under Marshal Bugeaud, could do nothing and the rebels after attacking the Palais Royal, bore down on the Tuileries. At half past twelve the King, losing heart, abdicated in favour of his grandson, the Comte de Paris, and fled to England. The radicals in the Chamber of Deputies hastily set up a provisional government. In order to proclaim it they went to the Hotel dè Villa, where they found a rival group of more left-wing radicals who had already proclaimed a provisional government of their own choosing. Somehow the two governments were blended together.

France from February 1848-December 1852

Such was the French Revolution of February 24, 1848. A stable regime was overthrown in a matter of hours with a minimum of bloodshed. After much negotiation a provisional government was set up in France whose leading members were Lamartine, poet and orator, and Louis Blanc, a socialist theorist. After abolishing monarchy and removing stamp duties and many other restrictions of the liberty of the citizen, the provisional government hastened to arrange for the establishment of a Republic on a regular basis. Accordingly, it announced on March 5 that elections for a new Parliament would be held in April and every Frenchman over twenty-one years of age should be entitled to a vote. To guard against the possibility of foreign intervention, the armed forces were strengthened. To prevent the recurrence of a mob violence, service in the National Guard was made compulsory for all adult males, and a new mobile guard of 15,000 men was set up in Paris. The new ministry proclaimed its belief in the right of all citizens to work. But it was not the intention of the government to promote socialistic experiments. It tried to meet the unemployment crisis with what may be called a caricature of Blanc's old idea of national workshops. The majority of the ministers, led by Lamartine, were staunch defenders of property and, therefore, they sidetracked Louis Blanc by putting him in charge of a commission. This Luxembourg Commission in its two months produced an amazing character of working standards—limitation of hours, minimum wages and controlled conditions of work.

The national workshops of 1848 were a failure. Thousands of workingmen were enrolled in these national workshops where they received wages at a rate of two francs a day when employed and one franc a day when not. The result was that, while the workshops did some useful work, the great majority of their members received wages for doing nothing. The irritation among the Frenchmen was reflected in the election results when France went to the polls in

April. The result, even in Paris, was a crushing defeat for the extreme Radicals and Socialists, who won only 100 out of 876 seats.

The National Constituent Assembly, elected by universal manhood suffrage, met for the first time in Paris on May 4. It entrusted executive power to a commission of five members, including Lamartine and Ledru-Rollin but without Louis Blanc. The Socialists, angry at losing all share in power, attempted a revolution by a sudden attack on the Assembly on May 15. They failed and their leaders, Raspail, Blanqui, Barbes, Albert, were arrested. Meanwhile persistent economic and financial crises thwarted the national workshops. There was insufficient work for a labour force exceeding 115,000. It was decided that the National workshops should be dissolved, that the workers should have the choice of dismissal or enrolment in the army, forcing others either to enter private industry or to undertake public works outside Paris.

This prompted counteraction on the part of national workshop leaders who, on June 18, issued a call for a democratic and social republic. On June 21, the National workshops were dissolved. The artisans of Paris rose in spontaneous revolt. The socialist party took up the challenge. Barricades were drawn across the narrow streets of Paris. There were no directors or organisers. Each man took his initiative. 'It was not a political struggle, but a class war'. But the National Assembly acted with ruthless efficiency. Having mobilised the National Guard, the Assembly directed other troops against the barricades and entrusted sole power to General Cavignac, who acted with great vigour. For four days (June 23-26) there was fierce fighting in the streets of Paris. More people were killed in Paris during these days than had been killed throughout the Great Revolution. Tocqueville called it truly 'the greatest slave war of modern times'. About fifteen thousand were killed during the June days, and many more afterwards. Twenty thousand were sent to prison. On June 26 the Assembly was again master of the city. The terrible 'June Days' was the first war between the bourgeoisie and proletariat, and it left a legacy of bitter antagonism between the two. When the Assembly applauded Cavaignac for his achievement in suppressing the insurrection Lamartine exclaimed 'The Republic is dead'.

After the June Days, the desire for order and stability was unmistakable and the Assembly busied itself in preparing a constitution. In November the new constitution was made public. It began with a vague Declaration of Rights and accepted universal, or manhood, suffrage. It gave the legislative power to a single Assembly of 750 representatives. France was to be a Republic, and to have a President. The Assembly declared that the President should be elected by manhood suffrage, should hold office for four years.

The presidential election took place on December 10, 1848. The results were unexpected. The progressive candidates—Raspail, the socialist, Lebrou Rollin, the democrat, received only a small number of votes. The real fight was between General Cavaignac, the republican candidate and Prince Louis Napoleon Bonaparte, a nephew of the great Napoleon. The name Napoleon cast a romantic spell on the people of France. Having lived most of his time outside France, Louis Napoleon had returned to France after the February revolution and been elected to the Assembly in June and September. An adroit politician as he was, Louis Napoleon appealed to the bourgeoisie, peasants, workers, the Catholic Church—all of whom voted in his favour. In the words of a contemporary, it was 'not an election, but an acclamation.' France, which nine months earlier had acclaimed the Republic, now entrusted her destiny to a Monarchist.

Possessed of a keen political intelligence, Louis Napoleon took an oath to remain faithful to the democratic republic. But his commitment to the Republic was fictitious. Swayed by tremendous popularity which manifested in his presidential election, he might have overthrown the Republic, but he considered it wiser to wait for an opportune moment. In May 1849, elections were held for the Legislative Assembly and the results showed a sharp decline of Republican influence. To please the Catholics, Louis Napoleon sent an expedition on behalf of the Pope against Mazzini's Roman Republic. In France, the republican leaders in the Assembly accused the President of violating the constitution of 1848 which stipulated that France should never use her arms against the liberty of any nation. Demonstrations and riots took place in Paris on June 13 and in Toulouse, Strasbourg and Lyon afterwards; but they were easily suppressed.

The Assembly, whose majority was now strongly monarchist, ordered the arrest of thirty-three republican deputies, enacted legislation closing the political clubs and curtailed the freedom of the press. In the months that followed they revised the franchise by introducing property and residence requirements, and thus deprived three million workingmen of the vote. Finally, Napoleon swept away the republican influence in the school, by passing the so-called Falloux Law (March 15, 1850), which largely subjected the educational system of the country to church control.

Meanwhile, in October 1849, Louis Napoleon had dismissed the ministers and chose new ones of his own choice. He announced the policy of the new cabinet: 'The name of Napoleon is itself a whole programme. It means order, authority, religion, popular welfare at home, national dignity abroad.' He now embarked on a campaign to appeal directly to the people by his appearance in public meetings where he was greeted with 'Vive Napoleon' and 'Vive la Empereur'. He also took care to ingratiate himself with the army. His name had a magical appeal to the rank and file and his position enabled him to place his supporters in the upper echelons of the command. But there were senior officers, headed by Changarnier, the Governor-General of Paris, who disliked the President's ambition. But in January 1851, Louis Napoleon managed to secure the dismissal of the general, a stroke that deprived the Assembly of its only hope of support against the soaring ambition of Louis Napoleon.

As time passed, the growing friction between the Executive and the Legislative became apparent. In February, the Assembly rejected a proposal to increase the President's civil list, and in July they defeated a proposal to revise the constitution so as to permit Louis Napoleon's re-election. From that moment, Louis Napoleon made up his mind of maintaining his position by force. To destroy the power of the Assembly by force, he took recourse to a stratagem by proposing the restoration of universal suffrage, which it had rejected earlier. Meanwhile, with his half-brother, the Duke of Morny, and with men like Mapas, the chief of police, and Saint-Arnaud, who had become minister of war in August 1851, Louis Napoleon executed a successful *coup d' etat* during the night of December 1-2, 1851. A presidential decree dissolved the Assembly, restored the universal suffrage and provided for the arrest of opposition leaders of the Assembly, including Cavignac and Thiers. There had been some street fighting in Paris, but it had been easily put down by General Magnan. 'In 1830 power had lain with the bourgeoisie; in 1848 with the people; in 1851 it lay with the army.'

On December 21, 1851, the nation was asked to vote in a plebiscite to confer upon Louis Napoleon constituent authority; and by an overwhelming vote he was sustained. It was the provinces' reply to Paris. The Second Republic lingered on for nearly a year in the guise of a dictatorship. Though the new Assembly extended his term of office as president for ten years, and vested him with absolute power, Louis Napoleon was not satisfied with this. He ventured on a second *coup d' etat,* and on December 2, 1852, he asked for another plebiscite, which gave him the title of Emperor, as Napoleon III.

Significance of the Revolution of 1848

The Revolution of 1848 was a momentous event in the history of Europe. "The revolutionary cry, 'All change' sounded across Europe. 'Hope lit the dawn of a new Europe; and mankind clambered into the trains of political and social upheaval."[1] 'The right to work', became the battle cry of the revolutionaries. The startling novelty of 1848 was the announcement of an economic programme.

Social upheaval overtook the countries situated in the east of Rhine. There were demonstrations and riots in Berlin and in Vienna. There was even talk of National Workshops. The peasants of central Europe also had their social discontents. The emancipation of the Austrian

1. Taylor, A.J.P. : *Europe: Grandeur and Decline* (1977), P. 46.

peasants from feudal dues and services was one of the few lasting achievements of the Revolution. Napoleon III was to give special attention to the condition of the workers. Though the class struggle put forward by the communists met with no response, the revolutionary legislation, however, everywhere freed workers from the bondage of tradition. By challenging the economic privilege of the owners of property, the events of 1848 heralded the arrival of a new revolutionary class, 'the proletariat.' In short, the revolution of 1848 hastened the proletarianisation of the masses.

The effect of the revolution on agraian problem was much deeper. This affected half Europe. The feudal system was abolished and the forces of reaction dared not oppose it. Though the land problem remained to be settled in the Austrian Empire, in central and southern Italy and in Prussia, the fact remains that the individual had been set free. '1848 did for Europe what 1789 had done for France. The abolition of serfdom and of all checks on individual freedom enabled both worker and peasant to move about at will'. This marked the beginning of the emigration of Europeans which was to change the face of the earth.

The legacy of the Revolution of 1848 was the assertion of the principle of sovereignty of the people against the sovereignty of kings. Though this had already served as inspiration to the French Revolution of 1789, its operation had been restricted. But the just act of the Revolution of 1848 in France was to abolish property qualification and to proclaim universal suffrage. Only Hungary held out against universal suffrage until the twentieth century.

National Revolution of 1848-50

The year 1848 was distinguished by revolutionary outbreaks in several countries of Europe. In Austria, Hungary, Italy, Germany and elsewhere popular risings took place against foreign rule and the repressive policy of Metternich. Despite important differences, the risings merged into one great European upheaval and brought to an end the Metternich system which had prevailed since 1815.

Austria: The fall of Louis Philippe in France in February 1848 fired the Austrians to demand the resignation of Metternich. On March 13, Metternich fled from Vienna to London signifying the collapse of his system which he had been rearing since 1815. At Vienna, Ferdinand I freed the press and promulgated a constitution. But the Liberals refused to accept the constitution, which, they feared, might be revoked by the King. They forced him to convene a Constituent Assembly which met in July 1848.

Hungary: Hungary came under Habsburg rule in the 16th century. Louis Kossuth, an Hungarian patriot, demanded a free parliament and self-government. The German liberals looked with favour of the idea of an independent Hungarian state. This was indeed the aim of the Hungarian revolutionaries in 1848 to establish a Hungary liberated from the Habsburg. Yet, ironically, the Hungarians or Magyars were themselves a minority in their national state. In 1848 Hungary fought two wars: one against the Habsburg Empire and the other against the lesser peoples—Serbs, Croats and Romanians—who were seeking to free themselves from Magyar rule. Early in 1849 Hungary won a pyrrhic victory. The Habsburgs were dethroned and Kossuth, the revolutionary leader, became supreme Governor.

Bohemia: In the non-German Habsburg province of Bohemia, nationalism caused the breakdown of central authority. In Prague the liberals set up a separate ministry for Bohemia and transformed the local Diet into a national Parliament. In April the Austrian Emperor felt compelled to recognise this liberal regime at Bohemia. But the German liberals at Vienna and the Hungarian liberals at Budapest were not eager to see the independence of either the Czech or the Slavs. Friedrich Engels, Marx's closet friend, observed: 'The natural and inevitable fate of these dying nations was to allow the process of dissolution and absorption by their stronger neighbours to complete itself.' In June 1848, therefore, a Pan-Slav Congress consisting of Czech, Slovak, Yugoslav, Polish and Russian delegates met at Prague demanding liberty and autonomy of the Slavic peoples.

Germany: In Germany the central revolutionary impulse was one of nationalism—for the overthrow of Austrian domination and for the unification of German territories into one State.

The revolution of 1848 discovered the German mission—the mission to extend German territory wherever German was spoken. The German liberal spokesman at Frankfurt said of western Poland : 'Our right is that of the stronger, the right of conquest.' In March 1848 the citizens of Berlin revolted. Frederick William IV of Prussia promised to convene a Prussian Parliament and to work for a national union of Germany. The first all-German parliament in history met at Frankfurt-on-the-Main in the Rhineland in May 1848. Its purpose was to formulate a constitution and to take direction of German affairs. This famous body, which sat for a whole year, had no executive authority or executive organs. It was the voice of the German nation, but it was a voice crying in the void.

The distinguishing feature of the German revolution was that its leaders were university professors, or at any rate academics. The German revolution did not aim at the overthrow of monarchs. Indeed no German dynasty was dethroned by the revolution. Only one prince, the King of Bavaria, lost his throne. The revolutionaries hoped that the monarchs would be peacefully converted to a mild liberalism. In the smaller German Sates—in Baden, Wurtemberg, Hesse, Hanover, Saxony, Nassau, Brunswick, the ruler granted freedom of the press and promised constitutional government.

Italy: Before the February Revolution of Paris, Ferdinand II of Naples was forced to accept a liberal constitution. Influenced by events in France, the King of Sardinia Piedmont, Charles Albert, promulgated a liberal constitution on March 4, 1848. At Milan, the populace expelled General Radetzky and his Austrian garrison. At Venice, under the leadership of Daniel Manin, a patriotic liberal, the people drove the Austrians and proclaimed the restoration of the Venetian republic. But the Austrian's still held on Lombardy with a large army. Charles Albert of Sardinia, therefore, declared war on Austria on March 23 1848. It looked as if Italy was on the road to national independence.

The lesser states which did not undergo a revolution reaped the most obvious benefit. Belgium gained a reduction of property qualification for the franchise; the Netherlands gained provincial autonomy; both countries achieved a parliamentary regime. The monarchies of norther Europe became constitutional—Denmark by the constitution of 1849, Sweden by the transformation of the Diet in 1851. Switzerland became a federal state keeping a delicate balance between the democratic freedom of the cantons and the assertion of the central power.

Sequel of the Revolutions

The summer of 1848 brought a change in the revolutionary movement. It was marked in most countries by counter-revolution. The first serious setback to the revolutionary movement occurred in Bohemia. In June 1848 the Austrian Governor and army commander, Prince Windischgratz, subdued Prague, dispersed the Pan-Slavic Congress and placed Bohemia under martrial law.

The next important setback was in Italy. The counter-offensive began by the Austrians whose General Radetzky decisively defeated the Italian army of Charles Albert at Custozza on July 23, 1848. Charles Albert was compelled to make an armistice and Radetzky reoccupied Milan and all Lombardy. But the cause of Italian unity assumed importance under leadership of Mazzini, the greatest prophet of radical nationalism. Mazzini also believed that the Italians would be the most inspired of all. Rome, the capital of Italy and the citadel of the Papacy, would become the leader of a new national Europe, a role Mazzini wanted to play in the winter of 1848-49 when he was virtual dictator of the short-lived Roman Republic. Pope Pius IX fled from Rome. The republicans also seized control of Florence and Naples. Charles Albert renewed the war with Austria. But, in March 1849, he suffered a severe defeat at Novara. In May 1849 the King of the Two Sicilies and the Grand Duke of Tuscany were restored to their thrones. Venice surrendered to the Austrians. At Rome, French troops reinstated Pope Pius IX. By the summer of 1849 nationalism was crushed.

In Hungary the nationalist movement aroused violent opposition not only of Austria but also of the Croats, Serbs, Slovaks and Rumanians, for it refused to make any concession to their nationalist sentiments. These anti-Hungarian nationalist found an able champion in Joseph Jellacic, a

Croatian patriot. But the Hungarians under Kossuth fought stubbornly against the Austrians and the Croatians. Kossuth proclaimed a republic in April 1849. The situation was saved by Tsar Nicholas I who believed that monarchs must help one another against revolutions. Once more Austrian authority was reestablished in Hungary which owed not a little to the Russian intervention. But the spirit of radicalism was not permanently arrested at the Russian frontier and Pan-Slavism became the delayed gift of 1848 to the Russian intellectuals.

The success of the conservative forces in the Habsburg Empire was felt as well in Germany. The feeble Frankfurt Assembly was placed in a awkward position. In order to save the situation, the Assembly offered the Imperial crown of a united Germany to the king of Prussia. Frederick William IV hesitated owing to the warnings he received from the Austrian Prime Minister Schwarzenberg and from the Russian Tsar Nicholas. In 1849 the Prussian King refused to 'pick up a crown out of the gutter'. Against the obvious failure of the Frankfurt Assembly, liberal extremists tried in May 1849 to instal republics in the Rhineland, Silesia, Saxony and Baden. But these were quickly suppressed by the Prussian troops.

But the movement for a united Germany was not at an end. Frederick proposed a plan for a German union under Prussian leadership. Some of the states sent delegates to a meeting of the Parliament of the new 'German Union' at Erfurt in 1850. But with reaction triumphant at home, Austria would not permit the union of Germany under Prussia. In 1850 it seemed that war would break out between Austria and Prussia owing to the disturbances in Hesse-Cassel. But Frederick William, as usual, gave way fearing that Russia would support Austria. In November 1850 he signed the treaty of Olmutz with Austria. By it the German Confederation, as established in 1815, was restored and the German union under Prussian leadership was dissolved. In a longer perspective, the bargain was made. The German liberals acknowledged the overlordship of the king of Prussia. In return the Prussian armies united all the German states. This was the work of Bismarck, the man who himself experienced the revolutions of 1848 and said to them; 'The great questions of our day will not be settled by resolutions and majority votes—that was the mistake of the men of 1848 and 1849—but by blood and iron.'

By the end of 1850 the fires of revolution had burned themselves out and the old order had been restored. The revoluntionary movements for Italian and German unification had been as totally frustrated as had the movements for Slav and Hungarian independence. Throughout Central and Eastern Europe absolutism had been restored. Even France, the home of revolution, moved in the same direction. In December 1851 Louis Napoleon secured the extension of his presidency of the Second Republic for another ten years; one year later he proclaimed the Second Empire.

Character of the Revolution

The character of the revolutionary movements in 1848 varied from place to place. In Germany the movement was based on a strong desire for national unity. In Austria the movement was similar, but the population was liberal rather than national in its outlook. In Hungary the impulse was always national. The Czechs of Bohemia fought for their rights against the Austrians. The Magyars struggled to free themselves altogether from Austrian rule, but they struggled to keep under their rule Slavs and Rumans. Consequently, the Serbs, Croats and Rumans ultimately fought for Austria against Hungary to secure their national rights.

Despite the varied character of the Revolution of 1848, its general feature was protests against the settlement of 1815. In Italy and Germany the revolutions were directed against the Vienna Settlement and the supremacy of the Habsburgs. In Austria and Prussia, people struggled for liberal self-government and greater constitutional liberties apart from struggle for national unification.

Paris was the storm-centre of revolutions which provided inspiration to the European movement in general. Once revolutionary movement had become general, Paris receded into the background and Vienna, Budapest, Turin, Rome, Florence and Venice came into limelight.

The revolutions of 1848 were the work of towns. Industrial development in most countries could not keep pace with the rapid growth of population. The result was that the towns experienced a low standard of life, acute hardship and unemployment. The conditions bred the revolutionary spirit. In France and Belgium, and to a certain extent in Germany and in Italy, socialism had found roots in the industrial working classes. Continental Socialism—which had its origins in 1848—accepted the doctrine of class war and 'the right to worker'.

Lewis Namier has called the revolution of 1848 'the revolution of intellectuals'. The leaders of the French and, to a certain extent, of the Italian revolutions, were mainly journalists or writers. The distinguishing feature of the German revolution was that its leaders were university professors or academics. In Germany the endless debates of the Frankfurt Assembly were the classic example of the dominance of the intellectuals. Thus the intellectuals—professors and students, journalists, poets and historians—provided inspiration to the revolutions. Poets like Lamartine and Petofi, journalists like Mazzini and Kossuth, historians like Palacky and Dahlmann lent inspiration and infused nationalism.

The events of 1848 demonstrated that nationalism was the most general force in European politics. It introduced great confusion in Italy, Germany, Hungary and the Rumans or various Slav races such as Croats, Serbs and Slovaks. Hungarian resisted Croatian and Serbian independence; German patriots denied Czech autonomy. With the exception of Hungarians, who had an historic nationality, the German liberals desired that lesser peoples should disappear. This answer was given by Friedrich Engels, Marx's closest friend : 'The natural and inevitable fate of these dying nations was to allow the process of dissolution and absorption by their stronger neighbours to complete itself'.

The great merit of the Revolution of 1848 was that it prevented the recurrence of the system of Metternich. Even at the height of his imperial power Napoleon III based his empire on a popular parliamentary foundation. Governments became increasingly more accountable to the people they governed. Moreover they had to provide solid material benefits if they were to survive.

The revolutionary movement brought notable gains to democracy and nationalism. Feudalism was abolished in the Habsburg dominions. The March Laws became the inspiration of Germany. Although it failed in its purpose, the Frankfurt Assembly was the first attempt to unite Germany. The year 1848 marked the emergence of the revolutionary proletariat. The appearance of the 'Communist Manifesto' frightened the bourgeois who feared the loss of their property. 1848 had inaugurated the age of the masses. Governments in future had to accept the fact that the masses held the master key of politics. 'The age which began in 1848 was the age of the masses: "the age of mass production, of mass migration and of mass war. In the pursuit of universal happiness everything became universal: universal suffrage, universal education, universal military service, finally universal destruction... The historic task of the intellectuals was to sever mankind from its roots and to launch it on its career of movement. This was the task which was accomplished in 1848."[2]

France Under Napoleon III

Born in 1808, Louis Napoleon was the son of Louis Bonaparte, younger brother of the great Napoleon. He had been educated in Switzerland and Germany and had gone to Italy in 1831. Here he took a minor part in the insurrectionary movement in the Papal States in 1831 in which his elder brother died of fever. Louis Napoleon was a man of energy and was determined to win his uncle's throne. He tried to utilise the Bonapartist sentiment which was being revived. In 1836 he made a foolhardy attempt to seize power by stiriring up a military insurrection in Strasbourg. He was arrested and was exiled to America. Subsequently he came to England and became an idol to the fashionable world. In August 1840, with companions, he landed at Boulogne; but again the enterprise met with a ludicrous failure. He was condemned to imprisonment for life in the fortress of Ham, near the Belgian border. After six years' imprisonment, he escaped in

2. Taylor, A. J. P.: *Europe Grandeur and Decline* (1977), PP. 58-9.

disguise in England, where he remained until the outbreak of the revolution of 1848 in France.

The fall of Louis Phillippe allowed him to return to Paris and he was elected to the Assembly. Apart from glory, Louis Napoleon seemed to offer security and stability under a strong Government. The magic of his name appealed to the middle-class, and the peasant proprietors who gave him the overwhelming vote in the Presidential election of 1848. Four years later he became Emperor of the French.

Before his rise to power, Louis Napoleon had published a series of writings in which he expounded his ideas. Famous among these were *Des Idees Napoleoniennes* published in 1839 and *De L' extinction du pauperisme* which appeared in 1844. The former developed the familiar theme that Bonapartism meant the reconciliation of authority and liberty. 'Order precedes liberty in historical sequence', for licence is not liberty, but the negation of liberty. The latter work propounded a scheme for the resttlement of the poor. In the true Napoleonic spirit he said in 1840: 'I represent before you a principle, a cause, a defeat. The principle is the sovereignty of the people; the cause is that of the Empire; the defeat is Waterloo.' Louis Napoleon was a political adventurer, bent on securing power and willing to retain it by devious means as long as he could. He really saw himself as a benevolent dictator, the Caeser who would reconcile all the classes in France and would remake the map of Europe. 'When a man of my name is in power, he must do great things'. "He thrashed about like a lion in a cage, convinced that it ought to be ranging the jungle always looking for great things to do, never finding them. He was no lion; he would have made an agreeable, though untrustworthy, domestic cat".[3]

Constitution of the Empire

The Emperor made little attempt to disguise his personal rule. He engrossed all the powers of the Executive, having supreme command of the army and navy, deciding peace or war and administering the laws. He appointed and dismissed at his own discretion the ministers and these were responsible to him as individuals. Even in the provinces all vestiges of self-government were done away with power vested in the prefects who were appointed by the Emperor. An arbitrary police system pervaded the administration and press laws controlled the publication of the newspaper and required heavy amount as surety. The judicial system was converted into an instrument of tyranny.

Legislature

The Legislature was composed of three bodies: the Legislative Body (*Corps Legislatif*), the Council, and the Senate. The Legislative Body of 250 members was elected on the basis of universal suffrage for a term of six years. Apart from electoral anomalies, the Legislative Body had not a shadow of power or independence; it could neither initiate laws nor even amend bills introduced by the Government. The President was chosen by the Emperor; the session lasted only three months in the year and the budget was voted *in bloc*. Indeed, the Legislative Body was kept as a show of consultative body, which had little to do in shaping the policy of the Government. The Council of State was allowed a larger share in legislation and it prepared measures for the Legislative Body; but its President was also appointed by the Emperor. The Senate—whose 150 members were all nominees of the Emperor—consisted mainly of those who had held high official rank. But its power was limited. It merely examined what the Legislative Body approved, although it might occasionally promulgate *senatus consulta* or constitutional rulings, which had to be approved by the President. An important feature of the new system was the use of the plebiscite by which the Emperor could appeal directly to the people over the heads of their representatives. This was intended to support the President's authority. This negative system of government was perpetuated till 1860.

Liberal Empire

After 1860, Napoleon was compelled to limit his autocracy and establish the Liberal Empire. In 1859 he exasperated the Catholic supporters by joining Piedmont in a war against Austria. At the same time he alienated the sympathy of the industrialists by signing a treaty of commerce

3. Ibid, P. 61.

(1860) with England which lowered the duties on imported commodities. The Emperor thus found himself in conflict with two powerful sections of the community—the Clericals and the Protectionists. His counsellors urged upon him to pursue a policy of moderation. By a decree of November 24, 1860, the Legislative Body and the Senate were allowed once a year to debate and criticise the policy of the Emperor. Publication of parliamentary discussion was also authorised. In 1861 Napoleon empowered the Assembly to vote on separate items of the budget and in 1867 to interpellate the ministers. The first step towards ministerial responsibility was taken in 1863 by authorising the President of the Council of State to sit regularly in the Legislative Body and the Senate. In May 1864 he legalised trade unions and the right to strike. In May 1868 he freed the Press from various restrictions and permitted public debate.

All these measures failed to appease the adversaries of the Empire. The elections of 1863 and 1869 saw successive increase in the number of republicans returned to the Legislative Body, while Thiers organised a conservative opposition, known as the 'Third Party'. In response the Emperor made new concessions to the left. In January 1870, he asked Emile Ollivier, one of the famous Five, the leaders of the republican opposition since 1857, to form a cabinet. It appeared that a new period of parliamentary government was about to dawn. This was proved by the great plebiscite of May 8, 1870 when, under the provisions of a new constitution, both the Legislative Body and the Senate were given the right to initiate legislation, as well as amend bills proposed by the Government and to criticise the actions of the executive. However, the Emperor still retained a number of important prerogatives. Apart from keeping control over the army and navy, he retained his hold over the ministers who were still appointed by him and remained accountable to him. Moreover, he alone could propose a revision of the constitution. But despite all these unfavourable trends, Napoleon III received an impressive vote of confidence in the plebiscite of May 8, 1870. But he could not invoke the right to return to absolutism for 'the Emperor of 1870 was not the adventurer of 1851'. His regime disappeared under the wave of a foreign invasion only a few months after the promulgation of the new constitution.

Social and Economic Policies

On September 2, 1852, Louis Napoleon adumbrated his policy by declaring:

> We have immense territories to cultivate, roads to open, canals to dig, rivers to render navigable, railway to complete... That is how I inerpret the Empire, if the Empire is to be restored.

This was not mere pious platitude. His reign was rendered memorable by remarkable economic advance. He undertook comprehensive economic programme and did everything possible to stimulate new investment. For the sake of raising funds, he took recourse to public bond issues. Always oversubscribed, these bond issues helped the state to intervene in every sector of the economy. Along with public investment, a new breed of private Financiers—Pereire, Could and later Germain—solicited public's saving for investment. The government encouraged a number of semi-public banking corporations like the *Credit Mobilier* (1852), the *Credit Foncier* (1852), the *Credit Lyennais* (1863) and The *Societe General* (1864). While the *Credit Mobilier*, which survived till 1867, was successful in financing large undertakings like railroad and public utilities, the *Credit Foncier*, till existing, advanced funds to peasants and town-dwellers on the security of their property.

The combined use of public and private investment under the guarantee of the state had striking results in railroad construction. In 1842 France possessed only 336 miles of railrorad (as against 1,650 in England); in 1850 she had 5,918; in 1870, 11.000. Transatlantic navigation companies were organised. The rapid development of communication gave a tremendous boom to the mining and metallurgical industries. The production of coal more than doubled and in the total production of iron and steel France was placed in the second rank, behind Britain, but ahead of Germany. Meanwhile, machine methods became widespread in the spinning and weaving of cotton goods, and, to a lesser extent, in the woollen industry. No less notable was the increase in foreign investment which rose from a total of about two billion francs to about twelve billion.

Being a convinced free trader, Louis Napoleon ingratiated with the greatest free-trading nation of the time, Britain. Along with his vision of the Europe of free nationalities living in interdependence, the Emperor hoped that free trade would bring high advantages to the French people. Between 1853 and 1855, Napoleon, therefore, effected reduction in the duties on iron steel, coal and certain other raw materials. In 1860, after much secret negotiations, he approved the so-called Cobden-Chevalier Treaty, which lowered duties on English goods entering France and opened the English market to French manufactures and wines. This Anglo-French treaty was the model of later agreement with other powers, and showed a sort of trend toward 'economic internationalism'.

Apart from his interest in industry, Napoleon gave equal attention to agriculture, still the occupation of most Frenchmen. He encouraged scientific farming, organised agricultural societies and model farms; he authorised projects that reclaimed waste land, drained swamps, and preserved forests.

The most impressive achievement of the Second Empire was undoubtedly the transformation of Paris. By a decree of 1860 the area of Paris was extended—increasing its administrative area from twelve to twenty administrative units. In 1851 Paris had just over one million inhabitants, but in 1870 it had more than 1,800,000. The imagination and daring of Napoleon and the city's prefect, Baron Haussmann, completely transformed the capital, dismantling the narrow winding streets and constructing wide boulevards, squares and parks with radiating avenues. He embellished the city with two architectural monuments—the central market and the new Opera—which were later imitated in numerous other cities. Paris became more than ever the economic, social and cultural centre of France. Napoleon made it the capital of Europe. Great exhibitions or world fairs were held in 1855 and 1867, and Napoleon's international showmanship derived satisfaction when the conference of powers, which ended the Crimean war, was held in Paris. Much of the development also took place in the outskirts of the city which was made possible by bankers like the Pereire brothers, Emile and Issac or the Paulin Talabot family. Apart from Paris, other cities also felt the reforming zeal of the Emperor. It has been said that Marseilles "owes more to the eighteen years of Napoleon III than to the preceding twenty-five hundred".

Arts and letter developed during the Second Empire. Though Victor Hugo was exiled, the historian Michelet lost his professorship in 1851, Renan in 1863, and Flaubert was prosecuted in 1857 for publishing Madame Bovary, there was no official policy of repression, much less persecution of literature. The period shed lustre when we remember that Flaubert and Baudelaire did their major works and Zola and Verlaine had their beginnings. The musical style of the empire was that of Offenbach whose operettas *Orpheus in the Underworld* (1858), Fair Helen (1865) and the Grand Duchess of Gerolotein became famous.

Colonial and Foreign Policy

Napoleon recognised the importance of indulging the national pride by adopting a vigorous foreign policy. His object was to restore France to her preeminent position in Europe. But he had no coherent policy to guide him and allowed himself to be swayed by popular impulse. 'He was vaguely aware', as Bismarck said, 'that he needed a war'. For a time his policy was eminently successful and raised the prestige of France to an amazing height of glory. But in the end it entangled him in serious embarrassment and landed France in disaster and disgrace.

Napoleon's reign marked the beginning of the huge colonial empire which had shrunk to the verge of extinction after Napoleon I had abandoned Louisinia in 1803. France strengthened her hold upon Algeria. It was largely through the French initiative that the Suez Canal between the Mediterranean and the Red Sea was constructed in 1869. If it had not been the French investors, who supplied the greater part of the capital needed, the canal could not have been completed. Settlements were established on the West coast of Africa. Between 1854 and 1864 the French created the port of Dakar and laid the basis for the flourishing colony of Senegal. In 1862 France penetrated into Somaliland and negotiated a treaty of friendship and commerce with the king of Madagascar. In the Far East, along with Britain, she secured concessions from the Chinese Government during 1858-60. In 1864 French troops helped the Chinese Government in putting down the Taiping rebellion. In the south-east Asia, the French influence rapidly grew. By 1860 Indo-China was under French influence which rapidly grew. By 1860 Indo-China was under French control, and the Emperor was Protector of Cambodia.

In the Eastern Question, France played a leading part. On behalf of the Catholic party in France, Napoleon III laid claim to the possession of the Holy Places in Jerusalem, a claim contested by Russia as the representative of the Greek Church. Russia widened the issue by demanding that the Turks should grant her a virtual protectorate over all orthodox Christians within their Empire. To Britain and to France, such claims were preposterous. The interests of both powers required that Constantinople and the Straits should be kept out of Russian hands. When in 1853-4 Russian troops entered the principalities of Wallachia and Moldavia and attempts to negotiate a settlement broke down, the two powers went to war to prevent the Turkish Empire from being crushed by Russia. Thus the Crimean War broke out. The war ended victoriously and the French Emperor had the satisfaction of dictating the Peace of Paris in his own capital. Moreover, it was at his insistence that the Sultan was required to concede self-rule to Moldavia and Wallachia which was to form as the Principality of Roumania in 1859. The war brought little gain, but great glory. It demonstrated that France was a considerable military power. In wiping out the stains of 1815 and the setback in Egypt in 1840-41, the Emperor propelled France to the pinnacle of greatness.

After re-establishing France as one of the arbiters of Europe, Napoleon embarked upon the Italian venture which was to prove the first in a series of blunders, culminating in his own ruin. He had a genuine sympathy with the nationalist aspirations of the Italians. Napoleon III also wanted to regain for France her natural boundary on the south-east by driving Austria out of Italy. In July 1858 he concluded an alliance with Cavour at Plombieres in which he promised to assist the Sardinian king Victor Emmanuel with an army should a war break out between Italy and Austria. In return for assistance against Austria, Napoleon III would acquire Nice and Savoy from Sardinia. In April 1857 he joined the Sardinian king and went to war with Austria. Once the French and Sardinians defeated the Austrians, it became impossible for Napoleon III to restrain the force of the Italian national movement. Napoleon III temporised and when Prussia took side against Italy, he signed an armistice with the Austrians at Villafranca (July 1859) without consulting his ally, the Sardinian king. Shortly afterwards he allowed the Papal States—Tuscany, Modena and the Romagna to be amalgamated with Kingdom of Sardinia and, as the price of his consent, obtained Nice and Savoy. But France could hardly regard this slight extension of her borders as an adequate compensation, especially as these annexations aroused deep suspicion in England. His abrupt withdrawal from the war and refusal to withdraw French forces from Rome, which every Italian regarded as the natural capital of the new kingdom, offended the Italians, as well as the liberals in France. He alienated Austria by his alliance with Sardinia and he alarmed Prussia by the revelation of his aggressive design.

Within a short time, Napoleon incurred the displeasure of Russia by intervening in support of Poland during the insurrection of 1863. In France, feeling ran high in favour of the Poles and the Emperor could have rallied all parties to his side by taking up arms on their behalf. But as England and Austria remained passive, Napoleon could do nothing except submitting a diplomatic protest which irritated Russia. The glory of the second Empire was fading fast; it set for ever after the Mexican fiasco.

Napoleon's great Mexican adventure contributed much to the loss of his popularity. 'There is no incident more characteristic of the man and his methods; of his brilliant but uncontrolled imagination; of his way of confusing fancy and fact; of his habit of taking up a project with enthusiasm and then dropping it with disgust, when the first difficulties showed themselves'. In 1861 the Government of Mexico, distracted by financial embarrassments, suspended payments to foreign creditors for two years. Taking advantage of the America Civil War, Napoleon, along with Britain and Spain, sent troops to enforce the rights of their subjects though they disclaimed any intention of interfering in the internal affairs of Mexico. Napoleon was goaded to this venture by his design of building up a Catholic and Latin Empire in the New World as a sort of counterpoise to Anglo-Saxon influences. He tried to ingratiate the favour of the Catholics who had been alienated by his Italian policy by attacking a Mexican regime that was notorious for its anticlericalism.

When it became evident that Napoleon was using intervention as a pretext to overthrow the Mexican Republic, England and Spain withdrew their forces and left France alone in the field. French troops took Puebla and Mexico City in the middle of 1863. Napoleon now set up an empire and offered the crown to Maximillian, the brother of the Austrian Emperor, Francis Joseph. Maximilian accepted the offer, but his government soon demonstrated a hopless ineptitude. The rebels remained in control of the northern and southern districts of the country; and it was only the French garrison that prevented them from withdrawing the new ruler. The French also began to lose interest owing to grave issues in Europe, posed by the Prussian challenge to Europe. At the close of the Civil War, the American Government invoked the Monroe Doctrine and demanded the withdrawal of the French troops. Not wishing war with the United States, Napoleon now deserted Maximilian as he had once deserted Cavour. The French withdrawal in 1867 was followed swiftly by the execution of Maximilian. Thus, Napoleon's most daring overseas adventure ended in fiasco which seriously impaired his prestige at home and weakened France's position in Europe.

Much more momentous in its consequences was Napoleon's failure to understand Prussia's ambition. He was not unaware of the French interest in maintaining an equilibrium of forces between Prussia and Austria. But unfortunately his judgement of the balance of forces went astray. He was indeed not alone in being amazed at the swiftness of Prussia's victory in the war of 1866. After this rude shock, Napoleon realised how serious was the problem before him. He could never permit without a challenge the further progress of Prussia towards German unification. But he failed to reveal his boldness to meet this eventuality. In a pitiful attempt to conciliate French public opinion he opened negotiations in 1867 for the purchase of Luxemburg from the King of the Netherlands. But nothing materialised. Meanwhile, to meet the Prussian challenge, he began to reorganise the French army. But little was accomplished owing to opposition in Parliament. His efforts to conclude an alliance with Austria and Italy also met with failure. The Italians refused to cooperate unless the Emperor withdrew French garrison from Rome, while the response of Vienna was lukewarm. The fateful climax was reached in the diplomatic crisis out of which came the war of 1870. In less than two months the French were defeated and the Emperor himself was taken prisoner in the battle of Sedan on September 2, 1870. Thereupon the Second Empire collapsed and a republic was proclaimed.

The downfall of Napoleon is rather amazing. His rise to his uncle's position was a brilliant performance; his foreign policy up to 1861 was a striking success. He had made France the arbiter of Europe, he had made possible the unification of Rumania and Italy, he had gained two coveted territories for France, and he had raised the national prestige both in the Near and Far East. Yet, from 1861, began his Mexican misadventure, of his foolish tampering with Poland, of the bungling policy towards the German unity and of the abysmal disaster of 1870.

The collapse of the Second Empire was due to its inherent contradictions. Internally, it had proved impossible to reconcile the Bonapartist principle of authoritarian rule with the growth of liberalism. In foreign policy, he failed to gauge the potential force of nationalism which completely altered the balance of power by producing powerful unitary states in Germany and Italy. He was something of an adventurer and, in an attempt to retrieve the prestige of the regime, he was driven to the desperate policy of diplomatic gambling in which he failed miserably. "The Second Empire claimed to be Wagner and turned out to be Offenbach—a frivolous echo of the past, not an inspiration for the future."[4]

4. Taylor, A. J. P: *Europe: Grandeur and Decline* (1977), P. 63.

CHAPTER 17

AUSTRIA-HUNGARY (1815-1867)

The history of Austria-Hungary is unique as it was not a nation but a 'monarchical machine' with as many nationalities. Moreover, the Austrian Empire was not built by the sword but it was the product of marriages. Its foundations were laid in the thirteenth century when Rudolf I, Count of Habsburg, was elected Emperor of the Holy Roman Empire. He added to the Empire Austria, Styria, Carinthia and Carniola, while his successors acquired Hungary and Bohemia. In 1526 the Hungarians, having been defeated by the Turks, invited Ferdinand of Austria to become elective King of Hungary. From that time till after the First World War (1914-1918). Hungary and Austria were united under one ruler.

During the seventeenth century the Turks were finally driven back and Hungary recovered most of what she had lost. In 1713 Charles VIs Pragmatic Sanction proclaimed that Hungary was an integral part of unified Habsburg administration.

Apart from Austria, the Austrian Empire comprised Bohemia, Galicia, the Kingdom of Hungary, Illyria on the Dalmation coast, and the northern Italian provinces of Lombardy and Venetia. The inhabitants of the Empire differed widely in racial origins, language, and custom. The Austrian duchies were peopled by Germans, Bohemia by Czechs and Slovaks, Galicia by Poles and Ruthenians, Hungary by the Magyars, Croats, Ruthenians, Rumarians and Slovaks, Illyria by Croats, Serbs and Solvenes, and Lombardy and Venetia by Italians.

It was a difficult problem to rule these widely scattered dominions. Emperor Joseph II (1765-90) had wished to introduce a centralised and unified Government into his dominions. He had tried to make German the official language everywhere; he had tried to bring all parts of his dominions under the direct rule of his officials and to introduce religious toleration. He had tried to emancipate the peasants from the remnants of serfdom. The peasants had been paying about 73 per cent of their gross incomes to Church, landlord and state. Joseph proposed to reduce it to 30 per cent. But he utterly failed to implement these reforms owing to the resistance of the privileged orders. In 1770 he died a disillusioned man. His administrative organisation, legal codification, emancipation of the peasants on the royal domains, survived the aristocratic counter-attack that followed. But his brother-successor Leopold II was a great contrast to his predecessor's impulsive and imaginative temperament. He adopted the traditional Austrian policy of maintaining the delicate balance by setting different forces against one another.

The unexpected death of Leopold on March 1, 1792 brought Francis I to the throne which he was to occupy for forty-three years. Like his uncle Joseph, he was by conviction a complete absolutist. Francis's philosophy, and the system of which it was the expression, took clear shape under the impact of two events—the first of which was the execution of his aunt and her consort in Paris, the second the discovery in 1794 of Jacobin conspiracies in Vienna and in Hungary. The Viennese conspiracy reflected real discontent with the war, which was widely unpopular. In Hungary the conspiracy was headed by a certain Abbe Martinovics, who himself had been a police spy for Leopold. Widespread arrests were made and, from this date on, the system became predominantly one of negation and repression. But during these years, the government exhibited energy by codifying the Criminal (1803) and the Civil Law (1811).

Francis held secret societies to be the chief hotbeds of subversive thought. But his control was prophylactic rather than punitive. Francis used the services of the police as a source of information. But his control over the professional and intellectual classes and over the civil servants and officers was minute. Education was at a low level. Though both primary and secondary schools increased and new technical schools were founded, the higher branches of knowledge languished. Francis found in abstract and speculative thought the chief source of subversion. According to him the purpose of education was the production of 'high-minded, religious and patriotic citizens'. It was, accordingly, entrusted chiefly to the Church, the latter itself being at the same time kept in strict subordination to the State. Francis also introduced the censorship which was rigidly enforced by the police.

The principles of constitutional government made little headway in the Habsburg monarchy. 'I also have my Estates', said Francis, 'I have maintained their constitution, and do not worry them; but if they go too far I snap my fingers at them and send them home.' The Estates of provinces thus led a shadowy existence. There was no coordination among the various governmental departments—the State Conference, the State Council and the Presidents of the Court Offices.

The most important social question afflicting the Habsburg Kingdom was whether the abolition of the *robot* (the forced labour or corvee) should be made compulsory. A committee appointed in 1796 was in favour of the retention of the *robot* as being 'a good school of obedience and humility'. However, a patent was issued in that year which sanctioned commutation by agreement with the landlord.

Trade and commerce did not flourish. The Church and the conservatives in general warned against the social dangers inherent with the growth of an industrial proletariat. But, as the wars proceeded, sheer necessity compelled Austria to expand her own manufactures. The Continental System gave a sudden fillip to industries.

Francis's 'system' became more systematic as the years went by. The Estates accepted the unsubstantial role assigned to them. The middle classes were content to remain subservient in the rapidly expanding bureaucracy. The peasants had returned to the old 'humility and submissiveness'. The only serious criticisms of Francis's conduct of affairs came from his close advisers—his tutor, Count Colloredo, his own brothers, Charles, John, and Rainer, and the most influential Baldacci. The result was that Francis tinkered endlessly with the machinery without ever surrendering his own personal authority, which had little practical effect.

Francis's policy remained unimpaired except for a brief interlude during which he sought from his subjects endorsement of his policy. This was in 1806, after Austria had been forced to sign the Peace of Pressburg (December 26, 1805) with Napoleon, a treaty which debased the monarchy. He now renounced the title of Holy Roman Emperor. Foreign policy was now placed in the hands of Count Philipp Stadion, who held that foreign policy could only succeed with popular approval. He accordingly produced a programme of reforms which Francis had to accept grudgingly. But this soft-pedalling was short-lived and he returned to an intensified orthodoxy when, after the disastrous defeat of 1809, he had to sign the Treaty of Schonbrunn (Vienna). Francis dismissed Stadion and Archdukes Charles and John fell from grace. Francis now listened to his new foreign minister, Metternich.

In 1815, however, peace at last returned to Austria. It had recovered all its old territories lost since 1792, except the Netherlands and the outlying possessions in West Germany. It had acquired Venetia, its position in Germany was more influential, and it dominated Italy through its own possessions. The decade which followed was, nevertheless, a very hard one. Inflation was rampant and, in July, the State had to repudiate a big fraction of its debt. 1815 and 1816 were black years for the poor, with harvests falling and prices soaring. There was extensive unemployment, accelerated by the demobilisation of armies. It was not until the late 1820s that production began to rise again.

It was to the credit of Francis that he had weathered so many years without loss of territory and without serious internal trouble. This was a convincing proof of the rightness of his own principle of government, which was abetted and encouraged by Metternich. He was an experienced and astute politician whose system was based on the exploitation of the disunity of Austrian Empire and the philosophy of conservatism. 'Govern and change nothing', was the basis of Austrian Government. Metternich was reported to have observed to an English statesman: 'We follow a system of prevention in order that we may be compelled to follow one of repression ... We are firmly convinced that any concession a Government may be induced to make strikes at the basis of its existence.' To Austria the spirit of nationalism might prove dangerous and, hence, her subjects must be insulated from this contagion.

'My nation', said the Emperor Francis II, 'is like a worm-eaten house, if one part is moved, one cannot tell how much of it will fall.' So long as Metternich was at the helm of Austrian affairs, nothing essential was changed—neither in Italy, nor in Hungary, nor in Bohemia, nor in the Slavonic and German possessions of the Austrian Crown. There was neither a free parliament, nor a free press, nor even an enlightened bureaucracy.

Metternich had a vision that transcended the boundaries of Austria. It was always to him 'to fight the revolution on the field of international politics.' Francis allowed Metternich a free hand so long as Austria was kept out of war. Metternich was the most anxious of allied statesmen to compromise with Napoleon. He hesitated to enter the last coalition and strove for an agreed peace. After 1815, Metternich reached the conclusion that the restored monarchs must stand together and there must be some machinery for concerted action. 'All I ask is a moral understanding between the five Great Powers. I ask that they take no important step, without a previous joint understanding.' He advocated a 'Concert of Europe' for settling disputes among powers. Periodic congresses were the device that he, more then anyone else, invented. Four such congresses met at Aix-la-Chapelle (1818), at Troppau (1820), at Liabach (1821), and at Verona (1822).

As long as Francis I was alive, Metternich retained complete control of affairs. Things changed when young Ferdinand I (1835-49), eldest son of Francis I, came to the throne. He was a man of feeble intelligence and power passed into the hands of a Council of State of three men : Archduke Louis, the late Emperor's brother, Metternich, and Kolowrat. The latter, who had been Minister of the Interior since 1826, had made himself indispensable by his financial ability. Soon the struggle for influence between Metternich and Kolowrat assumed such dimension that they had no time to think of reforms and the administration lapsed into apparent nothingness. It was only a question of time before the foundations of the monarchy were 'sucked away by the waves of pent-up discontents, national, political and social, which were now surging all around it.'

Causes of the Revolution of 1848

The efforts of the Government to stifle the intellectual life of Austria were only partially successful. The theologian Bernard Bolzano, Professor at the German University of Prague, emphasised the dictates of reason and morality rather than on revelation. Athanasius Grun suggested in 1831 that only the granting of public liberty could resolve the disturbing conflict between the various nationalities. The most moving testimony was that of Grillparzer who saw in the Habsburg dynasty the symbol of a great, powerful and prosperous Austria. Yet he bitterly denounced Metternich, the 'Don Quixote of legitimacy', stigmatising his lack of principles which led him to overlook the unmistakable signs of the times. In the years preceding the Revolution, opposition to the regime became more vocal. In 1842, a pamphlet by Baron Andrian, on Austria and her future, pointed to a decline in Austrian national feeling; his panacea was that the provincial Diets should be given increased autonomy and that a national Reichstag might be created with legislative powers. In short, enlightened public opinion became conscious that the machinery of government was operating to no purpose, for want of direction and control from above. The government had ended up by creating an administrative tyranny to smother all kinds of liberal tendencies. 'I have sometimes held Europe in my hands', Metternich admitted, 'but never Austria'.

The social and economic problems afflicting the country were no less serious. The population had increased by about 40 per cent. Though the country remained largely agricultural, the larger towns, headed by Vienna, were growing in space. Industrialisation, after its long setback, was making progress again. The use of machinery was spreading. The construction of railways made possible, for the first time, the large-scale development of heavy industry and mining. To the class structure of the monarchy was now added, on the one hand, a powerful independent mercantile class, and, on the other, the industrial proletariat. Landlords in the largest estates strove for greater production for profit which, in a way, altered the relation of the peasants with their landlords.

The driving force of the Austrian movement in 1848 was primarily agrarian discontent. The peasants aspired to release themselves from the yoke of feudal servitude. The value of *robot* unwillingly performed by the peasants and of dues had become so inferior to that of free hired labour that the more progressive landlords sought for the emancipation of this class. But the main question was that of compensation for the landlords, and the chief opponent of the reform was the government which declared that it could not itself finance the reform. Apart from the peasant farmers, the position of the rapidly growing agrarian class was worse, with their holdings below subsistence level or altogether landless. The increasing distress compounded by catastrophic harvests of 1846 and 1847 made their position almost unbearable. Thousands of people died of starvation and prices of foodstuff soared again. In addition, the textile industry faced suddenly an acute crisis of over-production which rendered thousands of persons out of employment. There were riots and the suburbs of Vienna, Prague and other industrial centres swarmed with desperate beggars.

Fall of Metternich

Upon a Government thus corroded the shock of the February Revolution in Paris fell with a shattering force. Crowds began to gather in the cafes of the Austrian capital and criticism of the government became vocal. Then on March 3, 1848, came reports of a speech delivered in Budapest by Kossuth, in which the gifted orator declaimed before the Hungarian Diet against the 'pestilential air' that 'breathes upon us from the charnel house of the cabinet in Vienna'. The effect of the speech was electrical. Petitions began to circulate demanding administrative changes, immediate convocation of a Diet, abolition of censorship and economic reform.

The leadership was provided by two professors of the University when on March 12 they presented a petition to the Emperor. On March 13 demonstrations began among the students of the University. A throng marched to the *Landlaus,* where the Estates of Lower Austria were meeting, and after some harangues, stormed the building. By mid-afternoon, the students joined by the frenzied mob, clashed with the troops, and there followed an uprising in the provinces. The first reaction of the Emperor Ferdinand was stupefaction. But when the situation deteriorated in the evening, the Emperor abandoned Metternich—announcing that the man who had held office uninterruptedly for 39 years had resigned. Metternich accepted his fate gracefully and made a dignified departure to London. The fall of Metternich was the first victory achieved by the revolution and marked the end of the era of despotism and reaction.

On March 15, the Emperor issued a manifesto which established freedom of the press, a National Guard, and promised a liberal constitution. A Committee of twenty-four citizens administered the affair of Vienna, the instruments of its authority being the National Guard and the Academic Legion. The new constitution was proclaimed on April 25. It asserted the indivisible unity of the Austrian State, which was to comprise all the dominions of the Habsburg Empire, exclusive of Hungary, Croatia and Transylvania. It converted an autocratic system of government into a constitutional monarchy, based upon the civil and religious freedom of the individual. Without abolishing the Provincial Estates, it created a *Reichstag* or General Parliament, composed of two Chambers and recognised the principle of ministerial responsibility. But the new Constitution aroused widespread dissatisfaction. Based on a limited franchise, it struck at one of the democratic organisations—The Central Political Committee—which was usurping the authority of the Executive. A fresh insurrection followed on May 15, panic gripped the Government, which not only restored the Central Political Committee, but also chastened the constitution by establishing universal suffrage and substituting a single chamber for a bicameral legislature. Alarmed for his safety, the Emperor and the Court fled from Vienna to Innsbruck on May 17. Hence the counter-revolutionary party found an asylum, while the important ministers in Vienna wrangled with the revolutionary masses.

It was the special weakness of the Austrian Empire that to the grievances of various classes there was added the factor of racial discord. There were many Germans in the Austrian Empire who desired to merge Austria in Germany and demanded that Austrian representatives should have a seat in the Frankfurt Assembly. But the Czechs of Bohemia, under the leadership of a great historian, Palacky resolutely refused to be merged in an all embracing German State. The Czechs had begun to dream of a nation of their own and took a leading part in the calling of a Pan-Slav Congress which met in Prague, early in July 1848. The Congress issued a ringing call for the conversion of the Habsburg Empire into a 'federation of nations all enjoying equal rights'. Such a union, could it be effected, would spell the immediate dissolution of the Habsburg Empire. The Imperial Court, true to its traditional policy of playing off one race against another, busily engaged Czech resistance to German Austrians. The Bohemian administration under Count Thun renounced the authority of Vienna and established an independent government. On June 12 the people of Prague imitated the people of Vienna and broke out in revolution. But the insurrection was speedily crushed by Windischgratz, the Austrian commander, who bombarded the city and forced the rebels to surrender (June 17).

The reaction had gained its first victory over the revolution. But at the same time it intensified the hostility of the rival nationalities. The Slavs, disappointed by their failure to establish a confederation, now became the instruments of the Austrian Government. It was in this atmosphere the Austrian Constituent Diet assembled at Vienna on July 22. But the Diet failed to work out a satisfactory constitution. The only enduring result of the protracted debates was the emancipation of the peasants from feudal servitude. The landlords were offered compensation for the loss of services paid them by the peasants.

The first success of Windischgratz was soon followed by the news of Radetzky's victory over the Sardinians in Italy (July 25) and the reoccupation of Milan (August 6). On August 12 the Emperor returned to Vienna. But the Emperor soon found himself in conflict with Hungary, where Kossuth, the Magyar leader who had been working for independence of Hungary, was challenged by an inveterate anti-Magyar, Colonel Jellachich, Governor of Croatia. The Austrian Crown welcomed this situation and, after dissolving the Hungarian Diet, gave Jellachich command of all imperial forces in Hungary.

These provocative actions inspired a wave of sympathy for the Magyars in Vienna. After two dangerous riots the disaffection of the masses culminated with an imperial decree on October 3, 1848, declaring war against Hungary. This touched off a bloody rising in Vienna, during which the minister of war, Count Latour, was murdered by the mob. The Emperor again fled from the capital on October 7, and set up his court at Olmutz. The rising, however, was doomed to failure as its leaders, bereft of political talent, alienated not only the bulk of the middle class but also the peasants by their senseless violence. Meanwhile, Windischgratz, who was given full power by an Imperial Edict on October 15, invested the capital on all sides. The general issued a forty-eight hours' ultimatum for surrender; on October 28, after an artillery barrage, his troops began assault on the city. There was possibility that the Hungarian forces might liberate their brother revolutionaries. In fact, Kossuth sent a Hungarian force of 25,000 men to their aid, but they were defeated on October 30 by Jellachich within sight of the capital. In spite of the heroic resistance of the Viennese, led by Joseph Bem, the city was taken on October 31.

The fall of Vienna brought a significant change in the government. In November a new ministry was formed under Prince Felix Schwarzenberg (1800-52), the brother-in-law of Schwarzenberg. A man of iron will and opposed to all reforms, Schwarzenberg's first objective was the restoration of the royal power. On December 2, 1848, Ferdinand was induced to abdicate in favour of his young nephew, Francis Joseph. While Schwarzenberg had been dealing with the Hungarian, Italian and Prussian challenges to imperial authority, he had brushed aside the constitutional experiments. The Austrian Constitutional Assembly, which, after the rising in Vienna in October, had removed to Kremsier in Bohemia, was busy in drafting a constitution for the whole empire.

The so-called Kremsier Constitution sought to solve the warring nationalities problem by providing for extensive provincial autonomy, while, at the same time, granting local self-government to towns and villages. But Schwarzenberg, who was opposed to decentralization of every kind, repudiated the draft constitution and dissolved the Assembly. But two fundamental principles, as laid down in the Kremsier constitution, survived and were incorporated in the 'Fundamental Laws' of 1867. 'All peoples of the empire are equal in rights. Each people has an inviolable right to preserve and cultivate its nationality in general, and its language in particular. The equality of rights in the school, administration and public life of every language in local usage is guaranteed by the State.' Some time later (March 4, 1849) the Emperor himself granted a Charter to his subjects which proclaimed the indissoluble unity of the monarch and forged heterogeneous dominions of the Austrian Empire into a centralised bureaucratic state.

The March Constitution introduced again a central parliament of two houses, and Landtags, though the competence of the latter were limited. A fairly extensive communal autonomy was promised and enacted by an order of March 11. An important addition was *Staatsrath,* the advisory body to the Crown, which had existed since the sixteenth century. Its new version, the *Reichsrath,* was to consist of twenty-one members, nominated by the Emperor. Francis Joseph's proclamation expressly declared that, in future, Austria was to be a unity, both political and economic. The practical effect of the proclamation was, however, to nullify the Hungarian constitution.

The unitary empire now established was mainly guided by Bach, the Minister of the Interior. Schwarzenberg was mainly occupied with foreign affairs. Bach formed a vigorous team along with Schmerling (Justice), Krausz (Firance), Bruck (Trade) and Thun (Education) and pressed forward with the reforms which he thought necessary. Bach suspended the Communal Autonomy Law. Under his guidance, the monarchy pursued a policy of naked absolutism. But it was not an era of blind reaction. Despite the stagnation of constitutional reform, administrative and economic reforms were vigorously undertaken.

The most grandiose of these reforms was to implement the programme of the emancipation of the peasants in which over three million persons received land. The whole judicial system was recast with higher courts in the provinces and a Supreme Court of Appeal. The old system of depositions taken privately gave way to a public procedure based on the oral examination of witnesses. The jury system was introduced for all crimes. Communications were greatly improved. The railways were taken over by the state and expanded, the merchant fleet doubled, and the postal services reorganised. Chambers of Trade and Industry were founded and attempts made to promote exports. The gymnasia were reformed, freedom of learning was introduced in the universities and technical education greatly developed. In elementary schools, instruction should be given in the mother tongue. It was laid down that German was to be the sole language of the administration. Two orders of December 16, 1854 and January 1, 1855, respectively, decreed that German must be an obligatory subject and instruction should be given in that language in the higher classes.

The all-powerful minister Bach's influence was not liked by Schwarzenberg and other members of Francis Joseph's entourage. It was in the hope of bridling Bach that they began to induce Joseph to assume unbridled power. The moving spirit in this episode was von Kubeck to whom absolutism seemed to be more important than any kind of innovation. On December 5, 1850, Kubeck was nominated president designate of the *Reichsrath* and, in the following April, he became Francis Joseph's special Adviser-in-Chief. He at once began to press on his young master the efficacy of abolishing ministerial responsibility and assuming full power.

Kubeck was the chief instrument to kindle the dying embers of Francis Joseph—the right to rule by divine right. On August 20, 1851, Francis Joseph issued a rescript relieving the ministers of all responsibility, except to himself. On December 31, 1851, the so-called 'Sylvester Patent' or proclamation of New Year's Eve revoked the March constitution and the Emperor now assumed sole and exclusive political responsibility. Complete absolutism—exercised through the bureaucracy and rigid centralisation—became the distinguishing features of the administration. Only the remnants of the communal autonomy survived, but the existing elected councillors became government servants, and there were to be no further elections.

The pre-revolutionary political condition was complete and political absolutism reached its climax. The next seven years saw, in fact, no major change in the political machine. The system hinged on the efficiency of Bach, who became more powerful after the resignation of Schmerling in January 1851, Bruck in May and Krausz soon after. When Schwarzenberg died suddenly, in April 1852, Francis Joseph appointed no new prime minister. Count Buol, a pupil of Metternich, was placed in charge of foreign affairs, Kubeck died in 1853 and the *Reichsrath* ceased to have any importance whatever.

An important move was made to renew the old alliance between the Habsburg Dynasty and the Holy See. In 1850 the powers and privileges of the Roman Catholic bishops were considerably enlarged. In June 1851, the Jesuits were reinstated. In April 1852 negotiations were opened for a concordat, and this was concluded in August. It put the church of Rome in an unenviable position. The Catholic Church was placed under the special protection of the state. The bishops took full charge of all Catholic education. The ecclesiastical courts were restored. The property of the Church was declared sacred and inviolable. A secret agreement was made that Austria would not alter any church laws without the previous consent of the Holy See.

The emancipation of the peasants gave a great impetus both to agriculture and trade. Bruck did all he could to foster free exchange; the trade-barriers with Hungary and Lombardy-Venetia were abolished. After him, Buol in 1853 concluded a commercial treaty with Prussia based on the most favoured nation clause. The new Chambers of Commerce and Industry did good work. The industrial boom which followed was made possible largely because industry began to operate largely or mainly on a credit basis. Large credit transactions were undertaken just by the *Credit Mobilier.* In 1853 an Austrian group founded the first important Austrian bank and in 1855 the Viennese Rothschilds founded the great *Creditanstalt.*

The constantly growing state expenditure owing to grandiose public works, extravagant army and the compensation of the landowners became a serious concern to the government. The State borrowed from the National Bank and met its deficits by floating loans. In 1855 Bruck again became Finance Minister; he tried to restore order by increasing taxation. Then in 1857 the great stock-exchange crash which overtook England and America, reached Vienna. From this movement onward finance and business gradually began to press for economy in state expenditure. The outbreak of war in April 1859 with Sardinia brought a change in the situation. Sardinia won the battles of Magenta and Solferino. Now Francis Joseph began his retreat from absolutism. Buol was replaced as Foreign Minister by Rechberg. In July 1859, Rechberg also took over the duties of Minister President. Bach was dismissed in favour of a new minister, Count Goluchowski. 'The Laxenburg Manifesto' of August 23, 1859 set out the Government's programme. It began with the promise that all government expenditure, civil and military, should be submitted to effective control, adding assurances that the non-Catholic religions should be allowed autonomy and freedom of worship. A measure of communal autonomy was to be restored.

HUNGARY

Developments in Hungary before 1848

Hungary was the only one of the Habsburg States which had cherished the traditions of self-government and constitutional rights. Joseph II, the greatest of the Enlightened Despots, came into conflict with these traditions on the eve of the French Revolution, in his attempt to weld heterogeneous dominions into a single compact State. In violation of the Hungarian constitution, he desisted from convoking the Diet, abolished the County Assemblies, carved out the country into ten provinces and enjoined the use of German as the official language. Though these drastic measures were revoked at the end of his reign, so violent was the storm of opposition that they crystallised in the revival of national feeling. Leopold II, the successor of Joseph, found himself compelled to recognise the freedom and independence of the Hungarian nation in 1791. Henceforth the Diet was to meet every three years, and without its assent no taxes could be levied. Hungary also should be governed according to its own laws and customs.

Francis followed the constitutional procedure of summoning the Diet fairly regularly. Henceforth, he had not to reckon with a threat of rebellion. The nobles in Hungary continued to enjoy their exemption from taxation and their unfettered control over their peasants and local affairs. The police was less omnipresent and intellectual freedom in general greater as to promote linguistic and cultural revival. The Hungarians demanded the extension of the use of Magyar in place of Latin, the latter being the official language. They also wanted the removal of the unequal economic policy which impelled Hungary to import manufactured goods from Austria at a heavy price with inflated import duty, and to export her agricultural produce to Austria at the latter's price. Francis made a few small concessions on the language question in 1805 and 1808, but refused to yield an inch on the economic issue.

The Napoleonic war put hardship to the Hungarians who refused to contribute to it. The Diet received the historic sobriquet of 'the Accursed.' Invasion, defeat and territorial cessions produced such economic hardships that the Austrian Finance Minister, Count Wallis, issued a Patent on February 20, 1811. The Government issued a new currency and pledged not to increase the note circulation. It, however, reduced by half all interest on government bonds. This drastic measure caused widespread dislocation. For decades thereafter the memory of the 'State bankruptcy' lingered and it was this memory, more than any other single factor, that touched off the revolution of 1848 in both Vienna and Hungary. The Hungarian Diet, which met in 1811, flatly denied the legality of the Patent. Francis, thereafter, dissolved it on May 18, 1812 and promulgated the Patent by royal decree.

For a period of thirteen years (1815-25), the Hungarian Diet was in abeyance. In 1820 and 1821—when the Hungarian countries refused to deliver men and supplies which Metternich wanted for suppressing the threat of revolution in Italy—the government collected it by force, but this operation proved so difficult that in 1825 Francis thought it expedient to reconvoke the Diet. The meeting was so stormy and so critical of the regime that the Emperor could not but agree to raise no taxes in the future without the consent of the Diet. At this Diet the cry was raised that Magyar should be established as the official language of Hungary, a thing which was accomplished in 1840.

It was at this Diet of 1825 appeared a remarkable person, Stephan Szechenyi, a former officer and one of the richest men in Hungary. An admirer of the British society and enriched by his travels in Western Europe, Szechenyi hoped for social reforms which would improve the status of the peasantry and induce the nobility to give up such privileges as its freedom from the land tax. He believed that feudalism had to give place to a commercial and capitalist system. Between 1825 and 1832 he carried through some economic reforms including the construction of a bridge between Buda and Pest and the inauguration of steam navigation on the Danube. In order to promote the intellectual emancipation of Hungary as well as the purification of the Magyar tongue, he founded the Budapest Academy.

Szechenyi made little practical headway at the Diet with his proposals, but he set in motion the national movement which was to develop with extraordinary rapidity. By 1836, Szechenyi was elbowed aside by the younger generation whose mouthpiece was the fiery and radical Louis Kossuth. An ardent advocate of every kind of liberal and democratic reform, Kossuth argued that the first necessity was to reduce the links with Vienna as the indispensable preliminary to any reform. He also urged the necessity of a national economy for Hungary with separate tariff and communication systems and autonomous institutions. Kossuth had achieved a great reputation as editor of the *Pesti Hirlap*, a political journal commanding a wide circulation. He was also in favour of emancipation of the serfs in return for compensation largely paid by the State.

All these aspirations, however, did not threaten the integrity of the Habsburg Empire. In 1837 Kossuth and some others were arrested and imprisoned. But the flare-up of the Eastern Question in 1840 introduced a policy of appeasement. Kossuth was released and became the idol of the nation. In this situation, a group of magnates, led by Count Greorge Apponyi and calling themselves 'progressive conservatives', evolved a programme of reforms to be enacted from above with safeguards for link with Austria. In 1843 this group was placed in charge of Hungary. But the opposition, under the leadership of Francis Deak, produced in 1847 a programme of democratic reform which included a Parliament based on wide franchise, complete liberation of peasants, imposition of taxes on the nobles, and union with Transylvania. When the Diet met in November 1847, the 'Government Party' itself accepted many of the reforms, although emphasising the retention of the vital link with Austria.

The news of the February Revolution at Paris made its influence felt in Hungary. Kossuth demanded a National Government and a ministry responsible to Parliament. On March 14, the revolution had triumphed at Budapest. Kossuth's followers now introduced the most extensive and far-reaching changes. The famous 'March Laws' of 1848 embodied the most sweeping reforms. Serfdom and feudal dues were abolished and the nobles had to forego their immunity from taxation. The franchise, hitherto the exclusive privilege of the nobility, was extended to every Hungarian. The Parliament was to be convoked annually and its duration was restricted to three years; while other measures included liberty of the press, religious freedom, a national guard and a National University. The separation of Hungary from Austria was rendered complete. An independent Hungarian Cabinet was created whose jurisdiction embraced not only the internal administration of Hungary, but also foreign affairs, war, finance, and control of the army. In addition, Transylvania was united with Hungary. The Government of Vienna, powerless to resist the nationalist demand of the Hungarians, conceded all the reforms. The Magyars had thus achieved a great triumph, but its permanence was jeopardised by chauvinistic nationalist sentiment of the Magyars.

The Magyars were only one among seven nationalities in Hungary and they numbered less than half the entire population. But the Magyar patriots resolved on complete Magyarization of their country, a policy which involved conflict with racial minorities under Hungarian rule. It was this Magyar policy of compulsory assimilation which inflamed the racial passion of other nationalities in Hungary. The North Hungarian Slavs, called Slovaks, resented the attitude of the Magyars. 'Rather the Russian knout than Magyar domination, for the one could only enslave our bodies while the other threatens us with moral ruin and death'. The French Revolution left its traces upon the Slovaks as upon the Magyars. The precursor of the Slavonic studies was Abbe Dobrovsky, who, starting with linguistics, demonstrated the close affinity of the Slav peoples. The greatest Slavonic scholar was P. J. Safarik, a professor, who depicted the Slav nation as peace-loving and hard-working. But the greatest influence was exerted by the national poet, Kollar, whose *Daughter of Slava* was published in 1824. This famous poem exalted the great memories of the Slav race and its departed glories. Kollar protested against the unjust decree 'that in Hungary the Slav should bury his language.' But he made clear that the Panslavism of his dreams was literary and not political. In a petition to the Crown in 1842, the Slavs represented that they 'form a peculiar nationality, which is only capable of further progress through the cultivation of its own language'. But the Slovak demands found no echo in Hungary: in 1847 the Magyar tongue was imposed on the Slovaks as their official language.

The linguistic monopoly asserted by the Magyars brought them also into conflict with the Southern Slavs—the Croats and the Serbs. The idea of a community of language and tradition—favoured by the existence of an independent Serbia and the provisional formation of an Illyrian State—found its most active representative in the person of Ljudevit Gaj, a disciple and rival of Kollar. In his *Illyrian National Gazette* and his *Danica,* he preached the doctrine of Illyrism, in other words the union of the Slavs of the south. The Croats, apart from their representation in the Hungarian Diet, had their own provincial Diet at Agram, where they resisted the forcible introduction of the Magyar language. The Vienna Government found in the Croats a weapon which could be used against the rebellious Magyars.

Hungarian nationalism committed a fatal blunder when it refused to conciliate the other races by timely concessions. As the apostle of narrow racial creed, Kossuth showed himself deficient in true statesmanship. As early as April 1848, he told the Serb deputation that "before there could be any question of an equal treatment of the Slavonian with the Magyar tongue, appeal would have to be made to the decision of the sword.' The Slav nationalities took up the challenge and began to agitate for their separation from Hungary.

The Vienna Government aggravated the racial passions by appointing an inveterate anti-Magyar, Colonel Jellachich, as Ban or Viceroy of Croatia. He was in favour of the Illyrian movement, whose object was now the formation of a Slav Kingdom under Habsburg rule. After summoning the Croatian Diet which met on June 5, 1845, at Agram, he decreed the separation of Croatia from Hungary. The Serbs also made common cause with the Croatians by summoning a Serb National Congress at Çarlowitz and setting up a provisional Government.

In this inflammable situation, the Hungarian Government tried to sow distrust between Vienna and Croatia. Batthyani, the President of the Hungarian Cabinet, tried to ingratiate the Emperor's favour by insinuating that the real object of the Illyrian movement was to establish an independent Slav Confederation. Jellachich was suspended from office. But he was an adroit intriguer, he visited the Emperor at Innsbruck, pointed out to him the advantage of conciliating the Slavs and was finally restored to power (September 4, 1848). The Hungarian Diet, under the influence of Kossuth, now pushed the Croatian question to a point of no return. For a time the Austrian Government refused to be drawn either on the side of the Magyars or the Slavs. But Kossuth's financial policy culminating in the issue of Hungarian paper money in place of Austrian notes and Radetzky's victory at Custozza (July 25), speedily forced the Vienna Government to a decision. Early in September, with the approval of the imperial Government, Jellachich opened the campaign by invading Hungary at the head of a Croatian army.

In the initial stage, the Austrian army obtained victories. Kossuth sent a Hungarian force of 25,000 men to relieve Vienna, but they were beaten off by Jellachich's Croats on October 30, 1848. On January 5, 1849, the Austrian General, Windischgratz, the conqueror of Vienna, occupied the Hungarian capital. This was followed a few weeks later by an over-whelming defeat of the Magyars at Kaplona. But in this hour of crisis, Hungary showed unexpected power of recuperation. Her resistance was even more remarkable as she had not only to fight armies superior in number, equipment and organisation, but she had also to encounter irregular levies of Serbs and Slovaks within her own territories. The achievements of the Hungarians astonished a world which had taken for granted the inevitability of their failure. In Transylvania, Bem drove the Austrians and Russians across the frontier of Wallachia and made himself master of the country. In the south, Perczel subdued the Serbs of Slavonia and the Croats; while the main army under Gorgei, who was now Commander-in-Chief, drove the Austrian forces of Windischgratz back to the frontiers of their own country. The recovery of Budapest was only a question of time. Windischgratz's position seemed precarious indeed as he had to hold Budapest as well as Vienna. He, therefore, made little effort to harass his opponents.

Undismayed by these reverses, the Austrian Government appealed to Russia for help and drove Kossuth into open rebellion. With Kossuth counsels of moderation had no weight and he might have obtained honourable terms of peace from the Austrian Government. On April 14, 1849, he took the most fatal step by issuing a Declaration of Independence, deposing the Habsburg dynasty and proclaiming a Republic. Kossuth even urged Gorgei to advance on Vienna, though the latter refused to undertake this hazardous enterprise. Early in May he moved on Budapest and on June 6, Kossuth triumphantly entered the city.

Meanwhile Bach, at that time Minister of Justice in the Austrian Government, promptly announced that the Declaration of Independence rendered the Hungarian constitution null and void. On April 12, Windischgratz was replaced by General Welden. On May 30, 1849, Welden was superseded by a new Commander-in-Chief Hayanu, to whom was attached, as civilian commissioner, Baron Geringer who was now invested with plenipotentiary power to introduce the order, issued a blue-print on July 4. Hungary was to be divided into five districts, each under a High Commissioner.

The issue was already decided. Tsar Nicholas—the relentless enemy of all progressive movements—had responded to Austria's call by sending 140,000 troops under Field-Marshal Paskievic. Hungary was invaded from three sides. While Jellachich again advanced from Croatia, and the Austrian army once more approached from the west, the Russians crossed the Carpathians from the east. On July 18th, the combined armies of Jellachich and Hayanu entered Budapest. Kossuth knew quite as well as Gorgie that resistance was impossible. On August 11 Kossuth abdicated in favour of Gorgei and took refuge across the Turkish frontier. On August 13, Gorgei with his 23,000 troops surrendered to the Russians at Vilagos.

Effects of the Revolution on Hungary

The Austrian Government proceeded to exact a barbarous penalty. Though Gorgei's life was spared owing to the intervention of the Tsar, thirteen of his generals were killed, and nearly 400 officers were imprisoned. Batthyani, the Prime Minister of Hungary, and over a hundred politicians were executed. Haynau's ruthless rule earned for him the nickname of 'Hyena'. Kossuth never returned to Hungary from Turkey where he had fled. 'He became an eloquent voice in the wilderness, displaying both in Britain and in the United States that marvellous gift of exciting human emotion which had made him the first man in Hungary. He lived for nearly fifty years and remained irreconcilably anti-Habsburg. In 1902 his bones were brought back to rest in his own land amid senses of emotion such as Hungary had never witnessed. He had indeed exercised a volcanic and incalculable power'.

The war dealt a heavy blow to the national aspirations of the Hungarians and other nationalities. The Magyars lost every vestige of their constitutional liberties, and Hungary became a province of Austria. For administrative purposes Hungary was divided into five districts. Croatia, Transylvania and Southern Hungary were made separate provinces. The Croats were deprived of their Diet, while the Serbs, the Saxons and Roumanians of Transylvania suffered loss of political privileges. Thus the political unity of the old Hungarin Kingdom was destroyed. German was also substituted for Magyar as the 'State language.'

Though the hand of reaction had been heavy on Hungary, the Vienna Government found it necessary to relax the pressure. There were a large number of amnesties and acts of grace. But the resentment of the Hungarians were not abated. The peasants persisted in maintaining that Kossuth, not Bach, had liberated them. The emancipation had acted as a cementing force between the social classes, uniting them against Vienna. Moreover, the new territories created as a counterweight to Hungary were hardly peaceful. In Transylvania, the Roumanians, although pleased to be free of the Magyar yoke, opposed the Austrian Government. The Croats were thoroughly disgruntled at finding Dalmatia kept apart from them and ruled by non-natives. Croatia was divided into six districts, each under a chief nominated from Vienna. The Serbs complained at the non-inclusion of the frontiers.

The Hungarian situation proved to be serious. The bureaucratic administration proved highly expensive which was accentuated by the 'Hungarians' reluctance to pay taxes. Moreover Kossuth, still the idol of the Hungarians, was touring the world, everywhere highlighting the misrule of the Habsburg and plotting their downfall. But it was not until 1859, when the defeat in Italy shook the prestige of the monarchy, that the Government began to consider reforms.

On March 5, 1860, Francis Joseph issued the so called 'March Patent'. The *Reichsrath* was to be enlarged and given a quasi-representative character by adding to its twenty-one original members thirty-eight more from the various Landtags. This body, the 'Reinforced *Reichsrath*' was convoked on May 31, 1860. The six Hungarian members, including their leaders, Counts Szeczen and Emil Dessewiffy, were the most skillful and experienced politicians who welded the aristocratic representatives from the Lands into a 'United Party of the Federalist Nobility'. Moreover, they also supported their colleagues from Bohemia and Galicia for their special rights. In return, the Bohemian nobles, as well as the Poles, supported the Hungarian demands for the restoration of their constitution. This meant, however, that the Slovaks, the Transylvanian Roumanians and the Serbs were not regarded as equals by the Hungarians.

Led by the Hungarians, the united nobility secured the adoption by the Reinforced *Reichsrath,* of a report recommending the reconstitution of the monarchy on the basis of the 'historic-political individualities of the various components'. Communal autonomy and the local institution of Hungary should be restored. All the Diets should be convoked. The Vienna Government granted a number of concessions to Hungary. Field-Marshal Benedek, a Hungarian, was made Governor-General and the predominance of the German language in education greatly reduced. None of these appeased public opinion.

Francis Joseph was now in earnest to reach a settlement. On October 20, 1860, he issued a hurriedly drafted document, known as the 'October Diploma'. The Diploma or Charter restored Hungary to the condition in which she was prior to the 1848 Revolution. It abolished the five administrative districts, and revived both the Diet and the system of self-government based on the County Assemblies. Francis Joseph agreed to exercise his power of legislation only with the cooperation of Diets in the Crown lands (Landtags) and of the central *Reichsrat* which would consist of delegates from these Diets. The new *Reichsrat* would control matters of economic policy while the local diets would control all other matters. The arrangement failed to satisfy the Hungarians as well as the Slav nationalities. Even in Austria there was raised the slogan that 'Austria must be treated as favourably as Hungary'. That is, if Hungary had a central constitutional Parliament, Austria must have one too.

To prevent Hungary from breaking away from the Empire, Francis Joseph dismissed Goluchowski in December and formed a new ministry under Anton Von Schmerling. The new minister represented at once German nationalism, centralism, and constitutionalism. He thought, that he would pave the way towards the dualism—a centralised constitutional Austria balancing a centralised constitutional Hungary. Schmerling, however, was not in reality a pro-Hungarian. He was as much of a centralist as Bach. So, on February 26, 1861, he issued the 'February Patent' which embodied his ideas. It reduced Hungary to the condition of a province and established a two-chamber parliament for the whole empire with an elaborate electoral geometry weighted in favour of the Germans. This was unanimously rejected by the Hungarian Diet, which refused to send deputies to the *Reichsrath* at Vienna. Schmerling dissolved the Diet and reincarnated the absolulist rule of the previous regime.

These measures not only aroused protests, but also had the effect of stimulating cultural movements that emphasised resistance to German domination. The establishment of a national theatre in Prague and the organisation throughout Bohemia of patriotic societies called Sokols, the foundation of a society of national culture by the Rumanians of Transylvania, and the beginning of a national press in Croatia heralded a new wave of dissatisfaction with the centralising policy of the Habsburg monarchy.

Most implacable in their resistance were the Magyars of Hungary, who found a leader in Francis Deak (1803-78) one of the noblest statesmen the nineteenth century produced. Deak was no extremist. He was not anti-Habsburg or unreasonable. The watchword of his policy was the restoration of a constitutional regime in Hungary such as the 1848 Laws had established. He asserted the historic principle that Austria and Hungary were joined only by 'personal Union' based on allegiance to a common ruler. On these grounds he claimed 'the complete restoration of our fundamental laws, our parliamentary government, and our responsible ministry'. In an address to the Hungarian Diet, Deak declared: 'We have no desire to endanger the existence of the Empire. We do not wish to dissolve the union'. He admitted the existence of certain affairs—foreign affairs, defence and finance—of common interest. But 'a forced unity will never make the Empire strong'. Deak upheld the free development of the individual nationalities, and the equal rights of Magyars and non-Magyars.

In 1864 the crisis in international situation—when Austria was threatened alike by France, Italy and Prussia—offered a basis of agreement. In December, Francis Joseph began secret negotiations with Deak. In the spring of 1865, Francis Joseph visited the Hungarian capital where he promised publicly 'to do everything possible to satisfy the peoples of my Hungarian Crown'. On September 20 he issued a manifesto suspending the operation of the October Diploma and February Patent. When the Hungarian Parliament met in December, it firmly refused to recognise either Diploma or Patent, or to enter any central *Reichsrath.*

In the middle of discussions, the Austro-Prussian war broke out in 1866. The war ended after a few days, with the defeat of the Austrians at Sadowa. Popular passion in Hungary tried to take advantage of Austria's predicament, but this was not Deak's view, nor that of Count Andrassy. When Deak was approached with the questions: 'What does Hungary demand?' He made the famous reply: 'Hungary asks no more after Konnigratz (Sadowa) than she asked before it.' Andrassy was more alive than Deak to the Slav danger and was convinced that the only safety for Hungary lay in a connection with Austria. Hungary found a powerful ally in the Austrian foreign minister, Baron Beust.

The final agreement was now reached in 1867 with the conclusion of the so-called Ausgleich or Compromise. It represented a system of government quite unique in the history of politics. It transformed the Habsburg Empire into a Dual Monarchy, comprising two independent and equal states with one ruler who would be Emperor of Austria and King of Hungary. Each half of this new Austria-Hungary would have its own parliament, its separate ministers, and its own civil service and administrative system. Nevertheless, a joint ministry (Common Ministry)—with responsibility for foreign affairs, defence and finance—was created. The acts of this ministry were supervised by two bodies, known as the 'delegations', one Austrian, one Hungarian, each composed of sixty members, elected annually by their respective legislatures. The two bodies were to meet separately in Vienna and Budapest, communicating with each in writing, and, very rarely, by means of joint sessions. Each side voted its quota towards the common expenses, this quota being fixed anew every ten years. A customs union was concluded, also renewable every ten years.

Effects of the Ausgleich

This elaborate compromise was a masterpiece of conciliatory statecraft, devised to perpetuate the Austo-Hungarian Empire, as a powerful unit in European politics. It was a league between the two strongest races, the Germans and the Magyars, who divided the monarchy between them, at the expense of all other people—the Czechs, the Slovaks, the Croats, the Serbs, the Poles and the Rumanians. Though Deak and Beust showed a spirit of realism by establishing the Dual Monarchy, their services were rendered to an ancient dynastic state and not to the cause of national integration.

Thus the settlement of 1867 contained within it the seeds of future discord. The Slavs advocated Federalism instead of Dualism. Bohemia claimed equality with Hungary. There was discontent among the Czechs and the Ruthenians. Galled by the Magyar domination, the discontent of the Croats, Serbs and Rumanians was a continuous menace to the dual state. In July 1868 such a violent anti-Habsburg demonstration occurred in Prague on the occasion of the anniversary of the birth of John Huss that the city had to be placed under martial law.

Deak exhibited a statesman-like grasp of the situation by his efforts to reconcile the non-Magyars to the *Ausgleich.* Croatia was given complete autonomy in all matters of administration; foreign affairs alone remained the province of the Hungarian Diet. Moreover, the celebrated 'Law of Nationalities' (1868) attempted to solve the vexed problem of the non-Magyar races in Hungary. Though Magyar was constituted the official language of Hungary— both in Parliament and in all branches of the administration— the use of other languages was permitted in the Country Assemblies, courts of law and schools. Actually the law of Nationalities was destined to remain inoperative. The condition of the Slovaks prior to the First World War was summed up in lucid light: 'Their language has been banished from all secondary schools, colleges and seminaries, and is being steadily expelled even from the primary schools... In Hungary the Magyar is the master. The other races are mere helots.' Thus the *Ausgleich,* instead of encouraging harmony and peaceful development of the Habsburg Empire, brought instead an exacerbation of the national differences that were to pull the empire to pieces.

CHAPTER 18

GROWTH OF THE GERMAN EMPIRE (1815-71)

One of the most remarkable changes of the nineteenth century was the transformation of Germany from a loose federation into an imposing powerful empire. Politically Germany was a divided land. Germany, like Italy, was long a geographical expression rather than a nation. Down to 1806, the German Empire comprised over three hundred separate political units, each with its own laws, bound together in a loose union called the Holy Roman Empire. Napoleon had created a territorial system in 1806—the Confederation of the Rhine—reducing the number to less than fifty. The Congress of Vienna carried Napoleon's work further. It established the Germanic confederation, composed of thirty-nine states, which survived less than half a century. The German settlement of 1815 was drawn up partly in the interests of the German princes, largely in the interests of the great powers, and not at all in the interests of the German people. The German confederation rested on the strength of the two powers, Austria and Prussia, and the lesser states of Germany played a second fiddle to the two powers.

The central body of the German confederation was the Diet which was vested with the control of all federal concerns. This Diet comprised two different forms of assembly. The ordinary or 'narrower' assembly contained 17 delegates, one each for the eleven large States, and the rest distributed among the remaining twenty-eight States. All important business, however, was reserved for the General Assembly composed of 69 delegates, in which every State had at least one vote, the chief States four, and a few others two or three. A unanimous vote was necessary for any changes affecting fundamental laws, organic institutions, individual rights or affairs of religion—a condition virtually impossible to attain. As an additional safeguard, the presidency of the Diet was entrusted to the Austrian delegate. The futility of the Diet for purposes of practical reform became unmistakable when the Austrian President of the Diet pronounced the fundamental laws of the constitution to be, like The Bible, incapable of change.

In 1815 Germany was constituted as a federated league of states *(Statebund)*, not as a United States of Germany *(Bundesstaat)*. She was without central organs capable of focusing national power. The Federal Diet was a negotiating body designed to coordinate the policy of the 39 governments. Instead of a supreme court, there were 39 separate judicial systems. Finally, the confederation failed to provide a German community. 'Germans remained politically in little watertight compartments, under their several governments'.

Article XIII of the Federal Constitution stipulated that all member states should set up representative assemblies. But with the exception of a few South German States (Saxe-Weimar, Bavaria, Wurtemberg. Baden, Hesse-Darmstadt) nowhere was that provision complied with. 'Judged by the requirements of a practical political organisation', says Von Sybel, 'this German Act of confederation, produced with so much effect, possessed about all the fauts that can render a constitution utterly useless'.

It is obvious that the confederation was incapable of giving Germany any real bond of unity. The famous Prussian General Clausewitz correctly diagnosed the situation when he observed 'Germany can achieve political unity only in one way, by the sword, by one of its states subjugating all the others'. The only states capable of such an act were Austria and Prussia. The Austrians wanted no change; the Prussians were satisfied with playing second fiddle to the Austrians. The cornerstone of Metternich's German policy was cooperation with Prussia. Frederick William III, the Prussian Emperor, who had experienced humiliation at the hands of Napoleon, was even more apprehensive than Metternich of any whisper of liberalism. Many nationalists had imagined the Habsburg Emperor as head of a new Germany; hardly any supposed that the king of Prussia would lead in the movement of national unity.

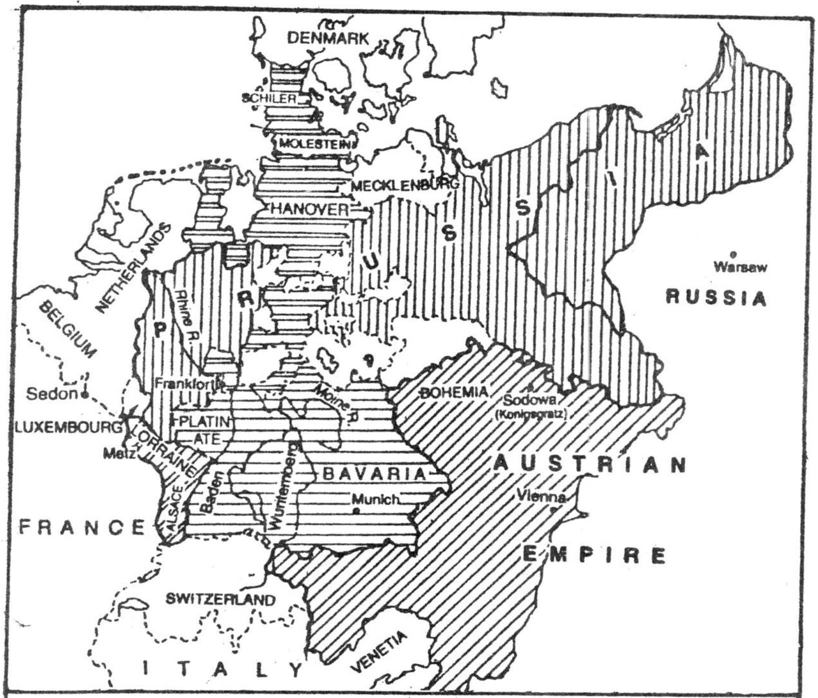

THE POLITICAL UNIFICATION OF GERMANY

Prussia 1815-1866
Annexation of 1866
South German States 1871
Austrian Section Excluded, 1866
Alsace-Lorraine, 1871
North german Confederation 1867
German Confederation, 1815-1866
German Empire, 1871

In spite of everything, the nationalist movement continued in university circles and within the German Societies. Students who had fought in the war of liberation came back to the universities to found a new kind of secret organisation *Burschenchaften*. By 1816 these secret societies were organised into a national federation with branches in 16 universities. In October 1817 the *Burschenchaft* of the University of Jena organised Warburg Festival to celebrate the anniversary of the Battle of Leipzig and the tercentenary of the Reformation. In this Festival, of course, there was no revolutionary plan but it ended with a bonfire in which various symbols of reaction were consigned to the flames.

Sporadic agitations of this nature continued for the next two years. But in 1819 the situation took a serious turn when a young student named Karl Sand murdered a reactionary journalist Kotzebue who was suspected as a Russian spy. This murder, which was followed by the attempted assassination of the head of the government of Nassau, provoked a violent reaction. Metternich, who was trying to establish reaction in Germany, summoned the representatives of nine states at Carlsbad in August 1819 and passed a series of decrees which were later approved by the Federal Diet. Inspectors were appointed for the universities, the *Burschenchaft* dissolved, censorship introduced, and a federal commission created at Mainz to coordinate the work of the separate commissions. The Carlsbad Decrees were the high-watermark of Austrian influence in Germany. From 1819 Prussia surrendered her independence to Austria and moved steadily under her umbrella.

The French Revolution of 1830 acted as a spur to the liberal movement in Germany. In Brunswick the sovereign was overthrown; in Hesse-Kassel, Hanover and Saxony, liberal constitutions had to be granted. In May 1832, at least 30,000 people gathered together at Hambach in Rhenish Bavaria where they demanded the destruction of absolutism in Austria and Prussia and the liberation of Poland, Hungary, and Italy as well. For want of coordination, the revolutionary movements failed to make any headway. In June 1832 Metternich persuaded the Diet to pass a series of repressive legislations. The unsuccessful attempt of a few liberals brought in fresh measures against the press and the universities. The culminating point of a reaction was reached in 1837 when the Hanover constitution was revoked and seven professors of the university of Gottingen were dismissed.

Two movements which greatly facilitated the transformation of German States were the *zollverein* and the Pan-Germanism.

Until 1818, Prussia had 67 different tariff systems in operation which inhibited commerce and industries. In 1818, under the influence of a great financial reformer, Maassen, all internal customs were abolished and free trade was established throughout all Prussia. This law was so successful that it was emulated by other German states. In 1819 Friedrich List (1789-1846) along with others established the *German Trade and Industry Union* to work for a single tariff for the whole of the Germanic confederation and the abolition of all customs duties inside it. In 1834 the Prussian Customs Union *(Zollverein)* were formed which included all German states except Hanover, the Hanse towns, Macklenburg, Oldenburg, Holstein, and Austria. The advantages of *Zollverein* were both economic and political. Industry grew rapidly by the application of the principle of free trade. Politically it made the member states increasingly dependent upon Prussia and gradually undermined Austrian influence in Germany. Prussia entered into a series of relationships with Britain, Belgium and France (1841-46) and 'thread by thread created a German network of commercial treaties'. Thus the *Zollverein* is generally considered in every real sense to have been the beginning of German Unity.

In Germany as in Italy, nationalism had made considerable progress in the realm of ideas. A great literary outburst had followed the French wars, and poets, philosophers and historians extolled the German idea. It began with Niebuhr (1776-1861). He was the historian of the peasantry, citizens and patricians of Republican Rome. He saw in Roman political history parallels to Prussia's mission in Germany. Niebuhr's contemporary was Savigny (1778-1861). For Savigny the true basis of law was the opinion of society. He distrusted arbitrary lawgiving by both parliaments and princes.

Hegel (1770-1831) was the predominant intellectual influence of the period. Hegel exalted conception of the State and the historic role of the Teutonic race. His doctrine that the state was the embodiment of the reason could be turned into a doctrine that if the existing state did not embody reason, it should be overthrown. Thus the 'young Hegelians' helped to inspire the revolution of 1848. Fichte gave his *Addresses to the German people.* Stein, the eminent Prussian statesman, founded the *Monumenta Germaniae* for the study of German history. Dahlmann, through his great work *Die Politik* (1836), put forward that true freedom consisted in self-government. Dahlmann exercised great influence on historians like Droysen, Waitz and Hausser who wanted to make the State, a *Rechstaat,* a 'judicial person' before which monarchical authority should bow. They admitted that without a modern parliament freedom remained a dead letter.

During the nineteenth century there arose a Prussian school of historians who believed that it was Prussia's historic mission to unite Germany.

These historians asserted the doctrine of 'historic necessity'. Among the best known were Ludwig Hausser, Gustav Droysen, Heinrich von Sybel and the famous Heinrich von Trietschke. German literature also reached its apex of creative power. A leading figure of the new Germany in literature was Heinrich Heine (1797-1856) who waged relentless war against despotic government and intellectual repression. Among the south German political thinkers, Paul Pfizer believed that if Germany were ever to be unified, Prussia must lead the way.

On the eve of the Revolution the principal source of discontent lay in the practice of absolutism and the general absence of freedom. The unjustifiable prosecutions brought against liberals and patriots antagonised the country as a whole. It was, therefore, the oppressive nature of the German governments which created a desire for change. This attitude assumed a new dimension in 1846 following the economic and social crisis. Many liberals considered that the time had come to obtain substantial reforms from the crown. The situation took a turn for the worse in Prussia when Frederick William IV decided, in spite of Metternich's protests, to summon a united Landtag consisting of all the deputies in the Provincial Diets (February 3, 1847). The United *Landtag* was to have the right of petition, and the king might consult it in regard to new legislation. There were to be two Chambers, meeting apart, the former a Chamber of Lords, the other of the three estates. The *Landtag* was not to meet at definite periods but only when the king should summon it. The Liberals were not satisfied with advisory powers for the *Landtag*, and they demanded regular meetings. They refused to vote a loan required for the building of the Berlin-Konigsberg railway. However, they failed to persuade the king to grant a constitution or even to agree to regular meetings of the *Landtag*. In June 1947, therefore, the *Landtag* was dissolved. Not being dispirited, the democrats held a congress at Offenburg in September 1847, where they called a national parliament common to all the Germanic countries.

The growing discontent was not confined to Prussia. In the industrial areas of Prussia and Saxony, workers were anxious to be rid of the surviving medieval restrictions; in the small states, the middle class were demanding a large share in the political activity. The local political situation varied. In some states, such as Hesse-Kassel and Brunswick, the demands were for constitutional guarantees against a despot. In Baden and Wurtemberg, the liberals were agitating for German unity.

Upon the news of the Parisian insurrection, the population of Berlin rose in revolt and erected barricades. The capitals of minor German states witnessed similar scenes. On March 5, 1848, a number of liberal leaders came together at Hidelberg and entrusted a Committee of seven with the task of summoning a parliamentary convention or *vorparlament.* This met at Frankfurt on March 31, 1848. It consisted of 500 members drawn from the parliamentary assemblies of the different German states. It achieved no results of any importance save to arrange for the election of an all-German assembly. Frederick William IV of Prussia issued a proclamation in which he promised to assume the leadership of the national movement.

The National Assembly met at Frankfurt-on-the-Main in the Rhineland on May 13, 1848. The Assembly consisted chiefly of the middle class, bourgeoisie, the patriotic class. Its first task was to set up a provisional Government. After a preliminary struggle the Austrian interest won a victory over the Prussian, and the Archduke John, a liberal and popular Habsburg, was nominated to the position of the imperial vicar, and his authority was recognised by the German princes.

From the start the Frankfurt Assembly exhibited its impotence to the whole German nation in connection with the Schleswig-Holstein question. The duchies of Schleswig and Holstein revolted against Denmark and attempted to unite themselves with Germany. Prussia intervened on their behalf, but the European powers declined to allow any dismemberment of Denmark, and they forced Frederick William to conclude the Convention of Malmoe (August 1848) and withdraw his troops. This Convention the Assembly was compelled to accept. When this became known, an insurrection broke out at Frankfurt. Order was finally restored (September 18) by the arrival of

Prussian and Austrian troops, but not before two popular deputies had been murdered.

From May until December the Frankfurt Parliament wasted precious time in drafting the new German constitution. The debates of the Assembly reflected two main conflicting points of unification. The Great German party believed that the empire must embrace all German states, including the German provinces of Austria whereas the small German party insisted that all of Austria must be excluded. Eventually, the majority agreed on the latter solution, while advocating a close connection with Austria. They concluded also that the king of Prussia must be invited to preside over the new German Reich. But Austria had made it clear, at Frankfurt in December 1848, that she intended to revive the old German *Bund*, in which Austria must remain as an organic part.

The Constitution as framed by the Frankfurt Parliament provided for a single hereditary Emperor to rule over all Germany and a legislature of two houses. A deputation was sent to offer the German crown to Frederick William IV, the King of Prussia. But the Prussian king, once more secure in his autocratic powers, refused the offer as it might lead to a war with Austria. Moreover, he disliked the idea of receiving a Crown from a revolutionary assembly ('pick up the crown from the gutter', as he expressed it) which had a doubtful right to make the offer. The Imperial Crown was the keystone of the arch of the German constitution, and, failing this, the whole structure collapsed.

This refusal was in effect the end of the Frankfurt Assembly. Austria and Prussia now withdrew their representatives. As the spring and summer of 1849 passed the members of the Assembly and the provisional government resigned. Revolts occurred in Baden, Bavaria, Saxony and were suppressed by Prussian troops. The Assembly, reduced to a rump, was removed to Stuttgart at the end of May, and in June 1849 was finally dispersed by order of the King of Wurtemberg. The Revolution of 1848 was at an end.

The causes of the momentous failure of German liberalism in 1848-49 are not hard to find. It was essentially a middleclass movement and it was largely confined to the cities. In 1848 these German cities were neither very large nor very influential. There was no 'Paris' in the centre of the country, the seizure of which would have given the movement a halo of national unity. The revolution won over neither the armies not the peasants; above all it failed to win over the princes. 'The voice of the people (at Frankfurt) which at one time had seemed to shake the seats of the mighty, ceased to alarm as soon as princes and governments knew that behind it was neither power nor national will.' Thus, 'this Assembly... was unable to accomplish its self-appointed task, and that the union of Germany was achieved, not by the give and take of Parliamentary argument, but by the blood and iron of civil and foreign war'.

Despite the failure of the Frankfurt Assembly, the King of Prussia did not wholly abandon the cause of German unity. This was due to the growing influence of General Joseph Maria von Radowitz, a Catholic nobleman, who called for an agreement by the German princes to join their territories in a union that would be led by Prussia and would exclude Austria. Radowitz secured the support of the two states adjacent to Prussia, Hanover and Saxony, and, on May 26, 1849, an 'Alliance of three kingdoms' was signed. It was arranged to convene a Diet at Erfurt in March 1850, to be composed of representatives from the north and central German states which were to form the new union.

Austria became highly suspicious. If Prussia solved the German problem, Austrian dominance would be reduced in Germany. The suppression of the Hungarian revolt set her free to devote attention to German affairs. The object of Schwarzenberg, the Austrian general, was to restore the old Germanic Confederation. During the winter of 1849-50, he succeeded in breaking up the Radowitz's union project even before the assembly of the Erfurt Congress. Hanover withdrew before the meeting, and Saxony, Wurtemberg and Hesse-Kassel began to waver. Henceforth, the Erfurt Congress came to nothing. Moreover, Schwarzenberg persuaded the Federal Diet in May 1850 to threaten sanctions against any state that attempted to break away from the confederation.

In the autumn of 1850, disturbance in Hesse-Kassel put a match to the powder magazine. The Elector of Hesse-Kassel was at bitter feud with his subjects, whom he had alienated by withdrawing from the Prussian League as well as by attack upon their parliamentary rights. He appealed to the Federal Diet where Austrian influence was paramount. On October 12, 1850, Austria—along with Bavaria and Wurtemberg issued a declaration that they would maintain the confederation and intervene in support of Hesse. On October 15, the Elector appealed for military help. Both Austria and Prussia sent troops into Hesse and, on November 8, a skirmish took place. The real issue at stake concerned something more than the pacification of Hesse. It involved the fundamental question whether the policy of the Union which comprised Prussia and the German states and professed constitutional principles should carry the day, or whether the policy of the Germanic confederation, which included Austria and was avowedly reactionary, should carry the day. Radowitz was ready to challenge; but the Prussian Government, having failed to get the support of the Tsar, decided to negotiate. Moreover, Prussian army was not reorganised and Bismarck was right when he wrote afterwards 'from the military point of view our hands were tied'. At the Convention of Olmutz (November 29, 1850), Prussia abandoned Hesse-Kassel to her fate and agreed to the dissolution of the Erfurt Union. This was followed by the Dresden Conferences (December 1850) (March 1851), which revived the old Germanic Confederation and the Federal Diet. The humiliation of Olmutz remained a symbol of shame until it was obliterated by the victory of Koniggratz in 1866. Thus, the efforts of the three years had been in vain and Austria emerged victorious.

A period of reaction in Germany began again, ever more far-reaching in its scope than that which had followed the Congress of Vienna, 1815. In most states the constitutions were revised in a reactionary way. The governing forces were the king and the landed nobility. Many liberal and radicals had been forced to emigrate. In Prussia, the Manteuffel ministry reintroduced political censorship and a political police. Prussian politics in the next decade held out little hope for national unity or constitutional reform. This despair filled the atmosphere of German liberal movement in the 1850s. 'The German nation', Julius Froebel said in 1859, 'is sick of principles and doctrines, literary existence and theoretical greatness. What it wants is Power, Power, Power! And whoever gives it power to him will it give honour, more honour than he can imagine.' This mood was to produce the National Liberalism of the 1860s and the admirable support for Bismarck's policy of forcible unification of Germany under Prussian leadership.

In 1859 political reaction began to be challenged both in Prussia and in Germany as a whole. In that year the war between France and Austria in Italy raised a host of questions about the solidarity of the German confederation. Public opinion in Germany was also deeply stirred by the Italian War of Liberation. To the liberals, Austria was the 'Hangman of Italy' and the 'Oppressor of Germany'. They saw in the war an opportunity for demonstrating German national solidarity against the hereditary enemy, France. Moreover, it raised the whole question of Austro-Prussian relations when the former tried to secure support from the whole confederation and, above all, the assistance of the Prussian army. But Prussia remained neutral which was a blow to Austria and to the confederation.

But signs were not lacking of the dawning of a new day. The economic evolution of the country was proceeding slowly—the transformation of Germany from an agricultural—feudal into a great industrial nation was rendered possible by Governmental measures and by the operation of the business laws. Great economic progress had been made in the Prussian kingdom. Berlin had grown in two decades and Cologne, Magdeburg and Breslau were growing fast. The discovery of gold in California in 1848 and in Australia in 1851 had an important result in Germany. Large number of banks and business corporations were created. In Bavaria, for instance, only six stock companies with a capital of five million marks had been founded between 1839 and 1848; but from 1849 to 1858 forty-four were established with a capital of one hundred and seventy million mark. In four years (1853-57) the capital of the banks accumulated to 750 millions. All this meant an immense increase in the resource available for industry. The low tariff imposed by Germany was the chief stimulant of the economy. The *Zollverein* was enlarged to include Hanover and in 1853 was renewed for twelve years. Hundreds of new industries were launched and such establishments as the dye work of Berlin and the steel industry of Albert Krupp became internationally famous.

The most remarkable thing about the development of German nationalism was the formation, in September 1859, of the German National Association (*Deutsche Nationalverein*). The *Nationalverein* was the first national political movement which had the support of liberal politicians of central and north Germany and included economists like Hermann Schulze-Delitsch and historians like Heinrich von Triestschke. The *Nationalverein* believed that Austria should be excluded from Germany and that the new Germany united under Prussian leadership. 'Better the stiffest Prussian military rule than the wretchedness of the small states' a leader of Hesse-Darmstadt is reported to have said.

The period from 1849 to 1859 was the most shameful in the history of Prussia. Even in 1859 Prussia did not take advantage of Austria's foreign difficulties to extend her influence and territory in Germany. Frederick William IV became insane and his brother William became Regent in 1858 and then became King in 1861. The accession of this ruler was hailed as the beginning of a 'new era'. He was a true Hohenzollern in his belief that Prussia's destiny was dependent upon his army and so he was bent upon strengthening the military power of the kingdom. He had never forgotten the humiliation of Olmutz. He became convinced of the necessity of military preparation if Prussia was to succeed in her competition with Austria for the leadership of Germany.

A soldier by profession, William I had long been critical of certain aspects of Prussia's military organisation; the restriction of the term of active service to two years, and the heavy reliance upon a civilian militia (*Landwehr*) which was largely independent of the regular army. In December 1859 he appointed General Albrecht von Roon, War Minister. Early in 1860 Roon accounced his proposals for reforms. These called for a marked increase in the annual number of conscripts, lengthened the term of service to three years, curtailed the independence of the *Landwehr* and asked for an enhanced military budget. When these proposals were placed before the Prussian Diet, the Prussian middle class, who now controlled the majority of seats in the Prussian Chamber of Deputies, opposed the proposed reform. Though the government withdrew the proposed legislation, it asked for extraordinary heavy sums to strengthen existing units of the army. The funds were sanctioned but William proceeded to use it to effect his cherished reforms. Not unnaturally, the liberal majority protested and refused to make any further grant of funds to the government unless the military innovations were withdrawn. The King dissolved the Chamber in March 1862. When the elections were held in May, however, the liberal majority opposed to reform was strengthened.

What followed was a complete deadlock. Emboldened by their electoral success and led by the new Progressive Party, the liberal opposition was now resolved to assert the right of parliament to control the executive. The deadlock was complete by September 1862. The king, in despair, seriously considered giving up his throne. Parliament rejected the whole military budget by 308 votes to 11. Roon resolved the impasse by dispatching telegraph to Bismarck on September 18, 1862, to hasten his return to Berlin. Bismarck arrived in Berlin on September 20, and two days later the King appointed him as his Minister President.

Bismarck's Political Ideas

The man who now entered upon the stage of European politics was one of the most original characters of his century. Bismarck was a wealthy Junker (country squire, member of the landowning aristocracy) but he had none of the provincialism of his fellow Junkers. Since 1850, he had been serving his country as a diplomat, first in the Diet at Frankfurt, later in St. Petersburg and Paris. As a determined reactionary, he opposed every liberal proposal. He deplored the events of 1848, welcomed the end of the Frankfurt Assembly, the defeat of the Erfurt Union of 1850, and the restoration of the old Bund.

Bismarck's political ideas centred in his ardent belief in the Prussian monarchy. 'The Prussian Crown', he said, 'must not allow itself to be thrust into the powerless position of the English Crown.' He had political sense and perhaps even political wisdom. At bottom he was a barbarian genius, but his genius gave him a sense of moderation. As a result, though his ultimate legacy to Germany was boundless tyranny and to Europe protracted war, his immediate achievement was to give Germany a long period of prosperity and Europe a long period of peace.

Bismarck had the sagacity to subordinate the lesser questions to the greater, and he had no ideal but Prussia's greatness. 'The healthiest basis of a state is a national selfishness', he said. He boldly denied in Parliament the favourite theory of the liberals, that Prussia was to be made great by a liberal, free parliamentary government. He made no secret of his feeling when in a historic speech he declared in 1863 that what Germans cared about was not the liberalism of Prussia but her power. 'Not by speeches and majority votes are the great questions of the day decided—that was the great blunder of 1848 and 1849—but by blood and iron.'

Bismarck's greatness lay not in mastering events, but in going with events. Sentimentally he would have preferred a return to the conservative order of the days of Metternich—Austria and Prussia cooperating to resist liberalism within Germany. But he was convinced that the friendship between Austria and Prussia was dead. He believed that if Prussia was to extend her power in Germany, this could be accomplished only at the expense of Austria. As early as 1856 Bismarck had recorded his opinion: 'Germany is clearly too small for us both... In the not too distant future, we shall have to fight for our existence against Austria ... since the course of events in Germany has no other solution.'

Bismarck united all the qualities of the consummate politician with the simplicity of purpose which are essential to the highest forms statesmanship. He was fertile in expedients. At one time or another, Bismarck made or planned alliances with every power in Europe—with England, France, Russia, Austria. Again, Bismarck worked or planned to work with every social and political force within Germany—with the great industrialists, with the Roman Catholics, with the anti-Catholics, and even with the Socialists.

Bismarck's accession to power in 1862 was therefore a turning-point in the history of nineteenth century Germany. His strategic mastery and firm grasp of political reality brought into play a new approach to the problem of German unity. The conflict with France did not constitute the essence of his original design; it was intended rather as the coping-stone to the German edifice. The details of his policy may be studied under the following heads: 1. his relations with the Prussian parliament; 2. his relations with Russia; 3. with Austria and 4. with France:

1. Bismarck had been called to the office when the popular chamber refused to vote the budget required for the army reform. This involved him in a struggle with the parliament that revealed his qualities of inflexible determination. Instead of persuading the Prussian House of Representatives to give assent to the military law, Bismarck invented a "gap theory'. The Prussian constitution, he said, had a gap in it, because it made no provision for the case in which the Crown and the Legislature failed to come to any agreement in regard to a budget. Therefore the King must fill this gap. The constitutional conflict followed. The House of Representatives refused, as before, to approve the government budget; whereupon Bismarck had the financial estimates voted by the House of Lords. The taxes were used to enlarge and reorganise the army. Bismarck's policy did not weaken the parliamentary opposition, which increased its strength in the elections of 1863. Undismayed, Bismarck believed that an active and successful foreign policy would break the opposition and to this purpose he directed his policy with great tenacity.

2. Bismarck cared nothing for the constitutional struggle in Prussia; his real anxiety was to preserve Prussia as a great power. 'Bismarck's first achievement in foreign policy was the consolidation of Russo-Prussian freindship over the body of Poland'. The Poles won the sympathy of half Europe when they revolted in 1863. Austria, estranged from Russia, supported the Poles. Bismarck, furiously anti-Polish, feared that the re-

volt would spread to Prussian Poland and proposed military cooperation to Russia. The anti-Polish agreement between Prussia and Russia—the Alvensleben Convention—was concluded on February 8, 1863. Bismarck claimed the Convention determined the character of future Germany. In the coming struggle with Austria, Prussia was at least assured of the neutrality of Russia; and this assurance was 'the first and not the least important step in Bismarck's advance against Austria'.

3. Secure in Russia's favour, Bismarck turned next to the conflict with Austria. Meanwhile the Austrian government made its last attempt to assert Austrian preponderance in Germany and to compensate Austria for her defeat in Italy. Popular support for the ideas of a 'Greater Germany' under Austria's leadership found expression in the organisation of Reform Association (*Reformverein*) in Munich in October 1862 to counteract the influence of the Pro-Prussian *Nationalverein* (Little German'). Count Rechberg, Austrian Foreign Minister from 1859 to 1863, believed in a policy of peaceful dual control of Germany, with Prussia and Austria each dominating its own sphere of influence. Other Austrians, like Anton von Schemerling, the Minister of the Interior, believed in some form of 'Greater Germany' with Austria predominant. The Austrian Emperor, Francis Joseph, summoned to Frankfurt on August 16, 1863, a Congress of Princes to discuss suggestions for the reform of the confederation. Francis Joseph in person invited the Prussian monarch to attend. William I found it hard to resist so tempting a bait. But Bismarck saw in the congress a blow aimed at Prussia. It was a threat of resignation that forced his will upon the reluctant King. With Prussia's refusal the Austrian reform plan was doomed. 'The failure of the Frankfurt meeting ended all chance of a Germany achieved by negotiation and so broke the last frail link of historic continuity.'[1]

Schleswig Holstein Question

In the autumn of 1863 the Schleswig-Holstein question occupied the attention of Bismarck. The two Duchies without being part of the Danish Kingdom, had long been united with Denmark by bond of personal union. Schleswig was predominantly Danish in character and was a fief of Denmark, while Holstein, whose population was almost entirely German, was a member of the Germanic confederation. In 1848 the Duchies tried to break away from Denmark and this was encouraged by a national feeling in Germany. The Danes might have been easily ousted from the Duchies, especially when Prussia took up the revolutionary cause. But the moral support of Britain, Russia, Sweden and even Austria, saved the Duchies. The Treaty of London (1852) recognised the integrity of Denmark, confirmed her possession of the Duchies, but prevented their absolute incorporation into the Danish Kingdom. Holstein was left as a member of the German confederation. The Treaty guaranteed the succession both to the Kingdom and to the Duchies, to Christian, Prince of Glucksburg.

The Treaty was not accepted by the German Diet, which had been unrepresented at London, nor by Frederick of Augstenburg, the rival claimant to the Danish throne. The terms of the Treaty, therefore, if 'a necessity for Europe, were a humiliation for Germany'. The Danes began to take advantage of their victory. A powerful section of the Danish opinion—known as the 'Eider Dane' party—demanded the extension of the Danish Kingdom to the river Eider, which meant the complete incorporation of Schleswig. In 1855 a new constitution was issued for the whole Kingdom and imposed upon the Duchies. Holstein protested and, upon the representation of the Prussian Diet, she was left out of the new constitutional arrangement.

In 1863 the dispute was revived by a disputed succession to the Danish throne and the desire of the Danes to incorporate Schleswig. The old king died in November 1863 and in accordance with the Treaty of London (1852) was succeeded by Prince Christian of Glucksberg. The new King promulgated a new Danish constitution which declared Schleswig an integral part of the Kingdom. As Schleswig, unlike Holstein, was not a member of the German confederation, this arrangement met with a nationalistic outcry from Germany. The Federal

1. Taylor, A. J. P.: *The Course of German History* (1978), P. 113.

Diet immediately protested and, when this was unavailing, ordered a federal army to prevent the execution of the terms of Denmark's new constitution. Bismarck had no intention that the Duchies should be won by Denmark. The Duchies were of great potential strategic importance to Prussia, especially Holstein, with its important position between the North and Baltic Seas and the excellent harbour of Kiel. He did not publish his true views but instead invoked the treaty of 1852 which guaranteed the autonomous position of the Duchies. Bismarck urged the Austrian government to join Prussia in upholding international law.

Bismarck was not oblivious of the dangerous possibilities of the situation: France, England and Russia might intervene at any movement. But the lack of any common policy among the great powers inhibited their joint action. Even England's offer to help Denmark proved to be only 'senseless and spiritless menaces'. Bismarck had been careful to associate Austria with every step against Denmark and a formal alliance was signed on January 17, 1864. A joint ultimatum was sent to Copenhagen demanding the repeal of the November constitution of 1863 within forty-eight hours. Denmark rejected the ultimatum and a joint Prussian-Austrian army overran Denmark in February.

Europe saw the step with alarm. The Treaty of London in 1852 had been signed by all five great powers, as well as by Denmark and Sweden. A conference was held in London in April 1864 for the purpose of arranging a settlement by diplomacy. But nothing was accomplished. Russia was grateful for Prussian aid in the recent Polish insurrection; France and England were full of reproaches for each other. Since 1861 France had become deeply involved in the difficult entanglement of the Mexican expedition. In Britain, Palmerston blustered but could do nothing against the determined opposition of the cabinet. The new Kingdom of Italy had no wish to engage herself against Prussia and Austria together. Norway and Sweden looked on with sympathy, but took no action.

So the war was quickly over. In October 1864 Austria, Prussia and Denmark signed the Treaty of Vienna. The Danish King renounced all right to Schleswig, Holstein and the little duchy of Lauenberg in favour of Austria and Prussia and agreed to recognise any disposition they should make of them. The claim of the Duke of Augustenburg, to the duchies was ignored. Bismarck later regarded his handling of the Schleswig-Holstein matter as the diplomatic masterpiece of his career. 'If Mr. Cobden (an avowed pacifist) had been Foreign Secretary', said Lord Robert Cecil, afterward Marquis of Salisbury, 'I believe this country would occupy a position proud and noble compared to that she occupies at this moment. She would at least have been entitled to the credit of holding out no hopes which she did not intend to fulfil, of entering into an engagement from which she was ready to recede.'

The Danish war is significant for several reasons. It provided a baptism of fire for the new Prussian army. It was in the campaign in Jutland that the architect of those later victories, Chief of the General Staff Helmuth von Moltke (1800-91) won the confidence of the King. It was in the successful assault of the formidable Danish strong point of Duppel that the army as a whole exhibited their skill. The victory in Duppel was described as 'one of the events that mark an epoch in a nation's history'. It aroused a degree of patriotic pride, strengthened Prussian claim for leadership in Germany and weakened liberal opposition to the army reform.

The rapprochement between Austria and Prussia was quickly broken down by the failure to agree to the future of the Duchies. The inhabitants of the Duchies wished to form a separate state under the Duke of Augustenburg and be admitted as such to the German confederation. The people of Germany were overwhelmingly in favour of this arrangement and Austria supported this. But Bismarck's aim was to annex Schleswig-Holstein and eliminate Austria from north Germany. The crux of the situation lay in the fact that Prussia coveted the Duchies, whereas Austria did not; but, at the same time, she could not allow Prussia any territorial advantage. Sources of friction were so numerous that in May 1865 the King and some of his ministers discussed the possibility of making war upon Austria. But Bismarck was not in favour of precipitating a war for fear of antagonising German public opinion. Consequently, after much involved haggling, the two Powers—Prussia and Austria—concluded the so-called Convention of Gastein on August 14, 1865. It was agreed that Schleswig was to be administered by Prussia and Holstein by Austria. This was regarded as a provisional arrangement rather than a definite one and gave Prussia a pretext for quarrel with Austria as the former reserved her rights in Holstein. Anyway, the Convention of Gastein was a diplomatic victory for Prussia as Austria had to repudiate the claims of Duke of Augustenburg.

The Convention of Gastein was highly disadvantageous to Austria. As Bismarck himself said, it 'merely papered over the cracks'. For he never forgot that war with Austria was necessary for the fulfilment of his great design—the unification of Germany under Prussia's leadership. Bismarck knew that his only problem was to time and stage the next war. He was sure of British inertia and Russian freindship; but he was uncertain of France's attitude. Bismarck met Napoleon III at Biarritz in October 1865 and reached an understanding that France would remain neutral in the case of a war, although she might receive territorial compensation which loomed large in Napoleon's mind. The war might last long and, if the decision remained in balance, Paris might play the role of arbiter and the arbiter might be able to profit. Napoleon's vacillation was reflected when, at the last moment in June 1866, he gambled on an Austrian victory and signed a secret treaty with Francis Joseph on June 12. He promised neutrality provided that no changes detrimental to France would be made in Germany. Austria agreed to cede Venetia to Napoleon for Italy and Napoleon would endeavour to secure Italian neutrality.

Bismarck strengthened the Prussian cause by making an offensive and defensive alliance with Italy on April 8, 1866. Italy agreed to fight on Prussias' side if war came within the next three months, and should receive Venetia from Austria. It was an arrangement of mutual 'insurance and suspicion', the time indicating Italy's distrust.

Bismarck still had to win popular support. Moreover, he did not wish to give the impression that he was so sordid as to go to war with Austria for territorial ambitions in Schleswig-Holstein. On April 9, 1866, Bismarck astonished everyone by proposing that a German Parliament elected by universal suffrage should meet to discuss constitutional reform. He allowed the inference that Austria was not to be included in the organisation. As a possible device for winning the South German liberals the measure was clever but hardly successful for no one believed that Bismarck's devotion to liberalism was genuine.

From April 1866 the Austrians were convinced that war was inevitable and after that they never tried to avoid it. They actually resigned themselves to the loss of Venetia and began the mobilisation of troops. Prussia mobilsed in the first week of May. Attempts at mediation were made by General Gablenz, brother of the Austrian Governor of Holstein, who proposed the creation of a separate duchy of Schleswig-Holstein under a Prussian prince, and the division of military leadership in Germany between Prussia and Austria. Napoleon III also proposed a European conference. Neither was successful.

Events now moved swiftly. On June 1, 1866, Austria placed the Schleswig-Halstein question before the Federal Diet. Bismarck promptly described this as a violation of the Gastein Convention and retaliated by occupying Holstein on June 7. On June 12, Austria broke off diplomatic relations with Prussia. On June 14, the Austrian Government demanded military action by the Federal forces against Prussia. The Federal Diet at Frankfurt, by a majority of nine to six, supported Austria's motion. Prussia declared that the German confederation was dissolved. On June 15, without any formal declaration of war, Prussia invaded Saxony.

The Seven Weeks' War

Thus the German civil war began. It proved to be one of the shortest wars in history for it began on June 16, 1866 and brought to a close by the definitive peace of Prague, August 13. The Austrian debacle was due to a number of factors. The Austrian army lacked training and discipline and a heterogeneous body where ten different languages were spoken. The officers were lazy and incompetent, a poor match for the self-sacrificing, hard-hitting Junker generals. The commanding Generals, including Benedek, the Commander-in-Chief on the Bohemian front, lacked confidence. The infantry had only the old muzzle-loading rifles instead of the new needle-guns, breach-loaders used by the Prussians that fired more rapidly. In addition, Austria had two enemies to fight—one in front, Prussia; one in the rear, Italy—a condition always full of danger. The decisive factor in the war proved to be Austria's deficiency in railroads which reduced Austrian mobility and made the movement of troops from the Italian front difficult. In contrast, the Prussians had a highly developed rail network that enabled the Chief of Staff, Moltke, to deploy his troops along an arc 600 miles wide, from the Elbe to the Neisse.

The Prussian military machine worked with fatal precision. Moltke could now demonstrate to Europe the full effectiveness of that war-machine which Roon and he had created since 1859. With a population of thirty-five million, Austria mobilised 540,000 men; but out of eighteen million inhabitants, Prussia moblisied 5,50,000, better disciplined, better equipped and better led. The Prussian plan of mobilisation enabled Moltke to begin the campaign with superior forces at all the decisive points. As it was, the object of the Prussian general was to crush the levies of the separate state before they should have time to concentrate.

The rapidity of the campaign struck Europe with amazement. Prussia had to deal with two enemy forces—Austrian army in Bohemia and the Hanoverian army. On June 29 the Hanoverian army was caught and crushed at Langensalza and capitulated the next day. Moltke sent three armies by different route into Bohemia and, on July 3, 1866, one of the great battles of history, that of Koniggratz Sadowa (Hredec Kralove by the Czechs) was fought. The battle was long and doubtful. The Austrians fought skilfully and stubbornly. The arrival of the Prussian Crown Prince with his army decided the fate of the day and gave victory to the Prussians. This encounter was a perfect illustration of the way in which Moltke's principle of dispersed advance by concentration on the battlefield could be applied to encircle and defeat an army. The trap did not succeed quite well as Benedek—with the skillful use of artillery and spirited rearguard action of his cavalry—extricated 180,000 men from the fateful field. The defeat was nonetheless shattering as Austrians and their allied had 44,313 casualties compared with 9,153 Prussians.

After the battle of Sadowa, Prussian troops marched into Bavaria as far as Wurzburg and Nuremburg. Nassau was occupied and also the free city of Frankfurt which had to pay a large war contribution. But Bismarck's Italian allies did not fare well in the battle. On June 24, they were defeated by the strong Austrian forces at Custozza in Lombardy. The Italian fleet was heavily defeated at the Battle of Lissa.

The news of Konnigratz came as a 'gunpowder explosion to Europe'. 'The extraordinary success of Prussia', wrote Lord Malmesbury, 'had alarmed all nations.' It was to the advantage of Bismarck to make peace as rapidly as possible in order to prevent European interference in German affairs. The views of Bismarck clashed with the military aspirations of Moltke and the King of Prussia who desired the continuation of war by marching into Vienna and dictating severe terms of peace. But the last thing Bismarck desired was the destruction of the Habsburg monarchy. The Habsburgs were his essential allies against Greater Germany. 'The dispute with Austria is decided, we have now to win back the ancient friendship', was his opinion.

Moreover, the questions of French interference was uppermost in Bismarck's mind. The French Emperor was anxious to act as a mediator and sent Benedetti, the French ambassador, to the Prussian headquarters at Nikolsburg. As Bismarck confessed in his *Reflections* and *Reminiscences*: 'We must finish off rapidly, before France has time to bring diplomatic action to bear on Austria.' England and Russia had already protested against any fundamental alteration of the German Federal Constitution without the approval of a European congress. Bismarck's reaction was sharp: he threatened to stir up the Poles.

It was not an easy task for Bismarck to win over the belligerent King William of Prussia to his views and to enlist the support of the Crown Prince. Bismarck threatened to resign; and he went so far as to contemplate suicide and consented 'to bite into this sour apple and accept the shameful peace.'

A preliminary peace was signed at Nikolsburg on July 26; the final Peace of Prague followed on August 23. Austria withdrew from German affairs, and the German confederation was dissolved. A North German Confederation was to be formed. Prussia—enlarged and consolidated by the annexation of the Kingdom of Hanover, the Elector of Hesse, a portion of Hesse-Darmstadt, and the free city of Frankfurt—became the acknowledged leader of a North German Confederation embracing all the states north of the Main. There was also formed south of that river an association with 'an independent international existence' of the states of southern Germany. But the independence of the southern states was compromised; for, immediately after the peace, Bismarck negotiated offensive and defensive alliances with all of them. Prussia got Schleswig and Holstein, subject to northern Schleswig's being returned to Denmark if decided by plebiscite. But no plebiscite was held and Prussia kept the territories till 1919. Finally, by the Peace of Vienna, October 3, 1866, Austria ceded Venetia to Napoleon for transfer to Italy.

The Austro-Prussian war was a landmark in the history of Europe. It dealt a sharp blow to French power and brought Italian unification one step closer. It helped to bring about the Dual Monarchy of Austria-Hungary in 1867.

Internally, Bismarck secured a significant tactical success over the Prussian Parliament. In the elections that were held on the day of the battle of Sadowa, the liberals were returned with a majority. The Progressive Party, which had opposed Bismarck's unconstitutional action in making war on Denmark without parliamentary financial sanction, lost support. The moderates broke away from the Progressive Party to form the National Liberal Party. Bismarck was aware that if Prussia was to pursue a policy of completing the unification of Germany, the support of the liberals was essential. To win the liberals Bismarck extended an olive branch by admitting that the government had acted in violation of the constitution by operating without a budget since 1862, if, in return, the Parliament would legitimize all past expenditure by an act of indemnity. After a protracted debate on the Indemnity Bill, the Prussian parliament, on September 3, 1866, passed the Bill by a vote of 230 to 75. 'The vote of September 3 was as decisive a landmark in the history of Germany as was the Bill of Rights in the history of England, or the oath of the Tennis Court in the history of France.'[2] It marked the end of liberalism in Germany. The socialist leader Wilhelm Liebknecht wrote that it was a personal triumph for Bismarck and added sardonically that 'the angel of darkness has become the angel of light, before whom the people lie in the dust and adore. The stigma of violation of the constitution has been washed from his brow and in its place the halo of glory rings his laurelled head.' Thus, in the struggle between the Crown and the Parliament, it was the Crown which won.

Bismarck further weakened his Parliamentary enemies by devising a new constitution. In July 1867, after months of drafting and debate, the constitution came into effect. The North German Confederation which was now created included all of Germany north of the river Main—22 states in all. Its president was the King of Prussia and his chief minister was the Chancellor, through whom he appointed and controlled all other ministers. Bismarck was the Chancellor of the Confederation who exercised great influence over the whole of Germany north of the river Main. The Confederation had a bicameral legislature : a parliament (*Reichstag*) elected by universal suffrage. But its powers were advisory only with no rights of legislative initiative and no effective control over foreign and military policy. The federal council (*Bundesrat*) was composed of delegates sent by the sovereigns of the different states. It could veto laws passed by the *Reichstag*. Prussian preponderance in the *Bundesrat* was ensured by giving her 17 votes out of the total 43, whereas no other state had more than 4 votes.

The creation of the new Confederation was never an end in itself to Bismarck. He had made it clear that 'the north German Bund was only a Provisorium, that his real energies were directed

2. Taylor, A. J. P.: *The Course of German History* (1978), P. 119.

toward the unification of the whole of Germany, and that this objective would be gained in the not too distant future.' The southern states could not join Austria, for she was permanently excluded from Germany; and if they remain alone, their economic and political position would suffer. Slowly, therefore, the sentiment for fusion with the north grew.

Franco-Prussian War

The Prussian victory over Austria and the subsequent establishment of the North German Confederation spurred Bismarck to bring to completion the unification of Germany. In his *Reminiscences* he avows that he entertained this belief as early as 1866: 'That a war with France would succeed the war with Austria lay in the logic of history'; and again 'I did not doubt that a Franco-German War must take place before the construction of a united Germany could be realised.'

'It is France that was beaten at Sadowa' said Marshal Randon. 'What has happened', said Thiers, 'is, for France, the greatest disaster that she has suffered for four hundred years'. King William later said that the war of 1866 was the ruin of France, because 'Napoleon should have attacked us in the rear.'

We cannot but admire the diplomatic skill with which Bismarck directed Prussian policy before the war. He did not want to do anything that would jeopardise the chances of success. He did not want to give the impression that Prussia wanted to change the situation created by the war. An appearance of satisfaction with the gain would have the advantage of reassuring Powers like Britain and Russia, which were disturbed by Prussia's victory. But Bismarck nevertheless wanted to make it appear that France was really responsible for the war. This would not only satisfy the European powers, but it would be a decisive importance in securing the adhesion of South Germany. It was at this point that France made one of her greatest blunders. Frenchmen were aware only that the population in South Germany had a feeling of strong antagonism toward Prussia; they were not aware that the feeling of hatred toward France was much stronger than the antipathy toward Prussia. In diplomatic finesse, Bismarck had no parallel. He knew what he wanted and had made up his mind how it was to be got. Napoleon III was a confused man and the French diplomats appeared as amateurs fighting against a master of fencing.

The French believed that they were entitled to compensation for the attitude of neutrality during the Austro-Prussian War. Early in August 1866, Benedetti, Napoleon's envoy to Berlin, presented Bismarck with a ultimatium. France demanded Mainz and the whole left bank of the Rhine as compensation for the great gains of Prussia. Bismarck demanded that the proposal be put in writing and then summarily rejected the proposal. It was not only a humiliating check for French diplomacy, but also denigrated the country when Bismarck publicised the French proposals through the correspondent of a French Newspaper, *Le Siecle*. The Southern Germans were thus taught to see in Napoleon a false friend and in Prussia the champion of German integrity. Baden, Bavaria and Wurtemberg made secret treaties with Prussia in mid-August by which they assured military cooperation in the event of a Franco-Prussian War.

From this time onward Napoleon III convinced himself that he could not afford to see a united Germany. He parted company with his Foreign Minister, Drouyn de Lhuys, who now regarded German unity as inevitable. Having failed to get compensation on the eastern front, Napoleon III tried his luck on the north. This time it was Luxemburg, a little Grand Duchy which had been conferred by exchange upon the King of Holland in 1815. The country had been a member of the German confederation until 1866 of the Prussian *Zollverein*. It possessed a strong French-speaking element and seemed to Napoleon a sound acquisition. The King of Holland—William III—who was in debt, declared himself willing to sell the Duchy on condition that France undertook to secure the consent of the King of Prussia. Bismarck's initial response was not at all hostile to the scheme. In March 1867, Napoleon III agreed with the King of Holland secretly to buy the grand Duchy outright. But the secret was not kept, and when it leaked out the German press protested strongly against the proposed transfer. The King of Holland took fright and withdrew his offer of sale.

The situation seemed ripe for war. But Bismarck did not desire to push matters to extremes. Napoleon also postponed it. The French Foreign Minister, M. Moustier, put forward the demand that Prussia should evacuate the fortress of Luxemburg. Again the possibility of war lay behind a refusal. But the Powers were working for peace. Queen Victoria wrote to the Prussian King. Russia also used her influence in favour of peace. Therefore, the affair was adjudicated at an international conference in London on May 17, 1867, which made Luxemburg a neutral and demilitarized state under the collective guarantee of the Powers. Prussian garrison was withdrawn. The Luxemburg affair advanced the cause of unity in southern Germany. At the height of the crisis Bismarck received assurances of support from Baden, Hesse-Darmstadt, Bavaria and Wurtemberg. It seemed to him that popular indignation against the French was as lively in the south as it was in the state of the North German Confederation.

After this rude blow, Napoleon's opposition to further Prussian growth hardened. His diplomats renewed their activities at the courts of South German States. Simultaneously, Napoleon tried to curry favour with Francis Joseph of Austria and Victor Emmanuel of Italy. The Austrian and Italian governments assured Napoleon III of their determination—in personal letters, not in formal diplomatic documents—to come to his aid in war. Napoleon placed a pathetic trust in these vague promises. Lord Acton, a contemporary, wrote that 'he made his preparations languidly, like a man in whom pain has extinguished resolution and activity and hopefulness, and he took so much time that he never concluded.'

Napoleon's projected triple alliance was doomed from the start. Even if the Austrian Germans were willing to contemplate a war against Prussia to regain the position lost in 1866, the Hungarians were doggedly opposed to it, for the simple reason that, if successful, it might lead to the loss of the gains secured by the Magyars by the compromise of 1867. The Italians were unwilling to commit themselves to go to war for a government which still denied them the possession of Rome.

Meanwhile, in Prussia, Bismarck had watched the French negotiations and had taken measures to counteract these schemings by making a secret agreement with Russia. In return for promise of Prussian support in event of an Austro-Hungarian threat to south-eastern Europe, the Russian government promised, in March 1868, to keep the Austrians neutral in a Franco-Prussian war by stationing enough troops in Galicia.

This does not mean that Bismarck was planning for war against France. For one thing, he was still uncertain of the attitudes of the South German States. Moreover, he had hopes that the new ministers in France would eventually reconcile themselves to the inevitable German unification. But his hopes were shaken by the French plebiscite of May 1870 which gave the Emperor such a resounding victory as to encourage his intransigence. The French Foreign Ministry was headed by Duc de Gramont (1819-80), who was conspicuous for his dislike of Bismarck. In June 1870 Napoleon III sent Lebrun, a military confidant, to Vienna, who got verbal assurances of military help from Austria. Gramont urged on Napoleon the futility of searching for allies in advance. If there was war with Prussia, he said, other powers would come to the assistance of France. 'It was with this counsellor at his elbow that Napoleon approached the final crisis of his reign.'

An unexpected affair broke out in Spain which threw France and Prussia into a vortex of war. In September 1868 the Spanish Queen Isabella II had been deposed. The Spanish throne was an uneasy seat and proved no attraction to the princes of Europe. Marshal Prim, the head of the Provisional Government in Madrid, offered the vacant throne to Prince Leopold of Hohenzollern, a kinsman of the King of Prussia. It was this candidature which provided the occasion for the Franco-German War. Throughout 1869 Bismarck was not concerned with this affair. When Prim actually offered the throne to Leopold in September 1869 and the latter refused it, Bismarck seemed satisfied with the result. Yet in February 1870, when the offer was renewed, Bismarck seized the occasion to induce Leopold to accept the candidature. On March 9, 1870 Bismarck urged on his reluctant monarch the importance of the strategic reasons for control of Spain. He pointed out that if Leopold did not assume the Crown, it might fall to the Wittelsbach dynasty, which would raise the danger of a future Catholic league against Prussia.

King William's attitude was so negative that, by the beginning of May 1870, Bismarck had almost given up the Spanish enterprise for lost. But a significant change in the political situation in France gave new colour to the whole atmosphere. By a plebiscite held on May 8, 1870, Napoleon's rule was approved overwhelmingly. To Bismarck this meant an end to liberal tendencies in foreign policy and this was borne out almost immediately, when Daru, the Foreign Minister, resigned and was replaced by the Duc de Gramont, a hardliner and an advocate of a military alliance with Austria. It seemed a matter of urgency to Bismarck to discredit the new tendency in French policy before it gathered momentum.

Bismarck and his agents Lothar Bucher and Major von Versen, therefore, begged Leopold to accept the Spanish offer. Leopold gave way and so did the irritated monarch. On June 21, 1870, the fateful telegram announcing Leopold's acceptance went off to Madrid. The remarkable news remained a secret for ten days. But by the beginning of July, when it became known, Gramont delivered an inflammatory speech in the French Assembly on July 6. He openly accused Prussia of threatening the balance of power and intimated plainly that his government was prepared to use force if the Prussian and Spanish Governments did not abandon their project at once. The speech alarmed and excited public opinion and let loose the flood of chauvinism which in the end the French Government was powerless to resist.

The Prussian king William was convinced that there was a genuine danger of a war, which he did not himself want to provoke. William himself suggested to Bismarck that an appeal might be made to the good offices of European powers. But Bismarck firmly rejected this suggestion. Gramont had already appealed to the other Powers. The Tsar disapproved of Leopold's acceptance, but was not inclined to protest at it. Austria did not take my effective measures for the support of either side, but counselled moderation on Gramont. In England, Gladstone's cabinet was so much preoccupied with domestic matters that it declared that the time was not ripe for European intervention but suggested the withdrawal of Prince Leopold in the interests of the peace of Europe. On July 9, Beneditti, the French ambassador to Prussia, talked to the Prussian King at Ems and remonstrated so eloquently that William was coaxed to persuade Leopold withdraw his candidature. On July 12, the Prince of Hohenzollern himself publicly renounced his candidature. William received the news with delight that a wearisome difficulty had been overcome.

'We have got our peace', cried Ollivier, the premier, 'and we will not let it go again'. 'We are satisfied', announced the *Constitutionnel,* an inspired paper, 'It is a great victory which has not cost a tear or a drop of blood.' Political opponents, like old Guizot said that it was the greatest diplomatic trumph he ever remembered. But the French Government was not content with it. Gramont and the French Military Party wanted war; Marshal Leboeuf, Minister of War, assured that the army was at the peak of preparedness. Gramont sent Benedetti back to the Prussian King at Ems on July 13 with request for assurance that the Hohenzollern candidature would never be renewed. William told Benedetti that he regarded the incident as closed; and he later sent word to the ambassador, who was expecting another interview, that he had nothing further to say. Moreover, the ambassador to Paris from the North German Bund, Baron Werther, was persuaded to forward to the Prussian king a draft letter of apology. The king refused firmly to give any such promise. He then had his aide Abeken telegraph a description of the conversation to Bismarck giving the latter authority to reveal the incident to the press.

It was the action of Bismarck which precipitated the war with France. But it was his intention that the French should appear as the aggressor. Bismarck and his two colleagues, Moltke and Roon, were much depressed by the king's conduct of the negotiations. But Bismarck found opportunity in the telegram and he used it cleverly to provoke the French to war. The form in which the Ems dispatch was published was intended by him to be 'a red rag for the Gallic bull' and certainly fulfilled his intention. He deliberately drew up a revised draft of the telegram which made it appear that Benedetti had discourteously pressed an unreasonable demand on William and had been rebuffed impolitely.

The effect of its publication on July 14 in sensational newspapers on both sides of the Rhine was instantaneous. At a council held on July 14, the French Cabinet decided on war, and the next morning a final cabinet met to settle details. Napoleon remarked later with anguish to an English friend : 'France has slipped out of my hand. I cannot rule unless I lead... I have no choice but to advance at the head of a public opinion which I can neither stem nor check.'

War was declared by France virtually on July 15, technically on July 19. Only Thiers and Fevre opposed it. Granville made a last minute appeal to both France and Russia to have recourse to the friendly offices of England. But events had moved too fast in which reason and compromise was impossible. "The immediate origins of the war of 1870 may be traced to short temper and excitement on the part of the peoples and statesmen of both belligerent nations: insensate bellowing for war in both capitals; the recklessness of Gramont, pitted against the calculation of Bismarck; the protracted irresolution of Napoleon III, and the hasty irresolution of William I."[3]

The diplomatic isolation of France was the first to reveal itself. France had counted upon the South German States. But the latter regarded the French demands—that the king of Prussia should pledge himself for all time to forbid the Prince of Hohenzollern's candidature—as insulting. At once Bavaria, Baden, Wurtemberg joined the campaign on the side of Prussia. Then Bismarck published the draft, in the handwriting of Benedetti, of a treaty with Prussia, the object of which was the acquisition of Luxemburg by France. In vain Benedetti protested that the treaty had been thrust on him by Bismarck himself. The English government, therefore, proclaimed its neutrality. Despite personal assurances of support by the Austrian Emperor, Francis Joseph, 'not a cartridge came from Vienna to help the French'. Russian threat to come to the support of Prussia in case Austria should support France, sufficed to keep Austria-Hungary neutral. France requested Italian aid. But the French refusal to evacuate Rome kept Italy neutral.

The superiority of Germany became manifest from the beginning. The German army outnumbered the French by nearly two to one. They also had the advantage of a better supply system as well as a superior staff system and a high command whose war plan had long been in readiness. Thanks to skillful staff planning and rail organisation, German forces were forwarded to the forward zone in 18 days. The French mobilisation broke down owing to lack of their transport and supplies. 'We are in want of everything', telegraphed Bazaine on July 21. Marshal Leboeuf, who had declared that everything was ready, soon lost his optimism and later declared that his troops had often 'no artillery, or baggage, ambulance or magazine.' Their officers were insufficient and the intelligence service poor. The staff was better provided with the maps of Germany they were supposed to invade than those of the French borders, which, as it turned out, they had to defend.

The Germans crossed into Alsace-Lorraine and between August 6 and September 2 the French suffered reverse after reverse. On the former day MacMahon was defeated in the battle of Worth who retreated rapidly towards Chalons, east of Paris. West of Worth, the Germans defeated the French on the same day (August 6) at Forbach and Spichern and drove the army back towards Metz, one of the strongest fortresses in France. The bad news from the frontier had overthrown the Ollivier Ministry, and power was entrusted to Count Palikao, an old soldier with no political experience. It was believed that a retreat on Paris would be fatal to the new Government. Bazaine and the Emperor were persuaded to attempt the defence of Metz. The German army pressed on, endeavouring to prevent Bazaine, now commander of Metz, from retreating and joining MacMahon. This they succeeded in doing in a series of very bloody battles, Borny to the east of Metz, on August 14; Mars-Ia-Tours, to the West, on August 16, and Gravellote, also to the west, on August 18. The result was that Bazaine

3. *The New Cambridge Modern History,* Vol. X: The Zenith of European Power (1830-70), P. 599.

was co-oped up with an army of nearly 200,000 men.

France was now threatened by a terrible catastrophe. MacMahon was at Chalons with a large force. The Emperor had abdicated the command into his hands. MacMahon resolved to retreat to Paris; but it was decided to move the army from Chalons to the relief of Metz. MacMahon got as far as Sedan on August 30 and all hope of reaching Metz disappeared as the Germans had occupied all the bridges. The Germans closed upon him from all sides. They took the offensive on the morning of September 1. There was still one line of retreat open. But MacMahon was wounded in the battle, and the command was taken over by Wimpffen, who was under the delusion of winning a victory. Late in the day, the French army surrendered to the Germans. Napoleon himself was taken prisoner of war. Sedan marked the end of *la grande nation,* dominating Europe, was shattered for ever. The Balance of Power was startlingly altered. Before 1866 the French had counted on a balance between Austria and Prussia in Central Europe; therefore it was they who had been beaten at Sadowa. Similarly, Great Britain and Russia had always counted on a Balance of Power on the Rhine; and it was they—Russia and other more than Great Britain—who were beaten at Sedan.[4]

The stunning German victory did not end the war, but brought down the Napoleonic regime. The Napoleonic dynasty lived on the traditions of military glory and the crowning defeat led to the proclamation of a Republic in Paris. A provisional government took over power, calling itself the Government of National Defence, with General Trochu as President, Jules Favre as Minister of Foreign Affairs and Gambetta the Minister of the Interior. Bismarck demanded Alsace and Lorraine and this demand stirred the depth of French resentment. Now the Franco-German war became the war of nations. Bismarck was also convinced that forbearance would have no political point. 'They did not forgive us for Sadowa,' Bismarck said on September 6, 'and they will be even less forgiving with respect to our present victory, no matter how generous we are when it comes to the peace.'

When the German troops appeared before Paris, Jules Favre met Bismarck at Ferrieres, near Paris, on September 18. The French, he suggested, would pay an indemnity, but could not afford to give up Alsace and Lorraine as the Germans demanded. 'Not an inch of our land, not a stone of our fortresses', he declared. The two men met again later but without any success, and the war went on.

The Germans made no attempt to take Paris by assault, but laid siege of that city on September 19 which lasted to January 28. The Parisians hoped to hold out long enough to enable new armies to be organised. To accomplish this end, Gambetta made his way from Paris to the provinces by balloon, raised an army of 600,000 men, established a branch seat of Government first at Tours, then at Bordeaux. But Gambetta's efforts were unsuccessful. On September 27, Strasbourg fell; on October 29 Bazaine capitulated with his army of 173,000. There was talk of treason. Bazaine was tried and found guilty, but he escaped to Spain. Elesewhere the French suffered reverses. Chanzy was beaten at La Mans. On January 18, 1871, Bourbaki's fine army, which had gone to the relief of Belfort, was driven back into Switzerland. On the same day, in the Hall of Mirrors in the Palace of Versailles, the King of Prussia was proclaimed German Emperor. Ten days later, on January 28, Paris finally capitulated after every scrap of food in the city had been eaten. Jules Favre met Bismarck at Versailles and an armistice was signed on January 28.

Bismarck refused to make peace with the Government of National Defence. In February 1871 elections were held for a National Assembly which elected Adolphe Thiers as chief of the executive power and authorised him to negotiate. The preliminaries of peace, signed at Versailles on February 26, 1871, were confirmed in the Peace of Frankfurt on May 10. France lost Alsace and Lorraine, including Metz and Strasbourg. The ceded land contained useful iron deposits. She undertook to pay an indemnity of five billion franc (200 million pounds sterling)

4. Taylor, A. J. P. : *The Struggle for Mastery of Europe* (1971), P. 210.

within a period of three years, during which period German troops were to remain in occupation of French soil. Meanwhile Bismarck used the occasion to complete the unification of Germany. The southern states of Bavaria, Baden and Wurtemberg were induced to join the German Confederation. 'The Franco-German war made Germany mistress of Europe and Bismarck master of Germany'. The political unification for which Bismarck had waged was at last complete.

There has been considerable disagreement among historians about whether the unification of Germany was due to one coherent plan conceived in the mastermind of Bismarck and then carried out with uncanny insight and clocklike precision. There is one remarkable piece of evidence which supports this view. Shortly before he came to power, Bismarck told Disraeli, at a dinner in London in 1862, about his whole scheme. Disraeli was reported to have remarked: 'What an extraordinary man Bismarck is; He meets me for the first time and he tells me all he is going to do. He will attack Denmark in order to get possession of Schleswig-Holstein; he will put Austria out of the German confederation; and then he will attack France—an extraordinary man'. Be that as it may, Bismarck was a brilliant opportunist, whose course of action always remained undecided and flexible until the last moment. First and foremost a Prussian nationalist as he was, he brought about the unification of Germany to subserve the Prussian interest.

Many years before 1871, the Prussian militarist, Clausewitz, had said that there remained 'only one way for Germany to attain political unity, and that is by the sword : one of the states must bring all others into subjection'. The wars of 1866 and 1870 seemed to prove him right. In many respects it is true that 'Germany was a Prussian conquest won at the expense of Austria and France.' And yet this is not the whole truth. Many factors were responsible for the unification of Germany and it has been said, perhaps with some justification, that 'Germany was practically united before Bismarck began to work at all'. First among these was the fact that Austria was on the defensive, seeking to check Prussia's ambitions, but unwilling herself to shoulder the burdens of German affairs. Secondly, the advent of the Industrial Revolution which began after 1850 were milestones along the road to the Bismarckian Empire of 1871. They enhanced the sense of German unity and greatly favoured Bismarck's policy. The establishment of German unity was inevitable. But for Bismarck the unification of Germany might have taken a radically different course. Hostility towards Prussia and fear of Prussian hegemony had been lively in 1848. But Bismarck, aided by social and economic developments, overcame their hostility after 1866.

It will be of interest to compare Bismarck, the maker of modern Germany, with Cavour, the maker of modern Italy. The comparison reveals striking points of resemblance, and of dissimilarity. Both sought the unification of their respective countries. Both were confronted by the same foe—Austria. In each case, superior statecraft overecame difficulties and achieved surprising success. Here the resemblance ends. The differences between Cavour and Bismarck were twofold. In the first place, Cavour was a liberal who believed in free institutions whereas Bismarck was a reactionary who believed in force. Although Cavour employed force to expel Austria from the Peninsula, the unification of Italy was essentially a popular movement. On the other hand, the German Empire which Bismarck established rested upon the sword. In the second place, Cavour was content to merge Prussia in a German national state. In a sense, Italy absorbed Piedmont, whereas Prussia absorbed Germany. Moreover, German unification posed problems for posterity as Prussia's predominance aroused resentment amount the other members of the union. When Cavour died, his work was substantially complete. Bismarck left behind him problems which seriously threatened the structure which he created.

Significance of the Settlement of 1871

The Settlement of 1871 transformed the balance of power. Germany became united under the auspices of Prussia. Italy also completed her unification for, when France had withdrawn her garrison from Rome, the Italians entered Rome and made it their capital. After the unification of

Italy and Germany the political map of Europe became simple. Six big states now dominated the scene. The Settlement of 1871 inaugurated a period of forty-three years during which there was no war between the major powers. Frontiers were less in dispute than at any time since 1815. But the Ottoman Empire remained the 'sick man of Europe'.

The territorial and political settlement rested primarily on the principle of nationality. But denying the French the possession of Alsace and Lorraine and the Danes of Schleswig violated the principle on which the Settlement of 1871 rested.

The Settlement of 1871 made Germany the new colossus in Europe. It soon made its impact felt throughout the whole continent. The great military power of Germany was ominous for the future. In short, it sowed many of the seeds which were bitterly reaped in the twentieth century.

CHAPTER 19

UNIFICATION OF ITALY

In the fifteenth and sixteenth centuries Italy reached the very heights of civilization and prosperity. The cities of Venice, Florence, Genoa and Rome attracted the whole world as they represented the best of the Italian Renaissance. But a great change was effected in the destiny of Italy by the discovery of America and of the Cape route to India. During the seventeenth century the Atlantic displaced the Mediterranean as the world's highway of commerce and gradually the importance of Italy declined. By the eighteenth century, Venice, Genoa, Florence and Milan, once great commercial centres, were sunk in decay. The history of Italy during the eighteenth century is almost a blank. In truth, there was no 'Italian people', but only various groups, under several governments.

The Napoleonic invasion of Italy awakened the Italian people. Napoleon's regime in Italy lasted from 1796 until 1814. During this period Italy made centuries of progress. The various states were organised as republics. Far-reaching social, political and economic reforms were also introduced. As in Germany, Napoleon's reduction in the number of states encouraged ideas of ultimate unification. The French even gave some encouragement to nationalism. In the Kingdoms of Italy and Naples the use of Italian language was promoted, and appeals were made to national feeling. After the French annexation of Nice and Savoy there were only three units in Italy: the Kingdom of Italy, the Papal States, and the Kingdom of Naples. Murat, the King of Naples, conceived the idea of uniting the whole of Italy under his rule and in 1815 proclaimed the union of Italy. He was defeated and killed, but his dramatic gesture was not forgotten by the Italian patriots.

With Murat, departed the last chance of an Italian solution to the Italian problem. At the Vienna Congress of 1815 Italy was treated as a pawn in the diplomatic game. Austrian influence was reinforced in the peninsula. The Kingdom of Lombardy and Venetia came under Austria which left her in a strong strategical position than ever before. In central Italy—Parma, Modena and Tuscany—princes of Austrian birth ruled. In the centre lay the Papal States which included Romagna, Bologna and Rome. In the south a Bourbon Dynasty governed the two Sicilies—Naples and Sicily. It was only the kingdom of Sardinia, which embraced the northwestern corner of the mainland, Genoa and Piedmont—that remained independent of foreign control. Everywhere there was censorship, popular ignorance and poverty. The strength of Metternich's system in Italy lay in the divisions so carefully maintained which provided safeguards against any concerted nationalist movement of independence. The Papal administration exhibited all the vices of tyranny, while Bourbon rule in Naples was later described by Gladstone as the 'negation of God'. Some elements of English opinion, including the parliamentary Whigs, opposed the treaty of Vienna on the ground that it ignored Italian aspirations. There was no capable leader, for the king of Piedmont and Sardinia was swayed by his intense desire of eliminating French influences than on resisting Austrian.

Despite the presence of Habsburgs and Bourbons in Italy, incipient national feeling was brewing in the country. There were, by 1796, some extreme Freemasons in Italy—whose leader was Filippo Buonarroti—who were the first advocates of an united Italian republic. The part played by Italians in the early Republics—Melzy d'Eril in the Cisalpine and Mario Pagano in the Parthenopian—stimulated liberal and patriotic ideas. In a new generation of dramatists (Alfieri and Niccolini), poets (Ugo Foscolo and Giacome Leopardi), novelists and historians (Alessandro Manzoni) there was a fresh flowering of Italian literature and an awakening sense of national pride. The political cohesion achieved during the Napoleonic period, the memories of the efficiency of French administration, and the liberalism of French legal codes made the people dissatisfied with the reactionary regimes that were restored in most Italian states in 1815. Moreover, the mercantile classes became interested in unification because it promised solid economic advantages. The desire for unity was also strengthened by a growing hatred of Austria, whose armies, based on the four great fortresses of Verona, Mantua, Peschiera and Legnano (the Quadrilateral) not only secured Lombardy and Venetia but dominated the whole peninsula.

Opposition to the foreigner became one of the social and political realities that shaped the outlook of the Risorgimento. The national aspirations drew inspiration from Napoleonic administration, the poetry of Berchet and Foscolo and the schemes of economic improvement of Gioia and Confalonieri. The greatest Italian writer of the age, Manzoni, contributed as powerfully to Italian nationality as any Carbonarist conspirator.

As no institutions existed through which discontent could be expressed, there sprang up secret societies, the *carbonari* or Society of Charcoal Burners, whose members pledged to revolt with signatures written in blood. As Mazzini observed: 'We Italians have neither Parliament, nor hustings, nor liberty of the press, nor liberty of speech, nor possibility of lawful public assemblage, nor a single means of expressing the opinion stirring within us.' The aims of the *Carbonari* were limited monarchy, administrative reform, attack on feudalism and mercantilism.

Inspired by the success of the Spanish uprising of 1820, the people of Naples, led by General Pepe, rose in revolt in July 1820. King Ferdinand I promised a constitution on the Spanish model. The Neapolitan revolution was followed a week later by a Sicilian separatist rising. But the rebels in Sicily were weakened by the rivalry of Palermo and they finally capitulated in September. King Ferdinand had no intention of keeping his word and asked for assistance at Laibach. General Pepe was defeated by an Austrian army which, on March 23, 1821, entered the capital. The revolution failed because of the divisions among the revolutionaries themselves, the distractions of the Sicilian revolt, and the use of the Austrian army against it. The Austrian army remained at Naples until 1827.

Hardly had the rebellion been suppressed when another occurred in Piedmont in 1821. It was not a popular rising as its leaders were officers and members of the court. The king, Victor Emmanuel, being unable to crush the rebellion, abdicated. He was succeeded by his brother Charles Felix who obtained Austria's aid in suppressing the uprising. Again, the overriding force had been Austrian and the revolutionaries had suffered from internal division. Moreover, there was no popular support behind the revolution. Balbo wrote that public opinion was neither for nor against it.

The events in Naples and Piedmont encouraged repression. The severity of the Austrian regime was intensified. The French Revolution of 1830 detonated a train of insurrections in Parma, Modena and the Papal States. The only practical outcome was a brief replacement of several governments. But ultimately the revolutions collapsed owing to the absence of coordinated aims and interests and presence of rivalry among the states. While Francis IV, Duke of Modena, hoped that revolution might be used for enlarging his own dominions, the silk merchant Menotti had visions of national unity based on Rome. Piacenza remained loyal out of rivalry with Parma and Bologna agreed that 'the affairs of Modena are not our concern.' By March 1831 Austrian intervention ruthlessly put down the insurrections. Menotti was executed and many national leaders fled into exile from Modena and Piedmont.

Mazzini: Young Italy

The failure of these risings demonstrated the weakness of the *Carbonari*. Its loose regional organisation and its failure to define its aims found little support among Italians generally. In 1831, a young Genoan, Giuseppe Mazzini (1805-72), founded a new society 'Young Italy'. As a student, Mazzini loved the great works of the romantic writers of Italy, France, Britain and Germany. He claimed that his favourite books were the Bible and Dante, Shakespeare and Byron.'His life is one of the best examples of how close became the affinities between romanticism and revolution.' He declared 'Place youth at the head of the insurgent multitude, you know not the secret of the power hidden in these youthful hearts, nor the magic influence exercised on the masses by the voice of youth. You will find among the young a host of apostles of the new religion.' Young Italy was to be a people's movement dedicated to the establishment of a free, independent, and republican Italian nation.

Mazzini's methods differed from those of the *Carbonari* and of Buonarroti in two main respects. First, he placed less emphasis on subterfuges and secrecy, and more on propaganda. His *Letter to Charles Albert* of 1831 was used for purposes of propaganda. It urged the king to come forward as the leader of Italian movements for freedom. Secondly, he addressed himself not to the educated clases only, but to the people as a whole.

Mazzini had a religious, almost a mystic enthusiasm for his work, for he loved Italy above everything else. Italy had a third life to lead. Once she had dominated the world through Rome; then through the Papacy; and now the Third Italy, the 'Rome of the People' 'radiant, purified by suffering, would move as an angel of the light among the nation'. Mazzini's patriotism was a genuinely cosmopolitan philosophy. As he said in his essay on *The Duties of Man*:

> Humanity is a great army moving to the conquest of unknown lands, against powerful and wary enemies. The peoples are the different corps and divisions of that army.
>
> Italy must, in short, be united so that she could play an effective part in leading the world to a better future.

The noble dream was bound to have only a limited appeal. The rural masses were generally unmoved by it and the middle classes were alienated by the kind of revolution that imperilled the social as well as political structure. The philosophy of Young Italy had its greatest effect upon the radical intelligentsia and the youth. But as years passed by, the futility of the movement became apparent even among these groups.

Nevertheless Mazzini must be regarded as one of the pioneers in forging Italy's national unity. His ceaseless propaganda created a vigorous public opinion in favour of national independence, without which the great plans of unification could not have succeeded. He had all the faith of a prophet and the courage of a crusader. His burning patriotism won thousands of followers. It was the kind of spirit that produced a Garibaldi. Even after his influence had begun to wane, it was strong enough to act as a spur to Cavour. His faith in liberation by popular insurrection had its greatest triumph in southern Italy in 1860. Among the makers of modern Italy, Mazzini holds an imperishable place as he laid the moral foundations of Italian unification. 'Mazzini's impact outside Italy was no doubt greatest after his country had been unified... Not only in England, but in other European countries and also outside Europe, he was regarded as a hero and a prophet... His significance as a symbol, as Italy incarnate, was immense. In his lifetime he was incomparably more effective than Marx.'[1]

The Neo-Guelf Movement

The first step in the movement of revolution came from the neo-Guelf writers, who, in the early 1840s associated Catholicism with the national movement and propagated the idea that the Papacy was the best instrument for uniting the Italian states. Manzoni, Rosmini and Tommasco had began to develop the idea of a liberal Catholicism. The neo-Guelf movement was given new strength by Gioberti by the publication in 1843 of a 700 page volume—*Del Primato morale a civile degli Italiani.* His object was to form a federation of all Italian states under the Papacy, with executive power being wielded by a college of princes. But the great drawback of Gioberti was that he did not offer any programme for freeing Italy from the Austrian. Two books followed quickly after Gioberti's *Primate*: Cesare Balbo's *Delle speranze d'Italia* ('Of the Aspirations of Italy') of 1844; and Massimo D'Azeglio's *Degli ultimi casi di Romagna* ('Of Recent Events in the Romagna') of 1846. Both were anti-revolutionary and displayed no faith in the ideal of unification. Unlike Gioberti, Balbo desired to displace the Austrians. He also advocated a customs union of Italian states.

In June 1846 Cardinal Mastai Ferritti became Pope Pius IX. For the next two years he became the centre of the hopes of the liberals of Europe. He issued political amnesties, allowed exiles to come back to Rome in freedom, granted limited freedom of speech, and the press. A Council of Ministers was appointed to discuss the action of the Papal Government. The Jews were released from their restrictions at Rome. A municipal council was established in Rome. Liberalism raised its head all over Italy. Everywhere in Sicily, in Naples, in Tuscany, in Parma, in Milan, in Venice, in Savoy the Pope was applauded. Mazzini approved of what the Pope had done: 'because it will shorten the way, and spare us dangers, bloodshed, and disasters, and because Italy will be at one stroke placed at the head of European progress'.

Metternich was much alarmed, as he saw Pius unwittingly raise up a monster which might prove uncontrollable. 'We were prepared for

1. Beales Derek: *The Risorgimento and the unification of Italy* (1971), PP. 56-7.

everything', said Metternich, 'except for a Liberal Pope, now we have got one, there is no answering for anything'. The Pope was no less alarmed by the consequences of his action. 'With the best intentions he struck a match to light a candle, and discovered to his horror that he was in a powder magazine.'

The year 1847 saw the sovereigns in Italy lying low owing to economic distress caused by bad harvest of 1846. The people became consicous of their power, and the revolution had effectively begun. In January 1848 occurred the tobacco riots in Milan as the people refused to smoke tobacco because it was a source of government revenue. Then a revolution broke out in Sicily in January 1848. Unrest then spread to Naples and Ferdinand II, King of Naples and Sicily, granted a constitution to his Kingdom. This abject surrender forced the hand of Leopold of Tuscany, Charles Albert of Sardinia and even Pius IX to concede more or less liberal constitutions.

Revolution of 1848 and its Impact on Italy

The news of the February Revolution of 1848 in France and the consequent fall of Metternich in Austria in March released serious revolutionary forces in Italy. The Habsburg Empire appeared after all but a house of cards which would turn asunder at the slightest touch of organised resistance.

Milan rose in revolt and, after five days of hard fighting, March 17-22, compelled the Austrian forces under Radetzky to evacuate the city. Venice immediately followed suit. Daniel Manin assumed the leadership of the movement, drove the Austrian garrison from the city and declared an independent republic. By the end of March, Parma, Modena, Lombardy had risen in revolt.

War was inevitable, but to wage war against the resourceful Austria seemed desperate by the weak Italian states. Everything now depended on Charles Albert, King of Sardinia, who happened to be the only prince who wanted to fight Austria. Reluctantly he assumed responsibility for the conduct of the war. All Italy flocked to his banner. The Piedmontese won the victory of Goito over the Austrian General Radetzky, but they failed to dislodge the Austrians from the famous Quadrilateral (Verona, Peschiera, Legnago and Mantua) which enabled them to receive reinforcements from their own country.

The impulse to unity proved to be short-lived. The Pope, Pius IX, torn by conflicting sentiments, as a Catholic Pontiff, declared in April 1848 his opposition to war with Catholic Austria. The announcement meant that the dream which had inspired Gioberti's *Primato* had collapsed. The King of Naples also overthrew the constitution and recalled his forces from the front. Moreover, there was no real union among the Italian states. The presence of strong local feeling in Milan, in Venice, in the Duchies of the Centre, in Naples and Sicily and the strife between the republicans and the royalists impeded the nationalist struggle of the Italians. Moreover, Charles Albert was as frightened of the radicals as of Austria. He refused Garibaldi's offer of cooperation. Many of the Lombards were suspicious of Piedmont and preferred rather the perpetuation of Austrian rule. Cattaneo denounced Charles Albert and added 'I should prefer the Austrians to recapture Milan than see a traitor in command of Lombardy'.

Apart from these, Charles Albert was a poor commander who dismally failed to mobilise the military resources and depended on officers, who did not know the basic principles of army discipline. His chronic indecision, pre-Napoleonic ideas of generalship, and initial slowness of advance gave the Austrians enough time for consolidation. On July 25, 1848, the Piedmontese were defeated at Custozza. After the capitulation of Milan, Charles Albert was forced to conclude the Salasco Armistice which restored to Austria his territorial possessions in upper Italy. Charles Albert was accused of having betrayed the national cause when he failed to defend Milan.

The withdrawal of Charles Albert from the national struggle did not mean the total collapse of the Italian movement; rather it stimulated a radical republican movement which grew rapidly during the summer months. By autumn, disorders were so great that the Pope was unable to control them. Many of the soldiers of the defeated armies flocked to Rome to take up the fight there. On November 15, 1848, the Pope's Chief Minister, Pellegrino Rossi, was stabbed to death. On November 24, Pius IX fled from Vatican to Gaeta, in the Kingdom of Naples.

With both Piedment and the Papacy losing the leadership for an anti-Austrian movement, initiative was seized by the republicans—by Mazzini in Rome and Daniel Manin in Venice. Mazzini proclaimed that now the war of kings was over; the war of the people must begin. Since June 1848 he had been joined by Garibaldi, whose red-shirted volunteers were trained in guerilla warfare. In its dying phase, the Italian revolutionary movement hinged upon the three pivots of Florence, Rome and Turin, with the independent island republic of Venice, under Manin, as peripheral centre. In February 1849, a Constituent Assembly met at Rome, proclaimed Rome a republic and called Mazzini to head its new government. The opposition of the Pope persuaded Tuscany not to unite with Rome as one Republic. Even Gioberti, now premier of Piedmont, refused to send representatives to the Assembly in Rome as opinion in Piedment was against a republicanism imposed on Italy from Rome. But it favoured the renewal of war with Austria and Charles Albert recklessly plunged once more into war. This time his defeat at Novara (March 23, 1849) being more disastrous, he abdicated in favour of his son, Victor Emmanuel, who became King. Charles Albert retired to Portugal and died there a few months later.

Only Rome and Venice held out faint hopes of struggle for liberation. Mazzini and Garibaldi challenged the power of Austria and of the Papcy. But the expulsion of the Pope aroused the whole of the Catholic world. To offset Austrian intervention in support of the Pope, France sent General Oudinot with ten thousand troops who landed in April at Civita Vecchia as the gateway to Rome. The French commander was sharply checked on his first advance but, strengthened by fresh reinforcements, he again advanced. The desperate and the heroic defence of the city for a month became an epic in the story of Italian nationhood. On June 30, 1849, Rome fell into the hands of the French and the cardinals and the Pope returned with the support of the French bayonets. Garibaldi left the city and appealed for volunteers to follow him. He tried to stir the nationalist sentiment in these ringing words : 'I offer neither pay nor quarters not provisions; I offer hunger, thirst, forced marches, battles and death. Let him who loves his country in his heart and not with his lips only follow me.'

Sicily had been overrun by King 'Bomba's' Swiss mercenaries in May; and when Manin's Venetian Republic collapsed in August, the struggle for Italian independence was over. The Peninsula again came under foreign occupation, Austria and the French remaining in Rome. The failure of the first phase of the nationalist movement was due in part to confusion of aims, in part to lack of coordinated efforts, but, above all, to lack of sound leadership. Mazzini could inspire and Garibaldi could fight. But they had not the ability to galvanise the latent forces of nationalism to constructive purpose. Thus, the revolutions of 1848 had a mainly negative influence for the unification of Italy. The most important single lesson to be derived from their failure was that the national movement could make little headway against reactionary forces in the international situation. 'It was only when the Austrian cat was distracted that the Italian mice could play.' Disillusioned politicians had to admit that the making of Italy demanded the active intervention of some other European states. Italy could not achieve her independence with her own efforts alone. The only hope was Piedmont whose last desperate attempt at Novara had restored her prestige.

But the efforts of 1848-9 were destined to have profound significance. Italy became conscious of her nationalism and the stirrings of socialism found expression in Carlo Pisacane, the first Italian socialist.

Cavour's Policy and Unification

Of all the established regimes in Italy, Piedmont had been the only one to fight wholeheartedly for freedom. The new ruler, Victor Emmanuel II, though lacking conspicuous political talent of his own, possessed a strategic shrewdness that served Italy well. With wise moderation, the King chose D' Azeglio of the right centre as premier. D' Azeglio, during his ministry of 1849-52 did much to restore confidence in the monarchy. One of his principal measures concerned the Piedmonese Church. In 1850, the Siccardi laws abolished ecclesiastical jurisdiction and forbade the Church from acquiring land without permission.

D' Azeglio was supported in his policy by Count Cavour, who joined the ministry in 1850. An extraordinarily farsighted statesman, an indefatigable worker, a daring opportunist, he was the man whom the Risorgimento needed. As a young man he had travelled widely in England, France, and Switzerland and became as enthusiastic admirer of parliamentary system of government and western methods of agriculture and industry. 'Parliamentary Government, like other governments', he once declared, 'has its inconveniences; yet, with its inconveniences, it is better than all the others'. The use of military force to suppress opposition was as repugnant to Cavour as was absolutism. Early in life, he was instrumental in founding the *Risorgimento,* a newspaper devoted to the cause of Italian unity.

Cavour was a nationalist to the core, whose greatest ambition was to increase the material and political strength of his country. After 1848, he was convinced that popular insurrection would be of little help in achieving Italian unity. Mazzini he regarded as a fanatic. Italy could achieve unity only by expelling the Austrians from northern Italy and absorbing Lombardy and Venetia. This was a difficult task and could not be achieved by Italians alone. The aid of a foreign power was considered essential.

In October 1850 Cavour joined the ministry of Piedmont as Minister of Agriculture, Commerce and Marine. Being a convinced free trader and with the loyal support of a growing middle class, Cavour negotiated commecial treaties with England, France and Austria and won the friendship of England. As Minister of Finance, which he also became, he raised capital by an internal loan, and an external loan from England. He spent a great deal on the navy and especially on improving the port of La Spezia. He also took keen interest in railway building so that by 1860 Piedmont, with 800 kilometres of the track, had a third of the tally for whole Italy. Piedmont's trade trebled during the fifties and her industries flourished.

Owing to D' Azeglio's indisposition, Cavour soon became leader of the house. D'Azeglio was an amateur in politics and an artist by profession. Cavour was a finer politician who could appreciate that honesty was not always the best policy. In February 1852. Cavour made an alliance or *connubio* with Rattazzi and the left centre, leaving D'Azeglio isolated. In November 1852, D'Azelio finally resigned, when the King refused to approve his bill for introducing civil marriage. When Cavour became Prime Minister in November 1852, his just task was to improve railways, roads and ports, expand her commerce and strengthen her finances. One of his first tasks had been the dissolution of the monasteries. To carry out these reforms in his eight years as Prime Minister, Cavour had to overcome opposition from the King and from the Senate as well as considerable unpopularity among the common people for heavy burden of taxes. Sometimes he used devious means to overcome opposition. Often he overrode his cabinet, bribed the press at home and abroad and set the tradition of taking action first and then asking parliament for ratification. To him a liberal end justified illiberal means. And yet he never tried to abolish Parliament, but rather preferred to disarm opposition peacably wherever possible.

With the vision of a true statesman, Cavour set himself to secure for Piedmont the active sympathy and cooperation of some great European powers and finally to take up arms against Austria. The diplomatic web—which he wove round Austria and finally outwitted her—was a master-stroke of statecraft. In 1853, Cavour made a dignified protest when Austria sequestrated the possessions of Lombards living in Piedmont. It was approved by England and France and revealed Piedmont as the champion of oppressed Italians. The real turning point came in 1855 when Cavour intervened in the Crimean War by fighting on the side of Britain and France. This decision enhanced the prestige of the Sardinian monarchy and earned the gratitude of the British and French Governments. At the same time it completed the isolation of Austria which estranged the Western Powers by her refusal to enter the war.

The Sardinian soldiers consisting of 17,000 men went to the Crimea, fought at the Battle of Techernaya with distinguished success. "Out of this mud" (the mud of the Sabastopol trenches), said a Sardinian soldier, 'Italy will be made.' Cavour's gamble bore fruit: Sardinia was allowed to participate at the Congress of Paris (1856). Here Cavour denounced the evils of Austrian oppression in Italy and gave it a publicity which at the time was particularly valuable. Cavour was supported by Clarendon, the British Foreign Minister. He won the sympathy of the French Emperor, Napoleon III, who exhibited his restless impetuosity to embark on foreign adventures in order to gain fresh prestige for his regime. Thus the Congress of Paris was for Cavour a big success. He had been able to focus the attention of the Western Powers on the conditions of Italy and to secure the sympathy of Napoleon III.

Cavour had to proceed warily. He was advised by Britain and France not to force the pace in Italy by any irresponsible action. The 1857 elections doubled the clerical opposition. But Cavour was able to find a pretext for annulling some of the opposition elections. He also forced the resignation of the anticlerical Rattazzi, Minister of the Interior, who had been implicated with Mazzini in 1856 over a rising in Lunigiana. The *connubio* thus ended in divorce, and Cavour decided to convince Louis Napoleon that Piedmont was a safe bulwark against revolution. Mazzini, therefore, was condemned to death.

To maintain Piedmont's ascendancy in the national movement, Cavour followed a deliberately anti-Austrian policy. Simultaneously, he gave secret support to the National Society, an organisation founded in 1856 by Daniel Manin, Giorgio Pallavicino and the Sicilian La Farine, the object of which was to unite different parties for making Victor Emmanuel King of Italy. For foreign support, Cavour turned back to Paris, where Napoleon III's sympathy with the doctrine of nationality, drew him to the side of Cavour. Napoleon III had taken part in the revolution of 1831 in the Romagna, as a sort of Carbonari. But it needed all Cavour's astuteness to turn the situation in his favour.

Things did not augur well when in January 1858 an attempt on Napoleon's life was made by an Italian, Orsini. He was unhurt but many others were killed or wounded. The plotters had been the supporters of Mazzini, though the latter was not in any way involved in the plot. As French support was essential, Cavour prosecuted the revolutionary party, expelled the suspected agitator and suppressed Mazzini's paper *Italia del Popolo*. These measures assuaged Napoleon's sentiment which got some fillip when Orsini from his prison made a pathetic appeal to him to free Italy. Henceforth the scheme matured in secret negotiations between Napoleon and Cavour.

The Plombieres Agreement

At last in July 1858 Napoleon took a decisive step by summoning Cavour to meet him secretly at Plombieres in the Vosges. 'The drama', Cavour wrote to a friend, 'approaches its crisis'. He met the Emperor on July 21-22 and the details were now worked out without great difficulty. France promised to support Sardinia in a war with Austria on condition that Cavour provided a justifiable pretext. In the event of victory, Piedmont would be allowed to annex Lombardy and Venetia, Parma and Modena, and part of the papal states. But Italy as a whole should be formed into a confederation under the presidency of the Pope, As reward for her service, France was to get Savoy (the original home of the Sardinian dynasty) and Nice (the birthplace of Garibaldi) which would give her natural boundaries in the south-east. The bargain would be sealed by the marriage of Victor Emmanuel's fifteen year old daughter Clotilde to Napoleon's cousin, Prince Jerome, a libertine of thirty-seven years. Though the pact was only oral, Cavour was confident that Napoleon would keep it. 'With this bargain, no easy one for his royal master to digest, but with the comfortable knowledge that the French Emperor was henceforth his accomplice, Cavour returned to Turin to work for war'.

The first step in fulfilling the pact of Plombieres was the announcement in mid-September 1858 that the marriage between Clotilde and Jerome was to take place. In January 1859 the pact was embodied in a formal treaty between the two Governments. Cavour meanwhile applied himself to make Austria declare war and give his ally an excuse for intervention. At the end of 1858 Austria had imposed military conscriptions upon Lombardy and Venetia, which proved to be so unpopular that hundreds of persons fled to Piedmont. Austrian demands for their extradition and Piedmontese refusals to comply led to mutual recrimination and mounting tension. This gave Cavour an excuse for military preparations.

By the beginning of 1859 it seemed that a crisis was impending. On the New Year's Day Napoloen told the Austrian ambassador that he regretted that his relation with Austria were not so good as they had been. This utterance created a profound impression. A few days later Victor Emmanuel spoke provocatively to parliament to 'the cry of pain which rises towards us from so many parts of Italy.' In February 1859 Napoleon issued a brochure—*The Emperor Napoleon and Italy*—in which he defended the principle of nationality and the idea of a federated Italy. A war of intervention was not suggested, but it was, in effect, an attack on the Vienna Settlement. The pamphlet produced a sensation and it appeared that there seemed little eagerness for war even in France. Britain and Russia tried to settle the Italian question that Italy should not be united if it had to be accomplished with French backing. In March and April 1859 it appeared that Napoleon III might have to withdraw from the Plombieres engagement owing to international pressure exerted upon him. Even on April 18, the French Emperor asked Cavour to consider the question of demobilisation. Things looked ominous for Cavour and the latter said in anguish 'Nothing remains for me but to put a bullet through my head.' Cavour was actually on the point of yielding. But events played into his hands when Austrian Chief Minister Buol-Schauenstein despatched to Turin an ultimatum demanding disarmament within three days. Austria provided the *casus belli* and the French troops marched again under a Bonaparte into the plains of Italy.

The War of 1859 and the Armistice of Villafranca

The War of Independence began in April 1859 and lasted less than three months. The Italian campaign of Austria is chiefly to be remembered as a catalogue of mistakes. Although the Austrians possessed able commanders, like Benedek, and competent strategists, like Hess, they lacked adequate supply and suffered from difficulties in communication owing to absence of railways. The choice for supreme command in Italy fell on Count Gyulai against his wishes. The French were no less slack as Napoleon III's schemes were far from settled when he took up the campaign. Yet since the Austrians were even less efficient than the French, everything succeeded with the army of invasion. On June 4, the Austrians were defeated at Magenta and driven from the plains of Lombardy. The Austrians retreated towards the 'Quadrilateral', but were again defeated at Solferino, just to the south of Lake Garda, on June 24. It was a protracted encounter in which the Italians gained a complete victory after sustaining heavy losses. But it was not a overwhelming blow as to decide the future course of war. The Austrian forces were still intact and further wars would be necessary if Napoleon was to free Italy from 'Alps to the Adriatic.'

Determined action on the part of Napoleon III might have achieved liberation of Italy from the Austrians. The effects of Magenta and Solferino on the Italians were electrical. The rulers of Modena, Parma, Tuscany and Romagna were driven from their possessions and Central Italy was prepared to join Sardinia. But at the height of success, as Mazzini had accurately foretold, Napoleon suddenly concluded an armistice with the Austrian Emperor, Francis Joseph at Villafranca, on July 11, 1859. The terms agreed upon provided for the transfer of Lombardy to Piedmont and the reinstatement of the rulers of Parma, Modena and Tuscany. An Italian federation would be established under the nominal presidency of the Pope in which Austria, by virtue of her retention of Venetia, would be member.

The reasons for Napoleon's abrupt withdrawal from the war were various. Shaken by the heavy losses at Solferino, the French Emperor found that the war was not popular at home, especially among the Catholics as it seemed to endanger the Pope. Moreover, Napoleon III feared that Prussia might enter the war at any moment in support of Austria in order to stop the extension of the French frontier on the Rhine. Napoleon had wanted an enlarged Sardinia as a convenient buffer state against Austria; he had never contemplated the political unity of the whole peninsula. He had discovered that Cavour, instead of working for a separate Kingdom of Central Italy as agreed at Plombieres, had tried to annex the duchies to Piedmont. Napoleon, therefore, felt justified in deserting his ally and he dropped the French claim to Nice and Savoy.

The Treaty of Villafranca came as a bolt out of the blue to Cavour, who resigned in disgust. 'Nothing can come of this Peace', he said, 'I will turn conspirator and revolutionary, but this treaty shall not be carried out'. The courtly Rattazzi took office with an interim ministry.

The episode which followed was one of spontaneous outbursts of national feeling which defied all calculations. After inflaming the force of nationalism to a high pitch of expectations, it was impossible to turn the clock back. The nationalist groups of Central Italy which had expelled petty rulers could not now afford to stop 'to allow 1859 to become a mere repetition of 1849'. In August constituent assemblies met in Parma, Modena, Tuscany and the Romagna and voted in favour of union with Piedmont. Officially, Victor Emmanuel could only express sympathy, but he could not accept them. By the Treaty of Zurich in November 1859, Austria ceded Lombardy to Sardinia and it was agreed that the petty sovereigns who had been dethroned should be restored. It was proposed to refer the final organisation of Italy to a congress which was forestalled by the settlement which Italy made for herself.

Central Italy refused to accept the decision that the rulers of Parma, Tuscany, Modena and the Romagna should be restored. Italy was helped by the warm sympathy of Great Britain as well as by the helpful attitude of the French Emperor. In January 1860 the British Government made it known that it favoured 'freedom from foreign interference by force of arms in the internal concerns of the people of Italy.' Napoleon also would allow no coercion on the part of Austria. The return of Cavour to power in January 1860 facilitated a solution of the problem. By direct secret negotiations with Napoleon, Cavour offered Nice and Savoy if the former would allow the annexation of Central Italy. In March 1860 plebiscites in the four areas of Central Italy were held which declared for union with the Kingdom of Piedmont. By the same expedient of a popular vote, Nice and Savoy passed into the possession of France. The Kingdom of Sardinia now included almost half the population of Italy. But the acquisition off Nice and Savoy by Napoleon III alienated the patriotic Italians and forfeited the friendship of Great Britain. Queen Victoria complained that England had been made a dupe. Even the so-called trade treaty with Cobden did not mitigate the unfavourable impression which the seizure of Nice and Savoy imprinted on the English mind.

Cavour had no plans for unifying Italy but hoped to consolidate his position in the north. Cavour had no faith in conspiracy as it was not to be viewed favourably either in Paris or in London. Moreover the situation in the south was so different from the north, in racial composition and social texture, that Cavour thought it wise not to assume the responsibility right now. But it was not possible for Cavour to direct the course of events. The success of the revolutionary movement in the north and central Italy stimulated the conspirators in the south.

Once again, Sicily proved to be the focal point. Crispi, a subtle republican conspirator, was stirring Sicily to rebel against its Bourbon king. But he needed a soldier who could fan conspiracy into rebellion and he found it in the person of Garibaldi. He could not forgive Cavour for bartering away his home town of Nice to France. After being twice expelled from Piedmont, Garibaldi had become a brilliant guerilla leader in his South American exile. He had returned in the hour of crisis, but in 1848 and 1859 he had been given a poor share in the war of independence. He had not anticipated the triumph of Italian Unity in a form that Cavour had wrought and he declared: 'I shall have no more joy in Italy; the country with its contempt for all ideals has killed the soul within me...' Though temperamental, Garibaldi was a honest, simple-minded egoist, a dauntless warrior and a loyal spirit. Garibaldi was a superb general for the sort of warfare involved. He was brilliant at sizing up the local situation, and his personality cast an extraordinary spell over his troops. When he was invited by the insurgents at Sicily to come to their aid Garibaldi readily assumed the leadership. In May 1860, with a tiny force of 1,000 red-shirted volunteers, he landed at Marsala, stormed Calatafimi, fought his way into Palermo, and at the end of three months cleared the island of royal troops. Cavour was not all sympathetic to Garibaldi's precipitate tactics. He was reported to have observed to the French ambassador: 'If the insurrection (in Sicily) is put down, we shall say nothing, if it is victorious, we shall intervene in the name of order and authority'.

Having taken Sicily, Garibaldi crossed the Strait of Messina on August 18 and in a few days became master of Naples. The Bourbon King Francis II did not even defend the capital, but fled to Gaeta. To have conquered a country of eleven million people in less than five months was a remarkable achievement. But it was Garibaldi's dream to free all Italy. He remembered his own defeat in the Holy City in 1849 and he began to plan an invasion of the Papal Marches.

Cavour was aware of Garibaldi's military preparations and the latter's intention to march on to Rome. This would mean war with France and with the whole of Catholic Europe; this might entail a further conflict with Austria. Cavour also feared that the nationalist movement in the south might abandon Piedmontese leadership and turn republican. There was a strong party who wanted to give to Naples and Sicily some independent standing in a free Italy. 'Cavour was blinded by his rigid hostility towards the radicals. He saw in them only the social peril, and was convinced that anarchy must follow their victory. His primary object was that Garibaldi should fail; only in the second place did he want Italy to be united.'[2] It was a serious crisis and could only be surmounted by Victor Emmanuel's taking an open part in the drama. Cavour turned to his old ally, Napoleon III, and after assuring him that the position of Rome itself would remain unaffected, sent the Piedmontese army to invade the Marches. On September 18, 1860, they defeated the Papal army at Castelfidardo, conquered Umbria and the Marches from the Pope to 'save them from the revolution'. The victorious forces then crossed into the state of Naples, defeated the Neopolitans at Capua, and bottled up the Bourbon forces in the fortress of Gaeta. Meanwhile, Garibaldi had also been involved in a series of dogged engagements with a large Neopolitan force. With his Red Shirts, he could carry the open country; he was helpless against an army in prepared position. Even before the military issue had been decided, plebiscites were held in October in Naples, Sicily, the Marches, and Umbria—which voted overwhelmingly in favour of union with Piedmont. In the face of this, Gaibaldi surrendered his conquests to Victor Emmanuel and, with a sublime simplicity, set sail for his island home on Caprera.

In February 1861, the first all Italian parliament met in Turin, repesenting the whole of the peninsula except Rome and Venetia, and Victor Emmanuel II was declared king of Italy. Cavour did not live long to see the completion of his dream. On June 6, 1861, he died at the age of fifty-one, after displaying uncommon political gift and political adroitness of the highest order. It was an extraordinary achievement on his part to achieve Italian unification but his contribution to the territorial and administrative cohesion of Italy seems somewhat less impressive. He showed scant respect for the wishes or the traditional usages of the southern provinces, preferring to impose a highly centralised administrative system on the country as a whole. He treated the Kingdom of Naples almost as if it were an African colony. As a result, there were frequent agitations which led to open brushes between Piedmontese troops and peasant bands. He had done little to mitigate the sufferings of the land-hungry peasant or the poor. 'Cavour always suspected Garibaldi; Garibaldi never suspected Cavour ... of course, Garibaldi disliked Cavour and resented his cession of Nice to Napoleon III ... Garibaldi put Italy first. Cavour put himself first. Therefore, Cavour was bound to win in the end, despite the great

2. Taylor, A. J. P.: Cavour and Garibaldi in *Europe: Grandeur and Decline* (1977), P. 84.

advantages which Garibaldi accumulated in Sicily and Naples'.[3]

The acquisition of Venetia and Rome from the hands of Austrians and the French, respectively, depended upon the expedients of diplomacy. The Italian Government took advantage of the growing friction between Prussia and Austria and concluded with the former a secret offensive and defensive alliance in April 1866. The Italians, however, despite their superior numbers, were defeated at Custozza again, and on sea at Lissa. The prize of Venetia was won on the field of Sadowa when the Austrians surrendered to their German rival.

Rome proved to be a more difficult problem. Most Italians regarded the unification incomplete as long as the city remained independent. Pope Pius IX refused to make any compromise with the new Italy. Napoleon III contended that the Papal States should be sensibly reduced, the Pope should retain Rome and the Roman Patrimony. In exchange for the temporal power Cavour offered to the Church complete spiritual independence, but he died in 1861. On two occasions, in August 1862 and in November 1867, Garibaldi, with his ill-equipped bands, tried to reach the Holy City. In the first attempt he was turned back by the Piedmontese and in the second he was defeated by the French while the royal army of Italy looked on in helpless neutrality. Finally, in 1870, the unexpected victory of Prussia over France brought a withdrawal of the French garrison and the Italians marched into Rome. With the acquisition of Rome, the Risorgimento seemed to be complete. Rome became the capital of the new Italian Kingdom, while the Pope, withdrawing behind the walls of the Vatican, continued his sullen opposition to the new regime.

Italy could not have been made one but for the help of France and Prussia and the moral support of England. 'France and her ruler paid more than lip-service to the nationalist theories inherited from Napoleon I. Britain... consistently upheld the Italians' right of self-determination. Even Prussia may have been actuated by the motive Cavour himself recommended to her, a readiness to see Piedmont and nationalism triumph in Italy as a precedent for a Prussian unification of Germany.'[4] During the first decade of the Kingdom, a remarkable body of conscientious statesmen stood round Victor Emmanuel II. Italy remembers with gratitude the names of Ricasoli and La Marmora, of Lauza and Sella, of Minghetti and Spaventa, who shouldered the heavy responsibility in the initial stage. In 1876 power passed from the right to the left and the foundations of the new Italy had been soundly laid. Despite strong separatist tendencies, there were unmistakable considerations of economic convenience which forced them together and bound them to a common yoke.

3. Taylor, A. J. P.: Cavour and Garibaldi in *Europe: Grandeur and Decline* (1977), P. 85.
4. Beales Derek: *The Risorgimento and the Unification of Italy* (1971), P. 91.

CHAPTER 20

REACTION AND REFORM IN RUSSIA

The size of Russia was so great that she constituted a separate continent wedged in between Europe and Asia. The Russian empire in 1815 stretched from Poland and Finland in the west to Siberia and the banks of the Amur in the Far East, and from the Arctic Ocean in the north to the shore of the Black, Caspian and Arab Seas in the south. Her population stood at about fourteen million in 1725, at the turn of the nineteenth century it had increased to forty million; on the eve of the 1848 revolution, it was close to seventy million.

Compared to other European nations, Russia was politically backward. During the thirteenth century, Russia was in part semi-barbaric, in part feudal; during the sixteenth and seventeenth centuries, when western Europe had passed from feudalism to national monarchy, Russia was in part feudal, in part monarchical; during the eighteenth and nineteenth centuries when western Europe was struggling for constitutional governments, Russia was a thoroughly absolute state.

The reasons for Russia's backwardness were that she had never been a part of the ancient Roman Empire, hence it did not receive advantages of the classical civilization. Secondly, Russia was outside the pale of the Catholic civilization of the Middle Ages. Thirdly, the semi-barbarous Tartars who conquered the country early in the thirteenth century and ruled for almost three centuries kept the country in utter backwardness. Having no sea coast and cut off from western Europe, Russia missed the enlightenment and stimulus of the Renaissance.

In 1800, ninety per cent of the population lived on agriculture, and well over half this percentage were serfs attached to the lands and owned by individual nobles. Most of the rest were so-called state peasants attached to public or imperial family domains. Besides the peasants there were about a million and half urban workers and dependants living in towns and some quarter of a million merchants and industrialists. Hereditary nobility counted at half a million in the first decade of the nineteenth century, the officials including life nobles amounting to a quarter of a million, the clergy half a million, and the armed forces with their dependants at well over a million.

The Russian economy was primarily agricultural. A thriving export trade was conducted through the Baltic ports; but it was discouraged by the high protective tariffs maintained by the government. As for industry, there were 5,261 manufacturing enterprises in 1825, with a total of 210,000 workers; but machinery was virtually unknown even in the most important firms.

The institution of serfdom dates from the middle of the sixteenth entury. By the turn of the next century the serfs became bound to the lords whose lands they occupied. Russian serfs were hardly indistinguishable from slaves. It has been observed that the Negroes of the American plantations were happier than the Russian private serfs. The serf had no right of redress against his master, who could deport him to Siberia, conscript him as a recruit for 25 years of military service, or put him up for public sale. Despite Catherine II's declaration in her instruction of 1765 that 'one must avoid making men slaves unless it is absolutely necessry for reasons of state', serfdom became a recognised institution. In sharp contrast to the Russian serf it is worthwhile to consider the humane precept laid down by Bracton for English serfs six hundred years before the Russian Edict of Emancipation (1861).

The great English jurist wrote, 'Serfs have a personal right of action in court against all persons for injuries done to themselves'. Serfdom hung like a deadweight over Russian society in the first half of the nineteenth century. If the institution was the mainstay of the Russian agriculture, it was to the Government the main agency for recruits in the army and for labour in industries.

There was no hereditary hierarchy among the Russian nobility. Place dependend almost wholly and promotion partly, upon social connections with the court. The greater offices went to generals and state servants of long-standing, lesser ones to members of rich cosmopolitan families. Local nobility exercised no power in the capital cities, St. Petersburg and Moscow, and even in the countryside was subordinate to the Governor. At the top the nobility were completely westernised and French had become an alternative official language. Noble privileges could also be withdrawn. Emperor Paul demoted a few hundred and a number of them received corporal punishment. Even a short while after the assassination of Paul I, a contemporary could write: 'I find in Russia only two estates, the slaves of the landlords and the slaves of the Emperor'.

The French Revolution influenced the two Russian men of letters—Novikov and Radishchev. One of Novikov's offences was his connection with Freemasonry, the latter being associated with non-conformist religiosity and hidden sympathy for revolution and cosmopolitanism. In 1792 he was sentenced to fifteen years' imprisonment by Catherine II but it was annulled by her successor, Paul. Radishchev, who received Werstern education and imbibed the egalitarian and republican ideas of some *philosophes* of the left, published in 1790 the *Journey from St. Petersburg to Moscow* which was to become a classic of Russian literature as well as social history. The *Journey* is a tirade against miserable conditions in the countryside, the agony of serfdom and the vices of the nobility and of the government. He was sentenced to Siberian exile whence Paul recalled him in the same way as Novikov.

When Catherine died in 1796 she left a heritage of priceless territorial acquisitions. If it can be said that Peter the Great made Russia a European power, it can be maintained with equal justice that Catherine the Great made Russia a great power. The Russian achievements in the Swedish and Turkish wars and the final liquidation of Poland were rightly identified with the personality of Catherine II. She was *Felitsiya,* the Russian equivalent of Glorina, immortalised in an ode by Derzhavin, the foremost Russian poet before Pushkin and a future minister of justice. Catherine died in November 1796 and was succeeded by Paul (1796-1801).

At first Paul showed some talent as a ruler. He activated the Senate as a court of appeal so that it settled 11,000 outstanding cases in the first year of his reign. He introduced regularity in the payment of troops. Though he prohibited week-work on Sundays and Feast Days, it became ineffective and led to peasant disturbances which Paul effectively suppressed. But Paul's sense of insecurity and his mania for discipline led him to harass the people by imposing vexatious rules of protocol. Nobles were deprived of their status and made liable to corporal punishment, and the lower clergy was deprived of its exemption from flogging. The fear of revolution led to the closure of all presses in Russia and the prohibition of any printed or manuscript works from abroad. But it was Paul's treatment of the military officers by transfers and demotions that imperilled the Tsar's position. In March 1801, the military governor of Moscow, O. Von der Pahlen, assassinated Paul. Alexander began his reign in tears. 'That is enough of acting like a child', Pahlen is reported to have said, 'Now go and reign, show yourself to the troops'.

Educated by a Swiss Jacobin tutor, La Harpe, Alexander was a late product of the enlightenment and of religious pietism. Surrounding himself with enlightened advisers, Alexander introduced various administrative reforms. But the constitutional reforms of 1801 and 1809, which were supposed to restrict Tsarist absolution, failed to become effective. His programme of expanding educational system at primary and secondary level in all provinces was hardly successful. New universities were founded at Kazan and Kharkov.

Alexander passed a decree permitting masters to emancipate their serfs through individual contract. But it had a limited success. The only positive measures came piecemeal in 1816 and 1817. Alexander forbade the advertisement of serfs for sale but their transportation by their master without legal process was not prohibited.

Alexander's impulse to domestic reform faded away with his going proeccupation with foreign and military affairs. The Polish question attracted him because of his liberal aspirations, and in 1804 he made the Pole Czartoryski Russian foreign minister. Since the last partition of Poland in 1795, the greater part of the country with the capital Warsaw had been incorporated in Prussia and the Poles, therefore, looked to Russia for aid.

The capitulation of Tilsit was regarded by the Russians as an affront to the national honour. The Russian nobility had never accepted the alliance with Napoleon with good grace, and the Continental System, to which Alexander had committed at Tilsit, faced them with economic ruin. The war of 1808 against Sweden was attributed to French pressure; patriotic officers avoided service in this and still more unjust struggle with Finnish national resistance which followed. The Emperor's mentor during this time was M. Speranskii (1772-1839) whose distinction in the ministry of the interior brought him to Alexander's notice in 1807. Meanwhile the war against Turkey and the Continental Blockade were exhausting Russia's national resource. The growing antipathy in Russian society to French connection led to the dismissal of Speranskii in March 1812. Alexander's refusal to interrupt all trade with neutrals and free entry for French luxury products led to war against Napoleon.

On June 25, 1812, with 450,000 men, Napoleon crossed the Niemen. But the Russians were compelled by sheer necessity to retreat and in retreating they adopted 'scorch-earth' policy. So Napoleon went on through Vilna and Vietbsk, and at Smolensk (a little over half-way to Moscow), only 160,000 of the invading force remained. At Borodino, Napoleon at last compelled the new Russian commander, Kutuzov, to fight a battle. But Napoleon's viictory did not alter the balance of forces, and Kutuzov abandoned Moscow. On September 14, 1812, Napoleon entered the deserted city only to find it in flames. For a month Napoleon made vain attempts to negotiate peace with the Tsar, 300 miles away at St. Petersburg. Alexander publicly declared, 'I would go and eat potatoes with the last of my peasants rather than ratify the shame of my fatherland'.

At the end of the Napoleonic wars, Alexander I went through a phase of mysticism. Under the influence of Prince Galitzin and Madame de Krudener, Alexander instituted the idea of Holy Alliance in international diplomacy. He behaved like a split personality. He still looked forward to the emancipation of the serfs and he introduced the reform into the Baltic provinces. In 1818 he introduced the constitutional regime in Poland which he wanted to extend to Russia. But these were fitful outbursts of his personal whims. His closest advisers were Arakcheev, the chairman of the department of military affairs in the State Council, a brutal, dissolute man and Photius, a fanatical cleric. Arakcheev was the brutal organiser of Russian military colonies. The villagers were subject to military discipline while the troops were liable to field labour in addition to drill. A revolt at Chuguev in 1819 was suppressed with exemplary brutality. Galitzin, the Minister of Education, emphasised the primacy of scientific teaching to the subordination of all others which exasperated the aristocratic intelligentsia.

Alexander was aware since 1816, of the seditious political groups among military officers. Tentative experiments resulted in 1818 a society known as the Union of Public Good. After 1820 there were three principal societies—the Society of the North, led by Prince Trubetskoi and the poet Ryleev and the Society of the South, led by Serge Muravev—Apostol, Bestuzhev-Rimin and Colonel Paul Pestel. The former drew its members from the army at Petrograd and favoured a constitutional monarchy. Its programme included the abolition of serfdom, equality before the law, and the granting of the principal liberties. The latter, which had its headquarters at Tulczyn, an important garrison town in the Ukraine, proposed not only the abolition of serfdom, but also the division of all land under cultivation and advocated a republic with broad administrative autonomy of the various regions.

A third society, afterwards amalgamated with the Society of the South, was that of the United Slavs, whose aim was to bring all Slavs together in a vast federal system. Though there was little coordination among the different groups, the so-called 'Decembrists' formed a huge organisation in 1825, many of whose members belonged to the highest ranks of the army and the navy. The Decembrists were inspired by an high ideal. In one of his poems in praise of liberty, the poet Ryleiev wrote; 'We know that death awaits those who are the first to rebel against the oppressors of the people'. But the Decembrists were a handful of patriots, a group of aristocratic revolutionaries, who had no contact with the masses. Moreover they had little agreement about their objectives. It was only Paul Pestel, a radical republican, who knew what he wanted.

The Decembrist Movement (1825)

On December 1, 1825, Alexander I died. He had three brothers, of whom Constantine, the eldest and the heir-apparent had been induced to renounce his claim in favour of his younger brother, Nicholas. But when news of Alexander's death reached the capital, people doubted the legality of Nicholas' succession. Hence Nicholas, to be on the safe side, proclaimed Constantine as Emperor, but the latter, however, disavowed this step. Finally, Nicholas I proclaimed himself Emperor. The three weeks' interregnum which followed Alexander's death gave the conspirators an opportunity to come out in the open. On December 14, 1825, three thousand troops at Petersburg mutinied and marched to the Senate Square, but they were easily dispersed by the Government troops. A few days later, the independent mutiny by the Society of the South was a forlorn hope and was suppressed with greater ease. The Decembrist Movement, thus, came to an untimely end. Five of the ring-leaders, including Pestel and Ryleev, were hanged in July 1825 and others were imprisoned or sent to Siberia. Paul Pestel confessed in the scaffold; 'My error has been that I tried to gather the harvest before I sowed the seed'. 'I knew beforehand', declared another patriot, 'that our enterprise had no chance of success. I know also that I must make a sacrifice of my life ... The harvest-hour will come later'.

Nicholas I (1824-55)

Mounting the throne in the shadow of a revolutionary conspiracy, Nicholas had a morbid fear of any kind of opposition. 'Revolution is at the gates of Russia', he said, 'but I swear that it shall not enter as long as I have a breath of life within me'. He, therefore, pursued a policy of resolute repression and put a dam upon revolutionary infection from Europe. In 1826, he issued the two famous repressive edicts—the edict reinstituting the political police and the censorship edict. He revived the secret police and their infamous record as the Department III of the Imperial Chancellory fills one of the darkest pages in Russian history. Its extra-legal action could lead to detention, deportation, or attachment of property without judicial process. This terrible institution 'rivalled, if it did not exceed, the horrors of the Spanish Inquisition'. The censorship edict, revised in 1828, continued with minor modifications till 1865. He forbade travel abroad without permission, prohibited the entry of subversive literature, and censored newspapers, journals and university lectures. He expunged the teaching of philosophy from the University curriculum and confined the ecclesiastics. So severe was the censorship of the press that the utterance of an unguarded word or the possession of a prohibited book might lead to exile.

The insurrection of the Kingdom of Poland in November 1830 hardened the repressive measures of Nicholas I. It was more or less anti-Russian, sparked off by news of the intervention of Russian troops in Belgium. The insurrection forced the Viceroy Constantine to leave Warsaw and the revolutionaries formed a national government. But the Diet failed to win the support of the peasant masses and, after some indecisive fighting, Warsaw fell in September 1831. A constitution was granted, but its bilateral provisions were violated; General Paskievitch subjected the country to a reign of terror and enforced Russianization.

After the Polish revolt of 1830, cultural repression became more systematic in Russia. The system is associated with the name of Count Uvarov, Minister of Education from 1833 to 1849. His triple formula of 'orthodoxy, autocracy and nationality' proposed in 1832 became the official ideology and survived into the last years of tsarism. The expansion of the University was checked, although Uvarov was responsible for a new one at Kiev. But the regime's cultural policy was not barren. Uvarov was a good patron to the Academy of Sciences.

The only notable innovations before 1848 were the successful codification of Russian laws, completed under the supervision of Speransky in 1833 and the stabilization of the currency and the elimination of depreciated paper money by the finance minister, Kankrin. Both reforms were long overdue; unfortunately, after Kankrin's retirement in 1844, his successors encouraged inflation and depreciation by issuing new money wherever they suffered financial crises. The autocratic character of Nicholas became more pronounced. There was a steady growth of the executive department—His Majesty's own Chancery—which absorbed new functions. With respect to serfdom, Nicholas studiously avoided anything that resembled reform. The increase in local peasant risings appeared ominous; official figure showed increases of over 50 percent in each decade of Nicholas's reign.

Nicholas's policy could not prevent the intellectual efflorescence culminating in the stupendous achievement of Lermontov and Pushkin. Two schools emerged—Slavophiles and Westerners. Its starting point was the publication in 1836 of P. Chaadaev's 'Philosophical Letters', the burden of which was the repudiation of Russian culture. 'We belong'. Chaadaev wrote 'to those nations who... exist only to teach the world some serious lesson'. The Slavophiles harked back to the Russia which had existed before Peter the Great, it was a country whose public and private life was based on faith, while Western civilization was influenced by rationalism, selfish individualism and a utilitarian spirit. The Slavophilês considered that government in Russia was based on a community of interests, harmony between the upper and lower classes, as opposed to the constitutionalism of the modern democracies. Against Catholicism and Protestantism, they set the indigenous strength of the orthodox church. Though conservatives in their outlook, the Slavophiles advocated a socialism consistent with agricultural collectivism. The Westerners were inspired by the French Revolution, with ideas of personal freedom and civil liberty. For the Westerners, Hegel was 'the algebra of revolution'. Among them, the literary critic, Belinski, turned in succession from idealism to Hegelianism, and then to revolutionary individualism. To Chaadaev it appeared that only the Roman Church could revive the country and link it with European culture. Despite their seeming differences, the Slavophiles and the Westerners felt a profound desire for change and recognised the necessity of solving the problem of serfdom. Combining the views of both sides, Alexander Herzen suggested that Russia was predestined to socialism. His ideas exerted considerable influence on Petrachevski's revolutionary circle, formed in St. Petersburg in 1845, which included in its ranks the young Dostoevsky. Petrachevski's group was arrested by the police in 1849. Thus the Russian Empire, unaffected by the revolutionary movement of 1848, remained a deadweight to liberal and democratic ideas. The historian Granovski, one of the leaders of the Western movement, was constrained to observe in 1849:

> Even the most stout-hearted give way to despair and contemplate with indifference the sad sight that meets their eyes. The dead are the lucky ones. If only one could wipe out this intolerable state of things.

Foreign Policy of Nicholas I

If Nicholas' domestic policy appeared unimpressive, his foreign policy till the outbreak of the Crimean War was crowned with success. His foreign policy was directed to achieve two important objects—the suppression of revolutionary movement on the Continent and the extinction of the Ottoman Empire in Europe. He championed the cause of the Greeks struggling for their independence from Turkish rule. In 1827, he joined with Britain and France and the result was the destruction of the Turkish fleet at Navarino in 1827. Nicholas followed up this victory by sending an army which advanced on Constantinople as far as Adrianople. Turkey was obliged to give in and consented to allow Greece to become an independent principality. Thus Russian influence became predominant at

Constantinople. The position was further strengthened when Turkey, hard pressed by Mehmet Ali, had to accept the Russian offer of help. By the treaty of Unkiar Skelessi (1833) Turkey allowed Russia to convert the Black Sea into a Russian sphere of influence.

From the Near East, Nicholas turned his attention to the West. In 1833 he formed a close alliance with Austria and Prussia for mutual defence against revolutionary movements. A few years later he joined England, Austria and Prussia in a Quadruple Alliance for counteracting the ambitious designs of Mehmet Ali. In 1849 he helped the Austrian Emperor, Francis Joseph, by sending him 400,000 men, in suppressing the Hungarian revolt. It was his uncompromising hostility that led Frederick William IV, king of Prussia, to refuse the crown offered him at Frankfurt.

Russia had a firm hold over Turkey and thus over the whole Balkan Peninsula. Nicholas was convinced that Turkey was a 'sick man' and that the Ottoman Empire was disintegrating. Britain was, he thought, his most probable opponent. He wanted to have Constantinople and, in return, Britain was to have Egypt and Crete. The offer was rejected. Russian ambition roused the fears of Britain and France and led to the Crimean War. England, France and Sardinia came to the aid of Turkey and succeeded in defeating the Russian armies. The campaign in the Crimea dispelled at one blow the illusion of the Russian might. Disappointed and broken-hearted, Nicholas died, in 1855, during the siege of Sebastopol, and was succeeded by his son, Alexander II.

Alexander II (1855-81)

Alexander II, who came to the throne during the Crimean War, realised the necessity of making peace which he did at Paris in 1856. He was convinced that the regeneration of Russian military and state power could not be done without social and economic modernisation. He was shrewd enough to realise that the imperial regime had lost prestige and it was better for the Government to forestall revolutionary activities by taking the initiative for reforms. After the Crimean War, Russia seemed in the words of the anarchist Kropotkin to 'awaken from the heavy slumber and the terrible nightmare of Nicholas' reign'. Alexander also recognised that it was better for change 'to come from above than to come from below'. He was still young and had the sagacity to introduce some preliminary measures which showed his reformist zeal.

The survivors of the Decembrist Movement were allowed to return home after thirty years of exile. He removed the galling restrictions imposed on the Universities and upon foreign travel. The censorship was relaxed and the press flooded with utopian schemes. The prevailing sentiment throughout Russia was not anti-monarchical and the eyes of the nation, therefore,were turned to the Tsar as the fountainhead of all reforms.

Emancipation of the Serfs

The condition of the serfs, comprising nearly one-half of the population, was degrading. Even Nicholas I had condemned serfdom. The educated classes, and especially the literary men, were in favour of abolition. Such novels as Gogol's *Dead Souls* and Turgenev's *Memoirs of a Huntsman* had made people realise the misery and helplessness of the serf's lot. During the Crimean War, peasant disorders became so serious that in some places whole regiment of troops had to be sent to quell them. Apart from moral grounds that it was unjustifiable, it was not even defensible on economic ones. Russia's export trade in wheat was inhibited by a system in which the majority of the landlords knew nothing about farming and the majority of the serfs employed traditional methods.

In March 1856, Alexander announced to the Moscow nobility that 'it is better to abolish serfdom from above than to await the time when its abolition would begin from below without action on our part.' The bureaucracy itself had no plan, but varying proposals were submitted by individuals. The leading spokesmen were now Herzen in London and Chernyshevskii in St. Petersburg. Herzen's influence began with the publication in London in 1857 of *Kolokol* (The Bell). Although nominally banned, it circulated widely in Russia demanding emancipation of the serfs with land and freedom of the press. Chernyshevski was an economist rather than a man of letters who felt impatient both with

Herzen's tolerance of reform from above and with the delay in its accomplishment. Plans were worked out in secret committees and the Council of State until finally, in March 1861, the coordinated plan was promulgated by decree. Indeed it was due to the progressive members of the civil service, especially Rostovtsev and Milyutin, that the reform took shape.

In 1861 the Edict of Emancipation abolished serfdom which kept more than forty million people in bondage to landowners or the State. This was an immense gain to Russia from the moral standpoint as it gave the Russian peasants legal freedom without economic freedom. The Edict was based on several principles. In the first place, it endowed the Russian serf with civil rights, conferring upon him the status of a free peasant and releasing him from bondage to his master. In the second place, it divided the ownership of the soil between the nobles and the peasants in order to prevent the growth of a landless proletariat. The third principle was that the lord was to receive a sum of money as compensation for the loss of the land; this was to be provided by the State and was to be repaid by the peasants in instalments extending over a period of 49 years. Another principle enjoined that the land was not to be bestowed upon the peasant in personal ownership, but in communal ownership upon the village group or *mir,* to which he was attached. The *mir* held the land, and the *mir* was collectively responsible for yearly payments which were to be given to the lord as compensation.

The sweeping character of these changes, however, failed to improve the economic condition of the peasants. In the first place, the lots assigned to the peasants were generally the poorest land and too small to provide for the sustenance of the growing families. As a peasant's holding shrank, he had no incentive to improve land. As productivity failed to keep pace with the growing population, famine became more frequent. In the second place, the peasants were forced to pay the price of their redemption. This financial burden, in addition to ordinary taxes, was greater than the *corvee* had been. Redemption had the effect of much heavier taxation, the money was advanced by the State and repaid by the peasant to the State in instalments. This additional burden proved vexatious, and by 1905 outstanding arrears had to be cancelled in order to offset revolution. In the third place, while technically free, the peasants were subjected to village communes which exercised considerable influence over them. What land they received they held through the commune or *mir* which paid the redemption money collectively. The peasants were not free to go elsewhere and to do so they needed permission from their *mir.* It was the government's policy to keep the mass of peasants where they were, as a stable element in society.

Though the nobility received equitable treatment than the peasant, thousands of middling gentry had been in debt before the emancipation. They now lost their free labour supply and their debts were paid out of their redemption fees. The nobles themselves were not materially helped by this reform. Accustomed to free labour, they found it hard to adapt themselves to the change and they soon discovered that the bonds they received as compensation money were not readily convertible into cash. A good many of them sold or leased their lands to the more enterprising peasants and thus was laid the peasant proprietorship. But the average peasant was not enterprising. No fresh wind of scientific agriculture blew through the farmlands of Russia. The abolition of serfdom failed to achieve the desired result. The situation of the Russian peasant was 'both better and worse' : he was relieved of certain disabilities, but was burdened with fresh obligations. The effects of the Emancipation upon the landowing classes varied in different parts of the country, but now they had to give serious attention to the administration of their estates. As one of the nobles said, 'Formerly we kept no accounts and drank champagne, now we keep accounts and content ourselves with beer'.

Other Reforms

The emancipation of the peasants brought other reform in its train. The decree of January 1864 instituted a measure of regional self-government—the *Zemstov* or local government. Three separate bodies of property holders—nobles, townsmen, and peasants respectively, elected the district assemblies and the latter nominated delegates to their provincial assembly. The *Zemstov* took over the responsibility for communications, famine relief, and hospitals, and, in addition, supervised local trade and agriculture and, above all, education. Described as a 'fragment of a constitution', they were introduced gradually in groups of provinces at a time. This formal co-operation of class amounted to a certain social revolution. But, as political tension lessened, the autocracy resisted the functions of the *Zemstovs* and forbade the intercourse between provincial *Zemstovs*. The latter, therefore, exercised nominal functions, but their practical achievement went far. Virtually all rural education—both primary and secondary—and all medical services in the countryside were indebted to them. Despite their inadequacies, the institution of these local and provincial assemblies was a first step towards representative government.

At the end of 1864, Alexander introduced the new judicial system. The old judicial system which contained no less than twenty-five radical defects, was replaced by new institutions remodelled—namely the separation of judiciary from the executive, independence of the judiciary and trial by jury. The country was divided into judicial circuits in which courts of first instance delivered final judgement. The sole higher court of appeal was the Senate. Justices of the Peace, chosen by popular election, were instituted to deal with minor cases. The independence of the judiciary was demonstrated in 1878, by the acquital of Vera Zasulich, a revolutionary underground, who had shot and wounded a police. More than the *Zemstov* reforms Alexander's legal innovations weakened the nobility.

A third reform in 1864 was the law providing for 'peoples' primary schools', controlled by the *Zemstovs*. A new establishment for secondary schools was introduced. The secondary education of girls had been brought under the ministry's control in 1862. Two other educational reforms were the nominal decontrol of University faculties in 1863, and the new censorship law of 1865.

The last major act in the era of reform was the introduction of military service, the work of Milyutin. In 1861, as Minister of War, Milyutin reduced the peasant's term of selective service from 25 to 16 years. In 1874 he fixed compulsory service for all classes at six years followed by nine in the reserve.

Having recognised the importance of co-ordinating the executive power, Alexander introduced a new body, the Council of Ministers (*Sovet Ministrove)*. The law of 1862 enabled the autocracy to shed some privileges by prescribing the annual publication of accounts of state income and expenditure. A series of financial reforms began with the creation of the Bank of Russia (1861) for stimulating trade and industry. Other measures provided for the abolition of liquor concessions in favour of an excise tax.

The Crimean War was followed by an economic surge which was reflected in foreign trade, the mechanisation of textile industry and, above all, railway building. In the sixties, industry picked up, and, in the next decade, the rise in output was some 60 per cent, compared to a rise from 8 to 11 in the United States and 14 to 18 in Germany in the same decade. The economic revolution also extended to foreign trade. Between 1860 and 1870 exports rose in value from 181 to 359 million roubles, and imports from 159 to 336 millions. As compared with incipient industrialisation, one can notice the economic failure of the agrarian revolution.

Foreign Policy

Poland had been in a state of ferment ever since the unsuccessful revolution of 1831. From 1855 to 1861, Poland went rapidly forward, and a great Agricultural Society took up the question of the serfs. In 1861 Alexander II suppressed the Agricultural Society. There followed violent demonstrations in the streets which were put down with ruthless severity. In 1862 the Tsar sent as Viceroy the Grand-Duke Constantine, who was well-known for his liberal views. By this time, however, Poland was ready for another revolution. But the Polish revolt of January 1863 was as ill-timed as it was heroic and hopeless. The Tsar had an excuse for war. While the contest lasted, Britain and France protested against the treatment of Poland, but Prussia upheld Russia. Brutal repression followed and the process known as the 'Russification' began. The Lithuanians, the

Livonians and the Finns soon suffered for the turbulence of the Poles.

Alexander II supported the Slav people of the Balkans in order to turn them into the satellites of the Russian planet. In 1858 Montenegro had beaten the Turks. But, during the following years, when her existence was threatened by Turkey, Russia came to her support. Rumania was assisted by Russia to complete her unity in 1861. In 1867 Russia interfered to remove the Turkish garrisons from Belgrade and other Serbian fortresses.

Alexander II became alienated with Napoleon III, ruler of France, owing to the latter's sympathy with the Polish insurgents. He turned to Prussia and this Prusso-Russian rapprochement proved advantageous to both countries. Russian neutrality enabled Prussia to expel Austria from Germany and Alexander's qualms were satisfied at this humiliation of Austria owing to the rebuff Russia received from her at the Crimean War. Strengthened by the Prussian support, Russia, in 1870, wiped out the Crimean humiliation by repudiating those clauses of the Treaty of Paris (1856) which had restricted her in the Black Sea. In her bid for the revival of Russian influence in the Balkans, Russia declared war on Turkey in 1877 and reaped substantial benefits from the Treaty of San Stefano. But she was not destined to reap the full fruits of her victory at the Treaty of Berlin as Russia was abandoned by Germany when the latter courted the alliance of Austria.

What Russia failed to achieve in Europe she was amply compensated by her consolidation beyond Europe—the Siberia, the Far East, the Causcasus and Central Asia. Even before the Crimean War, the Russian traders had penetrated into Chinese territory in the valley of the Amur River. In 1854 Nicholas Muravev, the Governor-General of Eastern Siberia, founded the city of Khabarovsk on that river. In 1860 Russian naval forces founded the port of Vladivostock. The Russian Government forced the Chinese Government to recognise these acquisitions. In the decade that followed, the Russians also occupied the province of Kuldja in the Chinese Turkestan and acquired the whole island of Sakhalin from Japan in 1875 in exchange for the Kuriles.

Russian interest in expansion in the Chinese mainland led the former to liquidate her holdings in North America. Having considered Alaska as a great strategic liability, Russia sold the territory to the USA for 7,200,000 dollars in 1867. But its reactions were not flattering as the purchase was unpopular in the United States and the sale regretted in Russia.

Along the southern border, Russian thrust had been evident when, in 1864, she succeeded in establishing her claim to all of the Western shore of the Caspian Sea north of Persia. In the same year a major drive was begun against the Moslem Khanates of Khokand, Khiva and Bokhara. In 1865 Tashkent was stormed and annexed. In 1868 Kaufmann occupied Samarkand. The conquest of Central Russia was regarded as a triumph of civilisation over barbarism, though it posed a threat to India. The integration of the region with Russia strengthened the economic resources of the country. Already in 1865 the annual turnover of Russian trade with the Khanates was nearly a million sterling. To many the Russian expansion in Central Asia appeared to offset the humiliation caused by the Crimean defeat.

The Intelligentsia: Nihilism

The reforms of Alexander II were autocratic reforms which disillusioned all classes of community. The real nationalist movement of Russia was a revolutionary movement, rooted in the intelligentsia which found inspiration in the West as well as inside Russia itself. Apart from the university students and graduates, as well as the literary men, the so-called intelligentsia included some of the nobles themselves. This important class of intellectuals was the outcome of remarkable cultural efflorescence of nineteenth-century Russia.

In music and literature Russia exercised tremendous influence on the culture of Europe. The symphonies of Borodin and Tchaikovsky, the programme-music of Rimsky-Korsakov, the songs of Musorgski, hearkened back to legends. The great novelists, Turgenev, Dostoevski, and Tolstoy reflected in their works the great social evils of Russian life and the psychological dilemmas that stemmed out of poverty. Thus the works of the Russian composers and novelists—by their profound concern for the welfare of the people—helped to give the intelligentsia unity and self-consciousness. Russian intelligentsia differed from the militant nationalism of Germany as they yearned not for national unity and independence, but for greater human happiness and an ideal social order.

In 1861, the year of the Emancipation of serfs and the violent measures taken against Polish nationalists, began agitation which was never again to subside under Tsarism. The first epoch-making illegal publication was the *Velikorus* (Great Russian) in the autumn of 1861 which appealed for the removal of the Tsar. It was followed by the more pregnant manifesto '*To the young Generation*' by Herzen which called for 'revolution, in aid of the people'. In 1862 appeared '*Young Russia*', written by Zaichnevskii in the Moscow prison. He divided society into haves and have nots and emphasised the need for a 'bloody and ruthless revolution'. This agitation crystallised into the formation of an organisation 'Land and Liberty' by Herzen's collaborator Ogarev. But the society petered out in 1864.

The active underground opposition was small, but it was winning converts—especially among students. Their abortive demonstration in 1861 in St. Petersburg and the great conflagrations in 1862 alienated liberal sympathisers and the word 'nihilism' came into use to denounce the left. The word was first used by Turgenev in the novel *Fathers and Sons* (1862) in his idealisation of revolutionary character Bazarov. He is represented as 'a man who does not bow before any authority whatsoever, does not accept a single principle on faith, with whatever respect that principle be endowed'. Bazarov is often supposed to embody 'the spirit of absolute negation and of barren criticism'. Nihilism, therefore, involved an uncompromising breach with the past, and the reconstruction of society on a *tabula rasa.* The idea of nihilism became more pronounced in the writings of Pisarev (1840-68). But the programme had also a positive side as was reflected in Chernyshevskii's novel *What is to be done* (1863). Socialism is part of the nihilist answer in the book, whose hero, Rakhmetov, became an even more popular model than Bazarov to Russian youth. Thus, in its first phase, Nihilism was mainly a philosophy of negation, but with the important difference that it was based on science. The author of *Underground Russia,* known under the name of Stepniak, described it as 'a struggle for the emancipation of intelligence from every kind of dependence... The fundamental principle of Nihilism, properly so called, was individualism.'

After a few years, Nihilism ceased to be a philosophical movement and developed into a revolutionary movement. An attempt to assassinate Alexander II by D.V. Karakozov on April 4, 1866, was a kind of signal for the government to unleash reactionary measures. This was apparent in the field of education where, under the inspiration of Count Dimitri Tolstoy, minister of education from 1866 to 1880, academic freedom in the universities was virtually extinguished. Simultaneously, Tolstoy tried to insulate the Russian youth from natural science and modern knowledge by putting greater emphasis upon classical and modern languages, history, geography, religion and other subjects considered to be politically innocuous. The Government, in an outburst of hysteria, indulged in all the excesses of reactionary measures. Its severity sowed the seeds of revolution which owed not a little to the Parisian Commune and the 'Internationale', a Socialist society at Zurich.

Out of the ferment of political ideas, emerged two strands of thought: Socialism and Anarchism. The socialists were represented by Lavroff whose programme was peaceful propaganda among the peasants. The Anarchists, on the other hand, were represented by Bakunin, an international terrorist and 'an apostle of universal destruction'. He was convinced that the goal of human endeavour was freedom which could only be achieved through anarchy.

In the year 1873 there began the Narod or 'Go-to-the People' movement which aimed to leaven the mass by a revolutionary propaganda among the peasants. It is vividly described by Stepniak in the following way : 'The time for talking was over : actual work was in contemplation... There were warm wishes for success and robust squeezings of hands ... And so like an electric spark, the cry 'To the people', ran through the youth'. The movement was carried on with the greatest difficulty. In Petrograd, Prince Kropotkin lectured secretly among the workers. But the Government was determined to crush the embers of revolution with a firm hand. Thousands of persons were imprisoned and deported to Siberia. The movement failed to make any headway as it found little response among the peasants, the latter too illiterate to comprehend its message.

The collapse of the movement to the people was succeeded by armed resistance. Populist leaders began to use methods advocated earlier by Serge Nechaev and Peter Tkachev. Nechaev, a former follower of Bakunin, had emphasised the uses of terror as a means of promoting revolutionary objectives. Tkachev, who has been considered a forerunner of Lenin, taught that success in revolutions depended upon the determination of a revolutionary elite. The years 1876-8 witnessed a number of street insurrections. But the Government was quick to react and suppressed with ease all popular outbreaks. Meanwhile the Government adopted severe reactionary measures and found itself in open conflict with the Russian intelligentsia. As a result of repression, Nihilism developed into a vast secret conspiracy and employed the deadly weapon of assassination. Deeds of violence were at first spasmodic but an organised system of terrorism began in February 1878 when Vera Zassulic, a woman, fired a revolver shot at General Trepoff. She was acquitted by the jury. But when the police tried to re-arrest her, she escaped over the frontier. This was followed shortly by the brutal murder of the head of the secret police in broad daylight in the streets of Petrograd, the assailant escaping arrest.

The main lever of the revolutionary movement was wielded by a society known as 'Land and Liberty' which had branches in different parts of Russia. Even in the heyday of terrorism, the Russian revolutionaries differed as to the methods. While the 'Black Partition', consisting of social democrats, advocated pacific methods, the 'Will of the People', relied on force. The latter, led by Andrew Zheliabov and Sophie Perovsky, marked Alexander II as their chief target and made at least seven attempts on his life. At last, in March 1881, he was killed by a bomb explosion while returning from a military review in St. Petersburg. The Revolutionary Party at once published a manifesto offering to refrain from revolutionary activities on condition of a national assembly elected on the basis of manhood suffrage and freedom of the press, freedom of speech and freedom of association.

CHAPTER 21

THE EASTERN QUESTION—PART I

In 1453 the Ottoman Turks captured Constantinople. They soon overran the Balkan Peninsula. The Ottoman Empire was at its height at the end of the seventeenth century. Its vast sprawling Empire included the Balkan Peninsula, Hungary and the lands bordering the Black Sea in Europe; the territories situated between the Mediterranean and the frontier of Persia in Asia; and, in Africa, all of the northern coast except Morocco. The Mediterranean had virtually been transformed into a Turkish lake. Tripoli, Tunis and Algeria, though semi-independent, however, acknowledged the suzerainty of Turkey. During the eighteenth century, the Turkish power suffered diminution as she was driven from Hungary by the Austrians, and from the northern shore of the Black Sea by the Russians.

In 1815 the Ottoman Empire included the Balkan Peninsula, Asia Minor as far as Persia, Syria, Egypt, Tripoli, Tunis and Algeria. Situated at the meeting place of three continents, the Ottoman Empire consisted of a conglomeration of races professing different faiths and speaking different languages. In Asiatic Turkey the majority of the inhabitants were Mohammedan. In European Turkey, the overwhelming majority were Slavic in race and Christian in faith.

The Eastern Question concerned itself mainly with the inhabitants of the Balkan Peninsula. The most important group were the Serbs and the Bulgarians. Dwelling in Serbia, Montenegro, Bosnia and Herzegovina, the Serbs were Slavic in speech. Included among the Balkan Peninsula, Rumania occupied the districts formerly known as Moldivia and Wallachia. Claiming their descent from the people of ancient Hellas, the Greeks were the leading nation of the Balkans and the most western in their customs. Albania, being the outlet of the Peninsula to the Adriatic, was inhabited by a nomadic and warlike people. Scattered all over the Balkans were Armenians and Jews. Constituting the middle class of the Peninsula, the Armenians, Greeks and Jews monopolised commerce. The upper class were the Turks most of whom were feudal lords and government officials. The Rumanians and Bulgarians were peasants, while the Greeks were a sea-faring people.

The great majority of the inhabitants were Christians, members of the Greek Church, which, in belief and ritual, was almost identical with the Orthodox Church in Russia. At its head was the Patriarch in Constantinople, who was always a Greek; but he was appointed by the Sultan, the head of Mohammedan faith and the oppressor of the Christians.

Until the twentieth century, Turkey was known as the Ottoman which denoted a dynasty. In the Ottoman Empire, Islam was the established religion. Christians were regarded with contempt and had to suffer various disabilities. Until the twentieth century Turkey was 'an alien, incompatible entity... attached to obsolete conceptions of theocratic feudalism, ignorant of the first principles of judicial administration, and addicted to making spasmodic efforts for welding together heterogeneous elements by means of brute force and massacre'.

The Government of Turkey was an absolute monarchy, all power vested in the Sultan. The Ulemas and the Janissaries, the Sultan's picked bodyguard, resisted Western ideas. The Sultan, Selim III (1789-1807), felt the necessity of introducing radical military reform, only to be impeded by a reaction which led to his deposition. Mahmud II (1808-39) had to wait until he felt strong enough to suppress the Janissaries (1826) and revive a reform of the army. But this came too late and the Greek revolt could not be averted. The Empire still had a medieval and feudal structure, capped by a top-heavy bureaucracy. Apart from inflation which hindered the economic growth of the country, agriculture and industry were crippled by taxes. Though Moslem recruits in the army were not negligible, the Sultans, no longer leaders in war, were prisoners of the bureaucracy.

The Eastern Question has always been an international question. The question took different shapes at different times. While the Ottoman Empire posed serious threat to Europe and Asia, European statesmen no longer feared the expansion of the Ottoman Empire. They feared its dismemberment and tried to take advantage of its weakness.

'The ambition of Russia at the expense of Turkey was a constant factor in the Eastern Question from the days of Peter the Great (1672-1725) to the war of 1914'. Russia was bound to the Balkan peoples by ties of religion and race and beneath the intention of protecting them from Turkish misrule lay the ostensible object of securing access to the Mediterranean. Russian policy in the Near East had been to seize Constantinople as an ultimate goal.

Between the years 1788 and 1791 Austria and Russia attacked Turkey in concert. On the plea of protecting the Christians in the Turkish Empire, Russia advanced as far as the port of Oczakov on the Black Sea. Pitt the younger—the then Prime Minister of England—was quick enough to realise the portents of the Russian advance and the menace to Turkey's integrity. Though Parliament did not support him over the incident, Britain with varying degree followed a pro-Turkish and anti-Russian policy. Austria, too, showed a moderate attitude to Turkey in 1791, returning all her conquests to the latter.

At the dawn of the nineteenth century Russia began to look covetuously on Constantinople. 'Austria crouched on Russia's flank, a suspicious hound threatening to spring when Russia was once engaged with Turkey'. In the eyes of Austria, Russia ascendancy in the Balkans foreshadowed a great Slav Empire. The growth of the Pan-Slavic movement in the Balkans, encouraged by the Russians, was a menace to the integrity of the Austrian Empire. After the expulsion of Austria from Italy and Germany, she sought to find compensation in the south-east at the expense of Turkey.

British policy in the Near East had not been consistently anti-Russian before the Crimean War. Canning, for instance cooperated with Russia throughout the Greek War of Independence. Though Palmerston projected an alliance with France against Russia in the Near East in 1833, he ended by working with Russia against France in 1839 and 1840. Until the beginning of 1853, British suspicions were turned against France both at Constantinople and in Egypt; and Britain and Russia often pitted themselves against French encroachment.

It is not easy to draw a dividing line in the attitude of the Great Powers to the Ottoman Empire. Though Russia wanted to break it up, Britain believed that the existence of Turkey in Europe as a barrier against Russia was necessary to safeguard her empire in India and her position in the Mediterranean. Ever since 1815, British statesmen had been obsessed with the thought that if France ceased to dominate Europe, Russia would take her place. Napoleon had visualised that in fifty years all Europe would be either Republican or Cossack. British policy, therefore, revolved round France by strengthening the latter against Russia's domination, yet keeping France harmless. Hence Castlereagh's rather absurd alliance with France and Austria in January 1815; hence Palmerston's welcome to the July Monarchy in France and his Quadruple Alliance with Spain and Portugal as well in 1834. Apart from this element, British policy was to develop the independence of Central Europe, so that it could hold its own against both Cossacks and Republicans. Britain's natural allies', therefore, were Austria and Prussia. Metternich and Palmerston, strange bed-fellows, pursued the same aims and served each other's needs.

The Revolutions of 1848 ended this diplomatic set-up. The fall of Metternich was a disaster to the British position. The Revolution of 1848 made France more powerful than before. On the other hand, the revolutions in Central

Europe were defeated only with Russian backing. By 1850 Austria and Prussia seemed to be Russian dependants. After 1848 the 'Russian bogey' appeared to be real to Britain. She now began to regard Russia as the tyrant of Europe, though fear of France still predominated in England until the spring of 1853.

Serbia was the first state in the Balkans which struggled for freedom. Serbia attained her zenith in the reign of Stephen Dusan (1336-56), who built up a great empire which covered nearly the whole of the Balkan Peninsula. But after his death the Serbian Empire rapidly fell to pieces and her power was finally shattered by the Turks in 1389 at the memorable battle of Kossovo. Serbia was allowed to maintain a separate existence for a period of seventy years, but in 1459 she was incorporated as an integral part of the Ottoman Empire.

After the battle of Kossovo, a large number of Serbs emigrated to Hungary and rendered valuable services to the Hungarians in their wars with Turkey. The independence of Serbia seemed to be imminent on the eve of the French Revolution. A Serbian poet, Obradovich, appealed to the Austrian Emperor Joseph II to 'protect the Serbian race which suffers miseries without number'. But the death of Joseph II in 1790 diverted Austrian policy into other channels. The Serbian people suffered disillusionment once more.

The founder of the modern Serbian State was Kara George, a peasant, who revolted in 1804 against the oppression of the Janissaries quartered in Serbia. The Janissaries were equally obnoxious to the Sultan of Turkey who combined with the Serbs in wresting Belgrade out of the hands of the Janissaries. The united forces achieved their objective. Flushed with their victory over the turbulent Janissaries, the Serbs made a bid for independence against the Turkish Government itself. Despite the overwhelming superiority of the Turkish arms, they could not make any headway against a country profoundly favourable to guerilla warfare. The result was the crushing defeat of the Turkish army at Mischar (1806). The Sultan granted favourable terms, complete autonomy, the evacuation of all Serbian fortresses except Belgrade and the expropriation of Turkish landowners.

For a few years Serbia enjoyed peace. In December 1808 Kara George was declared hereditary prince by the Senate. To counteract further aggression of Turkey, he made vain appeals to Napoleon and once more to Austria. In 1810 a Russian Resident returned to Belgrade with troops, to secure Russian influence and to save the Serbian people from reconquest. But Napoleon's approaching invasion made the Tsar to make peace with Turkey which produced the Treaty of Bucharest on May 28, 1812. Under Article 8, the Serbians were to have an autonomous status while allowing restricted Turkish garrisons in Belgrade and other fortresses. But the Serbians were deceived. Anticipating Russian defeat at the hands of Napoleon, the Sultan had no intention of giving effect to the Article voluntarily. Moreover, Kara George himself refused to submit to the terms. The result was the Turkish occupation of Belgrade in October 1813 and the flight into Austria of Kara George and thousands of persons.

The struggle for independence was carried on by another peasant, Milosh Obrenovich, the second founder of modern Serbia. A plea was advanced by Russia of European intervention on the novel ground that, although the Moslems were the Sultan's subjects, the Christians were only his tributaries, and entitled to place themselves under the protection of any European power. However, in 1815, after some partial succeses gained by the Serbians, and confronted by the prospect of Russian intervention, the Sultan conceded the right of self-government to Serbia (December 1815).

The rule of Milosh was sullied by avarice and tyranny. The emigrés who came back to Serbia were killed. In July 1817 Milosh procured the assassination of Kara George in order to remove a dangerous rival from his path. Nine years later, Kara George's son also shared the same fate. Milosh thwarted Russia's ambition in Serbia. He kept Serbia out of the long struggle of the Greeks and the Russo-Turkish war of 1828-9. His policy bore fruit when Turkey was required at the Peace of Adrianople (September 1829) to confirm the privileges promised to the

Serbians in Article 8 of the Treaty of Bucharest. Finally, in October 1830, Turkey recognised the autonomy of Serbia. In pursuing his own ambitions, Milosh had succeeded in gaining a real autonomy for Serbia and this he had achieved without any assistance of foreign powers. But his tyrannical rule made him unpopular and he was forced to abdicate in 1839.

Milosh was succeeded by his two sons, Milan Obrenovich II and Michael Obrenovich III, the former died immediately after his accession and the latter occupying the throne for a brief period of three years. The next ruler was Alexander Karageorgevich, the son of the great national leader. During the rule of sixteen years (1842-58), he did not initiate any reform and during the Crimean War he remained neutral despite overwhelming sympathies of the people with Russia. He was, therefore, deposed. Milosh was recalled and, at the age of 79, began his autocratic rule for the second time until his death in 1860. He was followed by his son, Michael Obrenovich III, the most efficient ruler Serbia had ever known. After inauguarating various economic reforms for his peasant subjects, he induced the Porte to withdraw the Turkish garrisons from all Serbian fortresses. But the irreconcilable dynastic feud between Obrenovich and Karageorgevich again flared up and Michael was brutally assassinated in 1868. A futile attempt was made to proclaim Pater Karageorgevich as ruler, but the crown devolved on Michael's cousin, Milan Obrenovich IV.

Greek War of Independence

The Greeks were the first to achieve their emancipation from Turkey. Though two-thirds of the land were occupied by the Moslems, they hardly exceeded one-tenth of the population. The Greeks enjoyed an exceptional degree of local autonomy and their Senate could appeal direct to the Sultan. The Christians were allowed a greater measure of liberty than that enjoyed by dissidents in any country in Europe. The importance of the Greek Church—both in resisting Islam and in providing the framework of an organised resistance—can hardly be exaggerated. The foreign powers, especially Russia, took some measures to safeguard the interests of the Balkan Christians. Russian prestige was enhanced in Greece when, by the Treaties of Kutchuk Kainardji (1774) and Jassay (1792), she secured some stipulations in favour of the Sultan's orthodox subjects. In 1783, Russia secured for Greek ships the privilege of trading under her flag. The wars left Greece unaffected, more populous and more prosperous than before. The revolutionary movement owed not a little to the merchants of the Aegean islands and the so-called captain-commanders of ships or bands of brigands.

The French Revolution stimulated national aspirations of the Greeks. As in Hungary, so in Greece, a linguistic and literary revival heralded a national uprising. Rhigas Pheraios (1757-98) who settled in Vienna, produced a number of rousing translations and poems. His professed aim was to unite the Greeks under the banner of liberty and equality proclaimed by the French. In 1797 he planned to start a rising in the Peloponnese, but he was seized at Trieste and executed by the Pasha of Belgrade. Another great literary figure was Adamantios Koraes (1748-1833), rightly honoured as architect of the written language. Through his edition of the Greek classics, Koraes expressed his patriotic, anti-clerical and republican opinions. Though Koraes declared that a violent solution was eventually unnecessary, he countenanced it through his occasional anonymous poems and tracts.

The activities of the *Philke Hetairia,* a widespread secret society, cannot be underrated in keeping alive the sparks of patriotism. Founded at Odessa in 1814, and, after a very slow growth till 1818, its membership spread rapidly from the lower Danube into Greece. 'The trickle became a stream and then a flood'. The society expected Russian support because the Greeks and the Russians belonged to the same branch of Christianity. It was generally believed that the Tsar's minister, Capodistrias, was at the head of the Society. But when Capodistrias repudiated the claim, the direction was accepted in June 1820 by Alexander Hypsilantes.

Taking advantage of the war between the Sultan and Ali Pasha, the Turkish Governor of Janina, the Greeks in the North revolted in March 1821 under the leadership of Ypsilanti. He thought that he could count on the support of the Russians as well as Greeks in the Danubian principalities. But Tsar Alexander I declared himself opposed to the movement and the Rumanians refused to be embroiled in this national uprising.

The news of the revolt and the massacres of the Turks perpetrated by the Greeks intensified Turkish reprisals. On Easter Sunday, 1821, the Patriarch, or head of the Greek Church, was hanged in his ecclesiastical robes at Constantinople and various bishops were also hanged.

This event deepened the ferocity of the conflict as the Greeks looked upon the Patriarch as Catholics look upon the Pope. Deprived of any help either from Russia or from his fellow brethren, Ypsilanti was defeated by the Turks in June 1821 and the movement fizzled out.

A month later, the peasants in Morea in the south rose which was not to subside until the Greek independence was won. On January 10, 1822, the assembly at Epidaurus proclaimed the independence of Greece and elected Mavrocordato Regent. For the first six years from 1821 the Greeks fought alone which was marked by savagery on both sides. Though Lord Byron, thinking that the spirit of Marathon was revived, joined in the struggle and died at Missolinghi for the cause of freedom, another poet, Pushkin, became disillusioned with a struggle that was vitiated with utmost barbarity on both sides. The best-known atrocity of the war was the massacre of 12,000 Turks at Tripolitza, hitherto the seat of the Turkish Government in Morea. A Greek leader said, 'as he rode from the gateway to the citadel his horse's hoof never touched the ground'. The Turks replied by blood-curdling massacre of the Greeks at Chios, where the population had been reduced from 120,000 to 30,000.

In the initial stage the Turks were handicapped by the fact that they were fighting on two fronts. Their best troops were locked up before the island fortress of Janina, where Ali maintained a desperate struggle against the Turks. Moreover, the Greeks, by their command of the sea, could hold out long against the Turks. But in 1824 the situation changed when the Porte summoned to its aid Mehmet Ali, the Pasha of Egypt who was promised Syria, Damascus and Morea as the price of his assistance against the Greeks. Early in 1825, Mehmet Ali's son, Ibrahim, landed at Morea with 11,000 well equipped forces and soon overran a greater part of the Peloponnese.

Attitude of European Powers

The war was of interest to the Great Powers, as it not only affected the general peace but also involved their political and economic stakes in the Near East. But in the beginning, the Great Powers were hesitant to take a positive attitude to the Greek War of Independence.

Metternich regarded the Greeks as rebels against the lawful sovereignty of the Ottoman Empire and the whole affair as 'placed beyond the pale of civilization'. At Laibach, Tsar Alexander had readily adopted Metternich's point of view. England, on her part, adhered strictly to the theory of non-intervention. At the same time, England and Austria were determined to preserve the integrity of the Ottoman Empire and were fully aware of the dangerous possibilities of the success of the Greek insurrection.

The Great Powers, however, could hardly remain unconcerned about Greek affairs when public opinion was overwhelmingly in favour of the struggle and the situation was charged with the possibilities of developing into a European conflagration. Britain took the initiative when George Canning recognised the Greeks as belligerents in March 1823. The pressure of Philhellenic societies in England and the popular upsurge caused by Byron's romantic death in the Greek struggle for independence were too strong to be ignored by British Government. Moreover, the fear of Russian intervention and support of Greece determined the British policy as Tsar Alexander made no secret of his feeling that he expected autonomous Greece to be a Russian protectorate. An increase in the Russian influence in the Balkans was the last thing England wanted to see. The St. Petersburg conferences held to restore peace in Greece came to nothing owing to the hostility of Austria and England. In the midst of such situation Tsar Alexander died in 1825.

In 1826 several factors altered the international situation completely. First of all, the surging tide of the Philhellenic Movement with its romantic taste for classical antiquity and the recollection of the Christian Crusade against

Islam, aroused universal sympathy for the Greek cause. Apart from London, Paris, Munich and Geneva became the chief centres of Philhellenism. Finally, the European living in the Middle East, originally suspicious of the Greeks, had now been turned in their favour by Turkish ferocity. However, the Philhellenic Movement would not have been successful had not the new Tsar, Nicholas I, been more sensitive than his brother to Russian expansion in the Balkans. Moreover, England could not remain aloof at the prospect of an increase in Russian power and the appeal of some Greek leaders for British protection (June 1825) provided the pretext for the latter's intervention.

In the existing circumstances, Canning thought it wise to act with Russia in solving the Balkan problem. The upshot was Protocol of Petrograd signed by England and Russia on April 4, 1826. According to the Protocol, Greece was to remain tributary to the Sultan; it was, however, to be governed by its own elected authorities and to be completely independent in its commercial relations. Even before the Protocol was signed, the new Tsar sent an ultimatum to the Sultan demanding settlement of outstanding Russo-Turkish disputes. The resulting convention of Akkerman (October 1826) was a diplomatic success of Russia as it secured the almost complete independence of Serbia and a share of the suzerainty over Rumania, but made no stipulation for the Greeks. The French Government, which had supported the Turks for a long time, spurred on by public sympathy for the Greeks, now entered the field.

The Protocol of April 4, 1826, now became the tripartite Treaty of London (July 6, 1827), by which Britain, France and Russia undertook to establish Greece as an autonomous State under Turkish suzerainty. The Mohammedan population of the Greek provinces was to be removed. Each of the three contracting parties agreed not to seek increase of territory in the East and any special commercial privileges. By an additional Article the powers were required an armistice on both parties 'without however taking any part in the hostilities'. Austria and Prussia refused, out of their hatred for liberty, their assent to the treaty.

Both parties accepted the armistice without fully observing it. A joint Anglo-French-Russian fleet under the command of the British admiral Codrington, while attempting to enforce an armistice between the Turks and the Greeks, encountered the Turkish and Egyptian fleets off Navarino on the west coast of Morea and destroyed it (October 20, 1827). The Battle of Navarino—regarded by Wellington, Canning's successor, as 'untoward event' and by Metternich as 'frightful catastrophe'—did not put an end to the conflict. It merely provoked the Sultan to declare a Holy War against the Christian Powers, whose ambassadors had to leave Constantinople, and afforded Russia a pretext for intervention in Turkey. While Wellington, the British Prime Minister, was opposed to coercive measures against Turkey, Russia declared war on Turkey alone in April 1828. The war that followed dragged on for two years, with French troops clearing the Morea of the Egyptian troops while one Russian army invaded Asia Minor and a second crossed the Balkan mountains. After preliminary reverses the Russian army reached Adrianople in August 1829. The Russian Commander, Diebitsch, summoned the Turks to make peace and the Treaty of Adrianople was promptly signed on September 14, 1829.

The Turks were forced to give up control of the mouths of the Danube, to cede part of the Black Sea coast to Russia and important territorial concessions in Armenia and the Caucasus. Serbia was to be occupied by the Russian army until a heavy indemnity had been paid. The rights of Russia in the Bosphorus and the Dardanelles were once more asserted. Moreover, all Moslems were to be evacuated from the Principalities and all Turkish fortresses to be destroyed.

With respect to Greece, the Treaty of Adrianople merely granted her autonomy under Turkish sovereignty. But Britain, France and Austria felt that the creation of an autonomous State would open the door to Russian intrigues in the Balkans. In fact, a year later, much to the reluctance of Russia, the second Treaty of London recognised the total independence of Greece. Serious differences arose among the Powers with regard to the boundaries of the new state. Haggling continued until March 1832 when the

Powers extended the boundaries of the country and elected Prince Otto of Bavaria in May 1832.

The Greek War of Independence was an important landmark in Balkan history. The event fired all the other Balkan people with the ambition to make themselves independent. Again, the Greek War of Independence gave a new turn to the foreign policy of Russia and started the famous Balkan question. Tsar Nicholas, on the basis of a report of a powerful committee of his Council (1829), decided to preserve for ten years the integrity of the Turkish Empire. The break-up of the Ottoman Empire would result in the creation of strong Balkan states which Russia would be unable to control. If Russia was to seek territory it should be in the direction towards Asia. But it should be remembered that whatever her intention might be, Russia had not the power in 1829 to seek alone a radical solution of the Eastern Question. Among the far-reaching results, the Greek revolt encouraged Turkey to take the first decisive step towards internal revivals. 'The first explosion of Greek nationalism kindled the first spark of its Turkish counterpart'. But it was not till a century later that the Turks appeared to be a 'nation rightly struggling to be free'.

Eastern Question: From 1830 to Outbreak of the Crimean War

The years immediately following 1830 witnessed the three eastern powers—Russia, Austria, and Prussia—ranging against Britain and France. This grouping, in the words of Palmerston, was 'not one of words but of things, not the effect of caprice or of will, but produced by the force of circumstances. The three and the two think differently and, therefore, they act differently'. It would be a mistake, however, to regard the two opposing combinations as a well-knit symmachy. In the years which spanned 1830 and the outbreak of the Crimean War, it would appear that the Powers ignored their ideological difference. Thus the cooperation was 'the axle' upon which Lord Palmerston based his policy. He found no hesitation in allying with the eastern powers in moments when French interests clashed with British interests. Similarly Metternich, the Austrian Chancellor, found occasion to discuss with Britain means of restraining the Near Eastern policy of Tsar Nicholas of Russia.

The rapprochement between England and France was revealed on the occasion of the first Egyptian crisis. There Mehmet Ali, the bold and ambitious Pasha, though in nominal subordination to the Sultan, had long aspired to extend his control over Palestine, Syria, and Arabia. Having decided to avert any possible design to expel him from Egypt, Mehmet Ali instructed his warlike son Ibrahim to start a 'preventive war' against the Sultan. In November 1831, Ibrahim invaded Palestine by land and sea. Jaffa, Gaza, Jerusalem fell in rapid succession and Acre, after heroic resistance, fell in May 1832. Sultan Mahmud II declared Mehmet a rebel and set out to crush him. In the subsequent campaigns which lasted throughout 1832, the Sultan's forces suffered a series of disastrous defeats. In Deccember 1832 the Sultan's last army was utterly routed at Koniah and it appeared that the Egyptians might overrun all Asia Minor and take Constantinople itself.

The Egyptian advance was a matter of serious concern to all European Powers. Despite Metternich's attempt to rally the European Powers to preserve the integrity of the Ottoman Empire, it aroused little enthusiasm either in London or in Paris. The French Government enjoyed cordial relations with Mehmet Ali and was more interested in mediation than in punitive measures. Unwilling to bring Britain to the aid of Turkey, Palmerston was inclined to agree to collective action, but wished London rather than Vienna to be the centre of diplomatic activity between the great Powers, a condition quite unacceptable to Metternich.

The Sultan, in despair, turned to Russia, his hereditary enemy, for help. To the dismay of the Western powers a Russian naval squadron anchored off Constantinople on February 20, 1833. In April, troops disembarked on the shores of the Bosphorus. The Russian intervention was the driving force in the Anglo-French diplomacy which succeeded in effecting peace between the belligerents. By the Treaty of Kutahia (May 1833), Mehmet Ali received Syria, Adana and Tarsus. But this could not prevent Russia from following up her advantages with Turkey. A new secret treaty was signed between Turkey and Russia at Unkiar Skelessi on July 8, 1833.The

Treaty was in reality an offensive and defensive alliance for a period of eight years between the two powers. By a separate Article, however, Russia waived her rights for Turkish military aid, and Turkey agreed in return to close the Dardanelles to all warships 'not allowing any foreign vessels to enter therein on any pretext whatever'. The Treaty was the highwater-mark of Russian influence in the Ottoman Empire.

Unkiar Skelessi raised a storm of protest among the European Powers. Apart from castigating the Treaty, Palmerston made a vain effort along with France to prevent ratification of the Treaty. At the same time, he became suspicious of Metternich, accusing him of having been privy to the Tsar's intentions. Though this proved to be false, Western suspicion about Austria's attitude was fully confirmed when Nicholas I met the Austrian Emperor Francis and Metternich at Munchengratz in Septembr 1833. At the meeting the Tsar tried to recreate with Austria and Prussia a sort of Holy Alliance, which tried to revive the principle of intervention in defence of monarchy.

In the growing complexities of the Eastern Question, the Anglo-French *entente* became less intimate. Although the *entente* lasted until 1840, it proved artificial and unfruitful after 1834. France wanted to support Mehemet Ali in the hope of developing her interests in Egypt and Syria. She also wanted to weaken British influence in the Mediterranean. This was as dangerous as the dominance which Russia had secured in the Ottoman Empire by the Treaty of Unkiar Skelessi. Moreover, colonial conflicts, especially in North Africa, embittered the relations between the two countries. The French had already conquered Algeria and the English seemed to fear a fresh attempt at French expansion from Algeria towards Morocco and Tunisia.

The basic weakness of Anglo-French *entente,* however, was that there was no real community of economic interests between the two countries. The menace of British competition alarmed the French industrialists who demanded tariff protection. British and French trading interests clashed not ony in Europe but also in more remote markets in Africa and the Pacific. In 1837 Palmerston was at pains to observe that France was jealous of the commercial prosperity of England and desired to arrest the progress of that prosperity. In the following year, when tariff negotiations between the two countries failed to provide any solution, the British ambassador in Paris warned the French Government that 'two nations cannot continue to be united politically unless they are bound directly together by the bond of commercial affair'. While the Anglo-French *entente* was in the process of becoming a dead letter, France found it impossible to enter into a new system of alliance. Her diplomatic isolation was complete in the course of the 1840 crisis.

Since 1834 British policy with regard to the Eastern Question had been based on a few principles. First of all, she was determined not to allow the St. Petersburg government to make use of the privileges it had acquired by virtue of the Treaty of Unkiar Skelessi. Even more than Russia, England feared the expansionism of Mehemet Ali, France's ally, whose ambitions could endanger British communications with India. After 1833 the British recognised the importance of the overland routes to India and it was Palmerston's determination that neither Russia nor Mehemet Ali should be allowed to dominate them. In the first half of 1838 Palmerston tried to persuade the other Powers to act in concert to check the aggression of Mehemet Ali. Both the Austrians and the French seemed ready to cooperate, but the Russians refused to do so. Palmerston made no secret of his feeling when he warned that Britain would resist unilateral action taken by Russia on the basis of the Treaty of Unkiar Skelessi.

The Near Eastern question approached a serious crisis by the soaring ambition of Mehemet Ali who regarded his settlement of 1833 with the Sultan as a mere truce. But it was Sultan Mahmud who took the initiative in opening hostilities against Mehemet Ali in April 1839. The Sultan's forces, however, fared badly. On June 24, 1839, the flower of the Turkish army was routed at Nezib. On July 1, Sultan Mahmud died and was succeeded by Abdul Mejid, an impetuous boy of sixteen. Immediately afterwards the Turkish fleet deserted to Mehemet Ali. Intoxicated by this success, Mehemet Ali could dream of exercising unfettered control over the Ottoman Empire.

With the outbreak of the war, Metternich began talks with four ambassadors at Vienna in May 1839 for resolving the crisis. Palmerston also acted at once. Fortified with his own resolution and indomitable British sea-power, Palmerston tackled the most urgent problem of forestalling the unilateral Russian intervention. He despatched the famous collective note of July 27 which was presented to the Sultan by the representatives of the five powers in Constantinople. It informed the Sultan that the powers were ready to intervene and urged him to make no concessions to Mehemet Ali.

Despite Nicholas's initial annoyance at the move of this collective *demarche,* the Tsar realised that unilatral action on his part might precipitate war with Britain. He had come to regard Unkiar Skelessi as a burdensome arrangement which the Turks might repudiate if they were assured of British support. Finally, the Tsar saw an opportunity of driving a wedge between Britain and France, the latter being regarded as the chief breeding ground of revolution. Accordingly, in September 1839, the Tsar showed his willingness to cooperate with Britain in maintaining the integrity of the Turkish Empire by sending an able diplomat, Barron Brunov, to London.

Britain and Russia found little difficulty in framing the outlines of the Near Eastern settlement which provided for forcing Mehemet Ali to give up most of his gains and, for an international agreement, closing both the Bosphorus and the Dardanelles to all warships. Austria and Prussia, refusing to be isolated in the diplomatic game, indicated their support to the terms agreed on. But France proved to be inflexible in her opposition to Anglo-Russian attitude towards the Near Eastern question. Palmerston was equally determined to act without France 'for the interests of England, the preservation of the balance of power and the maintenance of peace in Europe'. He was convinced that if he failed to do so, the result would be 'the practical division of Turkey into two separate states—one of the dependency of France and the other a satellite of Russia, in both of which our political influence will be annulled and our commercial interests sacrificed'. Palmerston had his views accepted by the British Cabinet and got Russia, Austria and Prussia to sign the London Convention of July 15, 1840. The terms were that Mehemet Ali was to become hereditary Pasha of Egypt and of Acre. He was required to give up all conquests and accept these terms within a period of ten days.

The French Government interpreted the London Convention as an outrageous insult to their country. Public opinion in Paris was exasperated by the isolation of France, and there was angry talk of war against England and of a thrust across the Rhine. Thiers embarked on a policy of military bluff. However, after the bombardment of Beirut, it became clear that the powers were detemined to enforce the decisions taken in London. Louis-Philippe did not want to be dragged into war by his 'little minister'. He replaced Thiers with Guizot, then French ambassador in London, who had disapproved of the policy pursued so far.

Meanwhile, on the appearance of a British fleet off Alexandria, Mehemet Ali capitulated at once. He signed a Convention on November 27, 1840, promising to submit and to evacuate Syria, provided that he was allowed to retain the hereditary Pasha of Egypt. The Great Powers demurred but Britain had her way and allowed Mehemet Ali to keep Egypt on a hereditary basis. The British triumph was completed when France joined in the so-called Straits Convention, July 13, 1841, which closed the Dardanelles and Bosphorus to all warships. Thus the crisis ended triumphantly for England. She secured the exit of Russia from the Straits and France from the Nile and ensured her own primacy in the Mediterranean. 'However brutal and discourteous Palmerston's diplomatic methods might be, there can be no doubt that he was one of the great promoters of English power in the world'[1] It should be remembered that throughout the critical months Metternich worked assiduously to promote moderate solutions. If France was able to find her way back to the concert, this was due in large part to Metternich who, aided by the Prussians, mediated between her and the other powers.

1. Droz Jacques: *Europe between Revolution*, P. 240.

The British triumph seemed to be complete but Russia could not forget the disappointment which she had to suffer in forgoing the privileges secured by her from the Treaty of Unkiar Skelessi. She tried to ingratiate Britain and sought a rapprochment. In the famous conversation which Tsar Nicholas had with Lord Aberdeen in 1844, the former expressed the view that the Turk was 'a dying man' and his Empire was disintegrating. A deal could be arranged by allowing Britain to have Constantinople or Crete as well provided Russia was given unfettered control over Constantinople. But the British policy had already been decided upon which found eloquent expression in the words of Palmerston in 1839: 'All that we hear everyday of the week about the decay of the Turkish Empire, and its being a dead body or a sapless trunk, and so forth, is pure and unadulterated nonsense'. No compromise was possible between England and Russia about their respective attitudes towards the Ottoman Empire. Therein lay the germ of the Crimean War.

THE CRIMEAN WAR

Causes of the War

The Crimean War had its immediate origin in a trifling dispute between Christians of different sects over their rights in the Holy Land of Jerusalem and Bethlehem. Its essential causes were, however, a test of prestige between France and Russia and a conflict between Russian attempts to control the Turkish Government and British fears of Russian expansion.

Religion was a potent element in the ferment of any country. The passions which aroused between the powers over the question of the Holy Land were serious. The French Government had a traditional right to be considered as the protector of the Latin Christians in the Holy Land. But the orthodox or Greek form of Christianity which prevailed in most countries found its protagonist in the person of the Tsar. The increasing ascendancy of the Orthodox pilgrims in the Holy Land—which outnumbered the Catholic by a hundred to one—inflamed the religious feeling.

The religious animosity, though trivial in itself, derived importance from the fact that the Greek claims were pressed upon Turkey by the Tsar, the Latin by the Emperor of the French. Harried from both sides. Turkey, in February 1852, made concessions to the Latin Christians in the Holy Land. Almost immediately afterwards, it secretly confirmed the privileges of the Greeks. By the end of 1852 the confusion was worse confounded when the Russian Government demanded that the Turkish Government give formal recognition to Russia's right to protect Greek Orthodox Christians throughout the Turkish dominions.

In January 1853 the Tsar moved Russian troops towards the borders of the Turkish provinces of Moldavia and Wallachia. The Tsar was probably banking upon British support. He was an old friend of Lord Aberdeen, the British Prime Minister, and was on friendly terms with Sir Hamilton Seymour, the British ambassador in St. Petersburg. Convinced of the imminent collapse of the Ottoman Empire, Tsar Nicholas suggested to Seymour in January and February 1853 various plans for reducing the Ottoman Empire to Asia, offering Egypt, Cyprus and Rhodes to England, making Constantinople a free city, with a Russian garrison on the Bosphorus and an Austrian on the Dardanelles. As for France, Nicholas affected to disregard her and for Austria, he could rely on—a fatal misconception.

There was, of course, more obvious cause of Russian confidence. A coalition ministry had been formed in England at the end of 1852 under Lord Aberdeen. Himself an old-fashioned Tory, Aberdeen had great confidence in the Tsar's good faith and great distrust of Napoleon III. 'If Aberdeen had his way there would have been no Crimean War. Russia would have strengthened her position in Turkey, consolidated her reactionary hold over Europe; and Great Britain would have consoled by taking Egypt.'[2] Instead, he was saddled with Whig colleagues, Palmerston and Russell, who were friendly to France and wished to draw a sharp line against any new Russian advance. They were both pretty clear that a firm line against Russia would compel the latter to

2. Taylor, A. J. P.: *Europe: Grandeur and Decline* (1977), P. 70.

observe the integrity of the Turkish Empire. If either course had been followed consistently, war might have been avoided.

As it was, the British Cabinet vacillated between the two extremes. It was then guided by a strong ambassador at Constantinople, Lord Stratford de Redcliffe, who had served a total of twenty-five years in Turkey. He was a man who could take a line of his own and commit his country owing to his long experience on the Eastern question. In unmistaken language he admired the Turk, distrusted the Tsar, and regarded Russia as England's most formidable enemy. He had a personal animus against Nicholas I, who had refused to accept him as ambassador to St. Petersburg in 1831. Clarendon, the Foreign Secretary, wrote in anguish:

> It is a misfortune and a complication that we cannot feel sure of Stratford acting with us for a peaceful solution... He is bent on war, and on playing the first part in settling the great Eastern Question. He seems just as wild as the Turks themselves, and together they may and will defeat every combination coming from the west, however well devised it may be.

The attitude of Napoleon III was hostile from the beginning. He wanted to overthrow the Balance of Power and to clear the way for a French domination. Alliance with England was dearest to his heart and the Crimean War was welcome to him as it gave him this alliance. 'The Russian was unpopular with French clericals as a schismatic, distasteful to French republicans as an autocrat and to the Emperor personallly'.

The situation became grave only when Tsar Nicholas sent to Constantinople a special envoy, Prince Menshikov (February 28, 1853). But he signally failed to settle matters and was caught in the prevailing vortex of intrigue and Turkish delaying tactics. He demanded from the Turks not merely concessions on the question of the Holy Land, but also a treaty guaranteeing for the future the Russian claim to be accepted as the Protector of the Christians of the Balkan Peninsula. The chief part in this negotiation, however, was played by Lord Stratford de Redcliffe who persuaded the Sultan to make concessions on the Holy Places, but to stand firm against guarantee for the future and to Russian protectorate of the Balkan Christians. Stratford de Redcliffe wrote to his wife on April 27, 1853 : 'If the Russians are in the wrong, as I believe they are, my business is to make the wrong appear, and to stand by the Porte, or rather make the P stand by me'. Menshikov left Constantinople in protest on May 21 and diplomatic relations were broken off.

Tsar Nicholas made another abortive attempt to reach an arrangement with the Porte, but it was accompanied by a threat to occupy the Principalities. At the same time, he asked Austria to occupy Bosnia and Harzegovina, an invitation that was declined. Both in London and Paris suspicions were aroused of Russia's intentions. On June 2 the Aberdeen Government ordered the British fleet to mobilise at Besika Bay, just outside the Dardanelles and Napoleon III followed suit. Palmerston was right when he observed that this was 'the crossing of the Rubicon'.

War clouds hung in the air. In July 1853 a Russian army crossed the Pruth and occupied Wallachia and Moldavia. Nicholas undertook to withdraw if the Western fleets also withdrew. A Russian circular made scathing remarks against Western support of Turkey. Meanwhile a maze of negotiations took place in Paris, Vienna and Constantinople to prevent war. Out of this emerged a main agreement among the Great Powers—Britain, France, Austria, and France—in Vienna. Known as the Vienna Note, it was designed to harmonise the integrity of the Turkish Empire. The Note with its amendments aimed at protection of the Christian population of the Balkans without admitting the right of Russia to interfere. Russian reaction to this Note was not flattering, as a confidential commentary on this Note revealed her policy of aggression. When this leaked out into the press on September 22, public outcry rent air in Britain and France—against Russia. By the end of September, the issue was decided. On October 4, 1853, Turkey demanded the withdrawal of the Russian troops from the Danubian Principalities within a fortnight. On their refusal, the Turks began hostilities on October 23. At the end of October the joint British and French fleets passed the Dardanelles to strengthen the cause of Turkey. A month later, the Turks crossed the Danube and won two minor successes. But a Russian squadron under Admiral Nakhimov wiped out a Turkish squadron near Sinope.

The 'massacre of Sinope' aroused immense indignation in England and France. The entire British press called for war and public sentiment now ran beyond control. There was prolonged outcry against the Prince Consort who was suspected of working for the Russian interest.

The effect of Sinope was equally strong in Europe. A huge loan to Turkey was immediatly sanctioned. A joint demand was made to St. Petersburg (December 22, 1853) that the British and French fleets must enter the Black Sea and that the Russian fleet must take no action against Turkey. This was followed on January 3 by the two fleets entering the Black Sea. On February 6, 1854, Russian ambassadors left London and Paris, respectively, and a fortnight later British (Seymour) and French (Castelbajac) left St. Petersburg. Acting on the suggestion of Austria, England and France presented an ultimatum (February 27) to Russia demanding the evacuation of Wallachia and Moldavia by April 30. Russia refused this ultimatum and England and France declared war on March 28.

Though war was declared, the military operations were slow to develop. Meanwhile, efforts were made to persuade Austria to join England and France. The presence of Russian troops in the Principalities gave a pretext for Austrian intervention. But the Russians withdrew from the principalties in July and the Austrians decided, for the time being, to remain neutral. Prussia remained neutral as she was indifferent to the affairs of the Near East.

Course of the War

The Allies decided to strike at Sebastopol, the great naval port of the Russian Empire in the Black Sea. This would lead to the destruction of the Russian preponderance in the Black Sea. But it was a mad enterprise, and, even if successful, would make no impression on the huge resources of Russia. In mid-September the Allies landed 50,000 troops on the Crimean peninsula. Determined action immediately after the landing would have enabled the Allies to take Sebastopol at once, for they broke the initial Russian resistance at the battle of the Alma River (September 20). Instead of driving straight for Sebastopol or even establishing a blockade on the north side of the river on which Sebastopol stands, they undertook to sail round to the south where there was better harbourage and thence to renew the attack. The precious time squandered by the Allies was utilised to the full by the Russians. Protected by the genius of Todleben, by the severity of a Crimean winter, by the constant accretions of relieving forces, the fortifications of Sebastopol were improved out of recognition.

The Russians tried to mount a counter-offensive that would clear the peninsula, but they failed at Balaclava in October 6 1854. The battle of Balaclava is memorable for the magnificent but useless charge of the famous Light Brigade. The Russian commander, Menshikov took the British by surprise on Inkerman ridge on November 5. This was an infantry battle. The Russians were defeated but Sebastopol was saved. After that, the conflict degenerated into a war of attrition, while the Allied troops suffered unspeakable miseries during winter.

As the campaign dragged on, a change made itself felt in the diplomatic scene. In December 1854 Austria intervened and, in conjunction with England and France, presented to Russia a Memorandum embodying the Four Points of Vienna. This called for the renunciation by Russia of her exclusive protectorate over Moldavia, Wallachia and Serbia, a similar renunciation of her claim to protect the Christian subjects of Turkey, free navigation of the Danube and the termination of Russian preponderance in the Black Sea. Austria bound herself to declare war if Russia failed to accept the Four Points by the end of the year. Austria had no intention to join the war and she tried to gain advantages from all sides including territorial *status quo* in the Italian peninsula. But the tripartite alliance became the starting point of fresh negoitations with Rusia, which began in Vienna on March 15, 1855.

Meanwhile, a series of events occurred which dramatically changed the diplomatic scene. In January 1855, Piedmont, under its astute leader Cavour, joined the allies. In Britain, an outcry aganist the mismanagement of the war brought down the coalition government. Palmerston became Prime Minister and the new cabinet faced the situation with boldness. On March 2, the temperamentally rigid Tsar Nicholas died, and the inexperienced Alexander II came to the throne. Palmerston deprecated negotiation 'in the middle of battle'. Russia was dilatory and the negotiation finally broke down on June 4.

Military operations were now moving towards a penultimate stage. Though the bombardment of Sebastopol in April 1855 proved to be fruitless, the Allied army captured Kerch on May 21 and made themselves complete masters of the Straits of Yenikale, which lead from the Black Sea into the sea of Azov. Despite the failure to caputure Sebastopol in June, the French and the Sardinians defeated the Russian field army at Tchernaya on August 16. The Sardinian contingent under general La Marmora contributed in no small degree to the defeat of the Russian army. 'Thus were Cavour's calculations precisely fulfilled. In the waters of the Tchernaya the stain of Novara was wiped out for ever; out of the mud of the Crimean trenches was modern Italy built up'. The final assault on Sebastopol was resumed and, on September 9, the Russians abandoned the town.

The Russians had been defeated but did not lose courage. The Allies also thought that a real victory meant another campaign. The war went on for some time and the Russians ended with a success when they captured the fortress of Kars (November 28, 1855) in Asia Minor from the Turks and the British officers. Though Palmerston desired to continue the war until a decision had been reached, Napoleon III was bent on peace. The fall of Sebastopol satisfied the French public and Napoleon was eager to repair his relations with Russia without losing the British friendship.

Diplomatic pourparlours began and Austria entered the scene. An acceptable memorandum was drafted on November 24 with the assistance of Seymour, the British ambassador in Vienna. Austria presented the terms to St. Petersburg in late December as an ultimatum expiring on January 18, 1856. Alexander II was no less keen for peace. The Russian armies were greatly weakened and her economic resources were strained. Moreover, rumblings of peasant discontent were surfacing. Alexander, however, disliked the Austrian mediation. This was Prussia's opportunity who, despite an army of 400,000 men, refused to be dragged at the heels of Austria. Alexander welcomed Prussia's intervention as a sort of counterpoise to Austria. But when Austria promised to include Prussia in the peace congress, the latter supported the Austrian ultimatum. Then followed Russia's acceptance of the Austrian ultimatum (January 16) and the choice of Paris as the place of the Congress.

The Congress continued its deliberations for nearly eight weeks from February 25 to April 16, 1856. The Settlement of 1856—the Peace of Paris—concerned partly with the immediate issues and partly with broader issues defining the relations between the Powers. Turkey was admitted to the family of nations and the European powers guaranteed Turkish integrity and independence. While the Powers repudiated the right to interfere in the internal affairs of Turkey, the latter sought to work for the welfare of his subjects 'without distinction of creed or race'. The Black Sea was neutralised, its water and ports thrown open to merchant ships of all nations, but closed to foreign warships. In similar spirit, the navigation of the Danube was to be open on equal terms to the ships of all nations.

The territorial settlement involved sacrifices on the parts of both Russia and Turkey. Russia ceded Southern Bessarabia to Moldavia. The principalities of Moldavia and Wallachia were to remain under the suzerainty of the Porte and under the guarantee of the contracting powers. Before the decade was over, the principalities were united under a ruler of their own choice. Similarly, Serbia was to remain under Turkey but under the collective guarantee of the power. After 1856 she enjoyed considerable autonomy though she did not become an independent kingdom until 1878.

By separate conventions which formed part of the main Treaty of Paris, Russia was forced to agree to leave the Aaland, in the Gulf of Finland, unfortified. The Straits of Dardenelles and Bosphorus were to be closed to foreign ships of war, while the Porte was at peace. Notwithstanding the neutralisation of the Black Sea, Russia and Turkey were authorised to maintain a specified number of light vessls of war for the services of their coasts.

By another addendum to the Treaty, known as the Declaration of Paris, the powers sought to codify the rules governing commerce during maritime wars. Privateering was abolished. Enemy goods could not be seized on a neutral vessel unless they came under the category of contraband of war. Neutral goods, except contraband, were not to be seized under an enemy's flag. A blockade to be effective must be maintained by an adequate force.

Significance of the Settlement

The chief significance of the settlement lay in its efforts to remove the sources of tension between Turkey and Russia and to prop up the Concert of Europe.

To Russia, the Treaty of Paris was a bitter disappointment. Russian schemes upon Turkey were not only checked, but she had to abandon all claims to a protectorate over the Orthodox Christain subjects of Turkey. The neutralisation of the Black Sea was an intolerable interference in the domestic concerns of the Russian Empire. She was kept back from the Danube by the cession of Bessarabia to Moldavia. The peace treaty represented 'a long line of circumvellation to confine the future extension of Russia... at any rate to her present circumference'. The treaty in the words of Gorchakov, Foreign Minister of Russia, was 'a screen full of holes' and Alexander II set himself to reverse the Bessarabian and Black Sea concessions. 'A treaty of peace can only define the conditions of the present; it cannot bind the future'. Thus the Russians, fifteen years later, repudiated the Black Sea clauses of the Treaty of Paris. In 1878 Russia completely wiped away the humiliation of Crimea by recovering Bessarabia.

The Crimean War saved Turkey from destruction. Her territorial integrity was not only guaranteed, but she was also admitted as a member of the Concert of Europe. But the hopes entertained to Turkey reforming herself proved deceptive. The Turks did not believe in reforms. Most of the Christian populations disliked military service and preferred instead to pay a tax. Despite the promise of many reforms by the new Sultan. Abdul Aziz, who succeeded in 1861, little, if anything, was done.

The Crimean War was 'an important chapter in the Eastern Question and the prelude to the most important political development of the nineteenth century'. The Peace of Paris reaffirmed the principle of collective responsibility by the Great Powers which believed that the European Concert would be effective in the years that followed. The Peace treaty gave to the powers acting in concert a general right of intervention in international disputes. Moreover, by permitting Cavour to bring the Italian question before the conference and to attack Austrian policy in the peninsula, the Peace of Paris seemed to imply that the future of Italy lay at the wise counsel of the Concert of Europe.

These apparent signs of collective action by the Great Powers proved to be misleading and the Concert was to prove generally ineffective in the next two decades. The old Russo-Austrian cooperation broke down. Both powers turned to France. But within three years Austria was at war with France, and Prussia seemed to Francis Joseph of Austria his only loyal friend. Similarly, Russia found France a difficult partner. In 1863 the Russo-French friendship foundered on the Polish rock and the Russo-Prussian association was revived. Palmerston had little confidence in the tripartite treaty which, in his words, was a 'summer seasons' partnership. Its value was exhausted by 1860 while the tripartite alliance was to prove a dead letter. The conflict between Britain and Russia had been suspended but not settled. In a new Eastern crisis Britain might find herself faced with a dilemma : the old anti-Russian course would entail opposition to nationalist course, while an anti-Turkish policy would allow Russia a free hand which was against Britain's interests. Turkey could never again rely upon the support of Britain or France or Austria against Russia.

The Crimean War was 'a fumbling war, probably unnecessary, largely futile, yet rich in unintended consequences'. It cleared the way for the unification of Italy and Germany by means of war. 'Cavour and Bismarck, not Napoleon III, were the real victors of the Crimean War'. Equally decisive was the action of Florence Nightingale who defined the conventions of the age for the relief of human suffering and raised the status of the nursing profession. The disappointing performance of the British forces in the Crimea had a sobering effect in England and had bred a desire for peace. And Britain refused to intervene in a continental war for sixty years thereafter.

Turkey

In 1815 the Ottoman Empire was a vast sprawling empire extending across the whole northern coast of Africa as far as Morocco, and into the Balkans as far as the rivers Danube and Pruth. In 1830 the process of disintegration set in with the French conquest of Algeria and the independence of Greece. This was further accelerated by the recognition of Serbia, Moldavia and Wallachia as autonomous principalities within the empire, and by the emergence of Egypt under Mehemet Ali as another autonomous region. In the Crimean War, Turkey was saved from disintegration by the Western Powers.

The Ottoman Empire between 1850 and 1870 resembled Russia in various aspects. The Crimean War injected an urgency of reform in both countries. Like Russia it comprised a great mixture of races, languages and religion bound together only by subservience to an arbitrary authority. But it differed from Russia in the important fact that the ruling class was Moslem, whereas many of the subject people were Christians and Jews.

'During the third quarter of the nineteenth century, the Eastern Question remained a cloud gathering for the future, rather than a storm immediately about to break'. From 1856 the Sultan Abdul Mejid seemed determined to inaugurate a series of reforms. He issued a reform edict known as the Hatt-i-Humayun. It created a universal Turkish national citizenship for all persons. It abolished the civil authority of the religious leaders and established equality before the law and equal eligibility for public office. The recruitment of the army, hitherto restricted to Moslems, were thrown open to Christian and Moslems alike. The system of taxation was reformed and judicial reforms were undertaken abolishing the use of torture. It not only provided complete security of property, but also tried to remove corruption from the administration.

But these far-reaching reforms were destined to end in disappointment. The pervading corruption of the Ottoman administration and the entrenched powerful class of legal religious orders inhibited any change for the better. In 1861 Sultan Abdul Mejid died and was succeeded by Abdul Aziz. He was an amiable and well-intentioned ruler who did something to modernise and secularise the administration of the State. He visited Vienna, London and Paris and opened Turkey to Western influence. He initiated useful public works, exploited the natural resources of the empire, and inaugurated a new system of education, free from ecelesiastical control and open to persons of every creed. A literary nationalist revival began. He set up a High Court of Justice and, in 1868, crowned the administrative edifice by establishing a Council of State. The Council, consisting of Christians and Moslems, was to have legislative and administrative functions. Its first President, Midhat Pasha, was a statesman of rare order.

But all these reforms were of no avail. The Ottoman Empire was a theocracy and it was impossible to secularise a theocracy. It was impossible to reform law which rested upon an unchangeable religious sanction or to secure good government where local officials were, in most cases, inefficient and corrupt. A person of exceptional ability was needed to restore a semblance of order in the administration. Unfortunately, Abdul Aziz had no such qualifications, and as his reign went on he plunged deeper into the grossest forms of financial extravagance.

While Turkey was on the road to decline Egypt, a part of the Empire, made rapid advance in Westernisation. Railroads were built mainly with British and French capitals. Between 1861 and 1865, while America was convulsed by the Civil War preventing the southern states from exporting raw cotton, Egypt's export of raw cotton multiplied fourfold. The Khedives modernised their administrative systems and encouraged the building of the Suez Canal. The completion of the Suez Canal in 1869 made the Middle East a focal point of world trade and of European rivalries.

Balkan Nationalism

Despite the effectiveness of the Sultan's power and the inefficacy of the reforms, a new spirit was beginning to stir the dry bones in the Balkan Peninsula. It was excited partly by the movement in the principalities, partly by the Pan-Slavist propaganda and not the least by the memory of the Napoleonic rule in the 'Illyrian Provinces'. During 1809-14, under Napoleon's auspices, the Yugoslavs of today were united under the name of the Illyrian Provinces which included Dalmatia, Istria, Trieste, Gorizia, Carinthia, Carniola and part of Croatia. The Union, achieved under an alien ruler, was an inspiration for future.

While Turkey floated on to destruction, the subject nationalities were showing a stirring vigour to assert their independence. The Greeks were the first to achieve independence in 1830 which was guaranteed by the European Powers. But she had disappointed many of the hopes that had been founded on her. Her territories were small, her economic resources were too meagre and her system of law and order too fragile, to ensure prosperity and security. King Otto, established in 1833, failed to win the loyal support of the nation, though he spared no pains to improve the well-being of the country. In 1843 he was forced by popular uprisings to grant a constitution.

During the Crimean War the general opinion of Greece was favourable to the Russians rather than the Allies. Otto became unpopular when he refused to take part in some abortive attempt of insurrection in Turkish territory. In 1862, a revolution broke out and, though it was suppressed in the initial stage, Otto thought it wise to abdicate. In the next year, a son of the King of Denmark was installed as George I. His reign was made memorable when Britain ceded to Greece the Ionian Islands, off its western coasts, which the former found costly and troublesome to maintain. But this only fuelled the ambition of the Greeks to gain, at Turkey's expense, the Aegean Islands of the east coast and Macedonia. Although philhellenic enthusiasm in Europe had ebbed considerably owing to aggressive fanaticism of independent Greece, it remained strong enough to enlist Western sympathies. Torn by internal dissensions and obsessed with hatred against the Turks, the Greeks by 1871 were the potential source of trouble in the Balkans.

In 1829 Serbia had become a semi-independent principality and her rights were reaffirmed by the Powers in 1856. To her south-west lay the sturdy mountain people of Montenegro, who had always maintained its independence of Turkey, though the latter refused to recognise that right. In 1858 the Turks tried to assert their control on the Montenegrins, but they were defeated among the mountains at Grahovo with immense loss. It was a heroic battle of Montenegrins defending their freedom against the Turkish invasion—a battle that deserves to rank with Marathon. But the Turkish danger was not eliminated. Michael of Serbia was aiming at closer union between Serbia and Montenegro when he was assassinated in 1868.

Making of Roumania

In Serbia and Montenegro the Turkish power ebbed and suffered a rebuff in the Principalities of Moldavia and Wallachia. The geographical situation of the two Principalities were such that the latter played the part of a shuttlecock between Russia on the one side and Turkey on the other. The Treaty of Kutchuk-Kainardji (1774) gave Russia the right of intervention in the Principalities and the latter in 1812 (Treaty of Bucharest) received the eastern portion of Moldavia known as Bessarabia. Under the Treaty of Adrianople (1829), the Principalities became protectorates of the Russia empire. At the Treaty of Paris (1856), Russia relinquished Bessarabia and Moldavia and Wallchia became autonomous States under Turkish suzerainty.

There was one progressive feature of the Treaty of Paris that the people of Moldavia and Wallachia were to be allowed to elect assemblies or 'divans', as they were called. But the elections were so manipulated by Turkey and Austria that the inhabitants had no option but to vote against union. But the French Emperor, Napoleon III, the champion of nationality, finally forced a crisis by demanding, on the threat of a diplomatic rupture, that the elections should be cancelled and that preparations be made for a fair plebiscite. Napoleon brought Russia round to his views. But Turkey, backed by Austria and Britain, rejected this demand. France, therefore, severed all diplomatic ties with Turkey, and Russia, Prussia and Sardinia immediately followed suit. Thus, in the summer of 1857, the Rouman question had brought an international crisis, and the Powers were divided into two camps.

In August 1857, however, the French Emperor paid a hurried visit to the English Court at Osborne. The result was the Pact of Osborne, by which it was apparently agreed that Napoleon should relinquish the idea of union and new elections should be held in the Principalities. New elections resulted in an overwhelming victory in favour of the 'union of the Principalities in a single neutral and autonomous state'. But the Powers still hesitated to accept the *fait accompli* and met in conference. After nearly six months' deliberation they resolved that the two Principalities must remain politically separate, that each should have its own parliament and its own prince, but that affairs common to both should be entrusted to a joint commission of 16 members.

To this arrangement, grossly insulting to the national sentiment of the Roumanians, the latter replied in early 1859, by each electing the same person, a Moldavian, Colonel Alexander Couza, as their prince. 'It was a striking retort of nationalism to an international protectorate' that had tried to keep its strings on a nation striving for consummation of national aspirations.

France was delighted, and, as Austria was being drawn into an Italian war, Britain could do nothing. Moreover, in Britain, men like Gladstone, Lord John Russell supported the nationalist sentiment of the people of Moldavia and Wallachia. Turkey had to accept quite reluctantly this act of revolution. But this was only the beginning of complications. Couza found it hard to govern with two legislatures and two ministries especially as he was involved in constant friction with the *boyards* or landlords. Couza felt that the only panacea for all these ills was the establishment of a union—an organic union in which there would be one legislature, one ministry, one administration. He appealed to Napoleon III and, after much negotiation, the powers agreed to the organic union of the two principalities. On December 23, 1861, the union of the principalities was formally proclaimed. The newborn state was named Roumania and Bucharest was selected as capital.

Prince Couza's tenure of power, which lasted only seven years (1859-66), did not prove to be a bed of roses. The *boyards* were still powerful to paralyse the government and the Roumanian leaders expressed a strong preference for a foreign prince. Despite much opposition, Couza carried through a series of far-reaching reforms. He founded two universitiers, at Jassy and at Bucharest, established a number of secondary and technical schools, and made elementary education compulsory. In 1863, he dissolved the monasteries, seized their property for national purposes, and converted the houses themselves into hospitals and jails. He abolished the feudal dues and handed over one-third of the land to the peasants, leaving two-thirds in possession of the landlords. All these reforms excited opposition of the feudal and military parties. In 1864 the prince, with French encouragement, was able to make himself a dictator with a constitution modelled on that of the Second Empire. The *boyards* never ceased to conspire against him, and, in February 1866, they were able to accomplish his overthrow. With Napoleon's connivance, the Rumanians chose a prince from a collateral branch of the House of Hohenzollern, the dynasty that ruled at Berlin. With the secret approval of Bismarck, the young Prince Charles of Hohenzollern-Sigmaringen accepted the offer and the Powers and the Porte duly recognised his position (1867). Thus ended the rule of Prince Couza who laid the foundation of modern Rumania. 'Hardly a voice was raised for Couza; not a drop of blood was shed on his behalf; he passed silently out of the land for which he had dared much, and seven years later he died in exile.'[3]

The decades between 1850 and 1870 therefore saw the creation or consolidation of three new Balkan States. There remained within Turkish territories two other peoples fretting with impatience to attain statehood. On the mountainous eastern coast of the Adriatic was the province of Albania, whose inhabitants, partly Moslem and partly Christain, were the most backward

3. Marriott J. A. R.: *The Eastern Question,* (1940), P. 303.

people of Europe. Turkish rule was weak in Albania owing to the ferocity and resistance of the tough barbaric mountain tribes. In the eastern Balkans lived a half-forgotten people, the Bulgars, whose nationalism was encouraged by Russia as a weapon against Turkey in the first half of the nineteenth century. When in 1860 the Bulgarians refused to acknowledge the eccelesiatical authority of the patriarch of Constantinople, the Sultan of Turkey, under Russian pressure, set up in 1870 an exarch in Bulgaria as head of the Bulgar Church. Although still under Turkish rule, the recognition of Bulgarians as a separate religious nation marked the first step towards national independence.

In 1871 it appeared that the whole Eastern Question was ready to burst into flames. The failure of reforms in Turkey, the weakening of Turkish rule in the Balkan Peninsula, the emergence of three restless new states and of other nationalist movements, all foreshadowed a fast-approaching upheaval. But events in western and central Europe absorbed the attention of the Great Powers. Austria and Russia made every effort to outbid each other in their expansionist plans. France and Italy were embroiled in the consolidation of new regimes. Britain still clung to the idea of maintaining the integrity of Turkey as a bulwark against Russian expansionism. Bismarck was so much preoccupied in completing the work of unifying the new German Reich that he treated the Eastern Questions as of negligible importance. Yet from this time onward the Eastern Question assumed a new dimension as to demand the attention of the Great Powers. The last quarter of the nineteenth century which was filled with frequent crises and wars owed not a little to this Eastern Question. "It contributed to the causing of two world wars in the twentieth century, one precipitated by events in Serbia and the other by events in Czechoslovakia and Poland."

CHAPTER 22

THE MAKING OF MODERN ENGLAND

Britain from 1789-1815

In the second half of the eighteenth century Britain became a modern industrial state. She ceased to be a land of peasant husbandry and small domestic industries. The wasteful scattered holdings in the open fields increasingly gave way to the enclosures of improving landlords, which increased the food supply, and consequently the population. First water power, then steam power, transformed the social and economic life. The iron industry found in the rich coal mines gave an unexpected impetus to vast developments. In the half century from 1760 population rose six and three-quarter million to twelve million. 'On the basis of iron, coal and textiles, Britain built up a civilization which has been copied all around the world.' To an atmosphere peculiarly favourable to industrialisation, there was added the incentive of the governing aristocracy of England, who, unlike the French nobility, was interested in commerce. Moreover, having successfully curbed the powers of the crown, they had no disposition to prop up an autocratic government in any form. The British parliaments of the eighteenth century may be criticised for doing too little, but they offered no resistance to the acquisitive spirit of the British mercantile class.

The central period of the Industrial Revolution in England—1789 to 1815—was occupied by European wars on a scale never before known. Britain entered these wars an agricultural and emerged from them an industrial country. In the initial stage, the French Revolution (1789) did not directly threaten the British interests. Britain was one of the last countries actually to join in the counter-revolutionary war, yet, once involved, she became the most determined enemy of France. Characteristically, it was Burke, a former Whig, whose *Reflections on the French Revolution* (1790) encouraged the ruling class of England, France and abroad to an unwise resistance.

It was the conquest of Belgium and the denouncing of the commercial treaties connected with that country that brought revolutionary France into conflict with Britain. Early in 1793, Britain entered the war, as a member of the First Coalition of Austria, Prussia, Spain and Piedmont.

Before war began the Radical and Republican agitation which arose in England as a result of the French Revolution had been suppressed. The Whig Party was soon split, the majority going over to Pitt and the reaction and only a handful under Fox demanding reform. But the period saw the first definitely working class political organisation—the Corresponding Society. Most of its members were republican disciples of Paine and its watchword was only universal suffrage and annual Parliaments. Thomas Paine, who had helped to formulate both the Declaration of Independence and the Declaration of the Rights of Man, asserted that government was only tolerable if it secured to the whole people 'Life, Liberty and the pursuit of happiness', and any government which failed by this test ought to be overthrown.

The movement was destined to end in failure owing to its limited character. The Government struck with a heavy hand. The *Rights of Man* was banned and Paine fled to France. In 1794 Pitt suspended *Habeas Corpus* and enacted laws which prohibited the holding of public meetings. In the years that followed, frequent strikes and bread riots kept the Government in a state of terror. The whole country was covered with a network of barracks. Troops were frequently used to suppress disorder.

From the formation of the First Coalition in 1793, Britain occupied a prime place in the various combinations against France. With one interlude after the Treaty of Amiens in 1802, Britain remained continuously at war with Napoleon till the capture of Paris in 1814. The main source of her strength was the capitalist economic organisation, her military resources, and the invincible navy. The war years gave a great fillip to England's rapidly expanding industry; its new urban centres—Manchester, Birmingham, Leeds, Sheffield, Bristol—grew feverishly.

The First Coalition collapsed in 1795 after Holland had been overrun and the Duke of York was trounced at Dunkirk. During this period, Ireland demanded her independence. Under the leadership of Wolfe Tone, the United Irishmen took the lead of the whole national movement. In 1796 Tone went to France to persuade the Directory to send an expedition to Ireland to act in co-operation with the rebels. While Ireland waited in vain for two years for French help, the policy of the British authorities goaded the peasants into a hopeless insurrection. In March 1798 the whole of Ireland was declared a state of insurrection and placed under martial law. The rising was suppressed after hard fighting and with great brutality. When a small French force landed in August 1798, they found that the rebellion was over. Tone was captured and committed suicide in prison. In 1803 a second insurrection led by Robert Emmet was crushed.

While the trouble in Ireland was going on, Napoleon had sailed for Egypt. But the destruction of his fleet at the Battle of the Nile (August 1798) smothered his prospect. With Napoleon out of the way, Pitt was able to form the Second Coalition with Russia and Austria. The Second Coalition broke up with Napoleon's decisive victory at Marengo in the last days of 1800. The years that followed left Britain alone in the war. The Treaty of Amiens brought hostilities to a close from 1802 to 1803. When war was resumed, Napoleon was preparing for a descent on England. But in October 1805 the French fleet was destroyed at Trafalgar. Before Trafalgar was fought, Pitt had persuaded Austria and Russia to join in the Third Coalition.

In 1807 the Tsar of Russia made peace with Napoleon. Finding the inflexible determination of England to carry on war, Napoleon tried to cripple her commerce by imposing a ban on her manufactured goods, England replied with a blockade, and, though neither the ban nor the blockade were completely effective, the alliance between France and Russia broke up. Before this happened, however, Portugal refused to recognise Napoleon's 'Continental System'. A French army was, therefore, sent to Portugal to coerce the latter to submission. At the same time Napoleon provoked Spain to insurrection by making his brother Joseph king of Spain. 'The Spanish proved to be the worst regular soldiers and the best guerrillas in Europe.' In 1808 Sir Arthur Wellesley, later Duke of Wellington, was sent with an army to defend Portugal and to encourage the Spanish insurrection. In 1811, when Napoleon had to withdraw part of his forces for his Russian venture, Wellington was able to take the offensive and flush out the French from the Peninsula. An attack on Russia by Napoleon in 1811, the march of the Grand Army to Moscow and its debacle, set Europe once more ablaze. Napoleon was decisively beaten at Leipzig in October 1813 and in April 1814 the Allies entered Paris. The Bourbons were restored and Napoleon exiled to Elba.

England, Russia, Austria and Prussia met at the Congress of Vienna to arrive at a settlement. Their deliberations were interrupted in 1815 by the sudden return of Napoleon to France and his valiant fight-back which ended with his defeat at Waterloo. England's gain in the Vienna Settlement was not inconsiderable. The foundations for a great Empire were laid by the acquisition of a number of strategic key points: Malta, Mauritius, Ceylon, Heligoland, and the Cape.

Postwar Depression : Years of Violence, 1815-19

Peace brought with it a general economic slump. Exports and imports fell and there was widespread unemployment. The heavy industries were the hardest hit. Wages fell, but prices were kept artificially high by the policy of inflation. Taxation was kept at a high level by the huge debt charges. Inflation and high taxes increased the misery of the people and prevented the rapid recovery of industry. In 1815 wheat prices fell sharply and, although Parliament immediately passed a Corn Law which imposed heavy duties upon foreign grains, domestic prices recovered very slowly. With the population curve still rising and the influx of Irish immigration, the industrial towns of England became centres of squalour and want, while the countryside was filled with paupers and unemployed handicraftsmen.

The monarchy was at a low ebb in its fortunes. The king, George III, was a hopeless maniac, while his son, the Prince Regent, was a cypher. Effective power lay in the Houses of Parliament and was wielded by the Cabinet. The Prime Minister was Lord Liverpool and his important colleagues were the Lord Chancellor Eldon, the Foreign Secretary Castlereagh, the Home Secretary Sidmouth, and the leader of the Tories in the House of Lords—the Duke of Wellington—all men of conservative ideas.

As the Depression continued, sporadic rioting began in various parts of the country. Strikes were widespread. A number of radicals and agitators appeared who distinguished themselves by the violence of their attacks. Jeremy Bentham (1748-1832), in his *An Introduction to the Principles of Morals and Legislation (1789)* developed his philosophy, which became known as Utilitarianism. In Bentham's view, the foundation of legislation is the 'greatest happiness of the greatest number'; hence government should concern itself primarily with the promotion of human welfare through legislative measures. In the House of Commons, Ricardo defended the liberal principles of the Benthamite group. But the principal role in these troubled years was played by the propagandists and men of action. The seventyfive year old Major Cartwright, who had previously called for universal suffrage and annual parliaments, founded an increasing number of clubs. William Cobbett (1762-1835), published and edited a radical newspaper, *The Weekly Political Register*, which was widely read by the working classes. Cobbett was a typical English agitator, virulently eloquent in denouncing the abuses of the day, but was opposed to revolutionary violence. He regarded parliamentary reform as all-important. 'Let us have this reform (universal suffrage) first, and all other good things will be given unto us', he once declared.

The most important figure in the movement was possibly Francis Place (1771-1854), whose house was the headquarters of the Reform Party and who directed the movements of the Radicals with great skill and shrewdness. Some were flamboyant agitators, like the fiery orator Hunt, and some were harmless fanatics. But there were dangerous agitators, like Arthur Thistlewood, who talked of overthrowing the monarchy by force and ruling England by a Committee of Public Safety on the French model.

In December, 1816, Thistlewood and his associates invaded a reform meeting at Spa Fields in London and made an attack upon the city of London. This foolish affair and a supposed attempt on the Regent's life a few days later hardened the attitude of the Government. There was rumour of widespread conspiracy against the Government. The Government became frightened and, early in 1817, suspended the *Habeas Corpus Act* and introduced the 'Gagging Bill' which banned seditious meetings and prevented the publication of pamphlets.

Despite all these repressive measures a band of petitioners (the Blanketeers) marched from Manchester to London in March 1817 with a petition against the suspension of *Habeas Corpus*. In June 1817, at Pentridge in Derbyshire, there occurred a muddled rising of the poor under the leadership of Jeremiah Brandreth. But the government dealt with the situation firmly and brutally. The Blanketeers' progress was broken up by troops; Brandreth and his associates were arrested and hanged. After a temporary lull, huge radical meetings were held all over the country, demanding reform and the repeal of the Corn Laws. On August 16, 1819, about 50,000 people gathered in St. Peter's Fields, Manchester, to hear Hunt and others talk about the need for government reform. The crowd was an orderly one. When Hunt began to speak he was arrested and the yeomanry suddenly charged into the crowd. In a few minutes eleven people were killed and about 400, including over 100 women, were wounded. 'Peterloo passed into popular mythology as an outrage on popular freedom and did much to offset the Tory credit for Waterloo.'

The 'Peterloo Massacre' let loose the forces of repression. Hunt, Bamford and others were arrested; Hunt sought refuge in America. In November 1819 the Government hurried through the Parliament the famous Six Acts which greatly limited the freedom of speech, of the press, and of assembly. Political agitation, nevertheless, was driven underground. Arthur Thistlewood spent the last month of 1819 devising a plot to murder the whole of the Tory Cabinet. The plotters were betrayed by a police spy and arrested in a loft in Cato Street and executed. Fortunately the Cato Street conspiracy was not initiated and the period of agitation died down when the government took up some remedial and progressive legislations.

The Reform Movement, 1820-32

The Tory Party, commanding the allegiance of the property-owning classes, had held power since 1793. Its uninspiring record in the years after 1815 were followed by a change of policy at home and abroad. After 1820, the party showed its inherent vitality by inducting a group of young and energetic leaders to direct the affairs of the state. Liverpool continued as Prime Minister, but his principal colleagues were now George Canning (1770-1827) at the Foreign Office, Robert Peel (1788-1850) at the Home Office, William Huskisson (1770-1830) as President of the Board of Trade and F. J. Robinson (1782-1859) as Chancellor of the Exchequer. These men did not belong to the old aristocracy and their horizon was not clouded by the sole consideration of landed interests. The bright young political leaders had received liberal education and were in touch with progressive ideas. The movement towards reform became more pronounced when Canning became Prime Minister in the spring of 1827 after Liverpool's retirement. Although Canning, who died in August 1827, was followed by the Tory Wellington, the wind of change was not halted. For a few years, Tory policy became progressive enough to win the approval of followers of Jeremy Bentham.

A number of reforms were put through that prepared the way for the great reform of 1832. Inspired by the proposals of the Whig jurist Mackintosh, Robert Peel, in 1823, reformed the criminal code by abolishing death penalty in certain cases and modernised the organisation of the police. The efforts of Robinson and Huskisson were directed to free the country from the restrictions of an outworn fiscal and commercial system. While the former overhauled the tax structure and reformed the national debt, Huskisson, a disciple of Adam Smith, freed the trade from artificial restrictions. He modified the Navigation Laws which required imports into the country to be carried in British ships or ships of the country of origin. He replaced them by a series of reciprocal trade agreements with foreign nations which increased British shipping by 50 per cent. He reduced the customs tariffs and by means of a sliding scale allowed the free entry of foreign corn in certain circumstances. 'National prosperity,' Huskisson said in 1825, 'would be most effectually promoted by an unrestrained competition.'

An attempt was made to repeal the Combination Laws of 1799 and 1800 which had forbidden association of various kinds including working-class organisations. Francis Place, 'Radical tailor of the Charing Cross' led a movement for the repeal of these laws. Place and his chief agent in Parliament, the radical Joseph Hume, succeeded in putting through Parliament a law allowing the workers to organise (1824). But an epidemic of strikes which immediately followed allowed the authorities to restrict the activities of trade unions. In 1825, a second act was, therefore, passed; it permitted workingmen to organise for regulating wages and hours of labour, but forbade them to strike.

More substantial progress was made in the field of religious liberty. In 1828, Parliament repealed the Test and Corporation Acts which made it possible for the Roman Catholics to hold most of the highest offices in civil government. But they were still barred from parliament by an Act of 1679. Roman Catholics in England numbered only 60,000. But the situation was anomalous in Ireland, where the bulk of the population was Roman Catholic, who were represented in Parliament by Protestants. The legal disabilities imposed on Roman Catholics kept the great majority of the Irish population from holding responsible civil or political office. However, a campaign for emancipation was organised by Daniel O'Connell, a Dublin barrister with remarkable gifts of oratory, who managed to unite the three noble causes—religion, freedom and patriotism. In 1823 he founded a Catholic Association in order to fight for the removal of Catholic disabilities. In 1828 O'Connell, though ineligible to stand as a candidate in a Parliamentary by-election in country Clare, was elected after defeating his opponent, a liberal Protestant. The Government of the Duke of Wellington was faced with a dilemma as, with the removal of legal disabilities on nonconformist Protestants (1828), it seemed impossible to refuse equal rights to Catholics alone. Faced with the formation in Ireland of Protestant Brunswick Clubs, which brought the country to the verge of civil war, the realistic Peel came round to the idea of emancipation. The Tory Government forced the bill through Parliament and, in March 1829, it was passed by Parliament. The Catholic Emancipation Act opened all offices to Roman Catholics, except those of Lord Chancellor and Viceroy of Ireland. However, by reducing the electorate in Ireland to only 26,000 voters, and by suppression of the Catholic Association, the Government took away with one hand a lot that they had given with the other. 'Religious equality was given but civil and political liberties were taken away. Goodwill was lost, and a rankling grievance remained to poison Anglo-Irish relations for another half century.'

The Reform Bill of 1832

By 1830 the economic crisis had reached its peak. Factories were closing down, unemployment increased rapidly. In the North, Trade Unions sprang up like mushroom. The revolution which took place in Paris in July and in Belgium in August helped to increase the tension. All events were conspiring in favour of reform. England's system of representative government had not altered despite the growth of population and the emergence of new industrial towns like Birmingham, Manchester, Leeds and Sheffield. Many Whig leaders had clearly spoken in favour of Parliamentary reform. The Radical circles—notably the Birmingham Political Union and the London Mechanics' Institute—demanded far-reaching electoral reforms. The National Union of the working classes and the other, known popularly as the Rotundists, regarded Parliamentary Reform as the first step towards social reform and economic equality.

The Tories refused to see this danger signal. In the fall of 1830, when the Parliamentary majority of the Tory party was dangerously slim, Wellington had the temerity to declare that he was 'not only prepared to bring forward any measure of Parliamentary reform', but that 'as long as he held any station in the Government of the country, he should always feel it his duty to resist such measures when proposed by others.' In the general election of August 1830 the Tories lost a few seats. In November Wellington was forced to resign and a Whig ministry took office.

In March 1831 the new Prime Minister Grey and his lieutenant, Lord John Russell, grandfather of Bertrand Russell, introduced the Reform Bill. When it was defeated on a technicality, Grey called new elections in April. The new elections gave the Whigs, led by Grey, a substantial majority. He then reintroduced the Bill, which, though carried through the Commons, was twice defeated in the House of Lords which had a Tory majority. This aroused widespread resentment which was expressed in riots and demonstrations throughout the country. The Bishops, who had voted against the Bill, were attacked. In the face of the King's refusal to create enough new peers to pass the Bill, Grey resigned in May 1832. Wellington, the Tory leader, tried to form a new Government but was unable to secure even the support of his own party. Grey returned with a promise from William IV to create enough new peers to force the Bill through the Lords. On June 4, 1832, the Great Reform Bill became the law of the land.

The major change effected by the Act of 1832 was to redistribute the strength of the constituencies. The House of Commons consisted, as before, of 658 members. But whereas the number of county members had been 188 it now became 253, and, instead of 262 boroughs returning 465 members, there were now only 257 boroughs returning 399. The Universities of Oxford and Cambridge and Trinity College, Dublin, each returned two representatives. The disfranchisement of 56 smaller boroughs (rotten boroughs) and the reduction of thirty others to one-member constituencies was a blow to the influence of the landowners. The increase of county representation of 65 members strengthened the power of the county gentry and the big towns at the expense of the landed proprietors and borough mongers. At the same time, the creation of 22 new boroughs with two members each, and of 20 more with one member each gave more power to the manufacturing and commercial interests. The House of Lords had become much larger by the lavish creation of peerages and by 1837 it numbered 456 members.

At the same time, the franchise was widened, but all depended on property qualifications. The county suffrage, no longer confined to landlords, was extended to long-term tenant farmers whose land yielded ten pounds of value annually and to tenants-at-will whose land was worth fifty pounds a year. In the boroughs, all special franchises were abolished and the vote was given to all men who owned a property with at least 10 pounds annual value. Throughout England and Wales, one man in five now had the vote; in Scotland, one man in eight; in Ireland, one in twenty. Thus a definite step was taken in the direction of perfecting democracy.

The Reform Bill of 1832 effected a great change in the politics and government of England as did the Revolution of 1689. The House of Lords lost its power and it was now established as a precedent that, in case of a disagreement between the two Houses, the Lords must yield. The Commons gained at the expense of the Lords and the former now claimed to be the representatives of the people against a clique of aristocrats. For the same reason the crown lost its means of direct interference in Parliamentary politics. Though the electoral system was far from perfect, it succeeded in returning to the Commons men who broadly represented the main interests and opinions of the country. The fact remains that the middle class could henceforth sit in Parliament beside the landed aristocracy.

It also marked the beginning of the kind of propaganda and pressure tactics that have become common place in our age. At critical junctures in the campaign, the London Radical Reform Association, in which Francis Place was most vocal, and Joseph Attwood's Birmingham Political Union, showed great restraint in mobilising public opinion. At the same time, the Reform Act marked the real beginning of modern party organisation in England. The Tory and Whig parties of the pre-1832 period gave way to modern Conservative and Liberal parties. Apart from these, the Act also heralded the growth of political clubs—like the Carlton Club, the Reform Club—which gave the parties their machinery. 'For the Act made legal enrolment of voters preliminary condition of voting, and this provision was a stimulus to such things as the formation of party associations in the local constituencies, the creation of central registration committees, the growth of election agents and party managers, and other features of the modern political party. In a real sense, the present political system of England dates from 1832.'

Nevertheless, it should be remembered that the Act of 1832 kept out of the electorate all the working classes which led the latter from parliamentary politics to revolutionary Trade Unionism. No provision was made for secret ballot, which meant that old methods of bribery, influence and intimidation remained entrenched in the system. Though the influence of wealthy classes diminished, there were still fifty boroughs and well over sixty members still depended on them.

Other Reforms

The Reform Bill of 1832 opened the floodgates of many reforms. One of the first acts of the reformed Parliament of 1833 was to abolish slavery as an institution throughout the Empire. The trade in slaves had been prohibited since 1807, and an Abolition Society, headed by Thomas Fowell Buxton and Zachary Macaulay, had been clamouring for its abolition. In 1833 Lord Stanley, backed by Buxton, succeeded in passing through Parliament a Bill that ended slavery throughout the Empire and provided for compensation to slave owners. The British example was followed by most other countries in the next fifty years: by France in 1848, Argentina in 1853, the United States in 1862-65, the Netherlands in 1863-69, Portugal between 1858 and 1878, Brazil in 1871-88.

In 1835, Parliament passed the Municipal Corporation Act which replaced the old Borough Corporations with New municipal Councils elected by rate-paying householders of three years' standing. A great agitation for factory reform was started by philanthropic people who were shocked at the miserable condition of industrial labour. Chief of these factory reformers was a prominent aristocrat, Lord Shaftesbury. Evangelical Tories and utilitarian reformers aroused the public conscience and secured laws regulating the hours and working conditions of women and children. Parliament's Health and Morals of Apprentices Act (1802) incidentally limited the workday for pauper children to 12 daytime hours. Another Act of 1819, applicable only to cotton mills, banned employment under 9 years of age and limited the work week for the youth between 9 and 19. In 1831 Michael Sadler headed another investigation that resulted in the Factory Act of 1833. This set a milestone along the path to modern factory codes because it provided four paid inspectors who were vested with enforcement powers. The factory reform was strengthened by the publication of the report of a Parliamentary Commission on Labour in the mines in 1842. A law enacted in the same year forbade the employment in the mines of women and girls, and of boys under ten. An Act of 1844 introduced the first safety regulations in cotton mills. In 1847 the workday for women and children was reduced to ten hours. Though the scope of these acts was limited to cotton mills and mines, the basis for the systematic Factory Code of 1901 was being built.

The Whig administration came to the view that the mass of the population will always live on the barest subsistence level and that their lot could not be improved by government action alone but only by self-help and personal discipline. This view was reflected in the new Poor Law of 1834. The practice of giving outdoor relief to supplement wages had done something to save the poor from destitution during the years of economic depression. But it had been wastefully—and often corruptly—administered. The new Poor Law passed in 1834 tried to reform the whole system. It checked payments to supplement wages, streamlined the operation of the workhouses and set up a central Poor Law Commission to supervise the system. It ended outdoor relief to the able-bodied and forced all recipients of relief to enter workhouses which were to be run by local Boards of Guardians elected by the ratepayers. The new system was, doubtless, more economical than the old, but the workhouse test, applied indiscriminately to all, struck terror in the life of the poor for the next generation. Charles Dickens in his *Oliver Twist* (1837) highlighted the human suffering in the workhouses. Even thirty years later Dickens did not change his view: 'I believe there has been in England since the days of the Stuarts no law so often infamously administered.'

The Trade Union Movement

The Combination Acts of 1790 and 1800 and other legislations made it impossible for the development of a strong trade union movement. At the end of the Napoleonic Wars, a 'Luddite' movement had grown up in Britain, denouncing starvation wages and miserable working conditions. In 1824, however, Parliament had repealed the Combination Laws and permitted the workingmen the right of combination for peaceful bargaining about wages and hours. The terms of the new Act, as amended in 1825, still made it difficult for workers to strike. But the following years witnessed a rapid progress for trade unionism. In 1829 John Doherty formed a single union for the whole cotton trade. In June 1830 he founded the National Association for the Protection of Labour, which catered for every trade and helped strikers. It disappeared the next year, but in 1832 the Builders' Union was revived. In the latter half of 1832, union membership in general began to grow and the climax was reached with the formation of the Grand National Consolidated Trade Union in October 1833, which had an estimated membership of half a million workers.

The leading spirit in this movement was Robert Owen (1771-1858), a born social reformer, who had made his New Lanark Mills a model establishment where workers were given good wages. His more ambitious experiment of 'New Harmony' in Indiana, in 1825, was a failure. But it stimulated the establishment of self-governing, non-profit cooperative shops and producers' societies to serve the needs of poor. Owen became a dreamer of dreams with the visionary ideal of establishing a socialist commonwealth.

But alarmed with these trade union activities, employers began to unite and to refuse employment to union members. At the same time, the Government's attitude also stiffened. Early in 1834, six Dorcetshire day labourers were sentenced to seven years' transportation as a warning to others. By 1835 the Grand National Union disintegrated. In the 1840s the miners set up a National Association and in 1845, a further attempt at a 'general union' met with temporary success. In 1851 the Amalgamated Society of Engineers was created with centralised control and, in 1886, the Trade Union Congress was formed.

The failure of revolutionary Trade Unionism made the working class realise that they could not win measures of social reform unless they had the right to vote. Abandoning the economic weapon, they now turned to political pressure—this was reflected in the agitation for the people's charter. However, Chartist agitation had been provoked in the first place by the passing of a new Poor Law in 1834 which obliged the unemployed to work in workhouses and made outdoor relief the exception instead of the rule. In 1836 William Lovett formed the London Workingmen's Association whose object was 'to seek by every legal means to place all classes of society in possession of equal political and social rights.'

Two years later, William Lovett and Francis Place drew up the People's Charter as a common political programme. Its six points called for universal male suffrage; equal electoral districts; removal of the property qualification for members of Parliament; payment of members of Parliament; secret ballot; and annual general elections.

Chartism found its mass support, as did the free trade movement, among the industrial population of northern England. The Birmingham Political Union (1816) sponsored the Charter and called for a National petition on its behalf. So, too, did the reformers of Leeds headed by the fiery Feargus O'Connor, whose paper the *Northern Star* became the official Chartist organ. Soon, the Chartists organised mass meetings and nationwide popular agitation. Highly inflammatory orators, like J. R. Stephens, Bronterre O'Brien and Richard Oastler, aroused popular enthusiasm for the 'Charter' which became the battle cry for a nationwide movement.

The climax of the movement was the calling of a National Convention which met in Westminster Palace Yard in London in February 1839. The Convention was marked by quarrels between moderates, led by Lovett, Place and their southern followers and the violent groups led by O'Connor and O'Brien and their northern followers. There was an air of civil war when pamphlets were sold to serve as guidelines for building barricades. In July 1839 the petition with nearly a million and a quarter signatures was rejected by the House of Commons. Riots, strikes and even an insurrection in South Wales, followed. The Government struck hard. In November 1839 it put down the Newport rising led by John Frost, and imprisoned the leaders including O'Connor, O'Brien and almost all the outstanding figures.

During the first half of 1840 the movement was forced underground. A National Chartist Association was formed in July 1840 to keep the movement alive. O'Connor was released in August 1841, and preparations were made for a second petition. The distress of the winter of 1841-42, and a slump in domestic and foreign trade—bringing unemployment to hundreds of thousand—intensified the Chartist agitation. Under O'Connor's leadership a new national petition, bearing 3,317,752 signatures, was submitted to the House of Commons in May 1842.

The House rejected the petition by 287 to 49. Again disorders gripped the country. A strike movement began in Staffordshire and spread rapidly over Lancashire, Yorkshire, Cheshire, Warwickshire and into Wales and Scotland. Troops were sent into the strike areas, and by the end of the year the movement petered out. After the French Revolution of 1848, O'Connor, who had been elected a Member of Parliament, tried to present the Commons with a monster petition in favour of the Charter; but it failed to materialise owing to repressive action of the Government.

The failure of Chartism was partly a result of the weaknesses of its leadership and tactics. Under O'Connor's leadership, it had become an anti-industrial movement. The revival of trade and increasing prosperity also smothered the Chartist agitation. Nevertheless, it was the first effective and spontaneous working class movement, shook the hardening complacency of Victorian England, and gave an eventual impulse to further reforms.

Queen Victoria

During the tumultuous years of trade union and Chartist agitation, King William IV died in 1837 and was succeeded by his niece, Queen Victoria, then a young girl of eighteen. After her marriage in 1840 to Prince Albert of Saxe-Coburg, she became a well-informed and conscientious ruler. Her reign (1837-1901) was to be the longest in English history and was to witness unprecedented prosperity.

The most distinguished man in public life during the early-Victorian period was Sir John Peel. 'Coming into office in 1841 at the head of a ministry of unparalleled ability, he made his government the instrument of a series of important social enquiries and reforms. If England during the latter part of the nineteenth century became a cheap place to live in, if her trade was worldwide, and the whole world was her granary, if a deficit had been turned into a surplus by the reduction of import duties, if her banking and currency had been placed on a firm foundation and her legal system relieved from many of the worst defects which had been pointed out by Jeremy Bentham, the great benefactor of legislators all the world over, the result is not a little owing to the extraordinary abilities of Sir Robert Peel.'[1]

New conditions began to appear after 1832 in English political life. The Whigs and Tories were followed by Liberals and Conservatives. Each party had a conservative right wing and a progressive left wing. Among the Tories, Lord George Bentinck and the Earl of Derby championed agricultural interests, while Peel advocated industrial reform. Among the Whigs, Palmerston was regarded as a rigid reactionary Liberal, while Lord John Russell was spokesman of the Radicals. The two parties influenced public opinion through high-quality independent newspapers: *The Times* and *The Morning Post* for the Conservatives, *The Morning Chronicle* and *The Examiner* for the Liberals. Until the end of the first half of the nineteenth century, the Whigs were responsible for the new political situation. Grey, then Melbourne, governed from 1830 to 1834, Melbourne from 1835 to 1841, and Russell from 1846 to 1852.

Repeal of the Corn Laws

Since the publication of Adam Smith's *Wealth of Nations* in 1776, there had been demands for free trade and a reduction of duties of imports and exports. The Corn Laws was the key to the protective system, and their removal, it was believed, would usher in a period of unexampled economic growth. In 1836, when the price of Corn was dear, the London Radicals founded the first Anti-Corn Law Association. But Lancashire of the cotton mills was destined to be the real home of the free trade movement. The prosperity of Lancashire depended largely on foreign trade; and the main impediment to foreign trade was the Corn Laws—designed primarily to keep the price of food high.

The leaders of the Anti-Corn Laws were Richard Cobden (1804-65), himself a cotton manufacturer, and John Bright (1811-89), the son of a Rochdale mill-owner. Although they wanted free trade in general, they thought it expedient to concentrate their attack upon the hated Corn Laws. In 1838 Cobden and Bright founded the famous Anti-Corn Law League with headquarters in Manchester. The Manchester Movement erected its own building, the Free Trade Hall, published its own papers and pamphlets, such as the *Free Trade Catechism,* and carried on intensive popular propaganda. Its motto 'give us our daily bread' struck the religious sentiment of the people. It represented Free Trade to Parliament as panacea capable of overcoming economic crisis.

On January 28, 1839, *The Times* declared in favour of free trade. In mass meetings, pamphlets and the press, protection was denounced as an economic evil because it artificially raised the

1. Fisher : *A History of Europe,* P. 901.

cost of food, and as a moral evil because it incited rivalries among nations, thereby causing wars. The movement spread to the countryside. By 1843 the weekly publication, the *League,* reached a circulation of over 20,000, and in London twentyfour mass meetings were held at Covent Garden Theatre. Cobden, Bright and the League orators had 'facilities for spreading the Free Trade gospel that Pym and even Cobbett could never even have imagined.'

In 1841 the Whigs were replaced by a Tory Cabinet under Sir Robert Peel who became convinced that the economic situation of the country was in need of reform. He expressed his belief in a letter to a friend: 'We must make this country a cheap country for living'. Peel showed his independence of mind by his gradual conversion of Free Trade. As early as 1842, he abolished export taxes and reduced import duties, and, in order to cover the losses incurred by the Treasury, he reintroduced the income tax. He also strengthened the monetary system and the credit facilities of the country by the Bank Charter Act of 1844 and other financial measures. In 1845 Peel reduced the import duties on sugar and silk.

Finally, in August 1845, the potato blight appeared in Ireland and since potatoes were the staple diet of Ireland, the country was faced with starvation. The English harvest had also been poor. The League demanded the immediate repeal of the laws which prohibited import of food when people were starving. Peel was bold enough to face realities and, in May 1846, the Bill for the repeal of the Corn Laws, prepared by Gladstone at the Board of Trade, was passed through the Commons by a coalition of liberals and Peelite conservatives. Peel was accused of treachery by his own partymen. But he proudly replied that those who earned their living by the sweat of his brow 'shall recruit their strength with abundant and untaxed food, the sweeter because it is no longer leavened by sense of injustice'. Free Trade in grain was followed by Free Trade in sugar, and finally in 1860, in timber. Now large and cheap supplies of corn were available from Russia, Germany and North America and Britain paid for them with export of manufactures.

The Repeal of the Corn Laws helped to make the period between 1845 and 1875 the golden age of the manufacturers. Engels sums up the whole period thus:

> The years immediately following the victory of Free Trade in England seemed to verify the most extravagant expectation of prosperity founded upon that event. British commerce rose to a fabulous amount: the industrial monopoly of England on the market of the world seemed more firmly established than ever: new iron works, new textile factories, arose wholesale, now branches of industry grew up on every side. The unparalleled expansion of British manufacturers and commerce between 1848 and 1866 was no doubt due, to a great extent, to the removal of protective duties on food and raw materials.

In 1849 the Navigation Laws—which had been designed to protect British shipping interests—were abandoned. So, by the middle of the nineteenth century, duties remained on imports and exports for reasons of revenue and not for purposes of protection.

Social and Material Progress

In the 1840s a series of reports of Royal Commissions revealed the deplorable conditions in factories and the abysmal condition in the mines. The effect of these admirable reports was to stimulate a demand for basic reform that cut across party-lines. A series of Acts were enacted improving the working conditions of the poor. Ashley's Act of 1842 excluded all women, girls and boys under ten from the mines. Graham's Factory Act of 1844 limited child labour and provided for inspection in the factories and mines. Fielden's Act of 1847 established a normal working day of ten and a half hours for all women and young people in the factories.

The Bank Charter Act of 1844 separated the Banking Department of the Bank of England from the Issue Department and required all notes to be backed by a reserve of bullion or coin. Another Act of the same year regulated the operation of joint-stock companies.

The ideals of voluntary cooperation for production were canvassed by Robert Owen and his followers. They founded the Cooperative and Economical Society in 1821. Similar Cooperative Societies were established in various places. They suffered by the general collapse of unionism in 1834. But the eighteen forties witnessed experiments in Cooperative villages when in 1844 the Rochdale Pioneers founded a successful cooperative store. It was based on democratic control by its members as consumers, giving the latter a dividend. In 1854 they also formed the Rochdale Cooperative Manufacturing Society and, a decade later, set up the Cooperative Wholesale Society. Industrial and Provident Societies Act, passed in 1852 and 1862, greatly facilitated their progress. By the 1870s the principles were rapidly extended to other sectors of economic life.

An era of railway building began with the construction, in 1830, of the Liverpool-Manchester Railway. In 1845, Parliament passed the first important law which established the principle of government supervision over rates and profits. In 1873 a permanent Railway Commission was appointed to supervise the railways. Steamship began in 1839-40 with the establishment of two famous lines, the 'P & O' (Peninsular and Oriental), running steamers to Asia and Africa, and the Cunard Line, running steamers to America.

The establishment of Free Trade, the repeal of the Navigation Laws, and the improvement of the means of communication made England pioneer in commerce and industry. She became the *entreport* or emporium of the world. An abundance of coal and iron, a large merchant marine, plenty of capital, and, above all, various scientific and technological inventions, gave the English people overwhelming advantages over all other nations in the race for economic supremacy. The London Stock Exchange was the chief centre of investment, and therefore the business barometer of the world. 'The extension of British trade to all countries, the growth of British shipping, the rise of British banking and insurance in a world in which British capitalists found themselves in a position of commercial dominance with the very minimum of foreign competition, all cooperated to produce a golden stream of almost boundless profits ... and a perpetual investment of the surplus in additional instruments of wealth production.'

Roman Catholics were predominant in England. The efforts of the Roman Catholics were confined to obtaining tolerance for themselves; they turned to the past more than to the present; they lived on 'memories and not on hope'. They cared little about the political and social problems that affected the mass of the population. In the first half of the nineteenth century a powerful intellectual movement revived the life and thought of the Church of England. Of the two parties within the Church, the Evangelicals did much to raise the moral standards of the age by preaching the 'Bible' Christianity. The High Church Party, on the other hand, was absorbed in doctrinal speculation that led, in the 1840s, to the Oxford Movement. It proclaimed the medieval ideas of the Church as the centre of all activity and of the importance of ritual in service and of holiness in life. A group of writers, among them John Kable, the author of *The Christian Year,* John Henry Newman, the famous preacher and writer, and Dr Pusey, the most eminent ecclesiastical scholar in England, advocated their ideas in a series of pamphlets called *Tracts for the Times*. The influx of University teachers and ecclesiastics of great ability raised the intellectual status and the vitality of the Catholic Church in England. The strongest of the dissenting sects in England was Wesleyanism—which was usually on the side of authority.

The established Church and the Non-conformists were pioneer in educational activities. The Societies established by them provided primary education for the masses. The British and Foreign School Society and its rival, the Anglican National Society, were pioneers in the field. But their methods were bad and their resources slender. The first government grant in education was made in 1833 with a grant of £ 20,000 to the two societies and was carried to a further stage by the establishment of a Committee of the Privy Council for Education in 1839. Not till 1846 was there any state provision for the training of teachers.

Secondary education was restricted to the upper and middle classes. Between 1818 and 1848, Thomas Arnold, the headmaster at Rugby, modernised and expanded the curriculum in this sphere with special emphasis on free enquiry. For the Universities this was not a distinguished period. Both Oxford and Cambridge were still clerical in character and governed by outworn statutes. The University of London, founded in 1825, was radical in origin with a wider curriculum. The University of Durban was established in 1832 and the Universities of St. Andrews, Glasgow, Aberdeen, and Edinburgh grew in size.

Much yet remained to be accomplished. England had to wait till 1870 for universal compulsory elementary education, and till 1902 for secondary education aided from public funds. But it is at least significant that as early as 1825 Henry Brougham, a great law reformer and a widely known political figure, published his *Observations on the Education of the People,* which at once went through twenty editions and led to the formation of the society for the diffusion of useful knowledge.

Foreign Policy

After 1815 England enjoyed a long period of peace. The Napoleonic Wars had forced the country out of its insularity and had created among the powers a diplomatic *esprit de corps.* Though Britain was not a party to the Tsar's nebulous Holy Alliance, she joined a much more practical Concert of Europe (November 20, 1815) in which the participating powers—Russia, Austria, Prussia, and Britain—agreed to meet frequently to discuss their common interests and matters affecting the peace and security of Europe.

It soon became evident that the union of the great powers was not based on solid foundations. Whereas Metternich wished the Quadruple Alliance to be an instrument for the suppression of liberal movements in Europe, Castlereagh, the British Foreign Minister, studiously maintained not to interfere in the internal affair of other states. The crushing of the Spanish Revolution in 1823 was the Concert's last victory. George Canning, the new Foreign Minister, welcomed the return to a situation of 'every nation for itself and God for us all.' Already he was involved in aiding the Greek and Latin American uprisings. To forestall intervention in Latin America, he turned to the United States. In reply, President Monroe issued a unilateral declaration later known as the Monroe Doctrine, in which he warned that the American continent was not to be considered subject to further colonisation. England, which played so large a part in the emancipation of the South American colonies, next contributed to the liberation of Greece from Turkish yoke.

Palmerston—who reigned almost without interruption at the Foreign Office from 1830 to 1865—was a liberal. While his aim was to avoid all serious entanglements in Europe, he nevertheless made it a point to prevent any power from securing a predominating position in Europe. Therefore he supported the revolutionary movements in Italy, Spain, Germany, and Hungary. So, while England was engaged in suppressing the Chartists at home, she gave countenance to revolutions in Europe. When the Belgians declared their independence of Holland, it was England's intervention that effected a settlement resulting in the neutralisation of Belgium. In the Near East he opposed Russia's plan to dismember Turkey and vigorously followed England's traditional policy of supporting the Sultan of Turkey. The outcome was the Crimean War which not only preserved the integrity of the Turkish Empire but had the effect of holding up the advance of Russia till 1870.

In the years that followed the Crimean War (1854-55), Britain was not seriously involved in continental affairs. During the Polish revolt of 1863, Britain made promises of assistance to the rebels that came to nothing. During the early stages of the Schleswig-Holstein War of 1864, Britain made a veiled threat to Prussia in case of an attack on Denmark. But the attack took place and the British Government acquiesced in the result. It was this 'policy of meddle and muddle' that came in for serious criticism in July 1864 which urged a return to the principle of Non-intervention.

Britain's policy was peaceful because war interfered with trade. Cobden and Bright popularised the idea of free trade which, it was believed, would bind nations together by bonds of mutual interest. This sincere and dynamic faith revolutionised Britain's colonial policy which made it possible for self-government in the dominions and gave birth to a new conception of Empire and Commonwealth.

With the achievement of American independence, British interests shifted from the Atlantic to the Indian Ocean resulting in the growth and consolidation of British trade and power in India, Ceylon and Burma. In consequence, Britain acquired extensive interests in the South

Atlantic and the Pacific Oceans. Cape Colony and a chain of Islands and West African ports bridged the Atlantic region and the Indian Ocean. In the South Pacific, Australia and New Zealand became a solid continent under British control.

In 1798 Jeremy Bentham had urged the French 'Emancipate your Colonies', and the early radicals were opposed to colonialism. But in the 1830s there grew up a group of younger radical reformers who saw in the colonies both an outlet for population explosion in the United Kingdom and an opportunity for administering colonies on humanistic principles. John Stuart Mill, Charles Buller, Edward Gibbon, Wakefield and Lord Durham were protagonists of this view. Through their influence the principles of responsible self-government were extended to all the overseas territories and the concept of 'Dominion Status' grew which made possible a new ideal of imperial cohesion founded on independence and freedom.

Meanwhile, rebellion in Canada attracted the attention of the radicals. By 1838 it appeared that the division between the predominantly British settlement of Upper Canada and the mainly French settlement of Lower Canada could no longer be preserved. At the end of 1837 violent disturbances took place in both provinces. In 1838 Lord Durham was sent out as High Commissioner with wide powers. He was accompanied by Buller and Wakefield. In the following year they produced the so-called Durham Report which has become the charter of British Commonwealth development. The Report recommended the reunion of Upper and Lower Canada and the grant of responsible government. Anything less, they felt, would lead eventually to the severance of ties between Canada and the home country, as had happened in the case of the United States.

The Durham Proposals were not immediately implemented. But in 1840 Upper and Lower Canada were united, and seven years later, when Lord Elgin became Governor-General of Canada, the attempt to apply the principle of responsible government began. It succeeded which was later applied to New Zealand (1854), Australia (1856), and the Cape Colony (1872). The Colonial Laws Validity Act of 1865 gave a general assurance of internal self-government to all the colonial legislatures. It was the 'charter of colonial legislative independence'. The direction was set for the establishment of the British Commonwealth of Nations in 1931.

British attention was diverted from Europe to America where Civil War began in 1861. The conflict aroused deeper passions in Britain, partly because it affected British economy by sharply reducing the imports of raw cotton to the mills of Lancashire and Yorkshire and it partly raised ideological and moral issues. There were sharp crises between Britain and the Union Government over the boarding of a British ship by a Union Commander (the famous Trent Affairs of 1861) and over the depredation of British commerce. The climax was reached when the privateer Alabama was allowed to get away from Liverpool and worked havoc upon the merchant shipping of the North. In the long run, the Civil War did much to destroy the monopoly of Lancashire.

Reform Act of 1867

In the field of politics the most important single event was the passage of the second Reform Bill of 1867. But this was preceded by a change in the nature and leadership of the political parties. Before 1832 the political parties had no programme at all and did not feel any need for them. The leader of the Tories, Lord Derby, was more interested in racing than in political issues; and Lord Palmerston, the Whig chieftain, busied himself in foreign affair to the exclusion of all.

The emergence of the Liberals (formerly known as the Whig) and the Conservatives (successors of the Tories) in the late fifties and sixties of the nineteenth century introduced a new element in party politics. In political reforms the Liberals were generally in the lead. The Conservatives, on the other hand, were content, as a rule, with the political *status quo*. In the second half of the nineteenth century, both parties favoured social reform, the Liberals taking the lead in parliamentary reform, the Conservatives trying to keep the Irish satisfied by economic concessions, while the Liberals came to advocate Home Rule, the Conservatives more inclined to promote imperial interests.

In 1866, a Liberal Ministry was in power with Lord Russell as Premier, and Gladstone as leader of the House of Commons. After a brilliant scholastic record at Oxford, Gladstone (1800-98) had turned to politics and served in Sir Robert Peel's last ministry as President of the Board of Trade and, later, as Secretary for War and the colonies. In the government of Aberdeen (1852-55) and Palmerston and Russell (1859-66), he was appointed Chancellor of the Exchequer and had distinguished himself by carrying forward the free-trade policy. The Reform Bill of 1832 had left much to be desired. In the 1860s only one adult male out of six had the vote. Gladstone favoured a broader suffrage and, in a famous speech in the House of Commons in May 1864, he expressed the belief that 'every man ... is morally entitled to come within the pale of the constitution.' Bright had also favoured the wider distribution of political power. In June 1866, Gladstone, as leader in the House of Commons in the Russell Cabinet, introduced a reform bill. Thanks to a combination of Conservatives and Palmerstonian Liberals, it met with defeat. The Russell Ministry fell, and was succeeded by a Conservative Ministry under Lord Derby, of which the most influential member was Disraeli (1804-81).

The defeat of the Reform Bill of 1866 suddenly made Reform a class question and almost a question of honour. In the autumn of 1866 the Government was alarmed at the outburst it had provoked. In scores of industrial towns huge demonstrations were held in which almost the whole working and lower middle class participated. In London there were huge gathering at Trafalgar Square and Hyde Park, the latter turning into a vast riot. Having sensed the public demand for reform, and having realised that extension of the suffrage was practically inevitable, Disraeli determined that his party should get the credit for it. In 1867, he introduced the Reform Bill and secured its passage.

The Reform Bill of 1867 gave the franchise to all householders of one year's residence in boroughs and all farmers in the countries paying an annual rent for their farms of £12 or more. It also redistributed fortyfive seats in the House of Commons giving preponderance to the countries and to the large industrial towns. The Second Reform Bill widened the franchise as it doubled the number of voters. It also provided the basis for the formation of an independent parliamentary party of the working class. The Labour Party grew up 'with one leg in the Trade Unions and the other in Parliament.'

Gladstone's Reforms

Gladstone's ministry—which lasted from 1868 to 1874—was characterised by a series of reforms. Gladstone, a great administrator and parliamentarian, set himself to the task of creating a better England through 'Peace, Retrenchment and Reform'.

Two measures that distinguished Gladstone's ministry were the Civil Service Reform of 1870 and the Education Act of the same year. In 1870, Gladstone abolished patronage and adopted the principle of recruitment by open competition. Even more important was the Forster Education Act (1870) which established a national system of popular education. Britain was divided into school districts, and new schools were built, known as 'Board Schools', which were supported by local taxation, and controlled by elected boards of education. Although religious instruction was to be permitted in both voluntary and board schools, in either case, parents could request that their children be excused from religious instructions on grounds of conscience. Another Liberal victory was recorded in 1870, when the English universities were made truly national for the first time by the abolition of the religious tests.

Gladstone and Ireland

The Irish problem absorbed the energies of the first Gladstone ministry. Their main grievances against England were mainly religious, political and economic. Predominantly Catholic, the Irish objected to tithes to the Anglican Church in Ireland. Politically, they opposed the Act of Emancipation of 1829 which had given the Catholics of Ireland parliamentary representation in the House of Commons. Economically, Ireland was plagued by several maladies. There was not enough land to support a rapidly growing population and the land was held by absentee English landlords. Lands were leased to the Irish by tenants of English landlords. Since leases were short, tenure was, at best, precarious. Most tenants could be evicted at moment's notice without any compensation.

Gladstone had announced in 1868 that his mission was to pacify Ireland. One of his first measures was the disestablishment of the Anglican Church in that country (1869), the Irish being no longer obliged to support an alien creed. In 1870, Gladstone secured the enactment of the Loan Act which recognised the principle of 'tenant right' by giving compensation for improvements to tenants who were evicted for causes other than the non-payment of rent.

The general character of British development during these years is epitomised in the system of imperial defence devised by 1870. The reorganisation of the army achieved by Edward Cardwell after 1868 produced a more efficient fighting force. Britain's worldwide interests and territories required a coherent system of imperial defence. The army was to act under cover of naval protection—a system best suited to the needs of a maritime commercial empire.

CHAPTER 23

CAPITALISM AND SOCIALISM

Economic Developments

In the first quarter of the nineteenth century Britain had all the prerequisites for the rapid growth of largescale factory production. She had undergone a certain degree of industrialization in cotton textiles and metallurgical industries. In the coming decades she was to become the workshop of the world.

English exports of cotton goods rose in value from 19 million pounds sterling in 1830 to 56 million in 1870. Similarly coal and iron production increased at a tremendous pace. The biggest advance took place in the methods of largescale conversion of iron into steel. Between 1856 and 1870 the price of steel was considerably reduced in Britain.

New industries came into existence. Gas was first used for cooking in 1832. Electricity, telegraph, photography, rubber industry made amazing progress. In the 1850s James Young discovered how to make naphtha, lubricating oils and kerosene by distilling crude oil.

The most striking feature of Britain's industrial growth was the decisive revolution in communication. In 1830 the common people still went on foot; in that year Liverpool and Manchester railway line was opened. By 1867 more than 12,000 railway lines were opened in Great Britain. The significance of the railways lay in the fact that they not only stimulated industrial growth but also provided the economy with a network of communication which enlarged its productive horizon. It has been said, 'It was the sheer scale of the railway investment boom of the 1840s that makes it so significant a feature of the industrial revolution in Britain'.

Along with the introduction of railways, improvement in ocean transportation took place. The opening of the Suez Canal in 1869 gave great impetus to sea-borne transport. Though it was built with French capital, more than half the shipping that passed through it was British.

The second phase of the Industrial Revolution in England was marked by the accumulation of capital in the hands of the British industrialists. They now invested in factories and shared the profits. As joint-stock companies grew in number, it became easy for the rich man to invest in industry and reap the profits. Industrialization increased the capital in England: from 2,500 million pound sterling in 1833, it rose to 6,000 million in 1865. Thus the English industrial revolution had brought a capitalist industry state. By 1880, the population of Britain had grown by leaps and bounds and four out of every five persons lived in towns; agriculture accounted for only about a tenth of the gross national product.

The first countries to industrialise rapidly after Britain were Belgium and France. The two countries had a history of technical skill and shared the rich mineral resources. Because they lacked credit and transport, their economic development proceeded slowly, but eventually they overcame these difficulties.

Belgium was the next to introduce railways, machine tools, mechanized textiles, and new banking institutions. These innovations made her preeminent in continental industrialization. By mid-century Belgium was keeping pace with England and its self-sustaining economy was much admired. But towards the end of the nineteenth century, Belgium's population increased tremendously and its mines failed to produce sufficient coal and iron for domestic use. Belgium then began to import more of both materials than it exported.

Compared to other countries, industrialization in France was slow in the beginning of the nineteenth century. This was due to war, disorder and inflation. The only sector to have made progress was cotton-spinning.

After the French Revolution, with the direct participation of the government, French industries developed behind a wall of tariffs. The construction of railways, begun in 1842, helped the process of industrialization. In 1848, 1,800 kilometres were opened to traffic as against 10,000 kilometres in England, Germany and even Belgium. The most active period of construction were between 1852 and 1860: About 9,000 kilometres were in use and their length had doubled in 1870.

From the middle of the nineteenth century several factors were responsible for the growth of the French industries: unification of the home market by railways, use of new techniques in metallurgy and other sectors and the development of foreign competition. The average annual rate of industrial growth in France between 1815 and 1913 was about 1.61 per cent. Although their achievements at home were not flattering, French capitalists and engineers promoted industrialization on the continent. By 1914 French foreign loans amounted to about 10 billion dollars. French capital and engineers also built the Suez Canal in 1869.

Despite vast resources of coal and iron, Germany was originally more backward than France. Most Germans were peasants. Capital was lacking and commercial banking was nonexistent. There was scarcely a beginning of industrialization in the first quarter of the nineteenth century. The formation of a customs union (*Zollverein*) in 1834 which embraced most German States by 1842 removed many trade barriers. Apart from enlarging markets for agricultural goods, it also served to stimulate commerce and to create a desire for improved means of communication. In 1839, with the aid from British capital, the first important German railway was built and by 1848 there were some 4,000 miles of railway connecting Berlin with Hamburg, Prague, and Vienna.

The political unification of Germany created the largest single market in Europe. After 1874, industrial investment took the lead. It rose from 14 per cent in the early 1850s to more than 56 per cent at the end of the nineteenth century. By exploiting the rich mineral resources of Ruhr, the Saar, as well as Alsace-Lorraine, Germany, by 1910, had become the greatest industrial producer in Europe and the second trading nation (after Britain) in the world.

Till 1870, 64 per cent of the population of Germany was still rural and agricultural. But after 1870 changes became so rapid that they defied description. The dazzling rate of growth was due to the adoption of latest technology as well as to the character and intelligence of the German people. Nineteenth century industry was founded on coal and iron, and the German Empire possessed much of these resources. The marriage of coal and iron enabled her to take the lead in iron and steel industry in Europe. The firms of Krupp, Thyssen, Stumm-Halberg and Donnersmark developed gigantic steel empires. As Keynes observed with some exaggeration: 'The German Empire has been built more truly on coal and iron than blood and iron.'

Behind this economic growth and industrialization lay a complex financial system. German banking vied equally with London, Paris and Amsterdam. German banks were very much concerned with 'production credit'. The Deutsche Bank, founded in 1870 and developed by George von Siemens, promoted foreign enterprises.

In sharp contrast, industrialization in Russia was slow and uneven. Russian resources were immense but its institutions were primitive. Emancipated but illiterate peasants constituted vast segments of the population, but a landed aristocracy dominated society. As late as 1900, about 80 per cent of the population derived its income from agriculture.

The Tsarist government, defeated militarily by industrial powers in 1856 and 1878, took interest in the economic development of the country. The Crimean War (1854-55) led to a rapid growth of railroads. By 1870 there were about 11,000 kilometres of track. The railroads did not cross Siberia until 1905. The government laid special emphasis on heavy industry rather than on consumer goods. At the opening of the twentieth century, Russia was fourth in the world in pig iron production. The period from 1906 to 1914 witnessed spectacularly rapid investment and growth.

Elsewhere, industrialization appeared slowly before 1870. Holland, Sweden, Spain, and Poland took the lead. Bohemia—specially Prague—and Austria—especially Vienna—became centres of the new mechanized industry. Cavour of Italy promoted industrialization by bringing a few steam engines into northern Italy (Piedmont). But by and large Europe, with the exception of Britain, France, Belgium and Germany, was—before 1870—more or less agricultural.

The United States—endowed with rich resources and her great potential—attracted foreign capital. Immigrants and the enterprisers built the superb railroad network that linked east and west into one gigantic market. By 1870 that network was tied with steamship lines on both oceans allowing the commerce of the world to flow in. After 1861, the United States forged ahead with the support of the government which was aware to the needs of industry, agriculture and finance.

Japan emerged rapidly after 1860 from feudalism and set out to modernise the country. Borrowing from advanced nations, the government sponsored industry and commerce. Despite serious shortages of raw materials, industry grew rapidly after 1890.

Dynamic Capitalism

The period of economic growth tended to be irregular and spasmodic. In France, for example, despite periodic spurts, progress was uneven. French businessmen were suspicious and believed in Baron Rothschild's dictum 'There are three ways to ruin: gambling, women, and engineers. The first two are more agreeable, but the last is more certain.' In industrialized countries, growth was accompanied by periodic crises. Some of the crashes were attributed to exuberance of investors or lackadaisical attitude of the entrepreneurs.

It was difficult, however, to avoid the economic glut. The outstanding characteristic of mature capitalism—in Schumpeter's view—is that it is engaged perpetually in a process of creative destruction. This process is effected by recurring surges of productive energy followed by paroxysm of collapse. Each surge forward brings activity in certain sectors of the economy. This is followed by increased investment which eventually leads to depression. Sweden offers a classical example of this kind of development. Her boom of productive activity came to an end in the 1890s; depression followed that shattered the country's economy. Sweden responded by switching from timber exports in favour of diversified production. Simultaneously, she developed hydro-electric sources of power which enabled her to establish an electrical machinery industry.

Government and Capitalism: Tariffs

As industrialist capitalism expanded after 1871, the entrepreneur began to rely increasingly on government aid. The English publicist, Herbert Spencer (1820-1903), decried state intervention and wrote: 'perpetually governments have thwarted and deranged growth, but have in no way furthered it, save by partially discharging their proper function and maintaining social order.' But this dogmatic utterance is far from truth. Economic growth is dependent in the first instance upon the creation of an efficient transportation system in which the government is called upon to play a leading part. The role of American federal government in the construction of transcontinental railway system is too well-known. The French Emperor Napoleon III issued public bonds to encourage railroad construction.

There were various kinds of aid that the government could give. It could facilitate investment by liberalising laws of incorporation. Thus, one of the important factors in Germany's industrial growth was the general company law of 1870-72, which lessened restrictions on corporate growth and extended the principle of limited liability. The result was a sudden spurt of joint-stock companies which rose in number from 2,100 in the early 1880 to 5,400 in 1912 and association with limited liability from 200 to 16,000. The government could also open up new opportunities for investment by acquiring overseas colonies. In time of war, it could protect those industries that were considered vital in war effort.

The most important form of government assistance was the protective tariff. After a period of virtual free trade—which had been inaugurated by the repeal of the British Corn Laws in 1846 and epitomised by the Cobden Treaty of 1860—most European countries took recourse to protectionism in the last quarter of the nineteenth century. The most important compelling forces were as follows:

In the first place, after 1871, some of the countries became apprehensive of the competition of advanced industrialised neighbours. When the cheap English goods flooded the German market, the latter became insistent on protection. The dumping of English goods at low prices in continental markets after 1873 gave rise to a policy of protection.

In the second place, apart from industrial advocates of protection, agriculturists also became warm advocates of the policy. After 1860, a boom in American grain production—owing to improved railway communication, lowering of freight rates and introduction of agricultural machinery—caused a crisis in the agriculture of Western Europe. Farmers of Central Europe were also affected owing to import of cheap grains of Rumania and Russia made possible by railway communication. Inevitably, agricultural pressure group came into existence and began to seek government protection.

This coalition between agriculture and heavy industry for protection found support from other groups. To many people it became evident that war was inevitable and, henceforth, dependence upon free trade was dangerous since imports might be cut off in time of war. As self-sufficiency seemed to be a desirable goal, most of the countries called for tariffs as a means of protecting their goods.

The pressure of these forces led the European powers to turn away from free trade. The passage of the German tariffs of 1879—preceded by the tariff schedules in Russia, Spain and Italy—had wide repercussions. The tariff laws of 1879 which imposed duties on grain, textiles, timber, meat and iron—were followed by similar laws in France, Austria, Sweden, Russia, Italy and other countries. In 1892, France passed the Tariff Act which increased agricultural duties about 25 per cent while giving protection to native industries like silk. Jules Meline, who piloted the bill through the Assembly, put forth the following argument in support of the bill:

> If we look over the table of our importations of the last fifteen years we find them perceptibly increasing in proportion as the principal countries of Europe raise their tariff barriers. If we do not give heed to this, we shall end by becoming the drain of the whole of Europe. Is it right, is it wise, to persist in keeping our doors open when all other are proceeding to close theirs?

As the old idea of international peace based on the economic interdependence of nations became a thing of the past, economic pressure in the form of tariffs came to occupy a potential force in the diplomatic relations.

Movement towards Combination : Trusts and Cartels

In every advanced industrial country, there took place a movement towards 'concentration of industry.' This was achieved by the amalgamation of large number of factories for the purpose of avoiding duplication of effort, lowering costs of production and dividing markets.

Various forms of combination were in vogue. In England and the United States, the most popular arrangements were amalgamation—in which several firms were put under one umbrella. These arrangements quickened technical progress which could hardly be achieved by rival competing units. However, this enabled the resulting combination to enjoy monopoly. The most famous of such trusts were Standard Oil in the United States, Bryant and May (the match trust) and the Imperial Tobacco Company in England. The Dynamite Trust formed in 1886 by the Swedish inventor of dynamite, Alfred Nobel, having collected a huge fortune, spent much of it to the advancement of learning and charity. The most powerful combination in Britain's largest combinations was Unilever and Imperial Chemical Industries which developed after 1914.

In Western Europe, the heavy industries were usually amalgamated. The French metal industries were owned by a trust, *Comite des Forges*. With a humble beginning in 1864, it had embraced, within half a century, most of the iron and steel in the country.

The German form of combination, no less popular in continental countries, was less compact in form. This was known as cartel, designed to restrict competition by association among rival producers in order to control output and prices. These combinations were not restricted to national frontiers; before World War I, there were agreements between German cartels and foreign trusts with regard to marketing production and price. The Allgemeine Elektrizitats-Gaesellschaft (AEG) had an arrangement with the General Electric Company of the United States. German manufacturers of steel rails and cartel made arrangements with their counterparts in Britain, France, Belgium and the United States which in a way, controlled the world market.

The most interesting phenomenon was the tendency of banking concerns to combine. The sharp decline of banking concerns in England from 600 in 1824 to 55 in 1914 and still further to 11 in 1937 was of special interest. The Big Five—the Midland Bank, the Westminster Bank, Barclay's, Lloyd's and the National Provincial—transacted five-sixths of England's banking business. The four so-called D Banks—*Disconto Geselleschaft* of Stuttgart (founded in 1851), the *Deutsche Bank* (1870), the *Darmstadtar Bank* (1870), and the *Dresdener Bank* (1872)—controlled the financial business of Germany. The D Banks—intended 'to foster commercial relations between Germany and other countries'—generally promoted greatest degrees of business amalgamation.

The beginning of commercial combinations had wide-ranging repercussions. There emerged new concentration of power behind trusts and cartels and no government could ignore such powerful combinations. Reciprocally, these new economic organizations tried to influence governmental policies only to reap huge profits. The Union of Economic Interests founded in France in 1911 exercised great influence in postwar France against governmental controls and state monopolies. In 1898 was created the German Navy League by the business magnates. It marked 'the entrance of the heavy industries, the mercantile interests, and the financiers into the ranks of the naval enthusiasts.' With the help of newspapers, they carried on propaganda in favour of naval armaments to counteract Britain's naval preeminence.

These economic combinations played a positive role in the expansion of the European economy by introducing new techniques and eliminating inefficiency. But the ordinary consumer was at the mercy of cartels and trusts owing to their monopolistic practices and high level price fixation. They became targets for socialist critics which, in turn, led to the growth of cooperative movements and trade unions.

Cooperative Movements

France took the lead in cooperative movements. France, the home of the producers' co-operative since the 1830s, made a sudden spurt between 1880 and 1914 when the number of such associations rose from 100 to 450. Britain, on the other hand, took the lead in the consumers' co-operatives. In 1863 was formed the English Cooperative Wholesale Society; five years later, the Scottish. In the 1870s their activities extended into production, landowning, insurance and banking. With the formation in 1899 of the Hamburg Society *Produktion*, cooperative movements began in Germany. In all the three countries, workers were induced to have a direct share in the business of profit sharing and copartnership.

Cooperative movements spread quickly to other countries—Denmark, Italy, the Low Countries, Finland and Ireland—mostly in the field of agriculture and dairies. By 1892 in Denmark there were 1,000 cooperative dairies. Italy had more than 400 such by the close of the century. Even masons and less skilled labourers formed cooperative associations. In Ghent in 1873 workmen set up a cooperative bakery. Eventually this gave rise in every large Belgian town to a great cooperative organisation running shops, cafes, bakery and breweries. In Sweden, the Wholesale Society (*Kooperative Forbundet*) was formed in 1899.

Apart from economic organisations, a large number of social and cultural associations grew up in various countries. Though they became closely linked with political parties as in Belgium and Germany, their functions were not political. The beginning of the twentieth century heralded a number of voluntary associations, ranging from the Workers' Educational Association in Britain (1903) to women's leagues and youth clubs; from the restless German youth movement (*Wandervogel)* to the French Catholic 'Popular Institutes'. They generated a new sense of community, a new urge to find intellectual and material improvement through self-help.

Trade Unions: The Labour Movement

Along with the large-scale combination of business, grew combination of labour. The condition of the workers was pitiable. Wages were low, hours of labour varied from twelve to fourteen. 'It is questionable', wrote John Stuart Mill, 'if all the mechanical inventions yet made have lightened the day's toil of any human being, they have enabled a greater population to live the same life of drudgery and imprisonment, and an increased number of manufacturers and others to make large fortunes.' Despite the hostile attitude of businessmen and governments to the formation of labour union, there were a few honest industrialists who believed with Andrew Carnegie: 'The right of the workingmen to combine is no less sacred than the right of the manufacturer to enter into associations and conferences with his fellows, and it must sooner or later be conceded.'

Out of these circumstances arose a new institution known as the Trade Union or Labour Union. The union asserted the principle of collective bargaining. It also claimed the right to strike. Trade Unions spread rapidly and a number of violent strikes took place. In 1799 and 1800 the British Parliament passed Combination Acts which forbade all working class movements. In spite of the law, numerous trade unions continued to exist. At last, in 1824-25, the law of 1799 was superseded by new acts which—though permitted combination of workmen—made it difficult for them to strike.

Between 1825 and 1832 there was a steady growth of union membership. In July 1830 John Doherty (1798-1854) founded the National Association for Protection of Labour. The Reforms Act of 1832—which disillusioned the working-class—encouraged the growth of unionism. In October 1833 was established the Grand National Consolidated Trade Union which had an estimated membership of half a million workers. Robert Owen (1771-1858) was the main spirit behind the Grand National. But financial mismanagement and unwise strike policy and government persecution contributed to the decay of the Grand National.

In 1836, a group of working class leaders in London, under the leadership of William Lovett, founded the London Workingmen's Association. This Association presented a petition known as the 'People's Charter' to the Parliament. The Chartist programme included universal suffrage, annual parliaments and the secret ballot. Unfortunately for the working class, Chartism did not produce any strong leader like William Cobbett. Meanwhile the granting of ten hour work to women and children in the textile mills in 1847 marked a big step forward to the workers' movement. The Reform Act of 1867 granted the right of suffrage to the working class. In 1871, Gladstone took steps to regularise the position of unions. In 1875, Disraeli widened their freedom of action by legalizing peaceful picketing. Trade unions were given legal recognition in Britain by 1871, in France in 1884, in Austria by 1870, in Germany in 1890, in Spain in 1881. Until the 1880s, labour unions were predominantly craft unions, mainly preoccupied with insurance against the hazards of accident, sickness and death—and occasionally engaged in strikes demanding better working conditions.

Most of the unions were essentially benevolent, using the strike weapon rarely. But in the last two decades of the nineteenth century, when the membership began to increase, trade unions became militant. The new unions were often influenced by the doctrines of Marxian socialism. This was evident in Germany. In Austria, Italy, the Scandinavian countries, Holland and Spain, Marxian socialists led the union movement. In England, the Labour Party championed the workers' movement.

The great increase in membership of the Trade Unions and the period of economic depression between 1882 and 1886 were responsible for a series of strikes leading to violence. The most important incidents were the strike of Belgian miners and glass workers in 1886, of the London Dock workers in 1889, of the Ruhr coal workers in 1889, of harbour workers of Hamburg in 1896. Gradually, the character of trade unionism had undergone changes with the entry of less skilled workers into it. There was a great proliferation of different types of labour organisation, often competing with one another for union allegiance. Moreover, there were not only demands for unified labour organisation but efforts were made to give international recognition to it.

The proliferation of different kinds of labour organisation weakened the trade union movement as a whole. In France, from 1887 onwards there grew up *bourses du travail*—a peculiar institution combining labour exchange, trades council and workers' club. In France and Germany, the Roman Catholic Church formed separate labour unions of Catholic workers.

Despite the proliferation of trade unions, there grew up a desire for national federation at the end of the century. The French unions in 1895 formed a national federation, the *Confederation Generale du Travail* (C.G.T.). It advocated a policy of industrial action through collective bargaining backed by strikes. It deliberately kept itself away from politics. Originating in 1868, the British Trade Union Congress represented some half a million members in the beginning of the twentieth century. In 1900 it set up a Labour Representation Committee to enable workers to participate in parliamentary elections. British unionism thus identified with politics and produced the modern Labour Party in the first decade of the twentieth century. In Italy was formed, in 1906, a General Italian Federation of Labour. In Germany, trade unionism was divided into three distinct segments: the liberal Hirsch-Duncker unions, the so-called free trade unions which were socialist in character; and the Christian unions. German unions were highly concentrated. In 1913 there were 1,000 unions in Britain representing four million persons, whereas in Germany 400 unions representing three millions.

To become an effective potent force and to put respectability in its movement, trade unionism evolved international affiliation. In 1895, the cooperative movement formed the International Cooperative Alliance. From 1889 onwards various trades formed international links, such as the leather workers' international federation of 1889. After concerted efforts the national federations of Britain, Germany and the Scandinavian countries set up by 1913 the International Federation of Trade Unions (IFTU).

Most of the labour organisations in other countries followed the patterns of development set up in Britain, France and Germany. In Austria, Italy, Spain and the Scandinavian countries, communists tried to get control of the unions. In Russia, before 1905, trade unionism was punished as a crime. In 1906, after the Revolution of 1905, both workers and employers were given the legal right to form unions. But the legal right to strike was yet to be achieved. Henceforth strikes occurred frequently. In 1913 alone there were more than 2,400 strikes.

Growth of Socialist Thoughts

While trade-unionism waged for better deal to workers, some intellectuals were envisaging a new social order. France was more fertile than any country in producing new socialistic theories. The early social thinker in France was Henri de Saint-Simon (1760-1825), an aristocrat by birth. He preached the gospel of work: 'man must work'. An oft-repeated sentence associated with him became popular in later days: 'From each according to his capacity, to each according to his work.' According to him the State should assume control of production and distribution and give loan to communities working on a cooperative basis. Saint-Simon and his followers believed that moral reform and education would, in the long run, promote better understanding among classes and usher in improved economic conditions of the working class. To achieve social justice, he proposed to establish a state bank to wield a monopoly of credit and abolish inheritance rights.

In his later years, Saint-Simon was influenced by the harmful effects of the Industrial Revolution. He was the precursor of the ideas of Karl Marx. 'The workers', he wrote, 'see themselves deprived of the enjoyment of their labour, which is the aim of their labour.' He, therefore, laid emphasis on improving the lot of the working class. He put forward the strikingly refreshing idea that society should be organised for the promotion of the well-being of the poorest class.

This idea found expression in his last work, *Noveau Christianisme* (1825), written shortly before his death.

Soon after Saint-Simon's death, some of his disciples put forth his ideas systematically in *La Doctrine Saint-Simonienne* (1828). This emphasised the importance of work for all, and advocated ambitious projects of public works. In order to implement these ideas, it was proposed that gigantic industrial companies be established. If the doctrine contained some features of a highly developed capitalism, it also anticipated some socialist ideas, such as the abolition of inheritance. Saint Amand Bazard and, later on, Pierre Leroux became advocates of these ideas.

Charles Fourier (1771-1837) attacked commercial civilization as it created conflict among classes. The great sources of evil are competition and greed; and the remedy is association and co-operation—to achieve social justice. But he did not look to the state but rather to the workers who should form themselves into self-sufficient communities. He had his peculiar conception of a so-called *phalanstere,* a community composed of about 1,600 persons on some 5,000 acres of land. He had some refreshing ideas, such as the need to render labour as attractive and joyous as possible. Each worker must share in its produce and be guaranteed a sufficient minimum to free him from anxiety. His cardinal doctrine that cooperation should replace competition had a wide appeal. Fourier pinned hope in the physical perfectibility of man and a long span of life—an average of 144 years. Fourier was eagerly read in France and Russia.

There were also revolutionary socialists in France. Philippe Buonarroti (1767-1837) preached the necessity of political revolution as a means of winning social reform. More extreme in his views was Auguste Blanqui (1805-81). He called upon the worker to wage ceaseless war against the bourgeoisie, since there could be no community of interests between the classes. In his emphasis on underground activity, Blanqui was a precursor of professional revolutionaries like Lenin and others. Anarchist in essence was the work of Pierre Joseph Proudhon (1809-65) whose famous book *What is Property*? appeared in 1840. He contributed to the vision of a future classless society which would operate under the motto 'from each according to his ability, to each according to his need.' To achieve an ideal society, small property holders and workmen should combine.

But the most influential of all the French socialists was Louis Blanc (1811-82). In 1839 appeared his famous book *Organization of Labour,* the most discussed book of the whole period. According to Blanc, competition was ruinous not only for the common people but also for the bourgeoisie. It must, therefore, be abolished. Blanc emphasised that political reform is the only means to achieve social reform, and that socialism must be state socialism. The state must acknowledge the 'right to work'. The government should organise national workshops in most industries which would eventually be controlled democratically by the workers themselves. Louis Blanc was to play an important role in the French Revolution of 1848 as his ideas were welcomed with enthusiasm by the French workers.

The leading socialist of England was Robert Owen (1771-1858). He was the manager of a well-known cotton factory in New Lanark, Scotland. He had made his mill a model establishment in which wages were good and social benefits were made available to workers. He abolished child labour under the age of ten and reduced the working hours in the factory from 16 to $10^1/_2$. Owen wanted general improvement of industrial conditions. In *New View of Society* (1813) he castigated the factory superintendents for giving care to machines while neglecting the workers. In an appeal *To the British Master Manufacturers* (1818) he condemned the employment of children in the factories. Owen tried to mobilise public opinion abroad for which he attended the Congress of Aix-la-Chapelle (1818) and submitted two *Memorials on Behalf of the Working Class* (1818). There he was rebuffed by the ultra-conservative Friedrich von Gentz, who ventilated his own reaction to Owen's schemes: 'We do not want the mass to become wealthy and independent of us. How could we govern them if they were?'

Believing that America would offer a fertile field for social experiments, Owen came to Indiana, in 1825, and founded a colony called New Harmony. From the beginning the colony was beset with internal dissensions which, ultimately, led to the collapse of the settlement. He returned to England and took part in the Trade Union Movement. His reformatory zeal owed in a greater part to his unflinching humanitarianism.

Despite the failure of the American experiment, the latter stimulated the establishment of self-governing non-profit cooperative shops and producers' societies which tried to mitigate the needs of the workers. Owen opposed the whole capitalistic profit system which exploited the workers. He was the main person behind the Grand National Consolidated Trades Union. He believed that it would enable the organised workers to gain control of the economic machinery of the country leading to the eventual replacement of capitalism with a cooperative system.

These earlier socialists are commonly known as the 'Utopians'. They had a very limited influence as they did not reach the hearts of the masses themselves. Utopian socialists were regarded as impractical, fantastic persons. They tried to teach mainly by examples. But most of these 'laboratory demonstrations of socialism' met with failure. However, their importance to the next generation must not be minimised. Paying tribute to the men whom he regarded as his own and Karl Marx's precursors, Friedrich Engels wrote:

> German socialism will never forget that it rests on the shoulders of Saint-Simon, Fourier and Owen—three men who, however fantastic and Utopian their teachings, belonged to the great minds of all times and by intuition of genius anticipated an incalculable number of truths which we now demonstrate scientifically.

Karl Marx and Socialism

Karl Marx was a German Jew who was born in 1818 at Trier in the Rhineland. He went to local schools and then studied at the Universities of Bonn and Berlin. He found philosophy and history more interesting than jurisprudence. He derived much inspiration from the German philosopher Hegel, who conceived of history as a struggle between opposing forces leading to constant change. He received his degree in 1841 and wished to join academic profession. But as the university opening did not materialise, he began to write philosophical articles for a newspaper called the *Rheinische Zeitung* and, in 1843, became its editor. The ferment of the times and the doctrines of French socialism influenced Marx so much that he began to write provocative articles on social questions. Before the year was over, the *Rheinische Zeitung* was banned by the government and Marx went to Paris.

Marx's Paris sojourn marked a new chapter in his life. Here he began to study socialism at its source. He fell under the influence of the Saint-Simonians. Here he met Friedrich Engels (1820-95) and their lifelong collaboration began. To Engels, Marx owed his practical knowledge of the working of the industrial system as well as a keen insight into military matters. Engels, on the other hand, admired Marx's power of analysis and conceptualization and observed eloquently: 'Marx was a genius; we others at best were talented.'

Marx was expelled from Paris in 1847 and went to Brussels, where he joined an association of radicals calling itself the Communist League. On the eve of the Revolution of 1848, Marx produced in collaboration with Engels his famous work *The Communist Manifesto.* When the Revolution of 1848 took place in Germany, Marx returned to his native land. He was promptly expelled from Germany and found asylum in Great Britain where he spent the remainder of his life working in the British Museum in study and researches until his death in 1883. In 1859 appeared his *Critique of Political Economy* and in 1867 the first volume of *Das Capital.* The second and third volumes of *Das Capital* were published after his death by Engels in 1885 and 1894, respectively.

Marx borrowed the idea of materialist history from Feuerbach, the class struggle from Saint-Simon, the dictatorship of the proletariat from Babeuf, the labour theory of value from Adam Smith, the theory of surplus value from Bray and Thompson, the principle of dialectical progress from Hegel. He marshalled all these ideas in a messianic doctrine: 'Marx was the Prophet; the Proletariat was the chosen people; the socialist movement was the Church; the Revolution was the second coming; Communism was the Promised Land.'

Karl Marx put together a synthesis of economics, history, philosophy, politics and sociology, which offered a total world view. Hegel's philosophy taught him to derive the fundamental law of nature from historical evolution but, unlike Hegel, Marx concluded that the purpose of philosophy was not to explain evolution, but to change the world. The extent to which change would be accomplished depended on circumstances, particularly on the prevailing 'mode of production' or the ownership. He traced the evolution of successive modes of production from traditional communal societies to a future classless socialist state.

Marx was one of the outstanding figures of the nineteenth century, and a world force like Luther and Voltaire. He possessed an unusual combination of qualities, profound learning, striking originality and discerning mind.

Marx's views on history were influenced by Hegel, who had believed that history is a logical process in which change is effected by the opposition of antagonistic elements. But whereas, in Hegel's view, the key to change was ideological, Marx believed that the basis of history and the key to historical change was materialistic. According to Marx, 'the mode of production in material life determines the general character of the social, political and spiritual processes of life.' When change takes place, it is because of the clash of competing economic groupings. As Engels once wrote: 'The whole history of mankind ... has been a history of class struggles, contests between exploiting and exploited, ruling and oppressed classes.' To the socialists, the economic interpretation of history is 'the one pass-key which will unlock all the secrets of the past.'

According to *The Communist Manifesto,* 'The history of all hitherto existing society is the history of class struggles. Freeman and slave, patrician and plebian, lord and serf, guildmaster and journeyman, in a word, oppressor and oppressed, stood in constant opposition to one another, carried on an uninterrupted fight, now hidden, now open, a fight that each time ended either in a revolutionary reconstitution of society at large, or in the common ruin of the contesting classes.' The struggle involved two classes that were engaged in industrial production: the upper middle-class, the bourgeoisie who owned the means of production and distribution and the proletariat or the propertyless worker. The class struggle, according to Marx, was bound to end in the victory of the proletariat and its dictatorship. 'What the bourgeoisie produces, above all, are its own gravediggers. Its fall and the victory of the proletariat are equally inevitable.' The *Manifesto* gave a clarion call to the labouring class in the inimitable language:

> 'the proletarians have nothing to loss but their chains. They have a world to win. Workers of all countries: unite.'

Marx borrowed crucial idea about the labour theory from the classical economists. Any object that man produces has a certain value. While the worker puts forth the labour to make something, he receives in wages only a fraction of the value of what he has created. The owner gets the remainder of the value in profits. The surplus value represented by profits should go to the man who puts in the labour that creates value; instead, it goes to the owner, who piles up capital while the worker gets the bare minimum. The capitalist, by pursuing a course of selfish exploitation, encouraged 'the boom-bust tendencies inherent in the system and hastened the coming of the final debacle.' Marx indicates the evil of a divided society and suggested the way to overcome that evil—by public ownership of the means of production and distribution. Marx tried to make the workers actually aware of their situation so that they would revolt and destroy the roots of class struggle.

Marx believed that the destruction of the capitalist system and the ushering in of a new age could be brought violently by the workers themselves. The proletariat must seize the right moment of revolution. To unite working class organisations into a common front was the primary duty of the socialist party. Its second task was to consolidate the revolution. Marx foresaw a violent revolution in which the partyled workers would seize the centres of bourgeoisie power and the means of production followed by a transitional period of the dictatorship of the proletariat. During this transitional stage, the party would lay the basis for the classless society in which the state withered away.

The Communist Manifesto called for the abolition of private landed property and the right of inheritance; a graduated income tax; the centralisation and control of credit, communications and the means of production in the hands of the state; equal obligations of all to work; abolition of distinction between industry and agriculture and free public education for children. Marx believed important changes would come both by evolution and revolution. *Das Capital* sought to demonstrate that capitalism would fall of its own weight.

Marx was more fertile in analysing the ills of contemporary society and delineating the forces that would overcome them and less perspicuous in drawing blueprints for the future. But the inexorable future would come. Marx and Engels denounced all socialist movements before their time. The Utopian socialists refused to believe the irreconciliable conflict between classes, and fondly pinned hope that socialism could be imposed from above. Marx based his theories upon the materialistic view of history and society, upon the inevitability of the class struggle, and the ultimate triumph of the proletariat by violence.

In 1848, Marx had attracted little attention, but as industrialisation progressed, he won followers. In 1864, Marx became the guiding spirit of an International Workingmen's Association, usually called the "First International". Though it succeeded in preaching the Marxist teaching, the "First International" met with no lasting success. It was weakened by differences between Marx on the one hand and the Anarchists like Bakunin on the other. But Marxian Socialism commanded the loyalty of workingmen. In 1889 the Second International met in Paris and held a series of congresses until the First World War (1914-18). In 1919, after the Russian Revolution, the Russian communists established the Third International.

Critical Analysis of Marxian Socialism

The premise of Marx that economic factor alone would determine every aspect of our life and action was fallacious as various other factors had a part to play in the drama of history and the life of man. Though economic factors encompassed human affairs, we need not ignore the interplay of such forces as human ambition, domestic politics, geographical condition, religious faith, administrative efficiency, military genius and so on. The question of causation is too complex to lead to conclusion that any single factor is more important than others in determining the course of history.

In determining the course of history, human factor or human initiative must be taken into account. The system of production was not a uniform or monolithic thing, as Marx would have us believe, but a composite of many ideas and institutions. In the same way, it would be too facile to assume—as Marx did—that individuals will act in accordance with their class allegiance. Apart from economic considerations, the behaviour of individuals is circumstanced by status, social aspirations, tradition. Throughout recent history, proletarians have turned more frequently to rightist political parties than to socialist or labour movements. Marx's claim that the 'proletarians in all countries had one and the same interest, one and the same enemy,' ignored the impact of nationalistic fervour on all classes.

If Marx's historical views were less scientific, so were his economic theories. His theory of surplus value took no cognition of the hidden costs of production—administration, advertising, interest payments and other things—that absorbed much of the profit which Marx claimed only enriched employers. Moreover, even in Marx's time, capitalists were enlightened and were prepared to make economic sacrifices.

The importance of Marx's work—either as historian or as economist—cannot be minimised. He provoked the historians to give more weight to the social and economic aspects of human evolution than on purely political factors. To economic thought he brought an emphasis upon class structure and attitude that was new and stimulating. While Marx's economic interpretation of history has had a far-reaching effect, it was his doctrine of the class struggle and of the inevitable triumph of the proletarian revolution which gave his teaching an immediate political appeal to the industrial workers. As Engels said, 'Just as Darwin discovered the law of evolution of organic nature, so Marx discovered the law of evolution of human history.'

To the suffering and the deprived, Marx held out the promise of a golden age, in which 'in place of the old bourgeois society with its classes and class antagonisms (would) come an association in which the free development of each individual (would) be the condition for the free development of all.' Yet the means he advocated were hardly to be accepted by all. The cult of violence which Marx advocated weakened the ideas of law, equity and compromise that were the hallmarks of nineteenth century liberalism and had been the best guarantee of progress towards freedom.

Anarchism

Anarchism is the very opposite of socialism. The latter favours the concentration of all authority in the State; and the former renounces all authority in whatever form—State, Church or family. The Anarchist believed that man was essentially good but had been corrupted by institutions. The anarchists wished to restore mankind to its state of primitive virtue by destroying the instruments of corruption—the state and the churches. The state, being the embodiment of the highest authority, must be destroyed because 'all government of man by man, under whatever name it may disguise itself, is tyranny.' As religion was another enemy of man's freedom, atheism formed as essential part of anarchism.

The early strand of Anarchism could be traced to the Anabaptists and Diggers of the seventeenth century. It came to fruition in England in the *Enquiry Concerning Political Justice* (1793) of William Godwin and in the soaring vision of *Prometheus Unbound* (1820) written by Shelley. A second strand appeared in France reflected in the writings of Proudhon and his disciple, Anselme Bellegarrigue. Their idea centred on the doctrine of *mutualite* (mutualism) which held that workers should dissociate themselves from parliamentary politics and should liberate themselves by direct action.

The most famous names in the history of anarchism are the Frenchman, Pierre Joseph Proudhon (1809-65) and the Russian, Michael Bakunin (1814-76). Proudhon, the father of modern anarchism, wrote one of the well-known pamphlets, *What is Property*? In which he observed that 'property is theft'. According to Proudhon, the individual derived little benefit from the government of his country:

> To be governed is to be watched over, inspected, spied on, directed, legislated, regulated, docketed, indoctrinated, preached at, controlled, assessed, weighed, censored ordered about ... Under pretext of the general interest, it is to be taxed, drilled, held to ransom, exploited, monopolised, extorted, hoaxed, squeezed, robbed; then at least resistance, at the first word of complaint, repressed, fined, abused, annoyed, followed, bullied, beaten, disarmed, imprisoned ... That's government, that's its justice, that's its morality.

He was an exponent of 'communist' anarchism which envisaged a system of cooperative production. Another advocate of this system was the Russian scientist and sociologist, Prince Peter Kropotkin.

The man who made anarchism a popular working class movement in Europe was Michael Bakunin. Born of an aristocratic family, he studied philosophy and became interested in the privations of subject nationalities like the Poles and the Italians. After becoming a professional revolutionary, he participated in the February Revolution of 1848 and was arrested in Dresden in 1849. Transported to his own country, Bakunin spent eight years in prison and four years in enforced exile in Siberia. He then escaped and, after brief sojourns in Yokohama, San Francisco and New York, returned to western Europe only to devote himself to revolutionary activity. In the 1880s he organised anarchist cells in Switzerland, Spain and Italy and founded a Social Democratic Alliance with its motto of 'Universal Revolution.' Being an ardent supporter of the Polish rising in 1863, he organised a commune in Lyon in 1871.

Bakunin formulated his anarchist creed in the following words:

> The State was born historically … of the marriage of violence, rapine, pillage … It has been from its origin … the divine sanction of brutal force and triumphant inequality … Even when it commands what is good, it hinders and spoils it just because it commands it … because the good, from the moment it is commanded, becomes evil from the point of view of true morality … and from the point of view of human respect and liberty.

Bakunin castigated capitalism, organised religion, modern science and all institutions, all laws that regulated human life.

Bakunin was vague in his generalisation. He preferred Proudhon's scheme for a society of small voluntary communities in which no one would be compelled to do anything except by his own will. But he failed to provide the details, preferring to believe that men would solve their own problems once they were free. Bakunin went further than Marx in deifying violence for the former dreamed of a gigantic conflagration that would accomplish what reason could not define. 'Unchain the popular anarchy in country and town,' he wrote 'magnify it, till it rolls like a raging avalanche, devouring and destroying.' He called for 'a phalanx of 40,000 strong of young folk of the educated classes' to lead the masses in acts of terrorism against authority until the goal of universal revolution had been achieved.

Bakunin's emphasis on the creation of a revolutionary elite might have influenced Marx on the necessity of a disciplined party. Lenin, who later elaborated this idea, owed as much to the anarchist as he did to the author of *The Communist Manifesto.* This is one of the slender bonds between Marx and Bakunin. Both of them disapproved of each other's ideas. Bakunin hated Marx's authoritarianism while the latter was highly critical of Bakunin's lackadaisical approach and individual terrorism.

Despite Marx's popularity, Bakunin's influence was not inconsiderable. In France he won many converts—especially those who were dissatisfied with the moderation of French socialism after 1871. Political assassinations took place in Paris, Lyons and other cities including the murder of the President of the Republic in 1894 and a bomb plot inside the Chamber of Deputies. In Italy and Spain, anarchism appealed to the rural classes who were most backward and impoverished. In the last decades of the nineteenth century, Bakunin's disciple, Malatesta fomented peasant discontent in the southern provinces of Italy, while, in Spain, anarchism spread rapidly among the landless peasantry of Andalusia and the industrial workers of Catalonia. By 1900, anarchism became the *raison d' etre* of the Spanish working class movement.

The Berlin journalist Max Stirner (1806-1856) emphasised the absolute rights of the individual to freedom from institutional control.

In practical terms, anarchism produced a baneful influence. Revolutionary anarcho-syndicalists dominated workers' movements in France, Italy, and Spain. Their major weapon was the general strike intended to paralyse all working institutions. Anarchism also inspired the birth of modern terrorism. The idea was to highlight injustice, and to engender fear among the ruling class. The list of victims included Tsar Alexander II (1881), President Sadi Carnot of France (1894), Empress Elizabeth of Austria (1896), Premier Canovas del castillo of Spain (1897), and King Umberto I of Italy (1900).

Syndicalism

At the end of the nineteenth century, a new revolutionary movement appeared, known as Syndicalism (which took its name from the French word for labour union, *syndicat).* Syndicalism had its roots in both socialism and anarchism. It was a protest against the growing tendency towards moderation in the European socialist parties after 1900. According to the Syndicalists, parliaments were essentially bourgeois institutions and emancipation of workmen would be won not in parliaments but by direct action. Such action should be exercised through trade union organisations and should take the form of sabotage and, above all, the strike. To enhance the effectiveness of such tactics, trade unions were to be organised on an industrial basis. Small craft unions within an industry were to amalgamate into an industrial union, comprising both skilled and unskilled workers. An industrial union would emphasise class solidarity and a general strike would instil into the workingmen a sense of the class war. Labourers should make no contracts or agreements with their employers and workingmen should strike to take possession of the means of production. General strike would weaken and paralyse the capitalist system and inaugurate the revolution. 'Poor work for poor pay' was the syndicalist alternative to a general strike.

The syndicalist movement was most active in France which produced its most brilliant exponent, George Sorel (1847-1922). An anarchist named Fernand Pelloutier founded the Confederation Generale du Travail (CGT) (September 1895). This federation adopted direct action as its policy which was embodied in the so-called Charter of Amiens of 1908. Before the First World War, the CGT organised strikes among civil servants and railway workers and encouraged disaffection among the army.

In other countries, syndicalism was no less popular. The cult of direct action won many followers in English unions and there was a wave of syndicalist activity in Ireland on the eve of the First World War. In Italy, the anarcho-syndicalist movement was led by Filippo Carridoni. His teachings influenced a young socialist named Benito Mussolini who wrote, in 1909: 'Syndicalism restores to its place in history the creative value of man, man who determines and is determined, who can leave the imprint of his force upon things and institutions.'

In Spain, a federation of syndicalist industrial unions, the *Confederacion Nacional del Trabajo* (CNT) was founded in 1910 and an agricultural federation, the *Federation Nacional de Agricultores Espanoles* (FNAE) in 1913. After the war, anarcho-syndicalists numbered more than a million workers. The cult of violence influenced both the rightist groups as well as labour organisations in Spain. So when the Spanish Civil War broke out in 1936, there were followers of Bakunin and Sorel on both sides.

If the methods of the syndicalists were concrete, their aims were full of abstract speculations. They preached a 'social myth', a universal strike of all labour. Although bitterly opposed to the state, the Syndicalists advocated relentless war against the capitalists directly. They ridiculed the idea that 'political action' through parliament would ever emancipate the workingmen. The supreme need, according to the syndicalists, was leadership by a group of revolutionary workingmen, the class conscious 'minority of a minority' to lead the masses against capitalism.

Revisionism

By 1890s, Socialist parties had been organised in most countries and were making considerable headway. Most of these parties were Marxist in inspiration and doctrine. But within the parties there developed splinter groups and dissident minorities. Before Engel's death in 1895 a profound division afflicted the socialist parties.

Some of the leading socialists proclaimed the doctrine of 'revisionism' when they saw a gap between Marx's predictions and the realities of European economic development. A prominent German Social Democrat, Eduard Bernstein (1850-1932), summed up the revisionist views pungently: 'Peasants do not sink; middle class does not disappear; crises do not grow ever longer; misery and serfdom do not increase.' As the collapse of the capitalist system was not imminent, Bernstein observed, the socialist parties must change their tactics, if not their goals. Bernstein and his followers urged that the Social Democrats work 'less for the better future and more for the better present.' They asserted that the mass of the workingmen were unwilling to wait 'until some fine day when the roast pigeons of the socialist revolution would fly into their mouths.' The logical course must be to seize opportunities for gradual reform in the interest of the working classes. They must adopt the evolutionary tactics favoured by the Fabian Society in Great Britain.

Bernstein's views, published in various articles and books between 1896 and 1899, were widely known. They appealed to those members of the socialist parties who had been disappointed with the negative parliamentary tactics of the past. They captivated the rank and file of the trade-union members who were opposed to sterile methods of opposition as that would weaken revolutionary fervour. They won wide acceptance in most countries and many of the orthodox Marxists began to act in the spirit of revisionism.

The great French Socialist leader Jean Jaures (1859-1914) found in revisionism nothing alien to the spirit of Marx's teaching, 'since Marxism itself contains the means by which it can be supplemented and revised.' Like Bernstein, Jaures rejected Marx's economic theories and the inevitability of revolution. The victory of the proletariat, he believed, was certain, but it would usher in by gradual degrees rather than by a sudden revolutionary movement. The important thing was 'to live always in a socialist state of grace, working each hour, each minute,' with the belief that the trade unions were to reshape the world in accordance with socialist ideals.

The revisionist point of view was bitterly assailed by the revolutionary socialists. Their most effective spokesman was V.I. Lenin who in his pamphlet *What is to be Done*? (1902) scathingly criticised the followers of Bernstein. Lenin argued that victory could never be won for proletariat by gradualist 'bread and butter socialism'. Instead of becoming bodies of parliamentarians, the Socialist parties must be disciplined bodies of professional revolutionaries who would strive to replace the 'trade-union mentality' with a renewed faith in the class struggle.

Bolshevism

Socialism came to Russia towards the last decade of the nineteenth century. The Russian Social Democratic Party was organised through the initiative of a lecturer named George Plekhanov. As the party was outlawed in Russia, there took place in 1903 a convention of the party in London. The convention was to have a profound influence upon world history.

Sharp differences arose in the Social Democratic Party which resulted in 1910, in splitting the party into two faction—the Bolshevists, led by Lenin and the Menshevists, led by Plekhanov. Both parties accepted the principles of Marxism, but they were poles apart with regard to the methods to be used by the socialists. The Menshevists believed that the road to socialism lay through democracy; hence the party should organise the workingmen politically. They decried the violent upsurge of the workingmen and upheld that in a democracy the transition from capitalism to socialism was to be through constitutional means.

The Bolshevists proposed a different plan. According to them, it was chimerical for any revolutionary party to gain political power through constitutional methods. Democracy, they asserted, was a cunningly devised system for maintaining the rule of the bourgeois. No parliamentary majority, declared the Bolshevists, can overthrow capitalism.

It was Lenin who developed new revolutionary methods for the attainment of socialism. Lenin, who was influenced by the writings of Marx, favoured the formation of small, well-organised groups to lead the masses in times of crisis. They must ruthlessly eliminate anyone who was opposed to Marxism.

The socialists should identify themselves with the aspirations of the workingmen and should infiltrate into the trade unions. They should make the trade unions, the centres of revolutionary agitation. Socialists should strive ceaselessly to get control of the machinery of every working-class political party by 'boring from within.' Unless socialists were geared up on these lines, declared Lenin, they would remain 'mere babblers' without any impact upon the masses.

No revolution is possible without a national crisis and the latter is inevitable because capitalist economy drives the nation to adopt imperialist policies, which, in turn, lead to war. War is the opportune moment for the working class to overthrow the existing system and to establish the dictatorship of the proletariat.

Once in power, the proletariat will destroy every existing institution and establish new ones in harmony with the new socialist thoughts. The dictatorship should give rights only to the workers and should liquidate all other classes, but its rule will be temporary. 'As the opposition of the bourgeois is broken, as it is expropriated and gradually absorbed into the working class the proletarian dictatorship disappears, until finally the State dies, and there are no longer any class distinctions.'

Bolshevism was practical and had nothing of the spirit of idealism that had characterised former revolutionists, the Jeffersons and Mazzinis. As Leon Trotsky observed in this connection:

> To accept the Workers' Revolution in the name of a high ideal means not only to reject it, but to slander it ... The Socialist Revolution tears the mask from illusions, from elevating as well as from humiliating illusions, and washes in blood the disguises assumed by reality. The Revolution is strong enough to the extent to which it is realistic, rational, strategic and mathematical.

The First and Second Socialist Internationals

The first attempt of the socialists was to found an international organisation of the proletariat. In 1864 there took place in London a meeting of workingmen in which were present English trade-unionists, Polish nationalists, Italian republicans, German socialists, Russian nihilists, and even anarchists. Among its prominent members was Marx, who provided the organisation a constitution. From time to time the International held Congresses and the organisation became a rallying centre of revolutionary workingmen throughout the world. In its manifesto the International declared that the economic dependence of the workingmen upon the capitalist was 'the basis of every kind of servitude, of social misery, of spiritual degradation, and political dependence.' The International was driven by factions led by Bakunin, the anarchist, and Marx, the socialist. The organisation was greatly weakened when the anarchists were expelled. In 1873, the First International went out of existence. But its undying influence as an international organisation of the working class was too deep to be effaced.

An important aspect of socialism was the failure of the Paris Commune of 1871. It weakened the enthusiasm of the revolutionary workingmen who were now convinced that all revolutionary upsurges were doomed to failure. The enfranchisement of the working class in England, the establishment of universal manhood suffrage in Germany, and of a democratic republic in France took away the edge of the revolutionary socialism. In every European parliament socialists challenged the existing order in a democratic way. 'The rostrum had displaced the barricade.'

In 1889, a socialist congress was held in Paris which came to be known as the Second International. It was attended by delegates from France, Germany, Britain, Belgium, Austria, Russia, Holland, Denmark, Sweden, Norway, Switzerland, Poland, Rumania, Italy, Hungary, Spain, Portugal, Bohemia and Bulgaria as well as observers from America, Argentina and Finland. The Second International rigidly excluded all those who favoured violence as against political action. It unequivocally declared:

> In a modern democratic state the conquest of the public power by the proletariat cannot be the result of an uprising; it must be the result of long and assiduous labour of proletarian organisation in both political and economic fields, of the physical and moral regeneration of the working class, and of the gradual conquest of municipal and legislative assemblies.

The main objective of the Second International was to facilitate contact among the various Socialist parties, to provide for mutual support, and on crucial issues, to speak for socialism as a whole. The International held a series of congresses—at Brussels in 1891, Zurich in 1893, London in 1896, Paris in 1900, Amsterdam in 1891 and in 1904, Stuttgart in 1907, Copenhagen in 1910, and Basle in 1912. In 1900 it set up a permanent International Socialist Bureau with headquarters at Brussels. The Second International grew rapidly and, by 1914, it embraced twentyseven countries. The Second International served to break down the barriers between the socialist leaders of different countries. It made the working class conscious of the political and social problems which confronted them. It helped to develop a real international working-class solidarity. The International tried to mobilise public opinion against the recrudescence of war, but its efforts were defeated by the forces of nationalism which proved too tempting for the socialists to ignore. The International failed to survive after the outbreak of the First World War (1914-1918).

Socialism in Germany

Germany was the home of the socialist movement which got inspiration from the philosophy of Karl Marx and the policies of the German

Social Democratic Party. The founder of this famous organisation was Ferdinand Lassalle (1825-64), who became the idol of the German working class. Son of a wealthy Jewish merchant, Lassalle received all the advantages that wealth and education could bestow. 'Every line that I write', he proudly declared, 'I do so fortified with the whole culture of my country.'

In his book *The Working Class Programme,* Lassalle divided history into three well-defined periods: (1) the phase of landed aristocracy which continued up to the outbreak of the French Revolution; (2) the phase of the bourgeois which dominated the period between the French Revolution and the Revolution of 1848; and (3) the aspirations of the working class which have been the dominant feature since 1848. As the workingmen were subject to the 'iron law of wages', Lassalle favoured the intervention of the State which alone could save them from degrading state. Under a socialist regime, in Lassalle's view, capital would be the servant, not the master, of labour. Unlike Marx, Lassalle was a staunch nationalist and infatuated with Prussia as a model state, competent to solve the problems of the working class, provided its direction was in their hands.

In 1863, Lassalle founded the General German Workers' Association (Allgemeiner Deut Scher Arbeiterverein) which however, attracted few followers. In 1864 after Lassalle's death, the organisation was left in a precarious state. In 1869, Wilhelm Liebknecht and August Bebel, both converts to Marxism, organised the Social Democratic Labour Party. It met at Eisenach and adopted a Marxian programme. The 'Eisenachers' as they were called, and the Lassalleans, though rivals at the outset, were united at Gotha in 1875 and formed the Social Democratic Party.

Bismarck became apprehensive of the rapid growth of socialism and waged war against the 'red flood'. But the outcome was a distinct triumph of the socialists. After the repeal of the anti-socialist laws, a congress of the Social Democrats was held at Erfurt in 1891. It adopted a programme (Erfurt Programme) which later became the model for the socialist parties throughout the world. Its basic demands were the abolition of private capital and the establishment of the Cooperative Commonwealth. Among the immediate minimum demands were included universal suffrage, proportional representation, freedom of speech and assembly, civil equality of men and women, separation of Church and State, free secular education, heavy income and inheritance taxes, a universal eight-hour working hours and factory reforms.

The growth of German socialism was phenomenal. Its best exponent was Bebel, a man of high ideals, a great parliamentary orator, who was greatly admired by his opponents as well as by his followers. His best-known associate was Karl Kautsky, who left an indelible impress by his writings on socialism and on history.

Socialism in France

The growth of socialism in France received a setback by the Paris Commune. Its leaders were imprisoned and exiled as a result of the bloody uprising of 1871. However, a vigorous socialist agitation began among the French working classes when the exiled communards were allowed to return. A prominent person was Jules Guesde, who had spent several years in Germany and developed fascination for Marxism and for German Social Democrats. A number of socialist factions appeared in the early eighties each with its own views. In 1893 a group calling itself the 'Independent Socialists' was organised by Jaures and Millerand, who believed in the graduated establishment of socialism. In general, the French socialists were of two kinds: Marxists, who were imbued with the ideas of the German Social Democrats; and 'possibilities' or 'reformists' who advocated a moderate and progressive form of socialism.

The two dominating personalities of French socialism were Guesde and Jaures. Guesde, an ardent follower of Marx, was profoundly convinced that the world was predestined to socialism. Therefore, a compromise with the bourgeois State was impossible. The socialist workingmen must ceaselessly toil until capitalism was abolished by a socialist national assembly. Jaures, the greatest orator of his day, favoured the peaceful penetration of democracy by socialism 'until the proletarian and socialist State shall have replaced the oligarchic and bourgeois State.'

The Dreyfus Affair[1] sharply divided the French socialists. Guesde believed that the socialists should remain neutral while Jaures upheld the socialist participation in the government. Alexander Millerand's acceptance of office in the republican government of France in 1890 raised a storm of controversy among the French socialists. The International Socialists Congress of Amsterdam (1904) decreed that no *bona fide* socialist should be permitted to hold office in a bourgeois cabinet. Jaures accepted the decision, and the outcome was a merger of the various socialist groups in the United Socialist Party.

Socialism in Britain

The pioneers of English socialism were Henry M. Hyndman and the poet William Morris, who founded the Social Democratic Federation (SDF) in 1884. Marxist in inspiration, it never received the formal blessing of Marx and Engels. Marx's emphasis on imminent revolution never appealed to the British common people and, by the late 1880s, it was already a spent force. A new organisation called the Independent Labour Party was formed in 1893, by Keir Hardie, a popular trade-unionist.

The British socialism received a great fillip when the Fabian Society was founded in 1883. It became a potent force in British politics as in 1945 there were 230 Fabians in the House of Commons, most of them associated with the Labour Party. The Society included the intellectual elite of England: Sydney Webb, its founder and his wife Beatrice, the dramatist George Bernard Shaw, the novelist H.G. Wells, the historian of socialism G.D.H. Cole. Acknowledging the contributions of Robert Owen and John Stuart Mill, they pledged themselves to the ideal of a reconstitution of society and analysed the industrial system of their day. In 1889 they published a collection called *Fabian Essays.*

The crux of the Fabian Socialism was based on two things: unlimited democracy in the political sphere and socialism in the economic sphere. Their philosophy of economic equality was to be accomplished by democratic means. They believed that the country had long been moving in the direction of collectivism and the government must be induced to take steps to nationalise the land and all key industries—public utilities, coal, electricity, railroads and other means of transport, communications, medical services, banks and the like.

The most eloquent champion of this philosophy was Bernard Shaw (1856-1950) when he wrote in 1896 that the Fabians aimed:

> to persuade the English people to make their political constitution thoroughly democratic and so to socialise their industries as to make the livelihood of the people entirely independent of private Capitalism ... Socialism, as understood by the Fabian Society, means the organisation and conduct of the necessary industries of the country, and the appropriation of all forms of economic rent of land and capital by the nation as a whole, through the most suitable public authorities, municipal, provincial or central.

During the early twentieth century another group of intellectuals sponsored a movement called 'Guild Socialism'. Its chief advocates were A.R. Orange and G.D.H. Cole. It favoured a scheme whereby the guilds would control the affairs of the industry and share in its product. It was to be vested with supreme power regulating such affairs as education, housing, roads and international affairs. Moreover, it was to regulate prices of goods produced by the guilds.

The most important event in the history of British socialism was the advent of the Labour Party. In 1893 James Keir Hardie (1856-1915), called a conference of labour leaders at Bradford and founded an organisation with the purpose of sponsoring independent candidates for parliament who would work for 'the collective ownership and control of production, distribution and exchange.' Thus was born the Independent Labour Party (ILP) with branches in other parts of the country. In February 1900, the Labour Party

1. Alfred Dreyfus, a French army officer whose trial on charges of spying for Germany caused a major political crisis in the Third Republic. Falsely accused of providing military secrets to the Germans in 1894, the trial, the imprisonment, and eventual—rehabilitation of the Jewish Dreyfus polarized deep-set anti-militarist and anti-semitic trends in a society still coming to terms with defeat and revolution in 1870-1. Notable among the supporters of Dreyfus was the novelist Emile Zola who exposed attempts to cover up official mistakes.

was formally established under the secretaryship of J. Ramsay MacDonald (1866-1937). It was not a single political organisation, but a federation of trade unions and socialist groups, such as the Independent Labour Party and the Fabians. In the decades that followed, the Labour Party succeeded in winning popularity and, on the eve of the First World War, it had become a strong political force in Britain. Its popularity owed not a little to supporting political action by the trade unions, but also by its appeal to religious Nonconformity.

Italian Socialism

In Italy, socialism found a rival in anarchy. The poverty of the country and the spirit of violence goaded the workingmen to favour methods of anarchists. A compromise was effected, in 1885, when socialists and anarchists organised a workingmen's party. Later on, the socialists were able to muster strength and to expel the anarchists. Prominent intellectuals, such as Enrico Ferri and Arturo Labriola joined the Socialist Party. A struggle between the extreme and the moderate elements weakened the organisation. A congress, held in 1906, for the time being, brought about a rapproachement between the two factions. But during the Turko-Italian War, 1911-12, the party was again split into two, when the reformist socialist leader Bonomi and Bissolati supported the war on nationalist grounds and were duly excommunicated from the party.

Despite their divergent views on many matters, the Socialists were uncompromising in their hostility to militarism. Everywhere they opposed standing armies and voted against military budget. In Germany, the socialists deprecated the influence of the army in the government. In France they raised a bogey against militarism which threatened the morals of the French army. Nevertheless, socialists were not impervious to defend their country against aggression.

The socialists discussed at length the strategy to be adopted in the event of war. Bebel, Jaures and most other socialists believed that the workers' interest lay in ending the war as quickly as possible. Lenin and the German Marxist Rosa Luxemburg argued that a war would weaken the capitalist state and usher in the socialist revolution. The Stuttgart Congress of 1907 condemned militarism and called for a national militia in place of standing armies. It cited instances of socialist action to prevent or end wars; and concluded with the omnibus statement of the role of the socialists in time of war:

> Should war break out in spite of all this, it is their duty to intercede for its speedy end, and to strive with all their power to make use of the violent economic and political crisis brought about by the war to rouse the people, and thereby to hasten the abolition of capitalist class rule.

CHAPTER 24

THE IMPERIAL EXPANSION

The Urge for Imperial Expansion

Imperialism may be defined as the extension of control or influence by one people over another. Throughout history it has assumed different forms and exerted varying degrees of influence on other events. From 1816 to 1870 imperialism did not play a vital factor in the policies of the great powers. By 1815 France had lost most of her colonial possessions in America and in the East. Bentham urged France to emancipate her colonies. In 1852 Disraeli made his famous declaration that 'these wretched colonies will be independent in a few years and are milestones around our necks.' But during the 1870s there was a shift in the attitude towards the colonies. By 1880 the new imperialism was gaining strength and there was scramble among the major powers to establish colonies.

The rivalries among the great powers led to the belief that the balance of power must be regarded as a worldwide question and not one limited to Europe alone. It opened the countries of Africa and Asia to European influence on a far greater scale than ever before. The effects of this movement on the peoples of Africa and Asia have been well summed up by the English political thinker Leonard Woolf:

> European civilisation, with its ideas of economic competition, energy, practical efficiency, exploitation, patriotism, power and nationalism descended upon Asia and Africa. But with it, it also carried, involuntarily perhaps, another set of ideas which it had inherited from the French Revolution ... These were the ideas of democracy, liberty, fraternity, equality and humanitarianism. They have had a profound effect upon the later history of Imperialism, for they have led to the revolt of the subject peoples against it.

Economic

Economic factors played an important role in the growth of imperial expansion. A famous British economist, J.A. Hobson, attributed the colonial expansion to economic forces at work in the industrialised nations of Europe. The accumulation of excess capital generated by industrialisation led the big nations to find new markets, new sources of raw materials and good investments. It is undeniable that the search for lucrative investment played a significant part in the European urge to acquire colonies.

Lenin elaborated the argument in his brilliant tract *Imperialism, the Highest Stage of Capitalism* (1917) that capitalist states must become imperialistic in their policies. He emphasised the importance of finance capital to find new outlets for investment. In the backward colonial peoples, Lenin argued, capitalism had found a new proletariat to exploit. But it should be remembered that much of the foreign investment of the European powers was not in colonial territories but in countries such as South America and Russia.

Industrialised nations sought new outlets for the 'glut of capital' and fresh markets for their products. After 1870 Germany, France, Belgium and other nations were able to satisfy their home markets and they began to look for more open markets overseas. For this purpose, Africa and Asia suited admirably. There was also the increasing need of raw materials for the industries at home. There was growing demand not only for cotton, wool and minerals, but for relatively new products such as palm oil, rubber and for older ones like coffee and tea.

Social

The pressure of population and growing unemployment in European countries were important factors in the imperialist expansion. The surplus population could earn its living in the colonies. In 1879 a delegation of workingmen petitioned Queen Victoria to make arrangement for the emigration of the unemployed to Britain's overseas possessions. Moreover, industrial economy in Great Britain and Germany reduced the opportunities of quick advancement at home for ambitious young men. Such men could find successful careers in colonial empires. In the century before the Second World War (1939-1945) more than sixty million people left Europe.

Political

Empire-building was an essential element in international prestige. France sought to recover her prestige after her humiliating defeat in the Franco-Prussian war by carving out an empire in Africa. Germany and Italy were young nations which felt that they must spread over the globe. After 1870 the idea had taken root that great powers earned respect only by demonstrating their power resources. The most dramatic way of doing this was to increase the overseas territory and failure to do this was the sign of decadence. Disraeli voiced the sentiment in 1872 when he fervently pleaded:

> I appeal to the sublime instinct of an ancient people... The issue is not a mean one. It is whether you will be content to be a comfortable England, modelled and moulded upon Continental principles and meeting in due course an inevitable fate, or whether you will be a great country, an imperial country, a country where your sons, when they rise, rise to paramount positions and obtain not merely the esteem of their countrymen but command the respect of the world.

The same argument was urged with vehemence by John Ruskin in his lectures at Oxford University:

> That is what England must do or perish. She must found colonies as fast and as far as she is able, formed of her most energetic and worthiest men, seizing every piece of fruitful waste ground she can set her foot on ... and that their first aim is to advance the power of England on land and sea.

The real impetus behind the new imperialism came from the rise of nationalism. France felt that it had great civilising mission to perform. Jules Ferry (1832-93), who had played a leading part in reviving French imperialism, talked much in the vein. In his book *The Expansion of England* which appeared in 1883, John Robert Seeley wrote of the great opportunities presented to England of extending the benefits of civilisation to backward races. Seeley also warned the growth of Russia and the United States which in fifty years would dwarf the pre-eminence of Britain, France and Germany. A similar argument had been put forward by Leroy-Beaulisu of France who passionately believed that colonial expansion was for his country 'a matter of life and death.' The same thoughts were expressed in Germany by a man like Schlieffen (Chief of Staff) and Holstein (foreign office counsellor) who warmly advocated a forward colonial policy. The German professor, Trietschke, championed imperialism as an agency for the spread of German culture.

Religion

The new imperialism also had a religious fervour. More often, the Christian missionaries were the purveyors of colonialism. In effect the flag tended to follow the Cross. One of the main incentives of the British and French policy in Africa, was the anti-slavery movement. The Scottish missionary, Dr. David Livingstone, who died in Africa in 1873, became an explorer to 'open a path of commerce and Christianity.' France sent organised missions into Africa to convert the heathen into Christianity. The Catholic missions of France under the Third Republic were very active. They were spread all over the world. In 1869 Cardinal Lavigerie founded the Society of African Missionaries. By 1875 they spread from Algeria to Tunisia and set up a religious protectorate as a prelude to political protectorate. Belgian missionaries worked zealously in the Congo as early as 1878.

Other Factors

Human factor must not be sidetracked in the growth of imperialism. Some persons who were not missionaries, but great administrators, played conspicuous role in bringing order in the distracted colonial territories. The great colonial proconsuls were Lord Cromer in Egypt, Lord

Lugard in Nigeria, Lord Milner at the Cape, Karl Peters in German East Africa. Without such men the consolidation of European control over Africa would have been impossible. Karl Peters, the German explorer, acquired for his country a domain of 60,000 square miles in East Africa, Cecil Rhodes was instrumental in advancing the power of England in Africa.

There were, however, a number of other motives which contributed to the imperialist movement. An urge for scientific discovery and for the exploration of unknown territory helped to open up Africa. But several motives merged into each other. In the words of the great explorer Livingstone 'Christianity, Commerce, Civilisation went hand in hand.' In 1874 the President of the French Society emphatically declared:

> It is not just in the interest of curiosity that exploration and geographical discoveries have been made. The discovery of America, the persevering exploration of the interior of Africa ... have had besides a scientific and, a political and commercial object.

Popularity of Imperialism

According to Schumpeter, a great portion of the whole human drama has been shaped by imperialism. He looked on nineteenth century imperialism as a cultural inheritance from primitive warring societies. Its primary aim was conquest for the sake of conquest spurred by a 'will for forcible expansion, without definite, untilitarian limits.'

The German Social Democrat Edward Bernstein stressed the humanitarian aspects of colonialism. In 1907 Bernstein agreed that even Marx had admitted that possession of colonies was of advantage to the European economy. He emphasized: 'The colonies are there—one ought to occupy them—and I estimate that certain tutelage of the civilised peoples over the uncivilised is a necessity.' Angust Babel, the leader of the German Social Democratic Party, acknowledged that 'the greatest guarantee of peace is the spread of international investments.'

Sometimes the governing class was actuated to embark on imperialistic policy owing to satisfy emotional urge of the masses who were susceptible to the appeals of imperialism. Moreover, the governing class adopted it as a sort of diversionary tactics to ward off the possibility of socialist revolution. The founder of the modern German navy, Admiral Tirpitz, advocated imperialism because he believed that apart from economic gains it would act as a strong palliative against potential Social Democrats.

The Capitalist Critique

Recently a new school of thought has emerged whose basic postulate is that capitalism is fundamentally opposed to imperialism. It rejected the claim that colonies made money for the home country. Rather, imperialist power spent far more in colonial territories on military and administrative upkeep than it received as profit from trade or capital investment.

A number of contradictory theses have been offered by imperialists to explain the sudden outburst of imperial expansion: 'the human yearn to aggrandize self, family, clan, nation; the white man's urge to share with the non-white world (at a price) his "advanced" culture; the desire to make Christianity truly catholic; the belief in the natural right of the strong to subjugate the weak; the need of bourgeois capitalists to export their surplus wealth; the impulse to escape from boredom created by the industrialization of society; objectless conquest rooted in atavistic drives; and the necessity to stabilize areas situated close to vital sea lanes.'

Colonial Rivalry and Colonial Collision

The simultaneous expansion of European powers overseas brought them into frequent collisions. The main tensions between powers may be listed as the six disputes; between Britain and France about Egypt; between Britain and Russia about Persia, between Germany and Russia about the Balkans; between Russia and Japan about China; and between Germany and France about Morocco. In addition to these disputes there were many others which were settled more amicably. The opening up of the great Congo basin, which involved the competing powers of Belgium, France, Britain, Germany and Portugal, were satisfactorily settled by the Berlin Conference of 1884-85. The Anglo-French entente of 1904 resolved their mutual conflicts in Egypt and Morocco, the Anglo-Russian entente settled their spheres of influence in Persia.

Rivalries of European powers in the Far East also involved the United States, Russia, and Japan. Until 1900, gains were chiefly made in the Southern Pacific. Thereafter tensions centred upon the North Pacific and China where Russians and Japanese competed for control of Manchuria and Korea. These tensions produced the Sino-Japanese War of 1894-1895, the Russo-Japanese war of 1904-05, the Boxer Rebellion of 1899 in China, and the Chinese nationalist revolution of 1911.

Imperialism in Africa

Before the middle of the nineteenth century Africa was the Dark Continent, a *terra incognita.* Nevertheless, European powers had been confined to Algeria (France), Cape Colony and Natal (Britain), the coastal regions of Angola and Mozambique (Portugal). From the middle of the nineteenth century occurred wonderful series of explorations which excited the curiosities of the Western powers and ultimately opened the heart of Africa to the world.

The British explorer, Speke, had discovered Lake Victoria in 1858; Baker, another Englishman, had reached Lake Albert in 1864. Among the host of explorers and adventurers, four merit special attention. In 1840 David Livingstone, a Scottish missionary, went to Africa. For thirty years he traversed the unchartered areas of south-central Africa and published two books that gave many Europeans an idea of the potential resources of this continent. When, in 1870, Livingstone seemed to have been lost while searching for the headwaters of the Nile, New York newspaper proprietors subsidized a search party, headed by the journalist-explorer Henry Stanley. The dramatic meeting between Livingstone and Stanley took place in 1871. Circumnavigating the great lakes of Tanganyika and Victoria, Stanley traced the course of the Congo river. By the publication of his *Through The Dark Continent* (1885), Stanley quickened the interest of King Leopold II of Belgium in the commercial possibilities of the Congo region.

Karl Peters, another famous adventurer in Africa, was the organizer of a German colonial society. In 1884 he landed on the east coast of Africa and by presenting gifts to the native chieftains, obtained from them about a dozen treaties ceding to his company about 60,000 square miles of territory. The next year he persuaded Bismarck to bring the vast territory under the formal protectorate of the German government. Within the next five years, German East Africa was expanded into a domain of 200,000 square miles.

The most successful empire-builder of Africa was Cecil Rhodes, an Englishman. In 1870 he came to Natal in South Africa and found wealth in the diamond fields at Kimberley. After returning to England and studying at Oxford, he came back to South Africa and acquired an astronomical fortune from mining and commercial activities. In 1886 he organised the British South Africa Company which obtained a vast area known later as Rhodesia. From 1890 to 1896, as Prime Minister of Cape Colony, Rhodes projected extension of the British influence along the whole length of Africa from the Cape of Good Hope to Alexandria on the Mediterranean. In 1902 he died, leaving a part of his fortune to Oxford University—Rhodes Scholarship as an endowment to provide for the education of young scholars.

It was Belgium's King Leopold II (1865-1909) who made the significant thrust into Africa. In 1876 he convened an international conference at Brussels to consider the possibility of opening up the interior of Africa to trade and commerce. Most of the European powers participated and established an 'International Association for the Exploration and Civilisation of Central Africa.' This body was never effective and instead became a forum for imperial rivalry. Through this organisation Leopold II financed a series of expeditions by Henry Stanley into the Congo basin and succeeded in bringing under his control a territory about eight times larger than Belgium.

The French had conquered Algeria in 1830. As Egypt commanded a route to India and Tunis counted in French Mediterranean policy, both the two countries had become a plaything for Anglo-French imperialism. In spite of the increase of European investment after 1830, the Bey (ruler) of Tunis fell into financial catastrophe. But the French were not enthusiastic to occupy Tunisia. But after 1877 the Italian encouragement to the ruler of Tunis to cancel the concessions which gave France dominance over economic and political future of the country, altered the situation. The French Government intervened, and, on April 22, 1881, the 'military promenade into Tunisia began.' Defining the war aims, Gambetta wrote:

> We ought to extort a large reparation from the Bey ... take a large belt of territory as a precaution for the future, sign a treaty with effective guarantees, and then retire... after having made a show of force sufficient to assure for ever a preponderant position there, in keeping with our power, our interests and our investments in the Mediterranean.

The Bey appealed to Europe for help; but no power, not even Italy, came to his rescue. By the Treaty of Bardo (May 12, 1881), the Bey had to recognise a French protectorate. However, the Treaty was not liked by Bey's Muslim subjects. They revolted after whipping up rage against the French invaders. Though the rebellion was crushed by October 1881, it brought obloquy upon its sponsors.

The French action in Tunis offended the Italians who occupied Assab on the Red Sea in 1882 and Massawa in the same area in 1885, thus laying the foundations of Italian East Africa. Germany also entered the race for territory in spite of Bismarck's reluctance. A Bremen merchant, Luderitz, purchased a strip of territory in South-West Africa and hoisted the German flag. This was followed by the formal annexation of a large area which, in 1884, became German South-West Africa. Simultaneously came the exploits of DR Nachtigal, a German explorer and scientist, who obtained Togoland and Cameroon. But the most spectacular achievement of Germany was in East Africa where the celebrated German explorer, DR Peters secured in 1884 necessary treaties and concessions from the Sultan of Zanzibar.

Britain's imperial expansion in Africa became manifest in the 1870s. Disraeli, as Prime Minister, advocated forward policy in Africa. Egypt, which became part of the Turkish Empire, asserted independence under Mehmet Ali in the first half of the nineteenth century. From the beginning, France and England who had the greatest interest in the development of North Africa, exercised control over Egypt. An English company built the first railroad from Cairo to Alexandria. A French engineer, De Lesseps, completed the Suez Canal in 1869. The overweening ambition of Mehmet Ali and the reckless extravagance of his successors had led Egypt into the brink of financial bankruptcy. In 1875 Khedive Ismail sold his Suez Canal shares to England which were purchased by Disraeli for £4,000,000. In 1875 the threatened financial crash came which led Khedive Ismail to suspend payment on large foreign loans. England and France, the greatest creditors, intervened—which eventually led to the dual control over Egyptian financial affairs. Khedive Ismail resented this tutelage. Consequently he was forced to abdicate and was succeeded by his son Tewfik, who ruled from 1879 to 1892.

The new Khedive was not hostile to the Dual Control, but a large section of the population resented the arrangement. A popular movement led by Arabi Bey surged forward with a cry for 'Egypt for the Egyptians.' A French consul in Cairo noted in February 1882 'an anti-European movement... destined to turn into fanaticism.' England and France urged moderation on Arabi Bey who refused to agree to dual financial control. France was not in a mood to armed intervention. Official mood in England was not in favour of intervention. Granville at the Foreign Office spoke with candour:

> Opposition of Egyptians; of Turkey; jealously of Europe; responsibility of governing a country of Orientals without adequate means and under adverse circumstances; presumption that France would object as much to our sole occupation as we should object to theirs.

Disraeli was equally forthright in his sentiments when he said, 'Constantinople (was still) the Key to India, not Cairo and the Canal.'

Arabi's *jihad* against the Europeans got fillip when an Anglo-French naval demonstration was made in June 1882. This provoked a massacre of Europeans at Alexandria. The British had no option but had to win by any means. On August 15, a British army under Sir Garnet Wolseley landed on the Suez Canal. They routed the Egyptian army at Tel el Kabir on September 13, 1882, and seized Cairo. The rebellion collapsed;

Arabi was imprisoned and Tewfik restored. A British army was left in occupation of Egypt in order to complete the restoration of order. Britain had no wish to remain in Egypt after accomplishing the task. As Lord Granville spoke in the House of Commons on January 3, 1883:

> We shall not keep our troops in Egypt any longer than is necessary; but it would be an act of treachery to ourselves, to Egypt and to Europe if we withdraw them without having a certainty or until there is reasonable expectation—of a stable, a permanent and a beneficial government established in Egypt.

But to their utter chagrin the British had found the Khedive a cypher who could not rule without the authority of British bayonets.

Britain was entangled with another crisis in Africa. Sudan was a dependency of Egypt and Khedive Ismail had imposed heavy tribute upon its people. But the Sudanese detested the imperialism of Cairo. In 1881 the Mahdi, Mohammed Ahmad, forged a sort of political unity of whipping up religious sentiment. In November 1883 the Mahdists had cut Egyptian troops in the Sudan to pieces. As the Mahdists threatened the frontiers of Lower Egypt, the British ministers complained: 'we have now been forced into the position of being the protectors of Egypt.'

Sir Evelyn Baring, who in September 1883 had returned to Egypt as Consul-General, counselled the relinquishment of Sudan. Gladstone ordered Tewfik to give up Sudan while sending General Gordon to withdraw the Egyptian garrisons. Having allowed himself to exceed his instructions, Gordon was killed by the Mahdists in Khartoum. The Mahdi set up a reign of terror. The British had found themselves in an untenable position owing to the loss of Sudan, the bankruptcy of the Khedive's authority and the refusal of the French to admit the British paramountcy in Cairo. Gladstone came to the mournful conclusion 'we have done our Egyptian business, we are an Egyptian government.'

By 1889 the British occupation of Egypt had become a necessity for imperial security in the world. As Salisbury said, 'the appetite had grown with the eating.' Eventually the occupation antagonised France and led her to ally with Russia. Therefore British resolution was to stay rather than withdraw. To keep the Suez Canal and Egypt under their control, they were to push their territorial claims up the Nile to Fashoda and from the Indian Ocean to Uganda.

On the western coast the European interest in the beginning was found to be lacking. Britain had been thinking of giving up Gambia, the Gold Coast, Lagos and Sierra Leone. The French Government had abandoned the Ivory Coast and in 1880 it was thinking of moving out of Dahomey and Gabon. But, by 1865, the French had carried their influence in Senegal.

In Western Africa the British merchants throve without the aid of colonial government. By 1881 George Goldie had amalgamated the Niger firms into the National African Company with the object of driving out French competitors. Though this created tension between Britain and France, this did not lead to an open rupture between them. It was only when the British ejected the French from Egypt in October 1882 that the latter tried to extend their control on West Africa. The French were allowed to expand their influence on the Ivory Coast. By November 1883 the British tried to bring the Niger districts under treaties of protection.

Anglo-French estrangement went so far that in November 1882 the French Government asserted its claim on the right bank of the Congo river. The British countered this by accepting Portugal's ancient claims to the Congo in return for guarantees of free trade. This Anglo-Portuguese agreement was interpreted in Paris as 'a security taken by Britain to prevent France... from setting foot in the Congo Delta.' In retaliation, France mounted a diplomatic onslaught and pressed the counter-claims of the Congo Free State.

In this situation, Britain and France both courted German favour. But Bismarck had no interest in bringing a rapprochement between England and France. Ferry—suspecting that Bismarck did not want to do anything to annoy England—negotiated an Egyptian agreement (June 1884) with Britain by which the latter promised to evacuate the country in 1888.

'With the Egyptian baton falling from his grasp,' Bismarck curried French favour by fomenting anti-British demonstration and denouncing the Anglo-Portuguese Treaty. He demanded an international conference to decide the Congo's future and proclaimed Togoland and the Cameroons to be German protectorates. At the London Conference of July 1884, Bismarck tried to wreck the Anglo-French agreement over Egypt by proposing a Franco-German *entente* on West African questions. In August, the French accepted the bait. 'After the bad treatment inflicted on us by England,' observed de Courcel, the French diplomat, 'this rapprochement is essential to us under penalty of utter and most dangerous isolation.' Shortly afterwards, the two powers agreed to decide the fate of the Niger as well as the Congo at an international conference in Berlin. To obviate a breach with Germany, Britain dropped the Anglo-Portuguese treaty and agreed to attend the conference.

The diplomats who met in Berlin from November 1884 to February 1885 had first to settle the conflicting claims in the Congo basin. The powers agreed to give Belgium the lion's share of the Congo basin, while 'contenting themselves with scraps.' For the rest, the Congo river was placed under an international region and its basin became a free-trade area. Having conceded the Congo, Britain was able to keep her control over the lower Niger while giving to France upper Niger. The Berlin Congress reduced international law to the convenient formula that any power could acquire territory in Africa by occupying it and notifying its fellow powers. As a result, the next ten years witnessed the shameless scramble of Africa among the European powers.

For the next few years the French were involved in headlong conquest in the western part of Africa. They penetrated into the region of Lake Chad and welded their settlements in Senegal, the Ivory Coast and Guinea into a great French West African empire, extending as far as Timbuktu. The French occupied the western Sudan. In 1888, the French founded the town of Djibouti on the Red Sea Coast.

Britain's priority in Africa lay in protecting Egypt. To disarm the French opposition, Salisbury offered compensation to France in West Africa. The Gambian hinterland was given to French Senegal; that of Sierra Leone to French Guinea. To compensate Paris for her acquisition of Zanzibar from Germany as a result of the Heligoland-Zanzibar Treaty of 1890, Salisbury assigned to France Sahara and Western Sudan. The French government accepted it without any demur. In the Foreign Ministry memorandum it has been written:

> Without any appreciable effort, without any large sacrifice, without the expense of exploration... without having made a single treaty... we have induced Britain to recognise... that Algeria and Senegal shall form a continuous belt of territory... Political access to Lake Chad seems important. But in striving to extend our activity towards Central Africa, there is a more important consideration, bound up with more pressing and concrete interests. We want to get it recognised once and for all that no European nation can ever resist our influence in the Sahara and that we shall never be taken in the rear in Algeria.

Unlike West Africa, East Africa had no large trade nor did it possess any large state on the mainland. However, Germany's most spectacular achievement was in East Africa. DR Peters, the celebrated German explorer, secured necessary treaties and concessions there in 1884 from the Sultan of Zanzibar. Britain acquiesced in Bismarck's claims for the former's sole interest was to keep Egypt in her tight control. As Gladstone put it: 'it is really impossible to exaggerate the importance of getting out of the way the bar to the Egyptian settlement... and winding up at once these small colonial controversies.'

Gladstone welcomed Germany's protectorates. The situation changed when British influence at Constantinople dwindled. France was now moving out of isolation and veering round Russia. 'As the margin of security shrank at Constantinople, Salisbury saw the need of broadening it at Cairo.' So, from 1890, Britain staked a claim along the whole Nile river and its approaches from Mombasa to Lake Victoria Nyanza.

Without much fuss, Germany decided to stay out of the Nile basin. In March 1890 she abandoned the Reinsurance Treaty with Russia and made rapprochement with Britain. Gaining Heligoland and the extension of their sphere from Dar-es-Salaam westward to Lake Tanganyika, Germany agreed to a British protectorate over Zanzibar. Salisbury had reason to congratulate himself:

> The effect of this (Heligoland-Zanzibar) agreement will be that … there will be no European competitor to British influence between the 1st degree of South latitude (running through the middle of Lake Victoria) and the borders of Egypt.

The Italians came late on the scene. The withdrawal of the British from the Sudan gave them an opportunity and they expropriated Eritrea in 1890. In the north-east part of Africa they secured a foothold in a part of the Somaliland coast. This became Italian Somaliland. Between them was the empire of Abyssinia or Ethiopia, a large and fertile region. In her designs upon Abyssinia, Italy incurred the displeasure of France. The Emperor of Abyssinia, Menelek, ingratiated France and the latter furnished arms to the kingdom. England, on the other hand, encouraged Italy to annex the kingdom. The Italians invaded Abyssinia, but suffered a crushing defeat at Adowa in 1896. It was not until 1935 that Italy succeeded in conquering Abyssinia. At the beginning of the twentieth century, Italy came to an understanding with France that Italy might penetrate into Tripoli with France's blessing. Tripoli, in-between Tunis and Egypt, belonged to Turkey. In 1908 a military revolution broke out in Turkey which made the country weak. It did not take long to conquer Tripoli and, in 1912, Turkey ceded that ancient possession to Italy. The Italians renamed it Libya.

There emerged a group in Paris who demanded that the colonial expansion of the French Empire in Africa should be taken seriously. Towards the end of 1890 was organised the *Comite de l' Afrique francaise.* It made eloquent appeal of turning Lake Chad into the linch-pin of French Africa. In 1891 Brazza, the Commissioner-General of the Republic in the Congo, suggested to the French Government that the expeditions towards Chad 'can produce a situation for us which will allow us to start negotiations with Britain about reciprocal concessions over the Egyptian question.'

Paris took the plunge. The French had expected a better deal from the Liberals, who came back to power in 1892. But Rosebery, the new Foreign Secretary, categorically told the French Government that the Egyptian question was a closed chapter. In 1893 the Khedive staged an anti-British coup. Though it was quickly put down, it encouraged Paris to fish in the troubled waters. In May 1893 Carnot, President of the Republic, advocated advance towards Chad. To pre-empt the French effort, the British were busy in fortifying their positions in the valley of the Nile. In the surcharged atmosphere appeared King Leopold II of Belgium, who declared an interest in the Nile. In 1891, he set up trading posts in Ubanghi, in 1893 in the Bahr-al-Ghazal and, in the same year, sent forces on the Upper Nile. The British tried to neutralise Leopold by the Anglo-Congolese agreement. By it Belgium was assigned Equatoria and much of the Bahr-al-Ghazal, so as to 'prevent the French who are about to send an expedition to (the Barh-al-Ghazal) from establishing themselves there, and to settle with the Belgians who are there already… The presence of the French there would be a serious danger to Egypt.'

The Anglo-Congolese Treaty provoked France and the latter revived the scheme of invading Fashoda by way of Ubanghi. However, the Treaty became ineffective when it was denounced by a joint Franco-German communique. Rosebery now opened negotiations with Paris. He was reported to have observed: 'Take all you want in Africa, provided that you keep off the Nile.' He offered to the French the hinterlands of the Gold Coast and some borderlands on the lower Niger. But the bargain failed to produce any effect in Paris. The British attitude also stiffened and Grey publicly warned France in March 1895 that any advance into the Nile valley would be taken as an 'unfriendly act.'

The defeat of the Italians at Adowa (March 1, 1896) at the hands of the Ethiopians hastily changed the politics of the Nile basin. Britain decided to conquer Sudan and ordered the mobilization of the army under Sir Herbert Kitchener. This decision, in the words of Salisbury, was 'to prevent the Dervishes from winning a conspicuous success which might have far-reaching result; and to plant the foot of Egypt rather further up the Nile.' This action provoked Paris to invade Sudan from the west. Captain Jean-Baptist Merchand left for Fashoda and the French General Lagarde came to Addis Ababa to forge an alliance with Menilek, the Abyssinian ruler. To forestall the French invasion from the south, the British General Macdonald was ordered in June 1897 to march from Uganda along the Nile to Fashoda 'before the French get there from the west.'

Menilek's response to the French was not heartening. He merely intended to play off the French against the British. It was reported that the Ethiopians did not help Marchand's mission; they did all they could to stop it from heading towards the Nile. In January 1898, apprehending Dervish counter-attack and the French movement, the British sent reinforcements to Kitchener with orders to capture Khartoum. On September 2, 1898, Kitchener's forces defeated the Sudanese dervishes at Khartoum. An Anglo-Egyptian condominium was clamped on Sudan.

Meanwhile, Marchand, with 150 men, reached the Nile and planted the French flag at Fashoda in late September 1898. A few days later Kitchener arrived with five gunboats and two thousand men and asked Marchand to evacuate the fortress. 'For two months it was touch and go whether France and Britain would fight each other.' However, in the turmoil of the Dreyfus Affair, the new Foreign Minister, Theophile Delcasse, realised the futility of going to war, even with Russian help. By the Anglo-French Declaration of March 1899, France was excluded from the entire Nile valley. As compensation she received the central Sudan from Darfur in the east to Lake Chad in the west. This settled the Egyptian question and paved the way for Anglo-French *entente* of 1904.

Apart from the central Anglo-French struggle for Egypt and the Nile, collateral disputes arose between them over the middle Niger. At the colonial office, Chamberlain was anxious to build an African empire for the sake of a new imperialism. He believed that a weak rival should not be left unmolested. In 1896 he annexed Ashanti and squeezed the French for possession of the Volta chiefdoms beyond. However, as both Britain and France had their interests elsewhere, they came to terms on June 14, 1898. While France gained the Upper Volta and Borgu, Britain secured Ilorin and Sokoto.

Meanwhile, France was organising a force to settle the Chad business once and for all. The Muslim leader Rabiti was found to be truculent and attacked the French force. On April 22, 1900, the French forces settled the Chad issue by overthrowing Rabiti.

South Africa

The Anglo-French quarrel over Egypt hardly affected South Africa. Occasionally the Germans tried to intervene but its impact was marginal. The partition of South Africa was essentially an affair between Boer and Briton in South Africa.

The nucleus of the British Empire in South Africa was Cape Colony, which was acquired from the Dutch during the Napoleonic wars. The simple, obstinate Dutch farmers called the Boers resented the British influence when the latter abolished indigenous forms of local government and made English the sole language. The abolition of slavery in 1833 also hurt the sentiments of the Boers. They resolved to leave the country and to settle in the interior. In 1836 they began their 'great trek' which continued for several years. This resulted in the establishment of two independent Boer republics to the north of Cape Colony, namely the Orange Free State and Transvaal. In 1848 the British annexed the Orange Free State, but it revolted and its independence was recognised by Britain in 1854.

The independence of Transvaal was also recognised in 1852. But with the diamond discoveries in Kimberley and the beginnings of investment, the British aim became specifically imperial. The Boers of the Transvaal were the most anti-British. Underestimating the strength of the Boers, Disraeli's colonial Secretary, Carnarvon, annexed Transvaal in 1876. His aim was to build up an imperial federation dominated by Cape Colony. In 1879 the Transvaalers took up arms in defence of their independence. Meanwhile, Disraeli was overthrown in 1880; the new Prime Minister Gladstone denounced the annexation and began negotiations with the Boers. But far from being pacified, the Boers rose in revolt in December 1880 and defeated a small detachment of British troops at Majuba Hill. Gladstone realised that:

> the Boers will resist our rule to the uttermost... if we conquer the country we can only hold it by the sword... the continuance of the war would have involved us in a contest with the Free State as well as the Transvaal Boers, if it did not cause a rebellion in the Cape Colony itself.

Britain swallowed the humiliation of Majuba and recognised the independence of the Transvaal.

The peace of the South African Republic was rudely shattered by the discovery of gold in 1884 which lay hidden in large quantity in the Rand. The discovery led to a great influx of foreigners—specially Englishmen—from the Cape. These foreigners or *Uitlanders* were soon involved in quarrels with the Boers when the latter, under Paul Kruger, President of the Transvaal, imposed political disabilities upon them. Meanwhile in 1894 Kruger opened his Delagoa Bay railway which, together with Rand placed him to be arbiter over the colonies' commercial future.

This was galling to Cecil Rhodes. Towards the end of 1895, he organised an invasion of the Transvaal by a few hundred troops under DR Jameson, the administrator of Rhodesia. The raid was a fiasco, it exposed the British conspiracy and caused worldwide sensation. The German Emperor, Kaiser Wilhelm II, sent Kruger a telegram congratulating him on his resounding success against Britain. The aim of Germany was to draw Britain closer to the Triple Alliance.

Jameson's raid encouraged the nationalist in the Cape, the Orange Free State and Transvaal to stand united in defence of republicanism. Early in 1896 Britain came to the painful conclusion that the Transvaal must be annexed quickly into 'a confederacy on the model of the Dominion of Canada... under the British flag', otherwise it would 'inevitably amalgamate (the Colonies) into a republican United States of South Africa.' But the British Cabinet were highly sceptical. Recalling the reactions of Afrikaner nationalism to the first Boer War, they suspected that a second war would inevitably lead to the fall of the whole of British South Africa.

Fortunately Salisbury was aware of the strength of Afrikaner nationalism. With clarity he predicted on the eve of the Second Boer War in August 1899:

> The Boer will hate you for a generation, even if they submit... if they resist and are beaten, they will hate you still more... What (Milner) has done cannot be effaced... and all for people whom we despise, and for territory which will bring no profit and no power to England.

In October 1899 war broke out between Britain on the one hand and the Transvaal and the Orange Free State on the other. The war, which lasted three years, was fought with great bravery on both sides. The English had to employ 350,000 soldiers to subdue the Boers. The war produced outstanding leaders like Lord Roberts and Lord Kitchener on the part of the English and Christian de Wet and Louis Botha on the part of the Boers. Britain annexed Transvaal and the Orange Free State. Though Britain gained important economic advantages, the war evoked sympathy for the Boers. The war also gave tremendous impetus to Anglo-German naval rivalry. Britain granted responsible government to the Transvaal Colony in 1906 and to the Orange River Colony in 1907. In 1908, a convention was held in which the four colonies were represented. This resulted in the passing of the Act of September 1909 which combined the Transvaal, the Orange Free State, Natal, and the Cape Colony into the South African Union.

British North America

In 1815 Great Britain possessed in North America six colonies: Upper Canada, Lower Canada, New Brunswick, Nova Scotia, Prince Edward Island and Newfoundland. The two most important of these colonies were Lower Canada, largely French, and Upper Canada, entirely English. Though each had a constitution granted in 1791, in neither colony did the constitution function properly. Britain had yet to learn any political lesson from the loss of her thirteen American colonies. In 1837 revolutionary movements broke out in both Upper and Lower Canada. Britain sent Lord Durham, a commissioner, to study the grievances of the colonists. In the report Durham suggested such significant changes in policy that entitles him to the rank of the greatest colonial statesman in British history. Durham struck the keynote in his Report: 'The crown must consent to carry on the Government by means of those in whom the representative members have confidence.' This was the first recognition by a responsible statesman of the principle of self-government in the colonies.

Durham's recommendations were not immediately followed. In 1847 the principle of ministerial responsibility was adopted. In 1867 a federation of all the North American colonies was brought about when the British North American Act was passed by the English parliament. By this Act, Upper and Lower Canada, Nova Scotia, New Brunswick were joined into a confederation called the Dominion of Canada. In 1869 the Dominion acquired by purchase (£ 300,000) the vast territories belonging to the Hudson Bay Company, out of which great provinces of Alberta and Sasketchewan were created and admitted into the Union (1907).

Australia

An eminent English historian, Sir Spencer Walpole, has written that 'the greatest fact in the history of England is that she is the mother of the United States. It may be similarly added, that the greatest fact in the history of the nineteenth century is the foundation of a new Britain—which may eventually prove a greater Britain—in the Southern Hemisphere.'

Australia was discovered by Captain Cook who made three voyages between 1768 and 1779. In 1788 the English established a penal settlement of Botany Bay (now Sydney), in Australia, to which only criminals were sent. A tremendous influx of settlers followed with the discovery of rich deposits of gold in Australia in 1851 and 1852. There gradually grew up six colonies—New South Wales, Queensland, Victoria, South Australia, Western Australia, and the neighbouring island of Tasmania.

The great political event in the history of these colonies was a movement for union. It found an energetic champion in the person of Henry Parkes who organised a number of conferences. A constitutional convention, held in 1897-98, drafted a constitution which was passed by the British parliament in 1900 under the title 'The Commonwealth of Australia Constitutions Act.' The constitution established a federation consisting of the six colonies which were henceforth to be called States.

New Zealand

The two islands of New Zealand, about a thousand miles away from Australia, are inhabited by the Maoris, who possess a high degree of culture. It was to pre-empt French influence that British colonisation of the islands began in 1839 largely through the influence of Gibbon Wakefield. In 1840 the British flag was hoisted on both islands. The discovery of gold and the potentialities of sheep-farming and agriculture attracted a huge influx of White settlers which the Maoris resented. As early as 1852, local autonomy was granted to the colony. In 1907 it was organised as a Dominion and acquired the status like Canada and Australia.

The First World War showed the strength of the British Empire. The self-governing Dominions—Canada, Australia, New Zealand and South Africa—took special pride in the military exploits during the First World War. They were represented in the Imperial War Cabinet, at the conference of Paris, in the ratification of the Peace Treaties, and the League of Nations. Their new status within the Empire was recognised by the creation of a post—Secretary for Dominion Affairs—in 1925. The Imperial Conference of 1926 recognised the Dominions as 'autonomous communities within the British Empire, equal in status, in no way subordinate, one to another, in any respect of domestic or foreign affairs, though united by a common allegiance to the Crown.' This principle was embodied in the Statute of Westminster which was passed by the British Parliament in 1931. The statute recognised the legal equality of the Dominions with the mother-country and their independence of one another. These new independent states—Canada, Australia, New Zealand and South Africa—became officially known as the "British Commonwealth of Nations."

The Pacific

As the Pacific islands had strategical values, Britain, Holland, France, United States and Germany showed increasing interest in acquiring these places.

Britain was primarily interested in New Guinea and Solomon Islands that stand as the natural gateway to Australia. Disraeli's first imperialistic coup was the acquisition of the Fiji group of islands. The Dutch, who held extensive possessions in Borneo, Celebes and Molucca Islands, also wished to acquire New Guinea. The Germans were not left behind as they were competetors of the British all over the south-west Pacific. This big island, therefore, was partitioned in 1885; Britain getting the territory of Papua in the south-eastern corner, Holland getting the western half, and Germany the north-eastern coast. Later on Britain took over Solomon Islands, Gilbert Islands. The British had settlements in Northern Borneo since the early 1880s.

French imperialism in the Pacific had begun with the annexation of Tahiti in 1880. In subsequent years France occupied the Society Islands, the Marquesas, and the Tuamoti Archipelago. Germany acquired the Bismarck Archipelago and the Marshall Islands. The disastrous defeat of Spain in her war with the United States in 1898 weakened her hold in the Pacific. Spain, therefore, sold to Germany the Carolines and the Marianas, including Guam, Saipen and Tinian. Finally, Germany had to share the Samoan islands with the United States. The earlier acquisition of the Hawaiian Islands had made the United States a Pacific power.

Asia

The progress of European imperialism in Asia was as competitive as it had been elsewhere. In the north Russia built up a great empire extending from the Urals to the Pacific, while in the south Britain consolidated her position in India and Burma. France appropriated Indo-China and the European powers penetrated into China. But the tide of European imperialism was checked by the rise of Japan who became a great power in Asia by her victory over Russia. Persia and Central Asia became European spheres of influence.

The greatest expansion of the European powers in Asia was made by Russia. She had long been seeking in Europe an access to the sea. Baffled in her attempts to secure this in the Crimean War, she turned towards Asia to obtain an outlet to an ice-free sea. From the middle of the nineteenth century, Russian attention was concentrated to two directions—southwards in the direction of Persia and Afghanistan and eastwards into China. In the course of her southward expansion she overran the Trans-Caspian region and came within striking distance of India. This embittered the Anglo-Russian relations which reached their high-water mark during the last three decades of the nineteenth century. The main stages of the Russian expansion in Central Asia were the occupation of Tashkhent (1814), Samarkand (1868) and Khiva (1873). By 1878 Russia had reached the frontier of Afghanistan. Russian menace in Afghanistan had influenced the British policy so much that the latter declared war against the Afghans (1878-79). The war checked Russian advance in the direction of India by placing a friendly Amir at Kabul. Moreover, Afghan foreign policy was to be controlled by Great Britain. Thus the frontier of British India was protected by the creation of a buffer state.

Thwarted in the region, Russia penetrated into other areas. She completed the conquest of Turkestan (1881) and occupied the Turcoman centre of Merv (1884), only 200 miles from Herat. In March 1885 the Russian forces occupied Pendjeh, a border district of Afghanistan. This brought Britain and Russia to the brink of war. But it was kept at bay by negotiations which left Pendjeh in Russian hands while setting a limit to their forward progress. It was not until the Anglo-Russian convention of 1907 that the Russian expansion ceased to be a cause of friction between the powers.

To the east of India, British expansion was somewhat checkmated by French advances in Indo-China. The reign of Napoleon III witnessed an active phase of French imperialism and, by 1868, they annexed the whole of Cochin-China. Then, after a short war with China in 1885, French protectorate was established over Annam and Tonkin. At first the various territories—Annam, Cambodia, Tonkin and Cochin-China—were united under 'The General Government of Indo-China.' French expansion in Indo-China was countered by a steady British advance into Burma. Between these two blocs of European territory lay the independent Kingdom of Siam. By the treaty of October 3, 1893, France compelled the King of Siam to cede the whole left bank of the Mekong river. The British reacted strongly. In 1896, an Anglo-French agreement defined the territorial jurisdiction of certain petty principalities of the upper Mekong, drew a common boundary between Burma and Tonkin, and agreed to a policy of non-intervention in Siam. In 1907, some southern provinces occupied by Siam were annexed by France so that French Indo-China formed a solid economic bloc. However, the independence of Siam was guaranteed by both Britain and France.

In the late 1880s, apart from India, Britain brought other Asian lands under her control. In 1885, she annexed Burma, an ancient state lying east of India. To the south of Burma, a melange of petty Sultanates drew the attention of the English East India Company. The great archipelago stretching from Sumatra to New Guinea had already been occupied by the Dutch East India Company. But such strategic ports as Singapore, Malacca and Penang were too tempting for Britain and, by the turn of the twentieth century, the whole bulge was under British control. Local Sultans were allowed to keep their thrones but they were closely supervised by the British High Commissioner of the Federated Malay States. Ceylon, just off the tip of India, was occupied by Britain in 1833.

Long before the advent of the new imperialism, Anglo-French rivalry in India had led to a series of clashes which ultimately forced the French to withdraw (1773). Thereafter the English East India Company brought many Indian powers like the Mysoreans, the Marathas and the Sikhs under their control. But in 1857 the Sepoys revolted which seriously threatened the rule of the British. The Sepoy Mutiny was, however, suppressed. In 1858 the East India Company was abolished and the Government of India passed into the hands of the Crown.

About the middle of the nineteenth century, the educated Indians became restless and denounced the British rule. In 1885 was born the Indian National Congress which galvanised the discontent of the people of India. It became a mighty weapon under Gandhi and Jawaharlal Nehru to fight the British imperialism. After World War I, in which Indian troops fought gallantly, Britain held out vague promise of self-government that led to full independence in 1947.

While these events were taking place, European penetration into the vast, rich empire of China got under way, Britain took the lead in breaking the isolation of China, waging two wars in 1839-41 and 1857-58, and forcing the Chinese to cede Hong Kong and part of the Kowloon peninsula. Russia also took advantage of Chinese embarrassments and, in 1858, acquired a considerable slice of territory further south and at its southern extremity built a ice-free port named Vladivostok.

For the next thirty years (1860-1890), European powers remained quiescent as their attention was diverted to Europe and the Near East. After 1890, Russia and Japan joined in the fray for the spoilation of Chinese territory.

The isolation of Japan was broken with the arrival of an American fleet under the command of Commodore Perry in 1853. A year later Japanese ports were opened to American ships and traders. Within twenty years the feudal structure of the state had been overthrown and a constitution modelled on Western charter of liberaties was adopted in 1889.

Imperialism became a necessity for Japan as she was a small country with a very large population. The most favourable area was Korea, which was claimed by China as well. In 1893 an internal disorder in Korea prompted a joint Sino-Japanese intervention which later on degenerated into a conflict between the two powers. The Japanese invaded Manchuria, and threatened to march on Peking. The Chinese surrendered, and, by a peace treaty, ceded to Japan the islands of Formosa and the Pescadores and the Liaotung Peninsula with Port Arthur and acknowledged the independence of Korea.

It was at this stage Russia came into the picture. Japan's preponderance in Korea endangered Russia's base at Vladivostok and a foothold on the Liaotung Peninsula would open the way into the province of Manchuria. In 1891, the Russians had begun to construct a trans-Siberian railway to Vladivostok which required traversing the Manchurian territory. This would not be feasible once Japan was established there. Russia intervened in the negotiations between China and Japan with the backing of France and Germany, and, by an elaborate series of cessions in 1895-96, Russia received the right to build railway lines not only across northern Manchuria to Vladivostok but also from Harbin. By the establishment of a commission house, the Russo-Chinese bank, Russia secured a preferred position in the economic development of Manchuria.

France obtained permission to run a rail line northward from Annam into China and secured valuable mining concessions in the provinces of Yuann, Kwangsi and Kwantung. In 1897, by a show of force, Germany persuaded the Chinese Government to grant to the former a ninetynine year lease of the harbour of Kiaochow and a virtual protectorate over the Shantung peninsula. This emboldened the Russians who, in 1896 compelled the Chinese into leasing Port Arthur to them for a period of twentyfive years. Russian influence was thus strengthened over Manchuria while Korea was placed between Russian pincers at Port Arthur and Vladivostok.

The rapid growth of Russian influence infuriated the Japanese and increased British apprehension. Russian expansion also prompted the United States government to defend the integrity of the Chinese Empire by circulating the so-

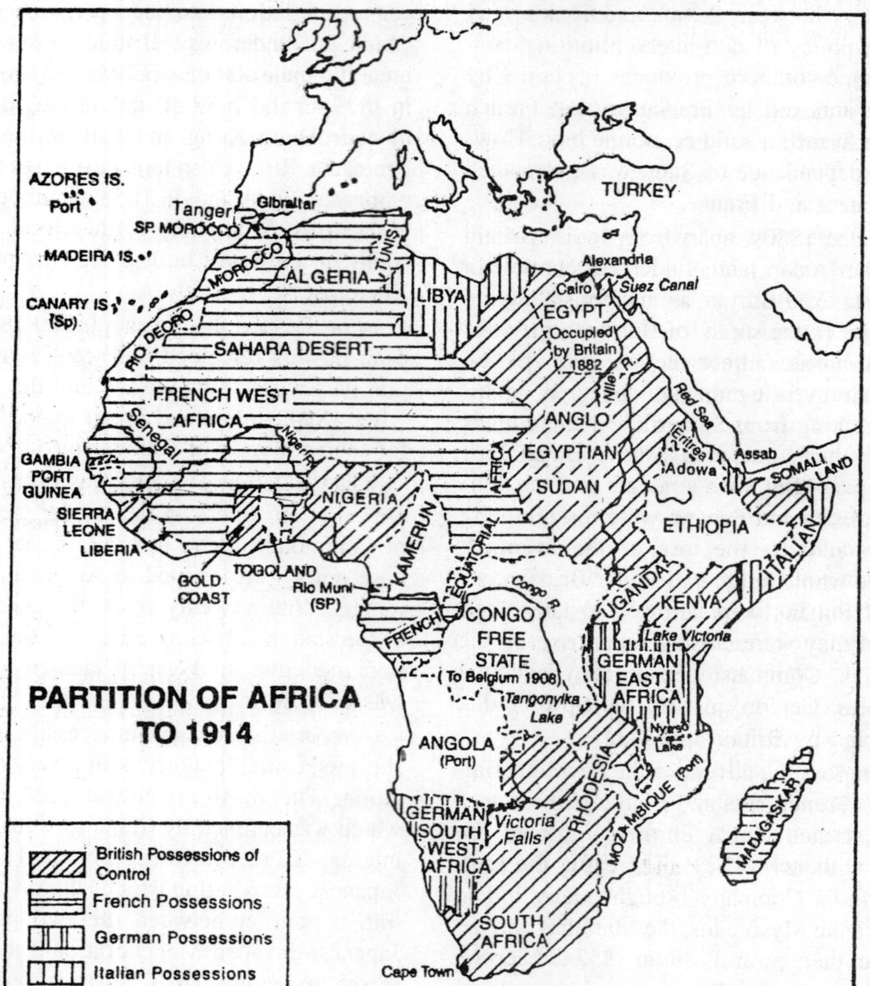

PARTITION OF AFRICA TO 1914

called Open-Door Note which required the powers to assert that they possessed no exclusive rights in China. Both Russia and Japan believed that no time should be wasted in claiming control over Manchuria and Korea. The result was a war (1904-05) in which the Russians were defeated. By the Treaty of Portsmouth, Russia agreed to evacuation of Manchuria and Korea and to give up her rights over Port Arthur to Japan.

Middle and Near East

The pressure of European imperialism was felt in Persia in the Middle East and Asiatic Turkey in the Near East. The southward expansion of Russia brought her to the frontier of Persia and, early in the twentieth century, she was able to establish her hold in northern Persia. But Britain, who was Russia's rival in Asia, could not view with equanimity the extension of Russia's influence in Persia. As a matter of fact, Britain was vitally interested in preventing the Persian Gulf from falling under the control of a hostile power as that would weaken her hold upon India. Hence Britain became active in southern Persia and succeeded in bringing it under her influence. Friction continued which was only to end by the Anglo-Russian convention of 1907. By it Russia was to have the northern half of Persia while Britain was assigned the south-eastern corner of the country, especially the Persian Gulf.

In the Near East, economic imperialism was in full swing in Asiatic Turkey. Commercial treaties, known as 'Capitulation', gave foreigners extra-territorial rights and financial control. Russian aggression at the expense of Turkey was ingrained in her policy and, in the course of expansion in the Caucasus region, Russia rounded off the eastern and the Black Sea. France, through her financial stronghold, was interested in Syria. Britain was keen in the Ottoman Empire as her communication with India lay across it.

In addition to these powers, there appeared Germany who tried to secure valuable concessions from Turkey. Since 1870s German banking and commercial establishments had been operating in the Turkish Empire. The Deutsche Bank and Wurttembergische Vereinsbank of Stuttgart offered loans to the Sultan in the 1880s.

In the same decade a syndicate was formed by the Siemens banking group to construct railway lines. This group envisioned a railway system running from Berlin to Constantinople and thence to Bagdad with branches running to Aleppo, Damascus, Smyrna, and, eventually, to Persia, Arabia and Egypt.

In 1898 the German Emperor paid a visit to the Sultan in Constantinople. Shortly afterwards, the government urged German bankers to go on with their railroad planning. So passionate was Germany in the projected railway that one of the German Emperor's advisers was reported to have said, 'With a bow to the British lion and courtesy to the Russian bear, we will worm our way, little by little, down to the Persian Gulf.' Had the project materialised, it would have opened Turkey to German exploitation. It caused great uneasiness in the diplomatic circles of Europe.

But the First World War (1914-1918) intervened and changed the situation dramatically.

CHAPTER 25

THE THIRD FRENCH REPUBLIC

Republicanism in France, born during the French Revolution, was regarded by the people as the repudiation of everything upheld by the Old Regime. But the First French Republic, associated with the glorious days of the Revolution, lasted only about a decade. The Second French Republic, an offshoot of the Revolution of 1848, lasted only four years. But the Third French Republic—which was the child of defeat, not of revolution—proved to be enduring.

The Third French Republic was proclaimed at Paris on September 4, 1870, two days after the disastrous defeat of the French army at Sedan. A Provisional Government of National Defence was immediately installed. This government gave way in February 1871, to a National Assembly of 650 deputies who were elected by universal manhood suffrage. A majority of the members of the National Assembly were Royalists and only about 250 were Republicans. The National Assembly, meeting at Bordeaux, naturally refused to sanction the Republic. The Assembly of Bordeaux made the truce with Germany ceding Alsace and Lorraine, and assuming the enormous war indemnity. The Assembly chose Adolphe Thiers as 'head of the executive power'.

Between the Government and the people of Paris serious disagreement arose over the activities of the Assembly. Tension rose high when the National Assembly moved in March 1871 from Bordeaux to Versailles, near Paris. People feared a restoration of the monarchy. They were disgusted when the Assembly refused to prolong the moratorium on rents, debts and promissory notes in spite of the economic dislocation still prevailing in the capital. Instead, the Assembly decreed that all arrears be made up within fortyeight hours. The decision of the National Assembly to suspend all payments to members of the National Guard deprived the latter of their only means of sustenance. The starting point of the insurrection was on March 18, 1871, when the Assembly tried to seize the guns from the National Guard. Violence immediately broke out in Paris. The National Guard marched on the centre of the city and seized the Hotel de Ville. The government forces fled from the city and the people proclaimed a commune in Paris.

So the commune led a revolt against the National Assembly. The programme of the commune was a protest against the centralised state. It summoned radicals in other localities to establish similar communes and to federate them with that at Paris. But it was only in a very few industrial town like Lyons, Mersailles, Limoges that communes were formed, but they were soon overthrown. 'The genius of the commune was rather that of Danton than of Lenin, its origin a sudden tempest of Republic patriotism rather than a deep-laid plot to overthrow society.' The leaders of the commune—a General Council of 90 members—had neither a coherent plan of action nor a sense of dedication that was needed. Their legislative activity was not remarkable. In the economic sphere they restored the moratorium on rents and debt payments. They never thought of seizing Versailles when the National Assembly was in disarray in the initial stage.

The National Assembly promptly took up the gauntlet. By the beginning of April, Thiers was able to mobilise 150,600 troops and immediately besieged Paris. Marshal MacMahon was given the supreme command. The commune had no chance of success as it was plagued by quarrels and jealousies of the authorities. The commune was confident of victory believing that a mighty upsurge might take place in other parts of France. But nothing of the sort happened. The great mass of the Parisians took no part in the conflict. MacMahon's careful preparation and incessant bombardment weakened the revolutionaries. On May 21, 1871, Thiers entered into the suburbs of Paris without encountering any resistance.

But the reconquest was a painful process. The real resistance began by the Communards who fought furiously. The Bloody Week of May 1871 had a particularly savage character. The conflict degenerated into violent reprisals, the defenders setting fire to famous buildings like Tuileries, the Palais Royal, the Hotel de Ville, Rue Royale, Rue de Rivoli. On May 24, the Archbishop of Paris and some others were killed by the Communards. It was not until May 28 that the organised resistance broke down. Then followed a horrible revenge, unparalleled in history. Nearly twenty thousand people were killed and thirtyeight thousand arrested, thousands being deported to New Caledonia. 'Paris after the commune was a different city.' The suppression of the commune with ruthless ferocity left an enduring bitterness between the two adversaries. The gulf created between class and class lasted into the twentieth century. The Republic was secured and the re-establishment of the monarchy was given a final burial.

Thiers as President

After the suppression of the Commune, the National Assembly turned to the work of reconstruction. France found in Thiers a statesman whose signal capacity and wise moderation admirably qualified him to guide the destiny of the nation in its hour of crisis. Appointed 'Chief of the Executive', Thiers defined his task as 'pacification, reorganisation, the restoration of credit and the revival of industry.' Though the definitive Peace with Germany had been signed at Frankfurt on May 10, 1871, German troops were to remain in France until the heavy war indemnity had been paid. Thiers had great financial knowledge and his appeal for three thousand million francs brought in fortytwo thousands. By September 1873 Thiers paid the entire indemnity and the German troops departed. The Assembly declared that Thiers 'had deserved well of the country'.

The war of 1870 had revealed the fundamental inefficiency of the French army. By the Army Law of July 1872 the French army was reorganised on the Prussian model. Compulsory military service for five years was introduced. The army was modernised which caused Bismarck serious concern.

In August 1871 was passed the Rivet Law whereby the National Assembly assumed full powers to prepare a constitution. It conferred on Thiers the interim title of 'President of the French Republic'. Though Thiers had been a royalist, he believed that the actual situation made a monarchy impossible. He found a happy formula in favour of the Republic: 'It is the form of government which divides us least.'

The Assembly, however, was predominantly monarchist. But the monarchists were divided into three parties, no one of which was in the majority. There were Legistimists, the Orleanists and the Bonapartists. The Legistimists supported the Bourbon claimant, the Count of Chambord, grandson of Charles X; the Orleanists, the Count of Paris, grandson of Louis Phillippe; the Bonapartists, Napoleon III or his son. In the National Assembly a motion was moved 'regretting that the policy of the Government was not resolutely conservative.' Thiers defended his policy of upholding the Republic 'My reason is that to-day for you and for me, in fact, the monarchy is absolutely impossible. There is only one Throne, and three people cannot sit on it at the same time.' On May 24, 1873, the Assembly, by a small majority, brought about Thiers' resignation, and elected Marshal MacMahon as the new President. MacMohan's intended role was the restoration of the monarchy.

For a time in 1873 the Royalist cause seemed to be successful. An agreement was reached in which the Legitimists and Orleanists agreed to support the Bourbaon candidate, the Count of Chambord (Henry V). Since he had no heirs, the Count of Paris, the Orleanist grandson of Louis Philippe, was promised the succession after his death. But unfortunately the monarchist unity proved to be short-lived. The Count of Chambord refused to give up the traditional lily flag of the Bourbon dynasty. The Orleanists, on the other hand, adhered to the tricolour, knowing its popularity with the people.

The flag issue killed the hopes of a restoration of the monarchy in 1873. As a way out of the impasse, the divided Monarchists extended MacMahon's term of office to seven years. But the country was tired of make-shift arrangements. Thiers' fall was provoking a republic reaction. The by-elections ran against the Monarchists. On January 30, 1875, by the slender margin of one vote, France was committed to a republic.

In 1875 the Monarchist Assembly passed a series of constitutional laws which established the permanent constitution of the Third Republic. France was to be a republic. The head of the Republic was the President elected by the two chambers—the Chambers of Deputies and the Senate—for a term of seven years. The President had initiative in introducing laws; he could force a second deliberation if a measure displeased him. He could dissolve the Chamber on the advice of the Senate. He chose the ministers who were, however, responsible to the Houses. The President had no real veto power over laws passed by parliament.

France was to be governed by a legislature of two Houses: a Senate of 300 members, a fourth of whom were to be appointed for a life term and the rest to be elected by departmental electoral colleges for a period of nine years. In 1884 the life term was abolished and all Senators were elected for a term of nine years. In theory, the Senate had equal legislative authority with the Chamber, in practice it served as a watch dog on the Chambers by revising, amending and sometimes defeating bills. The Chamber of Deputies was elected by universal male suffrage for four years. Modelled after the British House of Commons it was the 'sovereign voice' of the French people. The Chamber had power over all bills and it could overthrow the cabinet by a vote of no confidence. Joint sessions of Chamber and Senate could be called to amend the Constitution.

Parliamentary government on the English model was the gift of the constitution of 1875 to France. The President had little power as the authority was vested with a Cabinet responsible to the popular Chamber. The principle of ministerial responsibility was borrowed from the English. But the French cabinet was quite different from that of the British because of the multiplicity of political parties. The French Cabinet was composed of men belonging to various political groups. But parliamentary coalitions were based on loose ties and France had to witness frequent Cabinet crises. Between 1873 and 1888 there were nineteen Ministries in France.

Under the shadow of the new constitution, elections were held in December 1875 in the Chamber and the Senate. Republican majority was returned to the Chamber while the Royalists gained control of the Senate. The President, Marshal MacMahon, retained his office and tried to advance the Royalist cause. He encouraged army officers to demand the restoration of the monarchy and appointed Royalist protagonists to high church office. He gave moral support to the agitation of prominent Catholics for French intervention in Italy on behalf of the Pope.

Against the President, the republican majority in the Chamber of Deputies had a redoubtable leader in Gambetta, whose splendid gifts of oratory had been equal to those of Mirabeau and Danton. MacMahon's conviction that Republicanism would be the ruination of France led him to put the Presidential powers to the test. He conciliated the new Chamber of Deputies (elected in January 1876) by putting a new ministry in office under Jules Simon, an anti-clerical Republican, and an ally of Gambetta. But MacMahon pulled in opposite directions. On May 16, 1877, he dismissed the Republican Simon ministry and appointed a Monarchist Cabinet under the Duke of Broglie. Then with the sanction of the Senate he dissolved the Chamber and ordered the holding of new elections throughout France. The resulting electoral campaign was conducted by both sides with unusual enthusiasm. But Gambetta's impassioned appeal for the creation of one united Republic rallied the common people of France, peasant workers, and lower middle class. In the election held in October 1877, a solid republican majority was returned to the

Chamber and a Republican ministry was appointed. A year later, the new Senate elections gave the Republicans a majority, MacMahon's position became untenable. On January 28, 1879, he had to resign and was succeeded by Jules Grevy, a sincere Republican. Thus, nine years after its beginning the Third French Republic was at last secure in Republican hands. The government celebrated its triumph by moving the capital from Versailles to Paris and accepting July 14 the day of the storming of the Bastille, as the National Holiday and the Marseillaise as the National Anthem.

Reconstruction

During the next few years, the Republic was greatly strengthened. Most of the Republications were anti-clerical. They viewed the Catholics as their natural opponents. Their antipathy against the Catholics was strengthened by the publication in 1864 of Syllabus by Pope Pius IX which had been interpreted by many as Catholicism's declaration of war on modern thought and on democratic freedom. The Republicans now wanted to build a new world in which Science would replace faith. To attain that end they wanted to remove education from the control of the Church.

From the time of Napoleon, school education had been largely in the hands of the religious congregations. Under Napoleon III there had been a remarkable increase in the number of schools conducted by the Catholics. Only higher education remained within the ambit of state faculties. To assert the supremacy of the lay over clerical influence and indoctrinate the French boy and girl with Republican ideas, the government instituted a system of national education, free, secular, compulsory between the ages of six and thirteen. Between 1880 and 1885 the government carried through a comprehensive system of education. This was chiefly the work of Jules Ferry, a strong anti-clerical, and who was Minister of Education and Prime Minister. In 1880, he struck at Catholic schools and teaching orders by forbidding members of unauthorised congregations to teach. This was supplemented by a decree that no one could teach in the state schools without a state teacher's certificate. Primary education in state schools was made free in 1881 and an elementary education in some kind of school compulsory in 1882. State education was proclaimed in 1882 to be 'laic', *i.e.*, divorced from all religious ideas. Making primary education free and compulsory, it was thought, would enable the French to rival the Prussians as it was said that the Prussian schoolmaster had won the war with France. Laws were also passed which improved standards in state secondary schools and techincal schools. Efforts were made to restore the pristine glory of Sorborne, which it had held in the world of learning in the Middle Ages. Another anti-clerical law was the establishment of divorce in 1885.

Apart from the educational reforms, the government busied itself with other constructive activities. In the field of transportation, the work of Charles de Freycinet deserves special mention. Known as the 'white mouse' because of his shy manner, Freycinet was a brilliant engineer and administrator who came forward with a gigantic scheme of national reconstruction. Freyciner's comprehensive programme of improving railways, canals, roads and harbours was supported by parliament. This resulted in all-round development of France. Some 30,000 kilometres of new railway were constructed. New harbours were created at Le Havre and St. Nazaire. Paris became the intellectual and artistic capital of the world and great international expositions were held here in 1878, in 1889 and in 1900.

Colonial Expansion

Another significant development under the Third Republic was the reemergence of France as a colonial power. Despite the indifferent attitude of Clemenceau and his Radical followers to the colonial adventure, Jules Ferry was an ardent champion of building overseas empire. In this matter, he found allies in Catholic Conservatives, who found in French colonial expansion an opportunity to open up new areas for missionaries. In 1881 Jules Ferry established a French protectorate over Tunis after a show of force. In 1883-85, he compelled China to consent to the establishment of a French protectorate over its vassal states in Indo-China—Annam and Tonkin. Likewise, by effective bombardment, he secured Madagascar, the huge island in the Indian Ocean.

By similar means he brought under French control a part of Somaliland on the African Coast. Ferry, moreover, encouraged French exploratory expeditions and trading companies to chart into the interrior of Africa, particularly along the Congo and Niger rivers.

The expansion of the French colonial empire proceeded with accelerated speed. French Indo-China was steadily enlarged and rapidly consolidated with an area larger than the mother country's. In Africa, during the 1880s and 1890s French empire-building was taken up on a gigantic scale. Vast stretches of the Sahara and the western Sudan were explored. In 1892, Dahomey on the west coast of Africa was conquered. In 1896, a revolt in Madagascar led to its transformation from the protectorate into a colony. In 1912, a French protectorate was established over the greater part of Morocco. By 1913, the empire of republican France included not only Indo-China and Madagascar, but also a huge block of African territory constituting the five great administrative divisions of Algeria, Tunisia, Morocco, French West Africa, and French Equatorial Africa, comprising an area almost fourteen times the area of France. From its overseas empire, France reaped considerable advantage. The value of annual commerce between France and its colonies increased from 350 million francs in 1879 to nearly two billion in 1913. French capital investments in the colonies amounted to four billion francs.

Some Basic Problems

Despite the material prosperity and the vigour of the arts and science the rate of economic progress was lower in France. French economic system had to endure the worst crises. This crisis was linked with the depression that affected many countries from 1873 to 1896. In France the prosperity of the second Empire lasted until 1882. But that year heralded a process of stagnation and regression which lasted until 1895. French industrial exports were inconsiderable in 1895.

France's economy remained predominantly agricultural. Agriculture suffered acutely from the competition of new procedures, those of wheat specially. Another great agricultural industry—vine—suffered a grievous blow, when the vines were attacked with phylloxera, a deadly disease.

French industry was hit in various ways. French luxury and quality goods—which served an aristocratic clientele—suffered in the years of the depression. Expensive articles were abandoned in favour of mediocre articles costing less. The fabrics of pure silk or pure wool were rivalled by fabrics made of mixtures. But, above all, France was ill-equipped for mechanical producton. She had little coal. The consequence was that her metallurgical production was lowest before 1895, while that of Germany tripled. The economic stagnation of France was also due to decrease in population growth. 'France was caught in a descending spiral, so that population, markets and production all shrank.'

The effects of the great economic depression were felt in many fields. The landowners were chiefly hit by the collapse of land-values and the fall in rents. This led to the exodus to the towns of landless peasants and day labourers. The industrial workers suffered prolonged unemployment. Commercial professions became the refuge of persons who abandoned agriculture and industry. The crisis led to the decline of any enterprising spirit in France. This led to the triumph of protectionism. In 1892, a new tariff—the Meline Tariff—was introdúced which increased the customs dues on a large numbers of products.

Economic troubles breed discontent. After the middle 1880s, French Republic betrayed signs of stagnation and lack of direction. French parliamentary life was characterised by a pervasive malaise. The great ministry of Gambetta lasted only three months, and Ferry fell in 1885. The political parties underwent a steady process of fragmentation. The republican centre split up into a number of splinter groups.

There was no lack of critics of the regime. There were the inveterate anti-Republicans who were generally Monarchist in sympathy. The clerical wing of this group had many protagonists. The most important ones were Louis Veuillot, the editor of the Catholic organ *L Univers* who derided the Republic and Edouard

Drumont. This extreme right wing opposition found sanctuaries in certain salons in the Faubourg St. Germain.

Allied to the rightist opposition was the nationalist opposition who wanted to avenge the defeat of 1870 and to recover Alsace and Lorraine from Germany. To this belonged the members of Paul Deroulede's League of Patriots who regarded any deviation of the national effort was treason to the true France. Deroulede had no faith in Ferry's policy of imperialism as the former observed, 'I have lost two children and you offer me twenty servants.' Moreover, there were many in France who felt that the lack of patriotic spirit in the government prompted the growth of materialism and relativism and that would spell disaster for France. This attitude was reflected in Maurice Barres's fulminations against the decadence of his generations in his famous novel *Les Deracines* in 1897. Paul Bourget prefaced his novel *Le Disciple* in 1889 by appealing to the youth, 'Our generation' Bourget wrote, 'could never consider that the peace of 1871 was established for all time.'

The working classes were not satisfied with the middle class Republic. Labour unrest was common owing to bad working conditions, low wages and long hours. A violent strike in the Valenciennes coal-fields in 1884 inspired Zola to write his best novel *Germinal.* After 1890 the number of strikes increased sharply. Finally, the more educated working classes were infected with the ideas of Marxist socialism. In 1879, Jules Guesde founded a new Workers' Party which proclaimed itself to be Marxist.

Three Crises

The last fifteen years of the century saw the Republic endangered by three great crises. The two major forces of discontent against the Republic were the Catholics and the Socialists. The Catholics were convinced that the republican regime must be overthrown if the Church in France was to be saved. The Socialists added fuel to economic troubles by inflaming the workers to protest against their distress. The situation was congenial for the emergence of a dictator who would sweep away the malaise at home and lead France in a victorious war against Germany.

The man who was destined to play the role was General Georges Boulanger (1837-91) who had fought in the Franco-German war and in Tunis. Appointed as minister of war in 1886, he gradually became popular with the army by his dashing appearance and vague rhetoric. Boulanger made himself the spokesman of French rationalism who talked about a war of revenge against Germany. The increasing popularity of Boulanger alarmed Clemenceau and other Republic leaders who forced the General to resign his office in 1887.

Boulanger became a martyr to corrupt bourgeois politicians. There was a sudden swing in his favour which was strengthened by disclosure of financial scandals involving the family of the President of the Republic, Jules Grevy. The various Republican groups forced the resignation of Grevy which took place in December 1887. He was succeeded by Sadi Carnot, an eminently respectable man. A coup at any time in the months that followed might have succeeded, but Boulanger preferred to capture by legal means. Demanding a change in the whole constitution, he summed up his programme as 'Dissolution, and revision through a specially elected constituent assembly'. He became a candidate to the Chamber of Deputies for every vacant constituency and was elected in many with large majority. The climax was reached in January 1889 when he secured a big majority in Paris. It was thought by many that had Boulanger acted promptly after his electoral victory in Paris, he might have overthrown the Republic by a *coup d' etat.* But he allowed opportunities to slip, and the Republicans rallied against him. In the spring of 1889 the government ordered his arrest and trial on charges of conspiracy. He fled to Belgium where he committed suicide two years later.

The failure of Boulangism strengthened the Republic by discrediting its enemies. The prospect of monarchical restoration receded into the background. It also strengthened the socialist movement. Under the leadership of Paul Brousse, Joffrin and Benoit Malon, a 'Federation of Labour Socialists' of France was founded. The French parliament introduced some labour legislation in the 1890s. The great Act of 1892 regulated the employment of women, prohibited the employment of childern under thirteen years of age, fixed a maximum working day of ten hours and provided safeguards for miners. Free medical service to workmen and their families was provided in the Act of 1893. An Act of 1898 provided for the payment of compensation by the employers for personal injuries sustained by employees. During the Boulanger agitation, the Possibilists or Opportunists became very active against the military threat. They formed an alliance with the republican centre and declared:

> We workers are ready to forget the sixteen years during which the bourgeoisie has betrayed the hopes of the people. We are ready to defend and conserve by all means the weak germs of our republican institutions against military threats. Long live the social Republic.

Panama

If the Republic remained unscathed during the Boulanger crisis, its gains were largely dissipated by a scandal of great magnitude. The French Republican government had engaged Ferdinand de Lesseps (1805-84), the builder of the Suez Canal, in a project to build a canal across the Isthmus of Panama. But the work got bogged down by the unwise choice of a site, by defective engineering and by the terrible incidence of yellow fever. As a face-saving device, the canal promoters resorted to bribery of the press and the politicians. The corrupt attempts to hide the lapses of the government were exposed in the press in 1892 in a series of articles called "The Inside Story of Panama".

This and the fact that many of the company manipulators were Jews exposed the Republic with corruption, inefficiency and control by international Jewry. Though nothing spectacular happened in the elections of 1893, Panama contributed to the further development of French socialism. The elections increased socialist representation in the Chamber of 50 seats and inducted two men—Jean Jaures and Alexandre Millerand, both exponents of social reform by parliamentary means.

The Dreyfus Affair

'The Dreyfus affair can first of all be regarded as one of the best detective mysteries in history, one of the most complicated and most baffling.' In 1894, Captain Alfred Dreyfus, a Jewish officer with a good record, was supposed to have betrayed military secrets to Germany. In a trial marked by unsupported testimony, Dreyfus was found guilty and sentenced to life imprisonment on Devil's Island in French Guiana. Two years later, the head of the espionage section of the French army, Colonel Picquart, found to his utter astonishment that the officer who had sold military secrets to Germany was not Dreyfus but a Commandant Esterhazy, of foreign extraction, and a man of questionable integrity. Picquart immediately asked his superiors to arrest Esterhazy. But this was refused and, when Picquart insisted, he was transported to a post in Algeria. This steady refusal to the recognition of the truth was owing to the machinations of commandant Henry of the Intelligence Bureau, who was involved in the affair from the start. Henry did not scruple to forge documents in order to prove Dreyfus' guilt.

Luckily for Dreyfus, a small band of deputies, like Clemenceau and Jaures, as well as writers like Anatole France and Emile Zola, took up his cause and vindicated his innocence. To allay the public suspicion, the army, on January 11, 1898, arraigned Esterhazy before a packed court martial, swiftly acquitted him of all suspicion, and disgraced Picquart by imprisoning him. It was these events that led Emile Zola to release an open letter, entitled *J' Accuse,* to the President of the Republic. Zola denounced the verdict of the court-martial as 'a crime of high treason against humanity,' declared Dreyfus innocent and described the army's conduct corrupt and dangerous to the Republic. Instead, Zola was himself prosecuted for defamation and fled from France to avoid the sentence of imprisonment. But his action had brought the Dreyfus case into an issue of both national and international importance.

From 1899, however, the tide began to turn. Shortly afterwards Colonel Henry committed suicide having been charged with forging one of the most important documents in the case. This was followed by a confession of forgery from Esterhazy, who fled from the country.

In 1899 several groups, in support of Dreyfus, created in Parliament a political alliance or bloc and pledged to utilize their combined majority in 'Republican defense'. The bloc, with its parliamentary majority, secured the election of one of its supporters, Emile Loubet, as President of the Republic, and the choice of another, Waldeck-Rousseau, as head of a Republican ministry. The French Supreme Court ordered the army to reopen the Dreyfus case. The prisoner was brought before a manifestly biased military court at Rennes. The judges made a travesty of justice by excluding evidence that was clearly in Dreyfus's favour. He was, therefore, found guilty, but 'under extenuating circumstances', and the life imprisonment was reduced to ten years' imprisonment. But the verdict caused a new outburst of passion throughout the country and this was not mitigated when the President of the Republic Loubet pardoned the much-maligned officer. The supporters of Dreyfus were bent upon securing the assertion of his innocence. At last, in 1906, another revision of trial took place; Dreyfus was completely exonerated, promoted to the higher rank in the army, and was made a member of the Legion of Honour. Picquart was also promoted and became minister of war.

The vindication of Dreyfus meant the defeat of forces which were inimical to the Republic. It also enabled the civil authorities to purge the army command of a number of high officers who were not truly loyal to the Republic. The Dreyfus affair had captivated dozens of great French writers who dramatized the hero to vindicate his case. The Dreyfus case had taken a ugly form because everyone concerned in it had consciously or unconsciously recognised the weakness and corruption of the Republic.

A direct result of the Dreyfus case was a change in the system of recruitment. The law of 1872 had obligated all Frenchmen five years of active service but had allowed liberal exemptions. A law of 1889 had lowered the length of service to three years with few exemptions. In 1905 a new recruitment law stipulated two-years' service with virtually no exemptions. This reduction of the period of active training diminished the efficiency of the army. The Moroccan crisis in 1905 and other signs of mounting international tension exposed the weakness of the French army. The reduction of the length of service told upon the efficiency of the army. After the second Moroccan crisis the Chamber, in 1913, restored the three-year term of service.

Separation of Church and State

The controversies between Church and State had been chronic throughout French history. The Church as a organisation was not opposed to the Republic and Pope Leo XIII had sought to dissociate the Catholic Church from its Loyalist ties. Waldeck-Rousseau, Prime Minister of the Radical Republican and Socialist Coalition in 1899, came to the inescapable conclusion that clericalism was the Republic's real enemy. His successor Emile Combes said in 1902: 'Clericalism is to be found at the bottom of every agitation and every intrigue from which the Republican France has suffered during the last thirtyfive years.'

These sentiments led to a new spate of anti-clerical legislations. In 1901 an Association Law was passed which required that all congregations must apply for legal authorization or be dissolved. It was also provided in the law that no member of any unauthorised Congregation was to be permitted to teach. The law was described by the anti-clerical historian Debidour as 'the most decisive act of anti-clerical policy since 1870'. The enforcement of the law was entrusted to Emile Combes who, in 1901, succeeded Waldeck-Rousseau as Premier. Combes, who was an extreme anti-clerical, applied the law with unusual severity. By the end of 1902 about 12,000 schools conducted by unauthorised congregations had been closed. Most of the congregations were dissolved so that thousands of nuns and priests had to leave France. In 1904 a law was passed forbidding all congregations to give teaching of any kind. It also stipulated that all legally recognised teaching orders must give up their teaching work within ten years.

The policy of Combes annoyed the Vatican and once more brought the question of separation of church and state to the fore. Ever since the Concordat of 1801 between Napoleon and the Vatican, Church and State had been maintaining a happy co-existence. In November 1904, Combes introduced a bill for the separation of Church and State. The main task of piloting the bill through parliament belonged to Aristide Briand, then a young socialist Deputy. In his opinion the 'State must remain neutral in respect to all religions. It is not anti-religious, for it has not the right to be so; it is merely non-religious.' On December 9, 1905, the bill eventually became law. It declared null and void the Concordat and the Church was wholly separated from the State. It declared that the Republic ensured freedom of worship and guaranteed its free exercise. At the same time, however, the Republic ceased to recognise or subsidize any form of worship—Roman Catholic, Protestant, or Jewish. All Church revenues and endowments were to be handed over to religious corporations (*association cultuelles*). The State was henceforth not to pay the salaries of the clergy, on the other hand, it relinquished all rights over their appointment.

The separation of Church and State was deplored as the first serious breach made in the administrative fabric constructed by Napoleon. It was regrettable that an arrangement which had worked for over a century was terminated by the unilateral act of the State. The result was that Pope Pius X vehemently denounced the principle of separation and refused to recognise lay *associations cultuelles.* In consequence, the State sequestered Church property handing over its funds to public relief organisations and its buildings to the local municipalities.

Thus the Pope's uncompromising attitude led to extraordinary results—so much that 'the Catholic Church was without legal status of any kind, it could hold no property, it was literally an outlaw.' A new law of January 1907 revoked the privileges offered to the Roman Catholic Church by the law of 1905. The law reduced the amount of property to be used by the clergy, and stipulated that churches could be kept open for public worship by contracts between priests and the local authorities. Thus, 'by this separation of Church and State, France broke with the European tradition of Concordats, by which the state officially recognises religion; she adopted the American system which leaves the Churches to be organised by private initiative. This was a revolution in the ecclesiastical regime of France.'

Political History

The French Republic became stable in the decade after 1905. The Dreyfus affair had stengthened the republican parties and brought them into contact with the socialists. Officially this tie was terminated in 1905 when the different French Socialist parties coalesced with the name the French Section of the Workers International. Though they declared themselves to be a revolutionary party rather than a revisionist one, the French Socialists remained for the most part revisionist and supporters of the Republic. The spokesman of the republican parties was Aristide Briand who was to become France's longterm foreign minister after war.

The new vitality of the Republican centre was shown by the emergence of other leaders. Joseph Caillaux succeeded Waldeck-Rousseau and Combes as the chief of the Radical Republicans; and the Right Centre found a dynamic new leader in Raymond Poincare (1860-1934), who was to be President of the Republic in 1912.

To the left of the Socialists, the Syndicalists carried on their agitations through their militant trade unions, and their greatest theoretician, Georges Sorel, preached the uses of direct action. On the extreme Right, the forces of reaction sought a new rallying point and had found its leader in Charles Maurras (1868-1952). A powerful publicist, Maurras fulminated against the Republic as a hotbed by Jewry, Protestants and foreigners and called for the restoration of a king who would made France great once more.

Against the rising tide of social unrest, George Clemenceau, Prime Minister from 1906 to 1909, relentlessly set his pace. In this he was supported by Moderates and Conservatives and by a majority of the Radicals. But neither Conservatives nor Moderates liked his ecclesiastical policy, and when his finance minister, Joseph Caillaux, proposed the imposition of a progressive income tax, Clemenceau had to go out of power (1909). Briand, who stepped in, introduced a significant piece of social legislation, establishing a system of old-age pensions for the mass of wage-earners, but he was threatened with labour troubles culminating in a general strike of railwaymen in 1910. The strike was suppressed with the help of the army and Briand became the hero alike of the Right and the Radical and the villain of the extreme left. The republican Bloc was weakened and ministerial instability became a regular feature. In the three years 1911-14, nine ministries succeeded one another.

Foreign Policy

The strength of the Third Republic was manifest in foreign policy. Ever since 1870 France had been without a single ally. France was separated from England by colonial rivalries, any connection with Russia was unthinkable on both sides. But in the course of twenty years conditions had altered. The great prosperity of France which owed not a little to her wise economic policy had given her an incomparable importance to financial association. It was fortunate for France that her foreign policy during the years 1898 to 1905 was guided by Theophile Delcasse, a man of enormous industry, who showed remarkable pertinacity in pursuing his aims. In building France's diplomatic position, Delcasse set himself to the task of strengthening France against Germany as he believed that the most desirable objective of French policy was the recovery of Alsace and Lorraine.

Delcasse did his utmost to reinforce the Franco-Russian Alliance. The genesis of this alliance could be traced to 1888 when Russia had placed her first loan in Paris. Two years later, after the resignation of Bismarck, the plan for a Franco-Russian alliance took more definite form. The Russo-German "Reinsurance Treaty" lapsed and in its place an alliance was made between Russia and France in 1891. This was followed by a military convention between the two countries in 1892. The treaty laid down that if France was attacked by Germany or by Italy supported by Germany, Russia was to come to her aid. France undertook a similar obligation to aid Russia if the latter was attacked by Germany or by Austria supported by Germany. Thus was formed the famous Dual Alliance.

Relations with Italy, strained ever since France had established her protectorate in Tunisia, had deteriorated after Italy's adherence to the Triple Alliance in 1882. A tariff war had also been going on between Italy and France since 1887. In 1898 Delcasse concluded a new commercial treaty with Italy which put an end to this ruinous tariff war. In 1900 there took place a secret agreement whereby France promised Italy a free hand in Tripolitania in return for recognition of her own claims in Morocco. In 1902, when Italy renewed the Triple Alliance, she solemnly assured that she would not take part in any aggression against France under any circumstances whatever. The exchange of visits between the King of Italy and President Loubet strengthened ties between France and Italy. The German Chancellor, Prince Bulow, treated the rapprochement as an innocent flirtation. But as a French historian has remarked, 'the flirtation was to develop into a liaison.'

But the most important thing was the reconciliation with England. There were many causes of irritation between the two countries. England had occupied Egypt in 1882 and this France regarded with utmost dislike. British and French interests likewise clashed in Central Africa. In 1898 the two powers stood upon the brink of war over what is known as the Fashoda incident. In that year a French expedition under Marchand coming from West Africa occupied Fashoda on the Upper Nile in the British sphere of influence. England took up a resolute attitude and the French withdrew. A few months later a new Anglo-French Convention was concluded which decided that East Africa should remain predominantly British while West Africa would continue to be predominantly French.

Meanwhile, the French minister Delcasse was eager for a good understanding with Britain. The breakdown of Anglo-German alliance, French interests in Morocco, and the German menace on the other paved the way for a reconciliation between England and France. Both countries were served by new men, France by its new ambassador in London, Paul Cambon, and Great Britain by her new sovereign Edward VII who visited Paris in 1903. The result was the *Entente Cordiale* between England and France in April 1904. In return for a formal recognition of her position in Egypt, Britain gave France a free hand in Morocco. In an accompanying convention a series of long-standing disputes in Newfoundland and Africa and in Siam, Madagascar and the New Hebrides were settled. This *Entente* was extended to Russia in 1907 when England made up all her differences with Russia and signed conventions with regard to non-competition in Persia, Afghanistan and Tibet. Thus the Triple Alliance of Germany, Austria-Hungary and Italy was countered by a Triple Entente of France, Britain, and Russia.

The special position which France had secured in Morocco by the *Entente Cordiale* was challenged by Germany who had her treaty rights in Morocco. In March 1905 the Kaiser visited Tangier and declared that Germany regarded the future of Morocco as an international question. The vigour of the German intervention frightened the French government which brought about the resignation of Delcasse as the latter refused to grant any concessions to Germany. Though Delcasse's fall was a stunning victory for the Germans, in the ensuing conference, which met at Algeciras in 1906, Germany gained little. It was, on the whole, a victory for France as no essential change was made in the original Moroccan settlement. But in 1911 Germany issued another challenge by sending a gunboat, the *Panther,* to Agadir, which for a time threatened a European war. But the stiff attitude of Britain that she would go to France's help if she were attacked, led Germany to back out. A new Franco-German Convention was signed in November 1911. Germany gave France a free hand in Morocco, in return Germany got extensive territories in the French Congo and Cameroons.

France in 1914

By 1870, France could be reckoned a big industrial power. But unlike her industrialized neighbours such as Britain, Belgium and Germany, agriculture was still the biggest industry. Peasantry formed the backbone of the country. In comparison with many of her neighbours, France was handicapped in natural resources, especially coal. Though there were big industries, France was predominantly a land of small industries. 'As early as 1913,' it has been said, 'the ratio of industrial potential as between Germany, England and France was computed at Germany 3, England 2, France 1.' This did not mean that France was deficient in industrial development. France had developed chemical industries and electricity. One of the wonders of the 1889 Exhibition was soon to supersede gas as a widespread means of lighting. But compared with Britain and Germany, lack of coal and suitable raw materials put her at a disadvantage in the production of heavy chemicals. Although Paris had its first underground and the Paris-Lyons-Marseilles railway company began to electrify its lines in 1899, by 1914 France lagged behind Germany and Switzerland in her development of power. At the same time industrialization was facilitated by the growing improvement of communication. By 1890 the mileage of railway track had doubled since 1870, the canal system had been standardized and extended. About the same time motor-car had made its appearance. France did not lag behind in aviation, cinema and wireless.

In spite of the importance of industry, France still presented a rural society. Big industry was largely confined to five departments of the North, and to a few large cities such as Paris, Lyons and Marseilles. Elsewhere agriculture was the occupation of the majority of Frenchmen. As France had no enclosure movement like Great Britain, many of the peasant holdings were still widely scattered and were exceedingly small. After the long depression of the seventies and eighties, state encouragement followed in the form of protection accorded by the high Meline tariff of 1892. The French vineyards—encouraged and protected by the vine defence syndicate to combat the phylloxera prospered, so that by 1906—they suffered from over-production. The improvements in technique increased production and France became the greatest wheat-producing country in Europe outside Russia.

France was, as a whole, a singularly rich and prosperous country. The standard of living was above average for every class. In 1914 it was the bourgeoisie who dominated the scene, ruled the world of politics, industry, letters and the arts. The nobility had lost their separate political and social importance, although some of them still maintained a close circle in the Faubourg St. Germain in Paris. The great banking and industrial families were still more influential than before. After the British it was the French financiers who were the bankers of the world. Amid all changes the essential elements in the social structure, the family, stood firm, and the French women in general were satisfied with their position in the family.

During the Third Republic France attained such an intellectual pre-eminence in an extraordinary variety of subjects as to elicit wonders. Victor Hugo, the last and greatest of the Romantics, died in 1885. But the Romantic movement had long since given way to Realism and Realism, in turn, had passed into the scientific Naturalism, of which Zola was the leading spokesman. Meanwhile Guy de Maupassant had become the acknowledged master of the short story. Novels of men like Barres and Bourget marked, in their turn, a reaction from the Naturalist school, a reaction which was strengthened in another sphere by the work of Henry Bergson. Nationalists like Barres, Bourget Peguy and Maurras were challenged by internationalists like Anatole France and Romain Rolland. In theatre, Sardou was the most prolific and popular writer in which the famous actress Sarah Bernhardt became famous. The artists did not lag behind the men of letters. The Impressionists led by Manet, Monet, Renoir, Degas continued to exercise an extraordinary influence. The great figures of Cezanne, Van Gogh and Gauguin followed. Picasso, Braque and Matisse had begun to perplex, shock or delight a wide public with their new Cubist paintings. In sculpture Rodin, the greatest master of modern times, adorned France. In music too great composers of distinction—Massenet, Saint-Saens, Bizet, Faure, Vincent D'Indy and Debussy—made France their home. Furthermore, France was no less famous in the field of learning and sciences. Taine, Renan, continued their work as historians and were followed by men such as Sorel, Hanotaux and Lavisse. J. H. Fabre won recognition for his study of insects; Vidal de la Blache for his work as a geographer, Durkheim and Tarde for their studies of social psychology; and Marcel Bertrand as a geologist. Henri Poincare became the foremost mathematician of the age. In microbiology Pasteur became a legendary figure and the 'Institut Pasteur' was founded in 1888. The Father of Synthetic Chemistry was Marcellin Berthelot. Last but not the least, the Curies opened up a vast field of scientific and medical enquiry by their discovery of radium in 1898.

The Third Republic was distinguished by the creation of Universities, by the foundation of more specialized schools such as the Ecole des Sciences Politiques, and by a great improvement in the facilities for scientific study. The period witnessed a great battle between the champions of a classical and a modern education until, in 1902, the modernists won a notable victory.

First World War (1914-1918)

France became involved in the First World War as she had no intention of abandoning her Russian ally. German declaration of war on Russia on August 1, 1914, was followed by a general mobilization on the part of the French Government. On August 3, Germany declared war on France. On the August 4, all three powers of the Triple Entente were at war with Germany and Austria-Hungary. On Septemper 3, the Entente was converted into an Alliance by an agreement that each party would not conclude a separate peace.

Thus, for the third time within a century France was faced by a German invasion. The withdrawal of Russia after the Bolshevik Revolution in 1917 made the situation desperate for France. On November 14, 1917, the President called upon Clemenceau to take over the government of France. 'So long as victory is possible,' Poincare had written in August 1914, 'He (Clemenceau) is capable of upsetting everything. A day will perhaps come when I shall add: Now that everything seems to be lost, he alone is capable of saving everything.'

The effect of Clemenceau's accession to power was immediate. France now had a strong government. Such was the public trust in Clemenceau that he was able to impose his will upon Parliament without question. In May 1918 the Germans once more broke through the Marne and penetrated as far as Chateau Thierry, only fifty miles from Paris. The capital was again in danger. At such a moment Clemenceau was indomitable. He observed: 'The Germans may take Paris, but that will not prevent me from going on with the war. We will fight on the Loire, we will fight on the Garonne, we will fight even on the Pyrennes. And if at last we are driven off the Pyrennes, we will continue the war at sea.'

His confidence was fully justified. The Germans were held at the gates of Paris. Reinforcements poured in. By the beginning of September the German forces were in full retreat and on November 11, 1918, the armistice was signed. Through the help of her Allies, the tenacity of leaders such as Joffer and Poincare, Clemenceau and Foch, and the gallantry and courage of her people and soldiers, France had survived and emerged victorious. For four years she had to bear the brunt of German attacks on the western front; her troops had fought at the Dardanelles, in Serbia, in Italy, and at Murmansk; they had conquered Togoland and helped to take the Cameroons. Her ships acted as a sentinel in the Mediterranean. One million three hundred thousand of her men were lost and 740,000 injured; 289,000 houses had been destroyed. She was short of labour and raw materials. Her public debt had increased from 33 millions francs in 1913 to over 219 milliard in 1919. She owed 33 milliard francs to foreign countries.

Despite her heavy losses, France made considerable gains. She recovered Alsace-Lorraine. In Africa, France was given a mandate for the German colonies, Togoland and Cameroon. In western Asia, she got a mandate for Syria. By acquiring the iron of Lorraine, the potash of Alsace, and for fifteen years, the coal of the Saar, France became an industrialized nation.

But at the Paris Peace Conference, France was disappointed. The French government pleaded that the future security of their country depended upon the cession of the German Rhineland. But President Wilson of America had persuaded Clemenceau to give up the French demand. In return for France's surrender of the claims, the British and American governments had promised to guarantee France against German attack. But the United States Senate refused to ratify the Versailles Treaty and repudiated this pledge too and Britain also followed suit.

The event embittered relation between Britain and France for at least a decade. According to Arnold Toynbee:

> This was in effect a dissolution of the Anglo-French Entente of 1904, after the necessity of the Entente for the survival of Great Britain, as well as France, had been demonstrated, in the First World War, by a terrifying experience of Germany's military strength. The nonratification of the post-war British guarantee to France dealt a blow to Franco-British relations from which these never recovered.

French Search for Security

The disappointment suffered by France at the Paris Peace Conference led her to pursue a policy that was designed to give them security against Germany. In 1920, the French government concluded a defensive alliance with Belgium to render any future German invasion through Belgium impossible. The realisation that, in any future war, Germany would have to fight on two fronts, led France to find allies in Eastern Europe.

France, therefore, turned to Poland. In February 1921 a formal treaty was concluded in which the two powers agreed to 'consult each other in all questions of foreign policy' and in the event of unprovoked aggression upon the territory of either, 'to take concerted measures for the defence of their territories and the protection of their legitimate interests.' From a strategical point of view Czechoslovakia was a useful ally against Germany and in 1924 France concluded a military alliance with it. Czechoslovakia had already formed in, 1920-21, a 'Little Entente' with Rumania and Yugoslavia, and this arrangement helped France to draw into its own circle of alliance Rumania in 1926 and Yugoslavia in 1927.

The French alliance system seemed stronger than it was. The fundamental weakness of the system was that it was expensive and had to be buttressed by frequent loans. Moreover, most of the powers with whom France had contracted alliances were minor powers, widely scattered, whose fighting potentialities were very much in doubt. Besides, the alliances enmeshed France in all the controversies of eastern, as well as, western Europe. The French search for security alarmed Italy who ingratiated the favour of Austria, Hungary and Bulgaria as a counterpoise to the French alliances.

The French were aware that their recent victory had been won with the aid of other powers and they would have to build up their own resources. They could not regard the League of Nations, in its the then form, as a sufficient bulwark against future war. From the French point of view, the two fatal weaknesses which plagued the League were that it did not define 'aggression' and that it did not specify the action to be taken against an 'aggressor'.

The French government sponsored two plans for strengthening the League. The first was the Draft treaty of Mutual Assistance of 1923. It proposed that, once the Council had declared that a member state was the object of aggression, all other members would be obliged to come to its assistance. The second was the Geneva Protocol of 1924 which prescribed the settlement of every international dispute by arbitration or by conciliation. A state which refused to accept the award was, 'ipso facto', the aggressor, against whom each member of the League would be obliged to resist.

Both these proposals received wide support among League members. Both failed as a result of the opposition of the British government and the Dominions. Britain disliked the idea of obligating itself either to obey or to enforce each and every decision of an international body. Furthermore, it might involve them in war with the United States if the latter was regarded as an aggressor in any dispute with a League member. The real reason for British intransigence was their reluctance to accept obligations in Eastern Europe and other areas in which they had no vital interest.

In 1925 Franco-German relations showed some improvements owing to the conciliatory attitude of the foreign ministers of the two countries—Aristide Briand in France and Gustav Stresemann in Germany. The two statesmen believed that they could promote the security of their respective nations by direct agreements. Britain's Foreign Minister, Austen Chamberlain, encouraged the negotiations and persuaded the Italian government to do likewise. The outcome was a group of treaties, drafted in October 1925 at Swiss health resort of Locarno and collectively styled the Pact of Locarno. Of these the most important were (*a*) A treaty of mutual guarantee of Franco-German and Franco-Belgian frontiers, signed by Germany, France, Britain, Italy and Belgium, (*b*) A Franco-Polish and Franco-Czechoslovak treaty for mutual assistance in case of aggression by Germany. Germany agreed to seek readmission to the League of Nations. She also agreed to submit any disputes that it might have with its neighbours to arbitration or conciliation. The Pact of Locarno was important as it marked a beginning to the solution of European problems. Though it did not mark the 'real dividing point between the years of war and the years of peace,' it did produce a temporary atmosphere of goodwill and a period of conciliation.

In the afterglow of optimism produced by the Locarno Pact, the American Secretary of State, Frank Kellogg, acting on a suggestion of Briand, agreed to a mutual agreement, in which both parties renounced war as an instrument of policy. The Kellogg-Briand Pact was signed at Paris in August 1928. Being a pious declaration, it was signed by all nations including the Soviet Union.

Post-war Politics

From 1919 to 1924 the French government was controlled by a 'National Bloc.' Clemenceau, Prime Minister during the latter part of the war, retired from office in 1920. Alexandre Millerand, once a Socialist and now a conservative and nationalist, became Prime Minister and shortly afterwards was elevated to the Presidency.

The successive Bloc ministries worked with remarkable assiduity to reconstruct the ravages of the war and to restore economic prosperity. The reacquisition of Lorraine gave France one of the great iron fields of the world and enabled it to export steel; and the recovery of Alsace so strengthened the textile industry that France soon became the third largest producer of cotton goods. Since the markets of the world were clamouring for French articles—the wines of Burgundy and Beaune and the products of Chanel' and Mainbocher—French trade revived with astonishing rapidity.

The 'National Bloc' was less anti-clerical than the pre-war governments of France had been. It resumed diplomatic relations with the Papacy and left the relations of church and state in the recovered provinces of Alsace and Lorraine to be regulated by the Concordat of 1801. It also tolerated the revival of Catholic religious communities and became less rigid in the enforcement of the Associations Act of 1901.

In the elections of 1924 the Socialist Radicals deserted the 'National Bloc' and recreated with the Socialists a 'Cartel of the Left' which won a majority of seats in the Parliament, whereupon Millerand was forced out of the presidency of the Republic, and, under his successor, Gaston Doumergue, a Radical ministry was installed with Edouard Herriot as premier.

Herriot represented everything that was best in the Republican France. He had wide interests and a flexible mind. But his Radical ministry lasted barely a year. It withdrew French forces from the Ruhr and showed a soft attitude towards Germany. At the same time it began an anti-clerical campaign, breaking off diplomatic relations with the Papacy and threatening to repudiate the Concordat in Alsace-Lorraine. The result was an alienation of moderates who, along with many patriots, thought Herriot too conciliatory toward Germany. Herriot's recognition of Soviet Russia towards the end of 1924 gave the Right another pretext for agitation. But what brought about Herriot's downfall was the sorry state of public finance which the government proved incapable of rectifying. He was succeeded by a Cabinet led by Painleve. The significance of this change was reflected in the appointment of Aristide Briand to the Foreign Office, where he remained until 1930 despite fluctuating fortunes in French politics.

Although the President of the Council of Ministers seemed frequently to change, the actual Cabinets in France changed relatively little; they were rather 'transformed' into similar combinations. This fact, together with an enlightened civil service, gave the government of France greater stability than was appreciated. The most striking example of 'transformation' was the emergence in July 1926 of a ministry of 'National Union' headed by Poincare, with Briand as Foreign Minister, Painleve as Minister for War, and Herriot for Education. The coalition government, brought about by the threatened bankruptcy, faced the situation with grim determination.

Poincare's long experience in French politics and his abundant energy weathered the country through the grave financial crisis. He increased the taxation of all kinds and improved the system of collection. He did away with the former system of several different budgets and unified the accounting system. He negotiated a new loan with the Bank of France that enabled him to balance the budget and to stabilise the currency, with the franc at about a fifth of its pre-war value. It was not until June 1928, after the election in April of that year, that the franc was finally stabilised at 124 to the pound. Simultaneously, the government appeased the Catholics by restoring diplomatic relations with the Papacy and by rescinding the anti-clerical laws of the Herriot ministry. In 1928, the government enacted a comprehensive social insurance law for the benefit of workmen. Agriculture and industry flourished and so did small business from the influx of tourists. There was no unemployment problem.

The general election of 1928 was a decisive victory for Poincare and his ministry of National Union. But in the next year, he felt obliged to retire owing to his failing health. The impact of the World Depression that had started in New York in 1929 was felt in France as well. The curtailment of the tourist trade, the cancellation of orders for luxury goods, and the tendency towards economic nationalism eventually enfeebled the bases of French prosperity. Since France remained on the gold standard which Britain and the United States felt obliged to abandon, prices of goods soared and exports fell off. Unemployment and social distress made their appearance and, by 1932, the country seemed to be on the verge of bankruptcy.

The desperate situation demanded determined action, but the French Chamber failed to do so owing to the irreconcilable differences between different parties. The elections of May 1932 resulted in a victory for the parties of the Left, spearheaded by the Radical Socialists, led by Edouard Herriot and the United Socialists, led by Leon Blum. The two parties differed on the panacea for the economic ills of the country. To counteract the Depression, United Socialists advocated a programme that included nationalization of key industries and the Bank of France, increased taxation on the wealthy class of the society, and extensive government measures in the form of public works. The Radicals considered all these measures as mere empty gestures and preferred to rely upon a programme of rapid governmental economy. This incompatibility led to ministerial instability which reached its climax as there were four ministries in little more than a year.

This confused situation led to the growth of Communism and the resurgence of anti-Republican organisation of the right. In addition to the old *Action Francaise,* the most important of these was the *Croix de Feu.* Founded in 1927 as a society of war veterans, *Croix de Fue* had become, under the leadership of Colonel de la Rocque, a militant group of young conservatives. Besides these, there were the *Jeunesses Patriotes* which resembled Mussolini's Squadristi, the *Solidarite Francaise,* founded by the perfume manufacturer Coty, professed a preference for government by dictatorship, the *Francistes,* who wore uniforms similar to Hitler's S.A.; the Neo-Socialists of Marcel Deat, and others.

The rise of these groups was stimulated by the inefficacy of the French parliamentarism in contrast to the vigour and efficiency of the totalitarian regimes of Italy and Germany. These groups also received covert encouragement from self-seeking politicians represented in the *Comite des Farges* and the Bank of France, who were genuinely alarmed by the steady growth of socialism and the Blum's projected programme of nationalization and heavy corporate taxation.

In 1934, the Republic experienced another scandal which rocked the government to the brink of disaster. A stock manipulator named Serge Stavisky—who had enjoyed protection in high places—was arrested for having issued some fraudulent bonds. He committed suicide to escape punishment. The conservative press alleged that the government had been embroiled in a conspiracy with Stavisky in order to prevent him from divulging the names of his accomplices. In this atmosphere of suspicion, popular indignation began to grow. On January 27, 1934, the Prime Minister, Chautemps, and his Cabinet resigned. The ever maladriot Daladier undertook to form a new government, causing a storm by transferring the Prefect of the Paris Police and making another police official Director of the Comedie Francaise. Indignation knew no bounds. On February 6, in the Chamber, Daladier gained a vote of confidence after furious protests. The protests took an ugly turn and led to a major riot in Paris on February 6, 1934. According to one description, the Right denounced the government in the Chamber of Deputies, the *Croix de feu* assembled on the Esplanade des Invalides, *Action Francaise* militants in the Boulevard St. Michael, the *Jeuns Patriots* at the Hotel de Ville. The rioting caused twentyone deaths and 1,600 casualities. 'February 6th was a revolt against Parliament, an attack against the regime. It was hoped through a popular rising to disperse the deputies, to seize the Chamber and proclaim at the Hotel de Ville of Paris an authoritarian government.' Disturbances all over the country continued and a general strike was called for February 12. The government resigned. But on February 9, however, the former president, Gaston Doumergue, emerging from seclusion, formed a government of National Union. He achieved the distinction of combining Herriot of the left and Tardieu of the Right in the Cabinet; the veteran minister, Louis Barthou, went to the Foreign Office and Marshal Petain to the War Office.

In the middle of March 1934, the Government appointed an all-party commission of forty-four members to reform the state of France. They did good work, made several administrative changes by decree, but the crying necessity of constitutional reforms was postponed. Although Doumergue adopted a policy of direct contact with the people, he did not devalue the franc— which was required to tide over the fiscal crisis.

The most brilliant member of the Doumergue Cabinet was Louis Barthou. Despite his old age, he revivified French policy. He strengthened French security system—reinforcing her eastern alliance and by seeking to negotiate a sort of Eastern Locarno. He visited Warsaw, Prague, Bucharest and Belgrade and spoke in favour of the Russians joining the League of Nations which took place in September 1934. To strengthen French bonds with Yugoslavia, he invited King Alexander to visit France. While welcoming the king at Marseilles in October 1934, he was assassinated and the King fell with him.

The murder at Marseilles was one of the most appalling events of this inter-war period. Doumergue now entrusted the direction of foreign policy to Pierre Laval, a person who had Right-wing sympathies. The days of the Doumergue Cabinet were now numbered—it collapsed on November 7, 1934. A Flandin ministry succeeded, not really very different in membership. The internal condition of the Republic continued to deteriorate. Bitter rivalries, however, kept its enemies divided.

Laval continued Barthou's policy while altering the emphasis. He wanted an understanding with Germany; he cultivated the friendship of Italy; and he wanted to bring Britain into the same alignment. On January 7, 1935, he concluded with Mussolini a series of agreements which settled all the outstanding colonial issues between them, and recognised Italy's pre-eminence in Abyssinia. In April 1935 Laval summoned Britain and Italy to conference at Stresa to counteract Germany's growing strength. The outcome was the Stresa Declaration which committed its signatories to oppose the unilateral repudiation of treaties. On May 2, 1935, Franco-Soviet Pact of Mutual Assistance was signed in Paris. The Pact marked the high-water mark of French Policy against Germany.

In the Abyssinian crisis, when Italy attacked Abyssinia, the League of Nations denounced Italy as an aggressor and invoked economic sanctions against her. But Laval was in favour of compromise with Italy and was the author of Hoare-Laval Plan (December 1935) in which Britain and France envisaged the retention by Italy of most of the areas of Abyssinia. The plan, leaked to the Parisian press, caused such an outburst of indignation both in Britain and France as to lead to its ignominious burial.

The Radicals deserted the Ministry and Laval had to resign on January 22, 1936. The move towards a popular front had begun, and to fight the Election of 1936 the Communists, the Socialists, the Socialists Republican Union and the Radical party united. The aims of the popular front were to cleanse public life, economic reforms and social legislation. The Popular Front won the elections of 1936 and formed a government under the leadership of Leon Blum, a Socialist and one of the most capable republican figures of the period.

Leon Blum described the Popular Front as 'not merely a combination of parties, but a powerful mass movement.' When Blum took office in June 1936, he was overwhelmed by a wave of sitdown strikes by workers who thought that they were masters at last. The state was also threatened by a flight of gold from the country. Blum tried to face the grim economic crisis by reorganising the Bank of France and by negotiating international agreements for monetary co-operation. He tried to combat labour unrest by introducing the forty-hour maximum week and by promising annual holidays with pay. On October 1, 1936, he devalued the French franc. But this was merely a palliative. 'The basic cause of French financial and economic difficulties was the fact that the French national income was not large enough to maintain customary income standars at a time when the rapidly increasing burden of rearmament was superimposed upon a situation already rendered difficult by the attempt to achieve radical social reforms.' In truth, France was overtaken by a deep-seated malaise. Her production was inadequate and her fiscal system vicious. Within little more than a year the Blum Government fell and gave place to a ministry headed by M. Chautemps, a Radical. Once again Government were preoccupied by growing financial difficulties and the deterioration of the international situation. In April 1938 the second Blum Cabinet was replaced by a new Union National Ministry under Daladier. The need of the hour was national unity under a strong leader. 'But now she had no Poincare or Clemenceau, nor even a Doumergue; but only a mediocre Radical named Daladier.'

The successive Governments failed to give France the two things which might have united her; a stable economy and a unifying foreign policy. Each crisis served only to emphasize the division and confusion in the French politics. The outbreak of the Spanish Civil War in July 1936 brought to the fore the clashing interests of French political parties. While the militants and left wing of the popular Front (Front Populaire) were in favour of the Republican Government in Spain, the Right and the Catholics in France were equally in favour of General Franco, the rebel leader. With a divided nation behind him, a lukewarm Britain on his flank, and a hostile Germany and Italy in rear, Blum had to content himself with non-intervention. 'French intervention in the Spanish War,' *La Candide* explained, 'would be the beginning of the European conflagration wanted by Moscow.'

The Daladier Ministry issued a series of decrees which nullified the forty hour a week law; increased direct taxes on low income, and laid higher direct taxes on wine, tobacco, coffee and transportation fares. The General Confederation of Labour, led by Leon Jouhaux, ordered a general strike on November 30, 1938. The strike was a failure because the working class was weakened by feuds between those for and those against the Munich settlement, between Communists and anti-Communists, between pacifists and those in favour of resistance to Fascism. The division between the two major tendencies was too deep to be effaced. From 1935 onwards, both the Left and the Right differed widely in their attitudes towards the international problems. The Left, attached to the idea of the League of Nations, to Collective Security, and concerned with the defence of democracy, rejected pacifism. The Right, though violently anti-German and to the policy of appeasement, turned to pacifism since a war, even a victorious, could be ruinous. The Right attempted to direct Hitler's appetite for *Lebensraum* towards the plains of South-east Europe. The destruction of Czechoslovakia in March 1939 fully revealed the true nature of Hitlerism. National morale in France was debilitated when in August, National Socialist, Deat, refused to go to war over Danzig.

Germany invaded Poland on September 1, 1939 and, on September 3, Britain and France declared war on Germany. But in her peril France failed to produce a leader with sufficient impetus and drive to carry the nation forward in unity. 'The danger which threatened France after the outbreak of war in 1939 was still more terrible than that of August and September 1914. In the face of that earlier peril she had sunk her internal differences and achieved the impressive moral and political unity of *union sacree*; then she had the leadership of a Poincare, a Viviani and a Joffre, and had worked the miracle of the Marne. Now, however, she was still morally and politically divided and had only a Lebrun, a Daladier and a Gamelin, no miracle workers, but men of stature much too small for so great an emergency. The story of 1939-40 was to be different from that of 1914.'[1]

Initially all seemed to go well. The army was mobilised and there was an appearance of political unity. But the Russo-German Pact and the consequent Russian invasion of Eastern Poland on the one hand and the absence of any serious hostilities in the west had a debilitating effect. The Polish debacle was followed by the long winter months of the 'Phoney' war. The Communists continued its propaganda against the Government and insidious attempts were made by the extreme Left to undermine the morale of the troops and the worker. At the same time, there grew up a peace party headed by men of the Right such as Laval who questioned the wisdom of beginning a war in the West.

In March 1940, after having failed to send an expeditionary force to Finland, Daladier resigned and Paul Reynaud succeeded him as Prime Minister. Reynaud, who had condemned the Munich Agreement, and who had persistently demanded more dynamic leadership, seemed to be the man of the hour. He replaced the Commander-in-Chief, General Gamelin, with General Weygand, a close associate of Foch at the end of the First World War, while Marshal Petain, the defender of Verdun, was summoned from his post as Ambassador to Spain to take over the Ministry of Defence. Daladier was moved from the Ministry of Defence to the Foreign Office. A superficial optimism was generated by the assemblage of such traditional names. But the euphoria was soon to disappear.

The German Western offensive was planned with precision and was based upon the dynamic offensive. The French were not inferior in number of soldiers and artillery, their relative weakness was in the air. But the attitude of the French Command was purely defensive; faith in the

1. Bury J. P. T.: *France, 1814-1940*, P. 290.

Maginot Line had become the dogma of the French generals.

On June 5, 1940, the Germans began what was to be called the Battle of France. There was some stubborn French fighting which held up the German infantry, but the German armoured columns rushed on ahead. On the same day, June 5, Reynaud reshuffled his Cabinet again, dropping Daladier and inducting De Gaulle as Under-Secretary of Defence. By June 10, the signs of collapse were evident and Italy declared war on France and Britain. On June 11, the French Government withdrew from Paris to Tours. On the same day Churchill flew to Tours to persuade the French Cabinet to carry on the war from North Africa in collaboration with the British Empire. On June 12, in a dramatic Council of War at Cangey near Tours, Weygand declared that further resistance was impossible. But the majority of the ministers still refused to share his view that France should ask for an armistice. In the next three days, the arguements of Weygand gained ground. A Clemenceau would have replaced the defeatist generals, but Reynaud hesitated to do so.

On June 14, the Germans reached Paris and the Government retreated to Bordeaux. The majority of the members of the French were so convinced of the hopelessness of the situation that they refused to carry on the struggle. The dramatic British offer of a Franco-British union was turned down. Reynaud wanted to save the French fleet from the Germans and to continue the war from North Africa. On June 14, Reynaud sent a desperate appeal to President Roosevelt of America: 'The only chance of saving the French nation, vanguard of democracies, and through her to save England, by whose side France could then remain, with her powerful navy, is to throw into the balance, this very day, the weight of American power.' But at the moment the President could do nothing, except to make plans for continued economic aid.

It was at Bordeaux, on June 14, that the fateful decision of capitulation was taken. Laval, who had been out of office since the fall of his government in January 1936, appeared in Bordeaux and urged in strong terms in favour of surrender. Whereupon Reynaud resigned, and the French President Lebrun replaced him with the 84 year old Marshal Henri Petain, the hero of Verdun. On June 17, Petain asked the Germans for armistice terms. Twentyfour deputies including Mandel and Mendes-France, who refused to concur in, sailed to Casablanca where they were arrested on landing and sent back to Bordeaux.

On June 22, 1940, the Petain Government signed the most humiliating armistice in French history. By the armistice terms the northern half of France as well as the Atlantic Coast, was to be occupied by the Germans. Occupation costs were to be borne by the French. The military clauses included the disbanding of the French army and the demobilisation of the French fleet under German and Italian supervision. One of the most humiliating clauses obliged the French to hand over to the Germans the refugees from Nazi Germany who had fled to France. One million four hundred thousand men were to remain prisoners in German hands. Two days later an armistice followed with Italy. Only a small area of French territory along the Franco-Italian frontier was to be occupied by Italian troops under the armistice terms.

The eclipse of France seemed total. Yet the fact that part of her territory was left independent kindled a hope to the Frenchmen that a regenerated France might still regain a place in a new order in Europe. 'It is in military and internal troubles that other countries found strength to discover themselves and transform,' Petain declared. The feeling that Petain alone could achieve this transformation was widespread.

The fall of France was followed by events of far-reaching importance. It practically ended the Third French Republic for, on July 10, the Senate and Chamber met together at Vichy and granted Petain dictatorial power as 'Chief of the French State'. With Pierre Laval as his principal Lieutenant, Petain established an authoritarian regime. Political parties and trade unions were suppressed and the revolutionary watchwords of 'Liberty, Equality and Fraternity' substituted for 'labour, family, fatherland.'

The Vichy regime was accorded diplomatic recognition by the Western Powers, but it won no affection either abroad or at home. The real

France was represented by General De Gaulle who escaped to England, and, with British backing, formed a 'Free French' provisional government. In response, the Vichy Government condemned De Gaulle for treason and desertion. Thus began a long-drawn struggle between 'Vichy French' and 'Free French' for national predominance, first in the colonies, and, eventually, in the homeland. Thus the Third French Republic had lasted more than three times as long as any other since 1789 and the star of France, although dimmed, was not yet extinguished.

CHAPTER 26

THE GERMAN EMPIRE (1871-1914)

The imperial constitution, promulgated in April 1871, was a hotch-potch, hastily put together by Bismarck to serve his own ends. It possessed all trappings of constitutional government—the King-Emperor and his Chancellor, a federal state without being truly federal, and a parliamentary system based on universal suffrage which was rendered ineffective by limitation imposed on its responsibility.

The Empire was a union of eighteen German states of various sizes and one administrative territory, the so-called Reichsland. The federal government consisted of an executive, in the persons of the Emperor and his Chancellor, a Federal Council (*Bundesrat*) composed of delegations from the separate states, and a National Parliament (*Reichstag*), which was elected by universal manhood suffrage. The Federal executive was vested in the Prussian King with the title German Emperor. He directed Germany's foreign affairs, with the right to make treaties, as well as to declare war and conclude peace. He was empowered to appoint and dismiss the Chancellor and other officials of the Federal Government, to summon, prorogue, and close the two legislative bodies. Finally, he possessed the right to interpret the consitution. The fate of Germany was thus determined by the Emperor's absolute will.

The Federal Concil or *Bundesrat* composed of representatives of the states acted as the upper house of the legislature. The *Bundesrat* represented the states as separate units, not, however, as in the United States of America, on a basis of equality, but according to a quota agreed upon between the governments. Thus Prussia sent 17 members, Bavaria six, Saxony and Wurtemberg four each, and the other states even fewer. In the *Bundesrat,* Prussian influence was paramount as all legislation affecting the Reich was not legal until its affirmative vote had been secured. Prussian assent was necessary to make any change in military matters or customs and excise duties. And no amendment to the consitution could be accepted if fourteen votes were cast against it in the *Bundesrat*. Thus Prussia alone could block constitutional amendments that were not to its own interest.

The *Reichstag*, the lower house of the imperial parliament, represented the whole empire according to the respective population of each principality. It was elected by universal manhood suffrage, the legal voting age being twentyfive years. The *Reichstag* was demonstrably weak. It could hold debates and could pass laws: its consent was necessary to the expenditure of money. But it possessed little power. The *Reichstag* could indeed reject a proposal presented to it by the *Bundesrat* and could refuse to give its assent to a new appropriation, but its power was simply restrictive and, if recalcitrant, could be dissolved by the Emperor. It had little control over the Chancellor and his Secretaries of State, for the Chancellor was responsible only to the Emperor and the subordinate ministers responsible only to the Chancellor. Even its financial control was illusory. The revenue of the Reich was entirely derived from customs and excise dues, permanently fixed.

Despite the limitations the *Reichstag* occupied an important part in the constitutional system. It was a national political body, a living symbol of the nation's unity. In the management of Germany's foreign relations, it was a convenient and effective sounding board. Bismarck valued its cooperation to secure its backing for government policy as well as to demonstrate to the Emperor his own indispensability. The rights of debate and assent were not negligible powers, and the existence of the *Reichstag* was further strengthened by the stipulation that it could not be prorogued indefinitely and that new elections must follow upon dissolution. But the fact remains that members of the *Reichstag* were not like the members of Parliament in England or Congressmen in the United States. Because of this the *Reichstag* remained a body that reacted more than it acted.

Though sovereignty was vested in the Reich, considerable powers were left to the individual states. Thus education, health services, police, fiscal affairs, civil liberties were managed by the separate states rather than the federal government which controlled foreign affairs, posts and telegraphs, customs, and the colonies. But in the rights they enjoyed, the member states were not equal.

The Constitution of 1871 'was supposed to be federal, but its federalism was fraudulent, window dressing to make the dictatorship of Prussia more respectable.'[1] Prussia held 235 seats in the *Reichstag* and commanded twenty votes in the *Bundesrat* which gave her an absolute veto on all amendments to the constitution. Her King was hereditary Emperor. The German Empire was, in short, a Prussian hegemony. Thus the constitution of Germany, in the words of Theodore Mommsen, the great historian of Rome, was 'a pseudo-constitutional absolutism under which we live and which our spineless people has inwardly accepted.' 'The legislative system of Germany was outwardly democratic, the government of Germany was as autocratic as the government of Tsarist Russia.'

The Political Parties

From 1871 till the outbreak of the First World War (1914), the political activity of Germany centred in six main political parties, plus a number of splinter groups. On the extreme right was the German conservative party, the party of Prussianism, aristocracy and landed property. Opposed to liberalism and democratic reform, it had little understanding of industry. Originally a believer in free trade, it turned to become protectionist, taking its economic ideas from the Association of Landlords. It was a Protestant party which believed in maintaining the Christian foundations of the state. This led the party to take a genuine interest in social reform.

An offshoot of the Conservatives was the so-called *Reichspartei* or the Free Conservatives. Combining both landlords and industrialists in its membership, the Free Conservatives gave unflinching support to Bismarck's national policies and provided many officials for his ministries. The party never attained a mass following and eventually merged with the Conservatives.

Larger than either of these was the Catholic Centre Party that had been founded in 1870 to protect the rights of Roman Catholics. Embracing individuals and groups of varied political and social views, it showed a greater freedom of action than other parties. About 25 per cent of the German *Reichstag* members belonged to the Catholic party. Though conservative in defence of tradition, of the prerogatives of the Crown, it tended to be progressive in matters of social reform. It preached the necessity of combating the evils of capitalism by establishing workers' cooperatives, organising Christian trade unions, and otherwise helping the poor to raise their standard of living.

There were two liberal parties. The National Liberals, which had been the leading national party in Germany since 1867, represented the wealthy and educated middle class and the upper bureaucrats. They shared many of the characteristics of Liberals in other lands, being supporters of centralization, *laissez-faire* economics, constitutional government and material progress. The left liberals which formed the bulk of the Progressive Party, shared most of the economic views of the National Liberals, but was more vocal in demanding parliamentary rights, more critical of Government policy especially its military policy. Exhausted in mostly negative opposition the party never did anything positive to further the political aim of a monarchy under the control of parliament. In the first *Reichstag* of 1871, the National Liberals controlled less than

1. Taylor, A. J. P.: *The Course of German History,* P. 130.

half of the seats (168 out of 382). Even this majority was lost as early as 1874. Towards the end of 1870s Bismarck dissolved his alliance with the discredited National Liberal party and turned instead to the conservatives and those National Liberals who had seceded from their left wing. With these he achieved an absolute government majority at the *Reichstag* election of 1887.

Further, there was the Social Democratic Party which became unified after the Gotha Congress of 1875. Though declared 'enemies of the empire' by Bismarck on account of their revolutionary programme, the number of Social Democrats increased from election to election. In 1871 they amounted to only 2 per cent of the electorate, but in 1912 they had increased to 29 per cent of all electors. This rapid increase was due to the fact that the party drew its strength largely from the lower stratum of society. Despite its belief in the Marxist ideology, the Social Democratic Party was 'a revolutionary party, but not a party that makes revolution.'

The splinter groups—mostly comprising regional party groups—amounted to about 5 per cent of all electors and formed 5 to 10 per cent of the seats in the *Reichstag*. Guelf party from the former Kingdom of Hanover raised its voice of protests at Prussia's annexation of the Kingdom. The deputies from Alsace and Lorraine made solemn protest against the incorporation of their territory with the German Empire. A Dane or two from Northern Schleswig demanded the restoration of this province to Denmark. The Polish faction was of great importance accounting for fifteen to twenty members.

The National Liberal Period

In the *Reichstag* of 1871 the National Liberal Party was the largest majority party, with 155 seats out of a total of 399. With the support of the Progressives and the Free Conservatives, the National Liberal tried to strengthen the federal government against the divisive forces in the country as well by building a kind of economic infrastructure that would enable Germany to compete in the markets of the world. Germany was fortunate in securing the services of the Rudolf von Delbruck, the head of the Chancellor's office, who had done more to advance the unification of Germany than a dozen generals and diplomats. Among his numerous legislative achievements may be mentioned the standardisation of weights and measures, the establishment of a superior commercial court in Leipzig, new labour law that gave workers freedom of organisation and bargaining, and a law giving joint stock companies freedom to extend their operations. His economic legislation included a uniform coinage for the Empire, a new commercial code for trade and industry and an Imperial Bank (1875). In his desire to promote centralised government at the expense of the prerogatives of the separate states, the National Liberal Deputy Eduard Lasker, introduced a national civil and criminal procedure, established a supreme court of appeal at Leipzig and began a codification of the civil law. Though the Liberal pressure was successful in some broadening of the functions of provincial government, it could do nothing to make the provincial councils truly representative bodies with advisory functions. The press was also muzzled by the Press Law of 1874. 'If measured in terms of legislative success, therefore, the liberal record in the Empire's first years was a mixed one, most impressive in the economic and purely administrative spheres, much less so in matters that touched upon government prerogatives, the powers of the Crown, or even long-established social privilege. In one additional field, that of religion, the liberals' influence upon government policy was impressive but unfortunate in its results.'[2]

The Kulturkampf

Germany had, since the time of Luther, been divided among the Catholics and the Protestants, the latter predominating. The victories of Prussia over Austria and France were victories by a Protestant state over two strongly Catholic powers. The Roman Catholic Church was fundamentally hostile to the new German Empire as the Popes of history had been to the old German Emperors. It wielded considerable influence in the political life by creating a political organisation devoted to the Church, known as the Centre.

2. Craig Gordon A.: *Germany, 1866-1945*, P. 69.

The liberals saw Rome as a natural enemy which had declared its hostility to all forms of progress in Pius IX's *Syllabus of Errors* in 1864. German liberals had been particularly incensed by the doctrine of papal infallibility proclaimed in July 1870 during the war against France. Many Catholic professors and teachers protested against the doctrine and refused to teach it in the universities and schools. Trietschke saw the Church of Rome as a vampire.

Bismarck entertained deep antipathy against the existence of a confessional party (Centre) which owed allegiance to Rome. As Bismarck said: 'it is not a matter of struggle between faith and unbelief. What we have here is the age-old struggle for power, as old as the human race itself, betwen Kingship and the priestly class'. The conflict also fitted in with Bismarck's foreign policy. He believed that the foreign enemies of the Reich were Catholic France and Austria. Several groups within the Reich were also Catholic, the Poles and the Alsatians. Bismarck's aim was to obviate the danger of an alliance of all Catholic powers, both within and without, against his empire. Moreover by its adoption of a planned social policy, the Centre Party challenged the Liberalism of Bismarck's domestic policy. To Bismarck, the existence of a confessional party was likely to stimulate the appearance of an opposing Protestant party. Bismarck foresaw the establishment of a Catholic state within a state had a Protestant bias.

In his fight against the Catholic Church, Bismarck chose Adalbert Falk—he was appointed as Minister of Culture in Prussia in January 1871. It was Falk who drafted the new law on supervision of schools in February which abolished all Church supervision of schools. During the summer of 1872, a law was passed which dissolved the Jesuit establishments of any kind in Germany and expelled the Jesuits from the country. It was in the wake of this legislation the famous left wing liberal deputy Rudolf Virchow coined the term *Kulturkampf* in which he said that the struggle against the Roman Church was 'a great struggle for civilization in the interest of humanity'. In May 1873, the Prussian legislature enacted laws which limited the Catholic Church's control over the appointment of its clergy, the education of children and the training of priests, and empowered the state agencies disciplinary authority over the Church. A law of May 1874 gave the Prussian Government the power to expel all clerics who failed to satisfy state requirements and authorised the state to fill up sees and churches left vacant.

There was now open war between the Government and the Catholic Church. In 1875, Pope Pius IX condemned the May Laws root and branch and declared them null and void. The government responded by cutting off financial support, by banning all monastic orders, and imprisoning and expelling bishops and priests. By 1876 almost a third of parishes in Prussia were without incumbents. The severity of the Falk Laws was felt by many non-Catholics. A Protestant theologian, Christian Ernst Luthardt described the effects of the Kulturkampf:

> It is a bad thing when the state punishes actions that are considered as purely religious ones and as matters of conscience... In short, the state cannot conduct a war against a large part of its own population without causing, on all sides, profound injury to the moral consciousness.

An attempt on his life in July 1884 by a young and unbalanced Catholic and the dissatisfaction which continued to spread among all, made Bismarck uneasy. He also felt the futility of his campaign against the Centre when in the *Reichstag* elections of 1874 the party doubled its popular vote. In the elections of 1877 the Centre succeeded in returning 92 members and was the largest party in the *Reichstag*. This was sufficient in itself to convince Bismarck that the anti-Catholic crusade was a mistake. Moreover, he wanted to put an end to his long association with National Liberal Party which had grown overweening in its demands for a greater share in political power.

The death of Pope Pius IX in 1878, who was considered stubborn in his attitude and the succession of Leo XIII, a more conciliatory Pope, facilitated a change of policy. Bismarck began the process of repairing the damaged diplomatic relations with the Papacy, of revoking the May Laws and dismissing their author, Adalbert Falk. The last of the laws bringing religious peace to Prussia was passed in 1883 and the conflict was-over by 1887. Civil marriage and state inspection of schools were only retained.

The damage wrought by the Kulturkampf was great. Bismarck's religious policy may be compared with 'that of Earl of Cardigan who led the Light Brigade into the Russian guns at Balaclava and then retired in good order himself, leaving ruin and destruction behind him.' The cause of national unity that had been won during the Franco-Prussian war suffered when Germans had deliberately been set against Germans on confessional grounds. Apart from the distrust which the Roman Catholic entertained for the government, the latter was represented an instrument of the authoritarian state.

Fiscal Policy

The conversion of Germany form Free Trade to Protection was an event of great significance. The Free Trade movement, victorious in England, had rapidly gained adherents in continental states, and in the early seventies Germany became virtually a non-protectionist country. The cession of Alsace and Lorraine, the speedy payment of a huge indemnity by France and the currency reform of 1871 generated much heat in German economy. The speculative boom that followed was probably inevitable. Between 1871 and 1873, 726 new companies were founded, compared with only 276 in the period 1790 to 1870. Banks proliferated to an astonishing extent and played a major role in the stock market and the securities exchange. '...National prosperity rose to apparently unimagined heights. A shower of gold rained down on the drunken city.'

In 1873, the economic crisis or the crash occurred. The depression began with the collapse of the Vienna stock market in May 1873 and extended to Berlin stock exchange, to German industry, railways and mining. In Germany, iron industry was the worst hit. By 1878, cotton manufacturers complained of falling prices. By 1876 agriculture had entered upon a period of depression. Grain imports increased, grain prices fell and the income of farmers and landowners dropped. Heinrich von Trietschke criticised the policy of free trade. Eduard Lasker, one of the leaders of National Liberal Party, spoke against the Government's economic policy. Meanwhile a school of economists, led by Gustav Schmoller, Adolf Wagner, Lugo Brentano and E. Nasse, began a revolt in the Universities against *laissez-faire* and free trade.

It was the agricultural and industrial interests themselves that demanded protection. The farmers and landowners agitation for protection found expression through the *Association of Tax and Economic Reformers* (1876). The *Union of German Iron Foundries* demanded the retention of the duties on imported iron goods. The *Union of German Iron and Steel Manufacturers* (1873), opened a campaign for the same purpose in 1875. The manufacturers of cotton, linen, wool, paper, leather and soda also demanded increased protection. The iron manufacturers drew them into their own agitation through the *Central Association of German Industrialists,* founded in January 1876. Its first Secretary was Wilhelm Von Kardoff who in his book *Against the Current* demanded protection. Along with him Friedrich Stopel in his *Commercial Crisis in Germany* voiced the same demand. They argued that tariff protection was an element of national security, since without it a nation became dependent upon others. 'Let us.' Stopel wrote, 'show that Germany is no longer the step-child of foreign interests and that she can stand economically on her own feet, just as she has become independent in political matters.'

Bismarck's interest in financial reform was not new. In 1875 he had said: 'To give the German Empire a solid unshakeable financial basis which will give it a dominant position and yet bring it into an organic relationship with all public interests in state, province, country, and community that would be a great and worthy task, which could stimulate me to devote the last breath of my failing strength to it.' Bismarck's objective was to free the federal government from its financial dependence on the states as the German Empire had no separate finances.

Bismarck made long term preparations for his financial reforms. He first made sure of his finance minister, then of the Federal Council and finally of the *Reichstag*. The Centre was won over. While the National Liberals split over this question, the majority of them sided with Bismarck. This gave him an assured majority on the tariff question in the summer of 1879. In

December 1879, Bismarck announced moderate tariffs on iron and iron goods and grain and increases in the indirect taxes on tobacco, salt, coffee and other luxury items. Bismarck accepted the proposal of the Centre Party that only a portion of new tax yield and income from duties should go to the federal government and that the rest be distributed among the states.

The immediate effects of a shift to Protectionism were profound. There was an immediate drop in the value of imports and the gains made by German industrialists, particularly in the heavy industries, were important. The grain producers, particularly those east of the Elbe, profited. Their private gains, however, were made at the cost of technical progress. There emerged the great landowners—a group of about 25,000 men and their dependants—who occupied dominant position in the Reich after 1879. Henceforth the opinions of these landed proprietors of the *Junker* class determined the social and political attitudes of the higher bureaucracy. The result was a demoralization of German liberalism which prevented an effective consolidation of the forces for progress in Germany.

Bismarck and Socialism

In 1878, Bismarck turned his attention to the Social Democratic Party. As its aims were revolutionary and destructive of the existing order, it was a more serious enemy than the Centre. The German Social Democratic Party had its origin in the activities of Ferdinand Lassalle (1825-64). He argued that economic pressure and trade union activity alone were pointless. Only organised mass political action aimed at the conquest of state power would save the working class from capitalistic exploitation. Lassalle's contribution to German socialism was his emphasis on political action. His spirited activities in the last year of his life succeeded in founding the German Workingmen's Association. Its progress was impeded by the opposition of a new Social Democratic Labour Party founded by two followers of Marx—August Bebel (1840-1913) and Wilhelm Leibknecht (1826-1900). It was only after the two parties came together in 1875 at Gotha that the growth of German socialism became impressive. The Socialists adopted a programme of action that combined two strains of influence, being Marxist in its criticism of capitalist society, but Lassalean in its emphasis upon political action to secure practical objectives like universal manhood suffrage, abolition of inequalities of class and property, separation of church and state and free compulsory education.

In 1877 the Social Democratic Party counted nearly half a million adherents and sent twelve deputies into the Reichstag. This was a matter of concern to Bismarck who began to seek means of taking legal action against them. After two attempts on the life of the Emperor William I, Bismarck introduced a bill against the Social Democrats in 1879. This measure led to grave dissension among the National Liberals who had doubts about the efficacy of any Exceptional Law. It was not until after a dissolution and their electoral defeat that in the new Reichstag of 1878 they gave their support.

The Anti-Socialist Law of October 1878 forbade all associations and publications that supported socialist tendencies. Of the 47 leading party newspapers, 45 were suppressed immediately. All unions that had any association with Social Democracy in the past were crushed, many of the Party's leaders were forced to leave the country, and others were arrested. The Anti-Socialist Law proved to be an egregious failure. Socialist discontent was merely driven underground. Secret societies sprang up and meetings which could not be held in Germany were held outside in Switzerland. Bismarck was defeated by the Socialists as he had been by the Catholics. In 1890 the Exceptional Laws were not renewed. In 1890 the party polled a million and a half votes; while on the eve of the First World War the Socialists embraced one-third of the electorate.

Bismarck had a more positive method of combating socialism. As early as 1872 certain German economists known as 'Socialists of the professional chair' which included in their ranks the distinguished economic historian, Schmoller, had founded a 'Union for Social Politics'. They began to talk of State intervention in economic matters. In November 1881 Bismarck asserted the obligation of the State to improve the condition of the labouring classes and its moral duty to remove social evils. It was slowly that he carried them through, the Social Insurance Law in 1883, the Accident Insurance Laws in 1884 and the Old Age Insurance Law in 1889. In the case of accident insurance, the employers were to bear the burden alone. In the case of sickness insurance, as a rule, the employer must pay one-third and the employee two-thirds of the premium, and in the case of the old age and incapacity insurance, the premiums were to be paid by the employers, the employees, and by the state.

This system of social insurance was satisfactory as far as it went and was later improved in many respects. Britain followed the German example some twenty years later; France and the United States not until the nineteen thirties. No wonder, Bismarck has been called 'the first social reformer of the century'. But in other social welfare spheres Bismarck was not prepared to give one inch. Nothing was done for the health of workers, nothing to limit the hours of work, to determine minimum wages or to enforce the factory inspection which had long existed on paper. The workers took what the state offered and refused to be satisfied.

Foreign Policy, 1871-90

Bismarck was well aware of the fact that Germany's victory over France had been so shattering that it left all of its neighbours apprehensive. Even in England's Conservative Party there were doubts about Germany's intentions. The influential circles in Vienna still wanted revenge for Sadowa and the emerging Pan-Slav Party in Russia opposed the pro-German policy of the Tsar. Thus the outlook was hardly encouraging and called for circumspection.

In counteracting this trend, Bismarck invoked ideological affinity that had been markedly absent from his policy before 1870. It was an easy task for Bismarck to persuade Austria and Russia that the revolutionary unrest manifested in the Paris Commune, German Social Democracy and Russian Nihilism threatened the structure of autocracy in all monarchical countries alike. Hence as early as September 1870 Bismarck spoke of the desirability of a 'firm closing of the ranks of the monarchical conservative elements of Europe.'

Bismarck's policy was to manipulate the relations of nations to the advantage of German ascendancy. He, therefore, wanted to establish European relationships on the conflicting pulls of established interests. Hence an uneasy balance of power must have to be maintained between Britain and Russia, Austria and Russia, Austria and Italy or France and Italy. 'The initial principle of Bismarck's policy was simplicity itself; each great power must need Germany more than it needed any other. His object, therefore, was to keep quarrels open or, rather always just short of settlement.'[3]

In September 1872, Bismarck laid the basis of a long Three Emperors' League *(Dreikaiserbund)* consisting of Germany, Austria-Hungary and Russia. On October 22, 1873 an agreement was signed by which the Three Emperors agreed to cooperate in the preservation of peace and if necessary to protect each other in the event of a threat to peace. To Bismarck the Three Emperors' League had the advantage of protecting Germany against political isolation at little cost. Bismarck was not vainglorious when he observed: 'I have thrown a bridge across to Vienna, without breaking down the older one to Russia'. But the Three Emperors' League contained within it seeds of discord as the views of Austria-Hungary and Russia with regard to Balkan question and Near East differed essentially. Austria-Hungary wished to absorb Serbia, but to preserve the Turkish Empire if she could. Russia wished to dominate Bulgaria, to annex Constantinople, and to break up the Turkish Empire if she could.

The Triple Entente did not endure long. The emergence of a strong government in France bent upon military recovery, was not liked by Bismarck. Moreover, the Franco-German relations became embitterred by anti-church legislation in Germany. The French bishops attacked Bismarck's religious policy and offered prayers for the restoration of Lorraine to France. The increase of a number of battalions in the French infantry regiment from three to four in March 1873 was viewed with apprehension by Moltke who began immediately to think in terms of a preventive war. Bismarck launched a vigorous press campaign against

3. Ramm, Agatha; *Germany, 1789-1919: A Political History,* P. 327.

France in 1875. The French tried to take advantage of Bismarck's jingoism by publishing in the press of Radowitz's emissary to St. Petersburg to find out 'the attitude which Russia would take in the event of a new war between Germany and France'. The reaction, in all capitals, was one of shock, and in two of them, London and St. Petersburg, of resistance. With the personal encouragement of Queen Victoria, Tsar Alexander, accompanied by Gorchakov, paid a visit to Berlin. He had private talks with the German Emperor, authorising Gorchakov to inform the Press that he was 'leaving Berlin completely convinced of the conciliatory disposition that reigns there and that assures the maintenance of peace'. This effectively ended the war scare of 1875. For France the affair of 1875 was a minor triumph, proving that she could under certain circumstances, count upon the sympathy of other powers. For Bismarck it was a decided setback as his friends had decided not to support him over this issue. Thus, the so-called Three Emperors' League had now proved to be without real meaning.

Balkan Troubles, 1875-77

In the course of the next three years, the Three Emperors' League foundered on the conflicting ambitions of the Great Powers in the Eastern crisis of 1875-78. In August 1875, Bosnia and Herzegovina revolted against Turkey. The national consciousness of the two provinces had been encouraged by Serbian propaganda. The trouble spread rapidly to other Turkish part of the Balkans especially in Bulgaria. Both Austria-Hungary and Russia sought to avert the crisis by a programme of Balkan reforms. Andrassy, the Austro-Hungarian Foreign Minister, devised a note on December 30, 1875, containing reforms which the powers should recommend to Turkey. Next, at a meeting with Bismarck and Gorchakov, Andrassy produced the Berlin Memorandum of May 13, 1876, which contained not only reforms but a subtle hint of 'sanctions' to enforce them. All these schemes had no effect in moderating the Turkish government.

Though isolation had been the keystone of British policy, Britain was concerned to keep Russia away from dominating Constantinople or the Straits. Britain rejected the Berlin Memorandum and sent the fleet to Besika Bay to bolster up the Turks to defy the powers. In July 1876 the Austrians and Russians were able to sink their mutual suspicions in a plan for partitioning Turkey's European possessions in the event of her collapse. But the Turks did not collapse and in defence of the Serbs and Bulgarians the Russian Government opened hostilities in April, 1877.

Throughout 1875 and 1876 Bismarck played a negative role in Balkan affairs. He defined his policy in his famous statement: 'The whole of the Balkans is not worth the healthy bones of a single Pomeranian musketeer.' But Bismarck was aware that once Russia had intervened in the war, it would be difficult to remain neutral. Both Vienna and St. Petersburg would expect German support and neither would forgive either a neutral stance or assistance to its adversary. Gorchakov requested Bismarck to repay the supposed Russian service in 1870 by holding Austria-Hungary neutral. Apart from this, any major war would have widespread repercussion in the present state of Europe.

Bismarck was forced, therefore, to intervene and offered to act as a mediator by calling an international congress at Berlin. After initial hesitation on the part of Britain and Russia, the Great Powers met at Berlin on June 13, 1878. The Congress of Berlin was the distinguished diplomatic gathering between the Vienna Congress of 1814-15 and the Paris Peace Conference of 1919. Bismarck was in command of the Congress by his control of the direction and the pace of the negotiations. He knew the perils that lurked just below the surface of the Congress and warned the representatives of the Great Powers that their principal business was to reach a settlement among themselves.

The Treaty of Berlin produced a settlement of the Balkan troubles, at least for the time being. Russia was probably the most aggrieved member of the Congress except Turkey which lost half of its European territory. Though the Russian acquisiton of Bessarabia, Kars and Batum in Asiatic Turkey were more or less impressive, but her chagrin was increased by the fact that, without the loss of a man, Britain acquired Cyprus, Austria-Hungary gained Bosnia, and the French were encouraged to move into Tunis. No wonder the Tsar remarked that the Congress had been a 'European coalition against Russia under the leadership of Prince Bismarck'. The Russian chancellor Gorchakov pronounced the Congress of Berlin 'the darkest episode in his career'.

Bismarck's Alliance System

Russian resentment against Germany was the immediate problem that confronted Bismarck. Bismarck was convinced that relations might rapidly get worse and he was particularly unhappy about Russian troop movements in the spring of 1879. The exposed position of Germany in Central Europe forced Bismarck to adopt an insurance policy. He turned to Austria-Hungary and Andrassy, her able Foreign Minister, 'played the gigantic fish with a masterhand'. Andrassy knew that Bismarck feared a Franco-Russian combination; but in view of his good relations with Paris, he insisted that the new treaty mention Russia explicitly. Bismarck had to capitulate and it was only the threat of resignation by which Bismarck persuaded his sovereign, who had strong predilection for Russia, to accept the treaty.

The Austro-German Alliance, signed in Vienna on October 7, 1879, was directed against Russia and provided for mutual aid in the event of a Russian attack upon either signatory. In the event of an attack by any other Power, the allied country would remain neutral unless the attacking power received Russian support. It was the first of the secret treaties, whose terms were not known till 1888 and which encouraged other Powers to negotiate similar treaties in self-defence. Moreover, this alliance turned out to be a permanent one, lapsing only when both the powers bound by it collapsed in 1918.

Thus, secure in a firm alliance with Austria-Hungary, Bismarck made overture to Britain and actually suggested an alliance between Germany, Austria and Britain. Beaconsfield declined the overture. Now Bismarck's diplomacy was directed to stave off the inevitable consequence of the Austro-German alliance. The simplest way to achieve this was to reconcile Austria-Hungary and Russia. His unrivalled skill enabled him to perform these conjuring tricks with success. Bismarck's attempt was crowned with success when Saburov, the Russian ambassador in Berlin, advocated a defensive policy based on alliance with Germany. Austria resisted; her policy was the 'permanent blocking of Russia' with British assistance. But Anglo-Austrian relations steadily worsened after the advent of Gladstone and Granville. Hence, Bismarck found no difficulty in reviving the League, of the Three Emperors in June 1881. It pledged the three partners—Germany, Austria-Hungary and Russia—to neutrality in the event of a war between one of their members and a fourth European power and provided for mutual consultation in Balkan affairs.

The renewal of the Three Emperors' League gratified Bismarck because it gave him a measure of control over all European politics. 'Bismarck's grouping of three... appeared to isolate the forces of subversion in international affairs, Russian Pan-Slavism on the one hand and French *revanchisme* on the other.'[4]

The Alliance of 1881 effectively isolated France. The possibility of France seeking alliance with Great Britain and Italy was rendered nugatory by developments outside of Europe. The French seizure of Tunis in 1881 aroused indignation in Italy which had North African ambitions of its own. The Italian Government consulted Bismarck about the possibility of an alliance and were told by him that they must first reach an accommodation with Austria. The Italians felt that they must have to abandon the hope of winning the Trentino or Trieste, but the French danger obsessed them so much that they had no choice. In May 1882 they joined with Germany and Austria in the so-called Triple Alliance. The treaty may be described as one of neutrality and guarantee. Italy was assured of aid in the event of a French attack but obliged her to go to war if Germany were attacked by France or if either Germany or Austria were attacked by two more powers.

The Italian gains were illusory. France annoyed with this agreement, imposed tarrif on Italian goods which had ruinous effects upon the Italian economy. For Bismarck, on the other hand, the Triple Alliance provided insurance

4. Craig Cordon A: *Germany, 1866-1945,* P. 115.

against an Italian attack on Austria's southern border, while at the same time depriving France of an potential ally. Bismarck need not have to worry about Anglo-French combination as Britain's Egyptian venture kept the two nations apart until the beginning of the new century. Throughout all these diplomatic manoeuvres, Bismarck had shown his superiority by seizing the most of unforeseen opportunities always retaining the initiative. By 1882 he had established Germany's primacy in such a way that Berlin came to be regarded as the diplomatic capital of Europe. But even by that date the system by its inherent complications sowed the germs of future trouble.

In the mid-1880s Bismarck's security system was strained to the utmost by Balkan complications. A new national sentiment surged in Bulgaria which owed her independence not a little to Russia. Russian resentment was directed against Prince Alexander of Battenberg, the Bulgarian monarch and a nephew of the Tsar who showed his preference to Austrians to complete the projected Orient Railways, designed to run from Austria across Serbia and Bulgaria to Adrianople and Constantinople. The Russians, already alarmed by Austrian political and commercial treaties with Serbia (1881) and Rumania (1883), wanted to use force to thwart the projected rail link. The crisis became acute in early 1886 when the Austrians were making preparations to counter Russian moves. The thought of an Austro-Russian war filled the Chancellor with foreboding though he knew that, in that event, Germany would have to support Austria. As he observed in October 1886:

> We could certainly tolerate Austria's losing a battle but not that it should be destroyed or fatally wounded or made a dependency of Russia. The Russians do not possess the kind of self-restraint that would make it possible for us to live alone with them and France on the continent. If they had eliminated Austria or brought it to their heels, we know from experience that they would become so domineering towards us that peace with them would be untenable.

Meanwhile, Bismarck had to take into account the possibility of a Franco-Russian alliance. In 1886 there was a sharp increase in anti-German sentiment in France, bolstered up by her disappointments in the colonial field and the jingoism of war minister General Boulanger, who made menacing speeches for the liberation of the lost provinces of Alsace and Lorraine. On the other hand, Bismarck did not overlook the possibility of Franco-Russian alliance. Bismarck met the challenge by assuring the Russian Government of his sympathetic understanding of their Balkan interests. At the same time he discouraged French adventurism by increasing the armed strength from 427,000 to 468,000 men. He also declared that he would not attack France on the theory of 'preventive war', *i.e.,* because war was inevitable; but that if war did occur, the war of 1870 would be eclipsed by the war that would follow. This had a sobering effect in Paris. In February 1887 Bismarck renewed the Triple Alliance with Austria and Italy and the prospect of war with France disappeared.

Bismarck had a difficult task in alleviating tension in Eastern Europe. He had good reason to fear a Russian push that would invite Austrian retaliation. He also wanted that Britain should take interest in containing Russian design in Eastern Europe. It was also felt that there would be general deterioration of the situation in the Near East unless Britain reestablished its influence in Turkey. This move was expected to be supported by Austria and Italy and would succeed in bringing the Russians to reason. The British Premier Salisbury carried through a rapprochement with Austria-Hungary and Italy which ended in the First Mediterranean Agreement of February and March 1887. The Agreement was aimed at the preservation of the *status quo* in both the eastern and western Mediterranean and by implication, in the Balkans as well. 'By making England an associate of the Triple Alliance, it promised to be a deterrent to both French and Russian adventurism.'

In the complicated diplomatic manoeuvre, Bismarck had to forestall the Russians from concluding an alliance with France. The *Dreikaiserbund* of 1881 expired in 1887 and this provided Bismarck with an opportunity. On June 18, 1887, after two months of negotiation, Bismarck concluded with the Russians a new agreement—the Reinsurance Treaty. They agreed to maintain benevolent neutrality in the event that the other was at war, unless the conflict were caused by a Russian attack upon Austria or a German attack upon France. By its secret clauses, Germany promised to support Russian interest in Bulgaria and at the Straits.

In the summer and autumn of 1887 Austria-Hungary and Russia were on the brink of war on the issue of Bulgaria. Bismarck answered this threat by bringing about the second Mediterranean Agreement on December 12, 1887. Britain, Austria-Hungary and Italy agreed to maintain the *status quo* in the Near East, and more particularly in Bulgaria, Asia Minor, and the Straits. But the tension between Austria-Hungary and Russia over Bulgaria became so great in early 1888 that compelled Bismarck to intervene. In February 1888, he announced that the Austro-German Treaty of 1879 imposed on Germany an obligation to protect Austria, if attacked by Russia. 'Bulgaria is not an object of sufficient magnitude to set Europe aflame in a war whose issue none can foretell. I do not expect an early breach of the peace. But advise other countries to discontinue their menaces.'

The troublesome Bulgarian crisis had finally been liquidated by the beginning of 1888 when Russia accepted the inevitable. Bulgaria remained independent both of Russia and Turkey. Bismarck now had the satisfaction that his network of alliance was still in good repair. Germany still occupied the centre of the stage and there was no immediate prospect of new troubles in Europe.

Colonial Policy

In the initial stage, Bismarck was not much interested in overseas activity. He regarded colonialism as an activity for other nations. But by the beginning of the 1880s Bismarck came round to the view that the acquisition of colonies was an economic necessity for Germany. Moreover, his main motive was the desire to use colonial acquisition to solve the internal stresses within the Reich. In addition, Bismarck felt that a colonial policy, if properly directed, might serve to strengthen the system of elaborate alliances that he had built up since 1879.

By the beginning of the 1880s the spectacle of the French and the Italians and the British participating in the scramble for Africa and islands in the Pacific aroused fear lest Germany be excluded from the new markets. Writers like Ernst Von Weber and Friedrich Fabri propagated the view that colonies were not only an economic necessity but a form of insurance against a loss of standing among the nations of the world. In 1882 Kolonialverein (Colonial Union) was founded which had 9,000 members in 1884. Leading members of the academic community like Wagner, Schmoller, Sybel and Trietschke had concluded by 1884 that 'colonization was a matter of life and death'. Impressed by the popular enthusiasm for colonialism, Bismarck decided that Germany's debut as a colonial Power should be dramatic and, in the main, anti-English. From a political point of view, Bismarck's purpose was to defeat the Left Liberals associated with the Crown Prince and with the opposition to himself. With the election of 1884 in view, he strengthened his appeal to the Right in order to defeat the Left. The definitive proclamation of the German Protectorate in Africa came a fortnight before Germany went to the polls (October 28, 1884). In addition, the expansion of the German economy demanded new outlets.

By 1884 German missionary societies had hundreds of stations on the West African Coast. German trading stations in west, south-west and east Africa had begun to appear. In 1883, the Bremen merchant Luderitz had built up a factory on the west coast of south-west Africa at Angra Pequena. As the British had legal claims along the coast of South-West Africa, Bismarck tried to secure her recognition of German rights at Angra Pequena. Despite Britain's protest Bismarck succeeded in winning her recognition of the German protectorate over Angra Pequena and also of certain German claims in the Fiji islands. The British concession was due to her increasing interest in Egypt where they needed all the diplomatic support they could find.

Despite the British concession Anglo-German relations continued to deteriorate. In May 1884 the German explorer, Gustav Nachtigal, raised the flag over Togo and Cameroons, which threatened British interests in the Niger Delta. In East Africa, Carl Peters, inspired by his visit to

England to make his own country a world power—negotiated treaties with native chiefs which brought the protection of his Society for German Colonization enormous tract of territory. On the other side of the world, German protectorate in December 1884 over New Britain and the north-eastern part of New Guinea startled the British Government. Britain grudgingly welcomed Germany as a colonial power owing to her growing difficulties in Egypt and the Sudan. 'But the competition was a little too obvious to be comfortable.'

When France came into the African picture, Bismarck tried to build up a Franco-German entente. He objected to the Anglo-Portuguese Congo Treaty of 1884 and proposed to Paris in August for an agreement for mutual support in West Africa, the Congo, and Egypt. The British found it expedient to agree to attend a conference which was held at Berlin from November 1884 to February 1885. It recognised the vast and rich Congo Basin as a free state under the administration of King Leopold II of Belgium and opened it to traders of all nations. The conference gave a new stature to Germany for she now began to be recognised as a world as well as a continental power. The conference also marked the end of Franco-German entente for France proved more hostile to German interests in Africa even than Britain.

In retrospect, Bismarck's colonial ventures were disappointment or too expensive. Bismarck intended that the colonies should serve as an 'informal empire' in which the commercial gains would pay the costs of administration. But in West Africa and South West Africa, German protectorates became colonies in which the costs of empire were borne by the state. It was only in 1906 that the discovery of rich diamond and copper deposits in South West Africa began to redress an unhappy balance. In East Africa, the German East African Company proved more burdensome than financial strength. Bismarck had sufficient reason for disenchantment with the economic results of his colonial adventure. No wonder Bismarck observed to the Italian Prime Minister during the latter's visit in May 1889 that he offered to sell his guest all of his African holdings. Though Bismarck's colonial policy strengthened his position in the *Reichstag,* the anti-English tone and his flirtation with the French puzzled rather than gratified them. The memories of Sedan were too deep to be effaced. When Bismarck heard the ominous word *revanche* in France, he developed an interest in effecting a collaboration between the British Government and the Triple Alliance. It would have been easier to achieve this if his policy in 1884 had been less truculent.

Before his fall, Bismarck had built up for Germany a complicated system of alliance and counter-alliance. He had secured Russian neutrality in case of an Austrian attack, Italian support against a combined Russian and French attack. It has been said that Bismarck was like a rider on a horse who tossed five balls in the air and caught and threw them up again as they fell. But the incomparable wizard had reached a time when he could no longer keep up all five. For the German-Austro-Italian triangle contained implicit contradictions, as even before Bismarck's retirement, Russia was beginning to drift away from Germany towards France.

The Bismarckian system of alliance had other demerits. In 1879 Bismarck tied 'the trim Prussian frigate to the worm-eaten Austrian galleon', and surely this was not a triumph for his diplomacy. 'He set out to remake Central Europe. Instead he tied himself to the Habsburgs, and like everyone who follows this path ended up by believing that peace could be kept by tricks.'[5] The 1879 Treaty and the Triple Alliance Treaty ran counter to the Reinsurance Treaty. Bismarck ultimately had to make a choice and had to stand by the Triple Alliance of Germany, Austria-Hungary and Italy. 'Genius can make black look like white for a time, but not for ever, and Russia at last knew in 1888 that the great diplomatic artist had tricked her.' Bismarck's policy, therefore, ultimately drove Russia into the arms of France.

Another element of weakness of Bismarckian alliance was that there was no place for Britain in it. The Mediterranean Agreement of 1887

5. Taylor, A. J. P.: *Europe: Grandeur and Decline,* P. 112.

between Britain, Italy and Austria-Hungary might have been extended to Germany had not Bismarck supported Russia's Near Eastern interests to stand in the way. It is true that on his retirement Anglo-German relations were good. Britain was not then a member of an opposing camp, but Bismarck's system of alliances had engendered a lively sense of apprehension that compelled Britain later on to look for allies.

The mainspring of Bismarck's diplomacy after 1871 was fear—fear of an outburst of German national energy and fear of coalitions against Germany. That is why he negotiated with all and sundry and devised permutations and combinations to keep the Powers in good humour. He had taught the Germans that conquest was the only cure for danger; and he had whipped up that psychosis in order to maintain his power. 'The Bismarckian system aimed at security and peace; but it left the ruling classes of Germany no alternative—to preserve themselves they had to enter on a path of conquest which would be their ruin. Bismarck, the greatest of political Germans, was for Germany the greatest of disasters.'[6]

Bismarck's Fall

Towards the end of William I's reign, Bismarck scored another triumph in domestic policy with the so-called September Elections of 1887. The Chancellor was convinced that increased armaments were necessary in view of the Bulgarian Crisis of 1885-86 as well as the intensified *revanche* spirit in France. As the peace strength of the French army in 1886 exceeded that of Germany, Bismarck felt obliged to present a bill for a 10 per cent increase in the army. Like previous army bills it was to run for seven years, as a Septennate. Bismarck asked for a new Septennate a full year before the old one (1881) was due to expire. The Reichstag was willing to grant the increases asked for but insisted that the increased budget be for a term of three, rather than seven years. Bismarck dissolved the Reichstag. In the elections of 1887 the Conservatives, the Free Conservatives, and the National Liberals, forming the so-called Kartell, won an absolute majority of 220 of the 397 seats.

Thanks to his deft handling of the international situation and his commanding position in the Reichstag, Bismarck's reputation was at its height. Unfortunately the Emperor William I, over whom Bismarck had always imposed his superior will, died in March 1888. He was succeeded by the Crown Prince, known as Frederick III, who was too anglophile abroad and too liberal at home. But the Emperor, already mortally ill, died within three months of his accession. As soon as William II, still under thirty, came to the throne, the elaborate Bismarckian structure began to crumble.

An inexperienced and impetuous youth, William II had little patience with the politics of the past and no desire to be tied by the apron strings of Bismarck. He became critical of Bismarck's foreign policy and allowed himself to be persuaded that Bismarck had underestimated the Russian threat to German interests. Moreover, since he wanted to be popular, there was little scope for reconciliation between the Emperor and the Chancellor. The first indication of a breach between the two came in May 1889 when there was a massive strike in the Ruhr coalfields. The Emperor broke all precedent by receiving a delegation of miners and ordering the Westphalian coal-producers that they be forced to end the strike on the miners terms.

The clash between the two came in October 1889 when Bismarck decided to destroy the Social Democratic Party by passing a new Socialist Law. The Emperor, on the other hand, was opposed to this, obsessed as he was with a project of his own, a plan for legislation to improve working conditions and regulate working hours for all German labourers. On January 25, 1890, the Reichstag rejected the bill on the anti-Socialist Law. Bismarck then began to work up a state of international emergency reviving the demand for increase in the armed strength. He dissolved the Reichstag and the new elections in February brought a clear defeat for Bismarck and considerable success for the Social Democrats

6. Taylor, A. J. P.: *The Course of German History,* P. 154-55.

and left-wing Liberals. Bismarck observed in this connection:

> There is not the slightest prospect that future elections will ever again produce a majority as accommodating as the Kartell majority. I believe only if the diabolical means is used of terrifying petty bourgeois and rural circles by contrived pustsches.

In this crisis, Bismarck came to the conclusion that the best way of confronting the situation was by force of arms and he planned to destroy the Reichstag. In mid-March 1880, he alerted the Commanding-Generals to the possibility of risings indicating that the use of force might be necessary. But Bismarck failed to appreciate that the new Emperor wanted to be recognised as the real director of German policy. In order to create a body of subservient Ministers of State, who were secretly encouraging the Emperor to defy the Chancellor, the latter invoked a long-forgotten cabinet order of 1852 which forbade ministers to have access to the sovereign except with the permission of the Prime Minister. Finally, he made a last attempt to create a viable new parliamentary combination by trying to ingratiate the favour of his old enemy Ludwig Windthorst of the Centre party without the Emperor's knowledge. On March 15, 1890, William demanded the abrogation of the order of 1852 and reproached him for discussing parliamentary arrangements with the Centre without his knowledge. The crisis was accentuated when both the chiefs of Military cabinet and the General Staff abandoned Bismarck and urged the Emperor to dismiss him. On March 20, Bismarck tendered his resignation and the Emperor accepted it with relief.

For twentyfive years Bismarck has been Europe's first statesman, at times its arbiter. When the great star fell, it was felt that Germany had suffered an irreparable loss. On the other hand, many Germans heaved a sigh of relief at the Chancellor's dismissal, for they perceived that his political acumen had been blunted increasingly in his old age. As Theodore Fontane wrote on May 1, 1890, 'It is fortunate that we are rid of him, and many many questions will now be handled better, more honourably, more clearly than before.' But this expectation was to be disappointed. 'At the end of his career, Bismarck had no other answer for the problems of his society but violence. His successors proved to be no more fertile in expedients than he.'.[7]

William II: Domestic Politics

William II had attractive qualities and a quick intelligence. But he was ill-educated and infected with an overwhelming arrogance and forthrightness of speech which sometimes degenerated into vulgarity. He had a lofty conception of the prerogative of his office and sought to assert himself in every aspect of his country's policy, approaching all questions with an open mouth. He cultivated a military bearing and hobnobbed with the military officers and was more intimate with them than with the civilian officers. He was convinced that he had a special aptitude in foreign relations which in the end had deplorable results.

General Leo Von Caprivi (1831-99), succeeded Bismarck as Iron Chancellor and Minister President of Prussia. He had a reputation of administrative skill, energy and independence of mind. But Caprivi's talents were balanced by grave deficiencies. In both domestic and foreign affairs, he suffered from a lack of rudimentary knowledge and of that intuitive sense, the latter being the basic ingredient of a successful politician. He had integrity, but he was politically inexperienced.

Caprivi made it clear that he would work in the interest of efficiency and general welfare. He would conciliate the Left and the Centre and bring them into harmony with the conservatives and the state. Abroad, he wished to follow a policy of non-alignment while protecting Germany's interests and guarding her against the two enemies, France and Russia.

Caprivi succeeded in putting through labour legislation. Sunday became a holiday, female and child labour were restricted, minimum period for giving notice were fixed, and so on. As part of his programme and in response to worldwide economic malaise, Caprivi, in 1891, negotiated a series of trade treaties with Austria, Italy, Belgium

7. Craig Gordon A: *Germany, 1866-1945,* P. 179.

and Switzerland. Conspicuous feature of these treaties was a reduction of duties on imported wheat and rye in exchange for favourable rates for exports of German manufactured goods. The real significance of the trade policy is that it marked a deliberate choice by the Government in favour of industry against the agrarian interest. The Landowners' League was, therefore, founded in 1893 to agitate for a reversal of trade policy. The Farmers' Federation demanded protective tariffs, tax relief and finally a state grain monopoly and subsidies.

In the first months of 1892, in an attempt to conciliate the Centre, Caprivi introduced a new Prussian School Bill. Its purpose was to restore to the Catholic Church moneys confiscated during the Kulturkampf, the establishment of church control over education and the provision that all new schools should be confessional schools. The bill was opposed by the National Liberals, the moderate conservatives, the Progressive and Social Democrats; even Bismarck fulminated against its provisions from retirement. After attempts to water down the bill failed, it was withdrawn. But by giving it up, Caprivi had to lose the support of the Centre.

Caprivi's policy of divesting the office of Chancellor some power by giving his ministers and secretaries freedom of action brought unhappy consequences. He lost control over the Prussian ministers and some of them began to intrigue against him. The situation became worse when the Chancellor yielded the minister presidency to Count Botho Eulenburg in March 1892.

Since the lapsing of the Reinsurance Treaty and the rapprochement between France and Russia, there was a persistent demand for an increase in German armed strength. Caprivi was inclined to agree. On November 23, 1892, he introduced into the *Reichstag* the army bill which made the appropriate increase of the army, reduced the period of service from three to two years and arranged that the army should be voted for five instead of seven years. But Caprivi was incapable of manufacturing a war scare and he could carry through the bill only after a dissolution of the *Reichstag*, new elections and concessions to the opposition.

By 1894 the anarchist activities of the year—the assassination of Sadi Carnot, the French President, and the attempt on Caprivi's own life—had revived an agitation for legislation against anarchist and Social Democrats. In September 1894 the Emperor succumbed to those ideas and declared to wage 'war for religion, for morality and against the forces of revolution'. The Prussian Prime Minister, Count Eulenburg, enthusiastically shared these imperial fantasies and introduced a bill. Caprivi made a scathing attack in the Prussian Ministry of State upon Eulenburg's bill and theory of the *coup d' etat.* But he had lost the power to do what was right. In October 1894 he submitted his resignation in such a way as to force Eulenburg to do the same and the Emperor decided to let both men go.

Caprivi's successor was Prince Hohenlohe, who had a long and honourable career in German politics. He was 75 years old when he assumed office. His Chancellorship witnessed a further decline in the power of the office. The Emperor appointed him as a respectable figurehead who would be amenable to his will. But the Emperor overlooked Hohenlohe's reputation for stubbornness and evasiveness. But they were no substitute for the kind of firm leadership that Germany needed at this juncture.

Hohenlohe's Chancellorship was marked by an unending series of attempts to disable the Social Democratic Party. In January and February 1895 he suggested that Social Democrats should be deprived of all rights of suffrage and that their leaders should be arrested. He introduced an anti-revolutionary bill into the *Reichstag.* The bill would have amended the penal law and the press law to allow legal prosecution of agitators against the existing social order. The bill was referred to a committee and subjected to so many amendments that it was promptly voted down.

Almost from the beginning the Chancellor had to wrestle with intermittent conflicts of civil military relations that plagued the history of the Second Empire. The issue was that of military justice, because Hohenlohe's War Minister, Walter Bronsart von Schellendorf, undertook to revise the Prussian code of 1845 by modernizing trial procedures and providing for public hearings in most trials. The Emperor, however, steadfastly refused to accept the idea of reform. He was supported by the Chief of the Military Cabinet, Von Hahnke, who observed cryptically: 'The army must remain an insulated body into which no one dare peer with critical eyes'. Three whole years passed before the issue was resolved and in that period there were frequent cabinet crises that led to the dismissal of one War Minister (Bronsart), one Foreign Minister (Marshall von Biberstein) and two Prussian Ministers of the Interior—E. M. von Koller and H. von Boetticher. In December 1898 the reform was finally accepted owing to persistent pressure exerted by the Social Democratic, Progressive and Centre parties.

Bernard von Bulow replaced Hohenlohe as Chancellor on October 17, 1900. He had been in the Diplomatic Service since 1873 and in 1897 became Secretary of State for Foreign Affairs. Though Bulow ingratiated the favour of the Emperor, he was realistic enough to abandon the reactionary social politics of his predecessors. Instead of checking the advance of Social Democracy by force, Bulow tried to foster a union of the agrarian and industrials interests. To complement it and to provide the masses with an element of excitement, he embarked upon a spirited foreign policy, known as Weltpolitik. As he wrote in December 1907: 'Only a successful foreign policy can help to reconcile, pacify, rally, unite.' The Progressive politician Friedrich Naumann eagerly grasped at Weltpolitik as a means of social integration. In 1900 he wrote: 'The new era will be imperialist and proletarian... it is impossible at present to separate these two elements.'

The first tangible fruits of Bulow's policy were the passage of the Supplementary Naval Act of 1900 and the new tariff laws of 1902. The first was due partly to the hatred for England as a result of the Boer War and partly to the fear that a British victory in South Africa would herald a worldwide victory of industrialism over the agrarian way of life. The Tariff Law of December 1902 greatly increased the duties on imported grain that Russian grains were virtually excluded from the German markets. But the new Tariff Law did not relieve the mounting deficit which the Reich had to face after 1903 owing to heavy military expenditure and costly foreign adventures. The financial question proved to be Bulow's most intractable problem and in the end it brought him down.

The unpopularity of the new Tariff Law was so great that the Social Democratic Party which had fought against it, gained 25 seats in the national elections of 1903, while the left Liberals, which had remained neutral, lost 13 votes. The net result was a significant shift in the balance of forces in the *Reichstag,* which gave the Centre party a dominant position within the government coalition.

By 1905 the budgetary situation had grown so worse that Bulow had to declare that 'the Reich was in need of new income'. But Bulow was handicapped by the fact that the Centre and the left parties refused to agree to the kind of taxes that would increase the burden on the ordinary taxpayer. In 1907, with the help of the Left Liberals, Bulow built up a coalition called 'Bulow Bloc' and won the election. This had been achieved, however, at the cost of the Centre party. When it became evident that an increase of federal income was needed, Bulow decided to impose new taxes on articles of consumption, on the landholders as well as to increase the inheritance tax. Bulow emphasised the urgent necessity of tax reforms as a question of 'To be or not to be'. But his tax reform had no chance of success. Apart from the opposition of the Centre and the conservatives, a significant number of party leaders of Bulow Bloc were ready to counteract the measure.

Bulow's unassailable position was undermined in November 1908 by the publication in the *Daily Telegraph* of London of an interview with William II in which the Emperor made a number of comments about foreign affairs that were calculated to harm relations with Britain and Russia. In the fevered anxious atmosphere of 1908, every party seized on the *Daily Telegraph* interview as evidence of William II's incapacity. The *Reichstag* was in revolt; Bulow, ostensibly accepting responsibility, encouraged the uproar, and extracted from the Emperor a promise that he would in future respect his constitutional obligations. This event embittered the relations between the Emperor and the Chancellor.

Bulow held on his Chancellorship until the financial issue was resolved. The left liberals agreed to support him if he would introduce a direct tax on property. An inheritance tax was therefore proposed. The Conservatives opposed this. Bulow could now count only on support from National Liberals, Left Liberals and the Socialist Party. Bulow tried in vain to add the centre to this coalition. And he failed to carry the tax bill in 1909. The defeat of the bill dealt a death-warrant to Bulow. He offered his resignation, and William II was glad to get rid of him. Bulow was the last of the Imperial Chancellors who wielded the vast powers created by Bismarck for himself. 'The office and title of Chancellor remained; but it was not the Chancellorship of Bismarck's conception. The Chancellor became merely a superior clerk.'[8]

Bulow's successor was Bethmann-Hollweg. He had made his way from the provincial administration of Brandenburg to the Prussian Ministry of the Interior and, finally, in 1907 to the post of Secretary of State in the Imperial office of Internal Affairs. He was a careful and energetic administrator but he lacked creative talent and his political horizons were narrow. His ignorance of foreign affairs and military problems were profound. He was conservative in his views, and opposed in principle to the idea of parliamentary government. After some vain attempts to broaden his parliamentary backing, Bethmann became increasingly dependent upon non-parliamentary forces—the bureaucracy and the army.

The problems—both political and economic—which confronted Bethmann were most intractable. His attempt in 1910 to modify the existing law on Prussian suffrage by eliminating indirect voting and by diminishing aristocratic influence found few supporters. Bethmann became convinced that unless new taxes were levied the security of the nation would be jeopardized. But he found it difficult to reconcile the divergent interests of different parties. Meanwhile, he decided to follow the course charted out by his capable Secretary of State of the Treasury, Adolf Wermuth, a policy of vigorous retrenchment. This principle was followed until 1912. Even the Moroccan crisis of 1911 failed to defect the policy as Bethmann made it clear that he would resign if any military increases were brought in until after the elections.

The elections of 1912 gave the Socialists some advantages as they won 67 new seats, which increased their strength to 100 in the *Reichstag*. But the Socialists found it impossible to bring the liberals and other parties to their side. Hence there ensued a stalemate of the party system. The *Reichstag* ceased to become an effective body. Bethmann had little to do with the *Reichstag* bypassing it when he could and when this was impractical, creating majorities from issue to issue. William II derisively called the *Reichstag* as a 'troop of monkeys and a collection of blockheads and sleep-walkers.'

After the election, Bethmann found it impossible to tone up the imperial finance without any tax and this could be raised only by the introduction of inheritance tax. But when Bethmann began negotiations to lay the basis for such an innovation, it raised such a storm of protest that the idea was abandoned. In consequence, the Secretary of State of the Treasury resigned in disgust.

The increase of international tension after 1911 secured the passage of the Army Bill of 1912 which enabled the government to raise the necessary money to meet the army's needs. The vast sum—about £50 million—was to be raised not by loan, but by direct taxation, by means of a capital levy. It was welcomed by the *Reichstag* and supported even by the Social Democrats. For the first time in the history of the Reich, the federal government was given the right to tax property directly.

This popular demonstration did nothing to strengthen the position of Bethmann. It served only to reveal the inherent contradictions of German wishes. While the great majority of Germans wanted a Germany militarily strong, a place in the sun, they also wanted a constitutional system inside Germany and resented the dominating influence of the military clique. This

8. Taylor, A. J. P.: *The Course of German History,* P. 181.

particular mood was reflected in a great protest against militarism which united almost all Germany in the autumn of 1913. In November 1913 troops in the village of Zabern in Alsace became involved in a series of incidents with civilians which led to the suspension of civilian authorities and the wholesale arrest of people. All Germany was stirred. When the matter was raised in the *Reichstag*, the Minister of War supported the action taken in Zabern and was, in turn, defended by Bethmann. On December 4, 1913, a vote of no-confidence was passed by a majority of 293 to 54.

Despite this impressive victory of parliamentary government, Bethmann remained as Chancellor. Though the Socialists suggested that the Chancellor should resign, their view was rejected with indignation by the other parties. 'Like the *Daily Telegraph* affair, the Zabern case resulted in some rhetorical pyrotechnics and nothing more.' William II appreciated Bethmann's loyalty to the Crown and had scant regard for the *Reichstag*. 'The German parliamentarian and politician becomes daily more of a swine', observed William II but the latter thought of not superseding the body. Bethmann continued to remain as Chancellor till 1917 when his enemies brought him down.

Foreign Policy, 1890-1914

The period between Bismarck's fall and the inauguration of German Weltpolitik in 1897-98 is one of transition. The four years of Caprivi Chancellorship and the first two years under his successor Hohenlohe epitomised the period of transition. But even during this period there were different forces at work. On the one hand, there were those elements that stood for imperialist expansion, *i.e.*, for Weltpolitik—the Kaiser and his court, the National Liberals and the Pan-Germans—on the other hand, Caprivi's policy of restraint supported by the Catholic Centre Party, the left-wing Liberals and the Socialists.

Bismarck had largely succeeded in retaining his original policy of continental restraint. In his hands the Triple Alliance was a weapon of defence and even English statesmen welcomed its formation as a guarantee of European peace. Caprivi tried to keep the German foreign policy within rational bounds. 'General von Caprivi believed that Germany had no chance at all of becoming a world power, and consequently his policy was designed only to maintain Germany's position on the European continent. He was therefore ... seeking good relations with England as the natural ally against Russia, the country which threatened Germany's position in Europe.'

During the period 1890-97, German foreign policy was greatly influenced by Holstein. His importance was increased by the fact that he was the only one who had been in diplomatic service under Bismarck. Caprivi, and his Foreign Secretary, Marshall von Biberstein, had no experience at all in foreign policy. 'He was the one-eyed man in the country of the blind. He had great industry and experience, even great resolution, his weakness was that he tried to conduct foreign policy on a secretive basis, when in fact public opinion had to be increasingly considered.'[9]

Holstein's anti-Russian policy was reflected in Germany's refusal to prolong the Reinsurance Treaty with Russia. Moreover, the Treaty was incompatible with the Triple Alliance, and could therefore entangle Germany in a conflict. Russia reacted promptly and immediately turned to France who was more than ready to reciprocate. Once German policy had developed away from Russia after 1890, a corresponding rapprochement with Britain seemed the only alternative. In July 1890, the Caprivi Government concluded a colonial agreement with Britain. In return for a narrow strip of territory that gave German South West Africa access to the Zambezi River, and the island of Heligoland in the North Sea, the German Government accepted British claims to vast tracts of territory that gave them possession of the sources of the Nile. In England the government view was expressed in Stanley's words that a trouser button had been exchanged for a suit of clothes. The agreement helped to speed up the imminent Franco-Russian alliance.

In July 1891, a French naval squadron visited the Russian port Kronstadt and was received with great cordiality. In October 1893, a Russian

9. Taylor, A. J. P.: *The Struggle for Mastery in Europe*, 1848-1918, P. 328.

squadron visited Toulon. By the end of 1893 the Russians had concluded a military convention with France, and this was soon to be transformed into a defensive Alliance. The German press attacked the Caprivi Government for having brought the French press and the Russians together while following the will-o'-the-wisp of an alliance with Britain, an unreliable power. German foreign office believed that the logic of events would persuade Britain to come out of her isolationist stance. But Britain's difficulties with France over Siam (Thailand) and the Mekong Valley did not propel Britain any closer to the Triple Alliance. Germany's disillusionment with Britain led the former to conclude a trade treaty with Russia on terms favourable to the Russians. Holstein became disenchanted with Britain when the British electorate returned Gladstone to office in 1892. In the following year, he actually began to speculate upon leaving the British to their own policy, of allowing the Triple Alliance to expire without renewal, and of restricting Germany's commitment to alliances with Austria-Hungary and Russia.

The death of Tsar Alexander III and accession of Nicholas II marked a new turn in Russian policy. He had strong sentimental links to monarchical Germany, through his German wife. Both Russia and Germany protested against the Peace Treaty of Shimonoseki—imposed by Japan on China at the end of the Sino-Japanese War of 1894-95. Intervention in Shimonoseki in 1895 brought Germany in the Far East. The commander of the German Far East Squadron, Admiral von Tirpitz, was sent to the Far East.

The period of limited cooperation between Germany and Russia provoked new friction with Britain. The British Foreign Secretary Salisbury was irritated by the way in which the Kaiser rejected his idea of forming an agreement on the Near Eastern Question, once the Ottoman Empire disintegrated. The tense situation in 1895 was aggravated by the British policy in South Africa. In 1896 DR Jameson attempted without any authorization from the British Government to make an armed incursion into the Transvaal, an independent state. Although the British Government was quick to express its regret over the incident, the Kaiser, who at first wanted to declare a German protectorate over the Transvaal, sent a telegram to Kruger, President of the Transvaal. The message congratulated Kruger and his people for having repelled an invasion by armed bands and for succeeding in maintaining the independence of the country against attacks from without. This 'high explosive' was explicitly intended to teach Britain a lesson. But British resentment was very high as they regarded the Transvaal as lying within their sphere of influence. It was hoped by the German foreign policy experts that the Transvaal dispute might be used to bring Britain to terms with the Triple Alliance. The telegram had been designed as 'a warning to England that she could only find salvation in closer contact with Germany and her allies'. But *The Times* answered pungently, 'The paramount necessity of the moment is to bring home to the German mind the fact that England will concede nothing to menaces and will not lie down under insults'. In 1896 Anglo-German relations were at their lowest ebb.

Weltpolitik

The aims of German policy were expressed by the term 'Weltpolitik'—world policy. It means that Germany had by degrees ceased to regard exclusively the continent of Europe in framing her policy. This new development, we are told, was 'no chance outcome of the personality of a monarch possessed by exuberant scheme of world conquest, or of the excessive energy of the ambitious statesmen or even of the wild imaginings of small groups of Pan-German enthusiasts without political influence; rather it forms part of that strong tide of evolution which irresistibly bore the German state out beyond the bounds of its earlier policy.' It was claimed by Bulow that, at bottom, it was not ambitious restlessness which led Germany to embark upon a world-policy but the exigencies of her economic situation. Germany had changed from a predominantly rural to a predominantly urban society, from an inward-looking to an outward-looking country. The chief agents in this outward march were the great banking combinations which controlled about 40 percent of Germany's commercial deposits and whose chief purpose was to foster commercial relations between Germany and other countries.

The change in foreign policy was greeted with enthusiasm not only by patriotic societies like the Colonial Union and the Pan-German League, but by ordinary citizens who entertained visionary dream of Germany's greatness. Writers like Friedrick Naumann, Max Weber, Paul Rohrbach, the author of *The German Thought in the World and Onward to the Position of a World Power* were all believers in a German mission to play a worthy role.

The primary aim of German 'Weltpolitik' was to dominate the Near and Middle East. Bismarck had treated the whole Eastern Question as not worth the bones of a single Pomeranian grenadier, and, at the Congress of Berlin, he was content to play the part of honest broker. Over the mind of his successor, on the other hand, the Levant exercised an irresistible fascination, and the *Drang nach osten*—the advance eastwards—opened up a new phase of German foreign policy. As British influence at the Porte declined, Germany came forward as the champion of the Ottoman Empire and the Moslem creed. Apart from consideration of world power, the exploitation of Asia Minor was widely advocated on economic grounds. The well-known economist, Friedrich List, had long time earlier drawn attention to the vast fertile regions of Asia Minor and Mesopotamia which offered tempting field for German enterprise. 'Here the superfluous population of Germany might be dispersed in promising settlements; German capital could be profitably employed in railways and irrigation works, in mining and agriculture; increasing prosperity would provide growing markets for German produce ... Financial and economic control over Turkey ... meant also the control of South-eastern Europe and Eastern Mediterranean, the command of the Danube from source to mouth ... the practical possession of Baghdad, and a road to the Persian Gulf, whence it would be easy to bring pressure to bear not only on Persia but on Russian territory east of the Caspian and even on India.'[10] All these dazzling possibilities were foreshadowed in the far-reaching scheme for the Baghdad Railway, which was designed to connect Berlin with the Persian Gulf. The scheme was started in 1888, but the project of its extension to Baghdad and the Persian Gulf only took definite shape in 1903.

Growing Crisis

The two men who shaped the world policy and made it their own were Bernard von Bulow who became Secretary of State in 1897 and Chancellor in 1901 and Tirpitz, who became Secretary of State for the Navy in 1897. 'I am putting the main emphasis on foreign policy', Bulow wrote in December 1897, 'Only a successful foreign policy can help to reconcile, pacify, rally, unite'. Tirpitz dominated naval policy from 1897 to 1917. He believed that Britain was Germany's chief enemy and the necessary instrument for countering British influence in the world was the battleship.

The emergence of a world policy and the foundation of a first class navy made the years 1898 to 1901 a turning point in Germany's relations with Britain. In November 1897, Germany had seized Kiachow, thus obtaining a fine naval base in the Far East. This act infuriated the Russians, who regarded this as an intrusion into their sphere of influence. Both Germany and Britain recognised what they had in common. From March to April 1898, the British Colonial Secretary, Joseph Chamberlain, began unofficial talks with Count von Hatzfeldt, the German ambassador in London, for holding Russia back from China. The possibility of a defensive alliance or of treaty with the Triple Alliance was also discussed. Bulow, appointed Foreign Secretary in October 1897, rebuffed this approach, as he doubted Britain's sincerity. The next phase saw a revival of definite proposals for an alliance. The proposal by Britain for a defensive alliance involving neutrality, if she or a member of the Triple Alliance were attacked by a single member, and military assistance if either were attacked from two sides, failed to evoke any response from Germany. On August 20, 1898, Germany and Britain signed an agreement about the Portuguese colonies. They agreed on securities for a joint loan to Portugal whose finances were in bad shape: the customs revenue of Portugal's west-coast African colonies of Germany and of her east-coast colonies for Britain.

10. Prothero G. W.: *German Opinion and German Policy before the War,* P. 31-32.

It was also secretly arranged that if Portugal was obliged to renounce her own sovereignty each might take possession of its share. The Portuguese pact, however, remained a dead letter, for the country escaped financial collapse.

In November and December 1899, Germany and Britain made agreements which settled a number of minor disputes in Africa. In February 1900, Germany was able to proclaim her protectorate over the Samoan Island. This was followed by the Yangtse Treaty of October 16, 1900 between Britain and Germany. It upheld the American open door policy. But if other powers were to achieve territorial gains in China, Britain and Germany would take steps to prevent it.

Now, once again, Germany hoped to be able to bind Britain to the Triple Alliance. Lansdowne, the British Foreign Minister, on the other hand, favoured a separate alliance or a much looser agreement. Britain joining the Triple Alliance would have meant enormous advantages for Germany, while Britain would have been obliged to guarantee the territorial integrity of Austro-Hungary. British statesmen were reluctant to be enmeshed in the maze of Balkan problems and the disintegration of two dying Empires—Ottoman and Austria-Hungary. Germany, on the other hand, wanted to strengthen its position by winning Britain over to its side, without any intention of making any concession in the sensitive sphere—the questions of naval disarmament. As Bulow expressed at this time: 'The future task of the German Government in my opinion is to preserve good relations with both Britain and Russia and, in the possession of a strong fleet.'

By December 1901 the chances for a general agreement between Britain and Germany had faded away. One month later, on January 30, 1902, Britain entered into an alliance with Japan, the emerging power in the Far East. The Anglo-Japanese Alliance was an event of epoch-making importance. Britain left her policy of splendid isolation which was to have serious repercussions on German Foreign policy.

What Germany regarded as impossible soon happened. Thanks to King Edward VII and his Foreign Secretary, Lord Lansdowne, and the French Minister Delcasse, Britain and France signed a convention in April 1904. The most important feature of the 'Entente Cordiale' as it was called, was that Britain should have a free hand in Egypt and France should be free to restore order in Morocco. There were concessions by one side or another in the minor questions, Newfoundland, Siam (Thailand) and West Africa. The 'Entente Cordiale' represented the first major blow to German 'Weltpolitik'.

Germany tried to compensate her diplomatic defeat by drawing closer to Russia, when the latter had suffered defeat at the hands of Japan. After a new commercial treaty with Russia in July 1904, the Kaiser signed, in July 1905, the abortive Bjorke treaty with the Tsar. The Treaty was described by the Kaiser as 'a Continental combine … to block the way to the whole world becoming John Bull's private property'. Kaiser thought that the Treaty would have compelled France either to obey Germany or to abandon Russia, and have isolated Britain completely. But it came to nothing: the Treaty remained inoperative as it contravened the Dual Alliance between France and Russia. 'It took the Emperor some time to realise that his plan, though as brilliant as a soap bubble, was also a frail, and destined to the fate of all bubbles."

The strength of the Anglo-French Entente was soon to be tested in the question of Morocco. For some years France had been engaged in the peaceful penetration of Morocco—the preliminary to its political annexation. Moreover, France had a special interest in the development of affairs in Morocco on account of its proximity to her North African possessions and owing to the fact that French trade in Morocco had exceeded that of England or Germany. On the other hand, Germany could claim with fairness that she also had important economic interests in Morocco; and by virtue of the Madrid Convention on Morocco of 1880 of which Germany was a signatory, she had a right to be consulted affecting the integrity of Morocco. Finally as a result of the weakness of France's ally, Russia owing to her defeat by Japan (March 1905), Germany decided to challenge the Franco-British Entente. In March 1905 the Kaiser made a theatrical landing at Tangier and proclaimed in unequivocal language the independence and integrity of Morocco. In France there was a widespread feeling that war was very near. On April 11, 1905, Bulow issued a circular demanding the summoning of an international conference on Morocco. Despite the opposition of Delcasse, the French Minister of Foreign Affairs, the French Government accepted the German demand for an international conference. Delcasse thereupon resigned and the conference met at Algeciras (April 7, 1906). It has been said that the international conference was intended to create new opportunities for provocation. It is significant that the Schlieffen plan, the piece of German General Staff planning, designed to save Germany from a war on two fronts by the knockout blow against France, was given its final shape at this time.

Germany calculated to draw international support at the conference. But she obtained the support of Austria-Hungary alone. The French got exactly what they wanted. Though the French annexation of Morocco was forbidden and the 'open door' theoretically established, France was, nevertheless, left free to proceed with her peaceful penetration. Germany's action, instead of destroying, strengthened the Anglo-French Entente. In December 1905 and January 1906 some tentative and unofficial talks between the British and French General staffs about joint measures to be taken in the event of war with Germany took place. The talks might be unofficial, but they had a most serious meaning. It was Churchill's view that they constituted 'an exceedingly potent tie'.

The period that followed Algeciras saw the beginning of move by Russia towards London. Russia was prompted by the desire to protect her tie with France and also to secure British assistance in winning favourable terms in the Far East from Britain's ally, Japan. The Anglo-Russian rapprochement took place in August 1907. By it the paramount interest of Britain in Afghanistan was recognised. Both powers agreed to stay out of Tibet. Persia was divided into three zones: one Russian, one British, as well as a middle and neutral zone. Each power agreed not to seek concessions in the area allotted to the other; and both powers agreed to bar Germany from Persia as a whole. The Anglo-Russian Convention completed the entente of Britain with the Dual Alliance. The agreement of 1907 removed some of the immediate causes of friction between Britain and Russia. Even before the ratification of the agreement with Britain, Russia, in a secret agreement with Japan, got sphere of influence in Manchuria. Thus, the Triple Entente was brought into existence to balance the Triple Alliance. It was from this time that Germany began to bring forward against Britain the repeated charge of encirclement.

The Triple Entente did not involve military alliance against Germany and might soon have dissolved if the Germans had kept quiet. Instead, their actions turned it into a reality. The German by their naval activities alarmed Britain. There grew up the belief that Germany wished to challenge British naval supremacy. 'The military situation against England demands battleships in as great a number as possible.' The German Navy Law of 1898 had announced its intention to build a battle fleet and the 1900 law made it clear that this fleet was able to challenge the British in the North Sea. In November 1905 the German Government not only provided for an increase in the tonnage of the ships but called for the construction of six large cruisers and fortyeight destroyers. The British met this challenge by launching in February 1906 the HM5 *Dreadnought*—an 'all big-gunship' that was superior in speed and ability to manoeuvre. German public opinion was excited and paid scant regard to a British offer to cut down naval construction at the Hague Conference of 1907. Instead, Tripitz introduced a supplementary naval law in November 1907 which provided for more *Dreadnoughts*. The British Government had to increase their naval estimates in March 1908 which spiralled in the following year. Thus there began an endless naval competition which embittered Anglo-German relations.

In October 1908, Austria-Hungary annexed the territory of Bosnia and Herzegovina which it had administered since 1878. The annexation had been approved in advance by Izvolsky, the Russian Foreign Minister, in return for Austrian support to Russian claims in the Straits. But owing to adverse international reaction and under the pressure of his ministerial colleagues, Izvolsky now repudiated that bargain and asked that an international conference meet to undo the *fait-accompli*. The Serbs who had long coveted the seized area and encouraged by Pan-Slav agitation in Russia, began to prepare for action. The Austrians responded with a partial mobilization. Though the initial reaction of the German Government was of annoyance towards Vienna as the annexation of Bosnia had outraged the Turks, whom the Germans were bent on cultivating, still Bulow stood by the action of its ally. The Chancellor wrote:

> Our position would indeed be dangerous if Austria lost confidence and turned away. So long as we stand together, we form a bloc that no one will lightly attack. In eastern questions above all, we cannot place ourselves in opposition to Austria who has nearer or greater interests in the Balkan peninsula than ourselves. A refusal or a grudging attitude in the question of annexation of Bosnia and Herzegovina would not be forgiven.

The German Government not only supported Austria-Hungary in the Bosnian crisis but in March 1909 sent an ultimatum to Russia. Though the Russians caved in but their resentment was too deep to be effaced. They began to encourage the Serbian activists against Austria in the subsequent period.

Having suffered setback in two great diplomatic crises in 1905-06 over the first Moroccan affair and in 1908-09 over the Bosnian crisis, Germany seemed to have lost her moorings in foreign affairs. The successor of Bulow was Bethmann Hollweg who became Chancellor in 1909. Unlike his predecessors he had no experience either of politics or of foreign affairs. He had none of Bismarck's brutality or Bulow's shiftiness. He desired a reconciliation with Russia, good relations with England. All he lacked was any sense of power; henceforth this 'great gentleman' became, through his irresponsibility, responsible for various crises that engulfed Germany since 1909.

Soon after taking office as Chancellor, Bethmann began negotiations with Britain, for reducing the naval programmes or rather for retarding them. But the negotiations did not come to much. Bethmann demanded from Britain a definite political advantage 'in the case of an attack made on either power (Britain or Germany) by a third Power or a group of powers, the Power not attacked should stand aside'. This neutrality proposal was repeated in the next two years and again in 1912 and Germany always insisted that this must take precedence over the naval question. This proposal was evidently to the advantage of Germany for if Russia or France (or both) attacked Germany, Britain would be neutral. The fundamental fact in the neutrality proposal was that it ran counter to the assumptions underlying the Franco-British Entente. Despite this limitation, Britain offered to give assurances, in July 1910, that nothing in her agreements with any other Power was directed against Germany, and a similar agreement might be reached with Germany. On the naval side Grey now offered an exchange of information. In May 1911 Germany accepted it in principle, but insisted on a general political agreement. Bethmann expressed the view that the discussion of a naval agreement could lead to no practical result unless it formed part of a scheme for a general understanding and was based upon a conviction on the part, not only of the two governments but of public opinion in both countries, that neither country had any hostile or aggressive designs against the other. This cloudy formula caused irritation in Whitehall.

The irritation changed to anger when the Morocco Question once more became acute in the summer of 1911. A crumbling empire like China and Turkey, Morocco was bound to pose problems to the great powers. Owing to the anarchy in Morocco, the French sent an expedition to occupy Fez, the capital. Technically, the action was a violation of the terms of the Algeciras Treaty. Moreover this was interpreted by Germany as a sign that France intended to proclaim a protectorate as the British occupation of Egypt had begun in a similar way.

Instigated by the ebullient new Foreign Minister, Alfred von Kiderlen-Wachter, the German government, on July 1, 1911 sent *Panther*, a gunboat, to Agadir, on the pretext of looking after German interests, but ostensibly to frighten the French into compensation. This action was interpreted in the German press as 'the nightmares of reigning discontent being dispersed by the rays of the morning sun'. But contrary to Kiderlen's expectations, the French Government seemed reluctant to make any kind of territorial compensation. Henceforth, Kiderlen demanded that France cede all of the French Congo to Germany as compensation for its projected gains in Morocco.

Meanwhile Britain was resolved to thwart Germany at all costs. On July 21, the Chancellor of the Exchequer, Lloyd George stated publicly that Britain could not be treated as of no account in a question vitally affecting her interests. In the wake of that statement, everybody knew that Germany must either yield or fight. Despite the persuasion of Kiderlen that German prestige required that she should fight, the Emperor had no stomach for war. It may be that Germany was seeking to gain time that 'the war party in Germany had not yet gained complete ascendancy and that, in the opinion of their experts neither their military, their naval, nor their financial preparations had reached the stage of forwardness which would justify the invention of a *casus belli.*'[11] Kiderlen's policy was criticised in the Bundesrat and talk of war led to a sharp decline in the stock market. To add insult to injury, the French suspended short-term loans to Germany. In the end, an accord was reached in the second week of October 1911, and the final agreement signed on November 4, Germany agreed to the establishment of a French protectorate in Morocco on condition that the 'open door' was maintained; in return Germany obtained two large strips of French Congolese territory. The next year (1912) France formally declared Morocco a protectorate.

Agadir was more portentous than Algeciras and more critical than the Bosnian crisis. In the first place, it increased tension between Germany and the Entente Powers, accelerated the armaments race, and inculcated a belief in the ruling class that war was inevitable. Secondly, the French victory in Morocco galvanised the Italians moving into Tripoli. The Italian action touched off a war with Turkey which, in its turn, encouraged the Balkan states to join together to despoil Turkey of its European possessions. Finally, as a result of the setback in Morocco, Bethmann's ability began to be questioned. He was now regarded as a weakling who had allowed a 'new Olmutz to be imposed upon the country'. The contemporary situation was best described in the words of Moltke, the Chief of Staff, when he wrote to his wife in August 1911:

> If we creep out of this affair with our tails between our legs, if we cannot be aroused to an energetic set of demands which we are prepared to enforce by the sword, then I am doubtful about the future of the German Empire. And I will resign.

Moltke did not, of course, resign, but he and many other officers were determined that there must not be another climb-down like the one of 1911.

Meanwhile an attempt was made to bring about an Anglo-German accommodation. Both the German Chancellor, Bethmann-Hollweg, and the English Liberal Government of Asquith made efforts to achieve this. The key to improved relations was still the naval question and Bethmann came to believe that the British might be amenable to the suggestion of a mutual reduction in naval armament. In February 1912, the British Secretary of State for War, Lord Haldane, a man known for his sympathy for Germany, visited Berlin, to discuss a basis for an Anglo-German alliance. But the attempted rapprochement broke down, partly on the naval question, and partly because of the British refusal to give an assurance of neutrality in the case of a Franco-German war. So the Haldane Mission proved a fiasco. Having failed to arrive at a naval understanding with Germany, Britain concentrated her fleet in the North Sea and relied on France to protect the Mediterranean. In November 1912, Grey gave the French the assurance that if either Government had grave reason to expect an unprovoked attack by a third Power, or something that threatened the general peace, it should immediately discuss with the other whether both Governments should act together. In 1913, the new German Navy Bill became law. Anglo-German naval competition grew more tense. Winston Churchill, First Lord of the British Admiralty, proposed a 'naval holiday' which was rejected; in consequence, the British naval estimates went up by twenty-million pounds.

11. Oxford Earl of: *The Genesis of the War,* P. 95.

In October 1912, Europe was confronted with an extremely volatile situation in the Balkans. The four Balkan powers—Serbia, Montenegro, Bulgaria and Greece launched a concerted attack against Turkey. The two Great Powers who were interested in the Balkans were Austrtia and Russia. Austria was determined to prevent the acquisition by Serbia of access to the Adriatic. This raised the danger of Russian intervention who insisted that Serbia and Montenegro be granted such access. As Germany was Austria's ally, Lord Haldane, the British Minister of War, speaking on behalf of the Government, made it clear that, in the event of an Austrian invasion of Serbia, Britain could hardly remain a silent spectator. Haldane also added that the existing balance of forces in Europe should be maintained as it would not tolerate a defeat of France or the consolidation of all European power in the hands of a single state, *i.e.,* Germany. This warning infuriated William II who upbraided the British Government and declared that, in view of its attitude, Germany must declare war against France and Russia at once. Moltke, the Chief of Staff, was for war as soon as possible. But Bethmann Hollweg, the German Chancellor, took the opposite view and tried to solve the tangled Balkan situation 'through compromise with England without undermining the firmness of our alliance with Austria'. He also warned Berchtold, the Austrian Foreign Minister, against resorting to war. Grey and Bethmann Hollweg sponsored the London Conference which solved the Adriatic problem by creating an independent Albania and compensating Serbia with territory in interior. Peace was restored in May 1913 and lasted exactly one month. Although Serbia was the chief beneficiary of the new conflict and Austria's Bulgarian ally the victim, Bethmann restrained Austria from intervening by force of arms.

Bethmann's hope was that the fragile international balance could be maintained by striving for working relationship with Britain. His attitude was reciprocated by Grey who preserved in a pacific attitude towards Germany. In fact, during the winter of 1913 and the first half of 1914, negotiations took place with Germany over the Portuguese colonies and also over the Baghdad railway, which resulted in a considerable measure of agreement. Bethmann wrote in June 1914: 'If we both act together as guarantees of European peace ... war will be avoided'.

The fruitful cooperation, however, was not destined to endure. Bethmann was aware that the Balkan wars had left all of South-Eastern Europe in a state of unrelieved tension. The Austrians were critical of Germany's failure to support them. In the same way, the Russians blamed the British for the creation of Albania, which blocked Serbia from the sea; they were also highly critical of France for having done nothing to defeat this arrangement. Britain was haunted by the fear that 'Russia would become tired of us and strike a bargain with Germany'. Russian dissatisfaction had a sensible effect both in London and Prussia, and both powers tried to assure Russia that it could count on their future assistance.

Meanwhile, Germany's relations with Russia had become embittered in 1913 because of Russian fears for the control of the Straits. In April 1913 Turkey had appealed to Germany for a good officer to reorganise her army. Germany was anxious to develop her influence in Turkey. In October 1913, a German officer, Liman von Sanders, was put in charge of the Turkish army with headquarters at Constantinople. Russia protested and appealed to Britain and France. Sazanov, the Russian foreign minister, toyed with the idea of seizing the Straits by force but was held back. The Germans on their side shrank from the conflict and a face-saving compromise was arranged. Though the immediate crisis was over, the underlying conflict remained. 'In a sense, Constantinople was the key point in the conflicting ambitions of Russia and Germany.' In February 1914, Russia decided that the time had come to gain command of both Bosphorus and Dardanelles by force. In June 1914 a legislation was enacted for the strengthening of the Black Sea Fleet. No wonder the Emperor, William II remarked: 'Russo-Prussian relations are once for all dead, we have become enemies'. Bethmann remarked in the beginning of July, 1914: 'The future belongs to Russia. It grows and hangs upon us ever more heavily like a nightmare.'

Serbia also occupied a key position in the clash between Pan-Germanism and Pan-Slavism. Pan-Serb agitation was at boiling-point during 1913 and 1914. A feverish agitation ran through Serbia, Bosnia, Dalmatia, Croatia. Serbia was a land-locked country and her only practicable outlet lay through Austria-Hungary. This gave her powerful neighbour a lever for extorting economic concessions which were hardly to Serbia's interests. 'The Serbian peasantry was convinced that Austria-Hungary stood in the way of their prosperity and they came to have for the Dual Monarchy feelings of the most bitter hatred.'

Berchtold, the Foreign Minister of Austria-Hungary and Tisza, the Hungarian Premier, were well aware of the agitation. The defection of Rumania from Austrio-German alliance actuated both men to take action against Serbia. During April and May 1914 they moved steadily in this direction. The German Chief of the Staff, Conrad, concurred in their views and observed that a war with Serbia, though a desperate hazard in 1914, must be undertaken as there was no alternative. But Francis Ferdinand, the Emperor of Austria-Hungary, instead of concurring in Conard's views of an immediate attack on Serbia, agreed to a diplomatic offensive against Serbia. The object was to isolate Serbia and to win back Rumania. It was hoped to include Greece and Turkey in the new group, thereby countering the Russians in the Balkans. After many revisions, Berchtold had, on June 24, finished a memorandum and was about to forward it to Germany for approval when an unexpected event happened on June 18, 1914. This was the murder of Francis Ferdinand, nephew of the Emperor of Austria and heir to the throne and his wife at Sarajevo, a Bosnian town.

The assassination was the act of a young Serbian patriot named Gavrilo Princip. Vienna accused the Serbian Government of complicity in the plot, though 'It has not been proved that the Serbian Government had any share in the plot... To this extent Austria-Hungary must bear the responsibility for war in 1914.'[12]

The murder at Sarajevo did not automatically unleash the First World War. Nearly four weeks elapsed before Austria-Hungary presented her ultimatum to Serbia. The period saw a struggle between Berchtold, who was prepared to stake all, and Tisza made it clear that a war in Serbia was impossible while Rumania was a likely enemy. Despite Tisza's protest, official opinion in favour of war was general; but there must be no mistake about German cooperation. On July 5, 1914, Berchtold sent his emissary, Count Hoyos, to Berlin with a letter from Francis Joseph in which he told William II that Serbia must be eliminated. But the Austrian Government wished, before it acted, to be assured of German support. In the famous Council of War summoned by William II on July 5, 1914 it was decided that Austria should be encouraged to go ahead, with the assurance that Germany would come to its aid in the event of Russian intervention. On the following morning Bethmann gave the 'blank cheque' to Szogyeny, the Austrian ambassador, declaring that the Austrian government could count firmly on German support as ally and friend, whatever its decision might be. Bethmann clarified that the policy of supporting Austria arose out of sheer necessity: 'If we urge them ahead, then they will say we pushed them in; if we dissuade them, then it will become a matter of our leaving them in the lurch. Then they will turn to the Western Powers, whose arms are wide open, and we will lose our last ally, such as it is.'

A meeting of the ministerial Council in Vienna on July 7 became the scene of a conflict between Berchtold and Tisza. Berchtold was obliged to disavow Hoyos and his request for support from Berlin. Finally, Tisza won and decided to send an ultimatum to Serbia, hoping that Serbia would yield to it. He did so because Germany had made it clear that unless Austria now acted against Serbia, she would reconsider the attitude to the alliance. The true motive of German haste is clear. She wanted a local war between Austria-Hungary and Serbia in order to crush Serbia, humiliate Russia, irritate France and disrupt the Triple Entente.

Austria had originally decided to present the ultimatum on July 19, but delayed it until July 23

12. Ramm Agatha: *Europe in the Twentieth Century, 1905-70,* P. 51.

which was presented to Serbia with a time-limit of 48 hours. Lord Grey was shocked when he saw the ultimatum and remarked that he had never before seen 'a document of so formidable a character'. The Russian Foreign Minister, Sazanov, was aghast and exclaimed to the Austrian ambassador: 'This means a European war. You are setting Europe alight.'

On the day Serbia received the ultimatum, Sazanov warned the German Ambassador that 'if Austria swallows Serbia we will make war on her'. Thus encouraged, Serbia decided not to accept the ultimatum in full. Sending in her reply on July 25, she accepted outright about half the demands. Moreover, she also offered to submit the whole matter to the Hague Tribunal or to a Conference of the Powers. Kaiser rightly called this 'a brilliant achievement for a time limit of only 48 hours. A great moral success for Vienna; but with it all reason for war is gone.' The German Government rejected the conference proposal on the ground that for Austria it would amount to 'a court of arbitration'.

It has been held that the German Government were really against heeding the proposals for mediation. She apprehended that every delay in the beginning of war would invite foreign powers. The Austrians were also determined on war. Strengthened by the German support, Austria-Hungary declared war on Serbia on July 28. Even at the last moment Britain tried to persuade Germany to restrain Austria-Hungary from a foolhardly policy. Bethmann, therefore, asked Berchtold to moderate his further demands on Serbia and to make a conciliatory approach to Russia. Grey also suggested mediation.

On July 29, Russia ordered mobilisation against Austria-Hungary. The same day Germany warned Sazanov that 'further continuation of Russian mobilisation would force us to mobilise also'. Undeterred by this threat, Russia ordered general mobilisation along the German frontier on July 30. The French made a last-minute plea for caution and suggested that Russia should not immediately proceed to any measure which might offer Germany a pretext for a total or partial mobilisation of her forces. The German Government immediately declared a state of war emergency on July 31, and sent an ultimatum to St. Petersburg demanding cessation of mobilisation within twelve hours under threat of war. Russia failed to reply and a declaration of war followed on August 1. 'It was primarily Russia's general mobilisation made when Germany was trying to bring Austria to a settlement, which precipitated the final catastrophe causing Germany to mobilise and declare war.'

On August 1, Germany sent an ultimatum to France demanding answer in eighteen hours as to whether France would be neutral in a Russo-German war. Germany proposed to occupy Toul and Verdun, even if France remained neutral. Viviani, the French premier, merely replied: 'France will act in accordance with her interests'. The Germans had no justifiable cause for war against France. They, therefore, trumped up preposterous charges against France and declared war on August 3, 1914.

Britain had been trying to evolve a formula that would compose the Austro-Serb quarrel ever since the Austrian ultimatum. Grey warned the Germans not to count on British neutrality; equally he warned the French and Russians not to count on her support. On July 27 Lloyd George said: 'there could be no question of our taking part in any war in the first instance'. All that Grey had done was to warn Germany on August 2 that naval operations against France in the Channel would not be permitted. As the Germans had no plans for offensive naval operations against France this need have caused no trouble. But when, on August 3, Germany sent an ultimatum to Belgium, demanding free passage to invade France, Britain responded on the following day demanding that Belgian neutrality be respected. But German troops had already crossed the frontier and from midnight on August 4, Britain and Germany were at war. In a speech in the House of Commons on August 6, Asquith said:

> If I am asked what we are fighting for, I can reply in two sentences. In the first place, we are fighting to fulfil a solemn international obligation... Secondly, we are fighting to vindicate the principle that small nationalities are not to be crushed, in definance of international good faith, by the arbitrary will of a strong and overmastering Power.

Responsibility of Germany for World War I

The First World War was the unavoidable outcome of the basic instability of two states, Austria-Hungary and the Turkish Empire. It was also the unavoidable outcome of the two armed camps into which Europe was divided since 1907. The political situation was full of menacing possibilities. There were piling up of armaments by land and sea, and Germany's naval ambitions, which deeply affected British sentiments; there was the French desire for the recovery of Alsace-Lorraine, there was the periodical recrudescences, of embarrassing incidents like that of Morocco; there was continuous clash of interests of Austria and Russia in the Balkans, the restlessness of the Balkans themselves and the 'cloud of uncertainty that hung over the future of Turkey'. There were the chauvinists of all nations ready to light the fuel that was heaped up. Speaking of the years that preceded the Great War, Lord Oxford remarked: 'We were often conscious that we were skating on the thinnest of ice, and the peace of Europe was at the mercy of a chapter of unforeseen and unforseeable accidents'. Colonel House, the confidential adviser of the American President, Woodrow Wilson, who was on a peace mission to Europe in May 1914, found the atmosphere charged with electricity ready to ignite at any time.

The German military plans played a vital part. The German generals wanted a decisive victory for countering the 'encirclement'. Schlieffen, who died in 1913, had made it clear that any war in Europe must be a general war; it could not be localised; and he also believed that, once Germany began to mobilise, war was inevitable. The German diplomats had been told for years that only the Schlieffen Plan could save Germany. 'In this sense a dead man had the deepest responsibility of all for the European war.' In 1914, German security on the continent was at stake. She was divided from France by Alsace-Lorraine, divided from Russia by her Turkish policy. The Schlieffen Plan assumed that the war on two fronts—the French and the Russian—could be faced and could be won, after 1909, by concentrating on the West, while Austria-Hungary held Russia. War would give Germany ascendancy on the continent and strengthen her security.

Britain went to war because her survival depended on the survival of France. 'That Britain went to war only because Germany violated the neutrality of Belgium is untrue. That without the violation of Belgian neutrality Grey would have been unable to carry Parliament into war may be true. Britain went to war because her security would be destroyed if France was defeated.'

The war of 1914 could not have been averted. The Great Powers could have avoided war only by agreeing that Germany should become the dominant power of the Continent. None of these Powers decided on war. 'The three men who made the decisions—even if they too were the victims of circumstances—were Berchtold, Bethmann Hollweg, and the dead man Schlieffen.'[13] On August 4, when Britain entered the war, the British Foreign Secretary, Lord Grey, spoke words that have become classic. 'The lamps are going out all over Europe; we shall not see them lit again in our lifetime.'

Moral and Material Progress

During the period from 1871 to 1914, Germany was on the high road to economic transformation which owed not a little to her victory over France. The acquisition of Alsace-Lorraine gave a great fillip to Germany's industrial development. Germany soon possessed the most powerful iron and steel industry in Europe which enabled her to increase its domestic rail network, to build one of the greatest merchant fleets in the world, to expand the machine industry and to build up the armament industry with which the name of Krupp of Essen has been associated.

Germany's electrical and chemical industries were pioneers in the field. In 1847 Werner von Siemens founded the Berlin firm of Siemens and Halske which gave Germany its first telegraph net, its first electric railway, and its extensive trolley system. The expansion of German electric industry was due to Emil Rathenau, who secured the German rights to Thomas Edison's electric lamps in 1881. Simultaneously, the rapid strides

13. Taylor, A. J. P.: *Europe: Grandeur and Decline.* P. 189.

in the chemical industries were marked by the increased production of potash, sulphuric acid, potassium salts, ammonia, synthetic dyes, photographic supplies and pharmaceuticals, which made the name Bayer, Agfa and Farben as well known as Krupp.

German economy witnessed a spectacular development when her exports increased fourfold between 1871 and 1914. Her agricultural production increased by as much as fifty per cent in some crops, thanks to new techniques of cultivation and the agricultural chemistry introduced by Justus Liebig.

The vigour of the economy was matched by the unprecedented intellectual and artistic activity of Germany in these years. The natural and experimental sciences were enriched by the pioneering researches in chemistry of August Kekule, the invention of the opthalmoscope by Ludwig Helmholtz and the spectroscope by Gustev Robert Kirchhoff, the discovery of X-ray by Willhelm Konrad Roentgen, the formulation of the quantum theory by Max Planck, Einstein's first studies on relativity, the significant medical researches of Robert Koch (tuberculosis, cholera), Paul Ehrlich (syphilis) and Rudolf Virchow (pathology).

Even in the age of materialism, the humanistic tradition remained strong. Theodore Mommsen stoutly defended the University's freedom from domination by the State whose primary function was to help the students in the cultivation of the whole person. Defending academic freedom Mommsen wrote in 1901:

> There goes through German university circles a feeling of degradation. Our life impulse is uninhibited enquiry ... it should discover ... which logically and historically seems right to the conscientious researcher—in a word, the truth. Upon loyalty to the truth depends our self-respect, our professional honour, and our influence upon youth ... Who lays his hand on that puts an axe to the mighty tree in whose shade and protection we live and whose fruits benefit the world.

The late nineteenth century was a golden age of humanistic scholarship. In philosophy Eduard von Hartman's 'philosophy of the unconscious' appealed to an age that had turned away from Hegelian rationalism. Kuno Fischer, with Hermann Cohen and H. Rickert, revived Kantianism in the 1870s. Wilhelm Windelband's study marked a decisive breaking away from the materialism, mechanism and naturalism. In the historical sciences, the critical method became the hallmark, thanks to the influence of Leopold von Ranke.The period saw the publication of such monuments of historical scholarship as Wilhelm Hauck's *German Church History,* Eduard Meyer's *History of Antiquity,* the last volume of Theodore Mommsen's *History of Rome* and Ranke's unfinished *Universal History.* In Ranke's view of history, power and the state played a major role. The unification movement strengthened this tendency. This history of the modern period was dominated by political historians. Foremost among them were Heinrich von Sybel, author of multi-volume *Founding of the German Empire by William I* and Heinrich von Trietschke, author of *German History.* A new dimension was given to history by Wilhelm Dilthey who asked historians to develop analytical tools to investigate the world of ideas. The period was also adorned by sociologists like Ferdinand Tonnies, George Simmel and Max Weber, and economists like Adolf Wagner, Lujo Brentano and Werner Sombart.

The vigorous intellectual atmosphere was reflected in the growing prosperity of the city of Berlin which became the foyer of cultural activities. Berlin became the most important musical centre of Europe. The names of Johannes Brahms and Richard Strauss had been immortalised in the field of music. In the field of literature, the works of Spielhagen, Fontane and Sudermann won acclaim, while, in the theatre, a new era was inauguarated with the founding of *Freie Buhne* ('free stage'). Drama became a potent weapon of social criticism. Gerhart Hauptmann's *Vor Sonnenaufgang* (1889) shocked audiences when it turned to unconventional themes. In the field of novel, the period was illustrated by Theodore Fontane, the first German novelist since Goethe to enjoy a European reputation.

The 1890s saw the beginnings of Impressionism in Germany, which was reflected not only in the novels but also in the poems of Richard Dehmel, Stefan George, Richard von Schaukal, and Rainer Maria Rilke. Thier poems were apolitical, subordinating reality to feeling of momentary moods and vague perceptions.

Apart from Berlin, German cultural life was centred in other urban centres—Hamburg, Leipzig, Cologne, Frankfurt, Munich. Yet, beneath the glittering prosperity there lay misery, greed and lust for power. Stefan George, one of the greatest German poets, called Berlin 'the cold city of military and commercial serfs'. Friedrich Nietzsche wrote disdainfully of the culture of the great cities. Unimpressed by Germany's economic prosperity, Nietzsche exposed the mediocrity, vulgarity, materialism, love of power. 'Power', he wrote in the *Twilight of the Idols* (1889), 'makes stupid'. Conrad Alberti was more pungent in his novel *The Old and the Young* (1888). 'What we need,' he wrote: 'is a new Sedan in which we are the defeated ones, in order to be out of this stinking bed on which the stockbrokers and drill sergeants have thrown us.'

CHAPTER 27

AUSTRIA-HUNGARY (1867-1945)

In the compromise or Ausgleich of 1867 there were matters of concern to the whole empire—foreign affairs, war and finance. These were conducted by a joint ministry appointed by the monarch which met alternately in Vienna and Budapest. Austria contributed 70 per cent and Hungary 30 per cent to meet the common expenditures. The internal affairs of Austria and Hungary were in the hands of autonomous and distinct goverments.

The seventeen provinces which made up the province of Austria had individual Diets; they managed local affairs and were represented in the imperial parliament in Vienna. The parliament had two chambers—an upper one consisting of aristocrats, churchmen appointed by the Emperor and a lower house whose members were originally selected by the local diets but after 1873 the weightage was given to men of property and education. Parliament had been authorised to approve or reject any bill; the budget was discussed in the lower house, which also had the right to question and impeach ministers.

Ministers were appointed by the Emperor and the latter had the right to dismiss them. The Emperor had the right to dissolve or suspend the parliament. He could issue any decree when the parliament was not in session, which had to be approved by parliament. However, the Emperor preferred to work in collaboration with the legislature.

Throughout the first decade of its new existence, the destiny of Austria was guided by a strong Liberal Party. Like its German counterpart, this party stood for centralisation, constitutionalism and administrative efficiency and entertained prejudice against clerical influence. After 1867, when the country was beset with numerous problems, especially the financial difficulties caused by the crash of 1873, the Emperor found it expedient to curry favour with the Liberals. The effects of the collaboration were felt in various spheres; an improvement of judicial procedure, the relaxation of press laws, the abolition of laws restricting the rights of the Jews, and a series of laws calculated to promote economic growth of the state. Civil marriage was introduced and schools were freed from clerical control. In 1869 elementary education became free and compulsory for all children.

The most pressing problem of Austria was to satisfy the nationalistic aspirations of the non-German population of Austria, like the Poles of Galicia, the Serbs and Slovenes in the south and the Czechs of Bohemia. The ten million Germans of Austria constituted little more than one-third of the whole population. Emperor Francis Joseph was aware of the necessity of granting concessions to these nationalities but he was no less conscious of the need to maintain the ultimate authority of the central power. An auspicious beginning was made in 1871 by creating a special Austrian ministry for Galician affairs; Polish was recognised as the language of administration and secondary schools.

Austria, however, found it difficult to woo the Czechs who had been demanding since 1868 a status similar to that of Hungary. The Czech problem assumed such a crucial position that in 1871 Francis Joseph promised to elevate Bohemia to an autonomous position and promised to go to Prague to be crowned as king of Bohemia. However, the Czech demand was resisted by the Austrian Germans voiced by Beust and the root and branch opposition of the Magyars, voiced by Andrassy. The Emperor capitulated to German and Hungarian objection and unleashed a repressive policy, muzzling the press and restricting public meetings. The Czechs sulked and boycotted not only the imperial parliament *(Reichsrat)* but also the Diets. On top of this there came the financial crash of 1873.

To balance the losses of 1859 and 1866, Austria carried out a forward policy in foreign affairs. Andrassy, the Foreign Minister, was determined that Austria-Hungary must assert herself as the natural protector of the west Balkan peoples. Austria had dominated the external trade of European Turkey before the Crimean War and had lost much of her position to the British after it. The influential director of the commercial section of the Austrian Foreign Office, Baron Schwegel, was aware of the need and possibility of opening up of trade-routes from the north, and these were to be given definite shape during the eastern crisis of 1875-79. The main aim was to complete the great Orient Railway from Vienna to Constantinople and occupation of Bosnia.

Andrassy had the satisfaction when in 1878, Bosnia, Herzegovina came into Austria-Hungary's possession mainly due to Russia's exertions at the Congress of Berlin. But the occupation sharpened all political and strategical issues in the Balkan peninsula. The occupation was unsatisfying to those who wanted more of Turkish territory. It also disappointed the Emperor and the army leaders who felt that Andrassy had thrown away 'a heaven-sent opportunity not only to annex Bosnia-Herzegovina outright, but to dominate, and even possibly annex, the western Balkans as far as Salonika.'

Discontent was brewing in Austria-Hungary. The Liberals expressed violent alarm at the influx of two million Slavs and at the party's virtual exclusion from a voice in foreign policy. In Hungary there was a basic fear of the influx of Slavs. There was a genuine concern at any change in the political *status quo* which would imperil the relative strength of Hungary in imperial affairs.

Emperor Francis Joseph and Andrassy felt that they could dispense with the Liberal support and at the general election in June 1879 the party was defeated. Francis Joseph appointed Count Edward Taaffe, a loyal and accommodating person with great political gifts, premier, who remained in the post from 1879 to 1893. Taaffe created a political combination known as the Iron Ring which was composed of clericals, German conservatives, Slavs, Poles and Czechs. The Taaffe Government was called by one Italian deputy a *luogo di traffico* (a place for making deals) as the ill-assorted partners were kept in humour by concessions to their special inerests.

Throughout the 1880s, Taaffe succeeded in keeping together a bloc of supporters. In Galicia, the Poles were permitted to win special privileges over the Ruthenians; and in Carniola, the Slovenes were given free rein to the detriment of other nationalities. But the most crucial issue was the intransigence of the Czechs, and Taaffe succeeded in mollifying them and bringing the Czech deputies to the support of his ministry. The Czech language was given equality with German in the public affairs of Bohemia and Moravia. A national Czech university was founded in Prague in 1881. Some secondary Czech schools were established and the Czechs given some control in the state administration. In the meantime the Austrian state finances were put in order. The state resumed control of the railways. But all the empire's fundamental problems remained as beneath the apparent tranquillity the simmering irreconcilable nationalistic claims defied solutions.

Taaffe's policy of appeasement aroused the opposition of the Austrian Germans. It looked to Bismarck for assistance and emphasised its own exclusiveness which was fed by a demagogic leader, Schonerer. A new pan-German movement, led by Georg von Schonerer, preached the racial superiority of the Germans and called for a union of Austria's German provinces with the Reich. On the other hand, the moderate Czechs who had cooperated with Taaffe were supplanted by the rising young Czech party which gained control of the Diet of Bohemia in 1889. The Young Czech violently denounced Austria and one of their leaders, Edward Gregr, made no secret of his feeling in his diatribe in the imperial parliament in 1891:

> Bohemia is being sucked dry by Austria... The majority of the Czech population is utterly wretched in the midst of this alien empire ... Their nationality is oppressed and persecuted in this Austrian

> state, which is a state of violence and tyranny to all Slav races. The Bohemian people are made to hate this state—I repeat—hate this state, and mark my words, the day of reckoning will come.

The Slav people also grew restive and a movement of Pan-Slavism began which demanded a federation of Slavic peoples free from Austro-Hungarian control. It looked to Russia for assistance as the Russian Pan-Slav theorists like R. A. Fadeyev and N. Y. Danilevsky were vocal in future emancipation of the Slavs. The origin of Pan-Slavism lay in the nature of the constitution of the Dual Monarchy. As the great Czech leader, Palacky, had said in 1865:

> The day that Dualism is proclaimed will become, with irresistible natural necessity, the birthday of Pan-Slavism in its least gladdening form. The leaders of Dualism will be its sponsors. The result can be imagined. We Slavs will await it with justified pain, yet without fear. Before Austria was, we were, and after Austria we shall also be.

The growing opposition to Taaffe's policy was increased when he proposed universal suffrage. He thought that the enfranchising of the masses would sweep away the narrow issues that impeded the growth of the state. But the Emperor was not ready for the leap. Taaffe was, therefore, dismissed in 1893. Parliamentary confusion followed. The Emperor called to office Badeni, the Polish Governor of Galicia, who carried an electoral reform to satisfy the radicals. In 1897 Badeni decreed that Czech and German should be the languages for state service in Bohemia which assured a near-monopoly of administrative employment to the Czechs. The result was an outburst of German rioting which led the Emperor to dismiss Badeni. Non-parliamentary government began. Between 1897 and 1904 the special powers of legislation were used 97 times.

In the 1880s the Liberal Party was weakened by the rise of the Christian Socialist Party. This was a Catholic Party, organised by Karl Lueger, a Viennese lawyer. Appealing particularly to the urban petty bourgeoisie, it placed great emphasis upon democracy, social reform, and justice to subject nationalities. The party won adherents of the lower middle class and the peasantry and also of the Poles and the Czechs. Several enactments were made to better the lot of workmen. Thus in 1884-85, factories and mines were regulated; Sunday labour was abolished; and the employment of women and children was limited. In 1887-88, trade unions were legalised; accident and sickness insurance to workers, similar to Germay's, was adopted. Karl Lueger became Mayor of Vienna in 1897, a post which he retained till his death in 1907. He utilised his position to make the capital city a leading exemplar of municipal socialism that equalled those of Joseph Chamberlain in Birmingham.

The mass support of Christian Socialism owed in a large measure to its policy of anti-Semitism. One of the first effects of industrialism in Austria was the ruin of a number of small industrial concerns and a general depression among the independent artisan class. It was alleged that this economic dislocation was due to the influence of the Jews who played an important role in financing Austrian industry. Karl Lueger identified himself so closely with anti-Jewish feeling that in 1895, when he was tipped off as Mayor, the Liberal *Neue Freie Presse* lamented that, if this happens, 'Vienna will be the only great city in the world whose administration is in the hands of anti-Semitic fanatics.'

Incidentally, Lueger's success inspired two men who were to attain eminence. The first was Theodor Herzl, the greatest Jewish statesman who, in 1895, wrote a pamphlet in which he highlighted the Jewish problem as a universal one and initiated the programme soon to be called Zionism by proposing the reestablishment of the Jewish people as an independent nation on its own soil. The second was a young man from Linz, Adolf Hitler, whose obsession with the Jewish question was proverbial.

After the suffrage reform of 1907, the influence of the Christian Socialist Party waned and that of Social Democratic Party increased. Marxist in inspiration, the Socialist Party maintained close collaborations with the socialist parties in neighbouring countries. In the general election of 1907, the Social Democrats increased their strength in the lower chamber of Parliament from 11 to 87. The new parliament *Reichsrath* was still biased against some nationalities, but Ruthenians, Polish radicals, Czechs and Slovenes all won more seats. The two largest parties in the new parliament were the Social Democrats and the Christian Socialists.

The problems of Austria-Hungary assumed new dimension owing to her relations with the lesser states of south-eastern Europe, with the Turkish Empire, and with imperial Russia. The Habsburg Empire was drawn into this area by strategic and economic considerations. Its dependence upon the Danube as a trade route was menaced by Serbia, Bulgaria, and Rumania. In addition, her access to the sea depended upon its continued possession of the Istrian Peninsula at the head of the Adriatic, with its three important ports, Trieste, Pula, and Fiume (now Ryeka), and of the Dalmatian Coast with its ancient port of Regusa (now Dubrovnik). But these possessions became objects of Serbia where militant nationalism was actuated by the desire of building up of a united Yugoslavia of Serbs, Croats, and Slovenes.

Until 1903, there was a school of thought in Austria that envisaged a union of all the Serbs and Croats in Serbia, Montenegro, Dalmatia, Istria, Bosnia, Herzegovina and the Hungarian province of Croatia-Slavonia in a Yugoslav state within the Habsburg monarchy, a state analogous to that of Austria-Hungary. These 'trialists' thought that this would not only smother growing nationalism in Serbia but would give Austria the dominance of the western Balkans. This plan was bitterly opposed by the Magyars and by Serbian chauvinism.

The Habsburg Empire was still regarded as a great power. It had the firm alliance and backing of the powerful German Empire. For Germany was no less concerned than Austria-Hungary with the Balkans. Serbia's dependable ally was Russia, who was united with the sentimental tie of Pan-Slavism and had a common interest in weakening both the Ottoman and the Habsburg Empires.

The Dual Monarchy viewed with alarm the aggressive Serbian nationalism. But the feud between Austria and Serbia rested on fundamental factors. The chief clue to the feud was to be found more in geography than in history. Serbia was a land-locked country and her only practicable outlet lay through Austria-Hungary. This gave her powerful neighbour a lever for extorting economic concessions much to the detriment of Serbia's interest. Serbia's chief commodity was pigs which she exported to Austria-Hungary. When Serbia tried to explore other foreign markets, she at once encountered resistance from Austria-Hungary. 'The Serbian peasantry was convinced that Austria-Hungary stood in the way of their prosperity and they came to have for the (Dual) Monarchy feelings of the most bitter hatred.'

In 1906 a 'Pig War' began over the renegotiation of tariff agreements between Serbia and the Monarchy; Serbian agricultural produce was excluded and pressure was brought to bear upon the Serbs to buy arms from the Austrian Skoda factory. The tariff war was not ended until 1908 when attention was deflected to attempts of south Slav subjects of the Dual Monarchy to make common cause with their fellow-Slavs in Serbia. Unfortunately the statesmen of Austria-Hungary, especially the Magyars, magnified the danger and detected in Serbia a 'Piedmont of the South Slavs.'

This was the background of the Austrian annexation of Bosnia and Herzegovina in October 1908, the two Serb-speaking provinces which she had merely administered under an international mandate. The Austrian Foreign Minister, Aehrenthal, regarded Serbia 'a nest of revolution', which he was determined to snuff out. To Serbia the annexation was a bitter blow as it annihilated her prospect of reaching the Adriatic. Serbian nationalism was also outraged when two million Serbs and Croats of Bosnia and Herzegovina were now united under the Dual Monarchy.

Swept by a wave of popular indignation, Serbia immediately assumed a warlike attitude. She ordered mobilisation of her forces and summoned her parliament which voted war credits. Austria-Hungary strengthened her forces in Bosnia and Dalmatia. Serbia was encouraged by Russia which began mobilising its army. Whereupon Germany intervened in support of Austria-Hungary and sent a peremptory ultimatum to Russia to cancel its mobilisation.

Russia was in no position to risk war into the combined armies of the Austrian and German Empires. She persuaded Serbia and Montenegro to abandon their claims (on Bosnia and Herzegovina) in the interest of European peace. Early in March 1909 Serbia agreed to refer the case to the arbitration of the European powers and disclaimed hostility to Austria-Hungary. Unfortunately Aehrenthal vitiated the atmosphere by making a new diplomatic offensive to gain recognition of the annexation by the Powers. He declared the Serbian note unsatisfactory and created tension by ordering troop movements. However, Germany put pressure on Austria-Hungary and the whole crisis blew over. Eventually the annexation was recognised by all the Powers including Russia. The war party in Serbia had received a great blow. King Peter of Serbia had to admit that her rights were not infringed by the annexation. He also agreed to reduce her army, to abstain from further agitation, and to promise to live with Austria-Hungary as a good neighbour.

The relations of Austria-Hungary and Serbia were destined to influence the future course of events. In 1909 two notorious incidents occurred. The first was the trial at Zagreb of Serbo-Croat leaders accused of treason against Austria-Hungary. Convicted on forged evidence, they were acquitted on appeal. The next was a libel action brought by a number of Serbo-Croat politicians against the historian Professor Friedjung for an anti-Serb article. The documents, like the Zagreb trial, turned out to be forged. These trials served to emphasise the cause of Yugoslav unity and Habsburg trickery. The myth of Pan-Serbian conspiracy became a reality. A feverish agitation ran through Serbia, Bosnia, Dalmatia, Croatia. Hundreds of students dreamed of the days when Yugoslavia should be free. In 1910 a student, while trying to assassinate the Governor of Bosnia, committed suicide. He left a note, 'I leave it to Serbdom to aveng me' which inflamed the passions of the Serbians. This incident was glorified in a pamphlet which had a large circulation.

In the First Balkan War, Serbia had enough cause of hatred against Austria-Hungary. Primarily it was due to the threats of Austria-Hungary and Germany. Serbia had to relinquish various Adriatic ports it conquered from the Turks and to forego any outlet to the sea. But the war left her doubled in size and inflamed her pride. When the Russian Foreign Minister, Izvolski, was counselling moderation before the Second Balkan War, he said, 'Serbia's promised land lies in Austria-Hungary…Time is working for Serbia and for the destruction of her enemies, who already show clear signs of disintegration.' Serbia now became more determined to avenge itself on Austria-Hungary. Its Prime Minister Nicholas Pasic remarked: 'the first round is won, now we must prepare for the second, against Austria.'

In this tense atmosphere, terrorist organisations grew and began to carry out attacks on Habsburg officials. In 1911 was founded the most famous terrorist organisation, the Black Hand. It marked the beginning of an intense phase of Serbian terrorism. In 1912 a student-demonstration at Zagreb ended in bloodshed and the Ban or Governor of Croatia twice survived attempts on his life. Count Berchtold, successor of Aehrenthal (who had died in 1912), planned to launch an attack upon Serbia during the Second Balkan War. But as Russia was certain to come to Serbia's aid, he felt himself obliged to consult his allies, Germany and Italy, before taking such a drastic step. The response was not heartening. 'Should she (Austria-Hungary) try to do this,' warned Bethmann-Hollweg, 'it would mean a European War.' The Italian foreign minister later remarked to an Austrian diplomat, 'we shall hold you back by the coattails if necessary.'

The Balkan Wars opened a new stage and Austria felt that the integrity of the Empire was at stake. The secret societies with headquarters at Belgrade spread the gospel of revolutionary Pan-Serbism to the millions of Yugoslavs in the Dual Monarchy. In January 1913 two young Bosnians planned to murder their Governor. In March 1914 attempts were made at Zagreb to murder a Ban and an Austrian Archduke which were foiled. These attempts were due partly to propaganda, partly to terrorist organisations. But they were mostly the outbursts of emotions fed by new ideas. 'Thoughts burst forth, burning and irrepressible as lava.' The whole educational life of Bosnia, Croatia and Dalmatia was a seething mass of discontent inflamed by the students.

Berchtold, the Foreign Minister of Austria-Hungary, and Tisza, the Hungarian Premier, were not blind to potential threats. They felt that it could not go on for ever. But Istavan Tisza was not an impetuous man and moved cautiously. He was aware of the difficulties Hungary would have to encounter in case of a war that Berchtold dreamed of. But the defection of Rumania goaded both men to take action against Serbia. During April and May 1914 events moved rapidly in this direction. Conrad, Chief of the General Staff, advocated this policy as he felt that the Serbs were only amenable to force. He summed up his views in his own characteristic style that war with Serbia would have been a safe game in 1909, that a similar war in 1913 was a game which still offered chances, that in 1914, though a desperate hazard, it must be undertaken as there was no alternative. The Emperor Francis Joseph, on the other hand, agreed to a diplomatic offensive against Serbia and recommended it to inform Rumania of it. Serbia would thus be isolated, and Russia effectively countered in the Balkans. After many revisions a memorandum was prepared. On June 24, when it was about to be forwarded to Germany for approval, an event happened which altered the whole situation. On June 28, 1914, a young Serbian patriot, named Gavrilo Princip, killed the Austrian heir apparent, Archduke Francis Ferdinand and his wife at the Bosnian town of Serajevo.

The assassination was not a private act. But it was later proved that Princip and his fellow assassins were the tools of a colonel Dragutin Dimitrijevic, Chief of the Intelligence Staff and the moving spirit in the patriotic Black Hand Society. But there was no evidence of complicity of the Serbian Government in the assassination, as had been vouchsafed by the Chief Austro-Hungarian investigator. As reported by him that there was 'nothing to prove or even to cause suspicion of the Serbian Government's cognizance of the steps leading to the crime.' However, Vienna had the excuse it had long wanted for action against Belgrade.

The four weeks (June 28-July 23, 1914) saw a period of hectic activity between Berchtold, the Hungarian premier, Count Stephen Tisza, the Emperor Francis Joseph, and Kaiser William II. Berchtold was prepared to stake all for the war to which Tisza did not subscribe as the latter counselled moderation. However, Berchtold told Tisza that William II would stand behind any firm decision of Austria-Hungary. The hesitant and aged Emperor Francis Joseph was persuaded to sign a secret despatch to be forwarded to the German Emperor William II. The communication read:

> The crime against my nephew is the direct consequence of the agitation carried on by Russian and Serbian Pan-Slavists, whose sole aim is to weaken the Triple Alliance and shatter my Empire ... Though it may be impossible to prove the complicity of the Serbian Government, there can be no doubt that its policy of uniting all Yugoslavs under the Serbian flag promotes such crimes, and that a continuation of this situation endangers my dynasty and my territories. The aim of my government must henceforth be to isolate and diminish Serbia.

On July 5-6, 1914, the Austrian ambassador to Germany and a special emissary (Count Hoyos) of Berchtold bearing the communication from the Emperor Francis Joseph conferred secretly with the German Emperor at Potsdam. Hoyos returned to Vienna with an assurance of Germany's unqualified support of Austria in any action it might take against Serbia, even if such action involved war with Russia. But Hoyos was disavowed by Tschirschky, the German Ambassador in Vienna, who emphasised that the proposals Hoyos had made were not official. However, Germany confirmed her assurances of support. A meeting of the ministerial council in Vienna on July 7 witnessed a violent conflict between Berchtold and Tisza. Instead of peremptory attack on Serbia, Tisza advocated a diplomatic solution of the problem. He held out for delay and agreed that Serbia should be served with an ultimatum. Only July 19 the ultimatum was drawn up. By then Germany had lost patience. She threatened to withdraw if Austria-Hungary refused to take action against Serbia in the existing favourable circumstances. The German Emperor, William II, believed that it would be a limited Austro-Serbian war and that German threat would deter Russia from intervening. Even if Russia refused to remain neutral, Germany was prepared to fight both the Russian and their French allies.

While the Austrian Chief of Staff was planning the military campaign, Berchtold sent an ultimatum to Serbia on July 23, 1914. The ultimatum was so sweeping in its character that it would have deprived Serbia of independence. Serbia was asked unconditional acceptance of the ultimatum within fortyeight hours. Lord Grey was shocked and told the Austrian Ambassadar that he had never seen a 'document of so formidable a character.' Sazanov was aghast and cautioned the Austrian Ambassador, 'This means a European war. You are setting Europe alight.'

On July 25 the Serbian Government replied, accepting most of the terms excepting such as it would have compromised her sovereignty. But rightly sensing Austria's intentions, Serbia began to mobilize. Vienna was unmoved and declared war on July 28. So Berchtold lit the fuse when no one had time to extinguish it. The British Foreign Secretary, Sir Edward Grey spoke in anguish: 'The lamps are going out all over Europe; we shall not see them lit again in our lifetime.'

When Austria surrendered after the First World War, the doom of the Habsburgs was sounded. The Habsburg Empire had begun to disintegrate. The Monarchy made half-hearted attempts to satisfy the nationalist urge. On October 1, 1918, the Yugoslavs were offered national autonomy. The Social Democrats demanded a separate German-Austrian state on October 3, and three days later, a National Council of Serbs, Croats and Slovenes began to meet in Zagreb. On October 16, the Emperor-King Charles I published a manifesto promising to reorganise the monarchy on a federal basis. But it was too late for compromise and the collapse of the Habsburg Empire could not be staved off.

On October 18, Thomas Masaryk and Edward Benes, who had worked unremittingly for the cause of Czech independence, proclaimed the deposition of Charles of Habsburg as King of Bohemia and the creation of an independent Czechoslovakian republic. On October 29, the Croatian Diet announced the separation of the Kingdom of Croatia and Dalmatia from Hungary, thus paving the way for the fusion of these and other southern Slav provinces, including Bosnia-Herzegovina, with the Kingdom of Serbia, a month later. King Peter of Serbia assumed the kingship of the new Yugoslav kingdom with a ministry headed by the famous Serbian politician, Nicholas Pasic. The Poles of Austrian Galicia likewise seceded from the Habsburg Empire making it possible for the creation of an independent Poland. Simultaneously the national unification of Rumania was complete by her appropriation of Bessarabia from Russia, Transylvania from Hungary, and Bukovina from Austria.

Meanwhile Vienna witnessed a series of revolutions. On October 30, 1918, there occurred a series of demonstrations organised by workmen and students which threatened the existence of the monarchy. The Emperor Charles, being powerless to stem the tide, abdicated. The provisional government of the 'national German State of Austria' was constituted. On November 12, 1918, it proclaimed Austria a Republic. In the following February, a Constituent Assembly was elected by universal suffrage and eventually it adopted a democratic constitution.

The Treaty of St. Gemain, September 10, 1919, required Austria to recognise the independence of Czechoslovakia, Yugoslavia, Poland and Hungary. The treaty reduced Austria to a third of her old population of 26 millions. The Habsburg Empire, which had ruled over fifteen different races, was reduced to less than half of her former size. She was left an area and population smaller than Portugal's. Her new boundaries were confined to Upper and Lower Austria, Carinthia and Styria and the Tyrol without any access to the sea. She had to pay reparations to the Allies, and was forbidden to unite herself to Germany.

In 1920 the National Assembly met to draw up a constitution for the new Republic. It established a federal republic of eight small states, with a legislature similar to Germany's, and an executive like the French—a titular President elected for four years by the legislature and a ministry responsible to the legislature. In the beginning the government was carried on by a coalition of Social Democrats and Christian Socialists. Ignatius Seipel of Christian Socialists, was Chancellor of the Republic from 1922 to 1924 and again from 1926 to 1929. Despite their attachment to the Republic, the outlook of the two parties was different. The Christian Socialists were Catholic and chiefly rural whereas the Social Democrats were Marxian and urban. The former were jealous of provincial autonomy; the latter were eager to subordinate the interests of the countryside to affluent Vienna. To make matters worse, the Social Democrats had a left wing which became vociferous and critical of the government, while a right wing of the Christian Socialists was antagonistic to Marxian Socialists. Apart from the two parties, there were two types of Nationalists in Austria. The first was aristocratic aiming at a restoration of the Habsburg dynasty and an alliance with Germany. The second was embodied in a National Socialist (Nazi) party which subscribed to the entire programme of Hitler, including the fusion of Austria with a militant German Empire.

After the First World War, Austria had to pass through a period of economic bankruptcy. Her trade was ruined; her debts were increased and her people starving. The League of Nations tried to restore the economic health of the country by appointing a representative to supervise its finances. A loan was floated which greatly revived her credit. The currency was stabilized, and there were distinct signs of improvement.

The socialist administration of Vienna undertook a series of reforms. It established a magnificent system of public housing equipped with modern improvements. These municipal apartments were available to the workingmen at low rentals. Vienna also established municipal ownership of lighting, transportation, breweries and bakeries.

The success of the Nazis in Germany emboldened the Austrian Nazis to favour a union with Germany. Austria now became a scene of bitter struggle between the Nazis, supported by Germany, the Christian Socialists, supported by Italy, and the Social Democrats, backed by France. The most powerful of the three was Engelbert Dollfuss, the Christian Socialist leader, who became Premier in 1932.

When Hitler seized political power in Germany in 1933, he was eager to effect a union of Austria with Germany. Aided and abetted by him, the Austrian Nazis attacked the Dollfuss regime by unleashing terrorism and violence. The Socialists were concerned about the triumph of the Nazis in Germany and its impact on Austria and offered to cooperate with the Christian Socialists. But Dollfuss came to the conclusion that democracy must be sacrificed for the establishment of a fascist state. He put a ban on all political parties and sacked the Socialist officials of Vienna. But Dollfuss was bitterly opposed by the Christian Socialists and a desperate struggle ensued between the latter and *Heimwehr.* In February 1934 the proclamation of a general strike by Socialist leaders was met with an attack of government troops on Socialist strongholds in Vienna. The Social Democratic Party was outlawed and all trade unions were merged in a national union under government control. In April 1934 a new constitution was adopted which abolished the democratic Republic and set up a fascist state on the Italian model.

Dollfuss, who now became the dictator, fell under the influence of Mussolini. He was made to believe that it was only with Italy's backing, Austria could withstand Germany's demand for an *Anschluss.* The Austrian Nazis, though outlawed, carried on ceaseless propaganda which could have been countered by the powerful Socialist Party. But Dollfuss had suppressed the party and had lost the powerful counterweight against the Nazis.

The new order survived only for a few months when in July 1934 the National Socialists attempted a *coup.* Dollfuss was assassinated and widespread distrubances followed in the provinces. Hitler was ready to intervene but he did not dare to do so in the face of threats from Mussolini.

The successor of Dollfuss was Kurt von Schuschnigg who restored order and continued the policy of his predecessor. The Nazis, without being discouraged by their failure, continued their agitation. As Nazi Germany became strong and Rome-Berlin Axis a reality, Schuschnigg sought a *rapprochment* with Germany. In July 1936 Austria and Germany signed an agreement in which the latter recognised Austria's independence and Austria promised to conduct a policy favourable to Germany. The Austrian Nazis were offered amnesty and two of them were inducted into Schuschnigg's Cabinet.

Despite his soft attitude towards the Nazis, Schuschnigg allowed himself not to commit too far. He soon irritated Hitler by a public speech in November 1936 in which he spoke of Austrian Nazis as an enemy to the state. Meanwhile, his dependence on Mussolini eroded owing to the latter's entanglement with the Spanish Civil War and the consummation of the Rome-Berlin Axis.

In January 1937 Goering warned Mussolini that the Austrian government was 'neither Fascist nor National Socialist, but clerical.' He asked Mussolini to persuade Schuschnigg to adopt a policy more favourable to the Austrian Nazis. He did not forget to allude to the dangers which Austria might pose to the alignment of Italy and Germany. Mussolini was in a dilemma. In April he assured Schuschnigg that he still supported Austrian independence but cuationed him to pursue a policy that should be in harmony with the Axis. In September Mussolini's visit to Berlin profoundly disturbed Vienna. Moreover, other powers were found to be lukewarm to Austria's cause. The Yugoslav Prime Minister, Stoyadinovitch, believed an *Anschluss* inevitable. England seemed to be unconcerned about the fate of Austria. She foresaw the *fait accompli* when Eden told Ribbentrop at the end of 1937 that 'people in England recognize that a closer connection between Germany and Austria would have to come about some time.'

Schuschnigg tried to save the situation by paying a personal visit to Italy in April 1937. But he met with 'chilly gestures' from his patron. Hitler's attitude toward Austria hardened as it was to be part of the consolidation of German strength. Hitler received an unmistakable hint from Mussolini when the latter told Ribbentrop that he was 'tired of mounting guard over Austrian independence.' Events moved swiftly. In January 1938 a raid by the Austrian police on the headquarters of the Austrian Nazis revealed shocking disclosure of terrorist activity. Hardly had Schuschnigg begun to take effective measures, he was summoned by Hitler to meet him at Berchtesgaden which the former did on February 12, 1938. He was served with an ultimatum to submit to preparations for 'the assimilation of the Austrian into the German political system.' Under the threat of invasion, Schuschnigg yielded. He inducted Seyss-Inquart, the Austrian Nazi leader, into his cabinet as Minister of the Interior and another Nazi as Foreign Minister.

This marked the real end of the Austrian Empire, although it lingered on for a few weeks more. On February 13, Ciano wrote in his diary that 'the *Anschluss* is inevitable.' Hitler protested against imaginary violations of the new agreement. Encouraged by his speech on February 20, the Austrian Nazis began street demonstrations which the government failed to curb. The police under their new head collaborated with the Nazis against the government. At the beginning of March, huge demonstrations of Nazis took place at Graz and Linz. Schuschnigg belatedly tried to rally his people behind him but without any success. He played his trump card on March 9 that, a week hence, there would be a plebiscite to determine whether or not Austria should remain independent. This decided the issue. Hitler immediately announced that an attempt to hold plebiscite would result in immediate German invasion. When this was accepted, Schuschnigg was asked to resign. Some feeble resistance was put up by the Austrian President, Wilhelm Miklas, but was overcome by a subterfuge. The pro-Nazi Minister of the Interior, DR Arthur von Seyss-Inquart was asked to assume office and to requisition officially German troops to help the government establish peace and security. This was done and in the course of the night of March 11, German troops invaded Austria. On the following day, the army entered Vienna. On March 13, 1939, Austria was made a province of the German Reich.

Hitler arrived on March 13. A systematic persecution of the Jews, Socialists and Catholics—which had been launched by the Austrian Nazis—was strengthened by the arrival of the *Gestapo.* A huge purge began in which thousands of political opponents and suspects were liquidated. The Catholic Church, hitherto anti-Nazi, now changed its policy. The Cardinal—Archbishop of Vienna, Innitzer, now advised his followers to vote for the *Anschluss.* The plebiscite, which was held on April 10, showed an overwhelming vote in favour of the *Anschluss.*

During the Second World War the Allied foreign ministers had decided in their Moscow meeting of October 1943 that Austria should be restored as an independent state. But in 1945 Austria was separated from Germany. It was divided, like Germany, into four zones for military occupation. From the beginning, the Austrians possessed a central government at Vienna. Although this government had orginally been established under Soviet auspices, it received recognition from the Western powers. In May 1955, the Soviet Union, in alliance with the Western Allies, signed a peace treaty with Austria. This recognised Austria's independence with frontiers of 1938, prohibited political or economic union with Germany, and required it to uphold democratic institutions and to prevent the restoration of the Habsburg monarchical system. DR Karl Renner, a veteran Socialist, served as President until 1950 when he was succeeded by Theodore Koerner.

The Kingdom of Hungary

The settlement of 1867 contained within it the seeds of future discord. Out of Hungary's total population of fifteen million, the Magyars constituted less than a half, but the Magyars ruled big minorities of Rumanians, Ruthenians, Slovaks and Germans. Deak showed a statesman-like grasp of the situation when he tried to reconcile the non-Magyars to the *Ausgleich.* He gave Croatia complete autonomy in all matters of administration and made Croatian the language of the legislature and executive. Foreign affairs alone remained the province of the Hungarian Diet, to which Croatia contributed forty members, while she had her own Diet at Agram. Deak tried to solve the problem of non-Magyar races in Hungary of passing the celebrated Law of Nationalities in 1868 which guaranteed equal rights to all nationalities. For the sake of the political unity, Magyar was made the official language of Hungary in both the Parliament and in all branches of administration, but in the country Assemblies, courts of law and schools, the use of other langauages was permitted. From the beginning Law of Nationalities remained a dead letter. It has been said that in Hungary 'the Magyar is the master and the other races are mere helots.'

The *Ausgleich* gave Hungary the status of a quasi-independent State. The Emperor was crowned separately in Budapest, as king of Hungary. A constitution was adopted in 1867 which established a parliament of two houses—a House of Magnates and a House of Deputies, the latter controlling the ministers and taking initiative in legislation. The House of Deputies was, in a sense, a popular assembly, for the franchise was so restricted and so intricate were the electoral laws that, in 1910, out of a total population of over twenty million, only about one million were voters. Almost all of them were Magyar since the Magyar language was a qualification. A high illiteracy rate even excluded the poorer Magyars so that elections were in fact controlled by the aristocrats. In 1913, less than half the total Hungarian population was Magyars, and over 80 per cent high school graduates were Magyars, and over 95 per cent government officials.

Hungary was dominated by an agrarian society as 65 per cent of the people were engaged in agriculture. Small landowners were relatively few and poor. Most of them had less than twenty acres necessary for a family's livelihood. Most of the peasants were wage labourers who worked on the estates of the landlords, over 300 of which averaged more than 40,000 acres each. The Esterhazy estate had more than half a million acres and one bishopric possessed more than a quarter of a million. The lack of land of their own combined with the lack of industrial employment kept the peasants in crushing poverty. Landlords exploited this, exacting what was virtually forced labour. The social division even cut across racial ones. Magyar landlords sometimes employed Ruthenian labour to force down the wages of their Magyar labourers.

Hungarians were divided into two factions: those who wished to maintain the *Ausgleich* on the ground that Hungary had all self-government that she wished, and, in addition, the military aid of Austria, in case of war. On the other side was the Independence Party, led by Francis Kossuth, son of the great revolutionary Louis Kossuth, who began to agitate for virtual independence from Austria.

Koloman Tisza, Hungarian Premier from 1875 to 1890, relied mainly on the support of the gentry and led a liberal ministry. While pursuing a repressive policy towards the nationalities to preserve the dominance of the Magyars, Tisza remained loyal to the *Ausgleich* and the Emperor. Meanwhile the Hungarian magnates found a policy of their own in attacking Dualism itself. The Magyar nationalists deprecated the economic union of 1897 and refused to renew it. In 1902, the extremists, led by the irrepressible Kossuth, obstructed the passage of the budget unless their demands for further Magyarization of the army were met. In the face of this growing opposition, the army bill was withdrawn. Another Magyar, the son of Tisza, formed a government which found it impossible to tide over the parliamentary opposition. His defeat in the elections of January 1905 against a coalition led by Kossuth brought the Crown and Hungarian parliament into open conflict. At this point, the Monarchy suddenly showed its energy by forcibly dispersing the Hungarian parliament, and introducing the new commercial treaty by decree. When the Emperor threatened to introduce universal suffrage much to the detriment of the Magyar dominance, the ploy acted like a magic. Moreover, the Independence Party realised that a war with Russia might be disastrous to Hungary. The cry of Pan-Slavism, sounded by Russia, was heard by the Slavs as well as by those in Austria.

Terrified at the prospect of a new franchise law which might have given some justice to the subject nationalities, the coalition leaders agreed to assume office without insisting on the army reform. Hence the scheme for universal suffrage was dropped. A new suffrage bill for Hungary became law in 1908. It did not concede universal suffrage but by introducing literacy tests and plural voting kept the Magyars firmly entrenched in political power. Politics in Hungary became somewhat unruffled when, in 1910, a new party founded by Stephen Tisza (1861-1918) came into power. It smashed the Kossuth movement and dedicated to maintain the compromise of 1867. Tisza, who was to maintain his ascendancy in Hungarian politics till 1917, upheld the Emperor's military prerogative and ended parliamentary obstructionism by carrying a radical reform in 1912. However, it should not be forgotten that the Emperor had lost his chance of breaking the power of the Magyar oligarchy and that failure rendered the disintegration of the empire inevitable.

Hungary emerged as an independent kingdom following the break-up of the Habsburg monarchy. When Austria surrendered to the Allies a revolution broke out in Hungary. A provisional government was formed on October 24-25, 1918, with Count Machael Karolyi as its head. Two weeks later he proclaimed Hungary an independent republic with proposal to reorganise Hungary as a federal republic with full rights to the non-Magyar races. But the subject nationalities were determined to assert their complete independence; Karolyi was unable to prevent the secession of the Croats and Slovaks or to resist the occupation of Transylvania by the Rumanians.

In March 1919, unable to resist the Allies in fostering the aggrandisement of Czechoslovakia, Rumania and Yugoslavia, Karolyi resigned in despair. The government was seized by Bela Kun, a left-wing Socialist and Jewish journalist, who had recently returned from Russia.

Bela Kun proclaimed a communist State in Hungary and proceeded to stifle the Magyars by issuing decrees and to disarm the revolting colonies by employing force. A 'Red Army' was organised and was sent against the Slovaks and the Rumanians. Though the Slovaks gave way, the indefatigable Rumanian army overwhelmed the ragged communist forces of Hungary. Meanwhile, the Allies were alarmed at the rise of another communist State and in Hungary itself anti-communist movement was gathering momentum under Admiral Nicholas Horthy. As the Rumanians advanced on Budapest and domestic plots deepened against him, Bela Kun fled on August 1, 1919, into Austria. Budapest was occupied by the Rumanian troops. The communist regime was overthrown and the Hungarian government was controlled by a group of aristocrats, including Nicholas Horthy and Count Stephen Bethlen.

In January 1920 a general election was held in Hungary which proclaimed Hungary a monarchy with Horthy as Regent. Decrees issued by the Regent established a parliament with limited suffrage. The Horthy regime was compelled to sign the Treaty of Trianon (June 4, 1919), which left Hungary in a truncated form. To Czechoslovakia went Slovakia and Ruthenia; to Rumania went Transylvania. Yugoslavia took Croatia-Slavonia and some other strategical areas. Resentment was widespread among the people against the Treaty when the former Magyar kingdom lost three-fourths of its area to Czechoslovakia, Rumania and Yugoslavia. The Revisionists refused to accept the new frontiers by raising a slogan: 'No! No! Never!'

In April 1921, Count Bethlen began his ten-year term as premier and practical dictator. War and revolution had emasculated Hungary. The economic situation had become so deplorable that the League of Nations came to her rescue. A foreign loan was floated and the system of taxation was reformed. Hungary's government between the wars was undoubtedly in the interest of the traditional ruling class. The 'right radicals' were gradually converted by being given jobs. Bethlen, a great aristocrat, presided over a sort of Magyar Whig oligarchy, ruling by a judicious mixture of political corruption, jobbery and violence. He turned to Fascist Italy for help with whom a treaty of friendship was signed in 1927.

After the depression of 1931-1934, a right radical government came to power under Gombos. It lasted until 1936, Gombos pursuing anti-Semitic and anti-Habsburg policies. He found in Germany and Italy much-needed support for Hungary. However, the regent, Horthy, retained the main lever of the government, and Gombos found he could do little. He died in 1936, and this semblance of Fascism came to an end. During the great crisis of 1938, when Czechoslovakia was being torn asunder, Hungary asserted her claims over parts of Czechoslovakia. Being supported by Germany and Italy, she got a strip of territory from Czechoslovakia.

In the Second World War, Hungary became a puppet state under Germany permitting the latter's troops to use her territory as a corridor into the Balkan peninsula. In 1943, Hungary made overtures to the Allies which goaded Germany to tighten her control. In 1944 Horthy was waiting for a favourable opportunity to make peace with the British and Americans, but the Russians, who were in Rumania, seized the occasion. Therefore, in October 1944, he signed an armistice with Soviet Russia.

A 'provisional government' was organised in December 1944 by a group of Hungarian Communists. But in the free elections of November 1945, the Communists only gained 17 per cent of the vote, while the Peasants' party gained 57 per cent. The peasants were satisfied with the result as the land reform of the spring of 1945 had given them the land they wanted. Big landlords had been dispossessed without compensation and their estates had been sequestered and given to existing tenant farmers and peasants. The Hungarian National Assembly shortly afterwards adopted a liberal republican constitution and entrusted the premiership to Ferenc Nagy. Meanwhile, by the Peace Treaty of Paris, Hungary had to cede Northern Transylvania to Rumania and a small area to Czechoslovakia. But Rumania had to recognise the incorporation of Bessarabia and Bukovina in the Soviet Union and of Southern Dobruja in Bulgaria.

The communists, however, did not give away. Led by Matthias Rakosy, and assisted by troops and threats of the Soviet Union, the Communists infiltrated the government. They joined with the Socialists and the left wing of the Peasants' Party to undermine the position of the Prime Minister. In May 1947, while Nagy was in Switzerland, the Communists staged a coup at Budapest which eventually forced him to resign. The new Peasant Party Prime Minister made a change in electoral law. In 1948, in the elections under the new law, the communists gained 60 per cent of the vote. The communist leader Matthias Rakosy became Prime Minister, In February 1949, the popular Catholic primate, Cardinal Mindszenty, an outspoken patriot and bitter critic of the Nazis, was tried and sentenced to life imprisonment. By the middle of 1949, Hungary became a full-fledged 'people's republic', with a communist constitution, a single communist party and intimate bond with the Soviet Union.

Cultural Life of the Habsburg Empire

Beneath the hidden weaknesses of the Habsburg Empire lay the many-fangled splendours of the kingdom. The imperial capital, Vienna, exhibited

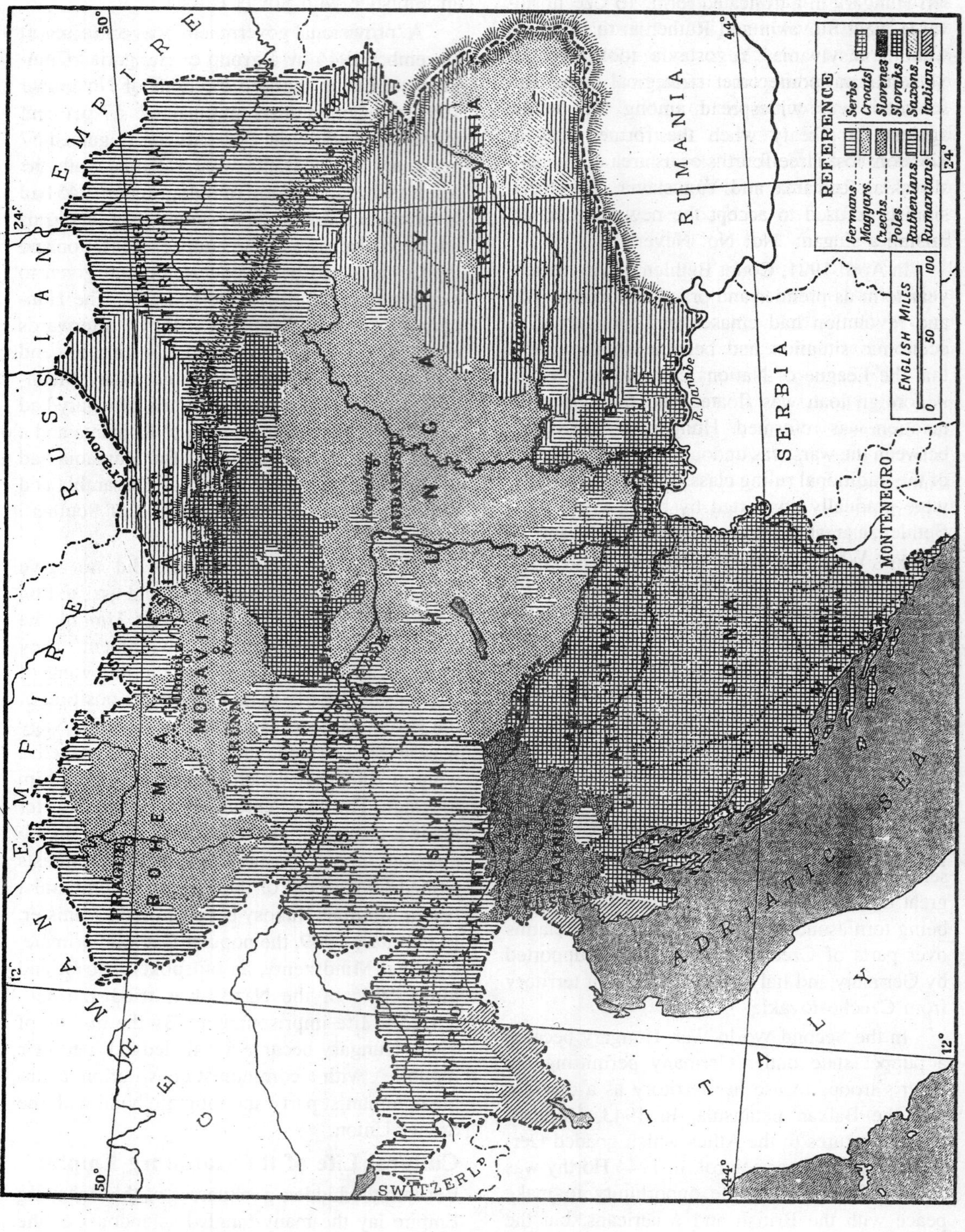
REFERENCE
Germans
Magyars
Czechs
Poles
Ruthenians
Rumanians
Serbs
Croats
Slovenes
Slovaks
Saxons
Italians
ENGLISH MILES
0
50
100
RUSSIAN EMPIRE
GERMAN EMPIRE
RUMANIA
SERBIA
MONTENEGRO
ITALY
SWITZERL'D
ADRIATIC SEA
BOHEMIA
PRAGUE
MORAVIA
BRUNN
SILESIA
WEST GALICIA
EASTERN GALICIA
LEMBERG
CRACOW
BUKOVINA
TRANSYLVANIA
HUNGARY
BUDAPEST
BANAT
R. Danube
CROATIA-SLAVONIA
BOSNIA
HERZEGOVINA
DALMATIA
CARNIOLA
CARINTHIA
STYRIA
TYROL
SALZBURG
LOWER AUSTRIA
UPPER AUSTRIA
VIENNA
AUSTRIA
12°
24°
44°
50°

joy and beauties which had been enhanced by its medieval wall, majestic Ringstrasse, one of the most beautiful avenues in the world, by the building of new bridges across the Danube, and by a series of architectural triumphs, the Rathaus, designed by Fredrick Schmidt, the new opera house, Theophil Hansen's Austrian parliament building, Karl Hasenauer's Burgtheater and many more. Arts and letters flourished in Vienna. Music was at its best with composers like Anton Bruckner, Gustav Mahler, Brahms, Hugo Wolf, the greatest composer of songs since Schubert, and Richard Strauss. Vienna was famous for light opera—thanks to the achievements of Johann Strauss, Karl Millocker and Franz Lehar.

The most popular painters of the period were men like Hans Makart. The country witnessed the emergence of a vigorous new movement called the Vienna Secession which anticipated some aspects of Expressionism and Surrealism. In literature, the Empire was adorned by Adelbert Stifter (1805-1868) whose novel *Nachsommer* (Indian Summer; 1857) won acclaim. Two Viennese dramatists won international reputations: Arthur Schnitzler (1862-1931) whose play *DR Bernhardi* exposed the social ills of his time and Strauss's collaborator Hofmannsthal (1874-1929) whose mystical dramas (*The Fool and Death, Elektra, Everyman*) were admired for their lyrical beauty and whose last play, *The Tower* (1925), looked to Europe's future with gloom and pessimism.

The University of Vienna produced outstanding personalities in different branches of knowledge. Medicine was distinguished by Theodor Billroth's pioneer work in antiseptic surgery and Theodor Meynert's in brain surgery; philosophy by Ernst Mach, economists like Carl Manger and historian like Heirnich Friedjung. Other scholars of great reputation were Rudolf von Ihering, Joseph Unger in legal studies and Rudolf Poch in anthropology. But the man who left imperishable imprint on European thought was the great psychiatrist Sigmund Freud (1856-1939).

Sigmund Freud

CHAPTER 28

THE EASTERN QUESTION—PART II

A new phase began in the Eastern Question when the Balkan nationalities continued their struggle for independence against Turkey with patriotic fervour. Until about 1830 the Balkan peoples were subjects of the Sultan of Turkey. In 1830 Greece won its independence and Serbs and parts of Rumania were granted autonomy.

In 1875 the oppressed peoples of Bosnia and Herzegovina revolted against their Turkish masters. The revolt rapidly spread to Serbia and Montenegro. For several months in the summer of 1875 the Turks busied themselves with savage reprisals against the rebel provinces. In December 1875, the Austrian Chancellor, Count Andrassy, with the approval of Russia and Germany, drew up a note which was presented to Turkey. The note demanded various kinds of reforms in the disaffected regions. But the Turkish Government had no intention of carrying out the proposed reforms. Meanwhile, Bulgaria defied Turkish authority in April 1876 and in Constantinople Sultan Abdul Aziz was deposed and replaced by Murad V. He occupied the throne for a few weeks and was deposed in August 1876 by his unscrupulous brother, Abdul Hamid II.

On May 11, 1876, the Austrian and Russian Chancellors met Bismarck at Berlin and proposed to impose an armistice upon Turkey. Though France and Italy agreed to the measure, Britain refused her assent. The British Government, led by Disraeli, was anxious to prevent Russian expansion in the Balkans. Hence the porposed intervention was given up. During May and June, the Turks adopted severe repressive measures and cruelly massacred twelve thousand Bulgars. Britain could not maintain her support of the Sultan in the face of such inhuman brutality. The question was taken up by Gladstone in a series of pamphlets on the 'Bulgarian Atrocities'. Meanwhile, the Turks inflicted such crushing defeats upon the Serbian forces in September and October that the latter appealed to the powers for protection. Under pressure, the Turkish Government convened an international conference which met at Constantinople in December 1876. The new Sultan, Abdul Hamid II drafted a general settlement which was to be honoured more in breaches. The Sultan was secretly encouraged by the British Government to defy the conference. Thereupon Russia, having secured the friendly neutrality of Austria, declared war on Turkey in April 1877.

In June, Russian forces crossed the Danube and advanced towards Constantinople. In July, a Turkish force of 12,000 men moved into the Bulgarian town of Plevna on the Russian flank. The Russians besieged Plevna and, reinforced by the Rumanian army, took the town in December. By the beginning of 1878 the Russian forces had taken Sofia and Adrianople and were advancing to the gates of Constantinople. At this point Turkey asked for an armistice and in March 1878 signed the Treaty of San Stefano. The Sultan recognised the independence of Rumania, Serbia and Montenegro. The Treaty provided for the creation of a large Bulgarian State. Russia was to acquire Kars, Batum and Dobrudja which were to be given to Rumania in exchange of Bessarabia.

The Treaty was extremely unpopular to Britain and Austria who feared that Russia would dominate the new Bulgaria. Lord Beaconsfield was unequivocal in his utterances. According to him the Treaty of San Stefano 'abolishes the dominion of the Ottoman Empire in Europe: it creates a large State which, under the name of Bulgaria, is inhabited by many races not

Bulgarian...all the European dominions of the Ottoman Ports are put under the administraton of Russia...the effect of all the stipulations combined will be to make the Black Sea as much a Russian lake as the Caspian.' Britain insisted that the treaty be submitted to a Congress to which Russia demurred. It was a war of nerves. Apart

THE BALKAN PENINSULA IN 1912

(The portion shaded Grey represents the Ottoman Empire in Europe)

from this, Greece, Serbia, Rumania were greatly dissatisfied with the Treaty of San Stefano. Britain made a move to mobilise her forces. An Austrian army was mobilised on the Russian flank in the Carpathians. The Austrian Emperor Francis Joseph demanded that the term of peace should be submitted to a Congress at Vienna. Austria might count on the support of Germany.

Bismarck had so long remained lukewarm in this tangled affair as he considered the Balkan Question 'not being the worth of a Pomeranian grenadier.' But he was concerned at the prospect of a war. He had an overriding interest in reconciling the two partners in the *Dreikaiserbund*—Austria and Russia. Bismarck assumed the role of a mediator. Accordingly, the Congress met in Berlin in June 1878 under the presidency of Bismarck, attended by Russia, France, Britain, Austria, Italy, and Turkey.

The Congress of Berlin was the most distinguished diplomatic gathering between the Vienna Congress of 1814-15 and the Paris Peace Conference of 1919. Apart from Bismarck, the Congress included great dignitaries like Disraeli and Salisbury of Great Britain, Gorchakov and Shuvalov of Russia, Andrassy of Austria-Hungary, Waddington of France, and Corti of Italy.

The Treaty of Berlin was signed on July 13, 1878. Russia's sole acquisition in Europe was Bessarabia and in Asia Batum, Ardahan and Kars. The Treaty recognised the complete independence of Rumania, Serbia, and Montenegro. The enlarged state of Bulgaria was reduced in size by exclusion of Rumelia and Macedonia, the latter being placed under direct Turkish rule. Austria-Hungary was allowed to occupy and administer Bosnia and Herzegovina. Britain gained the island of Cyprus. She was allowed to have free access to the Straits which greatly alarmed Russia. The spectre of a British fleet in the Black Sea haunted Russian policy for almost twenty years. Rumania received the province called the Dobrudja. Thessaly was promised to Greece, but only given up three years later. France was promised a free hand in Turkey's North African territory of Tunisia. Only Germany and Italy left the Congress without territorial gains. This comprehensive settlement was to be strengthened by reforms in European Turkey. The Turkish Government was to uphold religious liberty and equality.

The Treaty of Berlin forms an important landmark in the history of the Eastern Question. Russia's ambition in the south-eastern Europe had been checked much to the satisfaction of England who occupied the island of Cyprus. The treatment accorded to Russia by the Treaty of Berlin eventually strained her relations with Germany and she formed an alliance with France. Bismarck found in Austria-Hungary a valuable friend as the latter's interests were more closely interlinked with the Balkan peninsula.

The Congress of Berlin failed to settle the Eastern Question. If it prevented a localised European war in 1878, the Congress of Berlin sowed many of the seeds of a far greater conflict to come. It sacrificed the interests of the Balkan nationalities to the ambition of the great powers. On the other hand, it could not revive the Ottoman Empire as an independent power. The practical effects of the Congress were of little consequence. The British fleet never entered the Black Sea until after the collapse of the Russian empire. Bulgaria, which had been dismembered, was united within a few years. The Congress made a bad job by putting Macedonia under the Turks and Bosnia under Austria-Hungary. 'The first act caused the Balkan War of 1912; the second exploded the World War of 1914.'

Bulgaria

The new storm centre of the Eastern Question was Bulgaria which had been truncated in 1878. The Bulgarians looked upon their Russian protectors until it became clear to them that the Tsar intended to turn the state into a Russian protege. In 1879 the Bulgarians elected Prince Alexander of Battenberg, a nephew of the Tsarina. In 1881 he asserted himself by suspending the constitution and freeing himself from the hostility of the Bulgarian parliament (*Sobranjee*). Two years later he annoyed Russia by playing off nationalists and parliament against the Russians. He also incurred the displeasure of the Russians by allowing the Austrians to complete the projected Orient Railways, designed to run from Austria across Serbia and Bulgaria to Adrianople and Constantinople. These assertions of independence won British support, who wished to see Bulgaria a bulwark against Russian expansion.

Prince Alexander became popular owing to his anti-Russian posture. Then two events in 1885 increased his prestige. He annexed Eastern Rumelia, the south-eastern strip of Bulgaria which had been taken away in 1878 by Turkey. Britain restrained Turkey from protesting her loss of sovereignty over Rumelia. Tsar Alexander III prevaricated to coerce Bulgaria. The second event reinforced Bulgaria's prestige when the latter trounced the Serbian army after a desperate three-day battle. Serbia, who had been jealous of Bulgaria's rise to power, was forced to sign a treaty with Bulgaria in 1886 owing to pressure of the Austrians.

To the Russians, Prince Alexander was a bitter foe and they succeeded in deposing him in August 1886 and forcing him to leave the country. Against these blustering tactics, the Bulgarian Assembly stood firm. Eventually, in July 1887, a German prince, Ferdinand of Saxecoburg, a descendent of Louis Philippe of France and a relative of Queen Victoria of England, was chosen as ruler. Ferdinand consolidated his position partly by his own astuteness and partly with the aid of a resolute prime minister, Stefan Stambulov, and led Bulgaria to the high road of efficient administration. But he overreached himself when he took recourse to strong-arm tactics against the opposition. In 1894 Stambulov was forced out of office and in July 1895 the fallen statesman was finally removed from the scene by assassination.

Prince Ferdinand now became master in his own house and effected a reconciliation with Russia. The Tsar finally recognised him as the rightful ruler of Bulgaria. In 1908 Ferdinand proclaimed himself as an independent king by severing the nominal bond between Bulgaria and the Ottoman Empire.

The Armenian Massacres (1894-98)

The two million Christian Jews who lived in Armenia—an ill-defined geographical area lying between the Caspian, the Black Sea, the Caucasus and Kurdistan—were subjects of Turkey. In the Treaty of Berlin the Powers had exacted a promise from Turkey that the Armenians would be better treated and given security against 'the Circassians and Kurds.' The infectious spirit of nationalism which swept the Balkan Peninsula caught the Armenians who invoked support from foreign powers to achieve national independence. Assured by German support, the Turkish Sultan Abdul Hamid II undertook to stamp out Armenian agitation by launching his fanatical Moslem Kurds and Turkish troops against the Armenians. This resulted in massacres of the Armenians which by December 1895 numbered about 50,000. Britain tried hard to induce the European powers to intervene; but Russia resolutely refused. The refusal of Russia, Germany and Austria-Hungary to take any action emboldened the Sultan to complete his work with impunity.

Greece

Greece had a special grievance against the Berlin settlement because it had not granted her Thessaly and Epirus. In 1881 Greece gained Thessaly from Turkey by negotiation. Nevertheless, a large number of Greek people were still under Turkish rule, distributed through Macedonia, Epirus, the islands of the Aegean Sea, Crete and Asia Minor. A pan-Hellenic movement grew to wrest these lands from the Sultan. The most important organisation *Ethnike Hetaireia* (National Society), a secret society, was formed in 1894 to promote nationalist movement in the Greek territories.

In 1885 and 1886, the Greek Government threatened to attack Turkey, but was checked by the Great Powers. Crete, inhabited almost entirely by the Greeks, made many attempts to throw off Turkish thraldom. In 1896 the Cretans rose in revolt against Turkish administration and proclaimed union with Greece. Greek naval forces came to the aid of the insurgents. In April 1897, Turkey declared war on Greece. The 'Thirty Days' War' ensued which was over by May. The Powers intervened and imposed armistice on the combatants. A definitive peace was signed in December 1897.

Despite the failure of the Greeks to liberate Crete from Turkey, the event produced a remarkable figure Eleutherios Venizelos. A Cretan by birth, Venizelos had headed the revolutionary movement for the union of Crete with Greece. It was mainly through his initiative that Crete for the first time enjoyed real self-government. In 1905 the Cretans under Venizelos proclaimed union with the Hellenic Kingdom. The Powers again intervened.

By 1910 the popularity of Venizelos had reached such amazing height that King George I (1863-1913) was compelled to invite him to the mainland to assume the charge of premiership. He reformed the Greek government, modernised the army and navy and formed a Balkan League against the Ottoman Empire. 'He thus prepared Greece, internally and externally, just as Cavour had prepared Sardinia, or Bismarck had prepared Prussia, for wars of national unification.'

Rumania

In the Congress of Berlin, Rumania was recognised as an independent state. In 1881 she declared herself a Kingdom. The Rumanian Kingdom was ambitious to extend its control over a large portion of its own nationality scattered over Macedonia, Bessarabia, Transylvania and Bukovina. As anti-Russian sentiment prevailed, Rumania concluded in 1883 a secret alliance with Austria-Hungary and thus became a protege of the Triple Alliance of Austria-Hungary, Germany and Italy.

During the reign of Carol I (1881-1914), Rumania made notable progress. A predominantly agricultural country, Rumania suffered from inequitable land distribution which was largely in the hands of large proprietors, called 'boyars'. In 1907 a peasant uprising took place which became so violent and widespread that it required the deployment of 140,000 troops to restore order. The government undertook a series of reforms which, for a time, removed discontent. Exports of cereals and oil increased throughout Carol's reign. Simultaneously, through investment of foreign capital, began the exploitation of the country's rich mineral resources, especially coal and petroleum. In 1866 Rumania had no railways, but by 1914 it had 2,500 miles of railway. However, the persecution of the Jews, who constituted a large segment of the business class, caused many of them to emigrate to America.

Serbia

Serbia, which had been autonomous since 1830, became an independent principality in 1878. It was a backward country disturbed by the rivalry of opposing claimants to its throne and the interference of the foreign powers in its domestic affairs. The family of Karageorge, the peasant leader who revolted against the Ottoman Empire, was pitted against the family of Milos Obrenovitch, the soldier who had secured autonomy for Serbia. Though the latter was in power from 1859 to 1903, the relative calm was rudely shaken by the occasional insurrections of Karageorge faction. This dynastic feud kept the country in a state of perpetual disorder and made it a kind of football in the game of international intrigue between Russia and Austria-Hungary.

Milan Obrenovitch was the King of Serbia during the Russo-Turkish war of 1877-78. Pro-Austrian by sentiment, his reign was characterised by domestic disaffection, administrative incompetence and financial mismanagement. In 1881 he formed a secret alliance with Austria-Hungary and, in the following year, transformed Serbia from a principality into a kingdom. It was probably to disarm the opposition to his effete rule that the Serbian king went to war with Bulgaria in 1885. The war proved to be the death-knell of his decaying fortune and Serbia would have been overrun by Bulgaria had not Austria-Hungary intervened and stopped the war. The king held on for four years and tried to regain his fallen fortune by promulgating a liberal constitution in 1889. This action did not save his throne. Shortly afterwards he was forced to abdicate in favour of his son, Alexander I (1889-1903).

Alexander I was only thirteen at the time of his accession. Disorder and factionalism raged the country during his minority. Things did not improve when he assumed power in 1893 as he proved to be an impetuous young man. In 1900 he outraged a large part of the nation by marrying one of his mother's ladies-in-waiting, a woman of questionable integrity. In 1903, Alexander, his wife and several of her relatives were brutally murdered in Belgrade. Thereafter Peter I, the grandson of Karageorge, succeeded to the throne bringing to an end of Obrenovitch dynasty.

King Peter's accession marked a turning-point in Serbian history as it encouraged the development of Serbian nationalism much to the detriment of Austria-Hungary. The new king was an energetic ruler, eager to restore the prestige of the country by freeing Bosnia and Herzegovina from Austrian control. His dream was to make the kingdom of Serbia the nucleus of a Yogoslavia which should embrace Serbs, Croats and Slovenes in the Habsburg Empire.

A democrat in his sentiment, Peter restored the constitution of 1889. He depended upon the Ultra-patriotic party in the Parliament whose leader was Nicolas Pasic, an ardent patriot. While the King was engaged in carrying out reforms in the army, Pasic reorganised national finances and home. As Peter was hostile to Austria, the latter began a tariff war on Serbia by excluding her exports, mainly pig and farm products. The so-called 'Pig War' of 1905 brought great hardship to the Serbs and further antagonised them against Austria.

In 1908 there took place a serious crisis. Disquieted by Serb intrigue, Austria annexed Bosnia and Herzegovina, the two places which the former was allowed to administer by the Treaty of Berlin. It was alleged that the Russian Foreign Minister, Izvolski, had himself suggested the action anticipating to secure for Russia the coveted use of the Straits. But Russia had no chance of getting what she wanted without the assent of Britain. Moreover, the Young Turks had no intention of permitting Russian warships to manoeuvre in the Straits. To cap it all, the annexation of Bosnia with its large Serbian population was a direct challenge to their nationalistic aspiration. The possession of Bosnia was considered vital to Serbia for her expansion to the sea and her indignation knew no bounds at the unilateral action of Austria-Hungary. The outbreak of war seemed imminent for Russia encouraged the Serbs in their resistance. But when Germany took up the cause of Austria, Russia withdrew—exhausted as she was after her conflict with Japan. The weakness of Russia was revealed to the world and the Straits remained closed. On the other hand, the annexation of Bosnia and Herzegovina strengthened the Dual Monarchy providing a hinterland to the Dalmatian Coast by linking it up with Hungary and fortifying the Austrian position on the Adriatic.

Turkey (1878-1912)

In spite of the loss of Bosnia and Herzegovina, Turkey was still a European power retaining Macedonia, Albania, Thrace, and the Sandjak of Novi Bazar. The regime of Abdul Hamid II effected no change in the system of administration. It has been remarked 'The Turk changes not; his neighbours, his frontiers, his statute-books change, but his ideas and his practice remain the same.'

Abdul Hamid's regime aroused great discontent. The Young Ottomans believed that the ills of the regime could be cured only by the adoption of constitutional parliamentary government. Led by a high official and minister, Midhat Pasha, they persuaded the Sultan to promulgate a constitution in December 1876 which provided for a parliamentary democracy. The Parliament met in March 1877 only to be dissolved by the Sultan in February 1878. Despite the temporary success of the Sultan in stifling democratic movement, an uneasy feeling of unfulfilled promise haunted the official and intellectual classes.

The Hamidian period hastened the process of modernisation and centralisation in the Ottoman Empire. By promoting education and developing railways and telegraphs, the Sultan unconsciously sowed the seeds of discontent. Youngmen exposed to Western system of education became critical to the regime. Disaffection became widespread among the educated classes.

A group of radical young men, known as the 'Young Turks', formed secret societies and tried to win over the armed forces to their cause. Their aim was to revive the liberal constitution of 1876 which the Sultan had discarded. The main force behind the Young Turks was Enver Bey, an army lieutenant, who, with fellow officers, organised the revolutionary "Committee of Union and Progress". In July 1908 this committee executed a military coup at Salonica, revived the long-suspended constitution of 1876, and marched on Constantinople. Abdul Hamid II, thoroughly frightened, gave way. He abolished censorship of the press and ordered election on the basis of universal male suffrage. In December 1908 elections were held and the new Parliament met at Constantinople.

The new Parliament lacked any political experience. Meanwhile, the Turkish Empire was on the verge of disintegration. Troops revolted in Arabia and Mesopotamia. In Albania and Macedonia the situation was anarchical. Austria-Hungary and Bulgaria took advantage of the domestic difficulties of the Ottoman Empire and detached territories from its sovereignity. In October 1908 Austria-Hungary occupied Bosnia and Herzegovina. Simultaneously Bulgaria declared her independence. Abdul Hamid bided his time and staged a counter-revolution in April 1909. He occupied Constantinople and overthrew the Government. But Enver Bey and the Committee of Union and Progress rallied the army at Salonica and executed a second coup in April 1909. Abdul Hamid was deposed in favour of his younger brother, Mohammad V, who became a tool at the hands of the Young Turks. The liberal cabinet of Kamal Pasha was supplanted by a Young Turk ministry and the Parliament became a National Assembly.

The Young Turks disappointed liberal and nationalist hopes by adopting the policy of 'Turkification'. Turkish became the official language of the Empire and all citizens were henceforth liable for compulsory military service. Non-Turks like the Moslem Arabs and the Christian people in the Balkans resisted the Turkish regime. In September 1911 Italy declared war against Turkey and seized Tripoli.

In 1911 there was a split within the Committee of Union which invited opposition to its rule. This resulted in the dissolution of the Chamber of Deputies in January 1912 and the holding of a general election. The election was a staged affair known as the 'big-stick election' which saved the government. In July 1912 a group of officers known as the 'Saviour Officers' revolted and overthrew the Unionist Government. The Sultan, therefore, appointed a new government. In January 1913, a group of Unionist Officers, led by Colonel Enver Bey (1881-1922), executed a coup and shot the Minister of War dead. The Cabinet was forced to resign and until the end of the First World War, Unionist domination went unchallenged.

The weakness of Turkey was revealed when on September 25, 1911, she was attacked by Italy. In the following spring the Italian army attacked the Porte at various quarters and occupied Rhodes and the Dodecanese Archipelago. The situation became alarming when, simultaneously, Albania revolted against Turkey. A treaty was, therefore, signed at Lausanne on October 15, 1912, whereby Turkey relinquished Tripoli. Thus the process of the dismemberment of the Ottoman Empire, arrested since 1878, began with the Italian acquisiton of Tripoli. It also contributed directly to a more serious attack upon Turkey by the Balkans. The Balkan States believed that their hour had come. Russia and Austria, not yet ready for a showdown between themselves, warned the Balkan States not to attack Turkey.

The Balkan Wars

In 1912 an unprecedented development had taken place. Owing largely to the statesmanship of Venizelos of Greece, a league had been formed between Greece, Serbia, Montenegro, and Bulgaria. There were a number of factors which helped to bring about the unity of the Balkans against Turkey. The success of Austria in annexing Bosnia and Herzegovina created a sense of panic among the Balkan States. Their object was now to prevent any further increase in the threatening Austro-German control of the peninsula. Since the beginning of the nineteenth century Macedonia had been the storm-centre of the Balkan Peninsula in which a large number of Christians were inhumanely persecuted. On the triumph of the 'Young Turks' in Turkey (1908), the lot of the Christians in Greece grew worse. These events inflamed the people of the Balkan States with the desire to liberate their brothers in Macedonia.

For some years Russia had been active in bringing about a league of the Balkan States under her auspices—a weapon which might be used not only against Turkey but Austria as well. Also, it might enable Russia to gain the coveted control of Constantinople and the Straits. Poincare, the French Prime Minister who visited St. Petersburg in August 1912, said the agreement between the Balkan States contained 'the germ of a war not only against Turkey but against Austria. Poincare told Sazanov, Russian Foreign Minister, that 'France would not give Russia military aid over Balkan issues if Germany did not attack Russia.'

When Poincare was in St. Petersburg, a conflict in the Balkans appeared imminent. The Austrian Foreign Minister, Berchtold, took the initiative in solving the crisis. Ultimately his plan of issuing admonitions to the Turkish Government and warnings to the Balkans to keep the peace was accepted by Germany and Russia. Ultimately, on October 8, 1912, the Great Powers warned the Balkan States that they would not admit at the end of the conflict any modification of territorial *status quo* in European Turkey. On the same day Montenegro declared war against Turkey and this was followed by Serbia, Bulgaria and Greece ten days later.

The Greeks pushed northward into Macedonia and, on November 8, entered the important city and port of Salonica. Further west the Serbians and the Montenegrans were also successful. The Serbians won a great victory at Kumanovo, wiping out the ancient memories of the great defeat of Kossovo, which had ruined the Serbian Empire in the fourteenth century. The Serbs thus reached the Adriatic. Meanwhile, the Bulgarians defeated the Turks in the battles of Kirk Kilisse and Lule Burgas. The Bulgarians were stopped just outside Constantinople. The collapse of the Turkish power in Europe seemed imminent. It appeared that she ceased to exist with the exception of Constantinople, Adrianople, Janina, and Scutari.

On December 3, 1912 an armistice was concluded and a Peace Conference opened in London. At the same time, a conference of ambassadors of the great powers under the chairmanship of British Foreign Secretary, Sir Edward Grey, was held at London to supervise a Balkan settlement. But the Serbian victory and the creation of Albania became a source of contention between the Austrian and Russian governments. Germany tried to moderate Austrian policy. Bethmann observed prophetically that 'it was almost impossible for Russia to look on inactive in case of a military operation by Austria-Hungary against Serbia.' Moreover, Bulgaria demanded Adrianople which the Turks refused. In March 1913, the war was resumed. One after another the fortresses fell: Janina on March 6, Adrianople on March 26, Scutari on April 23. Turkey was now compelled to accept terms of peace. In April, the powers imposed their decisions against Montenegro who had seized Scutari, the latter being allocated to Albania. A naval demonstration forced Montenegro to withdraw.

On May 30, 1913, the Treaty of London was signed. By this Treaty Turkey lost all its European territory save Constantinople and a narrow strip along the Bosphorus and Dardenelles. Albania was set up as an autonomous state. Crete was allowed to unite with Greece. The danger that the Great Powers might be dragged into a general war had been averted because both Russian and Austrian interests had been safeguarded. Britain and Germany were satisfied with the improvement of their own relations in the process.

Second Balkan War

No sooner was peace concluded than the Balkan allies began to quarrel over the division of the spoils. The Great Powers were no less responsible for the Second Balkan War. Austria was determined to prevent Serbia from gaining Albania. In this determination Austria was backed by Germany and Italy. Albania was created as an independent state. Thus the hostile attitude of the powers checked Serbia from gaining an outlet on the Adriatic. 'It was the blocking of Serbia's outlet to the sea that caused the Second Balkan War between the allies.' In her disappointment Serbia demanded the part of Macedonia which had been assigned to Bulgaria. Bulgaria protested that the bulk of the Macedonian population were Bulgars. It had been her constant ambition ever since the Treaty of San Stefano to recover the Greater Bulgaria. Russia sought to intervene with offers of arbitration. The situation seemed to be saved when the Bulgarian cabinet accepted the Russian offer. But Austria had made up her mind to smash the Balkan League and she deliberately incited Bulgaria against her allies. 'We shall let the dogs devour one another,' an Austrian official was quoted as saying, 'and then we shall dominate the Balkans.'

On June 29, 1913, war broke out between Bulgaria on the one side and Serbia, Montenegro, Greece, and Rumania on the other. The Turks, hopeful of regaining some of their losses, fought against Bulgaria. In July the Turks recaptured Adrianople, while the Greeks, Serbs and Rumanians threatened the Bulgarian capital, Sofia. King Ferdinand of Bulgaria had to make peace and the Treaty of Bucharest (August 10, 1913) imposed a new settlement on the Balkans.

By this Treaty, Rumania gained the Silistrian plateau at the expense of Bulgaria. Serbia annexed northern and central Macedonia. Greece secured Crete, southern Epirus, southern Macedonia (including Salonica) and part of western Thrace. Turks wrested from Bulgaria the town of Adrianople and a larger part of Thrace, Bulgaria received a part of Thrace and Eastern Macedonia, with a few miles of the Aegean Coast. It was estimated that as a result of the

Treaty of Bucharest over a million Bulgarian people passed under foreign rule. Thus ended the Balkan War and seldom in history have any war changed their character so rapidly. 'The Balkan War,' it has been rightly remarked by Sir Edward Grey, 'began as a war of liberation, became rapidly a war of annexation, and has ended, if all the charges are true, in being a war of extermination.'

Disintegration of the Ottoman Empire and World War I

The results of the Balkan Wars were far-reaching in their consequence. Austria was not satisfied with the Balkan settlement. Serbia now regarded war against Austria-Hungary as inevitable. Extreme Serbian nationalists formed the Union of Death (commonly known as the Black Hand Society), a secret organisation dedicated to effecting the restoration of Bosnia and Herzegovina to the motherland. Covertly supported by Russian agents, their methods were terroristic. The Serbian government did not support such activities. Nevertheless, it continued to agitate for satisfaction of its nationalist claims. Bulgaria felt a deep grudge against her neighbours who had deprived her of territories and looked to Turkey and Austria-Hungary as possible allies. Russian influence in the Balkans was greatly strengthened since Turkey lay crushed and broken. She controlled Serbia and increased her influence on Rumania. Germany, realising the approaching decay of the Ottoman Empire, entered the political scene. By weakening Turkey, the Balkan Wars gave Germany an opening to become dominant in the Straits. 'In a sense Constantinople was the key point in the conflicting ambitions of Russia and Germany.' Thus the rivalry of the Great Powers in the Balkans and the growing nationalism of the Balkan peoples proved a prelude to much greater conflict. As the German Chief of Staff wrote in February 1913: 'A European war must come sooner or later in which ultimately the struggle will be one between Germany and Slavism ... but the aggression must come from the Slavs.'

The best commentary on the Balkan Wars of 1912-13 is that none of the contestants believed that the territorial decisions would be permanent. The victorious Serbs and Montenegrans thought that they would have to fight Austria-Hungary in future. The defeated Bulgars made overtures for an alliance both with Austria-Hungary and the Turks. The Greeks tried to cultivate relations with Austria-Hungary. All of them expected a new war. Turkey had been so weakened that in April 1913 she appealed to Germany for a good German officer to reorganise her army. General Liman Van Sanders was sent by Germany to Turkey. The news came as a shock to the Russians who were even prepared to go to war on this issue unless Turkey decided to drop Liman. The French also felt sore and protested to the Turkish Government against 'handing the keys of the Straits' to the Germans. But the British attitude was found to be evasive as they had their own adviser, Admiral Limpus, to the Turkish navy.

Nevertheless, the Liman episode produced a ministerial conference at St. Petersburg in January 1914. The Minister of War, Sukhomlinov, claimed that Russia was 'ready for a duel with Germany.' But without British and French support, Russia dared not risk war with Germany. The Liman episode embittered Russo-German relations. Soon the Allies, Austria-Hungary and France were drawn into a 'controversy which could hardly be more embittered if a war were on the point of breaking out'.

But the actual centre of the struggle lay in Serbia. It became a bone of contention to Austria. The annexation of Bosnia and Herzegovina with three million and a half Serbs by Austria had left in Serbia bitter feelings. But the most fundamental clue to the feud lay more in geography than in history. Serbia was a land-locked country, and her only practicable outlet lay through Austria-Hungary. This potential factor enabled her powerful neighbour to extort economic concessions from Serbia. Serbia's chief commodity was pigs; and when she tried to establish trade relations with other countries, she met with stiff resistance from Austria-Hungary. Denouncing the existing commercial treaty with Serbia, Austria temporarily put a ban to Serbia's pigs. This 'Pig War' antagonised Serbia as her peasants were convinced that 'Austria-

Hungary stood in the way of their prosperity (and) they came to have for the Dual Monarchy feelings of the most bitter hatred.'

In the First Balkan War, Serbia had been deprived of a window on the Adriatic owing to Austrian pressure. But the war left her doubled in size and population. When the Russian Foreign Minister was urging moderation before the Second Balkan War, he said, 'Serbia's promised land lies in Austria-Hungary ... Time is working for Serbia and for the destruction of her enemies, who already show clear signs of disintegration.' 'The first round is won,' the Serbian Premier prophetically observed, 'now we must prepare for the second, against Austria.'

In this tense situation occurred the murder of Archduke Francis Ferdinand (June 28, 1914), nephew of the Emperor of Austria, at the Bosnian town of Sarajevo. It was believed to have been done by a Serbian agent and Austria, backed by Germany, forced war and the First World War broke out.

CHAPTER 29

THE FIRST WORLD WAR

The century between the Napoleonic wars and the First World War was for Europe, as a whole, the longest period of tranquility ever experienced in the course of modern history. The wars for national unity in Germany and Italy, the Greek War of Independence, the Crimean War, the Russo-Turkish War, the Boer War and the Russo-Japanese War were more or less restricted to few powers and did not lead into a general conflagration.

The basic cause of the First World War was provided by German imperialism with its *Weltpolitik* or world policy. Germany under Bismarck had been a satiated power. But after 1871 the pressure of foreign trade and increasing participation in world markets created the demand for a German share in world domination or *Weltpolitik*. According to a German historian the term *Weltpolitik* means that 'Germany has ceased to regard exclusively the continent of Europe in framing her policy.'

Fully aware of the dangers of open German hegemony, Bismarck discouraged the idea of colonial expansion. Still Bismarck was unable to resist the irresistible demands for greater German power. She obtained South-West Africa, Togoland and the Cameroons (1884), as well as New Guinea and the Pacific Islands.

After the fall of Bismarck in 1890, the idea of a colonial Empire was embraced with vigour. The genesis of the ambitious restlessness of Germany was due to the exigencies of her economic situation. The industrial and commercial expansion of Germany between 1870 and 1914 was amazing. Germany now became preponderantly an industrial instead of agrarian state. In short 'industry, commerce and the shipping trade have transformed the old industrial life of Germany into one of international industry, and this has also carried the Empire in political matters beyond the limits which Prince Bismarck set to German statecraft.'

The primary aim of German *Weltpolitik* was to dominate the Near and Middle East. Bismarck had treated the whole Eastern Question as 'not worth the bones of a single Pomeranian grenadier.' But his successors zealously advocated the policy of *Drang nach osten*—the advance eastwards. Apart from considerations of the world, the exploitation of Asia Minor was widely advocated on economic grounds. 'Here the superfluous population of Germany might be disposed in promising settlements; capital could be profitably employed in railways and irrigation works, in mining and agriculture; increasing prosperty would provide growing markets for German produce ... Financial and economic control over Turkey... meant also the control of South-eastern Europe and eastern Mediterranean, the command of the Danube from source to mouth ... the practical possession of Baghdad, and a road to the Persian Gulf, whence it would be easy to bring pressure to bear not only on Persia but on Russian territory east of the Caspian, and even on India.'[1] All these dazzling possibilities were embodied in the far-reaching scheme for the Berlin-Baghdad Railway a scheme which originated in 1888 but took definite shape in 1903.

The most eloquent champion of *Weltpolitik* was Max Weber who, in 1895, pleaded for a new policy of striving for world power. Even more significant were the views of George Alexander von Muller, later Chief of the Imperial Naval

1. Prothero, G. W.: *German Opinion and German Policy before the War,* PP. 31-33.

Cabinet. In a private memorandum written in 1896 he maintained that out of international tensions 'war...must arise'. Muller clearly saw the two alternatives for Germany: 'Either to commit all the power of the nation, recklessly, not even shirking a great war, or else to limit ourselves to a continental Power.' The decision to plunge into the adventure of *Weltpolitik* was propagated even by a liberal conservative historian and publicist Hans Delbruck in November 1899:

> We want to be a World power and pursue colonial policy in the grand manner. That is certain. Here there can be no step backward. The entire future of our people among the great nations depends on it. We can pursue this policy with England or without England. With England means in peace; against England means—through war.

Triple Alliance and the Triple Entente

Germany's *Weltpolitik* had far-reaching effects. The Triple Alliance between Germany, Austria-Hungary and Italy, concluded in 1882, now became the basis for German ambitions. In 1871, there was no system of alliance in existence; in 1885, there existed only one alliance—the Triple Alliance. By 1907, however, the Triple-Entente between France, Russia and England had emerged. Among the first symptoms of the new development had been the Franco-Russian Alliance of 1892-94, which put an end to the isolation of France. It also ended for good the co-operation between Russia, Germany and Austria. Partly as a reaction to Germany's *Weltpolitik,* her naval armament, and her refusal to form a rapprochement with Britain, the latter ended her splendid isolation by concluding an alliance with Japan in 1902. Thereafter, in 1904, Britain concluded with France the *Entente Cordiale,* a cordial understanding. By this agreement France recognised British control over Egypt while Britain promised not to oppose French claims in Morocco, But this entente had grave political implications. Sir Edward Grey had declared as early as 1906 that this agreement would be morally as binding as a formal treaty of alliance: 'if there is war between France and Germany, it will be very difficult for us to keep out of it.' In 1907, Britain concluded a similar entente with Russia and they settled their conflicting interests in Persia, Afghanistan, and Tibet. Thus was born the Triple Entente between England, France and Russia. From 1907 Europe was grouped, somewhat artificially, into two armed camps. Speaking of the year that preceded the Great War, Lord Oxford remarked:

> We were often conscious that we were skating on the thinnest of ice, and the peace of Europe was at the mercy of a chapter of unforeseen and unforeseeable accidents.

It must be borne in mind that the Triple Entente was not conceived as an offensive alliance. Britain was opposed to any offensive war against Germay provoked by Russia or France. But Britain was disturbed and even frightened by the menace of the German fleet. This misgiving found strong expression in Sir Eyre Crowe's famous memorandum of January 1, 1907. But far from being anti-German, it was a balanced judgement of German intentions. Crowe summed up his policy in a remarkable passage:

> It would be of real advantage if the determination not to bar Germany's legitimate and peaceful expansion, nor her schemes of naval development, were made as patent and pronounced as authoritatively as possible, provided care was taken at the same time to make it quite clear that this benevolent attitude will give way to determined opposition at the first sign of British or allied interest being adversely affected.[2]

Crowe's analysis of the situation found its echo in the words of Kurt Reizler, the influential adviser of the Chancellor, Bethmann Hollweg. He wanted to make Germany pursue its *Weltpolitik* without any hindrance. Any attempt to contain this policy, Reizler concluded, would be brushed aside by Germany's effective power and its tremendous *elan vital.*

Growing Crisis

German *Weltpolitik* and the containment policy of the Entente made war inevitable. Germany's first political reaction of significance was the move against France over Morocco in 1905-06. France hesitated; the alternative seemed to be war. However, a conference was arranged at

2. Quoted in *The Origins of the First World War* (1985), Edited by H.W. Koch, P. 62.

Algeciras in 1906. The French annexation of Morocco was forbidden and the 'open door' theoretically established.

In 1908-09 occurred the Bosnian crisis. Disquieted by Serb intrigue, Austria annexed Bosnia and Herzegovina (October 6, 1908) which dashed all hopes of a great Serbian state to the ground. In the tension thus created the outbreak of war seemed imminent, for Russia encouraged the Serbs in their resistances. Izvolsky, however, tried to bring the question of annexation before an international conference to recover Russia's lost prestige. At this point, Germany supported Austria-Hungary without reserve. Military and economic weakness made the Russian government unwilling to fight. The French were frightened to support their ally. Therefore, Russia yielded and allowed Austria-Hungary to annex Bosnia and Herzegovina. The event had serious consequences. It antagonised Russia too deeply and the latter now devoted herself with pertinacity to revenging herself on Austria. It had even been felt by Bulow, the German Chancellor, that Russian humiliation was such that a repetition of the same manoeuvre was unlikely to be successful. Most serious of all, the event foreshadowed the Balkan Wars.

After the Bosnian crisis the relations between the great powers grew from bad to worse. The Agadir crisis was the first instance of this. On the plea of serious internal disorder, France sent her troops to Morocco in 1911 and then refused to withdraw them. Germany thereupon sent a gunboat Panther to Agadir, a Moroccan port. Britain took a resolute stand as Lloyd George in his famous Guildhall speech (21 July 1911) made it clear that Britain could not be treated as of no account in a question vitally affecting her interests. This was meant as a declaration of support for France in a war against Germany. When Italy and Austria refused to support Germany on her course of collision, Germany backed down and satisfied herself with some territorial concessions in the Cameroons.

The net effect of the Agadir crisis was to weld together the Triple Entente and to raise a new spirit of national defiance in France. Sir Edward Grey, the British Foreign Secretary, and Paul Cambon, the French Ambassador in London, now promised to coordinate the foreign policy of their countries in future period of crisis. The effect was even more dramatic in Germany. From now on, Germany loudly proclaimed that the Reich was encircled by a coalition of mischievous powers.

Tripoli and the Balkan Wars

Before the dust had settled in Morocco, Italy declared war on Turkey in September 1911 and invaded Tripoli. Germany and Austria were Italy's allies and could not object. The Italian navy bombarded the entrance to the Dardanelles and occupied Rhodes and Dodecenese Archipelago. This—and the fact that the Albanian revolution against the Turks was at the same time assuming serious proportions—made the latter to sign a treaty at Lausanne (October 15, 1912) whereby she relinquished Tripoli.

The success of Austria in annexing Bosnia and Herzegovina and the Italian action created fear among the Balkan States that Austria might seize the European possessions of Turkey. In 1912 a league was formed between Greece, Serbia, Montenegro and Bulgaria. 'There can be no doubt that behind this immediate and avowed aim lay the ulterior object of preventing any further increase in the threatening Austro-German control of the peninsula.' The two Great Powers—Austria and Russia—most interested in the Balkans intervened. An international conference which met at London in May 1913 restored peace by creating an independent Albania and compensating Serbia with territory in the interior. 'The first round is won,' the Serbian premier was quoted as saying, 'now we must prepare for the second against Austria.'

The creation of independent Albania cut off Serbia from the sea. 'It was the blocking of Serbia's outlet to the sea that caused the Second Balkan War among the allies.' During the Second Balkan War, Austria planned to launch an attack upon Serbia. But she was held back by Germany and Italy. 'Should she (Austria-Hungary) try to do this,' warned Bethmann Hollweg, 'it would mean a European War'. The Italian foreign minister later remarked to an Austrian diplomat: 'We shall hold you back by the coat-tails if necessary.'

The results of the Balkan Wars had direct bearing upon Europe. The Austro-Serbian feud was greatly aggravated. Russia's position, despite the collapse of the Balkan League, was increased, and Turkey lay prostrate. Germany had a great stake in Turkey. Her interests were in the heart of Turkey, at Constantinople, and in Asia Minor. 'The sweep of German imperialism from Berlin to Baghdad and the Persian Gulf might frustrate the designs of Russia to reach the Mediterranean and close the Straits to Russian trade.' The tension became inevitable when a German military mission to reorganise the Turkish armed forces was followed by the appointment of a German General, Limon van Sanders, to command at Constantinople. Sazanov, the Russian foreign minister, toyed with the idea of seizing the straits by force but it was abandoned. Germans, on their side, shrank from the conflict and in the end a face-saving compromise was arranged. The immediate crisis was over, but the underlying tension remained. William II recorded his voice of protest by observing: 'Russo-Prussian relations are dead once and for all. We have become enemies.'

The Final Crisis

From 1911 Germany was drifting towards war. On November 9, 1911, August Bebel, the veteran leader of the SPD, sounded a note of warning of a general war. On February 2, 1912, Spahn, the leader of the Catholic Centre Party, foretold of what was to happen in August 1914: Austria would attack Serbia, Russia would support Serbia, and *Casus foederis* would arise for Germany as well. After the Second Moroccan crisis the disposition towards war in Germany increased. During the crisis the Kaiser had chided Admiral Muller in not keeping the navy prepared for war. Muller himself was convinced that war with Britain could not be avoided in the long run. In December 1912, the Kaiser welcomed Haldane's warning that if Germany were to attack France, Britain would have to come to the aid of France. Moltke's reaction is typical: 'In my opinion war is inevitable, and the sooner the better'. But in early 1913 the German Government did not want to risk a great war. On February 10, 1913, both Moltke and Bethmann Hollweg warned their respective Austrian counter parts of the danger of making war with Serbia. Moltke also warned: 'When starting a world war one has to think very carefully.'

Meanwhile, the diplomatic crisis over the Second Balkan War provoked new outbursts of warlike sentiments in Germany. The Kaiser told the Austrian Chief of Staff, Baron Conrad, that he supported Austria against the Serbs:

> I am with you there. The other (*i.e.*, the other Powers) are not prepared, they will not do anything agianst it. Within a few days you must be in Belgrade. I was always a partisan of peace; but this has its limits. I have read much about war and know what it means. But finally a situation arises in which a Great Power can no longer just look on, but must draw the sword.

Moltke was also pressing more urgently than ever before for an early war. Fully aware of the military recovery of Russia, he told Conrad on May 12, 1914, about the possibility of a war. Conrad also believed that 'any delay meant a lessening of our chances; we could not compete with Russia in masses.'

The spark which set off the First World War was the assassination of the Austrian heir-apparent, Archduke Franz Ferdinand and his consort by a young Serbian patriot named Gavrilo Princip at the Bosnian town of Sarajevo on June 28, 1914. The murder was the act of a fanatic whose connection with Serbian Government could not be proved. But Berchtold, the Austro-Hungarian Foreign Minister, was determined to force war on Serbia, On July 5, 1914, he appealed to William II for assistance with the words: 'Serbia must be eliminated as a political factor in the Balkans ... friendly settlement is no longer to be thought of.' William II assured Szogyeny, the Austrian ambassador, of every help and the latter reported: 'Action against Serbia should not be delayed'. On July 6, Bethmann gave official confirmation: 'Austria must judge what is to be done to clear up her relations with Serbia; but whatever Austria's decision, she could count with certainty upon it, that Germany will stand behind her as an ally.' Bethmann added: 'If war must break out, better now than in one or two years' time when the Entente will be stronger.'

The Austrian Emperor, Francis Joseph, and the Hungarian Prime Minister, Tisza, on the other hand, were not in favour of a war. But Germany's firm assurance and the downright intolerable utterances of Serbian officials and newspapers finally converted Francis Joseph and Tisza to Berchtold's view. After an unusual delay—when the storm over the assassination had almost died down—Berchtold, on July 23, sent a fortyeight hour ultimatum to Serbia. On the day Serbia received the ultimatum, the Russian Foreign Minister, Sazanov, gave a solemn assurance to the Serbian ambassador at St. Petersburg that Russia would in no circumstances permit Austrian aggression against Serbia. Serbia accepted a number of the terms and expressed her willingness to refer the whole matter to the Hague Tribunal or to a Conference of the Powers. The Austrians declared this unsatisfactory and on July 28 declared war. They did this deliberately to make a peaceful solution impossible.

Now Russia had to do something. The Russians had no aggressive plan in Europe, but they could not allow the Balkans to fall under the control of the Central Powers. If they did, their economic life would be strangled. They warned Austria-Hungary off Serbia, when that failed, they announced their mobilisation, first against Austria-Hungary alone.

The determined attitude of Russia filled William II and Bethmann Hollweg with consternation. Moreover, the news on July 29 that Germany could not count on British neutrality if it attacked France shocked Bethmann, who had imagined that he could 'localize' the Austro-Serbian conflict. He pressed Austria to negotiate directly with Russia with a note of warning: 'As an ally we must refuse to be drawn into a world conflagration because Austria does not respect our advice.' William II also frantically wired the Tsar Nicholas II to avoid military measures which would 'precipitate a calamity we both wish to avoid'. Though the impressionable Tsar initially yielded by countermanding the order for general mobilisation, he could not resist for long the pleading of Sazanov. Hence, on July 30, Russia ordered general mobilisation.

When William II and Bethmann were trying to achieve impossible diplomatic success, Moltke on July 30 sent a telegram to Vienna, urging Conrad to start mobilization immediately and to reject compromise solutions that were being made by Lord Grey. On July 30, Russia ordered general mobilisation, and, on the next day, Germany began to mobilise. With this step effective diplomacy ceased. 'Once the German armies mobilised, war had to be brought on, not averted; and the German diplomats had to do what they were told by the German soldiers.'[3]

Bethmann Hollweg admitted on July 30, 'all direction had been lost and the stone had began to roll'. When he refused to be drawn into a worldwide conflagration by Vienna, it was too late to prevent escalation into a war.

On July 31 Germany presented a twelve-hour ultimatum to Russia demanding immediate demobilisation. Russia did not comply and Germany declared war on August 1. France was asked to stay neutral and to surrender her principal fortresses as security. The French evaded this demand and, on August 3, Germany declared war on France.

As to Britain, who had tried to avert the war, Bethmann on July 29 urged her to remain neutral and offered not to annex any French territory. Grey had never imagined military intervention on a continental scale. However, on August 2, he warned the Germans that their fleet would not be allowed to attack France in the Channel. The Germans would have gladly agreed to it, in exchange for British neutrality. But the German invasion of Belgium on August 3 brought Britain into war. The neutrality of Belgium had long been an important point in the foreign policy of Britain.

As the German army had actually entered Belgium, the issue had already been decided. On August 4, England sent an ultimatum to Germany demanding respect to Belgium neutrality. When the ultimatum was ignored, England declared war against Germany on August 4. It had been argued that Grey could have averted the war if he had defined his policy clearly. He had also been criticised for not acting earlier. But he could

---

3. Taylor, A. J. P.: *Europe: Grandeur and Decline,* P. 188.

not have averted the storm. Invasion of Belgium was an essential part of the German plan to knock out France. If Grey had acted earlier he would have achieved nothing; if he had delayed longer he would not have saved Belgium. 'The fact remains that but for the invasion of Belgium, British policy would have been much more confused and hesitant, the British people certainly not united.'[4]

Soon afterwards Montenegro joined Serbia against Austria-Hungary. On August 23, Japan declared war against Germany, partially to avenge itself on Germany and partially to fulfil its treaty obligations to Britain. The Ottoman Empire were arrayed against Russia, France, Britain, Japan, Belgium, Serbia, and Montenegro. Six of the eight great powers were immediately involved, and five of the six continents.

It is difficult to apportion the blame for the First World War to various sovereigns diplomats and chiefs of staff. 'The war was the child of the European anarchy, of the outworn system of sovereign states. The old World had degenerated into a powder-magazine, in which the dropping of a lighted match was almost certain to produce a gigantic conflagration.' It is a mistake to attribute war to any of the Governments which, in the words of Lloyd George, stumbled and staggered into war. The catastrophe could have been prevented, in the famous words of Lloyd George, the later British War Prime Minister:

> . . . had there been a Bismarck in Germany, a Palmerston or a Disraeli in Britain, a Roosevelt in America, or a Clemenceau in authority in Paris ... but there was no one of that quality visible on the bridge in any great State. Von Bethmann-Hollweg, Poincare, Viviani, Berchtold, Sazonov and Grey all able, experienced, conscientious; and respectable mariners, but distinctly lacking in the force, vision, imagination and resource which alone could have saved the situation. They were all handy men in a well-behaved sea, but helpless in a typhoon...[5]

The *Manchester Guardian*, Britain's leading Liberal paper, was dismayed when war was declared. 'For years,' it cried '[Grey] has been holding back the whole truth.' David Lloyd George, chancellor of the Exchequer, was also very critical. He assessed Grey as 'the most insular of our statesmen.' He exposed the fatal flaw of Grey: 'Had he warned Germany in time of the point at which Britain would declare war ... the issue would have been different.' In Germany, scathing criticism was made against him. He was portrayed as 'the bungler', 'the wily hypocrite', 'the chief architect of the war', who dragged Germany into war.

Bethmann Hollweg (1856-1920) the German Chancellor was no less responsible for the conflagration. He was criticised for his 'half-heartedness' and 'indecision'. His personal assistant, Kurt Reizler noted: 'His cunning is as great as his bungling.' After the war, Bethmann made a specious plea of collective guilt. In his memoirs he wrote: 'All nations are guilty, Germany, too, bears a large part of the blame.' He gave a blank cheque to Austria's war against Serbia by observing 'it can count safely on Germany's support of the Monarchy as an ally and a friend—whatever the decision.' He was obessed by fears of Russia. 'The future belongs to Russia, which grows and grows, looming above us as an increasingly terrifying nightmare, The Chancellor was suffering from paranoia with the idea that Germany's position would be imperilled by any further delay. On July 14, 1939, his personal assistant reported the Chancellor as saying 'our position is desperate ... this action is a leap in the dark and as such a most serious duty.' It appeared that Bethmann had already resigned himself to 'the calculated risk of a Continental War.'

On August 4 German troops invaded Belgium. In the mid-afternoon Bethmann was aware that the British ultimatum had arrived. The Kaiser spoke with equanimity of 'drawing the sword with a clear conscience and clean hands.' But Bethmann was aggressive. The Chancellor harangued the British Ambassador in the following words:

> The war is only turning into an unlimited world catastrophe through England's participation. It was in London's hands to curb French revanchism

4. Ibid.
5. Koch, H. W. (Ed.) *The Origin of the First World War,* P. 369 : War Guilt 1914 Reconsidered. A Balance of New Research by Erdmann Karl Dietrich.

> and pan-Slav chauvinism. Whitehall has not done so, but rather repeatedly egged them on ... All my attempts (for peace) have been wrested from me. And by whom? By England'. And why? For Belgian neutrality. Can this neutrality, which we violate from necessity, fighting for our very existence, really provide the reason for a world war? ... Germany, the Empire, and the Government are peace-loving. The Ambassador knows that as well as I do. We enter the war with a clear conscience. But England's responsibility is monumental.

The outbreak of war in 1914 provoked historical debate among scholars about the war's profound causes. The debate was spearheaded by A. J. P. Taylor whose incisive analysis and painstaking research led him to pass contradictory verdict on the issue. He squarely blamed three persons—Berchtold (the Austrian Foreign Minister), Bethmann Hollweg, and the dead man, Schlieffen, to have caused the war, even if they, too, were the victims of circumstances. But he said nothing about Sir Edward Grey. Perhaps he became sceptical when he observed: 'Perhaps the war that broke out in 1914 had no profound causes ... In July 1914, things went wrong. The only safe explanation is that things happen because they happen.' To illustrate the point, Taylor emphasizes the unforeseen and contingent factors when events move inexorably towards the critical point: 'Wars are much like road accidents. They have a general and a particular cause at the same time.'

Widening of the War

At the outbreak of the conflict, Italy refused to join the Allies on the ground that Austria was the aggressor. But her real purpose in staying out was to bargain for territory. As the Entente Powers promised Italy nearly all she wanted—Trentino and Trieste—she entered the war against its former ally (May 30, 1915). Italy's entrance was balanced to some degree by the fact that Bulgaria, still smarting from her losses in 1913, allied herself with the Central Powers in September 1915. Rumania remained neutral until August 1916, when in return for promise of territorial concessions, she declared war on Austria. By this time Portugal, on the basis of an old treaty alliance with Britain, declared war on Germany (March 9, 1916). Thus all Europe, save Scandinavia, Holland, Switzerland and Spain, was engaged in the struggle. Greece finally threw her lot with the Allies in July 1917.

At the outbreak of the war, the American President, Woodrow Wilson, had proclaimed the neutrality of the United States of America. But as the war progressed, America found it difficult to maintain the neutrality. The sinking of the British liner, Lusitania (May 7, 1916) in which about a hundred Americans lost their lives, reacted very unfavourably on American opinion. Wilson's protests had little effect on the policy of the German Government. On the other hand, in January 1917, Germany renewed her unrestricted submarine warfares. On April 6, 1917, with the support of the Congress, Wilson declared war on Germany. He intervened in the war with the historic statement: 'The world must be made safe for democracy.' In the following months a number of Latin American countries, together with Siam, Liberia and China took the lead of the United States. All together, before the guns fell silent, more that 60 nations were actively or passively involved in the war.

Comparison of the Belligerents

At the outset the advantage lay with the Central Powers. Next to Russia, Germany possessed the largest army and it was also the best equipped. There were no guns in the beginning which equalled those of the Germans in weight, precision or length of range. The Germans had gauged the potentialities of machine guns and heavy howitzers and were much better equipped with both than their enemies. Germany also had the advantage of greater unity of command. Whereas there was much jealousy between the French and the British, Germany was indisputably the leader of the Central Powers and her plans of coordination were practically unquestioned. The Central Powers enjoyed excellent internal lines of communication and hence could readily shift troops from one front to another. But the military superiority was offset by the fact that they had to carry on war on two fronts and on both of these the Germans were outnumbered. Hence the essence of the German strategy was to knock out the enemy to the west as quickly as possible before the enemy to the east could be fully mobilized.

Moreover Germany's ally, Austria-Hungary, did not possess a strong and well-equipped army. Its racial mixture was a source of weakness and Germany placed little reliance on them.

On paper the Entente Powers—France, Russia and Britain—appeared to be superior. France possessed the second-best army in the world. But there were grave deficiencies in equipment and weapons. The French relied heavily on the 75 mm field gun, which was, in fact, the best field piece in existence. But it proved to be inferior to the German machine gun and heavy artillery. Despite her immense resources, Russia's army was poor. Apart from bad leadership, it was ill-equipped and feebly supported by the home government. Britain was mistress of the seas and had a well trained professional army. But their number were only 120,000 compared to Germany's one and a half million arrayed against France in August 1914, while the French Field Army numbered over one million. But the strength of the Entente was scattered through the extremities of Europe and its efforts were inhibited by far-stretched and perilous lines of communication. Britain and France could not easily communicate with Russia.

Britain possessed the finest and largest navy in the world—65 battleships and 120 cruisers. Germany displayed a fleet of 40 battleships and 57 cruisers in 1914. Russia had a dozen battleships and a dozen cruisers. In 1914 France possessed 28 battleships and 34 cruisers. Although not considered a naval power, Austria-Hungary had a fleet which was only slightly smaller than that of Russia.

The use of submarine made its mark which few anticipated in 1914. Indeed, the sinking of three British cruisers on one day by a single German U-boat in September 1914 justified the British fear about the capacity of German submarine to 'render our position untenable'. Britain also built submarines and rendered inoperative the submarine activities by laying mines on the high seas. Yet, in the end, the submarine failed to achieve the desired result in the context of major naval operations. Moreover, the decision to use unrestricted submarine warfare precipitated the intervention of the United States which weakened the German war effort. On the other hand, the continuance of the British blockade constituted a constant problem to Germany.

Aircraft also played a vital part in combat operations. It was widely agreed that the initiative, both in technique and design, rested with the Central Powers. At the outbreak of war, Britain had a mere 37 planes while France had 136 and Germany 180. Germany depended heavily on Zeppelins which could fly higher than aeroplanes and could carry heavy loads or bombs.

1914

Germany's plan envisaged an overpowering thrust into France while maintaining a token force on the eastern front to contain Russia. The plan to overwhelm France within six weeks was largely the work of Count Schlieffen, Chief of the German General Staff from 1891 to 1906. After forcing the Western powers to sue for peace, an all-out offensive would be launched against Russia. For their part, the French planned to launch attack in the Metz-Strasbourg area, break through into Germany and join the Russians in Berlin. To hold the German thrust through Belgium, French and Belgian troops were required to link up with the British forces that would filter down from the Channel ports. The Allies also expected that the war would be a short affair. Both plans turned awry and the war turned first from one of thrust and movement into one of position and, finally, of attrition.

Seven German armies participated in the invasion of France. The three southernmost groups had two responsibilities—to turn back French invaders and to serve as anchor weights for the wide sweeping armies to the north. After entering Belgium on August 4, the northern German army captured the great fortress of Liege after four days of gallant resistance, forced the Belgian army to retire to Antwerp and threatened to engulf the left of General Lanrezac's Fifth French Army, which was holding grimly on the Sambre River. The Germans had not anticipated the arrival of the British forces which, under Sir John French, reached the Belgian frontier on August 21. By the delaying battles at Mons (August 23) and Le Cateau (August 26) the vastly outnumbered British prevented the encirclement of the French left wing.

The British and the French forces fell back upon Paris and put up stubborn resistance which slowed the momentum of the German drive. Kluck and Bulow, commanding the German First and Second Armies, began to doubt the feasibility of enveloping Paris. Now Moltke began to make mistakes which ended the possibility of a quick knock-out victory in the west. He kept his headquarters too far back; he permitted Kulck, commander of the First Army, to move his forces to the east of Paris, hoping that he would be able to smash Lanrezac's army, now engaged in bitter fighting with Bulow's forces near Guise. This was a fatal manoeuvre. As Kluck turned, General Gallieni, the Military Governor of Paris, ordered Joffre to make a general offensive on September 6. Thus began the battle of the Marne, which put the Germans on the defensive. It was at this juncture that Moltke made the mistake of committing his left wing to an offensive against Nancy. The Germans thus found themselves engaged in two violent and uncoordinated battles, on the Marne and in Lorraine, that proved too much for Moltke. The German army retreated to a position north of the River Aisne, the best defensive line in northern France. Here they entrenched themselves and began a trench warfare which continued till 1918.

For the next few months, the focus of military activity shifted to a series of battles—sometimes grandly described as the 'race to the sea'. Both sides extended their line northward from the Aisne, past Amiens and Arras to Flanders; each in turn, attempted to turn the others flank. Meanwhile, to complete the conquest of Belgium, the Germans turned upon Antwerp and occupied it on October 10. To prevent the Germans from reaching the Channel ports the British, Belgians and French fought stubbornly between mid-October and mid-November—known collectively as the first battle of Ypres. The German attempt had been thwarted, but the Allies lost heavily. It was at this point that the 'Western front' stablized in a line extending from the sea to the Swiss border.

The Eastern Front

In contrast to the western front, the war in the east was marked with great mobility. Russia, who had begun her mobilisation in a well-coordinated way, surprised both the Germans and the Austrians by throwing two armies into East Prussia and four against the Austrian lines in Galicia. The Russian army under Rennenkampf and Samsonov moved into East Prussia in mid-August. After some initial successes and the timorous behaviour of the German General Prittwitz who was replaced by Hindenburg and Ludendorff, the Russians suffered disaster at Tannenberg on August 29. Here 90,000 of their troops were taken prisoner before the fighting stopped on August 30. The unhappy commander Samsonov committed suicide. The stunning success was followed by Hindenburg's victory over Rennenkampf's isolated force in the battle of the Masurian Lakes. By the end of September, the Russians were pushed back from East Prussia. In these battles, the Russians lost a quarter of a million and a vast amount of war material.

While the Russians suffered disaster in East Prussia, four Russian armies confronted three Austro-Hungarian armies when the latter had invaded Poland. Between August 23 and the middle of September a series of hard battles were fought between them. After gaining some initial success, Conrad, the Austrian commander, ordered a retreat on September 11. The Austrians now turned their attention to this front. A German push in mid-October created apprehension that Warsaw would be captured. But this proved to be illusory and Russians were again to the German frontier. The Austrian attempt to capture Serbia also failed.

The campaign closed in December and was followed by a general stalemate. Though the Russian steam roller succeeded in immobilising masses of German and Austro-Hungarian troops, there was no hope of achieving the victory. 'It was the old story of Frederick the Great and the Russians, the battle of the athlete against the giant. The Titan was already severely punished, though his vast strength enabled him to prolong the struggle. The athlete was too agile to be knocked out, but still did not carry enough weight to knock out his opponent.'[6]

6. Grant and Temperely: *Europe in the Twentieth Century* (Edited by Agatha Ramm, 1984), P. 64.

1915

The year 1915 presaged that war would be protracted as none of the belligerents had achieved its initial war aims. It also appeared that in order to break the deadlock both sides were to spread the field of conflict, both politically and geographically. In 1915 attempts were made to find some way out of the stalemate. Falkenhayn, who took Moltke's place as Chief of the German Staff, believed that the Anglo-French armies would have to be beaten to end the war, but he did not want to subordinate the eastern front. The situation there had assumed a serious proportion with Turkey joining Germany in the autumn of 1914 and Britain preparing an expedition to the Dardanelles. Falkenhayn had to take into account the attitude of Italy. Though Italy had been Germany's ally, it became clear in the early months of 1915 that Italy would soon attack Austria-Hungary. Falkenhayn, therefore, decided to concentrate against Russia while standing generaly on the defensive on the west.

In January 1915 the Russians were hard pressed by the Turks and asked for British reinforcements. Britain, therefore, projected an attack on the Dardanelles which might relax Turkish pressure on the Caucasus and reopen the supply route to Russia through the Straits. Urged by Winston Churchill, the First Lord of the Admiralty, against the advice of Admiral Lord Fisher, a joint Anglo-French naval expedition was sent to the Dardanelles in March 1915 without adequate preparation. Churchill had visions of seizing Constantinople and, with one blow, winning the support of the doubtful Balkan States. But the expedition failed because of bad leadership in the early stages, remarkable Turkish resistance and almost incredible blunders in execution. The Turks fortified the Gallipoli Peninsula and successfully repulsed the naval attacks. Gallipoli rapidly degenerated into another 'trench front'. Towards the end of 1915 the bold decision was taken to withdraw from the peninsula. The withdrawal was the most brilliant achievement after suffering 252,000 casualties. Gallipoli was a fiasco. It was, as Liddell Hart believes, 'a sound and far-sighted conception marred by a chain of errors in execution almost unrivalled in British history.'

The Allied failure had repercussions in the Balkans. Though Greece and Rumania remained neutral, Bulgaria joined the Central Powers. In October 1915, the Bulgarian forces, along with Austrian division, invaded Serbia and overran that country before the end of the year.

Falkenhayn, who had made up his mind to make a thrust in the eastern front, found an admirable leader in Mackensen. On May 2, 1915, Mackensen's phalanx pierced the Russian line at Gorlice-Tarnow in Galicia. The Russians were completely routed. Falkenhayn exploited the success and diverted divisions from the west. Early in August Warsaw fell and the Russians were expelled from Poland altogether. The battered armies retreated behind a line that ran from Riga on the Baltic to the eastern end of the Carpathians. The Russian loss was estimated to be 300,000 men and 3,000 guns. Despite the shattering blow, the Russians could mount a new offensive in 1916 to relieve the German pressure on Verdun.

1916

At the opening of 1916, the situation was favourable to the Central Powers. In the West they held Belgium and the industrial area of France. In the east, they had a large part of Austria. On the other hand, the Allies were strengthened by Italy when the latter declared war in May 1915 against Austria.

In early December 1915 the military chiefs of Britain, France, Russia and Italy adopted the plan of a simultaneous general offensive in 1916. This would exhaust German resources while affording Britain sufficient time to build up her new armies. But the allied plan was wrecked by Falkenhayn who struck first. He identified Britain as Gemany's principal opponent. But it was useless to attempt to attack Britain herself or elsewhere in Suez or Mesopotamia. 'England, which had known how to swallow the humiliations of Antwerp and Gallipoli, will survive defeats in these distant theatres also.' But if France, Britain's best sword, was knocked out, Germany's arch-enemy would be deserted by her continental allies. Falkenhayn's choice, therefore, fell upon Verdun, a fortress on the Meuse, a place which had great strategic importance and endowed it with an emotional significance to the French. Falkenhayn's plan was to attract France's best forces at Verdun and to 'bleed her to death'.

On February 21, 1916, the German attack began with the greatest bombardment yet known in human history. For five months both sides amassed huge army, guns and ammunition into this inferno. The French defenders of Verdun, commanded by General Petain, created a legend of heroism by holding out at all costs. By mid-July the crisis was over and Verdun was saved. But it was at a heavy cost Verdun was saved. The French were badly shaken, and lost more than the Germans. Verdun marked the second failure of Germany to conquer France.

The French resistance at Verdun enabled the British to launch their first offensive. On July 1, the new fourth army, commanded by General Rawlinson, attacked on a fifteen-mile front north of the Somme river, while the French attacked on an eight-mile front south of the river. Desperate fighting took place for about five months. In November it gradually 'ran out in murder and rain'. For a net advance of six miles, the British and the French sacrificed about 600,000 lives. The German loss was estimated to be about 50,000. In the battle of Somme, the British employed a novel weapon—the armoured fighting vehicle called the tank—which was eventually to play a major role in breaking the trench deadlock. The battle of Somme caused greatest shock to the Germans. Falkenhayn was succeeded as Chief of Staff by Hindenburg by the end of August. The inexhaustible strength of Britain struck the Germans with amazement and dismay.

While the Germans were locked in grim battles in the West, the Russian General Brusilov mounted an offensive in the east. The great Brusilov offensive of June-July 1916 broke the Austrian front at Lutzk and took an entire army of 250,000 prisoners with its guns. It was a shattering setback from which Austria could never recover. Brusilov's success encouraged Rumania to join the Allies. In August Rumania invaded Austria-Hungary. But the Russo-Rumanian generals were no match for Falkenhayn and Mackensen. These two generals, the one marching through the Carpathians, and the other through the Dobrudja, converged on Bucharest on December 6. It was real victory. Henceforth the German Allies became masters of the resources of Rumania which, to a certain extent, restored the balance of German economy in 1917.

Brusilov's offensive exhausted Russia's resources in men and money. His huge losses—nearly a million in action and thousands more in desertion—broke Russia's strength and also brought revolution nearer. So, in Eastern Europe, the essential deadlock remained. Only against Turkey the Allies had scored some success. After defeating Turkey on her eastern frontier in January 1915, Russia captured Armenia a year later. The British, after suffering reverses at Gallipoli in 1916, took Baghdad in March 1917.

In Africa, a force of South Africans under Botha invaded and conquered German South West Africa in the late spring of 1915. In the following year, the Cameroons were occupied by Anglo-French forces. But the German East Africa defied Allied attack until almost the end of the war.

War at Sea

The maritime supremacy of Britain was the most important factor in the First World War. The British fleet blockaded Germany's coast, crippled her commerce and cleared the high seas of enemy warship. But the German fleet under Admiral Graf Spee sank two British cruisers off the Coast of Chile near Coronel in November 1914. Nevertheless, after a month, Spee's German Fleet was destroyed in the battle near the Falkland Island. Britain's naval supremecy was counteracted by German efforts to counter-blockade Britain by means of mines and submarines. In February 1915 the Germans declared the western approaches to the British Isles to be a zone of war and warned the neutral vessels not to enter the restricted field. In May 1915 a German submarine torpedoed off the Irish Coast the British liner, Lusitania, in which 1,200 persons lost their lives, of whom 118 were American citizens. The American President Wilson sent a sharp protest to Germany which, in a way, deterred the latter, for the next two years, from unrestricted submarine warfare.

Apart from blockade and counter-blockade, there was no major naval battle in the early phase of the war. A well-known analyst observes: 'The aim of German naval strategy, since August 1914, had been to avoid the risk of a decisive action until the British fleet was so weakened (by mines and torpedoes) that the prospect of success veered from gloomy to fair.'[7]

It was on May 31, 1916, that only one major encounter took place off the Norwegian Coast. In the Battle of Jutland, as it is called, both sides claimed victory. In point of numbers and tonnage the British loss was heavy, but the Germans failed to engage the whole of the British Grand Fleet and was fortunate to escape without great damage. After Jutland the great fleets played a secondary role. The Germans resorted to unrestricted submarine warfare mostly in the Mediterranean—on the calculation that they could fight Britain under the sea but not above it.

Crisis of the War, 1917-18

Despite the brilliant successes of the Central Powers against Russia and Serbia in 1915, and against Rumania in 1916, Germany was suffering from the British 'blockade' and its armies could apparently make no headway against France.

In January 1917 was talk of peace. In 1916 President Wilson of America had sent his emissary Colonel Edward H. House to Europe to explore the possibility of making peace. But nothing came out of it. Secret treaties had been concluded among the Allies which provided for the partition of the Austro-Hungarian and Ottoman Empires. Later in the year Wilson appealed to each side to announce negotiable terms. The Central Powers replied unspecifically, but the Allies issued, on January 30, 1917, their demands. They insisted on the restoration of lost territories and just reparation; they demanded the application of the principle of nationality as the basis of European reorganisation, and the liberation of the subject people of Austria-Hungary. These demands seemed unreasonable to Wilson who, however, entered into secret communications with the German government to elicit its demands. Wilson was disappointed when the German government made unreasonable claims.

The close of 1916 and the year 1917 heralded the appearance of new men with some new ideas. In Britain Lloyd George replaced Asquith as Prime Minister. Lloyd George's dynamic leadership infused new vigour in Britain's war efforts. He streamlined War Cabinet, secured vital appointments and recalled Churchill to the Ministry of Munitions. In France Joffre was replaced by a new Commander-in-chief, General Robert Nivelle, whose reputation had been made at Verdun. He converted Briand, the French President, and Lloyd George to his plan for a lightning offensive to end the war in the spring of 1917. Among the Central Powers, Ludendorff was in the ascendancy, both Falkenhayn and Conrad having been removed from the chief commands.

The year 1917 witnessed two important events—each destined to exercise a far-reaching influence on the course of the war; the entry of the United States into the war and the Russian Revolution.

For some time Ludendorff and his staff believed that only unrestricted submarine warfare would destroy Britain's supplies and end the war. It was believed that six or at most twelve months of such warfare would starve Britain into submission. Thus, on January 31,1917, the German government announced resumption of unrestricted submarine warfare. Three days later President Wilson of USA retaliated by breaking off diplomatic relations with Germany. In January the discovery of German intrigue with Mexico in order to help her to recover her lost territories and the severity of U-boat sinkings in February and March converted the reluctant Americans to enter into the war. On April 6, 1917, the United States declared war on Germany.

America's entry into the war changed the complexion of the war. The blockade was made more effective by the assistance of the American fleet. The Allied blockade of Germany became so severe that in 1917 food riots broke out in Berlin. The encirclement of Germany assumed a new and crippling form. The feeling grew in Germany that the war was a kind of cosmic curse. In July

7. Liddell Hart, B. H.: *The Real War, 1914-18,* P. 273.

1917 the Reichstag passed a resolution calling on the government to work for peace. Moreover, the financial burden of the war, mainly borne by Britain, was now shared with the wealthiest community in the world. As American loans relieved the financial anxieties of the Entente, so the appearance on the western front of a large well-equipped American army strengthened the Allies. The first contingent of American troops landed in France after two months of the Congress had declared war. Within a year two million American soldiers were in Europe.

Almost simultaneously with the intervention of the United States, a popular revolution in Russia overthrew the Tsar Nicholas II and set up a provisional form of Government. For a time the Russian front was not overwhelmed, but the Revolution had completely demoralised the army. Even Kerenski, the head of the provisional Government, became aware that Russia could not sustain both war and revolution at the same time. By July 1917, the Russian front had collapsed in the face of the enemy. 'No annexation, no indemnities', was the slogan of the new revolution. In October the Bolsheviks overthrew Kerensky and in December Trotsky opened peace negotiations with Germany. On March 3, 1918, Russia signed the Treaty of Brest-Litovsk. By the treaty Russia suffered immense territorial losses. it was forced to recognise Poland as an independent nation. The 'Ukraine' was set up as a 'sovereign' republic. The independence of Finland and the Baltic States—Estonia, Latvia and Lithuania—was conceded. Large territories in the Caucasus region were ceded to Turkey. By a supplementary treaty, Russia agreed to pay a heavy indemnity. By this treaty Russia lost nearly all the territory she had won since Peter the Great. Rumania was also compelled to accept a peace on most humiliating terms. Not only the whole of Dobrudja was given to Bulgaria but territories adjacent to Transylvania were ceded to Austria. Germany also took over all of Rumania's oil resource under 90-year lease.

The German generals Hindenburg and Ludendorff saw that their military effort was dangerously over-extended. They sprang a clever surprise on the Allies by withdrawing army to a new and shorter line which had been fortified with elaborate care and was known by the German as the Siegfried and by the English as the Hindenburg Line. While withdrawing the Germans adopted 'scorched earth' policy so that the Allies could not take advantage of the retreat. Neville, who had replaced Joffre as Commander-in-Chief, launched the major French offensive near Reims on April 16. The attacks which lasted until May 7, penetrated up to four miles on a sixteen-mile front. This limited success cost the French so dearly as to occasion a mutiny in half of the army. Neville was replaced on May 15 by Petain who quickly restored order.

Meanwhile, the British had already begun a massive bombardment around Arras. The British Third Army under Allenby dented the Hindenburg Line and the Canadians took Vimy ridge in one of the most brilliant assaults in the war. The British mounted offensives in April and May 1917 to distract attention from the French front. In July the British commander Haig launched his offensive in Flanders against the better judgement of Lloyd George, who called it an 'insane enterprise'. The long dreary battle of Passchandaele near Ypres in Flanders, lasting till November, brought an advance of five miles at a cost of 400,000 men. Both British and Germans regarded this battle as the worst of the whole war. Haig's optimism and policy of attrition sprang from the information which he had received from intelligence report. It suggested that: 'German civil and military morale were so near breaking point that a ruthless continuation of pressure might result not only in winning the battle but also in winning the war.' The cost of Passchendaele was to a certain extent retrieved by the brilliant British success at Cambrai in Flanders (November 1917) when tanks were used for the first time.

The catalogue of Allied reverses was completed when the Austrians, reinforced by picked German units, launched a massive attack on Italy at Caporetto (October 24, 1917) on the Isonzo River and smashed the Italian resistance. The Italians were driven back to Piave River, losing six thousand square miles of territory and 320,000 men. British and French divisions were rushed to the Italian front to sustain the sagging morale of the Italians.

While these disasters were sustained by the Allies, a wide-sweeping British thrust against the Turks brought the famous cities of Baghdad (March 11, 1917) and Jerusalem (December, 1917) under British control. These successes, though small, were significant as they secured important strategic advantages.

Victory of the Allies, 1918

Despite the collapse of Russia, the submission of Rumania, the Italian disaster and the French retreat to Marne, the position of the Central Powers had not been improved. The German submarine warfare proved to be ineffectual. Allied resistance received an impetus when in November 1917 a Supreme Allied War Council was created to coordinate the military efforts of France, Britain, Italy and the United States. In March 1918, the Allied Powers entrusted to Marshal Ferdinand Foch, the foremost military genius of the time, the central direction of their military operations in France. To Foch were subordinated the French armies under Marshal Petain and the British under Douglas Haig.

The popular morale of the Allied countries was heightened by the idealistic utterances of Woodrow Wilson, the American President. In his famous Fourteen Points laid before the Congress of January 8, 1918, President Wilson emphasised the principles that should guide a peace settlement, with a promise to grant the peoples of Austria-Hungary an autonomous status. Speaking of Germany, he said: 'We have no jealousy of German greatness... We do not wish to injure her or to block in any way her legitimate influence or power.'

By the end of 1917 Germany had become convinced that war with the Allied was not an easy affair. British blockade was sapping the resource of German economy. There were murmurs of disaffection among the German people and in July 1917 a resolution was passed in the Reichstag inviting government to consider peace by negotiation.

With Russia out of the war, Ludendorff made a last bid for victory in the West. His strategy was to split the Allied armies and roll up the British against the Channel Coast. His tactics were novel and brilliant. Picked groups of storm troops—armed with machine guns, light trench mortars and flame-throwers—were to penetrate enemy lines with surprising rapidity. Enormous reserves were necessary for the success of the manoeuvre which Ludendorff possessed. Ludendorff struck the keynote of his strategy in the following words:

> The manhood of Germany has been bleeding to death these four years and the strain cannot go on beyond a fifth. We are stinted not only in men but in everything—horses, goods, chemicals, metals, rubber. Austria-Hungary is in still worse need and is visibly perishing. Our ruthless submarine campaign has failed. Limitless supplies and overwhelming masses of men exist in America, and our submarines cannot prevent them from being brought to Europe in ever-increasing quantities. But we still have a chance of victory. Russia is at last out of the war, and the whole forces of Germany can be turned against France. Nearly forty divisions and four hundred thousand men can reinforce the western front. With these we have at least a superiority of force which will last for about four months. We will strike for victory at the point of junction of the Franco-British forces, separate their armies and win the war.

On March 21, 1918, Ludendorff launched a swift and massive bombardment over a sixty-mile line. The Germans carried everything before them but the British under Gough defended tenaciously in the Arras sector. When the fall of Amiens seemed imminent, the Allies made a supreme effort to extricate from the desperate situation by appointing Foch Supreme Commander to coordinate operations. On March 28 Ludendorff renewed the battering of Arras, but he failed to dislodge the British army. He switched his remaining reserves to support the advance on Amiens. A grim battle ensued but Amiens did not fall. The Germans had penetrated nearly forty miles and had captured many prisoners and guns and had caused around 150,000 casualties. It was a successful attack but the Germans failed to separate the British and French forces.

Ludendorff next shifted his attack to Flanders against the British and the Portuguese. The British suffered heavy losses, but they fought tenaciously and held Ypres. Haig issued his famous order: 'Every position must be held to the last man...With our backs to the wall and believing in the justice of our cause, each one of us must fight on to the end.' Foch sent French reinforcements. The Germans succeeded in capturing Kemmel hill from a French division, but broke off their offensive before April ended.

Slowly the tide of fortune began to turn against Germany. Despite heavy losses in men, reinforcements were rushed from England and divisions recalled from Italy, Salonika and Palestine. Despite the strength of 208 German divisions in France, time was running out. The arrival of 3,000,000 Americans every month from the end of April strengthened the Allied cause.

After a lengthy pause, Ludendorff burst over the Chemin des Dames on May 27 between Soissons and Reims. On May 29, Soissons fell. Next day, the Germans reached the Marne, only 37 miles from Paris. Panic seized the Parisians. Paradoxically, Ludendorff was already reaching the end of his resource. He had taken too long about his victory. The arrival of American forces in early June bolstered up the French troops. But Ludendorff still believed that he held the initiative. He decided to launch two more offensives on June 9; but this offensive ran into difficulties at an early stage and Ludendorff had to abandon it in the middle of the month.

Instead of sinking under despair, Ludendorff contemplated a final drive against the British in Flanders but decided to launch one more offensive against Reims. But when Ludendorff once more struck along the Marne west of Reims, Foch was ready for him. The Germans crossed the Marne, but that was all. On July 18 Foch ordered a counter-offensive along with nine American divisions. The Germans retreated hurriedly. This Second Battle of the Marne was an Allied victory. Not only was the German advance stopped, but like 'a gleam of sunshine dispersed the gloom that had settled on the Allies.'

After a most promising beginning Ludendorff had lost the last chance of German victory. Apart from the physical losses sustained by Germany during these offensives, the morale of the army ebbed when they found to their utter surprise that the Allied troops were basking with luxury as against their utter want.

On August 8, General Rawlinson's Fourth Army, supported by French units, made surprise attack near Amiens. This was as Ludendorff described 'the black day of the German army in the history of the war... it put the decline of our fighting power beyond all doubt.' Twenty thousand Germans were taken prisoner and they were evicted from positions which were held to be secure. Soon afterwards, Ludendorff asked his government to sue for peace.

By the beginning of September, the Allied armies mounted offensives in every sector, the British had hammered the formidable Hindenburg Line, the French were pushing forward in the Champagne and the Americans had won at St. Mihiel and were advancing in the Meuse-Argonne. From everywhere bad news began to filter through. In mid-September, the French commander at Salonika, Franchet d' Esperey, quickly overran Bulgaria, advanced to the liberation of Serbia and threatened Hungary from the rear. On September 29, Bulgaria surrendered. This meant the collapse of the whole south-eastern front as well as the indomitable will of Ludendorff. On October 3, he urged the new Chancellor, Prince Max of Baden, to sue for an armistice at once.

Germany's cause appeared to be hopeless. On October 1, the British General Allenby captured and destroyed the entire Turkish army in Palestine and entered Damascus. Turkey capitulated on October 30. By the end of October, the Italians avenged their defeat of Caporetto in 1917 by routing the Austrians at Vittoria Veneto. Austria signed an armistice on November 4.

In this predicament it was futile to expect that the Germans would hold out for long on the Western front. By the end of October, though they still remained on French soil, they were out numbered by 40 per cent. By early November the Allies were enveloping the German army from different directions. Though Foch still did not regard the war as finished, the morale of the German High Command was broken. On November 3, the German fleet at Kiel mutinied. From here the mutiny spread to the other seaports of northern Germany. Four days later, revolution broke out in Bavaria. On November 8, a German armistice commission met Foch. On November 9, the Kaiser and the Crown Prince fled to Holland and, on the same day, a republic was proclaimed at Berlin. The new German government signed an armistice at the eleventh hour of the eleventh day of the eleventh month.

The armistice brought to an end the terrible bloodletting of four years and more. The war was waged by thirty nations in which eight and a half million men were killed and twentynine million wounded. The war cost the exchequer over two hundred million dollars. A large part of France lay devastated. In Germany and Austria, the Allied blockade had played havoc. Throughout Central and Eastern Europe social revolution was either enthroned or encouraged. A by-product of the war had been Bolshevik Revolution of November 1917. 'Never before had there been a struggle so gigantic, so deadly and costly.'

Peace Settlement of Versailles

The Peace Conference opened at Paris on January 18, 1919. Twentyseven Allied and associated powers were represented by seventy delegates. In addition to the leaders of the 'Big Five', it included also Generals Botha and Smuts of South Africa, Willington Koo of China, Marquis Saionji of Japan. Because it was so large and its agenda so varied, the work of the conference was exercised by a Council of Ten composed of two representatives of each of the United States, Britain, France and Japan. It soon split into two organs; a council of four (Wilson, Lloyd George, Clemenceau and Orlando) with powers of ultimate decision. By the end of April 1919 when Orlando, the Premier of Italy departed, the most important decisions were taken by the famous 'Big Three'. A Council of Five, composed of the foreign ministers of the five principal Allied Powers, dealt with special problems assigned to it, especially economic questions and the reports of the Territorial Committee. Finally, there was a Plenary Conference, represented by lesser states, which dealt with the questions of war guilt, reparations, the League of Nations, international labour organisation, ports and railways.

Ostensibly the Powers met to translate the Wilsonian programme on the basis of which the Germans had surrendered, into a treaty of peace. The famous Wilson's Fourteen points are:

1. Renunciation by all powers of the practice of secret diplomacy.
2. Freedom of the seas.
3. Removal of all economic barriers.
4. Reduction of national armaments.
5. Settlement of all colonial claims according to the wishes of the colonial principles.
6. Evacuation of Russian territories by Germans and Austrians.
7. Restoration of Belgium.
8. Evacuation of French territory and restoration of Alsace-Lorraine.
9. Ethnic readjustments of the frontiers of Italy.
10. Self determination of the peoples of Austro-Hungarian Empire.
11. Evacuation and restoration of Rumania, Serbia and Montenegro; free access to the sea for Serbia and international guarantees of the economic and territorial integrity of the Balkan states.
12. Self-determination of the non-Turkish populations of the Ottoman Empire and internationalization of the Dardanelles.
13. An independent Polish State with assured access to the sea.
14. Creation of a League of Nations to protect the political independence and territorial integrity of all states, large and small.

During the preparatory Allied discussions of armistice terms in Paris and Versailles at the end of October 1918, England stipulated that 'freedom of the seas' must not be understood to restrict its naval supremacy. The Allied Powers also insisted on securing reparations for war damages caused by Germany. Moreover little attention was paid to Wilson's dictum of September 1918 that 'the impartial justice meted out must involve no discrimination between those to whom we wish to be just and those to whom we do not wish to be just.' The vanquished powers—Germany, Austria, Hungary, Bulgaria and Turkey—were not represented in the conference to plead their cause. In such circumstances, the 'Big Three' who made the final decisions could not mete out impartial justice to the vanquished. Moreover, the clashing personalities of Wilson, Clemenceau and Lloyd George militated against a happy solution of the war-weary world. Wilson, the idealist, was opposed by Clemenceau, the narrow nationalist filled with hatred of Germany and obsessed with the idea of the future security of France. Lloyd George, who possessed the instincts of a statesman, had to reconcile the two divergent forces, as well as to satisfy demands of the British public by the cries of 'hanging the Kaiser'. Of all three statesmen, Lloyd George used his influence to moderate the treaty in a liberal manner.

The draft treaty of peace was presented to Count Brockdorff-Rantzau, German Foreign Minister, on May 7, 1919. German plenipotentiaries were given three weeks time to present observations upon the draft terms. In several German memoranda, the main arguments were that 'the exactions of this treaty are more than the German people can bear' and that some of the terms were in flagrant violations of Wilson's Fourteen Points. The Foreign Minister Count Brockdorff-Rantzau spoke in anguish:

> We know the force of the hatred which confronts us here, and we have heard the passionate demand that the victors should both make us pay as vanquished and punish us as guilty, we are required to admit that we alone are war-guilty; such an admission on my lips would be a lie.

The draft treaty contained few provisions of Fourteen Points for which Wilson himself was to some extent responsible. He had failed to follow them up with a detailed plan and had transferred his enthusiasm to the League of Nations. Lloyd George took initiative in obtaining important modifications of the draft treaty which tried to reduce harshness on Germany, by giving minor concessions. On June 16, 1918 the Allied replied to the German observations and gave Germany a week's time to signify her acceptance of the revised treaty. Public opinion was inflamed in Germany where a cabinet crisis followed. Bauer became Chancellor and declared that the hand that signed such a treaty must wither. On the morning of June 23, the Supreme Council refused a German request for a 48-hour extension of the time limit. On June 28, 1919, at Versailles, the German plenipotentiaries signed the great treaty of 440 articles and sealed the defeat of the second German Empire which had been inaugurated in the same room, in victory.

The Treaty of Versailles

The territorial settlement contained few surprises for the Germans. In the West, Germany ceded to Belgium the small districts of Eupen and Malmedy subject to popular consultations. It also returned to France the provinces of Alsace and Lorraine which had unsettled the world for nearly fifty years.

In the east, Germany conceded to independent Poland a roughly ethnic frontier giving her Posen and West Prussia with a corridor to the Baltic. The German port of Danzig was constituted an outlet for Poland as a free city under the auspices of the League of Nations.

On the other side of East Prussia, Germany lost Memel, which eventually passed to Lithuania. Plebiscites were to determine the fate of Upper Silesia and of the East Prussian districts of Allenstein and Marienwerder. In July 1920 Allenstein and Marienwerder, by overwhelming votes, opted for Germany. In the Silesian plebiscite of March 1921 Germany secured 60 per cent of the votes against 40 for Poland. The consequent division of Upper Silesia provoked a Polish insurrection and an acute Anglo-French dissension. The matter was referred to the League of Nations Council. In October 1921 the League partitioned Upper Silesia leaving Germany more than half of the land area, but giving Poland the richer part of territory. As a result of these decisions Poland acquired the rich mineral wealth in Upper Silesia.

Though the determination of Germany's eastern frontier on ethnic lines was highly complex, this settlement, which afforded so much to the hated Poles, aroused bitter resentment in Germany—plebiscites should be held in Schleswig to determine her frontier with Denmark. As a result Denmark received northern Schleswig, while southern Schleswig voted to remain with Germany. The valuable coal region of the Saar passed under the administration of the League of Nations and the economic control of France for a period of fifteen years, after which its future would be determined by plebiscite.

In addition to territorial cessions in Europe, Germany surrendered all her colonial possessions. These regions were given the status of 'mandatories' and were distributed among the Allies. The Powers received German colonies as 'mandatories' of the League of Nations, to which they promised to give periodic accounts of their stewardship. Britain was given a mandatory over German East Africa, which was renamed Tanganyika Territory; the Union of South Africa, over German South-West Africa (Namibia); New Zealand, over the German Samoan Island; Japan, over the German New Guinea and over the German Pacific Islands South of the Equator, and Britain and France over Togo and Cameroon. The German control of Kia-chow and her privileged position in the Chinese province of Shantung were transferred to Japan. The League of Nations created a Permanent Mandates Commission to receive periodic reports on the administration of these mandated territories.

Germany recognised the independence of Belgium, Poland, Czechoslovakia and Austria, the latter being separated from Hungary. The two new independent states—Poland and Czechoslovakia—promptly allied themselves with France. Thus the creation of states in her flanks was intended to render Germany less dangerous in future. As an additional security, Germany was debarred from any political union with Austria without the consent of the League of Nations.

The Treaty of Versailles provided for the disarmament of Germany. Conscription was abolished chiefly at the instance of Lloyd George who limited the strength of the German army to 100,000 men. This small force was deprived of heavy artillery and tanks. As an additional precaution, the German Staff was to be strictly limited in number and power. The German navy was reduced to a specified number of warships, without submarines and an air force was forbidden. The disarmament was to be supervised by inter-allied commissions of control. Germany was to have no fortifications or troops on the left bank of the Rhine and in a zone fifty kilometres east of the river. The fortifications on Heligoland were to be dismantled as well as those on a zone bordering on the Baltic. The Allies expressed the fond hope that German disarmament would be followed by general disarmament. The pious hope was not fulfilled by the Allies and encouraged Hitler to violate the treaty terms.

The treaty also provided for the trial of the German Emperor who had taken refuge in Holland by an International Court for his offences against international morality. But the Dutch Government refused to extradite the ex-Emperor. Article 228 made provision for trial of German war criminals before Allied military tribunals. The German government from the first did its utmost to evade this obligation. Only a few war criminals were tried and they received light punishment.

The most galling provision of the treaty was the so-called 'war-guilt clause' (article 231), by which Germany was forced to agree to pay for damage done to the civilian population. The reparation clause was the most harshest and unrealistic part of the German settlement. The total figure for reparation was not laid down in the treaty as it was apprehended by Lloyd George that if figures were given now, they would frighten rather than reassure the Germans. A Reparation Commission was formed with powers to determine Germany's capacity to pay. The German people had to wait until 1921 to learn that in addition to the down payment of five billion dollars, they would have to pay thirtytwo billion dollars to their former enemies. Drafted by the future Secretary of State John Foster Dulles, the clause was interpreted by the Germans as an attempt to fasten guilt on them for having caused the war. As Dulles confessed later: 'it was the revulsion of the German people from this article of the treaty which, above all else, laid the foundation for the Germany of Hitler.'

Payments ceased when Adolf Hitler took power in 1933, with about 1/8 of the initial reparations paid. The final payments were made on October 4, 2010.

The remainder of the treaty disposed of miscellaneous matters like commercial relations, debts, property rights, contracts and judgments, industrial property, ports, waterways and railways. The Elbe, Oder, Niemen and Danube rivers were declared international. The Kiel Canal and its approaches were made free and open. To guarantee the execution of the treaty, the left bank of the Rhine, together with the bridgeheads on the right bank, was to be occupied by the Allies for fifteen years. Actually, the last of the occupying forces were withdrawn in 1930.

Criticism of the Treaty

The Treaty of Versailles was a dictated peace of victor powers on a vanquished nation. As Germany had not been consulted in drawing the treaty, she felt less obligation to keep to its terms. Germany was forced to admit that she was solely responsible for the war. The injustice and hypocrisy of the charge, confessed by Allied statesmen, created bitter resentment among all Germans. Truly did Wilson observe 'the real case was that justice had shown itself overwhelmingly against Germany.'

The most glaring defect of the settlement was that the principle of self-determination was not adhered to in the case of Germans. The creation of an independent Poland with secure access to the sea and the cession to Poland of a large slice of industrial area of Silesia, resulted in a geographically divided Germany. The Polish Corridor, separating East Prussia from the rest of Germany, proved a source of endless friction between the two states. Thus the Germans who lived in the Polish Corridor were sacrificed to Poland's economic need for a route to the Baltic. People in Germany agreed to the cession of Alsace and Lorraine to France, but they could not reconcile to the reshaping of the German-Polish frontier. 'That the conquests of the great Frederick should be thus abandoned through compulsion was of all the conditions of the Treaty that which German pride found it least easy to accept.'[8] Germany was not allowed the benefit of self-determination in the case of Sudetenland which was included in Czechoslovakia for geographical and defence reasons. German Austria was not allowed to become a part of the German Republic. Lloyd George had written in his Fontainebleau Memorandum:

> I cannot conceive any greater cause of future war than that the German people, who have certainly proved themselves one of the most vigorous and powerful races in the world, should be surrounded by a number of small States, many of them consisting of people who have never previously set up a stable government for themselves, but each of them containing large masses of Germans clamouring for reunion with their native land.

8. Fisher, H. A. L.: *A History of Europe,* P. 1165.

The reparation terms were the most unwise penalties inflicted upon Germany. Economically Germany was crippled when she was deprived of large territories and her rich mineral resources. Lloyd George remarked later 'was it sensible to treat her (Germany) as a cow from which to extract milk and beef at the same time?' J. M. Keynes, the noted economist, was the most vocal critic of the reparation question. He demonstrated that Germany had little capacity to pay, but that whatever resources she retained should be used by Germany not only in her own interests but in those of the European economy as a whole. Keynes also objected to the idea of longterm payments which would 'visit the sins of their fathers upon German children'. Winston Churchill described the reparation clauses as malignant and silly to an extent that made them obviously futile. Keynes' formulation provided the Germans with good excuses and they played it up fantastically for years.

The Allies tried to provide security to Europe by reducing not only German armament but also by carrying out a general disarmament programme. But the victors showed little inclination to implement the policy. While Germany's military strength was almost reduced to nullity, England continued to maintain a powerful navy, France kept a large army poised along the Rhine, and Poland raised an army more than twice as large as that of Germany. The Germans came to realise that the Wilsonian programme of disarmament was 'a sham, a trick to achieve by the pen what they (the Allies) never could have gained by the sword'.

From the beginning Germany was determined to evade the disarmament clause ingeniously and she found ample opportunity to do so through the instrumentality of Gereral von Seeckt, who became the Chief of the German Army Directorate in the second quarter of 1920. Seeckt found ways and means of circumventing the disarmament of Germany by developing paramilitary organisations, illegal militarisation of the police, and plans for general mobilisation. Seeckt, a far-sighted exponent of mobile warfare, observed with grim determination: 'Warlike is meant not in the sense of the imitation of the war, but in that of a preparation for a war.'

Seeckt got into touch with the Russian military authorities secretly and sent the Germans to receive military training in Russia. It was also arranged that war material, including aeroplanes and gas, should be jointly manufactured on Russian territory. Thus by all-round evasion of the treaty, Seeckt created a great army in miniature, full of potentialities.

The settlement created a power vacuum in Europe. Germany was strangled, politically and economically, but still possessed considerable potential strength. Russia became a communist State and found certain parts of settlement anything but satisfactory. In their anathema against Bolshevism, the Allies had concerted to detach from Russia large territories along Western frontier and to set them up as buffer states—Finland, Estonia, Latvia and Lithuania. Another weakness of the treaty was that on March 19, 1920, it finally failed to secure the ratification of the American Senate. America, having persuaded the European Allies to make peace upon the basis of an American programme, now withdrew from it. Only a greatly weakened France, with the half-hearted support of Britain, was left to counteract Germany's potential strength. Balfour had earlier prophesied that were Poland reconstituted 'France would be at the mercy of Germany in the next war, for this reason, that Russia could not come to her aid without violating the neutrality of Poland.'

The Versailles Settlement gave little satisfaction to Italy. Always the poorest of the Great Powers, the war left her economically prostrate. It came out of the war with colossal new debts piled into the old ones. Italy's territorial gains did not measure upto her expectations. She was particularly disturbed by the appearance of a new Yugoslav State in 1918. Italy saw in her only an obstacle to the satisfaction of Adriatic and Balkan ambitions. Moreover, Italians had been disappointed in not acquiring Fiume, a Dalmation port. The question of Fiume assumed significance when the Italian poet D' Annunzio seized it in a filibustering raid on 12 September 1919. But Wilson refused to concede it to Italy. This led to temporary withdrawal of Italian delegation from the Paris conference. It was not until 1924 when most of Fiume was secured by Italy. The minor concessions given to Italy in East Africa and Libya failed to satisfy her territorial aspirations. The Italian Prime Minister gave vent to his feeling on May 25, 1919:

> I cannot look forward without grave apprehensions to the future of continental Europe; the German longing for revenge must be considered in conjunction with the Russian position. We can thus see even now that the settlement to be arrived at will lack the assent of more than half the population of the European continent. If we detach from the bloc on which the new European system will have to rely for support forty million Italians, and force them into the ranks of the malcontents, do you think that the new order will rest on a firm basis?

The Treaty of Versailles rested on fragile foundation. To make the peace settlement durable, the victorious powers needed to cooperate as much as they cooperated in winning the war. After the peace settlement both Britain and France moved along divergent paths. While the British advocated a soft policy towards Germany after 1920, the French, anxious to keep Germany weak, advocated another. The situation enabled Germany to bring about a succession of treaty modifications winked at by one or another of Allies. Wilson who had sought to make the Treaty of Versailles the palladium of international democracy and had expected a radical change in the German attitude, found instead people burning with revenge. And they found a leader of deep and evil inspiration.

Thus, everybody felt that a great opportunity had been missed. 'The statesmen had not been equal to the grandeur of events. They had made a peace which was no peace ... Human nature, it was widely felt, had failed. Europe had not been made safe for democracy. The bright exhilaration of victory was soon blotted out by the fog of disillusion, resentment and despair.'[9]

OTHER TREATIES

Treaty of Saint-Germain (September 10, 1919)

The treaty of St. Germain dissolved the old Austro-Hungarian Empire and set up a republi-

9. Fisher, H. A. L.: *A History of Europe,* P. 1169.

can government in Austria. Moreover, Austria was made to accept responsibility for causing loss and damage to the Allies. Although Austria desired organic union with Germany, she was forbidden to do so.

The territorial redistribution of the former Habsburg dominion proved a ticklish problem. There were no clear-cut ethnic or national border lines and, therefore, in the end no one was happy. To Italy, Austria ceded South Tyrol, the Trentino, Trieste, Istria and some islands off Dalmatia. To Czechoslovakia she gave up Bohemia, Moravia, part of Lower Austria, and nearly all Austrian Silesia, these areas containing about three million Sudeten Germans, Poland received Austrian Galicia. Rumania was awarded Bukovina. Yugoslavia received Bosnia, Herzegovina and the Dalmatian coast and islands. 'The once proud Austria, which had ruled over fifteen different races, was reduced to less than half of her former size, and lost a third of her purely German population. She became miserably poor and dragged out a pathetic existence from this time until she was annexed by Germany in 1938. She was again separated in 1945.'

By other clauses of the treaty, Austria gave up all rights, privileges and concessions in non-European territories, assented to a blank reparation cheque; accepted special regulations governing navigation on the Danube and acknowledged the right of the Allies to try Austrian 'war criminals'. Austria herself was guaranteed free access to the Adriatic. Austria surrendered her entire naval force and her army was limited to 30,000 volunteers.

Treaty of Trianon (July 4, 1920)

The Treaty with Hungary took much longer. Like Austria, the armistice had cost her the occupation of large tracts of her prewar territory by Czechs, Yugoslavs and Rumanians. Being unable to get satisfaction on Allied decision to assign Transylvania to Rumania, Karolyi, the premier, resigned in March 1919. In the confusion that followed, Bolshevik-trained Bela Kun seized power. Unwisely, he alarmed the Allies by revolutionary propaganda outside Hungary. Czech and Rumanian attacks on his regime followed. The occupation of Budapest in August 1919 by the Rumanians and the failure of the Russians to help Bela Kun led to the collapse of his regime. A confused period was followed by the emergence of a stable government under Admiral Horthy (March 1, 1920). This government signed the treaty of Trianon (June 4, 1920), which rendered Hungary a truncated state, allowing her to retain only one-fourth of its old territories and one-third of its prewar population. To Czechoslovakia went Slovakia and Ruthenia; to Rumania went Transylvania. Yugoslavia took Croatia-Slavonia and some other strategic areas. Austria got Burgenland or West Hungary. Territorial cessions completely deprived Hungary of access to the sea. Like Austria, Hungary was made liable to reparation payments. Her army was also reduced to 35,000 men.

Treaty of Neuilly (November 27, 1919)

By the Treaty of Neuilly, Bulgaria lost its ascendancy in the Balkans which she had acquired as a result of the Second Balkan War. The treaty gave Yugoslavia four small regions in Western Bulgaria, Dobrudja was handed back to Rumania, western Thrace to Greece and with it Bulgaria's strip of Aegean Coast. Bulgaria was promised economic outlets to the Aegean Sea. She was also forced to pay a reparation debt (£ 100 million). Her navy was abolished and army was limited to 20,000 men.

Treaty of Sevres (August 10, 1920)

The Treaty of Sevres completely destroyed the Ottoman Empire. Palestine and Mesopotamia were mandated to Britain and Syria to France. Armenia in Asia Minor was declared independent. Turkey was compelled to give up Smyrna, Thrace, Adrianople, Gallipoli and the Aegean Islands to Greece, Dodecanese to Italy and Cyprus to Britain. Practically all that was left to Turkey were Anatolia and the city of Constantinople. Her population was reduced from twenty-one to five millions. Besides the usual punitive clause to be found in the other treaties, Turkey's finances were to be placed under the control of a commission. Though nothing was said in the treaty of spheres of interest, but France, Britain and Italy entered into a tripartite agreement to carve out their respective areas.

Nationalist forces under the leadership of Mustafa Kemal, refused to accept the settlement. In the civil war that followed, Kemal's revolutionary armies overthrew the Sultanate and set up a republic. Kemal was encouraged by the diplomatic recognition accorded to him by the Bolshevik regime in Russia. The French and the Italians were not happy with the terms of the Treaty of Sevres owing to undue gains secured by Britain and Greece.

The Lloyd George government in England encouraged the Greeks to invade Turkey. But Kemal met the situation with characteristic courage. In March 1921 the Italians agreed to withdraw from Anatolia. Kemal made a military agreement with Russia and in September 1922 he routed the Greek armies and drove them from Smyrna. The French came to terms. Kemal then turned his attention towards Constantinople, which was defended by a small British garrison. It was a serious crisis for British prestige and led to the downfall of Lloyd George. With French mediation an armistice was signed.

The final settlement was made at Lausanne on July 23, 1923, where the Sevres Treaty was completely revised. Britain retained most of the territorial gains made at Sevres, as did France. Greece lost to Turkey virtually everything and even had to turn the Dodecanese Islands back to Italy. Turkey recovered Anatolia, Cilicia, Adalia, Smyrna, eastern Thrace and Constantinople and secured complete independence in directing its internal affairs. The Straits of Dardenelles and Bosphorus were to be demilitarized, opened to neutral vessels and placed under the supervision of an international commission responsible to the League of Nations. It is not without significance that the Treaty of Lausanne was the only negotiated, rather than imposed, treaty and it proved to be the most durable one.

Criticism of the Settlement of Eastern Europe

The settlement of eastern Europe, though a vexed one, endured the test of time. The guiding principle in the territorial settlement was the principle of nationality and this was followed. But in redrawing the map of eastern Europe, it was impossible to eliminate national minorities. All the new countries had such minorities, and the new Czechoslovakia which was composed of multilingual people—Czechs, Slovaks, Germans, Poles, Hungarians, and Ruthenians—presaged future trouble.

The eastern settlement suffered from two inherent weaknesses. The increased political diversity of the area and the surging nationalism made economic interdependence among the states impossible and caused economic instability. This led to wasteful economic competition and military spending which contributed in no small degree to political instability of the area.

In the second place, the whole eastern settlement failed to come to grips with the Russian problem. The conference of Paris refused to explore the possibilities of and accomodation with the Bolshevik regime. After the Hungarian coup of Bela Kun, the Western Powers assumed anti-Bolshevik stance, countenanced the White armies of Denikin and Kolchak and tolerated the Polish invasion of the Ukraine. The Western Powers were under the delusion that by this policy they could contain Bolshevism and deny Russia a role in European affairs in the same way as they did with regard to Germany by imposing on the latter the Treaty of Versailles. 'But Russia and Germany were too large and potentially powerful to become political nullities.' Events were to prove that the failure of the peacemakers in Paris to integrate at least one of them into the new European system rendered the eastern settlement fragile and temporary.

Results of the First World War

The Great War was more than an international conflict; it was a revolution. Count Czernin, a leading Hungarian statesman predicted that 'the coming generation would not call the drama of the last five years the World War, but the World Revolution.' The German Conservative leader Gustav Stresemann saw 'the war as part of a world revolution which would profoundly stir all aspects of life and predicted that the revolution was destined to continue long after the formal end of hostilities.' There are some upheavals born of the War which have far-reaching effects: Communism in Russia, Fascism in Italy, Spain and a number of Central European States, Nazism in

Germany, faltering socialism in Britain and France and New Dealism in the United States.

Immediate Results

The First World War—lasting more than four years—left imperishable scars. More than eight million had been killed and a greater number disabled. All previous wars from the Napoleonic wars to the Balkan wars of 1913—had cost less than four and a half million lives. The material losses likewise were colossal. The countries which suffered most were Serbia, Rumania, Belgium, France and Poland. The Polish writer, Sienkiewicz wrote in anguish: 'Our country has been made the cockpit of Europe and been devastated from end to end.' In France about 8,000 square miles of agricultural land were laid waste, and 500,000 buildings damaged. The property loss in Europe reached an astronomical figure.

Economic Changes

The economic consequences of the war proved to be disastrous. Gold reserves were drawn upon, and large war loans were raised both at home and abroad. The whole process depleted Europe's overseas investment and strengthened the United States economy. America was the creditor of the Allies and emerged from the war as the economic dictator of the world. The internal balance of the economy of nearly every country in the world was affected. The blockade caused more damage to European neutrals than non-European countries.

The position of Britain was strong owing to her financial strength and accumulation of capital investment overseas. Yet even here the boom was temporary. Elsewhere, about 1920, business began to pick up but it was an utterly false prosperity, based on scarcity rather than plenty, and the bubble soon burst. In most of the countries, the currency lost its value by over-issuance of paper money. Prices soared and it became well nigh impossible to revamp the industries ravaged by the war. There was need of raw materials and machinery in order to produce; and credit was all but blocked by the chronic instability of exchange. The result was widespread unemployment especially in Central Europe. Economic prostration was also due to apathy of the working class and in some cases by famine which in Germany continued for more than a year after the war. Germany was burdened with heavy indemnities which acted as a deterrent to industrial recovery. A contemporary commented cryptically: 'It is far worse than the war. During the war we had hope. We knew it would end some day. Now there is no hope.' To make matters worse, nationalism created artificial barriers.

The peasant benefited greatly post-war conditions. In those countries where peasant proprietorship was widespread, the peasants greatly increased their holdings. A sweeping change occurred in eastern Europe. The large estates in Russia were confiscated and turned over to the peasant. In the Baltic States, in Poland, in Czechoslovakia, in Rumania, the large estates were expropriated and handed over to the tillers of the soil. Peasant proprietorship became the order of the day in Europe.

Meanwhile, competitive enterprise gave way to national controls and regulations. In Germany Walter Rathenau created 'war socialism' by requisitioning war materials, by efficient coordination, by finding substitutes for the natural resources of which the blockade deprived Germany. In the authentic tradition of Bismarck, Rathenau subordinated everything to state needs. Germany's 'war economy' set a model of economic planning for the whole of the post-war world. In France, special boards of industrialists were set up to plan production. In the United States, the War Industries Board, headed by Bernard Baruch accelerated production. In Britain, Asquith created a new Ministry of Munitions in May 1915 and put Lloyd George in charge of it.

Social Changes

The War marked the beginning of revolution in making the proletariat a powerful factor in politics. The triumph of the proletariat was complete in Russia. Trade-unions were now in a strong bargaining position. Laws were passed establishing systems of insurance against unemployment, sickness, accident and old age. The principle of minimum wage had been given a wide application both in England and France. There had been some experiment in what we call 'industrial democracy' in which the workers were 'co-workers with the employers and not merely living tools'. In Germany was adopted in 1923 a systematic plan of compulsory arbitration in wage disputes. The workers fought for a shorter day and they became successful. In most industries eight hours became the standard.

The importance of the working class was recognised at the Congress of Paris. An International Labour Bureau was established by the League of Nations to collect and disseminate information on Labour conditions. Some of its recommendations were adopted: (1) that labour should not be regarded as a commodity; (2) that it should have the right to organize for all lawful purposes; (3) that living wage should be maintained; (4) that child labour should be abolished; (5) that men and women should receive equal pay for equal work; and (6) that a system of factory laws be adopted.

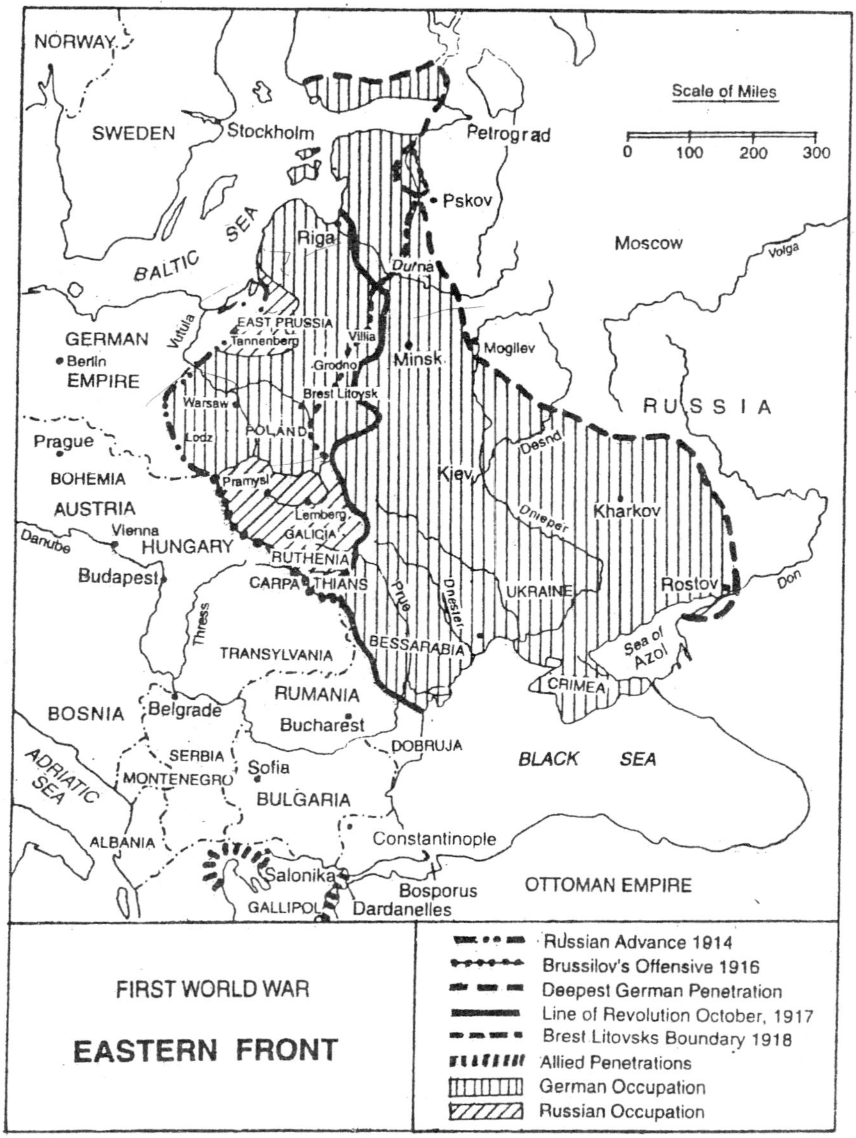

The growing importance of the working class led to a remarkable growth of the Labour Party in England. Even in France the strength of the socialists grew considerably. In Germany and Austria as well as in some of the new nations the socialists wielded an important influence.

The War also gave great impetus to the emancipation of women. Napoleon prescribed for women needlework and other innocent pursuits. Kaiser William II marked out women's sphere as 'church, children, cooking.' 'Feminism' as the movement for 'equal rights' has been called, had made considerable progress before the close of the war. After the war, women acquired equal rights with men in all the countries of Central Europe, as well as in Poland, Russia and the Baltic States. Woman now was more prone 'to face realities, more ready to think for herself, more apt to weigh conventions and to alter them as she pleases.'

The bursting of woman's fetters was somewhat paralleled by the outburst of youth. The war brought disillusionment to the youth. There was something of a revulsion against war as an instrument as barbarous as it was futile. There was a distinct note of pacifism among the English youth after the war. The Oxford Union resolved in 1933 that under no circumstance the youth was under obligation in fighting for King or country. In Germany, the *Wandervogel*, a student society, craved for freedom—freedom from the conventional. Though the organisations

FIRST WORLD WAR

WESTERN FRONT

of youth were patriotic in character, especially in China, Ireland, Germany and Russia—but they illustrated the lawless side of the restlessness which emanated from the war. 'With youth, as also with woman, the shock of that great upheaval tended to rouse a spirit of revolt against the sanctity of convention.'

Triumph of Democracy and Nationalism

The war brought about the end of the three of the oldest dynasties in history, the Romanovs, the Habsburgs and the Hohenzollerns and the establishment of democratic constitutions, in Germany and Austria. The war, whose object was to make the world safe for democracy, seemed to have achieved its aim. But as time went on, there was some reaction. Greece and Spain resorted to dictatorship temporarily; Italy erected her Fascist regime; Poland found autocracy more congenial than constitutional government; and Germany showed her allergy to democracy. The prevalence of dictatorships seemed to show that democracy was yet to gain ascendancy in post-war Europe—afflicted as it was with abnormal conditions.

The war spread the infection of European nationalism to a wider world. Japan's triumph in 1905 and her successful participation in the war encouraged her nationalist pride and imperial ambitions. India's collaboration in the Imperial cause inspired her people to demand independence. Similar reactions were evident among the self-governing Dominions.

Perhaps the most significant consequence of World War I was that it brought to a climax the process of the West's changing value patterns. Two divergent ideas enveloped the purpose of the Western society. One was characterised by political and economic liberalism and quest for universal peace. The other stressed the inevitability of violent force in the solution of human problems and chauvinistic nationalism. The war gave strong impetus to the second trend.

In 1922 Sigmund Freud said of the war: 'No event ever destroyed so much of the heritage of mankind ... or so thoroughly debased what is highest.'

But out of the ashes of the War was created the League of Nations—a unique experiment of sagfeguarding international peace and justice.

CHAPTER 30

REPARATION, INTER-ALLIED DEBTS

The payment of reparation by Germany after the First World War created a serious international problem. Article 232 of the Treaty of Versailles had specified that 'Compensation will be made by Germany for all damage done to the civilian population of the Allies and their property.' The basis of reparation was the famous War-Guilt Clause of Article 232 in which Germany accepted the responsibility 'for causing all the loss and damage to which the Allied and Associated Governments and their nationals have been subjected as a consequence of the war imposed upon them by the aggression of Germany and her allies.' This enforced acceptance of a very general responsibility was bitterly resented in Germany. Moreover, no sum was fixed by the treaty itself. It was left to an Allied Commission, called the Reparation Commission, to fix the total amount to be paid by Germany. The assessment was to be made by May 1, 1921. Prior to that date Germany was to pay the sum of £1,000,000,000.

The reparation issue was saddled with divergent political and economic interests of the powers. Belgium and France, which had suffered enormously as a result of the war, were insistent on claiming the maximum. Britain, more flexible in her attitude, began to look upon Germany as a potential customer of her commodities, which the heavy burden of reparation would impoverish. France, obsessed with the idea of keeping Germany weak, wanted to secure from reparation compensation from her losses. These differences of outlook and interest between France and Britain confused the reparation problem when their harmonious cooperation was needed to settle the issue.

While the Reparation Commission deliberated, the Allied statesmen met at Spain in July 1920 and agreed upon the allocation of reparation receipts. France was to take 52 per cent, Britain 22 per cent, Italy 10 per cent and Belgium 3 per cent, the balance being left for distribution among the minor Allies. Meanwhile, early in 1921, Germany announced that she had completed payment, in the form of coal, rolling stock and that further payments would be suspended until a final reparation total was fixed. The Reparation Commission declared the German claim false and accused Germany in default of her obligation. Thereupon the Allied troops occupied the three towns of Dusseldorf, Duisberg and Ruhrort on the east of the Rhine.

On April 27, 1921, the Reparation Commission fixed Germany's total liability at £6,600 million. On May 5, the Allied governments communicated to Germany a 'schedule of payments' prescribing methods for discharging her obligations which in practice mitigated them. But it included a demand for the payment of £50 million (one milliard marks) by the end of the month. The schedule was accompanied by an ultimatum that if a satisfactory reply were not made within six days, the Allies would occupy the Ruhr, the centre of Germany's metallurgical industry. After a Cabinet crisis in Germany, Wirth's administration accepted the Allied terms on May 11. By August 1921, Germany made the first payment under the schedule by means of a loan from London bankers. This was destined to be her last cash payment for more than three years.

Soon thereafter, Germany was in the throes of a currency crisis. The mark had lost its value. Before the war, 4.2 German marks equalled one American dollar; in 1919 the ratio was 8.9 to 1; by late 1921 it took nearly 250 marks to equal the buying power of one dollar. It became clear that Germany would require large amounts of foreign currency to meet her obligations under the schedule. At a conference at Cannes in January 1922, Lloyd George gave a sympathetic hearing to the arguments of Ratheneau, the leader of the German delegation. But the French Government, then headed by Raymond Poincare, was bent upon securing reparations. However, Germany had to be granted a moratorium on reparation payments for a year (May 31, 1922) because of collapse of the mark.

The British, who were sceptical about reparations offered in August 1922 annulment of all their reparations and Allied debt claims, if the United States would waive her claims to repayment by her Allies. Because the Americans would not consider this, the scheme failed. The remaining months of 1922 were spent in an exchange of notes between London, Paris and Berlin. Finally Poincare was convinced that Germany could pay, if only she was forced to do so. At the end of December 1922, the Reparation Commission, by a vote of the French, Italian and Belgium representatives declared Germany in default. Sir John Bradbury, the British representative in the Commission protested. On January 11, 1923 the French and Belgian forces began the invasion and occupation of the Ruhr.

The event proved disastrous for all concerned. The Germans, outraged by the hostile incursions, resorted to passive resistance. This measure created dislocation and severely hampered the French in their attempt to draw economic benefit from the occupation. The French, in turn, fostered separatist movement in the Rhineland and resorted to coercion by imprisoning local industrialists, who preferred inflation to providing reparation. The French eventually discovered that their expedition into the Ruhr cost them more money than they got out of it. The Germans also came to realise that passive resistance brought on more evils than the occupation itself.

The economic consequences to both sides were disastrous. The franc had lost nearly a quarter of its value and the mark had become to all intents and purposes worthless. Germany resorted to unrestricted printing of paper money. The inflation had a disastrous effect and the Government was forced to choose between complete surrender and total disintegration. On September 27, 1923, Germany unconditionally abandoned passive resistance and withdrew the ordinance suspending reparation deliveries. The new German government under Stresemann had an unusual sense of practical moderation. By the end of November the Schacht-Luther financial reforms had placed Germany on the road to recovery.

Fortunately the Allied Powers thought it wise to resume negotiations and a proposal was adopted for the appointment of an international commission of experts to study the whole problem of German reparation. On November 30, 1923 the French government agreed to participate and the Reparation Commission appointed a committee, consisting of two representatives each from the United States, Britain, France, Italy and Belgium to study various facts of Germany's financial problems. The committee, presided over by the American General Charles G. Dawes, met in Paris in January 1924 and presented its report on April 9.

Emphasising Germany's need for the resources of her whole territory, the report pointed out the two requisites of a stabilised currency and a balanced budget. The Dawes Committee recommended the creation of a new currency Rentenmark at the same parity, the Reichsmark, which would be controlled by a Bank of Issue independent of the German government. Germany was to pay amounts rising in five years from 1,000 million gold marks or £50 million to 2,500 million gold marks (£125 million), to be raised partly in the German budget, and partly from state railway bonds and industrial debentures. Payments were to be made in German currency, and that the responsibility for the transfer of these sums into foreign currencies should rest with the Allied Governments. There was to be an 'Agent for Reparation Payments' in charge of the whole plan. Finally, Ruhr should be evacuated. For the double purpose of creating a gold reserve requirements of the new bank and of helping her to pay reparations in 1924-25, Germany should receive a foreign loan of 800 million gold marks.

On August 16, necessary agreements for carrying out the Dawes Plan were signed. On September 1, 1924, the plan became effective. Evacuation of the Ruhr began at once. The proposed loan was floated with complete success, the largest portion being raised in the United States.

Under the supervision of Agent General Seymour Parker Gilbert, a United States financier, the plan worked well. German business picked up and reparation payments were promptly made. Above all, the Dawes Plan eased diplomatic tension between the Allies and the Germany, and between Britain and France. But the Dawes Plan had serious flaws. It provided for annual payments, but it failed to prescribe their duration or to fix the total amount of Germany's indebtedness. Worse still, the Dawes Plan set up the dangerous precedent of depending on foreign loans. German borrowing increased by leaps and bounds and the influx of capital was astonishing. 'Few people had the insight to realise that Germany was paying her debts out of American money, and that her solvency depended on the continued popularity of German loans in Wall Street.'[1]

The Dawes Plan was not a final settlement of the reparation problem. It was 'framed to facilitate a final comprehensive agreement as to all the problems of reparation and connected questions.' One of these connected questions was the occupation of the Rhineland. In September 1928 an agreement was reached among the Allied Powers in regard to the early evacuation of the Rhineland and for the appointment of a committee of financial experts to work out a final settlement of the Reparation problem.

The Committee of financial experts met in Paris in February 1929 under the chairmanship of the leading American expert, Owen D. Young. The Committee was known after him as the 'Young Committee.' After deliberations lasting for four months, the Committee submitted to the Governments the 'Young Plan'.

The Plan contemplated a new indemnity bill to be paid over a period of 58 years. For the first thirtyseven years Germany was to make annual payments averaging £100,000,000 (as against the maximum Dawes annuity of £125,000,000) followed by twentytwo smaller annual payments. The payments were divided into two categories, unconditional and conditional. About one-third of each annuity (£33,000,000) was to be treated as an unconditional obligation. In the case of conditional obligation, German Government was entitled to postpone transfer into foreign currencies for a maximum period of two years. The sums payable were to be paid in Reichsmarks. A Bank of International Settlements was created which was to act as trustee for the creditor countries and to act as the agency for the receipt and distribution of funds. By abolishing the Reparation Commission and other agencies of foreign control, the Young Plan gave financial autonomy to Germany.

The Allies met at the Hague in August 1929 to discuss the Young Report and to settle the details of the evacuation of the Rhineland. The Conference reached an agreement that all Allied troops should be withdrawn from the Rhineland by June 30, 1930. The first Hague Conference was followed, on January 3, 1930 by a second. It was mainly concerned with the question of establishing wilful default and with the imposition of sanctions in such an event. It was agreed to submit the question of default to the Permanent Court of International Justice, granting to the Allied states full liberty of action in the event of wilful default by Germany. On May 17, 1930, ratification of the Young Plan came into effect.

At the time of ratification of Young Plan, the United States was enjoying a period of unexampled prosperity. But in 1929 the Great Boom came to an abrupt end, and the long years of depression completely dried up the dollar flood to Germany. Deprived of this support, German economy collapsed. Because Germany was good customer of England, British economy seriously worsened. By 1930 and 1931 almost all of Europe was affected by the economic depression.

American economy in the twenties was anything but sound and basically served the greeds of its managers. In 1929 one-third of the nation's

1. Carr, E. H.: *International Relations between the Two World Wars*, 1919-39 (1963), P. 85.

income was siphoned off by 5 per cent of the population. With its small share of the total income, the general public could not buy the flood of goods which steadily poured into the market. Moreover, during the middle and late twenties the whole American population was engaged in a wild frenzy of speculation. In the last week of October 1929 the market collapsed. The Golden Twenties were over. 'As a result the world slipped with a crash from the shoulders of the Atlas who had been sustaining it.' As loans were no longer available, reparation and debt payments had to be made in gold. This abnormal flow to the United States created an artificial scarcity of gold. When gold is scarce, prices fall; prices fell accordingly reducing purchasing power and the capacity of debtors to pay.

Crisis in Germany

In Germany, the crisis was particularly acute. Germany was the largest debtor state. In the years 1927 and 1928, Germany had borrowed five times the amount payable in reparation. The surplus was spent in development work which left a substantial deficit in every year. The accumulated deficit in 1929, amounted to over 1,200 million Reichsmarks. To avert economic ruin, Chancellor Heinrich Bruning, issued between July 1930 and July 1931 dozens of emergency decrees increasing taxes, lowering salaries and unemployment benefits and effecting other economies. Foreign creditors withdrew their short term loans. In the first three weeks of June 1931 the Reichsbank lost 41 per cent of its gold holdings.

Throughout 1930 the crisis appeared to be a passing phase in the economic life of the world. 'But the winter of 1930-31 shattered the last defences of optimism; and serious people began to think of the impending collapse of civilization.' In May 1931 the most important private Austrian bank Credit-Anstalt, was threatened with liquidation. In June the Bank of England advanced £6,000,000 to the Austrian National Bank to tide over the crisis. But by this time worldwide bankruptcy and failure of confidence became manifest.

At this point on June 20, President Hoover of the United States proposed a one-year world moratorium by all important creditor Powers of 'all payments on intergovernmental debts, reparations, and relief debts, both principal and interest.' Of the Allied Powers, France alone objected to the Hoover moratorium. She at last agreed on condition that the unconditional reparation payments were to be paid by Germany to the Bank of International Settlements, and that the interest should be charged on the whole of the postponed payment.

Despite optimism in the United States, the moratorium negotiations revealed the total financial exhaustion of Germany. On July 13, first a week after the Hoover moratorium having been accepted by all concerned, the largest German bank Darmstadter and National bank failed. Thereupon all German banks were forced by governmental decrees to close their doors. To deal with the new financial crisis in Germany, a conference met in London. The whip hand was held by France who had few German investments. The Committee recommended that the existing shortterm credit be continued and recommended additional longterm credits. A 'Standstill Agreement' was reached whereby all shorttime credits to Germany were extended for six months. At the end of that time the Standstill was prolonged for another year, while Chancellor Bruning announced in January 1932 that Germany could not pay.

Meanwhile British finance had also crashed and Britain had to abandon the gold standard. The advisory committee of the Bank of International Settlements which met at Basle on December 7, 1931 reported that the conditioned reparation payment for the year beginning in July 1932 by Germany would not be possible. As a last resort, Britain, France, Germany, Italy, Belgium and Japan met at Lausanne in June 1932. The United States did not join as 'it was against the policy of Congress that any of the indebtedness of foreign countries to the United States should be in any manner cancelled or reduced.' Britain proposed a six months' moratorium. France opposed it because she thought it meant the end of Reparation. A basis of settlement was, however, arrived at Lausanne. The powers agreed to cancel all German reparation debt in return for a single payment by Germany of £150,000,000 in the form of 5 per cent redeemable bonds. But a contemporary agreement signed by the creditor governments on July 2, 1932 cancelled war debts as between themselves. But its ratification was to depend on a satisfactory settlement between the creditors and the United States. But the question of ratification or non-ratification of the Lausanne agreement was of little practical account. In fact, it was never ratified. The Lausanne Conference buried the Reparation question once and for all.

Inter-Allied War Debts

Inter-Allied War Debts were inextricably intertwined with the reparation problem and eventually shared its fate. In the first years of war Britain had advanced vast sums to her European Allies including Russia, and had in turn borrowed more than half the total amount from the United States. Soon after the entry of the United States into the war, Congress authorised the lending of $3,000,000,000 to the Allies at 5 per cent interest. Other loans followed during the remainder of war. Altogether the American advances to twenty nations totalled $10,338,000,000. During the Peace Conference in 1919, Britain announced their willingness to cancel the war debts owed them by the other Allies if the United States followed the same principle.

In 1922, when America insisted for repayment, France declared that she could only pay her war debts if Germany paid reparation. France, who had borne the brunt of the war, could not reconcile the idea of paying to the United States when defeated Germany failed to pay her.

America insisted that international good faith could be maintained only by the payment of the inter-Allied debts. From the very beginning of the controversy her thesis was that the debts owed by the Allies were in no way related to or dependent upon Reparation from Germany. Not all the money due her, America insisted, was spent for war purposes, some was loaned to pay maturities of previous debts; some to maintain the value of the franc and the pound, sterling and some was loaned after the armistice. America had no intention to cancel the debts and to burden their own tax-payers with European war-debts.

In view of the American attitude, the British Government decided to honour their obligations. American attitude also changed by deciding not to insist upon the full payment according to the terms of the contract. In February 1922, America appointed a World War Foreign Debt Commission to collect the Allied debts by 1947 and impose a rate of interest not less than 4 per cent. Britain's case was a special one, as being both debtor and creditor. After the entry of the United States into the war Britain acted as broker for her European Allies, contracting heavy debts in the United States, largely on their behalf. On August 1, 1922, Britain addressed to the Allied powers the famous Balfour Note. She reminded them that exclusive of interest, they together owed Britain about £1,300 million, in addition to the £650 million due to her from Russia and £1,450 million as German reparation; for her part Britain owed £850 to the United States. The Note explained that American insistence upon payment compelled Britain to abandon her liberal policy of remitting any Allied payment to her. But she still was prepared to remit all the debts due to Britain by her allies in respect of loans, or by Germany in respect of reparation. This would form part of an all round cancellation of war-indebtedness 'in one great transaction'. American opinion was highly inflamed by this statesman-like proposal. Both the Americans and the French opposed the linking of war debts with reparation. President Coolidge derisively remarked, 'They hired the money, didn't they?' The British Government accordingly sent Stanley Baldwin and Montagu Norman, Governor of the Bank of England, to Washington to assuage the feelings of the Americans. Nevertheless, the British Premier, Bonar Law, had to accept the stringent American terms. The British funded debt was fixed at 4,600 million (£ 33,000,000) dollars repayable over 62 years and subject to an average rate of $3^1/_3$ per cent interest. Until 1926, Britain received nothing from the European Allies. Then, following the model of British-American agreement, agreements were reached for the payment by annual instalment of the debts due from France, Italy, Rumania, Yugoslavia, Greece and Portugal to Britain and to the United States. Mention may be made that while the American settlement with Britain represented a reduction of less than 30 per cent of the original debt, the British settlement represented reductions, in the case of Italy, of more than 80 per cent in the case of the other Allies, of more than 60 per cent.

The Hoover moratorium caused intense feeling in Europe, especially in France and in England. However, in October 1931, America, for the first time, recognised the relationships between war debts and reparations. But the question became highly critical on the eve of the American Presidential Election which fell due in November 1932. In the election campaign however, both parties were pledged to oppose cancellation of the debts.

Meanwhile, opinion in the United States, as elsewhere, gathered momentum that complete cancellation would be in the interest of America as well as the rest of the world. The world depression hit the United States most and the loss was greater than the full amount receivable in respect of War debts. Since 1928-29, the United States had lost about 700 million pounds' worth of exports, as compared with a debt of £40 to £50 million payable to her by the world.

Immediately after the presidential elections, the British and French governments asked for a suspension of the instalments due in December, pending discussion of the whole question. American response was found to be unfavourable. This called forth, on December 1, 1932, a British statement of the whole case for remission. But the American Government, however, was adamant and insisted on the payment of the instalments due either from France or Britain. Thereafter Britain paid the whole instalment in gold. But the French Government refused to pursue a similar course and accordingly defaulted on the payment. In order not to disturb the Lausanne Agreement, Britain did not make any demand for payment from her own debtors.

Further negotiations on the question were resumed after Roosevelt's assumption of office in March 1933. Neville Chamberlain, however, made it clear that Britain was ready to discuss revision of war-debts on condition that the settlement must be final and that the Reparation question must not be reopened. America on her part, agreed to attend the forthcoming Economic Conference on condition that war-debt problem was not included in its agenda. The question, therefore, remained unsettled. When the next instalment became due on June 15, 1933, it was met by a token payment of 10 million dollars in silver. Six countries made no payment, and the only country paying in full was Finland. Thereafter, the British Government joined the French and others in defaulting on its payment.

The worldwide economic depression created a serious economic crisis in Germany. In September 1932 Britain had to suspend payment in gold; by the end of 1932 twelve countries had followed. The dollar went off gold in 1933. Owing to the inability of Germany to pay reparation, European states also failed to repay their debt to America. In June and December 1933 Britain made nominal payments of £2,000,000 each. Under such condition, the American Congress passed the 'Johnson Act' which forbade defaulting nations to float loans in the United States. Thus ended the problem of war-debts and reparation. 'The Lausanne Conference buried them both in the same unhonoured grave.' In the words of Churchill, 'All this is a sad story of complicated idiocy in the making of which toil and virtue was consumed.'

French Search for Security

The most important single factor that dominated European affairs in the years following 1919 was the French demand for security. The spectre of Germany haunted French minds since 1870. Despite her military defeat and territorial losses, Germany was still potentially a great power. To prevent Germany from doing mischief, France, therefore, embarked on a policy of protection. The leader in this hunt for security was Raymond Poincare. At the Paris Peace Congress, the French Government pleaded that the future security of their country depended upon the severance of the whole left bank of the Rhine from Germany. But the Allies refused to give France the security of the French frontier. Eventually, France reluctantly agreed to an alternative plan for its security. This was secured by the signing, on June 28, 1919, of two identical treaties between France and Britain, and France and the United States. These Guarantee Treaties provided that Britain and the United States, respectively, should 'come immediately to France's assistance in the event of any unprovoked attack against her being made by Germany.' But these treaties remained inoperative owing to the refusal of the American Senate to ratify it. Britain also was not willing to regard the violation by Germany of Articles 42 and 43 of the Treaty of Versailles (fortifications or armed forces in the demilitarized area near the Rhine) as a *casus belli.* The British argument is summed up by Lord Curzon in February 1922:

> In so far as British public opinion will endorse our guarantee, it will be in the belief that it can only become operative in the event of a German army actually crossing the French frontier.

France, therefore, turned to the smaller states. In 1920 the French government concluded a defensive alliance with Belgium with the object of devising joint plans to make any future German invasion through Belgium impossible. The alliance provided that each signatory should come to the support of the other in the case of attack by Germany. As the price for this alliance, France agreed to the inclusion of Luxemburg in a customs union with Belgium, although the Luxemburg had earlier voted for economic affiliation with France.

The treaty with Belgium was not in itself sufficient. Germany must be made to realize that, in any future war, it would have to fight on two fronts again. France, therefore, turned to Poland, the strongest military state in the east. An opportunity of winning Polish gratitude came in 1920 when Warsaw was in danger of being captured by the Red Army. The French help enabled the Poles to repel the Russian attack and to retrieve some lost territory. This collaboration led to the conclusion of a formal treaty in February 1921. It bound the two Governments to consult on all matters of mutual interest and to act in concert for the maintenance of treaties to which they were or might become parties. They also undertook to take concerted measures for the defence of their territories in the event of any unprovoked attack. This treaty was renewed in 1932 for a period of further ten years.

In January 1924, a Franco-Czechoslovak Pact was concluded. The signatories agreed to settle by pacific means any disputes that might arise between them, promised to consult with one another if Germany and Austria tried to unite and undertook to forge common measures in dealing with matters relating to their security or the peace treaties. Two years later (1926), France concluded a security agreement with Rumania. On November 11, 1927 France signed a similar treaty with Yugoslavia.

Meanwhile the eastern allies of France had formed a partnership among themselves. In 1920 and 1921, a Little Entente was organised by Czechoslovakia, Yugoslavia and Rumania for purposes of keeping intact the Treaty of Trianon, preventing a restoration of the Habsburgs and for purposes of common defence against a resurgent Hungary. The Entente was effected by the signing of three dual alliances, between Czechoslovakia and Yugoslavia, Czechoslovakia and Rumania, and Yugoslavia and Rumania. In 1921, moreover, Rumania signed a treaty of alliance with Poland. Each signatory agreed to give military aid to the other in case of unprovoked attack along their respective eastern frontier. Cordial relations were also established in 1922 between the members of the Little Entente and Poland. Periodic conferences were to be held by the foreign ministers of the Entente States for purposes of economic and diplomatic cooperation.

France's relations with the Little Entente rested on a tacit bargain. The three Little Entente Powers would assist France to enforce the Versailles Treaty. France would support the Little Entente as a whole against Hungary, and Yugoslavia in particular against Italy. By contracting the complex web of alliance, the French enlarged their conception of security. Their vision was not limited to the maintenance not only of the Versailles Treaty, but of the whole European peace settlement. It became a recognised French interest to support Poland against Lithuania, Czechoslovakia against Hungary, and Yugoslavia and Rumania against Bulgaria. The ties that bound these satellites to France were not alone of political expediency, but those of finance. For quite some time the French bankers lent the four states hundreds of millions of dollars and extended to them huge credits for munition purchases in France. During this period France reached the summit of the prestige and power in Europe. 'Her position was comparable to that of Metternich after the peace settlement of 1815.'

The French alliance system had many drawbacks. Eastern Europe could have been made a bulwark of collective security only by a joint Anglo-French commitment in that area. This was always an impracticable possibility as France's unilateral policy of alliance system alienated Britain. Most of the small powers involved in the French security system were minor powers whose fighting capabilities were doubtful. Besides, the alliance system entangled France in all the controversies of Eastern, as well as Western Europe and inflamed the jealousy of Italy. Apart from this, the French alliance system contributed to the weakening of the League in its formative years. Thus, in 1923, when Poland attacked Lithuania for possession of Vilna, the French Government prevented the intervention of the League and arranged to give the disputed area to her ally. Italy was not slow to emulate the example. In the same year, Mussolini refused to allow League interference in his dispute with Greece over Corfu and was allowed to have his way. Lastly, the new French hegemony contributed to the formation of two other systems centreing round the Soviet Union and Fascist Italy.

On April 10, 1922, the representatives of 34 nations including Germany and Russia met at Genoa to deliberate on improving the European economic situation. The discussions proved abortive. The only important outcome was the signature at Rapallo, on April 16, of a Russo-German treaty which normalised the diplomatic and commercial relations between the two countries. The two outcasts—Germany and Russia—now joined hands who were fearful of the possible designs of unfriendly Allied or French-controlled coalitions. The Treaty of Rapallo was momentous in its consequences. Germany was once again a big power—to be reckoned with diplomatically. Above all, the treaty involved the Germans in a 'network of schizophrenic activity'. As for the Russians, Stalin's 'Socialism in one country' became their motto and from this time onwards they offered international cooperation. Rapallo aroused utmost concern of Western powers. It presaged the Nazi-Soviet Pact of 1939 which heralded the Second World War.

Soon after the conclusion of the Rapallo Treaty, Russia, fearing encirclement by a European bloc, began to negotiate a series of non-aggression pacts with neighbouring countries. The first of its kind was the signing in 1925 of a treaty of friendship and neutrality with Turkey. On April 24, 1926, a similar covenant was signed at Berlin with Germany. The Berlin Treaty provided for mutual neutrality in the event of attack without provocation. Before the expiry of 1926, Moscow had concluded similar agreements with Afghanistan and Lithuania and, in 1927, a non-aggression treaty was negotiated with Persia.

The postwar period heralded a struggle between Italy and France for control of the western Mediterranean. The result was an armament race which was intensified on the Franco-Italian border. Italy had grievances against Britain and France as the former believed that she could not get more colonies in 1919 owing to the recalcitrant attitude of Britain and France. Besides, territorial problems strained the relations between the two countries as both the powers had land in Europe and North Africa. Britain and France divided Togoland and Cameroons between them. Italy had to be content with Jubaland in East Africa. Several times naval parleys between the two powers broke down because Rome insisted on parity with Paris which the latter refused to concede.

Into this surcharged atmosphere, steps to protect Italy against diplomatic manoeuvre were undertaken after Mussolini's advent to power. In 1924 were signed treaties of friendship and neutrality with Czechoslovakia and Yugoslavia. Similar agreements were contracted with Rumania and Spain in 1926. A treaty with Albania in 1926 was strengthened in the following year by a defensive alliance. An Italo-Hungarian Treaty was negotiated in 1927.

Thus, in 1927, nine years after the armistice, there took place the polarisation of Europe into two hostile camps. The two big prewar alliances—Triple Alliance and Triple Entente—were now substituted by three major groups. The outlook was hardly inspiring to generate confidence in the hearts of the people.

The three-cornered security system built up by France, the Soviet Union and Italy was destined to undergo changes with the rise of Germany. As Germany slowly regained strength, a demand for broad revision of the peace settlement was brewing among the powers. Italy, moreover, owing to her territorial ambitions, drew closer to her former enemies. By 1928 Italy began to emerge as the leader of a 'revisionist bloc'.

In 1928 Italy concluded treaties of friendship and neutrality with Turkey and Greece, and in 1930 one with Austria. Turkey and Greece negotiated non-agreession pact in 1933 owing largely through the instrumentality of Italy. A matrimonial alliance between the Italian princess Giovanna to King Boris of Bulgaria in 1930 eventually paved the way for friendship between the two countries. In 1933 Italy and the Soviet Union signed a pact of non-aggression. Thereafter, Italy encouraged a resumption of diplomatic relations between the Soviet Union and Hungary. In March 1934, Italy scored another diplomatic triumph. Italy, Austria and Hungary signed the Rome Protocols. The signatories agreed to maintain peace and to increase the facilities for their common trade and to develop traffic through the Adriatic ports. Italy guaranteed the independence of Austria in order to prevent its absorption by Germany.

The new German nationalism also affected the interrelations of the Little Entente, France and the Soviet Union. Already in 1929, Czechoslovakia. Yugoslavia and Rumania renewed the whole set of treaties. Now, in 1933, a 'pact of organisation' was signed which contemplated the transformation of the entente into a higher international unity directed by a permanent council. In 1933, the members of the Little Entente, wearied of being regarded as French satellites, signed the London Agreements with the Soviet Union and drew closer to Poland. The new shift in international relations was reflected when Poland signed a ten-year non-aggression pact with Nazi Germany. Soon thereafter, Poland renewed a non-aggression treaty with the Soviet Union.

The Third Republic also had to shift her policy in the changing diplomatic chessboard. This was owing to the aggressive nationalism of Nazi Germany which frightened both the French and the Bolsheviks. They threatened to repudiate the Versailles Treaty and sometimes referred to Russia as a suitable field for eastward expansion. Hence France in 1932 signed a neutrality treaty with the Soviet Union which was followed by a non-aggression pact in 1935.

Italy's diplomatic triumphs alarmed the Balkan States and the Little Entente. In 1934, the Balkan Pact was signed at Athens by Greece, Turkey, Rumania and Yugoslavia. Based on the principles of 'the Balkans for the Balkan peoples', the four states agreed to maintain the territorial *status quo* and promised not to take any action against any Balkan State (not a member of the Pact) without consulting the others. Bulgaria, having territorial claims against her neighbours, refused to join the pact. She was supported by Albania. Thus, without the adherence of Bulgaria and Albania, the Pact failed to stabilize the Balkan affairs. The Pact was criticised by Italy but welcomed by France.

Later, in 1934, America, Britain and Japan held consultations on the question of renewing the naval-limitation treaties. The question was complicated by Japan's demand of parity with the United States and Britain and the abolition of 5 : 5 : 3 ratio. As usual, the Western naval powers refused equality to Japan. Tokyo, therefore, gave (December 1934) the required two years' notice of the termination of the naval agreements. The matter assumed serious proportion by Germany's determination to build a sizable fleet. London, therefore, signed an agreement with Berlin in 1935 whereby the Nazis, regardless of the Versailles restrictions, might acquire a naval tonnage equal to 35 per cent of that of the British Commonwealth. Meanwhile, France and Italy had effected a reconciliation through the signing of another pact at Rome (Laval-Mussolini pact, 1935). The two powers settled some outstanding colonial differences and agreed to consult if Austrian independence were threatened. France ceded to Italy territories adjoining Libya and a small piece of French Somaliland touching Eritrea. It is alleged that Laval gave Mussolini a free hand to proceed as he wished in Ethiopia.

The autumn of 1935 saw the Italian invasion of Ethiopia and the imposition of limited League sanctions against the Fascist aggressor. Italy became annoyed with the allies who had come to act in the name of collective security. Henceforth, she began to veer towards Germany and Japan who had scant respect for existing territorial arrangements.

In November 1936, Mussolini decried the collective security in no uncertain terms. He observed: 'A virile people ... refuses to confide its destiny to the uncertain hands of third parties.' He hastened to add that Germany 'although surrounded and solicited, did not adhere to sanctions.' The recognition of the conquest of Ethiopia by Germany was cemented by the friendship between Italy and Germany. The friendship was bolstered by common opposition to Bolshevism and was in reality 'an axis around which all European states animated by the desire for peace might collaborate.'

Soon afterwards, Germany and Japan signed an Anti-Commintern Pact in November 1936. The signatories agreed 'to keep each other informed concerning the activities of the Third International, to consult upon the necessary defense measures and to execute these measures in close cooperation with each other.' One year later Italy adhered to the Pact and the 'Berlin-Rome-Tokyo axis' became a reality. The ideological conflict between the Axis and non-Axis worlds became pronounced with Mussolini's declaration:

> The struggle between two worlds can permit no compromise. Either we or they.

Era of Pacts 1923-33

In a memorandum dated March 25, 1919, Lloyd George urged for the limitation of armaments in the following words:

> The first condition of success for the League of Nations is, therefore, a firm understanding between the British Empire and the United States of America and France and Italy that there will be no competitive building up of fleets or armies between them. Unless this is arrived at before the covenant is signed the League of Nations will be a sham and a mockery.

In 1920, a general limitation of armaments was contemplated by the Allied Powers. Article 8 of the Covenant laid down the reduction of armaments 'to the lowest point consistent with national safety and the enforcement by common action of international obligations.' In its earlier efforts to cope with the problem, the League paid little or no attention to the controlling factor while putting undue emphasis on schemes for disarmament on a statistical and mathematical basis. A Permanent Advisory Commission was constituted in accordance with Article 9 of the Covenant, in May 1920. This was followed by the creation of the Temporary Mixed Commission in January 1921. These bodies did nothing except collecting information on existing armaments, while the Assembly recommended a drastic curtailment of expenditure on armaments in each national budget.

The Temporary Mixed Commission submitted to the 1923 Assembly a draft 'Treaty of Mutual Assistance', which contained vague provisions of future disarmament and precise guarantees for future security. Any outbreak of hostilities was to be followed within four days by a decision of the Council of the League which party was the aggressor and members of the League were then to be under an automatic obligation to render military assistance against the aggressor. Regarding armaments, it was stipulated that the Council should devise reductions to 'a point compatible with national security'. The draft incorporated, in short, the French thesis that absolute security should precede disarmament. It was rejected by Britain and the British Dominions, as well as by the Netherlands and the Scandinavian states, though it was welcomed by France and her allies. Most of the states protested against the absence of an adequate definition of aggression. Moreover, the treaty conferred large executive powers on the Council of the League which was not liked by Britain as well as by the Dominions.

The Geneva Protocol

Despite the defeat of the Draft Treaty, the paramount importance of security and disarmament had been recognised. It was felt that some acceptable alternative method of establishing the security might be found. In September 1924, Britain and France were represented by their Prime Ministers, Ramsay Macdonald and Edouard Herriot at the Fifth Assembly of the League.

They presented a joint resolution which became the basis of the Assembly's work. The Assembly unanimously approved a Protocol for the Pacific Settlement of International Disputes which came to be known as the Geneva Protocol.

The principal novelty of the Protocol was that it sought to close the existing gaps in the Covenant which still left open the possibility of war. These were mainly two: if the Council failed to pronounce an unanimous judgment on a dispute; and if the subject of the dispute was ruled to be a matter of domestic concern of the parties. Under the Protocol all disputes of a legal character should be submitted to the Permanent Court of International Justice, whose decision would be binding. On other disputes, if the Council should fail to reach a unanimous conclusion, it would refer the matter to a committee of arbitrators whose decision was binding. Disputes about matters of domestic jurisdiction, though still beyond the jurisdiction of the Council, were to be submitted to the procedure of conciliation under Aritcle 11. This article entitled the League to take 'any action that may be deemed wise and effectual to safeguard the peace of nations.' No Power should be judged an aggressor if it had brought the dispute before the League under Article 11. The whole plan, however, was to take effect only after a conference had adopted a disarmament plan.

The Protocol was accepted by the seventeen states. But the reaction set in. The most controversial clause relates to disputes on matters of domestic jurisdiction which might be brought before the League under Article 11 of the Covenant. Japan wanted to use the procedure to protest against the restrictions on Japanese immigrants introduced by Canada, Australia and New Zealand. The British overseas dominions were opposed to any idea of interference with their domestic sovereignty in matters on immigration question. Moreover, the Dominions viewed with dislike a prospect of European entanglements. Canada recorded her voice of protest in the debates of the Assembly:

> In this association of mutual insurance against fire, the risks assumed by the different States are not equal. We live in a fire-proof house, far from inflammable materials.

Britain did not reconcile herself to compulsory arbitration and sanctions had never been popular in any part of the British Empire. Britain advanced two specific objections to the Protocol. First, it might involve them in war with the United States which, being outside the League, might be deemed an aggressor in any dispute with a League member. Second, it would entail Britain to serve as a kind of police officer all over the world. Meanwhile, the Labour Government of Ramsay Macdonald, who had played a leading role in formulating the Geneva Protocol, was succeeded by a Conservative Government in November 1942. This sealed the fate of the Protocol and the *coup de grace* was administered in March by Austen Chamberlain, the new Foreign Secretary.

The Locarno Agreements

While rejecting the Geneva Protocol, Austen Chamberlain suggested that the Covenant might be supplemented by special arrangements 'Kniting together the nations most immediately concerned, and whose differences might lead to a renewal of strife, by means of treaties framed with the sole object of maintaining, as between themselves, an unbroken peace.' The prospects for a general pacification had been brightened by removal for the time being, of the question of German reparation and the consequent withdrawal of French and Belgian troops from the occupation of the Ruhr.

Meanwhile, during 1922-23, Berlin had several times suggested to Paris the negotiation of frontier guarantees, anti-war pledges and arbitration projects. Each time, France had been lukewarm to the proposals. Undismayed by these setbacks, Germany, through Foreign Minister Gustav Stresemann, in February 1925, once more broached the subject. Stresemann suggested:

1. a pact among Britain, Italy, France and Germany for guaranteeing the existing Rhine frontiers and settling future international disputes, by arbitration, and
2. a series of arbitration treaties between Germany and her neighbouring east and west.

Briand in France and Chamberlain in Britain welcomed the proposal, but before definite negotiations could be inaugurated the French insisted that:

1. Germany seek League Membership
2. that Belgium become a signer of the proposed pact
3. that nothing in the contemplated document interfere with France's obligation to Poland or with the Allies, obligations under the League Covenant, and
4. that Czechoslovakia and Poland be invited to attend the parleys.

Stresemann accepted the conditions. In October 1925, the delegates from Germany, France, Britain, Italy, Belgium, Poland and Czechoslovakia assembled at the Swiss lakeside town of Locarno. On October 15, 1925, the conference was brought to a happy conclusion by the initialling of a complex set of documents constituting the Locarno Pact:

(i) A treaty of mutual guarantee of the Franco-German and Belgo-German frontiers between Germany, Belgium, Britain and Italy.

(ii) Arbitration treaties between Germany and Belgium and between Germany and France.

(iii) Arbitration treaties between Germany and Poland and Germany and Czechoslovakia.

(iv) A Franco-Polish and Franco-Czechoslovak treaty for mutual assistance in case of aggression by Germany.

Locarno was widely hailed as precursor of a new era in world history. Austen Chamberlain described it with justifiable pride as 'the real dividing line between the years of war and the years of peace.' It struck for the first time a fair and impartial balance between French and German needs. It completed the process by which Germany was brought to the League of Nations in 1926 which increased new prestige and authority to that organisation. Action under the British and Italian guarantees was to be automatic only if violation of the treaties took the form of violent aggression. The sense of improved security which Locarno implanted in the minds of Frenchmen and Germans was important. The fear of British intervention had the effect of restraining the potential aggressors of both sides. 'The Locarno Pact was a most effective and formidable looking scarecrow.' Locarno also opened a prospect for a reconciliation between France and Germany, whose age-long hostility had endangered the peace of Europe. For the first time since the war, Germany had entered into treaty relations with the former enemies; she had accepted the loss of Alsace-Lorraine as final.

The enthusiasm generated by Locarno was not sufficient guarantees of peace. The security proved to be illusory unless the Rhineland Pact was supplemented by some kind of eastern Locarno. While agreeing to guarantee the Rhineland Pact, Britain was unwilling to defend frontiers in Eastern Europe. The British refusal to guarantee eastern frontiers with Germany denied the strategic unity of the Franco-Eastern Europe-Germany complex on which the French had always insisted.

The Locarno spirit proved to be temporary. Germany followed its ratification of the Pact by concluding a new treaty of friendship—the Treaty of Berlin, 1926—with the Soviet Union, a power antagonistic to the League system. Despite its adhesion to the Locarno Treaties, Italy plunged into a dangerous rivalry with France in the Danubian area. Britain was also generally opposed to the main line of French policy. 'In the long run, the Locarno Treaty was destructive both of the Versailles Treaty and of the Covenant. It encouraged both the view that the Versailles Treaty ... lacked binding force, and the view that governments could not be expected to take military action in defence of frontiers in which they themselves were not directly interested.'[2]

The Pact of Paris, 1928

The most important milestone in the history of international relations after the Treaty of Locarno was the Kellogg-Briand Pact. On April 6, 1927, French Foreign Minister Briand had sent a message to the American people, in which he suggested that the tenth anniversary of the entry of

2. Carr. E.H.: *International Relations between the Two World Wars,* 1919-39 (1963), P. 97.

the United States into the war might be celebrated by a mutual engagement in favour of 'the renunciation of war as an instrument of national policy.' The suggestion was followed in June by the despatch to Kellogg, American Secretary of State, of a draft treaty embodying this idea.

Instead of confining the Pact only to two powers, Kellogg, after a long delay, replied with a counter-proposal that the suggested pact should be universal. Briand agreed. Eventually, on August 27, 1928, representatives of the six great powers (America, Britain, France, Germany, Italy, and Japan), the other three Locarno powers (Belgium, Poland, and Czechoslovakia) and the British Dominions and India met in Paris and signed the pact. This was known as the Kellogg-Briand Pact or the Pact of Paris. Most of the independent states were invited to adhere to the Pact.

In the first article, the signatories condemned 'recourse to war for the solution of international controversies and renounced it as an instrument of national policy in their relations with one another.' In the second article the states agreed that 'the settlement or solution of all disputes or conflicts of whatever nature or whatever origin may be, which may arise among them. shall never be sought except by pacific means.' The third and last article outlined the terms of ratification and adherence. According to the preamble, 'any signatory power which shall hereafter seek to promote its national interests by resort to war should be denied the benefits furnished by the treaty.' Within a few years, sixtyfive nations, including the Soviet Union, signed the pact.

The Pact of Paris was not a far-reaching event. It renounced only wars of aggression. War was not outlawed (1) when resorted to in self-defence, (2) in the execution of obligations assumed under previous treaties, and (3) in fulfilment of responsibilities under the League Covenant or Locarno agreements. Though the Pact condemned aggressive wars, it made no provision for punishing the guilty. There was not even provision for consultation among the signatory powers in case of a breach of the Pact.

The assertion of self-defence by Britain and the United States brought into relief the hollowness of the Pact. The original authors of the Pact did not ban war in self-defence. In the name of self-defence, Britain made a special reservation with regard to certain regions of the world which materially affected her vital interest. The United States claimed a special privilege to act in order to preserve the Monroe Doctrine. France also reserved her previous treaty obligations, and emphasised the right of self-defence. Thus each state remained the sole judge of its own actions. The Pact made no provision for punishing the guilty. There was not even provision for consultation among the signatory powers in case of a breach of the Pact.

Nevertheless, the Pact of Paris was an important landmark. The universal repudiation of war as an instrument of policy seems to have a unique importance. 'As a gesture indicative of a new ethical attitude to war, it was undeniably impressive.' It constituted a great step forward on the road to international security. Flagrant violations of it were soon committed by Japan and Italy, but this did not minimise the significance of the Pact. The conception of banning war as a legitimate method of settling international disputes struck root in the political thought of the world.

Some attempts were made to combine the Pact of Paris and the Covenant of the League. But the task was fraught with difficulties. The Pact was a moral declaration which condemned all wars, but punished none. The Covenant allowed some wars and prohibited others; and in the latter case it punished the guilty. The only alternative was to make the sanctions envisaged by Article 16 applicable to all wars prohibited by the Pact of Paris as well as to wars prohibited by the existing Covenant. Britain and France put forward the proposal to the League Assembly in 1929. But the discussion was postponed till the Assembly of 1930. By that time strong opposition came from Japan and the Scandinavian countries after which it was abandoned.

Meanwhile the Assembly produced a plan in September 1928 for implementing the Pact of Paris without amending the Covenant by a General Act for the Pacific Settlement of International Disputes. The General Act provided for conciliation commissions to be set up by each of the parties with every other party, for legal disputes to be submitted to the Permanent Court and non-legal disputes to arbitration. The Act, though widely accepted, could not be implemented. It was a thoroughly doctrinaire document full of ambiguities. The conciliation commissions which the Act proposed were never found useful.

Pact of Rome and London Agreements

The suspicion and antagonism that characterised European relations in the early thirties produced among other things two additional peace agreements: the pact of Rome and the London Agreements. The first was born out of Mussolini's suggestion to the leading Western powers to guarantee peace at least for a certain fixed period. Henceforth a ten-year pact was signed at Rome in July 1933 by Britain, France, Germany, and Italy. The signatories agreed to consult on all important international political and economic questions, to work for the success of the disarmament proceedings at Geneva, and to acknowledge once more the principle of treaty revision as envisaged in Article 19 of the League Covenant.

The Soviet Union, far from welcoming the Pact, regarded it as another alliance against Bolshevism and proposed, therefore, a general non-aggression treaty to her neighbours. In July 1933, at the Soviet Embassy in London, the representatives of Afghanistan, Czechoslovakia, Estonia, Latvia, Lithuania, Persia, Poland, Rumania, the Soviet Union, Turkey, and Yugoslavia signed three conventions which together were called London Agreements. The signatories confirmed the inviolability of each other's territories, and expressed the conviction that the Kellogg Pact, to which they were parties, forbade all aggression. They formulated a specific definition of the term 'aggressor nation'. A nation was branded as an aggressor who declared war on another and invaded foreign lands without formal declaration of war.

Disarmament and Rearmament

In the Versailles Treaty, the Allied Powers had declared that by imposing drastic disarmament of Germany, their purpose was 'to render possible the initiation or a general limitation of the armament of all nations.' Article 8 of the Covenant placed on the Council of the League the duty of formulating plans for the reduction of armaments for the consideration and action of several governments. In November 1920, the Council appointed a 'Temporary Mixed Commission' to assist it in this task.

The first success in the field of disarmament was achieved in February, 1922 at the Washington Conference. It established the naval parity between the British Empire and the United States and fixed the strength of Japan in capital ships at 60 per cent of the British and American figures. The French and Italian quotas were 35 per cent. The Conference prescribed a ten-year naval holiday in the construction of capital ships. No limitation was placed on light cruisers, destroyers, submarines and auxiliaries chiefly owing to French obstruction which further strained Anglo-French relations.

In 1922, the British delegate on the Temporary Mixed Commission proposed a numerical scheme for the limitation of armies. Armies were to be divided into imaginary units of 30,000 men; and a certain number of units was to be allotted to each Power. Thus France was to have six units or an army of 180,000 men, Italy four units, Britain three, and so on. Unfortunately this plan failed to make any headway as it was almost universally condemned by nearly every European country.

Some concrete steps had to be adopted to implement Article 8 of the Covenant. It was at this point that the French delegate introduced the thesis of increased security as a necessary condition of disarmament. He succeeded in securing the assent of the British delegation to this view. The next three years were the years of the Draft Treaty of Mutual Assistance, the Geneva Protocol, and the Locarno Treaties. During this period nothing was done in the field of disarmament.

The signature of the Locarno Treaties once more brought the disarmament question into the fore. In the final protocol of the Locarno Conference, the signatories cherished the view that the conclusion of these agreements would hasten the process of disarmament as provided for in Article 8 of the Covenant. In December 1925, the Council appointed a Preparatory Commission for the Disarmament Conference.

The Preparatory Commission met at Geneva on May 18, 1926. Soviet Russia was still unrepresented. Opinion of the Commission was sharply divided on the vital question of disarmament. The French viewed with suspicion any measure of disarmament which was not controlled by effective international supervision. Italy and the United States refused to accept any such control, a view shared by Britain. Acute controversy arose in connection with naval disarmament and limitation of armed forces.

The real work of the Preparatory Commission began in March 1927 when the British and the French delegations submitted draft disarmament conventions. The drafts contained no figures, but provided a framework to show what should be limited and how. But they revealed fundamental differences:

(1) In matters of military personnel, the French delegation wished to limit only men in service; the British. American and German delegations wished to limit only trained personnel.

(2) In the question of military material, the German delegation demanded a specific numerical limitation of all categories of armament such as had been imposed on Germany by Versailles Treaty. The French delegation wanted to impose budgetary restrictions on military material. The British and American delegations deemed any limitation of armaments impracticable and preposterous.

(3) On matters of naval armament, the French and Italian delegations wanted only a limitation of the total tonnage of navies; the British and American delegations wanted separate limitations of each category of ship.

(4) On the question of international supervision, France was anxious to set up an elaborate system of international control. But the other states contended that the efficacy of the disarmament question must be based on the good faith of the parties concerned.

By the close of 1927, the labours of the Preparatory Commission proved to be illusory.

Meanwhile American President Calvin Coolidge invited Britain, France, Italy and Japan to attend, with the United States, a conference to consider the limitations of cruisers, destroyers and submarines. He reminded the Powers that the Washington Conference had imposed tonnage restrictions only on capital ships and aircraft carriers and the time had come to regulate other classes of war vessels. Only Britain and Italy accepted the invitation; and a Three-Power Conference assembled at Geneva in June 1927.

The United States proposed a total tonnage restrictions in each category of ship and suggested the ratio 5 : 5 : 3 with regard to capital ships. Japan was, on the whole, agreeable to the proposal. Britain held different views. She insisted that mathematical parity with the United States was by no means equivalent to practical parity. To protect 80,000 miles of trade and communication lines, Britain demanded, categorically, that there be no restriction on her right to build small (7,500 ton) cruisers. However, she was anxious to set a limit upon 10,000 ton cruisers, the best type that served American purpose. There was in short, a complete discrepancy between the doctrine of 'mathematical parity' advocated by the United States and the 'practical parity' insisted upon by the British. The irreconcilable difference between the two powers hastened the break-up of the conference without accomplishing anything.

While these events were taking place, the Preparatory Commission continued its deliberations. In the face of 'international wrath and ridicule… the delegates wrestled with arguments about the effect of fog and air and examined the history of international weather.' In 1928, the Russian representative M. Litvinov made his debut by making a passionate appeal for total and universal disarmament. The proposal met with no response; only Germany and Turkey supported the Soviet view. In these circumstances disarmament once more receded into the background.

During 1929, the prospect somewhat brightened when there occurred a rapprochment between the United States and Britain. The ratification of the Kellogg Pact and the assumption of office of President of the United States by Herbert Hoover and the office of the Prime Minister of

Britain by Macdonald hastened the process of reconciliation between the two Powers. In the autumn of 1929, MacDonald visited the United States. The outcome was the calling of a conference in London in January 1930 of the five great naval powers—Britain, the United States, Italy, France and Japan.

On April 22, 1930, the Five Powers signed a London Naval Treaty. Because of their irreconcilable differences on the question of mathematical parity, France and Italy withheld their signature from the really vital part of the pact. Because of their coastline on three seas and the extent of her overseas communication, France opposed the Italian claim to parity. She contested that all-round parity with Italy meant, in fact, inferiority in the Mediterranean. Italy, however, expressed her willingness to accept any naval figure, however low, provided it was not exceeded by any other Continental Power.

The Treaty to remain in force until the end of 1936 solved the problem of relative cruiser strength by compromise. The United States was to have 18 cruisers of the 10,000 ton type and 143,000 tons of smaller cruisers (total 323,500 tons). Great Britain was to have 15 of the large cruisers and 192,200 tons of smaller ones (total 339,000 tons). Japan accepted a maximum of 12 battle cruisers and smaller craft to the extent of 100,450 tons (total 208,850 tons). The tonnage allocations for destroyers were set at 150,000 tons each for the United States and Great Britain and 105,500 for Japan. Each of the three powers was given a submarine tonnage of 52,700, and no capital ships were to be constructed until 1936. The most-discussed section of the treaty was Article 21, the so-called safeguarding clause or the 'escalator' clause. This permitted any signatory to increase its tonnage in any category if, in its opinion, the requirements of national security demanded it. All five powers agreed at the same time to extend the Washington Treaty for a further five years.

While the London Naval Conference was in progress, the Preparatory Commission had adjourned. Discussions were resumed and in December 1930 a final draft convention for a general disarmament was adopted. The League Council now selected Geneva as the venue of the world's first disarmament conference to open in February 1932.

The draft convention that was placed before the conference was a general document which indicated the methods of limitation that might be adopted. It was 'a skeleton lacking flesh and blood' and it offered 'blanks and dashes in place of figures.' Among the specific recommendations were budgetary limitation of armaments; limitation of periods of military service, limitation of military, naval and air; effective prohibition of chemical and bacteriological warfare; acceptance of the London Naval Treaty; and the appointment of a permanent disarmament commission to sit at Geneva. But reservations were made to every one of these points. In addition to these, the success of the conference was foundered by the clash of French demands for security and German demands for equality. France steadfastly refused to vote for any general reduction of armaments unless adequate security were first guaranteed. Germany, on the other hand, maintained that the Versailles Treaty had created a right to demand that other nations should disarm to her own level.

Meanwhile, an American proposal for an all-round reduction of one-third in existing armed forces and armaments was coldly received by Great Britain, who saw in it a sinister design to reduce the number of British cruisers. On July 20, 1932, a resolution recording agreement was submitted to the conference: (1) to prohibit air bombardment and to limit the number of aircraft; (2) to limit heavy artillery and tanks, and (3) to prohibit chemical warfare. Fortyone delegations voted for this resolution, eight (including Italy) abstained, and two (Germany and the Soviet Union) voted against it. Thereafter, in September 1932, Germany withdrew from the Disarmament Conference and agreed to participate when the German claims for equality of rights were acknowledged.

When the Conference reassembled in October, Germany's place was vacant. For the moment the German issue dominated the scene. However, a formula was found on December 11. Britain, France and Italy recognised Germany's 'equality of rights in a system which would provide security for all nations.' This concession made it possible for Germany to return to the

Disarmament Conference. The concession came too late as on January 30, 1933, Adolf Hitler had become Chancellor of Germany. The new German government displayed no mood for temporising and once more differences, chiefly Franco-German differences, threatened to disrupt the proceedings of the conference.

A complete deadlock gripped the works of the conference when it resumed its sittings at the end of January 1933. To avert a crisis, Prime Minister MacDonald himself came to Geneva and presented a plan (MacDonald Plan) which tried to meet both the French demand for security and the German demand for equality. Unfortunately, nearly every Power had objections to the Plan and about 125 amendments were suggested. In June, the conference adjourned until October.

During the summer recess of 1933 France submitted a plan for dividing the disarmament convention into two periods. In the first period of four years, a system of international supervision over armaments would be established; limitation would come into force only in the second period. The British and the Italian Governments endorsed the proposal. But on October 14, 1933 Germany announced her withdrawal from the Disarmament Conference. While the Conference came to a standstill, Britain tried to revive the moribund body by sending Eden to Paris, Berlin and Rome in February 1934. Hitler made it known that Germany was willing to accept any limit for the German army which was equally accepted by the other Powers and so fix the German air force at 30 per cent of the combined strength of her neighbour or 50 per cent of the strength of the French Air Force, whichever figure was the lower. The French Government protested against the proposed 'Legalisation of German armament.' The British Government enquired whether, in the event of sufficient guarantees being given by Hitler, the French Government was disposed to change its views. But on April 17, the French Government put an end to the controversy by asserting the intention of Germany to rearm.

This answer was the real end of the Conference. It dragged on for a few months longer. But its sessions became intermittent and, after the end of 1934, it ceased to meet. 'The lingering death of the Disarmament Conference was the final episode in the period of post-war history.' The failure of the Allied Powers to carry out their promise to disarm emboldened Germany to rearm. This rearmament led to fear psychosis, and the vicious circle which the statesmen had hoped to break in 1919 was once more complete.

CHAPTER 31

THE LEAGUE OF NATIONS

The scheme for a League of Nations for the preservation of peace was first mooted by President Woodrow Wilson in his Fourteen Points. The scheme was elaborated by Lord Robert Cecil and General Smuts of England and Hurst and Miller, legal advisers of British and American legations, respectively. After discussions at the Paris Peace Conference (1919), the Covenant of the League of Nations was adopted on April 28, 1919, by the Congress as a whole. Wilson made the Covenant an integral part of the Treaty of Versailles.

The preamble to the Covenant stated that the object of the League was to 'promote international cooperation and to achieve international peace and security, by the acceptance of obligations not to resort to war.' The League of Nations was not a government of any kind but was an association more political than judicial in character, more in the tradition of the Concert of Europe.

The League had three principal organs: the Assembly, the Council and the Secretariat. The Assembly was a general body in which every nation had three members but had only one vote. The Assembly was to meet once in every year in September. It discussed various matters affecting the peace. It controlled the budget, admitted new members to the League, selected non-permanent members to the Council and, in conjunction with the Council, elected judges to the International Court. The Assembly became the dominant organ, partly because it controlled the budget and partly because the smaller powers were free to criticise the great in this forum.

The Council was a small body which was to meet thrice in a year; but there were frequent special meetings. It was made up of four permanent and eleven non-permanent members, the latter being elected from time to time by the smaller states. The presidency of the body was rotated in every successive session among the delegates in the alphabetical order. Except in matters of procedure, decisions of the Council had to be unanimous. Like the Assembly, the Council might consider any question affecting world peace. As it was a smaller body, it could meet frequently—especially in emergency situations. The Council served as a sort of executive committee of the Assembly, working out the details and supervising the execution of policies which the Assembly had accepted in principle. The Council was charged with the important task of mediating in international disputes as well as to approve sanctions against an offending state. Among its other duties included the formulation of plans for the reduction of armaments and the study of the annual reports submitted by the mandatories.

The Secretariat comprised the administrative machinery of the League. The Secretary-General was appointed by the Council though the formal approval of the Assembly was necessary. The Secretariat, divided into eleven sections, each of them being headed by a director, were concerned with such matters as mandates, disarmament, health, minorities, and economic and financial questions. The Secretariat was staffed by seven hundred employees drawn from more than fifty members.

The machinery of the League also contained two other major agencies: the Permanent Court of International Justice or World Court and the Industrial Labour Organisation.

The Permanent Court of International Justice came into existence in the later part of 1921. The

Court was originally composed of eleven judges chosen for nine-year terms by the Council and Assembly. The jurisdiction of the Court was of two kinds—voluntary and compulsory. A certain number of states, however, signed an 'Optional Clause'. By this clause, the members accepted the jurisdiction of the Permanent Court 'as compulsory, *ipso facto* and without special convention,' in all legal disputes concerning the interpretation of a treaty, any question of international law and a breach of a international obligation. Moreover, it was empowered to give an advisory opinion on any dispute or question referred to it by the Assembly or the Council. By 1940, the Court has given 31 decisions and 27 advisory opinions.

The International Labour Organisation (ILO) which had its seat at Geneva, came into existence in the interests of labour. The ILO consisted of a General Conference, a Governing Body, and an Intrernational Labour office. The General Conference consisted of four delegates from each member state, one chosen by labour, one by the employers, and two by the Government. The General Conference had no legislative powers. But it could focus attention upon certrain evils and, for their amelioration, could pass either recommendations or draft conventions. The Governing Body consisted of thirtytwo persons, eight representing the workers, eight the employers, and sixteen the governments. Its chief function was the election of a director of the International Labour Office.

The International Labour Office had its headquarters at Geneva. Its purpose was to collect and disseminate information, but its chief purpose was to frame international rules governing conditions of labour. Though its decisions were not binding, it succeeded in gaining adherence for rules governing such matters as nightwork of women and children and the rights of combination of agricultural workers. Apart from Germany and Austria who were members from the beginning, both the United States and the Soviet Union joined in 1934. After the end of the League of Nations, the ILO became one of the 'specialized agencies' affiliated with the United Nations.

At the time of its establishment in 1920, the League had fortyone members which rose to fifty in 1924. It was ironical that the United States, whose President had sponsored the Organisation, did not become a member. Germany was not admitted until 1926, nor the Soviet Union until 1934. By 1935 there were 62 members: 28 in Europe, 21 in America, 8 in Asia, 3 in Africa and 2 in Australia. Japan and Germany later on withdrew from the League. Soviet Union was expelled from the League in 1939, when the League was already in collapse. The outbreak of the Second World War brought its formal existence to a close.

Objects of the League

There were 34 specific engagements entered into by the members of the League, 19 of which dealt with the preservation of peace. Article 10 obligated members of the League to 'respect and preserve as against external aggression the territorial integrity and existing political independence' of one another. Article II empowered the League to 'take action that may be deemed wise and effectual to safeguard the peace of nations'. Article 12 required the members to submit disputes either to arbitration or to inquiry by the Council and 'in no case resort to war until three months after the award by the arbitrators or the report by the Council.' Article 13 bound the members to implement any arbitral award and not to resort to war against 'any member of the League that complies therewith.' Article 15 laid down that any dispute which could not be settled by arbitration must be submitted to the Council, and it prohibited any resort to war in contravention of a unanimous decision of the Council. Article 16 ordained that if a member resorted to war in disregard of the Covenant, 'it shall, *ipso facto* be deemed to have committed an act of war against all the other members of the League.' The offending nation was to be subjected to an economic boycott, and the Council might recommend military action. Members agreed to support one another in financial and economic sanctions against the breaker of the peace.

In respect of any dispute between a non-member and a member, Article 17 declared that the former was to be asked to accept the obligations of membersbip for purpose of such dispute. If the non-member refused and went to war, the penalties were to be the same as if it were a member. By Article 19 the Assembly was empowered 'from time to time to advise the reconsideration... of treaties which have become inapplicable and the consideration of the international conditions whose continuance might endanger the peace of the world.' Furthermore, the Covenant aimed at 'the reduction of national armaments to the lowest point consistent with national safety.'

Secret diplomacy was given a burial. Treaties, to be binding, must be published and registered with the Secretariat. All treaties, present and future, that were inconsistent with the Covenant, were to be declared null and void.

Achievements of the League of Nations

Despite its weakness, the League was able to solve some minor disputes. It settled disputes between Finland and Sweden over the Aland islands (1920); between Poland and Germany over their boundary in upper Silesia (1921); between Greece and Italy over the island of Corfu (1923); between Greece and Bulgaria over border incidents (1925); between Peru and Columbia over a border province (1933).

The League had to perform certain tasks of administrative character. Under Article 22 of the Covenant, the League was made responsible for the well-being and development of peoples inhabiting the German overseas possessions and Turkey's former dependencies. These territories were to be placed under the 'tutelage' of more advanced nations as 'Mandatories on behalf of the League'. The Covenant created a Permanent Mandates Commission to advise the Council and to receive an annual report for each of the mandatory powers. The Mandate system proved of considerable value in focussing public opinion on the 'sacred trust' of colonial administration. The first mandate to achieve independence was Iraq (1932) and the latter was elected a member of the League. The theory of League mandates ushered in a 'spirit of world politics'.

In addition to the peoples in the mandated areas, the League was entrusted with the task of supervising the observance of Minorities treaties made between the great powers and certain states, such as Poland, Czechoslovakia, Rumania and others. These treaties required the states concerned to accord certain rights to racial, religious or linguistic minorities within their territories. But the League was not authorised to enforce this guarantee. In 1929 the League Council revised its procedures for dealing with minority disputes. A Minorities Committee was established to which was assigned the duty of deciding whether or not questions regarding minority rights should be brought before the Council. This procedure was not effective and it was usually judged by its failures. Moreover, the treaties ran counter to the sentiments of nationalism as none of the great powers was expected to encourage irredentist feelings. Italy notoriously pursued an opposite policy in the territories acquired from Austria-Hungary. Confidence in the system was shaken when in 1934 Poland refused to recognise the jurisdiction of the Council in minority matters.

The Treaty of Versailles required Germany to renounce the Saar basin in favour of the League of Nations as trustee. The League successfully administered the Saar territory, through a governing commission, from 1920 to 1934 and the territory prospered economically and financially. In January 1935 a plebiscite was held which resulted in an overwhelming vote in favour of reunion with Germany. By discharging the delicate task successfully, the League had demonstrated that an efficient international government was not an insuperable task. Two of the greatest achievements of the League of Nations at this period were the settlement of upper Silesia and the prevention of war after Mussolini bombarded Corfu in the summer of 1933.

The League had a difficult task in the settlement of the Danzig area. Danzig was mainly a German city, but its situation made it the natural port for Poland. The Allies detached Danzig from Germany and constitued it a free city 'under the protection of the League.' The League guaranteed the constitution of the Free City of Danzig and was represented there by a High Commissioner. In view of the extreme complexity of the conflicting interests, Danzig-Polish relations became embittered and the Council had to intervene frequently. However, before 1939, Germany assumed the direction of affairs in Danzig.

The League provided a new and elaborate machinery for international cooperation in the economic sphere. A general financial conference was held at Brussels in 1920, and an economic conference at Geneva in 1927, the latter being concerned with the reduction of tariffs and other trade barriers. In the sphere of social and humanitarian work, the League broke fresh ground. After arranging a slavery convention at Geneva in 1925, the League set a Permanent Slavery Commission in 1932. Other League organisations dealt with world problems of health, narcotics, traffic in women, the protection of children, communications and transport. It rendered useful service with such problems as refugees and leprosy. One of its greatest services was to rescue Austria from economic ruin. It also promoted cultural cooperation among the nations by bringing together scholars and scientists from all parts of the world. The International Labour Office worked efficiently to improve the general position of labour. The Court of International Justice successfully arbitrated a number of disputes.

The League of Nations gave greater weight to the small powers which provided many of its most impressive figures, like Benes of Czechoslovakia and others. The League brought into focus the new Irish Free State. Norway and Sweden provided the great personalities of Branting and Nansen, the latter being for many years the League of Nations High Commissioner for Refugees. Thus the League of Nations was able to fulfil the aspirations of General Smuts. In a famous pamphlet, *The League of Nations: A Practical Suggestion,* Smuts urged that the League should be 'part and parcel of the common international life of states... an ever visible, living, working organ of the polity of civilization...' Finally,

> in its purposes and principles, its institutions and its methods, the United Nations bears at every point the mark of the experience of the League. In judgments upon the records of the League and all that it did, this truth must always be borne in mind.

Failure of the League of Nations

In spite of its promise, the League failed to fulfil the expectations of its most enthusiastic supporters. The rules of equality and unanimity gave even the smallest state of power of vote which prevented effective action in any emergency. The League also lacked the legal power to enforce peace. Members were free to ignore, if they wished, the recommendations of the Council. The absence of three major powers—United States, Russia and Germany—undermined the effectiveness of the League as an international organisation. The absence of the United States left Britain and France face to face in the League which had sharply opposed conceptions of what the League should be. In addition, the League appeared to be an organisation of those who were victorious in the First World War.

In the first years of the League's operation, the French government sponsored two schemes for strengthening the League. The first was the Draft Treaty of Mutual Assistance of 1923. It proposed that once the Council had declared that a member state was the object of aggression, all other members would be obliged to come to its assistance. The second was the Geneva Protocol of 1924 which provided that all disputes of a legal character should be submitted to the Permanent Court of International Justice, whose decision would be binding. Both failed as a result of opposition of the British Government and the Dominions. The British public opinion was opposed to compulsory arbitration as well as to accept automatic obligations under the Covenant in which they had no vital interests.

The League failed to implement Article 8 of the Covenant which provided plans for 'the reduction of national armaments to the lowest point consistent with national safety.' The only progress made towards such reduction was in naval armaments. But here the record was not impressive. The Washington Conference of 1921-22 provided some sort of naval parity among the United States, Britain, Japan, France and Italy for a period of ten years, but it failed to curb the building of cruisers or submarines. The Geneva Naval Conference of 1927 and the London Conference of 1930 did not improve the situation.

In November 1920 the Council appointed a Temporary Mixed Commission to assist in the task of the reduction of armaments. In 1922 the British delegate on the Temporary Mixed Commission proposed a numerical scheme for the limitation of armaments. Unfortunately the plan was rejected by most of the European powers. In December 1925 the Council appointed a Preparatory Commission for the Disarmament Conference which met for the first time at Geneva in May 1926. But the real work of the Commission began in March 1927 when the British and French governments submitted draft disarmament conventions. But they revealed wide differences of opinion and conflicted on nearly every vital issue.

When in 1932, after several years of preparatory work, a general conference was called at Geneva in February 1932, it revealed total disagreement. President Hoover proposed in vain a cut of one-third in the armies of all countries. The British Prime Minister, Macdonald, urged in vain a standard army of 200,000 men for each of the major powers. In October 1933, Germany, dominated by Adolf Hitler, withdrew from the conference, resigned from the League and proclaimed her intention of arming.

The weakness of the League was exposed when it failed to curb the aggression of the Great Powers. In 1931 Japan invaded Manchuria and set up a puppet state known as Manchukuo. This was an open challenge to the League. A Commission was appointed by the League, headed by an Englishman, Lord Lytton, to investigate the dispute between Japan and China. The report of the Commission condemned the Japanese aggression and recommended that China should be sovereign in Manchuria. In Frebruary 1933 the Assembly of the League accepted the report and a month later Japan withdrew from the League. The weakness of the collective security system had been mercilessly exposed and the confidence of the smaller powers in the League had been shaken.

Any hope that remained of the effectiveness of the League was destroyed on October 3, 1935 when Italy invaded Ethiopia. At once fifty nations assembled in the League Assembly, named Italy as an aggressor and put into force limited economic sanctions against her. Mussolini was at first surprised by the vigour of the League's reaction. But his apprehension was considerably lessened when the limited policy of sanction operated slowly on Italy as it did not include the prohibition of oil. The early collapse of Ethiopian resistance in May 1936—thanks to the indiscriminate use of poison gas by the Italians—decided the issue. It became clear that nothing short of military sanctions would affect the issue. In July 1937 the Assembly decided to lift the sanctions and in December Italy gave notice of resignation from the League. The League also demonstrated its weakness by its failure to prevent Germany from occupying the demilitarized zone of Rhineland in 1936.

The Spanish Civil War (1936-39) was another instance of the incapacity of the League to take effective action in the interest of peace. The League failed to prevent the Spanish conflict from developing into a general European war. In March 1938 Germany occupied and annexed Austria without the League doing anything to deter her.

In 1939-40 the League failed to protect Finland from Russia, although the latter was expelled from the League. During these years there was a general feeling that some revision of articles of the Covenant ought to be undertaken. 'But the fundamental question at issue was whether the League should still be armed with some sort of coercive powers... or whether it should henceforth be merely a machinery for facilitating consultation and cooperation.'[1]

Thus, in the political sphere, the League failed in its main purpose. The fundamental weakness of the League was to be found in the unwillingness of nations to subordinate their own interests to the peace of the world. 'What was everybody's business in the end proved to be nobody's business. Each one looked to the other to take the lead, and the aggressors got away with it.'

The League's founders overlooked the forces of nationalism. While they had the power, Italy, Japan and Germany refused to be bound by the limitations imposed on them by the Covenant of the League. Britain and France were the only major powers left to support the weak fabric of the League and even they were hesitant supporters of the League. Cecil, one of the British

1. *The New Cambridge Modern History,* Vol. XII (1968), P. 260.

founders of the League, wrote: 'Influential officials in the Foreign Office did not conceal their suspicion of the League. The League was officially tolerated. It was never liked.'

As a matter of fact the League existed to facilitate and to encourage cooperation among states. It could not make them cooperate if they did not want to.

CHAPTER 32

GREAT BRITAIN (1868-1945)

Gladstone's Ministry (1868-74)

The election of 1868 returned a substantial Liberal majority. Their leader, William E. Gladstone, formed a ministry which lasted from 1868 to 1874. He set himself to the task of creating a better England through 'Peace, Retrenchment and Reform.'

Gladstone began with education. Robert Lowe, the famous exponent of electoral reform in Britain, is quoted as saying 'now we must educate our masters.'

W. E. Forster, a Quaker, was given charge of Gladstone's measures for educational reform. Until 1870 there had been no real state schools in Britain, and children were not obliged to go to school. Since 1833 the state had been subsidizing elementary schools maintained by the Church. Forster's Education Act of 1870 established a national system of popular education. Britain was divided into school districts, and new schools were built, known as 'Board Schools'. They were supported mainly by local taxation and controlled by elected boards of education. In the Board Schools, no denominational religion should be taught, except the teaching of the Bible. Under the operation of these 'Board Schools' and with the added requirement in 1880 that every child must attend some school, illiteracy in England showed a marked decline from twentyfour per cent in 1871 to one per cent in 1910. In the matter of university education, improvement was made by abolishing the 'religious test' by the Repeal of the Tests Act of 1871. Hitherto no one could become a member of the Universities of Oxford and Cambridge unless he was a member of the Church of England.

The victory of Liberalism was also responsible for the reform of the Civil Service. In 1870 all posts were thrown open to be competed for by public examination. The Trade Union Act of 1871 finally legalised trade unions, by empowering them to hold property and to maintain and defend actions at law. But it contained drastic provisions against picketing and every form of violence and other trade disputes. Trade unionism grew rapidly in Britain after 1871.

In 1872 the Ballot Act made voting for members of Parliament secret, and voters no longer had to fear intimidation or reprisals. This supplemented the Reform Act of 1867 by enabling urban workers to vote as they pleased.

Gladstone carried through Edward Cardwell, the Secretary of War, reform in the Army. Britain had a professional army, liable to serve twenty years with the colours. This meant that the soldiers were too old for active service, and there were no reserves. Cardwell introduced short-term service, under which men enlisted for twelve years, and then went into the reserve. He rearmed the infantry with the Martini-Henry breach-loading rifle, divided Britain and Ireland into new regimental districts. He abolished the practice of purchasing commissions in the army. He also swept away separate authorities for different departments, and set up one Army Council, with the Secretary of War at its head.

Gladstone wanted to quicken the pace of reform. He wished to reform the trade in liquor and set to work on a Licensing Bill. He had already incurred the displeasure of the Nonconformists over education and the Church of England by his bill diestablishing the Church in Ireland (1869). Now this new Bill deprived him the workers' votes.

When Gladstone assumed office he declared that his mission was to pacify Ireland. He tried to carry out his mission through laws establishing religious equality, land reform, and Home Rule.

Disraeli and the Tory Democracy (1874-80)

In the election of 1874, Gladstone and the Liberal party lost their majority in Parliament. The Conservative party, under the leadership of Benjamin Disraeli, exploited a temporary economic depression and working-class dissatisfaction with Gladstone's Trade Union Act and the inglorious foreign policy. Disraeli now became the Prime Minister. He maintained amicable relations with Queen Victoria for which he was raised to the peerage as the Earl of Beaconsfield. He did much to render the Crown the outstanding symbol and object of British patriotism.

Cool, detached and a fiery debator, Disraeli was a statesman per excellence. Although admired by many he was trusted by few. Disraeli appreciated the need for reform and as Prime Minister from 1874 to 1880, he supported legislation dealing with labour conditions and trade unions, housing and merchant shipping. But it was in foreign affairs that Disraeli distinguished himself as he stressed imperial issues above all others. Hence he left the details of his domestic policy to be carried out by Sir Richard Cross, the Home Secretary.

In 1875 the Parliament repealed the restrictions which the Trade Union Act of 1871 had imposed on 'peaceful picketing'. The Act of 1878 codified the comprehensive code of Factory laws. In 1875 was passed the Public Health Act, which empowered the county and borough councils to take measures for public health. Provision was made for proper water sanitation and each district was now to have a Medical Officer of Health. The Artisans' Dwelling Act of 1875 gave local authorities power to pull down slums and rebuild them. To prevent the ships from being overloaded, the Merchant Shipping Act gave the Board of Trade the right to inspect all ships before they headed for sea.

In foreign affairs, Disraeli differed fundamentally from Gladstone. As he wanted to glorify the British Empire, he emphasised the idea of imperialism. In 1875, he acquired mastery of the Suez Canal which enabled Britain to control the route to India and led to the British occupation of Egypt. He arranged for the Prince of Wales to visit India and in 1877 Queen Victoria was proclaimed Empress of India.

Disraeli pursued the traditional policy of maintaining the integrity of Turkey against Russian design. In the Russo-Turkish war of 1877-78 he intervened in support of Turkey and did not allow Russia to settle the Eastern Question unilaterally. He compelled Russia to submit the Eastern Question to a European conference which met at Berlin in 1878. At the conference of Berlin, he played a conspicuous part to solve the baffling problems in the Near East. He acquired the island of Cyprus which safeguarded the route to India. He was not vainglorious when he said that he had brought 'Peace with Honour'.

The anti-Russian policy led Beaconsfield to further adventures. To prevent Russia from gaining control of Afghanistan, he sent his friend Lytton as Viceroy of India. A British mission was sent to Kabul. But within a few months the British agent was murdered at Kabul. Britain had to reverse her policy and did her best to win over Afghanistan by pacific means. Troubles in Africa with the Zulus and the Boers completed Beaconsfield's foreign entanglements.

In the general election of 1880 Gladstone undertook a vigorous propaganda, called 'Midlothian campaign'. He denounced Beaconsfield's policy towards the Turks, his misadventure in Afghanistan, and his failure in South Africa. In the election the Liberals won by a comfortable margin. Beaconsfield did not long survive after the defeat as he died the next year (1881).

Gladstone's Ministries (1880-85)

Gladstone was a staunch individualist, the masses had faith in him and his party. To them the Liberals stood for progress and Gladstone symbolised righteousness. Though Gladstone was a shrewd politician, his principles and prejudice conformed to mid-century liberalism than with progressive nationalism. He was still a 'little Englander,' dubious about foreign entanglements and interested in effecting domestic reforms.

Gladstone talked so much about reform that he alarmed the Conservative as well as Queen Victoria. Yet it was irony of fate that the only memorable reform which Gladstone effected during his second ministry was the extension of the parliamentary suffrage to farm tenants and agricultural labourers. Called the Country Franchise Act (1884), it added two million voters to the register, nearly half the total. Gladstone also redistributed members, limiting towns with less than 50,000 inhabitants to one member each. Finally, he tried to check corruption by limiting the amount of candidates' election expenses.

In British politics Ireland became a festering sore. English political leaders tried to sidetrack the Irish issue as long as possible, but after 1850 organised resistance made it a burning issue. The Fenian Society was formed at Kilkenny in 1857, which derived its inspiration from a group of revolutionary exiles in Paris. Irish veterans of the American Civil War strengthened the Fenian Society by instigating violence in English cities and in the Irish countryside. The Fenians were encouraged by agrarian discontent. The Land League was founded to defend the economic interests of the peasants. After the Irish Reform Act of 1868 enlarged the electorate, Charles Stewart Parnell became a member of Parliament in 1875 and demanded Home Rule for Ireland.

When Gladstone took office in 1880, Ireland was plagued by grave disorder. Evictions for failure to pay rent was followed by widespread disturbances. Gladstone passed the Land Act in 1881 which had been nicknamed the Act of the Three Fs—Fair Rent, Fixity of Tenure and Free Sale. The Act set up tribunals to fix rents for a period of fifteen years, during which time the tenants were not to be evicted. The object of the Act was to save the landlords from the ruin which the Land War was threatening them. This act was followed by a series of Land Purchase Acts by which tenants could buy their farms by a series of annual payments. T. P. O'Connor, then a quiet young revolutionary, summed up the object of the legislation by observing that 'Gladstone's policy was to fix a relation between landlord and tenant; the policy of the League was to abolish the relation and trample landlordism beneath its heels.'

Along with the Land Act, Gladstone passed his Coercion Act of 1881 which enabled the Government to detain any person without trials suspected of supporting the Land League. Parnell, Davitt and most of the League leaders were arrested. The mass struggle, now without any leadership, petered away in acts of individual terrorism. Parnell rejected an agreement with the Government by which violent methods were to stop in return for an amnesty and legislation to end eviction. Parnell was released in May 1882. But a few days later this understanding was wrecked by the murder of the new Irish Secretary, Lord Frederick Cavendish by a band of terrorists. Parnell at once condemned the assassins, but an English Government could not drop coercion after this. However, Ireland was quiet again when the 1884 Act gave the Irish peasant the vote on the same terms as the English country-dweller. Before a general election could take place, Gladstone was defeated; the Irish M.P.s voted against him because he wanted to renew the Crimes Act for Ireland.

A minority Conservative Government under Lord Salisbury took office in June 1885. Parnell gained the impression that Salisbury was willing to give Ireland some kind of autonomy. He, therefore, instructed the Irish in England to vote for Conservative candidates in the general election of 1885. It returned a slightly greater number of Liberals than of Conservatives but a sufficiently large number of Irish Nationalists to enable them a deciding factor between the two major parties. But Parnell was unable to achieve Home Rule for his country. Gladstone at once decided that Ireland must have Home Rule. In alliance with Irish Nationalists, he voted Salisbury out of office for the third time in February 1886.

Gladstone's third ministry did not last long. He stuck to his principles of granting Home Rule to Ireland. But he failed to convince all his followers and his most promising young Liberal, Joseph Chamberlain. So when the Home Rule Bill was presented in the House of Commons, a minority of Liberals—who called themselves 'Liberal Unionists'—joined the Conservatives in rejecting the bill. A general election quickly followed and Salisbury, with Liberal Unionists backing, again took office in July 1886.

The Liberal Party—which had been the major political party from 1846 to 1886—was now divided with the formation of the Liberal Unionist.

The most conspicuous leader of the Liberal Unionists was Joseph Chamberlain, a radical in religion and in the cause of social reform. During the next twenty years, the Conservatives, supported by Liberal Unionists, controlled the destiny of the country. There was only a brief interlude of three years (1892-95) when Gladstone was in office with a precarious majority in the House of Commons.

Salisbury's Conservative Ministry (1886-92)

The Conservative ministry of Salisbury, from 1886 to 1892, pursued a nationalist and imperialist policy. It celebrated, in 1887, with befitting pomp, the fiftieth anniversary of Queen Victoria's accession to the throne. It organised a series of colonial conferences and discussed with representatives of the home government matters of general concern to the British Empire as a whole. It sponsored in 1889 a sensational strengthening of the British navy. It greatly enlarged the territorial extent of the Empire by participating with Germany, France, Portugal in the general partition of Africa. In respect of Ireland, it consistently opposed all Home Rule. But in an effort to reconcile the Irish peasants, it advanced money to them on easy terms to purchase land. By a series of such 'land purchase acts', the number of peasant proprietors was increased.

Salisbury was less interested than Gladstone in social reform. Nevertheless, a group of young Conservatives, the so-called 'Tory Democrats', under the leadership of Lord Randolph Churchill, the father of Winston Churchill, and reinforced by the pressure of Joseph Chamberlain, took up the cause of the working class. The Salisbury ministry enacted in 1887 the Mines Act, forbidding the employment of children under 12 years of age. In 1891 it practically abolished tuition fees in elementary schools.

Government expenditure, however, on social services, was still meagre. Though working-class life was improving, distinctions between classes grew sharply. Above all, poverty meant appalling destitution. The Government could do little to remedy some of the obvious symptoms of such ills. And the blight of unemployment continued to plague the ministry. It is not really surprising, therefore, that these years were disturbed by violence. On November 13, 1887, there occurred a riot in London in which two people died later. The actual occasion of the riot was a demonstration about Ireland, but it followed weeks of agitation by the unemployed. Five years later soldiers opened fire in Yorkshire to protect property. The Dockers' Strike of 1889 brought important victory to the workers—a standard wage of six pence a hour.

The general election of 1892 gave the Liberals, in combination with the Irish Nationalists, a slight preponderance in the House of Commons. Gladstone, now at the age of 82, formed his fourth ministry. His mission was to grant Home Rule to Ireland. He passed the bill through the House of Commons, but the House of Lords rejected it by an overwhelming majority. In 1894 the 'Grand Old Man' of nineteenth century British liberalism retired—leaving the premiership to a younger colleague, Earl of Rosebery. He died in 1898.

Conservative Rule and Imperial Expansion (1895-1905)

The election of 1895 returned a coalition of Conservatives and Liberal Unionists. Salisbury resumed the premiership and appointed Joseph Chamberlain as colonial secretary. In 1900, another election prolonged the coalition's life till 1905. In 1902 Salisbury retired owing to his old age and infirmity giving place to Arthur J. Balfour, an academician and former disciple of Lord Randolph Churchill.

The ten years of Salisbury and Balfour government witnessed some social legislation, inspired mainly by Chamberlain. A workmen's Compensation Act enabled workmen to insure against accidents in certain specified trades. The Education Act of 1902 provided for state aid to Anglican and Roman Catholic schools as well as to undenominational ones.

The decade also witnessed an extraordinary advance of nationalism and imperialism. It was the time when economic rivalry was fast developing among the Great Powers. Britain began to feel the industrial competition of Germany and the United States and became alarmed by the ambitious projects of Russia in Asia, France in Africa, and Germany in the Near East and the Pacific. Britain became conscious of her 'manifest destiny' to rule Africa, Asia and other continents.

Despite their concern for imperial projects, the Conservatives found time to enhance popularity at home. They celebrated the Diamond Jubilee of Queen Victoria in 1897; they survived the disastrous war with the Boers which followed quickly upon that celebration. When the old Queen died in January 1901, they crowned her son and successor, Edward VII (1901-10).

The popularity of the Conservatives began to wane rapidly. The Boer War and the new continental troubles eroded the urge of imperialism. Balfour's Education Act of 1902 aroused the Non-conformist Churches with the fear that public money would be used to buttress the Established Church. Finally, in 1903—when Joseph Chamberlain began his campaign for imperial preferential tariffs in order to boost up England's already diminished foreign trade—he dealt a mortal blow to the party. Accustomed to free trade, a majority of the Conservatives were so afraid of the effect of tariff protection in raising the cost of living that they denounced his proposals. In vain did Balfour, the Prime Minister, try to prevent party warfare. The Tariff Reform League founded by the Tariff reforms was matched by the foundation of Free League of the Free traders. Balfour pressed on relentlessly until he resigned in December 1905.

In the elections of January 1906, the Liberal Party, the exponent of free trade, won a landslide victory. The Liberals won 377 seats in the Commons, a majority of 84 over all other parties combined. Young Liberals like Lloyd George and Winston Churchill looked upon the victory as a demand for social reform. The new Liberal cabinet was headed by Henry Campbell-Bannerman, a wise Scot with a long parliamentary experience. His cabinet included leading luminaries like Lord Morley at the India office, Lord Bryce at the Irish Secretaryship, H. H. Asquith (1852-1928) the Chancellor of the Exchequer, Sir Edward Grey (1862-1933) at the Foreign Office, R. B. Haldane (1856-1928) who became minister of war, David Lloyd George (1863-1945), who was at the Board of Trade and Winston Churchill (1874-1965), who succeeded him there when he went to the Exchequer in 1908.

The election of 1906 witnessed the emergence of a new Labour Party who won 29 seats. The appearance of Labour Party in Parliament marked a fundamental divide in British policies. The last quarter of the nineteenth century saw a revived interest in socialism. In 1881, a group of intellectuals, including William Morris and Henry Hyndman, formed the Social Democratic Federation for the propagation of revolutionary Marxian socialism among the masses. Its emphasis on imminent revolution, however, never appealed to the British common people. By the late 1880s it was already a spent force.

In 1883 the Fabian Society came into being. Apart from its founder, Sidney Webb (1859-1947) and his wife Beatrice, the Society included the dramatist George Bernard Shaw, Annie Besant, the novelist H. G. Wells, the historian of Socialism G. D. H. Cole and the future Prime Minister Ramsay MacDonald. Claiming as their spiritual predecessors, both Robert Owen and John Stuart Mill, the Fabians emphasised the necessity of a fundamental reorganisation of British society.

Two things were necessary to accomplish the objective—unlimited democracy in the political sphere and socialism in the economic sphere. The socialism the Fabians professed was a philosophy of economic equality to be achieved by democratic means. The philosophy of the Fabians was succinctly put forth by Bernard Shaw (1856-1950) when he wrote that the Fabians aimed to persuade the English people to make their political constitution thoroughly democratic and so to socialize their industries as to make the livelihood of the people entirely independent of private Capitalism. Fabianism was not attuned to working class philosophy. The Fabians hoped to 'permeate' the middle classes and the parties and parliament with the conviction that gradual transition to socialism was both necessary and practical.

In 1893, Keir Hardie, a Scottish miner, founded the Independent Labour Party which adopted a programme in harmony with revisionist Marxism. He put up candidates for Parliament who would work for the collective ownership and control of production, distribution and exchange. In 1899 a Trade Union Congress authorised a conference to investigate the question of labour's parliamentary representation. In February 1900, union delegations with representatives of the Fabian Society, the ILP and SDF, had founded a Labour Representation Committee (soon to be called the Labour Party) under the secretaryship of J. Ramsay MacDonald (1866-1937).

In the decade that followed, the new party gained increasing support from the rank and file of labour. Meanwhile, an event of great importance brought the whole trade union movement into limelight. In 1900 railwaymen working for the Taff Vale Railway Company in South Wales went on strike without prior approval of their union. The union nevertheless supported them, but was sued by the company for the losses incurred in the strike. The union eventually lost the case. The Taff Vale decision imperilled not only the right to strike but the whole trade union organisation.

Despite the adverse judgement, the Labour Party won 29 candidates in the elections of 1906. The Taff Vale decision was revoked by a new Trade Disputes Act in 1906. In 1909 it was declared illegal for any trade union to spend money in electing members of Parliament or in any other political activities. It was resented by the Labour Party and the unions alike. However, in the election of 1910, the Labour Party emerged with 42 seats. A year later it was stipulated that members of Parliament would be paid £ 400 a year. In 1913 Parliament legalised political action by the unions. On the eve of the war, a strong Labour Party had come into existence.

The new government gave up the imperialist policy. It conceded self-government to the Transvaal and laid the basis for the new constitution of the union of South Africa, which was ratified in 1909. Campbell Bannerman died in 1908 and Asquith became Prime Minister with Lloyd George as Chancellor of the Exchequer.

The central feature of the period was various reforms carried out by the ministry. The Merchant Shipping Act of 1906 prescribed standards of food and accommodations in the British ships. A new Patents Act of 1907 remedied deficiencies in the existing law. An Act set up a part of London authority to amalgamate existing dock authorities.

Haldane, Minister of War, carried out reforms in the armed forces. In the first Gladstone ministry, Edward Cardwell, the Secretary of War, had corrected important abuses in the army. But since then continental armies had moved forward with improved technique and innovative organisation, while the British army had been languishing. The Boer War had demonstrated shocking weakness in the British army and administrative bungling in the War Office itself. He introduced divisions of the continental type, established an Expeditionary Force of six infantry divisions and one cavalry division with supporting artillery, transport, medical units and adequate reserves and a Territorial Force. He established officer training corps at all public and secondary schools. He introduced first permanent general staff in the British army and inducted able men like Sir William Robertson, Henry Wilson, and Douglas Haig. While doing all this, Haldane actually reduced the military budget, thus silencing the opposition of the Radical wing of the party, which protested against military expenditure.

Under the care of the First Sea Lord, Admiral Sir John Fisher, reforms in the navy were undertaken. He advocated the disarming of all superannuated fleet units and inaugurated a building programme of dreadnought type of battleship. The building of the German navy posed such a threat that Fisher, in private conversation with the King, suggested the advisability of destroying the German navy before it began to cause trouble. Though the King indignantly refused the suggestion, the naval estimates had to be revised.

The cabinets of Henry Campbell Bannerman and Herbert Asquith inaugurated an era of domestic reforms. A comprehensive "Children's Act" of 1908 sought to regulate various phases of child's life, providing, among others, free medical examination and care of infants and young children. In the same year "Old-age Pensions Act" obligated the state to pay a subsidy to every needy old person. By 1913 about a million persons used to receive old-age pensions from the public exchequer. To improve the living conditions of the urban masses, a "Housing and Town Planning Act" of 1909 authorised the government to demolish condemned structures and unhealthy tenements and replace them with model dwellings.

Most of the social legislations were carried through the Parliament with little opposition. In some cases the Conservative majority in the House of Lords proposed amendments which rendered the measures less radical. The House of Lords, not subject to election, was a stronghold of privilege. To the Liberals the hereditary body with large powers was an anomaly in a progressive state. Though they had approved every Conservative measure during the years 1888-92, they had vetoed nearly every measure of social reform during the Liberal ministry of 1892-95. In 1906 the Lords vetoed a new Education Bill; in 1907 they mutilated four land-reform bills; in 1908 they rejected a liquor-licensing bill; and in 1909 they refused to approve the government's budget.

In 1909, the Welsh Chancellor of the Exchequer, David Lloyd George—who had a deep resentment against the aristocracy—introduced the People's Budget. It was 'a War Budget...to wage implacable warfare against poverty and squalidness.' 'In addition to customary stamp taxes and excise taxes, the budget levied a steeply graduated income tax, a heavy inheritance tax, special taxes on motor cars, and imposed four new land taxes, the most important of which was a tax on unearned increment.

The weight of taxation—imposed by the wish to finance social services and to build battleships—was unprecedented; 'almost revolutionary' in Woodward's description.[1] The Lords blundered in rejecting a financial measure, the budget of 1909, as it had been customary for the Upper House to give assent to finance bills adopted by the House of Commons. The Lords defended their action on the ground that the budget of 1909 was not an ordinary finance bill, but an extraordinary bill on which the whole nation should be consulted through a general election. The Liberal government appealed to the country with the declaration that the Lords had 'violated the British constitution.'

In the elections held in January 1910, the Liberals lost a considerable number of seats, but they were balanced by the Labour and Irish Nationalist support. The Budget became law. The Budget question was quickly overshadowed by a constitutional conflict over the House of Lords. Liberals were annoyed by the fact that however strong they might be in the House of Commons, any legislation passed by them could be stalled in the House of Lords. Therefore, the government proposed in February 1910 the Parliament Bill which provided that the Lords should neither amend nor reject a Money Bill, that the Lords could not hold up a Bill from the Commons for more than two years, and that the life of Parliament should be reduced to five years. The Parliament Bill, as usual, got through the House of Lords. Parliament was dissolved and a second general election was called in the year 1910—this time on the constitutional power of the House of Lords.

The election of December 1910 returned the same number of Liberals as in previous January; again the balance of power was held by Labourites and Irish Nationalists, both bent upon enacting the Parliament Bill into law. The Prime Minister, Asquith, pursued his objective with a determination. He secured a promise from the new King George V that, if the Lords refused to pass the Parliament Bill, he would create enough new peers to secure its passage. Under this threat the opposition collapsed and, after much bitter wrangling in both Houses, the Lords passed the Parliament Bill. By this act the democratically elected House of Commons imposed its will on the hereditary constituency of House of Lords and curbed the latter's power of obstruction. In this way, the Parliament Act of 1911 was almost as epochal in British constitutional history as the Reform Act of 1832.

Despite the great Liberal victory of 1911, Asquith's government lost prestige with different sectors of the British public. One sector was labour, fretting with discontent by rising taxes and prices. In 1910 and 1911, a series of strikes engulfed the country. In 1911 Parliament granted a national minimum wage to the miners but incurred displeasure of both the unions and employers. The government lost prestige, but the number of strikes declined.

1. Woodward, E. L. : *Great Britain and the German Navy,* P. 13.

Another sector was the militant Women's Suffrage Movement. Led by the redoubtable Ms. Emmeline Pankhurst, the militant Feminists indulged in a frenzy of vandalism and personal assault. They chained themselves to the railings of Buckingham Palace and then refused to eat when they were imprisoned. As Winston Churchill said in 1914, 'the civil parliamentary systems under which (Englishmen) (had) dwelt so long (seemed) to be brought to the rude challenge of force (and) to be exposed to menace and brutality.' Asquith's minister, however, refused to concede to their demands.

The third sector, made up of Conservatives and Unionists who opposed Irish Home Rule, threatened Britain with a civil war. As a price of support of the Irish Nationalists in 1910, Asquith introduced a bill in 1912 that granted Ireland a bicameral Parliament at Dublin, but subordinate to the British parliament in military, financial and certain other matters. But the Bill was opposed by a group of extreme nationalists, the Sinn Fein, who denounced it as a sorry compromise of Irish freedom. Moreover, the Protestants in the province of Ulster assailed the bill as a devious way to destroy the unity of the British Empire and set about enlisting a large militia to resist Home Rule by force. The prospect of rebellion and civil war was dramatically dispelled by the outbreak of the First World War.

The social reforms of Asquith Ministry constituted its chief title to fame. The National Insurance Act of 1911 insured workers against accident, sickness and unemployment. But like Bismarck's social insurance law of the 1880s, it was essentially a rigid one, since it was supported not by general taxation, but by contributions from employers and employees, with small additional state subsidy.

The British Empire

In the last quarter of the nineteenth century Britain played a leading part in international affairs. In 1870 the leading British statesmen believed that Britain was a satiated country. But in the next thirty years Benjamin Disraeli and Joseph Chamberlain advocated the expansion of the empire. After 1874, when industrialisation kindled overseas ambition, the British Empire grew by leaps and bounds. By the end of the nineteenth century, it embraced approximately a quarter of the globe and a quarter of its population.

The growth of the British Empire was partially a growth of such colonies—Canada, Australia, New Zealand, South Africa. Much more, however, it was the assertion of British political supremacy over Asia and Africa.

British India was declared an Empire and in 1877 Queen Victoria was proclaimed Empress of it. In the 1880s Burma was conquered. In 1874, Britain obtained the Malay States adjoining Singapore. From China were taken Hongkong in 1842 and Wei-hai-wei in 1898. In the Pacific Ocean, the Fiji Islands were annexed in 1874, southeastern New Guinea (Papua) in 1884, northern Borneo (Sarawak) in 1888, Tonga (or the Friendly Islands) in 1900. In the Mediterranean, Britain had occupied Cyprus in 1878.

In Africa especially, the British Empire expanded rapidly. Its possessions grew to such an enormous size that it covered an area 35 times greater than the homeland. Before 1880, Britain had a few trading posts on the west coast, and possessed Cape Colony and Natal in the extreme south. After 1880, British expansion proceeded rapidly in Africa. Here the Imperial East Africa Company, the Royal Niger Company, and the South Africa Chartered Company were the vehicles of expansion. Egypt was occupied in 1882. Protectorates were established in Bechauland in 1885, in Somaliland in 1887, in Zanzibar in 1890, in Uganda in 1896. Chartered commercial companies acquired Nigeria in 1886, British East Africa (Kenya) in 1888, and Rhodesia in 1889. The conquest of Zululand came in 1887, Ashanti in 1896, Egyptian Sudan in 1897, and the Dutch Republics of Tansvaal and Orange Free State in 1902.

It was not an easy task to govern such a large and heterogeneous Empire. There evolved three distinct types of dependency: (1) the self-governing colonies or 'dominions'; (2) Crown Colonies, naval stations and protectorates; and (3) the 'Empire' of India.

Self-governing colonies enjoying home rule were precisely the colonies in which large number of Britishers had settled—Canada, New Found-land, Australia, New Zealand and South Africa. In 1837, when Queen Victoria ascended the throne, there was no self-governing colony in the British Empire. But there were twentyone when Edward VII, Queen Victoria's son, died in 1907.

Canada

In 1867 was created the 'Dominion of Canada' by the British Parliament by enacting the British North America Act (1867). The government of the Dominion was modelled after the mother country. The growth of the Dominion was remarkably rapid. The new province of Manitoba was created in 1870 after purchasing extensive lands from the Hudson's Bay Company. Then British Columbia (1871) and Prince Edward Island (1873) joined the confederation. Finally in 1878 came a decree which declared that the Dominion of Canada should have jurisdiction over all British territory north of the United States, with the exception of Newfoundland. In 1905 the two last provinces to be created, Alberta and Saskatchewan, became members. Various disputes with United States over frontier questions were amicably settled.

Australia

In the early part of the nineteenth century the introduction of sheep-raising and, in the middle of the century, the discovery of gold, caused an influx of British immigrants to Australia. In addition to the original colony of New South Wales, which had been founded as a penal station in 1788, five others came into existence—Queensland, Victoria, South Australia, Western Australia, and Tasmania. A concerted move of maintaining British supremacy in the South Pacific against French and German infiltration took the shape of establishing a Federation. A constitutional convention, held in 1897-98, drafted a constitution which was incorporated in an Act passed by the British Parliament in 1900. The Act—Commonwealth of Australia Act—established a federal union of six 'States', modelled on that of the United States. New Zealand, physically separated from Australia, refused to join the Commonwealth.

Like the American Congress, the federal or Commonwealth legislature was composed of a Senate, representing the States equally, and a House of Representatives representing the people. Like the American Supreme Court, the High Court of the Commonwealth was the guardian and interpreter of the Constitution. The Australian Commonwealth was essentially British in character. The highest office was the Governor-General, who reigned but did not rule. The government was carried on by a cabinet of ministers, who was responsible to the Parliament rather than to the Governor-General.

Social reform occupied the attention of the government. Henceforth labour parties sprang up in the several states. Between 1890 and 1910, the state of Victoria enacted a series of laws which regulated the wages and hours of industrial labour. The Commonwealth Government established in 1904 a federal arbitration court for the settlement of interstate industrial disputes. In 1908 it also introduced a system of old-age pensions. In the general election of 1910 the Labour Party, under their leader Andrew Fisher, formed a ministry which—with a brief interruption—endured for the next seven years. In 1911, it introduced compulsory military training for all young Australians.

New Zealand

New Zealand, formally annexed to the British Empire in 1839, was granted local autonomy in 1852. In 1907 it was styled as a Dominion and accorded equal status with that of Canada and Australia. Here Parliament made more democratic through the popular election on the basis of Proportional Representation. In respect of socialistic legislation, New Zealand was more advanced than Australia. As early as 1893, women were granted voting rights. Public ownership of railways, telephones, and telegraphs was established. The government also provided fire and life insurance, granted old-age pension and rented model homes to workingmen.

South Africa

In South Africa, the two British colonies—Cape Colony and Natal—faced the two republics dominated by the Dutch—the so-called Boers—the Transvaal and the Orange Free State. For more than forty years considerable strife marked relations between Cape Colony and the Dutch

Republics. In 1877 hostilities were renewed when the British asserted their claims to sovereignty over the Transvaal. The country remained under British rule till the Boers regained their independence by the victory of Majuba Hill (27 February, 1881). Gladstone, who did not like the war, recognised the independence of the Boers in 1881. Three years later this was fully accepted with the recognition of the independence of the Transvaal as the South African Republic of the Transvaal.

When the Boers were dreaming the creation of all South Africa Dutch by absorbing Natal and Cape Colony, British imperial ambitions were stimulated by the activities of Joseph Chamberlain in England and sensational projects of Cecil Rhodes in Africa. Rhodes, a product of imperialism, took as his ideal the extension of British influence from 'Cape to Cairo.' Rhodes created the British South Africa Company in 1889 for the development of Rhodesia.

Relations between the Boers and the British became strained when thousands of British fortune hunters flocked into the Transvaal following the discovery of the world's richest gold mines. The British annexation of Zululand and the territory just south of Delagoa Bay blocked the Transvaal from all access to the sea. In 1895, DR Jameson, an associate of Rhodes, led a filibustering expedition into the Transvaal with the object of incorporating it in the British Empire. The 'Jameson Raid' bungled disastrously and its leader surrendered ingloriously with his whole force.

The Jameson Raid created intense bitterness. From 1895 to 1899 the Transvaal government, under Paul Kruger, adopted truculent attitude towards the British. He rejected the demand of the 'Uitlanders' (the British immigrant miners within the Transvaal). A special commissioner, Sir Alfred Milner, in his report denounced the Boer government. Thereupon Britain demanded the extension of the suffrage to the Uitlanders which was refused.

War was only a question of time and this was declared in 1899. In the initial stage, the Boers under their resourceful commanders—Louis Botha, De Wet, Jan Smuts—won astonishing victories. The British suffered heavy losses. But reinforced by volunteers from England and Scotland and by detachments from Canada, Australia and New Zealand, the British force, numbering about 350,000, under the command of Lord Roberts and Lord Kitchener, succeeded in vanquishing the Boers. President Kruger fled to Europe. Peace was concluded in May 1902; the two republics—the Transvaal and the Orange Free State—lost their independence and were annexed to the British Empire.

In 1909 the Union of South Africa was formed which included Cape Colony, Natal, the Transvaal and the Orange Free State. The British Government granted Dominion Status to the Union. It adopted a constitution which established a central government consisting of a parliament of two Houses with a responsible ministry. General Louis Botha, a Boer, the first Prime Minister of the Union, was now loyal to the British Empire.

Thus, by 1910, Britain was mistress of five 'colonial nations'—the union of South Africa, the Commonwealth of Australia, the Dominions of Canada, Newfoundland, and New Zealand. Politically, the bond between them and the mother country was not indissoluble. They managed their own internal affairs and the Governor-Generals sent out from Britain were mere symbols of British rule. The mother-country exercised certain control over the Dominions: to pass upon their constitution, to veto acts of their parliaments, and to regulate their foreign relations. In practice, however, the interference was minimal in so much as the Dominions could negotiate treaties with foreign countries.

Economically, too, the self-governing Dominions followed their own interests. To promote their own economic development, they did not hesitate to levy tariffs on imports from Great Britain and other countries. To raise the standard of living of their citizens, they imposed restrictions on immigration.

Despite the growing political and economic tension between the mother country and self-governing Dominions, there grew up a deep sense of attachment to the British Empire on the part of these Dominions. Most significant aspect of this new spirit of cooperation was the fact that

Canada could have a French Prime Minister in Laurier, Australia a socialistic Premier in Fisher, and South Africa a Dutch Premier in Botha, whose allegiance to Britain was beyond reproach.

Joseph Chamberlain, the Colonial Secretary and the chief spokesman of British imperialism, devised ways and means for forging a partnership between the Empire and the Dominion. The most famous was Chamberlain's triple scheme of imperial conference, imperial preference, and imperial defence. Formal imperial conferences were inaugurated in London in 1887; and in 1907 it was decided to meet at regular intervals of four years where the Prime Ministers of several Dominions would meet with the Prime Minister of the United Kingdom to discuss matters of mutual concern.

'Imperial preference' was recognised by some of the Dominions establishing preferential tariff rates, favouring British and colonial as against foreign goods. Chamberlain believed that the Empire could be made self-sustaining. 'We have an Empire,' he declared, 'which with decent organisation and consolidation, might be absolutely self-sustaining. There is no article of your food, no raw material of your trade, no necessity of your lives, no luxury of your existence, which cannot be produced somewhere or other in the British Empire.' 'Imperial defense' meant defending the mother country against war. It was purely voluntary but, at critical moments, as in the Boer War or in the World Wars, the Dominions responded to the call of the mother country with magnificent loyalty and devotion.

Colonies, Protectorates, and the Indian Empire

The 'Crown Colonies' were presided over by governors who were appointed by and responsible to the colonial ministry in London. The oldest group of crown colonies were in tropical America—British Honduras, British Guiana, and West Indian island; and the West African coastal lands—Gold Coast, Gambia, and Sierra Leone. All Crown Colonies were administered by the series of naval stations in the Mediterranean—Gibraltar, Malta, and Cyprus. Among other Crown Colonies were Ceylon, Hongkong, the Straits Settlements, the Falkland Islands and the British East Africa (Kenya).

The "Protectorates" represented, as a rule, larger areas, in which native rulers were allowed to exercise their power in consultation or with the 'advice' of a British Resident. In some instances, a Crown Colony acquired a protectorate over its hinterland, the notable example being the crown colonies in West Africa. In other instances, a commercial company, specially chartered by the British Government, gained a protectorate. Cecil Rhodes's British South African Company, chartered in 1898, actually governed the huge territory of Rhodesia. Moreover, the activities of the 'Royal Niger Company', chartered in 1886, added the huge tract of Nigeria to the British Empire. In other instances, protectorates were exercised from the beginning by the British government. The typical examples were the Federated Malay States, with Sarawak, with Tonga, with Zanzibar and Uganda and British Central Africa (renamed Nyasaland in 1907).

Egypt

Egypt had strategic importance to Britain as the region round Suez was the 'spinal cord' of the British Empire. The Suez Canal was the principal station on the highway to India; and much of Britain's foreign trade passed through it. From 1882, Egypt became virtually a British dependency. Under Lord Cromer, who was High Commissioner from 1883 to 1907, Egypt made considerable progress. Taxes were fairly levied and equitably collected. Forced labour was abolished. Important irrigation works were undertaken, the most important being the construction of the famous Aswan Dam to conserve the waters of the Nile for irrigation purposes. An advisory assembly was created in 1883, and in 1913 it was vested with limited legislative powers.

Despite various reform measures, the Egyptians clamoured for self-government. A new nationalist movement began to develop with the cry of 'Egypt for the Egyptians.' Under pressure of this movement small concessions had to be made. But the First World War which intervened placed Egypt under martial law. As Turkey entered the First World War on the side of Germany, England openly proclaimed Egypt a protectorate.

After the war, the nationalist agitation was resumed. In 1919 there were widespread riots and strikes and about one thousand persons were killed. After a struggle lasting for more than a decade, Britain was forced to grant Egypt a nominal independence.

India

The foundation of British supremacy in India had been laid by the empire builders of the English East India Company during the seventeenth, eighteenth and early nineteenth centuries. The Sepoy Mutiny of 1857 threatened to overthrow British rule in India. The Mutiny was suppressed and the East India Company ceased to function. In 1858, the Government of India passed into the hands of the Crown. A new system of administration was introduced which left the authority in the hands of the Viceroy, who was responsible only to the British Government. The Viceroy was assisted by two councils—one executive, the other legislative—appointed by the Crown. A Secretary of State for India was appointed in the British Cabinet, who was to look after all matters pertaining to India. On the other hand, there were fairly large number of Indian States, which were governed directly by the Indian Princes, though subject to supervision by the Viceroy.

After 1857, the British began to consolidate their power. A policy of expansion was pursued which resulted in the annexation of Burma. Early in the twentieth century, Baluchistan was conquered; and Afghanistan and Tibet were neutralised by special agreements. In 1911, the capital was transferred from Calcutta to Delhi, the ancient seat of the Mughal Empire.

India's economic resources strengthened Britain's determination to retain India. She was a cheap producer of foodstuffs and raw materials for export to Britain and a big consumer of manufactured goods imported from Britain. From 1857 to 1914, Britain had almost a monopoly of India's growing trade.

From the middle of the nineteenth century, a kind of nascent nationalism made its appearance among the educated Indians. They denounced the British exploitation of the economic resources of the country and demanded self-government. The demand of the nationalists crystallised in the formation of Indian National Congress in 1885. To reconcile the nationalist aspiration, Morley-Minto Reforms were passed by Parliament in 1909. Indians were now appointed to the Viceroy's Council. Provincial councils, already in existence, were made partly elective, and given large powers.

Britain from 1914 to 1939

When Britain entered the First World War, the Liberals, led by Asquith, controlled the government. The ministry became unpopular. There were clamours against Asquith's view that the war was a matter of the soldiers and that the ministry should interfere as little as possible. In May 1915 the failure of the Dardanelles expedition and the defeat at Gallipoli brought a political crisis. A coalition Ministry was formed in May 1915 under Asquith, in which all the parties united—Liberal, Conservative and Labour. Lloyd George, who became the first Minister of Munitions, succeeded in expanding the supply of war materials. He introduced conscription in January 1916 which enabled her to deploy seventy divisions in France. At Easter there was a rising in Dublin. Lloyd George wanted to grant Home Rule, excluding Ulster immediately, but this agreement was watered down by Asquith which ended in fiasco. In the summer the Somne offensive yielded nothing against colossal loss.

The political crisis that followed was the emergence of Lloyd George as Prime Minister on December 7, 1916. In November 1917 a Supreme Allied War Council was formed to coordinate the military efforts of Britain, France, Italy and the United States. In March 1918, the Germans launched a massive offensive on the British. The British loss was heavy, 400,000 killed and wounded, 80,000 taken prisoner. Then the attack was halted. With American assistance, the Allies, in their turn, attacked in July 1918. A series of counter-attacks began driving the German armies from position after position and inflicting heavy losses. On November 11, 1918, Germany was compelled to sign an armistice.

At the end of the war, Britain gained the German colonies, Most of Germany's African colonies passed under the control of the British Empire as mandates. Iraq, Hedjaz, Palestine and

Trans-Jordania became British mandates. British control was established over the Berlin-Baghdad railway.

The First World War witnessed a significant change in the British political life. In 1918 the great Reform Bill was passed which marked a triumph for woman suffrage. Its chief provisions were: (1) universal manhood suffrage; (2) women, over thirty were granted the franchise, and (3) plural voting was so greatly limited that it virtually fell into disuse.

Immediately after the armistice, the Coalition captured two-thirds of the seats in the House of Commons. The membership of the coalition was 70 per cent Conservative. The Liberals had 28 members and the Labour, with 63 members, became the official opposition.

The outstanding problems of Britain after the war were economic. During the war, Britain had borrowed heavily at home and aboard. Her outstanding debt to the United States amounted to over two billion dollars. Though there was a brief postwar boom, it was an artificial one. The country's foreign trade had been ruined by the war, and was quickly taken over by the United States. The 'unrationalised' state of British industry, *i.e.* lack of modern methods and implements which were in use in Germany and the United States, curtailed production. The backbone of the British economy, the coal industry, was badly hit by the lack of modern scientific techniques and the increasing use of oil in place of coal. Prices and wages rose, and unemployment began to mount. In 1921 there were about two million registered unemployed workers out of a total of about twelve million population.

Economic dislocation and depression caused widespread unrest. The coalition government under Lloyd George tried to meet the situation by passing tariff and other measures to protect key industries from competition. The Housing Act of 1919 enabled the government to enter into the housing business with subsidies and laid obligations on local authorities to meet housing needs. The Unemployment Insurance Act of 1920 covered everyone earning less than £ 250 a year. It was followed by 'dole'—as the relief payments came to be called—when heavy unemployment came back in 1921. This dole came in for sharp criticism by J. B. Priestley. 'The dole is part of no plan; it is a mere declaration of intellectual bankruptcy... nobody is getting any substantial benefit, any reasonable satisfaction out of it.' The dole was no solution for chronic unemployment. The government also encouraged the emigration of unemployed workers to other parts of the empire. In 1921 Britain, abandoning the long-established policy of free trade, imposed tariff duties of $33^1/_3$ per cent to protect certain key industries.

Throughout this period, Britain was preoccupied with the Irish problem. The political unrest in Ireland was accentuated by the rise of extremist groups, notably the Sinn Fein. When elections for the British Parliament were held in Ireland in 1918, seventyfive candidates elected belonged to Sinn Fein. They refused to go to Westminster and organised a separate parliament which proclaimed the Irish Republic with De Valera as President.

The British Government reacted to this self-styled Irish Republic and unleashed reprisals by an auxiliary force, the 'Black and Tans', recruited from ex-servicemen. There followed three years of violence until in December 1921 Lloyd George arrived at a truce. Ulster was to be part of the United Kingdom while providing for an Irish Free State as a self-governing Dominion. The truce of December 1921 did not give the Irish Free State formal independence. Though it was accepted by a narrow majority in the Irish Parliament, the nationalist minority, under De Valera, refused to submit and fought bitterly until the end of 1922.

Meanwhile, the Conservatives had grown tired of Lloyd George's leadership. British diplomacy in the Near East alienated the French and his irresponsible flirtation with the Greeks against the Turks dealt a mortal blow to the stability of the ministry. The Conservatives decided to withdraw their support from the coalition. The Conservative ministers resigned and Lloyd George had to do likewise. Lloyd George was a man of incomparable stature. 'He provided the leadership which enabled it to endure its greatest war and with the assistance of the only other men of comparable stature in twentieth century British politics, Winston Churchill, he founded the welfare state. Until 1940 England did not owe more to any other twentieth century statesman.'

After the resignation of Lloyd George, the Conservative leader, Andrew Bonar Law, formed a ministry. In the parliamentary elections of November 1922, the Conservatives won a clear majority though the Labour Party was now returned with 142 members. Bonar Law's failing health necessitated a change of prime minister and he was succeeded six months later by the comparatively obscure Stanley Baldwin.

Baldwin possessed few of the qualities that were expected of a prime minister. A modest man, 'honest to the point of simplicity,' he had little interest in foreign affairs and his economic and social ideas were even more rudimentary than those of Lloyd George. Baldwin faced an unemployment situation which by this time had grown to be a chronic malady. The remedy for unemployment, to him, was tariff protection.

On the tariff issue, Parliament was dissolved and elections held in December 1923. The Conservatives returned with reduced strength of 258 members against 159 Liberals and 191 Labours. The first Labour government, therefore, took office in January 1924 with Liberal support, under Ramsay MacDonald. The first Labour Government was a flimsy structure which could be sustained only with Liberal support. Ramsay MacDonald possessed the charismatic quality necessary to leadership, but he showed lamentable lack of clear thought. During his ten months of office from January to November 1924, MacDonald did little to ensure his continuation. He could do little to put through Labour policies. Earlier he had advocated a capital levy and other drastic socialist measures for dealing with the domestic situation. Once in office, he abandoned all such proposals and contented himself with obtaining from Parliament the repeal of some of the existing tariff duties. A new Housing Act expanded municipal housing schemes.

In foreign affairs, the Labour government achieved some success. It played a prominent role in the acceptance of the Dawes Plan. MacDonald supported the Geneva Protocol of 1924 and urged the admission of Germany into the League. The Soviet Union was recognised and soon thereafter the two governments agreed to a resumption of commercial relations. The Liberals saw the red peril and withdrew their support from the MacDonald government. The Labour government came to an end when MacDonald resigned in October 1924 on the issue of an alleged political interference with the prosecution of an editor of the Communist *Workers' Weekly.*

In the ensuing election the Conservatives exploited to the full the publication of the so-called Zinoviev letter, said to have been written by a Bolshevik leader, urging the British communists to prepare for revolution. Baldwin's promise of moderate, safe government carried him to high pitch of popularity. The Conservatives came back to power with a commanding majority. They won in all 415 seats against the Liberals 42 and the Labour Party's 142.

The second Baldwin ministry remained in office for five years, from November 1924 to May 1929. Along with Briand of France, Baldwin pursued a pacific policy in Europe. The Chancellor of the Exchequer, Winston Churchill, pursued a policy of deflation. In 1925 he reluctantly returned to the gold standard which set the pound at its former value once more. The pound was overvalued by at least 10 percent which meant a reduction in exports, raising their price on the world market. The government was forced to cut down wages.

The General Strike

The economic malaise which plagued Britain left its impress on industries. Particularly hard hit was the coal industry. After an artificial spurt in 1923 caused by the stoppage of coal production in the Ruhr during the French occupation, the industry suffered when the latter withdrew from the Ruhr in 1925. The resumpiton of German coal exports substantially diminished British exports. The mine-owners announced in June 1925 the termination of the previous wage agreements and the reduction of wages.

Supported by the General Council of the Trade Union Congress (TUC), the miners refused to accept pay cut and threatened comprehensive strike action. To avoid this, Baldwin appointed a commission, under the chairmanship of Sir

Herbert Samuel, to investigate the industry. Its report in March 1926 recommended substantial reorganisation of the industry and temporary reduction in wages. Both miners and owners rejected the report. Both sides showed rigidity and lack of statesmanship. A national coal strike began on April 30, 1926. It was supported by the General strike on May 3 involving one-sixth of the working population of England.

The strike lasted only nine days. Despite the remarkable demonstration of working class unity, the strike was ill-planned. It was interpreted to the great majority of the British people as an attmept to substitute revolutionary government for parliamentary democracy. Many of the trade union leaders had been dubious about the efficacy of the strike. Prime Minister Baldwin declared that the General Strike threatened 'the basis of ordered government'. The main thrust of the government forces came from Winston Churchill, Chancellor of the Exchequer. Through press and radio, he played up the 'insurrectionary threat' and demonstrated that the strike was controlled by the Soviet agents. The government succeeded in enlisting the whole-hearted support of Britain's middle and upper-middle classes. Within two weeks the strike collapsed and all workers returned to their jobs, with the exception of the miners. The miners desperately continued their strike for six months more before petering out in agreements which meant victory for the owners. In 1927 the government passed the Trade Disputes Act to prevent sympathetic strikes in the future.

The General Strike left a trail of bitterness. The militant phase of the Labour movement came to an end and the Labour Party now came to rely on other means—peaceful and parliamentary means—to gain their objectives. The Labour Party now sought to widen its appeal beyond the working class which paid them good dividend two years later.

The Conservative government under Baldwin made no serious efforts to improve the economic conditions. However, it made provisions for widows, orphans, and old-age pensions, and extended franchise to all women over twenty-one in 1928. In foreign policy, the government's activities were in low profile. Despite the conclusion of the Locarno Pact, friendship with the United States was strained over naval disarmament. In 1927 diplomatic relations with Moscow were severed.

Increasing unemployment and the chronic industrial depression eroded the popularity of the Conservative government. Higher tariff rates and the establishment of some new industries failed to revive industrial strength. British exports, from 1913 to 1927, fell by 21 per cent, although the world's total export rose in the same period by 18 per cent. Thus, the British economy continued to languish until it was overwhelmed by the world depression.

In the general elections of May 1929 the Labour Party regained power and Ramsay MacDonald once more became Prime Minister. But it was by a slender majority; the Labour had won with 288 seats, against the Conservatives 260 and the Liberals 59, However, the Labour Party had Liberal support. MacDonald formed his Cabinet with Snowden, as Chancellor of the Exchequer, J. H. Thomas, Minister in charge of Unemployment, Arthur Henderson, as Foreign Secretary and Margaret Bondfield, the first British woman, as Minister of Labour.

MacDonald pursued a pacific foreign policy. Diplomatic relations with the Soviet Union were resumed and the promise of a Russian market secured. Apart from accepting the Young Plan, MacDonald met President Hoover in the United States and prepared the way for the London Naval Conference of 1930. At the Imperial Conference of 1930 MacDonald refused the Canadian Premier's request for a preferential tariff arrangement as this would have adverse effect on Britain's economy. Throughout 1931 he supported the movement for world disarmament.

The efforts of the government to solve domestic problems proved ineffective when Britain was overtaken by the world depression of 1929. The Chancellor of the Exchequer, Snowden, adopted a policy of rigid orthodoxy and tried to meet the budget deficit. A small team consisting of J. H. Thomas (Minister in charge of Unemployment), Thomas Johnston, Sir Oswald Mosley and George Lanburg was formed to deal with the problem of unemployment. But Philip Snowden contented himself with palliative measures—the

Housing Act of 1930, to speed up slum clearance, and the Agricultural Marketing Act of 1931—to help the farming community.

The situation, however, did not improve. Destitution was widespread and the fiscal position of the country was imperilled by heavy withdrawals of gold from the Bank of England. In July 1931 the economic committee headed by Sir George May warned a deficit of £120 million and proposed increased taxes and drastic cut to government expenditure, specially the unemployment benefits. The publication of this report created panic and the value of the pound slumped. MacDonald and Snowden favoured the committee's report, but they were overruled by a majority of the Cabinet. MacDonald, therefore, resigned on August 24, 1931. But the King asked him to form a national government. The new ministry, as formed under MacDonald's leadership, comprised four Labourites, four Conservatives and two Liberals. As Prime Minister MacDonald solicited the cooperation of his party to support the coalition. But the Labour Party opposed the National Government when it was found that the latter intended to carry out the kind of programme that they had just repudiated.

The National Government reduced government salaries and unemployment benefits, but the budget showed no signs of improvement. Foreign bankers began to withdraw gold and, in 1931, Britain went off the gold standard. The pound fell from $4.86 to $3.40. The new government went to polls to ratify its mandate. It appealed to the country for a 'doctor's mandate' to cure the financial ills of England. The election of October 1931 returned the government with a massive majority—554 National Government candidates were returned out of 615 members of parliament. The Labour—with its depleted majority from 289 to 52—became the opposition party. As the Conservative alone had secured 472 seats, it became the mainstay of the National Government.

The new government, under MacDonald's leadership, included four National Labourites, five National Liberals and eleven Conservatives. Neville Chamberlain replaced Snowden as Chancellor of the Exchequer and the Liberal Sir John Simon as Foreign Secretary. The government made a determined effort to bolster up confidence in the country. It abandoned the gold standard and allowed the pound to find its own level. In 1932 Chamberlain introduced Tariff Reform; he abandoned free trade principles and levied preferential duties on imports. To support sagging farm prices, the government passed legislation that guaranteed a minimum price for some grains. Other legislations standardised the wages of industrial workers and stabilized price levels of various manufactured goods. Expenditure on social service rose. By 1935 the working class received £91 million more in social services than it paid in taxation. For a time, Britain was on the road to recovery. In foreign policy the government abandoned the pacific policy. In 1934, the enlarging of R.A.F. was begun in the teeth of violent opposition by Winston Churchill. In the following year, the government published a White Paper on Defence.

In 1935 MacDonald resigned owing to ill health. In the election campaign of 1935, Stanley Baldwin promised to the electorate, 'I give you my word that there will be no great armaments.' Baldwin won the elections with 387 seats. The Conservative leader, Baldwin, became the Prime Minister with Sir Samuel Hoare as Foreign Secretary, Neville Chamberlain as Chancellor of the Exchequer, and Anthony Eden as 'Minister for League of Nations Affair.'

Foreign affairs dwarfed domestic politics. The Hoare-Laval Pact of 1935 with regard to Italy's Abyssinian venture discredited Baldwin. The shock of German occupation of the Rhineland came next. Rearmament was accelerated; the Labour party voted against it. The Spanish Civil War muddied the political waters still further. Baldwin's attention was distracted by the crisis which affected the British royal family. In January 1936, George V, who had resigned since 1910, died and was succeeded by Prince of Wales, who became King Edward VIII. The new King became infatuated with an American woman Mrs. Wallis Simpson, who was about to obtain a divorce from her second husband. Baldwin interfered in the King's proposed marriage with Mrs. Simpson and made it a constitutional issue. Public attention was focussed on the British monarchy and for the time being from the Italio-

Abyssinian War. German rearmament and the Spanish Civil War receded into the background. On December 10, 1936, Edward abdicated. Some six months later he married the woman of his choice and retired to private life as the Duke of Windsor. In his farewell address, Edward VIII declared one of the finest love quotes in history. He said, 'I have found it impossible to carry the heavy burden of responsibility and to discharge my duties as king as I would wish to do without the help and support of the women I love.' He was succeeded by his brother, the Duke of York, as George VI and was crowned in May 1937.

After the coronation, Baldwin retired from politics and was succeeded by Neville Chamberlain. Apart from the perennial question of a budget and that of rapid rearmament, there was little in domestic administration that could demand Chamberlain's attenton. Foreign affairs demanded his particular concern, particularly after the resignation in 1938 of Foreign Secretary Eden. Chamberlain pursued a policy of appeasement in matters of foreign policy until the outbreak of the Second World War in 1939.

Chamberlain was convinced that economic recovery could come to Britain only through the return of a prosperous foreign trade. British foreign trade for 1937 was the highest for any year since 1930. In 1938, there came to an end a six-year old tariff and trade war with Ireland and there was signed with the United States a trade pact. While the United States, agricultural products obtained concessions from Britain, Washington modified its tariff schedules on British textiles, metals and books. Despite low wages and high taxes, unemployment declined. Under the new rearmament programme, some factories were set up. To tackle unemployment, an Overseas Settlement Board was set up to find means for encouraging migration within the Empire.

Ireland

Throughout this period, the British government was plagued with the rising tide of nationalism in certain of the British dependencies. Ireland was a centre of popular unrest which demanded Home Rule. In 1914 the British Parliament passed an Irish Home Rule Bill. It did not satisfy the aspirations of the people. Moreover, the outbreak of the First World War postponed the operation of the Home Rule. This led to the rise of extremist groups, notably the Sinn Fein party. In Easter week of 1916, these groups organised a rebellion which was put down with utmost severity. In the British parliamentary elections of December 1918, seventyfive per cent of the Irish constituencies elected Sinn Fein candidates. Instead of taking their seats in Westminster, they organised a separate parliament—*Dail Eireann*—at Dublin. This body proclaimed Ireland an independent republic with De Valera as President.

The British government resisted and there followed three years of unexampled violence perpetrated by both sides. The carnage was ended when Lloyd George passed another Home Rule Act in December 1920. The Act conceded more local autonomy to Ireland, but it set up separate parliaments for Ulster (Northern Ireland) and Southern Ireland. The scheme was rejected outright by the Republicans who aspired to a free and united country. But Lloyd George persisted and in December 1921 persuaded the southern leaders to sign a treaty that provided for an Irish Free State as a self-governing Dominion. Northern Ireland might join the Irish Free State or have a separate status.

As a result of the Anglo-Irish Treaty of 1921, two democratic governments were in operation in Ireland. One was the government of Northern Ireland which functioned at Belfast in subordination to the British Government at Westminster. The other was the government of the Irish Free State at Dublin which exercised control over the greater part of Ireland. In 1922 the British Government evacuated her army from Ireland, after an occupation lasting over seven hundred years.

However, the conflict between England and Ireland was yet to pass through final phase. After a decade in the political wilderness, Eamon De Valera became premier in 1932 at the head of a new party, the Fianna Fail (Soldiers of Destiny). He adopted a series of measures which led the Irish Free State on the road to independence. One law abolished the oath of allegiance to the British King. Laws passed by the Irish Parliament need not be submitted for approval by the Governor General. In 1932 De Valera refused to make annual payments of the land annuities owed by the Irish peasants to the British Government.

In 1937 De Valera promulgated a new constitution which was accepted by a popular referendum. The state was re-named Eire, the ancient name of Ireland which was declared a 'sovereign independent democratic state.' Its head was a President who was to continue in office for a term of seven years. Executive power was exercised by the President and by a ministry appointed by him that was responsible to Parliament. Legislative power was vested chiefly in the Dail, elected by universal suffrage according to proportional representation. Both Irish and English were declared official languages. Eire asserted independence by remaining neutral in the Second World War. The Irish Republic (Eire) secured its complete political independence from Britain in 1949.

CHAPTER 33

REFORM AND REVOLUTION IN RUSSIA

Alexander III (1881-1894)

Alexander III was a conscientious ruler, and a firm believer in orthodoxy, autocracy and rationalism. His reign is often referred to as the 'Age of Counter Reform.' He regarded the Russian Orthodox Church as a bulwark against subversive influence and asserted the prerogatives of the crown. He was a firm advocate of a policy of Russiafication at home, with respect to subject nationalities, and Pan-Slavism abroad.

The new Tsar's ideas were in large measures influenced by his ex-tutor and close confidant, Konstantine Pobedonostsev (1827-1907), procurator of the Holy Synod, that is, lay chairman of the governing body of the Russian Orthodox Church. He condemned all Western institutions root and branch and even attempted to give a philosophical basis to reaction. To him parliaments were nothing but breeding-places of personal ambition, vanity and self-interest of its members. Democracy was 'the most complicated and the most burdensome system of government recorded in the history of humanity.' Freedom of the press meant the free dissemination of lies and calumnies. Limited monarchy was a 'vain fancy' and trial by jury 'an invitation to the arts of casuistry.'

Pobedonostsev's policies were seconded by the former minister of education, Dmitry Tolstoy, who became minister of the interior in 1882. He reduced the autonomy of the Universities and put restrictions on the admission of students and their right of association. He placed reading rooms and libraries under stringent observations. The general educational policy inaugurated by Tolstoy was administered by Count Delianov, minister of education from 1882 to 1907. The principles guiding elementary education were designed to prevent social mobility. Little progress was made in the field of elementary education and, at the end of Alexander III's reign, only twentytwo per cent of the population of Russia could read and write.

The new government succeeded in restoring calm to the surface of Russian politics. Zhelyabov and four colleagues were hanged and others were sentenced to long terms of imprisonment and exile. Most young intellectuals with *narodnik* sympathies remained in low profile. With the tightening of the censorship regulation, many newspapers suspended publications. Most disastrous of all was the treatment meted out to the law courts and the *Zemstvos* (elected local government boards).

Tolstoy set out to integrate the cherished institutions into bureaucratic hierarchy. The law of June 1890 gave provincial governors and other officials increased powers. The electoral system was manipulated to reduce the franchise and increase the representation of the gentry. Tolstoy's policy reached its climax when, in July 1889, he abolished the 'Justices of the Peace', the class of elected magistrates, and introduced a new kind of officials, known as Land Captains. These officials, chosen by the Governor of the province from amongst local landowners, were responsible to the central government. The Justices of the Peace, elected by the *Zemstvos,* had shown themselves competent for their work. But the Land Captains, who had no legal training, proved hopelessly inferior to the Justices of the Peace. They possessed the most arbitrary powers and exercised the widest control over everything which concerned the peasants. Their unlimited authority was backed by the right to imprison without trial.

Along with bureaucratic hierarchy the government controlled the educational policy. In the elementary schools emphasis was laid upon religious instruction with the object of fostering a spirit of submissiveness to all authority. Though the Synod did not acquire control of the entire primary-school network, it established an educational administration of its own. Pobedonostsev made the secondary and higher education the preserve of the elite. The Universities lost their autonomy and acquired a barrack-like atmosphere. But Pobedonostsev's measures failed to win the students over the positive acceptance of his ideals.

Russiafication

Alexander III and his ministers pursued a policy of Russiafication. It involved repressive measures against any language other than Russian and any religion other than Russian orthodoxy. It was aimed primarily at the subject peoples in the Russian Empire who were to become good Russians obeying the Tsar. A virtual persecution was directed against both the Catholic Church in Poland and the Lutheran Church in the Baltic, as well as against the Russian sectarians who dessented from the Orthodox Church. Harsh measures were directed against the Poles who were not permitted to sell land to a non-Russian. Native language was prohibited in all educational institutions of Poland. Russian was made the official language in Finland. In the Baltic Provinces, Russian was prescribed as the official tongue in 1885.

Alexander's crushing blows also fell upon the Jews. A number of anti-Jewish laws were passed which put restrictions on Jews in respect of residence, occupation and education. Six million Jews were confined within the permitted zone of residence or 'Pale' of settlement. Residence within the Pale itself was not altogether unrestricted, Jews were forbidden to move from the cities to the villages. In 1882, Jews were prohibited from settling in rural districts even within the Pale itself. Foreign Jews were forbidden to travel in Russia. All public employment was closed to the Jews. Exception was made only in the case of the army doctors. Jews were denied the opportunity for higher education. Their numbers in the secondary schools and in the Universities were abnormally low. The privileged Jews who were still permitted to live in the cities outside the Pale suffered from various disabilities. Jews were not permitted to buy or lease land in the rural districts in Russia. Outside of the 'Pale' there were many 'unlicensed' Jews, who lived in constant fear of being hounded out. To this persecution, the Jews adopted a policy of passive resistance. Thousands fled to foreign lands, particularly to America. Those who remained lived in wretched poverty.

In Poland and Baltic provinces, the schools and the Orthodox Church became the principal instruments of Russiafication. The situation was particularly complex in the Baltic area where the Latvians, Lithuanians and Estonians were rapidly developing political aspirations of their own. Although local government was left in their hands, the educational system was placed under centralised control. Figes commented once, 'Trying to stamp out the native language was not just an insulting and demoralizing policy—it was ridiculous as well. Polish students at Warsaw University, for example, had to suffer the absurd indignity of studying their own native Literature in Russian translation.'

Fiscal Reforms and Industrialization

Russia's domestic resources were inadequate to provide the capital necessary for development. The Government also did little to overcome the country's economic backwardness. Alexander III's first Minister of Finance, N. Kh. Bunge, realised the importance of fiscal reform. In 1882, the amount of compensation to the ex-serfs was reduced; and, in 1885, the inequitable poll-tax was abolished. The treasury offset its losses by doubling the rent paid by peasants on state-owned land and by further increase in indirect taxation. Bunge's reformist measures, though moderate, aroused strong opposition from the government and he was forced to resign in January 1887. His successor, I. A. Vyshnegradsky, was an experienced financier whose attention was directed on the international money market.

The turning-point was the catastrophic famine of 1891-2 with the accompanying cholera epidemic and the arrival of Witte at the Ministry of Finance in 1892. Witte realised that Russia's role as a world power depended upon the rapid development of her rich natural resources. He abandoned liberal economics for direct state intervention in the economy. By undertaking an ambitious programme of guided economic development, Witte wanted to put the absolutist regime on a sound basis. He employed the means with greater sense of purpose to foster industrial progress. The government embarked upon a new spell of railway construction. The ambitious Trans-Siberian line commenced in 1891 and was completed within the short span of fourteen years. By 1905 the total length of railway track had reached 37,500 miles.

A new mining and metallurgical centre sprang up in the Donetz basin. By 1900 this supplied half of Russia's output of pig-iron; by this date coal production had reached 15 million tons. In the production of oil, Russia took first place as a result of rich discoveries in Transcaucasia. The textile industry made rapid strides. In the last fifteen years of 19th the century, total industrial output trebled.

This industrial expansion owed much to the government's adoption of the policy of protection. Duties on imported industrial products were continually raised in the 1880s and two large increases followed in 1890 and 1891. This incipient industrial revolution also owed much to foreign investment. In 1900, one-third of the capital of private industry in Russia was in foreign hands. Government borrowing, too, absorbed much foreign money. To attract foreign capital and reduce heavy interest charges Russia adopted the gold standard in 1897 which greatly strengthened her financial position.

The industrial expansion was accomplished at a heavy price of Russia's indebtedness. During the decade 1894-1903, annual payments to foreign creditors were some 300-400 million roubles. By 1904 the state debt alone exceeded $6^1/_2$ milliard roubles, of which almost half was owed abroad.

It became increasingly evident that the peasant taxpayer could not bear the increased burdens even in the worthy causes of industrial progress. The government's spirits monopoly, established in 1894, though fetched one-quarter of total receipts, perpetuated drunkenness, the worst bane of peasant life. The growing misery of the peasant families in the village became manifest. Russia's mortality rate was the highest in Europe. Perhaps the most ominous sign was the ever-increasing sum owed in tax arrears, which exceeded by one-fifth the average annual assessment.

The peasants tried to meet their obligations to the state by purchase of additional land. But it was rendered difficult by lack of adequate credit facilities and the restrictions imposed on the operations of the Peasant Land Bank, founded by Bunge in 1882. The heavy demand for land caused rents to soar and the peasants, driven by sheer need, tended to exhaust the soil. From the early 1890s the government began to facilitate migration to the untilled land of Asiatic Russia. However great the land shortage, the peasants preferred to seek employment nearer home.

The industrial climate was found to be uncongenial. Bunge regulated the working hours of women juveniles (1882) but the law was not enforced. It was only in 1897 that the working hours for men were limited to $11^1/_2$ hours. Wages were abnormally low. Strikes and any form of labour organisations were strictly prohibited. The resentment of the industrial workers found its outlet in violence and revolutionary activities. The famine of 1891 shook the Russian society from its enforced passivity.

A new self-confidence seized the intelligentsia who debated on the efficacy of populism (narodism) and communism. The former laid the blame for peasants' misery upon capitalism. For the Marxists, capitalism was a natural organic growth, an inevitable stage in social development. They condemned the populists as utopian and reactionary. A Social Democrat organisation was founded in exile in 1883 and there were a few other centres of Marxist influence. In the more frequent strikes of the 1890s, working-class leaders favoured direct action to achieve their ends. The labour movement was particularly strong in the border regions of Ukraine and Poland. The Ukrainian opposition was predominantly socialist. In Poland, the Polish Socialist Party placed independence in the forefront of its programme. Russia's strongest revolutionary organisation was the Jewish 'General Social-Democratic Union'—known as the *Bund* (established in October 1897). Further north, the Baltic provinces now became the scene of intense political activity. Thus there developed acute tensions in Russian society which posed a serious threat to the Tsarist regime.

Foreign Policy

In foreign policy, Alexander III, who pursued a traditionalist policy, had to change his policy according to exigencies of circumstances. By 1887, Russia had become estranged from Austria as a result of her hostile moves against France and her *rapprochement* with Britain, Russia's principle adversary. The *Dreikaiserbund* lapsed and the 'Reinsurance Treaty' with Germany, which replaced it, lasted only three years. To overcome her isolation Russia established a loose understanding with republican France in August 1891. In December 1893, Russia undertook to support France in the event of a German attack. The new alliance, however, did not impair the maintenance of good relations with Germany and Austria. Nevertheless, the change of alignment was a milestone in the decline of imperial Russia. She became increasingly dependent on the friendship and credit of France.

Nicholas II (1894-1917)

When Nicholas II, a youngman of twentysix ascended the throne, many hoped that a new era would usher in the nation. But he made it clear that he had no intention of granting concessions. He was weak in character and in intellect. He mistrusted ministers, preferring to rely on backstair advisers. He was always a tool in the hands of stronger individuals; Pobedonostsev, in the first ten years of his reign, as well as military advisers like Bezobrazov, General Kuropatkin and Admiral Alekseev; in later years, his wife and her favourites especially the monk Gregory Rasputin. There was thus ample scope for intrigues within the ruling group. In particular, a rivalry developed between the Ministries of the Interior and of Finance which, in the end, brought about Witte's exit in 1903.

Reforms and Revolutionaries

The accession of the new Tsar brought a revival of political activity. In the *Zemstvos* particularly, there was an upsurge of hope in liberal reform. Led by D. N. Shipov, leaders in these organs of local government wanted the creation of some kind of *Zemstvo* organisation that could play a role in the national government. But the Emperor paid scant regard to these proposals and forbade the holding of meetings of *Zemstvo*. Nevertheless, the *Zemstvos*, continued to serve as forums for liberal opinion.

By the nineties there grew up five groups of opposition against the Tsar. First was the Russian Social Democratic Labour Party. Its origin goes back to 1883 when George Plekhanov adopted the main tenets of Marxism and insisted that Russia must pass through capitalism before it could hope for a transition to socialism. He rejected the faith in the peasant masses. His literary gifts helped to contribute to the dissemination of Marxist ideas. In St. Petersburg alone, there were twenty Marxist groups in mid-1890. To one such belonged Vladimir Ilyich Ulyanov (Lenin) who had been expelled from the University of Kazan for his revolutionary activities. In 1898, the Russian Social Democrat Workers' Party held its first Congress at Minsk. It was poorly attended and some members of the Party at the Congress were arrested. Lenin was already in exile in Siberia. So it was that Plekhanov, Martov, Zasulich and others organised Russian Marxism from outside Russia. 'League of Russian Social Democrats Abroad' was located in Switzerland. Lenin became the first editor of the party newspaper *Iskra* (The Spark). At the second party congress that met in Brussels (and London) in 1903, personal and doctrinal differences split the party into two warring factions—Bolsheviks and Mensheviks. Both factions believed in the basic tenets of Marxism. Both believed that the fall of the imperial regime would be followed by a period of bourgeois democratic government before socialism could be ushered in. But whereas Lenin and the Bolsheviks argued that this period of bourgeois rule must be regarded as a purely transitional one, the Mensheviks regarded it as a period of long duration. The two factions held contrary views about the party organisation. Through his brilliant pamphlet *What is to be done*, published in 1902, Lenin advocated that the socialist movement must be led by an elite of professional revolutionaries. This implies a small party with a centralised and disciplined structure. On the other hand, the Mensheviks argued for a more comprehensive party, open not only to professional revolutionaries but to all workers and intellectuals who believed in its goals.

Inside Russia was a second group, called the Legal Marxists, who did much to make Marxism a matter of general interest. Avoiding social questions, they wrote on economics. One of their journals was popular largely owing to Maxim Gorky's contributions. Peter Struve, Tugan Baranovsky, Bulgakov, Frank, Berdaev, all belonging to universities, were the principal writers.

The third were the Social Revolutionaries who had many beliefs in common with the Social Democrats. They believed in the efficacy of political terrorism and had a combat brigade from 1902-7 for the purpose. They looked to the peasants, not to the industrial proletariat, to make the revolution. They were opposed both to capitalism and Marxian socialism; they did not believe that Russia had to be 'boiled in the cauldron of capitalism before she could attain socialism.' They believed that socialism would follow directly upon the fall of the monarchy.

Fourth were the so-called Economists, whose leader was Kuskova. The 'Imperial Free Economic Society' was set up by Catherine II for conducting research into various aspects of agricultural science. Its so-called Literary Committee sprang up after the famine of 1891. But in 1895 the Government closed it when it became a centre of progressive thought. They had a programme of democratic reform to be achieved in alliance with the liberals. 'For the Russian Marxist there was only one way: to support the economic struggle of the proletariat and to participate in liberal opposition activity.' The Economists were in touch with working men and were instrumental in passing the great law of June 2, 1897. This was the first piece of factory legislation limiting the working day to eleven and a half hours.

Lastly, there were the Liberals. They represented the progressive elements among the bourgeois and the nobility and who were led by Paul Miliukov, a well-known historian and sociologist. The Liberals aimed to establish in Russia a constitutional government on the model of England; hence they favoured a parliament elected by universal manhood suffrage and complete freedom of speech and of association. They were important also in the 'Imperial Free Economic Society' and participated in inquiries into trade unionism or the economic conditions of Russia. In June 1902, Struve, a convert from Marxism to liberal democracy, brought out an illegal newspaper, *Liberation* which played an important part in shaping moderate opinion.

Counter-Revolutionary Movement

The beginning of the twentieth century witnessed the Russian revolutionary movement in full swing. Strikes, demonstrations and mass meetings were of daily occurrence. Terror Squad organised by the Social Revolutionaries assassinated officials. Their ideal was the late 19th century revolutionary party which assassinated the then Tsar Alexander II (Nicholas' grandfather) in 1881. In fact, Lenin's elder brother was in that group, whose torture and hanging in 1881 inspired the 11-year old Lenin. Nicholas found in his Minister of the Interior, Plehve, a staunch supporter of autocracy. To counteract revolution, Plehve let loose a policy of retaliation which defied description. In 1903, there were as many as 12,000 political cases; many were imprisoned, exiled to Siberia, or executed. Plehve whipped up racial and religious animosities in order to distract the people from revolutionary activity. Bands of roughs called 'Black Hundreds' were encouraged to attack Jews and revolutionaries. A series of attacks on the Jews, called Pogroms, took place that culminated in the massacre of Kishinev in 1903.

The massacre of Kishinev shocked the world. To wreak vengeance, the revolutionaries assassinated Plehve in July 1904 by blowing him to pieces by a canon. Plehve was succeeded by Prince Mirsky, a more enlightened statesman, who invited the reformers to submit their grievances. The representatives of the *Zemstvos* meeting at Petrograd in November 1904 drew up the 'Eleven Points'. They demanded inviolability of person and domicile, freedom of conscience, of speech, and of the press, increased activity of the local government, an assembly of freely elected representatives and the immediate summoning of a Constituent Assembly to prepare a Constitution on these lines. Mirsky, finding that his efforts to introduce liberal measures were being rebuffed by Nicholas, resigned in disgust.

Collapse of the Autocracy

The Russo-Japanese War (1904-05) was unpopular with the nation. The defeat of the Russian army in the battles with the Japanese, the capture of Port Arthur and the destruction of the Russian fleet in the Straits of Tshushima utterly discredited the Government. By the fall of 1904 the atmosphere seemed charged with electricity. The liberals were holding banquets in St. Petersburg and Moscow similar to those in Paris in 1848.

The accumulated tension exploded at the beginning of 1905. A strike took place in St. Petersburg on January 15 over the dismissal of three workmen. The strikers demanded an eight hours' day, better wages, and arbitration boards. The strikers, led by an orthodox priest, Father Gapon, marched in procession on January 22, 1905, for the purpose of presenting a petition to the Tsar at the Winter Palace. The upshot was tragic. The security forces fired upon the pacific strikers, killing and wounding hundreds of people. This was the massacre of Bloody Sunday, January 22, 1905. A wave of strikes gripped the country and rapidly spread to Poland and the Baltic Provinces. In February serious peasant riots began which took the form of pillaging and burning of landlords' property. Innumerable assassinations also took place culminating in the murder of the hated Grand Duke Sergei, the Emperor's uncle, in Moscow (February 1905).

Faced with growing disorder, the Emperor announced on March 3, 1905 his intention of inviting persons to 'participate in the drafting and discussing of legislative proposals'. As a result of this invitation, the professional classes soon combined to form a huge Union of Unions. Everywhere the cry was raised for parliamentary government and the elementary rights of citizenship. The current of progressive opinion was strengthened at this juncture by the news of the naval disaster of the Baltic Fleet in the Straits of Tshushima (May 27). In June 1905 the sailors of the battleship Potemkin mutinied at Odessa. In July a congress of *Zemstvos* and municipality representatives met at Moscow defying police ban. It now became obvious that concessions had to be made.

On August 19, 1905, the Emperor announced that he would constitute a parliament to counsel with the government in the making of laws. The 'Bulyghin Constitution'—as it was termed—was received with great dissatisfaction. Instead of parliamentary assembly with full legislative powers, it set up an Imperial Duma with a restricted franchise. It also left the fundamental principles of Government unchanged. The result was the revival of riots and strikes. A general strike began in October which paralysed the railways. In October the first Soviet of Workers' Delegates was formed in St. Petersburg; others followed.

In the face of this deepening crisis, the Tsar seriously considered attempting to rule by military disctatorship, but was dissuaded by his advisers. He dismissed Pobedonostsev, Trepov and other reactionary ministers and appointed Witte as premier. On October 30, he issued the Manifesto. The October Manifesto guaranteed personal liberties and established a moderately popular franchise for the election of the Duma. The Duma was vested with legislative functions, and no law was to be valid without its approvals.

Hardly had the opposition gained success, when it was plagued with divisions and factional quarrels. Bolshevik communists quarrelled with Menshevik communists, and both with Socialist Revolutionaries. Socialist Revolutionaries were distrusted by Liberals and Liberals soon split into rival parties. A radical group of Liberals, known as the Constitutional Democrats, popularly known as Cadets, demanded a constitution in which the Tsar should remain as a mere figurehead and a ministry should be responsible to parliament. The Social Democrats rejected 'the police whip wrapped in the parchment of the constitution' and the Mensheviks began to suspect the Cadets as a bourgeois party. The Octobrists—comprising more conservative Liberals, especially the *Zemstvo* men—proposed to accept the Tsar's gift.

Once the unity of the revolutionary movement dissolved and its fire subsided, the reactionary elements plucked up courage. Orthodox clergymen and Slavophile patriots organised a 'Union of the Russian People' and inaugurated a counter-revolutionary movement early in 1906. 'Black Bands' or 'Black Hundreds', as the agents of the Union were popularly styled, unleashed violence against radical sympathizers and Jews. Leaders of the Union also exerted pressure on the Tsar to withdraw the concessions he had made. By the decree of March 5, 1906, he excluded from parliamentary discussions the constitutional laws of the state, asserted the Tsar's control over the army, navy and foreign policy, and even safeguarded the budget from parliamentary interference. A week before this, Witte had tendered his resignation. Nicholas was pleased to accept this and put an energetic conservative, Peter Stolypin, in the Ministry of the Interior.

The first Duma met on May 10, 1906. It contained over four hundred members. The progressive bloc, which was made up of the Constitutional Democrats or 'Cadets', numbered 153. Their chief rivals were Octobrists or Conservatives, who gained very few seats. The Labour group comprised 107 members. The Autonomists, who represented the minor nationalities, accounted for 63 members. The first Duma demanded parliamentary institutions on the English model, that is, a Cabinet responsible to the Duma, and not to the Emperor. It also wanted to assert its authority over legislation and finance. But this was strongly opposed by the Tsar who finally dissolved the Duma on July 21. In vain, half the members withdrew to Viborg in Finland, where they issued a Manifesto and called on the people to refuse taxes. The revolutionary tide had already ebbed and they were locked up. Capital punishment was enforced with more severity. More than six hundred persons suffered death penalty while in a single year as many as 35,000 persons were actually banished, without trial.

In the elections for the second Duma, every conceivable influence was exerted in favour of the official candidates. But in spite of these tactics, the opposition carried the great majority of seats. The Cadets were still in a majority and about 100 Socialist Revolutionaries (SR) and Social Democrats sat in it. The second Duma met on March 5, 1907. During its session, which lasted till June 16, the government arrested sixteen members for revolutionary activity. At the same time, the electoral law was modified to give more weightage to landlords than to any other class in Russia. Thus, the Duma was reduced to a purely consultative body.

The result was reflected in the third Duma which met on November 14, 1907. The overwhelming majority, made up of Conservatives and Octobrists, were in favour of the government while the Cadets, with their reduced strength to 54, abandoned obstructionist tactics. The Third Duma enlivened itself by liberating the peasant from the control of the commune. This resulted in individual ownership of peasant lands instead of communal ownership. The Third Duma completed its term of five years and, in 1912, it was dissolved. In the general election which followed, the Centre, composed of Nationalists and Octobrists, suffered a reverse. The victory was won by the Right which contained 155 members, while the Octobrists had 132 and the Cadets only 52. A change made itself manifest in the attitude of the Octobrists. Hitherto they had supported the government, but from this time they exhibited progressive attitude owing to the reactionary policy of the government. The formation of a Progressive Bloc in 1916 was significant in the history of Russia as it tried to induct into Russia the conceptions of democratic liberty—the essence of Western life.

The ablest of Nicholas' ministers was Stolypin—Prime Minister from 1906 to 1911. His greatest achievement was the agrarian reform which profoundly changed Russian life. He sought, by a series of laws passed in 1906, to liberate the peasants from the communes, which often destroyed their initiative and to promote communal redistribution of land so as to consolidate scattered holdings. By 1917 a change had taken place in the growth of individual ownership. About three million peasants had obtained proprietary rights over their lands and emancipation from the commune. This was a great achievement. Finally, Stolypin removed the legal hindrances which prevented the peasant from moving to the cities. Earlier, in 1906, he had cancelled arrears of redemption payments due to the State from emancipated serfs. Stolypin suffered the same treatment as had been meted out to Witte. It was widely rumoured in 1911 that he would be removed. Instead, while attending a theatre performance in Kiev in September 1911, he was shot and killed by Dimitry Bogrov. When he was assassinated, the Tsarina said, 'He is gone, let us hear no more of him.' Yet he had broken the back of the worst problems facing the country; under his rule grain production began to rise more quickly than population. He had tamed the left and restored order.

Meanwhile the Tsar Nicholas, who had proved utterly incompetent, submitted himself to his dominating wife, Tsarina Alexandra and an unscrupulous monk, Rasputin. Tsarina came to regard Rasputin as her mentor and no governmental appointment was made without his approval. It has been observed that Rasputin was 'the axis on which revolved the destinies of Russia.'

The best efforts of the government were spent in restoring the Empire's international prestige which had been badly impaired by the Russo-Japanese War. In 1907 was negotiated the friendly understanding with Britain which supplemented Franco-Russian Dual Alliance with a Triple Entente. After the treaty with Britain, Russia turned away from the Middle East as from the Far East. Under the guidance of Stolypin's brother-in-law Serge Sazonov, who became foreign minister in 1910, a spirited policy was undertaken in the Balkans which embittered her relations with Germany and Austria-Hungary.

The Russian Revolution

The autocratic government of Nicholas II continued in an atmosphere of growing corruption and decadence. The economic and social structrue of the country remained unchanged. About 30,000 landlords were still in possession of nearly 70 million *dessyatin* (1 *dessyatin* equals 2.7 acres) of land. On the other hand, about 10.5 million peasants owned only 75 million *dessyatin*. One-third of the peasantry was without any land. The technical level of agriculture was abysmally low. More than one-third of the farmsteads possessed no implements at all. The average yield of grain per acre was only one-third of that harvested by the German farmer. The grinding poverty was accentuated by the annual tributes which the peasantry had to pay to the landlords. The landlord's share was often 50 per cent of the crop. More than half a century after the emancipation of the serfs, traces of serfdom were still existent and 'temporary serfdom' openly existed in the Caucasus until 1912.

Agricultural poverty was followed by industrial backwardness. On the eve of the war, Russia's production of iron and coal was insignificant in comparison with Germany, Britain, and the United States. She was deficient in electrical and machine-building industries and had no machine-tool industry, chemical plants and motor-car factories.

It has often been what the Russians call 'a jolt from outside' that has brought about some radical changes in the domestic sphere of Russia. The Napoleonic Wars led to the first political movement of Russia—that of the Decembrists in 1825. The Crimean War of 1855-6 led to the institution of a representative and legislative assembly. The First World War (1914-1918) was to lead to the Revolution of 1917.

Russia's participation in the First World War proved to be her undoing. For Russia was not equal to a struggle such as this. Her losses in the first ten months of the war were reckoned as 3,800,000. By the end of 1914 the most successful of Russian generals, Brusilov, has written that the regular army was liquidated and had been replaced by a 'militia of ignoramuses'.

In August 1915, after military defeats which entailed the loss of Galicia and Poland, a progressive bloc was formed in the Duma. It embraced the Constitutional Democrats or Cadets led by Miliukov and Prince Lvov; the Octobrists led by Guchkov and a group of extreme right nationalists headed by Shulgin. The progressive bloc, instead of chastising the Tsar, requested the latter mildly to form a government 'enjoying the confidence of the country.' Alarmed by defeatist influences at the Court, the leaders of the bloc urged the Tsar to pursue the war with determination. But there were whispers of opposition in the supreme command. The Tsar was completely impervious to the crying needs of the nation. The courtiers did their best to prevent him from calling in a Russian Necker or Turgot. In September 1915 the Tsar decreed a 'temporary dispersal' of the Duma. He changed the government in such a way as to rebuff to the progressive bloc. Every reshuffling brought into the administration more and more odious figures. In two years of war, Russia had four Prime Ministers, six Ministers of Home Affairs, three Foreign Ministers and three Defence Ministers. Wrote Miliukov, the Cadet historian of the Revolution: 'They came one after another and passed like shadows, giving place to people who, like themselves, were only ... proteges of the court clique.'

Late in 1916 the Duma reassembled. Paul Miliukov, the leader of Constitutional Democrats (Cadets), scathingly attacked the government's policy and, for the first time, openly denounced the Tsarina herself. Once again the Tsar dispersed the Duma. 'The sluices were tightly locked against the tide of revolution, with the result that the flood was mounting ever higher until it would sweep away all barriers at once, and with them the age-old throne of the Romanovs.'[1]

In December 1916 a group of noblemen led by Prince Yusupov invited the Empress' favourite, Rasputin, to a private dinner party, shot him and threw his body into the freezing waters of the Neva. For a while the hopes for a change in the method of government rose. But the Tsar and the Tsarina refused to mend their ways. Their behaviour demonstrated that the removal of one clique of courtiers would not bring about the universally desired change. Meanwhile the country was drifting towards deeper chaos.

During the winter of 1916-17, popular disaffection overtook Russia. Patriots complained that the government was hampering the prosecution of the war. The subject nationalities grew restless. There were riots of peasants. Yet, when at last the revolution came, almost nobody gauged its elemental power. Like its great French predecessor, it was at first mistaken for a riot. All were overtaken by the march of events. The Octobrists and Cadet leaders pressed for a change of the Tsar's ministers. Then they urged the Tsar to abdicate in favour of his son or his brother. On the other hand, the group of socialists—Mensheviks, Bolsheviks and Social Revolutionaries—thought that they were just witnessing a bread riot which would prove to be ephemeral. When they were still wondering about the outcome of the whole struggle, they became suddenly aware of the intensity of the movement.

The die was cast. At the beginning of March 1917, there were widespread strikes in the national capital of Petrograd. On March 8, International Women's Day, a band of housewives attacked the bakeries. On the next day, demonstrators, breaking through police cordons, penetrated the centre of the city and demanded bread. Shouts of 'down with autocracy' filled the air. On March 10, all factories and industrial establishments in the capital were closed down. More often the soldiers, called upon to disperse the demonstrators, sympathised their cause.

On March 11, the Tsar issued an edict disbanding the Duma, and ordered the general commanding the Petrograd garrison to suppress the movement immediately. In the evening, the soldiers questioned the orders of their superiors to fire at workers' demonstrations. On March 12 the situation deteriorated further. The local garrisons, led by the Volhynian Guard, joined the revolutionary cause. The police disappeared from the streets. The authorities still hoped to crush the revolution with the help of troops. Late in the afternoon, delegates of factories and representatives of the socialist parties organised a Soviet of Workers' Deputies. By the following morning, the Soviet became the only *de facto* power in existence.

The creation of the Soviet resurrected the Duma. Hitherto reluctant to challenge the Tsar's authority, the Duma made itself into the Provisional Government on March 14. Prince Lvov was Prime Minister, Milukov was Foreign Minister, both Cadets; Guchkov from the Octobrists was War Minister and Kerenesky, a member of the Workers' and Soldiers' Soviet, became Minister for Justice. On the day of its formation, the Provisional Government sent representatives to the Tsar to persuade him to abdicate. On March 15

1. *The New Cambridge Modern History,* Vol. XII, P. 407.

the Tsar signed the act of abdication in favour of his brother, Grand Duke Michael. When the Grand Duke declined the honour, Russia virtually became a Republic. There is no evidence to show that the loss of his throne caused any grief to Nicholas II. He wrote in his diary: 'I had a long and sound sleep... I read much of Julius Caesar.' Five days later the Tsar and his family became prisoners. Thus the rule of the Romanovs, founded in 1613, came to an abrupt end. After months of detention, the Tsar and his family were murdered by the Communists in July 1918.

From the beginning the Provisional Government clashed with the Soviets. The Provisional Government, representing the upper and middle classes, hoped for the restoration of a constitutional monarchy. They were determined to continue the war in the hope that victory would give Russia control over the Turkish Straits and the Balkans. The Soviets, on the other hand, spoke in the name of the toiling and oppressed masses and the soldiers who had made the revolution. They were inclined to believe that the present revolution was the long-awaited bourgeoise revolution and the Mensheviks, the Socialist Revolutionaries and even the Bolsheviks agreed to tolerate the Lvov Government.

The honeymoon between the Provisional Government and the Soviet was soon shattered by Lenin's return to Russia in early April from his exile in Switzerland. Lenin combined 'variety of qualities, enormous scholarship, the passionate temperament of the revolutionary, tactical genius and great administrative ability.' Among the Bolsheviks, Lenin was the first to attack the assumption that the current upheaval in Russia was a bourgeois revolution and nothing more. It was a mass movement inspired by utopian visions of the emancipation of mankind from the shackles of a despotic power. This all—engulfing movement of revolt against authority presaged a new order of society. In his so-called 'April theses', Lenin described that the revolution in the first stage had given power to the bourgeois which would, in the second stage, transfer power to the workers and the poor peasants. The Provisional Government and the Soviets were not allies but antagonists. The end in view was not a parliamentary republic, but 'a republic of Soviets of Workers', Poor Peasants' and Peasants' Deputies all over the country, growing up from below.' Socialism could not be introduced immediately. But as a first step the Soviets should take control of 'social production and distribution.'

Lenin was the pillar of Bolshevik Party which, since 1912, had been a party distinct from the Mensheviks. He gave this Party an organisation and rigid discipline. The Mensheviks, equally a proletarian party, had the prestige of great names, such as Plekhanov and Martov, but not this monolithic structure. The Socialist Revolutionaries were not Marxists but belonged to the Populist tradition. They were the mouthpiece of the peasants.

The situation became more complex and piquant because behind the struggle between the Provisional Government and the Soviet for predominance was a struggle of the Bolsheviks against the Mensheviks and the Socialist Revolutionaries. In the struggle for predominance, the Soviet had gained the initiative by issuing its famous Order No. 1. This called upon the soldiers to take orders from the Soviet alone, to obey no directions contrary to its orders and, above all, to resist any attempt of the officers to disarm them. The Provisional Government received a setback when, on May 16, 1917, Miliukov and Guchkov resigned. This was the end of the first stage of the Revolution.

In the next phase from May 16 to July 15, the Provisional Government was under pressure from the Socialists and the Bolsheviks. Lenin had established his authority by reuniting the Social Democratic Workers' Party, whose Congress was in session from May 7-12, 1917. In June met the first All-Russian Congress of Soviets where Lenin made the pronouncement that the Bolsheviks were ready to take governmental power. As the prestige of the Provisional Government declined, the influence of the Bolsheviks grew correspondingly. In July a rising took place in Petrograd which was put down by the Provisional Government. That body, already under fire because of heavy losses suffered in a new Galician offensive, put the blame of its defeat upon Bolshevik agitators. Lenin was accused of being a German agent. Bolshevik headquarters were raided.

Trotsky and Kamenev were arrested, but Lenin fled to Finland. While continuing the war, the Provisional Government postponed the crucial land question. Under the direction of the Socialist Revolutionaries, the peasants attacked the landowners and seized the land. On July 15, the Provisional Government fell.

From July 16 to September 12, 1917—the third stage—a new Government under Kerenesky ruled. The capture of Riga by the Germans on September 3, was used as an excuse for his revolt against the government. The commander-in-chief of the army, General Kornilov, now attempted a counter-revolution and was supported by the liberal bourgeoisie. Kornilov's aim was not to restore the autocracy, but to set up a military disctatorship and to keep the Bolsheviks at bay. Kerenesky suppressed the revolt with the help of the Bolsheviks. On September 12, Kornilov was arrested, and Kerensky became commander-in-chief in his place. On September 14, Kerenesky formed a Directory composed of five ministers. The Bolsheviks, on the other hand, for the first time had obtained a clear-cut majority in the Petrograd Soviet. Trotsky, released from prison, was elected President of the Soviet. A few days later, the Bolsheviks were in a majority in the Soviet of Moscow and in most provincial Soviets.

The Bolshevik Revolution

Meanwhile Lenin, from his hiding-place in Finland, revived the slogan, 'All power to the Soviets'—a direct challenge to the Provisional Government. He concluded that the time had come to seize power by armed insurrection. On October 23, he returned in disguise to Petrograd to attend a meeting of the Bolshevik Central Committee. He urged that 'much time has been lost ...The question is very urgent and the decisive moment is near ... The majority is now with us ... The situation has become entirely ripe for power.' Under his persuasion the Committee decided, with only two dissidents. Zinoviev and Kamenev, to prepare for an immediate seizure of power. Lenin predicted that if the insurrection was speeded up, all proletarian Europe would rise.

The Bolsheviks were methodically making plans for their coup d' etat. The brain behind the operation was Leon Trotsky (1879-1940), who displayed uncommon strategical ability. A Revolutionary Military Committee had been set up by the executive committee of the Congress of Soviets. When Kerenesky ordered a reshuffling of armed forces in and around the capital, the Revolutionary Military Committee challenged this order. This was a challenge to the government. On November 5, Kerenesky ordered the suppression of Bolshevik newspapers and the arrest of the Bolshevik leaders. The next day, he indicted the Revolutionary Military Committee and ordered an enquiry into its activities.

Kerenesky' threats provided the Bolsheviks with a pretext for the insurrection. The Revolutionary Military Committee issued its orders: 'The Petrograd Soviet is in immediate danger ... You are hereby ordered to prepare your regiment for action. Await further orders. All procrastination and hesitation will be regarded as treason to the revolution.' The plan of the military operations had been laid with great precision by Trotsky, Podvoisky, Lashevich and other members of the Revolutionary Military Committee. During the night of November 6-7, the Red Guards and regular regiments occupied with lightning speed every key point in the city and besieged the Winter Palace, the seat of the Provisional Government. Within one night, almost without fight, the Provisional Government collapsed, Kerensky fled abroad.

The dazed population awakened in the morning to see this dramatic change:

> The Provisional Government has been overthrown. Governmental authority has passed into the hands of the ... Revolutionary Military Committee which leads the proletariat and the garrison of Petrograd. The cause for which the people have struggled: the immediate offer of a democratic peace, the abolition of the landlords' property of the land, workers' control over production and the formation of the Soviet Government—this cause is now secure. Long live the revolution of soldiers, workers, and peasants.

The coup synchronised with the opening of the Second All-Russian Congress of the Soviets. The Bolsheviks now had a majority—399 out of a total of 649 delegates. They became all-powerful when the Mensheviks and the right wing of the

Socialist Revolutionary Party walked out in protest against the insurrection. The Congress passed two decrees laid before them by **Lenin**. The first proposed to all the belligerent nations the conclusion of a peace without annexations and indemnities. The second abolished private property in land. Landlords' ownership of land was abolished without compensation. The Congress also set up, on November 8, the first Council of People's Commissars with Lenin as its head, Trotsky as Commissar for foreign affairs, Stalin as Commissar for nationalities, Rykov (home affairs), Lunacharsky (education) and Antonov-Obssenko, Krylenke and Dybenko, as the joint chief of the commissariats for military and naval affairs.

The programme of the new Government was still hazy. But its leaders were determined to establish a proletarian dictatorship and to assure the support of the vast mass of the peasantry. Their next objective was to conclude peace. Finally they set out to build up a proletarian socialist state.

Lenin's victory was yet a tenuous one. The Bolsheviks numbered at that time about 70,000

Lenin

members in a country of some 160 million men. Although they had gained control of the Petrograd and Moscow Soviets, they could not claim majority in the Russian political spectrum as a whole. In extensive outlying regions, such as the Caucasus and Siberia, they had little followers. Quite unexpectedly, the Bolsheviks had to face the demand of the Trade Union of Railway Workers for a coalition government. The railway-men wielded immense power, as they were disrupting communications. Moverover, there was protest at the suppression of the Liberal Press. Lenin, Trotsky and their allies successfully tided over the crises and, within a week, had defeated both.

Meanwhile, Lenin could not withstand the demand of the summoning of a Constituent Assembly to determine the future political system of the country. Between February and October 1917, the Provisional Government and the Soviet had both demanded a Constituent Assembly. November 25 was fixed for the election. Lenin did not wish to cancel them. In the elections the Socialist Revolutionaries gained an absolute majority—267 out of 520 deputies; the Bolsheviks had 161. The Assembly which met on January 18, 1918 showed itself hostile to the Bolshevik demands. But it was promptly suppressed and dispersed by force of arms. Bukharin spoke of 'the watershed which at this moment divides this assembly into ... two irreconcilable camps, camps of principle for socialism or against socialism.' It was a decisive moment. No one thought of opposing the Bolsheviks as the latter had a monopoly of force in the country.

The Bolsheviks now pursued a deliberate policy of crushing all centres of opposition. The members of the old Provisional Government were deported; the anti-Bolshevik municipal councils of Petrograd and Moscow were dissolved. In December, the Imperial Senate was abolished and, a month later, the *Zemstvos* shared the same fate. Meanwhile, a series of decrees removed the threat of military opposition by causing the army literally to disappear. In February 1918 complete separation of church and state was announced. Although no attempt was made to abolish the Russian Orthodox Church, its power and authority were curbed by expropriation of its lands, repeal of the old marriage and divorce laws. In December 1917, Lenin weakened the Socialist Revolutionary Party's stronghold over the peasants by creating an opportunity for effecting a fusion of the Peasant Soviets with the Workers and Soldiers.

Meanwhile, the confiscation of the great landed estates was carried out and other steps were taken to transform the national economy. In November, workers' committee were formed to supervise factory production, and the eight-hour day became universal. In subsequent months, the government created a Superme Economic Council, nationalised the banks, and cancelled the debts of the Tsarist regime.

While all this was going on, Russia's domain was being diminished. The Provisional Government had already recognised Poland's independence. Finland demanded independence which was recognised in the name of national self-determination by the Commissar of Nationalities, Stalin. Between December 1917 and February 1918, Lithuania, Latvia and Estonia declared their independence.

One of the first acts of the new government was to conclude peace with Germany. The Russian army had broken down completely. The few units that retained some semblance of discipline were generally anti-Bolshevik. The Commander-in-Chief, Dukhonin, was asked to negotiate for an armistice. When he refused to do this, he was dismissed at once. When his successor, Krylenke, arrived at the front, Dukhonin was lynched by the infuriated soldiers.

An armistice was concluded in December 1917. In February 1918 peace negotiations opened at Brest-Litovsk. Trotsky, who led the Soviet delegation, embarrassed the German delegation by pressing the demand for 'peace without annexations or indemnities.' He could not reconcile with his revolutionary principles to sign a humiliating treaty with an imperialist Power—a course which Lenin thought as inevitable. Trotsky demanded self-determination for the conquered Russian territory in vain. In the end he broke off the discussions with a vague and futile formula 'no war and no peace'. When Germany renewed the offensive in February 1918, Lenin used the argument that to renew resistance would militate against the revolutionary war. By a narrow margin Lenin had his way and the treaty was signed on March 3, 1918.

The terms of the Treaty of Brest-Litovsk were severe. Russia was forced to accept the loss of Poland, the Baltic States, Finland, large parts of Byelorussia, Ukraine, and part of Transcaucasia. Lenin found it hard to accept the mortifying conditions. But he was thinking not of Russian territory but of world revolution. He found a breathing space indispensable. According to Lenin, the reason for accepting the disgraceful peace was that Russia, needed 'a delay in order to put social reforms into effect; we need to consolidate, and for that we need time.'

The Civil War

The conclusion of the Peace of Brest-Litovsk was considered an act of betrayal by the Allied governments. Russia's defection from the war and the consequent transfer of German troops from the eastern to the western front and the opening up of the granary of Ukraine to Germany caused intense alarm to the Allies, especially to Britain and France. Wildest schemes were entertained in London and Paris for restoring some sort of fighting front in Russia. For a time, in March and April 1918, Trotsky, new People's Commissar for War, was not averse to this idea. He anticipated German attack in violation of the peace and, in such an eventuality, the Allied support would be of great help. But, by May, that fear was dissipated as Germany had no intention to renew incursions into Russian territory. The Bolshevik leaders, therefore, lost interest in Allied collaboration. The Allies swung to the idea of military intervention in Russia in collaboration with anti-Bolshevik forces. Extravagant claims were made in London and Paris as to the hearty response that would be accorded to the Allied troops by Russia. And out of these desperate hopes emerged the Allied intervention.

In March 1918, the British, followed by French and American forces, occupied the northern port of Murmansk. The position of Czechoslovak force, stationed along the Russian eastern frontier, theoretically under French command, became untenable after Russia's withdrawal from the war. When arrangements for its evacuation, via Siberia to the western front, were being made, a conflict broke out between certain of the Czech units and the Bolsheviks in western Siberia (May 1918). The Czechs succeeded in seizing large sections of the Trans-Siberian Railway. The Czechs, who enjoyed much sympathy in Washington, led President Wilson to send an expeditionary force to eastern Siberia. In April 1918, the Japanese Government landed troops in Vladivostok. The British occupied Archangal, Batum and Baku oil fields. A mixed force under French command took Odessa.

Despite the limited nature of these Allied expeditions, they served to stimulate military opposition to the communists. In this way, they helped to unleash the Russian Civil War. All along the boundaries of Bolshevik authority—from Siberia to the Ukraine—there grew up anti-communist forces. The southern borders of the country between the Black and Caspian Seas, became the base for a White Army—commanded first by General Kornilov and, after his death, by General Anton Denikin.

The Czech success not only heartened Denikin in the north, but soon led to a fusion of an anti-Bolshevik group in Siberia. This was effected in September 1918 with Omsk as headquarters where a national government—called the Directory—was set up. In November, after a military coup, the Siberian government handed supreme power to the former commander of the Black Sea Fleet, Admiral Alexander Kolchak.

At the beginning of 1919, the Tsarist general E. K. Miller occupied Archangel and placed himself and his forces in Kolchak's disposal. At the same time General Yudenich assembled a White Army at Estonia.

Despite the initial successes of the anti-Bolshevik forces, the latter failed miserably in the end. Unity of purpose and command strengthened the Bolshevik cause, while the situation was otherwise with their opponents. Disunity was so rampant among the latter that they often preferred fighting each other to fighting the Bolsheviks. Mutual antagonism among the opposing forces prevented any effective collaboration between them. The Bolsheviks, on the other hand, owing to Lenin's iron discipline, were determined fighters. But the chief cause of the Bolshevik success was the attitude of the peasants. They felt morally certain that a 'White' victory would mean the restitution of the land which they had seized. The town workers practically sided with the Red Army. But the main force behind the Bolsheviks was the enthusiasm of the youth which found a new sustenance in the Civil War.

Leon Trotsky, who had built up the Red Army, became the War Commissar. In April 1918, compulsory military service was introduced. Relying upon the former commanders in the imperial army, Trotsky inducted almost fifty thousand former Tsarist officers. To watch over the officers, Trotsky appointed political commissars who hardly interfered with military decisions. Iron discipline was introduced in the army as desertion and failure were punished with death. As Stalin quoted famously, 'In the Soviet army, it takes more courage to retreat than advance.'

The Bolsheviks had another advantage when they found that the Allied governments found it untenable at the close of the World War to conduct extensive military operations in Russia. Germany was impotent. France was too war-weary and too occupied with penalising Germany. Great Britain was handicapped by other imperial concerns and by the pacifist attitude of the Labour Party at home. Japan was more interested in the spoilation of China than in a far distant place like Russia.

The year 1919 saw the triumph of the Communist forces in different theatres of war. But there were fleeting moments of White supremacy. In October Denikin was in Kiev and Orel, and Yudenich was on the outskirts of Petrograd. But in the end both their thrusts miscarried. Kolchak's forces were routed by the Red Army under Michael Frunze and pushed back into Siberia. Kolchak was captured and executed in February 1920. In the summer of 1919, General Denikin, pushing up from the northern Caucasus, overran much of the territory between Moscow and the Black Sea. But, by the end of the year, the thrust of Denikin lost its momentum, his forces being driven back into the northern Caucasus. In early 1920 his force was finally shattered and did not pose any threat to the Communists.

Meanwhile, the Bolsheviks were faced with a threat on their north-western flank when Yudenich launched an attack from Estonia. The advances of Yudenich's forces in the vicinity of Petrograd, in October 1919, threatened the existence of the Soviet regime. But the turning-point came when Yudenich was driven back and his army dispersed. Only the forces of General Wrangel, after playing a part in the Polish war, fell back to Crimea, where he held out until the end of 1920.

The Polish War

The Russian Civil War found its curious sequel in the dramatic Soviet-Polish War of 1920. The Versailles Peace Conference, though created a new Poland, did not satisfy the territorial ambitions which the Poles had entertained. The Civil War in Russia provided the Poles favourable opportunity for realising their territorial ambitions. But it was only at the fag end of the Civil War, when the Bolshevik victory seemed assured, that the Poles took action. In the spring of 1920, the Poles, in conjuction with the Ukrainian nationalists led by Petlyura and the White Army of Wrangel, launched an attack.

The Poles advanced to Dnieper and captured Kiev in early May, 1920. The Red Army, relieved of the domestic trouble, met the challenge with great resolution. In June Kiev was retaken, and in July, Soviet forces under Tukhachevsky pursued the Poles to the gates of Warsaw. But it was at this point that Colonel Aleksander Yegorov opened a new front by deciding to march on L'vov, instead of backing the main drive against Warsaw. The gap thus created enabled the Polish Commander, Joseph Pilsudki, to assume the offensive. With the help of the French General Maxime Weygand, who came post-haste from Paris, Pilsudki turned the tide and drove the Reds back into Russia. The retreat was no less precipitate than had been their advance. The war ended with an agreement at Riga (March 18, 1921), making the Poles masters of a huge extent of White Russian and Ukrainian territory. The agreement endured up to 1939.

The New Soviet Order

In July 1918, a constitution of the Russian Socialist Federated Soviet Republic (RSFSR) had been promulgated. In January 1924 the Soviet Union, or Union of Soviet Socialist Republics, was formally established. According to the Constitution of 1924, the USSR comprised of seven republics: The RSFSR, the Ukraine, White Russia, the Transcaucasian Federation (Azarbaijan, Armenia and Georgia), Turkmen, Uzbeg, and Tajuk. The Constitution of 1936 increased the number to eleven. Of the eleven, three were in Europe: Russia proper, with its capital at Moscow; Ukraine with its capital at Kiev; and Byelorussia or 'White Russia' with its capital at Minsk. The other eight states were in Asia; Georgia, Armenia and Azerbaijan in Transcaucasia; Uzbekistan, Turkmenistan and Tadzhistan in southern Turkestan, Kirghizia in eastern Turkestan and Kazakhistan, stretching through northern Turkestan and southwestern Siberia to Mongolia. Of the eleven, the Russian state was by far the largest, containing nearly two-thirds of the population and two-thirds of the area.

The Soviet system was a great hierarchical structure with its base resting on the villages. Each had a soviet of its own, which elected delegates to the territorial soviets, which, in turn, sent representatives to provincial Soviets, which, in their turn, elected the Soviets of the republics, which, finally, elected the All-Union Congress of Soviets. All citizens over eighteen were eligible to vote on the local level.

The All-Union Congress, which, in theory, was the supreme governing body of the USSR, consisted of about two thousand delegates. It was, therefore, too unwieldy to discharge any real power. It met at two years' interval to listen to reports, to ratify acts of government, and to elect a Central Executive, the name of which was changed in 1936 to Supreme Soviet. A Central Committee of nineteen full members with eight candidates (who were entitled to attened meetings, but not to vote) constituted the Presidium of the Supreme Soviet. Its functions were largely ceremonial. The actual business of the state was in the hands of a ministry called the Council of People's Commissars, which was appointed by the Central Executive Committee.

The real sources of power lay in the Communist Party (Bolsheviks). It was so all-powerful that the governmental apparatus became the lifeless executive organ of the Party. In 1921 it had 730,000 members; in 1929 it had more than one million members. In January 1965, one-twentieth of the population were party members. A 3,000 member Party Congress met at Moscow annually. Each Congress elected a small Central Committee of the Party which was composed of a Secretariat, an Organisation Bureau and a Political Bureau or Politburo. The last body was the actual governing body of the country and was composed (in 1919) of five men; Lenin, Trotsky, Stalin, Kamenev and Bukharin, to whom Zinoviev and Tomsky were later added. In 1919, the Secretariat was composed of one man—the General Secretary. After 1922, Stalin, made it an increasingly important post. In 1920 the Secretariat was placed under the management of three permanent Secretaries, who were members of the party Central Committee. In the ensuing period the Secretariat acquired a staff of several hundred officials, divided into departments and entrusted with different branches of party activity. The Organisation Bureau or the Orgburo, together with the Secretariat, was responsible for all appointments. The Orgburo, which consisted in 1919 of five men, was later increased to seven. These two bodies—Orgburo and Politburo—together with the General Secretary, who was Stalin (after 1922), wielded the real power in the state appart.

The Communist Party had an extraordinary tribunal, the Cheka, for the summary trial and execution of its opponents. Established in 1917, it was believed to have liquidated as many as fifty thousand persons prior to 1922. The Cheka was replaced in 1922 by OGPU, as a 'third section of the police', with a staff of 45,000 agents. Like the Cheka, the OGPU was used to track down counter-revolutionaries; its duties also included the operation of various concentration camps. In the trials of the Stalin period, it played a key role, especially after 1936.

From Lenin to Stalin

Lenin, who had been a tower of strength to the Communist Party, suffered a stroke in May 1922 and a second one the same year. He was partially paralysed which affected his power of speech. There ensued a bitter succession struggle between Trotsky, the Commissar of War in the government, and **Stalin**, the Secretary of the Central Committee of the party. Disturbed by the prospect of a conflict Lenin wrote the famous political testament on December 25, 1922 with its postcript of January 4, 1923.. Dismissing a split between the two classes—the proletariat and the peasantry—as remote Lenin envisaged the irreconcilable differences between Trotsky and Stalin as a threat for the near future. Trotsky, though 'the most able man in the present Central Committee' exhibited too overweening self-confidence. Stalin concentrated an enormous power in his hands and did not always know how to use that power with sufficient caution.' Lenin referred to 'Stalin's hastiness and administrative impulsiveness' and severely censured him. In a postscript to the testament, Lenin added that Stalin should be replaced as General Secretary by someone 'more patient, more loyal, more polite, and more attentive to comrades, less capricious, etc.' He pointed to Trotsky as the most able of his associates, and, by inference, as the man best qualified to succeed him. Lenin would have effected this change at the Party Congress of 1923, but he suffered his third stroke before it met and was incapacitated from then until his death in January 1924.

Born in 1879 near Tiflis in Georgia, Stalin became involved in socialist politics. Adhering to the Bolshevik wing after the party division in 1903, he acquired a reputation for energy and

Stalin

resolution during the revolution of 1905. Carrying on underground work in Russia—marked by frequent arrests and escapes—he was exiled to Siberia in 1913. He returned in 1917 and played a conspicuous role in the Revolution and Civil War. Though described as a man of mediocrity by Trotsky, Stalin had uncommon intelligence and political finesse that enabled him to seize supreme political power by defeating his more brilliant rival. Once Lenin had been injured seriously by a woman assassin's bullet in 1918 as well as afflicted with incurable disease, a triumvirate composed of Zinoviev, Kamenev and Stalin, had been formed within the Politburo. They were all enemies of Trotsky. In this provisional triumvirate, Stalin was the junior partner. Kamenev had more intelligence than force of character. Zinoviev was weak, vain and ambitious. Stalin, by way of contrast, in the garb of calculated modesty, harped on the historic role of Lenin whom he described as his teacher. Trotsky, on the other hand, was a powerful personality owing to his record in the Civil War and his brilliant oratorical gift. In an open letter of October 8, 1923, Trotsky launched a bitter attack on the 'incorrect and unhealthy regime in the party'. He criticised the secretarial bureaucracy which should be replaced by 'party democracy'. It was a formidable indictment pointed unmistakably at Stalin.

Trotsky's chronic illness enabled his opponents to denigrate the former. Trotsky, dogged by illness, gave up the unequal struggle. At a party conference held in January 1924 an overwhelming majority held Trotsky personally responsible for the campaign against the party leaders. In January 1925, Trotsky was removed from the post of President of the Military Revolutionary Council and People's Commissar for War. He was too loyal to attempt a coup as he publicly avowed, 'one cannot be right against the party.' Within two years he had been expelled from the Central Committee and, in November 1927, from the party.

Having eliminated Trotsky as a rival for succession, Stalin now directed his attention to the destruction of the political position of Kamenev and Zinoviev. The last two leaders were, respectively, the heads of the Moscow and Leningrad organisations of the Party. In December 1925, at the fourteenth Party Congress, Stalin defeated Kamenev and Zinoviev by a majority of 559 to 65. Zinoviev's base at Leningrad was smashed and a new leader, Kirov, became the *de facto* head of the Leningrad organisation. Expelled from his base in Leningrad, Zinoviev lost all political power. Kamenev lacked the courage to assert his authority and he was soon ousted from the Moscow organisation. Both were expelled from the Party in 1927 and were exiled to various places. Later on, they apologised, lay low and were readmitted into the Party. Now, Stalin dealt with the old Bolsheviks—Rykov, Tomsky and Bukharin. At the beginning of 1929, Bukharin, the author of the '*ABC of Communism*', and Tomsky, head of the Trade Unions, demanded Stalin's resignation. In November, Bukharin was expelled from the Politburo and Rykov and Tomsky were given a warning. In the summer of 1930, Ryokov was replaced in the Premiership by one of the most able of Stalin's supporters, Molotov. Thus Stalin obtained absolute power, such as Lenin never claimed. But his brilliant success was achieved 'not by any momentary flash in the pan, not by any brilliant political improvisation, but by spadework.' He had behind him the rank and file of the party, especially the younger sections, who all looked to Stalin for the lead.

From War Communism to NEP

From 1918 to 1921, during the period of War Communism, the Supreme Council of National Economy (VSNK or Vesenkha) regulated the Soviet economy in all its aspects. Established on December 15, 1917, it developed several departments and a hierarchy of regional and local bodies through which it worked. In the period of War Communism, Vesenkha lacked power, which it later acquired. The most burning problem of the Soviet economy was the procurement of food. Deliveries of food by the peasants became compulsory. The practice promoted the despoiling of the rich. In June 1918 the government regularised the method of requisitioning grain and other supplies. Industry was nationalised and a ban was enforced on private trade and private manufacture. Central control of production was not effective. At this period there was complete disorder while free rations and free work was the rule. Production of largescale industry dropped in 1920 by twelve per cent of its pre-war level. Agricultural production declined by a third. The result was the collapse of the Soviet economy in 1920 and famine in 1921. Forty million persons suffered from malnutrition and at least five million died. The situation not only threatened the essential economic basis of the regime, but also engendered discontents and opposition to the Bolsheviks. At the end of February 1921, a widespread labour unrest broke out in Petrograd. In March, sailors of the great naval base at Kronstadt mutinied, which the government was able to suppress only by ruthless military action.

Lenin, with a deep sense of realism, adjusted his policy to meet these obstacles. In October 1921, Lenin frankly described 'the defeat we have suffered on the economic front at the beginning of 1921, in our attempt to make a transition to communism (was) much more serious than any we have suffered at the hand of Kolchak, Denikin or Pilsudski.' In 1921, he proclaimed a New Economic Policy—generally known as the NEP. It was a temporary halt in the revolutionary policy of socialism, a step back in order to move two steps forward later. The policy of forced grain collections was abandoned and was replaced by a single tax in kind on agricultural production. The peasant was allowed to trade on the open market with whatever further surplus he might have. This measure was supplemented by others—to restore a limited market economy in food and other consumer goods, to permit revival of the handicraft and cottage industries, and to make possible the operation of small industrial and commercial enterprises. The state retained complete control of banking, foreign trade and large-scale industry.

Hardly had the NEP been able to produce favourable economic results, when Russia was stricken with its worst famine in 1921. It not only took human lives by millions, but it also caused a shortfall in foodgrain of several million tons. With effective help from American Relief Administration and other foreign sources, as well as by the strong determination of the Soviet authorities, the disaster was eventually overcome. In 1922 and 1923 food production was satisfactory. There was revival of smallscale industry; although heavy industry, which remained under state control, took long periods for recovery.

The NEP served its purpose successfully. By the end of 1922, Soviet Russia made rapid progress. But in 1923 a sharp crisis—the so-called 'Scissors Crisis'—developed in the Soviet economy. Industrial prices rose dramatically at the expense of agricultural prices. At the Twelfth Party Congress in April 1923, Trotsky produced a diagram which showed how the 'scissors', representing the blades of agricultural and industrial prices—had opened more and more widely. In October 1923, the scissors opened to their widest extent, the ratio of industrial prices to agricultural prices was three times as high as in 1913. The crisis was overcome by the establishment of a system of price controls, under which prices on industrial goods were eventually brought down to satisfactory levels.

By the summer of 1924, a growing confidence was visible in Soviet economy. The recovery of Russian agriculture in the years of the mid-twenties was rapid and impressive. But this recovery proceeded on the basis of private interest, operating within a market economy which produced greater differentiation of income and greater inequalities in ownership. Industry steadily revived. The currency reform was completed in March 1924, when the gold-based currency was adopted, and the old Soviet rouble notes withdrawn. Foreign trade, managed by a separate Commissariat, reached favourable figures for the first time in the year 1923-4. Of exports, 75 per cent were agricultural products, including grain; of imports nearly 75 per cent were taken by industry. 'These impressive results had been achieved under the regime of NEP, and could not have been achieved without it; they were hailed as a triumphant vindication of NEP.'[2]

Collectivisation of Agriculture and the Five-Year Plans

The agrarian problem faced by the Soviet Union in the mid-1920s led Stalin to adopt the policy of

2. Carr, E. H.: *The Russian Revolution from Lenin to Stalin,* 1917-29 (1979), P. 59.

collectivisation. The government had no control over supply of grain for the feeding of the cities, the army, and for export. In the winter of 1927-28 it was estimated that over two million tons were being withheld by the peasants in the hope of a rise in the procurement price. In his speech at the Fifteenth Party Congress in December 1927, Stalin criticised the peasants. The way out of dependence on the peasants with their capitalist and individualist lifestyles, said Stalin, was to turn the small and scattered peasant farms into large united farms. So wealthier peasants were taxed more heavily; and the state grain procurement system was streamlined to favour collective farming. Next year, 1928, state procurements in crops and grain were abnormally low. Stalin began a largescale action with ruthless force. A task force of officials and police was sent with orders to close free markets, expropriate private traders, and to prosecute peasants who held back the grain as criminals. But the government encountered violent opposition—from the village community. This development caused tension between Stalin and the right wing of the Party. Stalin had to slow down the pace of reform.

With the removal of the Rightist leaders, Stalin proceeded to achieve not only the 'final liquidation of the *Kulaks* (rich peasants) as a class', but the immediate wholesale collectivisation of the peasantry. Force was used on the large scale which involved the destruction of the wealthy peasantry. Stalin struck to the basic theory as stated 'The Communist Manifesto': 'The theory of communism may be summed up in one sentence: Abolish all private property.' By a decree of 1929 the state machinery was adjusted so that it could impose the penalty of expropriation for individuals and even imprisonment. A decree of February 1930 systematised the attacks on the Kulaks. Concentration camps for the wealthiest, deportations to Siberia for others, was the rule. The Kulaks having been liquidated in 1930, the attack shifted to the middle peasants. The crisis of collectivisation came in 1931 when there was a crop failure. In 1932 the crop was again bad. In 1932 the peasants, demoralised and hungry, were found to be pilfering on socialised fields. The famine of 1933 gave a momentary pause to unchequed cruelty. But the villages were emptied and the land collectivised.

With the resistance of the Kulaks broken, the earlier excesses were unnecessary. By the outbreak (1939) of the Second World War, about 95 per cent of the farms had been collectivised. The basic type remained the regular collective or *Kolkhoz,* run by the peasants themselves, varying in size from 1,000 to more than 7,000 acres. There were also a much smaller number of state farms or *sovkhozes*. Finally, there were the machine tractor stations that could be rotated among the collectives in a given area.

The Fourteenth Congress in December 1925 proclaimed the goal of economic self-sufficiency. It meant converting the USSR 'from a country that imports machines and equipment into a country that produces machines and equipment.' The party conference in the following autumn called for the 'reconstruction of the economy on the basis of new and more advanced technology.' The draft of the plan was completed in March 1929 and finally approved by a large party conference in April.1929. It put first on the list of its aims 'the maximum development in production of the means of production as the foundation of the industrialization of the country.' As Stalin remarked later: 'We are fifty or a hundred years behind the advanced countries. We must make good this lag in ten years. Either we do it, or they crush us.'

Stalin began in 1928 the famous Five Year Plans in order to increase industrial output and agricultural production. It was an impressive and comprehensive review of the whole economy. 'The five year plan became the pivot round which the whole economy revolved.' It was directed by the State Planning Commission or *Gosplan* which had been in existence since 1921.

The First Five Year Plan, to run from 1928 to 1933, aimed to double Soviet production, concentrated on basic industry, which was scheduled to grow by 300 per cent, and on electrification, which was to grow more than five-fold. The most famous project executed as a vital part of the first Five Year Plan was the construction of a great dam and hydroelectric station on the

Dnieper river, known as Dneprostroi. It was built under the supervision of Cooper, the American engineer, who had built the Tennessee Valley dam. One-seventh of the industrial investment went into the production of iron and steel. Emphasis was laid on the manufacture of automobiles and tractors. The armament industry did not lag behind. The aircraft industry led the way, and was followed by the production of tanks. Much importance was attached to the development of a modern chemical industry. The 1,100 mile Turkestan-Siberian Railway was laid down.

The adoption of the first Five Year Plan was a landmark in Soviet history. The prestige of the Plan was enhanced by the economic crisis (the Great Depression) which engulfed the capitalist world in the autumn of 1929. It was widely felt that the Marxist prediction of the collapse of the capitalist order had been vindicated.

In 1933 the *Gosplan* announced that the 'achievement of the First Five Year Plan made it possible to set, in the Second Five Year Plan (January 1933 to December 1937), the task of finally abolishing the capitalist elements and classes generally...' The new Plan envisaged that the industrial output of 1937 was to be more than double that of 1932. Paying less attention to giant industries, the Second Plan put more emphasis on quality as well as on transportation facilities. New industries were set up in close proximity to the raw materials. Finally, to improve the standard of living and increase the real wages, greater emphasis was placed on the production of consumer goods. However, the Second Five Year Plan fell short of expectation. Neither the cost of production nor the price of goods fell so rapidly as had been anticipated. Hence the objective set to 'overtake and outstrip America' was far from being realised when the Second Five Year Plan gave way to the Third Five Year Plan in January 1938. Nevertheless, amazing progress had been accomplished during the ten-year period between 1928-38. Russia had finally become a major industrial power—after the United States and Germany. Materially, the Soviet experiment was successful, and from the choatic, famine-stricken land of 1919-21 there emerged a country economically almost self-sufficient.

The Great Purges

With the completion of the First Five Year Plan period in 1932, Stalin was determined to stamp out every trace of resistance to his personal rule. The violence of the years 1928-33 had caused growing opposition in the upper hierarchy of the Party and in certain of the army commands. It appears that at least one serious conspiracy was hatched to bring about Stalin's downfall. Stalin became convinced that totalitarian regimes can only be propped up by inventing conspiracies and culprits and liquidating them.

The events which touched off this insensate act of cruelty on the part of Stalin was the rebuff which the latter had received at the XVII Party Congress in January 1934. The immediate cause was the asassination, in December 1, 1934, of Sergai Kirov, Zinoviev's successor as head of the party in Leningrad and, in the opinion of some, Stalin's chosen heir. It is alleged that Stalin was involved in the assassination of Kirov. Stalin exploited the event as an excuse for the launching of that extraordinary process of liquidation which went by the name of the 'purges' of the thirties.

In 1935 the world was startled by news of a series of trials in Moscow. In January 1935 Zinoviev and Kamenev were arrested on a trumped up charge of plotting to murder Stalin. These old associates of Lenin and Stalin were allegedly implicated in a further plot to segregate Ukraine from the Soviet Union. To the astonishment of the world, they confessed their guilt in the public trial and were sentenced to be shot.

In January 1937, charges were levelled against Karl Radek, former editor of *Izvestia* and a former leader of the Third International; Grigori Sokolnikov, former ambassador to Great Britain; and Grigori Piatakov, vice-commissar for heavy industry. They were charged with having agreed to support Germany and Japan in a war against the USSR.

In June 1937, the hero of the Civil War, Marshal Tukhachevsky, and seven other Red Army generals were convicted and sentenced to death for military conspiracy.

The purge reached its crescendo in 1937 with the arrest of tens of thousands of people in all walks of life. Many old Bolshevik heroes like

Borodin and Bela Kun were imprisoned or deported. Even of the eight military judges who tried the Red Army generals in 1937, six were degraded by the end of 1938. The final purge was effected in 1938 with the elimination of Rykov, President of the Council of Commissars, and Bukharin, who, on the elimination of Rykov, was President of the Council of Commissars; Bukharin, who edited *Pravda*, Rakovsky who had been ambassador in London and Paris and even Yagoda, who was chief of the secret police. And this was only the tip of the iceberg. Hundreds of thousands of party officials and administrative officers were shot, deported or replaced. The majority of the delegates of the XVII Party Congress of 1934 were liquidated before another Congress could be convened in 1939. To cap the horrendous deeds, Trotsky, the arch-enemy of Stalin, was murdered in Mexico in 1940.

The number of men killed as a result of the purges were colossal. As many as 800,000 party members were killed, including six of the thirteen members of the Politburo, ninetyeight of the 138 members of the Central Committee, fourteen of the eighteen members of the Council of the People's Commissars, and nearly all the premiers and peoples' Commissars of the federated Republics. In the army also there was almost a thorough purge; the dead included three of the five marshals, fourteen of the sixteen army commanders, sixty of the sixtyseven corps commanders, 136 of the 199 divisional commanders and 221 of 397 brigade commanders. About half of the officers corps, some 35,000 in all, were liquidated. Stalin only said ironically! 'one death is a tragedy; one million is a statistic.'

The whole hysterical, unreal procedure was not produced by conspiracy alone. For no piece of evidence verifiable by legal procedure was even produced to justify the terror. The only organised power strong enough to dethrone Stalin was the army. They had ample motive for planning a *coup d' etat* to save themselves from the expected purge. But they did not do so with the help of the Nazis. The Nazi documents produced in 1947 at the Nuremburg trials revealed no hint of a Nazi fifth column in the Soviet Government or army. Stalin's central motive, in the words of his biographer, Isaac Deutscher, was 'to destroy the men who represented the potentiality of alternative government.' The purges were timed to forestall any combination of internal opposition with external enemy such as produced the Spanish Civil War.

Stalin now stood at the pinnacle of power. Lenin's apprehensions of his rough and arbitrary use of power had been justified. He had displayed an extraordinary ruthlessness in enforcing his will and in crushing all opposition to it. The horrors of the process of collectivisation, of the concentration camps, of the great show trials, and of the indiscriminate massacres—not only of those who had opposed him in the past, but of many who had assisted his rise to power—left a scar which could not be effaced by victory in the war.

Soviet Foreign Policy, 1917-39

The Bolshevik Government pledged itself to the overthrow of the capitalist regime everywhere. Lenin had said that the Bolsheviks would:

> Systematically start to incite rebellion among all the peoples now opposed... all the colonies and dependent countries of Asia (India, China, Persia and others). And we would also raise the socialist proletariat of Europe in rebellion against their governments.

Throughout the world of 1918, the Bolsheviks tried to exploit the unrest caused by the war in eastern Europe, in the Middle East, and elsewhere. In March 1919 was formed the Communist or, Third International or Comintern with headquarters at Moscow. Headed by Zinoviev and dominated by other Bolshevik leaders, the object of the Comintern was to overthrow the capitalist governments of other countries.

While the Soviet Government sought to overthrow or weaken by revolution the capitalist governments, it sought to establish normal relations with these same governments! These inherent contradictions marked the course of the Soviet foreign policy during the whole of this period. From 1918 to 1921 the policy of the Soviet Government in foreign affairs was to promote world revolution and aid communist uprisings wherever they might occur. The Bolsheviks denounced the Anglo-Russian Convention of 1907 that had divided Persia into foreign spheres of influence, surrendered all extraterritorial rights in Turkey, and encouraged the Afghans to resist British control. In September 1920 was held at Baku the First Congress of People of the East which was attended by nineteen hundred delegates.

Economic weakness was one of the most important factors that led Russia to establish normal diplomatic intercourse. By 1921 it was clear to the Bolsheviks that foreign capital was as necessary as it had been before 1914. The main difficulty was the distrust entertained by the foreign governments of a regime which had repudiated the large debts of the Tsarist governments. But a new thrust to Soviet foreign policy was given by Georgei Chicherin who felt that the best protection against foreign exploitation was a truce with the capitalist world. Chicherin began to hold out the prospect of acknowledging Tsarist debts, if further credits were made available.

In 1920, Russia concluded treaties of peace with Finland, Estonia, Latvia and Lithuania; and these were followed by the treaty with Poland next year. Early in 1921, the Soviet Union signed treaties of friendship with Turkey, Persia, and Afghanistan. A new turn in Soviet relation was taken when an Anglo-Soviet trade agreement was signed on March 16, 1921. Before the end of the year, Russia had completed similar trade pacts with eleven other states.

It was through the instrumentality of the then British Prime Minister Lloyd George that an economic conference was convened at Genoa in April 1922 to discuss the question of Russia's war debt and the extension of foreign cedit. The Soviet demanded the cancellation of war debts and asked for large foreign credits. But the French and Belgian delegates insisted on recognition of Russia's pre-war debts as a condition of any negotiations with the Soviet Union. From the beginning the Russian distrusted the conference as they feared that the Western powers would strangle Russia by economic means under the pretext of financial assistance. Chicherin insisted that his country was ready to enter into bilateral trade relations with any country. The Genoa Conference, therefore, foundered. To the dismay of all, the German and Soviet delegates met at Rapallo, a seaside resort a few miles from Genoa, and signed a treaty of friendship between the two countries. The two governments agreed to exchange ambassadors, mutually renounced claims against one another and set up preferential tariffs. In December 1920 Lenin had described Germany as 'naturally inclined in the direction of an alliance with Russia.' That prophesy was fulfilled. The agreement, according to *The Times,* was an 'unholy alliance.' From Russia's point of view it removed the dangers of an anti-Russian front in Europe and enabled her to win diplomatic recognition.

In 1923, at the Lausanne Conference, Chicherin won the sympathy of several small nations by championing the cause of Turkey. In the same year the foreign relations of the Soviet Union suffered setback when the British Government protested against the activities of the Soviet agents in Persia, Afghanistan, and India. The Anglo-Soviet trade agreement of 1921 contained a clause which prohibited the Soviet Government to carry on any form of revolutionary propaganda in any part of the British Empire. The British Government threatened to annul the trade agreement and withdraw its representative from Moscow. But the storm blew over as quickly as it had come as the Soviet Government agreed to comply with most of the demands.

In January 1924, when the British Labour Government took office, it granted *de jure* recognition of the Soviet Government on February 1. Italy followed suit. In August 1924 was signed a new Anglo-Soviet treaty, accompanied by the promise of a loan. But the treaty was not ratified. On the eve of the general election of October 1924, a conservative newspaper published 'Zinoviev letter'—a letter of instruction from the Comintern to the Communist Party of Great Britain to conduct propaganda in the armed forces and elsewhere. 'The letter was almost certainly a forgery.' However, the alleged letter brought about a perceptible cooling of Anglo-Soviet relations. The new Conservative Government, with Austen Chamberlain as its Foreign Secretary, virtually suspended all diplomatic relations with the Soviet Union throughout 1925. Franco-Soviet negotiations for a trade agreement reached a similar deadlock.

Meanwhile, in December 1924, Zinoviev encouraged an attack by a group of Russian officers upon the Estonian part of Reval. It failed miserably, but lowered the prestige of the Soviet Russia among the family of nations. Finally, in April 1925, the Comintern was believed to have engineered revolutionary activities in Bulgaria as a result of which 128 persons were killed in a cathedral in Sofia.

The signing of the Locarno Pact in October 1925 was regarded in Moscow as a conspiracy of the Western powers against Russia. The Pact was regarded as an attempt to detach Germany from the Rapallo and to bring her into the League of Nations. However, during the Locarno period, a German-Soviet trade agreement, carrying with it a substantial credit from German banks, was signed at Moscow. While denouncing British efforts to build up an anti-Soviet front, the Soviet Government established special relations with other states. It was designed to forestall combined action against the USSR by undertaking not to participate in hostile action against the other, and remain neutral in the event of a war. A treaty with Turkey on this basis was signed in December 1925. A similar treaty was signed with Germany on April 24, 1926. The treaty caused considerable annoyance in the West.

Anglo-Soviet friendship was further strained when the Soviet Government contributed large sums of money to the British General Strike of May 1926. But the British Trade Union Congress, fearing to be discredited, refused the sum. Public opinion—both within and outside Parliament—became increasingly critical of the Soviet Union. In February 1927, the British Government dispatched a Note to Moscow in which charges of subversive activities were made. In May matters reached a climax when the British police raided the private offices of Arcos Ltd., the Soviet Trading Corporation in London. On May 24, the British Government announced the severance of diplomatic relations with the USSR and the annulment of the trade agreement. Fears of war were rife in Moscow. The British Trade Union Congress dissolved the Anglo-Russian Trade Union committee. Even in Asia the Soviet fortune reached a low ebb.

The same year witnessed a crisis in Soviet-French affair. Despite the official recognition of Soviet Russia, the French adopted an unfriendly attitude towards Moscow. Apart from the Soviet-German rapprochement which frightened the French, the latter were annoyed by Moscow's continued ban on the importation of French luxuries. In 1927 the then French Prime Minister Poincare rejected a Soviet offer regarding debts and credits and demanded the recall of the ambassador. In June 1927, there was a recrudescence of anti-Soviet feeling in Poland, and the Soviet ambassador in Warsaw was murdered.

Throughout this period, the United States Government refused to recognise the Soviet Government. But a trickle of trade began to filter through. In 1924 the Soviet authorities set up a trading corporation in New York under the name Amtorg. An unofficial Soviet emissary resided in Washington. In 1925 an American financier was permitted to work the managanese mines in the Caucasus. But it was not till 1927 that American industrialists became seriously interested in the Soviet market.

Since 1923, the Soviet Union had maintained formal relations with the Kuomintang, the Chinese nationalist party founded by Sun Yat Sen and now led by Chiang Kai Shek. They were also on good terms with the Japanese Government which had interests in Manchuria and Korea. Now, in 1925 and 1926, when the Soviet position in Europe was at its nadir, it indulged in activities in the Far East that weakened her position in that region. Since the conclusion of Sino-Soviet agreement in May 1924, the USSR was determined to keep a firm control over the Mongolian People's Republic. Under Soviet influence, mainly under Borodin, was stimulated antagonism towards Western powers and Japan. However, the alliance between Moscow and Kuomintang had to some extent been artificial. When the Kuomintang split into two factions, the right wing, under the vigorous leadership of General Chiang Kai Shek, developed bitter hatred towards communism. In July 1927, Borodin and the Soviet military advisers took their departure. "Of four years of feverish effort directed from Moscow—nothing seemed to survive.'[3]

3. Carr, E. H.: *The Russian Revolution from Lenin to Stalin,* 1919-29, P. 103.

Soviet relations with Japan were also not favourable. In a treaty signed between the two countries in January 1925, the Japanese troops were withdrawn from the mainland of Siberia and northern Sakhalin. The first Japanese Communist Party disintegrated itself early in 1924. It was reconstituted as an unlawful organisation in December 1926. And the party was virtually wiped out by wholesale arrests in 1929.

For nearly two years after the break with Britain in May 1927, Soviet foreign relations were in doldrums. Relations with Germany had been temporarily strained by her signature of the Locarno Treaty and entry into the League of Nations. However, in May 1927, a large Soviet delegation attended the World Economic Conference at Geneva. Six months later, a Soviet delegation headed by Litvinov, the Deputy Commissar for Foreign Affairs, attended the session of the Preparatory Commission for Disarmament at Geneva. Litvinov stole the limelight by advocating the total abolition of all military, naval and air armaments. While acceding to the Kellogg Pact of August 1928, the Soviet Government concluded with its immediate neighbours a similar pact. This subsidiary pact was signed in Moscow on February 9, 1929, by the USSR, Poland, Latvia, Estonia and Rumania; Lithuania, Turkey and Persia joined later.

A new wind began to blow in Soviet foreign policy under the auspices of Litvinov, who virtually supplanted Chicherin as People's Commissar for Foreign Affairs, when the latter became ill in 1928. While Chicherin distrusted Western countries, especially Britain, Litvinov, who had spent many years in Britain, favoured rapprochement with the Western world.

The shift in foreign policy became evident when a party of businessmen visited Russia at the end of March 1929. When the Labour Party formed a government, it established full relations with the Soviet Union. At the same time France became worried at the growing Russian-German-Italian-Turkish friendship. In 1930, she raised the cry that the Bolsheviks were dumping their goods upon foreign markets to shatter the Western economic system. Soviet imports into France were put under restriction. Belgium also followed suit in putting embargoes on Soviet goods.

A change made itself felt in Russia's international relations owing to two factors of great importance. The first was the advent of the National Socialists to power in Germany. Moscow became suspicious of the anti-communist tactics of Hitler in Germany. The second factor was the conquest of Manchuria by Japan. This constituted a serious threat to Russia's military and strategic interests in the Far East. Without risking a military conflict, the Soviet Government compromised. While abandoning its claim to a special position in Manchuria, she adopted a stiff attitude in defence of the state frontiers of Siberia and also of Outer Mongolia, which had long been a Soviet protectorate. The threat posed by the presence of strong Japanese forces along the sensitive borders of Siberia and Mongolia was a source of constant irritation to the Soviet Russia till the final defeat (1945) of Japan in the Second World War.

A reorientation of international policy was given by Maxim Litvinov, Commissar for Foreign Affairs, at the Geneva conference of 1931. At this gathering Litvinov propounded a plan to negotiate an economic non-aggression pact between capitalism and communism. Although this suggestion was not adopted, a Franco-Soviet treaty of neutrality and non-aggression was signed in 1932.

The accession of Franklin Roosevelt to the American Presidency in 1933 broke the long diplomatic deadlock between the American and Soviet governments. Litvinov journeyed to Washington, and diplomatic relations between the two countries were formally established in November 1933.

Faced with the threat of a sweep of fascism over Europe, Moscow now began to collaborate with eastern Europe in opposing the advance of fascism. Under Litvinov's able direction as Foreign Minister, far-reaching changes were introduced into Soviet relations with other Western countries. In 1934, the Soviet Union entered the League of Nations. In 1935 was signed a Franco-Soviet Pact of mutual assistance.

The years 1936-38 marked new trends in Soviet foreign policy. By the middle of 1936, it had become clear to Moscow that the Western powers would have acquiesced in Hitler's repudiation of the Versailles Treaty and would not be likely to thwart German expansion in the east. This was evident by the reactions of the various powers to the Spanish Civil War. The Soviet Union at first adhered to the principle of non-intervention in the conflict. But when Germany and Italy despatched military aid to the rebels, the Soviet Government proceeded to give important military aid to the Republican cause. The initial defence of Madrid owed its success largely to Soviet assistance. But when the Soviet example was not followed by Western powers, Moscow began to lose interest.

It is not by accident that Moscow began to veer round Hitler. After the signing of the Munich Pact and then the Anglo-French acceptance of German protectorate over Czechoslovakia, Moscow lost faith in the leadership of London and Paris. Even in the summer of 1939, the Soviet leaders would have joined the Western powers in a common front against Hitler. But this was possible only if the Western powers would have agreed to the establishment of Soviet military ascendancy over the eastern European countries, with which the Western Allies were unwilling, at that moment, to agree. This was the background of the Soviet-German Non-Aggression Pact of August 1939. In the secret protocol of the Non-Aggression Pact, Stalin arranged what was, in effect, a partition of Eastern Europe with the Nazis. Stalin gained a breathing space by forestalling German attack on Russia. He also succeeded in checking any further Japanese aggression against the eastern frontiers of Soviet Russia. 'Stalin's motive was probably fear, not aggressiveness, for he knew Russia to be weak.'

Russian diplomacy had been fairly successful. Poland had been partitioned. The Baltic States became virtually Russian Protectorates. A war with Finland (Nov. 1939-March 1940) brought gains to Russia. She had obtained from Romania the cession of Bessarabia and north Bukovina.

The impressive record caused uneasiness to Germany. Then came the three-power (Axis) pact of September 1940 between Germany, Italy and Japan. In November, Russian Foreign Minister Molotov went to Berlin to negotiate Russian adherence to the pact. But Molotov demanded in exchange that Germany should not only withdraw support from Finland, but should put pressure on Japan to be more accommodating to Russian interests in the Far East. He also asked for Russian bases in the Dardanelles and the recognition of Russian hegemony over Bulgaria.

This was too much for Hitler to tolerate. On December 18, 1940, formal orders were issued for the invasion of Russia. In spite of a danger signal, Stalin clung to a policy of appeasement. When on June 22, 1941, the final blow fell, Russia was almost paralysed into non-resistance.

CHAPTER 34
RISE OF FASCISM IN EUROPE : ITALY

The unification of Italy established formal political unity, but not a really national unity. Localism and sectionalism were rife. Italy was described as a 'country in which two stages of civilization exist in the same state.' While the North was highly developed with many large cities, the South presented desolate region, with little semblance of law and order. Illiteracy was common in the region, while secret societies like *Mafia* and *Camorra* sprang up in Sicily and Naples.

The government of the Italian Kingdom which has been copied from England's, was embodied in the *Statute* of 1848. The King reigned but did not rule. His powers were practically exercised by a ministry responsible to a bicameral parliament consisting of a Senate and the Chamber of Deputies elected by the upper and middle classes.

The government began energetically to remove the various malaise that afflicted the country. Brigandage was suppressed and a compulsory education law was passed. A new law passed in 1904 required every commune to provide for public schools to be supported by local taxes. Illiteracy dropped to a considerable extent and, in 1914, it had fallen to about twenty-five per cent. A great reform in the finances by Luigi Luzzati in 1905-06 put the Italian economy in a good shape and the national treasury began to show a surplus instead of a deficit. Owing to high birth rate and the existence of widespread poverty, many Italians went to the United States and South America, even to France and Germany. Emigration drained off some of the surplus population while the riches sent by the emigrants stimulated a demand for better comforts at home.

State and the Papacy

The most crucial problem that confronted the country after 1870 was the hostility between Church and State. The Italian nation was Catholic by habit and tradition and the government maintained Catholicism as a kind of national institution. In 1871, the famous Law of Papal Guarantees tried to solve the relations between Church and the State. The Pope had reacted sharply at the seizure and occupation of Rome by troops of Victor Emmanuel II. The Law accorded to the Pope the ownership of the Vatican and Lateran Palaces and the villa of Castel Gandolfo, with full powers to conduct diplomatic affairs without any interference from the Italian government. The Pope was to receive an annual subsidy of three and a quarter million lire from the national treasury as compensation for the loss of temporal possessions. The Vatican was to be exempt from taxation and State interference in Church affairs was put to an end.

Pope Pius IX refused to accept the Law as it would have meant the recognition of a government which had unjustly invaded Rome. He shut himself up in the Vatican, regarding himself as a 'prisoner of Vatican'. His successors followed this policy until 1929, when the difficulty was settled. A Papal encyclical, known as the *non expedit,* forbade Italian Catholics to vote or hold office under the crown. At first the situation was embarrassing, and even dangerous, as it was feared that France might champion the cause of the Pope. With the passage of time, there began a rapprochement between the Pope and the Italian government, but a number of partiotic Italians became alienated from the Pope owing to his opposition to the nation's political unity. The greatest Italian writer since unification, Giosue Carducci (1835-1907), regarded the Church as the inveterate enemy of the United Italy. In his *Ode to Satan*, Carducci typified the Church as pagan in outlook and the cancer of the society.

Political History, 1870-1914

The political history of Italy after 1870 was a dismal tale of parliamentary intrigue and corruption. In general, there were two groups—those of the Right and those of the Left. The Right were aristocratic in composition embracing the industrial upper and middle classes of Piedmont, Lombardy and Tuscany while the Left included the intellectual bourgeoisie of Sicily and Naples.

From 1870 to 1878 the government was in the hands of the Right, who reorganised the administration, nationalised the railways and established military service. Popular discontent burst forth when heavy taxes were imposed on foodstuffs. The elections of 1876 were a triumph for the Left and the King summoned Agostino Depretis to form the ministry. He was to reform administration, balance the budget, lower taxation, and establish schools and lessen illiteracy. Depretis, who with Cairoli and Mancini dominated the decade 1876-87, failed to perform as much as he had promised. Nevertheless, the prime ministership of Depretis was memorable as during his stewardship there was an industrial spurt. But the economic heyday was over by 1887. In that year the Government introduced a protective tariff, giving protection to iron and steel and safeguarded the interests of the landowners by imposing duty on imported wheat.

The period of Depretis marked a new phase in Italy's foreign policy. The Italian army was reorganised and enlarged by the adoption of the principle of compulsory military training (1875). In 1881 Italian nationalism was stimulated by the French occupation of Tunis. Italy replied by contracting with Germany and Austria-Hungary Triple Alliance in 1882, which endured until 1915. Almost immediately Italy ventured to establish a colonial empire in eastern Africa along the Red Sea. She reconciled herself to France and acquired her first colonies in Eritrea and Somaliland. In 1887 she came to a close understanding with Britain by withering the Mediterranean Agreements.

Depretis was followed by Crispi who came to power in 1887. A fiery Sicilian, brilliant and erratic, and an old follower of Garibaldi, Crispi might have given prestige to the monarchy. But he was unscrupulous and impulsive and involved himself in the Bank of Rome scandal. A thorough probe revealed speculation of enormous amount, involving many prominent persons, including Crispi. A feeling of revulsion seized the country and many people turned to socialism to put an end to political corruption. Serious labour troubles broke out during Crispi's regime. Poverty and heavy taxes gave a fillip to revolutionary movement. In Sicily, agricultural labourers formed unions and began widespread agitation for better conditions. During 1893-94 serious labour riots took place in Sicily which were suppressed with ruthless severity.

After remaining out of office for two years, Crispi returned to power in 1893 with a vision of an imperialist Italy. Crispi tried to divert popular attention from domestic problems by pursuing an ambitious colonial policy. In his first ministry he had obtained Britain's consent to expansion in Ethiopia, and he now pushed this policy with zeal. But his misguided interference with the men on the spot and his impetuosity led General Baratieri into action. With 20,000 men, against 80,000 Ethiopians, the General met with stiff resistance. On March 1, 1896, under the leadership of the Emperor Menelek, the Ethiopians defeated the Italian army at Adowa. Over 6,000 soldiers were either killed or captured. This defeat drove Crispi from power and checked, for a time, Italian ambitions in Africa.

The year 1898 was marked by serious bread riots in Milan and elsewhere. The government adopted severe repressive measures and placed thirty provinces under military rule. Normal parliamentary life was suspended between 1898 and 1900. But that did not put an end to strikes and violent demonstrations. In 1900 King Humbert, who had succeeded to the throne on the death of his illustrious father Victor Emmanuel II in 1878, was assassinated by an anarchist.

The new king, Victor Emmanuel III, showed more initiative than his father. He took the important step of appointing Zanardelli as Prime Minister in February 1901; his right hand was Giovanni Giolitti, as Minister of the Interior. These two men were conscious of Italy's social problems. In the preceding decade, industrialization of northern Italy had begun. In 1899 the Fiat car factory was founded at Turin. The port of Genoa had been developed. Giolitti, who succeeded Zanardelli as Prime Minister in 1903, ruled Italy with few interruptions until she entered the war. He undertook important programmes of reform. He made it clear that henceforth the government would remain neutral in the struggle between capital and labour. In 1898 old-age pensions had been provided and workmen were insured against accidents and sickness. In 1902 an important factory law was enacted. In 1908 a weekly day of rest was provided for labour. In 1912 private insurance companies were nationalised. The government's reform policy was of many dimensions. It took over the operation of the railways from private companies. Municipalities were authorised to own and operate public utilities. Trade unions were legalised and cooperative societies were fostered, particularly in the rural districts. Some progress was made in the arbitration of labour disputes. In 1911 Giolitti broadened electoral reform by establishing universal manhood suffrage.

A major problem in Italy in 1900 was the relation between the state and the Roman Catholic Church. Though the Popes refused to recognise the Italian Kingdom many Catholics indeed criticised the policy of the Vatican. A particular group called the Modernist considered that Catholic dogma should adapt itself to social development. Soon after his election in 1903, Pope Pius X condemned the Modernists. He, however, modified the papal veto on voting in elections. Catholics were permitted to vote but only by special permission.

Catholic support was welcome to Giolitti, as he did not wish to allow socialists a decisive voice in government. From 1903 onwards the socialists were split into two factions—a minority, the 'Reformists' who were ready to work within the constitutional framework, while the majority, Syndicalists', were determined to forge class revolution. But the strength of the Socialist party in the parliament was small. Moreover, the government was strong to defeat the general strikes of 1904, 1907 and 1908. However, the political situation was rendered critical owing to the extreme poverty of the south. The situation became worse confounded by the appalling earthquake at Messina in 1908. The historian, Salvemini, who hailed from the south, spearheaded a campaign against Giolitti as a corrupter. The extremists, led by Lazzari and Mussolini, gained control of the Socialist party after defeating the moderate leadership in 1912. Shortly afterwards, Mussolini became editor of *Avanti*, the chief Socialist newspaper.

A new nationalist party appeared which demanded an aggressive foreign policy and more serious efforts to 'redeem' those provinces of *Italia irredenta*—Trent, Trieste and the eastern coast of the Adriatic. The new nationalism was fostered by literary and philosophical currents of which Gabriele D' Annunzio was a leading representative. Under the guidance of the Foreign Minister, San Guiliano, Italy declared war against Turkey in 1911, seizing Tripoli and occupying the Dodecanese islands in the Aegean.

In the general election of 1913, the Socialist party increased its representation in the Chamber from 43 to 78. Giolitti's position became weakened when there was intense urge among the Italians for participation in the First World War. Giolitti, who was against participation, resigned in March 1914. A new 'nationalist' ministry was formed under the leadership of Antonio Salandra. The Nationalists wished to join the Allies' side. So Sonnino, the new Foreign Minister, negotiated the Treaty of London (April 26, 1916) with the Allies and Italy declared war against Austria-Hungary.

Italy suffered much in the First World War. About 700,000 soldiers were killed and 1,000,000 wounded. She suffered a disastrous defeat at Caporetto in October 1917. The war had cost her an enormous sum, about twice as large as the total of all expenditure between 1861 and 1913. However, Italy gained from the war Trieste, Trentino, the South Tyrol up to the Brenner Pass and Istria, Zara and several Adriatic islands. Although *Italia Irredenta* was now achieved, Italians were disappointed not to achieve their desires in Dalmatia, Albania, the Near East and Africa. The Italians, therefore, accused their allies of faithlessness. They also denounced their statesmen by declaring that 'the war had been won and the peace lost.'

Widespread dissatisfaction with the government was fanned by dismal economic condition.

Apart from staggering debt and imbalance in foreign trade, inflation crippled Italian economy. The result was a number of a violent strikes in industry, and in rural areas, a series of spontaneous risings. The confusion was heightened by the number of returning soldiers, the *reduci*, who were demobilised.

The situation called for bold measures which were curiously lacking in the government. The first post-war government under Giovanni Giolitti, duly elected in November 1919, contained the three largest parties—the Socialists, the Catholic Popular Party (*Popolari*), and the Liberals. In the elections of 1919, the socialists captured 156 seats in the Chamber of Deputies out of a total of 574. Socialism received encouragement from the proletarian rule in Russia. Popular discontent took the form of strikes and riots. In 1919 and 1920 there was talk of the establishment of a dictatorship of the proletariat. Peasant tenants refused to pay taxes, large estates were broken up, and the workmen themselves took over the factories. The government remained supine and followed a policy of strict non-intervention. Industrial and agrarian disorders gave the Fascists the chance to pose as the custodian of law and order against the communist attack.

The Fascist movement was sponsored by Benito Mussolini. Born in 1883 and the son of a blacksmith and a schoolmistress, Mussolini eventually became a teacher. He gave up this career and went to Switzerland in 1902. Returning to Italy in 1904, he took up journalism and then went to Austria. In 1909 he was expelled from the Austrian district of Trent (Trentino) for his revolutionary journalism. In 1911 once more he returned to Italy but was jailed for five months for opposing the Tripolitan war of 1911-12. This made him a hero in Socialist circles. In 1912, he became editor of *Avanti*, the official paper of the Italian Socialist Party.

When the First World War broke out, he favoured Italian neutrality but soon afterwards he became a convert to the cause of intervention. He argued that the only way of converting the Italian masses to socialism was to identify it with a nationalist cause. This finished his career as a Socialist and thereupon he established at Milan an interventionist journal *Il Popolo d' Italic*. In 1915 he joined the army as a private, fought on the Isonzo front and rose to be corporal. In 1917 he was wounded.

Then, back on his newspaper, he displayed histrionic talent in combating pacifism. He possessed determination and imagination and worked for personal aggrandisement. His writings became popular and he spoke eloquently. He asserted that the war had been one of the finest chapters in Italian history, and that Italy had been deprived of the gains won by the blood of its sons. He enlisted the support of ex-soldiers, property owners and the intellectual proletariat. For his new movement, which he called 'Fascism', he borrowed communist methods.

In March 1919, **Mussolini** founded in Milan the first *Fascio di combattiments*, or fighting group, which was the nucleus of the Fascist party of the future. The Fascists adopted a programme which demanded proportional representation, an eight-hour day, a heavy capital levy and inheritance tax, confiscation of church properties, the calling of a national assembly to decide upon a new form of government, and annexation of Fiume and Dalmatia. The Fascists appealed to the demobilised soldiers the 'proletariat of the trenches'. Said Mussolini: 'It is we who have the right to succeed this government, for it was we who pushed the country into the war and led it to victory.'

Mussolini

In the beginning, the cause of Fascism progressed slowly. The collapse of D' Annunzio's Fiume adventure and the individualism of some of its local leaders threatened the organisation with disintegration. Men like Dino Grandi in Bologna,. Italo Balbo in Ferrarra, and Robert Farinacci in Cremona opposed Mussolini's centralised control. However, Mussolini had a charismatic personality who could flatter people by his oratory. He made Fascism a party with national support. The inept handling of agrarian and industrial disorders by Giolitti's Liberal government of 1920-1, gave the Fascists the chance of maintaining semblance of law and order and commended it to the middle class as their natural protector. Fascism fed on the growing atmosphere of violence and in early 1921 several people were killed in riots in Florence and Pisa. In the general election of March 1921, the Fascists won 35 seats. In November of the same year the Fascist political party was definitely constituted with a graded hierarchy headed by Mussolini, with a rigid discipline. As Garibaldi's volunteers had worn red shirts, so Mussolini's distinguished themselves with black shirts. The *fasces* or bundle of rods enclosing a battle-axe, symbolising strength and power, became the insignia of Fascism.

With mounting violence, the Fascist movement gathered momentum rapidly during 1921-22. Meanwhile the government was so unstable that there was talk of coalition with the Fascists which Mussolini refused. He found to his satisfaction that the situation was propitious for an all-out drive for seizure of power. In the spring of 1922, Mussolini openly hinted that he would start a full-scale revolt if any prime minister were appointed who stood for "anti-Fascist reaction." Even this threat did not influence the government to change its supine policy. The Socialists declared a general strike in August 1922. But the people, who were tired of strikes and agitations, gave the Fascists an excuse to declare open war on socialism. They destroyed all Socialist and union headquarters in Livorno, Genoa, and other key cities. In the weeks that followed, they took over the town councils of Ferrara, Cremona, Parma, Revenna and Livorno as well. Mussolini foiled every move of the government to suppress the Fascists. He decreed that all members of the Party should be members of the *fasci*, so that squads could not be suppressed without suppressing the Party as well. And a liberal Government could not suppress a political party.

Mussolini availed every opportunity to stage a national coup. Meanwhile, he appointed a small general staff to make an operational plan for the seizure of power. In October 1922, Mussolini reviewed some 40,000 Fascists at Naples and two days later began a march on Rome 'to cut the Gordian Knot and hand over to the king and the Army a renewed Italy.' King Victor Emmanuel III could have averted the crisis by declaring martial law demanded by the current Prime Minister, Luigi Facta. But the king refused to support him. On October 27, the Liberal Premier, Facta, resigned. A Fascist mission headed by Grandi persuaded the king to appoint Mussolini as the Premier. With Fascist men pouring into the capital and the government troops remaining inert, the king asked Mussolini to form a cabinet. On October 30, 1922, Mussolini formed a ministry containing representatives of the Popolari, Democratic, Liberal and nationalist parties. Only four of the fifteen portfolios ware placed in Fascist hands.

Mussolini owed his final success to the king and the politicians. The king could have used the regular army—12,000 men under General Pugliesi—against the Fascists. But the king avoided open confrontation when he found local administrations everywhere terrorised by the Fascist militia. 'Though militarily he might fight it out, political success might still elude him; for the events since the election of November 1921 had shown him that the Liberals had virtually abdicated power, and where else was he to look?' The majority acquiesced in the change because they wished to have the threat of social revolution removed.

Mussolini did not assume dictatorial powers. He told the Chamber of Deputies:

> With 300,000 youths, fully armed, fully determined and almost mystically ready to act at my command, I could have kicked out parliament and constructed a government exclusively of *Fascisti*. I could have done so, but I did not want to, at least not for the present.

Mussolini's assumption of dictatorship was gradual. During the first year of power, the prefectures, the offices of police and the key positions in the national bureaucracy were filled with Fascist nominees. He abolished the Royal Guards and transformed the Fascist militia *Squadristi* into a national party militia paid by the state. In April 1923, he broke with the Popolari, while retaining Liberals and Nationalists in his government. Then he secured the passage of bill—the so-called Acerbo Law of 1923—which changed the electoral law. By the law, whichever party obtained the largest number of votes in a national election was entitled to two-thirds of the seats in the Chamber of Deputies. The remaining seats were to be divided among the other parties on a proportional basis. In the elections of April 1924, the Fascists obtained four and a half million votes out of a total of seven and a half million. The Fascists, therefore, were given two-thirds of the seats in the new Chamber.

The drift toward totalitarianism now moved faster. On June 10, 1924, Giacomo Matteotti, leader of the Socialists in the Chamber, and the most virulent opponent of Mussolini, was murdered. The event aroused such national indignation that Mussolini felt it necessary to dismiss his chief of police and make other concessions. The opposition deputies, instead of taking advantage of this popular mood to curb Mussolini, withdrew from the Chamber of Deputies. This 'Aventine secession', as it was called, left Mussolini in absolute control of parliament. Secession was not the only remedy to oust Fascism.

Mussolini, however, was too quick to weather the political storm. In January 1925 he declared in the Chamber, 'I alone accept the political, moral and historical responsibility for everything that has happened.' In the course of 1925, Mussolini made himself supreme in Italy. Non-Fascist members of the ministry were dismissed and all other parties were dissolved. The law of May 18 allowed the dismissal of any official who differed from the policy of the Government. Local government was made subservient to Fascist control. All local elections were stopped and the power of the Prefect under the Minister of the Interior was made absolute. After 1925 the Prefects, like other civil servants, were purged of non-Fascists. Freedom of the press disappeared. The power of the Prefect was increased. He could dismiss any editor warned twice within a year. The Law on Public Security of November 1926 instituted the penalty of political exile, reintroduced the death penalty, and deprived the individual of any right to appeal against the state. Independence of the judiciary disappeared. After 1926 Italy became a police state as the Fascists believed that the individual had no rights against the state.

Machinery of Government

Mussolini had no intention to do away with the governmental machinery. The king was still the nominal sovereign. The bicameral legislature, composed of the Senate and Chamber of Deputies, was allowed to continue. But both Houses became exclusively Fascist and their powers were nominal. The Prime Minister or Mussolini was given the right to initiate all legislation and to govern by decree. He had extensive rights of appointment and all persons including the ministers of state were responsible to him.

As in the Soviet Union, the whole government was dominated by the Fascist party. The members of the party were distributed among some 10,000 local *fasci*, which were federated by provinces. At the head of the party pyramid was the Fascist Grand Council, a body of about twenty men. The Chairman of the Grand Council was the Prime Minister of the country. The Council not only ruled the party and shaped its policies, but also nominated candidates for parliament. In 1928 it was provided that the Council must be consulted on all matters affecting the constitution, the royal succession, the powers of the Prime Minister and other important issues. The Grand Council had at its disposal a special body of Fascist militia and a special tribunal of Fascist magistrates to impose its will. In reality, the real authority was wielded by the Grand Council's Chairman (Mussolini) and the party's Secretary General. Party membership was a prerequisite for a political career.

Corporate State

One of the chief objectives of the Fascist rule was to establish a corporate state in order to promote mutual understanding between capital and labour and to eliminate class conflict. An enactment of 1926 abolished the non-Fascist trade unions and political strikes and lockouts. At the same time it established thirteen "syndicates" (six of employers, six of employees, and one of professional men) under whose joint auspices labour courts were established to deal with labour disputes. In 1927 a "Charter of Labour" was enacted. The Charter dealt mainly with guarantees to the workers like eight hours a day or six days a week, and a broad social insurance programme. In 1928 the electoral law entrusted the thirteen syndicates to nominate parliamentary candidates numbering about 1,000. From this list, the Fascist Grand Council would select 400, the requisite number of the composition of the Chamber of Deputies. In 1930 Mussolini inaugurated a National Council of Corporations composed of representatives from the thirteen syndicates. The Council was to supervise the official employment bureaus and promote production. In 1934 were created 22 new corporations, each of which represented the state, capital and labour and embraced as well agriculture, industry and services. Their functions were to settle labour disputes, and to regulate production, distribution and prices. In 1938 a new legislative body called "the Chamber of Fasces and Corporations" was created by superseding the Chamber of Deputies. It was composed of 700 "National Councillors" representing the state, the Fascist Party, and 22 Corporations. All members were appointed by Mussolini.

The corporate activity of the state, in reality, was a fraud, a cloak to cover the harsh realities of totalitarianism. It satisfied the industrialists and landlords by putting a curb on effective labour organisation. The London *Economist* pointed out in 1935 that,

> the new corporative state only amounts to the establishment of new and costly bureaucracy, from which those industrialists who can spend the necessary amount can obtain almost anything they want and put into practice the worst kind of monopolistic practices at the expense of the little fellow who is squeezed out in the process.

Lateran Treaty and Concordat with Pope

The most important achievement of Mussolini was a settlement with the Catholic Church. The Pope occupied a preeminent position; he was the Vicar of Christ and, as such, the earthly head of the Roman Catholic Church, In February 1929 Mussolini healed a festering sore in the body politic by concluding the Treaty of the Lateran with Pope Pius XI. The Treaty recognised the Vatican as a State with access to the sea, and the Pontiff as an international person. In return the Pope recognised the Kingdom of Italy and renounced his claim to former papal estates. Supplementary agreements provided for the payment to the Pope a sum of about 100 million dollars. The Concordat established the future relations of Church and state. It gave the Pope the right to appoint all bishops in Italy in due consultation with the Italian government. The state continued to pay the salaries of bishops and priests and exacted an oath of loyalty from them. There were important clauses in the Concordat concerning education and marriage. Religious instruction was made compulsory in schools. Marriage was recognised as a sacrament by the state; no divorce was permitted.

Domestic Policies of Mussolini

Mussolini tried to improve the financial conditions of Italy. The budget was balanced by 1926 and foreign war debts were paid off. In 1932 Mussolini inaugurated the outlines of a planned economy. A board was established, without whose consent no new factories could be opened. Long-term loans were advanced to viable enterprises. New public works were started.

Mussolini tried to make the country self-sufficient by reducing the country's dependence on wheat, cotton and tobacco. To increase wheat production, he began a 'Battle of Wheat'. In 1933, he imposed heavy customs duties on the import of wheat. The railways were reorganised. Steamships were built for transoceanic service, and the Italian merchant marine reached in 1935 a tonnage almost equal to the French or the German. New cable lines were laid. The radio industry was encouraged. A law of 1930 doubled the duties on automobiles giving the Fiat Automobile Company a virtual monopoly of the Italian market. To offset her lack of coal and iron Italy developed a remarkable reservoir of hydroelectric power which was more than twice the developed water power of any other country.

Trade pacts were signed with many countries, including the then Soviet Union. Reclamation projects, especially in the Campagna and Pontine

Marshes, were undertaken. Airlines were subsidized. The imposition of limited League sanction during Italy's venture in Ethiopia, 1935-36, put a severe strain upon her economic structure. Mussolini, therefore, tried to secure "in the shortest possible time, the maximum degree of economic independence." In 1935 all foreign trade became a function of the state. Private commercial banks were converted into state institutions in 1936. Shipbuilding became a national enterprise in 1937. A ten per cent levy was imposed on the capital of stock companies in 1937. Drastic regulation of banking and currency was undertaken.

The Fascist regime achieved singular success in the field of popular education. Attendance in elementary schools increased from three million to four and a half million in the first decade of their power. Illiteracy was considerably reduced. In 1935 it was less than a fifth, and in northern Italy it was fast reaching zero. Great emphasis in elementary schools was laid on inculcating military virtues and 'Fascist culture'. Every teacher had to swear to uphold the existing government and refrain from anti-Fascist activity. The curricula and textbooks were Fascist in principle and aim.

Fascist Doctrine

Fascism was declared to be the antithesis of liberalism and democracy and socialism. Fascism elevated authoritarianism and destroyed man's essential nobility by promoting individualism and materialism. The most characteristic features of Fascism were national discipline and anti-Semitism. Mussolini lent an air to the first with his slogan 'Believe, obey and fight'. The philosopher Giovanni Gentile wrote: 'Fascism means to take life seriously. Life is toil, effort, sacrifice, hard-work; a life in which we know very well that there is neither matter nor time nor amusement.' In 1938 a group of Italian professors published a report that became the sheet-anchor for an anti-Semitic campaign. The glorifications of the state and the heroic virtues were emphasised with monotonous regularity by the Fascist leaders. The most vocal critic of the Fascist doctrines was Benedetto Croce, Italy's greatest philosopher. He declared on May 1, 1925, that Fascism was 'an incoherent and bizarre mixture of appeals ... flight from culture and sterile teachings toward a culture without a basis, mystical languors and cynicism.' In the actual practice of Fascism there was little that could be called noble virtue. The novels of Alberto Moravia (especially *The Indifferent Ones*) exposed the hollowness of Fascism and the devastating record of corruption.

Foreign Policy of Mussolini

Mussolini asserted that Italy must be an expanding power and that "imperialism is the basis of life for every people which tends to expand economically and spiritually." Italy did not like to be thwarted by its just desires by any treaty or by the League of Nations. Mussolini entertained the greatest contempt for the League of Nations. "Fascism", he said in 1921, "does not believe in the vitality and the principles of the so-called League of Nations". After assuming power, he warned Europe that Italy had no intention of maintaining the *status quo* just for the sake of peace. "We cannot afford the luxury of a policy of foolish altruism or of acing entirely in the interest of others."

Mussolini found a pretext for war when, in August 1923, an Italian general and his staff were killed on the Greco-Albanian border. Without ascertaining the real perpetrator of the deed, Mussolini sent an ultimatum to the Greek government and bombarded and occupied the Greek island of Corfu. When Greece appealed to the League of Nations, the Western Powers arranged the return of Corfu to Greece in return for the payment of damages to Italy.

Mussolini entertained deep animosity towards France as the latter disregarded Italy's legitimate claims at the peace conference. Moreover, some Italians maintained that Tunisia, Corsica, Savoy and Nice, all in the possession of France, belonged of right to Italy. Moreover, Franco-Italian relations became strained owing to quarrels between Italy and France's allies, especially Yugoslavia.

Without entering into needless competition with France, Mussolini tried to detach the Little Entente Powers from its security system. He made efforts to consolidate Italian power in Eastern Europe. In 1923, Italy acquired Dodecanese islands and, in 1924, Fiume. In 1925 Italy signed the Nettuno Convention with Yugoslavia. The Convention, while granting the citizens of Yugoslavia some commercial rights in Italy, permitted the Italians to hold land in certain parts of Yugoslavia. This provoked so much opposition in Yugoslavia that the treaty was not ratified till 1928. The Italo-Yugoslavia quarrel was heightened by the establishment of an Italian protectorate over Albania. On April 5, 1927, Italy concluded treaty with Hungary. This added apprehension to the powers of the Little Entente which was partially compensated by the signature of Franco-Yugoslavia treaty on November 11, 1927.

By 1927, Italy began to veer towards the revisionist powers. But the attitude, however, remained one of opportunistic vacillation until 1936. Franco-Italian relations took a new turn when negotiations on North African controversies were set afoot on November 30, 1927. Already on September 3, 1927, France and Italy had reached accord with regard to the anti-Fascist Italian refugees in France. On June 5, 1928, Mussolini referred with moderation to the possible revision of the Peace Treaties according to Article 19 of the Covenant of the League of Nations. In the spring of 1928, Britain, France and Spain invited Italy to participate in the international government of the free city of Tangier on the west coast of Africa.

In 1930 Mussolini announced a large increase in the Italian navy and disclosed the future programme of imperialism. He did not mince words when he told his Black Shirts in 1930:

> Words are very fine things, but rifles, machine-guns, warships, airplanes and cannon are still finer things. They are finer because right without might is an empty word.

On the occasion of the ninth anniversary of the March on Rome (1931), Mussolini advocated revision of the peace treaties in favour of Italy. In 1932 Foreign Minister Dino Grandi proclaimed the paramount necessity of a territorial redistribution in North Africa. In the same year, Mussolini dismissed his foreign minister Grandi and assumed his functions. In 1934 Britain took the initiative in readjusting the boundary between Egypt and Cyrnenaica (in north eastern Libya).

The World Depression (1929-1934) suited Mussolini. It gave Italy new opportunities to extend her influence, particularly over Austria and Hungary. The Rome Protocols of March 1934 provided Italy a much-needed market for their goods. In this year Mussolini took the initiative in championing Austrian independence against Hitler. The threat from Germany made him turn towards Abyssinia, the only independent native state left in Africa, except Liberia. Moreover, Abyssinia lay between the existing Italian colonies of Somaliland and Eritrea; and it was reputed to possess mineral wealth. Italy found pretext for intervention when in December 1934 took place a clash between the Abyssinian forces and a detachment of troops from Italian Somaliland near the village of Walwal. A few Italians were killed in that action; and the Italian Government demanded an apology and a substantial indemnity from Abyssinia.

Early in 1935 Abyssinia appealed to the League for arbitration. Before the League had time to take any decision, France and Italy signed a pact at Rome in January 1935. France was in desperate need of Italian friendship in Europe owing to political changes in Germany and threat to Austrian independence. The Laval-Mussolini Pact settled some outstanding colonial differences and agreed to consult if Austrian independence were threatened. Mussolini also secured Laval's acquiescence in a forward Italian policy in Abyssinia.

Abyssinia's request for the League's arbitration was dictated by the Italo-Abyssinian agreement of 1928 by which the two powers promised each other 'constant peace and perpetual friendship' and agreed to submit all disputes to a 'procedure of conciliation and arbitration.' On September 3, 1935, the arbitrators reached their unanimous decision that neither government was to be held responsible for the incident at Walwal.

Meanwhile at the League Council's suggestion, representatives of Britain, France and Italy met at Paris in August to seek a solution of the Abyssinian problem. All the three States were parties to the 1906 agreement in which they had declared to maintain intact the integrity of Abyssinia. Now Britain and France agreed to give Italy extensive economic rights in Abyssinia. Mussolini, however, rejected this offer. The League, therefore, took up the matter once more and appointed a neutral committee of conciliation. The conciliation committee drafted a plan for the international development of Abyssinia with a recognition of Italy's special interests. Though the Emperor Haile

Selassie accepted the plan in principle, Mussolini rejected it.

Britain took up a stern attitude towards Italy as she feared that Italy's Abyssinian venture might endanger British predominance along the Red Sea and in northeastern Africa. The new British Foreign Secretary, Sir Samuel Hoare, emphatically declared at the Assembly, on September 11, 1935, of the British Government's intention to carry out its obligation under the Covenant. On October 3, 1935, Italy invaded Abyssinia. On October 7, a Committee of the Council drafted a report pronouncing that Italy had "resorted to war in disregard of its obligation under Article 12 of the Covenant." Next day this report was adopted by the members of the Council, Italy alone dissenting from it. Two days later, the Assembly invoked the sanctions of Article 16 against Italy and set up a coordinating committee to implement it. Soon thereafter, the coordinating committee invited all members of the League (1) to prohibit all loans or credits from their respective countries to Italy, (2) to place an embargo on exports to Italy of war material, and (3) to place an embargo on all imports from Italy. These measures were approved by all members of the League, except Austria, Hungary and Albania. Though the rusty sanctions machinery of the League had for the first time been in operation, it fell far short of expectation. England and France were determined from the first to avoid putting any pressure upon Italy as might involve them in war. In December 1935, Sir Samuel Hoare had consulted with M. Laval, and the latter said in the French Chamber of Deputies:

> We found ourselves instantaneously in agreement upon ruling out military sanctions, not adopting any measure of naval blockade, never contemplating the closure of the Suez Canal—in a word ruling, out everything that might lead to war.

In December 1935 Hoare and Laval agreed on a plan whereby Italy was to keep most of the extensive territory she had conquered by that date, while Abyssinia was to get in exchange a narrow corridor to the Red Sea through Eritrea. The Chamberlain cabinet, in the face of unmistakable public condemnation, repudiated it. Hoare resigned and was succeeded by Eden. When Secretary Eden proposed oil sanctions in early 1936, French Foreign Minister Flandin suggested a policy of appeasement.

While all these events were taking place, Italian advance in Abyssinia proceeded at a quick pace. At last on May 1, 1936, the Emperor of Abyssinia left the country and on May 5 Italian troops entered Addis Ababa. On May 9, Italy formally annexed Abyssinia and King Victor Emmanuel was proclaimed Emperor of Abyssinia. 'It was the moment of his life in which he savoured his greatest triumph... possibly for the first time he was enjoying the unqualified admiration and support of the whole nation.'

A decree of 1936 united Ethiopia, Eritrea and Italian Somaliland into Italian East Africa. After the Abyssinian War, Italy drew closer to Germany as the latter had not participated in the sanctions against Italy. Moreover, Italy, along with Germany, supported General Franco in the Spanish Civil War that began in 1936. Italy and Germany, therefore, reached a general understanding which Mussolini first called an 'axis.' In 1937, Mussolini began to endorse Hitler's actions. He took less interest in the protection of Austria against Nazi advances and supported the German-Japanese Pact against communism. In 1938, he acquiesced in the German absorption of Austria and gave unqualified support over Germany's claim on Sudetenland. In 1939 he justified Germany's absorption of Bohemia, Moravia and Memel land and concluded a formal military alliance with Hitler. Italy had designs on Albania. On the Good Friday of 1939, Italian soldiers landed on the Albanian coast and on the next day entered Tirana. There was little resistance—King Zog fled. Albania was joined to Italy. Victor Emmanuel III added to his titles of King of Italy and Emperor of Ethiopia the title of King of Albania. Apart from Germany, who was Italy's ally, the other Powers acquiesced in this latest aggression.

CHAPTER 35

GERMANY : DRIFT TOWARDS WAR

Towards the end of the First World War, popular discontent in Germany spread far and wide. At the end of September 1918, Ludendorff demanded for an immediate armistice. Convinced that unless a civilian constitutional government was established, the Allies would not negotiate, Prince Max of Baden was appointed a new Chancellor. In the course of October the Reichstag passed a series of laws which not only provided for ministerial responsibility to parliament but virtually eliminated the royal power of command over the armed forces. These changes were followed by the dismissal of Ludendorff and the appointment of General Groener.

Despite the abdication of the kings of Saxony, Bavaria and Wurtemberg and of other German rulers, Emperor William II refused to abdicate believing that he had the support of the nation. This strengthened the belief that the government was not serious in its peace efforts. War-weariness, hunger, disillusionment led to a series of revolts. A naval mutiny at Kiel on October 28, 1918 spread to other coastal towns—Lubeck, Bremen, Hamburg and engulfed other areas like Hanover, Magdeburg, Oldenburg, Cologne, Dresden and Leipzig. On November 9, a Constituent Soldiers, Workers and Peasants Council was established in Munich under the leadership of the Independent Socialist Kurt Eisner. He proclaimed the establishment of a democratic and social republic of Bavaria. This event sealed the fate of the Hohenzollern dynasty. On the same day Prince Max announced the resignation of his government. Friedrich Ebert, the head of the Majority Socialist Party, was named as the Chancellor who announced his determination to establish a 'people's government' and to bring peace to the German people as soon as possible. William II resigned himself to the inevitable and fled across the border into Holland.

Ebert was a man who believed in the orderly methods towards the consolidation of democracy. He shared the views of Friedrich Stampfer, the editor of a Socialist newspaper: 'Socialism is organisation. Disorganisation is the worst enemy of socialism.' Ebert was challenged by the Spartacus Union, the German Communist Party which had two outstanding leaders, Kart Liebknecht and the remarkable Polish revolutionary, Rosa Luxemburg. To counteract the threat of the extreme left, Ebert allied himself with Groener, the supreme army Command.

The Communist menace was not real. Subsequent events proved the uncertainty of a leftist putsch. On November 25, the Prime Ministers of all German states met and opted for the Constituent Assembly. The Workers' and Soldiers' Council from all Germany met on December 16-21. It too came out for the Constituent Assembly and wished for a greater degree of demilitarisation and the restoration of economy.

From December 23, 1918, Germany witnessed a series of new disorders. On the same day, the People's Naval Division surrounded the Reich Chancellery and for the time held the government captive. On January 5, 1919, 200,000 workers, carrying flags and weapons, marched in the streets of Berlin. The Spartacist menace assuming serious proportion, Ebert abandoned the policy of vacillation and took the offensive against the Spartacists in Berlin. At the end of December, 1918 he appointed Gustav Noske, a Social

Democrat, as Minister of Defence and empowered him to raise a force capable of defending the government. Noske's instrument was 'Free Corps,' all composed of trained soldiers, 'true condottieri, without any principle or belief other than that of the bullet in the back'.

On the night of January 5-6, 1919, the Spartacists (now the Communist Party) made a serious attempt to capture the city of Berlin. For four days Ebert and his colleagues were besieged in the city. On January 10, the Free Corps began their advance into the city. The Reinhard Brigade (named after its commander) successfully assaulted Spartacist headquarters at Spandau. Other bands fanning out in different directions successfully liquidated the remaining centres of resistance. Among the communist casualties were Karl Liebknecht and Rosa Luxemburg who were murdered without any excuse. 'Those brutal murders inflicted a wound upon the German working-class movement from which it did not recover'. In February and March 1919 the Free Corps liquidated Spartacists' insurrections in Bremen, Cuxhaven, Dusseldorf and Halle. In March a second Spartacist rising in Berlin was crushed ruthlessly. On March 18, Groner wrote to Noske: 'The High Command has confidence in the Government, limited confidence in the Ministry of War, and unlimited confidence only in the Minister of Defence.' In April and May, Magdeburg, Dresden and Leipzig were purged of Spartacists and in June order was restored in Munich.

A National Assembly was elected in January 1919 and met at Weimar, the home of Goethe, on February 6, to work out a new constitution. Out of 423 deputies in the assembly only 187 were Socialists, the Catholic centre numbered 91 and the new Democratic Party 75. The new constitution guaranteed the basic personal liberties and introduced universal suffrage for men and women over twenty; it also introduced proportional representation which led to a proliferation of parties. It also introduced initiative and referendum, but unaccompanied by safeguards against misuse, it led to unfortunate results.

The first Article proclaimed the German Reich as a republic, and extolled the power of the people. The executive power was vested in the President, who was elected by direct vote of the people for a period of seven years and given wide powers. In addition to the command of the armed forces the President had the right to appoint and dismiss the Chancellor, to dissolve parliament and order new elections. Article 48 gave him absolute power in an emergency. Friedrich Ebert used Article 48 but never abused it. Only after his death in 1925 did the Article foreshadow danger. The President might be removed by a popular referendum following impeachment by a two-thirds vote in the Lower House.

The Constitution provided for a bicameral legislature. The Upper Chamber or Reichsrat had only nominal powers. All real authority was centred in the Reichstag, the members of which were elected by popular vote with proportional representation. All legislation was to originate in the Reichstag.

One of the striking features of the Constitution was that it diminished the powers of the separate states. The federal states lost their financial control over the Reich government. But while they acknowledged the Reich's exclusive jurisdiction over foreign and colonial affairs, national defence, currency, custom duties, posts, telegraphs and railways, the separate states retained much power. They had concurrent rights in civil and criminal law, religion, education and social welfare. 'The constitution-makers were anxious to preserve a united front of all parties in the face of the Allies and therefore allowed the states to continue in existence, but they phrased the constitution in such a way as to make them powerless'.[1]

Religious freedom was guaranteed and there was no state-supported church in the Reich. Teachers became public officials. Education was made compulsory until the age of eighteen. The constitution specified a uniform type of elementary school for all children. The most notable feature was to raise the status of women's secondary education. Provision was made for state insurance

1. Taylor, A. J. P.: *The Course of German History*, P. 213.

systems against sickness, accident, old age and unemployment.

Antirepublican Forces

In the four years that followed the promulgation of the Weimar Constitution the Republic was in throes of constant crises. At both extremes of the political spectrum stood the opposing forces. On the left were the Communists and the left wing of the Independent Socialists, who believed that the Majority Socialists had betrayed the revolution. On the right were the Nationalists composed of monarchists, landowners and industrialists, who regarded the Majority Socialists as being as dangerous as the Bolsheviks. Apart from the tiny group of Progressives, now called the Democratic Party, the Weimar Republic had few friends. The only hope of the Republic was the army—100,000 *Reichswehr* authorised by treaty whose patriotism could not be doubted. But they had a tendency to arrogate to themselves the right to determine what was the best interest of the Reich they served. Thus the army became a state within the state. General Hans Von Seeckt, Chief of the Army Command from 1920 to 1926, made every arrangement, even in collaboration with Russia, to strengthen the German army in violation of the military clauses of the Versailles Treaty.

The Treaty of Versailles (June 28, 1919) gave the final blow to the cause of democracy in Germany. Scheidemann, the Social Democrat who had become Chancellor when Ebert was elected President, burst forth in anger: 'May the hand wither that signs this treaty.' On June 20, therefore, Scheidemann submitted the resignation of his cabinet to Ebert.

The first Cabinet crisis that confronted the Republic was the soldiers' revolt. The Treaty of Versailles—which reduced the German army to 100,000 officers and men, without aircraft and offensive weapons—proved to be humiliating to the Germans. This led to resentment, secret conferences between the officers affected and hatching of plot to overthrow the regime. Under the leadership of General von Luttwitz and Wolfgang Kapp, an East Prussian politician, the army tried to overthrow the republican government. In February 1920, when the government ordered the disbandment of two first rate corps, their commanders appealed to Luttwitz, the commandant of Berlin, and the latter demanded from Ebert the revocation of the order. Ebert rejected the demand outright, and asked General Luttwitz to obey the government's order or to resign. On the morning of March 13, the rebel troops entered Berlin and met with no resistance from General Seeckt, the Army Chief of Staff. Seeckt's argument was that the army could not fire upon its wartime comrades. Ebert and his colleagues retreated to Stuttgart and the troops proclaimed a new government under Kapp's leadership.

The general strike that followed made a quick end of Kapp's government which had no clear idea of what it intended to do after the seizure of power. The general strike reawakened hopes of revolution among the Communists and spread to Ruhr, Dusseldorf and other industrial areas. Though Seeckt had failed to defend the Republic in March 1920, he was now quick to restore order. Gustav Noske lost his post and regular elections for a Reichstag were called. In the election (June 6, 1920) all three members of the Weimar coalition suffered severe losses. The Nationalists, People's Party, and Independent Socialists all gained seats, while the Communists won 4 seats. Finding no other alternative, as the Weimar coalition controlled only 205 of the Reichstag's 452 seats, Ebert formed the first all-bourgeois government leaning heavily on the People's Party, Centrists and Democrats. Konstantin Fehrenbach, a Centrist, became Chancellor. No wonder Rosen-berg, a distinguished historian of the Left, described the elections of June 1920 as 'a catastrophe for the Weimar Republic'.

The Kapp affair did not put an end to troubles of the Weimar Republic. All the ills of the time were blamed by the extremists on the Republic's acceptance of the Versailles Treaty. They, therefore, unleashed a veritable reign of terror against persons connected with the signing of the peace treaty. Jews and Catholics were attacked, and abortive attempts were made upon the lives of Ebert and Scheidemann. The Centrist leader, Erzberger, who had signed the Armistice in

November 1918, was murdered on August 26, 1921. In June 1922, a band of youngmen killed Walther Rathenau, a Jew and successful industrialist, who was considered by them to be the embodiment of the policy of fulfilment.

The year 1923 was highly critical as the Republic had to weather a severe storm. On August 13, 1923, President Ebert named Gustav Stresemann as Chancellor. He was genuinely shocked by the murders of Erzberger and Rathenau, but he was ready to face the challenge. There was a resurgence of Communism in Saxony and Thuringia. But the Chancellor had to worry about the situation in Bavaria. The Bavarian politics had been dominated since 1920 by Gustav von Kahr, a man of inflexibly reactionary views. His object was to strike a major blow against the Reich Government. But the situation was saved for the Berlin government by Adolf Hitler who, along with Ludendorff, attempted to seize power in Munich on November 9. 1923. Hitler declared that both the Reich and Bavarian governments were deposed and that the 'National Revolution' had begun. He compelled Kahr and his followers to pledge their support for his government. But the art of political hijacking was too much for the Bavarian leaders. They publicly repudiated their agreement with him, with the result that the plotters began to fight among themselves. The result was that Ludendorff, Hitler and his lieutenants were captured and imprisoned. 'The Beer Hall Putsch' (as it was called) of Hitler eliminated the last threat to republican authority. The restoration of order added much to the external prestige of the Reich government.

Reparation and Inflation

The normal state of the Weimar Republic was crisis. Apart from the humiliation of the peace terms the Republic was plagued with economic crises. The Republican government wrestled with the reparation payments and adverse trade balances. The inflation was due to the fiscal policy of the Imperial Government during the war years, and especially in its decision to finance the war by loans rather than taxes. As a result, paper money increased in circulation and the currency value of the mark had declined to about half of its gold parity by 1918. The situation became worse by the magnitude of the financial and economic burdens imposed upon Germany by the Allied powers. The purpose and scope of reparation of the Paris Conference embittered the relations of the Allied powers so much that an American expert, Norman H. Davis wrote:

> Some of the delegates wanted to destroy Germany, some wanted to collect reparations, and others wanted to do both. Some wanted to collect more than Germany had agreed to pay or could pay: and others wanted to take all her capital, destroy her, and then collect a large reparation bill.

The Allied Powers decided not to set a definite figure of reparation until the Reparation Commission had made a thorough study of the matter. Meanwhile some payments were to be made between August 1919 and May 1, 1921. In the spring of 1920, because of strikes and internal disorder, Germany failed to honour its commitment in the delivery of commodities. She was invited to offer alternate plans for payment at a conference at Spa in July 1920. The conference proved to be a fiasco owing to the arrogant attitude of German delegates. In January 1921, therefore, an impossible arrangement was made that required the Germans to make annual payment during the next forty-two years and a payment of 26 per cent of the proceeds of German exports. When Germany rejected this 'preposterous plan' the Allied governments resorted to sanctions, occupied the towns of Dusseldorf, Duisburg and impounded the customs receipts of the occupied territories.

Hardly had the German government recovered from the shock, when it was presented with the exact amount of reparation debt produced by the Reparation Commission in April 1921. Germany was informed that the total sum was 132 billion gold marks. The Allies sent an ultimatum to the German Government on May 5, 1921, demanding unconditional acceptance of the total obligation and the payment of a billion gold marks within twenty-five days. Germany paid but only by selling newly printed paper currency on the foreign currency exchanges. As a result, depreciation was accelerated and the inflation was now tremendously stimulated. By October 1921 Chancellor

Wirth with Rathenau's assistance had secured a revision of the arrangement, which at last lessened the amount to be paid in money and increased that to be paid in commodities. Cuno, a Director of the Hamburg-American Steamship Line, was then made Chancellor in the hope that his place in the business would secure greater degree of collaboration between government and business. But the reparation problem proved to be intractable and Cuno found that he was in no better a position in this regard than his predecessor. The Reparation Commission at the end of 1922 declared Germany in default. On January 12, 1923, French and Belgian troops occupied Ruhr simply to induce Germany to pay. German Government answered this action with a policy of passive resistance. This meant the stoppage of production and the eventual unemployment among the Germans.

The situation indeed was difficult when the government failed to raise new revenues. The crisis was heightened when the industrialists refused to subscribe to loans. It was not until August, when the country was experiencing a food riot, that representatives of industry agreed to a sizeable loan. The great defect of Cunos's tax policy was that it did not produce enough revenue to meet its obligations. The result was the excess of government expenditure over income. These deficits were covered by 'Floating debts' by recklessly printing notes. By the end of 1923, 1,783 printing presses were turning out Reichsbank notes at top speed. The effect of this upon the value of the mark was catastrophic. Inflation assumed such a menacing proportion that the protagonist of Erich Maria Remarque's *Drei Kameraden* says:

> In 1923 I was advertising chief of a rubber factory. That was during the inflation. I had a monthly salary of 200 billion marks. We were paid twice a day, and then everybody had a half-hour's leave so that he could rush to the stores and buy something before the next quotation on the dollar came out, at which time the money would lose half its value.

Though the inflation hit the self-employed middle class and the working class, it provided many opportunities for gifted speculators. Some of the largest of Germany's industries became larger as a result of the inflation. Among the many examples, the example of Hugo Stinnes could be cited. Stinnes was a man of substance before 1918, but when he died in April 1924, he had large shares in 69 construction companies, 66 chemical, paper and sugar works, 59 mines, 57 bank and insurance companies, 56 steel and iron works, 37 oil fields and petroleum factories, 100 metallurgical works, 389 commercial and transport concerns, 83 railway and shipping companies. The inflation had menacing social and political results. Between June and August 1923, a wave of strikes swept across the country. People turned to demagogues for salvation whom they would ordinarily have shunned.

Stresemann Era, 1923-29

With the appointment of Gustav Stresemann as Chancellor on August 13, 1923, the appearance of stability increased. He was the first German statesman since the time of Bismarck who had learnt wisdom and expediency from the pressure of events. His task was more difficult than that of Bismarck. Bismarck had won the support of the King of Prussia, but Stresemann had to govern a Germany that had been defeated. It was Stresemann's ambition to restore Germany to its pristine place, which he knew could not be accomplished by defying the Allies or by making empty threats. He once said the Nationalists would not 'learn that you can get nowhere by sabre-rattling, especially when you have no sabre in your scabbard'.

After his assumption of office, Stresemann called off the passive resistance to the French invasion of the Ruhr which was depleting the resources of the government by providing subsidies to the resisters. This courageous step which averted a total economic collapse in Germany was followed by Stresemann's assuming extraordinary powers to take any measures necessary for the economic health of the country. He was considerably helped in carrying out his policy by Hajalmar Schacht, the President of the Reichsbank, and Hans Luther, the Minister of Finance. Printing of paper currency was halted and a new currency, the so-called *Rentenmark*, was issued. The new currency had no gold basis and was not convertible; it was covered by mortgage bonds based on the assets of industry and agriculture. Schacht prevented the new currency from being devalued by imposing rigid limits on the amount issued, by cutting off new credits to industry and by compelling the speculators to sell the $1^1/_2$ billion dollars of foreign currency. The virtual doubling of the bank's gold foreign exchange reserves that followed from 1924, and the simultaneous cutback in government expenditure, balanced the budget and the inflation came to an end.

Meanwhile, Stresemann had appealed to the Western Powers for a new approach to the reparation problem. On October 12, 1923, the British Government had asked the United States whether it would be willing to take part in an enquiry of reparation problem by an international commission of financial experts. Despite French objections, the commission met under the Chairmanship of the American banker, Charles G. Dawes. The Dawes Plan regulated German reparation payments for the next five years. It laid down that Germany should meet reparation charges from her customs, railways and industry, and it organised their transfer to her creditors through the *Reichsbank*.

The schedule of payments was modified in the German interest. After a final conference in London in August, the Plan went into operation on September 1, 1924. The Plan offered tangible advantages—it freed the Ruhr from French occupation and encouraged the Western nations to advance new credit to Germany. Stresemann was not vainglorious when he said: 'The policy of the London conference carried with it not only the idea of an economic and financial settlement, but a settlement of the whole world-political situation'.

Stresemann's Foreign Policy

After a hectic three months as Chancellor, Gustav Stresemann was defeated in the Reichstag in November 1925; this was due to the defection of the Social Democrats. But in every succeeding cabinet from the time of his fall until his death in 1929, he occupied the post of Foreign Minister. It was in this particular field he accomplished his greatest work and in the words of Lord D' Abernon, the British Ambassador to Germany, "raised Germany from the position of a stricken and disarmed foe into that of a diplomatic equal". To D'Abernon, Stresemann seemed like a German Winston Churchill. He had resilience, finesse and great courage. "Probably he remained an intense, even a romantic nationalist, but he saw that German nationalism might be better served by subtle diplomacy than by showing one's teeth."[2]

The first stage in the accomplishment of the foreign policy was the negotiation of the Locarno Treaties. The Rapallo Treaty (1922) with Russia had given Germany her ally in the east. He, therefore, put forward a proposal to Britain for an international guarantee of the status quo in Western Europe. He found ready response from Chamberlain of Britain and Briand of France. After a series of Franco-British consultations the representatives of the Powers met on October 5, 1925, at Locarno in Switzerland. This eventuated in the conclusion of the Treaty of Mutual Guarantee. The states bordering on the Rhine abjured the use of force in their mutual relations and, together with Britain and Italy, guaranteed the demilitarization of the Rhineland and the existing western frontiers. Next, Germany was promised admission to the League of Nations with a permanent seat in the Council. In all these negotiations, 'Stresemann was forced to manoeuvre, in Bismarck's phrase, like a dog moving through a thick wood with a long stick in the jaws'.[3]

While welcoming the German renunciation of the use of force in the West, the French felt that a guarantee should be extended to their eastern allies. Stresemann refused to make any pledges as this would have prevented him not only to make any revision of the frontiers in the east, but also would have weakened public support of his policy. All that they obtained was Germany's signature of arbitration treaties with Poland and Czechoslovakia providing for arbitration over possible disputes. Similarly, Germany obtained exemption from the sanction obligations stipulated in Article 16 of the Covenant by which she was required to take military measures against any member of the

2. Wiskemann Elizabeth: *Europe of the Dictators*, PP. 56-57.
3. Craig Gordon A., *Germany*, 1866-1945, P. 517.

League who broke its obligations. Stresemann had reason to be satisfied with the results of Locarno. But the nationalist opinion sharply criticised the Foreign Minister.

This drew angry protest from the Chancellor, Hans Luther, who had accompanied Stresemann to Locarno:

> We have achieved one hundred per cent of what we undertook to achieve at Locarno. Never has a delegation had such a success. We were a people of helots, and today we are once more a state of world consequence!

Meanwhile, Germany's entry into the League was baulked by some states including the Soviet Union. To wean away the Soviet Government Stresemann found it expedient to sign a new agreement with her. The Treaty of Berlin (April 24, 1926) obliged each to remain neutral in the case of an attack upon the other and to consult in time of crisis. At last on September 8, 1926, Germany was voted unanimously into the League of Nations. The Treaty of Berlin was one of shock and outrage to Britain and France. Both the two Powers were now ready for further concession. The consequences were the reduction of the Allied occupation forces in Germany and the withdrawal of the International Military Control Commission in December 1926. In the beginning of 1927 Chamberlain became an eloquent champion of establishing cordial relations with Germany. In May 1927 he reminded Briand:

> We had won a success at Locarno. We had confirmed it when Germany entered the League, but the more difficult our relations with Russia became, the more important was it that we should attach Germany solidly to the Western Powers.

By August 1928 Stresemann had persuaded the French to think seriously of an early evacuation of the Rhineland and to agree to a fresh review of reparation. The outcome was the Hague Conference of 1929 which was presided over by the American banker, O. D. Young. The so-called Young Plan made a new arrangement for reparation payments by scaling down the schedule of payments set by the Dawes Plan. Under British pressure, the French agreed to evacuate the Rhineland by June 30, 1930. Stresemann—who died on October 3, 1929, at the age of fifty-one—did not live to see his cherished desire fulfilled. But during his five years tenure as Foreign Minister, Stresemann had accomplished a fair share of his objectives. His superb gifts as a negotiator, his intuitive sense to apprehend danger and to avoid it by seizing the initiative and the gift of maintaining perspective in the midst of a changing diplomatic situation accorded him an honoured place in the history of Germany.

Internal Weakness

Stresemann's impressive diplomatic achievements brought little peace to the ruffled sentiments of the Germans. His achievements did not shake the hostility of the 'national' parties to the Republic; instead they were eager to overthrow the Republic. On the death of Ebert in February 1925, the man who succeeded him as Reich President was Field Marshal von Hindenburg. Now in his seventy-seventh year, Hindenburg's election was widely regarded as a blow to the Republic. Though he took an oath to the Weimar Constitution, at heart he was anti-Republican. Moreover, 'what life was there in a republic which could find as president only a senile field-marshal of reactionary views?'

Another disturbing omen was that every diplomatic success won by Stresemann encountered deeper opposition at home. Though the Young Plan, liberating all Germany's territory, was the greatest of Stresemann's achievements, yet the strenuous exertions made by him to carry it through the Reichstag caused his death. But the greatest source of weakness of the Republic was the operation of the party system. The use of proportional representation multiplied the number of national parties and made inevitable the formation of the coalition governments. But to keep a coalition government intact requires magic wand and between February 1919 and January 1933 there were twenty-one different Reich cabinets!!

In 1924 the Reichstag that had been elected in 1920 was dissolved. In the elections of 1924, the moderate parties lost heavily, while the extremists, Right, and Left made sizable gains. Chancellor Wilhelm Marx (Centrist), therefore, resigned, but eventually effected another coalition. But when it became the target of attack of other parties, the Reichstag was dissolved and a second election was ordered in 1924. The formation of a government was rendered difficult by the election of a number of Nationalist delegates. Marx resigned owing to his antipathy towards the Nationalists, and a Centrist-people's-Nationalist coalition was formed under De Luther.

In December 1925, after eleven months in office, the Luther Ministry had to resign owing to the opposition of the Nationalists when the latter protested against the Locarno Pact. It also lost the support of other groups on domestic issues. A threat of presidential dictatorship led to the formation of another Cabinet, again by Luther. Soon this government, too, fell in May 1926. The succeeding Marx Ministry had to lead a delicate existence when it found it hard-pressed to reorganise ministry in 1927 and to admit some Nationalists. The delicate balance between the Nationalists, the Centrists and other parties did not prove satisfactory, and in 1928 the Reichstag was dissolved.

In the elections of May 1928 the Nationalists lost heavily, while the Social Democrats gained popularity. The Marx coalition, therefore, resigned, and the Social Democrat, Hermann Muller, became the first socialist Chancellor since 1920. Muller's regime was far from satisfactory. Along with economic difficulties came fierce nationalist opposition to the acceptance of the Young Plan. Then came the serious unemployment problem which affected the Germans in the winter of 1929-30. Germany was more immediately and sharply hit by the American depression than any other country in Europe. On the issue of unemployment insurance, Muller resigned in March 1930. Hindenburg forthwith appointed the leader of the Centre Party, Heinrich Bruening, to be Chancellor.

Bruening was an extremely able man who was known to stand for fiscal economics, lower salaries, and sterner taxes. He was a firm believer in the necessity of revising the arms clauses of the Versailles Treaty on Germany's behalf and he shared Field Marshal Schleicher's hostility towards Social Democracy. Groener, the Defense Minister in Muller's Cabinet, told a friend that he had never known 'a statesman, chancellor, minister, or general who combined in his head as much positive knowledge and political clarity and adaptability as Bruening'. But Bruening lacked some of the essential gifts of a statesman which politicians need if they are to be successful. To carry out a policy, he would admit of no compromise. Parliament must either accept it as a whole or see itself bypassed and the programme effected by other means. In June 1930, when he introduced the financial bill in the Reichstag, the latter refused to accept it. Bruening responded immediately by promulgating his budget with the help of the emergency decree. When the Reichstag majority passed a vote of no confidence in his policy, he dissolved the Reichstag and postponed the new election until September 14. Meanwhile he put his financial programme into effect by presidential authority.

The Chancellor and his military supporters were confident that the German people would support the policy by repudiating the Reichstag and electing a workable Reichstag. Outstanding feature of the election of September 1930 was the gain made by the Communist Party and the National Socialists. Obtaining 40 per cent more than it had polled in 1928, the Communist Party increased its membership from 54 to 77 seats. Even more amazing was the gain of the National Socialists who had increased their strength from 12 to 197 in the Reichstag. They now formed the second largest group in the Lower House, being led by the Social Democrats with 143 seats. "In 1930 parliamentary rule ceased in Germany. There followed, first, temporary dictatorship, then permanent dictatorship".[4]

Rise and Growth of National Socialism

The astonishing success of the National Socialists can be explained only in part by the prevailing economic distress of the country and the disenchantment with the Weimar party system. It was due to the political gifts and the magical appeal of their leader Adolf Hitler who had nurtured the party after the debacle of 1923.

Condemned to prison for five years in the fortress of Landsberg after the Beer Hall Putsch in Munich in 1923, Hitler was released in 1925. In his imprisonment he dictated his book *Mein Kampf* to Rudolf Hess, in which he defined his doctrine.

4. Taylor, A. J. P.: *The Course of German History*, P. 238.

It was a declaration of a belief in nothing but force. The strong, who were the Aryan or German race, were to be strengthened at the expense of the Jews and Slavs. While he took for granted that the Germans would dominate the Danubian world, he now urged that they should resume the colonisation of North-East Europe and Russia.

Adolf Hitler was, *sui generis*, a force without a real historical past. His magic force awed many who entered his presence. A political genius as he was, he combined in his own person indomitable will and self-confidence, a superb sense of timing, a mastery of the arts of propaganda and a ruthlessness in the execution of his designs. Hitler's faith and will generated a sense of confidence among his subordinates who came to believe in his mission as he did himself. Hitler had tremendous resources of patience and remarkable intuitive power. Otto Strasser, an early follower, who later broke with Hitler, said once: "Hitler responds to the vibrations of the human heart with the delicacy of a seismograph... (He possesses) an uncanny intuition, which infallibly diagnoses the ills from which his audience is suffering". Hitler showed a mastery of propaganda technique and directed his attack against the Versailles Treaty, the Young Plan, the League of Nations, the parliamentary democracy that sustained these things. In *Mein Kampf*, he stated that all propaganda must be popular and "all effective propaganda must be limited to a very few points and must harp on these in slogans"...

On emerging from prison, Hitler rebuilt his party of National Socialists, called Nazis for short. The party had a number of organs, like the political organisation which looked after foreign affairs, labour relations, agriculture, justice, and national economy. There was also a separate propaganda division, in which Hitler took personal interest, a department to study defence questions and youth organisation. He organised the party's paramilitary forces, the Storm Troopers (S.A.). There was also a second elite force, the Schutzstaffel or S.S. Originally designed as a personal bodyguard of Hitler, this body found its permanent Chief in Heinrich Himmler. At the head of the elaborate party organisation stood Hitler himself. He maintained his control of the party by sheer strength of will. Most of his close associates—Hess, Goebbles, Goering—regarded him with awe and veneration. Hitler sought to strengthen his influence among the people—especially the middle class youths who turned to National Socialism after 1929.

After a slow growth during the years 1925-29, the party gained considerably after 1929. The economic depression and the growing unemployment generated a sense of frustration among the people who sought salvation in National Socialism. Erich Kastner in his book *Fabian: The Story of a Moralist* (1932) analysed the conditions that helped to bring victory for National Socialism:

> The great unemployment, the spiritual depression that followed the economic one, the craving for oblivion, the activity of thoughtless parties, these were the storm signals of the coming crisis. Even the frightening calm before the storm was not absent—the laziness of the spirit that resembled an epidemic paralysis.

Bruening's position, after September 1930, was one of mounting difficulty. Along with growing employment, and his rigid economic programme which excited discontent and earned him the title 'Hunger Chancellor', he failed to secure diplomatic success. He sought concessions from other powers like the scaling down of the reparation payments and the regaining of his country's parity in armaments. He also demanded the abolition of the demilitarization restrictions in the Rhineland. In order to improve the economic situation, Bruening announced in March 1931 that the German and Austrian government intended to establish a customs union (*Zollunion*). France, supported by Italy and Little Entente, promptly invoked the ban of the Versailles Treaty on Austro-German union. The plan had to be submitted to the world court at Hague, where it was rejected. The rebuff which Bruening received was humiliating. The powers now blocked the concession that Bruening was seeking and led to the French Government's delay in accepting President Hoover's suggestion for a moratorium on war debts.

The result of this was a steady decline in Bruening's popularity which was reflected in an increase of domestic violence engineered by the Nazis and the Communists. In November 1931 the Frankfurt police came into possession of a set of incriminating papers for the seizure of power by the Nazis. The people were also disillusioned when Bruening failed to afford any relief and protection which they had expected from the Chancellor's emergency decrees.

President Von Hindenburg's term of office expired in the spring of 1932. To avoid a new election, Hindenburg wished that the Chancellor should persuade the Nazis and other parties to agree to prolong the presidential term. Bruening failed to achieve this owing to the truculence of Hitler. In the first poll held in March 1932, when Hitler himself stood as a candidate, the result was indecisive. In the run-off election on April 10, 1932, Hindenburg won easily with the help of the Centre and the Socialists. On the advice of the Defence Minister, Groener, the Chancellor banned by emergency decrees, Hitler's SA and SS. Schleicher, who had originally supported the ban, now complained along with other senior army officers that the dissolution of the SA was a serious blow to the country's military strength. In an attempt to divert the storm Groener himself assumed responsibility for the ban and resigned as Minister of Defence on May 13. When the Chancellor intended to push a plan for land settlement, Hindenburg refused to sign any emergency decree. This was a death sentence, and, at the end of May, Bruening resigned. Schleicher now urged Hindenburg to appoint Franz von Papen as Chancellor. Papen now headed what was quickly nicknamed the Cabinet of the Barons. His government was the high watermark of stupidity and reaction. He had a fair start when the Western Powers, at the Lausanne Conference, in June 1932, agreed to the abrogation of the Young Plan and the end of reparation. But the concessions came too late to do any good.

The first thing Papen did was to appease the Nazis by revoking the ban on the SA and SS and to promote a new election. The withdrawal of ban was followed by a spate of violence in the country. In five weeks, in Prussia alone, there were nearly 500 riots. On July 20, 1932, Papen dismissed the Prussian Government by decree on the grounds that it was incapable of maintaining public order. He now decreed himself to be Chancellor of the Reich and Reich Commissioner of Prussia at the same time. By this act Papen had sown the dragon's teeth. "Many experts felt that 20 July, 1932, was the day on which the Weimar Republic committed suicide, organised resistance to the Nazis was almost impossible after this."[5]

Neither the Prussian coup nor Papen's energetic foreign policy strengthened the government or had any effect on the Nazis at all. In the Reichstag elections of July 31, 1932, the Nazis increased the numbers of seats from 197 to 230. On August 5, Hitler demanded Chancellorship for himself and the Ministers of the Interior, Justice and Agriculture for his party; on August 13, Schleicher and Papen rejected all of his demands, offering him only the Vice-Chancellorship in the existing Cabinet. The events of August 13 alienated Hitler and he, therefore, refused to support the Government. Hitler, in revenge, forced a fresh dissolution of the Reichstag and fresh election. But his calculation went awry. In the election in November 1932 he had to give up 34 Reichstag seats. Papen was pleased, but Hitler had only lost a battle, not a war. At this juncture, 'the gentleman jockey Papen was seeking to become a real man on horseback'. He devised a constitutional reform that would transform the democratic Republic into an authoritarian state, in which popular sovereignty would be dispensed with. He gained such an ascendancy over the President Hindenburg that the latter was about to yield when Schleicher intervened. The general pointed out that Papen's scheme was both dangerous and superfluous as it might encourage Nazi and Communist rising to combat which the army was not adequately strong. Papen resigned and Schleicher became Chancellor on December 2, 1932.

Schleicher's idea was to build up a coalition between labour groups that would receive the strong backing of the army. He tried to split the Nazi party by winning the support of George Strasser, who was influential as the head of the party's political organisation. Schleicher offered Strasser the post of Vice-Chancellor in his cabinet and Strasser urged the party to consent to this. Hitler vetoed this suggestion and Strasser then

5. Wiskemann Elizabeth: *Europe of the Dictators,* 1919-45, P. 95.

resigned from the Nazi party. In the crisis of the party Hitler rose to the occasion by abolishing the political organisation that Strasser had dominated and set up a new central party office under Rudolf Hess. By this action Hitler terrified the vacillating members of the party into submission.

Unable to realise his grand design, Schleicher tried to mobilise labour support by introducing a new public works programme and by reviving land resettlement programme. But these measures failed to impress the people. On January 23, 1933, he asked for the dissolution of the Reichstag and the banning of the Nazi party by decree. Hindenburg refused and, when he learnt that the President had been conducting secret talks with Papen concerning the formation of a new government, Schleicher resigned his post.

There were two obvious successors—Papen and Hitler. Hindenburg, who did not like Hitler, made every effort to keep him out of power and wanted his favourite Papen back at his side. But Papen wavered because he believed that the only way to restore stability and stop the growth of Communism was to give Hitler the post he coveted. But Hitler must be forced to share power with other persons. By January 30, 1933, the reluctant President finally overcame his antipathy to Hitler. He agreed to accept Hitler as Chancellor of a coalition cabinet with Papen as Vice-Chancellor. The new Cabinet had only two Nazis besides Hitler, Wilhelm Frick as Minister of the Interior, and Hermann Goering as Minister without portfolio.

Consolidation of Nazi Power

Hitler had power, but he had not unlimited power which he wished to possess. Even with the support of the Nationalists, he did not command a majority of the Reichstag. Before seizing absolute power, Hitler had to move with circumspection. In the initial stage, his instrument was Hermann Goering, who, in his capacity as Prussian Minister of the Interior, supplemented the regular police with an auxiliary force of 50,000 men, four-fifths of whom were recruited from the SA and SS. Then came the presidential decree of February 4 which authorised the prohibition of newspapers or public meetings. In Joseph Goebbles, Hitler found a propagandist of genius, who manipulated press and radio to help secure a Nazi victory.

Despite this campaign of intimidation, Hitler had misgiving of Nazi party's electoral chances. He needed some pretext for frightening the other parties into giving him dictatorial power. He got it on February 27, 1933, when the Reichstag building caught fire, presumably through the initiative of the Nazi agents. Hitler laid the blame at the doorstep of the Communist Party. 4,000 Communist members were arrested. He also induced the President to sign on February 28 the most fateful of all the emergency decrees which suspended civil and individual liberties and authorised the Government to use any method it desired.

Despite all these terror tactics, the Nazis failed to secure an absolute majority in the elections of March 5, 1933. But Hitler still had powers granted by the decree of February 28. In the two weeks that followed the election, the Government sent units of the SA and SS into Wurtemberg, Baden, Bavaria, Bremen, Hamburg, Lubeck, Saxony, Hessen which replaced the legally constituted governments with Reich Commissioners. On March 23, Hitler passed on Enabling Act with necessary two-thirds majority in the Reichstag with stormtroopers howling vengeance outside the Reichstag on anyone who dared to oppose Hitler's will. Only the Socialists opposed it. The Act enabled the government to dispense with constitutional forms and limitations for a period of full years. Thus, on the afternoon of March 23, 1933, Hitler became dictator 'created by democracy and appointed by parliament,' free from any real control by his cabinet colleagues or by the President.

Then followed the process of regimentation under the guise of *Gleischaltung* or coordination (or putting into the same gear) whose purpose was to subordinate all independent agencies—administration, free press and trade unions—to his dictatorial power. In March he abolished the independent powers of the federal state. By promulgating a Law for the Restoration of the Professional Civil Service, on April 7, 1933, Hitler purged the civil service of Jews and recalcitrant elements. In Prussia, more than a quarter of the civil service was dismissed. No immediate attempt was made to purge the judiciary. But after March

1933 cases of political crime were tried before the *Sondergericht* or Special Court. Moreover, Hitler and Goering had the right to terminate criminal proceedings of which they did not approve. In addition, the Gestapo or Secret Police, created by Goering in April 1933, had the right to inflict arbitrary arrest, imprisonment in concentration camps and corporal punishment.

Hitler struck hard at all organisations that stood in his way, the trade unions especially : the autonomy of the *Lander* was suppressed, Germany becoming a highly centralised unitary state. 'The flowering of new art and literature in the Weimar period was killed by the frost of National Socialism'. On May 10, 1933, the Nazis consigned all books suspected of disseminating liberal thinking to fire. Thousands of great scholars and scientists lost or left their positions. The dismissed Jews—like Albert Einstein and a few German Christians including the Nobel prize winning writer Thomas Mann—left the country. In July 1933, Hitler concluded a Concordat with the Papacy that guaranteed the freedom of the Roman Catholic religion in Germany. But the Concordat included an article denying the Catholic clergy the right to engage in political activity. The Catholic Centre dissolved the party on July 5. During the course of summer of 1933, the remaining independent parties were disbanded. The Reich Press Law of October 4, 1933, laid down rigid censorship laws. By these methods, Hitler succeeded in annihilating "every institution that under democracy preserves remnants of human spontaneity".

By the beginning of 1934 the foundations of the totalitarian state had been truly laid. But still there were two sources of potential danger to his authority : the armed forces and his own party which had fallen prey to internal discontents. Criticism of Hitler was particularly vocal in the SA whose commander Ernst Rohm, who wished to make it the army of 'the new age', by replacing the old Reichswehr. Hitler had different views about a reorganisation of the armed forces. From the spring of 1934 Hitler was made aware of the growing dissatisfaction of the Reichswehr command over his failure to discipline Rohm. In a predawn sweep on June 30, 1934 known as Night of the Long Knives, Rohm and dozens of SA leaders were dragged out of their beds and shot. He also disposed of Gustav Kahr, who had broken with Hitler in 1923, Gregor Strasser, who parted company with Hitler in November 1932, two distinguished military officers, Kurt von Schleicher and General Von Bredow, and two of Papen's closest aides. On July 1, 1934, the Defence Minister, General Von Blomberg, congratulated Hitler in wiping out 'mutineers and traitors'.

On August 2, 1934, Hindenburg died and Hitler assumed the offices of both President and Chancellor. He became the head of state (Fuehrer) and Commander of the armed forces. Every officer and man in the armed forces were required to pay unconditional obedience to the Fuhrer.

The business of the government was performed in the various ministries of state by professional men. The Ministers of Finance and Economics had imaginative leaders in Count Schwerin von Krosigk and Hjalmar Schacht. The Reich Chancellery provided a link between Hitler and the Ministries. The government's authority was represented in the states by the Reichsstatthalter and the State Minister of the Interior Wilhelm Frick. The most effective instrument of power in the Third Reich was the SS. Accountable only to its commander and beyond him the Fuhrer himself, it exercised unfettered control over the lives and liberties of German citizens. Terror was thus the greatest of political realities in the Third Reich.

Hitler's respect for the senior army officer began to wane when he began to find murmurs of discontent among them against his ambitious foreign policy. At the beginning of February 1938, on the basis of trumped up charges, Hitler dismissed his Defence Minister, General Von Blomberg and Chief of the Army Command, General Von Fritsch, and reorganised the armed forces completely. He put the army under his immediate command by creating a new supreme command of the Armed Forces with General Keitel as his deputy.

Economic and Social Developments

Under Hitler, Germany emerged from the depression with amazing rapidity. Unemployment sank from six million in 1932 to less than one million four years later. Hitler was aware that without economic and social development Germany would not be elevated to a power of the first rank. In February 1933 he had announced that the 'national government would achieve the great task of reorganising the economy of our *Volk* by means of two great four-year plans'. He appointed in March 1933 Hjalmar Schacht as President of the Reichsbank. Under the Reinhardt Plan, named after the Secretary of State for the Finance Ministry, various public works—like the construction of roads, canals, housing complexes, machine tool and agricultural machinery—were undertaken. With the help of the private sector a national network of highways was created. The building of the autobahnen not only provided jobs for thousands of construction workers and engineers and architects but also stimulated the automotive industry and allied traders. As Hitler had intended to begin rearmament on a large scale as early as February 1933, state expenditure for this purpose rose sharply. This was enough to bring full employment in the country. He appointed a party official, Wilhelm Keppler, as special adviser on economic affairs for synthetic production.

Schacht, as President of the Reichsbank and as Minister of Economics, tried to overcome the unfavourable balance of payments. By means of the New Plan of September 1934, he increased German trade by means of bilateral agreements with various countries. Schacht increased Germany's export trade by 19 per cent between 1934 and 1936. Every effort was employed to create a self-sufficient 'balanced' economy, that is, to make Germany an autarkic state (Autarkie). A Four-Year Plan was adopted in 1936. "In four years", said Hitler, "Germany must be entirely independent of foreign countries with respect of all those materials which can in any way be produced through German capability, through German chemistry, or by our machine and mining industries'. The government put in force a system of agricultural planning by regulating production, prices and methods. Goering was made economic dictator to execute the plan, although Schacht was Minister of Economics. The two persons, Schacht and Goering, differed in their approaches to fundamental economic problem. While the former advocated greater economy, the latter emphasised the need for rearmament, i.e., 'the canon before butter'.

The economic goals laid down in Hitler's memorandum of August 1936 fell far below the target. Foreign exchange was in short supply and the Reich's debt, which had already reached the figure of 57 billion mark, went on increasing. In the words of the most authoritative analyst of the Four-Year Plan, Petzina "if the foreign governments had answered Hitler's foreign policy with a comprehensive economic blockade, the weaknesses of the economic mobilization would have become apparent." Finally, the Plan strengthened the monopoly of economic power by the largest firms. The 'Command Economy' suffered from a failure to command. Far from being totalitarian, there was a high degree of wasteful competition after 1936. Moreover, higher wages in the factories and industrial establishments set up inflationary pressures and encouraged a flight from the land that endangered the food supply.

With the exception of the Jews, work was found for every German. Skilled labour was well rewarded. German workers received significant supplementary benefits from the state. Working conditions were improved in industrial and commercial plants. The Law on the regulation of National Labour of January 20, 1934 subjected the workers under close party control. The Law provided equality of status as well as equality of opportunity. 'The worker is ever more aware that he has the opportunity to reach the highest levels in his plant commensurate with his merit'. Workers were required to join the German Labour Front (DAF), a Nazi-managed organisation set up in May 1933, after the liquidation of the trade unions. Wages and hours were regulated by the Labour Front. Recreational opportunities were provided to the workers by the Strength through Joy programme.

The attitude of the National Socialist towards women was somewhat reactionary. At the 1934 Party Convention Hitler drew the distinction between the world of man and 'the world of woman... a smaller world... her husband, her family, her children and her home.' After 1936, the restrictions against the employment of women in trade and industry were relaxed and the opportunities and rewards open to them steadily improved.

Hitler was obsessed with hatred and fear of the Jews. "The Jews inhibited Hitler's mind. He believed that they were the source of all evil, misfortune and tragedy." Hitler deprived the Jews of their positions in the state bureaucracy and stripped the German Jews of their nationality in September 1935. In November 1938 Goering issued a Decree on Eliminating the Jews from German Economic Life which deprived the Jews of their livelihood. But the attempt to drive the Jews out of their business was at best a half-solution. 'The main problem, namely, to kick the Jew out of German, remains'.

Weimar Culture

Weimar Germany has often been described as a cradle of modernity like Expressionism, Bauhas architecture, the physics of relativity, psychoanalysis, the sociology of knowledge and atonal music. Paul Ernst gave vent to his feeling in his book *The Collapse of German Idealism,* published in 1919, 'Our age is over. Thank God it is over. A new age dawns that will be different'.

Expressionism was described as 'the spiritual movement of a time that places inner experience above external life'. Expressionist dramatists relied heavily upon abstraction and symbolism accompanied by outbursts of ecstatic incantation, rather than in ordinary language. The Expressionist drama sought to advance the liberation of mankind from ancient error, from war and nationalism (Reinhardt Goering's *Seeschlacht),* from social malaise and economic dislocation (Toller's *Massemensch* and Georg Kaiser's *Gas*), and from false systems of values and religious superstitions (Bertolt Brecht's *Baal*).

The experimental theatre received some of its technical inspiration from a movement called Bauhaus. It owed its inspiration to Walter Gropius who, in 1919, announced the establishment of a new school of art, architecture and design at Weimar. Gropius in his inaugural address said in 1919, 'Let us create together the buildings of the future... as a crystalline symbol of a new and rising faith.' The Bauhaus students were encouraged to forget everything they had learned about art and to rely upon their spontaneous impulses in developing their sense to touch, colour and space. A faculty of talented artists like Lyonel Feininger, Paul Klee, Josef Albers, Hebert Bayer, Gerhard Marcks and Marcel Breurer adorned the Bauhaus.

In modern music Germany's contributions during the Weimar period were somewhat subdued. The great musical revolutionary of the prewar period, Richard Strauss, continued to produce works that were well received. The new forces were Hindemith and Schonberg. The former wrote string quartets, song-cycles based on the poetry of Rilke, jazz music and operas. Arnold Schonberg was the creator of the twelve-tone scale and of atonal music. As the musical capital of the country, Berlin, with three opera houses, with leading conductors like Wilhelm Furtwangler, Fritz Busch and Herbert von Karajan, showed the greatest variety.

The Weimar Republic struck against the pillars of orthodoxy. The churches had lost much of their former influence. Revolt against parental authority was a common place of Expressionist literature. Young people now became critical and flexible. But the liberation had its ambiguities. 'We are a generation that is united, so to speak, only by perplexity. As yet, we have not found the goal that might be able to dedicate us to common effort, although we all share the search for such a goal.'

German women were now freed from the fetters of the past. Women now had the vote. In the cultural sphere the role of women was very prominent. It was donned with names like Elisabeth Bergner, Tilla Durieux, Fritzi Massary in the theatre, Sigrid Onegin and Frida Leider in the opera, Mary Wigman in the dance, Else Laskerschular, Gertrud le Fort and Lichnowsky in literature, and Ricarda Huch in history. German women accepted as a model the indomitable heroine, Hellene Willfuer of Vicki Baum's novel *Stud Chem*, who makes her way to her goal despite financial want, personal tragedy, frustrated love, a child born out of wedlock. On the other hand, another respected writer, Ina Seidel, whose novels were widely read, emphasised the fundamental responsibilities of the German woman, motherhood, the family, the home, the soil.

Weimar democracy found few supporters in the world of literature. The country's two greatest writers—Thomas Mann and Hermann Hesse—though temperamentally disposed in favour of the Republic, entertained doubts about its existence. Mann in his impressive novel *Der Zauberberg* (1924) betrayed serious doubts about the ability of rationality to sustain society in an age of crisis.

Hesse also shared this doubt. In 1920 he wrote: 'For us in old Europe everything has died that was good and unique to us. Our admirable rationality has become madness, our art is suicide'.

Weimar Republic became the object of attack by a group of writers who were associated with the movements known as the New Objectivity or Matter-of-Factness. Inaugurated in the mid-twenties by Joseph Roth, Hermann Kesten and Erich Kastner, this group became violent critics of the ruling society, and had little hope about the future of mankind.The New Objectivists were, in Alfred Doblin's description, 'disenchanted and disillusioned people'. Erich Kastner's novel of the depression years *Fabian* (1931) took a pessimistic view of contemporary German society. About the capital of the Republic, Kastner wrote in *Fabian*: 'Insofar as this gigantic city consists of stone'. Some of the writers were also critical of the Republic and the parties that defended it. This was true, for example, of Kurt Tucholsky, the greatest German satirist since Heine. He was the most prolific writer, so much so that he used four noms de plume, and he was a relentless fighter against anti-democratic forces.

Apart from the Left intellectuals, there were the Right whose influence upon the German youth was pervasive. They repudiated both the Republic and the empire and dreamt of a new Reich of incomparable strength. In a real sense, they were the purveyors of the Rightist revolution that was to be effected in 1933. The most influential of these Right intellectuals or neo-conservatives were Arthur Moeller van den Bruck and Oswald Spengler. Both were cultural pessimists in the tradition of Nietzsche and Paul de Lagarde. Both were convinced that a society dominated by the debilitating philosophy of liberal democracy was degenerate and both called for the creation of an elite of heroes to save Germany from this impending fate.

In Moeller's view, the arch-enemy of German culture was liberalism. The war convinced Moeller that the Germans had not lost the heroic virtues, but that Germany had been robbed of victory by the cleverness of the Allies. Oswald Spengler's *The Decline of the West,* a morphological view of history, has been described as 'a sombre murky vision of the doom of our civilization.' After meeting Moeller, however, Spengler found gleams of hope. He veered round the view that Germany might emerge as the one vigorous power in an age of general decline. Urging the German youth to come forward, he supported Moeller's call for action. 'The beast in mankind is creeping upon us. The shadow of Africa darkens Europe. We must be the guardians at the threshold of our values'. Their teachings encouraged anti-intellectualism and the acceptance of violence.

In sharp contrast to the intellectuals of the left to whom war was an evil, the neo-conservatives glorified war and justified it as an instrument of national policy. About the First World War, Ernst Junger wrote: 'The war is not the end, but the chord that heralds new power. It is the anvil on which the world will be hammered into new boundaries and new communities'. Junger's eloquent pen gave a fillip to the revival of war literature in the Weimar period. The neo-conservatives encouraged a belief among the younger generation that the Republic was unworthy of support and that the sooner it fell the better. Another intellectual, Hans Zehrer, who edited *Die Tat* since 1929, encouraged the young academicians against the Republic.

Cultural·Decline

Adolf Hitler's distaste for intellectuals was expressed in his own words: 'Unfortunately one needs them. Otherwise, one might—I don't know—wipe them out or something. But unfortunately, one needs them'. Many distinguished writers went into exile during Nazi revolution. Hence Germany was deprived of the wisdom and skills of writers like Thomas and Heinrich Mann, and Arnold and Setfan Zweig and Franz Werfel and Jakob Wassermann, of all the important masters of the Bauhaus school, of painters like Beckmann, Kokoschka and Schwitters, of architects like Mies Van der Rohe and Marcel Breuer, of musicians like Kurt Weill. Those who remained, like Gerhard Hauptmann and Carl Schmitt and Martin Heidegger and Gottfried Benn, turned to National Socialism, out of fear.

Hauptmann, one of the Germany's greatest poets, became a warm advocate of Hitler when he was on the high road to success. To Hauptmann, Hitler was a complete Platonist, therefore a man of ideas, truly human, national, and both European and national. Hauptmann represented the bourgeois mentality. Carl Schmitt was the most widely read and respected political scientist of his day. A modern Machiavellian, Schmitt wasted no time on moral considerations. Schmitt had no faith in legal niceties. He argued that the actual situation creates its own legality, that emergencies obviate normative law, and that 'he is sovereign who makes the decisions regulating the emergency situation'.

Martin Heidegger, a philosopher, devoted himself to the investigation of the being and existence of the ordinary man. Concerned with the perennial problems of daily existence, Heidegger repudiated reason and science and technology. He was at once mystic of the soil, irrationalist and fatalist. He responded passionately to National Socialism and in 1933 hailed Hitler as a leader called by destiny. Gottfried Benn, a poet who has been compared with Eliot in scrupulousness of style, has a contempt for reason. He insisted that the writer could do nothing to affect the course of a stupid and criminal world and that his only activity was to accumulate experience. He hailed Hitler's regime as an expression of the 'complete identity of power and the spirit, of individuality and collectivity, of freedom and necessity'. The Fuehrer was the 'creative principle'. These intellectuals who supported Hitler were the victims of self-indulgence. To their utter chagrin they found that Hitler had none of the values they imputed to him and that his own cultural horizons were narrow. The writers were to conform top Nazi intellectual establishment.

In March 1933, when the new Ministry of Propaganda and Popular Education was created under Goebbles, the latter announced that all intellectuals life must be put in the same gear. To regulate this cultural regimentation, a law of September 1933 created a Reichskultuskammer, with separate sections for painting and sculpture, literature, music, theatre, film, radio and press, to which all 'makers of culture' must belong. Another office was created—'Office for the Supervision of Ideological Training and Education'. Its chief was Alfred Rosenberg, a man of pronounced views about cultural uniformity. A natural target for both Goebbles and Rosenberg was the prestigious Prussian Academy of Arts which had since the time of Frederick the Great been 'a living pantheon of German intellectual achievement.' The Academy lost its prestige in the Nazi regime as all its members were asked to foreswear their loyalty to National Socialist. Some of the members Alfons Paquet, Alfred Doblin, Thomas Mann and Ricarda Huch resigned their membership. Thus the Academy had no real function in the Nazi state and it lived in the shadow of the Reichskultuskammer.

Hitler detested Expressionism and any form of painting that was not realistic in the most banal sense. Goebbles, Rosenberg and many self-appointed local Nazi censors opened a full-scale attack upon modern art, which they equated with cultural anarchy. In 1939, hundreds and thousands of paintings were burned publicly in Berlin.

German musicians also received harsh treatment. Richard Strauss was tolerated because of his unassailable reputation, but he was always an object of suspicion to the Nazi censors. Paul Hindemith, a composer of remarkable originality, received shabby treatment. He was deprived of his leadership of the Philharmonic Orchestra and his post as Director of the State Opera.

There was little that the Nazi could do about the literary legacy of the past. The great satirist, Heinrich Heine, was a source of exasperation to them. The Nazi censors showed considerable circumspection in making public performances of the dead authors. Goethe and Shakespeare were regarded as safe authors, Schiller, on the contrary, was always a suspicious commodity.

It was Hitler's fondest hope that the achievements of National Socialism would find expression in masterpieces of architecture. The public buildings built after 1933 imitated classical forms without embodying grace and dignity. Indeed most of the creations of Hitler's architects Paul Ludwig Troost and Albert Speer convey 'a sense of power unenlightened by the spirit'.

It was in the domain of film that the Nazi contribution was considerable. Goebbles was convinced that 'films constitute one of the most modern and scientific means of influencing the masses. Therefore a government must not neglect them'. He created a Film Office in July 1933, and he maintained a special film section in the Propaganda Ministry as well. Hitler was the hero of the two Nazi films that are best known outside Germany. These were *Triumph des Willens* (1935) and *Olympia* (1937), directed by Leni Riefenstahl, a former dancer and actress.

The Universities and the press were made subservient to the state. Their normal state after January 1933 was one of demoralization. The universities never recovered from the expulsion of Jews from their faculties. Most of the scientists of the Max Planck Institute left their positions. In the field of history, the most promising scholars like Hajo Holborn, Hans Rothfels, Dietrich Gerhard, Theodor Ernst Mommsen, Felix Gilbert, Hans Kohn—left for America. Germany was filled with second-rate intellectuals like K.A. von Muller who commended himself to the Nazis by his idealization of youth.

In the last year before 1939 there grew up a resistance movement which was a movement of officers without soldiers. It was a large and uncoordinate collection of individual groups of intellectuals, civil servants, diplomats. Their objective was to save their country from the disaster that Hitler was destined to bring upon it. But they had no chance of success. As Franz Lehmann wrote in his diary in September 1939: 'the fanfares of victory are now drowning out every word of criticism and any thought of concern over the future'.

Hitler's Foreign Policy

The first pronouncements of Hitler's foreign policy were pacific. Hitler emphatically disclaimed any intention to revise the treaty settlement by force. But anyone who had read his autobiography *Mein Kampf* would be convinced that Hitler's policy was one of expansion and war. In his *Mein Kampf* he says:

> The oppressed lands are not to be brought back into the bosom of a common Reich by flaming protests, but by a sword strong to smite. To forge this sword is the object of a people's government in its internal policy, to safeguard the work of forging it and to seek for partners in arms is the task of its foreign policy.

The basic principles of foreign policy formulated in *Mein Kampf* was the acquisition of new living space in Eastern Europe which was essential to the future of the German race. Such a course entailed hostility with France. In another book which Hitler wrote in 1928 and which was not discovered until after the Second World War, he repeated the basic foreign policies for Germany—complete passivity, revision of the Versailles Treaty to restore the boundaries of 1914, and 'a clear, far-seeing territorial policy'. Moreover, the idea of war with France had run like a red thread through all his statements concerning foreign policy ever since 1919. To the Hungarian Prime Minister, Julius Gombos, Hitler told in June 1933, 'I will grind France to powder'.

European powers were not unconcerned about the aims of Hitler's policy. Andra Francois-Poncet, French ambassador in Berlin since 1931, had warned his government in February 1933 that Hitler was a man of action rather than of words. Sir Horace Rumbold, the British ambassador to Berlin since 1928, was perhaps the first foreign observer to perceive that the Fuhrer was a serious threat to his neighbours and to the peace of the world.

The First Years 1933-35

Tactical elasticity was the hallmark of Hitler's foreign policy in the initial stage lest the various powers took up arms to frustrate his designs. The limitation of armaments imposed on Germany by the Treaty of Versailles proved to be galling to Hitler and the latter wanted equality of status in armaments. He asserted that the German people wanted to see something done, 'because they were tired of being led by the nose'. By participating in the Disarmament Conference that had begun in Geneva in 1932, Hitler persuaded other powers to grant Germany equality of status in armaments. Then he made demands at Geneva that he was sure the other powers would not accept. Fully aware that the other powers were reluctant to reduce their forces to Germany's level, he insisted that all controls must be lifted so that it could seek actual equality in its own way. The French, supported by the British Government, refused to yield. This gave Hitler the excuse he needed. In October 1933, Hitler withdrew from the Disarmament Conference and from the League of Nations as well. On November 12, 1933, the German people supported his action by means of a plebiscite.

Simultaneously, Hitler assured the other powers that if they treated him humanely, he would return of his own accord to the League and the arms talks. This was the belief entertained by Neville Chamberlain of Britain who thought that there was a good chance of reopening Disarmament Conference with German participation, before the end of the year.

In January, the world was surprised by the announcement of a German-Polish Pact. By this, Hitler renounced German claims to Danzig and to the Polish corridor, the strip or territory separating East Prussia from the rest of Germany. It was no more than a temporary expedient. The Polish Pact reduced the potential danger of trouble in Germany's eastern flank, while simultaneously frustrating the French plan of forcing Germany back into a collective security. This was the plan of the French Foreign Minister Louis Barthou, for an 'Eastern Lacarno', whereby the Soviet Union, Germany, Poland, Czechoslovakia, the Baltic states and Finland would guarantee each other's territories and promise to assist one another. But the idea of an 'Eastern Locarno' was pure moonshine. The friction between the Czechs and the Poles and the reluctance of the latter to enter into any defensive arrangements that included the Russians as well the unwillingness of the British to make any commitment gave a death-knell to the plan. It was given a burial by Barthou's assassination in October 1934.

What was gained was unfortunately lost by Hitler's abrupt handling of the Austrian affair. Never from 1919 to 1933 had there been any doubt that the vast majority of the Austrian people desired union with Germany. But the Nazi revolution had alienated the large section of Austrian opinion. The encouragement and assistance given by the Nazi to the Austrian National Socialists led Dollfuss, the Austrian Chancellor, to suppress the Austrian Nazi party. Notwithstanding the resistance of the people, Austria might soon have yielded to German pressure but for the intervention of the Great Powers. Britain, France and Italy became insistent on the importance of maintaining Austrian independence. From this time, Italy became Austria's patron. Italy not only wanted treaty revision in Africa but she was concerned that if Germany was allowed to acquire Austria, she might be a dangerous neighbour for a power which had annexed the German-Austrian province of South Tyrol. On February 17, 1934, the governments of Britain, France and Italy made a joint declaration stating that they took a 'common view of the necessity of maintaining Austria's independence and integrity in accordance with the relevant treaties'. This announcement was strengthened by Sir John Simon's declaration in the House of Commons that the integrity and independence of Austria were an object of British policy.

Notwithstanding, Hitler quickened the pace. Meeting with Mussolini in Venice on June 15-16, 1934, Hitler believed that he had secured Italian support for his design on Austria. The result of this was the abortive Nazi putsch in Vienna in July 1934, which led to Dollfuss's death and the appearance of four Italian divisions at the Brenner pass.

The events of July 1934 proved a turning point. After meeting the rebuff, Hitler disclaimed any intention of threatening the independence of Austria. This policy was maintained for two years. In July 1936, when Italy's Abyssinian venture had weakened her hold on Central Europe, Austria concluded a pact of reconciliation with Germany. The result of these events was to establish a sort of German-Italian condominium over Austria. This laid the basis for the Rome-Berlin Axis of 1936.

Before launching his attack on the Versailles Treaty, Hitler had to settle one outstanding problem. This was the fate of the Saar which was to be decided by a plebiscite after fifteen years from the conclusion of Versailles Treaty. The plebiscite was duly held in January 1935 which resulted in an overwhelming pro-German vote and the return of the area to the Reich.

This success marked the beginning of a new phase in foreign policy. At the beginning of February 1935, British and French ministers met in London. They drew up a plan that promised Germany equality in armaments in return for adherence to conventions controlling air warfare, cooperation in new mutual assistance plans designed to give security to Eastern and Central Europe. While welcoming the air pact, Germany maintained her objections to entering into multilateral pacts in Eastern Europe. Sir John Simon, the Foreign Secretary and Anthony Eden, the

Minister for League of Nations Affairs, accepted an invitation to visit Berlin to discuss details of the scheme with Hitler. Meanwhile, on March 8, 1935, Hitler gave a stunning surprise by declaring that Germany had a new military air force. A week later, he dealt a mortal blow to the Anglo-French plan by announcing that he was no longer bound by the military clauses of the Versailles Treaty and was expanding the army from its treaty strength of 100,000 to a force of 55,50,000.

The British government made an official protest. The French and Italian governments also protested. The visit of the British Minister to Berlin took place as arranged on March 25, but achieved little. It was, therefore, in a concerned mood that the representatives of Britain, France and Italy sent representatives to Stresa on April 11, 1935 to consider the German action. The three powers jointly condemned Germany's repudiation of her obligation under the Versailles Treaty. A week later, the League of Nations issued strong words of condemnation of German policy. However, it was an empty gesture as there was no desire for joint military or economic action against Germany.

To counteract Germany's growing influence, France concluded an alliance with Soviet Russia on May 2, 1935. If either power were attacked by a European state, the other would come to its assistance. 'The conclusion of Franco-Soviet Pact marked the pinnacle of French policy against Germany'. But its efficacy was almost destroyed by the conclusion of Anglo-German Naval agreement of June 18, 1935. The British Government accepted Hitler's offer to limit German naval strength to 35 per cent of British strength. The British also agreed that Germany should be allowed a 45 per cent ratio in submarine strength. The Anglo-German Naval agreement legitimised Hitler's repudiation of the arms clauses of the Versailles Treaty. But European opinion—especially the French and Italian reaction—was particularly bitter.

Thanks to the Anglo-German naval accord, the short-lived Stresa front against Hitler collapsed. Taking advantage of the disunity of Europe, Italy sent troops into Abyssinia. By keeping aloof, Hitler won Mussolini's gratitude. More important, divisions among European powers gave Hitler an opportunity to repudiate the Locarno Treaty and to accomplish the remilitarization of the Rhine.

On March 7, 1936, Hitler sent his troops dramatically into the demilitarized zone of the Rhineland. He justified his action by accusing the French Government of having destroyed the Locarno Treaty by signing a pact with the Soviet Union that was clearly directed against Germany. Simultaneously he made an offer to negotiate with the French and Belgian government for the delineation of demilitarized zones, to conclude non-aggression pacts with those governments which could be guaranteed by Britain and Italy and to enter into similar pacts with the states of Eastern Europe. The Rhineland invasion which he did against the advice of his Chief army generals, was perhaps the biggest gamble of his career. There is little doubt that vigorous military reprisals adopted by the French Government would have thwarted Hitler for a time. Winston Churchill was perhaps correct when he wrote later that, if the French had taken military action immediately, the British could not have been an unconcerned spectator. But Camelin, the Chief of Staff of the French Army, had an exaggerated fear about the strength of the German forces. Moreover, France could not expect any assistance either from Soviet Russia or from Italy. Only little Belgium was ready to make common cause with France. Henceforth, the French Government gave up the thought of independent action and allowed itself to be persuaded by the British to take the road to negotiation.

The remilitarization of the Rhineland not only exhibited Germany's resources, that also had devastating consequences among France's allies. Belgium withdrew from the French security system and relapsed to strict neutrality. There were tremors in the Little Entente as well. All in all, Hitler had good reason to be jubilant. "The world belongs to the man with guts. God helps him." Hitler's success in the Rhineland also enabled Mussolini to complete his conquest of Abyssinia in the late spring of 1936.

Hitler had tried to cultivate good relations with Britain and appointed Ribbentrop as German ambassador in London. Ribbentrop tried in vain to bully the British into an alliance, in accordance with which they would give Germany a free hand in the East. But Britain received the proposal with coldness. Rebuffed by this attitude, Germany entered into an alliance with Italy in October 1936 which was styled as Rome-Berlin Axis. A month later Germany and Japan signed an Anti-Comintern Pact. A year later, in November 1937, this Anti-Comintern Pact was strengthened by Italy's adhesion, and a Berlin-Rome-Tokyo Axis created.

Thus, a new balance of power was set up between Germany, Italy and Japan, on the one side, and France, Britain and Soviet Union, on the other. But it was a precarious balance as between France and Britain there was no such solidarity as among the Axis powers. This dangerous state of international relations was illustrated in the Spanish Civil War (1936-39) which provided a test of strength between the opposing coalitions of great powers. Hitler and Mussolini, by taking up the cause of the Nationalist and helping it to victory, demonstrated the sabre-rattling tactics. Moreover, before embarking on aggressive policy, Hitler must make sure of his continental base. Thus, by 1937, Hitler had the satisfaction of bringing international prestige to the Third Reich.

On November 5, 1937, in a secret talk with his military chiefs, Hitler gave them a clear idea of the only logical and effective foreign policy. Germany would have to acquire living space (*Lebensraum*) in Eastern Europe which would be made possible only by the use of force. The first stages of the solution were to be the absorption of Austria and the destruction of Czechoslovakia. Hitler was aware that in carrying out such a policy 'German policy would have to reckon with the two hateful antagonists England and France'. He was resolved to solve Germany's problem of space at the latest by 1943-45.

The new British Prime Minister, Neville Chamberlain, who succeeded Stanley Baldwin in May 1937, pursued a policy of appeasement towards Germany. In November 1937 the new Foreign Secretary, Lord Halifax visited Hitler. He admitted that certain changes in Eastern Europe, notably in Austria, Czechoslovakia, and Danzig, could not probably be avoided in the long run. But 'England was only interested in seeing that such changes were brought about by peaceful development'. This green signal Hitler could hardly afford to ignore. With respect to France, Hitler had little to worry as Delbos, the Foreign Minister, was complacent about the possibility of changes in Austria's status.

Fortifying himself with the least resistance against Western powers Hitler decided to move against Austria.

Anschluss

Early in 1938, Hitler accused the Austrian government of violating the provisions of the Austro-German Pact of July 1936 and in February 1938 summoned the Austrian Chancellor, Schuschnigg, to Berchtesgaden. There Hitler browbeat him into legalizing the Austrian Nazi party and inducting Nazi representatives in his government. Suddenly, on March 9, 1938, Schuschnigg announced that a plebiscite on Austrian independence would be held on March 13. Hitler threatened to act unless the poll was cancelled. Thereupon Schuschnigg resigned. On March 12, Nazi Minister of the Interior Seyss-Inquart assumed power. He at once invited Hitler to send in the German army to preserve order and, on March 13, Austria was made a province of the German Reich. Hitler had reason to feel gratified when Mussolini, despite the strong anti-German reaction in Italy, gave him his blessing. Hitler declared, 'I will never forget him (Mussolini) for this... I shall be ready to go with him through thick and thin—through anything'.

The acquisition of Austria gave Germany important strategic and economic advantages. It enabled her to establish direct contact with Italy, Hungary and Yugoslavia and opened up the Bohemian and Moravian districts of Czechoslovakia. As Churchill said in the House of Commons : 'mastery of Vienna gives to Nazi Germany military and economic control of the whole of the communication of South-Eastern Europe, by road, by river and by rail.'

Czechoslovakia and Munich

Chamberlain's policy of appeasement once more became manifest when he signed an agreement with Italy in April 1938. Italy promised to get out of Spain as soon as possible and to stop anti-British propaganda. Britain promised, in return, to work for general recognition of Italy's conquest of Ethiopia. By this agreement Chamberlain expected to alienate Italy from Germany.

But no sooner was Italy appeased than Germany made further demands. Hitler demanded a substantial slice of Czechoslovakia—Sudetenland—where more than three million Germans lived. In March 1938, the leader of the Sudeten German Party, Konrad Henlein, visited Hitler and was instructed to ask for special rights and autonomy, which no self-respecting government could tolerate. In April, Henlein submitted the so-called Karlsbad Programme to the Czech government, asking for complete autonomy of the Sudeten area and a revision of Czech foreign policy amounting severance of treaty relations with France and Soviet Union.

The Czech Government made anxious attempt to reach a settlement with the Sudetens. France and Soviet Union were pledged to support the Czechs if they were attacked. Britain was under no obligation to act. In November 1937, Chamberlain had made it clear that Britain would not involve herself in a war with Germany over Czechoslovakia. In 1938, Britain was definitely not ready for war. On March 24, 1938, Chamberlain said in the Parliament that the Sudeten question was an internal problem of Czechoslovakia and Britain had no obligations to defend Czechoslovakia. At the same time, he warned Germany that if war should break out, it was unlikely that it would be confined to Central Europe. In April the French Prime Minister, Daladier and his minister Georges Bonnet visited London and tried to invoke British help against Germany. But Chamberlain flatly refused to do so as he did not believe that Hitler wanted to destroy Czechoslovakia but that, if he did, he 'did not see how that could be prevented'.

On May 30, 1938, Hitler announced his intention of crushing Czechoslovakia and made preparations for action which were to be ready by October 1. But in the initial stage, he suffered 'the worst brainstorm of the year'. Chamberlain, being alarmed, sent Lord Runiciman to Prague in early August to mediate between Czechs and Germans. In early September the Prague government accepted the so-called Karlsbad Programme, amounting to virtual German autonomy. Henlein rejected all these offers, while, on September 12, Hitler at the Nuremburg rally fulminated against the Czech government.'I have no intention of allowing a second Palestine to be formed here in the heart of Germany by the labours of other statesmen... The Germans in Czechoslovakia are neither defenceless nor abandoned. Of that you can rest assured.' On the following day Henlein demanded the complete separation of the Sudetenland from Czechoslovakia. On September 15, Chamberlain flew to Berchtesgaden and promised Hitler that he would try to persuade the Czech and the French Governments to accept the secession of the Sudetenland to Germany. On September 21, the Czech Cabinet finally accepted these proposals. On September 22, Chamberlain met Hitler at Godesberg and was told flatly by the latter that this was no longer enough. Hitler insisted that the Sudetenland be occupied by German military forces by October 1, and that the claims of all of Czechoslovakia's minorities and neighbours be settled immediately by plebiscites.

Both London and Paris rejected the Godesberg proposals. Daladier said that he would agree 'to the strangulation of a people' and the British reluctantly pledged their support if war should come. Sir Horace Wilson, Chamberlain's emissary, conveyed to Hitler the Anglo-French decision. The Fuhrer became furious and shouted: 'On the first of October I shall have Czechoslovakia where I want her. If France and England wanted to attack, let them do it. He was ready for any eventuality.'

Despite mobilizations on the part of France, Britain, Czechoslovakia on the one hand and Germany on the other, Hitler hesitated to take action. Simultaneously, Chamberlain made an appeal for peace in which he spoke of 'a quarrel in a faraway country among people of which we knew nothing.' On September 28, Chamberlain invoked the aid of Mussolini in proposing a four-power conference to settle the Sudeten question. On the following day, Hitler, Mussolini, Chamberlain and Daladier met at Munich and settled the terms which were to be imposed on the Czechs. Not only was Russia not invited to participate but she was not even informed beforehand! The Pact was signed by the Four Powers on October 1, 1938. Sudeten Province and the 'Little Maginot Line'—

the only effective defence of Czechoslovakia, with a third of its population and its most important industrial area—were handed over to Hitler.

'Peace with honour', 'Peace for our time', Chamberlain triumphantly announced on his return from Munich. 'A total and unmitigated defeat' observed Churchill in the House of Commons on October 5, 1938. 'They chose dishonour. They will have war'. The leader of the British Labour Party, Clement Attlee, gave vent to his feeling in the following words:

> The events of the last few days constitute one of the greatest diplomatic defeats that this country and France have ever sustained. Without firing a shot, by the mere display of military, he has achieved a dominating position in Europe which Germany failed to win after four years of war. He has destroyed the last fortress of democracy in eastern Europe that stood in the way of his ambition.

Hitler, in the meantime, moved in a calculated way to absorb the remaining portion of Czechoslovakia. In January 1939, Hitler made it clear to the Czech Foreign Minister that his country must be allied with Germany. On March 15, Hitler summoned the President of Czechoslovakia, Emil Hacha, to Berlin and forced the latter to place the destiny of the Czech people and their country into his hands. On the following morning, German troops entered Prague.

Immediately after making entry into Prague, Hitler presented an ultimatum to the Government of Lithuania, demanding the cession of Memel and the surrounding district. It was occupied on March 21 and the remilitarisation of the Baltic port began at once. About the same time, Ribbentrop demanded from the Polish ambassador, Lipski, the return of Danzig and a strip of territory connecting East Prussia across the corridor with the rest of Germany. Poland refused to accept these terms. She was fortified by the British offer of an Anglo-French guarantee against aggression, which the British Prime Minister, Chamberlain, made in the House of Commons on March 31, 1939. On April 6, Poland accepted the Franco-British guarantee as a mutual obligation and one week later Britain and France guaranteed the independence of Greece and Rumania. Meanwhile, President, Roosevelt on April 15, had asked Mussolini and Hitler to help the cause of peace by giving a ten-year pledge of non-aggression against thirty-one states. Both dictators rejected the proposal.

Meanwhile, in Britain, a bill was passed on April 20 introducing conscription. A week afterwards, Hitler denounced both the Anglo-German naval agreement of 1935 and the Nazi-Polish Pact of January 1935. As a result, the Rome-Berlin Axis drew closer. On May 6, 1939, Ribbentrop proposed to the Italian Foreign Minister Ciano that they should conclude a bilateral alliance. The German-Italian alliance, the 'Pact of Steel' was, in fact, signed on May 22, 1939. It provided for diplomatic cooperation and consultation and immediate military aid in case other signatory powers became involved in hostilities. On the following day, Hitler confidentially reported to his chief advisers that Poland must be attacked 'at the first suitable opportunity'.

Hitler, however, was deterred from any military action unless he was sure of the position of the Soviet Union. He was unwilling to risk an action eastwards that might embroil him with the Soviet Union and hearten the British and French to push through Holland and Belgium into the Ruhr, which he once described as 'our Achilles' heel'. He was reluctant, for ideological reasons, to make an agreement with the Soviet Union. Partnership with the great Communist state, he was to tell Mussolini in 1941, "seemed to me to be a break with my whole origin, my concepts, and my former obligations'. Therefore, despite obvious hints from Moscow, he was generally unresponsive.

It was western obduracy that made it impossible to reach an accord with the Soviet Union. Molotov, who succeeded Litvinov as Foreign Minister of Russia on May 4, tried to convince London and Paris that without Soviet aid this system of guarantees was pointless. Military representatives were sent to Moscow to discuss the negotiations. But there were perplexing delays. It became known that the Soviet Government was unwilling to enter into any pact unless it included a Soviet guarantee of the integrity of the Baltic States—Lithuania, Latvia, Estonia, and Poland. But Poland refused to contemplate under any condition the entry of Soviet troops into Polish territory. The

British and French Governments explained that they had no power to oblige Poland to accept the Russian proposal. But the paradoxical thing is in the following fact, as has been pointed out by Andrew Rothstein in his book, *History of Russia* :

> Thus pressure could be used in 1938 to force Czechoslovakia to surrender to Hitler, but pressure could not be used in 1939 to force Col. Beck to join in resisting Hitler.

It seemed as if the Western powers, equally afraid of Communists and the Nazis, wished the two to fight each other. Henceforth, when the Anglo-French delegation arrived in Moscow on August 11, 1939, they were informed by Marshal Voroshilov that he was empowered to sign a military convention. The Delegation had no power to conclude agreements.

Meanwhile, Hitler acted quickly. On August 11, 1939, he said candidly: "Everything I undertake is directed against Russia. If the West is too stupid and too blind to comprehend that, I will be forced to come to an understanding with the Russians, to smash the West, and then, after its defeat, to turn against the Soviet Union with my assembled forces". On August 21, Ribbentrop arrived in Moscow and two days later the Nazi-Soviet Non-aggression Pact was signed. The Pact which was to be effective for ten years embodied a secret protocol dividing Poland and eastern Europe into German and Soviet spheres of influence.

Events now moved swiftly to a violent conclusion. On August 22, Hitler said to his generals: "Now Poland is in the position in which I wanted her…. I am only afraid that at the last moment some swine or other will submit to me a plan for mediation". As a matter of fact, in mid-August, Ciano, the Italian Foreign Minister, had persuaded Mussolini to declare that Italian entry into war was impossible. About the same time, the Japanese Government broke off her alliance with Germany.

On August 25, Britain signed a formal alliance with Poland. But Hitler had gone too far to recoil. On August 29, Germany demanded from Britain that she arrange to have a Polish delegate with full powers to negotiate reach Berlin on the 30th. On the latter date, the British explained that such a procedure was unreasonable. Germany must follow the normal diplomatic procedure of transmitting her demands on Poland through the Polish ambassador. When Ribbentrop received these advices from the British ambassador at midnight, he replied with a sixteen-point proposal for the settlement of all German-Polish differences. But when Sir Neville Henderson asked for a copy of the text of these proposals, Ribbentrop asserted that it was now too late as the Polish representative had arrived in Berlin by midnight.

On August 31, the German Government broadcast the sixteen points. About five o'clock in the morning of September 1, Germany, without declaring war, invaded Poland. Both Britain and France sent warning notes to withdraw from the territory it had already occupied. Chamberlain declared war against Germany. Within a few hours France also declared war.

Thus, twenty-five years after the outbreak of the First World War, Europe entered the Second World War. Historian differ in their interpretation of causes of the war. Some trace the basic cause to harsh terms of the Treaty of Versailles imposed on Germany at the end of the First World War justifying Germany's policy to repudiate its terms. Others blame the policy of appeasement pursued by Britain and France in the thirties the climax of which was reached in the Munich Pact of 1938. Instead of counteracting Germany in 1936 when the latter invaded the Rhineland, Britain and France allowed Germany to arm to the teeth. It was too late in 1939 to resist Hitler's aggression. Amongst leading British politicians, Churchill raised his lone voice that Britain and France should move against Hitler as soon as he broke an international agreement. The British historian, A. J. P. Taylor, has argued that Hitler's aims were moderate and justifiable. 'In principle and doctrine, Hitler was no more wicked and unscrupulous than many other contemporary statesmen', Most historians, however, ascribe the responsibility of the Second World War to Hitler's aggression. As he said to his military chiefs in November 1939: 'Basically I did not organise the armed forces in order not to strike. The decision to strike was always in me'. The Second World War was Hitler's war. He planned it, began it and, ultimately, lost it.

The origins of the Second World War assumed a momentous turn when the Hossbach Memorandum was produced by the Allied prosecutors at the Nuremburg Trial. The Memorandum drafted on 5 November 1937 in a conference was addressed by Hitler. Hossbach, the man who took the minutes noted:

> The aim of German policy was to secure and preserve the Volksmasse, the racial community, and to enlarge it. It was a question of space..... German policy had to reckon with two hate-inspired antagonists, Britain and France, to whom a German collossus ... was a thorn in the flesh.. Germany's problem could only be solved by means of force and this was never without risk... There still remain the questions of 'when' and 'how'.

The significance of the Memorandum was deflated by apportioning the blame on Hitler. It would be too facile to conclude that Hitler was a war-monger. The Memorandum did not reveal any concrete plan for unleashing the war.

> The Memorandum tells us what we know already, that Hitler (like every other German statesman) intended to become the dominant power in Europe. It also tells us that he speculated how this might happen... They bear hardly any relation to the actual outbreak of war in 1939.

However, critics denounced Taylor's disregard for 'historical context.' They were of opinion that in mid-December 1937, the German army's directives were changed to envisage military aggression against Austria and Czechoslovakia. Nevertheless, Taylor was wrongly interpreted of absolving Hitler from war-game. What he wanted to demonstrate was the strange combination of the Fuhrer's jingoism and inability to put it into execution.

CHAPTER 36

THE SECOND WORLD WAR

The Second World War began in Europe in September 1939 between Germany on one side and England and France on the other. Until the entry of United States into the war in December 1941, the war remained essentially a European war. Italy remained neutral. Russia, too, remained neutral owing to Nazi-Soviet Pact of August 23, 1939 which was accompanied by a secret agreement under which Poland was to be partitioned between Germany and Russia. The war affected most of the nations in the world. The war was certainly global in character for it saw prolonged fighting in the Pacific as well as in the Atlantic, in Asia and Africa as well as in Europe.

The first phase of the war lasted from September 1939 until April 1940. It was one of unbroken German victories against Poland, Scandinavia and the Low Countries. The events of the second phase of the war (1940-41) were the defeat and fall of France, the Battle of Britain and the war in North Africa. The third phase of the war began in June 1941 and lasted until November 1942. The chief events were the German invasion of Soviet Russia, the Japanese war against the United States and Allies and the Allied landings in Morocco and Algiers. The fourth phase of the war (1942-44) was a phase of preparation for the final repulse of Germany, Italy and Japan. The final phase of the war (1944-45) witnessed the liberation of France, the surrender of Germany and Japan and the collapse of Eastern and Central Europe under Soviet influence.

1939-1940

The Second World War began on September 1, 1939 with a devastating attack on Poland. Germany demonstrated its coordinated tactics and speed with which their military machines were used. The Luftwaffe led the way by systematically destroying the Polish air force on the ground cutting supply lines and communication. This was followed by the tactics of *blitzkrieg* or lightning war. The tactics which the Germans were to use again and again in the next two years, were defined by Rommel, Germany's most gifted commander as 'the art of concentrating strength at one point, forcing a breakthrough, rolling up and securing the flanks on either side, and then penetrating like lightning, before the enemy has time to react, deep into his rear'. The bewildered Poles could not stand against this massive thrust of the Germans. By September 21, Western Poland had been completely overrun, while the Russian troops had occupied the eastern part of the country. Warsaw was occupied on September 27. On the following day a German-Russian Pact was signed which completed the fourth partition of Poland. Russia took the eastern half while Germany took the western half which contained Danzig and the Polish Corridor. In a broadcast on October 1, 1939, Churchill said: "Poland has again been overrun by two of the great powers which held her in bondage for a hundred and fifty years but were unable to quench the spirit of the Polish nation ... I cannot forecast to you the action of Russia. It is a riddle wrapped in a mystery inside an enigma; but there is a key. The Key is Russian Interest".[1]

German victory hustled the Russians into precipitate demands on Estonia, Lithuania and Latvia to establish military and naval bases. At the same time, Russia demanded from Finland

1. Churchill, *The Second World War*, Vol. 1, P. 35.

certain strategic areas—Karelian Isthmus and group of islands in the Gulf of Finland. While Estonia, Lithuania and Latvia succumbed to Soviet pressure, Finland took a rigid and unyielding position. Russia, therefore, invaded Finland on November 30, 1939. The Finns offered stubborn resistance. For a month or two it even appeared that Finland might force the Russians to sue for peace. At the turn of the year, Stalin streamlined the command of the northern army, put some of his best units and his modern equipment into the fight. Finland capitulated in March 1940 and ceded to Russia the city of Viborg and the whole of the Karelian peninsula.

The Phoney War

The rapid conquest of Poland was followed by a six months' lull—called the Phoney War or 'the Winter of Illusion'. Though Britain and France had gone to war in defence of Poland, they lacked determination and required strength to overcome Germany. They anticipated breaking of ties between Germany and Russia, the two mutually distrustful allies which would divert Hitler's explosive forces from westwards to eastwards. Though their anticipation proved true a year later, by then the strength of Britain and France had almost been exhausted.

In the first five months of the war, Britain sent 158,000 troops to France, assembled large combat force in the Middle East, and appealed to Australia and New Zealand to send troops to Egypt. But Britain sent no armoured division to France—which would have been far more effective in the circumstances. For the first six months Britain was under a false sense of security. In France also a certain sense of laxity prevailed which contributed to her eventual collapse. The French had 85 divisions as against 43 of the Germans on the western front, and it has been admitted later that German western front would have been broken if the French army had made a thrust to attack it. But France relied on her old-fashioned mobilisation and her successive military chiefs from Petain to Gamelin were all wedded to slow-motion ways of warfare. Instead of attacking the German defences in the west—the so-called Siegfried Line—or bombing German cities, the Allied Commander-in-Chief, General Maurice Gamelin of France, entrenched himself in the Maginot line fortifications which the French had been building since 1930 along their northeastern border from Switzerland to Belgium.

Though the winter of 1939-40 saw the sterile air-raids conducted by the Allies, serious naval action took place. The German submarines played havoc. They not only torpedoed the passenger ship S.S. *Athena* off the northwest coast of Ireland on September 8, sank the aircraft carrier *Courageous* on September 14, but the German U-47 passing through the harbour defenses of Scapa Flow torpedoed the *Royal Oak*, sinking her with a loss of 800 men on October 13-14. The British Royal Navy was heartened when their cruisers intercepted the pocket battleship *Graf Spee* off the coast of Uruguay and damaged her beyond repair. Moreover, from November onwards, both Britain and France replenished their military stocks from the United States under a so-called "cash and carry" amendment to American neutrality legislation. Yet neither the British Government of Neville Chamberlain nor the French Government of Edouard Daladier exhibited any such energy and tenacity of purpose as Lloyd George and Clemenceau had exhibited in the First World War. In vain did the French army officer, Charles de Gaulle, urge speedy mass production of tanks and other implements for waging the new type of war.

German Offensive in the West

In March 1940 the French Government was overhauled by the replacement of Daladier in the premiership by Paul Reynaud, though Daladier remained in the cabinet as minister of war.

Britain had been concerned over the use of Norwegian neutral waters by German ships carrying Swedish iron ore via Narvik, Norway. If these supplies were shut off, the German war effort would suffer. Churchill, as First Lord of the Admiralty, had pressed for this drastic action. He expected that this would provoke the Germans to 'fire back'. Moreover, Churchill wanted to open a new theatre of war in Scandinavia by attacking Germany's Baltic flank. But Hitler pre-empted the move by sending his own troops well ahead of the British. Early in February 1940 Hitler had observed that 'the English intended to land there, and I want to be there before them'. On April 9, 1940, Nazi forces overran the undefended frontier of Denmark and seized the capital. Simultaneously Hitler launched an air and naval attack on Norway. By employing the parachute troops and 800 operational planes and 250 transport planes, Hitler overawed the Norwegian people in the first phase. However, Allied forces were landed in several coastal areas, The Norwegian troops fought stubbornly and the coastal defence guns at Oslo sank the German Cruiser *Blucher*, damaged the pocket battleship *Deutschland*, and the cruiser *Emden*. Nevertheless, the Germans made good their landings and harried the Allied forces by air attack. The Allied troops held on tenaciously at Narvik till the end of May when dramatic events in western Europe led them to abandon Narvik, their last foothold in Norway. Hitler set up a puppet government under a man, Vidkun Quisling, whose name became a synonym for traitor.

The occupation of Norway and Denmark gave the Nazis an opportunity of dominating all Scandinavia and of imperilling North Atlantic shipping and Great Britain itself. The consequence of the British fiasco in Norway was the resignation of Neville Chamberlain and the appointment of Winston Churchill on May 10, 1940 as head of a coalition government. Churchill, who took charge of Britain's destinies, had brilliant achievements to his credit in the First World War, when he was in charge of the Admiralty. Fearless, possessed of a vivid imagination, imperturbable even in the midst of despair, he infused a new spirit into the whole conduct of Britain's greatest war. As Churchill observed in this connection: "At last I had the authority to give directions over the whole scene. I felt as if I were walking with destiny, and that all my past life had been but a preparation for this hour and for this trial."[2]

Instead of making a frontal attack on the Maginot Line, which would have been much too costly, Hitler chose a new plan. He decided to make the main thrust against the French through the hilly and wooded Ardennes, which the French believed to be impassable for tanks. The German invasion of the West opened with dramatic successes on the right flank, against strategic points in Holland and Belgium. Before dawn on May 10, German troops were dropped near Rotterdam and the Hague. Within four days, the backbone of the resistance was broken. On May 14, the Netherlands Commander-in-Chief surrendered, while Queen Wilhelmina escaped to England.

The invasion of Belgium had started at the same moment as the one on Holland. On May 11, the German troops occupied Fort Eben Emael, the key to Belgian defences. German Panzer divisions forced the Belgian forces to start a general retreat—just as the French and the British were striving to support them. But German armoured columns swept through the Ardennes and on May 14 broke into France at Sedan beyond the west end of the Maginot Line. The German commander, Guderian, with three armoured divisions supported by motorised infantry raced for the channel which he reached on May 20. The whole Belgian army and its supporting French and British units were caught in a girdle that now enveloped. An Allied plan to effect a breakthrough was frustrated by German pressure. The Allied forces were pushed slowly towards the coast. On May 28, the Belgian king, Leopold III, in despair, made an unconditional surrender without consulting France and Britain. The Belgian capitulation placed 400,000 British and French soldiers in a terrible predicament. Harried by the Germans on the south with their northern flank exposed, the Allied troops retreated to the sea at Dunkirk. For a week from May 27 to June 4, 1940, the British succeeded in evacuating 338,000 troops with the help of a miscellaneous armada of Royal Navy, ferry-craft, fire-floats and sloops. The evacuation was called "Operation Dynamo". It was an amazing feat on the part of the British navy. The miracle of Dunkirk made General Archibald Wavell to write: "At Dunkirk the true spirit of our people flashed out like a sword from its sheath". But Churchill warned: "We must be very careful not to assign to this deliverance the attributes of a victory. Wars are not won by evacaution."

2. Churchill, *Second World War*, Vol. 1, P. 526-27.

The battle for France began at once. German offensive was launched on June 5. Paul Reynaud, who had succeeded Daladier in March, was resolved to continue the fight. General Gemelin was succeeded by seventythree year old Weygand. Though the French had enough forces and superior artillery, they had no real battle plan. Their artillery was wearing out. On June 7, Weygand advised the French Government to ask for an armistice without delay. On the 9th the Government decided to leave Paris. On June 10, Italy declared war against France. On June 14, the Germans entered Paris. Two days later they breached the Maginot Line and pressed across the Loire. On June 16, Reynaud resigned. Marshal Petain formed a new government and asked the Germans for armistice which was granted on June 22. Under its terms German troops were to occupy more than half of France, including Paris. Occupation costs were to be borne by the French. French prisoners of war, numbering about two million, were to remain as hostages in German hands. Provisions were made for the immediate surrender of German prisoners, the disbanding of the French army, and demobilisation of the French fleet. A French totalitarian government under Petain and Pierre Laval was installed at Vichy. The Republican government was at an end. The Vichy regime enacted some of the most repressive laws. Political parties and trade unions were suppressed. The Vichy regime was accorded recognition by the Western powers. But the real France was represented by those Frenchmen who fled to England to join the Free French movement of General De Gaulle. The General announced from London: 'Whatever happens, the flame of French resistance must not and shall not die.'

Battle of Britain

The fall of France left Britain exposed to German attack separated only by the narrow water of the English Channel. Britain was also menacingly enveloped by a 2,000 mile (3,200 km) stretch of enemy-occupied coastline. Britain's land forces could have done little to stop the German forces if the latter had actually got ashore. Britain had only one division in the country and with great difficulty raised half a million Home Guards which had few rifles until the end of 1940.

Happily for Britain, Hitler and his service chiefs made no serious efforts to cripple Britain nor even worked out any plans for invasion of England. Though Hitler began preparations for an invasion of the British Isles, which was given the code name Sea Lion, this was abandoned, because the air battle that preceded it was lost. 'If Hitler had concentrated on defeating Britain, her doom would have been almost certain'. It seemed that Hitler became distracted by thoughts of an attack on Russia. He also thought that the only way to make Germany's rear secure was to attack and defeat Russia. He was also under the delusion that Britain would hasten to make peace once she was deprived of Russian intervention in the war.

Nevertheless, in early July 1940, the German Luftwaffe made air attacks on Britain. Thereafter a mass German air attack took place on British coastal towns. From the month of August wave after wave of German bombers spread destruction all over Britain. More than 20,000 civilians were killed in London alone; a few cities, such as Coventry, were almost obliterated. Yet the German attack on Britain failed. By the spring of 1941 Britain was retaliating with her efficient Royal Air Force and had shot down 2,400 German planes. The courage of Britain's fighter pilots, the spirit of the British people, and the radar network which provided early warning of the enemy's approach, had won the Battle of Britain. In paying tribute to British flyers, Churchill said: 'Never in the field of human conflict was so much owed by so many to so few.'

Perhaps England would not have held out if the United States had not furnished massive aid. At the outbreak of the war, most of the American people were anxious to keep out of it. But as Nazi aggression grew, President Roosevelt spoke out sharply against the aggressive dictatorships and in favour of all aid to Britain. In September 1940 he handed over to Britain fifty naval destroyers in return for leases on naval bases in Newfoundland and the West Indies. In March 1941 Congress passed the Lend-Lease Act authorising the President to put American resources at the disposal of any state whose defence he regarded as vital to the security of the United States. Under the terms of the Act, Britain received from the

United States vast quantities of goods of various kinds to meet both civilian and military needs.

Africa and the Mediterranean

While Britain was fighting for her existence, Mussolini threatened Britain's position in the Mediterranean and Africa. In August 1940, the Italians seized British Somaliland. The Italians next turned their attention to Egypt and the Suez Canal. In the middle of September 1940, an army of 250,000 under Marshal Graziani, an experienced desert fighter, moved from Libya to Egypt. He took Sollum and Sidi Burrani and then stopped. In December Wavell counterattacked and took Sidi Barrani and its whole garrison and rolled over the coast-fortress of Bardia. On January 6, 1941, Bardia, along with its whole garrison comprising 45,000 men, surrendered. The coastal fortress of Tobruk was occupied by the British on January 22. In early February, the British forces actually reached and captured Benghazi. Within three months the British had knocked out ten Italian divisions, taken 113,000 prisoners, captured hundreds of guns and tanks, and eliminated the threat to Suez. Meanwhile, in January 1941, the British forces, from both the Sudan and Kenya, advanced against Italian Somaliland and also entered Ethiopia. In May 1941, Haile Selassie reentered his capital at Addis Ababa.

So desperate was the plight of Italy that Hitler had to send his highly trained and armoured divisions under one of his best generals, Erwin Rommel, the Desert Fox as he was called. In April, 1941 Rommel appeared in North Africa, pushed the British out of Tripoli and Libya and forced Wavell to withdraw into Egypt.

Meanwhile, Italy tried her luck in the Balkan Peninsula. In October 1940, on trumped up charges, Italy declared war on Greece and attacked it with an army based in Albania. The British immediately offered their aid to the Greeks. But the Greeks were already in command of the situation. Under the leadership of General Metaxas, the Greek put up stiff resistance to the Italian invaders and in January 1941, after three months' fighting, drove them entirely out of Greece and back into Albania.

In the given situation, Churchill saw an opportunity of reviving his cherished Balkan project. On March 7, 1941, a British force of 50,000 landed in Greece. Churchill dreamed of opening up a new theatre of war in the Balkans and of marshalling the Balkan countries to deliver a thrust on Germany's flank. But Churchill's unrealistic project was soon shattered when the Germans promptly swept into Yugoslavia and Greece like a whirlwind and knocked over the opposing armies like ninepins. British forces were forced to retire to the island of Crete from where they were expelled by bombing attacks and parachute drops in May. But the German losses were heavy—this had an unforeseen effect on Hitler that turned out to Britain's benefit. For Hitler did not follow up his third Mediterranean victory by invasion of Cyprus, Syria, Suez, or Malta. A month later he launched the invasion of Russia which enervated him so much that he could afford little time for driving the British out of the Mediterranean and the Middle East.

Invasion of Russia

Despite the German-Soviet alliance, Hitler had taken the decision in June 1940 for a final break with Russia. Plans for the war were prepared between July 22 and December 5, 1940. In the beginning of 1941, Hitler had prepared 'Operation Barbarossa', a strategic plan for the invasion of Russia. In the middle of February, Hitler had confided that any large-scale operation in the Mediterranean must wait until the autumn of 1941, after Russia had been defeated. He was confident that the conquest of Russia would force the capitulation of Britain; it would enable him to command the immense resources of Russia and would bring to realisation his pan-German quest for expansion in the East. His lighting victories in Poland, Denmark and Norway, the Lowlands and France and now in the Balkans encouraged him to believe in the inevitability of the breakdown of Soviet resistance. On June 22, 1941, Hitler sent three large army groups across Russia's western frontier. The date is significant as it was exactly on this day (22 June 1812), a hundred and twenty-nine years ago, Napoleon had done so.

Stalin refused to believe that the attack was imminent and at first the Russians seemed to be overwhelmed by surprise and mobility of the

German troops. In the West, people spoke of Russia being finished by the end of six weeks. Russia's military strength in the western sector was estimated at 155 divisions, including sixty tank brigades, against 121 divisions of Germans. The supreme direction of the war was in the hands of a State Defence Committee consisting of Stalin, Molotov, Voroshilov, Berya, and Malenkov. After ten days of defeat and retreat, Stalin announced his scorched-earth policy. 'In occupied regions conditions must be made unbearable for the enemy and all his accomplices. They must be hounded and annihilated at every step, and all their measures frustrated'.

On the sixth day of the war, German Panzer divisions penetrated into Minsk, 200 miles (320 km) inside the frontier and after a few days captured 300,000 Russian troops. It is no wonder that Halder wrote in his diary on July 3: 'It is probably not an exaggeration when I contend that the campaign against Russia has been won in fourteen days'. On that day Guderian's troops had reached the Dneiper—320 miles (510 km) deep into Russia and halfway to Moscow. General von Leeb's army in the north occupied Riga in the first week of fighting and, by September, was poised before Leningrad. In the centre, the General von Bock's army advanced 500 miles (800 km) in the first month, but was held up in front of Smolensk. In the south, Rundstedt's army entered Kiev on September 19 and proceeded to conquer nearly all the Ukraine.

German advance on Moscow began on October 2. The prospects looked bright when Bock's armies captured 600,000 troops at Vyazma. But the first snow fell on October 6 and German troops with great difficulty arrived 20 miles (32 km) short of Moscow. In early December, Russian counter-offensives began which tumbled back the exhausted Germans and produced a critical situation. Russian winter proved a terrible drain on the German forces and they never fully recovered from it. But Hitler still had a good chance of victory in 1942 as the Red Army was seriously short of equipment.

In the late spring of 1942, Hitler planned a new offensive. It was to concentrate on the industrial resources of the Donetz basin, the grain of the Ukraine, and the oil of the Caucasus. Despite the resistance of the Russians, the German Army occupied the Don along its whole length in July, and Sebastopol fell. But Hitler, intoxicated with success, split his forces between the double objectives of the Caucasus and Stalingrad. Exhausted by the immense distances, with their supply lines over-lengthened, the Germans failed to capture Stalingrad and cross the Caucasus. Stalingrad witnessed the scene of worse fighting for over five months from August 23, 1942, until January 31, 1943. In mid-October 1942, Hitler decided to break off the offensive as he began to understand the magnitude of some of the frustrating problems which had proved the ruin of Napoleon.

War in the Pacific : 1941-1942

Since the beginning of the war, the ambitions of Japanese leaders for expansion had grown rapidly. In 1940 Japan planned the Greater East Asian Co-Prosperity Sphere which would include China, the Pacific Islands, French Indo-China, Thailand, British Burma, Dutch Indonesia. In preparation for her imperialist ambition, Japan signed a non-aggression pact with Soviet Russia (April 1941) and opened negotiations with the United States. Washington had opposed Japan's Asiatic ambitions ever since 1931. When in July 1941 Japan found pretexts for going into French Indo-China, the United States froze Japanese assets in the United States, imposed an oil embargo and appointed General MacArthur as Commander-in-Chief in the Far East.

On December 7, 1941, America was surprised when the Japanese fleet with 360 aircraft, without any warning, struck at the United States fleet at Pearl Harbour in the Hawaian Islands. Four of the American battleships were sunk. Soon afterwards the Japanese had gained control of the Pacific. On December 8, 1941, Britain and America declared war on Japan. On December 10, 1941, 80 Japanese bombers and torpedo-bombers from their base at Saigon struck at the British battleship *Prince of Wales* and the armoured cruiser *Repulse* near Singapore, and both ships were sunk.

By these strokes the way was cleared for the Japanese invasion of Malaya and Malaya Archipelago. By the middle of December the Japanese had taken Guam and Wake Islands from the United States, the Gilbert Islands and Hong Kong from Britain. A month later, Japan conquered the Malayan Peninsula. On February 15, 1942, Singapore, with a garrison of 60,000 men, surrendered. Even before the fall of Singapore, Japanese forces landed in Borneo, Celebes and New Guinea (14 January 1942). Three weeks later they launched an attack on Java, the core of the Dutch East Indies, which fell into their hands like a ripe plum after a few days. On March 8, Rangoon fell and, within two months, the British forces, driven out of Burma, took sanctuary in India. The Japanese had thus secured control of the western Pacific area 'between India and Hawaii and between Siberia and Australia". The Japanese position became so strong that it seemed well-nigh impossible for the Allies to recover their power. The only bright feature was the independence and preservation of Australia which provided the Allies with a large-scale base against the Japanese outposts.

The Grand Alliance

Despite the grand victories of the Axis Powers, there were signs of determination on the part of the Allied Powers to combat the forces of totalitarianism. The basis for cordial cooperation between England and America—which had been laid before the formal entrance of the United States into the war—was further strengthened in June 1941. The momentous decision was taken by Franklin Roosevelt and Winston Churchill that despite their ideological differences with the Soviet Union, they must strain every nerve to help the Russians withstand the German onslaught. This informal collaboration was given a concrete shape in January 1942 when the three major powers, with twenty-three others, issued the Declaration of the United Nations. It expressed their adhesion to the principles of the Atlantic Charter, which had been formulated by Churchill and Roosevelt in August 1941. The Charter had not only raised its voice against any form of aggression, but also had expressed the intention of creating a world free from fear and want.

The coalition was not an empty threat. Despite insuperable difficulties of supplying the fighting forces with war materials and of carrying military operations in two theatres of war, America poured indispensable supplies to the Allies. By the end of the war, the United States had produced 296,601 planes, 87,000 tanks, 2,434,553 trucks, 17,400,000 rifles, 315,000 pieces of field artillery. Under cover of Lend-Lease agreement, large amount of these materials went to America's allies.

The Pacific War

To contain the Japanese ambition of ruling over Asia, American resources were mostly concentrated in the Pacific. Japan's high road to victory was checked in 1942 in three great battles. The turning-point against Japan came with the Battle of the Coral Sea in May 1942, between Australia and the Solomon Islands. In this naval encounter, the American carrier-based planes enveloped Japanese fleet and sank a carrier, four cruisers, two destroyers, and crippled seven other ships. The second battle took place in early June 1942 in the Island of Midway in the Central Pacific. With a mighty naval contingent of 200 ships, together with 700 planes, the Japanese struck against Midway on June 4. In a four-day naval encounter, Japan suffered the greatest defeat, losing 5,000 men, 322 planes, four carriers and a heavy cruiser.

Undeterred by these reverses, the Japanese High Command planned a great pincers movement against Australia, the operations of which would cover a wide area from Port Moresby in New Guinea on the one hand and the Solomons Chain on the other. But the plan was too ambitious for Japan to execute. Under the command of General Douglas MacArthur, Australian and American forces defeated Japanese attempts to cross the mountains and seize Port Moresby. On August 7, 1942, the U.S. marines made a daring landing at the Japanese-built base of Guadalcanal in the Solomons. During the winter of 1942-3, these gains were consolidated and Australian and United States counterattack was launched on New Guinea which exposed the weakness of Japan. She suffered further important naval losses in a battle off the Solomon Islands during November 1942. By the middle of 1943 the Japanese dream of Pacific-wide empire was fading fast. The Allies had reconquered the southwest Pacific and General MacArthur and Admiral Nimitz made a deeper thrust into Japan's outlying rings of defence.

Western Europe

The Allies were fighting in Asia and the Pacific as well as in the Mediterranean. In this war, they were deprived of any help from the Soviet Union. Stalin, fully occupied in defending himself against Hitler's attack, maintained a strict neutrality in the war with Japan. However, in late 1941 and 1942, the Allies stepped up bombing offensive against German bases and installations in Norway and northern France and German industrial cities. In March 1942 a tiny British force carried by launches and torpedo boats crept into St. Nazaire harbour on the Bay of Biscay, rammed HMS *Campbeltown* and blew her and the dry docks up.

A second raid was on Dieppe, conducted by a force of 5,000 troops, mostly Canadian, in August 1942. The Dieppe raid, executed by a frontal assault on the port with infantry and tanks, combined with landings on the flanking beaches, was repulsed with heavy losses.

During these months plans had been going on among the Allies for the opening up of a Second Front. The Russians were pressing for a Second Front which would relieve German pressure on their armies. In May 1942 President Roosevelt had told Molotov that he hoped the creation of a Second Front would be possible in 1942. But Churchill needed time for a major cross-Channel invasion of France. Hence Churchill set out for Moscow in August 1942 to explain to Stalin that the Second Front must wait until 1943. Stalin bowed to the inevitable. The true Second Front was only to be opened until the very last year of the war.

North Africa: El Alamein and the 'Torch'

Meanwhile, in North Africa, a decisive battle was taking place. To retrieve the sagging Axis fortunes, Hitler sent Rommel in March 1941. His swift surprise advance on March 31 swept the British out of Cyrenaica and pushed them to the frontier of Egypt. Churchill then asked Wavell to make a fresh effort and when this 'Operation Battleaxe' failed in June, Wavell was replaced by Auchinleck.

The image of Rommel now filled Churchill's mind and to make a short work of the former Churchill poured most of Britain's available forces into Africa. The British offensive, strengthened by over 750 tanks, called 'Operation Crusader' (launched in November 1941), had the effect of pushing Rommel out of Cyrenaica. Rommel was handicapped by the weakness of his ally, Italy, and the lack of reinforcements, as Hitler was preoccupied with the main offensive against Russia. Moreover, the German General's supply lines were vulnerable to attacks by air and sea.

In December 1941, the British General Auchinleck launched a well-planned offensive against Rommel's lines and liberated Tobruk. But Rommel, 'a daring and skilful opponent, a great general', succeeded in retrieving his position. In May 1942 he began the great counter-attack that finally took Tobruk along with 33,000 men in it, together with an enormous amount of stores. 'It was the worst British disaster of the war except for the fall of Singapore'. Rommel rolled on into Egypt, past Sidi Barrani and Mersa Matruh, until he had reached Alamein, only 60 miles west of Alexandria. At El Alamein, Rommel's triumphant advance was stopped by Auchinleck in the middle of July. Now it became apparent to Rommel that he had advanced beyond his resources with his stock of fuel being depleted.

The Allies regrouped, Churchill dismissed Auchinleck and put General Montgomery in command of the Eighth Army. Montgomery husbanded his resources and reequipped the troops with new and heavier tanks sent from the United States. Rommel again attacked (August 31-September 7, 1942). This time the British lines held. A new spirit of confidence actuated the British forces. Tactically, the battle was decided by pure defence, without any counter-offensive.

At this point, Churchill shaken after a series of British disasters, used Montgomery to mount his own attack. But Montgomery was determined to wait until his preparations were complete. By October 1942, when the Eighth Army's fighting strength increased to 230,000 and a total of 1,440 tanks, Montgomery prepared himself for a death thrust. In comparison Rommel had less than 80,000 forces and had only 260 German tanks and 280 Italian tanks—so that the British started with a 6 to 1 superiority in numbers. On October 22 and 23 Montgomery opened a massive artillery barrage upon Rommel's line. For several days each side inflicted heavy casualties on the other. Finally, on November 5, Rommel began to give way. He began his retreat and did not pause until he had reached near El Agheila at the far end of Cyrenaica—700 miles back from El Alamein. Within three weeks Tobruk and Benghazi were again occupied by the British. Rommel withdrew further to the Mareth line inside the frontier of Tunisia. Rommel had to take this fatal decision not only owing to the weakness of his force, but also due to the new situation produced by the Anglo-American invasion of Morocco and Algeria in November under Eisenhower.

Hardly had Rommel begun his 1,000 mile (1,600 km) retreat, when the Allied landing took place at Casablanca, Oran and Algiers on French territory on November 8, 1942. This was the long-planned 'Operation Torch' whose success depended upon the cooperation of the French forces in Morocco and Algeria. Contrary to the Allied expectation, the French garrison resisted at Casablanca and Algiers. Hostilities were finally terminated on November 10 by a special agreement between Admiral Darlan, representing the Vichy regime in North Africa and General Eisenhower the Commander-in-Chief of the Anglo-American forces. Subsequently, Darlan was assassinated, and a "Free French" government was established at Algiers under General De Gaulle.

In January 1943, at a conference at Casablanca attended by President Roosevelt, Churchill and Gaulle Charles de, the Allies announced their determination to fight to the last to secure the unconditional surrender of Germany, Italy and Japan. It was also decided to make a thrust into Sicily. This would not only smash Italy, but also secure the Mediterranean supply routes and divert German pressure from the Russian front.

Meanwhile, despite his setback in the east, Hitler was able to send substantial reinforcement to Rommel at Tunisia. A new corps was formed under General Von Arnim. Thus strengthened, Rommel in January and February 1943 delivered a counter-stroke that gave the Allies a bad shock. In the middle of February, Rommel mounted an offensive on the American forces at the Kasserine Pass. The timely arrival of the British reserves relieved pressure on the Americans. On February 22, the Germans broke off the attack and began a gradual withdrawal. Rommel's attack on March 6, 1943 on Montgomery was repulsed with the German' loss of fifty tanks. Rommel, sick and frustrated, left Africa. He could do little against a double attack from Montgomery in the Libya on the West, and the combined Anglo-American-French forces under General Alexander on the West.

The final battle for Tunisia exhibited the superiority of Allied coordination. In March the Eighth Army broke the Mareth Line, a strong defensive position at the borders of Tunisia, by frontal attack. In this attempt the Eighth Army was helped by flanking movement from the south by the New Zealanders and by a French column under General Leclerc. This combined force joined hands with the armies from Algeria across the neck of the Tunisian peninsula on April 7. On May 6, 1943 the Allied army won a decisive victory. The city of Tunis and the naval base of Bizerta fell to them. On May 13, the Afrikakorps and the Italians numbering about 250,000 were taken prisoner. The German collapse was due to various causes: the aerial attack and the ground attack of the tank forces, the lack of reserves and disruption of supplies. Moreover, the Germans tried to hold in Tunisia too extensive a front for its resources—a 100-mile (160 km) perimeter—in the endeavour to preserve both Tunisia and Bizerta.

Invasion of Italy

The Nazi leaders tried to minimise the happenings in Tunisia. They deluded themselves with the idea of being invincible within 'Fortress Europe'. The nerve centre was Germany—protected by the outer screen of occupied or satellite states of Norway, Denmark, the Low Countries, France, the Pyrennes, Italy, the Balkans, Crete and the Crimea. But the German psychology of defensive warfare was soon dissipated by the rapidly mounting air attack of the Allies. On May 30, 1943 the Royal Air Force bombed Cologne and later on Essen and the Ruhr. Docks and shipping at Hamburg, submarine bases at Lorient and Saint-Nazaire in France, airfields and railway yards in France and Belgium, and, eventually, Berlin itself, became the target of Allied bombing. 'Fortress Europe' became vulnerable and pointless against the Allied air attacks. It has been said that a Second Front had been opened before the invasion of Europe, and from now on the combined bombing offensive was to prove itself 'the greatest lost battle on the German side'.

On July 9, 1943, the Allied forces landed on the coast of Sicily. The American forces took Palermo (July 22), the British Syracuse (July 12), and with some difficulty Catania (August 5), and the Americans Messina (August 16). The German forces were evacuated to the mainland during the first week of August.

On July 19, 1943, 700 Allied planes bombed Rome. On this fateful day Mussolini met Hitler at Feltre. He had received little assistance from Hitler and seemed henceforth a detached spectator of his own downfall. Mussolini's popularity had fallen to a low-water mark. "Everywhere in the trains, the theatres, the air-raid shelters people are denouncing the regime, and not only this or that party figure, but the Duce himself". On July 24, 1943, the Fascist Grand Council met for the first time after 1939 and disavowed Mussolini by 19 votes to 8, with one abstention. The next day the king, Victor Emmanuel, dismissed Mussolini and had him taken into custody. The king entrusted the government to Marshal Pietro Badoglio.

While assuring the Germans that Italy intended to remain in the war as their ally, Badoglio opened secret negotiations with the Allies. Hitler took the precaution of sending more troops into Italy. The German troops already deployed in the defence of southern Italy moved promtly to seize control of the entire peninsula. Meanwhile, on September 3, Badoglio signed an armistice, amounting to unconditional surrender. On the same day, the Eighth Army crossed the Straits of Messina into the toe of Italy. On September 9, General Mark Clark landed joint Anglo-American forces on the beaches at Salerno in Southern Italy. The army met strenuous German opposition until it was relieved by the Eighth Army. The united armies forced the Germans to retreat to Naples. On October 13, Badoglio declared war on the Germans, who, after wrecking the fine city of Naples, withdrew by the end of the month toward Rome. There, especially at Cassino, they held out until the end of the year.

Russian Offensive, 1943-1944

Even more disastrous was the fate of the Germans in Russia. With every month that passed, the Russian army was gaining notable successes. Hitler had set his heart on the capture of Stalingrad, a place of strategic importance. But Stalin was determined to hold on. In October and November 1942, the Russian pincers began to close. But Hitler refused to give the order for withdrawal for the psychological effect of a retreat would be intolerable. Hitler entrusted Goering with the task of keeping the Sixth Army supplied. As the Russian ring began to envelop the German army, a breakthrough was impossible. Hitler's decision condemned the German army to death. The German General Paulus who had begun the siege with 300,000 men, surrendered with ragged remnants of 123,000 officers and men on February 2, 1943.

After the victory of Stalingrad, the Red Army recaptured Rostov, Kussk and Kharkov. In July 1943 the Germans began their great offensive on the eastern front. But they were soon overwhelmed by a Russian counter-offensive. In November 1943, the Germans had to surrender the Ukrainian capital of Kiev. Hitler admitted the gravity of the situation when he wrote: 'The struggle for the existence of the German people and the future of Europe is reaching its culminating point ... The striking force of our Wehrmacht has suffered greatly in the battles of this summer, especially in the east'. The Russians pushed forward until, by March 1944, the Axis forces were expelled from most of the Ukraine. Meanwhile, in the north, Leningrad had succumbed after a siege of nearly two years and a half, and by mid-May 1944 the Crimea was once again in Russian possession.

Road to Victory, 1943-1945

From the German invasion of Russia, and especially after the entry of the United States into the war, the Soviet Union demanded the opening of a second front in Western Europe only to engage the Germans on two sides. The Allied statesmen tried to explain their difficulties and acknowledged the Soviet contribution to the war. In October 1943 the British Foreign Secretary, Anthony Eden and the United States Secretary of State, Cordell Hull, held talks with their counterpart, Molotov, at Moscow. They pledged to defeat Germany, to free Italy of Fascism and to liberate Austria from its forced union with Germany. They also proposed to establish a world organisation in the near future.

All these pledges were reaffirmed in November 1943 at Teheran where Churchill, Roosevelt and Stalin met. It was dominated by Stalin who emphasised the need for a major second front—preferably in France. This was also the desire of Roosevelt whose interest was to win the war in the shortest possible time by striking directly at Germany. Churchill was in favour of operations in the Mediterranean and the Balkans—'the soft underbelly of Europe'. But Roosevelt and Stalin overcame Churchill's objections and confirmed the tentative decision the British and Americans had reached six months earlier—a major landing would be made in France in May 1944. General Dwight D. Eisenhower was appointed Supreme Commander of the Allied Expeditionary Force to conduct operation 'aimed at the heart of Germany and at the destruction of her armed forces'. Stalin promised to open a simultaneous offensive on the Eastern Front.

The Liberation of Rome

The Teheran decisions had put the Italian campaign in a secondary position. Everything was subordinate to the grand task of building up strength in England for the cross-Channel operation in the spring. The year 1944 opened with heavy casualties in Italy. The German Supreme Commander in Italy, Marshal Kesselring, built a strong defensive position, called the Gustav Line, which had at its centre the 1,700-foot Monte Cassino. Kesselring, therefore, slowed the double-pronged advance of the British Eighth Army and the U.S. Fifth Army of Mark Clark.

To outflank the Gustav Line, the Allies, on January 22, 1944, made a landing at Anzio, about 33 miles (55 km) south of Rome. A simultaneous attack on the Germans was made in front of Cassino. This proved to be a disaster. In February another simultaneous attack was made on Anzio and Cassino. The Allied bombing on Benedictine Abbey of Monte Cassino which the Germans used for observation purposes was sharply criticised. In April 1944, Field Marshal Alexander, the Supreme Allied Commander in Italy, delivered a massive attack on Cassino and occupied it. But the victory was marred to a certain extent when General Clark detached his forces and sent them racing towards Rome. To be first in the Eternal City was the dream of Clark but it prevented the destruction of the German Tenth Army. On June 4, the Allies entered Rome in triumph. A real resistance movement grew up and in the last six months of the war, the Italians fought side by side with the Allies in the common cause.

Landings in Normandy and Southern France

In the early morning of June 6, 1944, the main Allied armies, under the supreme command of Eisenhower, landed in Normandy on a 60 miles (96 km) coast between Cherbourg and Le Havre. According to the report of the United States Chief of Staff, George Marshal, "the beaches of Normandy were chosen for the assault after long study of German coastal defenses and the disposition of German divisions". An armada of five thousand ships and landing craft supported by 12,000 planes, transported 150,000 soldiers, 1,500 tanks, and thousands of guns and vehicles to the Normandy coast. To facilitate landing and constant supply for this formidable army, artificial breakwaters and docks—the so-called Mulberries—were towed across the channel and installed along the beaches.

Throughout the spring of 1944 Field Marshal Rommel—the legendary 'desert fox' of North African fame—had been busy in the gigantic task of preparing the counter-stroke. But he was confronted with a hopeless task. Deprived of adequate forces with which to oppose the Allied thrust and without any naval forces and bedevilled by the lack of decision which left even the tactical matters in the hands of the Fuehrer in Berlin, Rommel found the task insuperable. The much advertised Atlantic Wall, in Rommel's eyes, was 'in its meaning and armaments ... no more than a thin line without depth or substantial reserves'.

The initial surprise was complete. Believing that the main attack would come in the Calais area, where the Channel was narrowest, Rommel had been calamitously deceived. Despite heavy initial resistance, especially on Omaha Beach, the British and American forces poured into the 80 miles (130 km) of the French coast between Cherbourg and Caen. The German defense was doomed to eventual collapse. The British under Montgomery bore the main burnt of German attacks and hammered away at the city of Caen. The Americans, under General Omar Bradley, were assigned the task of taking the Germans in the rear.

Cherbourg surrendered on June 27. On July 25, the American forces under General Omar Bradley broke out at St. Lo. From there they went on to the cathedral town of Coutanees. By early August, the dashing tank-commander General George Patton and his United States Third Army, aided by the French Forces of the Interior, flooded the open country. Meanwhile, on August 15, 1944, the United States Seventh Army, under Lieutenant-General Alexander Patch, with strong reinforcements of French, landed near Cannes in southern France and advanced northwards up the Rhine valley. Simultaneously, to the north, Montgomery had surrounded eight German divisions in 'Falaise pocket', and the Germans retreated to the Seine.

Lyon fell on September 3. On the same day one division of the British Second Army swept into Brussels. Next day another drove on the Antwerp and captured the vast docks. They were less than 100 miles (160 km) from the Rhine, at the gateway of the Ruhr, Germany's greatest industrial area. Paris fell to the Allies on August 15. By this time the Germans had suffered at least 400,000 casualties, of whom more than 200,000 were prisoners of war. But the Germans were yet to be defeated and, in the old Siegfried Line of the remilitarised Rhineland, they made a last stand.

Having realised the inevitability of an Allied victory, a group of frustrated German officers plotted to get rid of Hitler by assassinating him. On July 20, 1944, an attempt was made to kill Hitler. But the attempt miscarried. The conspirators were arrested and executed. July 20 had no effect in putting an end to war. Instead, Hitler said immediately after the failure of the conspiracy, 'We will fight until we get a peace that secures the life of the German nation for the next fifty or a hundred years'.

Germany's Collapse

In the late autumn and early winter of 1944, Germany made desperate efforts to check the advancing Allied army. In mid-September 1944, Montgomery's attempt to circumvent the Siegfried Line at its northern end, in Holland, by landing the Allied Airborne Army at Arnhem, met with disaster. The next month was spent by the U.S. First Army in breaking the German defences at Aachen, while Montgomery tried to clear out the two pockets of Germans which commanded the passage of Antwerp. But this was not completed until early in November. In mid-November a general offensive was launched by all six Allied armies on the western front. It yielded little result at heavy cost. In mid-December the Germans, under their experienced commander, Marshal von Runstedt, struck back at heavily forested area of Ardennes. Soon a whole sector of the Allied line in Belgium and Luxemburg was thrown into confusion: a great 'bulge' opened which had to be closed at all costs. In the so-called 'Battle of the Bulge', Runstedt cut 50 miles (80 km) through American lines and reinvaded Belgium. Supplementing this effect, Hitler employed small, unpiloted aircraft bombers which did considerable damage to the civilian population of London. Next were the longer-range rockets—so-called V-2s—a liquid-fuel of about twelve tons take-off weight—against which no effective defence could be found in time. But the Nazi offensive only caused a delay of about six weeks on the main Allied offensive in the North. By the end of January 1945 the Germans were again driven out of France with the loss of 120,000 men. The Ardennes offensive had exhausted the Fuehrer's last reserves—it hastened rather than delayed the fall of Germany.

Eastern Front

The opening of the 'Second Front' in June 1944 brought great advantage to the Russians. As the German front remained as wide as even, the superiority of the Russians in numbers was now nearly three to one. The Russian's summer offensive was launched on June 23, 1944, sweeping the Germans out of Belorussia and north-east Poland. By the end of July, the Russians also reached the Gulf of Riga while in the centre they penetrated to the suburbs of Warsaw, encouraging the Polish underground leaders to rise in revolt.

It was at this moment of general crisis, the Germans made an astonishing rally in August 1944. Three S.S. armoured divisions delivered a counter-stroke which threw back the Russian advance forces. This gave the Germans an opportunity to suppress the Polish rising. By the end of the first week of August, the Russians were held up almost everywhere. The Russians had advanced up to 450 miles (720 km) in five weeks and were now suffering the natural effect of overstretching their communications.

The temporary deadlock was broken by a change of direction. The Russians made a new move in the south, on the Rumanian front. On August 23, Rumania surrendered. On September 5, the Soviet Union declared war on Bulgaria and, within four days, Bulgaria surrendered. The Russians pushed through the Transylvanian Alps into Hungary. At the opening of 1945 the western half of Poland was still in Germany's grip. The Russian offensive opened on January 12, when Konev's armies were pitted against the German front in Southern Poland. After they had pierced the German defence, Zhukov's armies marched forward. On the 14th, Rokossovsky's armies struck north into East Prussia. By January 31, Zhukov's mechanised forces reached the Lower Oder, only 40 miles (64 km) from Berlin.

Meanwhile, in first half of February 1945, Churchill, Roosevelt and Stalin met at Yalta in Crimea. A certain sympathy existed between Roosevelt and Stalin which was not liked by Churchill. The British Prime Minister was afraid of Russian influence in Europe. However, they agreed upon the postwar control of Germany and the division of that country into states held together by some form of federal bond. She was to pay reparation totalling 20,000 million dollars of which half was to go to Russia. She was to be demilitarised. Russian claim to the occupation of Austria met with Churchill's opposition. But this was subsequently agreed to by General Eisenhower as a military decision. Stalin obtained control over Poland. The Allied concessions to the Soviet point of view were granted in order to secure Soviet participation in the war against Japan. The Powers also concluded agreements concerning the United Nations Organisation to be founded in accordance with the Atlantic Charter. Thus, at Yalta, the two super world-Powers appropriated different parts of the world and ignored the claims of the small states.

The Last Campaigns

Within three months of the Yalta conference, the war in Europe was over. In early March 1945, Eisenhower's armies began a general advance toward the Rhine. On reaching the river, they found to their utter astonishment that the railroad bridge at Remagen south of Bonn was in perfect order. This stroke of fortune changed the whole military outlook as the Americans crossed the river without any bloodshed. They were followed by the British to the north and the French to the south. On March 21, General Patton cleared the Germans along a seventy-mile (112 km) stretch between Coblenz and Mannheim. Next night, Patton's troops crossed the Rhine with little opposition. By this time Montgomery had concentrated 25 divisions for the grand assault on the Rhine near Wesel. When on the night of March 23 the massive attack was launched after a heavy bombardment by over 3,000 guns and by successive waves of bombers, the five exhausted German divisions could do nothing. The troops crossed the river and established bridgeheads. On April 11, the Allied armies reached the Elbe, 60 miles (96 km) from Berlin.

Hitler's escape from assassination in July 1944 helped to convince him of his providential role. So, when on April 12, the news reached Hitler that President Roosevelt had died suddenly, the former thought the event as a 'miracle'. The Fuehrer deluded himself.

In March and April, Russian armies under Marshals Zhukov and Konev took Danzig and Vienna, overran Czechoslovakia and rushed towards Berlin. By April 25, Berlin had been encircled by the armies of Zhukov and Konev. On the 27th, Konev's forces joined hands with the Americans on the Elbe.

Simultaneously, the Allied forces in Italy pierced the 'Gothic Line', captured Bologna and crossed the Po. By the end of April all Italy was free; the Germans laid down their arms. On April 28, 1945, Benito Mussolini, fleeing toward Switzerland with his mistress, was apprehended by members of the Resistance near Lake Como. A summary execution order was produced by the Committee of National Liberation in Milan. Mussolini and his mistress Claretta Petacci were shot dead. Their bodies, riddled with bullets and drenched with rain, were taken to Milan where they were displayed publicly.

Hitler escaped the humiliation of Mussolini's end. On April 30, Hitler shot his mistress and himself in a bunker in Berlin. Goebbles and his family also took their own lives. Of the other leading Nazis, Himmler committed suicide after being captured by the British.

On April 29, Italy surrendered while Hitler still lived and in disregard of his authority. On May 2, after desperate street-by-street resistance by the Germans, Berlin capitulated. On May 7, 1945, the Third Reich, under Admiral Karl Doenitz, surrendered unconditionally to the Allies. It was a formal ending of the Second World War. For the real ending took place on August 14, 1945, when Japan surrendered on the terms laid down by the Allies.

End of the War in the Pacific

The victory of Guadalcanal in February 1943 by the Allies marked the beginning of a protracted war in the Pacific. All of the great island cluster groups in the Pacific west of Hawaii still remained under Japanese control. Since the Pacific extends over more than half the surface of the globe, the strategy of the war involved immense difficulties. Its pivots were airfield and its chief weapons aircraft and aircraft-carriers. The Allied strategy in the Pacific involved the conquest of two key areas—the Philippines and the Burma. If the Philippines could be retaken, offensive operations by air and sea could be launched, via Formosa and Okinawa, against Japan itself. Reconquest of Burma would open the way into China. At the same time, efforts were made to supply China via India with the necessary war materials with the object of using China as a base for a successful allied invasion of the Japanese homeland.

To achieve the conquest of the Philippines, General MacArthur employed the so-called leap-frog approach. Instead of investing and capturing all the Japanese base along the New Guinea Coast which would have taken more time, the practice was adopted of attacking certain strategic points and then by-passing other bases to attack still farther. In this way, the by-passed stations were sealed off and allowed to wither. The second objective was to make amphibious landings among the Solomon Islands until the whole group was under Allied control. The burden of accomplishing the heavy responsibility fell upon the American and Australian troops who, under General MacArthur, began a long series of brilliant amphibious operations.

Between May and August 1943 the Japanese were dislodged from their holds on the Austrian Islands. In November 1943, the U.S. Marines struck at the Coral atoll of Tarawa in the Gilberts. The impregnable island fortress was taken after four days of hard fighting at the cost of 1,100 dead and 2,072 wounded. In January 1944 Kwajalein was seized and the Americans established control over the Marshalls. Eniwetok fell in February. From these bases, U.S. planes and ships were able to neutralise the fortress island of Truk and open the way to Saipan and Trinian in the Marianas. Saipan and Trinian fell in June and July. From the Marianas Japan was only 1,500 miles (2,400 km) away. In July American troops landed on Guam. In September the Americans reached the Pelelieu islands, 550 miles (880 km) from the southern tip of the Philippines.

On October 19, 1944 a great armada along with 250,000 men moved towards Leyte, the centre of the Philippine Archipelago. There took place the greatest naval battle of the whole war. The Japanese lost three battleships, six aircraft carriers and ten cruisers. The Americans lost two destroyers, a destroyer escort, one light carrier, two escort carriers. It was a decisive American victory and made possible the conquest first of Leyte and eventually of the whole of the Philippines. In November 1944 the first major strike was delivered on a Japanese island, Honshu. The ferocity of combat that accomplished the attack was tremendous. According to Marshall's report: 'Landing forces faced intense cross-fires. The enemy could be dislodged only by shattering bombardment and powerful hand-to-hand infantry assault'. In January 1945 MacArthur made another surprising landing on Luzon, the largest of the islands. Manila fell on February 23, 1945.

Meanwhile, the Americans, after heavy bombardment, took Iwo Jima (February), a volcanic island 750 miles (1,200 km) south of Japan. On April 1, 1945 divisions of the United States Tenth Army landed on Okinawa in the Ryukus, only 350 miles (560 km) from Japan. The shock of that news, along with Moscow's repudiation of the neutrality pact with Japan, precipitated the fall of Koiso's cabinet on April 5, and Suzuki became Prime Minister. Though Okinawa was not taken till mid-June, its fate had been sealed in the first week, when Japan's last and latest modern battleship, the *Yamato*, had been sunk by American aircraft on April 7. The war had come to the doorstep of Japan as the airfields were within less than 400 miles (640 km) of Japan. Since November 1944, Japan had been under heavy and continuous bombardment by the super-fortresses, B-29. In a single night's attack on March 9, 1945, more than 1,600 tons of incendiary bombs were dropped on Tokyo, damaging 15 square miles of the city and killing and injuring 185,000 people. By the end of May three million of Tokyo's population had been rendered homeless.

While the Allies made steady progress in the Pacific, there took place unrewarding jungle warfare in Burma and Malaya, and the land fighting in China. In August 1943, a South-East Asia Command (SEAC) was set up under Admiral Lord Louis Mountbatten. In northern Burma, the British Fourteenth Army under General Slim, guerrilla bands of British and Indian soldiers under Brigadier Wingate, General Stilwell's Chinese troops and General Merrill's American 'Galahad' fighters fought some of the toughest battles of the war during the winter of 1943-4. Braving impenetrable jungles and against tremendous odds, these forces eventually drove the Japanese from northern Burma and saved India from invasion. By 1944, Burma, like Italy, had become a minor theatre of war. But the Japanese in Burma were increasingly cut off when Rangoon was bombed with impunity by the British planes. By January 22, 1945, the Ledo Road in Burma had been cleared and the way opened to join forces with Generalissimo's Chiang Kai-shek's armies. This was accomplished in early spring, breaking Japan's hold on China. Meanwhile, the Australians had landed on Borneo and established control over the strategic bases from which Allied air and naval forces could cover the Asiatic Coast from Singapore to Shanghai.

The helplessness of the situation became apparent to Admiral Suzuki and his cabinet. Emperor Hirohito became convinced that further fighting was futile and that they should sue for peace. Eventually it was decided on June 20 that Prince Konoye should be sent on a mission to Moscow to negotiate for peace. On July 17, 1945, at Potsdam in Germany, President Truman of U.S.A., Premier Attlee of Britain and Chiang Kai-Shek issued a declaration demanding unconditional surrender of Japan as an alternative to complete destruction. Japan rejected this demand. Though Stalin did not participate in the declaration, he expressed the intention of entering the war against Japan after the close of hostilities in Europe.

The anticipated entrance of the Soviet Union in the war lest she might gain an advantageous position in the Far East led President Truman to take the hard decision of using the atom bomb to accelerate Japan's collapse. But there were some who hesitated to employ the destructive and deadly weapon of annihilation. Admiral Leah, Chief of Staff to President Roosevelt and President Truman, expressed his apprehension of employing such a weapon against the civilian population. 'My own feeling was that, in being the first to use it, we had adopted an ethical standard common to the barbarians of the Dark Age.'

On August 6, 1945, the first atomic bomb was dropped on Hiroshima in Japan which destroyed half the city and caused 80,000 deaths. Two days later, on August 8, Moscow declared war on Tokyo and sent troops into Manchuria and the Japanese half of the island of Sakhalin. On August 9, a second atomic bomb was dropped on Nagasaki in Kyushu, destroying the whole municipal area and killing tens of thousands of people. On the following day, Japan offered to surrender unconditionally which was accepted by the Allies on August 14. But the formal armistice was not signed until September 2, 1945.

Effects of the Second World War

The Second World War was a momentous event which changed the whole world. The loss in human life and in material goods was beyond any calculation. About 40 to 50 million people lost their lives—half of them were civilians. The destruction was greatest in the German-Soviet war and Russian losses were estimated at 20 million dead. France, which was twice a major battlefield, lost some 500,000 lives. The forces of the British Commonwealth lost some 445,000 of which well over half came from the United Kingdom. In addition, 60,000 civilians perished by aerial attacks. The United States estimated her loss at 300,000 military casualties. Germany lost over 4 million of whom 1 million were civilians. China's loses were estimated at between 6 and 8 million and Japan's at 3 million, including 600,000 civilians. On the other side, Italian loses were relatively small, about 310,000—of whom about half were civilians. Europe appeared a 'rubble heap, a charnel house, a breeding ground of pestilence and hate'—as Churchill described later.

The Second World War caused enormous uprooting and displacement of people. Bombing rendered millions homeless. German conscription of labour in the occupied countries displaced millions of Europeans from their homes. Each side took millions of prisoners. In the first three and a half years of the war, thirty million Europeans had left their original homes. Some twelve million Russians had left their homes for the interior of the country. In the Balkans and Hungary, several hundred thousand people had found themselves uprooted. To these must be added the forceful movements effected by Hitler and Stalin. Hitler 'brought home' German minorities from the South Tyrol, the Baltic States, the Bukovina and the Dobrudja. Hitler drove out Poles, Slovenes and Czechs from their homes and tried to replace them with Germans. Stalin moved Poles, Lithuanians, Estonians into Russia.

Displaced persons bequeathed to the postwar world vast problem of resettlement and rehousing. The settlement of frontiers at Yalta and Potsdam effected various transplantations. An increasing number of Germans sought asylum in the British and American Zones of Occupation. The problem of resettlement was protracted and beset with difficulties. A massive war weariness added to human suffering and distress.

The material and moral havoc wrought by the war was on a gigantic scale. Hundreds of harbours were destroyed, miles of railway line damaged, railway bridges, tunnels, road bridges and roads destroyed and damaged, buildings destroyed, material resources exhausted, agricultural crops lost or reduced. But the greatest moral damage done by the war was hatred and thirst for revenge. This was reflected in the Nuremberg Trial of War Criminals which opened on November 20, 1945.

The Trials proceeded through 403 open sessions in the Palace of Justice and the final sentences were pronounced on 1 October 1946. There were four Allied Judges, under their chairman, Sir Geoffrey Lawrence, QC, and 21 defendants present, who all pleaded Not Guilty. Lord Justice Lawrence pronounced 'We are here to judge major war criminals' and 'not to try the prosecuting powers'. The Nuremberg Trials confirmed the horror of Nazi crimes and documented the role played by Germany in the origins and conduct of the Second World War. However, the historical material furnished in the indictments were so selective that even the die-hard anti-Nazi could lament. A leading historian wrote: 'The published indictment reads like history written by non-historians'.

The economic consequences of the war were far-reaching. Though the United States, Canada, and the South American countries had been enriched, the rest of the world had been impoverished. Trade was at a standstill; transportation and communication systems had been disrupted; currencies were depreciated and credit facilities uncertain; food and fuel stocks were inadequate. The recovery from these conditions was slower in eastern Europe than in the west. Progress in western Europe was made easier owing to the loans land assistance rendered by the United States under the so-called Marshall Plan of 1947. Of all the participants in the war, the losses of the United States had been insignificant except in human terms. Her economic output, gold reserve, balance of trade were such that it turned out that no country in Europe could achieve reconstruction without American aid. This economic dependence of Europe upon the United States gave her the political primacy.

The political consequences of the war were immense. The immediate consequence was the disappearance of the German State. In accordance with the decisions reached at Yalta, Germany was divided into four zones, to be occupied and administered by Britain, France, the Soviet Union, and the United States. The Soviet Zone would cover the eastern part of the country, while the western part would comprise zones for Britain, the United States, and France, In each zone, authority was vested in the military commander of the occupying power, and the four commanders together would constitute a 'Control Council' for Germany as a whole.

Berlin was divided into four sectors and occupied by four powers. Each Power behaved in its own way in its own zone presaging the division of Germany into the German Democratic Republic and the German Federal Republic. Germany had to suffer great territorial losses, Russia getting the northern part of East Prussia including Konigsberg and Poland obtaining Danzig, Upper and Lower Silesia, eastern Brandenburg, most of Pomerania, and a southern strip of East Prussia. In addition, Alsace Lorraine was restored to France; Eupen and Malmedy to Belgium; the Sudetenland to Czechoslovakia. Austria was detached and divided into zones for Allied military occupation, and the Saar basin was put under French control.

Russia emerged from the war with enlarged territory. Apart from retaining all the territory—Karelia, the Baltic countries (Estonia, Latvia, Lithuania), Polish White Russia, Bessarbia, northern Bukovina, acquired as a result of the German-Soviet Pact, she added East Prussia and Ruthenia, East Germany, Austria, Poland, Hungary, Czechoslovakia, South Sakhalin, Dairen and Port Arthur. Russia showed tremendous resilience after the war.

The Second World War diminished Britain's strength and crippled her economic resources. A contemporary wrote with great pain—'The advantages which position, coal, skill and enterprise won for us in the nineteenth century have been liquidated, and we go back to scratch. With overseas debts amounting to a total of £ 3,355 million, Britain had no financial means for reconstruction.'

France had to suffer much during four years of Nazi occupation and in the difficult months after liberation. The situation was made worse by unusually severe winters in 1945-6 and 1946-7. The existence of various political groups and activities of the Communists weakened France. As a matter of fact, French politics after the Second World War continued to appear as "an interregnum of dissent between spells of chaos". The difficulty was increased by Gaulle Charles de resignation in January 20, 1946. It was not until the establishment of the second parliament of the Fourth Republic that France could become politically stable. Italy became a Republic (1946) with no overseas colonies, impoverished, but able to recover economically.

The Second World War shifted the balance of power, Out of the war emerged two great world powers—the United States and the Soviet Russia. Both had been strong states before the war; but in the years that immediately followed it they became the arbiters of international events. In the struggle between two ideologies—Democracy and Communism—the latter emerged with remarkable strength. During 1946-47 the governments of Poland, Yugoslavia, Bulgaria, Albania, Rumania, Hungary, Czechoslovakia were converted, step by step, into virtual Communist dictatorships. Democratic monarchies were restored in Norway, Denmark, the Netherlands, and Belgium.

SECOND WORLD WAR
Eastern Front

SECOND
WORLD WAR
Western Front
German advances
Allied advances
Major aerial conflict
Scale of Miles
0 100 200 300
Narvik
FINLAND
Helsinki
Leningrad
U.S.S.R.
Norway
Oslo
SWEDEN
Stockholm
Riga
April
1940
North Sea
Great
Britain
Baltic
Denmark
Copenhagen
Warsaw
IRELAND
1940-1942
Hamburg
POLAND
Atlantic Ocean
Potsdam
Berlin
Netherlands
1941-1945
Coventry
Rotterdam
Dresden
London
Dunkirk
Ostende
Bonn
Spring
1945
Prague
Calais
Remagen
CZECHOSLOVAKIA
Cherbourg
Le Havre
Abbeville
Falaise
Winter 1944/45
July 1944
Paris
Lexemburg
Vienna
Budapest
HUNGARY
AUSTRIA
Summer 1944
Switzerland
Spring 1945
Belgrade
FRANCE
Milan
Bolorna
YUGOSLAVIA
Bordezaue
Lyon
Turin
Florence
Fall 1944
Winter 1944/45
Marseille
Italy
Adriatic sea
Nice
Fall 1944
Albania
Summer 1944
Rome
Anzio
Cassino
Naples
Winter 1943/44
Fall 1943
Greece
Madrid
Portugal
Lisbon
SPAIN
Palenis
Summer 1943
Gibraltar
Mediterranea Sea
Malta

The division of the world into two ideologies led to significant new political alignments. During the war Britain, France, Russia, China, and the United States were allied against Germany, Italy and Japan. Not long after the war almost complete reversal of alignment took place. The United States came to lean heavily on the support of West Germany, Japan, and Italy. Conversely, Russia, Communist China, and their allies became another bloc. Thus, the postwar world saw a growing tension among the Allies—between East and West, and, more specifically, between Russia and the United States. In 1946 Churchill said at Fulton in the United States: 'From Stettin in the Baltic to Trieste in the Adriatic an Iron Curtain has descended across the continent'. Gradually the point of view developed that, as Truman put it, 'unless Russia is faced with an iron fist, and strong languages, another war is in the making'. To counteract Communism, the Western responses were the Truman Doctrine, the Marshall Plan, and the North Atlantic Treaty Organisation (NATO). The Warsaw Pact was the Soviet rejoinder. Thus old conflicts subsided into new discords and the result was not peace but 'Cold War'. After the Second World War, a third force emerged which refused to join either of the two sides in the Cold War. India became one of the two important leaders of the uncommitted or non-aligned powers, most of which were Afro-Asian.

The Second World War served to quicken national feeling among subject peoples throughout the Near East and Far East. The Atlantic Charter pledged to the restoration of 'sovereign rights and self-government to those who have been forcibly deprived of them'. Nationalist forces were at work in Burma, Malaya, Indo-China, Indonesia, India, and China. These movements had existed before the war, but they had been greatly encouraged by the demonstration that white nationals are not necessarily superior in military skill to colonial people. Once the process of liberation had started, it proceeded with a rush that defied all calculations. In 1947 Britain granted India complete independence and divided the country into self-governing states—India and Pakistan. Burma was accorded complete independence in 1948. Simultaneously, Britain made special concessions to the Arab States and also to the Jews in the Near East. Upon the withdrawal of British forces in 1947, an independent Jewish state, Israel, was set up. Even more important the war discredited the government of General Chiang Kai-Shek and the Kuomintang and paved the way for the Communist revolution of 1949.

The United States also granted to the Philippines the independence it had promised earlier. France was compelled to recognise the sovereign independence of Syria and Lebanon and to promise self-government to Indo-China (renamed Vietnam). Italy lost all her colonies. Ethiopia regained its independence. Libya was eventually made a sovereign state. It has been truly observed:

> Between 1945 and 1960 no less than forty countries with a population of eight hundred millions—more than a quarter of the world's inhabitants—revolted against colonialism and won their independence.

By 1965, African and Asian nations which had won their independence after 1945 made up more than half of the Assembly of the United Nations.

A sense of futility gripped Europe in the second half of the twentieth century. It was reflected in the post-war circle of Jean-Paul Sartre and the philosophers of Existentialism. It faded soon afterwards in most Western countries, that reappeared with much zest in the peace movement and anti-nuclear propaganda of later decades. In Eastern Europe, officialdom remained ingrained in people's inner lives until the revolution by reforms of 1989-91, when the two Germanies—East and West—were united (1990), and Soviet Russia broken up (1991).

Despite the divisions, the concept of Europe remained dormant among the citizens of former Soviet bloc. 'Europe has two lungs', declared a Slavonic Pope, 'it will never breathe easily until it uses both of them.'

Europe's destiny roughly comprises three periods. Beginning with the immediate post-war era (1945-48), when Allied unity was lost, it continued through four decades of the Cold War

(1948-89) and ended with the momentous reign in Moscow of Mikhail Gorbachev (1985-91). "Overall, they may be said to have begun on VE Day, 9 May 1945, and to have ended with the final disbandment of the Soviet Union in December 1991. By that time, almost all of Europe's peoples were free to determine their own destiny'.[3]

3. Norman Davies, *Europe*, P. 1058.

CHAPTER 37

MINOR EUROPEAN COUNTRIES

Belgium

Belgium was under Austrian occupation under Joseph II (1780-90). Inspired by the American revolution, a Congress of the Belgian Provinces proclaimed the independence of the 'United Belgian States' in January 1790. This proved to be short-lived. By the end of the year 1790 the Austrians reoccupied the Belgian provinces. However when war broke out between France and the continental powers on April 20, 1792, the French forces under Dumauriez overran Belgium, after a resounding victory at Jemappes (November 6, 1792). Many of the Belgians acted as the French General's advisers. They aimed at establishing an independent Belgian republic with a Girondist government. This was considered by Dumauriez as a step prelude to annexation. But the Convention decided to call in February 1793 a referendum by which it was anticipated the country's accession to the French Republic. Hardly had the referendum been over when the Austrian forces gained a victory at Neerwinden (March 18, 1793) and drove the French from Belgium. But the Austrian victory proved to be illusory. On June 26, 1794 the Battle of Fleurus sealed the fate of Belgium by placing it under French occupation for the next twenty years.

The Convention tried to exploit the country to relieve France's bankruptcy and shortages in essential commodities. Numerous works of art were appropriated and sent to museums in France. This vandalism antagonised the people. However it was during these years, France renovated the country's institutions by introducing administrative uniformity and efficient judicial, financial and postal organisation. On October 1, 1795 the Belgian departments became part of the Republic. Numerous laws especially those suppressing feudalism and clipping the powers of the nobles were introduced. Eventually, French legislation was imposed on Belgium on December 6, 1796.

The vicissitudes of French politics had their effect on Belgium. The election of March 1797 returned a conservative majority. The election helped to return nominees of the Right to the Five Hundred and to replace the officials by conservative elements. Anticipating the repeal of the laws on religion, they reopened closed churches. But the coup of 18 Fructidor (September 4, 1797) undid most of the works. Newly elected officials were removed and the old incumbents restored. The religious situation deteriorated rapidly. The oath of hatred of royalty was rigidly enforced; those who refused were sentenced to deportation. There was large-scale confiscation of Church property which antagonised the large section of the people. At the same time, the economic situation became more critical by depleted trade, bad harvests and unemployment. The introduction of conscription (September 1798) caused riots in Ghent which spread like wildfire over the whole of Flanders. But this 'Peasants War' lacked organisation and resources. By December 1798 the French were successful in suppressing the revolt. Hundreds of insurgents were executed and thousands of priests were prosecuted.

The attitude of the Belgians towards the French rule hardened. But they could do nothing against their new masters owing to the passivity of the European powers. A melancholy resignation seized the Belgians with hopes of liberation nourished by the varying fortunes of war. But their aspirations were clouded with uncertainty. Austrian restoration seemed chimerical. But a reunion of the Low Countries under the House of Orange seemed to the Belgians less attractive.

Despite the efficiency of the French administration, the educated people of Belgium resented the suppression of the representative Government. Only a few were soothed by prospects of promotion to higher offices, such as that of prefect. The only supporters of the French rule were buyers of the church property who believed that the regime was a guarantee against a restoration of the old order. However, during these years, Belgium became the birthplace of the new industry on the continent. Abundant and cheap manpower and ancient tradition of workmanship gave a fillip to Belgian manufacturers which commanded the whole continent. Ghent became the most thriving focus of cotton manufacturing industry on the continent. From 1799 on, the Lancashire engineer William Cookerill constructed textile equipment at Verviers. After 1807 he made Liege the premier centre of engine building. Trade was brisk and industrialists enjoyed prosperity till 1810 when a slump overtook the economy.

France's military setbacks in 1812-13 caused the first symptoms of unrest since 1798. Allied occupation between December 1813 and May 1814 was hailed with delight. Most noblemen and clergymen wanted the restoration of Habsburg rule. But Francis I of Austria was no longer interested in Belgium. The progressive industrialists saw the only alternative in a union with Holland which could with its colonies, provide outlet for Belgian industry. The solution was desired by King William of Holland, the latter being sponsored by the British Government. In June 1814 the big Powers through the instrumentality of Lord Castlereagh agreed to unite the Low countries in the 'most perfect amalgam'. A provisional Government was at once formed under William I.

Belgium was placed under Dutch rule as a matter of international convenience. There was little community of interests between the Belgium and the Dutch. They differed in language and religion—the Belgians being predominantly Roman Catholic, the Dutch Protestants. Economically, the Belgians were industrialists and believed in tariff protection while the Dutch were an agricultural and commercial people.

The main source of conflict between the Belgians and the Dutch was in the field of religion, which was included in the constitution. Another point of dispute with the Catholics was the building up of a state system of education. William wanted to reduce the excessive influence of the Church in matters of education which he thought incompatible with a modern state. In 1817 state universities were opened in the Belgian provinces at Ghent, Louvain and Liege and state 'athenaeums' for classical education were instituted in all main towns. This measure threatened the ecclesiastical predominance in Belgian schools.

The viability of the United Kingdom was also threatened by the Frenchification. In the Flemish provinces the language and culture were French. In Flanders, there was no substitute for French. The King considered it an affront when the Dutch remained nearly as foreign to his Flemish as to his Walloon subjects. To the King the amalgamation became incongruous when one-half of the realm kept aloof from the other's culture. To combat the French influence, the King in 1819 decreed that by 1823 the Dutch was to be used in Flanders for administration and justice. From 1823 it was also imposed in secondary schools. There arose a storm of protest from the bourgeoisie and the Church. Against this determined opposition, the King backed out. In fact, the law had been allowed to be ignored.

The King's supporters in Belgium were the industrialists and entrepreneurs who had welcomed the creation of the new state. However, a clash of interests occurred between the Dutch and the Belgian mercantilists. The Dutch advocated a return to free trade, while the Belgians clung tenaciously to Protectionism. Gradually, however, William shifted to industrial protection which, among other things, led to the beginnings of industrial revolution in Holland. In 1822 was established at Brussels a bank, the *Societe Generale des Pays-Bas*, to foster trade, the capital of which was subscribed up to four-fifths by the king himself.

With the passage of time, political strife became more acute. From 1824, a group of young lawyers, began to champion a new liberalism. The celebrities, Lebeau, Devaux and the

Rogiers—who were to be the makers of independent Belgium—demanded direct elections and ministerial responsibility. From 1828 the young liberals, united with the young Catholics, opposed royal despotism. Towards the close of 1828, people clamoured for the freedom of the press and of education. A liberal Catholic newspaper suggested administrative separation between Belgium and Holland under a common Crown. A series of bad harvests in the late 1820s hit the peasants. In the spring of 1830 the textile industry at Liege, Verviers and Tournai suffered over production and workers attributed this economic trouble unreasonably to the Dutch. The smouldering discontent of the Belgians burst forth after the July Revolution of France in 1830. On August 25, 1830, rioting began in Brussels. This was followed by widespread disturbances throughout the country. But it was too late to overcome revolutionary upsurge. A provisional government was formed on September 26, 1830 and, on October 4, it declared Belgium independent.

The declaration of independence was a clear violation of the Treaties of 1815 and it became a matter of concern to the great powers. The King of the Netherlands expected the intervention of the eastern powers on his behalf. In fact, Russia was ready to do so with 60,000 troops. The King of Prussia had also mobilised his army for the same purpose. Metternich also felt that intervention was the only way of preventing 'the universal shipwreck of Europe'.

In the face of this menacing threat, the western powers acted with commendable alacrity. Talleyrand, who had come to London in September 1830 as the French ambassador, declared categorically that France would not tolerate any intervention in Belgium. Wellington agreed and urged the powers to refrain from taking action until representatives of the five powers could meet in London to discuss Belgian affairs.

The eastern powers accepted the invitation hoping to convert Wellington to their point of view by persuasion. But before the London Conference would discuss the matter seriously, Wellington's government had made its exit. The new Foreign Secretary was Henry Temple Viscount Palmerston (1784-1865) who considered the union of the Low Countries 'the most advantageous to the general interests of Europe', but felt that it was too late to reverse the historical forces. Palmerston had many faults as a diplomat, but his accurate judgement, rapidity of decision and forces of will led him to insist the principle of non-intervention. Simultaneously he urged the powers to accept the *fait accompli*.

Palmerston was helped in this endeavour by the sudden rising of the Poles which absorbed the attention of Russia and diverted the energies of Austria and Prussia to their own Polish provinces. By the end of December 1830 Palmerston was able to secure the assent of all powers to Belgian independence. But the last stage was vitiated by Talleyrand's demand of some compensation for France and the stubborn efforts of the Dutch King to reimpose his will on Belgium. But in the face of Palmerston's firmness, Talleyrand beat a hasty retreat. On January 20, 1831, along with the other members, he signed a protocol which by delineating the boundaries of Belgium and Holland, established Belgium as a neutral state under the permanent guarantee of the powers. But the French government delayed in ratifying the protocol and tried to wreck it by securing the throne of Belgium for Louis Philippe's son, the duc de Nemours. Palmerston's irritation knew to bounds and observed categorically that the British occupied the position of 'impartial mediators between France on the one hand, and the three other powers on the other ... as long as both parties remain quiet, we shall be friends with both; but ... whichever side breaks the peace, that side will find us against them.'

The rebuff sobered the French government. When the Belgian National Assembly had elected Leopold of Saxe-Coburg as their future ruler, the two powers succeeded in securing the adhesion of the other members of the conference. But the French intrigue was not yet at an end. When the Dutch King sent his armies into Belgium in August 1831, the conference authorised Britain and France to drive away the force. The French troops refused to leave Belgium after accomplishing their work. Once more the British Foreign Secretary thundered: 'The French must go out of Belgium or we have a general war and war in a given number of days.' In the face of this grim resolution, the French gave way. On November 15, 1831 they joined with the other powers in the famous treaty by which Belgium was admitted to the family of nations as an independent state with Leopold of Saxe-Coburg as its ruler. The new nation was declared as a neutral state. The old barrier fortresses were destroyed and the Great Powers guaranteed the inviolability and integrity of the Belgium state. The treaty was ratified in May 1832, but not accepted by the Dutch King until April 1839. The Dutch intransigence became evident when, in December 1832, an Anglo-French force bombarded the citadel of Antwerp and forced the Dutch to surrender that stronghold to the Belgian King.

As a result of the Belgian revolution, a model constitution came into effect in 1831 which completely outbid practically every other constitution of the day. The country was to be governed by a truly liberal King who had to accept without any qualm the principles of limited monarchy and the sovereignty of the people. King Leopold of Belgium typified the best example of a limited constitutional monarchy. The Belgian constitution of 1831 became the beacon-light for liberals and radicals. In it were recognised the sovereignty of the people, a King owing allegiance to the constitution, a bicameral legislature completely elected by the people, an independent judiciary, a clergy paid by the state but independent of it and a declaration of the rights of the citizen based on the principles of 1776 and 1789. The constitution contained so many unique features that in the epoch-making period of 1848 it was very influential in Germany, Italy, Scandinavia, and elsewhere.

Belgium's first King, Leopold I (1830-65) helped consolidate the neutrality of the country by cultivating good relations with his royal neighbours and even by giving the European community the benefit of his advice. The mentor of Europe was succeeded by Leopold II (1865-1909), the founder of Belgium's rich colonial empire.

Like Britain, Belgium moved from liberalism to democracy. In 1893 the constitution was amended to give the vote to all male citizens who had reached the age of twenty-five. Until 1870, Belgium was the only continental country to keep pace with the industrial expansion of Britain. In 1834 the Belgian parliament endorsed a plan drawn up by George Stephenson for the construction of a national system of railways emanating from Liege and Brussels. With the help of British investments and engineers, Belgium became a nation of foundries, factories, and mines.

The domestic politics in Belgium was embittered by the relations between the Church and the State, particularly in regard to education. With the proliferation of schools, the question of imparting religious instruction assumed importance. On this question were formed, in 1847, two major political parties, the Catholic Party—enthusiastic in prescribing religious instructions in the schools, and the Liberal Party—denouncing 'clericalism'. Between 1847 and 1884 Liberals controlled parliament. They abolished religious instruction in the schools and severed diplomatic relations with the Papacy. In the latter part of the nineteenth century, the Liberal Party lost its ascendancy and gave way to an emerging Socialist Party.

Taking advantage of the rivalry between the Socialists and Liberals and by championing the cause of social reform, the Catholic Party obtained a parliamentary majority in 1884 which it retained for the next thirty years. Apart from restoring religious instruction in most of the public schools, the Catholic Party extended elementary education which considerably reduced the percentage of illiteracy in the country.

In 1894 the property qualification in the franchise was removed and every male Belgian who was over twenty-four years of age was accorded voting rights. Simultaneously, the principle of plural voting was introduced. In 1898 the Flemish language was put on an equal footing with the French thus removing the long-standing grievances of the lower classes in northern Belgium who knew Flemish but not French.

In 1899 proportional representation was introduced where several parties were accorded parliamentary seats in proportion to the number of votes polled by each. The Catholic Party had to undergo bitter opposition from the Socialists and the Liberals who decried the clerical influence in education and the system of plural voting. A general strike was conducted by the Socialists in 1913 with the rallying cry 'One man, One vote'. But the elections of 1914 returned a Catholic majority. After 1890 the Belgian parliament introduced some significant social legislation.

Apart from legalizing trade-unions in 1898, it adopted a system of old-age pensions. Steps were taken in providing decent houses to the working classes and in looking after their material well-being.

Largely influenced by an Anglo-American journalist and explorer, Henry Stanley, who pointed out the rich rubber resources of the huge Congo region in Central Africa, King Leopold II undertook colonial expansion. He organised a private commercial company with himself as President and chief stockholder and obtained international sanction (1884-85) for the creation of the 'Congo Free State' with himself as its personal sovereign. Leopold II invested heavily in the company and amassed huge fortunes. A startling disclosure of outrages and practical slavery inflicted upon the people of Congo to get rubber raised hue and cry against Belgium. Leopold II yielded to the pressure of public opinion and proposed the transformation of the Congo Free State into a Belgian colony in 1908. This was accepted by the Belgian government, thereby acquiring an overseas empire with an area almost eighty times its own.

On August 2, 1914, the German government presented a twelve-hour ultimatum to Belgium, demanding that German troops be permitted to cross into France. The Belgian government viewed the ultimatum as a gross violation of international law. They not only rejected the German requests, but appealed to Britain in maintaining the neutrality of Belgium.

The neutrality of Belgium had long been the corner-stone of British foreign policy. The British had fought against Napoleon I, denouncing the annexation of Belgium by France, and they had thwarted the ambition of Napoleon III in respect of Belgium. The last thing that Britain wanted was Belgium's incorporation with the German Empire. On August 4, 1914, no sooner had the German troops crossed the border into Belgium, than Sir Edward Grey, sent an ultimatum to Germany asking the latter to respect Belgian neutrality. Germany refused to comply. Bethmann-Hollweg, the German Chancellor, made no secret of his feeling when he berated the British ambassador: 'Just for a word neutrality, a word which in war time has so often been disregarded—just for a scrap of paper—Great Britain was going to make war on a kindred nation who desired nothing better than to be friends with her.' At midnight, Britain declared war on Germany.

Belgium made a determined stand against German onslaught. The gallant defense of the Liege fort surprised the Germans. But, by the latter part of August 1914, most of Belgium was under military occupation by Germany, and a German governor was installed at Brussels.

Despite economic troubles and some trying political disputes, Belgium showed no sign of political weakness. After long German occupation, Belgium was faced with problems of reconstruction and industrial reorganisation. However, recovery was not long in coming owing to careful planning and hard work. The growing labour movement led to the passage of social-insurance legislation. The government had to grapple with the old tension between the Flemings and the Walloons, being made more acute by the Germans encouraging the hope of Flemish separation. In 1921 the country was divided along language lines into two administrative sections. Some concessions were made to the Flamingos notably in the field of education.

After the First World War, political life in Belgium was disturbed. There was considerable governmental instability. Between 1928 and 1940, on an average, the government had to face two crises. The Socialist party, which won the 1920 election, had fulfilled the basic programme of universal suffrage, trade union liberty and progressive taxation of incomes. But later on it retreated and practically abandoned the socialisation of the means of production. The reconstituted Catholic Party was torn by working-class conflicts and by the Flemish question. The Liberal party, influenced by business circles and committed to traditional economic Liberalism, was anti-

Socialist. It was only at times of grave crisis that a coalition government was formed. In 1926 the Belgian Franc found itself in great difficulties. The Cabinet was taken over by a businessman, Emile Francqui. He was given full powers. He limited spending and introduced a new unit of currency, the *belga*, which he stabilised on the American dollar. All railway holdings were transferred to the state.

The Great Depression (1929-1934) brought with it severe crisis in Belgian economy. There was a serious budgetary deficit and unemployment figure rose to all time high. The government tried to surmount the crisis by applying orthodox measures: economies, customs tariffs, new taxes. The government of Theunis, Francqui and Gutt—the so-called 'Bankers' government' pursued a deflationary policy. It reduced buying power and, in March 1935, abandoned parity with gold. There began reaction against bourgeois conservation which assumed two dimensions: a nationalist upsurge in the Flemish area and of *Rexisme* in the Walloon area. The latter was a Fascist movement, founded by Leon Degrelle, who received active support from Hitler and Mussolini.

In the 1936 election the three traditional parties suffered defeat. The Liberals lost one seat, the Socialists and the Catholic Party lost three seats, respectively. On the other hand, the Communists won six seats, the Flemish Nationalists eight, and the Rexists twenty-one. But the electoral success of the Rexists was momentary. A few months later, Degrelle was defeated in Brussels by Van Zeeland. In 1939 the Rexists held only four seats.

Van Zeeland's government, with the cooperation of Henry de Man and Spaak, both Socialists, assumed special powers for twelve months. It devalued the franc once more, abandoned free exchange and adopted a Four-Year Plan. De Man, the most important figure in the political stage, showed sympathy towards Rexisme and began to talk of a national party 'of order and authority.' In 1930 he was succeeded by Spaak, the first Socialist to become Prime Minister. A new economic slump caused further unemployment and produced monetary crisis. Socialist unity was shattered by the opposition of Vandervalde and Brouckere to De Man. After the 1939 election the Catholic-Liberal government was formed under Pierlot.

At the Peace Conference of 1919, Belgium was freed from the restriction imposed upon it by the treaty of 1839 and was permitted to follow an independent foreign policy. After 1920 Belgium allied with France in a common defensive system. However, the German military occupation of the Rhineland in 1936 effected a change in the Belgium foreign policy. King Leopold III announced that Belgium must follow an exclusively national policy. Next year, she was released from her obligations under the Locarno Treaties. However, this retreat to neutrality did not save Belgium from German aggression in 1940.

Belgium resistance did not last long. On May 11, 1940, the German troops captured Fort Eben Emael, the key to Belgian defenses. On the same day armoured forces crossed the Albert Canal and forced the Belgians to retreat. The Belgians were supported by the British and French forces. However, the weakness of these forces was demonstrated when on May 13-14, General Ewald von Kleist penetrated through the impassable Ardennes and threw the Allied forces across the Meuse north of Sedan. Guderian, with three German armoured divisions supported by motorized infantry, raced for the coast which he reached on May 23. The whole Belgian army and its supporting French and British units were enveloped.

An Allied plan to break through the ring was frustrated by German pressure and by lack of vigour in the French command. The Allied forces were steadily pushed toward the coast. On May 27, the Belgian resistance collapsed and King Leopold III made an unconditional surrender to the German and was placed in 'protective custody' near Brussels. For this he was bitterly criticised by the Allies and by his own people. The Belgian capitulation exposed the north-eastern flank and forced the British and French back upon the beaches of Dunkirk. But, thanks to the combined power of navy and air force, the brave rearguard action of the French and the hundreds of little boats, the Allied troops evacuated from Denmark (May 27-June 4, 1940).

After the war, the two chief political parties—the Catholic and the Socialist—obtained an overwhelming majority in the parliament in election of 1946. They cooperated in governing the country. King Leopold III, who had surrendered to the Germans in 1940, was restored. But his predilection for authoritarianism and marriage to a commoner after the death of his wife, Queen Astrid, alienated Leopold III from his subjects. He, therefore, abdicated in favour of his son, Badouin, who ascended the throne in 1951. Belgium recovered its economic prosperity by checking inflation and stabilising the currency. Belgian politics were relatively quiet until 1960, when the decision to grant independence to its former colony in Africa caused discontent. However, discontent waned when it was found that the loss of Congo would have no adverse economic effect on Belgium. The country benefited from joining with other countries in a tariff union called 'Benelux'.

Holland

The Kingdom of the Dutch Netherlands—or Holland as the country is commonly called—was a land of burghers, farmers, and fishermen. The Dutch Netherlands possessed a large part of the colonial and commercial empire which had been acquired in the seventeenth century.

Dutch intervention in the American War of Independence (1780-84) had brought the country on the verge of economic bankruptcy. The stadholder William V was arraigned for naval reverses. Inspired by the ideology of Enlightenment, an opposition party grew up which demanded electoral reform as the Dutch government was based on selfish urban oligarchies. But the 'Patriot' movement was split into two sections: a conservative one, while dispensing with the stadholder, wanted to vest the superragotary power in the patrician oligarchy, and a democratic one, which sought for a limited progressive reform of power. The latter was more vocal and even organised militias to resist the stadholder.

The Democrats seized power in Utrecht in 1785 and gained ascendancy elsewhere. The conservatives became alarmed at the growing strength of the Democrats and tried to curry favour with the stadholder. An Organist party took shape, and civil war loomed large. Eventually, Prussia, with backing of the British government, invaded Holland on September 13, 1787. France refused to respond to Democrats' appeal for help. With the fall of Amsterdam on October 10, 1789, this civil war appeared to have ended.

After the collapse of the Patriot movement, the old institutions under the Stadholderate continued. The Grand Pensionary Van de Spiegel's courageous efforts to remove the flagrant abuses of administration met with violent opposition and foundered owing to William V's apathy. Meanwhile the Dutch attitude towards France hardened owing to the outbreak of the French Revolution. When Holland allied with Britain, the Convention declared war on the stadholder. The Dutch forces which took the field had to suffer defeat at Neerwinden.

In January 1795, Holland was in imminent danger of French occupation and the stadholder and his family fled to England. The French won over the Patriots by giving the latter the semblance of political power. Continuing the old institutions under the new facade, they proclaimed popular sovereignty and the Rights of Man and Citizen. But their main concern was to cultivate amicable relations with France.

But their honeymoon with France proved illusory. The new 'Batavian Republic' had to pay a heavy war contribution. It had to accept a permanent financial burden thrust upon it by France. Finally, instead of gaining any territory from Belgium, Holland had to cede to France Maastricht, Venlo and the left bank of the Scheldt, on which river the restrictions on free navigation were lifted by the Treaty of the Hague on May 16, 1795.

By autumn 1795, economic depression caused by British action against Dutch trade overtook the country with no will to adopt ameliorative measures. However the pressure of radical people's clubs forced an election for a National Assembly. But with restricted franchise hedged in with indirect voting system, a large majority of moderates were returned.

The Assembly which met on March 7, 1796, solved religious problem by granting full citizens' rights to the Catholics and the Jews. The

Reformed Church was disestablished. Voting was to remain indirect, and the franchise to be restricted to wealthy persons. The East India Company was brought under state control. After being adopted by the Assembly, the constitution had to be approved by a plebiscite. But the constitution was rejected on August 8, 1797 by an overwhelming majority.

However, a second National Assembly was constituted to consider the question of constitution. The growing economic distress and the naval disaster at Camperdown (October 11, 1797) strengthened radical opinion in the House. The Assembly was purged by a radical coup on January 22, 1798, whereupon it adopted a new constitution. It was primarily a unitarian one with two chambers and executive of five members. In April 1798 it was approved by a truncated electorate with great majority. However, the radical rule was not destined to last long. On June 12, 1798, a coup was carried out at the Hague by general Daendels. A third Assembly was elected which put into office a moderate Executive.

As Consul, Napoleon was anxious to obtain financial support from the Dutch. He, therefore, favoured a reconciliation with the old merchant class which had magnificent obsession with traditional regionalism. A new coup in September 1801 restored their preponderance in the provinces. A Legislative Assembly was to be elected by the wealthy persons which would appoint in turn an Executive of twelve members on a regional basis. The new system was to be approved by a plebiscite. Nevertheless, the new constitution was accepted. Though many Orangists accepted offices, William V virtually renounced his royal dignity. The new authorities had to contribute men and money to the French war efforts. But Napoleon was violently opposed to the plan. By the Peace of Amiens, the Dutch lost Ceylon, Essequibo and Demerara, and Napoleon made every effort to curb Batavian independence.

On April 29, Rutger Jan Schimmelpenninck became the head of the state with dictatorial powers. With abundant energy and the help of able ministers, he began the work of administrative and financial reform. Schimmelpenninck tried to preserve as much as he could of Dutch autonomy even to the extent of resisting French control on the Dutch coast over British goods. But, after Trafalgar, Napoleon in his crusade against British economic warfare, tried to woo the Batavian Republic to his policy. Instead of making direct annexation, Napoleon changed the republic into a monarchy under his younger brother Louis Bonaparte, who was proclaimed King of Holland in June 1806.

The new King, despite his physical weakness, took his new task rather seriously. While continuing Schimmelpennick's reforms, he tried to steer a middle course by reconciling his loyalty towards his brother with his duties towards his subjects. He defied Napoleon in recruiting Dutch troops and in applying the Continental System. He went to the length of admitting American vessels into Dutch ports in 1809. Napoleon's patience disappeared with English landing at the Dutch port of Walcheren in the same year and he began to dismember the Kingdom. Holland had to cede that island, and, soon, its whole territory south of the Rhine. French troops brought the other parts of the Kingdom under their occupation. On July 13, 1810 Holland was annexed to France. Louis abdicated the throne and a French Governor-General installed at Amsterdam.

Dutch people accepted with resilience the French sovereignty. They expected economic recovery which came at a time when the country was passing through great slump. Henceforth it could not bring great solace. Discontent of the people was stimulated by the introduction of conscription on February 3, 1811. Frequent riots broke out, particularly after the French disaster in Russia. Popular outcry rose at crescendo with Napoleon's defeat at Leipzig. On November 15, 1811, the people of Amsterdam rose in revolt and a provisional administration was formed under A. R. Falck, a former high official of King Louis. However, at the Hague, people, largely influenced by Hogendorp and Limburg Stirum, both Orangists, demanded the restoration of royalty. William VI, who had settled in England, came at an opportune moment on November 30, 1813. Two days later, he assumed the name and title of William I, Sovereign Prince of the Netherlands.

The new King had the good fortune of being guided by Hogendorp who by his unerring judgment and sagacity steered the state out of morass. Instead of adopting a policy of revenge against the former collaborators of the French rule or opponents of the House of Orange, it was decided to introduce a limited monarchy. It was decided that the sovereign should be controlled by elected States-General consisting of representatives of the nobility, the towns and the countryside, elected separately. In drafting the new constitution, centralisation was preferred to regionalism. The constitution was adopted by 600 notables on March 28, 1814. However, the new state, in the opinion of the King and Hogendorp, in order to act as a rampart against French imperialism, must be strengthened and this could only be possible by union with Belgium.

In June 1814, Castlereagh persuaded the powers to unite the Low countries in 'the most perfect amalgam' the provisional government of which was to be assumed by William I. After Napoleon's return from Elba, William assumed the title of King of the Netherlands. But it was a gigantic task to amalgamate the two Kingdoms of Holland and Belgium. Integration was rendered difficult when the prosperous Dutch despised the backward Belgians of the south, while the latter loathed the selfish heretics in the North. The viability of the United Kingdom was threatened by differences in matters of religion, education and economic policy.

The history of the Kingdom of the Netherlands, between 1815 and 1830, was one of abysmal failure to produce integration between Holland and Belgium. In the States-General, most of the Belgian representatives voted against the government. The state remained Dutch in its core, and its Belgian subjects nursed deep resentment against it. The Belgians were debarred from a multitude of offices owing to their ignorance of literary Dutch. Even in their own country, the linguistic laws debarred them for various offices. Apart for higher jobs which were usually manned by the Dutch, the latter was also preferred in lower jobs for their superior education. Among 119 generals and staff-officers in the army in 1830 only 18 were Belgians. The Dutchman's superiority over the Belgians which was zealously maintained aggravated the situation. No wonder that a contemporary newspaper of Liege *Le Politique* wrote that Belgium was no Dutch colony. In 1829 a Dutch observed that events in Belgium hardly made any impact in Amsterdam: 'Both peoples had entered their union in 1814 as foreigners to each other. When they dissolved it in 1830, they were, if possible, even more so.'

After the loss of Belgium in 1830, the Dutch Netherlands retained an East Indian Empire—Java, Sumatra, the Spice Islands, most of Borneo, and half of New Guinea, and, in addition, the colonies of Guiana (Surinam) in South America and Curacao in the West Indies. All these comprised a territory about sixty times as large as the mother country. The East Indies was an unfailing source of wealth to the Dutch. The commercial prosperity of the Dutch Netherlands was enhanced owing to the country's proximity to nations which were highly industrialised. It was at the crossroads of Britain, Germany and Belgium which was profitable to Dutch merchants. In these circumstances, the Dutch remained a free-trade country at a time when tariff protection and economic nationalism became the main plank of other countries of continental Europe.

Owing to the economic prosperity of the Netherlands, the Dutch remained satisfied with a conservative form of government. It was only in 1834 that the King, William II, acquiesced in a constitution which transformed the Estates General into a bicameral parliament and made the royal ministers responsible to it. However, the King retained an absolute veto over all legislation while the franchise was restricted to rich persons owing to heavy property qualification. It was not until 1913 that universal suffrage was introduced.

During the long reign of William III (1849-90) the chief political debate centred round education. The Liberal party advocated a system of free, public, secular schools in which no religious instruction should be given. But the Protestant Conservative Party and the Catholic Party made common cause in behalf of state sponsored schools which were to be directed by the Churches. In the beginning, the Liberals emerged triumphant; the state established a system of 'neutral' public schools. But in 1889, however, the government conceded to the Conservatives and Catholics by giving financial support for their respective denominational schools.

William III was succeeded on the throne by his daughter Wilhelmina. In 1898 she came of age and three years later married a German prince, Henry of Mecklenburg. This marriage along with close commercial and cultural relations between Germany and the Netherlands—stimulated apprehension among the Dutch of their country's security. A general conscription followed and large sums were spent on fortifications.

From 1815 to 1890, the Kings of the Netherlands, of the House of Orange, had been Grand Dukes of Luxemburg, a small state bordering on France, Belgium and Germany. However, it was arranged that, after the death of William III, the Grand Duchy should not pass to his daughter but to a kinsman, Adolphus of Nassau (1890-1905). Thus Luxemburg became an independent state, whose territorial integrity and neutrality had been guaranteed by the European powers since 1867.

The pressing problem of Dutch politics after 1867 was colonial. Throughout the 1920s, there was unrest in Far Eastern dependencies, with riots in Java and Sumatra. By the beginning of the next decade, there was a nationalist upsurge in Indonesia.

Despite the multiplicity of parties—seventeen in all—Dutch political life was relatively calm. Stability was guaranteed by proportional representation. The influence of the Liberal Party was gradually waning: from ten members in 1918 it had dwindled to four in 1937. The depression caused the devaluation of the Florin in 1936. A small Nationalist Socialist Party was founded by Mussert, an engineer.

On May 10, 1940, the German troops invaded Netherlands and the German Minister to the Hague demanded the surrender of the Netherlands. The government requested Britain and France to come to its rescue. Nazi airplanes made incessant bombings on Rotterdam, Amsterdam and the Hague and German mechanised forces seized strategic points everywhere. The conquest of the country was facilitated by some local traitors. The carnage was so terrible that after five days of fighting, a ceasefire took place. However, Queen Wilhelmina and the members of her family and government fled to Britain and put the rich resources of the vast Netherlands colonial possessions on the side of the Allies. Meanwhile, the Kingdom was placed under the commissioner-ship of Arthur Seyss-Inquart.

Seyss-Inquart introduced Nazi institutions and anti-Jewish laws and dissolved all political parties. The only party allowed was the *National Socialistische Beweging*, led by Mussert. The democratic spirit of the Dutch people spurred their resistance movement. But the persecution of the Jews stirred the Dutch conscience and helped in the resistance movement. Luxemburg was also incorporated into the German Reich. But tenacious resistance was offered by the people in the form of guerrilla activities.

After the Second World War, the governments of Luxemburg and the Netherlands were restored. Queen Wilhelmina of the Netherlands celebrated the fiftieth year of her anniversary to the throne in her own capital. But she abdicated, by reason of age, in 1948, in favour of her daughter, Juliana. Parliamentary life in the Netherlands was characterised by the division of power between the Catholic and Socialist Parties. Economic recovery was slow owing, in large part, to the loss of her rich East Indian empire. The loss of Holland's empire in Indonesia in 1954 caused some temporary economic dislocation. In 1954, furthermore, complete internal autonomy was accorded to Surinam and the Dutch West Indies. But in the end, Holland's economy recovered. Between 1958 and 1963, the country's gross national product increased by 34 percent and its export by 50 per cent.

Denmark

In the generation before the French Revolution, the two Scandinavian Kingdoms and their appendages enjoyed relative calm and prosperity. Copenhagen flourished as the political and economic capital of the twin Kingdoms of Denmark and Norway, with the duchies of Schleswig and Holstein attached to the Danish Crown. Stockholm, though dwarfed by St. Petersburg, was the centre of the foremost second-class power in Europe.

Since the death of Charles XII of Sweden, neither of the Scandinavian powers had been strong enough to conduct an independent foreign policy. But they were of importance to the European powers. Thus Catherine the Great in March 1765 concluded an alliance with Denmark which was to last more than forty years. For ten years (1762-72) Catherine held Sweden within her 'Northern System'.

During the American revolutionary war, the economic interests of the three Baltic Powers united them against Britain in the Armed Neutrality of the North. This league championed the principles of international law—the immunity of neutral goods in enemy ships and of enemy goods in neutral ships, except for contraband of war and the right to maintain an effective blockade. The league ended with the Peace of Versailles in 1783.

In Denmark, the autocratic monarchy became responsive to the wind of changes that was sweeping the continent. Between September 1770 and January 1772, hundreds of decrees, largely influenced by the most liberal ideas of the European Enlightenment, effected changes in the social and economic problems of country. The most important measures were the reorganisation of the law courts in Copenhagen which established uniformity and equality of treatment for different classes and a more humane poor-law system. In 1784 the Crown Prince Frederick gained mastery over his imbecile father, Christian II, and Denmark entered upon a phase of more durable reform under A.P. Bernstorff. He not only dominated the foreign affairs, but gave Denmark a free peasantry and a more liberal economy.

In 1787 the new government gave tenants full legal protection against the lord of the manor. In 1788, serfdom was finally abolished. The labour-services of tenant farmers were regulated which enabled the latter to buy their land. By 1807 the cultivation of crops increased by three times. Denmark, being an agricultural country, one-half of the farms were enclosed by 1807. A liberal policy rejuvenated commerce. Copenhagen was deprived of its special privileges thus enabling the other ports to thrive. There was to be free trade in corn. Slavery was abolished in 1803. All these measures strengthened the position of the absolutist monarchy.

The Scandinavian countries were big exporters. Sweden exported 50,000 tons of iron bar, half of it to England. Danish corn, Swedish copper and other naval stores were much in demand. By 1805 Copenhagen had achieved a trade turnover which was not exceeded until 1870. A common Scandinavian outlook developed which was not likely to be shaken by efforts of Britain and others. In 1793 a Danish historian, while visiting London, vaunted: 'What power on earth can endanger confederate Scandinavia'? In the first six and a half months of war Britain captured 189 Danish and Norwegian ships. But in March 1794, when a Danish-Swedish neutrality agreement was signed which provided for trade protection and the neutrality of the Baltic Sea, Britain abandoned its harsh attitude. Conversely, the French attitude became more stiff. This led Britain to inaugurate a convoy system in January 1788 which enabled her to enforce rules more strictly.

A series of small-scale conflicts ensued when Danish war-ships in charge of convoys resisted the British right of search. A British squadron came to Copenhagen and compelled the government to forego the use of convoys. But this proved to be temporary. In December 1800 the same three Powers (Denmark, Sweden and Russia) signed the Second Armed Neutrality and threw a challenge against Britain. The sequel was the seizure of their merchantmen stationed in British ports. The Danish West Indies were occupied; and on March 12, 1801, British navy sailed for Copenhagen. Britain acted with promptness and owed her success mainly to her naval strength and the weakness of her opponents. Moreover, the new Tsar Alexander had no wish to continue the conflict.

The Berlin Decree of December 1806 weakened the Scandinavian countries and had far-reaching effects. The Order-in-Council of January 7, 1807, which stopped the port-to-port trade in the Mediterranean, inflamed Danish feeling against British blockade regulations. An uneasy fear gripped Canning that Danish policy was now prejudiced in favour of the French. Anticipating a hypothetical French move against Denmark, Canning sent 30,000 troops which after bombarding Copenhagen, forced the Danes to surrender their seventeen ships of the line.

The Danes had to lose everything owing to their enforced enmity to Britain. Their last ship of the line was sunk in 1808; by 1814 some 1,560 ships had been captured or destroyed. In January 1813 the authorities were left with no alternative but to declare a formal bankruptcy. Apart from the shattered Danish economy, Denmark's relations with Norway were no less important. Sporadic outbursts in Norway against Danish officialdom had been quickly suppressed. In 1796-1804, R. N. Hauge, a powerful evangelist, began a national religious revival which awakened the common people. Meanwhile the upper classes in the towns were in favour of setting up certain national institutions. After 1807, the Danes appointed an administrative council for Norway, and eventually a Statholder. A feeling of separation from Denmark nourished the thought that Norway might be able to stand on its own feet.

At Vienna, in 1815, the Danes were punished for their allegiance to Napoleon by being forced to cede Norway to Sweden. In 1863-4 Denmark had to wage war against Prussia on the question of Schleswig and Holstein. The two Duchies had been included among the dominions of the Danish King. Holstein, whose population was almost entirely German, was a member of the Germanic Confederation, while Schleswig was not, although its German population comprising about two-thirds of the total, wished it to become so. But the Danish minority wanted Schleswig to be absorbed by Denmark.

In November 1863 the Danish King, Prince Christian of Glucksburg promulgated a new constitution which declared Schleswig an integral part of the Kingdom. The German Federal Diet decided to take action against Denmark. Frederick, Prince of Augustenburg, proclaimed himself the lawful heir to the Duchies and asked for federal help in establishing his claim. Federal contingents quickly entered Holstein in December 1863 followed by Prussian troops in January 1864. With the entry of Austro-Prussian force into Schleswig on February 1, war with Denmark began. By August 1864 the war was over. In October 1864, Denmark signed the Treaty of Vienna. By it the Danish King renounced all his rights over the Duchies of Schleswig and Holstein in favour of the King of Prussia and the Emperor of Austria.

Denmark—by ceding Norway to Sweden in 1815 and by surrendering the Duchies of Schleswig, Holstein to Germany in 1864, was restricted to the peninsula of Jutland and its adjacent islands—became the smallest of the three Scandinavian countries. However, of the three countries, Denmark alone possessed a colonial empire outside Europe: Iceland, Greenland, the Faroe Islands and some West Indian Islands. By the constitution of 1849, revised in 1866, the King of Denmark had to share political power with a parliament or the Lower House elected on a narrow franchise. The long reign of King Christian IX (1863-1906) was marked by a political contest between the monarch and the Upper House and the parliament or the Lower House. The King tried to democratise the government by making the royal ministers responsible to parliament. But the King refused to make himself subservient to parliament despite the latter's reluctance to vote the military appropriations. Henceforth the King deliberately ignored parliament and the constitution was hardly more than waste paper.

During these years, Denmark steadily improved her economic condition owing to intensive cultivation, dairy farming and cooperative enterprise. Economic prosperity led the people to political activities which gradually generated discontent against the arbitrary government of the Crown. In 1901, the aged King could not withstand popular pressure and installed a Liberal ministry. But democratic process was yet to be achieved and continued agitation led to constitutional amendments of 1914-15 which lowered the age-limit of voters from thirty to twenty-five, extended the franchise for the Lower House of the parliament to all men and woman and abolished the nominated members in the Upper House and the latter's veto power. Home Rule was granted to Faroe Islands and to Iceland. In 1917, Denmark sold the West Indian Islands, called the Virgin Islands, to the United States.

In the Peace Conference of Paris, 1919, Denmark obtained northern Schleswig. After the First World War, Socialists comprised the large majority in Danish parliament. Under Socialist premiers, Denmark banned strikes and lockouts in 1933. World Depression affected Denmark as well. Unemployment became acute in Denmark in the winter of 1932. Agriculture in Denmark was hard hit by customs barriers. The Depression also resulted in the creation of social tension which in turn led to the development of communism and to the creation of small fascist parties. The Social Democrats which had dominated the Danish parliament since 1929, allied themselves to the Radicals. The long economic crisis was capped by serious strikes in 1936.

In the beginning of the Second World War, the German occupation of Denmark was a simple affair. In the early morning of April 9, 1940, the Danish Government received a German note that Berlin had substantial evidence of Allied plans to use the Scandinavian territories and asked the latter to accept German rule. German forces actually entered Denmark without giving Copenhagen any time to reply. King Christian X and Premier Thorvald Stauning had to accept the situation under duress.

The Danish government under Stauning, a Socialist, favoured close collaboration with the Germans. The government went to the length of placing Danish economy under German control, accepting a very unfavourable rate of exchange, the strengthening of censorship and collaboration between the police and the Gestapo. In the election of March 1943, people recorded their protest to these measures: the Danish Nazis obtained 2 per cent of the total votes and only 3 seats, whereas the government coalition won 143; the Conservation Party won 40 per cent of the total votes. Resistance movement began in the form of sabotage and violence and distributing clandestine publications. The movement became universal with the beginning of persecution of the Jews and naval officers. A general strike on June 30, 1944 was followed by another in September. The result was disbandment and deportation of the entire Danish police force.

After the Second World War, the Danish government was carried on by a coalition of Socialists and Liberals. The King, Christian X, who had been placed under the tutelage of the Germans, died in 1947 and was succeeded by his son, Frederick IX.

Denmark's occupation by German troops led finally to the severance of Iceland from Denmark. The King of Denmark had so long been King of Iceland, but in 1944 a large majority of the Icelanders voted for separation of their Kingdom and to make it an independent republic. A new constitution of Denmark reduced the voting age from 25 to 23, and changed the status of Greenland from colony to self-governing member of a 'Danish Commonwealth'.

Norway

Norway, which had been placed under Danish rule, resented the rule of Danish bureaucracy. But the agitation centered round the improvement in local government. When Denmark was involved in conflict with Sweden in 1808-9, Swedish forces invaded east Norway which proved favourable to the Norwegian army.

Norway, roughly equal to Denmark in population and wealth, had its own army, and provided men and material against the common enemy. The peasants were usually inactive, and sporadic outbursts against Danish rule had been quickly suppressed. However, a peasant lay preacher, R.N. Hauge, began a national religious revival towards the end of the eighteenth century which did much to foster patriotism among the common people. The upper classes also became restive demanding the establishment of certain national institutions, like a bank and a university. In 1807 the Danes appointed an administrative council for Norway, and eventually a Stattholder; a university charter was also conceded. Helped by its strong ties with Britain, a separatist feeling grew in Norway that she might be able to stand on its own feet. There was also a small but influential group which favoured a union with Sweden instead of Denmark.

In April 1812 there was a joint plan between Sweden and Russia to wrest Norway from Denmark. But the plan was not carried out. On March 3, 1813, by the Treaty of Stockholm, Britain agreed to furnish large subsidies and naval assistance for the acquisition of Norway, while Sweden was to furnish 30,000 troops against Napoleon.

The Treaty of Kiel (January 14, 1814) between the Allies was disappointing to Norway. Her dependencies of Iceland, Greenland, and the Faeroes were left in Danish hands. Having obtained military support from Russia, Sweden now tried to acquire Norway. But the Norwegian people—which had obtained a brief taste of independence—now threw a challenge. Since May 1813 their Statholder had been Prince Christian Frederick, the heir-presumptive of the King of Denmark. He assumed office as provisional regent pending the election of representatives in the assembly where the official majority in one month adopted a constitution. On May 17, 1813, the regent accepted the throne of Norway as an independent constitutional monarchy. These events evoked considerable sympathy in Britain and elsewhere. But the Swedish King, Charles John, was not prepared to take the things lying down.

Charles John resorted to arms and in a week's encounter defeated the Norwegian forces and dictated terms to Norway. On November 4, 1813 the King of Sweden was elected to the throne of Norway vacated by Christian Frederick, thus leading to the union of the two Kingdoms. The Congress of Vienna recognised the *fait accompli*.

The Norwegian constitution was largely modelled on the French constitution of 1791. Legislative and financial power was concentrated in a single chamber. The principle of popular sovereignty, as asserted in 1814, led to a highly democratic, separate Norwegian monarchy in 1905. The most crucial factor that inhibited the union of Norway and Sweden was the constitutional differences.

The union of Norway and Sweden was not a happy one despite the fact that each had its own parliament, and administration. Norway was inhabited by fisherman, sailors, merchants and peasant proprietors while Sweden was an aristocratic country. Despite her union with Sweden, Norway began to assert that she was 'free, indivisible and independent'. Conversely, Sweden, with her feudal constitution, showed undue veneration to royal prerogatives. Differences between the two Kingdoms came to the fore when Sweden tried to regulate the foreign and military policy of Norway, and especially in 1864, when the King wished to give aid to the Danes which was opposed by the Norwegian Storting.

Apart from this, the two countries differed on economic viewpoints. While Sweden was moving rapidly towards industrialisation, Norway remained a predominantly agricultural and commercial state. However, as the Norwegian trade increased, the Norwegian parliament began to insist on the appointment of separate consular agents in foreign countries which was resisted by the Swedish government. After years of bitter conflict, in which the Norwegian universities and intellectuals like the poet and dramatist Bjarnstjerne Bjornson (1832-1910) played a conspicuous part, the Norwegian parliament declared unanimously, on June 7, 1905, that the union with Sweden was dissolved. For a time civil war threatened. However it was agreed to allow the Norwegian people to settle their national destiny by means of a plebiscite.

The plebiscite resulted in an overwhelming vote in favour of independence. Sweden grudgingly acquiesced in the verdict and Norway became an independent nation. She invited the younger son of the King of Denmark to assume the throne with the title Haakon VII. A treaty between Norway and Sweden provided that all disputes between them should be resolved by arbitration and prohibited the erection of fortification on their common frontier.

In Norway democratic reform struck a deep root. The universal manhood suffrage had already been introduced in 1898; direct elections replaced indirect in 1906. The suffrage was extended to women at first with property qualifications in 1907 and to men on a broad basis in 1913. Coronation and consecration ceremonies were abolished in 1908 and the royal veto in 1913.

The Liberal party, dominant in Norway, was divided into two sections. The more progressive, Venstre, joined forces with the Social Democratic Party and formed the government from 1908 to 1919, except for the period 1909-12. The government took up progressive legislation concerning the use of natural resources and foreign investments. The introduction of proportional representation in 1919 ended re-presentational inequality and favoured the Social Democrats.

During the Second World War, along with the invasion of Denmark on April 9, 1940, the German forces landed at half a dozen ports, from Oslo to Narvik. The Germans met little resistance owing to the fifth column activities of the Norwegians. The leading traitor, Major Vidkun Quisling, who had been minister of war for a brief period in 1932-3, induced the garrison commanders to surrender their charges to Nazi troops. The Germans set up a puppet government under Major Quisling, the word acquiring later a special connotation—meaning traitor. The Major failed to convert the people to his cause and was eventually removed from office.

It appeared that Britain, with her superior naval strength, would be able to free Norway. But the Germans with air superiority and control of the best ports, were able to frustrate several Allied plans for reconquest. In June 1940, the Allies left Norway and took King Haakon to London with them. There the King set up a government-in-exile. Most of the Norwegian merchant marine also escaped. Moreover, despite German occupation, the Norwegians showed great ingenuity in their resistance.

Resistance movement gathered momentum under Pascal Berg, the President of the Supreme Court and Bishop Berggrav. They put up opposition to the installation by the Germans of a puppet government under Gauleiter Josef Tarboven. In February 1942 Terboven named Vidkun Quisling, the head of the Norwegian National Socialist Party, as leader of a national government. However, resistance was not subdued as was evidenced by the resignation of senior civil servants and the formation of an 'Inner Front' which organised strikes and acts of sabotage. *Milorg*, the Military organisation, under General Ruge, surreptitiously sent agents to London and Stockholm and distributed clandestine publications. The Germans unleashed a policy of repression, introducing conscription, closing down the University of Oslo and arresting teachers and students and executing members of the Resistance. However, in the last stages of the war, the Germans faced tremendous hardships owing to the Russian advance and the attacks of Norwegian partisans.

Recovery from German military occupation was fairly rapid in commercial Norway. Norway had a peaceful change of reign when after ruling for fifty two years, King Hakkon VII died in 1957 and was succeeded by Olaf V. In Norway, the Workers' Party continued to maintain its parliamentary control in the first two postwar decades. The government, under the able leadership of Einar Gerhardsen and Halvard Lange, carried out new experiments in social insurance. The socialists, however, lost control in the elections of September 1965 and a coalition of middle class parties came into being. However, this did not affect the pace of social reform. A new wage-based pension plan came into effect in January 1967.

Sweden

Since the death of Charles XII, the predominance of Sweden suffered to a large extent. For ten years (1762-72), Catherine held Sweden within her 'Northern System'. But when the partition of Poland distracted her attention, the youthful Gustavus II broke the power of the Estates. He could do it with the support of France, an event which presaged the French influence in Sweden until the Revolution, while relations with Denmark and Russia continued strained.

During the American revolutionary war, Sweden together with Norway and Denmark united against Britain in the Armed Neutrality of the North. The league ended with the Peace of Versailles in 1783. Five years later mutual distrust culminated in Swedish attack on Russia, when the latter was involved in a war with Turkey. But the Swedish navy suffered defeat whereupon the recalcitrant elements in the army fanned a conspiracy of the nobles. Gustavus's position seemed untenable when Denmark as Russia's ally sent the Norwegian army to besiege Gothenburg. British mediation saved Sweden and Denmark also withdrew from the conflict. The next year, therefore witnessed the complete triumph of the King over the military conspirators. In August 1790, the Russians, hard pressed by the Turks, agreed to a peace which maintained *status quo*. The Russians also pledged not to intervene in the internal politics of Sweden.

Gustavus III, 'the enchanter on the throne', consolidated his authority by restoring the executive power of the crown and by making the Estates dependent upon him. The only limitation to his power that he could not continue a tax beyond a date fixed by the Estates in granting it or declare war except in defence. With political stability thus secured, there followed an era of brilliant cultural development tinged with French influence and of considerable improvements in administration. But the nobles who felt dissatisfied demanded the summoning of the Estates which had met only twice in sixteen years. But when they assembled in February 1789, it was the King who won the support of the clergy, bourgeoisie and peasants and forced the nobles to accept the Act of Union and Security.

The King succeeded in abolishing most of the privileges of the nobles by throwing open the government offices to the unprivileged classes and making lands available to the peasants. In return the King was vested with unfettered powers and the Estates remained subservient. This body had no right to initiate legislation. The King could impose any taxes pending the summoning of the Estates which he carried in defiance of the majority of the nobles. In 1792 he was assassinated in revenge; his son and successor was only thirteen at the time of his accession. But the consitution was left undisturbed.

In March 1794 a Dano-Swedish neutrality was signed, each signatory to provide eight ships of the line for protection of the trade and to maintain the neutrality of the Baltic Sea. There followed a series of small-scale conflicts with Britain. In December 1800 was signed the second Armed Neutrality, in which the three Scandinavian powers challenged the British right of search. But they proved no match for Britain owing to lack of cooperation among them. The Swedish fleet was detained at Karlskrona.

In the early nineteenth century Gustavus IV of Sweden joined the coalition against France. This was considered by Napoleon as a personal challenge to him. But Gustavus was no soldier. The Swedes surrendered to Marshal Bernadotte at the fall of Lubeck in November 1806. This led the Swedish King to sign an armistice with the French. In July 1807 the arrival of British forces could do nothing and the Swedes lost both Stralsund and Rugen. However, the British alliance of Sweden boosted the latter's commercial activities. It not only safeguarded her iron exports but doubled her imports to Gothenburg in 1808.

The British blockade regulations antagonised Denmark and the consequence was a Dano-Swedish war (March 1808-December 1809). The Danes had curried favour with the French; therefore, under Bernadotte, a French army entered Jutland; a British force under Sir John Moore also arrived at Gothenburg. But the British fleet under Sir James Saumarez played a leading part in protecting the Swedish coast. Bernadotte's force achieved nothing.

In February 1808 the Russian army with Napoleon's support began campaign against Finland. By the end of the year, the Russian forces had driven the Swedish army out of the country. Sweden's only ally was Britain, who controlled the Baltic; and the British advice was to make peace. In September 1809 the treaty of Friedrikshamn ceded Finland to Russia, together with Aaland Islands.

Sweden's diplomatic isolation and military failure were attributed to the King's incompetence. While the war was raging, he was dethroned by conspirators. The throne passed from Gustavus IV to the former Regent, the younger brother of Gustavus III. As Charles XIII was found to be old and childless, the choice of Crown Prince was of paramount importance. The ailing King survived for eight more years, and Bernadotte, the French Marshal, was chosen as regent from his arrival in Sweden in October 1810.

The new Crown Prince called Charles John faced with Napoleon's threats was forced to declare war on Britain in October 1810. However, the strategic advantage of keeping Gothenburg, and the passage to the Baltic open for her convoys, led Britain to adopt a soft policy toward Sweden before the Napoleonic invasion of Russia. Charles John decided to abandon the reconquest of Finland as it would be hazardous to attempt while Britain ruled the Baltic and, if successful, would incur the enmity of Russia. As an alternative Norway could be taken from Denmark as that would give Sweden a natural frontier.

In January 1812 Napoleon occupied Swedish Pomerania. This enraged the pro-French military circles in Sweden, making it easier for Charles John to turn against Napoleon as an ally of Russia. Both Sweden and Russia entered upon a joint plan which commenced in September 1812–the month of the French entry into Moscow. But the joint plan was delayed as Britain by the Treaty of Stockholm (March 3, 1813) became a party to the agreement. It was agreed that Britain would furnish naval assistance for the acquisition of Norway, while Sweden was to assist with 30,000 men for a 'direct mainland operation against the common enemy'.

Charles John undertook campaign against the French with 160,000 men, of whom only 30,000 were Swedes. His defeats of Oudinot at Grossbeeren (23 August) and of Ney at Dennewitz (6 September), however, prepared the way for the Allied triumph at Liepzig.

Sweden was dissatisfied at the Treaty of Kiel (January 14, 1814). Metternich was trying to restrict the gains of Sweden, and the British looked very coldly upon Charles John's claims upon Norway. However, Norway refused to be bound by the Treaty of Kiel. The Norwegians rejected the demand of the Allied commissioner and resorted to arms. Charles John was prompt to engage in a brief campaign that served his purpose. On November 4, 1814 the King of Sweden was elected to the throne of Norway vacated by Christian Frederick. The Congress of Vienna ratified the arrangement.

Sweden exhibited remarkable development for its representative institution. The Swedish Instrument of Government of 1809 vested the Estates with absolute control of taxation, participation in the legislative power, and the right to hold the advisers of the Crown accountable for their advice. Sweden also developed her separate national culture. She shared with Norway an important peasant art which embellished the churches and homes of the countryside. But she remained under the dominant French influence until the Romantic movement brought in the direct inspiration of the Scandinavian past. The first quarter of the nineteenth century included not only Sweden's national poet, Esaias Tegner, and her first modern historian, E. G. Geijer, but the father of Swedish gymnastics, P. H. Ling, who tried to revive the Viking heroes in flesh and blood.

Sweden emerged from the Napoleonic wars with the loss of Finland to Russia and with the addition of Norway from Sweden. Marshal Bernadotte of France who became Charles XIV ruled Sweden with absolute power from 1818 to 1844. The Bernadotte dynasty, despite its French and revolutionary origin, was royalist to the core and wedded to reactionary policies. The loss of Finland led to anti-Russian movement and pronounced militarism in Sweden.

Sweden and Norway were incompatible socially and politically. Sweden was a country of large landed estates which underwent considerable industrialisation, while Norway, a country of small farms, remained largely agricultural and commercial. Norway had a liberal constitution which vested supreme authority in a parliament. In Sweden, on the other hand, the only constitutional check upon royal authority until 1863 was the rusty Estates-General with its four houses of nobles, clergyman, burghers and peasants. The constitutional laws of 1863 abolished the Estates-General and set up a bicameral parliament with considerable power, although the deputies of the Lower House were elected exclusively by the propertied class.

The royal absolutism of Bernadotte had given way to a moderate liberalism under his successors Oskar I (1844-59), Charles XV (1859-72) and Oskar II (1872-1907). In 1905 Norway was separated from Sweden.

The influence of the aristocracy and the monarchy continued in Sweden till the beginning of the twentieth century. However, from 1906, the Liberal Party, created in 1901, secured a majority in the Lower Chamber. During the reign of Gustavus V (1907-50) important constitutional amendments were adopted. In 1907, the property qualification for election to the Upper House was reduced and universal manhood suffrage was introduced in elections for the Lower House. In subsequent years, voting rights were extended to women and proportional representation was introduced in elections for both Houses of Parliament.

Parliamentary regime had yet to strike a deep root in Sweden. On February 6, 1914, in the face of demonstration of 30,000 national peasants, the King defied the Liberal government of Staff and forced it to resign. In the First World War, Sweden remained neutral and censored the press to prevent it from expressing support for one side or the other. However, the Hammarskjold cabinet was forced to resign in 1917 owing to its pronounced pro-German stance and was replaced by a coalition of Liberals and Social Democrats led by Hjalmer Branting.

World Depression affected Sweden as well. Unemployment reached its peak. The Social Democrates regained the majority in Sweden in 1936. The Social Democrats were allied to the Agrarians in Sweden and tried to provide full employment and improve the peasants' lot. The three Scandinavian countries made a customs agreement, the Oslo Convention (1931). The economic crisis in Sweden was considerably lessened in 1934.

Sweden was the only state which maintained neutrality in the Second World War. But her position, pitchforked between Germany and Russia, was made difficult after the fall of Norway and Denmark. Completely isolated, she was forced to make military concessions to Germany, such as allowing the transit of troops and material and providing sanctuaries for German submarines in Swedish waters. However, with the improvement of the military situation of the Allies, the Swedish attitude became somewhat stiff towards Germany. Sweden even granted members of the Danish and Norwegian Resistance to be trained in Swedish camps.

Gustavus died in 1951 after a long reign and was succeeded by his son, Gustavus VI. The Socialist Party, under the able leadership of Tage Erlander, exercised uninterrupted power from 1945 to 1970. When Olaf Palme succeeded Erlander at the end of 1969, he announced that his government would seek to control technological progress and to work for a greater degree of social equality. Sweden's loss of German market was partly made up by a profitable economic agreement with the Soviet Union.

Poland

Poland was a country which, like Spain, had rich cultural heritage, but had fallen into decay. The Poles, like the Russians, were a Slavic people. The kingdom which they had founded in the tenth century lay between Lithuania and the Holy Roman Empire. In the fourteenth century Poland was enlarged by union with Lithuania under the Lithuanian dynasty of Jagello. The dynasty produced a succession of capable kings. It had been customary to elect the eldest son of a deceased Jagello; but the extinction of this line in 1570 weakened Poland. The Polish crown now became a pawn in the diplomatic game of the foreign powers and the national life was vitiated by the virus of political corruption. Foreign powers lost no opportunity in securing concessions from the puppet kings until the monarchy was left but a republic in disguise. All sovereignty was vested in a diet made up of nobles, most of whom were the underlings of foreign powers.

The most important factor which led to Poland's collapse was the overbearing attitude of the Polish nobles. Strongly entrenched in their exclusive privileges, the Polish nobles were a turbulent, undisciplined class who had kept the peasants in servile condition. They dominated the national diet and the constitution was rendered unworkable by the adoption of *liberum veto*. A member of the diet could not only prevent any bill from passing the assembly, but could force dissolution. Unanimity was impossible and sovereignty rested not with an assembly but with individual noble. No wonder the French philosopher, Rousseau, expressed pungently that whenever Poland moved, she had a fit of apoplexy. However, political impotence was not the only element of weakness. Out of a population of 11,500,000 in the eighteenth century, about a million were 'Dissidents', belonging not to the national religion, the Roman Catholic, but professing either the Lutheran or orthodox faith.

These Dissidents were a tempting wedge for foreign interference, already dominant through the corruption of the nobility. Finally, Poland, with no natural boundaries to protect her, was placed between strong and expansive powers. Thus, with her medieval polity, Poland was unable to maintain its existence in the face of the modern state.

The underlying weaknesses of Poland invited the intervention of three powerful neighbours—Austria, Prussia, and Russia. While Prussia was keen on Polish territory known as West Prussia to connect the two main divisions of her realm, Russia thought of acquiring as much of Poland to make herself a dominant European power. Austria was content with the *status quo* as long as the electors of Saxony, Austrian tools, were in possession of the Polish throne.

The partition of Poland had long been in the air. The pace was hastened when peace was signed between Austria and Prussia in 1763. In the following year when the Saxon king of Poland died without leaving any heir, Catherine II of Russia and Frederick the Great of Prussia were quick to seize the opportunity. A common candidate, Stanilass Poniatowski, a Polish nobleman, was chosen for the Polish throne. Both Russia and Prussia entered into a defensive alliance for eight years. With regard to Poland they agreed that the *liberum veto* should be maintained and that the Dissidents should be accorded equal rights with Roman Catholics. But when the Polish Diet refused to ratify the agreement, Catherine used force. Though the Diet yielded to compulsion, it could not prevent a civil war. The 'patriots', who hated foreign domination and religious toleration, rose in revolt. But they were no match for Catherine's Cossacks, the latter pursuing them across the frontier into Turkey. It was this encroachment on Ottoman Turkey that involved Turkey in war with Russia.

The Turkish war gave Catherine the opportunity to occupy the Danubian Principalities, Moldavia and Wallachia. Both Austria and Prussia were dismayed. Both powers wanted to arrest Catherine's victorious march by striking a bargain and this they found in Poland. So the first partition of Poland was effected in July 1772. Prussia acquired West Prussia, except Danzig and Thorn. Russia received territories on the east, peopled by Lithuanians and Little Russians. Austria obtained Galicia, the richest of the Polish provinces.

Sobered by the First Partition of 1772, the Poles attempted to organise themselves against the encroachments of the foreigners. But the Russians were too zealous to permit a Polish revival. In 1792 the Russian armies harried Poland which became a matter of concern of European powers. But Catherine could afford to ignore international pressure when she obtained Prussian assistance by offering a share of the spoils. In January 1793, a second partition was made which left one-third of Poland independent. Confronted by the French successes, Russia, Prussia and Austria divided the remaining fragment of Poland (third partition) in January 1795. As a consequence of the three partitions of Poland, the position of the Russians had been strengthened.

After his victories in 1805-06, Napoleon created the new Duchy of Warsaw in 1807, his satellite outpost in Eastern Europe. Outwardly it appeared to be a step towards the restoration of Poland. But Napoleon wanted to use Poland as a pawn in the diplomatic game. At Tilsit he threw the hint that Russia should have the whole of Poland and that Silesia should go to Jerome Bonaparte.

In the Congress of Vienna, Russia received most of the Grand Duchy of Warsaw. The territory that Russia received was later called "Congress", it was taken in part from the Polish territories of Prussia and Austria. The youthful and visionary Tsar Alexander granted a constitution to Poland. The Polish state was linked with Russia through personal union of the crowns. Although Czartoryski headed the provisional government, it was Zajaczek, a veteran nationalist, who became first viceroy. Alexander's brother Constantine became Commander-in-Chief of Poland's independent army. There was a Diet (*sejm*) of two houses and ministers were nominally responsible to the *sejm*. Catholicism was to be the religion and Polish the official language; but the Polish peasant remained a serf. The Poles fell increasingly under the influence of western liberal and democratic ideas. Alexander imposed a severe press censorship in 1819 and restricted the power of the Diet in 1825. The next Tsar, Nicholas, was an autocrat. He restricted some of the liberties previously granted to the Poles. Secret societies, therefore, sprang up and military insurrection was on the point of breaking out as early as 1828, during the Russo-Turkish war.

The French Revolution of 1830 greatly excited the Poles. In November 1830 a group of discontented officers and university students started a revolt in Warsaw. The Grand Duke Constantine, brother of the Tsar and the leader of the army in Poland, showed a great indecision and left the country. The rebels set up a provisional government which tried to bargain with the Tsar for reform. But the rebels which had 50,000 soldiers were no match for the Russians. Moreover, it was a revolt of aristocrats and intellectuals which failed to win the masses. In February 1831, a Russian army entered Poland. The only hope for the rebels was Western intervention which proved to be illusory. The Poles resisted but, by September, all was lost. The Russians entered Warsaw and suppressed the rebellion with utmost ferocity. Poland was subjected to severe suppression and was henceforth merged in the Russian Empire. Russian became the official language of the country and the Polish army was incorporated with the Russian imperial forces. While hundreds were put to death, thousands of intellectuals took refuge in western countries and America. It was in exile that a new Polish nationalism was born under the inspiration of Joachim Lelewel, a historian, and Adam Mickiewiez, a poet.

Polish national feeling was too strong to be subdued by the Russian repression. Though separated into three parts, Poland preserved her ideal of national unity. She remained 'three undigested fragments in three stomachs'. The annexation of Cracow by Austria in 1814 caused the outbreak of the Polish insurrection. Under the mild dominance of Austria, the Poles of Galicia had been enjoying something like home rule. Now the Polish nobles and intellectuals of Galicia revolted against Austria. But the revolt of 1846 was put down by Metternich in his characteristic way. The peasants were incited to revolt against their landowners. But in return the Austrian authorities had to abolish the hated *robot*, or labour rent.

The consequences of 1848 were also disappointing. Although the Polish cause gained widespread publicity and Polish exiles fought in every revolutionary or national army, but these were without any consequence for Poland herself. The disturbances in Galicia were followed by the bombardment of Cracow and Lwow. Thereafter the only disturbing spot was Russian Poland, which had not stirred in 1848. The Poles of Austria and Prussia, convinced of the futility of their struggles, preferred to work for social and economic reform and for parliamentary reforms by peaceful means.

The Poles had never lost their zeal for national independence. With the accession of Alexander II (1855-81), the Polish aspirations were revived. The national movement also received a powerful stimulus from the Crimean War. Emigrants like Mieroslawski, despite the setbacks of 1848, inflamed the national spirit. A new generation grew up fired by Mieroslawski's revolutionary ideas and the tales of the returning exiles, while the nationalist upsurge in Italy led many a young Pole to dream of emulating the deeds of Garibaldi.

After a popular demonstration in Warsaw in February 1861, Alexander introduced several administrative and educational reforms and entrusted Wielopolski to implement the measures. Within a week of the decree which emancipated the Russian serfs in 1861, Alexander II was presented with a memorandum from the Agricultural Society of Poland, to redress the grievances of the Polish serfs. This Society, composed of the old nobility of Poland, was committed to national independence. Alexander responded by setting up special bodies to deal with Polish grievances. Apart from the Agricultural Society, there was the Roman Catholic Church, which was vehemently opposed to the domination of Russia. Moreover, the middle and the professional classes, equally anti-Russian, had formed a secret committee. The crowning blow to the Russian domination was delivered when the Poles demanded the return of their eastern territories lost in 1772. The Tsar rejected outright the demand as these provinces were regarded as integral parts of the

Russian state. When the country was seething with discontent, the Tsar aggravated the situation by introducing conscription in Poland. Open revolt broke out in January 21, 1863, and the Revolutionary Party appointed a dictator.

The insurrection of 1863 was doomed to failure. There was no single political or military direction and by and large the people were apathetic to the revolutionary cause. The peasant remained inactive and were used by the Russians against the Polish nobles. 'Only in the cities, among the young officials and the sons of officials as well as in the artisan class, and in the country among the lower gentry, was the sentiment for war hearty and general.'[1] The result was a foregone conclusion. The rebels however, kept up a guerrilla warfare till their heroic resistance collapsed in March 1864. The British and French governments made a half-hearted attempt to intervene on the strength of the Treaty of Vienna. But Russia had the Prussian backing and succeeded in crushing the moves for Polish independence. The Polish peasants gained substantially from the revolt as they got more land and paid less compensation. The law of 1864 elevated the serf into a free peasant proprietor. A system of village commune was established to undermine the authority of the Polish nobles. A serious blow was struck at the Catholic Church by closing its monasteries and schools. In 1869 the University of Warsaw was suppressed and replaced by a Russian University. Russian became the language of Poland.

After the great disillusionment of 1863, a new generation of Poles settled down to a programme of 'organic work'. Land reform and the construction of railways enabled the Poles to develop industrially and capture many Russian markets. Textiles from Poland found their way to Turkey, China and Persia and this expansion was encouraged by the Russian government. It hoped to alienate the prosperous Polish industrial classes against the nationalistic Polish nobility. Russian expansion in the Far East at the turn of the century offered opportunities of employment for Polish engineers and managers.

At the same time an agricultural depression affected Poland along with most of the Europe. Landed estates went bankrupt and landlords were impoverished. They could find no alternative employment—blocked by Russians entrenched in the bureaucracy and by Jewish predominance in business. These changes stimulated a fresh spurt of nationalism among the nobility and the middle classes. Russian policy now had to adjust itself in the changed situation. It now began to favour the landlords against the growing middle class. Constitutional changes such as the introduction of *Zemstvo* institutions in 1911 and city councils in 1913 were introduced in order to placate the rural Polish elements against the urban Polish and Jewish elements. But these palliatives could not extinguish the nationalist sentiment which revived with tremendous force. The National Democratic Party, which represented the Polish middle classes had a leader in the person of Roman Dmowski whose teachings profoundly influenced the people in the war years. The Polish Socialist Party, founded in Paris in 1892, was headed by Rosa Luxemburg, who considered Polish independence as chimerical. But most of the Socialists took their lead from Joseph Pilsudski (1867-1935) whose burning desire for freedom was to achieve independence for Poland.

The impact was felt in the Polish territories of Austria, especially Galicia, which enjoyed a greater degree of autonomy than its Russian counterpart. In Galicia the bureaucracy was carried on by Poles, who also controlled the schools, together with the two universities of Lvov and Cracow. A separate Diet met at Lvov which was responsible for education, public health and agriculture. The Viceroy, head of the executive, was a Pole. A special minister for Galicia acted in the imperial parliament at Vienna.

The position of the Poles in the German Reich was not edifying. Just as Russia was colonizing her eastern borderlands, Prussia also was bent on Germanising the province of Poznan. Bismarck's quarrel with the Roman Catholic Church in the 1870s inevitably led him to imprison the Polish archbishop Ledochowski of

1. *The Cambridge History of Poland,* 1697-1935 (1941), P. 378.

Poznan in 1874. Bismarck, by his tirade against the Polish language and by his efforts to settle German families on the land in 1886, raised a storm of protest. Bismarck's successor, Caprivi, at first followed a soft policy towards the Poles, but from 1894 he had to reverse it at the insistence of Russia. The process of Germanisation was accelerated and until 1914 there continued a vigorous policy of colonisation.

During the First World War, Poland was invaded by Austro-German forces and Russian forces were too inadequate to stem the tide of the Austro-German advance. The Russian Commander-in-Chief, Grand Duke Nicholas, avoided confrontation and began to retreat. It was thus possible for the German General Falkenhayn to extend his line of advance in the East without weakening the Western Front. By September 1915 all Poland, together with the greater part of Lithuania, was occupied by the Central Powers.

In the early stages of the First World War, Polish patriots were oscillated between strategic calculation. One group, spearheaded by the celebrated musician, Ignace Paderewski, sympathised the Allied cause, hoping that the defeat of Austria and Germany would force them to surrender their respective Polish provinces. This group also anticipated the grant of autonomy from the Russian ally of France and Britain to reunited Poland. Another and larger group, headed by the radical Joseph Pilsudski, were not enamoured of Allied benevolence or of Russian altruism. As Austria had treated its Polish subjects humanely, the latter thought it prudent to assist the Central Powers in conquering Russian Poland and uniting it with Austrian Poland. Consequently, while Paderewski was hobnobbing with the Allies, Pilsudski had organised a Polish Legion and placed it at the disposal of the Central Powers.

Fortunately the conflicting efforts of Pilsudski and Paderewski were both crowned with success. The military debacle of Russia in 1915-16 enabled Pilsudski to secure from the Austrian and German Emperors a joint pledge on November 5, 1916, to set up an independent Polish Government. Pilsudski was admitted as Minister of War. He was, however, disillusioned about the motive of the Central Powers. They had no intention of granting independence to Poland and tried to woo the Polish support by holding out the lure of national independence. So Pilsudski turned against the Germans and was imprisoned by them. Paderewski had the satisfaction of galvanising the Polish support for the Allied cause and Polish volunteers joined the Allied armies in increasing numbers.

With the collapse of the Central Powers, Pilsudski, released from German prison, arrived in Warsaw in November 1918 and took over the provisional government of the country. In January 1919, with himself as President and Paderewski as premier and minister of foreign affairs, a Constituent Assembly was elected by universal suffrage. The Polish Constitution was modelled on the pattern of the Third French Republic.

The new Republic started its existence with geographical advantages and economic resources. But they were offset by territorial ambitions of Polish nationalists which, in the long run, shook the people's confidence in democratic institutions.

After more than a century of suppression, Poland now aspired to dominate Byelorussia (White Russia) and the Ukraine. Both Russia and Poland refused to accept the compromise boundary—the so-called 'Curzon Line'—proposed by the British Foreign Minister, Lord Curzon. Poland had great successes initially in 1919-20 and took Kiev and other centres. But these were followed by reverses. The Polish aggression kindled a genuine patriotic enthusiasm and the Red Army made a powerful counter-thrust. In June 1920 Kiev was recaptured and in July the Soviet forces under Tukhachevsky advanced to Warsaw. But instead of making a main thrust against Warsaw, Colonel Aleksander Yegorov, commanding the forces on Tukhachevsky's left flank, decided to march on Lvov. Before the gap thus created could be closed, the Polish commander, Pilsudski, in consultation with the French General Weygand, struck at the exposed flank and overpowered the Red Army. The Polish counterattack forced upon the Red army a precipitate retreat.

Both sides were weary of war and on March 18, 1921 was signed the treaty of Riga. Russia recognised the independence of Poland; strips of

Byelorussia and the Ukraine east of the Curzon Line went to Poland; and each party pledged itself not to engage in military activity against the other and not to interfere in the domestic affairs of the other. The Polish boundary line was to endure till 1939, a line more favourable to the Poles than that which the Allies had originally suggested.

Polish military expenditure strained the resources of the country and contributed to the financial distress of the country. Mounting budget deficit was aggravated by inflation which, by 1923, had reached a similar proportion as experienced by Germany in the same year. The key to economic growth in Poland was agrarian reform and the redistribution of large estates. But any fundamental change was not possible owing to the hostile attitude of the landlord class. The country grovelled in the same old way until it was engulfed in the world economic depression.

The Polish parliamentary system was too weak to deal with basic economic problems. The Polish constitution, which had been accepted in March 1921, elevated the legislature at the expense of the executive. The President, who was elected by the two legislative Houses (the Sejm and the Senate) could do little; the two Houses, elected by universal, secret and proportional vote, were vested with absolute powers which even the Presidential veto could not extinguish. At the same time, they shirked to discharge their functions with the result that they became battlegrounds for the too numerous parties and splinter groups. Joseph Pilsudski described the Sejm as "a sterile, jabbering, howling thing that engendered such boredom that the very flies on the walls died of sheer disgust." Between 1919 and 1926 there were thirteen governments without any visible change. Political conditions in Poland were reminiscent of earlier days of decadence. Proceedings in Parliament were deadlocked, land reform lagged, the financial condition was in doldrum, and corruption was widespread.

In May 1926 Pilsudski denounced the government for its weakness and corruption and marched on Warsaw with three regiments. After a three-day battle, Pilsudski forced the parliament to capitulate. Instead of setting up a dictatorship, Pilsudski kept up the semblance of republican government. His friend Professor Ignace Moscicki became President and he himself was content to become Minister of War in the cabinet of Casimir Bartel.

From this time Pilsudski was the real force in Polish politics. There were ministerial instability and eight different ministries guided the republic from 1928 to 1935. Pilsudski had a contempt for parliament by announcing that it was the deputies who endangered Poland most. Frequently the summoning of parliament was postponed by presidential decree, while opposition voices were throttled by arbitrary action. Pilsudski and his 'colonels' monopolised the premiership and other important offices and the governments were popularly known as the 'Cabinets of Colonels.' In 1933, President Moscicki, was reelected for another seven-year term.

In 1935 a new constitution came into operation which put an end to parliamentary democracy in Poland. The President was freed from parliamentary control and given a suspensive-veto power. He was empowered to appoint or dismiss ministers or to summon parliament at his discretion. 208 deputies in the Sejm were to be nominated. The Senate was to consist of 96 members, one-third appointed by the President and two-thirds elected by citizens over 30 occupying high military or civil posts. While the 'constitutional dictatorship' was continued, Pilsudski died in 1935. Early in 1937, it appeared Poland might veer round the totalitarian states. This trend had already been manifest when, in January 1934, Poland concluded a pact of friendship with the Nazis. The colonels were under the delusion that Poland had a chance to play power politics on a grand scale in the confused international scene and the German pact gave her an edge over both France and the Soviet Union.

Discontent was brewing and Ignace Paderewski issued a warning against the trend towards authoritarianism. During 1938, Moscicki expelled certain Fascist and anti-Semitic elements from the government and tried to establish a 'lawful and disciplined democracy.' However, in the parliamentary election of 1938, the candidates selected were nearly all government supporters.

The Paris Peace Conference of 1919 placed the German port of Danzig into a free city under

Poland and the general supervision of the League of Nations. The arrangement gave Poland access to the sea but embittered the relations with Germany. There were frequent disputes and in the first five years the League Commissioner handed down almost fifty decisions. To the west and south of Danzig was a stretch of territory 260 miles (416 km) long and 80 miles (128 km) in width which formerly comprised in part the provinces of West Prussia and Posen. The Versailles Treaty assigned this land to Poland which, consequently, divided Germany into two unconnected sections—Germany proper and East Prussia. The creation of this 'Polish Corridor' strengthened Poland economically while weakening Germany considerably. The Polish Corridor, therefore, generated much ill-will between Germany and Poland. In 1925, at Locarno, Germany declined to guarantee her Polish frontiers. Though the tension was somewhat relaxed by the German-Polish Non-aggression Pact of 1934, the situation was disturbing to the extent to induce H. G. Wells to prophesy in 1933 that the next great war would begin over the Polish Corridor in 1940.

Hitler's repudiation of the Versailles Treaty alarmed the Western Powers and Russia. In early March, he focussed his attention on Danzig and the Polish Corridor. On March 18, 1939, the Russian Foreign Minister Litvinov proposed a conference of the British, French, Rumanian, Polish, Turkish and Soviet governments to discuss common action. Britain considered the proposal lightheartedly and instead proposed a declaration by Britain, France, Poland and the Soviet Union on joint resistance to any threat to the political independence of any European state. By March 22, it had become clear that Poland was least of all interested in participating in a joint declaration with the Soviet Union.

On March 21, 1939, Hitler made a last bid to persuade Poland to join his camp. The next day German forces invaded Memel. In reply the Poles mobilised their forces. On March 23 and 28, while rejecting the German demand on Danzig, Poland asserted that any unilateral action over Danzig would lead to war. As Poland seemed destined to be Hitler's next victim, Chamberlain announced in the House of Commons on March 31, 1939, that in the event 'of any action which clearly threatened Polish independence, and which the Polish government accordingly considered it vital to resist with their national forces, His Majesty's Government would feel themselves bound at once to lend the Polish Government all the support in their power'. Chamberlain added that he was authorised to speak for France as well.

This extraordinary move, though taken seriously by the Poles, met with poor response either in Berlin or Moscow. It seemed incredible to them to save Poland from German aggression without Anglo-Soviet alliance or Soviet-Polish military cooperation.

At the end of March, Hitler instructed his Chief of Staff to prepare orders for war with Poland. The army was also ordered to prepare for a sudden *coup de main* against Danzig alone. On April 28, 1939 Hitler denounced the German-Polish Non-aggression Pact of 1934. On May 23, Hitler announced to his chief advisers that Poland must be attacked 'at the first suitable opportunity.'

In the meantime, attempts were made, though half-heartedly, by the Western powers to draw Soviet Union with them. Military representatives were sent to Moscow to discuss the negotiation. But there were unusual delays. It became known that the Soviet government was unwilling to enter into any pact unless it included a Soviet guarantee of the integrity of the Baltic States and Poland. But Poland refused to contemplate under any condition the entry of Soviet troops into Polish territory. The British and French Governments expressed their inability to oblige Poland to accept the Russian proposal. Andrew Rothstein, while commenting on this episode, observed wryly in his book *A History of the USSR*:

> Thus pressure could be used in 1938 to force Czechoslovakia to surrender to Hitler, but pressure could not be used in 1939 to force Col. Beck to join in resisting Hitler.

At the same time dispute over Danzig reached its alarming proportion. From May onwards tales of violence against Germans in the Polish Corridor infuriated Hitler. When he decided that the simple incorporation of Poland would not be enough, his diplomacy underwent transformation. Agreement with Moscow would insure against a two-front war. On August 23, 1939, a non-aggression treaty for ten years was signed. A secret protocol was also inserted dividing Poland and eastern Europe into German and Soviet spheres of influence.

Hitler decided to attack Poland on August 26. But prevarication followed when he heard on August 25 that Britain, far from being deterred by the conclusion of the Nazi-Soviet Pact, had signed a formal alliance with Poland. Moreover, Hitler learnt that Italy would not support him. Hitler, therefore, countermanded the orders for attack. Now he decided to isolate Poland diplomatically. The Poles were to be invited to negotiate in Berlin and the negotiations to be stage-managed in such a way as to put the blame on Poland for its breakdown. Hitler then would have no compunction in attacking Poland.

On August 29 Germany demanded from Britain that she arrange to have a Polish delegate with full powers reach Berlin on the thirtieth. On the following date, Britain explained the procedural difficulties and urged Germany to follow the usual diplomatic procedure of transmitting her demands on Poland through the Polish ambassador. At midnight, Ribbentrop replied by announcing a sixteen point proposal for the settlement of all German-Polish differences. On August 31, the German Government broadcast the sixteen points. The Polish ambassador tried to communicate the terms to Warsaw, but was unable to do so because of disruption of communication done deliberately by the Germans. This was interpreted by the Germans as a rejection of their overtures to Poland. At dawn on September 1, 1939, Germany, without declaring war, attacked Poland by land and air.

Hitler took only a month to conquer Poland. The clock-like precision and the coordinated tactics and speed with overwhelming superiority in arms destroyed the Polish resistance. The Luftwaffe led the way by destroying the Polish air force on the ground and disrupting communications. Aerial attacks were made over the towns and cities. Then the German armoured columns crossed the borders and cut their way into the interior, using the tactics of *blitzkrieg*. There were no fronts in this kind of warfare; the enemy was on every side. The bewildered Poles were scattered like chaffs in the wind. By September 21, western Poland had been completely overrun. Warsaw resisted till September 27 despite heavy aerial bombardment and then succumbed. Meanwhile Russian troops had occupied the eastern part of the country.

On September 28, Ribbentrop and Molotov arranged the fourth partition of Poland. The eastern half of Poland was joined to the Soviet Union. The industrial areas of the west were annexed by Germany and a separate protectorate was established round Cracow which was ruled over by the Nazi Hans Frank. A Polish government in exile was set up at Angers in France which later on moved to London after the defeat of France.

Poland had suffered much in the Second World War. In 1941, after a rupture with Germany, Russia resumed diplomatic relations with the Polish government with a promise to restore an independent Poland. Soon, however, Russia revealed her intention of retaining part of eastern Poland which it had acquired in 1939. When the exiled Polish Government objected, Stalin transferred his recognition to a provisional government, headed by the Polish Communist, Boleslav Beirut. It is alleged that, in order to weaken future resistance, the Soviet agents massacred several thousand imprisoned Polish army officers.

At the Yalta Conference in February 1945, Stalin prevailed upon Roosevelt and Churchill to recognise the Beirut government on condition that they would include some non-Communist members with a promise to hold free elections. Though an outward show was made of adding few non-Communist members to Beirut's regime like Stanislas Mikolajczyk, a representative of the government in exile, and Edward Morawski, leader of the Social Democratic Party, they had little influence in directing the state administration.

In the Potsdam Conference of July and August 1945, Stalin, Truman and Clement Attlee defined the Polish Kingdom as comprising the lands east of the Oder and Neisse river, the southern part of East Prussia (the rest of which went to Russia) and the free city of Danzig. The Poles took the Potsdam grant to be definitive. In August 1945, the Beirut government signed a treaty with the Soviet Union, ceding to it 70,000 square miles and obtaining by way of compensation 40,000 square miles to be taken from Germany. In January 1946 a decree abolished the capitalist system and nationalised all key industries. In January 1947, the National Assembly, backed by Russian forces, adopted a constitution similar to Soviet Union. Beirut became President and the virtual dictator. Both Morawski and Mikolajezyk were removed from office. Even the Secretary of the Communist Party, Wladyslaw Gomulka, was purged for submission to bourgeois influence and was jailed. So too was the Polish Catholic Primate, Cardinal Wyszynski. A Socialist economy took shape in 1948. Large land-owners were expropriated, key industries nationalised, and a three-year plan for economic reconstruction imposed. But farming was not collectivised. Hatred for the Russians and the strength of the Catholic Church influenced the Polish life.

The outbreak of a riot in Poznan (Posen) in June 1956 and widespread disaffection, frightened Eward Ochab, the Communist Party leader, into promising redress of grievances. Gomulka was released and reinstated as the party's general secretary. Khruschev paid a special visit to Warsaw in October 1956. In November Gomulka signed an agreement at Moscow with the Soviet Union whereby future relations between the two countries were to be based on 'complete equality, mutual respect for territorial integrity and national independence and non-interference in each other's internal affairs.' The Soviet Union should restrict its troop movements in Poland, cancel past Polish debts and grant long-term credits. In January 1957 elections were held which returned Gomulka with large majority. The regime, after 1968, became more rigid and out of touch with the country. In 1970 Gomulka signed a treaty with West Germany. But in that year Edward Gierek succeeded Gomulka as Party Secretary. Gomulka, who led a retired life in Warsaw, died, in 1982.

Switzerland

Switzerland, a confederation of diverse peoples, was a flourishing centre of political freedom and a refuge to political exiles. The great German-Swiss writer Gottfried Keller (1819-90) once wrote that Switzerland based its nationality upon the idea of liberty. He observed:

> Similar inclinations in a beautiful country, many neighbourly contacts, and a common tough determination to maintain independence, have produced in Switzerland a common federal life distinguished from any other national life. This ... has produced a far-reaching similarity of attitudes and character. In our common nationality we feel protected against the confusion which surrounds us on all sides.

Perched high upon the common Alpine watersheds of the Rhine, the Danube and the Rhone, Switzerland was a small country. In the Swiss federation there were twenty-two 'Cantons' with differing language, religion, and customs. In fifteen Cantons, embracing two-thirds of the whole population, the German language was predominant. Of the remaining seven Cantons, five were French and two Italian. Protestants were in a majority in twelve cantons, and Catholics in ten.

In April 1799, the French occupied Switzerland. They proclaimed a new Helvetic Republic which guaranteed the freedom of the press. However, Napoleon was not too liberal to guarantee democracy and imposed strict control. In the summer of 1799 the French suffered severe defeats in Switzerland at the hands of the Russians. But in October the French resistance gathered momentum and forced the Russians out of Switzerland. The Helvetic Republic survived two momentary withdrawals (1799 and 1802) and a sudden reoccupation in October 1802 but was dissolved by Napoleon's Act of Mediation (February 1803).

The Vienna Settlement of 1815 provided for a loose union among twenty-two Cantons and for adjusted frontiers. The Powers also guaranteed the neutrality of Switzerland. The Diet and Vorort created by the Federal Pact of 1815, like the Diet of the Germanic confederation, proved cumbersome. The Cantons' jealousy for their own political sovereignty was aggravated by the chaos of the country's economic arrangements. Swiss nationalists, like German, sought a more effective central government and a national and unified economic system to keep pace with rapid strides of industrialisation.

The French Revolution of 1830 gave an impetus to the doctrine of liberalism. The Swiss 'Regeneration' movement achieved its great success in the sphere of public education. It not only reformed the primary schools root and branch, but also established training colleges and founded universities at Zurich and Berne. The Revolution of 1830-31 led several Cantons to adopt liberal institutions and encouraged the radicals to demand the transformation of the federation of states (Staatenbund) into a federal state (Bundestaat) on liberal lines. But these proposals came to nothing owing to the opposition of conservative and predominantly Catholic and rural Cantons and reactionary Metternich.

In 1841 Lucerne experimented with a democratic form of government in alliance with the Catholic Church, and communicated a new constitution to the Pope. But this evoked a storm of protest and once more the *casus belli* centred in the religious problem. In 1844 the Great Council of Lucerne entrusted theological teaching in its seminary to the Jesuits. This action had repercussions throughout the confederation. In order to protect themselves the seven Catholic Cantons of Lucerne, Uri, Schwyz, Unterwalden, Zug, Fribourg and Valais concluded a defensive alliance, known as the *Sonderbund*. But the Radicals, which won an absolute majority in the Diet, demanded the dissolution of the *Sonderbund* on grounds that it militated the Federal Pact. When the *Sonderbund* refused to disband, civil war ensued. Once again Metternich and his conservative friends were eager to intervene. But their efforts were frustrated with the sweeping victory of the Radicals in 1847 within a few weeks. Moreover, a supreme self-confidence seized the government of the confederation. There was now a new tone of self-reliance in Swiss official documents and 'in foreign policy the *Sonderbund* war meant Switzerland's final release from tutelage and complete national independence.'

The military triumph of the nationalists in 1847 led to a revision of the national constitution in 1848. A bicameral legislature similar to that of the United States was established along with a Federal Tribunal and a Federal Council elected by the legislature. The historic tradition of Cantonal autonomy in regard to education, public health, religion and crime, was maintained. The central government controlled foreign and military affairs, commercial policy, post and coinage and fiscal policy. The Swiss form of government was to provide encouragement to liberals and democrats throughout the world.

In 1874 the federal constitution was revised which strengthened the federal authority. This authority was exercised through a federal assembly and the Council of the States representing the Cantons. Moreover, Article 89 of the revision of 1874 introduced plebiscite or referendum on the national as well as the Cantonal level. The constitution also underlined the individual's responsibility for protecting Swiss democracy by introducing compulsory military service. This 'militia' was strengthened by several subsequent laws, most notably by one in 1907. In 1891 was adopted the 'initiative', that is, the right of a specified number of citizens to demand referendum on any measure. Switzerland thus became a strong federal union, in which democracy made rapid progress than in any of the countries of continental Europe. The practice of direct democracy—that is, decisions being taken by the vote of all the affected citizens—continued in several of the smaller Swiss Cantons.

The growth of Swiss industry after 1870 was tremendous, especially in textiles, watchmaking, luxury goods and confectionery. The economic development of Switzerland was due to various factors. The habitual thrift of the hardy natives, the influx of foreign tourists to have a glimpse of enchanting views of Swiss Alps and lakes and the tariff legislation—all contributed to make the country industrially prosperous. The permissiveness of the political climate made Switzerland the refuge for political exiles from here. To escape the persecution of Bismarck, the German Social Democrats published their newspapers in Basel and smuggled them across the border. In the beginning of the twentieth century, a group of left wing socialists led by Lenin took sanctuary in Switzerland and began to think hopefully of their possible return to their native Russia.

During the First World War, Switzerland maintained her traditional neutrality. In domestic sphere, the tendencies were an increase of the powers of the national government at the expense of the cantons and a further extension of state socialism and government responsibility in the fields of agriculture and industry. In the Second World War, Switzerland clung to her traditional role as the servants of the humanitarian causes, and became intermediaries for the Red Cross and postal services. In the post-War period, Switzerland emphasised its traditional neutrality by refusing to become a member of the United Nations Organisation. She strengthened her economic resources by increasing its peacetime manufacture. The consequence was that the country enjoyed export surpluses.

Spain

Since the days of the Catholic Reformation in the sixteenth century, Spain has little to contribute in the cultural life of Europe. During the Napoleonic invasion, the Spanish people, proud of their cultural heritage, offered stiff resistance which cost Napoleon half a million men. In 1810 the Spanish parliament (Cortes) was summoned in response to popular demands. In 1812 it adopted a democratic constitution which enshrined the principles of the sovereignty of the people, freedom of the press, and individual liberty. The constitution of 1812 became the Magna Carta of Spanish liberalism.

In 1814 the Spanish Bourbon, King Ferdinand VII, was restored. He was cruel, incompetent and unscrupulous. He suppressed the constitution of 1812, restored the privileges of the nobles and clergy and reestablished the Inquisition. A group of favourities—known as the Camarilla or 'Kitchen Cabinet'—gathered around the King and conducted the administration in utter disregard of constitutional propriety. The despotic regime of Ferdinand VII roused every liberal element in the country. After his death in 1833, the country was riven by a dynastic conflict between the Carlists who supported Don Carlos, brother of King Ferdinand VII, and a pretender to the throne, and the Christinos, who supported the queen-mother Christina, who was Regent to Queen Isabella II.

The reign of Isabella II, who became of age in 1843, was a woeful tale of scandal and corruption. She was deposed in 1868 mainly engineered by army general Prim and Marshal Serrano. The vacant throne was offered to Prince Leopold of Hohenzollern, who declined the offer. In November 1870, Serrano's provisional government invited Amadeo, the younger son of Victor Emmanual of Italy, to become King of Spain. Amadeo accepted the offer; but he was opposed by the Legitimists, who sought the throne for Isabella' son Alfonso, the Carlists, who were striving for Don Carlos, the Catholic Church and the republicans. After two years of frustration, Amadeo abdicated.

There followed a brief republican interval (February 1873-December 1874) which plunged the country into chaos and anarchy. The European powers refused to recognise the new regime. Once more the army intervened, overthrew the Republic and, on Christmas Eve 1874, restored the Bourbon monarchy in the person of Alfonso, the son of Isabella II. A seeming stability ensued. The man behind the monarchical restoration was Don Antonio Canovas del Castillo, a conservative politician and an admirer of the English constitutional system. The constitution of 1876 established a responsible ministry and a parliament of two chambers. Canovas's conservative party was opposed by the Liberal party of Praxedes Sagasta. No patriotic feeling actuated either the conservatives or the Liberals; they vied only for political power. The fictitious political stability in which the privileged few enriched themselves at the expense of the nation, created a yawning gap between the governed and the governing class. By the Pact of EL Pardo in 1886, Canovas reached an understanding with Sagasta according to which both parties rotated in office by managing the elections through coercion and corruption. The system spread a deep scepticism about politics and, in 1897, Canovas was killed by an Italian anarchist.

Alfonso died in 1885 and his wife acted as regent until his son became King in 1902. The regency was marked by the loss of Spanish colonies. Already reduced in size by the loss of the Latin American colonies in 1820, Spain had retained Cuba and the Philippines. Chronic maladministration and exploitation led the Cubans to revolt in 1868 which took ten years to suppress on promises of reform. But these promises were sedulously thrown to the winds and Cuba erupted again in 1895. The brutal methods employed by the Spanish garrison in suppressing the rebellion led to the intervention of the United States. Spain was not only defeated but had to cede the Philippine Islands and Puerto Rico to the United States and to acknowledge the independence of Cuba. After four centuries, Spain ceased to be an oceanic power.

The loss of colonies, coupled with growing dissatisfaction on the part of the peasantry and the industrial masses, led to political instability. The disappearance of the two great statesmen—Canovas in 1897 and Sagasta in 1903—made the situation worse. Parties disintegrated and governments collapsed in quick succession; there were fifteen between 1901 and 1914. The country was plagued by a wave of strikes and rioting. All classes coaleasced and the Catalan movement emerged as a crusade of progress against the backwardness of Castilian hegemony.

In 1901, when a newly formed regional league won the general elections in Catalonia, the government struck back by employing terror tactics. The conservative Prime Minister, Maura, deplored these methods and observed with brutal frankness: 'Either we make the revolution from above or it will be made for us from below'. In 1905 the government again lost the elections. In 1907 a new coalition, *Solidaritat Catalana*, won an easy victory. An outburst of excitement followed in Barcelona. At the height of tension the government requisitioned the Catalan reserves. There were five days of rule during which twenty-two churches and thirty-four convents were burnt down. However, the troops restored order.

Amidst all these difficulties, the royal constitutional government introduced various social legislations, regulating factories, legalizing trade unions and imposing employers' liability. The educational law of 1902 provided for state supervision of elementary schools and another of 1909 entailed compulsory attendance of all children.

In 1910 Jose Camalejas, the leader of the Liberal party in parliament, became prime minister. To appease the Republicans and Socialists, he adopted a policy of anti-clericalism. The government passed the so-called Padlock Law in 1910 forbidding the establishment of any more religious houses without the consent of the government. He also broke off diplomatic relations with the Pope. But these measures failed to satisfy the people. A British observer in 1910 was forthright in his comment 'A sense of wrong, a wish to escape, and a tendency to revolt are spreading.' The assassination of Canalejas in 1912 and an attempt on the life of the King shortly afterwards, compelled the government to suspend the anti-clerical legislation and to resume diplomatic relations with the Papacy.

To distract attention from domestic problems, Alfonso XIII pursued an imperialist policy. As a result of an agreement with France and Britain, Spain established a protectorate over the northern coast of Morocco. But it was with great difficulty he retained her colony as the warlike 675 tribesmen, the Riffs, were too obdurate to be suppressed.

Spain remained neutral during the First World War. Her temporary prosperity not only strengthened Catalan nationalism, but accentuated the class warfare. The postwar slump brought unemployment and the situation became dangerous when Republicans, Socialists and Anarchists began their subversive activities. An epidemic of strikes immobilised the government. The situation was aggravated by Spain's involvement in Moroccan affair. In the battle of Anual (July 1921), the Spanish army was utterly routed. The Spanish parliament appointed an investigating commission to probe into the debacles. Its report was never published. But the Captain General of Catalonia, Don Miguel Primo de Rivera, seized power in September 1923 with the approval of the King. He suspended the constitution, banned the opposition parties and subjected the press and the universities to rigorous control. For seven years—from 1923 to 1930—he maintained a dictatorship which outwardly appeared successful.

Primo de Rivera adopted the slogan 'Country, Monarchy, Religion'. He established friendship with the Catholic Church. From 1925, he relaxed his dictatorship. He abolished the martial law and prescribed the compulsory arbitration of labour disputes. In September 1927 he convened a National Advisory Assembly and invested it with drafting a new constitution. He sought to appease the nationalists by pursuing a vigorous foreign policy. In 1926 Spain and Italy signed a treaty in which each promised to maintain a neutrality if the other were attacked by a third party. In cooperation with French armies, he finally bought the Moroccan conflict to a successful close in 1926.

Despite all these reforming activities, Primo de Rivera failed to allay popular discontent which expressed itself in mutiny, subversive activities in Catalonia and Barcelona, and student revolt. During all these years frequent attempts were made to assassinate both the King and the dictator. Eventually, in January 1930, disillusioned and broken in health, Primo de Rivera gave up his office. He was succeeded by General Damascus Berenguer. Despite his conciliatory attitude, he was unable, in the face of the World Depression, to introduce prosperity and provide employment for all labourers. There were renewed student strikes and riots. The Catalonians demanded 'Liberalism, Democracy and Republicanism.' Concessions and promise of a new parliamentary election in 1931 failed to stem the popular discontent. In February 1931 Premier Berenguer restored the constitution. The people reacted with indignation as they had no desire to participate in the resurrection of the 1876 constitution. Berenguer resigned and was succeeded by Admiral Juan Aznar, a loyal monarchist. In the municipal elections of April 1931, the Republicans won resounding success. Aznar resigned and Zamora, the leader of the Republicans, threatened revolution unless the King abdicated. Alfonso XIII fled and on April 14, 1931, Zamora proclaimed a republic and put himself at the head of provisional government.

The election of June 1931—the first national election since 1923—returned a majority of Socialists and Radicals with a motley of Communists, Syndicatists, Anarchists, Monarchists and Catalan and Basque Nationalists. In December 1931 this body adopted a republican constitution. Legislative power was vested in a single chamber or cortes, to which the ministry was responsible. The President was to be elected for six years by the members of the cortes and popularly chosen electors. The President was forbidden to contest for a second term. Alcala Zamora was elected President and Manuel Anzana became Prime Minister.

The new government immediately launched a programme that was mainly directed against the Church, the plutocracy and the army. In 1932 the Jesuit Order was dissolved, its property confiscated. Later legislation nationalised all ecclesiastical property. By an Act of 1933, members of religious Orders were forbidden to engage in industry, commerce or teaching. The church schools were closed and education was placed under government control. Pope Pius XI protested against the separation of Church and state. The Church had wide support in Spain and these measures alienated an important section of Spanish opinion. Large estates were confiscated and a beginning was made towards a more equitable distribution of arable land. High army officers lost their influence and their forces reduced. In response to demands of Catalian Nationalists, the Cortes in September 1932 granted home rule to Catabolia. The Basque Provinces, Galicia and other regions now made similar demands for autonomy.

The government was beset with opposition. Apart from the royalists, clericals and the landlords, there were the Communists, the Syndicalists and the Anarchists. In August 1932 a group of royalists seized Seville and a few small towns. The revolt was quickly suppressed and its leader exiled. In January 1933, a Syndicalist-Anarchist revolt took place at Barcelona and spread to other cities. The authorities were quick to put down the revolutionaries. The growing dissatisfaction became manifest in the municipal elections of spring and summer of 1933. When it showed a swing towards the right, the Azana ministry resigned. A succession of shaky coalitions followed.

In the elections of November 1933, in which women voted for the first time in Spain, the parties of the Right won. It was supported by the Church and the landowners which formed a government under Alejandro Lerroux, leader of the Radical Party. The government carried on a moderate policy and suspended the anti-clerical laws and the land laws. But this aroused the active hostility of the Communists, Syndicalists and Anarchists. In March 1934, the parties of the

Left called a general strike in protest against the drift to the right. The government proclaimed a national state of alarm; but the violence continued unabated. Finally, Lerroux resigned and was succeeded by the moderate Ricardo Samper.

The new premier, who held office from May to October 1934, failed to deal with the problem of Catalonia and the bloody independence movement in the Basque provinces. Samper resigned and once more Lerroux shouldered the responsibility. But he had to face a serious insurrection in October 1934 when a revolt of the miners of the Asturias destroyed the city of Oviedo and caused 3,000 deaths before it was suppressed. The Madrid Government triumphed over the demand of the independence of Catalonia and the separatist movement of the Basque Provinces. Lerroux held on until September 1935, but his successors could not govern in the teeth of a right-wing cortes. Elections were held in February 1936 which resulted in a victory of the 'Popular Front' comprising Socialists, Communists, Syndicalists and Left Republicans.

In April 1936, President Zamora was removed from office. Azana was chosen President and Santiago Quiroga became head of a new cabinet. The government at once resumed social reform, promising land reform and a restoration of Catalan autonomy. It adopted a tough attitude towards the Fascists and dissolved the Spanish Phalanx, the most aggressive anti-government group. It pensioned military officers, suspended pensions to politically-minded officers and effected a general shake-up in the high command. Suspected officers were either dismissed or transferred. General Franco, former commander of the Spanish Foreign Legion in Morocco, was exiled to Canary Islands.

But all these measures were unable to prevent political murder or to protect the Churches and monasteries from mob-fury. There were rumours of impending coups. On July 12, 1936, the Spanish Fascist Party, the *Falange*, murdered a Leftist police lieutenant in Madrid. The next day, Calvo Sotelo, who had been finance minister during Primo de Rivera's dictatorship, was killed in retaliation. On July 17, the military junta, headed by General Sanjurjo, revolted in Spanish Morocco and civil war began. Sanjurjo was killed in a plane accident. His place was taken by General Franco who flew from the Canary Islands to Morocco and quickly made himself master of Spanish Morocco. Strengthened with troops, Franco landed at Cadiz. The insurrection swept over southern and western Spain and enlisted about three-fourths of the regular army and half of the navy. In October, the rebellious army generals chose General Franco as their chief and the latter set up a provisional government at Burges.

Meanwhile, the Republican government had been transformed into a practical dictatorship under a new premier, Francisco Larfo Caballero. Himself a Socialist, he inducted Communists to his cabinet and raised new levies from among the Reds and Radical Republicans. He obtained help from the Soviet Union and its Comintern allies. He also gained much sympathy from the Popular Front government of France and from the Labour party in Britain. On the other hand, General Franco obtained help from Fascist Italy and Nazi Germany. Both powers furnished him with airplanes, pilots, armoured corps and munitions. As Britain, France and the United States were sympathetic to the Republican cause, the struggle appeared to be a fight between Democracy and Fascism. Thus, from a domestic struggle, the Spanish Civil War was transformed into an international conflict between rival powers—between Russia on the one side and Germany and Italy on the other.

By November 1936 the rebels reached the confines of Madrid and set up a government at Burgos. Germany and Italy thereupon recognised the Franco government. Meanwhile, the Caballero ministry resigned and was succeeded by a more moderate one under Juan Negrin. The established government moved from Valencia to Barcelona and under General Jose Miaza repulsed the rebel attack. During 1937 the rebel forces were pushed back to a safe distance and the Italian forces suffered a severe defeat at Brihuega, on the Guadalajara Front.

In the latter part of 1937 Franco strengthened his position by conquering the Basque provinces, Asturias, and Galicia. In March 1936 he turned east. Republican resistance petered out when the Soviet Union in mid-1930 decided to withdraw from Spain. With the end of Soviet aid to the Republic, General Franco achieved spectacular successes against the Republicans. Early in 1939, he conquered the whole of Catalonia, including Barcelona. President Azana fled to France in February. On March 26, Madrid surrendered. Franco became the undisputed master of Spain and the Spanish Republic came to an end after eight years of inglorious existence. The war, which cost Spain a million persons killed or wounded, established a military dictatorship and left a legacy of bitterness and disillusionment.

The Little World War

In its origin, the Spanish Civil War sprang from purely domestic causes. There is little or no evidence of prior knowledge of the event by either Germany or Italy. But when the rebels failed to overwhelm the Republican government, the former appealed to Italy and Germany for arms. The response was instantaneous and arms and aircraft poured into Spanish strongholds from both these countries. After the conquest of Abyssinia, Mussolini dreamt of making the Mediterranean a Roman Lake and the Spanish Civil War provided him an opportunity of accomplishing his objectives. The German motive was purely economic—the lure of Spain's coal, copper and other mineral resources. Hitler was interested in seeing that the Spanish War was prolonged, for it would not only keep Mussolini engaged but would create crises of which he could take advantage.

On the other hand, the Soviet Union intervened reluctantly and their help was limited to advisers, technicians and suppliers. Their aid was not regular and stopped a full year before the end of the war. It has been said that 'the number of Russians in Spain was certainly under 2,000 and probably never exceeded 500 at one time.' The Soviet Union was absorbed in its own problem, for during this period the great purges of Stalin's opponents began which stripped the Soviet military leadership of its senior members.

The Republican Government had hoped for assistance from the Popular Front Government in France. But the government itself was hopelessly divided over the issue and Premier Blum, despite his sympathy to the Republican cause, could take no decisive action. Moreover, France was increasingly dependent on British backing for its policies, and British policy was a policy of nonintervention in Spain. Even after Blum's fall in June 1937, his successors were less concerned about the fate of the Spanish Republic.

Officially, Britain was in favour of observing a strict neutrality in the Spanish affair. Stanley Baldwin, who succeeded Ramsay MacDonald as head of the National Government in 1935, was lukewarm in foreign affairs. Neville Chamberlain, who became head of the government in 1937, had a decided opinion to correct the imbalance of the world by enunciating a policy of appeasement. However, Britain had taken the initiative in September 1936 for a genial non-intervention agreement among the major European powers.

Eventually, twenty-seven European States, including Germany, Italy and the Soviet Union set up in London an 'international committee for the application of the agreement regarding Non-intervention in Spain.' The ostensible purpose of the committee was to prevent the despatch of soldiers and war materials to the belligerents and to withdraw any volunteers already there. But the objectives were far from being achieved. Large number of German and Italian troops continued to arrive in Spain. The German delegate to the committee commented pungently that the real purpose of the committee was to 'pacify the aroused feelings of the leftist parties in France and England'. Chamberlain, the British Prime Minister who inaugurated the appeasement policy, refused to take any action against Mussolini. Anthony Eden, the British Foreign Secretary, differed with Chamberlain's policy as this threatened the principle of collective security and resigned. Earlier Eden observed in the House of Commons that 'there are other Governments more to blame than either Germany or Italy.'

However, the non-intervention committee made a feeble effort to put an embargo on arms supplies to the rebel government in Spain by placing a cordon of British, French, Italian and German ships around Spain. But after many delays the patrol ships took up their duties—only to be withdrawn after a couple of months. Meanwhile, the non-intervention committee took up the question of withdrawal of volunteers already in Spain. But it was wrecked by a series of submarine attacks, apparently by Italy. Britain and France summoned a conference of Mediterranean and Black Sea Powers to meet at Nyon near Geneva. Germany and Italy refused to attend. Eventually a Nyon Agreement was signed on September 14, 1937 by nine states including the Soviet Union. An international patrol was established and patrol zones were assigned to several signatories with Britain and France doing the substantial work of supervising. An agreement was reached with Italy on September 30, 1937, under which she was allotted a patrol zone. The submarine attacks quickly ceased.

The ineffectiveness of the non-intervention committee became manifest in 1938 when it failed to find a satisfactory formula for the withdrawal of foreign 'volunteers'. It was only after the end of the Civil War that the last of the German and Italian troops departed from Spain.

The war led to the establishment of a new one-party dictatorship in Spain and the latter signed the Anti-Comintern Pact (April 1939) originally negotiated by Germany and Japan. It weakened France strategically by placing a potential enemy on its flank. It also strengthened the suspicion and mistrust already brewing between Western powers and Soviet Russia. Stalin, a supporter of collective security at the beginning of the war, observed in disgust at its close:

> Far be it for me to moralise on the policy of non-intervention, to talk of treason, treachery, and so ... It must be remarked, however, that the big and dangerous political game started by the supporters of the policy of non-intervention may end in a serious fiasco for them.

During the Second World War, Spain maintained a covert neutrality. However, grateful to Germany and Italy, Spain initially supported the cause of the Axis Powers. She sheltered their war vessels, and refuelled their airplanes. She sent labourers to Germany and sold war materials to Axis factories. In 1940 she occupied the free city of Tangier in North Africa.

As the Allied cause began to brighten, Franco veered round to the Allies. The USA ambassador, Carlton J. H. Hayes, was instrumental in bringing about this change. From 1943 Franco refused German requests for the passage of Nazi troops across Spain and permitted American planes to use Spanish airfields. In 1945 Spain withdrew from Tangier.

The majority of the Spanish people, fearing a recrudescence of the Civil War, rallied to the support of Franco. He consolidated his position and set up a virtual dictatorship. He suppressed Communism and all autonomy movements. He banned all political parties—the *Falange espanola* was the only political party being allowed to function. Economic situation was improved by war profits and welfare works were undertaken. Franco consolidated his position by establishing in 1942 a national parliament, or Cortes, partly appointitive and partly elective. In 1945 a charter of individual liberties was issued.

The end of the Second World War brought in its train inflation, black-marketeering, official corruption and lack of investment capital. Spain's international standing also suffered setback. In 1946 she was not allowed to join the General Assembly, and the latter urged United Nations members to withdraw their ambassadors from Madrid. This changed situation led the Spanish republican exiles to hope for a restoration of the republic. To this move, Franco enacted a Law of Succession in 1947, endorsed by referendum, which provided that in the event of a vacancy in the headship of the state, a Council of Regency would propose a King or Regent.

Gradually, when the differences between the Western world and the Soviet Union became pronounced, Spain came to be regarded in a changed perspective by the West. Despite her dictatorial political system, Spain's strategic location, her useful resources and her strong anti-Communism attitude made her acceptable to Western powers. In 1950 the General Assembly of the United Nations empowered its members to regulate its Spanish diplomatic relations according to their desire. Two years later, Spain obtained credits from the United States. In 1953 the United States agreed to provide further credits and military supplies in return for Madrid's consent to the establishment of US air bases on Spanish soil. In 1955, Spain was admitted to the

United Nations. In 1957, Spain surrendered most of its North African territory to newly independent Morocco.

Discontent was brewing against the Fascist rule of Franco. It gathered strength particularly among the workers and students. Demonstration of University students of Madrid in 1955 was firmly put down. But in 1967-68 student protest movement assumed European dimension.

Portugal

Portugal, like other countries, was deeply affected by Napoleon's aggression. In 1807 the French army under Marshall Junot, invaded the country to enmesh her into the Continental System of closing all Europe to English commerce. The King, John VI, fled with his family to the most important of the Portuguese colonies, Brazil. The actual authority in Portugal from 1808 to 1820 was that of Wellington or Beresford. After the fall of Napoleon, the Portuguese hoped for the return of the royal family. But the King, John VI, was reluctant to leave Brazil fearing that his departure would result in the independence of the country. The pride of the Portuguese was hurt when the mother country was relegated in importance at the expense of a colony. Moreover, Beresford remained in Portugal after 1814, and was the real force of the country. Discontent was brewing between the Portuguese and the English as most of the key positions were held by the latter. The army was disaffected as it was not promptly paid.

The Spanish Revolution of 1820 brought into focus the latent discontent of the Portuguese. The French Consul in Lisbon, de Lesseps, was convinced that the Spanish example would set off a revolution in Portugal. The expected revolution came with the revolt of the Oporto garrison and lower officers in Lisbon. The government was powerless to combat the radical euphoria of 1820. The Cortes adopted in 1822 the famous Spanish constitution of 1812 patterned after the French constitution of 1791. King John VI disliked the constitution, but he was unwilling to support an absolutist reaction. Meanwhile he had returned from Brazil leaving his eldest son, Dom Pedro, as regent of that country. In 1822 Brazil declared her independence under Dom Pedro I which was recognised by Portugal three years later.

Meanwhile, the Absolutists tried to regain control in Portugal and succeeded. Henceforth the constitutional experiment proved short-lived. The crisis in Portugal was accentuated by the succession dispute when John VI of Portugal died in 1826. Dom Pedro, Emperor of Brazil, tried to solve the Portuguese succession by the marriage of his seven-year old daughter, Donna Maria da Gloria, with Dom Miguel. Pedro decreed that the marriage should be consummated when Donna Maria became of age. He then appointed Dom Miguel as the regent. But in 1828 Miguel was declared king by the Absolutists. During the war of nerves between the two claimants, Britain, under the influence of Canning, took the side of Donna Maria because her party stood for constitutionalism, while her husband, Dom Miguel, was determined to be an Absolutist King.

Dom Pedro abdicated his position as Emperor of Brazil and took up the cause of his daughter's rights. With a mercenary army financed by Spain, he endured the siege of Oporto, captured Lisbon and forced Dom Miguel to renounce his claims by the Treaty of Evora Montes (May 1834).

Liberal Portugal was, however, unstable. Palmella, the Portuguese statesman, favoured an aristocratic constitution on the English model. His rival, Saldanha, was ready to ally with the radicals. Nevertheless, Dom Miguel was loved as a Dom Sebastian whose reappearance was announced by his supporters. But that was not possible as Mousinho, a Benthamite anti-Jacobin, tried to create by decree a liberal society that would sustain liberal institutions. A liberal society without prosperity is contradictory. After the loss of Brazil, Portugal suffered an acute deficit in its balance of payments.

Maria reigned until her death in 1853, a regime besmirched by frequent insurrections. The Septembrist Revolt (1836) gave way to the conservative Costa Cabral, an ex-radical who helped to establish liberalism by a brilliant policy of economic development. In 1852 the Charter of 1826, restored by Maria, was liberalised by important alterations.

Maria's successor, Pedro V, had a quiet and uneventful reign (1853-61). Portugal lagged behind in economic spheres compared to general development of Europe. Her finances were on the brink of collapse owing to inefficient and corrupt administration. During the reign of his brother, Louis I (1861-69), the country enjoyed orderly government and constitutional government seemed to have taken root. Nevertheless, the prevalence of corruption among officials, and the heavy burden of maintaining a large colonial empire, gravely impaired the national finances. Heavy taxes were imposed which compelled innumerable industrious and ambitious inhabitants of the country to emigrate to the more prosperous land of Brazil.

King Carlos I (1889-1908), a man of Absolutist temperament and an unscrupulous spendthrift, failed to avert the financial crisis. Opposition to his rule gathered strength and factional quarrels developed among its professed supporters. He frequently misused the royal prerogative by dissolving the parliament. In 1907 the king entrusted his faithful prime minister, Joao Franco, with dictatorial powers. In order to please the King, Franco tried to effect sweeping reforms. Franco ruthlessly suppressed dissent by filling the jails with political prisoners. On February 1, 1908 the King and the Crown Prince were killed in the streets of Lisbon. Franco escaped and Manuel II, second son of Carlos I, and an inexperienced youth, became king.

Manuel II was utterly incapable to cope with the situation. In the volatile situation came the murder of a prominent Republican physician in October 1910. This event precipitated the revolution. Soldiers, sailors and armed civilians put an end to the monarchy and proclaimed a Republic. King Manuel fled to England. A provisional government was formed under the presidency of DR Theophil Braga, a distinguished man of letters.

A new constitution was adopted in 1911 which was similar to that of the constitution of the Third French Republic. Manuel Arriaga was chosen first President of the Portuguese Republic. The Republican government decided to pursue a policy of anti-clericalism. One of the leaders of the government proudly declared that it would blot Catholicism out of Portugal within two generations. Church and State were separated, religious instruction was prohibited in schools and church schools were deprived of state aid. Under the pretence of safeguarding the secular Republic, most of the bishops were imprisoned and many churches were closed.

The Republic failed to create political stability the country badly needed. Like Spain, Portugal continued to suffer from a large debt, an unstable fiscal system, high-degree of illiteracy and the factious political parties. The fragile nature of the Republic bacame evident when there were eleven different ministries from 1911 to 1915. The Republic could achieve no constructive reform except in the field of education when, in 1911, elementary education was made compulsory. Domestic crisis was deepened when Portugal entered into the First World War in 1916 by joining the Allies.

Portugal's participation in the war yielded little dividend. Apart from loss of Portuguese lives in the battlefields, the war imposed crushing financial burden on an impoverished and bankrupt country. During and after the War Portugal was afflicted with seething unrest which provided opportunities to ambitious army officers.

In 1926, General Antonio Carmona seized power by a military coup. He inaugurated an era of constructive administrative reform and strengthened his position by securing his election in 1928 to the office of President for a term of four years; the term was extended to six years in 1932. Under a new constitution, which was approved by general plebiscite in 1933, Carmona was confirmed as President for an additional term of seven years. Meanwhile, in 1928, he called to his assistance Antonio de Oliveira Salazar, a reputed professor of economics at the University of Coimbra. Salazar proved himself so eminently successful as a reformer that he was vested with practically dictatorial authority. In 1932 Salazar became prime minister.

Under Salazar's stewardship, a steady improvement in different spheres was noticeable. Administration was geared up, national finances recognised, indebtedness reduced and credit restored. Relations between Church and State were improved when the anti-religious campaign ceased. Strikes and lockouts were prohibited and provision was made for the compulsory arbitration of labour disputes.

During the Second World War, Portugal benefited economically from its neutral position. However, after the war, the country suffered an appreciable slump owing to agricultural and industrial stagnation which failed to keep pace with the abnormal growth of population. Economic dislocation led to political opposition in the presidential elections that followed the death of Marshal Carmona in 1951. Francisco Craveiro Lopez was chosen as Carmona's successor. Actually, however, the government was carried on under the dictatorship of DR Salazar. He was strong enough to curb sporadic violence of students and workers and to restrict individual political rights. Portugal became a member of the U.N. in 1955. But even after Salazar's retirement in 1968, the country remained an authoritarian state.

Despite the anti-colonial movement that swept through the whole continent of Europe, the Portuguese colonies—Angola, Guinea and Mozambique—remained intact. In February 1981 terrorist outbreak in Angola was crushed by the Portuguese government. Though the French surrendered their Indian colonies, the Portuguese refused to hand over its three small sixteenth century posts of Goa, Daman and Diu. After years of border tensions and guerilla warfare, Indian troops occupied Goa, Damon, Diu in December 1961.

EMERGENCE OF NON-EUROPEAN COUNTRIES

CHAPTER 38

EMERGENCE OF THE UNITED STATES OF AMERICA

Foundation of the United States of America

A successful revolution against England gave the American people supreme self-confidence and an independent place in the family of nations. But the outlook was rather ominous. The thirteen states, torn with conflicting interests, had not yet succeeded in setting up a really national government. In March 1781, they had adopted certain Articles of Confederation, but this was simply a 'league of friendship' and nothing else. The Articles of Confederation failed to provide a real national government. As there was no central authority, most of the states acted independently. There were frequent quarrels among the states over boundary issues. Economic difficulties consequent to the war also fanned discontent. Washington summed up the situation in 1785: 'The wheels of government are clogged'.

In May 1787 the representatives of the thirteen states met at a convention at Philadelphia which was presided over by Washington. Among the leading members were Benjamin Franklin, James Madison and Alexander Hamilton. The convention adopted a constitution but some of the states refused to ratify it. Finally, a Bill of Rights was appended to the constitution in the form of amendments. These amendments have guaranteed to citizens of the United States freedom of religion, speech, the press and assembly; a militia instead of a standing army; the right to trial by jury; speedy trials by the law of the land and prohibition of general warrants. As a result of the adoption of the Bill of Rights, the wavering states ratified the constitution which was finally adopted on June 21, 1788.

George Washington (1789-97)

Under the new constitution, George Washington was unanimously elected President. He took office on April 30, 1789, pledging to 'preserve, protect and defend the constitutions of the United States'. But Washington had to grapple with enormous problems facing the country. Its internal economy was in a bad shape. There were no sources of revenue. Judiciary was yet to be established and the army was small.

In this hour of crisis the United States found the wise leadership of George Washington. He was a far-sighted statesman and had a capacity for taking infinite pains. He inspired respect and trust as well as humility and self-control.

Washington set himself to the task of creating governmental organisation. Congress created a Department of State, a Department of War and a Department of the Treasury. Washington appointed to the first post Thomas Jefferson, to the second Henry Knox and to the third Alexander Hamilton. Simultaneously, the Judiciary Act of 1789 set up not only a Supreme Court, with one Chief Justice and five associate justices, but also three circuit courts and thirteen district courts.

The administration of Washington produced two outstanding men—Alexander Hamilton and Thomas Jefferson, whose sterling qualities entitle them to a place in history. The keynote of Hamilton's policy was his love of efficiency, order and organisation. He was in favour of a strong national government and a closer union among the different states. His outlook was European rather than American and throughout his life he thought the English form the most admirable type of government. Politically, Jefferson's ideas were opposed to Hamilton's. He was not in favour of a strong national government which could be of value in foreign relations, but in favour of a loose federation making States as strong as possible. Hamilton's aim was to institute an efficient administration, Jefferson's to give individual men a wider liberty.

During the Presidency of Washington, Hamilton carried through a set of measures that made him the greatest finance minister in American history. He carried out a plan by which the Federal Government took over the unpaid debts of the states incurred in aid of the Revolution. He set up a Bank of the United States modelled on the Bank of England. He established a national mint. He argued in favour of imposing moderate tariff duties in order to develop national industries. He enacted a law in 1791 levying an excise tax to be collected upon all distilled liquors. All these measures encouraged commerce and industry. They also attached influential groups of men in every state to the national government. Hamilton's excise law of 1791 provoked resistance. Thereupon Washington, advised by Hamilton, took stern action by marching troops against the malcontents. Though the 'Whisky Rebellion' was suppressed, but it aroused much popular antagonism and distrust. When Jefferson came to power, the excise law was repealed.

The cornerstone of Washington's foreign policy was the preservaiton of peace. But his policy seemed to be threatened when, in 1793, war began in Europe between France and Britain. To the Americans the French Revolution seemed to be a contest between monarchy and republicanism, between autocracy and democracy. Washington wisely issued a proclamation of neutrality. But the hot-headed French minister to the United States, Genet, thought that he could disregard it. When he attempted to use American ports as base of operation for French privateers, he was ordered to return home.

Apart from incurring the displeasure of the French, Washington's relations with Great Britain were far from satisfactory. He had to settle a variety of disputes with Britain. To settle these matters, Washington sent John Jay, an experienced diplomat, who was now Chief Justice,.to London as envoy extraordinary. Jay negotiated a treaty in November 1794 whereby he secured the withdrawal of the British from the Northwest Territory. But Jay accepted the British position on neutral rights of trade and failed to secure any substantial commercial concession. Though the Senate accepted the treaty, it was vehemently denounced by the Republicans as a surrender to Britain. In 1795, the American minister, Thomas Pinckney, negotiated a treaty with Spain by which Americans could have unlimited use of the the Mississippi.

Washington retired at the end of his second term in 1797 and died two years later. He believed that the best interests of the United States would be served by remaining aloof from European entanglements. 'It is our true policy to steer clear of permanent alliances with any portion of the foreign world... We may safely trust to temporary alliances for extraordinary emergencies'.

The Adams Administration

After Washington's retirement, John Adams became the President (1797-1801). He was handicapped by having a divided party behind him and a divided Cabinet at his side. To make matters worse he had to deal with international situation which was surcharged with tension. France was annoyed with Jay's Treaty and regarded America as virtually an ally of Britain. French privateers, therefore, began to attack American merchant ships. When Adams sent a mission of three men to negotiate with the French Government, they were treated with discourtesy. American indignation reached to an excited pitch. Troops were enlisted and in 1798 a series of naval battles took place in which American ships were uniformly victorious. War seemed imminent; but war with France would mean war also with her ally Spain. In this crisis, Adams ignoring the advice of Hamilton, who wanted war, sent a new envoy to France. Napoleon, who had come to power received him cordially and the danger of war disappeared.

In home affairs, Adams was not popular with the American people. The Alien and Sedition Acts of 1798 passed in 1798 was a gross violation of personal and civil liberties. The year 1800 found the country ripe for a change. Though the Federalists had established a strong government, but they were not responsive to the wishes of the people. Jefferson, a born popular Republican leader, assumed the presidency in 1801 and the manner of his election emphasised the fact that democracy had triumphed.

Jefferson's Administration

Jefferson was a product of the Enlightenment. Throughout his long career he asserted that all men were endowed with rights and that the protection of these rights was the primary purpose of the government. He was, however, known as a thinker than as a man of action. In his policy he was supported by his two chief advisers, Madison as Secretary of State and Gallatin as Secretary of the Treasury.

He abolished the whisky excise and allowed the Alien and Sedition Acts to expire, while Gallatin severely cut government expenditure. He encouraged agriculture and westward expansion. He also encouraged immigration by a liberal naturalisation law. Most of the states abolished property qualifications for the ballot. By the end of 1807, Gallatin had reduced the national debt to less than seventy million dollars.

The most important achievement of Jefferson's administration was in diplomacy. Spain had long been in occupation of the country west of the Mississippi, with the port of New Orleans near its mouth. In 1800, by the Treaty of San Ildefonso, Louisinia was transferred from Spain to France. This alarmed the United States; for France was a vigorous and expansionist power and if she was allowed to control the mouth of the Mississippi, the development of the American West would be blocked. Jefferson asserted that if France took possession of Louisiana, 'from that moment we must marry ourselves to the British fleet and nation'. Finding the inflexible attitude of Jefferson, and the impending war with Britain, Napoleon made a bid to win American friendship by selling Louisiana to the United States. As a result, the United States, in 1803, obtained more than a million square miles and with it the port of New Orleans. 'The United States gained a sweep of rich plains that within eighty years was to become one of the world's granaries'.

During his second term of Presidency which began in 1805, Jefferson maintained American neutrality during the colossal struggle between Great Britain and Napoleon. Both Powers had set up blockades and thereby struck heavy blows at American commerce. Jefferson believed that European countries in general, and the British especially, were largely dependent upon American imports, particularly of foodstuffs. In December 1807, Congress passed an Embargo Act prohibiting foreign commerce altogether. The embargo, however, had disastrous effect upon the American economy, leading to commercial stagnation and falling prices. In 1809 the Congress, therefore, repealed it.

Madison's Administration

Jefferson was succeeded in the leadership of the Republican Party by his friend, James Madison in 1809. The most important event during his presidency (1809-17) was a war with England. The war arose out of England's hostilities with Napoleon. American feeling against England was hurt by the latter's right of search of American vessels to find out the English sailors who had deserted from the British ships. Moreover, northwestern settlers were subjected to frequent attacks by the Red Indians which were believed to have been abetted by the British agents in Canada. War was demanded by a group of youngmen in the Congress, known as 'War Hawks'—like Henry Clay and John C. Calhoun—who displayed an aggressive nationalism.

The War of 1812 was one of the most unfortunate events in American history. The war efforts suffered owing to internal divisions of the worst kind. The attempt to conquer Canada ended in a fiasco. As a British historian put it "the militia and volunteers do not seem to have made up their minds whether they wanted to fight or not". The British navy kept a close blockade of the American coast and crippled American commerce.

The war was brought to a close by the Treaty of Ghent in 1814. It merely provided for the cessation of hostilities, the restoration for conquests and a commission to settle boundary disputes. But the War of 1812 was of great significance. It was, in a measure, a second war of independence. It strengthened national unity and gave an impetus to patriotism.

During all these years, the national government was being greatly strengthened by the decisions of the Supreme Court. John Marshall of Virginia—who was made Chief Justice just before Jefferson entered the presidency and holding the office until his death in 1835—asserted categorically the true spirit of the constitution. He declared:

> That the United States form, for many and for most important purposes, a single nation, has not yet been denied. In war we are one people. In making peace we are one people. In all commercial regulations we are one and the same people. In many other respects the American people are one; and the government which is alone capable of controlling and managing their interests in all these respects is the government of the Union.

Actuated with these fundamental premises, Marshall reinforced the authority of the Federal Government, and of the Supreme Court. He established the right of the Supreme Court in Marbury vs. Madison (1803) to review any law of the Congress or of a state legislature.

Expansion of the United States

Before and after the War of Independence, American expansion had taken place towards the West. The westward movement has often been regarded as the central theme of American history down to the end of the nineteenth century. Essentially it was a spontaneous migration of individuals to take advantage of the rich lands in the interior, but this migration was directed by the Federal legislation. The North-West Ordinance of 1787 established the procedure whereby the western lands should be administered as territories. The Act of 1796—which attracted the speculative investor with a minimum price of 2 dollars an acre and a lot of 640 acres—was successfully modified until the Act of 1820 reduced the price to 1.25 dollar and the purchase to 80 acres. Easier conditions lured settlers to the west in land booms, in the 1790s, between 1816 and 1819 and in the mid-twenties. By 1796 Kentucky and Tennessee were full-fledged states and Ohio was to become one. Pioneers were settling in Indiana, admitted a State in 1816, and Illinois (1818), and planters in the rich alluvial cotton lands of Mississippi (1817) and Alabama (1819). The westward movement was then checked by the financial crisis of 1819 and was gradually resumed during the 1820s. By the middle of the 1830s Michigan and Arkansas were ready for statehood, and settlers had moved into Texas which was added to the Union in 1845.

After the depression years of 1837-40 the next pioneers moved into Iowa and Wisconsin in the North; in the South, the movement turned down into Florida. Meanwhile the central team approached the arid plains west of Missouri. The United States obtained California in 1848 but also the huge area between it and Texas called New Mexico, which included the present Nevada and Utah.

Rise of King Cotton

The most important element in the economic change was the rise of a great cotton-growing industry in the South. Prior to 1793 little cotton was produced in the United States. But the epochal invention of the gin by Eli Whitney in 1793 for cleaning the seeds from cotton greatly accelerated production. At the same time, the demand for raw cotton was spurred by the Industrial Revolution which made textile manufacture a large-scale industry. The opening of new lands in the west after 1812 greatly expanded the area available for cotton cultivation.

It is hardly possible to exaggerate the importance of cotton in the development of the United States as a whole. Cotton cultivation spread rapidly through the lower south to the Mississippi River and eventually on to Texas. At its greatest extent the cotton belt covered an area measuring 1,000 miles (1,600 km) from east to west and included parts of nine states. Cotton was the dominant factor in the friendly relations between British and the United States. By 1830 the greater part of raw cotton went to Britain, constituting nearly 50 per cent of the value of U.S. exports; and 76 per cent of the raw cotton imported into Britain came from the Southern States. By means of cotton, the United States and Britain were closely bound together and by 1830 the commercial relations between the two nations had become something unique.

The Monroe Doctrine

In 1817, President James Madison had been succeeded by James Monroe. His two exceptional qualities were his shrewd common sense and strong will. His administration took a momentous step by enunciating the so-called Monroe Doctrine.

Ever since the English colonies had gained their freedom, there were stirrings of nationalist aspirations among the people of the Spanish and Portuguese colonies in South America. Before 1821, Argentina and Chile had established their independence and in 1822 under the leadership of Jose de San Martin and Simon Bolivar, several other South American States achieved independence. In 1819 Bolivar united Granada, Panama, Venezuela and Ecquador into a single state called Columbia. In 1822 President Monroe recognised the new countries in South America as independent and accepted them as equal partners of a free America. About this time, a combination of Central European powers had taken steps to crush popular movements in Spain and Italy. Holding a Congress at Verona in 1822, they discussed sending forces across the ocean to South America to bring back some of the independent states to Spanish allegiance. Britain was alarmed and George Canning, the British Foreign Secretary, suggested that the United States and Great Britain take concerted steps to pre-empt such intervention. Jefferson and Madison who were in favour of joint action advised Monroe to do so. But John Quincy Adams, as Secretary of State, rightly insisted to move alone than to 'come in as a cock-boat in the wake of the British man-of-war'. Adams drafted that independent declaration warning the European Powers off the Western hemisphere which the world came to know as the Monroe Doctrine. In a message to the Congress on December 2, 1823, Monroe declared that the American continents were henceforth 'not to be considered as subjects for future colonisation by any European power'. Any European intervention in the American continent would be considered as 'dangerous to our peace and security'. The United States would not interfere in those parts of the colonies or dependencies of any European Power in the New World. The United States would not take part in the wars of the European Powers as it was inconsistent 'with our policy to do so'.

Monroe thus set up a new landmark in the history of American foreign policy which was destined to endure more than a century. 'It was a manifesto of political isolation and an appendix to the Declaration of Independence'. The Monroe Doctrine continued to be the guiding principle of American foreign policy till the First World War. The assumption of heavy responsibility—protecting the Spanish American colonies from European intervention—by the United States invested the latter with prestige and self-confidence.

In 1824 Monroe was succeeded by John Quincy Adams, a man of extraordinary talent but violent prejudices. Adams entered office with two great national achievements to his credit: the Monroe Doctrine was his handiwork and it was he who, in 1819, had pushed the Spanish government to cede Florida to the United States. Adams governed honestly and efficiently and tried in vain to institute a national system of roads and canals. His administration was one long campaign for the next election. The election of 1828 was like an earthquake with an overwhelming majority for Jackson.

Nullification Crisis

Jackson believed in political equality and in equal economic opportunity. The Government, he declared, should be administered for the benefit of the 'the planter, the farmer, the mechanic and the labourer' who form 'the great body of the people of the United States'. He was the very symbol of nationalism, but had no sympathy with the secessionist tendencies developing in South Carolina; but he was also opposed to the expansion of Federal power beyond the words of the constitution. Jackson vigorously carried these ideas into practice. In his first term he had to deal with the tariff question, which had first been adopted in 1816 and reinforced by subsequent acts in 1824 and 1828. The rates of 1828 were so high that they became known in the South as the 'Tariff of abominations'. South Carolina was particularly indignant as she had suffered a prolonged economic depression for which she blamed the tariff. When relief was not forthcoming under a new tariff law in 1832, she took recourse to a constitutional subtlety which had been developed by her Senator, John C. Calhoun. Calhoun, the foremost American political theorist of his generation, had worked out a defensive theory known as the Doctrine of Nullification. Calhoun argued that when, in the judgment of one of the states, the Central Government exeeded its powers, a state could adjudge an act of Congress to be null and void. In short, he regarded the individual state as the final arbiter of the limits of constitutional power of the Federal authority. South Carolina called a state convention which, in 1832, adopted an ordinance of Nullification to suspend the collection of duties. Jackson promptly asserted that nullification was 'incompatible with the existence of the Union' and that 'Disunion by armed force is treason'. He affirmed that instead of being 'a compact between sovereign states', the United States, was 'a government in which people of all the States, collectively, are represented'. Conflict appeared imminent and Jackson sent General Scott and a naval force to Charleston. Daniel Webster's peroration 'Liberty and Union, now and forever, one and inseparable', became a national rallying cry. But the crisis was averted when South Carolina agreed to suspend their ordinance pending the reconsideration of the tariff by Congress. Senator Henry Clay, introduced a compromise tariff bill which was quickly passed in 1833. This provided for the reduction of duties. South Carolina thereupon repealed her ordinance. The nullification episode left a profound impact on the later development of the state rights theory.

War on the Bank

Jackson had to fight a desperate battle with the Bank of the United States, the citadel of Eastern finance and monopolistic power. The bank was a corporation chartered by the United States but owned and controlled by private stockholders. It served as the sole bank of deposit for the government. The Bank virtually possessed a monopoly over the credit and currency of the country and in its operation, represented the interests of the wealthy few. The President of the Bank, Nicholas Biddle of Philadelphia, an overbearing aristocrat, did not adhere strictly to the rules and restrictions laid down in the original charter and began to seek political support by lending large sums to Congressmen and not pressing for repayment. To Jackson the Bank represented a dangerous 'concentration of power in the hands of a few men irresponsible to the people'.

Jackson decided to attack the bank immediately instead of waiting for the expiry of its charter in 1836. But Henry Clay secured the passage of a bill to recharter the Bank before the Presidential election of 1832. Without any ado, Jackson vetoed the bill. The Bank question became the overriding issue in the Presidential election and his adversaries chose Clay as the candidate to oppose him for the Presidency in 1832. Jackson won by heavy majorities. He now assumed the offensive at once, withdrawing the government funds from the Bank of the United States and transferring them to a number of state banks. The Bank of the United States retained its charter until 1836, and was then recognised as a state bank under the laws of Pennsylvania. With new funds in hands and with no central bank to control them, the 'pet banks' expanded their credit recklessly. The result was a crisis in 1837 in which most of the banks failed and the government lost its deposits. The country was plunged into a depression which lasted for several years.

Van Buren Harrison and Tyler

The political factions opposed to Jackson came together under a common party name—Whig—and contested the 1836 election. But in the election the Whigs were a poor force and Martin Van Buren, who was supported by Jackson, won the election. The period of economic depression which accompanied his term obscured much of his merits. Van Buren's public acts—like the ten-hour day for government workers—awakened no enthusiasm.

The depression gave the Whigs a good chance of winning the presidential election of 1840. William Henry Harrison of Ohio, the hero of the war of 1812, and a Whig candidate became the president. Within a month of his inauguration, the sixty-eight year old President died. The Presidency then passed on to John Tyler, who, as a Southerner, was opposed to most of the programme of the dominant Northern wing of the Whig party. Tyler was repudiated by the party which had elected him. The Cabinet resigned; Tyler then appointed Democrats to the Cabinet. After 1843, however, he was primarily concerned with the question of the annexation of Texas. For the next five years Western expansion was to dominate American politics.

Age of Reform

The period of the thirties and forties was characterised by infinite discontent and of infinite hope.

'A restless, prying, conscientious criticism broke out in the most unexpected quarter', wrote Emerson. There resulted an emancipation of the intellectual and spiritual as well as the material life of the people.

The period was marked by the beginning of labour organisations. In 1825, labour forces in Philadelphia succeeded in establishing a ten-hour work day. This was merely the beginning of similar reforms in other places—New Hampshire, Rhode Island, Ohio and California. The spread of manhood suffrage led to the demand of free education. In 1830 the working-men of Philadelphia said: 'There can be no real liberty without a wide diffusion of real intelligence ... until means of equal instruction shall be equally secured to all'. The outstanding figures in the fight for universal education were De Witt Clinton in New York, Abraham Lincoln in Illinois, and Horace Mann in Massachusetts. It was not until the middle decades of the nineteenth century that public education became free for everybody. The first compulsory education law was passed in Massachusetts in 1852 and other states did not follow this example until after the Civil War (1861-1865).

Superstition was a curse to religion and Clergymen like Emerson, Theodore Parker, William Ellery Channing and George Ripley, tried to rid the Church of dogma and ritual and return to the great principles of morality. A significant feature of the reform movement in America was the demand of women for political and legal rights. Lucretia Mott, Susan B. Anthony and Elizabeth Cady Stanton devoted their energies to **anti-slavery, feminism** and **labour welfare**. In 1848, a women's rights convention, the first in the history of the world, was held at Seneca Falls, New York. The delegates demanded equality with the male sex before the law in educational and economic opportunities and in voting. Although the feminist movement did not achieve its main goal, the right to vote, until the twentieth century, it improved the legal position of the women by giving them control of their own property after marriage.

The spirit of national self-confidence found expression in literature which, to a certain extent, was influenced by the doctrines of Romantic individualism. The decade of the thirties saw the emergence of Henry Wadsworth Longfellow, John Greenleaf Whittier, Oliver Wendell Holmes, and James Russell Lowell. Emerson preached the doctrine of individualism in immemorable verse and prose. Nathaniel Hawthrone and Edgar Allan Poe gave literary expression to the sombre and supernatural in men's experience. A number of writers took an active interest in the humanitarian and political struggles of the age. Whittier was the poet laureate of the anti-slavery crusade; Longfellow published his *Poems on Slavery* in 1842; Lowell acted as editor of the *Pennsylvania Freeman*. But it should be remembered, 'before the Civil War, American novelists made little attempt to produce realistic portrayals of American society; there were no American equivalents of Dickens or Balzac'.

Slavery: Causes of Conflict

The political conflicts between the North and the South which had plagued the country since the foundation of the Republic, owed their origin to different economic interests. Eli Whitney's invention of the cotton gin in 1793 gave new vigour to the southern plantation economy. In less than five decades after Whitney's invention, cotton advanced a thousand miles (1,600 km) across the lower South. Cotton cultivation was admirably suited to the employment of slaves as the work was done with the aid of primitive tools only.

The North, on the other hand, had become a centre of capitalist industry and finance. As the North grew steadily more urban, it embraced the values of progress and insisted upon the importances of social mobility. The North regarded a protective system as essential to the development of industry while the South, selling its cotton in the world market, resented restrictions.

Whatever fundamental economic issues may have been at stake, people differed about their attitudes toward slavery. While a majority of Southerners believed that slavery was a positive good, a growing number of Northerners insisted that it was an evil.

The Abolitionist Movement

The North, influenced by the natural-rights doctrine of the equality of men as reflected in the writings of Thomas Paine and Ralph W. Emerson, began to denounce slavery and to clamour for immediate abolition. Societies for the abolition of slavery began to increase after 1815. The abolition movement found an inspired leader in William Lloyd Garrison, who launched his weekly *The Liberator* on January 1, 1831. He announced:

> I shall strenuously contend for the immediate enfranchisement of our slave population ... On this subject I do not wish to think or speak, or write, with moderation ... I am in earnest—I will not excuse—I will not retreat a single inch—and I will be heard.

In 1831 Theodore Dwight Weld, an evangelist of intense fervour, began a crusade against slavery. In 1833 the American Anti-Slavery Society was established. By 1840 there were about 2,000 abolitionist societies, claiming a total membership of nearly 200,000 men.

Paradoxically, the people of the North as a whole held aloof from the anti-slavery movement. But as the movement gathered momentum and seemed to threaten the integrity of the Union, the matter became more important to them than the destruction of slavery. John Quincy Adams repeatedly warned the South that secession would mean war and that 'from the instant your slave-holding states become the theatre of war, from that moment the war-powers of the constitution extend to interference with the institution of slavery'.

At a time when Andrew Jackson left the presidency in 1837, the legal basis for determining the status of slavery lay exclusively with the states, thirteen of which sanctioned slavery while thirteen others forbade it. Slavery had been given limits by the Missouri Compromise of 1820; but it was not applicable to future acquisitions. Many northerners believed that, if kept within close bounds, it would ultimately die down. They pointed to the ordinance of 1787, which forbade the extension of slavery into North-West, as a binding precedent. As Texas already had slavery, she naturally entered the Union as a slave state in 1845. But when the United States prepared to take over California, New Mexico and Utah in 1846 which did not have slavery, controversy arose. A compromise was effected in 1850 through the instrumentality of Senator Henry Clay, in which it was decided that California be admitted as a free state, that New Mexico and Utah be left free to decide on slavery for themselves. The compromise also included legislation to secure the return of fugitive slaves. It guaranteed slavery but abolished the slave trade in the District of Columbia.

With the admission of California the North had, for the first time, a majority in both Houses of Congress, since there were now sixteen free and fifteen slave states. Thus the South could expect to be outvoted in Congress. This led some Southern extremists to advocate immediate secession.

The compromise of 1850 was only a patchwork. The tension was brewing and the new Fugitive Slave Law offended many Northerners. They refused to apprehend slaves with the result that the Northern states became honeycombed with shelters for runaways. Meanwhile, the publication of *Uncle Tom's Cabin* by Harriet Beecher Stowe in 1852—which depicted the seamy side of slavery—aroused deep feeling in both North and South. More than 300,000 copies were sold before the end of 1852.

The old issue of slavery flared up again in 1854. The region comprising the fertile states of Kansas and Nebraska was attracting settlers and the Northerners believed that a railroad could be built through it from Chicago to the Pacific. Under the Missouri Compromise, all this region was closed to slavery. However, dominant slave-holding elements in Missouri objected to letting Kansas, which adjoined her on the west, become a free territory. Backed by southern support, Senator Stephen Douglas proposed to repeal the anti-slavery restriction of the Missouri compromise and to apply popular sovereignty, leaving the inhabitants of Kansas and Nebraska free to determine whether they should enter the Union as free or slave states. Supported by Southern votes and applying extreme posture, Douglas drove this measure through 1854.

'The Kansas-Nebraska Bill proved to be one of the most catastrophic political blunders in American history'. Such a storm of indignation swept across the North that Salmon A. Chase prophesied: 'They celebrate a present victory, but the echoes they awaken shall never rest until slavery itself shall die'. The immediate result was the disintegration of the Whig party and the rise of a powerful new organisation, the Republican Party. In 1856 it nominated the dashing John C. Fremont, but it lost to the Democratic candidate, James Buchanan. Though the Republican Party lost the election, it swept a great part of the north and the popularity of its leaders—Chase, William Seward and, above all, Abraham Lincoln—rose to great height. Meanwhile, Kansas became a bleeding ground owing to the armed conflict between slave-holders and abolitionists.

Drift to War

'Year by year the nation moved closer to war. A great drum seemed to beat out the march to conflict, stroke after stroke'. Early in 1857, the Supreme Court announced its famous decision concerning a Negro slave named Dred Scott, who claimed freedom by virtue of former residence in free territory. The southern-dominated Court held that neither the Congress nor any State Legislature had the right to prohibit slavery in any part of the Union. According to the Supreme Court, the Missouri compromise had been unconstitutional and slavery was legal in all territories. This meant that the Northern theory of popular sovereignty for the territories was also void, and that all these areas were open to slavery.

The decision evoked a storm of protest throughout the North. Deprived of the popular sovereignty principle, the North came to the conclusion that it might, despite the Supreme Court, exclude slavery from all territories. For the southern Democrats, on the other hand, the decision was a great victory, since it gave judicial sanction to their theory of slavery. In 1858 the question of slavery assumed importance when Stephen Douglas and Abraham Lincoln became rival candidates for election to the Senate from Illinois. The two candidates engaged in a memorable series of debates which did much to awaken the country to the significance of the issues. On June 17, 1858, Lincoln struck the keynote of American history:

> A house divided against itself cannot stand. I believe this Government cannot endure permanently half slave and half free. I do not expect the Union to be dissolved—I do not expect the house to fall—but I do expect it will cease to be divided.

Lincoln succeeded in forcing Douglas to reiterate that people of a territory could exclude slavery in spite of the Dred Scott decision. Though Douglas was once again elected Senator, Lincoln became a national figure.

Throughout the year 1859 the country was visibly drifting towards a crisis. In 1859 John Brown, an anti-slavery fanatic, with eighteen companions, attempted a slave insurrection by means of a raid upon Harper's Ferry, Virginia. This quixotic enterprise completely failed and Brown and six of his followers were hanged. This episode, though trivial in nature, succeeded in widening the gulf between the North and the South. The Northerners regarded Brown as a martyr to liberty. Many Southerners concluded that if the abolitionists were going to instigate slave rebellions, then secession was preferable.

Apart from this incident, there remained deep-seated differences between the North and the South. While the South was almost wholly rural, the North had become urbanized. The Northerners believed in protective tariffs, while the rural South, wanting its manufactured goods cheaply, detested them. The North was in favour of a distribution of the public lands to small holders. The South wished to see the national domain held and sold only for good prices. Socially, the North was more democratic than the South, where the slave holding overlords held most of the wealth. Beneath these differences there lay an almost insoluble slavery problem. The abolitionist agitation engendered a fear that the North would attack slavery whereas the Northerners believed that radical Southerners would try to spread slavery over the whole nation.

The victory of Abraham Lincoln, a Republican candidate in the presidential election of 1860, precipitated the final crisis. As soon as the election results were known, South Carolina adopted an ordinance of secession on December 20. Before the end of February 1861, similar action had been taken by six other states—Mississippi, Florida, Alabama, Georgia, Louisiana and Texas. Early in February 1861, these seven seceding states formed a Southern Union—the Confederate States of America—and installed Jefferson Davis of Mississippi as President. Eight other slave states declined to follow them and remained in the old Union. Thus the dream of a faction of ardent secessionists who had urged disunion and had warned that the South could escape subjugation to an alien North only by seceding, now came to be fulfilled. They refused to be sobered by the Southern moderates who were, for the most part, lovers of the Union.

When Lincoln became President on March 4, 1861, he asserted that the Southern States had no constitutional right to secede. He also found a very tense situation at two Federal forts in the South—Pickens in Florida and Sumter in South Carolina—which were threatened with military force. Lincoln had no desire to plunge into war and urged the Southern states to change their mind before it was too late. He was reluctant to precipitate a crisis lest the eight slave states, still in the Union, might defect to the confederacy. However, he refused to withdraw the garrisons and, on April 6, sent relief expedition to the two forts. The Confederates, after much hesitation, bombarded and captured Fort Sumter on April 14. The fall of the fort provoked a burst of popular indignation in the North and Lincoln, on his own responsibility, entered into war. Of the eight slave states, Virginia, North Carolina, Tennessee and Arkansas, voted to join the Confederacy while the remaining four, Maryland, Delaware, Kentucky and Missouri, remained with the Union. Thus 'American nationalism moved into the phase of supreme crisis which was resolved only by four years (1861-1865) of Civil War'.

Both sides entered the war with hopes of a quick victory. The Northern states were numerically superior than the Southern. Twenty-three States were pitted against eleven. But though the North was capable of raising larger forces than the South, the former attained a clear numerical superiority only during the last year and a half of the war. But in material resources, the North enjoyed a decided superiority. It was apparent both in agricultural and industrial production. Even in military resources, the Northern States had abundant facilities for the manufacture of arms and ammunition, clothing and other supplies. By 1862 the thirty-eight largest gun factories in the North could produce 5,000 rifles a day, whereas the maximum for the South was only 300 a day. Confederate firearms were inferior to Northern weapons. The Southern economy, largely dependent on Europe, was unable to provide its military forces with uniforms, shoes, and medical supplies. After 1863 the South had exhausted its resources, while those of the North seemed inexhaustible.

In transport and communication, the North had an overwhelming superiority. The greatest advantages of the North was in its railways. 'The Civil war was one of the first in which railways played an important role'. In comparison with the North which had approximately 20,000 miles (32,000 km) of railways, the South, with an equal land-area, had only 10,000 miles (16,000 km). By 1864 the Southern railway system was almost on the brink of collapse. Some historians think that the railway breakdown aggravated the collapse of Southern resistance. Moreover, the North possessed a well-equipped navy. Numbering only 90 ships in 1861, the Federal navy increased to 670 ships in 1864. Apart from importing commodities, the navy supported the land forces in subjugating the vast western region between the Appalachian Mountains and the Mississippi rivers.

Despite the North's material advantages, it had to maintain long lines of communication and garrison—occupied territories. And because this was a civil war, the North had to conquer a people and convince them that their cause was hopeless. The Confederacy's hope was psychological. It was fighting for its independence. The North, on the other hand, was fighting an aggressive war in support of two abstract principles: the permanence of the Union, and, later, the emancipation of the slaves.

If the human factor eluded the South, there was still an almost certain promise of success—that of European intervention. Since the economic systems of England and France depended on Southern cotton, they would, therefore, force the North to stop the war and concede Southern independence. But the Southerners were disappointed when neither England nor France extended diplomatic recognition to the Confederacy or entertained any idea of intervention. Liberals like Bright and Cobden and the English workers expressed their sympathy for the Northern cause. Lincoln's Emancipation Proclamation (January 1, 1863) had an enormous influence in turning liberal opinion in Europe against the Confederacy.

A sturdy defiance animated the South even in disaster, but it was matched by Northern determination. The Southern generals were, on the whole, abler and more experienced than those of the North. But Robert E. Lee, one of the greatest military generals in American history, was not given of all the Confederate forces until almost the end of the war. Lincoln, on the other hand, gave full authority to his generals, and was able to pick up able leaders.

President Lincoln proved a far greater statesman than Jefferson Davis. But Lincoln's task seemed to be the most difficult ever confronted by an American statesman. He had to restore the Union, to direct a civil war, and, at the same time to animate his own people with unity of purpose. Lincoln was able to perform his great task because he had unbounded passion for democracy. The American Union was the symbol of the world's greatest example of democracy, 'the last, best hope of earth'. Confident in his own abilities, Lincoln boldly exercised his war powers. In his own cabinet, three of the members, Seward, Chase and the Secretary of War, Edwin M. Stanton, were first-rate men.

As director of war, Lincoln was superior to Davis, despite the latter's military experience. But Lincoln made up this deficiency by his superior mind and moral strength. He mobilised the maximum manpower resources of the North and urged his generals to better the strategic line of the Confederacy. His objective was to destroy the Confederate armies and not to occupy places. In contrast with Davis, who adopted a defensive strategy, Lincoln acted to implement a sound offensive strategy.

War

The war was mainly confined to three theatres: the eastern, the western, and the trans-Mississippi. The area between the mountains and the sea-coast became the eastern theatre, and the vast region between the mountain and the Mississippi became the western theatre. The trans-Mississippi theatre constituted the states of Arkansas, Louisiana and Texas.

Most of the fighting in the eastern theatre occurred in Virginia, where the chief Northern objective was to capture Richmond, the capital of the Confederacy. McClellan's attempt to capture Richmond from the east in the spring and summer of 1862 was unsuccessful. Union armies then tried to storm their way by south from Washington. Invasions of Virginia by Pope, Burnside and Hooker were defeated. Lee made two thrusts into the North and was checked at Antiem in September 1862 and at Gettysburg, in July 1863. Grant's slow and steady advance on Richmond in 1864 presaged its fall which was finally abandoned by Lee in April 1865.

In the western theatre the first objective of the Union was to capture the whole line of the Mississippi, thereby splitting the Confederacy into two. In the spring of 1862 forces led by Grant won control of western Tennessee. Simultaneously Admiral Farragut, after capturing New Orleans in a naval battle, took his ships as far as Vicksburg. By the summer of 1863, Vicksburg fell (July 1863) and the Federals were in possession of the river line They then started operations to secure their next objective, the line of the Tennessee River, which provided a base for invading the heart of the South. On the Tennessee the key position was Chattanooga, the most vital communication centre. They occupied Chattanooga in 1863 and from it, in 1864, General W. T. Sherman moved to North Carolina.

Action in the trans-Mississippi area was minor as neither side commanded large forces in this region. Federal forces occupied the northern half of Arkansas. In 1862 a Northern land and naval expedition seized New Orleans. After the fall of Vicksburg, it was felt unnecessary to conquer the states west of the Mississippi.

During the winter of 1864 the war came close to a conclusion. The Confederate Government, however, was still determined to continue fighting. On March 4, 1865, Lincoln began his second term, appealing to his countrymen 'with malice towards none, with charity for all to do all which may achieve and cherish a just and lasting peace'. On April 2, 1865 Lee evacuated Richmond, but Sheridan cut off his line of retreat. On April 9, hemmed in by overwhelming forces, Lee met Grant at Appomattox Court House in Virginia and agreed to surrender. On April 26 Johnston, feeling that further resistance was useless, capitulated to Sherman. Jefferson Davis, the last hope of the Confederate forces, was soon captured and this brought about the end of the Civil War.

But Lincoln did not live to enjoy the fruits of victory. On April 14, five days after Lee's capitulation, he was assassinated by a crazy fanatic, John Wilkes Booth, as he sat in his box in Ford's theatre. Thus perished an extraordinary man who combined in himself an inexhaustible patience, deep sagacity, and generosity of feeling. He desired above everything else that the war should result in 'a new birth of freedom, and that Government of the people, by the people, for the people, shall not perish from the earth'.

The Civil War was the greatest historical experience of the American people, comparable to the Revolution of 1789 in France. 'It settled certain differences, and it settled them permanently. It destroyed slavery, and assured the ascendancy of industrial capitalism. Furthermore, it preserved the Union and stabilised ... the modern American nation'. The United States now became 'the new nation, the guide and lawgiver of all nations'. Deeply touched by the impact of the war, Walt Whitman wrote emotionally: 'Today, ahead, though dimly yet, we see in vistas, a copious, sane, gigantic offspring'.

Impact of the War

The war left a hatred between North and South that lasted for decades. Most Southerners were willing to accept the supremacy of the Federal Government and the abolition of slavery. In the North there was a strong sentiment in favour of treating the South as conquered territory.

The immediate task after the war was the problem of reconstruction which raised two basic problems: the future of the Negro and the future of the Union. Before the war ended the Congress in March 1865 formalised the fact of Negro freedom by proposing the thirteenth constitutional amendment which abolished slavery and was ratified in December 1865.

Throughout the summer of 1865, Johnson proceeded to carry out Lincoln's plan of reconstruction. By presidential proclamation, he appointed a governor for each of the various Southern states and restored political rights to large number of Confederates. Conventions were held in the Southern states which replaced the ordinances of secession, abolished slavery and drafted new constitutions. Meanwhile, alarm was felt in the North when prominent ex-Confederates were elected to the Congress and by the passage of 'black Codes' which enshrined perpetual Negro inferiority.

The political atmosphere was tense when the momentous thirty-ninth Congress met in December 1865. While the abolitionists were profoundly shocked by the abandonment of the Negroes to their former masters, the Republicans feared that they might become a minority in the country. The situation brought to the fore the Radical Republicans, headed by Thadeus Stevens. The Radicals had a majority in both Houses of Congress and carried through the Congress in April 1866 a Civil Rights Bill, which declared that Negroes should have the same right as white people. Finally, Congress passed in the spring of 1866 the Fourteenth Amendment which effected a constitutional revolution by placing 'Civil rights under national protection'. It prohibited the states from making any law which 'abridged the privileges and immunities of the United States' or deprived any person of life, liberty or property without due process of law or denied 'to any person within its jurisdiction the equal protection of the laws'. But all the Southern States, with the exception of Tennessee, refused to ratify the Fourteenth Amendment.

Despite Johnson's opposition, the Radicals secured an overwhelming victory in the Congressional elections of 1866. The Radicals depicted Johnson as 'an ignorant boor and a Confederate sympathiser'. It ended the existing Southern State governments, divided the South into five districts, and placed them under military rule. The conditions on which a state could be readmitted to the Union were the inclusion of adult male suffrage in its constitution and the ratifica-

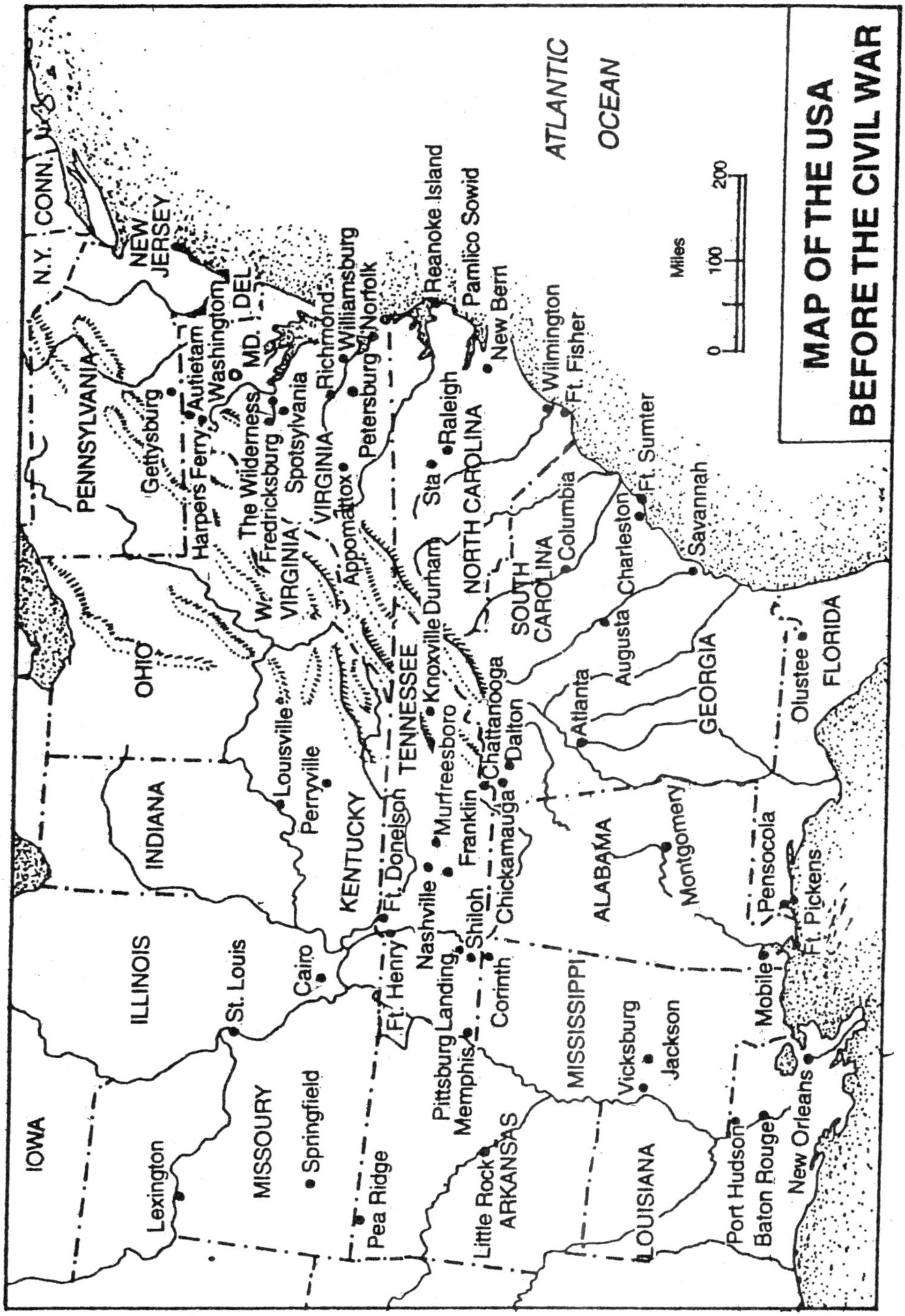

MAP OF THE USA BEFORE THE CIVIL WAR

tion of the Fourteenth Amendment by the legislature. In July 1868 the Fourteenth Amendment was passed by Congress and ratified in 1870 by state legislatures. The Fifteenth Amendment enacted that the right to vote could not be abridged 'on account of race, colour or previous condition of servitude'. Negroes took their places as state legislators, as executive officers, and even as Congressmen. By June 1868 seven states became eligible for readmission and, by June 1870, all the former rebel states were restored to the Union.

CHAPTER 39

CRISIS AND CONFIDENCE IN THE UNITED STATES OF AMERICA (1867-1945)

The War left a hatred between North and South that was difficult to be assuaged. The magnitude of the task was felt when two opposing sections—Republican North and the Democratic South—raised their respective viewpoints on Reconstruction. Republican demagogues appealed to the prejudice against Southern Democrats. The opposing section harked back to the past—slavery, the plantation system and the war.

The painful process of Reconstruction dominated the political scene up to 1877. Unfortunately, Andrew Johnson, for all his stubborn integrity, did not enjoy either the influence or the authority of Lincoln. In the North President Johnson maintained that after the war the only besetting problem was the restoration of normal government in the South and of normal relationship between the states and the Union. Lincoln had interpreted the struggle as one for free government. The first issue of the *Nation* (July 5, 1865), the principal organ of the Northern intelligentsia, declared that 'we utter no idle boast when we say that if the conflict of ages between law and power, between opinion and the sword, was not closed on the day on which Lee threw down his arms, the issue was placed beyond doubt.' These rhapsodies became clouded when rehabilitation of four million slaves who became free assumed pressing problem.

Johnson proceeded with his policy of reconstruction by amending the constitution. The first phase of Congressional Reconstruction was the promulgation of the Fourteenth Amendment in 1866. The first clause of the Amendment placed civil rights under national protection; it prohibited the states from making any law which 'abridged the privileges and immunities of the citizens of the United States', or deprived 'any person of life, liberty, or property without due process of law,' denied 'to any person the equal protection of the laws.' Congress was given power to enforce this amendment.

The amendment was rejected by overwhelming majorities in every Southern state save Tennessee. But the overwhelming victory of the Republicans in the Congressional elections of 1866, strengthened Radical leadership. The Reconstruction Acts passed in 1867 put an end to the existing Southern state governments, restored military rule, and instructed the military commanders to call constitutional conventions elected by all adult males. The work of Reconstruction was crowned by the Fifteenth Amendment which prohibited the states from disfranchising the Negro 'on account of race or colour.' Technically the era of Reconstruction achieved success. New constitutions on the best Northern models were introduced; Negroes became state legislators and even congressmen; and by June 1870 all the rebel states were restored to the Union. It seemed that the whole structure of the Union was knit together by a new grant of national power.

The political revolution, however, revealed serious weaknesses. The Negroes were legally free, but the Congress did nothing to provide them with political rights, social equality or economic security. Land was not distributed among the freed men. The majority of Negro farmers ended as share-croppers, occupying land but committing half their crop to the landowner for rent. Thus the economic ascendancy of the upper class was assured. While the majority of

Negroes remained poor peasants there emerged a small Negro middle class which antagonised the poorer whites. The history of Reconstruction became intertwined with a grim economic struggle which brought speculative Northerners to the South. New burdens were imposed on the South; in addition to national debt it was assessed a heavy excise duty on cotton. During the carpetbag regime, there was petty swindling, and a few major scandals, corruption and incompetence accounted for high taxes and indebtedness. Nevertheless, one should appreciate the constructive side of Radical reconstruction. Public schools and charitable institutions were established, immigration was encouraged and lands were distributed to the Negroes. Old factories were reopened and capital was attracted to new industries. Railroad tracks were re-laid, new roads sprang up in the Southwest, bridges rebuilt and banks and insurance companies began their operations. 'As ruin was never before so overwhelming, never was restoration swifter.'

With the restoration and extension of the railway system, the revival of cotton cultivation and the development of iron, steel and coal, the South entered upon an industrial revolution. As early as 1870 the counter-revolution was under way in most Southern states. Fear of force and economic coercion kept the Negroes from the polls or forced them to vote Democrats. By 1876 Republican governments survived in only three states.

Despite the passage of laws to enforce the Fourteenth and Fifteenth Amendments, radicalism made little headway. In 1875 the Congress passed a Civil Rights Act which was invalidated by the Supreme Court in 1883. In 1896 the Supreme Court decided that 'equal protection of the laws' of the Fourteenth Amendment was compatible with racial segregation. In 1890 the Senate refused to pass an act to enforce the Fifteenth Amendment. Behind the liquidation of radicalism lay the formation of a conservative alliance between Northern business and Southern business. This unwritten conservative alliance, which was to dominate Congress and the Senate, made a significant contribution to the restoration of national unity.

For the remainder of the century, Southern domestic politics did not stir the national scene. After 'redemption' Negroes continued to vote in some numbers and there were a few Negro members of state legislatures. This situation was ended by the imposition of suffrage qualification—like literacy, property and tax-paying qualifications—which disenfranchised Negroes while permitting poor whites to vote. In reaction against Reconstruction activity the state governments restricted their activities. Though the public education system made some headway, the results were not commensurate with the well-established systems of northern and western states. The South attracted few immigrants as the country still lived in an eighteenth century world. However, harsh discriminatory laws were often mitigated by friendly relations between the negroes and the Americans. Out of this kinship emerged a small Negro middle class to whom the great negro leader, Booker T. Washington, pinned the best hope for his race. The Negroes appealed to American traditions which were enshrined in American ideals.

Unlike the South, the Great Plains while accepting Northern superiority, rejected its economic control. The migrants who flooded west in great numbers after the Civil War were dependent on a capitalist economy. Though the farmer got 160 acres of land by the Homestead Act of 1862, he found himself at the mercy of forces which he could not control. The Western farmers opposed the intrusion of large-scale capitalism. Their main target were the great railway corporations which often sought quick profits instead of long-term development of the region they served.

Apart from attacking railway corporations, the western farmers had cause for resentment against the financial system, which they believed, restricted the flow of capital to their rural section. Agrarian west and the industrial east differed over the means by which capital could be supplied. The western demand for easy money had deep roots in American history. The Civil War had been financed by the issue of greenbacks, an inconvertible paper currency. Despite depreciation they were popular with businessmen. Immediately after the war, the greenbacks had the powerful support of radicals. But easy money was somewhat discredited by the Democratic adoption, in 1868, of the 'Ohio Idea' for the payment of the debt in paper currency. In spite of this, Republican majorities in Congress refused to sanction an immediate contraction of the greenbacks.

In the 40 years (1865-1914) between the two great wars—the Civil War and the First World War—America was transformed from a rural republic to an urban state. The period witnessed the emergence of giant factories, steel mills, inter-continental railroad lines, flourishing cities and vast agricultural holdings. 'The Civil War', observed one writer, 'cut a white gash through the history of the country; it dramatized in a stroke the changes that had begun to take place during the preceding twenty or thirty years.' War needs speeded up the economic process and pushed the nation to the march of science and invention.

From 1860 to 1890, 440,000 patents were issued—a gigantic leap from 36,000 patents granted before 1860. The principle of the dynamo, invented in 1831, revolutionised American life after 1880. Alexander Graham Bell invented a telephone system and within a short period millions of telephone connections accelerated the social and economic life of the nation. The pace was quickened by the invention of the typewriter in 1867, the adding machine in 1889, the cash register in 1897, the lino-type composing machine in 1886, and the rotary press. After 1880 Edison's incandescent lamp brought cheaper light to millions of homes. Edison, along with George Eastman, developed the motion picture. All these resulted a high level of productivity in various fields.

The basic industry of the nation—iron and steel—made rapid strides, protected by a high tariff. Though concentrated in the eastern states, new ore deposits were discovered in the western region. The great Mesabi iron range at the head of Lake Superior proved one of the greatest ore-producers in the world. Free of chemical impurities, it was processed under the new open-hearth methods into steel of superior quality at a cheap price.

Advances in steel production were to a large extent due to the enterprise and skill of Andrew Carnegie, a key figure in the history of the industry. The plant which he built in 1875 on the banks of the Monongahela was the greatest in the country. Carnegie's empire grew by leaps and bounds and, in 1900, it was turning out three million tons of steel a year with annual profits of forty million dollars. Although Carnegie had long dominated the industry, he had to face challenge from rival companies. Stung by competition and because of his old age, he merged his holdings with a new organisation out of which emerged the United States Steel Company in 1901.

A new concept of welding competing firms into a single organisation developed among the businessmen as it would enable the latter to control both production and markets. The primary instrument to achieve these ends was the corporation and the trust. The corporation enjoyed a permanent life, the power to float issues of stocks and bonds and limited liability for debts. The trust was a combination of corporations and managed by trustees. By virtue of their capital resources, they had greater power to expand, to compete with foreign business companies, and to bargain with labour.

The Standard Oil Company, which led the way, thrived under the superb genius of Rockefeller. By building an efficient marketing system the Standard Oil Company emerged as the first great trust in 1882. Before 1900 Rockefeller had harnessed the oil industry, eliminated most of his competitors and held the greatest monopoly in the country. This was followed by other trusts and combinations—in cottonseed oil, linseed oil, lead, sugar, tobacco and rubber. A survey of 1904 showed that more than five thousand independent concerns had been consolidated into 319 industrial trusts.

The process of combination was also felt in the field of transportation and communication. Western Union, the earliest large combination, was followed by the Bell Telephone System and, eventually, by the giant American Telephone and Telegraph. In the 1860s Cornelius, Vanderbilt knit some thirteen of fourteen separate railroads into a single line connecting New York City and

Buffalo, about 300 miles (480 km) away. During the next decade he acquired lines to Chicago and Detroit, and the New York Central system came into being. Soon most of the railroads were organized into trunk lines. E. H. Harriman created Illinois Central, the Union Pacific, the Southern Pacific and half a dozen other lines. He dreamed of creating a nation-wide network which nearly came to reality mainly through the efforts of a banker, J. P. Morgan. All through the eighties, Morgan reorganised and refinanced railroads. Apart from railroads, Morgan had exercised decisive influence in other major business. He had financed the Federal Steel Company and bought the United States Steel. Owing to his eff rts emerged the International Harvester Company. He helped finance General Electric, American Telephone and Telegraph, the New York Rapid Transit Company and a dozen other giant utilities.

It had been found in 1912 that the banking houses of Morgan and William Rockefeller held 341 directorships in railroads, shipping, utilities, banks, coal, copper, iron, steel and insurance with capital of twenty-two billion dollars. As Woodrow Wilson observed rhetorically, 'The great monopoly in this country is money monopoly.'

In this new industrial set-up, cities became the nerve centre. In 1860 hardly a city been inhabited by a million inhabitants. But thirty years later New York had a million and a half, and Chicago and Philadelphia each had over a million. In these three decades, Philadelphia and Baltimore doubled in population; Kansas City and Detroit grew fourfold, Cleveland sixold, Chicago tenfold.

The implication of these developments was felt in the political life of the period. The small businessmen complained of unfair competition from monopolistic giants. The most vocal critic of the New American order was Henry George whose *Progress and Poverty* was published in 1879. George held a passionate belief in the benefits of competitive-capitalism provided that its defects could be removed. Distrust of monopoly was an old American tradition which held that the constitution ought to provide for the inviolability of free enterprise.

George Cleveland, a Democrat, elected to the presidency in 1884, tried to grapple with the problems resulting from these economic changes. In 1873 the Court was of opinion that the privileges and immunities protected by the fourteenth amendment did not imply the right to pursue a trade without legislative interference. In 1886 another blow was struck at the commerce clause, giving Congress exclusive jurisdiction over interstate commerce. Some firm regulations were needed to protect the consumer against monopoly or the small businessman against 'unfair' competition. The railroads which followed discriminatory policy fanned popular resentment. It was felt that free competition was to be made compulsory by the abolition of monopoly. The problem was national in character and therefore required Congressional action.

The Interstate Commerce Act of 1887 set up a Federal Commission with the duty of supervising interstate railways and forbade excessive changes and rate discrimination. But Senator Nelson W. Aldrich said the Interstate Commerce Act of 1887 was 'a delusion and a sham . . . an empty menace to the great interests.' The Sherman Anti-Trust Act of 1890 was due to the monopoly enjoyed by the Rockefeller's Standard Oil Trust in the county's oil-refining. It declared that 'every contract, combination in the form of trust or otherwise, or conspiracy, in restraint of trade or commerce among the several states, or with foreign nations, is hereby declared to be illegal.' The Act of 1890 left its enforcement to the courts. However, great difficulty lay in the interpretation of the act and Cleveland's and McKinley's administrations failed to prosecute big business. The result was an acceleration rather than a check to consolidation of big business. Despite the disappointment history of these two great measures of the regulation of capitalist enterprise, the acts enshrined the principles for the conduct of business.

Despite these significant trends, the political trends of the period, were generally insipid. The main interest of the American people was focussed on the history of the West—a vast stretch of unoccupied land, unfenced prairies, plains that extended to the foothills of the Rockies and a thousand miles of mountain ranges. By the end of the century all the country had been carved into states. The Homestead Act of 1862 which granted free farms of 160 acres to citizens encouraged settlement. Miners had ranged over the whole of the mountain country, establishing themselves in Nevada, Montana and Colorado. Cattlemen found it convenient to settle in the vast region stretching from Texas to the upper Missouri River. Sheepmen found their way to the valleys and mountain slopes. The farmers swarmed into the plains and valleys. By 1890, the frontier had become a thing of the past. Railroads played a vital role in the process of colonization. The continental rail network speeded up the process and by 1884 four great lines joined the central Mississippi valley area with the Pacific.

In the west agriculture remained the country's basic industry. The decades following the war witnessed revolution in agriculture. From husbandry it had become machine farming and from subsistence to commercial farming. The number of farms increased three-fold, the area under cultivation doubled and the production increased. This extraordinary achievement was made possible owing to the application of machinery and science to the process of farming. In 1862, Congress appropriated public land to each state for the establishment of agricultural and industrial colleges. Agricultural experiment stations were created throughout the country and the Department of Agriculture received funds for research work.

Despite these advances, the American farmer had to face bouts of critical hardship. The factors that bedevilled him were exhaustion, the vagaries of nature, overproduction, lack of adequate legislative protection and unwieldy expansion of agricultural holdings. The problem of prices was no less complex to the farmer. He had to sell his product in a competitive world market and was compelled to purchase his supplies and equipment in a market protected against competition. From 1870 to 1890, prices of most farm productions showed downward tendency.

This economic imbalance led to the formation of farmers' organisations which were patterned after the Grange established in 1867. Within a few years, Granges appeared almost in every state. Many of the Granges set up cooperative marketing organisations, cooperative stores, and even factories. However, after the resurgence of prosperity in the late 1870s, the importance of the Grange dwindled. But its impact was felt in the formation of the Farmers' Alliances which began in the late eighties and early nineties. Because of drought and the consequent economic slump the Alliance movement spread quickly and by 1890 it had nearly two million members. These groups soon changed their character when they demanded political reform. They formed a political party, known as the Populists, and vigorously opposed the old Democratic and Republican parties.

The Populists became dominant in the prairies and cotton lands. Influenced by the impassioned oratory of their leaders, the Populists swept the elections of 1890 in a dozen southern and western states and sent a number of Senators to the Congress. The Populists now clamoured for extensive reforms, including a graduated income tax, loans for farmers, public ownership of railroads, and eight-hour day for labour, increase in the supply of currency by the free coinage of silver and the restriction of immigration in the interests of labour. Populist Party while meeting at Omaha, Nebraska on July 4, 1892 challenged the dominant forces in the American society by declaring that 'we meet in the midst of a country brought to the verge of moral, political and material ruin... The fruits of the toil of millions are boldly stolen to build up colossal fortunes for a few.'

During these years, American attention was engrossed in the currency question and in a demand for the unlimited coinage of silver. Before the Civil War the United States had been on a bimetallic standard but as the official ratio had overvalued silver, the coinage of silver was dropped in 1873. But with the discovery of new silver mines and demonetization of silver in several European countries, agrarian spokesmen in the west and south, demanded a return to the unlimited coinage of silver. The increase in the volume of money, they believed, would indirectly result in higher prices for farm crops and better wages in industry. Swayed by popular agitation, Congress passed in 1890 the Sherman Silver Purchase Act which legalized silver currency without adopting it as a standard. The measure was bitterly opposed by traditional economists who felt that any approach to bimetallism would be disastrous so long as London stuck to gold.

The growing demand for free silver completely overshadowed other things in the minds of the people. In the election campaign of 1892, the Populists had learned that of all the planks in their platform the silver plank had the widest appeal. But at the height of the Populist agitation, the Democratic candidate Grover Cleveland, was elected. In 1893 a sharp economic crisis drained gold reserve from the country. This was accentuated by the operation of the Silver Purchase Act, under which men could bring silver to the mint, sell it for legal-tender paper and convert the paper into gold. Cleveland forced the repeal of the act through Congress, and struck a deal with J. P. Morgan to replenish the country's gold reserve. This honeymoon with big financier led to a split in the Democratic Party. The dissident Democrats and old Populists found a leader in William Jennings Bryan of Nebraska. Bryan was obsessed with the idea of free silver to the exclusion of all. Bryan's oratory made a deep impression when he exhorted the party delegates that 'you shall not crucify mankind upon a cross of gold.'

The campaign of 1896 was more exciting than any since Jackson's day. The Republican candidate, William McKinley, won enthusiastic support from business interests, universities, press and a majority of trade unionists. In the end McKinley won by more than half a million votes. Republican victory settled the future course of American history and agrarian radicalism suffered a retreat. However, except for their monetary policies most of the ideas of the populists and the agrarian Democrats have subsequently been written into legislation.

Long before the Spanish-American War, the United States had charted her line of action in the international arena. After the purchase of Alaska in 1867, American sentiments became expansionist. A strong modern navy was built under the Presidency of Cleveland which became an object of keen national pride. The United States along with Britain asserted its rights over Samoa when it was threatened by German militarism. In Hawaii, the United States obtained in 1887 the exclusive right to use the priceless Pearl Harbour as a naval station. In 1889 was held the first Pan-American conference in Washington where the delegates of the southern republics met. In 1895, though United States was on the verge of a war on the boundary disputes between British Guiana and Venezuela, it was settled by arbitration. Anglo-American antagonism was thereafter replaced by Anglo-American harmony.

American expansionism found an opportunity when a bloody rebellion took place in Cuba in 1898. The Spanish Government was not chastened by the revolt of her major colonies in the Western hemisphere earlier in the century. She continued her tyrannical rule in Cuba draining the island two-fifths of its annual income and impoverishing the people. The reactionary Spanish rule made life and property of the Cubans unsafe. A smouldering discontent lay underneath which burst forth with all its fury in 1895 when the patriot Jose Marti raised his flag.

In the beginning America made earnest effort to keep neutral. But when it appeared that war was likely to be protracted and capital totalling fifty million dollars invested in Cuba would have to suffer, the United States intervened. The ruthless savagery with which the war was being carried out by the Spanish Government deeply stirred the American citizens. The Spanish General, Valeriano Weyler, turned the province into concentration camp where thousands of people perished.

By the beginning of 1898 the Spanish government had 200,000 soldiers in Cuba. Its attempt to organise a league of European powers to prevent the United States from interfering was not liked by Russia and Britain. American press and public outcry clamoured for war. War became unavoidable when the U.S. battleship Maine was destroyed in Havana harbour with a loss of 260 lives. McKinley recommended armed action on April 11, 1898.

The actual hostilities began on May 1 and all was over in ten weeks. On May Day at dawn Commodore George Dewey with his squadron of six vessels appeared at Manila Bay and destroyed the entire Spanish fleet without losing an American life. Troops were landed near Santiago and won a series of engagements. Four armoured Spanish cruisers were rendered ineffective at Santiago Bay. American troops landed at Puerto Rico. A surge of national feeling helped to remove the antagonism between the north and the south. The victory of the United States was, in large measure, due to the heroism of a dozen national heroes. Chief among them were George Dewey of Manila fame and Theodore Roosevelt, leader of the 'Rough Riders.' The Spanish weakness also contributed not a little to American victory. A treaty was signed on December 10, 1898 by which Spain transferred Cuba to the United States for temporary occupation destined to become a republic. Spain also ceded the entire Philippine Archipelago and the Puerto Rico. By this acquisition of overseas territories, America entered upon a new phase of world politics.

The Spanish-American War marked a turning point in American history. The country was suddenly transformed into a world power and it began to take more and more interest in international affairs. It undertook gigantic tasks of reorganisation and development in the Philippines, Cuba and Puerto Rico. The war gave birth to American navy and replaced the British navy required for maintenance of the Monroe Doctrine. Moreover, the war did something to increase Anglo-American friendship much to the chagrin of Germany.

The first postwar development of American foreign policy was the enunciation of Open Door Principle. Since China's defeat by Japan in 1894-95, various European powers had acquired economic privileges and territorial concessions. In September 1899, Secretary of State John Hay asked the powers concerned to adhere to the 'Open Door' doctrine—that is equality of trading opportunities in the areas they controlled. In 1900, during Boxer rebellion, the Chinese besieged the foreign legations in Peiping. Hay promptly announced his determination to oppose any violation of China's territorial integrity or of the 'Open Door.' Once the rebellion was quelled, Hay thwarted the attempt of the powers to subject China to crushing indemnities. In October 1900, Britain and Germany signified their adherence to the Open-Door policy which was later endorsed by other powers.

In the presidential election of 1900, McKinley was reelected, while Bryan was for second time repudiated. Theodore Roosevelt was nominated for the vice-presidency. On September 6, 1901, McKinley was shot down by an anarchist and Theodore Roosevelt became President of the United States. After Thomas Jefferson, he was the most versatile of Presidents. Graduating from Harvard, he had a varied stint as state legislator, as ranch owner, as Police Commissioner, as Civil Service Commissioner, as Assistant Secretary of the Navy. His interests and sympathies were wide. Like Andrew Jackson, he had a genius for winning the confidence of the people. He was aware of the great changes sweeping over America and confronted them in a statesmanlike way. He was a political realist. Without subverting the existing economic system, he weeded out the abuses that had crept into it. He was determined to give the people a 'square deal.'

Roosevelt made the federal government popular and strengthened the presidency. He initiated a policy of increased government supervision. He enforced the anti-trust laws, created the Bureau of Corporations as a vigilant watchdog and taught the big business a healthy regard for the government. The most notable achievement of his administration was the extension of governmental control over the railroads. In his *Autobiography*, Roosevelt argued with great force that regulation rather than dissolution was the answer to trusts and combinations. In 1902 the Northern Securities Company was prosecuted. However, though Roosevelt was against the abuses of big business, he was also sincerely against trust-bashing. Standard Oil, the best known, was stronger than ever and the United States Steel Corporation was created in 1901. Roosevelt wanted clean government and honest business. As he observed in his typical proverbial style: "We are neither for the rich man nor the poor man as such, but for the upright man, rich or poor."

In the domestic sphere, Roosevelt pushed through the Congress a Workmen's Compensation Act. In 1902 he intervened in the great Pennsylvania coal strike, but on the side of the miners. His most spectacular achievement was the conservation of the natural resources of the nation. In his far-reaching programme of Conservation and Reclamation, he earmarked some 150 million acres of land as a forest reserve and set aside another 95 million in Alaska and Northwest. In 1902 was passed the Reclamation Act, authorising large-scale irrigation projects and the construction of dams.

The abounding prosperity of the country and the captivating personality of Roosevelt enabled him to return to office in 1904 with great triumph. His reforming zeal received a fresh impetus. In June 1906 was passed the Hepburn Act which gave the Interstate Commerce Commission real authority in rate regulation and forced the railroads to surrender their interests in steamship lines and coal companies. By the end of the Roosevelt administration, public regulation of railroads became an accepted principle. His principle reforming zeal found expression in the Pure-Food Law of 1906 which prohibited the use of any 'deleterious drug, chemical or preservative' in medicines or foods.

The Roosevelt administration signalised the emergence of the United States as a world power. To make the United States a strong and great military power, he reformed the army and built a formidable army. He found an able supporter in his foreign policy in the person of his War Secretary, Elihu Root. Determined to construct an isthmian canal, Roosevelt opened negotiations with Britain for a new treaty. Negotiations between Secretary Hay and the British ambassador in Washington resulted in the Hay-Pauncefote Treaty of 1901. The Treaty represented a surrender by the British of all their treaty rights while permitting the United States 'construct, maintain and control' the canal.

In 1902, the Venezuelan debt question was settled with Britain much to the satisfaction of Washington. By a law in 1902 the Congress authorised the President to obtain from Colombia Panama Canal Zone—a strip of land from the Atlantic to the Pacific. As a result the Hay-Herran convention was negotiated in 1903. But the Colombian Senate refused to ratify the convention and the canal might have been constructed in Nicaragua, had not a revolution broken out conveniently in the province of Panama. American recognition was given immediately and the United States obtained the right to construct a canal in the territory of the new-born nation. Although Roosevelt boasted: 'I took Panama; it was the only way the canal could be constructed.' But his 'big stick' policy poisoned the relations of the United States with Latin America. He interpreted the Monroe Doctrine that while European powers were prevented from interfering in the southern republics, the United States was bound to impose its will on these republics. Thus the Dominican Republic was put under American supervision.

As the years passed, the United States became a world power. In the Russo-Japanese war of 1904-05, Roosevelt acted as a mediator and the Treaty of Portsmouth was concluded under American auspices in 1905. Thus it allowed something of a diplomatic defeat to be inflicted upon the Japanese Empire in spite of her victory. It participated in both the Hague conferences for the promotion of world peace. The United States also took part in the exclusively European question of Morocco in the Algeciras Conference of 1906.

Roosevelt represented something of the American sentiment as he understood the psychology of the people. He commanded the enthusiastic affection of people. The period of his ascendancy was a prosperous one in which popular discontent lacked the sharp edge. The general feeling was, as Roosevelt wrote in 1905, that "somehow or other we shall have to work out methods of controlling the big corporations without paralyzing the energies of the business community."

As the Presidential campaign of 1908 drew near, Roosevelt was at the height of his popularity. He, however, refused to stand for re-election as he did not want to break the convention by which no President should hold office for more than two terms. He chose his Secretary of War, William Haward Taft, as his successor. The Democrats nominated Bryan, but the country voted for Taft.

Before becoming President, Taft had held office as a federal judge, as Solicitor-General, as Governor-General of the Philippines and as Secretary of War. Though Taft was chosen by

Roosevelt, but the former got rid of the whole Roosevelt cabinet. While continuing the old programme, Taft made some forward steps. He prosecuted trusts, strengthened the Inter-State Commerce Commission, established a postal-savings bank, expanded the merit system in the civil service and sponsored the enactment of two amendments to the Federal constitution—one providing direct election of Senators, another authorising an income tax. But he outraged liberal opinion by revising tariff with protective schedules, by opposing the entry of Arizona into the Union because of her liberal constitution and his dependence on the ultra-conservative wing of the party.

By 1910, Taft's party was divided and a landslide swept the democrats back into control of the Congress. Public disenchantment brought Roosevelt back from Africa and European tour. The Republicans wanted to rally round Senator Robert Marion La Follette of Wisconsin. In 1911 La Follette began his campaign to win the Republican nomination. He got encouragement from Roosevelt, but was shocked when the ex-President threw his hat in the ring. Roosevelt became the candidate for the Republican nomination. But Taft was resolved to fight and succeeded in winning the blessings of the high command including the close friends of Roosevelt as Henry Cabot Lodge and Elihu Root. Instead of being dejected, Roosevelt organised a third party, the Progressives, and ran for the presidency on their ticket. This made a Democratic victory certain and with Bryan's support Woodrow Wilson, the governor of New Jersey, was nominated. He was a progressive liberal, campaigning for 'the New Freedom' and his sincerity and matchless eloquence carried him to victory.

Woodrow Wilson was the most illustrious figure in American politics since Jefferson. He set out a comprehensive programme to achieve the 'New Freedom'. 'We have itemised', said Wilson, 'the things that ought to be altered', and he mentioned 'a tariff which makes the government a facile instrument in the hands of private interests', a banking and currency system perfectly adapted to 'concentrating cash and restricting credits', an industrial system which 'restricts the liberties and limits the opportunities of labour', an agricultural economy thoroughly old and stereotyped and the exploitation of natural resources for private gain. Wilson affirmed that the government was to be 'put at the service of the humanity.'

Wilson's first task was tariff revision. 'The tariff duties must be altered', Wilson said, 'we must abolish everything that bears even the semblance of privilege'. The Underwood Tariff, signed on October 3, 1913, provided substantial reductions in the rates on important raw materials and foodstuffs, cotton and woollen goods, iron and steel and other commodities.

Secondly, Wilson made a thorough overhauling of the banking system. 'Control', said Wilson, 'must be public, not private, must be vested in the government itself, so that the banks may be the instruments, not the masters, of business and of individual enterprise and initiative'. The Federal Reserve Act of December 23, 1913 decentralised the banking system, affording better banking facilities to the neglected South and West and providing for a far more elastic currency and a much better organised federal banking system.

The third important legislation was the regulation of trusts. The Clayton Antitrust Act of 1914 prohibited discriminations in price which might tend to create monopolies and made corporation directors personally liable for infraction of the antitrust laws. At the same time a Federal Trade Commission was set up to investigate business operations and to prohibit unfair methods of competition. For the farmers a Federal Farm Loan Act was made available at low rates of interest. The Seamen's Act of 1915 provided for the improvement of living and working conditions of seamen. The Adamson Act of 1916 established an eight-hour day for railroad labour. The Federal Workingmen's Act in 1916 authorised allowances to civil service employees for disabilities suffered in harness.

Essentially the New Freedom was an attempt of the middle class, with agrarian and labour support, to arrest the concentration of wealth and to restore, as far as possible, competitive opportunities in business. Walter Lippmann described the New Freedom as 'the effort of small business and farmers to use the government against the larger collective organisation of industry'.

Wilson's foreign policy marked a departure from that of his predecessor. Roosevelt had wielded the 'big stick' in foreign affairs. Taft had followed a policy of 'Dollar diplomacy.' One of Wilson's first acts was to reject a proposed banker's loan to China. He also announced his purpose to cultivate the friendship of the Latin American republics. While repudiating 'Dollar diplomacy', he declared that the United States would never again seek territory by conquest.

Wilsonian policy had to encounter some difficulties while dealing with Mexico. As the country had been groaning under dictatorial rule of thirty-five years, Wilson was forced to intervene and to occupy Tampico to secure reparation for an insult to the flag. By invoking the mediation of Argentina, Brazil and Chile, Wilson succeeded in getting rid of the usurper, Huerta, from Mexico. Despite continued intervention in the Carribean, Wilson disfavoured full-scale intervention in Mexico, contenting himself in 1916 with sending a punitive expedition.

The First World War, however, brought about a dramatic change in the foreign policy of America. At the outset Wilson refused to be embroiled in the First World War as he held that America must be example of peace 'because peace is the healing and elevating influence of the world and strife is not.' In an early wartime letter, he wrote: 'It would be a calamity to the world at large, if we should be drawn actively into the conflict, and so deprived of all disinterested influence over the settlement.'

But the War left its impact on the United States. During 1914 a serious recession had overtaken the country but it was overcome in the next year by the stimulus of Allied war orders. In the spring of 1915 the sinking of the British liner, *Lusitania*, by the Germans in which 128 Americans lost their lives, inflamed American passion. When Wilson veered toward war with Germany, the German government, on May 4, 1916, gave a satisfactory pledge to restrict submarine warfare.

In 1916, Wilson was reelected President on the strength of his party's slogan, 'He kept us out of the war.' In January 1917, in a speech before the Senate, he called for a 'peace without victory.' But the resumption of unrestricted submarine warfare by Germany in which five American vessels were lost, led the United States to declare war on Good Friday, April 6, 1917. American supplies and reinforcement began to pour in abundance and, by October 1918, American army in France numbered about 1.75 million soldiers. In the battle of the Marne, the Germans encountered stubborn resistance of the American troops. In October 1918, an American army of over a million played a crucial role in the vast Meuse-Argonne offensive which, in the end, exposed the invulnerable Hinderburg line.

Meanwhile, Wilson strove to secure peace by his eloquent definition of the war aims of the Allies. In January 1918, he submitted to the Senate the famous Fourteen Points as the basis for a just peace. These embraced: open covenants; freedom of the seas in peace and in war; the removal of economic barriers between nations; the reduction of armaments; an impartial adjustment of colonial claims; cooperation with Russia in the establishment of her own national policy; a readjustment of the boundaries of Europe on the basis of the self-determination of peoples; and the establishment of a 'general association of nations' to afford 'mutual guarantees of political independence and territorial integrity.'

With the collapse of German resistance by the summer of 1918, the German government appealed to Wilson to negotiate on the basis of the Fourteen Points. Wilson attended the Peace Conference much against the will of the American people and under the shadow of party animosity and a sense of disillusionment. The Peace that was concluded at Versailles was a dictated—not a negotiated—peace. However, Wilson resisted Clemenceau's demand to detach the entire Rhineland from Germany, prevented France from annexing the Saar basin, and frustrated a proposal to burden Germany with the whole cost of the war. Wilson also succeeded, against the most formidable opposition, to embody the League of Nations into the treaty arrangements.

The League of Nations was Wilson's creation. In Article Ten, members of the League pledged themselves to 'respect and preserve as against external aggression the territorial integrity and existing political independence of all members, to submit all disputes to arbitration and to employ military and economic sanctions against nations resorting to war in violation of the League Covenant.'

But the Republicans were opposed to the League of Nations on the ground that Article 10 was an infringement on the rights of the Congress to declare war. Wilson's assurance that nothing could happen to the League Council without United States assent failed to remove misgivings from the mind of the antagonists. Even then two-thirds majority for ratification of the Treaty might have been obtained had Wilson been willing to compromise on Article Ten. But Wilson was unwilling to oblige. 'Article Ten', he said, 'seems to me to constitute the very backbone of the whole Covenant. Without it the League would hardly be more than an influential debating society.' Having decided to take the issue before the public, Wilson made a hurricane tour. On September 25, 1919, he suffered a paralytic stroke. In March 1920, the Senate rejected the Treaty and the League Covenant.

A sharp economic recession in 1920, blighted the election prospect of Democratic hopes. They nominated a former governor of Ohio, James M. Cox, a newspaper owner. The Republicans nominated Ohio Senator, Warren Gamaliel Harding, for Presidential candidate and the Governor of Massachusetts, Calvin Coolidge, for the vice-presidency. The League played a relatively minor part in the Presidential campaign being overshadowed by domestic issues. Harding won a landslide victory in 1920.

President Harding entrusted the State Department to Charles E. Hughes who made it possible to bring to a close the uneasy state of war that still existed between the United States on the one side and Germany, Austria and Hungary on the other. In July 1921 the Congress declared the war to be 'at an end.' A few months later the treaties of Berlin, Vienna and Budapest were signed and ratified. Despite his indifference to the League of Nations, President Harding urged membership in the World Court just to enable the United States to play a significant role in the selection of judges. With Russia, the United States maintained least relations as Secretary of Commerce, Hoover maintained that the Bolshevik economic system did not favour commercial growth.

In the Far East, the United States could not afford to remain passive onlooker. The close of the war enabled Japan to become the dominant power in the Pacific. By the Treaty of Versailles she had acquired from Germany the leased territory of Kiaochow and obtained mandate for Germany's former island possessions in the Northern Pacific. Japan had not only become the greatest naval power in the Far East, but the third naval power in the world. Meanwhile Japan's aggressive policy towards China and her bid for naval supremacy affected the foreign policy of the United States.

In the latter part of 1921 the United States invited Britain, Japan, France and Italy together with other powers (China, the Netherlands, Portugal and Belgium) 'to participate in a conference on the limitation of armaments, in connection with which Pacific and Far Eastern questions would also be discussed.' The Conference continued from November 1921 to February 1922 and concluded seven treaties. Two of these dealt with naval disarmament, the remaining five with Pacific and Far Eastern questions. Two additional treaties dealing with Shantung and Yap were signed outside the conference.

The Five Power Treaty concluded between the United States, Britain, Japan, France and Italy agreed to respect each other's rights in the Pacific and to consult together in the event of any controversy or any threat to them from the aggressive action of any power. Thus the United States for the first time was drawn into European alliance after their unceremonious rejection of the League Covenant. She also found a decent pretext to counteract the Anglo-Japanese alliance which had generated bitter feeling in the United States. The Five Power treaty drew up an extensive programme of naval disarmament by fixing naval parity between Britain and the United States and the strength of Japan in capital ships at 60 per cent of the British and American figures. Light cruisers, destroyers, submarines and other auxiliary crafts were exempted from any limitation.

By the Nine Power Treaty all the powers pledged themselves to respect the territorial integrity of China and to refrain from seeking special rights or privileges in the country. The treaty between the United States and Japan concerned Yap, a German possession which had been assigned as a mandate to Japan. Washington was anxious that the island be internationalised as the oceanic cable that passed through Yap formed one of the two channels of American communication with China. It was agreed to grant the economic rights of American citizens in all the Japanese mandates and guaranteed American access to Yap on an equal footing with Japan. In 1921 the United States showed increasing concern to have a share in the oil concessions of the Near Eastern mandates.

In the domestic sphere, the Harding administration inaugurated 'a policy of normalcy.' This was not pure *laissez faire*, but a happy combination of two policies—one, freedom of private enterprise and the other generous subsidies to private enterprise. In 1921 Congress replaced a war-time excess-profits tax and lowered the surtax maximum to 50 per cent. In 1922 Congress passed Fordney-McCumber Tariff which authorised the President to increase or decrease the tariff rates up to 50 per cent to protect the United States from the competition of foreign countries.

In 1922 the road back to normalcy was disrupted by the strikes of coal-miners and railway workers. There was violence in both fields and there was lack of public sympathy to the cause of the workers. Attorney-General Harry M. Daugherty, therefore, found no difficulty, in securing the passage of laws that virtually forbade the trade-union activities. Meanwhile, the plight of the farmers worsened after an unprecedented height of prosperity during the war. In the business slump that followed 1919 the farmers found themselves saddled with mortgage debt. As the farmers had no organisation for regulating production or fighting deflation, they turned to the government for relief. Between 1921 and 1923 several farm-relief measures were passed. But in the face of mounting competition from Canada, Australia and Russia, these measures failed to alleviate the country's agricultural problem.

The death of Harding in August 1923 relieved the Republicans of a burden that might have been fatal to their fortune in 1924. Harding had no serious executive of legislative experience and became a dupe of his corrupt friends. Never had the administration been the instrument of privileged group who exploited the government for personal gratification. Harding was too weak to arrest this corrupt trend of his officials like Attorney-General Harry Daugherty, Director of the Veterans' Bureau, Charles R. Forbes, Secretary of the Interior, Albert B. Fall, and other Federal officials. There were rumours of corruption even before Harding's death. But the storm broke in all its fury after the President's death. The Senate investigated scandals and found abundant and conclusive evidence against the officials. There had been no such plundering of the nation's wealth since Grant's time. The new President, Calvin Coolidge, sensing the public mood, gave way. Three cabinet officers resigned; Fall was imprisoned. 'The new administration cleaned house and the evil was interred with the bones of Harding.'

Calvin Coolidge had experience of administration as Mayor of Northampton and Governor of Massachusetts. He first attracted public attention when as Governor he had to tackle the policemen's strike at Boston in 1919. He issued a warning to the policemen that "there is no right to strike against the public safety by anybody, anywhere, any time." He was an embodiment of thrift and caution. In 1924 the income tax was further reduced and a highly restrictive immigration law was adopted. The Secretary of Commerce, Herbert Hoover, encouraged American business to look abroad for expanding markets. In domestic sphere, however, the situation was not propitious. The textile towns of New England were hit by southern competition. Many coalfields faced crippling competition from newer ones. There was no organised union and the radical forces were found to be disorganised. Communists were active in fomenting strikes. The Government found it difficult to enforce Prohibition as much profit was derived from violations of the law by bootleggers and smugglers.

In the 1928 Presidential election, Herbert Clark Hoover won as a Republic candidate against the Democrat candidate, Alfred E. Smith, four times Governor of New York. The campaign was exciting—punctuated with slander and character, assassination. In no campaign in modern times had the two candidates been closer in their programmes. The one exception was Governor Smith's strong antipathy towards prohibition while to Secretary Hoover it was 'a great social and economic experiment, noble in motive and far-reaching in purpose.'

Hoover, who came to the Presidency in 1929, was a hard worker and a man with a high sense of duty. But soon he showed his incapacity as a leader. It was said that "he could run a department or set of departments with great skill; he could organise forces to meet an emergency; but he could not direct a party... or guide public opinion." In politics he was conservative, and in business a neo-mercantilist, favouring high tariffs.

Initially, the Hoover administration seemed to be successful. But soon the President was confronted with problems of such magnitude that he had to convene special session of the Congress. In his inaugural address, Hoover had expounded limited changes in the tariff, farm relief and stricter enforcement of the law. As 'crime industry' had been entrenched, the government appointed a Law Enforcement Commission under the chairmanship of former Attorney-General George W. Wickersham, to make a thorough probe into the crime situation. The Wickersham Report, which was published in 1931, was disappointing. But it stressed the necessity of stricter enforcement of Prohibition law. The Congress, therefore, transferred the enforcement of the liquor laws from the Department of the Treasury to the Department of Justice.

In the matter of tariff, the government (Hawley-Smoot Tariff Act, 1930) lowered the rates on about 250 items, but raised it on about 900 items. The Act was passed in the face of the opposition of 1,000 economists and other experts. The consequence was the worsening of the foreign trade situation as most of the countries retaliated by raising their import duties on United States manufacture. The efforts of the government to provide farm relief were equally unsuccessful. In 1929 was created a Federal Farm Board with revolving fund to fight surplus production and to encourage the formation of Farmers' Cooperatives. But the measure was expensive and fostered over-production.

In the beginning Hoover boasted "We in America are nearer to the final triumph over poverty than ever before in the history of any land." But final triumph eluded Hoover and landed him in utter despair when a financial collapse occurred in October 1929. On October 24, the stock market in Wall Street crashed when uneasy speculators sold about twelve million shares. On the 29th came the catastrophe. Sound stocks like the American Telephone and Telegraph, General Electric, and General Motors lost their market value. By the end of the month stockholders had suffered a paper loss of about fifteen billion dollars! By the end of 1929 the shrinkage in securities of all kinds reached an all-time record of forty billion dollars. The spiral of depression affected business houses, banks, factories leading to mass unemployment. Foreign trade declined to an unprecedented loss. After the crash in the United States, disaster quickly gripped Europe. First came collapse in Austria and, finally, the economic depression became world-wide.

The causes of depression were manifold. In the first place the productive capacity of the nation far exceeded than its capacity to consume. In the second place, the tariff and war-debt policies of the Government severely curtailed foreign market for American goods. With the worldwide depression of the early thirties, the market collapsed. In the third place, easy credit policies had led to an inordinate expansion of credit and unrestrained speculation. Government and private debt totalled about one hundred and fifty billion dollars! Finally, the chronic agricultural depression and industrial unemployment and concentration of wealth in great corporations produced an unhealthy national economy.

The depression of 1929 that gripped the nation was the most ruinous depression in its history. Earlier instances of depression in the years 1837, 1873, 1893, 1904, 1907 and 1921 were short-lived affairs. But the financial crash of 1929 lasted almost a full decade. Moreover, it was the product of abundance and exhibited the collapse of the system of distribution of wealth and the failure of business leadership.

The President's initial reaction to this crisis was not serious. He wanted to delude himself with the idea that the crisis was due to uncontrolled speculation in securities and, hence; it was temporary. But the crisis deepened, Hoover explained that it was a global phenomenon and was caused by extraneous forces. Believing at first that the collapse of the market was merely a market collapse, Hoover embraced the theory that prosperity was 'just around the corner.'

When the depression enveloped the country's economy, remedial action became the main theme of politics. In order to speed economic revival, the President proposed an international moratorium from mid-1931 to mid-1932. To meet mounting unemployment, the government allotted large sums for the construction of public buildings and highways. National and local taxes were raised. In 1932 the Congress enlarged the credit facilities of the Federal Reserve System. The insolvency of many railways, the threatened insolvency of many banks, the drying up of local credits, forced the Government to underwrite the credit structure. One instrument of that underwriting was the creation of a Reconstruction Finance Corporation. It was authorised to lend money for three years for 'financing agriculture, commerce and industry, including facilitating the exploration of agricultural and other products.' Its lending powers eventually were extended to include relief loans to states.

The most important incident that occurred during the depression was a march of the war veterans in 1932 to Washington demanding bonus. The Bonus Expeditionary Force (B.E.F.) as it came to be called, remained encamped in Washington until they were dispersed by troops using gas bombs.

All these ameliorative measures failed to solve the pressing problem of economic malaise of the country. By 1932 unemployment figure soared to over twelve million; over five thousand banks liquidated; farm prices dropped to the lowest point in history and national income fell from eighty billion in 1929 to forty billion.

In this crisis the Americans looked for a different leadership. The obvious choice was for the Democrats. In 1930 they swept the Congressional elections and in 1932 they prepared to take the mantle of Presidency. They nominated the ebullient and magnetic Franklin Delano Roosevelt as their candidate. The Republican Old Guard renominated President Hoover. The Democratic platform proposed reduction in federal expenditure and support for the repeal of prohibition. The Democrats swept both Houses of Congress and Roosevelt carried 42 states. Meanwhile, the world situation grew worse. Hitler seized power in Germany (1933) and an attempt was made on the life of Roosevelt in Florida.

Foreign Affairs, 1923-33

Up to 1914, Europe had been the world's banker. But after the war the situation was radically transformed. The European war debts to the Washington Government and the interest payments to United States citizens amounted to astronomical figures. In 1927 United States were involved in political disturbances in Nicaragua by supporting the Conservative Party regime of President Adolfo Diaz. Coolidge eventually sent Colonel Henry L. Stimson to Nicaragua to effect a peaceful settlement. Despite the conclusion of an agreement between the Conservatives and the Liberal Party, the dissident Liberals, under General Augusto Sandino, continued to wage guerrilla warfare destroying American lives and property. After the withdrawal of the American marines in 1933, Sandino came to an agreement with the new Liberal President Juan Sarcasa.

United States also got herself involved in Mexican imbroglio when the President of Mexico decreed in 1926 that all owners of land who had secured their titles before 1917 must exchange these titles for new fifty-year concessions. A number of United States Oil companies protested against the land decrees. The State Department also denounced the decrees as infringement of United States property rights. Though the Secretary of State, Frank B. Kellogg, accused Mexico of propagating communism in the United States and Central America, the U.S. administration did not want to disrupt the amicable relations between the two countries that had been established after the settlement of the foreign-debt question in 1923. With the appointment of tactful Dwight W. Morrow as U.S. Ambassador to Mexico and the verdict of the Mexican Supreme

Court declaring unconstitutional (1927) some of the land and oil laws, both sides resumed peaceful relations.

In 1927 Washington sent armed forces to Nanking for the security and safety of American lives and property in China. But when the Chinese nationalists promised adequate protection, the American forces were withdrawn.

In 1923 was held at Santiago, Chile, Pan-American conference which was followed by another at Havana in 1928. At the latter, a resolution proposing that "no state has the right to intervene in the internal affairs of another" could not be carried through owing to the opposition of the United States. The Washington Conference in 1929 took adequate steps to adjust international disputes amicably by providing for the arbitration of all the disputes except those 'not controlled by international law.'

During the Coolidge and Hoover administration, the United States cooperated with the League of Nations by sending delegates to the League's disarmament and economic conferences. The same period also witnessed her efforts to promote world peace. Apart from employing financial experts in the formulation of reparation arrangements in 1924 and 1929, the Geneva Conference on the limitation of naval armaments was held in 1927 at the behest of President Coolidge. In 1928 Washington adhered to the Paris Pact which renounced war as an instrument of national policy. In 1930 the United States became a signatory to the London Naval Treaty and cooperated with the General Conference of 1932 on disarmament.

Roosevelt and the New Deal

Roosevelt had an instinctive faith in the common people and a rationalised faith in democracy. In his inaugural address, Roosevelt declared that 'there was nothing to fear but fear itself.' An effete administration was to be replaced by new faith, faith in new ways of doing things. The nation, he asserted, was fundamentally sound: 'Plenty is at our doorstep, but a generous use of it languishes in the very sight of plenty.' The task ahead was one of restoration. The task was not baffling and Roosevelt dedicated himself to this task with great optimism. "I am prepared", he said boldly, 'to recommend the measures that a stricken nation in the midst of a stricken world may require. These measures... I shall seek within my constitutional authority, to bring to speedy adoption.' He exuded confidence by concluding:

> We face the arduous days that lie before us in the warm courage of national unity, with the clear consciousness of seeking old and precious moral values; with the clean satisfaction that comes from the stern performance of duty by old and young alike. We aim at the assurance of a rounded and permanent national life. We do not distrust the future of essential democracy.

Roosevelt promised a "New Deal" and sought from the Congress "broad executive powers to wage a war against the emergency." To many contemporaries, the New Deal appeared like revolution. But in a sense it was deeply conservative as it aimed to protect the essentials of American democracy. In philosophy the New Deal was democratic, in method evolutionary. For fifteen years legislative reforms had proceeded haltingly, but now they burst upon the country with great fury leaving a precious legacy to future generations.

When Roosevelt assumed office on March 4, 1933, the country was on the verge of complete bankruptcy. Banks had failed in great numbers. Banks were closed in forty-seven states. One of the first acts of the new President was to close all banks in the United States. No banks could be reopened except by permission of the Federal Government and without Federal guarantee of deposits.

The first months of the "New Deal" came to be known as 'the Hundred Days.' 'But it was not a hundred days ending in Waterloo, but a hundred days ending in a feeling of hope and energy that the American people had not known since 1930.' The Congress passed an Economy Bill, and a bill establishing a civilian conservation corps to provide unemployment for hundred thousand young men on public works. Federal salaries were cut, the Federal Farm Bureau was closed, and all agricultural credit matters were centralised in the hands of a Farm Credit Administration. Pension to war veterans was reduced. The hoarding of gold was forbidden and an embargo was placed on the export of gold, thus taking the United States off the international gold standard.

The Agricultural Adjustment Act provided relief to farmers by giving compensation to farmers and by concluding agreements with producers and processors. The Tennessee Valley Authority (TVA) gave the government authority to develop power and natural resources. By the Securities Law the government took upon itself the regulatory powers over the sale of stocks and securities. The Glass-Steagall Act established a Federal Deposits Insurance Corporation. Railroad holding companies were placed under a federal railway coordinator.

On June 16, 1933, the National Industrial Recovery Act was passed. The NIRA empowered the President to set up machinery for 'a great cooperative movement throughout all industry in order to obtain wide reemployment, to shorten the work week... and to prevent unfair competition and disastrous overproduction.' The Act provided for codes of fair competition in industry, contained protective clause for labour and outlined a works programme.

To integrate the recovery measures the President created an executive council which included General Hugh S. Johnson, administrator of the National Recovery Administration (NRA), the agency responsible for the preparation and enforcement of the codes. Pending the formulation of individual codes for various industries, the administration provided a 'blanket code.' The 'codes of fair competition', by which NRA became best known, were originally planned for the big industries. But every type of business insisted on being protected against 'unfair competition'. Labour too wanted guaranteed wages and limitation of working hours. The N.R.A., however, proved a failure. Evasion of its obligations became more and more common. Labour, too, found that employment did not substantially increase, the NRA was already moribund even before the Supreme Court dealt it a mortal blow in 1935.

In 1935 Roosevelt signed a new work-relief bill. New instruments like Works Progress Administration (WPA) were created. The most far-reaching new projects were concerned with the electrification of rural areas and rural rehabilitation. Wagner or National Labour Relations Act of July 1935 required employers to bargain collectively with their workers and forbade them to interfere with the objectives of trade-unionism. A National Labour Relations Board (NLRB) was created to enforce the provisions of the act. A Social Security Act was adopted in August 1935. It provided unemployment insurance, administered by the states but largely financed by the federal government. The practice of grants-in-aid was extended to children, widows, the unemployed, the blind.

In 1936 Roosevelt was again re-elected. He defeated not only the Republican candidate but a Lincoln League which included such conservative Democrats as John W. Davis and Alfred E. Smith. Roosevelt carried every state but Maine and Vermont, with a percentage of the popular vote only exceeded by Hardinge's in 1920.

During his second term Roosevelt wanted to consolidate the changes of the New Deal. In order to effect this he wanted some changes in the judicial, administrative and legislative spheres. In 1937 the President sought from the Congress power to increase the number of judges to fifteen. It aroused storm of opposition who protested against the President's attempt to 'pack the Supreme Court.' Though he was defeated in the Congress, he found opportunity to nominate judges when vacancies arose after the retirement or death of nine judges. Before the end of his term as President, Roosevelt had nominated every member save one, and that one, Harlan F. Stone, was promoted to be Chief Justice. The Court ceased to be an obstacle to federal legislation.

Public opinion was alarmed by the wave of sit-down strikes. This came as a sequel to create effective trade unions in the mass industries mainly undertaken by the Committee for Industrial Organisation under the leadership of John L. Lewis. There were rumours of revolution and disorder everywhere. Thousands crowded into Washington. The great strikes were successful as had been evident by the recognition of unions by the United States Steel and other Steel companies. The Supreme Court validated the Wagner Act (1935) which armed the Unions with the support of the federal law. The victory for organised labour far outweighed the split in the labour movement. The American Federation of Labour expelled the unions which supported it. The

Committee for Industrial Organisation particularly successful in the coal, steel, automobile and textile, was reconstituted as Congress of Industrial Organisation, keeping the magic letters C.I.O.

In 1937 Farm Security Administration (FSA) was created to assist share croppers and tenant farmers. The FSA initially rehabilitated 13,000 families, specially in the south, by grants of land. The most important law of the second Roosevelt administration was the Fair Labour Standards Act of 1938 whose object was the universal establishment of forty-hour work week and a minimum wage. The Hatch Act of 1939 prohibited pernicious political activities on the part of government employees. A Second Hatch Act (1940) extended these prohibitions to state and local employees and struck at the corruption and extravagance of political parties.

The volume of relief expenditure, the mounting cost of administration owing to proliferation of various agencies and the added outlays made by the federal government, all tended to bring about a steady increase in the rational deficit and in taxes. As time went on, governmental activities expanded so much that it was feared that they might undermine the liberties of the people. President Roosevelt rebutted the criticism by defending New Deal measures—measures which fostered economic well-being—would strengthen liberty and democracy. In a broadcast to the nation in 1938 he said:

> Democracy had disappeared in several other great nations, not because the people of those nations disliked democracy, but because they had grown tired of unemployment and insecurity... Finally, in desperation, they chose to sacrifice liberty in the hope of getting something to eat. We in America know that our democratic institutions can be preserved and made to work. But in order to preserve them we need... to prove that the practical operation of democratic government is equal to the task of protecting the security of the people... The people of America are in agreement in defending their liberties at any cost, and the first line of the defence lies in the protection of economic security.

In the backdrop of unemployment and recession and the events of the Second World War came the Presidential election of 1940. The Republican candidate was Wendell Wilkie: 'Perhaps the darkest horse in American history.' The Democrats, abandoning the anti-third-term tradition, renominated Roosevelt as their candidate. The Republicans supported the President's foreign policy but condemned the extravagance of the New Deal. Wilkie made a gallant campaign and it is possible that if the war had ended before the election, he might have won it. But as war went on, people trusted their destiny to an experienced man in the White House. In the end Roosevelt won by securing the electoral votes of 38 States to Wilkie's 10.

Foreign Relations under Roosevelt

To stimulate domestic economic recovery, the government by 1939 had negotiated reciprocal trade relations with 21 foreign countries. To make the tariff wall more reasonable, the President was authorised to lower or raise by not more than 50 per cent any existing duty on imports. The United States participated in the abortive London Economic Conference of 1933. Diplomatic relations were also reestablished with the Russians in the same year. In 1934 the United States became a member of the International Labour Organisation. But Roosevelt's efforts in 1935 to persuade the government to adhere to the World Court failed to secure ratification of the Senate.

The first Roosevelt administration witnessed the collapse of the Geneva Disarmament Conference in 1934. After the expiration of the Washington and London naval-limitation armaments, Japan demanded naval parity with the United States and Britain. Both the powers rejected the demand and Tokyo renounced the restrictive treaties.

Roosevelt urged Congress to recognise Philippine independence. Earlier the Hawes-Cutting Act had provided that the islands were to become independent after a transitional period of twelve years. Earlier it had been rejected by the Manila Legislature; now it was accepted.

Defining his Latin American policy, Roosevelt made it clear that the 'world dedicate this nation to the policy of the good neighbour.' Later, he affirmed that "the definite policy of the United States from now on is opposed to armed intervention." To implement this policy, the United States withdrew his marines from Haiti. She also recognised the *de facto* government in EI Salvador.

In 1934 the United States relinquished her control over internal affairs in Cuba except for maintenance of a naval base at Guantanamo. In 1936 the United States relinquished the rights of intervention in Panama. In 1938 a new treaty was concluded with Mexico. In 1940 Roosevelt brought to an end the customs receivership in the Dominican Republic. He cooperated in the Settlement of the Chaco boundary dispute between Bolivia and Paraguay.

In 1936 American Republics met at Buenos Aires and signed an American Collective Security Convention. This provided for the obligatory arbitration of all disputes and consultation in any emergency arising out of a threat to the peace of the Western Hemisphere. The Eighth Pan-American Conference at Lima in 1938 reiterated these principles in a Declaration of the Solidarity of America.

Meanwhile the system of Collective Security which President Wilson had projected disintegrated. The League of Nations collapsed before Italian aggression in Abyssinia; Hitler occupied the Rhineland and undertook large-scale rearmament; Italy reduced Ethiopia to subjection in 1935-6. The American reaction to all this was one of wilful nonchalance. Disillusioned with the result of the last war, America at first adopted a policy of peace at any cost. She announced that under no circumstances could any belligerent look to them for aid. Neutrality legislation, enacted piecemeal from 1935 to 1937, embodied this principle.

As the international situation worsened, Roosevelt tried to awaken among the Americans a realisation of the shape of things to come. Speaking at Chicago in 1937, he called for a 'moral quarantine' against aggressor nations. He denounced Japanese aggression in China, bound the Latin American States and Canada with bonds of friendship and emphasised the necessity of arms build-up. "Peace by fear", Roosevelt warned the dictators, 'has no higher or more enduring quality than peace by the sword.'

Munich shocked the world but did not change American apathy. Roosevelt's efforts to get the Neutrality Act amended failed. With the outbreak of the Second World War in September 1939, Roosevelt made every effort to repeal the neutrality legislation. In November Roosevelt forced through an amendment of the Neutrality Acts permitting the belligerents to buy war supplies on a 'cash and carry business.' It made American resources available to the Allied countries.

The entry of Italy into the war, the rapid expansion of German control, led Washington to focus attention on defensive policies; the building up of the military resources of the United States; cooperation with other American countries in building organised defence and the provision of all possible aid to Britain against the Axis power. In 1940 astronomical sums were voted for rearmament. The President inducted into his Cabinet two Republican leaders—former Secretary of State Henry L. Stimson, who became Secretary of War and Colonel Frank Knox, who became Secretary of the Navy. To ensure efficient defence production, Roosevelt created an Office of Production Management (OPM) with William S. Knudsen as its head. To check inflation, the President created the Office of Price Administration (OPA). There came into existence an Office of Civilian Defence (OCD). To fix priorities and allocate supplies for defence and civilian purposes, a Supply Priorities and Allocation Board (SPAB) was created. In January 1942 the War Production Board (WPB) combined the functions of the OPM and SPAB. The Selective Training and Service Act of 1940 prescribed compulsory military service in time of peace.

To forge cooperation with the Latin American States, a meeting was held at Panama City in October 1939. Representatives of 21 states adopted a Declaration of Panama that set up a Neutral Zone extending from Canada to the tip of South America. They met once more at Havana (1940) and adopted a Convention on the Provisional Administration of European Colonies and Possessions in the America. Any attempt on the part of a non-American State to infringe the territorial or political sovereignty of any one of the republic was to be regarded as an act of aggression.

A defence deal was negotiated between the United States and Great Britain in September 1940. In exchange of fifty destroyers the United States acquired the right to lease naval and air bases in Newfoundland, and in the islands of

Bermuda, the Bahamas, Jamaica, St. Lucia, Trinidad, and Antigua, and in British Guiana. In April 1941, after renewed German air activity over Greenland, the latter was placed under the temporary protection of the United States. An Administration Bill with slight modifications to promote the defence of the United States became law in March 1941. It authorised the President to make available any defence article to 'the Government of any country whose defence the President deems vital to the defence of the United States.'

Meanwhile relation between the United States and Japan became unduly strained. In July 1941, when Japan acquired from Vichy France the right to set up naval and air bases in Indo-China, her assets in the United States were frozen. On August 14, 1941, Roosevelt and Churchill met in mid-Atlantic and there drew up the Atlantic Charter containing certain basic principles to inaugurate 'a better future for the world.' These principles were: no territorial aggrandizement, no territorial changes, the right of all people to choose their own form of government, freedom of the seas and the abandonment of the use of force as an instrument of international relations.

In November 1941 Churchill declared that 'should the United States become involved in war with Japan a British declaration will follow within the hour.' On November 19 a special Japanese envoy, Saburo Kurusu, arrived in the United States. His mission was ostensibly to arrive at a peaceful understanding with the Washington Government, but actually it was a prelude to the preparations for Japanese attack on the United States. On December 6, Roosevelt sent a personal appeal for peace to the Japanese Emperor. On December 7 came the news of Japanese aerial attack on the United States naval base at Pearl Harbour, Hawaii. On December 8, the Congress unanimously declared a state of war with Japan, three days later Germany and Italy declared war on the United States.

The war was a turning-point in the history of the United States. While dedicating the country into the vigorous prosecution of the war, President Roosevelt, on December 9, in his war message to the American people, reminded them that the ultimate goal was lasting peace. "The true goal we seek is far above and beyond the ugly field of battle. When we resort to force, as now we must, we are determined that this force should be directed towards ultimate good as well as against immediate evil. We Americans are not destroyers—we are builders."

The nation geared itself for mobilisation of its manpower and industrial resources. On January 6, 1942, President Roosevelt announced production goals which shattered all-time records. In five years from July 1940 to August 1945, American factories turned out almost 300,000 military planes, 36,000 tanks, three million machine guns, 71,000 naval ships of all kinds and 55 million tons of merchant shipping! The armed forces of the United States reached a staggering total of about 15 million.

Along with their attack on Pearl Harbour, the Japanese stormed the United States island bases of Guam and Wake. By Christmas 1941 Midway remained the only United States stepping stone between Hawaii and the Philippines. Meanwhile several British Pacific islands were occupied. The Japanese planes sank the British battleships *Repulse* and *Prince of Wales* off the eastern coast of Malaya. Thereafter the Japanese swept like a tidal wave occupying Hong Kong, Sarawak, Malaya, Singapore, Burma, the Philippines, the Netherlands East Indies, much of New Guinea, the Solomon Islands.

It was during this period occurred some spectacular rally which bolstered United States morale—the bombing of Tokyo in April 1942, the appointment of General Douglas MacArthur to supreme command in the south western Pacific and a naval victory over Japan in the Battle of the Coral Sea in May. A few weeks later came the decisive battle of Midway (June 4-6, 1942) in which American planes sank four of Japanese carriers, two heavy cruisers and three destroyers. It was the first major naval defeat Japan had ever suffered.

Eventually, in August 1942, the United States made gallant efforts to retrieve lost territories. On August 7, a small force of American marines landed on Guadalcanal. The Japanese reaction was sharp. There began gruelling fight for Guadalcanal and a decisive action followed in mid-November 1942 in which the Japanese suffered heavy losses. By February 1943, the Japanese had to evacuate Guadalcanal and, by the spring of 1943, naval supremacy in the Pacific passed to the United States. The Battle of the Bismarck Sea (March 2, 1943) destroyed the entire Japanese convoy and cost the life of Admiral Yamamoto.

In June 1942, Roosevelt and Churchill met at Washington with the combined Chief of Staff to build a strategy for Hitler's defeat. The Americans wanted to open a Second Front on the continent in 1942 or in 1943. The British hesitated. Finally, compromise was made in which it was decided to launch an offensive on the shores of North Africa. Command of Operation Torch, as it was known, was entrusted to General Dwight D. Eisenhower, hitherto Chief of the United States forces in Europe. Once started, the entire plan proceeded like a machine. Morocco and Algeria were soon brought under Allied control. Admiral Darlan, a top Vichy official in North Africa with his forces joined the Allies. After Darlan's assassination, Giraud, with Eisenhower's approval, assumed control. But the Allies recognised the claims of the heroic Charles de Gaulle to head the provisional government of French North Africa.

Meanwhile, on November 15, American troops had crossed into Tunisia. In January 1943, Roosevelt, Churchill and their staff met at Casablanca under auspicious circumstances. The Americans had won Guadalcanal. The Russians had scored a decisive victory at Stalingrad and were mounting massive counter-offensive. Montgomery had beaten Rommel. It was, as Churchill said, 'the end of the beginning.' Against this background, the Allied leaders took fateful decisions: to invade Sicily and Italy immediately, to step up anti-submarine warfare, to build up strength in the Pacific for a major offensive. On January 24, Roosevelt declared that the United Nations would fight until the Axis was ready to offer 'unconditional surrender.'

Early in June, General Eisenhower launched a major attack on Sicily and the British at Syracuse. Within forty days the Allies overran the entire island. On July 25, 1943 Mussolini was deposed and a provisional government opened peace negotiations with General Eisenhower. On September 3, 1943, Italy surrendered unconditionally. It was, as Roosevelt said, one down and two to go.

In 1943 the Allies worked out the grand strategy of the war. In August 1943, an Anglo-American conference surveyed the whole field of world operations and made the necessary decisions for the forward actions of fleets, armies and air forces. In September, Russia participated in a gathering of foreign ministers in Moscow. They set up a European advisory commission with headquarters in London for mutual collaboration in the international sphere and endorsed future cooperation in setting up a postwar international organisation for peace. At Cairo, Churchill and Roosevelt met with Chiang Kai-Shek and made plans for the war in the Pacific and the essential settlement of Far Eastern affairs. At Teheran on November 23, 1943, Roosevelt, Churchill and Stalin discussed the grand strategy of the war and mapped out the concerted Allied moves in the following year.

Operation Overlord—as the invasion came to be called—had been planned in detail a year in advance. It was decided that the United States would bear the main brunt and the supreme commander should be entrusted to an American. Eisenhower's success in Africa, Sicily and Italy made him the obvious choice for the formidable task. In January 1944, Eisenhower moved his headquarters to London and, with the assistance of General Sir Frederick Morgan, began minute planning for the coming onslaught.

It was a formidable task to counteract the Germans anywhere on the continent where Hitler had made himself insuperable by sheer force of numbers of mechanised units. To achieve this, the Allies had not only to build massive land and naval supplies but also to maintain command of the air.

The magnitude of the air-attack on Germany could be visualised when a thousand bomber raid on the great industrial area of Cologne took place on May 30, 1942. It was only in 1943 that the American air force participated in the air attack. In 1944 the Allied bombing rose to a crescendo. Most of the major cities in Germany suffered tremendous losses due to heavy aerial bombardment. Before the war was over Hamburg, Bremen, Cologne, Frankfurt, Essen and others were in shambles.

Despite heavy losses inflicted on Germany, air power alone could not win the war. Meanwhile, the target date, D-Day, for an attack on Normandy, was set for June 5, 1944. The Allies had gathered a vast concourse of about three million soldiers, sailors and airmen. As General Eisenhower wrote in *Crusade in Europe*: "The mighty host was as tense as a coiled spring, and indeed that is exactly what it was—a great human spring, coiled for the moment when its energy should be released and it would vault the English Channel in the greatest amphibious assault ever attempted."

Early in the morning of June 6, an armada of 4,000 ships carried the Allied men across the Channel. Aerial cover was provided by 11,000 planes. The Germans were taken by surprise, as they had anticipated main attack in the Pas de Calais area. However, the German defence was stubborn. The Americans struck westward, and, by June 26, captured the great port of Cherbourg. On July 25 the battle for Normandy was over, and the crucial battle for France began. On August 15, 1944, the United States Seventh Army landed near Cannes on August 25. A few days later the British captured Brussels and the great port of Antwerp. By September 11, the American army had liberated Luxemburg and penetrated into Germany at Aachen. By mid-September, France was under Allied occupation. The Allies achieved the most spectacular victories in the history of warfare.

In the autumn of 1944 began a triple invasion of Germany. On September 17, 1944, the Allied western offensive had launched an air-borne attack on the Netherlands flank. The operation achieved only partial success. With more than 3,000,000 troops on the continent, General Eisenhower attempted to penetrate the Siegfried Line and to cross the Rhine. On December 16, 1944, Field Marshal von Rundstedt launched a counter-offensive with the port of Antwerp as its objective. The resulting Ardennes counter-offensive or Battle of the Bulge created initial setback for the Allies. Rundstedt broke through the United States position and penetrated more than 50 miles into the Allied position. But the Americans swiftly rallied and threw the whole German strategy out of gear. By mid-January the Germans had lost their initiatives as they had lost hundreds and thousands of men, tanks and planes.

In February 1945, President Roosevelt, Prime Minister Churchill and Marshal Stalin met with their chiefs of staff at Yalta in Crimea. Here they drew out the general plan for the destruction of Nazi Germany. Then, as the Russians were advancing to the gates of Vienna and Berlin, the Allies prepared to plunge across the Rhine. The Germans retired across the river and, on March 7, 1945, an American task force was near Bonn. Within a few days five divisions of the American forces began to fan out north and south. Two weeks later, the whole Allied army crossed the Rhine, threw the German defence in disarray and proceeded at breakneck speed. The Americans First and Ninth armies drew a giant noose around Ruhr. With the Russians hemming in from the east and the south, and the Americans and British from the west, Germany began to crumble by sheer magnitude of Allied forces and their grand strategy. On April 25, 1945, the Russians and Americans met at Elbe. The Germans made a last-ditch fight for Berlin and Hitler committed suicide. Already Mussolini had been murdered. On May 7, the German army surrendered unconditionally.

One of the architects of victory, Franklin D. Roosevelt had died on April 12. Few figures in American history have been so deeply mourned. At Yalta, he was much more concerned about the postwar world. When Roosevelt and his military advisers returned from Yalta, they believed that:

> This was the dawn of the new day we had all been praying for and talking about for so many years. We were absolutely certain that we had won the first great victory for peace—and by we I mean all of us, the whole civilized human race.

The last words he wrote were a fitting epitaph to his own life: "The only limit to our realization of tomorrow will be our doubts of today. Let us move forward with strong and active faith."

The capture of Guadalcanal in February 1943 inaugurated a new strategy whereby enemy island outposts were isolated and conquered and used as springboards for further attacks with an eye to Japan. The process was directed by General MacArthur by strengthening the United States strength in the Pacific.

Between May and August, the Japanese were dislodged from their holds on the Aleutian Islands. By November 1943, the Gilbert Islands were in Allied hands. Three months later Kwajalein in the Marshall Group fell. From these bases, the United States marines and planes advanced to Saipan and Guam by July 1944. The first major strike on a Japanese island, Honshu, came from Saipan and Guam in November 1944.

The autumn of 1944 witnessed two major Allied offensives in the Far East. The first, under Rear Admiral Lord Louis Mountbatten, aimed at the reconquest of Burma and to reopen communications with China. The other campaign, led by General MacArthur, involved the reconquest of the Philippine Islands between October 1944 and June 1945. The Battle of Leyte Gulf (October 23-25, 1944) was the last desperate resistance of the Japanese fleet. The Japanese were defeated. MacArthur swiftly overran Leyte, and moved on to Luzon. Manila fell on February 23, 1945, and by April the Philippine Islands were freed from Japanese control.

While MacArthur was reconquering the Philippines, Iwo Jima, about 800 miles (1,280 km) from Tokyo, was taken by storm in February-March 1945. Then the army and navy moved on to Okinawa in the RyuKyus, and, after three months of fighting, this 'doorstep' of Japan was taken. On July 17, 1945, President Truman of America, Clement Attlee, Prime Minister of Britain, Chiang-Kai-Shek and Stalin met at Potsdam in Germany. The Potsdam Conference confirmed an occupational division of Central Europe and called upon Tokyo for an unconditional surrender. Japan ignored the ultimatum. Then, against the advice of seven scientists and urged by Secretary Stimson, Truman took the decision of using atom bombs to bring the war to a speedy conclusion. On August 6, 1945, a small atom bomb was dropped over the industrial city of Hiroshima, which wiped out more than half of the target area. Three days later, a second bomb was dropped on Nagasaki. Facing total destruction, Japan capitulated on August 14, and, on September 2, 1945 (V-J Day) signed an unconditional surrender aboard the battleship *Missouri*. Thus the war came to an end through untold suffering and mass destruction. But the agony of war did not put an end to civilising forces of humanity. President Roosevelt had said in his war message:

> The true goal we seek is far and above and beyond the ugly field of battle. When we resort to force... we are determined that this force shall be directed towards ultimate good as well as against immediate evil.

CHAPTER 40

THE LATIN AMERICA

Latin America covers almost fifteen per cent of the world's land surface. Towering civilizations like Aztecs, Mayas, Chibchas and Incas existed in that American sub-continent. Despite the existence of number of common characteristics, its unity is superficial. It was the colonial frontiers that ultimately provided the frontiers of its various nations, each jealously guarding its sovereignty.

The Napoleonic invasion of Portugal led to the peaceful dissolution of the Portuguese Empire in America. Along with it the break-up of the the Spanish Empire in America owed mainly to Napoleonic invasion of Spain.

Towards the end of November 1807, with the arrival of the French army under General Junot, the Royal House of Braganza fled from Lisbon to Rio de Janeiro. It is a tragedy that the king of Spain, Charles IV, had abetted France in the conquest of Portugal. By the Treaty of Fontainebleau (October 27, 1807), Charles IV and Napoleon had agreed to spoliate both Portugal and the Portuguese dominion. But after overthrowing Portugal, a French army under Murat entered Madrid. In May 1808, both Charles and Ferdinand were forced to renounce their rights and Joseph Bonaparte was proclaimed 'King of Spain and the Indies.'

Napoleon had to reckon with the Spanish national uprising. On July 4, 1808, Spain concluded treaty with England and soon afterwards Arthur Wellesley sailed to liberate Portugal and Spain from France. But the British Prime Minister Castlereagh made his views known that British interests would be best calculated to 'protect the independence of the Spanish dominions in South America against the designs of the common enemy.' In September 1808 came the unequivocal declaration from the Foreign Office that England could countenance no designs hostile to the Spanish colonies.

Despite the wave of sympathy for the captive king, Ferdinan VII, in Spanish America, the structure of colonial government, showed signs of strain. Apart from the age-old antagonism between Creoles (Spaniards born in America) and peninsulares (Spaniards born in Spain), the enmity between the Governor of Mentevideo and Viceroy at Buenos Aires added confusion to the volatile situation. In Upper Peru the Audiencia (High Court) of Caracas deposed and imprisoned the President in May 1809. At La Paz it was declared that the time had come to 'raise the standard of liberty in these unfortunate colonies.' The victory of the English colonies in the eighteenth century against England, emboldened the Spanish colonies to defy the sovereignty of the people of the peninsula. To this was added the doctrine of 'popular sovereignty' and the news of the dissolution of the Central Junta in Spain. Reinforced with these developments, Camilo Torres, one of the leaders of the revolutionary movement in New Granada wrote: 'The monarchy dissolved and Spain lost.'

The insurrectionary movement that followed in South America was essentially a movement for local autonomy, the capital cities, for the most part, taking the lead. The movement at the outset revealed a striking unity of action. Starting from Caracas on April 19, 1810, the movement spread to Buenos Aires on May 20 and at Santiago de Chile in September. Though the new authorities declared their loyalty to the Crown, the revolution at Buenos Aires and at Caracas was in effect a declaration of independence. And it was from Buenos Aires and Caracas that the revolutionary movements in South America drew their sustenance.

The imperial authorities in Spain were still wedded to old ideas of imperial monopoly and colonial subordination. The Spanish cortes which met in September 1810 produced the liberal constitution of 1812, declared that the Spanish dominions of both hemispheres formed a single monarchy. The colonial demands for equality of representation within the cortes and for freedom of trade were rejected. Even the proferred British mediation between the mother country and colonies was spurned by the cortes.

The wars of independence were, however, civil wars. Creoles fought Spaniards, Separatists and Loyalists unleashed forces of violence which enveloped the continent. Though a few regions, Paraguay and Central America escaped lightly, the Banda Oriental (later the Republic of Uruguay), some of the interior provinces of modern Argentina, upper Peru, the modern Bolivia and Venezuela, endured unspeakable horror and brutality. In general, the economic life of South America suffered a cruel blow. Thirteen states repudiated the authorities of Spain and Portugal. But except in Rio de la Plata, the early revolutionary movements failed.

The revolution at Rio de la Plata which embraced not only Argentina, but the modern states of Uruguay, Paraguay and Bolivia, had been the work of Buenos Aires. It was a *Parteno* (the name customarily given to the inhabitants of Buenos Aires) revolution who attempted to impose their will by force of arms. Their troops, in 1811, were twice defeated. In the same year Paraguay carried out its revolution and DR Jose Gaspar Rodriguez de Francia became its dictator in 1814. He remained dictator till his death in 1840.

Taking the cue from Paraguay, Montevedio also repudiated the authority of Buenos Aires. Montevedio remained the bastion of Spanish power till 1814, but it surrendered to the *partenos* in the same year. But the Portuguese crown in the neighbouring Viceroyalty of Brazil found an opportunity to intervene in Montevedio and made it their province.

Buenos Aires had spearheaded the revolutionary movement, but it was soon challenged by Artigas who dominated not only the Banda Oriental but the adjoining provinces of Corrientes, Entre Rios and Santa Fe. Temporarily, however, a semblance of unity was restored when the *Cabildo* of Buenos Aires convened a Congress at Tucuman in March 1816. Despite the absence of Artigas, the Congress proclaimed on July 9, 1816, the independence of the province of Argentina.

The revolutionary movement had disastrous consequence in Venezuela. Though the independence of Venezuela was proclaimed in July 1811, the royalist reaction was swift. Francisco de Miranda who became a dictator, was betrayed by his own officers, Bolivar among them, and died in a Spanish prison in 1816.

The revolutionary movement in New Granada was destined to suffer. It had been in a state of intermittent civil war, till January 1815. Meanwhile Spain had resolved on the reconquest of her colonies and made a clean sweep of Venezuela and New Granada.

Reaction was at its height in 1816. But the embers of revolt were still flickering. In its glow at Mendoza which divides Argentina from Chile, Jose de San Martin was organising his Army of the Andes. By fortunate coincidence in Spanish American history, when San Martin was about to launch his movement, Bolivar renewed his campaign by landing at Venezuela. He encouraged his compatriots in his inimitable words: "Our destinies call us to the uttermost parts of the American world."

San Martin, a strategist and a superb tactician, organised the expedition with clocklike precision. He invaded Chile by the high Andean passes and took the royalists by surprise at Chacabuco on February 12, 1817. Two days later San Martin entered Santiago. He refused to accept the reins of government himself leaving Bernardo O' Higgins, a leader of the earlier insurgent movement, to become the supreme director of Chile. But it was not till July 1821, the independence of Peru was proclaimed and San Martin assumed the title of the protector.

Endowed with extraordinary gifts, with talents amounted to genius, Bolivar had sworn to free his country from Spanish rule. He worshipped

Napoleon 'the bright star of glory, the genius of liberty.' His burning faith remained unshaken even in adversity. He wrote from Jamaica in 1835 when all seemed to be lost. 'The destiny of America has been settled irrevocably. The bond that held it to Spain has been sundered.'

In May 1819, with some three thousand men, Bolivar crossed the Andes, defeated the main Spanish army at Boyaca (August 7) and four days later entered the capital of New Granada, Bogota, in triumph. A proclamation of the union of New Granada and Venezuela in the Republic of Colombia soon followed. A constitution for the new state was drafted in 1821, Bolivar becoming the first President of the Republic.

Plagued by internal dissension, the Spanish king, Ferdinand VII, asked the Commander-in-Chief, General Morillo, to conclude an armistice (November 1820) with Bolivar. The armistice having expired, Bolivar again crossed the Andes finally to free Venezuela from Spanish control. The royalist province of Pasto and Quito which attracted his attention, now became part of the new Republic of Colombia. The port and province of Guayaquil, was also annexed to Colombia.

On July 26, 1822, Bolivar and San Martin met at Guayaquil. But while Bolivar's star was in the ascendant, San Martin's had begun to wane. Bolivar was the liberator of Venezuela and New Granada. San Martin had not yet been able to free Peru. He solicited Bolivar's assistance, but the latter refused to respond. Moreover they failed to reach agreement on the future form of the government in Peru.

On September, 20, 1822, San Martin resigned his protectorate to a constituent congress and sailed to Chile. From Chile, he moved to Argentina and then to Europe, where he died, more than a quarter of a century later.

Bolivar was destined to emancipate Peru. On August 6, 1824, Bolivar met and defeated his opponents at Junin in the high Andes. The end of Spanish domination came at Ayacucho on December 7. Though a few royalist strongholds held out till 1826, but what Yorktown had been to the British Empire in North America, Ayacucho was to the Spanish Empire in South America. In August 1825, the republic of Bolivia was born, taking the name of Bolivar in deference to him.

Liberator of Colombia, dictator of Peru, President of Bolivia—Bolivar had reached an amazing height of fame. He now began to dream of a Spanish American League of Nations with its seat at Panama. For Bolivia he drafted a constitution which was a thinly-veiled monarchy. As he wrote on July 8, 1826: 'I am convinced to the marrow of my bones, that our America can only be ruled through an able despotism.'

Bolivar's plan went awry. The Congress of Panama—which met in June 1826 and attended by delegates from Peru, Colombia, Mexico and Central America only, was a failure. Peru invaded both Bolivia and Colombia, and the latter was divided against itself. The liberator now became a dictator. At last he took to life of an exile and died in December 1830. Venezuela had seceded from Colombia and so also the old presidency of Quito under the new name of Ecuador. Bolivar was disillusioned before his death: his dream of a United South America had fallen to pieces. He said in anguish 'this country (Venezuela) is bound to fall into the hands of a crazy crowd of little tyrants, almost too small to notice, of all colours and all races.'

In Spanish America the problem of organising a stable government on the ruins of an imperial administrative system proved to be formidable. In Chile there were three constitutions between 1823 and 1829. It was only in 1830 the conservative forces put an end to the civil war and under its aristocratic constitution of 1833, Chile 'became an oasis of peace in a continent of despair.'

Argentina presented a sad spectacle of confusion. Though a constitution was promulgated in 1819 which provided a highly centralised, unitary state many provinces as well as military chieftains refused to submit to the authority of Buenos Aires. However, the country recovered its stability quickly. In September 1820 a Junta of Representatives appointed Martin Rodriguez as Governorship of the province (1820-24). Martin in turn appointed Bernardino Rivadavia, a 41 year old statesman, as Secretary of Government and Foreign Affairs. Within three years Rivadavia had changed the complexion of Argentina. Far-reaching measures were undertaken which established a representative assembly, founded a bank and a university, reorganised finance and judiciary. In January 1825, the constituent congress enacted a fundamental law which provided that the provinces should govern themselves until a national constitution should be approved. Finally, in February, 1826, the Congress appointed Rivadavia as President of the Republic. When in December the Congress enacted a constitution similar to the constitution of 1819, it was rejected outright by the provinces. The President resigned and there emerged the absolute rule of the greatest of the Argentina caudillos—Juan Manuel de Rosas.

Meanwhile, Argentina had entered into war with Brazil when the latter invaded the Banda Oriental—the future Uruguay. The war lasted three years with no decisive results. Finally, through the mediation of England, a peace treaty was signed in August 1828 between the rival powers. The treaty guaranteed the existence of the independent republic of Uruguay as a buffer state between them.

The war seriously impaired the position of the young Dom Pedro I of Brazil. A colony in 1807, Brazil had become an independent empire in 1822. Portugal had no intention to abdicate Brazil. Though the young impetuous Dom Pedro was ordered to return, he refused to leave. Instead, he became the symbol of the unity of Brazil and the hope of its native aristocracy. As his chief adviser he chose Jose Bonifacio de Andrada e Silva, the presiding genius of Brazilian independence. When Portugal annulled all his acts, he declared: 'The hour has come; Independence or death.' He became the Constitutional Emperor of Brazil on October 12, 1822, and, on December 1, was crowned. Portuguese troops were expelled. By the end of 1823 the independence of Brazil was complete.

Dom Pedro, who had dissolved the constituent assembly and had parted with Jose Bonifacio, promulgated by imperial decree, in March 1824, a new or revised constitution. The constitution, destined to survive for sixty-five years, turned Brazil into a highly centralised, unitary monarchy. But Pedro had dissolved the assembly. The constitution raised a storm of protest in Pernambuco (1824) and Estado Cisplatino (1825). Meanwhile Dom Pedro had signed treaties with Portugal and Britain. Portugal was Britain's ally and, due to Canning's persuasion, Portugal in August 1825 signed a treaty of recognition with her former colony. Dom Pedro signed two treaties with England. The one, a commercial treaty, signed in 1827, retained all those privileges which Britain had enjoyed in her trade with Brazil. The other was a convention (November 1826) promising to abolish the slave trade by 1830. But the rule of Dom Pedro had slowly become autocratic and his relations with parliament strained. The country's economy was in shambles and revolution was in the air. On April 7, 1831, he abdicated in favour of his infant son.

Two other countries—Haiti and Mexico—experimented with monarchy. Haiti, the old French colony of Saint Dominique, had become the first Negro republic in the modern world in January 1804. Spain's other insular possessions, Cuba and Puerto Rico, remained loyal to the mother country. On the North American mainland, New Spain and Guatemala both proclaimed their independence.

In Mexico the call for liberation was sounded by Father Miguel Hidalgo. Though it was unorganised, it spread with the rapidity of a pestilence. But Spanish repression was quick to launch counter-attack. Hidalgo, defeated was captured and shot on July 31, 1811. But the mantle of Hidalgo was inherited by Jose Maria Morelos, who was great as a war leader. He made himself the master of southern Mexico for nearly four years, summoned a congress and promulgated a constitution, before he was shot near Mexico City in 1815. His death left the guerrillas disorganised with the exception of Guerrero who continued the struggle. Paradoxically it was just when the disturbances seemed to be ebbing, that Spain at last recognised Mexican independence. On August 24, 1821, Spain gave formal recognition to Mexican independence. A federal republic on the American model was proclaimed and in August 1824, Guadalupe Victoria was inaugurated as its first President.

In July 1823, a 'national constituent assembly' declared that the provinces of which the kingdom was composed were free and independent. They formed the United Provinces of Central America—a federation which survived till

1838 and to end in the creation of component parts of Guatemala, Honduras, Nicaragua, El Salvador and Costa Rica.

The struggle for independence of the Spanish colonies was in main due to the heroic efforts of the colonial people without the active assistance of the foreign powers. But England took special interest owing to her trade and commerce with the Spanish America, to promote the reconciliation of Spain and her colonies. Castlereagh saw clearly that the separation of Spanish colonies from the parent state was 'inevitable and at hand.' By 1820 he was convinced that recognition of the independence of Spanish America was only a matter of time. In 1825, by the negotiation of commercial treaties, Britain accorded *de jure* recognition to Mexico, Colombia and the United Provinces of the Rio de la Plata.

The United States had taken earlier action, signing a treaty with Spain for the cession of the Floridas in 1819, and recognising Colombia and Mexico in 1822 and Buenos Aires and Chile in 1823. After a French army had restored despotism in Spain, Canning in 1823 sought the co-operation of the United States, preempting the French interference with the independence of Spanish America. But the American Secretary of State, John Quincy Adams, reacted quickly by observing that the idea of any 'active and substantial interposition' by Europe in Spanish America was "too absurd to be entertained." On December 2, 1823, President Monroe in a famous message to the Congress declared that since the policy of the United States was to accept as legitimate all *de facto* governments in Europe and not to interfere in their affairs, so too it would not interfere with existing European colonies or dependencies in America. The Monroe Doctrine meant more to the infant Spanish American republics than did recognition by the United States. France recognised them in 1830. Spain began the process of recognising her former colonies in 1836, a process which was completed in 1895.

The new Emperor of Brazil, Dom Pedro de Alcantara, was only six years old. The integrity of Brazil was threatened when Para in the north and Rio Grande do Sul defied the authorities at Rio de Janeiro. However, moderate opinion rallied the child emperor and in 1840 Dom Pedro was declared of age. A year later he was crowned, though he began to rule effectively from 1847.

From the middle of the nineteenth century, Brazil was emerging as a strong state. Despite the Anglo-Brazilian convention of 1826 and an anti-slave trade law of 1831, the slave-trade had not ceased. A million slaves had entered the country between 1831 and 1851. But in 1850, the trade was outlawed and ceased to exist after a few years. From this period began the economic transformation of Brazil. The prosperity of the country depended to a large extent on coffee, cotton and sugar. In the fifties and sixties, banks, railways, factories, steamships, telegraph lines appeared. The main spirit behind this economic transformation was Irenu de Souza, better known as the Baron of Maua.

The system of government was an oligarchy as only a small fraction of the population enjoyed the voting right. The model was that of the parliamentary government of England. The cabinet's existence was interwined with a majority in the Chamber of Deputies. The Upper House was called the Senate whose members enjoyed power for life. There were two main political parties— the Liberals and the Conservatives. The press was unfettered. However, behind the facade of parliamentary democracy, the emperor enjoyed absolute political power. The system worked as Dom Pedro exercised a general supervision over the whole political machinery and ensured the correct observance of constitutional niceties and the honesty and integrity of officials. Sometimes the exercise of Dom Pedro's personal power became irritating; nevertheless he was the 'schoolmaster of the nation' and gave the country the necessary political education.

The country reached its height of prosperity by the middle sixties. Volume of trade began to increase and foreign investment, especially British investment, began to pour in. Between 1852 and 1875, Brazilian loans were floated in London by N. M. Rothschild and Sons, rightly called 'the bankers of the empire.'

Despite the prosperity of the empire, Brazil had to undergo political tension by entering into the Paraguyan War of 1864-70. The imperial structure invited criticism from the Liberals and the new-born political Republican party. The question of negro slavery assumed great significance after Lincoln's emancipation proclamation of 1863. To this was added a growing rift between Church and State which antagonised a large section of the Brazilian clergy. The Paraguyan war itself caused friction between civil and military authorities and left a bitter trail of military discontent. Though the empire survived till 1889, signs of fissure had already appeared.

Among the Latin American States, Chile experienced a comparable evolution after 1830. The country, whose population in 1830 was little more than a million, was smaller than Great Britain. The landed estate—*hacienda*, formed the social and economic unit, to which the peasant was bound by contract and custom.

The dislocation wrought by the wars of independence was less severe in Chile. In 1830, after seven turbulent years, the conservative oligarchy found a leader in the person of Diego Portales. After prolonged debate a constitution was promulgated in 1833 which continued to be the sheet-anchor of Chilean political life. The constitution excluded from the suffrage the greater part of the population, made the Church subservient to the State and married local to central government. It vested the President with such extensive powers that he turned a virtual dictator. The system remained unchanged for forty years during which Chile knew only four Presidents—Joaquin Prieto, Manuel Bulnes, Manuel Montt, Jose Joaquin Perez. The constitution survived the civil war of 1891, which marked the downfall of the Presidential system and its replacement by a parliamentary system.

With the establishment of political stability in the thirties, the country's economic life underwent profound change. Despite the murder of Portales in 1837, the pace of change was quickened in the forties. New discoveries of mineral wealth, the stability of national finances and a rising foreign trade, especially with Britain, all foreshadowed economic prosperity. Like his counterpart Maua in Brazil, William Wheelwright, a native of Massachusetts, changed the economic spectrum of Chile. In 1840, he founded the Pacific Steam Navigation Company, linking the ports of Chile to those of Peru and Panama and Europe, introduced the electric telegraph and opened the first railway line in 1851. An advance was made in the far south which resulted in the effective occupation of the Straits of Magellan. German immigrants were encouraged to find new homes in Chile. The foundation of the University of Chile in 1842 with the great Venezuelan, Andres Bello, as its first Rector, heralded an intellectual awakening in the country.

A new wind was blowing in the political life of Chile in the late forties with the emergence of a Liberal Party. In 1851 it challenged conservative rule by force of arms. Though the President, Manual Montt, survived the crisis, he adjusted himself with the new spirit by abolishing, in 1852, the law of entail, thus facilitating the division of the estates. The election of Perez marked the beginnings of a progressive liberalisation of politics. With the cooperation of the Liberals, the President enacted a law permitting freedom of worship. A constitutional amendment in 1871 forbade the succession of the President.

A new era began both with political and economic life. In 1865 Chile went into war with Spain, in which Peru, Bolivia and Ecuador joined. A truce was signed in 1871. But Chile was soon to involve into war with Bolivia, when the latter disputed Chile's territorial claims over the Desert of Atacama. It was here that Chilean workers had developed the nitrate industry. 'Nitrate is to Chile what oil is to Venezuela or tin to Bolivia—a cause for permanent discord.' The claims and counter-claims soon developed into the War of the Pacific (1879-83). In the war Chile emerged the dominant power on the west coast of America by depriving Bolivia of her Pacific littoral and Peru of her southernmost provinces.

The vast territory of Bolivia stretched from the Pacific to the basin of the Amazon. Her one million population was confined among the lofty heights of the Andes. The city of La Paz lay on one of the great trade-routes of the Spanish empire, from Lima to Buenos Aires. Bolivia was destined to suffer economically and politically. During 1829-39, Andres Santa Cruz, and able *mestizo* soldier succeeded in uniting Bolivia and Peru in a short-lived federal state, the country's annals presented a sad spectacle of anarchy, misery and tyranny, culminating in the horrid rule of an illiterate and habitual drunkard, Mariano Melgarejo (1864-71).

Apart from Bolivia, Peru and Ecuador (the former Presidency of Quito), which had been incorporated between 1822 and 1830 in the neighbouring republic of Great Colombia, reflected the same deep-seated malaise. The scanty population with aboriginal stock were ill-equipped for statehood. Oscillating between anarchy and despotism, these countries found in autocracy the norm of government. In the struggle for power of rival *caudillos* in Ecuador, emerged the most remarkable and theocratic Gabrial Garcia Moreno, the dominant figure from 1860 to 1875. He turned in vain to the Church to supply the much-needed unifying force.

Peru found a master in Ramon Castilla (1845-51; 1855-62), a soldier 'brave as a lion, prompt in action, and beloved of his men.' By securing order from Europe for guano and the nitrate of soda, Castilla restored the country's shattered finances. But economic regeneration was followed by widespread corruption and a recrudescence of political disorder. The economic crisis was accentuated by reckless expenditure on public works, financed by extravagant loans. The War of the Pacific left Peru exhausted and dismembered.

Colombia and Venezuela, the two countries along with Ecuador, had formed a single state, Great Colombia, of which Bolivar was the founder. But after Bolivar's death, Great Colombia disintegrated. In Venezuela, a small oligarchy under the great guerrilla leader, Jose Antonio Paez, succeeded in maintaining a stable regime over a period of sixteen years (1830-46). The country thereafter relapsed into anarchy which continued till the advent of the long dictatorship of Guzman Blanco (1870-88). Colombia owed much of its prosperity to the organising genius of Francisco de Paula Santander (1832-37). But the country's economic development and political stability were disrupted by the strife between political parties, clericals and anti-clericals, and conservatives and liberals.

The United Provinces of the Rio de la Plata and of Uruguay also exhibited volatile situation. Embracing one of the greatest of the great plain regions of the Americas, the United Provinces of the Rio de la Plata contained in 1830 less than three-quarters of a million people. On the waters of the Rio de la Plata, Buenos Aires was the gateway to the sea, the link between Europe and the plains. As the political supremacy of Buenos Aires became galling to most of the provinces, the United Provinces had become by 1830 little more than a 'chain of petty republics.' However, the installation of Juan Manuel de Rosas, a landowner and a stock-farmer, as governor of Buenos Aires province in December 1829 inaugurated the most savage and unbridled of Latin American despotism. The years between 1829 and 1852 were the Age of the Rosas in which the constitutional machinery of Argentina was put in limbo. The period knew no peace as constant war raged within 'Argentine Confederation' and with other states. In 1837 Rosas entered into war with Bolivia. The struggle with Uruguay culminated in the long siege of Montevideo from 1843 to 1851. Meanwhile, a quarrel with France had resulted in a French blockade of Buenos Aires (1838-40). This was followed by another in 1845, when France and Britain jointly intervened to safeguard the independence of Uruguay. Needless to say, self-interest was the key to this kind of intervention.

The British and the French blockade were lifted in 1847 and 1848, respectively. Treaties were concluded between Argentina and England in 1849 and between Argentina and France in 1850. But the country's economy suffered heavily as a result of the blockade. Rosas, however, had given Buenos Aires a relatively honest and efficient administration. But his obsession with Buenos Aires at the cost of the interior provinces proved too heavy. In May 1851, Justo Jose de Urquiza, the governor of Entre Rios province, with the support of Uruguay and of Brazil, overthrew the dictator on February 3, 1852.

A Constituent Assembly promulgated on May 25, 1853, the constitution of the Argentine Confederation. But fearing to lose her preeminence, Buenos Aires refused to recognise the constitution. Instead she drew up, in 1854, the constitution of the 'State of Buenos Aires' and remained *de facto* independent. Henceforth two parallel governments—that of Buenos Aires and that of the Argentine Confederation—began to function.

Strained relations between the two governments culminated in open hostilities in 1859 and again in 1861. Buenos Aires prevailed in the long run and Bartolome Mitre became the first constitutional President of the undivided State in October 1862.

With the establishment of political unity, Argentina entered into a new lease of economic development. An economic revolution overtook the country with the construction of railways, the Baring loan of 1866 and the mounting flow of immigration.

The small republic of Paraguay, a sub-tropical land, owed much of its independent existence, to the absolute rule of three persons. The first dictator, DR Jose Gaspar Rodriguez de Francia, isolated Paraguay from the rest of the world, preserved her independence and made her self-sufficient. He ruled about thirty years and after his death in 1840, one despotism was succeeded by another. Carlo Antonio Lopez, who became President-Dictator in 1844, turned the country into a Police State. However, Lopez abandoned the isolationist policy of Francia, invited foreigners and encouraged foreign trade. Before his death in 1862, he bequeathed the presidency to his son, Francisco Solano Lopez, who undid whatever good his father had done for the country.

Vain, cruel and unprincipled, Lopez needlessly entered into war with the Triple Alliance of Argentina, Brazil and Uruguay (1864-70). The war should not have occurred had not Lopez wanted to 'make his voice heard in the affairs of Rio de la Plata.' The war led the country into a woeful tale of blood and terror and ended only with the near-extinction of the Paraguyan nation.

History barely records the names of the Presidents who held office from 1870 to 1932 as few among them could complete their four-year terms.

When Paraguay was beginning to come back to life a fresh blow struck it down, the horrible Chaco War. It lasted for three years from 1932-5. In theory the combatants were Bolivians and Paraguyans fighting for the exact determination of their frontiers, but the real combatants were the huge oil companies. Though a armistice was signed on June 12, 1935, the actual peace treaty was not ratified until 1938. The northern Chaco was divided more or less equally between Bolivia and Paraguay following an arbitration conference of the Presidents of Argentina, Brazil, Chile, Peru, Uruguay and the U.S.

Nineteenth-century South America had already been the scene of international conflicts. With the exception of Spanish war with Chile, Peru, Bolivia and Ecuador in the 1860s, most of the conflicts were confined among South American states themselves. Though Britain had occupied the Falkland Islands in 1832-33 after a show of force with an Argentine garrison, the territory was far away from the American mainland and its ownership was also disputable. Despite occasional intervention of France and Britain, these were not designed to further territorial ambition.

Mexico, Central America and the Caribbean Sea presented a different political scenario. Here competitive intervention, both from Europe and the United States, assumed a more threatening aspect.

Mexico which became independent in 1821, was a country half the size of Europe and contained a sparse population. Among the old colonies of Spain, Mexico began her independent life under a monarchy. Her first ruler, Augustin de lturbide, was an ambitious and unscrupulous soldier who was overthrown by a military conspiracy. In 1823 the Mexican Empire gave way to a republic and the federal system of government was established.

After a semblance of stability between 1823 to 1827, the country was soon after convulsed by countless revolts in which presidents, deputy-presidents and acting-presidents followed one another in bewildering rapidity. Political power was seized by the landowners; the Church and the Army, invested with privileges, contributed to the general impoverishment of the country. In thirty years the executive office changed hand forty-six times. But throughout that period the key figure in Mexican politics was an unscrupulous opportunist—Antonio Lopez de Santa Anna.

Mexico found it difficult to preserve her territorial integrity. Though a Spanish invasion from Cuba was repelled in 1829, Mexico found it hard to contain separatist movements. Yucatan seceded from the federation in 1839. But more serious still, Texas revolted in 1835, and proclaimed her independence in 1836. When, in 1845, Texas was annexed to the United States, the event sparked off a war between the United States and Mexico. The Treaty of Guadalupe Hidalgo in 1848 resulted not only in the surrender to the United State of Texas, but of California and of all the territory between them.

Mexico suffered a long period of decay and degeneration and trouble came, not from without, but from within. A small landed aristocracy, a vast mass of illiterate and famished peasants, a corrupt Church, an army of idle officers and a country riven by caste and class and between province and province, and financial chaos undermined the foundations of the republic.

The movement of reformation began in 1845 at the little town of Ayutla in the state of Guerrero rapidly became a national movement. It looked forward to the establishment of a new Mexico on the basic principles of nineteenth century liberalism. Finally it installed to the presidency a man of sterling quality and indomitable tenacity, Benito Juarez.

He issued a series of drastic measures. In November 1855, *Ley Juarez* reorganised the judicial system, limited the legal immunities of the clergy and the military and suppressed the Jesuit order. The *Ley Lerdo* in June 1856 forbade civil and ecclesiastical corporations to hold real property save for the purpose of public worship. Finally, in February 1857, he promulgated a new constitution which, though it provided a unicameral legislature, embodied a long bill of rights including *Ley Juarez* and *Ley Lerdo*. The constitution not only struck a blow at the communal ownership of the land by townships and villages, but also antagonised the privileged classes, both clerical and lay. Religious houses combined as the Pope had already condemned the new legislation. A long series of armed revolts culminated in a *coup d'etat* in Mexican city in December 1827. It swept away the new order and restored the old. A military dictatorship was installed in January while Juarez fled to the provinces and reestablished the liberal government in Vera Cruz, the country's chief port.

The civil war which lasted for three years, enfeebled Mexico. But Juarez was irrepressible. Even in this hour of crisis he proclaimed in July 1859 sweeping reforms—disestablishment of the Church, the confiscation of its property, reform of taxation, promotion of education, and encouragement of immigration. The United States had already recognised his government. In January 1861 he succeeded in regaining political power. He not only dismissed the Spanish minister and expelled the archbishop and some other ecclisiastics but also carried into effect his laws of reform. But guerrilla warfare still raged the country and, in July 1861, Juarez took the extreme step of putting a moratorium on all payments of the external national debt.

Mexico's repudiation of her international obligation to which the country was bound by agreements with Britain, Spain and France, raised a storm of protest. The three powers met and by the Convention of London (October 1861) agreed to enforce payment of their debts by military occupation of parts of the Mexican coast without infringing her political autonomy. In December 1861 a Spanish army landed at Vera Cruz. This was followed by the arrival of French troops and British marines.

Despite the withdrawal of the British and Spanish forces in April 1862, the French troops lingered. The French Emperor, Napoleon III, had deluded himself by believing that the French troops would be welcomed in Mexico as an army of liberators. Convinced that the United States, torn by civil war, would be unable to interfere, Napoleon III found in the person of Archduke Maximilian of Austria a ruler of Mexico. French forces overcame the tough opposition of the Mexican forces and once more, in May 1863, Juarez left the capital. Maximilian entered Mexico city in June 1864 and accepted the crown. Tolerant and romantic but deficient in common sense and ignorant of the country, Maximilian soon landed himself in trouble. His refusal to restore to the Church nationalised property, the hostility of the conservatives who were alienated by his liberal policy, the stubborn resistance of Juarez and the mounting pressure of the United States just freed from the incubus of the civil war, left

Maximilian with no other alternative but to surrender in May 1867.

Juarez once more became the undisputed President of Mexico. He now began the uphill task of reconstructing the war-torn country. Juarez realised the urgency of the fight for literacy and he decreed that every village must have its school. But his hopes were unfulfilled when he died in 1872. However, in the midst of gloom appeared the dawn of a national consciousness which was to gain lease of life under Porfirio Diaz, one of Juarez's trusted lieutenants.

The United Provinces of Central America, established a federation in 1823, consisted of five states—Guatemala, El Salvador, Honduras, Nicaragua and Costa Rica—whose total territory was little larger than that of Spain. The semblance of federation lasted till 1838 when it collapsed. Henceforth, Central America was plunged into internecine quarrels, each republic interfering in the affairs of its neighbours. Guatemala remained till 1865 under the control of a reactionary half-caste, Rafael Carrera. However, Costa Rica emerged as the most enlightened. But in all these states, authoritarianism was the chief form of government which could be overthrown only by revolution and civil war became the indispensable part of the political system.

Apart from the Central American republics, there remained few places in Central America over which Britain exercised sovereignty. On the Caribbean shores lay the British settlement of Belize and further southwards to San Juan River, the Mosquito Protectorate. In 1847 Britain announced that Mosquito Protectorate was under the protection of the British Crown. In 1848 the Nicaraguan authorities at the port of San Juan were dispossessed and the town itself was renamed Greytown. The place assumed great importance as it was the key to one of the most practicable routes for the construction of an interoceanic canal. In 1849, a canal company of the United States signed a contract with Nicaragua for the construction of a ship canal across Nicaragua with a terminal at Greytown. Britain immediately protested claiming that the San Juan River belonged to the Mosquito Kingdom over which Britain exercised jurisdiction. Britain had also claimed control over the island of Ruatan, the largest of the Bay Islands group in the Gulf of Honduras, which was occupied in 1838-39.

The diplomatic controversy carried with intense bitterness between Britain and the United States resulted in the signing, on April 19, 1850, of the Clayton-Bulwar Treaty. It was agreed that the proposed canal should be constructed under their joint protection and that neither party would 'occupy, or fortify, or exercise any dominion over Nicaragua, Costa Rica, the Mosquito Coast, or part of Central America.' The Treaty, however, did not affect British control over the Mosquito Protectorate. Neither did it create any impediment when in 1852 Ruatan and its neighbouring islands were erected into the colony of the Bay Islands.

This precipitated fresh controversy with forceful demands from Washington that Britain should keep its hands off from all places in Central America. Meanwhile, events in Central America were far from peaceful. Greytown was bombarded and destroyed by an American warship in 1854. Next year an American filibuster, William Walker, arrived in Nicaragua, captured the town of Granada and was elected President in 1836. Faced by the hostility of the Central American republics, he was forced to leave the country in 1857.

Into this distracted scene appeared the genuine desire of both London and Washington to settle their differences. However, instead of making direct treaty with the United States, Britain negotiated direct settlements with the Central American republics themselves. By the Anglo-Honduran Treaty of 1859 the Bay Islands were surrendered to Honduras. The Anglo-Guatemalan Treaty of 1859 redefined the frontiers of the Belize settlement, which was formally erected into the colony of British Honduras in 1862. By the Anglo-Nicaraguan Treaty of 1860, Nicaraguan sovereignty was recognised over the Mosquito Indians and Greytown became a free port.

The Monroe Doctrine seemed to be threatened by the actions of a European power. In 1822, the negro republic of Haiti, under the rule of Jean-Pierre Boyer, had annexed the neighbouring Spanish colony of Santo Domingo. Boyer ruled for about two decades in comparative peace when he was overthrown in 1843 by 'a revolution of the intellectuals.' The event was followed by the restoration of black supremacy under the savage dictatorship of an illiterate negro, who, as Emperor Faustin I, plunged the country into political and economic chaos. It was only in 1859, after his fall, that the republic was restored. But the restoration did not augur well. It remained till 1888 as a 'caricature of civilisation.'

After enduring twenty-two years of Haitian occupation, Santo Domingo had established its independence as the Dominican Republic in 1844. The stability of the new State was soon shattered by internal dissension and Haitiana ambitions. It appealed for protection to Britain, France and the United States. Finally, in 1861, the country's President implored Spain to resume her ancient dominion. Spanish troops arrived from Cuba and resumed her control over the dominion. However, Spanish rule proved to be incompetent and costly. In 1865 Spain abandoned her colony and the country was left to work out her salvation alone.

Despite the political convulsions and internal strife, a sense of national feeling had grown among the Latin American States. An unprecedented development began to take place after 1870. With the increasing flow of immigration from southern Europe came European investment which found new avenues of profit in Latin America. By 1897 the United States investment in Latin America totalled $ 300 million. At the end of the century total par value of Latin American securities traded on the London Stock Exchange was £ 540 million. Compared to other countries, British investments were the greatest, more than double those of the United States. Railway, mining enterprises, public utilities, and the Chilean nitrate industry accounted for most of the British investments. The inflow of foreign capitals revolutionised the greater part of Latin America. With modernisation of public services, like gas, electricity, water, public transportation, machines, steam-engines, generators and motors, the country witnessed a phenomenon of unparalleled development. During the three decades from 1870 to 1900, four million Europeans migrated to Latin America.

The period also witnessed the improvements in transportation and communication between Europe and Latin America and between the United States and the northern Caribbean. Submarine cables were laid between 1865 and 1890 connecting the whole of South America via the Pacific Coast with the United States. In the Caribbean, American lines served Central America, Mexico, Cuba. Foreign trade also received a boost with the establishment of corporate banking institutions. The London and River Plate Bank and the British Bank of South America were founded before 1870. Before 1900 banks were founded by Italian, French and Germans to finance trade between those countries and Buenos Aires.

Argentina outdid all other Latin American states in matters of economic growth. In the last three decades of the nineteenth century, immigration, railroad construction and foreign trade increased by leaps and bounds. The city of Buenos Aires underwent an amazing transformation. Between 1880 and 1900 the British investments rose from $ 20 million to over $ 200 million. The area of cultivated land increased from a million and a half acres in 1870 to over 17 million acres in 1901. In 1899 Argentina exported 100 million bushels of wheat and maize. Meanwhile the advent of refrigeration revolutionised the export of meat products. In 1883 the first modern packing plant was built near Buenos Aires.

The flow of immigration also played a major factor in transforming Brazil. By 1904, 10,000 miles (16,000 km) of rail track had been in operation. Coffee exports rose from 400 million pounds to 1,170 million pounds by the close of the nineteenth century. In Brazil coffee accounted for about two-thirds of the total value of exports. Among the minor items of export forest products, lumber, meat products and cacao were most important. By the beginning of the twentieth century Brazil expanded her cotton textile industry—over 100 mills employed about 40,000 workers. An industrial complex grew up in Sao Paulo. However, the pace of progress in Brazil was not so rapid as in Argentina.

Chile made some spectacular progress despite small foreign investment and less immigration. Chilean agriculture did not expand and population growth was not so marked as in Argentina and Brazil. However, all these handicaps were militated by the phenomenal development of the nitrate industry which accounted for three quarters of the total world production. This enhanced the government revenue and led to the growth of industry. By 1900, Chile was manufacturing a variety of consumer goods like shoes, cigarettes, flour, textiles, cement, soap, paper, tin, fertilisers and industrial chemicals.

Uruguay also made substantial economic gains. Livestock industry was the most important and, in 1900, there were twenty-one establishments engaged in exporting dried beef. Uruguay was pioneer in the production of meat extract since the establishment of the Liebig plant at Fray Bentos in 1863.

The export of guano derived from the rocky coasts and offshore islands led to the significant economic growth of Peru. Despite the receipt of large revenue derived form guano shipment, it led to waste of money, the enrichment of private individuals and the expansion of foreign debt. President Jose Balta tried to meet the threat of bankruptcy by ensuring the government monopoly of guano operations and making contract with a French banking firm to tide over the financial crisis.

The defeat of Peru in the war of the Pacific (1879-83) led to stagnation. Recovery was slow to come. However, the chief elements of strength in the Peruvian economy in 1900 were the expanding large-scale agriculture which produced sugar and cotton and the revival of mining industry.

In Northern Latin America, Mexico and Cuba also advanced progressively. Mexico contained over nine million inhabitants in 1870, second only to Brazil in population among Latin American countries, but its economic progress was somewhat tardy. The majority of the Mexicans had to depend on subsistence agriculture. The entry of foreign capital after 1876 and the consequent development of railroad put the country on a high road of prosperity. During the 1880s and 1890s mining industry became important. Foreign capital developed public utilities and, on a smaller scale, manufacturing industries. Mexican Petroleum Company came into existence in 1890. By 1900 the annual value of the foreign trade of the country increased fourfold. However, no distinct improvement was found in Mexican agriculture.

Cuba made great progress during the later decades of the nineteenth century, but it was offset to a great extent by two successive wars of independence—1868-78 and 1895-98. Cuba became independent in 1898 and hence its economic progress remained static till the end of the century. The influx of immigrants from Spain, Jamaica and other West Indian islands to develop her sugar industry and British investments in railroads and manufacturing gave a great fillip to her export trade. Cuba was the main source of sugar to the foreign countries.

Other Latin American countries made comparable economic progress. Coffee production expanded in Colombia and in several Central American countries. Cacao prospered in Venezuela and Ecuador as well as in Brazil. Mineral production increased in Bolivia since 1890 with the production of tin. Peru, Bolivia, Colombia and Venezuela also shared in the rubber boom which became evident in 1900 in Amazonia.

Till 1870 the Latin American countries witnessed political instability, frequent civil war and the emergency of charismatic leaders and conservative forces. After 1870 the political stability in some countries increased and enlightened oligarchies governed under the garb of a constitutional system. By 1870 Argentina gained political stability and a conservative oligarchy governed the country by establishing a federal government. In Chile, which witnessed the progressive weakening of the executive power, a parliamentary system of government was established in 1891 after the deposition of President Jose Manuel Balmaceda.

In Brazil, the major development was the downfall of the empire and the establishment of the United States of Brazil. New forces increased the power of the liberals providing an appearance of parliamentary system of government. In Mexico, the Diaz regime had established a highly authoritarian political order under the facade of a liberal policy. In Venezuela, Antonio Guzman Blanco's rule from 1870 to 1888 was more or less parallel to the Diaz regime in Mexico. In Guatemala, Justo Rufino Barrios (1871-85), while advocating liberal revolutionary ideas, became a benevolent despot. In Uruguay, power was exercised by a series of generals, mainly in their own interests. A succession of wars, revolutions and dictatorships plagued the body-politics of Bolivia, Ecuador, Peru, Colombia, Central America, the Dominican Republic, and Haiti.

Despite the establishment of oligarchic rule and dictatorship, murmurs of protest were not lacking in Latin American politics. These movements of protest owed their origin to democratic idealism, socialism and the labour movement. Liberal democratic idealism made considerable headway in Argentina. A protest group, known as Union Civica, under the leadership of Leandro Alem, was formed in Argentina. This group organised an uprising in 1890 which, though feeble in its impact, led to the resignation of the President. More aggressive in its approach, the Union Civica Radical, later known as the Radical Party, campaigned for electoral reform and won the support of public opinion.

Liberal democratic ideas found eloquent champion in some individual figures. The celebrated poet of Mexico, Ignacio Altamirano, spoke against the curtailment of the rights of man. In Cuba, Jose Marti championed the democratic doctrine which was enshrined in the future Chilean republic. In Peru, Manuel Gonzalez Prada gave a clarion-call to his countrymen for national welfare. In Uruguay, Jose Battle Y' Ordonez evoked sentiments that would transcend the traditional party politics of his country. The efforts of the individuals who stood for liberation and democracy were to bear fruits in many countries.

The period also marked the beginnings of left-wing radicalism in Latin America. Anarcho-Syndicalist agitation and the organisation of labour unions began in several countries in late nineteenth century. From 1892 Ricardo Flores Magon and his brother Enrique and others propagated the viewpoint in Mexico. In Argentina this ideology found an eloquent champion in the person of Pedro Abad de Santillan. After 1897, syndicalist unions appeared in the nitrate fields of northern Chile. Socialism, the chief rival of Syndicalism, made limited progress before 1900. However, in 1836, the Argentine Socialist Party was founded by Juan B. Justo and Alfredo Palacios. Unlike doctrinaire Marxist party, it was a reformist party favouring political action through legislation.

The labour movement and working class agitation had a delayed start in Latin America. In 1890 a union of railway workers was organised in Mexico. In Argentina Syndicalist and socialist unions were formed after 1891.

Cuba, the 'Pearl of the Antilles', remained in Spanish hands when other Spanish colonies became independent. After the end of the American Civil War, a revolutionary assembly in 1868 in Cuba had declared for independence. Led by the aristocratic Carlos Maria de Cespedes, the rebels mobilised the masses. However it failed to obtain recognition from the United States and European countries. The war degenerated into guerilla operations and the war hung on for ten years. Despite a compromise 'Pacto del Zanjon' between the rebels and the Spanish Governor-General Martinez Campos, the embers of revolutionary unrest were not extinguished. The Cuban spirit of nationality was fanned by the writings of Jose Marti who symbolized the passionate yearning of Cubans for freedom. Once more the revolution broke out in 1895. The death of Marti in the initial stage did not dampen the indomitable spirit of the Cubans who endured unspeakable hardships by the wanton destruction of life and property. The intervention of the United States in 1893 and the Spanish-American war led to the independence of Cuba.

Conflict and rivalry among the Latin American states grew out of boundary disputes and the aggressive attitude of more powerful states to dominate weaker neighbours. The rival ambitions of Argentina and Brazil to dominate Uruguay and Paraguay, the jealousy between Peru and Chile, the hostility between Chile and Bolivia, the inimical relations between Chile and Argentina and rivalry among Argentina, Brazil and Chile, vitiated the political atmosphere of the Latin American countries. Most of the controversies related to stubborn boundary questions which lingered throughout the first half of the twentieth century.

The period was enlivened by the development of literature in Latin America. There took place the evolution of the novel from romantic forms to realistic and later to the naturalist style. Brazil was pioneer in the field of novel. Joaquim Maria Machado de Assis is by far the greatest novelist of Latin America. At the close of the century, Euclydes da Cunha and Jose Pereira da Graca Aranha ushered in the naturalist school. In the early twentieth century, Spanish American prose took a naturalist form with the work of Gallegos, Rivera and host of others. The Mexican writer, Frederico Gamboa, also was a zealous follower of naturalism.

From the end of the nineteenth century, Spanish American literature showed some originality. The *modernista* movement derived inspiration from the French poets like Verlaine and Baudelaire. The founder of the movement was Ruben Dario of Nicaragua whose influence was felt in the work of other young poets—Leopoldo Lugones in Argentina, Jose Santos Chocano in Peru and Amado Nervo of Mexico.

Apart from these young men who were responsible for revitalising Latin American literature, a number of politicians, teachers and professional men exercised profound influence in moulding the character of the people. In the Caribbean, Marti's influence was responsible for the growth of a sense of brotherhood among the intellectuals. Another enemy of tyrants and enthusiast for education was Argentine Domingo Faustino Sarmiento. At the end of the nineteenth century the Uruguayan Jose Enrique Rodo cast a spell on young people throughout Spanish America. His famous essay *Ariel* (1900), which preached spiritual unity and exposed the materialistic culture of the United States, became the Bible of the succeeding generations. In the Caribbean area, Eugenio Maria de Hostos of Puerto Rico stood for the anti-imperialist cause—against Spain or United States. He worked zealously for the improvement of education in Puerto Rico and in the Dominican Republic. In Cuba, Enrique Jose Varona enjoyed great popularity as patriot, philosopher and poet.

The versatility of some Latin American men evoked admiration and wonder. The person who achieved distinction in this field was the Argentine Bartolome Mitre. He fought against the dictatorship of Rosas (1852) and successfully led the Argentine forces in the Paraguyan War. He was also an outstanding journalist and founded *La Nacion*—the most famous newspaper in Argentina. But his greatest achievement was in the field of historical literature and he was one of the few Spanish American historians who are still read today and comparable to that of Macaulay in England or George Bancroft in the United States.

Another example of versatility was to be found in the person of the Chilean, Diego Barros Arana. Primarily a historian whose monumental *Historia general de Chile*, the finest product of professional historical research, Barros was also an outstanding personality in the history of Chilean education. As a teacher in the celebrated Institute Nacional in Santiago and as a professor in the University of Chile he wielded immense influence on young Chilean intellectuals. He also served in the national congress as a staunch liberal and as a diplomat. He showed his historical acumen in championing Chile's case against Argentina for the ownership of Patagonia.

The twenty-odd nations in Latin America which achieved independence had one common characteristic: their dependence on foreign countries. As heirs of revolution many of them experienced European intervention while the United States upheld Latin American independence. The twentieth century, however, witnessed a dramatic change in the diplomatic role. While European influence ebbed, American influence increased.

In 1898 Spain, after a brief war with the United States, lost Cuba and Puerto Rico. After decolonisation, Spain became the object of respect and the centre of Pan-Hispanic feeling. Britain, a colonial power and the largest investor in Latin America, was not in favour of political interference. France was least present in Latin American countries. The United States, however, infected with a rising national feeling, cast a longing eye to Latin American countries. The slogan was Pan-Americanism. Though the first Pan-American conference had met at Washington in 1889, the second assembled at Mexico in 1901.

In the early twentieth century, Latin America was a land of promise and a fertile field for investors. Its economic progress was intertwined with outside world. Till the outbreak of the First World War, European wealth was pumped to

Latin America. However, during this period, portentous developments took place. Along with the peaceful and radical transition in Argentina came the violent upsurge in Mexico and aggressiveness of North American power and assertiveness in Central America.

The Radical Civic Union, the forerunner of the Radical Party of Argentina, formed in 1890, had strenuously attempted electoral reform. Yet reform was the product of a ruling aristocrat, Roque Saenz Pena, President from 1910 to 1913. A distinguished lawyer and a statesman, Saenz Pena inaugurated in 1912 a electoral law which provided universal male suffrage and secret compulsory voting. This revolutionary enactment changed the whole tenor of Argentine politics.

The Mexican revolution of 1910-11 was far-reaching in its consequences. Its origin lay in a financial crisis in 1907, crop failures in 1907-8, and a wave of anti-foreign agitation. The armed rising, led by a liberal theorist, Fancisco Madero, deposed Porfirio Diaz. However, it soon degenerated into a civil war when unscrupulous persons like Zapata, bandits like Pancho Villa, military adventurers like Huerta, the murderer and successor of Madero—joined the fray. The United States was soon drawn into the conflict—supplying arms to constitutionalist Carranza and denying them to Huerta. When American marines at Tampico were blockaded by the rebels, the United States intervened in 1914 and seized the port of Vera Cruz. The intervention helped to remove Huerta, but failed to restore order. Eventually Wilson withdrew.

Finally after much bloodshed, Carranza secured the presidency by accepting a programme of agrarian reform. While the First World War was raging, there emerged a new constitution in Mexico in 1917. Its political provisions expanded the radical and anti-clerical feature of 1857 constitution. But its economic provisions were far-reaching. It declared all land, water and minerals to be national property and certain types of mineral-bearing land, including oil-fields, being inalienable. It restricted ownership of land by individual or corporation and forbade ecclesiastical bodies to hold land. It promised the restoration of all village lands alienated since 1854 and authorised grants of land to villages. Agrarian bitterness had been so endemic that this was the only way of securing any semblance of peace. However, Carranza failed to seize the opportunity and was overthrown by his lieutenant, Obregon, in 1919 and murdered in the following year.

Obregon became President in 1920 and, on the expiration of his term, Calles succeeded him in 1924. For ten years till 1934 Calles dominated Mexican political scene. He assassinated Obregon when the latter secured the presidency in 1928. Calles ruled through the National Revolutionary Party which he organised and which dominated the army and the parliament. He earned the nickname the *Jefe Maximo*—the Big Boss.

Both Obregon and Calles were ardent nationalists and opposed to alien influence. Though they valued the friendship of the United States when the latter recognised their revolutionary regime in 1923, they were reluctant to grant any special concession to the United States. Mexico also did not join the League of Nations until 1931. Both of them waged war against the reactionary force of the Catholic Church. In 1926 Calles enacted a series of laws through the Parliament which altogether crippled the church establishment. The provincial governments went further by closing churches altogether. Against all this legislation, the Mexican clergy vehemently protested with bishops and priests refusing to conduct regular service in Mexico.

It was only in 1929, when the government gave an assurance that anti-clerical laws would be leniently enforced, that religious services were resumed. However, in 1931, the government again set in motion a strong anti-clerical policy which resulted in the expulsion of the papal delegate from Mexico.

The Mexican government was essentially a dictatorship. There existed only one political party—the National Revolutionary Party—which not only controlled the Presidency of the Republic, but also the army and the parliament. There were personal rivalries within the National Revolutionary Party. General Lazaro Cardenas, who had been the Secretary of the National Revolutionary Party and Minister of War during Calles's presidency, secured his nomination for a six-year term.

Cardenas was less concerned with the issue of anti-clericalism and more eager to forward the country to high road of prosperity. He zealously carried out the policy of expropriation of land with the result that forty-seven million acres of land were distributed among more than a million peasant families. His policy, influenced by Communism, favoured the grant of land of villages in common, rather than individual ownership. The hasty redistribution based on inadequate surveys caused a serious drop in production. A Land-bank was started to lend money but this was mostly confined to selected villages. Collection of interest from scattered borrowers became somewhat difficult. However, some villages achieved considerable success under the new system.

On the international level, Cardenas's government was a model democracy. It took a firm stand against Mussolini's fascism and Hitler's Nazism, and opened its gates to political exiles from Spain after Franco's victory. Another bold policy of Cardenas' administration was the expropriation of the foreign oil companies in 1938 after making compensation. Apart from incurring resentment of the foreigners, especially British, his measure caused a temporary dislocation of the industry. The Washington government announced economic sanctions against Mexico and demanded the payment in full of the debts incurred by its expropriations. Production declined to such an extent that it was only in the 1950s that a significant recovery was made.

Industrial working conditions were improved. Minimum-wage laws were introduced and unemployment figure was comparatively low. This was due to the efforts of the labour organisation *Confederation Regional Obrera Mexicana* (CROM) formed in 1917. Another union came up—*Confederation de Trabajadores Mexicanos* (CTM), whose leader Vicente Lombardo Toledano played a vital role in the Cardenas administration. The CTM leadership advocated socialization of Mexico and by 1940 played a crucial role in the management of railroads, petroleum companies, bus lines and sugar mills.

General Manuel Avila Camacho succeeded Cardenas in 1940. Camacho transferred the railroads from CTM control to government management, and struck a deal with the United States on the petroleum controversy. He inaugurated a new agrarian policy which replaced communal village landholdings with individual farm ownership. Under Camacho, the soldier, the Mexican revolution became more or less inactive. But under the civilian, Miguel Aleman, it decayed into a gradual corruption. In 1946 Miguel Aleman became President and inaugurated an ambitious plan of public works. In December 1952 Ruiz Cortenes became President and fought against corruption. His government was austere and honest.

Brazil, which was larger than the United States, was colonised by Portugal. A military revolution in 1889 had ousted the Braganza monarchy. The resulting constitution, inaugurated in 1891, was largely federal in which the provinces enjoyed large autonomy. The delicate balance of political power was shared between Sao Paulo and Minas Geraes, the coffee-producing and mining states of Central Brazil. Each of these states provided four presidents between 1894 and 1930.

The country's prosperity, which largely depended on coffee, required the construction of ports and railways. The much-needed capital, a £ 10,000,000 loan, was provided by the Rothschilds which helped the country to tide over the financial crisis in 1899. Rio de Janeiro and Santos grew as fine harbours in the beginning of twentieth century. However, the people of Brazil, who had little interest in politics, were largely illiterate.

In 1930, a revolt in October 1930, led by Vetulio Vergas and supported by army and liberal forces, against the dominance of the state of Sao Paulo, drove the president-elect, Julio Prestes, into exile and placed Vargas in power. Wading through conflicting political currents, Vargas suppressed a counter-revolt in Sao Paulo in 1932. He enlarged the system of social insurance, framed minimum wage laws and promulgated a new constitution in 1934. Though the constitution was federal in character, the powers of the central government were not circumscribed. While four-fifths of the Chamber of Deputies should be democratically elected by universal suffrage, the rest should be chosen by professional and trade unions. The constitution limited immigration and foreign investment. It also permitted religious instruction in the school and guaranteed the freedom of religious congregation. In 1934 the National Assembly formally elected Vargas as constitutional President.

In 1935 Vargas had to encounter a revolution which included Communists as well as capitalists. He suppressed the revolt and ruled through martial law for about two years. Meanwhile the rise of Fascism had disturbed the political scene of Mexico. A Fascist *Integralist Action* was formed in 1932 under the leadership of Plinio Salgado. The organisation grew in strength and carried on a vigorous propaganda. Fascist demonstrations frequently led to street fighting. On the plea of disorder, Vargas cancelled the election to be held in 1938 and issued an authoritarian constitution. It extended the presidential term from four to six years and allowed Vargas to continue until such time as a plebiscite might determine otherwise. In 1938 Vargas suspended all political parties. With limited ideas and a lot of empiricism, Vargas ruled the country upto 1945. In the 1945 general election General Gaspar Dutra won. The Dutra government decreed the Communist Party dissolved in 1947. In 1950 Vargas won by an impressive margin; people voted him to get things changed.

Chile was by far the smallest in area and in population. Most of the people lived by farming. But methods of farming were primitive and Chile had to import food. However, Chile is rich in copper mines and natural nitrates. Mainly financed by British and later North American capital, the nitrates were exported to the wheat-growing areas of the world. Political power was in the hands of the landowning aristocracy. Moreover, as a result of the Civil War in 1891, the powers of the President were severely curtailed. Most governments were coalitions whose stability was short-lived.

The First World War caused serious dislocations in the economic life of Chile. Sodium nitrate is required not only in fertiliser, but also in the manufacture of nitroglycerine. During the First World War, though the Allies purchased huge quantities of Chilean nitrate, the Germans, cut off from Chile by the blockade, met their own needs by manufacturing synthetic nitrate. As a result the production of nitrate fell from 70 per cent in 1900 to 35 per cent in 1924 and 11 per cent in 1931.

The post-war depression effected a change in the political life of Chile. Supported largely by middle-class and labour votes, the liberal-minded Arturo Alessandri assumed political power in 1920. He inaugurated a modicum of labour and social legislation and adopted a new constitution in 1925. The new constitution increased the powers of the President, vested the provinces with greater autonomy, and separated church and state. A series of coups followed which led to the establishment of a military quasi-dictatorship in 1927 in the person of General Carlos lbanez. The new President levied an income tax, introduced social welfare schemes, and reformed the educational system.

The Depression of 1930 deeply affected Chile and its export trade reached a low ebb. Ibanez tried to tide over the crisis by borrowing and stringent economic measures. But he was unable to weather the storm of opposition and his regime collapsed by political instability. The election of 1932 again brought Alessendri into the presidency for a six-year term. Liberal and upright, he was by far the most respected of Chilean statesmen. However, he gradually shifted away from old radicalism to a conservative policy. In his last years, he had to encounter the growing opposition of the Communists and the Socialists. His repressive policy against them helped to patch up their differences. Eventually, a coalition of Communists, Socialists and Radicals formed a popular Front and installed Pedro Aguirre Cerda to the presidency in 1938. His death in 1941 was followed by the presidency of Antonio Rios. In 1946 Gonzalez Videla won the presidential elections with the support of the extreme left. In 1948 the Communist Party was made illegal and for fifteen years Chile was in the curious situation of having the officially banned Communists in the forefront of public life. It was in part his promise to repeal that law that got General Carlos lbanez del Camps reelected in 1952.

A disturbing feature in the small republics of Central America was the increasing intervention of the United States. The Spanish-American War fuelled the colonial ambition of the United States.

Puerto Rico was annexed in 1899; but Cuba, after a temporary period of American occupation, became independent in 1902. But the United States retained a base at Guantanamo and under the Platt Amendment had the right to intervene in case of serious disorder. The Caribbean countries attracted the attention of America owing to the prospect of a ship canal through Central America. However Colombia objected to the project of a canal through Colombian territory. The outbreak of a revolution in the Panama province of Colombia in 1903 afforded the United States an opportunity to intervene against the Colombian authorities. The new republic of Panama gave the United States virtual sovereignty in the Canal Zone.

U.S. policy of intervention received a jolt by a decision of the Hague Court of Arbitration in the Venezuelan debt dispute. While upholding the legality of the British, German and Italian blockade of the Venezuelan coast, it discouraged the use of force as a means of collecting debts. However, it did not rule out the possibility of European armed intervention, sanctioned by international law. The only source left open to the United States was to employ police action to prevent defaults on debts. In 1904, Theodore Roosevelt elaborated the Monroe Doctrine by announcing that the United States might be forced to intervene in the affairs of Latin American States to pre-empt intervention by others.

In 1905 the United States concluded an agreement with the Dominican Republic in which the former obtained the right to collect the customs of the country. In 1906 Cuba was reoccupied as a measure to prevent internal anarchy. In 1909 the United States withdrew when an elected government came to power in Cuba. In 1906-07, the United States convened a conference at Washington to formulate proposals for peace in Central America. It was agreed to withhold recognition to governments which seized power by armed revolution. However, all these measures were viewed with suspicion by the Latin American states. Moreover, they were not enough to prevent the outbreak of any trouble in the states. Roosevelt's successor, President Taft, soon adopted a strong-arm policy in Central America. In 1909 Zelaya, the dictator of Nicaragua, was expelled and in 1912 American marines were landed at Nicaragua to prevent Zelaya from staging a comeback. Nicaragua remained under American tutelage till 1933. On the plea of internal disorder, America occupied Haiti from 1915 to 1934 and Santo Domingo from 1916 to 1924.

All these moves—which earned the phrase 'dollar diplomacy'—were pursued by the United States owing to strategic considerations. Taft's Secretary of State, Knox, however, found it hard in persuading New York bankers to make loans to Haiti, Nicaragua and the Dominican Republic.

In 1914 Latin America assumed increasing importance owing to its economic resources. Europe could hardly ignore the importance of food, livestock and raw materials if Latin America and Latin American friendship was courted by the belligerents. Germany, in particular, began to curry favour with them by elaborate propaganda and also by threatening to sink neutral ships. While Mexico, Venezuela and Chile were pro-German, they, along with Argentina, Colombia, Paraguay and El Salvador remained neutral throughout the war. However, Argentina and Uruguay gave material assistance to the Allies. The entry of the United States into the war changed the complexion of Latin American diplomacy. Most of the states of Central America and the Caribbean made formal declarations of war against the Axis ('Axis' in the First World War). Peru, Uruguay, Bolivia and Ecuador broke off relations with Germany. The sinking of Brazilian ships by German submarines led Brazil to declare war on Germany in October 1917. Brazilian warships along with the ships of the Allies scurried the Atlantic.

The close collaboration of the Latin American states with the Allies in the World War led to far-reaching results. Most of the Latin American States joined the League of Nations and used this body as a counterpoise to the power of the United States and a substitute for the Pan-American system. However, the absence of the United States from the League of Nations made the actions of the latter nugatory. Nevertheless, the League of Nations achieved distinct success—of course, with the cooperation of the United States—in settling a serious dispute between Colombia and Peru in 1933-34. Moreover, the technical organs of the League played important roles in various spheres of Latin America.

The War had administered a temporary setback to Latin American economy. The supply of European capital dwindled and the flow of immigrants ceased. Exports to Europe dropped temporarily, though it was offset by the sudden demand of the Allies for food and raw materials. Another significant development was an increase of trade between America and Latin American States. Direct American investments multiplied to a great extent and covered wide fields like mining, transport, and manufacturing industries. The consequence was not only economic independence, but also increase in apparent prosperity.

The twenties of the twentieth century witnessed the rapid development of Latin America to industrialised nations. In Brazil, along with export of coffee, appeared cotton and iron ore. In the republics of northern Andes, especially in Venezuela, rich oil-fields were discovered. Export of oil, which began in 1918, steadily accelerated and by 1930 Venezuela was meeting 10 per cent requirements of the total world supply. Peru, Colombia and Ecuador also developed oil-fields in the twenties, but nothing could be compared with the Venezuelan level of production which reached an amazing height. Colombia, of course, with its two important commercial cities, Cali and Madellin, enjoyed high level of prosperity. Its exports included coffee, cacoa, sugar and oil. Peru, with its capital Lima and port of Callao, exported cotton, copper, sugar, various agricultural products and oil.

The 1920s also saw a genuine concern of the Latin American countries over the wages, working conditions and general welfare of industrial labour. The International Labour Organisation of the League of Nations highlighted this problem. Argentina, Brazil and Chile established separate ministries of labour. Most of the states also enacted labour codes including eight-hour day, the right to strike, the minimum wage, and protection of women and children labour. Uruguay and Chile embarked on schemes of national insurance. However, in some industrial centres, such legislation made little headway owing to inadequacy of organisation and inability to put the law into effect. Labour movement suffered owing to the weakness of the trade union organisation. Socialist movements were in an embryonic stage and proscribed in some states.

The world economic depression of 1929-1934 affected Latin America with disastrous consequences. Their trade declined and were saddled with a heavy load of public and private debt. Faced with bankruptcy, all governments except Venezuela and Argentina suspended payment of interests to foreign countries. Unemployment plagued the countries, followed by labour unrest and violence. During 1930 and 1931, eleven of the twenty Latin American republics experienced revolution. These outbreaks, though relatively bloodless in character, were not due to economic depression alone, social and political grievances found outlet against bad government and dictatorship.

The administration of Irigoyen in Argentina came under heavy fire of the conservatives for its radicalism. Though his rule was not a dictatorship, the crippling maladministration added fuel to the public resentment. Irigoyen had incurred the displeasure of the labour forces by his uncompromising attitude towards strikes in 1930. In September of that year a massive demonstration of students and military compelled Irigoyen to resign. This was followed by a year's military rule under General Uriburu. An election in late 1931 established General Justo as the head of a National Democratic or Conservative government. The government tended towards oligarchic rule of the old type. Finally, during the Second World War, the oligarchy was displaced by a more or less Fascist regime.

Despite a tendency of the Latin American states in the 1930s to adopt authoritarian forms of government, the latest growth of self-conscious nationalism was not found lacking. In internal affairs it took the form of agitation against foreign capital—against the British investment in railways in Argentina, against the nitrate concerns in Chile, and the oil companies in Mexico. In some countries it took the form of racial discrimination against foreign employers. Apart from enacting legislation against immigration, most countries enacted anti-alien employment laws.

Throughout Latin America the driving force was to achieve a greater degree of economic independence. Governments attempted to control the principal products like Brazilian coffee, Argentine wheat, Chilean nitrate and Bolivian tin. In foreign trade, open competition was replaced by barter agreements. The most important was the Roca-Runciman Agreement between Argentina and Great Britain in 1931, followed by other similar pacts, which antagonised the United States. Nationalism also took overt forms in the case of disputes between states. The war between Paraguay and Bolivia over the possession of Gran Chaco ended in the latter's defeat. The resources of Bolivia suffered further diminution, in the early 1950s, by a revolution which distributed the land of the big estates and nationalised the mines.

In the 1930s nationalism in many countries took a new form. The outcome was the growth of Pan-American idea which owed not a little to Latin American disappointment with the League's achievement and reluctance to become embroiled with European quarrels. A new orientation in the foreign policy of the United States also contributed to the revival of Pan-Americanism.

The Union of American Republics, a voluntary association of sovereign states, has maintained since 1910 a permanent bureau at Washington. Though the United States has been the chief sponsor of the Union, she has been the object of distrust and suspicion to the Latin American states. Even the pronouncements of American statesmen, notably Woodrow Wilson, to respect the territorial sovereignty of its neighbours, failed to remove the cloud of suspicion of the Latin Americans. These suspicions were confirmed by the presence of the U.S. forces in Haiti, Santo Domingo and Nicaragua and by the Platt Amendment.

The end of the First World War removed the strategic excuse for American intervention in the Caribbean. The Havana Conference in 1928 voiced the resentment of the Latin American states against the political and economic policy of the United States. A wind of change was perceptible in the policy of the United States when the latter made a determined bid to improve relation with the Latin American States. A new policy of 'Good Neighbour' was inaugurated which found fullest expression when Roosevelt became President in 1933. In the seventh Pan-American Conference at Montevedio in 1933, the United States disclaimed the right of any state to interfere in the internal affairs of another state. The Buenos Aires Conference in 1936 enshrined this principle in unequivocal terms. The Conference outlined a pact providing for mutual consultation in the event of any threat to the peace and tranquillity of the Americas. The administrative organisation for implementing this consultative pact was created by the eighth Pan-American Conference at Lima in 1938.

In consonance to this policy, the United States withdraw its forces from Nicaragua and Haiti, abrogated the Platt Amendment in 1934 and gave up her right of intervention in Panama in 1936. This radical change of policy of the United States was reflected in her refusal to intervene in Cuba during the anarchy of Grau San Martin's administration. Meanwhile, a liberal trading policy was initiated by Cordell Hull under the Reciprocal Trade Agreement Act of 1934, the impact of which was felt in Latin America.

The 'good neighbour' policy met with not unqualified success. The Buenos Aires Conference refused to endorse the neutrality legislation of the United States. The Argentine proposals for non-aggression pacts with European states were not liked by the United States. Argentina looked with suspicion at the political leadership of the United States; moreover her economy was complementary to that of Europe.

Despite occasional pinpricks, the Pan-American movement grew in strength. Immediately after the outbreak of the Second World War, the American foreign ministers met to establish a 'Zone of neutrality.' In 1940 they met again at Havana and drafted a scheme for taking over the administration of European colonies in the Western hemisphere in case of German victory in Europe. It also affirmed that any attack by any non-American state would be construed as an act of aggression against all the Americas.

After the entry of the United States into the War in 1941, the American foreign ministers met at Rio de Janeiro early in 1942. This meeting

CARIBBEAN SEA
ATLANTIC OCEAN
PANAMA
Panama
Caracas
Orinoco R.
VENEZUELA
BRITISH GUIANA
Georgetown
Paramaribo
DUTCH GUIANA
FRENCH GUIANA
Cayenne
Bogota
COLOMBIA
Rio Negro
Quito
ECUADOR
River
Amazon
R.
B R A Z I L
Madeira R.
Araguaya R.
Sao Francisco R.
PERU
Lima
BOLIVIA
TACNA
ARICA
Sucre
CHACO
Pilcomayo R.
Paraguay R.
PARAGUAY
Paraná R.
Rio de Janeiro
Asuncion
PACIFIC OCEAN
CHILE
ARGENTINA
Paraná R.
Uruguay R.
Santiago
URUGUAY
Buenos Aires
Montevideo
ATLANTIC OCEAN
SOUTH AMERICA IN 1930
Shaded areas show territories in dispute.
Scale of Miles
0 200 400 600 800 1000

urged the Latin American states to sever relations with the 'Axis' powers. All the republics except Chile and Argentina broke off relations with the 'Axis' in 1942. Chile followed suit in 1943 and Argentina in 1944. The fourth conference of Foreign Ministers met in 1945 and acceded to the final Act of Chapultec. This Act reiterated the principle of American resistance to aggression which was to include aggression committed by one American state against another. While defining aggression, the Act committed states to the use of economic and military sanctions. The Act, thus marked a reciprocal system of regional security within the ambit of the United Nations.

Despite the 'Good Neighbour' policy of the United States, the Latin American states entertained feeling of hostility towards the United States. On the other hand, the United States scrupulously maintained a policy of non-intervention in the affairs of the Latin American states. However, this policy was dependent on good behaviours and could be set aside if there was a Communist upsurge in Latin America.

Communist influence, however, was relatively unimportant. The Mexican Revolution, which took cue from Marx, had little in common with Russian totalitarianism. APRA, the left-wing party which came into power in Peru in 1945, moved steadily to the right during its period of office. It recognised the importance of religion in social life and valued the support of the middle class in the reform of society. The APRA government was overthrown in 1948.

Until 1955 Argentina was governed by a radical dictatorship. General Peron seized political power by a military coup in 1943 and sanctified it by election in 1945. Riding on the crest of anti-American feeling, General Peron whipped up the left-wing nationalism by a promise to lead the workers against the capitalists and the foreigners.

However, dictatorship of the Argentine kind was rare in Latin America. The Second World War had given a powerful stimulus to industrial development of Latin America. Brazil, Mexico, Peru showed high level of industrial production. However, it was futile to compare the prosperity of Latin America with that of the United States. Agriculture was stagnant and technically backward. World demand for primary products remained sluggish. The country could hardly recover from the depression of the 1920s. In 1932 her export fell down considerably. The Latin American share of world trade declined from 1935 to 1940, recovered during the Second World War, and again declined in the post-War period. Unemployment was widespread and the tempo of industrialisation slackened owing to lack of foreign capital investment. However, the only relatively prosperous countries which were able to earn foreign exchange were Venezuela, from oil, Mexico, from tourism, and Panama, from the Canal. However, in spite of uneven economic growth, ruinous inflation and widespread distress, Latin America in 1950 was the most literate, and the most sophisticated in its leadership.

The second episcopal conference in Medellin in August 1968 drew the following conclusion:

> It is undeniable that there exists a revolutionary situation in many parts of the Latin American continent, a situation which calls for urgent, thoroughgoing and basically revolutionary changes... We Christians cannot stand aside or declare our neutrality as we see our people going forward to their historic destiny. The average *per capita* income is barely 300 dollars. This is a state of affairs which results from our continent's subjection to foreign capital, whose power never ceases to increase.'[1]

1. Quoted in *The Twenty Latin Americans* (Vol. I), 1971. P. 21, by Marcel Niedergang.

CHAPTER 41

ASIAN GIANTS—CHINA AND JAPAN

China

At the beginning of the nineteenth century, the vast area of the Far East, comprising China, Korea and Japan with almost a quarter of the population of the world, lived in a world of its own. In particular, the vast empire of China, set up by the Manchus in 1644, remained unaffected either by internal disintegration or by political changes that took place in major Asian powers since the end of the seventeenth century. The Mogul Empire had disappeared and had been replaced by the English East India Company; the Ottoman Empire had lost territory to Russia and had been weakened by the secession of Egypt; Persia also had lost territory to Russia. The Chinese Empire remained not only intact but had been strengthened by the incorporation of the Central Asian empire of the Kalmuk Mongols including Tibet. This was due to its traditional imperial structure associated with the teaching of Confucian scholar class which enveloped the Chinese ruling class with complacent self-sufficiency.

Sun-Yat-Sen

Mao-zedong-tsetung

The vast Chinese Empire extended to the north in eastern Siberia as far as the Sea of Okhotsk and in the west as far as Tibet. To the east and south Chinese held a vague sovereignty over a group of small states—Korea, Luchu, Annam, Siam and Burma. Farther to the east lay Japan. From 1757 Chinese trade with the Western powers was confined by law to the single port of Canton. Led by the Confucian philosophy that China was the unique source of true civilisation for mankind, she did not enter into diplomatic relations with any country trading with China.

Trade with China was hedged in with numerous regulations. Among Western nations, Britain took the leading part in the total volume of trade at Canton. Their business was conducted by the East India Company or by 'country' merchants from India operating under its licence. Influenced by the Industrial Revolution and the new production of textiles, as well as the competition in the Canton market, the British Government sent a mission under Earl of Macartney to the Emperor Chien-lung (1736-95) in 1793. Though the embassy was courteously received, Macartney observed:

> The Empire of China is an old, crazy first-rate Man of War... She may, perhaps, not sink outright; she may drift sometime as a wreck, and will then be dashed to pieces on the shore; but she can never be rebuilt on the old bottom.

A second embassy headed by Lord Amherst in 1816 was met with the same fate.

Meanwhile, China in the early nineteenth century stepped into the downward phase of deterioration. At the same time the expanding Western powers demanded the opening of the empire to Western diplomatic contact and trade. The administrative machine was completely subordinated to the personal rule of the Manchu autocrat. After Chien-lung (1736-95), no efficient ruler appeared in the Manchu line. Chia-Ching (1796-1820) and Tao-Kuang (1821-50) were not able rulers followed by Hsien-feng (1851-61), who has generally been described as an incompetent non-entity. To this inefficiency of the emperor must be added the static economy, inefficient administration and corruption among officials. In the Chinese empire corruption became a normal and recognised part of government.

Despite the irksome conditions, foreign merchants found it lucrative to carry on trade with China. During the eighteenth century the East India Company sold goods in China to pay for the tea and other Chinese products purchased there; for a long time the balance of trade was against the Europeans. But towards the end of the century the adverse balance was redressed to large extent by exports of opium from India. The opium had long been known in China and its product used as a drug. It was imported from India to China. From an average import of one thousand chests a year in the late eighteenth century, it rose to 4,500 chests a year between 1800 to 1821 and to some 40,000 chests by 1838.

Opium-smoking, a habit-forming narcotic, was considered as a social evil in China, 'even more serious than the gin that was considered an evil in contemporary Britain.' Selling and smoking opium had been prohibited by imperial edict in 1729, its importation in 1796, and after 1800 these bans were frequently repeated. But opium trade had been so entrenched in Chinese economic system and had become a source of corruption to officials, that it was found impossible to stop the trade. Foreign traders made big profits and Chinese smugglers likewise reaped advantage. As a result, the sales continually increased during the first decades of the nineteenth century, and spasmodic attempts of the Chinese authorities to enforce the law led to the beginning of the 'Coast trade' during the 1830s. The 'Coast trade' became worse as it was not susceptible to control.

With increase of habitual opium smokers and the large unofficial revenue which the government derived from the trade, the Ching Government had no real intention to check the evil. Similarly, as the British trade in China had become largely dependent on opium, it gave further impetus to British desire for commercial expansion in China. With the abolition of the East India Company's monopoly of British trade with China in 1834, the China trade was thrown open to free competition. The British Government, however, sent in 1834 an official Superintendent of Trade, Lord Napier, to Canton. Napier was instructed to deal directly with the Canton Viceroy. But when he reached Canton in July 1834, he was told by the local officials that he could not establish direct intercourse with the Viceroy as equals but must observe the regulation whereby foreigners could only communicate with the provincial administration through intermediaries (the Hong Merchants' Association). Soon afterwards, the local officials stopped the British trade and cut off all supplies to the British factory at Canton. Napier, however, decided to enforce his demands by force of arms. But the factory was surrounded by a strong force of Chinese troops and Napier had to retire to Macao, where he died of illness in October 1834. Thus Napier had 'raised the issue of diplomatic equality but not settled it.'

For the next four years, Napier's successors pursued a 'quiescent policy'. While a group of merchants headed by the enterprising firm of Jardine, Matheson and Company demanded reprisals against the Chinese, the rival group of merchants, headed by Dent and Company preferred to reap the profits of trade quietly. The Canton officials for their part demanded that England appoint a chief merchant (*tai-pan*) and not an official, to regulate British trade with China.

The Opium War

The First Anglo-Chinese War of 1839-42 was precipitated by the Chinese Government's effort to suppress a pernicious contraband trade in opium. In the first quarter of the nineteenth century, the economic condition of China became critical. Apart from the debasement of the copper coinage, the balance of trade was affected by the drain of silver from China owing to increase of imports of opium after 1821 and especially in the 1830s. This silver outflow was equal to half or more of the revenues received at Peking.

The opium evil had become so entrenched that its extirpation seemed an insuperable task. Though a proposal for legalisation of opium import had been mooted and implemented for a short period of four months in 1836, it was withdrawn by the Emperor who, instead, took recourse to legal prohibition. At the end of 1838 the Emperor Tao-Kuang adopted a root-and-branch policy against the evil and issued in 1839 a comprehensive statute which provided the death penalty for foreign importers of opium. The Emperor appointed an imperial high commissioner, Lin Tse-hsu, with special powers to go to Canton and enforce the legal prohibition.

In his efforts to wipe out the opium trade, he found it necessary to confine the foreign merchants numbering about 350 men for a period of six weeks and secured delivery of some 20,000 chests of British opium. As Captain Elliot, who was now superintendent, took personal responsibility for the surrender of the opium on behalf of the British Government, 'the Chinese have fallen into the snare of rendering themselves directly liable to the British Crown'. This incident gave the British Government a strong *casus belli*. The situation was further complicated by an incident which brought into fore the whole question of jurisdiction over foreigners of Chinese soil. In July 1839, when drunken English sailors killed a Chinese villager, the Chinese authorities demanded that the culprit be delivered up. Elliot refused to admit Chinese criminal jurisdiction over British subjects. Thereupon Lin forced the British community to leave successively from Canton to Macao and then to Hong Kong, a large island which was to become the chief port of call for European vessels reaching China.

On November 3, 1839, a naval battle took place between a Chinese fleet of 29 war junks and two British warships. Apart from the loss of four war junks, the Chinese fleet made a precipitate retreat. The First Anglo-Chinese war had begun. Military operations began with the blockading of Canton by the British. A British expeditionary force arrived in the summer of 1840. The British fleet moved directly to the Peiho requesting the appointment of a Chinese plenipotentiary for negotiations. Alarmed at the irresistible power of the British, the imperial government sent Kishen, the viceroy of Chihli, to negotiate with British envoys at Canton. An abortive convention was signed by them in January 1841 which would have ceded Hong Kong, given diplomatic equality and an indemnity to Britain and reopened Canton. But both governments refused to ratify this convention. Kishen was disgraced while Elliot was recalled.

In the second phase of the war, in 1841-42, Colonel Sir Henry Pottinger became the new plenipotentiary who received naval and military reinforcements. Amoy and Ningpo were taken. Reinforced from India in the spring of 1842, the British seized Chapu in the Hangchow Bay, occupied Shanghai, took Sinkiang and advanced to Nanking. The fall of Nanking seemed imminent and China concluded the Treaty of Nanking on August 29, 1842. Thus the Chinese capitulated owing to their effete military organisation, obsolete arms and corrupt civil government. It has been said that the land troops could neither ride nor shoot and the water troops could not sail or fire a cannon.

The Treaty of Nanking promised a fair and regular tariff, ceded Hong Kong to Britain and opened five ports to British trade—Canton, Amoy, Foochow, Ningpo and Shanghai. Consuls were to be opened at each port with the right of direct communication on a basis of equality with the local officials. A huge indemnity was to be paid by the Chinese government to Britain. Extra-territorial jurisdiction was introduced by a supplementary agreement which provided for the application of English law to British subjects charged with crimes in China, the law to be administered by consular courts. The extra-territoriality came to be regarded as the most galling feature of the 'unequal treaties', and its removal became the supreme objective of the Chinese.

The Treaty of Nanking opened China not only to England but stimulated other nations, like the United States and France to take advantage of the new situation. Caleb Cushing, the American plenipotentiary, who arrived at Macao early in 1844, negotiated with Kiying, the Chinese plenipotentiary. After initial reluctance on the part of Kiying, Cushing succeeded in securing the same formal equality which had already been conceded to Britain. The Americans also obtained the most favoured nation treatment—to trade on as good terms as anyone else. The first Sino-American treaty was signed on July 3, 1844, and three months later a treaty with France. The French succeeded in obtaining an edict of toleration for the Catholic faith, which was later extended to Protestantism.

For almost two decades after the Opium War, China by and large remained impervious to Western contact. Some feeble efforts were made by official to apprise the people of Western learning. The publication by the scholar-official Wei Yuan in 1844 of *Illustrated Gazetteer of the Countries Overseas*—a collection of materials on world geography and Western conditions—was widely read. In 1850, the Governor of Fukien, Tsu Chi-yu published a world geography, *A Brief Survey of the Maritime Circuit.*

Though the first treaties did not legalise the opium trade, opium trade expanded along the coast as far north as Shanghai without official protection. Tea exports rose above 100 million pounds and silk increased rapidly. A dynamic new order based on organised competition developed among the British, American and French at the five treaty ports and Hong Kong.

The activities of Western missionaries, both Catholic and Protestant, in the interior of China made little progress. The Chinese regarded the new religion not merely as a foreign faith but subversive and destructive of the ancestral way of life. During the Taiping rebellion strong anti-Christian feeling was aroused.

Internal Disorder: Taiping Rebellion

The Treaty of Nanking disgraced the imperial house of Ching. A strong anti-Manchu sentiment which had persisted in South China received its impetus from the numerous factors—the growth of population, flood, famine, poverty, corruption and the administrative inefficiency. Disorder became widespread in the late 1840s in South China—Kwangtung Kwangsi and southern Hunam. Stimulated by the Western example of patriotism, Canton became the focal point of resistance.

Along with the forces of discontent, a religious cult galvanised the rebel movement. Its founder was Hung Hsiu-Chuan (1814-64), a frustrated scholar and unsuccessful candidate in the competitive examination. He became a mystic and eventually became convinced that he had received a divine commission to regenerate China. His religious cult contained in it many elements of Christianity. In 1844 he began to preach his new doctrine of salvation, admitting converts by a ceremony of baptism. The members of the sect, who called themselves the Shangti Hui, denounced the existing religions of China. Hung moved as a wanderer preaching his new doctrine and gaining many adherents. When his preaching against idolatry became more violent and his followers began to destroy images in public temples, the government decided to take action. In the autumn of 1850, after an abortive attempt to arrest Hung, the latter at the head of an armed force openly challenged the existing government. Hung proclaimed himself as the 'Heavenly King', he declared his intention of founding a new rule, to be known as the 'Perfect Peace' (Tai Ping) dynasty. The followers of Hung became known to foreigners as Taipings.

The religious fanaticism of the Taipings made them a formidable fighting force, while the imperial troops failed to crush them. After being besieged in Yunganchow in Kwangsi, the Taiping army made its way through Hunan to the Yangtse and then captured Nanking, the second city of the empire, in March 1853. It seemed that Hung had China at his feet.

The Emperor Hsien Feng, who had succeeded to the throne in 1851, proved incapable of acting with vigour. But since the Taiping movement developed no constructive leadership and failed to set up administrative controls over the conquered regions, it collapsed because of its inherent weakness. The peasants, who had but moral support to the movement, were alienated by the ruthless foraging. The army, though relatively well-disciplined, was divided by quarrels among the generals. The jealousy among the chiefs who had been the original founders of the movement proved its undoing. When Hung's superiority was challenged by Yang Hsiu-Ching, the latter was assassinated with the help of the Northern King, Wei Chang Hui. But when Wei exceeded all limits of tolerance of killing thousands of Yang's followers, Hung felt obliged to have Wei assassinated in turn. Much more serious, however, was the fate of the Taiping cause doomed to failure owing to its religious fanaticism. The Taipings attack on Confucianism and the whole social order of the day made it impossible for them to obtain the services of the intellectuals. The Confucian opposition assumed the form of an armed counter-revolution which owed not a little to the intellectuals and the provincial gentry. The two most important leaders of this reaction against the Taiping were Tseng Kuo-fan and Li Hung-chang. Both of them raised provincial militia armies to fight against the Taipings.

Finally, the anti-foreign and feeble Emperor, Hsien Feng, died in August 1861. By a *coup d'etat* his brother, Prince Kung, and the young Empress Dowager, Tzu Hsi, mother of the new boy-emperor, came into power. The Empress Dowager was to be the dominant figure in Chinese politics for the next forty-seven years. The new regime strengthened the Manchu leadership by suppressing the Taiping rebellion and reunifying the empire under the Ching dynasty. The new regime followed a cautious policy of co-operating with the foreign powers in working of the treaty system and of giving full support to Tseng Kuo-fan and his lieutenants in the suppression of the rebellion. As Prince Kung put it: 'the rebels were a disease in China's vitals, the barbarians (foreigners) an affliction only of the limbs. It was more important to put down the rebellion than to keep out the foreigners.'

End of the Taiping Rebellion

The high noon of the Taiping rebellion was from 1856 to 1860 after which it petered out. Tseng and his able lieutenant Li Hung-chang built up the most powerful force in China and strengthened it with artillery. At Shanghai, a local corps made up of foreign adventurers, was organised under an American Frederick T. Ward. Despite Ward's initial success in mid-1860, the Taiping forces reached the outskirts of Shanghai early in 1862. As the Taiping rebellion seriously affected the trade of the foreign merchants, the Western Powers abandoned neutrality and intervened on behalf of the Peking Government against the Taipings. Ward was killed in action in September 1862 and his army was placed under the command of Major Charles George Gordon, a British officer. Operating in combination with the Chinese armies, Gordon won a series of victories over the Taipings. Finally, in July 1864, Nanking was captured by the Chinese army without foreign assistance and the rebellion came to an end. Thus this massive movement with all its burning idealism failed to achieve success owing to internal dissension, corruption, popular antagonism and foreign intervention. It would be too facile to ascribe the victory of the Ching dynasty over the Taipings only to Western aid. But the fact remains that the large Chinese armies mobilised under Tseng did most of the fighting against the rebels limiting the use of foreign forces to bare minimum. The imperial edict of 1862 clearly laid down:

> For the time being, we have to make use of foreigners to train our soldiers, as a scheme for self-strengthening ... It would be better to select our own officers and order them to learn the military methods of foreign countries.

Second Treaty Settlement

The Treaties of 1842-44 made great inroads into China's seclusion, but yet the foreign powers remained on sufferance. China as yet had not yielded on the question of opening regular diplomatic relations with foreign powers and nor had allowed the foreigners right of travel outside the five treaty ports and small surrounding areas. The Western nations also were not satisfied with the limited gain obtained from the Chinese and began to press demands for diplomatic representation in Peking and for freedom of travel throughout China.

In 1847 the British at Canton tried coercion. Their forces moved outside the walls and before withdrawing secured a promise of future entrance to the city. But in real sense, this accomplished nothing. The recall of Kiying from Canton in 1848 who had pursued a policy of conciliation with the Western powers brought about a change in the situation. The attitude of the new Emperor Hsien-feng, who ascended the throne in 1850, and opposed Western contact, accentuated the crisis. In 1854 Britain, the United States, and France tried to negotiate treaty revisions with Peking. By virtue of the most-favoured nation principle Britain insisted that the Treaty of 1842 should be revised in 1854. A clause in the American and French treaties of 1844 provided that they might be revised at the end of twelve years. But this legalism availed nothing as negotiation was refused or evaded by China.

The activities of the Christian missionaries both Catholic and Protestant—in the interior of China provided another sources of conflict. The Christian missionaries, protected by the principle of extra-terriroriality, claimed a right of propagating the various forms of the Christian faith throughout the country. The Chinese Government, on the other hand, maintained that no foreigners were entitled by the treaties to travel or reside in any part of the empire outside the five ports. In February 1856 a French Catholic missionary Chapdelaine and his converts were beheaded by Chinese authority in Kwangsi. The French envoy demanded from the Canton Viceroy redress for the action and the latter's refusal to grant it provided the *casus belli*. In the same year, the *Arrow*, a Chinese-owned but Hong Kong registered vessel, carrying an English master and flying the English flag, apparently engaged in a coasting smuggling trade, was seized by the Canton authorities. When full satisfaction for the incident was not obtained from the Canton Viceroy, Yeh Ming Chen, Britain began naval operations against Canton and other river forts. Thus both Britain and France found pretext to enter into hostilities with China.

In the beginning, the warfare was indecisive in character. Britain was handicapped by the outbreak of Sepoy Mutiny in India in May 1857. But, by the autumn of 1857, Britain had been joined by France and the two allies mustered enough forces to seize Canton in the beginning of 1858. Yeh, the Canton Viceroy, was captured and deported to Calcutta, where he died a year later. Stricken with civil war by the serious Taiping rebellion, China could not hold her own against the combined Anglo-French forces. The joint forces advanced to Tientsin and there, in June 1858, the Anglo-French negotiators—Lord Elgin and Baron Gros—secured their treaties. The American and Russian representative who as 'neutrals' accompanied the Anglo-French negotiators, secured almost identical treaties.

Tientsin Treaties which replaced the first agreements, provided for the opening to trade of eleven new ports, the right of travel in the interior and the right of diplomatic representation in Peking. Toleration for Christian missionaries and propagation of their faith was also incorporated into the treaties. Tariff schedules became fixed at a levy of five percent *ad valorem*. A duty was put on the importation of opium, thus legalizing and regulating the traffic. The cup of Chinese humiliation was completed by the grant of the right of 'extra-territoriality' which implied the exemption of the foreigners from the jurisdiction of the Chinese law-courts. 'Extra-territorial rights are the first instrument of the Imperialists for encroachment into foreign countries. Their function is not only to rob us of national pride, but also to enable the foreigners to regard Chinese sovereignty as nothing'. Meanwhile, even before the Tientsin Treaties were concluded, Russian representative, Muraviev concluded separately the Treaty of Aigun (May 1858) whereby all Chinese territory north of the Amur was ceded to Russia and the territory between the Ussuri and the sea was to be subject to a Russo-Chinese condominium.

The Chinese refusal to exchange ratifications of the treaty and their intransigence to grant the right of residence to the British envoy, led Britain and France to resume hostilities. The Allies entered Peking in October 1860, the Manchu court fleeing north to Jehol and the summer palace at Peking was destroyed as a measure of reprisal for the execution of some English prisoners. A few days later the ratifications of the British and French treaties of 1858 were exchanged and a supplementary convention was concluded. China had to pay increased indemnities and Britain secured the Kowloon Peninsula, opposite Hong Kong. France obtained the right for Catholic missions to hold property in the interior, as well as the restitution of all properties formerly confiscated.

Opening of China

China's acceptance of the second treaty settlement broke her seclusion and gave her opportunity to adapt to the new conditions. But it was curious that though the old civilisation seemed to be threatened by China's contact with the European powers, yet the traditional Chinese state and social order remained intact. But beneath these traditional hide-bound systems, the Chinese government was awakening to the fact that it must enter into permanent relations with the outside world. In 1861 a Foreign Office was founded. A College of Foreign Languages was created in Peking in 1862. A military school was established in Shanghai in 1863 where Western sciences and mathematics were taught by foreign instructors. But it was not until the seventies that students were sent abroad for training. In 1873 foreign ambassadors were received for the first time at the court of Peking. In 1877 a Chinese legation was set up in London and the next year Chinese agents were established in most of the capitals of Europe.

The defeat and humiliations of China had their repercussions in other areas of the Far East. In 1855 Sir John Bowring, the British Superintendent of Trade in China, negotiated a treaty with Siam on the model of the treaties which China had concluded with the Western powers. Three years later France extended her policy towards China to cover Annam. France also annexed the three eastern provinces of Cochin China, including the city of Saigon, and thus laid the foundations for her empire of Indo-China. In 1863 she established a protectorate over Cambodia; and in 1867 annexed the rest of Cochin China. But a French attempt in 1866 to subdue Korea was less successful. Korea was the only country in the Far East which defied Western powers for a long period, and Korea did not conclude a treaty with any foreign power until 1876. Then it was not with a Western nation, but with Japan.

Japan: Opening of Japan

The geographical isolation of Japan and its feudal society made the Japanese a separate identity which generated a feeling of nationalism. They made no claim to universal rule and developed a certain amount of pragmatism which explained Japan's active interest in the West and its science. While Chinese intellectuals generally excluded the West from their thinking, their Japanese counterparts were extremely curious about the West. In 1720 the ban was lifted on books about the Occident and owing to Japan's commercial contact with Holland, the Dutch language proved an important source of learning about the West.

From the thirteenth to the end of the sixteenth century, attempts were made to unite the country under the direction of the strongest of the feudal lords. After 1192, the Emperor became a puppet in the hands of the Daimyo or feudal chief. The Emperor invested the successful Daimyo with the office and title of Shogun or in full 'barbarian quelling-generalissimo'. The rule through the Shogunate continued when Hideyoshi, one of the great figures in the military annals of Japan, died at the end of the sixteenth century. Then Iyeyasu of Tokugawa family was created Shogun by the Emperor in 1603. He was the first in the long line of Tokugawa Shoguns who ruled Japan until the restoration of the Emperor in 1867.

Pre-Restoration Political System

At the head of the State stood the Emperor who lived in seclusion and obscurity at Kyoto. The actual power was in the hands of the Shogun who received his investiture from the Emperor. In 1603, the Tokugawa Shoguns established their supremacy as feudal lords over the whole country. The bulk of the country was divided into about 265 *han* or feudal domains. The *Daimyo* or lords of these *han* were divided into three categories. The majority were *fudai* or hereditary vassals who supplied the officials of the Shogunate and thus played an important role in the Tokugawa government. The other two categories of *Daimyo* were much more independent of the Shogunate. The collateral branches of the Tokugawa family, known as *Shimpan*, had large domains. The third category of lords, the *Tozama* or Outer *Daimyo* were in control of approximately half of Japan. The principle of 'divide and rule' was invoked by the Shogun to keep the powerful clans from conspiring to overthrow his power.

Next to the Shogun came the territorial nobility, the *Daimyo*. They were the heads of clans who ruled as feudal lords over territorial subdivisions of Japan. Their powers were supported by the *Samurai*, the warrior class of old Japan, who constituted some five or six per cent of the population. Most of the *Daimyo*, like the *Shoguns*, were little more than figureheads, and did not administer their fiefs. The administration of these was entrusted to family elders (*Karo*), who held office hereditarily in their respective clans. Not infrequently the chief formulators of policy were the lower officers inside the *Samurai* class.

During the period of the Tokugawa Shogunate money economy supplanted the 'rice economy'. Towns and cities such as Yedo, Sakai, Kyoto, Osaka and Nagasaki came into being to meet the heavy demands of the Shogunate for income. This transition added importance to the merchants and other 'service' classes in the towns. As early as 1700 the merchants became one of the strongest elements in the state supplanting in importance the military classes. But it was the interdependence of the merchant and *Samurai* classes which was responsible for causing 'a slow but irresistible revolution, culminating in the breakdown of feudal government and the resumption of intercourse with foreign countries after more than two hundred years of seclusion. What opened the doors was not a summons from without but an explosion from within'.

Early Foreign Contacts

In the early seventeenth century Japan adopted a seclusion policy and allowed the Chinese and Dutch merchants a small and carefully regulated trade confined to the single port of Nagasaki. A few individuals acquired a knowledge of the Dutch language and from Dutch books formed some conception of the outside world. Europeans also accepted Japan a mere political entity, a small, poor country of little interest.

The Russians were the first who took an active interest in Japan and established themselves on the Sea of Okhotsk in the seventeenth century. During the eighteenth century Russian traders had encounters with the Japanese in the Kuril Islands and Sakhalin, north of the island of Hokkaido. In 1739 Russian expedition under Spanberg discovered a route to Japan. In 1792 the Russian representative, Lieutenant Laxman arrived in Hokkaido and was told categorically that Nagasaki was the only port foreigners were allowed to enter. The next envoy, Rezanov, accordingly came to Nagasaki in 1804 but was disappointed when he was curtly informed that Japan had no need for foreign trade. The affront which Rezanov received promoted him to raid Sakhalin and the Kurils in 1806 and 1807. Alarmed by the Russian aggression, the Japanese forces in 1811 seized a Russian naval officer, Golovnin, and some of his companions in Kurils. The Russian prisoners were released in 1813.

Meanwhile, Britain began to take interest in Japan. The Macartney mission to Peking in 1793 had credentials to Japan, but failed to go there. In 1797, an English vessel, however, visited Hokkaido. In 1808 the British frigate *Phaeton* entered Nagasaki in search of Dutch ships. In 1818 a British trading ship entered Edo Bay (The present Tokyo Bay).

American Interest in Japan: Earlier attempts made by the United States to establish relations with Japan were somewhat half-hearted. But with the settlement of the American Pacific Coast and the establishment of a shipping route between San Francisco and Shanghai, the United States developed interest in opening Japan. Moreover, she needed a coaling station on the long trans-Pacific sea-route to Shanghai. In 1835 and twice again in the next ten years, America tried to open negotiations with Japan. In 1846 Commodore Biddle along with two ships arrived in Edo Bay, but received a curt refusal. His failure induced Commander Glynn to assume a bold stance when he came to Nagasaki in 1849. He was successful in this mission, but made no attempt to negotiate.

In July 1853 Commodore Perry, a forceful leader, with four American warships, arrived off Uraga, not far from Yedo, the modern Tokyo, at that time the seat of the Shogunate government. The objects of the Perry expedition were protection of the shipwrecked sailors, the opening of ports for trade, and the right to enter the ports for refuelling and obtaining coal. After a few days of diplomatic etiquette, Perry forwarded a letter from the President of the United States to the Emperor of Japan which the latter having been received, Perry departed, promising to return for the answer the next spring with adequate force.

The Shogun, alarmed at this menacing visit, referred the matter to feudal lords who debated the question whether to resist or submit to the American demands. The replies were overwhelmingly anti-foreign but ambiguous and vague. The result was that when Perry returned to Japan in February 1854 with eight ships—earlier than he had promised—in order to forestall the Russians and the French—he was well received. 'In the cold light of military reality, American determination appeared to be irresistible'. The Treaty of Kangawa was signed on March 31, 1854. The Treaty provided that, in addition to Nagasaki, two ports—Shimoda and Hakodate—were to be opened to American ships for provisioning and trade; shipwrecked Americans were to be protected; an American Consul was to be allowed to reside in Shimoda, and the most-favoured-nation clause stipulated that additional privileges granted to other nations should be equally applicable to the United States. The Treaty was 'the thin end of the wedge, and, as in China, there was soon pressure to drive the wedge in deeper'.[1] England negotiated a similar treaty on October 14, 1854, Russia on February 7, 1855, and Holland during the years 1855-57. The Russian treaty added Nagasaki as an open port and secured reciprocal extra-territoriality.

The Harris Treaty, 1858: Commodore Perry inserted the wedge with force, but it remained for another American, Townsend Harris, to win the good will of the Japanese authorities by his diplomatic tact and sincerity. Appointed in 1856 as the first American Consul to Japan, he was able to persuade the Japanese the advisability of a full commercial treaty with the friendly Americans. The treaty which was signed on July 29, 1858, resulted in the establishment of regular diplomatic and consular relations with Japan. In addition to Shimoda and Hakodate, four additional ports were to be opened to trade; moderate tariff duties were to be levied on export and import trade; Americans were to have extraterritorial privileges in Japan; and the United States agreed to provide Japan with ships, armaments and experts. Shortly afterwards Britain, Russia, Holland and France concluded similar commercial treaties, which together with the American treaty are known as the 'Treaties with the Five Nations.'

Effects of the Treaties

The treaties caused adverse economic impact on Japan. Permitted to export species, foreign traders dumped silver in Japan and exported gold, producing serious economic dislocations. Cotton fabrics, silk and other cheap manufactured goods from abroad affected domestic industries. The presence of foreigners in Japan, instead of producing amicable relations, caused distrust and hostility. In 1859 a Russian naval officer and a Dutch merchant captured were killed. The Shogunate finances, already in a poor state, suffered heavily owing to enormous indemnities for attacks on foreigners.

In the Japanese political system of the Tokugawa period the Emperor remained as a figurehead, the Shogun exercising powers which belonged to the Emperor. To the outer world the Shogun in Yedo appeared to be the only ruler of Japan and was often referred to as 'the Emperor'. But the Shoguns could only maintain their *de facto* authority by exercising effective power. But times had changed. Since the eighteenth century a romantic literary movement based on early Japanese literature and the Shinto religion, had inculcated belief that the real power belonged to the imperial dynasty and that the power of the Shogun could be revoked at any time by the *de*

1. *The New Cambridge Modern History*, Vol. X (1964), P. 711.

jure sovereign. The Shogun exhibited his weakness by invoking the imperial authority on the question of foreign relations. Even *daimyo* and their agents, and samurai, acting independently, tried to woo the Emperor to their views. Most of the Japanese became highly critical of the Shogunate which had signed the commercial treaties against popular wishes and the Emperor's reluctance.

The imperial court became the focal point for opposition to the unpopular foreign policies of the Shogunate. 'Down with the Shogunate', 'honour the Emperor' and 'expel the barbarians' became the rallying cries of the opposition. This was more pronounced among the samurai of Choshu and Satsuma in south-west Japan. The Harris Treaty of 1858, which gave generous concession to America, was signed without the Emperor's approval. A widespread feeling gained ground that this treaty and the subsequent treaties with Britain, France and Russia, were not binding on patriotic Japanese because they lacked the Emperor's sanction.

The anti-foreign agitation led to a series of murderous attacks on foreigners as well as on diplomatic mission at Yedo. Meanwhile, the Emperor, supported by Satsuma and Choshu which contained 27,000 *samurai* and 11,000 *samurai,* respectively, issued order to the Shogun in January 1863 to expel 'the barbarians'. Having been convinced of the strength of the foreigners, the Shogun could do nothing to carry out this directive. Hence he was summoned to Kyoto and asked to enforce the imperial order. Sensing the intransigence of the Shogun, the lord of Choshu unilaterally enforced the order by closing the Straits of Shimonoseki to foreign ships. In retaliation a combined fleet of English, French, Dutch and American vessels demolished the Choshu forts in September 1864. Meanwhile, the lord of Satsuma had his capital, Kagoshima, bombarded by a British squadron in reprisal for the murder of an Englishman and was forced to pay a heavy indemnity.

The strength of the foreign powers and the weakening of the anti-foreign attitude led the Emperor to doubt the wisdom of the old policy of isolation. The foreigners also realised the weakness of their position unless it was buttressed by the stamp of Imperial authority. Meanwhile, the growing disorder in the kingdom led the lord of Choshu to try to seize the person of the Emperor and to establish a new regency under its control—a new Shogunate. The attempt proved unsuccessful. Now wiser counsels prevailed and differences between Choshu and Satsuma disappeared when they felt that the best way to create a strong national government was to 'honour the Emperor'. The secret alliance between Choshu and Satsuma was effected in 1866. Their forces, aided by those of the collateral *han* of Echizen and Nagoya and of the outer domains of Tosa and of Hiroshima, seized the imperial palace of Kyoto on January 3, 1868 and announced another imperial restoration. Decrees were issued in the name of the boy-Emperor Mutsuhito, better known by his title, 'Meiji'—depriving the Shogun of his power. Almost at once Tokugawa adherents took up arms to defend their privileges, but they were defeated in February. In April 1868 the Shogun's surrender was negotiated and his capital Yedo (Edo) was occupied. A few months later the imperial court was transferred there and, renamed Tokyo. But it was not till May 1869 that the last centre of Tokugawa resistance collapsed and the whole of Japan came under the control of the revolutionaries.

The young Emperor was the personal symbol of the whole modernization of Japan. Freed from the yoke of tradition, the new regime was more capable of rapid change. More important, the turbulent fifteen years that followed the arrival of Perry convinced Japan that it was impossible to 'expel the barbarians'. Instead, a new idea crystallised to create a more centralised and modern government with innovative economic and social reforms to catch up with Western military and economic power. Japan had her reward. 'Within forty years, while China remained weak, passive and inert, Japan, emerging victorious from the ordeal of war against Russia, was accepted by the West as a great power.'

Japan in Transition: 1868-94

The New Government: On April 6, 1868, the young Emperor, Mutsuhito, issued a 'Five Articles Oath', known as the 'Charter Oath'.

The five articles were:

1. Deliberative assemblies shall be widely established and all matters decided by public discussion.

2. All classes, high and low, shall unite in vigorously carrying out the administration of affairs of state.

3. The common people, no less than the civil and military officials, shall each be allowed to pursue his own calling so that there may be no discontent.

4. Evil customs of the past shall be broken off and everything based upon the just laws of Nature.

5. Knowledge shall be sought throughout the world so as to strengthen the foundation of imperial rule.

Centralisation of power was basic policy of the new government. The first step in government was the creation of three offices on January 3, 1868. The three offices were (1) a General Director, a post held by an imperial prince, (2) a group of Conferees, consisting of Court nobles and some leading *Daimyo*, and (3) a group of Councillors, the most important as it included young *Samurai* leaders. Below them, there were added a deliberative assembly and a service of administrative departments.

With the Shogun's surrender in April, a constitution was issued on June 11, 1868 embodying the 'Five Articles Oath'. A Council of State was made the supreme organ of government. This council was divided into a legislative body, known as the Department of Deliberation, an executive section called the Department of Administration, and six other administrative departments. A complete revision of the government was made on August 15, 1869. The Council of State became the chief organ and six administrative departments, now called ministries, were placed under it. To the Council of State was attached a legislative assembly which was never convened after its second session in 1870. An office of Shinto Worship was created, an office no less important than the Council of State. Finally, on September 13, 1871, a further revision was made. The Council of State was divided into three chambers—a Left Chamber, which in theory was to determine legislation, a Right Chamber, which was to supervise the various ministries, and a Central Chamber which exercised control over legislation and supervision over the ministries.

The men who ran the administration were mainly exalted figureheads, drawn from among the court nobles and leading *Daimyo*. The actual work of government was largely in the hands of young Samurai leaders who served at first as advisers in the main organs of government. But when high-ranking court nobles and feudal lords were removed from the higher offices of state in August 1869, a number of *Samurai* and a small group of men of lower rank took up positions of trust and responsibility. In 1871, Okubo became minister of finance and, in 1872, it was laid down that the heads of ministries were to be the young *Samurai*.

End of the Feudal System

The new government was beset with difficult problems. It had to grapple with feudal separatism in order to create centralised rule. The new Government had to establish its authority over the 265 separate *han*, which, in theory, were autonomous. It had been realised by the Meiji leaders that 'the annihilation of centrifugal forces taking the form of autocratic feudal provinces was a necessary step to the unification of the country under a strong central Government, without which we would not have been able to offer a united front to the outside forces.'

In the constitution of June 1868, the new government had asserted the supreme authority of the Council of State and assumed the right to tax both *Daimyo* and *Samurai*. The economic autonomy of the *han* was ended in 1869 when customs duties were eliminated. Meanwhile, in early 1869 Kido, Okubo and other leaders persuaded the lords of Satsuma, Choshu Hizen and Tosa to return their domains to the Emperor. This was accomplished on March 5, 1869, by a dramatic act known as the 'return of the *han* registers'. Many other *Daimyo* followed suit, and in July the Central Government ordered the remainder to surrender their domains also. Then, on August 29, 1871, the new government suddenly abolished the *han*. Most of the *Daimyo* and *Samurai* grudgingly acquiesced in the measure incapable as they were of any organised resistance. All Japan was divided into three urban prefectures (*fu*) and 72 other prefectures (*Ken*) and were placed under governors. These local divisions have since been retained, though the number was reduced in 1889 to three urban and 42 other prefectures.

Financial Problem

By the abolition of the fiefs, the government had incurred the feudal dues debts and other commitments, greatest of which was the annual cost of stipends of *Daimyo* and *Samurai*. The *Daimyo* were guaranteed one-tenth and the Samurai one-half of their nominal revenues. This arrangement imposed an extraordinarily financial burden on the government. It had been argued that the government could have dispossessed the feudal classes without recompense. But it appeared to be risky to dispossess the *Samurai* class, who numbered about 1,900,000, constituting 5 to 6 per cent of Japan's population and monopolising the martial arts and political leadership. 'Actually, the government seems to have steered a successful course between the twin perils of financial bankruptcy on one side and the danger on the other side of pushing the *Daimyo* and *Samurai* to unified opposition, rebellion.' In 1873 the government offered the less affluent Samurai the option of a lumpsum payment of either four or six times their annual income. In 1876 all stipends were commuted into government bonds. Hereditary pensions were paid off at from five times their annual value for large pensions to fourteen times for the smallest one.

The government was saddled with heavy financial problem as its receipts from all sources in 1896 were hardly more than a third of its expenditure. Many of these receipts were in the forms of loans, some part of which by exacting forced loans from the great merchant houses. In 1869 a loan of £ 930,000 at 9 per cent was floated in London to finance the construction of a railway between Tokyo and Yakohama, and a second loan of £ 2,400,000 at 7 per cent in 1872 to meet the increased financial obligations of the Government. To cover its excess expenses, the government issued paper notes which had little backing.

The early 1870s brought a semblance of financial stability of the government. Stimulated by foreign trade and freed from the restrictions of feudal political divisions, the Japanese economy rapidly recovered from the slump it had fallen earlier. As a result, the government floated adequate bond issues at home. By 1871 it had repaid all the short-term debts. Meanwhile, the government carried out monetary, banking and tax reforms which helped stabilise its finances. These reforms were carried out largely by Okuma Shigenobu (1838-1922) and Ito. Both of them had critical acumen on financial matters. In 1871 Okuma and Ito revitalised the currency, adopting the decimal system and making the yen the standard coin. They also set up a modern mint in Osaka. In 1872, on Ito's advice, the American system of national banking was instituted.

The land tax was the chief source of government revenue and this was heavy in the early Meiji period. When Okuma became finance minister in 1873 he introduced a land tax. It was to be a cash payment of 3 per cent of the assessed value of the land in addition to 1 per cent to be levied by the local authorities. The fact that it had to be paid in cash in fixed amount and at a fixed date, whether harvests were good or bad, proved to be burdensome to the majority of the farmers. This was, however, reduced to $2^1/_2$ per cent in 1876. Despite its reduction, it provided approximately 78 per cent of ordinary revenue up to 1881. In 1873 Okuma started a modern budget system. In 1872 he also clearly established the ownership of all the land. Under the new law, it was established that the man paying the tax, whether the independent cultivator or the landlord, was the owner of the land.

Modernisation of Japan

One of the first tasks of the Meiji Government was to build up enough military strength to suppress domestic trouble and for defensive purpose. Omura, a leading military expert in the new government founded arsenals and military academics. Early in 1871 an Imperial Force was formed drawn from the *han* armies of Satsuma, Choshu and Tosa. Early in 1872 regulations were issued to enforce discipline over the disparate forces. The Imperial Force was renamed the

Imperial Guards, with Yamagata as commander who became army minister in 1873. The ministry of military affairs was divided into army and navy ministers. In 1874 Enomoto was made a Vice-admiral in the new Imperial Navy. In January 1873, a conscription law, prepared by Yamagata, came into effect. All men were made liable to three years of active military service followed by four in the reserves.

In November 1871 Iwakura led abroad a mission of forty-eight members which visited the United States and then to various countries in Europe to explore the possibilities of treaty revision. But the mission failed completely to persuade the Western powers to modify the treaties. After some eighteen months of travel, the mission became convinced that only through a programme of domestic reform, would Japan win the respect of foreign powers.

In the early 1870s Japan became involved in disputes with Korea, provoked by the latter's insistence on maintaining the same policy of national seclusion that Japan had abandoned. While Iwakura and his colleagues were abroad, the government, influenced by powerful members—Okuma, Saigo and Itagaki—decided to back its demands with force in the summer of 1873. But Iwakura and the members of the mission, who had returned, convinced of Japan's weakness, reversed the decision. Saigo, Itagaki and others resigned from the government in protest. Relations with Korea were soon settled. After a demonstration of force in 1875 and again the next year by the Japanese, the Koreans signed the Treaty of Kanghwa on February 27, 1876. Two ports were opened to Japanese trade in addition to Pusan, and Korea's independence was asserted though China continued to claim suzerainty.

New Educational Pattern: The Government realised the necessity to streamline education and to shape it to the changing needs of the nation. In 1871 was established a Ministry of Education. The next year on the model of the Centralised French System the country was divided into eight University districts, and subdivided into middle school and elementary school districts. Sixteen months of schooling were made compulsory for children of both sexes. Compulsory education was extended to three years in 1889 and later to six years. By 1905, 95 per cent of the children of statutory school age were in school. Elementary education was modelled on that of America.

In 1877 the Tokyo University was founded. Okuma founded in 1882 an institution that grew into Waseda University, one of the two leading private universities of Japan. Many private schools were also founded and some grew into large universities. Under Christian missionary societies women's education made rapid strides. Tsuda Umeko, who visited the United States as a student in 1871, founded Tsuda College in 1900 as an institution specialising in English language. In 1901 and 1908 were founded Japan Women's University and Tokyo Women's University.

Mori, who became minister of education in 1885, felt that an educational system should operate 'not for the sake of the pupils but for the sake of the country'. Tokyo University was reorganised into a multi-faculty university in 1886 and became the recruiting ground for future government officials. Other government universities sprang up—Kyoto in 1898, Tohoku in 1907, Kyushu in 1910, Hokkaido in 1918, and others later. The government universities were all named Imperial Universities.

Early in the twentieth century, the new Japanese educational structure took definite shape. There were three types of institutions: (1) five-year academic middle schools for boys, (2) various lower technical schools, and (3) the girls' higher schools. Above this level stood the three-year academic higher schools and the higher technical schools. The edifice was crowned by the three-year government universities (four-year in medicine).

Industries and Communications: The Meiji leaders inherited from their predecessors a number of recently established enterprises of Western type. The Shogunate had set up an imported iron foundry at Nagasaki in 1857 and established other foundries with French aid at Yokohoma and Yokosuka in 1865.

By time of the Restoration, Japan had owned 138 Western-style ships. The new government began to build up the strategic military industries instead of depending on foreign sources of supply. In addition to Nagasaki and Yokosuka which it had inherited from the Shogunate, it set up a shipyard at Hygo (the modern Kobe). The government operated large works in Tokyo and Osaka for making cannon, rifles and ammunition.

The government took interest in developing a modern network of communications. The government postal service, established in 1871, was extended in 1873. Telegraph being made a state monopoly, spread rapidly. Railway construction was difficult and costly in mountainous Japan. The first line from Tokyo to Yokohoma covering 19 miles was completed in 1872, a second line between Kobe and Osaka by 1874 and was extended to Kyoto in 1877.

In December 1870 a Ministry of Industry was established. In 1871 Ito took charge of it as vice-minister and in 1873 as minister, a post which he retained till 1878. Under Ito and his successors, the government sought to develop the non-strategic industries. The government took special care to develop mining industry, even by employing foreign technicians. In 1869 a modern coal mine came into operation in the Hizen domain. This was taken over by the new government in 1874. By 1880 eight other modern coal mines came into existence. The government made a large investment in a modern iron mine in 1881.

Tokyo became the centre of various industries—a machine tool factory (1871), a cement factory (1875), a glass factory (1876) and a white brick factory (1878). The most important industry was textiles which constituted half of Japan's imports between 1868 and 1882. The first textile plant was set up in 1868 in the Satsuma domain. Satsuma built a second mill in the Osaka area in 1870 and the central government added two other government mills in 1881 and 1882.

The costs of liquidating the old regime were a heavy financial burden, which was increased by the programme of modernisation. After 1877, however, inflation rapidly became serious. By 1880 paper currency depreciated to hardly more than half its face value; the price of rice more than doubled between 1877 and 1880, and inflation reduced the real value of the land tax on which the government largely depended.

The government adopted a policy of economic retrenchment and deflation. The first major step was the sale of government industrial enterprises. The chief executor of this retrenchment policy was Matsukata Masayoshi (1835-1924) who became finance minister in 1881, a position which he retained until 1892. Firm measures were introduced to restore stability to the public finances, including new taxes, stringent economy in administration and the reduction of government grants. Most of the government industries with the exception of war industries, communications and public services, were sold, at bargain prices, to a small group of giant corporation. They were able to develop into the great financial industrial combines (*Zaibatsu*) which was a conspicuous feature of later economic development.

Matsukata's retrenchment policies were successful. In 1882, the Bank of Japan, the chief fiscal agency of the government, was established, paper currency in circulation was reduced about one-quarter, interest rates dropped; specie reserves were increased to 35 per cent of notes outstanding, and, by 1886, paper money had regained its face value.

Based on a sound fiscal system, the Meiji Government surged ahead rapidly. Japan was ready for an industrial 'breakthrough'. Shibusawa's Osaka Spinning Mill heralded the new industrial development. A general boom overtook such diverse fields as mining, weaving, cement, gas and electricity, but the greatest growth came in cotton spinning and railway transportation. Between 1883 and 1890, government railways expanded from 181 (290 km) to 551 miles (880 km) and private railways from 63 (103 km) to 898 miles (1,440 km). The most noticeable improvement was in the production of cotton yarn. From substantial importer (90 per cent) of cotton yarn in the early 1880s Japan became a net exporter of cotton yarn by 1897.

The mid-eighties saw the emergence of joint business enterprises which produced a pooling of resources for financing large scale industries. In 1885 two emerging business giants, the Mitsubishi and Mitsui interests combined their steamship lines. The result was the creation of Japan Main Line (Nippon Yusen Kaisha, commonly known as the N.Y.K.), which has remained ever since the largest merchant marine of Japan.

Industrial growth in Japan was a painful process. The boom years of the 1880s were followed by a period of slow growth. But Japan's victory in the Sino-Japanese War in 1895 gave a sudden spurt in industrial development and in chemical fertilisers. The Russo-Japanese War of 1905 further accelerated the process of development. Thus, during the two and a half decades following Matsukata's financial reforms, Japan entered a period of sustained industrial growth.

Opposition to the Government

In 1873 there was a split in the government ranks over Korea which caused the resignation of Saigo Takamori and Eto Shimpei. In 1876 the government alienated the *Samurai* by forcing them to accept a lump sum in interest-bearing government bonds which yielded far less than their original stipends. These developments led to open *Samurai* rebellion. In February 1874 Eto Shimpei led a revolt in Hizen. Another followed immediately in Choshu. But the most important, however, occurred in Satsuma in 1877. This was led by Saigo Takamori who had resigned from the government in 1873. The government had to launch a vigorous military operation which lasted for six months before Satsuma rebellion was crushed.

After the suppression of the Satsuma rebellion, *Samurai* revolt broke out spasmodically, sometimes as leaders of peasant riots, but the main stream of opposition to the government thereafter was found in the so-called 'movement for freedom and people's rights'. A Radical group emerged which sought to increase their popularity with the people by demanding the creation of a representative assembly. In January 1874, Itagaki, Goto and other Tosa leaders submitted memorandum to the Emperor asking for the establishment of an elected assembly. Their immediate intention was not to make the franchise universal but to give the feudal governing classes an opportunity to express themselves.

The rank-and-file of the constitutional agitation were at first largely *Samurai*. This was evident in the formation of early political associations like the Public Party of Patriots (Aikoku Koto) in 1874, Society of Patriots (Aikokusha) in 1875. To meet the opposition, the government made a compromise in early 1875, called the Osaka compromise. These were the abolition of the Left and Right chambers and their replacement by a Supreme Court, designed to protect the independence of the judiciary, and a Senate or a Chamber of Elders. An assembly of Prefectural Governors was to be made part of the machinery of government so that the opinion of the people might be obtained. Itagaki and Saiko joined the government, but they were not satisfied with the manner in which this compromise was carried into effect and they soon left the government. Another concession was, therefore, made in July 1878 when elected prefectural assemblies were established to aid the Governor. 'These prefectural assemblies constituted a significant step toward democracy, for they were the first successful elected political bodies anywhere in the non-western world.'

Government Measures

Meanwhile the demand for parliamentary government known as 'the movement for freedom and people's rights' spread which was reinforced by the prosperous peasant landowners, who constituted the chief tax-paying group. The government leaders decided to keep the movement under control. In 1875, the new Press Law was issued which made it a punishable offence to criticise the government. In 1880, the government adopted a stringent law on public gatherings. The government leaders however, were convinced that some form of parliamentary government under a written constitution, was a necessity. They were willing to experiment with a limited national assembly. In March 1881, Count Okuma openly favoured the immediate establishment of a constitution on British lines. In June, at the instance of Ito and Iwakura, this proposal was rejected. In October they succeeded in getting Okuma himself removed from office, whereupon he founded in March 1882, the Constitutional Progressive Party (Rikken Kaishinto). Supported by urban intellectuals and businessmen (including the great Mitsubishi concern) the party advocated English parliamentary concepts. In October 1881, Itagaki with Goto founded a new party called the Liberal Party (Jiyuto). Sustained by the landowners, the Party demanded popular sovereignty.

After Okuma's enforced resignation, Ito and Iwakura procured an imperial edict promising that a constitution would be granted in 1889. Soon after, in March 1882, they founded the constitutional Imperial Rule Party (Rikken Teiseito) to support the government stand on the constitutional problem. It found little support and soon dissolved.

The new political parties faced formidable opposition from the government. In 1882, the laws on public meetings were made more stringent. In December 1887, came the Peace Preservation Law which armed the government to expel political suspects from the capital. Meanwhile the simmering discontent within the political parties sometimes culminated in violent outbreaks. The Liberal Party broke up in October 1884. At about the same time Okuma withdrew from the Kaishinto. The political parties became innocuous when Okuma became foreign minister in February 1888 and Goto communication minister in March 1889.

Prelude to Meiji Constitution

Meanwhile the government had made a start for writing a constitution and inaugurating a limited parliamentary government. Ito who became the real directive force in the government, went abroad in March 1882 at the head of a group to study European constitutions. After his return, Ito became the chairman of a special commission set up to draft a constitution (March 1884). In March 1884, he created a new House of Peers consisting of 500 persons who themselves were divided in five ranks prince, marquis, count, viscount and baron. Then in December 1885 the executive system was remodelled by the establishment of a Cabinet to replace the Council of State. The cabinet was made up of the heads of ministers under a Prime Minister. In 1887 Ito modernised the system of bureaucratic administration by adopting a civil service examination. Most important was the creation of Privy Council in April 1888 to approve the constitution then being drafted.

The Meiji Constitution

The Constitution was promulgated on February 11, 1889, the official anniversary of the supposed founding of the Japanese state in 660 B.C. The Constitution included an extensive series of popular rights, such as freedom of speech, freedom of religion, freedom of association, rights to property and due process of law, but these were hedged with restrictions. The Constitution established a bicameral parliament or the Diet consisting of the House of Peers and the House of Representatives, the latter being chosen by a strictly limited electorate. The Diet exercised the real powers as its consent was required for all laws. Ministers were not responsible to the elected House of Representatives, while the House of Peers had in effect a veto on all bills.

The Constitution, however, provided adequate safeguards against parliamentary domination. The constitution was a gift of the Emperor whose person was sacred and inviolable. The constitution confirmed the almost absolute powers of the monarchy. He had the right to appoint and remove both civil and military officers, and to declare war and peace and conclude treaties. The constitution specified that the Emperor was the supreme commander of the army and the navy and made the individual minister directly responsible to him. The Emperor could at any time prorogue the Diet or dissolve the House of Representatives. If the Diet failed to vote a new budget, the government was empowered to carry out the budget of the previous year. A judiciary branch of government was created, but it was little more than an extension of the Emperor's executive powers.

The Meiji Constitution contained various inconsistencies and ambiguities. The constitution left quite vague the degree of control the Diet could exercise over the administrative processes of government. Worst of all, it assumed moral leadership on the part of the Emperor, not only over the members of government but also over the Diet, but it failed to create a situation where emperors could give this leadership. The political parties controlled the House of Representatives, while the cabinet was controlled by the clan leaders. Though the Diet had been given sufficient power to obstruct but not to control legislation, yet no provision had been made for reconciliation between the two branches of the government. The constitution failed to provide cabinet responsibility to the House of Representatives.

Of the 300 representatives in the House of Representatives, the groups led by Itagaki, Goto and Okuma controlled 160 seats. They made immediate use of the one substantial power the constitution had given the Diet. They slashed the budget by about 11 per cent, curtailing particularly the salaries and perquisites of the bureaucrats. Yamagata, the Prime Minister, was not inclined to tolerate dictation by the Diet. Eventually Yamagata succeeded in effecting a compromise by which a quarter of the funds cut by the Diet was restored. Yamagata's successor, Matsukata, faced even greater difficulties and dissolved the House in December 1891. The struggle over the budget lingered. Ito, who succeeded Matsukata late in 1892, failed to control the Diet by his subtle and varied tactics and dissolved the House again in 1893 and June 1894.

Foreign Relations

While the work of reform was in progress, several attempts had been made to secure a revision of the treaties. In 1871 the Iwakura Mission was sent abroad to secure a modification of the treaties, but failed to achieve any success. In 1878 an attempt was made to secure revision of portions of American commercial treaty which became inoperative owing to the failure of other states to accept similar changes. In 1882 the Japanese Foreign Minister entered upon negotiations with foreign powers at Tokyo. As part of the agreement, the foreign powers demanded the establishment of 'Mixed Courts' composed of Japanese and foreign Jurists, to protect the interests of their nationals. The negotiation was wrecked as Japanese public opinion refused to acquiesce to this concession. In 1888 Count Okuma instead of negotiating collectively with foreign Powers, undertook unilateral negotiation. He was able to carry through a revision of the treaty with Mexico as well as with the United States. But owing to the intransigence of other states who demanded similar concessions and public apathy, the treaties failed to produce any effect. Success was finally attained in 1894, when England agreed to a revision of her treaty which was to become effective in 1899. England appeased the Japanese resentment by waiving the 'humiliation' of the 'Mixed Court'. The United States also agreed to revision of its treaties. The other states also followed suit in the course of the next three years.

Before 1894 Japan's frontiers had begun to take shape. China relinquished her claim to suzerainty over the Loochoo islands. In 1875 Japan gave up her claim to the southern half of Sakhalin in exchange of her title to the northern Kurile Islands. In 1876 she expanded her Empire by taking the Bonin islands.

Despite the various deficiencies that afflicted Japan in the late nineteenth century, it may truly be said that:

> By 1894 the crisis of the transition period had passed. The government had been completely organised and constitution had been given several years of trial. An Army and navy had been built up after approved Western models. A modern school system was in successful operation. Tariff and judicial autonomy were on the point of being granted. Industry and commerce were given promise of vigorous life. The reorganisation was not complete and its fruits were only beginning to be seen, but in the main the shock caused by internal adaptation to the modern world was over. From 1894 on, the .reorganised Japan was to expand and take her place an equal and increasingly important member in the family of nations.[2]

Sino-Japanese War (1894-95)

Ito's second dissolution of the Diet was followed by a period of unusual cooperation between Diet and Cabinet. A treaty signed with Britain on July 16, 1894, heralded the end in 1899 of extraterritoriality. But the most important event that overshadowed all others in the summer of 1894 was the outbreak of war with China over Korea. The new Diet, elected on September 1, voted all the war budgets unanimously.

2. Latourette: *Development of Japan*, P. 163.

Foreign policy remained an issue which was always likely to arouse emotion. Japan's dispute with China stemmed from the former's attempt to control Korea. Because of its geographical propinquity, the independence of Korea was more vital to Japanese security than that of Belgium to the national safety of Britain. Korea in hostile hands was 'a dagger thrust at the heart of Japan'. The peninsular had been recognised as a Chinese dependency since its conquest by the Manchus in the 17th century.

While Japan in the middle of the nineteenth century was ready to burst open with unbounded energy, Korea had to meet a challenge on two fronts, domestic and foreign. A large scale peasant based rebellion broke out in south-eastern Korea in 1862-63, the most serious revolt for several hundred years past. The Taewongun or Grand Prince, the regent (1864-73) and father of the boy-king Kojong, pursued a vigorous conservative reform programme. In keeping with established custom, the Taewongun left Korea's foreign relations for China to handle.

For twenty years before the outbreak of the Sino-Japanese conflict, Japan had meddled in Korean politics. In 1876 she concluded with Korea the treaty of Kanghwa which recognised the independence of Korea and opened three ports to trade. Despite this treaty, Korea continued to be loyal to China and sent a permanent representative in Tientsin. The Chinese government also shifted the Korean affairs from Peking to Li Hung Chang, the viceroy of Tientsin. Li's policy was that Korea should enter into treaties with Western powers as a counterpoise to Japan and Russia. The Koreans, therefore, concluded treaties with America at Chemulpo on May 6, 1882 and with England and Germany soon afterwards.

Meanwhile, Korea was convulsed by violent feuds between pro-Chinese conservative faction and pro-Japanese radicals. In July 1882, the conservative faction led by the Taewongun, attacked the Japanese legation and tried to seize control of the capital, Seoul. Both China and Japan collaborated in restoring order. Taewongun was arrested and was sent into exile in China. Ultimately an agreement was concluded between Japan and Korea which extended trade and residence privileges as well as giving an indemnity to Japan.

Japan's policy, however, was aimed at independence for Korea, to prevent China or any other power from dominating it. China, on the contrary, wanted openly to grasp control of Korea. Paradoxically, a number of Korean patriots, who wanted to Westernize on the Japanese model attempted a *coup d' etat* on December 4, 1884. Japan took an active part in their attempt to seize control. The chief minister was killed. After initial hesitation, the Chinese engaged the Japanese troops, seized the king, and compelled the Japanese to withdraw. China, however, was not in a position, to embark on a war against Japan. Neither did Japanese want war over this issue. A convention was, therefore, concluded between China and Japan, on April 18, 1885, at Tientsin. It provided for mutual withdrawal of forces, but both countries kept the right to send troops to Korea upon notifying the other.

The Convention put China and Japan on an equal footing, yet the former came to play a dominating role in the Korean politics. Only three weeks after the Tientsin convention, England suddenly occupied Port Hamilton, a harbour off the Korean coast, to offset Russian expansionism. Russia threatened to seize a Korean port in retaliation for the British occupation of Port Hamilton. At the same time she began negotiations with China for a joint guarantee of Korean independence. England withdrew from Port Hamilton at the end of 1886, on receiving Russia's assurance that she had no territorial ambition in Korea.

The withdrawal of England and Russia was followed by the ascendancy of China in Korean affair. But Japan had not abandoned her interest in Korea.

> During the five years from 1889 to 1894, China and Japan were left face to face at the court of Seoul. The party of content, those who supported the existing administration, found their support at the Chinese Residency; the party of discontent, the "Young Korea" party who demanded reform, found support at the Japanese legation. Plotting and counter-plotting, charge and counter-charge, advice and counter-advice, all were poured into the ears of the distracted puppet King, until nothing was left but final arbitrament of war.

The immediate cause of the war was the outbreak of a rebellion in Korea in 1894. The Tonghak party or 'party of Eastern learning' which was nationalistic, anti-Western, seized various provinces and defeated the government troops sent against them. The Korean King asked for Chinese help when the latter sent troops to Seoul. By the time the Chinese troops had reached Korea the revolt had been put down by the Korean army. But Japan was determined to force a solution to the troublesome Korean problem. China, dismayed by the prompt Japanese intervention, suggested a mutual withdrawal of troops and a common agreement not to interfere in Korean affairs. The Japanese Prime Minister, Hirobumi, rejected the suggestion and insisted that the two countries should join in carrying out internal reforms in Korea. China in her turn rejected the Japanese proposal and sent reinforcements to Korea. Japan seemed determined on war. She occupied Seoul after expelling the Chinese officials from the place. On July 25, 1894, the Japanese navy sank a British steamer *Kowshing* carrying Chinese reinforcements. On July 29 Japanese forces routed Chinese army stationed on the west coast of Korea. Japan seized control of the Korean government and had the Korean Regent declare war on China. Yuan Shih-Kai, the Chinese Resident fled and Japan declared war on August 1, 1894. Thus the eventual Sino-Japanese war broke out which was to some extent caused by Japan's desire to control Korea 'as the gateway to continental expansion, supplemented by a national fear lest Korea should come under the control of some strong foreign power'.

Course of the War

The war between China and Japan was a war between the giant and the dwarf and it was assumed that the Chinese Empire would win through sheer size. But the outcome of the war startled the world. Despite her superior resources, both in army and navy, China proved unequal to the Japanese who had better weapons and were masters of modern tactics and strategy.

On September 15, 1894, the Japanese army defeated the Chinese army before Pyongyang, the capital of northern Korea, and drove them back to the Chinese frontier, the Yalu river. On September 17, a major naval engagement took place off the Yalu. The Japanese fleet was faster and more up-to-date in battle tactics. In two columns it encircled the Chinese warship and sunk four of them while others fled. During October and November the Japanese advanced into South Manchuria and captured Port Arthur (November 21), the best harbour on that coast. The Japanese then gained a firm footing on the opposite coast in Shantung by storming Weihaiwei, where the remainder of the Chinese fleet remained bottled up. In March the conquest of South Manchuria was completed by a victory at Yingkou. The road to Peking now lay open, and China was now forced to sue for peace.

The Treaty of Shimonoseki (April 1895)

The Treaty of Shimonoseki was concluded on April 17, 1895. By its terms China recognised Korea's independence and ceded Formosa, the Pescadores and the Liaotung (South Manchuria) Peninsula to Japan. China also paid a large indemnity, opened four more ports to trade and negotiated a commercial treaty. The latter, signed in 1896, gave Japan all the privileges that the Western powers had in China and added the further privilege of carrying on 'industries and manufactures'.

The Sino-Japanese War was the most decisive event in the modern history of the Far East. As far as Japan was concerned, the unequal treaties imposed upon her by foreign nations in Japan were quashed. The extra-territorial rights of foreign nations in Japan were abolished; tariff autonomy was restored to her—*i.e.,* the right to impose her own customs duties on exports and imports.

Secondly, the treaty revealed the weakness of China. She had been compelled to give up a portion of her own territory. China was now about to become another Africa for the booty of the foreign powers. There followed the struggle for concessions, for leased territories, for spheres of influence.

Thirdly, the victory of 1895 inflamed Japan's imperialism on a large scale. The Sino-Japanese War ushered in a new phase of developments in the Far East. Japan's overwhelming victory upset the power balance in China. The war brought France and England to her borders on the south and south-west and Russia on the north. Hardly had Japan negotiated the Treaty of Shimonoseki when she was forced to relinquish part of the gains it had conferred upon her. Russia was alarmed by Japan's acquisition of a Liaotung Peninsula, with the strong ice-free harbour of Port Arthur which gave to Japan a strategic command of Peking. Russia advised Japan not to occupy the Liaotung Peninsula in perpetuity because such an occupation would 'destroy the political balance in the Far East'. Russia was backed by France and Germany. The intervention of the three powers forced victorious Japan to restore Liaotung peninsula and Port Arthur to China in return for a monetary compensation (April 1895).

Scramble for China

The Sino-Japanese War stimulated a scramble for Chinese territory by the European powers. Russia and France supplied the loan which China required in order to pay indemnity to Japan and as a consequence secured valuable concessions to build and extend railways as well as mining privileges. France actually was the first to act. On June 20, 1895 she extorted from China a border settlement concerning Tongking, a concession to open mines in south-west China and to extend her railways there from Tonkin. Three new frontier stations were opened to trade and reductions were made in China's tariffs. Thus, as it turned out, France acquired a sphere in Kwangtung-Kwangsi-Yunnan with a naval base at Kwang-Chow Bay (April 1898).

It was Russia that secured the greatest gain. In June 1896 a secret Russo-Chinese treaty of alliance was signed. By it, both powers agreed to cooperate with each other against any Japanese aggression, and the Russo-Chinese bank was to build the Chinese Eastern Railway across Manchuria. Russia followed up this treaty by obtaining from China a 25-year lease of the southern tip of the Kwantung Peninsula, including the port of Dairen and the Port Arthur naval base (March 1898) as also the right to carry the Trans-Siberian railway across Manchuria to Vladivostok. Port Arthur was also linked up by railway with the Trans-Siberian system.

In the ensuing melee for territorial scramble, Britain pragmatically followed a policy of compensation. In February 1897, Britain opened South-West China to trade up the West River from Canton and by a projected Burma railroad. Moreover Britain secured the entire Yangtze valley—the whole hinterland of Shanghai, half the China market and got concessions to build some 2,800 miles (4,480 km) of railways. In addition, Britain leased Weihaiwei in Shantung, opposite Port Arthur, as a naval base and acquired extension of her territory in Hong Kong.

Germany also participated in the so-called 'battle of the concessions' in China. In November 1897 two German missionaries were murdered in Shantung. Germany used the incident to secure the lease of the port and district of Kiaochow for 99 years, with concessions for two railways in Shantung.

The international scrambles for China took place with such bewildering rapidity that it threatened the Ching Empire with extinction. The process began when the powers began to delimit their 'spheres of influence'—a preliminary step towards making China into a congeries of outright European colonies. Thus, France in this way marked off Hainan and the territory bordering on Tonkin, Britain the Yangtze Valley, Japan Fukien, while Japan claimed priority in Shantung, and Russia in Manchuria, Mongolia and Chinese Turkestan.

American Expansion and the Open Door

The international scramble for concession in China led to new developments which in the long run saved the 'Celestial Empire', from impending dissolution. These were the 'Open Door' doctrine, the Boxer riots and the Anglo-Japanese alliance of 1902.

American activity in the Far East avoided 'imperialism' just as it avoided 'entangling alliances' in Europe. But she had been one of the first countries to enter into treaty relations with the Peking Government after the Opium War. She had secured the same commercial and diplomatic privileges as the other countries. But she had not joined the scramble for concession or for spheres of influence. The American expansion in the Far East was triggered by her war with Spain which took place in 1898. By a peace treaty in December 1898, the United States received the Philippines from Spain. Meanwhile Hawaii had been annexed in July, and the Western Pacific island of Guam had been taken from Spain. These American acquisitions in 1898-99 gave the United States potential naval bases at Pearl Harbour, Guam and Manila as well as the Hawaiian islands and the entire Philippine Archipelago.

The spoliation of the Chinese Empire by the Western Powers awakened in the Americans a lively sense of fear that she might be excluded from China. Moreover, the rise of cheap manufacturing export products and the disappearance of the frontier at home spurred the Americans in the search for markets, colonies and naval bases.

In September 1899, John Hay, Secretary of State, issued his first Open Door notes. He urged the powers to make a formal declaration in favour of equal opportunity for trade for all nations, of uniform tariffs and harbour dues and the maintenance of the Chinese treaty tariff and the Chinese collection of customs. In other words, Hay required a declaration of an 'open door' policy, that the Powers in their 'sphere of influence' would maintain an open market or an undiscriminating tariff toward all nations. America's demand cannot be regarded as other than self-interests. But it contained a protest against the spoliation of the Chinese Empire by the Powers. While advocating international cooperation, it pleaded for a guarantee of Chinese integrity. Britain, Germany, France, Italy and Japan all agreed to accept these provisions except Russia who remained silent on the question of the uniformity of harbour and railroad charges.

The Boxer Rebellion

These successive shocks produced a reform party in China. Among the individual reformers the best known was Dr. Sun Yat Sen, who led a revolutionary attempt against Canton in 1895. A more important figure in the early reform movement, however, was Kang Yu-Wei, known as the 'modern sage'. Unlike Sun Yat-sen, he advocated the gradual establishment of a constitutional monarchy. In 1889 the Emperor Kuang Hsu attained majority and the regent Empress Dowager retired to the Summer Palace near Peking. But the change was more nominal than real as the Empress Dowager still continued to interfere in state affairs. The imperial Court itself was divided into two factions—the so-called 'northern party' who, as patron of the Empress Dowager, insisted that she should resume the regency. The other, 'southern party', loyal to the throne, advocated a more liberal policy, then appealed to the Manchus and their northern colleagues.

The Sino-Japanese War revealed the impotence of China who became more sick than the 'Sick Man of Europe'. The unedifying episode known as the 'Battle for the Concessions' that followed presaged the dissolution of the empire. The young Emperor, then twenty-seven in 1898, who came under the dominance of K'ang, embarked on a policy of reform. 'China will soon perish', K'ang said. 'All that is caused by the conservatives' replied the Emperor. 'If Your Majesty wishes to rely on them for reform', said K'ang, 'It will be like climbing a tree to seek for fish'.

During the hundred days between June 11 and September 21, 1898, Kuang Hsu and others issued forty or more reform edicts dealing with almost every conceivable subject: setting up modern schools and remaking the examination system: establishment of an imperial university; modernisation of the army, secularisation of Buddhist monasteries, establishment of a National Board to promote commerce, agriculture, mining and the construction of railways, provision for sending students to study abroad, reform of the provincial administration and abolition of sinecure ministers and obsolete posts. Conservative opposition to the reform programme became vociferous as it affected nearly everyone in office. In short, the Emperor found himself as war with the whole establishment. During the Hundred Days, Chang Chih-tung published *Exhortations to Study,* in which he stated his anti-radical views. He vigorously opposed democracy, constitutional monarchy, the doctrine of the people's rights, parliaments and civil liberties of the western sort.

The Empress Dowager found her entire world shaken by the Emperor's reform programme. But she had to wait for an opportune moment. Finally, on September 21, 1898, with the help of the top Manchu military commander, she seized the Emperor in a *coup d'etat*. The reform movement was suppressed, K'ang and Liang escaped to Japan, and six of the reformers were executed. The Emperor remained in forced seclusion.

After the failure of the radical reforms, the initiative shifted to the Empress Dowager and the Manchu princes who offered determined opposition to the foreign powers. They eventually found a vehicle in a secret society called the 'Boxers'. As early as 1896, secret society activity had begun in Shantung. In May 1898 came the official report of the existence of the Boxer Movement. The most important factor that inspired the Boxer Movement was its anti-Christian hostility. 'Catholics and Protestants have villified our gods and sages, have deceived our emperors and ministers above and oppressed the Chinese people below ... This forces us to protect our country, expel the foreign bandits and kill Christian converts, in order to save our people from miserable sufferings.'

The Boxer Movement was fostered by current economic and political conditions. Widespread famine due to Yellow River floods overtook Shantung in 1898. North China suffered greatly from drought. The importation of foreign goods paralysed local industries, while plans for new railways were not welcomed. Throughout the empire, foreign encroachments on Chinese territory had spread a bitter discontent among the people. The late 1890s saw widespread disorder and local risings in every one of the eighteen provinces. In short, the Boxer Movement developed as a result of deepening crisis in the lives of the Chinese people. Finally, the Movement received its impetus from the patronage of Manchu and Chinese officials in order to counteract foreign aggression and local disorder.

During the first five months of 1900, Boxer bands of hundreds and even thousands spread over the countryside, burning missionary establishments and killing Chinese Christians. In May, they were terrorizing the countryside around Peking. The principal officials in the provinces and at Court urged suppression of the Boxers. But the attitude of the court was ambivalent rather than suppress the Boxers terror. But the final provocation was triggered off by the foreigners who agreed that the Boxers must be met by force.

In Peking foreign officials, missionaries and their families took refuge in the foreign legations and appealed to their home countries for help. On June 10, 1900, an international relief expedition of 2,100 troops under the British admiral, Seymour, started from Tientsin for the protection of the Peking legations. On June 13, the Boxer forces entered Peking, massacred Chinese Christians and burned foreign establishments outside the legations. On June 14, the Boxers swept into Tientsin and besieged the foreign settlements. On June 17, the foreign admirals attacked and seized the Taku forts on the coast. The next day Seymour's relief column was attacked. In Peking the German minister, Von Ketteler, was shot dead in the street on June 20. The next day the Ching dynasty declared war against foreign powers. But the southern viceroys and provincial governors agreed to suppress the Boxers' infiltration and maintain normal trade if the foreign powers refrained from landing troops or sending warships up the Yangtze. Thus the Boxer war remained localised in North China.

The eleven foreign legations in Peking were besieged from June 20. The foreign residents successfully repelled numerous Boxer assaults. Seventy-six foreigners died defending the legations. On July 14, the Allied forces captured the Chinese city of Tientsin. This success gave the reactionary party at the court a time to pause. Indeed there was a twelve-day truce between July 14 to 26. But the Empress Dowager once more changed her policy and resumed the attacks upon the legations. On August 4, the Allied forces entered Peking and relieved the besieged legations. The Empress Dowager and the Emperor left Peking in disguise. But late 1900, around 45,000 foreign troops were in North China, and Russia had already occupied Manchuria. Within a short time they defeated the Boxers and pacified the northern provinces. The court accepted in December the main points of a settlement but the Protocol was signed on September 7, 1901. The country suffered heavy penalties. China had not only to respect the privileges of the foreigners but had to pay a heavy indemnity. Foreign powers were given the right to occupy certain cities lying between Peking and the sea. The Boxer promise of a brighter tomorrow had come to a sad failure. 'The Boxer rising and the Protocol marked the nadir of the Ching dynasty's foreign relations.'

The Chinese Revolution (1911)

The Sino-Japanese War and the Boxer War had exhibited the bankruptcy of the Chinese Empire. Conservative reforms began early in the twentieth century, while the republican revolutionary movement grew up on the periphery. The final decade of the Ching dynasty from 1901 to 1911 was a period of metamorphosis. Institutional and social change began early and political disaster came only at the end.

In January 1901, the Empress Dowager repentantly announced a policy of adopting the 'strong points of foreign countries in order to make up China's shortcomings'. Under the guidance of Chang Chih-tung and Liu Kun-i, the Yangtze Viceroys and Yuan Shih-Kai, Viceroy of the Chihli province and Guardian of the Heir Apartment, the government inaugurated a policy of reform. They realised the necessity of establishing new school systems, sending students abroad, adopting western military methods, developing agriculture and industry, instituting better laws and taxes, abolishing sinecures and corruption.

The school system was modelled on the Japanese. Detailed regulations issued in 1904 followed Japan's example in leading students through higher elementary school (4 years), middle school (5 years), and higher school (3 years) to the Imperial University (3 years). Progress in building the school system was achieved at the provincial level. Chang Chih-tung had a great variety of small pilot-model schools operating in Hupei—a normal school to train teacher, five higher schools, and special schools for foreign languages, agriculture and industry, and the training of officials already in service. As Japan's language, literature and customs were close to China's, Chinese students and teachers visited Japan and received training in ever-increasing numbers. The intellectual content of the new education contained much from the West. After 1900 the Chinese scholar class began to absorb Western ideas by translating Dickens, Dumas, Scott, Balzac, Adam Smith, J. S. Mill and Montesquieu.

The government turned serious attention to military reform. Until after 1895 China had no real modern national army. Provincial troops were organised and controlled by provincial officials. After 1895 an attempt at reorganisation was made but without any salutary result. In 1901 an imperial edict again ordered reorganisation. Between 1903 and 1906 Yuan Shih-Kai created a model force of six divisions. A plan was also projected for the formation of a national army of 36 divisions, each of 125,000 men, on the Japanese model. But it lacked the essential ingredients of centralised direction and adequate financing. Russo-Japanese War of 1904-05 actuated the military growth of China when Chinese officers were sent to military academies in Japan.

Administrative reforms also began as China needed dynamic central organs to perform new functions. In 1903 a Ministry of Commerce was set up. In 1905 a Ministry of Police was inaugurated, forerunner of a Minister of Internal Affairs. In 1906 the old Board of War was expanded. In 1904 a law-compilation bureau began work under Shen Chiapen whose revision of the Ching Code was finally promulgated in 1910. This revision included civil and criminal law and procedures. It distinguished between civil and criminal law, reduced corporal punishment and torture, substituted individual for collective responsibility. The ancient Board of Revenue was reorganised in 1906 as a Ministry of Finance and a novel effort to make a national budget began with nationwide revenue surveys in 1908.

The old six Boards in November 1906 were expanded to make eleven ministries (Foreign Affairs, Civil Appointments, Internal Affairs, Finance, Rites, Education, War, Justice, Agriculture, Industry and Commerce, Posts and Communications and Dependencies). In August 1908 the Empress Dowager proclaimed a set of constitutional principles. But her death on November 14, 1908, weakened the Ching regime. Simultaneously the mysterious death of the Emperor Kuanghsu, at 37, destroyed the best chance of China's transition to a constitutional monarchy. However, in February 1910, representatives of all sixteen provincial assemblies met at Peking and demanded a national parliament. The demand for parliamentary government became intensified after the consultative national assembly, consisting of 100 representatives of the throne and 100 of the provincial assemblies, convened in October 1910. The regent, Prince Chun, promised a parliament and established a cabinet in April 1911.

Causes of Revolution

In the beginning of the nineteenth century, China became aware of the remarkable transformation wrought by the Westernisation of Japan. Japan's emergence as a great power between 1895 and 1905 made her the model for Asia. Because of geographical propinquity, a Japanese movement developed for the study of contemporary China, aimed at helping her achieve political reform and economic modernisation. Japan became the refuge for Chinese rebels and political exiles. Okuma, who had been Prime Minister of Japan briefly in 1898, formulated the famous 'Okuma Doctrine'—Japan, having modernised first, should repay her ancient cultural debt to China by guaranteeing her freedom.

The revolutionary elements in China were represented by and large, by two distinct protagonists—Liang Chi-Chao and Sun Yat-sen. Liang was a prolific writer and wrote in a forceful style that made him the most influential writer of the period. He urged the transfer of loyalty from ruler to nation and the establishment of new institutions—a constitution, a parliament and a responsible government. But he was a gradualist and the Political Culture Association which he organised in 1907 advocated orderly political processes.

While Liang was expounding the ideology of Chinese nationalism, Sun Yat-sen (1866-1925) sowed the seed of the early revolutionary movement. Son of a peasant, he studied medicine. In 1892 he began to practise medicine in Macao but was unsuccessful owing to lack of a diploma. Thwarted as a doctor, he now turned to a revolutionary. By 1894 he had a secret society of his own, the *Hsing-Chung hui (*Revive Chine Society). In 1895 his plot to seize Canton failed. He travelled widely in Japan, Britain and the United States. Sun became famous as the leading revolutionary.

Meanwhile, spurts of revolutionary activities were growing in China, but they lacked coordination and specific ideology. With his multicultural background, Sun propounded a set of ideas to usher in a republican government. This was the Three Principles of the People—Nationalism, Democracy and Socialism. Sun pleaded for his people the 'right to live' and 'the right to a living'. Bringing rival groups together, Sun founded in August 1905 the *Tung-meng hui* (United League) with branches in seventeen provinces as well as overseas offices in Singapore, Brussels, San Francisco and Honolulu. Sun became the chief executive of *Tung-meng hui*, Huang Hsing second in command, and Chang Ping-lin and others to key posts. In *Tung-meng hui*'s journal *Min-pao* ('The People'), Sun and his disciples vigorously attacked Liang Chi-Chao's ideas of gradualist reform. Sun advocated a three-stage programme (1) three years of military government, (2) six years under a provisional constitution—known as a period of tutelage, and (3) eventual constitutional government with an elected president and parliament.

Sporadic outbreaks occurred in China in 1906, 1907 and 1908 but these were destined to end in failure owing to revolutionists' lack of coordination. In 1910 an attempt to bomb the Prince Regent in Peking was foiled. After the suppression of army revolt at Canton in February 1910, another revolution took place at Canton in April 1911. This was also doomed to futility owing to general confusion and lack of coordination. Huang Hsing was at pains to observe: 'In instigating revolution, dictatorship is imperative. Once a dissenting voice is permitted, the revolution is bound to fail.'

Apart from sporadic outbreaks, the country was also endangered by worsening economic conditions. In September 1911 an uprising took place in the province of Szechwan, in the Yangtze valley, provoked by the railway scheme. In October 1911 three thousand soldiers revolted in Wuchang forcing the governor-general and the military commander to leave the city. Within a few weeks it inspired revolutionary outbreaks in two dozen other centres. By early December 1911 the outbreaks became general engulfing the southern, central and even the north-western provinces. On Sun Yat-sen's return from Britain, he was elected provisional president of the Chinese Republic.

Meanwhile, the imperial government recalled Yuan Shih-Kai who was made premier of a new cabinet government as well as commander of the armed forces. The revolutionaries also looked to Yuan as the chief hope of avoiding civil war, chaos and foreign intervention. Yuan negotiated with the provisional government at Nanking and reached a general settlement on February 12, 1912. The Emperor Hsuan-tung abdicated, ending the Ching dynasty. Thus, the Manchu rule came to an end after almost 270 years of rule.

Sun Yat-sen resigned as provisional president in favour of Yuan Shih-Kai in the hope that republican unity would be better strengthened under Yuan, the strong man, than under himself. But Yuan as president was later to betray the revolutionists just as he had betrayed the Ching court.

The new regime possessed an obvious source of strength, but its weaknesses were both numerous. Friction soon developed between Yuan and the revolutionaries. Yuan was an authoritarian who thought himself as the founder of a new dynasty. Sun Yat-Sen favoured a form of revolutionary totalitarianism. Another section of the *Tung-meng hui*, led by Sung Chiao-Jen, advocated the British system of parliamentary government. In pursuit of their objective, Sung formed a political party, the Kuomintang. National elections gave the Kuomintang a majority in the bicameral parliament by February 1913. But the prospect of a parliamentary democracy was blighted when Yuan Shih-Kai eliminated Sung Chiao-Jen by assassinating him (March 20, 1913). When the parliament met in April 1913, the Kuomintang, having the largest group of members, demanded a constitution in which executive power would be vested in a prime minister and cabinet responsible to parliament. The mutual ill-will increased steadily and after the President had concluded an unpopular huge loan with five foreign powers, an attempt was made in July and August 1913 to oust Yuan. Seven provincial governments declared their independence of Peking in the short-lived 'Second Revolution'. But this movement lacked popular support and was suppressed with ease. Sun Yat-Sen and other leaders fled to Japan.

Yuan kept up the facade of parliamentary government when he got himself elected President on October 6, 1913. In November he ordered the Kuomintang dissolved and in January he suspended the parliament and then the provincial assemblies. Yuan was now dictator. His monarchical ambition was fulfilled when he accepted the throne in December 1915 and began his reign under the title 'Grand Constitutional Era'. But all this came to nothing. Within six months he was undone by the military governors of the provinces. The precipitating factor was sparked by Liang Chi-Chao, the anti-revolutionist who yet saw 'history as irreversible and now advocated the continuity of the Chinese Republic'. He died a broken man on June 6, 1916. Yuan made a mistake in seeking imperial legitimacy as a prop to central power by forgetting that the people, the body-politic of the nation, were the active makers of history.

After Yuan's death, China soon relapsed again into political disorder. The former parliament was re-called and the constitution providing for an executive responsible to it was brought into force. But this did not resolve the fundamental conflict between the Kuomintang and the military. A compromise was effected: Li Huan-hung, the former Vice-President, became President and Tuan Chi-jui, a northern military leader, became Prime Minister.

This was only a patchwork. The country was split over questions of participation in the First World War and the further granting of foreign concessions. In mid-1917 the parliament was again dissolved and a group of monarchists attempted to restore the Manchus. Late in 1917, therefore, the Kuomintang along with Sun Yat-sen set up at Canton a Southern constitutional government in opposition to the northern government at Peking. The confusion was accentuated by the activities of a dozen military governors (*tuchuns*) who collected the local taxes and used their armies for personal aggrandisement. While the Canton government claimed to be the legitimate representative of the people, Peking obtained both recognition and funds from foreign powers. The end of World War I put both north and south under pressure to patch things up. The 1920s saw the height of disorder in Chinese politics and rise of a new revolutionary movement to reestablish central power.

Foreign Relations

The Chinese Revolution and the struggle of the Kuomintang introduced many changes in China's foreign relations. Russia immediately seized the opportunity of the Revolution to detach Outer Mongolia from China. Similarly China had to withdraw her troops from Tibet allowing Britain a permanent interest in that country. This expansion of great-power influence in China's borderlands was paralleled by a further growth of foreign control over China's trade and commerce. But the jealousy of the foreign powers put a restraining influence on the rapacity of any individual power.

The outbreak of World War I, however, removed these restraining influences and led Japan to embark on a course of aggression. In August 1914, China declared her neutrality. But Japan, as an ally of Britain, declared war on Germany on August 23, 1914, took over the whole German position in Shantung, seized Kiaochow and occupied the railway from Tsingtao to Tsinan. Japan followed this on January 18, 1915, by presenting to China a list of twenty-one Demands. These Demands, divided into five groups, were calculated to make China a Japanese protectorate. Under the threat of a Japanese ultimatum of May 7, 1915, China was forced to accept most of the first four groups of demands. Despite Britain's protest that 'Japan's action toward China is worse than that of Germany in the case of Belgium', no Western Power came to China's aid. These 'Demands' confirmed Japan's dominant position in Shantung and in South Manchuria and Eastern Inner Mongolia where her leases were now extended to 99 years. In addition, Japan was acknowledged to have a special interest in the Han-Yeh-Ping industrial base in Central China. But the Chinese Parliament refused to ratify these treaties. A widespread hostility to Japan developed in China thus fostering an incipient nationalism.

To counter Japan's expansion in China, the latter entered war in August 1917. But the result was disappointing. Japan's assistance was considered essential to protect the Allied navy from unrestricted German submarine attacks and in return for her help, Japan secured in the spring of 1917 the British, French and Italian agreement to her retaining rights in Shantung. She followed these moves by making with the United States the Lansing-Ishii agreement of November 1917. It was declared 'that territorial propinquity creates special relation between countries, and, consequently, the Government of the United States recognises that Japan had special interests in China.' The Japanese Government, on the other hand, reaffirmed that it would always adhere to the principle of the so-called 'Open Door' and disclaimed any intention to 'infringe in any way the independence or territorial integrity of China.'

After the war, China participated in the Paris Peace Conference in January 1919. Her representatives demanded the restoration of Shantung which was, to the Chinese 'the cradle of Chinese civilisation, the birth place of Confucius, and a Holy Land for the Chinese'. They also demanded the abolition of extra-territoriality and tariff autonomy, the cancellation of foreign 'spheres of influence' and the withdrawal of foreign troops. Not only did China experience disappointment from the great powers but she was rudely shaken when she found that President Wilson's doctrines of self-determination and open diplomacy did not apply to the Far East. Meanwhile Peking had signed secret agreements in 1918 confirming Japan's Shantung position. Thereupon China withheld her signature from the Versailles Treaty.

A wave of indignation swept China at the Paris decision and at the Peking Government's secret sell-out to Japan. On May 4, 1919, over 3,000 students of Peking assembled to observe 'National Humiliation Day' in order to commemorate the Twenty-one Demands. They endorsed a manifesto which concluded 'China's territory may be conquered, but it cannot be given away. The Chinese people may be massacred, but they will not surrender. Our country is about to be annihilated. Up, brethren!" The subsequent demonstration erupted into violence when students burned the house of a cabinet minister. The war-lord Peking Government struck hard and imprisoned some 1,150 students. But these repressive measures only accelerated the movement when Shanghaï merchants observed a week-long strike and workers struck in some forty Shanghai factories. The national movement won the day and the cabinet resigned.

Out of the political activity of May 4 incident came China's new nationalisation of the 1920s which was given the name 'New Culture Movement'. Numerous publications of books including translations of Western works exposed the hollowness of traditional culture and emphasised liberal ideas, individual rights and freedom. Political movements gathered momentum. Sun Yat-Sen reorganised the Kuomintang by recruiting students. The Soviet success in seizing power in 1917 exercised profound influence in China. Li Ta-Chao, a professor, hailed the 'Victory of Bolshevism'. In August 1920 a Socialist Youth Corps was founded in Shanghai. The First Congress of the Chinese Communist Party, held at Shanghai in July 1921, was attended among others by Mao Tse-tung. Small party branches sprang up in Peking, Changsa, Wuhan, Canton and elsewhere.

Despite the growth of political consciousness, China remained impoverished with her economy in the doldrum. Meanwhile calamities multiplied, like the great North-West Famine of 1920-21. While frustration gripped the Comintern, the Kuomintung could claim more the partial or temporary success.

The Washington Conference (November 12, 1921-February 1922)

Foreign powers who had interests in China looked with disfavour any violent change in the government. They wished to see China developing a stable central government like any other nation. Moreover, Washington had noticed with concern the predominance of Anglo-Japanese influence in China and the violation of the Open Door policy enunciated by John Hay in 1900. The situation was complicated by the existence of the Anglo-Japanese Alliance (1902) which was due to expire in July 1921. In the Far East, Japan seemed to be the potential opponent to America. The Washington Conference which was called on American initiative constituted the chief post-war development in the Far East. The treaties signed at the Washington Conference were:

(1) Limitation of naval armaments, the main business of the Conference, was accepted on a five-five-three ratio for Britain, the United States and Japan, with the proviso that no Anglo-American naval bases would be developed east of Singapore or West of Hawaii.

(2) The Anglo-Japanese Alliance was superseded by a Four-Power Treaty between Britain, America, France and Japan. They agreed to respect each other's rights in relation to their insular possessions in the Pacific, and consult together in the event of any controversy between them regarding these rights or any one of them 'threatened by the aggressive action of any other Power'. The Four-Power Treaty was little more than a diplomatic device to end the Anglo-Japanese alliance.

(3) The most important part of the Conference related to the position of China. By the Nine-Power Treaty (America, Britain, Belgium, France, Italy, China, Japan, the Netherlands and Portugal) all the Powers bound themselves to respect 'the sovereignty, independence and integrity of China', to provide the fullest opportunity to China to establish a stable government in China, to maintain the principle of equal opportunity for the commerce of all nations and to refrain from taking advantage of conditions in China for seeking any special right or privilege.

(4) By a separate agreement between Japan and China alone, Japan agreed to restore to China Kiachow territory, Shantung and the port of Tsingtao. Britain eventually restored Weihaiwei.

Though the decisions of the Conference were described as 'a blessing to all mankind', the settlement lacked any means of enforcement to maintain the arrangements it proclaimed. Moreover, China's internal disorder inhibited her growth as a nation state and checked the proposed revision of the unequal-treaty system.

Hardly had the Washington Conference been ended, when civil war broke out in northern and central China, which was divided between the authority of rival Tu-Chuns or provincial governors. In the extreme north, Manchuria became virtually independent under the energetic Chang-

Tso-Lin. In the Centre, Wu Pei-fu, the most powerful of several Tu-Chuns, failed to provide a national leadership. In the south, Canton was the headquarters of the Kuomintang (KMT) or nationalist party, led by Dr. Sun Yat Sen.

Sun's charismatic personality enabled him to emerge as a leader to mobilise the revolutionary forces for the unification of China. But his efforts were unavailing in the face of the dominating influence of the warlords. He soon made a working alliance between Soviet internationalism—Comintern—and Chinese nationalism. The Second Congress of the Chinese Communist Party (CCP) favoured an alliance with the Kuomintang (KMT). With Soviet advice Sun began the establishment of a party army and sent in August 1923 his military assistant Chiang Kai-Shek to the Soviet Union to gain first-hand knowledge of its military system. In September 1923, Sun took as his chief adviser an able Russian, Michael Borodin, who had been a Comintern agent in Mexico, Spain and Turkey. At Canton, Borodin, drafted the KMT's new constitution and began to organise mass support through a political institute. In 1924 the Soviet Union signed a treaty with the Peking Government and established close relations with the Nationalist movement at Canton. A military academy was established near Canton, under the direction of Chiang Kai-Shek. Thus, under Russian guidance, the government at Canton had been transformed into a powerful revolutionary organisation.

Sun's attitude was both self-confident and practical. He wrote a plan for material reconstruction, published in English as *The International Development of China*, which envisioned extensive foreign investment for China's economic growth. Sun did not accept the Leninist thesis that capitalism inevitably produces imperialism. He put forward a set of ideas to justify a republican revolution. This was the three Principles of the People—Nationalism, Democracy and Socialism. Sun piously hoped to make the government the machinery, and the people the engineer. Of the three principles, nationalism was the cardinal point. At the Kuomintang First Congress in January 1924, he emphasised the three cardinal principles—alliance with the Soviet Union, collaboration with the Chinese Communists and development of workers' and peasants' mass movement.

After his untimely death on March 12, 1925, Sun became the object of a revolutionary cult. His writings became a source of inspiration to the national movement against foreign control and his Three Principles of the People became the nationalist Bible. To promote his cause the National Government was formed at Canton on July 1, 1925 as a military-party dictatorship with Wang Ching-Wai, one of Sun's political heirs, as its chairman.

Meanwhile, both KMT and CCP saw the twin evils of 'Imperialism' and 'Warlordism' as the enemies of 'nationalism'. Early in 1925 strikes increased in Shanghai and elsewhere. On May 20, 1925, at Shanghai, Chinese students organised a peaceful demonstration against conditions of labour in the Japanese-owned mills. They were fired upon by the police of the International Settlement, commanded by an Englishman. The incident aroused a storm of protest throughout the country. This was followed on June 23, by a similar occurrence when the demonstrations were fired upon by the British police, the result being the so-called Shakee-Shameen massacre in the vicinity of Canton. The immediate reaction was a great 15-month strike and boycott against Hong Kong and against British trade in general.

These tumultous events marked the onset of high tide for the Nationalist Revolution. But the surging tide of nationalism was thwarted by the antagonism between supporters and opponents of links with the Communists. Despite obvious strains, the alliance between the Kuomintang (KMT) and the Chinese Communist Party (CCP) continued. Alarmed by the growth of the Communist influence, Chiang Kai-Shek on March 20, 1926, staged a *coup d'etat* at Canton, ousting part of the Communist leadership and some Soviet advisers while maintaining the link of Moscow-Canton alliance.

Chiang now launched in July 1926 the great military campaign against the warlords of the North (the Northern Expedition). The Nationalists had realised 'the ultimate cause of all the difficulties, and sufferings of the Chinese people lies with the aggression of the imperialists and the cruelty and violence of their tools, the nation-selling warlords.' As the army passed through the country, it was received as a force of liberation.

In the beginning of 1927, the Nationalist Government established itself in Hankow and tried to become the central authority for the whole of China. Meanwhile the preponderating anti-Communist view split the Kuomintang in two factions—the left wing supporting the communists and the right wing Chiang and his protagonists.

The confused events of early 1927 highlighted the rise of Chiang Kai-Shek. On March 10 at Hankow, the left wing of the party, by a resolution, deposed Chiang from the post of commander-in-chief. On April 6, the Peking authorities seized from the Soviet Embassy incriminating documents of subversion. Meanwhile, at Shanghai, on April 12, Chiang's forces destroyed the armed Chinese Communist organisation by a sudden coup. On April 18 Chiang set up his own government at Nanking. The Hankow Government retorted by expelling him from the party and appointed Feng Yu-Hsiang to the chief military command. But the left wing of the KMT, alarmed by the discovery, in June, of secret instructions to Borodin from Moscow, to supplant the Kuomintang by the Chinese Communist Party, broke in July with its Communist colleagues and expelled them. The Chinese Communists were arrested wholesale, and Borodin and his mission left for the Soviet Union. Communist putsches at Swatow in September and Canton in December 1927 both misfired.

The way was now open for Chiang Kai-Shek and the right-wing Kuomintang leaders to build up the Nanking Government as the central government of China. In the spring of 1928 the Chinese Nationalist army mounted its offensive against the North and threatened Manchuria, where the influence of Japan was paramount. In June the Nationalists occupied Peking. This marked the attainment of the objective towards which the revolutionary movement had been working since 1905. In July, the National Government received recognition from the United States and, by the end of 1928, general international recognition. Despite Japanese efforts to prevent the reunion of China and Manchuria, the end of 1928 saw its accomplishment. China's unity now became a reality, even though Japan and Russia still held special positions in Manchuria.

Decade of the Nanking Government

The Nanking period from the reunification of China in 1928 to the Japanese attack of 1937 forms a distinct epoch which found the Western world absorbed in its own problems. Simultaneously the mounting aggression of Japan and the militancy of the Chinese Communists kept alive the peasant unrest. Throughout its existence the Nationalists Government, under Chiang Kai-Shek, showed almost a dual personality. Neither democratic nor totalitarian, the regime looked both to the modern West and to the Chinese cultural heritage. But the government leaned heavily on its Westernization programme leaving the countryside in the hands of those landlord-warlords who had not yet been displaced in the outlying provinces.

In October 1928, a Government Organisation Law was promulgated by the Central Executive of the Kuomintang. Chiang Kai-Shek became the President. Since the party controlled the National Government, the Political Council, which usually headed the government, was merely a wing of the Central Executive Committee. A number of ministries—Organisation, Information, Social Affairs, Overseas Affairs—were formed under the Central administration. Sun Yat-sen's five-power system came into being under five yuans—Executive, Legislative, Judicial, Control or Censor, and Examination *i.e.* Civil Service. The Executive Yuan with its dozen big ministries of Foreign Affairs, Finance, Economic Affairs, Education, Justice, Communications, War, Navy became the most important. With little financial control, the Legislative Yuan had much less power than a parliament.

The authority of the National Government had yet to be established over the whole of China. The National Government directly controlled only the provinces at the mouth of the Yangtze River. Elsewhere, the authority of the government was dependent upon a combination of alliances with Feng Yu-hsiang, Yen Hsi-Shah and the Kwangsi generals who were in control of the region centering at Hankow. In the spring of 1929, a quarrel broke out between Chiang Kai-shek and Feng Yu-hsiang which led to the latter's expulsion from the Central Executive of the Kuomintang (May 23). From March to September 1930 a violence erupted in North China involving a million men in which Feng and Yen tried to usurp power. But Chiang Kai-Shek, with the support of the Young Marshal from Manchuria, Chang Hsueh-Ling, succeeded in putting down the revolt. Despite the victory of the National Government, embers of discontent were slow to die down. An anti-Chiang wing of the Kuomintang centred at Canton while the local militarists maintained control in Yunnan, Szechwan, Shansi, Sinkiang and other provinces. The Japanese in Manchuria became a source of irritation to China. Year after year central government forces had to grapple with these problems either by arms or by negotiation to maintain the facade of national unity.

Domestic Policy of the Nationalist Government

The National Government pursued a plan of development to strengthen the economy of the country. Finance was the government's most pressing need. More than thirty foreign banks still operated in the treaty ports, financing foreign trade and issuing, in some cases, their own bank notes. The biggest was the Hong Kong and Shanghai Banking Corporation. Meanwhile the hundred Chinese banks had issued great quantities of depreciating bank notes. In 1924 the Kuomintang had established the Central Bank of China at Canton. In 1928 it was reorganised in Shanghai to act as a central bank of issue and government treasury. At the same time the Bank of China was reorganised to deal with the foreign exchange business. In 1933 the Farmers Bank of China was set up to provide farm credit. In the same year was created the National Economic Council to initiate and coordinate economic development.

As finance minister until 1933, T. V. Soong carried through a fiscal revolution—recovery of tariff autonomy and increase of customs revenue, readjustment of foreign debts and domestic loans, and reforms of taxation. In November 1935 China nationalised all the old silver currency in the country and substituted a paper currency. Central Government revenues doubled between 1929 and 1936. But Nanking's policy was not designed to encourage production at home and the available resources went mainly to support the military or the 'bureaucratic capitalists'. More progress was perhaps made in transportation than in industry. Total mileage grew from 7,700 (12,320 km) in 1926 to 9,800 (15,680 km) by 1935. The building of 60,000 miles (96,000 km) of roads facilitated road transport. After depression of the early 1930s, China's economy by 1937, seemed more prosperous.

Foreign Policy of the Nationalist Government

In its foreign policy, the Nationalist Government tried to terminate all "unequal" treaties. The Western Powers signed new treaties that restored tariff autonomy to China. But in the case of the abolition of the extraterritorial rights for the foreigners, the Powers refused to consider anything except a gradual abolition of the system.

In 1929 the Nationalist Government had a serious quarrel with the Soviet Union. The dispute was due to the Bolshevik propagandist activities in Northern China and an attempt by the Governor of Manchuria, Chang Hsueh-Ling, to gain complete control of the Chinese Eastern Railway. In June and July, the Soviet Consular offices in a number of Manchurian cities were raided. The Soviet Union retaliated by arresting many of the visiting Chinese merchants in Russia. Diplomatic relations were severed and war appeared to be imminent. But the war was averted when the United States and forty one other signatories of the Kellogg Pact reminded the disputants of their obligations to settle the dispute by peaceful means. By the Khabarovsk Protocol of December 1929 the *status quo ante* was reestablished.

Manchurian Crisis

From the economic point of view, Manchuria assumed tremendous importance in China. The land not only grows numerous crops in abundance but her mineral resources include large quantities of coal, iron, gold, silver, lead, copper and asbestos. In 1928, Manchuria alone was responsible for almost one-third of exports of

China and about one-fifth of the imports. Apart from her economic importance, the Kuomintang Government regarded Manchuria as a vital outpost of Chinese culture. More than four million Chinese were reported to have entered Manchuria between 1923 and 1929. At the end of 1930 the numerical disparity between the Chinese and the Japanese was revealed when out of a population of 29 million, there were only 250,000 Japanese. The Nationalist Government, therefore, was anxious to restrict the encroachments of foreigners in the area.

Among the world's industrial powers, who had more or less commercial interests in Manchuria, the Soviet Union and Japan felt that they had special rights. The Soviet Government was half-owner of the Chinese Eastern Railway, a line more than a thousand miles (1,600 km) long, which offered the most direct route from the west to the Siberian port of Vladivostok. The Japanese, too, had control of a railroad, the South Manchuria Railway. This line, seven hundred miles (1,120 km) long, was economically important as more than half of the foreign trade of China passed through the line. Moreover, the foreign banking business of Manchuria was almost a monopoly of Japanese firms.

For some years after the Treaty of Versailles, Japan's balance of trade was in a favourable position, the United States being the heavy purchaser of silk. But with the appearance of the world depression and the increasing popularity of rayon and other silk substitutes there was a notable decline of Japan's export. Compared with 1929, Japanese raw silk exports in 1930 suffered a loss of 18 per cent in quantity and about 45 per cent in value. In an attempt to lower production costs, Japan abandoned the gold standard in 1931. The effect of the Japanese economy of falling prices and contracting markets was intensified by the problems of overpopulation. Japan found it impossible to obtain assistance from the United States or Britain, since they too were facing economic crises. In these circumstances, Manchuria, with its plentiful resources, undeveloped opportunities and strategic location offered a tempting field for exploitation to Japan. The idea became ingrained in Japanese thinking that "Manchuria was economically indispensable not merely to the well-being, but even to the continued existence of Japan. This view was based upon the apparent need of control of the coal and iron and other resources of Manchuria by an industrialised Japan."[3]

To counteract the Japanese influence in Manchuria, China built a separate railway system, with a total length of nearly 625 miles (1,000 km), and made efforts to route all freight through this line. Anti-Japanese feeling of the Chinese was heightened when it was felt that complete national unity could be attained only by terminating the special position of Japan in Manchuria.

Conditions in China in 1931 were volatile. The Kuomintang was rent by two factions—the right and left wing. Famines and floods added to the confusion while the Communist propaganda was rife. Japan, therefore, seized the opportunity for the realisation of her dreams in Manchuria.

The ascendancy of the army in the Japanese Government precipitated the crisis. During the years 1930 to 1932 the military held the lever of political control. High-ranking military officers, both in Tokyo and Manchuria, therefore, prepared to make a final show-down. Unfortunately for China, there occurred in 1931 two incidents which ignited the inflammable passions that were brewing between the two countries.

In August 1931 came the murder of Captain Nakamura, a Japanese officer, by Chinese soldiers in the interior of Manchuria. The Chinese alleged that he was either a military spy or an officer on a special military mission. The incident had a tremendous effect in inflaming Japanese opinion. China was also conscious of the extremely delicate situation as was evident from Chang Hsueh-Liang's telegram on September 6 to the garrison in Mukden:

> Our relations with Japan have become very delicate. We must be particularly cautious in our intercourse with them. No matter how they may challenge us, we must be extremely patient and never resort to force, so as to avoid any conflict whatever.

On September 18, 1931 the Japanese themselves blew up a short stretch of South Manchuria

---

3. Vinacke H. M.: *A History of the Far East in Modern Times* (1967), P. 505.

Railway and put the blame on the Chinese soldiers. On this flimsy pretext the Japanese army moved and occupied Mukden and its environs.

Meanwhile, the Chinese Government appealed to the League of Nations and the United States. But this did not deter Japan from extending her area of occupation in Manchuria. In February 1932, Japan set up a puppet state in Manchuria, which it called Manchukuo—and declared that the latter had severed all ties with China. Then it placed the ex-Emperor of China, Pu-yi, on the puppet throne as Emperor.

Japan's activities exerted a unifying influence upon Chinese politics. In December 1931 a reconciliation took place between the right and left wings of the Kuomintang. The Chinese People resorted to nationwide economic boycott of Japanese goods which crippled Japanese industry. In January 1932, the Tokyo government attempted to suppress anti-Japanese movement in Shanghai by a display of naval force. The Japanese marines inevitably clashed with the local Chinese garrison. The vigorous Chinese resistance and the approaching rainy season put a stop to the fighting and both sides accepted an armistice.

International Reactions

China had appealed to the League under Article XI of the Covenant. The Council endeavoured to persuade Japan to withdraw her troops within the railway zone. By mid-October 1931, however, when it appeared that far from withdrawing, Japan was advancing troops, the Council, on October 24, proposed to fix a date by which the withdrawal was to be complete. The resolution was rejected by the single adverse vote of the Japanese delegate. The ineffectiveness of Article XI conciliation procedure revealed the weakness of the League to impose its will on the recalcitrant state. As a last resort, in December 1931, the Council decided to send a commission of enquiry of the five major powers (Britain, France, Germany, Italy and the United States) under the chairmanship of Lord Lytton to investigate the whole Sino-Japanese relations and recommend possible solutions.

While the Commission was at work, the U.S. Secretary of State issued a famous statement on January 7, 1932, that became known as the 'Stimson Doctrine'. The United States, it declared, would not recognise any treaty or situation brought about in violation of the Kellogg Pact. In September 1932, before the report of the Lytton Commission was published, Japan affronted the League by officially recognising the 'State of Manchukuo'. The Lytton Report was received in Geneva in September and was considered successively by the Council and the Assembly. It was an authoritative document, which condemned in general the Japanese action, suggested the withdrawal of the Japanese troops, and the establishment of an autonomous regime in Manchuria under Chinese sovereignty. The Report skilfully avoided the application of the sanction under Article 16 of the Covenant. The only penalty recommended in the report was non-recognition of Manchukuo. In February 1933, these recommendations were accepted by the League Assembly and a month later Japan withdrew from the League. The weakness of the League and the efficacy of the collective security system were shamefully exposed.

During 1933 events moved rapidly. Despite her diplomatic defeats at Geneva, Japan continued to win military victories in northern China. From January to May the Japanese forces penetrated into the rich province of Jehol and into the regions south of the Great Wall. Since the League was impotent to prevent Japanese aggression, China accepted an armistice at Tangku (May 31). Under this agreement the Japanese were to return north of the Great Wall and China consented to the creation of a demilitarised zone south of the Wall.

The impotence of the League and the weakness of China gave Japan an opportunity to assert her position as the dominant power in the East Asia. In April 1934, Japan declared explicitly her special responsibilities in East Asia and observed that 'there is no country but China which is in a position to share with Japan the responsibility of peace in East Asia'. This declaration, which came to be known as 'Japan's Monroe Doctrine' was repeated in subsequent pronouncements. In 1935 Tokyo promoted 'friendship' with her neighbour by inciting a separatist movement in North China to set up an autonomous Hopei-Chahar State under Japanese tutelage. This effort collapsed in

December in the face of the Peiping student demonstration.

Meanwhile, Chiang Kai-Shek's attitude throughout was one of appeasement. He believed that the Kuomintang must first establish its power over the Chinese, and especially over the Communists, before it could launch a fullscale war against Japan. He, therefore, followed a strategy of 'unification before resistance' and mounted his anti-Communist campaigns in 1931-35. But his policy of fighting Chinese rebels and not Japanese invaders caused widespred discontent. A 'National Salvation Association' organised in 1936 by non-communist politicians and intellectuals, criticised Chiang's policy. Student strikes and demonstrations were organised calling for immediate resistance and a united front.

On December 12, 1936, took place a dramatic incident when Chiang was kidnaped by his own troops and threatened with execution unless he ceased the attacks on the Communists and began military operations against the Japanese. Chiang was about to be executed when he was released at the intercession of Mao Tse-tung and Chou En-Lai. For Mao believed that Chiang Kai-Shek was temporarily necessary to hold together the Kuomintang to fight back the Japanese. The Communists agreed to fight under Chiang Kai-shek in return for a promise of reform and a war of resistance against Japan.

Meanwhile, in Japan, the conflict between the civil and military branches of the government precipitated an election in April 1937. The moderate elements won an overwhelming victory. Sato, the Foreign Minister, urged the necessity of reduction of garrison in North China. This was promptly disregarded by the advocates of force who created a situation from which there was no point of return. Out of a clash between Japanese and Chinese at Marco Polo Bridge, a few miles from Peking in July 1937, there developed a full-scale war.

The Chinese announced their readiness to fight to the death and Tientsin and Peking became the scenes of bitter warfare. At Shanghai the Nationalist armies fought hard but suffered severe losses. Thousands of civilians and refugees were killed by Japanese bombs. In September 1937 the Communist armies in the north mobilised against the Japanese. Meanwhile the League of Nations referred a Chinese appeal to its Far Eastern Advisory Committee. This Committee unanimously condemned Japan's policy and urged a meeting of the signatories of the Nine-Power Treaties of 1922. Fifty members of the League endorsed the Committee's findings, expressed moral support of China and called a meeting at Brussels. The Brussels Conference, which met in November 1937, without any representative from Japan, achieved nothing except framing a resolution condemning Japan's aggression and a twelve-page innocuous report.

By the end of the year 1937 Nanking was in Japanese occupation and Yangtze was under their control. After the fall of Nanking in December 1937, Japan set up a puppet 'Provisional Government of China at Peking'. In Central China, Japan also installed a puppet 'Reform Government' at Nanking in March 1938. The Japanese armies carried everything before them. Hankow, which had become the temporary capital, fell in July 1938, and in October Canton was occupied. 'Foreign sympathy China appeared to have in abundance, but little foreign aid.'

The sinking of the United States naval vessel *Panay*, and damage to the British *Ladybird* in December 1937, brought the two powers in confrontation with Japan. But the Depression inhibited both the United States and Britain from contemplating war with Japan. After the Panay incident, Roosevelt would have liked to enforce economic sanctions against Japan. He was to return to this policy in 1940 and 1941 with crippling effects.

In November 1938 the Japanese Prime Minister Prince Konoe made it clear to Chiang Kai-Shek and the world that Japan would never leave China. Japan would establish a 'New Order in Asia' in which there would be no room for Western Powers. But Japan was concerned with the attitude of Soviet Russia whose military potential in the Far East might jeopardise Japan's spoliation of China. Moreover, the presence of the United States navy in the Pacific posed greatest threat to Japan.

It is not surprising that militarist Japan eventually became more sympathetic to Nazi Germany and Fascist Italy as both the powers were not critical of Japan's aggression in China. On September 27, 1940, a Three Power Pact was signed between Japan, Germany, and Italy. Japan recognised Germany's and Italy's new leadership in the establishment of a 'new order in Europe'. Germany and Italy recognised the 'leadership of Japan in the establishment of a new order in Greater Asia'. Japan expected that this pact would discourage the United States to take active interest in the Far East.

But the Tripartite Pact did not deter the United States from pursuing a dynamic policy in the Far East. Since 1931 the United States had espoused the principles of the Open Door, China's integrity and non-aggression, but avoided any military confrontation with Japan. But the Tripartite Pact made the United States more anti-Japanese than before. She indeed stepped up her support to Chiang Kai-Shek. Soon after Roosevelt declared 'No combination of dictator countries of Europe and Asia will stop the help we are giving to ... those who resist aggression, and who now hold the aggressors far from our shores'. Despite this bold statement of policy, Roosevelt was anxious to negotiate a settlement as he rejected Churchill's prompting of a joint Anglo-American forward policy against Japan.

Negotiations began in Washington between the Japanese ambassador Nomura and Secretary of State Cordell Hull in the spring of 1941. Meantime, Japan signed a neutrality pact with the Soviet Union and was extending her military base in Southern Indo-China. The United States reacted by placing a total embargo on all exports to Japan. This effectively cut Japanese oil imports and produced in Japan the 'Crisis of the dwindling stockpile'. In mid-August 1941, Nomura suggested a meeting between Prime Minister Konoe and the American President Roosevelt. But the American State Department insisted that, before any meeting took place, Japan should desist from a southern drive of conquest, and should agree to withdraw troops from China and to abrogate the Tripartite Pact. Japan was willing to halt its southern expansion, but not to make any withdrawal from China. Negotiations, therefore, dragged on through October and November 1941. In Japan opinion gained ground that war with the United States and Britain was inevitable and these negotiations were little more than window-dressing. The formation of a new government in Japan under General Tojo in October 1941 presaged that the moment for war was near at hand.

Meanwhile the American Secretary of State, Cordell Hull, was opposed to any compromise with Japan. The last chance to postpone the war came in November 1941 when Japan offered as a temporary *modus vivendi*: withdrawal of Japanese troops from Indo-China in return for oil and a United States 'hands off' policy towards China. Roosevelt was interested, but Hull refused to change. On November 26, 1941, he submitted to the Japanese the well-known Hull Note—a ten-point programme—requiring them to withdraw all their armed forces from Indo-China and China. Behind this uncompromising stand there lurked a belief that Japan would not dare to attack the United States. At Tokyo, the Japanese leaders considered the Hull Note as an ultimatum and decided to attack United States, Britain and the Netherlands simultaneously. On December 7, 1941, the Japanese attacked the United States fleet at Pearl Harbour.

With America's entry into the war against Japan, the Kuomintang Government received substantial military aid from the United States. But little effective use was made of these supplies. General Stilwell (who was in command of American forces in China, Burma and India) soon discovered that Chiang Kai-Shek was more concerned in combating the Chinese Communists than in defeating the Japanese.

Meanwhile, Britain and the United States signed treaties with China on January 11, 1943 abolishing extraterritorial rights and special privileges in China. The conception of equality gave China a position as a Great Power. And, finally, at the Cairo conference in 1943, it was agreed that the war would be waged until Japan had unconditionally surrendered.

With the increasing hold of the Communists on the north, Mao Tse-tung moved his headquarters at the end of 1936 to the town of Yenan. Here Mao spent much of his time in longterm planning for what he regarded as his inevitable victory. The Communists rarely attempted large scale fighting against the Japanese, but concentrated instead on guerrilla warfare.

It appeared to the United States that the best way to ensure the integrity of China was to bring the Communist Party into a coalition government with the Kuomintang. It was felt by the U.S. Government on November 14, 1944:

> In seeking to determine which faction we should support we must keep in mind these basic considerations: Power in China is on the verge of shifting from Chiang to the Communists. If the Russians enter North China and Manchuria we obviously cannot hope to win the Communists entirely over to us, but we can through control of supplies and post-war aid expect to exert considerable influence in the direction of Chinese nationalism and independence from Soviet Russia.

With Japan's surrender in August 1945, the long foreseen Chinese civil war began between the Kuomintang and the Communists. In the initial stage it appeared that the Kuomintang would emerge as the victors. They could field more divisions, they received generous American aid, and they controlled most of the cities and railways. The Communists hoped for support from Russia, but somewhat unexpectedly, the Soviet Government made a treaty with Chiang Kai-Shek's Government in August 1945. The Moscow Agreement between Britain, the United States and Russia of December 1945 urged 'a unified and democratic China under the National Government'. When the Japanese surrendered, a Russian army entered Manchuria, and remained in control until it was withdrawn in May 1946.

Meanwhile, the United states was trying to prevent the spread of the civil war and to seek a political solution of the question. Americans had come to realise that if civil war broke out 'the Communists would inevitably win ... because the foreign powers, including the United States, which would support the Government, could not feasibly supply enough aid to compensate for the organic weaknesses of the Government. In this unhappy dilemma, the United States should attempt to prevent the disaster of civil war ... The desirable means to this end is to encourage the reform and revitalisation of the Kuomintang so that it may survive as a significant force in a coalition government. If this fails, we must limit our involvement with the Kuomintang and must commence some cooperation with the Communists, the force destined to control China.'

With this end in view, General George C. Marshall was sent in December 1945 by President Truman to Chungking to seek a political solution of the Civil War. In January 1946 a cease-fire was issued by both armies and plans were drawn for a coalition government. In February a military merger was agreed to. But Marshall's efforts proved to be short-lived. Disillusioned with the rigid attitudes of both Chiang and Mao, he encouraged a third group, the Democratic League, which had the support of the intellectuals and middle classes. But the Democratic League was crushed by Chiang's secret police.

From the mid-1946 the civil war was renewed. The Nationalists' confidence in their superior armament and the Communists' shrewd calculation of the Nationalists' vulnerability made reconciliation impossible and plunged the country into a vortex of civil war. In the beginning it seemed that the Nationalist forces, by numerical superiority (numbering about three million) as by massive aid of the United States, must win this struggle. The United States aid to China between August 1945 to early 1948 amounted to over two billion dollars. The Nationalist forces spread out to major cities and provincial capitals and even into Manchuria. But behind the apparent superiority of the Nationalists lay the germs of their failure. The nationalist forces, much against American advice, became overextended and their stretched-out supply lines were the target of Communist guerrilla attacks. Corruption, demoralisation and desertion steadily depleted their armies. Moreover, the Nationalists failed to establish a sound economic base to sustain the military machine. There was rapid inflation. Prices doubled 67 times between January 1946 and August 1948 and then 85,000 times in six months. It has been said that a suitcase of bank-notes was required to pay for a meal.

Communist successes, however, were the result of their increased strength. Their armies manoeuvred in the countryside, recruiting among the populace and destroying railroads and strategic places. The superior discipline of the Communist armies was reflected when they respected peasant property rights than did the Nationalist troops. Supplies in the countryside were requisitioned, rather than looted. Communist propaganda was ever present. The unconcealed support given to the Nationalists by the United States was successfully interpreted as evidence of 'American imperialism'.

Early in 1948 the Communists controlled the northern half of China. Now Mao luanched large-scale military movements and one by one the cities were captured. In autumn 1948 the Nationalists lost the decisive battle for control of the Yangtze valley. The Nationalist forces surrendered on January 10, 1949. Dissension and jealousy among the commanders, failure to make effective use of air-force and American weapons illustrated the old adage that victory cannot be obtained by arms alone. In January 1949, Tientsin and Peking surrendered. In April the Communists overran the Yangtze, in May they occupied Shanghai, in October Canton and, in November, Chungking. In the summer of 1949 Chiang Kai-shek and the Nationalists fled to Taiwan which was recognised by the United States as the government of China.

On October 1, 1949 the People's Republic of China was proclaimed with Mao as Chairman of the Communist Party's Administrative Council and Chou En-Lai as Premier and Foreign Minister. The new regime was immediately recognised by the Soviet Union and its allies. The new government, Mao declared on July 1, 1949, should be a 'People's democratic dictatorship' based on democratic coalition under Communist leadership and, at the same time, a dictatorship directed against the reactionary classes or 'enemies of the people'.

Russo-Japanese War (1904-05): Causes and Effects

In the tangled politics of the Far East, the Russian attempt to absorb Manchuria threatened the territorial interests of both China and Japan and the commercial interests of Britain and the United States. The opening of the twentieth century saw a new course in the power relations among the Great Powers in the Far East. In Russia itself opinion was divided between the soft line of peaceful economic penetration of Manchuria, advocated by Witte as finance minister, and the hard line of military occupation advocated by the Russian military. Germany was also interested in Russian expansion in the Far East, anticipating that Britain's difficulties would lead to an Anglo-German alliance. Japanese counsels were divided between those who sought agreement with Russia, so that Japan could dominate Korea while Russia took Manchuria, and those who favoured armed action against Russia. The British were also not inclined to stop the Russian encroachment in Manchuria as the former considered Germany, more than Russia, as a potential rival for trade and naval power. An Anglo-Russian agreement of April 1899 and an Anglo-German agreement of October 1900, clearly revealed Britain's reluctance to stop Russian aggression in Manchuria.

Taking advantage of the Boxer War (1900) in China, Russia forced China to sign a sweeping draft agreement (the so-called Alexeiev-Tseng Agreement) which seemed to imply Russian absorption of Manchuria. Owing to the protests of the Great Powers, China refused to ratify the agreement and Russia finally withdrew it. The exposure of Russian militancy influenced the Japanese leaders to come closer to Britain. Public opinion in both countries had expressed support for a closer association. Anglo-Japanese alliance took place on January 30, 1902. The two powers declared that they recognised the independence of China and Korea. On the other hand, they recognised that both possessed special interests in China and that Japan was particularly interested in Korea. They agreed to safeguard those interests if threatened either by the aggressive action of any other Power or by disturbances arising in China or Korea. This alliance meant that Britain would help Japan against Russia. The alliance also would 'hold the ring', keeping France and Germany out of any Russian war against Japan. For Britain the alliance marked the end of her 'splendid isolation'. For Japan, it raised her prestige and placed her in the family of nations. It was also expected that the Alliance would stabilise the situation in the Far East.

The effect of this Alliance was that Russia agreed to withdraw her troops from Manchuria.

But the evacuation of troops was delayed. Moreover, Tsar Nicholas II, after dismissing gradualist Witte from power, created a Viceroyalty of the Far East. The situation demanded that Japan should take firm action. Japanese politics had also undergone changes after the Alliance of 1902. Yamagata Aritomo was the most authoritarian and aggressive statesman who was determined to achieve dominance over Korea and Southern Manchuria. Therefore, in the protracted Russo-Japanese negotiations of August 1903-February 1904, Japanese terms for a settlement were severe ones. Russian recognition of Japan's preponderant interests in Korea was to be qualified, while Japan offered to recognise only the Russian rights along the Manchurian railway. On the other hand, the attitude of Tsar Nicholas II appeared to be anything but conciliatory. He assumed that the Japanese would accept whatever concessions he chose to make rather than resort to war. Thus, by January 1904, both countries realised that an impasse had been reached when negotiations would be fruitless.

'At first sight the war appeared to be between two entirely unmatched antagonists, another case of the giant and the dwarf.'[4] Japan broke off diplomatic relations on February 6, 1904, surprised the Russian fleet at Port Arthur on the 8th and declared war on the 10th. In May, Japanese forces crossed the Yalu River into Manchuria, others invested Port Arthur and occupied Dairen. Port Arthur surrendered after a long siege in January 1905. In February and March 1905, the Japanese inflicted heavy defeats on the Russian forces in a 17-day battle for Mukden in Manchuria. The crowning disaster was the annihilation of Russia's European Baltic battle-fleet which had sailed halfway round the world to the straits separating Korea and Japan only to be sunk on May 27 by the Japanese fleet in the Straits of Tsushima.

After their resounding naval victory, Japan sought the mediation of the American President Theodore Roosevelt to bring the war to an end. With Roosevelt's diplomatic initiative, the peace conference met at Portsmouth, New Hampshire, in August and September 1905. The Treaty of Portsmouth (September 5, 1905) recognised Japan's paramount interests in Korea, restored China's sovereignty in Manchuria, gave Japan the Liatung Peninsula in South Manchuria and the southern half of Sakhalin Island. The Japanese people demanded reparation which the Russian refused to agree. With her financial resources weakened, Japan was in no position to continue the war. Even without an indemnity, the terms of the treaty established Japan as the foremost power in Asia. The Russo-Japanese war provided an opportunity for the nascent Japanese imperialism to grow—with far-reaching consequences in world politics. From a long-term point of view, Japan's victory stimulated the rise of Nationalism among Asian peoples. Not only in China but also in the Philippines, Vietnam, Indonesia and elsewhere, 1905 marked the dawn of organised freedom movements. Thus the stage was set for the end of Western dominance, the growth of Japanese imperialism, and the seed-time of indigenous Asian nationalism.

Japan exploited the new situation to her advantage. On August 12, 1905, the Anglo-Japanese alliance had been renewed for another five years. In June 1907 France and Japan agreed by treaty to respect the independence and integrity of China and to support each other's territorial rights and 'spheres of influence' in China. This was followed by Russo-Japanese convention of July 1907 by which they agreed to maintain China's independence and territorial integrity but secretly agreed to divide Manchuria into a northern sphere for Russian exploitation and a southern sphere for Japan.

Annexation of Korea (1910)

During the following years, Japan consolidated her position in Korea. In November 1905 a convention was made making Korea a Japanese protectorate and ending its diplomatic contact with other powers. Ito Hirobumi set up a Residency General to administer Korea, but leaving the Korean Emperor reigning. But when the Korean Emperor sent a secret mission to the Second Hague Peace Conference in 1907 to voice his protest against Japan's domination, he was forced to abdicate. Ito assumed wider pow-

4. Vinacke H. M. : *A History of the Far East in Modern Times* (1960), P. 182.

ers and disbanded the Korean army. Widespread riots followed and Ito had to suppress the riots with a heavy hand. But he held out against immediate annexation which was advocated by Yamagata and Katsura. But Ito was assassinated in Manchuria in October 1909 and the annexation of Korea took place in August 1910.

The early decades of the twentieth century were a golden age for Japan. By 1925 Japan was a far more industrialised country and a world power than at the close of the Russo-Japanese War. But it was during this golden age there appeared problems that were soon to overwhelm Japan. The Meiji leaders had been a close-knit group but, after achieving security for Japan, they gave way to a larger and more diverse leadership group. There was pressure from below among the influential merchants, administrators, landowners, and the educated elites, all claiming a share in the government machinery. They were not happy with an entrenched oligarchy which ruled Japan and monopolised all the important positions in the state. The army, its prestige raised after the Russo-Japanese war, demanded large share in the administration. The Meiji Constitution provided no clear mechanism for resolving difference of opinion. Though the Diet, the civil bureaucracy, and the army were knit together, no one of them was subordinate to any other. The demand for greater freedom, and a working parliamentary system became pronounced in Japanese politics in the 1920s. The educated Japanese became vulnerable to a cultural crisis of identity. Yet during the same period there were sufficient indications for the strengthening of the authoritarian control and in the 1930s Japan became a militarist state.

The First World War in Europe provided Japan an opportunity to strengthen her influence in Manchuria. Japan joined the Allied side in 1914 after mature deliberation. The oligarch, Yamagata, was convinced that the great war among the Western powers would be followed by a struggle between the 'yellow and white races'. He, therefore, ingratiated the favour of Russia and avoided confrontation with the United States. With China, he adopted a 'big brother' attitude and tried to foster an ethnic and cultural identity for competing with the 'so-called culturally advanced white races'. When the Japanese made their twentyone demands on China in 1915, the Western powers could do little to restrain Japan, beyond diplomatic pressure. Japan's policy of expansion seemed to be helped by the Communist Revolution in Russia in 1917. Accordingly, in 1918, Japan joined the Allies in the Siberian expedition ostensibly to crush the Russian Communists and secondarily to force Russia back into war against Germany. General Tanaka and other army officers had grandiose dreams of a Siberian empire as far as Lake Baikal, under Japanese influence. The expedition proved costly to Japan and in the end achieved nothing.

Japan's participation in the First World War brought no territorial gains apart from the German colonies in the Pacific. Moreover, the United States had viewed the Anglo-Japanese alliance with displeasure as it had enormously strengthened Japan's position in Asia. Japan's growing diplomatic isolation became evident at the Washington Conference in 1921-22. The Anglo-Japanese Alliance of 1902 was terminated and was replaced by a Four Power Treaty (Britain, France, United States and Japan). Japan agreed to return to China the Shantung province gained at the Paris Peace Conference. A naval limitation treaty placed Japan in a subservient position as she was allowed three battleships in comparison with five allotted to Britain and the United States, respectively. Finally, Japan became a signatory to the Nine-Power Treaty which pledged the territorial integrity of China. Thus, the Washington Treaties played a considerable check on Japan's aggressive imperialism in China.

Thwarted by the Great Powers, Japan's foreign policy underwent a change. The result was a change-over to internationalism and a thrust to pacific policy in Asia. This new policy is called 'Shidehara Diplomacy' after Shidehara Kijuro, Japan's foreign minister in 1924-27 and 1929-31. But the army which became dominant in Japan did not like the new foreign policy. Relations with the United States became sore by the passage of an immigration law in 1924 which excluded the Japanese from entering America. The rise of Chinese nationalism also posed a threat to Japan's position in Manchuria.

Domestic Affairs (1918-31)

The end of the First World War placed Japan in serious economic crisis. The phenomenal rise of the price of rice, Japan's staple food, led to serious riots all over Japan in 1918. Violent repression followed. The collapse of the war boom in 1921 led to left-wing movements. The devastating Tokyo earthquake in September 1923 added to the distress which was heightened by the attempts of the Communists and Socialists to seize power. The government pursued a repressive policy. The policy were given authority to arrest anyone suspected of subversive thoughts. Compulsory military training was resorted to by the authorities to counteract dangerous thoughts.

Along with economic troubles and political unrest appeared the weakness of the government. In 1921 Hara, the Prime Minister, an able politician, was assassinated. Two elder statesmen, Okuma and Yamagata, died in the following year. Their successors, with the possible exception of Kato, were found to be deficient in leadership. During the prime-ministership of Kato from 1924 to 1926, the government was both strong and apparently liberal. The suffrage was widened, thus increasing the electorate from 3 to 13 million. The administration of Kato was the highwatermark of parliamentary government in pre-war Japan.

The influence of the army, kept low for the time being, increased with the appointment of General Baron Tanaka as premier in 1927. More inclined to favour party government, and broader in outlook, Tanaka spoke of a positive foreign policy in Manchuria. This provoked an anti-Japanese reaction in China and Tanaka was compelled to abandon his Manchurian policy. In 1928 the Kwantung, the Japanese army in Manchuria, assassinated Chang Tso-lin, Japan's warlord in the area, with the hope that his son, Chang Hsueh-liang, would be more compliant with Japanese suggestions. Tanaka demanded the punishment of those responsible for the incident. But the Army High Command ignored the demand and Tanaka resigned.

Baron Tanaka was succeeded as premier in 1929 by Hamaguchi of the Minseito party. This was a return to a more committed constitutional government. At the London Naval Conference of 1930, Hamaguchi accepted a limitation of Japan's cruiser strength. This concession was considered reprehensible by the hawks. The army was split into factions. It ended tragically when a nationalist fanatic shot Hamaguchi in a Tokyo railway station who died a few months afterwards.

In the late twenties, Japan was beset by various problems. The domestic depression of 1926 was followed by a bank crisis of 1927 which wiped out a large number of small banks. The worldwide depression hit Japan early in 1930. The value of Japanese exports dropped 50 per cent from 1929 to 1931. Workers' real incomes dropped from an index of 100 in 1926 to 69 in 1931. Unemployment rose to about 3 million. In 1930 the 'bumper crop' famine occurred. This resulted in poverty in the countryside.

Party government acted effectively to counter the depression. Inukai of the Seiyukai, who became Prime Minister in December 1931, took Japan off the gold standard. This produced the boom in exports. By 1936 domestic consumption was up 20 per cent, unemployment dropped and the real wages of workers rose. Rural incomes recovered somewhat, the recovery came too late to benefit the parties.

Far more serious than the depression was the Manchurian incident of September 1931. For economic reasons Japan had to maintain her hold in China. Four-fifth of all Japan's overseas investment at the close of 1929 was in China. Japan's economic position was summed up by a journalist in 1929:

> Japan is a country whose territory is small and whose resources are scarce. It has to depend upon other countries for securing such materials. Furthermore, to sustain the livelihood of its excessive population, Japan finds it imperative to place a high priority upon exporting its products abroad.

Apart from economic considerations in Manchuria, where 75 per cent was Japanese investment and 40 per cent of Japan's China trade, the place had strategic importance to Japan. Ever since 1905, Manchuria had been looked upon by Japan as a buffer against Russian power in the north.

Despite economic and political considerations, Japan was not determined to reduce Manchuria to a colony. But the Kuomintang's unification of China and the rise of Chinese nationalism completely changed the situation. Contrary to Japan's political leaders, Wakatsuki and Shidehara, who argued for peaceful diplomacy, all groups in the army favoured bold action. In mid-September 1931, the Japanese troops invaded Mukden on the pretext of halting Chinese move in the Japanese owned South Manchurian Railway. By the end of the year, the whole of Manchuria was in Japanese hands. In February 1932, Japan set up a puppet state at Manchuria called Manchukuo and made the ex-Emperor of China, Henry Pu-yi, its puppet ruler. In 1933, the Lytton Commission appointed by the League of Nations condemned Japanese aggression and refused to recognise Manchukuo. Thereupon Japan withdrew from the League, while the army continued its expansion south of Manchuria.

In Japan itself the success of the Kwantung Army in Manchuria had important effects. In December 1931, the moderate Japanese cabinet which vacillated to take action, resigned. The next cabinet was formed by Inukai Tsuyoshi, the last party prime minister in pre-war Japan. Meanwhile, the army was gaining control in the decision-making functions of the cabinet. Inukai unsuccessfully sought to restrain the army in Manchuria. Therefore, he and others of his government were assassinated by ultra-nationalists on May 15, 1932. The days of the liberal were at an end and 'government by assassination' had taken their place.

The army did not have matters all its own way. The navy was less extreme and army activists were forced to accept two moderate premiers who were admirals, Saito Makato (prime minister May 1932-July 1934) and Admiral Okada Keisuke (July 1934-March 1936) for the years between 1932 and 1936. During the four years of government by the two moderate admirals there emerged patriotic societies which championed a wide range of ultra-nationalist doctrines. Fired with a keen sense of Japan's destiny, they all favoured Pan-Asianism and the exclusion of the West from continental Asia. They were opposed to the *Zaibatsu*, the bureaucracy and the political parties.

The period after the February Revolution of 1936 in Japan was the growing influence of the army and a resurgence of the political parties in opposition to the army-dominated government. In December 1936 Japan signed the Anti-Comintern Pact with Germany. Japan considered Soviet Union as her only serious enemy in the Far East and in the summer of 1937 she drew up a "Five-Year Plan for the production of War Material". The last thing Japan needed was a full-scale war with China. Despite these precautions, a clash between Japanese and Chinese troops near Peking in July 1937 developed into a general war, with disastrous results for Japan and the Far East.

War became the national cause and the Japanese Army obtained full national support. The Imperial Headquarters was formed in November 1937 to coordinate planning and operations between the army and the navy. A Liaison Council was formed in the same month which brought together for policy planning the prime minister, the service ministers, the foreign minister, the army and navy chiefs of staff. The National Mobilisation Law of April 1938 provided for the control of resources, labour, prices, wages and services, for censorship of the presses. Political parties were ended and a totalitarian state emerged.

In the early part of 1939 Japan sought to strengthen its position against Soviet Union. Most of the army and navy politicians favoured Germany. But Germany was not willing to ally with Japan against Russia alone but wished that Japan commit itself against Britain and America as well. The signing of a nonaggression pact between Germany and the Soviet Union in August 1939 upset Japanese calculation. 'Japan's foreign policy is in a state of having been practically betrayed'. Many leaders attempted to improve relations with the United States and Britain. But China remained the stumbling block. The American Secretary of State, Cordell Hull, was not willing to countenance Japanese aggression in China. Hence negotiations in this direction came to nothing.

The fall of France and the amazing German victories in Europe in the spring of 1940 completely changed the diplomatic situation. In

September 1940 Japan signed the Tripartite Pact with Germany and Italy. The Tripartite Pact made the United States more anti-Japanese than before. In April 1941 a neutrality agreement between Japan and Russia was signed and Japan felt she could breathe again. In June, Hitler attacked Russia without giving warning to Japan. Instead of honouring the Tripartite Pact with Germany, Japan decided to stick with the Russian agreement.

To carry forward policy in China, Japan needed strategic resources. The United States in 1940 banned exports to Japan of certain strategic materials. Japan feared that a total embargo might be put into effect by the United States at any moment, and Japan, therefore, looked to the oil-rich Dutch East Indies. With Russia neutralised, Japan decided to proceed south even at the risk of war with Britain and the United States. Japan attacked southern Indo-China in July 1941. America, together with Britain and the Dutch East Indies reacted by placing a total embargo on all exports to Japan. This produced in Japan a serious oil crisis. Tension now increased in Japan between the war party and those favouring negotiations. Premier Konoe tried to hold the balance between the two. Meanwhile negotiations went on in Washington. Secretary of State Cordell Hull submitted to the Japanese a ten-point programme requiring them to withdraw all their armed forces from Indo-China, China and Manchuria. The temporising Konoe was replaced by General Tojo Hideki who became premier in October 1941. On December 1, an Imperial Council voted to go to war with the United States. President Roosevelt made a last appeal to the Emperor, but without success.

On Sunday morning of December 7, 1941, the Japanese carrier-based planes destroyed the United States Pacific Fleet at its Pearl Harbour base in Hawaii. Immediately after Pearl Harbour, Japanese air force struck at the U.S. air base in Philippines. 'The crippling of the United States Pacific Fleet and the destruction of American air power in the Philippines, pulled the cork from the Southeast Asian bottle'. The way now lay open for the Japanese to sweep through Philippines, Borneo, and Celebes, and through Malaya and Sumatra, to Java. During the first few months of 1942, South-East Asia was overrun.

In the summer of 1942, Japan, however, experienced the first setbacks. Two inconclusive naval battles were fought, in the Coral Sea and near Midway Island. The Australians stopped the Japanese advance in New Guinea and the Americans gradually recaptured small islands in the Pacific.

After the Casablanca Conference in January 1943, the Allies agreed to harness their resources against Japan. From 1943 the tide of battle turned against Japan. During 1944 the Japanese were gradually pushed back. The British advanced in Assam and Burma, and in October the Americans under MacArthur landed in the Philippines. Japanese naval power was destroyed in the Battle of Leyte Gulf. Towards the end of July 1945, Britain, the United States and the Soviet Union at the Potsdam Conference called on Japan to surrender unconditionally. The Japanese response was a decision 'to press forward resolutely to carry the war to a quick end,' the Allies decided to use nuclear weapons. On August 6, 1945, the first atom bomb was dropped on Hiroshima, completely obliterating the city. Russia declared war on Japan on August 8, and began to invade Manchuria. The following day Nagasaki, major port, was destroyed by a second atomic bomb. On August 15, Emperor Hirohito said that Japan must 'endure the unendurable' and favoured unconditional surrender. Japan formally signed the Instrument of Surrender on September 2, 1945 on the American battleship *Missouri* in Tokyo Bay.

From September 1945 to April 1952, Japan was occupied, theoretically, by the Allied Powers who had defeated her, in practice by the Americans only. General Douglas MacArthur, a confirmed Republican, was in charge of occupation. Though lasting only seven years, the occupation was decisive for Japan's subsequent development. 'The Occupation was a success because it built on earlier trends, yet in crucial respects it produced changes which would not have occurred had Japan not fallen into American hands.' In some ways the changes were revolutionary, even though imposed from outside.[5]

5. Fairbank, Reischauer and Craig: *East Asia, The Modern Transformation* (1965), P. 811.

CHAPTER 42

ARAB NATIONALISM: THE MIDDLE EAST

The Middle Eastern policies in the nineteenth century were decided in the capitals of St. Petersburg, Paris and London, rather than those of Constantinople, Cairo and Teheran. In 1840-41, the Concert of Europe had curbed the ambition of the ambitious Mehmet Ali of Egypt of disturbing the peace of the Levant. Another concert in 1854-56 had taken appropriate steps to checkmate Tsar Nicholas I of Russia. The European 'spheres of interest' were mutually recognised, though expansion was objected to. For strategic reasons it was felt better to maintain the *status quo*.

Most of the European powers recognised the necessity of ensuring good government in these backward areas. This was vital to European commerce, strategy and communication. Its solution lay in garrisoning the area in sufficient strength. In the Middle East, the strength of the British navy, with the Indian army, gave the British an unassailable influence. But Britain was afraid of Russian influence as the latter appeared to the Asians the other imperial protector. This question bedevilled the British Foreign Office till the Anglo-Russian Convention of 1907.

From the end of the eighteenth century the crisis which gripped the Middle East emanated from the contact between the traditional orthodox Muslim society and Europe, which was militarily superior and full of reforming zeal. From the beginning of the nineteenth century, Middle Eastern governments were engaged in carrying discipline to their soldiers.

The Ottoman Empire was the first to introduce salutary military reforms. The two rulers—Selim III (1787-1807) and Mahmud II (1808-39)—replaced the traditional army with a European-model conscript army. The efficiency of the new army depended on a European-model centralised bureaucracy and a new type of officer trained in European discipline. Increasing centralisation not only pervaded the military affairs, but other spheres as well which enabled the Ottoman State to control its territory efficiently. The introduction of European military techniques encouraged absolutism in the Ottoman Empire which now dispensed with intermediary orders and institutions like the Janissaries.

The new class of military and civil official exposed to European ideas became increasingly disaffected towards the age-old traditional system with which the ruler was immersed. They were in favour of the adoption of constitutional parliamentary government, which, according to them, was the real foundation of European greatness. The vanguard of these progressive views was entertained by Midhat Pasha, a high official and minister of the Young Ottomans. Taking advantage of internal political dissension and external military threat, the Young Ottomans were responsible for persuading the new Sultan, Abdul Hamid II, to promulgate a new constitution in December 1876. The constitution provided for a parliament and made ministers responsible to it. The first parliament of 120 deputies proved to be short-lived. Convened in March 1877, it was dissolved by the Sultan in February 1878. However, the ghost of the parliamentary system of government haunted the intellectual classes for many years to come.

Despite the decent burial of the parliamentary system of government, the Hamidian period did not lag behind in its tendency towards modernisation and centralisation. As a modern writer, Bernard Lewis, writes: 'It would not be an exaggeration that it was in these early years of the reign of Abdul Hamid that the whole movement of the Tanzimat, of legal, administrative, and educational reform reached its fruition and its climax. And so, too, did the tendencies, already discernible under the Tanzimat regime, towards a new, centralised, and unrestrained despotism.'[1] It should, however, be remembered, that the progressive policies of the Hamidian period in promoting material welfare of the people—in promoting education and in developing railways and telegraphs—in a way brought about the downfall of the regime. Young men, steeped in Western ideas, as a result of proliferation of schools and colleges, began to question the efficiency of the despotic rule of the traditional Ottoman institutions. Thanks to over-centralisation and absolution of Hamidian rule, it now became easy to execute a successful *coup d' etat*, which could only be achieved by overthrowing the Sultan.

The Young Turk Revolution of 1908 was a culmination of the discontent of the intellectuals. In July a group of officers in the Third Army Corps stationed in Macedonia mutinied which, in a short while, became widespread. Troops loyal to the Sultan sympathised with the mutineers which compelled the former to capitulate and to restore the constitution of 1876 on July 24. But it was not destined to bring parliamentary system of government.

Until April 1904 there was an uneasy political truce between the officers organised into a Committee of Union and Progress and Abdul Hamid. A mutiny of the soldiers of the First Army Corps in Istanbul on 12 April enabled the Committee of Union and Progress to depose the Sultan and seize political power. Under the facade of parliamentary government, the officers began to rule with scant respect to constitutional government. Power lay at the hands of the officers who were not amenable to constitutional limitation. In 1911 there was split within the Committee and the Chamber of Deputies was dissolved in January 1912.

The general election, known as 'the big stick election', returned the Unionist. But in July a group of officers known as the 'Saviour Officers' engineered a conspiracy in the army which ultimately overthrew the Unionist government. The Sultan, Mehmed Reshad, Abdul Hamid's successor, appointed a new government much to the liking of the 'Saviour Officers'. But in January 1913 a group of Unionist officers, led by Colonel Enver Bey (1881-1922), stormed the cabinet meeting in which the Minister of War was fatally wounded. The cabinet was forced to resign and the Unionist domination was asserted which continued to remain till the end of the First World War. Thus the stable constitutional parliamentary government was replaced by unstable military rule which could only be propped up by appeal to the sword.

Iran

Iran was another country in the Middle East which proclaimed constitution before the First World War. Condition in Iran was somewhat different as, unlike the Ottoman Empire, she had not been subjected to radical Westernisation. Her army was weak and incapable of maintaining the internal security. Nasir al-Din Shah (1848-96) made a successful attempt at modernising the army. Iran largely remained a veritable symbol of oriental symbolism.

The country, however, felt the impact of the European influence in which Russia and Great Britain took the lead. Both powers tried to assert their supremacy in Iran as elsewhere in Central Asia. Long before political penetration, European economy brought Iran within its network through the activities of financiers. The telegraph, first introduced in 1858 and extended after 1862 by a British concern, the Indo-European Telegraph Company, marked the increasing European influence in Iran.

The impact of European diplomacy was felt in Iran. Both powers—Britain and Russia—had genuine concern in maintaining their respective influence in the country without antagonising each other. From the British standpoint, Iran had a strategic importance as it was an anteroom to India. After the Russian occupation of Khiva in 1874, the whole region to the north of Persia was placed under the administration of the Russian general, Lomakin. The fall of Khiva shifted the

1. Bernard Lewis: *The Emergence of Modern Turkey* (1961), PP. 174-75.

centre of gravity from Afghanistan to the Persian and Turkoman plains. It also exposed Herat—the 'key' not only to western Afghanistan, to Kabul, and to India, but also to Kandahar and the Persian Gulf.

The Shah of Iran was anxious to obtain British support in order to assert his sovereignty over the northern Turkoman. British statesmen evinced interest to occupy Merv—only twelve days' march from Herat—but Whitehall was not prepared to commit itself. British military agents in Khorasan viewed with concern the growing Russian influence. The Shah visited St. Petersburg in 1878 and inducted the Russian General Kosagovsky to organise a Cossack brigade. The British Foreign Secretary, Salisbury, wished to counteract the Russian influence before the situation got out of hand. To obtain the alliance or the neutrality of Persia, Salisbury offered Herat which Iran had long coveted. On 8 November 1879, a convention to that effect was drawn up, but Whitehall did not encourage the idea and the convention was dropped. The Liberal Government of England wanted to work amicably with Russia and stood aloof when a boundary agreement for part of the northern area was negotiated on December 21, 1881 between Russia and Iran. This Akhal-Khorasan Convention contained a secret clause in which Iran renounced any claim over Turkoman territory.

The India Office, till now obsessed with the Afghan situation, now became concerned with the recent convention which envisaged a Russo-Afghan clash. The British suggestion of occupying Merv and its dependencies for creating a buffer zone between the Russians and Afghans was rejected by the Shah. With the submission of Merv to the Russians in February 1884, Britain felt the absolute necessity 'to come to a clear understanding with Russia as to the exact line of the north and north-western frontiers of Afghanistan.' It was not until 1888 that the line was actually drawn.

While the Afghan frontier was being demarcated, Russian influence began to increase in Iran. In August 1887, the Shah agreed to consult the Tsar before he granted any commercial concessions to foreign companies. It appeared that Russia was intending to make Persia her sphere of influence, a policy which was not actively opposed by the Shah after the latter's failure to win the sympathy of Britain.

Meanwhile, the British Government was not enthusiastic of Iran's alliance. The conservative government had stuck to the Liberal's policy of Anglo-Russian amity. Refusing to compromise British foreign policy, Britain, in October 1887, sent to Iran Sir Henry Drummond Wolff to inaugurate a new era of Anglo-Russian friendship. But behind this policy there lay an inherent idea of partition of Iran into joint spheres of influence. Salisbury might dislike the idea, but Wolff was a zealous promoter of it. But it got a rebuff from Lansdowne, the British Viceroy of India, who pointed out that to permit Russia to build railways in northern Iran militated the principle of security on which the Raj had ever depended.

Alarmed by the financial exploitation of Iran by the British, in which Russia could play a low profile owing to her paucity of capital, the latter wanted to put a moratorium on any scheme for railway construction. In October 1890 the Shah, therefore, agreed to this proposition and put a ban on railway construction for a period of fifteen years.

The exploitation of Iran, however, came from a different source. The increasing intercourse between Europe and Iran had opened new avenues of exploiting Iran's resources which, in a way, drained her wealth. In 1890 the British were granted a monopoly of the production and export of Iranian tobacco. The concession aroused widespread opposition by the native merchants and moneylenders. They were supported by the Shia Ulama. The Shia's believed that the Hidden Imam would be resurrected to establish a reign of righteousness and the authority to interpret the Holy Law was vested in the *Mujtahids* or the theologians. The temporal ruler, who would recede into the background with the coming of the Hidden Imam, was bound to respect the authority of these *Mujtahids*.

The concerted opposition of the *Ulama* to the Shah appeared to grow with the active encouragement of the eminent *Mujtahids* of the Shia of the revered shrines of Karbala, Najaf and Kazimayn, that lay in the Ottoman Mesopotamia outside the control of the Shah. Fortified by *Fatwas* emanating from *Mujtahids* in Iran and Mesopotamia, the Iranian *Ulama* protested against the tobacco concession. They declared a boycott of tobacco and prohibited all forms of smoking.

Apart from the *Ulamas* and *Mujtahids*, another group—numerically inferior but potentially important—was drawn from the official and intelligentsia, who were themselves westernised. This group had to proceed very cautiously lest it might offend the religious susceptibilities of the Iranians. They adopted the method of presenting their European notions in a Muslim garb. One of these reformers, Malkam Khan, propagated these tactics in the following manner:

> As then Islam... is an ocean in which are accumulated all the sciences of the past times of Asia... As to the principles which are found in Europe, which constitute the root of your civilisation, we must get hold of them somehow, no doubt; but instead of taking them from London or Paris, instead of saying this comes from such an ambassador or that it is advised by such a government, ... it will be very easy to take the same principle, and to say that it comes from Islam, and that this can be soon proved.

Malkam Khan and his associate the famous Jamal-al-Din al-Afghani propagated this tactic in Iran. The protest against the tobacco concession was transformed into a protest against the Shah's regime.

All these elements including merchants found opportunities to act in concert. The agitation, thanks to the telegraph, spread like wildfire. Strengthened by the Russians who became suspicious of the growing British influence as a result of tobacco monopoly, the malcontents forced the Shah to cancel the concession. By this act the Shah implicitly admitted the changes of despotism and corruption. The tobacco protest exposed the weakness of the government and convinced the protesters that the government could be overthrown by a popular uprising. The murder of Nasir al-Din Shah in 1896 was the culmination of the protest. The murder took place at the instigation of Jamal al-Din Afghani whom the Shah had forcibly deported from Iran in 1891. The murderer, Mirza Muhammad Riza, a follower of Afghani, threatened Nasir al Din's successor with the same fate if he did not mend his policy. When asked that this bloodbath might precipitate disorder and confusion, he replied: 'Yes, that is true, but look at the histories of the Franks; so long as blood was not shed to accomplish lofty aims, the object in view was not attained.'

Conditions did not improve under Muzaffar al-Din Shah (1896-1907). Along with the smouldering discontent, Iran had to face the financial crisis that emanated mainly from her foreign debt. This evoked loud protest against foreign exploitation and effete administration. Secret societies or *anjumans* sprung up disseminating ideas of reform and modernisation. Some sixty activists met at a secret meeting on May 28, 1904, and drew up a programme of action consisting of eighteen articles, the main object being to bring about the revolution. But they were careful enough not to offend the Islamic regime by carrying out their programme. It required them to conform to the laws of Islam so that no member could be accused of heresy.

Very soon, another group, known as the Secret Society, was formed in February 1905—the object of which was to awaken the masses and to devise means of redressing abuses. In 1905 matters came to a head when popular agitation mounted against the Shah and his protegé and against the growing Russian influence. The Russo-Japanese War of 1904 and the revolution in Russia (1905) undoubtedly strengthened the hands of the revolutionaries. But the most potent source of trouble came from the new customs tariff introduced in 1903 which the merchants considered as oppressive. When the tariffs were enforced with rigour, there were widespread protests. A group of Teheran merchants took sanctuary in the shrine of Shah Abd al-Azim near the capital and demanded redressal of their grievances. Incidents of the ill-treatment of a *mullah* by the governor of Qazvin and the firing on a crowd demonstrating against the governor of Mashhad fanned the explosive situation.

In December 1905, the Prime Minister seized some of the merchants on the plea that they had raised the price of sugar. In consequence a group of merchants took refuge in a Teheran mosque and their number swelled by the *ulamas* and their followers. However, they were dislodged from the sanctuary by a rival *mulla*, who curried favour with the authorities. The protesters left the city and found sanctuary at Shah Abdal-Azim. There they remained and received encouragement from cross-sections of the people who were hostile to the Prime Minister. To put an end to the stalemate, the Shah issued a directive to the Prime Minister which promised equality before the law, a code, and the setting up of a ministry of justice for its implementation. The Shah's act pacified the protesters and the protesters soon got back to the capital.

But the Shah's act was a mere subterfuge with no intention to implement the promises. The secret societies and the *Ulama* revived their agitation and tried to win the allegiance of the people by exposing the Shah's treachery. In June 1906 riots ensued with the expulsion of two influential preachers from Teheran. Once again a large number of *ulamas* and merchants took refuge in Qum. Merchants of Teheran went on strike. On July 19, a large number of persons, about 12,000, took sanctuary in the gardens of the British Legation. The Shah now gave way and dismissed his unpopular minister. On August 5 he promised to convene a national consultative assembly. Elections were held in September and the assembly began its session on October 7. A Fundamental Law was promulgated on December 30, 1906 which was strengthened by a supplementary Fundamental Law on October 7, 1907.

The capitulation of the Shah was due to his dilatory policy. The two incompatible views—the Muslim traditionalist and the Western modernist—mingled in the Fundamental Laws. It has been emphatically declared in Article 2:

> At no time must any legal enactment of the Sacred National Consultative Assembly...be at variance with the sacred principles of Islam or the laws established by His Holiness the Best of Mankind (*i.e.,* the Prophet Muhammad).

In contrast, the constitution embodied provisions which were unmistakably European in character. Members of the National Consultative Assembly were to be elected by popular participation. And the Assembly represented the whole of the people of Iran. The sovereignty of the people was unequivocally expressed in some article. 'The powers of the realm are all derived from the people.' 'The sovereignty is a trust confided by the people to the person of the Shah.' The constitution provided separation of legislative, judicial and executive power and enjoined ministerial responsibility to the Assembly.

Later events were to prove the futility of such a constitution, which was the product of duress. Muzaffar al-Din, who opened the Assembly of October 7, 1906, died in the following January and was succeeded by his son Muhammad Ali Shah (1907-09). The new Shah and his minister could not reconcile themselves to the Assembly and their antipathy owed not a little to Russian intrigue. The net result was the breakdown of law and order which culminated in the assassination of the Prime Minister in August 1907 by a member of the secret society.

In December, the Shah tried to usurp untramelled authority by arresting the new Prime Minister and other ministers who were favourably disposed towards the Assembly. For the time being his efforts were foiled by popular clamour. In February 1908 the Shah narrowly escaped a bomb attack. In June the Cossack brigade stormed the Assembly, arrested popular leaders. On June 27 the Shah dissolved the Assembly and abolished the constitution. This provoked a rebellion in Tabriz, the capital of Azerbaijan, where the *Anjumans* rose in rebellion. Other pockets of resistance were Rasht and Isfahan and the Bakhtiari tribesmen of the latter by effecting junction with a force from Rasht, entered Teheran on July 13, 1909. On July 16, Muhammad Ali abdicated and the Assembly proclaimed his twelve-year old son, Ahmad Shah, as successor.

The Assembly, fortified by the new elections, met on December 5, 1905. Its record was uneventful as the Bakhtiari tribesmen wielding the political power, were not in a mood to perpetuate constitutionalism. The Russians were also trying to find an opportunity to exploit this volatile situation. Into this fluid situation appeared the ex-Shah who, in June 1911, landed at Teheran to regain his position. His attempt, however, met with a fiasco and the ex-Shah fled from the country. But the political turmoil plunged the country into anarchy and disorder. To safeguard their interests, the British landed troops in Bushire. The Russians did the same which they had commenced since the summer of 1909. The appointment of Morgan Shuster, an American, in May 1911 as Treasurer-General of Iran, antagonised the Russians and the latter demanded on November 24 his dismissal within 48 hours. Unable to resist the Russian pressure, the government wished to comply, but the Assembly refused to oblige. In this dilemma the government forcibly disbanded the Assembly and suspended the constitution. This sounded the death-knell of constitutionalism in Iran until the close of the Second World War.

Ahmad Shah, who attained his majority in July 1914, tried to resume parliamentary government. But the outbreak of the First World War affected Iran in various ways. The Germans and their Ottoman allies fanned popular opposition to the Russians and the British because of the latter's constant intervention in Iranian politics. The threat of Russian advance on Iran in November 1915 dispersed the Assembly which was not to meet again until 1921. By then, the war and its aftermath had thrown the country into vortex of anarchy out of which emerged a military adventurer, Riza Pahlavi.

Born in 1878, Riza Khan had been serving under Russian officers before the First World War and rose to the chief command in northern Persia with the withdrawal of the Russians during the war. In 1921 Riza suddenly appeared at Teheran at the head of a disciplined fighting force and set up a Nationalist government with himself as Minister of War. The absence of chronic interference by Britain and Russia in Iranian affairs gave him an admirable opportunity to modernise the army and put it under his personal control. The removal of the threat of partition of the country by foreign powers and the patriotic fervour that swept the country emboldened Riza to assert his authority over the capricious and weak ruler, Ahmed Shah. In 1923, Riza Pahlavi became the Prime Minister and taking advantage of the Shah's absence from the country, convoked the parliament or *Majlis* and forced the latter to grant him sweeping powers. Then in 1925 he caused the *Majlis* to depose the Shah *in absentia*. A special National Assembly was summoned towards the end of 1925 which elected Riza Pahlavi as Shah of Iran, with right of succession to his heirs. *The de facto* military dictator now became the *de jure* ruler of Iran.

Imitating the example of the Turkish leader Mustafa Kemal, Riza launched Iran into a wave of modernisation. He introduced various laws which curbed the influence of the Muslim religion and took steps to build up a modern secular state with European dress, calendar, weights and measures, and legal codes. He intensified the national patriotism by upholding the distinctive feature of its ancient heritage and by changing the unnational name of Persia to the ancient and racial name of Iran. He dismissed foreign military experts and made the army a well-knit disciplined unit. He also brought the autonomous desert tribes under the central authority. He tried to overcome the country's economic malaise by employing able foreign financial experts and made every effort to improve education and material well-being of the people. He undertook public works and railroad construction and placed women as equal to men in social status. Then he forced the Anglo-Persian Oil Company to accept a lease term (1933), cancelling the previous agreement of 1901. Apart from curtailing the company's sphere of interest, the agreement marked the triumph of a state which about a decade ago had been subjected to economic exploitation by foreigners. For more than a decade, from 1925 to 1941, Riza Khan ruled as an absolute ruler with the help of a subservient Assembly.

Egypt

Egypt, though in theory a vassal state of the Ottoman Empire, became practically independent in the first half of the nineteenth century when Mehmet Ali had wrung from Constantinople a privileged position for himself and his family. Under Mehmet Ali's grandson, Ismail (1863-79), Egypt made rapid strides. He assumed the title of Khedive in 1867 and inaugurated an era of reform with European culture as his model. He restructured the administrative system and helped Egyptian economy. He employed European engineers to build railways, telegraph lines, and breakwater at Alexandria. He encouraged the studies of Egyptian antiquities and founded a museum at Cairo. With great fanfare he celebrated the opening of the Suez in 1869, a project financed mainly by the French and constructed by a French engineer, Ferdinand de Lesseps. All these expensive undertakings involved huge sums obtained from foreign loans especially from Britain and France and by the imposition of heavy taxation on the Egyptians.

By 1870 Egypt had virtually become a European colony with 17 foreign consulates in the country, representing about 100,000 foreigners concentrated in Alexandria and Cairo. In the words of Cromer, Egypt 'must have been an earthly paradise for all who had money to lend at usurious rates of interest, or third-rate goods of which they wished to dispose at first-rate prices.'

France exercised immense influence over Khedive Ismail as a result of her financing the Suez Canal. Egypt had to bear the burden of heavy interest on sums borrowed for the canal's construction. Up to 1873 the total interest paid amounted to £ 6 million. The interest on Egypt's foreign loans amounted to about £ 5 million a year. In 1876 Stephen Cave, the British Pay-Master General, emphasised in his report that Egypt could not go on 'serving floating debts at 25 per cent and raising loans at 12 to 15 per cent to meet additions to her indebtedness which do not bring a single piastre into her single exchequer'.

As a way out of the impasse, Ismail gambled with the country's greatest asset, the Suez Canal, by offering to a French banker in 1874 the purchase of Egyptian 40 per cent ordinary shares, at a price of £ $3^1/_4$ million. In 1875 Disraeli bought these shares for over £ 4 million. The canal thus came under British control but financial relief was not forthcoming. In 1876 Ismail submitted Egyptian finances to a dual control of British and French agents. Financial crash came on April 8, 1878, when Ismail was forced to suspend payment on his Treasury bills. By a decree of May 2, he established an international *Caisse de la Dette Publique* consisting of representatives of France, Britain, Austria and Italy. A murky financial squabbles now vitiated the atmosphere in which self-interests of each nation became paramount.

When the *Caisse* funded the entire bonded and floating debt at £ 91 million, at $7^1/_2$ per cent interest, it raised opposition from the European bondholders. They reorganised the funding and recommended the appointment of two controllers, one to collect and one to control expenditure. An international board was constituted to supervise the railways, the telegraph and the harbour of Alexandria. This arrangement was not liked by the floating debt-holders—mainly British.

In March 1878 an Anglo-French Commission of Enquiry was instituted which transformed itself into the responsible ministry of the Egyptian government. Ismail, though a prisoner in the hands of his creditors, got rid of his ministers by April 1879. On May 18 Bismarck championed the cause of the European bondholders. From September Tewfik had to submit himself to an Anglo-French dual control. Although they passed a law of liquidation of the debt (July 17, 1880), interest charges on it took away 37 per cent of Egypt's revenue. To offset their bad economy, the Egyptian government sold its preference shares in the Canal Company to the *Credit Foncier* in 1880, entitling it to 15 per cent of the profits. Consequently, Egypt had to forfeit its revenue from the Canal till 1936.

Ahmed Arabi, anti-Turkish, anti-foreign and representative of disgruntled colonels, could not look with favour at the reduction of Egyptian army from 45,000 to 18,000. His victory over Tewfik in September 1881, forcing the latter to agree to a representative government and a larger army, ultimately brought a sharp rejoinder from Britain and France (January 8, 1882). This emphasised unstinted support to Tewfik and alienated public opinion. With growing deterioration of law and order, Tewfik appealed to the powers to rescue him from Arabi and his protagonists.

In May 1882, an Anglo-French naval squadron appeared off Alexandria. Turkey made an effort to resolve the crisis by sending two commissioners to Cairo, one of whom negotiated with the Khedive and the other with Arabi, but without any luck. On June 23 a conference of ambassadors was convened at Constantinople which ended in futility. Further riots brought about a British naval bombardment on July 11 and the mobilisation of a British army corps under Sir Garnet Wolseley. On September 13, Wolseley routed Arabi's forces at Tel-al-Kabir and became master of Egypt.

The British Foreign Office announced on January 3, 1883 that the occupation of Egypt was temporary. They found the continued occupation as an unnecessary burden on an already over-taxed empire. But their policy, in the words of their agent-general, Baring (later Lord Cromer), was not one 'capable of execution'. It was a difficult proposition, as Baring contended, to get out of Egypt. There was built 'a top-heavy and exotic superstructure, such as an enormous external debt, Western law courts, complete liberty of contract, and, in fact, all the paraphernalia of European civilisation, with some of its worst and not many of its best features.'

However, the British could hardly expect any sympathy from any European power to maintain her authority. Lord Lyons found 'the natural disposition of almost all Europe to side against us on the Egyptian question.' The French had vainly expected, after the battle of Tel-al-Kabir, the establishment of dual control over Egypt. When it was found that the French policy was hostile to British occupation of Egypt, Britain began to lean on Germany. The centre of gravity in Egyptian affairs now shifted from Cairo to Berlin. Bismarck now put pressure on British policy after the Russian venture in Central Asia.

Britain ultimately decided to withdraw from Egypt. Negotiation began at Constantinople where, on May 22, 1887, Drummond Wolff presented a convention for the Sultan's ratification. Under this convention Britain pledged to withdraw from Egypt within three years but with the right of re-entry 'upon the appearance of danger from without.' Moreover, if the Khedive misbehaved and disorder ensued in Egypt, both Turkey and Britain would have the right to intervene. But the most perplexing problem was that if one of the Mediterranean powers refused to ratify the convention, that refusal would amount to 'the appearance of a danger from without' implying that Britain would not leave Egypt.

The terms of this convention caused a diplomatic explosion and heightened Anglo-French colonial rivalry. France could never reconcile herself to the occupation of Egypt by Britain alone. Russian attitude was also similar. By this convention, Russia suffered a diplomatic defeat as she was deprived of making Egypt a pawn in return for English concession to Russian ambition in the Balkans. The Sultan was browbeaten by the French and Russian ambassadors that they be given the right to occupy provinces of empire like Syria and Armenia, and to vacate them only after a similar convention had been concluded. The net result of this diplomatic tension arising out of Wolff's convention was that the Sultan refused to ratify it and evacuation of Egypt by Britain was indefinitely postponed.

The British realised the strategic importance of the Suez Canal as they used the Canal as a military base in the military expedition of 1882. Though the Canal Company remained a French organisation, the British had overall control over it. In a circular of January 1883, Grenville proposed that the Canal must remain free to the passage of all shipping; that no troops should be disembarked in it; and that no hostilities should take place in the canal or anywhere in Egyptian waters. But these two last conditions were to be waived in cases which 'might be necessary for the defence of Egypt.' At the initiative of France an international commission had been summoned and by June 1885 an instrument had been drafted that embodied proposals from both Britain and France. But it was rendered nugatory by the British insistence to suspend the application of the clauses drawn up by the international commission so long as British forces occupied Egypt. The British view was expressed by Dilke in the House of Commons that this was a 'crazy and insane convention' under which Russian ships might pass through the Canal in any project against India. It was only in 1904—as a result of Anglo-French entente of 1904—that the British abandoned this attitude. Its main provision was that France was given a free hand in Morocco in return for the cession to Britain of her rights in Egypt.

Egypt, though under the occupation of the British since 1882, was virtually under sovereignty of the Ottoman Sultan. The aftermath of the war plunged Egypt in an agitation against the British who had proclaimed Egypt a protectorate in 1914. They deposed the Khedive and elevated his nephew, Hussein Kamel, to the throne as Sultan of Egypt. The British requisition of assistance in men and materials in the war alienated the Egyptians to which were added the general hatred for foreign rule and the traditional dislike of Muslims for Christians. Wilson's talk about self-determination quickened the demand for independence. While the leader of the Nationalist Party (Wafd), Saad Zaghlul Pasha, at the head of a delegation was on its way to Paris Peace Conference to present Egypt's case for independence, he was arrested. This provoked an insurrection in 1919 which was suppressed by General Edmund Allenby. Eventually the imprisoned delegates were released and Henry Milner was despatched to Egypt on a fact finding mission. After investigation the Milner Mission recommended that Egypt be given independence with certain restrictions. A treaty embodying the proposals was offered to Egypt in 1921 which was rejected by the Nationalists.

Rioting broke out again and Zaghlul was once more arrested. The British ultimately gave way to the agitation and by the Declaration of 28 February 1922 recognised Egyptian independence. But they reserved the following points absolutely to the discretion of His Majesty's Government: the defence of Suez, the protection of foreigners, and the control of the Sudan—for the supply of cotton and for regulating Egypt's water supply. In October 1922 a draft constitution was prepared which affirmed the sovereignty of the Egyptian people, and which provided for elections and a parliament to which ministers would be responsible. Sultan Ahmed Fuad, who had succeeded Hussein in 1917, vehemently opposed the draft constitution. It was only after making numerous changes which increased the royal power, and pressurised by Allenby, the British High Commissioner, that King Fuad approved the constitution in April 1923. Parliamentary elections were held in 1923 which went overwhelmingly in favour of the Wafdists. Its leader, Zaghlul, formed a government which lasted barely a year.

The murder of Sir Lee Stack, the Governor-General of the Sudan, at Cairo in November 1924 by terrorists belonging to the Wafdists, created tension. Zaghlul resigned. After dissolving the parliament, Fuad appointed a non-Wafdist ministry and ordered a new election. But the results did not prove to be satisfactory either to Zaghlul or to Fuad. The new parliament met in March 1925 only to be dissolved immediately. For a year the king ruled without any representative assembly. The British High Commissioner who succeeded Allenby, Lord Lloyd, whose influence was still paramount, persuaded the King to hold fresh elections. Fuad had to concede and the elections of May 1926 returned a Wafdist majority. But as Zaghlul was found to be unacceptable to Lloyd, the latter appointed a non-Wafdist as Prime Minister. Zaghlul having died in 1927, his successor, Mustapha Nahas Pasha, secured his nomination as Prime Minister by virtue of his parliamentary majority. Shortly afterwards, Nahas incurred displeasure of the British and was dismissed by Fuad. After dissolving the parliament, Fuad appointed as Prime Minister Muhammad Mahmud, the leader of the Liberal Constitutionalist party. Apart from suspending the constitution he ruled for a year without convening a parliament.

The return to power of a Labour Government in Britain in 1929 gave great encouragement to nationalist aspiration in Egypt. Subsequent elections returned a large Wafdist majority. But the King dismissed it and appointed Ismail Sidqi, a non-Wafdist, as Prime Minister. He promulgated a new constitution which vested the executive with wide power. Armed with dictatorial power, he ordered a new election which returned a non-Wafdist majority. Sidqi ruled with a heavy hand, convening the parliament at his discretion.

In 1933 there began a series of anti-Christian riots. Economic distress complicated the situation. In September 1933, Sidqi resigned owing to illness and constant interference by the King in administrative affairs. After fourteen troubled months, Mohammed Tewfik Nessim Pasha, a popular leader, came to the helm. He persuaded the King to abolish the undemocratic constitution of 1930. The Nationalists' expectation that the constitution of 1923 would be restored was not fulfilled. The situation grew portentous in the autumn of 1935 with Italy's attack on Ethiopia.

The adoption of precautionary measures by Britain in Egypt and the apprehension entertained by the people lest they be drawn into an Anglo-Italian conflict, hardened the Wafdist attitude. Anti-British riots took place in different places and Egyptian political parties coalesced by forming a United Front under Nahas. Britain announced her readiness to negotiate a treaty with an Egyptian government which could claim to be a representative government. Thereupon new elections were held in 1936 which gave the Wafdists an overwhelming majority in the parliament. Nahas again became premier. Meanwhile, Fuad having died in 1936, was succeeded by his sixteen-year old son, Faruq. After protracted negotiations an Anglo-Egyptian Treaty of Alliance was signed in London which was ratified before Christmas 1936.

The treaty provided for mutual assistance in case of war. The British promised to champion Egypt's candidacy for membership of the League of Nations, agreed to an exchange of ambassadors and undertook to limit their troops. Joint rule over the Sudan was to be reestablished. Britain was to use her good influence over other powers with extra-territorial rights in inducing them to surrender their privileged position in Egypt. Britain's initiative led to the meeting of the capitulatory powers at Montreaux in 1937. The Montreaux Convention provided for the complete abolition of extra-territoriality by 1949. Shortly afterwards, Egypt became a member of the League of Nations and Faruq became the first king of independent Egypt.

The young King joined himself at odds with Nahas when the former asserted his royal power much more than what had been provided in the constitution. At the end of 1936 the King dismissed the cabinet and appointed Muhammad Mahmud to the premiership. The new premier dissolved the parliament elected in 1936. The sequel was the outbreak of riots which were suppressed by Britain by rushing additional forces in Egypt. In the election held in 1938, the electorate returned a large anti-Wafdist party. The reasons for the defeat of the Wafdist were due to Nahas' differences with the King, the manipulation of the election machinery by the premier, and dissidence in the Wafdist rank.

The parliament lasted until 1942 when the British, suspecting the King's pro-Axis leanings, forced him to appoint Nahas Prime Minister. In the elections that were held in the changed set-up, a large Wafdist majority was returned. Hardly had the Second World War been over in 1945, when Faruq dismissed Nahas. His successor dissolved the 1942 parliament and a large anti-Wafdist majority was returned. The 1945 parliament completed its full term under the constitutional monarchy. The 1950 elections witnessed a change of fortune when the Wafdists again came to power. In 1951, Egyptian government denounced the Anglo-Egyptian treaty of 1936. In its wake rioting broke out in which much foreign property was destroyed in Cairo in January 1952. The King's influence eroded visibly owing to widespread corruption and his licentiousness. In July 1952 he was dethroned and exiled by General Muhammad Naguib, who, at the head of a nationalist army, made himself master of Egypt and made it a republic. The next year Naguib was replaced by another army officer, General Gamal Abdel Nasser. It was he who effected an agreement with Britain for the latter's evacuation of the Suez Canal zone.

Iraq

Iraq, which was formed out of three Ottoman provinces—Mosul, Baghdad and Basra—was occupied by the British during the First World War. The population of Iraq was composed of disparate elements. The Shiite semi-settled agricultural population occupied the south, the Kurds the north, and the Sunni Arab nomads the west and north-west. In 1921 the British government imposed a centralised government with its capital at Baghdad over which they placed as King, Faisal. Power was exercised by bureaucrats belonging to Sunni Arab minority whose model was the centralised absolutism of the Ottoman Empire. Along with this these men were wedded to an ideology, that of Arab nationalism. To all these complexities were added the British ideal of constitutionalism and responsible parliamentary government.

In 1925 a constitution was promulgated which incorporated the British ideal as Iraq was then under the supervision of Britain as a mandated territory. The mandate was terminated in 1932.

There followed unstable political condition in Iraq. Between 1921 and 1958, Iraq's constitutional monarchy had 58 cabinets. Political instability encouraged politicians to gain power by extra-constitutional means. Taking advantage of tribal dissidence in the South in 1934-36, they tried to effect a change of government in Baghdad. But the Iraqi army was too quick to put down these tribal rebellions. Conscious of their own importance, the army frequently intervened in state affairs, sometimes in combination with factious elements.

A succession of military coups enveloped the period 1936-41. In April 1941 when a pro-Axis government came into power, the British had to intervene and began to regulate Iraqi politics until 1945. After 1945, owing to centralisation and by continuous purges and strict control, the army was prevented from interference in politics. But such measures did not prevent a military *coup d' etat* in July 1958 which put a bloody end of the constitutional monarchy.

French conquest of Algeria in the nineteenth century marked a significant European penetration in the Middle East. But the balance of power in Europe and the Mediterranean acted as a deterrent to prevent annexations. It was not before the early 1880s that France could establish a protectorate over Algeria's western neighbour, Tunisia. Chagrined at this French behaviour, Italy sought compensation in Tripoli, an Ottoman province. Having obtained the consent of the Europeans powers, the Italian government presented a twenty-four hour ultimatum to Turkey on September 28, 1911, and declared war the following day. The Tripoli war dragged on for a year which was ended by Turkey's cession of the province to Italy in October 1912 by the Treaty of Ouchy.

Morocco

1912 also witnessed the establishment of a French protectorate over the greater part of Morocco. French interest in Morocco began with her conquest of Algeria. She could have conquered the country as the Sultan's authority over an extensive Berber-populated mountainous area was minimal. But she had to encounter the opposition of European powers, especially Britain, the latter insisting on the maintenance of Moroccan independence. But British opposition began to wear away with the signing of the Anglo-French Agreement in April 1904. France was given a free hand in Morocco in exchange for French acquiescence in the British occupation of Egypt. The Anglo-French entente was followed by a Franco-Spanish treaty (September 1904) which ceded to Spain a part of northern Morocco—opposite Gibraltar. Germany's opposition to French occupation was countered in 1911 by the French cession of a large tract of the Congo.

French process of pacification in Morocco continued till the mid-1930s. The centralisation of authority and the crushing of dissidence provoked a countrywide opposition which led to the collapse of the French authority in Morocco.

Turkey

The First World War and its aftermath saw the extension of European control over the whole Middle East. Britain had to abandon her traditional policy of maintaining the independence and integrity of the Ottoman Empire owing to the latter's involvement in war with the Central Powers. The immediate consequence of the war was the proclamation of British protectorates over Egypt and Kuwait. Russian demand for a share in the spoils of the Ottoman Empire became vocal after the Gallipoli expedition in early 1915. Despite British reluctance in the initial stage, Russia was involved, along with Britain, France and other Allies, in the process of partition of the Ottoman Empire. The partition scheme was embodied in the Sykes-Picot Agreement, which was signed in May 1916. Italy was lured to join the Allies by the promise of Smyrna and other territories. By mid-1917, Britain, France, Russia and Italy decided to spoliate the Ottoman Empire among themselves in the event of victory. The Sykes-Picot agreement conceded to France her foothold in Syria, and gave to Britain Baghdad and southern Mesopotamia. Apart from Constantinople and the Straits, Russia was to acquire eastern Anatolia. While the Holy Land was internationalised, Britain was given special interest in that region by her control of Haifa and Akka (Acre).

This secret arrangement was entangled with another grandiose scheme, which was the brainchild of Sir Henry McMahon, the British High Commissioner in Egypt. He bolstered the Sharif of Mecca to rebel against the Ottoman Empire. The price was too tempting to the Sharif: an independent Kingdom of the Hijaz, a transfer of the Caliphate from the Ottoman to his own dynasty, and the formation of an Arab state. The negotiation which continued intermittently throughout 1915 ended inconclusively in March 1916.

McMahon's offer was to lead to much trouble later on. Another undertaking, the Balfour Declaration of November 1917, later gave rise to many disputes. It was a unilateral declaration of the British in which they recorded that 'His Majesty's Government views with favour the establishment in Palestine of a national home for the Jewish people, and will use their best endeavours to facilitate the achievement of this object.' But the Balfour Declaration did not fit in well with the Sykes-Picot scheme as the latter proposed an international status for Palestine and 'the establishment in Palestine of a national home for the Jewish people.' Moreover, the Sykes-Picot scheme became highly unpopular in British eyes as Britain had to bear the main brunt in fighting against the Ottoman Empire. The British troops fought the Ottomans in Mesopotamia in 1914, in Gallipoli in 1915, in Sinai and Jerusalem in December 1917, and Damascus in October 1918. Britain, therefore, had justifiable reason to look with disfavour in any scheme which gave the French a dominant position in the Levant.

The Sykes-Picot scheme suffered another blow when the British encouraged the ambition of the Sharif. Allenby had made Faisal, the third son of the Sharif, the commander of a so-called 'Northern Arab Army' which served as an auxiliary to the British forces. The Sharifian troops entered Damascus and Faisal was appointed as military governor of Syria under Allenby's authority. Thus the French claim of their preponderant influence in Syria, under the Sykes-Picot scheme, was disregarded. The scheme also foundered with Russia's withdrawal from the war in November 1917. Britain and France, therefore, had to come to a new *modus vivendi* in the Middle East.

The process was protracted. It began from the Armistice of Mudros (October 30, 1918) between the Ottoman Empire and the Allied Powers and ended with the Treaty of Lausanne (July 24, 1923) between Turkey and Britain, France, Italy, Japan, Greece, Bulgaria and Rumania. The armistice found Britain in occupation of Palestine, Syria, the Lebanon, Cilicia, and parts of Mesopotamia including Basra, Baghdad and Mosul. Though the French gave up their claim to Palestine and to Mosul, they could not be persuaded to give up the others. A stalemate ensued which was only ended when the British agreed to withdraw from Syria, the Lebanon and Cilicia, allowing the French troops to occupy the last two places while Syria remained under Faisal's control. The change-over took place in November 1919. Earlier in April 1919, the Italians had occupied Adalia. This was followed in May 1920 by the landing of a Greek contingent in Smyrna, a territory containing a large Greek element and claimed by Venizelos, the Greek Prime Minister in the Paris Peace Conference.

The Greek occupation provoked widespread resentment among the Muslim Turkish-speaking

Mustafa Kemal

people of Smyrna. This was fanned by **Mustafa Kemal** (1881-1938), who spearheaded military resistance to the Greeks and the Allies. In 1919 Kemal was an Ottoman general and had distinguished himself in Gallipoli and in eastern Anatolia. In May he was appointed as Inspector-General of the 9th Army based on Samsun on the

Black Sea and from there mounted offensive operations against the Greeks. At the end of 1919 he established his dominant influence in Ankara which gradually became the effective seat of government. From April 1921, Kemal's troops struck heavy blows against the Greeks and routed them finally at Sakarya on August 24, 1921, and Smyrna reoccupied on September 9, 1922. The revival of the Turkish power had a dramatic effect. The Italians decided to withdraw from Adalia and the French from Cilicia. The British remained as the only power involved in the Turkish affair.

The occupation of Smyrna was not the only crowning glory of Mustafa Kemal. He also decided to expel the Greeks from eastern Thrace, which had been under their occupation. But to accomplish this object, he had to cross the Dardanelles, which was under Allied occupation. Despite the initial opposition of Britain not to allow the Turks to cross the Dardanelles, it finally gave way and agreed to the restoration of Istanbul and the Straits to Turkish sovereignty. The conclusion of the Treaty of Lausanne put an end to various schemes sponsored by the Allies for partitioning the Ottoman Empire.

Having obtained resounding victory over the Greeks and their protectors, Mustafa Kemal established himself at Ankara as the sole legitimate government of Turkey. In November 1922, the Grand National Assembly by a decree abolished the Sultanate, but retained the Caliphate as a purely spiritual office. The Sultan Muhammad VI Wahidal-Din was deposed and his cousin Abd al-Majid proclaimed Caliph. In January 1922 the Grand National Assembly passed a 'Law of Fundamental Organisation' which laid down that 'sovereignty belongs without reservation or condition to the nation.' In October 1923, the Grand National Assembly proclaimed Turkey a republic, the president of which was to be elected from among the members of the Assembly. As a republic was contradictory to the existence of Caliphate, it was abolished. Thus ended the most venerable political office in Islam. The great contribution of Mustafa Kemal was that he left a legacy to Turkish-speaking Muslims to consider themselves as the sovereign citizens of a republic and members of a Turkish nation.

In other areas of the Middle East, spectacular things happened in quick succession. In the autumn of 1919, French troops replaced British in the Lebanon and Faisal was left in control of Syria. After the withdrawal of the British, Faisal had to reach some accommodation with their rivals, the French. Influenced largely by his turbulent followers, Faisal adopted a foolhardy policy towards the French. In March 1920, Faisal proclaimed himself as King of the United Kingdom of Syria—*i.e.*, Syria, the Lebanon and Palestine. The French issued an ultimatum in July asking him to accept French control. Faisal wavered and the French troops marched on Damascus. A brief encounter near Damascus on July 24 led to the rout of Faisal's troops. The French occupied the city and expelled Faisal from Syria. Both Syria and Lebanon became French-administered mandated territories. Mandates were included in the Covenant of the League of Nations which was incorporated in the Treaty of Versailles (June 23, 1919). The idea of mandate and its mode of operation was explained in Article XXII of the Covenant:

> To those colonies and territories which as a consequence of the late war have ceased to be under the sovereignty of the states which formerly governed them ... there should be applied the principle that the well-being and development of such peoples form a sacred trust of civilisation and that securities for the performance of this trust should be embodied in this Covenant.
>
> The best method of giving practical effect to this principle is that the tutelage of such people should be entrusted to advanced nations ... and that this tutelage should be exercised by them as Mandatories on behalf of the League.

In April 1920, the Allied Supreme Council meeting at San Remo had given to France the mandate for Syria and the Lebanon. It also assigned to Britain the mandates for Mesopotamia and Palestine. The British administered Mesopotamia from Baghdad with the assistance of a Civil Commissioner and Political Officers. But the British government could not formulate a clear-cut policy. Apart from the alienation of the people, the southern part of the country presented a difficult problem of government. To all these factors were added the dissension between the two groups; by the Shiite divines and the

Sharifians. Both these two warring groups united in the summer of 1920 in fomenting a revolt against the British. Though the revolt was put down, Britain realised that sooner or later the occupation of the country would have to be ended. In 1921 they offered the throne to Faisal with the title of King of Iraq. Article XXII of the League Covenant required the Mandatories to facilitate the progressive development of Iraq, Syria and the Lebanon as independent states. But conflict arose when the Mandatory felt that the mandated territory was not yet ready to 'stand alone.' But the intensity of Arab nationalism was too strong to be brushed aside. Slowly Britain gave way, making concession after concession. In 1930 Britain concluded a treaty at Baghdad, recognising the independence of Iraq, promising to sponsor its admission to the League of Nations and to withdraw from Iraq within five years. In 1932 Iraq was admitted to the League of Nations and the British troops took their leave from Iraq in 1935. Meanwhile King Faisal died in 1933. His immediate successor was his son Ghazi, who in turn was followed by his son, Faisal II.

The impact of British policy in Iraq was felt in the French-mandated territories of Syria and Lebanon. In Syria the Arab population was large and relatively progressive. For the sake of convenience, the French separated from Syria the region around Beirut, which was predominantly Christian, and favourably disposed to a French protectorate. This truncated region was constituted as the autonomous 'Republic of Lebanon' with a native President and an elected Assembly. The rest of the territory was then consolidated into the 'State of Syria' with its capital at Damascus and under the direct rule of the French High Commissioner.

Despite the fact that the French did a great deal to develop the country, there was murmur of discontent among the Arab nationalists. The worst rioting occurred in 1925 during the High Commissionership of General Sarrail. The situation was rendered more difficult by a simultaneous Druze rebellion in 1925, a Moslem sect of warlike mountaineers in southern Syria. Druze turbulence and Sarrail's attempt to suppress the rioting at Damascus by brutal method provoked a general insurrection all over Syria. It was a national, Syrian, Arab revolt against French imperialism. Sarrail was recalled and a new High Commissioner was appointed who quickly restored order in 1927.

The ensuing election in the Assembly returned an overwhelming majority of the Arab Nationalists who demanded complete independence. But the French officials resisted such a sweeping demand and proposed instead a qualified autonomy. In 1930 the High Commissioner dissolved the Assembly and promulgated a constitution which—though provided for a Republic with a parliament and a native president—made it subservient to France. But the Syrian parliament was intensely nationalistic and the French attempt to rule without it met with a serious rebuff. Meanwhile the popular Front government came to power in France in 1936 and signed a treaty with Syria in 1936. The treaty provided for the gradual withdrawal of the French forces from Syria and the eventual admission of Syria to the League of Nations. But the treaty was not ratified owing to the objections by the French parliament. The Second World War affected profoundly the French position in the Levant.

Palestine

In Palestine, west of the Jordan, the situation was complicated by the Balfour Declaration to respect the national aspirations of the Jews as well as Arabs. In November 1917, when the World War was in a critical stage and just before the capture of Jerusalem by General Allenby, the British Foreign Secretary, Arthur Balfour, declared:

> His Majesty's Government views with favour the establishment in Palestine of a national home for the Jewish people and will use their best endeavours to facilitate the achievement of that object, it being clearly understood that nothing shall be done which may prejudice the civil and religious rights of existing non-Jewish communities in Palestine, or the rights and political status enjoyed by Jews in any other country.

Palestine had long been an Arab-speaking Muslim country. But after the installation of the British administration, the Jewish immigration overflowed Palestine, increasing from a barely 70,000 in 1920 to half a million in 1938.

The British administration of the Palestine mandate must be acknowledged as fairly successful. There was a remarkable achievement in the agricultural and industrial development of the country. Sir Herbert Samuel, the first British High Commissioner, did his job with strict impartiality without showing any undue favour to the Jews. Though the announcement of the mandate in April 1920 was immediately followed by anti-Jewish riots in Jerusalem, followed by other disturbances in 1921 and 1925, Herbert's tenure of office was peaceful. By 1925, he effected the reduction of British garrison to insignificant proportion. The British showed their conciliatory gesture in 1923 by granting autonomy to Transjordania, under the sovereignty of Abdulla. But in Palestine the irreconcilable antagonisms of Arabs and Jews remained a festering sore—making it impossible to create a parliamentary government.

In August 1929, the Arab-Jewish tension assumed a religious colour with the outbreak of violence at Wailing Wall, a place which had a peculiar sanctity in the eyes of each community. The violence left 133 Jews and 126 Arabs dead and a large number injured. The disturbances extended to other parts of the country which required the deployment of additional military and police forces. At the request of the British representative, the Council of the League in May 1930 appointed a neutral commission to enquire into the respective claims of Arabs and Jews to the Wailing Wall. Simultaneously, Sir John Hope Simpson was sent to Palestine with a fact-finding mission to study a question of Jewish immigration and land-settlement.

The Simpson Report was published in October 1930. The Report contained White Paper which sought to define the policy of the Mandatory Power. The latter document was interpreted in Zionist circles as being anti-Jewish in character. The Simpson Report dashed to the possibility of an eventual Jewish-majority in Palestine. Ramsay MacDonald tried to assuage the wounded sentiments of the Jews by writing a letter to DR Weizmann, the ex-President of the Zionist organisation, but this could only arouse the suspicion of the Arabs. In the long run, the prospect of self-government in Palestine which the terms of the mandate prescribed, appeared to be remote.

Though the continuance of the mandate was resented by the Arabs, the latter did not fear the increasing influx of Jews with their number restricted annually to less than 5,000. But with the advent of world economic depression, the situation was transformed. To this was added the anti-Semitic policy of Nazi Germany and her friends which accelerated the Jewish immigration. In 1935, according to official estimates, there were about 61,584 Jewish immigrants, but unofficial figure was much larger. Despite the growth of industrialism, the Arabs were faced with the prospect, in the foreseeable future, of being swamped by the Jewish majority. The Arabs expressed their anxieties in unequivocal terms. In the words of the Report of the Palestine Royal Commission: 'With almost mathematical precision, the betterment of the economic situation meant the deterioration of the political situation.'

In November 1935 the Arabs presented to the High Commissioner, Sir Arthur Wauchope, certain demands. These included the establishment of democratic government, the prohibition of the transfer of Arab lands to Jews and the immediate cessation of Jewish immigration. In reply to the last two points, the High Commissioner proposed an ordinance forbidding the sale of land to the Jews and a fresh check on Jewish immigration. He also proposed a scheme for a Legislative Council, to consist of five official and twenty-three unofficial members, of whom eleven were to be nominated and twelve elected. Among the unofficial members, eleven were to be Muslims, seven Jews, three Christians and the rest business representatives. This scheme, though received tardy acquiescence from the Arab leaders, was rejected by the Zionists.

The progress of events in Abyssinia due to Italy's aggression and the latter's propaganda conveyed an impression of waning British influence. Meanwhile the success achieved by the nationalists in Egypt and Syria fomented a state of unrest which culminated in April 1936. Beginning with sporadic violence, it rapidly assumed the proportion of a guerrilla warfare. Prompt measures were taken to suppress the disorder which induced the Arab Higher Committee to accept the mediatory advice proffered by the rulers of Iraq, Transjordan and Saudi Arabia in October 1936. In the beginning of November, a Royal Commission under Lord Peel was despatched to investigate the problem.

The Royal Commission published a report in July 1937. The report highlighted that the Mandate as it stood was unworkable. "We cannot—in Palestine as it now is—both concede the Arab claim to self-government and secure the establishment of the Jewish National Home." The Commission, therefore, proposed a scheme of partition which might give satisfaction to the nationalist aspiration of both communities. A small Jewish state occupying about one-fourth of the area of Palestine should be constituted. Jerusalem and Bethleham, Nazareth and the Sea of Galilee should remain under mandatory control as 'a sacred trust of civilisation.' The rest of the country would be fused with Transjordan.

The plan met with protests from all sections. The Jews considered it as an act of betrayal. The Arabs objected to the scheme by pointing out that "the richest zone is to be given to the Jews, the holiest to the British, and the most barren to the Arabs." The Arabs became violent and assassinated a British district commissioner. The recrudescence of Arab terrorism was accompanied by Jewish reprisal. The situation of the mandatory power was described by Sir John Shuckburgh as involving 'incessant war against terrorism, lawlessness and intimidation.'

In the face of hostile criticism, the British Government submitted the whole matter to the League for further consideration. The League appointed, in 1938, another Commission under the Chairmanship of Sir John Woodhead. He was directed to formulate a more precise and detailed scheme than the Peel Plan for solving the Palestine tangle. The Woodhead Commission unanimously opposed the partition scheme as it was found impracticable to delimit the boundaries of each zone. The British Government, therefore, came to the conclusion that "the surest foundation for peace and progress in Palestine would be an understanding between the Arabs and Jews." They, along with the Arabs of neighbouring states, were invited to a conference at London.

The proposal came at a time when Palestine became the scene of bomb outrages and guerrilla warfare. The leader of the rebel Arabs was the Grand Mufti of Jerusalem, who from the safe sanctuary of Syria, maintained contact with his followers. The situation became worse during the period of the European crisis over Czechoslovakia. The so-called Round Table Conference met in London in February-March 1939. The Arabs demanded the formation of an independent Arab state, proportionate representation for Arabs and Jews in the parliament, prohibition of Jewish immigration and stoppage of land sales to Jews. The Jews objected to each point. The British tried in vain to find a compromise formula. It issued a White Paper in May which drastically limited Jewish immigration into Palestine and put a limited ban on the Jews to buy land. The outbreak of the Second World War diverted the attention of Britain from Palestine to Europe.

The Round Table Conference marked a significant departure in British policy towards the Middle East. The Conference was attended not only by the Palestinian Arabs and the Jews, but also by the Arab world including Egypt, Iraq, Saudi Arabia, the Yemen and Transjordan. By inviting the Arab States to participate in the conference, the British recognised the claim of the Arab nationalists in shaping their own destiny.

The British had other stakes as well. They tried to wean away the Arab nationalist movement from the Axis powers and to curry favour with the Arab states by entering into treaty of friendship. This policy was enunciated by Anthony Eden, the Foreign Secretary, in May 1941 when he promised 'full support to any (Arab unity) scheme that commands general approval.'

British support to Arab nationalism was demonstrated in the Lebanon and Syria during the war. A year after the French capitulation to Germany, in June 1941, Britain quickly demanded the termination of the French-mandated territories in the Levant. The Free French authority replaced that of Vichy in the mandated territories. Under British pressure, the Free French issued a declaration promising complete independence to the Syrians and the Lebanese. But when the Free French dithered to implement the declaration and clashed with the Lebanese government in November 1943, the latter unilaterally ended the mandatory relation with France. The French had to accept the *fait accompli*.

Again, a year after the liberation of France, the French government clashed with the Syrians in May-June 1945. But when they found the British supporting the Syrians and even occupying Damascus, the French retraced their steps. The French were now eliminated and the British now became the dominant power in the Middle East.

The Palestine question became highly critical after the close of the Second World War. The situation became acute with the increased national feeling of the Arabs, the miserable plight of hundreds of thousands of Jews in post-war Central Europe, and their attempts to enter Palestine surreptitiously, the activities of Jewish terrorist groups and the importance of Palestine in the Near Eastern oil picture. The situation did not improve when an Anglo-American Committee recommended the immediate admission of 100,000 Jews persecuted by the Nazis, the removal of restrictions on land transfers, and the suppression of terrorism and violence. On the other hand, it urged continuance of the mandate until UN trusteeship agreement could be negotiated. Though the Report appeared to be flattering to President Truman and the Jewish Agency for Palestine, the Arab Higher Committee threatened to begin a countrywide agitation if any attempt was made to implement the report. Britain made it clear that it would not send reinforcement to enforce large-scale Jewish immigration. Foreign Secretary Bevin sarcastically wondered about the unwillingness of the United States to open its own doors to hapless Jewish refugees.

Meanwhile, the League of the Arab States extended support to the Palestinian Arabs. The League formed at Cairo in 1945 among Syria, Transjordan, Iraq, Saudi Arabia, Lebanon, Egypt and Yemen, demanded a cessation of Jewish immigration into Palestine. Anxious to end her Palestinian obligation, Britain, in the spring of 1947, sought UN intervention. In May 1947, the General Assembly appointed a Special Committee on Palestine with "widest powers to ascertain and record facts, and to investigate all questions and issues relevant to the problem of Palestine." In August 1947 the Committee submitted its report. The Committee unanimously recommended the early termination of the mandate, a transition period under UN supervision preceding independence, and safeguarding of the religious rights of the several communities. A majority of the Committee suggested a partition of Palestine into three spheres—an Arabic state, a Jewish state and the city of Jerusalem with one customs union.

In November 1947 the General Assembly accepted the partition plan and set up a Palestine Commission to implement the plan. The Commission, after convening 75 meetings, ceased to exist in May 1948. The announcement of Britain in the early months of 1948 that she would terminate her mandate in Palestine in May 1948 added fuel to the Palestine cauldron. When discussions were going on among the United States, Britain and Russia on the question of the application of international army to enforce compliance of the partition plan, the world was startled by the declaration in Tel-Aviv of a new independent state of Israel in the midnight of May 14-15, 1948. This was immediately followed by Britain's laying down of the Palestine mandate and the withdrawal of her forces. The new state was immediately recognised by the USA and Russia. The General Assembly now had nothing to do except to appoint a mediator in the person of Count Bernadotte, nephew of the King of Sweden, to ease tension between warring factions.

Meanwhile, a democratic parliamentary constitution was set up in the new state of Israel with DR Chaim Weizmann as President and David Ben-Gurion as Premier. Bernadotte made earnest efforts to find a peaceful solution of the most tangled problem bequeathed to the world by the First and Second World Wars. But unfortunately he was assassinated in September 1948. Disorderly fighting between Israel and the forces of the Arab League went on until the beginning of 1949. The handling of the whole Palestinian episode reflected little credit upon the United

Nations. Armistices were signed between February and July 1949.

Israel was recognised by the UN and was admitted to U.N. membership in May 1949. For the next seven years, the new state, under the leadership of its Prime Minister, David Ben Gurion, made rapid strides towards progress. With its vigorous foreign policy, Four-Year Plan for agricultural and industrial development, extensive programme of social welfare and with financial assistance from the United States, Britain and other countries, Israel was on the high road to prosperity. The Arab League could hardly reconcile to this setback. It exploited the grievances of the Palestinian Arabs, who had fled into the neighbouring countries and began to organise terrorist gangs. The Israelis began to train their armed forces on vigorous Western discipline to counteract this move. It had been observed:

> Both in the reserve and in the active army, training is more rigorous, puts heavier emphasis on field combat exercises, and makes heavier demand on the physical powers of the individual than in the United States army.

CHAPTER 43

INDIA AND SOUTH-EAST ASIA

During the administration of Warren Hastings (1772-85), the East India Company had no decided policy with regard to Indian States except that of using them as the first line of defence for the protection of Bengal, Bihar and Orissa. It was Wellesley (1798-1805) who evolved a definite policy towards the Indian States. By the application of Subsidiary Alliance, Wellesley, in fact, established British paramountcy over some of the Indian States. "The fundamental principle of the Governor-General's policy in establishing the Subsidiary Alliance is to place the States in such a degree of dependence on the British power as may deprive them of the means of prosecuting any measure hazardous to the security of the British Empire." But these states did not hereby become subject to British paramountcy as they retained their independence in matters of internal administration. Before Wellesley's departure, the Company, though not yet supreme, was still the predominant power in India. Mysore had been conquered, the Nizam had become a subsidiary ally and the Carnatic had been annexed. The Maratha Confederacy had been broken diplomatically at Bassein.

The Court of Directors disliked Wellesley's policy of annexation and recalled him in August 1805. The Company, therefore, withdrew from the proposed subordination alliances with the Maratha chiefs. Cornwallis postponed the negotiation of alliance with the Rajput States and left the Maratha States to themselves. Lord Minto (1807-13), who followed Barlow, continued the policy of non-intervention. It was only in the case of Ranjit Singh who was rapidly expanding his dominions that the Governor-General deviated from the settled policy and brought the Sutlej States under the Company.

Metcalfe described the policy of non-intervention as monstrous. It was Lord Hastings who effectively brought under British supremacy most of the Indian States. He compelled them to surrender their sovereign rights of making war or peace and negotiating treaties with other powers. The States retained their internal sovereignty, but frequent interference was resorted to by the Company. Though an aggressive champion of extending British authority in India, Hastings was not an annexationist. As he himself observed: 'our object ought to be to render the British Government paramount in effect, if not declaredly so. We should hold the other states as vassals, in substance, though not in name.'

The period of alliance practically came to an end with Marquis of Hastings. The Company had become predominant in India and had displaced the Mughal and the Maratha in the claim of a general supremacy over India. The Governor-Generals that followed were frankly annexationist in their policy. The period also saw the growth of the controlling authority of the Residents in the matter of internal administration. Though tied to the policy of 'let alone,' Bentinck (1828-35) did not hesitate to depart from it in some cases. In 1831, Mysore was put under British administration on the plea of misrule. The principality of Cachar was annexed in August 1832 on the charge of maladministration. Coorg, near Mysore, was annexed in 1834, at the request of its inhabitants, the latter being ruled by an insane tyrant.

In 1834, the Court of Directors formulated the policy of annexation and emphasised it more forcefully in 1841. Lord Auckland, Lord Ellenborough and Lord Dalhousie were ardent advocates of this policy of annexation. During their administration Sindh, Awadh, Satara, Nagpur,

Punjab, Jhansi, Tanjore, Jaipur and numerous other states were annexed. Sindhia was deprived of a large portion of his territories and brought within the subsidiary alliance. In executing the policy of annexation, the Company applied the claims of lapse, escheat and confiscation. Morvi was declared escheat in 1839; Kolaba lapsed in 1840; Surat was annexed in 1842.

The administration of Dalhousie saw the culmination of the policy of annexation. He did not want to miss any opportunity of bringing territories directly under British rule and permitted no considerations of treaty of law to stand in his way.

> Dalhousie certainly put the coping stone on the edifice, the foundation stone of which had been laid by Clive and which Warren Hastings, Wellesley and Marquis Hastings had reared up. The treaty map of India was complete and he had the satisfaction of knowing that the whole of India from Cape Comorin to Kashmir acknowledged the suzerainty of the Queen.

With the establishment of supremacy, the Company introduced free trade principles and humanitarian works in India. This ending of monopoly set up a ferment of ideas. The revenue system underwent profound changes and relations with the Indian princes were regularised. In the decade 1820-30, British Indian policy was largely influenced by the Utilitarians and Evangelicals. They were supported by enlightened public opinion led by Rammohun Roy and his friends in Calcutta. The decision to introduce British institutions and Western knowledge into India meant the inauguration of a new cultural policy. But this was to be introduced without brushing aside Indian institutions. Simultaneously, free-trade principle was gaining ground and India became a market for British industry.

Lord William Bentinck represented the ideas of the new age. He epitomised the phrase 'we have a great moral duty to perform in India,' which was coined by the brilliant Ellenborough. The social revolution began in the time of Lord Cornwallis. The Charter Act of 1793 excluded Indians from higher administrative posts. Still more important was the series of land settlements, beginning with Permanent Settlement. Its purpose was to do justice to peasant and landlord and to preserve the village communities. But in the long run it ruined the old landed aristocracy and extinguished the village communities. This process was reinforced by the widespread resumption of rent-free tenures. R. M. Bird and J. Thomson implemented this in the North-Western province and the Inam Commission in Bombay. By deprivation of land, the landed class was driven into a backwater of the national life.

Bentinck struck at the root of the social evils by abolishing *sati* or the burning of widows on the funeral pyres of the husbands and suppressing the ritual of child-sacrifice. Bentinck's progressive mind was reflected in other measures of reform: the abolition of transit duties in 1835, the development of steam transport by river and ocean, the beginnings of tea and coffee cultivation and of iron and coal production, the planning of a network of roads, projects for drainage and of irrigation canals.

In 1835, Bentinck took the momentous decision of making English the official language of the Company. This fateful decision gave a great impetus to the progress of English education in India. The Calcutta Medical College and Elphinstone Institution of Bombay were established in 1835. During the next twenty years, a network of schools spread throughout the country. In 1854 appeared the famous Education Despatch of Sir Charles Wood. Described as the Magna Carta of English education in India, it laid down the broad principle of English for the select few and vernaculars for the masses. It also introduced the system of grants-in-aid for running numerous institutions. In 1857 were founded the three Universities at Calcutta, Bombay and Madras. Efforts of the Christian missionaries led by William Carey, R. May and Alexander Duff and others for the spread of education were no less negligible.

Along with Western education came Western law. In 1861 the new penal code based on English law came into being. Perhaps more important was the introduction of the English judicial procedure. Though Hindu and Muslim private laws were preserved, doubtful cases were decided on the principles of English equity. Persian was replaced by English as the language of the court. This necessitated an urge for learning English as the latter provided the grand avenue of providing government jobs and equipping men with professional employment. The process was helped on by professional educational establishments such as the Medical College in Calcutta and Dalhousie's Engineering College at Roorkee.

Western influence was also felt in evolving a policy of public works. Dalhousie had been especially associated with this activity. It was Lord William Bentinck who realised the need of a trunk road connecting Calcutta with the Upper Provinces. The project was implemented by Thomson, Lieutenant-Governor of North-Western Provinces from 1843 to 1853. Road construction in India received greater attention during the administration of Lord Dalhousie (1848-56). In 1854 Dalhousie constituted the Public Works Department to work in the provinces under the Central Government. The first step towards the introduction of railways was taken by Lord Hastings, but it was Lord Dalhousie who took keen interest in its development. His Railway Minute of 1853 became the basis of an integrated system of rail communication. The first railway line from Bombay to Thane was completed for passenger traffic on 16 April 1853. Calcutta was connected with Ranigunje coalfields in 1855. By 1860, as many as eight railway companies had been entrusted with the task of construction.

It was during the Dalhousie administration that the first telegraph line was opened in 1854 from Calcutta to Agra, a distance of 800 miles (1300 km). By 1857 it was extended to Lahore and Peshawar. Another form of public work was irrigation. In 1820, Mughal and Tughluq Canal from the Upper Jumna to Delhi was restored. Major early works were the Grand Anicut across the river Cauvery in the south (1835-36) and the Ganges Canal, completed by Dalhousie in 1854.

The Indian response to all these innovations was significant. A small group which gathered round the remarkable figure of Rammohun Roy, welcomed the Western works. The *Brahmo Samaj*, founded by him in 1828, began the process of assimilation on the religious and social plane. Bodies like the Landholders' Association and the British India Association, though political, championed the cause of reform in Indian administration and in economic sphere.

The general framework of the British administration was provided in the last quarter of the eighteenth century. The traditional authority of the Mughal Emperor of Delhi collapsed with his surrender to the British in 1803. He became a pensionary of the British. Pitt's India Act of 1784 laid down the general framework in which the Company's administration was to be carried on till 1857. Minor changes were made by the Charter Acts of 1793, 1813, 1833 and 1853. The Charter Act of 1793 increased the powers of the Governor-General over the subordinate presidencies of Bombay and Madras. The Charter Act of 1813 abolished the monopoly of the Company's Indian trade, but it continued the Company's monopoly of the China trade. It also laid down the sovereignty of the Crown over the Company's possession in India. By the Charter Act of 1833 the Company lost its trading privileges—the monopoly of the China trade. The Governor-General of Bengal now became the Governor-General of India. The Charter Act of 1833 introduced open competition for entry into the covenanted service which, in a way, afforded the Indians an opportunity into the Company's service.

The wind of change introduced by the Company created a social and political tension. Dalhousie's aggressive policy, especially his annexation of Awadh on the plea of misgovernment, alienated Indian opinion. The Indian army, already disgruntled over their employment in distant regions, was shocked with the introduction of greased cartridges, smeared with cow's and pig's fat—unclean to both Hindus and Muslims. Originating at Meerut on May 10, 1857 and the seizure of Delhi the next day, the Mutiny virtually ended with the fall of Gwalior on June 20, 1858. For a time the British had their backs to the wall. The situation was saved by the defence of Lucknow, the investment of Delhi against superior forces, and the doggedness of John Lawrence in the Punjab. The government also owed much to the loyalty of the Sikhs and the Princes.

The Mutiny brought about fundamental change in the character of the Indian administration and the future development of the country. The Government of India Act of 1858 deprived the powers of the Company and transferred the Government of India directly to the Crown. The Governor-General received the title 'Viceroy', and became responsible to the Secretary of State in London. The Queen's Proclamation (November 1, 1858) promised religious tolerance, guaranteed the rights of the Indian princes and pledged equal treatment to her subjects—Indians and Europeans.

The Army was reorganised. The European troops were strengthened and the ratio of European to Indian troops in the Bengal Army was fixed at one : two. The Princes who had rendered valuable services in the Mutiny were rewarded. They were described by Canning as 'breakwaters to the storm which would otherwise have swept over us in one great wave.' Finance was reorganised. The new measures carried by James Wilson and his successor Samuel Laing included an income-tax for five years, a uniform tariff of 10 per cent, a convertible paper currency and additions to salt duty. The Government undertook a new land policy. The Rent Act of 1859 gave occupancy right to all cultivators who could prove possession for 12 years. After 1857, the Government adopted a non-interfering policy in the social system of India. Between the Indian Penal Code of 1861 and the Age of Consent (Sarda) Act of 1929 there was no social legislation. But public works did not lag behind. The two most important fields where progress was spectacular were railways and irrigation. In 1857 there were 200 miles (320 km) of track open to traffic; by 1905 the railway mileage was 33,000 (52,800 km). Irrigation was pushed ahead with the commissioning of the Sukkur barrage in Sind. The Government also took adequate steps to combat famine by creating the Famine Commission of 1880 and the Famine Code of 1883. Education was also not neglected. With the establishment of three Universities at Calcutta, Bombay and Madras in 1857, the Hunter Commission of 1882 and Curzon's educational reform, the country was covered with a network of schools and universities.

Large scale industry, based on the factory system, was introduced in India during the British rule. Its effect was felt in the exports and imports of India. Thus the proportion of manufactured exports to total exports of India rose from 8 per cent in 1879 to 53 per cent in 1907. Among the more important industries may be mentioned cotton, jute, coal, iron, steel and tea. The first cotton mill was established in Bombay in 1854. The opening of the Empress Mill at Nagpur in 1877 by the Parsi, J. N. Tata marked the beginning of a real progress in the industry. By 1914, India was reckoned to be fourth in the world list of cotton manufacturing countries. Dorabji, the son of J. N. Tata founded the Tata Iron and Steel Company at Jamshedpur in Bihar in 1907, producing the first iron in 1911 and steel in 1914. The value of the jute industry was first realised in 1838 when export started to Dundee in Scotland. The loss of Russian supplies as a result of the Crimean War of 1854 led to the establishment of the Indian jute industry around Calcutta about 1859. On the eve of the First World War (1914-1918), there were 64 mills. In 1947, India possessed 113 jute mills. Coal industry whose—operations in Bengal were carried with success from 1814—reached its output of 91,000 tons in 1846. The advent of the railways gave an impetus to the coal industry. From six million tons in 1900, production reached 38 millions in 1933, making India self-supporting in one of the key industries. Tea industry rapidly expanded after 1850. Britain's requirement of tea was met by India which reached from 10 million pounds in 1869 to 137 million pounds in 1900 as against China's 100 million pounds in 1869 to 24 million in 1900. Most of the industries were in the hands of European merchants. The Indian mercantile community established in 1887 the Bengal National Chamber of Commerce.

The British policy in India after 1857 was to a large extent influenced by her imperialistic designs and to counteract the foreign influence. The most important feature during the period was that foreign policy of British India was dictated by the Secretary of State. Britain had to face different European powers like France and Russia in their bid for colonial supremacy. The desire to defend their Indian empire and to promote their economic interests often led the British Government to commit aggression on India's neighbour.

The fear of Russia prompted the first Afghan War in 1839. The disaster of 1841 revealed the strength of Afghan resistance to interference. The conquest of Sind in 1843 and the annexation of the Punjab in 1849 carried the British boundaries beyond the Indus. The frontier policy of the British since 1849 was guided by the non-intervention school of Lord Lawrence. But the arrival of Lord Lytton in 1876 marked the end of 'masterly inactivity'. The Second Afghan War (1878-80) and the occupation of Afghan territory impressed upon the British statesmen the necessity for a scientific frontier. By the Anglo-Russian convention of August 1907, Russia disclaimed any jurisdiction over Afghanistan. By the treaty of November 1921 the British abandoned their claim to control Afghan foreign policy. With regard to North-West Frontier, Lord Curzon evolved a policy of withdrawal and concentration. He introduced an administrative change by creating the North-West Frontier Province in 1901 directly under the Government of India. Despite his best efforts, Lord Curzon could not solve the frontier problem.

The annexation of Burma was broadly due to the security motive. In 1852 Dalhousie annexed Lower Burma or Pegu. By the annexation of Lower Burma the entire coast of the Bay of Bengal from Chittagong to Singapore came under British control. Dalhousie considered Upper Burma as the real seat of the Burman race. But its final conquest was delayed till 1886 in the time of Lord Dufferein. The province of Burma was formed by the combination of Upper and Lower Burma with headquarters at Rangoon. Under the Act of 1935, Burma was separated from India with a separate constitution. The Tibetan campaign of 1904 was undertaken as a reply to imagined Russian activity. The move was ill-judged. By the Anglo-Russian Convention of August 1907 both Russia and England agreed to conduct their political relations with Tibet through China.

'The year 1857 may be looked upon as the great divide between the two great landmarks in Indian history—that of British paramountcy in the first half, and that of Indian nationalism in the second half of the nineteenth century.' The Viceroyalty of Lord Lytton (1876-80) formed an important landmark in the history in Indian National movement. The removal of import duties on British textile imports at the cost of Indian textile industry led to a widespread nationalist agitation. The second war against Afghanistan put heavy pressure on the Indian exchequer. The Vernacular Press Act and the Arms Act of 1878 were other reactionary measures of Lytton. In 1878 the Government reduced the age limit for the open competitive examination for the Indian Civil Service from 21 to 19. This was regarded as a deliberate attempt to 'blast the prospects of Indian candidates.' But the immediate factor was the introduction of the controversial Ilbert Bill of 1883. The Bill, introduced by Ilbert, the Law Member of the Viceroy's Council, abolished racial inequality by bringing Englishmen under the jurisdiction of Indian Magistrates or Sessions Judges. But the Europeans in India raised a hue and cry against this Bill and it was withdrawn. 'The response to the agitation of the Europeans against the Ilbert Bill was the National Congress.'

Before the birth of the Indian National Congress in 1885, there were other nationalist organisations like *Hindu Mela* (1867), the *Poona Sarvajanik Sabha* (1867), and the India League (1875). But the most important organisation was the Indian Association, headed by Surendranath Banerjee (1848-1925), who had earlier been dismissed from the Civil Service on frivolous grounds. To give it an all-India character, the Indian Association (1876) called an All-India National Conference, first at Calcutta and then at Bombay. In December 1886 the National Conference was merged with the Congress.

The foundation of the Indian National Congress in 1885 marked a new beginning in the history of Indian nationalism. The new body owed its existence largely to the vision and initiative of an Englishman, Allan Octavian Hume (1829-1912), a retired member of the Indian Civil Service. The most important demands of the Congress were the expansion of the Legislative Councils, appointment of a Royal Commission to enquire into the working of the Indian administration, reduction of military expenditure, holding of simultaneous Public Service Examinations in England and the raising of the age limit for the candidates for this examination.

Towards the end of the nineteenth century, the Congress became practically divided into two groups—the Moderates and the Extremists. The Moderates—Gopal Krishna Gokhale, Surendranath Banerjee, Pherozeshah Mehta, Sankaran Nair and others had unbounded confidence in the British sense of justice and demanded moderate reforms like administrative reorganisation, Indianisation of services, and admission of Indians into the Legislative Councils. The Extremists—Lala Lajpat Rai of Punjab, Bal Gangadhar Tilak of Maharashtra and Bipin Chandra Pal of Bengal (known as the famous Lal-Bal-Pal) contended that 'good' government is no substitute for self-government.

The attitude of the Government towards the development of the nationalist forces hardened as days passed by. The Congress was described as a 'factory of sedition.' In 1898 Elgin (1894-99), the Viceroy, openly declared 'India was conquered by the sword and by the sword it shall be held.' The arrival of Lord Curzon (1899-1905) as the new Viceroy added fuel to the burning fire of nationalism. Curzon's ambition was to assist the Congress 'to a peaceful demise.' He took recourse to a repressive policy to curb the rising tide of nationalism. His Municipality Act of 1899 gave greater representation to the European mercantile community in the municipal corporation of Calcutta. The Indian Universities Act of 1904 brought the Universities under Government control.

The crowning blunder of Lord Curzon was the Partition of Bengal in 1905. His object was to enfeeble the growing power and destroy the political tendencies of a patriotic spirit. The anti-Partition agitation galvanised the people of India for which 1905 was regarded as a landmark in the history of national progress. It had also achieved revolutionary techniques—Boycott and Swadeshi—to achieve its objects. The movement spread to the peasant classes—both Hindu and Muslim. The protest strengthened the Extremist wing of the Congress and created a small but active terrorist movement. Political murders took place and Tilak 'the father of Indian Unrest' was sentenced in July 1908 to six years' imprisonment.

An explosive situation faced Lord Minto in India and John Morley as the new Secretary of State in 1906. With repression in one hand and torch of political progress in the other the government carried through the Morley-Minto Reforms in 1909. An enlarged Imperial Legislative Council and the appointment of Indians to the Executive Councils were the distinguishing features of the Act. The Islington Commission (1912) grappled with the problem of the admission of more Indians into the public services. But the Morley-Minto reforms introduced for the first time in Indian politics the principle of communal electorate by giving the Muslims power to elect their own representatives to the Councils. This concession strengthened the Muslim League, which was founded on December 30, 1906.

The First World War broke out in Europe in July-August 1914. As a part of the British Empire, India automatically became involved in the war as a result of England's declaration of war against Germany. The ruling chiefs and the Indian nationalist leaders, including Tilak, decided to support the war-efforts of the Government. They deluded themselves with the belief that grateful Britain would repay India's loyalty with gratitude.

The entry of Annie Besant into the Indian political scene gave new zest to Indian politics. In September 1916, she founded the Home Rule League and demanded Home Rule for the Indians. The movement for Home Rule was strengthened by Tilak's participation when the latter toured different parts of the country. Tilak declared: 'Swaraj is my birthright and I will have it.'

The entry of Turkey against Britain roused the anti-British feeling of the Muslims. Apart from Muslim discontent, the Hindu middle class had become sore with the unsympathetic attitude of the British. The two streams of discontent met at Lucknow, where the Congress and the League held their annual sessions in December 1916. The Lucknow session of the Congress passed a resolution demanding self-government at an early date.

The need for a change in the Indian policy of the British Government was felt. On August 20, 1917, E. S. Montague, the Secretary of State for India, made the famous announcement of establishing responsible government in India and assisting Indians in every branch of the administration. The constitutional Rubicon was crossed and Montague-Chelmsford Report was published in July 1918. The Report formally announced responsible government as the goal for India. It introduced Dyarchy, a kind of double government, in the provinces. The provincial executive was to be divided into two parts, one to be responsible to the Indian electorate through the Legislature, and the other to the Governor. The Imperial Legislative Council was to be enlarged and given wider powers of discussion, but it was not to control the central executive.

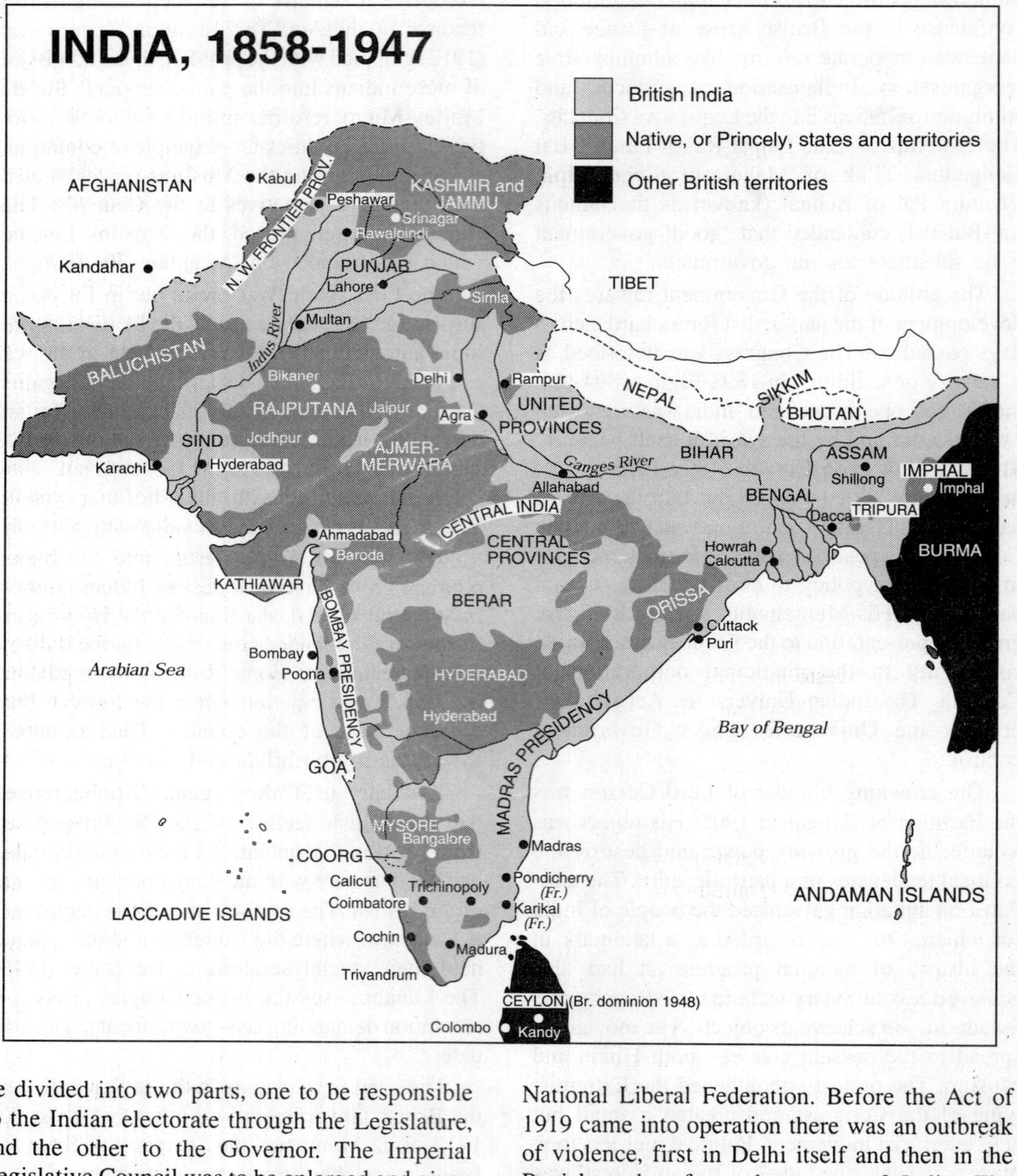

The Montford Report failed to satisfy the extremist section of the Congress. The Moderates, however, welcomed the proposal. This created a split in the Congress and the Moderates found a distinct political organisation known as Indian National Liberal Federation. Before the Act of 1919 came into operation there was an outbreak of violence, first in Delhi itself and then in the Punjab and a few other parts of India. The Rowlatt Act of 1919 and the indiscriminate firing by General Dyer on the unarmed crowd at

Jallianwalla near Amritsar on April 13, 1919 caused an outbreak of feeling all over India. The Hunter Commission, reporting on the event early in 1920, gave support to the general in command. **Gandhiji** who had pinned his faith in the British sense of justice, declared that there could be no cooperation with a satanic government. Meanwhile, the Muslims had been irritated by threats to dismember Turkey, the seat of the Caliphate. Militant Muslims like the Ali brothers, Muhammad Ali and Shaukat Ali organised a Khilafat Party, the avowed object of which was agitation for the restoration of the Sultan of Turkey as Khalifa (Caliph) of Islam. Gandhiji extended support to the *Khilafat* movement as this was to him an 'opportunity of uniting the Hindus and the Muslims.'

Mahatma Gandhi

Gandhiji began his Non-violent Non-cooperation Movement on August 1, 1920. Great emphasis was laid on the promotion of Swadeshi goods by means of reviving hand-spinning in every home. The movement evoked a hearty response from all sections of the people. The jail lost its terror and the people courted arrest voluntarily. On February 1, 1922, Gandhiji announced his decision to start mass Civil Disobedience at Bardoli, a small *tehsil* in the Surat district. But Gandhiji had to suspend the movement owing to an outbreak of mob violence at Chauri Chaura near Gorakhpur in which 22 policemen were killed. Gandhiji was arrested in early 1922 and sentenced to six years' simple imprisonment. Meanwhile, the outbreak of violence by the Moplahs on the Malabar Coast and the transformation of Turkey into a secular republican state under Kemal Pasha in 1922 led to the collapse of the Khilafat movement. The prospect of a Hindu-Muslim entente 'dissolved like a summer thundercloud.'

After Gandhiji's imprisonment there was a split in the Congress. A new faction under the leadership of Motilal Nehru and Chittaranjan Das formed a new Swarajya Party. The manifesto of the new organisation declared that 'while the goal of the party is the attainment of Swaraj, the immediate objective of the party is the speedy attainment of full Dominion Status.' The death of Das in 1925 weakened the Swarajya Party. In April 1926 Lord Irwin became the Viceroy. A commission, under the Chairmanship of Sir John Simon, was appointed in November 1927, to review the political situation in India. During its travels in India in 1928-29, it was subjected to hostile demonstrations and boycott by the Congress. The Madras session of the Congress (1927) declared complete independence as its goal. But the Calcutta session of the Congress (December 1928) agreed to accept Dominion Status if granted on or before December 31, 1929. In view of the Viceroy's unsatisfactory declaration of October 1929, the Lahore session of the Congress (December 1929) under the presidency of Jawaharlal Nehru, adopted complete independence as its goal.

Gandhiji started the Civil Disobedience Movement on March 12, 1930. On that day he left the Sabarmati Ashram on foot with 79 male and female members and reached the sea at Dandi, a small village on the Gujarat sea-coast on April 5. Here he ceremonially broke the Salt Law Regulations. Salt laws were broken in many places. Violation of laws, non-payment of taxes, boycott of foreign goods, mass strikes were adopted to paralyse the government. The movement evoked warm response from the masses, and women came out of their seclusion to participate in the movement.

The Government adopted severe repressive measures to curb the movement. According to official figures, 103 persons were killed, 420 injured and 60,000 imprisoned. But repression failed to unnerve the demonstrators. The Congress abstained from attending the First Round Table Conference, held in London from November 12, 1930 to January 19, 1931. On January 19, 1931, the British Prime Minister Ramsay Macdonald held out hopes of making a substantial transfer of power to India. The Viceroy Lord Irwin was anxious for a settlement and he took the novel step of holding direct talks with Gandhiji. The talks ended with the famous Gandhi-Irwin Pact of March 5, 1931. Gandhiji agreed to suspend the Civil Disobedience Movement and to participate in the next Round Table Conference, while the Government withdrew all repressive measures and released all political prisoners except those convicted of violent crime.

The Second Round Table Conference met in London in September 1931 under the dark shadow of the execution of Bhagat Singh in Punjab and the communal riots at Kanpur. While attending the Conference, Gandhiji demanded that Responsible Government must be established, immediately and in full, both at the centre and in the provinces. The communal question proved a baffling problem and Prime Minister Macdonald announced that the British Government should settle the dispute on its own authority.

On December 28, 1931 Gandhiji returned to India empty-handed. On January 1, 1932, the Congress adopted a resolution for the renewal of the Civil Disobedience. Tension mounted. Gandhiji was once more in prison and the Congress proscribed. Terrorism appeared in Bengal. The Government, with Lord Willingdon as its head, adopted repressive measures to suppress the outbreak. The number of political prisoners rose to 34,458 in April 1932. The announcement of Communal Award in August 1932 by Ramsay Macdonald provoked Gandhiji, then in jail, to undertake a fast. The result was the Poona Pact (September 24, 1932) by which the Depressed Classes were granted much larger representation. The third and the final Round Table Conference was held (November-December 1932) without the Congress.

The Civil Disobedience Movement was officially called off by Gandhiji on May 8, 1933. It caused intense disappointment to many. But the Civil Disobedience Movement was memorable in the struggle for India's freedom. It awakened a new feeling among the masses and increased the status and prestige of the Congress.

After the Third Round Table Conference, the British Government prepared a White Paper in March 1933. On the basis of the White Paper, a Bill was prepared and introduced in Parliament in December 1934. The Bill was finally passed as the Government of India Act on August 2, 1935. The Act was a blueprint for the constitution of independent India. A federal system replaced the unitary system which was designed to incorporate the princes in a single Indian state. There was to be full responsible government in the provinces and dyarchy or divided responsibility at the Centre. The franchise was extended so that a sixth of the adult population of India became eligible to vote. Women received the franchise on the same terms as men. The principle of communal representation, admitted in 1909 and extended in 1919, was accepted as regular feature in 1935.

The Hindu-Muslim fraternity, created by Gandhiji, faded away as soon as the Khilafat Movement came to an end. The acceptance of the Nehru Constitution by the Indian National Congress in 1928 was looked upon by Jinnah as a clear move to ignore the Muslim claims. In December 1930 at the Allahabad session of the Muslim League, Mohammad Iqbal justified the Muslim demand for the creation of a Muslim India within India. In 1933 Rahmat Ali prepared a plan for the establishment of a Pakistan incorporating the Punjab, North-West Frontier Province, Kashmir, Sind and Baluchistan. In 1938 Jinnah raised the cry for partition of India and in January 1940 referred to Hindus and Muslims as two nations.

The outbreak of the Second World War in September 1939 put the whole question of India's political future into a new perspective. The Congress declared that it could not associate with the war unless India was declared an independent nation. The fall of France exposed Britain to the danger of Nazi occupation. The Viceroy, in August 1940, offered an enlargement of his Executive Council and a Constituent Assembly after the

War. But the August offer failed to satisfy either the Congress or the League. Gandhiji opposed the war effort peacefully by initiating a policy of Individual Civil Disobedience. The first man to court arrest was Vinoba Bhave. Nehru was sentenced to four years rigorous imprisonment and more than 14,000 Congressmen were in prison.

The Japanese entry into the war (December 7, 1941) threatened India's integrity. Her cooperation was now considered vital. The British Government sent Sir Stafford Cripps with a new constitutional proposal in March and April 1942. A Constituent Assembly was to be called immediately after the war to draw up a constitution for an Indian Union with Dominion Status. The new state would have the right of secession. Cripps did not bring with him the promise of independence in the near future. Gandhiji described the Cripps' plan as 'a post-dated cheque upon a crashing bank.' The failure of the Cripps Mission ushered in a period of acute political anxiety in the country. In August 1942 the historic 'Quit India' resolution was taken at Bombay by the Congress Working Committee. This was followed by Gandhiji's historic utterance: 'I am not going to be satisfied with anything short of complete freedom. We shall do or die. We shall either free India or die in the attempt.' Gandhiji, Azad and other prominent leaders of the Congress were put under arrest. Serious disorder broke out in different parts of the country. By the end of 1942 the Government had been able to put down the rebellion in a ruthless manner.

Meanwhile **Subhas Chandra Bose,** who had become Congress President in 1938, and in 1939, parted company with the Congress and founded the Forward Bloc. He found the outbreak of the Second World War a convenient opportunity to strike a blow at the English for the freedom of India. In January 1941 he disappeared from Calcutta and found refuge first at Berlin and then at Tokyo. He formed the Provisional Government of Free India and assumed the command of the Indian National Army. In March 1944 the Indian flag was hoisted in Kohima. But with the final defeat of the Japanese, the INA movement collapsed.

Subhas Chandra Bose

The end of the war and the advent of the Labour Party under Clement Attlee as Prime Minister raised the hopes of the Indians. The Viceroy Lord Wavell called a conference in June 1945 to form an interim Cabinet, but this broke down on the League's claim to represent all Muslims. In the elections to the Central and Provincial Legislatures held in 1945-46, the Congress won the general seats and the Muslim League the Muslim seats. At the same time a short-lived naval mutiny in Bombay on February 18, 1946, exposed the weakness of the British authority in India. From March to June 1946 a Cabinet Mission consisting of Lord Pethwick-Lawrence, Sir Stafford Cripps and A. V. Alexander made efforts to find an agreed settlement. This broke down as neither the Congress nor the Muslim League was willing to give up its respective goals of union and partition. Recriminations led to Jinnah's Direct Action on August 16, 1946. The bloody riots which broke out in Calcutta enveloped different parts of India. Partition seemed to be the only solution.[1]

The British Prime Minister, Clement Attlee made the historic announcement on February 20, 1947 to wind up British rule by June 1948. The new Viceroy, Lord Mountbatten, realised that a partition was inevitable. He pushed forward with such speed that he could effect the transfer of power on August 15, 1947. To Pakistan was

1. *Cambridge History of South-East Asia* (Vol. 2), P. 365.

allotted the West Punjab, Sind, Baluchistan, North-West Frontier Province and the Muslim majority areas of East Bengal and Assam, to the new India the remainder. Thus 'the British period in India came to an end after nearly three and a half centuries of trading, two centuries of political power, and a hundred and thirty years of general supremacy.' Partition brought with it problems of great magnitude. About half a million people on both sides are said to have died and a mass migration of ten million was the price for the transformation of the undivided India.

South-East Asia

From the late eighteenth century, the Europeans deeply affected the whole of South-east Asia. But it took differing forms in different countries. Before the advent of the Europeans, Islam had increased its hold on south-east Asia. The coming of the Europeans altered the existing state structures and demarcation of territories were redrawn to suit the convenience of the European powers. The process of drawing the frontiers was not complete till the early twentieth century. Most of the main lines of demarcation were, however, made by 1870. The concept of a national frontier in South-East Asia was arbitrarily applied since it was designed to avoid conflict.

The nineteenth century was an age of migration. South-East Asia, always a recipient of Indians and Chinese, received them on large scale. There were also migrations within south-east Asia.

The Role of the British

In the nineteenth century, Britain was the predominant state in Europe and, thus, in the world. The French were defeated at sea in 1805 and on land in 1815. In southeast Asia, Britain sought security and stability. Britain's predominance did not eliminate its European rivals. The Netherlands and Spain were left with substantial holdings in southeast Asia. Even France was not obstructed in its Vietnam venture. Because of its predominance, Britain set the agenda for lesser European powers. Directly or indirectly, Britain's influence was often decisive in determining the frontiers of the new southeast Asian states.

The Dutch Kingdom in Indonesia

In the closing decades of the eighteenth century, the Dutch retained an Asia-wide empire, with Batavia (Jakarta) as its centre. Its failure to compete in the Asian textile and opium trades had led the Dutch East India Company to concentrate on Java. The Dutch were afraid of the British predominance but the latter were against alienating the Dutch lest they might seek the protection of the French. The Anglo-Dutch treaty of 1784 did not extend their political challenge to the Dutch, except by acquiring Penang in 1786.

In the wake of the Napoleonic Wars, when the Dutch Republic fell under French influence, the British took over the Dutch possessions in India, Ceylon and the Archipelago and, finally, Java (1811). The defeat of France and the establishment of the new Kingdom of the Netherlands made possible the restoration of all the Dutch territories except Ceylon. The opening of trade to the East under the Company's Charter of 1813, and the administration of Java by Stamford Raffles, had led to the establishment of British interest in the island. Meanwhile after the restoration of the colonies in 1816, the Dutch Commissioners-General embarked on renewal of treaties and contracts which aroused apprehensions of officials at Penang. In 1815 the Secret Committee of the Court of Directors disapproved the treaties Raffles made. The British authorities felt the necessity of arriving at a compromise with the Dutch. According to Castlereagh, the Foreign Secretary, the Dutch might hold 'Java and any other of his old possessions in direct colonial sovereignty ... but which after all, my opinion is, ought not in prudence to be one of the exclusive trade.' Beyond these limits, the Dutch should have an understanding with the British. The treaty of 17 March 1824 effected a compromise between Britain and the Dutch. As Canning wrote: 'The situation in which we and the Dutch ... stand to the rest of the world as exclusive Lords of the East, is one more reason for terminating our relative difficulties as soon as we can.' The treaty of 1824 excluded the Dutch from the peninsula, but admitted their predominance in the Archipelago. However, after 1824, an extension of Dutch influence in Bali and other regions was looked with disfavour by the British; but the British challenge never went far. In fact the Dutch expansion was preferred to the intervention of other powers in the Archipelago. As the Foreign office spokesman, Lord Wodehouse, reported in 1860:

> I believe the policy of Mr. Canning's treaty was much the wisest, *viz.*, to leave the Dutch the Eastern Archipelago... The French might, if they possessed such an eastern empire, be really dangerous to India and Australia, but the Dutch are and must remain too weak to cause us any alarm.

In the 1840s the British came back to Borneo and made a treaty with Brunei. In the 1880s British protectorate was established over Sarawak. The founding of the British North Borneo Company and a charter given to the Company in 1881 led to protectorate agreements in 1888 with Sarawak, North Borneo (Sabah) and Brunei.

Spain had, by the late eighteenth century, become a minor power as to cause any concern to the British. The Spanish claim to empire in the Philippines was respected, as they allowed the British real commercial opportunities. Only in Sulu the British opposed Spanish penetration and, ultimately, the powers agreed upon partition. Spanish authority in the Philippines was challenged by America in 1898. There was little chance of effectively opposing it. The British had to be content with American occupation as in their view American control was preferable to Spain.

The awakening process had begun earlier in the Philippines since the Filipinos had long been under Western subjection. In the nineteenth century, the growth of free trade led to the emergence of a prosperous middle class of Filipinos, whose leaders, Jose Rizal and Marcalo H. del Pilar, became the leaders of a nationalist movement. But Rizal's moderate *Liga Filipino* was suppressed. It was supplanted by a revolutionary secret society, *Katipunan* whose object was to secure independence by violent means. In 1897 it set up its own revolutionary government under Emilio Aguinaldo (1869-1963), but it proved to be short-lived. The outbreak of the Spanish-American war gave a new turn to the history of the Philippines which came under the occupation of the United States in 1902.

Sensing the intensity of Filipino nationalism, the United States adopted a policy of granting the Filipinos a measure of self-government. In 1913 Woodrow Wilson declared that the policy of the United States should be formulated 'with a view to the ultimate independence of the islands and as a preparation for that independence.' In 1916 was established in Philippines an administrative structure modelled on that of the United States with a strong executive and an independent judiciary along with the bicameral legislature.

By the thirties a strong move was set afoot in the United States Congress to offer full and immediate independence to the Philippines. In 1933, the Congress passed an Act providing for independence after a ten-year transition period. During this time a Commonwealth Constitution was to be drafted and elections held while permitting the United States to retain commercial rights and military bases in the Commonwealth. In 1935 the transition period commenced with a national plebiscite approving the new Constitution while electing Manuel L. Quezon as first President.

The outbreak of the Second World War and the Japanese occupation of the islands caused a setback to Filipinos' road to independence. With Japan's defeat, General Douglas MacArthur began to work through President Sergio Osmena, representing the pro-American leadership that had dominated Filipino politics before 1942. Meanwhile, Manuel Roxas and his Liberal Party mounted a challenge to Osmena's administration. In the elections that ensued the Liberals won in the House of Representatives and Senate and Roxas was elected President. The United States ensured free trade between the two countries and provided financial aid to the Philippines. The Philippines was proclaimed an independent republic on July 4, 1946. The grant of formal independence to the Philippines marked a significant departure on the policy of Washington than its counterparts in the Hague, London or Paris in her policy to post-war south-east Asia.

Indonesia

During the first two centuries of their rule in Indonesia, the Dutch maintained their commercial grip on the country. In the first half of the nineteenth century, the Dutch inaugurated a policy of exploitation of native production for their own benefit which yielded a vast colonial surplus. However, in 1901, the Dutch launched an 'ethical policy' to promote economic development and to encourage popular participation in social and administrative affairs. However, during the twenties, when relations between the Dutch administration and Indonesian nationalists became embittered, the 'ethical policy' was abandoned.

The first signs of Indonesian nationalism manifested in the early nineteenth century in the activities of Hadiningrat and his niece, Raden Adjang Kartini, whose interest in modernisation and in education made her a nationalist icon. Three organisations dominated Indonesian reformist activity during the 1910's: Sarekat Islam; Muhammadiyah, a modernist reforming Muslim organisation, and the *Indische Social-Demokratische Vereeniging* (ISDV), a radical Marxist group.

Constituted in September 1912, Sarekat Islam grew into a mass movement with its total membership of two million. Sarekat Islam became within a few years a revolutionary political party holding national congresses, organising strikes and demanding independence. The ISDV group which in 1920 formed the *Perserikatan Komunist India* (PKI) made futile efforts to stage revolts. Lacking widespread support, these were quickly put down. The Dutch administration suppressed the PKI so effectively that the party did not become a political force in Indonesia till 1945.

The most important development of the 1920s was the emergence of a second generation of political activists within Indonesia. The younger leadership was more volatile and adopted a radical stance. Study clubs provided a common meeting ground for students and local activists. The most important of these groups was the General Study Club of Bandung (1925) whose membership included leading figures like Dekker and Sukarno. **Sukarno**, who rapidly became one of the key nationalist figures, agreed to unity in opposing the Dutch. In 1927 was set up a new political organisation called *Perserikatan National Indonesia* (PNI, the Indonesian National Association). Its object was to promote the cause of Indonesian nationalism by fostering unity. Sukarno occupied a prominent place in its executive body. To avoid suppression, the leaders of the PNI adopted moderate demands. However, PNI's growing extremism led the Dutch to the detention of a number of leaders including Sukarno. In April 1931, PNI was dissolved and a new body came into being known as the *PNI Baru* or New PNI. It reflected Hatta's philosophy and sought to cultivate a political base among the proletariat and the peasantry. Sukarno, who considered unity to be of paramount importance was instrumental in creating a federation of anti-colonial parties called PPPKI, the Association of Political Organisations of the Indonesian People. The most important nationalist figure of the 1930s was Mohammed Husni Thamrin, Chairman of the PPPKI. His death in Dutch custody in January 1941 helped to mobilise anti-Dutch opinion before the Japanese invasion.

Sukarno

After the Japanese surrender, the Dutch, on November 15, 1946, recognised the Republican government's hold on Sumatra and Java and agreed to cooperate in establishing a sovereign, democratic and federal 'United States of Indonesia.' But she was in no mood to abandon her claims to the East Indies. The divisive tendencies of the nationalist movement encouraged the Dutch to maintain their hold in Indonesia. However, the pressure of world opinion and intervention of the Security Council precipitated the Renville Conference in January 1948. It was agreed to set up the United States of Indonesia before the Dutch withdrew their forces from the country. But the Dutch launched another offensive in 1948. The Dutch were subjected to international criticism which reached such a crescendo that it led to the decolonisation of Indonesia. The Security Council again intervened and induced the Hague to recognise a sovereign Republic of the United States of Indonesia (November 1949). On December 2, 1949, after the instruments of transfer had been signed, Sukarno entered Jakarta as President of the United States of Indonesia. Apart from UN actions, U. S. line on Indonesia partly guided the destiny of Indonesia and this was reflected in the UN resolutions. 'That Holland's colonial regime collapsed earlier than that of French Indo-China cannot be explained without reference to the international politics of 1948-50.'

Vietnam

The early French advance into Cochin-China in the south and then Tonkin in the north was met with sporadic armed resistance. In the mid-1880s a group of anti-French officials seized control of the court and fled inland with the Emperor, proclaiming general uprising against the French. The French immediately placed a pliant member of the imperial family on the throne and sent into exile his predecessor.

During the half century from 1870 to 1920 France went through two major wars with frequent changes in the Cabinet. This instability was reflected in some degree to Vietnam itself with twenty governors-general between 1887 and 1920. During this period France exploited the resources of Vietnam for her own benefit. It became one of the largest rice-exporting areas of the world and the most profitable of all France's overseas possessions.

The Vietnamese are culturally the most advanced peoples of Indo-China. To counteract nationalism the French introduced their own culture by establishing French vernacular schools and the University of Hanoi. But the French culture—instead of diminishing the embers of nationalism—actually fuelled it. Thus, when in 1907 the University of Hanoi was founded to counteract the growing tide of nationalism, such an outburst of national feeling took place that it had to be closed in the following year and was not reopened until 1917.

In early decades of the twentieth century, nationalism veered round the monarchy and republicanism. The second decade of the century was a period of relative calm. France was involved in the general conflict in Europe and the liberal Governor-General, Albert Sarraut, promised liberal reforms. The 1911 Revolution in China offered Indo-China a republican ideology. The man who was destined to become famous in the history of Vietnam, **Ho Chi Minh**, left the

Ho Chi Minh

country in 1911 and was drawn to Marxism. In the twenties secular forces came to the fore and played an important part in nationalist movement. The failure of the moderate parties like the constitutionalists marked a leftward swing in the nationalist movement.

French intrasigence and repression helped to foster subversive activity. In 1927 was founded a secret society *Viet Nam Quoc Dan Dang* (Vietnamese Nationalist Party). Without building a mass base, it hoped for revolutionary insurrection. An abortive uprising in February 1930 effectively put an end to the party. The way was left for the Communists to seize the leadership of the anti-colonial movement. After various vicissitudes, Ho Chi Minh succeeded in forging sev-

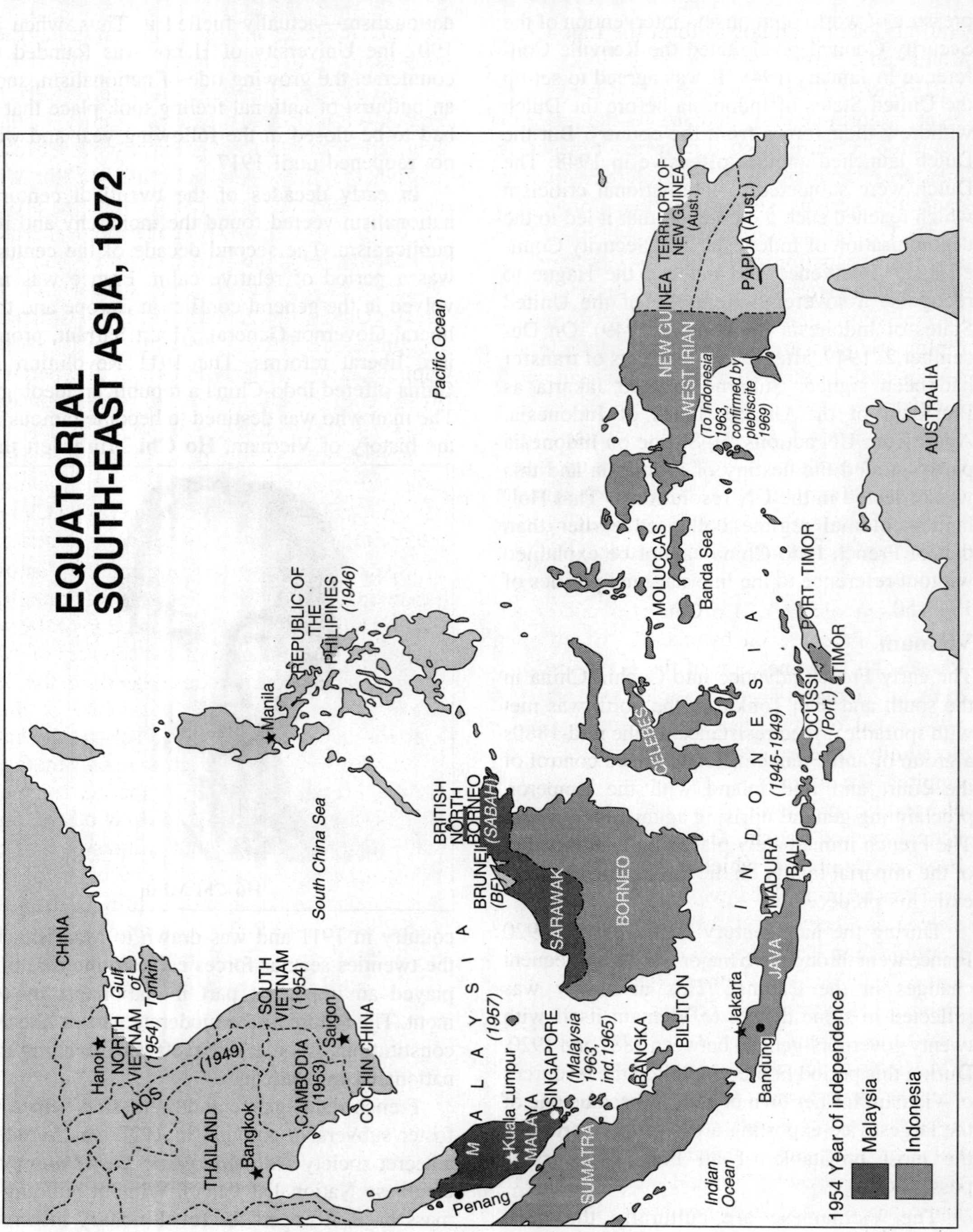
EQUATORIAL SOUTH-EAST ASIA, 1972
CHINA
Hanoi
NORTH VIETNAM (1954)
Gulf of Tonkin
LAOS (1949)
THAILAND
Bangkok
CAMBODIA (1953)
SOUTH VIETNAM (1954)
Saigon
COCHIN CHINA
South China Sea
REPUBLIC OF THE PHILIPPINES (1946)
Manila
Pacific Ocean
M A L A Y S I A
Penang
Kuala Lumpur
MALAYA (1957)
SINGAPORE (Malaysia 1963, ind.1965)
SUMATRA
BANGKA
BILLITON
Jakarta
Bandung
JAVA
MADURA
BALI
SARAWAK
BRUNEI (BR.)
BRITISH NORTH BORNEO (SABAH)
BORNEO
CELEBES
I N D O N E S I A (1945-1949)
OCUSSI (Port.)
TIMOR
PORT. TIMOR
MOLUCCAS
Banda Sea
NEW GUINEA
WEST IRIAN (To Indonesia 1963, confirmed by plebiscite 1969)
TERRITORY OF NEW GUINEA (Aust.)
PAPUA (Aust.)
AUSTRALIA
Indian Ocean
1954 Year of independence
Malaysia
Indonesia

eral left-leaning groups to form the Indo-China Communist Party.

In mid-1930 large-scale rural uprisings took place in north-central Vietnam. As the rebellion assumed Communist overtone, repressive measures mounted with great ferocity which caused a serious setback to the Communist Party. The outbreak of the Second World War and the occupation of France by Germany led Indo-China to recognise the Vichy regime. Indo-China soon came under strong Japanese diplomatic pressure which led to the stationing of Japanese military forces in north and south Vietnam.

Early in 1941 Ho Chi Minh crossed from China into northern Vietnam and set up a new organisation known as the *Vietminh.* Dominated by Communists, the Vietminh aimed at creating a broad coalition of anti-colonial and anti-Japanese elements.

The emergence of De Gaulle as undisputed leader of Free French by mid-1943 confirmed Roosevelt's apprehension of the French resolve to retain Vietnam. The Brazaville Declaration of 1944 ruled out 'all idea of autonomy and all possibility of development outside the French empire.' On March 24, 1945, De Gaulle proclaimed to create in future an Indo-Chinese Federation (of Tonkin, Cochin China, Annam, Laos and Cambodia) which would remain within the French Union. Meanwhile Ho Chi Minh was elected as Chairman of the National Liberation Committee in Hanoi and an independent Democratic Republic of Vietnam (DRV) was proclaimed. However, the French were quick to assert their control over Indo-China. Since Ho Chi Minh was consolidating his power, the French came to an agreement whereby the latter recognised the DRV as a free and self-governing state, but remained a part of the Indo-Chinese Federation and the French Union. However, the diplomatic phase ended in November 1946 with the French bombardment of Haiphong. Ho Chi Minh declared a war of nationwide resistance against the French. The first Vietnam War lasted until mid-February 1947 when the Vietnamese resistance collapsed. The battle committed France to seven and a half years war with the Vietnamese in which the latter showed profound strategy and mobilisation of rural people.

The aims of the Vietminh were to force the French out of Indo-China and to unify Vietnam as an independent sovereign state. When it became obvious that they could not crush Ho Chi Minh and the Vietminh, the French sought to project the ex-Emperor Bao Dai as the national leader. In February 1950 the USA recognised Bao Dai's Vietnam as 'an independent state within the French Union.' On January 18, 1950, China had recognised the DRV followed by the USSR and supplied arms and ammunition to the Vietminh. At the end of 1950 the French military position was desperate. In May 1950 the US entered into a momentous commitment to grant military assistance to the French. China's entry into the Korean War (November 1950) and fear of Chinese intervention stiffened the U.S. commitment.

Seeing the French flagging and the Vietminh expanding, the American Secretary of State, John Foster Dulles, took over the direction of the war. When the Navarre plan of the summer of 1953 to throw more French troops fizzled out, the USA began to contemplate the possibility of direct military involvement. In May 1954 at the battle of Dien Bien Phu, the French were outgeneralled. As the French reeled under the Vietminh onslaught, the US attempted to draw others, especially Britain, into a joint military operation. When it became clear at the end of April 1954 that Britain would not participate in joint military action over Indo-China, Eisenhower prevented US administration from acting unilaterally.

In July 1954, under the joint Chairmanship of Britain and Russia, armistice agreements were signed at Geneva—Vietnam was provisionally partitioned at the 17th parallel of latitude with the Democratic Republic in control of the north and the Saigon regime, headed by Bao Dai, in control of the south. The prospect of reunification of Vietnam was held out in the proposed elections in July 1956. France withdrew from Indochina and the independence and integrity of Cambodia and Laos became something more than a political formula. The Geneva settlement did not provide a lasting peace nor did it achieve the goal of national self-determination in Vietnam. The Vietminh struggle had only half succeeded.

Burma

The multiplicity of ethnic groups—the Mon, the Arakanese, the Karen, the Shan, and the Kachin, the Indians, and the Chinese—has been a centrifugal force in Burmese history. It resulted in political fragmentation and posed a constant obstacle to the establishment of any strong and unitary authority. In the twentieth century ethnic problems acted as a divisive force in the nationalist movement as many of the minority groups, fearful of the domination of ethnic Burman majority, looked to British colonial authority for protection.

Burma, annexed piecemeal between 1826 and 1886, became a province of British India at the time of the final annexation on January 1, 1886. The Third Anglo-Burmese War (1885-86) profoundly affected future political developments. Members of the deposed royal house and local chieftains led a disjointed series of rebellions, while various ethnic groups took advantage of upheaval at the centre to assert their autonomy. It took more than five years for the British to achieve the 'Pacification' of Burma, particularly in the newly-annexed upper regions.

In the early years of the twentieth century a new type of anti-colonial activity began in Burma. It was closely linked to the Buddhist religion which provided a powerful rallying focus against British rule. In 1906 was established the Young Men's Buddhist Association (YMBA). Initially the YMBA was non-political, focussing on cultural and religious revival. It became increasingly politicised in the 1910s as a result of the controversy whether British and other foreigners should be required to conform to the traditional practice of removing shoes when entering a Buddhist temple or monastery. The British grudgingly acquiesced to the traditional practice which was interpreted by the nationalists as a major victory.

Soon afterwards, factionalism reared head and there emerged in 1921 a new umbrella organisation, the General Council of Burmese Association (GCBA). It aimed to forge a broader anti-colonial movement and, to achieve this, it began a long tradition of political activism among university students.

The announcement by Montague in 1917 of his plan for the development of responsible government in India evoked from the Burmese a demand for separation from India. This step would bring with it the prospect of restrictions on Indian immigration. A wave of nationalist protests and strikes led the British Parliament in 1921 to extend dyarchy to Burma, a change which took effect two years later. In 1923 Burma received a new Legislative Council of 103 members, 79 of whom were elected on a democratic franchise. To it was assigned the overall charge of departments of education, public health, forests and excise.

The factional rivalries that had plagued the YMBA soon surfaced in the GCBA. Long-standing urban-rural divisions became more marked. Urban nationalists wanted to oust the British and take over the colonial state. Many of the rural constituencies wanted not only to oust the British but also to abolish the colonial institutions that had been established by the British.

The Great Depression of early 1930s marked a watershed on the nationalist movement in Burma and other areas of South-east Asia. In December 1930 full-scale rebellion broke out in the rice-producing region badly affected by the slump. It was led by an ex-monk, Saya San, proclaiming messianic prophecies with his professed goal of restoring the monarchy. The rebellion spread over wide areas of upper and lower Burma. Though it did not threaten British rule, it was not completely put down until 1932.

Influenced by socialism, Marxism and other currents of Western thought, an urban, secular, radical movement grew up in the 1930s. It was spearheaded by student leaders who appropriated to themselves the title *thakin* (master). They included charismatic **Aung San** and U Nu, the latter becoming the first prime minister of post-British Burma. The *thakin* sought to unite all ethnic groups in the Burmese nation and adopted as their slogan: 'Burma is our country; Burmese literature is our literature; Burmese language is our language. Love our country, raise the standards of our literature, respect our language.'

As the nationalist agitation increased in the late thirties, the British responded with another round of administrative reform. The Indian Statutory Commission (known as the Simon

Aung San

Commission) had recommended the separation of Burma from India, which was endorsed by the Second Round Table Conference held in London in 1931-32. In 1937 Burma achieved separation together with a bicameral parliament and cabinet government. Ba Maw, a veteran nationalist figure, became Prime Minister. Despite the retention of reserve powers by the Governor, the new government had effectual control over practically the whole range of the internal affairs of Burma.

The radicals, however, were dissatisfied with these limited British concessions and demanded full independence. The occupation of Burma by Japan by the end of May 1942 completely changed the struggle for independence by the Burmese. The appointment of Louis Mountbatten as Supreme Allied Commander of Southeast Asia in August 1943 breathed a new life. Allied troops entered Rangoon in early May 1945. After the war, the British grappled with the problem of economic rehabilitation and not its political advance. On May 17, 1945, the British government published a White Paper. While accepting Burma's full self-government within the British Commonwealth as Britain's long-term objective, it set no time-table for political advance. But Aung San, the commander of the National Army, and his associates of the *Dobama Asiayone* (We Burmans Association), demanded complete independence. They had organised the nation-wide Anti-Fascist Peoples Freedom League. The grant of independence of Japan to Burma on August 1, 1943 had sharpened their desire for real independence. They effectively opposed every ministry formed by the British Governor. Mountbatten recognised that it was imperative to reach an understanding with Aung San.

In August 1946 Dorman Smith was replaced by Sir Hubert Rance who was more sympathetic to nationalist aspirations than the former. In October 1946 he accepted an AFPFL-dominated Council of Ministers with Aung San as its leader. In January 1947 Aung San reached an agreement with Attlee's government on the election of a Constituent Assembly to draft the constitution for independent Burma. The overwhelming victory of AFPFL in the April elections seemed to settle the question of Burmese independence. But Aung San had to reconcile the non-Burman people—the Shans, Kachins, Karens and Chins. Aung San secured their agreement to join in the proposed Union of Burma. The Karens, however, held aloof and demanded a separate state under British protection. Britain rejected the demand. The assassination in July 1947 of Aung San and six of his cabinet colleagues exposed the weakness of the Burmese nationalist movement. Sir Hubert Rance at once nominated U Nu to the premiership and negotiated with him a treaty by which on January 4, 1948, the Union of Burma became a sovereign independent state. The end of British rule in India in August 1947 strengthened British desire to withdraw from Burma as well. The achievement of independence did not extinguish the civil war, Communist insurrection, and Karen secessionism which engulfed Burma following the achievement of independence.

Malay

British policy towards the Malay Peninsula was influenced to a certain extent to preempt foreign intervention. With Penang acquired in 1786, Melaka finally transferred in 1824, and Singapore occupied in 1819, Britain commanded the Straits. Britain's economic interest developed in the 1840s with a new demand for tin and for rubber at the turn of the century. Apart from the Malay States, Britain had to deal with Siam in establishing her influence over the area. British relationships differed from state to state.

In Johor, the British exerted more influence than in any other state. The German presence in Sulu from the early 1870's made Lord Kimberley to adopt precautionary steps in the peninsula: 'The Germans would be too powerful neighbours, and their presence in Borneo would exercise a disturbing influence in the Malay Peninsula.' Earlier British intervention in the Malay States was limited in form. The Pangkor engagement of 1874 involved the appointment of Residents, who were expected to give advice to the rulers. The murder of the first Resident in Perak, J. W. W. Birch, led to a punitive expedition. The installation of a Resident contributed to the success of the system and it was applied to Pahang in 1888. The system, however, produced tension and disturbances which led to the creation of the Federated Malay States in 1895.

Within Perak, Selangor and the Negri Sembilan, British rule brought important changes. Tin-mining was the principal source of income and government revenue until the second decade of the twentieth century when it was overtaken by the lucrative rubber industry. Technically Kedah, Kelantan, Terengganu and Perlis were client states of the Thai Kingdom until 1909 when Siam surrendered its rights to Britain.

In the first three decades of the twentieth century, reform in the Malay peninsula concentrated largely on religion and education. In 1905 a Malay College was established which fostered conservative opinion and produced candidates for Malay Administrative Service. A second institution, the Sultan Idris Training College, founded in 1922, attracted students from village vernacular schools. By promoting the study of Malay literature, the College created political awareness and its students became vocal critique of British rule in Malay. The press acted as a vehicle of discussions of religious issues. People were divided into a reformist *Kaum muda* (young group), seeking to purify Islam in Malaya, and a conservative *Kaum tua* (elder group) seeking to maintain the status quo. A writer on Malay nationalism earmarked 1926 as a watershed in the development of Malay political attitudes. In that year a group of activists formed a Malay political association called the *Kesatuan Melayu Singapura* (Singapore Malay Union)—the latter deriving inspiration from Indonesian radicals.

The obvious target of the Malay nationalists was the British administration which was generally sympathetic towards the Malays during the 1920s and 1930s. They stressed the need to ensure adequate representation of the local population in the administrative set-up and took steps to protect the interests of the Malays from the large segments of immigrant population. The British High Commissioner, Sir Shenton Thomas, sharply criticised the 1936 proposals that Malaya-born Indians be given a greater share in the administration. 'I do not know of any country in which what I might call a foreigner—that is to say, a native, not a native of the country or an Englishman—has ever been appointed to an administrative post.'

After the Great Depression, the government repatriated a number of Indians and Chinese, while an Aliens Enactment restricted new immigration. But this did not help the situation. So when the government began to explore the idea of maintaining a permanent Chinese and Indian population in the peninsula, it immediately provoked serious opposition among the Malays.

In the thirties anti-Japanese agitation among the Chinese population, as well as strikes and labour unrest, intensified Malay apprehension about foreign domination. In 1937 the Singapore Malay Union formed branches in Melaka and Penang. A Brotherhood of Pen Friends, to examine the political situation and particularly the position of the Malays, was formed in the same year, as was a radical group called the *Kesatuan Melayu Muda* or Malay Youth Union. The *Kesatuan Melayu Muda* 'neither professed loyalty to the Sultans and the British nor spoke of noncooperation, but worked to promote nationalist feelings and teaching among its members, whose strength lay in the lower classes.' A Pan-Malayan Conference met in Kuala Lampur in August 1939 to forge united movement by bringing the disparate Malay groups in a single movement. Though the efforts failed, it sowed the seed of the growth of a successful postwar organisation, the United Malays National Organisation.

In the Federated States the Chief Secretary at Kuala Lampur and his officials ruled with great efficiency. In the Unfederated States advisers had to coordinate policy by means of advice. In the Straits Settlement the Governor ruled with the assistance of an Executive Council and a small Legislative Council, members of which were nominated up to 1924. The non-official members included one Malay and three Chinese. Despite official majority, the government showed much deference to the views of the non-officials. Though there was little devolution of power to the Sultan, the British administrators were far from happy about the situation. With the adoption of the policy of decentralisation, the Chief Secretaryship was abolished in 1935 and the State Councils of the Sultans got additional powers. Up to the Japanese invasion in 1941 the Colonial office in London pursued the policy of decentralisation.

After the Japanese departure in 1945, Malay national sentiment assumed a new dimension and its rallying cry 'Malaya for the Malays' was directed against the Chinese. Accordingly, on April 1, 1946, all nine Malay states together with Penang and Malacca were joined to form the Malayan Union. The free port of Singapore was, however, excluded. The period of military occupation, however, was costly. Mountbatten was anxious to give autonomy to the Malayan Union. While the self-determination for the Malayan peninsula was Britain's ultimate objective, it still dithered. But the proposal to grant citizenship to non-Malays and the emergence of Communist-led opposition led the British to appease the Malay rulers. Finally, on February 1, 1948, the Federation Malaya was inaugurated. The Sultans regained their former powers and the British had to accept the restrictive citizenship scheme. Singapore remained as the headquarters of British military power in the region.

The beginning of armed struggle by the Malayan Communist Party (MCP), alienated the British. The High Commissioner, Gent, was blamed for failing first to anticipate and then to counter the violence. At the end of June 1948, he was recalled. During the next three and half years, the British had to deal with the menace of guerrilla attacks. Malay's strategic position and its economic importance stiffened British desire to retain her dominance. However, the increasing costs of the Emergency, Britain's shattered domestic economy, and the Korean War aggravated the problem. The new High Commissioner, Henry Gurney, like his predecessor Gent, failed to suppress the insurrection. The assassination of Gurney in October 1951 highlighted the futility of the British administration. With the return of the Conservatives under Churchill, General Templer was appointed High Commissioner and Director of Operation early in 1952.

Templer's 'hearts and minds' strategy was to resettle the Chinese squatters upon whom the Communists depended and to accelerate the political and social advance of the Malayan people. The British, however, were conscious of the fact that 'Communism in Asia cannot be checked by military means alone.' The British government declared that 'the policy of His Majesty's Government in the United Kingdom is that Malaya should in due course become a fully self-governing nation'; it expressed the hope that 'that nation will be within the British Commonwealth.'

From 1952, the counter-insurgency operations yielded results. The United Malaya National Organisation (UMNO) and MCA (Malayan Chinese Association) struck an ad hoc alliance which was reinforced by the accession of the Malayan Indian Congress in 1954. The pace of decolonisation hereafter gathered momentum. Malaya's first General Election was held only in 1955; full independence within the British Commonwealth came on August 31, 1957. Although Malaya was strategically important to Britain in the region, it was peripheral to the interests of other Great Powers. Henceforth, the country did not attract international attention to the same degree as did Indonesia and Indo-China. Although Malaya refused to join SEATO, it remained central to British interests for another decade. The remaining colonies of Singapore, Sabah and Sarawak were relinquished by Britain in 1963. Britain directly assisted Malaya in Emergency operations till 1960. It rushed to defence of Malaysia in its confrontation with Indonesia in 1963-66; it was the dominant partner in the Anglo-Malayan Defence Arrangement.

Thailand

Throughout the period of Western imperial expansion, Siam retained a formal—though circumscribed—independence. In the seventeenth century European powers, and particularly the French, had played a major role in Siam's economic development. For the next century and a half, European interests were focussed on other commercially promising states. Left largely to itself, Siam was engaged in traditional dynastic rivalries, a foreign trade particularly with China, and in counteracting her long-standing major rivals, Burma and Vietnam.

The Thai response to increasing Western activity in the early nineteenth century has been a balancing one, attempting to play the competing imperialist powers—one against another. In practice, it began to rely on Britain, a dominant power in the region and whose interests were largely economic. The French, on the other hand, were more interested with territorial expansion, especially after the European debacle of 1870-71. In a choice metaphor, the Siamese King Mongkut was reported to have observed that the choice facing Siam was whether 'to swim upriver and make friends with the crocodile (the French) or to swim out to sea and hang on to the whale (The British).' He and his successors down to 1932 opted for the whale and Britain exercised full control without declaring formal sovereignty.

In the middle of the nineteenth century a 'self-strengthening movement'—a programme of internal reforms intended to transform Siam into a modern country—began by Mongkut. The movement gathered momentum in the long reign of his successor Chulalong Korn (1868-1910). It covered various fields like finance, administration and communication. There was promoted 'official nationalism' focussing on loyalty to the throne. The reform movement was greatly intensified and institutionalised by his successor, Vajiravudh (1910-25), a king who received his education abroad. While continuing to promote Western science and technology, he stressed a kind of cultural nationalism with a romantic vision of the Thai past. He also began to look towards the sizeable Chinese minority as alien to Thai culture.

Vajiravudh sought to counteract Western or Chinese threats by religious fervour with an appeal to the Buddhist religion and by emphasising loyalty to the throne. His ideology was summed up in the motto 'King, Nation, Religion' and the programme was carried on zealously by Vajiravudh himself. In 1917 Vajiravudh joined the Allies in the First World War. Though he has been described by his admirers as 'Father of Thai Nationalism', critics have pointed out his lack of sympathy for other nationalist movements.

Vijiravudh's death in 1925 muted to a certain extent his 'state-sponsored nationalism.' His successor, Prajadhipok (1925-35), abandoned his predecessor's nationalist programme which was only to be revived following the 1932 coup that ended royal absolutism.

The social critic Thianwan (1842-1915) called for wide-ranging Westernisation and political modernisation. A series of rural rebellion in the 1890s and 1901-02 challenged the central authority and the political ideology of the state. In Chulalongkorn's reign such challenges were ignored or suppressed. But in the reign of Vajiravudh and Prajadhipok they became more overwhelming and ultimately swept the traditional order. There appeared the 'R. S. 130 Conspiracy' (1912), a plot among a group of lower-ranking military officers and few civilians to end the absolute monarchy. Though it was quickly aborted, the 'R. S. 130 Conspiracy' revealed a new disgruntled emerging middle class in the bureaucracy. The growing number of Thai students visiting France, particularly law and military studies, came into contact with republicanism and radical doctrines of French Socialist and Marxist thought. The student leaders found Siam relatively backward socially, politically and economically. The chief instigator-organiser of the Thai students in France was Pridi Phanomyong. To meet the growing discontent, Prajadhipok formulated a range of proposals for political change, including representative institutions. But the proposed reforms were overtaken by the economic crisis brought on by the Great Depression and then the 1932 coup itself.

In June 1932, a group calling itself the 'People's Party', overthrew royal absolutism. A six-point programme was issued by Pridi which alarmed the conservative elements in the People's Party. Pridi's economic plan was labelled Communistic and he was sent into exile in France. A second coup in June 1933 brought Pharya Phahon to the prime-ministership as leader of a more moderate military faction. In October an attempted counter-coup by conservative elements was unsuccessful. Phahon tried to serve as a moderating and balancing force between the rival and military factions. In late 1938 he stepped down from office.

After Phahon's resignation came the ambitious Phibun, who inaugurated a new phase of Thai nationalism. As Prime Minister-cum-Commander-in-chief, Phibun promoted the cult of 'The Leader' and downplayed 'King, Nation and the Constitution.' Early in 1942 he justified his policy by addressing the cabinet:

> The Japanese have the Emperor as their firm guiding principle. We have nothing. What we have are Nations, Religion, Monarch and Constitution. Nation is still a vision; Religion is not practised devoutly; the Monarch is still a child, only seen in pictures; the constitution is just a paper document. When the country is in a critical situation we have nothing to rely upon. Thus I ask you to follow the Prime Minister.

Phibun also harked back to cultural nationalism which included the promotion of traditional Thai values. Cultural nationalism was accompanied by economic nationalism, militarism, and propagation of the Buddhist religion. Phibun also fostered Pan-Thai movement which sought to recover lost territories. The irredentist drive became manifest in 1939 by changing the name Siam to Thailand, intended to assert Thai dominance over Chinese and Western influence and to proclaim Thailand as the natural home of all the Thai people. The 'greater Thailand' dream came to be fulfilled in a war against the weakened French regime in Indo-China in 1940-41, resulting in the recovery of former Thai territories in western and northern Cambodia and trans-Mekong Laos. With only brief interregnums—such as Pridi's return to power in 1944-47 or the democratic era of 1973-76—a form of conservative 'official' nationalism continued to be the focal ideology down through the 1980s.

The decline and fall of European empires in Southeast Asia is an interesting episode in history. The growth of the empires carries within them the seeds of their own destruction. Some empires succumbed to adversity, others more elaborate structures collapsed under their own weight. Difficulties in the mother country after 1945 had the effect of enhancing the value of overseas possession and of stiffening Britain, Dutch and French determination to hold on to them.

As war and peace swept across Southeast Asia in the 1940s and 1950s, there were dramatic twists in the fortunes of the colonial regimes and nationalist movements. Before World War II, colonialism had already become the target of protest in Southeast Asia. Wars in Java and Aceh, risings in Perak and Pahang, the disaffection of Vietnamese scholar-gentry and Saya San's millenarianism in the Irrawaddy Delta are symptoms of traditionalist resistance. With the extension of Western influence, educated elites wrestled with their colonial masters in the hope of wresting state power. Conditions oscillated between arbitrary rule and anarchy throughout Southeast Asia between 1942 and 1946 and in the decade that followed a host of communities struggle to survive by raising the bogey of identity and common cause.

Before the achievement of national independence, South-East Asia, in international spheres, was little more than a geographical expression. But in the 1940's for the first time in history, the area acquired a strategic and international importance. The Allies responded to the ideology and wishes of the nationalists with the principles of the United Nations and the machinery of South-East Asia Command. The emergence of nation-states in the 1950s was facilitated by the political, economic, and military assistance received from America, China or Russia. After the end of formal colonialism, 'the international relations of Southeast Asian countries now revolved round cold war rather than neo-colonial considerations.'

Africa

The First World War engulfed Africa as the warring nations sought to alter the colonial balance of power. Turkey attacked the Suez Canal and the

Allies fought at the Arab lands. By 1918 South African troops had overrun German Southwest Africa, and the British had invaded the German colonial territories of East and West Africa. In the aftermath of the war the British, French, Belgians and South Africans shared the spoils of the German African Empire. But the new colonies were placed under a mandate system of the League of Nations.

The First World War caused economic imbalance in Africa as it did throughout the world. The war also made many disruptive demands upon Africa by exploiting its manpower. However, ideological appeals of President Woodrow Wilson in which he emphasised the goal of self-determination had peripheral effect on the African countries. At the end of the First World War, nationalists in Egypt demanded the inclusion of an Egyptian national delegate at the Paris Peace Conference. Reverberations of nationalist aspirations were also felt in Tunsia and Syria. The feelings were so overwhelming in Syria that it led to a military confrontation between French troops and Syrian nationalists. Its effects were also felt when a Pan-African Congress met at Paris in 1919, and a group of West African intellectuals created a British West African Congress.

The fervour of nationalism that began at the end of First World War was accentuated after the end of the Second World War. Wilson's Fourteen points that emphasised self-determination and President Roosevelt and British Prime Minister Churchill's promulgation of the Atlantic Charter in 1941 which called for restoration of sovereign rights and self government, stirred nationalist hopes in the colonial world.

In response to these changing circumstances, the British and the French began certain palliative measures to smother the nationalist aspirations. However, they were convinced that the movement of the colonies for independence could not be postponed *sine die*. Hence, they made swift efforts to smother the movement by providing colonies with a modicum of self-rule and economic well-being. A Colonial Welfare Fund, created just before the war, was reactivated. The British formula for decolonisation was to enlarge the legislative bodies with enhanced functions and to foster an alliance between traditional leaders and the emerging educated elite.

The Burns Constitution in the Gold Coast in 1946 tried to foster such an alliance. The Legislative Council was composed of elected representatives and delegates appointed by the government. However, the tide of nationalism moved so swiftly that the Gold Coast became independent in 1957. Kwame Nkrumah (1909-1972) who led Ghana to independence, sets the tone of independence in twentieth century Africa by observing 'Seek ye first the political Kingdom.'

The French tried to stem the tide of nationalism by creating a special organ, the Investment Fund for the Economic and Social Development which provided subsidies for the welfare activities of the colonies. Rejecting the goal of ultimate independence, the French sought closer integration between France and the Empire. The Brazzaville Conference in 1944, under the leadership of Charles de Gaulle, took the decision of modifying legislation discriminating against colonial people. The changes envisioned were abolition of arbitrary powers (**indigenat**) of French administrators, and subject status, the granting of citizenship rights to all members of the French community and franchise rights for elections to the French National Assembly. The reforms enacted by the French in 1946 fell far short of the aspirations of the colonial people. But the changes were far-reaching—they abolished the hated **indigenat** and subject status and gave electoral powers to the colonial territories.

Early Political Protest

The political activity in Africa before the Second World War was in an embryonic stage. It strove for an equitable distribution of political power between the imperial power and the colonial people rather than independence. Nevertheless, opposition to European colonialism took the form of resistance movements which surprisingly were nurtured under European control. In general, the goal was to evict the Europeans and restore the traditional society. The Maji-Maji rebellion in German East Africa at the beginning of the twentieth century harnessed a number of disparate tribes. In North Africa, Islam served as a *point d' appui* for resisting European encroachment. Although the early resistance movement was defeated, it demonstrated the need to mobilise broad-based support.

Education acted as a catalyst in nationalist activity. A small educated elite comprising lawyers, doctors, teachers worked together to fight against the imperial system. Their demands were rather modest. They adopted a policy of petition and prayer just to persuade European authorities to make alterations in the colonial system. Despite the scant regard paid to them by the colonial administrators, this new intelligentsia charted out a new political goal of nationalism.

British West Africa nurtured a segment of nationalist-minded intelligentsia. At the end of the nineteenth century the educated elite had cooperated with the chiefs in the Gold Coast which resulted in the creation of the Aborigines Protection Society. This movement was subsequently supplanted by a British West African Congress under the leadership of a West African, J. Casely Hayford. He tried to harness intellectuals from all the British West African territories—Gold Coast, Nigeria, Sierre Leone and Gambia—to make them aware of more autonomy. In 1920s the intellectuals tried to mobilise a vast segment by moving from one colony to another but their success was peripheral. In the 1930s Nnamdi Azikiwe, the most dynamic Nigerian nationalist, settled in the Gold coast and started a newspaper, the **African Morning Post**. As the nationalist movements matured after the Second World War, the intellectuals built stronger political organisations in their respective territories.

The flicker of political consciousness first germinated in the voluntary associations. From a purely local body, they ranged to national politics. In Nigeria, the first important political party, Nigerian National Democratic Party, was founded in 1923 which was confined to Lagos. In 1944, a new party—the National Council of Nigeria and the Cameroons (NCNC), under the leadership of Azikiwe, came into being. It was a medley of 60 tribal unions or associations and articulated the feelings of nationalist discontent.

Religious Opposition

Religious revolt against Christian missionaries was another important factor in the growing nationalism. This revolt was intended to create independent African churches as the missionaries undermined traditional African practices. Many African churches accepted the new wave of African reformist zeal and incorporated many African customs as part of the creed. The European form of Christianity differed in many aspects with traditional African religious views. First, European Christianity propounded that suffering would be alleviated in afterlife, whereas traditional religion believed that suffering could be alleviated in the mundanic world by divine healers. Secondly, missionaries stressed that man was responsible for his own actions whereas Africans believed that witches and evil spirits hindered man's spiritual development. Thus the religious independence of the Africans emphasised such esoteric themes like healing and curing, and protection against witches.

Religious independence took political overtones in the radical, millenarian churches. The vanguard of an African millenarian movement was in the Belgian Congo led by Simon Kimbangu. He claimed to have prophetic and healing powers. With the proliferation of his followers, the colonial administrators became alarmed and arrested him in the early 1920s. However, the repressive measure did not deter his followers to preach his messages. Kimbangu was regarded as a messianic figure.

Islam, too, was embroiled in movements of political unrest. Jamal, al-Din al-Afghani, one of the most dynamic Middle Eastern political leaders of the nineteenth century, had preached Pan-Islamic unity. Before the First World War, the Muslim reformers, the **Salafis,** had imbibed his ideas. The Salafi reformers, especially prevalent in Egypt and North Africa, tried to revive the former glory of Islam in all its halo. The Salafi reformers, in Morocco and Algeria were pioneer in North African nationalism. To this was added the Muslim protest movements launched by the Muslim Brotherhood, with its headquarters in Egypt. Founded in 1929 by Hasan al-Banna, an Egyptian demagogue, exhorted its followers to repudiate evil Western practices and to embrace the teachings of Muhammad and the Koran. As it was a para military organisation, the Muslim Brotherhood advocated political assassination. Consequently a climate of political instabilities followed in Egypt which eventually led to the overthrow of the monarchy in Egypt in 1952.

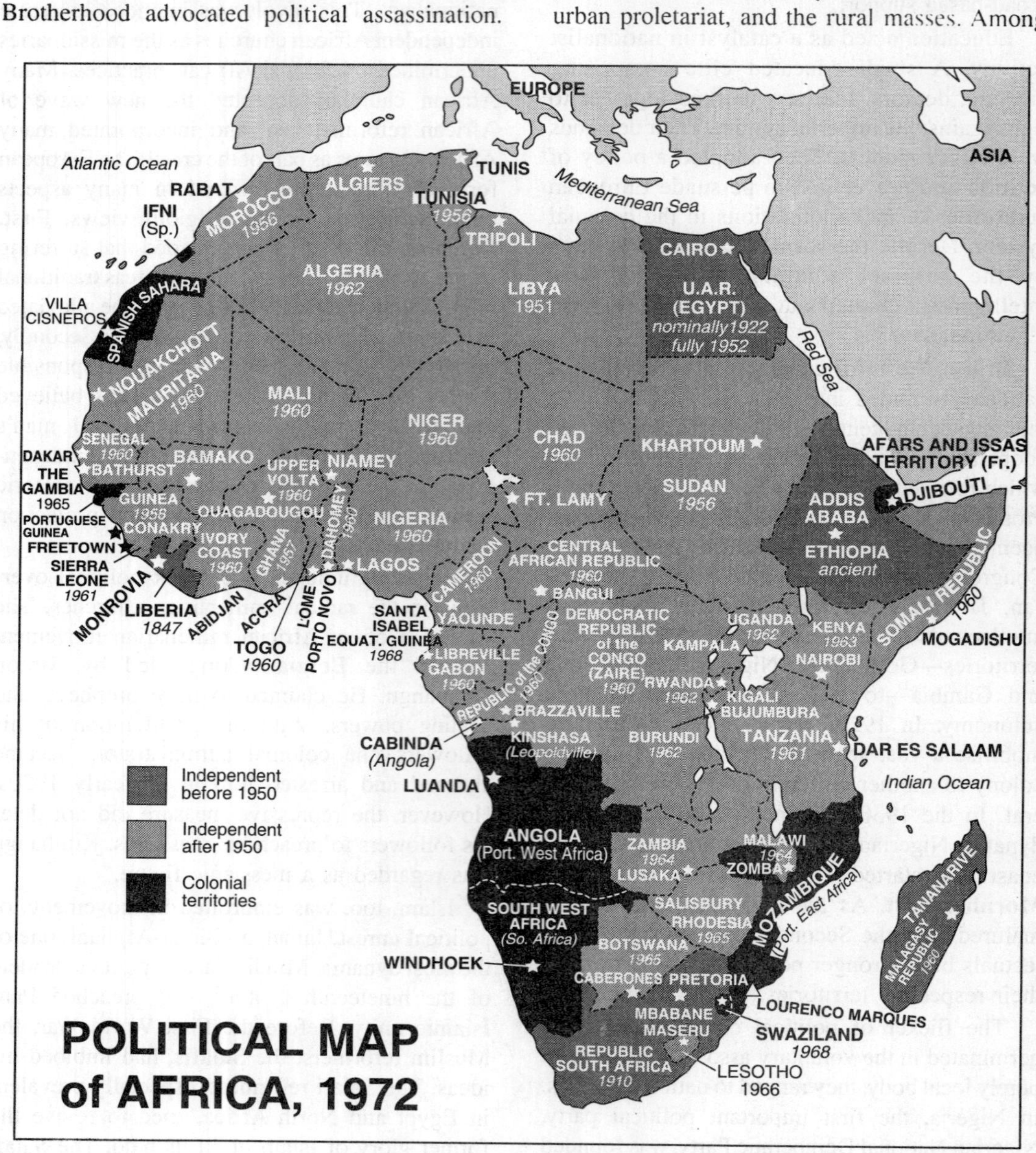

Political Parties

Apart from religious leaders, and the educated elites, political parties with broad base of support sprang up in the 1930s in the Arab world and in mid-twentieth century in Black Africa. These parties were sustained by educated elites, the urban proletariat, and the rural masses. Among the new nationalists, Nkrumah in the Gold Coast and Azikiwe in Nigeria came into limelight who advocated disciplined political action to smother colonialism.

The new parties such as Nkrumah's Convention People's Party (CPP), Azikiwe's National

Council of Nigeria and the Cameroons (NCNC) and Felix Houphouet-Boigny's Parti Democratique de la Cote d'lvorie (PDCI) were more broad-based—appealing to vast segment of the population. In the first election in the Gold Coast held in 1951, Nkrumah's CPP won a stunning victory, capturing 34 of the 38 seats. In 1956, just a year before independence, the CPP again emerged in flying colours, winning 71 out of the total 104 seats. However, the popular participation was not so flattering. 'Although nearly six out of ten adults who voted in the election cast their lot with the CPP—the party after many years of effort and in spite of [many] advantages... could mobilise ... only about one out of six or seven Ghanians.'

The political parties mobilised the intellingentsia and urban population. However, many intellectuals basking under the European standards had different perceptions for an independent Africa. Tunisia served as a glaring instance of the dichotomy. Occupied by the French in 1881, Tunisia expressed its resentment against French rule only in the beginning of the twentieth century. A strange combination of traditional religious elite and Western educated elite took place. They created a new political party, the **Destour** (meaning Constitution in Arabic) and demanded the introduction of representative and constitutional government in Tunisia.

By the 1930s a new generation of political leaders emerged in Tunisia which had a larger following than the old Destour. Their most dynamic figure was Habib Borguiba, a French-trained lawyer, who founded a political newspaper. The new leadership formed a new political party called the Neo-Destour. The party under the leadership of Borguiba carried on relentless campaign against the French which forced them to grant independence to Tunisia in 1956 along with its North African protectorate, Morocco.

The success of Ghana in attaining independence was contagious. In 1958 Guinea under Sekou Toure claimed complete independence after withdrawing from French Union. The other states followed suit and, by 1960, the former colonies in French West and Equatorial Africa had obtained independence.

THE TEXTURE OF EUROPEAN CULTURE

CHAPTER 44

SOCIAL TRANSFORMATION

The most far reaching of all longterm changes in the world was the rapid increase of population. During the twelve centuries before 1800 Europe's population accounted for 180 million. But within one century it more than doubled itself. This immense increase deeply affected social and political order and changed the course of world history. Between 1815 and 1914 about 40 million Europeans migrated to other countries like the United States, Canada, Australia, Africa, and many other parts of the world. In 1815 the population of Europe was only 200 million; but by 1914 it reached the staggering figure of 460 million.

There were many reasons for this fantastic growth of population, the most important being a decrease in death rates and an increase in birth rates. Improvements in public order and security came with the foundation of strong monarchies. They did much to relieve plague, famine and destitution. Significant advances in medical science in the eighteenth century freed Western countries from various epidemic and endemic diseases and plague. Child mortality decreased and expectation of life increased. Better transport like steamship and railway did much to end famines and shortages.

From the beginning of the nineteenth century there took place an agricultural revolution that increased food production. Adam Smith had observed that 'the cultivation and improvement of the country... must necessarily be prior to the increase of the town.' The increased agricultural productivity made it possible for Europe to feed its rapidly growing numbers. The increased productivity was due to various factors: enclosures, the reduction of fallow with crop rotation, cultivation of fodder crops, land reclamation, deeper ploughing, more manure, better harvesting. Modern pattern of agriculture was established in the century 1751 to 1850. Intensive cultivation of small farms became common in Belgium, Holland, French Flanders, Tuscany, Lombardy, Spain, and Portugal. Large farms were common in England, Russia, Poland, Hungary, southern Italy and southern Spain.

One striking social change was noticeable in the nineteenth century when attempts were made to strengthen the peasants' rights to the land and to remove feudal obligations. By the middle of the nineteenth century serfdom had become a thing of the past except in Russia and Rumania. The French Revolution by its liberal ideas strengthened the process of disappearance. Between 1790 and 1815 territories dominated by France like Holland, Prussia, Spain and Italy passed anti-feudal legislation. But the extent of reform varied. Moreover, there was some restoration of feudal rights after 1815—especially in Italy and Spain. However, the relaxation of feudal tenures broadened the distribution of landownership. In 1830 more land was held by *metayers* or tenants. Fragmentation of land was common except in England and Scandinavia where there were large farms. By 1900 more than one-third of Europe's farms were fragmented.

The Industrial Revolution (1760 on) which generated mechanised industry involved urbanism. Unskilled labour was mostly employed to run the new machines. Women and children were often employed at wages lower than those of men. Thousands of families, overworked and underpaid, huddled in factory towns, creating a new social problem. The transformation was a slow process and gained impetus only in the later half of the nineteenth century with the introduction of internal combustion engine and electricity. Relatively a small proportion of men lived in industrial towns as most of them lived in little towns and villages.

Industrialism created a new industrial proletariat. It also conferred power and wealth upon the growing middle class of enterprising traders, manufacturers and financiers. The energetic, thrifty and hardworking manufacturers of England, France and the Netherlands succeeded in carving their place with older families of business and industry. The established financial groups—such as the Rothschilds, Barings, Laffittes and Hopes—assumed increasing importance. The new wealth demanded greater political representation and power.

Meanwhile industrialism created new wage-earning classes who, in order to mitigate their growing problems, looked to the state for protection of their interests. Political pressures goaded the government to concern itself with working-class interests, the latter demanding votes and rights of free association. The activities of the government now transcended beyond general matters of public order and national security to the deepest levels of social and economic life.

Social unrest became common with unequal distribution of wealth. People began to question the existing ideas and institutions. Urbanisation and better communications fostered working-class association. Civil disorder followed as a result of economic discontent and due to the preaching of revolutionary ideas by Babeuf, Saint Simon and Fourier. Though reactionary hands were common in suppressing the disorders, there emerged the radicals and humanitarians who advocated social reform and pleaded for effective role by government for ameliorative measures. The remark of Lamartine is pertinent in this matter: 'The proletarian question is one that will cause the most terrible explosion in present-day society, if society and government decline to fathom and resolve it.' The first Factory Acts passed in England set an example for other countries to follow. Real wages in England in 1830 were 50 per cent higher than they had been before the Revolution.

The radicals like Edwin Chadwick and John Stuart Mill, disciples of Jeremy Bentham and aristocratic Tory humanitarians, like Lord Shaftesbury sought to make the government responsible to the needs of the people. The utilitarian philosophy expounded by Jeremy Bentham and his followers undermined the established order. He contended that the aim of the government should be to promote 'the greatest happiness of the greatest number.'

Working conditions became a burning topic in 1830 when Richard Oastler denounced the employment of children for long hours and began the agitation for a ten-hour working day. As a result the rudimentary Factory Acts of 1802, 1819 and 1825 were supplemented by the wide-ranging Act of 1833. It covered nearly all textile mills, forbade the employment of children under nine, fixed fortyeight hour working week for persons between nine and thirteen and a weekly maximum of 69 hours with no night work for persons between thirteen and eighteen. The Act included some safety precautions including the appointment of four fulltime inspectors. In Prussia was passed a decree in 1839 which prohibited the employment of children in mines and fixed a ten-hour day. But inspectors were not appointed till 1853. In 1841 the French Parliament passed a Factory Act restricting the use of child labour. But the French Act remained virtually ineffectual in the absence of factory inspectors which were done only in 1883. In the United States, by the early 1850s, half a dozen eastern states fixed a minimum age and maximum hours, including a ten-hour day for men.

The practice of giving relief to supplement wages came in vogue to mitigate the rigours of the early industrial revolution. But its widespread abuses led the Parliament to pass an Act in 1834 to reform the whole system. It checked payments to supplement wages and set up a central Poor Law Commission to supervise the system. Workhouses were to be run by local Boards of Guardians elected by the ratepayers. 'Workhouse test' was to be introduced so that only the needy would enter the workhouse. The reorganisation did not run smoothly as, in effect, the workhouses were controlled by undesirable elements, such as Charles Dickens satirized in *Oliver Twist*. But the fact is undeniable that the administration of poor relief became subject to democratic control.

The problem of public health and sanitation, street lighting, water supply and an adequate medical service had hitherto been left to the care of the local authorities. But usually these problems had been tackled perfunctorily with the result that the situation was deplorable in the large and growing industrial towns. A commission of enquiry appointed by the Parliament in 1846 in its report highlighted the lack of water supply in large towns. An Act of 1848 established a Central Board of Health on the lines of the Poor Law Commissioners with power to create local boards. A better perception of town life was accelerated by the recurrence of the dreaded Cholera in 1831-33 and in 1847-48. It also owed not a little to the pertinacity of Edwin Chadwick and his disciples which overcame official apathy. The growing concern of the government to social evils and to the welfare of the community as a whole found expression through state legislation to ensure minimum conditions of a civilised life.

The industrial world was born, according to Carlyle 'with infinite pangs.' Behind the facade lay the slums, the hovels of what Tocqueville in 1833 called 'this new Hades' of Manchester. In such places—like Manchester and Lille—there lived a race of men who had been labelled with a new name—'Proletariat.' The abysmal conditions in which they had to live produced physical and moral debasement. The growth of the proletariat seemed to make 'Two Nations' a reality. 'Two Nations' in Disraeli's famous phrase in *Sybil*, 'between whom there is no sympathy, who are as ignorant of each other's habits, thoughts and feelings, as if they were dwellers in different zones or inhabitants of different planets.'

The age-old mute warfare of the poor against the rich was now transmuted into a large scale of labour against capital. Appalled at these evils of the new industrialism, some ideas were being germinated of building of new societies in which there should be communal ownership and fair distribution of property. Hence the socialist utopias were characteristic products of the time. Others, more practical, tried to mitigate the evil through state intervention or the organisation of trade unions. Others like Marx propagated the theory of relentless class war between the proletariat and the bourgeoisie.

The *Communist Manifesto* proclaimed: 'All previous historical movements were movements of minorities, or in the interests of minorities. The proletarian movement is the movement of the immense majority.' Men now began to speak of 'the masses'. Western society had to reckon with numbers—both in peace and in war. As early as 1833 Tocqueville had prophesied: 'The century is primarily democratic. Democracy is like a rising tide; it only recoils to come back with greater force, and soon one sees that for all its fluctuations it is always gaining ground. The immediate future of European society is completely democratic.' Democracy also meant the rule of the majority acted as a levelling agent. 'The age of the common man' was looming large. In 1820 Thierry in France demanded 'a history of citizens, a history of subjects, a history of the people.' Michelet in 1846 responded readily in his *Le People*. In England, Carlyle in his *French Revolution* envisaged when 'History would be attempted on quite other principles, when the Court, the Senate and the Battlefield receding more and more into the background, the Temple, the Workshop and the Social Hearth will advance more and more into the foreground.' Besides Dickens, writers like Mrs Gaskell and George Sand exposed social injustice and the wrongs of the poor in their novels.

In spite of a growing literacy, progressive thinker like John Stuart Mill became apprehensive of the rule of the unenlightened and brute majority. Many compared the rise of the people to the incursion of the barbarian. This elemental force was impetuous and unpredictable and would sweep away all that was beautiful. 'Large sections of the society,' wrote Jacob Burckhardt, 'would readily give up all their individual literature and nationality.' This pessimism was voiced by the Swiss writer, Amiel, when in 1851 he wrote in his Journal after reading Tocqueville's masterpiece *Democracy in America*:

> Tocqueville's book has on the whole a calming effect upon the mind, but it leaves a certain sense of disgust behind. It makes me realise the necessity of what is happening around us... but it also makes it plain that the era of *mediocrity* in everything is beginning, and mediocrity freezes all desire. Equality engenders uniformity, and it is by sacrificing what is excellent, remarkable, and extraordinary

> that we get rid of what is bad. The whole becomes less barbarous, and at the same time more vulgar. The age of great men is going; the epoch of the anthill... is beginning. By continual levelling and division of labour, society will become everything and man nothing.

In the last quarter of the nineteenth century the governments undertook the comprehensive regulation of society. Rudimentary works had already been undertaken. But after 1870 the powers and function of the government increased so rapidly that a fundamental change took place in the relations between government and society. Before 1870 Britain was the only country where revolutionary changes took place in governmental activity. This was proved by the creation of the Metropolitan Police (1829), the appointment of the first factory inspectors (1833), and of the first emigration officers (1833), the assumption by the state of the responsibility for elementary education (1833), the setting up of the Poor Law Commissioners (1834) and the institution of prison inspection (1835).

With the complexities of social problems voluntary private organisations could only work with central assistance. The movement of population and the growth of urban areas also revealed the inadequacy of local authorities. Rapid advance in scientific and administrative knowledge made it necessary for central intervention. Enormous progress was made in the field of public health. After 1867 it was discovered that many diseases were caused by microbes and could be avoided by simple precautionary measures like asepsis and innoculation. The cumulative experience of the inspectors and epidemiologist in regulating factories, mines and public health acted as an incentive to government action. It was also felt that government action was more practicable and more necessary. Governments took steps to provide water, sanitation, hospitals and roads. The rapid progress in industrialisation, urbanisation and scientific knowledge forced governments in Europe, Japan and Latin America to respond to the needs of the people. Pressed by experts and officials, governments began to invoke special powers to enforce beneficial legislations for social and public ends and 'the grammar of common legislation acquired the novel virtue of the imperative mood.'

Between 1860 and 1875 there was continuous legislation and enforcement machinery in the cause of public health. Startling effects were visible with the falling incidence of plague, typhus, typhoid, small-pox, cholera, scarlet fever in 1880. Death rate declined in almost every quinquennium after 1870 and was brought down from 18.1 in the 1890s to 15.2 in the 1900s. The average expectation of life increased during the same period. However, by contrast, Russia's mortality rate remained as highest—35 per 1000.

With the improvement of public health, attention was paid to the provision of compulsory and free primary education. In Britain and Japan the development of national education proceeded so rapidly that by 1895 there was a school place for every child in Britain and 95 per cent were at school in Japan by 1906.

Along with rapid improvement in education and public health, state activities were geared to improve working conditions. In Britain, Factory Acts were supplemented by the Acts of 1878, 1886, 1891 and 1901 to deal with shops as well as factories and to regulate the working hours of men as well as women and children. In countries like Belgium, the Netherlands and Switzerland, Factory Laws were introduced in the 1870s, in Austria from 1883, in Italy and Spain from 1887 and in France from the 1890s. Germany took the lead in introducing compulsory insurance against accident and sickness for working men. Bismarck's insurance programme of 1883-89 set a standard for other countries like Austria, Switzerland, Belgium, Italy, where the scheme was introduced between 1887 and 1900.

The increase in population in the last three decades of the nineteenth century was phenomenal—Britain from 31 million (1871) to 41 million (1901), Germany from 40 (1870) to 56 (1900), Austria-Hungary from 35 (1869) to 45 (1900). Simultaneously there took place the expansion of industry in Europe. The surplus population crowded together in large industrial regions, like Ruhr, English Midlands, Saxony, the Bohemian frontier districts. After 1870 the process of urbanisation increased so rapidly that a sea-change was noticeable in the European industrial community. In 1871 there were 8 cities of 100,000 population in Germany; but the number rose to 33 in 1900. Similar growth was also seen in England after 1870. However, during the same period, the percentage of rural population remained static. The only exception was European Russia which showed a rapid rise in rural population after the emancipation of the serfs in 1861.

The concentration of European population owed not a little to the migratory movements of the people. The last three decades of the nineteenth century saw the emigration of twentyfive million to North America, South America and Australia. The migration took place not only in European countries as in France which received a considerable influx from Italy. Similarly, Polish agricultural labourers penetrated eastern Germany. But emigration overseas in the last three decades of the nineteenth century extended the white man's area of influence in the world. The motives for this emigration were largely economic and social. 10 million people of Europe emigrated to the United States during this period. Though the people in Europe maintained their respective identity, the United States was a shining example of a melting-pot of the nations as a whole.

Influenced by the radical-minded liberals, Parliament began to extend activities into social welfare measures. In Britain the Liberal Governments after 1905, led by Sir Henry Campbell-Bannerman and H. H. Asquith, undertook comprehensive reforms on social problems. In 1909, a Trade Boards Act objected to 'sweating' in certain trade. Shops Act of 1911 introduced the principle of a legal weekly half holiday. A Coal Mines Act consolidated mine laws to improve further the conditions of workers. In 1911 the National Insurance Act introduced a vast contributory scheme insuring the workers against sickness and insuring some categories of workers against unemployment. The scheme brought friendly societies and trade unions as 'approved societies' to help administer the money benefits for their members. The cooperation between the state and voluntary bodies marked a new British approach to social problems. In 1909 a start had been made in providing non-contributory old age pensions on a very limited scale.

Britain was largely influenced by Germany and other countries in initiating social welfare schemes. The Housing and Town Planning Act of 1909 which attempted to introduce effective town planning was prompted by German example. French example set in motion the Infants' Welfare Centre in the 1890s with schemes for supplying free clean milk to poor mothers. The Education Act of 1902, which established a national system of primary and secondary education, was modelled on the educational systems established either in France or Germany.

The fall of the Second Empire in France delayed the traditions of paternalist legislation. Moreover, France was not faced with the same social problems as those in Britain and Germany owing to her slow industrialisation. However, the traditions of Bonapartist paternalism set in motion a series of labour regulations. In the 1890s laws were passed regulating hygiene, limiting women's work to ten hours a day, and providing for pensions and accident insurance. In 1900 ten-hour working day was enforced, and in 1906 a six day work was started. Georges Clemenceau's seventeen-point programme for workers' welfare, though begun with great fanfare, practically achieved nothing. Nevertheless, labour legislation was codified between 1900 and 1902, old age pensions were instituted, and French industrial workers were given some protection from exploitation.

By 1914 most of the European countries—except Russia and the Balkans—had developed integrated codes of factory and labour legislation. Factory inspection was introduced in Austria in 1883. An elaborate industrial code was also introduced in 1907 that prohibited employment of children under twelve, limited an eleven-hour day in industry, and provided protection against injury. By 1877 Swiss cantons, led by Zurich, introduced similar legislation. In the same decade the Netherlands and Belgium introduced comparable laws. Between 1886 and 1904 Italy and Spain made some progress in labour legislation.

Germany made pioneering efforts in introducing systematic social legislation. Instead of emphasising on factory legislation and unemployment insurance, Bismarck aimed at a comprehensive national provision for security against sickness, accident, and old age. These three problems were successfully tackled by Acts of 1883, 1884 and 1889. In 1911 the whole law of social insurance was codified and benefitted various classes of non-industrial workers. By 1913 some fourteen and half a million persons were insured. Both workers and employers contributed to the sickness and pension funds, the latter being managed by both. In course of time free medical attendance and hospital care were extended. When the First World War began (1914), German workers were better off than those of any other country.

Examples of German insurance schemes influenced her neighbouring countries—Belgium, Denmark and the United Kingdom. Between 1887 and 1890, Austria, Italy and Switzerland adopted accident and sickness insurance. During these years Britain, France, Norway, Spain, and the Netherlands introduced legislations to protect workers from accidents.

During the first half of the twentieth century the world's population grew by more than 1,000 million. After 1940 the world's demographic balance widened between Europe and the other continents. The population of Europe increased from some 423 millions in 1900 to 573 millions in 1940, the largest accretion of 100 million took place within Russia. The period witnessed movements of people from one European country to another. Central and eastern Europe bore the chief brunt of this migratory movement. The war, redrawing of frontiers, political persecution contributed to this charge. The Bolshevik Revolution (1917) produced something between one and two million refugees. Germany after 1919 absorbed some three-quarter million of people from Poland while Hungary some 400,000 from its border regions. There was a largescale exchange between Greece and Turkey. The Nazi nightmare in Germany and the civil war in Spain led unnumbered people to seek refuge in other countries. With the imposition of restriction on immigration by the United States and by the British Dominion, the outflow was absorbed by France, under-populated as a result of war and a low birth rate. Between 1920 and 1923 France received more than a million and a half workers from Italy, Belgium and Poland. The exodus from Bolshevik and Nazi terror contributed in a way to the cultural fermentation in the societies of other countries.

Apart from this internal European migration, movement of people from countryside to town took place in response to rapid industrialisation. By 1831 some 16 per cent of British people lived in towns; after a century the number rose to 40 per cent. The situation was somewhat different in France where in 1936 only 16 per cent of its population lived in towns. As such, in 1939, there were only 17 towns in France as against 83 in the Soviet Union, 57 in the United Kingdom and 56 in Germany. Till the middle of the twentieth century, the population of London, Glasgow, Amsterdam, Vienna and Naples doubled; those of Birmingham and Lisbon trebled; those of Hamburg, Madrid and Milan grew fourfold; those of Barcelona, Prague and Rome more than fivefold.

In most countries, urbanisation became the chief feature of social change. While the growing numbers living in towns were absorbed into expanding industries and the tertiary sector of transportation or professional occupations, a small numbers were engaged in agriculture. Urban communities, developed around large industrial and business centers, became more susceptible to forces of social unrest and subject to different mass-pressures. On the other hand, the urban classes were receptive to new ideas and were in the vanguard of movements for demanding better conditions of life. It is undeniable that urban masses in twentieth century Europe have given the main momentum to movements of social reform.

Despite the various amenities in the town life the disparities between town life and country life did not assume serious proportion after the Second World War. After 1920 more and more people turned to agriculture which had become mechanised. Other factors like cheap rail and road transport, a yearning to nature, youth hostels in Britain, the Boy Scout movement everywhere and compulsory national service in peacetime, led the townsmen move into countryside. In France, Spain and in eastern Europe, massive urbanisation did not take place and disparities between rural and urban people were striking.

Social life underwent transformation with the improvement of communication. Better and fast communication was necessary for trade and commerce and for strategic purpose. The United States improved and extended their highways for the benefit of the automobiles. Europeans were slow to utilise the new invention of motorcar. It was in the 1930s that Germany began the famous national network of *Autobahnen*. In 1929 the Liberal Party in Britain adopted a large programme of public works including the construction of a national system of trunk roads. Europeans were ahead than Americans in developing aviation as a quick means of transport. In 1920 the Dutch introduced a regular air service between Amsterdam and London. Slowly European capitals came to be linked by a network of airlines. The eve of the Second World War saw the linking of Europe and the United States by a regular air service. The transatlantic telephone had been in operation since 1927.

With the development of transport and communication, Europeans showed varied interest in exploiting new avenues of resources and technology. Except in automobile industry, France lagged behind other countries in adopting new industrial techniques. The two large firms of Renault and Citroen and, to a lesser extent, Peugeot, adopted mass production of motor cars. Germany took the lead in developing chemical, electrical engineering and new textile industries. Sweden, changing from a predominantly agricultural to an industrial economy, developed new industries as pulp and paper making, electrical products and engineering. On the other hand, countries of southern and eastern Europe remained as producers of primary products.

The structure of each national society changed in highly complex ways. In western Europe the shrinkage of the Lumpenproletariat in favour of the skilled worker of professional field seemed to be the greatest social change that occurred during these years. This broad change became more evident with the applications of electronics and computers after the Second World War.

At the beginning of the century, Britain maintained her primacy as the world's most highly industrialised country—48 per cent of her population were engaged in manufacturing and mining, compared to 40 per cent of Germans, 31 per cent of Frenchmen and 30 per cent of Americans. The proportion of labour force engaged in agriculture declined sharply during these years. In a highly agricultural country like Denmark it fell from 40 per cent in 1911 to 28 per cent in 1931. It was only 6 per cent in Britain compared to 35 per cent in France in 1931. In the Soviet Union the decrease was dramatic owing to collectivisation and large scale mechanised farming. In terms of the total population engaged in agriculture, it dropped from 75 per cent to 56 per cent.

The thirties in Europe widened the gulf between the capitalist and the working class. In many countries outcry against economic oligarchies was raised. Hitler's National Social Party received vital backing from industrialists and financiers like Alfred Hugenberg, Hjalmar Schacht and Fritz Thyssen.

In Spain social conflicts resulted in prolonged civil war. The three years of bloodshed (1936-39) left Spain an impoverished and exhausted country:

> Here were ranged the masters of economic power in the country, led by the Army, and supported by the Church, that embodiment of Spain's past glory. All these believed that they were about to be overwhelmed. Opposed to them were 'the professors'—many of the enlightened middle class—and almost the entire labour force of the country, maddened by years of insult, misery and neglect, intoxicated by the knowledge of the better conditions enjoyed by their class comrades in France and Britain and by the actual mastery which they supposed that the working class had gained in Russia.[1]

Between the wars, the Republic of Austria experienced violent social changes. The Treaty of Saint-Germain forcibly fused together two radically different societies. This uneasy co-existence was shattered in 1932 in the wake of economic slump when Chancellor Dollfuss suspended parliamentary government in 1933.

The structure of society, despite its various hues, remained nationalist in character. The democracies which lacked national cohesion—Italy, Austria, Spain, Czechoslovakia—had to

1. Hugh Thomas: *The Spanish Civil War* (1965), P. 159.

succumb to authoritarian rule. In the 1930s the more nationalistic wings of the party triumphed over the reformist wings—Stalinists over the Trotskyists, Hitler over the second revolutionaries, and Mussolini over others in Abyssinia and Spain. In Britain, France and Belgium national coalitions maintained their existence by moderate reforms. In the colonial world movements of national independence—in India, Far East, Africa—coloured all social changes.

The most significant social change was felt in the standard of living. In terms of vital statistics, the United Kingdom made steady progress. Infant mortality fell significantly. In both United Kingdom and France, remarkable improvement came after 1945. From 49 in 1945 it dropped to 31 in U.K. in 1950. Sweden, with only 21 per thousand, could claim the lowest infant mortality rate in the world. The average expectation of life also increased. As a result the population of Europe (excluding Russia) grew from 310 to 396 million between 1900 and 1950.

Despite improvement in the standard of living there remained wide disparities in different countries and between Europeans and non-European countries. In terms of the national income per head of the population in 1938, the range was as wide from Great Britain (378) and the Netherlands (367) to France (236), Italy (127) and Greece (80). However, broadly speaking, there was a general advance in the material well-being of the masses. This included a shortening of the working day and working week and introduction of a conventional age for superannuation. The scale of migration overseas also slowed down considerably after 1914. In the Soviet Union, under the First Five Year Plan, and in the 'People's Democracies' of eastern Europe after 1945, emphasis on heavy industrialisation at the expense of agriculture kept down the standard of living.

The half century from 1900 to 1950 was filled with wars, revolutions and economic crises, each of which wrought great imbalance in distribution of wealth and social structure. The collapse of the dynastic empires of Austria-Hungary, Turkey and Russia after the First World War overthrew the aristocracy and landed nobility. Eastern Europe had to undergo dramatic changes in the wake of war and violence. In Russia, after 1917, property of all kinds were confiscated. The great currency crash in Germany in 1923 not only ruined the middle and *rentier* classes, it also wrought social upheaval of great magnitude. The world economic crisis of 1929-32 brought havoc to millions leading to bankruptcies and mass unemployment. Both World Wars and the political and racial persecution resulted in displacement of millions.

Social upheavals benefitted the peasantry. In eastern Europe they gained more land. Economic depression led the government to grant more assistance to agriculture. By 1939 agriculture was in a healthy state in most of the countries. The upheavals of war tended to hit urban rather than rural population and, with American help, European prosperity was restored to pre-war levels of production.

Landowners, industrialists and traders suffered most from the world economic depression. In Germany, between 1923 and 1933, members of the middle classes were reduced to poverty. Meanwhile debtors, speculative investors and farmers benefitted from inflation. Mass unemployment hit the industrial and agricultural workers. Growing unemployment reached a staggering figure in most of the countries. In Germany it exceeded 6 millions in 1932 and reached 3 millions in Britain in the years 1931-33.

Along with deprivation and destitution came the demand for social justice and systematic redistribution of wealth. Seats of government grappled with the problem by which greater social justice could be attained. But the problem involved several peripheral questions—like universal suffrage, civil liberties to all citizens, an attack on extremes of wealth and poverty, greater social security and providing safeguards against chronic unemployment. It meant also a new code of behaviour between different communities and greater coordination among international bodies for securing better standards of living. The demand became so persistent that by 1950 every European government made best efforts possible to implement programmes of social security, economic regulation, and full employment.

By 1900 most of the west European states had introduced universal suffrage. Universal male suffrage was introduced gradually in Sweden and Austria (1907), Turkey (1908), Italy (1912). In 1907 women gained the right to vote in Finland and Norway, in U.K. in 1918 and in Germany in 1919, in Turkey in 1934. By 1950, equal female suffrage gained acceptance throughout Europe. As a result, the size of the electorate was more than doubled. New electoral pressure of women brought changes in the promotion of welfare schemes.

The significance of social revolution was wider in its implications than the extension of the electorates. It emphasised the fundamental question of every human being to equal civil and political rights. It also signified comprehensive change of outlook in social life. This came with scientific facilities for birth control and desire for smaller families; with equal opportunities of employment of both men and women; with the extension of education to girls as well as boys. The average number of children per family in Britain was over five in 1870s, but it came down to about two in the 1930s. Women supplied a large additional labour force in both World Wars. But the change varied from one country to another. Female emancipation was often resisted by the Roman Church. The dictatorships of the inter-war years, especially in Germany, discouraged the progressive tendencies of women liberation and tried to raise the birth rate.

In most countries a far reaching transformation took place in the status and condition of women. She was not regarded only as the mother of children:

> It would seem that the typical mother of the 1890s, married in her teens or early twenties and experiencing ten pregnancies, spent about fifteen years in a state of pregnancy... She was tied, for the period of time, to the wheel of child bearing. Today, for the typical mother, the time so spent would be about four years. A reduction of such magnitude in only two generations in the time devoted to child bearing represents nothing less than a revolutionary enlargement of freedom for women brought about by the power to control their own fertility.[2]

The First World War effected a great change by involving women in men's work. The home became slightly less confining as less time was occupied in child-rearing. Formal political rights were widely extended after 1918. The Treaty of Versailles in Article 427 asserted the principle of equal pay. Meanwhile, the effect of trade union pressure, rapid population growth and industrial organisation led women to give up manufacturing employment. The effect was beneficial. It was accompanied by some increase of female employment in other industries as clerks, shop assistants and secretaries.

The family also underwent important changes. The 'extended family' or kinship was replaced by 'nuclear family' of parents and children. The movements of population and greater opportunities of labour destroyed the old bond of family life. The nuclear family itself underwent some changes owing to its smaller size and the personal freedom of the mother. In general, the family at all social levels was more independent of the wider connotation of kinship of grandparents, uncles and aunts.

The changes in family life were not the results of political enactments, but were the multitudinous effects of social and economic trends or world events. The two World Wars destroyed the finer textures of family life. Incidence of divorce—which remained low in the beginning of the century—suddenly increased after 1918. Then the incidence declined and remained steady until 1939; it increased again until 1947 after which it showed decline. In 1938 the French did away with the obligation of obedience to the husband which had been laid upon the wife by the Napoleonic code. The right to freedom from an intolerable tie was extended by the extension of divorce. Though its incidence was not high, except in Sweden, the growing acceptance of the idea is more significant than the extension of the practice. Wars are probably the greatest single factor that led to a spate of divorce.

Governmental policies intended to effect a change in family life had not succeeded. Mussolini's efforts to boost the birth rate met with limited success against the backdrop of lower birth rates in the general European trend. The rate of births actually fell from 29.5 per thousand in 1922-25 to 23.7 in 1938. The Bolshevik policy

2. R.M. Titmus: *Essays on 'The Welfare State'* (1958), P. 691.

was hostile to family life as it encouraged birth control, divorce and abortion. From 1936 the Soviet government reversed its policy and praised the traditional family life and decried free love. The French government elaborated in 1939 a *code de la Famille* which extended family benefits and allowances. Its purpose was also to strengthen the family and boost the birth rate. The system was incorporated into the wider system of *Securite sociale* of 1945.

Governmental measures effected significant change in social pattern by making provision of free public education and adopting comprehensive systems of 'social security.' Free compulsory primary education was introduced in most of the countries. England and France were pioneers in this endeavour, having introduced it in the eighties of the nineteenth century.

The increase of literacy was followed by the progress of secondary and technical education and the expansion of university education. Britain set up a Board of Education in 1900; the Act of 1902 gave a great fillip to secondary education. The Education Acts of 1918 and 1944 provided a complex system of national education. New universities were set up in various countries. Apart from the University of Wales (1903), six new Universities were set up at Birmingham (1900), Liverpool (1903), Leeds (1904), Sheffield (1905), Bristol (1909) and Reading (1926). In 1911 were founded the Portuguese Universities of Lisbon and Oporto. New Italian universities were founded in 1924 at Bari, Florence, Milan and Trieste and at Salerno in 1944. The first half of the twentieth century in Soviet Russia saw rapid increase of colleges and universities. In many countries, especially France, Germany, Italy, this rapid expansion of public education provoked confrontation with the Church which had been the chief instrument of education. The conflict in France precipitated the separation of Church from state in 1905.

These triumphs of liberal democracy in Europe created a well-informed and thoughtful public opinion in conformity with cherished democratic ideals. It also moved in the direction of mass hysteria owing to the manipulation of irrational impulses by the power of propaganda. Popular hysteria and violence of feeling generated in Britain by the Boer War, in France by the Dreyfus case, revealed capacities of insensate feeling endemic in urban societies.

Public opinion was moulded by the rise of demagogue like Hitler, Mussolini and the expansion of media of mass persuasion in the form of the cinema, the radio and large public meetings. The monolithic parties of Soviet Russia, Fascist Italy, National Socialist Germany clung to power by exploiting the irrational impulses of men and women. These forces, harnessed to politics and economics, threw a challenge to society.

Along with well-developed codes of factory and labour legislation and a comprehensive national system of social insurance against sickness, accident and old age, most of the governments had to seek fresh funds for social services. Progressive direct taxation, in proportion to income or wealth, was generally favoured. In 1909 Lloyd George included the whole gamut of fiscal devices: heavy duty on tobacco and liquor, death-duties on personal estates, heavier income tax, an additional supertax on incomes above certain level and a charge on the capital value of undeveloped land and minerals. With mounting expenditures on armaments and on social services, most of the European states introduced income tax: People were subjected to heavy taxation owing to war. In 1920 the French ambassador, M. Paul Cambon, conveyed to Churchill:

> In the twenty years I have been here I have witnessed an English revolution more profound and searching than the French Revolution itself. The governing class have been almost entirely deprived of political power and to a very large extent of their property and estates; and this has been accomplished almost imperceptibly and without the loss of a single life.[3]

Cambon seemed to be prophetic for, in 1937, five or six per cent of the national income were redistributed from rich to poor.

The publication of Lord Beveridge's *Report on Social Insurance and Allied Services* in 1942 marked a great landmark in the history of social

3. Churchill W.S.: *My Early Years* (1947), P. 90.

security in Europe. It was not only embodied in various Acts passed by the Labour Government, but won international acceptance. The British National Insurance Act of 1946, the National Health Service Act of the same year and the National Assistance Act of 1948 codified insurance laws against sickness, disability, unemployment and old age, extended the provision of free medical services and ended the old Poor Law. Family allowances were introduced in Britain and France in 1946. Thus the inter-war generated the social ideal which was to bear fruit in the forties.

There was no general pattern of social welfare scheme as each country adopted different methods to suit its own needs. The French system put a premium on family allowances and health provisions to encourage large families. The Spanish system followed the same pattern after the civil war. The British system put so much emphasis on the problem of unemployment that even old age pensions were regarded as appendages of unemployment relief. The Soviet system was unconcerned about population growth as in 1936 state aid was given to mothers only on the birth of the seventh child. In 1944 it was made available on the birth of the third child. In Soviet Russia social benefits were highly individual depending on skill and length of service. The United States was concerned with economic security rather than social security.

With general increase in national income came mounting expenditure on amenities, on luxuries. The whole gamut of business was influenced by the popular demand for consumer goods. Departmental stores multiplied. Originating in France and in the United States, the departmental store came to England when Gordon Selfridge opened his store in London in 1906. Meanwhile, the system of paying for goods on credit, popularly called 'hire-purchase', brought the articles of luxury within the reach of the ordinary men and women.

Radio was a great force in mass communication. By 1926 there were two million British sets. Other countries quickly followed. In England BBC enjoyed a monopoly. The political use of broadcasting was realised almost by all countries. In Russia the state's monopoly of the radio system was a great instrument of government. The cinema was a great educational force, diffusing notions of the desirable life which were often at variance with tradition and accepted practice.

Expenditure on luxuries and popular entertainment increased greatly. More and more people spent money on alcohol and tobacco, confectionery and entertainment, gambling and sports. The silent film of the twenties gave way in 1929 to 'talking film' which became the most important avenue of pastime even in small towns. In spite of the commercial dominance of Hollywood, the European film had great artistic achievements to its credit between 1918 and 1939. Italy had some 9,000 cinemas and Spain 4,000. By 1937 British cinemagoers spent £ 40 million a year. Dancing became popular. Such novelties like betting and gambling on horse-racing and on football pools began to appear. Much was spent on the pools in Britain as on cinemagoing. After the Second World War, new forms of mass entertainment—like television, ballet, concerts and group theatre—dethroned cinema from its pedestal.

The popular press and the cult of the sport provided insatiable appetite to the masses. The press with its importance of publicity in modern society have a mass interest owing to 'the pervasive force of politics in society.' France led the way in the establishment of a popular daily press in Europe. In 1905 the most important papers were *La Petit Parisien, La Petit Journal, La Journal, La Matin* and *La Echo de Paris* which reached some 5 million readers. British daily press did not achieve success until the 1930s which again was attained by some salesmanship stunts. The German press was avowedly political; in 1914 the Social Democrats alone had 110 daily newspapers. The modern newspaper buttressed by latest printing technology is the main vehicle of mass publicity.

Most of Europe's popular press was strongly political in attitude. In France, most of the papers were avowedly favourable to a particular political party, and leading politicians like Clemenceau, Jaures, Blum were associated with important newspapers. In Britain, too, popular papers were identified with a particular brand of politics and sometimes with the political views of the press barons who owned them. In Germany, Italy, Spain and elsewhere, most of the press had political affiliations though popularity of the press was not determined by political factors alone. The mass press thrived on sensational news and characteristic approach to national and international problems. However, the press maintained its ascendancy until coming of the mass television after 1945.

The popularity of sport attained such a dizzy height that it became a highly commercialised entertainment. Huge attendance at sports was made possible by the construction of huge stadiums in different countries with modern gadgets like flood-lighting. Modern Olympic Games were held in Athens in 1896, the Davis Cup in 1900, the French Grand Prix in 1906, the Tourist Trophy Race from 1905. National and international sports of various kinds—football, cricket, tennis, swimming, motor race—came into fashion at the turn of the century. It became a craze of every country to set up a national or international record in various events. Sport exercised such a tremendous influence in societal pattern that none of the mass media could ignore it. Special sporting papers came into circulation and sports champion became popular idols, sometimes outdistancing film-stars. Cricket was popular in many countries like U.K., Australia, West Indies, India except U.S.A. and Soviet Russia. But football, lawn tennis, golf proved to be infectious, encouraging millions of persons to be champions of these popular forms of entertainment. Mass attraction to sport reflects the peculiar mood of an industrial urban society:

> It is chiefly through sports (at any rate in peace time) that male industrial workers can submerge themselves, if only as roaring spectators, in the communal will that 'their' team, the group with which they are identified, should win... sport should in truth be recognised as the folk art of industrial communities in particular and of urban society in general.[4]

Sport in its mass forms serves the ends of nationalism as it involves contests between national teams, rather than individuals. Major national events have become a folk ritual as evidenced in the English Cup Final at Wembley. Sport transcends all regional and national barriers because it combines the strongest political, social and cultural tendencies of the age.

People began to expect more of life. At a moment when a cultural elite had lost faith in material progress, the masses came to regard it and its fruits for granted. One sign of this was the popular preoccupation with speed and records. A belief grew up that things could be changed rather than that they should be. There was an erosion of the acquiescence which had provided so much of the social cement of the past. People expected more from society and of its servant—government.

Industrial society seems to destroy individual's self-respect which is necessary to happiness. Work, as the great Rene Clair film *A nòus la liberte* (1930) showed, was often monotonous. Uncertainty about future employment grew as industrial operations became more complex. The relationship of young and old was revolutionised by the decline in the worker's value to the employer. There is much that must still be hypothetical in our assessment of such facts. We are told, 'we cannot so easily measure the complex sickness of a complex society; the prevalence of the stress diseases of modern civilisation, the instabilities of family relationships or the extent of mental ill-health.'

No thinker had much good to say of the society which had produced him. "Almost all bitterly attacked the social and political institutions they saw around them. Meanwhile the masses were profoundly alienated from market society, both its economic inefficiency and by the subtler pressures of uncertainty, fear and pointlessness which arose from urbanisation and industry. Men were left without guidance to face incomprehensible challenges. Church, family and locality had been so bettered by liberal civilisation that they were weaker than ever as steadying

4. Renee Haynes in A. Natan (ed.): *Sport and Society: A Symposium* (1958), PP. 60-61.

forces. Europeans were rootless as never before and less moved by custom and tradition. They were ready to follow men who promised security and a sense of purpose. Capitalism had been unprecedentedly successful in meeting material needs, but it appeared to have been unable to generate spiritual and intellectual purpose in any but a few."[5]

5. J.M. Roberts: *Europe 1880-1945* (1974), P. 474.

CHAPTER 45

ECONOMIC CHANGE

By the first half of the nineteenth century the powerful forces of economic liberalism arising largely from the French Revolution and the English Industrial Revolution, had made their impact on Europe. By 1830 England took the lead in transmitting to Europe and overseas new methods of production and new economic policies. England became 'the engine of growth that accelerated European and world economic development.' There began to grow increased international interdependence and the creation of a large network of trading and financial relations. However, except in England and Belgium, economic changes were not dramatic. In 1830, European economy was largely agricultural.

Nevertheless, cities and towns grew up and absorbed increasing population. By 1830 twenty-five cities in Europe accounted over 100,000 people. Towns served mainly as centers of industry, commerce and administration. While in Europe the main urban growth centred round capital cities, in England it was widely dispersed.

The most outstanding fact of the eighteenth century Europe was its growth of population. The primary cause of population increase was due to significant reduction in mortality. Before 1750 the average annual rate of growth had been 0.3 per cent; by 1900 it was 1.2 per cent. The increased agricultural productivity along with improved communication and industrialisation led to the growth of population.

The sustained economic development was reflected in increased production which was due to various factors: reclamation of land, enclosures, the reduction of fallow with better crop rotation. In the eighteenth century large estates played an important part in agricultural surplus. But in the nineteenth century the lead was taken by small farms. The intense cultivation of small farms in Belgium, Holland, French Flanders, in Tuscany and Lombardy, in Portugal and Spain accounted for large production. In Spain it had been said: 'where small farming prevails, the land is a garden; where estates are large, a desert.' However, farming on large estates was found in England, Prussia, Poland, Russia, Rumania, Hungary, Southern Italy. Gradually, cultivators' rights to the land were recognised. By 1850 serfdom had been extinct except in Russia and Rumania. However it is difficult to make generalisation of any kind. Fragmentation of land was common in most countries except in England and Scandinavian countries.

Improved communication is *sine qua non* for increased production. As Goethe observed in 1825: 'Railways, express mails, steamboats, and all possible means of communication are what the educated world seeks.' The increasing use of coal gave a fillip to improved communications. The canals formed an important element in the economic development in England. In Europe there was a great extension of waterways. There was widespread improvement of roads. But it was only after 1830 communication improved with the induction of locomotive and steamship.

Britain was the first country to experience the trauma of an industrial revolution. Britain had plenty of coal and iron. She had the advantages of a national unity and freedom of enterprise. The most plausible explanation of English industrial revolution was: the expansion of British commerce, conversion from mercantilism to *laissez-faire*, increase in production stimulated by new machines and the thrift of the early entrepreneurs. As Frankland Lewis declared in the House of Commons in 1816:

> This country was the first manufacturing state in the world not because labour was cheaper here than elsewhere, but because our persons and properties were secure—because we had good government—because we possessed some peculiar national advantages—because we had coals in abundance—because we had machinery and mechanical ingenuity—because, from our situation, we were not liable to the devastations of war which interrupt the progress of all improvement in countries exposed to its fury—and above all, because we had a vast accumulation of capital.

According to T. S. Ashton, the lower rate of interest at which capital could be obtained quickened the pace of economic development about the middle of the eighteenth century. Interest rates dropped from 7 or 8 per cent at the beginning of the century to 3 or 4 per cent in 1750. The development of British banking which provided capital was also remarkable. By 1800 there were 52 private banks in London and 400 in the provinces.

Amazing technical progress like the use of power-driven machinery gave tremendous boost to production. But the technical progress would have been sterile had there not been good market. Hence 'the greatest stimulus to English engineering has been Trade—the increase of our commerce at home and the extending of it abroad.' Between 1740 and 1780 large scale investment in agriculture and to a certain extent in communication, largely enhanced the industrial potential of the country. Between 1780 and 1855 the rate of growth of industrial output varied from 2 to 4 per cent per annum, more than double the rate before 1780. The volume of international trade doubled in the last decades of the eighteenth century, and after a retarded progress during the wars, doubled again by 1840. Although the contribution of manufacturing industry to national income increased 20 per cent in 1770 to 33 per cent in 1831, agriculture still accounted for one-third of the national income.

Britain's international trade after 1780 increased by leaps and bounds. British trade constituted about 27 per cent of world trade in 1800 and 24 per cent in 1840. While Britain had an unfavourable trade balance with the United States and Northern Europe, she had a favourable balance in Southern Europe, South America and Asia. The United States had a favourable balance with Europe while maintaining a precarious balance with the rest of the world.

In 1832 Nathan Rothschild observed that England became in general 'the Bank for the whole world... All the transactions in India, in China, in Germany, in the whole world are guided here and settled in this country.' By 1800 London became the hub of the commercial-financial capital of Europe. In 1780 a number of chartered public banks, private merchant banks and small private deposit banks fed the European banking services. In the eighteenth century banking, initially meant for the deposit and loan of money, enjoyed the right to issue bank-rates. But after 1800 governments imposed restrictions on this matter. In 1803 the Bank of France was given the monopoly of issue in Paris. By 1830 England, Netherlands, Norway, Sweden, Denmark, Prussia, France and Spain had national banks of issue.

The most significant development in the economic sphere was establishment of international banking houses which had its centre in London. The Rothschilds were pioneer to seize the opportunities afforded by the growth of international finance. Apart from London, it had branches in Paris, Vienna, Frankfurt and Naples in 1815. The need to protect the public from bank failures arose. In an attempt to control banking and currency England passed the Bank Charter Act in 1844.

Britain's foreign trade increased by leaps and bounds. This was followed by France and the United Netherlands. But other parts of Europe, especially southern, northern and eastern, remained unaffected before 1830. In the south—in Spain, Italy and Turkey—economies remained agricultural and stagnant. In Turkey there was some growth of enclosed farming owing to liberal trade policy. Italy until unification remained a backward country, only Lombardy and Piedmont, the natural gateways to the rest of Europe, showed some amount of progress in agriculture and industry. Elsewhere there was stagnation compounded by the growth of population. A contemporary reported in 1830: 'In innumerable cases families have occupied the same farms for hundreds of years, without adding a farthing to their wealth, or a fragment to their knowledge.'

Spain remained primarily an agricultural economy, a producer of raw materials for export. Industry languished because of the failure to exploit colonial market. Though the Spanish empire had a rapidly expanding economy in 1800, it was fed not by Spain, but by foreigners, especially the British. The empire had been the bulwark of Spanish fortunes. The loss of empire struck a grievous blow to Spain to which was added inflation which increased 60 per cent between 1770 and 1800.

In eastern Europe the rate of economic growth was slow. There took place a five-fold increase of population between 1720 and 1850. The industrial output was hampered by technological backwardness. Indeed the economic advance before 1830 was slow and precarious. In the Austrian empire, industrial development was slow. Despite large scale farming and agrarian reform after 1815, vast areas of rich land remained underdeveloped until 1848.

The Scandinavian economies were mainly agricultural. Industry, except for the Swedish iron industry, remained small in scale. Economic prosperity of Sweden was the most impressive. Apart from her self-sufficiency in agriculture, Sweden exported iron and timber, mostly to Britain. Norway, transferred from Denmark to Sweden in 1814, had an agricultural economy. Denmark controlled the entrance to the Baltic with Copenhagen as an important centre. Agricultural advance gave Denmark a relatively progressive economy by 1830. Denmark's need for British market led to a commercial treaty in 1824 on the basis of reciprocity.

The dominance of the Junkers in agriculture, and of guilds in industry hampered the economic growth of Germany. But with the abolition of serfdom, the erosion of guild power, the formation of the *Zollverein* or customs-union and state enterprise, Germany made notable progress before 1830.

Belgium was the first European country to experience an industrial revolution. It was the gateway through which England's industrial revolution radiated to the continent. Several factors were responsible for Belgium's industrial eminence: her favourable location that gave access to expanding markets of Britain, France and Germany, navigable rivers, rich coal and iron ore, skilled labour force, successive benevolent governments, a long period of peace, incorporation with Holland in 1815, a moderate tariff and rapid technological advance. But the main factors for Belgian expansion lay in the combination of coal and iron ores along the Meuse. Expansion of banking to provide credit and capital gave a great fillip to industrial development. By 1840, despite the separation of Holland, Belgium was technologically the most advanced country on the continent. It was 'the one country in Europe,' as J. H. Clapham points out, 'which kept pace industrially with England.'

The Dutch commercial economy was in a sorry state in the eighteenth century. The Napoleonic period saw the loss of colonies and the permanent eclipse of Dutch commerce. The abolition of feudal privileges in 1801 and 1804 led to the growth of a commercial agriculture which had been the strength of the Dutch trade by 1830.

France could not compete with Britain after 1780. Burdensome taxation, a restrictive system of commerce and the operation of the guild retarded the development. War also put the two countries in different perspectives. Michelet saw in 1800 that the masses in France were converging towards the barracks, and in England towards the factories. Agriculture dominated the French economy. The Physiocrats believed that 'the wealth of a country is in direct proportion to the fertility of its land.' Accordingly the government and the large landowners took measures to improve agriculture. But markets were mostly confined to provinces. Before 1789 proprietorship of land extended from landlord to peasants. The Revolution led to a great exchange of property. Before 1830 agriculture was primitive and industrial development was slow owing to technical backwardness. Whereas the war had stimulated Britain's industrialisation, it had left France without her colonial markets.

Thus the period 1750 to 1830 witnessed slow process of industrialisation in Europe. Generally it was a period of increasing population and growing British trade, the latter giving the main stimulus to economic growth. It has been aptly remarked: 'Where there is no English commerce, there is no commerce at all.' In 1830 Britain produced 80 per cent of Europe's coal and 50 per cent of Europe's iron and almost the whole of Europe's steam engines. Both the French Revolution and the Industrial Revolution encouraged a political and economic liberalism and to *laissez-faire* as the basis of public policy. Economic liberalism led to the withering away of the guild system and removal of restrictions on trade. Manufacturers and merchants soon organised themselves into pressure groups to influence public policy. Adam Smith and the classical economists expounded the advantages of free trade and of *laissez faire*. Adam Smith's *The Wealth of Nations* became so popular that translations in various European languages appeared before 1800. Smith not only attacked mercantilism but propounded the theory of the harmony of economic interests in a world of free competition. Smith's optimism was reinforced by J. B. Say's law of markets that emphasised supply. The influence of T. R. Malthus and D. Ricardo was not rosy. They explained how capital accumulation and population explosion would raise the rent of land until the law of diminishing returns reduced profits and resulted in a static subsistence-wage economy.

Social unrest was the product of economic growth. The working class attained economic and political self-consciousness. Existing ideas and institutions began to be questioned. Civil disorder, largely stemming from economic discontent, led to reaction. But it also helped the radicals to demand for more active role by the government in industrial sphere. There was no questioning when Lamartine wrote: 'the proletarian question is one that will cause the most terrible explosion in present-day society, if society and government decline to fathom and resolve it.' England introduced the first Factory Acts and inspired other countries to do the same. The condition of the working class showed improvement; real wages rose remarkably and the standard of life was distinctly better. To Macaulay England of 1830 appeared to be prosperous. He wrote: 'Yet is the country poorer than in 1790? We firmly believe that, in spite of all the misgovernment of her rulers, she has been almost constantly becoming richer and richer.'

By 1830 agriculture, Europe's largest occupation, showed improvement in methods and depended largely on capital. The supply of farm produce was increased by turning waste land into fertile soil in many western parts of the continent. The British landlords and enterprising farmers spent a lot in the improvement of estates. They exchanged information by holding meetings or through the Journal of the Royal Agricultural Society (founded in 1838).

Steps were taken in England and Germany for the completion of the enclosure of open arable fields, pastures and waste lands. Soil fertility was increased by deep drainage and fertilisers. Even before the publication of Liebig's *Organic Chemistry in its Relation to Agriculture and Plant Physiology* (1840), farmers were using bone dust, Chilean nitrate and artificial manure. Along with this, steps were taken for the improvement of farm equipment. McCormick patented his reaper in 1834.

The improvement in communication and reduction of customs barrier enabled the farmer to widen his market. The formation of the customs' union or *Zollverein* in Germany and customs amendments of 1842, 1848, 1853 and 1860 removed prohibitions. In 1842 the United States entered into the market and steadily expanded the volume of shipment.

The international grain trade thrived though each country tried to be self-sufficient. Belgium and Holland were regular net importers, Denmark and Prussia net exporters, while France hovered between exports and imports. Improved cultivation made Britain self-sufficient, but in the bad years 1838-42, she had to repeal the Corn Laws in 1846. From the middle of the nineteenth century, Russia's total exports more than trebled, establishing her primacy in the continental trade.

'Cotton was the single industry into which industrial revolution had cut really deep by the twenties.' During the next four decades more industries were influenced by technological know-how. New developments were evident in the heavy capital goods industries—mining, metallurgy and mechanical engineering. However, the textile industry still dominated because of the great demand for its products. The powerloom had replaced the handloom and began to produce much fine fabrics. In the United States the cotton industry grew fivefold between 1830 and 1860.

Improved technical methods made the products of Britain the cheapest in Europe. With the introduction of cheaper transport in 1850, French output of coal and iron ore trebled in two decades. During this period Germany forged ahead, thanks to cheap fuel from the new Ruhr mines. The United States, owing to its shift to coke, trebled iron production between 1830 and 1850.

In 1850 steel was a semi-precious metal. Its production was low, Britain contributing half of world's total output of 80,000 tons. But in 1856 Bessemer's method offered cheap mass-production by turning liquid iron into steel, without using any fuel. By 1870 the output increased at such a tempo that there was a glimpse of the Steel Age. The world's production of coal showed phenomenal increase between 1830 to 1870. In 1870 of world's total production, Britain constituted half, the United States a fifth, and Germany, France and Belgium together a quarter.

Economic growth is largely dependent on improved communication. By 1850 Britain and Belgium had the best waterways and best railways. The Western world became conscious of the benefits of good roads, improved river channels and steamboats. German engineers expanded the range of river navigation. French waterways received more attention and in the United States the number of steamboats plying the Mississippi rose from two hundred in 1830 to over a thousand in 1870.

The opening of railways gave encouraging growth of trade and commerce. By 1850 Britain had developed some major and many minor lines. Belgium in 1844 completed the core of its railway plan. The French Organic Law of 1842 authorised nine main lines. In Germany about 5,000 miles (8,000 km) of track were in service. In the United States some coastal cities were linked. By 1850 the best trains ran at an average speed of 35-40 miles (56-64 km) an hour.

By 1850 the railway world had explored various ways—public, private and mixed—of launching railway project. The British chose private enterprise in order to ensure flow of capital. Belgium chose public ownership followed by Austria. France decided on a mixture with state providing the land and leasing it for thirty or forty years to companies. In the United States the common practice was the purchase of railroad securities by states and cities.

From the middle of the nineteenth century railway construction went apace in Europe and other areas. Apart from Britain, France planned a network of branches. Quick followed Austria-Hungary, Italy, Holland, Switzerland, Spain and Russia. In the United States rails penetrated beyond the Mississippi, connecting east and west. Canada got its Grand Trunk line. Austria accomplished the first thousand miles (1,600 km) during the sixties. India was the first country in Asia to get railways. By 1870 the world had built one-sixth of the railways. It transformed the transport system, strengthened the old trade routes, and stimulated distribution system. Strategic considerations also influenced the construction of the railways.

In 1830 steam vessels began to ply on rivers, coastal routes and narrow seas. America built ships for every purpose. On 23 April 1838, the American vessels *Sirius* and *Great Western* reached New York after crossing the North Atlantic. A regular service was established by Cunard in 1840 between Liverpool, Halifax and Boston. During the fifties and sixties the steamship became more safe. Steamship dominated the carrying of cargoes.

Postal services became quicker and cheaper. The British reforms of 1840 set a worldwide pattern of using stamp. International Postal Union was established in 1874. Meanwhile domestic and international telegraph services developed. In 1851 a cable from Dover to Calais was hailed with delight as it provided the first of many links with the continent. Ocean cables followed linking New York in 1866, Calcutta in 1870 and Australia in 1871.

The economic results of improved communications were incalculable. A great world market was in the making owing to great mobility of goods and persons. Inter-state free trade led to expansion of trade in the United States and Germany, the latter merging 17 states into a Customs Union or *Zollverein.*

International trade policies were largely regulated by three countries—United Kingdom, France, and the United States. Most of the countries clung tenaciously to protection and opposed all attempts to lower tariffs. It was Britain who took the lead in changing her policy to world trade. In a phased way Britain dismantled the old system which combined protection, revenue and preferences. Peel found in the income tax a chief source of revenue. He repealed the Corn Laws and suspended the Navigation Laws, thus allowing foreign ships to bring grain. Gladstone carried on the cleaning operation so vigorously that by 1870 only seventeen dutiable imports remained, of which five (sugar, tea, wine, spirits and tobacco) contributed nine-tenths of the customs revenue. Britain and France made pioneering efforts in reciprocal concession by concluding a trade treaty of 1860 (Cobden-Chevalier Pact). By the treaty Britain imported French goods duty-free. France did away her prohibitions on some British goods included in the treaty.

The phenomenal increase of international trade opened up new areas of investment and enterprise on both sides of the Pacific. World trade rose by 40 per cent in the thirties to 80 per cent in the fifties.

Trade and business enterprises were largely financed by family or partnership firms. The alternative, corporate enterprise, raised large sums for various purposes. The prosperity of joint stock companies was largely due to investment-banks. Governments gave legal recognition to these companies either by decrees or by legislative charters. After 1840 general laws allowed any group to form a company. Limited liability was offered to any company. Joint Stock came in waves, some of them crashed soon afterwards. Same fate awaited the 5,000 limited liability corporations registered in London during 1855-65. In early nineteenth century most of the commercial banks were not adequate in expanding economies. The need for stronger banks became the chief concern for bankers and governments alike.

In 1832, a British Rothschild boasted: 'The country is in general, the Bank for the whole world. I mean that all transactions in India, in China, in Germany, in Russia, and in the whole world are all guided here and settled through this country.' But in the first quarter of the nineteenth century the widespread failures of private banks led the government to permit the establishment of joint stock banks in 1826 and 1833. By 1841 there were over a hundred of these in England and Wales which proliferated during the next three decades. At the head of the system was the Bank of England with branches in the provinces. It gradually became a central bank.

In France, the Bank of France and a few central banks provided commercial credit. This was supplemented by a small group of powerful banking houses—the Hopes, Rothschilds, Oppenheims, Hottinguers, Foulds and the like. The upheavals of 1848 did away with many weak banks and led to an outcrop of new joint stock banks, like *Credit Mobilier* in France and *Bank fur Handel and Industrie* in Darmstadt (1853). In the United States there was no national banking policy or note issue till 1863; therefore, service had to be provided by private bankers and merchant-bankers.

The right to issue notes came to be concentrated in a central bank and strictly regulated. The Bank of France regained that monopoly while the Bank Charter Act of 1844 entrusted the Bank of England with the sole bank of issue.

While the business world grappled with new problems, labour had to adjust itself to new opportunities of employment. Factory industries grew up rapidly of which textile industry occupied the prominent place. A wide variety of small producing units also grew up in London, Paris and other large cities. Other occupations like mining, smelting, building, ship-building grew in importance. By 1871 the industrial labour force equalled that of cloth-makers.

With the proliferation of industries, displacement of population took place, from village to town, from rural areas to mining regions, from country to country, or from Europe to America. Migration accounted for nearly half the growth of population in most of the English industrial counties between 1831 and 1841.

The problems of housing, sanitation and general public health began to emerge as pressing problems for employers and the government. Though Britain took some steps in that direction, little had been achieved by 1870. Working conditions with all their seamy sides became a burning topic in 1830. Social workers denounced the employment of children for long hours and began to agitate for ten-hour working day. This led to the passing of Factory Acts of 1802, 1819 and 1825. But the law of 1833 covered wide fields: it forbade the employment of children under nine, fixed a weekly maximum of sixty-nine hours for those between thirteen and eighteen years with some safety precautions and appointed factory inspectors. By 1870 most of the industrial establishments had to adhere to these regulations.

Factory Acts touched only the peripheral problems of the labour forces. The workers came to realise that their interests could best be protected by themselves through organised union. In Britain and the United States local societies or unions of skilled workers existed in 1830. The 'New Model' emerged with the Amalgamated Society of Engineers in 1851, which sought to settle disputes peacefully. The 'New Model' gained tardy recognition from employers. In Britain the union membership rose from a 100,000 in the forties to perhaps more than a million in 1873. In the sixties the German Radical Unions were formed by Max Hirsch (1868) while the first socialist unions appeared. But in 1870 the unions were not effective in achieving their objectives and their influence was minimal on the continent.

Despite the overwhelming influence of the capitalist classes in consuming 'the best part of the (income) cake', increased investment generated the demand for goods and labour. But economic buoyancy was sometimes followed by depression as had been witnessed during the years 1836-42. But the achievements were not negligible. The period was 'one of extraordinary development, perhaps the most rapid rate of development of domestic resources throughout the whole of Britain's economic history.' Comparable growth was also found in Belgium, France, Germany and the United States. Real wages rose after 1860: in Britain by 25 per cent in 1873; in France by 18 per cent in 1870.

The most powerful agent in revolutionising the national progress was the technology of transport. By 1870 the main railway system was completed in Europe. New links were forged and the Siberian railway was completed in 1900. Other nations like Belgium, Germany, Italy, Holland, Spain, France made similar progress in railway construction.

The tremendous advance in transport laid basis for industrial expansion. In Germany the great boom was due to Sidney Gilchrist Thomas who, with his cousin P. C. Gilchrist, discovered a new process for eliminating phosphorus from iron used in steel making. The Gilchrist-Thomas process utilised the iron ores of Alsace-Lorraine as well the rich deposits of Ruhr in the manufacture of steel. The result was the unprecedented development of steel output from 1.5 million tons in 1880 to 7.4 millions in 1900 comparable to Britain's 3.7 million tons to 6 million tons during the same period.

The opening up of the Suez Canal (1869) due to the efforts of the French engineer de Lesseps benefited not only France but also England and other countries. As the British became the principal shareholders, the canal was mainly used by British ships until the twentieth century. In 1872 Caland connected Rotterdam directly to the North Sea. The Kiel Canal, linking the North Sea with the Baltic, was completed by 1895. The world markets were linked with the laying of submarine cables. The pioneering work in this field was done by William Siemens, an immigrant German who settled in England in 1843. In 1871 the Indo-European cable was completed and five cables had been laid across the Atlantic by 1874.

The improved systems of communication and the motivation of capital investment revolutionised the nature and volume of world trade. Textiles and woollens of British export were now replaced by the export of metals and machinery. Germany's export of iron and steel had exceeded Britain's by the beginning of the twentieth century. European manufacturing nations had to depend on primary producers like the United States, India, Malaya, China, Australia, New Zealand and Russia.

With the disappearance of Britain-India-China trade, a new world economy began to emerge. Britain's deficit with one-half of the world was balanced by means of a surplus with the other half. From the 1880s her deficit with the United States rose steadily. America's deficits in Europe and Asia were paid for by Britain. As production and exports increased, the new nations, instead of turning to Britain, began to trade with other manufacturing nations. Britain, in turn, came to rely increasingly on the less developed countries like Turkey, Japan and India to offset her deficits in Europe and America. The key to Britain's success in world trade lay in her economic relations with India, whose exports to Europe and America helped to finance her deficit with Britain.

With expanding world trade, a visible change took place in the balance of economic power. Britain's supremacy of 1870 declined in the next few decades as her share fell from 25% to 21%, while Germany's share rose from 9 to 12 per cent and the United States' from 10 to 11 per cent.

Till the close of the nineteenth century American competition did not cause serious concern to British manufacturers in foreign markets. But American industries began to forge ahead as they were regarded as models of modernity and efficiency. In France, industrialisation moved at a lower pace. Though it picked up after mid-1890, the pace remained slow.

With France and the United States bogged down with domestic needs, Britain and Germany competed with each other in world market. The sudden metamorphosis of Germany into the most advanced industrial nation of Europe remains one of the wonders of economic history. Most of the factors that could stimulate industrial growth were present. Between 1871 and 1900 German output of coal increased from 38 million tons to 150 million tons. Her iron and steel industry outweighed Britain by 1900. Instead of putting emphasis on traditional industries like textile, woollen and cotton, Germany concentrated on iron and steel, machinery and coal. Efficient technical education enabled Germany to new fields like chemical industry and the electrical industry. The appearance of distinguished scientists like Liebig, Bunsen, Hoffman and many others gave a great fillip to scientific education. Henry Roscoe of Britain told the Select Committee on Scientific Instruction that in Germany 'a love of science and knowledge for its own sake is much more seen in those universities than it is in ours.' While in Britain and France chemical manufacturers were hamstrung with obsolete plants, Germany devised new methods which made possible the phenomenal increase of output of sulphuric acid, alkali and dyestuffs.

The greatest bequest of modern Germany was her electrical industry. Werner von Siemens constructed in 1849 the first major electric telegraph in Germany and invented the dynamo in 1867. Then came the electric lighting of the German cities and the electric trams. Like the chemical industry, the market for electrical industry was abroad, in countries like Italy, Switzerland, and Scandinavia.

German export trade acquired a special interest in foreign markets, especially in the Middle East and the Far East. This new mercantilism was due to the combination of many forces. It drew sustenance from the so-called 'Historical Economists' led by Gustav Schmoller, Professor at Berlin after 1882. For Schmoller and his school, there were no immutable economic laws. In Germany economic laws necessitated the intervention of the state to regulate economic affairs in the interests of national power and national wealth. Economic progress was linked with the nation's political institutions. The Navy Law of 1900 had a clear objective to further country's progress. As Schmoller wrote in 1884: 'It was precisely those governments which understood how to put the might of their fleets and admiralties, the apparatus of customs laws and navigation laws, with rapidity, boldness and clear purpose at the service of the economic interests of the nation and state, which obtained thereby the lead in the struggle and riches and industrial prosperity.'

From 1879 Germany had a planned economy, which she achieved largely on the basis of the tariff. German industry formed great combines for self-protection against depression. This trend towards neo-mercantilism was largely due to the alliance of Junkers, industrialists, bureaucrats and economists. After the crisis of 1900, the Darmstadter Bank observed: 'The community of interests of the great industrial groups, as expressed in cartels, protects industry from expenses and sudden collapses such as happened before their establishment.' In their mission for world market, the industrialists like Mevissen, the founder of the Darmstadter Bank, Werner von Siemens and others supported the German State policy like protective tariffs and preferential freight rates.

The effects of the new mercantilism in Germany were not congenial. The standards of living of German people did not register great increase compared to Britain. Between 1876 and 1900 the real wages in Britain rose by 32 per cent while in Germany it rose by 33 per cent. Trade unionism also suffered.

Meanwhile, the British industrialists since the 1870s noted with growing concern the rising competition of German industry. The Commission on the Depression in Trade and Industry wrote in 1885: 'The increasing severity of (German) competition in every quarter of the world, the perseverance and enterprise of the Germans are making themselves felt. In the actual production of commodities we have few, if any, advantages over them.'

Britain and the small western European countries were votaries of free-trade policy. France, Germany, Russia raised their tariffs. Britain's share in the expanding total of trade declined considerably. During the years 1871-75 the average annual deficit was offset by Britain's earnings through overall surplus of some £ 65 million. This deficit was offset by Britain's earnings through insurance, commission trading and shipping leaving an annual overall surplus of some £ 23 million a year. Late-Victorian governments supported the policy of foreign investments in India, Latin America and elsewhere.

In Britain there was improvement in the standard of living due to enterprise on the domestic front as well as investment abroad. Between 1860 and 1900 real wages improved by 75 per cent. The rise was due to the increased wealth that accumulated from the enterprise and from overseas investment, especially in railways. Sir Robert Giffen, the statistician, felt happy at the growing British economy. A new competition freed Britain from conservatism and she was 'preparing to prove that she was not decadent, though both enemies and friends often said that she was.'

The cyclical progress of European economy may be summarised as follows: from 1870 to 1873 Europe was 'at the tail end of a long upward trend of rising prices and profits.' Then followed depression with the collapse of the European markets. The depression was severe in the heavy industries as rail prices fell by 60 per cent from 1872 to 1881. Some revival took place between 1879 and 1882 owing to new American expansion. A new boom overtook the years 1887-90 as a result of gold in South Africa, the Panama Canal plans and expansion in America and in the British Empire. But this buoyancy proved to be short-lived as was evident in the fall of the House of Baring. It was not till 1896 that the economy revived largely due to new demand for rails in Europe, America and elsewhere. The impetus lasted till 1914.

To overcome economic fluctuations, British industry organised permanent type of association. The most important were the Salt Union of 1888 and the United Alkali Company of 1891. In 1895 J. and P. Coats, the sewing thread manufacturers, merged with four largest rivals. Germany proved to be more fertile soil for the growth of business association. The number of *Kartell* multiplied after 1873 and they gave protection to German industry against foreign competition.

America did not lag behind in the formation of business union. American oil industry was brought under the Standard Oil Alliance largely through the instrumentality of John D. Rockefeller. Carnegie and Morgan in steel, Harriman and Hill in railways created great trusts which restricted competition so rigidly as to create a great stir. The great anti-trust spokesman, Henry Demarest Lloyd, wrote in 1894: 'A small number of men are obtaining the power to forbid but themselves to supply the people with fire in nearly every form known to modern life and industry, from matches to locomotives and electricity.' The Sherman Anti-Trust Act of 1890 tried to restrict the movement, but it was nearly abandoned when Roosevelt came to power in 1900.

Banks, especially the joint stock banks played a great role in the formation of companies after 1870. By advancing capital, these banks converted Germany into an industrial state.

Economic development fostered the development of trade union. In Germany, trade union movement made progress between 1868 and 1875. In Belgium, unions were allowed from 1866, but strikers were penalised. In France, the *Confederation Generale du Travail* was formed in 1895. Stable unions were not formed in the United States till 1900. In England Disraeli's Act of 1875 legalised collective bargaining. The movement received impetus after the great dock strike of 1889.

The economic world of 1900 moved away from *laissez faire* and slowly gravitated towards collective or state interference. The outlook seemed to be more hopeful. Gold was coming into the bank. Trade was satisfactory in Germany. America was on the road to prosperity. *The Times* wrote on December 30, 1899:

> Trade was never better, wages were never so good, not were there ever fewer workmen unemployed.

The international economy before 1914 rested on free migration overseas of both men and capital, the use of machine industry, the development of communication and the expansion of multilateral trade. Though the United Kingdom secured a lead, other countries also went ahead. Germany began to challenge the pre-eminence of Britain in the industrial sphere. Russia experienced its first industrial revolution during the 1890s.

The industrialised west European countries after investing capital and labour increased their production by about a half between 1900 and 1913. During the last two decades of the nineteenth century huge areas were opened up for primary production like rubber in Malaya and the Dutch East Indies, minerals and chemicals in Chile, Canada and the Congo, sugar in Cuba and Java and meat in Australia, New Zealand and Argentina.

During the last two decades of the nineteenth century the industrialised countries were able to sell the products of their industry and to buy primary products from colonies at favourable terms of trade. Between 1900 and 1914 the quantum of world trade in manufactured goods doubled while that of primary products showed upward trends by two-thirds. Before the First World War (1914-1918), Europe occupied the central stage in economic power and the three countries—Britain, Germany and France monopolised Europe's manufacturing capacity in 1913.

The United States marched ahead and had a higher annual growth rate from 1870 to 1913 than Britain, France and Germany. But its activities were confined to expanding internal market rather than in international trade. In 1913 the three leading European countries had a monopoly in world export of manufactured articles. The British textile industry with its large overseas market surpassed that of France and Germany combined. London was to a great extent a world financial centre. It supplied long-term capital through the new issues and short-term capital through the bill market.

However in expanding world trade, the position of the United Kingdom was undermined in the face of United States competition. Its share of 19 per cent in 1880-85 declined to 14 per cent in 1911-13. Its rival, Germany, was ahead in steel as well as in new industries. Despite enormous capital exports before 1914, payments for imports outweighed current earnings from sale of goods. Nevertheless, in pre-war decades, the United Kingdom acted as 'the conductor of the orchestra' in the world economy. It was the world's largest creditor country. Bank of England's gold reserves rose from the mid-1890s. Unlike the restricted French and German capital movements, there was free export of capital from London. In the seven years before 1914, £ 600 million of British capital was provided for the construction of railways in other countries. Throughout the period before 1914, the United Kingdom adhered to free trade despite the appeal for imperial preference.

In 1907-08 the volume of economic activity showed recession. Britain suffered most and the United States shared the same fate. Governmental interference in economic matters before 1913 became frequent. The government pursued deliberate policies in foreign investment, central banking and railways. Economic planning was in its embryonic stage and tariffs were freely resorted to. While Britain clung to the principles of free trade, Germany and other countries adopted tariffs as instruments of general national policy.

Governmental interference in economic matters was to a large extent responsible for the growth of the welfare state in many countries of Europe. Social insurance in Germany, inaugurated by Bismarck in 1881 was crowned in 1911 by the promulgation of a Workmen's Insurance Code of 2,000 articles. By 1914 a wave of social insurance systems swept through the United Kingdom, France, Belgium, Holland, Italy, Denmark, Austria, Norway, Sweden, Switzerland.

While the underprivileged demanded state intervention for their own welfare, the business circles demanded protection for themselves. The demand was vocal from 1890 to 1914. In 1891 Switzerland favoured higher duties. Swedish farmers reverted to protection in 1894. In 1897 the German Emperor broached a general European Customs Union to protect against competition. Tariffs were conceived of, in some countries, as necessary instruments in the creation of national systems of political economy.

In some countries appeared cartels and business concentration. While the United States produced trusts, like the United States Steel Corporation (1901), Germany produced market-sharing cartels, like the Rhenish-Westphalian Coal Syndicate in 1893, controlling half the coal production of the country and the *Stahlwerk-verband* in 1904, controlling almost the whole of steel production. In France, six major firms regulated the *comte de forges*. In the United States, by the beginning of the twentieth century, trusts controlled two-fifths of the manufacturing capital of the country. During the First World War, in Germany, the United States, the United Kingdom and elsewhere, businessmen and business organisations exercised tremendous influence in influencing the policy of the state control. Walter Ratheneau, who wielded enormous influence in the economic apparatus of war-time Germany, was the director of sixty-eight business concerns.

During the period of interdependence, there was remarkable development of trade of overseas countries. Indian commerce greatly increased. South Africa with its rich mineral wealth was opened up. The employment of Dutch capital in Indonesia and American capital in the Philippines laid foundation of economic development of those countries.

With the happy marriage between old traditions and new techniques, Japan made rapid strides in economic sphere. The big labour force accompanied by machine production did much to promote exports of manufactured goods. Textiles accounted for 32 per cent of Japan's total exports.

War-time was largely controlled and market mechanism could not operate freely. However, with the end of autocratic empires in 1918, there began a demand for socialist planning.

During the First World War, the man behind the economic mobilisation of Germany was Ratheneau who wielded enormous power. In August 1914 was set up the war materials department (*Kriegs-Rohstoff Abteilung*) to deal with conservation, production of substitutes and planned distribution. War-work agencies acted as links between government and business. A Supreme War Office (*Oberster Kriegsamt*) was created in November 1916 to coordinate the various branches of centralised authority. The new economic structure engendered a robust attitude, largely through the influence of Ratheneau. He preached that economics was no longer the province of individuals, but for the whole community. It was not a war between two nations but a struggle between economic rivals. If Germany became successful, she should go forward from private to collective economy, *Gemeinwirtschaft*.

The First World War had brought about a change in Britain 'much of which is bound to be permanent.' In December 1916, a small War Cabinet provided a compact agency for central coordination. War-time planning like the Ministry of Munitions, Ministry of Shipping, Ministry of Food provided a great impetus and accomplished great work which could never have been done by private enterprise.

The most important facet of war-time planning was the emergence of international economic cooperation. There developed two main groups of commodity organisations, one under a Food Council and the other under a Munitions Council. In addition, the Allied Maritime Transport Council became the nucleus of the Allied machine of economic warfare. Such kind of international planning remained till the end of the war and the post-war period witnessed the re-establishment of freedom of business transaction.

After 1918 a general pressure was geared up against planning. In the United Kingdom and Germany, the governments during the war which had reached the commanding heights of economy through control, disappeared after the war. The brief war-time boom which continued till 1920 was followed by economic slump. The boom 'stirred starved appetites to new and clamorous life', the slump jettisoned all war-time schemes. The United States buoyed with economic regeneration, tried to abolish inter-Allied control of war materials. As Herbert Hoover wrote: 'This government will not agree to any programme that even looks like inter-Allied control of our resource after peace.' The dismantling of war-time controls aggravated many of the problems in the years to come.

Despite the disappearance of the control, many governments and people in general clamoured for its continuation. It was reflected in the constitution of the Weimar Republic which established workers' councils and economic councils with a National Economic Council at the top. In France attempt was made to convert war machinery to peace-time purposes. Apart from the creation of a new bank, the *Credit National,* a National Economic Council was set up in 1924 for deliberations between industrialists, workers and consumers.

The war-time experience left a legacy of planning campaigns of the 1920s and 1930s. In the Soviet Union there began battles of production in agrarian and industrial sectors. In Fascist Italy a 'Battle of the Grain' was proclaimed in 1925. In 1934 the National Socialist Germany announced a similar programme of agricultural production and replaced trade unions with regimented labour organisations.

Despite the apparent revival of multilateral trade, the post-war world witnessed drastic economic changes. The economic sphere was inherently unstable punctuated with shocks and confusions of the inter-war years culminating in the Great Depression of 1929-32. The dislocation caused by the war to the economic system showed no abatement during the inter-war period.

The devastation of war and economic dislocation caused heavy loss of manpower. As a result of the war, Europe lost about 20 to 22 million people and Russia about 28 million. Between 1913 and 1920 European manufacturing output fell by 23 per cent, while that of the United States rose by 22 per cent. European national income suffered. In economic terms European industrial development suffered an eight-year setback as a result of the war.

The post-war depression affected the United Kingdom, France and Belgium. Throughout the 1920s British staple industries stagnated and Japan made inroads into the British home market. The pattern of continued economic interdependence was broken up by the emergence of tariff walls in many countries.

The most disturbing phenomenon in the post-war period were internal inflation and a changed international balance of debtor-creditor relationships. Inflation reached at its height in central and eastern Europe and in Germany. By 1923 the German Mark became worthless. Savings were wiped out and Germany's capacity to pay reparations imposed by the peace settlement, had to be examined afresh. German financial collapse owed much to the country's lack of financial responsibility than to demands for reparation payment.

After the war, all European Allies were in debt to the United States and to the United Kingdom. Attempts by the United Kingdom in 1919 to wipe out the war debts or to reduce the burden of debt failed to make any progress owing to unsympathetic attitude of the United States and France. Henceforth the related problem of debts and of reparations remained a burning issue at international economic conferences till the 1930s.

Beneath the surface, fundamental changes occurred which were reflected in the fall of investment. Investment fell sharply. Meanwhile, the United States became the world's biggest creditor with its foreign investment reaching about seven times in 1930 than what it had been in 1913.

After the war, international economic system depended to a large extent on the United States. While the American Relief Association tried to rehabilitate Europe by supplying food, United States also furnished loans to European countries to pay reparations and war debts. German reparation payments to the Allies under the Dawes Plan of 1923 were met out of American loans. This enabled the Allies to pay their annual war debts to the United States. As Keynes wrote in 1926: 'Reparations and Inter-Allied debts are being mainly settled in paper and not in goods. The United States lends money to Germany, Germany transfers its equivalent to the Allies, the Allies pass it back to the United States Government. Nothing real passes—no one is a penny the worse.'

Nevertheless, the outlook of economic well-being was optimistic. From 1925 to 1929 there took place economic recovery over the whole world. The volume of international trade in Europe rose by 20 per cent. World manufacturing output rose by 26 per cent and food production by 11 per cent. The pound sterling went back on gold in 1925 and by 1928 most of the European countries adopted a gold exchange standard. In May 1927 the World Economic Conference was held at Geneva to consider removal of hindrances to international trade. The free flow of trade was reflected in the assertion of its President that 'international trade is normally and properly not a matter of victory and defeat or profit of one at the expense of the other, but of mutual benefit.' The new trend was sustained by a long boom in the United States which supplied the much needed capital.

However, beneath this apparent prosperity lay hidden danger. The gold standard never operated successfully. Most of the countries had little stock of gold in relation to their liabilities. London no longer held enough reserves to cover foreign currencies with gold if required. Simultaneously, the New York banks were reluctant to take over this role. The problem was accentuated by the increasing dependence of many European countries on loans which would have to be repaid quickly. Events in the United States hastened the process of economic crash.

From 1928 it appeared that the United States' boom was drawing to a close. It was found difficult to obtain short-term funds. These led to the withdrawal of American money from Europe. This meant not only a withdrawal of credit but that European banks had to meet their obligations in gold. A fall in American demand aggravated the crisis. Prices began to slump sharply. The crisis reached its climax on 24 October 1929, 'Black Thursday', by the Wall Street crash. On 29 October 'the most devastating day in the history of all markets', industrial index fell by 43 points. On November 11, 12 and 13, the index fell by another 50 points. The dramatic incident was followed by the lingering 'Great Depression'. The collapse became general and widespread affecting Europe and different parts of the world. Trade declined rapidly; unemployment reached alarming proportions and most of the countries tried to insulate the national economy from the debilitating effect of Depression.

The American crash was followed by financial collapse in Europe. The dollar went off gold in 1933, the franc in 1936. The struggle to remain on gold had further aggravated the slump. Despite a one year moratorium on reparation and war debt payments, the German *Reichsbank* was in the throes of crisis. In the United Kingdom gold reserves were being depleted at the rate of £ $2^1/_2$ million a day. The 'National' Government which replaced the Labour Government in August 1931 tried to put a brake on the withdrawals, but in two months £ 200 million of gold had been lost. In September 1931, Britain suspended the gold standard. This was followed by 23 countries and in 17 others the gold standard became inoperative.

Among other problems faced the countries the most serious was the abysmal fall in prices. In the United States, the wholesale price index fell from 100 in 1929 to 63 in March 1933, and in the United Kingdom it registered a fall in the same period from 100 to 72. The prices of primary products fell even more sharply. A sharp contraction of international trade followed. Between 1929 to 1932 the value of international trade shrank by more than 65 per cent. Most of the industrial countries witnessed a sharp fall in production, a rise in unemployment and a decline in exports.

Against the backdrop of economic dislocation, many countries adopted several expedients to offset its effects. By the Import Duties Act, the United Kingdom imposed a general 10 per cent tariff with protective duties on some manufactured goods of up to $33^1/_2$ per cent. Many countries adopted traditional economic weapons like tariffs and import quotas.

Apart from economic considerations, political approach played an important part in the choice of instruments for combating the malaise. In Germany, where unemployment rose to six millions in 1932, the National Socialists promised to abolish unemployment and guarantee national self-sufficiency. In Belgium and Holland, government interference to protect industrial capital was common. Attempts were made in 1932 to form a low-tariff zone in Benelux, only to be jettisoned by Britain. A Danubian Customs Union also suffered the same fate. Among the European countries, Sweden alone exhibited some economic resilience to achieve a 'definitely expansionist mentality.'

Despite a sharp slump in industrial construction from $ 949 million in 1929 to $ 74 in 1932, the United States made little attempt to recover from depression diaspora. She clung to war debts, despite its indirect rejection by the Lausanne Conference of July 1932. She followed a protectionist policy by raising the protective duties to a feverish height in 1930. Many countries adopted retaliatory measures. In 1930 the President of the Chase National Bank wrote: 'The debts of the outside world to us are ropes about their necks, by means of which we pull them towards us. Our trade restrictions are pitchforks pressed against their bodies, by means of which we hold them off.'

However, American economic nationalists were uninfluenced by business pressures. This was demonstrated in April 1933 when the new President, F. D. Roosevelt, stressed the need for international economic cooperation. The American government abandoned the gold standard and devalued the dollar by 41 per cent. Devaluation was intended to raise the American internal price level and to strengthen farm incomes. Yet in effect it raised United States tariff by 60 per cent and gave a 40 per cent bounty to American exports. The World Economic Conference of 1933 which met in London failed to reach an agreement on international cooperation. Its main achievement was to reinforce international commodity controls with regard to such products as wheat, tea, sugar, rubber, tin and copper.

In general, Roosevelt's economic policy was widely hailed in many countries in Europe. His vigorous actions to counteract the crisis situation in his country were widely hailed. The 'New Deal' which he offered to combat economic and social challenges brought to an end a period of stagnation. It was appreciated in all parts of the world, as did related American 'plans', like the Tennessee Valley Authority scheme.

The primary object of the New Deal was to rescue the United States out of the morass of slump and, secondarily, to widen the concept of social justice. The objectives did not involve any long-term planning, but necessitated governmental intervention. Nevertheless, the American experiment provided examples to many countries in Europe on the complex problems of planning. It struck a new note in economic planning. The view found wide acceptance that Roosevelt's 'strivings towards reconstruction and revival are as surely the outstanding example of reformed Capitalism as the Russian Five Year Plans are of Socialist planning in the world today.'

While the United States made bold efforts to achieve economic self-sufficiency, Sweden became known as 'the economic miracle' of the 1930s and New Zealand headed towards a 'welfare state'. It was in this context the well-known British economist Keynes wrote in 1934, 'we may not all be socialists now, but we are certainly (nearly) all planners.' However, the view might seem exaggerated when it was found that well-conceived planning was minimal compared to political interference with economies. Despite the publication in 1936 of Keynes's masterpiece *The General Theory of Employment, Interest and*

Money, there was little understanding of economics of unemployment. 'Planning' meant limited management usually concerned with particular problems of specific industries. 'Planning is forced upon us,' as observed by H. Macmillan, a young conservative politician. It was 'not for idealistic reasons but because the old mechanism which served us when markets were expanding naturally and spontaneously is no longer adequate when the tendency is in the opposite direction.' The founding of Iron and Steel Federation in 1934 fell far short of economic planning.

In Italy the Fascist economists evolved *Corporativismo* for planning the distribution of labour and capital and the system of production. In 1936 and 1937 Mussolini stressed the importance of state intervention in industry. But the corporation did little to coordinate the national economy. French economic policy relied more on import restrictions. A small country, Rumania, followed suit, where the number of quotas rose 120 in November 1932 to 500 in July 1933.

Sweden, thanks to the efforts of Ernst Wigforss and other economists, encountered dangers of deflation. Between 1933 and 1937 there was economic recovery in the United Kingdom which owed not a little to combination of devaluation, rationalisation, protection and cheap money. Britain's road to recovery had little to do with 'planning'.

Soviet Union was isolated from the 'Depression'. There a comprehensive planning scheme was in operation. The Soviet planning system was the product of national emergency. As Lenin observed after the October Revolution: 'There was nothing written about such matters in the Bolshevik textbooks, or even in those of the Mensheviks.' Initially the Soviet planning was hesitant but reinforced by experience it progressed rapidly effecting gigantic metamorphosis in economic life. There was continual adaptation and experimentation in the Supreme Council of National Economy or *Vesenkha*—a body which came into existence in December 1917 and continued till January 1932. There was no preconceived economic ideas. As an official report put it in 1929: 'socialist construction cannot proceed otherwise than gropingly.'

The most important agency for coordinating Soviet plans was *Gosplan* set up in February 1921. *Gosplan*'s earliest tasks were 'perspective' plans involving extensive electrification of industry or the nationalisation of the corn trade. It was only in 1925 that *Gosplan* began to take interest in the whole of the Soviet economy. From 1931 it began to collect statistics from different industries which laid the basis of an overall plan for the ensuing year. The calculation of the 'material needs' of the government was facilitated by the creation of a Central Department of Economic Accounting (TSUNKhu). In 1932 *Vesenkha* was eliminated and *Gosplan*'s coordinating powers increased. Despite the ramification of economic administration which increased in number from three in 1932 to twenty in 1939, Gosplan's primacy in Soviet planning remained unassailable.

The transformation of the Soviet economy from a relatively backward country into an industrialised modern state may be divided into three main phases. The first phase extended from the November 1917 to March 1921, during which the state ventured to reach the commanding heights of economic self-sufficiency. The second phase was a period of recovery and restoration accomplished by the so-called New Economic Policy **(NEP)** during the period 1922-27. The third phase was a period of industrialisation and agricultural collectivisation, begun with the First Five Year Plan in 1928.

The First Five Year Plan laid emphasis on a high rate of investment, particularly in heavy industry and in agriculture. Collectivisation in agriculture was pursued with great zeal. In 1927 state and cooperative farming covered only 2 per cent of the peasants. But by March 1930 the figure had risen to 55 per cent and by 1936 to 90 per cent.

During 1929-31 the state regulated the whole economic system of the Soviet Union. Apart from making agricultural changes, it introduced trade union reforms, tightened factory discipline and converted unions into governmental agencies. To these were added important fiscal and credit reforms, and the creation of specialised investment banks in 1932. The swan-song of the economic drive was 'There is no fortress the Bolsheviks cannot take.'

The Second Five Year Plan, extending from 1933 to 1937 put emphasis on consolidation rather than gigantic leap forward. After abandoning rationing in 1935, a collective Farm Statute of the same year brought to an end the period of rural turmoil. Along with increasing agricultural output, industrial productivity kept pace. Now factories were established which accounted for four-fifths of industrial output. The productive capacity of two metallurgical plants, Magnitogorsk and Stalinsk, was equal to that of the entire pre-1914 iron and steel industry.

The Soviet economic system concentrated more on internal economy rather than on foreign trade. From 1918 international trade was in the hands of the State Commissariat for Foreign Trade. This monopoly enabled the government to maintain the rouble at par with foreign currencies and impose restrictions on imports. In 1938 the total value of foreign trade amounted to only 24 per cent of the pre-war level. Soviet planning thus could steer away from world economic movements.

Throughout the whole of the inter-war years the entire planned economy of the Soviet Union was patterned after war economy. The whole economy was geared to fulfil the objective. Fulfilment was a practical task. As Molotov proclaimed in 1939: 'Planning is no mere piling up of tables and figures unrelated to the course of fulfilment of the plan.'

Soviet planning exercised fascination on both 'advanced countries' suffering from chronic unemployment and on 'backward countries' anxious for leap forward. Before 1939 the Soviet model influenced the Turkish Five Year Plan and the Mexican Six Year Plan. Since 1945 the influence had become general in Communist countries. Some of the non-Communist countries have acknowledged that the Soviet economic system has general relevance.

German planning under National Socialism was a mixture of private enterprise and capitalism. The government guided the economic machine for political purposes and to meet the exigencies of war. However, war economy was not developed in Germany until after 1942. Before the war there was certain vagueness about the criteria of German economic policy. 'Economic policy in the national socialist state is determined by considerations of expediency, and, without prejudice, applies such means as are necessary in every given case for the welfare of the people.' The effects of the government policy were pervasive: 'the state is for all practical purposes a partner in every German enterprise.'

The National Socialists made few economic innovations. Their objects were to reduce unemployment and to achieve national self-sufficiency. They devised their own institutional structure—the Central Committee of Entrepreneurial Associations (1920) and the National Union of German Industry (*Reichsverband*). The influence of the *Reichsverband* was enormous, and its organisation was both regional and functional. In 1932, the 29 industrial and 50 territorial organisations which belonged to it covered about 30 per cent of German industrial enterprise. The National Socialist government established the National Economic Chamber and the Cooperative Council of Chambers of Industry and Commerce to coordinate the German business administration.

The government had established in 1919 the Ministry of Economics. The Ministry under Hjalmar Schacht—from August 1934 to November 1937—controlled German banking and trade. Schacht favoured bilateral trade and opposed deficit financing. After 1938, however, the Ministry of Economics—under Walter Funk—was divested of power. In 1936 was set up the office of the Four Year Plan under General Goering to strengthen the hold of the National Socialist Party over the economy.

The main goal of economic planning of Germany between 1933 and 1939 was to achieve full employment. A Commissioner for the Creation of Employment had been set up in 1932. Meanwhile to generate employment major works were undertaken on building roads, houses, public utilities and inland water transport. Sizeable public expenditure and a revival of private investment increased total output and generated employment between 1933 and 1936. As a result unemployment fell appreciably.

The government also undertook extensive measures of labour and price control. In 1934 government replaced the trade union organisation with a Labour Front. To Trustees of Labour were delegated the power to regulate labour market. To control prices, a Reich Commissioner for the supervision of prices was created in December 1931 and a Reich Commissioner of Price Formation in 1936. A Price-Stop Decree of November 1936 prohibited all increase of prices.

The government exercised vigorous control of foreign trade. Imports were kept to a minimum and all foreign payments had to be debited to the Reichsbank. Foreign trade declined from 22.5 per cent in 1923 to 13.1 per cent in 1933.

German expenditure showed abnormal increase on rearmament—the proportion rising from 3.2 per cent in 1932 to 18.1 per cent in 1938. Increased expenditure on armament was an important factor in European economic recovery of the late 1930s. Despite some improvement in Europe's position in world market, the revival of world trade was not spectacular. The volume of world trade in 1937 was hardly commensurate with the twenties and attempts to reduce tariffs and to stimulate greater freedom of trade, met with little response. In the United Kingdom despite an increase of 24 per cent in the volume of industrial production between 1929 and 1937, the volume of exports was less than 16 per cent.

While the industrial countries enjoyed favourable balance of trade, the underdeveloped countries languished. The demand for planning, therefore, arose in poorer countries. The reports of the International Labour Organisation and of the League of Nations drew attention to the links between economic and social policy. In 1935 the League initiated an inquiry into 'nutrition in relation to health, agriculture, and economic policy.' Two years later the League's Economic Committee and the International Labour Organisation grappled with the broader problems of raising general standards of living. In 1938 the League appointed a committee to devise measures for preventing or mitigating trade depressions.

The market forces continued to vary. They were tampered with by governments, but not controlled. The prices of cocoa fell by 40 per cent in the recession years 1937-38.

> State intervention was being gradually extended into the field of price formation and income distribution. As a result, some of the market incentives to transformation were weakened; the idea of national planning was, on the other hand, not so far advanced that governments were prepared to steer the development of the economy in a particular direction; or that state directives took over the functions earlier exercised by private initiative.[1]

In this transitional period, there was no uniform monetary standard. The attempt made by a few countries to maintain the gold standard proved temporary. French effort to maintain the standard required deflation and put the country in an unfavourable position. In 1936 the new Popular Front Government was compelled to devalue the franc and abandoned the gold standard. France was thrown into economic disequilibrium and it was only after the Second World War could she succeed in regaining its 1919 peak level.

In the sphere of international economic system, Europe gained slightly over the United States because of the imposition of discrimination against United States goods. New industries in Europe like automobiles and electricity made up lost grounds. Yet in other industries, notably textiles, Japanese competition outweighed all others during the 1930s. In many parts of Europe there had been a move towards larger economic units in both old and new industries.

In the United Kingdom, great emphasis was laid on the necessity of the full employment and to propagate the idea of 'welfare state'. William Beveridge was the architect of a war-time plan for social security. He also popularised some of Keynes's ideas in his *Full Employment in a Free Society* (1944). The example of the Soviet Union attracted great attention in the 'underdeveloped world'. The concept of international interdependence had lost its meaning with the division

1. Svennilson: *Growth and Stagnation in European Economy*, P. 36.

of the world into two organised blocs in post-war world.

After the Second World War, the reconstruction of Europe proceeded. The high rate of economic growth in Europe during the 1950s swept away the record of inter-war years. The increase in productivity in the 1950s was twice the average for the whole period from 1913 to 1960. During the 1930s Europe had suffered from 'the arteriosclerosis of an old established, heavily capitalised economic system... (which) blocked the road towards general expansion.' But after the war, Europe reaped the benefit of a significant change.

The growth of independent states after 1945 transformed the economic world. During the 1950s the volume of trade in manufactures among industrial countries increased at a quick pace. At the same time imports of manufactures by non-industrial countries rose rapidly.

Significant changes had taken place in 'planning' since 1945. It has been agreed that planning is 'an activity of very recent origin, belonging to the 1960s rather than to the 1950s.' After 1950 long-term planning in years of peace became an obsession with the capitalist societies. In the changed atmosphere of the 1950s and 1960s, 'overall' planning in some countries began to grapple not only specific or short range problems but also long-term needs. In countries like Germany and the United States, there was a development of planning techniques within large business firms. A similar process began to emerge in the managerial practices and attitudes in the public and private sectors of most of the Western economies. There have been some planning processes common to both capitalist and Communist countries. The smaller underdeveloped countries face difficulties in introducing planning to their variegated problems.

CHAPTER 46

EDUCATION

The fundamental aim of education is that of freedom and moral spontaneity. Rousseau's idea was not to drill the child into regimented knowledge, but to release the power of independent life and power within him. In 1807 Freiherr von Stein wanted to elevate the people so that they might associate themselves in the work of the state. The Prussian reformers found the means in the person of Johann Heinrich Pestalozzi (1746-1827). After initial failures, he first achieved success in teaching a group of orphaned children at Stanz. He later ran several schools and pupils flocked to him from all parts of Europe. He was not interested in abstract theory of education and his fundamental idea was that education should start with the child himself. According to him, the vital part of all education was self-development. Pestalozzi was concerned for the education of the ordinary people and his emphasis was on the instruction of the poor man's child.

Pestalozzi's ideas were adopted by Fichte. The Prussian officials popularised the idea that it was the duty of the state to teach its people to read and write. Pestalozzi's work was familiar in England and influenced English thinkers of the period. Bentham's ideas about education were more practical than Pestalozzi. The Utilitarian school, spearheaded by James Mill, propagated the same idea of freedom and self-activity. Education should not be confined to select few, because it was the vehicle of knowing the art of happiness. Convinced of the value of education, Robert Owen believed that the best governed state would be that which concerned itself with education of its citizens. According to Owen, education must teach the people to become rational beings. He struck the practical idea: 'Train any population rationally and they will be rational. Furnish honest and useful employments to those so trained, and such employment they will greatly prefer to dishonest or injurious occupations.' The State must shoulder the responsibility of education. Sir James Kay-Shuttleworth, one of the founders of the popular education, found in education as an important remedy for the misery of the Manchester workers in 1832.

Pestalozzi and Owen were primarily concerned with the education of the people. To the German thinker Wilhelm von Humboldt fell the task of popularising the secondary and higher education. Fichte and the theologian Schleiermacher began to plan a new university in Berlin which should promote the higher culture of the mind. The State must tap new spiritual reserves. Wilhelm von Humboldt, who was Head of the Department of Religion and Education in the Ministry of the Interior, 1809-10, exemplified the idea. He believed that the goal of education was the all-round development of individuality. The great force in his mind and to his contemporaries like Herder, Goethe and Schiller, was that of the study of the Greek world. The appreciation of its language, history, culture and art, was the key to full self-development. It was Humboldt who infused the ideal of New Humanism into the mainstream of higher and secondary education.

Education to Humboldt was the key to the moral resources of the nation. The new University of Berlin, founded in October 1810, tried to develop the spirit of the whole German nation. Though it was a state institution, its autonomy was not impaired. In many German States some of the ancient universities underwent transformation. Heidelberg was reorganised in 1802-03. In Bavaria, a University at Munich was established in 1826. The Prussian government founded the

University of Bonn in 1818. In all these German universities, professors maintained high standard of learning and devoted themselves to research. In various branches of learning—in classical philology, Germanic studies, in law, in philosophy, in history and in science—the Germans attained a high degree of proficiency.

The excellence of German universities profoundly affected the secondary schools. New Humanism again became the motive force. Out of the old Latin schools developed the gymnasia, the secondary schools. In Prussia, a teachers' examination for secondary schools was adopted in 1810. Gradually an independent teaching profession came into existence. In 1812 the final school-leaving examination was reorganised. In the same year a standard plan of gymnasium studies was adopted, based on a ten year course of Latin, Greek, German and Mathematics. In 1817 a separate Ministry of Education was set up. However, the development was not satisfactory in the initial stage; a project for a general school law covering primary and secondary education was not successful in 1819. After the death of King Frederick William III in 1840, the Minister, Von Altenstein and his assistant Johannes Schutze completed the organisation of the Prussian gymnasium in its studies. With minor variations, development on more or less same lines happened in the other German states.

During the period of reaction (1815-30), governments became suspicious of academic freedom. The reforms made in Prussia and the other German states had been to tighten state control over the universities and schools. In the 1920s a number of edicts were issued in Prussia regulating the studies of schoolboys and asking the class teachers to maintain a report on the activities of their students. Naturally, such state control was found to be stifling.

German writers of the nineteenth century advocated cultural nationalism with Germany playing a leading role in an international activity of culture. Fichte in his *Addresses to the German Nation* (1807) disseminated such idea. Fichte propagated the idea of a national system of education embracing the whole people. It was the duty of State to carry this programme as it had done in introducing the system of compulsory military service. After 1815 the academic opinion of Germany was Liberal. Early Liberal leaders were professors like Rotteck and Dahlmann who believed in the free creative spirit which should transcend petty politics. 'I do not trouble myself about political matters', wrote Humboldt to Goethe in 1798. Absorption in philosophical matters reached its limit when it was adumbrated: 'In Germany, man who is not occupied with the comprehension of the whole universe, has really nothing to do.'

Napoleonic France witnessed state intervention in national education. Statesmen of the revolutionary period had seen education as a major function of the State. The First Consul took special care to regulate education, the object being to inculcate allegiance to the State. With the aid of Catholic religion, he wanted a teaching body with fixed principles. On May 1, 1802, he enacted a Law which created a lycee at the seat of each court of appeal. These were to be chiefly boarding schools, preference being given to sons of soldiers and officials. In addition, with proper authorisation, the communes or individuals might set up secondary schools. Primary education was practically neglected.

Napoleon wanted a national organisation of education which would depend entirely on the State. He formulated this idea in February 1805. Law was passed in 1806 for the formation of the university and it was set up in 1808. The University was a lay teaching corporation. At its head stood the Grand Master and the Council. France was divided into 'Academics' each presided over by a Rector. The Grand Master and Council laid down methods of instruction which the teachers were required to follow. Private education was not suppressed. All higher and secondary schools were linked together so that teachers could feel themselves to be members of one body. The basis of the teaching, according to the decree of 1808, was to be the precepts of the Catholic faith, allegiance to the emperor and compliance with the university statutes which aimed at producing citizens 'attached to their religion, to their prince, to their fatherland and to their family.'

The spirit of the new institutions was Catholic and was strongly anti-revolutionary. Efforts were made to maintain orthodoxy. The private schools suffered a great deal under the regime. They were forced to deposit a proportion of their fees into the funds of the University. Strict rules regulating private schools were enforced in 1811.

In higher education Napoleon preserved the professional schools. The *Ecole Normale* set up in 1795 for the training of teachers in secondary education was re-established in 1808. Apart from these schools, higher education was in the hands of the faculties of theology, law, medicine, science and letters. The purpose of higher education was to train men for state service. In the same way was established in 1808 the institution of the *baccalaureat*, a school examination designed to open the way to civil functions. University education in France was oriented to utilitarian ends. The Napoleon government evinced keen interest in the development of science. Napoleon derided critical thought and in 1803, he suppressed the class of moral sciences in the *Institut de France*.

State control of education was continued by the revived Bourbon monarchy. The countries of eastern and southern Europe maintained stricter state control over education. In the Habsburg Empire, the state exercised rigid control over teachers and syllabuses. In his sermon to the professors, the Emperor observed in 1821: 'There are now new ideas going about, which I never can nor will approve. Avoid them and keep to what is positive. For I need no savants, but worthy citizens. To form the youth into such citizens is your task. He who serves me must teach what I order.' Alexander I of Russia did much to promote education. He earmarked more funds for education and set up a department of education. New universities were created at Kharkov and Kazan and an institute of pedagogy was founded at St. Petersburg. A statute promulgated in 1804 gave the universities considerable autonomy. Poland also pursued a generous policy in education. The French-controlled Duchy of Warsaw in 1807 did much for primary and secondary schools. A new university was established at Warsaw in 1816-17. However, after 1815, forces of reaction undid much of this good work. The censorship was rigidly enforced, and the universities were carefully watched. The Polish rising of 1830-31 led to the closure of the universities of Vilna and Warsaw. Tsar Nicholas I of Russia by a statute of 1828 decreed that education was to be open only to the children of nobles and officials.

In contrast, education in England and the United States was left to private initiative. In the United States, progress in developing primary system of education had been slow. The colleges—Harvard, Yale and their contemporaries—were limited in their resources. But it was Thomas Jefferson who took a practical interest in the development of education. It was his aim to create a comprehensive structure in Virginia ranging from primary schools to higher schools and to the university. He was the father of the University of Virginia and recruited able professors from overseas.

In England the State had little to do in promoting education. This was left to ancient independent corporation or to the efforts of private individuals. Universities of Oxford and Cambridge and the ancient grammar schools came under the first category.

Secondary education was restricted to the upper and middle classes. Between 1813 and 1848 Thomas Arnold, the headmaster at Rugby, modernised and expanded the curriculum of the school. The old universities and grammar schools were Anglican in religion. The existence of the religious tests led to the creation of the non-sectarian London University in 1828. Both Oxford and Cambridge were still clerical in character and governed by outmoded statutes. However, the older universities served as centres of liberal education. The University of Durham was established in 1832; in the same decade colleges and technical schools were founded in Leeds, Birmingham and Sheffield.

The State began to exert a greater influence in regulating education. The great Utilitarian, Bentham, held that education 'is only government acting by means of the domestic magistrate.' The Select Committee of 1816 on the education of the poor unravelled many abuses in the management of charitable trusts which resulted in legislation for effective control. In 1827 a commission was appointed for visiting the Scottish universities. In the same year a Society for the Diffusion of Useful Knowledge came into being to bring education to adult members of the working class.

The period from 1870 to 1930 witnessed a great expansion of the activities of the schools and universities. The most complex problem which dominated the educational history of all European countries was that of the role of the state. Matthew Arnold castigated the English methods which left everything to private individuals and praised the state control of education in Germany, France, Holland and Switzerland. State intervention was not popular in England. Many Frenchmen welcomed a state system of education. According to Guizot, this system was imposed upon France by her 'history and national genius. We desire unity—the state alone can give it; we have destroyed everything—we must create a new.' Fichte had pinned his hopes for the greatness of Germany in a new national system of education. The Germans believed that the task of the state was to train its citizens by means of education. In Switzerland after 1830 the Liberals believed that education was the chief means of raising the level of national life.

The main purpose of state control of education was to serve its own interests. Napoleon III who controlled French education dismissed Michelet, the historian and Mickiewicz, the Polish poet, who were highly critical of him. Similarly Frederick William IV of Prussia controlled elementary schools in such a way as to keep them subservient to church and state. Russian education under Nicholas I (1825-55) was defined as that of 'Orthodoxy, Autocracy, Nationality.' But the reactionary system could not stem the tide of liberal ideas. Under Alexander II (1855-81) the universities were allowed more freedom. In Western countries, the policies of reactionary governments were unable to check academic liberalism. Professors and students played conspicuous part in both the German and Italian revolutions of 1848. In Germany, especially, the Universities were the repositories of national and liberal sentiments. In Switzerland, the spread of education promoted the growth of liberalism after 1830. Its manifestation was evident in the establishment of a federal technical university, the Zurich Polytechnikum in 1855.

With the expansion of the role of the state in education, there began a conflict between the state and the church. The spread of education was possible with the state's assistance but it inhibited the growth of new experiments or new ideas. Compared to the public system of education which was found to be efficient and extensive, the state system of education generated stagnant uniformity and killed individual initiative. State education also led to the immense increase of the power of the state over its citizens. A sharp conflict ensued between the claims of the secular and of the spiritual world in controlling education. However, in many countries—in Germany, in Austria and in the Scandinavian countries—state and church worked harmoniously in primary education. But the conflict became inevitable when the Christian church extended its arm over the secular education. The school question was the major issue that embittered the relations between the Roman Catholic Church and the new Italian state. It was one of the causes of *Sonderbund* war in Switzerland and it lingered even after 1848. Menaced by the fear of revolution, the Austrian state became subservient to the claims of the church in the Concordat of 1855.

The attitude of the Liberals towards the problem of education, varied from country to country. In France, Catholics challenged the monopoly of secondary education by the University. The result was the *Loi Falloux* of 1850 which enabled the Church to open secondary schools freely. Liberals, like Lamartine, disliked the monopoly of the university in education. One of the important causes of the revolution of 1830 in Belgium was the state monopoly of primary education under Dutch rule. The alliance between the Catholics and Liberals broke down soon when the former tried to assert their dominance. The primary-school law of 1842 was favourable to the Church, but the secondary-school law of 1850 strengthened the control of the state. Though the law of 1857 abrogated the state monopoly in education, but it failed to evoke sympathy from the Catholics and the Protestants.

Beneath the surface of educational controversy between the State and the Church there loomed a large number of theorists who delved deep into the educational problems. The greatest of them was the Swiss, Johan Heinrich Pestalozzi, who died in 1827. His belief that the potentialities of the child must have to be developed through his own latent power, exercised a strong force in popular education. One of Pestalozzi's contemporaries in Switzerland was Philipp Emanuel von Fellenberg, who established a series of schools for different classes of society. He continued his work with great zeal until his death in 1844. Pestalozzi exercised great influence over German thinkers Johann Friedrich Herbart (1776-1841) and Friedrich Wilhelm August Froebel (1782-1852). Herbart developed a science of education which put great emphasis on the importance of teaching method. His ideas gained wide currency among educational theorists in Germany, America and England. Froebel was a pioneer of devising methods of educating smaller children. According to him, children should be stimulated to creative activity through play, and he invented a series of 'gifts' and 'occupations' to develop their capacities. Based on these ideas, Froebel founded the first school for small children named *Kindergarten*. Though derided by the Prussian government, Froebel was popular in America and England.

In France and England, some of the political and social theorists grappled with educational problems. The English Utilitarians of 1830, were specially concerned with them. Both Jeremy Bentham and James Mill were optimistic about the ultimate aim of education. Another important English thinker, Herbert Spencer (1820-1903), valued the new scientific ideas which alone could train human beings for gainful occupation. In France, Auguste Comte (1798-1857) emphasised the importance of 'positive' education to suit the exigencies of modern time. Led by Charles Fourier and Henri de Saint-Simon, the earlier French Socialist schools, stressed the importance of bringing out the child's natural aptitudes.

Germany was pioneer in different facets of education like primary, secondary, technical and university. Horace Mann, Secretary of the Massachusetts State Board of Education, considered that Prussia, Saxony and some other German states, were pioneer in the education of the people. Prussia was called in 1831 by the French observer, Victor Cousin as that 'classic land of barracks and schools, of schools which civilise the people and the barracks which defend them.' In Prussia and in the German states, education was generally compulsory but it was yet to become free. Despite deficiencies in the provisions made for popular education, a large proportion of children went to school in the Habsburg empire.

Germany's neighbours, the Swiss, the Scandinavians and the Dutch, also made great advances in the field of education. In Holland, primary schools made great headway and were praised by Mann, Cousin and Matthew Arnold. Writing in the sixties, Arnold called some of the schools in Swiss cantons among the best in Europe. In the Scandinavian countries, the State undertook to establish and control a general system of primary education throughout the country. This was achieved in Sweden in 1842 and in Norway in 1860. The state system of education in Denmark, begun in 1814, was improved by a law of 1856. In all these three countries, education had been made compulsory. The Scandinavian countries produced some outstanding personalities in the field of education. In Denmark, Kristen Kold (1816-70) developed the 'Free Schools'. Sweden made gymnastics as a necessary part of school training while in Finland Ugo Cyganeus (1810-88) was a pioneer of manual training in schools.

In the advanced western Europe, general literacy was interlinked with advancing democracy. With the growth of factories, aided by the influence of humanitarianism, and the growing demand of education from below, there was a growing belief that education was the key to the betterment of the conditions of the factory workers. It should also be made free and compulsory. By the 1830s, the Lancastrian system of education, whereby the master taught monitors, who taught the other children, was over. In 1837 the French Society for Elementary Instruction found the deficiencies of the system in various countries. France took the lead in establishing a comprehensive primary-school organisation. The Education Law of 1833 provided each commune with a school and each department a college for training teachers. In 1833, the British Government for the first time allocated grant to two societies—the Church of England 'National' Society and the undenominational 'British' Society. These grants were gradually increased, but it received a setback when a law was passed in 1832 of providing conditional grants on the basis of performance in examination results. Forster's Education Act of 1870 while preserving the existing denominational schools, supplemented them by establishing new schools. In Scotland, the statutory system and voluntary schools of various kinds came under the state system set up by the Scottish Education Act of 1872.

Conditions in southern and eastern Europe were deplorable. Illiteracy was widespread. In Italy 72 per cent of the population were illiterate and in Hungary 63 per cent. The same problem also gripped Russia where *Zemstvo* or District Councils began rudimentary work in 1870.

Demands for education in science and technology outweighed classical education. In classical and in technical education German institutions were preeminent. Despite certain differences in the education system of the different German states, a basic similarity was evident in all of them.

In France and in England emphasis was given to classical education in secondary schools. When publicists like Herbert Spencer and T. H. Huxley drew attention to the deficiencies of the traditional course, a Royal Commission was appointed in 1870 to consider the problem of scientific education. Despite the introduction of a clear demarcation between literary and scientific studies in France in 1852, a specific plan for 'special scientific instruction' was introduced into the schools in 1855. The French schools or *lycees* and the *colleges communaux*, became adjunct of the Napoleonic University. After 1850 state control over private schools or church schools was relaxed. However, the state maintained its control over degrees. Voices were raised in protest in Germany and elsewhere against the exacting and stiff system of education required for higher professional schools. Strictly professional courses played an important part in higher education.

The French *lycees* provided excellent education at moderate cost. In England, the standard was very high in a few selected high schools, but the great mass of the middle class was not provided with any means of education. State organisation of secondary education was a far cry. There existed only private schools and ancient grammar schools, mostly inefficiently run and the smaller group of public schools. It was through the initiative of men like Thomas Arnold, Headmaster of Rugby (1828-42), the 'public school' system took its modern shape. However, England was still lagging behind her neighbours in 1870. There was proliferation of technical and professional courses in Germany. Zurich *polytechnikum* became the model for the German technical universities. The leading technical institutions of Karlsruhe (1825), Dresden (1828) and Stuttgart (1829) gradually assumed importance. But it was only after 1870 that full development of technical universities began to take place. In France, the famous *Ecole Centrale des Arts et Manufactures* was founded in 1828. But England was yet to catch up the new spirit. A rudimentary beginning was made when South Kensington became the headquarters of the Science and Art Department in 1853. Despite the efforts made by the Department to encourage science teaching, a Government enquiry of 1868 revealed England's weaknesses.

In most of the countries there existed Training Colleges for elementary school teachers or Normal Schools. In this sphere also Germany was most advanced. The most illustrious figure in the Prussian elementary education was F. A. W. Diesterweg (1790-1866), who was the principal of the college from 1832. Another prominent Swiss figure was Johann Jakob Wehrli (1790-1855), who advocated the combination of manual labour with ordinary classroom instruction. In England, a national Normal School could not be established before 1840, when DR Kay established a successful school at Battersea.

The University stood at the pinnacle of educational hierarchy. German universities were the model of institutions of modern research and scholarship. German professors were usually academics of higher excellence devoted to original investigation. In the universities, seminars or small class became popular where advanced work was done under the guidance of the eminent professors. To the students and teachers, the goal was the pursuit of learning for its own sake. The brightest jewels that adorned the portals of German universities were Muller in physiology, Gauss in mathematics and Liebig in chemistry.

The universities of Austria, Switzerland, Holland, and Scandinavia were largely modelled on the German type of organisation. Before 1848 little progress had been made in Austria. Schools and the universities were zealously controlled. The Director of Studies exercised control over the faculties. Even after 1849 the atmosphere was not favourable for academic freedom, though the Austrian universities had some distinguished teachers in their faculties. Two major schemes for higher education which came to nothing were Bishop Grundtvig's plan for a great Scandinavian university and a federal university in Switzerland. However, new universities were founded at Zurich (1833) and Berne (1834) and in 1835 Basle, the ancient university of German Switzerland was reorganised.

In France there was no real university life in the strict sense. Napoleon had created separate faculties of Theology, Law, Medicine, Science and Letters. Guizot, Minister of Public Instruction (1832-36), attempted to set up real universities with a full course of instruction which foundered; the same fate awaited later in the efforts of Victor Cousin to set up a university at Rennes. In contrast, the *College de France* in Paris became the most important centre of higher learning. It was adorned by distinguished men of letters like Michelet, Cuvier, Ampere and Berthelot. Higher education was improved to a certain extent under Napoleon III. In 1868, Minister Duruy organised *Ecole Pratique des Hautes Etudes* as a centre for research work in history, mathematics and natural sciences. Older professional institutions like *Ecole Polytechnique* continued to train men for the civil and military engineering services of the state, and the *Ecole Narmale Superieure* for the higher posts in secondary education.

Reforms in secondary and higher education in Italy made during the Napoleonic period lost momentum after 1815. The Normal School at Pisa was closed. Though there were numerous universities, including the famous universities of Bologna and Naples, the atmosphere was not congenial to the development of free thought. The Education Law of 1859 enforced state control of education on higher and secondary education. Few students took up literary or scientific subjects at the Universities, a majority of them crowded the professional faculties of law and medicine.

The English universities aimed at producing learned men and did little to foster research. They were, in Matthew Arnold's opinion, little more than higher schools. Yet the older English universities had a real tradition of their own, a tradition which had its own value.

America adopted European ideas of education. The general tendency in elementary and secondary education was towards a public and non-sectarian system. But it was bitterly opposed by many ecclesiastical and propertied interests. However, the demand for public schools led to the rise of the public High Schools. In higher education, state universities were established in southern and western states. At the end of the Civil War, the level of American higher education was much below general standard even in the prestigious Harvard, Yale, and Princeton. However, after 1870, great progress was made with the foundation of the Cornell University in 1868. Germany provided source of inspiration to America as most of the American students went to Germany for higher studies.

English educational ideas became potent source of influence in the self-governing colonies and in India. There was conflict between the advocates of a national and of a denominational system in New South Wales, Victoria and the Canadian provinces. English 'public school' became popular in Australia, New Zealand, and South Africa. In India, largely influenced by T. B. Macaulay, officials like C. E. Trevelyan, liberal thinkers like Rammohun and missionary educators like Alexander Duff, a fateful decision was taken in 1835 of introducing Western system of education. Sir Charles Wood's Education Despatch of 1854 planned a comprehensive system of education based on grants-in-aid from the government. The first universities at Bombay, Calcutta and Madras—modelled on the University of London—were opened in 1857.

Compared to the extension of secondary and university education, there was little enthusiasm for the public education of women. France was the most backward and state secondary schools did not come till the eighties. In England the Christian Socialists—F. D. Maurice, Hughes, Kingsley, founded Queen's College, London (1848). However, in the sixties, girls' schools received only 2 per cent of endowment from the state. In 1870 University College of London opened its doors to women. There were two Women's Colleges (1869-1871) at Cambridge. In Sweden girls were given the right to be admitted as university students in 1870. Russia made some progress in women's education as there were some 190 secondary schools of different grades in 1873. However, greatest progress was made in the United States where Mary Lyon and Emma Willard took the lead in founding schools for girls in the twenties and thirties of the nineteenth century. In the eastern states, separate colleges for women were opened. By 1870 several of the state universities in the western state opened their doors to women.

Adult education made some progress in England. Apart from the Christian Socialists, James Stuart in 1867 began the lectures in northern towns. Inspired by Bishop Grundtvig (1783-1872), People's High School Movement in Denmark touched the adult masses. The first Peoples' High School was opened at Schleswig in 1844 and the movement gradually spread through the untiring efforts of Kristen Kold. With no examinations, no fixed syllabus, the schools gave winter course to the peasant farmers.

Adult education movement, known as the Lyceum Movement in the United States, offered lecture courses. The movement was at its peak in the fifties and sixties and attracted lecturers like Emerson and Agassiz the scientist.

Libraries exercised profound influence on the growth of opinion. In England and the United States, library movement began about the middle of the century. 'Ewart's Act' of 1850 allowed boroughs to establish libraries and museums. The first library to be opened under the Act was the Manchester Library. In 1868 there were about fiftytwo libraries in existence, containing about 500,000 books. In the United States, the first state to legislate for setting up libraries was New York in 1835. It was followed by many others. English plan of allowing towns to establish state-supported libraries was followed in the United States. Boston took the lead to set up a public library in 1848. The first state to pass a general law was New Hampshire in 1849, followed by Massachusetts which had 82 libraries in 1872.

The 1870s was a decade of expanding public education and the 1880s witnessed such expansion consolidated. Public education was made free and compulsory. Education became free in Prussia in 1888. It was made compulsory in Switzerland in 1874, Italy in 1877, the Netherlands in 1878, Belgium in 1879. However, until the twentieth century, compulsory education was confined to the age group below nine or ten. Government spending on education was at first hesitant. But most of the governments became aware of its importance and university. In 1901 the Prussian government spent more than thirty times on primary education as it had done thirty years before. In 1914 despite heavy expenditure on armaments, education authorities in England and Wales spent twice on elementary education as they had spent in 1900.

In France, Napoleon I had evolved a single integrated system ranging from the village school to the *lycee* and the universities under the aegis of the Ministry of Public Instruction. However, the primary base of the pyramid had hitherto been neglected and there existed deep animosity between the Church and the State with regard to secular education. During Ferry's tenure of the Ministry of Public Instruction between 1879 and 1885, a real network of free, compulsory and primary schools was established.

With the expansion of education, school teachers became an influential element in the life of the community. They became apostles of the doctrines of secularism or nationalism. In a circular letter to primary teachers, Jules Ferry emphasised the role of the teacher as 'a natural aid to moral and social progress.' He also urged them 'to prepare a generation of good citizens for our country.'

Progress in education was also made in north-western Europe where after 1900 people became increasingly literate. Literacy was promoted in the Soviet Union after 1917, in Turkey under Mustafa Kemal Pasha and throughout southern and eastern Europe. However, complete success was not achieved in every country. In Portugal, in 1950 only 60 per cent of the population was literate; in Bulgaria, in 1946 about 25 per cent of the population was illiterate.

The increase of literacy was accompanied by a great development of secondary, technical and university education. In France number of students going to *lycees, colleges* and even to higher education were doubled in the first four decades of the twentieth century.

The Board of Education was established in Britain in 1900 and the Act of 1902 stimulated the growth of state sponsored secondary education. The Education Acts of 1918 and 1944 provided a complete system of national education. In comparison, the expansion of British universities was rather slow. Apart from the University of Wales (1903), six new universities came into being, at Birmingham (1900), Liverpool (1903), Leeds (1904), Sheffield (1905), Bristol (1909), and Reading (1926).

During these years new universities were also opened in other countries. In 1911 the Portuguese universities of Lisbon and Oporto were founded. In 1924 new Italian universities were founded at Bari, Florence, Milan and Trieste and in 1944 at Salerno. In 1928 was founded the Danish University of Aarhus and in 1946 the Norwegian University of Bergen. During this period many countries including Britain were forging ahead in the field of higher education and learning. Between 1917 and 1941, the Soviet Union increased the number of colleges and universities from 90 to 728. Education became more extensively subsidised and it was made available to many people.

CHAPTER 47

RELIGION

The romantic intellectuals placed little emphasis upon the essentials of religion. More serious was the fact that the aristocracy placed a conservative stamp upon the Churches. This was unfortunate, because, as a matter of fact, the Churches were not essentially conservative in the period before 1848 as the vigorous controversies between liberal and conservative groups inside both the Roman Catholic and the Protestant churches showed. In general, the major religions reflected strength and vigour and the masses were bound to their traditional faith.

The most divisive issue facing France during the Revolution proved to be religion. Tragically, the first principle of the Revolution, the sovereignty of the people, was opposed to the basic conception of catholicity. The Revolution made the Church a department of state and the resultant religious schism made the French Revolution an event of portentous significance in European history.

Initially, the first negative change in the position of the Church raised little controversy. On August 4, 1789 the Gallican Church voluntarily gave up its corporate status and its right to tax and to administer itself. In February 1790, certain religious orders were abolished with the consent of the higher clergy in the Assembly. Schemes to abolish ecclesiastical titles and to alienate ecclesiastical land were alike accepted without great demur. All these schemes were intended primarily to subordinate Church to the State and not to separate Church from State. But when the Civil Constitution of the Clergy which was approved by the King on August 24, 1790, separated Church from the Papacy and required the clergy to become paid officials of the State, the changes raised a storm of protest. By November 1790 the National Assembly declared the Civil Constitution of the Clergy to be in force and required a loyalty oath from bishops and priests. Only seven bishops took the loyalty oath, and in some parts of the country, 90 percent of the priests refused to join the new State Church. Pope Pius VI condemned the Civil Constitution of the Clergy in the spring of 1791. The newly elected constitutional clergy was regarded by the devout as blasphemous and the 'non-jurors' or refractory priests, were considered as potential counter-revolutionaries. However, the 'patriotic clergy' who took the oath fell foul of the Revolution after its pronounced radicalism in August 1792. On the other hand, the revolutionary leaders were disillusioned with the results of the Civil Constitution which had caused public disorder, and drove the non-juring priests to participate in the Vendee risings in 1793. In the hysteria of civil war and foreign war, fear of non-juring priests came as an incentive to debase Christianity itself.

The deliberate de-Christianisation began in the autumn of 1793. In their iconoclastic zeal which was not confined to Paris but spread to the provinces, the revolutionaries stopped the mass, desecrated Churches and executed non-jurors. The ancient clerical monopoly of education was swept away, and, in October 1793, France broke with her religious past by replacing the ancient Gregorian Calendar with the new calendar of the Revolution. The early de-Christianisation has been described as an 'expedient of national defence.' Its impetus came not only to restore public order but from military and economic crisis. But behind the destructive aim of de-Christianisation lay a positive purpose. The Jacobins sought to replace Christianity by a cult more congruous to changing circumstances. The basis of the cult, though religious, sought to usher in a new ideology of justice and fraternity. The cult of Reason propagated the worship of the revolutionary republic with less emphasis on worship of nature and reason. Robespierre tried to create a more unified form of worship which could provide a bridge between theists—Catholic and non-Catholic.

After the Thermidor, a widespread thaw set in and religious life revived in many parishes. Religious liberty was sanctioned in many localities. By a series of decrees between September 1794 and September 1795, the Convention brought about the separation of Church and State. The State was not to pay for any cult; freedom of worship was to be maintained and churches might be used for public worship.

The separation of 1794 marked an interesting experiment in European Church-State relations. The First Amendment of the American Constitution provided that 'Congress shall make no laws respecting an establishment of religion or prohibiting the free exercise thereof.' In France, separation was a policy of resignation. As Catholicism could not be eradicated, then it must be tolerated. Harsh laws against the non-juror remained on the statute-book. But in 1797 *coup d'etat* of Fructidor unleashed a persecution comparable to that of the Terror. However, many of the non-jurors preached counter-revolution, praying for the royal family. However, a minority group, led by the saintly Monsieur Emery, tried to separate the cause of Catholicism from that of the Bourbons. Thus, between the two sections of the Catholic clergy a rift appeared which bordered on the verge of schism.

The French Revolution imperilled the Italian peninsula, the heart of Catholicism. In February 1797, under the Treaty of Tolentino, France detached the Legations from the Papal States: the murder of General Duphot in Rome in December led to the occupation of the city in February 1798, and to the proclamation of Roman Republic. In 1799, Pope Pius VI was removed to France only to pass his time in bondage.

However, within two years, there was brought about the French Concordat on July 15, 1801. Bonaparte felt the necessity of reconciling the Church when he appreciated the hold of traditional religion on the masses and its value as a guarantee of social order. Napoleon's task of pacification required a religious peace, to mollify the warring divisions among the French clergy and to prepare the path for French hegemony in Italy. Napoleon diagnosed the situation in his proverbial style: 'A religion is necessary for the people. This religion must be in the hands of the government. ...The authority of the Pope is necessary for that.'

By the Concordat of 1801 the medieval Church-State was done away with. Rome was compelled to accept the mere recognition of Catholicism as 'the religion of the majority of Frenchmen.' She renounced her claims for the restitution of alienated Church property. The bishops and some of the clergy were to be paid by the State instead of by the endowment. Freedom of worship was guaranteed, but subjected to police regulations. Napoleon had the prerogative of nominating bishops and the clergy were ordered to take an oath of obedience to the government. The law which promulgated the Concordat also contained a number of Organic Articles, which curtailed the freedom of the Church. Communication between the French clergy and Rome was restricted. Organic Articles were also issued for the Reformed and Lutheran Churches and subsidised on a basis of parity with the Roman. The religious equality proclaimed by the Revolution was thus maintained. 'The essential for public order and morality is not all men should have the same religion, but that every man should be attached to his own.'

While the churches of France lay in unprecedented tranquillity, the Catholic Church in Germany suffered huge losses. 1803 marked an epoch in Church-State relation in Germany. The clergy of the old Church-States found themselves regimented by Protestant-princes and began to turn to Rome for protection. Moreover, the simplification of German political geography further undermined the crumbling principle of *cuius regio eius religio*. The upheaval in Germany was followed by a settlement between Rome and the Italian Republic in 1803. The Concordat, patterned on the broad lines of the French Concordat, was more favourable to Catholicism.

But the Concordat was accompanied by the Melzi Decrees, a more harsh version of the Organic Articles.

The entente between Rome and Paris was sealed by the Pope's officiation at Napoleon's coronation in Notre Dame (2 December 1804). This spectacular ceremony had hardly any parallel as even Charlemagne had to travel to Rome to be crowned. However, the entente was shattered when in October 1805 the French troops occupied the Papal port of Ancona. The Pope's letter of complaint threatened to break off diplomatic relations. In February 1806 Napoleon demanded the closure of the Papal ports to enemies of France which the Pope refused. After Tilsit, Napoleon was bold enough to dismember the Papal States. Rome was occupied in February 1808; in May 1809 the Papal States were absorbed within the Empire and on June 10, the Papal flag was pulled down and the tricolour hoisted. On July 6, a storming party entered the Church, seized the Pope and transported him in captivity at Savona. The neutrality of the Papal States threatened the French defensive system and the Pope must allow his Kingdom to become a French protectorate. Napoleon made no secret of his feeling when he observed: 'Your Holiness should have the same respect for me in the temporal sphere that I have for you in the spiritual ... Your Holiness is Sovereign of Rome, but I am its Emperor. All my enemies must be yours.' But Pope Pius VII insisted that the temporal power had a spiritual function and the head of a Church could never be subject to a single nation.

With the abduction of the Pope, the conflict assumed a new dimension—more especially when Napoleon made an attempt to turn Paris into the spiritual as well as the temporal capital of his Empire. But the Pope refused to perform the role of imperial chaplain. The imprisoned Pope applied an effective weapon: he refused to sanction the appointment of the bishops nominated by the emperor. By 1811 twentyseven Imperial Sees were without any bishop, and a new form of Investiture controversy shook the fabric of the Imperial Church. Napoleon tried to buttress his authority by consulting in 1809 and 1811 two small Ecclesiastical Councils on problems presented by his quarrel with the Pope. But, much to Napoleon's chagrin, the Councils expressed solidarity with the Holy See and implored to set at liberty the Holy Father. Even the grandiose National Council which assembled at Notre Dame in Paris with 95 'Fathers' of the Imperial Church took an oath of obedience to the imprisoned Pope. Henceforth, Napoleon was driven to the desperate effort of bullying the Pope. Debilitated by illness, Pope Pius VII was on the point of making concession, when Napoleon's military defeat released him from his ordeal.

By 1815 a religious awakening swept across many parts of Europe. Traditional conception of revelation seemed discredited by the Enlightenment. Miracles now needed explanation. Old proofs of God's existence were compromised by Hume and Kant. Chateaubriand, Schleirmacher and Lamennais tried to present theology in a fresh light that would strike the imagination. A new generation of defenders sought to show the Church as a living organism; religion not as superstition but as an expression of life; doctrine not as a static, but as progressive, developing revelations in history. Through Romanticism the Roman Church found new defenders in the world of literature and art. In Catholicism many Romantics found symbols for the imagination. Chateaubriand's *Genie du Christianisme* (1802) heralded an aesthetic approach to religion. His conversion from Stoic scepticism had been a matter of emotion: 'I wept and I believed.' The traditionalists—like Bonald, de Maistre and Lamennais—were mainly concerned with the value rather than the truth of religion. Traditionalism was united with a new Ultramontanism, which rested more on the need for social order than on doctrinal proofs. The new Ultramontanes made the Pope the keystone of a Christian polity which could resolve the antithesis between liberty and order. He was the rightful arbiter of Christendom. 'Without the Pope', ran Lamennais's famous dictum, 'no Church; without the Church no Christianity, without Christianity ... no society.'

The prolonged European wars excited among the Protestants a moral fervour and a sense of spiritual need. The War of Liberation was preached as a crusade. In the early nineteenth century 'rational Christianity' found many exponents.

But there were many Protestants who believed that the spiritual life could not be explained by abstract conceptions of nature and reason. Traditional forms of piety revived. The Protestant revival was associated with a conservative neo-confessionalism, which looked back wistfully to the heroic days of the Reformation.

The chief feature of the Protestant revivals was a concern for 'practical piety' which found expression in the growth of voluntary societies. Bible Societies propagated translations of the Scriptures throughout the globe. In England, Evangelicals lured many people into the service of moral reform. The Baptist Missionary Society (1792) and a cluster of societies were formed in Europe and America for the conversion of the heathen.

Evangelicanism shaped English society most significantly. Anglicans and Dissenters built new Churches in old parishes and in teeming streets. In North America the revivalist tradition ushered in another Great Awakening in the last years of the eighteenth century. By 1830, Charles G. Finney, the greatest revivalist of the century, transmitted Western fervour to many areas. Finney's *Lectures on Revivals* (1835) marked an important stage in the development of modern mass evangelism. Wesley's circuit system with its itinerant preaching was successful in the frontier and by 1844 the Methodists had become the largest Protestant denomination in the United States.

The theology of Schleirmacher (1768-1834), Hegel's colleague at the University of Berlin, gave a great boost to Protestantism. His *On Religion: Addresses to Cultural Despisers* (1799), marked a new epoch in theology. He was the greatest Protestant theologian since the sixteenth century. Religion, according to him, was not a set of dogmatic propositions or an ethical code, but an inward experience. His appeal was not to the Bible, prophecies and miracles, but to the living religious consciousness. The essence of religion lay in 'the immediate consciousness of the universal existence of all finite things in and through the Infinite.'

The forces of religion were sometimes used in the work of social restoration. Napoleon himself had set a precedent. On a diplomatic level the Holy Alliance of Christian princes as projected by the Tsar was a grandiose gesture. Some of the aristocratic sceptics now saw the value of the Church as a bulwark against future revolutions. Pietism flourished even among Prussian Junkers.

Needs of the Churches were not ignored in the political reorganisation in 1815. The Congress of Vienna restored temporal power to Pius VII. A series of agreements reestablished the Catholic Church in most of the European states. The bonds of Church and State, jeopardised by war and revolution, were drawn closer together again. Rome continued to curry favour with the princes. Pope Pius VII wisely refused to join the Congress System. But the cause of legitimacy found eloquent champion at Rome. Pius VII and his successors tied themselves to the chariot wheels of reaction. After the death of Pius VII in 1823, Leo XII issued the first of the series of doctrinal condemnations of political liberalism. However, a number of Catholic leaders began to question the principle of throne and altar. The fall of an unpopular regime, like that of Ferdinand of Spain in 1820, or Charles X of France in 1830, with which the Church had been associated intimately, discredited the clergy. But the advent of constitutional form of government found the Catholics an ardent champion of it. The Catholics, therefore, carried on relentless struggle against the princes who were not only heretics but aliens—Ireland, Belgium, the Prussian Rhineland and Russian Poland.

France witnessed the high-water mark of the fusion of legitimism and Catholicism. Disillusioned with the so-called Union of Throne and Altar, Lamennais began to move towards the Liberal Catholicism. In 1829 he called upon the Church to cut asunder the political entanglements and to 'isolate herself completely from a politically atheist society.'

In Protestant States, one could see the main varieties of Church-State relations. At one extreme stood Sweden, Norway and Denmark, overwhelmingly Lutheran, where separation from the national Church was illegal. At the other end stood the United States where existed a multiplicity of denominations, free and equal in the eyes of the federal government. The American system provided a working model of religious freedom. It was a paradox that religion flourished much more in the free atmosphere in North America than it did in Europe, where it was protected.

Britain was regarded a Christian Commonwealth in which Church and State were 'one and the same thing, being different integral parts of the same whole.' Politicians, Whig and Tory, regarded Westminster Abbey as 'part of the British constitution.' In 1818, Parliament granted a million pounds, and in 1824 half a million, to build new Churches. However, in Britain, as elsewhere, the demand for religious equality became vocal. In 1829 Catholic Emancipation struck a blow at the idea of the 'Protestant Constitution' of Britain. In 1828 Non-Conformists secured the repeal of the Test and Corporation Acts. In the thirties, a formidable army ranged against the establishment—Chartists, Dissenters, Irish Catholics, Utilitarians, the latter inveighing against the misuse of Church property. In a famous aphorism Thomas Arnold cried 'the Church as it now stands no human power can save.'

There grew up in France a Liberal-Catholic movement, begun by Lamennais and gathering to its support Lacordaire, Montalembert and Gerbet. The maxim of his new policy was 'Men tremble before liberalism; make it Catholic and society will be reborn.' The anti-clerical disturbances of 1830 did not augur well for this new evangel. But in a daily newspaper, *L'Avenir* which Lamennais and his disciples had launched in Paris in October 1830, he demanded the union of religion and liberty. The only alternative, however, to alliance with the state was reliance on the Papacy. The French episcopate took alarm at the demand for four freedoms: freedom of education, freedom of the press, freedom of association and freedom of worship. In November 1831 Lamennais took the bold step of appealing to the Pope himself for recognition of his principles. Unfortunately for the reformers, Gregory VII dared not affronting the civil princes. Instead he issued a Bull on August 15, 1832 which sounded the death-knell of their hopes. The Bull repudiated the suggestion that the Church needed regeneration; it fulminated against freedom of conscience and it denounced freedom of the press.

Despite the humiliation of Lamennais, his followers, Lacordaire and Montalembert, continued to uphold the standard of liberal Catholicism. For the time being, the Liberal-Catholic sentiment became more insistent. Montalembert's campaign for freedom of Catholic education grew more strong and the administration was compelled to take cognisance. Accordingly, a new bill was introduced in 1847 which curtailed the control by the University over voluntary schools. The controversy aroused thereby was not settled until the *Loi Falloux* was passed in 1850. This statute was a victory for the Church. Within a year of the passing of the *Loi Falloux* over 250 educational establishments were opened, mainly by religious orders.

Meanwhile, in Switzerland, the Revolution of 1830 revived the doctrines of liberalism and the stage was set for conflict between Radicals and Conservatives in the religious sphere. Friction between the Radical government and the Catholics in some Cantons led to the dissolution of the monasteries. But within the other Swiss cantons and outside the Confederation, this secularisation of the monasteries evoked loud protests from the Catholics. The conflict now assumed a new dimension from the traditional rivalry of Protestant and Catholic cantons, to a rivalry between a militant ultramontanism and free thinking. In 1844 the Great Council of Lucerne invited the Jesuits to undertake theological teaching in the seminary. The Radicals organised an anti-Jesuit campaign. Armed clashes followed. The Catholic cantons of Lucerne, Uri, Schwyz, Unterwalden, Zug, Fribourg and Valais concluded a defensive alliance, known as the *Sonderbund*. In the civil war in 1847, the *Sonderbund* was decisively defeated. A spirit of reconciliation followed and the relationship of Church and state was to remain peaceful until the old Catholic schism, as a result of the proclamation of papal infallibility in 1870.

'Men tremble before Liberalism; make it Catholic and Society will be reborn', this was the view of Lamennais in 1830. For Newman and the leaders of the Oxford Movement in England the remedy lay elsewhere. Newman enunciated the remedy in the following words: 'The real ground on which our authority is built—our Apostolical descent.' The main principle of the Oxford Movement was to combat Liberalism by asserting the dogmatic basis of Christianity. Before its rise the Evangelicals held sway in the Church whose leaders played a conspicuous part in the abolition of slavery and other humanitarian works. The Oxford Movement proved to be a complement to the evangelical revival by its doctrine of the Church, the ministry and the sacraments. 'All we who have been ordained clergy, in the very form of our ordination, acknowledged the doctrine of the Apostolical Succession. And for the same reason we must necessarily consider none to be really ordained, who have not thus been ordained.' This principle became the foremost eccelesiastical shibboleth in England and elsewhere. The Oxford Movement wrought a far-reaching religious revival by its emphasis on holiness of life and its restoration of religious orders and its ceremonial and liturgical interests.

Meanwhile, the strife between the established Church and the Non-Conformists centred on education. With the steady increase of state subvention on education, there began a friction between the established and the free churches concerning the use of public funds for denominational teaching. At first the Nonconformists were not in favour of state intervention in education as expressed by Edward Baines in 1843: 'It is not the province of a government to educate the people.' But the growing interest in education evinced by the state, led to a change of attitude. By the middle of the century, the Dissenters were in favour of state education, whilst the Anglicans, being in possession of largest number of primary schools, were opposed to it. Forster's Educational Bill of 1870 marked a substantial victory for the established church and drew the criticism of radical Free-churchmen. The supremacy of the British parliament was demonstrated when steps were taken to open the ancient universities like Oxford and Cambridge to non-Anglicans. Gladstone's University Tests Act of 1871 threw open to non-Anglicans all offices in the Universities of Oxford, Cambridge and Durham, with the exception of clerical fellowships and divinity professorships.

The accession of Pius IX to the Papacy in 1846 witnessed hostile relations between Church and State in various European countries. The Revolution of 1848 caused the flight of the Pope to Gaeta, whence he returned in 1849 under the protection of the French troops. This ended the papal flirtation with Liberalism. On December 8, 1854, Pius IX formally elevated the doctrine of Immaculate Conception to the status of a dogma of faith. During the decade beginning from 1854, the relations between Church and State in Italy grew steadily worse. On December 8, 1864, Pope Pius IX issued the *Syllabus Errorum* with an attendant encyclical, *Quanta Cura*. In the encyclical, Pope condemned the modern liberal ideas of extreme individualism and of the supremacy of the secular State over the Church. The encyclical concluded with a warning against non-believers and with an exhortation to prayer and invocation of the Virgin Mary.

The Syllabus or Collection of Modern Errors contained eighty propositions. Fourteen propositions condemned pantheism, naturalism and moderate and absolute nationalism. Four propositions censured indifferentism and latitudinarianism. A single proposition condemned socialism, Communism and secret societies. Twenty propositions relating to the rights and authority of the church were arraigned, especially the denials that the Catholic religion is the only true religion, and that the church has any temporal power. Seventeen erroneous propositions concerning the power of the civil authority to regulate religion and education were reproved. A further nine concerning natural and Christian ethics were condemned. Ten propositions relating to Christian marriage were reproved including the assertion of the legitimacy of divorce. Two propositions contained erroneous opinions about the temporal power of the Papacy. Finally, four articles condemned false opinions concerning modern liberalism especially the denial that Catholicism alone should have the position of an established religion and that liberty should be granted to all citizens to propagate their own religious beliefs.

The Encyclical was one of a series of papal pronouncements against modern errors; the Syllabus a brief compendium and summary of various propositions taken from previous papal allocutions. Both were accompanied by a covering letter to the episcopate. 'The Pope has already in encyclicals and allocutions condemned the principal errors of this most unhappy age. But all of you may not have received all the pontifical acts. Therefore the Pope wished a Syllabus of these errors to be drawn up for the use of all the Catholic bishops, that they may have before their eyes the pernicious doctrines that he has proscribed.' Taken as a whole, the Syllabus attacked the basic principles of modern society and as such the Ultramontanes welcomed it. The Syllabus evoked loud protests from liberals and prominent statesmen.

In 1869, while controversy about the *Syllabus* was raging, Pope Pius IX convened a general council of the Catholic church at the Vatican. The Vatican Council, attended by nearly eight hundred prelates all over the world, elaborated the relationship between faith and reason, but its most outstanding achievement was the definition of the dogma of papal infallibility. It solemnly proclaimed as 'a dogma divinely revealed, that the Roman Pontiff, when he speaks *ex cathedra* to define a doctrine regarding faith or morals to be held by the universal church, is possessed of that infallibility bestowed by Christ on church, and therefore such definitions of the Roman Pontiff are irreformable of themselves and not from the consent of the church.'

While the Vatican Council was in session, the Franco-Prussian war broke out. The French garrison was withdrawn from Rome and in September 1870, Italian troops took possession of Rome and made it the new national capital of United Italy. Pius IX protested and in October 1870 prorogued the Council *sine die*. On November 1, the Pope placed the King and the government of Italy under the ban of the church for their invasion of Rome and refused all offer of compromise. This dissension remained a festering sore until it was healed by the Concordat with Mussolini in 1929.

The overthrow of the Pope's temporal power was viewed with favour by the opponents of the Catholic Church. They feared that the doctrine of Papal Infallibility might undermine liberalism and nationalism. But the majority of the Catholic intellectuals defended the doctrine. All the bishops accepted it, and only a small minority in Germany and Switzerland formed a dissident 'Old Catholic' sect. On the other hand, the Protestants, liberals and patriots, denounced the doctrine. In Prussia, Bismarck waged a war with the Catholic Church—*Kulturkampf*, a 'struggle for civilisation.' Between 1870 and 1880, the Jesuits were expelled from Germany, religious orders were dissolved, civil marriage was made obligatory and Prussia withdrew its financial support from Catholic churches. It was only in 1879 that Bismarck began to ponder to conciliate the Papacy, a process which took several years.

In England Gladstone propagated the idea that Catholics could not be 'good citizens'. In France, anti-clericalism led to a confrontation between church and state and was to end in disestablishment. In Italy, the quarrel with the Papacy led to the formation of an anticlerical league of governments in 1880. The Spanish anti-clericals fought stubbornly against the church. In Austria Emperor Joseph was prevailed upon to repudiate his Concordat with Pius IX. In Belgium the clerical party won the 1880 elections and held power for the next twentyfive years.

Pope Pius IX died in 1878 leaving behind a disastrous tradition for the Catholic church. But the succeeding pontificate of Leo XIII (1879-1903) marked a recovery in the political fortunes of the Papacy. Leo XIII was a scholar and had sympathy with democratic and social-reform movements. He felt that it was possible to break with disastrous tradition without compromising on essentials. Meanwhile, embittered relations between church and state were threatening the welfare of millions of Roman Catholics. Leo quickly began to apply emollients counselling the French Catholics to accept and cooperate with the republican government of their country (the policy known as *Ralliement*). 'None of the several forms of government is condemned in itself', preached the encyclical *Immortale Dei* (1855), 'in as much as none of them contains anything contrary to Catholic doctrine, and all of them are capable, if wisely and justly managed, of ensuring the welfare of the state'. Even in Italy, where Leo clung tenaciously to his claim to the Temporal Power, there appeared a fair prospect of rapprochement between Church and State in the mid-1880s. He expressed admiration for the constitution of the United States.

Leo XIII was not blind to the social problems concommitant with industrialisation. In 1880 St. Thomas Aquinas was acknowledged the patron of all Catholic schools and learning and a great revival took place which was to integrate Catholic dogma with the advances of natural science. Leo XIII commended the efforts of clergymen to build up a Catholic social movement which denouncing economic liberalism and Marxian socialism, aimed at Christianising modern industrial society. In 1891 the Pope reinforced the movement by the publication of the encyclical *Rerum Novarum*. This document defended private property as a natural right, emphasised the importance of the family life, protested against the omnipotence of the state, condemned the doctrine of economic determinism, and declared that 'class is not antagonistic to class.' Against economic liberalism, it held that labour was not a commodity and the state prevent the exploitation of labour, encourage collective bargaining and enact social legislation. The state was accorded the right and the duty to encourage free associations of workers. Consequently, Christian unions were formed in Germany, Belgium and France. The encyclical urged a wider distribution of private property, a restriction of the hours of employment and the assurance of a living family wage. From these developments sprang much constructive social thinking chiefly pronounced in France by men like Marc Sangnier, Albert de Mun and Rene da la Tour-du Pin. In Germany, a confessional Centre Party emerged in 1870 with a complete programme of constructive social reforms. In Austria-Hungary, Christian socialism found a powerful advocate in Baron Karl von Vogelsang, whilst in Vienna the redoutable Karl Lueger denounced socialism and capitalism, Marxists and Jews.

The pontificate of the Leo XIII did not realise the hopes it awoke. The Catholic Christianity, while maintaining its existence in several countries, became relatively weaker in 1903 than in 1878. In Italy there was no settlement of the 'Roman question' between King and Pope and during Crispi's first ministry (1887-91) the Pope even considered leaving Rome. In France, there was a marked growth of anti-clerical agitation and legislation. Sporadic and sometimes violent attacks on ecclesiastical property, schools and monasteries took place in Spain, Portugal and in Latin America. On the other hand, Catholics put a stop to the *Kulturkampf* in Germany, reestablished primacy in Austria, and obtained control of the Belgian government. Moreover, there was noticeable increase in their numbers and influence in Switzerland, in the Dutch Netherlands and in English-speaking countries.

The pontificate of Pius X (1903-14) witnessed the rise of 'modernism' within the Catholic Church. In Italy, earlier tensions which had marked the relations between Church and State were relaxed. The Pope relaxed the ban on Catholic participation in Italian politics. In France, however, a bitter conflict led to annulment of Napoleonic Concordat (1905) and to the enactment of drastic anti-clerical legislation. The Pope reacted with new disciplinary measures and recommendations which asserted his authority over clericals and lay Catholics.

Into this volatile situation appeared a considerable number of Catholic priests and laymen. Influenced by 'Darwinism' and by the 'higher criticism' of the Bible, they propagated the idea that the Church must modernise its teachings and discipline. These 'Modernists' held that dogma is not immutable but evolutionary, that the basic apology for the church is less its divine origin than its human utility, that ecclesiastical authority should be reformed and 'science' should be independent of the church.

Pius X was implacably opposed to 'Modernists'. The encyclicals *Lamentabili* and *Pascendi* in 1907 denounced Modernism as a summation of heresies. The Pope excommunicated some of its leaders and obliged all Catholic priests to take a special oath against it. The Catholic Church was thus purged, and its traditional beliefs reasserted. It has been said that a 'reign of terror' began in the intellectual life of the Roman Church. 'Since the death of Pope Leo the Roman Curia has assumed towards the world of thought a reactionary attitude reminiscent of the days of Pius IX, when the church was at war with everything and everybody.'

'Modernism' became a potent force within Protestant Christianity. Protestantism seemed more adaptable than Catholicism to modern civilisation. Industrialisation began in Protestant Britain and spread rapidly in Protestant Germany and America. Moreover, the major Protestant churches had always been national churches and responsive to patriotic emotions—the Anglicans in England, the Presbyterian in Scotland, the Dutch Reformed in Holland, the Lutheran in Scandinavia. They supported the nationalism of the nineteenth century more naturally than could the supra-national Catholic Church. Most important of all, Protestants were liberal in their own interpretations on the relationship between religion and science.

The conflict between Church and State which had been a bane of the Catholic Church was not marked in Protestantism; and anti-clericalism was exceptional in countries traditionally Protestant. However, Protestantism had to face a challenge when it questioned the distinctive historic principle of religious authority. For Protestantism, while rejecting the Papacy as the supreme ecclesiastical authority, had insisted that the Bible itself was the main source of faith for Christians. However, 'Darwinism' and 'higher criticism' assailed the authenticity of the Bible and shook Protestantism to its foundations.

By the end of the nineteenth century, there were evident among Protestants three different trends. A minority of Protestants, including a large segment of intellectuals, unable to accept Catholicism, repudiated historic Christianity altogether. At the opposite extreme stood a large number of Protestants who took a fundamentalist position and regarded the Bible as the literally inspired 'Word of God.' 'Fundamentalists' were to be found among Lutherans and Calvinists and in the evangelical section of the Anglican Church, especially among the Methodists and Baptist.

There emerged in the beginning of the twentieth century a powerful body of Protestant Christians who subjected church creeds and the Bible itself to scientific speculation and 'higher criticism.' In Britain, America, Germany and most of the European states they had adopted a theology which is named Liberal Protestantism. The principal features of this type of Christian belief were the debasement of the supernatural and 'a return to the Gospels.' The dominant idea among them was that of the Kingdom of God. The greatest name associated with Liberal Protestantism is that of Harnack, whose *History of Dogma* largely influenced the intellectual ferment of the time. In this work, Harnack sustained the thesis that the New Testament had been transformed from its primitive simplicity into a series of theological propositions. Harnack's popular *Das Wesen des Christentums* was an eloquent plea for a simplified Christian faith with main emphasis on the fatherhood of God and the brotherhood of men. Harnack and the liberal theologians in their quest for new explanation of Christianity did not ignore such weighty matters as sin, redemption and the Incarnation; they aimed at a revolution of these doctrines in the light of simple message of Jesus.

Liberal Protestantism evinced a special regard for such good works as social uplift, popular education, and public health. Numerous Europeans and Americans who were Protestant decried outworn dogmas and spoke in favour of 'the good life.' To realise such an ideal the Modernist movement contributed to the development of several comprehensive organisations half religious and half social. One of these was the 'Young Men's Christian Association,' founded in England in 1844 for the union of evangelical Christians in social and religious works. Another was the 'Salvation Army' founded in England by William Booth in 1880 for rescuing slum-dwellers.

Another organisation, Freemasonary—primarily a social and benevolent organisation—flourished in the latter part of the nineteenth century. Though it had been condemned by the Pope, its membership were numerous and practically restricted to Protestants, Jews and agnostics. Freemasonary provided a common platform for various opponents of Catholic Christianity.

The First World War dealt a heavy blow to the optimism of Liberal Protestantism. The dream of the leavening of society by the principles of Christianity was shattered, though not destroyed. The League of Nations was based on Christian idealism, but it failed to sustain it owing to conflicting interests. The hopes of the 1920s and the disillusionment of the 1930s had their impact on religious thought. Some changes also occurred in theology itself.

The 'historical Jesus' occupies a central figure of idealistic Christianity. He is a universal figure made out of the Gospels which are consonant with our ways of thinking. The Apocalyptic School of New Testament interpretation protested against this picture on the ground that it ignored the most important element in the story. They pointed out that the first three Gospels are permeated with the ideas and imagery of Jewish Apocalyptic. Albert Schweitzer created sensation when he produced his book, *The Quest of the Historical Jesus*, in which he insisted that Jesus was 'a Jew of the first century.' Other works, *The Mysticism of St. Paul*, followed the clue of Apocalyptic. Though the extreme Apocalyptic view of the Gospels has been rejected by many eminent scholars, yet it has left a permanent mark on New Testament interpretation.

In the welter of conflicting theories, some magnificent efforts were made to restate the orthodox doctrines for contemporary minds. DR Gore defended the Christian beliefs about God, Christ and the Church. DR A. C. Hedlam, apart from his *Life and Teaching of Jesus and The Atonement*, produced the first volume of a system of theology. William Temple, Archbishop of Canterbury, was the most effective exponent of a liberal kind of orthodox theology. Three of his books, *Mens Creatrix, Christus Veritas,* and *Nature, Man and God* reflect his changing mood from a 'broad church' to a more traditional viewpoint.

Along with theological controversy appeared the growth of mysticism where man found refuge when he could find no reassuring answer in the idea of progress or in the dogmas of the church. The basis of Mysticism was inner Self and many found it there. Among the distinguished students of mysticism, Dean. W. R. Inge, did much to widen the understanding of mysticism in his *Christian Mysticism* and in his lectures on *The Philosophy of Plotinus*. Evelyn Underhill, in her *Mysticism* exercised great influence through her spiritual conferences. Baron F. von Hugel, a religious thinker, in his memorable book, *The Mystical Element of Religion,* brought out the nature and significance of the mystical experience. The London Society for the Study of Religion, founded by von Hugel, was a centre of religious thinkers of the twenties and thirties of the twentieth century. Among them must be mentioned Claude Montefiore, the Jewish scholar and student of the Gospels, and Edwyn Bevan, the author of a valuable book on *Symbolism*.

Despite universal progress of secularisation and gradual decline of ecclesiastical influence on society, dictatorial attempts to muffle religion, its roots are embedded in human minds. The Catholic church continued to maintain its antagonistic trend to new winds of change in religion. Pope Benedict XV (1914-22), on August 1, 1917, called upon the belligerent countries to end 'the Fratricidal conflict' and to negotiate 'a just and durable' peace. But his peace overtures fell on deaf ears. However, the war years proved to be advantageous to the church. In 1917 the codification of canon law, begun under his predecessor Pius X, was completed. The political map of Europe which emerged after the war enhanced the prestige of the church. Numerically Catholics were preponderant in the newly created nations of Poland, Lithuania, Czechoslovakia, the Irish Free State as well as in the enlarged states of Yugoslavia and Rumania. For several years after the war, Catholic political parties held sway in the governments of Austria, Belgium, Germany, Hungary and the Netherlands. This improved position of the Catholic Church owed not a little to the untiring efforts and intellectual qualities of Pope Pius XI (1922-39), the worthy successor of Benedict XV.

Pius XI rehabilitated, after the lapse of fifty-nine years, an independent temporal sovereignty for the Papacy by concluding the Lateran Treaty (1929) with the Italian government. Vatican City, a tiny part of Rome and the seat of the Papal sovereignty, symbolised to the world that the Pope was no longer a 'prisoner' of Italy, but a supranational figure, revered throughout the world whose position was fortified by an international treaty. 'We have given back God to Italy and Italy to God', said the Pope, adding that 'perhaps the times called for a man such as he whom Providence has ordained we should meet.' With most nations, Pius XI established friendly relations.

He concluded Concordats with Latvia (1922), Poland (1925), Lithuania (1927), Czechoslovakia (1928), Italy, Portugal, Rumania (1929) and Germany (1933). Through these Concordats the Pope secured the right to appoint bishops within the countries concerned including the right to impart religious instruction.

Catholicism, however, suffered serious setbacks in Communist countries and totalitarian regimes. The anti-religious policies of the Communist Russia dealt a heavy blow to the Catholic minority largely concentrated in Ukraine and Byelorussia. Repeated protests of Pius XI went unheeded. The Pope also could do nothing to stem the anti-clerical tide in Mexico. The humiliation of the Pope was rendered complete when a Papal delegate was expelled from Mexico City. In Spain, the Republican Government in 1931 precipitated conflict between Church and State; the civil war in Spain also enfeebled the clergy. Moreover, the new Concordats were not scrupulously adhered to; the glaring infraction was in the case of the Nazi Germany which, despite the Concordat of 1933, pursued an anti-Catholic policy.

The missionary activities of the Church especially in Asia and Africa made tremendous strides under Pius XI. In several encyclical letters, Pius XI laid down the basic postulates which Christians should adopt while dealing with burning questions. While condemning totalitarian nationalism and atheistic Communism, these letters urged pacific settlement of international disputes and limitation of armaments. They supported the principles and programme of Catholic social reform, denounced artificial method of birth-control, and reaffirmed the traditional rights of the Church.

After the death of Pius XI in 1939, his Secretary of State, Cardinal Pacelli, succeeded him with the title of Pius XII. The new Pope laboured hard to maintain traditional policies in the midst of extraordinary difficulties attending World War II. Despite the defeat of totalitarian nationalism and a resurgence of Catholic activity in Italy and western Europe, the Pope had to witness the religious persecutions perpetrated by the Communists in Russia, Yugoslavia, Hungary, Rumania, Czechoslovakia, Poland, and China.

Protestant Christianity has developed since First World War with greater flexibility. On the one hand, 'high-Church' Anglicanism came into being, and a similar 'high-Church' trend in Lutheranism had become prominent in most Protestant churches. The Protestant faith and practice of the sixteenth century had lost its relevance and a sharp reaction against Puritanism had developed.

While Protestant sectarianism lost most of its earlier distinctiveness, attempts had been made to federate various Protestant denominations in particular countries. In 1922 was created an international council for coordinating Protestant missionary activities. In 1925 an ecumenical Christian conference at Stockholm was attended by thirtyone non-Catholic bodies. In 1938 an international federation of all these bodies was founded. Like the Catholic, the Protestant missionary enterprise made considerable progress in Asia and Africa.

The most refreshing feature of the times is that the Ecumenical movement for Christian unity has emerged from two world wars. In the sphere of theological thinking, the Ecumenical spirit has become evident in the spirit of understanding rather than in controversy. Second Vatican Council (1962-64) stimulated restatement of doctrinal positions in the Roman Catholic Church. Memorable studies of Systematic Theology by Rienhold Niebuhr and Paul Tillich exercised profound influence in Protestant thought in America and Britain. Cooperation in religious thinking has been increasingly felt in the central concern of theology—the doctrine of the Being of God and the man's salvation.

Apart from Catholicism and Protestantism, the Orthodox communion of eastern Europe was not a single ecclesiastical organisation, but a federation of Churches in close communion with one another. Originally, it had been a single ecclesiastical organisation headed by the Greek Patriarch of Constantinople. But later, with Russia in the vanguard, some countries became practically independent of the Ottoman Empire. In this way, so-called 'autocephalous' Orthodox Churches were established for Greece in 1850, and in the 1870s for Serbia, Rumania and Bulgaria. One of the main features of Orthodox

Christianity was its organisation on national lines. Another distinguishing feature was its doctrinal unity and conservatism. Several churches clung tenaciously to the ritual and observances of the mother-church at Constantinople.

The countries in which Orthodox Christianity was prevalent, were relatively backward. Its main adherents were agricultural and illiterate. There was no serious conflict in these countries between Church and State, between Christianity and nationalism. However, the disintegration of the Ottoman Empire and the rise of Mustafa Kemal Pasha deprived the Orthodox Patriarch of Constantinople of any privileged position. In addition, the Russian Revolution affected the large majority of the Orthodox communion.

At the opening of the twentieth century, two other religious minorities—Islam and Judaism—exercised considerable influence in Europe and elsewhere. The Muslim minority was concentrated in south-eastern Europe and in the Middle East, South Asia, Africa and the East Indies. Moreover, Islam was treated with tenderness by the Christian powers of Europe as the latter, in pursuit of the 'new imperialism', acquired large Muslim territories.

The Jewish minority was dispersed all over Europe, especially in eastern Europe, America, northern Africa and western Asia. Though they maintained a community life of their own, they had to suffer various restrictions and sometimes persecution. However, the Jews of central and western Europe had undergone a gradual emancipation from restrictive legislation and had adapted themselves to modern civilisation. In Britain, the Netherlands, France, Italy and, to a lesser extent, in Germany and Austria, they had to enjoy full rights of citizenship by the end of the nineteenth century. The Jews exerted tremendous influence in business in capitalistic industry, trade and banking—and in science and technology. Three of them—who revolutionised modern thinking—were Marx, Freud, and Einstein.

In the face of growing liberalism, traditional Judaism was divided into three camps:

(1) The Jews of eastern Europe remained rigidly orthodox and loyal to traditional Jewish laws and observances.

(2) The majority in central and western Europe and in America became 'reformed', approximating their religion to the contemporary Unitarian and 'Ethical Culture' movements in Protestant Christianity.

(3) A small number, without disarming their Jewish identity, severed any connection with the synagogue and became agnostic or Marxian.

European liberalism had been favourable for Jewish emancipation and absorption with cultural milieu. But by 1880s an extreme and illiberal nationalism overtook European states and the latter reacted against Jews. Such pugnacious behaviour was not confined to Germany. Its echoes were felt in Russia, Rumania, Austria, France and elsewhere. This reaction against the Jews, called anti-Semitism, was especially directed against the Jewish race. It preached the doctrine that the Semitic inheritance of Jews endows them with physical and mental traits quite different from Aryans or true Europeans. This racialism was accepted with zeal by zealous nationalists who fanned anti-Jewish propaganda. Suffering from Governmental oppressions in eastern Europe and in Germany, numerous Jews migrated to America and elsewhere.

Some of the Jews formulated a nationalism of their own, called Zionism. Its chief proponent was Theodore Herzel, who urged that the Jews were a distinct nationality and that an independent national state should be created for them in Palestine. Zionism was political and cultural as it clearly subordinated religion to politics. In 1897 the Zionist Congress was held at Basle. The first wave of Jewish migration marked an epoch in the history of Jewry. Zionism was a challenge to liberal culture as it fed both on a new nationalism, and a revivification of orthodoxy.

CHAPTER 48

PROGRESS IN SCIENCE AND TECHNOLOGY

The eighteenth and nineteenth centuries were the formative period of the modern world as they represented the road to prosperity and unlimited progress. Science became an indispensable feature in a new industrial civilisation. The application of science infused the great transformation of the means of production which we call the Industrial Revolution. By itself the Industrial Revolution stimulated and supported a new outburst of scientific activity. Not only in England, Scotland and France, but as the century wore on, in Russia, Italy and Germany as well, the movement towards a utilisation of science spread among the bourgeoisie.

The most eminent forerunner of the scientific movement was Benjamin Franklin. Born in 1706, he laid the foundations of electrical theory, and invented the lightning conductor and the iron stove. During his stay in Paris and Versailles he exercised the greatest influence on the direction of politics and science. Franklin was the Bacon of the eighteenth century.

Franklin's younger contemporaries in Britain made his ideas popular. The value of science was fully grasped and began to be taught systematically. It found a place in the dissenting academics and independent foundations, next to the Scottish universities which provided the best scientific education in the world. This was the age of the 'Lunar Society' of Birmingham which counted among its members John Wilkinson (1728-1808), Wedgwood (1744-1817), Dr. Erasmus Darwin (1731-1802), Joseph Priestley (1733-1804), James Watt (1736-1819), Murdock (1754-1839), the inventor of coal-gas lighting and finally the main inspirer of the whole movement, Mathew Boulton (1728-1809), who, as the first manufacturer of steam-engines, became literally the prime mover of the Industrial Revolution.

Closely linked with them was the more serious group of the Scottish renaissance of the eighteenth century, the philosopher Hume (1711-96), the economist Adam Smith (1723-90), Dr. Black (1728-99) the originator of the pneumatic revolution, Dr. Hutton, (1726-97), the founder of modern geological theory.

The most important scientific contribution of the period of the Industrial Revolution was the foundation of modern chemistry. It was an event of great significance in the history of science comparable with the great astronomical-mechanical synthesis of a century before. It marks the result of the rapid development of the chemical industry, largely as an ancillary to the new large scale mechanical textile industry.

The scientists of the later eighteenth century were predominantly radical and liberal in their ideas. The leading figure who combined the pursuit of science and radical politics was Joseph Priestley (1733-1804). Immersed in the new spirit of enlightenment, he came into contact with Benjamin Franklin, who inspired him to write a *History of Electricity*. At Leeds, he carried out his experiments on carbon dioxide. The most fruitful period of his life was 1773-1780 when he was provided with a laboratory by Lord Shelburne. Here he made his discovery of oxygen which won him international recognition. His radical political and religious views were not liked by the Puritans. He emigrated to America where he died in 1804.

Priestley's name is indissolubly linked in the history of science with that of Lavoisier, the Father of Chemistry. This Frenchman made chemistry once and for all a rational and quantitative science. Lavoisier began his scientific career in the 1760s in geology. This led him to chemical experiments. By the late 1770s he was convinced that air was a compound of some kind. In 1779 he claimed the combustible part of air was a constituent of all acids, and he named it the acid principle or 'principe oxygine'. He investigated the precise action of acids on metals and the production of 'inflammable air'. Lavoisier showed how oxygen and hydrogen each played a part and was able to formulate a whole new chemistry. His successors, Claude Bertholett, Guyton de Morveau and Antonie de Foureroy reorganised the whole of chemical nomenclature in the light of the new theory, giving each substance a name that described its chemical composition. In 1789 Lavoisier produced his famous *Elementary Treatise on Chemistry* which popularised the new ideas.

The French Revolution left its impact on the progress and development of science. Condorcet (1743-94), last of the *philosophers,* wrote a treatise *Sketch for a Historical Picture of the Progress of the Human Mind*—which appeared in 1795 after his death. In that book, science is represented as the bearer of progress. Positivism in scientific thinking was a product of the Revolution.

The greatest gift of the Revolution was the creation of the *Institut national de France* which opened on April 4, 1796. The *Institut* consisted of three classes—science coming first in precedence, moral and political science second and literature and fine arts third. The *Institut* was the summit under which there were founded several establishments. In *Ecole centrale* which provided secondary education, science was taught for the practical importance in the affairs of a modern nation. In higher education, the Directory followed pragmatic principles. The *Observatorie de Paris* was restored to the astronomers. A new *Bureau des Longitudes* busied itself in preparing the astronomical almanac. The prestige of the ancient *College de France* was enhanced by its hospitality to science. Two useful institutions were revived—*Ecole des mines* and *Ecole des ponts et chaussees.* The *Conservatoire des arts metiers* became the first national museum of science and technology. New medical faculties were created in the old Universities of Paris, Strasbourg and Montpellier.

The two nurseries of the intellectual life of nineteenth century France were *Ecole normale superieure* and the *Ecole Polytechnique.* The latter school, the nursery of all engineering science, opened on December 21, 1794. The revolutionary governments sought the assistance of the scientists in war production. For the first time, a scientific community emerged to serve the nation in arms. The guiding spirit in the whole war effort was Lazare Carnot (1753-1823) and the moving spirit in technology was Gaspard Monge (1746-1818). *Polytechnique* offered four year rigorous course where students went through a systematic scientific and mathematical curriculum. Among the graduates many celebrities of nineteenth century science were found—Cauchy, Poncelet, Poisson, Sadi Carnot and Fresnel. Among its students was Auguste Comte, who founded in Positivism the most influential modern philosophy of science.

Polytechnique and the other schools gave the scientists opportunities to produce systematic treatises. They published their courses—Lagrange his theory of analytical functions, Monge his descriptive geometry, Laplace his essay in probabilities, Cuvier his comparative anatomy, Lamarck his zoological philosophy. Science thus became a profession, a profession entwined in educational institutions and scientists became professors. Thus France with her modern set of scientific institutions became the scientific schoolmistress of Europe.

The light from Paris drew scientists to its emanating glow. In 1804 Alexander von Humboldt came to Paris with his rich collections and specimens gathered during his pioneering geographical, botanical and anthropological exploration. In 1801 Alessandro Volta and his assistant Brugnatelli came to Paris to demonstrate the experiments of electric current. On November 7, 1801, he read a paper on current and static electricity. Napoleon awarded him a gold medal and created a prize for further discoveries with this new phenomenon. Napoleon awarded a prize to Humphry Davy for his electrochemical discoveries in 1807.

Napoleon was not vainglorious when he observed on May 19, 1796: 'All men of genius, all who have won distinction in the republic of letters are French, whatever be the country which has given them birth.' Napoleon wanted to make Paris, the cultural capital of Europe, a republic of science rather than letters. He chose his favourites among the scientists. Bertholett and Monge were his favourites. Laplace served briefly as Minister of the Interior, Cuvier as Minister of Education. In the afterglow of the Empire, the Academy of Sciences continued to dominate the European scene. The pattern of *Polytechnique* was followed in Germany in the foundation of *Techniche Hochschulen*, Prague in 1806, Vienna in 1815, Munich in 1827, Oresen in 1828, Stuttgart in 1829 and Hanover in 1831.

The great legacy of the French Revolution was the metric system which was complete by 1799. But the new units were not used before 1840. The replica of French institutions were established in Italy. Napoleon exercised a benign patronage over Italian science. *Institute de Scienze, Letters ed Arti* at Milan became an *Institute della Republica Italiana* in 1802 with its seat at Bologna. It was turned into the *Imperiale Regio Institute* when Italy became a Kingdom in 1805. The Florentine Academy revived with special emphasis on science. The Institute was decentralised in 1810 with branches at Venice, Padua, Verona with Milan as foyer of the spirit of progress.

The impact of France was felt in Prussia and Russia. Around the Royal Academy of Sciences of Berlin gravitated its satellite of St. Petersberg. Berlin became the most important city where science had a tremendous growth. After a shattering defeat at Jena, Frederick William III declared in 1806 'The State must make up in intellectual force what she has lost in physical.' French remained the language of Prussia's Academy and many members of the Academy were French. The Humboldt brothers—Wilhelm von Humboldt, the humanist and Alexander von Humboldt, the naturalist—reorganised the Prussian Academy in the spirit of exact science.

The University of Berlin was founded in 1809-10. It incorporated all the learned institutions of Berlin into a single great foundation. It disseminated science to the educated class as a whole. Without eclipsing the older and smaller centres of learning—Hiedelberg and Gottingen, Marburg and Giessen, Konigsberg and Tubingen, Leipzig and Wurzberg, the University of Berlin 'glows like a burning point whereon all rays stream together.' By mid-century Germany established her scientific preeminence. Though laboratories had developed in England and France at an institutional stage by the end of the eighteenth century but in Germany the laboratory became an instrument of research and instruction combined and the foyer of the doctorate. In 1826 Justus Liebig opened the laboratory of research and instruction at the University of Giessen. In 1828 Friedrich Wohler accomplished the synthesis of urea.

Britain presents quite another prospect as it was a story of scientists and not of science. During the Napoleonic era there was a spasmodic outburst of scientific effort—Thomas Young and the wave model of light, Humphry Davy and the inauguration of electrochemistry, John Dalton and the atomic hypothesis of chemical combination, and Faraday's discovery of inducing electric current by magnetism. The critical minds while appreciating the ingenuity of British scientists, agreed upon the unwholesome state of British science. In England the French Revolution came late to science. Science had grown up in Britain outside the Establishment. The public schools taught neither science nor any modern subjects. Oxford and Cambridge also lagged behind. Science was taught in dissenting academies, in Scottish Universities, or by themselves. It is astonishing to think that despite this handicap Britain achieved so much.

Meanwhile, Russia and the United States developed comparable scientific institutions. The Imperial Academy of Sciences of St. Petersburg was reorganised in 1803, but recovered its vitality only after 1815. America depended primarily upon British scientific associations and upon the voluntary pattern. Professors and physicians in Philadelphia and Boston continued the American Philosophical Society and the American Academy of Arts and Sciences. The colleges—Harvard, Yale, Columbia, Princeton, Pennsylvania—modelled themselves on eighteenth century dissenting academies.

Evolution and the Age of the Earth

The crowning scientific achievement of the nineteenth century was the demonstration of the universal process of evolution. In the middle of the eighteenth century, the ill-defined conception of a slowly developing natural world assumed in the mind of the naturalist, Buffon (1707-88), a quasi-scientific character. In his monumental *Systeme de la Nature*, Buffon claimed that the relationship implied by the classification of animals and plants was a real one.

The problem of evolution was well explained by two different men, **Erasmus Darwin** (1731-1802) and Lamarck (1744-1829). Darwin formulated ideas about the evolution of animal

Erasmus Darwin

species, ideas which he published in two volumes as *Zoonomia* or the *Laws of Organic Life* (1794 and 1796). He concluded that living things possessed a spirit of animation and drew a parallel between their embryonic changes and possible earlier evolution. He subscribed to the view that life began with a filament from the male and that the female's job was to provide the nourishment for subsequent growth. He believed in the inheritance of acquired characteristics.

Lamarck's best-known works are his *Zoological Philosophy* (1809) and the seven- volume *Natural History of Invertebrate Animals* which came out between 1815 and 1822. He introduced the valuable classification of vertebrates and invertebrates. He came to the firm conclusion that there was a natural sequence for all living creatures. He advanced the theory that, in adaptation to changing conditions of life, each organism was to some extent modified during the course of its life.

The influence of Georges Cuvier (1769-1832) was so immense that he had earned the nickname 'dictator of biology'. After settling in France, he gained a reputation by his anatomical description of animals. He also studied fossils and laid the foundations of palaeontology. He denied the existence of fossil men and believed that after each catastrophe the remaining species repopulated the earth. His most significant work was *The Animal Kingdom, Distributed According to its Organization* (1817).

Cuvier's views stimulated a positive interest in comparative anatomy and in palaeontology. Of those who followed him was Richard Owen. In 1856 he was appointed superintendent of the Natural History department of the British Museum. Owen's scientific work lay mainly in palaeontology, though he did dissect a great number of rare animals in order to identify species. His palaeontological interests led him to reconstruct many prehistoric animals and also to undertake research on mammal teeth.

While the main techniques of palaeontology and the succession of strata had been determined, many parts of the world were surveyed. Charles Lyell, a Scotsman, believed that a slow change was a characteristic geological phenomenon. He produced his monumental three volume *Principles of Geology* (1830-33). In it he renounced early catastrophic theories of the formation of the earth's crust; rather its configuration should be attributed solely to the same slow process of elevation and depression, deposition and erosion that operate still. He enunciated the *Uniformitarian theory*, the uniform course of nature throughout the Earth's history in changing the Earth's crust. He claimed each species had grown up in a particular centre from which it spread, and showed how it became extinct and was replaced by another species. Thus he held that the emergence of new species was a continuous process throughout geological history.

The theory of evolution reached a synthesis in the writings of Charles Darwin (1809-82).

Enriched by the geological ideas of Charles Lyell, the ideas of Malthus relating food supply and population growth, his own researches carried out during a long voyage in H.M.S. Beagle, and his later researches Charles Darwin (grandson of Erasmus Darwin) made a decisive breakthrough in evolutionary theory.

In 1859 Darwin published his famous book '*On the origin of species by Means of Natural Selection or the Preservation of Favoured Races in the Struggle for Life*.' The *Origin* argued that both within and between species there was a struggle for life, that each creature differed slightly from its parents, and that in the struggle for life those most suited to cope with environment were naturally selected to survive. Ultimately the accumulative preservation of differences produced new species, a process facilitated by the geographical isolation of variant forms of life. Thus Darwin's law of nature offered a thesis to explain the mechanism that had produced different species and their variations during vast spans of geologic time. Progress and differentiation were rooted in nature, where they were exempt from divine or human intervention. Yet on the fundamental point of natural selection Darwin wavered.

Darwin conceived his hypothesis of evolution as a naturalist. He was well aware of the opposition it would encounter. He continued to gather fresh materials which he incorporated in successive volumes of which the *Descent of Man* (1871) was the most famous. The survey of the whole of natural history for this new purpose was a tremendous undertaking. The comparative development of single structures; the sexual physiology of plants; behaviour in animals; the geographical distribution of species; the selective mechanism of inheritance; ecology and palaeontology—all these were branches of science which Darwin welded into a harmonious synthesis. Darwin did more than assert evolution; he provided a mechanism—natural selection—which shook the basis of Aristotelian category of final causes.

Darwin's theory evoked furious criticism. Scientists like Hooker, Huxley, Lyell had accepted Darwinism, but others like Louis Agassiz, Lord Kelvin, Owen could not accept the theory on purely scientific grounds. Darwin's science also drew resentment from religious spokesmen who considered his account of human origin irreconcilable with a liberal reading of the Book of Genesis. Even more shocking was the idea that man himself was nothing more than a remarkably successful ape. This seemed not only to shatter the doctrine of religion but also the eternal values of rational philosophy. In 1864 Pope Pius IX plainly denounced in the *Syllabus* of modern errors the Roman Catholics' opposition to modern civilisation and influence of science. But the Protestant Churches gradually came to terms with Darwinism.

As an innovator Darwin was, quite justly compared to Copernicus. The fundamental importance of the theory of evolution was that it introduced a historical element into the field of science. But in its stress on the kinship of man and the animals, the social evolution of humanity was obscured in favour of a purely biological one, which was in turn lead to the justification of race theories and imperialism.

In the last quarter of the nineteenth century an increasing number of finds of the fossil remains of Neanderthal man helped to establish the fact of human evolution. In 1891 was found in Java *Pithecanthropus* and afterwards *Sinanthropus* near Peking. In 1900 it was generally believed that Neanderthal man arose at some point between *Pithecanthropus*, the most ancient fossil form, and *homo sapiens*, or modern man. The Steinheim skull, found in 1933, and the Swanscombe (Kent) skull found in 1935 led to the rejection of Neanderthal man from the line of descent of *homo sapiens*.

Biology

Pure biology made great strides in the nineteenth century. At the same time, however, different branches were formed in the laboratory—histology, embryology, physiology, cytology and pathology. Xavier Bichat (1771-1802), in his short life, virtually refounded pathology. He identified no less than twentyone types of tissues—nervous, arterial, venous, muscular, fibrous, glandular, epidermal—in organs and noted their distribution. In his *Anatomia generale* of 1801 he wrote:

> All animals are assembled of diverse organs which, each performing its own function, cooperates in conserving the whole. They are so many particular machines in the general machine which constitutes the individual. But these particular machines are themselves formed of several tissues of very different types which form the true elements of the organs. Chemistry has its simple bodies... Anatomy has its simple tissues which, by their combination... form the organs.

The practice of experimental biology was consolidated by Francois Magendie who installed the first laboratory in the *College de France*. He published a corrected edition of Bichat. He himself left a collection of fine discoveries, especially in neuro-physiology. He set an example of experimental discipline and fidelity to fact. Claude Barnard was his great pupil in whose hand experiment reached the high degree of precision. In 1824 Prevost and J.B. Dumas established the role of spermatozoa in the fertilisation of frogs' eggs.

The study of biology was facilitated by the advent of achromatic microscopes. In 1830 the microscopes enabled a greater insight to be obtained into the fine structure of tissues—*histology*. This revealed that the tissues in turn were composed of cells.

Knowledge of cell was more highly developed for plants than for animals when in 1831 the botanist Robert Brown discovered the nuclei of cells. In 1838 Schleiden (1804-81) represented the plants as a community of cells. In 1839 Schwann (1810-82) enunciated the concept of the cell as the unit in the animal and vegetables kingdoms.

The main triumphs of cell theory came in the second half of the nineteenth century. Rudolf Virchow, Professor of Pathological Anatomy at Berlin University, produced in 1858 his important *Cellular Biology*. He stressed that cells 'are the last link in the great chain of subordinated formations that form tissues, organs, systems and the individual.' He also emphasised the importance of pathological cells in disease. There still remained much more to be done to demonstrate that the cell really was the fundamental functional unit. The French physiologist Claude Bernard elaborated it in his medical research as he did valuable work in the digestion, the physiology of the nerves, and on toxic substances.

It was at this stage that the embryologists made significant contributions. They enunciated the doctrine of epigenesis, in which, starting with the more or less simple egg there was a straightforward development. This new theory had been helped by the observation in 1843 of the presence of sperm within the egg. In 1876 and 1877 things changed when Oskar Hertwig and Hermann Fol showed the presence of not one but two nuclei—one male and one female—in the fertilised egg.

Microbiology began as a science in close collaboration with organic chemistry and chemical industry. **Louis Pasteur** (1822-95), a chemist by profession, was responsible for nearly all the advance in this direction during the period. In 1855 his studies of the tartaric acids led him to investigation of fermentation, at the conclusion of which he had proved that they were invariably due to the presence of living microorganisms. Wine makers and brewers were benefitted by his investigation of ferments and his method of arresting degeneration by a gentle heat known as pasteurisation. Pasteur made a far-reaching analogy between fermentation and putrefaction, which was universally believed to take place spontaneously in dead organic matter. Pasteur asserted that nothing could putrefy unless living agents were introduced into it.

Louis Pasteur

In 1865 when Pasteur was asked to investigate a disease that was killing off millions of silkworms in the south of France, he found that the disease was a bacterial infection. He suggested remedies which saved the industry. Encouraged by his success with silkworms, Pasteur combated two deadly diseases—anthrax and chicken cholera. He turned to the innoculation work of Jenner (1749-1823) as the latter had long before taken the first practical step to control smallpox by vaccination, which presupposed the presence of an active virus of disease. Pasteur found safe vaccines first in 1881 against anthrax and, a year later, against the dreaded disease of rabies. Soon vaccines against tetanus and diptheria were available.

The great age of bacteriology opened after 1870. In 1876 Robert Koch initiated those bacteriological researches which resulted in the successive isolation of various pathogenic organisms, and in the establishment of the science of immunology. Meanwhile the British physician, Lord Lister (1827-1912), found the possibility of preventing death from infection in surgery and childbirth. Infections were first prevented from developing by antiseptic techniques—by the use of carbolic acid. Lister also developed the practical techniques of antisepsis that began to reduce the appalling mortality in hospitals. Lister's work coincided with the introduction of anaesthetics. Ether was first used during a tooth extraction in 1846 and its use was taken up at Edinburgh by the surgeon James Simpson. But in 1847 he substituted chloroform which he found more satisfactory. Chloroform was administered to Queen Victoria by John Snow during the birth of Prince Leopold in 1853. With the use of anaesthesia and asepsis the whole practice of surgery was revolutionised.

By the end of the nineteenth century most of the important pathogenic bacteria had been identified, as well as some of the disease-causing protozoa. In 1880 was discovered the malarial parasites and seventeen years later Sir Ronald Ross identified the Anopheles mosquito as the carrier of the disease. These discoveries not only materially reduced suffering but greatly lowered the death rate. As a great physician, Sir William Osler has said:

> Measure as we may the progress of the world—materially in the advantages of steam, electricity and the mechanical appliances; intellectually in the diffusion of education; morally in the possibly higher standard of ethics—there is no one measure that can compare with the decrease of physical suffering in man, woman and child when stricken by disease or accident. This is the one fact of supreme personal import to every one of us. This is the Promethean gift of the century to man.

Biology in the Twentieth Century

Darwin's theory of evolution deeply influenced biology. It created such an amount of interest in the development of plants and animals that during the second half of the nineteenth century this formed the focal point of biological research. Darwin's theory of evolution focussed great attention on the principles of the variation of inheritance. He thought that species might vary in response to environment and that selection would operate on those variations. But Darwin's ideas on heredity were not immediately fruitful as they were not fortified by quantitative experimental basis.

From the 1860s to 1880s great efforts were made in morphology—the study of the forms of living things. Morphologists wanted to discover common ancestors for two or more groups of organisms, and to construct family trees to indicate the history of the development of a particular animal. Their leader was Ernst Haeckel, a votary of Darwin. Being interested in the comparative anatomy of men and animals, Haeckel constructed a tree or pedigree for man; during its development, he suggested, an embryo goes through the major adult stages of its ancestors in this evolutionary pedigree—known as Haeckel's 'biogenetic law'.

Darwin's theory had been expressed in terms of small continuous variations. But by the beginning of the twentieth century, biologists recognised the discontinuous variations. Bateson (1861-1926) in 1894 claimed that it was these sharp variations that was significant in evolution. In 1901 Hugo de Vries (1848-1935) discovered abrupt changes—mutations—among evening primroses. Both found credence in the experiments done between 1857 and 1868 and laws of Mendel (1822-84). Mendel had explained that 'particulate inheritance' was conveyed and controlled by the mechanism of genes—inherited factors, one derived from each parent. The genes were carried into *chromosomes* of the cells and followed the Mendelian laws of inheritance.

The Mendelian assumed importance when a connection was established between the unit genetic characters and the chromosomes. This was essentially the work of T. H. Morgan, an American. Beginning in 1910, he made an extensive study of the whole range variation of one small fly, *Drosophila Melanogaster*. It was discovered that various characters that were often inherited together could be associated with certain parts of the chromosomes. Each inherited character that appeared in the adult organism corresponded a material particle, the *gene* in one of the chromosomes of its parents. Each cell of every organism contains a set of pair of chromosomes, one derived from each parent.

During the 1930s advances in biology were due to synthesis between the sciences of biological heredity (genetics) and of cell structure (cytology). These specialised sciences were developed in Britain and the United States by C. D. Darlington, J. B. S. Haldane, T. Dobzhansky and other biologists. They showed that 'during the history of life there must have been an evolution of evolutionary mechanism.' During and after the Second World War biology assumed new dimension. Attention was given not only to evolutionary change produced by environment but also to causes of mutation. In 1927 H. J. Muller showed the increased production of mutants by means of X-rays. Since then it has been shown that other agents also produce mutations. These observations have since become of crucial importance to humanity because of the production of such mutations in plants, animals, and human beings, through the effect of radiation produced by atomic and hydrogen bombs and their active fall-out.

Physiology

It was especially through the influence of Bernard that physiology became, in the modern sense, an experimental science. Before him, the botanist N. T. de Saussure, the chemist Liebig and others had applied the quantitative methods of chemistry to the study of physiological processes. Experimental physiology was concentrated particularly in studies of nerve condition and nervous system. The English and French researchers looked at the nervous system as a whole and came to the conclusion that there was a difference between those nerves leading to the spiritual column and those leading from it. They made a particular study of the reflex system. By 1880 reflexes were acknowledged to be a function of the spinal cord which Pierre Flourens had demonstrated to be of very intricate nature.

The Russian Ivan Pavlov and the Englishman Charles Sherrington made a critical analysis of the problem. Pavlov observed that the repeated use of particular stimulus would give rise to a response—a conditioned reflex. Pavlov's work was of great significance as it showed the important relationship between behaviour and the physiology of the nervous system. Sherrington's research was concerned with the transmission of nerve impulses, being based on studies by the Spanish tissue expert, Ramon Cajal, who, in the 1880s, had discovered that the nerves of all animals are made up of individual units or neurons, each distinct from the next. In 1906 he published his *Integrative Action of the Nervous System*, a book which made a deep impact on the succeeding generations. Sherrington gave an integrated picture of the nervous system of an organism right down to the neuron level. More comprehensive was the latter work of Lawrence Henderson of the Harvard Medical School in the United States. He analysed the way the body regulates its chemical balance, so that its fluids are neither too acid nor too alkaline. He also made clear that the blood and the other tissue fluids could also help the body to adjust its acid-alkali balance.

Until the second half of the twentieth century, the advance of biological science had been somewhat tardy. However, advances were made in the discoveries of antibiotics and hormones. The phenomena studied in biology are so varied and complex that progress in biology in the twentieth century has been one of the continuous interactions of the advances in different fields.

The approaches to modern biology have undergone tremendous changes. The influences of systematic zoology and botany, medicine and agriculture have become much more potent. The influence of medicine has been profound in biology. The nineteenth century pioneer work of

Pasteur and Claude Bernard began to make itself felt on a large scale. Medicine has become dependent for its supplies on important chemical industries. Thus pharmacy has become a scientific industry. The development of antibiotics revolutionised biological science.

In the early twentieth century the science of nutrition assumed importance. Its study led to a major scientific discovery—the vitamins. Nutrition is one of the new aspects of public health that have given fillip to biological science. The triumph over waterborne diseases by the introduction of sanitation was a great landmark in the nineteenth century. The triumph over the insect-borne diseases—malaria, typhus, yellow fever and plague—is a great twentieth century achievement. Many biological sciences such as entomology, epidemiology and parasitology were stimulated. The outbreak of war led to a great scientific effort in preventive and palliative medicine. War medicine—particularly blood transfusion and plastic surgery—have added new dimension in medical science.

Agriculture became a powerful stimulus to biological research. Remarkable change in the twentieth century agriculture have been made—the tractor, the constant struggle against the forces of nature, the battle against insects and viruses and the conservation of soil against erosion. Indeed, the whole new science of the soil—pedology—founded by the Russian pioneers V. V. Dokuchaev (1846-1903) and K. D. Glinka (1867-1927)—is the basis of scientific agriculture.

Since the 1950s some of the major branches of biology have made greatest advances. These are biochemistry, molecular biology, microbiology, biochemistry in medicine, cytology and embryology, the organism as a whole, heredity and evolution, ecology.

Biochemistry

Biochemistry is concerned with the chemical reactions involved in living processes such as respiration or the metabolism of proteins. The major breakthrough in biochemistry was made by Gowland Hopkins, a British biochemist with international reputation. Hopkins discovered many substances important in animal metabolism and found that some essential protein fragments known as amino acid, had to be obtained from food. These vital substances are now called vitamins.

Another study in biochemistry is concerned with the way in which living cells break down the molecules of fats and carbohydrates to produce energy for the organism. The technical name for this breakdown is 'respiration' (which is quite unrelated to breathing air). Two types are known: one is 'aerobic respiration' which requires oxygen and occurs in all the cells of higher animals; the other is 'anaerobic respiration', known as fermentation and occurs in yeast, in some bacteria and some muscle cells. Another aspect concerns that class of proteins now known as enzymes, which act as catalysts as their presence makes chemical reactions.

The motive force behind biochemistry had always been to improve medicine, on the one hand, and industrial processes, on the other. The establishment of biochemistry as a separate science may be traced in 1897 when Edward Buchner (1860-1917) found that crushed yeast could cause sugar to ferment. This showed that a dead chemical substance, called enzyme, was responsible for fermentation.

By the beginning of the twentieth century, it became clear that when proteins were broken down by acids or by certain enzymes a number of chemically separate amino acids were produced. A German chemist, Emil Fischer, believed that proteins were like molecules of other substances. Fischer made it clear that amino acids were the building blocks from which protein molecules were constructed. By 1909, Fischer was able to synthesise a unit of eighteen amino acids which he called a 'polypeptide' (a peptide is the type of chemical bond that exists between amino acids). In the mid 1940s, a group of British biochemists at Cambridge, under the leadership of Frederick Sanger, came to the conclusion that proteins were in fact long-chain molecules of amino acids linked together by peptide bonds. This was a result of great significance.

The importance of very small quantities of chemicals in biological processes was a unique discovery in modern times. It was Hopkins who first discovered that in the absence of small quantities of substances in full diet growth and development of human body became, inadequate. These accessory factors, later known as *vitamins*, gave an immediate impetus to the study of biochemistry. Szent-Gyorgyi defined vitamin in a paradoxical way as 'a substance that makes you ill if you don't eat it.' The discovery of the vitamins and the determination of the quantities of each necessary to maintain health is a gift of twentieth century science.

The importance of special molecules in very small quantities was not confined to food. It became apparent that many bodily conditions were dependent on the existence of minute quantities of substances produced inside the body itself. Thus a new group of substances was discovered, the *hormones*, as E. H. Sterling (1866-1927) first called them in 1905, such as oestrone and its related ovarian hormones. Another is thyroxine, the failure to produce which may cause goitre. Iodine is the key element in thyroxin and its absence is the basic cause of many diseases.

Apart from the impact of molecules in organisms, there are others having another property, which is peculiarly associated with proteins. Pasteur had discovered how a harmless vaccine taken from dead bacteria could immunise a patient against an attack by the same bacteria in a virulent state. This became the foundation of the new science of *Immunology*. The first scientific use of the principle of protective immunisation was made by Jenner in 1796 when he made use of the practice of vaccination.

The principle of immunity found a wide range of application in twentieth century. The study of blood groups by Landsteiner was to prove of such inestimable value in saving lives in war and in peace.

One of the crucial problems of biology is metabolism. Though the processes of metabolism have been more or less worked out, but the study of the constructive part of metabolism or *anabolism* had hardly started. But one thing is apparent, that is, both the *anabolism*—or building up of compounds from simple structures in the body, and the *Katabolism*—breaking them down, are taking place at regular intervals.

Biochemical discoveries have had a great impact on the treatment of diseases. Frequently, symptoms can be alleviated by drug, and the discovery and mode of action, are the major areas of study in biochemistry. Bacterial infections can be treated with sulfonamides, penicillins and tetracyclines. Recent interest has developed in the details of carcinogenesis and cancer chemotherapy. Chemistry has developed methods for determining the structure of proteins and DNA.

Molecular Biology

Molecular Biology, the most exciting branch of biological science, deals with the structure and functions of entities of dimensions below those of the cells, and in particular with the molecules of proteins and the nucleic acids. The study of the particular branch has begun in an evolutionary way, the study of the structures of protein molecules, fibrous and crystalline, of nucleic acid and of viruses.

The protein molecules could be crystallised, that is millions of protein molecules of the same kind could fit together. Both muscle and nerve are made of fibrous proteins. Meanwhile, nucleic acids and molecular genetics had begun to be studied with the help of X-ray analysis. The study in the Cavendish Laboratory at Cambridge by Max Perutz and John Kendrew showed the immense complexity of protein molecules such as haemoglobin.

The picture of heredity was now emerging in full colour. In 1938 Max Delbruck, an atomic physicist who had turned to biology, introduced a new research 'animal', the 'bacteriophage', a virus which attacks bacteria. Viruses consist only of two types of molecule, a protein and a nucleic acid. It was found that if living, benign types of bacteria together with dead but virulent types are injected into a living creature, some of the benign types also become virulent. The change is due to the fact that the virulent bacteria was found to be a particular nucleic acid, DNA (deoxyribonucleic acid).

Chemistry

The modern science of chemistry owed its origin to Robert Boyle, whose critical work *The Skeptical Chemist* (1661), first defined method in this field of research. The eighteenth century was a period remarkable for chemical discovery; a large number of new substances were isolated and classified by their chemical relationships. The names of Boerhaave, Mayow, Stahl, Bergman, Scheel and Priestley are associated with these works.

The chemical knowledge of the late eighteenth century was theoretically interpreted by the chemists in terms of an old alchemical idea. It meant that all combustibles contained a substance that they lost on burning. It was given a new lease of life by Becher (1635-82) and his disciple Stahl (1660-1734) by christening it phlogiston, the principle of phlex or flame. A body with much phlogiston, like coal, could transfer it to a body that had lost it, like iron ore, and by permeating it with phlogiston turn it into metallic iron.

The first distinguished research in chemistry was that of Black on the alkaline earth, in 1753. The next important advance was made by Joseph Priestley who digressed from the field of physics to that of chemistry. Priestley felt that there was not only one kind of air. He played with many gases as he could find. His first success was the preparation of soda water containing fixed air in solution. The discovery of Oxygen in 1774 was the culminating point in the field of chemistry.

Chemistry was raised to the status of exact science by Lavoisier's principle of conservation of mass and his conception of oxidation and reaction. Lavoisier also explained the process of respiration and founded the modern science of chemical physiology.

The next crucial step in the understanding of chemistry was taken by John Dalton (1766-1844), an Englishman. His scientific work embraced observation of the aurora, trade winds, and the cause of rain. He was concerned with the physical behaviour of gases, in diffusion and in solution. Dalton also made the first systematic study of colour blindness. But it is his atomic theory which was his most important contribution. Knowing that air was composed of at least two gases of different weights, Dalton posed some fundamental questions about the atmosphere. Dalton's experience led him to conclude that the gases were mixed but not chemically combined. As heat surrounded all the gas particles (or atoms as he called them), he thought of keeping them apart and thus preventing them settling down into separate groups. Dalton expanded this idea by assuming that each gas was composed of its own kind of atoms; the heavier the gas the heavier its atoms, with atoms of one kind attracting one other. Dalton's theory was published in 1808 in his *New System of Chemical Philosophy*.

Dalton's theory explained the quantitative laws of chemistry. Since he did not know how many billions of atoms there were in a particular piece of material, he was able to measure their relative weights by assuming that the same number were always present in a given volume. This gave chemists a firm ground. Though atomic theory was not new, it was now propounded with a degree of precision.

Dalton's work was followed by the Frenchman Gay-Lussac (1778-1850) and the Italian Aredeo Avogadro (1776-1856). Gay-Lussac carried out research on the combining properties of gas in which he was assisted by the Prussian scientist, Alexander von Humboldt (1769-1859). In 1811 Gay-Lussac had come to the conclusion that water was composed of two parts hydrogen and one part oxygen and that all gases combine in volumes that are in simple relation to one another.

Avogadro is remembered for what is called 'Avogadro's hypothesis'. He realised that the atoms might combine together when the gases were mixed to give group of atoms. Thus in the case of water two volumes of pairs of hydrogen atoms combined with one volume of pairs of oxygen atoms gave two volumes of water. The word 'molecule' (Latin *molecula*, small mass) was used by Avogadro to describe groups of atoms. To Avogadro atoms were 'elementary molecules' and combination of atoms were 'integral molecules'. His hypothesis paved the way for measurement of atomic weights with great degree of precision.

It was left to the Swedish chemist Jons Jakob Berzelius (1779-1848) to devise an effective chemical symbolism. His chemical shorthand is still the basis of the method in use today. The atom of each element was represented by the first letter of its name. Thus H represented a hydrogen atom, O an oxygen atom, Zn a Zinc atom, and so on. Berzelius also made a serious attempt to measure atomic weights. He also discovered some new substances himself while he was analysing a large number of chemical compounds.

Humphry Davy, who is famous for his invention in 1815 of the miner's safety lamp,

Humphry Davy

found time to engage in pure chemical research. He discovered a number of new substances and did pioneering work on agricultural chemistry, though his important work was his study of electrochemistry. The new electric current discovered by Volta was found to decompose not only water but also salts. Davy in 1807 prepared the new metals sodium, potassium and calcium from the previously undecomposed alkalis and earth, and dividing all elements into metals and non-metals. It was found that metallic atoms were charged positively and non-metallic negatively. Davy was convinced that electricity could be generated by a purely chemical process, and further research led him to the conclusion that 'chemieal and electrical attractions are produced by the same cause.'

Davy's young assistant, **Michael Faraday**, demonstrated that the electrical effect worked throughout the liquid. Faraday was able to establish the laws of chemical and electrical actions inside a battery. In 1833 he made a statement that showed his rare scientific insight. 'The atoms in matter,' he wrote, 'are in some way endowed or associated with electrical powers, to which they owe their most striking qualities, and amongst them their chemical affinity.'

As the years passed by, chemistry had developed enormously. But the most important progress was in organic chemistry which opened a new vista. Organic chemistry was originally concerned with wide range of substances that can

Michael Faraday

be obtained from plant or animal material. The German chemist Wohler's discovery in 1828 that he could prepare urea artificially—'without requiring a kidney or an animal, either man or dog'—opened a new era. Virtually all the constituents of living matter are compounds of the element carbon, the latter being associated with only a limited number of the other ninety-one elements, the principal ones being nitrogen, oxygen, hydrogen, sulphur and phosphorus.

It was the German chemist, Justus von Liebeg, who gave an impetus to organic chemistry by new methods of chemical analysis. He was a prolific author, writing about 300 scientific papers, a book on organic chemistry, and an encyclopedia of chemical science. Liebeg's dedicated pupil August Hofmann, who took charge of the Royal College of Chemistry, London, began research into the organic chemistry of coal tar substances. Hofmann's pupil, William Perkin (1838-1909), carried out similar work. Perkin tried to synthesise the important drug quinine, but without any success. He did, however, synthesise mauveine, the first synthetic aniline dye, which laid the foundations of chemical industry and gave a great stimulus to organic chemical research.

Hofmann had extracted benzene from coal tar, and this substance lay at the basis of all the aniline dyes. But the baffling problem was not the chemical composition but the way in which the atoms were arranged within their molecules. The problem was solved by August Kekule von Stradonitz (1829-96). In the 1850s Kekule came to the conclusion that although chemists had been placing different substances into groups according to their chemical behaviour, it would be preferable to classify them according to the way atoms, or groups of atoms in them were structured. Later, he developed this idea into an important concept combining power or 'valency' (Latin *valens*, strength).

It was Kekule who elucidated the structure of benzene. This substance is of utmost importance, for from it derive tens of thousands of different chemical substances, the so-called 'aromatics', such as dyes and drugs. The molecules of benzene consist only of six carbon atoms and six hydrogen atoms. It was Kekule who found that the six carbon atoms were arranged not in a straight or branched chain but in a circle. This minor suggestion revolutionised chemical thought in the last half of the nineteenth century. Kekule's discoveries were important as they gave chemists a basis on which to construct the atomic layout of a host of other organic molecules. In the twentieth century this was to lead to the vast petrochemical industry and the development of plastics.

Another important field was the development of stereochemistry. The classic researches of Louis Pasteur (1822-95) had established the fundamentally important fact that certain substances, such as tartaric acid, could exist in two forms that were chemically indistinguishable but nevertheless had important physical differences. Such scarce differences are profoundly important, especially in the chemistry of vital processes. Thus the human body derives much of its energy from one stereoisomer of the sugar 'glucose'.

The proper interpretation of Pasteur's discovery was done by two young chemists, J. A. Le Bel (1897-1930) and J. H. Van't Hoff (1852-1911). They established that the atoms that make up molecules are arranged according to a strict geometric pattern. The name of Hoff is also associated with another important chemical development, that of the theory of solution. His experiments on Osmosis proved clearly that when a solid is dissolved in a liquid its particles behave in much the same way as if they were the particles of a gas occupying the same volume as the solution. This conception, however, presented difficulties when applied to solutions of the important substances known as electrolytes, so-called because their aqueous solutions conduct electricity. Typical of such substances is common salt, sodium chloride. To explain the properties of such substances the Swedish chemist Svante Arrhenius (1857-1927) advanced the revolutionary hypothesis that in solution the molecules of such substances dissociate into what are called ions. For the first half of the twentieth century, chemistry was seen by many as the science of the future. The potential use of chemical products for enriching society appeared to be unlimited. On the reverse side, the negative aspects of chemistry have come to the fore. Disposal of chemical by-products has resulted in environmental and health hazards. However, chemical products are essential for humanity. The world's reserves of fossil fuels (e.g. oil, natural gas and coal) will eventually be exhausted, and new chemical processes and materials will provide alternative energy sources. The conversion of solar energy to useful forms, for example, will rely heavily on discoveries in chemistry.

Physics

During the nineteenth century physics forged ahead and subjects which had once been separate disciplines began to converge.

As early as 1620 Francis Bacon had inferred that heat was an internal motion of the smallest particles of substances. In 1695 the German mathematician and philosopher, Gottfried Liebniz (1646-1716) first suggested that heat and kinetic energy, or the energy of motion, had some connection. In 1761, the Scottish chemist Black, first measured the heat absorbed in fusion and ebullition, and the temperatures of different substances. He defined the fundamental concepts of latent and specific heat; and his technique which measured quantities rather than intensities of heat, were the first of those which we call 'Calorimetric'. His epoch-making works are important for two reasons. First, his investigation led to the establishment of the universal science of thermodynamics; second, it stimulated the scientific techniques which perfected the steam engine. Watt, who constructed the first practical steam engine, was Black's assistant and collaborator.

At the turn of the century Count Rumford in his famous cannon-boring experiments of 1798 discovered that enough heat was generated to melt blocks of ice floating in it or to boil the water. After Rumford, the Frenchman Sadi Carnot made a searching analysis of machines that produce mechanical power from heat, focussing mainly on the energy and heat losses of a steam engine. Carnot who died at the early age of thirty-six came to the conclusion that 'heat is nothing else than motive power, or rather motion which has changed its form.' He thus laid the foundation of a Kinetic (vibratory) theory of heat.

The researches of three men, James Joule, Lord Kelvin and Rudolf Clausius contributed to the development of a modern theory of heat. Joule (1818-89) studied the work done by a gas when it expands and the heat generated when it is compressed. In 1847 his famous experiment of paddle-wheel in water gave a precise determination of how much work is required to generate a given amount of heat.

Joule's work was taken up by William Thompson, later Lord Kelvin, a brilliant mathematician and physicist. He was involved with the laying of the first Atlantic telegraph cable in 1866 and made great improvements in the accuracy of the magnetic compass. Kelvin tried to find the appropriate mathematical laws to explain Joule's work, and realised that to formulate them he needed some absolute scale of temperature rather than an arbitrary one.

In 1850 the German physicist Rudolf Clausius made a mark with a famous paper on the theory of heat. He formulated the first two laws of thermodynamics. The first stated that in any closed system (a steam engine, for example), the total amount of energy is constant. The second law stated that heàt cannot pass from a colder to a hotter body; for this to happen some external cause must come into operation. The work of Clausius and Kelvin made it clear that heat was no mysterious weightless fluid but was instead a form of energy. So, too, was mechanical work. It also became clear that neither form of energy could be destroyed, though one could be converted into the other. This led him to formulate that became known as the conservation of energy, a principle that had been stated in 1847 by the German physicist Hermann von Helmholtz.

Electricity and Magnetism

The first new science to develop after the end of the Newtonian period was electricity. During the 1760s it became clear from the experimental work by Benjamin Franklin, by the chemist and physicist Joseph Priestley and Henry Cavendish that electric attractions varied according to the inverse square of the distance between charges. In 1785, Coulomb, by measurements with a torsion balance, established the inverse-square law for both electric and magnetic attractions. In 1791 the Italian physiologist Galvani made the first artificial electric current flow around a circuit including as fundamental elements the nerves of a frog's leg and a metallic couple. In 1799 the Italian physicist Alessandro Volta reexamined these phenomena and found that electricity could be produced by constructing a device—a pile of copper and zinc discs separated by discs of moist pasteboard. This was not only the first electric battery, it was also the first source giving a continuous flow of electricity. Galvanic batteries at first were expensive. It fell to Humphry Davy in 1802 to produce the new metals, sodium and potassium, by the use of the world's largest battery at the Royal Institution. The first arc light was also made by Davy.

Soon afterwards, a remarkable discovery made possible the mechanical measurement of electric currents, and consequently the definition of a group of new concepts. In 1820 Hans Christian Oersted discovered that the electric current would deflect a magnetic needle. His experiments led to the manufacture of galvanometer, used to define the strength of currents. In 1826 a German school teacher Ohm discovered the relation between this strength, the intensity of the current, and the resistance of the circuit. Meanwhile, the French physicist Ampere had carried out an even more important work. He discovered that an electric current had mechanical effect, not only on the magnet, but on other currents. These phenomena which were developed mathematically with exactitude, laid the foundation of the science of electromagnetism.

Before the full interaction of electricity and magnetism could be understood, one more decisive step had to be taken. It had been demonstrated how electric currents produced magnetism; it remained to show how magnetism could produce electric currents. This discovery was the result of a planned research by Faraday. In 1831, Faraday showed that relation between magnetism and electricity was dynamic and not static—that a magnet had to be moved near an electric conductor for the current to arise. The most crucial observation showed that not only was magnetism equivalent to electricity in motion but also, conversely, electricity was magnetism in motion.

Faraday's discovery was of much greater practical importance. These led to the development of the electric motor and the electric generator and thus to electric trams, tramways and a public electric supply, as well as to the electric telegraph and the telephone. Faraday was one of that rare class of physicists who had a deep understanding of the forces with which he was dealing. His conception of electric fields as regions of stress, which could be graphically defined by lines and tubes of force, was the basis of the masterly final development of electrical theory in the nineteenth century. This, primarily, was the work of Clark Maxwell (1831-79), which was summarised in his classical *Treatise on Electricity and Magnetism* (1881). With extraordinary skill and insight, Maxwell gave them precise mathematical definition, and thus elaborated equations which are fundamental in modern theory. Thus Maxwell showed that light must be an electromagnetic wave of some kind, and, conversely, that electromagnetic waves should undergo reflection, refraction and all the other effects which light waves experience. Moreover, his results showed that radiation of shorter and greater wavelengths than light should exist. In 1888, long electromagnetic waves were indeed discovered. The brilliant researches of German physicist Heinrich Hertz led to the discovery of electric (radio) waves whose existence Maxwell had deduced. Hertz established the essential similarity of electric and light waves and showed that they travelled at the same speed. The practical importance of Hertz's work lies in the fact that it firmly established the wave theory of light which represented the first break in Newtonian physics.

Light

Newton's famous 'emission theory' which pictured a beam of light as a stream of invisible corpuscles held the field in the eighteenth century. In 1801 the English physicist Thomas Young explained the bands of colour, produced by diffraction or otherwise, was caused by the interference of trains of waves in different phase. In 1808 Laplace claimed that the splitting of light into two rays could be explained on the corpuscular theory by assuming that the corpuscles were split into two rays each with different velocities.

It was Augustin Fresnel (1788-1827) who overthrew corpuscular theory. Considering that each light wave gives rise to secondary wavelets, Fresnel then suggested that most of such wavelets are absorbed at the edge of a body and only a few remain to give rise to others. It is the interference of these that we observe as diffraction. Fresnel's work was supported by Francois Arago.

Meanwhile the emission theory had been elaborated satisfactorily by Biot, Brewster and other adherents. But its growing complication by the multiplication of hypotheses, lost it much support. Its fundamental premises were invalidated by the crucial experiment of Foucault in 1853. According to the emission theory, the velocity of light in water must be greater than its velocity in air; according to the wave theory, the velocity in water must be less. In 1849 Fizeau had determined the velocity of light for the first time by measurement over terrestrial distances. By Foucault's method, it was possible to lead one beam for a sufficient distance through water while another traversed the same distance through air; a comparison of their displacements then showed that the velocity of light was greater in air, and this finally put an end to the controversy.

Another question about light that required investigation was the true nature of the spectrum. Newton had shown how sunlight was composed of light of all colours and the subject was opened up again by William Wollaston. In 1802 he expected to separate the colours from each other. To this end, he built an instrument—a spectroscope. But, contrary to his expectations, no separation of colours was shown by this technique. At the beginning of the century, the German technician Fraunhofer was engaged with experiments designed for the improvement of lenses. He discovered and located dark lines in the spectrum of sunlight and characteristic lines in flame spectra.

The presence of the dark lines was to remain a mystery for some time. Meanwhile other spectroscopic investigations were taking place. Investigations by the astronomer John Herschel and his friend W. H. Fox Talbot, remembered for pioneering work in the development of photography, showed that when certain chemical substances were heated and their flames examined in a spectroscope, each element gave its own characteristic bright lines. In 1833 William Allen Miller, Professor of Chemistry at King's College, London, investigated the spectra of many materials. His experiments revealed that if sunlight was passed through various gases in the laboratory, some additional dark lines appeared.

The whole subject of spectroscopy was finally put on a more precise footing by two physicists, Balfour Stewart at Manchester University and Gustav Kirchoff in Hiedelberg. In 1858 Stewart showed that if a body emitted radiation at specific wavelengths then it also absorbed radiation best at those wavelengths. This discovery was also made by Kirchoff, who was then working with the chemist, Robert Bunsen, inventor of the bunsen burner. It was made clear that different substances in the state of a gas or vapour had characteristic spectra which consisted of lines and bands; that the continuous spectra of glowing liquids and solids were characteristically modified when viewed through layer of different gases and liquids; notably, that the dark lines of the solar spectra were caused by such absorption. Thus was founded the science of spectrum analysis. The most astounding implications of spectrum analysis were in the field of astronomy.

Atomic Physics and the Quantum Theory

A deep understanding of the elements of the nature of atoms themselves arose out of the practice of passing electricity through rarefied gases. The experiments of William Crookes in 1870-74 in London showed that in electrical discharges streams from the negative electrode which produced fluorescence when they fell on glass—cathode rays, as they were later called. Crookes tried to explain these cathode rays by suggesting that they were due to the few gas molecules still remaining in the tube becoming electrified and then being repelled from the cathode. But the accidental discovery of X-rays in 1895 by W. K. Roentgen (1845-1923) led not only to demolition of Crooke's explanation but also to the beginning of revolutionary ideas about atom. Roentgen discovered that the electric discharges through gases generated, upon impact with matter, radiations of a new type, which penetrated many substances that were opaque to light. Roentgen called them 'X-rays', though many preferred to call them 'Roentgen rays.'

John Joseph Thomson of the Cambridge University began to study the new rays with a research student Ernest Rutherford. They noticed that when the rays passed through a gas it was able to conduct electricity, a result that led Thomson to speak of the gas as 'ionised'. In 1897-99 J. J. Thomson detected the first component to be known in the structure of the atom. This had since been known as the electron. It is some 1,800 times less than that of hydrogen—the lightest atom. The significance of the discovery was that it proved atoms were not the smallest particles.

In 1895, while Thomson was working on cathode rays, the French physicist Henri Becquerel discovered that the heavy element uranium was continuously emitting rays. Once radioactivity was discovered, scientific progress was fast. Pierre Curie (1859-1906) and his Polish wife Marie Curie (1867-1934), had found sources very much stronger than the original uranium.

They isolated elements of a new kind such as *polonium* and *radium*.

Rutherford (1871-1937) who had been studying radioactivity in detail, soon discovered that two sets of rays—alpha and beta rays—were being emitted. His further research with the English physicist, Frederick Soddy, led to the realisation that these were not in fact rays at all but particles. By 1903 they came to the conclusion that atoms of radioactive substances were spontaneously breaking up. In 1907 Rutherford, with the assistance of the young German physicist Hans Geiger (later developer of the Geiger Counter for measuring radioactivity), discovered that from whatever radioactive element they came, the alpha-ray particles gave the same spectrum as atoms of the gas helium. Clearly, the alpha-ray particles were helium atoms. Further investigation showed that the beta-ray particles were high-speed electrons.

In 1910, William Bragg found that when the rays struck atoms in a rarefied gas, they caused these atoms to emit high-speed electrons which, in their turn, 'knocked off' electrons from other atoms. The gas thus became electrically conducting or ionised. In 1911 Rutherford suggested that every atom has a central core or nucleus; this has a positive electrical charge and contains most of the mass of the atom. In 1912, Niels Bohr, a young Danish scientist, laid the foundations of powerful theory of the atom. Basically, Bohr's model, which replaced Rutherford's, consisted of a nucleus with a positive charge, but with the electrons orbiting around it like the solar system—the electrons in orbit round the protons and neutrons in the nucleus.

Bohr's atomic model was supported by other researches that had been carried out earlier. It corresponded with some work by the German physicists Max Planck and Albert Einstein. In 1900 Planck had put forward the suggestion that radiation does not appear in a continuous stream but in discrete packets or 'quanta' of energy, the number of quanta being greater the shorter the wavelength of the radiation. This had been confirmed by Einstein in 1905, who analysed the 'photoelectric' effect in which short-wave ultra-violet radiation falling on a metal surface causes electrons to be emitted. Thus the observed fact and a theoretical analysis made it clear that light and all electromagnetic radiation should be considered as both a wave and a particle.

The quantum theory was developed in great detail by a number of mathematical physicists—Louis de Broglie, Erwin Schrodinger, Paul Dirac, and Werner Heisenberg. In 1927 the German scientist, Heisenberg, described the 'principle of indeterminacy.' He showed that the very act of assuming that energy moves in discrete quanta means that certain pairs of variables that constantly affect one another, such as time and energy, cannot be determined with complete accuracy.

Bohr's theory of the atom provided a theoretical background to the Periodic Table of chemical elements, drawn up by the Russian chemist, Domitri Mendeleyev. The table displays the chemical elements arranged according to atomic weight, and lays out in vertical columns those with similar chemical properties.

The explanation of the Mendeleyev Table drew attention to the nucleus, some ten thousand times smaller than the atom itself. By 1919 Francis Aston had discovered that the gas neon could exist in different forms, having different atomic weights though similar chemical properties. This was true of other elements which also possessed such 'isotopes.' In 1919, Rutherford bombarded nitrogen atoms with alpha particles and disintegrated the nitrogen nucleus. The products of this disintegration were positively charged particles, called 'protons'. By 1920 it had been proved that the atoms certainly consisted of still smaller components, the electron and the proton. Moreover, Rutherford's bombardment of the nitrogen nucleus had initiated a new technique, the artificial atomic-disintegration methods to be used by John Cockfort and Ernest Wolton in 1932.

In 1932 James Chadwick discovered the neutron, a nuclear particle with the same large mass as the proton but having no electric charge. In 1932 Carl Anderson at the California Institute of Technology observed a new sub-atomic particle which were created at the moment the beta particles left the nucleus. It was named the 'positron'. Yet beta particle production presented problems which were solved in 1934 by Enrico Fermi, an Italian physicist. He gave a complete explanation using a particle known as the neutrino. Fermi's theory of beta particle production raised new questions, in particular neutrons and protons were held together in the nucleus. In 1935, the Japanese physicist Hideki Yukawa attributed this to a hypothetical intermediate particle, the meson.

In six brief years, from 1932 to 1938, the effects of neutrons on different nuclei were studied. The first crucial discovery was that of Joliot-Curie—that nearly all atoms bombarded with neutrons become themselves radioactive. In 1937 Hahn (1879-1968) and Strassman discovered that some of the products produced by irradiating uranium with neutrons were of an altogether lower atomic mass. This time it was realised that the atom had been split and this knowledge was to have the most tremendous impact.

The twentieth century has affected fundamental changes in scientific outlook. During its first

Einstein

two decades the entire foundations of everyday physics were shaken by the theory of relativity. **Einstein**, born at Ulm in Germany in 1879, concluded that that velocity of light was the greatest velocity in Nature; nothing could travel faster than this. Known later as the 'Special Theory of Relativity', it restricted itself to the motion of bodies moving at uniform velocities relative to each other.

Einstein next dealt with the far more difficult situation in which bodies are moving relative to one another in accelerated motion, a thing we find in the natural world. In 1905 he proposed his new famous equation $E = mc^2$—a formula that expresses the relationship between energy and mass. This energy equation forms the basis of nuclear-power generation and, of course, of the atomic bomb; it has almost important implications in astronomy.

His general theory of relativity of 1915 marked a great step forward in man's understanding of Nature. Because the theory dealt with accelerated motion, and since gravity caused bodies to fall at an accelerated pace, general relativity was also a theory of gravity. It showed that while gravity is associated with the mass of the body, this is because space is distorted by the presence of a large mass.

Discoveries in modern physics are converted into technical innovation and analytical tools for associated disciplines. There are, for example, such nascent fields as nuclear and biomedical engineering, quantum chemistry and quantum optics and radio, X-ray and gamma-ray astronomy, as well as such analytical tools as radioisotopes, spectroscopy, and lasers which all stem directly from basic physics. The relationship of physics to its bordering disciplines is a reciprocal one. Mathematics has always been the primary tool of the theoretical physicist.

Astronomy

The science of astronomy was completely summarised in the monumental *Mecanique Celeste* of Laplace, the first and the greatest astronomical treatise of the nineteenth century (1799-1825). The first dramatic achievement of astronomy in the nineteenth century was that of Bessel who, in 1838, determined for the first time the distance of a fixed star. According to Bessel's calculation, his star was so far away that light, which traversed the earth's orbit in almost sixteen minutes, would take more than six years to cover the distance; or otherwise, the star was about 600,000 times the distance of the sun.

Another dramatic event was the discovery of Neptune. In 1781, F. O. Herschel had identified a new planet, Uranus. Later analytic studies of its motion suggested to several astronomers that its perturbations might be due to the gravitational action of a still more distant planet. In 1843

Adams in England calculated the orbit and relative position of this hypothetical body, and in 1846, shortly after Leverrier in France had independently arrived at like results.

The newly improved techniques of observation resulted in the discovery of still other bodies within the planetary system. Prior to the observations of Herschel, four satellites of Jupiter, discovered by Galileo, and five satellites of Saturn, discovered by Huygens and Cassini, were known; to these were now added one to the system of Jupiter, three to that of Saturn; two were discovered attending Uranus, one attending the new planet Neptune; and two very close to Mars, revolving rapidly. More interesting were the discoveries of the small minor planets, which revolve between Mars and Jupiter. The largest of these called Ceres, a body only five hundred miles in diameter, was discovered on the first day of the nineteenth century; and in 1807, three others were known. By the end of the nineteenth century over four hundred had been discovered and their orbits traced. Finally, of the more than two hundred comets whose paths were calculated, fifty or more belonged to the solar system.

The momentous development that took place in nineteenth century astronomy concerned the studies that were made of the spectra of stars. The pioneering astronomical work on this subject was done by an amateur astronomer, William Huggins. His spectroscopic work laid the foundation of astrophysics. In 1868 Huggins, with improved apparatus, was able to measure the velocity of Sirius, the brightest star in the northern skies. This opened up a new technique of observation, for previously velocities of stars—radial velocities—could not be detected.

Astronomy had made great strides during this century, most significantly in the field of stellar astronomy. The main advances in the field were associated in the first half of the century with the Danish astronomer, Ejnar Hertzprung, the American Henry Norris Russell, and the Englishman Arthur Eddington. Their work was based on the foundations laid by Huggins and the Italian Jesuit Angelo Secchi and the American Edward Pickering. In the late 1860s Secchi devised what seemed a workable classification, dividing the stars into five classes. It later turned out that the system devised by Edward Pickering was the more satisfactory. Based on the work started by Henry Draper, it became known as the Draper classification.

Hertzprung's main interest was to measure stellar distances. Russell's aim was to gain an insight into the stars themselves. The Hertzprung-Russell approach was based on vastly improved evidence and the graph they produced, known as the Hertzprung-Russell or H.R. diagram, was productive of all kinds of useful astrophysical results. In Russell's hands the H-R diagram gave a clue to the life cycle or 'evolution' of stars.

Coupled with the question of stellar evolution was the problem of the source of stellar energy. In the late nineteenth century Kelvin had suggested that the Sun's energy came from heat generated by its contraction, and this view was strongly advocated by the English astronomer, James Jeans. In 1919 Russell made some suggestions about energy locked up in stellar atoms. But the man who turned the scales was Eddington, who, in 1920, strongly supported atomic energy as a source of power. Eddington made a pregnant remark: 'If, indeed, sub-atomic energy in the stars is being freely used to maintain their great furnaces, it seems to bring a little nearer to fulfilment our dream of controlling this latent power for the well-being of the human race—or for its suicide;' and he died some eight months before the first atom bomb was dropped on Hiroshima. Later research by George Gamow has shown that nuclear energy is indeed the power source of the Sun and all other stars.

Astronomical research has always been limited by the available means of observation. The introduction of the telescope brought a new dimension into astronomy. The twentieth century has seen vast improvements in telescopic power. The pioneer in this effort was George Ellery Hale, an American born in 1868. His first notable success was the establishment in 1897 of the Yerkes Observatory with world's largest refractor of 40 inches (1 metre) aperture as its main instrument. In 1908 a 60 inch (1.5 metre) reflector was set up at Mount Wilson in California, to be followed in 1917 by the Mount Wilson 100 inch

(2.5 metre) reflector and then in 1948 by the 200-inch (5 metre) reflector at Palomar.

The value of Hale's large 100 inch reflector emerged in the 1920s with the discovery of the existence of galaxies. The initiative in proving that the universe was composed of myriads of galaxies similar to our own containing either stars, dust or gas, was taken by Edwin Hubble, an American.

The most spectacular advances in astronomy during the twentieth century have been in the field of space exploration. Travel to the Moon and planets was always a dream. But with the launching of the Russian 'Sputnik', a small body put into orbit round the Earth in October 1957, space technology has developed rapidly. In 1959, for the first time in human history, man saw the rear face of the Moon, and he obtained an actual foothold on the lunar surface in July 1969.

The expanding universe observed by Hubble leads one to suppose that the universe began a long time ago—about twenty thousand million years ago. It has been held by the Belgian astronomer Georges Lemaitre that the universe began as a concentrated lump, a super-atom of material which disintegrated and then expanded outwards. On the other hand, in 1939, George Gamow, Ralph Alpher and Hans Bethe in the United States considered a 'hot' nuclear explosion of highly concentrated material to have started the expansion. This 'hot bang theory' is now the favoured view.

Gamow proposed that the universe began in a state of extremely high temperature and density and exploded outward—the so-called 'big bang.' Matter was originally in the form of neutrons, which quickly decayed into protons and electrons; these then combined to form hydrogen and heavier elements.

Mathematics

During the nineteenth century, mathematics developed in every field, in geometry, in algebraic analysis and the use of the calculus. It also opened up the new field of statistics. Mathematical statistics were developed by the Belgian Lambert Quetelet. In 1845 Quetelet mentioned what is known as a 'normal' or 'Gaussian' distribution (the latter after the German mathematician Carl Friedrich Gauss). It was an important result which shows mathematically and in graphical form the distribution of normal variations.

Earlier, the French mathematical physicist Simeon Poisson made important contributions to the mathematics of perturbations in the solar system, worked on a mathematical analysis of the theory of heat and in 1937 tackled the questions of probability. It is to him we owe the term 'Law of large numbers.'

The work of Quetelet and Poisson was to bear fruit in many branches of science. The study of statistics played a considerable part in genetics, the study of inherited characteristics. The man who had much to do with the latter was Francis Galton (a grandson of Eramus Darwin) who had no formal education. His interests were multi-faceted. He introduced the use of fingerprints for identification and did some research in meteorology. But his main interests were in genetics and psychology. These were based on his conviction that everything was quantifiable.

Galton realised that statistical methods were of great importance to study genetics and inheritance. He sowed the seeds of mental testing and the measurement of the acuteness of the senses. In the field of mathematical statistics, he introduced the concepts of correlation and regression.

Galton also became much concerned with the inheritance of talent. But his views were contradicted by others who claimed that the children of talented families owed their gifts to their environment. But Galton stood his ground. This led him to advocate a programme of 'eugenics' to 'foster talent and health and suppress sickness and stupidity.' Just after the turn of the century, a eugenics laboratory was established which had close ties with the University College of London. In 1911 Karl Pearson, a Cambridge trained mathematician, was appointed as the Professor of Eugenics. He laid down firm mathematical foundations for the whole of twentieth century statistical science, but especially as applied to biological questions.

The second field of mathematics was geometry. During the nineteenth century two quite new geometrical systems were proposed. These arose out of the failure of the theorems in Euclidean geometry. In the eighteenth century, Giorolamo Saccheri, the Jesuit Professor of Mathematics at Pavia, tried to prove the theorems. The great mathematician and physicist Carl Friedrich Gauss tried to replace the theorem by a simpler one, but failed. The first steps in developing non-Euclidean geometry were developed in the 1820s and early 1830s by two mathematicians, Nikolni Lobachevsky in Russia and Janos Bolyai in Hungary. In 1866, the last year of his short life, Bernard Riemann, entered the field of non-Euclidean geometry.

Increasing knowledge of the atom and of its structure has largely removed the barriers between the sciences of physics and chemistry. Geology is another science in which techniques of physics and chemistry have been used.

In the first part of the twentieth century a new dimension was given to geology. An ever-increasing demand for oil, coal, and metals, has revolutionised the methods of survey. A new science of geophysics has arisen which give us information about the nature of strata thousands of metre down the earth. The greatest of these, the so-called 'moholes', are already in operation. They are drilled both by United States and Soviet geophysicists in the thinner parts of the crust of the earth. Their object is to reach below the discontinuity found by A. Mohorovicic (1857-1936) by seismic methods, separating the light from the heavy rocks of the crust. An interesting development of geological thought was propounded by Wegener's (1880-1930) theory of continental drift in 1915, to explain the distribution of the great land masses, on the earth's surfaces.

In the early years of the present century the study of radioactivity has provided the geologist with a reliable means of dating the formation of various strata. The use of isotopes in tracking down the origin and dates of different formations has begun. It has already shown that life is more than half as old as the earth itself—2,700 million years. The geologist is now concerned in the location of sources of uranium and other elements of high atomic weight.

In the early twentieth century the study of oceanography was more extensive. Data on the physical conditions of the oceans have been steadily accumulating. The greatest advances have been made on the edges of the ocean basins, the continental shelf which have been studied with the anti-submarine device—the piezo-electric echo sounder. But the most exciting study has been that of the deep-sea bottom.

The study of the atmosphere has shown that it consists of three very different layers, the troposphere, or lowest layer, extending from the surface of the earth to a vertical height of about six miles (9 km); the stratosphere, above the troposphere and at a uniform temperature; and above this, the ionosphere, beginning about thirty miles (48 km) above the earth's surface and extending a further one hundred and twenty miles (192 km). The circulation of the atmosphere and the formation of clouds have been increasingly studied. The next crucial discovery was in 1918 with Bjerknes' (1862-1951) polar-front theory of Cyclones. The crucial idea which Bjerknes added was the concept of separate masses of warm and cold air with the production of clouds and rains. By introducing a third dimension into meteorology, Bjerknes anticipated the importance of the physics of the upper air vitally important for aviation. The overall range of meteorological information has been immensely increased through the use of weather satellites. In 1945 a new aspect of meteorology was revealed by the use of crystal seeding for promoting rain formation in clouds.

Medical Science

Medical science had made phenomenal growth in the first half of the twentieth century. The discovery of vitamins by Sir F. Gowland Hopkins in 1912, and of hormones by Bayliss and Starling (1902) added a new dimension to medical science. Adrenaline was isolated by Takamine in 1901 from the suprarenal glands and thyroxine from the thyroid gland by Kendall in 1915. Insulin, isolated by Banting and Best from the pancreas in 1922, proved of great value in the treatment of diabetes mellitus; cortisone, from the adrenal cortex, isolated by Kendall in 1936, is being applied in the treatment of rheumatoid arthritis.

Apart from germs, there are minute agents of disease, namely the viruses, which can reproduce themselves only in living tissues. Some of these viruses, from plants, were isolated by Stanley in 1935 as crystals. A number of investigations in this half century succeeded in the preparation of new drugs with the property of being deadly to bacteria, while generally being harmless to the host. The component that would deal with the bacteria must be combined with some other molecular group to form a new molecular grouping that would be innocuous to the host but deadly to bacteria. One of the first of these new drugs to be prepared was salvarsan, an organic compound of arsenic, for the treatment of syphilis, by Paul Ehrlich in 1909. In 1935 Domagk showed that streptococcal infections could be treated in a similar way by means of prontosil, a red organic dye-substance. As the prontosil molecule was the sulphonamide group, the new drug, known as 'M and B 693', or sulphapyridine, was synthesised by Ewins and Phillips and applied in 1938 in the treatment of pneumonia and other fatal diseases. The sulphonamide drugs have also proved an effective remedy in puerperal fever.

The discovery of antibacterial properties of penicillin by Fleming in 1929, and its successful development as an antibiotic by Chain and Florey in 1940, proved to be a milestone in medical science. Other antibiotics followed, including streptomycin, choloramphenicol and aureomycin used, respectively, in the treatment of tuberculosis, typhus and of virus diseases.

Cancer research made some headway after 1945. Surgery made considerable progress owing to improvement of anaesthatics and the use of radioactivity for diagnosis. Improved methods of blood transfusion enabled the surgeon to operate on heart, lungs, brain and the central nervous system. Physiotherapy and occupational therapy made recovery after injuries or operations quicker.

The emphasis now shifted from curative treatment to preventive measures. Preventive medicine required not only more hygienic conditions in towns, houses, factories and schools, but also vigil by state and local authorities and international cooperation through the World Health Organisation (**WHO**).

Psychology made less progress as it lacked firm theoretical foundations. The basic work of Freud and Jung, valuable as it was, lacked the profundity of a Darwin or an Einstein. Psychology made rapid progress where it was able to link up with the allied sciences of physiology and medicine. The result was a great increase in knowledge of neurology and of the role of the nervous system in human behaviour, a better understanding, through laboratory experiments, of the working of memory and of skill.

The application of science on industry has become so general that science is quickly becoming an integral and inseparable part of industry. Men realised the importance of scientific knowledge and its application in the modern world. A. J. Balfour was right in his observation about the scientists: 'They are the people who are changing the world and they don't know it. Politicians are but the fly on the wheel—the men of science are the motive power.'

The first half of the twentieth century witnessed the development of chemical and electrical industries and even in the most traditional industries such as agriculture and building science had now more to contribute to industry. The essential change was in the methods of production from machine-aided craftsmanship to mass production.

The twentieth century witnessed a dramatic change in the communications revolution. The most astounding revolution that took place in communications in twentieth century was in electronics. The scientific examination of the relationship between light waves and electromagnetic waves had already revealed the possibility of transmitting electromagnetic signals between widely separated points. After Marconi's successful transmission of first wireless message on December 12, 1901 across the Atlantic, striking progress was made in improving the means of transmitting and receiving coded messages. Particularly important was the development of thermionic valve, a device for rectifying an electromagnetic wave. The idea of harnessing the flow of electrons was applied in the electron microscope, radar, the electronic computer, and in the cathode-ray tube of the television set. By the outbreak of World War II, television services were being introduced in several countries, although the war put a brake on their extension. The emergence of television as a universal medium of mass communication is, therefore, a revolutionary phenomenon of the post-war years.

In military affairs, the technological innovations have transformed the character of the war itself. Though the principle of rocket propulsion was known earlier, German war effort in the 1930s succeeded in developing a rocket capable of delivering a warhead hundreds of miles away. At an island in the Baltic, Wernher von Braun and his team created the V-2. Weighing about 14 tons, it was 40 feet (13 metres) long and propelled by a mixture of alcohol and liquid oxygen. Reaching a height of more than 100 miles (160 kilometres), the V-2 marked the beginning of the space age.

Technology had revolutionised the society during the period 1900-45. The automobile and electric power caused a sea-change in the social life and quickened the process of rapid urbanisation. The rapid development of the airplane, the cinema and radio made the world seem smaller.

The machine that transformed both industry and conditions of life in the twentieth century was the internal-combustion engine. The practical pioneers Lenoir (1822-1900), Otto (1832-91) and Diesel (1852-1913), the latter adding compression ignition, were able to make efficient engines, but during the nineteenth century their use was limited. Their use for road locomotives or automobiles grew, slowly in the last decades of the century. Henry Ford (1863-1947) became the most successful of the manufacturers of the new car. Mass production of the car began which gave an enormous impetus to its further development. The automobile industry became the largest concern that could meet the market demand.

The internal combustion engine led to the development of aviation industry. The maiden flight powered by petrol was that made by the Wright brothers in 1903; they flew 284 yards (250 m). In 1909 Colonel Bleriot flew across the Straits of Dover. The First World War led to the development and design in aircraft. In 1919 Alcock and Brown flew the Atlantic from west to east, while in the same year was started a passenger service between London and Paris. In 1927 Lindberg flew solo 3,100 miles (5,800 km) non-stop from New York to Paris in $33^1/_2$ hours. Helicopters and jet-engined aircraft began from the Second World War. In 1947 an aeroplane flew faster than sound travels in air. Long flights became common. During the Second World War flying bombs and rocket bombs were devised. Since then flight to the moon and of space travel became common.

The use of electricity has revolutionised the lives of men in the present century. It has become the usual source of power in the home and in the factory. Electricity has brought broadcasting and television to town and country. The progress was phenomenal. In 1897 Marconi sent a message by wireless telegraphy to a distance of eighteen miles (29 km). In 1901 signals were transmitted across the Atlantic. In the 1920s radio-broadcasting became general and it was followed by television after the Second World War.

The rapidity of modern technological advance became evident in the tapping of the vast sources of atomic energy. A team of physicists, American, British and Canadian discovered atomic fission for use in war. The first atomic bomb was dropped on Hiroshima on August 6, 1945, and the second on Nagasaki three days later. The manufacture of these atomic bombs was kept secret, yet, after five years, the Soviet Union successfully tested it. Human civilisation faced a menacing problem of annihilation. On the reverse side, the discovery of atomic energy unleashed a new source of power which proved beneficial to humanity—producing electricity to nucleor-powered ships and submarines.

Developments in technology have made rapid strides. Metallurgical progress brought a great variety of alloy steels. The special use of silicon steel in electromagnets effected economies in electric power. Stainless steel, an alloy with chromium, served domestic needs and medical science. Alloys with manganese, tungsten, nickel, vanadium, cobalt and molybdenum have served modern engineering. Aluminium alloys have been particularly useful in aircraft industry.

The pneumatic tyre, essential to motor transport, has been developed and a wide range of synthetic rubber substitutes came into being since 1930. The production of plastic and bakelite marked the beginning of a new industry. Perspex, the first plastic to replace glass, was discovered in 1930, and polythene came into being in 1939. Nylon, which replaced artificial silk as a fabric, dates from 1935.

Atmospheric nitrogen in the form either of nitric acid or of ammonia proved of great benefit to agriculture and to the explosives industry. The manufacture of improved dyestuffs has added colour and variety to fabrics. Photography has been greatly improved. Colour cinematography and sound films were introduced in 1920. Insecticides have been invented, the best known being DDT.

While the agricultural production has increased by the application of scientific knowledge, population has multiplied even faster, increasing annually by 20 million. In the preservation of food, progress has been achieved by the use of deep freezing. The domestic refrigerator is another invention.

Ships have passed from coal to oil and from the steam engine to the steam turbine. Time signals broadcast by wireless telegraphy have greatly helped the navigator. Other radio aids to navigation, particularly radar, were developed during the Second World War.

The application of science to technology has been effected by the labours of the professional scientist. In the eighteenth century there were, however, a few special colleges in France and Germany for teaching science. The Ecole Polytechnique, founded in Paris in 1794, was the first of its kind. Developments in the nineteenth century were gradual, Germany was pioneer in multiplying technical schools of increasing standard. In Britain, the home of the Industrial Revolution, the teaching of science developed slowly during the nineteenth century. The foundation of the University College, London, in 1826, heralded the teaching of different branches of science.

The twentieth century opened with scientific education already well-established in Germany. In France the situation was much the same. Generally there was an increasing awareness of the use of science to industry. The application of science in certain war industries during the First World War coupled with the rapid strides of German industry, led various countries to take various steps for the promotion of science. In 1896 practically the whole of world science was concentrated in Germany, Britain and France. By 1954, while the science of the old centres had grown considerably, that growth was eclipsed by the phenomenal growth of science in the United States and the then Soviet Union including Japan, China and India.

The establishment of official or semi-official institutions gave great encouragement to technical or industrial research. In Britain the Department of Scientific and Industrial Research was instituted; various research boards were organised; and the National Physical Laboratory was taken over. In the United States a National Research Council was set up and National Research Fellowships were instituted. In the then Soviet Union and China, great attention was paid to the setting up of scientific institutions in large numbers. In the early 1920s, scientific research received a great impetus from one or other of such bodies. In Britain this kind of academic research was financed by the Department of Scientific and Industrial Research, the Medical Research Council and the various research associations.

The advance of science and technology has increased immeasurably in the twentieth century. In 1896 there were perhaps in the works some 50,000 people who belonged to the discipline of science, of whom not more than 15,000 were devoted to research activities. Sixty years later there were at least a million active research workers. The expenditure on science has increased many fold with an average rate of growth of ten percent per annum. Science, however, is still a long way behind, as this only forms twelve per cent of military expenditure.

Science has now entered industry in an intimate and operational way. The increasing scale of scientific application has involved science even more closely with governments. Science has become an inseparable part of society. It is not without hope that Descartes in the seventeenth century declared that through science we could become 'the masters and possessors of Nature.'

The potentiality of science to affect the life of man is an unchallenged fact. The First World War, which fostered the development of war plane, tank and poison gas, gave some foretaste of what science could do in war. The Second World War, with the production of atom bomb, revealed more strikingly the abuse of science. The advent of the Cold War gave a further impulse to science in the service of destruction.

War generated the application of science in various fields which was very much evident in the twentieth century. Industry, agriculture, medicine, and even science itself began to be planned. The new efflorescence of science with new discoveries and inventions are, however, continuations of scientific experiment and thought that have been progressing ever since the Renaissance.

It is unfortunate that the mankind's achievement in the scientific and technological knowledge has been a tragic failure. The wide 'morality gap' was a cause of concern before the invention and use of the atomic weapon. Since that epoch-making event the spectacle of the gaping 'door of death' has been terrifying.[1]

1. Arnold Toynbee: *Experiences* (1970), P. 301.

CHAPTER 49
LITERATURE

Enlightenment had its roots in science and the new humanism of the eighteenth century which tried to improve the social and political texture of contemporary Europe. Enlightenment had its home in France but reached out to all Europe. The literature it created was a by-product. The French Revolution owed much to the philosophies of the Enlightenment. The most prolific of the French philosophers were Montesquieu, Voltaire, Condillac, Diderot, Rousseau and Condorcet who set the Enlightenment's basic tone.

The philosophies attacked inherited institutions. They were in favour of freedom of thought instead of authoritarian censorship and indoctrination by the Church. They condemned the priesthood and attacked clerical obscurantism as the most serious threat to social progress. Education, the main plank of the philosophers' programme, should be divested of Church control and entrusted to state. They denounced arbitrary government and the violations of the rights of property and person. They also opposed economic regulations and systems of forced labour. Against the divine prerogative of the monarchy and the Church, they appealed to nature, and the innate goodness of men. Along with 'reason' the word 'natural' became the philosophers' touchstones for testing institutions. They reiterated that men should discover the laws of nature. According to the philosophies, 'nature' untarnished by arbitrary authority, would operate harmoniously as a unifying force.

Most of the philosophers considered 'social science' as instrument of progress. They looked to the future as heralding the golden age for man rather than in a past era of excellence. They believed that knowledge of nature would make men virtuous and advocated sweeping humanitarian reforms. They attacked slavery, arbitrary imprisonment and the inferior status of women. They also inveighed against war and militarism. Their patriotism was cultural and not based on emotional hatred.

Rational criticism of Louis XIV in France had begun with Montesquieu (1689-1755). In 1721 appeared Montesquieu's The *Persian Letters* in which he sharply criticised the French government and religion. In 1748 appeared his famous work *The Spirit of Laws*. He expounded the virtues of the British system of government as he found in England a political freedom that contrasted with the tyranny of Louis XIV. That freedom, he observed, was guaranteed by a separation of the executive, legislative and judicial powers. 'There is no liberty', he remarked 'if the judicial power be not separated from the legislative and the executive.' He showed a deep insight in arguing that laws were often the product of circumstances.

Voltaire

While Montesquieu represented the enlightened nobility, **Voltaire** (1694-1778) expressed the aristocratic viewpoint of the middle class. Thanks to his brilliant pen, he enjoyed a celebrity rarely surpassed by any one of the philosophers. His energy and copiousness were as formidable as his reputation. Plays, poems, histories, essays, letters by the thousands, came in an unending stream from him. He used his pen to expose the cruelties, irrational privileges and follies of Church, State and society. His chief target was the Church. 'Annihilate the infamous thing,' he wrote, as he looked upon it as a privileged nuisance. In one of his forceful works, *The Letters on the English*, he pointed out that the Church and the nobility in England were not exempt from direct taxation. In his vitriolic attack on the Church and other pillars of the Old Regime, he was something of a crusader.

He popularised Newton, Locke and the whole English social system in sharp contrast to contemporary French thought and institutions. His work disseminated the Enlightenment's message of free thought, and hatred of fanaticism, ignorance, persecution and war. Hostile to revolution, he urged the rulers to enact the philosophers' programme of civil rights and freedoms for their citizens. His masterpiece is *Candide*. He generally held the view that if men made sensible Church and State reforms, put an end to persecution, adopted rational institutions, and reason as against prejudice, then a good life might be ushered in. But in *Candide* the possibility seemed to have vanished 'cracking like thin ice to give us a glimpse of the black depths.'

The next most important figure of the Enlightenment after Voltaire is Denis Diderot. The great instrument of the Enlightenment was the 17-volume *Encyclopedia* published between 1751 and 1780 under the principal editorship of Denis Diderot (1713-84). Its chief purpose was to "bring together all the knowledge scattered over the face of the earth, to lay its general system before the men with whom we live ... so that our children will know more, and so that they may at the same time be greater in virtue and in happiness." Its contributors included men like Montesquieu, Turgot, Rousseau, d'Alembert, Holbach, Voltaire and, especially, Diderot. His editorial labours and his tremendous zeal for ideas produced in him a profound intuitive feeling for what was germinal and of deepening influence. Though educated by the Jesuits, he became a thorough materialist. Much of his thought anticipated the dialectical materialism afterwards elaborated by Marx and Engels. The *Encyclopedia* was much more than a philosophic compilation; it popularised the Newtonian revolution and Bacon's ideas of inductive science. The *Encyclopedia* was too large, too unwieldy a work to be as effective as Voltaire's tracts. Nevertheless as a vehicle for spreading the Enlightenment, it reinforced the activities of the salons, the scientific societies, public libraries and museums that appeared both in Europe and America.

Jean Jacques Rousseau (1712-78) "possessed one quality which cut him off from his contemporaries, which set an immense gulf betwixt him and them: he was modern ... he belonged to another world." The Romantics discovered in him their prophet. He was the prophet of revolt against rationalism and materialism. In 1749 he leapt into fame by winning an essay contest on the question 'Has the Restoration of Science and Arts tended to corrupt or purify Morals?' By charging that luxuries and cities had corrupted man, he shook the cherished notion that increased knowledge automatically brought progress. In the *Discourse on Inequality* (1755), he indicted the morally corrupting influence of society and rule by and for the rich. According to Rousseau, a moral revolution was the first prerequisite for revolution.

Jean Jacques Rousseau

He adumbrated his principal theory that man was essentially good, but corrupted by civilisation. He felt that it was in the people that sovereignty should properly rest. He imagined that a prince usurped this sovereignty, but that it still resided in the people which could overthrow the prince if he failed to do his duty. This was the main tenet of the *Social Contract* (1762), destined to be the gospel of radical revolutionaries. For Rousseau, only the 'general will' could legitimately bind man to law and government.

Rousseau's *Confessions* provided a possible key to his thought and personality. In this autobiographical sketch he portrays at length his sentiments and feelings. Rousseau's approach admirably suited the tastes of those who wanted governments responsive to their peoples. As a prolific writer, he stands as the fountainhead of such nineteenth century movements as the religious revival, democracy, romanticism, socialism, and nationalism. He was the founder of modern methods of education. His tract on education, *Emile,* advocated a natural spontaneous education of youth.

Among the romantic young writers, Francois-Rene de Chateaubriand towered above all. Already in his early *Essai historique, politique, at moral sur les Revolutions,* published in 1797, he declared about the inevitability of the French Revolution. He wrote about almost everything except the theatre, but there is a theatrical element in his writing. His best legacy in his posthumously published autobiography, *Memoires d'Outre—Tombe*. After the July Revolution of 1830, he lamented the complete disappearance of respect for authority of any kind. 'Nothing more exists,' he wrote in anguish in his *Memoires* 'authority of experience and age, birth or genius, talent or virtue; all are denied, contested and despised.'

Comte de Rivarol, who travelled widely, was a shrewd observer of the revolutionary scene. Burke called him the Tacitus of the French Revolution. He was appalled at the new political fanaticism. To combat the new ideas, arms were ineffective; it was new ideas that were needed. Rivarol also observed that man was not a rational creature; he was frequently swayed by a non-rational and even anti-rational quest for power. He was pioneer who tried to make a psychological study of mass behaviour. He showed his talent as a writer in his famous indictment of the Terror which later influenced profoundly the literary critic Sainte Beuve. He had a preference for a strong constitutional monarchy as he foresaw that the Revolution was destined to end in the emergence of a despot.

Mme de Stael, who died in 1817, was known more as a critic and novelist. She had a considerable influence in French romanticism. Her maiden venture was a study of Rousseau. But her best known work was an account of Germany that introduced many of the German Romantics to French readers.

Henri Boyle had many enthusiastic admirers. His reputation rests on two long novels—*The Red and the Black* and *The Chartreuse of Parma*. But his novels lack the breadth and balance. 'They blow as too hot and cold, like winds in an unhealthy climate.'

The great popularity of Lamartine is his graceful and melodious verse which expresses certain tender and sentimental mood of man. In his *Meditations Poetiques* (1820) and *Nouvelles Meditations* (1823) a young man wanders in enchanting natural surroundings of woods and mountains. In his *Les Harmonies poetiques at religioues* (1830) God and Nature are one.

Despite his small output of verse, de Vigny had romantic versatility. He contributed several prose plays, of which the most successful was *Chatterton*. He wrote the historical romance, *Cinq-Mars*, and some admirable memoirs of both military and literary life.

One of the best incarnations of Romanticism is Victor Hugo. He occupies a central position in the literary history of France. In 1830 he took the Paris stage by his plays *Hernani* and *Ruy Blas*. His huge novel *Notre-Dame de Paris* (1831) is the most spectacular survival of 'historical novel.' Hugo has a kingdom of his own, and in it he towers majestically, through the sheer force of his poetical ability, power of language and imaginative inventiveness. He is the first and one of the most ambitious of realistic modern novelists, the architect of *Human Comedy*, the novelist of society itself (*Les Miserables*—1862), the man who has stupendous energy and abundant self-confidence.

Mention may be made of two other novelists—George Sand, whose real name was Aurore Dupin, and Alexandre Dumas. George Sand represented romanticism in its militantly feminist aspect. Alexandre Dumas was a tremendous character who monopolised the Parisian life for quarter of a century (1825-50), after which he left the city. His *Three Musketeers* (1844) has always been popular together with more ambitious tales of like *Maguerite de Valois* and The *Count of Monte Cristo* (1845). His popular plays, *Antony and Kean* and the rest held the stage throughout the country.

Prosper Merimea wrote comparatively little. He has one of the best prose narrative styles of the century. He is at his best in the *nouvelle*, a long short story and more direct form of the novel, as in *Matteo Falcone* and *Carmon*. Theophile Gautier (1811-72) holds an important place in the history of romantic poetry. His poetry has not much weight or penetration but is exquisitely beautiful and splendidly pictorial. Among others, Baudelaire has been his ardent admirer.

Alfred de Musset (1810-57), the youngest member of Hugo's circle, was astonishingly productive. He was a poet in the Byronic style which reached a higher level of beauty and romantic exaltation. His prose tales were more immediately successful than his plays. But after his death, he was acknowledged as one of the finest French dramatists of the century. His drama is both original and delightful. Musset represented the final phase of the French Romantic movement from which he broke away in 1837. With him romanticism dwindles into something poised between wistfulness and mockery.

Balzac has been called the literary portraitist par excellence. He became the master of the social novel (La Pere Goriot) and the founder of the new conception of man, according to which "the individual exists only in relation to society." Balzac is not only a thoroughly bourgeois writer, but attacks everything that threatens the stability of the *status quo*. Balzac is a revolutionary writer without knowing that he is. His real sympathies make him an ally of the rebels and nihilists. Victor Hugo asserts that whether he wanted to or not he was a revolutionary writer, and that his works revealed the heart of a genuine democrat.

In Germany, the intellectual circles were deeply moved by the Revolution. In 1798 Kant predicted that such a phenomenon could never be obliterated from the memory of mankind. Kant firmly believed in the inevitability of the human progress. He was greatly impressed by the attempt on the part of the French to set up a representative government. He envisaged an ever growing respect for public international law which was reflected in his famous essay *On Perpetual Peace* (1795).

It was hoped that the French Revolution would usher in the Age of Reason. Human Reason was sought to be the panacea for all the political and social ills of mankind. Kant and Hegel dreamt of a Kingdom of Reason. Hegel, in his *Lectures on the Philosophy of History* (1830) enthusiastically observed:

> All of a sudden, the idea, the conception of Right, asserted its authority, and old framework of injustice could offer no resistance to its onslaught. In this way, a constitution was established in harmony with the idea of Right, and everything was henceforth to be based on this foundation.

If the French Revolution proved to be the high watermark of enlightened expectations, the wave began to ebb from 1793. Kant in his essay *Der Streit der Fakultaten* (1798), though appalled by the Jacobin Terror, predicted that Revolution was bound to prove a blessing to mankind. Fichte also expressed similar views. Friedrich Schiller realised that the idea of liberty too could be abused. In the drama *Die Reuber*, Schiller expressed his violent antipathy to the Revolution. The German poet Holderlin showed his insight by observing: 'What has transformed the State into a hell is precisely that man had tried to transform it into his heaven.'

The Romantic movement in Germany began about 1770 when Herder met Goethe at Konigsberg. Herder had a passion for poetry which he regarded as the mother-tongue of mankind. The greater poetry full of passion and feeling came from the people.

Apart from Goethe and Schiller, there were intellectuals who typified the Romantic movement in Germany. But their reputations blazed and then fizzled out. The Universities and university towns—Strassburg and Gottingen, Jena and Hiedelberg—played an important part in the German Romantic Movement. The chief names associated with this Romantic Movement are these: Tieck and Novalis; Brentano and Arnim; dramatists Werner and Von Kleist; later storytellers and poets, Eichendorff, Uhland, Kerner, Chamisso and Fouque; master of queer tales, Hoffmann and Hauff and Heine. Many of these writers were poets and wrote short lyrical poems, ballads and songs. The movement made use of folklore and the folktale, the *Marchen*, the fairy or dream tale. Heinrich Heine must be ranked as one of the masters of lyrical poets.

Schiller (1759-1805), who became professor of history at Jena in 1789, produced the poetic drama that had an enduring reputation. He was a good dramatist and the theatre in Germany owed much to Schiller. But his philosophical bent of mind blunt the edge of his drama.

The greatest European man of letters of the Romantic Age is **Goethe** (1749-1832). He was

Goethe

the most many-sided and complete man of his time. In his later years he was much concerned with the idea of 'world literature'. As a writer, his versatility is more remarkable than what he actually achieved. He cannot be considered a great dramatist—*Faust* is too complicated and demanding. Nor was he a great novelist—for *Werther* has vanished in the thin air of sentimentalism.

But when all this had been said, his greatness remains. In a time of vast upheaval, he had to create his own world in which to create his own work. It is this that really sets him apart making him appear to be the detached Olympian. A wonderful poet, Goethe may never have reached the supreme creative achievements of the earlier masters, his *Wilhelm Maister, Faust* and *Mephistocles* falling short of a *Hamlet* or *Don Quixote*; but his act of creation was deep, and strong and abiding. In his last years, Goethe wrote his memoirs, composed the remarkable cycle called the *Westostlicher Divan* and finished the second part of his masterpiece *Faust*, which had been called an 'electrocardiogram of the German character.'

Victor Hugo has his equal in Heinrich Heine (1797-1856), the *enfant terrible* of German romanticism. His first collection of poems, *Das buch dar Leider* (1827) had established Heine's fame. He satirised the political conditions of Germany in his *Deutschland-ein Winter-marchen* (1844). Heine has a claim to greatness which is based on the immensity of his talent. Heine develops his method to high degrees of virtuosity in such volumes as *Atta Troll* (1847) and *Romanzero* (1851). Of all the German poets of this period, only Heine has gained a secure place in the literary consciousness of the world. Compared to him, other poets like Eichendorff, Morike and Annette Von Drosta-Hulshoff are provincial. In a strictly poetic sense, Morike may be one of the finest poets of the period. Nikolas Lenau is another embodiment of romantic poet. His real talent is lyrical, and some of his nature-poems are superb by virtue of their intensity and poignancy.

Early Romantic Period

The great novelist Jane Austen wrote *Sense* and *Sensibility* (1811), *Pride* and *Prejudice* (1813), *Mansfield Park* (1814), *Emma* (1815), *Persuasion* (1817). She observed and described very closely the subtleties of personal relationships, while like Wordsworth and Coleridge she believed to be threatened in a fragmenting society. The debate concerning the nature of society is reflected in the novels of Walter Scott. After his early success as a poet in narrative historical romances as *The Lay of the Last Minstrel* (1805),

Marmion (1908), and *The Lady of the Lake* (1810), he turned to prose and wrote more than 20 novels.

The Romantic emphasis on individualism is reflected in much of the prose of the period. Among the most vigorous and forthright writer is William Hazlitt whose characteristic work is seen in the works like *On the English Poets* (1818), *On the English Comic Writers* (1819) and in the *Spirit of the Age* (1825), a series of valuable portraits of his contemporaries. In the *Essays of Elia* (1823) and *The Last Essays of Elia* (1833), Charles Lamb wrote with apparent artlessness, a carefully managed portrait of himself. Thomas De Quincey produced a colourful account of his early experiences in *Confessions of an English Opium Eater* (1821). Leigh Hunt, expressed his independent journalism by attacking many kinds of prejudice and abuse in his *Examiner* (begun 1808).

Robert Burns stands outside the Romantic Movement, though there are romantic elements in his work. Burns was a poet of the people—both the virtued and the wicked. His songs have both satirical sharpness and lyrical beauty. Another poet who is outside the Romantic movement is William Blake. He lived and died in poverty. His writing consists of poems, largely lyrical, his aphorisms and critical notes in prose are very profound. His creative imagination revived the fundamental religious attitudes. His works look beyond the immediate ages of Reason and Romance.

Scott and **Byron** dominated the Romantic Movement throughout the Western world. Scott is the father of nineteenth century romantic and historical prose fictions. He was described as one of the wonders of the age. In *Ivanhoe* or the *Talisman* he shone forth brilliantly with his breadth and sweep. Byron was a prolific and glorious poet. He worshipped the wild beauty of Nature and man's liberty, for which he fought and died in Greece. His best work, *Don Juan*, is one of the great romantic poems.

Byron was praised for his political radicalism. Yet Byron had no love for democracy, which he once called 'an aristocracy of blackguards.' Byron's satirical poems—*Don Juan, The Age of*

Byron

Bronze and *the Vision of Judgment*—helped to inflame revolutionary sentiments both in England and abroad. It was in Italy, Germany, Poland, Russia and the Balkans that Byron's impact was keenly felt. 'The day will come,' Mazzini wrote in 1835, 'when Democracy will remember all that it owes to Byron.'

Byron was the first English poet to play a leading role in European literature, Walter Scott the second. Through them what Goethe described as 'world literature' became a reality. Their school embraced the whole literary world, introduced new forms and new values. The vogue of Byron was perhaps more feverish, but the influence of Scott was more profound.

Wordsworth, Coleridge and Robert Southey were frequently called the 'Lake Poets'. Wordsworth's poetry is original as he is the supreme poet of passion. Wordsworth is the prophet and high priest of his time. In one of the greatest poems, *Intimations of Immortality*, he suddenly soars out of the dull surroundings. He does not see Nature as God but as the symbol of God. Wordsworth felt that the French Revolution opened a new world. He immortalised that frame of mind in *The Prelude*:

> Bliss was it in that dawn to be alive
> And to be young was very heaven

Coleridge must be considered the first critic in the whole European Age of Romance. The few gems of his poetry are *The Ancient Mariner,*

Kubla Khan and *Christabel.* Coleridge condemned the economic approach to the problem of human

Wordsworth

labour. He attacked the system which considered 'man as things, instruments, machines and property.' In *The Friend* (1809) he declared unequivocally: 'The economists who are willing to sacrifice men to the creation of national wealth are forgetting that even for patriotic purposes no person should be treated as a thing.' The enormities of the French Revolution disillusioned Coleridge which left imprint in the magnificent ode, *Recantation*. A year later he was constrained to observe that 'rulers are much the same in all ages, and under all forms of government; they are as bad as they dare to be.'

Southey was a rigid conservative. He was profoundly disturbed at the seamy side of the Industrial Revolution. His pseudonymous *Letters from England* contains some of the harsh observations on the human aspect of the Industrial Revolution. 'In commerce, even more than in war, both men and beasts are considered mainly as machines, and sacrificed with even less compunction.'

Shelley is one of the supreme poets of and for impetuous and enthusiastic youth. Shelley was profoundly influenced by Godwin's *Inquiry Concerning Political Justice. Queen Mab, The Revolt of Islam* and *Prometheus Unbound* propagate Godwin's ideas; perfectibility of the human race, egalitarianism, and anarchism. Since Shelley rejected an organised religion he declared that the existing system of marriage was hostile to human happiness. He championed the cause of Irish Repeal and Catholic Emancipation and advocated equal rights for women. His strong dislike of cruelty and tyranny inspired the bitter poem *The Mask of Anarchy* (1819). He remains a lyrical genius, a romantic figure of eager revolt and poetry that completely captures the imagination.

John Keats was the youngest of these great Romantic poets, who died in 1821 at the age of twentysix. His letters and poems are of enduring beauty, giving him a place of equality beside Wordsworth, Coleridge, Byron, Shelley. His poetry achieved its own originality through its richness, its unusual evocative quality, undertones and overtones.

England's poetry is next occupied by Tennyson, the Victorian poet Laureate. Tennyson wrote his poems with highly respectable and aesthetically convenient idea of the poet. 'His fire is not of the volcano; it is of the fireplace, and gently warms the surface of the soul.' He has a very fine sense of language and lyrical precision. The *Princess* (1847) and *Enoch Arden* (1864) exhibit the moments of lyrical exaltation. He rises to the standard of poetic seriousness in his confessional poem *In Memoriam* (1850) written on the death of a friend.

Second to Tennyson is Robert Browning, the romantic hero of Wimpole Street. He was a controversial figure. His rhymes are often harsh and crude. His chosen form was the lyrical drama or the 'dramatic monologue'. The best examples are *Paracelsus* (1835), *Pippa Passes* (1841) and the three volumes of *Dramatic Lyric* (1842), *Men and Women* (1855) and *Dramatis Personae* (1864) in which many figures from the Bible and the Italian Renaissance are crowded. By endowing poetic life upon his philosophy in *The Ring and the Book* (1868-69), he exposes the problem of evil.

The most romantic contribution to English poetry is Edward Fitzgerald's The *Rubaiyat of Omar Khayyam* (1869). Fitzgerald might have remained unknown, had he not been discovered by the literary circle around D. G. Rossetti. Because of a few popular poems like *The Blessed Damozel* and the romanticism of his paintings,

Rossetti is too often considered a soft poet. Algernon Charles Swinburne has remained a controversial poet with the pagan sensuality of his rhythms. He seems to have been influenced by Baudelaire, whom he acknowledged as his master.

The American poet and writer Edger Allan Poe might have remained a shadowy figure had he not been transmuted by Baudelaire. It was Poe's insistence upon the need for brevity which endeared him to Baudelaire and many French poets. While Poe enjoyed a limited reputation among his fellow countrymen, he was hailed by the French as an essentially 'pure poet.' 'There are some facts in the physical world which have a really wonderful analogy with others in the world of thought,' Poe wrote. He added to poetic language the dimension which was to be exploited by the Symbolist Movement and such poets as Verlaine, Rimbaud, and Mallarme.

The American Walt Whitman is probably the oddest of all great poets. His form, manner and attitude of mind are fully displayed in his first book *Leaves of Grass* (1855). Whitman's boisterous, vital, lyrical oratory, dedicated to the soul of the people, is a lonely voice amidst multitudes of romantic loneliness.

The most famous poet, Charles Baudelaire, declared that poetry has no other end but itself. His poetic force brings together a classical strength and an ultra-romantic evocative quality. His *Les Fleure du Mal* (1857) are nourished by the finest substances of romantic soil. The poem symbolises superb workmanship as it assimilates both sublimity and degradation, beatitude and anger. The rare combination of aesthetic exquisiteness and spiritual intensity has made Baudelaire preeminent among modern poets.

Rimbaud believed that the poet had to become a *voyant*, a seer. Behind Rimbaud's sensitiveness to his own world, which his poetry reveals, there is something not belonging to that world, but rather our history. Verlaine with his flexible technique, succeeded simply by dropping out what he felt to be superfluous, but Mallarme, the authentic Symbolist, worked laboriously to create a new poetry. Mallarme believed that poetry could be made to behave like music, that words used symbolically could bring the mind into some eternal realm. According to Mallarme, the basic feature of all great poetry is the incommensurable. His poetry owes its attraction to the compression of the idea and the leaps and bounds of the images.

The influence of the French Symbolists was immediate and wide. They were responsible for the sudden rise of Belgian poetry, for Fontainas, Gilkin, Ginaud, Lerberghe, Mockel and Maeterlink. Symbolism makes inroad into German literature through Stefan George and Rilke, English literature through Yeats, Russian literature through Blok and moves on to Latin America. Without this French Movement, modern poetry would have been barren.

The miracle of the Russian novel consists in the fact that in spite of its youth, it not only reaches the heights of the French and English novel, but takes over the lead from them and represents the most progressive literary form of the age. Major Russian writers like Pushkin, Lermontov and Gogol owe little to anybody outside Russia. The Russian writers were explorers and pioneers in literature, doing everything for the first time. A strange fatality pervaded the earliest phase of Russian literature as most of them died young. Pushkin died before he was forty and Lermontov before he was thirty. Griboyedov, the dramatist, was killed when he was thirtyfour. Belinsky, the most influential critic, died in his late thirties. Gogol wrote all his masterpieces in his twenties and died at the age of fortythree. "It is like a hurried but brilliant procession to the graveyard."[1]

Pushkin was a mature artist, influenced early by Voltaire and later by Byron. A great deal of Russian fiction and drama really stems from him. The main achievement of his poetic period, *Eugene Onegin*, with all the variety, the rich atmospheres and verbal felicity of a poem, must be regarded as one of the masterpieces of this whole Romantic Age. Pushkin made a strong appeal in *The Village* (1819) for the abolition of serfdom.

Lermontov's short life was bound up with the Caucasus, a land of enchanting beauty. Caucasus

1. Priestley J. B.: *Literature and the Western Man* (1960), P. 175.

is the background of his famous novel, *A Hero of our Time*, and of his narrative poem *The Demon*. Like his great idol Byron, Lermontov waged a state of war with the debasing Russian society. In his *Ode on the Death of Pushkin* (1837), he showed nothing but utmost contempt to Tsar Nicholas I.

Gogol was Russia's great realist. Gogol was endowed with a rich creative imagination, enabling him to invent and then describe, in a equally exuberant style. His *Dead Souls* (1842) is a work designed after the model of Dante's *Divine Comedy*. His wonderful comedy, *Government Inspector*, is a satire on political corruption. Though Dostoevsky paid Gogol a handsome tribute—'we (Tolstoy, Turgenev, Dostoevsky) have all come out of Gogol's 'overcoat' pocket Gogol has limited influence both within and outside Russia.

Turgenev spent much of his time abroad in Paris. The publication of his famous novel, *Fathers and Sons*, dominated by its nihilist hero, Bazaroz, cost him his popularity with the radicals. From 1862 onwards, Turgenev remained abroad, except for occasional visits. His novels, *Rudin, A Nobleman's Nest, On the Eve, Fathers and Sons*—all published between 1856 and 1862—had a considerable influence on the fiction of western Europe, especially in France and England. In addition to these central novels, the best of his shorter and poetic novels and the exquisite *Sportsman's Notebook* and his play *A Month in the Country* testify that his legacy has been substantial in bulk. Like Chekhov, who probably owes as much to Turgenev as Turgenev does to Pushkin, Turgenev represents the rich Russian character and its tender poetic side.

Dostoevsky was profoundly influenced by the various problems and movements of the time and tormenting questions to which he found no answer. He himself swung widely between the opposites. It is the divided men, torn between the opposites that he creates Ivan Karamazov; and next to them those terrible and prophetic figures, still in the underworld and victims of a moral and spiritual anaesthesia. Concentration camps, torture chambers, violence, cruelty and death must be haunted by the accusing fingers of Dostoevsky.

Dostoevsky

According to Dostoevsky the meaning of existence is not contained in its temporality, but in those high moments in which human souls are stripped bare, in which they feel they are their real unquestionable selves and in which they declare themselves one with their destiny. That there are such moments is the basis of Dostoevsky's tragic optimism of that reconciliation with fate, which the Greeks called 'catharsis' in their tragedies. Dostoevsky represents the highly developed form of the naturalistic novel. He himself declares unequivocally 'I am called a psychologist, that is wrong, I am only a realist on a higher level, in other words, describe all the depths of the human soul.'

Religion becomes a forte in the books—*Crime and Punishment* (1866), *The Idiot* (1868), *The Possessed* (1871-72) and *The Brothers Karamazov.* For him religion is not a religion of transcendental felicity, it is a religion of flesh and blood and ecstasy and suffering. Dostoevsky's Saviour has not come to set man free from pain, but to ennoble it in all its hideousness. There can be no doubt whatever about Dostoevsky's genius. If he can be the cruellest of novelists, he can also be the most compassionate. He is also more than an artist. No intuitions into the maladies of the age, not even those of Neitzsche, were more searching than this.

Count Leo Tolstoy (1828-1910) attained the greatest international reputation of any living man of letters. His world fame was based on two

Count Leo Tolstoy

pieces of fiction—the epic *War and Peace* and the magnificent novel, *Anna Karenina. War and Peace* is an epic with an extra dimension. Behind the manifold characters, as widely different as Natasha, Kutuzov and many others, we are made to feel the presence of a nation, and—behind the nation—Man himself. *Anna Karenina* is no epic, no river of life. It is not another panorama of instinctive life in which the scene seems to vanish in the distance into a misty brightness. By the end of the century he was venerated as no man of letters had been since Goethe. If Dostoevsky's novels have a dramatic structure, then Tolstoy's have an epic. He was not merely a great novelist, but, above all, the social reformer and the founder of a new religion. Tolstoy enjoyed the fame of Voltaire, the popularity of Rousseau, the authority of Goethe and, more than that, he became a legendary figure.

Born of his personal conflicts, Tolstoy decided that he must demonstrate what such a religious basis and framework could be. But a man cannot do this by himself; it must rise from the living depths of the society itself. His diagnosis was right, but he was wrong in thinking he could supply the remedy. Tolstoy's absolute condemnation of civilised society, his intolerance of everything which fell short of his particular ideal, turned even Chekhov against him. Evil may be overcome by saints, but can it be overcome by writers? In trying to do this, he denied the world the creative personality responsible for his two masterpieces. Though his flickering genius appears in some fine peasant tales and in *The Death of Ivan Ilych, The Kreutzer Sonata* and *Resurrection,* the prodigious creator of *War and Peace* and *Anna Karenina* has vanished.

Gustave Flaubert and Emile Zola are the dominating figures in the French fiction. Guy de Maupassant—who made the intelligent short story so popular—owes his superb naturalistic technique to Flaubert. There were some others—notably Barbey d' Aurevilly, perhaps the last of the true Romantics, and Huysmans. There was also Villiers de L'Isla-Adam, who began as a Symbolist poet.

Flaubert showed his dislike to bourgeois class to which he himself belonged. His work may be seen as an oscillation between a direct criticism of this society in *Madame Bovary, L'Education Sentimentale, Bouvard et Pecuchet*, and an escape from it in *Salammbo, La Legende de Saint Julien L'Hospitalier* and *La Temtation de Saint Antoine*. Flaubert was at heart a Romantic, and, indeed, a wildly rebellious Romantic. *Madame Bovary* is his most representative piece of work, his masterpiece. With his interpretation of Romanticism, Flaubert is one of the great revealers of the century, and, therefore, one of the founders of the modern reflexive outlook on life.

Zola believed that the novelist could work in a spirit of scientific determinism. His plan of the huge *Rougon-Macquert* series in twenty volumes was conceived in that spirit. He is a world figure in modern fiction. He is the representative novelist of French naturalism of seventies and eighties. His originality lies in his genuine feeling for people in the mass and his sense of social justice. The *Germinal* is his masterpiece. But by writing a novel on the basis of a scientific experiment, he forgot what literature is. For literature does not put life under a microscope. Literature thinks and feels and imagines its way into life. In his own day he was accused of deliberate sensationalism and pornography, but it was he who finally risked everything by intervening in the Dreyfus affair. In spite of its sombre notes, Zola's work exposes a new hope. He is, as he himself declares, a determinist, but not a fatalist. He considers the real task of the social science to transform and improve the external conditions of human life—to plan society.

Along with the French, German, and Russian Romantics, the English took the lead again. By the end of the 1830s, with *Pickwick Papers* and *Nicholas Nickleby* behind him, **Dickens** was already a great literary figure and read all over Europe. The forties brought Thackeray and the Bronte sisters to join Dickens.

Dickens

The Bronte sisters both died young—Emily at thirty, Charlotte before she was forty. The secret of Charlotte is that she combines an ultra-romanticism of spirit with an essentially feminine realism. In her first novel, *Jane Eyre*, and the three that followed it—*Shirley, Villette* and *The Professor*—she visualises a plain little woman, very different from the ladies of romance who symbolises an inner world of gigantic hopes, fears, passion, tenderness and joy. Emily's solitary masterpiece, *Wuthering Heights*, is somewhat turgid and confused.

William Makepeace Thackeray is one of the best English essayists. His historical novel, *Esmond*, is a remarkable *tour de force*, recreating the age of Queen Anne. His best novel, *Vanity Fair*, is unquestionably a masterpiece. In *Pendennis, The Newcomes, Denis Duval* and other works, we catch occasional glimpses of a great novelist. But his work on the whole is unsatisfactory as he lacks the creative will that lifts an artist from the mundanic world.

Dickens typifies in abundance the creative will in which Thackeray is deficient. He is not only a great prose novelist, closely observing man in society; he is a maker, a dramatic and epic poet of inns and parlours, fog and street lamps. After *David Copperfield*, a semi-autobiographical novel, his novels—*Bleak House, Little Dorrit, Our Mutual Friend*—are deeply concerned with society itself. In fact he is one of vitriolic critics of the age. Though he is never an immaculate artist, his positive qualities are gigantic and rare, those of a great creator. As Santayana wrote: 'I think Dickens is one of the best friends mankind has ever had.' Dickens enjoys a popularity for which there is no parallel since Shakespeare. Dickens is not merely a representative of truth to life, but the artist to whom English literature owes the most important naturalistic achievements. The whole modern English novel derives its art of description, its character drawing, and its mastery of dialogue from him.

During the decade immediately before the Civil War, Dickens' popularity was challenged by new American novelists. One of them, Susan B. Warner writing as 'Elizabeth Wetherell', discovered a vein of sentimental religiosity in *The Wide, Wide World*. Another woman novelist, Harriet Beechar Stowe, had an international success through her *Uncle Tom's Cabin*. She followed it with many other novels but never could repeat her first sensational triumph. Along with these best-selling ladies, there appeared Nathaniel Hawthrone whose *The Scarlet Letter* was the first and best of his novels. Apart from three other novels, Hawthrone produced other volumes of short stories and some *Notebooks*. If Emerson represents the bright side of New England life, Hawthrone offers us the shadowy side.

A great admirer of Hawthrone, Herman Melville wrote his masterpiece *Moby Dick*. But he is not really a novelist, not even his sea stories, powerful *Billy Budd* or romanticised travel books *Typee* and *Omoo*.

It was after the Civil war that America produced her own literature and was no longer dependent on England and Europe. Samuel Langhorne Clemens, better known as Mark Twain, made his own contribution in American writing. He wrote two masterpieces whose heroes are children—*The Adventures of Tom Sawyer* (1876) and *Huckleberry Finn* (1884). Twain was influenced by the vast Mississippi river which flows through *Huckleberry Finn* and brings vitality to the first half of his *Life on the Mississippi.*

Set against the mature social and political consciousness of Stendhal, Balzac and Dickens, the literature of 'Young Germany' is politically immature. If we compare Anthony Trollop's *The Warden* (1855) with Gustav Fraytag's *Soll and Haben* (1855) or Otto Ludwig's *Zwischen Himmol and Erde* (1856), we shall be struck in the Englishman's work by a vitality and spontaneity of imagination which is absent from the German works. On a higher level, Immermann's *Munchhausen* (1838) can hardly bear comparison with the contemporary *Pickwick Papers.*

The major novelists in English, French, Russian represented communities of greater size, wealth and power. It was not until the seventies was there a genuinely unified German community. The novelists of Paris, London and Moscow led the way, while novelists elsewhere were still groping through the spirit of romanticism.

We enter different realm of imagination in the works of Conrad Ferdinand Meyer (1825-98), Gottfried Kellar (1819-90) and Theodor Storm (1817-88). This is known as 'poetic realism' and it maintains and develops an artistic tradition of language. Keller is undoubtedly one of the finest and most original writers in the language. He is also the foremost poet among this group of novelists. Theodor Storm had established his fame by his song-like poetry in the German romantic style. Fontane is concerned with social and psychological problems of marriage and infidelity. In all his better works, *L'Adultera* (1882), *Graf Petofy* (1884), *Stine* (1890), he shows love in conflict with the conventions of a society. It is the dignity of underserved suffering, rather than the actual nature of passion, which concerns Fontane and reflected in his best novel *Effi Briest* (1895). As a realist, Fontane is astonishingly discreet and indirect. Marie Von Ebner-Eschenbach (1830-1916) commands respect as he depicts a finer world with natural nobility.

Naturalism had a decisive effect in Germany upon drama. It fostered a generation of ingenious stage producers like Otto Brahm and Max Reinhardt. The movement attained its height in the person of Gerhart Hauptmann (1862-1946). Fontane, admiring the works of the young Gerhart Hauptmann, points out that 'what seems to the layman a mere recording of life represents a degree of sheer artistry which can scarcely be surpassed.' Hauptmann succeeded in creating moments of pure and deeply moving tragedy out of the rawest material. This is true in *Die Weber* (1892), a play that had no hero and hardly a plot, and yet invades the mind with pity and terror. In a series of naturalist plays, including masterpieces like *Fuhrmann Henschel* (1898) and *Rose Bernd* (1903), Hauptmann bestows the dignity of character even upon small figures. His imagination is further demonstrated by his mixture of poetry and prose in *Henneles Himmalfahrt* (1893). He experimented with poetic drama in *Die Versunkene Glocke* (1896), a composition in which light and darkness, spiritual freedom and demonic bondage oscillate through symbolic representatives.

The Symbolist poetry of George Stefan (1868-1939) was indebted to Mallarme and Baudelaire. He believed that to serve the 'pure spirit' of poetry was to regenerate the nation. Though his poems form a kind of spiritual pilgrimage—beginning with the *Hymnen* (1890), then travellings through the various domains of art (*Algabal*, 1892) and exploring the moods of the soul (*Das Jahr der Seele*, 1877)—they are all short lyrical pieces. In comparison with Stefan's achievement, the works of Detlev Von Liliencron (1844-1909), Richard Dehmel (1863-1920) or Max Dauthendey (1867-1918) are poor. But great poems are rare; George's style stands out with firm distinction, a pattern inspired by his lifelong crusade against decadence.

The poetry of Hugo Von Hofmannsthal (1874-1929) provides a sharp contrast. He displayed a lyrical genuine of the first order in a brief collection of poems. His inspiration is deeply associated with a sense of disintegration, which culminates in the famous 'Letter' (*Ein Brief*, 1902).

Dramatic writing fell far below the level of excellence reached by the novel and by poetry.

Victor Hugo, after having romantically succeeded in *Hernani* and *Ruy Blas,* was eventually driven off the stage when his *Les Burgraves* collapsed in 1843. The Russian drama is mostly represented by non-dramatists—Pushkin and later Tolstoy—while Dostoevsky dominates the Petersburg stage.

The German and Austrian contribution to drama is not negligible. Grillparzer and Hebbel are dramatic poets of high purpose. Although Grillparzer is too pessimistic and too introspective to write great drama, his work is, nevertheless, pervaded by the sense of dramatic greatness. Hebbel attempted to write great poetic drama on the foundation of a comprehensive mythology or metaphysical interpretation of life and the world. Like his contemporary Richard Wagner, Hebbel was obsessed with the 'problem of the drama.'

The second half of the nineteenth century drama is dominated by the Norwegian poet and playwright, **Henrik Ibsen** (1828-1906). Ibsen is the greatest theatrical talent of the century, because

Henrik Ibsen

he gives the most intense dramatic expression to the moral problems of his age. It was his gospel of individualism, his glorification of the sovereign personality that made the deepest impression on the younger generation, and that was not only akin to Nietzsche's ideal of the superman and Bergson's vitalism, but, also found an echo in Shaw's idea of the 'life-force'. He was a great dramatist because he made a technical discovery of the highest importance—a method of construction that had been followed by dramatists since his time. Ibsen realised that all that matters in a drama is the climax, the final flare-up, the end result of entangled life-stories. So he devised for himself what has been called his 'retrospective method.' His *Peer Gynt* (1867), *A Doll's House* (1879) and *Ghosts* (1881) are masterpieces. To Ibsen the crucial issue is to have a moral character, a soul worth saving or damning. The need to be a 'real' person provides the central idea for two of his first plays—*Hedda Gabler* (1890) and *John Gabriel Borkman* (1896). The revolutionary plays, *Pillars of Society* (1877) and *An Enemy of the People* (1882), are concerned with the tragic conflict encountered by an idealistic passion for truth. This theme finds its best expression in *The Wild Duck* (1884). In *Brand* (1866), *The Master Builder* (1892) and *When We Dead Awaken* (1899), Ibsen emphasises the artist's need to be true to his inspiration. He gave to the theatre an appearance of strict realism, giving prose drama depth and penetration, and transforming and enriching the modern playhouse.

No sooner had Ibsen established himself as the master dramatist of the age than another genius arrived from Sweden. He was August Strindberg (1849-1912), Ibsen's twentyone year's junior. Unlike Ibsen, Strindberg's canvas was broad. Apart from plays, he poured out novels, volumes of autobiography, essays and treatises and in Sweden he is regarded as a great all-round man of letters. But he owes his international reputation almost entirely to his plays. In the theatre he is recognised to be one of the rare masters. His characters are immersed in hell, which is 'described with a realism that seems to preclude all thought of metaphors, poetical or otherwise.' So it appears in *The Dance of Death* (1901). *Creditors* presents the most accomplished display of slow spiritual torture in literature. A similar technique is used in *The Father* (1887) where defeat is acknowledged with equanimity. There is no escape for Strindberg's men and women, who are 'bound together by guilt and crime' (*The Ghost Sonata*, 1907). In one of his famous plays, *Miss Julia* (1888), the highly strung, neurotic daughter of a land-owning family succumbs to the valet, where nature is not weakened by any 'superstitions about honour.'

In drama, **Chekhov** (1860-1904), is one of its most original and gifted sons. He is perhaps

Chekhov

the most startlingly original dramatist of the whole age. He was a doctor and a liberal; but he was also an artist of his time as detached as Maupassant. Drama, we are told, is created out of the conflict between two or more leading characters. This central conflict and the familiar stage characters are not to be found in Chekhov. Chekhov's characters are not single-minded and strong-willed; they have rather less determination and direct purpose. They are never moving towards some great thundering clash and climax. Chekhov's characters are filled with the feeling of absolute helplessness and hopelessness. This philosophy of passivity and indolence has considerable formal consequences.

In *The Cherry Orchard,* Chekhov takes more risks of appearing artificial or descending into bathos. In *The Seagull* and *Uncle Vanya* he is sometimes nearly off the tightrope he is walking; and even in *The Three Sisters* there are a few moments of danger. By avoiding tight construction, by keeping his action fluid, he is able to allow his characters to reveal themselves in different ways. He suggests the complexity and richness of life, all its overtones and undertones. Though written in prose, Chekhov's drama is essentially poetic. Each play and even each act of a play has its own rich atmosphere. What is finally communicated to us by his drama is an immense brooding tenderness, unequalled by any other modern dramatist, which never lapses into sentimentality.

The literature of the late nineteenth century shows unmistakable signs of decay. In the style and form, language and ideas of many works of the period there is something affected, artificial, intellectual.

Henry James (1843-1916) holds a pride of place in late-Victorian literature. He came to Europe as an American in search of a tradition. Although he acquired all its late refinements, he never lost his native moral vigour. This rare combination of qualities produced such masterpieces as *The Portrait of a Lady* (1881) and *The Ambassadors* (1903). His tragedies are not of the conventional kind. There is little direct contact with violence, either of action or of passion. The actual subject-matter of *The Wings of the Dove* (1902) and *The Golden Bowl* (1904) amounts to almost no more than an elaborate play of consciousness. The aim of a literary manoeuvre is to redeem the wickedness of the world by sheer beauty of spirit. In *The Spoils of Poynton* (1897) and *What Maisie Knew* (1897), the love of heroines transcends treachery and death. But in the case of the earlier novels like *The American* (1877), *The Princess Casamassima* (1886) and *The Portrait of a Lady* the evil eventually breaks loose into melodrama.

In contradistinction of James, the style of Thomas Hardy (1840-1928) is simple, his setting rural, and his tragedies down to earth. His outstanding gift is a sense of dramatic occasion. He argued that art consisted in a 'disproportioning of reality,' at which he showed his own skill of contriving plots. *A Pair of Blue Eyes* (1873) contains the most fantastic examples and it is the secret of all his best short stories, for example *The Three Strangers* (1888). Hardy thought that the universe was essentially chaotic and senseless, but his imagination spontaneously felt that there was drama and significance in all those extraordinary happenings. What this significance is cannot perhaps be formulated theoretically. There are glimpses of lyrical beauty and idyllic charm in *Under the Greenwood Tree* (1872) and *The Trumpet Major* (1880), of the mystery of myth and the terror of tragedy in the two finest novels, *The Return of the Native* (1870) and *The*

Mayor of Casterbridge (1886), and of heroic strength and eternal folly in *Far from the Madding Crowd* (1874) and *The Woodlanders* (1887). Hardy's poetic vision is marred by prosaic insights which is revealed in his *Wessex Poems* (1898).

George Meredith (1828-1909) established his claim as one of the great novelists in his *Beauchamp's Career* (1876), *The Egoist* (1879), and *Diana of the Crossways* (1885). His novels have an air of unreality about them; but in his big scenes, he is often magnificent—perhaps matchless—in the penetration, fire and wit of his mind, his intellectual high spirits lit by flashes of poetry. In a famous essay, *On the Idea of Comedy* (1877), he explicitly prescribes the 'comic spirit' to encounter the world's errors. Meredith's prose and poetry preach spiritual temperance. Even while disbelieving in any God, Meredith claims that prayer is psychologically beneficial. His style is not only scintilatingly vigorous; but it is also philosophical, epigrammatic, lyrical and it combines comedy, romance, tragedy and satire. Meredith championed the cause of feminine emancipation which is reflected in all his last novels—*One of Our Conquerors* (1891), *Lord Orment and his Amanita* (1894), and *The Amazing Marriage* (1895).

The works of other novelists cannot be ranked as among the national classics. The increasing mass of minor talent is apt to be forgotten—Mark Rutherford (1831-1913) or Ms Humphrey Ward (1851-1920). There are hints of a disillusioned theologian in Samuel Butler (1835-1902) and frustrated scholar in George Gissing (1857-1903). The famous adventure stories of R. L. Stevenson (1850-1914) are like fantasies, and even Joseph Conrad (1857-1924) brings back his tales from remote and secret places. From the bright satire of Butler's *Erewhon* novels (1872 and 1901) to the dark tragedy of Conrad's *Lord Jim* (1900), the reader is confused or unsure about what is true. The truth lies in escape from tyrannical convictions and hypocritical assurance—the theme of Butler's *The Way of all Flesh* (1903).

Mathew Arnold had tried to achieve the revival of faith with the assistance of great literature which John Ruskin strengthened by his rediscovery of painting and architecture and which culminated in the work of Walter Pater (1839-94). His *Studies in the History of the Renaissance* (1873) and the philosophical romance *Marius the Epicurean* (1885) mark the climax of his perfection. His scholarly style is an essay in perfection, striving 'towards the vision—the beatific vision—of our actual experience.'

Echoes of Pater's thought are found in the work of many contemporaries. The extreme realism of ugliness and mediocrity is found in Gissing's *Demos* (1886), *The Nether World* (1889) or *New Grub Street* (1891) which has unexpected kinship with the cult of beauty and brilliance which George Moore (1852-1933) and Oscar Wilde (1854-1900), derive directly from Pater. Moore's *The Confessions of a Young Man* (1888) has a character of self-conscious affectation; he produced a minor scandal by straying into forbidden subjects in *Esther Waters* (1894). Even Wilde's notorious *The Picture of Dorian Gray* (1891) is second-rate fiction, while his most moving prose work *De Profundis* proclaim the virtual renunciation of aesthetic adventure. Wilde's social comedies—*Lady Windermere's Fan* (1892) and *An Ideal Husband* (1894)—are clever jests in a conventional world of make-believes. *The Importance of Being Earnest* (1895) is Wilde's masterpiece.

Henry James is consciously devoted to the art of fiction. It is he who composes a novel as if it were a sonata, organises it as if it were a landscape on canvas. He brings to fiction exquisitely civilised standards—European in their depth of culture, American in their candid purity. Undoubtedly he had a passion for literature and especially for the art of fiction. As he wrote: "The only reason for the existence of a novel is that it does attempt to represent life." Among the catalogue of James' masterpieces are: *What Maisie Knew* (1897), *The Spoils of Poynton* (1897), *The Awkward Age* (1899), *The Sacred Fount* (1901), *The Wings of the Dove* (1902), *The Ambassadors* (1903) and *The Golden Bowl* (1905). He worked wonders, especially during the eighties, when he gave us among other things *The Portraits of a Lady, The Bostonians, The Princess Casamassima.*

John Galsworthy, who won Nobel Prize in Literature in 1932, enjoyed a large international reputation after the war. His *Forsyte Saga* was regarded as a representative portrait of England. He was a creative writer and a crisis in his conjugal life, in 1905, gave his work character and force. Both his first novel, *The Man of Property* and his best play, *The Silver Box,* first appeared in 1906.

A different writer was E. M. Forster whose most ambitious novel, *A Passage to India*, did not appear until 1924. His first novel *Where Angels Fear to Tread* (1905) was followed by *The Longest Journey* (1907), *A Room with a View* (1908), and *Howard's End* (1910). Forster rejected from the first any idea of being a solid chronicler of a society. He works in brilliant flashes, sudden revelation of character, action that is not realistic but symbolic. This creative method probably explains why Forster in his later years abandoned fiction for the essay, which he wrote with unusual charm. Although he may be said to have changed the direction of the English novel, he is never entirely satisfactory. There is an uneasy tremor in his narrative. It is like looking at life through glass that is clear in some places and hazy in others.

The first English writer to be given the Nobel Prize Award in 1907 was Rudyard Kipling. His major works include—*The Second Jungle Book* (1895), *Stalky and Co.* (1899), *Kim* (1901), *Just So Stories* (1902), *They* (1905), *Puck of Pook's Hill* (1906), *The Brushwood Boy* (1907), *and Actions and Reactions* (1907). And though Kipling's reputation suffered a decline in his lifetime, he is now being regarded as a major figure. The secret of Kipling's success is that the artist in him was born in and nourished by his deep attachment to India. His sheer literary ability was astonishing. He was a poet, though he wrote a good deal of journalism turned into verse. The prose of his tales is at once economic and effective though glittering and brash in manner. He remains a melancholy example of a writer who failed to grow in stature. If he could have returned to the fountainhead, India, he might have written more masterpieces. He declares that East and West can never meet. They could have met in him.

The other major British novelist of pre-War period is Conrad, a lone wolf in the English novel tradition. Though he was a Pole, he lived in England and wrote in English. His literary influences were largely French, while in temperament and outlook he is closer to Eastern Europe than to the West. His first novel, *Almayer's Folly,* was published in 1895, and the next thirty years saw, among other works, *An Outcast of the Islands* (1896), *Nigger of the Narcissus* (1897), *Lord Jim* (1900), *Typhoon* (1903), *Nastromo* (1904), *The Secret Agent* (1907), *Under Western Eyes* (1911), *Chance* (1913), *Victory* (1915), *The Shadow Line* (1917), *The Rescue* (1920), *Suspense* (1925). Conrad seldom writes about the domestic and middle-class scenes. He portrays the moments when individuals are tested by circumstances and challenged to survive. The challenge is to develop courage and endurance. The heroic virtues become both the means of victory, and their best reward. He was a pessimist, but he was not an ignoble pessimist, believing that a man by self-mastery should by ready to face the worst.

Hilaire Belloc and G. K. Chesterton were two other personalities in the literary world. Belloc began as a young man of great promise, but after producing some excellent verse and a few satirical novels, books of travel, he wasted his energy in polemics and in histories from the Catholic point of view. Chesterton, an essayist, critic and fantastic story-teller, became a popular figure. Belloc and Chesterton were the dominating figures in Edwardian England and its afterglow until 1914.

H. G. Wells, who died in 1946, belongs as a novelist to the period before the First War. Some of his best science fictions, dates back to the 1890s including his little masterpiece, *The Time Machine* (1895). After the First World War, with his *Outline of History* and similar work, Wells became a popular figure on a world scale. Even before the war, he had declared that he was not a literary man, but a journalist. It was at this time that he began writing novels, of which *The New Machiavelli* is the best example. His earlier novels, outside his science fiction, are of different character. *Kipps and Mr. Polly* were essentially new and modern because they looked at life and contemporary society from the standpoint of a deprived class. *Tono Bungay,* probably his masterpiece, is a sociological fiction. His ample two-volume *Experiment in Autobiography* deserves special mention, for it is in fact a remarkably good account of this whole age, particularly the period up to 1914. He was a writer among writers, and artist among artists: his background, he felt, was science. His scientific training and outlook—coupled with his literary genius—brought a new tone and temper belonging to his own time.

George Bernard Shaw or G.B.S. is one of the master dramatists of the period. Shaw is

George Bernard Shaw

Ibsen's only real disciple and successor—the only one to continue the fight against Romanticism. The unmasking of the romantic hero, the shattering of the belief in the great, is consummated by him. Shaw is at the same time the most progressive and the most modern writer of his generation. The originality and splendid vitality of his drama entitle him to be recognised as the greatest comic dramatist since Moliere. Shaw was a great believer in reason. He pioneered ceaselessly on a wide variety of social topics, as a selection from his titles amply shows: *Plays Pleasant and Unpleasant* (1898), *Three Plays for Puritans* (1900), *Man and Superman* (1903), *Major Barbara* (1905), *The Doctor's Dilemma* (1911), *Pygmalion* (1912), *Androcles and the Lion* (1916), *Heartbreak House* (1919), *Back to Methuselah* (1921), *St. Joan* (1924), *The Apple Cart* (1930), *The Millionairess* (1936). He invented a new comedy, a comedy not of situation and character, but of debate, of intellectual conflict and high spirits. He approached his plays as if they were a kind of opera without music. His dramatic method is far from being subtle. He makes few experiments in form and technique, is not afraid of wildly improbable situations. His range of characters is limited. He is uneasy with life on irrational, instinctive, intuitive levels. But he is inequitable in his own kind of intellectual comedy. The sheer vitality of his drama is demonstrated by the fact that his earliest plays do not yet seem faded and out-moded. G.B.S. of the Theatre, with his wonderful intellectual high spirits, fills our playhouses with delight and laughter, and is alive.

In the beginning of the twentieth century there was the *Jungwien* group, led by Hermann Bahr, who wrote scores of plays, of which one, *The Concert,* was the best of his Viennese comedies. The Spanish dramatists, with Unamuno in their midst and with Jacint Benavante (who received the Nobel Prize in 1922) and Martinez Sierra, translated foreign plays and produced plays, usually with success, outside Spain. Many of the English translations of these dramatists were the work of Harley Granville-Barker who himself was a dramatist and worked in close association with Shaw as a director and actor. He brought to the London stage an intelligence and a sense of society in both its breadth and depth that was keener than Galsworthy's.

In the early twentieth century, the theatre was dominated by Irish dramatists. During the Edwardian years there were the highly poetic plays of Yeats, and the plays of John Millington Synge. Synge's main dramas fall within a very short period: *In the Shadow of the Glen* (1905), *Riders to the Sea* (1905), *Well of the Saints* (1905), *Playboy of the Western World* (1907), *Deirdre of the Sorrows* (1910). They are characterised by a highly stylised rhetoric woven with general tragic music of life. In his plays, Synge brought forth the wildness of nature and the lives of simple people mingled with the inevitability of transience.

Equally Irish was Sean O'Casey, whose most famous dramas are: *Shadow of a Gunman* (1923), *June and the Paycock* (1925) and *The Plough and the Stars* (1926). His plays have more realism than Synge's. He brings into his plays tremendous freshness and vitality—the lives of the poor in the Dublin tenements, the human fickleness and courage, humour and resilience.

Shortly before the First World War, Expressionism arrived. The Expressionist playwrights wanted to bring the drama into line with the whole contemporary movement, to give the drama the breadth of the novel and the subjective depth of poetry and the new fiction. The Expressionists deliberately made their drama more obviously theatrical. During the twenties and thirties of the 20th century, Expressionism appears in various places. But in its first vivacity it was entirely German. The outstanding playwright of the original Berlin group, which included Sarge, Hasenclever, Unruh, Sternheim, Kornfield, Toller, Brecht, was Georg Kaiser. He was a prolific playwright, whose *From Morn to Midnight*, has been accepted as the standard Expressionist play. Bertolt Brecht aroused divided opinion because of his Communist background. But he has created a drama that meets the challenge of the age, because of its broad social basis and significance and its unique mixture of epic and ballad.

The twenty years (1919-1938) between the Wars were crowded with playwrights of talent. Of these, the Swedish Hjalmar Bergman and Par Lagerkvist are good examples, as well as the Norwegians, from Gunnar Heiberg and Hans Kinck to Helge Krog and Nordahl Grieg. During this period the most accomplished Hungarian playwright was Ferenc Molnar.

The period also witnessed the emergence of many figures in the French theatrical scene. The most important figures were Raynal, Pagnol, Romains, Vildrac, Marcel, Crommelynck, Giraudex. But the most outstanding figures who gave prose drama a new subjective depth were Henri Rene Lenormand and Jean Jacques Bernard. Lenormand is chiefly the dramatist of inevitable degeneracy, as in *Les Rates* (produced in English as *Failures*), of a sinister determinism and fatalism, as in his *Time is a Dream*. His central characters are not unreal. The world of Jean Jacques Barnard's drama is not tragic but tenderly wistful and pathetic.

The Italian theatre had, in the 1920s, a number of ingenious and experimental playwrights—Chiarelli, Antonelli, Bontempelli, de Stephani, Rosso de San Secondo and the popular Ugo Betti. But the Italian theater was represented largely by Luigi Pirandello, Nobel Prize winner in 1934. Among his most famous dramas may be mentioned—*Six Characters, Right You are, As You Desire Me*. His drama deserves our attention because it is satisfying in theatrical terms, grapples successfully with all that is solidly objective in stage performance, and yet contrives to reflect the inner bewilderment, the broken vision of our age.

It was not until the 1920s that drama in America caught up the imagination. The most famous dramatist was Elmer Rice, whose *Street Scene* had an international success. Among the lesser celebrities may be mentioned Sidney Howard and Robert Sherwood. But America's leading dramatist was Eugene O'Neill. His earlier plays were oversimplified. But with the passage of time, his tragic vision deepened and his exploration of human failure became more moving. From early plays like *The Emperor Jones* (1921) and *Anna Christie* (1922), his brilliance radiated through *Desire under the Elms* (1924) and the *Great God Brown to Strange Interlude* (1928) and *Mourning Becomes Electra* (1931). His two greatest plays—*The Iceman Cometh* (1946) and *Long Day's Journey into Night*—were discovered after his death. His dogged courage and a dour integrity, a determination to make the theatre obey his will, raise the level of his drama as a whole and to give it a quality of massive endurance.

The 1930s saw the revival of poetic drama. Apart from one or two interesting left wing plays, *The Dog Beneath the Skin* (1935) and *The Ascent of F.6.* (1936) by Auden and Isherwood, and the *Trial of a Judge* (1938) by Stephen Spender, the only major plays to leave indelible impress were T.S. Eliot's *Murder in the Cathedral* (1935) and *The Family Reunion* (1939). The poetic texture in the *Murder in the Cathedral* is immensely rich—which makes it the best Christian play in the English tongue.

In 1939 Christopher Fry wrote *Boy with a Cart*, but neither his later plays nor Eliot's could bring vibrancy in the poetic drama. About two decades were to pass before the rebirth in England of drama with the imaginative intensity of poetry through the works of Beckett and Pinter.

The literary greatness of the late Victorian and the Edwardian periods was usually measured in the novel. The poets were considered insignificant against the backdrop of their great European contemporaries. Though there were some talented English poets, the one that shone forth brilliantly was Thomas Hardy who transformed himself from a great novelist of one century into a great poet of the next. Apart from his early poems, including some fine ones, Hardy's memorable poems began to appear soon after the death of his wife, Emma, in 1912. Poems such as *After a Journey* and *The Shadow on the Stone* express the agony of bereavement in a moving fashion.

The Great War produced some famous poets. While Rupert Brooke celebrated the old romantic concept of patriotism and glory, Wilfred Owen—in *Futility* and other masterpieces—exposed the horrid images of death and violence. Owen's voice is 'the pity of war' which has now become more relevant in the atomic age.

In Europe, the most striking war poet was Guillaume Apollinaire (1880-1918). The other most important British poet of the period was Edward Thomas, a writer of great charm, who wrote vivid images of the fleeting world. Before the war, a minor revolt took place in the realm of poetry. A group of poets, usually referred to as 'Georgians', under Sir Edward Marsh, denounced the more stuffy and didactic aspects of versifying. They valued lyricism, music, and poetic themes and believed that the poet's chief task is to ennoble the human spirit by his creation of beauty. Edward Marsh gathered around him many famous poets of his time, including Walter de la Mare, Edward Thomas, W. H. Davies and D. H. Lawrence.

A group of young poets known as the Imagists challenged the Georgian taste. In a Manifesto in 1913, the Imagists proclaimed that in this materialistic world the poetry must encompass the whole of reality. The credo of the Imagists was that the poet must seek truth even before beauty. So the demand of the Manifesto was for freedom, of style and content. As **T. S. Eliot** observes in his essay on Hamlet, the poet seeks an 'objective correlative' for his experience.

T. S. Eliot

Eliot and Pound were the only distinguished poets associated with the Imagist movement. Pound's *Canzoni* (1911) and subsequent volumes, and Eliot's *Prufrock* (1917) typify Imagism to the highest level. The relevance of Imagism was confirmed by the work of two important novelists—James Joyce and Virginia Woolf.

The period was enriched by Halldor Laxness's modern *Lyrics in Iceland*, Chilean Nobel Prize-winner Gabriela Mistral's poems and Pablo Neruda's strange poetry where French Symbolism and Surrealism are mixed with some earthly feeling. Paul Valery was a key figure in the poetry of this period. He largely created certain ideas about poetry and a general attitude towards the art which influenced later poets. 'We make poetry,' Yeats said, 'out of the quarrel with ourselves.'

Of the three German poets who came out of the Symbolist Movement, only one, Stefan George, belonged to Germany. Hugo von Hofmannsthal, very much a Viennese, had in his ancestry almost every Central European element. The third, Rainer Maria Rilke, was born in Prague. They did much for German literature, but from the standpoint of world literature they are not great poets. The lyrical poetry of Hofmannsthal belongs to his youth until he turned to the theatre. Stefan George is a magnificent poet until he turns almost completely didactic. Here was indeed a masculine force and dignity about this poet. Rilke offers whatever he discovers exploring his inner world to its further recesses. Away from the humdrum world, poetry with its symbols can create a real enduring world. Rilke's *Elegies* contain some magnificent poetry, but it is poetry shining through a crack in the mind of the age. He transformed the German language into an astonishing new poetic instrument and provided a strange disturbing voice.

Symbolism found its way to Russia and suffered a change there. Among the Russians may be mentioned—Balmont, Bryusov, Sologub, Hippius, Annesky, Byely, Ivanov, and the greatest of them, Alexander Blok. The movement may include Boris Pasternak. Blok is generally held to be the greatest Russian poet of the 20th century. He has the instinctive power of creation. He writes under the impulse of overwhelming emotional drives. Blok is much nearer to the old Romantics in spirit but making full use of modern effects. The significant details, of which he is a master, are realistic. And there are prophetic glimpses and warnings of terror and misery to come, as in *A Voice from the Chorus*. His greatest poem, *The Twelve*, centered around the abortive revolution of 1905.

Yeats was also a symbolist poet, and he became not only a great poet but probably the

Yeats

greatest poet of the 20th century. Blok and Rilke had genius but were deficient in character. Yeats had both, to a high degree. He lived much longer and he wrote directly and profoundly out of what he thought and felt at each stage of his life. Once he is past his youth, his poetry becomes vibrant. He created his poetry with an air of direct realism. He believed in poetry and the life of the imagination. His verse is an attempt to reveal what he believes; it is poetry in the service of ideas. In 1937 Yeats published *Lapis Lazuli*. This wonderful poem explores the resilience of man and of art. In the artist's gaiety there is a hope beyond tragedy. But this gaiety is not escapism; it is a supreme conquest transcending the death of a civilisation. He was not a mystic or a seer; he was entirely an artist, committed to the "supreme theme of Art and Song", the life of the imagination, using whatever was supernatural to give depth and illumination to his poetry. Yeats, born in Ireland, left us a kind of poetry which is incomparable in its combination of quantity, range and power.

There are other lesser poets—Bridges, Gerard Manley Hopkins, George Barker, Auden, Day Lewis, Spender, MacNeice, whom Yeats considered more 'modern' than himself. In America, among the crowded personalities, one may refer to Carl Sandburg and Lee Masters, William Carlos Williams, Wallace Stevens, Marianne Moore. However, in this milieu, Robert Frost is widely recognised as a major poet. He is a 'country poet'. Out of this rusticity comes almost everything, that the modern poet is trying to express—bewilderment and horror, wonder and compassion and a tragic sense of life.

The two American poets—Ezra Pound and T.S. Eliot—who left America were destined to leave major influence in the poetry of the 1920s and thirties. Pound's odd combination of learning and wide culture, seriousness and cheerful impudence impressed his fellow-poets. His range is wide, adding economics, history, philosophy to literature and linguistics, to create his own framework. He is capable of compressing a poem which has encouraged an unnecessary obscurity.

T. S. Eliot, in spite of his collaboration with Pound in the beginning, is entirely different. Eliot achieved a highly distinctive verse, low in tone, slow but subtle of movement, at once easy and yet tense, that justifies his claim to be modern. His has been one of the major voices of the age, proclaiming its disgust and despair. A major poet in a bad time should make powerful enemies.

Eliot left despair—if not disgust—behind, passed through the wasteland, but the trumpets—either of battle or victory—never sounded on the other. He turned to drama and there made some experiments. But he lacks the breadth of sympathy, the constant dramatic invention within the main structure, that a drama needs. With his technical mastery, he is the best-remembered poet of the early 1920s.

Eliot's *The Waste Land* is a great masterpiece, a free-verse poem. The poem is essentially an account of modern London. But London related to other great cities, and also to Dante's Hell. The main framework of Eliot's poem is in death-and-resurrection cycles, the ordinary round of months and seasons. The temporal cycle in the poem holds no hope for salvation. The modern world is a scene of staleness, delirium, and broken images. No hope for man is envisaged except through a religious dimension. With hindsight one can read the poem as a movement towards faith. But faith is engulfed in enigma; the positive experience is of sickness in society. But a number of intellectuals appreciated the poem as it found an echo in so many hearts. Fear of the future, and of international chaos, must be one answer. Nevertheless, creative writers tried to find salvation. Some writers, like Eliot himself and, later, Auden, turned to Anglo-Catholicism; some, like Aldous Huxley, Yeats and Lawrence, to a variety of mysticisms and some others to Marxism.

In the thirties, as the storm clouds darkened, a group of young poets became famous. They were W.H. Auden (*Poems* 1930, *The Orators* 1932, *Dance of Death* 1933, *Look Stranger* 1936); Louis MacNeice (*Blind Fireworks* 1929, *Poems* 1935, *Vienna* 1934, *Still Centre* 1939); C. Day Lewis, *Beechen Vigil* 1925, *Country Comets* 1928. *Transitional Poem* 1929, *From Feathers to Iron* 1931, *Magnetic Mountain* 1933, *Time to Dance* 1935, *Overtures to Death* 1928. These 'poets of the 30s' were all very youthful and exuberant with strong social commitment. Spender depicts in a poem the unemployed as the drifting floatsam of society. The Spanish Civil War became the dominating theme of these poets. Auden's *Spain 1937* is the best of several poems written on this war.

These poets of the thirties were exciting and influential rather than outstanding. The poetic aura of Auden and MacNeice is often metrical and verbal. But Dylan Thomas's (*Eighteen Poems*, 1934) mastery over language is more original. The other two poets who achieved great fame at a later time were Robert Graves and Edwin Muir. In America the modern movement was reflected in the works of important poets—Conrad Aiken, Marianne Moore, Wallace Stevens, John Crowe Ranson, Allen Tate, Hart Crane, E. E. Cummings and Richard Eberhart.

Along with the poetry, the novel was holding its sway. D. H. Lawrence died in the thirties. Men need human relationships—especially family relationships—to fulfil themselves, and, in studying these manifestations, Lawrence is at his best. Both through his senses and an intuitive perception he is in direct contact with life—in all its natural manifestations. This gives his fiction a strange quality that many readers find as fascinating as it is original. Like some other writers of his age, Lawrence was violently anti-intellectual. He knew in his heart of hearts that our society was hurtling to disaster, but had not the temperament and tenacity to find out what exactly was wrong. An unsatisfactory novel like *Kangaroo* is a good example of the two opposing strains, the creative poetic and the prophetic-egoistical, at work in him. Apart from the short stories in which he is at his best, his famous novels were *Sons and Lovers* (1913) and *Women in Love* (1920). His most posthumously controversial novel is *Lady Chatterley's Lover* (1928). Lawrence was a messianic writer who became bitterly critical as he judged himself rejected by the world. Towards the end of his life, he became fascinated with death and resurrection and his writings assumed religious overtones of a mystical kind. He is regarded by some as one of the greatest novelists of the age, while others find him unsatisfying and often irritating.

There is the same division of opinion with regard to another English novelist, Virginia Woolf. Although she was herself a perceptive and delightful critic, she was arrogantly narrow in asserting that it is the task of the novelist to record life itself. In her masterpiece *To The Lighthouse* (the next best as pieces of fiction are

Mrs. Dalloway and *Between the Acts*) she is experimental. She is not a major novelist, she has the depth, but her vision is unusually narrow. She also represents the cultivated section of the English upper-middle class.

Aldous Huxley made some experiments in his fiction but his novels are made, not really created. Huxley wrote many novels—*Crome Yellow* (1921), *Antic Hay* (1923), *Point Counter Point* (1928), *Brave New World* (1932), *Eyeless in Gaza* (1936), *After Many a Summer* (1939). In Huxley the satire is pungent bordering on fear. He found salvation, through renunciation of the flesh, in mystical faith. Evelyn Waugh (*Decline and Fall* 1928, *Vile Bodies* 1930, *Black Mischief* 1932, *Handful of Dust* 1934, *Scoop* 1938) is always in love with the world. Waugh strongly influenced a whole generation by creating a new kind of humour; it is hard and coolly impudent but superbly comic. An eccentric often richly rewarding novelist is John Cowper Powys. Among the women novelists who gained wider recognition during the 1930s was probably Elizabath Bowen. In modern British literature, L. H. Myers may be mentioned who is devoted to historical novels.

From the early 1920s the American novel gained prominence. Willa Cather wrote an indifferent war novel that became popular, *One of Ours*. She also wrote *A Lost Lady* and the *The Professor's House*, the novels which are essentially symbolic. Her writing reaches a sober charm hardly found in modern American fiction.

Another famous American novelist was Sinclair Lewis who received the Nobel in 1930. As a writer he was bewildered, confused, and restless who could not identify himself with any kind of life. His masterpiece is *Babbit*, which is something more than a novel, just as *Moby Dick* and *Huckleberry Finn* are. The real Sinclair Lewis, the enduring writer, should not be looked for in *Martin Arrowsmith, Dodsworth, Ann Vickers*, but in *Babbit, Elmer Gantry*, The *Man Who Knew Coolidge* and *It Can't Happen Here*. He is one of those creators who do not make works of art for the limited few, but myths for the multitude. Both Ring Lardner and Sherwood Anderson strongly influenced American writing in the post—First World War period. London opened the way for later sardonic realists. Sherwood Anderson opened a way too, but in a different fashion.

The four representative novelists of the then younger generation were Scott Fitzerald, Ernest Hemingway, William Faulkner and Thomas Wolfe. Among others may be mentioned Dos Passes, a genuine innovator with an appreciation of social forces; John Steinbeck, for his *Grapes of Wrath* and J. G. Cozzens, through his two best novels—*The Just and the Unjust* and *Guard of Honour*. Scott Fitzerald had a natural talent, but was a shockingly divided man. Among his masterpieces may be mentioned *The Great Gatsby, Tender is the Night, The Last Tycoon*. He is fundamentally concerned in his serious work with society itself.

Hemingway's style stems from the art of literature to which he is devoted tenaciously. He became master of the magic style soon to be imitated by others. But he was incapable of any great further effort. His style reaches perfection in *A Farewell to Arms*.

William Faulkner has a love for violent situations. His novels are at once so powerful and so confused. He is one of the best and one of the worst novelists in the world. Critics find meaning, significance, emotional depth, in much of Faulkner that seems to the rest of us merely violent, confused, embittered and cruel.

The then youngest was Thomas Wolfe—born in 1900 and died in 1938. He wrote gigantically but he never learnt how to construct a novel. He is monstrously rhetorical and oratorical. Yet we may discover something infinitely worth saying, once and for all: 'Man was born to live, to suffer, to die, and what befalls him is a tragic lot. There is no denying this in the final end. But we must, dear Fox, deny it all along the way.' Wolfe is one of the most satisfying and rewarding of all the American novelists. He explores the scene with astonishing thoroughness. He is able to give life, down to the last flicker, to an amazing range of scenes. He remains one of the few major young writers of this age, a giant of the morning; and everything about him belongs essentially to an America that is still a giant of the morning.

In the early 1930s Graham Greene received recognition in Europe than most of his English contemporaries. He offered a series of grim entertainments which culminated notably in 1938—*Brighton Rock*. As a novelist, Greene has the rare gift of combining plots with complex moral and religious concern. The quality of compassion in the novels is deepened by the sense of evil.

George Orwell

In temperament and values, **George Orwell** seems the antitheses of Greene, but he produced visions of evil. Like many other twentieth-century figures, Orwell seems oddly contradictory. Yet he produced the *Animal Farm* and *1984*. According to Sir Richard Rees four conflicting strands are visible in Orwell—the rebel, the paternalist, the rationalist, and the romantic. It was in Orwell that a passionate love of justice and a passionate bitterness mingled. The hero of *Keep the Aspidistra Flying* is reminiscent of the 'angry young man' of the 1950s—a man whose social anger turns to bitterness as an 'evil mutinous mood.' However, in the early Orwell, there is clear common sense as well as impassioned honesty. The mood of the 1930s is evoked in Orwell's following novels—*Down and Out in Paris and London* (1933), *Burmese Days* (1934), *A Clergyman's Daughter* (1935), *Keep the Aspidistra Flying* (1936), *The Road to Wigan Pier* (1937), *Homage to Catalonia* (1938), *Coming up for Air* (1939).

The new Dark Age is reflected in other European chronicles—Antonie de Saint Exupery's *Vol de ruit* (1931), Louis Ferdinand Coline's *Voyage au bout de la ruit* (1932), Andre Malraux's *La Condition humaine* (1933) and Christopher Isherwood's *Mr. Norris Changes Trains* (1935) and *Goodbye to Berlin* (1939).

CHAPTER 50

MUSIC

Towards the end of the eighteenth century and the beginning of the nineteenth century, the art of music attained greater freedom and individuality. Symphonies now gave way to the seductive call of Romanticism and the composer became an independent artist. A growing self-consciousness pervaded the composers and many expressed their views on music and aesthetics. Schumann, Berlioz and N. W. Wagner have each left behind extensive critical writings.

The late eighteenth and early nineteenth centuries witnessed the foundation of various concert societies in London, Paris, Vienna, Berlin, Liepzig. Most of the institutions like Royal Philharmonic Society (1813) in London are still in existence today. The leadership of the German-speaking countries in instrumental music is evident by the prominence of Vienna, Berlin and Liepzig.

Haydn's patron was Prince Nicholas Esterhazy who died toward the end of 1790. Esterhazy's son, Prince Anton, had little musical interests and Haydn took full advantage of a new freedom by visiting England in 1791-92 and again in 1794-95. It was in England that Haydn composed his last twelve symphonies and the two great choral works—*The Creation* and *The Seasons*. The character of the tunes made Haydn the most popular instrumental composer of the early nineteenth century. Haydn gained in England a true enthusiasm for Handel's music. Haydn's use of contrasting themes gave his works a plastic clarity. Haydn's influence moulded Mozart's model, which Beethoven followed in all of his nine symphonies.

Vienna was a musical city that enjoyed the patronage of music-loving nobles. Born in Bonn in 1770, Beethoven lived in Vienna from 1792 till his death in 1827. In 1803 the Archduke Rudolph, son of Emperor Leopold II, became a pupil of Beethoven and his patron. Beethoven's earlier compositions reflected the style of his two great predecessors—Haydn and Mozart. By 1800 he had written several piano sonatas, the first two concertos for piano, the six string quartets (Opus 18) and the First Symphony. In 1804 he attained the height of glory in the *Eroica* symphony. This symphony in E-flat begins a new era in the history of symphony as a whole. The magnitude of the symphony exceeds any composed by Haydn or Mozart. *Eroica* is characterised by the propulsive force and rhythmic drive. The impetus is fully evident in the Fifth Symphony, completed in 1808. In Beethoven's Fifth and Seventh symphonies great importance is attached to rhythm. The finale of the Fifth Symphony lacks the melodic beauty of Mozart or Schubert, but it has an immediate appeal owing to its simplicity of expression with strong rhythmic impulses. The finale of the Ninth Symphony proclaims the brotherhood of mankind.

Beethoven sublimated music through his personal emotions. His Fifth Symphony saw the

Beethoven

fury that lay behind the notes. As early as 1798-1800, Beethoven wrote a set of six quartets, Opus 18. In 1806-07 Beethoven wrote Opus 59, a set of three quartets which he dedicated to the Russian ambassador in Vienna, Count Andrey Kryillovich Razumovsky. The Count maintained the celebrated Razumovsky Quartet which later became the Schuppanzig Quartet. The Schuppanzig ensemble set a tradition of Chamber music for public performance.

The last quartets of Beethoven are remarkable for their wide range of expression. *The Alla Danza Tedesca* of Opus 130 is of great simplicity. The same is true of the *Alla Marcia* of Opus 132 which lends to the music an ethereal quality. Beethoven wished to encircle the force of his expression by an ancient and almost impersonal technique of composition. He died in 1827 and Europe had lost the greatest musician of its time.

Beethoven's only opera, *Fidelio*, shares many characteristics with contemporary French operas. *Fidelio* held the operatic stage for a century and a half. By integrating absolute music such as Canon and Sonata form into the framework of the opera as a whole, Beethoven anticipated the future course of music.

Despite the ultimate success of *Fidelio*, the supremacy of Italian and French opera in Vienna remains unchallenged. Italian opera achieved fame under Rossini's (1792-1868) composition of *Tancredi*. He was complimented by Beethoven on his 'excellent opera' (*Il Barbiere*). His chief forte were his infectious melodies, his thorough grasp of the operatic metier and its potentialities and his sense of humour.

Compared with the operatic developments in Italy and France, the German opera evolved slowly. It came into limelight owing to Carl Maria von Weber whose *Der Freischutz* was performed in the Berlin theatre in 1821. Weber's bold imagination—coupled with superior technical musical equipments like clarinets, flutes and horns—captivated the public mind. *Der Freischutz* is a successful romantic opera. In his last opera, *Oberon*, written for London in 1826, Weber carried his Romantic ideas to further heights of glory.

Romantic songs reached their perfection in the person of Viennese school-teacher, **Franz Schubert** (1797-1828). Schubert venerated

Franz Schubert

Goethe's poetry which found expression in some of his songs. At eighteen he composed the *Erlkonig* in 1815. Schubert wrote exquisite songs at a surprisingly early age. But his early symphonies followed the tradition of his predecessors. But between 1820 and his death in 1828, he wrote his significant works. He achieved new colour by restating his melodies, either in a different key or in another scoring.

Hector Berlioz (1803-1860) was a French composer of outstanding virtuosity and the founder of musical romanticism. Berlioz was a link between Beethoven and Wagner, whose opera *Tristan and Isolde* (1859) was strongly influenced by the new world of tonal colour. Berlioz had little influence on opera, the most popular composers being less original minds like Auber and Meyerbeer, the latter finding Paris more congenial than Berlin for musical world. The great Polish pianist and composer Frederick Chopin (1810-49) also made Paris the home of his musical genius. Paris was also the home of Franz Liszt (1811-86), who gave pianoforte lessons and enraptured the audiences with his virtuosity at the keyboard until 1848.

It was during the July Monarchy that Paris became the centre of European ballet, adorned by the great ballerinas Carlotta Grisi, Marie Taglioni and Fanny Elsser. The musical style of the Second

French Empire was that of Offenbach (1819-80). His operettas *Orpheus in the Underworld* (1868). *Fair Helen* (1865) and the *Grand Duchess of Gerolstein* won tremendous applause during the exposition year 1867. The French ballet had a brilliant revival which began with the debut of the enchanting Emma Livry in 1858 and ended with the production of Delibes' *Coppelia* in 1870.

It was in music that Germany most held her own. Richard Wagner, who lived until 1883, represented a peculiarly Germanic revolt against Western traditions. The creative genius of German music showed itself at its best in the persons of Franz Liszt and Johannes Brahms. In opera, Wagner's penchant for the grandiose was carried further by Richard Strauss, whose first operas—*Saloma* (1905) and *Elektra* (1909)—created sensation.

In music France stole a march. There was an impressive galaxy of younger composers in the persons of Massenet and Saint-Saens, Cesar Franck, Gabriel Faure and Claude Debussy. The French music reached a new height in 1902 with the first presentation of Maurice Ravel's *Pavane Pour une enfante defunte* and of Claude Debussy's opera *Pelleas at Melisande* "the summit of musical impressionism, catching every faint nuance of the words always suggesting rather than saying, but always tense and direct and full of throbbing beauty."

Italy bequeathed her operatic tradition with the work of Pietro Mascagni, whose *Cavelleria Rusticana* was first performed in 1890; Ruggiero Leoncavallo, whose *Pagliacci* won acclaim shortly afterwards. But the most towering personality was Giacomo Puccini whose *Manon Lescaut* (1893) and *La Boheme* (1896) and operatic heroines Manon, Mimi, Tosca and Madame Butterfly acquired unprecedented fame. Russia continued the past legacy through the works of Tchaikovsky, Rinski-Korsakov, Rachmaninoff, Scriabin and Glazounov.

Everywhere composers found inspiration in the folklore and in a new national consciousness. In Britain there were Frederick Delius, Edward Elgar, Gustave Holst, and Ralph Vaughan Williams; in Finland Jean Sibelius; in Poland, Jan Paderewski; in Bohemia, Bedrich Smetana and Anton Dvorak; in Hungary, Bela Bartok; in Norway, Greig; in Spain, Manuel de Falla and Enrique Granados. The comic operas of W. S. Gilbert and Arthur Sullivan carved a permanent place in the English life from the last quarter of the nineteenth century.

In the immediate postwar period there emerged in Paris a group of young composers who came to be called 'The Six.' Of these, three eventually attained international fame: the Swiss Arthur Honegger, the Provencal Darius Milhand and, finally, the Parisian Francis Poulenc, the latter known for his songs and his works for piano. John Coeteau, who sponsored 'The Six' wanted to shake off the pervasive influence of modern French music and to introduce a new type of music—brief, sharp and precise. Maurice Ravel tried to keep pace with his juniors. He had met the Russian composer, Igor Stravinsky shortly after 1910, the latter having already established himself in the world of ballet. Along with Ravel, Stravinsky attracted younger talents like Milhand and Poulenc and the Russian exile Sergei Prokofiev. Prokofiev by his *Classical Symphony* (1917) won fame. He was a musical craftsman, whose clarity and simplicity served as a beacon-light to later composers.

In was in Germany and Austria that the great musical revolution took place. This was the invention and systematic development of the twelve-tone scale, by Arnold Schonberg, a contemporary of Ravel. Schonberg inaugurated a new era by substituting twelve-note atonality for the tonal style that had characterised the two greatest centuries of Western music. Schonberg's legacy was carried on by his two pupils who were themselves to become influential composers: Anton Webern and Alban Berg. However, the vast majority of composers continued to work in traditional style. In Germany and Austria, the memory of the old masters was still popular. Richard Strauss was still Germany's best known composer. The majestic symphonies of the Finnish national composer, Jean Sibelius, still lingered on. Italy, with her popular obsession with the Opera, began to take interest in instrumental music in the early twentieth century. The most popular twentieth century Italian composer was

Ottorino Respighi whose *Fountains of Rome* (1917) and *Pines of Rome* (1924) became standard pieces in the symphonic repertory.

The composers whose orchestral music reflected their allegiance to classical forms is represented by Beethoven, Franz Schubert, Robert Schumann, Johannes Brahms and Anton Bruckner. The romantic contingent was centred round Berlioz, Liszt, Gustav Mahler and **Richard Strauss**.

Richard Strauss

Another group, chiefly rationalists, reacting against Germanic domination of instrumental music as well as reflecting the socio-political developments of the era, emerged in Hungary, Poland, Spain and England. The most outstanding of those who sought to reflect rational distinctiveness were the Russian Five—Cesar Cui, Mily Balakirev, Aleksandr Borodin, Modest Mussorgsky and Nikoky Rimsky Korsakov—the Bohemians Bedrich Smetana and Antonin Dvorak, and the Scandinavians Edvard Grieg, Carl Nielsen, and Jean Sibelius.

One of the most popular media of the Romantic era was piano music. Chopin, Schumann, Liszt and Brahms were the major composers of piano music after Beethoven. The solo song with piano accompaniment became popular in Germany, France, and Russia and composers produced a song literature of universal appeal. The most prolific composer was Schubert, who in his short life of 31 wrote more than 600 songs. His chief successors were Karl Loewe, Mendelssohn, Schumann, Brahms, Hugo Wolf and Richard Strauss. The great Viennese tradition of chamber music reached its apogee in the works of Beethoven. Mendelssohn, Schumann, and Brahms.

The last decades of the nineteenth century witnessed the diffusion of Romanticism when significant departures appeared in the works of nationalist composers. The experimental works of Arnold Schoenberg and Igor Stravinsky about 1910 inaugurated a new epoch in music. Schoenberg was the pioneer of the Expressionist movement that resulted in his discarding traditional harmonic concepts of consonance and dissonance. Stravinsky's revolutionary style, variously labelled 'dynamism' 'barbarism', introduced a decade of extreme experimentation.

In contrast with Schoenberg's and Stravinsky's experiments during the second decade of the century, a general return to the aesthetic ideals appeared in 1920. Following the leadership of Stravinsky, Paul Hindemith, Bela Bertok and Sergey Prokofiev, most composers entered a Neo-classical period characterised by restraint of emotional content and a greater attention to craftsmanship. Neo-classicism continued to be the dominant trend throughout the period form 1920 to the Second World War.

CHAPTER 51

ART AND ARCHITECTURE

The Renaissance marked a landmark in the history of architecture. The Renaissance began in Italy where a romantic feeling in architecture existed. Rome and Florence became the centres of Renaissance art. This was followed by a brief period of High Renaissance architecture in Italy (1495-1520) exemplified by the work of Bramante. The largest palace of the High Renaissance is the Palazzo Farnese (1517-89) at Rome. Another charming building of the period is the Villa Farnesina (1509-11) at Rome. From 1520-1600—period of late Renaissance, a new form of style, Mannerism, appeared mainly in Italy. In place of harmony, clarity and repose it was characterised by sophistication, complexity and novelty. Mannerist architects were also interested in ancient classical architecture. The period of free and decorative Mannerism was followed by a more restrained classical architecture perfected by one of the greatest architects of the Renaissance, Andrea Palladio. The most important architect of the period in Rome is Giacomo da Vignola who wrote a treatise *Regola delli cinque ordini d' architettura* (*1562:* Rule of the Five orders of Architecture).

Baroque and Rococo terms are applied by common consent to European art of the period from early seventeenth century to mid-eighteenth century. During the Baroque period (1600-1750), architecture, sculpture and painting were integrated into decorative ensembles. Rococo refined the robust architecture of the seventeenth century to suit elegant eighteenth century tastes. Vivid colours were replaced by pastel shades; diffuse light flooded the building volume and surface relief was replaced by smooth flowing masses. In Rococo architecture, decorative sculpture and painting are inseparable from the structure. The classicism that flourished in the period 1750-1830 is often known as Neo-Classicism. The architects of Neo-Classicism interested themselves as much in the picturesque aspects of nature and objects in nature in rational procedures. Neo-Classicism and Romanticism share the same roots.

The architectural movement commonly associated with Romanticism is the Gothic Revival. The second half of the nineteenth century saw the active and productive period of the Gothic Revival. Its contribution was the encouragement of freedom and honesty of structural arrangement. The Gothic Revival survived into the twentieth century largely for ecclesiastical architecture. The modern movement began in the twentieth century as a reaction against the stylistic pluralism of the twentieth century.

The outstanding artistic achievements of the last quarter of the eighteenth century was Jacques Louis David's *Oath of the Horatii*. The Horatii was described as the most beautiful picture of the century. The work appeared to the contemporary world as the perfect realisation of the classic ideal. In this picture the monumental style dominated French art. Its grave, simplified manner, its extreme clarity of space ended the Rococo taste which had survived so long. David was a great master—'the father of the whole school of painting and sculpture.' His talent is evident in the *St. Roch begging the Virgin to intercede for the Plague-stricken* which clearly point to the influence of Rubens. His merging of scientific realism with baroque principles reaches its climax in the *Dead Marat* of 1793. Under Directorate and Napoleonic patronage, David's work acquired a certain grace and delicacy of contour. David's gifts led to two distinct lines of development in

French painting—classical or romantic, and realist. He is the founder of a school, the authority and extent of which are almost without parallel in the history of art.

David's pupil Antoine-Jean Gros (1771-1835) achieved fame as a painter of Napoleon's campaigns. He was in fact the first to portray war from a humanitarian point of view. Gros, like his master, admired Rubens who influenced the neo-Classic framework of his work.

Paris became the art capital of Europe and took over the role played by Italy since Renaissance in the artistic life of western Europe. In 1793 David founded the "Commune des Arts", a free and democratic artists' association. It was replaced in the next year by the *Societe populaire at republicans des Arts*. In the same year the *Club revolutionaire des Arts* arose to which—amongst others—David, Prudhen, Gerard belonged.

Gros's fellow-pupil Anne-Louis Girodet (1757-1824) adapted the forms of re-classicism to imaginative and legendary subjects. His *Sleep of Endymion* (1792, Louvre) is a unique combination of a classical form and a romantic mood. Girodet's achievements are relegated by the work of a more original artist Pierre-Paul Prud'hon (1758-1823) who studied the paintings of Leonardo, Raphael, Correggio and Pietro de Cortona in Italy. However, he gained little official recognition until the turn of the century. His Italian training enabled him a powerful manipulator of figures in action. His masterpiece is perhaps the *Justice and Divine. Vengence pursuing Crime* in which Prud'hon adapts the biblical theme of Cain and Abel as a basis for secular work. A favourite of the Bonaparte family, Prud'hon paints the portrait of the Empress Josephine (Louvre). It was only after completing the great religious work, the great *Crucifixtion* of 1822, that his career came to a tragic end.

Theodore Gericault (1791-1824) was an innovative artist endowed with creative imagination and the power of his hand. Gros was his real exemplar. Gericault's large *Officer of the Guard* (1812, Louvre) resembles Gros's *Murat on Horseback. The Wounded Cuirassier* (1814, Louvre) takes a personal view of battle. In 1816 he went to Rome and was influenced by Michelangelo, Raphael and Caravaggio. Gericault leapt into fame with his *Raft of the Medusa* (1819). Among his early works are *Marino Falieri*, the *Death of Sardanapalus*, the *Murder of the Bishop of Liege*. In 1820 he came to England and painted dynamic pictures of racing at Epsom and made his lithographs and drawings of life in London.

Eugene Delacroix (1798-1863) was Gericault's spiritual heir. With him French romantic painting reaches some sort of perfection employing Symbolism and abstraction. In Delacroix the conception of art is expressed in the fact that man still stands in the centre of his world. He is in fact and perhaps the only painter since Rubens and the greatest artistic personalities of the Renaissance to combine the highest intellectual culture with the mode of life of a grand seigneur. To Delacroix, Rubens was the Homer of painting and was influenced by his 'verve which is both of the blood and the head.' In 1822 Delacroix produced *Dante and Virzil in the Infernal Regions* which shows unmistakable influence of Rubens and Michelangelo. In his later work, Delacroix shows an understanding of Venetian colouring. Like Gericault, he adopted the new medium of lithography.

Jean-Auguste-Dominque Ingres (1780-1867) a follower of academic painting, developed an unshakeable taste for Raphael. Ingres pursued linear purity with fanatical zeal which is evident in his *Jupiter and Thetis* in 1805. His portrait drawings were excellent, mainly done during his eighteen years stay in Italy. He produced some masterly figure paintings like the Valpincon *Bather* of 1808 and the *Grande Odalisque* of 1814 (Louvre).

The English tradition of portraiture, deriving from Titian and Van Dyck but modified by Naturalism continued unchanged. Most of the artists of repute like William Beachey (1753-1839), John Hoppner (1758-1910), George Romney (1734-98), John Opie (1761-1807) and Sir Henry Raeburn (1756-1823) were first and foremost portrait painters. Joshua Reynold's most gifted successor was Sir Thomas Lawrence (1769-1830) who had made a brilliant debut at the Royal Academy in 1789 with a full-length portrait of Queen Charlotte.

The art of William Blake (1757-1827) portrayed the primary characteristics of Romanticism. Blake produced an encylopaedic system of Symbolism. He derived inspiration from Gothic tomb-sculpture, Michelangelo's frescoes, and contemporary works of Mortimer and Fuseli. These characteristics are reflected in *The Ancient of Days* (1794), *in Pity* and in the *Prophetic Books*. In his later years Blake devoted himself on the subject of man's redemption and of the sacrifice of Christ on the Cross. This can be illustrated by *Albion before the Crucified Christ* and the *Soul embraced by God* (1818) and *Jerusalem*. In 1821 appeared his seventeen wood-engravings for Virgil's *Eclogues* which was to influence the work of Blake's followers—Samuel Palmer, Edward Calvert, and George Richmond.

Joseph Mallord William Turner established with the Royal Academy an Art which defied all canons. He made intense study at the Louvre of Italian masters, especially Titian. His supermacy in English landscape was assured when large sea-pieces appeared between 1801 and 1805. In 1819 Turner visited Italy and Venice became his primary source of material. Many large oils of his 1820s are of Mediterranean subjects. After 1820 Turner ceased to emulate earlier masters and typified the potentialities of fire, air and water, atmospheric conditions, rain, clouds, mountains and waves. Turner fully exploited the anatomy of nature and produced masterpieces from 1830. In the group of seascapes of the 1840s, Turner bases his pictorial effects entirely on atmospheric and colour perspective.

Turner died in 1851 but left a generation of artists who did not regard landscape as an inferior branch of painting. John Constable (1776-1837) made important contribution to romantic art by transforming the familiar by dew or sunlight or cloud-shadow. Influenced by Rubens, his canvases after 1810 became more ambitious in scale and content. While his large canvases are successful, his small sketches are among the most delightful works of the whole century. In Constable, man becomes a thing amongst other things, and is absorbed by his material environment. Hence Constable is the most progressive artist of his time.

The first important German painter of the period, Asmus Jakob Carstens (1754-98) was influenced by the turbulent art of Guilio Romano. Though his forms are in the Neo-Classic mould, he was a forerunner of Romanticism.

Among his followers, Eberhard Wachter (1762-1862) and Gottlieb Schick (1776-1812) imbibed the teaching of David. The portraits of Schick possess something of French breadth and humanity. Joseph Arton Koch (1768-1839) was a leading exponent of landscape in the Neo-Classic manner.

By far the greatest of the German romantic landscape painters was Caspar David Friedrich (1774-1840). His exaggeration of scale and distance was heightened by efforts of light and silhouette to create a sense of stillness and vastness. Friedrich's *Cathedral in the Mountains and Moon Rising over the Sea* reflect his highly individual manner. One of his followers. Johann Christian Dahl (1788-1857), a Norwegian, made important contribution to landscape painting.

The art of Philip Otto Runge (1777-1810), the most ambitious of the German romantics, is suffused with complexity of his pictorial schemes. However, his talent as a master craftsman is evident in his well-known portraits, such as that of his parents and children (1806, Hamburg).

The Spanish Francisco Jose de Goya Lucientes (1746-1828) belongs unquestionably to the first rank among painters. In early years he carried out religious paintings in oil and fresco. From 1775 he worked for seventeen years for the Royal tapestry workshops. In 1778 he discovered the art of Velazquez which contributed greatly to the directness and simplicity of his portraits. By 1780 he was one of the king's painters. All his portraits display a universality and simplicity. In his later years he began to paint subjects in which fantasy and invention were given free play.

Among the Neo-Classic sculptors John Flaxman (1755-1826) was known in England for his exquisitely-contoured relief and soft modelling. Antonio Canova (1757-1822) made large figure sculptures of the leaders of Napoleonic Europe. Bertel Thorwaldsen (1770-1844) failed to achieve lasting influence on European art. His figures betray a rather superficial aspect of the romanticism of their age.

A great dramatic force tempered by a new Realism in European sculpture overtook France.

Theodore Gericault was the founder of this school. FranÇois Rude (1804-1855) executed the splendid relief of the *Departure of 1792* on the Arc de Triomphe in Paris. Antoine-Louis Barye (1796-1875) produced his masterly bronze animal groups. David d'Angers (1788-1856) and Jean-Jacques Pradier (1790-1852) were the most successful Romantic sculptors.

In the history of architecture a radical change took place in the structure of the building. The finest buildings of the period include Soane's Bank of England and in France the Bourse.

In France an interest in structural engineering was evident. The *Corps des Ponte at Chaussees* and its school founded in 1750 were haven for the architects. Abbe Laugier urges the reduction of architectural elements. The theorists Algarotti and Milizia adopted a similar rationalism, and several architects adopted these principles with main thrust on a scientific study of structures and materials. The famous among these were J. R. Perronet (1708-94) and J. G. Soufflot (1713-80), one of the first students of Gothic structural techniques. The great theorists Rondelet (1743-1829) and Durand (1760-1834) are the heirs of these pioneers.

The beginning of the French Revolution witnessed the designs of C. L. Ledoux (1736-1806) and E. L. Boullee (1728-99). Ledoux who had built thirtyfive gatehouses round Paris, had shown a mastery both of pure form and Neo-Classicism. Boullee's plans for a museum and amphitheatre anticipate the mass scale of nineteenth century public architecture. Boullee used every device to enhance the scale of his works.

Napoleon emphasised the importance of architecture and undertook gigantic programmes of public works, roads, bridges, quays and markets. The two men who shared his patronage were Pierre-Francois Leonard Fontaine (1762-1853) and Charles Percier (1764-1838). Percier and Fontaine showed their brilliance in the completion of the Louvre and in the highly-wrought Arc de Triomphe du Carrousel. Fontaine achieved his masterpiece in the Chapelle Expiatoire (1816-21).

Francois Joseph Belanger (1745-1818) in 1779 designed the miniature palace of Bagatelle as well as many other buildings. His style shows an indication of the swift association by French architects of current technology. The Bourse was completed by Alexander-Theodore Brongniart in 1826. The Church of Madeleine, begun in 1764, was redesigned at Napoleon's wish by Pierre-Alexander Vignon. This gigantic building, with its Corinthian style, was finally consecrated in 1842. Church-building was resumed at the Restoration, the most outstanding works being the Chapelle Expiatoire and the Church of Notre Dame de Lorette (1823-36) by Hippolyts Lobas.

The greatest architects of the post-Napoleonic period were Jacques Hittorf and Henri Labrouste. The works of P. M. Letarouilly (1795-1855), a pupil of Percier, mark a revival of interest in the architecture of the High Renaissance.

While French architects received active patronage from the State, their counterparts in England derived support from landlords and speculators. The English architects owed much to the theorists of the so-called 'picturesque', among them Richard Payne Knight and Uvadale Price. Their views were given shape by Humphrey Repton (1752-1812) who became associated with another architect John Nash (1752-1835). Nash used Palladian elements in his individual buildings. Repton favoured elegant informality, broken skylines and curving paths. Nash at first designed cottages and ancillary buildings. Before 1800 he worked for the Prince of Wales and the Court. But his real talent was revealed in the layout of Regent's Park and its magnificent links with Carlton House and St. James's. He succeeded in imposing on London an urban scheme worth comparing with those of Napoleon I. This was achieved in the face of a hostile Parliament. Nash's later additions included Carlton House Terrace, Trafalger Square, the Haymarket Theatre, the first scheme for Buckingham Palace, the new British Museum, and the National Gallery.

Sir John Soane (1753-1837), the contemporary of Nash, is remembered for his enclosed space of labyrinthine subtlety. Soane is distinguished by severe modelling of internal space. He was one of the few Romantic architects of high rank. Soane's originality is revealed in the private house and museum which started at Lincoln's Inn Fields in 1812.

Nash and Soane are by far the most important personalities in English architecture. Gothic architecture had also developed whose best manifestations are probably the churches of St. Mary, Bathwick, St. Luke, and Chelsea.

Greek styles found support in Scotland and its protagonists were A. Elliot, T. Hamilton and, later, W. H. Mayfair. St. Pancreas Church in England was its best product. Its major practitioners were William Wilkins (1778-1839) and Robert Smirke (1781-1867). Buildings like Wilkin's National Gallery and Smirks's General Post Office (1824-29) and the gigantic scale of Smirks's British Museum (1823-47), are new in function.

In the arts of architecture and painting England was ahead at least until the closing years of the eighteenth century. In the more intimate arts of landscape, portrait and genre painting, England led the way. From 1760, when Reynolds and Gainsborough were nature artists, to 1800, when Crome, Girtin, Turner and Constable began to work, England's chief contributions were to portrait and landscape painting. The English portrait painters gave up the grand formality of French and Italian style and replaced it by the free asymmetrical layouts. Their freedom and their naturalness impressed the Continent enormously.

In the field of architecture, English leadership appears again. Variety of style or a 'Carnival of Architecture' is the distinguishing feature of architecture for the whole of the nineteenth century. England took the lead in the wide range of public and private buildings as well as Church buildings owing to her great prosperity. The most important building of the period is the Crystal Palace, designed by Joseph Paxton (1801-65). The use of iron and glass opened a new style in architecture. The celebrated architect of the period, Sir George Gilbert Scott (1811-78), wrote that this modern metallic construction 'opens out a perfectly new field for architectural development.'

'Ornamentation is the principal part of architecture' observed Ruskin. In Scott's words, the general principle of architecture was to decorate construction. Up to 1830, churches were mostly Classical but Gothic was also present. The same two styles were evident in private houses. The new Houses of Parliament were evidently Gothic. This style was strengthened by the theories of A. W. N. Pugin (1812-52), and popular theories of John Ruskin (1819-1900). Apart from the Gothic and the Elizabethan, another style—the Italian Palatial—began to flourish. It was first established by Charles Barry (1795-1860), the architect of the Houses of Parliament. For private houses besides Gothic, Elizabethan and Jacobean were highly popular as well as a debased Italian style.

In the nineteenth century architecture, eclecticism is a principle of the highest value. Ruskin formulated the same thought in his inimitable works: 'We want no style of architecture... The forms of architecture already known are good enough for us, and far better than any of us... A man who has the gift, will take up any style that is going.' Ruskin was the first person in England to emphasise the fact that art is a public concern and its cultivation one of the most important tasks of the state. He was the first to proclaim the gospel that art is not the privilege of artists and the educated classes, but is part of every man's inheritance.

The architectural development in Great Britain between 1830 and 1870 is more or less similar as has been found in France, Germany, Italy, the Netherlands and the other European countries. Everywhere, including Russia, the 1830s witnessed the Neo-Greek style in the building activities. The Moscow Gate (1833-38) at St. Petersburg (later Leningrad), by Vassill Petrovich Stasso (1769-1849), is the finest example.

Gothic, on the other hand, was more diversified and won greater recognition. England and Germany were in the vanguard of this style. In Germany, Goethe was the first to appreciate its true greatness. The Romantics, Schlegal and others followed suit. Karl Friedwich Schinkel (1781-1841), the greatest German architect of the first quarter of the nineteenth century, was a follower of the Gothic style. In 1840 the *Domverien* was founded at Cologne to complete the gigantic fragment of the cathedral. From 1842 and 1880 the huge building rose above the roofs of the medieval city.

Gothic style had a competitor, called the Roundarched Style—a style composed of the Early Christian and the Italian Romanesque. It was established by Schinkel and his successor Persius (1805-45) in Prussia and by Gartner (1792-1842) and others in Munich. It was more suitable in the secular field. But most of the public buildings preferred a Gothic style, like the town-halls of Vienna (1872) and of Munich (1874) and the Houses of Parliament at Budapest (1885-1902).

Anglo-German passion for Neo-Gothic was peculiarly absent in Italy. Though France was not enamoured of the Gothic revival, yet the latter survived. Henri Labrouste (1801-75) built the Library of Ste Genevieve (1844-50) and then the Bibliotheque Nationale (1868) on Gothic principle.

In America most large scale public buildings was Neo-Classical—like state Capitals everywhere and the administrative buildings at Washington. The leading churches, on the other hand, like Holy Trinity, New York, by Richard Upjohn (1802-1879) and St. Patrick's Cathedral, New York, by James Renwick (1792-1863), are Gothic.

Apart from the Classical and the Gothic phases there was added the Italian High Renaissance and the Elizabethan-Jacobean which was then called the Native Renaissance. It began in England and France and spread to Germany. The highwater marks of this Neo Renaissance are the works of Gottfried Semper (1803-79) at Dresden, the first Opera House of 1838-41, and the State Gallery of 1847. In France the extension to the Paris Town Hall began in 1836. But far more spectacular was the extension of the Louvre begun in 1852 by L. Visconti (1791-1853) and continued by H. M. Lefuel (1810-81). Other countries tended to revert to their own forms of Renaissance. In Russia a growing Byzantine revival was noticeable. Showiness and pomposity began to adorn the more freely classical designs from the middle of the nineteenth century. In America the Capital at Washington was completed by Thomas U. Walter (1804-87) between 1855 and 1865 with a huge dome and extension colonnades.

Nineteenth century architecture was entirely a matter of facades. But the whole period was very poor in sculpture and rich in painting. There are names of sculptors to remember. In England Alfred Stevens (1817-75), Thomas Woolner (1825-92), Alexander Munro (1825-71) were most popular. John Ball (1811-95) and J. H. Foley (1816-74) had their share in the decoration of the Albert Memorial. In Germany the works of Ernst Rietschel (1804-61) and August Kiss (1802-65) are worth mentioning, the latter's *Amazon* being regarded as 'the noblest work of art now existing.' The French contribution is aesthetically important with Francois Rude's (1784-1855) dramatic groups, Louis Barye's (1796-1875) animals and the lively and graceful Neo-Rococo nudes of J. B. Carpeaux (1827-75).

During the nineteenth century the French painting is undoubtedly the most important in Europe. Jacques Louis David, the exponent of classical painting, who died in 1825, had painted portraits of martyrs of the Revolution, e.g. *Marat assassinated in his Bath*. He voted for the abolition of the Academie de Peinture at de Sculpture and extolled Napoleon in vast compositions. With the Restoration, the academy was revived as the Academie des Beaux Arts, a part of the Institut de France. The leading personality in the academy was Jean Auguste-Dominique Ingres (1780-1867) who was an admirer of classical subject.

Realism is the hallmark of the mid-nineteenth century. In French painting Realism appears in various hues—in Paul Gavarni's (1804-66) lithographs of Parisian life, in Honore Daumier's (1808-74) political and social caricatures and vivid oil sketches, in J. L. E. Meissonnier's (1815-91) painting of contemporary battle scenes, and in early landscapes of Corot. The untutored artists of the nineteenth century, Camille Corot (1796-1875), who struggled with nature quite alone, painted Italian landscapes with all their freshness and spontaneity. Baudelaire, the most sensitive art critic, places Corot 'at the head of the modern school.'

Theodore Rousseau (1812-67), a great landscape painter, breaks new ground. More important is Jean-Francois Millet (1814-75) who discovered the farmer and the farm labourer of the nineteenth century. He monumentalised his subjects. Henceforth realism in art might easily mingle with socialism. Such was the case of Gustave Courbet (1819-77) who was proud of being 'without ideals and without religion.' He was robust, self-confident and gross. His work of early maturity is *Stonebreakers* about which he wrote: 'I have invented nothing. I saw the wretched people in this picture everyday as I went on my walks.' Courbet revealed the animal nature of man in the *Bathers, Girls on the Banks of the Seine*, the *Hammock*. The brutal vigour of Courbet's paint enabled him to create some of the most wonderful landscapes and seascapes of the nineteenth century.

The Industrial Revolution and the age of the railways have left little impact on contemporary painting. Turner's *Rain, Steam and Speed*, the *Great Western Railway* of 1844, Karl Blechen's (1798-1845) *Rolling Mill* and of Adolf Menzel's (1813-1900) *Berlin-Potsdam Railway* of 1847 are more or less an atmospheric and not a social study.

Menzel was a man of brilliant talent and was influenced by pre-Impressionism. His landscapes near Berlin, or a corner of a church with the pastor in the pulpit, are brilliant specimens. He also worked meticulously on a series of wood engravings to illustrate Krugler's *Life of Frederick the Great*. He also embarked on some oil paintings of subjects from the life of the King with a blend of realism and historicism. In his later years Menzel adopted the same technique while depicting scenes from contemporary society. His *The Supper at the Imperial Palace* of 1878 and the *Piazza d'Erbe at Verona* of 1884 are always entertaining.

Menzel's English counterpart, William P. Frith (1819-1901) is famous all over Europe from his *Ramsgate Sanda* of 1854, *Derby Day* of 1858 and *Paddington Station* of 1862.

In Belgium, Antwerp had become a centre of academic art in Europe. Here a kind of melodramatic history painting was developed in the hands of Wappers (1803-74), Gallait (1810-67) and de Keyser (1813-87).

Ford Madox Brown (1821-93), who had studied at Antwerp, Paris and Rome, produced in 1847 his painting *Chaucer at the Court of Edward III*. The picture is entirely pre-Raphaelite in style and painted several months before the formation of the Brotherhood. Its founder—chiefly Rossetti, Holman, Hunt and Millais—were all younger than Brown. The aims of the Brotherhood are enunciated in some wise counsels: 'Without the pure heart nothing can be done worthy of us'; 'exaggerated action, false sentiment, voluptuousness, poverty of invention' must be avoided and 'an entire adherence to the simplicity of nature' is to be aimed at. Madox remained faithful to these principles to the end whether he painted Wyclif or Cordelia or green landscape. Among his pictures may be mentioned *The Last of England*—depicting the departure of emigrants for Australia—and *Work* in 1852 and *John Dalton collecting Marsh-gas*. *Work* remains the most important document of social reform in European painting.

Among the pre-Raphaelites, Holman Hunt (1827-1910), Dante Gabriel Rossetti (1828-82) and John Everatt Millais (1829-96) are the most important figures. Rossetti's colours are hotter and richer but equally repulsive. Millais is a painter who is oscillated between the worlds of conscientious art and social success.

The English painter appealed to sentiment, the French to the senses. Cabanel (1823-89) and Bouguereau (1825-1905) produced seductive nudes. Manet's *Olympia* in 1865 evoked strident press comments—'a deliberate manifestation of inconceivable vulgarity,' 'This Olympia, a kind of female gorilla', 'This yellow-bellied odalisk'. Cabanel's *Birth of Venus,* which appeared in 1863 was the sensation of the salon.

The art of Impressionism—suggesting that all phenomena are regarded purely as they affect the eye—is decidedly of the late nineteenth century. While Naturalism marked an increase in the elements of the composition, the Impressionistic method, on the other hand, involves a series of reductions, a system of restrictions and simplifications. A turn towards refinement and aesthetic aspects was given by William Morris and Norman Shaw of England. Morris's style developed when he designed the dining room of 1867 for Victoria and Albert Museum. Norman Shaw's mature style is reflected in the New Zealand Chambers in Leadenhall Street in London. In 1875, at Bedford Park near London, the first of all garden suburbs was built. In 1877 William Morris compared the London of the Middle Ages with its 'pretty, carefully whitened houses' with the London of his day of 'hideous hovels, big, middle-sized and little.' Morris defines art as 'man's expression of his joy in labour'. Its real value lies in the creative process.

Impressionism usually starts with Edouard Manet (1832-83). Manet painted with full aesthetic detachment. Manet called Velasquez 'the painter of painters' when he visited Spain in 1865. Manet became the subject of hostile criticism. Rossetti called his art 'Putrescence', Jules Claretie 'jokes or parodies'. Nevertheless, the young Impressionists like Edgar Degas (1834-1917), Claude Monet (1840-1926) and Auguste Renoir (1840-1919), Camille Pissarro (1830-1903) and Alfred Sisley (1839-99) began to rally round him. Most of them were landscape painters. 'Impression' is rendering of what meets the eye and the everyday subject, whether landscape or still-life or portrait or genre.

The Impressionists were not revolutionaries but their technique opened a new vista. They stand at the end of a golden age of painting and were influenced by their ancestors like Titian, Velasquez, Rembrandt, Goya and Constable. The skill of the Impressionists is breathtaking and the pleasure is infectious. Monet observed that he could wish 'he had been born blind and then suddenly regained sight so that he could paint what he saw without knowing what the objects were.'

Impressionism in the end spread to all countries. Walter Sickert (1860-1942) of England, Max Liebermann (1847-1935), Giuseppe de Nittis (1846-84) of Italy became famous Impressionists. Among the Americans, James McN Whistler (1834-1904) settled in London in 1859. His *At the Piano in 1859,* his *White Girl* of 1862 and his *Valpariso Harbour* of 1866 strike one as impressionist. But Whistler contradicts the doctrine of the Impressionists by calling his landscape not Impressions but Harmonies, Symphonies or Nocturnes—Symphony in grey and green, Nocturne in grey and gold, and so on. As Whistler said: 'painting is the poetry of sight, as music is the poetry of sound.'

The Impressionists had no taste in their own houses. Whistler's house, the White House in Tite Street, Chelsea, designed by his friend Godwin (1833-86) in 1878, was a challenge to the historicism of nineteenth century architecture. Whistler was fascinated by Japanese art which formed the focal point of the celebrated Peacock Room in 1877. Godwin also looked to Japan for pure, clear colours and delicacy of compositions. In the field of decorative arts, Whistler and Godwin turns from refined Realism to refined decoration and from the gloom of Victorian furnishing to the light colours of the post-Victorian style.

Decorative arts found an eloquent champion in the person of William Morris (1834-96). Influenced by the pre-Raphaelites and Ruskin, the latter preaching craftsmanship and social reform, Morris added a robust aggressiveness and an artistic genius. Morris formulated his theory of artistic and social reform and thus achieved universal fame. Morris believed that every artist had been a craftsman and every craftsman an artist. 'Art is the expression by man of his pleasure in labour.'

Morris was of course a designer and made socialism his creed. 'I do not want art for a few,' he observed. Art in the end, he believed, was both work done as 'a happiness to the maker and the user' and work done 'by the people, for the people.'

Philip Webb (1831-1915) was one of the two most important English architects of his generation. Webb did not build much, his Red House being the most important one. Richard Norman Shaw (1813-1912), who had a livelier imagination, built houses in the 1870s, mostly in Hampstead and Chelssa, with motifs from the Dutch and English elegantly mixed. This style was known by the name Queen Anne. The style was a domestic architecture of a refinement in full contrast to the grossness of the High Victorian decades.

The 1870s must be regarded as the centrepiece of the Domestic Revival, as it is highlighted by Impressionism. Norman Shaw's New Zealand Chambers, Royal Geographical Society near the Albert Hall, Swan House, Chelsea—are among the best examples. He designed the garden suburbs in 1875 for Bedford Park, Turnham Green, London.

Architecture outside Britain before the turn of the century was not as rich as had been witnessed with the Domestic Revival in Britain. It is mostly Neo-Baroque, whether one goes to Rome or to Berlin. Only America took the lead. The American houses of the 1880s by Henry Hobson Richardson (1838-86) and Stanford White (1853-1906) enriched Western art. Even in official architecture the United States assumed a distinction by imitating Italian Renaissance and a classical Re-Revival which was reflected in Public Library, Boston (1888-92) and Pennsylvania Station, New York (1906-10).

As against Impressionism, a noble classicism appears in France in the cool grey murals of Pierre Puvis de Chavannes (1824-98) and culminates in Germany in the mysterious, sombre paintings of Hans Von Mareas (1837-87). In France Georges Seurat (1859-91) established his position by his system of colouration instead of his composition. Seurat's was a clear logical mind and his converts were Paul Signac (1863-1935) and some Frenchmen and Belgians including Henri Van de Velde. Signac wrote in 1887: 'Our formula is certain and demonstrable, our paintings are logical, and no longer done haphazardly.'

Paul Cezanne

This group, known as Neo-Impressionists, was so obsessed with the science of painting that they took an interest in rules of composition, direction of lines and their emotional meanings.

If Seurat was a master of stylisation forcing nature into elementary patterns, he must also be regarded as a complementary figure to **Paul Cezanne** (1839-1906). Despite his simplification of the 'motif', Cezanne never lost sight of nature. Cezanne emphasised that for the painter all drawings is colour and all modelling is colour. Henceforth all his landscapes, still-lives and portraits are suffered with a calm, reposeful nobility.

Emile Bernard (1868-1941), a disciple of Gauguin, came into limelight with a few religious paintings and with work in the decorative arts. Bernard's pictures focussing on subject-matter of emotional value are of great significance. In Gauguin's own religious pictures, the *Jacob wrestling with the Angel,* the *Yellow Christ* and the *Deposition*, the intensity of form and colour are exquisitely blended. Gauguin's world has a greater weight and nobility with direct emotional appeal.

While **Paul Gauguin** toyed only with Christian themes, **Vincent Van Gogh** (1853-90) was intensely religious and essentially Christian. Influenced by the Impressionists in Paris in 1868,

Paul Gauguin

Van Gogh found warm interest in the Neo-Impressionists and Japan as well. He remarked truly: 'All my works is in a way founded on Japanese art.' He worked doggedly with a 'terrible lucidity,' 'wrung with enthusiasm ... like a Greek oracle on the tripod.' Van Gogh painted the landscapes that surrounded him with the burning sense of religious mission. He wanted to represent ordinary men and women 'with that something of the eternal halo.' **Vincent Van Gogh** was a true Symbolist. Whatever he painted has a meaning beyond itself.

But while his portraits aim at peace, his mature landscapes are turbulent throughout. Nature to Van Gogh was not serene, it was chaos. As he observed he wanted 'to exaggerate the essential.'

Vincent Van Gogh

In the later 1880s there are two principal aspects of the change: from realism to a new faith in subject-matter and expression and to a new faith in decoration. Mystical subjects and disembodied swaying figures appear in the paintings of the Dutchman Jan Toorop (1859-1928); sharply drawn, more realistic figures in Ferdinand Hodler's (1853-1918) large allegorical panels, and subjects of elementary passion in Edward Munch's paintings and lithographs.

The most interesting movement in purely decorative art of the last decade of the nineteenth century is the movement known in English and French as *Art Nouveau*. Britain was pioneer in the field. Arthur H. Mackmurdo's (1851-1942) *Wren's City Churches* is internationally recognised as the first work in the Art Nouveau style. Another striking example is the bronze sculpture and decoration of Albert Gilbert (1854-1934), best known as the sculpture of the Eros foundation in Piccadilly Circus (1887-93). Art Nouveau decoration can indeed be vegetal or abstract. The former is seen especially in the glass of Emile Galle (1846-1904), the latter in Van de Valde, the Belgian architect Victor Horta (1861-1946), the French architect Hector Guimard (1867-1942) and the great Scotsman Charles Rennie Mackintosh (1868-1928).

Art Nouveau is strongest in the graphic arts. The best contribution was made by Henri de Toulouse-Lautrec (1864-1901) and the Beggarstaff Brothers (Sir William Nicholson, 1872-1949 and James Pryde (1866-1941).

Mackintosh epitomised the most brilliant of all Art Nouveau inventors. Between 1895 and 1900 Mackintosh and a number of others made Glasgow one of the centers of European art. The Glasgow school worked in wood, in glass, in metal. Art Nouveau glass outside Britain is best known in the person of the American Louis C. Tiffany (1848-1933).

The credit of having applied Art Nouveau in architecture goes to an architect, Antoni Gaudi (1852-1926), who lived at Barcelona. In its re-establishment of originality, Art Nouveau heralds the twentieth century. But the very radicalism of Art Nouveau was the cause of its decline. It happened in Viennese Art Nouveau, and the outcome was the strictly cubic style of the early twentieth century. It also happened in Berlin in the weightier style of Peter Behrens, an industrial designer.

The commercial architecture of Chicago is the most interesting event of the 1880s and the 1890s. The architect who handled it with the greatest aesthetic mastery was Louis Sullivan (1856-1924). Because of the high prices of the ground, America took recourse to skyscrapers. It was at first simply a high masonry building, but in 1884, at Chicago, iron frame construction was applied along with glass and other light material in the interstices. As masters of iron and glass European engineers were preeminent. The Crystal Palace had been built in 1851, and the train-shed at St. Pancreas Station in London in 1863-65. It was outdone by the Galerie des Machines of the International Exhibition in Paris in 1889 and the **Eiffel Tower**—the then highest building ever created by man, by Gustave Eiffel.

Eiffel Tower

In England, Peter Ellis designed Oriel Chambers at Liverpool in 1864 in which iron and glass play a prominent part. But the technical possibilities of this new method found their champion in the person of Sullivan. His Wainwright Building at St. Louis of 1890-1 is the best specimen. Though not strictly averse to ornamentation, Sullivan recommended his contemporaries to 'refrain entirely from the use of ornament for a period of years in order that our thought might concentrate acutely upon the production of buildings comely in the nude.'

The great reactionary movement of the century in the realm of art is a rejection of Impressionism. Cubism, Futurism, Expressionism, Dadaism and Surrealism turn away from nature-bound and reality—affirming Impressionism. The aversion to the sensualism of the older art, the desire to destroy its illusions, goes so far that artists now refuse to use even its means of expression and prefer to create an artificial language of their own.

The first half of the twentieth century saw the creation of modern art. The first modern art was created by the Fauves between 1904 and 1908. Colour, used in raw, was their chief characteristic. Fauvism was represented by two schools, one by Viaminck, the other by Matisse. Viaminck adopted the swift strokes and burning colour while Matisse sought—by juxtaposing colours—a new pictorial architectonic. For the Fauves nature was a starting point and the picture an end in itself.

The logical counterpart of Fauvism was Cubism, a revolution of form and an intellectual rebellion against a sensuous art. There were three phases of Cubism—proto-Cubism 1907-09, analytical Cubism 1901-12 and synthetic Cubism. Proto-cubism began with Picasso's *Demoiselles d'Avignon* (1907), a large picture of five nudes. Perspective and chiaroscuro are replaced by a play of surface planes. During 1909, **Georges Braque** experimented with constructing pictures

Georges Braque

from low-toned colour planes. In 1909 Picasso concentrated on emphasising the surface planes so that the figure appeared faceted like a crystal. In 1911-12, the climax of analytic Cubism was reached in pictures such as Picasso's *'Clarinet Player'* and Braque's *'Portuguese'* in which the object could be glimpsed through the pattern of interpenetrating and translucent planes.

In 1911-12 **Picasso** and Braque introduced into their pictures pieces of wall-paper, newspaper, etc. 'Papier Colle' as this was called carried Cubism into pictorial reality. Picasso and Braque remained empirical, and very often ignored theory. The masterpiece of synthetic Cubism is probably *'Three Musicians'* (1921) of Picasso. It achieves everything—image, space and recession by manipulating the coloured planes.

Expressionism is associated with Germany. In 1905 the group 'die Bruck ' was formed at Dresden. It created an art like that of the Fauves and drew inspiration from African sculpture and Gothic woodcuts. Expressionism was applied by

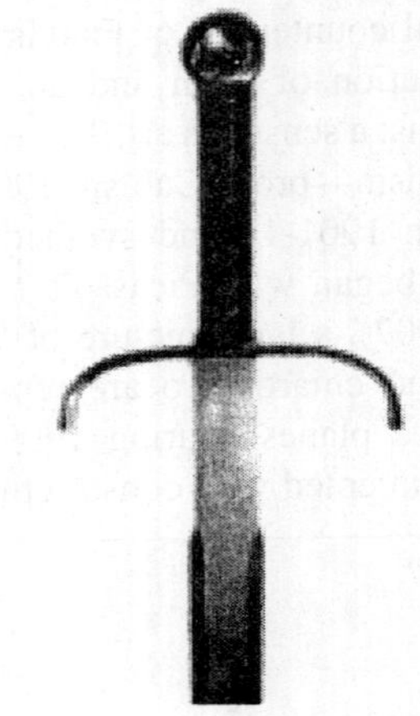

Picasso

Nolde to religious art and by Kokoschka to the portrait. The greatest Expressionist was perhaps the Parisian Rouault.

Pre-1914 abstraction resulted logically from the formal preoccupations of Fauves and Cubists and emerged in several countries to demonstrate that pictures could be made from form alone. Abstraction was various. For Dalauney it symbolised light, for Boccioni movement, and in Kandinky's hands it was freed from geometrical as well as natural form.

Cubism came under heavy fire and it was Marcel Duchamp who attacked it. Between 1911 and 1914 he debunked many accepted norms. His scepticism became the nihilism of Dada which demanded a romantic anarchy for both art and society. Defeated Germany gave this philosophy a ready welcome. Dadaism not only questions the value of art but of the whole human situation. For, as it is expressed in one of its manifestos 'measured by the standard of eternity, all human action is futile'. But in Germany and in Paris the Dadaists made nonsense verse and nonsense pictures to mark rationality. Finally an idea emerged that Dada nonsense was not nonsense but symbolised unconscious desires. At this point Dada evolved into Surrealism.

The origin of Surrealism was literary. The poets sought to explore the subconscious by automatic writing and the artists looked for equivalent techniques by presenting irrational imagery. The Surrealists take their refuge in the rationalisation of the irrational and the methodical reproduction of the spontaneous. Its true artist-poet was Catalon Miro who rejected Illusionism for abstract shapes. Miro transcended Surrealism, and in his hieroglyphs developed a range of expression. But his particular gift was to preserve the insights and spontaneous reactions of primitives and children in a precise and subtle art. Miro owed something to Paul Klee whose art was rooted in the subconscious. His method was to begin with formal elements—lines, tone and colour—until an image suggested itself which he would consciously perfect.

Against Surrealism and Expressionism, there emerged in the early post-First World War years an ultra-rational trend which sought discipline in a stricter geometry. Mondriaan reduced his forms to a grid and his colours to primes. His 'Neo-Plasticism' was an art of pure contemplation whose aim was to render visible a universal harmony. Kandinsky, stimulated by the Constructivists, turned to free arrangement of geometric forms. All these trends were institutionalised by the German Bauhaus which Gropius founded in 1919. Here artists were to design buildings with all their contents so that art should rejoin craft under the aegis of architecture. Thus Bauhaus created art-training while its two greatest teachers—Kandinsky and Klee—strove to formulate the laws of form.

From 1918 Bonnard, Matissa and Braque continued to develop their personal styles—Bonnard on the basis of Impressionism, Matisse of Fauvism and Braque of Cubism. Their pictures are among the finest of the period. Picasso was Cubist, Neo-classic, Surrealist and Expressionist by turn. But from 1927 Surrealism became a major element in his art.

In Britain complacency was absolute in the twenties. But in 1933 'Unit One' was formed with Read as spokesman, *Axis* as its magazine and Nicholson, Hepworth and Moore among its members. Joined by notable refugees like Mondriaan, Gabo, Gropius they generated the most exciting artistic atmosphere in Europe. The threat of Fascism led a return to Impressionist realism. 'Unit One' dissolved, but Nicholson continued geometrical abstraction and—along with the sculptors Moore and Hepworth—preserved British art in its vivacity.

Artistic American looked to Europe as a source of inspiration. They established a small gallery for modern French works—the New York '291', in 1909. In the inter-war wars an isolationist and characteristic reaction took place. A romantic and regionalist naturalism became the vogue. The New Deal patronised artists. But two events were more important—the foundation in 1929 of the Museum of Modern Art (MOMA) in New York, and the coming of artist refugees in America. An exciting artistic climate was born—led by Jackson Pollock which generated the American 'Action Painting' soon to burst upon the world.

Modern history of sculpture began with **Rodin** who personified Romanticism, Realism and Impressionism along with a French understanding of Michelangelo. Rodin preserved not only the Renaissance technique but its full heroic humanism.

Rodin

Maillol led a reaction to Neo-classism but his revival of humanism kept him within the nineteenth century. The most talented exponent of German sculpture was Lahmbruck. The protagonist of Fauve sculpture is Matisse, who metamorphosed composition by colour into composition by plastic force.

A departure to the traditional sculpture was made by Cubism, Futurism and Brancusi. The Cubist phase was represented by Lipchitz and Laurens. Futurist sculptures were the most important creations. Brancusi's organic abstraction tried to express an idea through fewest and simple shapes.

Dada produced sculpture such as Marcci Duchamp's *'Ready-Mades'*. Surrealist sculptures are better than Surrealist painting. In his sculptural activity Picasso used many styles which made his creation a rich quarry of ideas. Matisse, by contrast, produced few surprises. Naum Gabo, a poineer of Russian Constructivism, added transparent plastics to wood and metal. Jean Arp and Henry Moore were the two leading figures in the biomorphic wing. Less refined than Brancusi, Arp's 'Human concretions' are suggestive. Moor's wide range and powers of development are reflected in the *'Recumbent Figure'*, *'Green Hornton stone'* (1930). Moore not only founded the English school of sculpture but also projected England to the mainstream of Western art.

In the twentieth century, architecture was lighter and more suburban. William Morris opined that the present age should imitate the methods and not the style of the Middle Ages. Machine-age architecture began in Chicago, where Louis Sullivan built his *'Guaranty Building'* (1895). It expresses both its function (shops in the basement and offices above) and its structural steel cage.

About the same time Europe made contribution by the creation of 'Art Nouveau'. This was a decorative style of free-flowing curves owing much to Morris. Though it was applied to objects, furniture, china, jewellery, it could also be truly architectural. Thus Harta's *Maison de peuple* (Brussels, 1896-99) by using iron and glass, effected a light spatial transparency. In Barcelona, Guadi built a stone palace of swaying forms like sea-hollowed caves (*Casa Mila*, 1905-10).

In 1893 the Chicago Fair launched a new phase of new-classicism which largely dominated America and Europe till 1945. Sullivan's famous pupil, Frank Lloyd Wright, showed his skill before 1914, in the field of suburban villa. Wright's *'Robic Houses'* (Chicago, 1909) shows its modernity in sweeping horizontals.

As Art Nouveau declined, a Scotsman, Mackintosh, brought a new approach to modern architecture by developing two main premises—the subjective or expressionist and the objective or rational.

It was in Germany that modern architecture matured. Hermann Mathesius founded the 'Deutsche Werkbund' in 1907 where art and craft were reoriented towards industry and a mass society. Peter Behrens, the chief designer to the electrical combine A.E.G., built his Turbine Factory (Berlin, 1909) which was a masterpiece. It was a classical and expressionist, rational and irrational—at once.

The masters of contemporary architecture—Gropius, Mies Van der Rohe and Le Corbusier—all worked in Behren's studio. The result was that the first modern or the so-called 'international' style came into being. The workshop of Gropius's *'Fagus Factory'* (1911-13) is the first entirely modern building. It continues the work of Behrens. If Gropius represented the rational-classical wing of German architecture, Poelzig, Berg and Taut constituted its so-called expressionist.

Modern architecture in France found its expression in the development of reinforced concrete. The best specimen was the *'Tourcoing Spinning Mill'* (1895) by Francois Hennabique. But it was Auguste Perret who gave an aesthetic touch to the reinforced concrete in his *'25 bis Rue Franklin'* (Paris 1903).

The two architects—the Frenchman Garnier and the Italian Sant Elia—are most modern. Garnier in his blueprint *'Cite Industrielle'* (1901-04) shows not only house blocks but their setting—work, residence, leisure and transport. The futurist Sant Elia in his *'Projects 1914'* gave romantic glimpses of a skyscraper city with multi-level circulation.

Actual town-planning was advanced in Holland. Berlage's South Amsterdam begun in 1915 was based on the broad street residential block. But the more significant was the work of **Le Corbusier** who worked with his projects in Paris. His conception of the house converted Sant Elia's visions into a precise and revolutionary plan.

The exhibition at Weissenhof in 1927 with flats by Gropius, Oud, Corbusier and others revealed a new style. Called as the 'International

Le Corbusier

Style', it was rectangular with black roofs and terrace gardens, flat facades with balconies and windows. It rejected decoration and relied on base geometry and good proportions.

In England there were signs of activities when Owen Williams erected a modern factory for Boots Ltd. (1930-32). The arrival of refugees changed the atmosphere. Gropius along with Fry designed Impington College (Cambridgeshire, 1933) while Lubetkin inspired two other modern buildings'—Highpoint Flats (Highgate, 1933) and 'Finsbury Health Centre' (London, 1938).

Architecture in America was commercial. Wright's *'Çalifornian Houses'* were brilliant rather than modern. The *'Rockefeller Centre'* (New York, 1931-40) marked an advance. The Swiss Lescaze shaped the first skycraper in the international style (*Saving Fund Society Building*, Philadelphia, 1932), while the Viennese Neutra brought the same style to the domestic house (*Lovelle House*, Los Angeles, 1927-29).

The exhibition by the Museum of Modern Art in New York in 1932 made a great impact. Wright, influenced by it, designed *'Usonian'* houses which characterised simplicity, standardisation and low-cost production. These achievements were consolidated by the arrival of Gropius and Mies, the latter designing the campus of the Illinois Institute of Technology.

Scandinavia developed a style of tasteful compromise of which the masterpiece was *'Stockholm Town Hall'* (1909-23). Denmark made inroads by Arne Jacobsen's *Bella Vista Flats* (1923). But it was Finland who produced a new master in Alvar Aalto. In his *'Vipuri Library'* (1927-35), he demonstrated more forcibly than Corbusier how curving forms could be rational.

Mussolini's dictatorship did not impede modern architecture in Italy. Narvi's *'Florence Stadium'* (1930-32) has a cantilevered roof which is poised apparently on air—a feat exceeded by the Spaniard Torroja in his *'Madrid Grandstand'* (1935).

Architects are dependent upon expensive patronage. Contemporary masters like Corbusier abandons his earlier style of weightlessness, machine polish and even square forms, and his architectural sculpture becomes free and irrational. At Chandigarh (Punjab, 1954-65) he planned a city and the emphasis was on individual great buildings and their mutual relations. Similarly Mies in his *'Crown Hall'* of 1952 on the Illinois Campus develops his industrial temple to its ultimate perfection. He applied the precision of the Parthenon architects in his *'Seagram Building'* (New York, 1958). Thus the international begins to take its place among traditional styles and the fundamentals of function, material, and structure remain unchanged.

CHAPTER 52

EPILOGUE

It would be mistake to regard the history of Europe as an age of conflict; it was an age of creative accomplishment. Our view of the world and the universe has been changed as a result of the Theory of Relativity and the development of atomic research. Tremendous advances in medicine, physiology and surgery have been made possible by the contribution of biophysics and biochemistry to genetics, germ cell and gland research, and particularly by the discovery of vitamins, of insulin (1922) and cortisone (1936) and of effective antidotes of virus diseases like penicillin (1929) and such antibiotics like streptomycin and aureomycin. Irrational behaviour of human being has been improved by the development of clinical neurology and psychiatry. Material life has undergone sea change by the invention of automobile, the airplane, motion pictures, radio, television, computers, internet etal.

The achievements of pure and applied science were equally great. The new physics received its initial impulses from the German Max Planck's Quantum Theory of 1900 and found its comprehensive exposition in Theory of Relativity formulated by Albert Einstein. The development of atomic research began in 1911 with Rutherford's deduction from his studies of radioactivity. In 1913 the Dane Niels Bohr formulated his general theory of atomic structure. This provided inspiration to distinguished European physicists as Warner Heisenberg of Germany and Erwin Schrodinger of Austria, Enrico Fermi of Italy and the Englishmen Cockcroft, Walton and Chadwick. In other sciences like clinical and social psychiatry, the period was distinguished by the Austrian Sigmund Freud and the Swiss Carl Jung.

In the field of arts, the same vitality and high achievement were to be noted. In the field of architecture emphasis was laid on functionalism—non-decorative beauty of form, and the use of new materials and techniques of construction. The new architectural style combined beauty with a directness of design. A fine example was the famous *Bauhaus at Dessau*, built in 1925 by German architect Walter Gropius. Another pioneer of the modern movement was the French-Swiss architect, Le Corbusier, who combated urban sprawl by preaching that towns should be built upward rather than outward. Cities like Rio de Janeiro, Berlin, Marseilles and Chandigarh exhibit Le Corbusier's masterpieces in ferro-concrete. They are the epitomes of his belief that 'the materials of city planning are sky, space, trees, steel and cement in that order and hierarchy.'

In painting and sculpture, a deliberate repudiation of any kind of naturalism was noticeable. The impressionist school of the nineteenth century was followed by a new outlook which renounced all illusions of reality. The expressionist paintings of Chagall, the works of Picasso's Cubist period, the Surrealist paintings of Chirico, Delvaux, Escher and Dali, the sculpture of Epstein and Henry Moore portrayed worlds or fragments of worlds not easily comprehended by the viewer.

The period was distinguished by men of literary distinction. This included novelists like Thomas Mann, Hermann Hesse, Alfred Doblin, Marcel Proust, Andre Gide, Andre Malraux, Franz Kafka, D. H. Lawrence and James Joyce; poets like A. E. Housman, William Butler Yeats, T. S. Eliot, W. H. Auden, Paul Valery; dramatists like George Bernard Shaw, Paul Claudel, Luigi

Pirandello, Bertold Brecht; in the film Sergei Eisenstein, Rene Claire and Fritz Lang.

Most of these men paid scant respect to past tradition. They showed utter contempt of commonly acepted values and institutions. The latter tendency was to be found in the Fabian frivolities of Shaw, the militant reformism of plays like Ernst Toller's *Man and the Masses* (1920), the cynicism of Brecht's *Threepenny Opera* (1928) and Kafka's *The Trial* (1920) and *The Castle* (1926). In many cases, the writers sought to with draw from contemporary realities, seeking inspiration from unconventional quarters. Gide looked for inspiration to Africa and Hesse turned to the East as a result of Europe's 'deep spiritual devastation.' "For us in old Europe", he wrote, "everything has died that was good and unique to us. Our admirable rationality has become madness, our gold is paper, our machines can only shoot or explode, our art is suicide. We are going under, friends" (Klingsor's *Last Summer).*

In literature emphasis was placed upon the inadequacy of reason to control life. The idea was influenced by the Freudian theory that man can be free if he will loose himself from old burdens and repression. This was reinforced by writers like Dostoevsky and the theologian Soren Kierkegaard, who had emphasised the irrational as a regenerative force. On the other hand, Proust, Joyce, Thomas Mann stressed that man's life was determined by external compulsions over which he had no control. The same reaction against rationalism was in vogue among the philosophers which was to bear fruit in the growth of existentialism. This was offset to some extent by the strong revival of Aquinian rationalism. In philosophy of history, *The Decline of the West* (1918) by Oswald Spengler sought to demonstrate that cultures pass through stages from birth to death like living organisms. Spengler's much shorter essay *Prussianism and Socialism* (1919)—which popularised the belief that the ideals of Frederick the Great were the real alternative to Socialism—exercised profound influence upon the revival of Neoconservatism in Germany.

The progress of urbanisation and the success of secular religions raised serious problems for the established churches. There took place a more stubborn and convincing defense of the elements of religious faith. Roman Catholicism had two eloquent spokesmen in the persons of Pope Pius XI (1922-39) and Pope Pius XII (1939-58). Protestantism found in the person of Karl Barth a sworn enemy of rationalistic theology. Under his leadership and the influence of writers like Albert Schweitzer, Dean Inge and Emil Brunner, Christianity found its anchorage.

Despite the vitality and the diversity of European thought, the years after 1919 presented a confusing picture—a 'Waste Land'! There was much truth in the words of Paul Valery:

> All the fundamentals of our life have been affected by the war... You know how greatly the general economic situation has been disturbed, and the polity of states and the very life of the individual; you are familiar with the universal discomfort, hesitation, apprehension. But among these injured things is the Mind. The Mind has indeed been cruelly wounded; its complaint is heard in the hearts of intellectual man; it passes a mournful judgement on itself. It doubts itself profoundly.

In March 1944, the Italian philosopher Benedetto Croce wrote in his diary:

> We must not expect the rebirth of that world (the pre-1914 world), its revival and improvement, but we must expect an interminable sequence of clashes, and upsets and ruin due to revolutions and wars. We must get accustomed to living a life without stability...Upon this scene, faltering at every step, we must do the best we can to live with dignity.

Croce's prognostications were proven correct in the first post second World War years when there was conflict between two power blocs headed by the United States of America and the then Soviet Union, and social and economic dislocation. The Truman Doctrine, the Marshall Plan, and the establishment of the North Atlantic Treaty Organisation were aimed at the supremacy of the United States of America; the Warsaw Pact was the then Soviet rejoinder.

The aftermath of the Second World War included a sequence of secondary wars—wars in Palestine, in Indo-China, in Korea, in Algeria. It included, too, a series of revolutions, in the internal structure of western European states and their colonial territories and in the whole fabric of international relations.

Within ten years of the outbreak of the Second World War, a new world organisation, dedicated to peace and human organisation, came into being. Though it began to play a significant role in the web of world affairs, its overall influence rarely prevailed against the opposing forces of traditional power politics.

In 1918 Oswald Spengler denounced the myopic view of history prevailing in the West. He felt the need to substitute for the "empty figment of one linear history, the drama of a number of mighty cultures". A few decades later Toynbee denounced the parochialism and impertinence of the West manifested in the "egocentric illusions" that the world revolved around it. Like Spengler, he discarded the notion that 'there is only one river of civilisation, our own, and that all others are either tributary to it or lost in the desert sands.' Forty years after Toynbee, Braudel urged the need to understand 'the great cultural conflicts in the world and the multiplicity of its civilisation'.

However, the warnings which these scholars have articulated still linger and have blossomed forth 'in the widespread and parochial conceit that the European civilisation is now the universal civilisation of the world.' Toynbee was not parochial when he inferred in 1968 that the civilisation was not immune against the possibility of a holocaust. He quoted the grim lines of Lucretius: 'So the door of death is not tight shut... No, it stands hideously wide-open, eyeing us expectantly with an enormous gape.'

BIBLIOGRAPHY

GENERAL WORKS

Albrecht-Carrie, R. : *A Diplomatic History of Europe since the Congress of Vienna* (1958)

Anderson Pauline : *Political Institutions and Social Changes in Continental Europe in the Nineteenth Century* (1968)

Ashworth, W. : *A Short History of International Economy, 1850-1950* (1952)

Bury, J.P.T. : *France, 1814-1940* (1949)

Cameron Rondo, E. : *France and the Economic Development of Europe, 1800-1914* (1961)

Carr, E.H. : *A History of Soviet Russia*

Charques, R.D. : *A Short History of Russia* (1956)

Clapham, J.H. : *An Economic History of Modern Britain,* 3 Vols., (1926-28)

: *The Economic Development of France and Germany, 1815-1914* (1936)

Clark, Sir George (Edited by) : *The New Cambridge Modern History* Vols. VII-XII

Clough, S.B. and Cole, C.W. : *An Economic History of Europe* (1941)

Cobban, A. : *National Self-determination* (1948)

Craig Gordon, A. : *Europe since 1815*

: *War, Politics and Diplomacy: Selected Essays* (1966)

Croce Benedetto : *History of Europe in the Nineteenth Century* (1933)

Davies Norman : Europe (1996)

Ensor, R.C.K. : *England, 1870-1914* (1936)

Fisher, H.A.L. : *A History of Europe* (1936)

Flenley, R. : *Modern German History* (1953)

Ford Franklin, L. : *Europe 1780-1830* (1989)

Forster, E.S. : *A Short History of Modern Greece*, 1921-56 (1957)

Fueter Eduard : *World History, 1815-1920* (1920)

Grant and Temperley (Edited by Agatha Ramm) : *Europe in the Nineteenth Century, 1789-1905*

: *Europe in the Twentieth Century, 1905-1970* (1984)

Habbakuk, H.J. : *The Cambridge Economic History of Europe,* Vol. VI (1978)

Halevy Elie : *A History of English People in the Nineteenth Century*, 6 Vols. (1927-47) Translated by E.I. Watkin

Hartman, F.H. : *Basic Documents of International Relations* (1951)

Hayes, C.H.J. : *The Historical Evolution of Modern Nationalism* (1938)
: *A Generation of Materialism, 1871-1900* (1941): *Contemporary Europe since 1870*

Hearnshaw, F.J.C. : *Main Currents of European History*

Hobsbawm, E.J. : *The Age of Revolution, Europe, 1789-1848* (1964)

Hobsbawm, E.J. : *The Age of Capital, 1848-1875* (1975)
: *The Age of Empire, 1875-1914* (1987)

Hobsbawm, E.J. : *Nations and Nationalism since* 1780, 1990

Holborn Hojo : *The Political Collapse of Europe* (1951)

Laidler, H.W. : *Social-Economic Movements: An Historical and Comparative Survey of Socialism, Communism, Cooperation, Utopianism and the other forces of Reform and Reconstruction* (1944)

Langer William, L. : *Political and Social Upheaval, 1832-52* (1969)

Langsam, W.C. : *World since 1914* (1964)

Lewis, W.A. : *Economic Survey 1919-39* (1949)

Lipson, E. : *Europe in the Nineteenth Century, 1815-1914* (1946)
: *Europe, 1914-1939*

Moraze Charles : *The Triumph of the Middle Classes* (1961)

Mosse George, L. : *The Culture of Western Europe* (1961)

Namier, L.B. : *Vanished Supremacies: Essays on European History, 1812-1918*, *1958*

Oakeshott, M. : *Social and Political Doctrines of Contemporary Europe* (1939)

Petrie Charles : *Diplomatic History, 1713-1933* (1947)

Pinson, K.S. : *Modern Germany: Its History and Civilization* (1954)

Postan, M. (Edited by) : *The Industrial Revolution and After* (1966)

Ramm Agatha : *Germany 1789-1919, A Political History* (1967)

Riker, T.W. : *A Short History of Modern Europe* (1935)

Roberts, J.M. : *Europe 1880-1945* (1977)

Ropp Theodore : *War in Modern World* (1959)

Seaman, L.C.B. : *From Vienna to Versailles* (1956)

Seton-Watson, H. : *Eastern Europe between the Wars* 1918-41 (1945)

Seton-Watson, R.W. : *A History of Roumenians* (1936)
: *Britain in Europe 1789-1914, A Summary of Foreign Policy* (1937)
: *Britain and the Dictators: A Survey of Post-War British Policy* (1938)

Stearns Peter : *European Society in Upheaval: Social History since 1800* (1967)

Strang Lord : *Britain in World Affairs* (1961)

Taylor, A.J.P. : *The Struggle for Mastery in Europe, 1848-1918* (1954)

Temperley, H.W.V. : *History of Serbia* (1917)

Thompson David: : *Europe Since Napoleon* (1966)
: *World History from 1914 to 1961* (1963)

Tracy Michael : *Agriculture in Western Europe: Crisis and Adoption since 1880* (1964)

Ward, A.W. and Gooch, G.P. : *Cambridge History of British Foreign Policy 1866-1919* (1923)

Woodward, E.L. : *War and Peace in Europe, 1815-70* (1931)
: *The Age of Reform, 1815-70* (1938)
Wright Gordon : *The Ordeal of Total War, 1939-45* (1969)

ADVENT OF MODERN AGE

CHAPTER 1
GEOGRAPHICAL DISCOVERIES

Cary, M. and Warmington, E.H. : *The Ancient Explorers,* 1963
Cordier Henri : *The Travels of Marco Polo,* 1993
Guillemard, F.H.H. : *Life of Ferdinand Magellan,* 1971
Hakluyt, Richard : *The Principal Navigations, and Discoveries of the English Nation,* 2 Vols., 1965
Jane Cecil (ed.) : *Select Documents Illustrating the Four Voyages of Columbus,* 2 Vols., 1967
Newton, A.P. (ed.) : *Travel and Travellers of the Middle Ages,* 1968
Parryna, J.H. : *The Age of Reconnaissance,* 1981
Penrose Boise : *Travel and Discovery in the Renaissance 1420-1620,* 1975
Roditi Edouard : *Magellan of the Pacific,* 1972
Scammel, G.V. : *The First Imperial Age : European Overseas Expansion, 1400-1715,* 1989

CHAPTER 2
DECLINE OF FEUDALISM—RISE OF CAPITALISM

Bloch Marc : *Feudal Society,* Translated by **L.A. Manyon,** 2 Vols, 1961
Dawson Christopher : *The Making of Europe,* 1946
Ganshof, F.L. : *Feudalism,* translated by P. Grierson, 1961
Latouche Robert : *The Birth of Western Economy,* translated by E.M. Wilkinson, 1961
Pirenne Henri : *Economic and Social History of Mediaeval Europe,* 1956
Previte-Orton, C.W. : *Shorter Cambridge Medieval History,* 1952
Seignobos, C. : *The Rise of European Civilization,* 1939
Trevor-Roper Hugh : *The Rise of Christian Europe,* 1966

CHAPTER 3
RENAISSANCE IN EUROPE

Burckhard Jacob : *The Culture of the Renaissance in Italy,* 1878
Burke Peter : *Popular Culture in Early Modern Europe,* 1988
Butterfield Herbert : *The Origins of Modern Science, 1300-1800,* 1947
Cassirer, Ernst, Kristeller, Paul O., Randall, John, H. (edited) : *The Renaissance Philosophy of Man,* 1955
Garin Eugenio (ed.) : *Renaissance Characters,* 1991
Harman, P.M. : *The Scientific Revolution,* 1983

Hay, Denys : *The Italian Renaissance in Its Historical Background,* 1977
Holmes George : *Florence, Rome and the Origins of the Renaissance,* 1986
Jacob, E.F. (Ed.) : *Italian Renaissance Studies,* 1960
Kristeller Paul Oskar : *Renaissance Thought: The Classic, Scholastic, Humanistic Strain,* 1961
: *Renaissance Thought II: Papers on Humanism and the Arts,* 1980
Pater Walter : *The Renaissance,* 1959
Stinger Charles, L. : *The Renaissnance in Rome,* 1985

CHAPTER 4

THE REFORMATION

Bainton Roland, H. : *The Age of the Reformation,* 1956
: *Here I Stand : A Life of Martin Luther,* 1959
Bodensieck Julius (Ed.) : *The Encyclopaedia of the Lutheran Church,* 3 Vols., 1965
Bouwsma William, J. : *John Calvin : A Sixteenth Century Portrait,* 1988
Burns Edward Mc Nall : *The Counter-Reformation,* 1964
Chadwick, Owen : *The Reformation,* 1964
Dickens, A.G. : *The Counter Reformation,* 1968
Dillenberger and Claude Welch : *Protestant Christianity Interpreted Through Its Development,* 1988
Elton Geoffrey, R. : *Reformation Europe, 1557-1559,* 1966
: *Reform and Reformation England, 1509-1558,* 1977
Evenett, H. Outram : *The Spirit of the Counter-Reformation,* 1968
Grimm Harold, J. : *The Reformation Era, 1500-1650,* 1965
Hillebrand Hans, J. (Ed.) : *The Reformation, A Narrative History Related by Contemporary Observers and Participants,* 1964
Hughes Philips : *A Popular History of the Reformation,* 1960
Kidd, B.J. : *The Counter-Reformation, 1550-1600,* 1958
Marty Martin, E. : *Protestantism,* 1974
Mcneil, John, T. : *History and Character of Calvinism,* 1954
Mosse George, L. : *The Reformation,* 1953
Ritter Gerhard : *Luther, His Life and Work,* 1963
Trevor-Roper, H.R. : *Religion, the Reformation, and Social Change,* 1968
Troeltsch Ernst : *Protestantism and Progress: The Significance of Protestantism for the Rise of the Modern World,* 1986

CHAPTER 5

THE NEW ABSOLUTE MONARCHIES—EMERGENCE OF THE NATIONAL STATE

Cipolla Carlo, M. : *Guns, Sails and Empires: Technological Innovation and the Early Phases of European Expansion,* 1968
Nef. John, U. : *Western Civilizaton Since the Renaissance,* 1963
Parry, J.H. : *The Establishment of European Hegemony: Trade and Expansion in the Renaissance,* 1966
Rice Eugene, F. : *The Foundations of Early Modern Europe,* 1970

CHAPTER 6
COMMERCIAL REVOLUTION IN WESTERN EUROPE—MERCANTILISM

Furber Holden : *Rival Empires of Trade in the Orient, 1600-1800,* 1976
Gillespie, J.E. : *A History of Europe, 1500-1815*
Horrocks, J.W. : *A Short History of Mercantilism*
Ogg, F.A. : *Economic Development of Modern Europe*
Rich, E.E. and Wilson C.H. (Ed.) : *The Cambridge Economic History of Europe,* Vol. 4, **1967**
Tracy James, D. (Ed.) : *The Rise of Merchant Empires; Long Distance Trade in the Early Modern World, 1350-1750,* 1990
The Political Economy of Merchant Empires, 1991

CHAPTER 7
GROWTH OF PARLIAMENTARY INSTITUTION IN ENGLAND

Adams, E.B. : *Constitutional History of England*
Clark, G.N. : *The Later Stuarts, 1660-1714*
Davies, R.G. and Denton, J.H. (Ed.) : *The English Parliament in the Middle Ages,* 1981
Gillespie, J.E. : *History of Europe, 1500-1815*
Gooch, G.P. : *English Democratic Ideas in the Seventeenth Century*
Holt, J.C. : *Magna Carta,* 1965
Jacob, E.F. : *The Fifteenth Century, 1399-1485,* 1978
Prothero, E.W. : *Statutes and Constitutional Documents, 1558-1625*
Sayles, G.O. : *The King's Parliament of England,* 1974

CHAPTER 8
THE THIRTY YEARS' WAR—ITS SIGNIFICANCE IN EUROPEAN HISTORY

Cooper, J.P. (Ed.) : *The Decline of Spain and the Thirty Years' War, 1609-48/59,* 1970
Parker Geoffrey (Ed.) : *The Thirty Years' War,* 1987
Europe in Crisis, 1598-1648, 1979
Wedgwood, C.V. : *The Thirty Years' War,* 1957

CHAPTER 9
ASCENDANCY OF FRANCE

Bonney Richard : *Society and Government in France under Richelieu and Mazarin, 1624-61,* 1988
Hamscher Albert, N. : *The Parliament of Paris after the Fronde 1653-73,* 1976
Lublinskaya, A.D. : *French Absolutism: The Crucial Phase, 1620-1629,* 1968
Mettam Roger (Ed.) : *Government and Society in Louis XIV's France,* 1977
Parker David : *The Making of French Absolutism,* 1983
Ranum Orest : *Richelieu and the Councillors of Louis XIII,* 1976

Rule John, C. (Ed.) : *Louis XIV and the Craft of Kingship,* 1969

Wolf, John, B. : *Louis XIV,* 1968

CHAPTER 10

THE EMERGENCE OF A SCIENTIFIC VIEW OF THE WORLD—THE AGE OF ENLIGHTENMENT

Anchor Robert : *The Enlightenment Tradition,* 1979

Boas Marie : *The Scientific Renaissance, 1450-1630,* 1962

Bronowski, J. and Mazlish, B. : *The Western Intellectual Tradition from Leonardo to Hegel,* 1962

Brown, S.C. (Ed.) : *Philosophers of the Enlightenment,* 1979

Bury, J.B. : *The Idea of Progress, An Inquiry into Its Growth and Origin,* 1955

Butterfield Herbert : *The Origins of Modern Science: 1300-1800,* 1965

Cassirer, Ernst : *The Philosophy of the Enlightenment,* 1955

Cobban, Ernst : *In Search of Humanity, the Role of the Enlightenment in Modern History,* 1960

Gay Peter : *The Enlightenment : An Interpretation,* Vol. 1 *The Rise of Modern Paganism,* 1966

: *The Party of Humanity, Essays in the French Enlightenment,* 1964

Hall, A.R. : *The Scientific Revolution: 1500-1800 The Formation of the Modern Scientific Attitude,* 1954.

: *From Galileo to Newton, 1630-1720,* 1981

Hampson Norman : *The Enlightenment, Vol. IV of the Pelican History of European Thought*

Krieger Leonard : *Kings and Philosophers, 1689-1789,* 1970

Smith Preserved : *The History of Modern Culture,* Vol. 2

: *The Enlightenment,* 1934

Venturi France : *Italy and the Enlightenment: Studies in a Cosmopolitan Century,* 1972

Wolf, A. : *A History of Science, Technology and Philosophy in the Sixteenth and Seventeenth Centuries,* 1950

CHAPTER 11

THE AMERICAN REVOLUTION—ITS SIGNIFICANCE

Alden, John, R. : *The American Revolution, 1775-1783,* 1962

Bailyn Bernd : *The Ideological Origins of the American Revolution,* 1967

Boorstin Daniel, J. : *The Americans : The Colonial Experience,* 1988

Countryman Edward : *The American Revolution,* 1985

Greene Jack, P. (Ed.) : *The American Revolution,* 1987

Higginbotham, Don : *The War of American Independence*

Hofstadter Richard : *The Idea of Party System,* 1969

Mackesy Piers : *The War for America, 1775-1783,* 1964

Pocock, J.G.A. (Ed.) : *Three British Revolutions: 1641, 1688, 1776;* 1980.

Rogers Alan : *Empire and Liberty: American Resistance to British Authority, 1755-1763*, 1974

Thomas, P.G.D. : *British Politics and the Stamp Act Crisis,* 1975

White Morton : *The Philosophy of the American Revolution,* 1978

Wood Gordon, S. : *The Creation of the American Republic, 1776-1787*, 1969

EUROPE IN FERMENT

CHAPTER 12

INTRODUCTION

Barraclough Geoffrey : *An Introduction to Contemporary History,* 1964

Bishop George: : *Witness to Evil,* 1971

Contemporary Civilisations, 3 Vols. (Chicago) : *Scott, Foresman and Co.* 1959-64

Craig Gordon : *Europe Since* 1815

Regler Gustav : *The Owl of Minerva,* 1959

Toynbee Arnold, J : *Acquaintances,* 1967

: *Experiences,* 1969

CHAPTER 13

THE FRENCH REVOLUTION

Acton, Lord : *Lectures on the French Revolution* (1910)

Blanning, T.C.W. : *The Origins of the French Revolutionary Wars* (1986)

Bruun, G. : *Europe and the French Imperium, 1799-1814* (1938)

Butterfield, H. : *The Peace Treaties of Napoleon, 1806-08* (1928)

Cobban Alfred : *A History of Modern France,* Vols. I and II

: *The Debate on the French Revolution, 1789-99* (1945)

: *The Social Interpretation of the French Revolution* (1964)

: *Rousseau and the Modern State* (1934)

Farmer, P. : *France—Reviews its Revolutionary Origins* (1944)

Geyl, P. : *Napoleon—For and Against* (1949)

Gooch, G.P. : *Germany and the French Revolution* (1953)

Goodwin, A. : *The French Revolution* (1953)

Greer, D. : *The Incidence of the Terror* (1935)

: *The Incidence of the Emigration during the French Revolution* (1951)

Hampson Norman : *A Social History of the French Revolution* (1963)

Hecksher, E.F. : *The Continental System: An Economic Interpretation* (1922)

Lobanov Rostovsky, A.A. : *Russia and Europe, 1789-1925* (1947)

Lefebvre Georges : *The Coming of the French Revolution* (1947) (English translation by R.R. Palmer)

: *The French Revolution,* 2 Vols. (1962-64)

Markham, F.M.H. : *Napoleon and the Awakening of Europe* (1954)

Palmer, R.R. : *Twelve Who Ruled* (1941)
Rose Holland : *Life of Napoleon I,* 2 Vols. (1902)
: *The Personality of Napoleon* (1912)
Salvemini, G. : *The French Revolution, 1788-1792* (English translation by I.M. Rawson, 1954)
Shennon, J.H. : *France before the Revolution* (1989)
Soboul, Albert : *The French Revolution* (1989)
Tarle, E. : *Napoleon's Invasion of Russia,* 1812 (1942)
Thompson, E. : *Popular Sovereignty and the French Constituent Assembly, 1789-91* (1952)
Thompson, J.M. : *Leaders of the French Revolution* (1932)
: *Robespierre,* 2 Vols. (1935)
: *The French Revolution* (1943)
: *Napoleon Bonaparte: His Rise and Fall* (1952).
Watson, S.J. : *Carnot* (1954)
Woodword, E.L. : *French Revolution* (1934)

CHAPTER 14
THE INDUSTRIAL REVOLUTION

Ashton, T.S. : *The Industrial Revolution,* 1760-1830 (1948)
: *An Economic History of England: The Eighteenth Century* (1955)
Flinn, M.W. : *Origins of the Industrial Revolution*
Fontana Economic History of Europe : *Editor Carlo M. Cipolla*, 3 Vols, 1973
Habbakkuk, H.J. and Postan, M. : *The Cambridge Economic History of Europe,* Vol. VI: *The Industrial Revolution and After* (1978)
Mathias Peter : *The First Industrial Revolution: An Economic History of Britain, 1700-1914* (1969)
Montoux, P. : *The Industrial Revolution in the Eighteenth Century* (1937)
Rostow, W.W. : *British Economy of the Nineteenth Century*
: *Growth and Fluctuations of the British Economy, 1790-1850* (1975)

CHAPTER 15
RESTORATION AND REACTION

Kissinger Henry : *A World Restored: Metternich, Castlereagh and the Problems of Peace, 1812-22* (1964)
Mowat, R.B. : *Concert of Europe* (1931)
Nicholson Harold : *The Congress of Vienna* (1945)
Palmer, A. : *Metternich* (1972)
Philipps, W. Alison : *The Confederation of Europe: A Study of the European Alliance, 1813-23* (1920)

Rolo, P.J.V. : *George Canning* (1965)

Schenk, H.G. : *The Aftermath of the Napoleonic Wars: The Concert of Europe—An Experiment* (1947)

Temperley, H.W.V. : *The Foreign Policy of Canning, 1822-27* (1925)

Webster, C.K. : *The Congress of Vienna* (1937)

: *The Foreign Policy of Castlereagh* (1937)

CHAPTER 16
FRANCE (1815-70)

Agulhon Maurice : *The Republican Experiment 1848-52* (1983) (*Cambridge History of Modern France*)

Bury, J.P.T. : *France, 1814-1940* (1949)

Dabbs Autrey : *The French Army in Mexico, 1816-67* (1962)

Duveau Georges : *1848: The Making of a Revolution* (1967) (Translated from the French by Anne Carter)

Fejto, F (Edited by) : *The Opening of an Era: 1848* (1948)

Guedella Philip : *The Second Empire* (1922)

Guerard, A. : *Napoleon III* (1943)

Jardin Andre and Andre Jean Tudesq : *Restoration and Reaction, 1815-48* (1983) (*Cambridge History of Modern France*)

Kulstein David : *Napoleon III and the Working Class* (1969)

Manuel, F.E. : *The Prophets of Paris* (1962)

Marriott, Sir J. : *The French Revolution of 1848 in its Economic Aspect,* 2 Vols. (1913)

McKay, D.C. : *The National Workshops: A Study in the French Revolution of 1848* (1933)

Namier, L.B. : *1848: The Revolution of the Intellectuals* (1946)

Pinkney David, S. : *Napoleon III and the Reconstruction of Paris* (1958)

Plamenetz, J. : *The Revolutionary Movement in France 1815-71* (1952)

Plessin Alain : *The Rise and Fall of the Second Empire, 1852-71* (1979) (*Cambridge History of Modern France*)

Postgate, R. : *Story of a Year: 1848* (1955)

Rath John, R. : *The Viennese Revolution of 1848* (1957)

Resnick Daniel Philip : *The White Terror and the Political Reaction of the Waterloo* (1967)

Robertson Priscilla : *Revolution of 1848* (1952)

Simpson, F.A. : *The Rise of Louis Napoleon* (1909)

: *Louis Napoleon and the Recovery of France, 1848-56* (1951)

Thompson, J.M. : *Louis Napoleon and the Second Empire* (1954)

Whitridge Arnold : *Men in Crisis : The Revolution of 1848* (1949)

Williams Roger, L. : *Gaslight and Shadow: The World of Napoleon III* (1957)

Wright Gordon : *Modern France* (1960)

Zeldin, T. : *The Political System of Napoleon III* (1958)

CHAPTER 17

AUSTRIA-HUNGARY (1815-1867)

Kohn Hans : *The Habsburg Empire, 1804-1918* (1961)

Palmer, A. : *Metternich* (1972)

Schroeder Paul, W. : *Metternich's Diplomacy at its Zenith, 1820-33* (1962)

Taylor, A.J.P. : *The Habsburg Monarchy* (1948)

CHAPTER 18

GROWTH OF THE GERMAN EMPIRE (1815-71)

Anderson, E.N. : *The Social and Political Conflict in Prussia, 1858-1864* (1954)

Bonnin, G. : *Bismarck and the Hohenzollern Candidature for the Spanish Throne* (1957)

Craig Gordon, A. : *Germany, 1866-1945*

: *Politics of the Prussian Army* (1965)

Eyck Erich : *Bismarck and the German Empire* (1950)

Friedjung, H. : *The Struggle of Supremacy in Germany, 1859-66* (1955)

Hamerow Theodore, S. : *Restoration, Revolution, Reaction: Economics and Politics in Germany, 1815-71* (1958)

: *The Social Foundation of German Unification, 1858-71: Ideas and Institutions* (1969)

Henderson, W.O. : *The Zollverein* (1939)

Holborn Hajo : *A History of Modern Germany, 1648-1840* (1964)

: *A History of Modern Germany, 1840-1945* (1969)

Kohn Hans : *The Mind of Germany: The Education of a Nation* (1961)

Medlicott, W.N. : *Bismarck and Modern Germany* (1965)

Mosse, G.E. : *The European Powers and the German Question, 1848-71* (1958)

Pflanze Otto : *Bismarck and the Development of Germany,* Vol. I: *The Period of Unification (1815-71)* (1963)

Richter Werner : *Bismarck* (1964)

Robertson Grant, C. : *Bismarck* (1964)

Steefel, L.D. : *The Schleswig-Holstein Question* (1932)

Taylor, A.J.P. : *Bismarck* (1955)

: *Struggle for Mastery in Europe, 1848-1918* (1954)

: *The Course of German History* (1978)

: *Europe, Grandeur and Decline* (1977)

CHAPTER 19

UNIFICATION OF ITALY

Albrecht-Carrie, R. : *Italy from Napoleon to Mussolini* (1950)

Beales Derek : *The Risorgimento and the Unification of Italy* (1971)

Case, L.M. : *Franco-Italian Relations, 1860-63: The Roman Question and the Convention of September* (1932)

Crew Raymond : *A Sterner Plan for Italian Unity: The Italian National Society in the Risorgimento* (1963)

Hales, E.E.Y. : *Mazzini and the Secret Societies* (1956)

King Bolton : *A History of Italian Unity* (2 Vols., 1899)

Salvemini Gaetano : *Mazzini* (1957)

Smith Mack Denis : *Cavour and Garibaldi in 1860* (1954)

: *Garibaldi* (1956)

Taylor, A.J.P. : *The Italian Problem in European Diplomacy, 1847-49* (1934)

Thayers William : *The Life and Times of Cavour,* 2 Vols. (1914)

Trevelyan, G.M. : *Garibaldi and the Defence of the Roman Republic* (1907)

: *Garibaldi and the Thousand* (1911)

: *Garibaldi and the Making of Italy* (1911)

CHAPTER 20

REACTION AND REFORM IN RUSSIA

Almedingen, E.M. : *The Emperor Alexander I* (1963)

Blum Jerome : *Lord and Peasant in Russia* (1961)

Lovanov-Rostovsky, A.A. : *Russia and Europe, 1789-1825* (1947)

Seton-Watson Hugh : *The Decline of Imperial Russia, 1855-1914* (1952)

: *The Russian Empire, 1801-1917* (1967)

CHAPTER 21

THE EASTERN QUESTION—PART I

Henderson, G.B. : *Crimean War Diplomacy* (1947)

Marriott, J.A.R. : *The Eastern Question* (1940)

Mosse, W.E. : *The Rise and Fall of the Crimean System* (1963)

Temperley, H.W.V. : *England and the Near East: The Crimea* (1936)

Puryear, V.J. : *A Study of British Commercial Policy* (1935)

: *England, Russia and the Straits Question 1844-56* (1931)

Woodham-Smith, C. : *Florence Nightingale* (1951)

Woodward, E.L. : *War and Peace in Europe, 1815-70* (1931)

CHAPTER 22

THE MAKING OF MODERN ENGLAND

Bell, H.C.F. : *Lord Palmerston,* 2 Vols. (1936)

Briggs Asa : *The Age of Improvement* (1959)

: *Chartist Studies* (1959)

Davis, H.W.C. : *The Age of Grey and Peel* (1929)

Gash Norman : *Politics in the Age of Peel: A Study in the Technique of Parliamentary Representation 1830-50* (1953)

: *Reaction and Reconstruction in English Politics 1832-52* (1964)

Guedalla, P. : *Palmerston, 1784-1865* (1942)
Halevy Elie : *A History of the English People in the Nineteenth Century* (Vols. I-IV, 1927-47)
Hill, R.L. : *Toryism and the People, 1832-46* (1929)
Hovell, M. : *The Chartist Movement* (1925)
Thompson, E.P. : *The Making of the English Working Class* (1963)
Trevelyan, G.M. : *Lord Grey of the Reform Bill* (1929)
Webb, R.K. : *Modern England* (1969)
Woodward. E.L. : *The Age of Reform* (1938)

CHAPTER 23
CAPITALISM AND SOCIALISM

Beer, M. : *A History of British Socialism* (1940)
Berlin Isaiah : *Karl Marx, His Life and Environment* (1948).
Carr, E.H. : *Studies in Revolution* (1950)
Cole, G.D.H. : *Socialism in Evolution* (1938)
: *British Working Class Politics, 1832-1914* (1941)
Gay, P. : *The Dilemma of Democratic Socialism* (1952)
Hobsbawm, E.J. : *Labouring Man* (1964)
Joll, J. : *The Anarchists* (1964)
Kindelberger Charles, P. : *Economic Growth in France and Britain 1851-1950* (1964)
Lichtheim George : *Marxism: An Historical and Critical Study* (1964)
Pelling Heary : *A History of British Trade Unionism* (1963)
Rostow, W.W. : *Stage of Economic Growth* (1960)
Russell, B. : *Proposed Roads to Freedom: Socialism, Anarchism and Syndicalism* (1919)
Schumpeter, A. : *Capitalism, Socialism and Democracy* (1950)
Wolfe Bertram, D. : *Marxism: 100 years in the Life of a Doctrine* (1965)
Woodcock, G. : *Pierre Joseph Proudhon* (1956)

CHAPTER 24
THE IMPERIAL EXPANSION

Belloff Max : *Imperial Sunset,* Vol. I: *Britain's Liberal Empire 1897-1921*
Coupland, R. : *The Exploitation of East Africa, 1856-90* (1939)
Crowe, S.E. : *The Berlin West African Conference, 1884-85* (1942)
Dubois, W.E.B. : *The World and Africa* (1947)
Hobsbawm, E.J. : *Industry and Empire* (1968)
Hobson, J.A. : *Imperialism, A Study* (1938)
Hofmeyer, J.H. and Cope, J.P. : *South Africa* (1952)
Johnston Harry : *History of the Colonisation of Africa by Alien Races* (1930)

Koebner Richard and Schmidt Helmut Dan : *Imperialism: The Story and Significance of a Political World (1840-1960)*, (1963)

Langer, W.L. : *The Diplomacy of Imperialism* (1951)

Lenin, V.I. : *Imperialism, The Highest Stage of Capitalism* (1918)

Moon, P.T. : *Imperialism and World Politics* (1926)

Morris James : *Pax Britannica* (1968)

Muir, R. : *The Expansion of Europe* (1939)

Pratt, Sir J.T. : *The Expansion of Europe in the Far East* (1947)

Prosser Gifford and Louis William, R. : *Britain and Germany in Africa* (1967)

Summer, B.H. : *Tsardom and Imperialism in the Far East and the Middle East, 1880-1914*, (1942)

Thornton, A.P. : *The Imperial Idea and its Critics* (1959)

Viekke, B.H.M. : *The Story of the Dutch East Indies* (1945)

CHAPTER 25

THE THIRD FRENCH REPUBLIC

Azema Jean Pierre : *From Munich to the Liberation 1938-44* (1979) (*The Cambridge History of Modern France*)

Bernard Philippe and Dubief Henri : *The Decline of the Third Republic 1914-38* (1985) (*Cambridge History of Modern France*)

Brogan, D.W. : *The Development of Modern France, 1870-1939* (1940)

Carroll, E.M. : *French Public Opinion and Foreign Affairs, 1870-1914* (1930)

Chapman, G. : *The Dreyfus Case: A Reassessment* (1955)

Clapham, J.H. : *The Economic Development of France and Germany, 1815-1914* (1921)

Joughin, J.T. : *The Paris Commune in French Politics 1871-80* (2 Vols., 1956)

Thomson David : *Democracy in France: The Third Republic* (1952)

Weber Eugen : *The Nationalist Revival in France, 1905-14* (1959)

: *Action Francaise: Royalism and Reaction in Twentieth Century France* (1962)

CHAPTER 26

THE GERMAN EMPIRE (1871-1914)

Balfour Michael : *The Kaiser and His Times* (1964)

Barlow Ima, C. : *The Agadir Crisis* (1940)

Brandenberg, E. : *From Bismarck to the World War: A History of German Foreign Policy 1870-1914* (1927)

Bruck, W.F. : *Social and Economic History of Germany from William II to Hitler, 1888-1938* (1938)

Carroll, E.M. : *Germany and the Great Powers, 1866-1914: A Study in Public Opinion and Foreign Policy* (1939)

Hale, O.J. : *Publicity and Diplomacy with special reference to England and Germany, 1890-1914* (1940)

Hoffmann, R.J.S. : *Great Britain and the German Trade Rivalry, 1875-1914* (1933)

Kohn Hans : *The Mind of Germany: The Education of a Nation* (1931)

Langer, W.L. : *European Alliances and Alignments, 1871-1940* (1931)

: *The Diplomacy of Imperialism, 1890-1902,* 2 Vols. (1950)

Mosse George, L. : *The Crisis of German Ideology: Intellectual Origins of the Third Reich* (1966)

Rich Norman : *Friedrich von Holstein,* 2 Vols. (1965)

Schmitt, B.E. : *Triple Alliance and Triple Entente* (1934)

Simon, W.M. : *Germany in the Age of Bismarck* (1968)

Sontag, R.J. : *Germany and England: Background of Conflict, 1848-1894* (1938)

Stolper, G. : *German Economy, 1870-1940* (1940)

Taylor, A.J.P. : *The Struggle for Mastery in Europe, 1848-1918* (1954)

Woodward, E.L. : *Great Britain and the German Navy* (1935)

CHAPTER 27
AUSTRIA-HUNGARY (1867-1945)

Jaszi, O : *The Dissolution of the Habsburg Monarchy* (1929)

May Arthur, J : *The Passing of the Habsburg Monarchy, 1914-18,* 2 Vols. (1966)

Mansergh, N : *The Coming of the First World War 1878-1914* (1949)

Spender, J.A. : *Fifty Years of Europe: A Study in à Pre-War Documents* (1936)

CHAPTER 28
THE EASTERN QUESTION—PART II

Earle, E.M. : *Turkey, the Great Powers and the Baghdad Railway* (1923)

Helmreich, E.C. : *The Diplomacy of the Balkan Wars, 1912-13* (1938)

Marriott, J.A.R. : *The Eastern Question, An Historical Study in European Diplomacy* (1940)

Medlicott, W.N. : *The Congress of Berlin and After 1878-1880* (1938)

Miller, W : *The Ottoman Empire and its Successors 1801-1927* (1936)

Schevill Ferdinand : *History of the Balkan Peninsula* (1933)

Seton-Watson, H : *Eastern Europe between the Wars 1918-1941* (1945)

: *The East European Revolution* (1952)

Seton Watson, R.W. : *Rise of Nationality in the Balkans* (1917)

: *Disraeli, Gladstone and the Eastern Question: A Study in Diplomacy and Party Politics* (1935)

Sumner, B.H. : *Russia and the Balkans, 1870-80* (1947)

CHAPTER 29

THE FIRST WORLD WAR

Albertini Luigi : *Origin of the War of 1914* (English Translation, 3 Vols.,) (1952-57)

Baldwin Hanson, W. : *World War I: An Outline History* (1962)

Birdsall Paul : *Versailles Twenty Years After* (1941)

Churchill, W.S. : *The Unknown War* (1931)

: *World Crisis, 1911-18,* 5 Vols. (1923-29)

Cruttwell, C.R.M.F. : *A History of the Great War, 1914-18* (1934)

Dedijer Vladimir : *The Road to Sarajevo* (1966)

Edmonds Sir James : *A Short History of World War I* (195[illegible])

Falls Cyril : *The Great War, 1914-18* (1959)

Fay, S.B. : *Origins of World War,* 2 Vols. (1930)

Fritz Fischer : *Germany's Aim in the First World War* (1967)

Gooch, G.P. : *Before the War: Studies in Diplomacy* (2 Vols., 1936-38)

Kennedy Paul : *The Rise of Anglo-German Antagonism 1860-1914* (1980)

Koch, H.W. (Edited by) : *The Origins of the First World War* (1985)

Lafore Lawrence : *The Long Fuse: An Interpretation of the Origins of World War I* (1965)

Liddell Hart, B.H. : *History of the World War, 1914-18* (1935)

: *The War in Outline* (1938)

Marshall, S.L.A. and Taylor, A.J.P. : *World War I: An Illustrated History* (1964)

Remak Joachim : *Sarajevo* (1959)

Schmitt, B.E. : *The Coming of the War, 1914,* 2 Vols. (1930)

Seymour Charles : *American Neutrality, 1914-17* (1935)

: *American Diplomacy during the World War* (1934)

Steiner Zara, S. : *The Foreign Office and Foreign Policy, 1898-1914* (1969)

Taylor, A.J.P. : *Politics in Warfare and other Essays* (1965)

Temperley, H.W.V. (Ed.) : *History of the Peace Conference at Paris* 6 Vols. (1920-24)

Trumpener Ulrich : *Germany and the Ottoman Empire 1914-18* (1968)

Wheeler-Bennett, J.W. : *Brest-Litovsk: The Forgotten Peace* (1939)

Woodward Sir Llewellyn : *Great Britain and the War of 1914-18* (1967)

CHAPTER 30

REPARATION, INTER-ALLIED DEBTS

Birdsall Paul : *Versailles Twenty Years After* (1941)

Bowley, A.L. : *Some Economic Consequences of the Great War* (1930)

Carr, E.H. : *The Twenty Years Crisis* (1956)

Cobban, A. : *National Self-Determination* (1944)

Craig Gordon, A. and Gilbert Felix (Edited) : *The Diplomats* (1953)

Doll, R. : *The Geneva Racket, 1920-39* (1941)

Fraser, L.	:	*Germany Between Two Years: A Study of Propaganda and War-Guilt* (1944)
Galbraith, J.K.	:	*The Great Crash* (1929)
Gathorne-Hardy, G.M.	:	*A Short History of International Affairs, 1920-39* (1950)
Hodson, H.V.	:	*Slump and Recovery, 1929-1937: A Survey of World Economic Affairs* (1938)
Jordon, W.M.	:	*Great Britain, France and the German Problem, 1918-39* (1943)
Keynes John Maynard	:	*The Economic Consequences of the Peace* (1920)
Rappard, W.E.	:	*The Quest for Peace since the World War* (1940)
Robbins, L.C.	:	*The Great Depression* (1934)
Weeter Dixon	:	*The Age of the Great Depression, 1929-41* (1948)
Wheeler Bennett, J.W.	:	*Wreck of Reparations* (1933)
	:	*Disarmament and Security since Locarno* (1932)
	:	*Brest-Litovsk : The Forgotten Peace* (1939)

CHAPTER 31

THE LEAGUE OF NATIONS

Butler, Sir H	:	*The Lost Peace: A Personal Impression* (1941)
Cecil Viscount	:	*A Great Experiment : An Autobiography* (1941)
Gathorne Hardy, G.M.	:	*A Short History of International Affairs 1920-39* (1950)
Hill, M.	:	*The Economic and Financial Organisation of the League of Nations: A Survey of Twenty-Five Years Experience* (1945)
Hudson, M.O.	:	*The Permanent Court of International Justice* (1943)
Miller, D.H.	:	*The Drafting of the Covenant,* 2 Vols. (1928)
Walters, F.P.	:	*A History of the League of Nations,* 2 Vols. (1952)
Zimmern, Sir A.	:	*The League of Nations and the Rule of Law, 1918-35* (1936)

CHAPTER 32

GREAT BRITAIN (1868-1945)

Campion, G. and others	:	*British Government since 1918* (1950)
Ensor, R.C.K.	:	*England 1870-1914* (1936)
Grelton, R.H.	:	*A Modern History of the English People 1880-1922* (1930)
Hancock, W.K.	:	*Survey of British Commonwealth Affairs,* 2 Vols. (1942)
Jenkins Roy	:	*Asquith: Portrait of a Man and an Era* (1964)
Kindleberger Charles, P.	:	*Economic Growth in France and Britain, 1851-1950* (1964)
Mansergh Nicholas	:	*The Commonwealth Experience* (1969)
Mowat, C.L.	:	*Britain between the Wars, 1918-40* (1955)
Nowell-Smith (ed.)	:	*Edwardian England, 1901-1914* (1964)
Ponsonby Lord	:	*Recollections of Three Reigns* (1951)
Pribram, A.F.	:	*England and the International Policy of the European Great Powers, 1871-1914* (1931)
Rostow Walt Whitman	:	*British Economy in the Nineteenth Century*

Somervell, D.C. : *British Politics since 1900* (1950)
Taylor, A.J.P. : *English History, 1914-45* (1965)

CHAPTER 33
REFORM AND REVOLUTION IN RUSSIA

Aragon Louis : *A History of the USSR from Lenin to Khruschev* (1964)
Beloff Max : *Foreign Policy of Soviet Russia, 1929-41*, 2 Vols., (1947, 1952)
Carmichael Joel : *A Short History of the Russian Revolution* (1964)
Carr, E.H. : *History of Soviet Russia,* 7 Vols.
: *Studies in Revolution* (1950)
: *The Bolshevik Revolution, 1917-23*, 3 Vols. (1951-53)
: *The Russian Revolution: From Lenin to Stalin (1917-1929)* (1979)
Carroll Malcom, D : *Soviet Communism and Western Opinion 1919-21* (Edited by Frederick B.M. Hollyday) (1965)
Chamberlain William Henry : *The Russian Revolution,* 2 Vols (1987)
Charques Richard : *The Twilight of Imperial Russia* (1959)
Cohen F, Cohel, Stephen, F : *Rethinking of the Soviet Experience: Politics and History since 1917* (1985)
Conquest Robert : *The Great Terror: Stalin's Purge of the Thirties* (1968)
Dallin, D.J. : *The New Soviet Empire* (1951)
: *From Purge to Co-existence* (1964)
Deutscher Issac : *The Prophet Armed: Trotsky, 1879-1921* (1954)
: *The Prophet Unarmed: Trotsky, 1921-29* (1959)
: *The Prophet Outcast: Trotsky, 1929-40* (1963)
: *Stalin : A Political Development since 1917* (1948)
Dobb M. : *Soviet Economic Development since 1917* (1948)
Ehrenburg Ilya : *Men, Years, Life* 5 Vols. (1963-65)
Erikson John : *The Soviet High Command* (1962)
Ferro Marc : *The Russian Revolution of February 1917* (1972)
Fischer Louis : *Lenin* (1964)
: *Soviet Foreign Relations, 1917-41* (1969)
Fitzpatrick, Sheila : *The Russian Revolution, 1917-32* (1982)
Haimson, L.H. : *The Russian Marxists and the Origins of Bolshevism* (1955)
Kenan George, F : *Soviet Foreign Policy, 1917-41* (1960)
: *Russia and the West under Lenin and Stalin* (1961)
Lane Theodore Von : *Why Lenin? Why Stalin? A Reappraisal of the Russian Revolution, 1900-1930* (1964)
Lederer Ivo, J. (Ed. by) : *Russian Foreign Policy* (1962)
McCauley Martin (Ed. by) : *The Soviet Union since* 1917
: *The Russian Revolution and the Soviet State 1917-21, Documents* (1975)
Mohrenschildt Dimitri Von (Ed. by) : *The Russian Revolution of 1917: Contemporary Accounts* (1971)

Payne Robert : *The Life and Death of Lenin* (1964)
Possony Stefan, T. : *Lenin: The Complete Revolutionary* (1964)
Rushter John, S. : *A Concise History of the Communist Party of the Soviet Union* (1960)
Seton Watson Hugh : *The Decline of Imperial Russia* (1952)
: *From Lenin to Khruschev* (1960)
Schwarz Solomon, M : *The Russian Revolution of 1905* (1967)
Tempkins, S.R. : *The Russian Intelligentsia* (1957)
Toynbee Arnold : *The Impact of the Russian Revolutions, 1917-1967* (1967)
Treadgold Donald : *Twentieth Century Russia* (1959)
Trotsky Leon : *The History of the Russian Revolution* (1965) (Translated from the Russian by Max Eastman)
Ulam Adam, B. : *Expansion and Coexistence: The History of the Soviet Foreign Policy 1917-67* (1968)
Vernadsky George : *The Russian Revolution, 1917-21* (1932)
Vusinich Wayne, S. (Ed.) : *The Peasant in Nineteenth Century Russia* (1968)
Warth Robert, D. : *Soviet Russia in World Politics* (1963)
Wolfe, B. : *Three who Ruled: A Biographical History* (1948)

CHAPTER 34
RISE OF FASCISM IN EUROPE: ITALY

Albrecht Carrie Rene : *Italy from Napoleon to Mussolini* (1950)
Badoglio, P. : *The War in Abyssinia* (1937)
Blinkhorn, M. : *Mussolini and Fascist Italy*
: *Fascists and Conservatives: The Radical Right and the Establishment in Twentieth Century Europe* (1990)
Borgini Luigi : *The Italians* (1964)
Chabod Frederice : *A History of Italian Fascism* (1963)
Cremona, P. : *Italy's Foreign and Colonial Policy, 1914-37* (1938)
Halperin, S.W. : *Mussolini and Italian Fascism* (1964)
Kirkpatrick Ivone : *Mussolini: A Study in Power* (1964)
Macartney, M.H.H. : *The Rebuilding of Italy* (1946)
Nolte Ernst : *Three Faces of Fascism* (1967)
Salvemini, G. : *Under the Axe of Fascism* (1936)
Wiskemann Elizabeth : *Fascism in Italy: Its Development and Influence* (1969)
: *Rome-Berlin Axis: A Study of Relations between Hitler and Mussolini* (1949)

CHAPTER 35
GERMANY: DRIFT TOWARDS WAR

Bloch, M. : *Ribbertrop* (1992)
Brook Shephard Gordon : *Anschluss: The Rape of Austria* (1963)
Bullock Alan : *Hitler: A Study in Tyranny* (1964)

Carr, E.H. : *German-Soviet Relations between the Two World Wars* (1951)

Churchill, W.S. : *The Gathering Storm* (1948)

: *The Second World War,* 6 Vols. (1948-53)

Craig Gordon, A : *From Bismarck to Adenauer* (1965)

: *Germany, 1866-1945* (1978)

: *The Germans* (1982)

Dorpalen Andreas : *Hindenburg and the Weimar Republic* (1963)

Eschenburg Theodor and others : *The Path to Dictatorship* (1966)

Eubank Keith : *Munich* (1963)

Eych Erich : *History of the Weimar Republic*, 2 Vols. (1962-63)

Fest Joachim, C. : *The Face of the Third Reich* (1963) (Translated from the German by Michael Bullock)

Fleming Gordon : *Hitler and the Final Solution*

Furnia, A.H. : *The Diplomacy of Appeasement: Anglo-French Relations, 1931-38* (1960)

Gilbert Martin : *The Roots of Appeasement* (1961)

Greenberger Richard : *The Twelve-Year Reich* (1971)

Kater Michael : *The Nazi Party: A Social Profile of Members of Leaders 1919-45* (1983)

Lafore Laurence : *The End of Glory: An Interpretation of the Origins of World War II* (1970)

Namier, L.B. : *Diplomatic Prelude*, 1938-39 (1948)

: *Europe in Decay: A Study in Disintegration, 1936-40* (1950)

: *In the Nazi Era* (1952)

Parker, R.A.C. : *Europe 1919-45* (1968)

Rossi, A : *Russo-German Alliance, 1939-41* (1951)

Rowse, A.L. : *All Souls and Appeasement* (1961)

Schoenbaum David : *Hitler's Social Revolution: Class and Status in Nazi Germany, 1933-39* (1966)

Schuman, F.L. : *Europe on the Eve: The Crisis of Diplomacy, (1933-39)* (1939)

: *Night over Europe: The Diplomacy of Nemesis, 1939-40* (1941)

Scott William : *Alliance against Hitler* (1962)

Seton-Watson R.W. : *Britain and the Dictators: A Survey of Post-War British Policy* (1938)

Shirer William : *The Rise and Fall of the Third Reich* (1960)

Taylor, A.J.P. : *The Origins of the Second World War* (1961)

Walt Richard, M. : *The Kings Depart: The Tragedy of Germany at Versailles and the German Revolution* (1969)

Wheeler-Bennett, J.W. : *Wooden Titan, Hindenburg in Twenty Years of German History, 1914-34* (1936)

: *The Nemesis of Power: The German Army in Politics, 1918-45* (1953)

Wiskemann Elizabeth : *The Rome-Berlin Axis* (1949)

CHAPTER 36
THE SECOND WORLD WAR

Bradley, O.N. : *A Soldiers' Story* (1951)
Bullock Alan : *Hitler, A Study in Tyranny* (1952)
: *Ernest Bevin* (1967)
Calvocoressi Peter, Guy Wint and John Pritchard : *The Causes and Courses of the Second World War* (1989)
Churchill, W.S. : *History of the Second World War*, 6 Vols. (1948-53)
: *The Memoirs of Anthony Eden: The Reckoning* (1965)
Draper, T. : *The Six Weeks' War: France, May 10-June 25, 1940* (1944)
Eisenhower, D.D. : *Crusade in Europe* (1948)
Feis Herbert : *Churchill, Roosevelt, Stalin: The War they Waged and the Peace they Sought* (1957)
: *Between Peace and War, The Potsdam Conference* (1960)
Fuller, J.F.C. : *The Second World War: A Strategical and Tactical History* (1949)
Hoffmann Peter : *The History of German Resistance, 1933-45* (1988)
Liddell Hart, B.H. : *The Rommel Papers* (1953)
Marshall, G.C. : *The Winning of the War in Europe and the Pacific* (Biennial Report of the U.S. Chief of Staff, 1945)
Nicholson Harold : *The War Years 1939-45* (1968)
Shirer, William L. : *The Complete War Memoirs of Charles de Gaulle* (1964)
: *The Collapse of the Third Republic* (1969)
Stettinius, E.R. : *Lend-Lease: Weapon for Victory* (1944)
Taylord Telford : *The March of Conquest* (1958)
: *The Breaking Wave* (1967)
Trevor-Roper, H.R. : *Last Days of Hitler* (1947)
Wilmot Chester : *Struggle for Europe* (1952)
Wright Gordon : *The Ordeal of the Total War, 1939-45* (1968)
Young Desmond : *The Desert Fox* (1950)
Young Peter, Brigadier : *A Short History of World War II* (1966)

CHAPTER 37
MINOR EUROPEAN COUNTRIES

Arneson, B.A. : *The Democratic Monarchies of Scandinavia* (1939)
Birch, J.M.S. : *Denmark in History* (1938)
Blinkhorn, M. : *Democracy and Civil War in Spain* (1988)
Carr, E.H. : *The Commintern and the Spanish Civil War* (1984)
Carr Raymond : *Spain, 1808-1975* (1982)
Cleugh James : *Spanish Fury* (1962)
Davies Norman : *God's Playground: A History of Poland* (1981)
Derrick, M. : *The Portugal of Salazar* (1939)
Eppstein, J. (Ed.) : *Denmark* (1945)

Gorin, J.A. (Ed.) : *Belgium* (1945)
Jackson Gabriel : *The Spanish Republic and the Civil War 1931-39* (1965)
Jackson, J.H. : *The Post-War Decade: A Short History of the World 1945-55* (1955)
Keren Larsen : *A History of Norway* (1948)
Leslie, R.F. (Ed. by) : *The History of Poland Since 1863* (1980)
Louis Bertrand Louis and Patric Sir Charles : *History of Spain* (1952)
Machray, R. : *The Poland of Pilsudski* (1937)
Martin, P.F. : *Greece of the Twentieth Century* (1913)
Pattee Richard : *Portugal and the Portuguese World* (1957)
Payne Robert : *The Spanish Civil War* (1962)
Payne Stanley, G. : *Politics and the Military in Modern Spain* (1967)
Peers Allison : *The Spanish Tragedy, 1930-36* (1936)
: *Spain in Eclipse, 1937-43* (1943)
Puzzo Dante, A. : *Spain and the Great Powers, 1936-41* (1962)
Rafael Altamira : *A History of Spain* (English translation), (1949)
Reddaway, W.F. and others (Edited) : *Cambridge History of Poland, Vol. II: From Augustus II to Pilsudski* (1941)
Schmitt, B.E. (Ed.) : *Poland* (1945)
Seton-Watson Hugh : *The East European Revolution* (1951)
Stromberg, A.A. : *The History of Sweden* (1931)
Sweet-Escott, B. : *Greece, A Political and Economic Survey, 1939-53* (1955)
Thomas Hugh : *The Spanish Civil War* (1961)
Verney, D. : *Parliamentary Reform in Sweden,* 1866-1921 (1957)

EMERGENCE OF NON-EUROPEAN COUNTRIES

CHAPTER 38

EMERGENCE OF THE UNITED STATES OF AMERICA

CHAPTER 39

CRISIS AND CONFIDENCE IN THE UNITED STATES OF AMERICA (1867-1945)

Bailey, T.A. : *A Diplomatic History of the American People* (1950)
Beard Charles and Mary : *Rise of American Civilisation,* Vols. I, II
Fairbank, J.K. : *The United States and China* (1948)
Fleming, D.F. : *The United States and the League of Nations 1918-20* (1932)
Kenan, G.F. : *American Diplomacy, 1900-1950* (1951)
Navins Allan and Commager Henry Steels : *A Short History of the United States*
Perkins Dexter : *America and Two Wars* (1944)
: *Evolution of American Foreign Policy* (1948)

Rhodes, J.F. : *History of the United States,* 7 Vols. (1893-1918)
: *History of the Civil War,* 1861-65 (1919)
Seymour Charles : *American Diplomacy during the World War* (1934)
: *American Neutrality, 1914-17* (1935)
Nevins Allan : *The Emergence of Lincoln* (1950)
: *The Emergence of Modern America, 1865-1878* (1927)
: *The New Deal and World Affairs: A Chronicle of International Affairs, 1933-45* (1951)

CHAPTER 40
THE LATIN AMERICA

Bernstein Harry : *Venezuela and Colombia* (1964)
Boxer Charles, R. : *The Golden Age of Brazil* (1962)
Burns, E. Bredford : *A History of Brazil* (1970)
Cumberland Charles, C. : *Mexico: The Struggle for Modernity* (1968)
Diffie Bailey, W. : *Latin American Civilisation: Colonial Period* (1945)
Gibson Charles : *Spain in America* (1967)
Hering, C.H. : *The Spanish Empire in America* (1952)
Humphreys, R.A. and Lynch John (Ed.) : *The Origins of Latin American Revolution, 1808-1826*
Madariaga Salvador de : *The Rise of the Spanish Empire in America and the Fall of the Spanish Empire in America* (1947)
Masur Garhard : *Simon Boliver* (1948)
Parkers Henry Bamford : *A History of Mexico* (1970)
Parry, J.H. : *The Spanish Seaborne Empire* (1966)
Poppino Rollie, F. : *Brazil: The Land and People* (1968)
Rippy, J.F. : *Latin America in World Politics* (1938)
Rodriguez Mario : *Central America* (1965)
Scobie James, R. : *Argentina, A City and a Nation* (1964)
Stein Stanley, J. and Barbara, H. : *The Colonial Heritage of Latin America* (1970)
Wilkie James, W. and Michaels Albert, L. (Ed.) : *Revolution in Mexico: Years of Upheaval, 1910-40* (1969)

CHAPTER 41
ASIAN GIANTS—CHINA AND JAPAN

Ch'en Jerome : *Mao and the Chinese Revolution* (1965)
Fairbank, J.K. : *The United States and China* (1948)
Fairbank, Reischauer and Craig : *East Asia, the Modern Transformation* (1965)
Fitzerald, C.P. : *The Birth of Communist China* (1964)
Gasster Michael : *Chinese Intellectuals and the Revolution of 1911* (1969)

Hall John Whitney and Marius B. Jansen : *Studies in the Institutional History of Early Modern Japan* (1968)
Hsu, C.Y. Immanuael : *The Rise of Modern China* (1990)
Johnson Chalmers : *Peasant Nationalism and Communist Power: The Emergence of Revolutionary China, 1937-45* (1962)
Jones, F.C. : *Manchuria since 1931* (1949)
Langer William, L. : *The Diplomacy of Imperialism, 1890-1902* (1960)
Latourette, K.S. : *A History of Modern China* (1954)
Latourette, K.C. : *The History of Japan* (1953)
Prett, Sir J.T. : *The Expansion of Europe into the Far East* (1947)
Purcell, V. : *China* (1962)
Smith Sara, R. : *The Manchurian Crisis, 1931-32* (1948)
Teng Sou-Yu and John K Fairbank : *China's Response to the East, A Documentary Survey, 1839-1923* (1965)
Toland John : *The Rising Sun: The Decline and Fall of the Japanese Empire, 1936-45* (1970)
Tse-tsung Chow : *The May Fourth Movement: Intellectual Revolution in Modern China* (1964)
Vinacke, H.M. : *A History of the Far East in Modern Times* (1960)
Waley Arthur : *The Opium War Through Chinese Eyes* (1958)
Wright Mary, C. (Ed.) : *China in Revolution: The First Phase, 1900-13* (1968)

CHAPTER 42

ARAB NATIONALISM: THE MIDDLE EAST

Antonius, G. : *The Arab Awakening* (1946)
Armstrong, H.C. : *Grey Wolf*
Avery Peter : *Modern Iran* (1965)
Gaury, G. de : *The New State of Israel* (1952)
Hoskins Holford, L. : *The Middle East: Problem Area in World Politics* (1957)
Hourani, A.H. : *Syria and Lebanon: A Political Essay* (1946)
Kirk, G.E. : *A Short History of the Middle East: From the Rise of Islam to Modern Times* (1957)
Lawrence, T.E. : *Revolt in the Desert* (1927)
Lewis Bernard : *Emergence of Modern Turkey* (1961)
: *Arabs in History* (1966)
Royal Institute of International Affairs : *The Middle East: A Political and Economic Survey* (1950)
Smith, W.C. : *Islam in Modern History* (1957)

CHAPTER 43

INDIA AND SOUTH-EAST ASIA

Hall, D.G.E. : *A History of South-East Asia* (1968)
Kahin, G.M. : *Nationalism and Revolution in Indonesia* (1952)

Legge, J.D. : *Indonesia* (1964)
Marr David, G. : *Vietnamese Anti-Colonialism, 1885-1925* (1971)
McLane John, R. : *The Political Awakening in India* (1970)
Metcalfe, T.R. : *The Aftermath of Revolt, India, 1857-70* (1964)
Moon Pendral : *Divide and Quit* (1961)
Seal Anil : *The Emergence of Modern Nationalism* (1968)
Spear Percival : *The Twilight of the Mughals* (1951)
: *The Nabobs* (1963)
: *India, A Modern History* (1961)

THE TEXTURE OF EUROPEAN CULTURE

CHAPTER 44

SOCIAL TRANSFORMATION

Cipolla Carlo : *The Economic History of World Population* (1962)
Cole, G.D.H. : *A History of Socialist Thought,* 4 Vols. (1953-60)
Flinn, M.W. : *Essays in Social History* (1974)
Graves Robert and Allan Hodge : *The Long Weekend: A Social History of Great Britain, 1918-39* (1963)
Tarling Nicholas (Ed. by) : *The Cambridge History of South-East Asia,* 2 Vols. (1992)
Hughes, H.S. : *Consciousness and Society, The Reorientation of European Social Thought, 1890-1930* (1958)
Myrdal, G. : *Beyond the Welfare State* (1960)
Schumpeter Joseph, A. : *Capitalism, Socialism and Democracy* (1942)

CHAPTER 45

ECONOMIC CHANGE

Birnie, A. : *An Economic History of Europe, 1760-1939* (1951)
Bowley, A.L. : *Some Economic Consequences of the Great War* (1930)
Clapham, J.H. : *An Economic History of Modern Britain,* 3 Vols. (1936-38)
: *Economic Development of France and Germany 1815-1914* (1936)
Cole, G.D.H. : *Introduction to Economic History, 1759-1950* (1952)
Day, J.P. : *An Introduction to World Economic History Since the Great War* (1939)
Hodson, H.V. : *Slump and Recovery, 1929-37: A Survey of World Economic Affairs* (1938)
Keynes J.M. : *Economic Consequences of the Peace* (1920)
Kindelberger Charles, P. : *Economic Growth in France and Britain, 1851-1950* (1964)

CHAPTER 46

EDUCATION

Kandal, I.L. : *Comparative Education* (1933)
Wodehouse, H.M. : *A Survey of the History of Education* (1924)

CHAPTER 47
RELIGION

Dawson Christopher : *Progress and Religion* (1931)
: *Religion and the Modern State* (1935)
: *Religion and Culture* (1948)
Figgis, J.N. : *Churches in Modern State* (1914)
Halperin, S.W. : *Italy and the Vatican at War* (1939)
Routh, H.V. : *Towards the Twentieth Century: Essays in the Spiritual History of the Nineteenth* (1937)
Wallace, L.P. : *The Papacy and European Diplomacy 1869-78* (1948)

CHAPTER 48
PROGRESS IN SCIENCE AND TECHNOLOGY

Chase, C.T. : *The Evolution of Modern Physics* (1947)
Dampier, Sir W.C.D. : *History of Science* (1948)
Findlay, A. : *A Hundred Years of Chemistry* (1937)
Goldston, L. (Edited) : *Social Medicine: Its Derivations and Objectives* (1949)
Harman, P.M. : *The Scientific Revolution* (1983)
Himmelfarb, G. : *Darwin and the Darwinian Revolution* (1959)
Hughes, D.J. : *The Nuclear Energy, its potential for peaceful uses* (1957)
Infeld, L. : *Albert Einstein, his work and its influence* (1950)
Jeans James, H. : *The Physical Universe* (1930)
: *Through Space and Time* (1934)
: *Growth of Physical Science* (1948)
Lieber, L.R. and H. : *The Einstein Theory of Relativity* (1945)
Shryock, R.H. : *Development of Modern Medicine* (1947)
Zimmer, E. : *The Revolution in Physics* (1936)

CHAPTER 49
LITERATURE

Brandes, G. : *Main Currents in Nineteenth Century Literature,* 6 Vols. (1901-06)
Chesterton, G.K. : *Victorian Age in Literature* (1913)
Croce, B. : *European Literature in the Nineteenth Century* (1924)
Eliot, T.S. : *Selected Prose* (1953)
Geyl, P. : *From Ranke to Toynbee* (1952)
Mosse, G.L. : *The Culture of Western Europe* (1963)
Priestley, J.B. : *Literature and Western Man* (1960)
Pritchett, V.S. : *The Living Novel* (1947)
Simmons, E.J. : *Outline of Modern Russian Literature 1880-1940* (1943)
Smith H. (Edited) : *Columbia Dictionary of Modern European Literature* (1947)

CHAPTER 50
MUSIC

Einstein, A. : *A Short History of Music* (1938)
Finney, T.M. : *A History of Music* (1947)
Lang, P.M. : *Music in Western Civilisation* (1941)

CHAPTER 51
ART AND ARCHITECTURE

Cherey : *The Story of Modern Art* (1941)
Craven Thomas : *Modern Art, The Man, The Movement, The Meaning* (1934)
Pevsner, N. : *Pioneers of Modern Movement from William Morris to Walter Gropius* (1936)
Raynal, M. : *The 19th Century, Goya to Gauguin* (1951)
Read, H. : *Art and Society* (1937)
Richards, J.M. : *An Introduction to Modern Architecture* (1951)
Richardson, F.P. : *The Way of Western Art*, 1776-1914 (1939)
Valentiner, W.R. : *Origins of Modern Sculpture* (1946)

CHAPTER 52
EPILOGUE

Boulding Kenneth : *The Meaning of the Twentieth Century,* (1965)
Heilbroner Robert, L. : *The Great Ascent* (1963)
Pryce-Jones, A. (Ed.) : *The New Outline of Modern Knowledge,* (1956)
Toynbee Arnold : *Experiences* (1970)

INDEX

A

A Doll's House 790
A Farewell to Arms 799
A Pair of Blue Eyes 791
A. E. Housman 820
A. Elliot 809
A. J. Balfour 774
A. Mohorovicic 773
A. V. Alexander 681
A. W. N. Pugin 809
A.R. Orange 279
Aaland Islands 532
Abbe Dobrovsky 180
Abbe Laugier 808
Abdul Aziz 242, 243
Abdul Hamid 365, 655
Abdul Hamid II 360, 365, 654
Abdul Mejid 236, 243
Aberdeen 258
Aborigines Protection Society 695
Aboukir 109
Aboukir Bay 108
Abraham Lincoln 561, 563
Abyssinia 288, 312, 470, 471, 490, 548, 668, 708
Academia dei Lincei 62
Academic del Ciments 62
Academie des Beaux Arts 810
Academie des Sciences 62
Academy of France 55
Accident Insurance Laws in 1884 322
Acerbo Law 467
Act of 1819 135
Act of Chapultec 612
Act of Settlement 44
Act of Supremacy 29
Adages 14
Adalbert Falk 319
Adalia 391
Adam Mickiewiez 536
Adam Smith 37, 66, 91, 135, 138, 250, 270, 701, 717, 753
Adam Smith's Wealth of Nations 255
Adamantios Koraes 232
Adams 146, 771
Addington 109
Addis Ababa 289, 471, 500
Admiral Alekseev 440
Admiral Alexander Kolchak 450
Admiral Darlan 504, 588
Admiral Graf Spee 380
Admiral Horthy 390
Admiral Karl Doenitz 509
Admiral Leah 510
Admiral Limpus 368
Admiral Muller 373
Admiral Nicholas Horthy 356
Admiral Nimitz 503
Admiral Tirpitz 283
Admiral von Tirpitz 334
Adolf Hitler 348, 387
Adolf Menzel 811
Adolf Wagner 320, 344
Adolf Wermuth 332
Adolfo Diaz 582
Adolph Thiers 151, 203
Adolphus of Nassau 526
Adowa 288, 463
Adrianople 222, 234, 325, 360, 362, 367, 390
Adriatic 245, 369, 390
Adriatic littoral 35
Adventures of Tom Sawyer 789
Aegean 390
Aegean Coast 367
Aegean Islands 232, 390
Aegean Sea 363, 390
Aehrenthal 349, 350
Afghanistan 292, 306, 337, 371, 403, 409, 420, 430, 458, 656, 676

Africa 3, 53, 86, 87, 137, 153, 168, 236, 257, 281, 282, 283, 284, 286, 300, 305, 326, 327, 336, 414, 420, 422, 426, 463, 464, 470, 471, 486, 496, 504, 523, 588, 694, 697, 701, 708, 751, 752
African Missionaries 282
Agadir 306, 338, 339, 372
Agassiz 739
Age of Consent (Sarda) Act of 1929 675
Agfa 344
Agostino Depretis 463
Agra 674
Agriculture 760, 761
Ahmad Shah 658, 659
Ahmed Arabi 660
Aix-la-Chapelle 144, 145, 174
Akhal-Khorasan Convention 656
Alabama 259, 558, 563
Alaska 576
Alban Berg 245, 340, 365, 367, 372, 403, 404, 470, 471, 500, 512, 803
Albert Einstein 483, 769, 820
Albert Gilbert 814
Albert Krupp 192
Albert Memorial 810
Albert Museum 811
Albert Sarraut 685
Albert Speer 487
Alberta 291, 427
Alberti 15
Alberto Moravia 469
Albrecht Altdorfer of Regensburg 18
Albrecht Durer 18
Albrecth von Wallenstein 46
Alcaba 13
Alciati 19
Alcock 775
Aldous Huxley 798, 799
Alejandro Lerroux 546
Aleksandr Borodin 804
Aleppo 295
Alessandro Manzoni 207
Alessandro Volta 754, 766
Alexander 140, 219, 220, 221, 225
Alexander Blok 797
Alexander Duff 673, 738
Alexander Graham Bell 571
Alexander Hamilton 78, 555
Alexander Hypsilantes 232
Alexander I 221, 364
Alexander II (1855-81) 536, 735, 223, 225, 226, 227, 241
Alexander III 437, 438, 440
Alexander Karageorgevich 232
Alexander Millerand 279
Alexander Munro 810
Alexander VI 21, 24
Alexander von Humboldt 754, 755, 763
Alexander-Theodore Brongniart 808
Alexandre Dumas 781
Alexandre Millerand 302
Alexandria 108, 237, 284, 285, 503, 659, 660
Alfieri 207
Alfonso XIII 545, 546
Alfred de Musset 781
Alfred Doblin 486, 487, 820
Alfred E. Smith 580, 584
Alfred Nobel 265
Alfred Rosenberg 487
Alfred Sisley 812
Alfred von Kiderlen-Wachter 338
Alfredo Palacios 603
Algarotti 808
Algeciras 306, 337, 339, 372
Algeciras Conference of 1906 576
Algeciras Treaty 338
Algeria 168, 229, 243, 282, 284, 287, 300, 302, 504, 588, 664, 695, 821
Algernon Charles Swinburne 785
Algiers 35, 152, 157, 496
alkaline 760
Allan Octavian Hume 676
Allen Tate 798
Allenby 662
Alonso de Ojeda 5
Alps 543
Alsace 48, 49, 53, 133, 203, 205, 296, 301, 308, 309, 318, 320, 333, 386, 388
Alsace and Lorraine 49, 512, 202, 263, 308, 310, 343, 385, 407, 720
Alvar Aalto 819
Alvensleben Convention 194
Alvise Ca' da Mosto 3
Amado Nervo 604
Amazon 596
America 5, 6, 10, 32, 53, 58, 70, 130, 147, 178, 257, 259, 277, 281, 389, 400, 404, 408, 414, 438, 488, 556, 571, 591, 622, 653, 693, 718, 722, 723, 736, 738, 749, 751, 752, 755, 788, 798, 813, 817, 818

America Civil War 170
American 258
American Civil War 83, 85, 421
American Declaration 95
American President Wilson 380
American Secretary 309
American War of Independence 523
Amerigo Vespucci 5
Amiens 113, 383
Amoy 615
Ampere 738, 767
Amsterdam 10, 63, 64, 263, 277, 523, 706, 707
Anabaptist movement 26, 273
anabolism 762
Anarchism 273
Anarchists 227, 280
Anatole France 307
Anatolia 390, 391, 665
Ancona 743
Andalusia 274
Andes 593
Andra Francois-Poncet 488
Andrassy 323, 346, 347, 362
Andre Gide 820
Andre Le Notre 55
Andre Malraux 800, 820
Andrea Mantegna 18
Andrea Palladio 805
Andres Bello 596
Andres Santa 596
Andrew Bonar Law 432
Andrew Carnegie 571
Andrew Fisher 427
Andrew Jackson 562, 575
Andrew Johnson 569
Angelo Secchi 771
Anglican Church 27, 29, 260, 261
Anglicans 744
Anglo-Congolese Treaty 288
Anglo-Egyptian treaty of 1936 663
Anglo-French Agreement in April 1904 664
Anglo-French Convention 305
Anglo-French Entente 336
Anglo-French entente of 1904 283, 661
Anglo-German agreement of October 1900 648
Anglo-German Naval agreement of June 18, 1935 490
Anglo-Honduran Treaty of 1859 600
Anglo-Japanese Alliance of 336, 632, 648, 650
Anglo-Nicaraguan Treaty of 1860 600
Anglo-Persian Oil Company 659
Anglo-Portuguese Congo Treaty of 1884 327
Anglo-Portuguese Treaty 287
Anglo-Russian agreement of April 1899 648
Anglo-Russian Convention of 1907 457, 654, 292, 295, 676
Angola 284, 552
Angust Babel 283
Anjumans 658
Ankara 666
Anna Bijns 18
Anna Karenina 787
Annam 292, 294, 299, 613, 687
Anne Boleyn 28
Anne-Louis Girodet 806
Annette Von Drosta-Hulshoff 782
Annie Besant 423
Anopheles 759
Anschluss 353, 354
Antartica 6
Anthony Eden 434, 489, 506, 548, 669
Anthony Trollop 789
Anti-Comintern Pact (April 1939) 405, 491, 549, 652
Anti-Trust Act of 1890 572
Antibiotic 774
Antigua 587
Antoine-Jean Gros 806
Anton Bruckner 804
Anton Von Schmerling 183, 194
Anton Webern 803
Antonelli 795
Antoni Gaudi 814
Antonie de Foureroy 754
Antonie de Saint Exupery 800
Antonin Dvorak 804
Antonio Allegri 18
Antonio Canova 807
Antonio Guzman Blanco 602
Antonio Lopez de Santa Anna 598
Antonio Salandra 464
Antonio Serra 37
Antwerp 10, 377, 379, 507, 520, 589, 811
Apocalyptic School 750
Apostolical Succession 746
Appalachian Mountains 564
April theses 446
Arab League 670, 671

Arab nationalism 663, 669
Arabi Bey 285
Arabia 295
Arabs 20, 668
Aragon 33
Arakcheev 220
Arc de Triomphe du Carrousel 808
Arc de Triomphe in Paris 808
Archangal 450
Archbishop of Canterbury 28
Archduke Albert 45
Archduke Charles 45, 119
Archduke Francis Ferdinand 351, 369, 373
Archduke John 189
Archduke Louis 174
Archduke Maximilian of Austria 599
Archduke Rudolph 801
Archimedes 19, 59
Architecture 813
Archives Nationales 112
Ardennes 498, 507, 522
Aredeo Avogadro 763
Argentina 252, 277, 559, 578, 592, 593, 594, 597, 598, 601, 603, 604, 605, 609, 612, 723, 612
Aristide Briand 304, 309, 310
Aristotle 32, 61
Arkansas 558, 564, 565
Armed Neutrality 527
Armed Neutrality of the North 531
Armenia 390, 451
Armenians 363
Armistice of Plestwitz 122
Arms Act of 1878 676
Arndt 122, 127
Arne Jacobsen 819
Arnold Schoenberg 803, 804
Arnold Toynbee 308
Arras 383
Art Nouveau 814, 817
Art of War 15
Arthur Balfour 667
Arthur Eddington 771
Arthur H. Mackmurdo 814
Arthur Henderson 433
Arthur Honegger 803
Arthur J. Balfour 422
Arthur Moeller 486
Arthur O'Connor 127
Arthur Schnitzler 359
Arthur Seyss-Inquart 526
Arthur Sullivan 803
Arthur Thistlewood 249, 250
Arthur Wellesley 591
Arthur Young 89
Articles of Confederation 77
Artisans' Dwelling Act of 1875 420
Arturo Labriola 280
Ashanti 289, 426
Ashley's Act of 1842 256
Asia 84, 86, 137, 257, 281, 414, 496, 636, 646, 649, 721, 751, 752
Asia Minor 229, 326, 335
Asmus Jakob Carstens 807
Asquith 342, 381, 392, 424, 425, 426, 430
Assam 653
assignats 96
Astrakhan 35
Asturias 117, 547
Aswan Dam 429
Athens 404, 712
Atlantic 6, 720, 774
Atlantic Charter 502, 508, 515, 587
Atlantic Charter in 1941 694
atom bomb 777
Attlee 510
Attorney-General Harry M. Daugherty 580
Auchinleck 503
Auden 795, 797, 798
Auerstadt 114
Augsburg Settlement 48
August Bebel 278, 321, 373
August Hofmann 764
August Kekule 344
August Kiss 810
August Strindberg 790
Auguste Blanqui (1805-81) 157, 269
Auguste Comte 736
Auguste Renoir 812
Auguste-Dominique Ingres 810
Augustenberg 195
Augustin de lturbide 598
Augustin Fresnel 767
Aung San 688, 689
Aurore Dupin 781
Ausgleich 184, 185, 346, 355, 356
Austen Chamberlain 309, 406, 407, 458
Austerlitz 113, 114, 119, 125
Australasia 6

Australia 84, 85, 259, 291, 406, 414, 426, 427, 428, 497, 502, 580, 701, 705, 712, 718, 720, 723, 738
Austria 29, 58, 81, 84, 85, 98, 99, 100, 103, 107, 109, 113, 114, 115, 119, 120, 122, 123, 128, 139, 140, 141, 142, 143, 144, 145, 146, 147, 158, 162, 164, 169, 170, 173, 174, 176, 180, 182, 183, 184, 186, 187, 188, 190, 191, 193, 194, 195, 196, 197, 199, 200, 210, 211, 212, 213, 223, 230, 231, 237, 239, 242, 244, 246, 247, 248, 258, 264, 265, 267, 277, 318, 319, 322, 325, 326, 329, 338, 340, 341, 346, 347, 349, 350, 352, 353, 354, 355, 356, 360, 361, 362, 365, 368, 369, 371, 372, 379, 384, 385, 387, 390, 393, 395, 404, 414, 416, 440, 471, 489, 491, 495, 512, 535, 579, 581, 704, 705, 706, 707, 709, 724, 738, 748, 750, 752, 803
Austria-Hungary 84, 172, 306, 307, 323, 324, 326, 328, 336, 337, 349, 350, 351, 362, 363, 364, 368, 371, 374, 377, 379, 381, 383, 415, 444, 463, 464, 708, 718, 748
Austrian Emperor 214
Austrian Emperor Joseph II 231
Austrian Emperor, Francis Joseph 202
Austrian General Radetzky 210
Austro-German Alliance 324
Austro-German Treaty of 1879 326
Autobahnen 707
Avanti 464, 465
Avignon 21, 139
Awadh 672, 674
Axel Oxenstierna 47
Azana 547
Azerbaijan 451, 658
Azikiwe 695, 696
Aztec 6, 591

B

Ba Maw 689
Babbit 799
Babeuf 107, 270, 702
Bach Bach's 182
Bacon 64, 66, 779
Baden 153, 163, 164, 186, 190, 199, 200, 202, 204, 482
Badeni 348
Badoglio 505
Bagdad 295, 335, 370, 380, 383, 663, 664, 665, 666
Baghdad railway 340
Bahamas 587
Bahr-al-Ghazal 288
Bailly 95
Baker 284
Baku 450
Bakunin 227, 228, 272, 273, 274
Bal Gangadhar Tilak of Maharashtra 677
Balaclava 240
Baldwin 434
Balfour 389, 423
Balfour Declaration 665, 667
Balfour Note 400
Balfour Stewart 768
Bali 683
Balkan 244, 404
Balkan League 367, 373
Balkan Peninsula 229, 231, 244, 246, 363, 366, 500, 347
Balkan wars of 1913 392
Balkans 19, 234, 246, 374, 446, 504, 511, 705, 783
Ballot Act 419
Baltic 379, 386, 387, 489, 532
Baltic Provinces 438
Baltic Sea 532
Baltic States 26, 392, 394, 449, 511
Baltimore 572
Baluchistan 430, 680, 682
Balzac 561, 781, 789
Banda 592
Bank 263
Bank Charter Act of 1844 256, 719
Bank of Amsterdam 10
Bank of England 10, 110, 256, 434, 556, 719, 808
Bank of France 110, 310, 311, 312, 719
Bank of the United States 560
Banking 10
Banting 773
Bao Dai 687
Baptist 27, 749
Baptist Missionary Society 744
Barbary Pirates 144
Barcelona 545, 546, 706, 814
Bardoli 679
Barings 137, 661, 702
Baron Beust 184
Baron Conrad 373
Baron F. von Hugel 750
Baron Geringer 182
Baron Gros 618
Baron Karl von Vogelsang 748
Baron Rothschild's dictum 264
Baron Schwegel 347
Baron Werther 201
Baroque 31, 805

Barres 307
Barthelemy 107
Bartholomew Diaz 3
Barthou 312
Bartolome Mitre 598
Basil III 36
Basle 277
Basque Provinces 546, 547
Basra 35, 663, 665
Bastille 94, 95, 105
Bastille Day 100
Batavia (Jakarta) 682
Batavian Republic 523
Bateson 759
Batthyani, 181, 182
Battle of Britain 496, 499
Battle of Fleurus 517
Battle of Jutland 381
Battle of Leipzig 139, 187
Battle of Lepanto 35
Battle of Lutter 46
Battle of Nordlingen 48
Battle of the Bismarck Sea 588
Battle of the Bulge 589
Battle of the Nile 248
battle of Somme 380
battle of the Marne 378
Batum 323, 450
Baudelaire 82, 604, 781, 785, 789
Bauhaus 485, 816
Bauhaus at Dessau 820
Bautzen 122
Bavaria 113, 115, 153, 186, 190, 191, 197, 199, 200, 202, 204, 316, 472, 482, 732
Bay Islands 600
Bay of Bengal 676
Bayer 344
Bayle 63
Baylen 117
Bayonne 117
Bazaine 202, 203
Bazarov 227
Bazaroz 786
Beaconsfield 324, 420
Beatrice 279, 423
Bebel 280
Beccaria 68, 91
Becher 763
Bechualand 426
Bedford Park 811, 813
Bedrich Smetana 804
Beer Hall Putsch 479
Beethoven 801, 802, 804
Beggarstaff Brothers 814
Beirut 542, 667
Bela Bartok 803
Bela Kun 356, 390, 391, 457
Belgian Congo 695
Belgian independence 153
Belgium 84, 85, 107, 109, 110, 113, 114, 115, 123, 124, 132, 133, 142, 153, 155, 165, 221, 262, 263, 264, 266, 277, 281, 283, 284, 287, 301, 306, 329, 343, 374, 375, 377, 385, 386, 387, 392, 396, 397, 399, 402, 460, 490, 493, 498, 505, 507, 512, 517, 518, 519, 520, 521, 522, 523, 525, 526, 579, 701, 704, 705, 706, 708, 714, 716, 717, 718, 720, 723, 724, 725, 727, 744, 747, 748, 750, 811
Belgrade 351
Belinski 222
Belinsky 785
Bell Telephone System 571
Benedek 183, 197, 214
Benedetti 199, 201, 202
Benedetto Croce 469, 821
Benedict XV 750
Benelux 523, 727
Benes of Czechoslovakia 416
Bengal 672
Bengal National Chamber of Commerce 675
Benito Juarez 599
Benito Mussolini 275, 465
Benits Montenego 68
Benjamin Disraeli 138, 426
Benjamin Franklin 72, 74, 90, 555, 753, 766
Bentham 281, 734
Bentinck 672, 673
Berchtesgaden 492
Berchtold 340, 341, 343, 351, 352, 366, 373, 374, 375, 376
Beresina 121
Berg 818
Bergman 763
Berlage 818,
Berlin 85, 114, 161, 163, 192, 263, 320, 323, 335, 344, 354, 377, 381, 384, 397, 406, 412, 420, 461, 472, 474, 485, 488, 490, 493, 505, 506, 508, 509, 512, 579, 589, 661, 681, 732, 755, 801, 802, 820
Berlin Conference of 1884-85 283

Berlin Congress 287
Berlin Decree 116
Berlin Decree of December 1806 527
Berlin Memorandum of May 13, 1876 323
Berlin University 758
Berlin-Baghdad railway 431
Berlin-Rome-Tokyo axis 405
Berlioz 801, 802, 804
Bermuda 587
Bernadotte 122, 533, 670
Bernard Bolzano 174
Bernard de Fontenelle 62
Bernard Shaw 279, 423
Bernard von Bulow 331
Bernardino Rivadavia 593
Bernardo O' Higgins 592
Berne 543, 738
Bernstein 275, 276
Bertel Thorwaldsen 807
Berthelot 738, 755
Bertold Brecht 821, 485
Berya 501
Besika Bay 239, 323
Bessarabia 242, 244, 323, 352, 357, 364, 461
Bessel 770
Bessemer 131, 132
Best 773
Bethleham 238, 669
Bethmann 333, 338, 341, 342
Bethmann Hollweg 332, 338, 339, 340, 343, 371, 372, 373, 374, 375, 376, 350, 521
Beust 184, 346
Bevin 670
Bezobrazov 440
Bhagat Singh 680
Biarritz 196
Bible 749
Bibliotheque Nationale (1868) 104, 112, 810
Bichat 758
Bihar 672
Bill of Rights 44, 78, 555
Billeting Act 72
Biochemistry 761
biology 760
Bipin Chandra Pal 677
Birmingham 130, 134, 136, 248, 251, 706, 710, 734
Birmingham Political Union 251
Bishop Fisher 28
Bishop George Berkeley 63
Bishop Grundtvig 739
Bismarck 84, 85, 86, 164, 168, 191, 192, 193, 194, 195, 196, 197, 198, 199, 200, 201, 202, 203, 204, 242, 246, 278, 284, 286, 287, 316, 318, 319, 320, 321, 322, 323, 324, 325, 326, 327, 328, 329, 330, 333, 347, 360, 361, 362, 363, 370, 476, 477, 537, 538, 660, 661, 705, 724, 747
Bissolati 280
Bjarnstjerne Bjornson 530
Bjerknes 773
Bjorke treaty 336
Black Hand 350
Black Hand Society 351
Black Hundreds 443
Black Sea 240, 242, 361, 362, 363, 450, 666
Black Shirts 470
Blake 807
Blanc 159
Blanqui 160
blitzkrieg 496, 541
Bloch 9
Blok 797
Bloody Sunday 442
Blucher 123, 124
Blum 313, 548, 711
Board Schools 260, 419
Boccaccio 12, 16
Boer 370
Boer War 423, 424, 429, 710
Boerhaave 763
Boers 289, 427, 428
Bogota 593
Bohemia 45, 48, 162, 163, 164, 172, 174, 177, 183, 184, 197, 264, 277, 347, 352, 390, 471
Boileau 55
Boleslav Beirut 541
Bolivar 592, 593, 597
Bolivia 586, 592, 593, 596, 597, 598, 602, 608, 610
Bologna 14, 68, 206, 755
Bolshevik 579, 728
Bolshevik policy 709
Bolshevik Revolution (1917) 706, 385
Bolsheviks 404, 440, 442, 445, 446, 447, 448, 450, 451, 474
Bolshevism 276, 389
Bombay 674, 738
Bonald 128, 743
Bonaparte 106, 108
Bonar Law 400

Bonn 733
Bonnard 816
Bonomi 280
Bontempelli 795
Booker T. Washington 570
Bordeaux 102, 203, 296, 314
Boris Pasternak 797
Borneo 292, 502, 525, 653, 683
Borodin 121, 226, 457, 459, 641
Bosnia 229, 323, 324, 337, 338, 341, 347, 349, 350, 360, 362, 364, 365, 366, 368, 372, 390
Bosnia and Harzegovina 239, 347, 352
Bosphorus 234, 237, 238, 367
Boston 74, 580, 718, 739, 755, 813
Botany Bay 291
botany 760
Botha 429
Boticelli 12, 15, 17
Bouguereau 811
Boulanger 301, 302
Boulogne 113
Bourbon 298
Bourbon Dynasty 206
Bourbon King Francis II 216
Bourbons 47, 126, 248
Bourse 808
Bousset 65
Boxer 635
Boxer Movement 634
Boxer rebellion 284, 575, 633
Boxer War (1900) 648
Boxers 634
Boy Scout 706
Boycott 677
Braganza 591
Brahmo Samaj 674
Brahms 359, 804
Bramante 17, 805
Brancusi 817
Brandenburg 26, 28, 332
Branting 416
Braque 307, 815, 816
Braque's 'Portuguese' 815
Braudel 822
Brave New World (1932) 799
Bray 270
Brazaville Declaration of 1944 687
Brazil 3, 6, 85, 116, 117, 252, 550, 578, 594, 595, 597, 598, 601, 602, 603, 606, 609
Brazza 288
Brazzaville Conference 694
Brecht 795, 821
Bremen 49, 116, 472, 473, 482, 589
Brentano 122, 782
Breslau 191
Briand 305, 309, 381, 407, 477
Bridges 797
Brienne 93
Brigadier Wingate 510
Bright 255, 258, 260, 565
Bright Brothers' 86
Brissot 99, 101, 103
Bristol 5, 248, 710
Britain 58, 70, 74, 75, 76, 84, 101, 107, 108, 111, 114, 115, 116, 123, 125, 129, 130, 131, 132, 135, 139, 140, 141, 142, 144, 145, 146, 153, 154, 158, 167, 169, 170, 194, 199, 212, 214, 217, 222, 223, 225, 230, 233, 235, 237, 238, 239, 240, 242, 243, 245, 246, 247, 248, 258, 259, 260, 262, 264, 267, 268, 277, 280, 283, 286, 287, 289, 290, 291, 292, 293, 295, 306, 309, 312, 313, 314, 322, 323, 324, 325, 326, 327, 328, 333, 334, 335, 336, 337, 338, 339, 342, 343, 362, 365, 371, 372, 375, 377, 379, 380, 381, 383, 387, 389, 390, 392, 397, 399, 400, 401, 403, 404, 405, 406, 407, 408, 409, 410, 411, 412, 416, 417, 419, 422, 426, 430, 433, 434, 440, 444, 449, 460, 470, 471, 477, 478, 489, 490, 491, 492, 493, 494, 497, 499, 500, 502, 512, 515, 520, 521, 525, 526, 527, 528, 529, 530, 532, 533, 541, 545, 547, 548, 549, 550, 556, 558, 574, 575, 576, 579, 585, 586, 594, 596, 598, 600, 601, 615, 618, 619, 621, 622, 629, 632, 633, 639, 643, 644, 645, 646, 647, 648, 650, 653, 655, 656, 660, 661, 663, 664, 665, 666, 667, 669, 670, 675, 677, 680, 682, 687, 689, 690, 691, 692, 693, 704, 705, 706, 707, 708, 709, 710, 711, 715, 716, 717, 719, 720, 721, 722, 723, 724, 727, 740, 745, 749, 751, 752, 755, 760, 776, 813, 814
British Columbia 427
British Commonwealth of Nations 291
British East Africa (Kenya) 426
British General Allenby 384
British Guiana 429, 574, 587
British High Commissioner 690
British Honduras 429
British India Association 674
British Museum 756, 808, 809
British South Africa Company 284

British Trade Union Congress 268
Brittany 57
Broglie 155
Broglie Ministry 156
Bronte sisters 788
Brown 775
Bruckner 359
Bruening 479, 480, 481
Brugnatelli 754
Brumoire 104
Brunei 683
Brunelleschi 15, 16
Bruni 12
Brunswick 100, 163, 189
Brussels 45, 277, 416, 507, 518, 645
Bucharest 245, 380
Buckingham 808
Budapest 175, 180, 181, 182, 184, 346, 356, 357, 390, 579, 810
Buenos Aires 591, 592, 593, 596, 597, 598
Buenos Aires Conference in 1936 610
Buffalo 572
Buffon 756
Bukharin 452, 453, 457
Bukovina 352, 357, 364, 390, 461, 511, 512
Bulgaria 85, 246, 277, 308, 323, 325, 326, 340, 349, 357, 360, 362, 363, 364, 366, 367, 372, 382, 384, 385, 390, 415, 508, 512, 665, 740, 751
Bulgarian Atrocities 360
Bulow 332, 335, 337, 338, 372, 378
Bundesrat 198, 316, 317, 339
Bunge 439
Bunsen 721
Buonarotti 107, 127, 208
Burgenland 390
Burgoyne 76
Burgundy 18
Burke 74, 128, 247
Burma 259, 292, 293, 426, 430, 501, 502, 509, 510, 515, 587, 590, 613, 646, 653, 688, 689, 692
Burns Constitution 694
Burschenchaften 187
Bushire 659
Butler 792
Byelorussia 449, 451, 538, 539, 751
Byron 208, 784, 785, 786
Byzantine 810

C

C. D. Darlington 760
C. E. Trevelyan 738
C. L. Ledoux 808
Cabanel 811
Cabinet Mission 681
Cacao 602
Cachar 672
Cadet 442, 443, 444, 445
Cadiz 547
Caen 507
Cairo 285, 286, 588, 654, 660, 661, 663, 670
Calais 40, 507
Calcutta 430, 674, 718, 738
Calcutta Medical College 673
Caleb Cushing, 616
Calicut 3, 5
California 191, 558, 561, 562
California Institute of Technology 769
Calonne 92
Calvin 28
Calvin Coolidge 579, 580
Calvinism 28
Calvinists 51
Calvo Sotelo 547
Cambodia 292, 687, 693
Cambrai 382
Cambridge 251, 257, 734, 739, 746, 755, 761
Cambridge University 768
Camelin 490
Cameroon 308, 387, 287, 308, 326, 380, 403, 695, 697
Camille Corot 810
Camille Pissarro 812
Camilo Torres 591
Camp Formio 109
Campbell Bannerman 424
Camperdown 524
Canada 70, 76, 84, 290, 291, 406, 426, 427, 428, 429, 511, 557, 580, 586, 701, 718, 723
Cancasus 363
Cancer 774
Candide 65, 779
Cannes 397, 589
Canning 146, 147, 230, 234, 250, 258, 527, 595, 675, 682
Canovas 545
Canovas del castillo of Spain 274
Canton 614, 615, 616, 618, 636, 637, 642, 645, 648
Canton River 5
Cape 284
Cape Colony 84, 140, 259, 284, 290, 426, 427, 428
Cape of Good Hope 6
Cape Verde 6

Cape Verde Islands 3
Capitalism 9
Capodistrias 232
Caporetto 382, 384
Caprivi 329, 330, 333, 334, 538
Captain Cook 291
Captain Elliot 615
Captain Jean-Baptist Merchand 289
Captain Nakamura 643
Caracas 591
Caravaggio 31, 806
Carbonari 127, 208, 213
Cardenas 606
Cardinal de Brienne 92
Cardinal de Richelieu 52
Cardinal Lavigerie 282
Cardinal Mastai Ferritti 209
Cardinal Mazarin 49, 53
Cardinal Pacelli 751
Cardinal Richelieu 47
Cardinal Wyszynski 542
Cardinal Ximenes 13
Caribbean 87
Caribbean 601, 604, 608
Caribbean Sea 598
Carinthia 244, 352
Carl Anderson 769
Carl Friedrich Gauss 772, 773
Carl Jung 820
Carl Maria von Weber 802
Carl Nielsen 804
Carl Peters 326
Carl Sandburg 797
Carl Schmitt 486, 487
Carlo Antonio Lopez 598
Carlo Pisacane 211
Carlos I 551
Carlos Maria de Cespedes 603
Carlotta Grisi 802
Carlsbad 188
Carlsbad Decrees 188
Carlton Club 252
Carlton House 808
Carlton House Terrace 808
Carlton J. H. Hayes 549
Carlyle 83, 703
Carnarvon 289
Carnatic 672
Carniola 244
Carnot 103, 104, 107, 288
Carol I 364
Carpathians 379, 380
Carranza 605
Carribean 578
Cartwright's 130
Casablanca 314, 588
Casimir of Brandenburg 26
Casimir Perier 155
Caspar David Friedrich (1774-1840) 807
Caspian 361, 363, 370
Cassel 141
Cassini 771
Cassino 506
Castel Gandolfo 462
Castelfidardo 216
Castlereagh 140, 141, 145, 146, 249, 258, 525, 595, 682, 139, 230
Catabolia 546
Catalon Miro 816
Catalonia 274, 546, 547, 548
Catherine 219, 531
Catherine II 218, 219, 441, 535
Catherine II of Russia 68, 69
Catherine of Aragon 28
cathode ray 768, 774
Catholic 27, 31, 260
Catholic Church 304, 749
Catholic Emancipation 251, 784
Catholic Reformation 544
Catholicism 30, 31, 751
Catholics 44, 518
Cato Street conspiracy 250
Caucasus 448, 450, 459, 501
Cauchy 754
Cavendish Laboratory at Cambridge 762
Cavignac 152, 161
Cavour 83, 84, 169, 204, 209, 212, 213, 214, 215, 216, 217, 240, 242, 264, 363
Cecil 417
Cecil Rhodes 283, 284, 290, 428
Celebes 292, 502, 653
Cellular Biology 758
Central America 592, 598, 603, 605, 608
Centre Party 319, 321
Ceres 771
Cesar Cui 804
Cesar Franck 803
Ceylon 110, 248, 258, 293, 429, 524, 682

Cezanne 307
Chaadaev 222
Chad 289
Chadwick 820
Chain 774
Chamberlain 289, 407, 477, 478, 491, 492, 493, 540, 548
Chambers' Cyclopaedia 91
Chambord (Henry V) 297
Chamisso 782
Champagne 89
Chancellor Bruning 399
Chancellor Heinrich Bruning 399
Chancellor of the Exchequer 434
Chancellor Wilhelm Marx 478
Chandigarh 819, 820
Chang Chih-tung 633, 635
Chang Hsueh-Liang 642, 643
Chang Tso-lin 639, 651
Charcoal Burners 208
Charlemagne 120, 125, 743
Charles Albert 163, 210, 211
Charles Barry 809
Charles Baudelaire 785
Charles Buller 259
Charles d' Albert 52
Charles Darwin 82, 756, 757
Charles de Freycinet 299
Charles de Gaulle 497, 499, 588, 694
Charles Dickens 82, 94, 253, 702
Charles E. Hughes 579
Charles Felix 208
Charles Fourier (1772-1837) 136, 157, 269, 736
Charles G. Dawes 477
Charles G. Finney 744
Charles Goodyear 132
Charles I 43, 44, 352
Charles II 33, 44, 57, 149
Charles IV 117, 591
Charles IX 34
Charles James Fox 95
Charles John 530, 533
Charles Lamb 783
Charles Le Brun 55
Charles Lyell 756, 757
Charles Maurras 304
Charles Percier 808
Charles Rennie Mackintosh 814
Charles Sherrington 760
Charles Stewart Parnell 421
Charles Townshend 73
Charles V 25, 28, 35
Charles VIs Pragmatic Sanction 172
Charles Wood 673
Charles X 34, 151, 152, 153, 155, 297, 744
Charles XII 120, 531, 526
Charles XIII 532
Charles XIV 533
Charles XV 533
Charleston 560
Charlotte 788
Charter Act of 1793 673, 674
Charter of Amiens of 1908 275
Chartism 254, 255
Chartist 254
Chartist programme 267
Chartists 135, 137, 745
Chase 563, 565
Chateaubriand 81, 88, 150, 152, 153, 743
Chatham 74
Chatillon 123
Chaucer 134
Chauri Chaura 679
Chautemps 311
Cheka 452
Chekhov 786, 787, 791
Chelsea 809, 812
Chemistry 762
Cherbourg 507
Chernyshevskii 223, 227
Cheshire 254
Chia-Ching 614
Chiang Kai Shek 459, 510, 588, 590, 640, 641, 642, 645, 646, 647
Chiarelli 795
Chicago 572, 814, 817
Chicherin 460
Chien-lung 614
child-sacrifice 673
Chile 380, 578, 583, 591, 592, 593, 596, 598, 601, 602, 603, 607, 608, 609, 612, 723
China 6, 20, 30, 84, 85, 87, 131, 134, 138, 283, 284, 292, 293, 294, 295, 299, 336, 376, 395, 417, 426, 501, 509, 510, 511, 515, 575, 579, 580, 586, 590, 613, 614, 615, 616, 617, 618, 630, 632, 634, 638, 639, 641, 642, 643, 645, 646, 647, 648, 650, 652, 674, 676, 685, 691, 693, 715, 719, 720, 751, 776

Chinese Communist Party (CCP) 639, 640
Chinese Eastern Railway 643
Chinese Turkestan 632
Ching Empire 632
Chins 689
Chios 233
Chirico 820
Chittaranjan Das 679
Cholera 703, 704
Chopin 804
Choshu 622, 624
Choshu Hizen 623
Chou En-Lai 645, 648
Christian IV of Denmark 46
Christian Socialists 349
Christian X 529
Christofels 19
Christopher Columbus 3, 5
Christopher Fry 795
Christopher Isherwood 800
Chulalong Korn 692
Chungking 647
Church-building 808
Churchill 314, 401, 494, 496, 497, 498, 499, 500, 503, 504, 506, 508, 511, 515, 587, 588, 691, 710
Ciano 354, 493, 494
Cicero 12, 63
Cilicia 391, 666
cinema 711
Cisalpine Republic 107
Citroen 707
Ciudad Rodrigo 118
Civic humanism 12
Civil 788
Civil Constitution of the Clergy 97, 741
Civil Disobedience 679, 680, 681
Civil Rights Bill 566
Civil Service Reform of 1870 260
Civil War 259, 566, 570, 571, 573, 738
Clarendon the British Foreign Minister 213, 239
Clark Maxwell 767
Classical Symphony (1917) 803
Classicism 55
Claude Bernard 758, 761
Claude Bertholett 754
Claude Debussy 803
Claude Helvetius 66
Claude Monet 812
Claude Montefiore 750
Claus Sluter 18
Clausewitz 204
Clayton Antitrust Act of 1914 577
Clayton-Bulwar Treaty 600
Clemenceau 53, 299, 301, 302, 304, 307, 308, 309, 312, 314, 375, 385, 386, 497, 711
Clement Attlee 493, 541, 681
Clive 673
Coal 675
Coal Mines Act 705
coal 718
Cobban 89
Cobbett 256
Cobden 255, 256, 258, 565
Cobden Treaty 135, 265
Cobden-Chevalier Pact 719
Cobden-Chevalier Treaty 168
Cochin 3
Cochin China 619, 292, 685, 687
Cockcroft 820
Code Napoleon 111, 112, 115, 126
Codrington 234
Colbert 39, 54, 55, 111
Cold War 515, 777
Coleridge 127, 782, 783, 784
Collective Security 586
College de France 758
Colloquies 14
Cologne 23, 191, 345, 472, 588, 589, 809
Colombia 6, 576, 593, 595, 597, 602, 603, 608, 609
Colonel Alexander Couza 245
Colonel Bleriot 775
Colonel Enver Bey 366
Colonel Frank Knox 586
Colonel Henry 302
Colonel Henry L. Stimson 582
Colonel House 343
Colonel Jellachich 181
Colonel Picquart 302
Colonel Thomas Pride 44
Colorado 573
Coluccio Salutati 12
Columbia 415, 559, 755
Columbus 5, 6
Combes 304
Combination Acts 253, 267
Combination Laws 253
Comintern 457, 458, 459
Comite des Forges 265

Committee of Public Safety 102
Commodore Biddle 620
Commodore George Dewey 574
Commodore Perry 84, 293, 621
Common Law 40, 42, 78
Common Sense 74
Commonwealth 44
Communal Award in August 1932 680
Commune 101
Communism 391, 691, 746, 751
Communist Manifesto 6, 83, 165, 272, 274, 703
Communist Party 452, 479, 482, 542, 607, 647
Communist Revolution in Russia in 1917 650
Communists 357, 480, 515, 546, 580, 645, 646, 647, 685
company law of 1870-72 264
computers 820
Comte de Rivarol 780
Concert of Europe 86, 87, 242, 258, 413
Concordat 112, 310, 743, 747, 748
Concordat of 1801 303, 309, 735
Concordat of Bologna 33
Concordat on July 15, 1801 742
Condillac 778
Condorcet 66, 778
Confederacion Nacional del Trabajo (CNT) 275
Confederation Generale du Travail 268, 275
Confederation of the Rhine 114, 123, 186
Confucius 638
Congo 284, 287, 288, 300, 327, 521, 523, 664, 723
Congo basin 283, 287
Congo Free State 521
Congo River 3
Congress at Troppau 145
Congress at Verona 146, 559
Congress of Aix-la-Chapelle 269
Congress of Berlin 323, 335, 347, 362
Congress of Paris 213
Congress of Verone 146
Congress of Vienna 49, 140, 142, 191, 248, 530, 535
Congress of Westphalia 49
Conrad 341, 351, 374, 378, 793
Conrad Aiken 798
Conrad Alberti 345
Conrad Ferdinand Meyer 789
Conservatives 259
Constable 809, 812
Constantine 221, 535
Constantinople 11
Constantinople 35, 120, 222, 223, 229, 230, 235, 237, 238, 239, 285, 287, 295, 323, 325, 340, 347, 360, 362, 365, 366, 367, 373, 379, 390, 391, 654, 660, 661, 751, 752
Constituent Assembly 96, 98
Constitutionalists 99
Consul 109
Consulate 113
Continental Blockade 220
Continental Congress 74, 75, 77
Continental System 115, 116, 117, 120, 123, 125, 173, 248
Convention 101, 102, 104, 105, 106, 109, 112, 517, 742
Convention of Akkerman (October 1826) 234
Convention of Cintra 117
Convention of Erfurt 118
Convention of Gastein on August 14 196
Convention of London 599
Convention of Malmoe 189
Convention of Olmutz 191
Convention People's Party (CPP) 696
Coolidge 583
Cooper 456
Coorg 672
Copenhagen 109, 277, 526, 527, 716
Copernicus 19, 32, 59, 63, 757
Coral Sea 653
Corbusier 818, 819
Cordell Hull 506, 610, 646, 652
Corfu 403, 415, 469
Corn Law 249, 82, 255, 256, 717
Cornelius 571
Cornelius Jansen 30
Cornell University 738
Cornwallis 76, 672
Corot 810
Correggio 806
Corsica 469
Cortes 544, 546
Corti 362
cortisone 820
Cossack 535, 658
Costa Cabral 550
Costa Rica 6, 595, 600
Cotton 717
Coulomb 766
Council of Constance 21
Council of the People's Commissars 457

Council of Trent 30
Count 297
Count Andrassy 184
Count Andrey Kryillovich Razumovsky 802
Count Berchtold 350
Count Bernadotte 670
Count Bethlen 357
Count Buol 178
Count Czernin 391
Count Dimitri Tolstoy 227
Count Eulenburg 330
Count Gyulai 214
Count Hoyos 341, 351
Count Latour 176
Count Machael Karolyi 356
Count of Chambord 297
Count of Habsburg 172
Count of Monte Cristo 781
Count Okuma 627, 629
Count Oxenstierna 53
Count Palikao 202
Count Philipp Stadion 173
Count Rumford 766
Count Schlieffen, Chief of the German General Staf 377
Count Schwerin von Krosigk 483
Count Stephen Tisza 351
Count Thun 176
Count Tilly 46
Count Wallis 179
Counter Reformation 32, 35, 29, 30, 58
Court of Directors 672
Court of the Star Chamber 34
Covent Garden Theatre 256
Cracow 119, 536, 537, 541
Credit Foncier 167
Credit Mobilier 167, 178, 719
Creoles 591, 592
Crete 223, 363, 367, 504
Cricket 712
Crime and Punishment 786
Crimea 212, 243, 504, 505
Crimean War (1854-55) 83, 169, 212, 222, 223, 225, 226, 230, 232, 235, 238, 239, 242, 244, 258, 263, 292, 370, 536
Crimean War of 1855-6 444
Cripps Mission 681
Cripps' plan 681
Crispi 215, 463
Critique of Pure Reason 67
Croatia 114, 175, 181, 182, 183, 185, 244, 341, 350, 352
Croatia-Slavonia 390
Croats 172, 184, 349
Crome 809
Cromer 660
Cromwell 31, 39
Crown Prince Frederick 527
Crusades 9
Crystal Palace 809, 814
Cuba 5, 6, 85, 544, 574, 575, 586, 601, 602, 603, 604, 608, 723
Cubism 815, 816, 817
Cunard Line 257
Cuno 476
Curia Regis 41
Curzon Line 538, 539
Curzon's 675
Customs Union or Zollverein 719
Custozza 197, 210, 217
Cuvier 738, 755
Cyprus 238, 323, 362, 390, 420, 426, 429, 500
Cyrenaica 470, 503, 504
cytology 761
Czar Alexander 113, 143
Czar Paul 109
Czechoslovakia 246, 308, 313, 352, 356, 357, 387, 388, 390, 391, 392, 402, 403, 409, 415, 477, 489, 491, 492, 493, 495, 512, 669, 707, 750, 751
Czechs 184, 346, 347, 349, 390
Czechs of Bohemia 176

D

'Deutsche Werkbund' in 1907 818
D' Annunzio 389, 465
D' Azeglio 211, 212
d' Alembart 63, 66, 779
D-Day 589
D. G. Rossetti 784
D. H. Lawrence 796, 798
D. H. Lawrence 820
D. N. Shipov 440
D. Ricardo 717
Dada 817
Dadaism 815, 816
Daguerre 132
Dahlmann 165, 188, 733
Dahomey 300
Daily Telegraph 331, 333
Daimyo 619, 620, 623, 624

Dairen 512
Dakar 168
Daladier 311, 312, 313, 314, 492, 499
Dalhousie 673, 674, 676
Dalmatia 114, 182, 341, 349, 350, 352, 390, 464, 465
Daman 552
Damascus 233, 295, 384, 667, 670
Damascus Berenguer 546
Dance of Death (1901) 790, 798
Dandi 679
Daniel Manin 163, 210
Daniel Manin in Venice 211
Daniel O'Connell 251
Dante 16, 19, 208, 798
Dante Gabriel Rossetti 811
Danton 53, 99, 100, 101, 103, 104, 296, 298
Danube 119, 148, 179, 239, 240, 242, 243, 335, 349, 359, 387, 390
Danzig 34, 35, 313, 386, 415, 489, 491, 493, 496, 539, 540, 541
Dar-es-Salaam 287
Dardanelles 234, 236, 237, 238, 239, 308, 372, 379, 430, 461, 666, 367
Darien 5
Darmstadtar Bank 266
Darmstadter Bank 721, 722
Darwin 273, 757, 759, 774
Darwinism 748, 749
Das Capital 270, 272
David 18, 806
David Ben-Gurion 670, 671
David Hume 63, 66, 91
David Livingstone 284
David Lloyd George 423, 425
David Lloyd George, chancellor of the Exchequer 375
David Ricardo 135
Davis Cup in 1900 712
Dawes Committee 397
Dawes Plan 398, 432, 477, 478
DDT 776
De Gaulle 314, 499, 504, 512, 687
De Lesseps 285
De Luther 479
De Man 522
De Valera 436
de Courcel 287
de Maistre 743
de Stael 153
de Stephani 795
de Tocqueville 157
Dead Marat 805
Deak 184, 185, 355
Debussy 307
Decazes 150
Decembrist Movement 221, 223
Decembrists 127, 221
Declaration 75
Declaration of Independence 77
Declaration of Independence and the Declaration of the Right of Man 247
Declaration of Pillnitz 99
Declaration of the Rights 125
Declaration of the Rights of Man and
Declaratory 72
Degrelle 522
Delacroix 806
Delagoa Bay 428
Delaware 564
Delbos 491
Delcasse 53, 289, 305, 336, 337
Delhi 674
Delvaux 820
Democrats 444
Denikin 391, 450, 454
Denis Diderot 63, 66, 91, 779
Denmark 26, 46, 47, 48, 49, 69, 85, 100, 109, 115, 123, 133, 142, 144, 189, 194, 195, 204, 266, 277, 386, 498, 500, 504, 512, 522, 526, 527, 529, 531, 533, 706, 707, 715, 716, 717, 724, 736, 744, 818
Depression of 1930 581, 607
Der Freischutz 802
Descartes 62, 63, 64, 776
Descent of Man 757
Desiderius Erasmus 22
Destour 697
Deutsche 263
Deutsche Bank 266, 295
Devaux 518
Devil's Island 302
diabetes mellitus 773
Dickens 561, 703, 788, 789
Diderot 66, 92, 778, 779
Diego Barros Arana 604
Diego Portales 596
Diego Velasquez 31
Dien Bien Phu 687
Diesel 775
Diet at Erfurt 190

Diet of Augsburg 26
Diet of Speyer 26
Diet of Vasteras 34
difficult 323
Diggers 273
Dimitry Bogrov 444
Dimitry Tolstoy 437
Dino Grandi 466, 470
Diogo Cao 3
Directory 106, 107, 108, 111
Disarmament Conference 412, 417, 488, 489
Disraeli 83, 85, 204, 260, 267, 281, 282, 285, 289, 360, 420, 660, 703, 723
Diu 552
Divine Comedy 16
Djibouti 287
DNA 762
Dneiper 451, 501
Dobrudja 362, 380, 382, 390, 511
Dockers' Strike of 1889 422
Doctor's Dilemma 794
Dodecanese 390
Dodecanese Archipelago 366, 372
Dodecanese Islands 391
Dollar diplomacy 578
Dollfuss 353, 489, 707
Dom Miguel 550
Dom Pedro 550
Dom Pedro 594
Dom Pedro de Alcantara 595
Dom Pedro I of Brazil 594
Domagk 774
Domenico Theotocopuli 18
Domingo Faustino Sarmiento 604
Dominican Republic 608
Dominion Status 259, 679, 681
Domitri Mendeleyev 769
Don Antonio Canovas del Castillo 544
Don Balthasar de Zuniga 46
Don Carlos 544
Don Juan 783
Don Miguel Primo de Rivera 545
Donatello 12, 15, 16
Donation of Constantine 12
Donetz basin 439, 501
Donna Maria da Gloria 550
Donnersmark 263
Dorman Smith 689
Dos Passes 799
Dostoevsky 82, 226, 786, 787, 790, 821
Douglas Haig 383, 424
Doumergue 311, 312
DR A. C. Hedlam 750
DR Arthur von Seyss-Inquart 354
DR Chaim Weizmann 668, 670
DR Gore 750
DR Jameson 290, 334
DR Jose Gaspar Rodriguez de Francia 598
DR Karl Renner 355
DR Kay 737
DR Nachtigal 285
DR Peters 285, 287
DR Theophil Braga 551
Dr Pusey 257
Dr. Black 753
Dr. David Livingstone 282
Dr. Erasmus Darwin 753, 756
Dr. Hutton 753
Dr. Sun Yat Sen 633, 640
Draft Treaty of Mutual Assistance 309, 409, 416
Drama 791
Drang nach osten 335, 370
Dreadnought 337
Dred Scott 563
Dreikaiserbund 361, 440
Dresden 472, 473, 737, 810, 815
Dresden Conferences 191
Dresdener Bank 266
Dreyfus 303, 787
Dreyfus
Dreyfus Affair 279, 302, 304
Dreyfus case 710
Driekaiserbund 322, 325
Drouyn de Lhuys 199
Droysen 188
Drummond Wolff 661
Dual Alliance 305, 336
Dublin 426, 430, 435, 795
Duc de Gramont 200, 201
duc de Nemours 519
Duchy of Parma 124
Due de 156
Duisberg 396
Duke 195
Duke d' Orleans 52, 94
Duke de Sully 51
Duke of Augustenburg 195
Duke of Bordeaux 155

Duke of Broglie 298
Duke of Cadiz 158
Duke of Coburg 103
Duke of Marlborough 58, 113
Duke of Orleans 152
Duke of Wellington 121, 146, 248, 249, 251
Duke of Windsor 435
Dukhonin 449
Duma 442, 443, 444
Dumauriez 99, 101, 517
Dundee 675
Dunkirk 103, 248, 498, 522
Dupont 117
Dupont de Nemours 91
Duport 96
Durand 808
Durham 291, 746
Durham Proposals 259
Durham Report 84
Durkheim 307
Dusseldorf 396, 473, 474
Dutch 5, 33, 39, 46, 47, 292, 293, 682, 683, 684, 685, 693
Dutch East India 38, 502, 653, 723
Dutch Republic 45, 47, 48, 49, 100, 129
Dutch West 526
Dwight D. Eisenhower 506
Dwight W. Morrow 582
Dyarchy 678
dyarchy 680
Dybenko 448
Dynamite 265
dynamos 132

E

E. E. Cummings 798
E. H. Harriman 572
E. H. Sterling 762
E. K. Miller 450
E. L. Boullee 808
E. M. Forster 793
E. S. Montague 677
Earl of Beaconsfield 420
Earl of Derby 255
Earl of Macartney 614
Earnest Renan 83
East Africa 283, 287, 326, 327
East Asia 87
East India Company 293, 430, 613, 614, 672
Eastern Lacarno 489
Eastern Question 86, 180, 230, 236, 242, 246, 360, 362, 370, 420
Eastern Thrace 391
Eberhard Wachter 807
Ebert 474, 478
Ecole centrale 754
Ecole Normale 734
Ecole Normale Superieure 112, 738, 754
Ecole Polytechnique 112, 738, 754, 776
Ecquador 559, 596, 597, 598, 603, 608, 609
Eddington 771
Eden 412, 471
Edgar Degas 812
Edger Allan Poe 785
Edict 56
Edict of Emancipation 224
Edict of Nantes 51, 53, 55, 56
Edict of Restitution 47, 48
Edinburgh 258, 759
Edison 132, 571
Edmund Burke 88, 99, 103
Edmund Cartwright 130
Edo Bay 620
Edouard Daladier 497
Edouard Herriot 310, 405
Edouard Manet 812
Eduard Lasker 318, 320
Eduard Meyer 344
Education Act 260, 705, 740
Education Law of 1833 736
Edvard Grieg 804
Edward 42
Edward Baines 352, 746
Edward Bernstein 283
Edward Buchner 761
Edward Calvert 807
Edward Cardwell 261
Edward Elgar 803
Edward Fitzgerald's 784
Edward Gibbon 63, 259
Edward Gierek 542
Edward Gregr 347
Edward Grey 367
Edward I 42
Edward III 42
Edward Morawski 541
Edward Munch's 814
Edward Pickering 771
Edward Taaffe 347

Edward Thomas 796
Edward VI 28, 34, 43
Edward VII 305, 423, 427
Edward VIII 435
Edwin Chadwick 702, 703
Edwin M. Stanton 565
Edwin Muir 798
Edwyn Bevan 750
Egypt 3, 108, 110, 223, 229, 230, 236, 237, 238, 243, 248, 282, 283, 284, 285, 286, 287, 288, 289, 295, 305, 327, 338, 371, 426, 429, 430, 470, 497, 500, 503, 613, 659, 660, 661, 662, 663, 664, 668, 669, 670, 694, 695, 696
Ehrlich 86
EI Salvador 585
Eichendorff 782
Eiffel Tower 132, 814
Einstein 86, 752, 770, 774
Eisenhower 504, 588, 687
Ejnar Hertzprung 771
El Alamein 503
El Salvador 595, 600, 608
Elba 124, 143, 248, 525, 321, 387
Eldon 249
Elector John of Saxony 26
Elector-Palatine Frederick III 28
Eleutherios Venizelos 363
Elgin 677
Eli Whitney 558, 561
Elihu Root 576, 577
Eliot 798
Elisabeth Bergner 485
Elizabath Bowen 799
Elizabeth 39, 43
Elizabeth Cady Stanton 561
Elizabeth I 29, 34
Ellenborough 672
Elliot 615
Elphinstone Institution 673
Emden 498
Emerson 561, 739, 788
Emil Fischer 761
Emil Hacha 493
Emil Rathenau 343
Emile 780
Emile Bernard 813
Emile Combes 303
Emile Galle 814
Emile Loubet 303
Emile Ollivier 167
Emile Zola 81, 82, 302
Emilio Aguinaldo 683
Emily's 788
Emma Livry 803
Emma Willard 739
Emmeline Pankhurst 426
Emperor 25
Emperor Faustin 601
Emperor Francis Joseph 351
Emperor Hirohito 653
Emperor Kuanghsu 635
Emperor Mutsuhito 622
Emperor Paul 219
Emperor William 328
Emperor William II 472
Empress Dowager 633, 634, 635
Empress Elizabeth of Austria 274
Ems 201
Ems dispatch 201
Enabling Act 482
Enclosure 129
Encyclical 746
Encyclopaedia 66
Encyclopedia 779
Encyclopédie 91
Engel's 275
Engelbert Dollfuss 353
Engels 82, 256, 270, 273, 279
Engineering College at Roorkee 674
England 5, 8, 14, 22, 28, 33, 34, 39, 40, 42, 43, 45, 46, 57, 58, 59, 63, 70, 81, 82, 103, 109, 110, 113, 114, 115; 116, 117, 122, 123, 125, 127, 129, 130, 136, 138, 147, 152, 153, 156, 157, 158, 159, 166, 167, 169, 178, 195, 197, 198, 202, 212, 223, 235, 236, 237, 238, 239, 240, 243, 247, 248, 249, 252, 258, 263, 265, 270, 273, 277, 279, 284, 285, 286, 287, 305, 306, 325, 327, 333, 337, 338, 354, 374, 376, 384, 385, 392, 393, 398, 429, 435, 492, 496, 499, 527, 551, 564, 591, 594, 597, 621, 629, 630, 632, 656, 701, 710, 711, 714, 715, 716, 717, 719, 720, 723, 732, 734, 736, 737, 739, 744, 747, 749, 753, 755, 771, 778, 786, 788, 793, 801, 804, 806, 808, 809, 810, 815
England Alfred Stevens 810
Englightenment 62
English 5
English Channel 499

English East India Company 38, 293
Enlightenment 63, 64, 66, 68, 69, 78, 88, 527, 778, 779
Enrico Fermi 280, 769, 820
Enrique Jose Varona 604
Entente Cordiale 305, 336, 371
Enver Bey 365, 655
Epirus 363
Epstein 820
Erasmus 14, 19, 26
Erasmus of Rotterdam 14
Erfurt 23, 164
Erfurt Congress 190
Erfurt Union 191, 192
Erich Kastner 480, 486
Erich Maria Remarque 476
Eritrea 404, 463, 470
Ernest Hemingway 799
Ernest Wolton 769
Ernst Haeckel 759
Ernst Junger 486
Ernst Rietschel 810
Ernst Rohm 483
Ernst Toller 821
Ernst Von Weber 326
Eroica 801
Erwin Schrodinger 769
Erwin Schrodinger 820
Erzberger 474, 475
Essen 589
Estates-General 96
Esterhazy 302
Estonia 382, 389, 409, 449, 450, 458, 460, 493, 496, 497, 512
Ethiopia 3, 288, 404, 417, 469, 500, 515, 662
Ethnike Hetaireia 363
Eto Shimpei 627
Eugene Delacroix 806
Eugene O'Neill 795
Eugenio Maria de Hostos 604
Eupen 386, 512
Europe 7, 9, 727
Evangelicals 744, 746
Evelyn Underhill 750
Evelyn Waugh 799
Eward Ochab 542
Ewins 774
Existentialism 515
Expressionism 359, 485, 795, 815, 816
Exsurge Domine 24
Extremists 677
Ezra Pound 797

F

F. A. W. Diesterweg 737
F. D. Roosevelt 727
F. J. Robinson 250
F. O. Herschel 770
Fabian Socialism 279
Fabian Society 275, 279
Fabians 279, 423
Facta 466
Factory Act of 1833 135, 253, 256, 702, 704, 720
Factory Laws 704
Fair Helen 803
Faisal 666
Falange 547
Falk Laws 319
Falkenhayn 379, 380, 381
Falkland Island 380, 429
Falloux Law 161
Famine Code of 1883 675
Famine Commission of 1880 675
Fancisco Madero 605
Fanny Elsser 802
Far East 169, 218, 226, 284, 335, 337, 460, 461, 515, 579, 590, 619, 632, 645, 646, 648, 708
Far from the Madding Crowd 792
Faraday 755, 767
Faruq 663
Fascism 357, 391
Fascist party 465, 466
Fashoda 286, 289, 305
Father Gapon 442
Father Miguel Hidalgo 594
Faubourg St. Germain 306
Faust 782
Fauve 817, 815, 816
Fauvism 815, 816
Feargus O'Connor 254
February Patent 184
February Revolution 180
February Revolution in Paris 175
February Revolution of 1848 210
February Revolution of 1848 273
Federated Malay States 293, 690
Federated Soviet Republic 451
Federation Malaya 691

Federation Nacional de Agricultores Espanoles (FNAE) 275
Fenian Society 421
Ferdinand 13, 33, 46, 162, 175, 177, 302, 363
Ferdinand de Lesseps 302
Ferdinand Hodler 814
Ferdinand I 174
Ferdinand II 46, 47
Ferdinand II of Naples 163
Ferdinand II, King of Naples and Sicily 210
Ferdinand III 47, 48
Ferdinand Lassalle 278, 321
Ferdinand Magellan 6
Ferdinand of Aragon 33
Ferdinand of Austria 172
Ferdinand of Saxecoburg 363
Ferdinand of Spain 744
Ferdinand VII 544, 591, 593
Ferenc Molnar 795
Ferenc Nagy 357
Fernand Pelloutier 275
Ferry 286, 300, 739
feudalism 7, 8, 40
Feuerbach 270
Feuillant Club 98
Feuillants 99
Fianna Fail 435
Fiat Automobile 468
Fiat car 463
Fichte 83, 127, 188, 732, 733, 735, 781
Fidelio 802
Field Marshal Alexancer 506
Field Marshal Rommel 506
Field Marshal Schleicher 479
Field Marshal von Hindenburg 478
Field Marshal von Rundstedt 589
Field-Marshal Paskievic 182
Fielden's Act of 1847 256
Fifteenth Amendment 570
Fifth Symphony 801
Fiji Islands 326, 426
Filarte 15
Filippo Buonarroti 206
Filippo Carridoni 275
Filippo Lippi 12
Fillippo Brunelleschi 16
Finland 26, 141, 218, 266, 313, 389, 401, 415, 417, 438, 447, 449, 458, 461, 489, 497, 533, 819
Finland Jean Sibelius 803
Finland Ugo Cyganeus 736
First Anglo-Chinese War 615
First Balkan War 350, 369
First Coalition in 1793 248
First Five Year Plan 455, 456, 708, 728
First International 272
First Lord of the Admiralty 379
First Mediterranean Agreement of February and March 325
First Peace of Paris 143
First Reform 137
First Round Table Conference 680
First Symphony 801
First World War (1914) 86, 133, 172, 185, 272, 275, 277, 280, 291, 295, 307, 317, 321, 341, 343, 353, 369, 370, 392, 396, 416, 429, 431, 444, 465, 472, 486, 497, 521, 528, 538, 543, 545, 551, 559, 571, 578, 604, 605, 607, 650, 659, 663, 664, 675, 677, 692, 693, 694, 695, 706, 708, 723, 724, 749, 751, 775, 777, 793, 795
first Afghan War in 1839 676
first battle of Ypres 378
Fiume 349, 389, 465, 469
Flanders 382, 517, 518
Flandin 471
Flaubert 168
Fleming 774
Flemish language 520
Floreal 104
Florence 12, 13, 16, 164, 206, 211, 710, 740, 805
Florence Cosimo de Medici 13
Florence Nightingale 242
Florentine 14
Florentine Academy 755
Florentines 9, 12
Florey 774
Florida 558, 559, 563, 564
Foch 313, 383, 384
Fontainebleau 33, 116, 117
Fontainebleau Memorandum 388
Fontane 344, 789
Fontenelle 63
Foochow 615
Ford Madox Brown 811
Formosa 509
Forster Education Act 260, 419, 737, 746
Forsyte Saga 792
Fort Sumter 564
Forward Bloc 681

Foucault 767
Fouque 782
Four-Power Treaty 639
Fourier 269, 702
Fourteen Points 383
Fourteen Points 413, 578
Fourteenth Amendment 566, 568, 570
Fowell Buxton 252
Fox 247
Fra Angelico 15
Fracasto-rious 19
France 8, 9, 14, 22, 26, 33, 39, 40, 46, 47, 48, 49, 50, 51, 52, 54, 55, 59, 65, 70, 75, 81, 84, 85, 88, 89, 98, 99, 100, 106, 107, 108, 109, 110, 113, 114, 115, 116, 117, 118, 122, 123, 125, 126, 130, 131, 132, 133, 135, 139, 140, 141, 142, 143, 144, 145, 146, 151, 153, 156, 157, 158, 159, 160, 162, 165, 166, 169, 191, 195, 199, 201, 202, 204, 210, 212, 217, 222, 223, 225, 230, 235, 236, 237, 238, 239, 240, 242, 246, 248, 252, 262, 263, 264, 265, 266, 267, 268, 269, 273, 275, 277, 281, 282, 283, 286, 287, 288, 289, 291, 293, 294, 297, 298, 302, 305, 306, 307, 308, 312, 313, 314, 318, 319, 320, 322, 324, 325, 326, 327, 329, 334, 336, 337, 338, 342, 362, 371, 375, 377, 379, 383, 385, 388, 389, 390, 392, 393, 396, 397, 399, 400, 401, 402, 403, 404, 405, 406, 407, 408, 409, 410, 411, 416, 422, 449, 460, 462, 469, 470, 477, 478, 488, 489, 490, 491, 492, 496, 497, 499, 504, 505, 512, 515, 517, 519, 523, 526, 545, 547, 548, 549, 556, 557, 564, 579, 589, 597, 598, 601, 616, 619, 621, , 632, 633, 644, 648, 652, 660, 661, 664, 665, 667, 670, 680, 682, 685, 687, 692, 694, 702, 703, 705, 706, 707, 708, 710, 711, 715, 716, 718, 719, 720, 721, 722, 723, 724, 725, 730, 733, 735, 736, 737, 738, 739, 741, 745, 748, 752, 753, 771, 776, 786, 803, 804, 807, 809, 810, 818
France Georges Seurat 813
Francis 13, 100, 158, 173, 341
Francis Aston 769
Francis Bacon 62, 63, 129, 765
Francis Deak 180, 184
Francis Ferdinand, the Emperor of Austria-Hungary 341
Francis Galton 772
Francis I 32, 33, 34, 56, 172, 174
Francis II 174
Francis IV, Duke of Modena 208
Francis Joseph 170, 177, 178, 183, 184, 194, 196, 200, 223, 242, 346, 347, 351, 374
Francis Joseph at Villafranca 214
Francis Kossuth 355
Francis Place 249, 250, 254
Francis Xavier 30
Francisco Craveiro Lopez 552
Francisco de Miranda 592
Francisco Jose de Goya Lucientes 807
Francisco Larfo Caballero 547
Francisco Solano Lopez 598
Franco 549, 550, 551
Franco-German Convention 306
Franco-Prussian War 199, 200, 282, 320
Franco-Russian 305
Franco-Soviet Pact of Mutual Assistance 312
Franco-Spanish treaty (September 1904) 664
FranÇois Rude 808
Francois Arago 767
Francois Guizot 154
Francois Hennabique 818
Francois Joseph Belanger 808
Francois Magendie 758
Francois Quesnay 68
Francois Rabelais 13
Francois-Rene de Chateaubriand 780
Frank B. Kellogg 582
Frank Kellogg 309
Frank Lloyd Wright 817
Frankfurt 131, 194, 196, 198, 223, 345, 589, 715
Frankfurt Assembly 164, 176, 189
Frankfurt on May 10, 1871 297
Frankfurt Parliament 190
Frankland Lewis 131, 714
Franklin Delano Roosevelt 582, 589
Franklin Roosevelt 460, 502
Franz Kafka 820
Franz Lehmann 488
Franz Liszt 802, 803
Franz Schubert 804
Franz Werfel 486
Fraunhofer 768
Frederick 46, 535
Frederick Barbarossa 49
Frederick Chopin 802
Frederick Delius 803
Frederick II 37, 65
Frederick III 328
Frederick IX 529
Frederick of Augstenburg 194
Frederick Sanger 761
Frederick T. Ward 617

Frederick the Great 378, 487, 821
Frederick V of the Palatinate 45
Frederick William 114, 122, 163, 189
Frederick William III 122, 140, 187, 755
Frederick William IV 189, 192, 223, 735
Frederick William IV of Prussia 189
Frederico Gamboa 604
Fredrick Schmidt 359
Free Trade 137, 257, 320, 84
Freemasonary 749
Freiherr von Stein 732
French East India Company 38
French Emperor 213
French Foreign Minister Briand 407
French Grand Prix in 1906 712
French Organic Law of 1842 718
French Revolution 81, 83, 88, 89, 90, 127, 143, 219, 222, 247, 556, 701, 714, 742, 754, 755, 778, 780, 781, 784, 162, 188, 208, 536, 543, 254, 269
French West African empire 287
Freud 752, 774
Fribourg 745
Frida Leider 485
Friedrich 326, 335
Friedrich Ebert 472, 473
Friedrich Engels 6, 136, 162, 165, 270
Friedrich List 188
Friedrich Naumann 331
Friedrich Schiller 781
Friedrich Stopel 320
Friedrich von Gentz 269
Friedrich Wilhelm August Froebel 736
Friedrick Naumann 335
Fritz Busch 485
Fritz Lang 821
Fructidor 104, 742
Fuad 662
Fukien 632
functionalism 820
Fuseli 807
Futurism 815, 817

G

G. D. H 423
G. Dawes 397
G. K. Chesterton 793
G.D.H 279
G.D.H. Cole 279
Gabo 816
Gabriel Faure 803
Gabriela Mistral's 796
Gabriele D' Annunzio 464
Gaeta 211
Gagging Bill 249
Gainsborough 809
Galicia 172, 183, 200, 348, 390, 444, 535, 536, 537, 546, 547
Galileo 19, 32, 63, 771
Galileo Galilei 60, 61
Galitzin 220
Gallatin 557
Gallipoli 379, 380, 390, 430, 664, 665
Galsworthy's 794
Galvani 766
Gambetta 203
Gambetta 285, 298, 300
Gambia 3, 286, 429, 695
Gamelin 313, 497
Gandhi M. K. 293
Gandhi-Irwin Pact of March 5, 1931 680
Gandhiji 679, 681
Gargantua 13
Garibaldi 127, 210, 211, 213, 215, 216, 217, 463, 536
Garnier 818
Gartner 810
Gas 262
Gaskell 703
Gaspard Monge 754
Gaston de France 52
Gaston Doumergue 310
Gaudin 110
Gauguin 307, 813
Gauss 738
Gavrilo Princip 341, 351, 373
Gay-Lussac 763
General Alexander 504
General Allenby 667
General Anton Denikin 450
General Antonio Carmona 551
General Archibald Wavell 498
General Assembly 549
General Augusto Sandino 582
General Baron Tanaka 651
General Bonaparte 107
General Botha 385
General Boulanger 325
General Bourmont 151
General Carlos lbanez 607
General Cavignac 160

General Charles 397
General Chiang Kai-Shek 515
General De Gaulle 315
General Douglas MacArthur 502, 587, 653, 683
General Duphot 742
General Dwight D. Eisenhower 588
General Dyer 678
General Eisenhower 588, 589
General Electric 572, 581
General Electric Company 266
General Ewald von Kleist 522
General Franco 313, 471, 547, 548
General Gablenz 196
General Gallieni 378
General Gamal Abdel Nasser 663
General Gamelin 313
General Gaspar Dutra 607
General Gates 76
General Gemelin 499
General George C. Marshall 647
General German Workers' Association 278
General Goering 729
General Gordon 286
General Hans Von Seeckt 474
General Hugh S. Johnson 584
General Jose Miaza 547
General Joseph Maria von Radowitz 190
General Keitel 483
General Kornilov 450
General Kuropatkin 440
General Lamarque 155
General Lazaro Cardenas 605
General Leo Von Caprivi 329
General Louis Botha 428
General MacArthur 501, 503, 509, 590
General Manuel Avila Camacho 606
General Mark Clark 505
General Marmont 152
General Maurice Gamelin 497
General Metaxas 500
General Montgomery 503
General Omar Bradley 507
General Patton 508
General Paulus 505
General Peron 612
General Petain 380
General Radetzky 163
General Rawlinson' 384
General Sanjurjo 547
General Scott 560
General Seeckt 474
General Serrano 158
General Sir Frederick Morgan 588
General Smuts 413, 416
General Stilwell 510, 646
General Tanaka 650
General Templer 691
General Tojo 646
General Tojo Hideki 653
General Trochu 203
General Uriburu 609
General Von Blomberg 483
General Von Bredow 483
General Von Fritsch 483
General von Luttwitz 474
General W. T. Sherman 565
General Weygand 313
General Yudenich 450
Geneva 27, 28, 29, 234, 409, 410, 412, 414, 416, 488, 549, 687, 726
Geneva Disarmament Conference in 1934 585
Geneva Naval Conference of 1927 416
Geneva Protocol 406, 409, 416, 432
Genoa 5, 35, 114, 142, 206, 464, 466
Genovesi 68
Gensonnet 101
Gent 691
Gentz 128, 142
Geology 773
Georg Kaiser 795
George Alexander 370
George Bancroft 604
George Barker 797
George Bernard 423, 794
George Bernard Shaw 820
George Canning 146, 233, 250, 258, 559
George Clemenceau 304
George Cleveland 572
George Dewey 575
George Eastman 571
George Eliot 82
George Ellery Hale 771
George Gamow 771, 772
George Gissing 792
George Goldie 286
George Grenville 70

George III 74, 249
George Lanburg 433
George Marshal 506
George Meredith 792
George Moore 792
George Orwell 800
George Plekhanov 276, 440
George Richmond 807
George Romney 806
George Sand 82, 155, 703, 781
George Sorel 275
George Stefan 789
George Stephenson 130, 132, 520
George V 434
George VI 435
George W. Wickersham 581
George Washington 72, 74
Georgei Chicherin 458
Georges Bonnet 492
Georges Braque 815
Georges Cadoudal 113
Georges Clemenceau's 705
Georges Cuvier 756
Georges Lemaitre 772
Georges Sorel 304
Georgia 451, 452, 563
Gerard 806
Gerard Manley Hopkins 797
Gereral von Seeckt 388
Gerhard Hauptmann 344, 486, 789
German 133
German Communist Party 472
German Conrad Pickel 19
German East 387
German East Africa 283
German Empire 263
German Navy League 266
German Social Democrat, Eduard Bernstein 275
German Social Democratic Party 321
German-Polish Non-aggression Pact of 1934, 540
Germany 8, 14, 18, 19, 21, 22, 23, 24, 26, 34, 46, 47, 49, 52, 70, 84, 85, 86, 103, 109, 113, 114, 115, 116, 124, 128, 131, 132, 133, 134, 135, 137, 138, 139, 142, 143, 154, 162, 163, 165, 167, 171, 173, 176, 186, 187, 191, 192, 193, 196, 198, 199, 200, 204, 205, 230, 242, 258, 263, 264, 266, 267, 268, 277, 280, 281, 282, 283, 287, 291, 295, 301, 305, 306, 307, 309, 311, 312, 313, 314, 316, 317, 320, 324, 328, 332, 333, 334, 335, 336, 337, 342, 349, 350, 353, 355, 363, 368, 369, 370, 371, 372, 373, 375, 376, 380, 381, 384, 385, 386, 387, 388, 389, 390, 392, 393, 394, 395, 396, 397, 398, 399, 400, 402, 403, 404, 405, 407, 408, 409, 410, 411, 412, 414, 415, 416, 417, 422, 429, 431, 432, 444, 449, 456, 458, 460, 461, 462, 463, 470, 471, 472, 475, 476, 477, 483, 484, 488, 489, 490, 491, 492, 496, 506, 511, 520, 521, 525, 526, 534, 547, 548, 575, 578, 579, 587, 632, 633, 638, 644, 646, 648, 652, 687, 705, 706, 707, 708, 709, 710, 712, 716, 717, 718, 720, 721, 722, 723, 724, 725, 727, 735, 736, 737, 738, 742, 747, 748, 749, 750, 751, 752, 753, 776, 781, 782, 783, 803, 804, 809, 810, 813, 815, 816, 820, 821, 104
Germinal 787
Gestapo 354, 483, 529
Gettysburg 565
Ghana 694, 697
Ghent 517
Ghiberti 15, 16
Giacomo Puccini 803
Gibbon 90
Gibbon Wakefield 291
Gibraltar 58, 429, 664
Gide 821
Gilbert Islands 292, 502
Gilchrist-Thomas 720
Gioberti 209, 211
Giolitti 464, 466
Giorolamo Saccheri 773
Giosue Carducci 462
Giotto 16
Giovanna 404
Giovanni Giolitti 463, 465
Girolamo Cardano 19
Girondins 101, 102, 103, 105
Girondists 127
Girtin 809
Giuseppe de Nittis 812
Gladstone 78, 206, 245, 256, 260, 261, 267, 287, 289, 290, 324, 360, 419, 420, 421, 428, 747
Glasgow 258, 706, 814
Glorious Revolution 44, 152
Goa 5, 552
Gobelins 55
Godesberg 492
Godoy 117
Godwin 784, 812
Goebbles 487, 509

Goering 484, 485, 505
Goethe 90, 473, 487, 714, 732, 733, 781, 782, 787, 802
Gogol 223, 785, 786
Gold Coast 286, 288, 429, 694, 695
Golden Bull 46
Goluchowski 183
Gombos 357
Gomulka 542
Gonzalez Videla 607
Good 284
Gopal Krishna Gokhale 677
Gorchakov 83, 323, 362
Gorchakov, Foreign Minister of Russia 242
Gordon Selfridge 711
Gorgei 181
Gorizia 244
Gosplan 455, 456, 728
Gotha 278, 321
Gothenburg 532
Gothic 16, 18, 809
Gothic architecture 809
.Gothic art 18
Gothic Line 509
Gothic style 809, 810
Goto 627, 628
Gottfried Benn 487
Gottfried Kellar 542, 789
Gottfried Liebniz 765
Gottfried Semper 810
Gottingen 755, 782
Gottlieb Schick 807
Gottlief Daimlar 132
Gough 383
Gournay 91
Government of India Act on August 2, 1935 680
Governor-General Martinez Campos 603
Gowland Hopkins 761
Goya 812
Graham Greene 800
Gramont 201
Gran Chaco 610
Granada 33, 559
Grand Duchy of Warsaw 115, 119, 120, 122, 141
Grand Duke Constantine 536
Grand Duke Michael 446
Grand Duke Nicholas 538
Grand Duke of Tuscany 163
Grand Duke Sergei 442
Grand National Consolidated Trade Union 253, 267, 270
Grand National Union 254
Grand-Duke Constantine 225
Grandes Ecoles 112
Grandi 466
Granovski 222
Granville 202, 285, 324
Great Britain 39, 70, 72, 74, 76, 90, 92, 113, 125, 203, 215, 275, 282, 290, 292, 324, 362, 428, 456, 458, 557, 559, 586, 596, 610, 708, 809
Great Council of Lucerne 745
Great Depression (1929-1934) 86, 522, 688, 690, 692, 725
Great Reform Bill 251
Great Wall 644
Greece 84, 146, 147, 153, 154, 222, 232, 233, 234, 244, 340, 360, 361, 363, 366, 367, 376, 379, 390, 391, 395, 400, 403, 404, 415, 469, 493, 500, 665, 706, 708, 751
Greek 12, 13, 733
Greek independence 151
Greek War 370
Greek War of Independence 230, 232, 233, 235
Greenland 530
Gregor Strasser 483
Gregorian Calendar 741
Gregory Rasputin 440
Gregory VII 745
Gregory XIII 31
Greig 803
Gremmelshausen 19
Grenville 72
Greorge Apponyi 180
Grey 251, 255, 288, 374, 375
Greytown 600
Grillparzer 790
Gropius 816, 818
Gros 806
Grouchy 124
Grover Cleveland 574
Guadalajara Front 547
Guadalcanal 502, 587, 588, 589
Guadalupe Victoria 594
Guadet 101
Guadi 817
Guam 6, 292, 502, 509, 587, 590, 633
Guantanamo 586, 608
Guatemala 6, 595, 600
Guchkov 446

Guerrero 594
Guesde 278, 279
Guiana (Surinam) 525
Guild Socialism 279
Guilio Romano 807
Guillaume 13
Guillaume Apollinaire 796
Guillaume Bude 13
Guinea 3, 287, 552, 697
Guizot 156, 158, 159, 237, 738
Gulf of Finland 497
Gulf of Honduras 600
Gulf of Paria 5
Gunnar Heiberg 795
Gustav Droysen 189
Gustav II Adolf of Sweden 53
Gustav Kahr 483
Gustav Kirchoff 768
Gustav Nachtigal 326
Gustav Noske 472
Gustav Schmoller 320, 721
Gustav Stresemann 309, 391, 406, 476, 477
Gustav von Kahr 475
Gustavas IV of Sweden 142
Gustave Courbet 811
Gustave Eiffel 814
Gustave Flaubert 82, 787
Gustave Holst 803
Gustavus 34
Gustavus Adolf 47
Gustavus Adolphus 34
Gustavus II 531
Gustavus III 532
Gustavus IV 532
Gustavus IV of Sweden 532
Gustavus V (1907-50) 533
Gustavus VI 534
Gustev Robert Kirchhoff 344
Guyton de Morveau 754
Guzman Blanco 597
Gwalior 674

H

H. G. Wells 423, 793
H. H. Asquith 423, 705
H. J. Muller 760
H. M. Lefuel 810
H. Macmillan 728
H.G. Wells 279
Haakon VII 530
Habib Borguiba 697
Habsburg 52, 162, 352, 353
Habsburg Dynasty 178
Habsburg Empire 176, 210
Habsburg monarchy 173, 183
Habsburgs 33, 46, 47, 50, 53, 395
Hague 63, 480, 683
Hague Tribunal 342
Hahn 770
Haile 470
Haile Selassie 500
Haiphong 687
Haiti 5, 585, 594, 608, 610
Hajalmar Schacht 476
Hajo Holborn 488
Hakodate 621
Haldane 373, 424
Haldane Mission 339
Halder 501
Hale's 772
Halifax 718
Halldor Laxness 796
Halley's 64
Hamaguchi 651
Hamburg 116, 263, 268, 345, 472, 482, 504, 589, 706
Hamilton 556
Hamilton Seymour 238
Hankow 641
Hanoi 687
Hanotaux 307
Hanover 113, 141, 153, 163, 188, 198, 318
Hans Bethe 772
Hans Christian Oersted 82, 766
Hans Delbruck 371
Hans Geiger 769
Hans Holbein of Augsburg 18
Hans Kohn 488
Hans Luther 478
Hans Von Mareas 813
Hans Zehrer 486
Hara 651
Hardenberg 122
Harding 580
Hardy 792
Hargreaves' Jenny 130
Harlan F. Stone 584
Harley Granville-Barker 794
Harnack 749
Harriet Beechar Stowe 562, 788
Harris Treaty of 1858 622

Harta 817
Harvard 734, 738, 755
Harvey 19
Hasan al-Banna 695
Hasenclever 795
Hatch Act of 1939 585
Hauff 782
Hausser 188
Havana 583
Havana Conference 610
Hawaian Islands 501
Hawaii 509, 639, 653
Hawaiian Islands 292, 633
Hawes-Cutting Act 585
Hawley-Smoot Tariff Act, 1930 581
Hay 575
Hayanu 182
Haydn 801
Hebbel 790
Hebert 102
Hebertists 104
Hector Berlioz (1803-1860) 802
Hector Guimard 814
Hedjaz 430
Hegel 128, 188, 222, 270, 271, 781
Heidelberg 732
Heilbronn League 47
Heimwehr 353
Heine 82, 486, 782
Heinrich Bruening 479
Heinrich Heine 156, 189, 782
Heinrich Hertz 767
Heinrich Himmler 480
Heinrich Mann 486
Heinrich von Sybel 189, 344
Heinrich von Trietschke 189, 192, 320, 344
Heirnich Friedjung 359
Heister Eckehart 22
Heligoland 248, 333
Heligoland-Zanzibar Treaty of 1890 287
Helmuth von Moltke 195
Helvetic Republic 542
Helvetic Republic in Switzerland 109
Helvetius 91
Henlein 492
Henri Becquerel 768
Henri Boyle 780
Henri de Saint-Simon 156, 736
Henri de Talleyrand 52
Henri de Toulouse-Lautrec (1864-1901) 814
Henri Labrouste 808, 810
Henri Poincare 307
Henri Rene Lenormand 795
Henri Van de Velde 813
Henrik Ibsen 790
Henry Bergson 307
Henry Bessemer 130
Henry Brougham 258
Henry Cabot Lodge 577
Henry Campbell Bannerman 424
Henry Cavendish 766
Henry Clay 557, 560
Henry de Man 522
Henry Demarest Lloyd 722
Henry Draper 771
Henry Ford 775
Henry George 572
Henry Gurney 691
Henry Hobson Richardson 813
Henry Hyndman 423
Henry I 40
Henry II 40
Henry III 41
Henry IV 42, 51, 52, 53, 56
Henry James 791, 792
Henry Knox 555
Henry L. Stimson 586
Henry M. Hyndman 279
Henry Milner 662
Henry Moore 817, 820
Henry Norris Russell 771
Henry of Mecklenburg 526
Henry Parkes 291
Henry Pirenne 9
Henry Roscoe 721
Henry Stanley 284
Henry Temple Viscount Palmerston 519
Henry the Navigator 3
Henry Valois 35
Henry VII 43
Henry VIII 14, 34, 43
Henry Wilson 424
Henry Wordsworth Longfellow 561
Herat 656
Herbert Asquith 424
Herbert Clark Hoover 580
Herbert Hoover 410, 580, 725

Herbert Samuel 433
Herbert Spencer 264, 736, 737
Herbert von Karajan 485
Herbrew 13
Herder 99, 122, 127, 732, 781
Herman Melville 788
Hermann Fol 758
Hermann Goering 482
Hermann Helmholtz 82
Hermann Hesse 485, 820
Hermann Kesten 486
Hermann Mathesius 818
Hermann Muller 479
Hermann von Helmholtz 766
Hernando 6
Herriot's 310, 311
Herriot's ministry 310
Herschel 771
Hertzprung-Russell 771
Herzegovina 229, 323, 337, 338, 349, 350, 360, 362, 364, 365, 366, 368, 372, 390
Herzen 83
Herzen 223, 227
Hesse 163, 486
Hesse-Cassel 153, 164
Hesse-Darmstadt 186, 192, 198, 200
Hesse-Kassel 188, 189, 190, 191
Hidalgo 594
Hideki Yukawa 770
Hideyoshi 619
Hiedelberg 755, 768, 782
Hieronymus Bosch 18
High Commission 43, 691
High Renaissance 17, 18, 805, 808
Hilaire Belloc 793
Hilton 9
Hindenburg 378, 380, 382, 384, 479, 482, 481
Hindenburg Line 382
Hindu Mela 676
Hiroshima 511, 590, 622, 653, 771, 775
histology 758
Hitler 86, 120, 311, 353, 354, 460, 461, 471, 475, 479, 480, 481, 482, 483, 484, 486, 487, 489, 491, 492, 493, 494, 495, 498, 505, 507, 508, 511, 522, 540, 541, 588, 606, 653, 708, 710
Hjalmar Bergman 795
Hjalmar Schacht 483, 484, 707, 729
Hjalmer Branting 534
Ho Chi Minh 685, 687
Hoare-Laval Pact of 1935 434
Hoare-Laval Plan 312
Hobbes 68
Hoffman 721, 782, 765
Hofmannsthal 359, 796
Hogendorp 524
Hohenlinden 109
Hohenlohe 333
Hohenzollern 192, 200
Hohenzollern dynasty 472
Hohenzollern-Sigmaringen 245
Hohenzollerns 28, 395
Hokkaido 620, 625
Holbach 66, 779
Holderlin 781
Holland 22, 31, 34, 39, 57, 58, 101, 103, 107, 110, 114, 115, 116, 123, 130, 142, 248, 258, 264, 267, 277, 291, 376, 384, 387, 493, 498, 518, 519, 523, 524, 619, 621, 685, 701, 714, 717, 718, 720, 724, 727, 735, 736, 738, 749
Holman 811
Holman Hunt 811
Holstein 188, 189, 194, 195, 196, 198, 282, 333, 526, 528
Holy Alliance 143, 144, 147, 220, 236, 258
Holy Land 8, 664
Holy Roman 25
Holy Roman Emperor 45, 57, 23, 32, 113, 172, 186, 534
Holy Trinity 810
Home Rule 421, 422, 426, 430, 435, 677
Home Rule for Ireland 421
Home Rule League 677
Homestead Act of 1862 570, 573
homo sapiens 757
Honduras 5, 6, 595, 600
Hong Kong 502, 587, 615, 616, 619, 642, 429
Honore Daumier 810
Honshu 510
Hooker 757
Hoover 582, 583
Hoover moratorium 401
Hopei-Chahar State 644
Hopes 702
Hopkins 761
Horace Mann 561, 736
Horatii 805
hormones 762
Hormuz 5

Horthy 357
Hossbach Memorandum 495
Hotel de Ville 296, 297
House of Commons 43, 279, 422, 425
House of Hohenzollern 245
House of Lords 42, 252, 425
House of Orange 141, 517, 525, 526
Hoyos 341
Hsien-feng 614, 617
Hsing-Chung hui 636
Hsuan-tung 637
Huang Hsing 636
Huckleberry Finn 789, 799
Hudson Bay Company 291
Hudson River 76
Hudson's Bay Company 427
Huerta 578, 605
Hugo 153
Hugo de Vries 759
Hugo Stinnes 476
Hugo Von Hofmannsthal 789
Hugo Wolf 804
Hugowolf 359
Huguenots 31, 39, 51, 53, 55
Huldrych Zwingli 26
Hull Note 646
Humanism 11, 13
Humboldt 140, 733
Hume 90, 743, 753
Humphrey Repton 808
Humphry Davy 130, 754, 755, 764, 766
Hunan 616
Hung Hsiu-Chuan 616
Hungarian Prime Minister 374
Hungary 20, 85, 162, 163, 164, 165, 172, 174, 175, 176, 179, 180, 181, 182, 183, 184, 185, 188, 229, 258, 277, 308, 323, 346, 351, 352, 355, 377, 384, 385, 387, 390, 404, 470, 471, 511, 512, 579, 701, 706, 737, 750, 751, 773, 803, 804
Hunt 249, 811
Hunter Commission 675, 679
Huskisson 250
Hussein Kamel 662
Huxley 757
Huygens 771
Hyde Park 260

I

I. A. Vyshnegradsky 438
Ianus Pannonius 19
Ibsen 790
Iceland 529, 530
Ignace Moscicki 539
Ignace Paderewski 538
Ignacio Altamirano 603
Ignatius of Loyola 29
Ignatius Seipel 352
Igor Stravinsky 803, 804
Il Principe 32
Ilbert Bill 676
Illinois 563
Illyria 172
Illyrian State 181
Immanuel Kant 62
Immunology 762
Imperial Chemical Industries 265
Imperial Conference 291
Imperial Tobacco Company 265
Impressionism 811, 812, 817
INA 681
Incas 591
Independence 75
Independence of Greece 234
independence 258
Independent Labour Party 279
India 30, 108, 133, 137, 259, 293, 458, 509, 515, 646, 708, 712, 719, 720, 722, 776
India Act of 1858 675
India League 676
Indian Association (1876) 676
Indian National Congress 293, 293, 430, 676
Indian National Liberal Federation 678
Indian Ocean 3, 6, 35, 259, 299
Indian Penal Code of 1861 675
Indian Statutory Commission 688
Indian Universities Act of 1904 677
Indiana 558
Indo-China 169, 292, 293, 299, 300, 501, 515, 646, 653, 685, 687, 821
Indonesia 501, 515, 649, 684, 685
Indulgences 24
Industrial Labour Organisation 413
Industrial Revolution 82, 83, 127, 129, 131, 134, 136, 204, 247, 262, 268, 558, 613, 701, 714, 717, 753, 784, 811
Infanta Louisa Duc de Montpensier 158
Innocent VIII 21
Innsbruck 176
Institut de France 734
Institut national de France 754

Insulin 773, 820
Inter-Allied War Debts 400
International 277
International Federation of Trade Unions (IFTU) 268
International Labour Bureau 393
International Labour Organisation 414, 585, 609, 730
International Postal Union 718
International Socialists Congress of Amsterdam (1904) 279
Inukai 651
Inukai Tsuyoshi 652
Ionian Islands 244
Iran 655, 659
Iraq 430, 663, 669, 670
Ireland 34, 70, 126, 248, 251, 256, 260, 266, 395, 419, 421, 426, 435, 744
Irigoyen 609
Irish Free State 431
Irish problem 260
Irish Republic (Eire) 436
Isaac Newton 59, 61, 64
Isabella 13, 33, 158
Isabella II 544
Isabella of Castile 33
Isfahan 658
Isherwood 795
Islam 695, 752
Island of Midway 502
Isle de France 139, 140
Islington Commission 677
Ismail 659
isotopes 769
Israel 671
Isthmus 5
Istria 114, 244, 390
Itagaki 625, 627
Italia Irredenta 464
Italian Renaissance 18, 813
Italo Balbo 466
Italy 13, 14, 20, 30, 34, 85, 86, 115, 116, 123, 124, 127, 134, 137, 143, 153, 154, 155, 162, 169, 170, 171, 174, 184, 186, 188, 191, 195, 196, 202, 204, 206, 209, 215, 230, 242, 246, 265, 266, 267, 273, 274, 275, 277, 280, 282, 288, 305, 308, 311, 313, 314, 322, 325, 328, 329, 362, 366, 371, 372, 376, 379, 382, 383, 389, 390, 391, 395, 397, 399, 403, 404, 408, 410, 411, 415, 416, 461, 462, 463, 464, 467, 470, 480, 489, 491, 500, 504, 510, 512, 515, 520, 546, 547, 548, 579, 587, 588, 633, 644, 645, 646, 662, 664, 665, 701, 704, 706, 707, 708, 709, 710, 712, 721, 724, 747, 748, 751, 752, 753, 783, 803, 806, 807, 809, 812, 819
Ito 628
Ito Hirobumi 649
Ivan III 35
Ivan IV 36
Ivan Karamazov 786
Ivan Pavlov 760
Ivory Coast 286, 287
Iwakura 625, 627
Iwo Jima 510, 590
Iyeyasu 619
Izvestia 456
Izvolski 337, 350, 365, 372

J

J. A. Le Bel 765
J. and P. Coats 722
J. B. Carpeaux 810
J. B. Priestley 431
J. B. S. Haldane 760
J. Casely Hayford 695
J. G. Soufflot 808
J. H. Clapham 132, 716
J. H. Fabre 307
J. H. Foley 810
J. H. Thomas 433
J. H. Van't Hoff 765
J. J. Thomson's 86
J. L. E. Meissonnier 810
J. M. Keynes 133, 388
J. N. Tata 675
J. P. Morgan 572, 574
J. R. Perronet 808
J. Ramsay MacDonald (1866-1937) 280, 424
J. Thomson 673
J. W. W. Birch 690
J.A. Hobson 281
J.B. Dumas 758
Jacint Benavante 794
Jackson 559, 560
Jackson Pollock 817
Jacob Burckhardt 11, 703
Jacobin 105
Jacobin Club 98, 99
Jacobin Terror 781
Jacobins 101, 106
Jacopo Zabarella 19

Jacques Benigne Bousset 64
Jacques Hittorf 808
Jacques Laffitte 155
Jacques Louis David 805, 810
Jacques Pierre Brissot 99
Jacques Rousseau 90
Jaipur 673
Jallianwalla 679
Jamaica 587, 593, 602
Jamal, al-Din al-Afghani 657, 695
James 43
James Buchanan 563
James Chadwick 769
James Hargreaves 129
James I 39
James II 152
James Joule 766
James Joyce 796, 820
James Keir Hardie 279
James M. Cox 579
James Madison 78
James Madison 555, 557
James McN Whistler 812
James Mill 732, 736
James Monroe 558
James Otis 73
James Pryde, (1866-1941) 814
James Russell Lowell 561
James Simpson 759
James Watt 130, 753
James Young 132, 262
James, Duke of York 44
Jameson Raid 428
Jan Hus 21
Jan Kochanowski 18
Jan Paderewski 803
Jan Smuts 428
Jan Toorop 814
Jane Austen 782
Jane Eyre 788
Janina 367
Janissaries 35, 230, 231
Japan 30, 84, 87, 134, 264, 283, 284, 292, 293, 294, 295, 336, 365, 375, 387, 395, 399, 404, 408, 410, 411, 414, 416, 417, 456, 459, 460, 461, 491, 496, 501, 502, 503, 509, 510, 515, 579, 580, 587, 590, 613, 620, 621, 622, 625, 630, 632, 633, 638, 639, 644, 645, 646, 648, 649, 650, 651, 652, 653, 665, 704, 776, 813
Japan Main Line 626
Japan's 87
Japan's Monroe Doctrine 644
Jassy 245
Jaures 278, 279, 302, 711
Java 502, 525, 653, 682, 684
Jawaharlal Nehru 293, 679
Jay's Treaty 556
Jean Arp 817
Jean Bodin 33
Jean d' Alembart 63
Jean Jacques Bernard 795
Jean Jacques Rousseau 779
Jean Jaures 276, 302
Jean Le Rond d'Alembert 91
Jean Sibelius 803, 804
Jean-Auguste-Dominque Ingres 806
Jean-Baptiste Colbert 37, 54
Jean-Baptists Lully 55
Jean-Francois Millet (1814-75) 810
Jean-Paul Sartre 515
Jean-Pierre Boyer 600
Jefferson 66, 74, 556, 557, 559
Jefferson Davis 564, 565, 566
Jellachich 176, 181, 182
Jemappes 154
Jena 114, 117, 755, 782
Jeremy Bentham 68, 91, 249, 250, 259, 736
Jerome 114
Jerome Bonaparte 114, 123
Jerusalem 29, 383, 665, 669
Jesuits 543
Jews 44, 128, 484, 485, 668, 669, 748, 752
Jhansi 673
Joachim Lelewel 536
Joaquin Prieto 596
Joffer 308, 378, 381
Johann Christian Dahl 807
Johann Friedrich Herbart 736
Johann Fust 20
Johann Heinrich Pestalozzi 732, 736
Johann Jakob Wehrli 737
Johann Reuchlin 13
Johann Strauss 359
Johann Struensee 69
Johann Tauler 22
Johann Tetzel 24
Johannes Brahms 344, 803, 804
Johannes Guttenberg 20
Johannes Kepler 59
Johannes Reuchlin 21

Johannes Schutze 733
John Adams 73, 74, 556
John Ball 810
John Bradbury 397
John Brown 563
John C. Calhoun 557, 559
John C. Fremont 563
John Cabot 5
John Calvin 27
John Cockfort 769
John Coeteau 803
John Colet 14
John Constable 807
John Cowper Powys 799
John D. Rockefeller 722
John Dalton 755, 763
John Dickinson 73, 74
John Doherty 253, 267
John Donne 63
John Everatt Millais 811
John Flaxman (1755-1826) 807
John Foster Dulles 387
John Foster Dulles, American Secretary of State 687
John Fox 29
John Galsworthy 792
John Greenleaf Whittier 561
John Hay 633
John Henry Newman 257
John Herschel 768
John Hoppner 806
John Hus 24
John Huss 185
John III 34
John Jay 78, 556
John Joseph Thomson 768
John Kay 129
John Keats 784
John Kendrew 762
John Knox 28
John L. Lewis 584
John Lawrence 674
John Locke 63, 64
John Marshall of Virginia 557
John McAdam 130
John Millington Synge 794
John Morley 677
John Nash 808
John Opie 806
John Quincy Adams 559, 562, 595
John Robert Seeley 282
John Ruskin 282, 809
John Snow 759
John Steinbeck 799
John Stuart 135
John Stuart Mill 134, 259, 267, 279, 423, 702, 703
John Tyler 560
John VI 550
John W. Davis 584
John Wilkes Booth 566
John Wilkinson 753
John Wycliffe 21
Johnson Act 401
Joliot-Curie 770
Jons Jakob Berzelius 82, 763
Joost Van den Vondel 18
Jordan 667
Jose Bonifacio 594
Jose Bonifacio de Andrada e Silva 594
Jose Camalejas 545
Jose de San Martin 559
Jose Enrique Rodo 604
Jose Joaquin Perez 596
Jose Maria Morelos 594
Jose Marti 574, 603
Jose Pereira da Graca 604
Jose Santos Chocano 604
Joseph 118, 304
Joseph Arton Koch 807
Joseph Attwood's 252
Joseph Bonaparte 115, 117
Joseph Caillaux 304
Joseph Chamberlain 335, 421, 422, 423, 426, 428, 429
Joseph Conrad 792
Joseph de Maistre 128
Joseph Goebbles 482
Joseph Hume 250
Joseph II 126, 172, 179, 517
Joseph Jellacic 163
Joseph Mallord William Turner 807
Joseph Pilsudki 451, 537, 538, 539
Joseph Priestley 753, 766
Joseph Roth 486
Josephine 120
Joshua Reynold 806
Jourdan 103
Joyce 821
Juan B. Justo 603
Juan Luis—Vives 13

Juan Manuel de Rosas 594, 597
Juan Sebastian de Elcano 6
Juarez 600
Jubaland 403
Judaism 752
Jules de Polignac 151
Jules Favre 203
Jules Ferry (1832-93) 282, 299
Jules Grevy 301
Jules Guesde 278, 301
Jules Meline 265
Jules Michelet 88, 155
Jules Simon 298
Julius Froebel 191
Julius Gombos 488
Julius II 24
Julius Mayer 82
July Revolution 153, 780
July Revolution of France 519
Jung 774
Junker 321, 716, 721
Jupiter 771
Justo Rufino Barrios 602
Justus Liebig 82
Justus von Liebig 755, 760, 764
Jutland 381

K

K. D. Glinka 761
K.A. von Muller 488
K.F. Gauss 82
Kabul 292, 420, 656
Kachins 688, 689
Kafka 821
Kaiser Wilhelm II 290, 351, 394
Kamal Pasha 366
Kamenev 447, 452, 453, 456
Kandahar 656
Kandinsky 816
Kang Yu-Wei 633
Kangaroo 798
Kanpur 680
Kansas 562
Kansas City 572
Kansas-Nebraska Bill 562
Kant 63, 67, 68, 90, 99, 127, 128, 743, 781
Kapp 474
Kara George 231
Karageorge 364
Karageorgevich 232
Karbala 656
Karen 688, 689
Karl 187
Karl Blechen 811
Karl Friedwich Schinkel 809
Karl Liebknecht 472, 473
Karl Loewe 804
Karl Lueger 348, 748
Karl Marx 6, 136, 268, 270, 271
Karl Pearson 772
Karl Peters 283, 284
Karl Radek 456
Kartell 328
Kartell 722
Kashmir 680
Katabolism 762
Kato 651
Kaufmann 226
Kazakhistan 451
Kazan 36, 219, 734
Kedah 690
Keir Hardie 279, 423
Kekule 765
Kellogg 408
Kellogg Pact 410, 642, 644
Kellogg, American Secretary of State 408
Kellogg-Briand Pact 309, 407, 408
Kelvin 771
Kemal 391
Kemal Pasha 679
Kendall 773
Kentucky 558, 564
Kenya 429, 500
Kepler 19, 32, 60
Kerenesky 382, 445, 447
Kerner 782
Kesatuan Melayu Muda 690
Keynes 263, 388, 726, 727, 730
Kharkov 219, 734
Khartoum 289
Khedive 659, 660, 661, 662
Khedive Ismail 285, 286, 660
Khedives 243
Khilafat movement 679
Khilafat Party 679
Khiva 292, 655
Khorasan 656
Khruschev 542
Kia-chow 335, 387

Kiao-Chou 294, 632, 638
Kiderlen 338, 339
Kido 623
Kiel 384, 472
Kiel Canal 387, 720
Kiev 222, 444, 450, 451, 501, 505, 538
Kilkenny 421
Kimberley 284, 289
Kindergarten 736
Kinetic 766
King 118
King Alexander 311
King Boris of Bulgaria 404
King Carlos I 551
King Christian IX 528
King Christian X 529
King Edward 336
King Edward VIII 434
King Faisal 667
King Ferdinand 146, 367
King Ferdinand VII 544
King Frederick William III 733
King Fuad 662
King George 74, 425
King George I 363
King Haakon 531
King Hakkon VII 531
King Henry VIII's 28
King John 40, 41
King John II of Portugal 3
King John VI 550
King Leopold II 284, 521
King Leopold II of Belgium 284, 288, 327
King of Naples 206, 210
King of Spain, Ferdinand VII 145
King Otto 244
King Peter of Serbia 350, 352
King Umberto I of Italy 274
King William IV 255
King William of Prussia 197
Kingdom of Naples 211
Kingdom of Sardinia 142, 169, 215
Kingdom of Westphalia 114, 123
Kirov 453
Kishen 615
Kitchener 289
Klee 816
Kluck 378
KMT 641
Knox 608
Kobe 626
Kohima 681
Kokoschka 816
Kolchak 391, 454
Kolkhoz 455
Kollar 180
Kolokol 223
Koloman Tisza 355
Konev 509
Koniggratz 191
Koniggratz Sadowa 197
Konigsberg 114, 512, 755
Konnigratz (Sadowa) 184
Konoe 646
Konrad Henlein 492
Konstantin Fehrenbach 474
Konstantine Pobedonostsev 437
Koran 696
Korea 293, 294, 295, 459, 613, 619, 625, 627, 630, 648, 649, 821
Korean War 687, 691
Kornfield 795
Kosagovsky 656
Kossovo 231, 367
Kossuth 127, 164, 165, 175, 176, 180, 181, 182, 183, 356
Kotzebue 187
Kowloon Peninsula 619
Kremsier Constitution 177
Kristen Kold 736, 739
Kronstadt 333, 454
Kruger, President of the Transvaal 334
Krugler's 811
Krupp 263, 343
Krylenke 448, 449
Kuala Lampur 690
Kuang Hsu 633
Kubeck 178
Kulaks 455
Kulturkampf 319, 330, 747, 748
Kuomintang (KMT) 640, 459, 515, 637, 638, 639, 640, 641, 642, 643, 644, 645, 647, 652
Kuomintang Government 646
Kuril Islands 620, 629, 630
Kurils 620
Kurt Riezler 371, 375
Kurt Tucholsky 486
Kurt von Schleicher 483

Kurt von Schuschnigg 353
Kuskova 441
Kutchuk Kainardji 232
Kutuzov 121, 220, 787
Kuwait 664
Kwame Nkrumah 694
Kwangsi 616, 618
Kwangtung Kwangsi 616
Kwantung Peninsula 632
Kyoto 619, 620, 622, 625, 626
Kyushu 625

L

L. H. Myers 799
L. Visconti 810
La Bourdonnaye 152
La Fontaine 55
La Harpe 219
La Marmora 217, 241
La Paz 591, 596
Labedoyere 150
Labour 280
Labour Party 260, 268, 279, 393, 423, 424, 427, 433, 434, 493
Lacordaire 745
Lady Chatterley's Lover 798
Lady Windermere's Fan 792
Lafayette 92, 95, 98, 99, 100
Laffittes 702
Laffittes and Hopes 137
Lagos 286, 695
Lagrange 754
Lahmbruck 817
Laibach 146, 147, 233
laissez-faire 39, 68
Lake Albert 284
Lake Baikal 650
Lake Chad 287, 288, 289
Lake Poets 783
Lake Superior 571
Lake Tanganyika 287
Lake Victoria 284
Lake Victoria Nyanza 287
Lal Rochelle 53
Lala Lajpat Rai of Punjab 677
Lamarck 754, 756
Lamartine 127, 136, 153, 155, 158, 159, 165, 702, 735, 780
Lambert Quetelet 772
Lamennais 743, 744, 745
Lamoignon 93
Lancashire 254, 255, 259, 518
Lancastrian system of education 736
Lander 483
Landholders' Association 674
Landsteiner 762
Landtag 189
Lansdowne 656
Laos 687
Laplace 754, 755, 767, 770
Lassalle 278
Last Judgement 18
Lateran Treaty 468, 750
Latin 12, 13, 19, 733
Latin America 84, 85, 258, 576, 591, 601, 602, 603, 605, 608, 609, 612, 704, 722, 748, 785, 585
Latin American literature 604
Latin American States 596, 601
Latin Literature 12
Latvia 382, 389, 409, 449, 458, 460, 493, 496, 497, 512, 751
Lauenberg 195
Lausanne 366, 399
Lausanne Conference 400, 401, 458, 481
Lausanne Conference of July 1932 727
Laval 312, 404
Laval-Mussolini 470
Laval-Mussolini pact, 1935 404
Lavisse 307
Lavoisier 128, 753, 763
Lavroff 227
Law of Maximum 103
Lawrence Henderson 760
Laws 250
Lazare Carnot 754
Lazzari 464
Le Corbusier 818, 820
Le Havre 299
Le Tellier 54
Leadenhall Street 811
League Covenant 667
League of Nations 87, 144, 291, 312, 309, 353, 385, 386, 387, 391, 393, 395, 405, 407, 413, 414, 415, 416, 460, 469, 470, 477, 488, 490, 540, 578, 579, 586, 605, 608, 644, 645, 652, 663, 666, 667, 694, 730, 749
League of the Arab States 670
Leandro Alem 603

Leaves of Grass 785
Lebanon 665, 666, 667, 669, 670
Lebeau 518
Lebensraum 313, 491
Lebrun 200
Lectures on the Philosophy of History 781
Ledochowski 537
Lee 565
Lee Masters 797
Leeds 134, 136, 248, 251, 710, 734
Lefebre 89
Lefebvre d' Etaples 13
Legislative Assembly 99, 100, 101
Legitimists 297
Legnano 207
Leigh Hunt 783
Leipzig 122, 123, 248, 318, 345, 472, 473, 755
Lend-Lease Act 499
Leni Riefenstahl 488
Lenin 100
Lenin 228
Lenin 269, 274, 276, 280
Lenin 281, 296, 440, 441, 446, 447, 448, 449, 452, 453, 454, 456, 457, 458, 543, 728
Leningrad 453, 456, 505
Lenoir 775
Leo X 25
Leo XII 744
Leo XIII 319, 747, 748
Leon Ballista Alberti 16
Leon Blum 310, 312
Leon Degrelle 522
Leon Jouhaux 313
Leon Trotsky 277, 447, 450
Leonard Woolf 281
Leonardo 17, 806
Leonardo Bruni 12
Leonardo da Vinci 12, 15, 16, 17
Leopold I 520
Leopold II 98, 172, 179, 284, 520, 801
Leopold III 498, 522, 523
Leopold of Saxe-Coburg 519, 520
Leopold of Tuscany 69, 210
Leopold von Ranke 34
Leopoldo Lugones 604
Lermontov 222, 785, 786
Lerroux 547
Les Miserables 149
Les Miserables—1862 780
Lescaze 818
Lessing 90
Levant 667
Leverrier 771
Leviathan 33
Lexington 74
Leyden 63
Leyte 509, 510, 590
Li Huan-hung 637
Li Hung Chang 617, 630
Liabach 174
Liang Chi-Chao 636, 637
Liaotung Peninsula 293, 632, 649
Liberal Party 421
Liberals 259
Liberia 376, 470
liberum veto 534
Library of Ste Genevieve (1844-50) 810
Libya 288, 389, 404, 515
Liddell Hart 379
Liebig 717, 721, 738
Liege 377, 518, 521
Liepzig 533, 801
Lieutenant Laxman 620
Lieutenant-General Alexander Patch 507
Lille 90, 703
Lima 586, 596
Liman Van Sanders 368
Limoges 296
Limon van Sanders 373
Lin Tse-hsu 615
Lincoln 564, 565, 566, 569
Lindberg 775
Lionne 54
Lipski 493
Lisbon 118, 550, 591, 706, 710, 740
Lister's 82
Liszt 804
Lithuania 35, 382, 389, 402, 403, 409, 449, 458, 460, 493, 496, 497, 512, 534, 538, 750, 751
Little Entente 308, 402, 404, 469, 470, 480, 490
Little Maginot Line 492
Litvinov 460, 493, 540
Liverpool 250, 259, 262, 710, 718
Liverpool-Manchester Railway 257
Livingstone 283
Livy 32

Lloyd George 339, 342, 375, 381, 382, 385, 386, 387, 388, 391, 392, 397, 423, 424, 430, 431, 432, 435, 458, 497, 710

Locarno 478

Locarno Pact 407, 433, 459

Locarno Treaties 409

Locarno Treaty 460, 490

Locke 65, 67, 90, 91, 95, 779

Loi Falloux 735, 745,

Lomakin 655

Lombardy 163, 172, 197, 210, 212, 213, 214, 463, 701, 714, 715

Lombardy-Venetia 178

London (Virginia) 70

London 131, 204, 234, 239, 243, 249, 260, 263, 277, 397, 399, 449, 461, 477, 492, 507, 527, 531, 574, 595, 619, 624, 654, 663, 683, 689, 706, 707, 715, 719, 723, 739, 764, 768, 775, 776, 789, 794, 798, 801, 802, 808, 811, 812

London Conference 519

London Conference of 1930 416

London Convention of July 15, 1840 237

London Naval Conference 411

London Naval Conference of 1930 433, 651

London Naval Treaty 411, 583

London Stock Exchange 257, 601

London University 734

London Workingmen's Association 254

Loochoo islands 629

Lord Aberdeen 238

Lord Acton 200

Lord Amherst 614

Lord Auckland 672

Lord Beaconsfield 360

Lord Beveridge's 710

Lord Byron 233

Lord Castlereagh 518

Lord Chancellor 249

Lord Cornwallis 673

Lord Cromer 282, 429, 661

Lord Curzon 402, 538, 676, 677

Lord D' Abernon 477

Lord Dalhousie 672, 674

Lord Derby 259, 260

Lord Dufferein 676

Lord Durham 259, 290

Lord Elgin 259, 618

Lord Frederick Cavendish 421

Lord George Bentinck 255

Lord Granville 72, 286

Lord Grey 342, 352, 374

Lord Haldane 339, 340

Lord Halifax 491

Lord Hastings 672, 674

Lord Irwin 679

Lord John Russell 245, 251

Lord Justice Lawrence 511

Lord Kelvin 757, 766

Lord Kimberley 690

Lord Kitchener 290, 428

Lord Lansdowne 336

Lord Lawrence 676

Lord Lister 759

Lord Liverpool 249

Lord Lloyd 662

Lord Louis Mountbatten 510

Lord Lugard 282

Lord Lyons 661

Lord Lytton 417, 644, 676

Lord Milner 283

Lord Minto 672, 677

Lord Morley 423

Lord Mountbatten 681

Lord Napier 614

Lord North 74

Lord Oxford 343, 371

Lord Palmerston 235, 259, 137

Lord Peel 669

Lord Pethwick-Lawrence 681

Lord Randolph Churchill 422

Lord Robert Cecil 413

Lord Roberts 290, 428

Lord Runiciman 492

Lord Russell 260

Lord Salisbury 421

Lord Shaftesbury 253, 702

Lord Shelburne 753

Lord Stanley 252

Lord Stratford de Redcliffe 239

Lord Wavell 681

Lord William Bentinck 673, 674

Lord Wodehouse 683

Lorenzetti 15

Lorenzo 12

Lorenzo Ghiberti 16

Lorenzo Valla 12, 14, 21

Lorraine 49, 89, 133, 203, 205, 296, 301, 309, 318, 320, 386, 388

Lothar Bucher 201
Loubet 303
Louis 56
Louis Agassiz 757
Louis Barthou 311, 489
Louis Barye 810
Louis Blanc 136, 155, 269
Louis Bonaparte 524
Louis Botha 290, 428
Louis C. Tiffany 814
Louis de Broglie 769
Louis Kossuth 162
Louis Kossuth 180, 355
Louis MacNeice 798
Louis Mountbatten 689
Louis Napoleon 160, 161, 164, 165, 166, 167, 168
Louis Napoleon Bonaparte 160
Louis Pasteur 758, 765
Louis Philippe 152, 153, 154, 156, 157, 158, 162, 363, 519, 155, 166, 297
Louis Sullivan 814, 817
Louis XIII 47, 48, 52
Louis XIII
Louis XIV (1643-1715) 50, 51, 53, 54, 57, 65, 91, 110, 125, 778
Louis XV (1715-74) 91
Louis XVI 92, 101, 109, 149, 154
Louis XVIII 124, 139, 141, 143, 149, 150, 151
Louis's Religious Policy 56
Louis-Philippe 237
Louisburg 52
Louisiana 113, 168, 557, 563, 565
Louvre 104, 806, 807, 810
Lovett 254
Low Countries 14, 49, 504, 517, 519
Lower Canada 259, 290
Lubeck 116, 472, 482
Lucas Cranach 18
Lucerne 543, 745
Luchu 613
Lucknow 674
Lucretius 822
Ludendorff 378, 381, 382, 383, 384, 472, 475
Luderitz 285, 326
Ludovico Ariosto 18
Ludwig Hausser 189
Ludwig Helmholtz 344
Ludwig Windthorst 329
Luftwaffe 496, 499
Lugo Brentano 320
Luigi Facta 466
Luigi Luzzati 462
Luigi Pirandello 795
Luix de Camoens 18
Lujo Brentano 344
Lule Burgas 367
Lusitania 376, 380, 578
Luther 19, 24, 25, 26, 271, 479
Lutheran 749
Lutheran Church 438
Lutherans 28
Luttwitz 474
Lutzen 122
Luxemburg 199, 200, 402, 526, 589
Lvov 536, 537
lycee 112, 737, 739
Lyceum Movement 739
Lyell 757
Lyons 90, 103, 155, 274, 296, 306
Lytton 420
Lytton Commission 644, 652

M

M and B 693 774
M. Chautemps 312
M. Laval 471
M. Litvinov 410
M. Moustier 200
M. Paul Cambon 710
M. Speranskii (1772-1839) 220
Macao 614, 615, 616
MacArthur 510, 590
Macaulay 134, 604
MacDonald 434
MacDonald Plan 412
Macdonald 289, 411, 417
Macedonia 362, 363, 364, 365, 366, 367, 655
Machiavelli 14, 15
Mackensen 379, 380
Mackintosh 250, 814, 817
Macklenburg 188
MacMahon 202, 203, 297, 298, 299
Madagascar 169, 299, 300, 305
Madame Bovary 168, 787
Madame de stael 153
Madame Roland 99, 103
Madison 557, 559
Madras 738
Madrid 45, 47, 118, 201, 461, 547, 548, 549, 550, 591, 706

Magdeburg 191, 473
Magellan 6
Magenta 178, 214
Maginot 497, 498
Maginot Line 498, 499
Magna Carta 40, 41
Magnificent 35
Magyar 179, 185, 355
Magyar language 181
Magyars 162, 164, 180, 181, 182, 200, 346, 349, 355, 356
Magyars of Hungary 184
Mahdists 286
Mahmud II 229, 654
Maillol 817
Mainz 23, 199
Maison de peuple 817
Maitland 124
Maji-Maji rebellion 694
Major Barbara 794
Major Cartwright 249
Major Charles George Gordon 617
Major Quisling 531
Majuba Hill 290, 428
Malacca 5, 293, 691
malaria 761
Malatesta 274
Malay 426, 690, 691
Malay States 429
Malaya 30, 501, 510, 515, 587, 653, 720, 723
Malayan Indian Congress in 1954 691
Malenkov 501
Malkam Khan 657
Mallarme 82, 785, 789
Malmedy 386, 512
Malta 108, 139, 140, 248, 429, 500
Malthus 135, 757
Man and Superman 794
Man and the Citizen 126
Manchester 134, 136, 248, 249, 251, 262, 703
Manchester Guardian 375
Manchester Movement 255
Manchester University 768
Manchu 614, 617
Manchukuo 417, 644, 652
Manchuria 87, 284, 293, 294, 295, 337, 417, 459, 632, 641, 642, 643, 644, 647, 648, 649, 650, 651, 652
Manchurian railway 649
Manchus 613, 637
Manet 811
Manila 510, 590, 633
Manila Bay 574
Mankind 91
Mannerism 18, 805
Mantegna 17
Manteuffel ministry 191
Mantua 207
Mantuan Succession 53
Manuel Anzana 546
Manuel de Falla 803
Manuel Gonzalez Prada 603
Manuel II 551
Manuel L. Quezon 683
Manuel Montt 596
Manuel Roxas 683
Manzoni 207, 209
Mao 647, 648
Mao Tse-Tung 645, 647
Marat 99, 101, 102, 103
Marcel Bertrand 307
Marcel Duchamp 816
Marcel Proust 820
Marcellin Berthelot 307
March Laws 180
March Patent 183
Marchand 289, 305
Marco Polo Bridge 645
Marconi 86, 774, 775
Marengo 114, 248
Margaret Bondfield 433
Marie Ampere 82
Marie Antoinette 98, 103
Marie Curie 768
Marie de Medicis 52
Marie Louise 119, 124
Marie Taglioni 802
Marie Von Ebner-Eschenbach 789
Mark Clark 506
Mark Rutherford 792
Mark Twain 788
Marlowe 18
Marne 307, 383, 384
Marquis Hastings 673
Marquis of Rockingham 72
Marquis Saionji of Japan 385
Marseilles 102, 103, 168, 306, 312, 820
Marshal 150
Marshal Bugeaud 159

Marshal Carmona 552
Marshal Ferdinand Foch 383
Marshal Graziani 500
Marshal Kesselring 506
Marshal Leboeuf 201, 202
Marshal MacMahon 296, 297, 298, 299
Marshal Ney 124
Marshal Petain 313, 383
Marshal Randon 199
Marshal Serrano 544
Marshal Soult 155, 156
Marshal Stalin 589
Marshal Tukhachevsky 456
Marshal von Runstedt 507
Marshal Voroshilov 494
Marshall 512
Marshall Junot 550
Marshall Plan 821
Marshall von Biberstein 331, 333
Marsilio 13
Martignac 151
Martin Bucer 25
Martin Heidegger 487
Martin Luther 23
Martin Rodriguez 593
Martin Van Buren 560
Martinez Sierra 794
Marx 82, 89, 165, 209, 272, 273, 274, 276, 278, 279, 283, 479, 612, 703, 752
Marxism 276, 278, 423, 440, 688
Marxists 89
Mary (1553-58) 29
Mary I 34, 43
Mary Lyon 739
Mary Wollstonecraft 90
Maryland 564
Masaccio 15, 16
Massachusetts 70, 72, 77, 580, 739
Massachusetts Government Act 74
massacre of Sinope 240
Massena 118
Massimo D' Azeglio 209
Mathematics 19, 770
Mathew Arnold 738, 792
Mathew Boulton 130, 753
Matissa 307, 815, 816, 817
Matsukata 629
Matsukata Masayoshi 626
Matteo Palmieri 11
Matthew Arnold 735, 736
Matthias Rakosi 357
Maupassant 791
Maura 545
Maurice Ravel 803
Mauritius 248
Maurras 307
Max Delbruck 762
Max Hirsch 720
Max Liebermann 812
Max Perutz 762
Max Planck 344
Max Planck 488, 769
Max Reinhardt 789
Max Stirner 274
Max Weber 335, 370
Maxim Gorky 441
Maxim Litvinov 460
Maxime Weygand 451
Maximilian 46, 48, 170
Maximilian of Bavaria 45, 46, 48
Maximilian Robespierre 98
Maxwell 767
May Laws 319
Mayas 591
Mayor of Casterbridge 792
Mazarin 49, 51, 53, 54, 127, 163, 165, 208, 209, 211, 213, 214
Mazzini 160, 783
Mazzini in Rome 211
McCormick 717
McKinley 572, 574, 575
Mecca 665
Mecklenburg 46, 49
Medici 13
medicine 760
Mediterranean 35, 140, 145, 153, 157, 168, 230, 236, 237, 339, 381, 403, 411, 426, 429, 500, 504, 527, 548, 664
Mediterranean Agreement of 1887 327
Meerut 674
Mehemet Ali 236, 237, 243
Mehmed Reshad 655
Mehmet 158
Mehmet Ali 223, 235, 285, 659
Mehmet Ali, Pasha of Egypt 157
Mehmet Ali, the Pasha of Egypt 233
Meiji 622
Meiji Constitution 628, 650
Meiji Government 624

Meiji revolution 85
Mein Kampf 479, 488
Mekong 293
Mekong Valley 334
Melaka 689, 690
Melbourne 255
Meline tariff 306
Memel 471, 493, 540
Mendel 759
Mendeleyev Table 769
Mendelssohn 804
Mendes-France 314
Mendoza 592
Menelek 288, 289
Menno Simons 27
Mensheviks 276, 440, 442, 445, 446, 728
Menshikov 239, 240
Mentevideo 591
Mercantilism 37, 38, 39, 55
Merseilles 296
Merv 292, 656
Mesopotamia 335, 379, 390, 664, 665, 666
Messina 464, 505
Metcalfe 672
meteorology 773
Methodists 744, 749
Methuen 39
Mettconich 189, 81, 119, 122, 123, 139, 140, 141, 142, 144, 145, 146, 147, 153, 162, 165, 173, 174, 175, 179, 187, 188, 189, 193, 209, 210, 230, 235, 236, 237, 258, 402, 519, 533, 536, 543
Metternich's system 128
Metz 202, 203
Mevissen 722
Mexico 170, 381, 457, 578, 582, 586, 593, 594, 595, 598, 599, 600, 601, 602, 604, 605, 608, 609, 612, 640
Michael Bakunin 273
Michael Borodin 640
Michael de Montaigne 63
Michael Faraday 82, 764
Michael Obrenovich 232
Michael Sadler 253
Michelangelo 12, 15, 16, 17, 18, 31, 806, 807, 817
Michelet 88, 703, 716, 735, 738
Michelozzo 15
Michigan 558
Mickiewicz 735
microbiology 761
Middle Age 7, 9, 32
Middle East 243, 335, 457, 497, 500, 654, 655, 664, 666, 752
Midhat Pasha 243, 365, 654
Midway Island 653
Mies 818, 819
Mies Van der Rohe 818
Mignet 88
Miguel Aleman 606
Miguel Cervantes 18
Mikhail Gorbachev 516
Mikolajezyk 542
Milan 163, 176, 206, 209, 210, 463, 465, 509, 706, 710, 740, 755
Milan Obrenovich II 232
Miliukov 444, 445, 446
Milizia 808
Millais 811
Millerand 278, 310
Milos Obrenovitch 364
Milosh 231, 232
Milyutin 225
Minas Geraes 606
Minister Maupeou 91
Mirabeau 91, 98, 298
Mirsky 442
Mirza Muhammad Riza 657
Mississippi 72, 76, 558, 563, 564, 565, 718
Missolinghi 233
Missouri 558, 564
Missouri Compromise of 1820 562, 563
Mitsubishi concern 627
Mme de Krudener 143
Mme de Stael 780
Model Parliament 42
Modena 141, 142, 153, 169, 206, 208, 210, 214, 215
Moderates 677, 678
Moeller 486
Mogul Empire 613
Mohammad 365
Mohammad Iqbal 680
Mohammed Ahmad 286
Mohammed Husni Thamrin 684
Mohammed Tewfik Nessim Pasha 662
Moldavia 35, 169, 229, 238, 240, 241, 242, 244, 245, 535
Moldavia and Wallachia 244
Mole Ministry 156
Molecular Biology 761, 762

molecule 763
Moliere 55
Molotov 461, 493, 501, 506, 541, 729
Moltke 197, 201, 322, 339, 340, 373, 374, 378, 379
Molucca Islands 292
Moluccas 5
Mombasa 287
Mommsen 344
Mona Lisa 17
monasticism 26
Monge 755
Mongkut 692
Mongolia 451, 632
Mongols 3, 613
Monroe Doctrine 170, 258, 408, 558, 559, 595, 600, 608
Montague 688
Montague-Chelmsford Report 678
Montalembert 745
Montana 573
Montenegro 226, 229, 244, 340, 350, 360, 366, 367, 372, 375, 385
Montereau 123
Montesquieu 65, 66, 90, 95, 778, 779
Montevedio 592, 597
Montgomery 504, 507, 508
Montreaux Convention 663
Moplahs 679
Moravia 347, 390, 471
Morawski 542
Morea 153, 233
Morgan 722
Morgan Shuster 659
Morike 782
Morley-Minto Reforms 430, 677
Moroccan 332
Moroccan crisis in 1905 303
Morocco 243, 283, 300, 305, 306, 336, 337, 338, 339, 371, 372, 496, 504, 547, 550, 576, 588, 661, 664, 695, 697
Morris 817
Mortimer 807
Moscow 34, 35, 121, 122, 219, 355, 403, 442, 448, 451, 453, 456, 457, 459, 460, 461, 493, 501, 506, 511, 533, 540, 542, 789
Mosquito Protectorate 600
Mosul 663, 665
Motilal Nehru 679
Mount Wilson in California 771
Mountain 101, 127
Mountbatten 689
Mozambique 284, 552
Mozart 801
Mr. Cobden 195
Ms Humphrey Ward 792
Muhammad Ali 679
Muhammad Ali Shah 658
Muhammad Mahmud 662, 663
Muhammad Naguib 663
Mujtahids 657
Mukden 643, 649
Muller 371, 738
Munich 45, 194, 234, 345, 479, 492, 732, 810
Munich Pact 461, 494
Munich settlement 313
Municipality Act of 1899 677
Murat 117, 120, 121, 123, 139, 591
Murat, the King of Naples 206
Murder in the Cathedral 795
Murdock 753
Murmansk 308
Museum of Modern Art (MOMA) 817, 818
Music 359
Muslim League 677, 680, 681
Musset 153
Mussolini 311, 312, 354, 403, 404, 405, 409, 415, 464, 466, 467, 468, 469, 471, 489, 490, 491, 492, 500, 505, 509, 522, 548, 588, 589, 606, 710, 728, 819
Mussorgsky 804
Mustafa Kemal 391, 659, 665, 666
Mustafa Kemal Pasha 740, 752
Mustapha Nahas Pasha 662
Mutiny 674, 675
Mutsuhito 622
Muzaffar al-Din 658
Muzaffar al-Din Shah 657
Mysore 672

N

N. Kh. Bunge 438
N. M. Rothschild 595
N. T. de Saussure 760
N. W. Wagner 801
N. Y. Danilevsky 348
N.Y.K. 627
Nagasaki 511, 590, 620, 621, 625, 626, 653, 775
Nagpur 672
Nahas 663
Namibia 387
Nanking 583, 615, 617, 645
Nansen 416

Nantes 56, 103
Naples 68, 101, 107, 113, 115, 117, 127, 131, 147, 206, 208, 209, 210, 216, 462, 463, 505, 706, 715
Napoleon 50, 53, 81, 97, 106, 107, 108, 109, 110, 111, 112, 113, 116, 117, 118, 119, 120, 121, 123, 124, 125, 139, 140, 143, 144, 150, 152, 161, 168, 170, 186, 202, 203, 214, 215, 220, 231, 248, 394, 500, 501, 524, 529, 532, 544, 556, 557, 591, 593, 733, 734, 738, 742, 743, 754, 755
Napoleon I 521, 739
Napoleon II 124
Napoleon III 83, 119, 162, 165, 167, 168, 169, 196, 199, 202, 206, 213, 216, 217, 238, 239, 241, 242, 244, 245, 264, 292, 297, 299, 599, 735, 738
Narod 227
Narvi 819
Narvik 498, 531
Nash 808, 809
Nasir al-Din Shah 655, 657
Nassau 163, 197
Natal 290, 426, 427, 428
Natasha 787
Nathan Rothschild 131, 715
Nathaniel Hawthrone 788
National 160
National African Company 286
National Assembly 94, 98, 296
National Convention 101
National Economic Council 725
National Gallery 808, 809
National Health Service Act 711
National Industrial Recovery Act 584
National Insurance Act 705, 711
National Liberal 318
National Liberal Party 319
National Liberals 317
National Recovery Administration (NRA) 584
National Social Party 707
National Socialism 487
National Socialist 480, 484
National Socialist Party 729
Naturalism 811
Naum Gabo 817
Navarino 222
Navigation Acts 39, 70
Navigation Laws 256, 257, 719, 721
Nazareth 669
Nazi-Soviet Pact 403, 496
Nazis 404, 480, 481
Neanderthal man 757
Near East 230, 293, 295, 420, 422, 431, 515
Nebraska 562, 573
Nechaev 228
Necker 93, 94, 152, 445
Neerwinden 101, 517, 523
Negro 566, 569, 570
Neitzsche 786
Nelson 108, 109, 113
Neo Renaissance 810
Neo-Baroque 813
Neo-Classical 810
Neo-Classicism 805, 808, 8 7
Neo-Destour 697
Neo-Gothic 810
neo-Guelf movement 209
Neo-Impressionists 813
Neo-Rococo 810
NEP 728
Neptune 770
Nesselrode 140
Netherlands 28, 47, 49, 57, 53, 163, 173, 252, 512, 519, 526, 579, 682, 702, 704, 705, 706, 708, 715, 752, 809
Nettuno Convention 469
Nevada 573
Nevada and Utah 558
Neville 382
Neville Chamberlain 401, 434, 435, 489, 491, 497, 498, 548
New Brunswick 290, 291
New Caledonia 297
New Deal 583, 584, 585, 727, 817
New Economic Policy (NEP) 454, 728
New England 580
New Granada 6, 592, 593
New Guinea (Papua) 426
New Guinea 293, 327, 370, 502, 525, 587
New Hampshire 561, 649, 739
New Hebrides 305
New Humanism 732, 733
New Lanark 131
New Lanark Mills 253
New Mexico 558, 562
New Orleans 565
New South Wales 291, 738
New Testament 14, 750
New World 6, 70, 85
New York 77, 273, 608, 718, 726, 739, 810, 813, 817
New York City 571, 572

New Zealand 84, 85, 259, 291, 387, 406, 426, 427, 428, 497, 720, 723, 727, 738
Newfoundland 336, 427, 428, 586
Newman 745
Newton 19, 60, 62, 65, 68, 767, 779
Ney 120
Nicaragua 582, 595, 600, 604, 608, 610
Niccolini 207
Niccolo Machiavelli 32
Niccolo Tertaglia 19
Nice 54, 101, 114, 169, 206, 213, 215, 469
Nicholas 221, 222, 443, 536
Nicholas Biddle 560
Nicholas Horthy 356
Nicholas I 221, 222, 223, 234, 236, 735
Nicholas II 334, 446
Nicholas Pasic 350, 352
Nicholas's 237
Nicolas Pasic 364
Nicolaus Copernicus 59
Nicolo Machiavelli 14
Niebuhr 188
Niels Bohr 769, 820
Niemen 121, 387
Nietzsche 345, 486, 790
Niger 287
Niger Delta 326
Nigeria 283, 426, 695, 696, 697
Nihilism 226, 227
Nikoky Rimsky Korsakov 804
Nikolas Lenau 782
Nikolni Lobachevsky 773
Nikolsburg 198
Nile 286, 288, 289, 333, 429
Nine Power Treaty 579
Nine-Power Treaties of 1922 639, 645
Ningpo 615
Nizam 672
Nkrumah 696, 697
Nnamdi Azikiwe 695
Nobel 84
Non-violent Non-cooperation Movement 679
Nordlingen 47, 48, 49
Normal School 737
Norman Shaw 811
Normandy 57, 589
North Africa 236, 403, 549, 588
North African 35
North America 38, 52, 226, 593, 705, 744
North Atlantic Treaty Organisation (NATO) 515, 821
North Borneo 683
North Carolina 564
North German Confederation 198, 200
North West Ordinance 77
North-West Frontier 676, 682
Northern Borneo (Sarawak) 292, 426
Norway 26, 120, 133, 142, 154, 195, 277, 416, 498, 500, 504, 512, 526, 528, 529, 530, 531, 533, 706, 709, 715, 724, 736, 744, 803
Notre Dame 104, 743
Notre-Dame de Paris 780
Nova Scotia 290, 291
Novara 211
November-December 1932 680
Novikov 219
now Sydney 291
Nuremberg Trial of War Criminals 511
Nuremburg 18, 197
Nuremburg trials 457
Nutrition 761
Nyon 549

O

O'Brien 254
O'Connor 254, 255
O. D. Young 478
Oberon 802
Obradovich 231, 232
Obregon 605
October 7, 1879 324
October Diploma 184
October Manifesto 442
October Revolution 728
Octobrist 442, 443
Oder 387
Odessa 232
Of Crimes and Punishments 68
Offenbach 168, 171, 803
Offenburg 189
OGPU 452
Ohio 561, 579
Ohio Valley 77
Ohm 766
Okinawa 509, 510
Okubo 623
Okuma 624, 625, 628, 636
Okuma Doctrine 636
Okuma Shigenobu 624
Olaf Palme 534
Olaf V 531
Old Age Insurance Law in 1889 322

Old-age Pensions Act 424
Oldenburg 188
Oliver Cromwell 44
Oliver Twist 253, 702
Oliver Wendell Holmes 561
Ollivier Ministry 202
Olmutz 164, 191, 192
Olympic Games 712
On May 2 312
Open Door 632
Open Door Principle 575
Opera House of 1838-41 810
Operation Barbarossa 500
Operation Crusader 503
Operation Overlord 588
Opium War 616, 632
Oporto 550, 710, 740
Oprichnina 36
Oprichnina 36
Orange Free 427
Orange Free State 289, 290, 426, 428
Organic chemistry 764
Organic Laws 112
Organisation of Labour 157
Orgburo 452
Orient Railways 325, 362
Origin of the Species 82
Orissa 672
Orlando 385
Orleanists 297, 298
Orpheus in the Underworld 803
Orsini 213
Osaka 620, 624, 626
Osborne 245
Oscar Wilde 792
Oskar Hertwig 758
Oskar I (1844-59) 533
Oskar II (1872-1907) 533
Oslo 498, 531
Oslo Convention 534
Osmosis 765
Oswald Spengler 486, 821, 822
Otto 775
Otto Brahm 789
Otto Strasser 480
Ottoman 655
Ottoman Empire 35, 205, 223
Ottoman Empire 229, 230, 231, 233, 235, 236, 238, 243, 360, 366, 375, 390, 613, 654, 659, 664, 665, 666, 752, 752
Ottoman Sultan 36
Ottoman Turkey 535
Ottoman Turks 3
Ottomans 35
Ottorino Respighi 804
Outer Mongolia 460, 638
Outline of History 793
Owen 254
Owen D. Young 398
Owen Williams 818
Oxenstierna 48
Oxford 257, 260, 734, 746, 755
Oxford Movement 745, 746
Oxford Union 394
Oxford University 284

P

P & O 257
P. C. Gilchrist 720
P. J. Safarik 180
P. M. Letarouilly 808
Pablo Neruda 796
Pacific 6, 236, 292, 326, 422, 502, 509, 510, 590
Pacific Islands 370, 501
Pacific Steam Navigation Company 596
Pact of EL Pardo 544
Pact of Locarno 309
Pact of Osborne 245
Pact of Paris 408
Pact of Rome 409
pact of Plombieres 213
Paderewski 538
Padua 68
Pahang 693
Pahlavi 659
Paine 66, 128, 247
Painleve 310
Pakistan 681
Palacky 165, 176
Palais Royal 297
Palazzo Farnese 805
Palermo 208, 505
Palestine 235, 384, 390, 430, 666, 667, 668, 669, 670, 752, 821
Palestine question 670
Palladio 15
Palmerston 158, 230, 235, 236, 237, 238, 239, 240, 242, 255, 258, 260, 519
Pan-American Conference at Lima in 1938 610
Pan-German League 335

Pan-Slav Congress 176
Pan-Slavic movement 230
Pan-Slavism 341, 348, 349, 356
Panama 5, 6, 302, 576, 586, 593, 596, 608, 610
Panama Canal 722
Panama City 586
Pancho Villa 605
Panslavism 180
Pantagruel 13
Panther 306, 338, 372
Panzer divisions 501
Paolo Uccello 18
Papacy 107
Papal Bull 25
Papal States 208
Papen 481
Papua 292
Paraguay 586
Paraguay 592, 598, 603
Paraguyan War 604
Paraguyan War of 1864-70 595
Paris 34, 54, 85, 89, 94, 95, 100, 101, 104, 106, 124, 131, 151, 155, 156, 158, 159, 160, 164, 168, 196, 202, 203, 234, 237, 239, 243, 263, 274, 277, 286, 287, 288, 289, 296, 299, 306, 308, 311, 314, 385, 397, 412, 421, 449, 451, 461, 470, 492, 499, 654, 683, 715, 719, 738, 743, 753, 754, 775, 789, 801, 802, 803, 806, 811, 813, 814, 818
Paris attacked 159
Paris Commune 277, 278, 322
Paris Peace Conference 308, 413, 539, 638, 694
Parlement 93, 96
Parma 107, 117, 141, 142, 153, 206, 208, 209, 210, 213, 214, 215, 466
Parthenon 819
Partition of Bengal in 1905 677
Partition of Poland in 1772 69
Pasha of Egypt 157
Passage to India 793
Passchandaele 382
Pasteur 307, 759, 761
Patagonia 6, 604
Paul (1796-1801) 219
Paul Bourget 301
Paul Cambon 305, 372
Paul Cezanne 813
Paul Claudel 820
Paul de Lagarde 486
Paul Deroulede's 301
Paul Dirac 769
Paul Ehrlich 344, 774
Paul Ernst 485
Paul Gavarni 810
Paul I 219
Paul III 29
Paul Klee 816
Paul Kruger 290, 428
Paul Ludwig Troost 487
Paul Miliukov 441, 445
Paul Pestel 221
Paul Pfizer 189
Paul Reynaud 313, 499
Paul Rohrbach 335
Paul Rubens 31
Paul Signac 813
Paul Valery 796, 820, 821
Peace 50, 119, 198
Peace Conference of 1919 522, 528
Peace of Adrianople (September 1829) 231
Peace of Alais 53
Peace of Amiens 110
Peace of Augsberg 26, 31, 46
Peace of Campo Formio 107
Peace of Frankfurt 203
Peace of Prague 47, 48
Peace of Pressburg 113, 173
Peace of Westphalia 50, 54
Peace Treaty at Paris 124
peace of Prague 196
Pearl Harbour 501, 574, 587, 633, 646, 653
Peasant's Revolt 26
Pedro Aguirre Cerda 607
Pedro Alvarez Cabral 3
Pedro V 551
Peel 250, 256
Peel Plan 669
Pegu 676
Peking 619, 620, 630, 633, 634, 636, 637, 638, 639, 641, 648, 757
Penang 293, 689, 690, 691
Pendjeh 292
Peninsular War 120, 121
Pennsylvania 73, 575, 755
Pennsylvania Station 813
People's Charter 267
People's Republic of China 648
Perak 690, 693
Pericles 63
Permanent Court of International Justice 398, 406

Permanent Court of International Justice or World 413
Permanent Mandates Commission 387, 415
Pero da Cavilha 3
Perry 622
Persia 35, 229, 283, 292, 295, 306, 370, 371, 403, 409, 458, 460, 656, 659
Persian Gulf 295, 335, 370, 656
Persian Letters 65
Persius 810
Peru 6, 415, 592, 593, 596, 597, 598, 602, 603, 604, 608, 609
Petain 314, 382, 497, 499
Peter Behrens 818
Peter Ellis 815
Peter I 364
Peter Stolypin 443
Peter Struve 441
Peter the Great 219, 222
Peter the Great 230
Peterloo 249
Peterloo Massacre 250
Petersburg 222
Petition of Right 43
Petofi 165
Petrach 12, 16, 19
Petrograd 220, 228, 441, 445, 447, 448, 451
Peugeot 707
Pharya Phahon 693
Pherozeshah Mehta 677
Phibun 693
Philadelphia 74, 76, 555, 572, 755
Philadelphia Convention 77
Philharmonic Orchestra 487
Philhellenic Movement 234
Philhellenic societies 233
Philip II 30, 33
Philip III 33, 45
Philip IV 33
Philip IV of Spain 47, 49
Philip of Anjou 57
Philip of Hesse 26
Philip Otto Runge 807
Philip the Fair 8
Philip Webb (1831-1915) 812
Philippe Buonarroti (1767-1837) 157, 269
Philippine 575
Philippine Archipelago 509, 510, 633
Philippine Islands 590
Philippines 6, 544, 545, 575, 576, 587, 633, 649, 653, 683
Philke Hetairia 232
Phillips 774
Photography 132
Physiocrats 68, 91, 716, 39
Physiotherapy 774
Piacenza 208
Picasso 815, 817
Picasso's 'Clarinet Player' 815
Pichegru 103, 107
Pickwick Papers 788
Pico della Mirandola 13
Picquart 303
Piedment 211
Piedmont 101, 146, 147, 204, 206, 208, 212, 215, 217, 240, 247, 463, 715
Piero de Cosimo 17
Piero della Francesca 15
Pierre Bayle 64
Pierre Curie 768
Pierre Flourens 760
Pierre Joseph Proudhon 269, 273
Pierre Laval 314, 499
Pierre Puvis de Chavannes 813
Pierre-Alexander Vignon 808
Pierre-Francois Leonard Fontaine 808
Pierre-Joseph Proudhon (1809-65) 157, 806
Pieta 18
Pieter Bruegel the Elder 18
Pietro de Cortona 806
Pietro Mascagni 803
Pig War 349, 364, 368
Pilsudski 454
Pirandello 821
Pisano 15
Pisarev 227
Pithecanthropus 757
Pitt 247, 248
Pitt the younger 230
Pius IX 210, 211, 319, 746, 747
Pius VII 744
Pius X 748, 750
Pius XI 751
Pius XII 751
Pizaro 6
Place 254
plague 701, 761
Planck 86, 820
Plantation Act 70
Plato 63

Platt Amendment 608, 610
Plays Pleasant and Unpleasant 794
Plehve 441
Plekhanov 276, 440
Plombieres 169, 213, 215
PNI, the Indonesian National Association 684
Pobedonostsev 438, 442
Poelzig 818
Poincare 53, 308, 310, 312, 366, 375, 397
Point Counter Point (1928) 799
Poisson 754
Poland (third partition) 535
Poland 18, 20, 31, 35, 45, 48, 100, 126, 127, 143, 153, 154, 155, 169, 188, 193, 194, 218, 220, 221, 225, 246, 264, 277, 308, 313, 352, 378, 382, 386, 387, 388, 389, 390, 392, 394, 395, 402, 403, 404, 409, 415, 438, 439, 442, 444, 449, 451, 458, 459, 460, 477, 489, 493, 494, 496, 497, 500, 512, 531, 535, 536, 537, 538, 539, 540, 541, 542, 701, 706, 714, 744, 750, 751, 783, 803, 804
Poland-Lithuania 31
Poland-Lithuania 32, 34, 35
Poles 184
Poles Dantiscus 19
Polignac 152
Polish 489, 540
Polish Corridor 388, 496, 540
Politburo 452, 453
polypeptide 761
Polytechnique 754, 755
Pombal 69
Poncelet 754
Poona Sarvajanik Sabha 676
Poor Law 253, 711
Poor Law passed in 1834 253
Pope 13, 116, 210, 543
Pope Alexander 13
Pope Benedict 750
Pope Clement VII 28
Pope Innocent X 50
Pope John XXII 21
Pope Julius 17
Pope Leo 748
Pope Leo X 24, 33
Pope Leo XIII 303
Pope Nicholas 13
Pope Paul III 18, 30
Pope Pious VI 97
Pope Pious VII 113, 144
Pope Pius IX 83, 163, 209, 217, 299, 319, 462, 746, 747, 757
Pope Pius VI 741, 742
Pope Pius VII 743
Pope Pius X 304, 464
Pope Pius XI 468, 546, 750
Pope Pius XII 821
Popolari 467
Porfirio Diaz 605
Port Arthur 293, 294, 295, 442, 512, 632, 649
Port Hamilton 630
Portsmouth 649
Portugal 39, 69, 85, 86, 107, 115, 116, 117, 118, 119, 140, 142, 145, 146, 154, 211, 248, 252, 277, 283, 335, 336, 400, 422, 550, 552, 579, 591, 594, 701, 740, 748, 751
Portuguese 5
Portuguese Navigator Dinis Dias 3
Posen 386
Potsdam 351, 510, 541
Potsdam Conference 541, 590, 653
Pound 796, 797
Poznan (Posen) 537, 542
Pparlement 92
Prague 46, 162, 163, 176, 183, 185, 263, 347, 492, 493, 706
Prairial 104
Prajadhipok (1925-35) 692
Pravda 457
pre-Raphaelites 812
Prelude 127
Premier Konoe 653
Premier Thorvald Stauning 529
Presbyterian 749
President 493
President Calvin Coolidge 410
President Coolidge 400, 583
President Ebert 475
President Hoover 417
President Hoover of the United States 399
President James Madison 558
President Jose Balta 602
President Juan Sarcasa 582
President Loubet 305
President Monroe 147, 258, 595
President Moscicki 539
President of the Transvaal 290
President Roosevelt 314, 499, 503, 504, 506, 508, 510, 587, 589, 694

President Sadi Carnot of France 274
President Taft 608
President Truman 510, 590, 647
President Wilson 308, 450, 586, 638
President Zamora 547
Pressburg 119
Prevost 758
Pridi 692
Pridi Phanomyong 692
Priestley 99
Priestley 763
Prim 200
Prime Minister Baldwin 433
Prime Minister Castlereagh 591
Prime Minister Churchill 589
Prime Minister Grey 251
Prime Minister MacDonald 412
Prime Minister of Hungary 182
Primo de Rivera 546, 547
Prince Albert of Saxe-Coburg 255
Prince Alexander 362, 363
Prince Alexander of Battenberg 325
Prince Anton 801
Prince Bernadotte 154
Prince Bernadotte of Sweden 120
Prince Blucher 122
Prince Bulow 305
Prince Charles 245
Prince Christian of Glucksberg 194, 528
Prince Chun 636
Prince Couza 245
Prince Edward Island 290, 427
Prince Ferdinand 117
Prince Henry 3
Prince Hohenlohe 330
Prince Konoe 510, 645
Prince Kropotkin 228
Prince Leopold 200, 201
Prince Lvov 444, 445
Prince Max 472
Prince Max of Baden 384, 472
Prince Menshikov 239
Prince Metternich 140
Prince Mirsky 441
Prince Nicholas Esterhazy 801
Prince of Hohenzollern 201
Prince of Wales 420, 501, 587, 808
Prince Otto of Bavaria 235
Prince von Schwarzenberg 122
Prince Windischgratz 163
Princeton 738, 755
printing 20
Prittwitz 378
Privy Council 42
Professor Friedjung 350
Prosper Merimea 781
Protection 320
Protestant 27, 31, 741, 743, 749, 751
Protestant Reformation 23, 28, 32
Protestant Revolt 21
Protestantism 56
Protestants 250
Proudhon 136, 273
Proust 821
Provence 57
Provisions of Oxford 41
Prussia 26, 39, 40, 99, 100, 107, 109, 114, 115, 119, 120, 122, 123, 125, 126, 127, 139, 140, 141, 143, 144, 145, 146, 157, 164, 170, 184, 186, 187, 188, 189, 190, 191, 193, 194, 195, 196, 197, 198, 201, 202, 204, 214, 217, 223, 225, 231, 237, 242, 245, 247, 248, 258, 316, 318, 476, 482, 535, 537, 714, 715, 717, 733, 736, 739, 747, 755, 810
Psychology 774
Ptolemy 32, 59
Public Library 813
Puerto Rico 575, 604
Punjab 673, 674, 676, 680
Pushkin 222, 233, 785, 786, 790
Pygmalion 794
Pym 256
Pyrennes 504

Q

Quadruple Alliance 144, 223, 230, 258
Quakers 27, 65
Quanta Cura 746
Quantum Theory 820
Quartering 74
Quartre Bras 124
Quebec 52
Quebec Act 74
Queen Anne 788, 812
Queen Christina 34
Queen Elizabeth 28
Queen Isabella 158
Queen Isabella II 544
Queen Isabella of Castille 3
Queen Victoria 200, 255, 282, 323, 363, 420, 423, 426, 427, 759

Queen Wilhelmina 498, 526
Queen's College 739
Queen's Proclamation (November 1, 1858) 675
Queensland 291, 427
Quesnay 91
Quincy Adams 559
Quit India 681
Quito 593

R

R. B. Haldane 423
R. L. Stevenson 792
R. M. Bird 673
R. May 673
R.A.F 434
Racine 55
Radetzky 176, 210
Radio 138, 711, 820
radioisotopes 770
Radishchev 219
Radowitz 191, 323
Rafael Carrera 600
Rainer Maria Rilke 344, 796
Rakovsky 457
Ralph Alpher 772
Ralph Vaughan Williams 803
Ralph W. Emerson 562
Rammohun 738
Rammohun Roy 673, 674
Ramon Cajal 760
Ramon Castilla 597
Ramsay MacDonald 405, 406, 423, 432, 433, 548, 668, 680
Rangoon 502, 676, 689
Ranjit Singh 672
Rapallo Treaty 403
Raphael 15, 16, 17, 806
Raspail 160
Rasputin 445
Rathenau 397, 476, 724
Rattazzi, Minister of the Interior 212, 213
Raymond Poincare 304, 397, 401
Razumovsky Quartet 802
Reading 710
Realism 817
Rear Admiral Lord Louis Mountbatten 590
Red Army 450, 451, 501, 505, 538
Red Cross 544
Red Sea 3, 285, 463, 471
Reform Act 137, 252, 259, 260, 267, 425
Reform Bill of 1867 259, 260
Reform Club 252
Reformation 21, 26, 28
Reformation In England 28
Reforms Act of 1832 267
Regent's Park 808
Reichsbank 399, 476, 477, 726
Reichsland 316
Reichstag 174, 175, 198, 316, 317, 318, 319, 320, 321, 327, 328, 330, 331, 332, 333, 473, 477, 478, 479, 481
Reichswehr 474, 483
Reign of Terror 105
Reinhardt Plan 484
Reinsurance 325
Reinsurance Treaty 305, 327, 333
Reinsurance Treaty with Russia 287
Rembrandt 812
Renaissance 11, 12, 15, 19, 21, 23, 59, 63, 218, 777, 805, 810, 817
Renault 707
Rene Clair 712, 821
Rene Descartes 61, 63
Rennes 738
Rent Act of 1859 675
Rentenmark 397, 476
Reparation Commission 396, 397, 398, 475
Reparations 726
Republic of China 86
Republican Calendar 104
Repulse 501, 587
Revolution 39, 153, 163, 230, 270, 444
Revolutionary 104
Rexists 522
Reynaud 314
Reynolds 809
Rezanov 620
Rheims 90
Rheinische Zeitung 270
Rhine 215
Rhineland 270, 398, 417, 434, 478, 480, 490, 494, 507
Rhineland Pact 407
Rhode Island 561
Rhodes 284
Rhodesia 284, 426, 428, 429
Ribbentrop 490, 493, 494, 541
Ricarda Huch 485, 487
Ricardo 135, 249
Ricardo Samper 547

Richard Arkwright 130
Richard Cobden 135, 255
Richard Dehmel 789
Richard Eberhart 798
Richard Norman Shaw (1813-1912) 812
Richard Oastler 702
Richard Owen 756
Richard Payne 808
Richard Simon 65
Richard Strauss 344, 485, 487, 803, 804
Richard Upjohn 810
Richard Wagner 790, 803
Richelieu 48, 51, 52, 53, 125, 150
Richmond 565, 566
Riga 34, 447, 451, 501, 538
Rilke 485, 785, 797
Rimbaud 785
Rio de Janeiro 591, 606, 610, 820
Rio de la Plata 595, 597, 598
Risorgimento 207, 212, 217
Rivadavia 594
Riza Khan 659
Riza Pahlavi 659
Robert Boyle 762
Robert Brown 758
Robert Browning 784
Robert Bunsen 768
Robert Burns 783
Robert Cecil 195
Robert E. Lee 565
Robert Farinacci 466
Robert Frost 797
Robert Giffen 722
Robert Graves 798
Robert Koch 344, 759
Robert Lowe 419
Robert Owen 131, 136, 253, 256, 267, 269, 279, 423, 732
Robert Peel 250
Robert Schumann 804
Robert Sherwood 795
Robert Smirke 809
Robert Southey 783
Robertson 90
Robespierre 88, 99, 101, 104, 105
Robinson 250
Roca-Runciman Agreement 610
Rochdale Pioneers 257
Rockefeller 84, 571
Rockefeller Centre 818
rocket 775
Rococo 805
Rodin 307, 817
Romagna 169, 206, 213, 214, 215
Romain Rolland 307
Roman Catholic Church 83, 268
Roman Catholicism 25
Roman Catholics 250, 257
Roman Law 14, 42
Romania 84, 85
Romanov 36, 446
Romantic Movement 782, 783
Romanticism 780, 801, 807, 817
Rome 11, 16, 17, 18, 24, 25, 29, 31, 45, 57, 97, 164, 169, 178, 202, 204, 206, 209, 211, 216, 217, 319, 412, 462, 466, 506, 706, 805, 806, 811
Rome-Berlin Axis 489, 491, 493
Rommel 496, 500, 503, 504, 507
Rondelet 808
Roon 192, 201
Roosevelt 401, 493, 506, 508, 575, 576, 577, 578, 583, 584, 585, 586, 587, 588, 610, 645, 646, 722
Rosa Luxemburg 280, 472, 473, 537
Rosas 604
Rosebery 288
Rosenberg 474, 487
Rosmini 209
Rossetti 785, 811, 812
Rossini 802
Rothschild 137, 606, 702, 719
Rotterdam 720
Rotundists 251
Rouault 816
Rouen 90
Roumania 169
Round Table Conference 669
Rousseau 49, 66, 67, 68, 95, 534, 732, 778, 779, 780
Rowlatt Act of 1919 678
Royal Agricultural Society (founded in 1838) 717
Royal Air Force 499, 504
Royal College of Chemistry 764
Royal Geographical Society near the Albert Hall 812
Royal Niger Company 426, 429
Royal Philharmonic Society 801
Royal Society of London 62
Royal Society of London for the Promotion of Natur 62

Rubaiyat of Omar Khayyam 784
Ruben Dario 604
Rubens 805, 806, 807
Rudolf Claussius 766
Rudolf Hess 479, 482
Rudolf I 172
Rudolf Virchow 319, 344, 758
Rudolf von Delbruck 318
Rudyard Kipling 793
Ruhr 263, 310, 396, 397, 432, 477, 504, 507, 704, 720
Ruiz Cortenes 606
Rumania 170, 265, 277, 308, 341, 400, 402, 403, 404, 409, 415, 460, 493, 508, 512, 665, 701, 714, 728
Rumanians 183
Rundstedt 501
Runnymede 40
Rupert Brooke 796
Ruskin 809, 812
Russell 238, 255, 260
Russell Cabinet 260
Russia 8, 19, 31, 49, 85, 87, 100, 108, 109, 113, 114, 115, 116, 118, 119, 120, 122, 123, 125, 126, 138, 139, 140, 141, 143, 144, 145, 146, 147, 157, 169, 194, 197, 199, 202, 203, 214, 218, 219, 220, 222, 223, 225, 226, 230, 231, 234, 236, 237, 238, 239, 240, 241, 242, 245, 246, 248, 256, 258, 263, 265, 269, 277, 281, 282, 283, 284, 286, 292, 294, 295, 305, 306, 317, 322, 323, 324, 325, 326, 327, 329, 333, 334, 336, 337, 340, 400, 416, 417, 420, 422, 439, 441, 445, 446, 449, 453, 454, 458, 465, 496, 497, 499, 500, 501, 503, 512, 515, 519, 527, 529, 532, 535, 537, 538, 541, 543, 574, 579, 580, 588, 613, 621, 622, 632, 633, 634, 641, 642, 647, 648, 650, 652, 655, 656, 657, 670, 687, 693, 701, 705, 706, 708, 711, 714, 720, 722, 723, 725, 737, 753, 755, 773, 783, 804, 809, 810
Russian Edict of Emancipation (1861) 218
Russian foreign minister 340
Russian Revolution 128, 272
Russian Social Democratic Party 276
Russo-German 313
Russo-Japanese wars 85, 134, 284, 442, 444, 576, 627, 635, 648, 689, 550, 657
Russo-Turkish war 420, 536
Rutger Jan Schimmelpenninck 524
Rutherford 86, 769, 820
Rykov 453

S

Saad Zaghlul Pasha 662
Saar 308, 386, 489
Saar basin 415, 512
Sabah 691
Saburo Kurusu 587
Saburov 324
Sadi Carnot 301, 330, 754, 766
Sadowa 184
Saftey Lamp 130
Sagasta 544, 545
Sahara 300
Saigo 625
Saigo Takamori 627
Saigon 501, 619, 687
Saint Simon 702
Saint-Just 105
Saint-Simon 268, 270
Sainte Beuve 780
Saipan 292, 509, 590
Sakhalin 460, 511, 620
Sakhalin Island 649
Salazar 551
Salerno 710, 740
Salisbury 286, 287, 288, 325, 334, 421, 422, 656
Salmon A. Chase 562
Salonica 365, 366, 367, 384
Salvation Army 749
Salzburg 119, 140
Sam Adams 73
Sam Adams of Massachusetts 73
Samarkand 292
Samoa 574
Samoan Island 336, 387
Samuel Crompton 130
Samuel Langhorne Clemens 788
Samuel Palmer 807
Samurai 620, 622, 623, 624, 627
San Francisco 273, 620
San Giovanni 16, 464
San Juan 600
San Martin 592, 593
San Salvador 5
Sandro Botticelli 18
Sankaran Nair 677
Sans-culottes 104
Sant Elia 818
Santa Lucia 139
Santiago 583, 592
Santiago Bay 575
Santiago Quiroga 547

Santo Domingo 600, 601, 608, 610
Sao Paulo 601, 606
Sarajevo 341, 369, 373
Saratoga 76
Sarawak 429, 587, 683, 691
Sardinia 101, 107, 206, 213, 214, 223
Sardinia 245, 363
Sardinia-Piedmont 142
Sarekat Islam 684
Saskatchewan 291, 427
Satara 672
Satsuma 622, 623, 624
Satsuma rebellion 627
Saturn 771
Saudi Arabia 669, 670
Savigny 188
Savonarola 13
Savoy 46, 52, 54, 101, 114, 123, 169, 206, 213, 215, 469
Saxe-Weimar 186
Saxony 107, 141, 163, 164, 188, 190, 316, 472, 482, 704, 736
Sazanov 340, 342, 352, 366, 373, 374, 375
Scandinavia 20, 376, 520, 701, 721, 738, 749, 818
Scandinavian countries 408, 735
Scapa Flow 497
Schacht 477, 484
Scheel 763
Scheidemann 474
Schelling 127
Schiller 90, 732, 782
Schinkel 810
Schlegal 809
Schleicher 481
Schleiden 758
Schleiermacher 732, 743, 744
Schleswig 189, 194, 195, 196, 198, 205, 318, 386, 526, 528, 739
Schleswig-Holstein 194, 195, 196, 204, 258
Schlieffen 282, 343, 376
Schlieffen Plan 337, 343
Schmerling 178
Schmoller 326
scholasticism 12
Schonerer 347
Schubert 359, 801
Schumann 801, 804
Schumpeter 264, 283
Schuppanzig Quartet 802
Schuschnigg 354, 491
Schwann 758
Schwarzenberg (1800-52) 123, 164, 177, 178, 190
Scissors Crisis 454
Scotland 31, 43, 70, 130, 252, 753
Scott Fitzerald 799
scutage 8
Scutari 367
Sea of Okhotsk 620
Seagram Building 819
Seamen's Act of 1915 577
Sean O'Casey 794
SEATO 691
Sebastian Brant 19
Sebastian Cabot 5
Sebastopol 223, 240, 241, 501
Second 26
Second Afghan War (1878-80) 676
Second Balkan War 350, 367, 369, 372, 373
Second Battle of the Marne 384
Second Boer War 290
Second Continental Congress met in Philadelphia 74
Second Estate 89
Second Five Year Plan 456, 729
Second Front 505, 508, 588
Second Hague Peace Conference in 1907 649
Second International 277
Second Mediterranean Agreement on December 12, 187, 326
Second Peace of Paris 143
Second Republic 161
Second Round Table Conference 680, 689
Second World War 86, 87, 282, 355, 414, 460, 488, 494, 496, 511, 512, 529, 531, 534, 544, 549, 552, 585, 586, 609, 612, 659, 663, 667, 669, 670, 680, 687, 694, 695, 706, 707, 711, 731, 760, 775, 776, 777, 822
second Armed Neutrality 532
Secretary Hay 576
Secretary Hoover 581
Secretary Stimson 590
Sedan 90, 203, 327, 498, 522
Seeckt 389
Sejm (parliament) 35
Sekou Toure 697
Selassie 471
Selim III 654
Senator Henry Clay 560, 562
Senegal 169, 286

Seoul 630
Sepoy Mutiny 430, 618
September 2, 1945 (V-J Day) 590
September Laws 156
Serajevo 351
Serbia 84, 181, 229, 231, 232, 240, 241, 243, 244, 246, 308, 322, 325, 340, 341, 342, 349, 350, 351, 352, 360, 361, 362, 366, 367, 368, 369, 372, 373, 374, 375, 378, 381, 384, 385, 392, 751, 164, 172, 182, 184, 346, 349, 365, 368
Sergai Kirov 456
Serge Nechaev 228
Serge Sazonov 444
Serge Stavisky 311
Sergei Eisenstein 821
Sergey Prokofiev 803, 804
Sergio Osmena 683
Setfan Zweig 486
Settlement of 1871 204, 205
Seven Years' War 70, 72
seventh Pan-American Conference at Montevedio in 1933 610
Seville 6, 546
Sevres 391
Sevres Treaty 391
Seward 565
Seymour 238, 634
Seymour Parker Gilbert 398
Seyss-Inquart 354, 491
Shafetsbury 63
Shakespeare 18, 208, 487, 788
Shan 688, 689
Shanghai 510, 615, 616, 617, 619, 620, 639, 640, 641
Shanghai Banking Corporation 642
Shangti Hui 616
Shantung 387, 579, 632, 634, 638, 639
Shantung peninsula 294
Shaukat Ali 679
Sheffield 134, 136, 248, 251, 710, 734
Shelley 784
Sheridan 566
Sherman Anti-Trust Act of 1890 722
Shidehara 652
Shidehara Kijuro 650
Shimoda 621
Shimonoseki 334
Shinto religion 621
Shinto Worship 623
Shogun 620, 621, 622
Shogunate 619, 625, 626
Shuvalov 362
Siam (Thailand) 336
Siam 293, 305, 334, 376, 613, 689, 692, 693
Siberia 226, 263, 273, 448, 449, 450, 451, 453, 455, 502, 613
Siberian railway 720
Sicily 115, 208, 209, 210, 216, 462, 463, 588
Sidmouth 249
Sidney Gilchrist Thomas 720
Sidney Howard 795
Sidney Webb 423
Siegfried Line 497, 507, 589
Siemens 263, 295, 343
Siemens-Martins 132
Sienkiewicz 392
Sierra Leone 286, 287, 429, 695
Sieyes 108
Sigismund III 35
Sigismund III Vasa 31
Sigismund Vasa 35
Sigmund Freud 359, 395, 820
Silesia 164, 388, 390, 415, 512
Silistrian plateau 367
Simeon Poisson 772
Simon Bolivar 559
Simon de Montford 41
Simon Kimbangu 695
Simpson Report 668
Sinclair Lewis 799
Sind 672, 676, 680, 682
Sindhia 673
Singapore 426, 501, 502, 510, 587, 639, 676, 689, 690, 691
Sinkiang 642
Sinn Fein 431, 435
Sino-Japanese 134
Sino-Japanese conflict 630
Sino-Japanese War (1894-95) 284, 334, 627, 629, 632, 633, 635
Sir Alfred Milner 428
Sir Arthur Wauchope 668
Sir Arthur Wellesley 117
Sir Charles Wood 673, 738
Sir Edward Grey 367, 368, 371, 372, 376, 423, 521
Sir Evelyn Baring 286
Sir Eyre Crowe 371
Sir F. Gowland Hopkins 773
Sir Garnet Wolseley 285, 661

Sir Geoffrey Lawrence 511
Sir George Gilbert Scott 809
Sir George May 434
Sir Henry Campbell-Bannerman 705
Sir Henry Drummond Wolff 656
Sir Henry McMahon 665
Sir Henry Raeburn 806
Sir Herbert Kitchener 288
Sir Herbert Samuel 668
Sir Horace Rumbold 488
Sir Hubert Rance 689
Sir James Kay-Shuttleworth 732
Sir James Mackintosh 127
Sir James Saumarez 532
Sir John Bowring 619
Sir John Fisher 424
Sir John Fortescue 42
Sir John French 377
Sir John Hope Simpson 668
Sir John Moore 118
Sir John Peel 255
Sir John Simon 434, 489, 679
Sir John Soane 808
Sir John Woodhead 669
Sir Lee Stack 662
Sir Neville Henderson 494
Sir Oswald Mosley 433
Sir Richard Cross 420
Sir Robert Peel 256
Sir Ronald Ross 759
Sir Samual Hoare 471, 434
Sir Shenton Thomas 690
Sir Spencer Walpole 291
Sir Stafford Cripps 681
Sir Thomas 28
Sir Thomas Lawrence 806
Sir William Howe 75
Sir William Nicholson, 1872-1949 814
Sir William Osler 759
Sistine Chapel 18
Slavophiles 222
Slavs 176, 347
Sleep of Endymion 806
Slovakia 357, 390
Slovaks 184, 355
Slovenes 346, 349
Smolensk 36, 121, 220, 501
Smuts of South Africa 385
Smyrna 295, 390, 391, 666
Snowden 433
Soane 809
Social Contract 67, 780
Social Contract
Social Democratic Party 278, 328, 331, 332, 348, 349, 353
Social Insurance Law in 1883 322
socialists 280
Society of Jesuits 29
Socotra 5
Sofia 360, 367, 459
Solferino 178, 214
Solomon 292, 502, 587
Solvenes 172
Somaliland 169, 288, 300, 404, 426, 463, 470, 471
Somme 380
Sonderbund 543, 735, 745
Sorel 307
Soren Kierkegaard 821
Soult 118
South Africa 84, 291, 334, 420, 424, 426, 427, 722
South America 6, 147, 281, 559, 591, 592, 593, 598, 705, 715
South Asia 752
South Australia 291, 427
South Carolina 72
South Kensington 737
South Manchuria 649
South Tyrol 390
South West Africa 327
South-East Asia 653, 682, 683, 688, 693
South-West 370
Southey 127, 784
Soviet Russia 310, 357, 410, 459, 496, 549, 645, 710, 711, 712
Soviet Union 357, 404, 409, 414, 432, 456, 460, 467, 489, 491, 492, 493, 508, 512, 516, 534, 542, 548, 643, 648, 652, 653, 707, 725, 728, 730, 740, 775, 776
Soviet-German Non-Aggression Pact of August 1939 461
Spaak 522
Spain 5, 8, 20, 29, 30, 33, 35, 37, 43, 46, 47, 48, 49, 52, 54, 57, 58, 69, 75, 76, 84, 85, 86, 98, 100, 103, 107, 113, 115, 116, 117, 118, 119, 122, 125, 140, 142, 146, 147, 153, 154, 170, 247, 258, 264, 265, 267, 268, 273, 274, 275, 277, 292, 376, 391, 395, 491, 544, 545, 546, 548, 549, 550, 556, 557, 591, 592, 595, 601, 602, 606, 633, 640, 682, 701, 704, 706, 707, 708, 712, 715, 716, 718, 720, 744, 748, 751, 803, 804

Spanish 592
Spanish America 591, 593, 595
Spanish Civil War 417, 491, 312, 354, 434, 435, 457, 461, 471, 547, 548, 798
Spanish colonies in America 137
Spanish Queen Isabella II 200
Spanish Revolution in 1823 258, 550
Spanish Succession 57
Spanish-American War 574, 575, 607
Spartacist 472, 473
Spartacus Union 472
spectroscope 768, 770
Speke 284
Spender Stephen 797, 798
Spenser 18
Spice Islands 525
Spinoza 63
Sputnik 772
St. Augustine 12, 24
St. Bernardine 21
St. Casimir 21
St. Francis 15
St. Helena 111, 124, 143
St. James 808
St. Lucia 140, 587
St. Mary 809
St. Nazaire 299
St. Pancreas Church 809
St. Pancreas Station 814
St. Peter 17, 18, 21
St. Peter's Fields, Manchester 249
St. Petersburg 121, 147, 192, 219, 220, 227, 228, 233, 239, 240, 241, 323, 342, 366, 440, 442, 654, 656, 734, 755
St. Simon 136
St. Thomas Aquinas 748
St. Vincent 21
Staatenbund 543
Stadholderate 523
Stalin 403, 450, 452, 453, 454, 455, 456, 457, 461, 500, 501, 503, 506, 508, 510, 511, 541, 549, 588
Stalingrad 501, 505, 588
Stamford Raffles 682
Stamp Act 72, 73
Standard Oil 265
Standard Oil Company 571
Stanford White 813
Stanislas Mikolajczyk 541
Stanley 284, 774
Stanley Baldwin 400, 432, 548
Stanley's 333
Stapleton 147
Star Chamber 43
State 309
State Gallery of 1847 810
Statebund 186
Stattholder 528, 530
Statute of Westminster 291
steel 718
steel empires 263
Stefan Batory 35
Stefan George 344, 345, 785, 796
Stefan Stambulov 363
Stein 122
Stendhal 789
Stephan Szechenyi 179
Stephen A. Douglas 562, 563
Stephen Bethlen 356
Stephen Cave 660
Stephen Dusan 231
Stephen Tisza 356
Stepniak 227
sterdam 103
Sternheim 795
Stimson Doctrine 644
Stockholm 751
Stolypin 443, 444
Storm Troopers (S.A.) 480
Stoyadinovitch 354
Stradonitz 765
Strait of Gibraltar 113
Strait of Messina 216
Straits 326
Straits Convention, July 13, 1841 237
Straits of Dardenelles 391
Straits of Dardenelles and Bosphorus 241
Straits of Magellan 596
Straits Settlements 429
Strassburg 782
Strasser 481, 482
Strassman 770
Stratford de Redcliffe 239
Stravinsky 804
Stresa 490
Stresa Declaration 312
Stresemann 407, 477, 478
Stumm-Halberg 263
Stuttgart 277, 474, 737
Stuttgart Congress of 1907 280

Styria 352
Subhas Chandra Bose 681
Subsidiary Alliance 672
Sudan 286, 287, 288, 289, 327
Sudetenland 471, 492, 512
Suez 35, 379, 500, 662
Suez Canal 168, 243, 262, 263, 285, 420, 500, 660, 661, 693
Sugar Act 70, 72
Sukarno 684
Sukhomlinov 368
Suleiman the Magnificent 34
Sullivan 815
Sully 51, 53
Sultan Abdul Hamid II 363
Sultan Abdul Mejid 243
Sultan Ahmed Fuad 662
Sultan Mahmud 236
Sultan Mahmud II 235
Sultan Muhammad VI Wahidal-Din 666
Sultan Suleiman I 35
Sumatra 293, 525, 653, 684
Sumter 564
Sun Yat-Sen 86, 636, 637, 641
Supreme Court 558, 570, 584
Surendranath Banerjee 677
Surinam 526
Surrealism 359, 815, 816
Surrealist 817, 820
Susan B. Warner 788
Suzuki 510
Svante Arrhenius 765
Swadeshi 677
Swan 132
Swan House 812
Swanscombe 757
Swarajya Party 679
Sweden 26, 31, 34, 46, 47, 48, 49, 57, 85, 98, 109, 113, 114, 115, 120, 133, 140, 142, 144, 154, 163, 194, 195, 220, 264, 265, 266, 277, 415, 416, 527, 528, 529, 530, 533, 534, 707, 709, 715, 716, 724, 728, 736, 744, 790
Swinburne 82
Swiss Confederation 141
Switzerland 14, 26, 31, 63, 70, 108, 115, 123, 139, 163, 165, 203, 212, 273, 277, 306, 321, 330, 357, 376, 440, 446, 465, 477, 497, 542, 543, 544, 704, 706, 718, 721, 724, 735, 736, 738, 739, 745, 747, 748
Sybel 326
Sybil 83, 138
Sydney Webb 279
Sykes-Picot 665
Sykes-Picot Agreement 664, 665
Syllabus Errorum 746
Sylvester Patent 178
Symbolism 750, 807
Symbolist Movement 785, 796
Symphony 801, 812
Syndicalism 274, 275
Syndicalists 464, 546
Syracuse 505, 588
Syria 229, 233, 295, 308, 500, 665, 666, 667, 668, 670, 694
Szechenyi 180
Szechwan 636, 642
Szent-Gyorgyi 762
Szogyeny 341, 373

T

T. Dobzhansky 760
T. H. Huxley 737
T. H. Morgan 760
T. Hamilton 809
T. P. O'Connor 421
T. R. Malthus 717
T. S. Ashton 715
T. S. Eliot 796, 797, 820
T. V. Soong 642
Tabriz 658
Tadzhistan 451
Taewongun or Grand Prince 630
Taff Vale Railway Company 424
Taft 577
Tage Erlander 534
Tahiti 292
Taiping 617
Taiping rebellion 616, 617, 618
Taipings 616
Tajuk 451
Takamine 773
Talavera 118
Talleyrand 118, 119, 141, 519
Tanganyika 284
Tangier 306, 336, 549
Tanjore 673
Tannenberg 378
Tansvaal 426
Tanzimat 655

Tao-Kuang 614, 615
Tarde 307
Tardieu 311
Tashkhent 292
Tasmania 291, 427
Taut 818
Tchaikovsky 226, 803
Tchernaya 241
Tea 675
Tea Act 73
Techernaya 212
Teheran 506, 588, 65-, 657, 658, 659
Tel el Kabir 285
Tel-Aviv 670
Tel-el-Kebir 661
telegraph 138, 138
television 138, 820
Temporary Mixed Commission 405, 409, 416
Tennessee 564, 566
Tennessee Valley Authority 584, 727
Tennessee Valley dam 456
Tennyson 82, 784
Terrible 36
Terror 103
Tests Act of 1871 419
Tewfik 285, 286, 660
Texas 558, 562, 563, 565, 573, 599
Thadeus Stevens 566
Thailand 501, 693
thakin 688
The Act of Supremacy, 1534 28
The Babylonian Captivity 25
The Balkan Wars 366
The Battle of Navarino 234
The Beer Hall Putsch 475
The Book of Common Prayer 29
The Brothers Karamazov 786
The Cherry Orchard 791
The Committee of Public Safety 103
The Communist Manifesto 136, 270, 271
The Croats 182
The David 18
The Decline and Fall of the Roman Empire 63
The Decline of the West 821
The Diet of Speyer 26
The East India Company 524
The Fifteenth Amendment 568
The Five Power treaty 579
The Fronde 54
The Geneva Protocol 405
The Harris Treaty, 1858 621
The House of Commons 136
The Idiot 786
The Jews 669
The King of Holland 199
The King of Rome 124
The Last Supper 17
The Luxenburg Manifesto 178
The Monroe Doctrine 147
The Morning Post 255
The Picture of Dorian Gray 792
The Portrait of a Lady (1881) 791
The Praise of Folly 14
The Prince 15
The Rapallo Treaty 477
The Red Sea 168
The Revolution of 1848 161
The Rights of Man 128
The Scarlet Letter 788
The Sepoy Mutiny 293
The Septembrist Revolt 550
The Spirit 65
The Spirit of Laws 90, 778
The Suez Canal 429
The Sultan, Selim III (1789-1807) 229
The Three Sisters 791
The Three Strangers 791
The Time Machine (1895) 793
The Times 255, 334
The Truman Doctrine 821
The United States 715
The Waste Land 798
The Working Class Programme 278
Theobold Dillon 100
Theodor Billroth 359
Theodor Ernst Mommsen 488
Theodor Storm 789
Theodore Dwight Weld 562
Theodore Fontane 329, 344
Theodore Gericault 806, 808
Theodore Herzel 752
Theodore Koerner 355
Theodore Mommsen 317, 344
Theodore Roosevelt 575, 608
Theodore Rousseau (1812-67) 810
Theophile Delcasse 305
Theophile Gautier 781
Theory of Relativity 820

theory of heat 766
Thermidor 104, 742
Thermidorian Reaction 105
Thermodynamics 82
thermodynamics 766
Thessaly 363
Thianwan 692
Thierry 83, 703
Thiers 88, 152, 156, 161, 167, 237, 297, 298
Third Anglo-Burmese War 688
Third Coalition 248
Third Estate 89, 93, 94, 98
Third Five Year Plan 456
Third French Republic 296, 299, 315
Third International 272, 456
Third International or Comintern 457
Third Reich 483, 491, 509
Third Republic 298, 305
Third Republic France 307
third and the final Round Table Conference 680
Thirty Years' 50, 53
Thirty Years' War 31, 33, 45, 49
Thomas Arnold 257, 734, 737, 745
Thomas Cranmer 28
Thomas Cromwell 28, 34
Thomas De Quincey 783
Thomas Edison's 343
Thomas Hardy 791, 796
Thomas Hobbes 33
Thomas Jefferson 75, 555, 734
Thomas Kuhn 19
Thomas Mann 483, 485, 487, 820, 821
Thomas Masaryk 352
Thomas More 13, 14
Thomas Mun 37
Thomas Muntzer 25
Thomas Newcomer 130
Thomas Paine 66, 74, 99, 127, 247, 562
Thomas Pinckney 556
Thomas Robert Malthus 135
Thomas U. Walter 810
Thomas Wolfe 799
Thomas Woolner 810
Thomas Young 755, 767
Thompson 270
Thomson, Lieutenant-Governor of North-Western Prov 674
Thrace 367, 390
Three Emperors' League 323
Three Musketeers 781
Three Power Pact 646
Tibet 306, 371, 613
Tieck 122
Tientsin 634
Tientsin convention 630
Tientsin Treaties 618
Tilsit 115, 220, 535
Timbuktu 287
Tirana 471
Tirpitz 335, 337
Tisza 341, 351, 356, 374
Titian 15, 18, 806, 807, 812
Tiziano Vercelli 18
Tkachev 228
Tobago 139, 140
Tobruk 500, 503
Tocqueville 83, 88, 159, 160, 703
Todleben 240
Togo 326, 387
Togoland 287, 308, 370, 403
Tohoku 625
Tokugawa period 621
Tokugawa Shogunate 620
Tokugawa Shoguns 619
Tokyo 404, 511, 585, 587, 624, 626, 643, 644, 646, 651
Tokyo University 625
Toleration Act 44
Toller 795
Tolstoy 82, 226, 786, 787, 790
Tomsky 453
Tonga (or the Friendly Islands) 426
Tonkin 292, 293, 299, 632, 687
Torquato Tasso 18
Torres Vedras 118
Torricelli 62
Tory Cabinet 256
Tosa 624
Toulon 102, 103
Townshend Act 73
Townshend Duties 73
Toynbee Arnold 822
Trade Union 267
Trade Union Act of 1871 419
Trade Union Congress 432
Trafalgar 113, 248, 260, 524
Trafalgar Square 808
Trans-Siberian line 439
Trans-Siberian Railway 450, 632
Transcaucasia 439, 451

Transcaucasian Federation 451
Transjordan 669, 670
Transjordania 668
Transvaal 289, 290, 334, 427, 428
Transylvania 35, 175, 180, 183, 352, 364, 382, 390
Treaty of 1842 618
Treaty of Adrianople 234
Treaty of Aigun 618
Treaty of Amiens 248
Treaty of Bardo 285
Treaty of Barwalde 47, 53
Treaty of Basel 103
Treaty of Berlin 226, 323, 362, 363, 365, 407, 478
Treaty of Brest-Litovsk 382, 449
Treaty of Bucharest 232, 367
Treaty of Bucharest on May 28 231
Treaty of Campo Formio 109
Treaty of Chaumont 123, 139
Treaty of Evora Montes 550
Treaty of Fontainebleau 117, 123, 591
Treaty of Ghent in 1814 557
Treaty of Guadalupe Hidalgo 599
Treaty of Hamburg 48
Treaty of Kalisch 122
Treaty of Kanghwa 625, 630
Treaty of Kiel (January 14, 1814) 530, 533
Treaty of Kutahia (May 1833) 235
Treaty of Kutchuk-Kainardji 244
Treaty of Lausanne 372, 391, 665, 666
Treaty of London 194, 195, 234, 464
Treaty of Lyons (1601) 52
Treaty of Nanking 615, 616
Treaty of Neuilly 390
Treaty of Oliva (1660) 34
Treaty of Paris 70, 226, 242
Treaty of Paris, May 1814 139
Treaty of Portsmouth 295
Treaty of Rapallo 403
Treaty of Ryswick 57
Treaty of Saint-Germain 707
Treaty of San Ildefonso 557
Treaty of San Stefano 226, 360, 361, 367
Treaty of Schonbrunn 173
Treaty of Sevres 390
Treaty of Shimonoseki 334
Treaty of St. Gemain 352, 389
Treaty of Stockholm 529, 533
Treaty of the Lateran 468
Treaty of the Pyrennes 54
Treaty of Tilsit 114, 125
Treaty of Trianon 357, 390, 402
Treaty of Unkiar Skelessi 236, 238
Treaty of Versailles 387, 388, 389, 391, 402, 415, 474, 494, 579, 643, 666
Treaty of Vienna 528, 537
Treaty of Villafranca 215
Treaty of Zurich in November 1859 215
Trent 465
Trentino 324, 376, 390, 464
Triennial Act 43
Trieste 232, 244, 324, 349, 376, 390, 464, 515, 710, 740
Trietschke 282, 319, 326
Trinidad 5, 110, 140, 587
Trinity College 251
Tripartite Pact 653
Triple 371
Triple Alliance 57, 290, 305, 324, 325, 327, 333, 334, 335, 336, 337, 364, 371, 403, 598
Triple Alliance Treaty 327
Triple Entente 307, 322, 337, 341, 372, 403, 444
Triple-Entente between France, Russia and England 371
Tripoli 36, 229, 288, 339, 366, 372, 464, 664
Tripoli war 664
Triumvirate 107
Troppau 145, 174
Trotsky 447, 448, 449, 450, 452, 453, 457
Truman 510, 515, 541
Truman Doctrine 515
Tsar 233, 234
Tsar Alexander 144, 145, 146, 147, 233, 535
Tsar Alexander I 232, 233
Tsar Alexander II 274, 441
Tsar Alexander III 334, 362
Tsar Nicholas 164, 182, 235, 238, 239, 241, 444
Tsar Nicholas I 786
Tsar Nicholas I of Russia 654
Tsar Nicholas II 374, 382, 649
Tsar Nicholas of Russia 235
Tschirschky 351
Tseng Kuo-fan 617
Tsuda Umeko 625
Tu-Chuns 639, 640
Tuan Chi-jui 637
Tubingen 755
Tudor Dynasty 34
Tudor monarchy 8
Tudors 43, 44

Tuileries 100, 297
Tukhachevsky 451, 538
Tung-meng hui 636, 637
Tunis 35, 229, 284, 285, 288, 299, 324, 463
Tunisia 282, 300, 305, 362, 469, 504, 588, 664, 697
Turgenev 82, 223, 226, 227, 786
Turgot 66, 91, 92, 445, 779
Turin 164, 211, 214, 216, 464
Turkestan 292
Turkestan-Siberian Railway 456
Turkey 85, 108, 114, 116, 144, 146, 147, 157, 222, 223, 226, 229, 230, 231, 234, 235, 237, 238, 239, 240, 241, 242, 243, 244, 245, 246, 258, 295, 339, 340, 343, 347, 360, 362, 363, 365, 366, 368, 370, 372, 373, 379, 380, 382, 385, 390, 404, 409, 410, 429, 458, 459, 460, 531, 640, 660, 665, 677, 693, 706, 708, 709, 715, 740
Turkmenistan 451
Turko-Italian War, 1911-12 280
Turkoman 656
Turks 5
Turner 809, 811
Turnham Green 813
Tuscany 45, 141, 142, 206, 209, 214, 215, 463, 701, 714
Twenty-one Demands 87
Twenty-one Demands 638
Tycho Brahe 59
typhus 761
Tyrol 140, 141, 352

U

U Nu 688, 689
U-boat 377, 381
U. S. A. 712
U.K. 708, 552
Uganda 286, 429
Uhland 782
Uitlanders 290
Ukraine 220, 382, 391, 439, 449, 451, 456, 538, 539, 751
Ulrich Zwingli 23
Ulster 426
Ultramontane 31
Ultramontane Party 31
Ultramontanes 747
Ultramontanism 743
Umbria 216
UN 670
Uncle Tom's Cabin 562, 788
Under the Greenwood Tree 791
Unemployment Insurance Act of 1920 431
Unilever 265
Union of Lublin 35
Union of South Africa 387
Unitarians 27, 44
United Alkali Company of 1891 722
United Kingdom 431, 518, 708, 719, 723, 724, 725, 726, 727, 730
United Nations 414, 549, 550, 588, 612, 693
United Nations Organisation 508, 544
United Provinces 595
United States 83, 84, 85, 86, 87, 133, 134, 225, 226, 252, 264, 265, 266, 282, 284, 291, 292, 309, 310, 377, 381, 382, 383, 392, 397, 398, 399, 400, 401, 406, 408, 410, 411, 414, 416, 422, 427, 431, 433, 435, 444, 456, 462, 496, 499, 500, 501, 502, 511, 512, 515, 543, 545, 547, 549, 555, 557, 558, 559, 560, 573, 574, 576, 578, 579, 580, 582, 583, 585, 586, 587, 590, 595, 598, 599, 601, 604, 605, 606, 607, 608, 610, 612, 616, 618, 620, 621, 625, 629, 633, 639, 642, 643, 644, 645, 646, 647, 648, 650, 653, 670, 671, 683, 701, 702, 705, 706, 707, 711, 715, 717, 718, 719, 720, 721, 723, 724, 725, 726, 727, 730, 731, 734, 739, 744, 755, 760, 772, 776, 813
United States of America 78, 316, 821
United States Steel Company 571, 575
Universities of Oxford 251
Universities of St. Andrews 258
University College 776
University College of London 772
University of Berlin 744, 755
University of Chile 604
University of Durban 258
University of Hanoi 685
University of Kazan 440
University of London 257, 738
University of Oslo 531
University of Paris 14, 151
University of Wittenberg 23
University Tests Act of 1871 746
Unkiar Skelessi 223, 236, 237
Unkiar Skelessi on July 8, 1833 235
Unruh 795
Unterwalden 745
Upper Canada 259, 290
Upper Silesia 386
Uranus 770
Urbain Leverrier 82
Uruguay 592, 594, 597, 598, 602, 603, 608

USSR 451, 456, 687
Utah 562
Utilitarian 734
Utilitarianism 249
Utilitarians 673
Utopia 14
Utrecht Settlement 58
Uvadale Price 808
Uvarov 222
Uzbeg 451

V

V-2 775
V. V. Dokuchaev 761
V.I. Lenin 276
Vajiravudh 692
Valais 745
Valla 13
Valmy 101, 117, 154
Van de Spiegel 523
Van Dyck 806
Van Eyck brothers 18
Van Gogh 307, 813
Van Zeeland 522
Vanderbilt 571
Vanity Fair 788
Vargas 607
Vasco da Gama 3, 5
Vasco Nunez de Balbao 6
Vatican 21, 31, 211, 303, 462
Vatican City 750
Vatican Council 747
Velasquez 807, 812
Vendee risings in 1793 741
Vendemiaire 104
Venetia 142, 172, 173, 212, 213, 214, 216, 217
Venetian Republic 211
Venezuela 5, 6, 559, 574, 592, 593, 596, 597, 602, 608, 609
Venice 18, 29, 34 35, 107, 164, 206, 209, 210, 211, 807
Venizelos 363, 655
Venstre 530
Ventose 104
Vera Cruz 599
Vera Zassulic 225, 228
Verdun 100, 379, 380, 381
Verlaine 82, 604, 785
Vernacular Press Act 676
Verona 147, 174, 207
Verrocchio 15, 16
Versailles 94, 95, 203, 296, 299, 385, 386, 480, 578, 753
Versailles Peace 451
Versailles Settlement 389
Versailles Treaty 404, 407, 409, 411, 461, 474, 479, 480, 488, 489, 490, 494, 540, 638
Vesenkha 728
Viaminck 815
Vicente Lombardo Toledano 606
Vichy 314, 669
Vichy Government 315
Vichy regime 499
Vicki Baum's 485
Vicksburg 565
Vico 68
Victor Cousin 736
Victor Emmanuel 169, 208, 211, 214, 471, 505, 544
Victor Emmanuel II 211, 217, 462
Victor Emmanuel III 463, 471
Victor Emmanuel King of Italy 213
Victor Emmanuel of Italy 200
Victor Emmanuel's 216
Victor Horta 814
Victor Hugo 149, 168, 780, 781, 782
Victoria 284, 291, 427, 738, 811
Vidkun Quisling 531
Vienna 26, 35, 45, 58, 81, 85, 109, 113, 119, 124, 131, 140, 143, 145, 147, 154, 161, 162, 164, 170, 172, 175, 176, 177, 178, 179, 180, 181, 182, 184, 206, 240, 241, 243, 263, 264, 320, 341, 346, 347, 348, 351, 353, 354, 355, 357, 359, 374, 491, 528, 579, 589, 706, 715, 748, 801, 802, 810
Vienna Congress of 1815 206
Vienna Note 239
Vienna Settlement 81, 83, 143, 164, 542
Vienna, October 3, 1866 198
Vietminh 687
Vietnam 649, 685, 687, 692
Vigny 153
Villafranca 169
Villele 150, 151
Vilna 220, 403
Vimiero 117
Vincent Van Gogh 813, 814
Vinoba Bhave 681
Virgin Islands 528

Virginia 77, 563, 564, 565
Virginia Assembly 72
Virginia Woolf 796, 798
virus 820
Viruses 762, 774
vitamins 761, 762, 820
Viviani 375
Vladimir Ilyich Ulyanov (Lenin) 440
Vladivostok 226, 293, 294, 450, 632
Volta 764
Voltaire 64, 65, 66, 90, 151, 271, 778, 779, 785
Von Altenstein 733
Von Hahnke 331
Von Ketteler 634
Von Kleist 782
Von Sybel 186
von Muller 370
Voroshilov 501
VSNK or Vesenkha 453

W

W. E. Forster 419
W. H. Auden 820
W. H. Davies 796
W. H. Fox Talbot 768
W. H. Mayfair 809
W. K. Roentgen 768
W. R. Inge 750
W. S. Gilbert 803
W.H. Auden 798
Waddington 362
Wafdist 662
Wagner 171, 326, 802, 803
Wagner or National Labour Relations Act of July 1935 584
Wagram 118, 119
Wailing Wall 668
Waitz 188
Wakatsuki 652
Wake 587
Wakefield 259
Walachia 35
Waldeck-Rousseau 303, 304
Wales 34, 252, 739
Wall Street 581, 726
Wallachia 169, 229, 238, 240, 241, 245, 535
Wallachia and Moldavia 239
Wallenstein 46, 53
Wallis Simpson 434
Walt Whitman 566, 785
Walter Bronsart von Schellendorf 330
Walter de la Mare 796
Walter Funk 729
Walter Gropius 485, 820
Walter Lippmann 577
Walter Pater (1839-94) 792
Walter Prescot Webb 6
Walter Rathenau 392
Walter Scott 782
Walter Sickert 812
Walther Rathenau 475
Walton 820
Walwal 470
Wandervogel 267, 394
War and Peace 787
war of American Independence 88
Warburg Festival 187
Warner Heisenberg 820
Warren Gamaliel Harding 579
Warren Hastings 672, 673
Wars of the Roses 43
Warsaw 220, 221, 379, 402, 451, 508, 536, 538, 539, 541, 734
Warsaw Pact 515, 821
Warsaw University 438
Warwickshire 254
Washington 75, 76, 459, 460, 555, 556, 574, 576, 583, 584, 588, 604, 810
Washington Conference 410, 416, 583, 650
Waterloo 124, 144, 250, 583
Watling Island 5
Watt 766
Wavell 500, 503
Wealth of Nations 37, 135
Wedgwood 753
Wegener 773
Wei Chang Hui 617
Weihaiwei 632, 639
Weimar 473
Weimar Constitution 474, 478
Weimar Republic 474, 475, 481, 485, 486
Weissenhof 818
Wellesley 672, 673
Wellington 118, 124, 152, 234, 248, 251
Wellington, the British Prime Minister 234
Weltpolitik 331, 333, 334, 335, 370, 371
Wembley 712
Wendell Wilkie 585
Werner 782

Werner Heisenberg 769
Werner Sombart 344
Werner Von Siemens 343
Wernher von Braun 775
Werther 782
West Africa 327, 333, 429
West Germany 542
West Indies 712
Western Australia 291, 427
Westminster Abbey 745
Westphalia 48, 50, 114
Weygand 314, 499, 538
Whig Party 247
Whigs 256
Whisky Rebellion 556
Whistler 812
White 105
White Russia 451, 538
Wielopolski 536
Wilfred Owen 796
Wilhelm Dilthey 344
Wilhelm Frick 482, 483
Wilhelm Furtwangler 485
Wilhelm Keppler 484
Wilhelm Leibknecht 321, 198, 278
Wilhelm Miklas 354
Wilhelm Von Kardoff 320
Wilhelm von Humboldt 732, 755
Wilhelmina 526
Willhelm Konrad Roentgen 344
William Allen Miller 768
William Beachey 806
William Beveridge 730
William Blake 783
William Booth 749
William Bragg 769
William Butler Yeats 820
William Carey 673
William Cobbett 137, 249, 267
William Cockeril 132, 518
William Crookes 768
William E. Gladstone 419
William Faulkner 799
William Godwin 128
William Harvey 47
William Hazlitt 783
William Henry Harrison 560
William Henry Perkin 132
William Howard Taft 576
William Huggins 771
William Huskisson 250
William I 202, 524, 525
William II 328, 332, 333, 340, 351, 373, 374, 525
William III 199, 525, 526
William Jennings Bryan 574
William Johnson 72
William Lloyd Garrison 562
William Lovett 254, 267
William Makepeace Thackeray 788
William McKinley 574
William Morris 279, 423, 811, 812
William of Holland 518
William of Ockham 21
William of Orange 44, 57, 152
William P. Frith 811
William Perkin 764
William Pitt, the Younger 109
William Robertson 424
William Rockefeller 572
William S. Knudsen 586
William Seward 563
William Siemens 720
William Temple 750
William the silent 33
William Thompson 766
William V 523, 524
William VI 524
William Wheelwright 596
William Wilkins (1778-1839) 809
William Wollaston 768
William Wordsworth 127
Willington Koo of China 385
Wilna 120
Wilson 578
Wilson's Fourteen Points 385, 386
Wilsonn 381, 383, 385, 388, 389
Windischgratz 176, 181
Winston Churchill 339, 379, 422, 423, 426, 431, 432, 434, 490, 498, 502
Winston Churchill, Chancellor of the Exchequer 433
Wirth 396
Wisconsin 577
Wit Stwosz 18
Witenagemot 41
Witte 438, 443, 648
Wohler 764
Wolfe Tone 248
Wolfgang Kapp 474

Women's Suffrage Movement 426
Woodrow Wilson 343, 376, 383, 413, 572, 577, 610, 683, 694
Wordsworth 99, 782, 784
Workers' Revolution 277
World Court 585
World Economic Conference of 1933 727
World Health Organisation 774
World War I 266, 395, 637
World War II 751, 774
Wright brothers 775
Wu Pei-fu 639
Wurtemberg 26, 113, 115, 153, 163, 186, 89, 191, 199, 200, 202, 204, 316, 472, 482
Wurzberg 755, 197
Wuthering Heights 788

X

X-ray 762, 760, 768, 770
Xavier Bichat 757
Xiemenes' 13

Y

Yakohama 624
Yale 734, 738, 755
Yalta 508, 589
Yalta Conference 541
Yamagata 625, 629
Yamagata Aritomo 649
Yamamoto 588
Yang Hsiu-Ching 617
Yangtse Treaty 336
Yangtze 634, 645, 648
Yangtze valley 636
Yap 579, 580
Yeats 794, 797, 798
Yedo 621, 622
Yeh Ming Chen 618
yellow fever 761
Yemen 669, 670
Yerkes Observatory 771
Yokohama 273, 626
Yokosuka 626
Yorkshire 254, 259
Young Committee 398
Young Italy 208, 209
Young Men's Buddhist Association (YMBA) 688
Young Men's Christian Association 749
Young Plan 398, 433, 478, 479, 480, 481
Young Turks 365, 366
Ypres 382, 383
Ypsilanti 232
Yuan Shih-Kai 635, 637
Yudenich 450, 451
Yugoslavia 308, 311, 349, 352, 356, 390, 400, 402, 403, 404, 409, 469, 470, 512, 751
Yugoslavs 390
Yunnan 642

Z

Zachary Macaulay 252
Zagreb 350, 352
Zaibatsu 626, 652
Zajaczek 535
Zamora 546
Zanardelli 463, 464
Zanzibar 285, 287, 288, 426, 429
Zapata 605
Zelaya 608
Zemstov 225
Zemstov or local government 224
Zemstovs 225
Zemstvo 440
Zemstvo 437, 441, 448, 537, 737
Zeppelins 377
Zhukov 508, 509
Zinoviev 447, 452, 453, 456, 457, 458
Zinoviev letter 432, 458
Zionism 348, 752
Zola 168, 301, 307, 787
Zollunion 480
Zollverein 131, 133, 135, 154, 188, 192, 199, 263, 716, 717
zoology 760
Zululand 426, 428
Zulus 420
Zuniga 46
Zurich 26, 227, 277, 543, 705, 737, 738
Zygmunt I 35
Zygmunt-August 35

Some exciting gifts are up for grabs with this book!!

EUROPE AND THE WORLD

Sailendra Nath Sen

FREE Gifts Rs. 1000/-

Dear Readers

By now you must have gone through this book in the entirety. So we invite your assessment on this title with absolute impartiality and candid observations. After all, we publishers blindly depend on your benchmarking. Friends, please fill up the open spaces below with CAPITAL LETTERS. You may add some extra sheets of paper if the space provided is not sufficient for you.

i. What are the important topics of your syllabus which are not adequately covered in this book?

ii. In which chapters and on what topics the treatment of the subject-matter by the author is not satisfactory and why?

iii. Have you come across the typos, factual inaccuracies, inconsistencies, and other forms of mistakes in the book? If yes, then please specify the mistakes and page numbers.

iv. Name top three books on the same subject, which, in your consideration, are better than this book. Could you provide some reasons?

Your 1st Preference: ....

Your 2nd Preference: ....

Your 3rd Preference: ....

v. Any suggestion to improve the quality of illustrations, diagrams, etc.?

vi. How did you like the cover design? Any suggestion on colours?

vii. Suggestions for further improvement of production-standard:

viii. Who recommended you this book:

☐ Teacher ☐ Friend ☐ Parents ☐ Bookseller ☐ Librarian

ix. Name of the person who has recommended:

Designation: ....

Address: ....

Phone No.: ....

e-mail: ....

x. Name and address of the bookseller from whom you have purchased this book:

....

....

....

xi. Name and address of the library where you would like to find the book:

....

....

xii. Name and address of your institution (Please mention the University or Board):

....

....

xiii. Your name, e-mail, and complete postal address:

....

....

....

xiv. A few other titles published by us that you would like to read:

....

....

The best assessment will be rewarded half-yearly. The award will be in the form of our publications, as decided by the Editorial and Marketing Operations Division, amounting to Rs. 1000/- (Rupees one thousand) only.

....

Please mail the filled up coupon at your earliest to :

Editorial & Marketing Operations Division

NEW CENTRAL BOOK AGENCY (P) Ltd

8/1 Chintamoni Das Lane, Kolkata 700 009

West Bengal, INDIA

Phone + Fax: 033 + 2241 8411, 2241 8573, 2241 9094

e-mail: ncbapvtltd@eth.net, ncba@cal2.vsnl.net.in

Website: www.centralgroup.com

Studies in Fuzziness and Soft Computing

Volume 401

Series Editor

Janusz Kacprzyk, Systems Research Institute, Polish Academy of Sciences, Warsaw, Poland

The series "Studies in Fuzziness and Soft Computing" contains publications on various topics in the area of soft computing, which include fuzzy sets, rough sets, neural networks, evolutionary computation, probabilistic and evidential reasoning, multi-valued logic, and related fields. The publications within "Studies in Fuzziness and Soft Computing" are primarily monographs and edited volumes. They cover significant recent developments in the field, both of a foundational and applicable character. An important feature of the series is its short publication time and world-wide distribution. This permits a rapid and broad dissemination of research results.

Indexed by ISI, DBLP and Ulrichs, SCOPUS, Zentralblatt Math, GeoRef, Current Mathematical Publications, IngentaConnect, MetaPress and Springerlink. The books of the series are submitted for indexing to Web of Science.

More information about this series at http://www.springer.com/series/2941

Muhammad Akram · Musavarah Sarwar ·
Wieslaw A. Dudek

Graphs for the Analysis of Bipolar Fuzzy Information

Springer

Muhammad Akram
Department of Mathematics
University of the Punjab
Lahore, Pakistan

Musavarah Sarwar
Department of Mathematics
Government College Women University
Sialkot, Pakistan

Wieslaw A. Dudek
Faculty of Pure and Applied Mathematics
Wrocław University of Technology
Wrocław, Poland

ISSN 1434-9922 ISSN 1860-0808 (electronic)
Studies in Fuzziness and Soft Computing
ISBN 978-981-15-8758-0 ISBN 978-981-15-8756-6 (eBook)
https://doi.org/10.1007/978-981-15-8756-6

This Springer imprint is published by the registered company Springer Nature Singapore Pte Ltd.
The registered company address is: 152 Beach Road, #21-01/04 Gateway East, Singapore 189721, Singapore

We dedicate this book to the memory of Professor Lotfi Zadeh!

Foreword

Graphs are considered as one of the fundamental structures studied in combinatorics. The subject started with the paper published by Euler on the seven bridges of Königsberg in 1736. Graph theory is highly applied in other areas of mathematics and other branches of science. However, "crisp graphs" are not appropriate for describing all of the existing relations between objects. Thus, Kauffman (1973) presented the first definition of fuzzy graphs based on Zadeh's fuzzy relations. In addition, Rosenfeld (1975) introduced "fuzzy analogs" of several basic graph-theoretic concepts.

In many real-world problems, "bipolarity" plays a role when it is important to distinguish between positive information representing satisfaction degree and negative information indicating dissatisfaction degree. Both types of information cannot be understood simultaneously by the fuzzy model, leading to the existence of bipolar information. This type of information cannot be well-represented by means of fuzzy graphs. In these situations, bipolar fuzzy set theory is applied to the graphs in order to describe the relationships. Muhammad Akram (2011) first introduced the notion of bipolar fuzzy graphs and published different papers with his colleagues and students on a wide variety of bipolar fuzzy graph-theoretic structures. This book presents some fundamental theories of such types of bipolar fuzzy graphs, complex bipolar fuzzy graphs, Cayley bipolar fuzzy graphs, bipolar fuzzy planar graphs, bipolar fuzzy matroids, double dominating energy of bipolar fuzzy graphs, bipolar single-valued neutrosophic competition graphs, and bipolar single-valued neutrosophic graph structures.

The authors are well-known researchers in the field of fuzzy graphs. They have presented all concepts of bipolar fuzzy graph theory with applications in a variety of diverse fields and have paid careful attention to algorithmic issues. Therefore, the book can contribute to the development of fuzzy graph theory for students and researchers.

Rajab Ali Borzooei
Shahid Beheshti University
Tehran, Iran

Preface

The motivation of this monograph can be traced back to the work of late Lotfi A. Zadeh (1921–2017). Professor Zadeh introduced fuzzy set theory in 1965, as a model for the representation of uncertainty and vagueness in real-world systems. A mathematical framework—fuzzy logic—was initiated in order to give formal support to the notion of partial truth between "absolute true" and "absolute false." This meant one of the most important, creative, and fruitful concepts introduced in science and technology during the second half of the twentieth century. One of its interactions with other branches of mathematics produced the concept of fuzzy graphs, which is based on Zadeh's fuzzy relations, originated with Kafmann. In 1975, Rosenfeld laid the foundations for fuzzy graph theory. Mordeson and Nair also made early contributions to that field.

Some aspects of data uncertainty are likely to appear in many contexts and scientific disciplines. Thus, different forms of vagueness have been recognized in applied fields. Some come from conflicting or incomplete information, as well as from multiple interpretations of some phenomena. In applications including expert systems, belief systems, and information fusion, it is not only convenient to use the one real value from the unit interval [0, 1] supported by the evidence, but also useful to consider the counter-membership against the evidence. Such 'bipolarity' is a core feature in many domains of information processing, both from the point of view of knowledge representation and from the perspective of processing and reasoning. Bipolarity appears whenever it is important to distinguish between (*i*) positive information that represents what is possible or preferred and (*ii*) negative information that represents what is impossible or forbidden. Both inputs cannot be simultaneously discerned by the fuzzy model. Motivated by this concern, Zhang introduced in 1994 a new component that expresses a negative degree of membership in addition to the structure of a fuzzy set. This idea launched the concept of bipolar fuzzy set that inspires the concept to which this monograph is devoted. With this work we aim at filling a gap, to wit, the lack of a mathematical approach towards bipolar information, that is, the coexistence of positive and negative information.

This volume is based on a number of papers by the authors that have been published in various scientific journals. They are part of a long-lasting research program that concerns decision-making methods under bipolar fuzzy graphical models. Now they are wrapped together in a book that may be useful for researchers in mathematics, computer scientists, and social scientists alike. Let us describe its content.

In Chap. 1, we review the notion of bipolar fuzzy sets. Then, we present the concept of bipolar fuzzy graphs and describe various methods of their construction. We discuss the concept of isomorphism of bipolar fuzzy graphs and investigate their fundamental properties. We present certain types of bipolar fuzzy graphs, complex bipolar fuzzy graphs, bipolar fuzzy walk, bipolar fuzzy bridge, strength of connectedness, and weak and strong bipolar fuzzy edges. We also endorse the importance of bipolar fuzzy digraphs with a number of real-world problems.

In Chap. 2, we discuss certain properties of distance functions in bipolar fuzzy graphs. We establish the formulae of distance in complete bipolar fuzzy graphs, complete bipartite bipolar fuzzy graphs and products of bipolar fuzzy graphs. We present an algorithm for computing the distance matrix, eccentricity of the vertices, radius, and diameter in bipolar fuzzy graphs. We study the concepts of self-centered bipolar fuzzy graphs and antipodal bipolar fuzzy graphs. We describe applications of bipolar fuzzy graphs in product manufacturing.

In Chap. 3, we present certain types of bipolar fuzzy graphs with various methods of construction. We discuss the concept of degree and isomorphism of irregular bipolar fuzzy graphs. We describe the concepts of bipolar fuzzy line graphs and the Cayley bipolar fuzzy graphs.

In Chap. 4, we present different types of concepts concerning bipolar fuzzy competition graphs and their extensions. Various methods for the construction of bipolar fuzzy competition graphs of certain products of bipolar fuzzy digraphs are studied with theoretical proofs. We study certain types of competition graphs under complex bipolar fuzzy environment. We describe applications of bipolar fuzzy competition graphs in different domains.

In Chap. 5, we apply the powerful technique of bipolar fuzzy sets to multigraphs and planar graphs. We present the notions of bipolar fuzzy multigraphs, bipolar fuzzy planar graphs, and bipolar fuzzy dual graphs. Chapter 6 considers various types of dominations in bipolar fuzzy graphs and their importance in decision-making models.

In Chap. 7, we study the theory of matroids and circuits in bipolar fuzzy environment, soft environment, and bipolar fuzzy soft environment. We present certain applications of bipolar fuzzy matroids in decision support systems, secret sharing problems, and network analysis.

Chapter 8 is concerned with various energy-like quantities of bipolar fuzzy graphs. In particular, we study Laplacian energy, signless Laplacian energy, dominating energy, and double dominating energy of bipolar fuzzy graphs. Two case studies illustrate these concepts.

In Chap. 9, we present the concepts of bipolar single-valued neutrosophic competition graphs, bipolar neutrosophic single-valued p-competition graphs, and m-step bipolar single-valued neutrosophic competition graphs. We describe some applications of bipolar single-valued neutrosophic competition graphs and m-step bipolar single-valued neutrosophic competition graphs in economics, organizational designations, and business competition.

In Chap. 10, we apply the concept of bipolar single-valued neutrosophic set to graph structures and study a framework to handle bipolar neutrosophic information by combining bipolar neutrosophic sets with graph structures. We study several operations on bipolar single-valued neutrosophic graph structures with interesting properties. We describe the isomorphism properties of various types of bipolar single-valued neutrosophic graph structures with φ-complement. We explain the importance of bipolar single-valued neutrosophic graph structures with real-world applications in international relations, psychology, and global terrorism.

Acknowledgements: The authors are grateful to the administration of University of Punjab, Lahore, for providing the facilities, which were required for successful completion of this monograph. Musavarah Sarwar is also thankful to the administration of Government College Women University, Sialkot, Pakistan, for providing the facilities which were required for writing this book.

Lahore, Pakistan — Muhammad Akram
Sialkot, Pakistan — Musavarah Sarwar
Wrocław, Poland — Wieslaw A. Dudek

Contents

1 Bipolar Fuzzy Sets and Bipolar Fuzzy Graphs 1
1.1 Introduction 1
1.2 Bipolar Fuzzy Graphs 7
1.3 Isomorphism of Bipolar Fuzzy Graphs 26
1.4 Complex Bipolar Fuzzy Graphs 42
1.5 Bipolar Fuzzy Digraphs 51
1.6 Applications of Bipolar Fuzzy Digraphs to Decision Making 60
1.6.1 Bipolar Fuzzy Neurons in Medical Diagnosis 61
1.6.2 Social Networking 63
1.6.3 Bipolar Fuzzy Organizational Model 64
1.6.4 Bipolar Fuzzy Graphs in Marketability 66
1.6.5 Vulnerability Assessment of Gas Pipeline Networks 68
1.6.6 Bipolar Fuzzy Digraph in Travel Time 70
1.6.7 Comparison Analysis 74
1.7 Conclusions 74
Exercises 1 75
References 78

2 Distance Measures in Bipolar Fuzzy Graphs 81
2.1 Introduction 81
2.2 Distance in Bipolar Fuzzy Graphs 82
2.3 Metric in Bipolar Fuzzy Graphs 96
2.4 Self-centered Bipolar Fuzzy Graphs 103
2.5 Antipodal Bipolar Fuzzy Graphs 112
2.6 Applications of Bipolar Fuzzy Graphs 122
2.6.1 Product Manufacturing 122
2.6.2 Safe Route and Shortest Path Problem 122

2.7 Conclusions 124
Exercises 2 125
References 126

3 **Special Types of Bipolar Fuzzy Graphs** 127
3.1 Introduction 127
3.2 Regular and Irregular Bipolar Fuzzy Graphs 128
3.3 Bipolar Fuzzy Line Graphs 141
3.4 Cayley Bipolar Fuzzy Graphs 147
3.5 Conclusions 157
Exercises 3 158
References 158

4 **Bipolar Fuzzy Competition Graphs** 161
4.1 Introduction 161
4.2 Bipolar Fuzzy Competition Graphs 163
4.3 Bipolar Fuzzy *k*-competition Graphs 187
4.4 Complex Bipolar Fuzzy Competition Graphs 191
4.5 Applications of Bipolar Fuzzy Competition Graphs 195
4.5.1 Variants of Bipolar Fuzzy Competition Graphs in Food Webs 196
4.5.2 Competitive Market 205
4.5.3 Political Competition 206
4.5.4 Social Competition in Bipolar Fuzzy Environment 210
4.5.5 Interactions and Conflicts in Communication Networks 213
4.6 Conclusions 219
Exercises 4 220
References 221

5 **Bipolar Fuzzy Planar Graphs** 223
5.1 Introduction 223
5.2 Bipolar Fuzzy Planar Graphs 225
5.3 Bipolar Fuzzy Bridges 234
5.4 Bipolar Fuzzy Cut Vertices and Bipolar Fuzzy Blocks 238
5.5 Bipolar Fuzzy Cycles and Bipolar Fuzzy Trees 241
5.6 Applications of Bipolar Fuzzy Planar Graphs 246
5.6.1 Road Network Model to Monitor Traffic 247
5.6.2 Modeling of Electrical Connections 248
5.7 Conclusions 249
Exercises 5 250
References 250

6 Domination in Bipolar Fuzzy Graphs ... 253
6.1 Introduction ... 253
6.2 Types of Domination in Bipolar Fuzzy Graphs ... 254
6.3 Irredundance in Bipolar Fuzzy Graphs ... 272
6.4 Applications of Domination in Decision-Making Problems ... 274
6.4.1 Facility Location Problem ... 274
6.4.2 Representatives in Youth Development Council ... 275
6.4.3 Transmission Tower Location Problem ... 277
6.5 Conclusions ... 278
Exercises 6 ... 279
References ... 279

7 Bipolar Fuzzy Circuits ... 281
7.1 Introduction ... 281
7.2 Bipolar Fuzzy Circuits ... 282
7.2.1 Circuit Rectangles ... 294
7.3 Bipolar Fuzzy Soft Circuits ... 295
7.4 Decision Support Systems ... 301
7.4.1 Ordering of Machines Using Bipolar Fuzzy Matroids ... 301
7.4.2 Network Analysis ... 303
7.4.3 Ordering of Tasks Using Bipolar Fuzzy Soft Matroids ... 304
7.5 Conclusions ... 305
Exercises 7 ... 305
References ... 306

8 Energy of Bipolar Fuzzy Graphs ... 309
8.1 Introduction ... 309
8.2 Energy of Bipolar Fuzzy Graphs ... 311
8.3 Laplacian Energy of Bipolar Fuzzy Graphs ... 317
8.4 Signless Laplacian Energy of Bipolar Fuzzy Graphs ... 324
8.5 Dominating and Double Dominating Energy of Bipolar Fuzzy Graphs ... 328
8.6 Applications of Energy to Decision-Making Problems ... 335
8.6.1 Smooth Communication Problem ... 335
8.6.2 Selection of a Business Partner ... 338
8.7 Conclusions ... 343
Exercises 8 ... 343
References ... 347

9 Bipolar Neutrosophic Competition Graphs 349
9.1 Introduction 349
9.2 Certain Types of Bipolar Neutrosophic Competition Graphs 350
9.3 Bipolar Neutrosophic Neighborhood Graphs 369
9.4 Applications of Competition Graphs in Bipolar Neutrosophic Environment 377
9.4.1 Designation Competition in an Organization 379
9.4.2 Competition in Textile Market 382
9.4.3 Competition in Sports 385
9.5 Conclusions 389
Exercises 9 390
References 390

10 Bipolar Neutrosophic Graph Structures 393
10.1 Introduction 393
10.2 Operations on Bipolar Neutrosophic Graph Structures 394
10.3 Isomorphism in Bipolar Neutrosophic Graph Structures 416
10.4 Applications of Bipolar Single-Valued Neutrosophic Graph Structures 427
10.4.1 International Relations 427
10.4.2 Psychological Improvement of Patients 433
10.4.3 Uncovering the Undercover Reasons of Global Terrorism 438
10.5 Conclusions 444
Exercises 10 444
References 446

Index 447

About the Authors

Muhammad Akram is Professor at the Department of Mathematics, University of the Punjab, Lahore, Pakistan. He previously served at Punjab University College of Information Technology as Assistant Professor and Associate Professor. He earned his Ph.D. in Fuzzy Mathematics from Government College University, Lahore, Pakistan. His research interests include numerical algorithms, fuzzy graphs, fuzzy algebras, and fuzzy decision support systems. He has published 9 books and over 365 research articles in peer-reviewed international journals and supervised 12 Ph.D. students.

Musavarah Sarwar is Assistant Professor at Government College Women University, Sialkot, Pakistan. A gold medalist in academic excellence, Dr. Sarwar received her Ph.D. in Mathematics from the University of the Punjab, Lahore, Pakistan. Her research interests include graph theory, fuzzy graphs and fuzzy decision support systems/decision-making models. She has published 18 research articles in international peer-reviewed journals.

Wieslaw A. Dudek is Professor at the Department of Pure and Applied Mathematics, Wrocław University of Science and Technology, Wrocław, Poland. He completed his Ph.D. in Mathematics at the Department of Higher Algebra, State University of Chisinau, Republic of Moldova, under the supervision of Prof. V. D Belousov. He received his Degree of Habilitated Doctor from the Warsaw University of Technology. The main areas of his scientific interests include polyadic groups, quasigroups, fuzzy algebras, fuzzy graphs and their applications. Professor Dudek has authored 2 monographs, 4 textbooks, and published 200 research articles in international peer-reviewed journals. He is Editor-in-Chief of the journal *Quasigroups and Related Systems* and on the editorial board of several international journals. He has promoted 4 doctors of mathematics.

List of Figures

Fig. 1.1 Order of magnitude ($\geq\geq$) of crisp and bipolar fuzzy logic 4
Fig. 1.2 Bipolar fuzzy graph 9
Fig. 1.3 Union of bipolar fuzzy graphs 10
Fig. 1.4 Bipolar fuzzy graph G_1 11
Fig. 1.5 Bipolar fuzzy graph G_2 11
Fig. 1.6 Union $G_1 \cup G_2$ of bipolar fuzzy graphs 1
Fig. 1.7 Intersection of bipolar fuzzy graphs G_1 and G_2 13
Fig. 1.8 Join of bipolar fuzzy graphs G_1 and G_2 14
Fig. 1.9 Cartesian product $G_1 \Box G_2$ 17
Fig. 1.10 Direct product $G_1 \times G_2$ 18
Fig. 1.11 Strong product $G_1 \Box G_2$ 19
Fig. 1.12 Bipolar fuzzy path $\mathcal{P}_5$ 21
Fig. 1.13 Strong bipolar fuzzy graph G 22
Fig. 1.14 Complete bipolar fuzzy graph 22
Fig. 1.15 Bipartite bipolar fuzzy graph 23
Fig. 1.16 Complete bipartite bipolar fuzzy graph 24
Fig. 1.17 Bipolar fuzzy graph G 24
Fig. 1.18 Complement of G 25
Fig. 1.19 Union of strong bipolar fuzzy graphs 26
Fig. 1.20 Bipolar fuzzy graph G 28
Fig. 1.21 Bipolar fuzzy graph $G^{'}$ 28
Fig. 1.22 Bipolar fuzzy graph G_3 34
Fig. 1.23 Bipolar fuzzy graph G_4 34
Fig. 1.24 Bipolar fuzzy graph G_1 36
Fig. 1.25 Bipolar fuzzy graph G_2 36
Fig. 1.26 Strength of connectedness 40
Fig. 1.27 Strongest bipolar fuzzy path 40
Fig. 1.28 Phase term in bipolar fuzzy set 43
Fig. 1.29 Phase term in complex bipolar fuzzy set 44

Fig. 1.30 Complex bipolar fuzzy graph . . . 46
Fig. 1.31 Complex bipolar fuzzy graph G . . . 52
Fig. 1.32 Complement of G . . . 52
Fig. 1.33 Bipolar fuzzy digraph $\vec{G} = (A, \vec{B})$ . . . 53
Fig. 1.34 Union of bipolar fuzzy digraphs . . . 54
Fig. 1.35 Intersection of bipolar fuzzy digraphs $\vec{G}_1$ and $\vec{G}_2$ . . . 54
Fig. 1.36 Join of bipolar fuzzy digraphs $\vec{G}_1$ and $\vec{G}_2$ . . . 55
Fig. 1.37 Cartesian product $\vec{\mathcal{P}}_4 \Box \vec{\mathcal{P}}_4$ . . . 56
Fig. 1.38 Direct product $\vec{G} \times \vec{\mathcal{P}}_3$ . . . 57
Fig. 1.39 Strong product $\vec{\mathcal{P}}_4 \boxtimes \vec{\mathcal{P}}_4$ . . . 58
Fig. 1.40 Lexicographic product $\vec{\mathcal{P}}_3 \bullet \vec{\mathcal{P}}_3$ . . . 59
Fig. 1.41 Bipolar fuzzy influence graph . . . 64
Fig. 1.42 Bipolar fuzzy organizational model. . . . 66
Fig. 1.43 Bipolar fuzzy digraph of marketability . . . 67
Fig. 1.44 Weighted digraph of a gas pipeline network. . . . 69
Fig. 1.45 Bipolar fuzzy graph of a road network . . . 71
Fig. 1.46 Weighted digraph of bipolar fuzzy road network . . . 72
Fig. 2.1 Cartesian product $G_1 \Box G_2$ . . . 83
Fig. 2.2 Direct product $G_1 \times G_2$. . . . 84
Fig. 2.3 Strong product $G_1 \boxtimes G_2$ . . . 85
Fig. 2.4 Bipolar fuzzy path $\mathcal{P}_5$. . . . 86
Fig. 2.5 Cartesian product $\mathcal{P}_4 \Box \mathcal{P}_4$. . . . 89
Fig. 2.6 Direct product $\mathcal{P}_3 \times \mathcal{P}_3$ . . . 91
Fig. 2.7 Direct product $\mathcal{P}_3 \times \mathcal{C}_3$ . . . 92
Fig. 2.8 Strong product $\mathcal{P}_3 \boxtimes \mathcal{P}_3$ . . . 94
Fig. 2.9 Lexicographic product $\mathcal{P}_3 \circ \mathcal{P}_3$. . . . 96
Fig. 2.10 Radius and diameter of a bipolar fuzzy graph G. . . . 98
Fig. 2.11 Eccentric vertices in bipolar fuzzy graph G . . . 101
Fig. 2.12 Center of bipolar fuzzy graph G. . . . 101
Fig. 2.13 Distance in bipolar fuzzy graph G . . . 104
Fig. 2.14 Self-centered bipolar fuzzy graph G . . . 105
Fig. 2.15 Self-centered bipolar fuzzy graph . . . 107
Fig. 2.16 Bipolar fuzzy graph G . . . 113
Fig. 2.17 Antipodal bipolar fuzzy graph $A(G)$ . . . 113
Fig. 2.18 Bipolar fuzzy graph G . . . 117
Fig. 2.19 Antipodal bipolar fuzzy graph $A(G)$ . . . 117
Fig. 2.20 Complement G^c . . . 118
Fig. 2.21 Antipodal bipolar fuzzy graph $A(G^c)$ . . . 118
Fig. 2.22 $\overline{(A(G))^c}$ . . . 118
Fig. 2.23 Bipolar fuzzy graph G . . . 119
Fig. 2.24 Antipodal bipolar fuzzy graph $A(G)$ . . . 119
Fig. 2.25 Complement G^c . . . 119
Fig. 2.26 Antipodal bipolar fuzzy graph $A(G^c)$ . . . 120

Fig. 2.27	$(A(G))^c$	120
Fig. 2.28	Self-median bipolar fuzzy graph	121
Fig. 2.29	Bipolar fuzzy model of product manufacturing	123
Fig. 2.30	Bipolar fuzzy model of shortest path problem	124
Fig. 2.31	Bipolar fuzzy graphs	125
Fig. 3.1	Regular bipolar fuzzy graph	129
Fig. 3.2	Totally regular bipolar fuzzy graph	130
Fig. 3.3	Regular and totally regular bipolar fuzzy graph G	130
Fig. 3.4	Irregular bipolar fuzzy graph G	132
Fig. 3.5	Totally irregular bipolar fuzzy graph	132
Fig. 3.6	Complete bipolar fuzzy graph	132
Fig. 3.7	Neighborly irregular bipolar fuzzy graph	134
Fig. 3.8	Neighborly totally irregular bipolar fuzzy graph	135
Fig. 3.9	Highly irregular bipolar fuzzy graph	135
Fig. 3.10	Bipolar fuzzy graph G	136
Fig. 3.11	Neighborly irregular bipolar fuzzy graph	137
Fig. 3.12	Neighborly totally irregular bipolar fuzzy graph	138
Fig. 3.13	Neighborly irregular bipolar fuzzy graph	140
Fig. 3.14	Bipolar fuzzy subgraph H which is not neighborly irregular	140
Fig. 3.15	Totally irregular bipolar fuzzy graph G	141
Fig. 3.16	Bipolar fuzzy subgraph which is not totally irregular	141
Fig. 3.17	Bipolar fuzzy graph G	142
Fig. 3.18	Bipolar fuzzy line graph $L(G)$	143
Fig. 3.19	Cayley bipolar fuzzy graph	149
Fig. 4.1	Bipolar fuzzy digraph	164
Fig. 4.2	Bipolar fuzzy competition graph	164
Fig. 4.3	Bipolar fuzzy digraph	165
Fig. 4.4	Bipolar fuzzy competition graph	166
Fig. 4.5	Bipolar fuzzy digraphs $\vec{G}_1$ and $\vec{G}_2$	170
Fig. 4.6	Bipolar fuzzy competition graphs	171
Fig. 4.7	Bipolar fuzzy graph $G_{\mathcal{C}(\vec{G}_1)^*\Box\mathcal{C}(\vec{G}_2)^*} \cup G^{\Box}$	173
Fig. 4.8	Cartesian product $\vec{G}_1 \Box \vec{G}_2$	173
Fig. 4.9	Bipolar fuzzy competition graph $\mathcal{C}(\vec{G}_1 \Box \vec{G}_2)$	174
Fig. 4.10	Bipolar fuzzy digraphs $\vec{G}_5$ and $\vec{G}_6$	174
Fig. 4.11	Bipolar fuzzy competition graphs $\mathcal{C}(\vec{G}_5)$ and $\mathcal{C}(\vec{G}_6)$	175
Fig. 4.12	Bipolar fuzzy graph $G_{\mathcal{C}(\vec{G}_5)^*\Box\mathcal{C}(\vec{G}_6)^*} \cup G^{\Box}$	177
Fig. 4.13	Cartesian product $\vec{G}_5 \Box \vec{G}_6$	178
Fig. 4.14	Bipolar fuzzy competition graph $\mathcal{C}(\vec{G}_5 \Box \vec{G}_6)$	178
Fig. 4.15	Bipolar fuzzy digraphs $\vec{G}_3$ and $\vec{G}_4$	181
Fig. 4.16	Bipolar fuzzy competition graphs $\mathcal{C}(\vec{G}_3)$ and $\mathcal{C}(\vec{G}_4)$	181
Fig. 4.17	Bipolar fuzzy graph $[\mathcal{C}(\vec{G}_3) \times \mathcal{C}(\vec{G}_4)] \cup G^{\times}$	182

Fig. 4.18 Direct product $\vec{G}_3 \times \vec{G}_4$ . . . 183

Fig. 4.19 Bipolar fuzzy competition graph $\mathcal{C}(\vec{G}_3 \times \vec{G}_4)$ . . . 183

Fig. 4.20 Bipolar fuzzy digraphs $\vec{G}_5$ and $\vec{G}_6$ . . . 184

Fig. 4.21 Bipolar fuzzy competition graphs $\mathcal{C}(\vec{G}_5)$ and $\mathcal{C}(\vec{G}_6)$ . . . 184

Fig. 4.22 Bipolar fuzzy graph $[\mathcal{C}(\vec{G}_5) \times \mathcal{C}(\vec{G}_6)] \cup G^{\times}$ . . . 185

Fig. 4.23 Cartesian product $\vec{G}_5 \times \vec{G}_6$ . . . 186

Fig. 4.24 $\mathcal{C}(\vec{G}_5 \times \vec{G}_6)$ . . . 186

Fig. 4.25 Bipolar fuzzy food web . . . 197

Fig. 4.26 Bipolar fuzzy competition graph of bipolar fuzzy food web . . . 198

Fig. 4.27 Bipolar fuzzy common enemy graph . . . 200

Fig. 4.28 Bipolar fuzzy food web . . . 202

Fig. 4.29 Bipolar fuzzy competition common enemy graph . . . 203

Fig. 4.30 Bipolar fuzzy niche graph . . . 204

Fig. 4.31 Bipolar fuzzy marketing digraph . . . 206

Fig. 4.32 Bipolar fuzzy competition graph of business network . . . 207

Fig. 4.33 Bipolar fuzzy digraph of political seats . . . 209

Fig. 4.34 Bipolar fuzzy political competition graph . . . 210

Fig. 4.35 Bipolar fuzzy social digraph . . . 212

Fig. 4.36 Bipolar fuzzy influence graph . . . 214

Fig. 4.37 Communication over a noisy channel . . . 215

Fig. 4.38 Bipolar fuzzy conflict graph . . . 216

Fig. 4.39 Bipolar fuzzy noisy channel . . . 218

Fig. 4.40 Bipolar fuzzy confusion graph . . . 219

Fig. 4.41 Bipolar fuzzy graphs . . . 220

Fig. 4.42 Bipolar fuzzy digraphs $\vec{G}_1$ and $\vec{G}_2$ . . . 221

Fig. 5.1 Bipolar fuzzy multigraph . . . 226

Fig. 5.2 Bipolar fuzzy complete multigraph . . . 227

Fig. 5.3 Bipolar fuzzy planar graph . . . 228

Fig. 5.4 Bipolar fuzzy faces in G . . . 231

Fig. 5.5 Bipolar fuzzy dual graph . . . 233

Fig. 5.6 Connected bipolar fuzzy graph . . . 235

Fig. 5.7 Bipolar fuzzy bridges . . . 236

Fig. 5.8 Bipolar fuzzy cut vertices in $G = (A, B)$ . . . 238

Fig. 5.9 Bipolar fuzzy block . . . 240

Fig. 5.10 Bipolar fuzzy block which is not a firm . . . 241

Fig. 5.11 Bipolar fuzzy cycle . . . 242

Fig. 5.12 Partial bipolar fuzzy graph cycle . . . 242

Fig. 5.13 Bipolar fuzzy road model . . . 247

Fig. 5.14 Electrical connections . . . 248

Fig. 5.15 Bipolar fuzzy planar graph . . . 249

Fig. 6.1 Bipolar fuzzy graph G . . . 255

Fig. 6.2 Domination numbers of bipolar fuzzy graph . . . 256

Fig. 6.3 EN degree of vertices in G 260
Fig. 6.4 Equitable isolated vertex 260
Fig. 6.5 Equitable dominating set of G 261
Fig. 6.6 Degree equitable bipolar fuzzy graph 261
Fig. 6.7 EI set of G 262
Fig. 6.8 Strong equitable dominating set of G 263
Fig. 6.9 Total ED set of G 265
Fig. 6.10 Total 2-dominating set of G 266
Fig. 6.11 Restrained dominating set of G 267
Fig. 6.12 Global RD set of G 267
Fig. 6.13 Direct product of G_1 and G_2 269
Fig. 6.14 Irredundant sets of G 273
Fig. 6.15 Bipolar fuzzy graph of towns 275
Fig. 6.16 Bipolar fuzzy graph of representatives 276
Fig. 6.17 Bipolar fuzzy graph of cities 277
Fig. 7.1 Bipolar fuzzy graph 284
Fig. 7.2 3−polar fuzzy multigraph 289
Fig. 7.3 Bipolar fuzzy soft graph $G = \{H(e_1), H(e_2)\}$ 297
Fig. 7.4 Wireless communication 304
Fig. 8.1 Bipolar fuzzy graph G 312
Fig. 8.2 Bipolar fuzzy digraph 317
Fig. 8.3 Bipolar fuzzy graph G 318
Fig. 8.4 Bipolar fuzzy digraph $\vec{G}$ 323
Fig. 8.5 Bipolar fuzzy graph 325
Fig. 8.6 Signless Laplacian energy of bipolar fuzzy digraph 327
Fig. 8.7 Bipolar fuzzy graph G 329
Fig. 8.8 Bipolar fuzzy graph G 334
Fig. 8.9 Bipolar fuzzy digraphs 337
Fig. 8.10 Bipolar fuzzy digraphs 339
Fig. 8.11 Cartesian product $\vec{G}$ 343
Fig. 8.12 Bipolar fuzzy digraph $\vec{G}$ 344
Fig. 8.13 Bipolar fuzzy digraph G 344
Fig. 9.1 Bipolar neutrosophic graph G 353
Fig. 9.2 Bipolar neutrosophic digraph 354
Fig. 9.3 Bipolar neutrosophic digraph $\vec{G}$ 355
Fig. 9.4 Bipolar neutrosophic competition graph 356
Fig. 9.5 Bipolar neutrosophic digraph 357
Fig. 9.6 Bipolar neutrosophic 3-competition graph 357
Fig. 9.7 Bipolar neutrosophic digraph $\vec{G}$ 359
Fig. 9.8 Bipolar neutrosophic digraph $\vec{G}$ 360
Fig. 9.9 Bipolar neutrosophic digraph $\vec{G}$ 360
Fig. 9.10 2-step bipolar single-valued neutrosophic competition graph 361

Fig. 9.11 Bipolar neutrosophic graph G . . . 370
Fig. 9.12 Bipolar neutrosophic open neighborhood graph $\mathcal{N}(G)$ . . . 371
Fig. 9.13 Bipolar neutrosophic closed neighborhood graph $\mathcal{N}[G]$ . . . 371
Fig. 9.14 Bipolar neutrosophic digraphs . . . 374
Fig. 9.15 Bipolar neutrosophic competition graphs . . . 375
Fig. 9.16 Bipolar neutrosophic graph $G_{\mathcal{C}(\vec{G}_1)^* \Box \mathcal{C}(\vec{G}_2)^*} \cup G^{\Box}$ . . . 376
Fig. 9.17 Cartesian product $\vec{G}_1 \Box \vec{G}_2$ . . . 377
Fig. 9.18 Bipolar neutrosophic competition graph $\mathcal{C}(\vec{G}_1 \Box \vec{G}_2)$ . . . 378
Fig. 9.19 Bipolar neutrosophic organization model . . . 379
Fig. 9.20 Bipolar neutrosophic competition graph . . . 381
Fig. 9.21 Bipolar neutrosophic market model . . . 384
Fig. 9.22 Bipolar neutrosophic market competition graph . . . 384
Fig. 9.23 Bipolar neutrosophic digraph of players . . . 387
Fig. 9.24 4-step bipolar single-valued neutrosophic competition graph . . . 388
Fig. 10.1 Bipolar neutrosophic graph structure no. 1 . . . 396
Fig. 10.2 Bipolar neutrosophic graph structure no. 2 . . . 397
Fig. 10.3 Bipolar neutrosophic subgraph structure . . . 397
Fig. 10.4 Bipolar neutrosophic induced subgraph structure . . . 398
Fig. 10.5 Bipolar neutrosophic spanning subgraph structure . . . 399
Fig. 10.6 Strong bipolar single-valued neutrosophic graph structure . . . 400
Fig. 10.7 Complete bipolar neutrosophic graph structure . . . 401
Fig. 10.8 Bipolar neutrosophic graph structures . . . 402
Fig. 10.9 Lexicographic product $\check{G}_{b1} \bullet \check{G}_{b2}$ . . . 403
Fig. 10.10 Strong product $\check{G}_{b1} \boxtimes \check{G}_{b2}$ . . . 407
Fig. 10.11 Strong product $\check{G}_{b1} \boxtimes \check{G}_{b2}$ . . . 407
Fig. 10.12 Union $\check{G}_{b1} \cup \check{G}_{b2}$ . . . 411
Fig. 10.13 Join $\check{G}_{b1} + \check{G}_{b2}$ . . . 417
Fig. 10.14 Bipolar single-valued neutrosophic graph structure $\check{G}_{b1}$ . . . 418
Fig. 10.15 Bipolar neutrosophic graph structure $\check{G}_{b2}$ . . . 419
Fig. 10.16 Bipolar neutrosophic graph structure $\check{G}_{b1}$ . . . 420
Fig. 10.17 Bipolar neutrosophic graph structure $\check{G}_{b2}$ . . . 421
Fig. 10.18 $\check{G}_{bn}$ and φ-complement $\check{G}_{bn}^{\psi c}$ . . . 421
Fig. 10.19 Bipolar neutrosophic graph structure . . . 424
Fig. 10.20 International relations of countries . . . 432
Fig. 10.21 Psychological behaviors of patients in a Mental Hospital . . . 437
Fig. 10.22 Highlighting undercover reasons of global terrorism . . . 443

List of Tables

Table 1.1 Operation $\oplus$ in bipolar space . . . 2
Table 1.2 Operation $\otimes$ in bipolar space . . . 2
Table 1.3 Bipolar fuzzy set A on $\{x_1, x_2, x_3\}$ . . . 9
Table 1.4 Bipolar fuzzy relation B in $\{x_1, x_2, x_3\}$ . . . 10
Table 1.5 Bipolar fuzzy set A on $\{x, y, z\}$ . . . 21
Table 1.6 Bipolar fuzzy relation B in $\{x, y, z\}$ . . . 22
Table 1.7 Complex bipolar fuzzy set A . . . 46
Table 1.8 Complex bipolar fuzzy relation D . . . 46
Table 1.9 Bipolar fuzzy set A on $\{v_1, v_2, v_3, v_4\}$ . . . 52
Table 1.10 Bipolar fuzzy relation $\vec{B}$ in $\{v_1, v_2, v_3, v_4\}$ . . . 53
Table 1.11 Bipolar fuzzy relation $Q(D \rightarrow S)$ . . . 62
Table 1.12 Bipolar fuzzy relation $R(S \rightarrow P)$ . . . 62
Table 1.13 Composition $T = R \circ Q(D \rightarrow P)$ . . . 62
Table 1.14 Names of employees in the organization with their designations . . . 64
Table 1.15 Bipolar fuzzy set A of employees . . . 65
Table 1.16 Adjacency matrix corresponding to Fig. 1.42 . . . 65
Table 1.17 Bipolar fuzzy set F . . . 68
Table 1.18 Bipolar fuzzy relation P . . . 69
Table 1.19 Adjacency matrix of ranks of edges . . . 69
Table 1.20 Bipolar fuzzy relation on the set of crossings . . . 71
Table 1.21 Weights of directed edges in Fig. 1.45 . . . 71
Table 1.22 Bipolar fuzzy relation $Q(D \rightarrow S)$ . . . 76
Table 1.23 Bipolar fuzzy relation $R(S \rightarrow P)$ . . . 76
Table 3.1 Bipolar fuzzy set A on $\{a, b, c, d\}$ . . . 129
Table 3.2 Bipolar fuzzy relation B in $\{a, b, c, d\}$ . . . 129
Table 3.3 Bipolar fuzzy set on $\{v_1, v_2, v_3\}$ . . . 130
Table 3.4 Bipolar fuzzy relation in $\{v_1, v_2, v_3\}$ . . . 130
Table 3.5 Bipolar fuzzy set A . . . 131
Table 3.6 Bipolar fuzzy relation B . . . 131

Table 3.7 Bipolar fuzzy set A on X 142
Table 3.8 Bipolar fuzzy relation B in X 142
Table 3.9 $R(a,b)$ for Cayley bipolar fuzzy graph. 148
Table 4.1 Bipolar fuzzy out neighborhoods of vertices 164
Table 4.2 Adjacency matrix of bipolar fuzzy relation $\vec{B}$. 165
Table 4.3 Bipolar fuzzy out neighborhoods of vertices 165
Table 4.4 Bipolar fuzzy out neighborhoods 170
Table 4.5 Bipolar fuzzy out neighborhoods 171
Table 4.6 Membership values of constructed edges 172
Table 4.7 Bipolar fuzzy out neighborhoods of vertices in $\vec{G}_1 \square \vec{G}_2$. 173
Table 4.8 Adjacent vertices of $G_{\mathcal{C}(\vec{G}_5)^* \square \mathcal{C}(\vec{G}_6)^*} \cup G^{\square}$. 176
Table 4.9 Adjacent vertices of $[\mathcal{C}(\vec{G}_3) \times \mathcal{C}(\vec{G}_4)] \cup G^{\times}$ 182
Table 4.10 Membership values of constructed edges 185
Table 4.11 Bipolar fuzzy in neighborhoods of species. 198
Table 4.12 Strength of competition between species 198
Table 4.13 Bipolar fuzzy out neighborhoods of species. 200
Table 4.14 Strength of common enemies between species. 201
Table 4.15 Bipolar fuzzy out and in neighborhoods of species 203
Table 4.16 Strength of competition between species 204
Table 4.17 Bipolar fuzzy out neighborhoods of companies 207
Table 4.18 Strength of competition between companies. 208
Table 4.19 Bipolar fuzzy out neighborhoods of candidates 209
Table 4.20 Strength of competition of candidates for political seats 211
Table 4.21 Bipolar fuzzy in neighborhoods of families in social network 213
Table 4.22 Strength of competition in social network 214
Table 4.23 Bipolar fuzzy out neighborhoods of noisy channel. 216
Table 4.24 Strength of conflict between wireless devices. 216
Table 4.25 Communication over a noisy channel. 217
Table 4.26 Bipolar fuzzy out neighborhoods of noisy channel. 218
Table 4.27 Strength of confusion. 219
Table 5.1 Bipolar fuzzy vertex set 226
Table 5.2 Bipolar fuzzy multiedge set 226
Table 5.3 Bipolar fuzzy vertex set A 229
Table 5.4 Bipolar fuzzy multiedge set A 229
Table 6.1 Bipolar fuzzy set A on set X 259
Table 6.2 Bipolar fuzzy relation B in X. 260
Table 7.1 Bipolar fuzzy set A on $\{x_1, x_2, x_3\}$ 284
Table 7.2 Bipolar fuzzy relation B in $\{x_1, x_2, x_3\}$. 284
Table 7.3 Bipolar fuzzy soft vertex set 297
Table 7.4 Bipolar fuzzy soft edge set. 297
Table 7.5 Decision Support System 302
Table 7.6 Bipolar fuzzy soft information 306
Table 9.1 Bipolar neutrosophic set A 352

Table 9.2 Bipolar neutrosophic relation A 353
Table 9.3 Bipolar neutrosophic out-neighborhoods of vertices 355
Table 9.4 Bipolar neutrosophic out- and in-neighborhoods of $\vec{G}_1$ 375
Table 9.5 Bipolar neutrosophic out- and in-neighborhoods of $\vec{G}_2$ 375
Table 9.6 Adjacent vertices of $G_{\mathcal{C}(\vec{G}_1)^*\Box\mathcal{C}(\vec{G}_2)^*} \cup G^{\Box}$ 376
Table 9.7 Bipolar neutrosophic out-neighborhoods of $\vec{G}_1\Box\vec{G}_2$ 378
Table 9.8 Bipolar neutrosophic out-neighborhoods 380
Table 9.9 Strength of competition of applicants for particular designations 381
Table 9.10 Strength of competition of brands for particular quality 385
Table 9.11 4-step bipolar single-valued neutrosophic out-neighborhoods 387
Table 9.12 Strength of competition of players for international games 387
Table 10.1 Bipolar neutrosophic set B 395
Table 10.2 Bipolar neutrosophic sets B_1, B_2, and B_3 395
Table 10.3 Bipolar neutrosophic information of countries 428
Table 10.4 Types of relations between countries 428
Table 10.5 Types of relations between countries 428
Table 10.6 Types of relations between countries 428
Table 10.7 Types of relations between countries 429
Table 10.8 Types of relations between countries 429
Table 10.9 Types of relations between countries 429
Table 10.10 Types of relations between countries 429
Table 10.11 Types of relations between countries 430
Table 10.12 Types of relations between countries 430
Table 10.13 Bipolar neutrosophic information of patients 433
Table 10.14 Psychological behavior of Albert with other patients 434
Table 10.15 Psychological behavior of Charles with other patients 434
Table 10.16 Psychological behavior of Burton with other patients 434
Table 10.17 Psychological behavior of Calvert with other patients 435
Table 10.18 Psychological behavior of Christopher with other patients 435
Table 10.19 Psychological behavior of David with other patients 435
Table 10.20 Psychological behavior of Chapman with other patients 435
Table 10.21 Psychological behavior of Joseph with other patients 436
Table 10.22 Various psychological behaviors of patients 436
Table 10.23 Bipolar neutrosophic information of terrorism in various countries 439
Table 10.24 Reasons of terrorism due to relationships of Pakistan with other countries 440
Table 10.25 Reasons of terrorism due to relationships of India with other countries 440

Table 10.26 Reasons of terrorism due to relationships of Afghanistan with other countries 440
Table 10.27 Reasons of terrorism due to relationships of America with other countries 440
Table 10.28 Reasons of terrorism due to relationship of Iraq with other countries 441
Table 10.29 Reasons of terrorism due to relationship of Israel with other countries 441
Table 10.30 Reasons of terrorism due to relationship of Palestine with other countries 441
Table 10.31 Reasons of terrorism due to relationship of Kashmir with other countries 441
Table 10.32 Reasons of terrorism due to relationship between countries..... 442

Chapter 1
Bipolar Fuzzy Sets and Bipolar Fuzzy Graphs

In this chapter, we first review the notion of bipolar fuzzy sets and present several basic concepts concerning bipolar fuzzy graphs and bipolar fuzzy digraphs. We discuss different methods of construction of bipolar fuzzy graphs and their isomorphism properties. We describe certain types of bipolar fuzzy graphs, bipolar fuzzy walk, bipolar fuzzy bridge, strength of connectedness, weak and strong bipolar fuzzy edges. We establish the relations on bipolar fuzzy graphs, complement of bipolar fuzzy graphs, and crisp graphs with different operations, $\alpha-$cuts and $(\alpha, \beta)-$cuts. We also study certain operations and properties of complex bipolar fuzzy graphs. Moreover, with the help of composition of bipolar fuzzy relations, connectivity, and weighted matrices, we study the importance of bipolar fuzzy digraphs with a number of real-world problems. This chapter is basically adapted from [1–3, 45, 46, 51].

1.1 Introduction

Set theory and logic systems are strongly coupled in the development of modern logic. Classical logic corresponds to the crisp set theory, and fuzzy logic is associated with the fuzzy set theory, which owes its origin to the pioneering work of Zadeh [48] in 1965. The theory of fuzzy sets has become a vigorous area of research in different disciplines. A fuzzy set, as a superset of a crisp set, has been introduced to deal with the notion of partial truth between "absolute true" and "absolute false". The notion of a fuzzy set is an essential mathematical structure, whose boundaries are vague. The membership degree range of a fuzzy set is [0, 1]. Considering fuzzy relations studied by Zadeh [49], Kaufmann [20] introduced the powerful notion of a fuzzy graph. The fuzzy relations constructed using fuzzy sets were additionally considered by

M. Akram et al., *Graphs for the Analysis of Bipolar Fuzzy Information*, Studies in Fuzziness and Soft Computing 401,
https://doi.org/10.1007/978-981-15-8756-6_1

Rosenfeld [41] for developing the structure of a fuzzy graph, proposing mainframe of several graph theoretical ideas.

It comes to no surprise that bipolarity in data and information plays a vital role in various domains of science and technology. A wide variety of human decision-making, especially multiagent decision analysis, is based on bipolar judgmental thinking on a positive side and a negative side. Although 2-valued Boolean logic provides a theoretical basis for digital computer technology and fuzzy logic provides one way for dealing with vagueness and uncertainty both lack the representational and reasoning capabilities for directly modeling the coexistence and interaction of bipolar relationships. This is because the logical values in the two classical logical models lie in the positive interval [0, 1] and these are unipolar models in nature. Since positive and negative causal factors can be interactive but not counteractive at the same time, it is misleading to bury them into a summation; on other hand, it is neither cognitive nor convenient to represent bipolar perceptions with a unipolar structure. For instance, (large negative effect) $\vee$ (large positive effect) $\neq$ (neutral effect). Therefore, a system based on unipolar variables can be rather misleading or less effective for modeling bipolar perceptions involved in the decision processes. In qualitative reasoning, decision has often been made by considering the bipolar space $\{0, 1\} \times \{-1, 0\}$ (cf. [57]) which makes up what is usually referred to as the Quantity Space or the Universe of Description. Two internal operations $\oplus$ and $\otimes$ on the space can be defined as in Tables 1.1 and 1.2.

Similar to unipolar crisp values, the real-valued bipolar representation in the bipolar space $\{0, 1\} \times \{-1, 0\}$ suffers from the deficiency that it cannot be used to represent high-order fuzziness. To overcome this limitation, a negative-positive-neutral (NPN) fuzzy logic (cf. [56]) was defined in the space $[-1, 1]$. The two internal operators $\oplus$ and $\otimes$ are defined as

Table 1.1 Operation $\oplus$ in bipolar space

$\oplus$	(0, 0)	(0, −1)	(1, 0)	(1, −1)
(0, 0)	(0, 0)	(0, −1)	(1, 0)	(1, −1)
(0, −1)	(0, −1)	(0, −1)	(1, −1)	(1, −1)
(1, 0)	(1, 0)	(1, −1)	(1, 0)	(1, −1)
(1, −1)	(1, −1)	(1, −1)	(1, −1)	(1, −1)

Table 1.2 Operation $\otimes$ in bipolar space

$\otimes$	(0, 0)	(0, −1)	(1, 0)	(1, −1)
(0, 0)	(0, 0)	(0, 0)	(0, 0)	(0, 0)
(0, −1)	(0, 0)	(1, 0)	(0, −1)	(1, −1)
(1, 0)	(0, 0)	(0, −1)	(1, 0)	(1, −1)
(1, −1)	(0, 0)	(1, −1)	(1, −1)	(1, −1)

$$(x, y) \oplus (u, v) = (\max(x, u), \min(y, v)) \tag{1.1}$$

$$(x, y) \otimes (u, v) = (\max(x \otimes u, x \otimes v, y \otimes u, y \otimes v), \min(x \otimes u, x \otimes v, y \otimes u, y \otimes v)), \tag{1.2}$$

where $x, y, u, v \in [-1, 1]$ and $x \leq y, u \leq v$. This definition is not strictly bipolar because the allowance of $(x, x) \in [-1, 1]$ violates the principle of polarity and fuzziness. Note that when real value pairs in the bipolar space $[0, 1] \times [-1, 0]$ are used, neutrality of (u, v) can be measured as $u + v$. Therefore, any bipolar logical value can be represented as a pair $(x, y) \in [0, 1] \times [-1, 0]$. With bipolar fuzzy variables $(x, y), (u, v) \in [0, 1] \times [-1, 0]$, we have

$$(y, x) \oplus (v, u) = (\min(y, v), \max(x, u)) \tag{1.3}$$

$$(y, x) \otimes (v, u) = (\max(x \otimes u, y \otimes v), \min(x \otimes v, y \otimes u)) \tag{1.4}$$

$$\text{Complement}: (\neg a, b) = (1 - a, b), (a, \neg b) = (a, -1 - b), \neg(a, b) = (1 - a, -1 - b) \tag{1.5}$$

$$\text{Negation}: \neg(x, y) = (-y, -x) \text{ or } (0, -1) \otimes (x, y) = (-y, -x). \tag{1.6}$$

$A = (\oplus, \otimes, \neg)$, where $A = \{\forall\ (x, y) \mid (x, y) \in [0, 1] \times [-1, 0]\}$ defines a bipolar fuzzy logic in the strict sense and inevitable for dealing with both polarity and fuzziness principles (cf. [57]) as follows:

1. Representation principle: A bipolar fuzzy logic variable should have both a positive pole and a negative pole. It should be able to capture the nature of a positive side, a negative side, and the coexistence of both sides in different degrees of gray levels.

2. Computation principle: A bipolar fuzzy logic should be able to support bipolar reasoning by allowing computational interactions between the positive and negative sides of bipolar fuzzy variables.

The max and min operators in (1.3) and (1.4) enable causal effects to propagate through a pair of strongest (maximal in absolute value) causal chains (a positive one and a negative one). This provides a basis for assessing both positive and negative factors. In bipolar fuzzy logic, $\leq\leq$, $\geq\geq$, $\leq\geq$ or $\geq\leq$ are used as bipolar comparison operators. The order of magnitude of crisp and bipolar fuzzy variables is depicted and compared in Fig. 1.1. The bipolar comparison is applied to the absolute values of the two poles, respectively. For instance, with bipolar comparison we have $(0.4, -0.5) \geq\geq (0.3, -0.5)$ is true because $0.4 \geq 0.3$ and $|-0.5| \geq |-0.5|$; $(0.3, -0.8) \leq\geq (0.4, -0.5)$ is true because $0.3 \leq 0.4$ and $|-0.8| \geq |-0.5|$; $(0.4, -0.5) \geq\leq (0.3, -0.8)$ is true because $0.4 \geq 0.3$ and $|-0.5| \leq |-0.8|$; and $(0.3, -0.5) \leq\geq (0.4, -0.5)$ is true because $0.3 \leq 0.4$ and $|-0.5| \leq |-0.5|$.

Bipolarity plays a vital role in many research domains and gives more precision, flexibility, and comparability to the system as compared to the classical and fuzzy models. In 1994, Zhang [51] initiated the concept of bipolar fuzzy sets. Bipolar fuzzy sets are an extension of fuzzy sets, whose membership degree range is $[-1, 1]$.

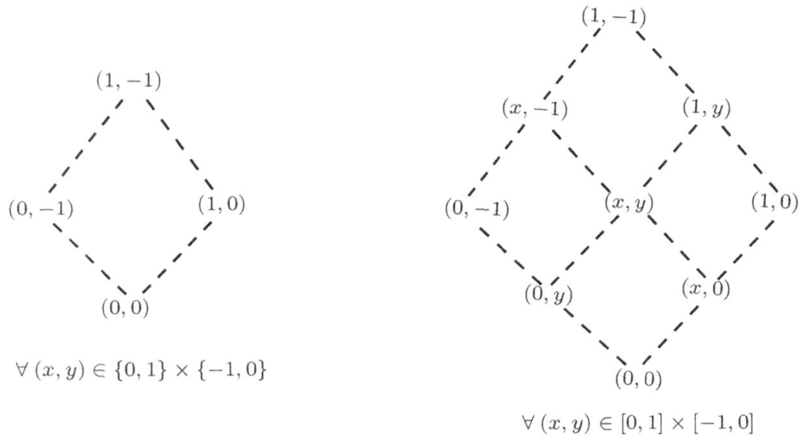

Fig. 1.1 Order of magnitude ($\geq\geq$) of crisp and bipolar fuzzy logic

In a bipolar fuzzy set, the membership degree 0 of an element means that the element is irrelevant to the corresponding property, the membership degree (0, 1] of an element indicates that the element somewhat satisfies the property, and the membership degree $[-1, 0)$ of an element indicates that the element somewhat satisfies the implicit counter property. The idea which lies behind such description is connected with the existence of "bipolar information" (e.g., positive information and negative information) about a set under consideration. Positive information represent what is granted to be possible, while negative information represents what is considered to be impossible. Actually, a wide variety of human decision-making is based on double-sided or bipolar judgmental thinking on a positive side and a negative side. For instance, cooperation and competition, friendship and hostility, common interest and conflict of interest, effect and side effect, likelihood and unlikelihood, feedforward and feedback, and so forth are often the two sides in decision and coordination. In the traditional Chinese medicine, "yin" and "yang" are the two sides. Yin is the feminine or negative side of a system and yang is the masculine or positive side of a system. The coexistence, equilibrium, and harmony of the two sides are considered a key for the mental and physical health of a person as well as for the stability and prosperity of a social system. This idea motivates the necessity of bipolar fuzzy sets. Bipolar fuzzy sets indeed have potential impacts on many fields, including artificial intelligence, computer science, information science, cognitive science, decision science, management science, economics, neural science, quantum computing, medical science, and social sciences. In recent years, bipolar fuzzy sets seem to have been studied and applied a bit enthusiastically and a bit increasingly.

Definition 1.1 **A lattice** L on a non-empty set X is a triple $(X, \vee, \wedge)$, where $\wedge$ and $\vee$ are binary operations on X, both $\vee$ and $\wedge$ are commutative, associative, idempotent, and satisfy absorption law, that is,

1. Commutative Law: $x \vee y = y \vee x$, $x \wedge y = y \wedge x$,
2. Associative Law: $x \vee (x \vee z) = (x \vee y) \vee z$, $x \wedge (x \wedge z) = (x \wedge y) \wedge z$,
3. Absorption Law: $x \vee (x \wedge y) = x$, $x \wedge (x \vee y) = x$,
4. Idempotent: $x \vee x = x$, $x \wedge x = x$ for all $x, y, z \in X$.

Example 1.1 1. $L = [0, 1]$ (unit closed interval) is an example of a lattice with binary operations: $x_1 \vee x_2 = \max(x_1, x_2)$ and $x_1 \wedge x_2 = \min(x_1, x_2)$.
2. $L = [0, 1]^2$ (unit closed square) is a lattice with binary operation $(x_1, y_1) \vee (x_2, y_2) = (\max(x_1, x_2), \max(x_1, y_2))$ and $(x_1, y_1) \wedge (x_2, y_2) = (\min(x_1, x_2), \min(x_1, y_2))$.

Definition 1.2 An L-**subset** (or an L-set) on the set X is a mapping $\mu : X \to L$, where L is a lattice. When $L = [0, 1]$ (the closed unit interval with ordinary relation), then $[0, 1]$-set on X will be called a fuzzy set on X. When $L = [0, 1]^2$, then it is a $[0, 1]^2$-set.

Definition 1.3 A **bipolar fuzzy set** A on a non-empty set X is an object of the form $A = \{(x, \mu_A^P(x), \mu_A^n(x)) \mid x \in X\}$, where $\mu_A^P : X \to [0, 1]$ and $\mu_A^n : X \to [-1, 0]$ are mappings.

The positive membership degree $\mu_A^P(x)$ denotes the truth or satisfaction degree of an element x to a certain property corresponding to bipolar fuzzy set A and $\mu_A^n(x)$ represents the satisfaction degree of an element x to some counter property of bipolar fuzzy set A. If $\mu_A^n(x) \neq 0$ and $\mu_A^P(x) = 0$, it is the situation that x is not satisfying the property of A but satisfying the counter property to A. If $\mu_A^P(x) \neq 0$ and $\mu_A^n(x) = 0$, it is the case when x has only positive satisfaction for A. It is possible for x to be such that $\mu_A^P(x) \neq 0$ and $\mu_A^n(x) \neq 0$ when x satisfies the property of A as well as its counter property in some part of X.

Question: Is bipolar fuzzy set equivalent to intuitionistic fuzzy set?

The answer to Question 1 is negative. The intuitionistic fuzzy set theory is an extension of fuzzy set theory initiated by Atanassov [10] in 1986. An **intuitionistic fuzzy set** on the universe of discourse X is an object of the form $A = \{(x, \mu_A(x), \nu_A(x)) \mid x \in X\}$, where the functions $\mu_A : X \to [0, 1]$ and $\nu_A : X \to [0, 1]$ define the degrees of membership and non-membership, respectively, of the element $x \in X$ to the set A, and for every $x \in X$, $0 \leq \mu_A(x) + \nu_A(x) \leq 1$. When we compare a bipolar fuzzy set $A = \{(x, \mu_A^P(x), \mu_A^n(x)) \mid x \in X\}$ with an intuitionistic fuzzy set $A = \{(x, \mu_A(x), \nu_A(x)) \mid x \in X\}$ under the conditions $\mu_A^P(x) = \mu_A(x)$ and $\mu_A^n(x) = -\nu_A(x)$, both the sets look similar to each other. However, they are different from each other in terms of modeling of problems: In bipolar fuzzy set A, the positive membership degree $\mu_A^P(x)$ characterizes the extent that the element x satisfies the property A, and the negative membership degree $\mu_A^n(x)$ characterizes the extent that the element x satisfies the **implicit counter property** of A. On the other hand, in intuitionistic fuzzy set A, the membership degree $\mu_A(x)$ denotes the extent to which the element x satisfies property A, and the membership degree $\nu_A(x)$ denotes the extent to which the element x does not satisfy property A, that is, **not-property** of

A. Since a **counter property** is not usually equivalent to **not-property**, both bipolar fuzzy set and intuitionistic fuzzy set are different extensions of fuzzy sets.

This difference can also be manifested in the interpretation of an element x to be indifferent (i.e., neutral). In the perspective of bipolar fuzzy set A, it is interpreted that the element x does not satisfy property A and its implicit counter property and so its membership degree is $(0, 0)$. In case of intuitionistic fuzzy set, the element x is neutral if it does not satisfy property A, that is, it completely satisfies **not-property** of A, and so the degree of membership is $(0, 1)$. The intuitionistic fuzzy set representation is useful when there are some uncertainties in assigning membership degrees as illustrated in the following practical examples.

1. The bipolar fuzzy set representation is useful when irrelevant elements and contrary elements are needed to be discriminated. For example, when we want to express effect and side effect of a drug, we can use bipolar fuzzy valuations. Because side effect is a negative effect. In an intuitionistic fuzzy set, we can not model negative effect. The non-membership degree of an element doesn't correspond to negative effect.

2. In modeling the profit and loss of a product, we can use bipolar fuzzy set because loss is implicit counter property to profit and is treated as negative effect of product. In an intuitionistic fuzzy set, this scenario can be treated as "profit" and "no profit". Clearly, the property "no-profit" is not equivalent to "loss", that is, the intuitionistic fuzzy set cannot be used to model negative effect (loss).

Definition 1.4 Let A and B be two bipolar fuzzy sets on X and Y, respectively. A **bipolar fuzzy relation** R from A to B is a mapping $R : A \to B$ defined as $R = \{((x, y), \mu_R^p(x, y), \mu_R^n(x, y)) \mid (x, y) \in X \times Y\}$ such that

$$\mu_R^p(x, y) \leq \mu_A^p(x) \wedge \mu_B^p(y) \text{ and } \mu_R^n(x, y) \geq \mu_A^n(x) \vee \mu_B^n(y).$$

R is also a bipolar fuzzy relation in $X \times Y$ defined by the mapping $R : X \times Y : [0, 1] \times [-1, 0]$. A bipolar fuzzy relation R in X is defined by a mapping $R : X \times X : [0, 1] \times [-1, 0]$.

Definition 1.5 Let R and S be two bipolar fuzzy relations in $X \times Y$. The **union** of R and S is defined as a bipolar fuzzy set $R \cup S = \{((x, y), \mu_{R\cup S}^p(x, y), \mu_{R\cup S}^n(x, y)) \mid (x, y) \in X \times Y\}$ such that

$$\mu_{R\cup S}^p(x, y) = \mu_R^p(x, y) \vee \mu_S^p(x, y) \text{ and } \mu_{R\cup S}^n(x, y) = \mu_R^n(x, y) \wedge \mu_S^n(x, y).$$

The **intersection** of R and S is denoted by $R \cap S$ such that for all $(x, y) \in X \times Y$,

$$\mu_{R\cap S}^p(x, y) = \mu_R^p(x, y) \wedge \mu_S^p(x, y) \text{ and } \mu_{R\cap S}^n(x, y) = \mu_R^n(x, y) \vee \mu_S^n(x, y).$$

Definition 1.6 Let R be a bipolar fuzzy relation in X. Then R is called a **bipolar fuzzy equivalence relation** on X if it satisfies the following conditions.

1. R is bipolar fuzzy reflexive, i.e., $R(x, x) = (1, -1)$, for each $x \in X$.

2. R is bipolar fuzzy symmetric, i.e., $R(x, y) = R(y, x)$, for any $x, y \in X$.
3. R is bipolar fuzzy transitive, i.e., $R(x, z) \geq \bigvee_y (R(x, y) \wedge R(y, z))$.

Definition 1.7 Let R be a bipolar fuzzy relation in X. Then R is called **a bipolar fuzzy partial order relation** on X if it satisfies the following conditions.

1. R is bipolar fuzzy reflexive, i.e., $R(x, x) = (1, -1)$, for each $x \in X$.
2. R is bipolar fuzzy antisymmetric, i.e., $R(x, y) \neq R(y, x)$, for any $x, y \in X$.
3. R is bipolar fuzzy transitive, i.e., $R(x, z) \geq \bigvee_y (R(x, y) \wedge R(y, z))$.

Definition 1.8 Let R be a bipolar fuzzy relation in X. Then R is called **a bipolar fuzzy linear order relation** on X if it satisfies the following conditions.

1. R is bipolar fuzzy partial order relation.
2. $R(x, y) \neq (0, 0)$ or $R(y, x) \neq (0, 0)$, for all $x, y \in X$.

For further terminologies and studies on fuzzy sets, bipolar fuzzy graphs and complex bipolar fuzzy graphs, readers are referred to [5–9, 11–19, 21–36, 38–40, 42–44, 47, 50, 52–55, 58].

1.2 Bipolar Fuzzy Graphs

Graph theory was first initiated by Euler during the course of finding solution to the problem of "Königsberg bridge" in 1736. Graph theory is a conceptual framework to study and analyze the units that are intensely or frequently connected in a network. It is used to study the mathematical structures of pairwise relations among objects. Graphs are used to model various practical processes and relations in social, physical, information, and biological systems.

A **graph** is a figure consisting of points, called vertices, which are connected by lines, called edges. Mathematically, a pair $G^* = (X, E)$ is a **crisp graph**, where $E \subseteq X \times X$ is a collection of 2−element subsets of a non-empty universe X.

However, in some cases, the crisp graphs do not study the uncertain behavior and degree of dependence among the objects. In such cases, it is important to deal with uncertainty using the methods of fuzzy sets. The approach of fuzzification to crisp graph is called a fuzzy graph. Graphical models can be studied more precisely when two-sided behavior of objects are to be dealt with, emphasizing the need for a mathematical approach toward graphs under bipolar fuzzy environment. Considering bipolar fuzzy relations studied by Zhang [51], bipolar fuzzy graphs were introduced by Akram [1], in 2011, to overcome the limitations entailed in crisp graph theory and fuzzy graph theory. Akram and Dudek [4] considered regular bipolar fuzzy graphs. The concept of a bipolar fuzzy graph is obtained as a generalization of a fuzzy graph which is an extension of the term crisp graph. Its construction depends on the mathematical structure of a bipolar fuzzy set which is more a convenient, intuitive, and computationally tractable notation.

Definition 1.9 Let A be a bipolar fuzzy set on a non-empty set X. A **bipolar fuzzy relation** B on A is a mapping $B : A \to A$ such that

$$\mu_B^p(xy) \le \mu_A^p(x) \wedge \mu_A^p(y) \text{ and } \mu_B^n(xy) \ge \mu_A^n(x) \vee \mu_A^n(y), \qquad \text{for all } x, y \in X.$$

B is also a bipolar fuzzy relation in X defined by the mapping $B : X \times X \to [0, 1] \times [-1, 0]$.

Definition 1.10 The **support** of a bipolar fuzzy set $A = (\mu_A^p, \mu_A^n)$, denoted by $supp(A)$, is defined as $\text{supp}(A) = supp^p(A) \cup supp^n(A)$, where $supp^p(A) = \{x \mid \mu_A^p(x) > 0\}$, $supp^n(A) = \{x \mid \mu_A^n(x) < 0\}$. We call $supp^p(A)$ as **positive support** and $supp^n(A)$ as **negative support**.

Definition 1.11 Let $A = (\mu_A^p, \mu_A^n)$ be a bipolar fuzzy set on X and $\alpha \in [0, 1]$. The α-**cut** of bipolar fuzzy set A is denoted by A_α and defined as $A_\alpha = A_\alpha^p \cup A_\alpha^n$, where $A_\alpha^p = \{x \mid \mu_\alpha^p(x) \ge \alpha\}$, $A_\alpha^p = \{x \mid \mu_\alpha^n(x) \le -\alpha\}$. We call A_α^p as positive α-cut and A_α^n as negative α-cut. The **height** of a bipolar fuzzy set $A = (\mu_A^p, \mu_A^n)$ is defined as $h(A) = \max\{\mu_A^p(x) | x \in X\}$. The **depth** of a bipolar fuzzy set $A = (\mu_A^p, \mu_A^n)$ is defined as $d(A) = \min\{\mu_A^n(x) | x \in X\}$. We shall say that bipolar fuzzy set A is **normal**, if there is at least one $x \in X$ such that $\mu_A^p(x) = 1$ or $\mu_A^n(x) = -1$.

Definition 1.12 A **bipolar polar fuzzy graph** G on a non-empty set X is a pair $G = (A, B)$, where $A : X \to [0, 1] \times [-1, 0]$ is a bipolar fuzzy set on the set X and $B : X \times X \to [0, 1] \times [-1, 0]$ is a bipolar polar fuzzy relation in X such that

$$\mu_B^p(xy) \le \mu_A^p(x) \wedge \mu_A^p(y) \text{ and } \mu_B^n(xy) \ge \mu_A^n(x) \vee \mu_A^n(y), \qquad \text{for all } x, y \in X.$$

Remark 1.1
1. Clearly, $B(xy) = (0, 0)$ for all $xy \in X \times X - E$, where $E \subseteq X \times X$ is the set of edges. A is called a bipolar fuzzy vertex set of G and B is a bipolar fuzzy edge set of G.
2. In Definition 1.12, B is called a bipolar fuzzy relation on A. A bipolar fuzzy relation B on A is **symmetric** if $B(xy) = B(yx)$ for all $x, y \in X$.
3. In a bipolar fuzzy graph G, the support of a bipolar fuzzy relation B is the set of edges in G. We will use the notation E to write the support of bipolar fuzzy relation B, that is, $supp(B) = E$.

The following example illustrates the above definition.

Example 1.2 Consider a bipolar fuzzy set A on the vertex set $X = \{x_1, x_2, x_3\}$ as given in Table 1.3 and a bipolar fuzzy relation B in X as defined in Table 1.4. The bipolar fuzzy graph $G = (A, B)$ on set X is demonstrated in Fig. 1.2.

Definition 1.13 Let $G = (A, B)$ be a bipolar fuzzy graph on X and $(\alpha, \beta) \in (0, 1] \times [-1, 0)$. Define (α, β)-**cut** of a bipolar fuzzy set A as, $A_{(\alpha,\beta)} = \{x \in X \mid \mu_A^p(x) \ge \alpha, \mu_A^n(x) \le \beta\}$. If $B_{(\alpha,\beta)} = \left\{xy \in E \mid \mu_B^p(xy) \ge \alpha, \mu_B^n(xy) \le \beta\right\}$ is (α, β)-cut of bipolar fuzzy relation B, then the (α, β)-level graph of G is a crisp graph denoted by $G_{(\alpha,\beta)}$ and defined as a pair $G_{(\alpha,\beta)} = (A_{(\alpha,\beta)}, B_{(\alpha,\beta)})$.

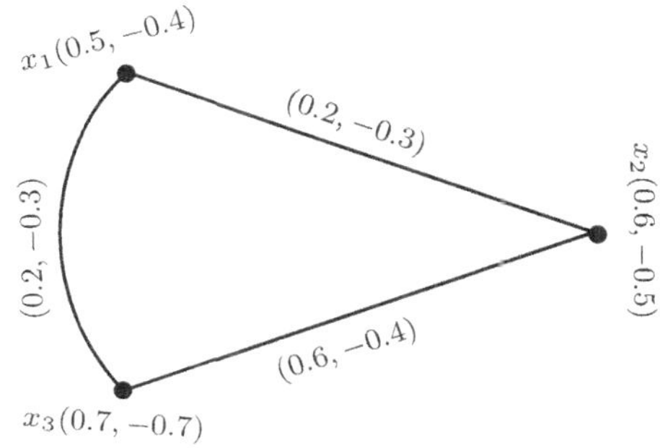

Fig. 1.2 Bipolar fuzzy graph

Definition 1.14 Let $G_1 = (A_1, B_1)$ and $G_2 = (A_2, B_2)$ be two bipolar fuzzy graphs on non-empty sets X_1 and X_2, respectively. The **union** of G_1 and G_2 is defined as a pair $G_1 \cup G_2 = (A_1 \cup A_2, B_1 \cup B_2)$ such that for all $x, y \in X_1 \cup X_2$,

1. If $x \in X_1, x \notin X_2$, then $(A_1 \cup A_2)(x) = A_1(x)$,
2. If $x \notin X_1, x \in X_2$, then $(A_1 \cup A_2)(x) = A_2(x)$,
3. If $x \in X_1 \cap X_2$, then $(A_1 \cup A_2)(x) = (\mu^p_{A_1}(x) \vee \mu^p_{A_2}(x), \mu^n_{A_1}(x) \wedge \mu^n_{A_2}(x))$.

If $supp(B_1) = E_1$ and $supp(B_2) = E_2$ are the sets of edges in G_1 and G_2, then $B_1 \cup B_2$ can be defined as

1. If $xy \in E_1, xy \notin E_2$, then $(B_1 \cup B_2)(xy) = B_1(xy)$,
2. If $xy \in E_1, xy \notin E_2$, then $(B_1 \cup B_2)(xy) = B_2(xy)$,
3. If $xy \in E_1 \cap E_2$, then $(B_1 \cup B_2)(xy) = (\mu^p_{B_1}(xy) \vee \mu^p_{B_2}(xy), \mu^n_{B_1}(xy) \wedge \mu^n_{B_2}(xy))$.

Example 1.3 Consider two bipolar fuzzy graphs G_1 and G_2 as shown in Fig. 1.3. The union $G_1 \cup G_2$ is also given in Fig. 1.3.

Example 1.4 Consider bipolar fuzzy graphs G_1 and G_2 as shown in Fig. 1.4 and 1.5, respectively. $G_1 \cup G_2$ is a bipolar graph with set of vertices $X_1 \cup X_2 = \{a, b, c, d, e, f\}$. The membership values of the vertices in $G_1 \cup G_2$ can be computed as:

1. $(A_1 \cup A_2)(a) = (\mu^p_{A_1}(a) \vee \mu^p_{A_2}(a), \mu^n_{A_1}(a) \wedge \mu^n_{A_2}(a)) = (0.2 \vee 0.$[illegible]$, -0.4 \wedge -0.4) = (0.2, -0.4)$,
2. $(A_1 \cup A_2)(d) = (\mu^p_{A_1}(d) \vee \mu^p_{A_2}(d), \mu^n_{A_1}(d) \wedge \mu^n_{A_2}(d)) = (0.3 \vee 0.2, -0.7 \wedge -0.6) = (0.3, -0.7)$
3. $(A_1 \cup A_2)(f) = A_2(f)$ as $f \notin X_2$.

Table 1.3 Bipolar fuzzy set A on $\{x_1, x_2, x_3\}$

A	x_1	x_2	x_3
$\mu^p_A(x)$	0.5	0.6	0.7
$\mu^n_A(x)$	−0.4	−0.5	−0.7

Table 1.4 Bipolar fuzzy relation B in $\{x_1, x_2, x_3\}$

B	x_1	x_2	x_3
x_1	(0, 0)	(0.2, −0.3)	(0.2, −0.3)
x_2	(0.2, −0.3)	(0, 0)	(0.6, −0.4)
x_3	(0.2, −0.3)	(0.6, −0.4)	(0, 0)

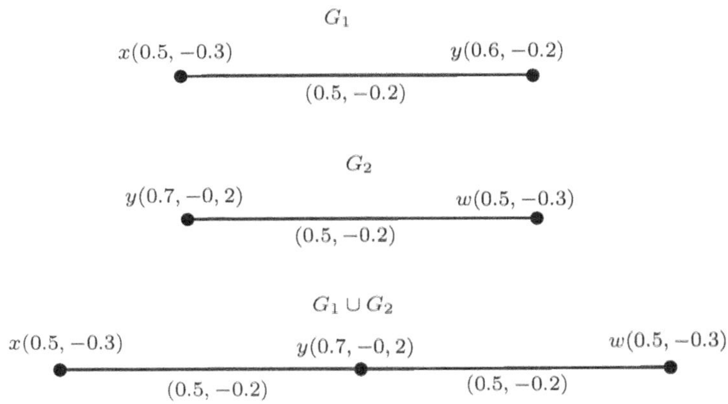

Fig. 1.3 Union of bipolar fuzzy graphs

The membership values of the other vertices can be computed similarly. The membership values of the edges in $G_1 \cup G_2$ can be computed as:

1. $(B_1 \cup B_2)(bc) = (\mu^p_{B_1}(bc) \vee \mu^p_{B_2}(bc), \mu^n_{B_1}(bc) \wedge \mu^n_{B_2}(bc)) = (0.2 \vee 0.1, -0.4 \wedge -0.4) = (0.2, -0.4)$,
2. $(B_1 \cup B_2)(bd) = B_2(bd)$ as bd is not an edge in G_1,
3. $(B_1 \cup B_2)(ad) = B_1(ad)$ as ad is not an edge in G_2.

The union $G_1 \cup G_2$ is shown in Fig. 1.6.

Proposition 1.1 *If G_1 and G_2 are bipolar fuzzy graphs, then $G_1 \cup G_2$ is a bipolar fuzzy graph.*

Proof Let $G_1 = (A_1, B_1)$ and $G_2 = (A_2, B_2)$ be two bipolar fuzzy graphs on X_1 and X_2, respectively. Also let E_1 and E_2 be the set of edges in G_1 and G_2, respectively. If $xy \in E_1 \cap E_2$, then

$$\begin{aligned}
\mu^p_{B_1 \cup B_2}(xy) &= \mu^p_{B_1}(xy) \vee \mu^p_{B_2}(xy) \\
&\le \left(\mu^p_{A_1}(x) \wedge \mu^p_{A_1}(y)\right) \vee \left(\mu^p_{A_2}(x) \wedge \mu^p_{A_2}(y)\right) \\
&= \left(\mu^p_{A_1}(x) \vee \mu^p_{A_2}(x)\right) \wedge \left(\mu^p_{A_1}(y) \vee \mu^p_{A_2}(y)\right)
\end{aligned}$$

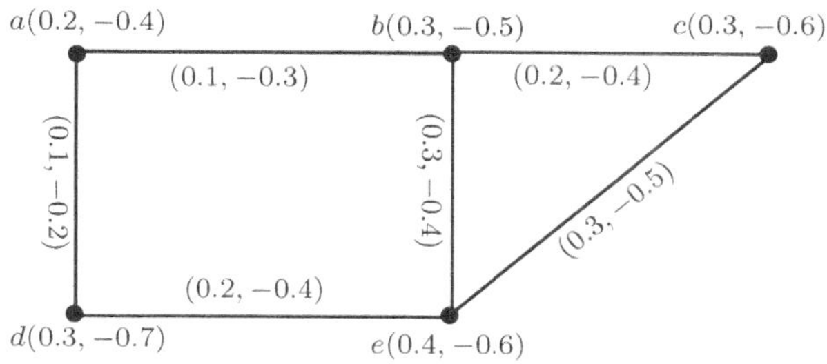

Fig. 1.4 Bipolar fuzzy graph G_1

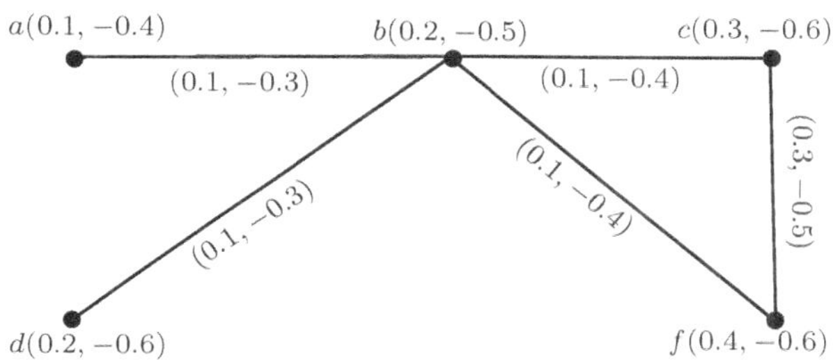

Fig. 1.5 Bipolar fuzzy graph G_2

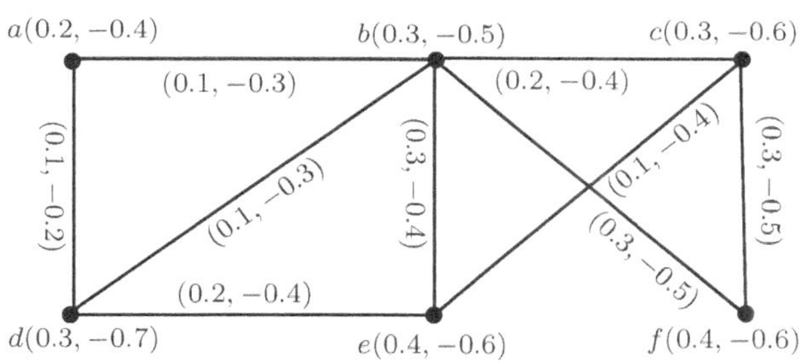

Fig. 1.6 Union $G_1 \cup G_2$ of bipolar fuzzy graphs

$$\begin{aligned}
&= \mu^p_{A_1\cup A_2}(x) \wedge \mu^p_{A_1\cup A_2}(y),\\
\mu^n_{B_1\cup B_2}(xy) &= \mu^n_{B_1}(xy) \wedge \mu^n_{B_2}(xy)\\
&\geq \left(\mu^n_{A_1}(x) \vee \mu^n_{A_1}(y)\right) \wedge \left(\mu^n_{A_2}(x) \vee \mu^n_{A_2}(y)\right)\\
&= \left(\mu^n_{A_1}(x) \wedge \mu^n_{A_2}(x)\right) \vee \left(\mu^n_{A_1}(y) \wedge \mu^n_{A_2}(y)\right)\\
&= \mu^n_{A_1\cup A_2}(x) \vee \mu^n_{A_1\cup A_2}(y).
\end{aligned}$$

If $xy \in E_1 \cap \overline{E_2}$, then

$$
\begin{aligned}
\mu^p_{B_1\cup B_2}(xy) &= \mu^p_{B_1}(xy)\\
&\le \mu^p_{A_1}(x) \wedge \mu^p_{A_1}(y)\\
&\le \big(\mu^p_{A_1}(x) \vee \mu^p_{A_2}(x)\big) \wedge \big(\mu^p_{A_1}(y) \vee \mu^p_{A_2}(y)\big)\\
&= \mu^p_{A_1\cup A_2}(x) \wedge \mu^p_{A_1\cup A_2}(y),\\
\mu^n_{B_1\cup B_2}(xy) &= \mu^n_{B_1}(xy)\\
&\ge \mu^n_{A_1}(x) \vee \mu^n_{A_1}(y)\\
&\ge \big(\mu^n_{A_1}(x) \wedge \mu^n_{A_2}(x)\big) \vee \big(\mu^n_{A_1}(y) \wedge \mu^n_{A_2}(y)\big)\\
&= \mu^n_{A_1\cup A_2}(x) \vee \mu^n_{A_1\cup A_2}(y).
\end{aligned}
$$

Similarly, it can be proved that if $xy \in E_2 \cap \overline{E_1}$, then

$$\mu^p_{B_1\cup B_2}(xy) \le \mu^p_{A_1\cup A_2}(x) \wedge \mu^p_{A_1\cup A_2}(y),$$

$$\mu^n_{B_1\cup B_2}(xy) \ge \mu^n_{A_1\cup A_2}(x) \vee \mu^n_{A_1\cup A_2}(y).$$

This completes the proof. □

Definition 1.15 The **intersection** of two bipolar fuzzy graphs $G_1 = (A_1, B_1)$ and $G_2 = (A_2, B_2)$ is a pair $G_1 \cap G_2 = (A_1 \cap A_2, B_1 \cap B_2)$, where $A_1 \cap A_2$ and $B_1 \cap B_2$ are defined as

1. $(A_1 \cap A_2)(x) = \big(\mu^p_{A_1}(x) \wedge \mu^p_{A_2}(x), \mu^n_{A_1}(x) \vee \mu^n_{A_2}(x)\big)$, for all $x \in X_1 \cap X_2$,
2. $(B_1 \cap B_2)(xy) = \big(\mu^p_{B_1}(xy) \wedge \mu^p_{B_2}(xy), \mu^n_{B_1}(xy) \vee \mu^n_{B_2}(xy)\big)$, for all $xy \in E_1 \cap E_2$.

Example 1.5 Consider bipolar fuzzy graphs G_1 and G_2 as shown in Fig. 1.4 and 1.5, respectively. $G_1 \cap G_2$ is a bipolar graph with set of vertices $X_1 \cap X_2 = \{a, b, c, d\}$. The membership values of the vertices in $G_1 \cap G_2$ can be computed as:

1. $(A_1 \cap A_2)(a) = (\mu^p_{A_1}(a) \wedge \mu^p_{A_2}(a), \mu^n_{A_1}(a) \vee \mu^n_{A_2}(a)) = (0.2 \wedge 0.1, -0.4 \vee -0.4) = (0.1, -0.4)$,
2. $(A_1 \cap A_2)(d) = (\mu^p_{A_1}(d) \wedge \mu^p_{A_2}(d), \mu^n_{A_1}(d) \vee \mu^n_{A_2}(d)) = (0.3 \wedge 0.2, -0.7 \vee -0.6) = (0.2, -0.6)$
3. $(A_1 \cap A_2)(f) = (0, 0)$ as $f \notin X_1 \cap X_2$.

The membership values of the other vertices can be computed similarly. The membership values of the edges in $G_1 \cap G_2$ can be computed as:

1. $(B_1 \cap B_2)(bc) = (\mu^p_{B_1}(bc) \wedge \mu^p_{B_2}(bc), \mu^n_{B_1}(bc) \vee \mu^n_{B_2}(bc)) = (0.2 \wedge 0.1, -0.4 \vee -0.4) = (0.1, -0.4)$,
2. $(B_1 \cap B_2)(bd) = (0, 0)$ as $bd \notin E_1 \cap E_2$,
3. $(B_1 \cap B_2)(ad) = (0, 0)$ as $ad \notin E_1 \cap E_2$.

The intersection $G_1 \cap G_2$ is shown in Fig. 1.7.

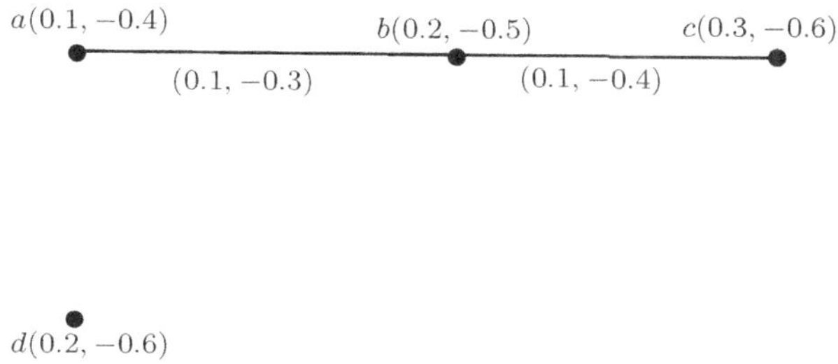

Fig. 1.7 Intersection of bipolar fuzzy graphs G_1 and G_2

Proposition 1.2 *Let $\{G_i \mid i \in \Lambda\}$ be a family of bipolar fuzzy graphs on non-empty set X. Then $\bigcap_{i\in\Lambda} G_i$ is a bipolar fuzzy graph.*

Proof Let $G_i = (A_i, B_i), i \in \Lambda$, be bipolar fuzzy graphs on X. For any $x, y \in X$,

$$\begin{aligned}
\mu^p_{\cap_{i\in\Lambda} B_i}(xy) &= \inf_{i\in\Lambda} \mu^p_{B_i}(xy) \le \inf_{i\in\Lambda} \big(\mu^p_{A_i}(x) \wedge \mu^p_{A_i}(y)\big)\\
&= \inf_{i\in\Lambda} \mu^p_{A_i}(x) \wedge \inf_{i\in\Lambda} \mu^p_{A_i}(y)\\
&= \mu^p_{\cap_{i\in\Lambda} A_i}(x) \wedge \mu^p_{\cap_{i\in\Lambda} A_i}(y),\\
\mu^n_{\cap_{i\in\Lambda} B_i}(xy) &= \sup_{i\in\Lambda} \mu^n_{B_i}(xy) \ge \sup_{i\in\Lambda} \big(\mu^n_{A_i}(x) \vee \mu^n_{A_i}(y)\big)\\
&= \sup_{i\in\Lambda} \mu^n_{A_i}(x) \vee \sup_{i\in\Lambda} \mu^n_{A_i}(y)\\
&= \mu^n_{\cap_{i\in\Lambda} A_i}(x) \vee \cap\mu^n_{\cap_{i\in\Lambda} A_i}(y).
\end{aligned}$$

Hence $\bigcap_{i\in\Lambda} G_i$ is a bipolar fuzzy graph. □

Definition 1.16 The **join** of two bipolar fuzzy graphs $G_1 = (A_1, B_1)$ and $G_2 = (A_2, B_2)$ is defined as a pair $G_1 + G_2 = (A_1 + A_2, B_1 + B_2)$ such that $A_1 + A_2 = A_1 \cup A_2$, for all $x \in X_1 \cup X_2$, and the membership values of the edges in $G_1 + G_2$ are defined as

1. $B_1 + B_2 = B_1 \cup B_2$, for all $xy \in E_1 \cup E_2$.
2. Let E' be the set of all edges joining the vertices of G_1 and G_2, then for all $xy \in E'$, where $x \in X_1$ and $y \in X_2$, $(B_1 + B_2)(xy) = \big(\mu^p_{A_1}(x) \wedge \mu^p_{A_2}(y), \mu^n_{A_1}(x) \vee \mu^n_{A_2}(y)\big)$.

Example 1.6 The join of two bipolar fuzzy graphs G_1 and G_2 is shown in Fig. 1.8.

Proposition 1.3 *If G_1 and G_2 are the bipolar fuzzy graphs, then $G_1 + G_2$ is a bipolar fuzzy graph.*

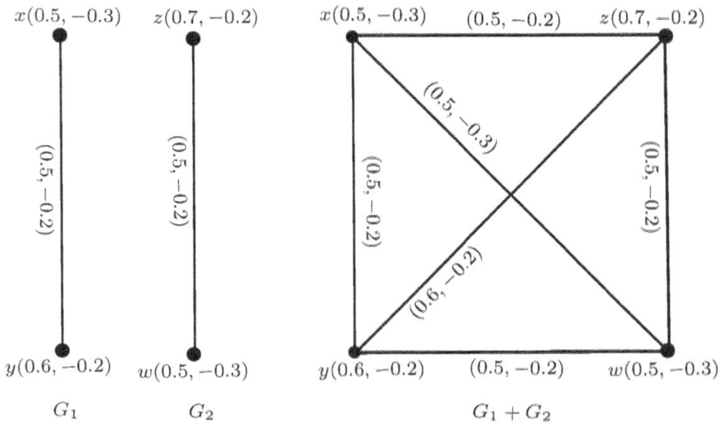

Fig. 1.8 Join of bipolar fuzzy graphs G_1 and G_2

Proof Let $G_1 = (A_1, B_1)$ and $G_2 = (A_2, B_2)$ be two bipolar fuzzy graphs on X_1 and X_2, respectively. If $xy \in E'$, then

$$\begin{aligned}
\mu^p_{B_1+B_2}(xy) &= \mu^p_{A_1}(x) \wedge \mu^p_{A_2}(y) \\
&\le \mu^p_{A_1\cup A_2}(x) \wedge \mu^p_{A_1\cup A_2}(y) \qquad \because \text{By Proposition 1.1.} \\
&= \mu^p_{A_1+A_2}(x) \wedge \mu^p_{A_1+A_2}(y), \\
\mu^n_{B_1+B_2}(xy) &= \mu^n_{A_1}(x) \vee \mu^n_{A_2}(y) \\
&\ge \mu^n_{A_1\cup A_2}(x) \vee \mu^n_{A_1\cup A_2}(y) \\
&= \mu^n_{A_1+A_2}(x) \vee \mu^n_{A_1+A_2}(y).
\end{aligned}$$

If $xy \in E_1 \cup E_2$, then the result follows from Proposition 1.1. It completes the proof. □

Proposition 1.4 *Let $G_1^* = (X_1, E_1)$ and $G_2^* = (X_2, E_2)$ be crisp graphs such that $X_1 \cap X_2 = \emptyset$. Let A_1 and A_2 be bipolar fuzzy sets on X_1 and X_2 and B_1, B_2 be bipolar fuzzy relations in X_1 and X_2, respectively. Then $G_1 \cup G_2 = (A_1 \cup A_2, B_1 \cup B_2)$ is a bipolar fuzzy graph on $X_1 \cup X_2$ with underlying graph $G_1^* \cup G_2^*$ if and only if $G_1 = (A_1, B_1)$ and $G_2 = (A_2, B_2)$ are bipolar fuzzy graphs with underlying graphs G_1^* and G_2^*, respectively.*

Proof Suppose that $G_1 \cup G_2$ is a bipolar fuzzy graph. Let $xy \in E_1$, then $xy \notin E_2$ and $x, y \in X_1 - X_2$,

$$\begin{aligned}
\mu^p_{B_1}(xy) &= \mu^p_{B_1\cup B_2}(xy) \le \mu^p_{A_1\cup A_2}(x) \wedge \mu^p_{A_1\cup A_2}(y) = \mu^p_{A_1}(x) \wedge \mu^p_{A_1}(y), \\
\mu^n_{B_1}(xy) &= \mu^n_{B_1\cap B_2}(xy) \ge \mu^n_{A_1\cup A_2}(x) \vee \mu^n_{A_1\cup A_2}(y) = \mu^n_{A_1}(x) \vee \mu^n_{A_1}(y).
\end{aligned}$$

It shows that $G_1 = (A_1, B_1)$ is a bipolar fuzzy graph. Similarly, we can show that $G_2 = (A_2, B_2)$ is a bipolar fuzzy graph. The converse part of the proposition is given by Proposition 1.1. □

Proposition 1.5 *Let $G_1^* = (X_1, E_1)$ and $G_2^* = (X_2, E_2)$ be crisp graphs such that $X_1 \cap X_2 = \emptyset$. Let A_1 and A_2 be bipolar fuzzy sets on X_1 and X_2 and B_1, B_2 be bipolar fuzzy relations in X_1 and X_2, respectively. Then $G_1 + G_2 = (A_1 + A_2, B_1 + B_2)$ is a bipolar fuzzy graph on $X_1 \cup X_2$ with underlying graph $G_1^* + G_2^*$ if and only if $G_1 = (A_1, B_1)$ and $G_2 = (A_2, B_2)$ are bipolar fuzzy graphs with underlying graphs G_1^* and G_2^*, respectively.*

Definition 1.17 The **composition** of two bipolar fuzzy graphs $G_1 = (A_1, B_1)$ and $G_2 = (A_2, B_2)$ is denoted by the pair $G_1 \circ G_2 = (A_1 \circ A_2, B_1 \circ B_2)$ (or $G_1[G_2] = (A_1[A_2], B_1[B_2])$), where $A_1 \circ A_2 = (\mu^p_{A_1 \circ A_2}, \mu^n_{A_1 \circ A_2})$ and $B_1 \circ B_2 = (\mu^p_{B_1 \circ B_2}, \mu^n_{B_1 \circ B_2})$ are defined as

1. $(A_1 \circ A_2)(x_1, x_2) = \big(\mu^p_{A_1}(x_1) \wedge \mu^p_{A_2}(x_2), \mu^n_{A_1}(x_1) \vee \mu^n_{A_2}(x_2)\big)$, for all $(x_1, x_2) \in X_1 \times X_2$,
2. $(B_1 \circ B_2)((x, x_2)(x, y_2)) = \big(\mu^p_{A_1}(x) \wedge \mu^p_{B_2}(x_2y_2), \mu^n_{A_1}(x) \vee \mu^n_{B_2}(x_2y_2)\big)$, for all $x \in X_1$, $x_2y_2 \in E_2$,
3. $(B_1 \circ B_2)((x_1, z)(y_1, z)) = \big(\mu^p_{B_1}(x_1y_1) \wedge \mu^p_{A_2}(z), \mu^n_{B_1}(x_1y_1) \vee \mu^n_{A_2}(z)\big)$, for all $z \in X_2$, $x_1y_1 \in E_1$,
4. $(B_1 \circ B_2)((x_1, x_2)(y_1, y_2)) = \big(\mu^p_{A_2}(x_2) \wedge \mu^p_{A_2}(y_2) \wedge \mu^p_{B_1}(x_1y_1), \mu^n_{A_2}(x_2) \vee \mu^n_{A_2}(y_2) \vee \mu^n_{B_1}(x_1y_1)\big)$,
   for all $x_2, y_2 \in X_2$, $x_1y_1 \in E_1$.

Proposition 1.6 *If G_1 and G_2 are bipolar fuzzy graphs, then $G_1 \circ G_2$ is a bipolar fuzzy graph.*

Proof Let $G_1 = (A_1, B_1)$ and $G_2 = (A_2, B_2)$ be two bipolar fuzzy graphs on X_1 and X_2, respectively. Let $x \in X_1$ and $x_2y_2 \in E_2$, then

$$\begin{aligned}
\mu^p_{B_1 \circ B_2}((x, x_2)(x, y_2)) &= \mu^p_{A_1}(x) \wedge \mu^p_{B_2}(x_2y_2) \\
&\leq \mu^p_{A_1}(x) \wedge \big(\mu^p_{A_2}(x_2) \wedge \mu^p_{A_2}(y_2)\big) \\
&= \big(\mu^p_{A_1}(x) \wedge \mu^p_{A_2}(x_2)\big) \wedge \big(\mu^p_{A_2}(x) \wedge \mu^p_{A_2}(y_2)\big) \\
&= \mu^p_{A_1 \circ A_2}(x, x_2) \wedge \mu^p_{A_1 \circ A_2}(x, y_2), \\
\mu^n_{B_1 \circ B_2}((x, x_2)(x, y_2)) &= \mu^n_{A_1}(x) \vee \mu^n_{B_2}(x_2y_2) \\
&\geq \mu^n_{A_1}(x) \vee \big(\mu^n_{A_2}(x_2) \vee \mu^n_{A_2}(y_2)\big) \\
&= \big(\mu^n_{A_1}(x) \vee \mu^n_{A_2}(x_2)\big), \big(\mu^n_{A_1}(x) \vee \mu^n_{A_2}(y_2)\big) \\
&= \mu^n_{A_1 \circ A_2}(x, x_2) \vee \mu^n_{A_1 \circ A_2}(x, y_2).
\end{aligned}$$

Let $z \in X_2$ and $x_1y_1 \in E_1$, then

$$\mu^p_{B_1 \circ B_2}((x_1, z)(y_1, z)) = \mu^p_{B_1}(x_1y_1) \wedge \mu^p_{A_2}(z)$$

$$
\begin{aligned}
&\le \big(\mu^p_{A_1}(x_1) \wedge \mu^p_{A_1}(y_1)\big) \wedge \mu^p_{A_2}(z) \\
&= \big(\mu^p_{A_1}(x) \wedge \mu^p_{A_2}(z)\big) \wedge \big(\mu^p_{A_1}(y_1) \wedge \mu^p_{A_2}(z)\big) \\
&= \mu^p_{A_1 \circ A_2}(x_1, z) \wedge \mu^p_{A_1 \circ A_2}(y_1, z), \\
\mu^n_{B_1 \circ B_2}((x_1, z)(y_1, z)) &= \mu^n_{B_1}(x_1 y_1) \vee \mu^n_{A_2}(z) \\
&\ge \big(\mu^n_{A_1}(x_1) \vee \mu^n_{A_1}(y_1)\big) \vee \mu^n_{A_2}(z) \\
&= \big(\mu_{A_1}(x) \vee \mu^n_{A_2}(z)\big) \vee \big(\mu^n_{A_1}(y_1) \vee \mu^n_{A_2}(z)\big) \\
&= \mu^n_{A_1 \circ A_2}(x_1, z) \vee \mu^n_{A_1 \circ A_2}(y_1, z).
\end{aligned}
$$

Let $x_1 y_1 \in E_1$, $x_2, y_2 \in X_2$, $x_2 \neq y_2$, then

$$
\begin{aligned}
\mu^p_{B_1 \circ B_2}((x_1, x_2)(y_1, y_2)) &= \mu^p_{A_2}(x_2) \wedge \mu^p_{A_2}(y_2) \wedge \mu^p_{B_1}(x_1 y_1) \\
&\le \big(\mu^p_{A_2}(x_2) \wedge \mu^p_{A_2}(y_2)\big) \wedge \big(\mu^p_{A_1}(x_1) \wedge \mu^p_{A_1}(y_1)\big) \\
&= \big(\mu^p_{A_1}(x_1) \wedge \mu^p_{A_2}(x_2)\big) \wedge \big(\mu^p_{A_1}(y_1) \wedge \mu^p_{A_2}(y_2)\big) \\
&= \mu^p_{A_1 \circ A_2}(x_1, x_2) \wedge \mu^p_{A_1 \circ A_2}(y_1, y_2), \\
\mu^n_{B_1 \circ B_2}((x_1, x_2)(y_1, y_2)) &= \mu^n_{A_2}(x_2) \vee \mu^n_{A_2}(y_2) \vee \mu^n_{B_1}(x_1 y_1)) \\
&\ge \big(\mu^n_{A_2}(x_2) \vee \mu^n_{A_2}(y_2)\big) \vee \big(\mu^n_{A_1}(x_1) \vee \mu^n_{A_1}(y_1)\big) \\
&= \big(\mu^n_{A_1}(x_1) \vee \mu^n_{A_2}(x_2)\big), \big(\mu^n_{A_1}(y_1) \vee \mu^n_{A_2}(y_2)\big) \\
&= \mu^n_{A_1 \circ A_2}(x_1, x_2) \vee \mu^n_{A_1 \circ A_2}(y_1, y_2).
\end{aligned}
$$

This completes the proof. □

Definition 1.18 The **Cartesian product** of two bipolar fuzzy graphs $G_1 = (A_1, B_1)$ and $G_2 = (A_2, B_2)$ is denoted by the pair $G_1 \square G_2 = (A_1 \square A_2, B_1 \square B_2)$, where $A_1 \square A_2 = (\mu^p_{A_1 \square A_2}, \mu^n_{A_1 \square A_2})$ and $B_1 \square B_2 = (\mu^p_{B_1 \square B_2}, \mu^n_{B_1 \square B_2})$ are defined as

1. $(A_1 \square A_2)(x_1, x_2) = \big(\mu^p_{A_1}(x_1) \wedge \mu^p_{A_2}(x_2), \mu^n_{A_1}(x_1) \vee \mu^n_{A_2}(x_2)\big)$, for all $(x_1, x_2) \in X_1 \times X_2$,
2. $(B_1 \square B_2)((x, x_2)(x, y_2)) = \big(\mu^p_{A_1}(x) \wedge \mu^p_{B_2}(x_2 y_2), \mu^n_{A_1}(x) \vee \mu^n_{B_2}(x_2 y_2)\big)$, for all $x \in X_1$, $x_2 y_2 \in E_2$,
3. $(B_1 \square B_2)((x_1, z)(y_1, z)) = \big(\mu^p_{B_1}(x_1 y_1) \wedge \mu^p_{A_2}(z), \mu^n_{B_1}(x_1 y_1) \vee \mu^n_{A_2}(z)\big)$, for all $z \in X_2$, $x_1 y_1 \in E_1$.

Example 1.7 The Cartesian product of two bipolar fuzzy graphs G_1 and G_2 is shown in Fig. 1.9.

Proposition 1.7 *The Cartesian product of two bipolar fuzzy graphs is a bipolar fuzzy graph.*

Proof Let $G_1 = (A_1, B_1)$ and $G_2 = (A_2, B_2)$ be two bipolar fuzzy graphs on X_1 and X_2, respectively. Let $x \in X_1$, $x_2 y_2 \in E_2$, then

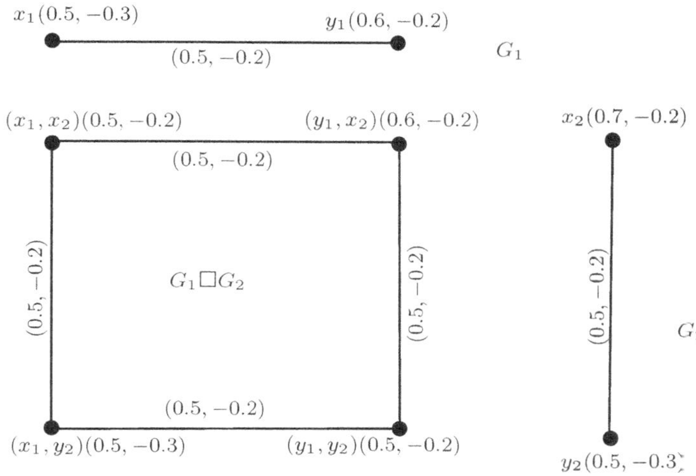

Fig. 1.9 Cartesian product $G_1 \Box G_2$

$$\begin{aligned}
\mu^p_{B_1\Box B_2}((x,x_2)(x,y_2)) &= \mu^p_{A_1}(x) \wedge \mu^p_{B_2}(x_2y_2)\\
&\le \mu^p_{A_1}(x) \wedge \left(\mu^p_{A_2}(x_2) \wedge \mu^p_{A_2}(y_2)\right)\\
&= \left(\mu^p_{A_1}(x) \wedge \mu^p_{A_2}(x_2)\right) \wedge \left(\mu^p_{A_2}(x) \wedge \mu^p_{A_2}(y_2)\right)\\
&= \mu^p_{A_1\Box A_2}(x,x_2) \wedge \mu^p_{A_1\Box A_2}(x,y_2),\\
\mu^n_{B_1\Box B_2}((x,x_2)(x,y_2)) &= \mu^n_{A_1}(x) \vee \mu^n_{B_2}(x_2y_2)\\
&\ge \mu^n_{A_1}(x) \vee \left(\mu^n_{A_2}(x_2) \vee \mu^n_{A_2}(y_2)\right)\\
&= \left(\mu^n_{A_1}(x) \vee \mu^n_{A_2}(x_2)\right) \vee \left(\mu^n_{A_1}(x) \vee \mu^n_{A_2}(y_2)\right)\\
&= \mu^n_{A_1\Box A_2}(x,x_2) \vee \mu^n_{A_1\Box A_2}(x,y_2).
\end{aligned}$$

Let $z \in X_2$, $x_1y_1 \in E_1$, then

$$\begin{aligned}
\mu^p_{B_1\Box B_2}((x_1,z)(y_1,z)) &= \mu^p_{B_1}(x_1y_1) \wedge \mu^p_{A_2}(z)\\
&\le \left(\mu^p_{A_1}(x_1) \wedge \mu^p_{A_1}(y_1)\right) \wedge \mu^p_{A_2}(z)\\
&= \left(\mu^p_{A_1}(x_1) \wedge \mu^p_{A_2}(z)\right) \wedge \left(\mu^p_{A_1}(y_1) \wedge \mu^p_{A_2}(z)\right)\\
&= \mu^p_{A_1\Box A_2}(x_1,z) \wedge \mu^p_{A_1\Box A_2}(y_1,z),\\
\mu^n_{B_1\Box B_2}((x_1,z)(y_1,z)) &= \mu^n_{B_1}(x_1y_1) \vee \mu^n_{A_2}(z)\\
&\ge \left(\mu^n_{A_1}(x_1) \vee \mu^n_{A_1}(y_1)\right) \vee \mu^n_{A_2}(z)\\
&= \left(\mu^n_{A_1}(x_1) \vee \mu^n_{A_2}(z)\right) \vee \left(\mu^n_{A_1}(y_1) \vee \mu^n_{A_2}(z)\right)\\
&= \mu^n_{A_1\Box A_2}(x_1,z) \vee \mu^n_{A_1\Box A_2}(y_1,z).
\end{aligned}$$

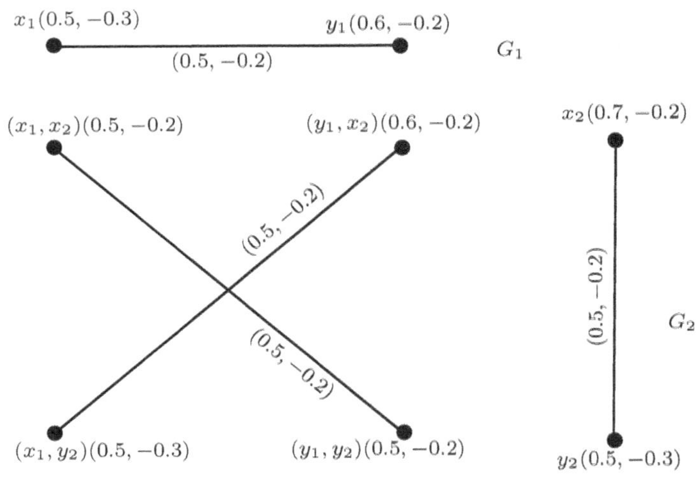

Fig. 1.10 Direct product $G_1 \times G_2$

This completes the proof. □

Definition 1.19 The **direct product** of two bipolar fuzzy graphs $G_1 = (A_1, B_1)$ and $G_2 = (A_2, B_2)$ is a pair $G_1 \times G_2 = (A_1 \times A_2, B_1 \times B_2)$, where $A_1 \times A_2 = (\mu^p_{A_1\times A_2}, \mu^n_{A_1\times A_2})$ and $B_1 \times B_2 = (\mu^p_{B_1\times B_2}, \mu^n_{B_1\times B_2})$ are defined as

1. $(A_1 \times A_2)(x_1, x_2) = \big(\mu^p_{A_1}(x_1) \wedge \mu^p_{A_2}(x_2), \mu^n_{A_1}(x_1) \vee \mu^n_{A_2}(x_2)\big)$, for all $(x_1, x_2) \in X_1 \times X_2$,
2. $(B_1 \times B_2)((x_1, x_2)(x_1, y_2)) = \big(\mu^p_{B_1}(x_1y_1) \wedge \mu^p_{B_2}(x_2y_2), \mu^n_{B_1}(x_1y_1) \vee \mu^n_{B_2}(x_2y_2)\big)$,

   for all $x_1y_1 \in E_1$, $x_2y_2 \in E_2$.

Example 1.8 The direct product of two bipolar fuzzy graphs G_1 and G_2 is shown in Fig. 1.10.

Proposition 1.8 *The direct product of two bipolar fuzzy graphs is a bipolar fuzzy graph.*

Proof Let $G_1 = (A_1, B_1)$ and $G_2 = (A_2, B_2)$ be two bipolar fuzzy graphs on X_1 and X_2, respectively. Let $x_1y_1 \in E_1$ and $x_2y_2 \in E_2$, then

$$\begin{aligned}
\mu^p_{B_1\times B_2}((x_1, x_2)(y_1, y_2)) &= \mu^p_{B_1}(x_1y_1) \wedge \mu^p_{B_2}(x_2y_2)\\
&\le \big(\mu^p_{A_1}(x_1) \wedge \mu^p_{A_1}(y_1)\big) \wedge \big(\mu^p_{A_2}(x_2) \wedge \mu^p_{A_2}(y_2)\big)\\
&= \big(\mu^p_{A_1}(x_1) \wedge \mu^p_{A_2}(x_2)\big) \wedge \big(\mu^p_{A_1}(y_1), \mu^p_{A_2}(y_2)\big)\\
&= \mu^p_{A_1\times A_2}(x_1, x_2) \wedge \mu^p_{A_1\times A_2}(y_1, y_2),
\end{aligned}$$

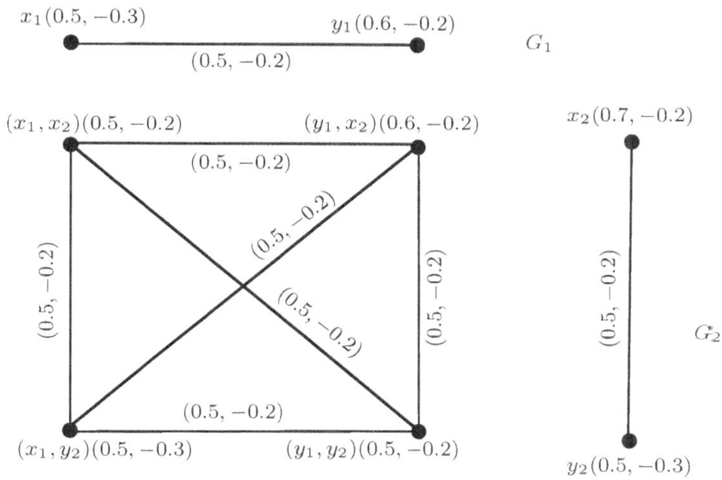

Fig. 1.11 Strong product $G_1 \boxtimes G_2$

$$\begin{aligned}
\mu^n_{B_1 \times B_2}((x_1, x_2)(y_1, y_2)) &= \mu^n_{B_1}(x_1 y_1) \vee \mu^n_{B_2}(x_2 y_2) \\
&\geq \left(\mu^n_{A_1}(x_1) \vee \mu^n_{A_1}(y_1)\right) \vee \left(\mu^n_{A_2}(x_2) \vee \mu^n_{A_2}(y_2)\right) \\
&= \left(\mu^n_{A_1}(x_1) \vee \mu^n_{A_2}(x_2)\right) \vee \left(\mu^n_{A_1}(y_1) \vee \mu^n_{A_2}(y_2)\right) \\
&= \mu^n_{A_1 \times A_2}(x_1, x_2) \vee \mu^n_{A_1 \times A_2}(y_1, y_2).
\end{aligned}$$

The proof is complete. □

Definition 1.20 The **strong product** of two bipolar fuzzy graphs $G_1 = (A_1, B_1)$ and $G_2 = (A_2, B_2)$ is denoted by the pair $G_1 \boxtimes G_2 = (A_1 \boxtimes A_2, B_1 \boxtimes B_2)$ and defined as

1. $(A_1 \boxtimes A_2)(x_1, x_2) = \left(\mu^p_{A_1}(x_1) \wedge \mu^p_{A_2}(x_2), \mu^n_{A_1}(x_1) \vee \mu^n_{A_2}(x_2)\right)$, for all $(x_1, x_2) \in X_1 \times X_2$,
2. $(B_1 \boxtimes B_2)((x, x_2)(x, y_2)) = \left(\mu^p_{A_1}(x) \wedge \mu^p_{B_2}(x_2 y_2), \mu^n_{A_1}(x) \vee \mu^n_{B_2}(x_2 y_2)\right)$, for all $x \in X_1$, $x_2 y_2 \in E_2$,
3. $(B_1 \boxtimes B_2)((x_1, z)(y_1, z)) = \left(\mu^p_{B_1}(x_1 y_1) \wedge \mu^p_{A_2}(z), \mu^n_{B_1}(x_1 y_1) \vee \mu^n_{A_2}(z)\right)$, for all $z \in X_2$, $x_1 y_1 \in E_1$,
4. $(B_1 \boxtimes B_2)((x_1, x_2)(x_1, y_2)) = \left(\mu^p_{B_1}(x_1 y_1) \wedge \mu^p_{B_2}(x_2 y_2), \mu^n_{B_1}(x_1 y_1) \vee \mu^n_{B_2}(x_2 y_2)\right)$, for all $x_1 y_1 \in E_1$, $x_2 y_2 \in E_2$.

Example 1.9 The strong product of two bipolar fuzzy graphs G_1 and G_2 is shown in Fig. 1.11.

Proposition 1.9 *The strong product of two bipolar fuzzy graphs is a bipolar fuzzy graph.*

Proof Let $G_1 = (A_1, B_1)$ and $G_2 = (A_2, B_2)$ be two bipolar fuzzy graphs on X_1 and X_2, respectively. Let $x \in X_1$ and $x_2y_2 \in E_2$, then

$$\begin{aligned}
\mu^p_{B_1 \boxtimes B_2}((x, x_2)(x, y_2)) &= \mu^p_{A_1}(x) \wedge \mu^p_{B_2}(x_2y_2)\\
&\leq \mu^p_{A_1}(x) \wedge \big(\mu^p_{A_2}(x_2) \wedge \mu^p_{A_2}(y_2)\big)\\
&= \big(\mu^p_{A_1}(x) \wedge \mu^p_{A_2}(x_2)\big) \wedge \big(\mu^p_{A_2}(x) \wedge \mu^p_{A_2}(y_2)\big)\\
&= \mu^p_{A_1 \boxtimes A_2}(x, x_2) \wedge \mu^p_{A_1 \boxtimes A_2}(x, y_2),\\
\mu^n_{B_1 \boxtimes B_2}((x, x_2)(x, y_2)) &= \mu^n_{A_1}(x) \vee \mu^n_{B_2}(x_2y_2)\\
&\geq \mu^n_{A_1}(x) \vee \big(\mu^n_{A_2}(x_2) \vee \mu^n_{A_2}(y_2)\big)\\
&= \big(\mu^n_{A_1}(x) \vee \mu^n_{A_2}(x_2)\big) \vee \big(\mu^n_{A_1}(x) \vee \mu^n_{A_2}(y_2)\big)\\
&= \mu^n_{A_1 \boxtimes A_2}(x, x_2) \vee \mu^n_{A_1 \boxtimes A_2}(x, y_2).
\end{aligned}$$

Let $z \in X_2$ and $x_1y_1 \in E_1$, then

$$\begin{aligned}
\mu^p_{B_1 \Box B_2}((x_1, z)(y_1, z)) &= \mu^p_{B_1}(x_1y_1) \wedge \mu^p_{A_2}(z)\\
&\leq \big(\mu^p_{A_1}(x_1) \wedge \mu^p_{A_1}(y_1)\big) \wedge \mu^p_{A_2}(z)\\
&= \big(\mu^p_{A_1}(x_1) \wedge \mu^p_{A_2}(z)\big) \wedge \big(\mu^p_{A_1}(y_1) \wedge \mu^p_{A_2}(z)\big)\\
&= \mu^p_{A_1 \Box A_2}(x_1, z) \wedge \mu^p_{A_1 \Box A_2}(y_1, z),\\
\mu^n_{B_1 \Box B_2}((x_1, z)(y_1, z)) &= \mu^n_{B_1}(x_1y_1) \vee \mu^n_{A_2}(z)\\
&\geq \big(\mu^n_{A_1}(x_1) \vee \mu^n_{A_1}(y_1)\big) \vee \mu^n_{A_2}(z)\\
&= \big(\mu^n_{A_1}(x_1) \vee \mu^n_{A_2}(z)\big) \vee \big(\mu^n_{A_1}(y_1) \vee \mu^n_{A_2}(z)\big)\\
&= \mu^n_{A_1 \Box A_2}(x_1, z) \vee \mu^n_{A_1 \Box A_2}(y_1, z).
\end{aligned}$$

Let $x_1y_1 \in E_1$ and $x_2y_2 \in E_2$, then

$$\begin{aligned}
\mu^p_{B_1 \boxtimes B_2}((x_1, x_2)(y_1, y_2)) &= \mu^p_{B_1}(x_1y_1) \wedge \mu^p_{B_2}(x_2y_2)\\
&\leq \big(\mu^p_{A_1}(x_1) \wedge \mu^p_{A_1}(y_1)\big) \wedge \big(\mu^p_{A_2}(x_2) \wedge \mu^p_{A_2}(y_2)\big)\\
&= \big(\mu^p_{A_1}(x_1) \wedge \mu^p_{A_2}(x_2)\big) \wedge \big(\mu^p_{A_1}(y_1), \mu^p_{A_2}(y_2)\big)\\
&= \mu^p_{A_1 \boxtimes A_2}(x_1, x_2) \wedge \mu^p_{A_1 \boxtimes A_2}(y_1, y_2),\\
\mu^n_{B_1 \boxtimes B_2}((x_1, x_2)(y_1, y_2)) &= \mu^n_{B_1}(x_1y_1) \vee \mu^n_{B_2}(x_2y_2)\\
&\geq \big(\mu^n_{A_1}(x_1) \vee \mu^n_{A_1}(y_1)\big) \vee \big(\mu^n_{A_2}(x_2) \vee \mu^n_{A_2}(y_2)\big)\\
&= \big(\mu^n_{A_1}(x_1) \vee \mu^n_{A_2}(x_2)\big) \vee \big(\mu^n_{A_1}(y_1) \vee \mu^n_{A_2}(y_2)\big)\\
&= \mu^n_{A_1 \boxtimes A_2}(x_1, x_2) \vee \mu^n_{A_1 \boxtimes A_2}(y_1, y_2).
\end{aligned}$$

This completes the proof. □

Definition 1.21 The **lexicographic product** of two bipolar fuzzy graphs $G_1 = (A_1, B_1)$ and $G_2 = (A_2, B_2)$, denoted by $G_1 \bullet G_2$, is defined as a pair $(A_1 \bullet A_2, B_1 \bullet B_2)$ such that

1. $(A_1 \bullet A_2)(x_1, x_2) = \big(\mu^p_{A_1}(x_1) \wedge \mu^p_{A_2}(x_2), \mu^n_{A_1}(x_1) \vee \mu^n_{A_2}(x_2)\big)$, for all $(x_1, x_2) \in X_1 \times X_2$,
2. $(B_1 \bullet B_2)((x, x_2)(x, y_2)) = \big(\mu^p_{A_1}(x) \wedge \mu^p_{B_2}(x_2y_2), \mu^n_{A_1}(x) \vee \mu^n_{B_2}(x_2y_2)\big)$, for all $x \in X_1$, $x_2y_2 \in E_2$,
3. $(B_1 \bullet B_2)((x_1, x_2)(x_1, y_2)) = \big(\mu^p_{B_1}(x_1y_1) \wedge \mu^p_{B_2}(x_2y_2), \mu^n_{B_1}(x_1y_1) \vee \mu^n_{B_2}(x_2y_2)\big)$, for all $x_1y_1 \in E_1$, $x_2y_2 \in E_2$.

Definition 1.22 Let $G = (A, B)$ be a bipolar fuzzy graph on X. A **bipolar fuzzy walk** in a bipolar fuzzy graph G is an alternating sequence of vertices and edges y_o, $e_1, y_1, e_2, \ldots, e_{n-1}, y_{n-1}$ such that $B(e_k) \neq (0, 0)$, for all $1 \leq k \leq n-1$.

Definition 1.23 A **bipolar fuzzy path** in a bipolar fuzzy graph $G = (A, B)$ is a sequence of distinct vertices $y_1, y_2, \ldots, y_n$ such that either $\mu^p_B(y_ky_{k+1}) > 0$ or $\mu^n_B(y_ky_{k+1}) < 0$, for all $1 \leq k \leq n-1$. It is denoted by $\mathcal{P}_n$. If $y_1 = y_n$ and $A(y_1) = A(y_n)$, the bipolar fuzzy path is known as a **bipolar fuzzy cycle** denoted by $\mathcal{C}_n$. A bipolar fuzzy graph G is **connected** if there exists a bipolar fuzzy path between each pair of distinct vertices.

An example of a bipolar fuzzy path $\mathcal{P}_5$ is shown in Fig. 1.12.

Definition 1.24 A bipolar fuzzy graph $G = (A, B)$ on a non-empty set X is known as a **strong bipolar fuzzy graph** if

$$B(xy) = \big(\mu^p_B(xy), \mu^n_B(xy)\big) = \big(\mu^p_A(x) \wedge \mu^p_A(y), \mu^n_A(x) \vee \mu^n_A(y)\big), \quad \text{for all } xy \in E.$$

Example 1.10 Let A be a bipolar fuzzy set on $X = \{x, y, z\}$ given in Table 1.5 and B be a bipolar fuzzy relation in X defined in Table 1.6. By routine computations, it is easy to see that the bipolar fuzzy graph $G = (A, B)$, shown in Fig. 1.13, is a strong bipolar fuzzy graph.

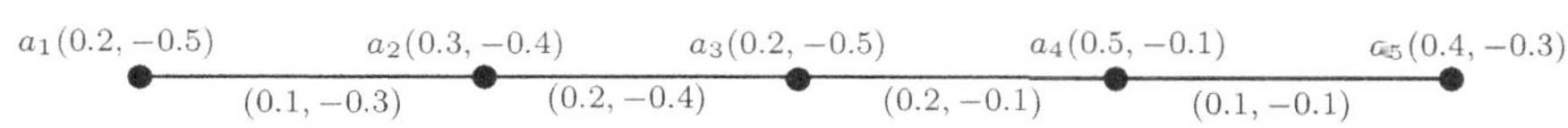

Fig. 1.12 Bipolar fuzzy path $\mathcal{P}_5$

Table 1.5 Bipolar fuzzy set A on $\{x, y, z\}$

A	x	y	z
μ^p_A	0.2	0.3	0.4
μ^n_A	−0.4	−0.5	−0.5

Table 1.6 Bipolar fuzzy relation B in $\{x, y, z\}$

B	x	y	z
x	(0, 0)	(0.2, −0.4)	(0.2, −0.4)
y	(0.2, −0.4)	(0, 0)	(0.3, −0.5)
z	(0.2, −0.4)	(0.3, −0.5)	(0, 0)

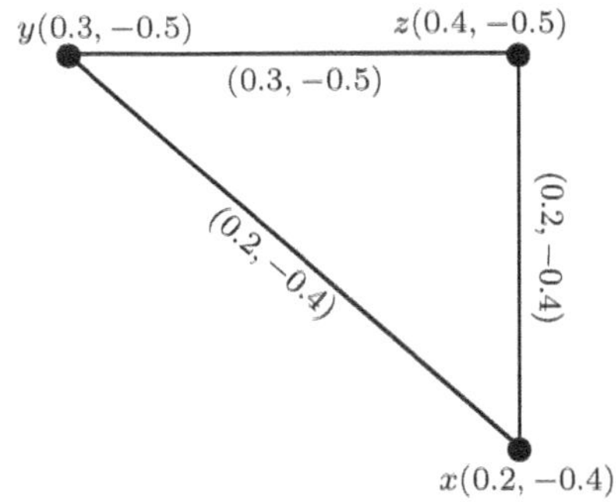

Fig. 1.13 Strong bipolar fuzzy graph G

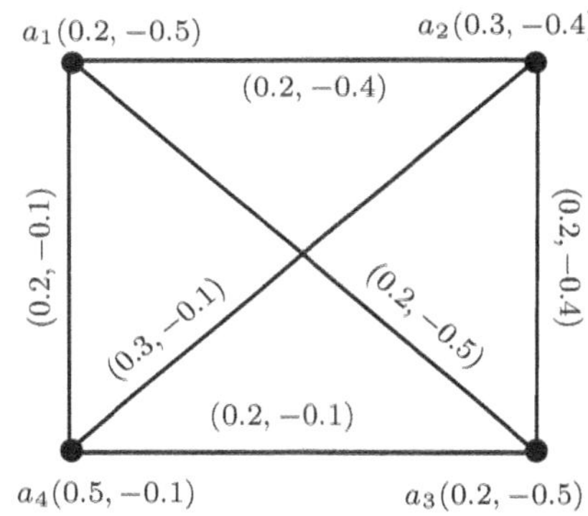

Fig. 1.14 Complete bipolar fuzzy graph

Definition 1.25 A bipolar fuzzy graph $G = (A, B)$ on a non-empty set X is known as a **complete bipolar fuzzy graph** if

$$B(xy) = \left(\mu_B^p(xy), \mu_B^n(xy)\right) = \left(\mu_A^p(x) \wedge \mu_A^p(y), \mu_A^n(x) \vee \mu_A^n(y)\right), \quad \text{for all } x, y \in X.$$

Example 1.11 Consider a bipolar fuzzy graph G on $X = \{a_1, a_2, a_3, a_4\}$ as shown in Fig. 1.14. Routine calculations show that G is a complete bipolar fuzzy graph.

Definition 1.26 A bipolar fuzzy graph $G = (A, B)$ on a non-empty set X is known as a **bipartite bipolar fuzzy graph** if the set of vertices X can be written as the union of two disjoint sets X_1 and X_2 such that for some k and j,

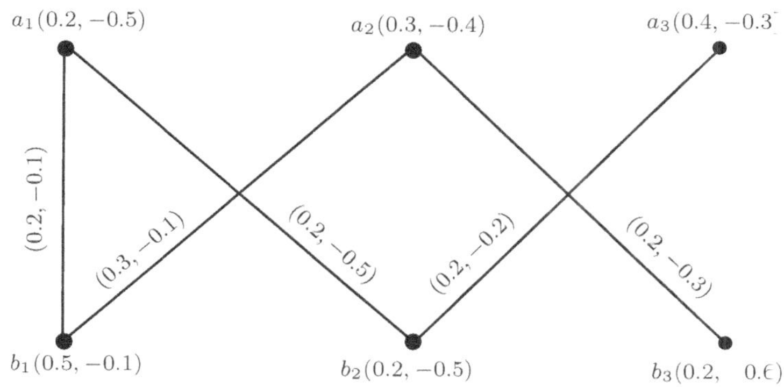

Fig. 1.15 Bipartite bipolar fuzzy graph

1. $B(x_k x_j) = (0, 0)$, if $x_k, x_j \in X_1$ or $x_k, x_j \in X_2$,
2. $B(x_k x_j) \neq (0, 0)$, if $x_k \in X_1$ and $x_j \in X_2$ or $x_k \in X_2$ and $x_j \in X_1$.

Example 1.12 Let G be a bipolar fuzzy graph on $X = \{a_1, a_2, a_3\} \cup \{b_1, b_2, b_3\}$ as shown in Fig. 1.15. By Definition 1.26, G is a bipartite bipolar fuzzy graph.

Definition 1.27 A bipolar fuzzy graph $G = (A, B)$ is said to be **n-partite (multipartite)** bipolar fuzzy graph if the vertex set X can be partitioned into n disjoint subsets $X_1, X_2, \dots X_n$ such that

1. $B(xy) = (0, 0)$, for every $x, y \in X_k$, $1 \leq k \leq n$.
2. $B(xy) \neq (0, 0)$, if $x \in X_i$, $y \in X_j$, $X_i \neq X_j$, $1 \leq i, j \leq n$.

Definition 1.28 A bipolar fuzzy graph $G = (A, B)$ on a non-empty set X is called a **complete bipartite bipolar fuzzy graph** if the set of vertices X can be written as the union of two disjoint sets X_1 and X_2 such that, for all $x, y \in X$,

1. $B(xy) = (0, 0)$, if $x, y \in X_1$ or $x, y \in X_2$,
2. $B(xy) = \big(\mu_A^p(x) \wedge \mu_A^p(y), \mu_A^n(x) \vee \mu_A^n(y)\big)$, if $x \in X_1$ and $y \in X_2$ or $x \in X_2$ and $y \in X_1$.

Example 1.13 A complete bipartite bipolar fuzzy graph on $X = \{a_1, a_2, a_3\} \cup \{b_1, b_2, b_3\}$ is shown in Fig. 1.16.

Definition 1.29 A bipolar fuzzy graph $G' = (A', B')$ on a non-empty set X is known as a **bipolar fuzzy subgraph** of bipolar fuzzy graph $G = (A, B)$ if

1. $A' \subseteq A$, that is, $\mu_{A'}^p(x) \leq \mu_A^p(x)$ and $\mu_{A'}^n(x) \geq \mu_A^n(x)$, for all $x \in X$.
2. $B' \subseteq B$, that is, $\mu_{B'}^p(xy) \leq \mu_B^p(xy)$ and $\mu_{B'}^n(xy) \geq \mu_B^n(xy)$, for all $xy \in E$. A **spanning subgraph** of a bipolar fuzzy graph $G = (A, B)$ is a bipolar fuzzy graph $H = (C, D)$ such that $C(x) = A(x)$, for all $x \in X$.

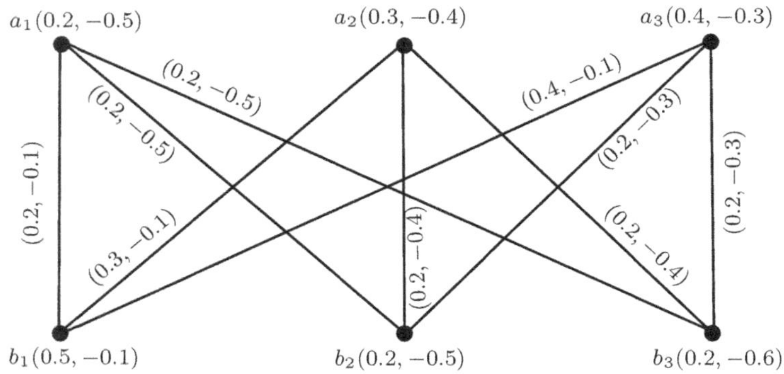

Fig. 1.16 Complete bipartite bipolar fuzzy graph

Definition 1.30 The **complement** of a bipolar fuzzy $G = (A, B)$ is a pair $G^c = (A^c, B^c)$ or $\overline{G} = (\overline{A}, \overline{B})$, where $A^c = A$ and $B^c = (\mu^p_{B^c}, \mu^n_{B^c})$ is defined as $\mu^p_{B^c}(xy) = \mu^p_A(x) \wedge \mu^p_A(y) - \mu^p_B(xy)$ and $\mu^n_{B^c}(xy) = \mu^n_A(x) \vee \mu^n_A(y) - \mu^n_B(xy)$.

Definition 1.31 The **complement** of a strong bipolar fuzzy graph $G = (A, B)$, on a non-empty set X, is a strong bipolar fuzzy graph $G^c = (A^c, B^c)$ on X such that $A^c = A$ and $B^c = (\mu^p_{B^c}, \mu^n_{B^c})$ is defined as

$$\mu^p_{B^c}(xy) = \begin{cases} 0 & \text{if } \mu^p_B(xy) > 0, \\ \mu^p_A(x) \wedge \mu^p_A(y) & \text{if } \mu^p_B(xy) = 0, \end{cases}$$

$$\mu^n_{B^c}(xy) = \begin{cases} 0 & \text{if } \mu^n_B(xy) < 0, \\ \mu^n_A(x) \vee \mu^n_A(y) & \text{if } \mu^n_B(xy) = 0. \end{cases}$$

Example 1.14 Consider a bipolar fuzzy graph $G = (A, B)$ on $X = \{a, b, c\}$ as shown in Fig. 1.17. The complement of G is given in Fig. 1.18.

Fig. 1.17 Bipolar fuzzy graph G

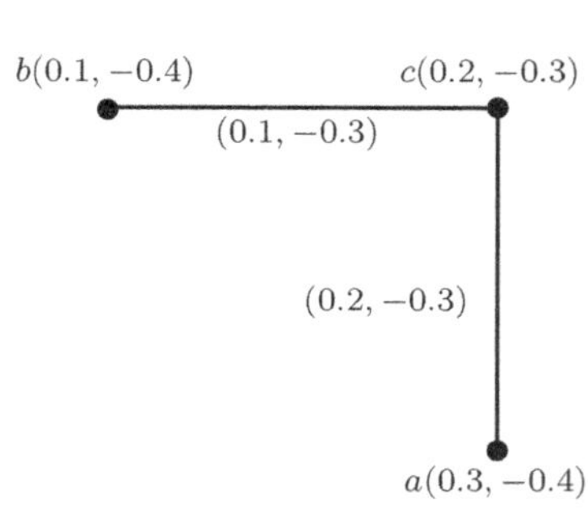

Fig. 1.18 Complement of G

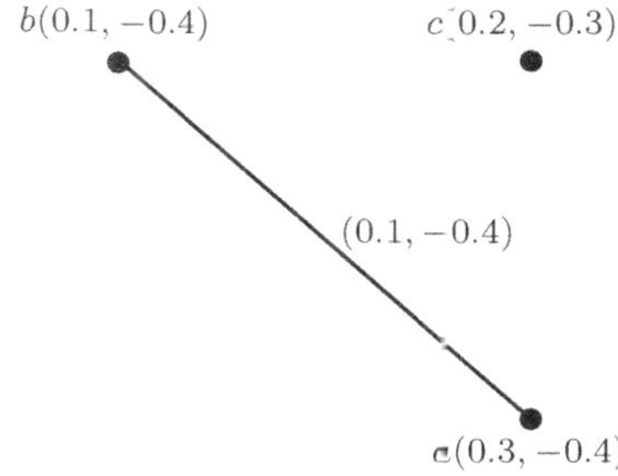

Proposition 1.10 *If G_1 and G_2 are strong bipolar fuzzy graphs, then $G_1 \Box G_2$, $G_1 \circ G_2$, $G_1 \times G_2$, $G_1 \boxtimes G_2$ and $G_1 \bullet G_2$ are strong bipolar fuzzy graphs.*

Remark 1.2 The union of two strong bipolar fuzzy graphs is not necessarily a strong bipolar fuzzy graph as it can be seen in Example 1.15.

Example 1.15 Let G_1 and G_2 be two strong bipolar fuzzy graphs on $X = \{a, b, c\}$. The union $G_1 \cup G_2$ shown in Fig. 1.19 is not a strong bipolar fuzzy graph.

Proposition 1.11 *If $G_1 \Box G_2$ is a strong bipolar fuzzy graph, then at least one of G_1 or G_2 must be strong.*

Proof Suppose that $G_1 = (A_1, B_1)$ and $G_2 = (A_2, B_2)$ are not strong bipolar fuzzy graphs. Then there exist $x_1y_1 \in E_1$ and $x_2y_2 \in E_2$ such that

$$\mu^p_{B_1}(x_1y_1) < \mu^p_{A_1}(x_1) \wedge \mu^p_{A_1}(y_1),\ \mu^p_{B_2}(x_1y_1) < \mu^p_{A_2}(x_2) \wedge \mu^p_{A_2}(y_2),$$

$$\mu^n_{B_1}(x_1y_1) > \mu^n_{A_1}(x_1) \vee \mu^n_{A_1}(y_1),\ \mu^n_{B_2}(x_1y_1) > \mu^n_{A_2}(x_2) \vee \mu^n_{A_2}(y_2).$$

Assume that $\mu^p_{B_2}(x_2y_2) \leq \mu^p_{B_1}(x_1y_1) < \mu^p_{A_1}(x_1) \wedge \mu^p_{A_1}(y_1) \leq \mu^p_{A_1}(x_1)$ and $E = \{(x, x_2)(x, y_2) | x \in X_1, x_2y_2 \in E_2\} \cup \{(x_1, z)(y_1, z) | z \in X_2, x_1y_1 \in E_1\}$. Consider $(x, x_2)(x, y_2) \in X_1 \times X_2$ such that $x \in X_1$ and $x_2y_2 \in X_2$, then

$$\mu^p_{B_1 \Box B_2}((x, x_2)(x, y_2)) = \mu^p_{A_1}(x) \wedge \mu^p_{B_2}(x_2y_2) < \mu^p_{A_1}(x) \wedge \mu^p_{A_2}(x_2) \wedge \mu^p_{A_2}(y_2),$$

$$\mu^p_{A_1 \Box A_2}(x, x_2) = \mu^p_{A_1}(x) \wedge \mu^p_{A_2}(x_2),\ \mu^p_{A_1 \Box A_2}(x, y_2) = \mu^p_{A_1}(x) \wedge \mu^p_{A_2}(y_2),$$

$$\Rightarrow \mu^p_{A_1 \Box A_2}(x, x_2) \wedge \mu^p_{A_1 \Box A_2}(x, y_2) = \mu^p_{A_1}(x) \wedge \mu^p_{A_2}(x_2) \wedge \mu^p_{A_2}(y_2),$$

$$\Rightarrow \mu^p_{B_1 \Box B_2}((x, x_2)(x, y_2)) < \mu^p_{A_1 \Box A_2}(x, x_2) \wedge \mu^p_{A_1 \Box A_2}(x, y_2).$$

Similarly, it can be easily shown that $\mu^n_{B_1 \Box B_2}((x, x_2)(x, y_2)) > \max(\mu^n_{A \Box A_2}(x, x_2), \mu^n_{A_1 \Box A_2}(x, y_2))$. That is, $G_1 \Box G_2$ is not a strong bipolar fuzzy graph, a contradiction.

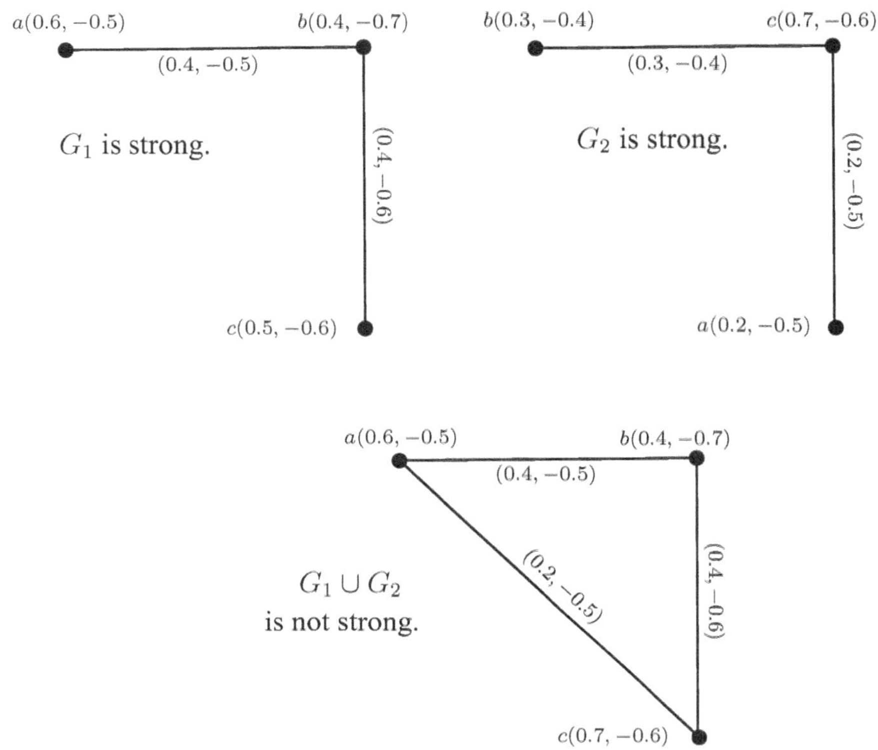

Fig. 1.19 Union of strong bipolar fuzzy graphs

Hence if $G_1 \square G_2$ is strong bipolar fuzzy graph, then at least one of G_1 or G_2 must be strong. □

Proposition 1.12 *If $G_1 \circ G_2$ is a strong bipolar fuzzy graph, then at least one of G_1 or G_2 must be strong.*

1.3 Isomorphism of Bipolar Fuzzy Graphs

In this section, the concept of isomorphism in bipolar fuzzy graphs is studied with certain properties which remain invariant between isomorphic bipolar fuzzy graphs.

Definition 1.32 Let $G_1 = (A_1, B_1)$ and $G_2 = (A_2, B_2)$ be two bipolar fuzzy graphs on X_1 and X_2, respectively. A **homomorphism** of bipolar fuzzy graphs G_1 and G_2, written as G_1 is homomorphic to G_2, is a mapping $f : X_1 \to X_2$ that satisfies

1. $\mu^p_{A_1}(x_1) \leq \mu^p_{A_2}(f(x_1))$, $\mu^n_{A_1}(x_1) \geq \mu^n_{A_2}(f(x_1))$, for all $x_1 \in X_1$
2. $\mu^p_{B_1}(x_1y_1) \leq \mu^p_{B_2}(f(x_1)f(y_1))$, $\mu^n_{B_1}(x_1y_1) \geq \mu^n_{B_2}(f(x_1)f(y_1))$, for all $x_1, y_1 \in X_1$.

Definition 1.33 A **weak isomorphism** of bipolar fuzzy graphs G_1 and G_2 is a bijective homomorphism $f : X_1 \rightarrow X_2$ that satisfies

$$\mu^p_{A_1}(x_1) = \mu^p_{A_2}(f(x_1)), \quad \mu^n_{A_1}(x_1) = \mu^n_{A_2}(f(x_1)), \quad \text{for all } x_1 \in X_1$$

Definition 1.34 A bijective homomorphism $f : X_1 \rightarrow X_2$ is called a **co-weak isomorphism** from a bipolar fuzzy graph G_1 to a bipolar fuzzy graph G_2 if it satisfies

$$\mu^p_{B_1}(x_1y_1) = \mu^p_{B_2}(f(x_1)f(y_1)), \quad \mu^n_{B_1}(x_1y_1) = \mu^n_{B_2}(f(x_1)f(y_1)),$$
$$\text{for all } x_1, y_1 \in X_1.$$

Definition 1.35 Let $G_1 = (A_1, B_1)$ and $G_2 = (A_2, B_2)$ be two bipolar fuzzy graphs on X_1 and X_2, respectively. An **isomorphism** of bipolar fuzzy graphs G_1 and G_2, written as $G_1 \cong G_2$, is a bijective mapping $f : X_1 \rightarrow X_2$ that satisfies

1. $\mu^p_{A_1}(x_1) = \mu^p_{A_2}(f(x_1))$, $\mu^n_{A_1}(x_1) = \mu^n_{A_2}(f(x_1))$, for all $x_1 \in X_1$
2. $\mu^p_{B_1}(x_1y_1) = \mu^p_{B_2}(f(x_1)f(y_1))$, $\mu^n_{B_1}(x_1y_1) = \mu^n_{B_2}(f(x_1)f(y_1))$, for all $x_1, y_1 \in X_1$.

Remark 1.3
1. If $G_1 = G_2 = G$, then the homomorphism f over itself is called an **endomorphism**. An isomorphism f over G is called an **automorphism**.
2. Let $A = (\mu^p_A, \mu^n_A)$ be a bipolar fuzzy graph with an underlying set X. Let Aut(G) be the set of all automorphisms $f : X \rightarrow X$ of G. Let $e : X \rightarrow X$ be a map defined by $e(x) = x$, for all $x \in X$. Clearly, $e \in Aut(G)$.
3. If $G_1 = G_2$, then the weak and co-weak isomorphisms actually become isomorphisms.
4. If $f : X_1 \rightarrow X_2$ is a bijective map then $f^{-1} : X_2 \rightarrow X_1$ is also bijective map.

Example 1.16 Consider bipolar fuzzy graphs $G = (A, B)$ and $G^{'} = (A^{'}, B^{'})$ on $X = \{a, b, c, d, e, f\}$ and $X' = \{a', b', c', d', e', f'\}$ as shown in Figs. 1.20 and 1.21, respectively. Define a mapping $f : X \rightarrow X^{'}$ by $f(a) = c^{'}$, $f(c) = a^{'}$, $f(b) = d^{'}$, $f(d) = b^{'}$, $f(e) = e^{'}$ and $f(f) = f^{'}$. Clearly, $A(a) = (0.2, -0.3) = A^{'}(c^{'}) = A'(f(a))$, $A(b) = (0.5, -0.4) = A^{'}(d^{'}) = A^{'}(f(b))$ $A(c) = (0.5, -0.6) = A^{'}(a^{'}) = A^{'}(f(c))$, $B(ab) = (0.2, -0.3) = B^{'}(c^{'}d^{'}) = B^{'}(f(a)f(b))$. Similarly, $A(x) = A^{'}(f(x))$ and $B(xy) = B^{'}(f(x)f(y))$, for all $x, y \in X$. Hence G and $G^{'}$ are isomorphic bipolar fuzzy graphs.

Definition 1.36 A bipolar fuzzy graph G is called **self-complementary** if $G^c \cong G$.

Theorem 1.1 *Let $G = (A, B)$ be a self-complementary bipolar fuzzy graph on X, then*

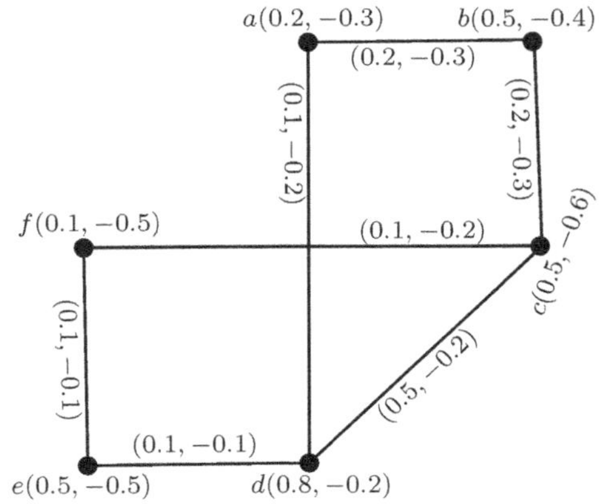

Fig. 1.20 Bipolar fuzzy graph G

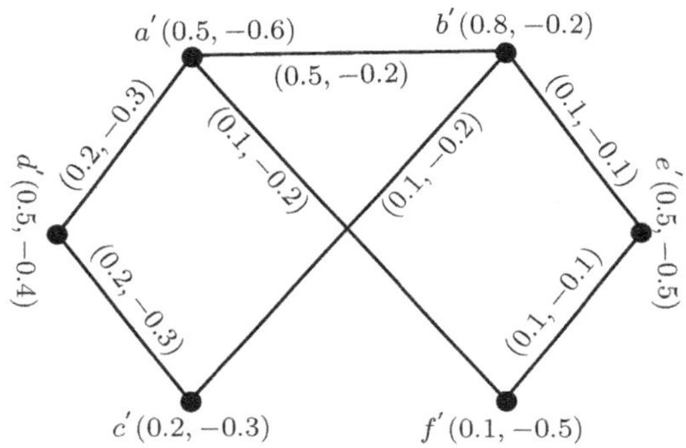

Fig. 1.21 Bipolar fuzzy graph G'

$$\sum_{x\neq y}\mu_B^p(xy)=\frac{1}{2}\sum_{x\neq y}\mu_A^p(x)\wedge\mu_A^p(y),\qquad \sum_{x\neq y}\mu_B^n(xy)=\frac{1}{2}\sum_{x\neq y}\mu_A^n(x)\vee\mu_A^n(y).$$

Proof Since $G=(A,B)$ is a self-complementary bipolar fuzzy graph, there exists an isomorphism $f:X\to X$ from G to $G^c=(A^c,B^c)$ such that

1. $\mu_A^p(x)=\mu_{A^c}^p(f(x)),\ \ \mu_A^n(x)=\mu_{A^c}^n(f(x)),$ for all $x\in X$
2. $\mu_B^p(xy)=\mu_{B^c}^p(f(x)f(y)),\ \ \mu_B^n(xy)=\mu_{B^c}^n(f(x)f(y)),$ for all $x,y\in X$.

Now by Definition 1.30,

$$\begin{aligned}
\mu_{B^c}^p(f(x)f(y))&=\mu_{A^c}^p(f(x))\wedge\mu_{A^c}^p(f(y))-\mu_B^p(f(x)f(y))\\
\Rightarrow\ \mu_B^p(xy)&=\mu_A^p(x)\wedge\mu_A^p(y)-\mu_B^p(f(x)f(y))\\
\Rightarrow\ \sum_{x\neq y}\mu_B^p(xy)+\sum_{x\neq y}\mu_B^p(f(x)f(y))&=\sum_{x\neq y}\mu_A^p(x)\wedge\mu_A^p(y)\\
\Rightarrow\ 2\sum_{x\neq y}\mu_B^p(xy)&=\sum_{x\neq y}\mu_A^p(x)\wedge\mu_A^p(y)
\end{aligned}$$

$$\Rightarrow \sum_{x\neq y} \mu_B^p(xy) = \frac{1}{2}\sum_{x\neq y} \mu_A^p(x) \wedge \mu_A^p(y).$$

Similarly,

$$\begin{aligned}
\mu_{B^c}^n(f(x)f(y)) &= \mu_{A^c}^n(f(x)) \vee \mu_{A^c}^n(f(y)) - \mu_B^n(f(x)f(y)) \\
\Rightarrow \mu_B^n(xy) &= \mu_A^n(x) \vee \mu_A^n(y) - \mu_B^n(f(x)f(y)) \\
\Rightarrow \sum_{x\neq y} \mu_B^n(xy) + \sum_{x\neq y} \mu_B^n(f(x)f(y)) &= \sum_{x\neq y} \mu_A^n(x) \vee \mu_A^n(y) \\
\Rightarrow 2\sum_{x\neq y} \mu_B^n(xy) &= \sum_{x\neq y} \mu_A^n(x) \vee \mu_A^n(y) \\
\Rightarrow \sum_{x\neq y} \mu_B^n(xy) &= \frac{1}{2}\sum_{x\neq y} \mu_A^n(x) \vee \mu_A^n(y).
\end{aligned}$$

The proof is complete. □

Theorem 1.2 *Let $G = (A, B)$ be a bipolar graph such that for all $x, y \in X$,*

$$\mu_B^p(xy) = \frac{1}{2}(\mu_A^p(x) \wedge \mu_A^p(y)) \ \ and \ \ \mu_B^n(xy) = \frac{1}{2}(\mu_A^n(x) \vee \mu_A^n(y)),$$

then G is a self-complementary bipolar fuzzy graph.

Proof Let $G^c = (A^c, B^c)$ be the complement of a bipolar fuzzy graph $G = (A, B)$, then by Definition 1.30,

$$\begin{aligned}
\mu_{B^c}^p(xy) &= \mu_A^p(x) \wedge \mu_A^p(y) - \mu_B^p(xy), & \mu_{B^c}^n(xy) &= \mu_A^n(x) \vee \mu_A^n(y) - \mu_B^n(xy), \\
\mu_{B^c}^p(xy) &= \mu_A^p(x) \wedge \mu_A^p(y) - \frac{1}{2}(\mu_A^p(x) \wedge \mu_A^p(y)), & \mu_{B^c}^n(xy) &= \mu_A^n(x) \vee \mu_A^n(y) - \frac{1}{2}(\mu_A^n(x) \vee \mu_A^n(y)), \\
\mu_{B^c}^p(xy) &= \frac{1}{2}(\mu_A^p(x) \wedge \mu_A^p(y)), & \mu_{B^c}^n(xy) &= \frac{1}{2}(\mu_A^n(x) \vee \mu_A^n(y)), \\
\mu_{B^c}^p(xy) &= \mu_B^p(xy). & \mu_{B^c}^n(xy) &= \mu_B^n(xy).
\end{aligned}$$

It follows that $B = B^c$, that is, G is a self-complementary bipolar fuzzy graph. □

Proposition 1.13 *Let G_1 and G_2 be strong bipolar fuzzy graphs, then $G_1 \cong G_2$ if and only if $G_1^c \cong G_2^c$.*

Proof Assume that G_1 and G_2 are isomorphic to each other, then there exists a bijective map $f : X_1 \to X_2$ satisfying

$$\mu_{A_1}^p(x) = \mu_{A_2}^p(f(x)),\ \mu_{A_1}^n(x) = \mu_{A_2}^n(f(x)), \quad \text{for all } x \in X_1,$$

$$\mu_{B_1}^p(xy) = \mu_{B_2}^p(f(x)f(y)),\ \mu_{B_1}^n(xy) = \mu_{B_2}^n(f(x)f(y)), \quad \text{for all } xy \in E_1.$$

Case 1. If for $x, y \in X_1$, $B_1(xy) = (0, 0)$, then $B_2(f(x)f(y)) = (0, 0)$. By Definition 1.30,

$$\mu^P_{B_1^c}(xy) = \mu^P_{A_1}(x) \wedge \mu^P_{A_1}(y) = \mu^P_{A_2}(f(x)) \wedge \mu^P_{A_2}(f(y)) = \mu^P_{B_2^c}(f(x)f(y)),$$

$$\mu^n_{B_1^c}(xy) = \mu^n_{A_1}(x) \vee \mu^n_{A_1}(y) = \mu^n_{A_2}(f(x)) \vee \mu^n_{A_2}(f(y)) = \mu^n_{B_2^c}(f(x)f(y)), \quad \text{forall } xy \in E_1.$$

Case 2. If for $x, y \in X_1$, $B_1(xy) \in (0, 1] \times [-1, 0)$, then $B_2(f(x)f(y)) \in (0, 1] \times [-1, 0)$. By Definition 1.30, $B_1^c(xy) = (0, 0) = B_2^c(f(x)f(y))$. Hence $G_1^c \cong G_2^c$.

Conversely, let $G_1^c \cong G_2^c$, then there exists a bijective mapping $g : X_1 \to X_2$ which satisfies

$$\mu^P_{A_1^c}(x) = \mu^P_{A_2^c}(g(x)), \ \mu^n_{A_1^c}(x) = \mu^n_{A_2^c}(g(x)), \quad \text{for all } x \in X_1,$$
$$\mu^P_{B_1^c}(xy) = \mu^P_{B_2^c}(f(x)f(y)), \ \mu^n_{B_1^c}(xy) = \mu^n_{B_2^c}(f(x)f(y)), \quad \text{for all } xy \in E_1.$$

Case 1. If for $x, y \in X_1$, $B_1(xy) = (0, 0)$, then $B_1^c(xy) \in (0, 1] \times [-1, 0)$. It implies that $B_2^c(f(x)f(y)) \in (0, 1] \times [-1, 0)$. By Definition 1.30, $B_2(f(x)f(y)) = (0, 0)$.

Case 2. If $B_1(xy) \in (0, 1] \times [-1, 0)$, then by Definition 1.30, $B_1^c(xy) = (0, 0) = B_2^c(f(x)f(y)) = (0, 0)$. Thus we have

$$\begin{aligned}
\mu^P_{B_2}(f(x)f(y)) &= \mu^P_{A_2}(f(x)) \wedge \mu^P_{A_2}(f(y)) \\
&= \mu^P_{A_2}(f(x)) \wedge \mu^P_{A_2}(f(y)) \\
&= \mu^P_{A_2^c}(f(x)) \wedge \mu^P_{A_2^c}(f(y)) \\
&= \mu^P_{A_1^c}(x) \wedge \mu^P_{A_1^c}(y) \\
&= \mu^P_{A_1}(x) \wedge \mu^P_{A_1}(y) \\
&= \mu^P_{B_1}(xy), \\
\mu^n_{B_2}(f(x)f(y)) &= \mu^n_{A_2}(f(x)) \vee \mu^n_{A_2}(f(y)) \\
&= \mu^n_{A_2}(f(x)) \vee \mu^n_{A_2}(f(y)) \\
&= \mu^n_{A_2^c}(f(x)) \vee \mu^n_{A_2^c}(f(y)) \\
&= \mu^n_{A_1^c}(x) \vee \mu^n_{A_1^c}(y) \\
&= \mu^n_{A_1}(x) \vee \mu^n_{A_1}(y) \\
&= \mu^n_{B_1}(xy).
\end{aligned}$$

It follows that $G_1 \cong G_2$. □

Proposition 1.14 *Let G_1 and G_2 be strong bipolar fuzzy graphs. If there is a weak isomorphism between G_1 and G_2, then there is a weak isomorphism between G_1^c and G_2^c.*

Proof Let f be a weak isomorphism between G_1 and G_2 then $f : X_1 \to X_2$ defined by $f(x_1) = x_2$, for all $x_1 \in X_1$, is a bijective map that satisfies

$$\mu^p_{A_1}(x_1) = \mu^p_{A_2}(f(x_1)),\ \mu^n_{A_1}(x_1) = \mu^n_{A_2}(f(x_1)), \quad \text{for all } x_1 \in X_1,$$

$$\mu^p_{B_1}(x_1y_1) \le \mu^p_{B_2}(f(x_1)f(y_1)),\ \mu^n_{B_1}(x_1y_1) \ge \mu^n_{B_2}(f(x_1)f(y_1)), \quad \text{for all } x_1y_1 \in E_1.$$

Since $f : X_1 \to X_2$ is a bijective map, $f^{-1} : X_2 \to X_1$ is also bijective map such that $f^{-1}(x_2) = x_1$, for all $x_2 \in X_2$. Thus $\mu^p_{A_1}(f^{-1}(x_2)) = \mu^p_{A_2}(x_2)$, $\mu^n_{A_1}(f^{-1}(x_2)) = \mu^n_{A_2}(x_2)$, for all $x_2 \in X_2$.

Case 1. If for $x, y \in X_1$, $B_1(xy) = (0, 0)$, then by Definition 1.30 $\mu^p_{B_1^c}(f^{-1}(x_2) f^{-1}(y_2)) = \mu^p_{B_1^c}(x_1y_1) = \mu^p_{A_1}(x_1) \wedge \mu^p_{A_1}(y_1) = \mu^p_{A_2}(f(x_1)) \wedge \mu^p_{A_2}(f(y_1)) \ge \mu^p_{B_2^c} (f(x_1)f(y_1)) = \mu^p_{B_2^c}(x_2y_2)$ because,

1. If $\mu^p_{B_2}(f(x_1)f(y_1)) = 0$, then $\mu^p_{B_2^c}(f(x_1)f(y_1)) = \mu^p_{A_2}(f(x_1)) \wedge \mu^p_{A_2}(f(y_1))$.
2. If $\mu^p_{B_2}(f(x_1)f(y_1)) > 0$, then $\mu^p_{B_2^c}(f(x_1)f(y_1)) = 0 < \mu^p_{A_2}(f(x_1)) \wedge \mu^p_{A_2} (f(y_1))$.

Analogously, it can be proved that $\mu^n_{B_1^c}(f^{-1}(x_2)f^{-1}(y_2)) \le \mu^n_{B_2^c}(x_1y_1)$.

Case 2. If for $x, y \in X_1$, $B_1(xy) \ne (0, 0)$, then on the same lines as case 1, it can be proved that $\mu^p_{B_2^c}(x_2y_2) \le \mu^p_{B_1^c}\left(f^{-1}(x_2)f^{-1}(y_2)\right)$ and $\mu^n_{B_2^c}(x_2y_2) \ge \mu^n_{B_1^c} \left(f^{-1}(x_2)f^{-1}(y_2)\right)$. Thus, $f^{-1} : X_2 \to X_1$ is a bijective map which is a weak isomorphism between G_1^c and G_2^c. The proof of converse part is straightforward. □

Proposition 1.15 *Let G_1 and G_2 be strong bipolar fuzzy graphs. If there is a co-weak isomorphism between G_1 and G_2, then there is a homomorphism between G_1^c and G_2^c.*

Theorem 1.3 *Let $G_1 = (A_1, B_1)$ and $G_2 = (A_2, B_2)$ be two bipolar fuzzy graphs on X_1 and X_2, respectively, such that $X_1 \cap X_2 = \emptyset$, then*

1. $(G_1 + G_2)^c \cong G_1^c \cup G_2^c$,
2. $(G_1 \cup G_2)^c \cong G_1^c + G_2^c$.

Proof 1. To prove that $(G_1 + G_2)^c$ and $G_1^c \cup G_2^c$ are isomorphic to each other, it is to be shown that the identity mapping $I : X_1 \cup X_2 \to X_1 \cup X_2$ is the required isomorphism, that is, for all $x, y \in X_1 \cup X_2$, $(A_1 + A_2)^c(x) = A_1^c(x) \cup A_2^c(x)$ and $(B_1 + B_2)^c(xy) = B_1^c(xy) \cup B_2^c(xy)$.

$$\begin{aligned}(A_1 + A_2)^c(x) = (A_1 + A_2)(x) &= (A_1 \cup A_2)(x)\\ &= (\mu^p_{A_1}(x) \vee \mu^p_{A_2}(x), \mu^n_{A_1}(x) \wedge \mu^n_{A_2}(x))\\ &= (\mu^p_{A_1^c}(x) \vee \mu^p_{A_2^c}(x), \mu^n_{A_1^c}(x) \wedge \mu^n_{A_2^c}(x))\end{aligned}$$

$$= (A_1^c \cup A_2^c)(x),$$

$$\begin{aligned}
\mu^p_{(B_1+B_2)^c}(xy) &= \mu^p_{A_1+A_2}(x) \wedge \mu^p_{A_1+A_2}(y) - \mu^p_{B_1+B_2}(xy) \\
&= \begin{cases} \mu^p_{A_1\cup A_2}(x) \wedge \mu^p_{A_1\cup A_2}(y) - \mu^p_{B_1\cup B_2}(xy), & \text{if } xy \in E_1 \cup E_2 \\ \mu^p_{A_1\cup A_2}(x) \wedge \mu^p_{A_1\cup A_2}(y) - \mu^p_{A_1}(x) \wedge \mu^p_{A_2}(y), & \text{if } xy \in E' \text{ and } x \in X_1, y \in X_2 \end{cases} \\
&= \begin{cases} \mu^p_{A_1}(x) \wedge \mu^p_{A_1}(y) - \mu^p_{B_1}(xy), & \text{if } xy \in E_1 \\ \mu^p_{A_2}(x) \wedge \mu^p_{A_2}(y) - \mu^p_{B_2}(xy), & \text{if } xy \in E_2 \\ \mu^p_{A_1}(x) \wedge \mu^p_{A_2}(y) - \mu^p_{A_1}(x) \wedge \mu^p_{A_2}(y), & \text{if } xy \in E' \text{ and } x \in X_1, y \in X_2 \end{cases} \\
&= \begin{cases} \mu^p_{B_1^c}(xy), & \text{if } xy \in E_1 \\ \mu^p_{B_2^c}(xy), & \text{if } xy \in E_2 \\ 0, & \text{if } xy \in E' \text{ and } x \in X_1, y \in X_2 \end{cases} \\
&= \mu^p_{B_1^c\cup B_2^c}(xy),
\end{aligned}$$

$$\begin{aligned}
\mu^n_{(B_1+B_2)^c}(xy) &= \mu^n_{A_1+A_2}(x) \vee \mu^n_{A_1+A_2}(y) - \mu^n_{B_1+B_2}(xy) \\
&= \begin{cases} \mu^n_{A_1\cup A_2}(x) \vee \mu^n_{A_1\cup A_2}(y) - \mu^n_{B_1\cup B_2}(xy), & \text{if } xy \in E_1 \cup E_2 \\ \mu^n_{A_1\cup A_2}(x) \vee \mu^n_{A_1\cup A_2}(y) - \mu^n_{A_1}(x) \vee \mu^n_{A_2}(y), & \text{if } xy \in E' \text{ and } x \in X_1, y \in X_2 \end{cases} \\
&= \begin{cases} \mu^n_{A_1}(x) \vee \mu^n_{A_1}(y) - \mu^n_{B_1}(xy), & \text{if } xy \in E_1 \\ \mu^n_{A_2}(x) \vee \mu^n_{A_2}(y) - \mu^n_{B_2}(xy), & \text{if } xy \in E_2 \\ \mu^n_{A_1}(x) \vee \mu^n_{A_2}(y) - \mu^n_{A_1}(x) \vee \mu^n_{A_2}(y), & \text{if } xy \in E' \text{ and } x \in X_1, y \in X_2 \end{cases} \\
&= \begin{cases} \mu^n_{B_1^c}(xy), & \text{if } xy \in E_1 \\ \mu^n_{B_2^c}(xy), & \text{if } xy \in E_2 \\ 0, & \text{if } xy \in E' \text{ and } x \in X_1, y \in X_2 \end{cases} \\
&= \mu^n_{B_1^c\cup B_2^c}(xy).
\end{aligned}$$

2. To prove that $(G_1 \cup G_2)^c$ and $G_1^c + G_2^c$ are isomorphic to each other, it is to be shown that $(A_1 \cup A_2)^c(x) = A_1^c(x) + A_2^c(x)$ and $(B_1 \cup B_2)^c(xy) = B_1^c(xy) + B_2^c(xy)$.

$$\begin{aligned}
(A_1 \cup A_2)^c(x) = &= (A_1 \cup A_2)(x) \\
&= (\mu^p_{A_1}(x) \vee \mu^p_{A_2}(x), \mu^n_{A_1}(x) \wedge \mu^n_{A_2}(x)) \\
&= (\mu^p_{A_1^c}(x) \vee \mu^p_{A_2^c}(x), \mu^n_{A_1^c}(x) \wedge \mu^n_{A_2^c}(x)) \\
&= (A_1^c \cup A_2^c)(x) \\
&= (A_1^c + A_2^c)(x)
\end{aligned}$$

$$\mu^p_{(B_1\cup B_2)^c}(xy) = \mu^p_{A_1\cup A_2}(x) \wedge \mu^p_{A_1\cup A_2}(y) - \mu^p_{B_1\cup B_2}(xy)$$

$$= \begin{cases} \mu^p_{A_1}(x) \wedge \mu^p_{A_1}(y) - \mu^p_{B_1}(xy), & \text{if } xy \in E_1 \\ \mu^p_{A_2}(x) \wedge \mu^p_{A_2}(y) - \mu^p_{B_2}(xy), & \text{if } xy \in E_2 \\ \mu^p_{A_1}(x) \wedge \mu^p_{A_2}(y) - 0, & \text{if } x \in X_1, y \in X_2 \end{cases}$$

$$= \begin{cases} \mu^p_{B_1^c}(xy), & \text{if } xy \in E_1 \\ \mu^p_{B_2^c}(xy), & \text{if } xy \in E_2 \\ \mu^p_{A_1^c}(x) \wedge \mu^p_{A_2^c}(y), & \text{if } x \in X_1, y \in X_2 \end{cases}$$

$$\mu^p_{(B_1 \cup B_2)^c}(xy) = \mu^p_{B_1^c + B_2^c}(xy),$$

$$\mu^n_{(B_1 \cup B_2)^c}(xy) = \mu^n_{A_1 \cup A_2}(x) \vee \mu^n_{A_1 \cup A_2}(y) - \mu^n_{B_1 \cup B_2}(xy)$$

$$= \begin{cases} \mu^n_{A_1}(x) \vee \mu^n_{A_1}(y) - \mu^n_{B_1}(xy), & \text{if } xy \in E_1 \\ \mu^n_{A_2}(x) \vee \mu^n_{A_2}(y) - \mu^n_{B_2}(xy), & \text{if } xy \in E_2 \\ \mu^n_{A_1}(x) \vee \mu^n_{A_2}(y) - 0, & \text{if } x \in X_1, y \in X_2 \end{cases}$$

$$= \begin{cases} \mu^n_{B_1^c}(xy), & \text{if } xy \in E_1 \\ \mu^n_{B_2^c}(xy), & \text{if } xy \in E_2 \\ \mu^n_{A_1^c}(x) \vee \mu^n_{A_2^c}(y), & \text{if } x \in X_1, y \in X_2 \end{cases}$$

$$\mu^n_{(B_1 \cup B_2)^c}(xy) = \mu^n_{B_1^c + B_2^c}(xy).$$

The proof is complete. □

Definition 1.37 If $G = (A, B)$ is a bipolar fuzzy graph on a non-empty set X, then the **order** of G is denoted by $O(G)$ and defined as

$$O(G) = \sum_{x \in X} \left(\mu^p_A(x), \mu^n_A(x) \right).$$

The **size** of a bipolar fuzzy graph G is denoted by $S(G)$ and defined as

$$S(G) = \sum_{xy \in E} \left(\mu^p_B(xy), \mu^n_B(xy) \right).$$

Theorem 1.4 *The order and size of isomorphic bipolar fuzzy graphs are the same.*

Proof Let $G_1 = (A_1, B_1)$ and $G_2 = (A_2, B_2)$ be two bipolar fuzzy graphs on X_1 and X_2, respectively. Let $f : G_1 \to G_2$ be an isomorphism from G_1 to G_2, then

$$O(G_1) = \sum_{x_1 \in X_1} \left(\mu^p_{A_1}(x_1), \mu^n_{A_1}(x_1) \right) = \sum_{x_1 \in X_1} \left(\mu^p_{A_2}(f(x_1)), \mu^n_{A_2}(f(x_1)) \right)$$

$$= \sum_{x_2 \in X_2} \left(\mu^p_{A_2}(x_2), \mu^n_{A_2}(x_2) \right) = O(G_2).$$

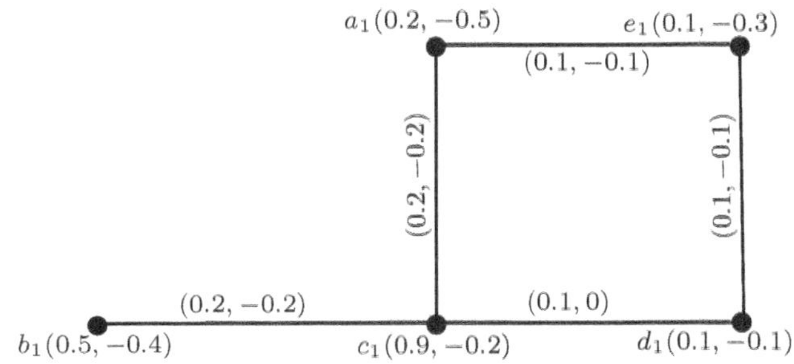

Fig. 1.22 Bipolar fuzzy graph G_3

Fig. 1.23 Bipolar fuzzy graph G_4

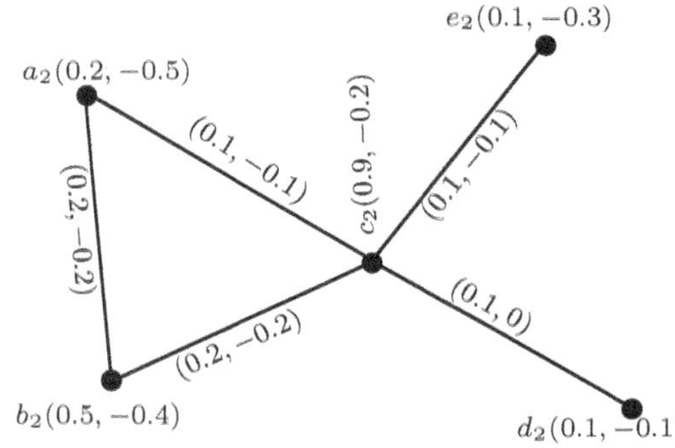

$$
\begin{aligned}
S(G_1) &= \sum_{x_1y_1 \in E_1} \left(\mu^p_{B_1}(x_1y_1), \mu^n_{B_1}(x_1y_1)\right) \\
&= \sum_{x_1y_1 \in E_1} \left(\mu^p_{B_1}(f(x_1)f(y_1)), \mu^n_{B_1}(f(x_1)f(y_1))\right) \\
&= \sum_{x_2y_2 \in E_2} \left(\mu^p_{B_2}(x_2y_2), \mu^n_{B_2}(x_2y_2)\right) = S(G_2).
\end{aligned}
$$

The proof is complete. □

Remark 1.4 The converse of Theorem 1.4 is not true in general as it can be seen in Example 1.17.

Example 1.17 Consider bipolar fuzzy graphs $G_3 = (A_3, B_3)$ and $G_4 = (A_4, B_4)$ as shown in Figs. 1.22 and 1.23. Clearly $O(G_3) = O(G_4) = (1.8, -1.5)$ and $S(G_1) = S(G_4) = (0.7, -0.6)$. The order and size of G_3 and G_4 are the same but these are not isomorphic to each other.

Remark 1.5 1. If bipolar fuzzy graphs are weak isomorphic to each other, then orders are the same but the converse of this statement is not true in general.

2. If bipolar fuzzy graphs are co-weak isomorphic to each other, then sizes are the same but the converse of this statement is not true in general.

Definition 1.38 Let $G = (A, B)$ be a bipolar fuzzy graph on a non-empty set X then the **degree** of any vertex $x \in X$ is a pair $\deg(x) = (\deg^p(x), \deg^n(x))$, where $\deg^p(x) = \sum_{u \in X} \mu_B^p(xu)$ and $\deg^n(x) = \sum_{u \in X} \mu_B^n(xu)$.

Theorem 1.5 *If G_1 and G_2 are isomorphic bipolar fuzzy graphs, then the degrees of corresponding vertices are preserved.*

Proof Let $G_1 = (A_1, B_1)$ and $G_2 = (A_2, B_2)$ be two bipolar fuzzy graphs on X_1 and X_2, respectively. Let $f : X_1 \to X_2$ be an isomorphism of bipolar fuzzy graphs, then by Definition 1.38

$$\begin{aligned} deg(x_1) &= \sum_{y_1 \in X_1} (\mu_{B_1}^p(x_1y_1), \mu_1^n B(x_1y_1)) \\ &= \sum_{y_1 \in X_1} (\mu_{B_1}^p(f(x_1)f(y_1)), \mu_1^n B(f(x_1)f(y_1))) \\ &= \sum_{y_2 \in X_2} (\mu_{B_2}^p(x_2y_2), \mu_2^n B(x_2y_2)) = deg(x_2). \end{aligned}$$

This completes the proof. □

Remark 1.6 If the degrees of vertices of bipolar fuzzy graphs are preserved, then they may not be isomorphic to each other as it can be seen in Example 1.18.

Example 1.18 Consider the example of bipolar fuzzy graphs $G_1 = (A_1, B_1)$ and $G_2 = (A_2, B_2)$ on $X_1 = \{a_1, b_1, c_1, d_1, e_1\}$ and $X_2 = \{a_2, b_2, c_2, d_2, e_2\}$ as shown in Figs. 1.24 and 1.25, respectively. Define a mapping $f : X_1 \to X_2$ by $f(a_1) = a_2$, $f(b_1) = c_2$, $f(c_1) = b_2$, $f(d_1) = d_2$ and $f(e_1) = e_2$. By routine calculations, $\deg(a_1) = (0.2, -0.2) = \deg(f(a_1))$, $\deg(b_1) = (0.3, -0.3) = \deg(c_2) = \deg(f(b_1))$. Similarly, the degrees of all the vertices are preserved. But $B_1(a_1b_1) \neq B_2(f(a_1)(b_1))$, i.e., the edges are not preserved which shows that f is not an isomorphism.

Definition 1.39 A bipolar fuzzy set $A = (\mu_A^p, \mu_A^n)$ on a semigroup S is called a **bipolar fuzzy subsemigroup** of S if it satisfies

$$\mu_A^p(xy) \geq \mu_A^p(x) \wedge \mu_A^p(y), \quad \mu_A^n(xy) \leq \mu_A^n(x) \vee \mu_A^n(y), \quad \text{for all } x, y \in S.$$

A bipolar fuzzy set $A = (\mu_A^p, \mu_A^n)$ on a group G is called a **bipolar fuzzy subgroup** of a group G if it is a bipolar fuzzy subsemigroup of G and satisfies

$$\mu_A^p(x^{-1}) = \mu_A^p(x), \quad \mu_A^n(x^{-1}) = \mu_A^n(x), \quad \text{for all } x \in G.$$

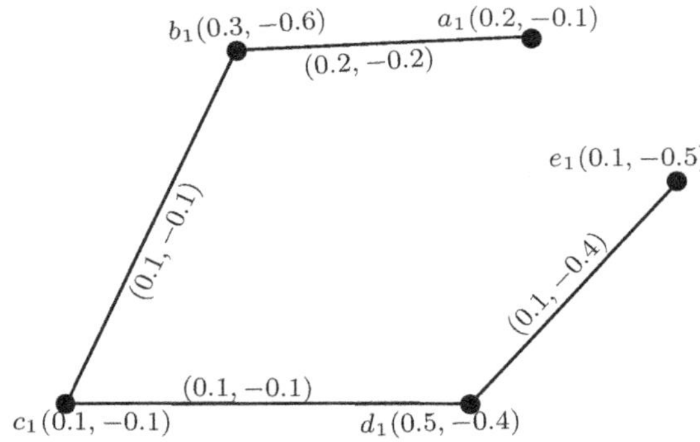

Fig. 1.24 Bipolar fuzzy graph G_1

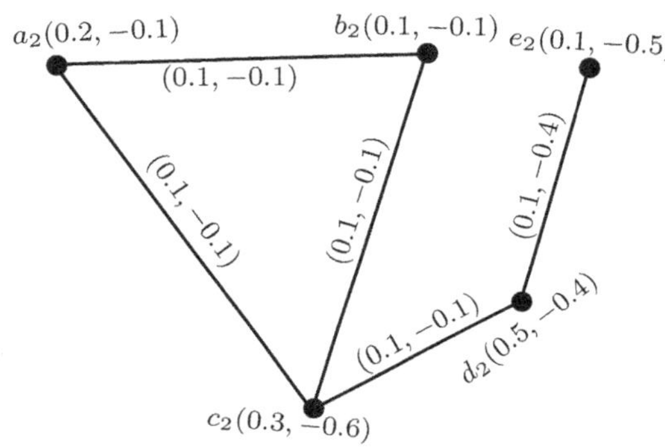

Fig. 1.25 Bipolar fuzzy graph G_2

Consider the case to associate a bipolar fuzzy group with a bipolar fuzzy graph in a natural way.

Proposition 1.16 *Let $G = (A, B)$ be a bipolar fuzzy graph and $Aut(G)$ be the set of all automorphisms of G, then $(Aut(G), \circ)$ forms a bipolar fuzzy group.*

Proof Let $\phi, \psi \in Aut(G)$ and $x, y \in X$, then

$$\begin{aligned}
\mu_B^p((\phi \circ \psi)(x)(\phi \circ \psi)(y)) &= \mu_B^p((\phi(\psi(x))(\phi(\psi))(y)) \\
&\geq \mu_B^p(\psi(x)\psi(y)) \geq \mu_B^p(xy), \\
\mu_B^n((\phi \circ \psi)(x)(\phi \circ \psi)(y)) &= \mu_B^n((\phi(\psi(x))(\phi(\psi))(y)) \\
&\leq \mu_B^n(\psi(x)\psi(y)) \leq \mu_B^n(xy). \\
\mu_B^p((\phi \circ \psi)(x)) &= \mu_B^p((\phi(\psi(x))) \geq \mu_B^p(\psi(x)) \geq \mu_B^p(x), \\
\mu_N^p((\phi \circ \psi)(x)) &= \mu_B^n((\phi(\psi(x))) \leq \mu_B^n(\psi(x)) \leq \mu_B^n(x).
\end{aligned}$$

Thus $\phi \circ \psi \in Aut(G)$, that is, $Aut(G)$ satisfies associativity under the operation $\circ$, $\phi \circ e = \phi = e \circ \phi$, $\mu_A^p(\phi^{-1}) = \mu_A^p(\phi)$, $\mu_A^n(\phi^{-1}) = \mu_A^n(\phi)$, for all $\phi \in Aut(G)$. Hence $(Aut(G), \circ)$ forms a bipolar fuzzy group. The proof is complete. □

Proposition 1.17 *Let $G = (A, B)$ be a bipolar fuzzy graph and $Aut(G)$ be the set of all automorphisms of G. Let $g = (\mu_g^P, \mu_g^n)$ be a bipolar fuzzy set on $Aut(G)$ defined by*

$$\mu_g^P(\phi) = \sup\{\mu_B^P(\phi(x)\phi(y)) \mid x, y \in X\} \text{ and}$$
$$\mu_g^n(\phi) = \inf\{\mu_B^n(\phi(x)\phi(y)) \mid x, y \in X\},$$

for all $\phi \in Aut(G)$. Then $g = (\mu_g^P, \mu_g^n)$ is a bipolar fuzzy group on $Aut(G)$.

Proposition 1.18 *Every bipolar fuzzy group has an embedding into the bipolar fuzzy group of the group of automorphisms of some bipolar fuzzy graph.*

Proposition 1.19 *The relation of isomorphism between bipolar fuzzy graphs is an equivalence relation.*

Proof Let $G_1 = (A_1, B_1)$, $G_2 = (A_2, B_2)$ and $G_3 = (A_3, B_3)$ be bipolar fuzzy graphs on non-empty sets X_1, X_2 and X_3, respectively.

1. Reflexivity: Define $I : X_1 \to X_1$ by $I(x_1) = x_1$, for all $x_1 \in X_1$. Then I is a bijective homomorphism and $A_1(x_1) = A_1(I(x_1))$ and $B_1(x_1y_1) = B_1(I(x_1)I(y_1))$, for all $x_1, y_1 \in X_1$. I is an isomorphism of a bipolar fuzzy graph to itself.
2. Symmetry: Let $f : X_1 \to X_2$ be an isomorphism defined by $f(x_1) = x_2$. Since f is a bijective mapping, $f^{-1} : X_2 \to X_1$ exists and $f^{-1}(x_2) = x_1$, for all $x_2 \in X_2$. Then,

$$A_2(x_2) = A_2(f(x_1)) = A_1(x_1) = A_1(f^{-1}(x_2)).$$
$$B_2(x_2y_2) = B_2(f(x_1)f(y_1)) = B_1(x_1y_1) = B_1(f^{-1}(x_2)f^{-1}(y_2)),$$
$$x_1, y_1 \in X_1,\ x_2, y_2 \in X_2.$$

   Hence f^{-1} is an isomorphism.
3. Transitivity: Let $f : X_1 \to X_2$ and $g : X_2 \to X_3$ be the isomorphisms from G_1 into G_2 and G_2 into G_3 defined by $f(x_1) = x_2$ and $g(x_2) = x_3$, respectively. By Definition 1.35,

$$A_1(x_1) = A_2(f(x_1)) = A_2(x_2) = A_3(g(x_2)) = A_3(g(f(x_1))) = A_3(g \circ f(x_1)),$$
$$B_1(x_1y_1) = B_2(x_2y_2) = B_3(g(x_2)g(y_2)) = B_3(g(f(x_1))g(f(y_1)))$$
$$= B_3(g \circ f(x_1)g \circ f(y_1)),$$

   where $x_1, y_1 \in X_1$, $x_2, y_2 \in X_2$ and $x_3, y_3 \in X_3$. Clearly, $g \circ f$ is an isomorphism from G_1 into G_3.

Hence isomorphism of bipolar fuzzy graphs is an equivalence relation. □

Proposition 1.20 *Let G_1, G_2 and G_3 be bipolar fuzzy graphs, then the weak isomorphism between these bipolar fuzzy graphs is a partial order relation.*

Proof The reflexivity is obvious. To prove the antisymmetry, let $f : X_1 \to X_2$ be a weak isomorphism from G_1 into G_2. Then f is a bijective map defined by $f(x_1) = x_2$, for all $x_1 \in X_1$, satisfying,

$$\mu^p_{A_1}(x_1) = \mu^p_{A_2}(f(x_1)), \quad \mu^n_{A_1}(x_1) = \mu^n_{A_2}(f(x_1)), \quad \text{for all } x_1 \in X_1,$$

$$\mu^p_{B_1}(x_1 y_1) \le \mu^p_{B_2}(f(x_1) f(y_1)), \quad \mu^n_{B_1}(x_1 y_1) \ge \mu^n_{B_2}(f(x_1) f(y_1)), \quad \text{for all } x_1 y_1 \in E_1. \tag{1.7}$$

Let $g : X_2 \to X_1$ be a weak isomorphism from G_2 into G_1, then g is a bijective map defined by $g(x_2) = x_1$, for all $x_2 \in X_2$, satisfying,

$$\mu^p_{A_2}(x_2) = \mu^p_{A_1}(g(x_2)), \quad \mu^n_{A_2}(x_2) = \mu^n_{A_1}(g(x_2)), \quad \text{for all } x_2 \in X_2,$$

$$\mu^p_{B_2}(x_2 y_2) \le \mu^p_{B_1}(g(x_2) g(y_2)), \quad \mu^n_{B_2}(x_2 y_2) \ge \mu^n_{B_1}(g(x_2) g(y_2)), \quad \text{for all } x_2 y_2 \in E_2. \tag{1.8}$$

The inequalities (1.7) and (1.8) hold on the finite sets X_1 and X_2 only when G_1 and G_2 have the same number of edges and the corresponding edges have same weight. Hence G_1 and G_2 are identical. To prove the transitivity, let $f : X_1 \to X_2$ and $g : X_2 \to X_3$ be weak isomorphisms from G_1 into G_2 and G_2 into G_3, respectively. Then $g \circ f : X_1 \to X_3$ is a bijective map from X_1 to X_3, where $(g \circ f)(x_1) = g(f(x_1))$, for all $x_1 \in X_1$. Since the map $f : X_1 \to X_2$ defined by $f(x_1) = x_2$, for $x_1 \in X_1$, is a weak isomorphism

$$\mu^p_{A_1}(x_1) = \mu^p_{A_2}(f(x_1)) = \mu^p_{A_2}(x_2), \quad \mu^n_{A_1}(x_1) = \mu^n_{A_2}(f(x_1)) = \mu^n_{A_2}(x_2), \quad \text{for all } x_1 \in X_1, \tag{1.9}$$

$$\begin{aligned} &\mu^p_{B_1}(x_1 y_1) \le \mu^p_{B_2}(f(x_1) f(y_1)) = \mu^p_{B_2}(x_2 y_2), \\ &\mu^n_{B_1}(x_1 y_1) \ge \mu^n_{B_2}(f(x_1) f(y_1)) = \mu^n_{B_2}(x_2 y_2), \quad \text{for all } x_1 y_1 \in E_1. \end{aligned} \tag{1.10}$$

Since the map $g : X_2 \to X_3$ defined by $g(x_2) = x_3$, for $x_2 \in X_2$ is a weak isomorphism,

$$\mu^p_{A_2}(x_2) = \mu^p_{A_3}(g(x_2)) = \mu^p_{A_3}(x_3), \quad \mu^n_{A_2}(x_2) = \mu^n_{A_3}(g(x_2)) = \mu^n_{A_3}(x_3), \quad \text{for all } x_2 \in X_2, \tag{1.11}$$

$$\begin{aligned} &\mu^p_{B_2}(x_2 y_2) \le \mu^p_{B_3}(g(x_2) g(y_2)) = \mu^p_{B_3}(x_3 y_3), \\ &\mu^n_{B_2}(x_2 y_2) \ge \mu^n_{B_3}(g(x_2) g(y_2)) = \mu^n_{B_3}(x_3 y_3), \quad \text{for all } x_2 y_2 \in E_2. \end{aligned} \tag{1.12}$$

From (1.9), (1.11) and $f(x_1) = x_2$, $x_1 \in X_1$,

$$\begin{aligned} &\mu^p_{A_1}(x_1) = \mu^p_{A_2}(f(x_1)) = \mu^p_{A_2}(x_2) = \mu^p_{A_3}(g(x_2)) = \mu^p_{A_3}(g(f(x_1))), \\ &\mu^n_{A_1}(x_1) = \mu^n_{A_2}(f(x_1)) = \mu^n_{A_2}(x_2) = \mu^n_{A_3}(g(x_2)) = \mu^n_{A_3}(g(f(x_1))), \quad \text{for all } x_1 \in X_1. \end{aligned}$$

From (1.10) and (1.12),

$$\begin{aligned}
\mu^p_{B_1}(x_1y_1) &\le \mu^p_{B_2}(f(x_1)f(y_1)) = \mu^p_{B_2}(x_2y_2)\\
&\le \mu^p_{B_3}(g(x_2)g(y_2)) = \mu^p_{B_3}(g(f(x_1))g(f(y_1))),\\
\mu^n_{B_1}(x_1y_1) &\ge \mu^n_{B_2}(f(x_1)f(y_1)) = \mu^n_{B_2}(x_2y_2)\\
&\ge \mu^n_{B_3}(g(x_2)g(y_2)) = \mu^n_{B_3}(g(f(x_1))g(f(y_1))),
\end{aligned}$$

for all $x_1y_1 \in E_1$.

Thus $g \circ f$ is a weak isomorphism between G_1 and G_3. This completes the proof. □

Definition 1.40 Let $G = (A, B)$ be a bipolar fuzzy graph on X. The **strength** of a bipolar fuzzy path $x_1, e_1, x_2, e_2, x_3, \ldots, e_{r-1}, x_r$ between any two distinct vertices x_1 and x_r is defined as a pair $S_G(x_1, x_r) = \big(S^p_G(x_1, x_r), S^n_G(x_1, x_r)\big)$, where $S^p_G(x_1, x_r) = \wedge_{i=1}^{r-1}\mu^p_B(e_i)$ and $S^n_G(x_1, x_r) = \vee_{i=1}^{r-1}\mu^n_B(e_i)$. A **strongest bipolar fuzzy path** between any two distinct vertices is a bipolar fuzzy path with maximum positive strength and minimum negative strength. If $\mathbb{P} = \{P_i \mid i = 1, 2, 3, \ldots\}$ is the collection of all bipolar fuzzy paths between x and y, then the strength of the strongest bipolar fuzzy path $x - y$ is defined as the pair $S^\infty_G(x, y) = \big(S^{\infty^+}_G(x, y), S^{\infty^-}_G(x, y)\big) = (\vee_{\mathbb{P}} S^p_G(x, y), \wedge_{\mathbb{P}} S^n_G(x, y))$. It is referred as **strength of connectedness** between x and y.

Definition 1.41 Let $G = (A, B)$ be a bipolar fuzzy graph and $x, y \in X$ be any two distinct vertices of G. Let $G' = (A, B')$ be a subgraph obtained by deleting the edge xy from G, that is, $B'(xy) = (0, 0)$ and $B' = B$ for all other edges. Then xy is said to be a **bipolar fuzzy bridge** in G if either $S^{\infty^+}_{G'}(x, y) < S^{\infty^+}_G(x, y)$ and $S^{\infty^-}_{G'}(x, y) \ge S^{\infty^-}_G(x, y)$ or $S^{\infty^+}_{G'}(x, y) \le S^{\infty^+}_G(x, y)$ and $S^{\infty^-}_{G'}(x, y) > S^{\infty^-}_G(x, y)$, for some $x, y \in X$.

In other words, deleting an edge xy reduces the strength of connectedness between some pair of vertices. Thus, xy is a bipolar fuzzy bridge if and only if there exist $u, v \in X$ such that xy is an edge of every strongest bipolar fuzzy path from u to v.

Definition 1.42 An edge xy in a bipolar fuzzy graph $G = (A, B)$ is said to be a **strong edge** if $\mu^p_B(xy) \ge S^{\infty^+}_G(x, y)$ and $\mu^n_B(xy) \le S^{\infty^-}_G(x, y)$. In this case, x, y are called **strong neighbors**. A vertex x is called a **bipolar fuzzy end vertex** of G if it has at most one strong neighbor in G. A bipolar fuzzy path consisting of only strong edges is called a strong bipolar fuzzy path in G. An edge with least positive membership value and greatest negative membership value is called a **weakest bipolar fuzzy edge** of G.

Example 1.19 Consider a bipolar fuzzy graph on $X = \{a, b, c, d\}$ as shown in Fig. 1.26. The strength of bipolar fuzzy path $b - a - c$ is $(0.3 \wedge 0.1, -0.2 \vee -0.3) = (0.1, -0.2)$ and that of $b - d - c$ is $(0.2 \wedge 0.2, -0.3 \vee -0.4) = (0.2, -0.3)$. The strength of connectedness between the vertices b and c is $(0.2, -0.3)$.

Example 1.20 Consider a bipolar fuzzy graph G on $X = \{a, b, c, d\}$ as shown in Fig. 1.27.

By routine computations, it is easy to see that

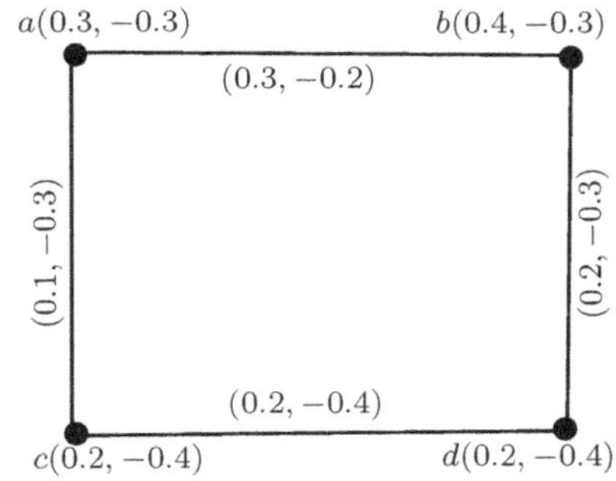

Fig. 1.26 Strength of connectedness

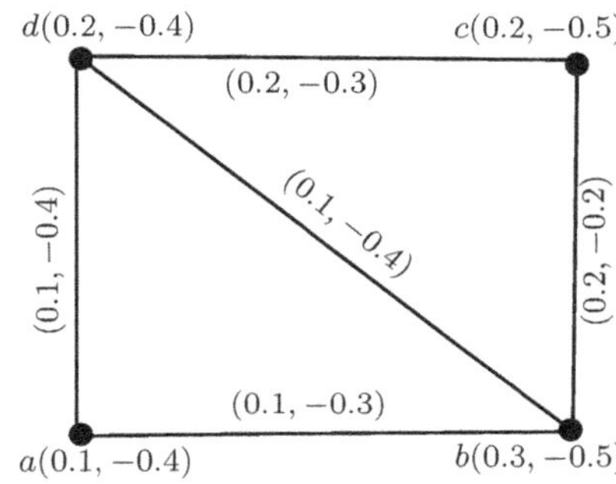

Fig. 1.27 Strongest bipolar fuzzy path

1. $a - d$ is a bipolar fuzzy path of strength $(0.1, -0.4)$.
2. The bipolar fuzzy path $a - b - d$ has strength $(0.1, -0.3)$.
3. $a - b - c - d$ is a bipolar fuzzy path of strength $(0.2, -0.2)$.
4. A strongest bipolar fuzzy path joining a and d is $a - b - c - d$ with strength of connectedness $(0.2, -0.2)$.

Theorem 1.6 *Let $G = (A, B)$ be a bipolar fuzzy graph, then G is connected if and only if $S^{\infty}(x, y) \neq (0, 0)$, for all $x, y \in X$.*

Proof Assume that G is connected, then for every $x, y \in X$, there exists at least one bipolar fuzzy path such that

$$
\begin{aligned}
& \text{Either } S_G^p(x, y) > 0 \text{ or } S_G^n(x, y) < 0 \\
\Rightarrow\ & \text{Either } \vee_{\mathbb{P}} S_G^p(x, y) > 0 \text{ or } \wedge_{\mathbb{P}} S_G^n(x, y) < 0 \\
\Rightarrow\ & (\vee_{\mathbb{P}} S_G^p(x, y), \wedge_{\mathbb{P}} S_G^n(x, y)) \neq (0, 0) \\
\Rightarrow\ & S_G^{\infty}(x, y) \neq (0, 0).
\end{aligned}
$$

Conversely, suppose that for all $x, y \in X$,

$$S_G^{\infty}(x, y) \neq (0, 0)$$

$$\begin{aligned}
&\Rightarrow \quad (\vee_{\mathbb{P}} S_G^p(x, y), \wedge_{\mathbb{P}} S_G^n(x, y)) \neq (0, 0) \\
&\Rightarrow \quad \text{Either } \vee_{\mathbb{P}} S_G^p(x, y) > 0 \text{ or } \wedge_{\mathbb{P}} S_G^n(x, y) < 0 \\
&\Rightarrow \quad \text{Either } S_G^p(x, y) > 0 \text{ or } S_G^n(x, y) < 0.
\end{aligned}$$

It follows that there exists at least one bipolar fuzzy path between each pair of distinct vertices x and y, that is, G is a connected bipolar fuzzy graph. □

Theorem 1.7 *Let G_1 and G_2 be two isomorphic bipolar fuzzy graphs, then G_1 is connected if and only if G_2 is connected.*

Proof Let $G_1 = (A_1, B_1)$ and $G_2 = (A_2, B_2)$ be two bipolar fuzzy graphs on X_1 and X_2, respectively. Let $f : X_1 \to X_2$ be an isomorphism from G_1 to G_2. Assume that G_1 is connected, then for any $x_1, y_1 \in X_1$,

$$\begin{aligned}
(0, 0) \neq S_{G_1}^{\infty}(x_1, y_1) &= (\vee_{\mathbb{P}} S_{G_1}^p(x_1, y_1), \wedge_{\mathbb{P}} S_{G_1}^n(x_1, y_1)) \\
&= \left(\vee_{\mathbb{P}} S_{G_2}^p(f(x_1), f(y_1)), \wedge_{\mathbb{P}} S_{G_2}^n(f(x_1), f(y_1))\right) \\
&= S_2^{\infty}(f(x_1), f(y_1)) \\
\Rightarrow (0, 0) \neq S_2^{\infty}(x_2, y_2).
\end{aligned}$$

Conversely, let G_2 is connected, then $S_{G_2}^{\infty}(x_2, y_2) \neq (0, 0)$. Since $f^{-1} : X_2 \to X_1$ is an isomorphism from G_2 into G_1, for every $x_2, y_2 \in X_2$

$$\begin{aligned}
(0, 0) \neq S_{G_2}^{\infty}(x_2, y_2) &= (\vee_{\mathbb{P}} S_{G_2}^p(x_2, y_2), \wedge_{\mathbb{P}} S_{G_2}^n(x_2, y_2)) \\
&= \left(\vee_{\mathbb{P}} S_{G_1}^p(f^{-1}(x_2), f^{-1}(y_2)), \wedge_{\mathbb{P}} S_{G_1}^n(f^{-1}(x_2), f^{-1}(y_2))\right) \\
&= S_1^{\infty}\left(f^{-1}(x_2), f^{-1}(y_2)\right) \\
\Rightarrow (0, 0) &\neq S_{G_1}^{\infty}(x_1, y_1).
\end{aligned}$$

Hence G_1 is connected. □

Theorem 1.8 *Let G_1 and G_2 be to isomorphic bipolar fuzzy graphs then G_1 is strong if and only if G_2 is strong.*

Proof Let $G_1 = (A_1, B_1)$ and $G_2 = (A_2, B_2)$ be two bipolar fuzzy graphs on X_1 and X_2, respectively. Let $f : X_1 \to X_2$ be an isomorphism from G_1 into G_2. Assume that G_1 is strong, then for any $x_1 y_1 \in E_1$ and $x_2 y_2 \in E_2$,

$$\begin{aligned}
B_2(x_2 y_2) &= B_2(f(x_1) f(y_1)) = B_1(x_1 y_1) \\
&= \left(\mu_{A_1}^p(x_1) \wedge \mu_{A_1}^p(y_1), \mu_{A_1}^n(x_1) \vee \mu_{A_1}^n(y_1)\right) \\
&= \left(\mu_{A_2}^p(f(x_1)) \wedge \mu_{A_2}^p(f(y_1)), \mu_{A_2}^n(f(x_1)) \vee \mu_{A_2}^n(f(y_1))\right) \\
&= \left(\mu_{A_2}^p(x_2) \wedge \mu_{A_2}^p(y_2), \mu_{A_2}^n(x_2) \vee \mu_{A_2}^n(y_2)\right).
\end{aligned}$$

Hence G_2 is a strong bipolar fuzzy graph. Conversely, suppose that G_2 is a strong bipolar fuzzy graph, then for every $x_1 y_1 \in E_1$,

$$\begin{aligned}B_1(x_1y_1) &= B_1\left(f^{-1}(x_2)f^{-1}(y_2)\right) = B_2(x_2y_2)\\ &= \left(\mu^p_{A_2}(x_2)\wedge\mu^p_{A_2}(y_2), \mu^n_{A_2}(x_2)\vee\mu^n_{A_2}(y_2)\right)\\ &= \left(\mu^p_{A_1}(f^{-1}(x_2))\wedge\mu^p_{A_1}(f^{-1}(y_2)), \mu^n_{A_1}(f^{-1}(x_2))\vee\mu^n_{A_1}(f^{-1}(y_2))\right)\\ &= \left(\mu^p_{A_1}(x_1)\wedge\mu^p_{A_1}(y_1), \mu^n_{A_1}(x_1)\vee\mu^n_{A_1}(y_1)\right).\end{aligned}$$

Thus G_1 is a strong bipolar fuzzy graph. □

Theorem 1.9 *Let G_1 and G_2 be isomorphic bipolar fuzzy graphs, then G_1 is complete if and only if G_2 is complete.*

Proof Let $G_1 = (A_1, B_1)$ and $G_2 = (A_2, B_2)$ be two bipolar fuzzy graphs on X_1 and X_2, respectively. Let $g : X_1 \to X_2$ be an isomorphism from G_1 to G_2. Assume that G_1 is complete, then for all $x_1, y_1 \in X_1$ and $x_2, y_2 \in X_2$

$$\begin{aligned}B_2(x_2y_2) &= B_2(g(x_1)g(y_1)) = B_1(x_1y_1)\\ &= (\mu^p_{A_1}(x_1)\wedge\mu^p_{A_1}(y_1), \mu^n_{A_1}(x_1)\vee\mu^n_{A_1}(y_1))\\ &= (\mu^p_{A_2}(g(x_1))\wedge\mu^p_{A_2}(g(y_1)), \mu^n_{A_2}(g(x_1))\vee\mu^n_{A_2}(g(y_1)))\\ &= (\mu^p_{A_2}(x_2)\wedge\mu^p_{A_2}(y_2), \mu^n_{A_2}(x_2)\vee\mu^n_{A_2}(y_2)).\end{aligned}$$

Hence G_2 is a complete bipolar fuzzy graph. Conversely, let G_2 is a complete bipolar fuzzy graph, then for every $x_1, y_1 \in X_1$

$$\begin{aligned}B_1(x_1y_1) &= B_1\left(g^{-1}(x_2)g^{-1}(y_2)\right) = B_2(x_2y_2)\\ &= \left(\mu^p_{A_2}(x_2)\wedge\mu^p_{A_2}(y_2), \mu^n_{A_2}(x_2)\vee\mu^n_{A_2}(y_2)\right)\\ &= \left(\mu^p_{A_1}(g^{-1}(x_2))\wedge\mu^p_{A_1}(g^{-1}(y_2)), \mu^n_{A_1}(g^{-1}(x_2))\vee\mu^n_{A_1}(g^{-1}(y_2))\right)\\ &= \left(\mu^p_{A_1}(x_1)\wedge\mu^p_{A_1}(y_1), \mu^n_{A_1}(x_1)\vee\mu^n_{A_1}(y_1)\right).\end{aligned}$$

Thus G_1 is a complete bipolar fuzzy graph. □

1.4 Complex Bipolar Fuzzy Graphs

The extension of crisp sets to fuzzy sets and then to bipolar fuzzy sets, in terms of membership functions, is mathematically comparable to the extension of the set of integers, Z, to the set of real numbers, $\mathbb{R}$, and to the real plane, $\mathbb{R}^2$. That is, expanding the range of the membership function from $\{0, 1\}$ to $[-1, 0] \times [0, 1]$ is mathematically analogous to the extension of Z to $\mathbb{R}^2$.

Of course, the development of number system did not end with the set of real numbers. Historically, the introduction of real numbers was followed by their extension to the set of complex numbers, **C**. Based on this extension, the notion of a fuzzy set was extended to a complex fuzzy set, by Ramot et al. [37], as a fuzzy set characterized by a complex-valued membership function.

Definition 1.43 A **complex fuzzy set** S defined on a universe of discourse X is characterized by a membership function that assigns any element $x \in X$, a complex-valued grade of membership in S. By definition, the values $\mu_S(x)$ may receive all lying within the closed unit disk in the complex plane, and are thus of the form $\mu_S(x) = r_S(x)e^{iw_S(x)}$, where $i = \sqrt{-1}$, $r_S(x)$and $w_S(x)$ are both real numbers, $r_S(x) \in [0, 1]$ and $w_S(x) \in [0, 2\pi]$. The complex fuzzy set may be represented as the set of ordered pairs

$$S = \left\{\left(x, r_S(x)e^{iw_S(x)}\right) \mid x \in X\right\}.$$

The term $r_S(x)$ is called **amplitude** and $w_S(x)$ is called **phase** term of the complex grade of membership $\mu_S(x)$. Note that the amplitude $r_S(x)$ is equal to $\mid \mu_S(x) \mid$.

Complex numbers have applications in many scientific areas, including signal processing, control theory, electromagnetism, fluid dynamics, thermodynamics, theory of relativity, and vibration analysis. The signals that change periodically are expressed in terms of sine or cosine function or a group of these together, that is, as a complex number $e^{i\theta} = \cos\theta + i\sin\theta$. However, adding a polarity perspective, we may represent signals as complex bipolar fuzzy sets for identifying a particular signal of interest out of a large number of signals received by a TV, radio, or digital receiver. A power factor correction uses a lot of complex numbers and phase vectors. Using a suitable method, complex bipolar fuzzy sets can be used to represent the power factors to find the optimal device to reduce power bills and save money. The notion of a complex bipolar fuzzy set can be implemented to represent the uncertainty and periodicity problems having bipolar information in complex geometry as shown in Figs. 1.28 and 1.29. The notion of complex bipolar fuzzy set represents bipolar behavior of uncertainty and periodicity semantics simultaneously by applying the notion of bipolar fuzzy set in complex geometry to illustrate various phenomena in

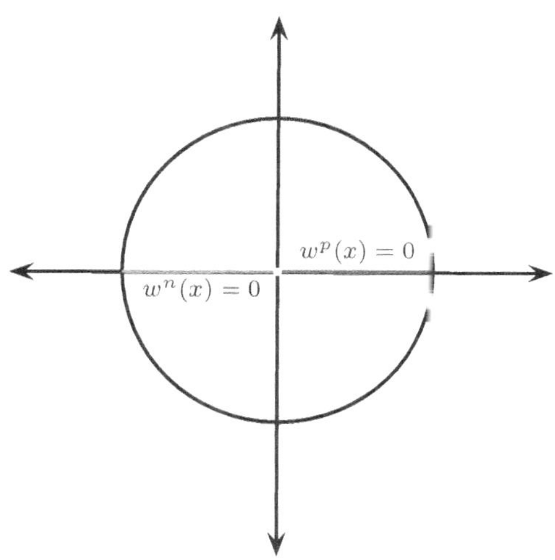

Fig. 1.28 Phase term in bipolar fuzzy set

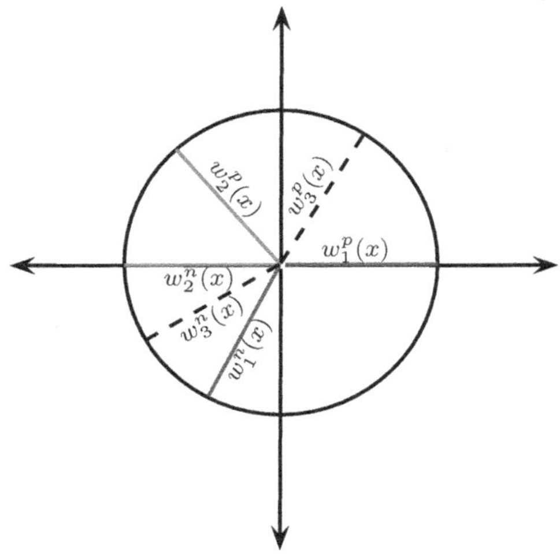

Fig. 1.29 Phase term in complex bipolar fuzzy set

different phases or levels. The bipolarity of uncertainty semantics can be represented in the form of amplitude terms as $r^p(x)$ and $r^n(x)$ and the bipolarity of periodicity semantics in the form of phase terms $w^p(x)$ and $w^n(x)$ corresponding to complex numbers $r^p(x)e^{iw^p(x)}$ and $r^n(x)e^{iw^n(x)}$. The following definition illustrates the notion of complex bipolar fuzzy set.

Definition 1.44 A **complex bipolar fuzzy set** A on a non-empty set X is an object of the form

$$A = \left\{(x, r_A^p(x)e^{iw_A^p(x)}, r_A^n(x)e^{iw_A^n(x)}) \mid x \in X\right\},$$

where $i = \sqrt{-1}$, $r_A^p : X \to [0, 1]$ and $r_A^n : X \to [-1, 0]$ are mappings, $w_A^p(x) \in [0, \pi]$ and $w_A^n(x) \in [\pi, 2\pi]$ or $w_A^n(x) \in [-\pi, 0]$. For any element $x \in X$, $r_A^p(x)$ and $r_A^n(x)$ are called amplitude terms, $w_A^p(x)$ and $w_A^n(x)$ are called phase terms.

The complex bipolar fuzzy set can also be written as

$$A = \left\{(x, r_A^p(x)e^{i\arg_A^p(x)}, r_A^n(x)e^{i\arg_A^n(x)}) \mid x \in X\right\}.$$

1. If $r_A^p(x) = r_A^n(x) = 0$, then x is considered as neutral with no positive or negative satisfaction for A.
2. If $r_A^p(x) = 0$ and $r_A^n(x) \neq 0$, it is the case when x is observed as having only positive satisfaction for A effected by positive phase value $w_A^p(x)$.
3. If $r_A^p(x) = 0$ and $r_A^n(x) \neq 0$, it is the situation that x is not satisfying the property of A but satisfying the counter property to A with negative phase quality $w_A^n(x)$.
4. If $r_A^p(x) \neq 0$ and $r_A^n(x) \neq 0$, then the membership function of given property overlaps that of its counter property in some parts of X effected by both positive and negative phase values $w_A^p(x)$ and $w_A^n(x)$.

Example 1.21 Every 11 years the sun undergoes a period of activity called the "solar maximum", followed by a period of quiet called the "solar minimum". During the solar maximum, there are many sunspots, solar flares, and coronal mass ejections, all of which can affect communications and weather on Earth. During the solar minimum, there are few sunspots. One way solar activity may be tracked is by observing sunspots. Sunspots are relatively cool areas that appear as dark blemishes on the face of the sun, and are sites where solar flares are observed to occur. Let A denote the complex bipolar fuzzy set with **rising or decreasing solar activity** in which each month is associated with a bipolar complex-valued grade of membership consisting of amplitude terms and phase terms. The role of amplitude terms is simple: it signifies the degree to which a particular month x has rising or decreasing solar activity. The phase term contains information regarding the position of the month under consideration in the solar cycle. Accordingly, any position between the solar minimum and the solar maximum is associated with a membership phase in the range $(0, \pi)$ if solar activity is on the rise, or a value in the range $(\pi, 2\pi)$ if solar activity is decreasing.

Definition 1.45 Let $A = \left\{(x, r_A^p(x)e^{iw_A^p(x)}, r_A^n(x)e^{iw_A^n(x)}) \mid x \in X\right\}$ be a complex bipolar fuzzy set on a non-empty set X. A **complex bipolar fuzzy relation** D on A is a mapping $D : A \to A$ such that, for all $x, y \in X$,

$$r_D^p(xy) \leq r_A^p(x) \wedge r_A^p(y) \quad \text{and} \quad r_D^n(xy) \geq r_A^n(x) \vee r_A^n(y), \quad \text{(for amplitude terms)}$$
$$w_D^p(xy) \leq w_A^p(x) \wedge w_A^p(y) \quad \text{and} \quad w_D^n(xy) \geq w_A^n(x) \vee w_A^n(y), \quad \text{(for phase terms)},$$

where $\mu_D^p(xy) = r_D^p(xy)e^{iw_D^p(xy)}$, $\mu_D^n(xy) = r_D^n(xy)e^{iw_D^n(xy)}$ and $i = \sqrt{-1}$.

Note that D is also a complex bipolar fuzzy relation in X defined by $D = \{(xy, r_D^p(xy)e^{iw_D^p(xy)}, r_D^n(xy)e^{iw_D^n(xy)}) \mid xy \in X \times X\}$, where $r_D^p : X \times X \to [0, 1]$ and $r_D^n : X \times X \to [-1, 0]$ are mappings, $w_D^p \in [0, \pi]$, $w_D^n \in [\pi, 2\pi]$ or $w_D^n \in [-\pi, 0]$.

We will use the notations $A = \left(r_A^p e^{iw_A^p}, r_A^n e^{iw_A^n}\right)$ and $D = \left(r_D^p e^{iw_D^p}, r_D^n e^{iw_D^n}\right)$ for a complex bipolar fuzzy set and a complex bipolar fuzzy relation, respectively.

Definition 1.46 A **complex bipolar fuzzy graph** on a non-empty set X is a pair $G = (A, D)$, where $A = (r_A^p e^{w_A^p}, r_A^n e^{w_A^n}) : X \to \{z \mid z \in C, |z| \leq 1\}^2$ is a complex bipolar fuzzy set on X and $D = (r_D^p e^{w_D^p}, r_D^n e^{w_D^n}) : X \times X \to \{z \mid z \in C, |z| \leq 1\}^2$ is a complex bipolar polar fuzzy relation in X such that, for all $x, y \in X$,

$$r_D^p(xy) \leq r_A^p(x) \wedge r_A^p(y) \quad \text{and} \quad r_D^n(xy) \geq r_A^n(x) \vee r_A^n(y), \quad \text{(for amplitude terms)}$$
$$w_D^p(xy) \leq w_A^p(x) \wedge w_A^p(y) \quad \text{and} \quad w_D^n(xy) \geq w_A^n(x) \vee w_A^n(y), \quad \text{(for phase terms)},$$

where $i = \sqrt{-1}$, $r_A^p : X \to [0, 1]$, $r_A^n : X \to [-1, 0]$, $r_D^p : X \times X \to [0, 1]$ and $r_D^n : X \times X \to [-1, 0]$ are mappings, $w_A^p, w_D^p \in [0, \pi]$, $w_A^n, w_D^n \in [\pi, 2\pi]$ or $w_A^n, w_D^n \in [-\pi, 0]$.

Note that $D(xy) = (0, 0)$ for all $xy \in X \times X - E$, where $E \subseteq X \times X$ is the set of edges. A is called a complex bipolar fuzzy vertex set of G and D is a complex bipolar fuzzy edge set of G. A bipolar fuzzy relation D on X is **symmetric** if $D(xy) = D(yx)$ for all $x, y \in X$. Notice that $D(xy) = (0, 0)$ for $xy \notin E$.

The following example illustrates the above definition.

Example 1.22 Consider a complex bipolar fuzzy set A on the vertex set $X = \{x, y, z\}$ as given in Table 1.7 and a complex bipolar fuzzy relation D in X as defined in Table 1.8. The complex bipolar fuzzy graph $G = (A, D)$ on X is shown in Fig. 1.30.

Definition 1.47 Let $G_1 = (A_1, B_1)$ and $G_2 = (A_2, B_2)$ be two complex bipolar fuzzy graphs on non-empty sets X_1 and X_2, respectively. The **union** of G_1 and G_2 is a pair $G_1 \cup G_2 = (A_1 \cup A_2, D_1 \cup D_2)$ such that for all $x, y \in X_1 \cup X_2$,

Table 1.7 Complex bipolar fuzzy set A

A	x_1	x_2	x_3
$\mu_A^p(x)$	$0.7e^{0.9\pi i}$	$0.5e^{0.5\pi i}$	$0.8e^{0.8\pi i}$
$\mu_A^n(x)$	$0.6e^{-0.8\pi i}$	$-0.7e^{-0.9\pi i}$	$-0.6e^{-0.9\pi i}$

Table 1.8 Complex bipolar fuzzy relation D

D	x	y	z
x	$(0, 0)$	$(0.4e^{0.5\pi i}, -0.6e^{-0.7\pi i})$	$(0.7e^{0.8\pi i}, -0.5e^{-0.7\pi i})$
y	$(0.4e^{0.5\pi i}, -0.6e^{-0.7\pi i})$	$(0, 0)$	$(0.5e^{0.5\pi i}, -0.6e^{-0.8\pi i})$
z	$(0.7e^{0.8\pi i}, -0.5e^{-0.7\pi i})$	$(0.5e^{0.5\pi i}, -0.6e^{-0.8\pi i})$	$(0, 0)$

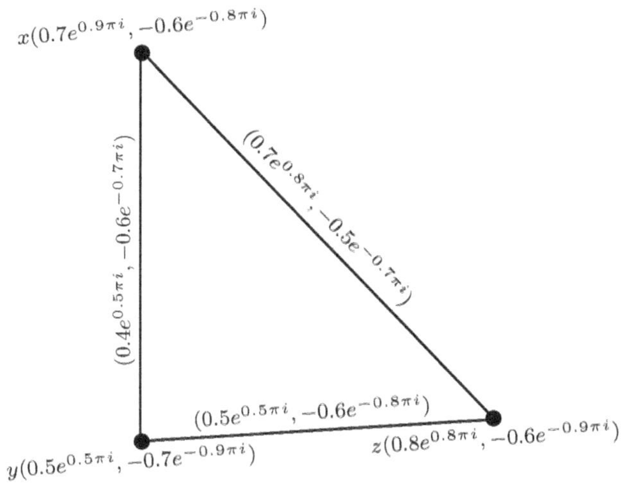

Fig. 1.30 Complex bipolar fuzzy graph

1. If $x \in X_1 \setminus X_2$, $(A_1 \cup A_2)(x) = A_1(x)$,
2. If $x \in X_2 \setminus X_1$, $(A_1 \cup A_2)(x) = A_2(x)$,
3. If $x \in X_1 \cap X_2$,

$$\begin{aligned}&(A_1 \cup A_2)(x)\\&= \left(\left(r^p_{A_1}(x) \vee r^p_{A_2}(x)\right) e^{i\left(w^p_{A_2}(x) \vee w^p_{A_2}(x)\right)}, \left(r^n_{A_1}(x) \wedge r^n_{A_2}(x)\right) e^{i\left(w^n_{A_2}(x) \wedge w^n_{A_2}(x)\right)}\right).\end{aligned}$$

If E_1 and E_2 are the sets of edges in G_1 and G_2, respectively, then $D_1 \cup D_2$ can be defined as

1. If $xy \in E_1 \setminus E_2$, $(D_1 \cup D_2)(x) = D_1(xy)$,
2. If $xy \in E_2 \setminus E_1$, $(D_1 \cup D_2)(x) = D_2(xy)$,
3. If $x \in E_1 \cap E_2$, $(D_1 \cup D_2)(xy) = \left(\mu^p_{D_1 \cup D_2}(xy), \mu^n_{D_1 \cup D_2}(xy)\right)$, where

$$\mu^p_{D_1 \cup D_2}(xy) = \left(r^p_{D_1}(xy) \vee r^p_{D_2}(xy)\right) e^{i\left(w^p_{D_1}(xy) \vee w^p_{D_2}(xy)\right)},$$
$$\mu^n_{D_1 \cup D_2}(xy) = \left(r^n_{D_1}(xy) \wedge r^n_{D_2}(xy)\right) e^{i\left(w^n_{D_1}(xy) \wedge w^n_{D_2}(xy)\right)}.$$

Definition 1.48 The **intersection** of two complex bipolar fuzzy graphs $G_1 = (A_1, D_1)$ and $G_2 = (A_2, D_2)$ is a defined as a pair $G_1 \cap G_2 = (A_1 \cap A_2, D_1 \cap D_2)$, where $A_1 \cap A_2$ and $D_1 \cap D_2$ are defined as

1. For all $x \in X_1 \cap X_2$, $(A_1 \cap A_2)(x) = \left(\mu^p_{A_1 \cap A_2}(x), \mu^n_{A_1 \cap A_2}(x)\right)$ such that

$$\mu^p_{A_1 \cap A_2}(x) = \left(r^p_{A_1}(x) \wedge r^p_{A_2}(x)\right) e^{i\left(w^p_{A_2}(x) \wedge w^p_{A_2}(x)\right)},$$
$$\mu^n_{A_1 \cap A_2}(x) = \left(r^n_{A_1}(x) \vee r^n_{A_2}(x)\right) e^{i\left(w^n_{A_2}(x) \vee w^n_{A_2}(x)\right)}.$$

2. For all $xy \in E_1 \cap E_2$, $(D_1 \cap D_2)(xy) = \left(\mu^p_{D_1 \cap D_2}(xy), \mu^n_{D_1 \cap D_2}(xy)\right)$ such that

$$\mu^p_{D_1 \cap D_2}(xy) = \left(r^p_{D_1}(xy) \wedge r^p_{D_2}(x)\right) e^{i\left(w^p_{D_2}(xy) \wedge w^p_{D_2}(xy)\right)},$$
$$\mu^n_{D_1 \cap D_2}(xy) = \left(r^n_{D_1}(xy) \vee r^n_{D_2}(x)\right) e^{i\left(w^n_{D_2}(xy) \vee w^n_{D_2}(xy)\right)}.$$

Definition 1.49 The **join** of two complex bipolar fuzzy graphs $G_1 = (A_1, D_1)$ and $G_2 = (A_2, D_2)$ is a defined as a pair $G_1 + G_2 = (A_1 + A_2, D_1 + D_2)$ such that $A_1 + A_2 = A_1 \cup A_2$, for all $x \in X_1 \cup X_2$, and the membership values of the edges in $G_1 + G_2$ are defined as

1. $D_1 + D_2 = D_1 \cup D_2$, for all $xy \in E_1 \cup E_2$,
2. Let E' be the set of all edges joining the vertices of G_1 and G_2, then for all $xy \in E'$, where $x \in X_1$ and $y \in X_2$

$$(D_1 + D_2)(xy)$$

$$= \left(\left(r^p_{A_1}(x) \wedge r^p_{A_2}(y)\right) e^{i\left(w^p_{A_1}(x) \wedge w^p_{A_2}(y)\right)}, \left(r^n_{A_1}(x) \vee r^n_{A_2}(y)\right) e^{i\left(w^n_{A_1}(x) \vee w^n_{A_2}(y)\right)} \right).$$

Proposition 1.21 *If G_1 and G_2 are complex bipolar fuzzy graphs, then $G_1 \cup G_2$, $G_1 \cap G_2$ and $G_1 + G_2$ are complex bipolar fuzzy graphs.*

Definition 1.50 The **composition** of two complex bipolar fuzzy graphs $G_1 = (A_1, D_1)$ and $G_2 = (A_2, D_2)$ is denoted by the pair $G_1 \circ G_2 = (A_1 \circ A_2, D_1 \circ D_2)$, where $A_1 \circ A_2 = (\mu^p_{A_1 \circ A_2}, \mu^n_{A_1 \circ A_2})$ and $D_1 \circ D_2 = (\mu^p_{D_1 \circ D_2}, \mu^n_{D_1 \circ D_2})$ are defined as

1. $(A_1 \circ A_2)(x_1, x_2) = (\mu^p_{A_1 \circ A_2}(x_1, x_2), \mu^n_{A_1 \circ A_2}(x_1, x_2))$

$$\mu^p_{A_1 \circ A_2}(x_1, x_2) = \left(r^p_{A_1}(x_1) \wedge r^p_{A_2}(x_2)\right) e^{i\left(w^p_{A_1}(x_1) \wedge w^p_{A_2}(x_2)\right)}$$
$$\mu^n_{A_1 \circ A_2}(x_1, x_2) = \left(r^n_{A_1}(x_1) \vee r^n_{A_2}(x_2)\right) e^{i\left(w^n_{A_2}(x_1) \vee w^n_{A_2}(x_2)\right)},$$
$$\text{for all } (x_1, x_2) \in X_1 \times X_2,$$

2. $(D_1 \circ D_2)((x, x_2)(x, y_2)) = (\mu^p_{D_1 \circ D_2}((x, x_2)(x, y_2)), \mu^n_{D_1 \circ D_2}((x, x_2)(x, y_2)))$

$$\mu^p_{D_1 \circ D_2}((x, x_2)(x, y_2)) = \left(r^p_{A_1}(x) \wedge r^p_{D_2}(x_2 y_2)\right) e^{i\left(w^p_{A_1}(x) \wedge w^p_{D_2}(x_2 y_2)\right)}$$
$$\mu^n_{D_1 \circ D_2}((x, x_2)(x, y_2)) = \left(r^n_{A_1}(x) \vee r^n_{D_2}(x_2 y_2)\right) e^{i\left(w^n_{A_1}(x) \vee w^n_{D_2}(x_2 y_2)\right)},$$
$$\text{for all } x \in X_1,\ x_2 y_2 \in E_2,$$

3. $(D_1 \circ D_2)((x_1, z)(y_1, z)) = (\mu^p_{D_1 \circ D_2}((x_1, z)(y_1, z)), \mu^n_{D_1 \circ D_2}((x_1, z)(y_1, z)))$

$$\mu^p_{D_1 \circ D_2}((x_1, z)(y_1, z)) = \left(r^p_{D_1}(x_1 y_1) \wedge r^p_{A_2}(z)\right) e^{i\left(w^p_{D_1}(x_1 y_1) \wedge w^p_{A_2}(z)\right)}$$
$$\mu^n_{D_1 \circ D_2}((x_1, z)(y_1, z)) = \left(r^n_{D_1}(x_1 y_1) \vee r^n_{A_2}(z)\right) e^{i\left(w^n_{D_1}(x_1 y_1) \vee w^n_{A_2}(z)\right)},$$
$$\text{for all } x_1 y_1 \in E_1,\ z \in X_2,$$

4. $(D_1 \circ D_2)((x_1, x_2)(y_1, y_2)) = (\mu^p_{D_1 \circ D_2}((x_1, x_2)(y_1, y_2)), \mu^n_{D_1 \circ D_2}((x_1, x_2)(y_1, y_2)))$

$$\mu^p_{D_1 \circ D_2}((x_1, x_2)(y_1, y_2))$$
$$= \left(r^p_{D_1}(x_1 y_1) \wedge r^p_{A_2}(x_2) \wedge r^p_{A_2}(y_2)\right) e^{i\left(w^p_{D_1}(x_1 y_1) \wedge w^p_{A_2}(x_2) \wedge w^p_{A_2}(y_2)\right)}$$
$$\mu^n_{D_1 \circ D_2}((x_1, x_2)(y_1, y_2))$$
$$= \left(r^n_{D_1}(x_1 y_1) \vee r^n_{A_2}(x_2) \vee r^n_{A_2}(y_2)\right) e^{i\left(w^n_{D_1}(x_1 y_1) \vee w^n_{A_2}(x_2) \vee w^n_{A_2}(y_2)\right)},$$
$$\text{for all } x_1 y_1 \in E_1,\ x_2, y_2 \in X_2.$$

Definition 1.51 The **Cartesian product** of two complex bipolar fuzzy graphs $G_1 = (A_1, D_1)$ and $G_2 = (A_2, D_2)$ is denoted by the pair $G_1 \Box G_2 = (A_1 \Box A_2, D_1 \Box D_2)$, where $A_1 \Box A_2 = \left(\mu^p_{A_1 \Box A_2}, \mu^n_{A_1 \Box A_2}\right)$ and $D_1 \Box D_2 = \left(\mu^p_{D_1 \Box D_2}, \mu^n_{D_1 \Box D_2}\right)$ are defined as

1. $(A_1 \Box A_2)(x_1, x_2) = \left(\mu^p_{A_1 \Box A_2}(x_1, x_2), \mu^n_{A_1 \Box A_2}(x_1, x_2)\right)$

$$\mu^p_{A_1 \Box A_2}(x_1, x_2) = \left(r^p_{A_1}(x_1) \wedge r^p_{A_2}(x_2)\right) e^{i\left(w^p_{A_1}(x_1) \wedge w^p_{A_2}(x_2)\right)}$$
$$\mu^n_{A_1 \Box A_2}(x_1, x_2) = \left(r^n_{A_1}(x_1) \vee r^n_{A_2}(x_2)\right) e^{i\left(w^n_{A_2}(x_1) \vee w^n_{A_2}(x_2)\right)},$$
$$\text{for all } (x_1, x_2) \in X_1 \times X_2,$$

2. $(D_1 \Box D_2)((x, x_2)(x, y_2)) = \left(\mu^p_{D_1 \Box D_2}((x, x_2)(x, y_2)), \mu^n_{D_1 \Box D_2}((x, x_2)(x, y_2))\right)$

$$\mu^p_{D_1 \Box D_2}((x, x_2)(x, y_2)) = \left(r^p_{A_1}(x) \wedge r^p_{D_2}(x_2 y_2)\right) e^{i\left(w^p_{A_1}(x) \wedge w^p_{D_2}(x_2 y_2)\right)}$$
$$\mu^n_{D_1 \Box D_2}((x, x_2)(x, y_2)) = \left(r^n_{A_1}(x) \vee r^n_{D_2}(x_2 y_2)\right) e^{i\left(w^n_{A_1}(x) \vee w^n_{D_2}(x_2 y_2)\right)},$$
$$\text{for all } x \in X_1, \ x_2 y_2 \in E_2,$$

3. $(D_1 \Box D_2)((x_1, z)(y_1, z)) = \left(\mu^p_{D_1 \Box D_2}((x_1, z)(y_1, z)), \mu^n_{D_1 \Box D_2}((x_1, z)(y_1, z))\right)$

$$\mu^p_{D_1 \Box D_2}((x_1, z)(y_1, z)) = \left(r^p_{D_1}(x_1 y_1) \wedge r^p_{A_2}(z)\right) e^{i\left(w^p_{D_1}(x_1 y_1) \wedge w^p_{A_2}(z)\right)}$$
$$\mu^n_{D_1 \Box D_2}((x_1, z)(y_1, z)) = \left(r^n_{D_1}(x_1 y_1) \vee r^n_{A_2}(z)\right) e^{i\left(w^n_{D_1}(x_1 y_1) \vee w^n_{A_2}(z)\right)},$$
$$\text{for all } x_1 y_1 \in E_1, \ z \in X_2,$$

Definition 1.52 The **direct product** of two complex bipolar fuzzy graphs $G_1 = (A_1, D_1)$ and $G_2 = (A_2, D_2)$ is denoted by the pair $G_1 \times G_2 = (A_1 \times A_2, D_1 \times D_2)$, where $A_1 \times A_2 = \left(\mu^p_{A_1 \times A_2}, \mu^n_{A_1 \times A_2}\right)$ and $D_1 \times D_2 = \left(\mu^p_{D_1 \times D_2}, \mu^n_{D_1 \times D_2}\right)$ are defined as

1. $(A_1 \times A_2)(x_1, x_2) = \left(\mu^p_{A_1 \times A_2}(x_1, x_2), \mu^n_{A_1 \times A_2}(x_1, x_2)\right)$

$$\mu^p_{A_1 \times A_2}(x_1, x_2) = \left(r^p_{A_1}(x_1) \wedge r^p_{A_2}(x_2)\right) e^{i\left(w^p_{A_1}(x_1) \wedge w^p_{A_2}(x_2)\right)}$$
$$\mu^n_{A_1 \times A_2}(x_1, x_2) = \left(r^n_{A_1}(x_1) \vee r^n_{A_2}(x_2)\right) e^{i\left(w^n_{A_2}(x_1) \vee w^n_{A_2}(x_2)\right)},$$
$$\text{for all } (x_1, x_2) \in X_1 \times X_2,$$

2. $(D_1 \times D_2)((x_1, x_2)(y_1, y_2)) = \left(\mu^p_{D_1 \times D_2}((x_1, x_2)(y_1, y_2)), \mu^n_{D_1 \times D_2}((x_1, x_2)(y_1, y_2))\right)$

$$\mu^p_{D_1 \times D_2}((x_1, x_2)(y_1, y_2)) = \left(r^p_{D_1}(x_1 y_1) \wedge r^p_{D_2}(x_2 y_2)\right) e^{i\left(w^p_{D_1}(x_1 y_1) \wedge w^p_{D_2}(x_2 y_2)\right)}$$
$$\mu^n_{D_1 \times D_2}((x_1, x_2)(y_1, y_2)) = \left(r^n_{D_1}(x_1 y_1) \vee r^n_{D_2}(x_2 y_2)\right) e^{i\left(w^n_{D_1}(x_1 y_1) \vee w^n_{D_2}(x_2 y_2)\right)},$$
$$\text{for all } x_1 y_1 \in E_1, x_2 y_2 \in E_2.$$

Definition 1.53 The **strong product** of two complex bipolar fuzzy graphs $G_1 = (A_1, D_1)$ and $G_2 = (A_2, D_2)$ is denoted by the pair $G_1 \boxtimes G_2 = (A_1 \boxtimes A_2, D_1 \boxtimes D_2)$, where $A_1 \boxtimes A_2 = \left(\mu^p_{A_1 \boxtimes A_2}, \mu^n_{A_1 \boxtimes A_2}\right)$ and $D_1 \boxtimes D_2 = \left(\mu^p_{D_1 \boxtimes D_2}, \mu^n_{D_1 \boxtimes D_2}\right)$ are defined as

1. $(A_1 \boxtimes A_2)(x_1, x_2) = \left(\mu^p_{A_1 \boxtimes A_2}(x_1, x_2), \mu^n_{A_1 \boxtimes A_2}(x_1, x_2)\right)$

$$\mu^p_{A_1 \boxtimes A_2}(x_1, x_2) = \left(r^p_{A_1}(x_1) \wedge r^p_{A_2}(x_2)\right) e^{i\left(w^p_{A_1}(x_1) \wedge w^p_{A_2}(x_2)\right)}$$
$$\mu^n_{A_1 \boxtimes A_2}(x_1, x_2) = \left(r^n_{A_1}(x_1) \vee r^n_{A_2}(x_2)\right) e^{i\left(w^n_{A_2}(x_1) \vee w^n_{A_2}(x_2)\right)},$$
$$\text{for all } (x_1, x_2) \in X_1 \times X_2,$$

2. $(D_1 \boxtimes D_2)((x, x_2)(x, y_2)) = \left(\mu^p_{D_1 \boxtimes D_2}((x, x_2)(x, y_2)), \mu^n_{D_1 \boxtimes D_2}((x, x_2)(x, y_2))\right)$

$$\mu^p_{D_1 \boxtimes D_2}((x, x_2)(x, y_2)) = \left(r^p_{A_1}(x) \wedge r^p_{D_2}(x_2 y_2)\right) e^{i\left(w^p_{A_1}(x) \wedge w^p_{D_2}(x_2 y_2)\right)}$$
$$\mu^n_{D_1 \boxtimes D_2}((x, x_2)(x, y_2)) = \left(r^n_{A_1}(x) \vee r^n_{D_2}(x_2 y_2)\right) e^{i\left(w^n_{A_1}(x) \vee w^n_{D_2}(x_2 y_2)\right)},$$
$$\text{for all } x \in X_1,\ x_2 y_2 \in E_2,$$

3. $(D_1 \boxtimes D_2)((x_1, z)(y_1, z)) = \left(\mu^p_{D_1 \boxtimes D_2}((x_1, z)(y_1, z)), \mu^n_{D_1 \boxtimes D_2}((x_1, z)(y_1, z))\right)$

$$\mu^p_{D_1 \boxtimes D_2}((x_1, z)(y_1, z)) = \left(r^p_{D_1}(x_1 y_1) \wedge r^p_{A_2}(z)\right) e^{i\left(w^p_{D_1}(x_1 y_1) \wedge w^p_{A_2}(z)\right)}$$
$$\mu^n_{D_1 \boxtimes D_2}((x_1, z)(y_1, z)) = \left(r^n_{D_1}(x_1 y_1) \vee r^n_{A_2}(z)\right) e^{i\left(w^n_{D_1}(x_1 y_1) \vee w^n_{A_2}(z)\right)},$$
$$\text{for all } x_1 y_1 \in E_1,\ z \in X_2,$$

4. $(D_1 \boxtimes D_2)((x_1, x_2)(y_1, y_2)) = \left(\mu^p_{D_1 \boxtimes D_2}((x_1, x_2)(y_1, y_2)), \mu^n_{D_1 \boxtimes D_2}((x_1, x_2)\right.$ $(y_1, y_2)))$

$$\mu^p_{D_1 \boxtimes D_2}((x_1, x_2)(y_1, y_2)) = \left(r^p_{D_1}(x_1 y_1) \wedge r^p_{D_2}(x_2 y_2)\right) e^{i\left(w^p_{D_1}(x_1 y_1) \wedge w^p_{D_2}(x_2 y_2)\right)}$$
$$\mu^n_{D_1 \boxtimes D_2}((x_1, x_2)(y_1, y_2)) = \left(r^n_{D_1}(x_1 y_1) \vee r^n_{D_2}(x_2 y_2)\right) e^{i\left(w^n_{D_1}(x_1 y_1) \vee w^n_{D_2}(x_2 y_2)\right)},$$
$$\text{for all } x_1 y_1 \in E_1, x_2 y_2 \in E_2.$$

Definition 1.54 A complex bipolar fuzzy graph $G = (A, D)$ on a non-empty set X is known as a **strong complex bipolar fuzzy graph** if

$$\begin{aligned}\mu^p_D(xy) &= r^p_D(xy)e^{iw^p_D(xy)} = \left(r^p_A(x) \wedge r^p_A(y)\right) e^{i\left(w^p_A(x)\wedge w^p_A(y)\right)}\\ \mu^n_D(xy) &= r^n_D(xy)e^{iw^n_D(xy)} = \left(r^n_A(x) \vee r^n_A(y)\right) e^{i\left(w^n_A(x)\vee w^n_A(y)\right)}, \quad \text{for all } xy \in E.\end{aligned}$$

Definition 1.55 A complex bipolar fuzzy graph $G = (A, D)$ on a non-empty set X is known as a **complete complex bipolar fuzzy graph** if

$$\begin{aligned}\mu^p_D(xy) &= r^p_D(xy)e^{iw^p_D(xy)} = \left(r^p_A(x) \wedge r^p_A(y)\right) e^{i\left(w^p_A(x)\wedge w^p_A(y)\right)}\\ \mu^n_D(xy) &= r^n_D(xy)e^{iw^n_D(xy)} = \left(r^n_A(x) \vee r^n_A(y)\right) e^{i\left(w^n_A(x)\vee w^n_A(y)\right)}, \quad \text{for all } x, y \in X.\end{aligned}$$

Definition 1.56 The **complement** of a strong complex bipolar fuzzy graph $G = (A, D)$, on a non-empty set X, is a strong complex bipolar fuzzy graph $\overline{G} = (\overline{A}, \overline{D})$ on X such that $\overline{A} = A$ and $\overline{D} = (\mu^p_{\overline{D}}, \mu^n_{\overline{D}})$ is defined as

$$\mu^p_{\overline{D}}(xy) = \begin{cases} 0 & \text{if } \mu^p_D(xy) \neq 0,\\ \left(r^p_A(x) \wedge r^p_A(y)\right) e^{i\left(w^p_A(x)\wedge w^p_A(y)\right)} & \text{if } \mu^p_D(xy) = 0,\end{cases}$$

$$\mu^n_{\overline{D}}(xy) = \begin{cases} 0 & \text{if } \mu^n_D(xy) \neq 0,\\ \left(r^n_A(x) \vee r^n_A(y)\right) e^{i\left(w^n_A(x)\wedge w^n_A(y)\right)} & \text{if } \mu^n_D(xy) = 0,\end{cases}$$

Definition 1.57 The **complement** of a complex bipolar fuzzy graph $G = (A, D)$ is a pair $\overline{G} = (\overline{A}, \overline{D})$, where $\overline{A} = A$ and $\overline{D} = (\mu^p_{\overline{D}}, \mu^n_{\overline{D}})$ is defined as

$$\begin{aligned}\mu^p_{\overline{D}}(xy) &= \left(r^p_A(x) \wedge r^p_A(y) - r^p_D(xy)\right) e^{i\left(w^p_A(x)\wedge w^p_A(y) - w^p_D(xy)\right)},\\ \mu^n_{\overline{D}}(xy) &= \left(r^n_A(x) \vee r^n_A(y) - r^n_D(xy)\right) e^{i\left(w^n_A(x)\vee w^n_A(y) - w^n_D(xy)\right)}.\end{aligned}$$

Example 1.23 Consider a complex bipolar fuzzy graph $G = (A, D)$ on $X = \{a, b, c\}$ as shown in Fig. 1.31. The complement of G is given in Fig. 1.32.

1.5 Bipolar Fuzzy Digraphs

A **directed graph**, also known as **digraph** is a pair $\overrightarrow{G}^* = (X, \overrightarrow{E})$, where X is the set of vertices and $\overrightarrow{E}$ is the set of directed edges. Note that the edges (or arcs) in $\overrightarrow{G}^*$ have directions and arrows on these edges are used to encode the directional information: an arc from vertex x to vertex y indicates that one may move from x to y but not from y to x.

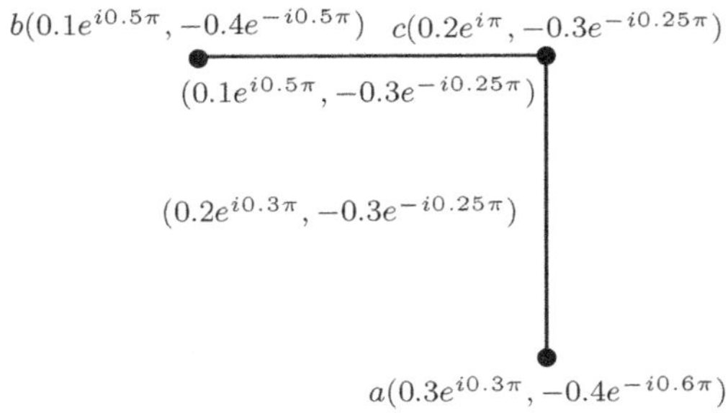

Fig. 1.31 Complex bipolar fuzzy graph G

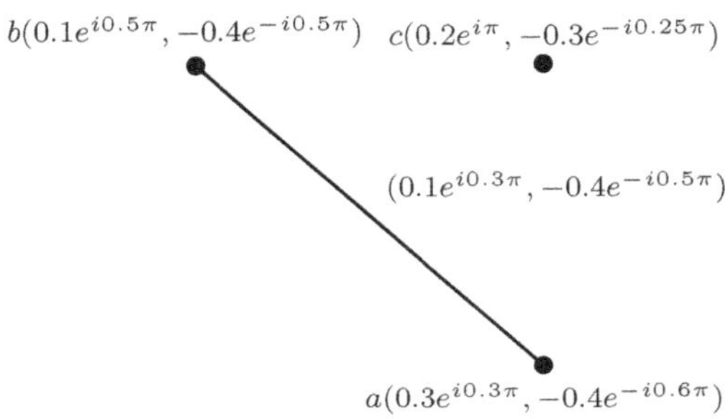

Fig. 1.32 Complement of G

In this section, we will write $\overrightarrow{xy} \in \overrightarrow{E}$ and say x and y are **adjacent** such that x is a starting node and y is an ending node.

Definition 1.58 A **bipolar fuzzy digraph** on a non-empty set X is a pair $G = (A, \overrightarrow{B})$, where $A = (\mu_A^p, \mu_A^n)$ is a bipolar fuzzy set on X and $\overrightarrow{B} = (\mu_{\overrightarrow{B}}^p, \mu_{\overrightarrow{B}}^n)$ is a bipolar fuzzy relation in X such that

$$\mu_{\overrightarrow{B}}^p(xy) \leq \mu_A^p(x) \wedge \mu_A^p(y) \text{ and } \mu_{\overrightarrow{B}}^n(xy) \geq \mu_A^n(x) \vee \mu_A^n(y), \text{ for all } x, y \in X.$$

Note that $\overrightarrow{B}$ is not a symmetric bipolar fuzzy relation. Throughout this book, we denote $\overrightarrow{G}^*$ a crisp digraph and $\overrightarrow{G}$ a bipolar fuzzy digraph.

Example 1.24 Let A be a bipolar fuzzy set on $X = \{v_1, v_2, v_3, v_4\}$, given in Table 1.9, and $\overrightarrow{B}$ a bipolar fuzzy relation defined in Table 1.10. Figure 1.33 shows that $\overrightarrow{G} = (A, \overrightarrow{B})$ is a bipolar fuzzy digraph.

Table 1.9 Bipolar fuzzy set A on $\{v_1, v_2, v_3, v_4\}$

A	v_1	v_2	v_3	v_4
μ_A^p	0.4	0.6	0.5	0.5
μ_A^n	−0.2	−0.3	−0.2	−0.3

Table 1.10 Bipolar fuzzy relation $\overrightarrow{B}$ in $\{v_1, v_2, v_3, v_4\}$

$\overrightarrow{B}$	v_1	v_2	v_3	v_4
v_1	(0, 0)	(0.1, −0.1)	(0, 0)	(0, 0)
v_2	(0, 0)	(0, 0)	(0.2, −0.1)	(0, 0)
v_3	(0, 0)	(0, 0)	(0, 0)	(0.3, −0.1)
v_4	(0.5, −0.1)	(0, 0)	(0, 0)	(0, 0)

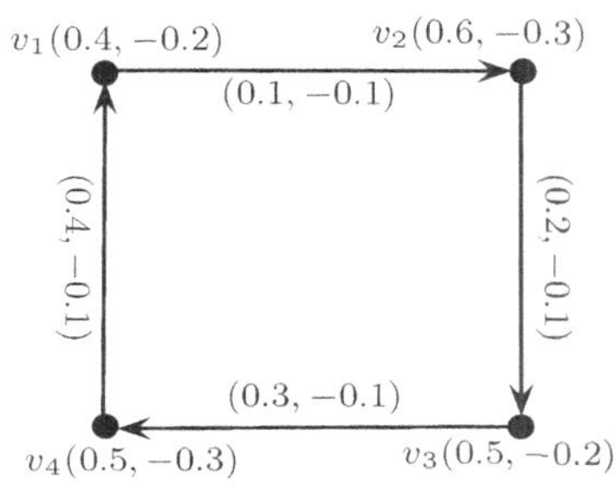

Fig. 1.33 Bipolar fuzzy digraph $\overrightarrow{G} = (A, \overrightarrow{B})$

Definition 1.59 A **bipolar fuzzy directed walk** in a bipolar fuzzy digraph is an alternating sequence of vertices and directed edges $y_0, \overrightarrow{e}_1, y_1, \overrightarrow{e}_2, \ldots, \overrightarrow{e}_{n-1}, y_{n-1}$ such that $\overrightarrow{B}(e_k) \neq (0, 0)$, for all $1 \leq k \leq n$.

Definition 1.60 A **bipolar fuzzy directed path** in a bipolar fuzzy digraph is a sequence of distinct vertices $y_1, y_2, \ldots, y_n$ such that either $\overrightarrow{B}(y_k y_{k+1}) \neq (0, 0)$, for all $1 \leq k \leq n-1$. It is denoted by $\overrightarrow{\mathcal{P}}_n$. If $y_1 = y_n$ and $A(y_1) = A(y_n)$, the bipolar fuzzy directed path is known as a **bipolar fuzzy directed cycle**, denoted by $\overrightarrow{\mathcal{C}}_n$.

Definition 1.61 Let $\overrightarrow{G}_1 = (A_1, \overrightarrow{B}_1)$ and $\overrightarrow{G}_2 = (A_2, \overrightarrow{B}_2)$ be two bipolar fuzzy digraphs on non-empty sets X_1 and X_2, respectively. The **union** of $\overrightarrow{G}_1$ and $\overrightarrow{G}_2$ is defined as a pair $\overrightarrow{G}_1 \cup \overrightarrow{G}_2 = (A_1 \cup A_2, \overrightarrow{B}_1 \cup \overrightarrow{B}_2)$ such that for all $x, y \in X_1 \cup X_2$,

1. $(A_1 \cup A_2)(x) = (\mu^p_{A_1}(x) \vee \mu^p_{A_2}(x), \mu^n_{A_1}(x) \wedge \mu^n_{A_2}(x))$,
2. If $\overrightarrow{xy} \in \overrightarrow{E}_1, \overrightarrow{xy} \notin \overrightarrow{E}_2$, then $(\overrightarrow{B}_1 \cup \overrightarrow{B}_2)(xy) = \overrightarrow{B}_1(xy)$,
3. If $\overrightarrow{xy} \in \overrightarrow{E}_1, \overrightarrow{xy} \notin \overrightarrow{E}_2$, then $(\overrightarrow{B}_1 \cup \overrightarrow{B}_2)(xy) = \overrightarrow{B}_2(xy)$,
4. If $\overrightarrow{xy} \in \overrightarrow{E}_1 \cap \overrightarrow{E}_2$, then $(\overrightarrow{B}_1 \cup \overrightarrow{B}_2)(xy) = (\mu^p_{\overrightarrow{B}_1}(xy) \vee \mu^p_{\overrightarrow{B}_2}(xy), \mu^n_{\overrightarrow{B}_1}(xy) \wedge \mu^n_{\overrightarrow{B}_2}(xy))$.

Example 1.25 Consider two bipolar fuzzy digraphs $\overrightarrow{G}_1$ and $\overrightarrow{G}_2$ as shown in Fig. 1.34. The union $\overrightarrow{G}_1 \cup \overrightarrow{G}_2$ is also given in Fig. 1.34.

Definition 1.62 The **intersection** of two bipolar fuzzy digraphs $\overrightarrow{G}_1 = (A_1, \overrightarrow{B}_1)$ and $\overrightarrow{G}_2 = (A_2, \overrightarrow{B}_2)$ is a pair $\overrightarrow{G}_1 \cap \overrightarrow{G}_2 = (A_1 \cap A_2, \overrightarrow{B}_1 \cap \overrightarrow{B}_2)$, where $A_1 \cap A_2$ and $\overrightarrow{B}_1 \cap \overrightarrow{B}_2$ are defined as

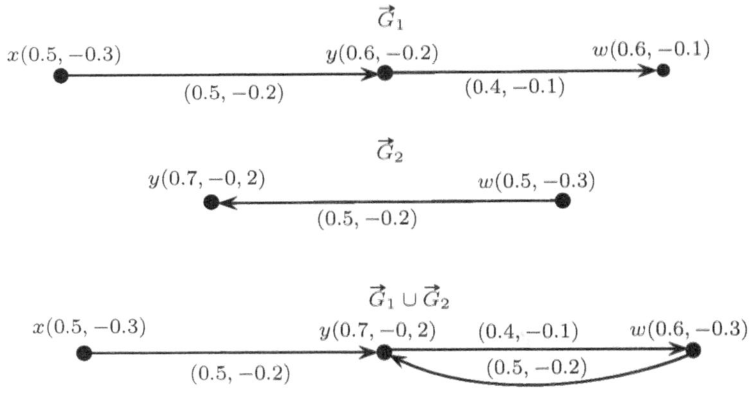

Fig. 1.34 Union of bipolar fuzzy digraphs

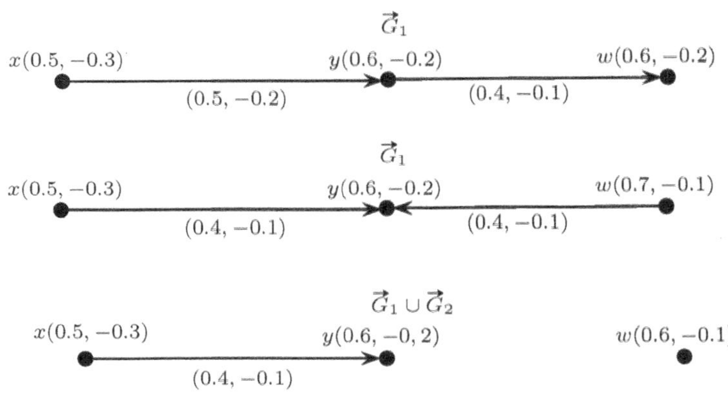

Fig. 1.35 Intersection of bipolar fuzzy digraphs $\vec{G}_1$ and $\vec{G}_2$

1. $(A_1 \cap A_2)(x) = (\mu^p_{A_1}(x) \wedge \mu^p_{A_2}(x), \mu^n_{A_1}(x) \vee \mu^n_{A_2}(x))$, for all $x \in X_1 \cap X_2$,
2. $(\vec{B}_1 \cap \vec{B}_2)(xy) = (\mu^p_{\vec{B}_1}(xy) \wedge \mu^p_{\vec{B}_2}(xy), \mu^n_{\vec{B}_1}(xy) \vee \mu^n_{\vec{B}_2}(xy))$, for all $\vec{xy} \in \vec{E}_1 \cap \vec{E}_2$.

Example 1.26 The intersection of two bipolar fuzzy digraphs $\vec{G}_1$ and $\vec{G}_2$ is shown in Fig. 1.35.

Definition 1.63 The **join** of two bipolar fuzzy graphs $\vec{G}_1 = (A_1, \vec{B}_1)$ and $\vec{G}_2 = (A_2, \vec{B}_2)$ is defined as a pair $\vec{G}_1 + \vec{G}_2 = (A_1 + A_2, \vec{B}_1 + \vec{B}_2)$ such that $A_1 + A_2 = A_1 \cup A_2$, for all $x \in X_1 \cup X_2$, and the membership values of directed edges in $\vec{G}_1 + \vec{G}_2$ are defined as

1.]1.] $\vec{B}_1 + \vec{B}_2 = \vec{B}_1 \cup \vec{B}_2$, for all $\vec{xy} \in \vec{E}_1 \cup \vec{E}_2$.

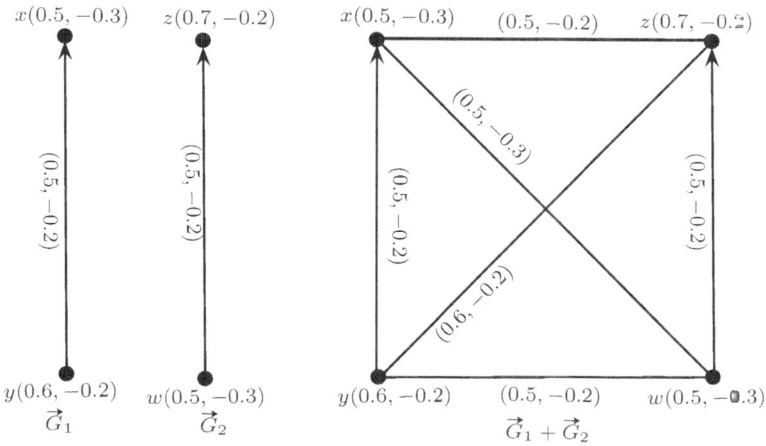

Fig. 1.36 Join of bipolar fuzzy digraphs $\vec{G}_1$ and $\vec{G}_2$

2.]2.] Let E' be the set of all edges joining the vertices of $\vec{G}_1$ and $\vec{G}_2$, then for all $xy \in E'$ where $x \in X_1$ and $y \in X_2$, $(\vec{B}_1 + \vec{B}_2)(xy) = (\mu^p_{A_1}(x) \wedge \mu^p_{A_2}(y), \mu^n_{A_1}(x)$
$\vee\, \mu^n_{A_2}(y))$.

Example 1.27 The join of two bipolar fuzzy digraphs $\vec{G}_1$ and $\vec{G}_2$ is shown in Fig. 1.36.

Definition 1.64 The **composition** of two bipolar fuzzy digraphs $\vec{G}_1 = (A_1, \vec{B}_1)$ and $\vec{G}_2 = (A_2, \vec{B}_2)$ is denoted by the pair $\vec{G}_1 \circ \vec{G}_2 = (A_1 \circ A_2, \vec{B}_1 \circ \vec{B}_2)$, where $A_1 \circ A_2 = (\mu^p_{A_1 \circ A_2}, \mu^n_{A_1 \circ A_2})$ and $\vec{B}_1 \circ \vec{B}_2 = (\mu^p_{\vec{B}_1 \circ \vec{B}_2}, \mu^n_{\vec{B}_1 \circ \vec{B}_2})$ are defined as

1. $(A_1 \circ A_2)(x_1, x_2) = (\mu^p_{A_1}(x_1) \wedge \mu^p_{A_2}(x_2), \mu^n_{A_1}(x_1) \vee \mu^n_{A_2}(x_2))$, for all $(x_1, x_2) \in X_1 \times X_2$,
2. $(\vec{B}_1 \circ \vec{B}_2)((x, x_2)(x, y_2)) = (\mu^p_{A_1}(x) \wedge \mu^p_{\vec{B}_2}(x_2 y_2), \mu^n_{A_1}(x) \vee \mu^n_{\vec{B}_2}(x_2 y_2))$,

   for all $x \in X_1$, $\overrightarrow{x_2 y_2} \in \vec{E}_2$,
3. $(\vec{B}_1 \circ \vec{B}_2)((x_1, z)(y_1, z)) = (\mu^p_{\vec{B}_1}(x_1 y_1) \wedge \mu^p_{A_2}(z), \mu^n_{\vec{B}_1}(x_1 y_1) \vee \mu^n_{A_2}(z))$,

   for all $z \in X_2$, $\overrightarrow{x_1 y_1} \in \vec{E}_1$,
4. $(\vec{B}_1 \circ \vec{B}_2)((x_1, x_2)(y_1, y_2)) = (\mu^p_{A_2}(x_2) \wedge \mu^p_{A_2}(y_2) \wedge \mu^p_{\vec{B}_1}(x_1 y_1), \mu^n_{A}(x_2) \vee \mu^n_{A_2}(y_2) \vee \mu^n_{\vec{B}_1}(x_1 y_1))$,

   for all $x_2, y_2 \in X_2$, $\overrightarrow{x_1 y_1} \in \vec{E}_1$.

Definition 1.65 The **Cartesian product** of two bipolar fuzzy digraphs $\vec{G}_1 = (A_1, \vec{B}_1)$ and $\vec{G}_2 = (A_2, \vec{B}_2)$ is denoted by the pair $\vec{G}_1 \square \vec{G}_2 = (A_1 \square A_2, \vec{B}_1 \square \vec{B}_2)$, where $A_1 \square A_2 = (\mu^p_{A_1 \square A_2}, \mu^n_{A_1 \square A_2})$ and $\vec{B}_1 \square \vec{B}_2 = (\mu^p_{\vec{B}_1 \square \vec{B}_2}, \mu^n_{\vec{B}_1 \square \vec{B}_2})$ are defined as

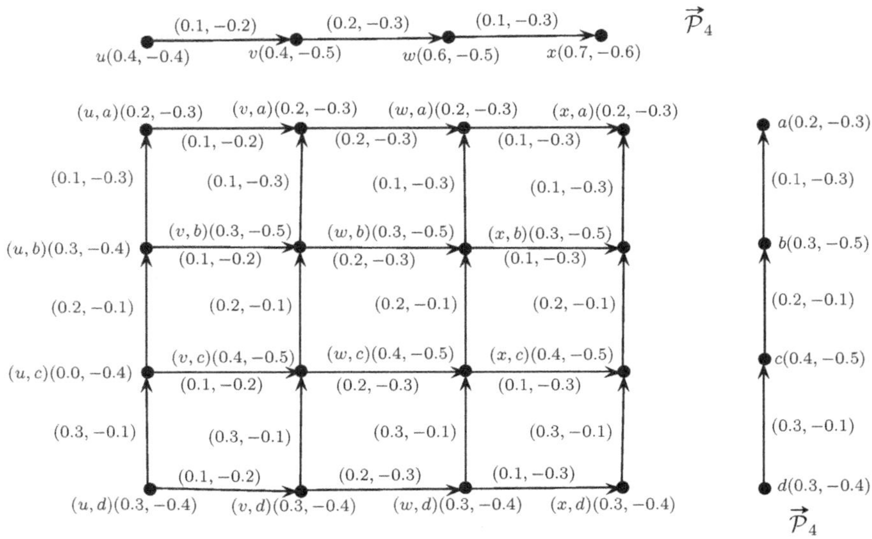

Fig. 1.37 Cartesian product $\vec{\mathcal{P}}_4 \Box \vec{\mathcal{P}}_4$

1. $(A_1 \Box A_2)(x_1, x_2) = (\mu^p_{A_1}(x_1) \wedge \mu^p_{A_2}(x_2), \mu^n_{A_1}(x_1) \vee \mu^n_{A_2}(x_2))$, for all $(x_1, x_2) \in X_1 \times X_2$,
2. $(\vec{B}_1 \Box \vec{B}_2)((x, x_2)(x, y_2)) = (\mu^p_{A_1}(x) \wedge \mu^p_{\vec{B}_2}(x_2 y_2), \mu^n_{A_1}(x) \vee \mu^n_{\vec{B}_2}(x_2 y_2))$, for all $x \in X_1$, $x_2 y_2 \in \vec{E}_2$,
3. $(\vec{B}_1 \Box \vec{B}_2)((x_1, z)(y_1, z)) = (\mu^p_{\vec{B}_1}(x_1 y_1) \wedge \mu^p_{A_2}(z), \mu^n_{\vec{B}_1}(x_1 y_1) \vee \mu^n_{A_2}(z))$, for all $z \in X_2$, $x_1 y_1 \in \vec{E}_1$.

Example 1.28 The Cartesian product of two bipolar fuzzy directed paths is shown in Fig. 1.37.

Definition 1.66 The **direct product** of two bipolar fuzzy digraphs $\vec{G}_1 = (A_1, \vec{B}_1)$ and $\vec{G}_2 = (A_2, \vec{B}_2)$ is a pair $\vec{G}_1 \times \vec{G}_2 = (A_1 \times A_2, \vec{B}_1 \times \vec{B}_2)$, where $A_1 \times A_2 = (\mu^p_{A_1 \times A_2}, \mu^n_{A_1 \times A_2})$ and $\vec{B}_1 \times \vec{B}_2 = (\mu^p_{\vec{B}_1 \times \vec{B}_2}, \mu^n_{\vec{B}_1 \times \vec{B}_2})$ are defined as

1. $(A_1 \times A_2)(x_1, x_2) = (\mu^p_{A_1}(x_1) \wedge \mu^p_{A_2}(x_2), \mu^n_{A_1}(x_1) \vee \mu^n_{A_2}(x_2))$, for all $(x_1, x_2) \in X_1 \times X_2$,
2. $(\vec{B}_1 \times \vec{B}_2)((x_1, x_2)(x_1, y_2)) = (\mu^p_{\vec{B}_1}(x_1 y_1) \wedge \mu^p_{\vec{B}_2}(x_2 y_2), \mu^n_{\vec{B}_1}(x_1 y_1) \vee \mu^n_{\vec{B}_2}(x_2 y_2))$, for all $\overrightarrow{x_1 y_1} \in \vec{E}_1$, $\overrightarrow{x_2 y_2} \in \vec{E}_2$.

Example 1.29 The direct product of two bipolar fuzzy digraphs is shown in Fig. 1.38.

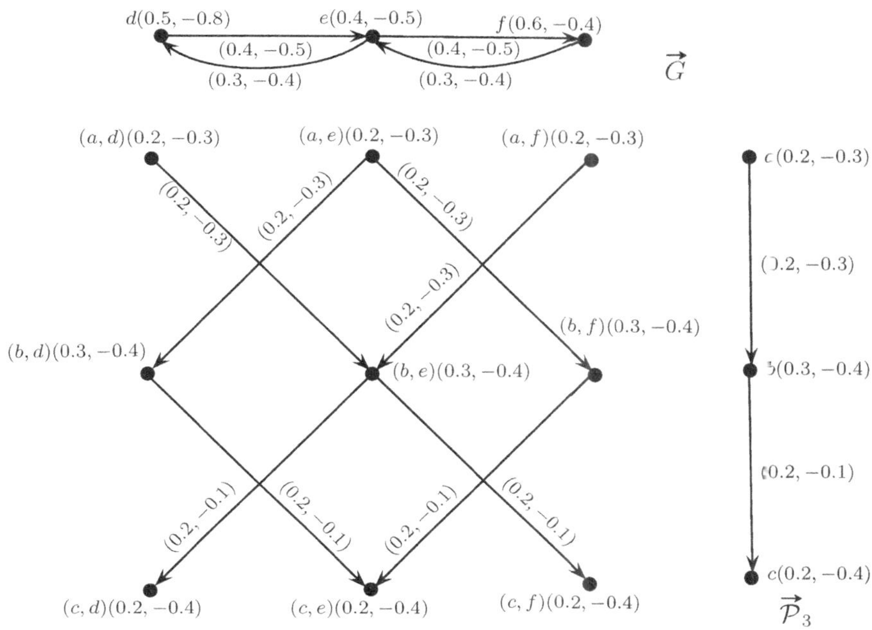

Fig. 1.38 Direct product $\vec{G} \times \vec{\mathcal{P}}_3$

Definition 1.67 The **strong product** of two bipolar fuzzy digraphs $\vec{G}_1 = (A_1, \vec{B}_1)$ and $\vec{G}_2 = (A_2, \vec{B}_2)$ is denoted by the pair $\vec{G}_1 \boxtimes \vec{G}_2 = (A_1 \boxtimes A_2, \vec{B}_1 \boxtimes \vec{B}_2)$ and defined as

1. $(A_1 \boxtimes A_2)(x_1, x_2) = (\mu^p_{A_1}(x_1) \wedge \mu^p_{A_2}(x_2), \mu^n_{A_1}(x_1) \vee \mu^n_{A_2}(x_2))$, for all $(x_1, x_2) \in X_1 \times X_2$,
2. $(\vec{B}_1 \boxtimes \vec{B}_2)((x, x_2)(x, y_2))=(\mu^p_{A_1}(x) \wedge \mu^p_{\vec{B}_2}(x_2y_2), \mu^n_{A_1}(x) \vee \mu^n_{\vec{B}_2}(x_2y_2))$, for all $x \in X_1$, $\overrightarrow{x_2y_2} \in \vec{E}_2$,
3. $(\vec{B}_1 \boxtimes \vec{B}_2)((x_1, z)(y_1, z)) = (\mu^p_{\vec{B}_1}(x_1y_1) \wedge \mu^p_{A_2}(z), \mu^n_{\vec{B}_1}(x_1y_1) \vee \mu^n_{A_2}(z))$, for all $z \in X_2$, $\overrightarrow{x_1y_1} \in \vec{E}_1$,
4. $(\vec{B}_1 \boxtimes \vec{B}_2)((x_1, x_2)(x_1, y_2)) = (\mu^p_{\vec{B}_1}(x_1y_1) \wedge \mu^p_{\vec{B}_2}(x_2y_2), \mu^n_{\vec{B}_1}(x_1y_1) \vee \mu^n_{\vec{B}_2}(x_2y_2))$, for all $\overrightarrow{x_1y_1} \in \vec{E}_1$, $\overrightarrow{x_2y_2} \in \vec{E}_2$.

Example 1.30 The strong product of two bipolar fuzzy directed paths is shown in Fig. 1.39.

Definition 1.68 The **lexicographic product** of two bipolar fuzzy digraphs $\vec{G}_1 = (A_1, \vec{B}_1)$ and $\vec{G}_2 = (A_2, \vec{B}_2)$, denoted by $\vec{G}_1 \bullet \vec{G}_2$, is defined as a pair $(A_1 \bullet A_2, \vec{B}_1 \bullet \vec{B}_2)$ such that

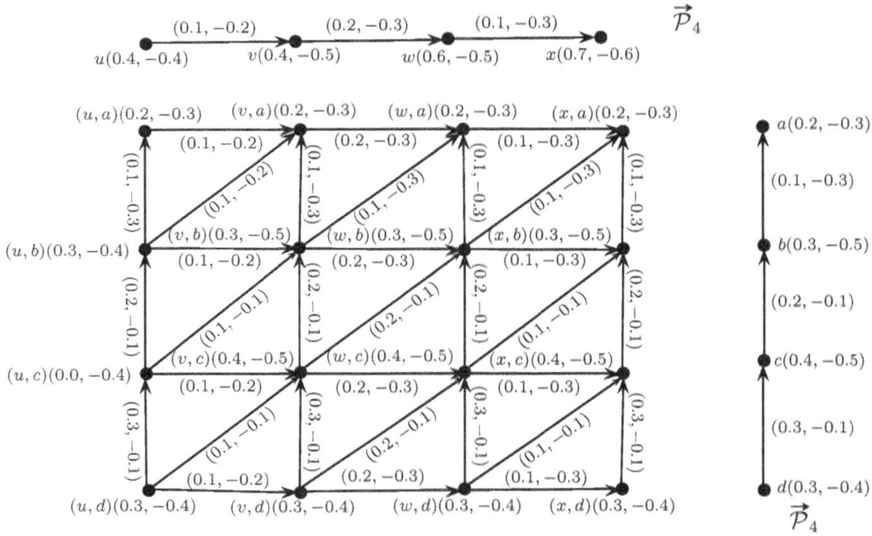

Fig. 1.39 Strong product $\vec{\mathcal{P}}_4 \boxtimes \vec{\mathcal{P}}_4$

1. $(A_1 \bullet A_2)(x_1, x_2) = (\mu^p_{A_1}(x_1) \wedge \mu^p_{A_2}(x_2), \mu^n_{A_1}(x_1) \vee \mu^n_{A_2}(x_2))$, for all $(x_1, x_2) \in X_1 \times X_2$,
2. $(\vec{B}_1 \bullet \vec{B}_2)((x, x_2)(x, y_2)) = (\mu^p_{A_1}(x) \wedge \mu^p_{\vec{B}_2}(x_2y_2), \mu^n_{A_1}(x) \vee \mu^n_{\vec{B}_2}(x_2y_2))$, for all $x \in X_1$, $\overrightarrow{x_2y_2} \in \vec{E}_2$,
3. $(\vec{B}_1 \bullet \vec{B}_2)((x_1, x_2)(x_1, y_2)) = (\mu^p_{\vec{B}_1}(x_1y_1) \wedge \mu^p_{\vec{B}_2}(x_2y_2), \mu^n_{\vec{B}_1}(x_1y_1) \vee \mu^n_{\vec{B}_2}(x_2y_2))$, for all $\overrightarrow{x_1y_1} \in \vec{E}_1$, $\overrightarrow{x_2y_2} \in \vec{E}_2$.

Example 1.31 The lexicographic product of two bipolar fuzzy directed paths is shown in Fig. 1.40.

Theorem 1.10 *The union, intersection, join, composition, Cartesian product, direct product, lexicographic product, and strong product of two bipolar fuzzy digraphs is also a bipolar fuzzy digraph.*

Definition 1.69 A bipolar fuzzy digraph $\vec{G}' = (A', B')$ is called a **bipolar fuzzy subdigraph** of a bipolar fuzzy digraph $\vec{G} = (A, \vec{B})$, written as $\vec{G}' \subseteq \vec{G}$, if $A' \subseteq A$ and $\vec{B}' \subseteq \vec{B}$, i.e.,
1. $\mu^p_{A'}(x) \leq \mu^p_A(x)$, $\mu^n_{A'}(x) \geq \mu^n_A(x)$, for all x ∈ X,
2. $\mu^p_{\vec{B}'}(xy) \leq \mu^p_{\vec{B}}(xy)$, $\mu^n_{\vec{B}'}(xy) \geq \mu^n_{\vec{B}}(xy)$, for all x, y ∈ X.

Definition 1.70 A bipolar fuzzy digraph $\vec{G} = (A, \vec{B})$ is called **strong** if

$$\mu^p_{\vec{B}}(xy) = \mu^p_A(x) \wedge \mu^p_A(y) \text{ and } \mu^n_{\vec{B}}(xy) = \mu^n_A(x) \vee \mu^n_A(y), \quad \text{for all } \overrightarrow{xy} \in \vec{E}.$$

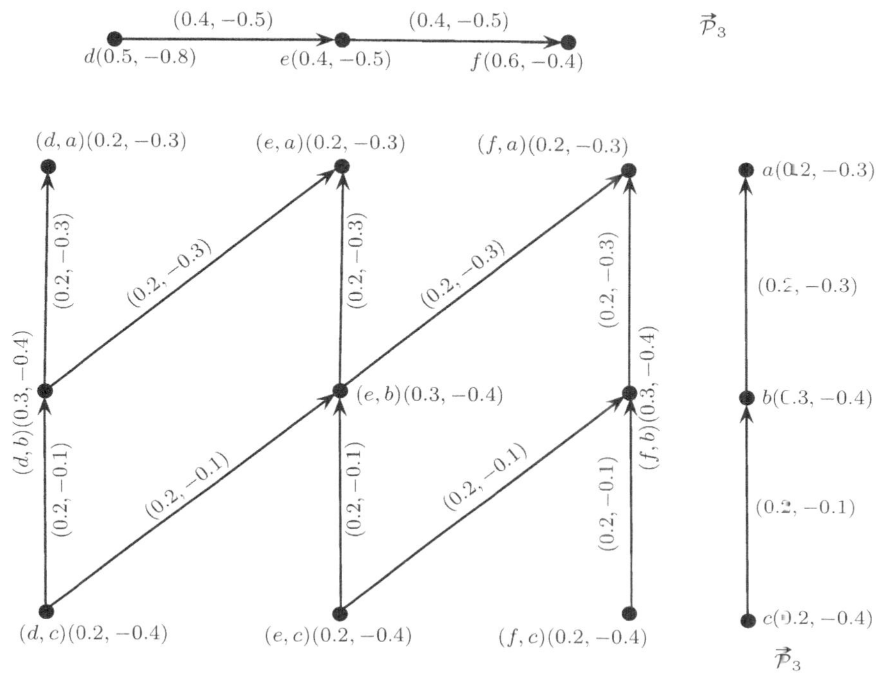

Fig. 1.40 Lexicographic product $\vec{\mathcal{P}}_3 \bullet \vec{\mathcal{P}}_3$

Proposition 1.22 *If $\vec{G}_1$ and $\vec{G}_2$ are strong bipolar fuzzy digraphs, then $\vec{G}_1 \square \vec{G}_2$, $\vec{G}_1 \times \vec{G}_2$ and $\vec{G}_1 \boxtimes \vec{G}_2$ are strong bipolar fuzzy digraphs.*

Definition 1.71 Let $Q(X \to Y)$ and $R(Y \to Z)$ be two bipolar fuzzy relations. The **max-min-max composition** $R \circ Q(X \to Z)$ is the bipolar fuzzy relation defined by the membership functions

$$\mu^p_{R\circ Q}(x, z) = \bigvee_y \left(\mu^p_Q(x, y) \wedge \mu^p_R(y, z)\right),$$

$$\mu^n_{R\circ Q}(x, z) = \bigwedge_y \left(\mu^n_Q(x, y) \vee \mu^n_R(y, z)\right), \quad \text{for all } (x, z) \in X \times Z,\ y \in Y.$$

Definition 1.72 Let $Q(X \to Y)$ and $R(Y \to Z)$ be two bipolar fuzzy relations. The **max-product−min-product composition** $R \circ Q(X \to Z)$ is the bipolar fuzzy relation defined by the membership functions

$$\mu^p_{R\circ Q}(x, z) = \bigvee_y (\mu^p_Q(x, y) \cdot \mu^p_R(y, z))$$

$$\mu^n_{R\circ Q}(x, z) = \bigwedge_y (\mu^n_Q(x, y) \cdot \mu^n_R(y, z)), \quad \text{for all } (x, z) \in X \times Z,\ y \in Y.$$

1.6 Applications of Bipolar Fuzzy Digraphs to Decision Making

Decision-making refers to making decisions in the presence of multiple, usually conflicting criteria. Decision-making problems are common in everyday life. Graph theory is a useful tool in solving the combinatorial and decision-making problems in different areas of science and technology. To expand the base of applications, fuzzy graphs were introduced to model complex systems arising in computer science and operation research. Fuzzy models are becoming useful because of their aim in reducing the differences between the traditional numerical models used in engineering and sciences and the symbolic models used in expert systems. In some cases, when the complex models are fuzzy in nature and contain bipolar information, it becomes necessary to make judgments with two opposite agreements. Decision-making situations can be categorized in different groups according to certain characteristics, sources of information and preference representations.

1. **Single-criteria decision-making** carries a situation, where we have only one source of information (or criteria) to solve a decision problem. In these situations, the solution to the problem comes directly and exclusively from the information provided.
2. In decision-making process, an expert mostly needs to compare a finite set of alternatives $x_i (i = 1, 2, \dots, n)$ and construct a preference relation. However, decision-making is not only the case for a single expert, whereas some decision problems have to be explained by a group of experts which work together to find the best alternative(s) from a set of feasible alternatives under certain characteristics. The nature of decision-making with multiple experts is called **group decision-making (GDM)** which is also known as **multi-person decision-making**.
3. Real-world decision-making problems are usually too complex and ill-structured to be considered through the examination of a single criterion, attribute, or point of view that will lead to the optimum decision. In fact, such a unidimensional approach is merely an oversimplification and can lead to unrealistic decisions. A more appealing approach would be the simultaneous consideration of all pertinent factors that are related to the problem. **Multi-criteria decision-making** (MCDM) is a discipline in its own right, which deals with decisions involving the choice of the best alternative from several potential candidates in a decision, subject to several criteria or attribute that may be concrete or vague.

Using different criteria of decision-making, real-world applications of bipolar fuzzy sets and bipolar fuzzy digraphs in medical diagnosis, social networks, marketing, and decision support systems are discussed here in detail.

1.6.1 Bipolar Fuzzy Neurons in Medical Diagnosis

Medical science has drawn much attention due to its recent advances in research in the past few years. Diseases are often misdiagnosed because the symptoms and their interrelationships are usually not considered during computations. Diseases can also be caused by the wrong medical treatments and the lack of information and ignorance of incompleteness of patient's disease information. Bipolar fuzzy relations are one of the most fruitful and interesting mathematical techniques to study the relations of diseases and their causes. In the **discrimination analysis** for diagnosis of an illness, the symptoms are ranked according to the grade of discrimination of each disease by a particular symptom. In this application, the procedure for the diagnosis of diseases of patients with particular symptoms is discussed in detail. Let $D = \{d_1, d_2, \ldots, d_n\}$ be the set of diseases, $S = \{s_1, s_2, \ldots, s_r\}$ the set of symptoms and $P = \{p_1, p_2, \ldots, p_m\}$ be the set of patients. Let $Q : D \to S$ and $R : S \to P$ be the bipolar fuzzy relations. The method for calculating the disease of each patient is given in Algorithm 1.6.1.

Algorithm 1.6.1 Algorithm for the medical diagnosis of patients

Begin
    Input the bipolar fuzzy relations $Q = [(q^p_{ij}, q^n_{ij})]_{n\times r}$ and $R = [(\xi^p_{jk}, \xi^n_{jk})]_{r\times m}$.
    for i from $1 \to n$
        for k from $1 \to m$
            $t^p_{max} = 0$
            $t^n_{min} = 0$
            for j from $1 \to r$
                $\alpha^p_j = q^p_{ij} \times \xi^p_{jk}$
                $\alpha^n_j = q^p_{ij} \times \xi^p_{jk}$
                $t^p_{max} = \max\{t^p_{max}, \alpha^p_j\}$
                $t^n_{max} = \max\{t^n_{max}, \alpha^n_j\}$
            end for
            $t^p_{ik} = t^p_{max}$
            $t^n_{ik} = t^n_{min}$
        end for
    end for
    for i from $1 \to n$
        $S_{max} = 0$
        for k from $1 \to m$
            $d_{ik} = \sqrt{(t^p_{ik})^2 + (t^n_{ik})^2}$
            $p_{ik} = t^p_{ik} + t^n_{ik} \times d_{ik}$
            $S_{max} = \max\{S_{max}, p_{ik}\}$
            if $S_{max} = p_{ik}$ then
                print: Patient p_k is suffering from disease d_i.
            end if
        end for

```
27     end for
28 End
```

Description of Algorithm 1.6.1: Line 1 passes the input of bipolar fuzzy relations Q(diseases $\rightarrow$ symptoms) and R(symptoms $\rightarrow$ patients) with n number of diseases, r symptoms, and m patients. Lines 3−−16 calculate the max-product-min-product composition $T = R \circ Q$. Lines 17−−26 calculate and print the symmetry index of diseases corresponding to each patient.

Time complexity: Line 1 corresponds to the input of the algorithm, its time complexity is O(1). The for loop on line 7 runs r times, and therefore its complexity is O(r). The nested loop on line 3 runs nmr times, and therefore its time complexity is O(nmr). The time complexity of lines 17 and 19 is O(nm) and O(m), respectively. The net time complexity of the algorithm is O(nmr).

To illustrate Algorithm 1.6.1, consider the example of set of diseases $D =$ {Diabetes, Dengue, Tuberculosis} and the set of symptoms $S =$ {Temperature, Insulin, Blood pressure, Blood platelets, Cough}. The bipolar fuzzy relation $Q(D \rightarrow S)$ is shown in Table 1.11. Consider the set of patients as P = {Fayyaz, Amir, Aslam}. The bipolar fuzzy relation $R(S \rightarrow P)$ is given in Table 1.12. Using Definition 1.72, the max-product-min-product composition $T = R \circ Q$ is shown in Table 1.13.

Table 1.11 Bipolar fuzzy relation $Q(D \rightarrow S)$

Q	Temperature	Insulin	Blood pressure	Blood platelets	Cough
Diabetes	(0.2, −0.8)	(0.9, −0.1)	(0.1, −0.8)	(0.1, −0.8)	(0.1, −0.8)
Dengue	(0.9, −0.1)	(0.0, −0.8)	(0.8, −0.1)	(0.9, −0.1)	(0.1, −0.8)
Tuberculosis	(0.6, −0.2)	(0.0, −0.9)	(0.4, −0.4)	(0.0, −0.8)	(0.9, −0.1)

Table 1.12 Bipolar fuzzy relation $R(S \rightarrow P)$

R	Fayyaz	Amir	Aslam
Temperature	(0.8, −0.1)	(0.6, −0.2)	(0.4, −0.4)
Insulin	(0.2, −0.6)	(0.9, −0.1)	(0.2, −0.7)
Blood pressure	(0.4, −0.4)	(0.1, −0.8)	(0.1, −0.7)
Blood platelets	(0.8, −0.1)	(0.2, −0.7)	(0.3, −0.6)
Cough	(0.3, −0.4)	(0.5, −0.4)	(0.8, −0.2)

Table 1.13 Composition $T = R \circ Q(D \rightarrow P)$

T	Fayyaz	Amir	Aslam
Diabetes	(0.18, −0.06)	(0.81, −0.01)	(0.18, −0.07)
Dengue	(0.72, −0.01)	(0.54, −0.02)	(0.36, −0.04)
Tuberculosis	(0.48, −0.02)	(0.45, −0.04)	(0.72, −0.02)

By applying Algorithm 1.6.1, it is identified that Fayyaz is suffering from Dengue, Amir is suffering from Diabetes, and Aslam is a patient of Tuberculosis.

1.6.2 Social Networking

Social influence is a widespread mechanism to figure out a best-suited group economically, politically, educationally, etc. Social conflict and influence occur when individual opinions, decisions, and behaviors are influenced by others. In social networking problems, it is often observed that graphical models need to incorporate more structure than simply the adjacencies between vertices. In studies of group behavior, it is a common social issue that certain people can influence the thinking of others. A directed graph, called an influence graph, can be used to model this behavior. Each person of a group is represented by a vertex. There is a directed edge from vertex x to vertex y when the person represented by vertex x influences the person represented by vertex y. This digraph does not contain loops. In influence graph, the vertex (node) represents a power (authority) of a person and the edge represents the influence of a person on another person in the social group. The influence of the person has a fuzzy boundary, which gives a better representation in the fuzzy digraph.

In a fuzzy influence graph, the degree of membership of nodes depicts the degree of power of a person belonging to the social group. The degree of membership can be interpreted as how much power a person posses in a group. The degree of membership of directed edges can be interpreted as the influence of one person onto another person.

The influence of a person cannot always be positive. If two persons in a social group have some conflicts, then the influence between these persons can be negative. Similarly, if a person is not in the good books of the other person, the influence is negative on the other person. The coexistence of the positive and negative behavior of people can only be studied using a bipolar fuzzy digraph known as bipolar fuzzy influence graph. Consider the example of a bipolar fuzzy influence graph given in Fig. 1.41.

In a bipolar fuzzy influence graph, the degree of membership of vertices is defined in terms of its positive and negative membership value. The positive degree of membership can be interpreted as how much power a person posses and negative membership value depicts as how much power a person losses, e.g., Tanzel has 70% power within the social group but he losses 60% power in the same group. The degree of membership of directed edges can be interpreted as the percentage of positive and negative influence, e.g., Amir follows 80% Naila's suggestions but he does not follow 20% of her suggestions. Thus, bipolar fuzzy influence graphs are more compatible as compared to fuzzy influence graphs and can be used to study the influence and conflict among objects more precisely.

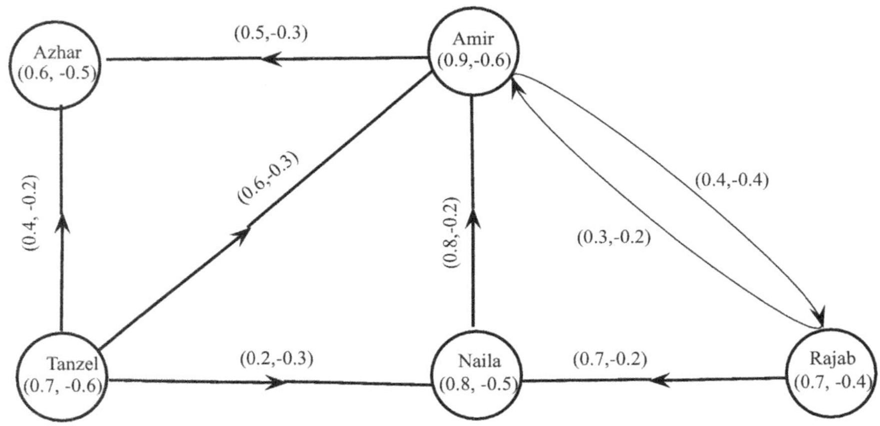

Fig. 1.41 Bipolar fuzzy influence graph

1.6.3 Bipolar Fuzzy Organizational Model

Bipolar fuzzy influence graph can also be used to study the most influential person within an organization. In this bipolar fuzzy graphical model, vertices represent employees and directed edge represents the influence of an employee to another employee of the company. Such bipolar fuzzy digraphs have applications in modeling social structures, communication, and distributed computing. Consider the example of an organization having employees and their designation as shown in Table 1.14.

For this organization, the set of employees is $E = \{BOD, MQ, TM, MZ, AK, RB, St\}$. The work environment within the organization is observed as follows:

- Mujeeb Qayyum has worked with Munib Zia for over 10 years, and he values his input on strategic initiatives.
- The board of directors is chaired by a long time associate of Munib Zia. Like Mujeeb, the chair of board also values Munib.

Table 1.14 Names of employees in the organization with their designations

Name	Designation
Board of Director (BOD)	Board of director
Mujeeb Qayyum (MQ)	CEO
Tahir Mahmood (TM)	CTO
Munib Zia (MZ)	Director of marketing
Arif Kaleem (AK)	Director of product development
Rizwan Bashir (RB)	Director of human resources
Staff (St)	Staff

- For organization, the entire Marketing and HR team is very important. Rizwan Bashir is especially centered in the organization.
- Tahir Mahmood and Rizwan Bashir have a history of conflict.
- Tahir Mahmood has a great influence on the development team.

Considering the above points, an influence graph can be constructed but such a directed graph cannot represent the power of employees within the organization and the degree of influence of employees on each other. As the power and influence have no defined boundaries, it is desired to represent them in the form of a fuzzy set. The fuzzy digraph represents the influence of employees on each other. To represent both power and conflict at the same time, we apply here the concept of bipolar fuzzy set, which is more precise about the influence and conflicts between the employees. The bipolar fuzzy set of the employees is shown in Table 1.15.

The bipolar fuzzy relation among employees is shown in Table 1.16. The resultant bipolar fuzzy digraph is shown in Fig. 1.42.

The positive membership value of a vertex in Fig. 1.42 represents the percentage of influence and negative membership value represents the percentage of conflict of one employee to the other, e.g., MQ possesses 90% power within the organization or MZ has 70% power and 20% conflicts. The positive degree of membership and negative degree of membership can also be interpreted as the percentage of positive and negative influence respectively, e.g., BOD is 60% influenced by MZ's opinions but ignores 10% of his opinions. In Fig. 1.42, it is clear that MZ has influenced both BOD and MQ. He can influence both of them equally as the degree of membership in

Table 1.15 Bipolar fuzzy set A of employees

A	BOD	MQ	TM	MZ	AK	RB	St
μ_A^p	0.9	0.9	0.8	0.7	0.6	0.6	0.5
μ_A^n	−0.1	0.0	−0.3	−0.2	−0.5	−0.4	−0.5

Table 1.16 Adjacency matrix corresponding to Fig. 1.42

Employees	BOD	MQ	TM	MZ	AK	RB	St
BOD	(0, 0)	(0.8, 0.0)	(0, 0)	(0, 0)	(0, 0)	(0, 0)	(0, 0)
MQ	(0, 0)	(0, 0)	(0.7, 0.0)	(0, 0)	(0, 0)	(0, 0)	(0.5, 0.0)
TM	(0, 0)	(0, 0)	(0, 0)	(0, 0)	(0, 0)	(0, 0)	(0.4, −0.3)
MZ	(0.6, −0.1)	(0.6, 0)	(0, 0)	(0, 0)	(0, 0)	(0, 0)	(0.4, −0.2)
AK	(0, 0)	(0, 0)	(0, 0)	(0, 0)	(0, 0)	(0.5, −0.3)	(0.5, −0.5)
RB	(0, 0)	(0, 0)	(0, 0)	(0, 0)	(0, 0)	(0, 0)	(0.5, −0.3)
St	(0, 0)	(0, 0)	(0, 0)	(0, 0)	(0, 0)	(0, 0)	(0, 0)

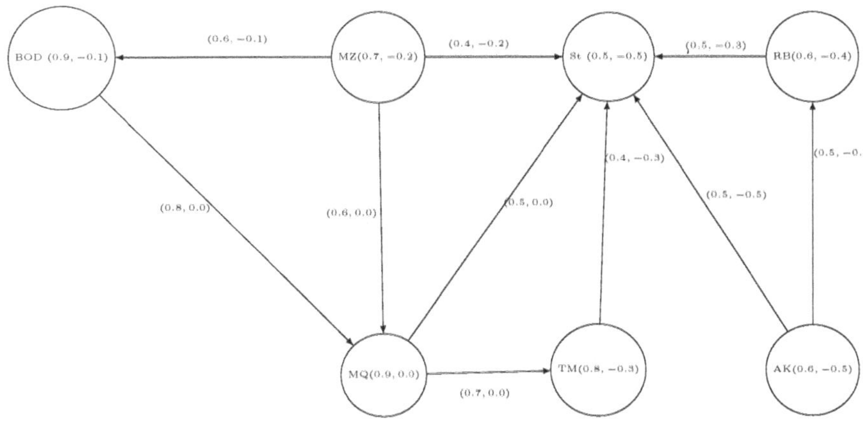

Fig. 1.42 Bipolar fuzzy organizational model

both cases is 0.6. But in the case of MQ, there is no negative degree of membership but in the case of BOQ there is a bit conflict which is 0.1. It is quite obvious that MZ is the most influential employee in the organization and possesses 70% power within the organization.

1.6.4 Bipolar Fuzzy Graphs in Marketability

The marketability of science books is based on three criteria, i.e., pictures P, cost C, and examples E. It is known that if a book has more examples, low cost and a large number of pictures, the sale of the book improves. Here we assume that the sale of 60 percent of books in any stock is considered as a good sale. Consider the bipolar fuzzy set of criteria $Cr = \{(P, 0.6, -0.3), (C, 0.1, -0.8), (E, 0.6, -0.3)\}$. The degree of membership of E and P can be interpreted as 60% of books contain examples and pictures and 30% are theory based. The degree of membership of C depicts that 10% of the books have a low price but 80% are expensive. Cr can be written in the form of a matrix as

$$C = \left[\, (0.6, -0.3)\ (0.1, -0.8)\ (E, 0.6, -0.3) \,\right]$$

To determine a better sale, we present it in bipolar fuzzy digraph given in Fig. 1.43 and apply Algorithm 1.6.2 to it.

The bipolar fuzzy digraph in Fig. 1.43 shows a typical three-layered architecture of bipolar fuzzy neuron, i.e., input, hidden, and output layer. In a bipolar fuzzy neuron the input, hidden, and output weights are defined in terms of positive degree of membership and negative degree of non-membership. The aggregation, or activation,

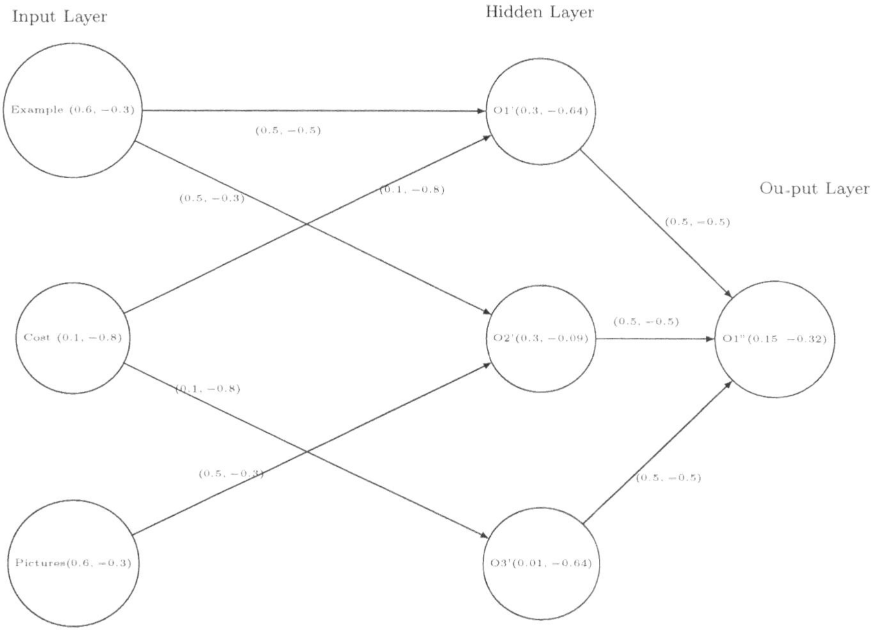

Fig. 1.43 Bipolar fuzzy digraph of marketability

of a neuron involves both positive and negative degrees of membership. A node in the input layer represents the criteria C of sales. A node in the hidden layer shows the aggregation/activation of the neuron, and the output layer shows the expected sales. The bipolar fuzzy relation IH between the input and hidden layers and the bipolar fuzzy relation HO between the hidden and output layers are given in Eq. (1.13).

$$IH = \begin{bmatrix} (0.5,-0.5) & (0.5,-0.3) & (0.0,0.0) \\ (0.1,-0.8) & (0.0,0.0) & (0.1,-0.8) \\ (0.0,0.0) & (0.5,-0.3) & (0.0,0.0) \end{bmatrix}, \quad HO = \begin{bmatrix} (0.5,-0.5) \\ (0.5,-0.5) \\ (0.5,-0.5) \end{bmatrix}. \tag{1.13}$$

The output on the hidden layer can be computed by taking composition between IH and C, i.e., $O' = C \circ IH = \big[\,(0.3,-0.64)\ (0.3,-0.09)\ (0.01,-0.64)\,\big]$. Similarly, the final output is calculated by taking the composition of O' and HO i.e., $O'' = O' \circ HO = \big[\,(0.15,-0.32)\,\big]$. The bipolar fuzzy digraph output layer in Fig. 1.43 shows that the sale is about 15 percent. The method to calculate the percentage sale of books is described in Algorithm 1.6.2.

Algorithm 1.6.2 Algorithm to check the marketability of books

```
Begin
    C := Criteria of sale
    IH := Relation between input and hidden layer
```

```
04      HO := Relation between hidden and output layer
05      O' := C ∘ IH
06      O'' := O' ∘ HO
07      if O'' is not expected
08          Modify C using backpropagation and goto line 4
09      end if
10    print O''
11 End
```

Description of Algorithm 1.6.2: The first three lines of the algorithm set the required input. At lines 5 and 6, output on the hidden layer is calculated by taking the composition of bipolar fuzzy relations C and IH. The final output is calculated on line 5 by taking the composition of the output of hidden layer and bipolar fuzzy relation HO. Lines 7–10 check whether the results are in the desirable limits or not. If they are not within limits, the positive and negative membership degrees are modified using backpropagation.

Time complexity of Algorithm 1.6.2: The net time complexity of the algorithm depends on lines 5 and 6 only. Line 5 is the composition of C and IH whose running time is cn, where c is the number of criteria and n is the number of activations in the hidden layer. Line 6 is the composition of O' and HO with n complexity. The complexity of algorithm is $O(cn)$ or $O(n)$. Since n is smaller than cn, the net complexity is $O(cn)$.

1.6.5 Vulnerability Assessment of Gas Pipeline Networks

The vulnerability assessment of a gas pipeline network can be categorized into structural components: reliability, connectivity reliability, flow performance reliability, and/or inter-dependent reliability. These reliabilities depend on the type of pipe and fittings used, their aging, and the connection between fittings and pipe. In most of the cases, we don't know the exact age and condition of connectivity. We can present these factors as a bipolar fuzzy set. Any gas network can be represented as a bipolar fuzzy digraph $\overrightarrow{G} = (F, P)$, where F is the bipolar fuzzy set of pipe fittings, presenting their ages and connectivity conditions as positive and negative degree of membership $\mu_F^p(x)$ and $\mu_F^n(x)$, respectively, and P is a bipolar fuzzy relation of pipeline fittings. Consider the bipolar fuzzy set F of pipe fittings in Table 1.17 and

Table 1.17 Bipolar fuzzy set F

A	$C1$	$C2$	$C3$	$C4$	$C5$	$C6$
μ_A^p	0.7	0.5	0.6	0.7	0.5	0.5
μ_A^n	−0.1	−0.3	−0.3	−0.2	−0.4	−0.3

Table 1.18 Bipolar fuzzy relation P

P	$C1$	$C2$	$C3$	$C4$	$C5$	$C6$
C_1	(0, 0)	(0.5, −0.1)	(0, 0)	(0, 0)	(0, 0)	(0, 0)
C_2	(0, 0)	(0, 0)	(0.5, −0.3)	(0, 0)	(0, 0)	(0, 0)
C_3	(0, 0)	(0, 0)	(0, 0)	(0, 0)	(0.5, −0.2)	(0.3, −0.3)
C_4	(0.6, −0.1)	(0, 0)	(0, 0)	(0, 0)	(0.5, −0.2)	(0.6, −0.2)
C_5	(0.6, −0.1)	(0, 0)	(0, 0)	(0, 0)	(0, 0)	(0, 0)
C_6	(0, 0)	(0, 0)	(0, 0)	(0, 0)	(0, 0)	(0,0)

Table 1.19 Adjacency matrix of ranks of edges

Weights	$C1$	$C2$	$C3$	$C4$	$C5$	$C6$
C_1	0	0.4490	0	0	0	0
C_2	0	0	0.3251	0	0	0
C_3	0	0	0	0	0.3923	0.1727
C_4	0.5392	0	0	0	0.3923	0.4735
C_5	0.5392	0	0	0	0	0
C_6	0	0	0	0	0	0

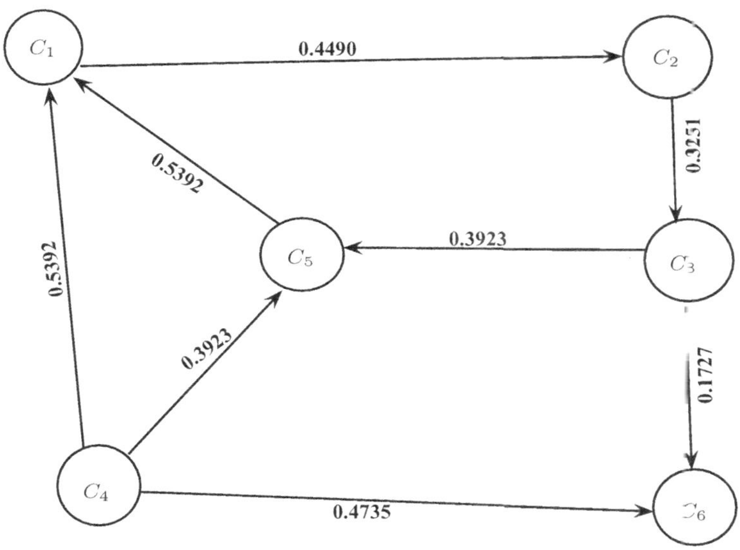

Fig. 1.44 Weighted digraph of a gas pipeline network

bipolar fuzzy relation P of the gas pipeline network is represented by the adjacency matrix in Table 1.18.

Calculate the rank S_i of each membership value of directed edge from bipolar fuzzy relation P as, $S_i = {\mu_i}^p + {\mu_i}^n * d_i$, where d_i is the distance between membership poles of the directed edge, i.e., $d_i = \sqrt{(\mu^p)^2{}_i + (\mu^n)^2{}_i}$. The final adjacency matrix of weights (ranks) of directed edges is shown in Table 1.19 and weighted digraph developed based on these weights is given in Fig. 1.44. This weighted digraph $\overrightarrow{G}_w$ can be used for analyzing different kind of vulnerabilities in gas pipeline networks.

The overall procedure to determine vulnerability of pipeline network in explained in Algorithm 1.6.3 with net complexity $O(f^2)$.

Algorithm 1.6.3 Algorithm to determine vulnerability of pipeline network

Algorithm	Complexity
01 Begin	
02 Input the bipolar fuzzy set $F = \{C_1, C_2, \ldots, C_f\}$ of f number of fittings.	f
03 Input the bipolar fuzzy relation $P = [(\mu^p_{ij}, \mu^n_{ij}]_{n\times n}$	f^2
04 for i from $1 \rightarrow f$	f
05 for j from 1 to f	f^2
06 $d_{ij} := \sqrt{(\mu^p_{ij})^2 + (\mu^n_{ij})^2}$	f^2
07 $S_{ij} := \mu^p_{P(i)} + \mu^n_{P(i)} * d_i$	f^2
08 end for	f^2
09 end for	f
10 Print $W = [S_{ij}]_{f\times f}$	f^2
11 End	

Description and complexity of Algorithm 1.6.3: The algorithm first takes a bipolar fuzzy set and bipolar fuzzy relation of pipeline fittings as an input. Lines 4–9 calculate the adjacency matrix of weights corresponding to bipolar fuzzy relation based on the degree of membership of directed edges. This weighted matrix is printed in line 10. Since nested loop on lines 5−8 runs f^2 times, the running time of Algorithm 1.6.3 is $O(f^2)$.

1.6.6 Bipolar Fuzzy Digraph in Travel Time

Communication graphs are used in many network models, such as transportation, as a natural mathematical tool to identify problems and, then calculating the most beneficial solution. These network models are mostly used to find the shortest path between end nodes. The optimality criteria is often evaluated in terms of weights of arcs/edges between two adjacent vertices in the network. In case of transportation and road networks, the travel time is mostly used as a weight. The travel time is a function of the traffic density on the road and/or the length of the road. The length of a road is a crisp quantity but the traffic density is fuzzy in nature. In a road network, we represent crossings as nodes and roads as directed edges. The traffic density is mostly calculated on the road between adjacent crossings and can be represented as bipolar fuzzy membership values. Figure 1.45 shows the model of a road network represented as a bipolar fuzzy digraph $\overrightarrow{G} = (C, L)$, where $C = \{(C_1, 0.8, -0.1), (C_2, 0.5, -0.3), (C_3, 0.6, -0.3), (C_4, 0.7, -0.2), (C_5, 0.5, -0.3)\}$

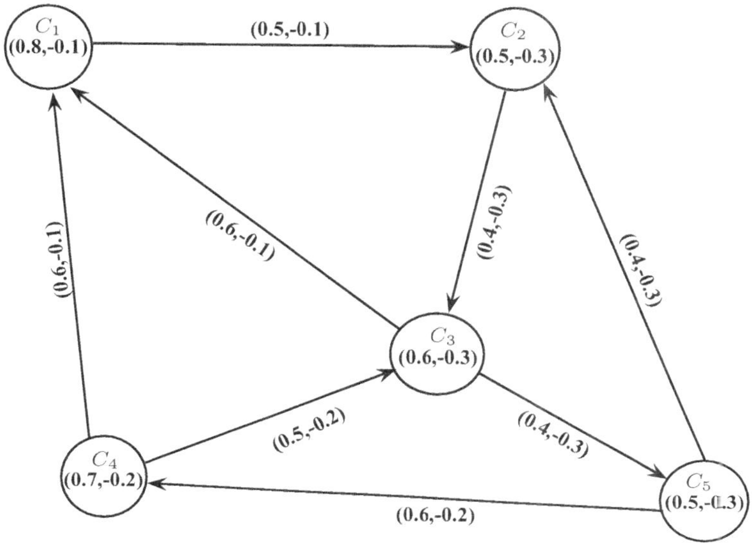

Fig. 1.45 Bipolar fuzzy graph of a road network

Table 1.20 Bipolar fuzzy relation on the set of crossings

L	C_1	C_2	C_3	C_4	C_5
C_1	(0, 0)	(0.5, −0.1)	(0, 0)	(0, 0)	(0, 0)
C_2	(0, 0)	(0, 0)	(0.4, −0.3)	(0, 0)	(0, 0)
C_3	(0.6, −0.1)	(0, 0)	(0, 0)	(0, 0)	(0.4, −0.3)
C_4	(0.6, −0.1)	(0, 0)	(0.5, −0.2)	(0, 0)	(0, 0)
C_5	(0, 0)	(0.4, −0.3)	(0, 0)	(0.6, −0.2)	(0, 0)

Table 1.21 Weights of directed edges in Fig. 1.45

L_{iw}	C_1	C_2	C_3	C_4	C_5
C_1	0	0.4490	0	0	0
C_2	0	0	0.2500	0	0
C_3	0.5392	0	0	0	0.25
C_4	0.5392	0	0.3923	0	0
C_5	0	0.25	0	0.4735	0

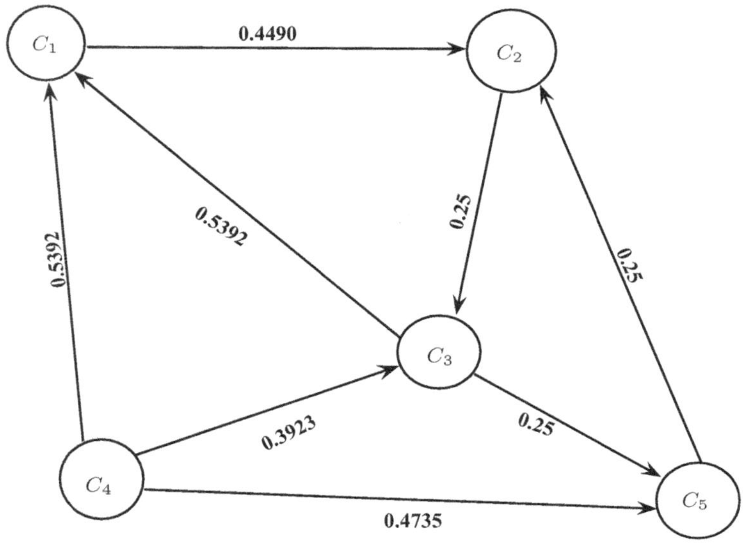

Fig. 1.46 Weighted digraph of bipolar fuzzy road network

is a bipolar fuzzy set of crossings at which the traffic density is calculated and L is a bipolar fuzzy relation of crossings given in Table 1.20.

The final weights of directed edges L_i can be calculated by finding the rank as $L_{iw} = \mu_i{}^p + \mu_i{}^n * d_i$, where d_i is the distance between membership poles of directed edge, i.e., $d_i = \sqrt{(\mu^p)^2{}_i + (\mu^n)^2{}_i}$. The final adjacency matrix is shown in Table 1.21 and the weighted digraph is shown in Fig. 1.46.

The above weighted adjacency matrix represents the final weighted digraph $\overrightarrow{G}_w$, which can be used to find the shortest/optimal path between two vertices by any of the known methods, including Dijkstra, A star, etc. Algorithm 1.6.4 generates the weighted digraph, $\overrightarrow{G}_w$, for the given bipolar fuzzy digraph $\overrightarrow{G}$ and can be used to calculate the optimal path from a source node to any other node.

Algorithm 1.6.4 Computing adjacency matrix of weighted digraph of a road network

Algorithm	Complexity
01 Begin	
02 C := Bipolar fuzzy set of crossings	1
03 R := Bipolar fuzzy relation (Adjacency matrix of $C \times C$)	1
04 for each adjacent crossing x in C	c
05 for each adjacent crossing y in C	c^2
06 if (C(x) is adjacent to C(y))	c^2
07 $\mu^p_{R(xy)} := \min(\mu^p_{C(x)}, \mu^p_{C(y)})$	c^2
08 $\mu^n_{R(xy)} := \max(\mu^n_{C(x)}, \mu^n_{C(y)})$	c^2
09 end if	c^2
10 end for	c^2
11 end for	c
12 L := Bipolar fuzzy set of edges	1
13 WR := Weighted relation (Adjacency matrix of $C \times C$)	1
14 for each bipolar fuzzy element i in L	l
15 $d_i := \sqrt{(\mu^p_{L(i)})^2 + (\mu^n_{L(i)})^2}$	l
16 $S_i := \mu^p_{L(i)} + \mu^n_{L(i)} * d_i$	l
17 $WR_{xy} := S_i$	l
18 end for	l
19 print WR	1
20 Calculate Optimal path using WR	
21 End	

Description and complexity of Algorithm 1.6.4: This algorithm is quite similar to Algorithm 1.6.3. This algorithm initially sets a bipolar fuzzy set of crossings. Lines 3−6 calculate the membership values for roads which are assigned to bipolar fuzzy set of edges in line 7 and, then the adjacency matrix is prepared in line 3. Finally, a weighted adjacency matrix is calculated in lines 9−12 using rank techniques based on membership values. This weighted matrix, which is printed on line 19, can be used for calculating the shortest path using any known algorithm like Dijkstra or A star in line 20. On a similar argument as in Algorithm 1.6.3, this algorithm can also be divided into two blocks, lines 4−11 and lines 14−18. The blocks of lines 4−11 which are calculating positive membership function and negative membership function of edges are nested between two loops of size c each, where c is the number of crossings in the road network. The running time of this block is c^2. The other block of lines 14−18, calculating the weight of edges, consists of one loop of size l, where l is the number of roads. The running time of this block is l. The running time of the algorithm can be determined using these two blocks. Since $O(c^2)$ is greater than $O(l)$, the running time of the algorithm is $O(c^2)$.

1.6.7 Comparison Analysis

Decision-making is a procedure to make an ideal decision that has the highest level of achievement from a set of alternatives which are characterized regarding various conflicting criteria. The bipolar fuzzy graph is a conceptual framework to study and analyze the bipolar fuzzy units that are intensely or frequently connected in a network. These are used to study the mathematical structures and model various practical processes and pairwise bipolar fuzzy relations among objects in social, physical, information, and biological systems. In most of the real-world problems, there are situations when an object can travel from point x to point y but not from y to x. That is, the relation among objects is non-symmetric and bipolar in nature, for instance,

1. capacity of water in pipeline networks,
2. studying the various phenomena on roads networks such as density of traffic, severity of accidents at ongoing and incoming roads, dangers of robbery, etc.,
3. modeling leadership and incapacity of candidates competing for different political seats,
4. communication network of server and client computers,
5. strength of predator-prey relations in ecological niches.

Bipolar fuzzy digraphs play a vital role in studying such problems and representing non-symmetric bipolar fuzzy relations. These mathematical structures not only study multi-attribute data but also conflicting parameters of the data which can increase the accuracy of the results. Moreover, it is difficult to deal with data given in the form of symmetric bipolar fuzzy matrices as compared to non-symmetric bipolar fuzzy matrices in which most of the entries are (0, 0). Thus, the concept of bipolar fuzzy digraphs is more reliable in many decision-making problems because they decrease the calculation complexity and time consumption when the data is given in the form of higher order matrices.

1.7 Conclusions

Mathematical modeling is an important aspect of apprehending the discrete and continuous physical systems. Bipolar uncertainty in data and information incorporates a significant role in various abstract and applied mathematical modeling and decision analysis. Graphical networks can be studied more precisely when two opposite linguistic properties are to be dealt with, emphasizing the need for a mathematical approach toward bipolar fuzzy information. Bipolar fuzzy graph has been introduced, using Zhang's powerful bipolar fuzzy set, to overcome the limitations entailed in classical graph theory and fuzzy graph theory. In this chapter, we have illustrated the notion of bipolar fuzzy sets and presented several basic concepts concerning bipolar fuzzy graphs and bipolar fuzzy digraphs. We have discussed the isomorphism properties of bipolar fuzzy graphs and various methods of their construction. We have studied certain types of bipolar fuzzy graphs, bipolar fuzzy directed walk, bipolar fuzzy bridge, connectedness in bipolar fuzzy graphs, weak and strong bipolar fuzzy edges, and properties of $\alpha-$cuts in bipolar fuzzy graphs. We have also elaborated certain operations and properties of complex bipolar fuzzy graphs. We have discussed the importance of bipolar fuzzy graphical models in various real-world phenomenon with the help of composition of bipolar fuzzy relations, connectivity and weighted matrices.

Exercises 1

1. What do you mean by $(1, -1)$, $(1, 0)$, and $(0, -1)$ in bipolar fuzzy environment?
2. If B is a bipolar fuzzy reflexive relation on A, then show that $B_{(s,t)}$ is a reflexive relation on $A_{(s,t)}$, for $s \in [0, 1]$, $t \in [-1, 0]$.
3. If B_1 and B_2 are bipolar fuzzy reflexive relations, then show that $B_1 \circ B_2$ is bipolar fuzzy reflexive relation.
4. Discuss transitive closure of a bipolar fuzzy relation.
5. If B_1 and B_2 are bipolar fuzzy symmetric relations, then $B_1 \circ B_2$ is a bipolar fuzzy symmetric relation if and only if $B_1 \circ B_2 = B_2 \circ B_1$.
6. Give an example to show that bipolar fuzzy sets and intuitionistic fuzzy sets are not the same.
7. Determine whether the following bipolar fuzzy relation R is an equivalence relation. Also calculate R^{-1}.

$$R = \begin{bmatrix} (1,-1) & (1,-0.5) & (0.6,-0.6) & (0.4,-0.7) & (0.2,-0.4) \\ (1,-0.7) & (0.5,-0.5) & (0.2,-0.6) & (0.4,-0.4) & (0.2,-0.5) \\ (0,-1) & (1,0) & (0.6,-0.5) & (0.6,-0.3) & (0.5,-0.8) \\ (0.1,-0.1) & (1,-0.4) & (0.2,-1) & (0.1,-0.7) & (0.2,0) \\ (0,-1) & (1,0) & (0.6,-0.5) & (0.6,-0.3) & (0.5,-0.8) \end{bmatrix}.$$

8. Consider the following set of diseases/diagnoses D, and set of symptoms S,

$$D = \{\text{Diabetes, Dengue, Tuberculosis}\},$$

$$S = \{\text{Temperature, Insulin, Blood pressure, Blood platelets, Cough}\}.$$

   The bipolar fuzzy relations $Q(D \to S)$ and $R(S \to P)$ are shown in Tables 1.22 and 1.23.
   Calculate **(a)** Composition and **(b)** Disease of each person.

9. Let G and H be two isomorphic bipolar fuzzy graphs.

   (a) If $G = \mathcal{P}_n$ is a bipolar fuzzy path of length n, then prove that H is also a bipolar fuzzy path of length n.

Table 1.22 Bipolar fuzzy relation $Q(D \to S)$

Q	Temperature	Insulin	Blood pressure	Blood platelets	Cough
Diabetes	(0.5, −0.8)	(0.9, −0.5)	(0.4, −0.8)	(0.6, −0.8)	(0.61, −0.8)
Dengue	(0.9, −0.5)	(0.4, −0.8)	(0.8, −0.6)	(0.9, −0.3)	(0.4, −0.8)
Tuberculosis	(0.6, −0.5)	(0.5, −0.9)	(0.4, −0.4)	(0.6, −0.8)	(0.9, −0.5)

Table 1.23 Bipolar fuzzy relation $R(S \to P)$

S	Fayyaz	Amir	Aslam
Temperature	(0.8, −0.6)	(0.6, −0.5)	(0.4, −0.4)
Insulin	(0.4, −0.6)	(0.9, −0.1)	(0.4, −0.7)
Blood pressure	(0.4, −0.6)	(0.5, −0.8)	(0.5, −0.7)
Blood platelets	(0.8, −0.5)	(0.5, −0.7)	(0.3, −0.6)
Cough	(0.3, −0.4)	(0.5, −0.4)	(0.8, −0.2)

(b) If $G = C_n$ is a bipolar fuzzy cycle with n vertices, then prove that H is also a bipolar fuzzy cycle with n vertices.

10. The **degree sequence** of a bipolar fuzzy graph consists of degrees of vertices written in increasing order, with repeats where necessary. Classify whether the following statements are true or false.

    (a) Any two isomorphic bipolar fuzzy graphs have the same degree sequence.
    (b) Any two bipolar fuzzy graphs with same degree sequence are isomorphic.

11. Let G_1 be a disconnected bipolar fuzzy graph and ϕ be an isomorphism from G_1 onto a bipolar fuzzy graph G_2, then prove that G_2 is also disconnected. If ϕ is a weak isomorphism, then what about G_2?
12. A **null bipolar fuzzy graph** is a bipolar fuzzy graph with no edges. Let f from G_1 into G_2 be a one-to-one homomorphism.

    (a) If G_1 is a complete bipolar fuzzy graph, then prove that $f(G_1^c)$ is a null bipolar fuzzy graph. Give an example to show that if f is not onto, then $f(G_1^c)$ may not be a null bipolar fuzzy graph.
    (b) If G_1 is a null bipolar fuzzy graph, then prove that $f(G_1^c)$ is a complete bipolar fuzzy graph. Give an example to show that if f is not onto, then $f(G_1^c)$ may not be a complete bipolar fuzzy graph.

13. If G_1 and G_2 are two complex bipolar fuzzy graphs, then prove that $G_1 \cup G_2$, $G_1 \cap G_2$, $G_1 \Box G_2$, $G_1 \times G_2$, $G_1 \boxtimes G_2$, $G_1 \bullet G_2$, and $G_1 \circ G_2$ are complex bipolar fuzzy graphs.
14. If G_1 and G_2 are two strong complex bipolar fuzzy graphs, then prove that $G_1 \Box G_2$, $G_1 \times G_2$, $G_1 \boxtimes G_2$, $G_1 \bullet G_2$ and $G_1 \circ G_2$ are strong complex bipolar fuzzy graphs.

15. Give an example to show that the union of strong complex bipolar fuzzy graphs may not be strong.
16. If $G_1 \Box G_2$ is a strong complex bipolar fuzzy graph, then prove that at least one of G_1 or G_2 must be strong.
17. If $G_1, G_2, G_1^{'}, G_2^{'}$ are bipolar fuzzy graphs and $G_1 \cong G_2, G_1^{'} \cong G_2^{'}$, then classify whether the following statements are true or false.

    (a) $G_1 \Box G_1^{'} \cong G_2 \Box G_2^{'}$
    (b) $G_1 \boxtimes G_1^{'} \cong G_2 \boxtimes G_2^{'}$
    (c) $G_1 + G_1^{'} \cong G_2 + G_2^{'}$
    (d) $(G_1 + G_1^{'})^c \cong G_2^c \cup (G_2^{'})^c$
    (e) $(G_1 + G_2)^c \cong (G_1^{'})^c \cup (G_2^{'})^c$
    (f) $(G_1 \cup G_1^{'})^c \cong G_2^c + (G_2^{'})^c$
    (g) $(G_1 \cup G_2)^c \cong (G_1^{'})^c + (G_2^{'})^c$

18. Let X, Y, and Z be three disjoint sets with $|X| = p$, $|Y| = q$ and $|Z| = r$. If $K_{p,q}$, $K_{q,r}$, $K_{p,r}$ are complete bipartite bipolar fuzzy graphs on $X \cup Y$, $Y \cup Z$, $X \cup Z$, respectively, and $K_{p,q,r}$ is tripartite bipolar fuzzy graph on $X \cup Y \cup Z$, then describe the conditions under which the following statements are true.

    (a) $K_{p,q} \cup K_{q,r} \cong K_{p,q,r}$
    (b) $K_{p,q} \cup K_{q,r} \ncong K_{p,q,r}$
    (c) $K_{p,q} \cup K_r \cong K_{p,q,r}$
    (d) $K_{p,q,r}$ is a null bipolar fuzzy graph.

    Here K_r is a complete bipolar fuzzy graph on Z.
19. Give an example of a bipolar fuzzy graph G such that

$$\sum_{x \neq y} \mu_B^p(xy) = \frac{1}{2} \sum_{x \neq y} (\mu_A^p(x) \wedge \mu_A^p(y)),$$

$$\sum_{x \neq y} \mu_B^n(xy) = \frac{1}{2} \sum_{x \neq y} (\mu_A^n(x) \vee \mu_A^n(y)),$$

    but G is not self-complementary.
20. If G is a self-complementary strong bipolar fuzzy graph, then show that

$$\sum_{x \neq y} \mu_B^p(xy) = \sum_{x \neq y} (\mu_A^p(x) \wedge \mu_A^p(y)),$$

$$\sum_{x \neq y} \mu_B^n(xy) = \sum_{x \neq y} (\mu_A^n(x) \vee \mu_A^n(y)),$$

    do not hold.
21. Let G be a strong bipolar fuzzy graph such that

$$\sum_{x \neq y} \mu_B^p(xy) = \sum_{x \neq y} (\mu_A^p(x) \wedge \mu_A^p(y)),$$

$$\sum_{x \neq y} \mu_B^n(xy) = \sum_{x \neq y} (\mu_A^n(x) \vee \mu_A^n(y)).$$

Then G is not a self-complementary.

22. Let G_1 and G_2 be two strong bipolar fuzzy graphs, then show that $G_1 \circ G_2$ is a strong bipolar fuzzy graph. Determine whether or not $(G_1 \circ G_2)^c = {G_1}^c \circ {G_2}^c$.
23. Let G_1 and G_2 be two bipolar fuzzy graphs. Give an example to show that $(G_1 \circ G_2)^c \neq (G_2 \circ G_1)^c$.
24. Give an example of a connected bipolar fuzzy graph G such that $G - xy$ has at most two components, for any edge xy in G.

References

1. Akram, M.: Bipolar fuzzy graphs. Inf. Sci. **181**(24), 5548–5564 (2011)
2. Akram, M.: Bipolar fuzzy graphs with applications. Knowl.-Based Syst. **39**, 1–8 (2013)
3. Akram, M., Alshehri, N., Davvaz, B., Ashraf, A.: Bipolar fuzzy digraphs in decision support systems. J. Multiple-Valued Logic Soft. Comput. **27**(5–6), 531–551 (2016)
4. Akram, M., Dudek, W.A.: Regular bipolar fuzzy graphs. Neural Comput. Appl. **21**(supp 1), 197–205 (2012)
5. Akram, M., Farooq, A.: Bipolar fuzzy trees. New Trends Math. Sci. **4**(3), 58–72 (2016)
6. Akram, M., Feng, F., Saeid, A.B., Leoreanu-Fotea, V.: A new multiple criteria decision-making method based on bipolar fuzzy soft graphs. Iranian J. Fuzzy Syst. **15**(4), 73–92 (2018)
7. Akram, M., Karunambigai, M.G.: Metric in bipolar fuzzy graphs. World Appl. Sci. J. **14**(12), 1920–1927 (2011)
8. Akram, M., Samanta, S., Pal, M.: Application of bipolar fuzzy sets in planar graphs. Int. J. Appl. Comput. Math. **3**(2), 773–785 (2017)
9. Alkouri, A.U.M., Massa'deh, M.O., Ali, M.: On bipolar complex fuzzy sets and its application. J. Intell. Fuzzy Syst. (Preprint) (2020)
10. Atanassov, K.: Intuitionistic fuzzy sets. Fuzzy Sets Syst. **20**(1), 87–96 (1986)
11. Bhattacharya, P.: Some remarks on fuzzy graphs. Pattern Recogn. Lett. **6**(5), 297–302 (1987)
12. Bhutani, K.R.: On automorphisms of fuzzy graphs. Pattern Recogn. Lett. **9**(3), 159–162 (1989)
13. Bhutani, K.R., Mordeson, J., Rosenfeld, A.: On degrees of end nodes and cut nodes in fuzzy graphs. Iranian J. Fuzzy Syst. **1**(1), 57–64 (2004)
14. Bhutani, K.R., Rosenfeld, A.: Strong arcs in fuzzy graphs. Inf. Sci. **152**, 319–322 (2003)
15. Chen, J., Li, S., Ma, S., Wang, X.: $m-$polar fuzzy sets: An extension of bipolar fuzzy sets. Sci. World J. (2014). https://doi.org/10.1155/2014/416530
16. Dubois, D., Kaci, S., Prade, H.: Bipolarity in reasoning and decision, an introduction. In: International Conference on Information Processing and Management of Uncertainty, IPMU04, pp. 959966 (2004)
17. Ghorai, G., Pal, M.: Certain types of product bipolar fuzzy graphs. Int. J. Appl. Comput. Math. **3**(2), 605–619 (2017)
18. Harary, F.: Graph Theory. Addison-Wesley, Reading (1969)
19. Hwang, C.L., Yoon, K.: Multiple attribute decision-making-methods and applications. In: A State of the Art Survey. Springer, New York (1981)
20. Kaufmann, A.: Introduction la thorie des sous-ensembles flous l'usage des ingnieurs (Fuzzy sets theory). Masson, Paris (1973)

21. Lee, K.M.: Bipolar valued fuzzy sets and their basic operations. In: Proceedings of the International Conference, Bangkok, Thailand, pp. 307–317 (2000)
22. Ma, X., Zhan, J., Khan, M., Zeeshan, M., Anis, S., Awan, A.S.: Complex fuzzy sets with applications in signals. Comput. Appl. Math. **38**(4), 150 (2019)
23. Mathew, S., Mordeson, J.N.: Fuzzy influence graphs. New Math. Nat. Comput. **13**(3), 311–325 (2017)
24. Mathew, S., Sunitha, M.S.: Types of arcs in a fuzzy graph. Inf. Sci. **179**(11), 1760–1768 (2009)
25. Mathew, S., Sunitha, M.: Strongest strong cycles and θ-fuzzy graphs. IEEE Trans. Fuzzy Syst. **21**(6), 1096–1104 (2013)
26. Mathew, S., Sunitha, M.S., Anjali, N.: Some connectivity concepts in bipolar fuzzy graphs. Ann. Pure Appl. Math. **7**(2), 98–108 (2014)
27. Mordeson, J.N., Nair, P.S.: Cycles and cocycles of fuzzy graphs. Inf. Sci. **90**(1–4), 39–49 (1996)
28. Mordeson, J.N., Nair, P.S.: Successor and source of (fuzzy) finite state machines and (fuzzy)directed graphs. Inf. Sci. **95**(1–2), 113–124 (1996)
29. Mordeson, J.N., Nair, P.S.: Fuzzy graphs and hypergraphs. Studies in Fuzziness and Soft Computing. Springer, Berlin (1998); 2nd edn (2001)
30. Mordeson, J.N., Chang-Shyh, P.: Operations on fuzzy graphs. Inf. Sci. **79**(3–4), 159–170 (1994)
31. Nagoorgani, A.: Properties of $\mu-$complement of a fuzzy graph. Int. J. Algorithms Comput. Math. **2**(3), 73–83 (2009)
32. Nagoorgani, A., Chandrasekaran, V.T.: A First Look at Fuzzy Graph Theory. Allied Publishers, Chennai (2010)
33. Nagoorgani, A., Malarvizhi, J.: Isomorphism on fuzzy graphs. Int. J. Comput. Math. Sci. **2**(4), 190–196 (2008)
34. Nagoorgani, A., Radha, K.: The degree of a vertex in some fuzzy graphs. Int. J. Algorithms Comput. Math. **2**(3), 107–116 (2009)
35. Radha, K., Arumugam, S.: On strong product of two fuzzy graphs. Int. J. Sci. Res. Publ. **4**(10), 1–6 (2014)
36. Radha, K., Arumugam, S.: On lexicographic products of two fuzzy graphs. Int. J. Fuzzy Math. Arch. **7**(2), 169–176 (2015)
37. Ramot, D., Milo, R., Friedman, M., Kandel, A.: Complex fuzzy sets. IEEE Trans. Fuzzy Syst. **10**(2), 171–186 (2002)
38. Rao, R.V.: A decision-making framework model for evaluating flexible manufacturing systems using digraph and matrix methods. Int. J. Adv. Manuf. Technol. **30**(11–12), 1101–1110 (2006)
39. Rashmanlou, H., Samanta, S., Pal, M., Borzooei, R.A.: A study on bipolar fuzzy graphs. J. Intell. Fuzzy Syst. **28**(2), 571–580 (2015)
40. Rashmanlou, H., Samanta, S., Pal, M., Borzooei, R.A.: Bipolar fuzzy graphs with categorical properties. Int. J. Comput. Intell. Syst. **8**(5), 808–818 (2015)
41. Rosenfeld, A.: Fuzzy graphs. In: Zadeh, L.A., Fu, K.S., Shimura, M. (eds.) Fuzzy Sets and Their Applications, pp. 77–95. Academic, New York (1975)
42. Samanta, S., Pal, M.: Irregular bipolar fuzzy graphs. Int. J. Appl. Fuzzy Sets **2**, 91–102 (2012)
43. Samanta, S., Pal, M.: Some more results on bipolar fuzzy sets and bipolar fuzzy intersection graphs. J. Fuzzy Math. **22**(2), 253–262 (2014)
44. Sunitha, M.S., Vijayakumar, A.: Complement of a fuzzy graph. Indian J. Pure Appl. Math. **33**(9), 1451–1464 (2002)
45. Talebi, A.A., Rashmanlou, H.: Complement and isomorphism on bipolar fuzzy graphs. Fuzzy Inf. Eng. **6**, 505–522 (2014)
46. Yang, H.-L., Li, S.-G., Yang, W.-H., Lu, Y.: Notes on "Bipolar fuzzy graphs". Inf. Sci. **242**, 113–121 (2013)
47. Yaqoob, N., Gulistan, M., Kadry, S., Wahab, H.A.: Complex intuitionistic fuzzy graphs with application in cellular network provider companies. Mathematics **7**(1), 35 (2019)
48. Zadeh, L.A.: Fuzzy sets. Inf. Control **8**(3), 338–353 (1965)
49. Zadeh, L.A.: Similarity relations and fuzzy orderings. Inf. Sci. **3**(2), 177–200 (1971)
50. Zadeh, L.A.: The concept of a lingusistic variable and its application to approximate reasoning. Inf. Sci. **8**, 199–249 (1975)

51. Zhang, W.-R.: Bipolar fuzzy sets and relations: a computational framework for cognitive modeling and multiagent decision analysis. In: Proceedings of IEEE Conference, pp. 305–309 (1994)
52. Zhang, W.R.: YinYang bipolar lattices and $L-$sets for bipolar knowledge fusion, visualization and decision. Int. J. Inf. Technol. Decis. Making **4**(4), 621–645 (2005)
53. Zhang, W.-R.: Bipolar fuzzy sets. In: Proceedings of FUZZ-IEEE, pp. 835–840 (1998)
54. Zhang, W.-R., Zhang, L.: YinYang bipolar logic and bipolar fuzzy logic. Information Sciences. **165**(3–4), 265–287 (2004)
55. Zhang, W.-R.: YinYang bipolar relativity: a unifying theory of nature, agents and causality with applications in quantum computing, cognitive informatics and life sciences. Information Sciences Reference, Hershey (2011)
56. Zhang, W.-R.: NPN fuzzy sets and NPN qualitative algebra: a computational framework for bipolar cognitive modeling and multiagent decision analysis. IEEE Trans. Syst. Man Cybern. Part B (Cybernetics). **26**(4), 561-574 (1996)
57. Zhang, W.-R.: (YinYang) Bipolar fuzzy sets. In: IEEE International Conference on Fuzzy Systems, pp. 835–840 (1998)
58. Zhang, G., Dillon, T.S., Cai, K.Y., Ma, J., Lu, J.: Operation properties and δ-equalities of complex fuzzy sets. Int. J. Approx. Reason. **50**(8), 1227–1249 (2009)

Chapter 2
Distance Measures in Bipolar Fuzzy Graphs

In this chapter, we discuss the notion of distance in bipolar fuzzy graphs and present certain properties concerning distance functions in complete bipolar fuzzy graphs, complete bipartite bipolar fuzzy graphs, and products of bipolar fuzzy graphs. We establish certain formulae of distance and degree of vertices of bipolar fuzzy graphs $G_1 * G_2$ in terms of distance and degree of vertices of bipolar fuzzy graphs G_1 and G_2, where $*$ is any given operation. We obtain a characterization of self-centered bipolar fuzzy graphs using eccentric vertices, peripheral vertices, and central vertices. We describe the notions of bipolar fuzzy path cover and edge cover of a bipolar fuzzy graph and, establish a necessary and sufficient condition for a complete bipolar fuzzy graph to have a bipolar fuzzy bridge. We discuss certain properties of self-centered, antipodal, and self-median bipolar fuzzy graphs when the bipolar fuzzy graph is complete or strong. Moreover, using the techniques of distance function, we describe the importance of bipolar fuzzy graphs with real-world applications in traveling and product manufacturing. This chapter is due to [4, 5, 18].

2.1 Introduction

The mathematical field of graph theory is growing rapidly in recent times with a lot of research activities. In the past few decades, at the international level, one-third of the Mathematics research papers are from graph theory and combinatorics. Most of the real-world networks come with a spatial embedding, as they exist in three-dimensional Euclidean space and have a natural notion of distance. The applications of distances in graph theory arise in various domains including drug discovery, robotic navigation, routing internet traffic, scheduling and planning, social networking and determining aircraft routes. The distance $d_G(x, y)$ between two vertices x and y in a graph G is the number of edges in the shortest path (also called a graph geodesic) connecting them. This is also known as the geodesic distance [9]. If there is no path

M. Akram et al., *Graphs for the Analysis of Bipolar Fuzzy Information*, Studies in Fuzziness and Soft Computing 401,
https://doi.org/10.1007/978-981-15-8756-6_2

connecting the two vertices, i.e., if the vertices x and y belong to different connected components, then conventionally the distance is defined as infinite. Fuzzy set theory owes its remarkable origin to the work of Zadeh [22] in 1965. The theory of fuzzy sets has been introduced to solve real-life problems having uncertainty and vagueness. It has become a vigorous area of research in different disciplines. The advantage of replacing classical sets by Zadeh's fuzzy sets is that it gives more accuracy and precision in theory and more efficiency and system compatibility in applications. In 1975, Rosenfeld [15] obtained fuzzy analogues of several basic graph-theoretic concepts like bridges, paths, cycles, trees, connectedness, and established some of their properties. The author has defined μ-length of any $u - v$ fuzzy path P as the sum of reciprocals of edge weights in P and the distance between u and v, called μ-distance, is defined as the smallest μ-length of P. Based on this μ-distance, Bhattacharya [7] introduced the concepts of eccentricity and center in fuzzy graphs and the properties of this distance are further studied by Sunitha and Vijyakumar [19]. The concept of sum distance in fuzzy graphs is studied in [21] as the smallest sum of edge weights of any fuzzy path P and proved that it is a metric. The concept of length, distance, eccentricity, radius, diameter of a bipolar fuzzy graph, and self-centered bipolar fuzzy graphs are studied in [4]. Bhutani and Rosenfeld introduced the concepts of strong arcs [8], fuzzy end nodes [11], and geodesics in fuzzy graphs [10]. Further studies based on g-distance are carried out by Sameena and Sunitha in [16] and [17]. The concepts of g-peripheral nodes, g-boundary nodes, and g-interior nodes based on g-distance were introduced by Linda and Sunitha [14]. In 1994, Zhang [23] introduced bipolar fuzzy set theory as an extension of fuzzy set theory in which the membership degree range is $[-1, 1]$. The main idea behind such characterization is linked with the existence of "bipolar information" (such as positive information and negative information) about the given set. Bipolar fuzzy sets not only have applications in mathematical theories but also in real-world problems [25, 26]. The notion of a bipolar fuzzy graph was introduced by Akram [1] in 2011 and, Akram and Dudek [3] discussed regular bipolar fuzzy graphs.

2.2 Distance in Bipolar Fuzzy Graphs

In this section, the concept of distance function in bipolar fuzzy graphs is introduced and applied to various classes of bipolar fuzzy graphs.

Definition 2.1 Let $G = (A, B)$ be a bipolar fuzzy graph on a non-empty set X then the **degree** of any vertex $x \in X$ is a pair $\deg(x) = (\deg^p(x), \deg^n(x))$, where $\deg^p(x) = \sum_{u \in X} \mu_B^p(xu)$ and $\deg^n(x) = \sum_{u \in X} \mu_B^n(xu)$.

Definition 2.2 The **Cartesian product** of two bipolar fuzzy graphs $G_1 = (A_1, B_1)$ and $G_2 = (A_2, B_2)$ is denoted by the pair $G_1 \square G_2 = (A_1 \square A_2, B_1 \square B_2)$, where $A_1 \square A_2 = (\mu^p_{A_1 \square A_2}, \mu^n_{A_1 \square A_2})$ and $B_1 \square B_2 = (\mu^p_{B_1 \square B_2}, \mu^n_{B_1 \square B_2})$ are defined as

1. $(A_1 \square A_2)(x_1, x_2) = \big(\mu^p_{A_1}(x_1) \wedge \mu^p_{A_2}(x_2), \mu^n_{A_1}(x_1) \vee \mu^n_{A_2}(x_2)\big),$ for all $(x_1, x_2) \in X_1 \times X_2$,

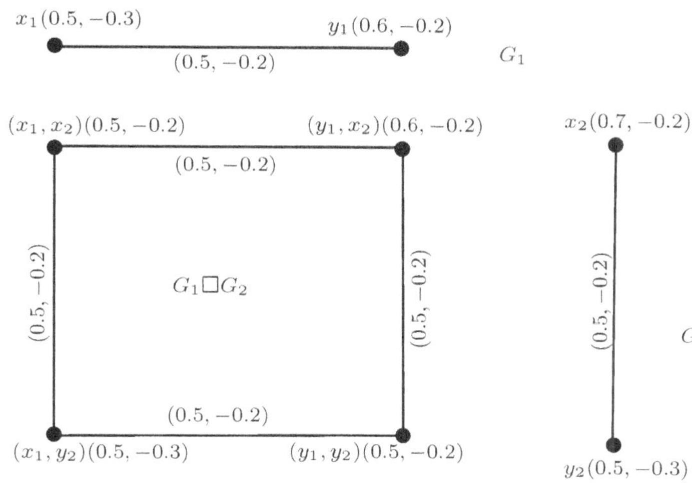

Fig. 2.1 Cartesian product $G_1 \Box G_2$

2. $(B_1 \Box B_2)((x, x_2)(x, y_2)) = \big(\mu^p_{A_1}(x) \wedge \mu^p_{B_2}(x_2y_2), \mu^n_{A_1}(x) \vee \mu^n_{B_2}(x_2y_2)\big)$, for all $x \in X_1$, $x_2y_2 \in E_2$,
3. $(B_1 \Box B_2)((x_1, z)(y_1, z)) = \big(\mu^p_{B_1}(x_1y_1) \wedge \mu^p_{A_2}(z), \mu^n_{B_1}(x_1y_1) \vee \mu^n_{A_2}(z)\big)$, for all $z \in X_2$, $x_1y_1 \in E_1$.

Example 2.1 The Cartesian product of two bipolar fuzzy graphs G_1 and G_2 is shown in Fig. 2.1.

Definition 2.3 The **direct product** of two bipolar fuzzy graphs $G_1 = (A_1, B_1)$ and $G_2 = (A_2, B_2)$ is a pair $G_1 \times G_2 = (A_1 \times A_2, B_1 \times B_2)$, where $A_1 \times A_2 = (\mu^p_{A_1 \times A_2}, \mu^n_{A_1 \times A_2})$ and $B_1 \times B_2 = (\mu^p_{B_1 \times B_2}, \mu^n_{B_1 \times B_2})$ are defined as

1. $(A_1 \times A_2)(x_1, x_2) = \big(\mu^p_{A_1}(x_1) \wedge \mu^p_{A_2}(x_2), \mu^n_{A_1}(x_1) \vee \mu^n_{A_2}(x_2)\big)$, for all $(x_1, x_2) \in X_1 \times X_2$,
2. $(B_1 \times B_2)((x_1, x_2)(x_1, y_2)) = \big(\mu^p_{B_1}(x_1y_1) \wedge \mu^p_{B_2}(x_2y_2), \mu^n_{B_1}(x_1y_1) \vee \mu^n_{B_2}(x_2y_2)\big)$, for all $x_1y_1 \in E_1$, $x_2y_2 \in E_2$.

Example 2.2 The direct product of two bipolar fuzzy graphs G_1 and G_2 is shown in Fig. 2.2.

Definition 2.4 The **strong product** of two bipolar fuzzy graphs $G_1 = (A_1, B_1)$ and $G_2 = (A_2, B_2)$ is denoted by the pair $G_1 \boxtimes G_2 = (A_1 \boxtimes A_2, B_1 \boxtimes B_2)$ and defined as

1. $(A_1 \boxtimes A_2)(x_1, x_2) = \big(\mu^p_{A_1}(x_1) \wedge \mu^p_{A_2}(x_2), \mu^n_{A_1}(x_1) \vee \mu^n_{A_2}(x_2)\big)$, for all $(x_1, x_2) \in X_1 \times X_2$,

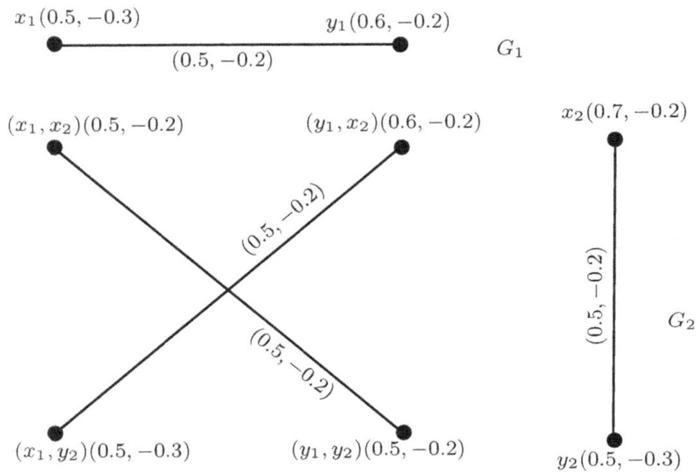

Fig. 2.2 Direct product $G_1 \times G_2$

2. $(B_1 \boxtimes B_2)((x, x_2)(x, y_2)) = \big(\mu^p_{A_1}(x) \wedge \mu^p_{B_2}(x_2y_2), \mu^n_{A_1}(x) \vee \mu^n_{B_2}(x_2y_2)\big)$, for all $x \in X_1$, $x_2y_2 \in E_2$,
3. $(B_1 \boxtimes B_2)((x_1, z)(y_1, z)) = \big(\mu^p_{B_1}(x_1y_1) \wedge \mu^p_{A_2}(z), \mu^n_{B_1}(x_1y_1) \vee \mu^n_{A_2}(z)\big)$, for all $z \in X_2$, $x_1y_1 \in E_1$,
4. $(B_1 \boxtimes B_2)((x_1, x_2)(x_1, y_2)) = \big(\mu^p_{B_1}(x_1y_1) \wedge \mu^p_{B_2}(x_2y_2), \mu^n_{B_1}(x_1y_1) \vee \mu^n_{B_2}(x_2y_2)\big)$, for all $x_1y_1 \in E_1$, $x_2y_2 \in E_2$.

Example 2.3 The strong product of two bipolar fuzzy graphs G_1 and G_2 is shown in Fig. 2.3.

Definition 2.5 The **lexicographic product** of two bipolar fuzzy graphs $G_1 = (A_1, B_1)$ and $G_2 = (A_2, B_2)$, denoted by $G_1 \bullet G_2$, is defined as a pair $(A_1 \bullet A_2, B_1 \bullet B_2)$ such that

1. $(A_1 \bullet A_2)(x_1, x_2) = \big(\mu^p_{A_1}(x_1) \wedge \mu^p_{A_2}(x_2), \mu^n_{A_1}(x_1) \vee \mu^n_{A_2}(x_2)\big)$, for all $(x_1, x_2) \in X_1 \times X_2$,
2. $(B_1 \bullet B_2)((x, x_2)(x, y_2)) = \big(\mu^p_{A_1}(x) \wedge \mu^p_{B_2}(x_2y_2), \mu^n_{A_1}(x) \vee \mu^n_{B_2}(x_2y_2)\big)$, for all $x \in X_1$, $x_2y_2 \in E_2$,
3. $(B_1 \bullet B_2)((x_1, x_2)(x_1, y_2)) = \big(\mu^p_{B_1}(x_1y_1) \wedge \mu^p_{B_2}(x_2y_2), \mu^n_{B_1}(x_1y_1) \vee \mu^n_{B_2}(x_2y_2)\big)$, for all $x_1y_1 \in E_1$, $x_2y_2 \in E_2$.

Definition 2.6 Let $G_1 = (A_1, B_1)$ and $G_2 = (A_2, B_2)$ be two bipolar fuzzy graphs on nonempty sets X_1 and X_2, respectively. The **union** of G_1 and G_2 is defined as a pair $G_1 \cup G_2 = (A_1 \cup A_2, B_1 \cup B_2)$ such that for all $x, y \in X_1 \cup X_2$,

1. If $x \in X_1, x \notin X_2$, then $(A_1 \cup A_2)(x) = A_1(x)$,

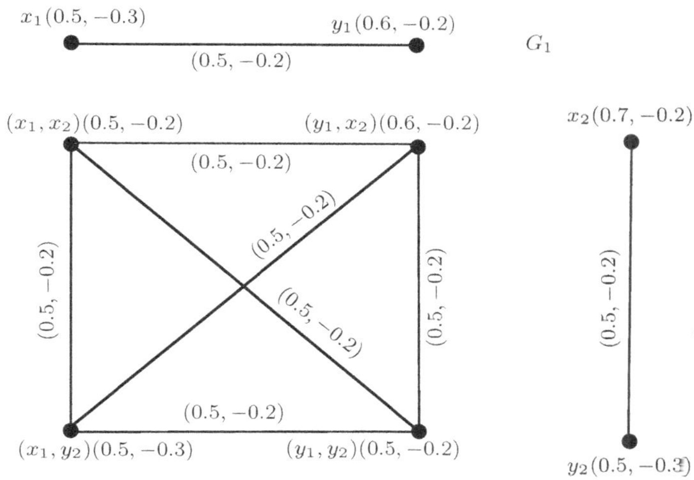

Fig. 2.3 Strong product $G_1 \boxtimes G_2$

2. If $x \notin X_1, x \in X_2$, then $(A_1 \cup A_2)(x) = A_2(x)$,
3. If $x \in X_1 \cap X_2$, then $(A_1 \cup A_2)(x) = (\mu^p_{A_1}(x) \vee \mu^p_{A_2}(x), \mu^n_{A_1}(x) \wedge \mu^n_{A_2}(x))$.

If $supp(B_1) = E_1$ and $supp(B_2) = E_2$ are the sets of edges in G_1 and G_2, then $B_1 \cup B_2$ can be defined as

1. If $xy \in E_1, xy \notin E_2$, then $(B_1 \cup B_2)(xy) = B_1(xy)$,
2. If $xy \in E_1, xy \notin E_2$, then $(B_1 \cup B_2)(xy) = B_2(xy)$,
3. If $xy \in E_1 \cap E_2$, then $(B_1 \cup B_2)(xy) = (\mu^p_{B_1}(xy) \vee \mu^p_{B_2}(xy), \mu^n_{B_1}(xy) \wedge \mu^n_{B_2}(xy))$.

Definition 2.7 The **join** of two bipolar fuzzy graphs $G_1 = (A_1, B_1)$ and $G_2 = (A_2, B_2)$ is defined as a pair $G_1 + G_2 = (A_1 + A_2, B_1 + B_2)$ such that $A_1 + A_2 = A_1 \cup A_2$, for all $x \in X_1 \cup X_2$, and the membership values of the edges in $G_1 + G_2$ are defined as

1. $B_1 + B_2 = B_1 \cup B_2$, for all $xy \in E_1 \cup E_2$.
2. Let E' be the set of all edges joining the vertices of G_1 and G_2, then for all $xy \in E'$, where $x \in X_1$ and $y \in X_2$, $(B_1 + B_2)(xy) = \left(\mu^p_{A_1}(x) \wedge \mu^p_{A_2}(y), \mu^n_{A_1}(x) \vee \mu^n_{A_2}(y)\right)$.

Definition 2.8 A **bipolar fuzzy path** in a bipolar fuzzy graph $G = (A, B)$ is a sequence of distinct vertices $y_1, y_2, \ldots, y_n$ such that either $\mu^p_B(y_k y_{k+1}) > 0$ or $\mu^n_B(y_k y_{k+1}) < 0$, for all $1 \leq k \leq n - 1$. It is denoted by $\mathcal{P}_n$. If $y_1 = y_n$ and $A(y_1) = A(y_n)$, the bipolar fuzzy path is known as a **bipolar fuzzy cycle**, denoted by $\mathcal{C}_n$. A bipolar fuzzy graph G is **connected** if there exists a bipolar fuzzy path between each pair of distinct vertices.

An example of a bipolar fuzzy path $\mathcal{P}_5$ is shown in Fig. 2.4.

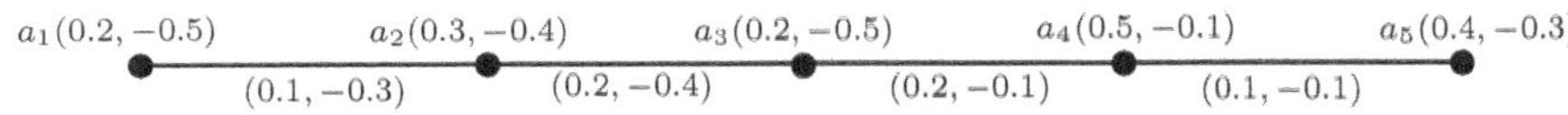

Fig. 2.4 Bipolar fuzzy path $\mathcal{P}_5$

Definition 2.9 Let $G = (A, B)$ be a bipolar fuzzy graph on X. For any bipolar fuzzy path R: $y_1 - y_2 - \ldots - y_n$ in G, the μ^p–length of R is defined as the sum of μ^p-values of the edges and μ^n–length of R is defined as the sum of μ^n-values of the edges, that is,

$$L^p(R) = \sum_{i=2}^{n} \mu_B^p(y_{i-1}y_i), \quad L^n(R) = \sum_{i=2}^{n} \mu_B^n(y_{i-1}y_i).$$

The **length** of bipolar fuzzy path R is represented by the ordered pair $L(R) = (L^p(R), L^n(R))$. For any two vertices x, y of G, let $\mathbb{R} = \{R_i \mid R_i \text{ is an } x - y \text{ bipolar fuzzy path}, i = 1, 2, 3, \ldots\}$ be the set of all bipolar fuzzy paths from x to y. Then the **distance** from x to y is denoted by $d(x, y)$ or $d_G(x, y)$ and defined as the ordered pair $d(x, y) = (d^p(x, y), d^n(x, y))$, where

$$\begin{aligned} d^p(x, y) &= \min\left\{L^p(R_j) \mid R_j \in \mathbb{R},\ j = 1, 2, 3, \ldots\right\}, \quad d^n(x, y) \\ &= \max\left\{L^p(R_j) \mid R_j \in \mathbb{R},\ j = 1, 2, 3, \ldots\right\}. \end{aligned}$$

Theorem 2.1 *Let $G_1 = (A_1, B_1)$ and $G_2 = (A_2, B_2)$ be two bipolar fuzzy graphs. If (x_1, x_2) and (y_1, y_2) are vertices of the Cartesian product $G_1 \Box G_2$, then*

$$\begin{aligned} d^p_{G_1 \Box G_2}((x_1, x_2), (y_1, y_2)) &\le d^p_{G_1}(x_1, y_1) + d^p_{G_2}(x_2, y_2), \\ d^n_{G_1 \Box G_2}((x_1, x_2), (y_1, y_2)) &\ge d^n_{G_1}(x_1, y_1) + d^n_{G_2}(x_2, y_2). \end{aligned}$$

Proof Assume that $d_{G_1}(x_1, y_1)$ and $d_{G_2}(x_2, y_2)$ are finite. Let R_1 and R_2 be the bipolar fuzzy paths in G_1 and Q_1, Q_2 be bipolar fuzzy paths in G_2, where $R_i : x_1 = x_{i1}, x_{i2}, \ldots, x_{in} = y_1$ is such that

$$d_{G_1}(x_1, y_1) = (L^p(R_1), L^n(R_2)),$$

and $Q_i : x_2 = y_{i1}, y_{i2}, \ldots, y_{in'} = y_2$ be a bipolar fuzzy paths in G_2 such that

$$d_{G_2}(x_2, y_2) = (L^p(Q_1), L^n(Q_2)).$$

This establishes the following bipolar fuzzy paths in $G_1 \Box G_2$:

$$\begin{aligned} R_i \times \{y_{i1}\} &= (x_{i1}, y_{i1}), (x_{i2}, y_{i1}), \ldots, (x_{in}, y_{i1}) \\ \{x_{in}\} \times Q_i &= (x_{in}, y_{i1}), (x_{in}, y_{i2}), \ldots, (x_{in}, y_{in'}), \qquad i = 1, 2, \end{aligned}$$

whose join are the bipolar fuzzy paths of length $L(R_i \times \{y_1\}) + L(\{x_n\} \times Q_i)$. It is clear that

$$d^p_{G_1 \Box G_2}((x_1, x_2), (y_1, y_2)) \le L^p(R_1 \times \{x_2\}) + L^p(\{y_1\} \times Q_1), \tag{2.1}$$

$$d^n_{G_1 \Box G_2}((x_1, x_2), (y_1, y_2)) \ge L^n(R_2 \times \{x_2\}) + L^n(\{y_1\} \times Q_2). \tag{2.2}$$

$$\begin{aligned} L^p(R_1 \times \{x_2\}) &= \mu^p_{B_1}(x_{11}x_{12}) \wedge \mu^p_{A_2}(x_2) + \mu^p_{B_1}(x_{12}x_{13}) \wedge \mu^p_{A_2}(x_2) \qquad (2.3)\\ &\quad + \cdots + \mu^p_{B_1}(x_{1\overline{n-1}}x_{1n}) \wedge \mu^p_{A_2}(x_2) \\ &\le \mu^p_{B_1}(x_{11}x_{12}) + \mu^p_{B_1}(x_{12}x_{13}) + \cdots + \mu^p_{B_1}(x_{1\overline{n-1}}x_{1n}) = L^p(R_1), \\ L^p(R_1 \times \{x_2\}) &\le L^p(R_1) = d^p_{G_1}(x_1, y_1) \qquad (2.4)\\ \Rightarrow L^p(R_1 \times \{x_2\}) &\le d^p_{G_1}(x_1, y_1). \qquad (2.5) \end{aligned}$$

By using similar argument, it can be proved that

$$\begin{aligned} L^p(\{y_1\} \times Q_1) &\le L^p(Q_1) = d^p_{G_2}(x_2, y_2), \qquad (2.6)\\ L^n(R_2 \times \{x_2\}) &\ge L^n(R_2) = d^n_{G_1}(x_1, y_1), \qquad (2.7)\\ L^n(\{y_1\} \times Q_2) &\ge L^n(Q_2) = d^n_{G_2}(x_2, y_2). \qquad (2.8) \end{aligned}$$

From (2.1), (2.4), and (2.6), we conclude that $d^p_{G_1 \Box G_2}((x_1, x_2), (y_1, y_2)) \le d^p_{G_1}(x_1, y_1) + d^p_{G_2}(x_2, y_2)$.

From (2.2), (2.7), and (2.8), it follows that $d^n_{G_1 \Box G_2}((x_1, x_2), (y_1, y_2)) \ge d^n_{G_1}(x_1, y_1) + d^n_{G_2}(x_2, y_2)$.

Definition 2.10 Let $G_1^* \bullet G_2^* \bullet \ldots \bullet G_k^*$ be any product of the graphs $G_1^*, G_2^*, \ldots, G_k^*$, where $\bullet$ represents any product including Cartesian product, direct product, strong product, or lexicographic product. The mapping $f_{G_i} : G_1^* \bullet G_2^* \bullet \cdots \bullet G_k^* \to G_i^*$ defined by

$$f_{G_i}(x_1, x_2, \ldots, x_k) = x_i, \qquad x_i \in X_i, \ 1 \le i \le k,$$

is called the **projection** of G_i^* onto $G_1^* \bullet G_2^* \bullet \cdots \bullet G_k^*$.

Theorem 2.2 *Let S be a bipolar fuzzy path in $G_1 \Box G_2$ and the membership values of both bipolar fuzzy graphs $G_1 = (A_1, B_1)$ and $G_2 = (A_2, B_2)$ have the following relations: $\mu^p_{A_1} \ge \mu^p_{B_2}$, $\mu^n_{A_1} \le \mu^n_{B_2}$, $\mu^p_{A_2} \ge \mu^p_{B_1}$ and $\mu^n_{A_2} \le \mu^n_{B_1}$, then $L(S) = L(f_{G_1}(S)) + L(f_{G_2}(S))$.*

Proof Let $P : x_1 - x_2 - \cdots - x_n$ be a bipolar fuzzy path in G_1 and $Q : y_1 - y_2 - \cdots - y_{n'}$ be a bipolar fuzzy path in G_2. Let S be a bipolar fuzzy path in $G_1 \Box G_2$

which is established as follows:

$$S: (x_1, y_1) - (x_2, y_1) - \cdots - (x_n, y_1) - (x_n, y_2) - \cdots - (x_n, y_{n'}).$$

Clearly, $f_{G_1}(S) = P$, $f_{G_2}(S) = Q$ and $L(S) = (L^P(S), L^n(S))$. It follows that

$$\begin{aligned} L^P(S) &= \mu^P_{B_1}(x_1x_2) \wedge \mu^P_{A_2}(y_1) + \mu^P_{B_1}(x_2x_3) \wedge \mu^P_{A_2}(y_1) + \cdots + \mu^P_{B_1}(x_{n-1}x_n) \wedge \mu^P_{A_2}(y_1) \\ &\quad + \mu^P_{A_1}(x_n) \wedge \mu^P_{B_2}(y_1y_2) + \cdots + \mu^P_{A_1}(x_n) \wedge \mu^P_{B_2}(y_{n'-1}y_{n'}) \\ &= \mu^P_{B_1}(x_1x_2) + \mu^P_{B_1}(x_2x_3) + \cdots + \mu^P_{B_1}(x_{n-1}x_n) + \mu^P_{B_2}(y_1y_2) + \cdots + \mu^P_{B_2}(y_{n'-1}y_{n'}) \\ &= L^P(P) + L^P(Q) = L^P(f_{G_1}(S)) + L^P(f_{G_2}(S)). \end{aligned}$$

Similarly, it can be proved that $L^n(S) = L^n(f_{G_1}(S)) + L^n(f_{G_2}(S))$. Hence,

$$L(S) = (L^P(S), L^n(S)) = \Big(L^P(f_{G_1}(S)) + L^P(f_{G_2}(S)), L^n(f_{G_1}(S)) + L^n(f_{G_2}(S))\Big),$$
$$L(S) = \Big(L^P(f_{G_1}(S)), L^n(f_{G_1}(S))\Big) + \Big(L^P(f_{G_2}(S)), L^n(f_{G_2}(S))\Big) = L(f_{G_1}(S)) + L(f_{G_2}(S)).$$

□

Lemma 2.1 *Let $G_1 = (A_1, B_1)$ and $G_2 = (A_2, B_2)$ be two bipolar fuzzy graphs and (x_1, y_1) and (x_2, y_2) are vertices of the Cartesian product $G_1 \square G_2$. If the membership values of both bipolar fuzzy paths G_1 and G_2 have the following relations: $\mu^P_{A_1} \geq \mu^P_{B_2}$, $\mu^n_{A_1} \leq \mu^n_{B_2}$, $\mu^P_{A_2} \geq \mu^P_{B_1}$ and $\mu^n_{A_2} \leq \mu^n_{B_1}$, then*

$$d_{G_1 \square G_2}((x_1, x_2), (y_1, y_2)) = d_{G_1}(x_1, y_1) + d_{G_2}(x_2, y_2).$$

Proof Let $G_1 = (A_1, B_1)$ and $G_2 = (A_2, B_2)$ be bipolar fuzzy graphs on X_1 and X_2, respectively, and $(x_1, y_1), (x_2, y_2) \in X_1 \times X_2$. By Theorem 2.1,

$$d^P_{G_1 \square G_2}((x_1, x_2), (y_1, y_2)) \leq d^P_{G_1}(x_1, y_1) + d^P_{G_2}(x_2, y_2), \tag{2.9}$$
$$d^n_{G_1 \square G_2}((x_1, x_2), (y_1, y_2)) \geq d^n_{G_1}(x_1, y_1) + d^n_{G_2}(x_2, y_2). \tag{2.10}$$

Let R_1 and R_2 be the shortest bipolar fuzzy paths between vertices (x_1, x_2) and (y_1, y_2) such that $d_{G_1 \square G_2}((x_1, x_2), (y_1, y_2)) = (L^P(S_1), L^n(S_2))$. The projections $f_{G_1}(S_i)$ and $f_{G_2}(S_i), i = 1, 2$ are the bipolar fuzzy paths between the vertices x_1 and y_1 in G_1, x_2, and y_2 in G_2. Consider

$$\begin{aligned} d^P_{G_1}(x_1, y_1) + d^P_{G_2}(x_2, y_2) &\leq L^P(f_{G_1}(S_1)) + L^P(f_{G_2}(S_1)) = L^P(S_1) \\ &= d^P_{G_1 \square G_2}((x_1, x_2), (y_1, y_2)). \end{aligned} \tag{2.11}$$

Similarly it can be proved that $d^n_{G_1}(x_1, y_1) + d^n_{G_2}(x_2, y_2) \geq d^n_{G_1 \square G_2}((x_1, x_2), (y_1, y_2))$. (2.12)

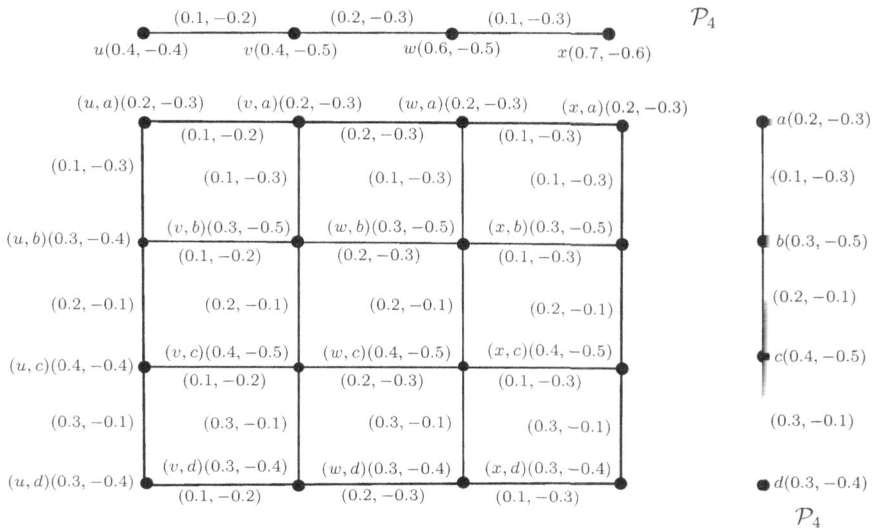

Fig. 2.5 Cartesian product $\mathcal{P}_4 \square \mathcal{P}_4$

By combining (2.9), (2.11), (2.10), and (2.12), the required result is obtained. □

Example 2.4 Consider the Cartesian product of two bipolar fuzzy paths in Fig. 2.5. It can be easily seen that $d_{\widetilde{P}_4 \square \widetilde{P}_4}((u,a),(v,b)) = (0.2, -0.5) = d_{\widetilde{P}_4}(u,v) - d_{\widetilde{P}_4}(a,b)$, $d_{\widetilde{P}_4 \square \widetilde{P}_4}((u,a),(u,c)) = (0.3, -0.4) = d_{\widetilde{P}_4}(u,u) + d_{\widetilde{P}_4}(a,c)$. Similarly, for the other vertices.

Theorem 2.3 *Let $G_1 = (A_1, B_1)$ and $G_2 = (A_2, B_2)$ be two bipolar fuzzy graphs on X_1 and X_2, respectively. If $x_1 \in X_1$, $x_2 \in X_2$ and the membership values of G_1 and G_2 have the following relations: $\mu^p_{A_1} \ge \mu^p_{B_2}$, $\mu^n_{A_1} \le \mu^n_{B_2}$, $\mu^p_{A_2} \ge \mu^p_{B_1}$ and $\mu^n_{A_2} \le \mu^n_{B_1}$, then*

$$deg_{G_1 \square G_2}(x_1, x_2) = deg_{G_1}(x_1) + deg_{G_2}(x_2).$$

Proof By Definition 2.1,

$$\begin{aligned}
\deg_{G_1 \square G_2}(x_1, x_2) &= \sum\nolimits_{(y_1,y_2)\in X_1 \times X_2} \left(\mu^p_{B_1 \square B_2}((x_1,x_2)(y_1,y_2)), \mu^n_{B_1 \square B_2}((x_1,x_2)(y_1,y_2))\right) \\
&= \sum\nolimits_{x_1=y_1, x_2y_2\in E_2} \left(\mu^p_{B_1 \square B_2}((x_1,x_2)(y_1,y_2)), \mu^n_{B_1 \square B_2}((x_1,x_2)(y_1,y_2))\right) \\
&\quad + \sum\nolimits_{x_1y_1\in E_1, x_2=y_2} \left(\mu^p_{B_1 \square B_2}((x_1,x_2)(y_1,y_2)), \mu^n_{B_1 \square B_2}((x_1,x_2)(y_1,y_2))\right) \\
&= \sum\nolimits_{x_1=y_1, x_2y_2\in E_2} \left(\mu^p_{A_1}(x_1) \wedge \mu^p_{B_2}(x_2y_2), \mu^n_{A_1}(x_1) \vee \mu^n_{B_2}(x_2y_2)\right) \\
&\quad + \sum\nolimits_{x_1y_1\in E_1, x_2=y_2} \left(\mu^p_{B_1}(x_1y_1) \wedge \mu^p_{A_2}(x_2), \mu^n_{B_1}(x_1y_1) \vee \mu^n_{A_2}(x_2)\right) \\
&= \sum\nolimits_{x_2y_2\in E_2} \left(\mu^p_{B_2}(x_2y_2), \mu^n_{B_2}(x_2y_2)\right) + \sum\nolimits_{x_1y_1\in E_1} \left(\mu^p_{B_1}(x_1y_1), \mu^n_{B_1}(x_1y_1)\right) \\
&= \deg_{G_2}(x_2) + \deg_{G_1}(x_1).
\end{aligned}$$

Theorem 2.4 *Let $G_1 = (A_1, B_1)$ and $G_2 = (A_2, B_2)$ be two bipolar fuzzy graphs such that membership values of edges have the following relations: $\mu^p_{B_1} \leq \mu^p_{B_2}$ and $\mu^n_{B_1} \geq \mu^n_{B_2}$. Let $x_1, y_1 \in X_1$, $x_2, y_2 \in X_2$, and R_1, R_2 be the shortest bipolar fuzzy paths between (x_1, x_2) and (y_1, y_2) such that $d_{G_1 \times G_2}((x_1, x_2), (y_1, y_2)) = (L^p(R_1), L^n(R_2))$, then*

$$d_{G_1 \times G_2}((x_1, x_2), (y_1, y_2)) = (L^p(f_{G_1}(R_1)), L^n(f_{G_1}(R_2))).$$

Proof Assume that for $i = 1, 2$,

$$R_i : (x_1, x_2) = (x_1^{(i1)}, x_2^{(i1)}) - (x_1^{(i2)}, x_2^{(i2)}) - \cdots - (x_1^{(in)}, x_2^{(in)}) = (y_1, y_2)$$

are the shortest bipolar fuzzy paths between (x_1, x_2) and (y_1, y_2). Clearly,

$$d_{G_1 \times G_2}((x_1, x_2), (y_1, y_2)) = (L^p(R_1), L^n(R_2)). \tag{2.13}$$

If E is the set of edges in $G_1 \times G_2$, then

$$\begin{aligned} L^p(R_1) &= \sum_{(x_1^{(1j)}, x_2^{(1j)})(x_1^{(1\overline{j+1})}, x_2^{(1\overline{j+1})}) \in E} \mu^p_{B_1 \times B_2}\left((x_1^{(1j)}, x_2^{(1j)})(x_1^{(1\overline{j+1})}, x_2^{(1\overline{j+1})})\right) \\ &= \sum_{x_1^{(1j)} x_1^{(1\overline{j+1})} \in E_1, x_2^{(1j)} x_2^{(1\overline{j+1})} \in E_2} \mu^p_{B_1}\left(x_1^{(1j)} x_1^{(1\overline{j+1})}\right) \wedge \mu^p_{B_2}\left(x_2^{(1j)} x_2^{(1\overline{j+1})}\right) \\ &= \sum_{x_1^{(j)} x_1^{(j+1)} \in E_1} \mu^p_{B_1}\left(x_1^{(1j)} x_1^{(1\overline{j+1})}\right) \\ &= L^p\left(f_{G_1}(R_1)\right). \end{aligned} \tag{2.14}$$

It is easy to show that

$$L^n(R_2) = L^n\left(f_{G_1}(R_2)\right). \tag{2.15}$$

From (2.13), (2.14), and (2.15), $d_{G_1 \times G_2}((x_1, x_2), (y_1, y_2)) = \left(L^p(f_{G_1}(R_1)), L^n(f_{G_1}(R_2))\right)$. □

Remark 2.1 If membership values of edges have the relation: $\mu^p_{B_2} \leq \mu^p_{B_1}$ then Theorem 2.4 takes the form as

$$d_{G_1 \times G_2}((x_1, x_2), (y_1, y_2)) = \left(L^p(f_{G_2}(R_1)), L^n(f_{G_2}(R_2))\right).$$

Example 2.5 In Fig. 2.6, the shortest bipolar fuzzy path between the vertices (a, d) and (a, f) is $S : (a, d) - (b, e) - (a, f)$. $f_{\mathcal{P}_3}(S) = a - b - a = P$. It can be easily seen that $d_{\mathcal{P}_3 \times \mathcal{P}_3}((a, d), (a, f)) = (0.4, -0.6) = L(P)$. For the vertices (a, d) and (c, f), the shortest bipolar fuzzy path is $S : (a, d) - (b, e) - (c, f)$. Therefore, $d_{\mathcal{P}_3 \times \mathcal{P}_3}((a, d), (c, f)) = (0.4, -0.4)$. The projection of S in $\mathcal{P}_3$ is $a - b - c$, whose length is equal to $d_{\mathcal{P}_3 \times \mathcal{P}_3}((a, d), (c, f))$.

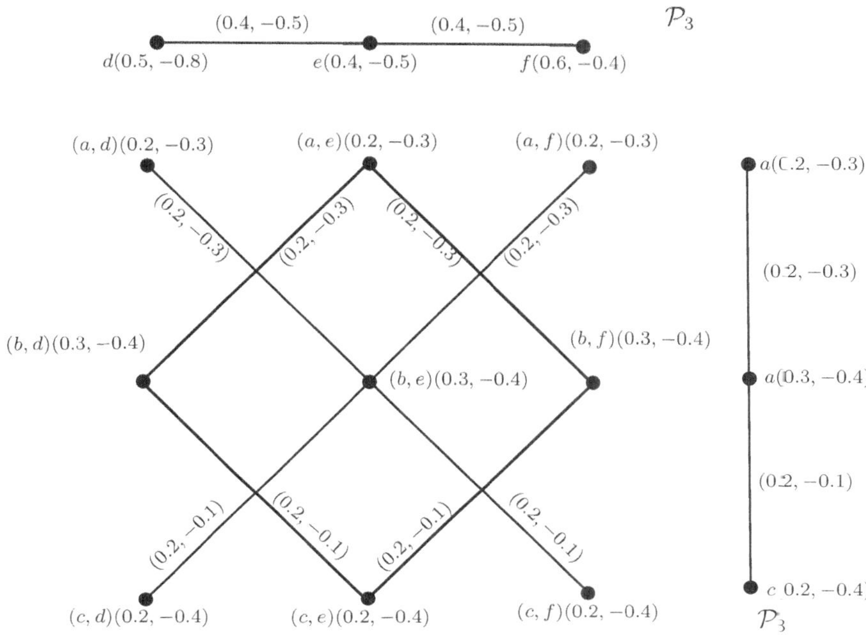

Fig. 2.6 Direct product $\mathcal{P}_3 \times \mathcal{P}_3$

Theorem 2.5 *Let $G_1 = (A_1, B_1)$ and $G_2 = (A_2, B_2)$ be two bipolar fuzzy graphs such that the membership values of edges have the following relation: $\mu^p_{B_1} \le \mu^p_{B_2}$ and $\mu^n_{B_1} \ge \mu^n_{B_2}$. For any two vertices (x_1, x_2) and (y_1, y_2) of the direct product $G_1 \times G_2$, let k be a smallest positive integer such that G_1^* has a x_1, y_1-walk of length k and G_2^* has a x_2, y_2-walk of length k. The positive distance between (x_1, x_2) and (y_1, y_2) is the smallest μ^p-length of any bipolar fuzzy walk between x_1 and y_1, whose length in the crisp graph G_1^* is k. The negative distance between (x_1, x_2) and (y_1, y_2) is the largest μ^n-length of any bipolar fuzzy walk between x_1 and y_1, whose length in the crisp graph G_1^* is k.*

Example 2.6 The bipolar fuzzy graph in Fig. 2.7 is the direct product of $\mathcal{P}_3$ and $\mathcal{C}_3$. Take the vertices (a, d) and (c, e), the smallest $a - c$ and $d - e$ walks are of length 2. Therefore, the positive and negative distances between (a, d) and (c, e) must be the smallest and largest, respectively, lengths of a bipolar fuzzy walk in $\mathcal{P}_3$ whose length in crisp path P_3 is 2. Such a bipolar fuzzy walk in $\mathcal{P}_3 \times \mathcal{C}_3$ is $(a, d) - (b, f) - (c, e)$. Hence $d_{\mathcal{P}_3 \times \mathcal{C}_3}((a, d), (c, e)) = (0.4, -0.4)$.

Theorem 2.6 *Let G_1 and G_2 be two bipolar fuzzy graphs such that the membership degrees of edges have the following relation: $\mu^p_{B_1} \le \mu^p_{B_2}$ and $\mu^n_{B_1} \ge \mu^n_{B_2}$. If $x_1 \in X_1$ and $x_2 \in X_2$, then*

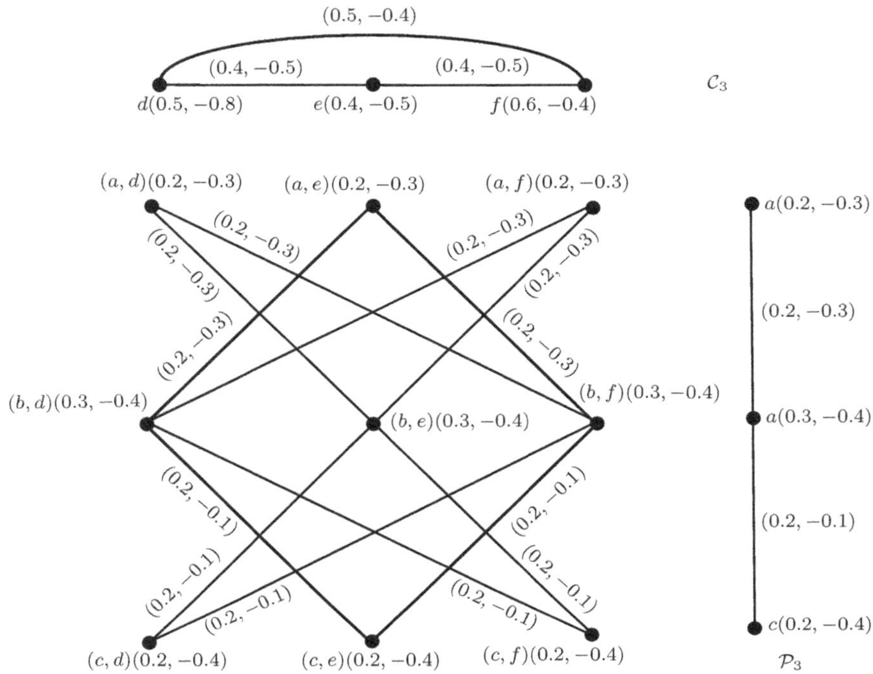

Fig. 2.7 Direct product $\mathcal{P}_3 \times \mathcal{C}_3$

$$deg_{G_1 \times G_2}(x_1, x_2) = (number\ of\ vertices\ adjacent\ to\ x_2) deg_{G_1}(x_1).$$

If for all the edges $\mu^p_{B_2} \leq \mu^p_{B_1}$ and $\mu^n_{B_2} \geq \mu^n_{B_1}$, then

$$deg_{G_1 \times G_2}(x_1, x_2) = (number\ of\ vertices\ adjacent\ to\ x_1) deg_{G_2}(x_2).$$

Proof If membership values of the edges in G_1 and G_2 satisfy the relation: $\mu^p_{B_1} \leq \mu^p_{B_2}$ and $\mu^n_{B_1} \geq \mu^n_{B_2}$ then by Definition 2.1

$$\begin{aligned}
\deg_{G_1 \times G_2}(x_1, x_2) &= \sum\nolimits_{(y_1, y_2) \in X_1 \times X_2} \Big(\mu^p_{B_1 \times B_2}((x_1, x_2)(y_1, y_2)), \mu^n_{B_1 \times B_2}((x_1, x_2)(y_1, y_2))\Big) \\
&= \sum\nolimits_{x_1 y_1 \in E_1, x_2 y_2 \in E_2} \Big(\mu^p_{B_1 \times B_2}((x_1, x_2)(y_1, y_2)), \mu^n_{B_1 \times B_2}((x_1, x_2)(y_1, y_2))\Big) \\
&= \sum\nolimits_{x_1 y_1 \in E_1, x_2 y_2 \in E_2} \Big(\mu^p_{B_1}(x_1 y_1) \wedge \mu^p_{B_2}(x_2 y_2), \mu^n_{B_1}(x_1 y_1) \vee \mu^n_{B_2}(x_2 y_2)\Big) \qquad (2.16) \\
&= \sum\nolimits_{x_1 y_1 \in E_1, x_2 y_2 \in E_2} \Big(\mu^p_{B_1}(x_1 y_1), \mu^n_{B_1}(x_1 y_1)\Big) \\
&= (\text{number of vertices adjacent to } x_2) \deg_{G_1}(x_1).
\end{aligned}$$

If for all the edges $\mu^p_{B_2} \leq \mu^p_{B_1}$ and $\mu^n_{B_2} \geq \mu^n_{B_1}$, then (2.16) takes the form

$$\begin{aligned}\deg_{G_1\times G_2}(x_1,x_2) &= \sum\nolimits_{x_1y_1\in E_1, x_2y_2\in E_2}(\mu^p_{B_2}(x_1y_1), \mu^n_{B_2}(x_1y_1))\\ &= (\text{number of vertices adjacent to } x_1)\deg_{G_2}(x_2).\end{aligned}$$

The proof is complete. □

Theorem 2.7 *Let $G_1 = (A_1, B_1)$ and $G_2 = (A_2, B_2)$ be two bipolar fuzzy graphs such that the membership values of vertices and edges in G_1 and G_2 satisfy the following relations: $\mu^p_{A_1} \geq \mu^p_{B_2}$, $\mu^n_{A_1} \leq \mu^n_{B_2}$, $\mu^p_{A_2} \geq \mu^p_{B_1}$, $\mu^n_{A_2} \leq \mu^n_{B_1}$, $\mu^p_{B_1} \leq \mu^p_{B_2}$ and $\mu^n_{B_1} \geq \mu^n_{B_2}$ then the following conditions are satisfied:*

1. *If $x_2 = y_2$, $d_{G_1\boxtimes G_2}((x_1, x_2), (y_1, y_2)) = d_{G_1}(x_1, y_1)$.*
2. *If $x_1 = y_1$ and $x_2 \neq y_2$ or $x_1 \neq y_1$ and $x_2 \neq y_2$. Then*
   $d_{G_1\boxtimes G_2}((x_1, x_2), (y_1, y_2)) = (L^p(W) \wedge L^p(T), L^n(W) \vee L^n(T))$, where
   (a) W is a bipolar fuzzy walk of smallest μ^p−length and largest μ^n−length in $G_1 \times G_2$ from (x_1, x_2)
   to (y_1, y_2) whose length in crisp strong product is the positive integer k such that
   $k = d_{G_1^*}(x_1, y_1) \vee d_{G_2^*}(x_2, y_2)$.
   (b) $L^p(T)$ is the smallest μ^p−length of any bipolar fuzzy walk T from x_1 to y_1 in G_1 such that the length
   of T^* is greater than k.
   (c) $L^n(T)$ is the largest μ^n−length of any bipolar fuzzy walk T from x_1 to y_1 in G_1 such that the length
   of T^* is greater than k.

Example 2.7 Consider the strong product of two bipolar fuzzy paths in Fig. 2.8,
1. $d_{\mathcal{P}_3\boxtimes\mathcal{P}_3}((a, u), (c, u)) = (0.3, -0.7) = d_{\mathcal{P}_3}(a, c)$.
2. $d_{\mathcal{P}_3\boxtimes\mathcal{P}_3}((a, u), (a, w)) = (0.4, -0.6) = L(W)$, $W : a - b - a$.
3. $d_{\mathcal{P}_3\boxtimes\mathcal{P}_3}((a, u), (c, w)) = (0.3, -0.7) = L(W)$, here $W = (a, u) - (b, v) - (c, w)$. It is clear that $k = L(W^*) = d_{P_3}(a, c) \vee d_{P_3}(u, w)$.

4. $d_{\mathcal{P}_3\boxtimes\mathcal{P}_3}((a, u), (b, w)) = (0.4, -0.9) = \big(L_1(f_{\mathcal{P}_3}(W_1)), L_2(W)\big)$, where $W = (a, u) - (b, v) - (b, w)$, $d_{P_3}(a, b) \vee d_{P_3}(u, w) = 2 = L(W^*)$ and similarly $W_1 = (a, u) - (b, v) - (c, w) - (b, w)$. Clearly, $f_{\mathcal{P}_3}(W_1) = a - b - c - b$ whose crisp length is 3 which is greater than k and $L_1(f_{\mathcal{P}_3}(W_1)) < L_1(W)$.

Theorem 2.8 *Let $G_1 = (A_1, B_1)$ and $G_2 = (A_2, B_2)$ be two bipolar fuzzy graphs such that the membership values of vertices and edges in G_1 and G_2 satisfy the following relations: $\mu^p_{A_1} \geq \mu^p_{B_2}$, $\mu^n_{A_1} \leq \mu^n_{B_2}$, $\mu^p_{A_2} \geq \mu^p_{B_1}$, $\mu^n_{A_2} \leq \mu^n_{B_1}$, $\mu^p_{B} \leq \mu^p_{B_2}$ and $\mu^n_{B_1} \geq \mu^n_{B_2}$. If $x_1 \in X_1$ and $x_2 \in X_2$, then*

$$deg_{G_1\boxtimes G_2}(x_1, x_2) = deg_{G_1}(x_1) + deg_{G_2}(x_2) + r_2 deg_{G_1}(x_1),$$

where r_2 is the number of vertices adjacent to x_2.

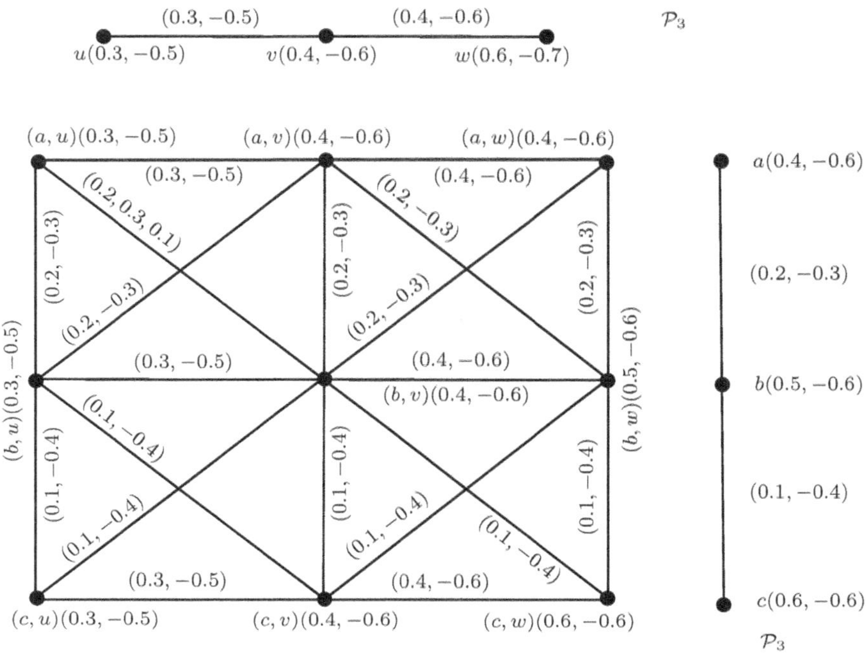

Fig. 2.8 Strong product $\mathcal{P}_3 \boxtimes \mathcal{P}_3$

Proof By Definition 2.1,

$$
\begin{aligned}
\deg_{G_1 \boxtimes G_2}(x_1, x_2) &= \sum\nolimits_{(y_1, y_2) \in X_1 \times X_2} \left(\mu^p_{B_1 \boxtimes B_2}((x_1, x_2)(y_1, y_2)), \mu^n_{B_1 \boxtimes B_2}((x_1, x_2)(y_1, y_2))\right) \\
&= \sum\nolimits_{x_1 = y_1, x_2 y_2 \in E_2} \left(\mu^p_{B_1 \boxtimes B_2}((x_1, x_2)(y_1, y_2)), \mu^n_{B_1 \boxtimes B_2}((x_1, x_2)(y_1, y_2))\right) \\
&\quad + \sum\nolimits_{x_1 y_1 \in E_1, x_2 = y_2} \left(\mu^p_{B_1 \boxtimes B_2}((x_1, x_2)(y_1, y_2)), \mu^n_{B_1 \boxtimes B_2}((x_1, x_2)(y_1, y_2))\right) \\
&\quad + \sum\nolimits_{x_1 y_1 \in E_1, x_2 y_2 \in E_2} \left(\mu^p_{B_1 \boxtimes B_2}((x_1, x_2)(y_1, y_2)), \mu^n_{B_1 \boxtimes B_2}((x_1, x_2)(y_1, y_2))\right) \\
&= \sum\nolimits_{x_1 = y_1, x_2 y_2 \in E_2} \left(\mu^p_{A_1}(x_1) \wedge \mu^p_{B_2}(x_2 y_2), \mu^n_{A_1}(x_1) \vee \mu^n_{B_2}(x_2 y_2)\right) \\
&\quad + \sum\nolimits_{x_1 y_1 \in E_1, x_2 = y_2} \left(\mu^p_{B_1}(x_1 y_1) \wedge \mu^p_{A_2}(x_2), \mu^n_{B_1}(x_1 y_1) \vee \mu^n_{A_2}(x_2)\right) \\
&\quad + \sum\nolimits_{x_1 y_1 \in E_1, x_2 y_2 \in E_2} \left(\mu^p_{B_1}(x_1 y_1) \wedge \mu^p_{B_2}(x_2 y_2), \mu^n_{B_1}(x_1 y_1) \vee \mu^n_{B_2}(x_2 y_2)\right) \\
&= \sum\nolimits_{x_2 y_2 \in E_2} \left(\mu^p_{B_2}(x_2 y_2), \mu^n_{B_2}(x_2 y_2)\right) + \sum\nolimits_{x_1 y_1 \in E_1} \left(\mu^p_{B_1}(x_1 y_1), \mu^n_{B_1}(x_1 y_1)\right) \\
&\quad + \sum\nolimits_{x_1 y_1 \in E_1, x_2 y_2 \in E_2} \left(\mu^p_{B_1}(x_1 y_1), \mu^n_{B_1}(x_1 y_1)\right) \\
&= \deg_{G_2}(x_2) + \deg_{G_1}(x_1) + r_2 \deg_{G_1}(x_1).
\end{aligned}
$$

□

Theorem 2.9 *Let $G_1 = (A_1, B_1)$ and $G_2 = (A_2, B_2)$ be two bipolar fuzzy graphs such that the membership values of vertices and edges in G_1 and G_2 follow the relations: $\mu^p_{A_1} \geq \mu^p_{B_2}$, $\mu^n_{A_1} \leq \mu^n_{B_2}$, $\mu^p_{A_2} \geq \mu^p_{B_1}$, $\mu^n_{A_2} \leq \mu^n_{B_1}$, $\mu^p_{B_1} \leq \mu^p_{B_2}$ and $\mu^n_{B_1} \geq \mu^n_{B_2}$. If $x_1 \in X_1$ and $x_2 \in X_2$ then the following conditions are satisfied:*

1. *If $d_{G_1^*}(x_1, y_1) = k$, where k is even (or odd) and $d_{G_2^*}(x_2, y_2)$ is also even (or odd), then $d_{G_1 \bullet G_2}((x_1, x_2), (y_1, x_2)) = (L^p(W), L^n(W))$, where W is a bipolar fuzzy walk of smallest μ^p-length and largest μ^n-length in G_2 such that W^* is a walk of length k in G_2^*.*
2. *If $d_{G_1^*}(x_1, y_1) = k$, where k is even (or odd) and $d_{G_2^*}(x_2, y_2)$ is odd (or even), then $d_{G_1 \bullet G_2}((x_1, x_2), (y_1, x_2)) = (L^p(W), L^n(W))$, where W is a bipolar fuzzy walk of smallest μ^p-length and largest μ^n-length in G_2 such that W^* is a walk of length $k + 1$ in G_2^*.*

Example 2.8 The lexicographic product of two bipolar fuzzy paths $\mathcal{P}_3$ and $\mathcal{P}_3$ is given in Fig. 2.9.

In Fig. 2.9,

1. $d_{\mathcal{P}_3 \bullet \mathcal{P}_3}((d, a), (f, c)) = (0.4, -0.4) = L(W)$, $W = a - b - c$. It is clear that $L(W^*) = d_{P_3}(d, f)$ because both $d_{P_3}(d, f)$ and $d_{P_3}(a, c)$ are even.
2. $d_{\mathcal{P}_3 \bullet \mathcal{P}_3}((d, a), (f, b)) = (0.6, -0.5) = L(W)$, $W = a - b - c - b$. Here $L(W^*) = d_{P_3}(d, f) + 1$ because $d_{P_3}(d, f)$ is even and $d_{P_3}(a, b)$ is odd.

Theorem 2.10 *Let $G_1 = (A_1, B_1)$ and $G_2 = (A_2, B_2)$ be two bipolar fuzzy graphs such that the positive and negative degrees of membership of edges and vertices in G_1 and G_2 follow the relations: $\mu^p_{A_1} \geq \mu^p_{B_2}$, $\mu^n_{A_1} \leq \mu^n_{B_2}$, $\mu^p_{A_2} \geq \mu^p_{B_1}$, $\mu^n_{A_2} \leq \mu^n_{B_1}$, $\mu^p_{B_1} \leq \mu^p_{B_2}$ and $\mu^n_{B_1} \geq \mu^n_{B_2}$. If $x_1 \in X_1$, and $x_2 \in X_2$, then*

$$deg_{G_1 \bullet G_2}(x_1, x_2) = deg_{G_2}(x_2) + r_2 deg_{G_1}(x_1),$$

where r_2 is the number of vertices adjacent to x_2.

Proof By Definition 2.1,

$$\begin{aligned}
\deg_{G_1 \bullet G_2}((x_1, x_2)) &= \sum\nolimits_{(y_1, y_2) \in X_1 \times X_2} \left(\mu^p_{B_1 \bullet B_2}((x_1, x_2)(y_1, y_2)), \mu^n_{B_1 \bullet B_2}((x_1, x_2)(y_1, y_2))\right) \\
&= \sum\nolimits_{x_1 = y_1, x_2 y_2 \in E_2} \left(\mu^p_{B_1 \bullet B_2}((x_1, x_2)(y_1, y_2)), \mu^n_{B_1 \bullet B_2}((x_1, x_2)(y_1, y_2))\right) \\
&\quad + \sum\nolimits_{x_1 y_1 \in E_1, x_2 y_2 \in E_2} \left(\mu^p_{B_1 \bullet B_2}((x_1, x_2)(y_1, y_2)), \mu^n_{B_1 \bullet B_2}((x_1, x_2)(y_1, y_2))\right) \\
&= \sum\nolimits_{x_1 = y_1, x_2 y_2 \in E_2} \left(\mu^p_{A_1}(x_1) \wedge \mu^p_{B_2}(x_2 y_2), \mu^n_{A_1}(x_1) \vee \mu^n_{B_2}(x_2 y_2)\right) \\
&\quad + \sum\nolimits_{x_1 y_1 \in E_1, x_2 y_2 \in E_2} \left(\mu^p_{B_1}(x_1 y_1) \wedge \mu^p_{B_2}(x_2 y_2), \mu^n_{B_1}(x_1 y_1) \vee \mu^n_{B_2}(x_2 y_2)\right) \\
&= \sum\nolimits_{x_2 y_2 \in E_2} \left(\mu^p_{B_2}(x_2 y_2), \mu^n_{B_2}(x_2 y_2)\right) + \sum\nolimits_{x_1 y_1 \in E_1, x_2 y_2 \in E_2} \left(\mu^p_{B_1}(x_1 y_1), \mu^n_{B_1}(x_1 y_1)\right) \\
&= \deg_{G_2}(x_2) + r_2 \deg_{G_1}(x_1).
\end{aligned}$$

The proof is complete. □

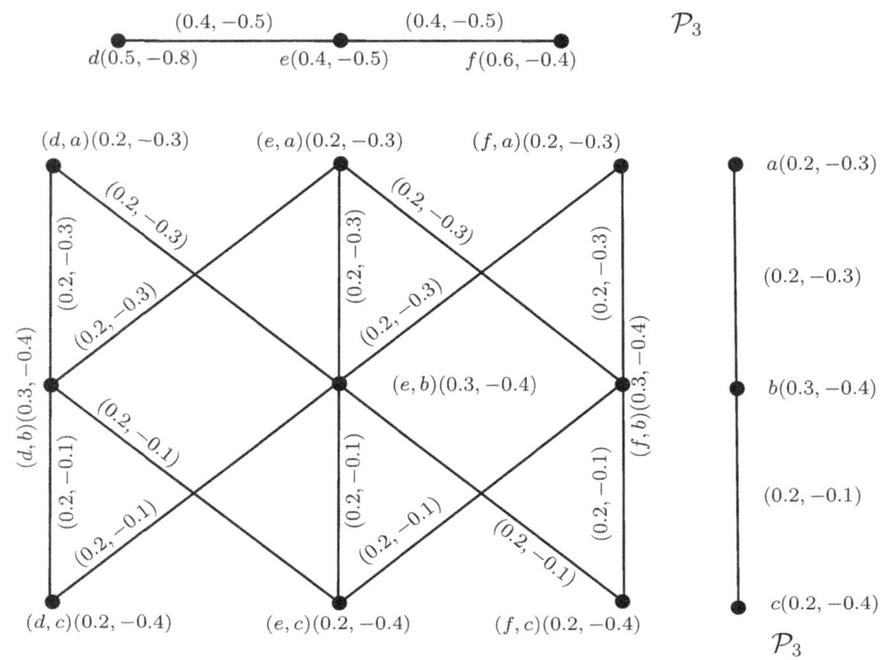

Fig. 2.9 Lexicographic product $\mathcal{P}_3 \circ \mathcal{P}_3$

2.3 Metric in Bipolar Fuzzy Graphs

In this section, the concept of metric, radius, diameter, and self-centered bipolar fuzzy graphs is discussed in detail.

Theorem 2.11 *For a bipolar fuzzy graph $G = (A, B)$, $d = (d^P, d^n) : X \times X \to [0, 1] \times [-1, 0]$ defines a* **metric** *on X with the following conditions:*

1. $d^P(x, y) \geq 0$ *and* $d^n(x, y) \leq 0$,
2. $d(x, y) = (0, 0) \Leftrightarrow x = y$,
3. $d(x, y) = d(y, x)$,
4. $d^P(x, z) \leq d^P(x, y) + d^P(y, z)$ *and* $d^n(x, z) \geq d^n(x, y) + d^n(y, z)$ *for all* $x, y, z \in X$.

Proof It is clear from Definition 2.9 that $L^P(x, y) \geq 0$ and $L^n(x, y) \leq 0$ for all $x, y \in X$. Therefore, $d^P(x, y) \geq 0$ and $d^n(x, y) \leq 0$.

If $x = y$, then $d(x, y) = d(x, x) = (d^P(x, x), d^n(x, x)) = (0, 0)$. The inverse of any $x - y$ bipolar fuzzy path is a $y - x$ bipolar fuzzy path and vice versa of same distance. Let P_1, P_2 be two $x - y$ bipolar fuzzy paths and Q_1, Q_2 be $y - z$ bipolar fuzzy paths such that

$$d(x, y) = (d^P(x, y), d^n(x, y)) = (L^P(P_1), L^n(P_2)),$$
$$d(y, z) = (d^P(y, z), d^n(y, z)) = (L^P(Q_1), L^n(Q_2)).$$

P_1 followed by Q_1 and P_2 followed by Q_2 are $x - z$ bipolar fuzzy walks, each of which contains only one bipolar fuzzy path whose length cannot exceed $d^P(x, y) + d^P(y, z)$ and $d^n(x, y) + d^n(y, z)$, respectively. Thus, we can write $d^P(x, z) \leq d^P(x, y) + d^P(y, z)$ and $d^n(x, z) \geq d^n(x, y) + d^n(y, z)$. □

Definition 2.11 Let $G = (A, B)$ be a bipolar fuzzy graph on X. The **eccentricity** of a vertex x in G is denoted by the ordered pair $e(x) = (e^P(x), e^n(x))$ and defined as the distance to a vertex farthest from x, that is,

$$e(x) = \left(\max_{y \in X} d^P(x, y), \min_{y \in X} d^n(x, y) \right).$$

Definition 2.12 The **radius** of a bipolar fuzzy graph G, denoted by the ordered pair $r(G) = (r^P(G), r^n(G))$, is the minimum and maximum of all the positive and negative eccentricities of the vertices in G, respectively, that is,

$$r(G) = \left(\min_{x \in X} e^P(x), \max_{x \in X} e^n(x) \right).$$

Definition 2.13 The **diameter** of a bipolar fuzzy graph G is defined as an ordered pair $diam(G) = (diam^P(G), diam^n(G))$, where $diam^P(G)$ and $diam^n(G)$ are the maximum and minimum values of all positive and negative eccentricities of the vertices in G, respectively, that is,

$$diam(G) = \left(\max_{x \in X} e^P(x), \min_{x \in X} e^n(x) \right).$$

Definition 2.14 A vertex y in a bipolar fuzzy graph G at a distance $e(z)$ from x is called **eccentric vertex** of x.

Definition 2.15 A vertex x in a bipolar fuzzy graph G is called a **central vertex** of G if $e(x) = r(G)$.

Definition 2.16 A bipolar fuzzy subgraph induced by the central vertices is known as **center** of a bipolar fuzzy graph G, denoted by $C(G)$. If the center of G is G itself then G is called a **self-centered bipolar fuzzy graph**.

Definition 2.17 A vertex x in a bipolar fuzzy graph G is called a **peripheral vertex** if $e(x) = diam(G)$.

Example 2.9 Consider a bipolar fuzzy graph as shown in Fig. 2.10.

The distance between all the vertices is calculated as

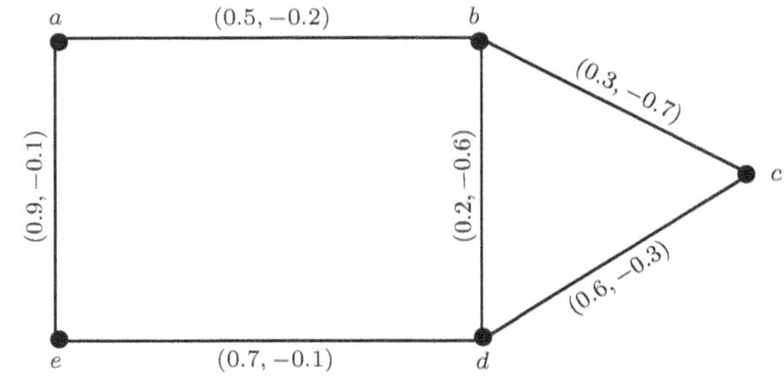

Fig. 2.10 Radius and diameter of a bipolar fuzzy graph G

$$d(a,b)=(0.5,-0.2),\quad d(a,c)=(0.8,-0.5),\quad d(a,d)=(0.7,-0.2),\quad d(a,e)=(0.9,-0.1),$$
$$d(b,c)=(0.3,-0.7),\quad d(b,d)=(0.2,-0.4),\quad d(b,e)=(0.9,-0.3),\quad d(c,d)=(0.5,-0.3),$$
$$d(c,e)=(1.2,-0.4),\quad d(d,e)=(0.7,0.1,0.1).$$

Therefore the eccentricities of the vertices using above distances are computed as follows:

$$e(a)=(0.9,-0.5),\quad e(b)=(0.9,-0.7),\quad e(c)=(1.2,-0.7),\quad e(d)=(0.7,-0.4),\quad e(e)=(1.2,-0.4).$$

Hence $r(G)=(0.7,-0.4)$, $diam(G)=(1.2,-0.7)$, d is a central vertex and c is a peripheral vertex.

Theorem 2.12 *For any bipolar fuzzy graph G, radius and diameter satisfy the inequalities:*

$$r^p(G)\le diam^p(G)\le 2r^p(G)\quad and\quad r^n(G)\ge diam^n(G)\ge 2r^n(G).$$

Proof By Definitions 2.12 and 2.13, we have

$$r^p(G)\le diam^p(G) \text{ and } r^n(G)\ge diam^n(G).$$

Let u, v be central vertices of G then $e(u)=r(G)$ and $e(v)=r(G)$. Let x be a peripheral vertex of G. Since d defines a metric, for some vertices $y_1, y_2\in X$,

$$diam^p(G)=d^p(x,y_1)\le d^p(x,u)+d^p(u,y_1)\le 2r^p(G),$$

and

$$diam^n(G)=d^n(x,y_1)\ge d^n(x,u)+d^n(u,y_1)\ge 2r^n(G) \text{ for some } u,v\in X.$$ □

The following theorem gives an absolute difference between the eccentricities of any two adjacent vertices in a bipolar fuzzy graph.

Theorem 2.13 *For any two adjacent vertices x and y in a bipolar fuzzy graph G,*

$$|e(x) - e(y)| \leq (1, 1).$$

Proof Let $G = (A, B)$ be a bipolar fuzzy graph on X. Without loss of generality, assume that $e^p(x) \leq e^p(y)$ and $e^n(x) \geq e^n(y)$. For any vertices $z_1, z_2 \in X$,

$$e^p(y) = d^p(y, z_1) \leq d^p(y, x) + d^p(x, z_1) \leq 1 + e^p(x).$$

Hence

$$-(e^p(x) - e^n(y)) \leq 1. \tag{2.17}$$

Also

$$e^n(y) = d^n(y, z_2) \geq d^n(y, x) + d^n(x, z_2) \geq -1 + e^n(x).$$

Thus

$$e^n(x) - e^n(y) \leq 1. \tag{2.18}$$

For any vertices $u_1, u_2 \in X$

$$e^p(x) = d^p(x, u_1 \leq d^p(x, y) + d^p(y, u_1) \leq 1 + e^p(y).$$

So,

$$e^p(x) - e^n(y) \leq 1. \tag{2.19}$$

Similarly,

$$e^n(x) = d^n(x, u_2) \geq d^n(x, y) + d^n(y, u_2) \geq -1 + e^n(y).$$

Hence,

$$(e^n(x) - e^n(y)) \leq 1. \tag{2.20}$$

Combining inequalities (2.17), (2.19), (2.18), and (2.20), the required result is obtained. □

By assuming any two arbitrary vertices x and y in Theorem 2.13, we obtain the following result.

Remark 2.2 For any two vertices x and y in a bipolar fuzzy graph G,

$$|e^p(x) - e^p(y)| \leq d^p(x, y) \text{ and } |e^n(x) - e^n(y)| \leq -d^n(x, y).$$

Theorem 2.14 *For any two adjacent vertices x and y in a bipolar fuzzy graph G*

$$|d(x, z) - d(y, z)| \leq (1, 1)$$

for every vertex z in G.

Proof Let G be a bipolar fuzzy graph on X. Since d defines a metric on X,

$$d^P(x,z) \le d^P(x,y) + d^P(y,z) \le 1 + d^P(y,z).$$

Hence,

$$d^P(x,z) - d^P(y,z) \le 1. \tag{2.21}$$

Similarly,

$$d^n(x,z) \ge d^n(x,y) + d^n(y,z) \ge -1 + d^n(y,z).$$

Thus

$$-(d^n(x,z) - d^n(y,z)) \le 1. \tag{2.22}$$

For the vertex y we have $d^P(y,z) \le d^P(y,x) + d^P(x,z) \le 1 + d^P(x,z)$, which gives

$$-(d^P(x,z) - d^P(y,z)) \le 1. \tag{2.23}$$

Analogously, $d^n(y,z) \ge d^n(y,x) + d^n(x,z) \ge -1 + d^n(y,z)$, implies

$$d^n(x,z) - d^n(y,z) \le 1. \tag{2.24}$$

The required result is clear from inequalities (2.21), (2.23), (2.22), and (2.24). □

For any two arbitrary vertices x and y, Theorem 2.14 can be generalized in Remark 2.3.

Remark 2.3 For any two vertices x and y in a bipolar fuzzy graph G,

$$|d^P(x,z) - d^P(y,z)| \le d^P(x,y) \text{ and } |d^n(x,z) - d^n(y,z)| \le -d^n(x,y).$$

Theorem 2.15 *If G is a self-centered bipolar fuzzy graph, then each vertex of G is an eccentric vertex.*

Proof Let y be an eccentric vertex of x, then $e(x) = d(x,y)$. Since G is self-centered therefore, $e(x) = e(y) = r(G)$. It follows that $e(y) = d(x,y)$. It clearly shows that x is an eccentric vertex of y . Since x was taken to be arbitrary, the given statement is true for all vertices. □

Remark 2.4 The converse of Theorem 2.15 is not true in general as it can be seen in Example 2.10.

Example 2.10 Consider a bipolar fuzzy graph as shown in Fig. 2.11.

From routine calculations, $e(x) = (0.9, -0.5)$, $e(y) = (0.9, -0.5)$, $e(z) = (0.8, -0.5)$ $e(w) = (0.8, -0.5)$, $r(G) = (0.8, -0.5)$, $diam(G) = (0.9, -0.5)$. All vertices of G are eccentric but G is not self-centered bipolar fuzzy graph because the center of G is shown in Fig. 2.12.

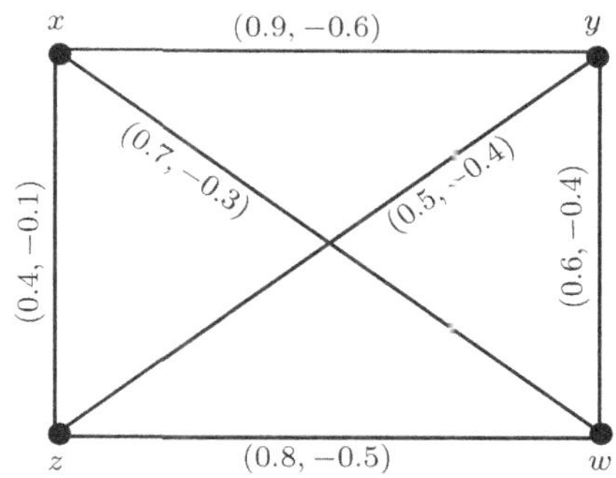

Fig. 2.11 Eccentric vertices in bipolar fuzzy graph G

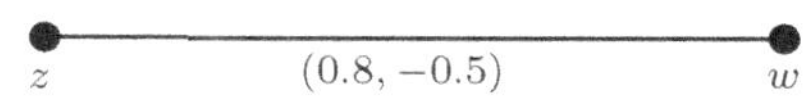

Fig. 2.12 Center of bipolar fuzzy graph G

Theorem 2.16 *Let G be a self-centered bipolar fuzzy graph. For every two vertices $x, y \in X$, if $x \in Y^*$ then $y \in X^*$, where X^* is the set of all eccentric vertices of x and Y^* is the set of all eccentric vertices of y.*

Proof Since x is a eccentric vertex of y, $e(x) = d(x, y) \Rightarrow x \in Y^*$. It is given that G is a self-centered bipolar fuzzy graph so $e(y) = e(x) = d(y, x)$, i.e., y is an eccentric vertex of x. Hence $y \in X^*$. □

Remark 2.5 The converse of Theorem 2.16 is not true in general. In Example 2.10, $x \in Y^*$, $y \in X^*$, $z \in W^*$, and $w \in Z^*$ but G is not self-centered.

Theorem 2.17 *Let G be a bipolar fuzzy graph then all peripheral vertices are eccentric vertices.*

Proof Let x be a peripheral vertex and y be its eccentric vertex, then $diam(G) = e(x) = d(x, y) = d(y, x)$. It is only possible if $diam(G) = d(y, x) = e(y)$. It shows that x is an eccentric vertex of y. Hence the proof. □

Remark 2.6 The condition in Theorem 2.17 is not sufficient. In Example 2.10, z and w are eccentric vertices of each other but these are not peripheral vertices.

Theorem 2.18 *Let G be a complete bipolar fuzzy graph on X such that $\mu_A^p(x_1) \le \mu_A^p(x_2) \le \mu_A^p(x_3) \le ... \le \mu_A^p(x_n)$ and $\mu_A^n(x_1) \ge \mu_A^n(x_2) \ge \mu_A^n(x_3) \ge .. \ge \mu_A^n(x_n)$, then the distance between any two vertices x_i and x_j is $d(x_i, x_j) = \big(\mu_B^p(x_ix_j) \wedge 2\mu_A^p(x_1), \mu_B^n(x_ix_j) \vee 2\mu_A^n(x_1)\big)$.*

Proof Let x_i and x_j be any two vertices of G then for some $x_k^{(1)}, x_k^{(2)} \in X$, the distance between x_i and x_j can be defined as

$$d(x_i, x_j) = (d^p(x_i, x_j), d^n(x_l, x_j)),$$
$$= \left(\min\{\mu_B^p(x_ix_j), \mu_B^p(x_ix_k^{(1)}) + \mu_B^p(x_k^{(1)}x_j)\}, \max\{\mu_B^n(x_ix_j), \mu_B^n(x_ix_k^{(2)}) + \mu_B^n(x_k^{(2)}x_j)\}\right). \quad (2.25)$$

Since G is a complete bipolar fuzzy graph, $\mu_B^p(x_i x_k^{(1)}) = \mu_A^p(x_i) \wedge \mu_A^p(x_k^{(1)})$ and $\mu_B^n(x_i x_k^{(1)}) = \mu_A^n(x_i) \vee \mu_A^n(x_k^{(1)})$. Considering the conditions of membership values given in the statement, if we take $x_k^{(1)} = x_k^{(2)} = x_1$, then $\mu_B^p(x_i x_k^{(1)}) = \mu_A^p(x_k^{(1)}) = \mu_A^p(x_1)$ and $\mu_B^n(x_i x_k^{(2)}) = \mu_A^n(x_k^{(2)}) = \mu_A^n(x_1)$.

Similarly, $\mu_B^p(x_k^{(1)} x_j) = \mu_A^p(x_k^{(1)}) = \mu_A^p(x_1)$ and $\mu_B^n(x_k^{(2)} x_j) = \mu_A^n(x_k^{(2)}) = \mu_A^n(x_1)$. Equation (2.25) takes the form $d(x_i, x_j) = \big(\mu_B^p(x_i x_j) \wedge 2\mu_A^p(x_1), \mu_B^n(x_i x_j) \vee 2\mu_A^n(x_1)\big)$. □

Theorem 2.19 *Let $G = (A, B)$ be a complete bipartite bipolar fuzzy graph on $X \cup Y$, where $X = \{x_1, x_2, \ldots, x_n\}$ and $Y = \{y_1, y_2, \ldots, y_{n'}\}$ such that*

$$\mu_A^p(x_1) \le \mu_A^p(x_2) \le \mu_A^p(x_3) \le \cdots \le \mu_A^p(x_n), \quad \mu_A^n(x_1) \ge \mu_A^n(x_2) \ge \mu_A^n(x_3) \ge \cdots \ge \mu_A^n(x_n),$$

$$\mu_A^p(y_1) \le \mu_A^p(y_2) \le \mu_A^p(y_3) \le \cdots \le \mu_A^p(y_{n'}), \quad \mu_A^n(y_1) \ge \mu_A^n(y_2) \ge \mu_A^n(y_3) \ge \cdots \ge \mu_A^n(y_{n'}).$$

If $\mu_A^p(x_1) \le \mu_A^p(y_1)$, $\mu_A^n(x_1) \ge \mu_A^n(y_1)$, $\mu_A^p(y_1) \le \mu_A^p(x_j)$ and $\mu_A^n(y_1) \ge \mu_A^n(x_j)$, for each $2 \le j \le n$, then

$$d(u, v) = \begin{cases} 2A(x_1), & \text{if } u, v \in Y \\ A(x_1) + A(y_1), & \text{if } u, v \in X, u = x_1 \text{ or } v = x_1 \\ 2A(y_1), & \text{if } u, v \in X, u \ne x_1 \text{ and } v \ne x_1 \\ \big(\mu_B^p(uv) \wedge (2\mu_A^p(x_1) + \mu_A^p(y_1)), & \\ \quad \mu_B^n(uv) \vee (2\mu_A^n(x_1) + \mu_A^n(y_1))\big) & \text{if } u \in X \text{ and } v \in Y. \end{cases}$$

If $\mu_A^p(y_1) \le \mu_A^p(x_1)$, $\mu_A^n(y_1) \ge \mu_A^n(x_1)$, $\mu_A^p(x_1) \le \mu_A^p(y_j)$ and $\mu_A^n(x_1) \ge \mu_A^n(y_j)$, for each $2 \le j \le n'$, then

$$d(u, v) = \begin{cases} 2A(y_1), & \text{if } u, v \in X \\ A(y_1) + A(x_1), & \text{if } u, v \in Y, u = y_1 \text{ or } v = y_1 \\ 2A(x_1), & \text{if } u, v \in Y, u \ne y_1 \text{ and } v \ne y_1 \\ \big(\mu_B^p(uv) \wedge (2\mu_A^p(y_1) + \mu_A^p(x_1)), & \\ \quad \mu_B^n(uv) \vee (2\mu_A^n(y_1) + \mu_A^n(x_1))\big) & \text{if } u \in X \text{ and } v \in Y. \end{cases}$$

Proof Consider the case $\mu_A^p(x_1) \le \mu_A^p(y_1)$, $\mu_A^n(x_1) \ge \mu_A^n(y_1)$, $\mu_A^p(y_1) \le \mu_A^p(x_j)$ and $\mu_A^n(y_1) \ge \mu_A^n(x_j)$, for each $2 \le j \le n$. Assume that $u, v \in X$ are two arbitrary vertices of G then for some $y_k^{(1)}, y_k^{(2)} \in X$, the distance $d(u, v)$ between u and v is given as

$$d(u, v) = (d^p(u, v), d^n(u, v)) = \left(\mu_B^p(u y_k^{(1)}) + \mu_B^p(y_k^{(1)} v), \mu_B^p(u y_k^{(2)}) + \mu_B^p(y_k^{(2)} v)\right). \quad (2.26)$$

If $u = x_1$, then for $y_k^{(1)} = y_k^{(2)} = y_1$ we have, $\mu_B^p(uy_k^{(1)}) = \mu_A^p(x_1)$ and $\mu_B^n(uy_k^{(2)}) = \mu_A^n(x_1)$. Similarly, $(\mu_B^p(y_k^{(1)}v), \mu_B^n(y_k^{(2)}v)) = (\mu_A^p(y_k^{(1)}), \mu_A^n(y_k^{(2)})) = (\mu_A^p(y_1), \mu_A^n(y_1))$. Equation (2.26) takes the form as

$$d(u, v) = \left(\mu_A^p(x_1) + \mu_A^p(y_1), \mu_A^n(x_1) + \mu_A^n(y_1)\right).$$

If $u, v \neq x_1$, then for $y_k^{(1)} = y_k^{(1)} = y_1$, $\mu_B^p(uy_k^{(1)}) = \mu_A^p(y_k^{(1)}) = \mu_A^p(y_1)$ and $\mu_B^n(uy_k^{(2)}) = \mu_A^n(y_k^{(2)}) = \mu_A^n(y_1)$. Similarly, $\mu_B^p(y_k^{(1)}v) = \mu_A^p(y_k^{(1)}) = \mu_A^p(y_1)$ and $\mu_B^n(y_k^{(2)}v) = \mu_A^n(y_k^{(2)}) = \mu_A^n(y_1)$. Equation (2.26) takes the form as $d(u, v) = 2A(y_1)$. If $u, v \in Y$, there exist some $x_k^{(1)}, x_k^{(2)} \in X$ such that

$$d(u, v) = (d^p(u, v), d^n(u, v)) = (\mu_B^p(ux_k^{(1)}) + \mu_B^p(x_k^{(1)}v), \mu_B^n(ux_k^{(2)}) + \mu_B^n(x_k^{(2)}v)). \tag{2.27}$$

Since $\mu_A^p(x_1) \leq \mu_A^p(y_1)$ and $\mu_A^n(x_1) \geq \mu_A^n(y_1)$, for $x_k^{(1)} = x_k^{(2)} = x_1$, $\left(\mu_B^p(ux_k^{(1)}), \mu_B^n(ux_k^{(2)})\right) = A(x_1)$. Similarly, $\left(\mu_B^p(x_k^{(1)}v), \mu_B^n(x_k^{(2)}v)\right) = A(x_1)$. Equation (2.27) takes the form $d(u, v) = 2A(x_1)$. If $u \in X$ and $v \in Y$, then

$$\begin{aligned} d(u, v) &= \left(d^p(u, v), d^n(u, v)\right) \\ &= \left(\mu_B^p(uv) \wedge (\mu_B^p(uy_1) + \mu_B^p(y_1x_1) + \mu_B^p(x_1v)), \mu_B^n(uv) \wedge (\mu_B^n(uy_1) + \mu_B^n(y_1x_1) + \mu_B^n(x_1v))\right) \\ &= \left(\mu_B^p(uv) \wedge (2\mu_A^p(x_1) + \mu_A^p(y_1)), \mu_B^n(uv) \wedge (2\mu_A^n(x_1) + \mu_A^n(y_1))\right). \end{aligned}$$

Similar argument can be used for other cases. □

2.4 Self-centered Bipolar Fuzzy Graphs

A notion of distance in bipolar fuzzy graphs is already given in Definition 2.9. In this section, self-centered bipolar fuzzy graphs are discussed with another notion of distance in Definition 2.18.

Definition 2.18 Let $G = (A, B)$ be a bipolar fuzzy graph. For any bipolar fuzzy path, P: $y_1 - y_2 - ... - y_n$ in G, the μ^p**−length** of P is defined as the sum of reciprocals of μ^p-values (positive membership values) of the edges and μ^n**−length** of P is determined as the sum of reciprocals of μ^n-values (negative membership values) of the edges, that is,

$$l^p(P) = \sum_{i=2}^{n} \frac{1}{\mu_B^p(y_{i-1}y_i)}, \quad l^n(P) = \sum_{i=2}^{n} \frac{1}{\mu_B^n(y_{i-1}y_i)}.$$

The **length** of bipolar fuzzy path P is represented by the ordered pair $l(P) = (l^p(P), l^n(P))$. For any two arbitrary vertices $x, y \in X$, let

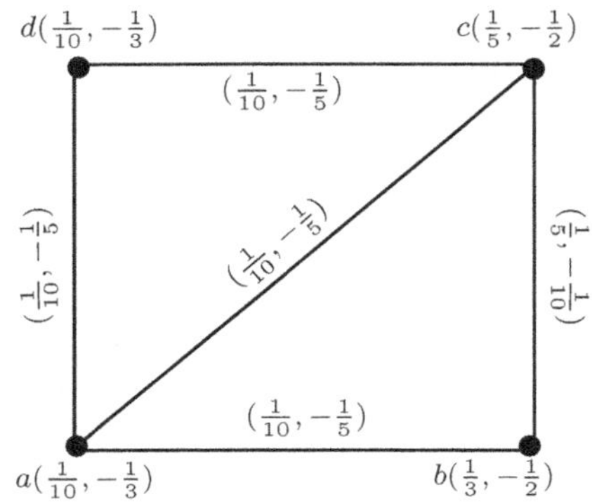

Fig. 2.13 Distance in bipolar fuzzy graph G

$$\mathbb{P} = \{P_i \mid P_i \text{ is an } x - y \text{ bipolar fuzzy path}, \; i = 1, 2, 3, ...\}$$

be the set of all bipolar fuzzy paths from x to y. Then the **distance** from x to y is denoted by $\delta(x, y)$ or $\delta_G(x, y)$ and defined as the ordered pair $\delta(x, y) = \big(\delta^P(x, y), \delta^n(x, y)\big)$, where

$$\delta^P(x, y) = \min\{l^P(P_j) \mid P_j \in \mathbb{P}, j = 1, 2, 3, ...\}, \quad \delta^n(x, y) = \max\{l^n(P_j) \mid P_j \in \mathbb{P}, j = 1, 2, 3, ...\}.$$

Example 2.11 Consider a bipolar fuzzy connected graph G on the set $X=\{a, b, c, d\}$ as shown in Fig. 2.13.

By routine computations, it is easy to see that

1. $a - d$ is a bipolar fuzzy path of length $(10, -5)$, $a - c - d$ is a bipolar fuzzy path of length $(20, -10)$, $a - b - c - d$ is a bipolar fuzzy path of length $(25, -20)$.
2. The distances are calculated as

$$\delta^P(a, d) = 10, \; \delta^P(a, b) = 10, \; \delta^P(a, c) = 10, \; \delta^P(b, c) = 5, \; \delta^P(b, d) = 15,$$
$$\delta^P(c, d) = 10, \; \delta^n(a, d) = -5, \; \delta^n(a, b) = -5, \; \delta^n(a, c) = -5, \; \delta^n(b, c) = -10,$$
$$\delta^n(b, d) = -10, \; \delta^n(c, d) = -5,$$
$$\delta(a, d) = (10, -5), \; \delta(a, b) = (10, -5), \; \delta(a, c) = (10, -5),$$
$$\delta(b, c) = (5, -10), \; \delta(b, d) = (15, -10), \; \delta(c, d) = (10, -5).$$

3. The eccentricity of each vertex is calculated as

$$e(a) = (10, -5), \; e(b) = (15, -10), \; e(c) = (10, -10), \; e(d) = (15, -15).$$

4. The radius of G is (10, -5) and diameter of G is (15, -15).

Example 2.12 Consider $G = (A, B)$, a bipolar graph, on the set $X = \{a, b, c\}$ as given in Fig. 2.14.

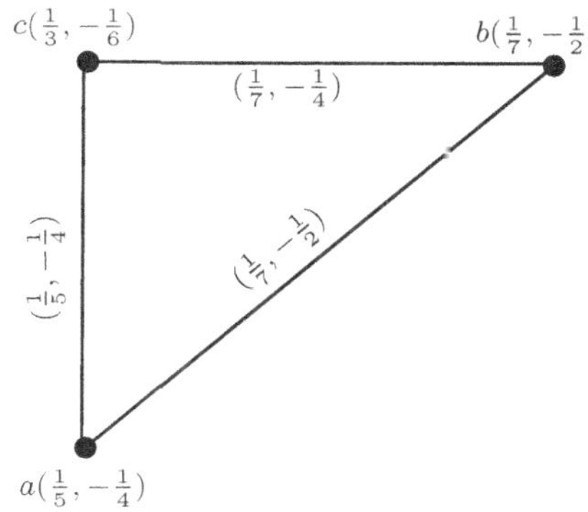

Fig. 2.14 Self-centered bipolar fuzzy graph G

1. The distances between vertices are calculated as

$$\delta^P(a,b) = 7,\ \delta^P(a,c) = 5,\ \delta^P(b,c) = 7,\ \delta^n(a,b) = -2,\ \delta^n(a,c) = -4,$$
$$\delta^n(b,c) = -4,\ \delta(a,b) = (7,-2),\ \delta(a,c) = (5,-4),\ \delta(b,c) = (7,-4).$$

2. The eccentricity of each vertex is (7, -4).
3. The radius of G is (7, -4). Hence G is a self-centered bipolar fuzzy graph (see Definition 2.16).

Theorem 2.20 *Every complete bipolar fuzzy graph G is a self-centered bipolar fuzzy graph and $r^P(G) = \frac{1}{\mu^P(v_i)}$, $r^n(G) = \frac{1}{\mu^n(v_i^{'})}$, where $\mu^P(v_i)$ and $\mu^n(v_i^{'})$ are the least and greatest membership values, respectively, for some vertices v_i and $v_i^{'}$ of G.*

Proof To prove that G is a self-centered bipolar fuzzy graph, it is to be shown that every vertex of G is a central vertex. Let $v_i, v_i^{'} \in X$ such that $\mu^P(v_i)$ and $\mu^n(v_i^{'})$ are the least and greatest membership values, respectively.

Case 1: Consider all the $v_i - v_j$ bipolar fuzzy paths P of length n in G, for all $v_j \in X$.
1. If $n = 1$ then μ^P−length of $P = l^P(P) = \frac{1}{\mu^P(v_i)}$.
2. If $n > 1$ then one of the edges of P possesses the positive membership value equal to $\mu^P(v_i)$ and hence, μ^P−length of a $v_i - v_j$ bipolar fuzzy path will exceed $\frac{1}{\mu^P(v_i)}$. That is, $l^P(P) > \frac{1}{\mu^P(v_i)}$. Hence,

$$\delta^P(v_i, v_j) = \min_{P \in \mathbb{P}} l^P(P) = \frac{1}{\mu^P(v_i)} \text{ for all } v_j \in X. \tag{2.28}$$

Case 2: Let $v_k \neq v_i \in X$. Consider all $v_k - v_j$ bipolar fuzzy paths Q of length n in G, for all $v_j \in X$.
1. If $n = 1$, then $l^P(Q) = \frac{1}{\mu_B^P(v_k v_j)} \leq \frac{1}{\mu^P(v_i)}$.

2. If $n = 2$, then $l^P(Q) = \frac{1}{\mu_B^p(v_k v_{k+1})} + \frac{1}{\mu_B^p(v_{k+1} v_j)} \leq \frac{2}{\mu^p(v_i)}$, since $\mu^p(v_i)$ is the least.
3. If $n > 2$, then $l^P(Q) \leq \frac{n}{\mu^p(v_i)}$, since $\mu^p(v_i)$ is the least. Thus,

$$\delta^P(v_k, v_j) = \min_{Q \in \mathbb{P}} l^P(Q) \leq 1/\mu^p(v_i), \text{ for all } v_k, v_j \in X. \tag{2.29}$$

From (2.28) and (2.29),

$$e^p(v_i) = \max_{y_j \in X} \delta^P(v_i, v_j) = \frac{1}{\mu^p(v_i)}, \text{ for all } v_i \in X. \tag{2.30}$$

$$\begin{aligned} Now,\ r^p(G) &= \min_{v_i \in X} e_{\mu^+}(v_i) \\ &= \frac{1}{\mu^p(v_i)}, \quad \text{since } by \qquad (2.34) \\ r^p(G) &= \frac{1}{\mu^p(v_i)}. \end{aligned}$$

Choose a vertex $v_i^{'} \in X$ such that $\mu^n(v_i^{'})$ is the greatest membership value of G.

Case 1: Consider all the $v_i^{'} - v_j$ bipolar fuzzy paths P of length n in G, for all $v_j \in X$.
1. If $n = 1$ then μ^n−length of $P = l^n(P) = \frac{1}{\mu^n(v_i^{'})}$.
2. If $n > 1$ then one of the edges of P possesses negative membership value equal to $\mu^p(v_i^{'})$ and hence $l^n(P) > \frac{1}{\mu^n(v_i^{'})}$. Thus,

$$\delta^P(v_i^{'}, v_j) = \min_{P \in \mathbb{P}} l^n(P) = \frac{1}{\mu^n(v_i^{'})}, \text{ for all } v_j \in X. \tag{2.31}$$

Case 2: Let $v_k \neq v_i \in X$. Consider all $v_k - v_j$ bipolar fuzzy paths paths Q of length n in G, for all $v_j \in X$.
1. If $n = 1$ then $l^n(Q) = \frac{1}{\mu_B^n(v_k v_j)} \geq \frac{1}{\mu^n(v_i^{'})}$.
2. If $n = 2$ $l^n(Q) = \frac{1}{\mu_B^n(v_k, v_{k+1})} + \frac{1}{\mu_B^n(v_{k+1}, v_j)} \geq \frac{2}{\mu^n(v_i^{'})}$, since $\mu^n(v_i^{'})$ is the greatest.
3. If $n > 2$ then $l^n(Q) \geq \frac{n}{\mu^n(v_i^{'})}$. Thus,

$$\delta^n(v_k, v_j) = \min_{Q \in \mathbb{P}} l^n(Q) \geq 1/\mu^n(v_i^{'}), \text{ for all } v_k, v_j \in X. \tag{2.32}$$

From (2.31) and (2.32),

$$e^n(v_i) = \min_{v_j \in X} \delta^n(v_i, v_j) = \frac{1}{\mu^n(v_i^{'})}, \text{ for all } v_i \in X. \tag{2.33}$$

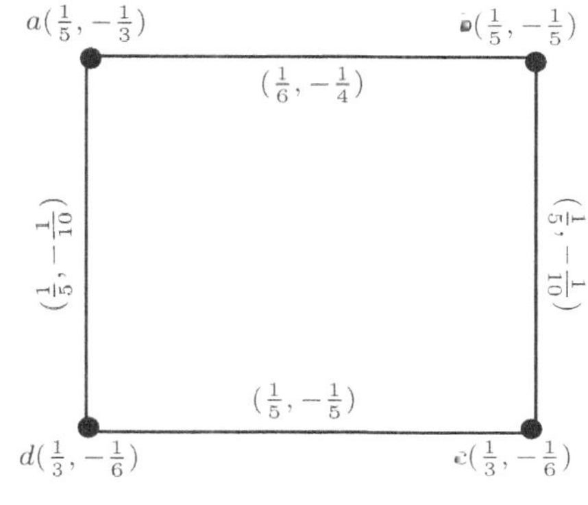

Fig. 2.15 Self-centered bipolar fuzzy graph

$$
\begin{aligned}
Now, r^n(G) &= \min_{v_i \in X} e_{\mu^-}(v_i) \\
&= \frac{1}{\mu^n(v_i^{'})}, \text{ since by (2.33)} \\
r^n(G) &= \frac{1}{\mu^n(v_i^{'})}.
\end{aligned}
$$

Equations (2.30) and (2.29) imply that every vertex of G is a central vertex. Hence G is a self-centered bipolar fuzzy graph. □

The following example shows that the converse of Theorem 2.20 is not true in general.

Example 2.13 Consider a bipolar fuzzy graph G on $X = \{a, b, c, d\}$ as shown in Fig. 2.15.

Clearly, G is a self-centered bipolar fuzzy graph but not complete.

Lemma 2.2 *A bipolar fuzzy graph G is a self-centered bipolar fuzzy graph if and only if* $r^p(G) = diam^p(G)$ *and* $r^n(G) = diam^n(G)$.

Definition 2.19 A **bipolar fuzzy path cover** of a bipolar fuzzy graph G is a set P of bipolar fuzzy paths such that every vertex of G is incident to some bipolar fuzzy path in P. If a bipolar fuzzy path between two vertices v_i and v_j belongs to P then it can be written as $(v_i, v_j) \in P$.

Definition 2.20 An **edge cover** of a bipolar fuzzy graph G is a set L of edges such that every vertex of G is incident to some edge in L.

Definition 2.21 A **maximal connected bipolar fuzzy subgraph** of a bipolar fuzzy graph G is a bipolar fuzzy subgraph that is connected and not contained in any other connected bipolar fuzzy subgraph of G. The components of a disconnected bipolar fuzzy graph G are its maximal connected bipolar subgraphs.

Theorem 2.21 *Let G be a connected bipolar fuzzy graph with path covers P_1 and P_2. The necessary and sufficient condition for a bipolar fuzzy graph to be self-centered is that*

$$\delta^{p}(v_i, v_j) = diam^p(G), \quad \text{for all } (v_i, v_j) \in P_1 \tag{2.34}$$

$$\delta^{n}(v_i, v_j) = r^n(G), \quad \text{for all } (v_i, v_j) \in P_2. \tag{2.35}$$

Proof Assume that G is a self-centered bipolar fuzzy graph. Suppose that (2.34) and (2.35) do not hold then $\delta^{p}(v_i, v_j) \neq diam^p(G)$, for some $(v_i, v_j) \in P_1$ and $\delta^{n}(v_i, v_j) \neq r^n(G)$, for some $(v_i, v_j) \in P_2$. Lemma 2.2 follows that $\delta^{p}(v_i, v_j) \neq r^p(G)$, for some $(v_i, v_j) \in P_1$ and $\delta^{n}(v_i, v_j) \neq r^n(G)$, for some $(v_i, v_j) \in P_2$. Then $e^p(v_i) \neq r^p(G)$, $e^n(v_i) \neq r^n(G)$, for some $v_i \in X$, which implies G is not a self-centered bipolar fuzzy graph, a contradiction. Hence $\delta^{p}(v_i, v_j) = diam^p(G)$, for all $(v_i, v_j) \in P_1$ and $\delta^{n}(v_i, v_j) = r^n(G)$, for all $(v_i, v_j) \in P_2$.

Conversely assume that (2.34) holds. It is to be shown that G is a self-centered bipolar fuzzy graph. If (2.34) and (2.35) hold then $e^p(v_i) = \delta^{p}(v_i, v_j)$, for all $(v_i, v_j) \in P_1$ and $e^n(v_i) = \delta^{p}(v_i, v_j)$, for all $(v_i, v_j) \in P_2$. It implies $e^p(v_i) = r^p(G)$ and $e^n(v_i) = r^n(G)$, for all $v_i \in X$. Hence G is a self-centered bipolar fuzzy graph. □

Theorem 2.22 *Let $H = (A, B)$ be a connected self-centered bipolar fuzzy graph on X then there exists a connected bipolar fuzzy graph $G = (A', B')$ on X' such that $C(G)$ is isomorphic to H. Also $diam^p(H) = 2r^p(G)$ and $diam^n(H) = 2r^n(G)$.*

Proof Given that H is a connected self-centered bipolar fuzzy graph. Let $diam^p(H) = l$ and $diam^n(H) = m$. Then construct G from H as follows:

Take two vertices $v_i, v_j \in X$ with $\mu^p(v_i) = \mu^p_A(v_j) = \frac{1}{l}$, $\mu^n_A(v_i) = \mu^n(v_j) = \frac{1}{2m}$ and join all the vertices of H to both v_i and v_j with $\mu^p_B(v_i v_k) = \mu^p_B(v_j v_k) = \frac{1}{l}$, $\mu^n_B(v_i v_k) = \mu^n_B(v_j v_k) = \frac{1}{2m}$ for all $v_k \in X'$. Put $\mu^p_A = \mu^p_{A'}$, $\mu^n_A = \mu^n_{A'}$ for all vertices in H and $\mu^p_B = \mu^p_{B'}$, $\mu^n_B = \mu^n_{B'}$ for all edges in H.

Claim: G is a bipolar fuzzy graph. First note that $\mu^p_A(v_i) \leq \mu^p_A(v_k)$, for all $v_k \in H$. If possible, let $\mu^p_A(v_i) > \mu^p_A(v_k)$ for at least one vertex $v_k \in H$. Then $\frac{1}{l} > \mu^p_A(v_k)$, that is, $l < \frac{1}{\mu^p_A(v_k)} \leq \frac{1}{\mu^p_B(v_k v_l)}$, where the last inequality holds for every $v_k \in X'$, since H is a bipolar fuzzy graph. That is, $\frac{1}{\mu^p_B(v_k, v_l)} > l$, for all $v_k \in H$ which contradicts that $diam^p(H) = l$. Therefore $\mu^p_A(v_i) \leq \mu^p_A(v_k)$ for all $v_k \in X'$ and $\mu^p_B(v_i v_k) \leq \min(\mu^p_A(v_i), \mu^p_A(v_k)) = \frac{1}{l}$. Similarly, $\mu^p_B(v_j v_k) \leq \min(\mu^p_A(v_j), \mu^p_A(v_k)) = \frac{1}{l}$ for all $v_k \in X'$. Note that $\mu^n_A(v_i) \geq \mu^n_A(v_k)$, $\mu^n_A(v_j) \geq \mu^n_A(v_k)$, for all $v_k \in X'$, since $diam^n(H) = m$. Therefore $\mu^p_B(v_i v_k) \geq \max\left(\mu^p_A(v_i), \mu^p_A(v_k)\right) = \frac{1}{2m}$. Similarly, $\mu^p_B(v_j v_k) \geq \max(\mu^p_A(v_j), \mu^p_A(v_k)) = \frac{1}{2m}$. Hence G is a bipolar fuzzy graph.

Also, $e^p(v_k) = l$, for $v_k \in X'$ and $e^p(v_i) = e^p(v_j) = \frac{1}{\mu^p_B(v_i v_k)} + \frac{1}{\mu^p_B(v_k v_l)} = 2l$, $r^p(G) = l$, $diam^p(G) = 2l$. Next, $e^n(v_k) = m$ for all $v_k \in X'$ and $e^n(v_i) = e^n(v_j)$

$= \frac{1}{\mu^n_B(v_l v_k)} = 2m$ for all $v_k \in X'$. Therefore, $r^n(G) = m$, $diam^n(G) = 2m$. Hence $C(G)$ is isomorphic to H. □

Theorem 2.23 *A bipolar fuzzy graph G is self-centered if and only if* $\delta^P(v_i, v_j) \leq r^P(G)$ *and* $\delta^n(v_i, v_j) \geq r^n(G)$ *for all* $v_i, v_j \in X$.

Proof Assume that G is a self-centered bipolar fuzzy graph. That is, $e^P(v_i) = e^P(v_j)$, $e^n(v_i) = e^n(v_j)$, for all $v_i, v_j \in X$, $r^P(G) = e^P(v_i)$, $r^n(G) = e^n(v_i)$, for all $v_i \in X$. It is to be shown that $\delta^P(v_i, v_j) \leq r^P(G)$, $\delta^n(v_i, v_j) \geq r^n(G)$, for all $v_i, v_j \in X$. By Definition 2.11,

$$\delta^P(v_i, v_j) \leq e^P(v_i) \text{ and } \delta^n(v_i, v_j) \geq e^n(v_i), \tag{2.36}$$

for all $v_i, v_j \in X$. This is possible only when $e^P(v_i) = e^P(v_j)$, $e^n(v_i) = e^n(v_j)$, for all $v_i, v_j \in X$. Since G is a self-centered bipolar fuzzy graph, (2.36) takes the form as $\delta^P(v_i, v_j) \leq r^P(G)$, $\delta^n(v_i, v_j) \geq r^n(G)$.

Conversely, let $\delta^P(v_i, v_j) \leq r^P(G)$, $\delta^n(v_i, v_j) \geq r^n(G)$, for all $v_i, v_j \in X$. It is to be shown that G is a self-centered bipolar fuzzy graph. Suppose that G is not self-centered then $e^P(v_i) \neq r^P(G)$ and $e^n(v_i) \neq r^n(G)$, for some $v_i \in X$. Assume that $e^P(v_i)$ and $e^n(v_i)$ are the least and greatest values among all other eccentricities, respectively. That is,

$$r^P(G) = e^P(v_i), \quad r^n(G) = e^n(v_i), \tag{2.37}$$

where $e^P(v_i) < e^P(v_j)$, $e^n(v_i) < e^n(v_j)$ for some $v_i, v_j \in X$, and

$$\delta^P(v_i, v_j) = e^P(v_j) > e^P(v_i), \tag{2.38}$$

$$\delta^n(v_i, v_j) = e^n(v_j) < e^n(v_i) \text{ for some } v_i, v_j \in X. \tag{2.39}$$

Hence from (2.37), (2.38), and (2.39), $\delta^P(v_i, v_j) > r^P(G)$ and $\delta^n(v_i, v_j) < r^n(G)$, for some $v_i, v_j \in X$. A contradiction to the fact that $\delta^P(v_i, v_j) \leq r^P(G)$, $\delta^n(v_i, v_j) \geq r^n(G)$, for all $v_i, v_j \in X$. Hence G is a self-centered bipolar fuzzy graph. □

Definition 2.22 Let $G = (A, B)$ be a bipolar fuzzy graph and $x, y \in X$ be any two distinct vertices of G. Let $G' = (A, B')$ be a subgraph obtained by deleting the edge xy from G, that is, $B'(xy) = (0, 0)$ and $B' = B$ for all other edges. Then xy is said to be a **bipolar fuzzy bridge** in G if either $S^{\infty^+}_{G'}(x, y) < S^{\infty^+}_G(x, y)$ and $S^{\infty^-}_{G'}(x, y) \geq S^{\infty^-}_G(x, y)$ or $S^{\infty^+}_{G'}(x, y) \leq S^{\infty^+}_G(x, y)$ and $S^{\infty^-}_{G'}(x, y) > S^{\infty^-}_G(x, y)$, for some $x, y \in X$.
In other words, deleting an edge xy reduces the strength of connectedness between some pair of vertices. Thus, xy is a bipolar fuzzy bridge if and only if there exist $u, v \in X$ such that xy is an edge of every strongest bipolar fuzzy path from u to v.

Theorem 2.24 *Let G be a bipolar fuzzy graph on X then the following conditions are satisfied.*

1. *If $B : X \times X \to [-1, 0] \times [0, 1]$ is a constant function then G has no bipolar fuzzy bridge.*
2. *If $B(xy)$ is not constant for all $xy \in E$, then G has at least one bipolar fuzzy bridge.*

Proof 1. Let $B(v_i v_j) = (c_1, c_2)$, for all $v_i, v_j \in X$ such that $0 \leq c_1 \leq 1$ and $-1 \leq c_2 \leq 0$. Since each edge has the same membership value, deleting any edge does not reduce the strength of connectedness between any pair of vertices. Hence G has no bipolar fuzzy bridge.

2. Given that $B(v_i v_j)$ is not constant for all $v_i v_j \in E$. Choose an edge $v_x v_y \in E$ such that

$$\mu_B^p(v_x v_y) = \max\{\mu_B^p(v_i v_j) | v_i, v_j \in X\},$$
$$\mu_B^n(v_x v_y) = \min\{\mu_B^n(v_i v_j) | v_i, v_j \in X\}.$$

There exists at least one edge $v_s v_t$ distinct from $v_x v_y$ such that $\mu_B^p(v_s v_t) < \mu_B^p(v_x v_y)$ and $\mu_B^n(v_s v_t) > \mu_B^n(v_x v_y)$. We claim that $v_x v_y$ is a bipolar fuzzy bridge of G. For, if we delete the edge $v_x v_y$ then the strength of connectedness between v_x and v_y in the bipolar fuzzy subgraph $G' = (A, B')$ thus obtained is decreased. In other words, $S_{G'}^{\infty^+}(x, y) < S_G^{\infty^+}(x, y)$ and $S_{G'}^{\infty^-}(x, y) > S_G^{\infty^-}(x, y)$. Hence by definition of a bipolar fuzzy bridge, $v_x v_y$ is a bipolar fuzzy bridge of G. □

Theorem 2.25 *Let $G = (A, B)$ be a bipolar fuzzy graph. If $B : X \times X \to [-1, 0] \times [0, 1]$ is a constant function then an edge $v_i v_j$ is a bipolar fuzzy bridge in G if $\mu_B^p(v_i v_j)$ is maximum and $\mu_B^n(v_i v_j)$ is minimum in G.*

Definition 2.23 A bipolar fuzzy cycle C in a bipolar fuzzy graph G is called a **strong bipolar fuzzy cycle** if all edges of C are strong edges (see Definition 2.8).

Theorem 2.26 *If G is a bipartite bipolar fuzzy graph then it has no strong bipolar fuzzy cycle with odd number of vertices.*

Proof Let G be a bipartite bipolar fuzzy graph on $X_1 \cup X_2$. Suppose that it contains a strong bipolar fuzzy cycle say $v_1, v_2, \ldots, v_n, v_1$ for some odd n. Without loss of generality, let $v_1 \in X_1$. Since (v_i, v_{i+1}) is strong for $i = 1, 2, \ldots, n-1$ and the vertices are alternatively in X_1 and X_2, we have $v_n, v_1 \in X_1$. It implies that $v_n v_1$ is an edge in X_1, which contradicts the assumption that G is a bipartite bipolar fuzzy graph. Hence a bipartite bipolar fuzzy graph has no strong bipolar fuzzy cycle with odd number of vertices. □

Theorem 2.27 *If $G = (A, B)$ is a complete bipolar fuzzy graph then there exists at least one edge $v_i v_j$ such that $\mu_B^p(v_i v_j) = S_G^{\infty^+}(v_i, v_j)$ and $\mu_B^n(v_i v_j) = S_G^{\infty^-}(v_i, v_j)$.*

Proof Consider a vertex v_i whose positive membership value is $\mu_A^p(v_i)$ and negative membership value is $\mu_A^n(v_i)$.

Case 1: Let $\mu_A^p(v_i)$ be the least and $\mu_A^n(v_i)$ be the greatest for the vertex $v_i \in X$. Let $v_i, v_j \in X$ then $\left(\mu_B^p(v_i v_j), \mu_B^n(v_i v_j)\right) = (\mu_A^p(v_i), \mu_A^n(v_i))$ and $S_G^{\infty}(v_i, v_j) =$

$(\mu_A^p(v_i), \mu_A^n(v_i))$. The strength of all the edges which are incident with vertex v_i is $(\mu_A^p(v_i), \mu_A^n(v_i))$ since G is a complete bipolar fuzzy graph.

Case 2: Let $\mu_A^p(v_i)$ be the least and $\mu_A^n(v_k)$ be the greatest, where $v_i \neq v_k$, then $(\mu_B^p(v_i v_k), \mu_B^n(v_i v_k)) = (\mu_A^p(v_i), \mu_A^n(v_k))$. Since it is a complete bipolar fuzzy graph, there will be an edge between v_i and v_k such that $S_G^\infty(v_i, v_k) = (\mu_A^p(v_i), \mu_A^n(v_k))$. □

Theorem 2.28 *Let G be a complete bipolar fuzzy graph with n vertices. Then G has a bipolar fuzzy bridge if and only if there exist an increasing sequence of real numbers* $\{t_1, t_2, \ldots, t_{n-1}, t_n\}$ *such that* $t_i \in [0, 1]$ *and* $t_i = \mu_A^p(v_i)$, *for every* $i = 1, 2, \ldots, n$ *and a decreasing sequence* $\{s_1, s_2, \ldots, s_{n-1}, s_n\}$ *such that* $s_i \in [-1, 0]$ *and* $s_i = \mu_A^n(v_i)$, *for all* $i = 1, 2, \ldots, n$. *Also the edge* $v_{n-1}v_n$ *is a bipolar fuzzy bridge in G.*

Proof Assume that G is a complete bipolar fuzzy graph and that G has a bipolar fuzzy bridge $v_i v_j$. Without loss of generality, let $t_{n-1} = \mu_A^p(v_i), t_n = \mu_A^p(v_j)$ and $\mu_A^p(v_i) \leq \mu_A^p(v_j)$, that is, $t_{n-1} \leq t_n$ and, $s_{n-1} = \mu_A^n(v_i)$, $s_n = \mu_A^n(v_j)$, $\mu_A^n(v_i) \geq \mu_A^n(v_j)$, that is, $s_{n-1} \geq s_n$. So $\mu_B^p(v_i v_j) = \mu_A^p(v_i)$, $\mu_B^n(v_i v_j) = \mu_A^n(v_i)$.

Assume on contrary that there is at least one vertex $v_i \neq v_k$ such that $\mu_A^p(v_i) \leq \mu_A^p(v_k)$, that is, $t_{n-1} \leq t_k$, where $k \neq n$, $t_{n-1} = \mu_A^p(v_i)$, $t_k = \mu_A^p(v_k)$, and $\mu_A^n(v_i) \geq \mu_A^n(v_k)$, $s_{n-1} \geq s_k$, where $k \neq n$, $s_{n-1} = \mu_A^n(v_i)$, $s_k = \mu_A^n(v_k)$. Now consider the bipolar fuzzy cycle $C : v_i - v_j - v_k - v_i$ in G such that $\mu_B^p(v_i v_j) = \mu_B^p(v_i v_k) = \mu_A^p(v_i)$ and $\mu_B^n(v_i v_j) = \mu_B^n(v_i v_k) = \mu_A^n(v_i)$.

$$\mu_B^p(v_j v_k) = \begin{cases} \mu_A^p(v_j) & \text{if } \mu_A^p(v_i) = \mu_A^p(v_j) \text{ or } \mu_A^p(v_i) < \mu_A^p(v_j) \leq \mu_A^p(v_k), \\ \mu_A^p(v_k) & \text{if } \mu_A^p(v_i) < \mu_A^p(v_k) \leq \mu_A^p(v_j), \end{cases}$$

$$\mu_B^n(v_j v_k) = \begin{cases} \mu_A^n(v_j) & \text{if } \mu_A^n(v_i) = \mu_A^n(v_j) \text{ or } \mu_A^n(v_i) > \mu_A^n(v_j) \geq \mu_A^n(v_k), \\ \mu_A^n(v_k) & \text{if } \mu_A^n(v_i) > \mu_A^n(v_k) > \mu_A^n(v_j). \end{cases}$$

In either case, it is seen that $\mu_A^p(v_i)$ is the least and $\mu_A^n(v_i)$ is the greatest among all other edges. But by Theorem 2.25, it is a contradiction to the fact that $v_i v_j$ is a bipolar fuzzy bridge.

Conversely, let $t_1 < t_2 < \ldots < t_{n-1} \leq t_n, t_i = \mu_A^p(v_i)$ and $s_1 > s_2 > \ldots > s_{n-2} > s_{n-1} \geq s_n$, $s_i = \mu_1^n(v_i)$.

Claim: (v_{n-1}, v_n) is a bipolar fuzzy bridge of G.

Now $\mu_B^p(v_{n-1}v_n) = \mu_A^p(v_{n-1})$ and $\mu_B^n(v_{n-1}, v_n) = \mu_1^n(v_{n-1})$ and clearly by hypothesis, all other edges of G will have μ^p- strength strictly less than $\mu_A^p(v_{n-1})$ and μ^n-strength strictly greater than $\mu_A^n(v_{n-1})$. Hence the edge $v_{n-1}v_n$ is a bipolar fuzzy bridge by Theorem 2.25. □

Theorem 2.29 *Let G be a complete bipartite bipolar fuzzy graph then the complement of G is self-centered.*

Proof A bipolar fuzzy graph $G = (A, B)$ on $X_1 \cup X_2$ is said to be complete bipartite if

1. $B(xy) = (0, 0)$, if $x, y \in X_1$ or $x, y \in X_2$,
2. $B(xy) = (\mu_A^p(x) \wedge \mu_A^p(y), \mu_A^n(x) \vee \mu_A^n(y))$, if $x \in X_1$ and $y \in X_2$ or $x \in X_2$ and $y \in X_1$.

By the above definition, the complement of G has two components and each component is a complete bipolar fuzzy graph, which are self-centered bipolar fuzzy graphs by Theorem 2.26.

2.5 Antipodal Bipolar Fuzzy Graphs

In this section, the concept of antipodal bipolar fuzzy graphs is discussed with certain theoretical properties.

Definition 2.24 Let $G = (A, B)$ be a bipolar fuzzy graph. An **antipodal bipolar fuzzy graph** of G is defined as a pair $A(G) = (C, F)$ such that

1. The bipolar fuzzy vertex set of G is taken as bipolar fuzzy vertex set of $A(G)$, that is, $\mu_C^p(x) = \mu_A^p(x)$ and $\mu_C^n(x) = \mu_A^n(x)$, for all $x \in X$.
2. If $\delta(x, y) = diam(G)$, then

$$\mu_F^p(xy) = \begin{cases} \mu_B^p(xy), & \text{if } x \text{ and } y \text{ are neighbors in } G, \\ \min(\mu_A^p(x), \mu_A^p(y)), & \text{if } x \text{ and } y \text{ are not neighbors in } G, \end{cases}$$

$$\mu_F^n(xy) = \begin{cases} \mu_B^n(xy), & \text{if } x \text{ and } y \text{ are neighbors in } G, \\ \max(\mu_A^n(x), \mu_A^n(y)), & \text{if } x \text{ and } y \text{ are not neighbors in } G. \end{cases}$$

That is, two vertices in $A(G)$ are made as neighborhood if the distance between them is diameter of G.

Example 2.14 Consider a bipolar fuzzy graph G on $X = \{v_1, v_2, v_3\}$ as shown in Fig. 2.16. By routine calculations, $\delta^P(v_1, v_2) = 6$, $\delta^P(v_1, v_3) = 3$, $\delta^P(v_2, v_3) = 3$, $\delta^n(v_1, v_2) = -5$, $\delta^n(v_1, v_3) = -4$, $\delta^n(v_2, v_3) = -2$, $e^p(v_1) = 6$, $e^p(v_2) = 6$, $e^p(v_3) = 3$, $e^n(v_1) = -5$, $e^n(v_2) = -5$, $e^n(v_3) = -4$. Clearly, $diam(G) = (6, -5)$, $\delta(v_1, v_2) = (6, -5) = diam(G)$. Hence $A(G) = (C, F)$, shown in Fig. 2.17, is an antipodal bipolar fuzzy graph of G.

Theorem 2.30 *Let $G = (A, B)$ be a complete bipolar fuzzy graph where (μ_A^p, μ_A^n) is constant function then G is isomorphic to $A(G)$.*

Proof Given that $G = (A, B)$ is a complete bipolar fuzzy graph with $(\mu_A^p, \mu_A^n) = (k_1, k_2)$, where k_1 and k_2 are constants. It implies that $\delta(v_i, v_j) = (l_1, l_2)$, for all $v_i, v_j \in X$, where $(l_1, l_2) \in [0, 1] \times [-1, 0]$. Therefore, $e(v_i) = (l_1, l_2)$, for all $v_i \in X$, that is, $diam(G) = (l_1, l_2)$. Hence $\delta(v_i, v_j) = (l_1, l_2) = diam(G)$, for all $v_i, v_j \in X$. Hence every pair of vertices are made as neighbors in $A(G)$ such that

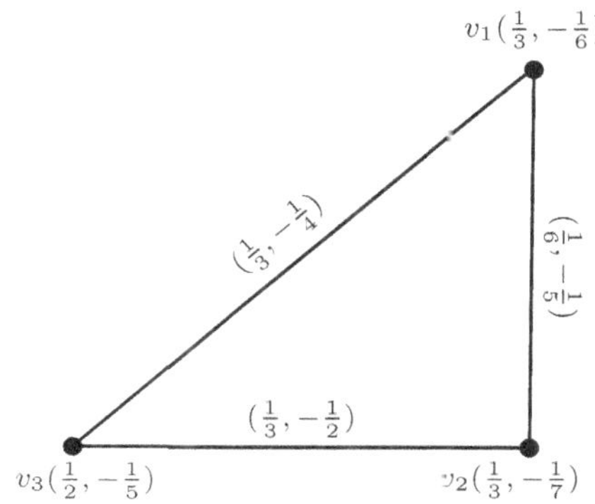

Fig. 2.16 Bipolar fuzzy graph G

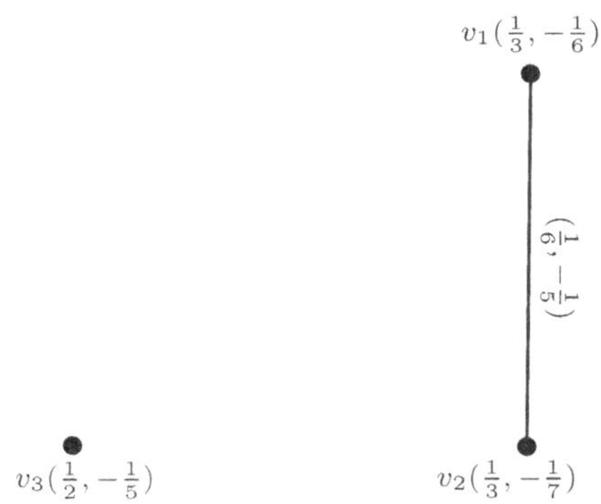

Fig. 2.17 Antipodal bipolar fuzzy graph $A(G)$

1. The bipolar fuzzy vertex set of G is taken as bipolar fuzzy vertex set of $A(G)$, that is, $\mu_C^p(v_i) = \mu_A^p(v_i)$ and $\mu_C^n(v_i) = \mu_A^n(v_i)$ for all $v_i \in X$,
2. $\mu_F^p(v_iv_j) = \mu_B^p(v_iv_j)$, since v_i and v_j are neighbors in G. $\mu_F^n(v_iv_j) = \mu_B^n(v_iv_j)$, since v_i and v_j are neighbors in G.

Hence G and $A(G)$ have same number of vertices, edges and their degree of memberships are preserved. The degrees of vertices are also preserved. Hence $G \cong A(G)$.

Lemma 2.3 *Let $G = (A, B)$ be a connected bipolar fuzzy graph then the antipodal bipolar fuzzy graph of G is a spanning subgraph of G.*

Proof By Definition 2.24, $A(G)$ contains all the vertices of G. That is.

1. $\mu_C^p(x) = \mu_A^p(x)$ and $\mu_C^n(x) = \mu_A^n(x)$ for all $x \in X$, and
2. if $\delta(x, y) = diam(G)$, then

$$\mu_F^p(xy) = \begin{cases} \mu_B^p(xy), & \text{if } x \text{ and } y \text{ are neighbors in } G, \\ \min(\mu_A^p(x), \mu_A^p(y)), & \text{if } x \text{ and } y \text{ are not neighbors in } G, \end{cases}$$

$$\mu_F^n(xy) = \begin{cases} \mu_B^n(xy), & \text{if } x \text{ and } y \text{ are neighbors in } G, \\ \max(\mu_A^n(x), \mu_A^n(y)), & \text{if } x \text{ and } y \text{ are not neighbors in } G. \end{cases}$$

Hence $A(G)$ is spanning subgraph of G. □

Theorem 2.31 *Let $G = (A, B)$ be a bipolar fuzzy graph such that the crisp graph G^* is an even or odd cycle. If alternate edges have same membership values then G is self-centered bipolar fuzzy graph.*

Theorem 2.32 *Let G be a bipolar fuzzy graph where crisp graph G^* is an even or odd cycle. If alternate edges have same positive and negative membership values then $A(G)$ is the edge induced bipolar fuzzy subgraph of G^c, whose end vertices (see Definition* 1.42) *are with maximum μ^p−eccentricity and minimum μ^n−eccentricity in G.*

Proof If alternate edges have same positive and negative membership values then positive distance between nonadjacent vertices is greater than the adjacent vertices and negative distance between nonadjacent vertices is lesser than the adjacent vertices. Let $\mu_B^p(v_i v_j)$ be the least among all other edges then $\delta^P(v_i, v_j) = \frac{1}{\mu_B^p(v_i v_j)}$.

Claim (i): Neighbors in G are not neighbors in $A(G)$.
Consider an arbitrary bipolar fuzzy path connecting v_k and v_t such that

$$v_k v_t \notin supp(B). \tag{2.40}$$

If P is a bipolar fuzzy path of length 2 between v_k and v_t, then

$$l^p(P) \geq \frac{1}{\mu_B^p(v_i v_j)}. \tag{2.41}$$

Hence $\delta^P(v_k, v_t) \geq \frac{1}{\mu_B^p(v_i v_j)}$, by (2.40) and (2.41), which implies that $\delta^P(v_i, v_j) < \delta^P(v_k, v_t) \leq diam^p(G)$, where $\delta^P(v_k, v_t) \notin supp(G)$ and $v_i v_j \in supp(G)$. That is, $\delta^P(v_i, v_j) < diam^p(G)$ if $v_i v_j \in supp(B)$. Therefore, if $v_i v_j \in supp(B)$ then v_i and v_j are not neighbors in $A(G)$.
Claim (ii): Edges in $A(G)$ are edges in G^c.
If $v_m v_n \in supp(F)$, then by claim (i), $v_i v_j \notin supp(B)$. So $\mu_F^p(v_m v_n) = \min(\mu_A^p(v_m), \mu_A^p(v_n))$, by Definition 2.24, which implies that the edges in $A^p(G)$ are induced by the edges of G^c whose end vertices are with maximum μ^p−eccentricity in G.

Consider the statement for negative membership values. Let $v_i v_j \in supp(B)$ then $\delta^n(v_i, v_j) = k$.
Claim (i): Neighbors in G are not neighbors in $A(G)$.
Consider an arbitrary bipolar fuzzy path connecting v_k and v_t such that,

$$v_k v_t \notin supp(B) \tag{2.42}$$

If Q is a bipolar fuzzy path of length 2 between v_k and v_t, then

$$\delta^{p}(P) \leq k. \tag{2.43}$$

Hence $\delta^{n}(v_k, v_t) \leq \delta^{n}(v_i, v_j)$, by (2.42) and (2.43), which implies that $\delta^{n}(v_k, v_t) \geq diam^n(G)$ where $v_k v_t \notin supp(B)$ and $v_i v_j \in supp(B)$. That is, $\delta^{n}(v_i, v_j) \geq diam^n(G)$, if $(v_i, v_j) \in supp(B)$. Therefore, if $(v_i, v_j) \in supp(B)$ then v_i and v_j are not neighbors in $A(G)$.

Claim (ii): Edges in $A(G)$ are edges in G^c.

If $v_m v_n \in supp(F)$, then by claim (i), $v_i v_j \notin supp(B)$. So $\mu^n_F(v_m v_n) = \max(\mu^n_A(v_m), \mu^n_A(v_n))$, by Definition 2.24, which implies that edges in $A^n(G)$ are induced by the edges of G^c whose end vertices are with minimum μ^n-eccentricity in G.

Conclusively, the edges in $A(G)$ are edges in G^c. Hence $A(G)$ is a bipolar fuzzy subgraph of G^c induced by the edges of G^c whose end vertices are with maximum μ^p-eccentricity and minimum μ^n-eccentricity in G.

Theorem 2.33 *Let G be a bipolar fuzzy graph, where crisp graph G^* is an even or odd cycle. If alternate edges have same membership values then $A(G)$ is a bipartite bipolar fuzzy graph.*

Theorem 2.34 *Let $G = (A, B)$ be a connected strong bipolar fuzzy graph where crisp graph G^* is an even or odd cycle such that $A(v_i) = (k_1, k_2)$, for all $v_i \in X$. Then $A(G)$ is the spanning bipolar fuzzy subgraph of G^c induced by the edges of G^c whose end vertices are with maximum μ^p-eccentricity and minimum μ^n-eccentricity in G.*

Proof Let $v_i v_j \in supp(B)$, $\delta^{p}(v_i, v_j) = \frac{1}{k_1}$. But for any $v_i v_j \notin supp(B)$, $\delta(v_k, v_m) \geq \frac{2}{k_1}$. That is, $\delta^{p}(v_i, v_j) = \frac{1}{k_1} < \frac{2}{k_1} \leq \delta^{p}(v_k, v_m)$, where $v_i v_j \notin supp(B)$. It follows that v_i, v_j are vertices in $A(G)$ but these are not neighbors in $A(G)$. Now let $v_i v_j \in supp(B)$, $\delta^{n}(v_i, v_j) > \frac{1}{k_1}$. But for any $v_i v_j \notin supp(B)$, $\delta^{n}(v_i, v_j) \geq \delta^{n}(v_k, v_m)$, where $v_i v_j \notin supp(B)$. It implies that v_i, v_j are vertices in $A(G)$ but are not neighbors in $A(G)$. The remaining proof is similar to claim (ii) of Theorem 2.32. □

Theorem 2.35 *If G_1 and G_2 are isomorphic to each other then $A(G_1)$ and $A(G_2)$ are also isomorphic.*

Proof Let $G = (A_1, B_1)$ and $G_2 = (A_2, B_2)$ be two bipolar fuzzy graphs on X_1 and X_2 and, $h : X_1 \to X_2$ be an isomorphism between G_1 and G_2 (see Definition 1.35). As G_1 and G_2 are isomorphic, membership degree of edges, length, and distance between corresponding vertices will be preserved. If the vertex v_i has the maximum μ^p-eccentricity and minimum μ^n-eccentricity in G_1 then $h(v_i)$ has the maximum μ^p-eccentricity and minimum μ^n-eccentricity in G_2. So G_1 and G_2 will have the same diameter. If the distance between v_i and v_j is (k_1, k_2) in G_1, then $h(v_i)$ and $h(v_j)$ will also have their distance as (k_1, k_2). The same mapping h itself is a bijection between $A(G_1)$ and $A(G_2)$ satisfying the isomorphism conditions.

1. $\mu^p_{C_1}(v_i) = \mu^p_{A_1}(v_i) = \mu^p_{A_2}(h(v_i)) = \mu^p_{C_2}(h(v_i))$, for all $v_i \in X_1$,
2. $\mu^n_{C_1}(v_i) = \mu^n_{A_1}(v_i) = \mu^n_{A_2}(h(v_i)) = \mu^n_{C_2}(h(v_i))$, for all $v_i \in X_1$,
3. $\mu^p_{F_1}(v_i v_j) = \mu^p_{B_1}(v_i v_j)$, if v_i and v_j are neighbors in G_1,
4. $\mu^p_{F_1}(v_i v_j) = \min(\mu^p_{C_1}(v_i), \mu^p_{C_1}(v_j))$, if v_i and v_j are not neighbors in G_1,
5. $\mu^n_{F_1}(v_i v_j) = \mu^n_{B_1}(v_i v_j)$, if v_i and v_j are neighbors in G_1,
6. $\mu^n_{F_1}(v_i v_j) = \max(\mu^n_{C_1}(v_i), \mu^n_{C_1}(v_j))$, if v_i and v_j are not neighbors in G_1.

As $h : X_1 \to X_2$ is an isomorphism,

$$\mu^n_{F_1}(v_i v_j) = \mu^n_{B_2}(h(v_i)h(v_j)), \quad \text{if } v_i \text{ and } v_j \text{ are neighbors in } G_1,$$
$$\mu^n_{F_1}(v_i v_j) = \max(\mu^n_{A_2}(v_i), \mu^n_{A_2}(v_j)), \quad \text{if } v_i \text{ and } v_j \text{ are not neighbors in } G_1,$$
$$\mu^n_{F_1}(v_i v_j) = \mu^n_{B_2}(h(v_i)h(v_j)), \quad \text{if } v_i \text{ and } v_j \text{ are neighbors in } G_1, .$$
$$\mu^n_{F_1}(v_i v_j) = \max(\mu^n_{A_2}(v_i), \mu^n_{A_2}(v_j)), \quad \text{if } v_i \text{ and } v_j \text{ are not neighbors in } G_1.$$

Hence $\mu^p_{F_1}(v_i v_j) = \mu^p_{F_2}(h(v_i)h(v_j))$ and $\mu^n_{F_1}(v_i v_j) = \mu^n_{F_2}(h(v_i)h(v_j))$. So the same h is an isomorphism between $A(G_1)$ and $A(G_2)$. □

Theorem 2.36 *If G_1 and G_2 are complete bipolar fuzzy graphs such that G_1 is co-weak isomorphic to G_2 then $A(G_1)$ is co-weak isomorphic to $A(G_2)$.*

Proof As $G_1 = (A_1, B_1)$ is co-weak isomorphic to $G_2 = (A_2, B_2)$, there exists a bijection $h : X_1 \to X_2$ satisfying (see Definition 1.34),

$$\mu^p_{B_1}(x_1 y_1) = \mu^p_{B_2}(h(x_1)h(y_1)), \quad \mu^n_{B_1}(x_1 y_1) = \mu^n_{B_2}(h(x_1)h(y_1)), \quad \text{for all } x_1, y_1 \in X_1.$$

If G_1 has n vertices $v_1, v_2, \ldots, v_n$ then arrange the vertices of G_1 in such a way that $\mu^p_A(v_1) \le \mu^p_A(v_2) \le \mu^p_A(v_3) \ldots \mu^p_A(v_n)$ and $\mu^n_A(v_1) \ge \mu^n_A(v_2) \ge \mu^n_A(v_3) \ldots \mu^n_A(v_n)$. As G_1 and G_2 are complete and co-weak isomorphic bipolar fuzzy graphs, $\mu^p_{B_1}(v_i v_j) = \mu^p_{B_2}(h(v_i)h(v_j))$, for all $v_i, v_j \in X_1$. By Theorem 2.35 and Definition 2.24, $A(G_i)$ contains all the vertices of G_i, for $i = 1, 2$. That is, $\mu^p_{C_i}(x) = \mu^p_{A_i}(x)$ and $\mu^n_{C_i}(x) = \mu^n_{A_i}(x)$ for all $x \in X_i$, $i \in \{1, 2\}$, and $\mu^p_{F_1}(v_k v_j) = \mu^p_{F_2}(h(v_k)h(v_j))$, for all $v_k, v_j \in X_1$. So h is a co-weak isomorphism between $A(G_1)$ and $A(G_2)$. □

Remark 2.7 If G is a self-complementary bipolar fuzzy graph then its antipodal bipolar fuzzy graph may not be self- complementary as it can be seen in Example 2.15.

Example 2.15 Consider a bipolar fuzzy graph G in Fig. 2.18.

By routine calculations, $\delta(a, b) = (15, -4)$, $\delta(a, c) = (10, -2)$, $\delta(a, d) = (10, -2)$, $\delta(b, c) = (5, -2)$, $\delta(b, d) = (25, -6)$, $\delta(c, d) = (20, -4)$, $e(a) = (15, -2)$, $e(b) = (15, -2)$, $e(c) = (20, -2)$, $e(d) = (25, -2)$, $diam(G) = (25, -2)$. Since $diam(G) \ne \delta(x, y)$ for all $x, y \in X$, $A(G)$ is an antipodal bipolar fuzzy graph of G having same vertices as in G and no two vertices in $A(G)$ are made as neighbors since the distance between them is not equal to the diameter of G (Fig. 2.19). Consider the complement G^c of bipolar fuzzy graph G as given in Fig. 2.20.

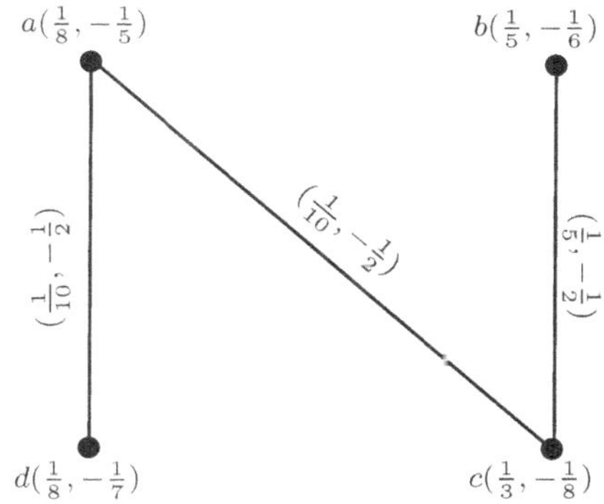

Fig. 2.18 Bipolar fuzzy graph G

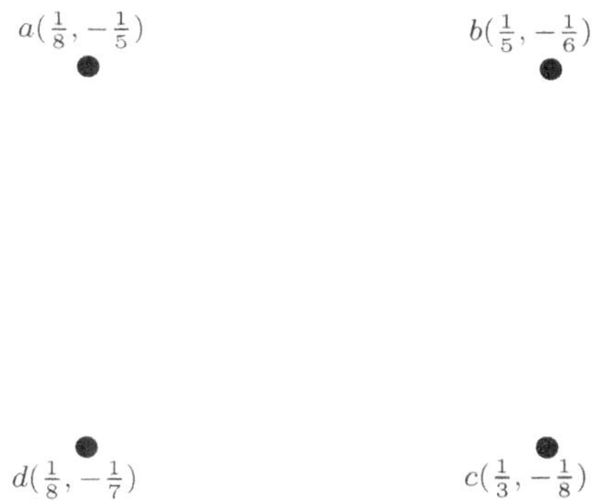

Fig. 2.19 Antipodal bipolar fuzzy graph $A(G)$

By routine calculations, $\delta(a, b) = (8, -5)$, $\delta(a, c) = (24, -18)$, $\delta(c, d) = (16, -11)$ $\delta(b, c) = (16, -13)$, $\delta(b, d) = (8, -6)$, $\delta(c, d) = (8, -7)$, $e(a) = (24, -5)$, $e(b) = (16, -5)$, $e(c) = (24, -7)$, $e(d) = (16, -6)$, $d(G^c) = (24, -5)$. Since $diam(G^c) \neq \delta(x, y)$ for all $x, y \in X$ in G^c, $A(G^c)$, in Fig. 2.21, is an antipodal bipolar fuzzy graph of G^c having same vertices as in G^c but no two vertices in $A(G^c)$ are made as neighbors.

Clearly, $A(G)$ is not isomorphic to $(A(G))^c$ as shown in Fig. 2.22. Hence G is self-complementary but its antipodal bipolar fuzzy graph $A(G)$ is not a self-complementary bipolar fuzzy graph.

Example 2.16 Consider a bipolar fuzzy graph G in Fig. 2.23.

By routine calculations, $\delta(a, b) = (5, -4)$, $\delta(a, c) = (11, -7)$, $\delta(a, d) = (17, -10)$, $\delta(b, c) = (6, -3)$, $\delta(b, d) = (12, -6)$, $\delta(c, d) = (6, -3)$, $e(a) = (17, -4)$, $e(b) = (12, -3)$, $e(c) = (11, -3)$, $e(d) = (17, -3)$, $diam(G) = (17, -3)$. Since $diam(G) \neq \delta(x, y)$, for all $x, y \in X$. Hence $A(G)$, in Fig. 2.24, is an antipodal bipolar fuzzy graph of G having same vertices as in G and no two vertices in $A(G)$ are made as neighbors since the distance between them is not equal to the diameter of G.

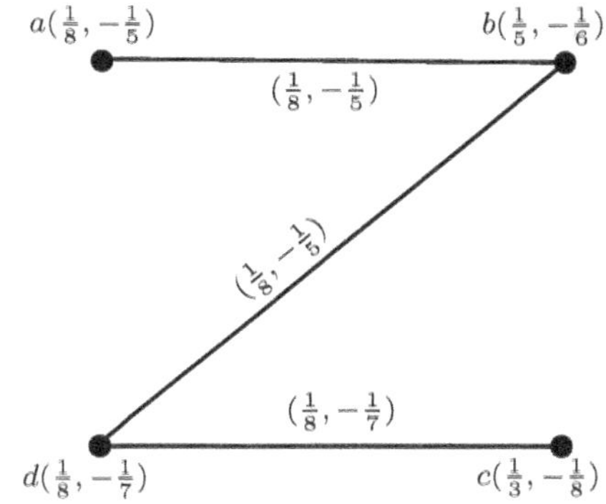

Fig. 2.20 Complement G^c

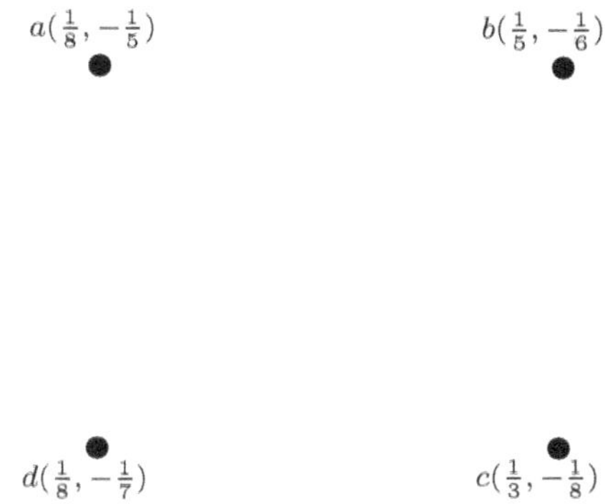

Fig. 2.21 Antipodal bipolar fuzzy graph $A(G^c)$

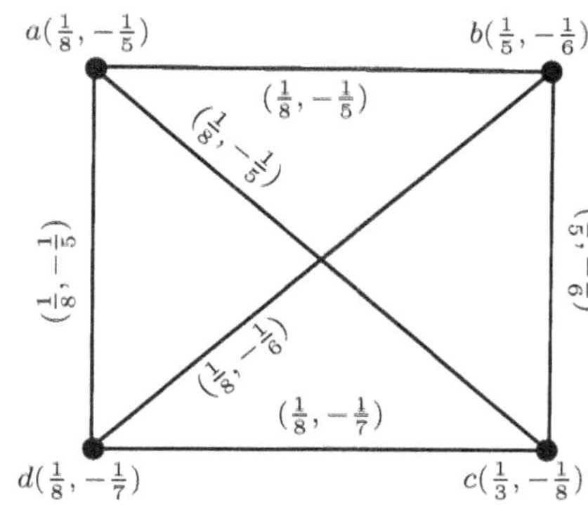

Fig. 2.22 $\overline{(A(G))^c}$

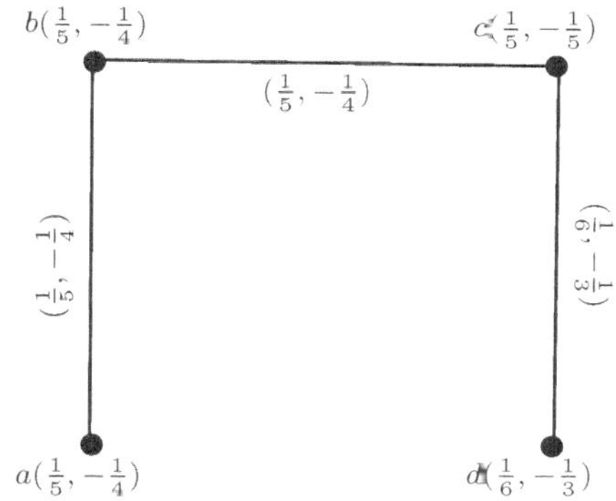

Fig. 2.23 Bipolar fuzzy graph G

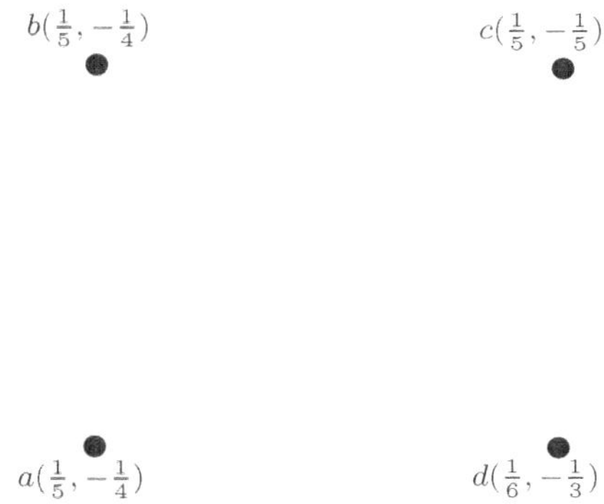

Fig. 2.24 Antipodal bipolar fuzzy graph $A(G)$

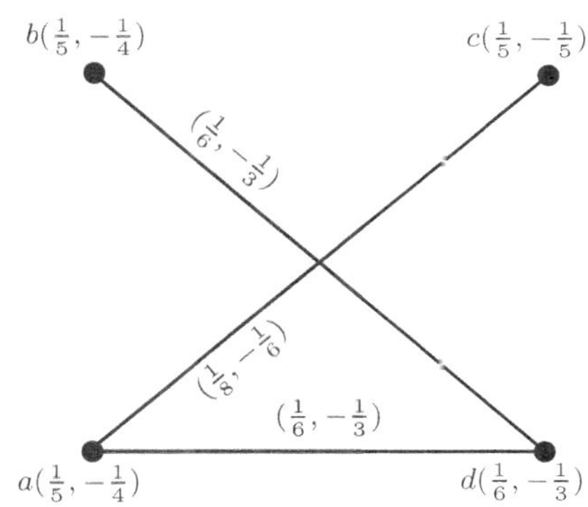

Fig. 2.25 Complement G^c

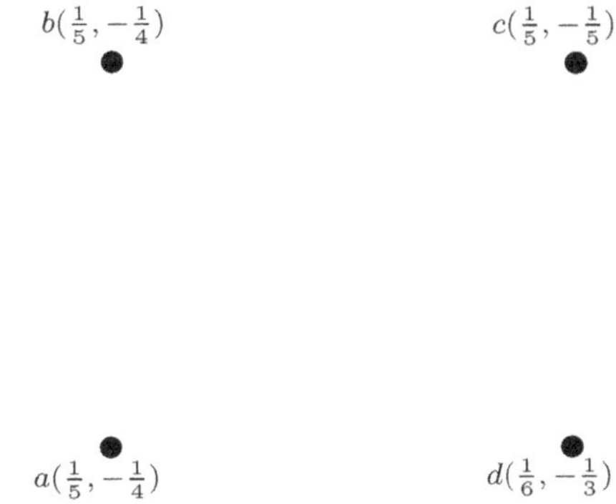

Fig. 2.26 Antipodal bipolar fuzzy graph $A(G^c)$

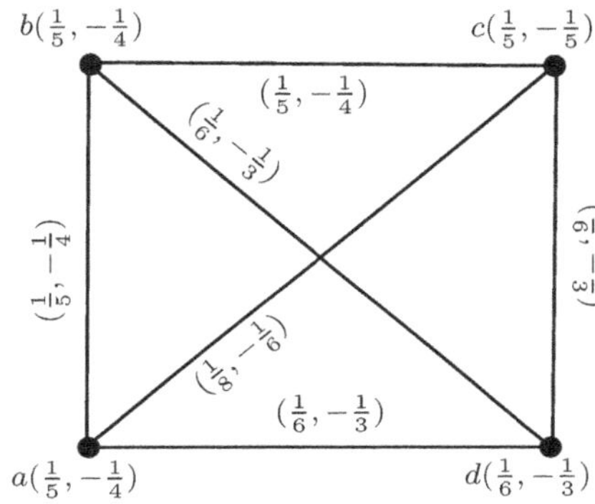

Fig. 2.27 $(A(G))^c$

By routine calculations, $\delta(a,b) = (12, -6)$, $\delta(a,c) = (5, -4)$, $\delta(a,d) = (6, -3)$, $\delta(b,c) = (17, -10)$, $\delta(b,d) = (6, -3)$, $\delta(c,d) = (11, -7)$, $e(a) = (12, -3)$, $e(b) = (17, -3)$, $e(c) = (17, -4)$, $e(d) = (11, -3)$, $d(G^c) = (17, -3)$. Since $d(G^c) \neq \delta(x, y)$, for all $x, y \in X$ in G^c. Hence $A(G^c)$, in Fig. 2.26, is an antipodal bipolar fuzzy graph of G^c, given in Fig. 2.25, having same vertices as in G^c and no two vertices in $A(G^c)$ are made as neighbors.

Clearly $A(G)$ is not isomorphic to $(A(G))^c$ as shown in Fig. 2.27, though $A(G)$ is isomorphic to $A(G^c)$. Hence G is a self-complementary bipolar fuzzy graph but $A(G)$ is not a self-complementary bipolar fuzzy graph.

Definition 2.25 Let G be a connected bipolar fuzzy graph. The μ^p-**status** of a vertex v_i is denoted by $s^p(v_i)$ and defined as $s^p(v_i) = \sum_{v_j \in X} \delta^p(v_i, v_j)$. The μ^n-**status** of a vertex v_i is denoted by $s^n(v_i)$ and defined as $s^n(v_i) = \sum_{v_j \in X} \delta^n(v_i, v_j)$. The **status** of a vertex $v_i \in X$ is defined as $s(G) = (s^p(G), s^n(G))$. The **minimum status** of G is denoted by $m[s(G)]$ and defined as $m[s(G)] = (\min_{v_i \in X} s^p(v_i), \max_{v_i \in X} s^n(v_i))$. The **maximum status** of G is denoted by $M[s(G)]$ and defined as $M[s(G)] = (\max_{v_i \in X} s^p(v_i), \min_{v_i \in X} s^n(v_i))$. The **total** μ^p-**status** of a bipolar fuzzy graph G

is denoted by $t[s^p(G)]$ and defined as $t[s^p(G)] = \sum_{v_i \in X} s^p(v_i)$. The **total** μ^n-**status** of a bipolar fuzzy graph G is denoted by $t[s^n(G)]$ and defined as $t[s^n(G)] = \sum_{v_i \in X} s^n(v_i)$. The **total status** of a bipolar fuzzy graph G is denoted by $t[s(G)]$ and is defined as $t[s(G)] = (t[s^p(G)], t[s^n(G)])$. The **median** of a bipolar fuzzy graph G is denoted by $M(G)$ and is defined as the set of vertices with minimum status. A bipolar fuzzy graph G is said to be **self-median** if all vertices have same status. In other words, G is self-median if and only if $m[s(G)] = M[s(G)]$.

Example 2.17 Consider a bipolar fuzzy graph in Fig. 2.28. By routine calculations, $\delta^p(v_1, v_2) = 3, \delta^p(v_1, v_3) = 6, \delta^p(v_1, v_4) = 3, \delta^p(v_2, v_3) = 3, \delta^p(v_2, v_4) = 6$, $\delta^p(v_3, v_4) = 3, \delta^n(v_1, v_2) = -11, \delta^n(v_1, v_3) = -7, \delta^n(v_1, v_4) = -10, \delta^n(v_2, v_3) = -10$, $\delta^n(v_2, v_4) = -7$, $\delta^n(v_3, v_4) = -11$. $s^p(v_1) = 12$, $s^p(v_2) = 12$, $s^p(v_3) = 12$, $s^p(v_4) = 12$, $s^n(v_1) = -28$, $s^n(v_2) = -28$, $s^n(v_3) = -28$, $s^n(v_4) = -28$. Therefore, $s(v_1) = (12, -28)$, $s(v_2) = (12, -28)$, $s(v_3) = (12, -28)$, $s(v_4) = (12, -28)$ and $t[s(G)] = (48, -112)$. Here $s(v_i) = (12, -28)$, for all $v_i \in X$. Hence G is a self-median bipolar fuzzy graph.

Theorem 2.37 *Let G be a bipolar fuzzy graph where crisp graph G^* is an even cycle. If alternate edges have same membership values then G is a self-median bipolar fuzzy graph.*

Proof Let $G = (A, B)$ be a bipolar fuzzy graph on $X = \{v_1, v_2, \ldots, v_n\}$ such that the crisp graph G^* is an even cycle and alternate edges of G have same membership values. So $\delta(v_1, v_2) = \delta(v_3, v_4) = \delta(v_1, v_2) = \cdots = \delta(v_{n-1}, v_n)$ and similarly, $\delta(v_2, v_3) = \delta(v_4, v_5) = \cdots = \delta(v_n, v_1)$, $\delta(v_1, v_3) = \delta(v_2, v_4) = \delta(v_3, v_5) = \cdots = l$ and so on. Thus $s^p(v_i) = k$ and $s^n(v_i) = m$, for all $v_i \in X$. Hence G is a self-median bipolar fuzzy graph. □

Remark 2.8 Let G be a bipolar fuzzy graph where crisp graph G^* is an odd cycle. If alternate edges have same membership values then G may not be self-median bipolar fuzzy graph.

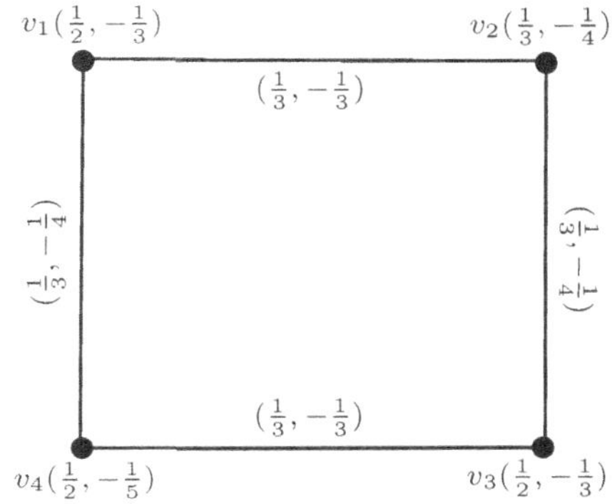

Fig. 2.28 Self-median bipolar fuzzy graph

2.6 Applications of Bipolar Fuzzy Graphs

In this section, the importance of bipolar fuzzy graphs is studied with example applications in decision support system and safe traveling.

2.6.1 *Product Manufacturing*

A product can increase the profit of a company if it is sold in multiple areas. Before manufacturing a product, engineers and manufacturers test several important things in a product. Bipolar fuzzy graphs are used on a wide range in decision-making problems when it is necessary to make decisions with opposite agreements. Suppose a multinational enterprise (MNE) has to decide to manufacture a product among four products P_1, P_2, P_3, and P_4 to market it in different countries. Every company considers various points before manufacturing a product. The most important thing is the demand for the product in the respective area. Here we consider the following two points in every product.

1. The product is appealing to people.
2. The product does not follow the mass market demands.

We gather the above two points in a set as {Appealing, Not demanding}. Let the set of products be $P = \{P_1, P_2, P_3, P_4\}$. This phenomenon can be represented by a bipolar fuzzy graph $G = (A, B)$ taking P as the set of vertices and $A(P_1) = (0.5, -0.8)$, $A(P_2) = (0.8, -0.2)$, $A(P_3) = (0.4, -0.6)$, $A(P_4) = (0.6, -0.8)$. The positive degree of membership of each product represents the percentage to which the product appeal the public and negative degree of membership shows the percentage that the product is not needed in the respective area. Take $B(P_1 P_2) = (0.5, -0.5)$, $B(P_1 P_3) = (0.1, -0.3)$, $B(P_1 P_4) = (0.2, -0.3)$, $B(P_2 P_3) = (0.3, -0.4)$, $B(P_2 P_4) = (0.6, -0.2)$. The positive degree of membership of the edge between any two products shows that if these two products are manufactured then it would be beneficial for the company. The negative degree of membership depicts that it can harm company's finance. The description of degree of membership of each edge can be gathered in a set as {Profit, Loss}. This means that the manufacturing of P_1 and P_2 can give 50% profit and 50% loss. It can be easily verified that it is a bipolar fuzzy graph as shown in Fig. 2.29.

By observation, it is easy to see that the production of P_2 has more demand and attraction. Also, its manufacturing with other products can be beneficial.

2.6.2 *Safe Route and Shortest Path Problem*

Graphs are used as a common source to model communication networks such as transportation, calculating traffic density, intensity of accidents on various roads, or

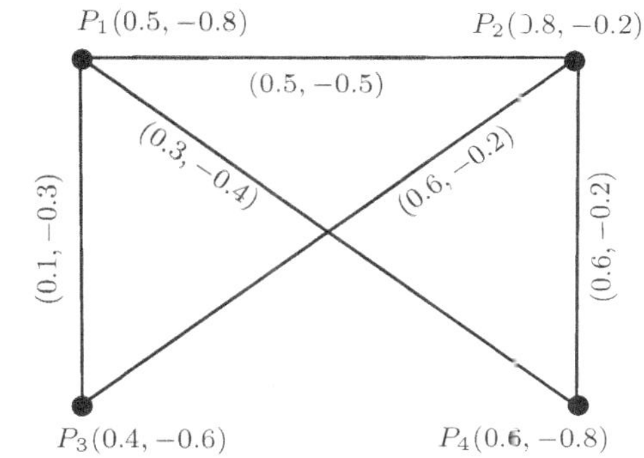

Fig. 2.29 Bipolar fuzzy model of product manufacturing

to find the shortest paths between any two points of the network. Bipolar fuzzy graphs can be used to find the shortest paths when it is required to consider two opposite agreements. An agency wants to deliver a secret envelope from Astana Kazakhstan to British Columbia through delivery. The delivery car can only travel 4000 kilometers before refilling the tank. The agency requires to deliver the envelope with safety. From Astana to Columbia, there are 17 fuel stations, namely, Moscow Russia, London England, Barcelona Spain, Algiers Algeria, San Juan, Boston, Houston Texas, Helena Montana, Beijing China, Delhi India, Tokyo, Singapore, Australia, Honolulu, Alaska, and California. The agency demands to consider the following points during travel.

1. Refill the tank at a station having less danger of robbery.
2. Take into account the distance traveled (in kilometers) between two fuel stations.
3. Use a path which is safe and confidential.

We represent the fuel stations by vertices. The negative membership value of each vertex represents the degree of safety at the fuel station and positive membership value shows the danger at the node. The degree of membership of edge between two stations represents the degree of danger and safety. As we are dealing with two opposite agreements, that is, danger and safety, this situation can be represented by a bipolar fuzzy graph in Fig. 2.30. Since in calculating the distance there is no use of membership value of vertices, we do not write these values in the bipolar fuzzy graph.

It is necessary to travel through the bipolar fuzzy path with the least positive degree of membership and maximum negative degree of membership. For this, calculate the length of all bipolar fuzzy paths from Astana to British Columbia and travel through a bipolar fuzzy path with minimum danger. By routine calculations, it can be easily seen that the minimum danger between Astana and British Columbia is through the path Astana–Moscow–Barcelona–Boston–British Columbia. The same procedure can be used to find the shortest path between any two points on a bipolar fuzzy graph if the degrees of memberships are given in terms of distance traveled, traffic density, etc.

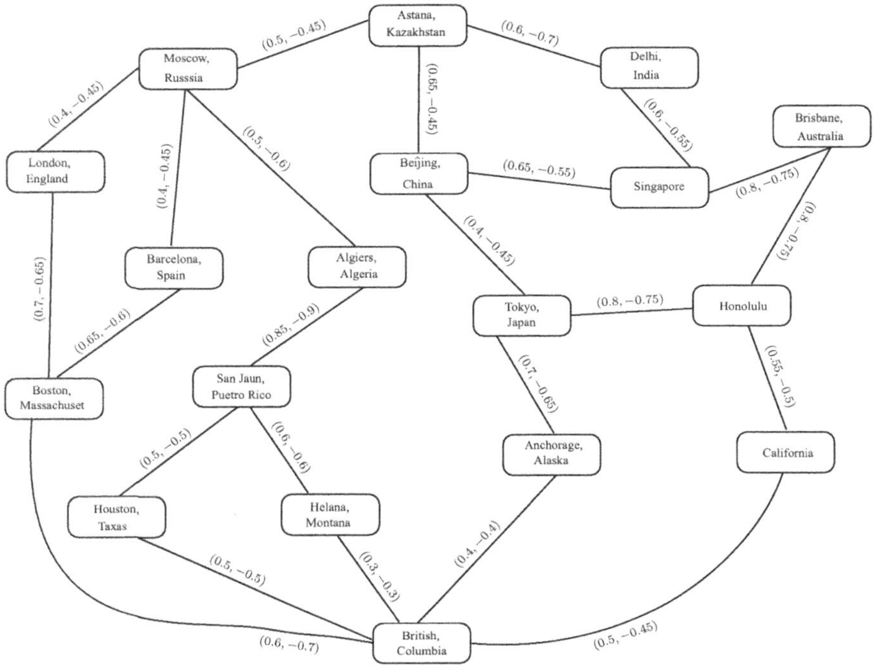

Fig. 2.30 Bipolar fuzzy model of shortest path problem

2.7 Conclusions

The notion of distance function in bipolar fuzzy graphs plays a significant role to solve shortest path problems in communication networks in the presence of various conflicting criteria. In this chapter, we have illustrated different types of distance functions in bipolar fuzzy graphs and established formulae of degree and distance of higher order bipolar fuzzy graphs including complete bipolar fuzzy graphs, complete bipartite bipolar fuzzy graphs, and products of bipolar fuzzy graphs. Using eccentric vertices, peripheral vertices, and central vertices, we have described certain properties and characterizations of self-centered bipolar fuzzy graphs. We have studied relations of self-median, antipodal, and self-centered bipolar fuzzy graphs when the bipolar fuzzy graph is complete or strong. We have described the notions of bipolar fuzzy path cover and edge cover of a bipolar fuzzy graph and presented a necessary and sufficient condition for a complete bipolar fuzzy graph to have a bipolar fuzzy bridge. We have also discussed the importance of the distance function of bipolar fuzzy graphs with real-world applications in traveling and product manufacturing.

Exercises 2

1. Consider two bipolar fuzzy digraphs $\vec{G}_1$ and $\vec{G}_2$ as shown in Fig. 2.31. Calculate the values of $d_{\vec{G}_1 \Box \vec{G}_2}((u, a), (v, a))$, $d_{\vec{G}_1 \Box \vec{G}_2}((w, d), (v, c))$ and $d_{\vec{G}_1 \times \vec{G}_2}((u, d), (v, c))$.
2. If $C_{2k+1} = (A, B)$ is an odd bipolar fuzzy cycle on X with $A(x) = (0.5, -1)$ and $B(xy) = (0.2, -0.5)$, for all $x, y \in X$. Determine whether $C_{2k+1} \times C_{2k+1}$ and $C_{2k+1} \Box C_{2k+1}$ are isomorphic or not? What happens if we replace odd bipolar fuzzy cycles by even bipolar fuzzy cycles?
3. Let $G = (A, B)$ be a bipolar fuzzy graph, where A and B are constant functions. Calculate the value of $d_{G \Box G}((x, u), (y, v))$, for all $x, y, u, v \in X$.
4. Let G_1 and G_2 be two bipolar fuzzy graphs, then show that $G_1 \Box G_2$ is connected if and only if G_1 and G_2 are both connected.
5. Let G_1, G_2, and G_3 be three bipolar fuzzy graphs, then prove or disprove that $G_1 \times (G_2 + G_3) = G_1 \times G_2 + G_1 \times G_3$.
6. Determine whether or not the Cartesian product of antipodal bipolar fuzzy graphs is antipodal.
7. If $G = \prod_{i=1}^{n} \vec{G}_i$ is the Cartesian product or strong product of bipolar fuzzy digraphs $\vec{G}_i$, then show that G is connected is and only if each factor $\vec{G}_i$ is connected.
8. Prove that the lexicographic product $G = \vec{G}_1 \bullet \vec{G}_2 \bullet \ldots \bullet \vec{G}_n$ of nontrivial bipolar fuzzy digraphs is connected if and only if each factor $\vec{G}_i$ is connected.
9. Let $(\alpha_1^p, \alpha_1^n), (\alpha_2^p, \alpha_2^n), \ldots, (\alpha_k^p, \alpha_k^n) \in [0, 1] \times [-1, 0]$, then $\max_{i=1}^{k}(\alpha_i^p, \alpha_i^n) = (\max_{i=1}^{k} \alpha_i^p, \min_{i=1}^{k} \alpha_i^n)$. Determine whether or not the diameter of strong product of k bipolar fuzzy graphs is the maximum of the diameters of the factors.
10. Let $(\alpha_1^p, \alpha_1^n), (\alpha_2^p, \alpha_2^n), \ldots, (\alpha_k^p, \alpha_k^n) \in [0, 1] \times [-1, 0]$, then $\min_{i=1}^{k}(\alpha_i^p, \alpha_i^n) = (\min_{i=1}^{k} \alpha_i^p, \max_{i=1}^{k} \alpha_i^n)$. Determine whether or not the radius of strong product of k bipolar fuzzy graphs is the minimum of the radii of the factors.

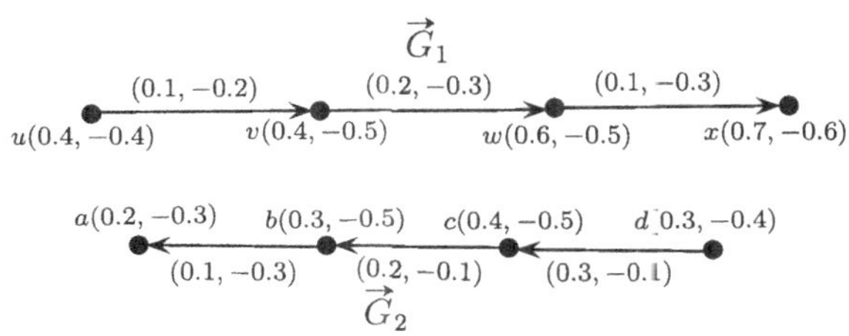

Fig. 2.31 Bipolar fuzzy graphs

References

1. Akram, M.: Bipolar fuzzy graphs. Inf. Sci. **181**(24), 5548–5564 (2011)
2. Akram, M.: Bipolar fuzzy graphs with applications. Knowl.-Based Syst. **39**, 1–8 (2013)
3. Akram, M., Dudek, W.A.: Regular bipolar fuzzy graphs. Neural Comput. Appl. **21**(supp 1), 197–205 (2012)
4. Akram, M., Karunambigai, M.G.: Metric in bipolar fuzzy graphs. World Appl. Sci. J. **14**(12), 1920–1927 (2011)
5. Akram, M., Li, S.-G., Shum, K.P.: Antipodal bipolar fuzzy graphs. Ital. J. Pure Appl. Math. **31**, 97–110 (2013)
6. Akram, M., Yousaf, M.M., Dudek, W.A.: Self centered interval-valued fuzzy graphs. Afr. Math. **26**(5–6), 887–898 (2015)
7. Bhattacharya, P.: Some remarks on fuzzy graphs. Pattern Recogn. Lett. **6**(5), 297–302 (1987)
8. Bhutani, K.R., Rosenfeld, A.: Strong arcs in fuzzy graphs. Inf. Sci. **152**, 319–322 (2003)
9. Bouttier, J., Di Francesco, P., Guitter, E.: Geodesic distance in planar graphs. Nucl. Phys. B **663**(3), 535–567 (2003)
10. Bhutani, K.R., Rosenfeld, A.: Geodesics in fuzzy graphs. Electron. Notes Discret. Math. **15**, 49–52 (2003)
11. Bhutani, K.R., Rosenfeld, A.: Fuzzy end nodes in fuzzy graphs. Inf. Sci. **152**, 323–326 (2003)
12. Dudek, W.A., Talebi, A.A.: Operations on level graphs of bipolar fuzzy graphs, Buletinul Academiei de Stiinte a Republici Moldova. Mathematica. **81**(2), 107–126 (2016)
13. Hammack, R., Imrich, W., Kalvžar, S.: Handbook of Product Graphs. Discrete Mathematics and its Applications, pp. 49–60. CRC Press, Taylor & Francis Group (2011)
14. Linda, J.P., Sunitha, M.S.: On $g-$eccentric nodes $g-$boundary nodes and $g-$interior nodes of a fuzzy graph. Int. J. Math. Sci. Appl. **2**(2), 697–707 (2012)
15. Rosenfeld, A.: Fuzzy graphs. In: Zadeh, L.A., Fu, K.S., Shimura, M. (eds.) Fuzzy Sets and Their Applications, pp. 77–95. Academic Press, New York (1975)
16. Sameena, K., Sunitha, M.S.: Characterisation of $g-$self centered fuzzy graphs. J. Fuzzy Math. **16**, 787–791 (2008)
17. Sameena, K., Sunitha, M.S.: On g-distance in fuzzy trees. J. Fuzzy Math. **19**, 787–791 (2011)
18. Sarwar, M., Akram, M.: Representation of graphs using m-polar fuzzy environment. Ital. J. Pure Appl. Math. **38**, 291–312 (2017)
19. Sunitha, M.S., Vijayakumar, A.: Some metric aspects of fuzzy graphs. In: Proceedings of the Conference on Graph Connections. Cochin University of Science and Technology, Cochin, pp. 111–114 (1998)
20. Tom, M., Sunitha, M.: Strong sum distance in fuzzy graphs. SpringerPlus **4**(1), 1–14 (2015)
21. Tom, M., Sunitha, M.: Sum distance in fuzzy graphs. Ann. Pure Appl. Math. **7**(2), 73–89 (2014)
22. Zadeh, L.A.: Fuzzy sets. Inf. Control **8**(3), 338–353 (1965)
23. Zhang, W.-R.: Bipolar fuzzy sets and relations: a computational framework for cognitive modeling and multiagent decision analysis. In: Proceedings of IEEE Conference, pp. 305–309 (1994)
24. Zhang, W.-R., Zhang, L.: YinYang bipolar logic and bipolar fuzzy logic. Inf. Sci. **165**(3–4), 265–287 (2004)
25. Zhang, W.-R.: YinYang bipolar relativity: A unifying theory of nature, agents and causality with applications in quantum computing, cognitive informatics and life sciences. Information Sciences Reference, Hershey (2011)
26. Zhang, W.-R.: NPN fuzzy sets and NPN qualitative algebra: A computational framework for bipolar cognitive modeling and multiagent decision analysis. IEEE Trans. Syst., Man, Cybern., Part B (Cybern.) **26**(4), 561–574 (1996)
27. Zhang, W.-R.: (YinYang) Bipolar fuzzy sets. In: IEEE International Conference on Fuzzy Systems, pp. 835–840 (1998)

Chapter 3
Special Types of Bipolar Fuzzy Graphs

In this chapter, we discuss the concept of irregularity in bipolar fuzzy graphs and present isomorphism properties of regular, m-totally regular, neighborly irregular, totally irregular, highly irregular and neighborly totally irregular bipolar fuzzy graphs. We present certain characterizations under which, regular and totally regular bipolar fuzzy graphs, highly irregular and neighborly irregular bipolar fuzzy graphs are equivalent. We discuss certain formulae of order and size of $m-$totally regular bipolar fuzzy graphs. We study the concept of bipolar fuzzy line graphs and establish a necessary and sufficient condition for a bipolar fuzzy graph to be isomorphic to its corresponding bipolar fuzzy line graph. Using algebraic structures, we discuss the notions of regularity, vertex transitivity, and connectedness in Cayley bipolar fuzzy graphs. We describe the relations of connected, weakly connected, semiconnected, locally connected, and quasi-connected Cayley bipolar fuzzy graphs. The work in this chapter is from [1, 2, 9].

3.1 Introduction

Graph theory was first initiated by Euler during the course of finding a solution to the problem of "Königsberg bridge" in 1736. Graph theory is a conceptual framework to study and analyze the units that are intensely or frequently connected in a network. Graphs can be classified on the basis of number of vertices, number of edges, order, size, connectivity, distance, degree, and their overall structure. Alavi [8] investigated several properties concerning the existence and enumeration of highly irregular graphs and extended this concept to $k-$path irregular graphs [7]. Most of the real-world problems ranging from engineering to medical and medical to social fields involve uncertainty in data. Fuzzy graphs occur when the uncertainty

M. Akram et al., *Graphs for the Analysis of Bipolar Fuzzy Information*, Studies in Fuzziness and Soft Computing 401,
https://doi.org/10.1007/978-981-15-8756-6_3

is observed in real-life situations. Structures of both crisp graphs and fuzzy graphs are similar but fuzzy graphs deal with uncertainty on vertices and/or edges. Several graph-theoretic concepts like paths, connectedness, bridges, cycles, and trees were obtained by Rosenfeld [16]. Nagoorgani and Radha [15] introduced regular fuzzy graphs, total Degree, and totally regular fuzzy graphs. Nagoorgani and Latha [13] initiated the concept of irregular fuzzy graphs, neighborly irregular fuzzy graphs, and highly irregular fuzzy graphs, and discussed isomorphism properties of these fuzzy graphs in [13]. An antipodal graph $A(G)$ of a graph G, introduced by Smith [19], is a graph with the same set of vertices as of G, two vertices being adjacent if the distance between them is equal to the diameter of G. As a fuzzy analog to this, Nagoorgani [14] discussed the nature of antipodal fuzzy graph when the given fuzzy graph is complete or strong.

In many everyday situations, a single-valued membership function fails to express the support evidence and counter-evidence simultaneously. In several practical situations, an appropriate level of information of the problem domain may not exist due to some uncertainty over the object consideration, which shows the characteristic of satisfaction and dissatisfaction. Zhang [20] extended fuzzy set theory to bipolar fuzzy sets and discussed the bipolar behavior of objects. The concept of bipolar fuzzy set can be observed as another approach, where existing information is not sufficient to define the uncertainty by using a fuzzy set. A fuzzy set gives the degree of membership of an element in a given set, while bipolar fuzzy set gives both a positive degree of membership and a negative degree of membership which are independent of each other; the only requirement is that one is opposite to the other. Bipolar fuzzy set can describe two-sided fuzzy characteristics of the objects more comprehensively, thus a more powerful and effective tool in dealing with fuzzy information. The concept of regular and totally regular bipolar fuzzy graphs was introduced by Akram and Dudek [2]. The same author Akram in collaboration with other researchers studied various types of irregular bipolar fuzzy graphs and bipolar fuzzy influence graphs in [1], antipodal and self-median bipolar fuzzy graphs in [5], and self-centered bipolar fuzzy graphs in [4]. Samanta and Pal [18] introduced the notion of bipolar fuzzy intersection graphs and proved that any bipolar fuzzy graph can be expressed as a bipolar fuzzy intersection graph of some bipolar fuzzy sets.

3.2 Regular and Irregular Bipolar Fuzzy Graphs

The degree of a vertex x in a graph G is the number of edges incident to x. If each vertex in a graph G has the same degree then it is called a **regular** graph otherwise it is an irregular graph. In this section, different types of irregular bipolar fuzzy graphs are studied with certain interesting properties.

Definition 3.1 The **degree** of a vertex x in a bipolar fuzzy graph G is defined as a pair $\deg(x) = (\deg^p(x), \deg^n(x))$, where $\deg^p(x) = \sum_{y \in X} \mu_B^p(xy)$ and $\deg^n(x) = \sum_{y \in X} \mu_B^n(xy)$.

Table 3.1 Bipolar fuzzy set A on $\{a, b, c, d\}$

A	a	b	c	d
μ_A^p	0.5	0.4	0.7	0.5
μ_A^n	−0.3	−0.2	−0.3	−0.5

Table 3.2 Bipolar fuzzy relation B in $\{a, b, c, d\}$

B	a	b	c	d
a	(0, 0)	(0.2, −0.1)	(0, 0)	(0.4, −0.1)
b	(0, 0)	(0, 0)	(0.2, −0.1)	(0, 0)
c	(0, 0)	(0.2, −0.1)	(0, 0)	(0.4, −0.1)
d	(0.4, −0.1)	(0, 0)	(0.4, −0.1)	(0, 0)

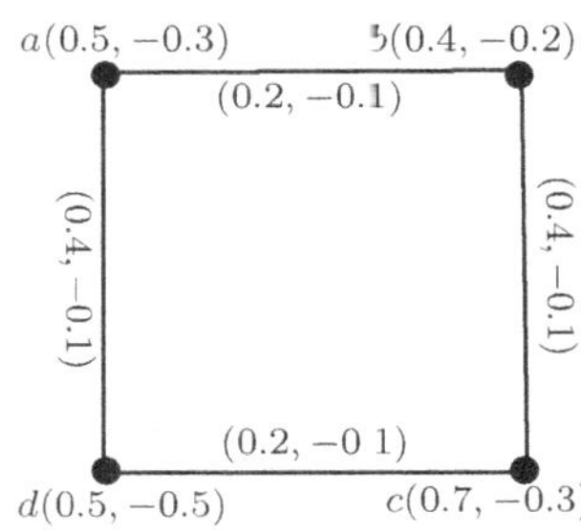

Fig. 3.1 Regular bipolar fuzzy graph

Definition 3.2 Let $G = (A, B)$ be a bipolar fuzzy graph on X. If all vertices of G have same degree then G is called a **regular bipolar fuzzy graph** , that is, $\deg(x) = \deg(y)$, for all $x, y \in X$.

Example 3.1 Let A be a bipolar fuzzy set on $X = \{a, b, c, d\}$, given in Table 3.1, and B be a bipolar fuzzy relation in X defined in Table 3.2. Routine computations show that the bipolar fuzzy graph G, in Fig. 3.1, is regular.

Definition 3.3 The **total degree** of a vertex x in a bipolar fuzzy graph G is denoted by $T\deg(x) = (T\deg^p(x), T\deg^n(x))$ and defined as

$$T\deg^p(x) = \sum_{xy\in E} \mu_B^p(xy) + \mu_A^p(x) = \deg^p(x) + \mu_A^p(x),$$

$$T\deg^n(x) = \sum_{xy\in E} \mu_B^n(xy) + \mu_A^n(x) = \deg^n(x) + \mu_A^n(x).$$

If each vertex of G has same total degree, say $m = (m^p, m^n)$, then G is called an m-**totally regular bipolar fuzzy graph**.

Table 3.3 Bipolar fuzzy set on $\{v_1, v_2, v_3\}$

A	v_1	v_2	v_3
μ_A^p	0.4	0.8	0.7
μ_A^n	−0.1	−0.7	−0.6

Table 3.4 Bipolar fuzzy relation in $\{v_1, v_2, v_3\}$

B	v_1	v_2	v_3
v_1	(0, 0)	(0.3, −0.5)	(0.4, −0.6)
v_2	(0.3, −0.5)	(0, 0)	(0, 0)
v_3	(0.4, −0.6)	(0, 0)	(0, 0)

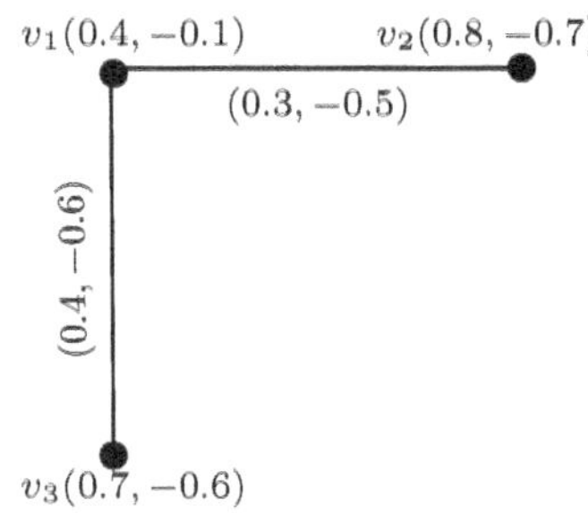

Fig. 3.2 Totally regular bipolar fuzzy graph

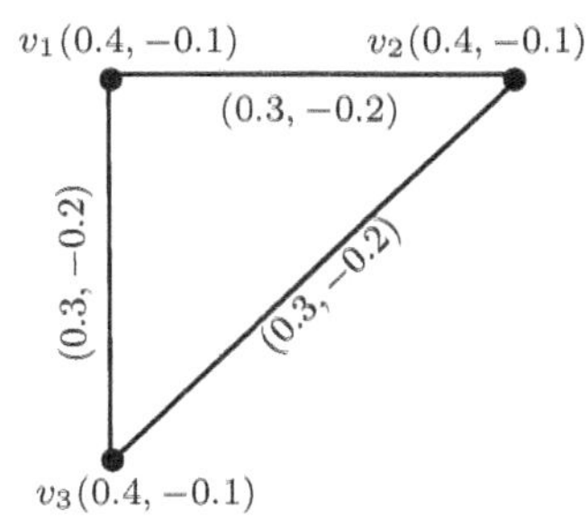

Fig. 3.3 Regular and totally regular bipolar fuzzy graph G

Example 3.2 Let A be a bipolar fuzzy set on $X = \{v_1, v_2, v_3\}$ and B be a bipolar fuzzy relation in X as given in Table 3.3 and 3.4, respectively. Routine computations show that the bipolar fuzzy graph G, shown in Fig. 3.2, is totally regular but not regular.

Example 3.3 Consider a bipolar fuzzy graph G on $X = \{v_1, v_2, v_3\}$ as given in Fig. 3.3. It is easy to check that G is both regular and totally regular bipolar fuzzy graph.

Table 3.5 Bipolar fuzzy set A

A	v_1	v_2	v_3
μ_A^p	0.2	0.2	0.3
μ_A^n	−0.6	−0.7	−0.4

Table 3.6 Bipolar fuzzy relation B

B	v_1	v_2	v_3
v_1	(0, 0)	(0.1, −0.2)	(0.1, −0.2)
v_2	(0.1, −0.2)	(0, 0)	(0.2, −0.3)
v_3	(0.1, −0.2)	(0.2, −0.3)	(0, 0)

Definition 3.4 The **neighborhood** of a vertex x in a bipolar fuzzy graph $G = (A, B)$ is defined as a set $N(x) = \{y \in X \mid B(xy) \neq (0, 0)\}$.

Definition 3.5 The **neighborhood degree** of a vertex x in $G = (A, B)$ is defined as a pair $N\deg(x) = (N\deg^p(x), N\deg^n(x))$, where $N\deg^p(x) = \sum_{y \in N(x)} \mu_A^p(y)$ and $N\deg^n(x) = \sum_{y \in N(x)} \mu_A^n(y)$.

Definition 3.6 Let $G = (A, B)$ be a bipolar fuzzy graph on X. If there is a vertex which is adjacent to vertices with distinct neighborhood degrees then G is called an **irregular bipolar fuzzy graph**, that is, $\deg(x) \neq (r^p, r^n)$, for all $x \in X$.

Definition 3.7 The **closed neighborhood degree** of a vertex x in a bipolar fuzzy graph G is defined as a pair $N\deg[x] = (N\deg^p[x], N\deg^n[x])$ such that

$$N\deg^p[x] = N\deg^p(x) + \mu_A^p(x),$$

$$N\deg^n[x] = N\deg^n(x) + \mu_A^n(x).$$

If there is a vertex which is adjacent to vertices with distinct closed neighborhood degrees then G is called a **totally irregular bipolar fuzzy graph**.

Example 3.4 Let A be a bipolar fuzzy set on $X = \{v_1, v_2, v_3\}$ as given in Table 3.5 and B be a bipolar fuzzy relation defined in Table 3.6. The bipolar fuzzy graph $G = (A, B)$ is shown in Fig. 3.4.

From Fig. 3.4, $N\deg(v_1) = (0.5, -1.1)$, $N\deg(v_2) = (0.5, -1.0)$, and $N\deg(v_3) = (0.4, -1.3)$. It is clear that G is an irregular bipolar fuzzy graph.

Example 3.5 Consider a bipolar fuzzy graph G on $X = \{v_1, v_2, v_3, v_4, v_5\}$ as shown in Fig. 3.5. From usual calculations, $N\deg[v_1] = (1.4, -2.4)$, $N\deg[v_2] = (1.4, -2.4)$, $N\deg[v_3] = (1.4, -2.4)$, $N\deg[v_4] = (1.6, -2.9)$, and $N\deg[v_5] = (0.6, -0.7)$. Clearly G is a totally irregular bipolar fuzzy graph.

Fig. 3.4 Irregular bipolar fuzzy graph G

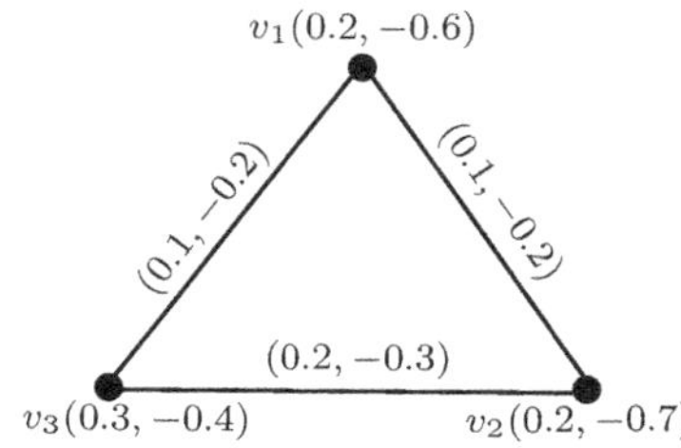

Fig. 3.5 Totally irregular bipolar fuzzy graph

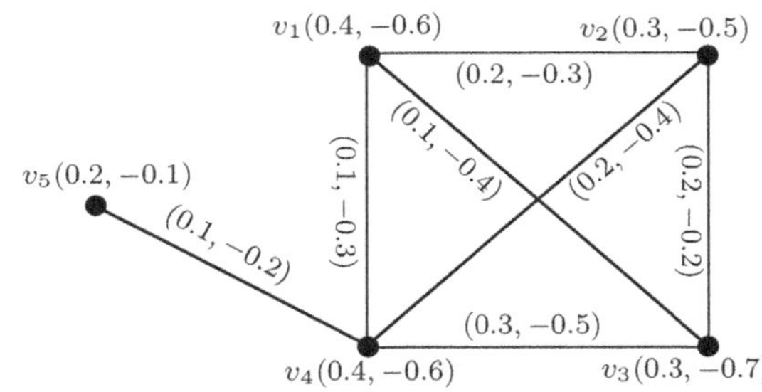

Fig. 3.6 Complete bipolar fuzzy graph

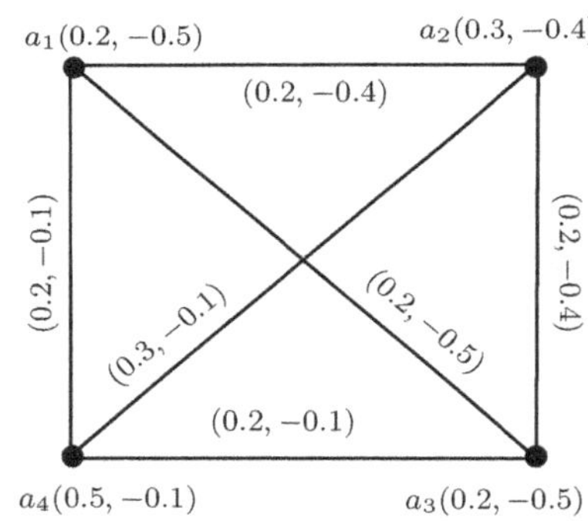

Definition 3.8 If $G = (A, B)$ is a bipolar fuzzy graph on a nonempty set X then the **order** of G is denoted by $O(G))$ and defined as $O(G) = \sum_{x \in X} \left(\mu_A^p(x), \mu_A^n(x)\right)$. The **size** of G is denoted by $S(G)$ and defined as $S(G) = \sum_{x,y \in X} \left(\mu_B^p(xy), \mu_B^n(xy)\right)$.

Definition 3.9 A bipolar fuzzy graph $G = (A, B)$ on a nonempty set X is known as a **complete bipolar fuzzy graph** if

$$B(xy) = \left(\mu_B^p(xy), \mu_B^n(xy)\right) = \left(\mu_A^p(x) \wedge \mu_A^p(y), \mu_A^n(x) \vee \mu_A^n(y)\right), \quad \text{for all } x, y \in X.$$

Example 3.6 Consider a bipolar fuzzy graph G on $X = \{a_1, a_2, a_3, a_4\}$ as shown in Fig. 3.6. Routine calculations show that G is a complete bipolar fuzzy graph.

Theorem 3.1 *Let $G = (A, B)$ be a bipolar fuzzy graph of X. Then $A = (\mu_A^p, \mu_A^n)$ is a constant function if and only if the following statements are equivalent.*

(1) *G is a regular bipolar fuzzy graph.*
(2) *G is a totally regular bipolar fuzzy graph.*

Proof Suppose that $A = (\mu_A^p, \mu_A^n)$ is a constant function and $A(x) = (c_1, c_2)$, for all $x \in X$.
(1) $\Rightarrow$(2): Assume that G is an (n_1, n_2)-regular bipolar fuzzy graph, for all $x \in X$, then

$$T\deg^p(x) = \deg^p(x) + \mu_A^p(x), \quad T\deg^n(x) = \deg^n(x) + \mu_A^n(x) \text{ for all } x \in X,$$
$$\Rightarrow T\deg^p(x) = n_1 + c_1, \quad T\deg^n(x) = n_2 + c_2, \quad \text{for all } x \in X.$$

Hence G is a totally regular bipolar fuzzy graph.
(2) $\Rightarrow$ (1): Suppose that G is a totally regular bipolar fuzzy graph then for all $x \in X$,

$$\begin{aligned} & T\deg^p(x) = k_1, \quad T\deg^n(x) = k_2, \\ \Rightarrow\ & \deg^p(x) + \mu_A^p(x) = k_1, \quad \deg^n(x) + \mu_A^n(x) = k_2, \\ \Rightarrow\ & \deg^p(x) + c_1 = k_1, \quad \deg^n(x) + c_2 = k_2, \\ \Rightarrow\ & \deg^p(x) = k_1 - c_1, \quad \deg^n(x) = k_2 - c_2. \end{aligned}$$

Thus G is a regular bipolar fuzzy graph.

Conversely, assume that G is both (n_1, n_2)-regular and (t_1, t_2)-totally regular bipolar fuzzy graph, then for all $x \in X$,

$$\begin{aligned} & T\deg^p(x) = t_1, \quad T\deg^n(x) = t_2, \\ \Rightarrow\ & \deg^p(x) + \mu_A^p(x) = t_1, \quad \deg^n(x) + \mu_A^n(x) = t_2, \\ \Rightarrow\ & n_1 + \mu_A^p(x) = t_1, \quad n_2 + \mu_A^n(x) = t_2, \\ \Rightarrow\ & \mu_A^p(x) = t_1 - n_1, \quad \mu_A^n(x) = t_2 - n_2. \end{aligned}$$

It follows that $A = (\mu_A^p, \mu_A^n)$ is a constant function. □

Proposition 3.1 *If a bipolar fuzzy graph G is both regular and totally regular, then $A = (\mu_A^p, \mu_A^n)$ is a constant function.*

Proof Let G be a regular and totally regular bipolar fuzzy graph, then

$$\begin{aligned} \deg^p(x) = n_1, \deg^n(x) = n_2, &\quad \text{for all } x \in X \\ T\deg^p(x) = k_1, T\deg^n(x) = k_2, &\quad \text{for all } x \in X. \\ \Rightarrow T\deg^p(x) &= k_1 \\ \Leftrightarrow \deg^p(x) + \mu_A^p(x) &= k_1 \\ \Leftrightarrow n_1 + \mu_A^p(x) &= k_1 \\ \Leftrightarrow \mu_A^p(x) &= k_1 - n_1 \quad \text{for all } x \in X. \end{aligned}$$

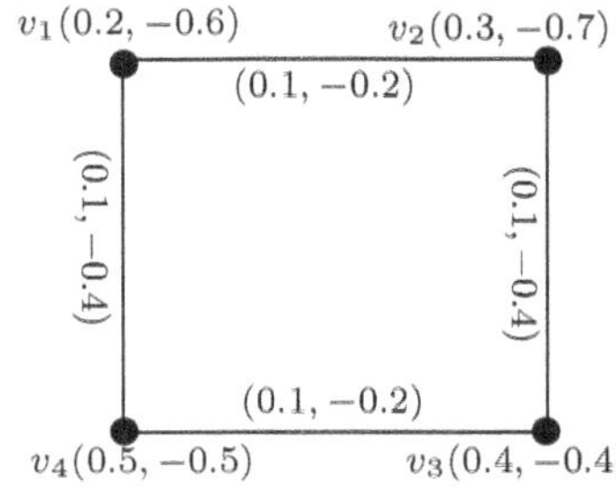

Fig. 3.7 Neighborly irregular bipolar fuzzy graph

Likewise, $\mu_A^n(x) = k_2 - n_2$, for all $x \in X$. Hence $A = (\mu_A^p, \mu_A^n)$ is a constant function. □

Remark 3.1 The converse of Proposition 3.1 is not true in general. Let $G = (A, B)$ be a bipolar fuzzy graph on $X = \{v_1, v_2, v_3\}$ such that

$$\mu_A^p(v_1) = \mu_A^p(v_2) = \mu_A^p(v_3) = 0.4,\ \mu_A^n(v_1) = \mu_A^n(v_2) = \mu_A^n(v_3) = -0.2,$$

$$\mu_B^p(v_1v_2) = 0.2,\ \mu_B^p(v_1v_3) = 0.1,\ \mu_B^n(v_1v_2) = -0.1,\ \mu_B^n(v_1v_3) = -0.1.$$

Clearly $A = (\mu_A^p, \mu_A^n)$ is a constant function but G is neither regular nor totally regular bipolar fuzzy graph.

Definition 3.10 A connected bipolar fuzzy graph G is said to be a **neighborly irregular bipolar fuzzy graph** if every two adjacent vertices of G have distinct neighborhood degrees.

Example 3.7 Consider a bipolar fuzzy graph G on $X = \{v_1, v_2, v_3, v_4\}$ as shown in Fig. 3.7 such that $N\deg(v_1) = (0.8, -1.2)$, $N\deg(v_2) = (0.6, -1.0)$, $N\deg(v_3) = (0.8, -1.2)$, and $N\deg(v_4) = (0.6, -1.0)$. It is clear from calculations that G is neighborly irregular bipolar fuzzy graph.

Definition 3.11 A connected bipolar fuzzy graph G is said to be **neighborly totally irregular bipolar fuzzy graph** if every two adjacent vertices of G have distinct closed neighborhood degrees.

Example 3.8 Consider a bipolar fuzzy graph G on $X = \{v_1, v_2, v_3, v_4\}$ as given in Fig. 3.8.

From the figure, $N\deg[v_1] = (1.2, -1.5)$, $N\deg[v_2] = (1.4, -1.3)$, $N\deg[v_3] = (1.6, -1.1)$ and $N\deg[v_4] = (1.5, -1.2)$. It is easy to see that G is a neighborly totally irregular bipolar fuzzy graph.

Definition 3.12 A connected bipolar fuzzy graph G is called **highly irregular bipolar fuzzy graph** if every vertex of G is adjacent to vertices with distinct neighborhood degrees.

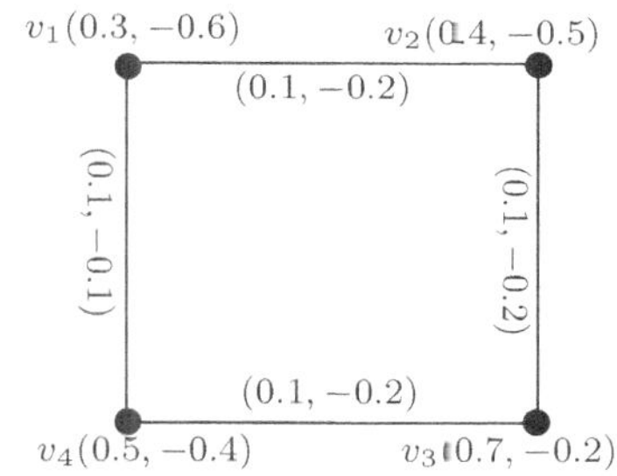

Fig. 3.8 Neighborly totally irregular bipolar fuzzy graph

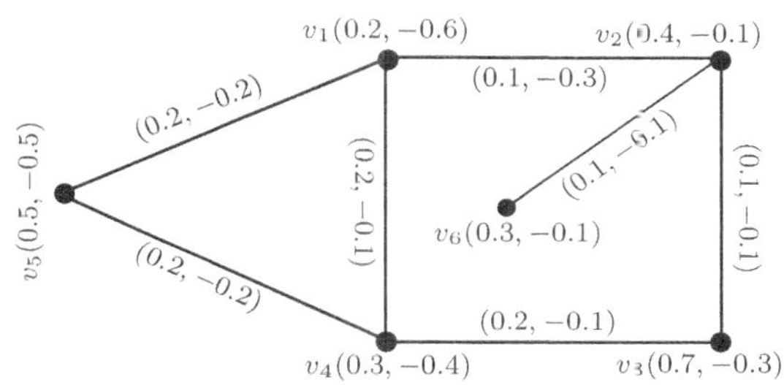

Fig. 3.9 Highly irregular bipolar fuzzy graph

Remark 3.2 A highly irregular bipolar fuzzy graph may not be a neighborly irregular bipolar fuzzy graph.

There is no relation between highly irregular bipolar fuzzy graph and neighborly irregular bipolar fuzzy graph as explained in Example 3.9.

Example 3.9 Consider a bipolar fuzzy graph G as shown in Fig. 3.9. Clearly $N\deg(v_1) = (0.7, -0.5)$, $N\deg(v_2) = (1.2, -1.0)$, $N\deg(v_3) = (1.2, -1.0)$, $N\deg(v_4) = (1.0, -0.7)$, $N\deg(v_5) = (1.4, -1.4)$, and $N\deg(v_6) = (0.4, -0.1)$. Consider a vertex $v_2 \in X$ which is adjacent to vertices v_1, v_3, and v_6 with distinct neighborhood degrees but $N\deg(v_2) = N\deg(v_3)$. So G is highly irregular but it is not a neighborly irregular bipolar fuzzy graph.

Remark 3.3 A neighborly irregular bipolar fuzzy graph may not be a highly irregular bipolar fuzzy graph as shown in Example 3.10.

Example 3.10 Consider a bipolar fuzzy graph G on set $X = \{v_1, v_2, v_3, v_4\}$ given in Fig. 3.10 such that $N\deg(v_1) = (0.6, -0.8)$, $N\deg(v_2) = (0.8, -0.9)$, $N\deg(v_3) = (0.6, -0.8)$, $N\deg(v_4) = (0.8, -0.9)$. It is easy to see that every two adjacent vertices have distinct neighborhood degrees. Consider a vertex v_2 which is adjacent to vertices v_1 and v_3 but $N\deg(v_1) = N\deg(v_3)$. Hence G is neighborly irregular bipolar fuzzy graph but not a highly irregular bipolar fuzzy graph.

Theorem 3.2 *If all the vertices of a bipolar fuzzy graph G are of distinct neighborhood degrees, then G is highly irregular and neighborly irregular.*

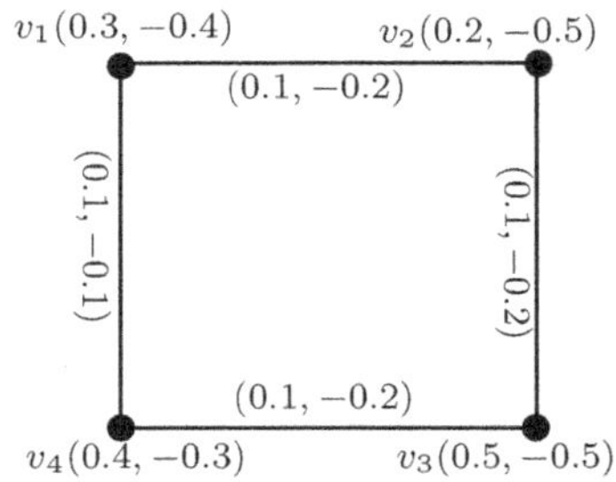

Fig. 3.10 Bipolar fuzzy graph G

Proof Assume that the neighborhood degrees of all the vertices of G are distinct.
Claim: G is highly irregular and neighborly irregular bipolar fuzzy graph.

Let $\deg(v_i) = (k_i, l_i), i = 1, 2, ..., n$. Given that $k_1 \neq k_2 \neq k_3 \neq ... \neq k_n$ and $l_1 \neq l_2 \neq l_3 \neq ... \neq l_n$, which implies that every two adjacent vertices have distinct neighborhood degrees, and to every vertex the adjacent vertices have distinct neighborhood degrees. It completes the proof. □

Theorem 3.3 *If G is highly irregular and neighborly irregular such that G^* is a complete graph, then all the vertices of a bipolar fuzzy graph G are of distinct neighborhood degrees.*

Proof Let G be a bipolar fuzzy graph with n-vertices $v_1, v_2, \ldots, v_n$. Assume that G is highly irregular and neighborly irregular bipolar fuzzy graph.
Claim: The neighborhood degrees of all vertices of G are distinct.

Let $\deg(v_i) = (k_i, l_i)$ for all $i = 1, 2, \ldots, n$. The adjacent vertices of v_1 are $v_2, v_3, \ldots, v_n$ with neighborhood degrees $(k_2, l_2), (k_3, l_3), \ldots, (k_n, l_n)$, respectively. As G is highly irregular so $k_2 \neq k_3 \neq \ldots \neq k_n$ and $l_2 \neq l_3 \neq \ldots \neq l_n$. Also by assumption G is neighborly irregular, $k_1 \neq k_2 \neq k_3 \neq \ldots \neq k_n$ and $l_1 \neq l_2 \neq l_3 \neq \ldots \neq l_n$. Hence the neighborhood degrees of all the vertices of G are distinct. □

Theorem 3.4 *Let G a bipolar fuzzy graph such that the underlying graph G^* is a cycle with 3 vertices then G is neighborly irregular and highly irregular bipolar fuzzy graph if and only if the positive membership and negative membership values of the vertices between every pair of vertices are all distinct.*

Proof Assume that positive membership and negative membership values of the vertices are all distinct.
Claim: $G = (A, B)$ is neighborly irregular and highly irregular bipolar fuzzy graph.
Let $v_i, v_j, v_k \in X$. Given that, $\mu_A^p(v_i) \neq \mu_A^p(v_j) \neq \mu_A^p(v_k)$ and $\mu_A^n(v_i) \neq \mu_A^n(v_j) \neq \mu_A^n(v_k)$, which implies that

$$\sum_{v_i \in N(x)} \mu_A^p(v_i) \neq \sum_{v_j \in N(x)} \mu_A^p(v_j) \neq \sum_{v_k \in N(x)} \mu_A^p(v_k)$$

and

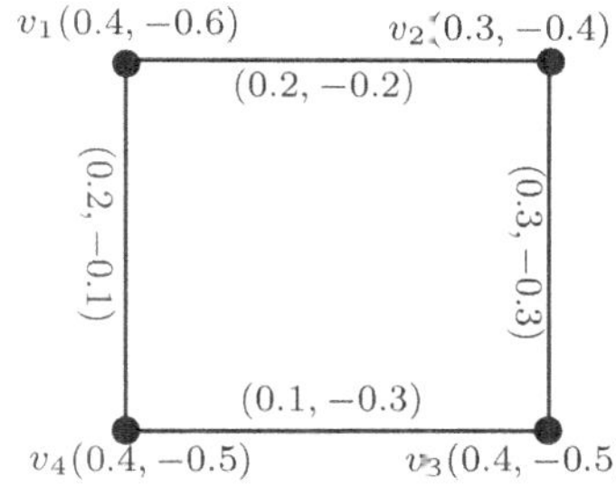

Fig. 3.11 Neighborly irregular bipolar fuzzy graph

$$\sum_{v_i \in N(x)} \mu_A^n(v_i) \neq \sum_{v_j \in N(x)} \mu_A^n(v_j) \neq \sum_{v_k \in N(x)} \mu_A^n(v_k).$$

That is, $N\deg(v_i) \neq N\deg(v_j) \neq N\deg(v_k)$. Hence G is neighborly irregular and highly irregular bipolar fuzzy graph.

Conversely, assume that G is neighborly irregular and highly irregular bipolar fuzzy graph.
Claim: The positive membership and negative membership values of the vertices are all distinct.
Let $N\deg(v_i) = (k_i, l_i), i = 1, 2, \ldots, n$. Suppose that positive membership and negative membership values of any two vertices are same. Let $v_1, v_2 \in X$ such that $\mu_A^p(v_1) = \mu_A^p(v_2)$ and $\mu_A^n(v_1) = \mu_A^n(v_2)$ then $N\deg(v_1) = N\deg(v_2)$. Since G^* is cycle which is a contradiction to the fact that G is neighborly irregular and highly irregular bipolar fuzzy graph. Hence the positive membership and negative membership values of the vertices are all distinct. □

Remark 3.4 A neighborly totally irregular bipolar fuzzy graph may not be neighborly irregular.

Remark 3.5 A neighborly irregular bipolar fuzzy graph may not be neighborly totally irregular as it can be seen in Example 3.11.

Example 3.11 Consider a bipolar fuzzy graph G as shown in Fig. 3.11. From the figure, $N\deg(v_1)$=(0.7, −0.9), $N\deg(v_2) = (0.8, -1.1)$, $N\deg(v_3) = (0.7, -0.9)$, $N\deg(v_4) = (0.8, -1.1)$ and $N\deg[v_1] = (1.1, -1.5)$, $N\deg[v_2] = (1.1, -1.5)$, $N\deg[v_3] = (1.1, -1.4)$, $N\deg[v_4] = (1.2, -1.6)$. It is easy to see that $N\deg[v_1] = N\deg[v_2]$. Hence G is neighborly irregular but not a neighborly totally irregular bipolar fuzzy graph.

Example 3.12 Consider a bipolar fuzzy graph G as given in Fig. 3 13. Clearly $N\deg[v_1] = (1.2, -1.5)$, $N\deg[v_2] = (1.3, -1.4)$, $N\deg[v_3] = (1.5, -1.2)$, $N\deg[v_4] = (1.4, -1.3)$. But $N\deg(v_1) = N\deg(v_2) = N\deg(v_2) = (0.9, -0.9)$. Hence G is neighborly totally irregular but not a neighborly irregular bipolar fuzzy graph (Fig. 3.12).

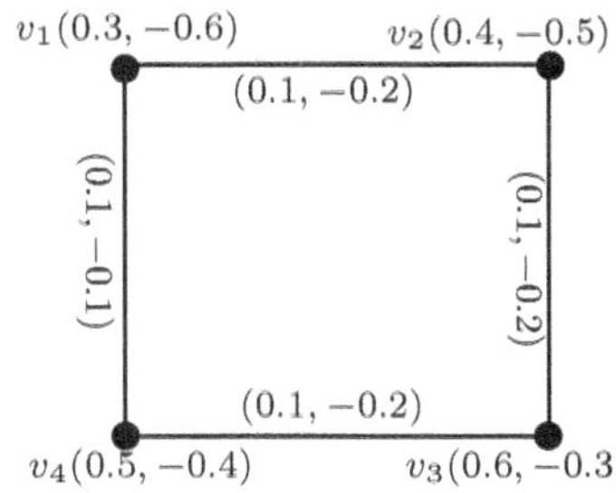

Fig. 3.12 Neighborly totally irregular bipolar fuzzy graph

Proposition 3.2 *Let G be a bipolar fuzzy graph. If G is neighborly irregular bipolar fuzzy graph and* (μ^P_A, μ^n_A) *is a constant function then G is a neighborly totally irregular bipolar fuzzy graph.*

Proof Assume that G is a neighborly irregular bipolar fuzzy graph, that is, the neighborhood degrees of every two adjacent vertices are distinct. Let $v_i, v_j \in X$, where v_i and v_j are adjacent vertices with distinct neighborhood degrees (k_1, l_1) and (k_2, l_2), respectively. That is, $N\deg(v_i) = (k_1, l_1)$ and $N\deg(v_j) = (k_2, l_2)$, where $k_1 \neq k_2$, $l_1 \neq 1_2$. Let us assume that $A(v_i) = A(v_j) = (c_1, c_2)$, where c_1, c_2 are constant and $(c_1, c_2) \in [0, 1] \times [-1, 0]$. Therefore, $N\deg^P[v_i] = N\deg^P(v_i) + \mu^P(v_i) = k_1 + c_1$, $N\deg^n[v_i] = N\deg^n(v_i) + \mu^n(v_i) = l_1 + c_2$, $N\deg^P[v_j] = N\deg^P(v_j) + \mu^P(v_j) = k_2 + c_1$, and $\deg^n[v_j] = \deg^n(v_j) + \mu^n(v_j) = l_2 + c_2$.
Claim: $N\deg^P[v_i] \neq N\deg^P[v_j]$ and $N\deg^n[v_i] \neq N\deg^n[v_j]$.
On contrary, assume that $N\deg^P[v_i] = N\deg^P[v_j]$ and $N\deg^n[v_i] = N\deg^n[v_j]$.
Consider

$$\begin{aligned} N\deg^P[v_i] &= N\deg^P[v_j] \\ k_1 + c_1 &= k_2 + c_1 \\ k_1 - k_2 &= c_1 - c_1 = 0 \\ k_1 &= k_2, \text{ which is a contradiction.} \end{aligned}$$

So, $N\deg^P[v_i] \neq N\deg^P[v_j]$.

$$\begin{aligned} \text{Similarly, } N\deg^n[v_i] &= N\deg^n[v_j] \\ l_1 + c_2 &= l_2 + c_2 \\ l_1 - l_2 &= c_2 - c_2 = 0 \\ l_1 &= l_2, \text{ which is a contradiction.} \end{aligned}$$

Thus $N\deg^n[v_i] \neq N\deg^n[v_j]$. Hence G is a neighborly totally irregular bipolar fuzzy graph. □

Theorem 3.5 *Let G be a bipolar fuzzy graph. If G is neighborly totally irregular and* (μ^P_A, μ^n_A) *is a constant function, then G is a neighborly irregular bipolar fuzzy graph.*

Proof Assume that G is a neighborly totally irregular bipolar fuzzy graph. That is, the closed neighborhood degree of every two adjacent vertices are distinct. Let $v_i, v_j \in X$ and $N\deg[v_i] = (k_1, l_1)$ and $N\deg[v_j] = (k_2, l_2)$, where $k_1 \neq k_2$ and $l_1 \neq l_2$. Assume that $A(v_i) = A(v_j) = (c_1, c_2)$, where $(c_1, c_2) \in [0, 1] \times [-1, 0]$ and $N\deg[v_i] \neq N\deg[v_j]$.
Claim: $N\deg(v_i) \neq N\deg(v_j)$.
Given that $N\deg[v_i] \neq N\deg[v_j]$ which implies that $N\deg^p[v_i] \neq \deg^p[v_j]$ and $\deg^n[v_i] \neq \deg^n[v_j]$. Now,

$$\begin{aligned} N\deg^p[v_i] &\neq N\deg^p[v_j] & \quad N\deg^n[v_i] &\neq N\deg^n[v_j] \\ k_1 + c_1 &\neq k_2 + c_1 & l_1 + c_2 &\neq l_2 + c_2 \\ k_1 &\neq k_2. & l_1 &\neq l_2. \end{aligned}$$

Hence the neighborhood degrees of every pair of adjacent vertices are distinct in G. □

Remark 3.6 If G is neighborly irregular bipolar fuzzy graph then bipolar fuzzy subgraph $H = (A', B')$ of G may not be neighborly irregular bipolar fuzzy graph.

Example 3.13 Consider a bipolar fuzzy graph $G = (A, B)$ as given in Fig. 3.13, where A is a bipolar fuzzy set on $X = \{v_1, v_2, v_3, v_4, v_5\}$ and B is a bipolar fuzzy relation in X such that $supp(B) = E = \{v_1v_2, v_2v_3, v_3v_1, v_3v_4, v_4v_1, v_4v_5, v_5v_1\}$. Consider the bipolar fuzzy subgraph, in Fig. 3.14, $H = (A', B')$ of G such that $X' = \{v_1, v_2, v_3\}$ and $supp(B') = E' = \{v_1v_2, v_2v_3, v_3v_1\}$.

1. For G: By routine computations, $N\deg(v_1) = (2.0, -1.4)$, $N\deg(v_2) = (0.7, -0.8)$, $N\deg(v_3) = (1.9, -0.6)$, $N\deg(v_4) = (1.3, -1.2)$ and $N\deg(v_5) = (1.3, -0.4)$.
2. For H: By routine computations, $N\deg(v_1) = (0.7, -0.8)$, $N\deg(v_2) = (0.7, -0.8)$ and $N\deg(v_3) = (1.2, -0.4)$. It is easy to see that v_1 and v_2 are adjacent vertices with the same neighborhood degrees in H. Hence, H is not a neighborly irregular bipolar fuzzy graph but G is neighborly irregular bipolar fuzzy graph.

Remark 3.7 If G is totally irregular then the bipolar fuzzy subgraph $H = (A', B')$ of G may not be totally irregular bipolar fuzzy graph.

Example 3.14 Consider a bipolar fuzzy graph $G = (A, B)$, shown in Fig. 3.15, on set $X=\{v_1, v_2, v_3, v_4\}$ such that $supp(B) = E=\{v_1v_2, v_2v_3, v_2v_4, v_3v_4, v_3v_1, v_4v_1\}$. Consider the bipolar fuzzy subgraph, in Fig. 3.16, $H = (A', B')$ of G such that $X' = \{v_1, v_2, v_3\}$ and $supp(B') = E' = \{v_1v_2, v_2v_3, v_3v_1\}$.

1. For G: By routine computations, $N\deg[v_1] = (1.4, -2.4)$, $N\deg[v_2] = (1.0, -1.8)$, $N\deg[v_3] = (1.4, -2.4)$, $N\deg[v_4] = (1.1, -1.9)$. Here there is a vertex v_3 which is adjacent to v_1, v_2 and v_4, where $N\deg[v_1] \neq N\deg[v_2]N \neq N\deg[v_4]$.

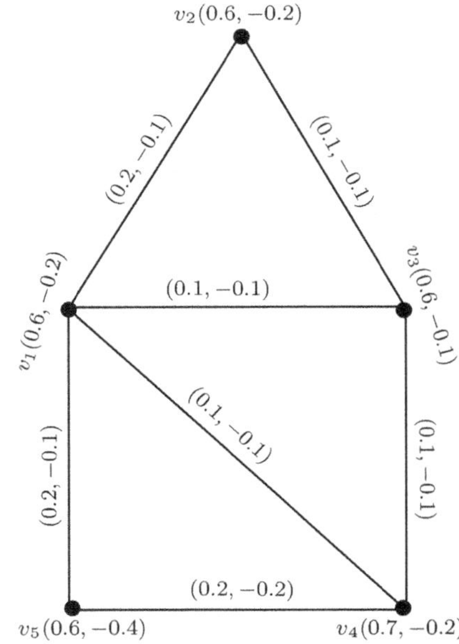

Fig. 3.13 Neighborly irregular bipolar fuzzy graph

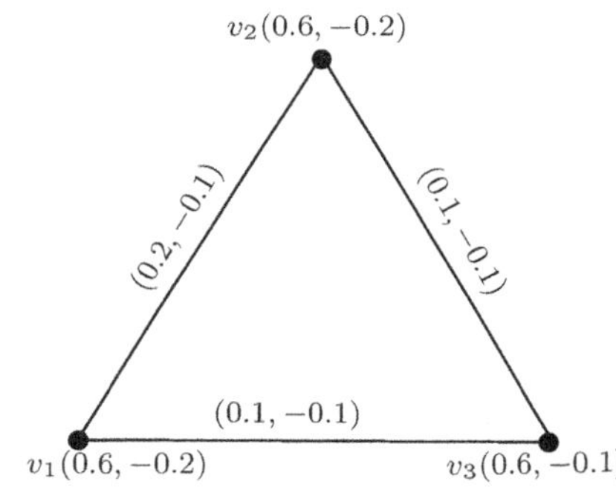

Fig. 3.14 Bipolar fuzzy subgraph H which is not neighborly irregular

2. For H: By routine computations, $N\deg[v_1] = (1.0, -1.8)$, $N\deg[v_2] = (1.0, -1.8)$ and $N\deg[v_3] = (1.0, -1.8)$. Here, there is a vertex v_1 which is adjacent to the vertices v_2 and v_3 with same closed neighborhood degrees. Also, v_2 which is adjacent to the vertices v_1 and v_3 with same closed neighborhood degrees and v_3 which is adjacent to the vertices v_1 and v_2 with same closed neighborhood degrees. Hence H is not a totally irregular bipolar fuzzy graph but G is totally irregular bipolar fuzzy graph.

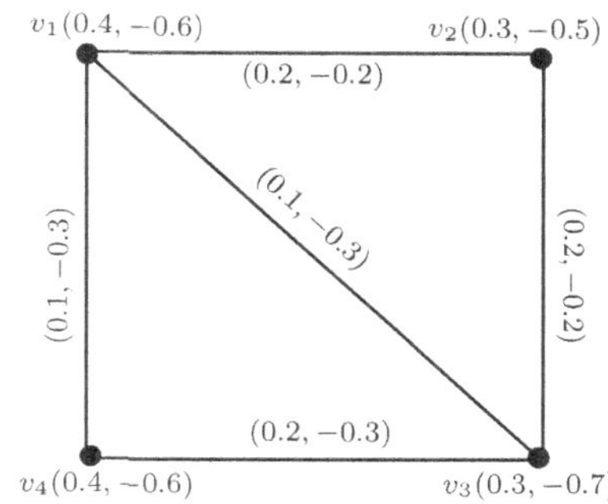

Fig. 3.15 Totally irregular bipolar fuzzy graph G

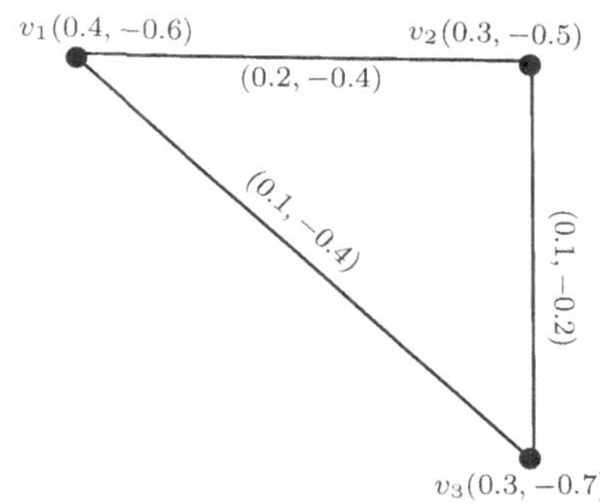

Fig. 3.16 Bipolar fuzzy subgraph which is not totally irregular

3.3 Bipolar Fuzzy Line Graphs

The line graph of a simple graph G^* is a graph $L(G^*)$ that represents the adjacencies between edges of G^*. Let $G^* = (X, E)$ be a graph then its line graph $L(G^*)$ is such that

1. Each vertex of $L(G^*)$ represents an edge of G^*.
2. Two vertices of $L(G^*)$ are adjacent if and only if their corresponding edges share a common endpoint in G^*.

Definition 3.13 Let $G = (A, B)$ be a bipolar fuzzy graph on X and $supp(B) = \{S_{xy} \mid x, y \in X\}$. The bipolar fuzzy line graph $L(G) = (A_L, B_L)$ of G is a bipolar fuzzy graph, where $A_L = B$ and there is an edge between two vertices S_{xy} and S_{yz} in $L(G)$ if S_{xy} and S_{yz} share a common vertex in y in G. The degree of membership of vertices and edges in $L(G)$ is defined as

1. $\mu^p_{A_L}(S_{xy}) = \mu^p_B(xy)$,
2. $\mu^n_{A_L}(S_{xy}) = \mu^n_B(xy)$,
3. $\mu^p_{B_L}(S_{xy}S_{yz}) = \mu^p_B(xy) \wedge \mu^p_B(yz)$,
4. $\mu^n_{B_L}(S_{xy}S_{yz}) = \mu^n_B(xy) \vee \mu^n_B(yz)$.

Table 3.7 Bipolar fuzzy set A on X

A	v_1	v_2	v_3	v_4
μ_A^p	0.2	0.3	0.4	0.2
μ_A^n	−0.5	−0.4	−0.5	−0.3

Table 3.8 Bipolar fuzzy relation B in X

B	x_1	x_2	x_3	x_4
μ_B^p	0.1	0.2	0.1	0.1
μ_B^n	−0.2	−0.3	−0.2	−0.2

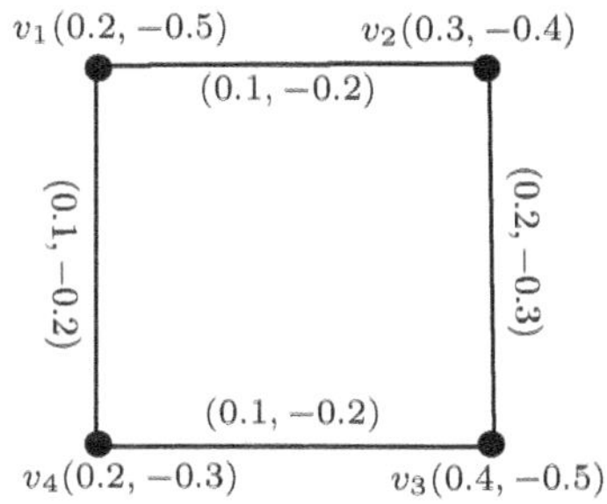

Fig. 3.17 Bipolar fuzzy graph G

Example 3.15 Consider the set of vertices $X = \{v_1, v_2, v_3, v_4\}$ and the set of edges $E = \{x_1 = v_1v_2,\ x_2 = v_2v_3,\ x_3 = v_3v_4,\ x_4 = v_4v_1\}$. Let A be a bipolar fuzzy set on X, in Table 3.7, and B a bipolar fuzzy set on E defined in Table 3.8. It is easy to see, from Fig. 3.17, that G is a bipolar fuzzy graph.

The bipolar fuzzy line graph $L(G) = (A_L, B_L)$ of G is shown in Fig. 3.18, where $A_L = B$ and the membership values of edges in $L(G)$ are computed as

$$\mu_{A_L}^p(S_{x_1}) = 0.1,\ \mu_{A_L}^p(S_{x_2}) = 0.2,\ \mu_{A_L}^p(S_{x_3}) = 0.1,\ \mu_{A_L}^p(S_{x_4}) = 0.1,$$

$$\mu_{A_L}^n(S_{x_1}) = -0.2,\ \mu_{A_L}^n(S_{x_2}) = -0.3,\ \mu_{A_L}^n(S_{x_3}) = -0.2,\ \mu_{A_L}^n(S_{x_4}) = -0.2.$$

$$\mu_{B_L}^p(S_{x_1}S_{x_2}) = 0.1,\ \mu_{B_L}^p(S_{x_2}S_{x_3}) = 0.1,\ \mu_{B_L}^p(S_{x_3}S_{x_4}) = 0.1,\ \mu_{B_L}^p(S_{x_4}S_{x_1}) = 0.1,$$

$$\mu_{B_L}^n(S_{x_1}S_{x_2}) = -0.2,\ \mu_{B_L}^n(S_{x_2}S_{x_3}) = -0.2,\ \mu_{B_L}^n(S_{x_3}S_{x_4}) = -0.2,\ \mu_{B_L}^n(S_{x_4}S_{x_1}) = -0.2.$$

$L(G)$ is a regular bipolar fuzzy graph but not totally regular bipolar fuzzy graph since $\mathrm{Tdeg}(S_{x_2}) \neq \mathrm{Tdeg}(S_{x_4})$.

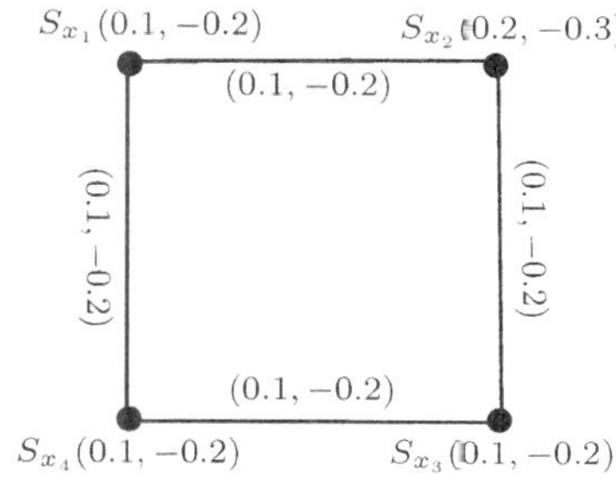

Fig. 3.18 Bipolar fuzzy line graph $L(G)$

Proposition 3.3 *If $L(G)$ is a bipolar fuzzy line graph of a bipolar fuzzy graph G, then $L(G^*)$ is the line graph of G^*.*

Proof Let $G = (A, B)$ be a bipolar fuzzy graph and $L(G) = (A_L, B_L)$. Let (Z, W) be a crisp graph corresponding to $L(G) = (A_L, B_L)$. Clearly, $\mu_A^p(S_{xy}) = \mu_B^p(xy)$, $\mu_A^n(S_{xy}) = \mu_B^n(xy)$, for all $xy \in E$ and so $S_{xy} \in Z \Leftrightarrow x \in E$. By definition of bipolar fuzzy line graph,

$$\mu_{B_L}^p(S_{xy}S_{yz}) = \mu_B^p(xy) \wedge \mu_B^p(yz)$$

$$\mu_{B_L}^n(S_{xy}S_{yz}) = \mu_B^n(xy) \vee \mu_B^n(yz),$$

for all $S_{xy}, S_{yz} \in Z$, and so $W = \{S_{xy}S_{yz} | S_{xy} \cap S_{yz} \neq \emptyset, x, y \in E, x \neq y\}$. It completes the proof. □

Proposition 3.4 *$L(G)$ is a bipolar fuzzy line graph of some bipolar fuzzy graph G if and only if*

$$\mu_{B_L}^p(S_{xy}S_{yz}) = \mu_{A_L}^p(S_{xy}) \wedge \mu_{A_L}^p(S_{yz}), \quad \text{for all } \mathrm{S_{xy}S_{yz}} \in \mathrm{W}, \tag{3.1}$$

$$\mu_{B_L}^n(S_{xy}S_{yz}) = \mu_{A_L}^n(S_{xy}) \vee \mu_{A_L}^n(S_{yz}), \quad \text{for all } \mathrm{S_{xy}S_{yz}} \in \mathrm{W}. \tag{3.2}$$

Proof Assume that $\mu_{B_L}^p(S_{xy}S_{yz}) = \mu_{A_L}^p(S_{xy}) \wedge \mu_{A_L}^p(S_{yz})$, for all $S_{xy}\ S_{yz} \in W$, then

$$\mu_{B_L}^p(S_{xy}S_{yz}) = \mu_{A_L}^p(S_{xy}) \wedge \mu_{A_L}^p(S_{yz}) = \mu_B^p(xy) \wedge \mu_B^p(yz),$$

$$\mu_{B_L}^n(S_{xy}S_{yz}) = \mu_{A_L}^n(S_{xy}) \vee \mu_{A_L}^n(S_{yz}) = \mu_B^n(xy) \vee \mu_B^n(yz).$$

A bipolar fuzzy set $A = (\mu_A^p, \mu_A^n)$ that yields the property

$$\mu_B^p(xy) \leq \mu_A^p(x) \wedge \mu_A^p(y),$$

$$\mu_B^n(xy) \geq \mu_A^n(x) \vee \mu_A^n(y)$$

will suffice. Thus (A_L, B_L) is a bipolar fuzzy line graph of $G = (A, B)$.

Conversely, suppose that $L(G) = (A_L, B_L)$ is a bipolar fuzzy line graph of $G = (A, B)$, then $\mu^p_{B_L}(S_{xy}S_{yz}) = \mu^p_B(x) \wedge \mu^p_B(y)$, hence consequently, $\mu^p_{B_L}(S_{xy}S_{yz}) = \mu^p_{A_L}(S_{xy}) \wedge \mu^p_{A_L}(S_{yz})$. Similarly, $\mu^n_{B_L}(S_{xy}S_{yz}) = \mu^n_B(x) \vee \mu^n_B(y)$ implies $\mu^n_{B_L}(S_{xy}S_{yz}) = \mu^n_{A_L}(S_{xy}) \vee \mu^n_{A_L}(S_{yz})$. □

Proposition 3.5 *$L(G)$ is a bipolar fuzzy line graph of G if and only if $L(G^*)$ is a line graph of G^* and*

$$\mu^p_{B_L}(uv) = \mu^p_{A_L}(u) \wedge \mu^p_{A_L}(v)$$
$$\mu^n_{B_L}(uv) = \mu^n_{A_L}(u) \vee \mu^n_{A_L}(v), \quad \text{for all uv} \in \text{W}.$$

Definition 3.14 Let $G_1 = (A_1, B_1)$ and $G_2 = (A_2, B_2)$ be two bipolar fuzzy graphs on X_1 and X_2, respectively. A **homomorphism** of bipolar fuzzy graphs G_1 and G_2 is a mapping $f : X_1 \to X_2$ such that

1. $\mu^p_{A_1}(x_1) \leq \mu^p_{A_2}(f(x_1)),\ \ \mu^n_{A_1}(x_1) \geq \mu^n_{A_2}(f(x_1)),$ for all $x_1 \in X_1$,
2. $\mu^p_{B_1}(x_1y_1) \leq \mu^p_{B_2}(f(x_1)f(y_1)),\ \mu^n_{B_1}(x_1y_1) \geq \mu^n_{B_2}(f(x_1)f(y_1)),$ for all $x_1, y_1 \in X_1$.

Definition 3.15 A **weak isomorphism** of bipolar fuzzy graphs G_1 and G_2 is a bijective homomorphism $f : X_1 \to X_2$ that satisfies

$$\mu^p_{A_1}(x_1) = \mu^p_{A_2}(f(x_1)),\ \ \mu^n_{A_1}(x_1) = \mu^n_{A_2}(f(x_1)), \quad \text{for all } x_1 \in X_1.$$

Definition 3.16 A **co-weak isomorphism** of bipolar fuzzy graphs G_1 and G_2 is a bijective homomorphism $f : X_1 \to X_2$ that satisfies

$$\mu^p_{B_1}(x_1y_1) = \mu^p_{B_2}(f(x_1)f(y_1)),\ \ \mu^n_{B_1}(x_1y_1) = \mu^n_{B_2}(f(x_1)f(y_1)), \quad \text{for all } x_1, y_1 \in X_1.$$

Definition 3.17 Let $G_1 = (A_1, B_1)$ and $G_2 = (A_2, B_2)$ be two bipolar fuzzy graphs on X_1 and X_2, respectively. An **isomorphism** of bipolar fuzzy graphs G_1 and G_2, written as $G_1 \cong G_2$, is a bijective mapping $f : X_1 \to X_2$ that satisfies

1. $\mu^p_{A_1}(x_1) = \mu^p_{A_2}(f(x_1)),\ \ \mu^n_{A_1}(x_1) = \mu^n_{A_2}(f(x_1)),$ for all $x_1 \in X_1$,
2. $\mu^p_{B_1}(x_1y_1) = \mu^p_{B_2}(f(x_1)f(y_1)),\ \mu^n_{B_1}(x_1y_1) = \mu^n_{B_2}(f(x_1)f(y_1)),$ for all $x_1, y_1 \in X_1$.

Proposition 3.6 *Let G_1 and G_2 be bipolar fuzzy graphs. If f is a weak isomorphism from G_1 into G_2, then f is an isomorphism from G_1^* into G_2^*.*

Theorem 3.6 *Let $L(G) = (A_L, B_L)$ be a bipolar fuzzy line graph corresponding to bipolar fuzzy graph $G = (A, B)$. If the crisp graph $G^* = (X, E)$ corresponding to G is connected, then*

1. *There exists a week isomorphism from G into $L(G)$ if and only if G^* is a cycle and, $A = (\mu^p_A, \mu^n_A)$ and $B = (\mu^p_B, \mu^n_B)$ are constant functions.*
2. *If f is a weak isomorphism from G into $L(G)$ then f is an isomorphism.*

Proof Assume that f is a weak isomorphism of $L(G)$ into G. From Proposition 3.6, it follows that $G^* = (X, E)$ is a cycle. Let $X = \{v_1, v_2, \ldots, v_n\}$ and $E = \{x_1 = v_1v_2, x_2 = v_2v_3, \ldots, x_n = v_nv_1\}$, where $v_1v_2v_3\ldots v_nv_1$ is a cyclic. Define bipolar fuzzy sets A and B as

$$\mu_A^p(v_i) = s_i,\ \mu_A^n(v_i) = \acute{s}_i$$

$$\mu_B^p(v_iv_{i+1}) = r_i,\ \mu_B^n(v_iv_{i+1}) = \acute{r}_i,\ i = 1, 2, \ldots, n,\ v_{n+1} = v_1.$$

Then for $s_{n+1} = s_1$, $\acute{s}_{n+1} = \acute{s}_1$,

$$\begin{cases} r_i \le s_i \wedge s_{i+1}, \\ \acute{r}_i \ge \acute{s}_i \vee \acute{s}_{i+1},\ i = 1, 2, \ldots, n. \end{cases} \tag{3.3}$$

It follows that $Z = \{S_{x_1}, S_{x_1}, S_{x_2}, \ldots, S_{x_n}\}$ and $W = \{S_{x_1}S_{x_2}, S_{x_2}S_{x_3}, \ldots, S_{x_n}S_{x_1}\}$. Also for $r_{n+1} = r_1$,

$$\mu_{A_L}^p(S_{x_i}) = \mu_A^p(x_i) = \mu_A^p(v_iv_{i+1}) = r_i,$$

$$\mu_{A_L}^n(S_{x_i}) = \mu_A^n(x_i) = \mu_A^n(v_iv_{i+1}) = \acute{r}_i,$$

$$\begin{aligned} \mu_{B_L}^p(S_{x_i}S_{x_{i+1}}) = & \qquad \mu_B^p(x_i) \wedge \mu_B^p(x_{+1}) \\ &= \mu_B^p(v_iv_{i+1}) \wedge \mu_B^p(v_{i+1}v_{i+2}) \\ &= r_i \wedge r_{i+1}, \\ \mu_{B_L}^n(S_{x_i}S_{x_{i+1}}) = & \qquad \mu_B^n(x_i) \vee \mu_B^n(x_{+1}) \\ &= \mu_B^n(v_iv_{i+1}) \vee \mu_B^n(v_{i+1}v_{i+2}) \\ &= \acute{r}_i \vee \acute{r}_{i+1} \end{aligned}$$

for $i = 1, 2, \ldots, n$, $v_{n+1} = v_1$, $v_{n+2} = v_2$. Since f is an isomorphism from G^* into $L(G^*)$, f maps X one-to-one and onto Z. Also f preserves adjacency. Hence f induces a permutation π of $\{1, 2, \ldots, n\}$ such that

$$f(v_i) = S_{x_{\pi(i)}} = S_{x_{\pi(i)}}S_{x_{\pi(i+1)}}$$

$$x_i = v_iv_{i+1} \to f(v_i)f(v_{i+1}) = S_{v_{\pi(i)}}S_{v_{\pi(i+1)}}S_{v_{\pi(i+2)}},\ i = 1, 2, \ldots, n-1.$$

$$s_i = \mu_A^p(v_i) \le \mu_{A_L}^p(f(v_i)) = \mu_{A_L}^p(S_{v_{\pi(i)}v_{\pi(i+1)}}) = r_{\pi(i)},$$

$$\acute{s}_i = \mu_A^n(v_i) \ge \mu_{A_L}^n(f(v_i)) = \mu_{A_L}^n(S_{v_{\pi(i)}v_{\pi(i+1)}}) = \acute{r}_{\pi(i)},$$

$$\begin{aligned}
r_i = \mu^p_B(v_i v_{i+1}) &\le \mu^p_{B_L}(f(v_i)f(v_{i+1}))\\
&= \mu^p_{B_L}(S_{v_{\pi(i)}} S_{v_{\pi(i)+1}} S_{v_{\pi(i+1)+1}})\\
&= \mu^p_B(v_{\pi(i)}v_{\pi(i)+1}) \wedge \mu^p_B(v_{\pi(i)+1}v_{\pi(i+1)+1})\\
&= r_{\pi(i)} \wedge r_{\pi(i+1)},\\
\acute{r}_i = \mu^n_B(v_i v_{i+1}) &\ge \mu^n_{B_L}(f(v_i)f(v_{i+1}))\\
&= \mu^n_{B_L}(S_{v_{\pi(i)}} S_{v_{\pi(i)+1}} S_{v_{\pi(i+1)+1}}\\
&= \mu^n_B(v_{\pi(i)}v_{\pi(i)+1}) \vee \mu^n_B(v_{\pi(i)+1}v_{\pi(i+1)+1}))\\
&= \acute{r}_{\pi(i)} \vee \acute{r}_{\pi(i+1)}
\end{aligned}$$

for $i = 1, 2, \ldots, n$. That is, $s_i \le r_{\pi(i)}$, $\acute{s}_i \ge \acute{r}_\pi(i)$ and,

$$\begin{cases} r_i \le r_{\pi(i)} \wedge r_{\pi(i+1)},\\ \acute{r}_i \ge \acute{r}_{\pi(i)} \vee \acute{r}_{\pi(i+1)}. \end{cases} \tag{3.4}$$

From (3.4), we get $r_i \le r_{\pi(i)}$, $\acute{r}_i \ge \acute{r}_{\pi(i)}$, for $i = 1, 2, \ldots, n$ and so $r_\pi(i) \le r_{\pi(\pi(i))}$, $\acute{r}_\pi(i) \le \acute{r}_{\pi(\pi(i))}$, for $i = 1, 2, \ldots, n$. Continuing this process,

$$r_i \le r_{\pi(i)} \le \ldots \le r_{\pi^j(i)} \le r_i,$$

$$\acute{r}_i \ge \acute{r}_{\pi(i)} \ge \ldots \ge \acute{r}_{\pi^j(i)} \ge \acute{r}_i.$$

So $r_i = r_{\pi(i)}, \acute{r}_i = \acute{r}_{\pi(i)}$, $i = 1, 2, \ldots, n$, where π^{j+1} is the identity map. From (3.4),

$$r_i \le r_{\pi(i+1)} = r_{i+1}, i = 1, 2, \ldots, r_{n+1} = r_1,$$

$$\acute{r}_i \ge \acute{r}_{\pi(i+1)} = \acute{r}_{i+1}, i = 1, 2, \ldots, \acute{r}_{n+1} = \acute{r}_1.$$

From Eqs. (3.3) and (3.4),

$$r_1 = \ldots = r_n = s_1 = \ldots = s_n,$$

$$\acute{r}_1 = \ldots = \acute{r}_n = \acute{s}_1 = \ldots = \acute{s}_n.$$

It is not only proved that A and B are constant functions, but condition (2) is also satisfied. □

Theorem 3.7 *Let G and H be two bipolar fuzzy graphs such that the corresponding crisp graphs G^* and H^* are connected. Suppose that it is not the case that one of G^* and $H*$ is a complete graph K_3 and the other is complete bipartite graph $K_{1,3}$. If $L(G)$ and $L(H)$ are isomorphic then G and H are co-weak isomorphic.*

3.4 Cayley Bipolar Fuzzy Graphs

In this section, the concept of Cayley bipolar fuzzy graphs is discussed with connectedness properties. Some interesting properties of bipolar fuzzy graphs are presented in terms of algebraic structures. Let G be a finite group and S be a minimal generating set of G. A **Cayley graph** (G, S) has elements of G as its vertices, the edge-set is given by $\{(g, g_s) \mid g \in G, s \in S\}$. Two vertices g_1 and g_2 are adjacent if $g_2 = g_1.s$, where $s \in S$. Note that a generating set S is minimal if S generates G but no proper subset of S does. All Cayley graphs are vertex transitive.

Definition 3.18 Let $(V, *)$ be a group and A be any subset of V. Then the Cayley graph induced by $(V, *, A)$ is the graph $G = (V, R)$, where $R = \{(x, y) \mid x^{-1}y \in A\}$.

Definition 3.19 Let A and B be two bipolar fuzzy sets on X and Y, respectively. A **bipolar fuzzy relation** R from A to B is a mapping $R : A \to B$ defined as $R = \{(x, y, \mu_R^p(x, y), \mu_R^n(x, y)) \mid (x, y) \in X \times Y\}$ such that

$$\mu_R^p(x, y) \leq \mu_A^p(x) \wedge \mu_B^p(y) \text{ and } \mu_R^n(x, y) \geq \mu_A^n(x) \vee \mu_B^n(y).$$

R is also a bipolar fuzzy relation in $X \times Y$ defined by the mapping $R : X \times Y : [0, 1] \times [-1, 0]$. A bipolar fuzzy relation R in X is defined by a mapping $R : X \times X : [0, 1] \times [-1, 0]$.

Definition 3.20 Let R be a bipolar fuzzy relation in X. Then R is called a **bipolar fuzzy equivalence relation** on X if it satisfies the following conditions:

1. R is bipolar fuzzy reflexive, i.e., $R(x, x) = (1, -1)$, for each $x \in X$.
2. R is bipolar fuzzy symmetric, i.e., $R(x, y) = R(y, x)$, for any $x, y \in X$.
3. R is bipolar fuzzy transitive, i.e., $R(x, z) \geq \bigvee_y (R(x, y) \wedge R(y, z))$.

Definition 3.21 Let R be a bipolar fuzzy relation in X. Then R is called **a bipolar fuzzy partial order relation** on X if it satisfies the following conditions:

1. R is bipolar fuzzy reflexive, i.e., $R(x, x) = (1, -1)$, for each $x \in X$.
2. R is bipolar fuzzy anti-symmetric, i.e., $R(x, y) \neq R(y, x)$, for any $x \ y \in X$.
3. R is bipolar fuzzy transitive, i.e., $R(x, z) \geq \bigvee_y (R(x, y) \wedge R(y, z))$.

Definition 3.22 Let R be a bipolar fuzzy relation in X. Then R is called a **bipolar fuzzy linear order relation** on X if it satisfies the following conditions:

1. R is bipolar fuzzy partial order relation.
2. $R(x, y) \neq (0, 0)$ or $R(y, x) \neq (0, 0)$, for all $x, y \in X$.

Table 3.9 $R(a, b)$ for Cayley bipolar fuzzy graph

a	0	0	0	1	1	1	2	2	2	2
b	0	1	2	0	1	2	0	1	2	
$a^{-1}+b$	0	1	2	2	0	1	1	2	0	
R(a,b)	(0.5, −0.4)	(0.3, −0.2)	(0.3, −0.2)	(0.3, −0.2)	(0.5, −0.4)	(0.3, −0.2)	(0.3, −0.2)	(0.3, −0.2)	(0.5, −0.4)	

Definition 3.23 Let $\mathbf{G} = (A, \mathbf{B})$ be a bipolar fuzzy digraph. The in-degree of a vertex x in $\mathbf{G}$ is defined by $ind(x) = (ind^p_\mu(x), ind^n_\mu(x))$, where $ind^p_\mu(x) = \sum_{y \neq x} \mu^p_{\mathbf{B}}(xy)$ and $ind^n_\mu(x) = \sum_{y \neq x} \mu^n_{\mathbf{B}}(xy)$. Similarly, the out-degree of a vertex x in $\mathbf{G}$ is defined by $outd(x) = (outd^p_\mu(x), outd^n_\mu(x))$, where $outd^p_\mu(x) = \sum_{y \neq x} \mu^p_{\mathbf{B}}(xy)$ and $outd^n_\mu(x) = \sum_{y \neq x} \mu^n_{\mathbf{B}}(xy)$. A bipolar fuzzy digraph in which each vertex has same out-degree r is called **an out-regular digraph** with index of out-regularity r. In-regular digraphs are defined similarly.

Definition 3.24 Let $(V, *)$ be a group and $A = (\mu^p_A, \mu^n_A)$ be the bipolar fuzzy subset on V. The bipolar fuzzy relation R defined on V by

$$R(x, y) = (\mu^p_R(x^{-1} * y), \mu^n_R(x^{-1} * y)), \quad \text{for all x,y} \in V$$

induces a bipolar fuzzy graph $G = (V, R)$ called **Cayley bipolar fuzzy graph**, denoted by by $(V, *, \mu^p_R, \mu^n_R)$.

Definition 3.25 Let $(V, *)$ be a group and $A = (\mu^p_A, \mu^n_A)$ be an bipolar fuzzy subset on V. Then the bipolar fuzzy relation R on V defined by

$$R(x, y) = \{(\mu^p_R(x^{-1} * y), \mu^n_R(x^{-1} * y)) \mid x, y \in V\}$$

induces a bipolar fuzzy graph $G = (V, R)$, called **Cayley bipolar fuzzy graph**. It is denoted by $(V, *, A)$.

Example 3.16 Consider the group Z_3 and take $V = \{0, 1, 2\}$. Define $\mu^p_A : V \to [0, 1]$ and $\mu^n_A : V \to [-1, 0]$ by $\mu^p_A(0) = \mu^p_A(1) = \mu^p_A(2) = 0.5, \mu^n_A(0) = \mu^n_A(1) = \mu^n_A(2) = -0.4$. Then the Cayley bipolar fuzzy graph $G = (V, R)$ induced by $(Z_3, +, A)$ is given by the following Table 3.9 and Fig. 3.19.

We see that Cayley bipolar fuzzy graphs are actually bipolar fuzzy digraphs. Furthermore, the relation R in the above definition describes the strength of each directed edge.

Theorem 3.8 *The Cayley bipolar fuzzy graph G is vertex transitive.*

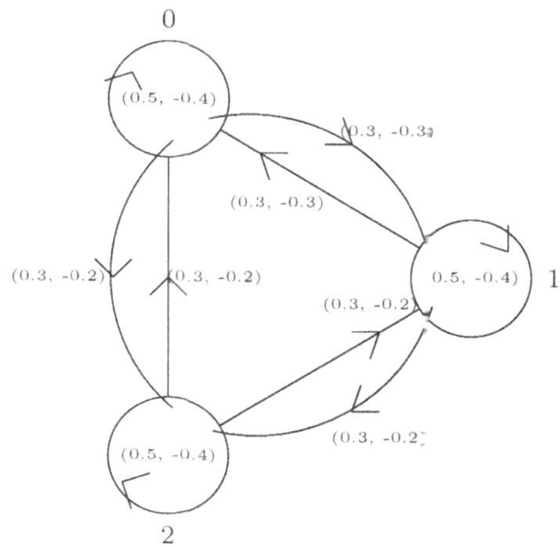

Fig. 3.19 Cayley bipolar fuzzy graph

Proof Let $a, b \in V$. Define $\psi : V \to V$ by $\psi(x) = ba^{-1}x\ \forall x \in V$. Clearly, ψ is a bijective map. For each $x, y \in V$,

$$
\begin{aligned}
R(\psi(x), \psi(y)) &= (R_{\mu^p}(\psi(x), \psi(y)), R_{\mu^n}(\psi(x), \psi(y))). \\
\text{Now } R_{\mu^p}(\psi(x), \psi(y)) &= R_{\mu^p}(ba^{-1}x, ba^{-1}y) \\
&= \mu_A^p((ba^{-1}x)^{-1}(ba^{-1}x)) \\
&= \mu_A^p(x^{-1}y) \\
&= R_{\mu^p}(x, y). \\
R_{\mu^n}(\psi(x), \psi(y)) &= R_{\mu^n}(ba^{-1}x, ba^{-1}y) \\
&= \mu_A^n((ba^{-1}x)^{-1}(ba^{-1}x)) \\
&= \mu_A^n(x^{-1}y) \\
&= R_{\mu^n}(x, y).
\end{aligned}
$$

Therefore, $R(\psi(x), \psi(y)) = R(x, y)$. Hence ψ is an automorphism on G. Also $\psi(a) = b$. Hence G is vertex transitive. □

Theorem 3.9 *Every vertex-transitive bipolar fuzzy graph is regular.*

Proof Let $G = (V, R)$ be any vertex-transitive bipolar fuzzy graph. Let $u, v \in V$. Then there is an automorphism f on G such that $f(u) = v$. Note that

$$\begin{aligned} ind(u) &= \sum_{x\in V} R(x,u) = \sum_{x\in V} (R_{\mu^p}(x,u), R_{\mu^n}(x,u)) \\ &= \sum_{x\in V} (R_{\mu^p}(f(x), f(u)), R_{\mu^n}(f(x), f(u)) \\ &= \sum_{x\in V} (R_{\mu^p}(f(x), v), R_{\mu^n}(f(x), v)) \\ &= \sum_{x\in V} (R_{\mu^p}(y, v), R_{\mu^n}(y, v) \\ &= ind(v), \end{aligned}$$

$$\begin{aligned} outd(u) &= \sum_{x\in V} R(x,u) = \sum_{x\in V} (R_{\mu^p}(u,x), R_{\mu^n}(u,x)) \\ &= \sum_{x\in V} (R_{\mu^p}(f(u), f(x)), R_{\mu^n}(f(u), f(x)) \\ &= \sum_{x\in V} (R_{\mu^p}(v, f(x)), R_{\mu^n}(v, f(x)) \\ &= \sum_{x\in V} (R_{\mu^p}(v, y), R_{\mu^n}(v, y) \\ &= outd(v). \end{aligned}$$

Hence G is regular. □

Theorem 3.10 *Cayley bipolar fuzzy graphs are regular.*

The proof of Theorem 3.10 follows from the Theorems 3.8 and 3.9.

Theorem 3.11 *Let $G = (V, R)$ be a bipolar fuzzy graph then bipolar fuzzy relation R is reflexive if and only if $\mu_A^p(1) = 1$ and $\mu_A^n(1) = -1$.*

Proof R is reflexive if and only if $R(x, x) = (1, -1)$, for all $x \in V$.

$$\begin{aligned} R(x,x) &= (\mu_A^p(x^{-1}x), \mu_A^n(x^{-1}x)) \\ &= (\mu_A^p(1), \mu_A^n(1)) \text{ for all x} \in V. \end{aligned}$$

Hence R is reflexive if and only if $\mu_A^p(1) = 1$ and $\mu_A^n(1) = -1$. □

Theorem 3.12 *Let $G = (V, R)$ denotes bipolar fuzzy graph. Then bipolar fuzzy relation R is symmetric if and only if $(\mu_A^p(x), \mu_A^n(x)) = (\mu_A^p(x^{-1}), \mu_A^n(x^{-1}))$ for all $x \in V$.*

Proof Suppose that R is symmetric. Then for any $x \in V$,

$$\begin{aligned}(\mu_A^p(x), \mu_A^n(x)) &= (\mu_A^p(x^{-1}x^2), \mu_A^n(x^{-1}x^2)) \\ &= R(x, x^2) = R(x^2, x), \quad \text{since R is symmetric} \\ &= (\mu_A^p((x^2)^{-1}x), \mu_A^n(x^2)^{-1}x) \\ &= (\mu_A^p((x^{-2}x), \mu_A^n(x^{-2}x) \\ &= (\mu_A^p((x^{-1}), \mu_A^n(x^{-1}).\end{aligned}$$

Conversely suppose that $(\mu_A^p(x), \mu_A^n(x)) = (\mu_A^p(x^{-1}), \mu_A^n(x^{-1}))$ for all $x \in V$. Then for all $x, y \in V$,

$$\begin{aligned}R(x, y) &= (\mu_A^p(x^{-1}y), \mu_A^n(x^{-1}y)) \\ &= (\mu_A^p(y^{-1}x), \mu_A^n(y^{-1}x)) \\ &= R(y, x).\end{aligned}$$

Hence R is symmetric. □

Theorem 3.13 *A bipolar fuzzy relation R is anti-symmetric if and only if $(\mu_A^p(x), \mu_A^n(x)) = (\mu_A^p(x^{-1}), \mu_A^n(x^{-1})) = (1, -1)$, for all $x \in V$.*

Proof Suppose that R is anti-symmetric and $x \in V$, then $(\mu_A^p(x), \mu_A^n(x)) = (\mu_A^p(x^{-1}), \mu_A^n(x^{-1}))$, which implies $R(1, x) = R(x, 1)$. Hence $x = 1$, since R is anti-symmetric.

Conversely suppose that $\{x \mid (\mu_A^p(x), \mu_A^n(x)) = (\mu_A^p(x^{-1}), \mu_A^n(x^{-1})) = \{1, 1\}\}$. Then for any $x, y \in V$, $R(x, y) = R(y, x) \Leftrightarrow (\mu_A^p(x^{-1}y), \mu_A^n(y^{-1}x))$. This implies that $(\mu_A^p(x^{-1}y), \mu_A^n(y^{-1}x)) = (\mu_A^p((x^{-1}y)^{-1}), \mu_A^n((x^{-1}y)^{-1}))$. That is $x^{-1}y = 1$. Equivalently, $x = y$. Hence R is anti-symmetric. □

Definition 3.26 Let $(S, *)$ be a semigroup. Let $A = (\mu_A^p, \mu_A^n)$ be a bipolar fuzzy subset of S. Then A is said to be a *bipolar fuzzy subsemigroup* of S if for all $x, y \in S$, $\mu_A^p(xy) \geq \mu_A^p(x) \wedge \mu_A^p(y)$ and $\mu_A^n(xy) \leq \mu_A^p(x) \vee \mu_A^n(y)$.

Theorem 3.14 *A bipolar fuzzy relation R is transitive if and only if $A = (\mu_A^p, \mu_A^n)$ is a bipolar fuzzy subsemigroup of $(V, *)$.*

Proof Suppose that R is transitive and let $x, y \in V$. Then $R^2 \leq R$. Now for any $x \in V$, we have $R(1, x) = (\mu_A^p(x), \mu_A^n(x))$. This implies that $\{R(1, z) \wedge R(z, xy) \mid z \in V\} = R^2(1, xy) \leq R(1, xy)$. That is $\vee\{\mu_A^p(z) \wedge \mu_A^p(z^{-1}xy) \mid z \in V\} \leq \mu_A^p(xy)$ and $\wedge\{\mu_A^n(z) \vee \mu_A^n(z^{-1}xy) \mid z \in V\} \geq \mu_A^n(xy)$. Hence $\mu_A^p(xy) \geq \mu_A^p(x) \wedge \mu_A^p(y)$ and $\mu_A^n(xy) \leq \mu_A^p(x) \vee \mu_A^n(y)$. Hence $A = (\mu_A^p, \mu_A^n)$ is a bipolar fuzzy subsemigroup of $(V, *)$.

Conversely, suppose that $A = (\mu_A^p, \mu_A^n)$ is a bipolar fuzzy subsemigroup of $(V, *)$. That is, for all $x, y \in V$ $\mu_A^p(xy) \geq \mu_A^p(x) \wedge \mu_A^p(y)$ and $\mu_A^n(xy) \leq \mu_A^p(x) \vee \mu_A^n(y)$. Then for any $x, y \in V$,

$$\begin{aligned}
R^2(x, y) &= (R^2_{\mu^p}(x, y), R^2_{\mu^n}(x, y))\\
R^2_{\mu^p}(x, y) &= \vee\{R_{\mu^p}(x, z) \wedge R_{\mu^p}(z, y) \mid z \in V\}\\
&= \vee\{\mu^p_A(x^{-1}z) \wedge \mu^p_A(z^{-1}y) \mid z \in V\}\\
&\leq \mu^p_A(x^{-1}y)\\
&= R_{\mu^p}(x, y).
\end{aligned}$$

$$\begin{aligned}
R^2_{\mu^n}(x, y) &= \wedge\{R_{\mu^n}(x, z) \vee R_{\mu^n}(z, y) \mid z \in V\}\\
&= \wedge\{\mu^n_A(x^{-1}z) \vee \mu^n_A(z^{-1}y) \mid z \in V\}\\
&\geq \mu^n_A(x^{-1}y)\\
&= R_{\mu^n}(x, y).
\end{aligned}$$

Hence $R^2_{\mu^p}(x, y) \leq R_{\mu^p}(x, y)$ and $R^2_{\mu^n}(x, y) \geq R_{\mu^n}(x, y)$. Hence R is transitive. □

Theorem 3.15 *A bipolar fuzzy relation R is a partial order if and only if $A = (\mu^p_A, \mu^n_A)$ is a bipolar fuzzy subsemigroup of $(V, *)$ satisfying the following properties:*

1. $\mu^p_A(1) = 1$ *and* $\mu^n_A(1) = -1$,
2. $(\mu^p_A(x), \mu^n_A(x)) = (\mu^p_A(x^{-1}), \mu^n_A(x^{-1})) = (1, -1)$, *for all* $x \in V$.

Theorem 3.16 *A bipolar fuzzy relation R is a linear order if and only if (μ^p_A, μ^n_A) is a bipolar fuzzy subsemigroup of $(V, *)$ satisfying the following properties:*

1. $\mu^p_A(1) = 1$ *and* $\mu^n_A(1) = -1$,
2. $\{x \mid (\mu^p_A(x), \mu^n_A(x)) = (\mu^p_A(x^{-1}), \mu^n_A(x^{-1})) = (1, -1)\}$ *and*
3. $\{x \mid \mu^p_A(x) \vee \mu^p_A(x^{-1}) > 0, \mu^n_A(x) \wedge \mu^n_A(x^{-1}) < 0\} = V$.

Proof Suppose R is a linear order then clearly by Theorem 3.15 conditions 1,2, and 3 are satisfied. For any $x \in V$, $(R \vee R^{-1})(1, x) > 0$. This implies that $R(1, x) \vee R(x, 1) > 0$. Hence $\{x \mid \mu^p_A(x) \vee \mu^p_A(x^{-1}) > 0, \mu^n_A(x) \wedge \mu^n_A(x^{-1}) < 0\}$.

Conversely, suppose that the conditions 1,2, and 3 hold. By Theorem 3.15, R is partial order. Now for any $x, y \in V$, we have $(x^{-1}y), (y^{-1}x) \in V$. Then, $\{x \mid \mu^p_A(x) \vee \mu^p_A(x^{-1}) > 0, \mu^n_A(x) \wedge \mu^n_A(x^{-1}) < 0\}$. Therefore R is linear order. □

Theorem 3.17 *A bipolar fuzzy relation R is an equivalence relation if and only if (μ^p_A, μ^n_A) is a bipolar fuzzy subsemigroup of $(V, *)$ satisfying*

1. $\mu^p_A(1) = 1$ *and* $\mu^n_A(1) = -1$,
2. $(\mu^p_A(x), \mu^n_A(x)) = (\mu^p_A(x^{-1}), \mu^n_A(x^{-1}))$ *for all* $x \in V$.

Theorem 3.18 *G is a Hasse diagram if and only if for any collection $x_1, x_2, x_3, \ldots, x_n$ of vertices in V with $n \geq 2$ and $\mu^p_A(x_i) > 0$, $\mu^n_A(x_i) < 0$, for $i = 1, 2, 3, \ldots, n$, we have, $\mu^p_A(x_1x_2 \ldots x_n) = 0$ and $\mu^n_A(x_1x_2 \ldots x_n) = 0$.*

Proof Suppose G is a Hasse diagram and let $x_1, x_2, \ldots, x_n$ be vertices in V with $n \geq 2$ and $\mu_A^p(x_i) > 0, \mu_A^n(x_i) < 0$, for $i = 1, 2, \ldots, n$. Then it is obvious that $R(x_1x_2 \ldots x_{i-1}, x_1x_2 \ldots x_i) = (\mu_A^p(x_i), \mu_A^n(x_i))$, for $i = 1, 2, \ldots, n$, where $x_0 = 1$. Therefore $(1, x_1, x_1x_2, \ldots, x_1x_2 \ldots x_n)$ is a path from 1 to $x_1x_2 \ldots x_n$. Since G is a Hasse diagram, we have $R(1, x_1x_2 \ldots x_n) = 0$. This implies that $\mu_A^p(x_1x_2 \ldots x_n) = 0$ and $\mu_A^n(x_1x_2 \ldots x_n) = 0$.

Conversely, suppose that for any collection $x_1, x_2, \ldots x_n$ of vertices in V with $n \geq 2$ and $\mu_A^p(x_i) > 0, \mu_A^n(x_i) < 0$, for $i = 1, 2, \ldots, n$, we have, $\mu_A^p(x_1x_2 \ldots x_n) = 0$ and $\mu_A^n(x_1x_2 \ldots x_n) = 0$. Let $(x_0, x_1, x_2, \ldots x_n)$ be a path in G from x_0 to x_n with $n \geq 2$. Then $R(x_{i-1}, x_i) > 0$, for $i = 1, 2, \ldots, n$. Therefore $\mu_A^p(x_{i-1}^{-1}x_i) > 0, \mu_A^n(x_{i-1}^{-1}x_i) < 0$, for $i = 1, 2, \ldots, n$. Now consider the elements $x_0^{-1}x_1, x_1^{-1}x_2, \ldots, x_{n-1}^{-1}x_n$ in V. Then by assumption $\mu_A^p(x_0^{-1}x_1x_1^{-1}x_2 \ldots x_{n-1}^{-1}x_n) = 0$ and $\mu_A^n(x_0^{-1}x_1x_1^{-1}x_2 \ldots x_{n-1}^{-1}x_n) = 0$. That is, $\mu_A^p(x_0^{-1}x_n) = 0$ and $\mu_A^n(x_0^{-1}x_n) = 0$. Hence, $R(x_0, x_n) = 0$. Thus G is a Hasse diagram. □

Let $G = (V, R)$ be any bipolar fuzzy graph, then G is connected (weakly connected, semiconnected, locally connected, or quasi- connected) if and only if the induced fuzzy graph (V, R_0^+) is connected (weakly connected, semiconnected, locally connected, or quasi-connected).

Definition 3.27 Let $(S, *)$ be a semigroup and $A = (\mu_A^p, \mu_A^n)$ be a bipolar fuzzy subset of S. Then the subsemigroup generated by A is the meet of all bipolar fuzzy subsemigroups of S which contain A. It is denoted by $< A >$.

Lemma 3.1 *Let $(S, *)$ be a semigroup and $A = (\mu_A^p, \mu_A^n)$ be a bipolar fuzzy subset of S. Then bipolar fuzzy subset $< A >$ is precisely given by*

$$< \mu_A^p > (x) = \vee\{\mu_A^p(x_1) \wedge \mu_A^p(x_2) \wedge \ldots \wedge \mu_A^p(x_n) \mid x = x_1x_2 \ldots x_n \; with \; \mu_A^p(x_i) > 0 \; for \; i = 1, 2, \ldots, n\},$$

$$< \mu_A^n > (x) = \wedge\{\mu_A^n(x_1) \vee \mu_A^n(x_2) \vee \ldots \vee \mu_A^n(x_n) \mid x = x_1x_2 \ldots x_n \; with \; \mu_A^n(x_i) < 0 \; for \; i = 1, 2, \ldots, n\},$$

$x \in S$.

Proof Let $A' = (\acute{\mu}_A^p, \acute{\mu}_A^n)$ be a bipolar fuzzy subset of S defined by

$$\acute{\mu}_A^p(x) = \vee\{\mu_A^p(x_1) \wedge \mu_A^p(x_2) \wedge \ldots \wedge \mu_A^p(x_n) \mid x = x_1x_2 \ldots x_n \; with \; \mu_A^p(x_i) > 0 \; for \; i = 1, 2, \ldots, n\},$$

$$\acute{\mu}_A^n(x) = \wedge\{\mu_A^n(x_1) \vee \mu_A^n(x_2) \vee \ldots \vee \mu_A^n(x_n) \mid, x = x_1x_2 \ldots x_n with \mu_A^n(x_i) < 0 \; for \; i = 1, 2, \ldots, n\}$$

for any $x \in S$.

Let $x, y \in S$. If $\mu_A^p(x) = 0 \; or \; \mu_A^p(y) = 0$, then $\mu_A^p(x) \wedge \mu_A^p(y) = 0$ and $\mu_A^n(x) = 0 \; or \; \mu_A^n(y) = 0$, then $\mu_A^n(x) \vee \mu_A^n(y) = 0$. Therefore, $\acute{\mu}_B^p(xy) \geq \mu_A^p(x) \wedge \mu_A^p(y)$ and $\acute{\mu}_B^n(xy) \leq \mu_A^n(x) \vee \mu_A^n(y)$. Again , if $\mu_A^p(x) \neq 0, \mu_A^n(x) \neq 0$, then by definition of $\acute{\mu}_A^p(x)$ and $\acute{\mu}_A^n(x)$, we have $\acute{\mu}_B^p(xy) \geq \mu_A^p(x) \wedge \mu_A^p(y)$ and $\acute{\mu}_B^n(xy) \leq \mu_A^n(x) \vee \mu_A^n(y)$. Hence $(\acute{\mu}_A^p, \acute{\mu}_A^n)$ is a bipolar fuzzy subsemigroup of S containing (μ_A^p, μ_A^n). Now let L be any bipolar fuzzy subsemigroup of S containing (μ_A^p, μ_A^n). Then for any

$x \in S$ with $x = x_1x_2 \ldots x_n$ *with* $\mu_A^p(x_i) > 0$, $\mu_A^n(x_i) < 0$, for $i = 1, 2, \ldots, n$, we have $\mu_L^p(x_i) \geq \mu_L^p(x_1) \wedge \mu_L^p(x_2) \wedge \ldots \wedge \mu_L^p(x_n) \geq \mu_A^p(x_1) \wedge \mu_A^p(x_2) \wedge \ldots \wedge \mu_A^p(x_n)$ and $\mu_L^n(x_i) \geq \mu_L^n(x_1) \wedge \mu_L^n(x_2) \wedge \ldots \wedge \mu_L^n(x_n) \geq \mu_A^n(x_1) \wedge \mu_A^n(x_2) \wedge \ldots \wedge \mu_A^n(x_n)$. Thus $\mu_L^p(x) \geq \vee\{\mu_A^p(x_1) \wedge \mu_A^p(x_2) \wedge \ldots \wedge \mu_A^p(x_n) \mid x = x_1x_2 \ldots x_n \; with \; \mu_A^p(x_i) > 0 \; for \; i = 1, 2, \ldots, n\}$, $\mu_L^n(x) \leq \wedge\{\mu_A^n(x_1) \vee \mu_A^n(x_2) \vee \ldots \vee \mu_A^n(x_n) \mid x = x_1x_2 \ldots x_n \; with \; \mu_A^n(x_i) < 0 \; for \; i = 1, 2, \ldots, n\}$, for any $x \in S$. Hence $\mu_L^p(x) \geq \acute{\mu}_A^p(x)$, $\mu_L^n(x) \leq \acute{\mu}_A^n(x)$, for all $x \in S$. Thus $\acute{\mu}_A^p(x) \leq \mu_L^p(x)$, $\acute{\mu}_A^n(x) \geq \mu_A^p(x)$. Thus $A' = (\acute{\mu}_A^p, \acute{\mu}_A^n)$ is the meet of all bipolar fuzzy subsemigroup containing (μ_A^p, μ_A^n). □

Theorem 3.19 *Let $(S, *)$ be a semigroup and $A = (\mu_A^p, \mu_A^n)$ be a bipolar fuzzy subset of S. Then for any $\alpha \in [0, 1]$, $(< \mu_\alpha^p >, < \mu_\alpha^n >) = (< \mu^p >_\alpha, < \mu^n >_\alpha)$ and $(< (\mu^+)_\alpha^p >, < (\mu^+)_\alpha^n >) = (< \mu^p >_\alpha^+, < \mu^n >_\alpha^+)$, where $(< \mu_\alpha^p >, < \mu_\alpha^n >)$ denotes the subsemigroup generated by $(\mu_\alpha^p, \mu_\alpha^n)$ and $< (\mu^p, \mu^n) >$ denotes bipolar fuzzy subsemigroup generated by (μ^p, μ^n).*

Proof Let $x \in S$, then

$$\begin{aligned} x \in (< \mu^p >_\alpha, < \mu^n >_\alpha) &\Leftrightarrow \text{there exists } x_1, x_2, \ldots, x_n \; in \; (\mu_\alpha^p, \mu_\alpha^n) \text{ such that } x = x_1x_2 \ldots x_n \\ &\Leftrightarrow \text{there exists } x_1, x_2, \ldots, x_n \text{ in S such that } \mu^p(x_i) \geq \alpha, \mu^n(x_i) \leq \alpha, \\ &\quad \text{for all } i = 1, 2, \ldots, n \text{ and } x = x_1x_2 \ldots x_n \\ &\Leftrightarrow < \mu^p > (x) \geq \alpha \text{ and } < \mu^n > (x) \leq \alpha \\ &\Leftrightarrow x \in < \mu^p >_\alpha \text{ and } x \in < \mu^n >_\alpha . \end{aligned}$$

Therefore $(< \mu_\alpha^p >, < \mu_\alpha^n >) = (< \mu^p >_\alpha, < \mu^n >_\alpha)$.

Similarly, $(< (\mu^+)_\alpha^p >, < (\mu^+)_\alpha^n >) = (< \mu^p >_\alpha^+, < \mu^n >_\alpha^+)$. □

Remark 3.8 Let $(S, *)$ be a semigroup and $A = (\mu_A^p, \mu_A^n)$ be a bipolar fuzzy subset of S. Then by Theorem 3.19, we have $< supp(A) = A^+ >= supp < A >$.

Let G denote the Cayley bipolar fuzzy graphs $G = (V, R)$ induced by $(V, *, \mu^p, \mu^n)$. Then we have the following results.

Theorem 3.20 *Let A be any subset of V' and $G' = (V', R')$ be the Cayley graph induced by $(V', *, A)$. Then G' is connected if and only if $< A > \supseteq V - v_1$.*

Theorem 3.21 *G is connected if and only if $supp < A > \supseteq V - v_1$.*

Proof Indeed,

$$\begin{aligned} G \text{ is connected} &\Leftrightarrow (V, R_0^+) \text{is connected} \\ &\Leftrightarrow < A_0^+ > \supseteq V - v_1 \\ &\Leftrightarrow < supp(A) > \supseteq V - v_1 \\ &\Leftrightarrow supp < A > \supseteq V - v_1, \end{aligned}$$

as expected. □

Theorem 3.22 *Let A be a nonempty subset of a set V' and $G' = (V', R')$ be the Cayley graph induced by the triplet $(V', *, A)$. Then G' is weakly connected graph if and only if $< A \cup A^{-1} > \supseteq V - v_1$, where $A^{-1} = \{x^{-1} \mid x \in A\}$.*

Definition 3.28 Let $(S, *)$ be a group and A be a bipolar fuzzy subset of S. Then we define A^{-1} as bipolar fuzzy subset of S given by $A^{-1}(x) = A(x^{-1})$ for all $x \in S$.

Theorem 3.23 *G is weakly connected if and only if $supp\,(< A \cup A^{-1} >) \supseteq V - v_1$.*

Proof Indeed,

$$\begin{aligned} G \text{ is weakly connected} &\Leftrightarrow (V, R_0^+) \text{is weakly connected} \\ &\Leftrightarrow < A_0^+ \cup (A_0^+)^{-1} > \supseteq V - v_1 \\ &\Leftrightarrow < supp(A) \cup supp(A)^{-1} > \supseteq V - v_1 \\ &\Leftrightarrow supp < A \cup (A)^{-1} > \supseteq V - v_1 \\ &\Leftrightarrow supp < A \cup A^{-1} > \supseteq V - v_1, \end{aligned}$$

as expected. □

Theorem 3.24 *Let A be any subset of a set V' and $G' = (V', R')$ be the Cayley graph induced by the triplet $(V', *, A)$. Then G' is semiconnected if and only if $< A > \cup < A^{-1} > \supseteq V - v_1$, where $A^{-1} = \{x^{-1} \mid x \in A\}$.*

Theorem 3.25 *G is semiconnected if and only if $supp\,(< A > \cup < A^{-1} >) \supseteq V - v_1$.*

Proof Observe that

$$\begin{aligned} G \text{ is semiconnected} &\Leftrightarrow (V, R_0^+) \text{is semiconnected} \\ &\Leftrightarrow < A_0^+ > \cup < (A_0^+)^{-1} > \supseteq V - v_1 \\ &\Leftrightarrow < supp(A) > \cup < supp(A)^{-1} > \supseteq V - v_1 \\ &\Leftrightarrow supp < A > \cup < (A)^{-1} > \supseteq V - v_1 \\ &\Leftrightarrow supp(< A > \cup < A^{-1} >) \supseteq V - v_1, \end{aligned}$$

which completes the proof. □

Theorem 3.26 *Let $G' = (V', R')$ be the Cayley graph induced by the triplet $(V', *, A)$. Then G' is locally connected if and only if $< A > = < A^{-1} >$, where $A^{-1} = (x^{-1} \mid x \in A)$.*

Theorem 3.27 *Let G is locally connected if and only if $supp(< A >) = supp(< A^{-1} >)$.*

Proof Note that

$$\begin{aligned} G \text{ is locally connected} &\Leftrightarrow (V, R_0^+) \text{ is locally connected} \\ &\Leftrightarrow < A_0^+ >=< (A_0^+)^{-1} > \\ &\Leftrightarrow < supp(A) >=< supp(A)^{-1} > \\ &\Leftrightarrow supp < A >= supp < A^{-1} >, \end{aligned}$$

which completes the proof. □

Theorem 3.28 *Let $G' = (V', R')$ be the Cayley graph induced by the triplet $(V', *, A)$, where V' is finite. Then G' is quasi-connected if and only if it is connected.*

Theorem 3.29 *A finite Cayley bipolar fuzzy graph G is quasi-connected if and only if it is connected.*

Proof Indeed, G is quasi-connected $\Leftrightarrow (V, R_0^+)$ is Quasi-connected $\Leftrightarrow (V, R_0^+)$ is connected $\Leftrightarrow G$ is connected. □

Definition 3.29 The μ^p- **strength** of a path $P = v_1, v_2, \ldots, v_n$ is defined as $\min(\mu_2^p(v_i, v_j))$ for all i and j and is denoted by S_μ^p. The μ^n- **strength** of a path $P = v_1, v_2, \ldots, v_n$ is defined as $\max(\mu_2^n(v_i, v_j))$ for all i and j and is denoted by S_μ^n.

Definition 3.30 Let $G = (V, \mu^p, \mu^n)$ be a bipolar fuzzy graph, then

1. G is called α**-connected** if for every pair of vertices $x, y \in G$, there is a path P from x to y such that strength $(P) \geq \alpha$,
2. G is called **weakly** α**-connected** if a bipolar fuzzy graph $(V, R \vee R^{-1})$ is α-connected,
3. G is called **semi** α**-connected** if for every $x, y \in V$, there is a path of strength greater than or equal to α from x to y or from y to x in G,
4. G is called **locally** α**-connected** if for every pair of vertices x and y, there is a path P of strength greater than or equal to α from x to y whenever there is a path P' of strength greater than or equal to α from y to x,
5. G is called **quasi** α**-connected** if for every pair $x, y \in V$, there is some $z \in V$ such that there is directed path from z to x of strength greater than or equal to α and there is a directed path from z to y of strength greater than or equal to α.

Remark 3.9 Let $G = (V, R)$ be any bipolar fuzzy graph, then G is α-connected (weakly α-connected, α-semiconnected, locally α-connected, or quasi- α-connected) if and only if the induced fuzzy graph (V, R_0^+) is connected (weakly connected, semiconnected, locally connected, or quasi-connected).

Theorem 3.30 *G is α-connected if and only if $< A >_\alpha \supseteq V - v_1$.*

Proof Indeed, G is connected $\Leftrightarrow (V, R_\alpha)$ is connected $\Leftrightarrow < A_\alpha > \supseteq V - v_1 \Leftrightarrow < A >_\alpha \supseteq V - v_1$.

Theorem 3.31 *G is weakly α-connected if and only if $< A \cup A^{-1} >_\alpha \supseteq V - v_1$.*

Proof G is weakly connected $\Leftrightarrow (V, R_\alpha)$ is weakly connected $\Leftrightarrow < A_\alpha \cup (A_\alpha)^{-1} > \supseteq V - v_1 \Leftrightarrow < (A \cup A^{-1})_\alpha > \supseteq V - v_1 \Leftrightarrow < A \cup (A)^{-1} >_\alpha \supseteq V - v_1$.

Theorem 3.32 *G is semi α connected if and only if $(< A >_\alpha \cup < A^{-1} >_\alpha) \supseteq V - v_1$.*

Proof G is α-semiconnected $\Leftrightarrow (V, R_0^+)$ is α-semiconnected $\Leftrightarrow < A_\alpha > \cup < A_\alpha^{-1} > \supseteq V - v_1 \Leftrightarrow < A >_\alpha \cup < A^{-1} >_\alpha \supseteq V - v_1$.

Theorem 3.33 *Let G is locally α-connected if and only if $< A >_\alpha = < A_\alpha^{-1} >$.*

Proof G is locally α-connected $\Leftrightarrow (V, R_\alpha)$ is locally connected $\Leftrightarrow < A_\alpha > = < A_\alpha^{-1} > \Leftrightarrow < A >_\alpha = < A^{-1} >_\alpha$. □

Theorem 3.34 *A finite Cayley bipolar fuzzy graph G is quasi α-connected if and only if it is α-connected.*

Proof G is quasi α-connected $\Leftrightarrow (V, R_\alpha^+)$ is quasi-connected $\Leftrightarrow (V, R_\alpha^+)$ is connected $\Leftrightarrow G$ is α-connected. □

3.5 Conclusions

Bipolar fuzzy graphs can be categorized on the basis of the number of vertices, number of edges, connectivity, distance, degree, and their overall structure. Different classifications of bipolar fuzzy graphs play an important role in modeling graphical structures under certain conditions of regularity, irregularity, transitivity, and connectedness. In this chapter, we have discussed, in detail, the concept of irregularity in bipolar fuzzy graphs and extended this notion, with more strong constraints, to neighborly irregular, totally irregular, highly irregular, and neighborly totally irregular bipolar fuzzy graphs. We have discussed isomorphism properties of regular, m-totally regular, and different kinds of irregular bipolar fuzzy graphs. We have presented the conditions under which a regular bipolar fuzzy graph and a totally regular bipolar fuzzy graph are equivalent. We have described the idea of bipolar fuzzy line graph and established the characterizations under which a bipolar fuzzy graph is isomorphic to its bipolar fuzzy line graph. We have discussed the notions of regularity, vertex transitivity, and connectedness in Cayley bipolar fuzzy graphs using various algebraic structures.

Exercises 3

1. Give an example of a regular bipolar fuzzy graph G such that $G_{(\alpha,\beta)}$ is not a regular graph, for any $(\alpha, \beta) \in [0, 1] \times [-1, 0]$.
2. Let $G = (A, B)$ be a regular bipolar fuzzy graph, then determine whether or not G^c is a regular bipolar fuzzy graph.
3. Let $G = (A, B)$ be an irregular bipolar fuzzy graph, then determine whether or not G^c is an irregular bipolar fuzzy graph.
4. Let $G = (A, B)$ be an (r^p, r^n)-regular bipolar fuzzy graph with k number of vertices then prove that $S(G) = \frac{k}{2}(r^p, r^n)$.
5. Let $G = (A, B)$ be an (m^p, m^n)-totally regular bipolar fuzzy graph with k number of vertices then prove that $2S(G) + O(G) = (m^p, m^n)k$.
6. Let $G = (A, B)$ be an $r = (r^p, r^n)$-regular and $m = (m^p, m^n)$-totally regular bipolar fuzzy graph with k number of vertices then prove that $O(G) = k(m^p - r^p, m^n - r^n)$.
7. Let $G = (A, B)$ be a bipolar fuzzy graph such that G^* is an odd cycle. Prove that G is regular if and only if B is a constant function.
8. Prove that every complete bipolar fuzzy graph is a totally regular bipolar fuzzy graph.
9. Give an example to show that a highly irregular and neighborly irregular bipolar fuzzy graph G need not have all the vertices of distinct neighborhood degrees.
10. Give examples of two regular bipolar fuzzy graphs G and H such that the strong product $G \boxtimes H$ is not a regular bipolar fuzzy graph.
11. Let xy be an edge of a connected bipolar fuzzy graph G. Show that $G - xy$ is connected if and only if xy is an edge of a bipolar fuzzy cycle in G.

References

1. Akram, M.: Bipolar fuzzy graphs with applications. Knowl.-Based Syst. **39**, 1–8 (2013)
2. Akram, M., Dudek, W.A.: Regular bipolar fuzzy graphs. Neural Comput. Appl. **21**(1), 197–205 (2012)
3. Akram, M., Dudek, W.A., Sarwar, S.: Properties of bipolar fuzzy hypergraphs. Ital. J. Pure Appl. Math. **31**, 426–458 (2013)
4. Akram, M., Karunambigai, M.G.: Metric in bipolar fuzzy graphs. World Appl. Sci. J. **14**, 1920–1927 (2011)
5. Akram, M., Li, S.-G., Shum, K.P.: Antipodal bipolar fuzzy graphs. Ital. J. Pure Appl. Math. **31**, 97–110 (2013)
6. Akram, M., Yousaf, M.M., Dudek, W.A.: Self centered interval-valued fuzzy graphs. Afr. Math. **26**(5–6), 887–898 (2015)
7. Alavi, Y., Boals, A.J., Chartand, G., Oellermann, O.R., Erdos, P.: $k-$path irregular graphs. Congr. Numer. **65**, 201–202 (1988)
8. Alavi, Y., Chung, F.R.K., Erdos, P., Graham, R.L., Oellermann, O.R.: Highly irregular graphs. J. Graph Theory **11**(2), 235–249 (1987)
9. Alshehro, N.O., Akram, M.: Cayley bipolar fuzzy graphs. Sci. World J. **2013**, Article ID 156786 (2013)

10. Aravamudhan, R., Rajendran, B.: On antipodal graphs. Discret. Math. **49**, 193–195 (1984)
11. Bhutani, K.R., Battou, A.: On M-strong fuzzy graphs. Inf. Sci. **155**(1–2), 103–109 (2003)
12. Nagoorgani, A., Latha, S.R.: Isomorphism on irregular fuzzy graphs. Int. J. Math Sci. Eng. Appl. **6**(3), 193–208 (2012)
13. Nagoorgani, A., Latha, S.R.: On irregular fuzzy graphs. Appl. Math. Sci. **6**(11), 517–523 (2012)
14. Nagoorgani, A., Malarvizhi, J.: On antipodal fuzzy graph. Appl. Math. Sci. **4**(43), 2145–2155 (2010)
15. Nagoorgani, A., Radha, K.: On regular fuzzy graphs. J. Phys. Sci. **12**, 33–44 (2008)
16. Rosenfeld, A.: Fuzzy graphs. In: Zadeh, L.A., Fu, K.S., Shimura, M. (eds.) Fuzzy Sets and their Applications, pp. 77–95. Academic Press, New York, USA (1975)
17. Samanta, S., Pal, M.: Irregular bipolar fuzzy graphs. Int. J. Appl. Fuzzy Sets **2**, 91–102 (2012)
18. Samanta, S., Pal, M.: Some more results on bipolar fuzzy sets and bipolar fuzzy intersection graphs. J. Fuzzy Math. **22**(2), 253–62 (2014)
19. Smith, D.H.: Primitive and Imprimitive graphs. Q. J. Math. **22**(4), 551–557 (1971)
20. Zhang, W.-R.: Bipolar fuzzy sets and relations: a computational framework for cognitive modeling and multiagent decision analysis. In: Proceedings of IEEE Conference. pp. 305–309 (1994)
21. Zhang, W.-R., Zhang, L.: YinYang bipolar logic and bipolar fuzzy logic. Inf. Sci **165**(3–4), 265–287 (2004)
22. Zhang, W.-R.: (YinYang) Bipolar fuzzy sets. In: IEEE International Conference on Fuzzy Systems, pp. 835–840 (1998)
23. Zhang, W.-R.: Equilibrium relations and bipolar cognitive mapping for online analytical processing with applications in international relations and strategic decision support. IEEE Trans. Syst., Man, Cybern., Part B (Cybern.) **33**(2), 295–307 (2003)

Chapter 4
Bipolar Fuzzy Competition Graphs

In this chapter, we discuss the concept of bipolar fuzzy competition graphs and present several notions concerning bipolar fuzzy out neighborhoods, bipolar fuzzy in neighborhoods, bipolar fuzzy open neighborhood graphs, bipolar fuzzy closed neighborhood graphs, bipolar fuzzy $\boldsymbol{k}$−competition graphs, and underlying bipolar fuzzy graphs. We describe various methods for the construction of bipolar fuzzy competition graphs of certain products of bipolar fuzzy digraphs. Using various constraints, we study the relations of bipolar fuzzy $[\boldsymbol{k}]$−competition graphs, bipolar fuzzy $(\boldsymbol{k})$−competition graphs, and underlying bipolar fuzzy graphs. We elaborate certain algorithms to compute the strength of competition with a number of real-world applications in different fields including food webs, business marketing, politics, wireless communication networks, and social networking. We also study different types of competition graphs under complex bipolar environment. We illustrate the concepts of bipolar fuzzy common enemy graph, bipolar fuzzy competition common enemy graph, bipolar fuzzy niche graph, bipolar influence graph, bipolar fuzzy conflict graph, and bipolar fuzzy confusion graph using these applications. The work in this chapter is from [4, 15, 16].

4.1 Introduction

Digraphs are the important mathematical structures to represent point-to- point interconnections for distributed and parallel systems. A digraph is a generalized case of a graph, whose edges have directions. In a digraph, a directed edge from x to y shows that the object can travel from point x to point y but not from y to x. Competition graphs arose in the work of Cohen [7] in connection with an application in ecosystems. Based on this analog, Cohen defined the notion of a competition graph

M. Akram et al., *Graphs for the Analysis of Bipolar Fuzzy Information*, Studies in Fuzziness and Soft Computing 401,
https://doi.org/10.1007/978-981-15-8756-6_4

to represent the competition between species in a food web. Competition graphs have many applications including modeling of economic systems, communication over a noisy channel, phylogenetic tree reconstruction, and channel assignment. After the primary motivation of ecological application of competition between species, a lot of work has been done on competition graphs. These representations are crisp graphs, which do not describe all the competitions of real-world problems. In a competition graph, it is assumed that vertices and edges are defined clearly. But in some cases, it is observed that vertices and edges are not defined precisely. For instance, over a noisy channel, a communication channel may have a different network range, radio frequency, bandwidth, and latency. To describe the competition in politics, a politician may have different positions according to leadership quality, public voting, education, and political power. In a social network, the influence rate of different people may be different with respect to socialism, proactiveness, and trading relationship. In a food web, species may be of different types including strong, weak, vegetarian, nonvegetarian, and preys may be energetic, harmful, and digestive.

The predator–prey relations can not only be represented by competition graphs but also by the dependence of a specie onto a prey as compared to other species. The terms tasty, digestive, harmful, etc., have no precise meanings and are fuzzy in nature. Fuzzy competition graphs, fuzzy $k-$competition, and fuzzy $p-$competition graphs were introduced by Samanta and Pal [13]. Samanta et al. [12] studied various properties of $m-$step fuzzy competition graphs. Sahoo and Pal [14] studied intuitionistic fuzzy competition graphs, intuitionistic fuzzy $p-$competition graphs, intuitionistic fuzzy closed neighborhood graphs and applied this idea to ecosystems. Pramanik et al. [10] investigated interesting properties of fuzzy tolerance graphs and fuzzy $\phi-$tolerance competition graphs for particular cases of ϕ (minimum, maximum, and sum). But all the predator–prey relations can not only be represented by fuzzy competition graphs. For example, a specie is at the same time strong and weak, a prey may be energetic and harmful. Similarly harmony and noise, eligibility and legal disqualification, friend and enemy are bipolar information, which are fuzzy in nature. This idea motivates the necessity of bipolar fuzzy competition graphs. Akram and Dudek [1] discussed certain properties of regular bipolar fuzzy graphs and bipolar fuzzy line graphs. Akram and Dudek, in collaboration with other researchers discussed self-centered interval-valued fuzzy graphs [3]. Alshehri and Akram [6] initiated the concept of bipolar fuzzy competition graphs, studied their application in economic markets, and identified the subscribers or facilitators from a company. Akram and Sarwar studied decision support systems in $m-$polar fuzzy competition graphs [4], bipolar fuzzy competition graphs of certain products of bipolar fuzzy digraphs, bipolar fuzzy $k-$competition graphs, underlying bipolar fuzzy graphs, bipolar fuzzy open neighborhood graphs, and bipolar fuzzy closed neighborhood graphs in [16], designed and implemented algorithms for computing the strength of competition in bipolar fuzzy graphs [15]. For further terminologies and studies on complex fuzzy graphs, readers are referred to [2, 5, 8, 9, 11, 17–19].

4.2 Bipolar Fuzzy Competition Graphs

Let $\vec{G} = (X, \vec{E})$ be a digraph corresponding to a food web in which vertices represent the species. There is a directed edge $\vec{yz}$ between two species y any z if y preys on z. A **competition graph** $C(\vec{G}) = (X, E)$ of a digraph $\vec{G} = (X, \vec{E})$ is an undirected graph with the same vertex set X and there is an edge between two vertices y and t if there exists $z \in X$ such that $\vec{yz}, \vec{tz} \in \vec{E}$, i.e., y and t has a common prey

Definition 4.1 Let $\vec{G} = (A, \vec{B})$ be a bipolar fuzzy graph on a nonempty set X. A **bipolar fuzzy out neighborhood** of a vertex $x \in X$ in a bipolar fuzzy digraph $\vec{G}$ is a bipolar fuzzy set $\mathcal{N}^+(x) = (X_x^+, \mu^p_{\mathcal{N}^+(x)}, \mu^n_{\mathcal{N}^+(x)})$, where $X_x^+ = \{y \in X \mid \vec{B}(xy) \neq (0, 0)\}$ and $\mu^p_{\mathcal{N}^+(x)} : X_x^+ \to [0, 1]$ and $\mu^n_{\mathcal{N}^+(x)} : X_x^+ \to [-1, 0]$ are defined as $\mu^p_{\mathcal{N}^+(x)}(y) = \mu^p_{\vec{B}}(xy)$ and $\mu^n_{\mathcal{N}^+(x)}(y) = \mu^n_{\vec{B}}(xy)$.

A **bipolar fuzzy in neighborhood** of a vertex $x \in X$ in a bipolar fuzzy digraph $\vec{G}$ is a bipolar fuzzy set $\mathcal{N}^-(x) = (X_x^-, \mu^p_{\mathcal{N}^-(x)}, \mu^n_{\mathcal{N}^-(x)})$, where $X_x^- = \{y \in X \mid \vec{B}(yx) \neq (0, 0)\}$ and $\mu^p_{\mathcal{N}^-(x)} : X_x^- \to [0, 1]$ and $\mu^n_{\mathcal{N}^-(x)} : X_x^- \to [-1, 0]$ are defined as $\mu^p_{\mathcal{N}^-(x)}(y) = \mu^p_{\vec{B}}(yx)$ and $\mu^n_{\mathcal{N}^-(x)}(y) = \mu^n_{\vec{B}}(yx)$.

Definition 4.2 Let $B = (\mu^p_B, \mu^n_B)$ be a bipolar fuzzy set on a nonempty set X. The **height** of B is defined as $h(B) = \max\{\mu^p_B(x) \mid x \in X\}$. The **depth** of $B = (\mu^p_B, \mu^n_B)$ is defined as $d(B) = \min\{\mu^n_B(x) \mid x \in X\}$.

Definition 4.3 Let $\vec{G} = (A, \vec{B})$ be a bipolar fuzzy digraph on a nonempty set X. A **bipolar fuzzy competition graph** of a bipolar fuzzy digraph $\vec{G}$ is an undirected bipolar fuzzy graph $\mathcal{C}(\vec{G}) = (A, R)$, which has the same vertex set as in $\vec{G}$ and there is an edge between two vertices x and y, $x, y \in X$, if $\mathcal{N}^+(x) \cap \mathcal{N}^+(y)$ is nonempty, i.e., x and y prey on at least one common specie. The positive membership and negative membership values of the edge xy are defined as

$$\mu^p_R(xy) = (\mu^p_A(x) \wedge \mu^p_A(y))h(\mathcal{N}^+(x) \cap \mathcal{N}^+(y)),$$

$$\mu^n_R(xy) = (\mu^n_A(x) \vee \mu^n_A(y))h(\mathcal{N}^+(x) \cap \mathcal{N}^+(y)).$$

Example 4.1 Let $\vec{G} = (A, \vec{B})$ be a bipolar fuzzy digraph on $X = \{a, b, c, d, e, f, g\}$ as shown in Fig. 4.1. The bipolar fuzzy out neighborhoods of the vertices are given in Table 4.1.

The construction of bipolar fuzzy competition graph $\mathcal{C}(\vec{G})$ from $\vec{G}$ is given as follows: Consider the vertices a_1 and a_7 as

$$\mathcal{N}^+(a_1) \cap \mathcal{N}^+(a_7) = \{(a_4, 0.2, -0.3)\},$$

$$\mu^p_R(a_1a_7) = (\mu^p_A(a_1) \wedge \mu^p_A(a_7))h(\mathcal{N}^+(a_1) \cap \mathcal{N}^+(a_7)) = 0.04,$$

$$\mu^n_R(a_1a_7) = (\mu^n_A(a_1) \vee \mu^n_A(a_7))h(\mathcal{N}^+(a_1) \cap \mathcal{N}^+(a_7)) = -0.08.$$

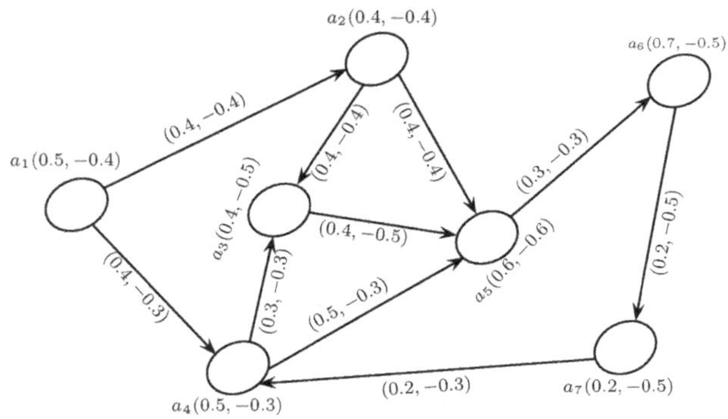

Fig. 4.1 Bipolar fuzzy digraph

Table 4.1 Bipolar fuzzy out neighborhoods of vertices

x	$\mathcal{N}^+(x)$	x	$\mathcal{N}^+(x)$
a_1	$\{(a_2, 0.4, -0.4), (a_4, 0.4, -0.3)\}$	a_3	$\{(a_5, 0.4, -0.5)\}$
a_2	$\{(a_3, 0.4, -0.4), (a_5, 0.4, -0.4)\}$	a_5	$\{(a_6, 0.3, -0.3)\}$
a_4	$\{(a_5, 0.5, -0.3), (a_3, 0.4, -0.5)\}$	a_6	$\{(a_7, 0.2, -0.5)\}$
a_7	$\{(a_4, 0.2, -0.3)\}$		

Fig. 4.2 Bipolar fuzzy competition graph

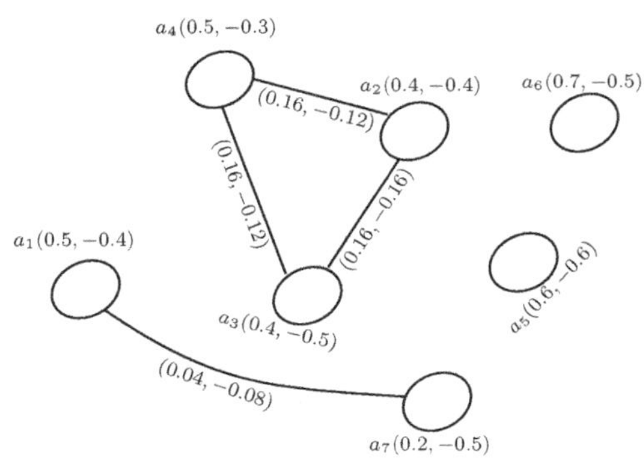

Therefore, $R(a_1a_7) = (0.04, -0.08)$. Similarly, the membership values of other edges can be calculated. The bipolar fuzzy competition graph of $\vec{G}$ is given in Fig. 4.2.

Example 4.2 Let $\vec{G} = (A, \vec{B})$ be a bipolar fuzzy digraph on $X = \{a, b, c, d, s, f, g\}$ with $A = \{(a, 0.3, -0.4), (b, 0.5, -0.6), (c, 0.4, -0.7), (d, 0.6, -0.5), (e, 0.8, -0.4), (f, 0.7, -0.6), (g, 0.7, -0.8)\}$. The membership values of the directed edges are represented by the adjacency matrix in Table 4.2. The bipolar fuzzy digraph is shown in Fig. 4.3.

Table 4.2 Adjacency matrix of bipolar fuzzy relation $\vec{B}$

$x \in X$	a	b	c	d	e	f	g
a	$(0, 0)$	$(0.3, -0.4)$	$(0.3, -0.4)$	$(0, 0)$	$(0.3, -0.4)$	$(0, 0)$	$(0, 0)$
b	$(0, 0)$	$(0, 0)$	$(0, 0)$	$(0, 0)$	$(0, 0)$	$(0.5, -0.5)$	$(0, 0)$
c	$(0, 0)$	$(0, 0)$	$(0, 0)$	$(0.4, -0.5)$	$(0, 0)$	$(0.4, -0.6)$	$(0.4, -0.6)$
d	$(0, 0)$	$(0, 0)$	$(0, 0)$	$(0, 0)$	$(0.5, -0.4)$	$(0, 0)$	$(0, 0)$
e	$(0, 0)$	$(0, 0)$	$(0, 0)$	$(0, 0)$	$(0, 0)$	$(0.7, -0.4)$	$(0.7, -0.4)$
f	$(0, 0)$	$(0, 0)$	$(0, 0)$	$(0, 0)$	$(0, 0)$	$(0, 0)$	$(0, 0)$
g	$(0, 0)$	$(0, 0)$	$(0, 0)$	$(0, 0)$	$(0, 0)$	$(0, 0)$	$(0, 0)$

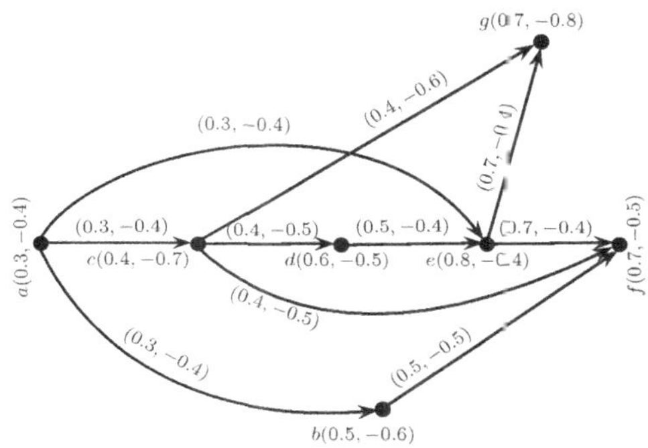

Fig. 4.3 Bipolar fuzzy digraph

Table 4.3 Bipolar fuzzy out neighborhoods of vertices

$u \in X$	$\mathcal{N}^+(u)$
a	$\{(b, 0.3, -0.4), (c, 0.3, -0.4), (e, 0.3, -0.4)\}$
b	$\{(f, 0.5, -0.5)\}$
c	$\{(d, 0.4, -0.5), (f, 0.4, -0.5), (g, 0.4, -0.6)\}$
d	$\{(e, 0.5, -0.4)\}$
e	$\{(f, 0.7, -0.4), (g, 0.7, -0.4)\}$
f	$\emptyset$
g	$\emptyset$

The bipolar fuzzy out neighborhoods of the vertices are given in Table 4.3.

The bipolar fuzzy competition graph of bipolar fuzzy digraph, in Fig. 4.3 is shown in Fig. 4.4.

The method for the construction of a bipolar fuzzy competition graph is given in Algorithm 4.2.1.

Algorithm 4.2.1 Construction of bipolar fuzzy competition graph

1. Competition(X, C, $M = [x_{ij}]_{n\times n}$)
2. Begin
3. **do** i from $1 \to n$
4. Take $\mathcal{N}^+(x_i) = \emptyset$
5. **do** j from $1 \to n$
6. **if**$(\vec{B}(x_i x_j) \neq (0,0))$**then**
7. $(x_j, \mu^p_{\vec{B}}(x_i x_j), \mu^n_{\vec{B}}\vec{D}(x_i x_j)) \in \mathcal{N}^+(x_i)$
8. **else**
9. $(x_j, \mu^p_{\vec{B}}(x_i x_j), \mu^n_{\vec{B}}\vec{D}(x_i x_j)) \notin \mathcal{N}^+(x_i)$
10. **end if**
11. **end do**
12. **end do**
13. **do** i from $1 \to n$
14. **do** j from $i+1 \to n$
15. **if**$(\mathcal{N}^+(x_i) \cap \mathcal{N}^+(x_j) \neq \emptyset)$**then**
16. $R(x_i x_j) = \inf\{A(x_i), A(x_j)\} \times h(\mathcal{N}^+(x_i) \cap \mathcal{N}^+(x_j))$
17. **else**
18. $R(x_i x_j) = (0,0)$
19. **end if**
20. **print***, $R(x_i x_j)$
21. **end do**
22. **end do**
23. End

Description: Line 1 passes the input of bipolar fuzzy set C and adjacency matrix $M = [x_{ij}]_{n\times n}$ of a bipolar fuzzy digraph $\vec{G} = (A, \vec{B})$ on n vertices $x_1, x_2, \ldots, x_n$. Lines 3–12 calculate bipolar fuzzy out neighborhood of each vertex. Lines 13–22 calculate and print the adjacency matrix R of bipolar fuzzy competition graph of $\vec{G}$.

Time Complexity: Line 1 corresponds to the input of the algorithm, its time complexity is O(1). The do loop on line 3 runs n times, therefore its complexity is O(n).

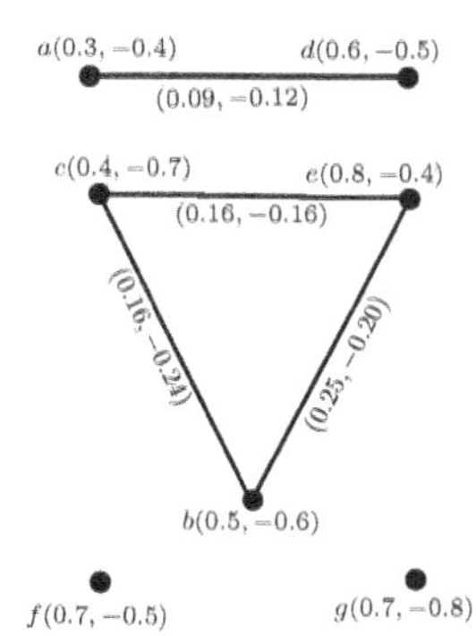

Fig. 4.4 Bipolar fuzzy competition graph

The nested loop on line 5 runs n^2 times, its complexity is $O(n^2)$. Ignoring the constant, the if conditional on line 6 has complexity $O(n^2)$. The complexity of lines 10, 11, and 12 is $O(n^2)$, $O(n^2)$ and $O(n)$, respectively. Similarly, the time complexity of line 13 is $O(n)$, lines 14 − −21 is $O(n(n-1))$, line 22 is $O(n)$. The net time complexity of the algorithm is $O(n^2)$.

Proof of Correctness: The loop initializes by taking the value $i = 1$ of do loop which is always true, i.e., the loop runs for the first iteration. As the elements in the adjacency matrix are always zero or nonzero-ordered pairs, therefore for any ith iteration of do loop on line 3, the do loop on line 4 runs n times. If the membership value of x_{ij} is positive, then line 7 is executed otherwise line 9 is executed. For every ith iteration of the loop on line 3, this process continues n times and then increments i for the next iteration maintaining the loop throughout the algorithm. For $i = n$, the loop calculates the bipolar fuzzy out neighborhood of every vertex and terminates successfully at line 12. Similarly, the loops on lines 13 and 14 maintain and terminate successfully.

Theorem 4.1 *Let G be a bipolar fuzzy graph then adding a sufficient number of isolated vertices to G produces a bipolar fuzzy competition graph of some bipolar fuzzy digraph.*

Proof Let $G = (A, R)$ be a bipolar fuzzy graph on nonempty set X, where $A = (\mu_A^p, \mu_A^n)$ is a bipolar fuzzy set on the set of vertices X and $R = (\mu_R^p, \mu_R^n)$ is a bipolar fuzzy relation in X. Construct the bipolar fuzzy digraph $\vec{G} = (A, \vec{B})$ as follows: Let $x, y \in X$ be any two vertices of G such that $R(xy) \neq (0, 0)$. Add a vertex β_{xy}, remove the edge xy, and draw directed edges from x and y to β_{xy} such that

$$\mu_A^p(\beta_{xy}) = \mu_A^p(x) \wedge \mu_A^p(y), \quad \mu_{\vec{B}}^p(x\beta_{xy}) = \mu_{\vec{B}}^p(y\beta_{xy}) = \frac{\mu_R^p(xy)}{\mu_A^p(x) \wedge \mu_A^p(y)},$$

$$\mu_A^n(\beta_{xy}) = \mu_A^n(x) \vee \mu_A^n(y), \quad \mu_{\vec{B}}^n(x\beta_{xy}) = \mu_{\vec{B}}^n(y\beta_{xy}) = -\frac{\mu_R^n(xy)}{\mu_A^n(x) \vee \mu_A^n(y)}.$$

Continuing this process, we obtain a bipolar fuzzy digraph $\vec{G}$ such that $\mathcal{C}(\vec{G}) = G \cup I$, where I is the bipolar fuzzy set of isolated vertices added to G. □

The method for the construction of bipolar fuzzy competition graph of the Cartesian product of bipolar fuzzy digraphs is elaborated in Theorem 4.2.

Theorem 4.2 *Let $\mathcal{C}(\vec{G}_1) = (A_1, R_1)$ and $\mathcal{C}(\vec{G}_2) = (A_2, R_2)$ be two bipolar fuzzy competition graphs of bipolar fuzzy digraphs $\vec{G}_1 = (A_1, \vec{B}_1)$ and $\vec{G}_2 = (A_2, \vec{B}_2)$, respectively. Then*

$$\mathcal{C}(\vec{G}_1 \Box \vec{G}_2) = G_{\mathcal{C}(\vec{G}_1)^* \Box \mathcal{C}(\vec{G}_2)^*} \cup G^{\Box},$$

where $G_{\mathcal{C}(\vec{G}_1)^* \Box \mathcal{C}(\vec{G}_2)^*}$ is a bipolar fuzzy graph on the crisp graph $(X_1 \times X_2, E_{\mathcal{C}(\vec{G}_1)^*} \Box E_{\mathcal{C}(\vec{G}_2)^*})$, $\mathcal{C}(\vec{G}_1)^*$ and $\mathcal{C}(\vec{G}_2)^*$ are the crisp competition graphs of $\vec{G}_1$ and $\vec{G}_2$, respectively. $G^{\Box}$ is a bipolar fuzzy graph on $(X_1 \times X_2, E^{\Box})$ such that

(1) $E^{\square} = \{(a_1, a_2)(b_1, b_2) \mid b_1 \in \mathcal{N}^-(a_1)^*, b_2 \in \mathcal{N}^+(a_2)^*\}$,
$E_{\mathcal{C}(\vec{G}_1)^*} \square E_{\mathcal{C}(\vec{G}_2)^*} =$
$\{(a_1, a_2)(a_1, b_2) \mid a_1 \in X_1, a_2b_2 \in E_{\mathcal{C}(\vec{G}_2)^*}\} \cup \{(a_1, a_2)(b_1, a_2) \mid a_2 \in X_2, a_1b_1 \in E_{\mathcal{C}(\vec{G}_1)^*}\}$.

(2) $\mu^p_{A_1 \square A_2}(a_1, a_2) = \mu^p_{A_1}(a_1) \wedge \mu^p_{A_2}(a_2)$, $\mu^n_{A_1 \square A_2}(a_1, a_2) = \mu^n_{A_1}(a_1) \vee \mu^n_{A_2}(a_2)$, $(a_1, a_2) \in X_1 \times X_2$.

(3) $\mu^p_R((a_1, a_2)(a_1, b_2)) = [\mu^p_{A_1}(a_1) \wedge \mu^p_{A_2}(a_2) \wedge \mu^p_{A_2}(b_2)] \times \vee_{x_2}[\mu^p_{A_1}(a_1) \wedge \mu^p_{\vec{B}_2}(a_2x_2) \wedge \mu^p_{\vec{B}_2}(b_2x_2)]$,
$(a_1, a_2)(b_1, a_2) \in E_{\mathcal{C}(\vec{G}_1)^*} \square E_{\mathcal{C}(\vec{G}_2)^*}$, $x_2 \in (\mathcal{N}^+(a_2) \cap \mathcal{N}^+(b_2))^*$,

(4) $\mu^n_R((a_1, a_2)(a_1, b_2)) = [\mu^n_{A_1}(a_1) \vee \mu^n_{A_2}(a_2) \vee \mu^n_{A_2}(b_2)] \times \vee_{x_2}[\mu^p_{A_1}(a_1) \wedge \mu^p_{\vec{B}_2}(a_2x_2) \wedge \mu^p_{\vec{B}_2}(b_2x_2)]$,
$(a_1, a_2)(b_1, a_2) \in E_{\mathcal{C}(\vec{G}_1)^*} \square E_{\mathcal{C}(\vec{G}_2)^*}$, $x_2 \in (\mathcal{N}^+(a_2) \cap \mathcal{N}^+(b_2))^*$,

(5) $\mu^p_R((a_1, a_2)(b_1, a_2)) = [\mu^p_{A_1}(a_1) \wedge \mu^p_{A_1}(b_1) \wedge \mu^p_{A_2}(a_2)] \times \vee_{x_1}[\mu^p_{A_2}(a_2) \wedge \mu^p_{\vec{B}_1}(a_1x_1) \wedge \mu^p_{\vec{B}_1}(b_1x_1)]$,
$(a_1, a_2)(b_1, a_2) \in E_{\mathcal{C}(\vec{G}_1)^*} \square E_{\mathcal{C}(\vec{G}_2)^*}$, $x_1 \in (\mathcal{N}^+(a_1) \cap \mathcal{N}^+(b_1))^*$,

(6) $\mu^n_R((a_1, a_2)(b_1, a_2)) = [\mu^n_{A_1}(a_1) \vee \mu^p_{A_1}(b_1) \vee \mu^n_{A_2}(a_2)] \times \vee_{x_1}[\mu^p_{A_2}(a_2) \wedge \mu^p_{\vec{B}_1}(a_1x_1) \wedge \mu^p_{\vec{B}_1}(b_1x_1)]$,
$(a_1, a_2)(b_1, a_2) \in E_{\mathcal{C}(\vec{G}_1)^*} \square E_{\mathcal{C}(\vec{G}_2)^*}$, $x_1 \in (\mathcal{N}^+(a_1) \cap \mathcal{N}^+(b_1))^*$,

(7) $\mu^p_R((a_1, a_2)(b_1, b_2)) =$
$[\mu^p_{A_1}(a_1) \wedge \mu^p_{A_1}(b_1) \wedge \mu^p_{A_2}(a_2) \wedge \mu^p_{A_2}(b_2)] \times [\mu^p_{A_1}(a_1) \wedge \mu^p_{\vec{B}_1}(b_1a_1) \wedge \mu^p_{A_2}(b_2) \wedge \mu^p_{\vec{B}_2}(a_2b_2)]$,
$(a_1, b_1)(a_2, b_2) \in E^{\square}$,

(8) $\mu^n_R((a_1, a_2)(b_1, b_2)) =$
$[\mu^n_{A_1}(a_1) \vee \mu^n_{A_1}(b_1) \vee \mu^n_{A_2}(a_2) \vee \mu^n_{A_2}(b_2)] \times [\mu^p_{A_1}(a_1) \wedge \mu^p_{\vec{B}_1}(b_1a_1) \wedge \mu^p_{A_2}(b_2) \wedge \mu^p_{\vec{B}_2}(a_2b_2)]$,
$(a_1, b_1)(a_2, b_2) \in E^{\square}$.

Proof Consider an edge $(a_1, a_2)(b_1, b_2)$ of $G_{\mathcal{C}(\vec{G}_1)^* \square \mathcal{C}(\vec{G}_2)^*} \cup G^{\square}$. Then there are three cases,

Case 1: $a_1 = b_1, a_2 \neq b_2$, then $(a_1, a_2)(a_1, b_2) \in E_{\mathcal{C}(\vec{G}_1)^*} \square E_{\mathcal{C}(\vec{G}_2)^*}$. By conditions (3) and (4),

$$\begin{aligned}
\mu^p_R((a_1, a_2)(a_1, b_2)) &= [\mu^p_{A_1}(a_1) \wedge \mu^p_{A_2}(a_2) \wedge \mu^p_{A_2}(b_2)] \\
&\quad \times \vee_{x_2}[\mu^p_{A_1}(a_1) \wedge \mu^p_{\vec{B}_2}(a_2x_2) \wedge \mu^p_{\vec{B}_2}(b_2x_2)], \qquad (4.1)\\
\mu^p_R((a_1, a_2)(a_1, b_2)) &= [\mu^p_{A_1}(a_1) \wedge \mu^p_{A_2}(a_2)\} \wedge \{\mu^p_{A_1}(a_1) \wedge \mu^p_{A_2}(b_2)] \\
&\quad \times \vee_{x_2}[\{\mu^p_{A_1}(a_1) \wedge \mu^p_{\vec{B}_2}(a_2x_2)\}, \wedge\{\mu^p_{A_1}(a_1) \wedge \mu^p_{\vec{B}_2}(b_2x_2)\}], \\
\mu^p_R((a_1, a_2)(a_1, b_2)) &= [\mu^p_A(a_1, a_2) \wedge \mu^p_A(a_1, b_2)] \\
&\quad \times \vee_{x_2}[\mu^p_{\vec{B}}((a_1, a_2)(a_1, x_2)) \wedge \mu^p_{\vec{B}}((a_1, b_2)(a_1, x_2))], \\
\mu^p_R((a_1, a_2)(a_1, b_2)) &= [\mu^p_A(a_1, a_2) \wedge \mu^p_A(a_1, b_2)] \times \vee_{x_2}[\mu^p_{\mathcal{N}^+(a_1,a_2) \cap \mathcal{N}^+(a_1,b_2)}(a_1, x_2)], \\
\mu^p_R((a_1, a_2)(a_1, b_2)) &= [\mu^p_A(a_1, a_2) \wedge \mu^p_A(a_1, b_2)] \times h(\mathcal{N}^+(a_1, a_2) \cap \mathcal{N}^+(a_1, b_2)). \qquad (4.2)
\end{aligned}$$

$$\mu^n_R((a_1,a_2)(a_1,b_2)) = [\mu^n_{A_1}(a_1) \vee \mu^n_{A_2}(a_2) \vee \mu^n_{A_2}(b_2)] \times \vee_{x_2}[\mu^p_{A_1}(a_1) \wedge \mu^p_{\vec{B}_2}(a_2x_2) \wedge \mu^p_{\vec{B}_2}(b_2x_2)],$$

$$\mu^n_R((a_1,a_2)(a_1,b_2)) = [\{\mu^n_{A_1}(a_1) \vee \mu^n_{A_2}(a_2)\} \vee \{\mu^n_{A_1}(a_1) \vee \mu^n_{A_2}(b_2)\}] \times \vee_{x_2}[\{\mu^p_{A_1}(a_1) \wedge \mu^p_{\vec{B}_2}(a_2x_2)\}, \wedge\{\mu^p_{A_1}(a_1) \wedge \mu^p_{\vec{B}_2}(b_2x_2)\}],$$

$$\mu^n_R((a_1,a_2)(a_1,b_2)) = [\mu^n_A(a_1,a_2) \vee \mu^n_A(a_1,b_2)] \times \vee_{x_2}[\mu^p_{\vec{B}}((a_1,a_2)(a_1,x_2)) \wedge \mu^p_{\vec{B}}((a_1,b_2)(a_1,x_2))],$$

$$\mu^n_R((a_1,a_2)(a_1,b_2)) = [\mu^n_A(a_1,a_2) \vee \mu^n_A(a_1,b_2)] \times \vee_{x_2}[\mu^p_{\mathcal{N}^+(a_1,a_2)\cap\mathcal{N}^+(a_1,b_2)}(a_1,x_2)],$$

$$\mu^n_R((a_1,a_2)(a_1,b_2)) = [\mu^n_A(a_1,a_2) \vee \mu^n_A(a_1,b_2)] \times h(\mathcal{N}^+(a_1,a_2) \cap \mathcal{N}^+(a_1,b_2)). \tag{4.3}$$

From Eqs. (4.2) and (4.3), $(a_1,a_2)(a_1,b_2)$ is an edge of $\mathcal{C}(G_1 \Box G_2)$.
Case 2: If $a_1 \neq b_1, a_2 = b_2$, then $(a_1,a_2)(b_1,a_2) \in E_{\mathcal{C}(\vec{G}_1)^*} \Box E_{\mathcal{C}(\vec{G}_2)^*}$. Using conditions (5) and (6),

$$\mu^p_R((a_1,a_2)(b_1,a_2)) = [\mu^p_{A_1}(a_1) \wedge \mu^p_{A_1}(b_1) \wedge \mu^p_{A_2}(a_2)] \times \vee_{x_1}[\mu^p_{A_2}(a_2) \wedge \mu^p_{\vec{B}_1}(a_1x_1) \wedge \mu^p_{\vec{B}_1}(b_1x_1)], \tag{4.4}$$

$$\mu^p_R((a_1,a_2)(b_1,a_2)) = [\{\mu^p_{A_1}(a_1) \wedge \mu^p_{A_2}(a_2)\} \wedge \{\mu^p_{A_1}(b_1) \wedge \mu^p_{A_2}(a_2)\}] \times \vee_{x_1}[\{\mu^p_{A_2}(a_2) \wedge \mu^p_{\vec{B}_1}(a_1x_1)\}, \wedge\{\mu^p_{A_2}(a_2) \wedge \mu^p_{\vec{B}_1}(b_1x_1)\}],$$

$$\mu^p_R((a_1,a_2)(b_1,a_2)) = [\mu^p_A(a_1,a_2) \wedge \mu^p_A(b_1,a_2)] \times \vee_{x_1}[\mu^p_{\vec{B}}((a_1,a_2)(x_1,a_2)) \wedge \mu^p_{\vec{B}}((b_1,a_2)(x_1,a_2))]$$

$$\mu^p_R((a_1,a_2)(b_1,a_2)) = [\mu^p_A(a_1,a_2) \wedge \mu^p_A(b_1,a_2)] \times \vee_{x_1}[\mu^p_{\mathcal{N}^+(a_1,a_2)\cap\mathcal{N}^+(b_1,a_2)}(x_1,a_2)],$$

$$\mu^p_R((a_1,a_2)(b_1,a_2)) = [\mu^p_A(a_1,a_2) \wedge \mu^p_A(b_1,a_2)] \times h(\mathcal{N}^+(a_1,a_2) \cap \mathcal{N}^+(b_1,a_2)). \tag{4.5}$$

$$\mu^n_R((a_1,a_2)(b_1,a_2)) = [\mu^n_{A_1}(a_1) \vee \mu^n_{A_1}(b_1) \vee \mu^n_{A_2}(a_2)] \times \vee_{x_1}[\mu^p_{A_2}(a_2) \wedge \mu^p_{\vec{B}_1}(a_1x_1) \wedge \mu^p_{\vec{B}_1}(b_1x_1)], \tag{4.6}$$

$$\mu^n_R((a_1,a_2)(b_1,a_2)) = [\{\mu^n_{A_1}(a_1) \vee \mu^n_{A_2}(a_2)\} \vee \{\mu^n_{A_1}(b_1) \vee \mu^n_{A_2}(a_2)\}] \times \vee_{x_1}[\{\mu^p_{A_2}(a_2) \wedge \mu^p_{\vec{B}_1}(a_1x_1)\}, \wedge\{\mu^p_{A_2}(a_2) \wedge \mu^p_{\vec{B}_1}(b_1x_1)\}],$$

$$\mu^n_R((a_1,a_2)(b_1,a_2)) = [\mu^n_A(a_1,a_2) \vee \mu^n_A(b_1,a_2)] \times \vee_{x_1}[\mu^p_{\vec{B}}((a_1,a_2)(x_1,a_2)) \wedge \mu^p_{\vec{B}}((b_1,a_2)(x_1,a_2))],$$

$$\mu^n_R((a_1,a_2)(b_1,a_2)) = [\mu^n_A(a_1,a_2) \vee \mu^n_A(b_1,a_2)] \times \vee_{x_1}[\mu^p_{\mathcal{N}^+(a_1,a_2)\cap\mathcal{N}^+(b_1,a_2)}(x_1,a_2)$$

$$\mu^n_R((a_1,a_2)(b_1,a_2)) = [\mu^n_A(a_1,a_2) \vee \mu^n_A(b_1,a_2)] \times h(\mathcal{N}^+(a_1,a_2) \cap \mathcal{N}^+(b_1,a_2)). \tag{4.7}$$

Equations (4.5) and (4.7) show that $(a_1,a_2)(b_1,a_2)$ is an edge of $\mathcal{C}(G_1 \Box G_2)$.
Case 3: $a_1 \neq b_1, a_2 \neq b_2$, then $(a_1,a_2)(b_1,b_2) \in E^{\Box}$. Using conditions (7) and (8),

$$\mu^p_R((a_1,a_2)(b_1,b_2)) = [\mu^p_{A_1}(a_1) \wedge \mu^p_{A_1}(b_1) \wedge \mu^p_{A_2}(a_2) \wedge \mu^p_{A_2}(b_2)] \times [\mu^p_{A_1}(a_1) \wedge \mu^p_{\vec{B}_2}(a_2b_2) \wedge \mu^p_{A_2}(b_2) \wedge \mu^p_{\vec{B}_1}(b_1a_1)],$$

$$\mu^p_R((a_1,a_2)(b_1,b_2)) = [\mu^p_A(a_1,a_2) \wedge \mu^p_A(b_1,b_2)] \times [\mu^p_{\vec{B}}((a_1,a_2)(a_1,b_2)) \wedge \mu^p_{\vec{B}}((b_1,b_2)(a_1,b_2))],$$

$$\mu^p_R((a_1,a_2)(b_1,b_2)) = [\mu^p_A(a_1,a_2) \wedge \mu^p_A(b_1,b_2)] \times \mu^p_{\mathcal{N}^+(a_1,a_2)\cap\mathcal{N}^+(b_1,b_2)}(a_1,b_2),$$

$$\mu^p_R((a_1,a_2)(b_1,b_2)) = [\mu^p_A(a_1,a_2) \wedge \mu^p_A(b_1,b_2)] \times h(\mathcal{N}^+(a_1,a_2) \cap \mathcal{N}^+(b_1,b_2)). \tag{4.8}$$

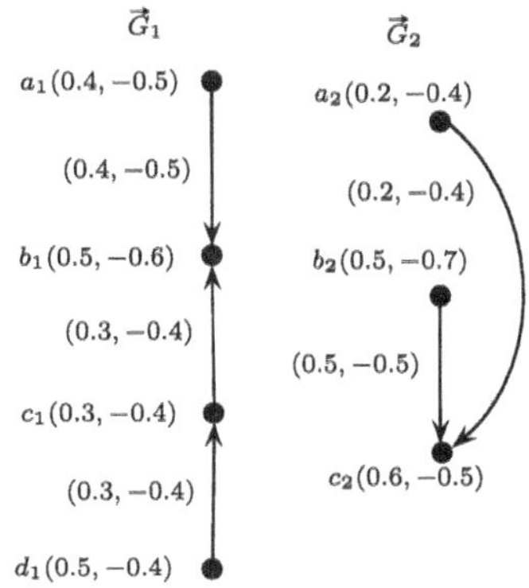

Fig. 4.5 Bipolar fuzzy digraphs $\vec{G}_1$ and $\vec{G}_2$

Table 4.4 Bipolar fuzzy out neighborhoods

$u \in X_1$	$\mathcal{N}^+(u)$
a_1	$\{(b_1, 0.4, -0.5)\}$
b_1	$\emptyset$
c_1	$\{(b_1, 0.3, -0.4)\}$
d_1	$\{(c_1, 0.3, -0.4)\}$

$$\begin{aligned}
&\mu_R^n((a_1, a_2)(b_1, b_2)) = \\
&\quad [\mu_{A_1}^n(a_1) \vee \mu_{A_1}^n(b_1) \vee \mu_{A_2}^n(a_2) \vee \mu_{A_2}^n(b_2)] \times [\mu_{A_1}^p(a_1) \wedge \mu_{\vec{B}_2}^p(a_2 b_2) \wedge \mu_{A_2}^p(b_2) \wedge \mu_{\vec{B}_1}^p(b_1 a_1)], \\
&\mu_R^n((a_1, a_2)(b_1, b_2)) = [\mu_A^n(a_1, a_2) \vee \mu_A^n(b_1, b_2)] \times [\mu_{\vec{B}}^p((a_1, a_2)(a_1, b_2)) \wedge \mu_{\vec{B}}^p((b_1, b_2)(a_1, b_2))], \\
&\mu_R^n((a_1, a_2)(b_1, b_2)) = [\mu_A^n(a_1, a_2) \vee \mu_A^n(b_1, b_2)] \times \mu^p_{\mathcal{N}^+(a_1, a_2) \cap \mathcal{N}^+(b_1, b_2)}(a_1, b_2), \\
&\mu_R^n((a_1, a_2)(b_1, b_2)) = [\mu_A^n(a_1, a_2) \vee \mu_A^n(b_1, b_2)] \times h(\mathcal{N}^+(a_1, a_2) \cap \mathcal{N}^+(b_1, b_2)). \qquad (4.9)
\end{aligned}$$

Equations (4.8) and (4.9) imply that $(a_1, a_2)(b_1, b_2)$ is an edge of $\mathcal{C}(G_1 \Box G_2)$. Hence $\mathcal{C}(G_1 \Box G_2) \subseteq G_{\mathcal{C}(\vec{G}_1)^* \Box \mathcal{C}(\vec{G}_2)^*} \cup G^{\Box}$. Conversely, it can be proved on the same lines that $G_{\mathcal{C}(\vec{G}_1)^* \Box \mathcal{C}(\vec{G}_2)^*} \cup G^{\Box} \subseteq \mathcal{C}(G_1 \Box G_2)$. It completes the proof. □

The idea of the construction of bipolar fuzzy competition graph of the Cartesian product is explained with the following two examples.

Example 4.3 Let $\vec{G}_1 = (A_1, \vec{B}_1)$ and $\vec{G}_2 = (A_2, \vec{B}_2)$ be two bipolar fuzzy digraphs X_1 and X_2, respectively, as shown in Fig. 4.5. The bipolar fuzzy out neighborhoods of vertices of $\vec{G}_1$ and $\vec{G}_2$ are given in Tables 4.4 and 4.5.

The bipolar fuzzy competition graphs $\mathcal{C}(\vec{G}_1)$ and $\mathcal{C}(\vec{G}_2)$ are given in Fig. 4.6. Now construct the bipolar fuzzy competition graph $G_{\mathcal{C}(\vec{G}_1)^* \Box \mathcal{C}(\vec{G}_2)^*} \cup G^{\Box} = (A, R)$ from $\mathcal{C}(\vec{G}_1)^*$ and $\mathcal{C}(\vec{G}_2)^*$ using Theorem 4.2, where $A = (\mu_A^p, \mu_A^n)$ and $R = (\mu_R^p, \mu_R^n)$. The two sets of edges according to condition (1) are computed as follows:

Table 4.5 Bipolar fuzzy out neighborhoods

$v \in X_2$	$\mathcal{N}^+(v)$
a_2	$\{(c_2, 0.2, -0.4)\}$
b_2	$\{(c_2, 0.5, -0.5)\}$
c_2	$\emptyset$

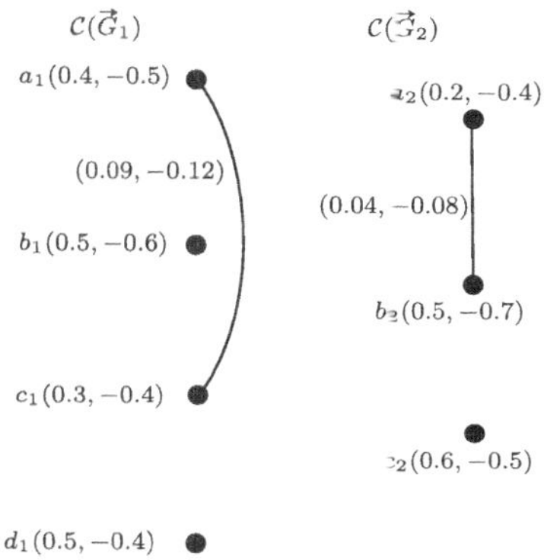

Fig. 4.6 Bipolar fuzzy competition graphs

$$E_{\mathcal{C}(\vec{G}_1)^*}\Box E_{\mathcal{C}(\vec{G}_2)^*} = \{(a_1, a_2)(a_1, b_2), (b_1, a_2)(b_1, b_2), (c_1, a_2)(c_1, b_2), (d_1, a_2)(d_1, b_2), (a_1, a_2)(c_1, a_2), (a_1, b_2)(c_1, b_2), (a_1, c_2)(c_1, c_2)\},$$

$$E^{\Box} = \{(b_1, a_2)(a_1, c_2), (b_1, a_2)(c_1, c_2), (b_1, b_2)(a_1, c_2), (b_1, b_2)(c_1, c_2), (c_1, a_2)(d_1, c_2), (c_1, b_2)(d_1, c_2)\}.$$

The degrees of membership of the edges can be calculated according to conditions (3)–(8) as

$$\begin{aligned}
R((a_1, a_2)(a_1, b_2)) &= [A_1(a_1) \wedge A_2(a_2) \wedge A_2(b_2)] \times [\mu^p_{A_1}(a_1) \wedge \mu^p_{\vec{B}_2}(a_2c_2) \wedge \mu^p_{\vec{B}_2}(b_2c_2)\} \\
&= (\mu^p_{A_1}(a_1) \wedge \mu^p_{A_2}(a_2) \wedge \mu^p_{A_2}(b_2), \mu^n_{A_1}(a_1) \vee \mu^n_{A_2}(a_2) \vee \mu^n_{A_2}(b_2)) \\
&\times [\mu^p_{A_1}(a_1) \wedge \mu^p_{\vec{B}_2}(a_2c_2) \wedge \mu^p_{\vec{B}_2}(b_2c_2)\} \\
&= (0.2, -0.4) \times 0.2 \\
&= (0.04, -0.08). \\
R((b_1, a_2)(a_1, c_2)) &= [A_1(b_1) \wedge A_1(a_1) \wedge A_2(a_2) \wedge A_2(c_2)] \times [\mu^p_{\vec{B}_1}(a_1b_1) \wedge \mu^p_{\vec{B}_2}(a_2c_2)] \\
&= (\mu^p_{A_1}(b_1) \wedge \mu^p_{A_1}(a_1) \wedge \mu^p_{A_2}(a_2) \wedge \mu^p_{A_2}(c_2), \mu^n_{A_1}(b_1) \vee \mu^n_{A_1}(a_1) \vee \\
&\mu^n_{A_2}(a_2) \vee \mu^n_{A_2}(c_2)) \times [\mu^p_{\vec{B}_1}(a_1b_1) \wedge \mu^p_{\vec{B}_2}(a_2c_2)] \\
&= (0.2, -0.4) \times 0.2 \\
&= (0.04, -0.08).
\end{aligned}$$

The membership degrees of all the adjacent vertices of $G_{\mathcal{C}(\vec{G}_1)^*\Box\mathcal{C}(\vec{G}_2)^*}$ and $G^{\Box}$ are given in Table 4.6.

Table 4.6 Membership values of constructed edges

$(x_1, x_2)(y_1, y_2)$	$R((x_1, x_2)(y_1, y_2))$
$(b_1, a_2)(b_1, b_2)$	$[A_1(b_1) \wedge A_2(a_2) \wedge A_2(b_2)] \times [(\mu^P_{A_1}(b_1) \wedge \mu^P_{\vec{B}_2}(a_2c_2) \wedge \mu^P_{\vec{B}_2}(b_2c_2)] = (0.04, -0.08)$
$(c_1, a_2)(c_1, b_2)$	$[A_1(c_1) \wedge A_2(a_2) \wedge A_2(b_2)] \times [\mu^P_{A_1}(c_1) \wedge \mu^P_{\vec{B}_2}(a_2c_2) \wedge \mu^P_{\vec{B}_2}(b_2c_2)] = (0.04, -0.08)$
$(d_1, a_2)(d_1, b_2)$	$[A_1(d_1) \wedge A_2(a_2) \wedge A_2(b_2)] \times [\mu^P_{A_1}(d_1) \wedge \mu^P_{\vec{B}_2}(a_2c_2) \wedge \mu^P_{\vec{B}_2}(b_2c_2)] = (0.04, -0.08)$
$(a_1, a_2)(c_1, a_2)$	$[A_1(a_1) \wedge A_1(c_1) \wedge A_2(a_2)] \times [\mu^P_{A_2}(a_2) \wedge \mu^P_{\vec{B}_1}(a_1b_1) \wedge \mu^P_{\vec{B}_1}(c_1b_1)] = (0.04, -0.08)$
$(a_1, b_2)(c_1, b_2)$	$[A_1(a_1) \wedge A_1(c_1) \wedge A_2(b_2)] \times [\mu^P_{A_2}(b_2) \wedge \mu^P_{\vec{B}_1}(a_1b_1) \wedge \mu^P_{\vec{B}_1}(c_1b_1)] = (0.09, -0.12)$
$(a_1, c_2)(c_1, c_2)$	$[A_1(a_1) \wedge A_1(c_1) \wedge A_2(c_2)] \times [\mu^P_{A_2}(c_2) \wedge \mu^P_{\vec{B}_1}(a_1b_1) \wedge \mu^P_{\vec{B}_1}(c_1b_1)] = (0.09, -0.12)$
$(b_1, a_2)(c_1, c_2)$	$[A_1(b_1) \wedge A_1(c_1) \wedge A_2(a_2) \wedge A_2(c_2)] \times [\mu^P_{A_1}(b_1) \wedge \mu^P_{\vec{B}_1}(c_1b_1) \wedge \mu^P_{A_2}(c_2) \wedge \mu^P_{\vec{B}_2}(a_2c_2)] = (0.04, -0.08)$
$(b_1, b_2)(a_1, c_2)$	$[A_1(b_1) \wedge A_1(a_1) \wedge A_2(b_2) \wedge A_2(c_2)] \times [\mu^P_{A_1}(b_1) \wedge \mu^P_{\vec{B}_1}(a_1b_1) \wedge \mu^P_{A_2}(c_2) \wedge \mu^P_{\vec{B}_2}(b_2c_2)] = (0.16, -0.20)$
$(b_1, b_2)(c_1, c_2)$	$[A_1(b_1) \wedge A_1(c_1) \wedge A_2(b_2) \wedge A_2(c_2)] \times [\mu^P_{A_1}(b_1) \wedge \mu^P_{\vec{B}_1}(c_1b_1) \wedge \mu^P_{A_2}(c_2) \wedge \mu^P_{\vec{B}_2}(b_2c_2)] = (0.09, -0.12)$
$(c_1, a_2)(d_1, c_2)$	$[A_1(c_1) \wedge A_1(d_1) \wedge A_2(a_2) \wedge A_2(c_2)] \times [\mu^P_{A_1}(c_1) \wedge \mu^P_{\vec{B}_1}(d_1c_1) \wedge \mu^P_{A_2}(c_2) \wedge \mu^P_{\vec{B}_2}(a_2c_2)] = (0.04, -0.08)$
$(c_1, b_2)(d_1, c_2)$	$[A_1(c_1) \wedge A_1(d_1) \wedge A_2(a_2) \wedge A_2(b_2)] \times [\mu^P_{A_1}(c_1) \wedge \mu^P_{\vec{B}_1}(d_1c_1) \wedge \mu^P_{A_2}(c_2) \wedge \mu^P_{\vec{B}_2}(b_2c_2)] = (0.09, -0.12)$

The bipolar fuzzy graph obtained using this method is given in Fig. 4.7, where solid lines show the part of bipolar fuzzy graph obtained from $G_{\mathcal{C}(\vec{G}_1)^*} \Box G_{\mathcal{C}(\vec{G}_2)^*}$ and dotted lines represent the part $G^{\Box}$.

The Cartesian product $\vec{G}_1 \Box \vec{G}_2$ of bipolar fuzzy digraphs $\vec{G}_1$ and $\vec{G}_2$ is shown in Fig. 4.8. The bipolar fuzzy out neighborhoods of vertices of $\vec{G}_1 \Box \vec{G}_2$ are calculated in Table 4.7.

The bipolar fuzzy competition graph of $\vec{G}_1 \Box \vec{G}_2$ is shown in Fig. 4.9. It is clear from Figs. 4.7 and 4.9 that $G_{\mathcal{C}(\vec{G}_1)^* \Box \mathcal{C}(\vec{G}_2)^*} \cup G^{\Box} \cong \mathcal{C}(\vec{G}_1 \Box \vec{G}_2)$.

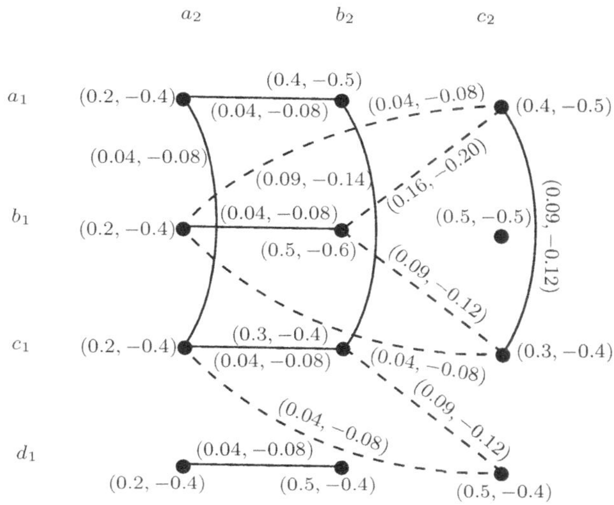

Fig. 4.7 Bipolar fuzzy graph $G_{\mathcal{C}(\vec{G}_1)^*\square\mathcal{C}(\vec{G}_2)^*} \cup G^{\square}$

Fig. 4.8 Cartesian product $\vec{G}_1\square\vec{G}_2$

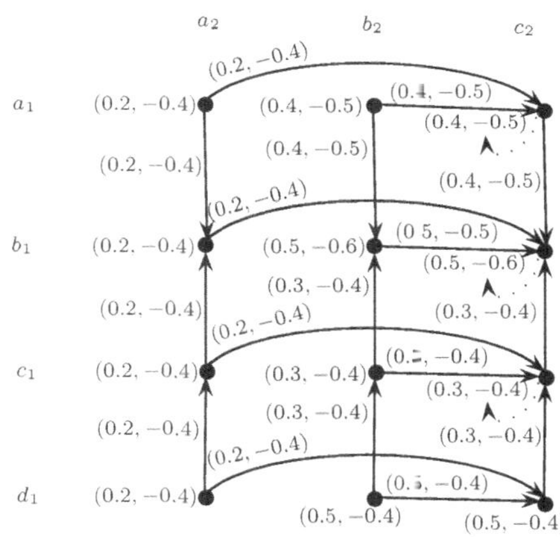

Table 4.7 Bipolar fuzzy out neighborhoods of vertices in $\vec{G}_1\square\vec{G}_2$

(x, y)	$\mathcal{N}^+((x, y))$	(x, y)	$\mathcal{N}^+((x, y))$
(a_1, a_2)	$\{(a_1, c_2), 0.2, -0.4), (b_1, a_2), 0.2, -0.4)\}$	(b_1, a_2)	$\{(b_1, c_2), 0.2, -0.4)\}$
(a_1, b_2)	$\{(a_1, c_2), 0.4, -0.5), (b_1, b_2), 0.4, -0.5)\}$	(a_1, c_2)	$\{(b_1, c_2), 0.4, -0.5)\}$
(c_1, b_2)	$\{(b_1, b_2), 0.3, -0.4), (c_1, c_2), 0.3, -0.4)\}$	(b_1, b_2)	$\{(b_1, c_2), 0.5, -0.5)\}$
(d_1, a_2)	$\{(d_1, c_2), 0.2, -0.4), (c_1, a_2), 0.2, -0.4)\}$	(c_1, a_2)	$\{(c_1, c_2), 0.2, -0.4)\}$
(d_1, b_2)	$\{(d_1, c_2), 0.5, -0.4), (c_1, b_2), 0.3, -0.4)\}$	(b_1, a_2)	$\{(b_1, c_2), 0.2, -0.4)\}$
(d_1, c_2)	$\{(c_1, c_2), 0.3, -0.4)\}$	(c_1, c_2)	$\{(b_1, c_2), 0.3, -0.4)\}$

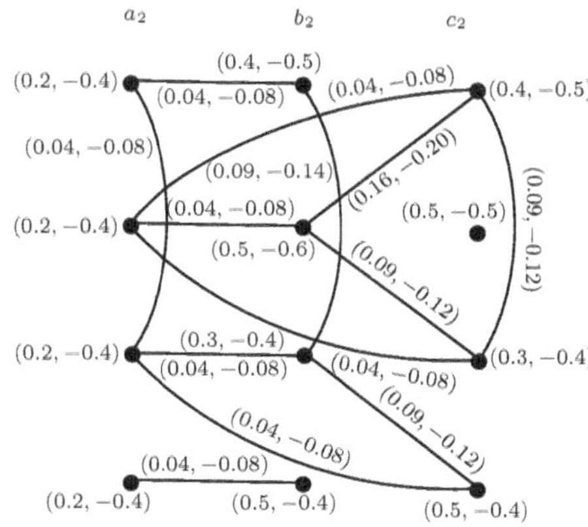

Fig. 4.9 Bipolar fuzzy competition graph $\mathcal{C}(\vec{G}_1 \Box \vec{G}_2)$

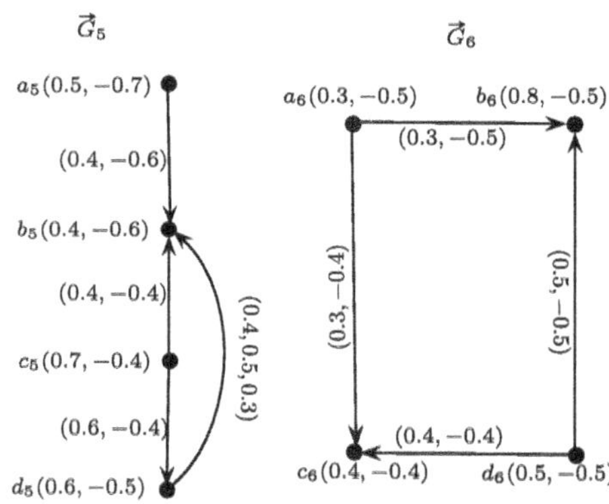

Fig. 4.10 Bipolar fuzzy digraphs $\vec{G}_5$ and $\vec{G}_6$

Example 4.4 Consider another example of bipolar fuzzy digraphs $\vec{G}_5 = (A_5, \vec{B}_5)$ and $\vec{G}_6 = (A_6, \vec{B}_6)$ on X_5 and X_6 as given in Fig. 4.10. The bipolar fuzzy competition graphs $\mathcal{C}(\vec{G}_5)$ and $\mathcal{C}(\vec{G}_6)$ are given in Fig. 4.11.

Apply Theorem 4.2 to construct bipolar fuzzy competition graph $\mathcal{C}(\vec{G}_5 \Box \vec{G}_6) = (A, R)$ from $\mathcal{C}(\vec{G}_5)^*$ and $\mathcal{C}(\vec{G}_6)^*$. The sets of edges constructed using condition (1) are

$$\begin{aligned}E_{\mathcal{C}(\vec{G}_5)^*} \Box E_{\mathcal{C}(\vec{G}_6)^*} = \{&(a_5, a_6)(a_5, d_6), (b_5, a_6)(b_5, d_6), (c_5, a_6)(c_5, d_6), (d_5, a_6)(d_5, d_6), (a_5, a_6)(d_5, a_6),\\ &(a_5, b_6)(d_5, b_6), (a_5, c_6)(d_5, c_6), (a_5, d_6)(d_5, d_6), (c_5, a_6)(d_5, a_6), (c_5, b_6)(d_5, b_6), (c_5, c_6)(d_5, c_6),\\ &(c_5, d_6)(d_5, d_6), (a_5, a_6)(c_5, a_6), (a_5, b_6)(c_5, b_6), (a_5, c_6)(c_5, c_6), (a_5, d_6)(c_5, d_6)\}.\\ E^{\Box} = \{&(b_5, a_6)(a_5, b_6), (b_5, a_6)(a_5, c_6), (b_5, d_6)(a_5, b_6), (b_5, d_6)(a_5, c_6), (b_5, a_6)(c_5, b_6), (b_5, a_6)(c_5, c_6),\\ &(b_5, d_6)(c_5, b_6), (b_5, d_6)(c_5, c_6), (d_5, a_6)(b_5, b_6), (d_5, a_6)(b_5, c_6), (d_5, d_6)(b_5, b_6), (d_5, d_6)(b_5, c_6),\\ &(d_5, a_6)(c_5, b_6), (d_5, a_6)(c_5, c_6), (d_5, d_6)(c_5, b_6), (d_5, d_6)(c_5, c_6)\}.\end{aligned}$$

The degrees of membership of the edges according to conditions (3) to (8) are calculated as follows:

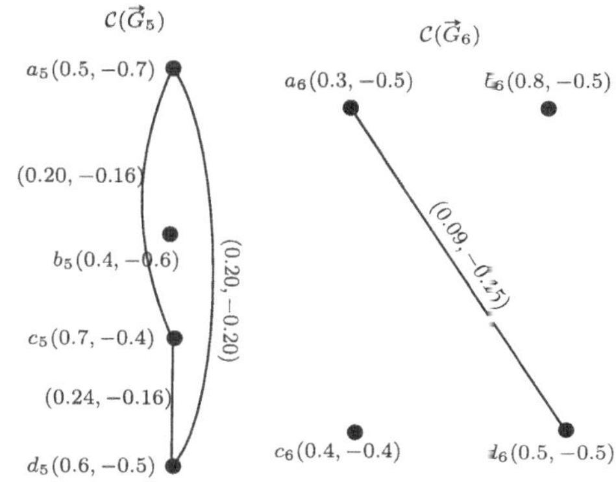

Fig. 4.11 Bipolar fuzzy competition graphs $\mathcal{C}(\vec{G}_5)$ and $\mathcal{C}(\vec{G}_6)$

$$\begin{aligned}
R((a_5, a_6)(a_5, d_6)) &= [A_5(a_5) \wedge A_6(a_6) \wedge A_6(d_6)] \times [\{\mu^p_{A_5}(a_5) \wedge \mu^p_{\vec{B}_6}(a_6c_6) \wedge \mu^p_{\vec{B}_6}(d_6c_6)\} \\
&\quad \vee \{\mu^p_{A_5}(a_5) \wedge \mu^p_{\vec{B}_6}(a_6b_6) \wedge \mu^p_{\vec{B}_6}(d_6b_6)\}] \\
&= [(\mu^p_{A_5}(a_5) \wedge \mu^p_{A_6}(a_6) \wedge \mu^p_{A_6}(d_6), \mu^n_{A_5}(a_5) \vee \mu^n_{A_6}(a_6) \vee \mu^n_{A_6}(d_6))] \\
&\quad \times [\{\mu^p_{A_5}(a_5) \wedge \mu^p_{\vec{B}_6}(a_6c_6) \wedge \mu^p_{\vec{B}_6}(d_6c_6)\} \vee \{\mu^p_{A_5}(a_5) \wedge \mu^p_{\vec{B}_6}(a_6b_6) \wedge \mu^p_{\vec{B}_6}(d_6b_6)\}] \\
&= (0.3, -0.5) \times 0.3 = (0.09, -0.15). \\
R((b_5, a_6)(a_5, c_6)) &= [A_5(b_5) \wedge A_5(a_5) \wedge A_6(a_6) \wedge A_6(c_6)] \times [\mu^p_{A_5}(b_5) \wedge \mu^p_{\vec{B}_5}(a_5b_5) \wedge \\
&\quad \mu^p_{A_6}(c_6) \wedge \mu^p_{\vec{B}_6}(a_6c_6)\} \\
&= (\mu^p_{A_5}(b_5) \wedge \mu^p_{A_5}(a_5) \wedge \mu^p_{A_6}(a_6) \wedge \mu^p_{A_6}(c_6), \mu^n_{A_5}(b_5) \vee \mu^n_{A_5}(a_5) \vee \mu^n_{A_6}(a_6) \\
&\quad \vee \mu^n_{A_6}(c_6)) \times \{\mu^p_{A_5}(b_5) \wedge \mu^p_{\vec{B}_5}(a_5b_5) \wedge \mu^p_{A_6}(c_6) \wedge \mu^p_{\vec{B}_6}(a_6c_6)\} \\
&= (0.3, -0.4) \times 0.3 = (0.09, -0.12).
\end{aligned}$$

The way of calculating the membership degrees of the edges from $E_{\mathcal{C}(\vec{G}_1)^*} \Box E_{\mathcal{C}(\vec{G}_2)^*}$ and $E^{\Box}$ is described in Table 4.8.

The bipolar fuzzy graph obtained using this method is shown in Fig. 4.12. The solid lines show the part of the bipolar fuzzy graph obtained from $G_{\mathcal{C}(\vec{G}_5)^*} \Box G_{\mathcal{C}(\vec{G}_6)^*}$ and dashed lines show the part of the bipolar fuzzy graph obtained from $G^{\Box}$.
The Cartesian product of $\vec{G}_5$ and $\vec{G}_6$ is shown in Fig. 4.13 and its bipolar fuzzy competition graph is given in Fig. 4.14, which clearly shows that $G_{\mathcal{C}(\vec{G}_5)} \Box \mathcal{C}(\vec{G}_6)^* \cup G^{\Box} \cong \mathcal{C}(\vec{G}_5 \Box \vec{G}_6)$.

The method for the construction of bipolar fuzzy competition graph of the direct product of bipolar fuzzy digraphs from respective bipolar fuzzy competition graphs of the bipolar fuzzy digraphs is discussed in Theorem 4.3.

Theorem 4.3 *Let $\vec{G}_1 = (A_1, \vec{B}_1)$ and $\vec{G}_2 = (A_2, \vec{B}_2)$ be two bipolar fuzzy digraphs. $\mathcal{C}(\vec{G}_1) = (A_1, R_1)$ and $\mathcal{C}(\vec{G}_2) = (A_2, R_2)$ are the bipolar fuzzy competition graphs without isolated vertices such that neither is a bipolar fuzzy empty graph. Then*

Table 4.8 Adjacent vertices of $G_{C(\vec{G}_5)^*\Box C(\vec{G}_6)^*} \cup G^{\Box}$

$(x_1, x_2)(y_1, y_2)$	$R((x_1, x_2)(y_1, y_2))$
$(b_5, a_6)(b_5, d_6)$	$[A_5(b_5) \wedge A_6(a_6) \wedge A_6(d_6)] \times [\{\mu^P_{A_5}(b_5) \wedge \mu^P_{\vec{B}_6}(a_6c_6) \wedge \mu^P_{\vec{B}_6}(d_6c_6)\} \vee \{\mu^P_{A_5}(b_5)$ $\wedge \mu^P_{\vec{B}_6}(a_6b_6) \wedge \mu^P_{\vec{B}_6}(d_6b_6)\}] = (0.09, -0.15)$
$(c_5, a_6)(c_5, d_6)$	$[A_5(c_5) \wedge A_6(a_6) \wedge A_6(d_6)] \times [\{\mu^P_{A_5}(c_5) \wedge \mu^P_{\vec{B}_6}(a_6c_6) \wedge \mu^P_{\vec{B}_6}(d_6c_6)\} \vee \{\mu^P_{A_5}(c_5)$ $\wedge \mu^P_{\vec{B}_6}(a_6b_6) \wedge \mu^P_{\vec{B}_6}(d_6b_6)\}] = (0.09, -0.12)$
$(d_5, a_6)(d_5, d_6)$	$[A_5(d_5) \wedge A_6(a_6) \wedge A_6(d_6)] \times [\{\mu^P_{A_5}(d_5) \wedge \mu^P_{\vec{B}_6}(a_6c_6) \wedge \mu^P_{\vec{B}_6}(d_6c_6)\} \vee \{\mu^P_{A_5}(d_5)$ $\wedge \mu^P_{\vec{B}_6}(a_6b_6) \wedge \mu^P_{\vec{B}_6}(d_6b_6)\}] = (0.09, -0.15)$
$(a_5, a_6)(c_5, a_6)$	$[A_5(a_5) \wedge A_5(c_5) \wedge A_6(a_6)] \times [\mu^P_{A_6}(a_6) \wedge \mu^P_{\vec{B}_5}(a_5b_5) \wedge \mu^P_{\vec{B}_5}(c_5b_5)] = (0.09, -0.12)$
$(a_5, b_6)(c_5, b_6)$	$[A_5(a_5) \wedge A_5(c_5) \wedge A_6(b_6)] \times [\mu^P_{A_6}(b_6) \wedge \mu^P_{\vec{B}_5}(a_5b_5) \wedge \mu^P_{\vec{B}_5}(c_5b_5)] = (0.20, -0.16)$
$(a_5, c_6)(c_5, c_6)$	$[A_5(a_5) \wedge A_5(c_5) \wedge A_6(c_6)] \times [\mu^P_{A_6}(c_6) \wedge \mu^P_{\vec{B}_5}(a_5b_5) \wedge \mu^P_{\vec{B}_5}(c_5b_5)] = (0.16, -0.16)$
$(a_5, d_6)(c_5, d_6)$	$[A_5(a_5) \wedge A_5(c_5) \wedge A_6(d_6)] \times [\mu^P_{A_6}(d_6) \wedge \mu^P_{\vec{B}_5}(a_5b_5) \wedge \mu^P_{\vec{B}_5}(c_5b_5)] = (0.20, -0.16)$
$(a_5, a_6)(d_5, a_6)$	$[A_5(a_5) \wedge A_5(d_5) \wedge A_6(a_6)] \times [\mu^P_{A_6}(a_6) \wedge \mu^P_{\vec{B}_5}(a_5b_5) \wedge \mu^P_{\vec{B}_5}(d_5b_5)] = (0.09, -0.15)$
$(a_5, b_6)(d_5, b_6)$	$[A_5(a_5) \wedge A_5(d_5) \wedge A_6(b_6)] \times [\mu^P_{A_6}(b_6) \wedge \mu^P_{\vec{B}_5}(a_5b_5) \wedge \mu^P_{\vec{B}_5}(d_5b_5)] = (0.20, -0.20)$
$(a_5, c_6)(d_5, c_6)$	$[A_5(a_5) \wedge A_5(d_5) \wedge A_6(c_6)] \times [\mu^P_{A_6}(c_6) \wedge \mu^P_{\vec{B}_5}(a_5b_5) \wedge \mu^P_{\vec{B}_5}(d_5b_5)] = (0.16, -0.16)$
$(a_5, d_6)(d_5, d_6)$	$[A_5(a_5) \wedge A_5(d_5) \wedge A_6(d_6)] \times [\mu^P_{A_6}(d_6) \wedge \mu^P_{\vec{B}_5}(a_5b_5) \wedge \mu^P_{\vec{B}_5}(d_5b_5)] = (0.20, -0.20)$
$(c_5, a_6)(d_5, a_6)$	$[A_5(c_5) \wedge A_5(d_5) \wedge A_6(a_6)] \times [\mu^P_{A_6}(a_6) \wedge \mu^P_{\vec{B}_5}(c_5b_5) \wedge \mu^P_{\vec{B}_5}(d_5b_5)] = (0.09, -0.12)$
$(c_5, b_6)(d_5, b_6)$	$[A_5(c_5) \wedge A_5(d_5) \wedge A_6(b_6)] \times [\mu^P_{A_6}(b_6) \wedge \mu^P_{\vec{B}_5}(c_5b_5) \wedge \mu^P_{\vec{B}_5}(d_5b_5)] = (0.24, -0.16)$
$(c_5, c_6)(d_5, c_6)$	$[A_5(c_5) \wedge A_5(d_5) \wedge A_6(c_6)] \times [\mu^P_{A_6}(c_6) \wedge \mu^P_{\vec{B}_5}(c_5b_5) \wedge \mu^P_{\vec{B}_5}(d_5b_5)] = (0.16, -0.16)$
$(c_5, d_6)(d_5, d_6)$	$[A_5(c_5) \wedge A_5(d_5) \wedge A_6(d_6)] \times [\mu^P_{A_6}(d_6) \wedge \mu^P_{\vec{B}_5}(c_5b_5) \wedge \mu^P_{\vec{B}_5}(d_5b_5)] = (0.20, -0.16)$
$(b_5, a_6)(a_5, b_6)$	$[A_5(b_5) \wedge A_5(a_5) \wedge A_6(a_6) \wedge A_6(b_6)] \times [\mu^P_{A_5}(b_5) \wedge \mu^P_{\vec{B}_5}(a_5b_5) \wedge \mu^P_{A_6}(b_6) \wedge \mu^P_{\vec{B}_6}(a_6b_6)]$ $= (0.09, -0.15)$
$(b_5, d_6)(a_5, b_6)$	$[A_5(b_5) \wedge A_5(a_5) \wedge A_6(d_6) \wedge A_6(b_6)] \times [\mu^P_{A_5}(b_5) \wedge \mu^P_{\vec{B}_5}(a_5b_5) \wedge \mu^P_{A_6}(b_6) \wedge \mu^P_{\vec{B}_6}(d_6b_6)]$ $= (0.16, -0.20)$
$(b_5, d_6)(a_5, c_6)$	$[A_5(b_5) \wedge A_5(a_5) \wedge A_6(d_6) \wedge A_6(c_6)] \times [\mu^P_{A_5}(b_5) \wedge \mu^P_{\vec{B}_5}(a_5b_5) \wedge \mu^P_{A_6}(c_6) \wedge \mu^P_{\vec{B}_6}(d_6c_6)]$ $= (0.16, -0.16)$
$(b_5, a_6)(c_5, b_6)$	$[A_5(b_5) \wedge A_5(c_5) \wedge A_6(a_6) \wedge A_6(b_6)] \times [\mu^P_{A_5}(b_5) \wedge \mu^P_{\vec{B}_5}(c_5b_5) \wedge \mu^P_{A_6}(b_6) \wedge \mu^P_{\vec{B}_6}(a_6b_6)]$ $= (0.09, -0.12)$
$(b_5, a_6)(c_5, c_6)$	$[A_5(b_5) \wedge A_5(c_5) \wedge A_6(a_6) \wedge A_6(c_6)] \times [\mu^P_{A_5}(b_5) \wedge \mu^P_{\vec{B}_5}(c_5b_5) \wedge \mu^P_{A_6}(c_6) \wedge \mu^P_{\vec{B}_6}(a_6c_6)]$ $= (0.09, -0.12)$
$(b_5, d_6)(c_5, b_6)$	$[A_5(b_5) \wedge A_5(c_5) \wedge A_6(d_6) \wedge A_6(b_6)] \times [\mu^P_{A_5}(b_5) \wedge \mu^P_{\vec{B}_5}(c_5b_5) \wedge \mu^P_{A_6}(b_6) \wedge \mu^P_{\vec{B}_6}(d_6b_6)]$ $= (0.16, -0.16)$
$(b_5, d_6)(c_5, c_6)$	$[A_5(b_5) \wedge A_5(c_5) \wedge A_6(d_6) \wedge A_6(c_6)] \times [\mu^P_{A_5}(b_5) \wedge \mu^P_{\vec{B}_5}(c_5b_5) \wedge \mu^P_{A_6}(c_6) \wedge \mu^P_{\vec{B}_6}(d_6c_6)]$ $= (0.16, -0.16)$
$(d_5, a_6)(b_5, b_6)$	$[A_5(d_5) \wedge A_5(b_5) \wedge A_6(a_6) \wedge A_6(b_6)] \times [\mu^P_{A_5}(b_5) \wedge \mu^P_{\vec{B}_5}(b_5d_5) \wedge \mu^P_{A_6}(b_6) \wedge \mu^P_{\vec{B}_6}(a_6b_6)]$ $= (0.09, -0.15)$

(continued)

Table 4.8 (continued)

$(x_1, x_2)(y_1, y_2)$	$R((x_1, x_2)(y_1, y_2))$
$(d_5, a_6)(b_5, c_6)$	$[A_5(d_5) \wedge A_5(b_5) \wedge A_6(a_6) \wedge A_6(c_6)] \times [\mu^P_{A_5}(b_5) \wedge \mu^P_{\vec{B}_5}(b_5d_5) \wedge \mu^P_{A_6}(c_6) \wedge \mu^P_{\vec{B}_6}(a_6c_6)]$ $= (0.09, -0.15)$
$(d_5, d_6)(b_5, b_6)$	$[A_5(d_5) \wedge A_5(b_5) \wedge A_6(d_6) \wedge A_6(b_6)] \times [\mu^P_{A_5}(b_5) \wedge \mu^P_{\vec{B}_5}(b_5d_5) \wedge \mu^P_{A_6}(b_6) \wedge \mu^P_{\vec{B}_6}(d_6b_6)]$ $= (0.16, -0.20)$
$(d_5, d_6)(b_5, c_6)$	$[A_5(d_5) \wedge A_5(b_5) \wedge A_6(d_6) \wedge A_6(c_6)] \times [\mu^P_{A_5}(b_5) \wedge \mu^P_{\vec{B}_5}(b_5d_5) \wedge \mu^P_{A_6}(c_6) \wedge \mu^P_{\vec{B}_6}(d_6c_6)]$ $= (0.16, -0.16)$
$(d_5, a_6)(c_5, b_6)$	$[A_5(d_5) \wedge A_5(c_5) \wedge A_6(a_6) \wedge A_6(b_6)] \times [\mu^P_{A_5}(c_5) \wedge \mu^P_{\vec{B}_5}(c_5d_5) \wedge \mu^P_{A_6}(b_6) \wedge \mu^P_{\vec{B}_6}(a_6b_6)]$ $= (0.09, -0.12)$
$(d_5, a_6)(c_5, c_6)$	$[A_5(d_5) \wedge A_5(c_5) \wedge A_6(a_6) \wedge A_6(c_6)] \times [\mu^P_{A_5}(c_5) \wedge \mu^P_{\vec{B}_5}(c_5d_5) \wedge \mu^P_{A_6}(c_6) \wedge \mu^P_{\vec{B}_6}(a_6c_6)]$ $= (0.09, -0.12)$
$(d_5, d_6)(c_5, b_6)$	$[A_5(d_5) \wedge A_5(c_5) \wedge A_6(d_6) \wedge A_6(b_6)] \times [\mu^P_{A_5}(c_5) \wedge \mu^P_{\vec{B}_5}(c_5d_5) \wedge \mu^P_{A_6}(b_6) \wedge \mu^P_{\vec{B}_6}(d_6b_6)]$ $= (0.25, -0.20)$
$(d_5, d_6)(c_5, c_6)$	$[A_5(d_5) \wedge A_5(c_5) \wedge A_6(d_6) \wedge A_6(c_6)] \times [\mu^P_{A_5}(c_5) \wedge \mu^P_{\vec{B}_5}(c_5d_5) \wedge \mu^P_{A_6}(c_6) \wedge \mu^P_{\vec{B}_6}(d_6c_6)]$ $= (0.16, -0.16)$

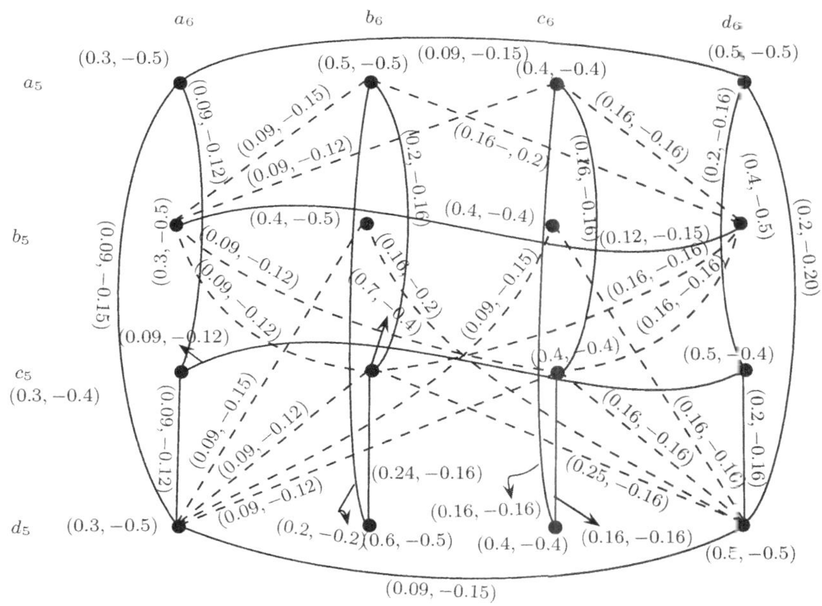

Degree of membership of vertices is shown in red colour.

Fig. 4.12 Bipolar fuzzy graph $G_{C(\vec{G}_5)^* \square C(\vec{G}_6)^*} \cup G^{\square}$

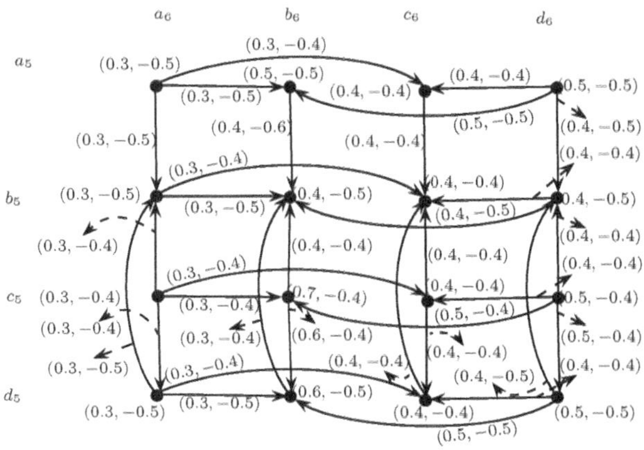

Degree of membership of vertices is shown in red colour.

Fig. 4.13 Cartesian product $\vec{G}_5 \Box \vec{G}_6$

Fig. 4.14 Bipolar fuzzy competition graph $\mathcal{C}(\vec{G}_5 \Box \vec{G}_6)$

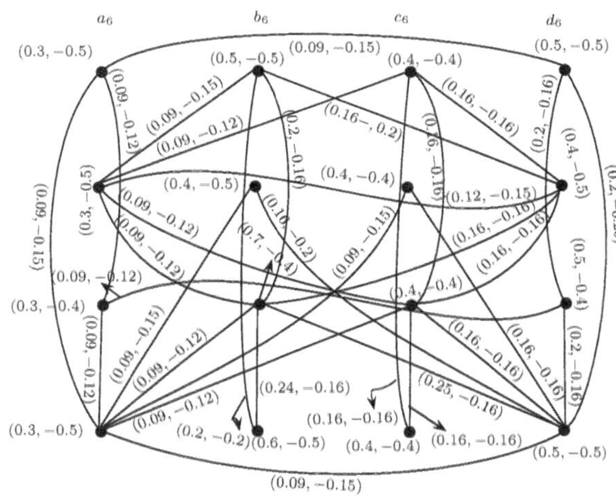

$\mathcal{C}(\vec{G}_1 \times \vec{G}_2) = [\mathcal{C}(\vec{G}_1) \times \mathcal{C}(\vec{G}_2)] \cup G^{\times}$, *where* $G^{\times} = (A, R)$ *is a bipolar fuzzy graph on the crisp graph* $(X_1 \times X_2, E^{\times})$ *defined as*

(1) $C((a_1, a_2)) = (\mu^p_{A_1}(a_1) \wedge \mu^p_{A_2}(a_2), \mu^n_{A_1}(a_1) \vee \mu^n_{A_2}(a_2)), \quad a_1 \in X_1, a_2 \in X_2,$

(2) $E^{\times} = \{(a_1, a_2)(a_1, b_2) | a_1 \in X_1, a_2, b_2 \in X_2, \mathcal{N}^+(a_1) \neq \emptyset, a_2 b_2 \in E_{\mathcal{C}(\vec{G}_2)^*}\} \cup \{(a_1, a_2)(b_1, a_2) | a_1, b_1 \in X_1, a_2 \in X_2, a_1 b_1 \in E_{\mathcal{C}(\vec{G}_1)^*}, \mathcal{N}^+(a_2) \neq \emptyset\},$

(3) $\mu_R^p((a_1, a_2)(a_1, b_2)) = [\mu_{A_1}^p(a_1) \wedge \mu_{A_2}^p(a_2) \wedge \mu_{A_2}^p(b_2)] \times \vee_{c_1 \in X_1, c_2 \in X_2}\{\mu_{\vec{B}_1}^p(a_1c_1) \wedge \mu_{\vec{B}_2}^p(a_2c_2) \wedge \mu_{\vec{B}_2}^p(b_2c_2) | c_1 \in \mathcal{N}^+(a_1)^*, c_2 \in \mathcal{N}^+(a_2)^* \cap \mathcal{N}^+(b_2)^*\}, \quad (a_1, a_2)(a_1, b_2) \in E^\times$,

(4) $\mu_R^n((a_1, a_2)(a_1, b_2)) = [\mu_{A_1}^n(a_1) \vee \mu_{A_2}^n(a_2) \vee \mu_{A_2}^n(b_2)] \times \vee_{c_1 \in X_1, c_2 \in X_2}\{\mu_{\vec{B}_1}^p(a_1c_1) \wedge \mu_{\vec{B}_2}^p(a_2c_2) \wedge \mu_{\vec{B}_2}^p(b_2c_2) | c_1 \in \mathcal{N}^+(a_1)^*, c_2 \in \mathcal{N}^+(a_2)^* \cap \mathcal{N}^+(b_2)^*\}, \quad (a_1, a_2)(a_1, b_2) \in E^\times$,

(5) $\mu_R^p((a_1, a_2)(b_1, a_2)) = [\mu_{A_1}^p(a_1) \wedge \mu_{A_1}^p(b_1) \wedge \mu_{A_2}^p(a_2)] \times \vee_{c_1 \in X_1, c_2 \in X_2}\{\mu_{\vec{B}_1}^p(a_1c_1) \wedge \mu_{\vec{B}_1}^p(b_1c_1) \wedge \mu_{\vec{B}_2}^p(a_2c_2) | c_2 \in \mathcal{N}^+(a_2)^*, c_1 \in \mathcal{N}^+(a_1)^* \cap \mathcal{N}^+(b_1)^*\}, \quad (a_1, a_2)(a_1, b_2) \in E^\times$,

(6) $\mu_R^n((a_1, a_2)(b_1, a_2)) = [\mu_{A_1}^n(a_1) \vee \mu_{A_1}^n(b_1) \vee \mu_{A_2}^n(a_2)] \times \vee_{c_1 \in X_1, c_2 \in X_2}\{\mu_{\vec{B}_1}^p(a_1c_1) \wedge \mu_{\vec{B}_1}^p(b_1c_1) \wedge \mu_{\vec{B}_2}^p(a_2c_2) | c_2 \in \mathcal{N}^+(a_2)^*, c_1 \in \mathcal{N}^+(a_1)^* \cap \mathcal{N}^+(b_1)^*\}, \quad (a_1, a_2)(a_1, b_2) \in E^\times$.

Proof Let $(a_1, a_2)(b_1, b_2)$ be an edge of $[\mathcal{C}(G_1) \times \mathcal{C}(G_2)] \cup G^\times$. Then there are three cases.

Case 1: $a_1 = b_1, a_2 \neq b_2$, then $(a_1, a_2)(a_1, b_2) \in E^\times$. Using conditions (3) and (4),

$$
\begin{aligned}
\mu_R^p((a_1, a_2)(a_1, b_2)) =& [\mu_{A_1}^p(a_1) \wedge \mu_{A_2}^p(a_2) \wedge \mu_{A_2}^p(b_2)] \times \vee_{c_1 \in X_1, c_2 \in X_2}[\mu_{\vec{B}_1}^p(a_1c_1) \wedge \mu_{\vec{B}_2}^p(a_2c_2) \wedge \\
& \mu_{\vec{B}_1}^p(a_1c_1) \wedge \mu_{\vec{B}_2}^p(b_2c_2)], \\
\mu_R^p((a_1, a_2)(a_1, b_2)) =& [\mu_C^p(a_1, a_2) \wedge \mu_C^p(a_1, b_2)] \times \vee_{c_1 \in X_1, c_2 \in X_2}[\mu_{\vec{B}}^p((a_1, a_2)(c_1, c_2)) \wedge \\
& \mu_{\vec{B}}^p((a_1, b_2)(c_1, c_2))], \\
\mu_R^p((a_1, a_2)(a_1, b_2)) =& [\mu_A^p(a_1, a_2) \wedge \mu_A^p(a_1, b_2)] \times \vee_{c_1 \in X_1, c_2 \in X_2}[\mu_{\mathcal{N}^+((a_1, a_2)) \cap \mathcal{N}^+((a_1, b_2))}^p], \\
\mu_R^p((a_1, a_2)(a_1, b_2)) =& [\mu_A^p(a_1, a_2) \wedge \mu_A^p(a_1, b_2)] \times h(\mathcal{N}^+((a_1, a_2)) \cap \mathcal{N}^+((a_1, b_2))).
\end{aligned} \tag{4.10}
$$

$$
\begin{aligned}
\mu_R^n((a_1, a_2)(a_1, b_2)) =& [\mu_{A_1}^n(a_1) \vee \mu_{A_2}^n(a_2) \vee \mu_{A_2}^n(b_2)] \times \vee_{c_1 \in X_1, c_2 \in X_2}[\mu_{\vec{B}_1}^p(a_1c_1) \wedge \mu_{\vec{B}_2}^p(a_2c_2) \wedge \\
& \mu_{\vec{B}_1}^p(a_1c_1) \wedge \mu_{\vec{B}_2}^p(b_2c_2)], \\
\mu_R^n((a_1, a_2)(a_1, b_2)) =& [\mu_C^n(a_1, a_2) \vee \mu_C^n(a_1, b_2)] \times \vee_{c_1 \in X_1, c_2 \in X_2}[\mu_{\vec{B}}^p((a_1, a_2)(c_1, c_2)) \wedge \\
& \mu_{\vec{B}}^p((a_1, b_2)(c_1, c_2))], \\
\mu_R^n((a_1, a_2)(a_1, b_2)) =& [\mu_A^n(a_1, a_2) \vee \mu_A^n(a_1, b_2)] \times \vee_{c_1 \in X_1, c_2 \in X_2}[\mu_{\mathcal{N}^+((a_1, a_2)) \cap \mathcal{N}^+((a_1, b_2))}^p], \\
\mu_R^n((a_1, a_2)(a_1, b_2)) =& [\mu_A^n(a_1, a_2) \vee \mu_A^n(a_1, b_2)] \times h(\mathcal{N}^+((a_1, a_2)) \cap \mathcal{N}^+((a_1, b_2))).
\end{aligned} \tag{4.11}
$$

Equations (4.10) and (4.11) show that $(a_1, a_2)(a_1, b_2)$ is an edge of $\mathcal{C}(G_1 \times G_2)$.

Case 2: $a_1 \neq b_1, a_2 = b_2$, then $(a_1, a_2)(b_1, a_2) \in E^\times$. It can be proved on the same lines as Case 1.

Case 3: $a_1 \neq b_1, a_2 \neq b_2$, then $(a_1, a_2)(a_1, b_2)$ is an edge of $\mathcal{C}(\vec{G}_1) \times \mathcal{C}(\vec{G}_2)$. By definition of direct product of bipolar fuzzy digraphs,

$$
\begin{aligned}
\mu^p_R((a_1,a_2)(b_1,b_2)) =&\mu^p_{R_1}(a_1b_1)\wedge\mu^p_{R_2}(a_2b_2),\\
\mu^p_R((a_1,a_2)(b_1,b_2)) =&[\mu^p_{A_1}(a_1)\wedge\mu^p_{A_1}(b_1)\wedge\mu^p_{A_2}(a_2)\wedge\mu^p_{A_2}(b_2)]\times\vee_{c_1\in X_1,c_2\in X_2}[\mu^p_{\vec{B}_1}(a_1c_1)\\
&\wedge\mu^p_{\vec{B}_1}(b_1c_1)\wedge\mu^p_{\vec{B}_2}(a_2c_2)\wedge\mu^p_{\vec{B}_2}(b_2c_2)],\\
\mu^p_R((a_1,a_2)(b_1,b_2)) =&[\mu^p_{A_1}(a_1)\wedge\mu^p_{A_1}(b_1)\wedge\mu^p_{A_2}(a_2)\wedge\mu^p_{A_2}(b_2)]\times\vee_{c_1\in X_1,c_2\in X_2}[\mu^p_{\vec{B}_1}(a_1c_1)\\
&\wedge\mu^p_{\vec{B}_2}(a_2c_2)\wedge\mu^p_{\vec{B}_1}(b_1c_1)\wedge\mu^p_{\vec{B}_2}(b_2c_2)],\\
\mu^p_R((a_1,a_2)(b_1,b_2)) =&[\mu^p_A(a_1,a_2)\wedge\mu^p_A(b_1,b_2)]\\
&\times\vee_{c_1\in X_1,c_2\in X_2}[\mu^p_{\vec{B}}((a_1,a_2)(c_1,c_2))\wedge\mu^p_{\vec{B}}((b_1,b_2)(c_1,c_2))],\\
\mu^p_R((a_1,a_2)(b_1,b_2)) =&[\mu^p_A(a_1,a_2)\wedge\mu^p_A(a_1,b_2)]\times\vee_{c_1\in X_1,c_2\in X_2}[\mu^p_{\mathcal{N}^+((a_1,a_2))\cap\mathcal{N}^+((b_1,b_2))}(c_1,c_2)],\\
\mu^p_R((a_1,a_2)(a_1,b_2)) =&[\mu^p_A(a_1,a_2)\wedge\mu^p_A(b_1,b_2)]\times h(\mathcal{N}^+((a_1,a_2))\cap\mathcal{N}^+((b_1,b_2))). \qquad (4.12)
\end{aligned}
$$

$$
\begin{aligned}
\mu^n_R((a_1,a_2)(b_1,b_2)) =&\mu^n_{R_1}(a_1b_1)\vee\mu^n_{R_2}(a_2b_2),\\
\mu^n_R((a_1,a_2)(b_1,b_2)) =&[\mu^n_{A_1}(a_1)\vee\mu^n_{A_1}(b_1)\vee\mu^n_{A_2}(a_2)\vee\mu^n_{A_2}(b_2)]\times\vee_{c_1\in X_1,c_2\in X_2}[\mu^p_{\vec{B}_1}(a_1c_1)\\
&\wedge\mu^p_{\vec{B}_1}(b_1c_1)\wedge\mu^p_{\vec{B}_2}(a_2c_2)\wedge\mu^p_{\vec{B}_2}(b_2c_2)],\\
\mu^n_R((a_1,a_2)(b_1,b_2)) =&[\mu^n_{A_1}(a_1)\vee\mu^n_{A_1}(b_1)\vee\mu^n_{A_2}(a_2)\vee\mu^n_{A_2}(b_2)]\times\vee_{c_1\in X_1,c_2\in X_2}[\mu^p_{\vec{B}_1}(a_1c_1)\\
&\wedge\mu^p_{\vec{B}_2}(a_2c_2)\wedge\mu^p_{\vec{B}_1}(b_1c_1)\wedge\mu^p_{\vec{B}_2}(b_2c_2)],\\
\mu^n_R((a_1,a_2)(b_1,b_2)) =&[\mu^n_A(a_1,a_2)\vee\mu^n_A(b_1,b_2)]\times\vee_{c_1\in X_1,c_2\in X_2}[\mu^p_{\vec{B}}((a_1,a_2)(c_1,c_2))\\
&\wedge\mu^p_{\vec{B}}((b_1,b_2)(c_1,c_2))],\\
\mu^n_R((a_1,a_2)(b_1,b_2)) =&[\mu^n_A(a_1,a_2)\vee\mu^n_A(a_1,b_2)]\times\vee_{c_1\in X_1,c_2\in X_2}[\mu^p_{\mathcal{N}^+((a_1,a_2))\cap\mathcal{N}^+((b_1,b_2))}(c_1,c_2),\\
\mu^n_R((a_1,a_2)(a_1,b_2)) =&[\mu^n_A(a_1,a_2)\vee\mu^n_A(b_1,b_2)]\times h(\mathcal{N}^+((a_1,a_2))\cap\mathcal{N}^+((b_1,b_2))). \qquad (4.13)
\end{aligned}
$$

Equations (4.12) and (4.13) imply that $(a_1, a_2)(b_1, b_2)$ is an edge of $\mathcal{C}(G_1 \times G_2)$. Hence $[\mathcal{C}(\vec{G}_1) \times \mathcal{C}(\vec{G}_2)] \cup G^\times \subseteq \mathcal{C}(G_1 \times G_2)$. The converse part is similar. □

The construction of bipolar fuzzy competition graphs of the direct product using Theorem 4.3 is explained with the following two examples.

Example 4.5 Consider bipolar fuzzy digraphs $\vec{G}_3 = (A_3, \vec{B}_3)$ and $\vec{G}_4 = (A_4, \vec{B}_4)$ on X_3 and X_4 as shown in Fig. 4.15 and their bipolar fuzzy competition graphs are given in Fig. 4.16.

It is to be shown that $\mathcal{C}(\vec{G}_3 \times \vec{G}_4) = [\mathcal{C}(\vec{G}_3) \times \mathcal{C}(\vec{G}_4)] \cup G^\times$, where $G^\times$ is a bipolar fuzzy digraph on $(X_3, \times X_4, E^\times)$. The edge set $E^\times$ using condition (2) is constructed as follows:

$$
\begin{aligned}
E^\times =\{&(a_3,a_4)(a_3,c_4), (c_3,a_4)(c_3,c_4), (d_3,a_4)(d_3,c_4), (a_3,a_4)(c_3,a_4),\\
&(a_3,c_4)(c_3,c_4), (a_3,d_4)(c_3,d_4)\}.
\end{aligned}
$$

The degree of membership of all the edges from $E^\times$ using conditions (3) and (4) are calculated as follows:

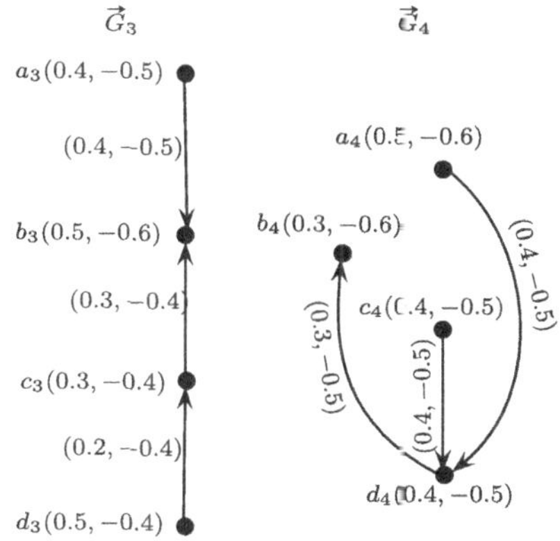

Fig. 4.15 Bipolar fuzzy digraphs $\vec{G}_3$ and $\vec{G}_4$

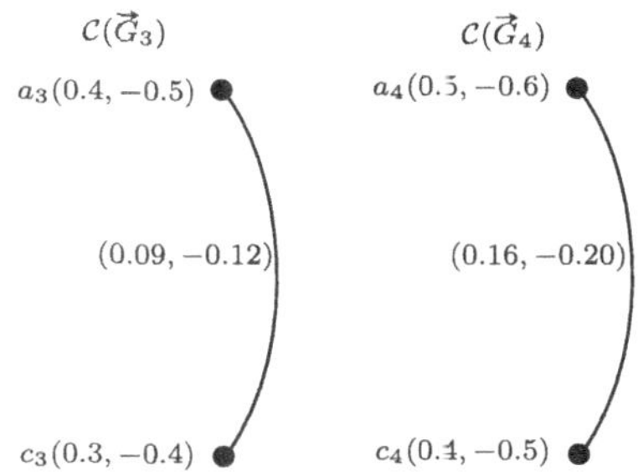

Fig. 4.16 Bipolar fuzzy competition graphs $\mathcal{C}(\vec{G}_3)$ and $\mathcal{C}(\vec{G}_4)$

$$
\begin{aligned}
R((a_3, a_4)(a_3, c_4)) &= [A_3(a_3) \wedge A_4(a_4) \wedge A_4(c_4)] \times [\mu^p_{\vec{B}_3}(a_3b_3) \wedge \mu^p_{\vec{B}_4}(a_4d_4) \wedge \mu^p_{\vec{B}_4}(c_4d_4)] \\
&= (\mu^p_{A_3}(a_3) \wedge \mu^p_{A_4}(a_4) \wedge \mu^p_{A_4}(c_4), \mu^n_{A_3}(a_3) \vee \mu^v_{A_4}(a_4) \vee \mu^n_{A_4}(c_4)) \\
&\times [\mu^p_{\vec{B}_3}(a_3b_3) \wedge \mu^p_{\vec{B}_4}(a_4d_4) \wedge \mu^p_{\vec{B}_4}(c_4d_4)] \\
&= (0.4, -0.5) \times 0.4 = (0.16, -0.20).
\end{aligned}
$$

Other membership values are given in Table 4.9.

The bipolar fuzzy graph constructed using Theorem 4.3 is shown in Fig. 4.17.

The part of bipolar fuzzy graph obtained from $\mathcal{C}(\vec{G}_3) \times \mathcal{C}(\vec{G}_4)$ is shown with solid lines and $G^\times$ is shown with dashed lines. The direct product of $\vec{G}_3$ and $\vec{G}_4$ is shown in Fig. 4.18 and its bipolar fuzzy competition graph in Fig. 4.19, which is the same as Fig. 4.17. Clearly, $[\mathcal{C}(\vec{G}_3) \times \mathcal{C}(\vec{G}_4)] \cup G^\times \cong \mathcal{C}(\vec{G}_3 \times \vec{G}_4)$.

Example 4.6 Let $\vec{G}_5 = (A_5, \vec{B}_5)$ and $\vec{G}_6 = (A_6, \vec{B}_6)$ be two bipolar fuzzy digraphs as given in Fig. 4.20 and their bipolar fuzzy competition graphs without isolated vertices are shown in Fig. 4.21.

Construct $[\mathcal{C}(\vec{G}_5) \times \mathcal{C}(\vec{G}_6)] \cup G^\times = (A, R)$ using Theorem 4.3, where $G^\times$ is a bipolar fuzzy graph on $(X_5 \times X_6, E^\times)$.

Table 4.9 Adjacent vertices of $[\mathcal{C}(\vec{G}_3) \times \mathcal{C}(\vec{G}_4)] \cup G^{\times}$

$(x_3, x_4)(y_3, y_4)$	$R((x_3, x_4)(y_3, y_4))$
$(a_3, a_4)(a_3, c_4)$	$[A_3(a_3) \wedge A_4(a_4) \wedge A_4(c_4)] \times [\mu^p_{\vec{B}_3}(a_3b_3) \wedge \mu^p_{\vec{B}_4}(a_4d_4) \wedge \mu^p_{\vec{B}_4}(c_4d_4)]$ $= (0.16, -0.20)$
$(c_3, a_4)(c_3, c_4)$	$[A_3(c_3) \wedge A_4(a_4) \wedge A_4(c_4)] \times [\mu^p_{\vec{B}_3}(c_3b_3) \wedge \mu^p_{\vec{B}_4}(a_4d_4) \wedge \mu^p_{\vec{B}_4}(c_4d_4)]$ $= (0.09, -0.12)$
$(d_3, a_4)(d_3, c_4)$	$[A_3(d_3) \wedge A_4(a_4) \wedge A_4(c_4)] \times [\mu^p_{\vec{B}_3}(d_3c_3) \wedge \mu^p_{\vec{B}_4}(a_4d_4) \wedge \mu^p_{\vec{B}_4}(c_4d_4)]$ $= (0.08, -0.08)$
$(a_3, a_4)(c_3, a_4)$	$[A_3(a_3) \wedge A_3(c_3) \wedge A_4(a_4)] \times [\mu^p_{\vec{B}_3}(a_3b_3) \wedge \mu^p_{\vec{B}_3}(c_3b_3) \wedge \mu^p_{\vec{B}_4}(a_4d_4)]$ $= (0.09, -0.12)$
$(a_3, c_4)(c_3, c_4)$	$[A_3(a_3) \wedge A_3(c_3) \wedge A_4(c_4)] \times [\mu^p_{\vec{B}_3}(a_3b_3) \wedge \mu^p_{\vec{B}_3}(c_3b_3) \wedge \mu^p_{\vec{B}_4}(c_4d_4)]$ $= (0.09, -0.12)$
$(a_3, d_4)(c_3, d_4)$	$[A_3(a_3) \wedge A_3(c_3) \wedge A_4(d_4)] \times [\mu^p_{\vec{B}_3}(a_3b_3) \wedge \mu^p_{\vec{B}_3}(c_3b_3) \wedge \mu^p_{\vec{B}_4}(d_4b_4)]$ $= (0.09, -0.12)$

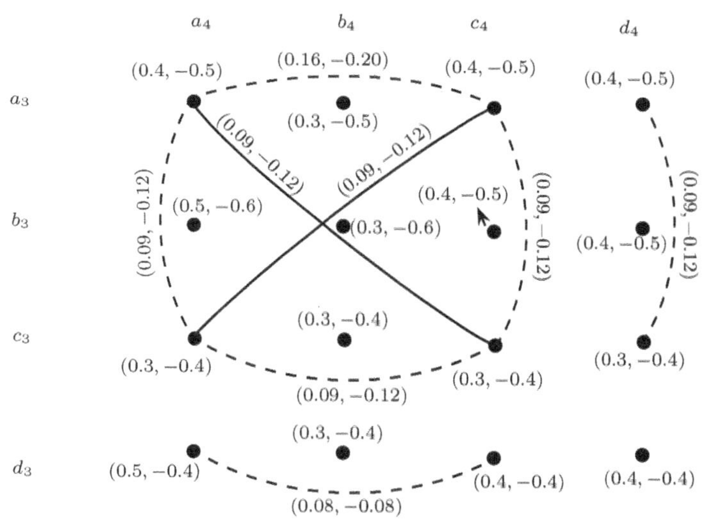

Fig. 4.17 Bipolar fuzzy graph $[\mathcal{C}(\vec{G}_3) \times \mathcal{C}(\vec{G}_4)] \cup G^{\times}$

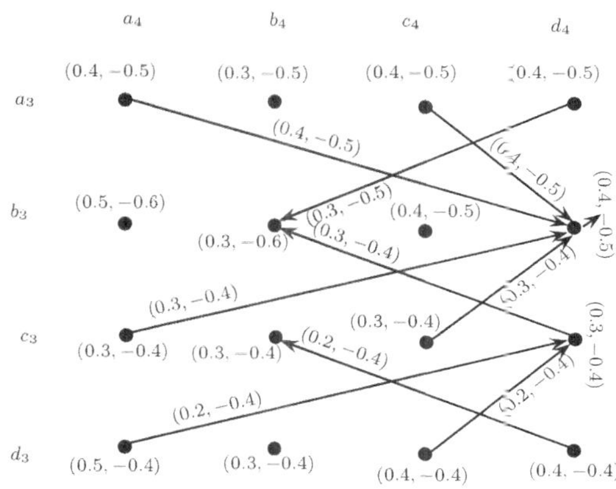

Fig. 4.18 Direct product $\vec{G}_3 \times \vec{G}_4$

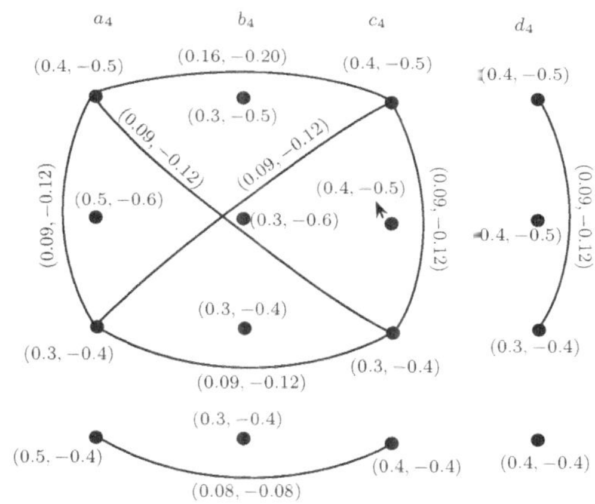

Fig. 4.19 Bipolar fuzzy competition graph $\mathcal{C}(\vec{G}_3 \times \vec{G}_4)$

$$E^{\times} = \{(a_5, a_6)(a_5, d_6), (b_5, a_6)(b_5, d_6), (c_5, a_6)(c_5, d_6), (a_5, a_6)(c_5, a_6), (a_5, d_6)\\ (c_5, d_6), (b_5, a_6)(c_5, a_6), (b_5, d_6)(c_5, d_6)\}.$$

The degree of membership of all the edges from $E^{\times}$ can be calculated as

$$\begin{aligned} R((a_5, a_6)(a_5, d_6)) =& (\mu^p_{A_5}(a_5) \wedge \mu^p_{A_6}(a_6) \wedge \mu^p_{A_6}(d_6), \mu^n_{A_5}(a_5) \vee \mu^n_{A_6}(a_6) \vee \mu^n_{A_6}(d_6)) \times [\{\mu^p_{\vec{B}_5}(a_5b_5) \\ & \wedge \mu^p_{\vec{B}_6}(a_6b_6) \wedge \mu^p_{\vec{B}_6}(d_6b_6)\} \vee \{\mu^p_{\vec{B}_5}(a_5b_5) \wedge \mu^p_{\vec{B}_6}(a_6c_6) \wedge \mu^p_{\vec{B}_6}(d_6c_6)\}] \\ =& (0.3, -0.5) \times 0.3 = (0.09, -0.15). \end{aligned}$$

Other membership values are given in Table 4.10.

The bipolar fuzzy graph constructed using Theorem 4.3 is shown in Fig. 4.22.

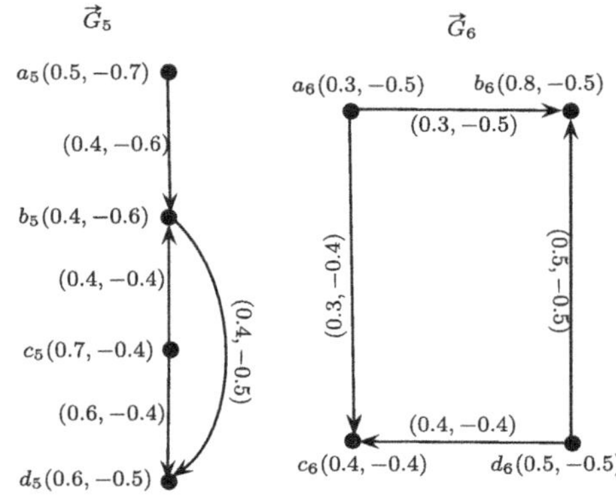

Fig. 4.20 Bipolar fuzzy digraphs $\vec{G}_5$ and $\vec{G}_6$

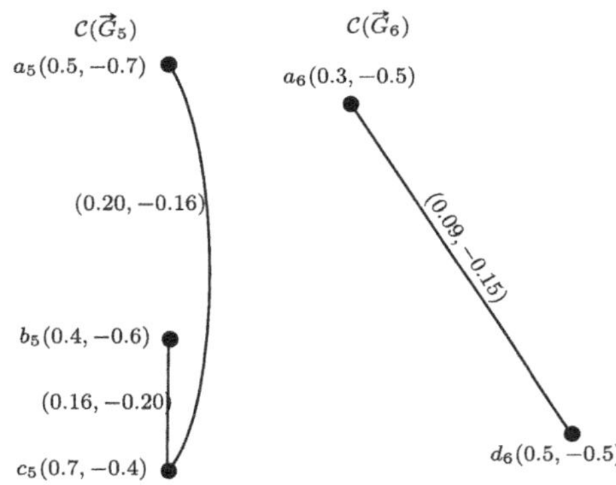

Fig. 4.21 Bipolar fuzzy competition graphs $\mathcal{C}(\vec{G}_5)$ and $\mathcal{C}(\vec{G}_6)$

The part of bipolar fuzzy graph obtained from $\mathcal{C}(\vec{G}_3) \times \mathcal{C}(\vec{G}_4)$ is shown with solid lines and $G^\times$ is shown with dashed lines. The direct product of $\vec{G}_5$ and $\vec{G}_6$ is shown in Fig. 4.23 and its bipolar fuzzy competition graph in Fig. 4.24 which clearly shows that $\mathcal{C}(\vec{G}_5 \times \vec{G}_6) \cong [\mathcal{C}(\vec{G}_5) \times \mathcal{C}(\vec{G}_6)] \cup G^\times$.

Proposition 4.1 *Let $\vec{G}_1 = (A_1, \vec{B}_1)$ and $\vec{G}_2 = (A_2, \vec{B}_2)$ be two bipolar fuzzy digraphs on X_1 and X_2 with $\mathcal{C}(\vec{G}_1) = (A_1, R_1)$ and $\mathcal{C}(\vec{G}_2) = (A_2, R_2)$ as the bipolar fuzzy competition graphs, respectively. Then $\mathcal{C}(\vec{G}_1 \cup \vec{G}_2) = (A_1 \cup A_2, R)$ can be constructed from $\mathcal{C}(\vec{G}_1) = (A_1, R_1)$ and $\mathcal{C}(\vec{G}_2) = (A_2, R_2)$ in the following way.*

1. *If $X_1 \cap X_2 = \emptyset$, then $\mathcal{C}(\vec{G}_1 \cup \vec{G}_2) = \mathcal{C}(\vec{G}_1) \cup \mathcal{C}(\vec{G}_2)$,*

2. *if $X_1 \cap X_2 \neq \emptyset$, then $R : E_{\mathcal{C}(\vec{G}_1)^*} \cup E_{\mathcal{C}(\vec{G}_2)^*} \cup \breve{E} \to [0,1] \times [-1,0]$ is a bipolar fuzzy set, where*

$$\breve{E} = \{a_1a_2 \mid e \in X_1 \cap X_2 \text{ and } \vec{a_1e} \in \vec{E}_1, \vec{a_1e} \notin \vec{E}_2, \vec{a_2e} \in \vec{E}_2, \vec{a_2e} \notin \vec{E}_1\},$$

Table 4.10 Membership values of constructed edges

$(x_3, x_4)(y_3, y_4)$	$R((x_3, x_4)(y_3, y_4))$
$(b_5, a_6)(b_5, d_6)$	$[A_5(b_5) \wedge A_6(a_6) \wedge A_6(d_6)] \times [\{\mu^P_{\vec{B}_5}(b_5d_5) \wedge \mu^P_{\vec{B}_6}(a_6b_6) \wedge \mu^P_{\vec{E}_6}(d_6b_6)\}$ $\vee\{\mu^P_{\vec{B}_5}(b_5d_5) \wedge \mu^P_{\vec{B}_6}(a_6c_6) \wedge \mu^P_{\vec{B}_6}(d_6c_6)\}] = (0.09, -0.15)$
$(c_5, a_6)(c_5, d_6)$	$[A_5(c_5) \wedge A_6(a_6) \wedge A_6(d_6)] \times [\{\mu^P_{\vec{B}_5}(c_5d_5) \wedge \mu^P_{\vec{B}_6}(a_6b_6) \wedge \mu^P_{\vec{B}_5}(d_6b_6)\}$ $\vee\{\mu^P_{\vec{B}_5}(c_5d_5) \wedge \mu^P_{\vec{B}_6}(a_6c_6) \wedge \mu^P_{\vec{B}_6}(d_6c_6)\} \vee \{\mu^P_{\vec{B}_5}(c_5b_5) \wedge \mu^P_{\vec{B}_6}(c_6b_6) \wedge$ $\mu^P_{\vec{B}_6}(d_6b_6)\}$ $\vee\{\mu^P_{\vec{B}_5}(c_5b_5) \wedge \mu^P_{\vec{B}_6}(a_6c_6) \wedge \mu^P_{\vec{B}_6}(d_6c_6)\}] = (0.09, -0.15)$
$(a_5, a_6)(c_5, a_6)$	$[A_5(a_5) \wedge A_5(c_5) \wedge A_6(a_6)] \times [\{\mu^P_{\vec{B}_5}(a_5b_5) \wedge \mu^P_{\vec{B}_5}(c_5b_5) \wedge \mu^P_{\vec{E}_6}(a_6b_6)\}$ $\vee\{\mu^P_{\vec{B}_5}(a_5b_5) \wedge \mu^P_{\vec{B}_5}(c_5b_5) \wedge \mu^P_{\vec{B}_6}(a_6c_6)\}] = (0.09, -0.12)$
$(a_5, d_6)(c_5, d_6)$	$[A_5(a_5) \wedge A_5(c_5) \wedge A_6(d_6)] \times [\{\mu^P_{\vec{B}_5}(a_5b_5) \wedge \mu^P_{\vec{B}_5}(c_5b_5) \wedge \mu^P_{\vec{E}_6}(d_6b_6)\}$ $\vee\{\mu^P_{\vec{B}_5}(a_5b_5) \wedge \mu^P_{\vec{B}_5}(c_5b_5) \wedge \mu^P_{\vec{B}_6}(d_6c_6)\}] = (0.20, -0.16)$
$(b_5, a_6)(c_5, a_6)$	$[A_5(b_5) \wedge A_5(c_5) \wedge A_6(a_6)] \times [\{\mu^P_{\vec{B}_5}(b_5d_5) \wedge \mu^P_{\vec{B}_5}(c_5d_5) \wedge \mu^P_{\vec{E}_6}(a_6b_6)\}$ $\vee\{\mu^P_{\vec{B}_5}(b_5d_5) \wedge \mu^P_{\vec{B}_5}(c_5d_5) \wedge \mu^P_{\vec{B}_6}(a_6c_6)\}] = (0.09, -0.12)$
$(b_5, d_6)(c_5, d_6)$	$[A_5(b_5) \wedge A_5(c_5) \wedge A_6(d_6)] \times [\{\mu^P_{\vec{B}_5}(b_5d_5) \wedge \mu^P_{\vec{B}_5}(c_5d_5) \wedge \mu^P_{\vec{E}_6}(d_6b_6)\}$ $\vee\{\mu^P_{\vec{B}_5}(b_5d_5) \wedge \mu^P_{\vec{B}_5}(c_5d_5) \wedge \mu^P_{\vec{B}_6}(d_6c_6)\}] = (0.16, -0.16)$

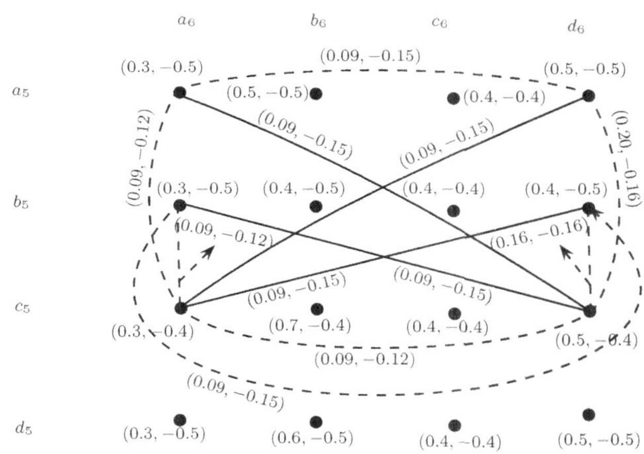

Fig. 4.22 Bipolar fuzzy graph $[\mathcal{C}(\vec{G}_5) \times \mathcal{C}(\vec{G}_6)] \cup G^{\times}$

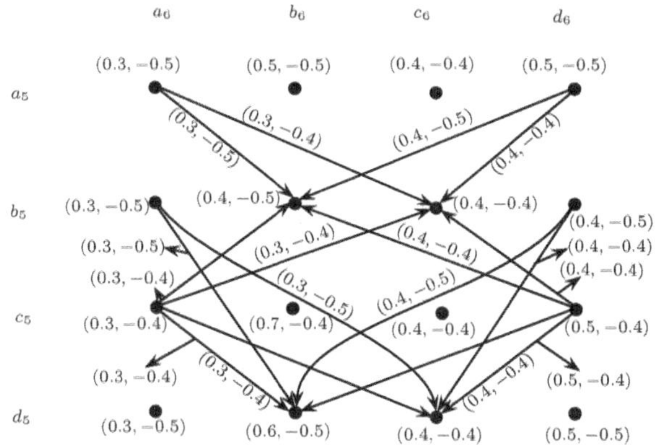

Fig. 4.23 Cartesian product $\vec{G}_5 \times \vec{G}_6$

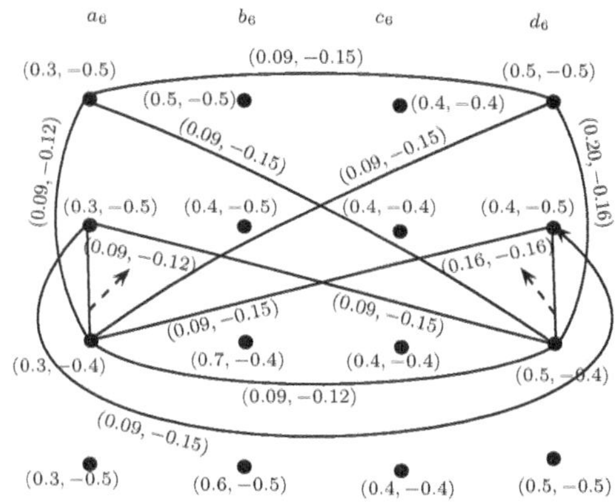

Fig. 4.24 $\mathcal{C}(\vec{G}_5 \times \vec{G}_6)$

3. $\mu_R^p(ab) = [(\mu_{A_1}^p(a) \vee \mu_{A_2}^p(a)) \wedge (\mu_{A_1}^p(b) \vee \mu_{A_2}^p(b))] \times \max_c\{(\mu_{\vec{B}_1}^p(ac) \vee \mu_{\vec{B}_2}^p(ac)) \wedge (\mu_{\vec{B}_1}^p(bc) \vee \mu_{\vec{B}_2}^p(bc)) \mid c \in \mathcal{N}^+(a) \cap \mathcal{N}^+(b)\}$, $ab \in E_{\mathcal{C}(G_1)^*} \cup E_{\mathcal{C}(G_2)^*}$,

4. $\mu_R^n(ab) = [(\mu_{A_1}^n(a) \wedge \mu_{A_2}^n(a)) \vee (\mu_{A_1}^n(b) \wedge \mu_{A_2}^p(b))] \times \max_c\{(\mu_{\vec{B}_1}^p(ac) \vee \mu_{\vec{B}_2}^p(ac)) \wedge (\mu_{\vec{B}_1}^p(bc) \vee \mu_{\vec{B}_2}^p(bc)) \mid c \in \mathcal{N}^+(a) \cap \mathcal{N}^+(b)\}$, $ab \in E_{\mathcal{C}(G_1)^*} \cup E_{\mathcal{C}(G_2)^*}$,

5. $\mu_R^p(ab) = [(\mu_{A_1}^p(a) \vee \mu_{A_2}^p(a)) \wedge (\mu_{A_1}^p(b) \vee \mu_{A_2}^p(b))] \times \max_c\{\mu_{\vec{B}_1}^p(ae) \wedge \mu_{\vec{B}_2}^p(be) \mid e \in \mathcal{N}^+(a) \cap \mathcal{N}^+(b)\}$, $ab \in \breve{E}$,

6. $\mu_R^n(ab) = [(\mu_{A_1}^n(a) \wedge \mu_{A_2}^n(a)) \vee (\mu_{A_1}^n(b) \wedge \mu_{A_2}^p(b))] \times \max_c\{\mu_{\vec{B}_1}^p(ae) \wedge \mu_{\vec{B}_2}^p(be) \mid e \in \mathcal{N}^+(a) \cap \mathcal{N}^+(b)\}$, $ab \in \breve{E}$.

4.3 Bipolar Fuzzy k-competition Graphs

In this section, the concepts to bipolar fuzzy open neighborhood graphs, bipolar fuzzy closed neighborhood graphs and bipolar fuzzy $\boldsymbol{k}$-competition graphs are discussed with the underlying bipolar fuzzy graphs.

Definition 4.4 Let $\vec{G} = (A, B)$ be a bipolar fuzzy digraph on a nonempty set X. An edge $\vec{xy} \in \vec{E} = supp(\vec{B})$ is called **strong** if $\mu_B^p(xy) \geq \frac{1}{2}(\mu_A^p(x) \wedge \mu_A^p(y))$ and $\mu_B^n(xy) \leq \frac{1}{2}(\mu_A^n(x) \vee \mu_A^n(y))$.

Remark 4.1 If all the edges of a bipolar fuzzy digraph are strong, then all the edges of the corresponding bipolar fuzzy competition graph may not be strong.

Definition 4.5 Let $A = (\mu^p, \mu^n)$ be a bipolar fuzzy set on X, then the **cardinality** of A is denoted by $|A|$ and defined as

$$|A| = (\mid \mu_A^p \mid, \mid \mu_A^n \mid) = \left(\sum_{x\in X} \mu^p(x), \sum_{x\in X} \mu^n(x)\right).$$

Definition 4.6 Let $\boldsymbol{k} = (k^p, k^n)$ be an ordered pair such that $k^p \in [0, 1]$ and $k^n \in [-1, 0]$. The **bipolar fuzzy $\boldsymbol{k}$−competition graph** of a bipolar fuzzy digraph $\vec{G} = (A, \vec{B})$ is an undirected bipolar fuzzy graph $\mathcal{C}_{\boldsymbol{k}}(\vec{G}) = (A, R)$ which has the same bipolar fuzzy vertex set as in $\vec{G}$ and there is an edge between two vertices x and y if $|\mu^p_{\mathcal{N}^+(x)\cap\mathcal{N}^+(y)}| > k^p$ and $|\mu^n_{\mathcal{N}^+(x)\cap\mathcal{N}^+(y)}| < k^n$. The membership value of the edge xy is defined as

$$\mu_R^p(xy) = \frac{l^p - k^p}{l^p}(\mu_A^p(x) \wedge \mu_A^p(y)) \times h(\mathcal{N}^+(x) \cap \mathcal{N}^+(y)),$$
$$\mu_R^n(xy) = \frac{l^n - k^n}{l^n}(\mu_A^n(x) \vee \mu_A^n(y)) \times h(\mathcal{N}^+(x) \cap \mathcal{N}^+(y)), \qquad \text{for all } x, y \in X$$

where $|\mathcal{N}^+(x) \cap \mathcal{N}^+(y)| = (l^p, l^n)$.

Theorem 4.4 *Let $\vec{G} = (A, \vec{B})$ be a bipolar fuzzy digraph. If $h(\mathcal{N}^+(x) \cap \mathcal{N}^+(y)) = 1$, $|\mu^p_{\mathcal{N}^+(x)\cap\mathcal{N}^+(y)}| > 2k^p$, and $|\mu^n_{\mathcal{N}^+(x)\cap\mathcal{N}^+(y)}| < 2k^n$ for some $x, y \in X$, then the edge xy is strong in $\mathcal{C}_{\boldsymbol{k}}(\vec{G})$.*

Proof Let $\mathcal{C}_{\boldsymbol{k}}(\vec{G}) = (A, R)$ be a bipolar fuzzy $\boldsymbol{k}$−competition graph of the bipolar fuzzy digraph $\vec{G} = (A, \vec{B})$. Suppose for $x, y \in X$, $|\mathcal{N}^+(x) \cap \mathcal{N}^+(y)| = (l^p, l^n)$, then

$$\mu_R^p(xy) = \frac{l^p - k^p}{l^p}(\mu_A^p(x) \wedge \mu_A^p(y))h(\mathcal{N}^+(x) \cap \mathcal{N}^+(y)),$$
$$\mu_R^p(xy) = \frac{l^p - k^p}{l^p}(\mu_A^p(x) \wedge \mu_A^p(y)), \quad \because h(\mathcal{N}^+(x) \cap \mathcal{N}^+(y)) = 1$$
$$\Rightarrow \quad l^p\mu_R^p(xy) = (l^p - k^p)(\mu_A^p(x) \wedge \mu_A^p(y)) > k^p(\mu_A^p(x) \wedge \mu_A^p(y)),$$

$$\Rightarrow \qquad 2k^p\mu_R^p(xy) > k^p(\mu_A^p(x) \wedge \mu_A^p(y)),$$
$$\Rightarrow \qquad \mu_R^p(xy) > \frac{1}{2}\left(\mu_A^p(x) \wedge \mu_A^p(y)\right).$$

$$\mu_R^n(xy) = \frac{l^n - k^n}{l^n}(\mu_A^n(x) \wedge \mu_A^n(y))h(\mathcal{N}^+(x) \cap \mathcal{N}^+(y)),$$
$$\mu_R^n(xy) = \frac{l^n - k^n}{l^n}(\mu_A^n(x) \wedge \mu_A^n(y)), \quad \because h(\mathcal{N}^+(x) \cap \mathcal{N}^+(y)) = 1$$
$$\Rightarrow \qquad l^n\mu_R^n(xy) = (l^n - k^n)(\mu_A^n(x) \wedge \mu_A^n(y)) < k^n(\mu_A^n(x) \wedge \mu_A^n(y)),$$
$$\Rightarrow \qquad 2k^n\mu_R^n(xy) < k^n(\mu_A^n(x) \wedge \mu_A^n(y)),$$
$$\Rightarrow \qquad \mu_R^n(xy) < \frac{1}{2}\left(\mu_A^n(x) \wedge \mu_A^n(y)\right).$$

Thus the edge xy is strong in $\mathcal{C}_k(\vec{G})$. □

Definition 4.7 Let $G = (A, B)$ be a bipolar fuzzy graph. A **bipolar fuzzy open neighborhood**, $\mathcal{N}(u)$, of a vertex u in G is a bipolar fuzzy set $\mathcal{N}(u) = (X_u, \mu^p_{\mathcal{N}(u)}, \mu^n_{\mathcal{N}(u)})$ where $X_u = \{v | B(uv) \neq (0, 0)\}$ and $\mu^p_{\mathcal{N}(u)} : X_u \to [0, 1]$, $\mu^n_{\mathcal{N}(u)} : X_u \to [-1, 0]$ are the membership functions defined by $\mu^p_{\mathcal{N}(u)}(u) = \mu^p_B(uv)$ and $\mu^n_{\mathcal{N}(u)}(u) = \mu^n_B(uv)$. The **bipolar fuzzy closed neighborhood**, $\mathcal{N}[u]$, is defined as $\mathcal{N}[u] = \mathcal{N}(u) \cup \{(u, \mu^p_A(u), \mu^n_A(u))\}$.

Definition 4.8 Let $G = (A, B)$ be a bipolar fuzzy graph. A **bipolar fuzzy open neighborhood graph** of G is a bipolar fuzzy graph $\mathcal{N}(G) = (A, R')$, whose set of vertices is the same as G and there is an edge between two vertices u and v if $\mathcal{N}(u) \cap \mathcal{N}(v) \neq \emptyset$ and $R' = (\mu^p_{R'}, \mu^n_{R'})$ is a bipolar fuzzy set, where $\mu^p_{R'} : X \times X \to [0, 1]$ and $\mu^n_{R'} : X \times X \to [-1, 0]$ are the membership functions defined as

$$\mu^p_{R'}(uv) = (\mu^p_A(u) \wedge \mu^p_A(v)) \times h(\mathcal{N}(u) \cap \mathcal{N}(v)),$$
$$\mu^n_{R'}(uv) = (\mu^n_A(u) \vee \mu^n_A(v)) \times h(\mathcal{N}(u) \cap \mathcal{N}(v)), \qquad \text{for all } u, v \in X.$$

The bipolar fuzzy closed neighborhood graph is defined on the same lines in Definition 4.9.

Definition 4.9 Let $G = (A, B)$ be a bipolar fuzzy graph. The **bipolar fuzzy closed neighborhood graph** of G is a bipolar fuzzy graph $\mathcal{N}[G] = (A, R')$ whose set of vertices is the same as G and there is an edge between two vertices u and v if $\mathcal{N}[u] \cap \mathcal{N}[v] \neq \emptyset$ and $R' = (\mu^p_{R'}, \mu^n_{R'})$ is a bipolar fuzzy set, where $\mu^p_{R'} : X \times X \to [0, 1]$ and $\mu^n_{R'} : X \times X \to [-1, 0]$ are the membership functions defined as

$$\mu^p_{R'}(uv) = (\mu^p_A(u) \wedge \mu^p_A(v)) \times h(\mathcal{N}[u] \cap \mathcal{N}[v]),$$
$$\mu^n_{R'}(uv) = (\mu^n_A(u) \vee \mu^n_A(v)) \times h(\mathcal{N}[u] \cap \mathcal{N}[v]), \qquad \text{for all } u, v \in X.$$

Considering the bipolar fuzzy open and closed neighborhood of the vertices, another type of bipolar fuzzy graphs are introduced in the following definitions.

Definition 4.10 Let k be an ordered pair (given in Definition 4.6) then a **bipolar fuzzy (k)−competition graph** of a bipolar fuzzy graph $G = (A, B)$ is a bipolar fuzzy graph $\mathcal{N}_k(G) = (A, R')$ which has the same vertex set as in G and there is an edge between two vertices u and v if $|\mu^p_{\mathcal{N}(u)\cap\mathcal{N}(v)}| > k^p$ and $|\mu^n_{\mathcal{N}(u)\cap\mathcal{N}(v)}| < k^n$. The membership value of the edge uv is defined as

$$\mu^p_{R'}(uv) = \frac{l^p - k^p}{l^p}(\mu^p_A(u) \wedge \mu^p_A(v)) \times h(\mathcal{N}(u) \cap \mathcal{N}(v)),$$
$$\mu^n_{R'}(uv) = \frac{l^n - k^n}{l^n}(\mu^n_A(u) \vee \mu^n_A(v)) \times h(\mathcal{N}(u) \cap \mathcal{N}(v)), \qquad \text{for all } u, v \in X$$

where $|\mathcal{N}(u) \cap \mathcal{N}(v)| = (l^p, l^n)$.

Definition 4.11 Let k be an ordered pair (given in Definition 4.6) then a **bipolar fuzzy $[k]$− competition graph** of a bipolar fuzzy graph $G = (A, B)$ is a bipolar fuzzy graph $\mathcal{N}_k[G] = (A, R')$ which has the same vertex set as in G and there is an edge between two vertices u and v if $|\mu^p_{\mathcal{N}[u]\cap\mathcal{N}[v]}| > k^p$ and $|\mu^n_{\mathcal{N}[u]\cap\mathcal{N}[v]} < k^n$. The membership value of the edge uv is defined as

$$\mu^p_{R'}(uv) = \frac{l^p - k^p}{l^p}(\mu^p_A(u) \wedge \mu^p_A(v)) \times h(\mathcal{N}[u] \cap \mathcal{N}[v]),$$
$$\mu^n_{R'}(uv) = \frac{l^n - k^n}{l^n}(\mu^n_A(u) \vee \mu^n_A(v)) \times h(\mathcal{N}[u] \cap \mathcal{N}[v]), \qquad \text{for all } u, v \in X$$

where $|\mathcal{N}[u] \cap \mathcal{N}[v]| = (l^p, l^n)$.

Theorem 4.5 *For every edge of a bipolar fuzzy graph G, there exists one edge in $\mathcal{N}[G]$.*

Proof Let $\mathcal{N}[G] = (A, R')$ be a bipolar fuzzy closed neighborhood graph corresponding to the bipolar fuzzy graph $G = (A, B)$. Let uv be an edge in G, then $u, v \in \mathcal{N}[u]$ and $u, v \in \mathcal{N}[v]$. So, $u, v \in \mathcal{N}[u] \cap \mathcal{N}[v]$ and therefore $h(\mathcal{N}[u] \cap \mathcal{N}[v]) \neq 0$. Hence,

$$\mu^p_{R'}(uv) = \frac{l^p - k^p}{l^p}(\mu^p_A(u) \wedge \mu^p_A(v)) \times h(\mathcal{N}[u] \cap \mathcal{N}[v]) > 0,$$

$$\mu^n_{R'}(uv) = \frac{l^n - k^n}{l^n}(\mu^n_A(u) \vee \mu^n_A(v)) \times h(\mathcal{N}[u] \cap \mathcal{N}[v]) < 0.$$

That is, uv is an edge of $\mathcal{N}[G]$ which completes the proof. □

Definition 4.12 Let $\vec{G} = (A, \vec{B})$ be a bipolar fuzzy digraph on X such that $\vec{E} = supp(\vec{B})$. The **underlying bipolar fuzzy graph** of $\vec{G}$ is a bipolar fuzzy graph $\mathcal{U}(\vec{G}) = (A, B)$ where $B = (\mu^p_B, \mu^n_B)$ is defined as

$$B(uv) = (\mu_B^p(uv), \mu_B^n(uv)) = \begin{cases} (\mu_{\vec{B}}^p(uv), \mu_{\vec{B}}^n(uv)), & \text{if } \vec{uv} \in \vec{E}, \vec{vu} \notin \vec{E}, \\ (\mu_{\vec{B}}^p(vu), \mu_{\vec{B}}^n(vu)), & \text{if } \vec{vu} \in \vec{E}, \vec{uv} \notin \vec{E}, \\ (\mu_{\vec{B}}^p(uv) \wedge \mu_{\vec{B}}^p(vu), \mu_{\vec{B}}^n(uv) \vee \mu_{\vec{B}}^n(vu)), & \text{if } \vec{uv}, \vec{vu} \in \vec{E}. \end{cases}$$

The relations between bipolar fuzzy neighborhood graphs and bipolar fuzzy competition graphs are established in the following theorems.

Theorem 4.6 *Let $\vec{G} = (A, \vec{B})$ be a symmetric bipolar fuzzy digraph without any loops then $\mathcal{C}_k(\vec{G}) = \mathcal{N}_k(\mathcal{U}(\vec{G}))$, where $\mathcal{U}(\vec{G})$ is the underlying bipolar fuzzy graph of $\vec{G}$.*

Proof Let $\mathcal{U}(\vec{G}) = (A, B)$ be an underlying bipolar fuzzy graph corresponding to a bipolar fuzzy digraph $\vec{G} = (A, \vec{B})$. Also, let $\mathcal{N}_k(\mathcal{U}(\vec{G})) = (A, R')$ and $\mathcal{C}_k(\vec{G}) = (A, R)$. The bipolar fuzzy $\boldsymbol{k}$−competition graph $\mathcal{C}_k(\vec{G})$ as well as the underlying bipolar fuzzy graph have the same vertex set as $\vec{G}$. Hence $\mathcal{N}_k(\mathcal{U}(\vec{G}))$ has the same vertex set as $\vec{G}$. It remains only to show that $R(uv) = R'(uv)$, for every $u, v \in X$. There are two cases.

Case 1: If for all $u, v \in X$, $R(uv) = (\mu_R^p(uv), \mu_R^n(uv)) = (0, 0)$ in $\mathcal{C}_k(\vec{G})$, then either $|\mu^p_{\mathcal{N}^+(u)\cap\mathcal{N}^+(v)}| \ngtr k^p$ or $|\mu^n_{\mathcal{N}^+(u)\cap\mathcal{N}^+(v)}| \nless k^n$. Since $\vec{G}$ is symmetric, either $|\mu^p_{\mathcal{N}(u)\cap\mathcal{N}(v)}| \ngtr k^p$ or $|\mu^n_{\mathcal{N}(u)\cap\mathcal{N}(v)}| \nless k^n$ in $\mathcal{U}(\vec{G})$. Hence, $R'(uv) = (0, 0)$ and so $R(uv) = R'(uv)$, for all $u, v \in X$.

Case 2: If for some $u, v \in X$, $(\mu_R^p(uv), \mu_R^n(uv)) \neq (0, 0)$ in $\mathcal{C}_k(\vec{G})$, then $|\mu^p_{\mathcal{N}^+(u)\cap\mathcal{N}^+(v)}| > k^p$ and $|\mu^n_{\mathcal{N}^+(u)\cap\mathcal{N}^+(v)}| < k^n$. Since $\vec{G}$ is a symmetric bipolar fuzzy digraph, $h(\mathcal{N}(u) \cap \mathcal{N}(v)) = h(\mathcal{N}^+(u) \cap \mathcal{N}^+(v))$. Then for all $u, v \in X$,

$$\mu_R^p(uv) = \frac{l^p - k^p}{l^p}(\mu_A^p(u) \wedge \mu_A^p(v))h(\mathcal{N}^+(u) \cap \mathcal{N}^+(v)) = \mu_{R'}^p(uv),$$
$$\mu_R^n(uv) = \frac{l^n - k^n}{l^n}(\mu_A^n(u) \wedge \mu_A^n(v))h(\mathcal{N}^+(u) \cap \mathcal{N}^+(v)) = \mu_{R'}^n(uv), \qquad (l^p, l^n) = |\mathcal{N}^+(u) \cap \mathcal{N}^+(v)|.$$

Hence $R(uv) = R'(uv)$. Since u and v were taken to be arbitrary, the result holds for all edges uv of $\mathcal{C}_k(\vec{G})$.

Theorem 4.7 *Let $\vec{G} = (A, \vec{B})$ be a symmetric bipolar fuzzy digraph having loops at every vertex, then $\mathcal{C}_k(\vec{G}) = \mathcal{N}_k[\mathcal{U}(\vec{G})]$, where $\mathcal{U}(\vec{G})$ is the underlying bipolar fuzzy graph of $\vec{G}$.*

Proof Let $\mathcal{U}(\vec{G}) = (A, B)$ be an underlying bipolar fuzzy graph corresponding to bipolar fuzzy digraph $\vec{G} = (A, \vec{B})$. Also, let $\mathcal{N}_k(\mathcal{U}(\vec{G})) = (A, R')$ and $\mathcal{C}_k(\vec{G}) = (A, R)$. The bipolar fuzzy $\boldsymbol{k}$−competition graph $\mathcal{C}_k(\vec{G})$ as well as the bipolar fuzzy underlying graph have the same vertex set as $\vec{G}$. Hence $\mathcal{N}_k(\mathcal{U}[\vec{G})]$ has the same vertex set as $\vec{G}$. It remains only to show that $R(uv) = R'(uv)$ for every $u, v \in X$. As the bipolar fuzzy digraph has a loop at every vertex therefore, the bipolar fuzzy out neighborhood contains the vertex itself. There are two cases.

Case 1: If for all $u, v \in X$, $R(uv) = (0, 0)$ in $\mathcal{C}_k(\vec{G})$, then either $|\mu^p_{\mathcal{N}^+(u)\cap\mathcal{N}^+(v)}| \ngtr k^p$ or $|\mu^n_{\mathcal{N}^+(u)\cap\mathcal{N}^+(v)}| \nless k^n$. Since $\vec{G}$ is symmetric, either $|\mu^p_{\mathcal{N}[u]\cap\mathcal{N}[v]}| \ngtr k^p$ or $|\mu^n_{\mathcal{N}[u]\cap\mathcal{N}[v]}| \nless k^n$ in $\mathcal{U}(\vec{G})$. Hence, $R'(uv) = (0, 0)$ and so $R(uv) = R'(uv)$ for all $u, v \in X$.

Case 2: If for some $u, v \in X$, $\mu^p_R(uv) > 0$ and $\mu^p_R(uv) < 0$ in $\mathcal{C}_k(\vec{G})$, then $|\mu^p_{\mathcal{N}^+(u)\cap\mathcal{N}^+(v)}| > k^p$ and $|\mu^n_{\mathcal{N}^+(u)\cap\mathcal{N}^+(v)}| < k^n$. Since $\vec{G}$ is a symmetric bipolar fuzzy digraph with loops, $|\mathcal{N}[u] \cap \mathcal{N}[v]| = |\mathcal{N}^+(u) \cap \mathcal{N}^+(v)|$ and $h(\mathcal{N}[u] \cap \mathcal{N}[v]) = h(\mathcal{N}^+(u) \cap \mathcal{N}^+(v))$. Thus for all $u, v \in X$,

$$\mu^p_R(uv) = \frac{l^p - k^p}{l^p}(\mu^p_A(u) \wedge \mu^p_A(v))h(\mathcal{N}^+(u) \cap \mathcal{N}^+(v)) = \mu^p_{R'}(uv),$$

$$\mu^n_R(uv) = \frac{l^p - k^p}{l^p}(\mu^n_A(u) \wedge \mu^n_A(v))h(\mathcal{N}^+(u) \cap \mathcal{N}^+(v)) = \mu^n_{R'}(uv), \quad (l^p, l^n) = |\mathcal{N}^+(u) \cap \mathcal{N}^+(v)|.$$

Hence $R(uv) = R'(uv)$. Since u and v were taken to be arbitrary, the result holds for all edges uv of $\mathcal{C}_k(\vec{G})$. □

4.4 Complex Bipolar Fuzzy Competition Graphs

In this section, the concept of complex bipolar fuzzy competition graphs is discussed with several notions concerning complex bipolar fuzzy out neighborhoods, complex bipolar fuzzy in neighborhoods, complex bipolar fuzzy open neighborhood graphs, complex bipolar fuzzy closed neighborhood graphs, complex bipolar fuzzy $k-$competition graphs, and underlying complex bipolar fuzzy graphs.

Definition 4.13 A **complex bipolar fuzzy digraph** on a nonempty set X is a pair $G = (A, \vec{D})$, where $A = (r^p_A e^{w^p_A}, r^n_A e^{w^n_A}) : X \to \{z \mid z \in C, |z| \leq 1\}^2$ is a complex bipolar fuzzy set on X and $\vec{D} = (r^p_{\vec{D}} e^{w^p_{\vec{D}}}, r^n_{\vec{D}} e^{w^n_{\vec{D}}}) : X \times X \to \{z \mid z \in C\ |z| \leq 1\}^2$ is a complex bipolar polar fuzzy relation in X such that, for all $x, y \in X$,

$$r^p_{\vec{D}}(xy) \leq r^p_A(x) \wedge r^p_A(y) \quad \text{and } r^n_{\vec{D}}(xy) \geq r^n_A(x) \vee r^n_A(y), \quad \text{(for amplitude terms)}$$

$$w^p_{\vec{D}}(xy) \leq w^p_A(x) \wedge w^p_A(y) \quad \text{and } w^n_{\vec{D}}(xy) \geq w^n_A(x) \vee w^n_A(y), \quad \text{(for phase terms)}$$

where $i = \sqrt{-1}$, $r^p_A : X \to [0, 1]$, $r^n_A : X \to [-1, 0]$, $r^p_{\vec{D}} : X \times X \to [0, 1]$ and $r^n_{\vec{D}} : X \times X \to [-1, 0]$ are mappings, $w^p_A, w^p_{\vec{D}} \in [0, \pi]$, $w^n_A, w^n_{\vec{D}} \in [\pi, 2\pi]$ or $w^n_A, w^n_{\vec{D}} \in [-\pi, 0]$.

Note that $\vec{D}$ is not a symmetric complex bipolar fuzzy relation.

Definition 4.14 A **complex bipolar fuzzy graph** on a nonempty set X is a pair $G = (A, D)$, where $A = (r^p_A e^{w^p_A}, r^n_A e^{w^n_A}) : X \to \{z \mid z \in C, |z| \leq 1\}^2$ is a complex bipolar fuzzy set on X and $D = (r^p_D e^{w^p_D}, r^n_D e^{w^n_D}) : X \times X \to \{z \mid z \in C, |z| \leq 1\}^2$ is a complex bipolar polar fuzzy relation in X such that, for all $x, y \in X$

$$r^p_D(xy) \le r^p_A(x) \wedge r^p_A(y) \text{ and } r^n_D(xy) \ge r^n_A(x) \vee r^n_A(y), \quad \text{(for amplitude terms)}$$
$$w^p_D(xy) \le w^p_A(x) \wedge w^p_A(y) \text{ and } w^n_D(xy) \ge w^n_A(x) \vee w^n_A(y), \quad \text{(for phase terms)},$$

where $i = \sqrt{-1}, r^p_A : X \to [0, 1], r^n_A : X \to [-1, 0], r^p_D : X \times X \to [0, 1]$ and $r^n_D : X \times X \to [-1, 0]$ are mappings, $w^p_A, w^p_D \in [0, \pi], w^n_A, w^n_D \in [\pi, 2\pi]$ or $w^n_A, w^n_D \in [-\pi, 0]$.

Note that $D(xy) = (0, 0)$ for all $xy \in X \times X - E$, where $E \subseteq X \times X$ is the set of edges. A is called a complex bipolar fuzzy vertex set of G and D is a complex bipolar fuzzy edge set of G. A bipolar fuzzy relation D on X is **symmetric** if $D(xy) = D(yx)$ for all $x, y \in X$. Notice that $D(xy) = (0, 0)$ for $xy \notin E$.

Definition 4.15 Let $\vec{G} = (A, \vec{D})$ be a complex bipolar fuzzy graph on a nonempty set X. A **complex bipolar fuzzy out neighborhood** of a vertex $x \in X$ in a complex bipolar fuzzy digraph $\vec{G}$ is a complex bipolar fuzzy set $\mathcal{N}^+(x) = (X^+_x, \mu^p_{\mathcal{N}^+(x)}, \mu^n_{\mathcal{N}^+(x)})$, where $X^+_x = \{y \in X \mid (\mu^p_{\vec{D}}(xy), \mu^n_{\vec{D}}(xy)) \neq (0, 0)\}$ and $(\mu^p_{\mathcal{N}^+(x)}, \mu^n_{\mathcal{N}^+(x)}) : X^+_x \to \{z \mid z \in C, |z| \le 1\}^2$ is defined as

$$\mu^p_{\mathcal{N}^+(x)}(y) = \mu^p_{\vec{D}}(xy) = r^p_{\vec{D}}(xy)e^{iw^p_{\vec{D}}(xy)}, \quad \mu^n_{\mathcal{N}^+(x)}(y) = \mu^n_{\vec{D}}(xy) = r^n_{\vec{D}}(xy)e^{iw^n_{\vec{D}}(xy)}.$$

A **complex bipolar fuzzy in neighborhood** of a vertex $x \in X$ in a complex bipolar fuzzy digraph $\vec{G}$ is a complex bipolar fuzzy set $\mathcal{N}^-(x) = (X^-_x, \mu^p_{\mathcal{N}^-(x)}, \mu^n_{\mathcal{N}^-(x)})$, where $X^-_x = \{y \in X \mid (\mu^p_{\vec{D}}(yx), \mu^n_{\vec{D}}(yx)) \neq (0, 0)\}$ and $(\mu^p_{\mathcal{N}^-(x)}, \mu^n_{\mathcal{N}^-(x)}) : X^-_x \to \{z \mid z \in C, |z| \le 1\}^2$ is defined as

$$\mu^p_{\mathcal{N}^-(x)}(y) = \mu^p_{\vec{D}}(yx) = r^p_{\vec{D}}(yx)e^{iw^p_{\vec{D}}(yx)}, \quad \mu^n_{\mathcal{N}^-(x)}(y) = \mu^n_{\vec{D}}(yx) = r^n_{\vec{D}}(yx)e^{iw^n_{\vec{D}}(yx)}.$$

Definition 4.16 Let $A = \left(r^p_A e^{iw^p_A}, r^n_A e^{iw^n_A}\right)$ be a complex bipolar fuzzy set on a nonempty set X. The **height** of A is defined as $h(A) = r_{h(A)}e^{iw_{h(A)}}$, where

$$r_{h(A)} = \max\{r^p_A(x) \mid x \in X\} \quad \text{and} \quad w_{h(A)} = \max\{w^p_A(x) \mid x \in X\}.$$

Definition 4.17 Let $\vec{G} = (A, \vec{D})$ be a complex bipolar fuzzy digraph on a nonempty set X. A **complex bipolar fuzzy competition graph** of a complex bipolar fuzzy digraph $\vec{G}$ is an undirected complex bipolar fuzzy graph $\mathcal{C}(\vec{G}) = (A, R)$ which has the same vertex set as in $\vec{G}$ and there is an edge between two vertices x and y, $x, y \in X$, if $\mathcal{N} = \mathcal{N}^+(x) \cap \mathcal{N}^+(y)$ is nonempty. The complex bipolar fuzzy set $R = \left(r^p_R e^{iw^p_R}, r^n_R e^{iw^n_R}\right)$ is defined as

$$r^p_R(xy) = (r^p_A(x) \wedge r^p_A(y)) \times r_{h(\mathcal{N})},$$
$$r^n_R(xy) = (r^n_A(x) \vee r^n_A(y)) \times r_{h(\mathcal{N})}, \quad \text{(for amplitude terms)}$$
$$w^p_R(xy) = \pi\left[\left(\frac{w^p_A(x)}{\pi} \wedge \frac{w^p_A(y)}{\pi}\right) \times \frac{w_{h(\mathcal{N})}}{\pi}\right],$$

$$w_R^n(xy) = \pi\left[\left(\frac{w_A^n(x)}{\pi} \vee \frac{w_A^n(y)}{\pi}\right) \times \frac{w_{h(\mathcal{N})}}{\pi}\right], \quad \text{(for phase terms)}.$$

Theorem 4.8 *Let G be a complex bipolar fuzzy graph then adding sufficient number of isolated vertices to G produces a complex bipolar fuzzy competition graph of some complex bipolar fuzzy digraph.*

Proof Let $G = (A, R)$ be a complex bipolar fuzzy graph on nonempty set X, where $A = (r_A^p e^{iw_A^p}, r_A^n e^{iw_A^n})$ is a complex bipolar fuzzy set on the set of vertices X and $R = (r_R^p e^{iw_R^p}, r_R^n e^{iw_R^n})$ is a complex bipolar fuzzy relation in X. Construct the complex bipolar fuzzy digraph $\vec{G} = (A, \vec{D})$ as follows: Let $x, y \in X$ be any two vertices of G such that $R(xy) \neq (0, 0)$. Add a vertex β_{xy}, remove the edge xy and draw directed edges from x and y to β_{xy} such that

$$A(\beta_{xy}) = \left((r_A^p(x) \wedge r_A^p(y))e^{i(w_A^p(x) \wedge w_A^p(y))}, (r_A^n(x) \vee r_A^n(y))e^{i(w_A^n(x) \vee w_A^n(y))}\right)$$

$$r_{\vec{D}}^p(x\beta_{xy}) = r_{\vec{D}}^p(y\beta_{xy}) = \frac{r_R^p(xy)}{r_A^p(x) \wedge r_A^p(y)}, \quad r_{\vec{D}}^n(x\beta_{xy}) = r_{\vec{D}}^n(y\beta_{xy}) = -\frac{r_R^n(xy)}{r_A^p(x) \vee r_A^n(y)}$$

$$w_{\vec{D}}^p(x\beta_{xy}) = w_{\vec{D}}^p(y\beta_{xy}) = \frac{w_R^p(xy)}{\frac{w_A^p(x)}{\pi} \wedge \frac{w_A^p(y)}{\pi}}, \quad w_{\vec{D}}^n(x\beta_{xy}) = w_{\vec{D}}^n(y\beta_{xy}) = -\frac{w_R^n(xy)}{\frac{w_A^n(x)}{\pi} \vee \frac{w_A^n(y)}{\pi}}.$$

Continuing this process, we obtain a complex bipolar fuzzy digraph $\vec{G}$ such that $\mathcal{C}(\vec{G}) = G \cup I$, where I is the complex bipolar fuzzy set of isolated vertices added to G. □

Definition 4.18 Let $\vec{G} = (A, D)$ be a complex bipolar fuzzy digraph on a nonempty set X. An edge $\vec{xy}$ in $\vec{G}$ is called **strong** if

$$r_D^p(xy) \geq \frac{1}{2}(r_A^p(x) \wedge r_A^p(y)),$$
$$r_D^n(xy) \leq \frac{1}{2}(r_A^n(x) \vee r_A^n(y)),$$
$$w_D^p(xy) \geq \frac{1}{2}\left(w_A^p(x) \wedge w_A^p(y)\right),$$
$$w_D^n(xy) \leq \frac{1}{2}\left(w_A^n(x) \wedge w_A^n(y)\right).$$

Definition 4.19 Let $A = (r^p e^{iw^p}, r^n e^{iw^n})$ be a complex bipolar fuzzy set on X then the **cardinality** of A is denoted by $|A|$ and defined as

$$|A| = \left(|\mu_A^p|, |\mu_A^n|\right) = \left(\sum_{x\in X} r^p(x)e^{i\sum_{x\in X} w^p(x)}, \sum_{x\in X} r^n(x)e^{i\sum_{x\in X} w^n(x)}\right).$$

Definition 4.20 Let $\boldsymbol{k} = (k^p e^{i\theta^p}, k^n e^{i\theta^n})$ be an ordered pair of complex numbers such that $k^p \in [0, 1], k^n \in [-1, 0], \theta^p \in [0, \pi], \theta^n \in [-\pi, 0]$. The **complex bipolar fuzzy k−competition graph** of a complex bipolar fuzzy digraph $\vec{G} = (A, \vec{D})$ is an undirected complex bipolar fuzzy graph $\mathcal{C}_k(\vec{G}) = (A, R)$ which has the same complex bipolar fuzzy vertex set as in $\vec{G}$ and there is an edge between two vertices x and y if

$$l^p > k^p, \quad \phi^p > \theta^p, \quad l^n < k^n, \quad \phi^n < \theta^n,$$

where $|\mathcal{N}| = |\mathcal{N}^+(x) \cap \mathcal{N}^+(y)| = \left(l^p e^{i\phi^p}, l^n e^{i\phi^n}\right)$. The membership values of the edge xy are defined as

$$\begin{aligned}
r_R^p(xy) &= \frac{l^p - k^p}{l^p}(r_A^p(x) \wedge r_A^p(y)) \times r_{h(\mathcal{N})},\\
r_R^n(xy) &= \frac{l^n - k^n}{l^n}(r_A^n(x) \vee r_A^n(y)) \times r_{h(\mathcal{N})}, \quad \text{(for amplitude terms)}\\
w_R^p(xy) &= \frac{\pi(\phi^p - \theta^p)}{\phi^p}\left[\left(\frac{w_A^p(x)}{\pi} \wedge \frac{w_A^p(y)}{\pi}\right) \times \frac{w_{h(\mathcal{N})}}{\pi}\right],\\
w_R^n(xy) &= \frac{\pi(\phi^n - \theta^n)}{\phi^n}\left[\left(\frac{w_A^n(x)}{\pi} \vee \frac{w_A^n(y)}{\pi}\right) \times \frac{w_{h(\mathcal{N})}}{\pi}\right], \quad \text{(for phase terms)}
\end{aligned}$$

for all $x, y \in X$.

Definition 4.21 Let $G = (A, D)$ be a complex bipolar fuzzy graph on a nonempty set X. A **complex bipolar fuzzy open neighborhood** of a vertex $x \in X$ in a complex bipolar fuzzy graph G is a complex bipolar fuzzy set $\mathcal{N}(x) = (X_x, \mu^p_{\mathcal{N}(x)}, \mu^n_{\mathcal{N}(x)})$, where $X_x = \{y \in X \mid D(xy) \neq (0, 0)\}$ and $(\mu^p_{\mathcal{N}(x)}, \mu^n_{\mathcal{N}(x)}) : X_x \rightarrow \{z \mid z \in C, |z| \leq 1\}^2$ is defined as

$$\mu^p_{\mathcal{N}(x)}(y) = \mu^p_D(xy) = r^p_D(xy)e^{iw^p_D(xy)}, \quad \mu^n_{\mathcal{N}(x)}(y) = \mu^n_D(xy) = r^n_D(xy)e^{iw^n_D(xy)}.$$

The **complex bipolar fuzzy closed neighborhood**, $\mathcal{N}[x]$, is defined as $\mathcal{N}[x] = \mathcal{N}(x) \cup \left\{(x, r^p_A(x)e^{iw^p_A(x)}, r^n_A(x)e^{iw^n_A(x)}\right\}$.

Definition 4.22 Let $G = (A, D)$ be a complex bipolar fuzzy graph on a nonempty set X. A **complex bipolar fuzzy open neighborhood graph** of a complex bipolar fuzzy graph G is an undirected complex bipolar fuzzy graph $\mathcal{N}(G) = (A, R')$ which has the same vertex set as in G and there is an edge between two vertices x and y, $x, y \in X$, if $\mathcal{N} = \mathcal{N}(x) \cap \mathcal{N}(y)$ is nonempty. The complex bipolar fuzzy set $R' = \left(r^p_{R'}e^{iw^p_{R'}}, r^n_{R'}e^{iw^n_{R'}}\right)$ is defined as

$$\begin{aligned}
r^p_{R'}(xy) &= (r^p_A(x) \wedge r^p_A(y)) \times r_{h(\mathcal{N})},\\
r^n_{R'}(xy) &= (r^n_A(x) \vee r^n_A(y)) \times r_{h(\mathcal{N})}, \quad \text{(for amplitude terms)}\\
w^p_{R'}(xy) &= \pi\left[\left(\frac{w^p_A(x)}{\pi} \wedge \frac{w^p_A(y)}{\pi}\right) \times \frac{w_{h(\mathcal{N})}}{\pi}\right],
\end{aligned}$$

$$w^n_{R'}(xy) = \pi\left[\left(\frac{w^n_A(x)}{\pi} \vee \frac{w^n_A(y)}{\pi}\right) \times \frac{w_{h(\mathcal{N})}}{\pi}\right], \quad \text{(for phase terms)}$$

for all $x, y \in X$.

The bipolar fuzzy closed neighborhood graph is defined on the same lines in Definition 4.23.

Definition 4.23 Let $G = (A, D)$ be a complex bipolar fuzzy graph on a nonempty set X. A **complex bipolar fuzzy closed neighborhood graph** of a complex bipolar fuzzy graph G is an undirected complex bipolar fuzzy graph $\mathcal{N}[G] = (A, R^*)$ which has the same vertex set as in G and there is an edge between two vertices x and y, $x, y \in X$, if $\mathcal{N} = \mathcal{N}[x] \cap \mathcal{N}[y]$ is nonempty. The complex bipolar fuzzy set $R^* = \left(r^p_{R^*}e^{iw^p_{R^*}}, r^n_{R^*}e^{iw^n_{R^*}}\right)$ is defined as

$$r^p_{R^*}(xy) = (r^p_A(x) \wedge r^p_A(y)) \times r_{h(\mathcal{N})},$$
$$r^n_{R^*}(xy) = (r^n_A(x) \vee r^n_A(y)) \times r_{h(\mathcal{N})}, \quad \text{(for amplitude terms)}$$
$$w^p_{R^*}(xy) = \pi\left[\left(\frac{w^p_A(x)}{\pi} \wedge \frac{w^p_A(y)}{\pi}\right) \times \frac{w_{h(\mathcal{N})}}{\pi}\right],$$
$$w^n_{R^*}(xy) = \pi\left[\left(\frac{w^n_A(x)}{\pi} \vee \frac{w^n_A(y)}{\pi}\right) \times \frac{w_{h(\mathcal{N})}}{\pi}\right], \quad \text{(for phase terms)}$$

for all $x, y \in X$.

Definition 4.24 Let $\vec{G} = (A, \vec{D})$ be a complex bipolar fuzzy digraph on X such that $\vec{E}$ is the crisp set of edges in $\vec{G}$. The **underlying complex bipolar fuzzy graph** of $\vec{G}$ is a complex bipolar fuzzy graph $\mathcal{U}(\vec{G}) = (A, D)$ such that $D = (\mu^p_D, \mu^n_D) = (r^p_D e^{iw^p_D}, r^n_D e^{iw^n_D})$ is defined as,

$$D(uv) = \begin{cases} (\mu^p_{\vec{D}}(uv), \mu^n_{\vec{D}}(uv)), & \text{if } \vec{uv} \in \vec{E}, \vec{vu} \notin \vec{E} \\ (\mu^p_{\vec{D}}(vu), \mu^n_{\vec{D}}(vu)), & \text{if } \vec{vu} \in \vec{E}, \vec{uv} \notin \vec{E} \\ (f^p, f^n), & \text{if } \vec{uv}, \vec{vu} \in \vec{E} \end{cases}$$

where $f^p = (r^p_{\vec{D}}(uv) \wedge r^p_{\vec{D}}(vu))e^{i(w^p_{\vec{D}}(uv) \wedge w^p_{\vec{D}}(vu))}$ and $f^n = (r^n_{\vec{D}}(uv) \vee r^n_{\vec{D}}(vu))$ $e^{i(w^n_{\vec{D}}(uv) \vee w^n_{\vec{D}}(vu))}$.

4.5 Applications of Bipolar Fuzzy Competition Graphs

In this section, certain algorithms are elaborated to compute the strength of competition among objects with a number of real-world applications in different fields including food webs, business marketing, politics, wireless communication networks, and social networking.

4.5.1 Variants of Bipolar Fuzzy Competition Graphs in Food Webs

Food webs are the graphical representations of natural interconnection of food chains between different species. Competition graphs arose in connection with an application in food webs. In a food web, vertices represent species and there is a directed edge between two species x and y if y is a food for x. Bipolar fuzzy graphs are more realistic to represent the competition between species. There are many interesting variations of the notion of bipolar fuzzy competition graphs in ecological interpretation. For instance, two species may have a common prey, a common enemy, both common prey and common enemy, or either a common prey or a common enemy. All of these notions are discussed in two different ecological niches.

1. Bipolar fuzzy competition graph in food webs

Let $\vec{G} = (A, \vec{B})$ represents a bipolar fuzzy food web on the set of species X in which $\vec{xy} \in \vec{E}$ if x preys on y. Bipolar fuzzy food webs can play an important role for investigating the flow of energy and predator—–prey relationship in ecosystem. Bipolar fuzzy competition graph can be constructed from bipolar fuzzy food web (Definition 4.25) to study the extent to which species compete for common prey.

Definition 4.25 Let $\vec{G} = (A, \vec{B})$ be a bipolar fuzzy food web. The bipolar fuzzy competition graph $\mathcal{C}(\vec{G}) = (A, R)$ has the same set of vertices as $\vec{G}$ and there is an edge between two vertices x and y if $\mathcal{N}^-(x) \cap \mathcal{N}^-(y) \neq \emptyset$. The membership function R is defined as

$$\mu_R^p(xy) = (\mu_A^p(x)(x) \wedge \mu_A^p(y))h\left(\mathcal{N}^-(x) \cap \mathcal{N}^-(y)\right),$$

$$\mu_R^n(xy) = (\mu_A^n(x)(x) \vee \mu_A^n(y))h\left(\mathcal{N}^-(x) \cap \mathcal{N}^-(y)\right).$$

The method for calculating the strength of competition between species in ecosystem in given in Algorithm 4.5.1.

Algorithm 4.5.1 Bipolar fuzzy competition graph in ecosystem

1. Input the number n of species $x_1, x_2, \ldots, x_n$.
2. Input the adjacency matrix of bipolar fuzzy food web.
3. Construct the table of bipolar fuzzy in neighborhoods of all the species.
4. Construct the bipolar fuzzy competition graph $\mathcal{C}(\vec{G}) = (A, R)$ using Definition 4.25.
5. If $\mathcal{N}^-(x) \cap \mathcal{N}^-(y) \neq \emptyset$ for any two species x and y then the strength of competition between x and y for common food can be calculated using Formula (4.14) as

$$S(x, y) = \frac{\mu_A^p(x) + \mu_A^p(y) + \mu_R^p(xy) + (3 + \mu_A^n(x) + \mu_A^n(y) + \mu_R^n(xy))}{6}. \tag{4.14}$$

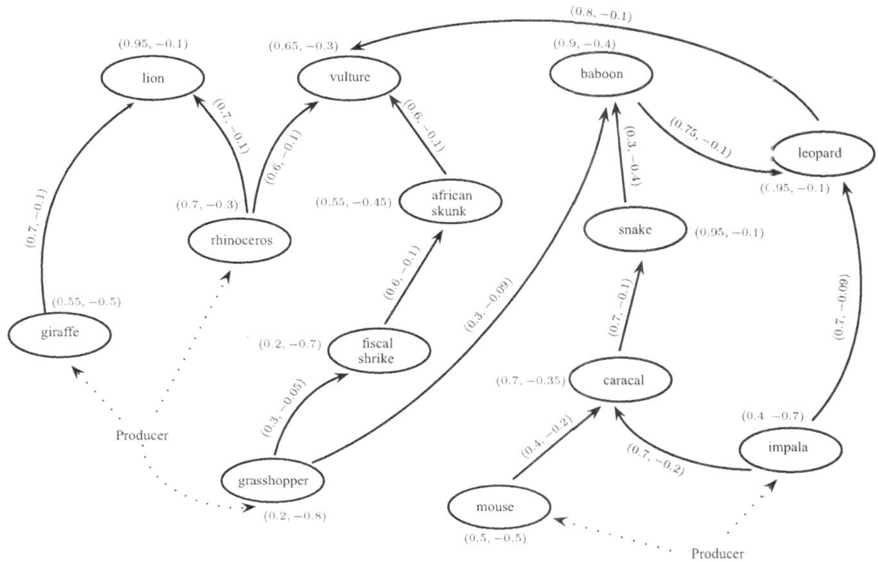

Fig. 4.25 Bipolar fuzzy food web

Consider the example of bipolar fuzzy food web of 13 species giraffe, lion, vulture, rhinoceros, African skunk, fiscal shrike, grasshopper, baboon, leopard, snake, caracal, mouse, and impala. The positive degree of membership of each specie represents the extent to which a specie is strong according to its power and can defend itself to exist in the animal kingdom. The negative degree of membership of specie represents its weakness that it can be killed or dominated by other species. The bipolar fuzzy food web is shown in Fig. 4.25.

The degree of membership of lion is (0.95, −0.1), which shows that lion is 95% strong in its kingdom according to hunting power and 10% weak because a group of animals together can dominate a lion. The directed edge between giraffe and lion has degree of membership (0.7, −0.1), which represents that lion obtains 70% energy from giraffe and a giraffe is 10% harmful to lion because it can kill a lion with its long legs. This is an acyclic bipolar fuzzy digraph. A bipolar fuzzy competition graph can be constructed to investigate the strength of competition between species for common food\prey. The bipolar fuzzy in neighborhoods are given in Table 4.11.

The bipolar fuzzy competition graph is shown in Fig. 4.26. There is a food competition between lion and vulture, fiscal shrike and baboon, snake and caracal, leopard and caracal. The membership value of an edge between two species represents the degree of benefits and harm of common food.

The strengths of competition between species x and y calculated using Formula (4.14) are given in Table 4.12.

According to Table 4.12, there is a strong competition between caracal and leopard for common food with respect to hunting powers and weaknesses.

Table 4.11 Bipolar fuzzy in neighborhoods of species

Species	$\mathcal{N}^-(u)$: u is a specie
giraffe	∅
lion	{(giraffe, 0.7, −0.1), (rhinoceros, 0.7, −0.1)}
rhinoceros	∅
vulture	{(rhinoceros, 0.6, −0.1), (African skunk, 0.6, −0.1), (leopard, 0.8, −0.1)}
African skunk	{(fiscal shrike, 0.6, −0.1)}
fiscal shrike	{grasshopper, 0.3, −0.05}
grasshopper	∅
baboon	{(grasshopper, 0.3, −0.09), (snake, 0.3, −0.4)}
leopard	{(baboon, 0.75, −0.1), (impala, 0.7, −0.09)}
snake	{(caracal, 0.7, −0.1), (mouse, 0.5, −0.4)}
caracal	{(mouse, 0.4, −0.2), (impala, 0.7, −0.2)}
mouse	∅
impala	∅

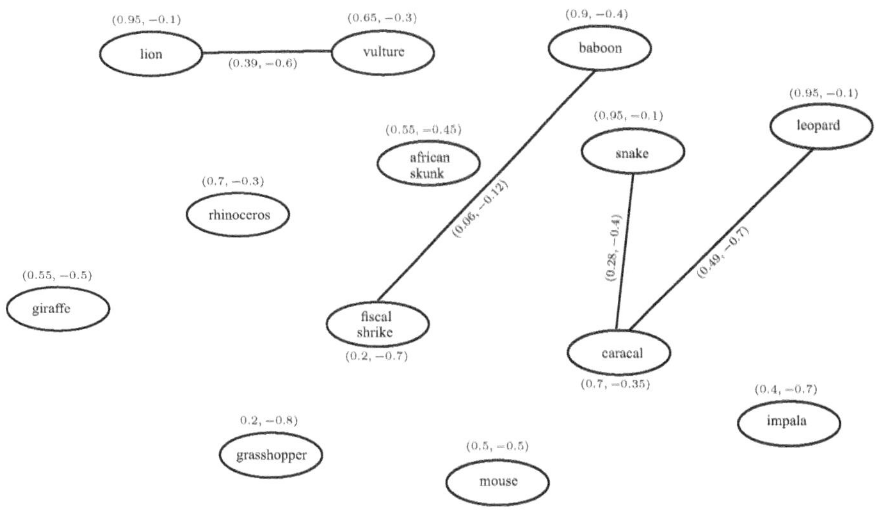

Fig. 4.26 Bipolar fuzzy competition graph of bipolar fuzzy food web

Table 4.12 Strength of competition between species

Species	Strength of competition	Species	Strength of competition
lion, vulture	0.9983	shrike, baboon	0.855
snake, caracal	0.9633	caracal, leopard	1.0483

2. Bipolar fuzzy common enemy graph

Bipolar common enemy graphs can be constructed from bipolar fuzzy food webs to study the strength of common enemies between species as given in Definition 4.26.

Definition 4.26 Let $\vec{G} = (A, \vec{B})$ be a bipolar fuzzy food web. The bipolar fuzzy common enemy graph $\mathcal{C}(\vec{G}) = (A, R)$ has the same set of species as $\vec{G}$ and there is an edge between two species x and y if $\mathcal{N}^+(x) \cap \mathcal{N}^+(y) \neq \emptyset$, i.e., x and y has a common predator and the membership function R is defined as

$$\mu_R^p(xy) = (\mu_A^p(x) \wedge \mu_A^p(y))h(\mathcal{N}^+(x) \cap \mathcal{N}^+(y)),$$

$$\mu_R^n(xy) = (\mu_A^n(x) \vee \mu_A^n(y))h(\mathcal{N}^+(x) \cap \mathcal{N}^+(y)).$$

The method for calculating the strength of common enemies between species in ecosystem is presented in Algorithm 4.5.2

Algorithm 4.5.2 Bipolar fuzzy common enemy graph

1. Input the number of species.
2. Input the bipolar fuzzy set A of species.
3. Construct the table of bipolar fuzzy out neighborhoods of all the species.
4. Construct the bipolar fuzzy competition graph $G = (A, R)$ using Definition 4.26.
5. If $\mathcal{N}^+(x) \cap \mathcal{N}^+(y) \neq \emptyset$ for any two species x and y then the strength of competition between x and y for common food can be calculated using Formula (4.15) as

$$S(x, y) = \frac{\mu_A^p(x) + \mu_A^p(y) + \mu_R^p(xy) + (3 + \mu_A^n(x) + \mu_A^n(y) + \mu_R^n(xy))}{6}. \tag{4.15}$$

Consider the example of a bipolar fuzzy food web of 13 species as shown in Fig. 4.25.The bipolar fuzzy out neighborhoods are given in Table 4.13.

The bipolar fuzzy common enemy graph is shown in Fig. 4.27. There are common enemies between giraffe and rhinoceros, rhinoceros and African skunk, rhinoceros and leopard, African skunk and leopard, grasshopper and snake, mouse and impala and baboon and impala. The positive membership value of an edge between two species represents the degree of energy both provide to common predator/enemy and the negative degree of membership shows the extent to which the species can harm their common enemy.

Let x and y be two species then the strength of common enemies between x and y is calculated using Formula (4.15). The strength of having common enemies between all the species is given in Table 4.14, which shows that impala and baboon have the largest number of common enemies.

Table 4.13 Bipolar fuzzy out neighbohoods of species

Species	$\mathcal{N}^+(u)$: u is a specie
giraffe	{(lion, 0.7, −0.1)}
lion	∅
rhinoceros	{(lion, 0.7, −0.1), (vulture, 0.6, −0.1)}
vulture	∅
African skunk	{(vulture, 0.6, −0.1)}
fiscal shrike	{(African skunk, 0.6, −0.1)}
grasshopper	{(fiscal shrike, 0.3, −0.05), (baboon, 0.3, −0.09)}
baboon	{(leopard, 0.75, −0.1)}
leopard	{(vulture, 0.8, −0.1)}
snake	{(baboon, 0.3, −0.4)}
caracal	{(snake, 0.7, −0.1)}
mouse	{(caracal, 0.4, −0.2)}
impala	{(caracal, 0.7, −0.2), (leopard, 0.7, −0.09)}

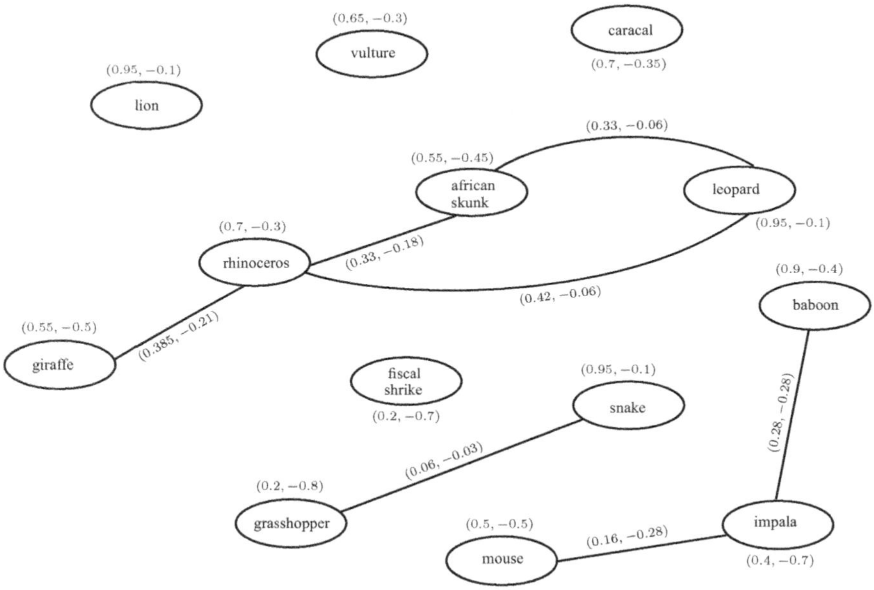

Fig. 4.27 Bipolar fuzzy common enemy graph

Table 4.14 Strength of common enemies between species

$x,\ y$	$S(x, y)$	$x,\ y$	$S(x, y)$
giraffe, rhinoceros	0.9408	grasshopper, snake	0.8567
rhinoceros, African skunk	0.91	impala, baboon	0.9933
African skunk, leopard	0.9067	mouse, impala	0.9233
rhinoceros, leopard	0.9217		

3. Bipolar fuzzy competition common enemy graph

Bipolar fuzzy competition common enemy graphs can be constructed from bipolar fuzzy food webs to study the relationship of common enemies as well as competition for prey between species as given in Definition 4.27.

Definition 4.27 Let $\vec{G} = (A, \vec{B})$ be a bipolar fuzzy food web. The bipolar fuzzy competition common enemy graph $\mathcal{C}(\vec{G}) = (A, R)$ has the same vertices as $\vec{G}$ and there is an edge between two vertices x and y if $\mathcal{N}^+(x) \cap \mathcal{N}^+(y) \neq \emptyset$ and $\mathcal{N}^-(x) \cap \mathcal{N}^-(y) \neq \emptyset$, that is, x and y has a common predator and a common prey. The membership function R is defined as

$$\mu_R^p(xy) = (\mu_C^p(x) \wedge \mu_C^p(y))[h(\mathcal{N}^-(x) \cap \mathcal{N}^-(y)) \wedge h(\mathcal{N}^+(x) \cap \mathcal{N}^+(y))],$$

$$\mu_R^n(xy) = (\mu_C^n(x) \vee \mu_C^n(y))[h(\mathcal{N}^-(x) \cap \mathcal{N}^-(y)) \wedge h(\mathcal{N}^+(x) \cap \mathcal{N}^-(y))].$$

The method for calculating the strength of power of each specie according to competition for common prey and common enemies is elaborated in Algorithm 4.5.3.

Algorithm 4.5.3 Bipolar fuzzy competition common enemy graph

1. Given any bipolar fuzzy food web.
2. Construct the table of bipolar fuzzy out neighborhoods and bipolar fuzzy in neighborhoods of all the species.
3. Construct the bipolar fuzzy competition graph $G = (A, R)$ using Definition 4.27.
4. If $\mathcal{N}^+(x) \cap \mathcal{N}^+(y) \neq \emptyset$ and $\mathcal{N}^-(x) \cap \mathcal{N}^-(y) \neq \emptyset$, for any two species x and y then calculate the degree of each specie x using Eq. (4.16).

$$(\deg^p(x), \deg^n(x)) = \sum_{\mathcal{N}^+(x)\cap\mathcal{N}^+(y)\neq\emptyset,\ \mathcal{N}^-(x)\cap\mathcal{N}^-(y)\neq\emptyset} \left(\mu_R^p(xy), \mu_R^n(xy)\right). \tag{4.16}$$

5. The strength of power of each specie x can be computed using Formula (4.17) as

$$S(x) = \frac{\deg^p(x) + 1 + \deg^n(x)}{2}. \tag{4.17}$$

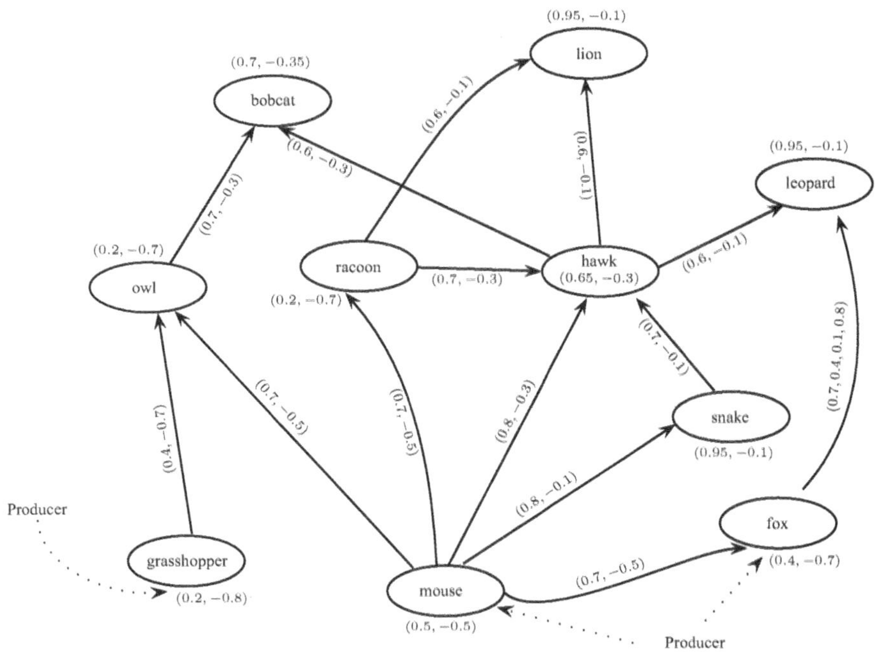

Fig. 4.28 Bipolar fuzzy food web

Consider the example of a bipolar fuzzy food web of 10 species as shown in Fig. 4.28. The description of degrees of membership of vertices and directed edges is the same as in Fig. 4.25.

The bipolar fuzzy out neighborhoods and bipolar fuzzy in neighborhoods of species are given in Table 4.15.

The bipolar fuzzy competition common enemy graph is shown in Fig. 4.29.

The strength of power of each specie according to food competition and common enemies using Formula (4.17) is calculated in Table 4.16, which depicts that hawk is the most powerful animal in this bipolar fuzzy food web.

4. Bipolar fuzzy niche graph

Niche graphs are important to study the behavior of species in ecological networks. Since all the species have different characteristics with respect to each other, bipolar fuzzy niche graphs can play a substantial role to study ecological networks more precisely. A bipolar fuzzy niche graph is defined in Definition 4.28.

Definition 4.28 Let $\vec{G} = (A, \vec{B})$ be a bipolar fuzzy food web. The bipolar fuzzy niche graph $\mathcal{C}(\vec{G}) = (C, R)$ has the same vertices as $\vec{G}$ and there is an edge between two vertices x and y if $\mathcal{N}^+(x) \cap \mathcal{N}^+(y) \neq \emptyset$ or $\mathcal{N}^-(x) \cap \mathcal{N}^-(y) \neq \emptyset$, i.e., x and y has a common predator or a common prey, where

Table 4.15 Bipolar fuzzy out and in neighborhoods of species

x is a specie	$\mathcal{N}^-(x)$ and $\mathcal{N}^+(x)$
grasshopper	$\mathcal{N}^-(\text{grasshopper}) = \emptyset$, $\mathcal{N}^+(\text{grasshopper})=\{(\text{owl}, 0.4, -0.7)\}$
owl	$\mathcal{N}^-(\text{owl})=\{(\text{grasshopper}, 0.4, -0.7), (\text{mouse}, 0.7, -0.5)\}$ $\mathcal{N}^+(\text{owl}) = \{(\text{bobcat}, 0.7, -0.3)\}$
bobcat	$\mathcal{N}^-(\text{bobcat})=\{(\text{hawk}, 0.6, -0.3)\}$, $\mathcal{N}^+(\text{bobcat}) = \emptyset$
lion	$\mathcal{N}^-(\text{lion})=\{(\text{racoon}, 0.6, -0.1), (\text{hawk}, 0.6, -0.1)\}$, $\mathcal{N}^+(\text{lion}) = \emptyset$
leopard	$\mathcal{N}^-(\text{leopard})=\{(\text{fox}, 0.7, -0.1), (\text{hawk}, 0.6, -0.1)\}$, $\mathcal{N}^+(\text{leopard}) = \emptyset$
racoon	$\mathcal{N}^-(\text{racoon})=\{(\text{mouse}, 0.7, -0.5)\}$ $\mathcal{N}^+(\text{racoon}) = \{(\text{lion}, 0.6, -0.1), (\text{hawk}, 0.7, -0.3)\}$
hawk	$\mathcal{N}^-(\text{hawk})=\{(\text{racoon}, 0.7, -0.3), (\text{mouse}, 0.8, -0.3), (\text{snake}, 0.7, -0.1)\}$ $\mathcal{N}^+(\text{hawk}) = \{(\text{lion}, 0.6, -0.1), (\text{leopard}, 0.6, -0.1), (\text{bobcat}, 0.6, -0.3)\}$
mouse	$\mathcal{N}^-(\text{mouse}) = \emptyset$, $\mathcal{N}^+(\text{mouse})=\{(\text{owl}, 0.7, -0.5), (\text{racoon}, 0.7, -0.5),$ $(\text{hawk}, 0.8, -0.3), (\text{snake}, 0.8, -0.1), (\text{fox}, 0.7, -0.5)\}$
fox	$\mathcal{N}^-(\text{fox}) = \{(\text{mouse}, 0.7, -0.5)\}$, $\mathcal{N}^+(\text{fox}) = \{(\text{leopard}, 0.7, -0.1)\}$
snake	$\mathcal{N}^-(\text{snake}) = \{(\text{mouse}, 0.8, -0.1)\}$, $\mathcal{N}^+(\text{snake}) = \{(\text{hawk}, 0.7, -0.1)\}$

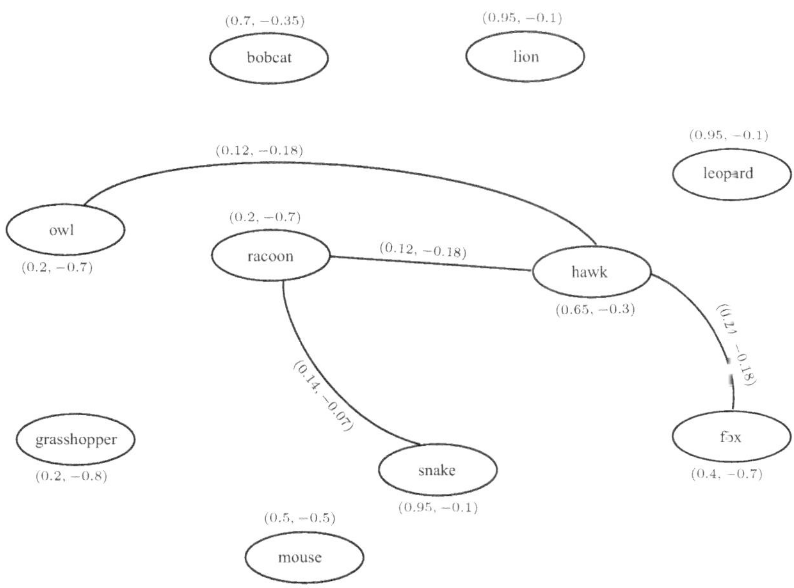

Fig. 4.29 Bipolar fuzzy competition common enemy graph

Table 4.16 Strength of competition between species

Specie	Degree of each specie	Power in food web
owl	(0.12, −0.18)	$(0.12 + 1 + 0.18)/2 = 0.65$
racoon	(0.26, −0.25)	0.755
hawk	(0.48, −0.54)	1.01
snake	(0.14, −0.07)	0.605

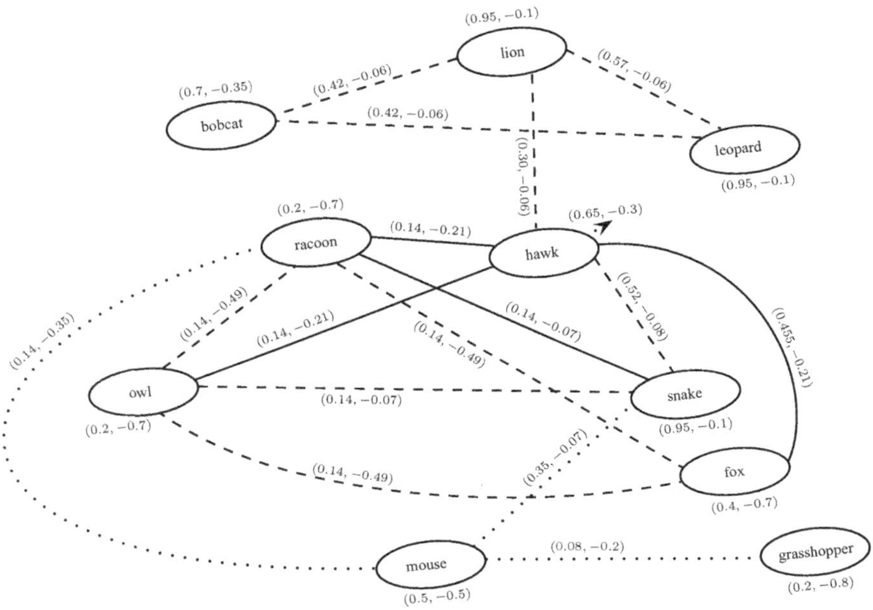

Fig. 4.30 Bipolar fuzzy niche graph

$$\mu_R^p(xy) = (\mu_A^p(x) \wedge \mu_A^p(y))[h(\mathcal{N}^-(x) \cap \mathcal{N}^-(y)) \vee h(\mathcal{N}^+(x) \cap \mathcal{N}^+(y))],$$

$$\mu_R^n(xy) = (\mu_A^n(x) \vee \mu_A^n(y))[h(\mathcal{N}^-(x) \cap \mathcal{N}^-(y)) \vee h(\mathcal{N}^+(x) \cap \mathcal{N}^+(y))].$$

The bipolar fuzzy niche graph of Fig. 4.28 is shown in Fig. 4.30. The edge between species which have only common prey is represented by dashed lines and dotted line represent the species relationship having only common enemies and solid lines represent the species which have both common prey and common enemies.

4.5.2 Competitive Market

In business marketing, there are rivalry competitions among companies which are trying to increase the profit and demand of their products. There are more than one companies which sell the identical products to retailers and other companies. As different companies often market the same types of products, every company tries to attract consumer's attention to its product. There is always a competitive environment in business marketing. Graph theory is a key approach to study the competition between buyers and sellers using graphical structures. But sometimes these graphical structures cannot be defined precisely. For example, companies are different according to annual profit and loss. These are bipolar information, which are fuzzy in nature. This idea motivates the necessity of bipolar fuzzy competition graphs.The method for calculating the strength of competition between companies is explained in Algorithm 4.5.4.

Algorithm 4.5.4 Algorithm for computing the strength of competition in business market

1. Input the bipolar fuzzy set A of n companies.
2. Input the adjacency matrix of bipolar fuzzy relation $\vec{B}$ of companies.
3. Construct the table of bipolar fuzzy out neighborhoods of all the companies.
4. Construct the bipolar fuzzy competition graph $G = (A, R)$ using Definition 4.3.
5. If $\mathcal{N}^+(x) \cap \mathcal{N}^+(y) \neq \emptyset$ for any two companies x and y then calculate the degree of each specie x as,

$$(\deg^p(x), \deg^n(x)) = \sum_{\mathcal{N}^+(x)\cap\mathcal{N}^+(y)\neq\emptyset} (\mu_R^p(xy), \mu_R^n(xy)).$$

6. The strength of competition of each company x can be computed using formula:

$$S(x) = \frac{\deg^p(x) + 1 + \deg^n(x)}{2}. \tag{4.18}$$

Consider the example of a business competition between 7 companies DEL, CB, HW, AK, LR, RP, SONY, RA, LR, 3 retailers, 1 retailer outlet, and 1 multinational brand as shown in Fig. 4.31. The vertices represent companies, retailers, Outlets, and brands. The positive degree of membership of each vertex represents the degree of annual loss of each company\retailer\industry and the negative degree of membership represents the annual profit. These characteristics can be collected in the form of a set as,

$$\{\text{annual lose, annual profit}\}.$$

The positive degree of membership of each directed edge $\vec{xy}$ represents the degree of rejectability of the product of company x by company y. The negative degree of membership represents the quantity of product purchased by the company y from x. The relationship between the companies can be written in a set as,

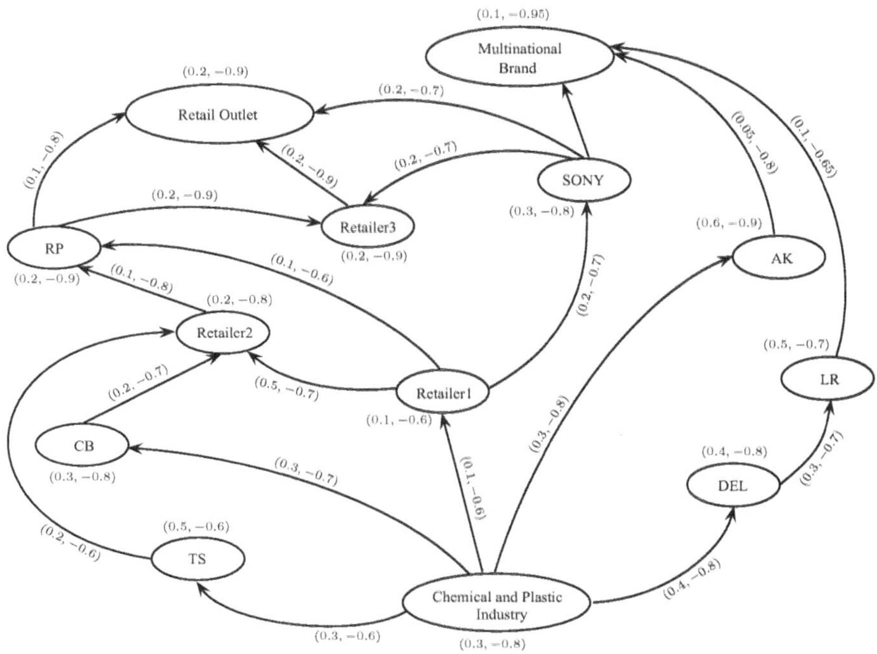

Fig. 4.31 Bipolar fuzzy marketing digraph

{rejectability, product quantity purchased}.

The strength of competition between companies can be discussed using bipolar fuzzy competition graph. The bipolar fuzzy out neighborhoods are calculated in Table 4.17.

The bipolar fuzzy competition graph of Fig. 4.31 is shown in Fig. 4.32. The degree of membership of each edge between companies shows the strength of competition between the companies for rejectability and purchase of their product.

The strength of competition of each company is calculated in Table 4.18, which shows its competitive value within business market. Table 4.18 shows that AK is the most competitive company in market.

4.5.3 Political Competition

Local governments are the public administration in towns, districts, and cities to govern a specific geographic area. Many countries have local governments in their cities. Local governments are important because the people of the area have much contact with local officials as compared to the federal government. The selection criteria of local government officials are different in different countries. Some countries

Table 4.17 Bipolar fuzzy out neighborhoods of companies

Company	$\mathcal{N}^+(u)$: u is a company
chemical and plastic industries	{(DEL, 0.4, −0.8), (AK, 0.3, −0.8), (Retailer1, 0.1, −0.6), (CB, 0.3, −0.7), (TS, 0.3, −0.6)}
DEL	{(LR, 0.3, −0.7)}
AK	{(Multinational Brand, 0.05, −0.8)}
LR	{(Multinational Brand, 0.1, −0.65)}
Retailer1	{(SONY, 0.2, −0.7), (RP, 0.1, −0.6), (Retailer2, 0.5, −0.7)}
CB	{(Retailer2, 0.2, −0.7)}
TS	{(Retailer2, 0.2, −0.6)}
Retailer2	{(RP, 0.1, −0.8)}
SONY	{(Retailer3, 0.2, −0.7), (R. Outlet, 0.2, −0.7), (M. Brand, 0.1, −0.7)}
Retailer3	{(R.Outlet, 0.2, −0.9)}
RP	{(Retailer3, 0.2, −0.9), (R. Outlet, 0.1, −0.8)}
M. Brand	∅
R. Outlet	∅

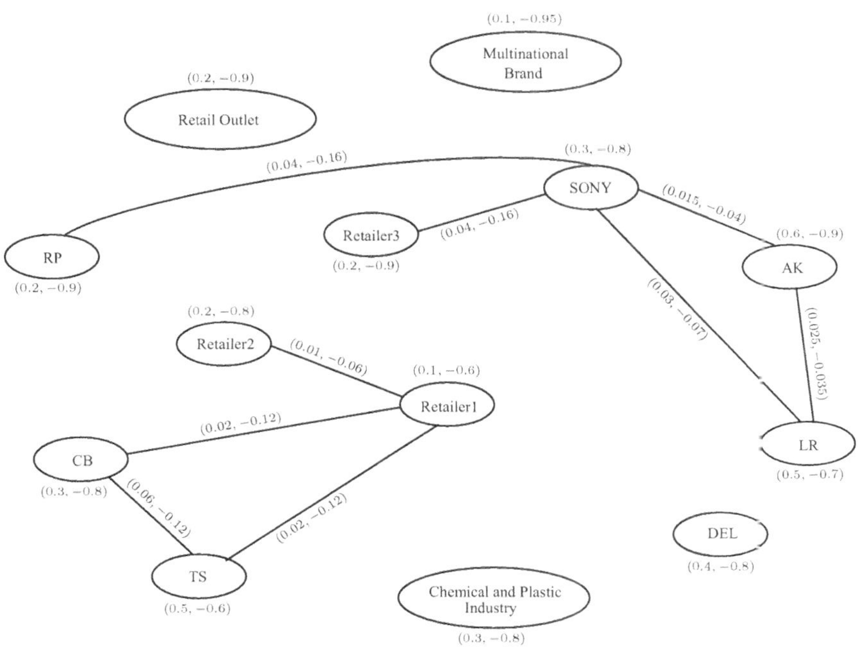

Fig. 4.32 Bipolar fuzzy competition graph of business network

Table 4.18 Strength of competition between companies

Company	Degree of company	Competition strength
LR	(0.055, −0.105)	0.475
AK	(0.04, −0.075)	0.4825
SONY	(0.125, −0.43)	0.3475
Retailer3	(0.04, −0.16)	0.44
RP	(0.04, −0.16)	0.44
Retailer2	(0.01, −0.06)	0.475
Retailer1	(0.05, −0.30)	0.375
CB	(0.08, −0.24)	0.42
TS	(0.08, −0.24)	0.42

have direct public elections and some countries elect the local government officials by the decisions of a governing council. Usually, there are five common positions in a local government, namely, mayor, city manager, city council member, county commissioner, and city attorney. A procedure for the governing council to select the politicians on the basis of leadership quality, eligibility, and incapacity of candidates is explained in Algorithm 4.5.5.

Algorithm 4.5.5 Algorithm for calculating the strength of competition for political seats

1. Given a bipolar fuzzy digraph of candidates and political seats.
2. Construct bipolar fuzzy out neighborhoods of all the candidates.
3. Construct bipolar fuzzy competition graph using Definition 4.3.
4. Calculate the strength of competition $A(x, p)$ of each candidate x for a particular seat p. If $x, a_1, a_2, \ldots, a_n$ are the candidates, which are competing for political seat p, then

$$A(x, p) = (A^p(x, p), A^n(x, p)) = \frac{1}{n}\left(\mu_R^p(xa_1) + \mu_R^p(xa_2) + \cdots + \mu_R^p(xa_n), \mu_R^n(xa_1) + \mu_R^n(xa_2) + \cdots + \mu_R^n(xa_n)\right).$$

5. Calculate $S(x, p)$, the strength of competition of each candidate x for seat p as,

$$S(x, p) = A^p(x, p) + 1 + A^n(x, p).$$

Consider the example of 7 persons in a country named Jeorge Estregan, Ramil, Dave Miranda, Jaun Menzoda, Maria Evita, Neil Andrew, and Bresies Jackson competing for different positions. A bipolar fuzzy digraph is shown in Fig. 4.33, which represents the candidates competing for particular seats. The positive degree of membership of each candidate represents the degree of leadership quality and negative degree of membership represents the incapacity to manage public affairs. The candidate characteristics can be represented in a set as {leadership, incapacity}. The positive degree of membership of each directed edge between a candidate and a position

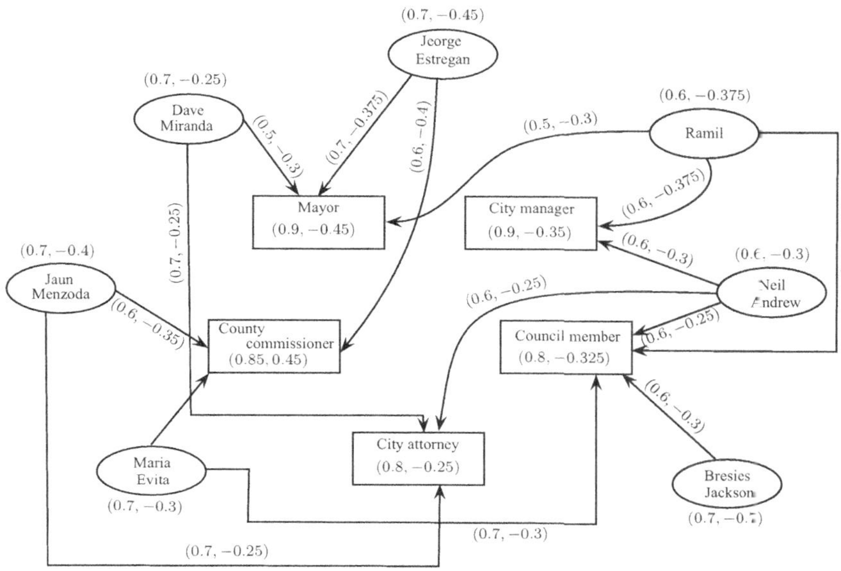

Fig. 4.33 Bipolar fuzzy digraph of political seats

indicates the degree of eligibility for the position. The negative degree of membership represents the degree of legal disqualification for that position. These membership properties can be written in a set as {eligibility, legal disqualification}. The positive and negative degrees of membership of each political position represent the average past leadership quality and incapacity of politicians for these positions.

A bipolar fuzzy competition graph can be constructed to describe the competition between candidates for the political positions. The bipolar fuzzy out neighborhoods are given in Table 4.19.

Table 4.19 Bipolar fuzzy out neighborhoods of candidates

Candidate	$\mathcal{N}^+$(candidate)
Bresies Jackson	{(Council member, 0.6, −0.6)}
Neil Andrew	{(Council member, 0.6, −0.25), (City manager, 0.6, −0.3), (City attorney, 0.8, −0.25)}
Ramil	{(City manager, 0.6, −0.375), (Mayor, 0.5, −0.3)}
Jeorge Estregan	{(Mayor, 0.7, −0.375), (County commissioner, 0.6, −0.4)}
Dave Miranda	{(Mayor, 0.5, −0.3), (City attorney, 0.7, −0.25)}
Jaun Menzoda	{(County commissioner, 0.6, −0.35), (City attorney, 0.7, −0.25)}
Maria Evita	{(County commissioner, 0.7, −0.3), (Council member, 0.7, −0.3)}

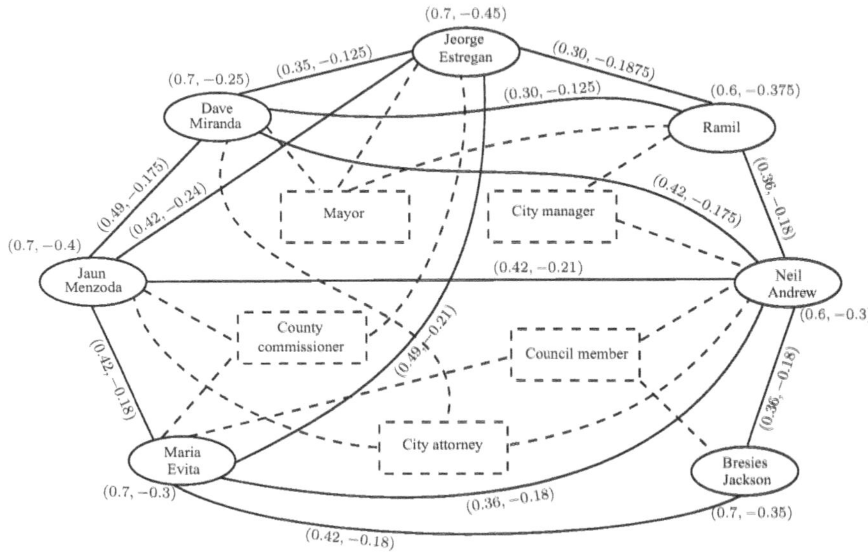

Fig. 4.34 Bipolar fuzzy political competition graph

The bipolar fuzzy competition graph is shown in Fig. 4.34. The solid lines show the strength of competition between two candidates. The dashed lines indicate the candidates competing for particular seats. For example, Neil Andrew and Ramil both are competing for the seat of the City manager. The strength of competition between them is (0.36, −0.18). In Table 4.20, $A(x, p)$ represents the competition of candidate x for seat p with respect to leadership quality and incapacity to manage public affairs. The strength of competition of all the candidates with respect to particular seats is calculated in Table 4.20.

From Table 4.20, Bresies Jackson and Neil Andrew are equally eligible to be selected for the seat of Council member, Dave Miranda for city attorney, Maria Evita for County commissioner, Jeorge Estregan for Mayor and Neil and Ramil for the seat of the City manager.

4.5.4 *Social Competition in Bipolar Fuzzy Environment*

Social competition is a widespread mechanism to figure out a best-suited group economically, politically, or educationally. Social competition occurs when an individual's opinions, decisions, and behaviors are influenced by others. Graph theory is a conceptual framework to study and analyze the units that are intensely or frequently connected in a network. Bipolar fuzzy networks can be used to study the influence and competition between objects more precisely. The strength of influence between

Table 4.20 Strength of competition of candidates for political seats

(Candidate, seat)	In competition	A(candidate, seat)	S(candidate, seat)
(Bresies, Council member)	Neil, Maria	(0.39, −0.18)	1.21
(Neil, Council member)	Bresies, Maria	(0.36, −0.18)	1.18
(Maria, Council member)	Bresies, Neil	(0.39, −0.18)	1.21
(Neil, City attorney)	Jaun, Dave	(0.42, −0.1925)	1.2275
(Jaun, City attorney)	Neil, Dave	(0.455, −0.1925)	0.64875
(Dave, City attorney)	Neil, Jaun	(0.455, −0.175)	1.28
(Maria, County commissioner)	Jeorge, Jaun	(0.455, −0.195)	1.26
(Jaun, County commissioner)	Jeorge, Maria	(0.42, −0.21)	1.21
(Jeorge, County commissioner)	Jaun, Maria	(0.455, −0.225)	1.23
(Neil, City manager)	Ramil	(0.36, −0.18)	1.18
(Ramil, City manager)	Neil	(0.36, −0.18)	1.18
(Ramil, Mayor)	Jeorge, Dave	(0.30, −0.15625)	1.14375
(Jeorge, Mayor)	Ramil, Dave	(0.325, −0.15625)	1.16875
(Dave, Mayor)	Ramil, Jeorge	(0.325, −0.125)	1.2

different objects in a bipolar fuzzy influence graph can be calculated by the method presented in Algorithm 4.5.6.

Algorithm 4.5.6 Algorithm for calculating the strength of influence in a social network

1. Given any bipolar fuzzy digraph $\vec{G}$ of social relationship among families.
2. Construct the table of bipolar fuzzy in neighborhoods of all the families.
3. Construct the bipolar fuzzy influence graph $G = (A, R)$ as,
   G has the same set of vertices as $\vec{G}$ and there is an edge between two vertices x and y if $\mathcal{N}^-(x) \cap \mathcal{N}^-(y) \neq \emptyset$.
4. If $\mathcal{N}^-(x) \cap \mathcal{N}^-(y) \neq \emptyset$ for any two vertices x and y then calculate the average strength of competition of each vertex x as,

$$(\text{Average}^p(x), \text{Average}^n(x)) = \frac{(\deg^p(x), \deg^n(x))}{\text{number of vertices adjacent to } x}.$$

5. Find the total strength of competition of each vertex x as

$$S(x) = \text{Average}^p(x) + 1 + \text{Average}^n(x).$$

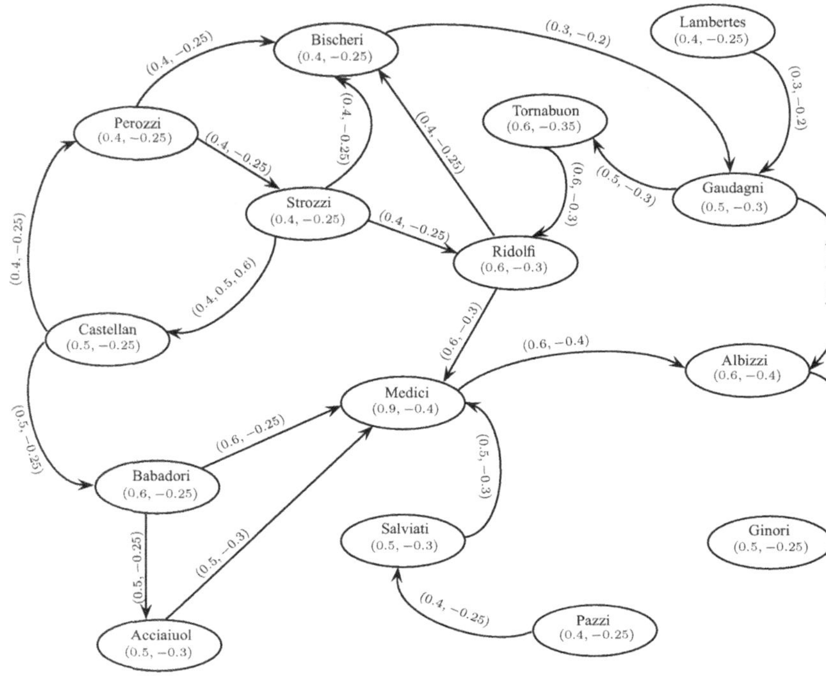

Fig. 4.35 Bipolar fuzzy social digraph

Consider a bipolar fuzzy social network of Florentine trading families Peruzzi, Lamberts, Bischeri, Strozzi, Guadagni, Tornabuoni, Castellan, Ridolfi, Albizzi, Barbados, Medici, Acciaiuol, Salviati, Ginori, and Pazzi. The vertices in bipolar fuzzy digraph represent the name of trading families. The positive degree of membership of each family represents the strength of centrality and negative degree of membership represents the strength of weak position of each family in the network. The description of the degree of membership value families can be written in the form of a set as {centrality, weak position}. The directed edge $\vec{xy}$ indicates that the family x is influenced by y. The degree of membership of each directed edge indicates the extent to which the opinions and suggestions of one family influence the others and negative membership value represents the strength of suggestions ignored by family x. The influence factors can be written in the form of a set as {followed suggestions, ignored suggestions}. The degree of membership of Medici is (0.9, −0.4), which shows that Medici has 90% central position in trading network and 40% weak position. The degree of membership between Redolfi and Medici is (0.7, −0.3), which indicates that Redolfi follows 70% of the suggestions of Medici and ignore 30% of its suggestions. The bipolar fuzzy influence graph is shown in Fig. 4.35.

Table 4.21 Bipolar fuzzy in neighborhoods of families in social network

Family	$\mathcal{N}^-$(family)	Family	$\mathcal{N}^-$(family)
Acciaiuol	{(Babadori, 0.5, −0.25)}	Pazzi	∅
Ginori	{(Albizzi, 0.5, −0.25)}	Salviati	{(Pazzi, 0.4, −0.25)}
Babadori	{(Castellan, 0.5, −0.25)}	Castellan	{(Strozzi, 0.4, −0.25)}
Tornabuon	{(Gaudagni, 0.5, −0.3)}	Perozzi	{(Castellan, 0.5, −0.25)}
Lambertes	∅	Strozzi	{(Perozzi, 0.4, −0.25)}
Medici	{(Babadori, 0.6, −0.25), (Acciaiuol, 0.5, −0.3), (Salviati, 0.5, −0.3), (Ridolfi, 0.6, −0.3)}		
Bischeri	{(Perozzi, 0.4, −0.25), (Strozzi, 0.4, −0.25), (Redolfi, 0.4, −0.25)}		
Albizzi	{(Medici, 0.6, −0.4), (Gaudagni, 0.5, −0.3)}		
Redolfi	{(Strozzi, 0.4, −0.25), (Tornabuon, 0.6, −0.3)}		
Gaudgani	{(Bischeri, 0.3, −0.2), (Lambertes, 0.3, −0.2)}		

A bipolar fuzzy influence graph can be constructed to show that which family is the most influential in the bipolar fuzzy network. The bipolar fuzzy in neighborhoods are given in Table 4.21.

The bipolar fuzzy influence graph is given in Fig. 4.36, which shows the strength of social competition between families to influence other families in the social network.

The strength of competition of families is calculated in Table 4.22, where Average(x) represents the strength of influence of family x according to its suggestions followed and ignored by other families. $S(x)$ represents the total strength of competition of each family to influence other families.

4.5.5 Interactions and Conflicts in Communication Networks

Due to the increase of wireless devices, signal conflicts and confusions over communication networks are a common issue. Since the air is shared by all transmitters, transmissions by any device at an equivalent frequency will cause interference. The interference of signals is highly dependent on the strength of interference of physical objects, environment factors, and electronic devices. The phenomenon of signal conflicts and confusions in communication networks are discussed in the following two example applications.

1. Bipolar fuzzy conflict graph

In wireless networking, signals are transmitted through the air. Some channels are operating signals at the same frequencies and range that can cause conflict with each other and it affects the network performance badly. Competition graphs arise in the theory of network interference but these graphical representations do not include all the competitions between signals. The crisp competition graphs cannot

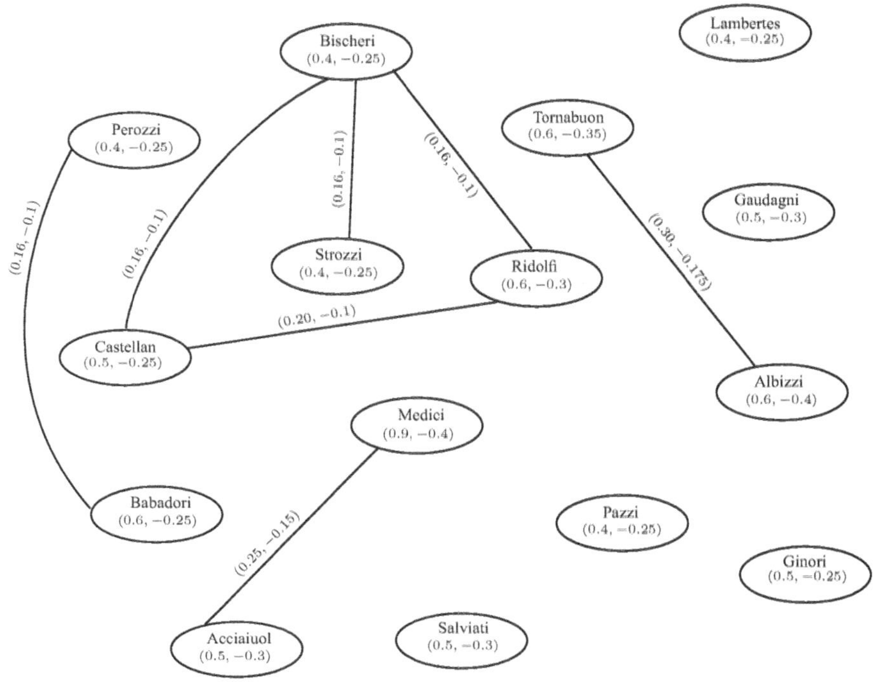

Fig. 4.36 Bipolar fuzzy influence graph

Table 4.22 Strength of competition in social network

family	Average(family)	S(family)	family	Average(family)	S(family)
Acciaiuol	(0.25, −0.15)	1.1	Medici	(0.25, −0.15)	1.1
Babadori	(0.16, −0.1)	1.06	Perozzi	(0.16, −0.1)	1.06
Castellan	(0.18, −0.1)	1.08	Redolfi	(0.18, −0.1)	1.08
Strozzi	(0.16, −0.1)	1.06	Besceri	(0.16, −0.1)	1.06

represent the degree of conflict between signals. To reduce this limitation, bipolar fuzzy competition graphs can be used to study the degree of conflict of signals. The method to calculate the strength of signal conflict between wireless devices in a bipolar fuzzy conflict graph is given in Algorithm 4.5.7.

Algorithm 4.5.7 Algorithm for the calculation of the strength of conflict between signals

1. Given a bipolar fuzzy network of n wireless devices.
2. Construct bipolar fuzzy conflict graph using Definition 4.3.
3. Calculate the strength of signal conflict of each sender device in wireless connection as follows: If $x, a_1, a_2, \ldots, a_n$ are the sender devices such that

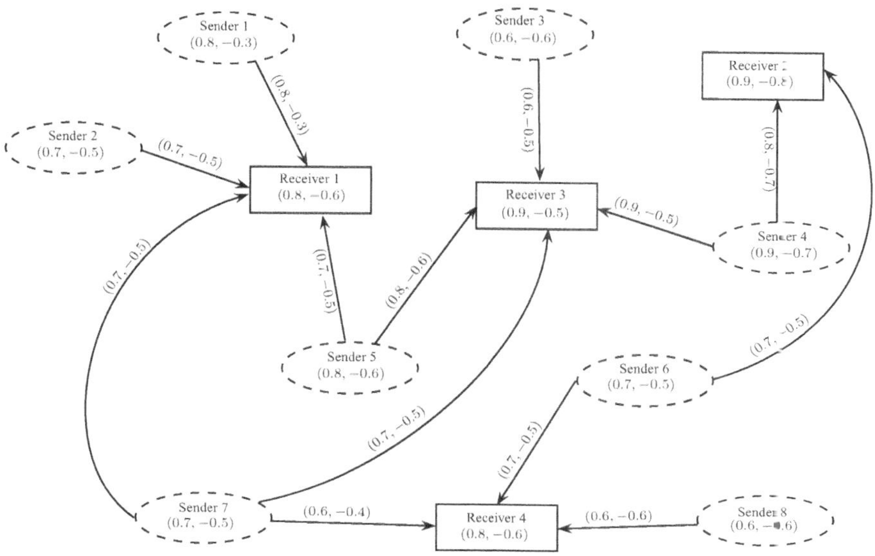

Fig. 4.37 Communication over a noisy channel

$(\mu_R^p(xa_i), \mu_R^n(xa_i)) \neq (0, 0)$, for each $1 \leq i \leq n$, then the average degree of conflict $A(x) = (A^p(x), A^n(x))$ of each sender device x is,

$$A(x) = \frac{(\mu_R^p(xa_1) + \mu_R^p(xa_2) + \cdots + \mu_R^p(xa_n), \mu_R^n(xa_1) + \mu_R^n(xa_2) + \cdots + \mu_R^n(xa_n))}{n}.$$

4. Calculate the strength of conflict of device x to other nearby devices as

$$S(x) = A^p(x) + 1 + A^n(x).$$

Assume that there are 8 sender devices and 4 receiver channels. The bipolar fuzzy digraph is shown in Fig. 4.37 in which vertices represent senders and receivers. The positive degree of membership of each vertex represents the degree of strength of the signal. The negative degree of membership represents the degree of weakness of the signal because the signal spread apart as it gets weaker. These factors can be represented in a set as {strength, weakness}. The positive degree of membership of each directed edge between sender and receiver represents the degree of continuity of signal and negative degree of membership represents the degree of interference of physical objects, environmental interference, and electronic devices. These characteristics can be collectively written as {continuity, interference}.

The bipolar fuzzy conflict graph (A, R) can be used to study the strength of signal conflict of sender devices in the wireless network. For this, the bipolar fuzzy out neighborhoods are given in Table 4.23.

Table 4.23 Bipolar fuzzy out neighbohoods of noisy channel

Sender	$\mathcal{N}^+$(Sender)	Sender	$\mathcal{N}^+$(Sender)
Sender1	{(Receiver1, 0.8, −0.3)}	Sender2	{(Receiver1, 0.7, −0.5)}
Sender3	{(Receiver3, 0.6, −0.5)}	Sender8	{(Receiver4, 0.6, −0.6)}
Sender4	{(Receiver2, 0.8, −0.7), (Receiver3, 0.9, −0.5)}		
Sender5	{(Receiver1, 0.7, −0.5), (Receiver3, 0.8, −0.6)}		
Sender6	{(Receiver2, 0.7, −0.5), (Receiver4, 0.7, −0.5)}		
Sender7	{(Receiver1, 0.7, −0.5), (Receiver3, 0.7, −0.5), (Receiver4, 0.6, −0.4)}		

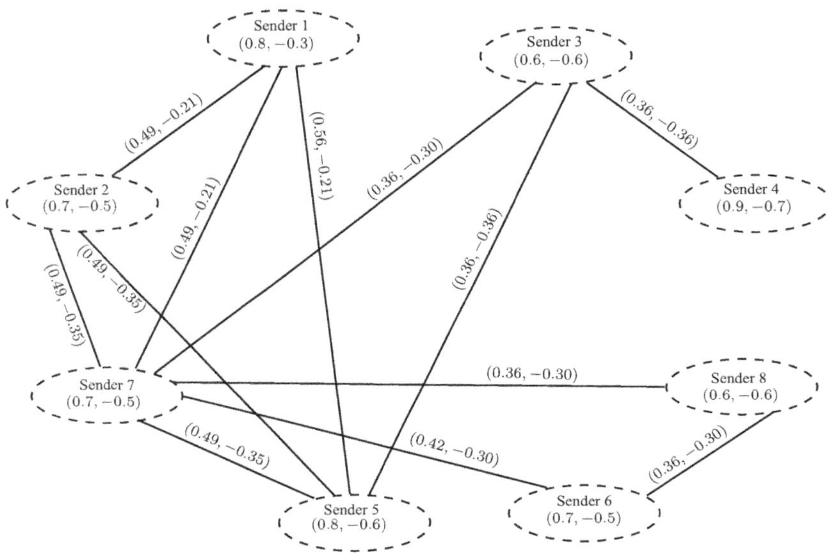

Fig. 4.38 Bipolar fuzzy conflict graph

Table 4.24 Strength of conflict between wireless devices

Sender	A(Sender)	S(Sender)	Sender	A(Sender)	S(Sender)
Sender1	(0.51, −0.21)	1.3	Sender2	(0.49, −0.30)	1.19
Sender3	(0.36, −0.34)	1.02	Sender4	(0.36, −0.36)	1.00
Sender5	(0.475, −0.3175)	1.1575	Sender6	(0.39, −0.30)	1.09
Sender7	(0.435−, 0.3017)	1.13	Sender8	(0.36, −0.3)	1.06

The bipolar fuzzy conflict graph is shown in Fig. 4.38. The degree of membership of each edge represents the degree of conflict between two devices for strength and weakness of signals due to the interference of different physical and electronic objects. The strength of conflict of all the devices is given in Table 4.24.

2. Bipolar fuzzy confusion graph

Another application of bipolar competition graphs is in the communication network over a noisy channel. Through a noisy channel, a message A may be received as A' due to atmospheric noise, transit-time noise, or electronic noise. Assume that a transmitting device transmits three signals a, b, c and the receiving channel receives the signals as α, β, γ. Unfortunately, due to noise over the channel, confusion in receiving the signals is possible: a could be received as α or β, b could be received as β or γ, c could be received as γ or α. Graphical models can be used to study the confusion of signals in message strings but these models do not take into consideration the degree of noise because every path may have a different degree of noise. Therefore, bipolar fuzzy confusion graphs are more effective to study the strength of confusion in message strings. A method in Algorithm 4.5.8 is given to calculate the strength of confusion between signals in a bipolar fuzzy confusion graph.

Algorithm 4.5.8 Algorithm for computing the strength of confusion between signals

1. Given a bipolar fuzzy communication network of sender and receiver communication devices.
2. Construct the bipolar fuzzy confusion graph using Definition 4.3.
3. If xy and uv are two message strings in a bipolar fuzzy confusion graph, then calculate the strength of confusion that xy could be received as uv as

$$S(xy, uv) = \mu_R^p(xyuv) + 1 + \mu_R^n(xyuv).$$

Consider the example that Bob sends a message of two letter strings, namely, aa, ab, ac, bc, bb, cc. The possible strings aa could be received as are: $\alpha\alpha$, $\alpha\beta$, $\beta\alpha$, $\beta\beta$. The possible receiving strings for each sent string are given in Table 4.25.

The bipolar fuzzy digraph is shown in Fig. 4.39. The set of vertices is the set of strings. The positive degree of membership of each vertex represents the degree of strength of signals and negative degree of membership represents the weakness of signals. These properties of signals can be written collectively as {strength, weakness}. There is a directed edge between between two strings xy and uv if xy is sent and uv could be received. The positive degree of membership of each directed edge

Table 4.25 Communication over a noisy channel

Sent string	Possible received strings
aa	$\alpha\alpha, \alpha\beta, \beta\alpha, \beta\beta$
ab	$\alpha\beta, \alpha\gamma, \beta\beta, \beta\gamma$
ca	$\gamma\alpha, \gamma\beta, \alpha\alpha, \alpha\beta$
bb	$\beta\beta, \beta\gamma, \gamma\beta, \gamma\gamma$
cc	$\gamma\gamma, \gamma\alpha, \alpha\gamma, \alpha\alpha$

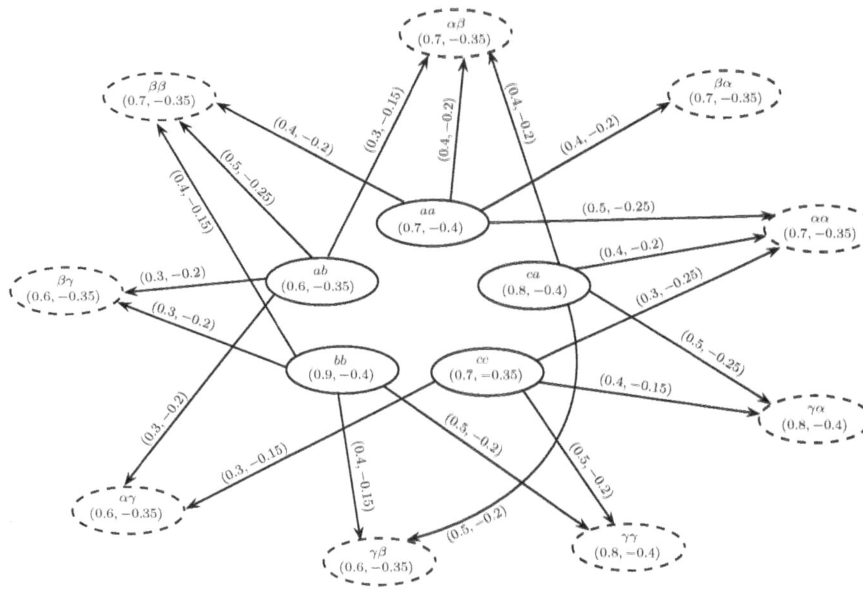

Fig. 4.39 Bipolar fuzzy noisy channel

Table 4.26 Bipolar fuzzy out neighborhoods of noisy channel

xy	$\mathcal{N}^+(xy)$
aa	$\{(\alpha\alpha, 0.5, -0.25), (\alpha\beta, 0.4, -0.2), (\beta\alpha, 0.4, -0.2), (\beta\beta, 0.4, -0.2)\}$
ab	$\{(\alpha\beta, 0.3, -0.15), (\alpha\gamma, 0.3, -0.2), (\beta\beta, 0.5, -0.25), (\beta\gamma, 0.3, -0.2)\}$
ca	$\{(\gamma\alpha, 0.5, -0.25), (\gamma\beta, 0.5, -0.2), (\alpha\alpha, 0.4, -0.2), (\alpha\beta, 0.4, -0.2)\}$
bb	$\{(\beta\beta, 0.4, -0.15), (\beta\gamma, 0.3, -0.2), (\gamma\beta, 0.4, -0.15), (\gamma\gamma, 0.5, -0.2)\}$
cc	$\{(\gamma\gamma, 0.5, -0.2), (\gamma\alpha, 0.4, -0.15), (\alpha\gamma, 0.3, -0.15), (\alpha\alpha, 0.3, -0.25)\}$

represents the degree of harmony of the signal and negative degree of membership represents the degree of noise. The noise categories can be written in the form of a set as {harmony, noise}.

A bipolar fuzzy confusion graph can be constructed to study the strength of confusion between message strings. For this, the bipolar fuzzy out neighborhoods given in Table 4.26.

The bipolar fuzzy confusion graph (A, R) is shown in Fig. 4.40. The edge between aa and ab has a degree of membership $(0.24, -0.14)$, which shows that the harmony of signal aa is 24% and 14% surity for aa to be received as ab due to channel noise.

The strength of confusion of each pair of message string is given in Table 4.27, which shows that aa could be confused with bb or ca, ab could be received as aa or bb, bb and cc can confuse with each other, ca can confuse with bb.

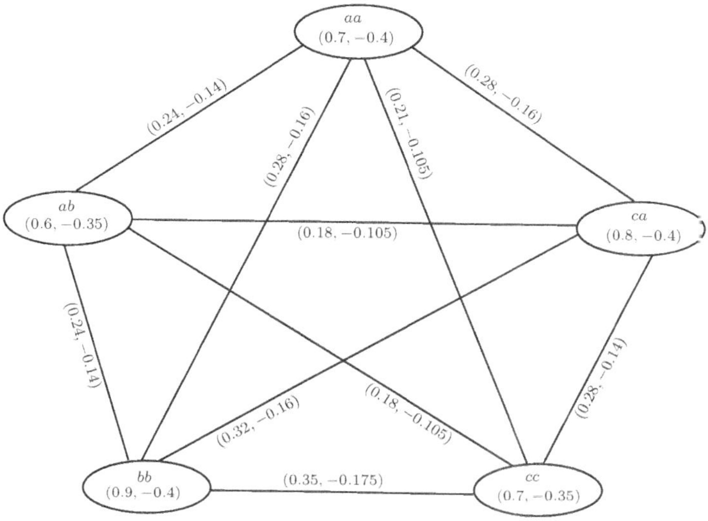

Fig. 4.40 Bipolar fuzzy confusion graph

Table 4.27 Strength of confusion

(xy, uv)	$S(xy, uv)$	(xy, uv)	$S(xy, uv)$	(xy, uv)	$S(xy, uv)$	(xy, uv)	$S(xy, uv)$
(aa, ab)	1.10	(aa, bb)	1.12	(aa, cc)	1.105	(aa, ca)	1.12
(ab, bb)	1.1	(ab, cc)	1.075	(ab, ca)	1.075	(bb, ca)	1.16
(bb, cc)	1.175	(ca, cc)	1.12				

4.6 Conclusions

Bipolar fuzzy competition graphs are the important mathematical structures to represent point to point interconnections, conflicts, confusions, and competitions among objects in economic systems, ecological niches, noisy channels, and other conflicting networks. In this chapter, we have discussed different concepts such as bipolar fuzzy out neighborhoods, bipolar fuzzy in neighborhoods, bipolar fuzzy competition graphs, bipolar fuzzy k−competition graphs, bipolar fuzzy open neighborhood graphs, bipolar fuzzy closed neighborhood graphs, and underlying bipolar fuzzy graphs. We have described the construction of bipolar fuzzy competition graphs of certain products of bipolar fuzzy digraphs from their respective bipolar fuzzy competition graphs and illustrated these fundamental techniques with graphical examples. We have also elaborated the relation of underlying bipolar fuzzy graphs with bipolar fuzzy $[k]$−competition graphs and bipolar fuzzy (k)−competition graphs in the existence and nonexistence of loops. We have also studied different types competition graphs under complex bipolar fuzzy environment. We have presented algorithms to compute the strength of competition, the strength confusion and conflict, and the strength of influence using application examples of food webs, business marketing, political rivalry, and communication over noisy channels.

Exercises 4

1. Let $\vec{G}_1$ and $\vec{G}_2$ be two bipolar fuzzy digraphs as shown in Fig. 4.41. Construct $\mathcal{C}(\vec{G}_1 \square \vec{G}_2)$ using Theorem 4.2.
2. Let $\vec{G}_1$ and $\vec{G}_2$ be two bipolar fuzzy digraphs as shown in Fig. 4.42. Construct $\mathcal{C}(\vec{G} \times \vec{H})$ using Theorem 4.3.
3. Derive a method for the construction of bipolar fuzzy competition graph $\mathcal{C}(\vec{G}_1 \boxtimes \vec{G}_2)$ of the strong product of bipolar fuzzy digraphs $\vec{G}_1$ and $\vec{G}_2$ using $\mathcal{C}(\vec{G}_1)$ and $\mathcal{C}(\vec{G}_2)$.
4. If all the edges of a complex bipolar fuzzy digraph are strong then prove using a contradiction example that all the edges of corresponding complex bipolar fuzzy competition graph may not be strong.
5. Derive a method for the construction of bipolar fuzzy competition graph $\mathcal{C}(\vec{G}_1 \circ \vec{G}_2)$ of the composition of bipolar fuzzy digraphs $\vec{G}_1$ and $\vec{G}_2$ using $\mathcal{C}(\vec{G}_1)$ and $\mathcal{C}(\vec{G}_2)$.
6. Derive a method for the construction of bipolar fuzzy competition graph $\mathcal{C}(\vec{G}_1 \bullet \vec{G}_2)$ of the lexicographic product of bipolar fuzzy digraphs $\vec{G}_1$ and $\vec{G}_2$ using $\mathcal{C}(\vec{G}_1)$ and $\mathcal{C}(\vec{G}_2)$.
7. Let $\vec{G} = (A, \vec{D})$ be a complex bipolar fuzzy digraph, $\boldsymbol{k} = (k^p e^{i\theta^p}, k^n e^{i\theta^n})$ be an ordered pair of complex numbers such that $k^p \in [0, 1], k^n \in [-1, 0], \theta^p \in [0, \pi]$, $\theta^n \in [-\pi, 0]$. If for some $x, y \in X$,

$$h(\mathcal{N}^+(x) \cap \mathcal{N}^+(y)) = (e^{i\pi}, -e^{-i\pi}), \quad |\mathcal{N}^+(x) \cap \mathcal{N}^+(y)| = \left(l^p r^{i\phi^p}, l^n e^{i\phi^n}\right)$$

$$l^p > 2k^p, \;\; \phi^p > 2\theta^p, \;\; l^n < 2k^n, \;\; \phi^n < 2\theta^n$$

then prove that the edge xy is strong in $\mathcal{C}_{\boldsymbol{k}}(\vec{G})$.

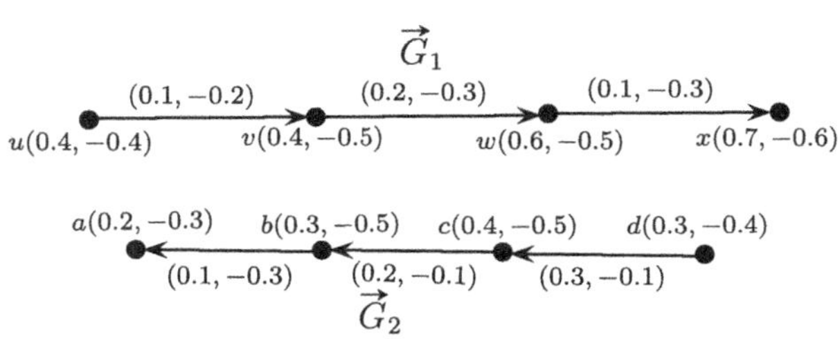

Fig. 4.41 Bipolar fuzzy graphs

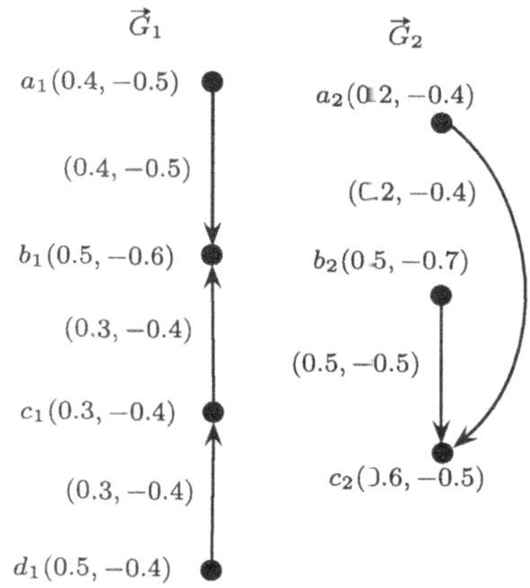

Fig. 4.42 Bipolar fuzzy digraphs $\vec{G}_1$ and $\vec{G}_2$

8. Prove or disprove that for every edge of a complex bipolar fuzzy graph G, there exists an edge in $\mathcal{N}[G]$.
9. Define a complex bipolar fuzzy $(\boldsymbol{k})$-competition graph, $\mathcal{N}_k(G)$, of a complex bipolar fuzzy graph $G = (A, D)$. Let $\vec{G} = (A, \vec{D})$ be a symmetric complex bipolar fuzzy digraph without any loops then prove that $\mathcal{C}_k(\vec{G}) = \mathcal{N}_k(\mathcal{U}(\vec{G}))$, where $\mathcal{U}(\vec{G})$ is the underlying complex bipolar fuzzy graph of $\vec{G}$.
10. Define a complex bipolar fuzzy $[\boldsymbol{k}]$-competition graph, $\mathcal{N}_k[G]$, of a complex bipolar fuzzy graph $G = (A, D)$. Let $\vec{G} = (A, \vec{D})$ be a symmetric complex bipolar fuzzy digraph having loops at every vertex, then prove that $\mathcal{C}_k(\vec{G}) = \mathcal{N}_k(\mathcal{U}(\vec{G}))$, where $\mathcal{U}(\vec{G})$ is the underlying complex bipolar fuzzy graph of $\vec{G}$.
11. Derive the methods for the construction of complex bipolar fuzzy competition graphs $\mathcal{C}(\vec{G}_1 \Box \vec{G}_2)$, $\mathcal{C}(\vec{G}_1 \times \vec{G}_2)$, $\mathcal{C}(\vec{G}_1 \bullet \vec{G}_2)$, $\mathcal{C}(\vec{G}_1 \cup \vec{G}_2)$ and $\mathcal{C}(\vec{G}_1 \cap \vec{G}_2)$ of complex bipolar fuzzy digraphs $\vec{G}_1$ and $\vec{G}_2$ using $\mathcal{C}(\vec{G}_1)$ and $\mathcal{C}(\vec{G}_2)$.

References

1. Akram, M., Dudek, W.A.: Regular bipolar fuzzy graphs. Neural Comput. Appl. **21**(supp 1), 197–205 (2012)
2. Akram, M., Sattar, A.: Competition graphs under complex Pythagorean fuzzy information. J. Appl. Math. Comput. 1–41 (2020)
3. Akram, M., Yousaf, M.M., Dudek, W.A.: Self centered interval-valued fuzzy graphs. Afrika Mathematika **26**(5–6), 887–898 (2015)
4. Akram, M., Sarwar, M.: Novel applications of $m-$polar fuzzy competition graphs in decision support system. Neural Comput. Appl. **30**, 3145–165 (2018)
5. Alkouri, A.U.M., Massa'deh, M.O., Ali, M.: On bipolar complex fuzzy sets and its application. J. Intell. Fuzzy Syst. (Preprint) (2020)
6. Alshehri, N.O., Akram, M.: Bipolar fuzzy competition graphs. Ars Combinatoria **121**, 385–402 (2015)
7. Cohen, J.E.: Interval graphs and food webs: a finding and a problem. Document 17696-PR, RAND Coporation, Santa Monica, CA (1968)

8. Dudek, W.A., Talebi, A.A.: Operations on level graphs of bipolar fuzzy graphs, Buletinul Academiei de Stiinte a Republici Moldova. Mathematica. **81**(2), 107–126 (2016)
9. Ma, X., Zhan, J., Khan, M., Zeeshan, M., Anis, S., Awan, A.S.: Complex fuzzy sets with applications in signals. Comput. Appl. Math. **38**(4), 150 (2019)
10. Pramanik, T., Samanta, S., Sarkar, B., Pal, M.: Fuzzy ϕ−tolerance competition graphs. Soft Comput. **21**(13), 3723–3734 (2017)
11. Ramot, D., Milo, R., Friedman, M., Kandel, A.: Complex fuzzy sets. IEEE Trans. Fuzzy Syst. **10**(2), 171–186 (2002)
12. Samanta, S., Akram, M., Pal, M.: m-step fuzzy competition graphs. J. Appl. Math. Comput. **47**(1–2), 461–472 (2015)
13. Samanta, S., Pal, M.: Fuzzy k−competition and p−competition graphs. Fuzzy Inf. Eng. **5**(2), 191–204 (2013)
14. Sahoo, S., Pal, M.: Intuitionistic fuzzy competition graphs. J. Appl. Math. Comput. **52**(1), 37–57 (2016)
15. Sarwar, M., Akram, M.: Novel concepts of bipolar fuzzy competition graphs. J. Appl. Math. Comput. **54**(1–2), 511–547 (2017)
16. Sarwar, M., Akram, M.: Certain algorithms for computing strength of competition in bipolar fuzzy graphs. Int. J. Uncertain. Fuzziness Knowl.-Based Syst. **25**(6), 877–96 (2017)
17. Zhang, W.-R.: (YinYang) Bipolar fuzzy sets. In: IEEE International Conference on Fuzzy Systems. pp. 835–840 (1998)
18. Zhang, W.-R.: Bipolar fuzzy sets and relations: a computational framework for cognitive modeling and multiagent decision analysis. In: Proceedings of IEEE Conference, pp. 305–309 (1994)
19. Zhang, G., Dillon, T.S., Cai, K.Y., Ma, J., Lu, J.: Operation properties and δ-equalities of complex fuzzy sets. Int. J. Approx. Reason. **50**(8), 1227–1249 (2009)

Chapter 5
Bipolar Fuzzy Planar Graphs

In this chapter, we study the concepts of bipolar fuzzy multisets, bipolar fuzzy multigraphs, strong and complete bipolar fuzzy multigraphs, bipolar fuzzy planar graphs, and bipolar fuzzy dual graphs. We discuss different types of bipolar fuzzy edges, intersection value and planarity value of bipolar fuzzy graphs, strong and weak bipolar fuzzy faces, and the relation of planarity and duality in bipolar fuzzy graphs. We elaborate various properties of bipolar fuzzy bridges, bipolar fuzzy cut vertices, bipolar fuzzy blocks, bipolar fuzzy cycles, and bipolar fuzzy trees in terms of level graphs. We describe the importance of bipolar fuzzy planar graphs with a number of real-world applications in road networks and electrical connections. The main results of this chapter are from [6, 7].

5.1 Introduction

Graph theory is a conceptual framework to study and analyze the units that are intensely or frequently connected in a network. Graphs are used to model various practical processes in which crossing between edges is a nuisance including design problems for circuits, subways, and utility lines. The crossing of two connections normally means that the communication lines must work at different heights. This is not a big issue for electrical wires, but it creates extra expenses for some types of lines. Circuits, in particular, are easier to manufacture if their connections can be constructed in fewer layers. These applications are designed by the concept of planar graphs. Circuits where the crossing of lines is necessary cannot be represented by planar graphs. Numerous computational challenges can be solved by means of cuts of planar graphs. Planar graphs are essential in city planning, subway tunnels, pipelines, and metro lines. Due to crossing, there is a chance for an accident. Also, underground routes reduce traffic jam but the cost of the crossing of these routes is high. In a city

M. Akram et al., *Graphs for the Analysis of Bipolar Fuzzy Information*, Studies in Fuzziness and Soft Computing 401,
https://doi.org/10.1007/978-981-15-8756-6_5

planning, routes without crossing are perfect for safety. But due to lack of space, the crossing of such lines is allowed. It is easy to observe that the crossing between one congested and one non-congested route is better than the crossing between two congested routes. The term "congested" has no definite meaning. We generally use "congested", "very congested", "highly congested" routes, etc. These terms are called linguistic terms and they have some membership values. A congested route may be referred to as a strong route and a low congested route may be called a weak route. Thus crossing between a strong route and a weak route is more safe than the crossing between two strong routes. That is, crossing between a strong route and a weak route may be allowed in city planning with a certain amount of safety. The terms strong route and weak route lead to the strong edge and weak edge of a fuzzy graph, respectively. And the crossing between strong and weak edges leads to the concept of fuzzy planar graphs.

One of the earliest questions concerning planarity was presented by Möbius during a lecture in about the year 1840, where Möbius presented the following problem: There was once a king with five sons. In his will, he stated that after his death the sons should divide the kingdom into five regions so that the boundary of each region should have a frontier line in common with each of the other four regions. Can the terms of the will be satisfied? [19]. This question can be rephrased using the geometric dual of the land regions. The geometric dual of a map G, denoted by G^*, can be formed by replacing each face of G with a vertex and connecting vertices if the faces of G share an edge. Then, the question of Möbius can be posed in a graph theoretic context as the problem of asking if each of the five sons has a road connecting his capital city to all his other brothers' capital cities in such a way that no two roads intersect. The problem of the five princes can be solved if the complete graph of the five vertices, denoted by K_5, is a planar graph. The second puzzle, sometimes called the gas-water-electricity problem requires to join three houses to three gas, water, and electricity facilities using pipes so that no two pipes cross. This problem reduces to the planarity of the complete bipartite graph $K_{3,3}$ obtained by connecting each of the three independent vertices to each of the three other independent vertices. It appears that these two puzzles are unfeasible.

Rosenfeld [13] introduced the fuzzy analog of several basic graph-theoretic concepts including bridges, cut-nodes, connectedness, trees, and cycles. Sunitha and Vijayakumar [18] characterized fuzzy trees. Bhutani and Rosenfeld [11] introduced the concepts of strong arcs, fuzzy end nodes, and geodesics in fuzzy graphs, and types of arcs in a fuzzy graph are described in [8]. Various concepts of fuzzy planar graphs, special fuzzy planar graphs, fuzzy trees, fuzzy cycles, fuzzy co-cycles, fuzzy dual graphs, strongest strong cycles, θ-fuzzy graphs, and strong arcs in fuzzy graphs are studied in [1, 9, 10, 12, 15, 17]. Zhang [20] introduced the notion of a bipolar fuzzy set as a powerful technique to discuss the bipolar behavior of objects. Bipolar fuzzy graph theory [2–5] is finding an increasing number of applications in modeling real-time systems and gives more precision, flexibility, and compatibility to the system as compared to the fuzzy and crisp models. The concepts of planar graphs, fuzzy planar graphs, and fuzzy trees are extended to bipolar fuzzy planar graphs, bipolar fuzzy cycles, and bipolar fuzzy trees in [6, 7] which is the main discussion of this chapter. For further terminologies and studies on fuzzy graphs and bipolar fuzzy systems, readers are referred to [14, 16, 21–23].

5.2 Bipolar Fuzzy Planar Graphs

A **multiset** is a modification of the concept of a set that, unlike a set, allows multiple instances for each of its elements. The number of instances given for each element is called the **multiplicity** of this element in the multiset. A **multigraph** is a graph that can have more than one edge between a pair of vertices. That is, $G = (X, E)$ is a multigraph if X is a set of vertices and E is a multiset of 2−element subsets of X. A **fuzzy multiset** A drawn from a non-empty set X can be characterized by a function $CM_A : X \to Q$, where Q is the set of all crisp multisets drawn from the unit interval.

Definition 5.1 A **bipolar fuzzy multiset** A drawn from a non-empty set X is characterized by two functions: "count positive membership" of A (CM_A) and "count negative membership" of A (CN_A) given by $CM_A : X \to Q_1$ and $CN_A : X \to Q_2$, where Q_1 and Q_2 are the sets of all crisp multisets drawn from the intervals $[0, 1]$ and $[-1, 0]$, respectively, such that for each $x \in X$,

1. The positive membership sequence is defined as a decreasingly ordered sequence of elements in $CM_A(x)$ which is denoted by $(\mu_A^p(x)_1, \mu_A^p(x)_2, \mu_A^p(x)_3, \dots, \mu_A^p(x)_m)$, where $\mu_A^p(x)_1 \geq \mu_A^p(x)_2 \geq \mu_A^p(x)_3 \geq \cdots \geq \mu_A^p(x)_m$,

2. The corresponding negative membership sequence is defined as an increasingly ordered sequence of elements in $CN_A(x)$ which is denoted by $(\mu_A^n(x)_1, \mu_A^n(x)_2, \mu_A^n(x)_3, \dots, \mu_A^n(x)_m)$, where $\mu_A^n(x)_1 \leq \mu_A^n(x)_2 \leq \mu_A^n(x)_3 \leq \cdots \leq \mu_A^n(x)_m$.

A bipolar fuzzy multiset A is denoted as

$$A = \left\{\left(x : (\mu_A^p(x)_1, \mu_A^p(x)_2, \mu_A^p(x)_3, \dots, \mu_A^p(x)_m), (\mu_A^n(x)_1, \mu_A^n(x)_2, \mu_A^n(x)_3, \dots, \mu_A^n(x)_m)\right) \mid x \in X\right\}$$

$$\text{or } A = \left\{\left(x : \mu_A^p(x)_i, \mu_A^n(x)_i\right)\right), i = 1, 2, \dots, m \mid x \in X\}.$$

Definition 5.2 A **bipolar fuzzy multigraph** on a non-empty set X is a pair $G = (A, B)$, where $A = (\mu_A^p, \mu_A^n)$ is a bipolar fuzzy set on X and $B = \{(xy, \mu_B^p(xy)_i, \mu_B^n(xy)_i), i = 1, 2, \dots, m \mid xy \in X \times X\}$ is a bipolar fuzzy multiset on $X \times X$ such that for all $x, y \in X$,

$$\mu_B^p(xy)_i \leq \min\{\mu_A^p(x), \mu_A^p(y)\} \text{ and } \mu_B^n(xy)_i \geq \max\{\mu_A^n(x), \mu_A^n(y)\}, \quad \text{for all } i = 1, 2, \dots, m.$$

Note that there may be more than one edge between the vertices x and y. Here, $\mu_B^p(xy)_i$ and $\mu_B^n(xy)_i$ represent the positive membership value and negative membership value of the ith edge xy in G. m denotes the number of edges between the vertices x and y. In a bipolar fuzzy multigraph G, B is said to be a bipolar fuzzy multiedge set. Also, $\mu_A^p(xy)_i = 0 = \mu_A^n(xy)_i$ for all $xy \in X \times X - E$.

Table 5.1 Bipolar fuzzy vertex set

	a	b	c	d
μ_A^p	0.5	0.4	0.5	0.4
μ_A^n	−0.3	−0.4	−0.3	−0.4

Table 5.2 Bipolar fuzzy multiedge set

	ab	ab	ab	bc	bd
μ_B^p	0.2	0.1	0.2	0.3	0.1
μ_B^n	−0.2	0	−0.2	−0.3	−0.2

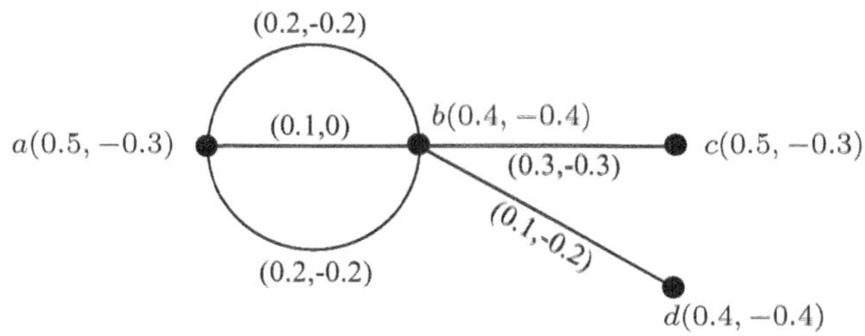

Fig. 5.1 Bipolar fuzzy multigraph

Example 5.1 Let $A = (\mu_A^p, \mu_A^n)$ be a bipolar fuzzy set on $X = \{a, b, c, d\}$, shown in Table 5.1, and $B = (\mu_B^p, \mu_B^n)$ be a bipolar fuzzy multiedge set of $X \times X$ given in Table 5.2.

The bipolar fuzzy multigraph is shown in Fig. 5.1.

Definition 5.3 Let $B = \{(xy, \mu_B^p(xy)_i, \mu_B^n(xy)_i), i = 1, 2, \ldots, m \mid xy \in X \times X\}$ be a bipolar fuzzy multiedge set in a bipolar fuzzy multigraph G. The **degree** of a vertex $x \in X$ is denoted by $deg(x)$ and defined as

$$\deg(x) = \left(\sum_{y \in X} \sum_{i=1}^{m} \mu_B^p(xy)_i, \sum_{y \in X} \sum_{i=1}^{m} \mu_B^n(xy)_i\right).$$

Example 5.2 In Example 5.1, the degree of the vertices a, b, c, d are calculated as $\deg(a) = (0.5, -0.4)$, $\deg(b) = (0.9, -0.9)$, $\deg(c) = (0.3, -0.3)$, and $\deg(d) = (0.1, -0.2)$.

Definition 5.4 Let $B = \left\{(xy, \mu_B^p(xy)_i, \mu_B^n(xy)_i), i = 1, 2, \ldots, m \mid xy \in X \times X\right\}$ be a bipolar fuzzy multiedge set in a bipolar fuzzy multigraph G. A multiedge xy of G is **strong** if $\frac{1}{2}\min\{\mu_A^p(x), \mu_A^p(y)\} \le \mu_B^p(xy)_i$ and $\frac{1}{2}\max\{\mu_A^n(x), \mu_A^n(y)\} \le \mu_B^n(xy)_i$ for each $i = 1, 2, \ldots, m$.

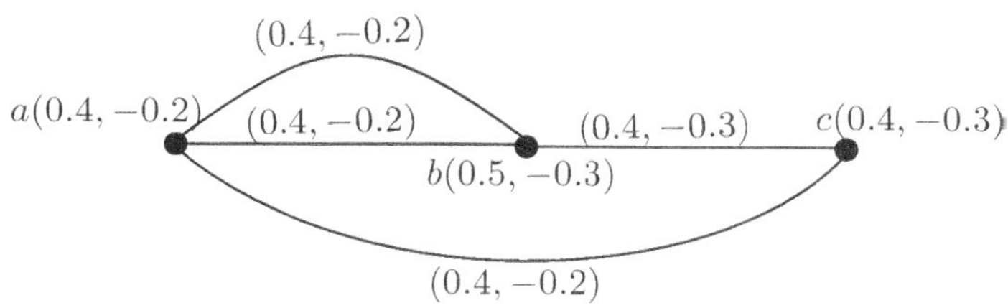

Fig. 5.2 Bipolar fuzzy complete multigraph

Definition 5.5 Let $B = \{(xy, \mu^p_B(xy)_i, \mu^n_B(xy)_i), i = 1, 2, \ldots, m \mid xy \in X \times X\}$ be a bipolar fuzzy multiedge set in a bipolar fuzzy multigraph G. A bipolar fuzzy multigraph G is **complete** if $\min\{\mu^p_A(x), \mu^p_A(y)\} = \mu^p_B(xy)_i$, $\max\{\mu^n_A(x), \mu^n_A(y)\} = \mu^n_B(xy)_i$ for each $i = 1, 2, \ldots, m$, for all $x, y \in X$.

Example 5.3 Consider a bipolar fuzzy multigraph G as shown in Fig. 5.2. By routine computations, it is easy to see from Fig. 5.2 that it is a complete bipolar fuzzy multigraph.

Definition 5.6 The **strength** of a bipolar fuzzy edge $(ab)_i$, for some $i \in \{1, 2, \ldots, m\}$, is denoted by the ordered pair $I_{(ab)_i} = (M_{(ab)_i}, N_{(ab)_i})$ and can be measured by the value,

$$I_{(ab)_i} = (M_{(ab)_i}, N_{(ab)_i}) = \left(\frac{\mu^p_B(ab)_i}{\mu^p_A(a) \wedge \mu^p_A(b)}, \frac{\mu^n_B(ab)_i}{\mu^n_A(a) \vee \mu^n_A(b)} \right).$$

Definition 5.7 Let $G = (A, B)$ be a bipolar fuzzy multigraph. A bipolar fuzzy edge $(ab)_i$, for some $i \in \{1, 2, \ldots, m\}$, is said to be **strong** if $M_{(ab)_i} \geq 0.5$ or $N_{(ab)_i} \leq 0.5$. Otherwise it is called a **weak** bipolar fuzzy edge.

Definition 5.8 Let $G = (A, B)$ be a bipolar fuzzy multigraph such that B contains two bipolar fuzzy edges $(ab, \mu^p_B(ab)_i, \mu^n_B(ab)_i)$ and $(cd, \mu^p_B(cd)_j, \mu^n_B(cd)_j)$ intersecting at a point P, where i and j are fixed integers. The **intersecting value** at point P is defined as

$$\mathcal{I}_P = (M_P, N_P) = \left(\frac{M_{(ab)_i} + M_{(cd)_j}}{2}, \frac{N_{(ab)_i} + N_{(cd)_j}}{2} \right), \quad \text{for some } i, j.$$

If the number of points of intersection in a bipolar fuzzy multigraph increases, planarity decreases. Thus, for a bipolar fuzzy multigraph, $\mathcal{I}_P$ is inversely proportional to the planarity. The concept of a bipolar fuzzy planar graph in introduced in Definition 5.9.

Table 5.3 Bipolar fuzzy vertex set A

A	a	b	c	d	e
μ_A^p	0.5	0.4	0.3	0.6	0.6
μ_A^n	−0.2	−0.1	−0.1	−0.2	−0.1

Table 5.4 Bipolar fuzzy multiedge set A

B	ab	ac	ad	ad	bc	bd	cd	ae	ce	de	be
μ_B^p	0.2	0.2	0.2	0.3	0.2	0.2	0.2	0.2	0.2	0.2	0.2
μ_B^n	−0.1	−0.1	−0.1	−0.1	−0.1	−0.1	−0.1	−0.1	−0.1	−0.1	−0.1

Definition 5.9 Let $G = (A, B)$ be a bipolar fuzzy multigraph such that $P_1, P_2, \ldots, P_n$ are the points of intersection between the edges for a certain geometrical representation, then G is said to be a **bipolar fuzzy planar graph** with bipolar fuzzy **planarity value** $f = (f^p, f^n)$ which is defined as

$$f = (f^p, f^n) = \left(\frac{1}{1+\{M_{P_1} + M_{P_2} + \cdots + M_{P_n}\}}, \frac{-1}{1+\{N_{P_1} + N_{P_2} + \cdots + N_{P_n}\}}\right).$$

Clearly, $f = (f^p, f^n)$ is bounded and $0 < f^p \leq 1$, $f^n, -1 \leq f^n < 0$. If there is no point of intersection for a certain geometrical representation of a bipolar fuzzy planar graph, then its planarity value is $(1, -1)$. In this case, the underlying crisp graph of this bipolar fuzzy graph is the crisp **planar graph**. If f^p decreases (f^n increases), then the number of points of intersection between the edges increases (decreases) and the nature of planarity decreases (increases). Thus, every bipolar fuzzy graph is a bipolar fuzzy planar graph with certain planarity value.

Example 5.4 Consider a bipolar fuzzy multigraph $G = (A, B)$ as shown in Fig. 5.3, where $A = (\mu_A^p, \mu_A^n)$ is a bipolar fuzzy set on $X = \{a, b, c, d, e\}$ and $B = (\mu_B^p, \mu_B^n)$ is a bipolar fuzzy set on $E = \{ab, ac, ad, ad, bc, bd, cd, ce, ae, de, be\}$ as given in Tables 5.3 and 5.4, respectively.

The bipolar fuzzy multigraph, shown in Fig. 5.3, has two points of intersection P_1 and P_2. P_1 is a point of intersection between $(ad, 0.2, -0.1)$ and $(bc, 0.2, -0.1)$ while P_2 is the point of intersection between $(ad, 0.3, -0.1)$ and $(bc, 0.2, -0.1)$.

1. For bipolar fuzzy edge $(ad, 0.2, -0.1)$, $I_{ad} = (0.4, 0.5)$.
2. For bipolar fuzzy edge $(ad, 0.3, -0.1)$, $I_{ad} = (0.6, 0.5)$.
3. For bipolar fuzzy edge $(bc, 0.2, -0.1)$, $I_{bc} = (0.67, 1)$.

For the first point of intersection P_1, intersecting value $\mathcal{I}_{P_1}$ is $(0.53, 0.75)$ and that for the second point of intersection P_2, $\mathcal{I}_{P_2} = (0.63, 0.75)$. Therefore, the planarity value for the bipolar fuzzy multigraph shown in Fig. 5.3 is $(0.46, -0.4)$.

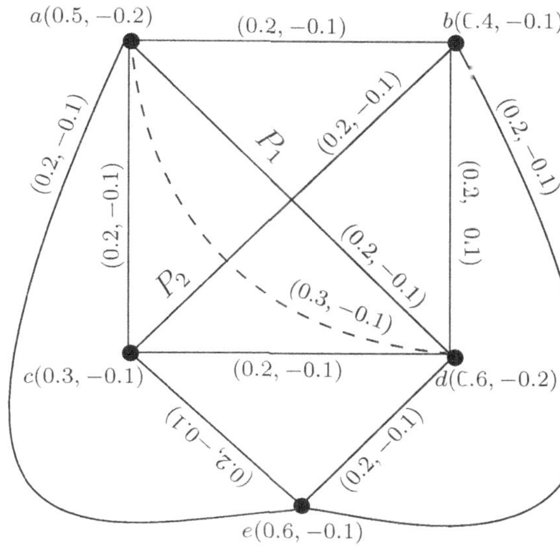

Fig. 5.3 Bipolar fuzzy planar graph

Definition 5.10 An bipolar fuzzy planar graph $G = (A, B)$ is called **strong bipolar fuzzy planar graph** if the planarity value $f = (f^p, f^n)$ of G is such that $f^p \geq 0.5$ and $f^n \leq -0.5$.

Theorem 5.1 *Let G be a strong bipolar fuzzy planar graph, then the number of points of intersection between strong bipolar fuzzy edges is at most one.*

Proof Let $G = (A, B)$ be a strong bipolar fuzzy planar graph on X. Assume that G has at least two points of intersection P_1 and P_2 between two strong bipolar fuzzy edges in G. For any strong bipolar fuzzy edge $(ab, \mu_B^p(ab)_i, \mu_B^n(ab)_i)$,

$$\mu_B^p(ab)_i \geq \frac{1}{2}\min\{\mu_A^p(a), \mu_A^p(b)\} \text{ and } \mu_B^n(ab)_i \leq \frac{1}{2}\max\{\mu_A^n(a), \mu_A^n(b)\}.$$

This shows that $M_{ab} \geq 0.5$ or $N_{ab} \leq 0.5$. Thus, for two intersecting strong bipolar fuzzy edges $(ab, \mu_B^p(ab)_i, \mu_B^n(ab)_i)$ and $(cd, \mu_B^p(cd)_j, \mu_B^n(cd)_j)$,

$$\frac{M_{ab} + M_{cd}}{2} \geq 0.5, \quad \frac{N_{ab} + N_{cd}}{2} \leq 0.5.$$

That is, $M_{P_1} \geq 0.5$, $N_{P_1} \leq 0.5$. Similarly, $M_{P_2} \geq 0.5$, $N_{P_2} \leq 0.5$. This implies that $1 + M_{P_1} + M_{P_2} \geq 2$, $1 + N_{P_1} + N_{P_2} \leq 2$. Therefore, $f^p = \frac{1}{1+M_{P_1}+M_{P_2}} \leq 0.5$, $f^n = \frac{-1}{1+N_{P_1}+N_{P_2}} \geq -0.5$. It contradicts the fact that the bipolar fuzzy graph is a strong bipolar fuzzy planar graph. Thus, the number of points of intersection between strong bipolar fuzzy edges cannot be two. Obviously, if the number of points of intersection of strong bipolar fuzzy edges increases, the planarity value decreases. Similarly, if the number of points of intersection of strong bipolar fuzzy edges is one, then planarity value $f^p < 0.5$, $f^n > -0.5$. Any bipolar fuzzy planar graph without any crossing between edges is a **strong bipolar fuzzy planar graph**. Thus, we conclude that the maximum number of points of intersection between the strong bipolar fuzzy edges in G is one. □

Theorem 5.2 *Let G be a bipolar fuzzy planar graph with planarity value $f = (f^p, f^n)$. If $f^p \geq 0.67$, $f^n \leq -0.67$, then G does not contain any point of intersection between two strong bipolar fuzzy edges.*

Definition 5.11 Let $G = (A, B)$ be a bipolar fuzzy planar graph and $B = \{(xy, \mu_B^p(xy)_i, \mu_B^n(xy)_i), i = 1, 2, \ldots, m \mid xy \in X \times X\}$ be a bipolar fuzzy multiedge set of G. A **bipolar fuzzy face** of G is a region bounded by the set of the bipolar fuzzy edges $E' \subset E$ of a geometric representation of G. The positive and negative membership values of the bipolar fuzzy face are defined as

$$\min\left\{\frac{\mu_B^p(xy)_i}{\min\{\mu_A^p(x), \mu_A^p(y)\}}, i = 1, 2, \ldots, m \mid xy \in E'\right\},$$

$$\max\left\{\frac{\mu_B^n(xy)_i}{\max\{\mu_A^n(x), \mu_A^n(y)\}}, i = 1, 2, \ldots, m \mid xy \in E'\right\}.$$

Definition 5.12 A bipolar fuzzy face is called a **strong bipolar fuzzy face** if its positive membership value is greater than 0.5 or the negative membership value is lesser than −0.5. Otherwise, it is called a **weak bipolar fuzzy face**. Every bipolar fuzzy planar graph has an infinite region which is called **outer bipolar fuzzy face**. Other faces are called **inner bipolar fuzzy faces**.

Example 5.5 Consider a bipolar fuzzy planar graph $G = (A, B)$ as shown in Fig. 5.4. Then G has the following bipolar fuzzy faces.

1. The bipolar fuzzy face F_1 is bounded by bipolar fuzzy edges $(v_1v_2, 0.5, -0.1)$, $(v_2v_3, 0.6, -0.1)$,$(v_1v_3, 0.5, -0.1)$.
2. The outer bipolar fuzzy face F_2 is surrounded by bipolar fuzzy edges $(v_1v_3, 0.5, -0.1)$, $(v_1v_4, 0.5, -0.1)$, $(v_2v_4, 0.6, -0.1)$, $(v_2v_3, 0.6, -0.1)$.
3. The bipolar fuzzy face F_3 is bounded by bipolar fuzzy edges $(v_1v_2, 0.5, -0.1)$, $(v_2v_4, 0.6, -0.1)$, $(v_1v_4, 0.5, -0.1)$.

Clearly, the positive and negative membership values of a bipolar fuzzy face F_1 are 0.833 and −0.333, respectively. The positive membership value and negative membership value of a bipolar fuzzy face F_3 are also 0.833 and −0.333, respectively. Thus, F_1 and F_3 are strong bipolar fuzzy faces.

The concept of dual of a bipolar fuzzy planar graph is given in Definition 5.13. In a bipolar fuzzy dual graph, vertices are corresponding to the strong bipolar fuzzy faces of the bipolar fuzzy planar graph and each bipolar fuzzy edge between two vertices is corresponding to each edge in the boundary between two bipolar fuzzy faces of the bipolar fuzzy planar graph as explained in Definition 5.13.

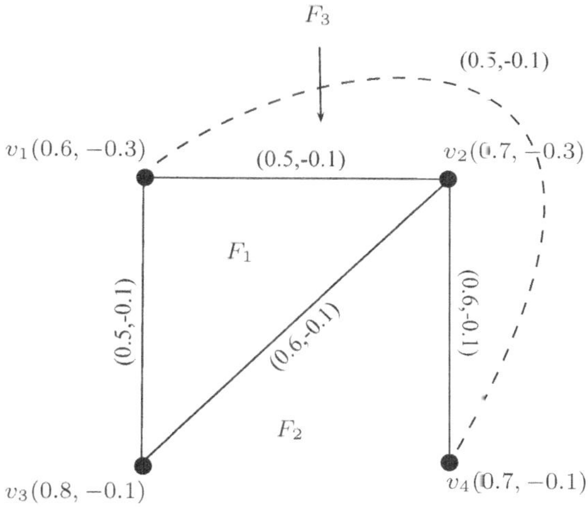

Fig. 5.4 Bipolar fuzzy faces in G

Definition 5.13 Let $G = (A, B)$ be a bipolar fuzzy planar graph and $B = \{(xy, \mu_B^p(xy)_i, \mu_B^n(xy)_i), i = 1, 2, \ldots, m \mid xy \in X \times X\}$ be a bipolar fuzzy multiedge set of G. Let $F_1, F_2, \ldots, F_k$ be the strong bipolar fuzzy faces of G. The **bipolar fuzzy dual graph** of G is a bipolar fuzzy planar graph $G' = (X', A', B')$, where $X' = \{x_i, i = 1, 2, \ldots, k\}$, and the vertex x_i of G' is considered for the face F_i of G. The positive and negative membership values of the vertices are given by the mapping $A' = (\mu_{A'}^p, \mu_{A'}^n) : X' \to [0, 1] \times [-1, 0]$ such that $\mu_{A'}^p(x_j) = \max\{\mu_{B'}^p(uv)_i, i = 1, 2, \ldots, p \mid uv$ is an edge of the boundary of the strong bipolar fuzzy face $F_j\}$, $\mu_{A'}^n(x_j) = \min\{\mu_{B'}^n(uv)_i, i = 1, 2, \ldots, p \mid uv$ is an edge of the boundary of the strong bipolar fuzzy face $F_j\}$.

There may exist more than one common edge between two bipolar fuzzy faces F_i and F_j in G. Thus, there may be more than one edge between two vertices x_i and x_j in a bipolar fuzzy dual graph G'. Let $\mu_B^p(x_i x_j)_l$ denote the positive membership value of the lth edge between x_i and x_j, and $\mu_B^n(x_i x_j)_l$ denote the negative–positive membership value of the lth edge between x_i and x_j. The positive membership and negative membership values of the edges of the bipolar fuzzy dual graph are given by $\mu_{B'}^p(x_i x_j)_l = \mu_B^p(uv)_l$, $\mu_{B'}^n(x_i x_j)_l = \mu_B^n(uv)_l$, where $(uv)_l$ is an edge in the boundary between two strong bipolar fuzzy faces F_i and F_j and $l = 1, 2, \ldots, s$, where s is the number of common edges in the boundary between F_i and F_j or the number of edges between x_i and x_j. If there is any strong **pendant edge** in the bipolar fuzzy planar graph, then there will be a self-loop in G' corresponding to this pendant edge. The positive and negative membership values of the self-loop are equal to the positive and negative membership values of the pendant edge. The bipolar fuzzy dual graph of the bipolar fuzzy planar graph does not contain the point of intersection of edges for a certain representation, so it is a bipolar fuzzy planar graph with planarity value $(1, -1)$. Thus, the bipolar fuzzy face of the bipolar fuzzy dual graph can be similarly described as in bipolar fuzzy planar graphs.

Example 5.6 Consider a bipolar fuzzy planar graph $G = (X, A, B)$ as shown in Fig. 5.5 such that $X = \{a, b, c, d\}$, $A = \{(a, 0.6, -0.2), (b, 0.7, -0.2), (c, 0.8, -0.2), (d, 0.9, -0.1)\}$, and

$$B = \{(ab, 0.5, -0.01), (ac, 0.4, -0.01), (ad, 0.55, -0.01), (bc, 0.45, -0.01), (bc, 0.6, -0.01), (cd, 0.7, -0.01)\}.$$

The bipolar fuzzy planar graph has the following bipolar fuzzy faces.

1. The bipolar fuzzy face F_1 is bounded by $(ab, 0.5, -0.01)$, $(ac, 0.4, -0.01)$, $(bc, 0.45, -0.01)$.
2. The bipolar fuzzy face F_2 is bounded by $(ad, 0.55, -0.01)$, $(cd, 0.7, -0.01)$, $(ac, 0.4, -0.01)$.
3. The bipolar fuzzy face F_3 is bounded by $(bc, 0.45, -0.01)$, $(bc, 0.6, -0.01)$.
4. The outer bipolar fuzzy face F_4 is surrounded by $(ab, 0.5, -0.01)$, $(bc, 0.6, -0.01)$, $(cd, 0.7, -0.01)$, $(ad, 0.55, -0.01)$.

Routine calculations show that all bipolar fuzzy faces are strong bipolar fuzzy faces. For each strong bipolar fuzzy face, consider a vertex for the bipolar fuzzy dual graph. So the vertex set is $X' = \{x_1, x_2, x_3, x_4\}$, where the vertex x_i is taken corresponding to the strong bipolar fuzzy face F_i, $i = 1, 2, 3, 4$. Thus,

$$\mu^p_{A'}(x_1) = \max\{0.5, 0.4, 0.45\} = 0.5, \mu^p_{A'}(x_2) = \max\{0.55, 0.7, 0.4\} = 0.7,$$

$$\mu^n_{A'}(x_1) = \min\{-0.01, -0.01, -0.01\} = -0.01, \mu^n_{A'}(x_2) = \min\{-0.01, -0.01, -0.01\} = -0.01,$$

$$\mu^p_{A'}(x_3) = \max\{0.45, 0.6\} = 0.6, \mu^p_{A'}(x_4) = \max\{0.5, 0.6, 0.7, 0.55\} = 0.7,$$

$$(mu^n_A)'(x_3) = \min\{-0.01, -0.01\} = -0.01, (\mu^n_{A'}(x_4) = \min\{-0.01, -0.01, -0.01, -0.01\} = -0.01.$$

There are two common edges ad and cd between the bipolar fuzzy faces F_2 and F_4 in G. Hence, between the vertices x_2 and x_4, there exist two edges in the bipolar fuzzy dual graph of G. The positive and negative membership values of these edges are given as

$$\mu^p_{B'}(x_2x_4) = \mu^p_B(cd) = 0.7, \mu^p_{B'}(x_2x_4) = \mu^p_B(ad) = 0.55,$$

$$\mu^n_{B'}(x_2x_4) = \mu^n_B(cd) = -0.01, \mu^n_{B'}(x_2x_4) = \mu^n_B(ad) = -0.01.$$

The positive and negative positive membership values of other edges of the bipolar fuzzy dual graph are calculated as

$$\mu^p_{B'}(x_1x_3) = \mu^p_B(bc) = 0.45, \mu^p_{B'}(x_1x_2) = \mu^p_B(ac) = 0.4,$$

$$\mu^p_{B'}(x_1x_4) = \mu^p_B(ab) = 0.5, \mu^p_{B'}(x_3x_4) = (\mu^p_B)'(bc) = 0.6,$$

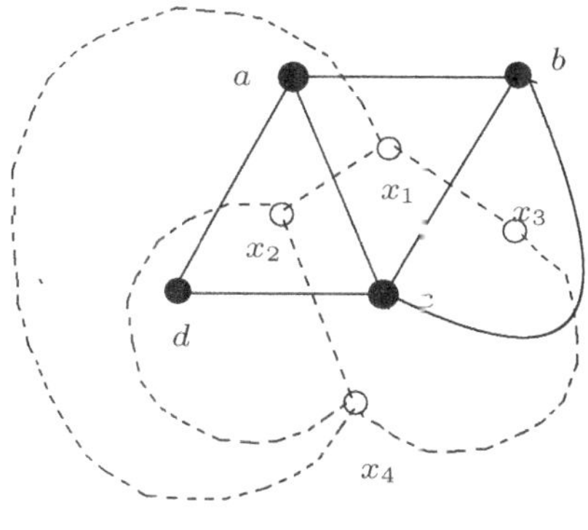

Fig. 5.5 Bipolar fuzzy dual graph

$$(\mu_B^n)'(x_1x_3) = \mu_B^p(bc) = -0.01, \mu_{B'}^n(x_1x_2) = \mu_B^n(ac) = -0.01,$$

$$\mu_{B'}^n(x_1x_4) = \mu_B^n(ab) = -0.01, (\mu_B^n)'(x_3x_4) = \mu_B^n(bc) = -0.01.$$

Thus, the edge set of the bipolar fuzzy dual graph is $B' = \{(x_1x_3, 0.45, -0.01), (x_1x_2, 0.4, -0.01), (x_1x_4, 0.5, -0.01), (x_3x_4, 0.6, -0.01), (x_2x_4, 0.7, -0.01), (x_2x_4, 0.55, -0.01)\}$. In Fig. 5.5, the bipolar fuzzy dual graph $G' = (X', A', B')$ of G is drawn by dotted lines.

Theorem 5.3 *Let G be a bipolar fuzzy planar graph whose number of vertices, number of bipolar fuzzy edges, and number of strong faces are denoted by n, p, and m, respectively. Let G' be the bipolar fuzzy dual graph of G, then the following conditions are satisfied.*

1. *The number of vertices of G' is equal to m.*
2. *The number of edges of G' is equal to p.*
3. *The number of bipolar fuzzy faces of G' is equal to n.*

Theorem 5.4 *Let $G = (X, A, B)$ be a bipolar fuzzy planar graph without weak edges and the bipolar fuzzy dual graph of G be $G' = (X', A', B')$. The positive and negative membership values of edges in G' are equal to positive and negative membership values of the bipolar fuzzy edges of G.*

It is known that the isomorphism between bipolar fuzzy graphs is an equivalence relation (see Definition 1.35). If there is an isomorphism between two bipolar fuzzy graphs such that one is a bipolar fuzzy planar graph, then the other will also be a bipolar fuzzy planar graph.

Theorem 5.5 *Let G be a bipolar fuzzy planar graph and H be a bipolar fuzzy graph. If there exists an isomorphism $f : G \to H$, then H can be drawn as a bipolar fuzzy planar graph with the same planarity value as G.*

Two bipolar fuzzy planar graphs with the same number of vertices may be isomorphic. But the relations between planarity values of two bipolar fuzzy planar graphs are discussed in the following theorems.

Theorem 5.6 *Let G_1 and G_2 be the isomorphic bipolar fuzzy graphs with planarity values f_1 and f_2, respectively, then $f_1 = f_2$.*

Theorem 5.7 *Let G_1 and G_2 be weak isomorphic bipolar fuzzy graphs with planarity values f_1 and f_2, respectively, then $f_1 = f_2$ if the positive and negative membership values of corresponding intersecting edges are the same.*

Theorem 5.8 *Let G_1 and G_2 be co-weak isomorphic bipolar fuzzy graphs with planarity values f_1 and f_2, respectively, then $f_1 = f_2$ if the minimum of positive membership values and maximum of negative membership values of the end vertices of corresponding intersecting edges are the same.*

5.3 Bipolar Fuzzy Bridges

A **path** in a crisp graph G^* is an alternating sequence of vertices and edges $v_0, e_1, v_1, e_2, \ldots, v_{n-1}, e_n, v_n$. The path with n vertices is denoted by P_n. A path is sometimes denoted by $P_n : v_0 v_1 \cdots v_n$ $(n > 0)$. The **length** of a path P_n in G^* is n. A path $P_n : v_0 v_1 \cdots v_n$ in G^* is called a **cycle** if $v_0 = v_n$ and $n \geq 3$. Note that path graph, P_n, has $n - 1$ edges and can be obtained from cycle graph, C_n, by removing any edge. An undirected graph G^* is **connected** if there is a path between each pair of distinct vertices. A **block** is a maximal **biconnected** (if any one vertex is removed, then the graph remains connected) subgraph of a crisp graph G^*. An edge e in a connected graph G^* is a **bridge** (cut edge or cut arc) if $G - e$ is disconnected. A vertex v in a connected graph G is a **cut vertex** if $G - v$ is disconnected. The graphs with exactly $n - 1$ bridges are exactly the **trees** (connected acyclic undirected graph), and the graphs in which every edge is a bridge are exactly the **forests** (disjoint union of trees). A **spanning tree** in a connected graph G is a subgraph of G which includes all the vertices of G and is also a tree.

Let $G = (A, B)$ be a bipolar fuzzy graph. The μ^p**-strength** of a bipolar fuzzy path $P : v_1, e_1, v_2, e_2, v_3, \ldots, e_{k-1}, v_k$ is defined as $(\mu^p)^k(v_1, v_k) = \wedge_{i=1}^{k-1} \mu_B^p(e_i)$. The μ^n**-strength** of P between v_1 and v_n is defined as $(\mu^n)^k(v_1, v_k) = \wedge_{i=1}^{k-1} \mu_B^n(e_i)$. If $x, y \in X$, the $\boldsymbol{\mu^p}$**−strength of connectedness** between x and y is defined as

$$(\mu_B^p)^\infty(x, y) = \max\{(\mu_B^p)^k(x, y) \mid k = 1, 2, \ldots\},$$

$$(\mu_B^p)^\infty(x, y) = \max\{\mu_B^p(x, v_1) \wedge \mu_B^p(v_1, v_2) \wedge \ldots \wedge \mu_B^p(v_{k-1}, y) \mid x, v_1, v_2, \cdots, v_{k-1}, y \in X,\ k = 1, 2, \ldots\}.$$

The $\boldsymbol{\mu^n}$**−strength of connectedness** between x and y is

$$(\mu_B^n)^\infty(x, y) = \min\{(\mu_B^n)^k(x, y) \mid k = 1, 2, \cdots, n\},$$

$$(\mu_B^n)^\infty(x, y) = \min\{\mu_B^n(x, v_1) \vee \mu_B^n(v_1, v_2) \vee \ldots \vee \mu_B^n(v_{k-1}, y) \mid x, v_1, v_2, \cdots, v_{k-1}, y \in X,\ k = 1, 2, \cdots, n\}.$$

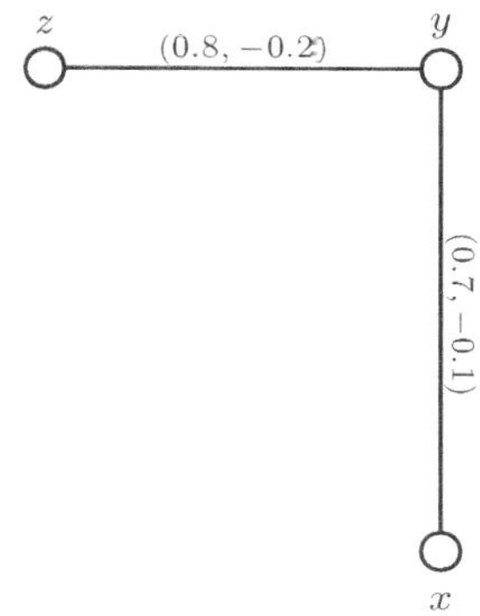

Fig. 5.6 Connected bipolar fuzzy graph

Also, $(\mu_B^p)'^{\infty}(x, y)$ and $(\mu_B^n)'^{\infty}(x, y)$ denote $(\mu^p_{G-(x,y)})^{\infty}(x, y)$ and $(\mu^n_{G-(x,y)})^{\infty}(x, y)$, where $G - (x, y)$ is obtained from G by deleting the arc (x, y).

Definition 5.14 A **bipolar fuzzy edge graph** on a non-empty set X is an ordered pair of the form $\widehat{G} = (X, B)$, where X is the crisp vertex set and B is defined by the functions $\mu_B^p : X \times X \to [0, 1]$ and $\mu_B^n : X \times X \to [-1, 0]$.

Definition 5.15 An edge xy in bipolar fuzzy graph G is said to be **μ^p-bridge** if deleting xy reduces the μ^p-strength of connectedness between some pair of vertices. An edge xy is said to be **μ^n-bridge** if deleting xy increases the μ^n-strength of connectedness between some pair of vertices. An edge xy is said to be a bipolar fuzzy **bipolar fuzzy bridge** if it is μ^p-bridge and μ^n-bridge.

Definition 5.16 Let $G = (A, B)$ be a bipolar fuzzy graph on a non-empty set X, then

1. xy is called a **weak bipolar fuzzy bridge** if there exists $(s, t) \in (0, h(B)] \times [d(B), 0)$ such that xy is a bridge of $G_{(s,t)}$ (see Definitions 7.10 and 4.2).
2. xy is called a **partial bipolar fuzzy bridge** if xy is a bridge of $G_{(s,t)}$, for all $(s, t) \in (0, h(B)] \times (d(B), 0] \cup \{(h(B), d(B))\}$.
3. xy is called a **full bipolar fuzzy bridge** if xy is a bridge for $G_{(s,t)}$, for all $(s, t) \in (0, h(B)] \times [d(B), 0)$.

Example 5.7 Consider a connected bipolar fuzzy graph as shown in Fig. 5.6. By routine computations, $d(B) = -0.2$, $h(B) = 0.8$. Thus, $(s, t) \in (0, 0.8] \times [-0.2, 0)$. For $0 < s \leq 0.7$, $-0.2 \leq t < 0$, $G_{(s,t)} = (X, \{xy, yz\})$. For $0.7 < s \leq 0.8$, $-0.2 \leq t < 0$, $G_{(s,t)} = (X, \{yz\})$. Hence, yz is a full bipolar fuzzy bridge and xy is a weak bipolar fuzzy bridge but not a partial bipolar fuzzy bridge. Both xy and yz are bridges and bipolar fuzzy bridges.

Example 5.8 Consider a connected bipolar fuzzy graph as shown in Fig. 5.7. By routine calculations, $d(B) = -0.4$, $h(B) = 0.9$. For $0 < s \leq 0.1$, $-0.4 \leq t < 0$,

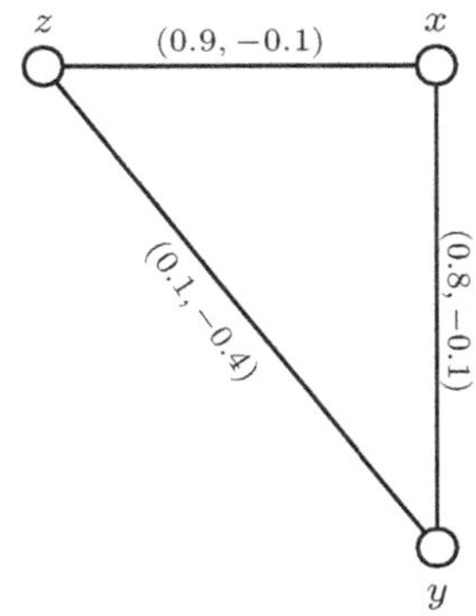

Fig. 5.7 Bipolar fuzzy bridges

$G_{(s,t)} = (X, \{xy, xz, yz\})$. For $0.1 < s \leq 0.8, -0.1 \leq t < 0, G_{(s,t)} = (X, \{xy, xz\})$. For $0.8 < s \leq 0.9, -0.1 \leq t < 0$, $G_{(s,t)} = (X, \{xz\})$. Thus, xz is a bipolar fuzzy bridge and a partial bipolar fuzzy bridge but not a bridge. The edge yz is not any type of bipolar fuzzy bridge.

Example 5.9 Let A be a bipolar fuzzy set on $X = \{x, y, z\}$ and B be a bipolar fuzzy relation in X defined by

$$\mu_A^p(x) = \mu_A^p(y) = \mu_A^p(z) = 1, \quad \mu_A^n(x) = \mu_A^n(y) = \mu_A^n(z) = -1,$$

$$\mu_B^p(xy) = \mu_B^p(yz) = \mu_B^p(xz) = 0.9, \quad \mu_B^n(xy) = \mu_B^n(yz) = \mu_B^n(xz) = -0.1.$$

Clearly, $G = (A, B)$ has no bipolar fuzzy bridges of any type.

Example 5.10 Let A be a bipolar fuzzy set on $X = \{x, y, z, w\}$ and let B be a bipolar fuzzy relation in X defined by

$$\mu_A^p(x) = \mu_A^p(y) = \mu_A^p(z) = \mu_A^p(w) = 1, \quad \mu_A^n(x) = \mu_A^n(y) = \mu_A^n(z) = \mu_A^n(w) = -1,$$

$$\mu_B^p(xy) = \mu_B^p(yz) = 0.1, \ \mu_B^p(xz) = \mu_B^p(wz) = 0.9, \ \mu_B^n(xy) = \mu_B^n(yz) = -0.5, \ \mu_B^n(xz) = \mu_B^n(wz) = -0.1.$$

Here, $d(B) = -0.5$, $h(B) = 0.9$. For $0 < s \leq 0.1$, $-0.5 \leq t < 0$, $G_{(s,t)} = (X, \{xy, yz, xz, zw\})$. For $0.1 < s \leq 0.9$, $-0.1 \leq t < 0$, $G_{(s,t)} = (X, \{xz, zw\})$. Thus, zw is a full bipolar fuzzy bridge and xz is a partial bipolar fuzzy bridge but not a full bipolar fuzzy bridge.

Proposition 5.1 *Let $G = (A, B)$ be a bipolar fuzzy graph on a non-empty set X such that G^* is a crisp graph corresponding to G. If xy is a bridge in G^*, then xy is a bipolar fuzzy bridge in G if and only if $\mu_B^p(x, y) > (\mu_B^p)'^{\infty}(x, y)$ and $\mu_B^n(x, y) < (\mu_B^n)'^{\infty}(x, y)$.*

Proposition 5.2 *Let $G = (A, B)$ be a bipolar fuzzy graph on a non-empty set X, then xy is a bipolar fuzzy bridge in G if and only if xy is not a weakest bipolar fuzzy edge of any bipolar fuzzy cycle.*

Proposition 5.3 *An edge xy in a bipolar fuzzy graph is a bipolar fuzzy bridge if and only if xy is a bridge of G^* and $\mu_B^p(x, y) = h(B)$, $\mu_B^n(x, y) = d(B)$.*

Proof Suppose xy is a full bipolar fuzzy bridge of a bipolar fuzzy graph G. Then xy is a bridge for $G_{(s,t)}$, for all $(s, t) \in (0, h(B)] \times (0, d(B)]$. Hence, $xy \in B_{(h(B),d(B))}$ and so $\mu_B^p(x, y) = h(B)$, $\mu_B^n(xy) = d(B)$. Since xy is a bridge for $G_{(s,t)}$ for all $(s, t) \in (0, h(B)] \times (0, d(B)]$, it follows that xy is a bridge for G^*.

Conversely, suppose that xy is a bridge for G^* and $\mu_B^p(xy) = h(B)$, $\mu_B^n(xy) = d(B)$. Then $xy \in B_{(s,t)}$, for all $(s, t) \in (0, h(B)] \times [d(B), 0)$. Since xy is a bridge for G^*, therefore, xy is a bridge for $G_{(s,t)} \forall (s, t) \in (0, h(B)] \times [d(B), 0)$ since each $G_{(s,t)}$ is a subgraph of G^*. Hence, xy is a full bipolar fuzzy bridge. □

Proposition 5.4 *Let $G = (A, B)$ be a bipolar fuzzy graph on X and xy is not contained in a cycle of G^*, then the following conditions are equivalent.*

1. $\mu_B^p(xy) = h(B)$, $\mu_B^n(xy) = d(B)$.
2. *xy is a partial bipolar fuzzy bridge.*
3. *xy is a full bipolar fuzzy bridge.*

Proof Since xy is not contained in a cycle of G^*, xy is a bridge of G^*. Hence by Proposition 5.3, 1⇔ 3. Clearly, 3⇔ 2. Assume that condition 2 holds, then xy is a bridge for $G_{(s,t)}$, for all $(s, t) \in (d(B), 0] \times (0, h(B)]$. So, $xy \in B_{(h(B),d(B))}$. Thus $\mu_B^p(xy) = h(B)$, $\mu_B^n(xy) = d(B)$, i.e., condition 1 holds. □

Proposition 5.5 *Let $G = (A, B)$ be a bipolar fuzzy graph on X and xy is a bridge of G^*, then xy is a weak bipolar fuzzy bridge and a bipolar fuzzy bridge.*

Proposition 5.6 *Let $G = (A, B)$ be a bipolar fuzzy graph on X, then xy is a bipolar fuzzy bridge if and only if xy is a weak bipolar fuzzy bridge.*

Proof Suppose xy is a weak bipolar fuzzy bridge, then there exists $(s, t) \in (0, h(B)] \times [d(B), 0)$ such that xy is a bridge for $G_{(s,t)}$. Hence, removal of xy disconnects $G_{(s,t)}$. Thus, any path from x to y in G has an edge uv with $\mu_B^p(uv) < s$, $\mu_B^n(uv) > t$. Thus, the removal of xy results in $(\mu_B^p)'^{\infty}(x, y) < s \leqslant (\mu_B^p)^{\infty}(x, y)$, $(\mu_B^n)'^{\infty}(x, y) > t \geqslant (\mu_B^n)^{\infty}(x, y)$. Hence, xy is a bipolar fuzzy bridge

Conversely, suppose xy is a bipolar fuzzy bridge. Then there exists uv such that removal of xy results in $(\mu_B^p)'^{\infty}(u, v) < (\mu_B^p)^{\infty}(u, v)$, $(\mu_B^n)'^{\infty}(u, v) > (\mu_B^n)^{\infty}(u, v)$. Hence, xy is on every strongest path connecting u and v and in fact, $\mu_B^p(uv) \geqslant \mu_B^p(xy)$ and $\mu_B^n(uv) \leqslant \mu_B^n(xy)$. Thus, there does not exist a bipolar fuzzy path (other than xy) connecting x and y in $G_{(\mu_B^p(xy),\mu_B^n(xy))}$, else the other bipolar fuzzy path without xy would be of strength greater or equal to $\mu_B^p(xy)$, less or equal to $\mu_B^n(x, y)$ and would be a part of a bipolar fuzzy path connecting u and v of strongest length, contrary to the fact xy is on every such bipolar fuzzy path. Hence, xy is a bridge of $G_{(\mu_B^p(xy),\mu_B^n(xy))}$ and $0 < \mu_B^p(xy) \leq h(B)$, $d(B) \leq \mu_B^n(xy) < 0$. Thus, $\mu_B^p(xy) = s$ and $\mu_B^n(xy) = t$. □

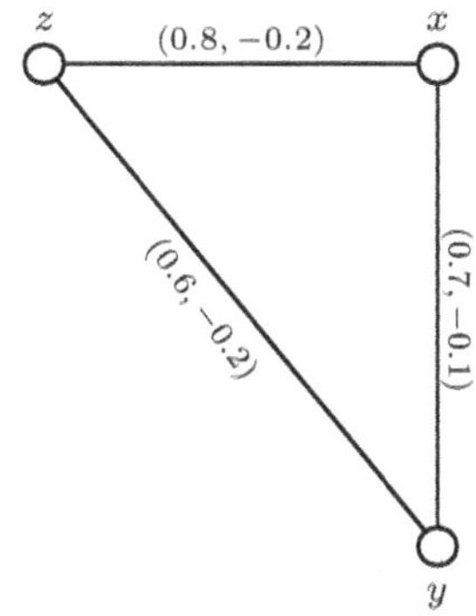

Fig. 5.8 Bipolar fuzzy cut vertices in $G = (A, B)$

5.4 Bipolar Fuzzy Cut Vertices and Bipolar Fuzzy Blocks

Definition 5.17 A vertex $x \in X$ in a bipolar fuzzy graph $G = (A, B)$ is called **μ^p-cut vertex** if deleting x from G reduces the μ^p-strength of connectedness between some pair of vertices. A vertex $x \in X$ in called a **μ^n-cut vertex** if deleting x increases the μ^n-strength of connectedness between some pair of vertices. A vertex $x \in X$ is a **bipolar fuzzy cut vertex** if it is μ^p-cut vertex and μ^n-cut vertex.

Definition 5.18 Let $G = (A, B)$ be a bipolar fuzzy graph on a non-empty set X with crisp graph $G^* = (X, E)$, then

1. a vertex $x \in X$ is called a **bipolar fuzzy cut vertex** if $(\mu_B^p)'^{\infty}(u, v) < (\mu_B^p)^{\infty}(u, v)$ and $(\mu_B^n)'^{\infty}(u, v) > (\mu_B^n)^{\infty}(u, v)$, for some $u, v \in X$,
2. x is called a **weak bipolar fuzzy cut vertex** if there exists $(s, t) \in (0, h(B)] \times [d(B), 0)$ such that x is a cut vertex of $G_{(s,t)}$,
3. x is called a **partial bipolar fuzzy cut vertex** if x is a cut vertex of $G_{(s,t)}$, for all $(s, t) \in (0, h(B)] \times (d(B), 0] \cup \{(h(B), d(B))\}$,
4. x is called a **full bipolar fuzzy cut vertex** if x is a cut vertex of $G_{(s,t)}$, for all $(s, t) \in (0, h(B)] \times [d(B), 0)$.

Example 5.11 Consider a connected bipolar fuzzy graph $G = (A, B)$ as shown in Fig. 5.8. Here $d(B) = -0.2$, $h(B) = 0.8$. Thus, $(s, t) \in (0, 0.8] \times [-0.1, 0)$. For $0 < s \leq 0.6$, $-0.2 \leq t < 0$, $G_{(s,t)} = (X, \{xy, yz, xz\})$. For $0.6 < s \leq 0.7$, $-0.2 \leq t < 0$, $G_{(s,t)} = (X, \{xy, xz\})$. For $0.6 < s \leq 0.8$,$-0.1 \leq t < 0$, $G_{(s,t)} = (X, \{xz\})$. Thus, x is a bipolar fuzzy cut vertex and a weak bipolar fuzzy cut vertex, but not a partial bipolar fuzzy cut vertex.

Example 5.12 Let A be a bipolar fuzzy set on $X = \{x, y, z\}$ and B be a bipolar fuzzy relation in X defined by

$$\mu_A^p(x) = \mu_A^p(y) = \mu_A^p(z) = 1, \quad \mu_A^n(x) = \mu_A^n(y) = \mu_A^n(z) = -1,$$

$\mu_B^p(xy) = \mu_B^p(xz) = 0.9,\ \mu_B^p(yz) = 0.5\ \mu_B^n(xy) = \mu_B^n(xz) = -0.1,\ \mu_B^n(yz) = -0.4.$

Here $d(B) = -0.4$, $h(B) = 0.9$. For $0 < s \leq 0.5$, $-0.4 \leq t < 0$, $G_{(s,t)} = (X, \{xy, yz, xz\})$. For $0.5 < s \leq 0.9, -0.1 \leq t < 0, G_{(s,t)} = (X, \{xy, xz\})$. Thus, x is a bipolar fuzzy cut vertex and a partial bipolar fuzzy cut vertex but neither a cut vertex of G^* nor a full bipolar fuzzy cut vertex.

Example 5.13 Let A be a bipolar fuzzy set on $X = \{x, y, z\}$ and B be a bipolar fuzzy relation in X defined by

$$\mu_A^p(x) = \mu_A^p(y) = \mu_A^p(z) = 1,\quad \mu_A^n(x) = \mu_A^n(y) = \mu_A^n(z) = -1,$$

$$\mu_B^p(xy) = \mu_B^p(xz) = 0.9,\quad \mu_B^n(xy) = \mu_B^n(xz) = -0.1.$$

Clearly, $d(B) = -0.1$, $h(B) = 0.9$. For $0 < s \leq 0.9$, $-0.1 \leq t < 0$ $G_{(s,t)} = (X, \{xy, xz\})$. Thus, x is a full bipolar fuzzy cut vertex of G, bipolar fuzzy cut vertex of G, and a cut vertex of G^*.

Proposition 5.7 *Let G be a bipolar fuzzy graph such that G^* is a cycle. Then a vertex is a bipolar fuzzy cut vertex of G if and only if it is a common vertex of two bipolar fuzzy bridges.*

Proposition 5.8 *If z is a common vertex of at least two bipolar fuzzy bridges, then z is a bipolar fuzzy cut vertex.*

Proposition 5.9 *If G is a complete bipolar fuzzy graph, then $(\mu_B^p)^\infty(u, v) = \mu_B^p(uv)$ and $(\mu_B^n)^\infty(u, v) = \mu_B^n(uv)$.*

Proposition 5.10 *A complete bipolar fuzzy graph has no bipolar fuzzy cut vertices.*

A bipolar fuzzy graph G is **biconnected** if a vertex is removed from G, then G remains connected (see Definition 1.23).

Definition 5.19 Let $G = (A, B)$ be a bipolar fuzzy graph on X, then

1. G is called a **bipolar fuzzy block** if it has no bipolar fuzzy cut vertices.
2. G is called a **weak bipolar fuzzy block** if there exists $(s, t) \in (0, h(B)] \times [d(B), 0)$ such that $G_{(s,t)}$ is a block.
3. G is called a **partial bipolar fuzzy block** if $G_{(s,t)}$ is a block, for all $(s, t) \in (0, h(B)] \times (d(B), 0] \cup \{(h(B), d(B))\}$.
4. G is called a **full bipolar fuzzy block** if $G_{(s,t)}$ is a block, for all $(s, t) \in (0, h(B)] \times [d(B), 0)$.

Example 5.14 Consider a connected bipolar fuzzy graph $G = (A, B)$ as shown in Fig. 5.9. By routine calculations, $d(B) = -0.3, h(B) = 0.7$. Thus, $(s, t) \in (0, 0.7] \times [-0.2, 0)$. For $0 < s \leq 0.5$, $-0.3 \leq t < 0$, $G_{(s,t)} = (X, \{xy, yz, xz\})$. For $0.5 < s \leq 0.7, -0.2 \leq t < 0, G_{(s,t)} = (X, \{xz\})$. Thus, G^* is a block, G is a bipolar fuzzy block and a weak bipolar fuzzy block. G is not a partial bipolar fuzzy block since $G_{(s,t)}$ is not a block for $0.5 < s \leq 0.7, -0.2 \leq t < 0$.

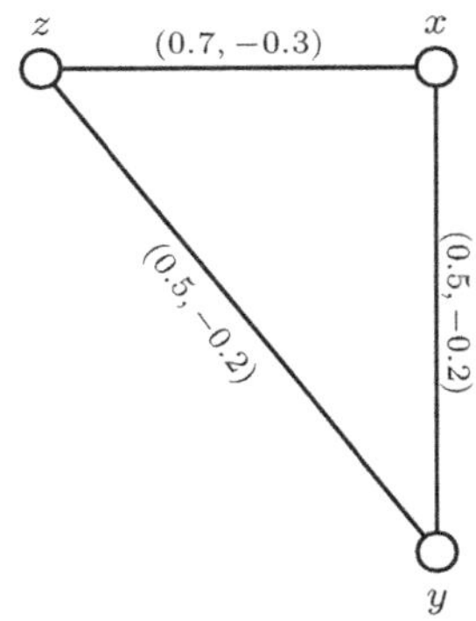

Fig. 5.9 Bipolar fuzzy block

Example 5.15 Consider a bipolar fuzzy graph $G = (A, B)$ on $X = \{x, y, z\}$, where A is a bipolar fuzzy set of X and let B is a bipolar fuzzy relation in X defined by

$$\mu_A^p(x) = \mu_A^p(y) = \mu_A^p(z) = 1, \quad \mu_A^n(x) = \mu_A^n(y) = \mu_A^n(z) = -1,$$

$$\mu_B^p(xy) = \mu_B^p(x, z) = 0.9, \mu_B^p(y, z) = 0.5 \;\; \mu_B^n(x, y) = \mu_B^n(x, z) = -0.1, \mu_B^n(y, z) = -0.4.$$

Clearly, $d(B) = -0.4$, $h(B) = 0.9$. For $0 < s \leq 0.5$, $-0.4 \leq t < 0$, $G_{(s,t)} = (X, \{xy, yz, xz\})$. For $0.5 < s \leq 0.9$, $-0.1 \leq t < 0$, $G_{(s,t)} = (X, \{xy, xz\})$. Thus, G^* is a block and G is a weak bipolar fuzzy block. However, G is not a bipolar fuzzy block since x is a bipolar fuzzy cut vertex of G. Also, G is not a partial bipolar fuzzy block since x is a cut vertex of $G_{(s,t)}$ for $0.5 < s \leq 0.9$, $-0.1 \leq t < 0$.

Example 5.16 Consider a bipolar fuzzy graph $G = (A, B)$ on $X = \{x, y, z\}$, where A is a bipolar fuzzy set of X and B is a bipolar fuzzy relation in X defined by

$$\mu_A^p(x) = \mu_A^p(y) = \mu_A^p(z) = 1, \quad \mu_A^n(x) = \mu_A^n(y) = \mu_A^n(z) = -1,$$

$$\mu_B^p(xy) = \mu_B^p(x, z) = \mu_B^p(y, z) = 0.9 \;\; \mu_B^n(x, y) = \mu_B^n(x, z) = \mu_B^n(y, z) = -0.1.$$

By routine computations, $d(B) = -0.1$, $h(B) = 0.9$. For $0 < s \leq 0.9$, $-0.1 \leq t < 0$, $G_{(s,t)} = (X, \{xy, yz, xz\})$. Thus, G^* is a block, G is a bipolar fuzzy block and a full bipolar fuzzy block.

Definition 5.20 A connected bipolar fuzzy graph $G = (A, B)$ is said to be a **firm** if

$$\min\{\mu_A^p(x) \mid x \in X\} \geq \max\{\mu_B^p(xy) \mid xy \in E\},$$

$$\max\{\mu_A^n(x) \mid x \in X\} \leq \min\{\mu_B^n(xy) \mid xy \in E\}.$$

The bipolar fuzzy graph shown in Fig. 5.7 is a firm.

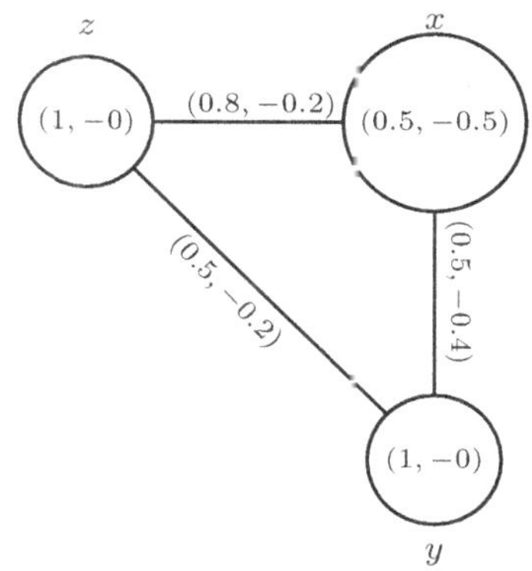

Fig. 5.10 Bipolar fuzzy block which is not a firm

Example 5.17 Consider a connected bipolar fuzzy graph as shown in Fig. 5.10.

Here $d(B) = -0.4$, $h(B) = 0.8$. Thus, $(s, t) \in (0, -0.8] \times (0, -0.2]$. For $0 < s \leq 0.5$, $-0.4 \leq t < 0$, $G_{(s,t)} = (X, \{xy, yz, xz\})$. For $0.5 < s \leq 0.8$, $-0.2 \leq t < 0$, $G_{(s,t)} = (X, \{xz\})$. Thus, G is a bipolar fuzzy block and full bipolar fuzzy block but not a firm.

5.5 Bipolar Fuzzy Cycles and Bipolar Fuzzy Trees

The concept of a bipolar fuzzy cycle is already elaborated in Definition 1.23. In this section, the notions of bipolar fuzzy cycles and bipolar fuzzy trees are discussed with level graphs.

Definition 5.21 Let $G = (A, B)$ be a bipolar fuzzy graph on a non-empty set X, then

1. G is called a **bipolar fuzzy cycle** if G^* is a cycle and there does not exist unique $xy \in E$ such that $\mu_B^p(xy) = \min\{\mu_B^p(uv) \mid uv \in E = supp(B)\}$, $\mu_B^n(xy) = \max\{\mu_B^n(uv) \mid uv \in E\}$.
2. G is called a **weak bipolar fuzzy cycle** if there exists $(s, t) \in (0, h(B)] \times [d(B), 0)$ such that $G_{(s,t)}$ is a cycle.
3. G is called a **partial bipolar fuzzy cycle** if $G_{(s,t)}$ is a cycle, for all $(s, t) \in (0, h(B)] \times (d(B), 0] \cup \{(h(B), d(B))\}$.
4. G is called a **full bipolar fuzzy cycle** if $G_{(s,t)}$ is a cycle, for all $(s, t) \in (0, h(B)] \times [d(B), 0)$.

Example 5.18 Consider a connected bipolar fuzzy graph $G = (A, B)$ as shown in Fig. 5.11.

By routine computations, $d(B) = -0.2$, $h(B) = 0.9$. Thus $(s, t) \in (0, -0.9] \times (0, -0.1]$. For $0 < s \leq 0.5$, $0 \leq t < -0.2$, $G_{(s,t)} = (X, \{xy, xw, yz, wz\})$. For 0.5

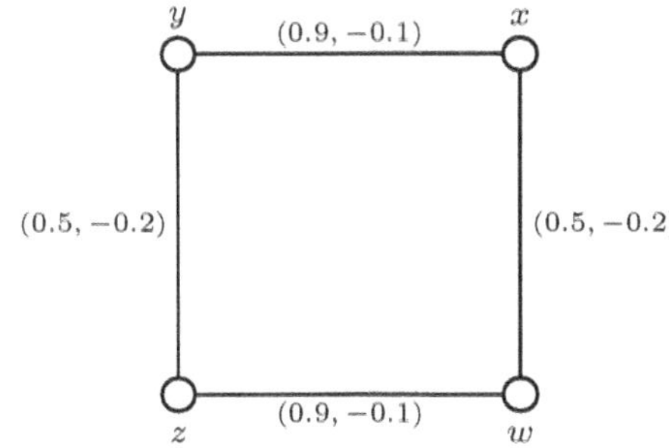

Fig. 5.11 Bipolar fuzzy cycle

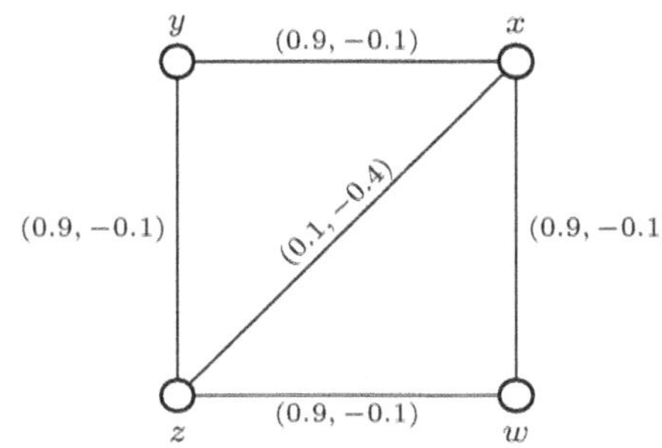

Fig. 5.12 Partial bipolar fuzzy graph cycle

$< s \leq 0.9$, $-0.1 \leq t < 0$, $G_{(s,t)} = (X, \{xy, zw\})$. Thus, G is a bipolar fuzzy cycle and weak bipolar fuzzy cycle but G is not partial bipolar fuzzy cycle.

Example 5.19 Consider a bipolar fuzzy graph $G = (A, B)$ as shown in Fig. 5.12. Here $d(B) = -0.4$, $h(B) = 0.9$. Thus, $(s, t) \in (0, h(B)] \times [d(B), 0)$ means $(s, t) \in (0, -0.9] \times [-0.1, 0)$. For $0 < s \leq 0.1$, $-0.4 \leq t < 0$, $G_{(s,t)} = (X, \{xy, yz, wz, wx, xw\})$ which is not a cycle. For $0.1 < s \leq 0.9$, $-0.1 \leq t < 0$, $G_{(s,t)} = (X, \{xy, yz, zw, wx\})$ which is a cycle. Thus, G is not a bipolar fuzzy cycle. G is a partial bipolar fuzzy cycle but not a full bipolar fuzzy cycle.

The proofs of the following propositions are trivial.

Proposition 5.11 *Suppose G is a bipolar fuzzy cycle, then G is a partial bipolar fuzzy cycle if and only if G is a full bipolar fuzzy cycle.*

Proposition 5.12 *A bipolar fuzzy graph $G = (A, B)$ is a full bipolar fuzzy cycle if and only if G is a bipolar fuzzy cycle and B is a constant function.*

Definition 5.22 A connected bipolar fuzzy graph $G = (A, B)$ is a **bipolar fuzzy tree** if it has a bipolar fuzzy spanning subgraph $H = (A, C)$ such that H^* is a tree and for all edges xy not in H, $\mu_B^p(xy) < (\mu_C^p)^\infty(x, y)$, $\mu_B^n(xy) > (\mu_C^n)^\infty(x, y)$.

Definition 5.23 Let $G = (A, B)$ be a bipolar fuzzy graph on X, then

1. G is called a **bipolar fuzzy forest** if G has a bipolar fuzzy spanning subgraph $H = (A, C)$ such that H^* is a forest and for all edges uv not in F, $\mu_B^p(uv) < (\mu_C^p)^\infty(u, v)$ and $\mu_B^n(uv) > (\mu_C^n)^\infty(u, v)$. In this case, the bipolar fuzzy graph G need not be connected.
2. G is called a **weak bipolar fuzzy forest** if for all $(s, t) \in (0, h(B)] \times [d(B), 0)$, $G_{(s,t)}$ is a forest.
3. G is called a **partial bipolar fuzzy forest** if $G_{(s,t)}$ is a forest, for all $(s, t) \in (0, h(B)] \times (d(B), 0] \cup \{(h(B), d(B))\}$.
4. G is called a **full bipolar fuzzy forest** if $G_{(s,t)}$ is a forest, for all $(s, t) \in (0, h(B)] \times [d(B), 0)$.

Example 5.20 Consider a connected bipolar fuzzy graph $G = (A, B)$ on $X = \{x, y, z, w\}$, where A is a bipolar fuzzy set on X and B is a bipolar fuzzy relation in X defined by

$$\mu_A^p(x) = \mu_A^p(y) = \mu_A^p(z) = \mu_A^p(w) = 1, \quad \mu_A^n(x) = \mu_A^n(y) = \mu_A^n(z) = \mu_A^n(w) = -1,$$

$$\mu_B^p(xy) = \mu_B^p(w, z) = 0.9, \ \mu_B^p(xw) = \mu_B^p(yz) = 0.5, \ \mu_B^n(xy) = \mu_B^n(wz) = -0.1, \ \mu_B^n(xw) = \mu_B^n(yz) = -0.4.$$

By routine computations, $d(B) = -0.4$, $h(B) = 0.9$. For $0 < s \leq 0.5$, $-0.4 \leq t < 0$, $G_{(s,t)} = (X, \{xw, yz, xy, wz\})$ and for $0.5 < s \leq 0.9$, $-0.1 \leq t < 0$, $G_{(s,t)} = (X, \{xy, wz\})$. Thus, G is a partial bipolar fuzzy forest but neither a bipolar fuzzy forest nor a full bipolar fuzzy forest.

Proposition 5.13 *A bipolar fuzzy graph $G = (A, B)$ is a full bipolar fuzzy forest if and only if G^* is a forest.*

Proof Suppose that G is a full bipolar fuzzy forest, then G^* is a forest.

Conversely, let G^* be a forest, then $G_{(s,t)}$ is a forest for all $(s, t) \in (0, h(B)] \times [d(B), 0)$ and each such $G_{(s,t)}$ is a subgraph of G^*. It completes the proof. □

Example 5.21 Consider a connected bipolar fuzzy graph $G = (A, B)$ on $X = \{x, y, z\}$ such that

$$\mu_A^p(x) = \mu_A^p(y) = \mu_A^p(z) = 1, \quad \mu_A^n(x) = \mu_A^n(y) = \mu_A^n(z) = -1,$$

$$\mu_B^p(xy) = 0.9, \ \mu_B^p(yz) = 0.5, \ \mu_B^n(xy) = -0.1, \mu_B^n(yz) = -0.4.$$

Clearly, $d(B) = (0.5, -0.4)$, $h(B) = (0.9, -0.1)$. For $0 < s \leq 0.5$, $-0.4 \leq t < 0$, $G_{(s,t)} = (X, \{xy, yz\})$. For $0.5 < s \leq 0.9$, $-0.1 \leq t < 0$, $G_{(s,t)} = (X, \{xy\})$. Thus, G is a full bipolar fuzzy forest without B being a constant function. Note that $G(h(B), d(B))$ has more connected components than G^*.

Proposition 5.14 *A bipolar fuzzy graph $G = (A, B)$ is a weak bipolar fuzzy forest if and only if G does not contain a bipolar fuzzy cycle whose edges are of strength $(h(B), d(B))$.*

Proof Suppose G contains a bipolar fuzzy cycle whose edges are of strength $(h(B), d(B))$. Then $G_{(s,t)}$, $(s, t) \in (0, h(B)] \times [d(B), 0)$ contains this bipolar fuzzy cycle and so G^* is not a forest. Thus, G is not a weak bipolar fuzzy forest.

Conversely, suppose G does not contain a bipolar fuzzy cycle all of whose edges are of membership value $(h(B), d(B))$. Then $G_{(h(B),d(B))}$ does not contain a cycle and so is a forest. □

Corollary 5.1 *If G is a bipolar fuzzy forest, then G is also a weak bipolar fuzzy forest.*

Theorem 5.9 *Let $G = (A, B)$ be a bipolar fuzzy graph, then G^* is a forest and B is a constant function if and only if G is a full bipolar fuzzy forest, G^* and $G_{(h(B),d(B))}$ have the same number of connected components and G is a firm.*

Proof Suppose that G^* is a forest and B is a constant function. Then for all $(s, t) \in (0, h(B)] \times [d(B), 0)$, $G_{(s,t)} = G^*$ and so G is a full bipolar fuzzy forest and G^* and $G_{(h(B),d(B))}$ have the same number of connected components. Clearly, G is a firm since B is a constant function.

Conversely, suppose G is a full bipolar fuzzy forest, G^* and $G_{(h(B),d(B))}$ have the same number of connected components and G is a firm. Suppose there exists $(s_1, t_1), (s_2, t_2) \in [0, 1] \times [-1, 0]$ such that $\mu^p_B(xy) = s_1$, $\mu^n_B(xy) = t_1$, and $xy \in B_{(s_1,t_1)}$, $xy \notin B_{(s_2,t_2)}$. Hence, $G_{(s_2,t_2)}$ has more connected components than $G_{(s_1,t_1)}$ since G is a firm, i.e., no vertices were lost. Thus, $G_{(h(B),d(B))}$ has more connected components than G^*, a contradiction. □

Corollary 5.2 *Let $G = (A, B)$ be a bipolar fuzzy graph, then G^* is a forest and B is constant function if and only if G is a full bipolar fuzzy tree and G is a firm.*

Definition 5.24 Let $G = (A, B)$ be a bipolar fuzzy graph on X, then

1. G is called a **bipolar fuzzy tree** if G has a bipolar fuzzy spanning subgraph $H = (A, C)$ which is a tree such that for all edges uv not in H, $\mu^p_B(uv) < (\mu^p_C)^\infty(u, v)$ and $\mu^n_B(uv) > (\mu^n_C)^\infty(u, v)$.
2. G is called a **weak bipolar fuzzy tree** if for all $(s, t) \in (0, h(B)] \times [d(B), 0)$ $G_{(s,t)}$ is a tree.
3. G is called a **partial bipolar fuzzy tree** if $G_{(s,t)}$ is a tree, for all $(s, t) \in (d(B), 0] \times (0, h(B)] \cup \{(h(B), d(B))\}$.
4. G is called a **full bipolar fuzzy tree** if $G_{(s,t)}$ is a tree, for all $(s, t) \in (0, h(B)] \times [d(B), 0)$.

Example 5.22 Consider a bipolar fuzzy graph $G = (A, B)$ on $X = \{x, y, z\}$, where A and B are defined as

$$\mu^p_A(x) = \mu^p_A(y) = 1,\ \mu^p_A(z) = 0.5,\ \ \mu^n_A(x) = \mu^n_A(y) = 0,\ \mu^n_A(z) = -0.2,$$

$$\mu^p_B(xy) = 0.9,\ \mu^p_B(yz) = 0.5,\ \ \mu^n_B(xy) = 0.1, \mu^n_B(yz) = -0.4.$$

By usual calculations, $d(B) = -0.4$, $h(B) = 0.9$. For $0 < s \leq 0.9$, $-0.1 \leq t < 0$, $G_{(s,t)} = (X, \{xy, yz\})$ and for $0.5 < s \leq 0.9$, $-0.1 \leq t < 0$, $G_{(s,t)} = (X, \{xy\})$. Thus, G^* is a tree, G is a full bipolar fuzzy tree, and G^* and $G_{(h(B),d(B))}$ have the same number of connected components. However, G is not a firm and $B = (\mu_B^p, \mu_B^n)$ is not a function.

Example 5.23 Consider a bipolar fuzzy graph $G = (A, B)$ on $X = \{x, y, z\}$, where A and B are defined as

$$\mu_A^p(x) = \mu_A^p(y) = 1,\ \mu_A^p(z) = 0.5,\ \ \mu_A^n(x) = \mu_A^n(y) = -1,\ \mu_A^n(z) = -0.2,$$

$$\mu_B^p(xy) = 0.9,\ \mu_B^p(xz) = \mu_B^p(yz) = 0.5,\ \ \mu_B^n(xy) = -0.1,\ \mu_B^n(xz) = \mu_B^n(yz) = -0.4.$$

Here $d(B) = -0.4$, $h(B) = 0.9$. For $0 < s \leq 0.5$, $-0.4 \leq t < 0$, $G_{(s,t)} = (X, \{xy, xz, yz\})$, and for $0.5 < s \leq 0.9$, $-0.1 \leq t < 0$, $G_{(s,t)} = (\{x, y\}, \{xy\})$. Thus, G is a partial bipolar fuzzy tree, but not a full bipolar fuzzy tree. G is also not a bipolar fuzzy tree.

Proposition 5.15 *If G is a bipolar fuzzy tree, then G is not a complete bipolar fuzzy graph.*

Proposition 5.16 *If G is a bipolar fuzzy tree, then edges of spanning bipolar fuzzy subgraph H are the bipolar fuzzy bridges of G.*

Proposition 5.17 *Let $G = (A, B)$ be a bipolar fuzzy graph, then G is a bipolar fuzzy tree if and only if the following are equivalent.*

1. *xy is a bipolar fuzzy bridge.*
2. *$(\mu_B^p)^\infty(x, y) = \mu_B^p(xy)$ and $(\mu_B^n)^\infty(x, y) = \mu_B^n(xy)$.*

Proposition 5.18 *A bipolar fuzzy graph is a bipolar fuzzy tree if and only if it has a unique maximum bipolar fuzzy spanning tree.*

Proposition 5.19 *Let $G = (A, B)$ be a firm. If G is a weak bipolar fuzzy tree, then G is a bipolar fuzzy tree.*

Proof There exist $(s, t) \in (0, h(B)] \times [d(B), 0)$ such that $G_{(s,t)}$ is a tree. Since G is a firm, $G_{(s,t)}$ is a spanning subgraph of G^* which is a tree. If $uv \in E\ B_{(s,t)}$, then $\mu_B^p(uv) < s$, $\mu_B^n(uv) > t$ and so it follows that G is a bipolar fuzzy tree. □

Definition 5.25 Let $G = (A, B)$ be a bipolar fuzzy graph on X, then

1. G is called **weak bipolar fuzzy connected** if there exists $(s, t) \in (0, h(B)] \times [d(B), 0)$ such that $G_{(s,t)}$ is connected.
2. G is called **partial bipolar fuzzy connected** if $G_{(s,t)}$ is connected, for all $(s, t) \in (d(B), h(B)] \cup \{h(B)\}$.
3. G is called **full bipolar fuzzy connected** if $G_{(s,t)}$ is connected, for all $(s, t) \in (0, h(B)] \times [d(B), 0)$.

Proposition 5.20 *If G is a connected bipolar fuzzy graph, then G is weakly connected.*

Proof Let $G = (A, B)$ be a connected bipolar fuzzy graph, then G^* is connected, then there exists some $(s, t) \in (0, h(B)] \times [d(B), 0)$ such that $G_{(s,t)} = G^*$ and so G is weakly connected. □

Proposition 5.21 *Let $G = (A, B)$ be a bipolar fuzzy graph, then the following conditions are satisfied.*

1. *If G is a weak bipolar fuzzy tree, then G is weakly connected and G is a weak bipolar fuzzy forest. Conversely, if $\exists (s_1, t_1), (s_2, t_2) \in (0, h(B)] \times [d(B), 0)$ with $s_1 < s_2$, $t_1 > t_2$ such that $G_{(s_1,t_1)}$ is a forest and $G_{(s_2,t_2)}$ is connected, then G is a weak bipolar fuzzy tree.*
2. *G is a bipolar fuzzy tree if and only if G is a bipolar fuzzy forest and G is connected.*
3. *G is a partial bipolar fuzzy tree if and only if G is a partially connected partial bipolar fuzzy forest.*
4. *G is a full bipolar fuzzy tree if and only if G is a full bipolar fuzzy forest and G is fully connected.*

Proof 1. If $G_{(s,t)}$ is a tree for some $(s, t) \in (, h(B)] \times [d(B), 0)$, then $G_{(s,t)}$ is connected and is a forest. For the converse, if $G_{(s_1,t_1)}$ is a forest and $G_{(s_2,t_2)}$ is connected, then $G_{(s_2,t_2)}$ is a tree.

The proofs of 2, 3, and 4 are immediate. □

5.6 Applications of Bipolar Fuzzy Planar Graphs

Graph theory is considered an important part of Mathematics for solving countless real-world problems in information technology, psychology, engineering, combinatorics, and medical sciences. Everything in this World is connected, for instance, cities and countries are connected by roads, railways are linked by railway lines, flight networks are connected by air, electrical devices are connected by wires, web pages on the Internet by hyperlinks, components of electric circuits by various paths, and many more. Scientists, analysts, and engineers are trying to optimize these networks to find a way to save millions of lives by reducing traffic accidents, plane crashes, and circuit shots. Planar graphs are used to find such graphical representations of networks without any crossing or the minimum number of crossings. But there is always a bipolar uncertainty in data which can be dealt with using bipolar graphs. The applications of bipolar fuzzy planar graphs in road networks and electrical connections are discussed in this section.

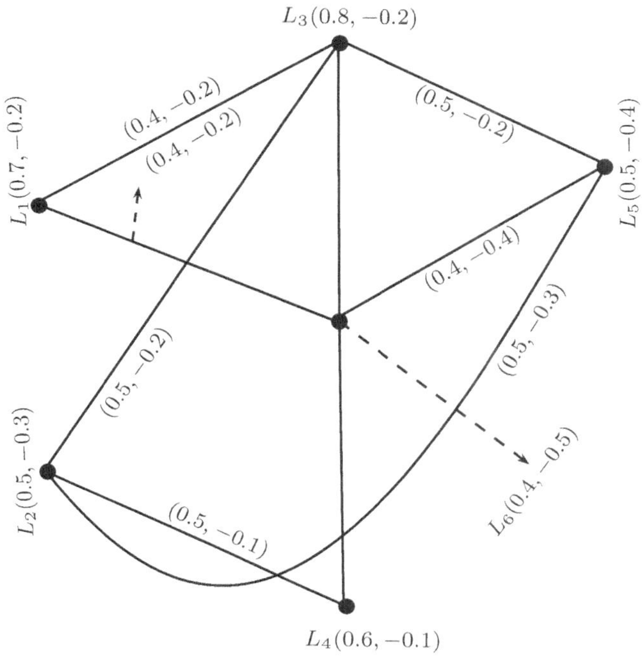

Fig. 5.13 Bipolar fuzzy road model

5.6.1 *Road Network Model to Monitor Traffic*

Roads are a means of a frequent and unacceptable number of fatalities every year. Road accidents are increasing due to dense traffic, negligence of drivers, and speed of vehicles. Traffic accidents can be minimized by modeling road networks to monitor the traffic, apply quick emergency services, and by taking action against overspeeding. The practical approach of bipolar fuzzy planar graphs can be applied to construct road networks. Consider the problem of road networks between 6 locations $L_1, L_2, L_3, L_4, L_5, L_6$ as shown in Fig. 5.13.

The positive degree of membership $\mu^p(x)$ of each vertex x represents the percentage that vehicles traveling to or from this city are dense. The negative degree of membership $\mu^n(x)$ represents the percentage that traffic is not dense. The positive degree of memberships of each edge xy indicates the percentage of road accidents through this road and the negative degree of memberships of xy shows the percentage that the road is safer. This bipolar fuzzy model can be used to check and monitor the percentage of annual accidents. Also, by monitoring and taking special security actions, the total number of accidents can be minimized.

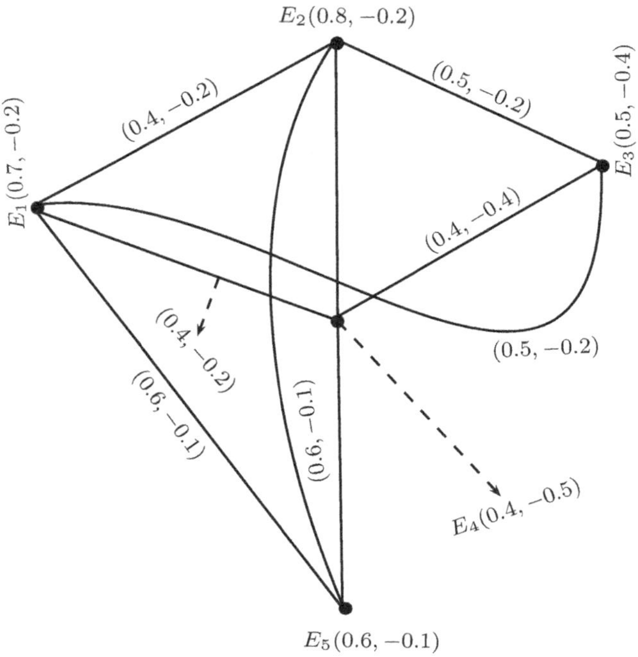

Fig. 5.14 Electrical connections

5.6.2 *Modeling of Electrical Connections*

Graph theory is extensively used in designing circuit connections and installation of wires in order to prevent crossing which can cause dangerous electrical hazards. The twisted and crossing wires are a serious safety risk to human life. There is a need to install electrical wires to reduce crossing. Bipolar fuzzy planar graphs can be used to model electrical connections and to study the degree of damage that can cause due to the connection. Consider the problem of setting electrical wires between 5 electrical utilities and power plugs E_1, E_2, E_3, E_4, E_5 in a factory as shown in Fig. 5.14.

The positive degree of membership $\mu^p(E_i)$ of each vertex E_i represents the percentage of faults and electrical sparks of utility or power plug E_i and the negative degree of membership $\mu^n(E_i)$ represents the percentage that E_i is updated and safer. The positive degree of membership of each edge E_iE_j indicates the percentage of electrical hazards through this connection. The negative degree of membership of E_iE_j shows the percentage that the connection is safer. The crossing of wires can be reduced if we change the geometrical representation of Fig. 5.14. The other representation is shown in Fig. 5.15 which has only one crossing, at point P_1, between the edges E_1E_4 and E_2E_5. The electrical damage at the crossing point P_1 can be reduced by using better electrical wires between E_1 and E_4, E_2 and E_5.

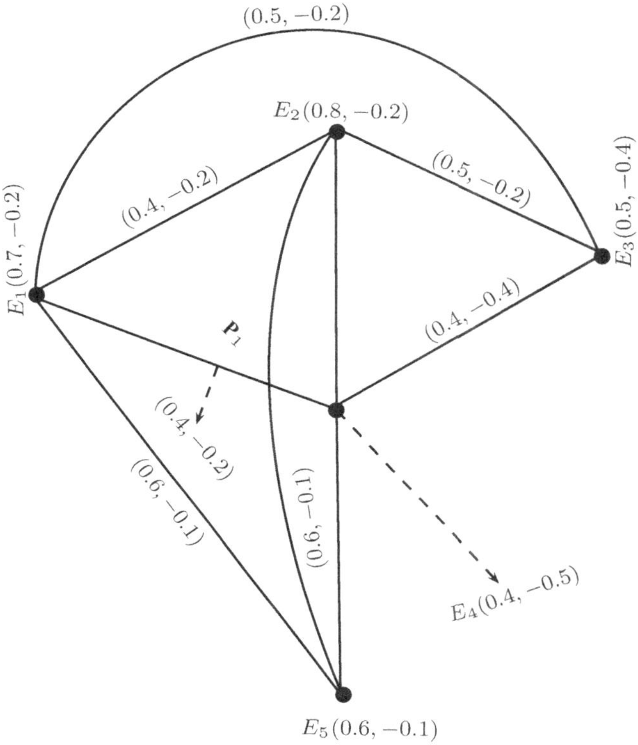

Fig. 5.15 Bipolar fuzzy planar graph

5.7 Conclusions

Bipolar fuzzy planar graphs are used to model various practical problems in which the crossings between any two lines are prohibited with certain bipolar uncertainty. In this chapter, we have studied the concepts of bipolar fuzzy multisets, bipolar fuzzy multigraphs, strong and complete bipolar fuzzy multigraphs, bipolar fuzzy planar graphs, and bipolar fuzzy dual graphs. We have discussed the strong and weak properties of bipolar fuzzy edges, bipolar fuzzy faces, and bipolar fuzzy planar graphs. We have described the relation of planarity and duality in bipolar fuzzy graphs using different characterizations of intersection value and planarity value of bipolar fuzzy graphs. We have elaborated various properties of bipolar fuzzy bridges, bipolar fuzzy cut vertices, bipolar fuzzy blocks, bipolar fuzzy cycles, and bipolar fuzzy trees in terms of level graphs. We have presented the importance of bipolar fuzzy planar graphs with a number of real-world applications in road networks and electrical circuits.

Exercises 5

1. Let G and H be connected bipolar fuzzy fuzzy graphs different from K_1 and K_2, then prove or disprove that $G\Box H$ is a bipolar fuzzy planar graph if and only if both factors are bipolar fuzzy paths, or one is a bipolar fuzzy path and other is a bipolar fuzzy cycle.
2. If $G = (A, B)$ is a bipolar fuzzy graph with p vertices, then show that G has at most $p - 1$ bipolar fuzzy bridges.
3. Prove that a nontrivial bipolar fuzzy tree H has at least two bipolar fuzzy end nodes.
4. If H is a bipolar fuzzy tree, then show that every vertex of H is either a bipolar fuzzy cut-node or a bipolar fuzzy end node. Also, show that the converse is not true.
5. If G is a bipolar fuzzy tree, then prove or disprove that the arcs of G are bipolar fuzzy bridges.
6. Show that a bipolar fuzzy cut vertex of a bipolar fuzzy tree is the common vertex of at least two bipolar fuzzy bridges.
7. If G is a bipolar fuzzy tree, then show that every vertex of G is either a bipolar fuzzy cut vertex or a bipolar fuzzy end node.
8. If G is a bipolar fuzzy tree, then show that it has at most $n - 1$ number of bipolar fuzzy bridges where n is the number of vertices in G.
9. Show that every bipolar fuzzy bridge is strong, but a strong edge need not be a bipolar fuzzy bridge.

References

1. Abdul-jabbar, N., Naoom, J.H., Ouda, E.H.: Fuzzy dual graph. J. Al. Nahrain Univ. **12**(4), 168–171 (2009)
2. Akram, M.: Bipolar fuzzy graphs. Inf. Sci. **181**(24), 5548–5564 (2011)
3. Akram, M.: Bipolar fuzzy graphs with applications. Knowl.-Based Syst. **39**, 1–8 (2013)
4. Akram, M., Dudek, W.A.: Regular bipolar fuzzy graphs. Neural Comput. Appl. **21**(supp 1), 197–205 (2012)
5. Akram, M., Alshehri, N., Davvaz, B., Ashraf, A.: Bipolar fuzzy digraphs in decision support systems. J. Multiple-Valued Logic Soft. Comput. **27**(5–6), 531–551 (2016)
6. Akram, M., Farooq, A.: Bipolar fuzzy trees. New Trends Math. Sci. **4**(3), 58–72 (2016)
7. Akram, M., Samanta, S., Pal, M.: Application of bipolar fuzzy sets in planar graphs. Int. J. Appl. Comput. Math. **3**(2), 773–785 (2017)
8. Mathew, S., Sunitha, M.S.: Types of arcs in a fuzzy graph. Inf. Sci. **179**(11), 1760–1768 (2009)
9. Mathew, S., Sunitha, M.S.: Strongest strong cycles and θ-fuzzy graphs. IEEE Trans. Fuzzy Syst. **21**(6), 1096–1104 (2013)
10. Mordeson, J.N., Nair, P.S.: Cycles and cocycles of fuzzy graphs. Inf. Sci. **90**(1–4), 39–49 (1996)
11. Nagoorgani, A., Radha, K.: Degree of fuzzy graph. Int. J. Algorithms Comput. Math. **2**(3), 1–9 (2009)
12. Pal, A., Samanta, S., Pal, M.: Concept of fuzzy planar graphs. In: Proceedings of Science and Information Conference, pp. 557–563. IEEE (2013)

13. Rosenfeld, A.: Fuzzy graphs. In: Zadeh, L.A., Fu, K.S., Shimura, M. (eds.) Fuzzy Sets and Their Applications, pp. 77–95. Academic, New York (1975)
14. Samanta, S., Pal, M.: Fuzzy planar graphs. IEEE Trans. Fuzzy Syst. **23**(6), 1936–1942 (2015)
15. Samanta, S., Pal, M., Pal, A.: New concepts of fuzzy planar graph. Int. J. Adv. Res. Artif. Intell. **3**(1), 52–59 (2014)
16. Shinoj, T.K., John, S.J.: Intuitionistic fuzzy multisets and its application in medical diagnosis. World Acad. Sci. Eng. Technol. **6**(1), 1418–1421 (2012)
17. Sunitha, M.S., Vijayakumar, A.: A characterization of fuzzy trees. Inf. Sci. **113**, 293–300 (1999)
18. Sunitha, M.S., Vijayakumar, A.: Complement of a fuzzy graph. Indian J. Pure Appl. Math. **33**(9), 1451–1464 (2002)
19. Wilson, R.J.: Graph theory. History of Topology. Elsevier Science, Amsterdam (1999)
20. Zhang, W.-R.: Bipolar fuzzy sets and relations: a computational framework for cognitive modeling and multiagent decision analysis. In: Proceedings of IEEE Conference, pp. 305–309 (1994)
21. Zhang, W.-R., Zhang, L.: YinYang bipolar logic and bipolar fuzzy logic. Inf. Sci. **165**(3–4), 265–287 (2004)
22. Zhang, W.-R.: (YinYang) Bipolar fuzzy sets. In: IEEE International Conference on Fuzzy Systems, pp. 835–840 (1998)
23. Zhang, W.-R.: The road from fuzzy sets to definable causality and bipolar quantum intelligence-To the memory of Lotfi A. Zadeh. J. Intell. Fuzzy Syst. **36**(4), 3019–3032 (2019)

Chapter 6
Domination in Bipolar Fuzzy Graphs

In this chapter, we discuss different concepts of dominating, total dominating, equitable dominating, total equitable dominating, and independent and equitable independent sets in bipolar fuzzy graphs. We present certain properties concerning the relationship of domination, total domination and independence numbers in complete bipolar fuzzy graphs, complete bipartite bipolar fuzzy graphs, and products of bipolar fuzzy graphs. We study the notions of private neighbor, lower and upper irredundant sets, and irredundance number in relation to independence and dominating numbers of bipolar fuzzy graphs. We describe the importance of domination in bipolar fuzzy graphs with a number of real-world applications in facility location problem, finding the set of representatives, and transmission tower location problem. The main discussion of this chapter is from [5, 14].

6.1 Introduction

Domination in graph theory has a wide range of applications in different fields including, school bus routing, facility location problem, finding the set of representatives, land surveying, coding theory and, monitoring communication and electrical networks. The idea of domination first arose in the chessboard problem. The classical problems of covering chessboards with the minimum number of chess pieces were important in motivating the revival of the study of dominating sets in graphs, which commenced in the early 1970s. These problems certainly date back to de Jaenisch [11] and have been mentioned in the literature frequently since that time (cf. [9, 12]). In 1962, Ore [17] was the first to use the term "domination" for undirected graphs, and he introduced the concepts of minimal and minimum dominating sets of vertices in a graph. Somasundaram and Somasundaram [19] introduced domination and independent domination in fuzzy graphs. Gani and Chandrasekaran [15] studied the notion of fuzzy domination and independent domination using strong

M. Akram et al., *Graphs for the Analysis of Bipolar Fuzzy Information*, Studies in Fuzziness and Soft Computing 401, https://doi.org/10.1007/978-981-15-8756-6_6

arcs. The independent domination number and irredundance number in graphs are introduced by Cockayne [10] and Hedetniemi [13]. Nagoorgani and Vadivel [16] discussed domination, independent domination, and irredundance in fuzzy graphs using strong edges. The concept of domination in intuitionistic fuzzy graphs was investigated by Parvathi and Thamizhendhi [18]. Zhang [20] introduced the theory of bipolar fuzzy sets (also known as YinYang bipolar fuzzy sets, Yang depicts the positive side while Yin represents the negative side in a system). The concept of bipolar fuzzy sets was applied to graphs in [1–4]. The concept of certain types of dominating and independent sets in bipolar fuzzy graphs and m-polar fuzzy graphs is discussed in [5–7, 14] which is the main discussion of this chapter.

6.2 Types of Domination in Bipolar Fuzzy Graphs

A **dominating set** of a crisp graph $G^* = (X, E)$ is a subset D of X such that every vertex not in D is adjacent to at least one member of D. The **domination number** is the number of vertices in a smallest dominating set for G^*. An **independent set** of G^* is a subset I of vertices such that no two vertices of I are adjacent in G^*. That is, for every two vertices $x, y \in I$, $xy \notin E$. A **maximal independent set** is an independent set of a graph containing the largest possible number of vertices for the given graph, and the cardinality of this set is called the **independence number** of the graph.

Definition 6.1 Let $G = (A, B)$ be a bipolar fuzzy graph on X, then the **vertex cardinality** of G is denoted by $|A|$ and defined as

$$|A| = \sum_{v_i \in X} (\mu_A^p(v_i), \mu_A^n(v_i)).$$

Definition 6.2 Let $G = (A, B)$ be a bipolar fuzzy graph on X, then the **edge cardinality** of G is denoted by $|B|$ and defined as

$$|B| = \sum_{v_i, v_j \in X} (\mu_B^p(v_i v_j), \mu_B^n(v_i v_j)).$$

Example 6.1 Consider a bipolar fuzzy graph $G = (A, B)$ on $X = \{v_1, v_2, v_3, v_4\}$ as shown in Fig. 6.1.

The vertex cardinality of G is $(0.8, -2.3)$ and the edge cardinality is $(0.7, -1.8)$ cardinality.

Definition 6.3 The **degree** of a vertex v in a bipolar fuzzy graph $G = (A, B)$ is defined as the sum of weights of strong edges incident to v. It is denoted by $d_G(v)$. The **minimum degree** of G is $\delta(G) = \min \{d_G(v) \mid v \in X\}$. The **maximum degree** of G is $\Delta(G) = \max \{d_G(v) \mid v \in X\}$.

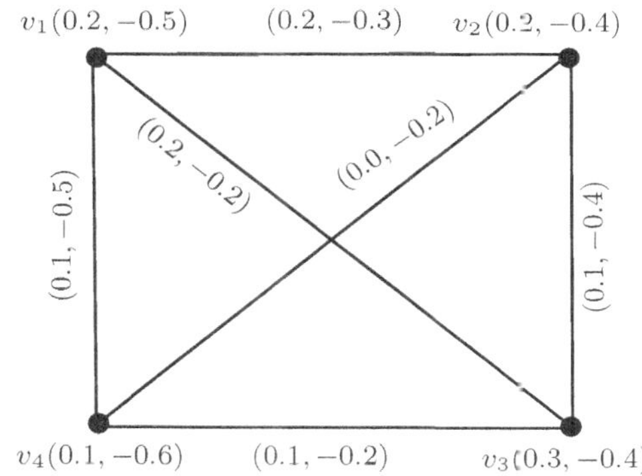

Fig. 6.1 Bipolar fuzzy graph G

Definition 6.4 Two vertices v_i and v_j in a bipolar fuzzy graph $G = (A, B)$ are said to be **neighbors** if either one of the following conditions is satisfied.

1. $\mu^p_B(v_i v_j) > 0$ and $\mu^n_B(v_i v_j) \leq 0$,
2. $\mu^p_B(v_i v_j) \geq 0$ and $\mu^n_B(v_i v_j) < 0, \quad v_i, v_j \in X$.

The set of all neighbors of u is denoted by $N(u)$.

Definition 6.5 An edge uv in a bipolar fuzzy graph $G = (A, B)$ is said to be a **strong edge** if $\mu^p_B(uv) \geq (\mu^p_B)^\infty(u, v)$ and $\mu^n_B(uv) \leq (\mu^n_B)^\infty(u, v)$.

Definition 6.6 A vertex $u \in X$ in a bipolar fuzzy graph $G = (A, B)$ is said to be an **isolated vertex** if $\mu^p_B(uv) = 0$ and $\mu^n_B(uv) = 0$, for all $v \in X$, $u \neq v$. That is, $N(u) = \emptyset$.

Definition 6.7 Let $G = (A, B)$ be a bipolar fuzzy graph on a non-empty set X. Let $u, v \in X$ then u **dominates** v in G if there exists a strong edge between u and v.

Remark 6.1 Let $G = (A, B)$ be a bipolar fuzzy graph on a non-empty set X, then the following statements are satisfied.

1. For any $u, v \in X$, if u dominates v, then v dominates u and hence domination is a symmetric relation on X.
2. For any $v \in X$, $N(v)$ is precisely the set of all vertices in X which are dominated by v.
3. If $\mu^p_B(uv) < (\mu^p_B)^\infty(u, v)$ and $\mu^n_B(uv) > (\mu^n_B)^\infty(u, v)$, for all $u, v \in X$, then the dominating set of G is X itself.
4. An isolated vertex does not dominate any other vertex of G.

Definition 6.8 A subset S of X is called a **dominating set** in G if for every $v \in X - S$ there exists $u \in S$ such that u dominates v.

Definition 6.9 A dominating set S of a bipolar fuzzy graph G is said to be a **minimal dominating set** if no proper subset of S is a dominating set.

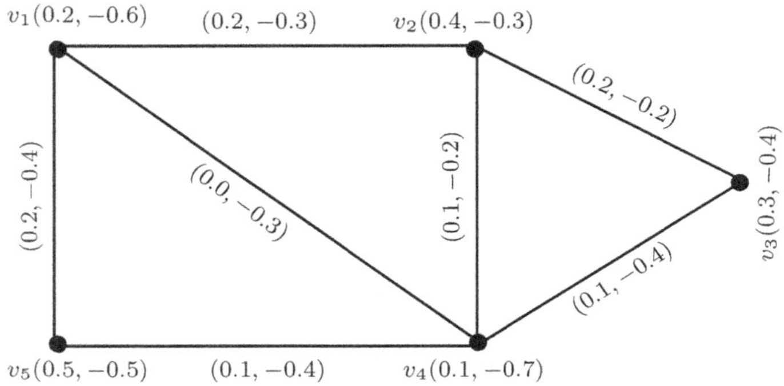

Fig. 6.2 Domination numbers of bipolar fuzzy graph

Definition 6.10 The minimum cardinality among all minimal dominating sets is called **lower domination number** of G and is denoted by $d_B(G)$ or $d(G)$.

Definition 6.11 The maximum cardinality among all minimal dominating sets is called **upper domination number** of G and is denoted by $D_B(G)$.

Example 6.2 Consider a bipolar fuzzy graph $G = (A, B)$ on $X = \{v_1, v_2, v_3, v_4, v_5\}$ as shown in Fig. 6.2.

In Fig. 6.2, $\{v_1, v_2, v_4, v_5\}$, $\{v_2, v_4\}$, $\{v_2, v_3, v_4\}$ are dominating sets but $\{v_3, v_4\}$ is not a dominating set. Also, $\{v_1, v_3\}$, $\{v_1, v_4\}$, $\{v_2, v_4\}$, $\{v_2, v_3, v_5\}$ are minimal dominating sets, and $\{v_1, v_4\}$ has minimum cardinality among all minimal dominating sets, therefore, $d_B(G) = 2$. As $\{v_2, v_3, v_5\}$ has maximum cardinality among all minimal dominating sets, $D_B(G) = 3$.

Definition 6.12 Two vertices in a bipolar fuzzy graph $G = (A, B)$ are said to be an **independent** if there is no strong edge between them.

Definition 6.13 Let $G = (A, B)$ be a bipolar fuzzy graph on X. A subset S of X is said to be an **independent set** if $\mu_B^p(uv) < (\mu_B^p)^\infty(u, v)$ and $\mu_B^n(uv) > (\mu_B^n)^\infty(u, v)$, for all $u, v \in S$.

Definition 6.14 An independent set S of bipolar fuzzy graph $G = (A, B)$ is said to be **maximal independent set** if for every vertex $v \in X - S$, the set $S \cup \{v\}$ is not an independent set.

Definition 6.15 The minimum cardinality among all maximal independent sets is called **lower independence number** of G and it is denoted by $i_B(G)$.

Definition 6.16 The maximum cardinality among all maximal independent sets is called **upper independence number** of G and it is denoted by $I_B(G)$ or $I(G)$.

Example 6.3 In Fig. 6.2, $\{v_1\}$, $\{v_2, v_5\}$, $\{v_2, v_3, v_5\}$ are independent sets. $\{\{v_1, v_3\}$, $\{v_1, v_4\}$, $\{v_2, v_4\}$, $\{v_2, v_3, v_5\}\}$ are maximal independent sets; among all maximal independent sets, $\{v_1, v_4\}$ has minimum cardinality and so $i_B(G) = 2$, $\{v_2, v_3, v_5\}$ has maximum cardinality among all maximal independent sets and $I_B(G) = 3$.

Definition 6.17 Let $G = (A, B)$ be a bipolar fuzzy graph on X without isolated vertices. A subset $S \subseteq X$ is a **total dominating set** if for every vertex $v \in X$, there exists a vertex $u \in S$, $u \neq v$ such that u dominates v.

Definition 6.18 A total dominating set S of a bipolar fuzzy graph $G = (A, B)$ is said to be a **minimal total dominating set** if no proper subset of S is a total dominating set.

Definition 6.19 The minimum cardinality of a minimal total dominating set is called the **lower total dominating number** of G and it is denoted by $t_B(G)$.

Definition 6.20 The maximum cardinality of a minimal total dominating set is called the **upper total dominating number** of G and it is denoted by $T_B(G)$.

Example 6.4 In Fig. 6.2, $\{v_1, v_4, v_5\}$, $\{v_1, v_2, v_3, v_4\}$ are minimal total dominating sets; $\{v_1, v_4, v_5\}$ has minimum cardinality among all minimal total dominating sets and $t_B(G) = 3$; $\{v_1, v_2, v_3, v_4\}$ has maximum cardinality among all minimal total dominating sets and $T_B(G) = 4$.

Theorem 6.1 *A dominating set D of a bipolar fuzzy graph $G = (A, B)$ is a minimal dominating set if and only if for each $d \in D$, one of the following conditions holds.*

1. *d is not a strong neighbor of any vertex in D,*
2. *there is a vertex $v \in X - D$ such that $N(v) \cap D = \{d\}$.*

Proof Assume that D is a minimal dominating set of G, then for every vertex $d \in D$, $D - d$ is not a dominating set. Hence, there exists $v \in X - (D - \{d\})$ which is not dominated by any vertex in $D - \{d\}$. If $v = d$, v is not a strong neighbor of any vertex in D. If $v \neq d$, v is not dominated by $D - \{v\}$ but is dominated by D. Then the vertex v is a strong neighbor only to d in D, that is, $N(v) \cap D = \{d\}$.

Conversely, assume that D is a dominating set and for each vertex $d \in D$, one of the two conditions holds. Suppose D is not a minimal dominating set, then there exists a vertex $d \in D$ such that $D - \{d\}$ is a dominating set. Hence, d is a strong neighbor to at least one vertex in $D - \{d\}$, that is, condition 1 does not hold. If $D - \{d\}$ is a dominating set, then every vertex in $X - D$ is a strong neighbor to at least one vertex in $D - \{d\}$, condition 2 does not hold which contradicts our assumption that at least one of the conditions hold. So D is a minimal dominating set. □

Theorem 6.2 *Let $G = (A, B)$ be a bipolar fuzzy graph without isolated vertices and D is a minimal dominating set of G, then $X - D$ is a dominating set of G.*

Proof Let D be a minimal dominating set and $d \in D$. Since G has no isolated vertices, there is a vertex $v \in N(d)$ such that v must be dominated by at least one vertex in $D - \{d\}$, that is, $D - \{d\}$ is a dominating set. Theorem 6.1 follows that $v \in X - D$. Thus, every vertex in D is dominated by at least one vertex in $X - D$ and so, $X - D$ is a dominating set. □

Theorem 6.3 *Let G^* be a crisp graph corresponding to a bipolar fuzzy graph $G = (A, B)$, then $d_B(G) + d_B(G^c) < 2O(G^*)$, where $d_B(G^c)$ is the lower domination number of G^c and equality holds if and only if $0 < \mu_B^p(v_iv_j) < (\mu_B^p)^\infty(v_i, v_j)$ and $0 > \mu_B^n(v_iv_j) > (\mu_B^n)^\infty(v_i, v_j)$, for all $v_i, v_j \in X$.*

Proof The result is trivial when $d_B(G) + d_B(G^c) < 2O(G^*)$. Also $d_B(G) = O(G^*)$ if and only if $\mu_B^p(v_iv_j) < (\mu_B^p)^\infty(v_i, v_j)$ and $\mu_B^n(v_iv_j) > (\mu_B^n)^\infty(v_i, v_j)$, for all $v_i, v_j \in X$. Clearly, $d_B(G^c) = O(G)$ if and only if $\overline{\mu_B^p(v_iv_j)} - \mu_B^p(v_iv_j) < (\mu_B^p)^\infty (v_i, v_j)$ and $\overline{\mu_B^n(v_iv_j)} - \mu_B^n(v_iv_j) > (\mu_B^n)^\infty(v_i, v_j)$, for all $v_i, v_j \in X$ which gives $\mu_B^p(v_iv_j) > 0$ and $\mu_B^n(v_iv_j) < 0$. Hence, $d_B(G) + d_B(G^c) \leq 2O(G^*)$. □

Corollary 6.1 *For any bipolar fuzzy graph $G = (A, B)$ without isolated vertices $d_B(G) = \dfrac{O(G^*)}{2}$, where $O(G^*)$ is the order of crisp graph G^* corresponding to G.*

Theorem 6.4 *Let $G = (A, B)$ be a bipolar fuzzy graph, then $d_B(G) \leq O(G^*) - \Delta(G^*)$, where $\Delta(G^*) = \max\{deg_{G^*}(x) \mid x \in X\}$.*

Proof Let v be a vertex in a bipolar fuzzy graph $G = (A, B)$. Assume that $|N(v)| = \Delta(G^*)$, then $X - N(v)$ is a dominating set of G, so that $d_B(G) \leq |X - N(v)| = O(G^*) - \Delta(G^*)$. □

Theorem 6.5 *An independent set of bipolar fuzzy graph $G = (A, B)$ is maximal if and only if it is an independent set and a dominating set.*

Proof Let D be a maximal independent set of a bipolar fuzzy graph, then for every vertex $v \in X - D$, the set $D \cup \{v\}$ is not an independent set. For every vertex $v \in X - D$, there is a vertex $u \in D$ such that u is a strong neighbor to v. Thus, D is a dominating set. Hence, D is both a dominating and independent set.

Conversely, assume that D is both an independent and dominating set. Suppose that D is not a maximal independent set, then there exists a vertex $v \in X - D$ such that the set $D \cup \{v\}$ is an independent set. If $D \cup \{v\}$ is an independent set, then no vertex in D is a strong neighbor to v. Thus, D cannot be a dominating set which is a contradiction. Hence, D is a maximal independent set. □

Theorem 6.6 *Every maximal independent set in a bipolar fuzzy graph $G = (A, B)$ is a minimal dominating set.*

Proof Let S be a maximal independent set in a bipolar fuzzy graph. By Theorem 6.5, S is a dominating set. Suppose S is not a minimal dominating set, then there exists at least one vertex $v \in S$ for which $S - \{v\}$ is a dominating set. But if $S - \{v\}$ dominates $X - \{S - \{v\}\}$, then at least one vertex in $S - \{v\}$ must be a strong neighbor to v. This contradicts the fact that S is an independent set of G. Therefore, S must be a minimal dominating set. □

Table 6.1 Bipolar fuzzy set A on set X

A	u	v	w	x	y	z
μ_A^p	0.3	0.2	0.2	0.1	0.3	0.3
μ_A^n	−0.7	−0.8	−0.7	−0.9	−0.6	−0.5

Theorem 6.7 *Let $G = (A, B)$ be a bipolar fuzzy graph, then $t_B(G) = O(G^*)$ if and only if every vertex of G has a unique neighbor.*

Proof If every vertex of G has a unique neighbor, then X is the only total dominating set of G and $t_B(G) = O(G^*)$. Conversely, assume that $t_B(G) = O(G^*)$. If there exists a vertex u with neighbors v and w, then $X - \{u\}$ is a total dominating set of G. So $t_B(G) \leq O(G^*)$ which leads to a contradiction, hence every vertex of G has a unique neighbor. □

Definition 6.21 Let $G = (A, B)$ be a bipolar fuzzy graph on a non-empty set X. The **equitable neighborhood** (EN, in short) of a vertex $v \in X$, denoted by $EN(v)$, is defined as $EN(v) = (EN^P(v), EN^n(v))$, where $EN^p(v) = \{u \in X \mid u \in N(v), |deg^p(u) - deg^p(v)| \leq 1, \mu_B^p(uv) = \min\{\mu_A^p(u), \mu_A^p(v)\}$ and $EN^n(v) = \{u \in X \mid u \in N(v), |deg^n(u) - deg^n(v)| \geq 1, \mu_B^n(uv) = \max\{\mu_A^n(u), \mu_A^n(v)\}$.

Definition 6.22 The **EN degree** of a vertex $v \in X$, denoted by $deg_{EN}(v)$, is defined as $deg_{EN}(v) = (deg_{EN}^p(v), deg_{EN}^n(v))$, where $deg_{EN}^p(v) = \sum_{u\in EN(v)} \mu_B^p(vu)$ and $deg_{EN}^n(v)=\sum_{u\in EN(v)} \mu_B^n(vu)$.

The **minimum EN degree**, denoted by $\delta_{EN}(G)$, is defined as $\delta_{EN}(G) = (\delta_{EN}^p(G), \delta_{EN}^n(G))$, where $\delta_{EN}^p(G) = \min\{deg_{EN}^p(v) \mid v \in X\}$ and $\delta_{EN}^n(G) = \min\{deg_{EN}^p(v) \mid v \in X\}$.

The **maximum EN degree**, denoted by $\Delta_{EN}(G)$, is defined as $\Delta_{EN}(G) = (\Delta_{EN}^p(G), \Delta_{EN}^n(G))$, where $\Delta_{EN}^p(G) = \max\{deg_{EN}^p(v) \mid v \in X\}$ and $\Delta_{EN}^n(G) = \max\{deg_{EN}^n(v) \mid v \in X\}$.

Example 6.5 Let $G = (A, B)$ be a bipolar fuzzy graph on $X = \{u, v, w, x, y, z\}$ such that $A = (\mu_A^p, \mu_A^n)$ is a bipolar fuzzy subset of X, in Table 6.1, and $Y = (\mu_B^p, \mu_B^n)$ is a bipolar fuzzy relation in X defined in Table 6.2. The bipolar fuzzy graph is shown in Fig. 6.3.

By routine verification, it is clear from Fig. 6.3 that $EN(u) = \{v, w\}$ $EN(v) = \{u, x, y\}$, $EN(w) = \{u, x, z\}$, $EN(x) = \{w, v\}$, $EN(y) = \{v\}$, and $EN(z) = \{w\}$. The EN degrees of vertices are calculated as $deg_{EN}(u) = (0.4, -1.4)$, $deg_{EN}(v) = (0.5, -2.1)$, $deg_{EN}(w) = (0.5, -1.9)$, $deg_{EN}(x) = (0.2, -1.5)$, $deg_{EN}(y) = (0.2, -0.6)$, and $deg_{EN}(z) = (0.2, -0.5)$. The minimum EN degree of a bipolar fuzzy graph G is $\delta_{EN}(G) = (0.2, -2.1)$, and the maximum EN degree of a bipolar fuzzy graph G is $\Delta_{EN}(G) = (0.5, -0.5)$.

Definition 6.23 Let $G = (A, B)$ be a bipolar fuzzy graph on a non-empty set X. A vertex $v \in X$ is called an **equitable isolated vertex** in G if, for every

Table 6.2 Bipolar fuzzy relation B in X

B	uv	uw	wx	xv	vy	wz	vw
μ_B^p	0.2	0.2	0.1	0.1	0.2	0.2	0.1
μ_B^n	−0.7	−0.7	−0.7	−0.8	−0.6	−0.5	−0.6

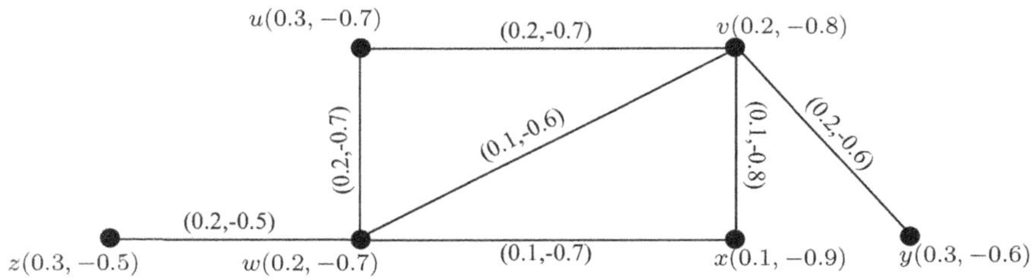

Fig. 6.3 EN degree of vertices in G

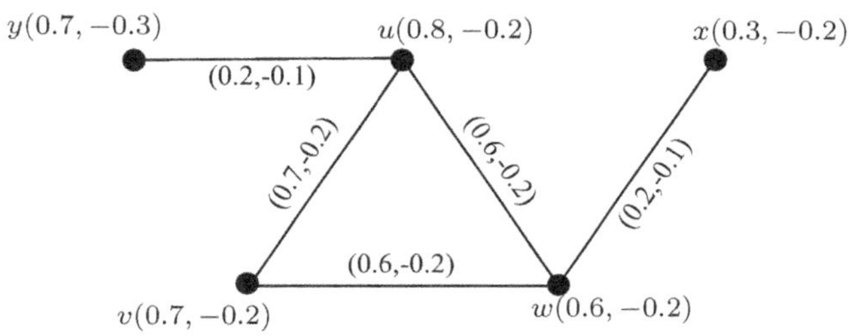

Fig. 6.4 Equitable isolated vertex

$u \in X$, $|deg^p(u) - deg^p(v)| > 1$, $\mu_B^p(uv) < \min\{\mu_A^p(u), \mu_A^p(v)\}$, and $|deg^n(u) - deg^n(v)| < 1$, $\mu_B^n(uv) > \max\{\mu_A^n(u), \mu_A^n(v)\}$, i.e., $EN(v) = \emptyset$.

Example 6.6 Consider a bipolar fuzzy graph $G = (A, B)$ on $X = \{u, v, w, x, y\}$, as shown in Fig. 6.4.

From Fig. 6.4, it is clear that $deg(u) = (1.5, \ -0.5)$, $deg(y) = (0.2, \ -0.1)$, $deg(w) = (1.4, -0.5)$, and $deg(x) = (0.2, -0.1)$. Since $|deg^p(u) - deg^p(y)| > 1$, $\mu_B^p(uy) < \min\{\mu_A^p(u), \mu_A^p(y)\}$ and $|deg^n(u) - deg^n(y)| < 1$, $\mu_B^p(uy) > \max\{\mu_A^p(u), \mu_A^p(y)\}$, i.e., $EN(y) = \emptyset$. Also, $|deg^p(w) - deg^p(x)| > 1$, $\mu_B^p(wx) < \min\{\mu_A^p(w), \mu_A^p(x)\}$ and $|deg^n(w) - deg^n(x)| < 1$, $\mu_B^n(wx) > \max\{\mu_A^n(w), \mu_A^n(x)\}$, i.e., $EN(x) = \emptyset$. Therefore, y and x are equitable isolated vertices in G.

Definition 6.24 Let $G = (A, B)$ be a bipolar fuzzy graph on a non-empty set X. A subset $S \subseteq X$ is called an **equitable dominating (ED) set** of G if for every vertex $v \in X - S$, there exists a vertex $u \in X$ such that $uv \in E$, $|deg^p(u) - deg^p(v)| \leq 1$, $\mu_B^p(uv) = \min\{\mu_A^p(u), \mu_A^p(v)\}$, and $|deg^n(u) - deg^n(v)| \geq 1$, $\mu_B^n(uv) = \max\{\mu_A^n$

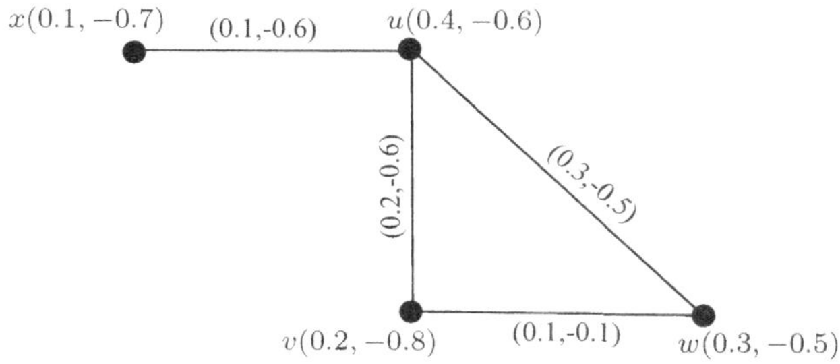

Fig. 6.5 Equitable dominating set of G

Fig. 6.6 Degree equitable bipolar fuzzy graph

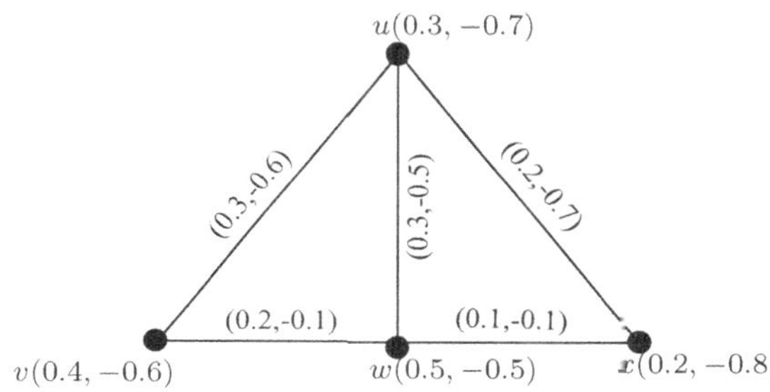

$(u), \mu_A^n(v)\}$. The **ED (equitable domination) number** of G, denoted by $\gamma_e(G)$, is defined as the minimum cardinality of an ED set S.

Definition 6.25 An ED subset $S \subseteq X$ of a bipolar fuzzy graph G is called a **minimal ED set** of G if for every vertex $v \in S$, the set $S - \{v\}$ is not an ED set, i.e., no proper subset of S is an ED set of G.

Example 6.7 Consider a bipolar fuzzy graph $G = (A, B)$ on $X = \{u, v, w, x\}$, as shown in Fig. 6.5.

By Definition 6.24, it is easy to see from Fig. 6.5 that the minimal ED set of a bipolar fuzzy graph G is $S = \{u\}$. The ED number of G is $\gamma_e(G) = 0.4$.

Definition 6.26 Let $G = (A, B)$ be a bipolar fuzzy graph on a non-empty set X. G is called a **degree equitable** if for every vertex $v \in X$, there exists a vertex $u \in X$ such that $uv \in supp(B)$, $|deg^p(u) - deg^p(v)| \leq 1$, $\mu_B^p(uv) = \min\{\mu_A^p(u), \mu_A^p(v)\}$, and $|deg^n(u) - deg^n(v)| \geq 1$, $\mu_B^n(uv) = \max\{\mu_A^n(u), \mu_A^n(v)\}$.

Example 6.8 Consider a bipolar fuzzy graph $G = (A, B)$ on $X = \{u, v, w, x\}$, as shown in Fig. 6.6.

Routine computations show that G is a degree equitable bipolar fuzzy graph.

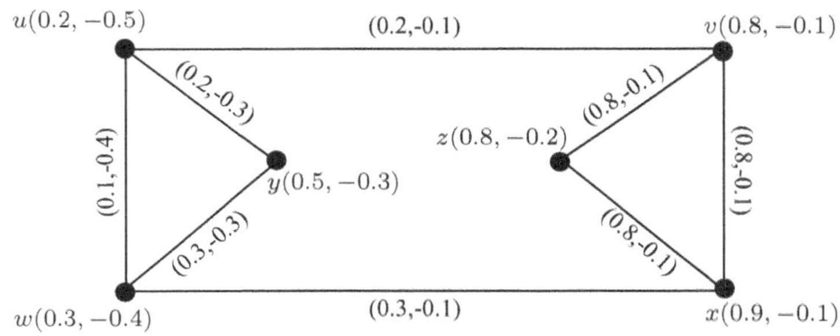

Fig. 6.7 EI set of G

Definition 6.27 A subset $I \subseteq X$ is called an **equitable independent (EI) set** of a bipolar fuzzy graph $G = (A, B)$ if $|deg^p(u) - deg^p(v)| > 1$, $\mu_B^p(uv) < \min\{\mu_A^p(u), \mu_A^p(v)\}$, and $|deg^n(u) - deg^n(v)| < 1$, $\mu_B^n(uv) > \max\{\mu_A^n(u), \mu_A^n(v)\}$, for all $u, v \in I$. The **EI (equitable independence) number** of G, denoted by $\gamma_{ie}(G)$, is defined as the minimum cardinality of an EI set of G.

Definition 6.28 An EI set I is called a **maximal EI set** of G if for every vertex $u \in X - I$, the set $I \cup \{u\}$ is not an EI set.

Example 6.9 Consider a bipolar fuzzy graph $G = (A, B)$ on $X = \{u, v, w, x, y, z\}$ as shown in Fig. 6.7.

By routine verifications, it is easy to see from Fig. 6.7 that $S_1 = \{u, x\}$ and $S_2 = \{v, w\}$ are maximal EI sets of G. The EI number of G is $\gamma_{ie}(G) = 2$.

Definition 6.29 Let $G = (A, B)$ be a bipolar fuzzy graph on X. For any two vertices $u, v \in X$, u **strongly dominates** v in G if $\mu_B^p(uv) = \min\{\mu_A^p(u), \mu_A^p(v)\}$, $\mu_B^n(uv) = \max\{\mu_A^n(u), \mu_A^n(v)\}$, $d_G^p(u) \geq d_G^p(v)$, and $d_G^n(u) \leq d_G^n(v)$. Similarly, u **weakly dominates** v if $\mu_B^p(uv) = \min\{\mu_A^p(u), \mu_A^p(v)\}$, $\mu_B^n(uv) = \max\{\mu_A^n(u), \mu_A^n(v)\}$, $d_G^p(v) \geq d_G^p(u)$, and $d_G^n(v) \leq d_G^n(u)$.

Definition 6.30 An ED set $S \subseteq X$ is called a **weak (strong) ED (equitable dominating) set** of G if for every vertex $v \in X - S$, there is at least one vertex $u \in S$ such that u weakly (strongly) dominates v. The **weak (strong) ED (equitable domination) number** of G, denoted by $\gamma_{we}(G)$ ($\gamma_{se}(G)$), is defined as the minimum cardinality of a weak (strong) ED set of G.

Example 6.10 Consider the example of a bipolar fuzzy graph $G = (A, B)$ as shown in Fig. 6.8. By routine computations, it is easy to see from Fig. 6.8 that the strong ED set of G is $S = \{u, v\}$. The strong ED number of G is $\gamma_{se}(G) = 2$.

Definition 6.31 Let $G = (A, B)$ be a connected bipolar fuzzy graph on X. A **connected ED (equitable dominating) set** is a subset $X' \subseteq X$ of G if it satisfies the following conditions.

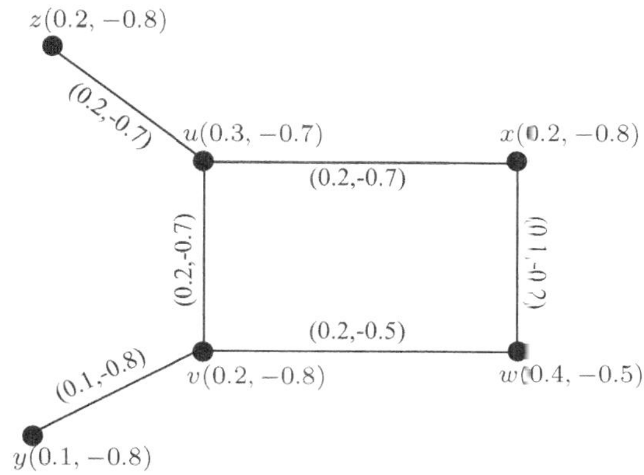

Fig. 6.8 Strong equitable dominating set of G

1. For every $v \in X - X'$, there exists a vertex $u \in X'$ such that $vu \in E$, $|deg^p(u) - deg^p(v)| \leq 1$, $\mu^p_B(uv) = \min\{\mu^p_A(u), \mu^p_A(v)\}$ and $|deg^n(u) - deg^n(v)| \geq 1$, $\mu^n_B(uv) = \max\{\mu^n_A(u), \mu^n_A(v)\}$.
2. The subgraph $H = (A', B')$ of $G = (A, B)$ induced by X' is connected.

Theorem 6.8 *Let $G = (A, B)$ be a bipolar fuzzy graph on X. An ED set D of G is called a minimal ED set if and only if for each $v \in D$, one of the following conditions is satisfied.*

(i) *v is an isolated vertex in D,*
(ii) *$EN(v) \cap (X - D) \neq \emptyset$,*
(iii) *there exists a vertex $u \in X - D$ such that $EN(u) \cap D = \{v\}$.*

Proof Let $G = (A, B)$ be a bipolar fuzzy graph with minimal ED set D, then for each vertex $v \in D$, the set $D' = D - \{v\}$ is not an ED set. Thus, there is at least one vertex u in $X - D'$ such that u is not dominated by any vertex in D'. There arise two cases.

If $u = v$, then v is an isolated vertex in D, that is, v is not adjacent to any vertex $w \in D$ such that $\mu^p_B(vw) = 0 = \mu^n_B(vw)$. So, $EN(v) \cap (X - D) \neq \emptyset$, that is, each vertex in D has a neighbor in $X - S$.

If $u \neq v$, i.e., $u \in X - D$, then u is dominated by some vertex of D but not dominated by any vertex in D'. Thus, u is adjacent only to one vertex $v \in D$, hence $EN(u) \cap D = \{v\}$.

Conversely, assume that D is an ED set of a bipolar fuzzy graph G and for each vertex $v \in D$, one of the given conditions is satisfied. Suppose that D is not a minimal ED set, then clearly there exists a vertex $v \in D$ such that $D - \{v\}$ is an ED set of G. Hence, v is adjacent to at least one vertex of set $D - \{v\}$, i.e., v is not an isolated vertex in D, so condition (i) is false. Also, if we take $D' = D - \{v\}$ as an ED set of G, then every vertex of $X - D'$ is adjacent to at least one vertex in D'. Thus, conditions (ii) and (iii) are also false which is a contradiction. □

Theorem 6.9 *Let $G = (A, B)$ be a bipolar fuzzy graph with order $O(G)$, then*

1. $\gamma_e(G) \leq \gamma_{se}(G) \leq O(G^*) - \Delta^p_{EN}(G)$,
2. $\gamma_e(G) \leq \gamma_{we}(G) \leq O(G^*) - \delta^p_{EN}(G)$.

Proof As, by definition, every weak (strong) ED set of a bipolar fuzzy graph G is an ED set of G, $\gamma_e(G) \leq \gamma_{se}(G)$ and $\gamma_e(G) \leq \gamma_{we}(G)$. Let u and v be two arbitrary vertices of G. If $deg^p_{EN}(v) = \Delta^p_{EN}(G)$ and $deg^p_{EN}(u) = \delta^p_{EN}(G)$, then $X - EN(v)$ is a strong ED set of G and $X - EN(u)$ is a weak ED set of G. Thus, $\gamma_{se}(G) \leq |X - EN(v)|$ and $\gamma^p_{we}(G) \leq |X - EN(u)|$, i.e., $\gamma_{se}(G) \leq O(G^*) - \Delta^p_{EN}(G)$ and $\gamma_{we}(G) \leq O(G^*) - \delta^p_{EN}(G)$. □

Theorem 6.10 *Let $G = (A, B)$ be a bipolar fuzzy graph without isolated vertices and S be a minimal ED set of G, then $X - S$ is an ED set of G.*

Proof Let G be a bipolar fuzzy graph with minimal ED set S, then for every vertex $v \in S$, there is at least one vertex $u \in X - S$ such that $|deg^p(u) - deg^p(v)| \leq 1$, $\mu^p_B(uv) = \min\{\mu^p_A(u), \mu^p_A(v)\}$ and $|deg^n(u) - deg^n(v)| \geq 1$, $\mu^n_B(uv) = \max\{\mu^n_A(u), \mu^n_A(v)\}$. Thus, $X - S$ dominates every element of S. Hence, $X - S$ is an ED set of G. □

Theorem 6.11 *If H is a spanning subgraph of a bipolar fuzzy graph G, then $\gamma_e(G) \geq \gamma_e(H)$.*

Theorem 6.12 *Let G be a bipolar fuzzy graph with EI dominating set I, then I is both a minimal ED set and a maximal EI set of G. Conversely, any maximal EI set I of a bipolar fuzzy graph G is an EI dominating set of G.*

Proof Let G be a bipolar fuzzy graph with EI dominating set M, then for every vertex $v \in X - M$, the set $M \cup \{v\}$ is not an EI set and the set $M - \{v\}$ is not an ED set of G. Hence, M is both a minimal ED set and a maximal EI set of G.

Conversely, suppose that M is a maximal EI set of G, then for every vertex $v \in X - M$, the set $M \cup \{v\}$ is not an EI set of G. Thus, the set M dominates every vertex $u \in X - M$ and so M is an ED set of G. Hence, M is an EI dominating set of G. □

Theorem 6.13 *A subset $I \subseteq X$ is an EI set and an ED set of a bipolar fuzzy graph G if and only if I is a maximal EI set of G.*

Proof Suppose that M is both an ED set and an EI set of a bipolar fuzzy graph G. Assume that M is not a maximal EI set of G, then clearly there exists a vertex $u \in X - M$ such that $M \cup \{u\}$ is an EI set, that is, u is not dominated by any vertex $v \in M$ showing that M is not an ED set of G, a contradiction, hence M is a maximal EI set of G.

Conversely, let M be a maximal EI set of G, then for every vertex $u \in X - M$, the set $M \cup \{u\}$ is not an EI set of G. Thus, the set M dominates every vertex $u \in X - M$, that is, M is an ED set of G. Hence, M is both an ED set and an EI set and an ED set of G. □

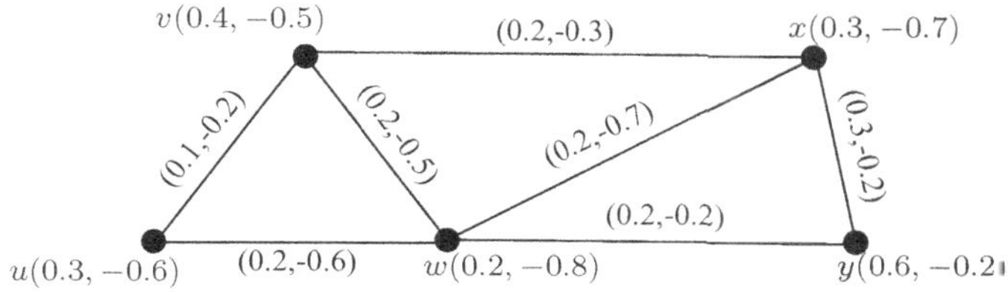

Fig. 6.9 Total ED set of G

Definition 6.32 A **total ED set** of a bipolar fuzzy graph $G = (A, B)$ is a subset $S \subseteq X$ if for every vertex $v \in X$, there is at least one vertex $u \in S$ such that $uv \in E(G)$, $|deg^p(u) - deg^p(v)| \leq 1$, $\mu_B^p(uv) = \min\{\mu_A^p(u), \mu_A^p(v)\}$, and $|deg^n(u) - deg^n(v)| \geq 1, \mu_B^n(uv) = \max\{\mu_A^n(u), \mu_A^n(v)\}$. The **total ED (equitable domination) number** of G, denoted by $\gamma_{te}(G)$, is defined as the minimum cardinality of a total ED set S.

Definition 6.33 A total ED set S of a bipolar fuzzy graph G is called a **minimal total ED set** if for every vertex $v \in S$, the set $S - \{v\}$ is not a total ED set, i.e., no proper subset of S is a total ED set of G.

Example 6.11 Consider a bipolar fuzzy graph $G = (A, B)$ on a crisp set $X = \{u, v, w, x, y\}$, as shown in Fig. 6.9.

By Definition 6.32, it is easy to see from Fig. 6.9 that $S = \{w, y\}$ is a total ED set of G.

Remark 6.2 If G has an equitable isolated vertex, then $\gamma_{te}(G) \to \infty$.

Theorem 6.14 *Let $G = (A, B)$ be a bipolar fuzzy graph on a non-empty set X. A total ED set S of G is called a minimal total ED set if and only if for each $v \in S$, one of the following conditions is satisfied.*

1. *There exists a vertex $u \in X - S$ such that $N(u) \cup S = \{v\}$.*
2. *$< S - \{v\} >$ contains an isolated vertex.*

Theorem 6.15 *Let G be a bipolar fuzzy graph with no isolated vertices, then $\gamma_t(G) \leq \gamma_{te}(G)$.*

Proof As every total ED set of a bipolar fuzzy graph $G = (A, B)$ is also a total dominating set, $\gamma_t(G) \leq \gamma_{te}(G)$. □

Definition 6.34 Let $G = (A, B)$ be a bipolar fuzzy graph on a non-empty set X and $k \geq 1$ be an integer. A subset $S \subseteq X$ is called a **k-dominating set** of G if for every vertex $u \in X - S$, there exists a $u - v$ bipolar fuzzy path which contains at least k effective edges for $v \in S$. The **k-domination number** of G, denoted by $\gamma_k(G)$, is defined as the minimum cardinality among all k-dominating sets in G.

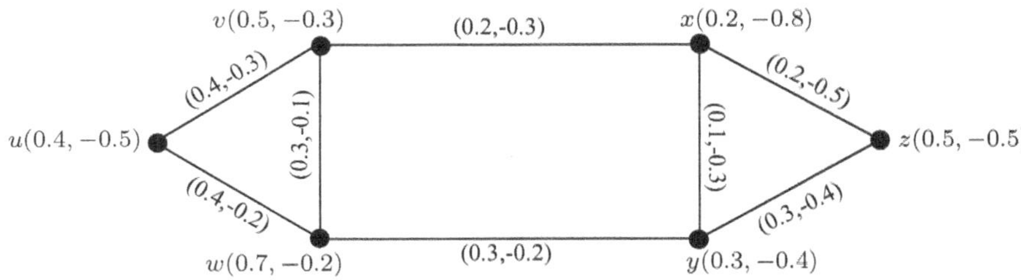

Fig. 6.10 Total 2-dominating set of G

Definition 6.35 Let $G = (A, B)$ be a bipolar fuzzy graph on a non-empty set X and let $k \geq 1$ be an integer. A subset $S \subseteq X$ is called a **total k-dominating set** of G if for every vertex $u \in X$, there exists a $u - v$ bipolar fuzzy path which contains at least k effective edges for $v \in S$. The **total k-domination number** of G, denoted by $\gamma_{tk}(G)$, is defined as the minimum cardinality among all total k-dominating sets in G.

Example 6.12 Consider an example of a total 2-dominating set of a bipolar fuzzy graph G shown in Fig. 6.10.

By Definition 6.35, it is clear from Fig. 6.10 that $S = \{u, z\}$ is a minimal total 2-dominating set of a bipolar fuzzy graph G. The total 2-domination number of G is $\gamma_k(G) = 2$.

Definition 6.36 Let $G = (A, B)$ be a bipolar fuzzy graph on X. A subset $S \subseteq X$ is called a **k-independent dominating set** of G if for every vertex $u \in X - S$, there exists a $u - v$ bipolar fuzzy path which contains at least $k + 1$ effective edges for $v \in S$. The **k-independent domination number** of G, denoted by $\gamma_{ik}(G)$, is defined as the minimum cardinality among all k-independent dominating sets in G.

Definition 6.37 Let $G = (A, B)$ be a bipolar fuzzy graph on X. A subset $S \subseteq X$ is called a **restrained dominating (RD) set** of G if every vertex in $X - S$ dominates a vertex in S and also a vertex in $X - S$. The **RD (restrained domination) number** of G, denoted by $\gamma_r(G)$, is defined as the minimum cardinality among all RD sets in G.

Example 6.13 Let $G = (A, B)$ be a bipolar fuzzy graph on $X = \{u, v, w, x\}$ as shown in Fig. 6.11.

From Fig. 6.11, it is clear that $S = \{w, x\}$ is an RD set of G. The RD number of G is $\gamma_r(G) = 2$.

Definition 6.38 Let $G = (A, B)$ be a bipolar fuzzy graph on X. A subset $S \subseteq X$ which is an RD set of both bipolar fuzzy graph G and its complement G^c is called a **global RD (restrained dominating) set** of G. The minimum cardinality among all global RD sets in G is called a **global RD (restrained domination) number** of G, denoted by $\gamma_{gr}(G)$.

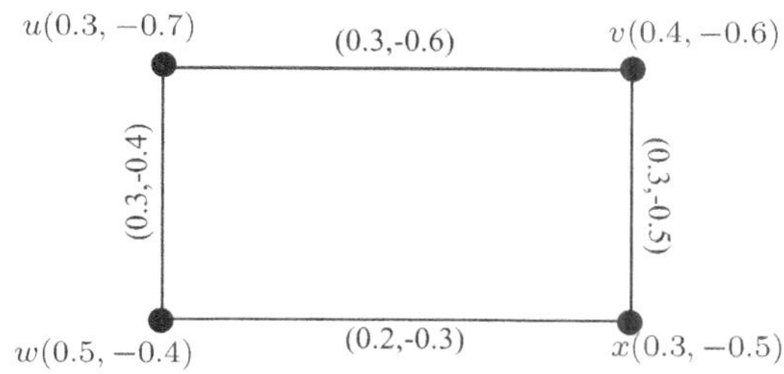

Fig. 6.11 Restrained dominating set of G

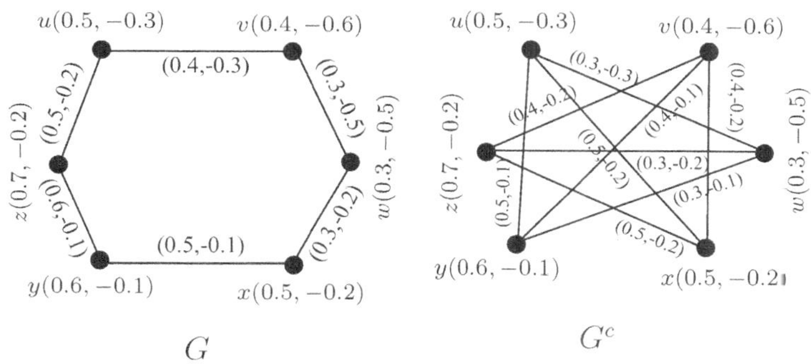

Fig. 6.12 Global RD set of G

Example 6.14 Consider a bipolar fuzzy graph G and its complement G^c on $X = \{u, v, w, x, y, z\}$ as shown in Fig. 6.12.

By direct calculations, it is easy to see that $S_1 = \{v, y\}$, $S_2 = \{u, x\}$, and $S_3 = \{w, z\}$ are global RD sets of G. The global RD number of G is $\gamma_{gr}(G) = 2$.

Definition 6.39 An edge xy of a bipolar fuzzy graph $G = (A, B)$ is called an **effective edge** if $B(xy) = (\mu_A^p(x) \wedge \mu_A^p(y), \mu_A^n(x) \vee \mu_A^n(y))$. Otherwise, it is called a **noneffective edge**.

Theorem 6.16 *Let $G = (A, B)$ be a complete bipolar fuzzy graph on X, then $\gamma_r(G) = |X|$.*

Proof Suppose that $G = (A, B)$ is a complete bipolar fuzzy graph. Then $\mu_B^p(uv) = \min(\mu_A^p(u), \mu_A^p(v))$ and $\mu_B^n(uv) = \max(\mu_A^n(u), \mu_A^n(v))$, i.e., each edge in G is an effective edge. Let S be the minimal RD set of G. Then every vertex in $X - S$ dominates a vertex in S and also a vertex in $X - S$. Thus, every vertex dominates all other vertices. Hence, $\gamma_r(G) = |X|$. □

Note 6.1 For a complete bipartite bipolar fuzzy graph, the RD number is $\gamma_r(G) = |X_1| + |X_2|$.

Theorem 6.17 *Let $G = (A, B)$ be a bipolar fuzzy graph on X with $|X| = n$, then $\gamma_{gr}(G) = n$ if and only if $G = K_n$ or K_n^c.*

Proof Let $G = K_n$ be a complete bipolar fuzzy graph on X, then for each edge $uv \in E$, $\mu_B^p(uv) = \min\{\mu_A^p(u), \mu_A^p(v)\}$ and $\mu_B^n(uv) = \max\{\mu_A^n(u), \mu_A^n(v)\}$. Thus, the complement K_n^c, having no edges, is a null bipolar fuzzy graph. Each vertex in the null bipolar fuzzy graph K_n^c is an isolated vertex. Therefore, RD set of K_n and K_n^c is the vertex set X. Hence, global RD set of $G = K_n$ is equal to set X, i.e., $\gamma_{gr}(G) = O(G^*)$. If $G = K_n^c$, then the RD set of K_n is the singleton set $\{v\}$, for all $v \in X$, but it is not the RD set of K_n^c. Since every vertex in K_n^c is an isolated vertex, the only RD set of both K_n and K_n^c is the vertex set X.

Conversely, assume that $\gamma_{gr}(G) = n = O(G^*)$ but $G \neq K_n$ or $G \neq K_n^c$, then there exists a vertex v which is not dominated by u. Thus, $X - \{v\}$ is a global RD set containing $n - 1$ vertices. Hence, $\gamma_{gr}(G) \neq O(G^*)$ which is a contradiction. □

Theorem 6.18 *Let $G_1 = (A_1, B_1)$ and $G_2 = (A_2, B_2)$ be two bipolar fuzzy graphs with $X_1 \cap X_2 = \emptyset$, then the strong product $G = G_1 \boxtimes G_2$ remains connected even after removal of all noneffective edges in it.*

Proof Suppose that $G = G_1 \boxtimes G_2 = (A, B)$ is a strong product of two bipolar fuzzy graphs $G_1 = (A_1, B_1)$ and $G_2 = (A_2, B_2)$. Let $e = (u, u_1)(v, v_1)$ be a noneffective edge in G, i.e., $\mu_B^p((u, u_1)(v, v_1)) < \min\{\mu_A^p(u, u_1), \mu_A^p(v, v_1)\}$ and $\mu_B^n((u, u_1)(v, v_1)) > \max\{\mu_A^n(u, u_1), \mu_A^n(v, v_1)\}$. Let $G' = G - e$ and assume that G' is disconnected. The edge e disconnects the bipolar fuzzy graph into more than one components. Thus, there does not exist any path between (u, u_1) and (v, v_1) except the edge $e = (u, u_1)(v, v_1)$ in G'. It implies that $\mu_B^p((u, u_1)(v, v_1)) = \min\{\mu_A^p(u, u_1), \mu_A^p(v, v_1)\}$ and $\mu_B^n((u, u_1)(v, v_1)) = \max\{\mu_A^n(u, u_1), \mu_A^n(v, v_1)\}$ which is a contradiction. Hence, $G' = G - e$ is connected. □

Theorem 6.19 *The strong product $G_1 \boxtimes G_2$ of two complete bipolar fuzzy graphs is a complete bipolar fuzzy graph.*

Proof Let $G_1 = (A_1, B_1)$ and $G_2 = (A_2, B_2)$ be two bipolar fuzzy graphs such that E is the set of edges in $G_1 \boxtimes G_2$. If $(u, u_1)(u, v_1) \in E$, then since G_2 is complete,

$$\begin{aligned}\mu^p_{B_1 \boxtimes B_2}((u, u_1)(u, v_1)) &= \min\{\mu^p_{X_1}(u), \mu^p_{B_2}(u_1 v_1)\}\\ &= \min\{\mu^p_{X_1}(u), \min\{\mu^p_{A_2}(u_1), \mu^p_{A_2}(v_1)\}\\ &= \min\{(\mu^p_{B_1 \boxtimes B_2})(u, u_1), (\mu^p_{B_1 \boxtimes B_2})(u, v_1)\}.\end{aligned}$$

If $(u, u_1)(v, u_1) \in E$, then since G_1 is complete,

$$\begin{aligned}\mu^p_{B_1 \boxtimes B_2}((u, u_1)(v, u_1)) &= \min\{\mu^p_{B_1}(u, v), \mu^p_{X_2}(u_1)\}\\ &= \min\{\min\{\mu^p_{X_1}(u), \mu^p_{A_1}(v)\}, \mu^p_{A_2}(u_1)\}\\ &= \min\{(\mu^p_{B_1 \boxtimes B_2})(u, u_1), (\mu^p_{B_1 \boxtimes B_2})(v, u_1)\}.\end{aligned}$$

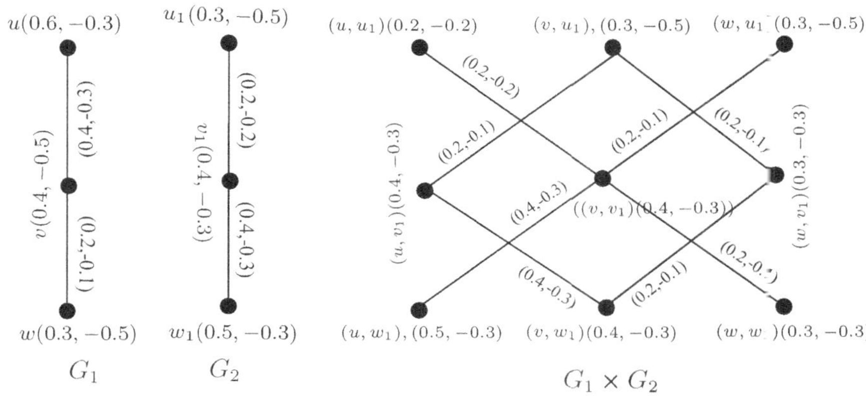

Fig. 6.13 Direct product of G_1 and G_2

If $(u, u_1)(v, v_1) \in E$, then since G_1 and G_2 are complete,

$$\begin{aligned}\mu^p_{B_1 \boxtimes B_2}((u, u_1)(v, v_1)) &= \min\{\mu^p_{B_1}(u, v), \mu^p_{B_2}(u_1 v_1)\}\\ &= \min\{\min\{\mu^p_{X_1}(u), \mu^p_{X_1}(v)\}, \min\{\mu^p_{X_2}(u_1), \mu^p_{X_2}(v_1)\}\\ &= \min\{(\mu^p_{B_1 \boxtimes B_2})(u, u_1), (\mu^p_{B_1 \boxtimes B_2})(v, v_1)\}.\end{aligned}$$

Similarly, it is so for other cases. Hence, $G_1 \boxtimes G_2$ is a complete bipolar fuzzy graph.□

Theorem 6.20 *If a vertex u dominates a vertex v in $G_1 = (A_1, B_1)$ and the vertex u_1 dominates a vertex v_1 in $G_2 = (A_2, B_2)$, then the vertex (u, v) does not dominate the vertex (u_1, v_1) in $G_1 \Box G_2 = (A, B)$.*

Proof Assume that u dominates v in G_1. Then there exists an effective edge uv in G_1, i.e., $\mu^p_{B_1}(uv) = \min\{\mu^p_{A_1}(u), \mu^p_{A_1}(v)\}$ and $\mu^n_{B_1}(uv) = \max\{\mu^n_{A_1}(u), \mu^n_{A_1}(v)\}$. Similarly, assume that a vertex u_1 dominates a vertex v_1 in G_2 such that $\mu^p_{B_2}(u_1 v_1) = \min\{\mu^p_{A_2}(u_1), \mu^p_{A_2}(v_1)\}$ and $\mu^n_{B_2}(u_1 v_1) = \max\{\mu^n_{A_2}(u_1), \mu^n_{A_2}(v_1)\}$. Now by Definition 1.18, there does not exist any edge between the vertices (u, u_1) and (v, v_1) in $G_1 \Box G_2$, i.e., $\mu^p_B((u, u_1)(v, v_1)) = 0$ and $\mu^n_B((u, u_1)(v, v_1)) = 0$. Thus, (u, u_1) does not dominate (v, v_1) in $G_1 \Box G_2$. □

Note 6.2 If a vertex u dominates a vertex v in G_1 and a vertex u_1 dominates a vertex v_1 in G_2, then the vertex (u, u_1) dominates the vertex (v, v_1) in $G_1 \times G_2$. It can be seen in Fig. 6.13

Example 6.15 Consider a bipolar fuzzy graph as shown in Fig. 6.13.

From Fig. 6.13, it is clear that the vertex u dominates v in G_1 and v dominates w_1 in G_2. Also, the vertex (u, v_1) dominates the vertex (v, w_1) in $G_1 \times G_2$.

Theorem 6.21 *Let G_1 and G_2 be bipolar fuzzy graphs on a non-empty sets X_1 and X_2, respectively, then*

$$\gamma_e(G_1 \times G_2) \leq \min(|S_1 \times X_1|, |S_2 \times X_2|),$$

where S_1 and S_2 are ED sets of G_1 and G_2, respectively.

Proof Let $G_1 = (A_1, B_1)$ and $G_2 = (A_2, B_2)$ be two bipolar fuzzy graphs with direct product $G_1 \times G_2 = (A, B)$. Suppose S_1 and S_2 are ED sets of G_1 and G_2, respectively, with minimum cardinality. Then for every vertex $v \in X_1 - S_1$, there exists a vertex $u \in S_1$ such that $|deg^p(v) - deg^p(u)| \leq 1$, $\mu^p_{B_1}(uv) = \min\{\mu^p_{A_1}(u), \mu^p_{A_1}(v)\}$ and $|deg^n(v) - deg^n(u)| \geq 1$, $\mu^n_{B_1}(uv) = \max\{\mu^n_{A_1}(u), \mu^n_{A_1}(v)\}$. Similarly, for every vertex $x \in X_2 - S_2$, there exists a vertex $w \in S_2$ such that $|deg^p(w) - deg^p(x)| \leq 1$, $\mu^p_{B_2}(wx) = \min\{\mu^p_{A_2}(w), \mu^p_{A_2}(x)\}$ and $|deg^n(w) - deg^n(x)| \geq 1$, $\mu^n_{B_2}(wx) = \max\{\mu^n_{A_2}(w), \mu^n_{A_2}(x)\}$. That is, u dominates v in G_1 and w dominates x in G_2. Thus, by Note 6.2, the vertex (u, w) dominates the vertex (v, x) in $G_1 \times G_2$. So $|deg^p((u, w)) - deg^p((v, x))| \leq 1$, $\mu^p_B((u, w)(v, x)) = \min\{\mu^p_A(u, w), \mu^p_A(v, x)\}$ and $|deg^n((u, w)) - deg^n((v, x))| \geq 1$, $\mu^n_B((u, w)(v, x)) = \max\{\mu^n_A(u, w), \mu^n_A(v, x)\}$. Hence, $\gamma_e(G_1 \times G_2) \leq \min(|S_1 \times X_1|, |S_2 \times X_2|)$. □

Theorem 6.22 *Let S_1 and S_2 be k-dominating sets of connected bipolar fuzzy graphs $G_1 = (A_1, B_1)$ and $G_2 = (A_2, B_2)$, respectively, then*

1. *$G_1 \Box G_2$ is connected.*
2. *If S_1 is a connected k-dominating set of G_1, then $S_1 \times X_2$ is a connected k-dominating set of $G_1 \Box G_2$.*
3. *If S_2 is a connected k-dominating set of G_2, then $X_1 \times S_2$ is a connected k-dominating set of $G_1 \Box G_2$.*

Proof To prove that $G_1 \Box G_2$ is connected, consider any two arbitrary distinct vertices (u, w), (v, x) of $X_1 \times X_2$. Then by Definition 1.18, there exists a bipolar fuzzy path between these two vertices in the following cases.

1. If $u = v$, then, since G_2 is a connected bipolar fuzzy graph, there exists a bipolar fuzzy path $P : w, w_1, w_2, \ldots, x$ such that $\mu^p_{B_2}(rs) > 0$ and $\mu^n_{B_2}(rs) < 0$ for any two vertices r, s of bipolar fuzzy path P. Thus, $\mu^p_B((u, w)(u, x)) = \min\{\mu^p_{A_1}(u), \mu^p_{B_2}(wx)\}$ and $\mu^n_B((u, w)(u, x)) = \max\{\mu^n_{A_1}(u), \mu^n_{B_2}(wx)\}$. Therefore, $P' : (u, w), (u, w_1), (u, w_2), \ldots, (u, x)$ is the bipolar fuzzy path between (u, w), (v, x) in $G_1 \Box G_2$.
2. If $w = x$, then, since G_1 is a connected bipolar fuzzy graph, there exists a bipolar fuzzy path $Q : u, u_1, u_2, \ldots, v$ such that $\mu^p_{B_1}(uv) > 0$ and $\mu^n_{B_1}(uv) < 0$ for any two vertices r, s of bipolar fuzzy path Q. Thus, $\mu^p_B((u, w)(v, w)) = \min\{\mu^p_{B_1}(u, v), \mu^p_{A_2}(w)\}$ and $\mu^n_B((u, w)(v, w)) = \max\{\mu^n_{B_1}(u, v), \mu^n_{A_2}(w)\}$. Therefore, $Q' : (u, w), (u_1, w), (u_2, w), \ldots, (v, w)$ is the bipolar fuzzy path between (u, w), (v, x) in $G_1 \Box G_2$.
3. If $u \neq v$, $w \neq x$, then by case 1, there exists a bipolar fuzzy path between the vertices (u, w) and (u, x) in $G_1 \Box G_2$. Also by case 2, there exists a bipolar fuzzy

path between the vertices (u, w) and (v, w) in $G_1 \Box G_2$. Thus, the union of these two disjoint bipolar fuzzy paths is a bipolar fuzzy path between the vertices (u, w) and (v, x) in $G_1 \Box G_2$.

Now, if S_1 and S_2 are k-dominating sets of G_1 and G_2, respectively, then $\gamma_k(G_1 \Box G_2) = \min\{|S_1 \times X_2|, |S_1 \times X_2|\}$. Hence, $X_1 \times S_2$ and $S_1 \times X_2$ are k-dominating sets of $G_1 \Box G_2$ and the connectivity can be proved similarly. □

Theorem 6.23 *Let G_1 and G_2 be bipolar fuzzy graphs on non-empty sets X_1 and X_2, respectively. Let S_1 and S_2 be k-dominating sets of G_1 and G_2, then*

(1) *$S_1 \times X_2$ is an independent k-dominating set of $G_1 \Box G_2$ if and only if S_1 is k-independent and,*

1. *$\mu^p_{B_1}(uv) < \mu^p_{A_2}(w)$ and $\mu^n_{B_1}(uv) > \mu^n_{A_2}(w)$, for $u, v \in S_1$, $w \in X_2$,*
2. *$\mu^p_{B_2}(wx) < \mu^p_{A_1}(u)$ and $\mu^n_{B_2}(wx) > \mu^n_{A_1}(u)$, for $u \in S_1$, $w, x \in X_2$,*
3. *$\mu^p_{B_2}(wx) < \min\{\mu^p_{A_2}(w), \mu^p_{A_2}(x)\}$ and $\mu^n_{B_2}(wx) > \max\{\mu^n_{A_2}(w), \mu^n_{A_2}(x)\}$, for $w, x \in X_2$.*

(2) *$X_1 \times S_2$ is an independent k-dominating set of $G_1 \Box G_2$ if and only if S_2 is k-independent and,*

1. *$\mu^p_{B_1}(uv) < \mu^p_{A_2}(w)$ and $\mu^n_{B_1}(uv) > \mu^n_{A_2}(w)$, for $u, v \in X_1$, $w \in S_2$,*
2. *$\mu^p_{B_2}(wx) < \mu^p_{A_1}(u)$ and $\mu^n_{B_2}(wx) > \mu^n_{A_1}(u)$, for $u \in X_1$, $w, x \in S_2$,*
3. *$\mu^p_{B_1}(uv) < \min\{\mu^p_{A_1}(u), \mu^p_{A_1}(v)\}$ and $\mu^n_{B_1}(uv) > \max\{\mu^n_{A_1}(u), \mu^n_{A}(v)\}$, for $u, v \in X_1$.*

Proof To prove that every two distinct vertices $(u, w), (v, x)$ in $S_1 \times X_2$ are not adjacent. If $u = v$, then

$$\begin{aligned}
\mu^p_B((u, w)(u, x)) &= \min\{\mu^p_{A_1}(u), \mu^p_{B_2}(wx)\} \\
&< \min\{\mu^p_{A_1}(u), \min\{\mu^p_{A_2}(w), \mu^p_{A_2}(x)\}\} \\
&< \min\{\mu^p_X(u, w), \mu^p_X(u, x)\}, \\
\mu^n_B((u, w)(u, x)) &= \max\{\mu^n_{X_1}(u), \mu^n_{Y_2}(wx)\} \\
&> \max\{\mu^n_{X_1}(u), \max\{\mu^n_{X_2}(w), \mu^n_{X_2}(x)\}\} \\
&> \max\{\mu^n_X(u, w), \mu^n_X(u, x)\}.
\end{aligned}$$

If $w = x$, the result is obtained by independence of u, v in S_1. If $u \neq v$, $w \neq x$, then $\mu^p_B((u, w)(v, x)) = 0$ and $\mu^n_B((u, w)(v, x)) = 0$. Hence, $(u, w), (v, x)$ are not adjacent in $G_1 \Box G_2$.

Conversely, suppose that (1) and (2) are false. That is, there exist vertices $y, z \in X_2$ such that $\mu^p_{B_2}(yz) = \min\{\mu^p_{A_2}(y), \mu^p_{A_2}(z)\}$ and $\mu^n_{B_2}(yz) = \max\{\mu^n_{A_2}(y), \mu^r_{A_2}(z)\}$. Let $u \in S_1$, then

$$\begin{aligned}
\mu_B^p((u,y)(u,z)) &= \min\{\mu_{A_1}^p(u), \mu_{B_2}^p(yz)\}\\
&= \min\{\mu_{A_1}^p(u), \min\{\mu_{A_2}^p(y), \mu_{A_2}^p(z)\}\}\\
&= \min\{\mu_X^p(u,y), \mu_X^p(u,z)\},\\
\mu_B^n((u,y)(u,z)) &= \max\{\mu_{A_1}^n(u), \mu_{B_2}^n(yz)\}\\
&= \max\{\mu_{A_1}^n(u), \max\{\mu_{A_2}^n(y), \mu_{A_2}^n(z)\}\}\\
&= \max\{\mu_X^n(u,y), \mu_X^n(u,z)\}.
\end{aligned}$$

Thus, $S_1 \times X_2$ is not independent. Hence, condition (1) is true, i.e., $\mu_{B_2}^p(yz) < \min\{\mu_{A_2}^p(y), \mu_{A_2}^p(z)\}$ and $\mu_{B_2}^n(yz) > \max\{\mu_{A_2}^n(y), \mu_{A_2}^n(z)\}$. Similarly (2) can be proved. □

6.3 Irredundance in Bipolar Fuzzy Graphs

In this section, the notions of private neighbor, lower and upper irredundant sets, and irredundance number are discussed in relation with independence and domination numbers of bipolar fuzzy graphs.

Definition 6.40 Let $G = (A, B)$ be a bipolar fuzzy graph and S be a set of vertices. A vertex v is said to be a **private neighbor** of $u \in S$ with respect to S if $N[v] \cap S = \{u\}$. Furthermore, a **private neighborhood** of $u \in S$ with respect to S is denoted by a set as $PN[u, S] = \{v \mid N[v] \cap S = \{u\}\}$. Also, $PN[u, S] = N[u] - N[S - \{u\}]$.

Definition 6.41 A vertex u in a subset $S \subseteq X$ is said to be a **redundant vertex** if $PN[u, S] = \emptyset$. Equivalently, u is redundant in S if $N[u] \subseteq N[S - \{u\}]$. Otherwise u is said to be an **irredundant vertex**.

Definition 6.42 A subset $S \subseteq X$ is said to be an **irredundant set** if $PN[u, S] \neq \emptyset$, for every vertex u in S.

Definition 6.43 An irredundant set $S \subseteq X$ in a bipolar fuzzy graph $G = (A, B)$ is called a **maximal irredundant set** if for every vertex $v \in X - S$, the set $S \cup \{v\}$ is not an irredundant set which means that there is at least one vertex $w \in S \cup \{u\}$ which does not have any private neighbor.

Definition 6.44 The maximum cardinality among all maximal irredundant sets is called the **upper irredundance number** and is denoted by $IR_B(G)$.

Definition 6.45 The minimum cardinality among all maximal irredundant sets is called the **lower irredundance number** and is denoted by $ir_B(G)$.

Example 6.16 Consider a bipolar fuzzy graph $G = (A, B)$ on $X = \{v_1, v_2, v_3, v_4, v_5, v_6\}$ as shown in Fig. 6.14. Clearly, $S_1 = \{v_5, v_6\}$, $S_2 = \{v_2, v_3, v_5\}$, $S_3 = \{v_1, v_4, v_6\}$, $S_4 = \{v_1, v_2\}$, and $S_5 = \{v_3, v_4\}$ are maximal irredundant sets, $PN[v_5,$

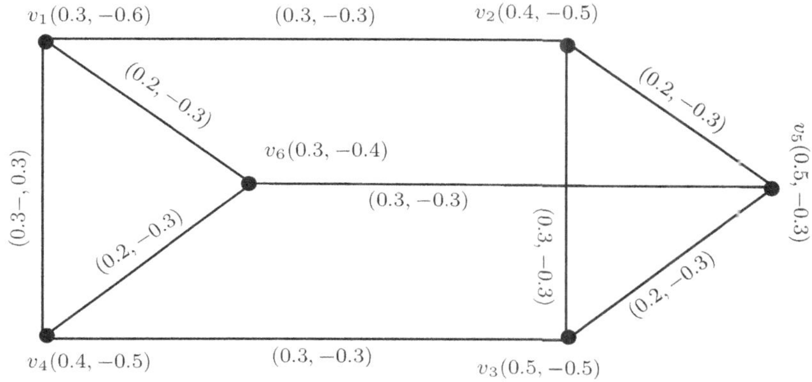

Fig. 6.14 Irredundant sets of G

$S_1] = \{v_2, v_3\}$, $PN[v_6, S_1] = \{v_1, v_4\}$, $PN[v_2, S_2] = \{v_1\}$, $PN[v_3, S_2] = \{v_4\}$, $PN[v_5, S_2] = \{v_6\}$, and so on. The set $\{v_1, v_2\}$ has minimum cardinality among all maximal irredundant sets and $ir_B(G) = 2$, $\{v_2, v_3, v_5\}$ has maximum cardinality among all maximal irredundant sets and $IR_B(G) = 3$.

Theorem 6.24 *Let $G = (A, B)$ be a bipolar fuzzy graph on X, then $ir_B(G) \leq O(G^*) - \delta(G^*)$.*

Proof Let S be an irredundant set in a bipolar fuzzy graph $G = (A, B)$. Let v be a vertex in S which is a strong neighbor to a set of vertices in S with cardinality $|k|$. Since the neighborhood degree of v in G^* is at least $\delta(G^*)$, v must be a strong neighbor to a set of vertices in $X - S$ with cardinality $\delta(G^*) - |k|$. Here $\delta(G^*) - |k| \leq |X - S|$. If $|k| = 0$, then $\delta(G^*) \leq |X - S|$. That is, $\delta(G^*) \leq O(G^*) - ir_B(G)$ or $ir_B(G) \leq O(G^*) - \delta(G)$. If $|k| > 0$, then each neighbor of v in S must be distinct and has a private neighbor in $X - S$. Hence, $|X - S| \geq (\delta(G^*) - |k|) + |k| = \delta(G^*)$. Thus, $ir_B(G) \leq O(G^*) - \delta(G^*)$. □

Corollary 6.2 *Every maximal independent set in a bipolar fuzzy graph G is a maximal irredundant set, that is, $ir_B(G) \leq i_B(G) \leq d_B(G) \leq IR_B(G)$.*

Theorem 6.25 *Let $G = (A, B)$ be a bipolar fuzzy graph on X, then $ir_B(G) + IR_B(G) \leq 2(O(G^*) - \delta(G*))$. The equality holds if and only if $O(G^*) - \delta(G^*)$ divides $O(G^*)$.*

Proof By Theorem 6.24 and Corollary 6.2,

$$ir_B(G) \leq IR_B \leq O(G^*) - \delta(G^*) \tag{6.1}$$
$$\Rightarrow ir_B(G) + IR_B(G) \leq 2(O(G^*) - \delta(G^*)).$$

If $O(G^*) - \delta(G^*)$ divides $O(G^*)$, then there exists a complete multipartite bipolar fuzzy graph, each of whose defining independent sets is of size $O(G^*) - \delta(G^*)$. Hence, $i_B(G) = IR_B(G) = O(G^*) - \delta(G^*)$. It follows that $ir_B(G) + IR_B(G) = 2(O(G^*) - \delta(G^*))$.

Conversely, if $ir_B(G) + IR_B(G) = 2(O(G^*) - \delta(G^*))$, from Eq. (6.1), $i_B(G) = IR_B(G) = O(G^*) - \delta(G^*)$. It follows that every vertex of G lies in a maximal independent set of cardinality $O(G^*) - \delta(G^*)$. Since $\delta(G^*)$ is the minimum neighborhood degree, every vertex in such a maximal independent set is a strong neighbor to every vertex outside the set. It follows that the vertex set X can be partitioned into maximal independent sets of size $O(G^*) - \delta(G^*)$, and hence $O(G^*) - \delta(G^*)$ divides $O(G^*)$. It follows that G is a complete multipartite bipolar fuzzy graph. □

6.4 Applications of Domination in Decision-Making Problems

In this section, the applications of domination in bipolar fuzzy graphs are discussed in facility location problem, finding the set of representatives, and in transmission tower location problem .

6.4.1 Facility Location Problem

Suppose that a provincial government has decided to build some colleges which must serve all the towns in a province. In order to decide the location of a college in a town, it is very important to analyze the educational situation in a town. The educational situation depends on many factors including the availability of skilled teachers, availability of transportation, urbanization, rate of literacy, flow rate, and drop-out rate of students. Now the government wants to locate a college in such a way that every town has a college or is a neighbor of a town which has a college, i.e., the government wants to build a minimum number of colleges to save money. We can present this problem as a bipolar fuzzy graph $G = (T, R)$, where T is a bipolar fuzzy set of towns presenting the literacy rate and drop-out rate as positive and negative membership degrees and R is a bipolar fuzzy set of roads between the towns. The positive and negative membership degrees can be calculated as

$$\mu_B^p(uv) \leq \min\{\mu_A^p(u), \mu_A^p(v)\}, \quad \mu_B^n(uv) \geq \max\{\mu_A^n(u), \mu_A^n(v)\}.$$

Consider the example of a bipolar fuzzy graph of various towns as shown in Fig. 6.15.

By direct computations, it is easy to check that the minimum dominating set of a bipolar fuzzy graph is $S = \{Tonopah, Beatty, Oasis\}$. Thus, the government

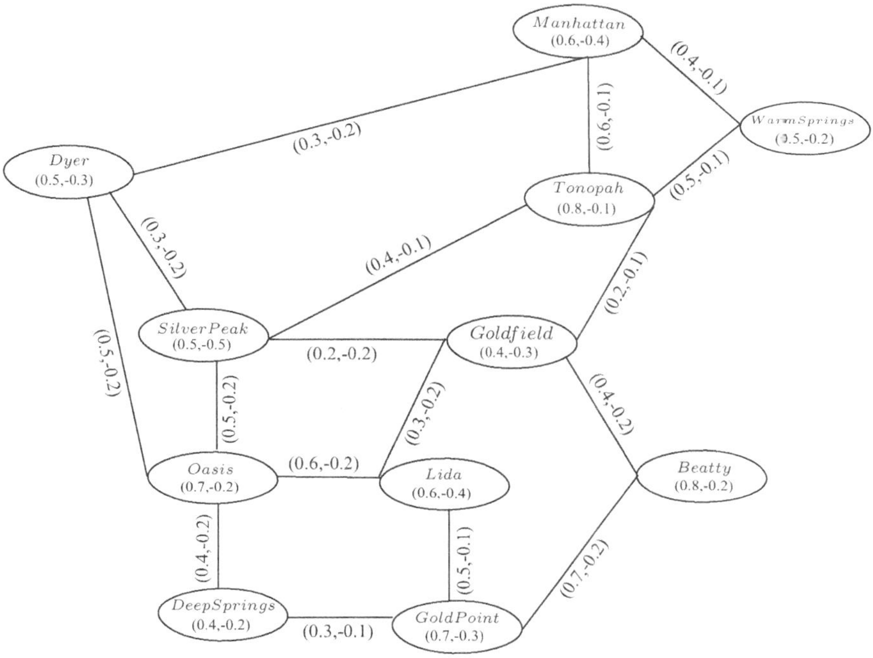

Fig. 6.15 Bipolar fuzzy graph of towns

needs to build colleges in three towns to save money and provide college facility to all towns of the province.

6.4.2 Representatives in Youth Development Council

A bipolar fuzzy graph can be used to find the set of representatives in a youth development council of a university. Consider a group of students who wants to become a member of the youth development council. Each student has some good and some bad leadership qualities. Bad leadership is characterized by lack of enthusiasm, poor communication skills, incompetency, inflexibility, and poor decision- making skills. A member of the youth development council must be a good listener, honest and fair, good communicator, and approachable. All these qualities are fuzzy in nature. We want to form a council with as a few members as possible. Form a council in such a way that every member not in the council has something in common with the member in the council, that is, finding a minimum dominating set. The method for computing the youth development council is explained in Algorithm 6.4 1.

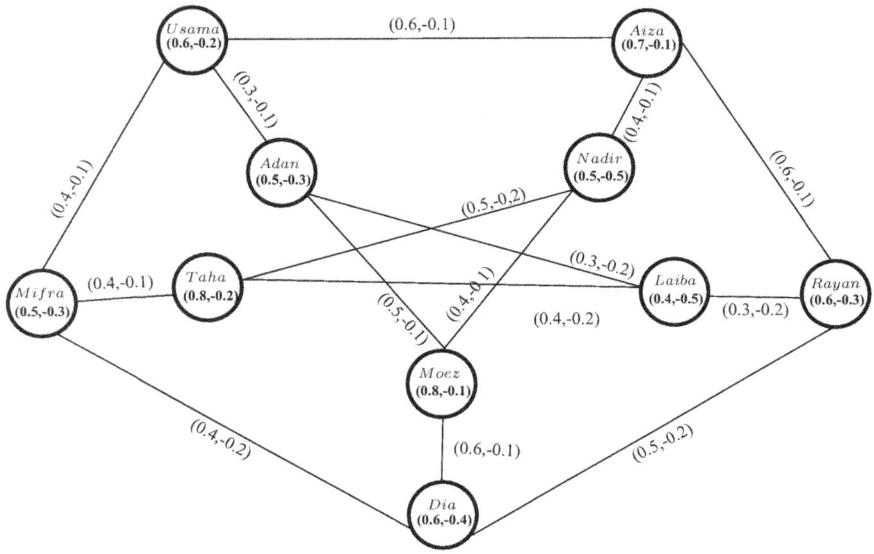

Fig. 6.16 Bipolar fuzzy graph of representatives

Algorithm 6.4.1 Computing the representative of youth development council.

1. Input the bipolar fuzzy A set of students $u_1, u_2, \ldots, u_n$.
2. Compute the bipolar fuzzy graph $G = (A, B)$ from given data.
3. Find the vertices u_i such that $\mu_B^p(u_i, u_j) = \min\{\mu_A^p(u_i), \mu_A^p(u_j)\}$ and $\mu_B^n(u_i, u_j) = \max\{\mu_A^n(u_i), \mu_A^n(u_j)\}, i \neq j$.
4. Form the set $S_i \subseteq X$ of vertices u_i.
5. If $\cup_j\{u_j\} = X - S_i$, then S_i is a dominating set otherwise, S_i is not a dominating set.
6. Repeat the steps from 3 to 5 and find all the dominating sets S_i of X.
7. The decision is S_i if S_i is a minimal dominating set.

Consider the example of a bipolar fuzzy graph as shown in Fig. 6.16.
The nodes of the bipolar fuzzy graph represent the students and their leadership qualities in terms of the positive membership degree and its counter property, bad leadership by a negative membership degree, e.g., Usama has 60% leadership qualities and lacks 20% leadership qualities. The edges of a bipolar fuzzy graph represent the common qualities between the students. The positive and negative degree of membership can be interpreted as the percentage of common leadership qualities and the qualities which are not common between the students, e.g., Usama and Aiza have 60% qualities in common but 10% qualities are different. From Fig. 6.16, it is clear that the dominating set of a bipolar fuzzy graph G is $S = \{Taha, Moez, Aiza, Mifra\}$ and it is also the minimal dominating set of G. The domination number of a bipolar fuzzy graph G is $\gamma(G) = 4$. Thus, Taha, Aiza, Moez, and Mifra are the members of a youth development council.

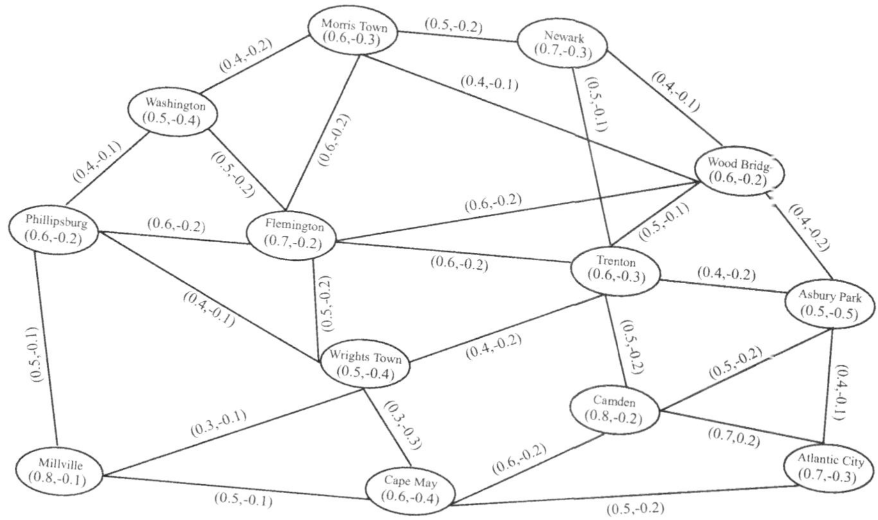

Fig. 6.17 Bipolar fuzzy graph of cities

6.4.3 *Transmission Tower Location Problem*

Consider the problem of locating transmission towers in selected cities so that the transmission can be broadcasted to all cities. The selection of the location of a transmission tower depends on many factors including the availability of electrical power, telecommunication network connectivity, etc. Also, for better transmission signals, it is necessary to avoid electromagnetic interferences. The strength of the transmission signal decreases as the distance between two towers increases. Since each transmission tower has a limited transmission range, there is a need to locate several transmission towers so that the transmission can reach to each city. But transmission towers are costly. Therefore, we want to locate as few transmission towers as possible.

This problem can be modeled by using a bipolar fuzzy graph, and an example is given in Fig. 6.17.

The vertices of the bipolar fuzzy graph represent the cities. The positive and the negative membership degrees of the vertices can be interpreted as the availability of electrical power and electromagnetic interferences, respectively, e.g., Washington has 50% availability of electrical power and 40% electromagnetic interferences. The edge between two cities indicates that a transmission from a tower at one of these cities reaches the other. The positive and the negative membership degree of the edges represent the transmission strength and transmission range, respectively. The problem is to find the minimum number of towers so that each city either has a tower or is a neighbor of a city that has a tower. This is equivalent to finding a minimum dominating set of locations that covers all the cities. By routine calculations, it is easy to see that the minimum dominating set is $S = \{Flemington, Newark, Millville, Camden\}$. Thus, it is sufficient to place the transmission towers at these four cities for better transmission coverage and minimum cost. The method for finding the desired set of cities is presented in Algorithm 6.4.2.

Algorithm 6.4.2

Transmission tower location problem

---

1 Begin
2 Input the set of locations(vertices) $X = \{a_1, a_2, \ldots, a_n\}$
3 Input the positive $\{u_i^p : i = 1, 2, 3, \ldots, n\}$ and negative $\{u_i^n : i = 1, 2, 3, \ldots, n\}$ membership values of vertices
4 Input the adjacency matrices $A^p = [u_{ij}^p]_{n\times n}$ and $A^n = [u_{ij}^n]_{n\times n}$ of positive and negative membership values
5 Take $S = \emptyset$ and $T = \emptyset$
6 **do** i from 1 to n
7 **do** j from 1 to n
8 **if**($i \neq j$ and $u_{ij}^p = \min\{u_i^p, u_j^p\}$, $u_{ij}^n = \max\{u_i^n, u_j^n\}$)**then**
9 $a_i \in S$ and $a_j \in T$
10 **end if**
11 **if**($S \cup T = X$)**then**
12 Print that S is a dominating set
13 goto step 19
14 **else if** ($i = n$)**then**
15 Print that there is no dominating set
16 **end if**
17 **end do**
18 **end do**
19 Stop

6.5 Conclusions

The term domination has a wide range of applications in graph theory for the analysis of bipolar fuzzy information. In this chapter, we have discussed different concepts of dominating and independent sets in bipolar fuzzy graphs and used these concepts to solve real-world problems for finding the minimum number of locations in any bipolar fuzzy network and a team of representatives for any organization. We have presented certain properties concerning the relationship of domination, total domination, and independence numbers in complete bipolar fuzzy graphs, complete bipartite bipolar fuzzy graphs, and products of bipolar fuzzy graphs. We have studied the notions of EN degree, equitable isolated vertices, private neighbors, irredundant sets, and irredundance number in bipolar fuzzy graphs and elaborated their relation with independence and domination numbers.

Exercises 6

Let $G_1 = (A_1, B_1)$ and $G_2 = (A_2, B_2)$ be two bipolar fuzzy graphs on X_1 and X_2, respectively, then prove or disprove the following statements.

1. If $D_1^{'}$ and $D_2^{'}$ are dominating sets of G_1 and G_2, then $d(G_1 \cup G_2) = d(G_1) + d(G_2) - |D_1^{'} \cap D_2^{'}|$.
2. If for $y_1 \in X_1$, $A_1(y_1) \neq (0, 0)$, and y_2 dominates z_2 in G_2, then (y_1, y_2) dominates (y_1, z_2) in $G_1 \Box G_2$.
3. If for $z_2 \in Y_2$, $A_2(z_2) \neq (0, 0)$, and y_1 dominates z_1 in G_1, then (y_1, z_2) dominates (z_1, z_2) in $G_1 \Box G_2$.
4. If $D_1^{'}$ and $D_2^{'}$ are minimal dominating sets of G_1 and G_2, respectively, then $D_1^{'} \times X_2$ and $X_1 \times D_2^{'}$ are dominating sets of $G_1 \Box G_2$ and $d(G_1 \Box G_2) \leq |D_1^{'} \times X_2| \wedge |X_1 \times D_2^{'}|$.
5. Let $D_1^{'}$ and $D_2^{'}$ be the dominating sets of G_1 and G_2, respectively, then $D_1^{'} \times D_2^{'}$ is a dominating set of the direct product $G_1 \times G_2$ and $d(G_1 \times G_2) = |D_1^{'} \times D_2^{'}|$.
6. If y_1 dominates z_1 in G_1 and y_2 dominates z_2 in G_2, then (y_1, z_1) dominates (y_2, z_2) in $G_1 \times G_2$.
7. If $X_1 \cap X_2 = \emptyset$, then $I(G_1 \cup G_2) = I(G_1) + I(G_2)$.
8. If N_1 and N_2 are maximal independent sets of G_1 and G_2, respectively, and $X_1 \cap X_2 = \emptyset$, then $I(G_1 \Box G_2) = |N_1 \times N_2| + |N|$, where $N = \{(y_i, z_i) : y_i \in X_1 \setminus N_1, z_i \in X_2 \setminus N_2, y_i y_{i+1} \in E_1, z_i z_{i+1} \in E_2, \quad i = 1, 2, 3, \ldots\}$.
9. If $D_1^{'}$ and $D_2^{'}$ are minimal dominating sets of G_1 and G_2, then $X_1 \times X_2 \setminus D_1^{'} \times D_2^{'}$ is a maximal independent set of $G_1 \times G_2$ and $I(G_1 \times G_2) = n_1 n_2 - d(G_1 \times G_2)$, where n_1 and n_2 are the number of vertices in G_1 and G_2, respectively.

References

1. Akram, M.: Bipolar fuzzy graphs. Inf. Sci. **181**(24), 5548–5564 (2011)
2. Akram, M.: Bipolar fuzzy graphs with applications. Knowl.-Based Syst. **39**, 1–8 (2013)
3. Akram, M., Dudek, W.A.: Regular bipolar fuzzy graphs. Neural Comput. Appl. **21**(supp 1), 197–205 (2012)
4. Akram, M., Alshehri, N., Davvaz, B., Ashraf, A.: Bipolar fuzzy digraphs in decision support systems. J. Multivalued Log. Soft Comput. **27**(5–6), 531–551 (2016)
5. Akram, M., Waseem, N.: Novel applications of bipolar fuzzy graphs to decision making problems. J. Appl. Math. Comput. **56**(1–2), 73–91 (2018)
6. Akram, M., Waseem, N.: Novel decision making method based on domination in m-polar fuzzy graphs. Commun. Korean Math. Soc. **32**(4), 1077–1097 (2017)
7. Akram, M., Waseem, N., Davvaz, B.: Certain types of domination in m-polar fuzzy graphs. J. Multivalued Log. Soft Comput. **29**(5), 619–646 (2017)

8. Bauer, D.B., Harary, F., Nieminen, J., Suffel, C.L.: Domination alteration sets in graphs. Discret. Math. **47**, 153–161 (1983)
9. Ball, W.W.R.: Mathematical Recreations and Problems of Past and Present Times. Macmillan and Company, New York (1892)
10. Cockayne, E.J., Favaron, O., Payan, C., Thomason, A.C.: Contribution to the theory of domination and irredundance in graphs. Discret. Math. **33**(3), 249–258 (1981)
11. De Jaenisch, C.F.: Applications de l'Analyse Mathematique an Jeu des Echecs (Applications of mathematical analysis in chess games). Petrograd (1862)
12. Guy, R.K.: Unsolved Problems in Number Theory, vol. 1. Springer, Berlin (1981)
13. Haynes, T.W., Hedetniemi, S., Slater, P.: Fundamentals of domination in graphs. CRC Press, Boca Raton (2013)
14. Karunambigai, M.G., Akram, M., Palanivel, K., Sivasankar, S.: Domination in bipolar fuzzy graphs. In: IEEE International Conference on Fuzzy Systems (FUZZ-IEEE), pp. 1–6 (2013)
15. Nagoorgani, A., Chandrasekaran, V.T.: Domination in fuzzy graphs. Adv. Fuzzy Sets Syst. **I**(1), 17–26 (2006)
16. Nagoorgani, A., Vadivel, P.: Fuzzy independent dominating set. Adv. Fuzzy Sets Syst. **2**(1), 99–108 (2007)
17. Ore, O.: Theory of Graphs, vol. 38. American Mathematical Society Publications, Providence (1962)
18. Parvathi, R., Thamizhendhi, G.: Domination in intuitionistic fuzzy graphs. Notes Intuit. Fuzzy Sets **16**(2), 39–49 (2010)
19. Somasundaram, A., Somasundaram, S.: Domination in fuzzy graphs. Pattern Recognit. Lett. **19**(9), 787–791 (1998)
20. Zhang, W.-R.: (YinYang) Bipolar fuzzy sets. In: IEEE International Conference on Fuzzy Systems, pp. 835–840 (1998)

Chapter 7
Bipolar Fuzzy Circuits

In this chapter, we discuss the notions of bipolar fuzzy rank function, bipolar fuzzy vector spaces, bipolar fuzzy basis, bipolar fuzzy matroids, bipolar fuzzy circuits, and describe certain characterizations concerning the linear independence of linear bipolar fuzzy matroids, uniform bipolar fuzzy matroids, partition bipolar fuzzy matroids, and cycle bipolar fuzzy matroids. We establish the relation of crisp matroids and bipolar fuzzy matroids using $(\alpha, \beta)-$cuts. We study the concepts of closure of bipolar fuzzy matroids, $\mathcal{M}-$induced matroid sequence, fundamental sequence, circuit rectangles, and put special emphasis on bipolar fuzzy circuits. We also introduce the concepts of matroids and circuits in a soft environment and bipolar fuzzy soft environment. We present certain applications of bipolar fuzzy matroids and bipolar fuzzy soft matroids in decision support systems and network analysis. The main results of this chapter are from [25].

7.1 Introduction

Matroid theory laid down its foundations in 1935 after the work of Whitney [28]. This theory constitutes a useful approach for linking major ideas of linear algebra, graph theory, combinatorics, and many other areas of Mathematics. Matroid theory has been a focus for active research during the last few decades. The resurgence of work in combinatorics during the last few decades has resulted in an increased interest in matroids, and matroid theory remains a focus for much active research. In 1988, Goetschel [10] presented the approach of fuzzification to matroid theory and discussed the uncertain behavior of matroids. The same authors introduced the concept of bases of fuzzy matroids, fuzzy matroid structures and greedy algorithm in fuzzy matroids, fuzzy circuits, fuzzy rank functions and fuzzy matroid sums in [10–16]. Hsueh [17] proposed one possible fuzzification of matroids which entended the independence axioms of matroids from set systems to fuzzy set systems and

M. Akram et al., *Graphs for the Analysis of Bipolar Fuzzy Information*, Studies in Fuzziness and Soft Computing 401,
https://doi.org/10.1007/978-981-15-8756-6_7

preserves the most basic properties of matroids. Novak [20] presented two assertions concerning a regular pair of crisp matroids in order to clarify an important step of the proof of Lemma 2.5 of the paper by Goetschel and Voxman [11]. Novak [21, 22] also presented the concepts of fuzzy pre-independence set system, fuzzy independence set system, fuzzy pre-matroid, and hereditary fuzzy pre-matroid. Shi [26, 27] generalized the concept of closed fuzzy pre-matroids to L-fuzzy set theory when L is a complete lattice, called L-fuzzifying matroid and (L, M)-fuzzy matroid. It comes as no surprise that bipolarity in data and information plays a vital role in various fields of science and technology. As an extension of the fuzzy set theory, Zhang [30] introduced the theory of bipolar fuzzy sets (also known as YinYang bipolar fuzzy sets, where Yang depicts the positive side while Yin represents the negative side in a system), which illustrate the bipolar behavior of objects. The coexistence, equilibrium, and harmony of the two sides are considered a key for the mental and physical health of a person as well as for the stability and prosperity of a social system. In recent years, bipolar fuzzy sets seem to have been studied and applied a bit enthusiastically and a bit increasingly. The concept of bipolar fuzzy sets was applied to graphs in [2, 3, 5, 7]. The idea of bipolar fuzzy matroids and bipolar fuzzy circuits is discussed in [25] with a number of real-world applications in decision support systems.

7.2 Bipolar Fuzzy Circuits

In this section, the notion of bipolar fuzzy vector spaces, bipolar fuzzy matroids, and bipolar fuzzy circuits is given with certain properties. The term crisp matroid has various equivalent definitions but we are using here the simplest definition of a matroid.

Definition 7.1 If X is a non-empty set and I is any subset of $P(X)$, the power set of X, satisfying the following conditions:

1. If $B_1 \in I$ and $B_2 \subset B_1$, then $B_2 \in I$,

2. If $B_1, B_2 \in I$ and $|B_1| < |B_2|$, then there exists $B_3 \in I$ such that $B_1 \subset B_3 \subseteq B_1 \cup B_2$,

then the pair $M = (X, I)$ is called a **matroid** and I is known as the family of **independent subsets** of M.

Definition 7.2 If $M = (X, I)$ is a matroid, then the mapping $R : P(X) \to \{0, 1, 2, \ldots, |X|\}$ defined by

$$R(B) = \max\{|E| | E \subseteq B, E \in I\}$$

is a **rank function** for M. If $B \in P(X)$, R is known as the rank of B.

Definition 7.3 A **bipolar fuzzy set** A on a non-empty set X is an object of the form $A = \{(x, \mu_A^p(x), \mu_A^n(x)) \mid x \in X\}$, where $\mu_A^p : X \to [0, 1]$ and $\mu_A^n : X \to [-1, 0]$ are mappings.

The positive membership degree $\mu_A^p(x)$ denotes the truth or satisfaction degree of an element x to a certain property corresponding to the bipolar fuzzy set, A and $\mu_A^n(x)$ represents the satisfaction degree of an element x to some counter property of the bipolar fuzzy set A. If $\mu_A^n(x) \neq 0$ and $\mu_A^p(x) = 0$, it is the situation that x is not satisfying the property of A but satisfying the counter property to A. If $\mu_A^p(x) \neq 0$ and $\mu_A^n(x) = 0$, it is the case when x has only positive satisfaction for A. It is possible for x to be such that $\mu_A^p(x) \neq 0$ and $\mu_A^n(x) \neq 0$ when x satisfies the property of A as well as its counter property in some part of X.

Definition 7.4 Let A be a bipolar fuzzy set on a non-empty set X. A **bipolar fuzzy relation** B on A is a mapping $B : A \to A$ such that

$$\mu_B^p(xy) \leq \mu_A^p(x) \wedge \mu_A^p(y) \quad \text{and} \quad \mu_B^n(xy) \geq \mu_A^n(x) \vee \mu_A^n(y), \qquad \text{for all } x, y \in X.$$

B is also a bipolar fuzzy relation in X defined by the mapping $B : X \times X \to [0, 1] \times [-1, 0]$.

Definition 7.5 The **support** of a bipolar fuzzy set $A = (\mu_A^p, \mu_A^n)$ is denoted by $supp(A)$ and defined as $\text{supp}(A) = supp^p(A) \cup supp^n(A)$, where $supp^p(A) = \{x \mid \mu_A^p(x) > 0\}$, $supp^n(A) = \{x \mid \mu_A^n(x) < 0\}$. We call $supp^p(A)$ as **positive support** and $supp^n(A)$ as **negative support**.

Definition 7.6 Let $A = (\mu_A^p, \mu_A^n)$ be a bipolar fuzzy set on X and $\alpha \in [0, 1]$. The α**-cut** of a bipolar fuzzy set A is denoted by A_α and defined as $A_\alpha = A_\alpha^p \cup A_\alpha^n$, where $A_\alpha^p = \{x \mid \mu_\alpha^p(x) \geq \alpha\}$, $A_\alpha^n = \{x \mid \mu_\alpha^n(x) \leq -\alpha\}$. We call A_α^p as positive α-cut and A_α^n as negative α-cut. The **height** of a bipolar fuzzy set $A = (\mu_A^p, \mu_A^n)$ is defined as $h(A) = \max\{\mu_A^p(x) | x \in X\}$. The **depth** of a bipolar fuzzy set $A = (\mu_A^p, \mu_A^n)$ is defined as $d(A) = \min\{\mu_A^n(x) | x \in X\}$.

Definition 7.7 A **bipolar polar fuzzy graph** on a non-empty set X is a pair $G = (A, B)$, where $A : X \to [0, 1] \times [-1, 0]$ is a bipolar fuzzy set on the set of vertices X and $B : X \times X \to [0, 1] \times [-1, 0]$ is a bipolar polar fuzzy relation in X such that

$$\mu_B^p(xy) \leq \mu_A^p(x) \wedge \mu_A^p(y) \text{ and } \mu_B^n(xy) \geq \mu_A^n(x) \vee \mu_A^n(y), \qquad \text{for all } x, y \in X.$$

Note that $B(xy) = (0, 0)$ for all $xy \in X \times X - E$, where $E \subseteq X \times X$ is the set of edges. A is called a bipolar fuzzy vertex set of G, and B is a bipolar fuzzy edge set of G. A bipolar fuzzy relation B on A is **symmetric** if $B(xy) = B(yx)$ for all $x, y \in X$.

Example 7.1 Let A be a bipolar fuzzy set on the set of vertices $X = \{x_1, x_2, x_3\}$ and B be a bipolar fuzzy relation in X as shown in Tables 7.1 and 7.2, respectively. The bipolar fuzzy graph $G = (A, B)$ is shown in Fig. 7.1.

Table 7.1 Bipolar fuzzy set A on $\{x_1, x_2, x_3\}$

A	x_1	x_2	x_3
$\mu_A^p(x)$	0.5	0.6	0.7
$\mu_A^n(x)$	−0.4	−0.5	−0.7

Table 7.2 Bipolar fuzzy relation B in $\{x_1, x_2, x_3\}$

B	x_1	x_2	x_3
x_1	(0,0)	(0.2,−0.3)	(0.2,−0.3)
x_2	(0.2,−0.3)	(0,0)	(0.6,−0.4)
x_3	(0.2,−0.3)	(0.6,−0.4)	(0,0)

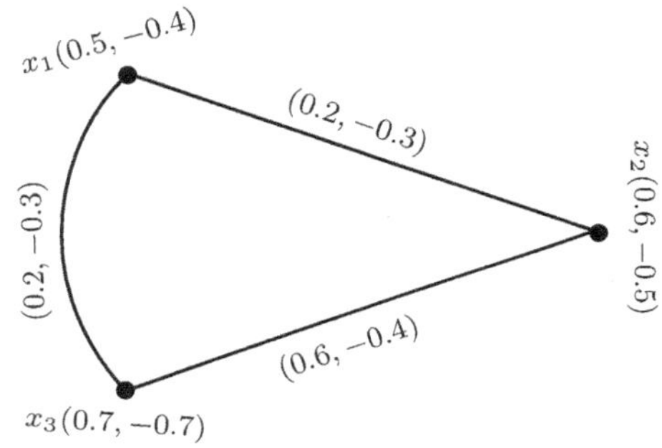

Fig. 7.1 Bipolar fuzzy graph

Definition 7.8 The **order** or **cardinality** of a bipolar fuzzy set $A = (\mu^p, \mu^n)$, on a non-empty set X, is defined as $|A| = (|A|^p, |A|^n) = \sum_{x \in X} \left(\mu_A^p(x), \mu_A^n(x)\right)$.

Definition 7.9 Let $(t^p, t^n), (r^p, r^n) \in [0, 1] \times [-1, 0]$ be two ordered pairs, then we denote $(t^p, t^n) < (r^p, r^n)$ if $t^p < r^p$ and $t^n > r^n$. If A and B are two bipolar fuzzy sets, then
1. $|A| < |B|$ if $|A|^p < |B|^p$ and $|A|^n > |B|^n$,
2. $|A| \leq |B|$ if $|A|^p \leq |B|^p$ and $|A|^n \geq |B|^n$.

Definition 7.10 Let $G = (A, B)$ be a bipolar fuzzy graph on X and $(\alpha, \beta) \in [0, 1] \times [-1, 0]$. Define (α, β)**-cut** of a bipolar fuzzy set A as $A_{(\alpha,\beta)} = \{x \in X \mid \mu_A^p(x) \geq \alpha, \mu_A^n(x) \leq \beta\}$. The crisp graph $G_{(\alpha,\beta)} = (A_{(\alpha,\beta)}, B_{(\alpha,\beta)})$ is called an (α, β)-level graph of G, where $B_{(\alpha,\beta)} = \left\{xy \in E \mid \mu_B^p(xy) \geq \alpha, \mu_B^n(xy) \leq \beta\right\}$ is (α, β)-cut of B.

Definition 7.11 Let β be any bipolar fuzzy set on X and $\boldsymbol{t} = (t^p, t^n)$, $t^p \in [0, 1]$, $t^n \in [-1, 0]$, then

$$\beta_t = \{y \in X \mid \mu^p_\beta(y) \geq t^p, \mu^n_\beta(y) \leq t^n\},$$
$$R^p(\beta) = \{\mu^p_\beta(y) \mid \mu^p_\beta(y) > 0\},$$
$$R^n(\beta) = \{\mu^n_\beta(y) \mid \mu^n_\beta(y) < 0\}.$$

Definition 7.12 A **bipolar fuzzy vector space** over a field F is defined as a pair (X, B), where $B = (\mu^p_B, \mu^n_B) : X \to [0, 1] \times [-1, 0]$ is a mapping and X is a vector space over F such that for all $c, d \in F$ and $y, z \in X$,

$$\mu^p_B(cy + dz) \geq \min\{\mu^p_B(y), \mu^p_B(z)\},$$
$$\mu^n_B(cy + dz) \leq \max\{\mu^n_B(y), \mu^n_B(z)\}.$$

Example 7.2 Let X be a vector space of 2×1 column vectors over $\mathbb{E}$. Define a mapping $B : X \to [0, 1] \times [-1, 0]$ such that for each $z = \begin{bmatrix} x & y \end{bmatrix}'$,

$$B(z) = \begin{cases} (1, -1), & z = \begin{bmatrix} 0 & 0 \end{bmatrix}' \\ (\frac{1}{3}, -\frac{2}{3}), & z = \begin{bmatrix} x & 0 \end{bmatrix}' \text{ or } z = \begin{bmatrix} 0 & y \end{bmatrix}' \\ (1, -1), & x \neq 0 \text{ and } y \neq 0 \end{cases}.$$

First show that (X, B) is a bipolar fuzzy vector space. For $z = \begin{bmatrix} 0 & 0 \end{bmatrix}'$, the case is trivial. So the following cases are to be discussed.

Case 1: Consider two column vectors $z = \begin{bmatrix} x & y \end{bmatrix}'$ and $\boldsymbol{u} = \begin{bmatrix} u & v \end{bmatrix}'$, then for any scalars c and d,

$$B(cz + d\boldsymbol{u}) = B\left(\begin{bmatrix} cx + du \\ cy + dv \end{bmatrix}\right).$$

If either exactly one of c or d is zero or both are non-zero, then $cx + du \neq 0$ and $cy + dv \neq 0$ and so $\mu^p_B(cz + d\boldsymbol{u}) = 1 \geq \min\{\mu^p_B(z), \mu^p_B(\boldsymbol{u})\}$ and $\mu^n_B(cz + d\boldsymbol{u}) = -1 \leq \max\{\mu^n_B(z), \mu^n_B(\boldsymbol{u})\}$.

Case 2: If $z = \begin{bmatrix} x & 0 \end{bmatrix}'$ and $\boldsymbol{u} = \begin{bmatrix} 0 & v \end{bmatrix}'$, then $B(cz + d\boldsymbol{u}) = B(\begin{bmatrix} cx & dv \end{bmatrix}')$. If both c and d are non-zero, then

$$\mu^p_B(cz + d\boldsymbol{u}) = 1 > \min\{\mu^p_B(z), \mu^p_B(\boldsymbol{u})\} \quad \text{and}$$
$$\mu^n_B(cz + d\boldsymbol{u}) = -1 < \max\{\mu^n_B(z), \mu^n_B(\boldsymbol{u})\}.$$

If exactly one of c or d is zero, then

$$\mu^p_B(cz + d\boldsymbol{u}) = \frac{1}{3} = \min\{\mu^p_B(z), \mu^p_B(\boldsymbol{u})\} \quad \text{and}$$
$$\mu^n_B(cz + d\boldsymbol{u}) = -\frac{2}{3} = \max\{\mu^n_B(z), \mu^n_B(\boldsymbol{u})\}.$$

Hence, (X, B) is a bipolar fuzzy vector space.

Definition 7.13 Let (X, B) be a bipolar fuzzy vector space over F. A set of vectors $\{y_k\}_{k=1}^n$ is known as **bipolar fuzzy linearly independent** in (X, B) if

1. $\{y_k\}_{k=1}^n$ is linearly independent,
2. $B(\sum_{k=1}^{n} c_k y_k) = (\bigwedge_{k=1}^{n} \mu_B^p(c_k y_k), \bigvee_{k=1}^{n} \mu_B^n(c_k y_k))$, for all $\{c_k\}_{k=1}^n \subset F$ and distinct $y_i \in X$, $1 \le i \le n$.

Definition 7.14 A set of vectors $\mathcal{B} = \{y_k\}_{k=1}^n$ is said to be a **bipolar fuzzy basis** in (X, B) if condition 2 of Definition 7.13 holds and $\mathcal{B}$ is a basis in X.

Proposition 7.1 *If (X, B) is a bipolar fuzzy vector space, then any set of vectors with distinct positive and negative degrees of membership is linearly independent and bipolar fuzzy linearly independent.*

Proof This proposition can be proved by induction on the number of vectors, n, with distinct degree of membership. For $n = 1$, $\{y_1\}$, the statement is trivial. Assume that the statement is true for k vectors. Let $\{y_j\}_{j=1}^{k+1}$ be the set of vectors with distinct positive and negative degrees of membership. Suppose $\{y_j\}_{j=1}^{k+1}$ are not linearly independent and hence not bipolar fuzzy linearly independent. Then there exist scalars $c_1, c_2, \ldots, c_k$ such that $y_{k+1} = \sum_{j=1}^{k} c_j y_j$ and

$$B(y_{k+1}) = \left(\bigwedge_{j=1}^{k} \mu_B^p(c_j y_j), \bigvee_{j=1}^{k} \mu_B^n(c_j y_j)\right) = (\bigwedge_{j=1}^{k} \mu_B^p(y_j), \bigvee_{j=1}^{k} \mu_B^n(y_j)).$$

It clearly shows that $\mu_B^p(y_{k+1}) \in \{\mu_B^p(y_j)\}_{j=1}^k$ and $\mu_B^n(y_{k+1}) \in \{\mu_B^n(y_j)\}_{j=1}^k$, a contradiction to the fact that y_{k+1} has distinct positive and negative degrees of membership. Thus, $\{y_j\}_{j=1}^{k+1}$ are linearly independent. The bipolar fuzzy linear independence of the vectors can be proved similarly.

Proposition 7.2 *Let (X, B) be a bipolar fuzzy vector space, then*

1. $B(0) = (\max_{y\in X} \mu_B^p(y), \min_{y\in X} \mu_B^n(y))$,
2. $B(ay) = B(y)$ *for all* $a \in F \setminus \{0\}$ *and* $y \in X$,
3. *If* $B(y) \neq B(z)$ *for some* $y, z \in X$, *then* $B(y + z) = (\mu_B^p(y) \wedge \mu_B^p(z), \mu_B^n(y) \vee \mu_B^n(z))$.

Proof The proof of conditions 7.2.1 and 7.2.3 is enough.
1. For any $y \in X$, $B(0) = B(0y) = (\mu_B^p(0y), \mu_B^n(0y))$. By Definition 7.12, $\mu_B^p(0) = \mu_B^p(0y) \ge \mu_B^p(y)$, for every $y \in X$. Hence, $\mu_B^p(0) = \max_{y\in X} \mu_B^p(y)$. Similarly, it can be proved that $\mu_B^n(0) = \min_{y\in X} \mu_B^n(y)$.
3. Suppose for $y, z \in X$, $B(y) \neq B(z)$. Without loss of generality, assume that $\mu_B^p(y) > \mu_B^p(z)$. By Definition 7.12, $\mu_B^p(y + z) \ge \mu_B^p(y) \wedge \mu_B^p(z) = \mu_B^p(z)$. Also, $\mu_B^p(z) = \mu_B^p((y + z) - y) \ge \mu_B^p(y + z) \wedge \mu_B^p(y) = \mu_B^p(y + z)$. Hence, $\mu_B^p(y + z) = \mu_B^p(z)$. Other cases can be proved similarly.

Remark 7.1 If $\mathcal{B}$ is a bipolar fuzzy basis of (X, B), then the membership value of every element of X can be calculated from the membership values of basis elements, i.e., if $u = \sum_{k=1}^{n} c_k u_k$, then

$$B(u) = B\left(\sum_{k=1}^{n} c_k u_k\right) = \left(\bigwedge_{k=1}^{n} \mu_B^p(c_k u_k), \bigvee_{k=1}^{n} \mu_B^n(c_k u_k)\right)$$
$$= \left(\bigwedge_{k=1}^{n} \mu_B^p(u_k), \bigvee_{k=1}^{n} \mu_B^n(u_k)\right).$$

Definition 7.15 Let X be a non-empty finite set and $\mathcal{I} \subseteq \mathcal{BF}(X)$ be a family of bipolar fuzzy subsets; $\mathcal{BF}(X)$ is a bipolar fuzzy power set of X, satisfying the following conditions.

1. If $\beta_1 \in \mathcal{I}$, $\beta_2 \in \mathcal{BF}(X)$, and $\beta_2 \subset \beta_1$, then $\beta_2 \in \mathcal{I}$.
2. If $\beta_1, \beta_2 \in \mathcal{I}$ and $|supp(\beta_1)| < |supp(\beta_2)|$, then there exists $\beta_3 \in \mathcal{I}$ such that
   $a.$ $\beta_1 \subset \beta_3 \subseteq \beta_1 \cup \beta_2$,
   $b.$ $m^p(\beta_3) \geq \min\{m^p(\beta_1), m^p(\beta_2)\}$, $m^p(\beta_i) = \min\{\mu_{\beta_i}^p(y) | y \in supp(\beta_i)\}$, $i = 1, 2, 3$,
   $c.$ $m^n(\beta_3) \leq \max\{m^n(\beta_1), m^n(\beta_2)\}$, $m^n(\beta_i) = \max\{\mu_{\beta_i}^n(y) | y \in supp(\beta_i)\}$, $i = 1, 2, 3$.

Then the pair $\mathcal{M}(X) = (X, \mathcal{I})$ is called a **bipolar fuzzy matroid** on X, and $\mathcal{I}$ is a family of **independent bipolar fuzzy subsets** of $\mathcal{M}(X)$.

Note 7.1 $\{\alpha : \alpha \in \mathcal{BF}(X), \alpha \notin \mathcal{I}\}$ is the family of dependent bipolar fuzzy subsets in $\mathcal{M}(X)$. A minimal dependent bipolar fuzzy set is called a **bipolar fuzzy circuit**. Equivalently, a bipolar fuzzy set $\alpha \in \mathcal{BF}(X)$ is a bipolar fuzzy circuit in $\mathcal{M}$ if $\alpha \notin \mathcal{I}$ and $\beta \in \mathcal{I}$ for each $\beta \subset \alpha$. The family of all bipolar fuzzy circuits is represented by $C_r(\mathcal{M})$. A bipolar fuzzy $n-$circuit is a bipolar fuzzy circuit which has n number of elements. Since the elements of $\mathcal{I}$ are those members of $\mathcal{BF}(X)$ which are mutually disjoint with the members of $C_r(\mathcal{M})$, a bipolar fuzzy matroid can be uniquely determined from $C_r(\mathcal{M})$.

Definition 7.16 Let X be a non-empty universe. For any bipolar fuzzy matroid, the **bipolar fuzzy rank function** $\lambda_r : \mathcal{BF}(X) \to [0, \infty) \times (-\infty, 0]$ is defined as

$$\lambda_r(\beta) = \left(\lambda_r^p(\beta), \lambda_r^n(\beta)\right) = \left(\max_{\gamma \subseteq \beta} |\gamma|^p, \min_{\gamma \subseteq \beta} |\gamma|^n\right),$$

where $\beta \in \mathcal{I}$. Clearly, the bipolar fuzzy rank function of a bipolar fuzzy matroid possesses the following properties.

1. If $\beta_1, \beta_2 \in \mathcal{BF}(X)$ and $\beta_1 \subseteq \beta_2$, then $\lambda_r^p(\beta_1) \leq \lambda_r^p(\beta_2)$ and $\lambda_r^n(\beta_1) \geq \lambda_r^n(\beta_2)$,
2. If $\beta \in \mathcal{BF}(X)$, then $\lambda_r^p(\beta) \leq |\beta|^p$ and $\lambda_r^n(\beta) \geq |\beta|^n$,
3. If $\beta \in \mathcal{I}$, then $\lambda_r(\beta) = |\beta|$.

The concept of certain types of bipolar fuzzy matroids is described in the following examples.

Example 7.3 A simple example of a bipolar fuzzy matroid, known as a **uniform bipolar fuzzy matroid** is defined as $\mathcal{I} = \{\beta \in \mathcal{BF}(X) \mid |supp(\beta)| \leq k\}$. If $|X| = n$ and k is any positive integer, then the uniform bipolar fuzzy matroid is denoted by $\mathcal{U}_{k,n} = (X, \mathcal{I})$. The bipolar fuzzy circuit of $\mathcal{U}_{k,n}$ is a bipolar fuzzy subset β such that $|supp(\beta)| = k + 1$.

Consider the example of a uniform bipolar fuzzy matroid $\mathcal{M} = (X, \mathcal{I})$, where $X = \{e_1, e_2, e_3\}$ and $\mathcal{I} = \{\beta \in \mathcal{BF}(X) : |supp(\beta)| \leq 2\}$ such that for any $\beta \in \mathcal{BF}(X)$, $\beta(y) = \tau(y)$, for all $y \in X$, where

$$\tau(y) = \begin{cases} (0.2, -0.3), & y = e_1 \\ (0.4, -0.5), & y = e_2 \\ (0.1, -0.3), & y = e_3 \end{cases}.$$

$$\begin{aligned}\mathcal{I} =\{&\emptyset, \{(e_1, 0.2, -0.3)\}, \{(e_2, 0.4, -0.5)\}, \{(e_3, 0.1, -0.3)\}, \{(e_1, 0.2, -0.3), (e_2, 0.4, -0.5)\},\\ &\{(e_2, 0.4, -0.5), (e_3, 0.1, -0.3)\}, \{(e_1, 0.2, -0.3), (e_3, 0.1, -0.3)\}\}. \end{aligned} \tag{7.1}$$

The bipolar fuzzy circuit of $\mathcal{M}$ is $\{(e_1, 0.2, -0.3), (e_2, 0.4, -0.5), (e_3, 0.1, -0.3)\}$. For $\beta = \{(e_2, 0.4, -0.5), (e_1, 0.2, -0.3)\}$, $\lambda_r(\beta) = (0.6, -0.8)$.

Example 7.4 A bipolar fuzzy matroid derived from a bipolar fuzzy matrix is called a **linear bipolar fuzzy matroid**. If X is the set of all column labels of a bipolar fuzzy matrix and β_x represents a bipolar fuzzy submatrix having those columns which are labeled by X, then the bipolar fuzzy linear matroid is defined as $\mathcal{I} = \{\beta_x \in \mathcal{BF}(X) \mid$ columns of β_x are bipolar fuzzy linearly independent$\}$, $\mathcal{BF}(X)$ is the power set of all bipolar fuzzy submatrices labeled by elements in X. For any $\beta_x \in \mathcal{BF}(X)$,

$$|\beta_x| = \sum_{k=1}^{r} \left(\sup_{i=1}^{c} \mu^p_{\beta_x}(a_{ki}), \inf_{i=1}^{c} \mu^n_{\beta_x}(a_{ki}) \right), \beta_x = [a_{ij}]_{r \times c}.$$

Let $X = \{\mathbf{1}, \mathbf{2}, \mathbf{3}, \mathbf{4}\}$ be a set of column labels of bipolar fuzzy 2×1 vectors over $\mathbb{R}$ such that for any $\beta_x \in \mathcal{BF}(X)$, $\beta_x(y) = A(y)$, where

$$A = \begin{bmatrix} \mathbf{1} & \mathbf{2} & \mathbf{3} & \mathbf{4} \\ (0.2, -0.3) & (0.4, -0.5) & (0.6, -0.7) & (0.8, -0.9) \\ (0.3, -0.4) & (0.5, -0.6) & (0.7, -0.8) & (0.9, -1.0) \end{bmatrix}.$$

Take $\mathcal{I} = \{\emptyset, \{\mathbf{1}\}, \{\mathbf{2}\}, \{\mathbf{4}\}, \{\mathbf{1}, \mathbf{2}\}, \{\mathbf{2}, \mathbf{4}\}\}$, then $\mathcal{M}(A) = (A, \mathcal{I})$ is a bipolar fuzzy matroid on X. The family of dependent bipolar fuzzy subsets of $\mathcal{M}(A)$ is $\{\{\mathbf{3}\}, \{\mathbf{1}, \mathbf{3}\}, \{\mathbf{1}, \mathbf{4}\}, \{\mathbf{2}, \mathbf{3}\}, \{\mathbf{3}, \mathbf{4}\}\} \cup \{\eta : \eta \subseteq A, |supp(\eta)| \geq 3\}$. For $\beta = \{\mathbf{2}, \mathbf{4}\}$, $\mu_r(\beta) = (1.7, -1.9)$.

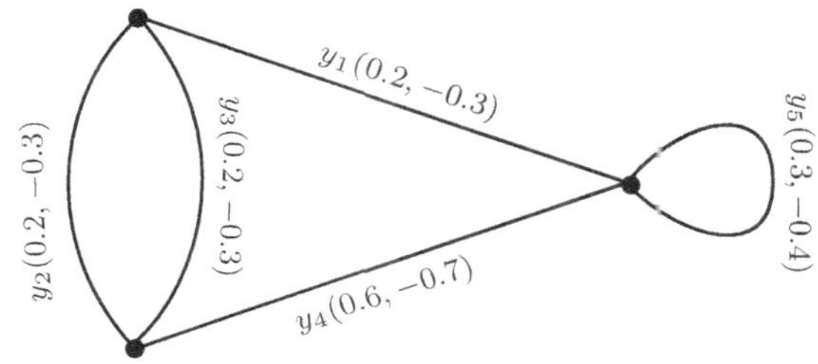

Fig. 7.2 3−polar fuzzy multigraph

Example 7.5 A bipolar fuzzy matroid in which the universe X is partitioned into sets $\delta_1, \delta_2, \ldots, \delta_r$ such that $\mathcal{I} = \{\beta \in \mathcal{BF}(X) \mid |supp(\beta) \cap \delta_i| \leq l_i,$ for all $1 \leq i \leq r\}$ for given positive integers $l_1, l_2, \ldots, l_r$ is called a **partition bipolar fuzzy matroid**. The circuit of a partition bipolar fuzzy matroid is a bipolar fuzzy subset α such that $|supp(\alpha) \cap \delta_i| = l_i + 1$.

Example 7.6 A significant class of bipolar fuzzy matroids derived from bipolar fuzzy graphs is known as a **cycle bipolar fuzzy matroid**. The detail is illustrated in Proposition 7.3. The cycle bipolar fuzzy matroid derived using Proposition 7.3 is denoted by $\mathcal{M} = (X, \mathcal{I})$, where $X = \{y_1, y_2, \ldots, y_n\}$ is the set of edges and $\mathcal{I}$ is defined as $\mathcal{I} = \{\beta \in \mathcal{BF}(X) \mid \beta$ is a bipolar fuzzy set on $U \subseteq X\}$. Clearly, $\beta \in \mathcal{I}$ is an independent set of $\mathcal{M}(G)$ if and only if $supp(\beta)$ is not the set of edges of any crisp cycle. Alternatively, the elements of $\mathcal{M}$ are bipolar fuzzy graphs β such that $supp(\beta)$ is a crisp forest.

As an example, consider a cycle bipolar fuzzy matroid $(X, \mathcal{I})$, where $X = \{y_1, y_2, y_3, y_4, y_5\}$ and for any $\beta \in \mathcal{I}$, $\beta(y) = D(y)$, (C, D) is a bipolar fuzzy multigraph with edge set X as shown in Fig. 7.2.

By Proposition 7.3, $C_r(\mathcal{M}) = \{\{(y_5, 0.3, -0, 4)\}, \{(y_2, 0.2, -0.3)\ (y_3, 0.2, -0.3)\}, \{(y_1, 0.2, -0.3), (y_2, 0.2, -0.3), (y_4, 0.6, -0.7)\}, \{(y_1, 0.2, -0.3), (y_3, 0.2, -0.3)\}\}$.
$\mathcal{I} = \{\emptyset, \{(y_1, 0.2, -0.3)\}, \{(y_2, , 0.2, -0.3)\}, \{(y_3, 0.2, -0.3)\}, \{(y_4, 0.6, -0.7)\}, \{(y_1, 0.2, -0.3), (y_2, 0.2, -0.3)\}, \{(y_1, 0.2, -0.3), (y_4, 0.6, -0.7)\}\ \{(y_2, 0.2, -0.3), (y_4, 0.6, -0.7)\}, \{(y_1, 0.2, -0.3), (y_3, 0.2, -0.3)\}, \{(y_3, 0.2, -0.3), (y_4, 0.6, -0.7)\}\}$.
For $\beta = \{(y_2, 0.2, -0.3), (y_4, 0.6, -0.7)\}$, $\lambda_r(\beta) = (0.8, -1.0)$.

Proposition 7.3 *For any bipolar fuzzy matroid $(X, \mathcal{I})$, if $C_r(\mathcal{M})$ is the class of bipolar fuzzy edge sets α such that $supp(\alpha)$ is the set of edges of a cycle, then $C_r(\mathcal{M})$ is the class of bipolar fuzzy circuits on $\mathcal{M}$.*

Example 7.7 For any bipolar fuzzy graph $G = (C, D)$ and $\boldsymbol{t} = (t^p, t^n), 0 \leq t^p \leq 1$, $-1 \leq t^n \leq 0$ define
$E_t = \{yz \in supp(D) | \mu_D^p(yz) > t^p, \mu_D^n(yz) < t^n\}$,
$F_t = \{F \mid F$ is a forest in the crisp graph $(X, E_t)\}$,
$\mathcal{I}_t = \{E(F) | F \in F_t\}$, where $E(F)$ is the edge set of F.
Then $(E_t, \mathcal{I}_t)$ is a matroid for each $\boldsymbol{t}$.

Define $\mathcal{J} = \{\beta \in \mathcal{BF}(X) | \beta_t \in \mathcal{I}_t$, for each $\boldsymbol{t} = (t^p, t^n), 0 \le t^p \le 1, -1 \le t^n \le 0\}$, then $(X, \mathcal{J})$ is a cycle bipolar fuzzy matroid.

Theorem 7.1 *Let* $\mathcal{M} = (X, \mathcal{I})$ *be a bipolar fuzzy matroid and, for each* $\boldsymbol{t} = (t^p, t^n), 0 \le t^p \le 1, -1 \le t^n \le 0$, *define* $\mathcal{I}_t = \{\beta_t \mid \beta \in \mathcal{I}\}$. *Then* $(X, \mathcal{I}_t)$ *is a matroid on* X.

Proof We prove conditions 1 and 2 of Definition 7.1. Assume that $\beta_{1t} \in \mathcal{I}_t$ and $\alpha \subseteq \beta_{1t}$. Define a bipolar fuzzy set $\beta_2 \in \mathcal{BF}(X)$ as

$$\beta_2(y) = \begin{cases} \boldsymbol{t}, & y \in \alpha \\ (0, 0), & \text{otherwise} \end{cases}.$$

Clearly, $\beta_2 \subseteq \beta_1$, $\beta_2 \in \mathcal{I}$, and $\beta_{2t} = \alpha$, therefore $\alpha \in \mathcal{I}_t$. To prove condition 2, let $\alpha_1, \alpha_2 \in \mathcal{I}_t$ and $|\alpha_1| < |\alpha_2|$. Then there exist β_1 and β_2 such that $\beta_{1t} = \alpha_1$ and $\beta_{2t} = \alpha_2$. Define $\hat{\beta}_1$ and $\hat{\beta}_2$ as

$$\hat{\beta}_1(y) = \begin{cases} \boldsymbol{t}, & y \in \alpha_1 \\ (0, 0), & \text{otherwise} \end{cases} \quad \hat{\beta}_2(y) = \begin{cases} \boldsymbol{t}, & y \in \alpha_2 \\ (0, 0), & \text{otherwise} \end{cases}.$$

It is clear that $supp(\hat{\beta}_1) < supp(\hat{\beta}_2)$. As $\mathcal{M}$ is a bipolar fuzzy matroid, there exists β_3 such that $\hat{\beta}_1 \subseteq \beta_3 \subseteq \hat{\beta}_1 \cup \hat{\beta}_2$. Since

$$\hat{\beta}_1 \cup \hat{\beta}_2(y) = \begin{cases} \boldsymbol{t}, & y \in \alpha_1 \cup \alpha_2 \\ (0, 0), & \text{otherwise} \end{cases},$$

there exists a set α_3 such that

$$\beta_3(y) = \begin{cases} \boldsymbol{t}, & y \in \alpha_3 \\ (0, 0), & \text{otherwise} \end{cases}.$$

Also, $\alpha_1 \subseteq \alpha_3 \subseteq \alpha_1 \cup \alpha_2$, $\alpha_3 \in \mathcal{I}_t$. Hence, $\mathcal{M}_t$ is a matroid on X.

Remark 7.2 Let $\mathcal{M} = (X, \mathcal{I})$ be a bipolar fuzzy matroid and, for each $\boldsymbol{t} = (t^p, t^n)$, $0 \le t^p \le 1, -1 \le t^n \le 0$, $\mathcal{M}_t = (X, \mathcal{I}_t)$ be a matroid on a finite set X as given in Theorem 7.1. As X is finite, there is a finite sequence $\boldsymbol{t}_0, \boldsymbol{t}_1, \boldsymbol{t}_2, \ldots, \boldsymbol{t}_m$, $0 < t_1^p < t_2^p < \cdots < t_m^p$, $0 > t_1^n > t_2^n > \cdots > t_m^n > -1$ such that $\mathcal{M}_{t_i} = (X, \mathcal{I}_{t_i})$ is a crisp matroid, for each $1 \le i \le m$, and

1. $\boldsymbol{t}_0 = (0, 0)$, $t_m^p \le 1$ and $t_m^n \ge -1$,
2. $\mathcal{I}_{\boldsymbol{w}} \ne \emptyset$ if $\boldsymbol{w} = (w^p, w^n)$, $0 \le w^p \le t_m^p$ and $t_m^n \le w^n \le 0$,
3. If for $\boldsymbol{s} = (s^p, s^n)$, $t_i^p < w^p, s^p < t_{i+1}^p$ and $t_i^n > w^n, s^n > t_{i+1}^n$, then $\mathcal{I}_{\boldsymbol{w}} = \mathcal{I}_{\boldsymbol{s}}$, $0 \le i \le m-1$,
4. If $t_i^p < w < t_{i+1}^p < s^p < t_{i+2}^p$ and $t_i^n > w > t_{i+1}^n > s^n > t_{i+2}^n$, then $\mathcal{I}_{\boldsymbol{w}} \supset \mathcal{I}_{\boldsymbol{s}}, 0 \le i \le m-2$.

The sequence $\boldsymbol{t}_0, \boldsymbol{t}_1, \boldsymbol{t}_2, \ldots, \boldsymbol{t}_m$ is known as a **fundamental sequence** of $\mathcal{M}$. Let $\bar{\boldsymbol{t}}_i = \frac{1}{2}(\boldsymbol{t}_{i-1} + \boldsymbol{t}_i)$ for $1 \le i \le m$. The decreasing sequence of crisp matroids $\mathcal{M}_{\bar{t}_1} \supset \mathcal{M}_{\bar{t}_2} \supset \cdots \supset \mathcal{M}_{\bar{t}_m}$ is known as $\mathcal{M}-$**induced matroid sequence**.

Definition 7.17 Let $\boldsymbol{t}_0, \boldsymbol{t}_1, \ldots, \boldsymbol{t}_m$ be the fundamental sequence of a bipolar fuzzy matroid. For any $\boldsymbol{t} = (t^p, t^n)$, $0 < t^p \le 1$ and $-1 \le t^n < 0$, define $\overline{\mathcal{I}}_{\boldsymbol{t}} = \mathcal{I}_{\bar{t}_i}$, where $\bar{\boldsymbol{t}}_i = \frac{1}{2}(\boldsymbol{t}_{i-1} + \boldsymbol{t}_i)$ and $t^p_{i-1} < t^p \le t^p_i$, $t^n_{i-1} > t^n \ge t^n_i$. If $t^p > t^p_m$ and $t^n < t^n_m$ take $\overline{\mathcal{I}}_{\boldsymbol{t}} = \mathcal{I}_{\boldsymbol{t}}$. Define $\overline{\mathcal{I}} = \{\beta \in \mathcal{BF}(X) : \beta_{\boldsymbol{t}} \in \overline{\mathcal{I}}_{\boldsymbol{t}}$, for each $\boldsymbol{t} = (t^p, t^n)$, $0 < t^p \le 1$ and $-1 \le t^n < 0\}$. Then $\overline{\mathcal{M}} = (X, \overline{\mathcal{I}})$ is known as **closure** of $\mathcal{M} = (X, \mathcal{I})$.

Example 7.8 We now explain the concept of closure by an example of a bipolar fuzzy uniform matroid $\mathcal{M} = (X, \mathcal{I})$, where $X = \{y_1, y_2, y_3\}$ and $\mathcal{I} = \{\beta \in \mathcal{BF}(X) : |supp(\eta)| \le 1\}$ such that for any $\beta \in \mathcal{BF}(X)$, $\beta(y) = \tau(y)$, for all $y \in X$, where

$$\tau(y) = \begin{cases} (0.2, -0.3), & y = y_1 \\ (0.3, -0.4), & y = y_2 \\ (0.4, -0.5), & y = y_3 \end{cases}.$$

$$\mathcal{I} = \big\{\emptyset, \{(y_1, 0.2, -0.3)\}, \{(y_2, 0.3, -0.4)\}, \{(y_3, 0.4, -0.5)\}\big\}.$$

The fundamental sequence of $\mathcal{M}$ is $\{\boldsymbol{t}_0 = (0, 0), \boldsymbol{t}_1 = (0.2, -0.3), \boldsymbol{t}_2 = (0.3, -0.4), \boldsymbol{t}_3 = (0.4, -0.5)\}$. From routine calculations, $\bar{\boldsymbol{t}}_1 = (0.1, -0.15)$, $\bar{\boldsymbol{t}}_2 = (0.25, -0.35)$, $\bar{\boldsymbol{t}}_3 = (0.35, -0.45)$. Now $\mathcal{I}_{\bar{t}_1} = \{\{y_1\}, \{y_2\}, \{y_3\}\}$, $\mathcal{I}_{\bar{t}_2} = \{\{y_2\}, \{y_3\}\}$, $\mathcal{I}_{\bar{t}_3} = \{\{y_3\}\}$. Hence, the closure of $\mathcal{I}$ can be defined as $\mathcal{I} = \{\emptyset, \{(y_1, 0.2, -0.3)\}, \{(y_2, 0.3, -0.4)\}, \{(y_1, 0.2, -0.3), (y_2, 0.3, -0.4)\}, \{(y_1, 0.2, -0.3), (y_3, 0.4, -0.5)\}, \{(y_2, 0.3, -0.4), (y_3, 0.4, -0.5)\}, \{(y_3, 0.4, -0.5)\}\}$.

Theorem 7.2 *The closure $\overline{\mathcal{M}} = (X, \overline{\mathcal{I}})$ of a bipolar fuzzy matroid $\mathcal{M} = (X, \mathcal{I})$ is also a bipolar fuzzy matroid.*

The proof of Theorem 7.2 is a clear consequence of Theorem 7.1.

Definition 7.18 A bipolar fuzzy matroid with fundamental sequence $\boldsymbol{t}_0, \boldsymbol{t}_1, \ldots, \boldsymbol{t}_m$ is known as a **closed bipolar fuzzy matroid** if for each $\boldsymbol{t} = (t^p, t^n)$, $t^p_{i-1} < t^p \le t^p_i$ and $t^n_{i-1} > t^n \ge t^n_i$, $\mathcal{I}_{\boldsymbol{t}} = \mathcal{I}_{t_i}$.

Remark 7.3 The closure $\overline{\mathcal{M}}$ of a bipolar fuzzy matroid $\mathcal{M}$ is closed and the smallest closed bipolar fuzzy matroid containing $\mathcal{M}$ is $\overline{\mathcal{M}}$. Also note that the fundamental sequences of $\overline{\mathcal{M}}$ and $\mathcal{M}$ are same.

Theorem 7.3 *Let $\mathcal{M} = (X, \mathcal{I})$ be a bipolar fuzzy matroid and suppose $\beta \in \mathcal{BF}(X)$, then $\beta \in \mathcal{I}$ if and only if for each $\boldsymbol{t} = (t^p, t^n)$, $\beta_{\boldsymbol{t}} \in \mathcal{I}_{\boldsymbol{t}}$, where $t^p \in R^p(\beta)$, $t^n \in R^n(\beta)$.*

Theorem 7.3 follows from the proof of Theorem 7.1.

Theorem 7.4 *If $\mathcal{M} = (X, \mathcal{I})$ is a closed fuzzy matroid, then each dependent bipolar fuzzy set in $\mathcal{M}$ properly contains a dependent bipolar fuzzy subset.*

Proof Assume that α is a dependent bipolar fuzzy set in $\mathcal{M}$ and $R^p(\alpha) = \{t_1^p, t_2^p, \ldots, t_m^p\}$, $R^n(\alpha) = \{t_1^n, t_2^n, \ldots, t_m^n\}$, where $t_1^p < t_2^p < \cdots < t_m^p$ and $t_1^n > t_2^n > \cdots > t_m^n$. By Theorem 7.3, there exists $\boldsymbol{t}_i$, $1 \leq i \leq m$, such that $\alpha_{\boldsymbol{t}_i} \notin \mathcal{I}_{\boldsymbol{t}_i}$. Since $\mathcal{M}$ is a closed bipolar fuzzy matroid, there is an $\varepsilon = (\varepsilon^p, \varepsilon^n)$, $\varepsilon^p > 0$, $\varepsilon^n < 0$ such that for each $\boldsymbol{t} = (t^p, t^n)$, $t_i^p - \varepsilon^p \leq t^p \leq t_i^p$, $t_i^n - \varepsilon^n \geq t^n \geq t_i^n$,

$$\alpha_{\boldsymbol{t}} = \alpha_{\boldsymbol{t}_i} \quad \text{and} \quad \mathcal{I}_{\boldsymbol{t}} = \mathcal{I}_{\boldsymbol{t}_i}.$$

Let γ be a proper bipolar fuzzy subset of α defined by

$$\gamma(y) = \begin{cases} \boldsymbol{t}_i - \varepsilon, & \mu_\alpha^p(y) \geq t_i^p \text{ and } \mu_\alpha^n(y) \leq t_i^n \\ (0, 0), & \text{otherwise} \end{cases}.$$

Note that $\gamma_{\boldsymbol{t}_i - \varepsilon} \notin \mathcal{I}_{\boldsymbol{t}_i - \varepsilon}$ and hence by Theorem 7.3, $\gamma \notin \mathcal{I}$.

As a consequence of Theorem 7.10, we adopt the following definition of a bipolar fuzzy circuit.

Definition 7.19 Let $\mathcal{M} = (X, \mathcal{I})$ be a bipolar fuzzy matroid. Then $\alpha \in \mathcal{BF}(X)$ is a bipolar fuzzy circuit in $\mathcal{M}$ if $\alpha \notin \mathcal{I}$ and $\alpha \backslash\backslash z \in \mathcal{I}$ for each $z \in supp(\alpha)$, where $\alpha \backslash\backslash z$ is defined as

$$(\alpha \backslash\backslash z)(y) = \begin{cases} \alpha(y), & y \neq z \\ (0, 0), & y = z \end{cases}.$$

Now characterizing the properties of bipolar fuzzy circuits in the form of crisp circuits.

Theorem 7.5 (Characterization Theorem) *Assume that $\mathcal{M} = (X, \mathcal{I})$ is a bipolar fuzzy matroid and $\alpha \in \mathcal{BF}(X)$. Let $R^p(\alpha) = \{t_1^p, t_2^p, \ldots, t_m^p\}$ and $R^n(\alpha) = \{t_1^n, t_2^n, \ldots, t_m^n\}$, where $t_1^p < t_2^p < \cdots < t_m^p$ and $t_1^n > t_2^n > \cdots > t_m^n$. Then α is a bipolar fuzzy circuit in $\mathcal{M}$ if and only if*

(1) $\alpha_{\boldsymbol{t}_1}$ is a crisp circuit in $(X, \mathcal{I}_{\boldsymbol{t}_1})$,
(2) $\alpha_{\boldsymbol{t}_i} \in \mathcal{I}_{\boldsymbol{t}_i}$, for $2 \leq i \leq m$.

Proof Let α be a bipolar fuzzy circuit, then $\alpha \notin \mathcal{I}$. By Theorem 7.3, there exists at least one i, $1 \leq i \leq m$, (say, $i = i'$) such that $\alpha_{\boldsymbol{t}_{i'}} \notin \mathcal{I}_{\boldsymbol{t}_{i'}}$. We now show that $i' = 1$. On contrary, assume that $2 \leq i' \leq m$. Since $t_1^p < t_{i'}^p$ and $t_1^n > t_{i'}^n$, $\alpha_{\boldsymbol{t}_{i'}} \subset \alpha_{\boldsymbol{t}_1}$. Then there exists, $z \in \alpha_{\boldsymbol{t}_1} \setminus \alpha_{\boldsymbol{t}_{i'}}$. Clearly, $(\alpha \backslash\backslash z)_{\boldsymbol{t}_{i'}} = \alpha_{\boldsymbol{t}_{i'}} \notin \mathcal{I}_{\boldsymbol{t}_{i'}}$. It follows from Theorem 7.3 that $\alpha \backslash\backslash z \notin \mathcal{I}$ which is a contradiction to the supposition that α is a bipolar fuzzy circuit. Thus, for $2 \leq i \leq m$, $\alpha_{\boldsymbol{t}_{i'}} \in \mathcal{I}_{\boldsymbol{t}_{i'}}$ and it establishes (2).

We now prove (1). It is clear that $\alpha_{\boldsymbol{t}_1} \notin \mathcal{I}_{\boldsymbol{t}_1}$. If $\alpha_{\boldsymbol{t}_1}$ is not a circuit, then there exist $B \subset \alpha_{\boldsymbol{t}_1}$ such that $B \notin \mathcal{I}_{\boldsymbol{t}_1}$. If $x \in \alpha_{\boldsymbol{t}_1} \setminus B$, then $B \subseteq (\alpha \backslash\backslash x)_{\boldsymbol{t}_1} \Rightarrow (\alpha \backslash\backslash x)_{\boldsymbol{t}_1} \notin \mathcal{I}_{\boldsymbol{t}_1}$.

So, by Theorem 7.3, $\alpha\backslash\backslash x \notin \mathcal{I}$, a contradiction to the fact that α is a bipolar fuzzy circuit and it establishes (1).

Conversely, let $\alpha \in \mathcal{BF}(X)$ satisfy (1) and (2). By Theorem 7.3, $\alpha \notin \mathcal{I}$. Suppose that $y \in supp(\alpha)$, then $\mu_\alpha^p(y) \geq t_1^p$ and $\mu_\alpha^n(y) \leq t_1^n$. Hence, $(\alpha\backslash\backslash y)_{t_1} = \alpha_{t_1} \setminus y \in \mathcal{I}_{t_1}$ and for $2 \leq i \leq m$ $\alpha_{t_i} \supseteq (\alpha\backslash\backslash y)_{t_i} \in \mathcal{I}_{t_i}$. Clearly, by Theorem 7.3, $\alpha\backslash\backslash y \in \mathcal{I}$ and so α is a bipolar fuzzy circuit.

We can say that a bipolar fuzzy circuit α is **elementary** if it is an elementary bipolar fuzzy set, i.e., α is single valued on $supp(\alpha)$.

Corollary 7.1 *Let $\mathcal{M} = (X, \mathcal{I})$ be a bipolar fuzzy matroid, then α is a bipolar fuzzy circuit in $\mathcal{M}$ if and only if $\alpha = \lambda \cup \gamma$, where λ is an elementary bipolar fuzzy circuit, $\gamma \in \mathcal{I}$ and $supp(\gamma) \subset supp(\lambda)$.*

Proof Assume that α is a bipolar fuzzy circuit in $\mathcal{M}$, $R^p(\alpha) = \{t_1^p, t_2^p, \ldots, t_m^p\}$, and $R^n(\alpha) = \{t_1^n, t_2^n, \ldots, t_m^n\}$, where $t_1^p < t_2^p < \cdots < t_m^p$ and $t_1^n > t_2^n > \cdots > t_m^n$. Define λ and γ as

$$\lambda(y) = \begin{cases} t_1, & y \in supp(\alpha) \\ (0,0), & otherwise \end{cases} \quad \text{and} \quad \gamma(y) = \begin{cases} \alpha(y), & \text{if } y \in \alpha_{t_2} \\ (0,0), & otherwise \end{cases}.$$

Consequently, λ is an elementary bipolar fuzzy circuit, $\gamma \in \mathcal{I}$, $supp(\gamma) \subset supp(\lambda)$ and $\alpha = \lambda \cup \gamma$.

Conversely, let $\alpha = \lambda \cup \gamma$, λ is elementary, $\gamma \in \mathcal{I}$ and $supp(\gamma) \subset supp(\lambda)$. If $R^p(\alpha) = \{t_1^p, t_2^p, \ldots, t_m^p\}$ and $R^n(\alpha) = \{t_1^n, t_2^n, \ldots, t_m^n\}$, where $t_1^p < t_2^p < \cdots < t_m^p$ and $t_1^n > t_2^n > \cdots > t_m^n$, then $R^p(\lambda) = \{t_1^p\}$, $R^n(\lambda) = \{t_1^n\}$, $R^p(\gamma) = \{t_2^p, \ldots, t_m^p\}$, and $R^n(\gamma) = \{t_2^n, \ldots, t_m^n\}$. It follows from Theorem 7.5, that 1) α_{t_1} is a circuit in $\mathcal{I}_{t_1}$ and for $2 \leq i \leq m$, $\alpha_{t_i} \in \mathcal{I}_{t_i}$. Thus, by Theorem 7.5, α is a bipolar fuzzy circuit.

Note 7.2 Corollary 7.1 implies that every bipolar subset of a bipolar fuzzy circuit is either a bipolar fuzzy circuit or an independent bipolar fuzzy set.

Corollary 7.2 *Suppose that $\mathcal{M} = (X, \mathcal{I})$ is a bipolar fuzzy matroid and $\gamma \in \mathcal{BF}(X)$. If $\gamma \notin \mathcal{I}$, then there exists a bipolar fuzzy circuit α such that $\alpha \subseteq \gamma$.*

Proof Let $\mathcal{R}^p(\gamma) = \{t_1^p, t_2^p, \ldots, t_m^p\}$ and $\mathcal{R}^n(\gamma) = \{t_1^n, t_2^n, \ldots, t_m^n\}$. By Theorem 7.3, there exists t_i such that $\gamma_{t_i} \notin \mathcal{I}_{t_i}$. Let $B \subseteq \gamma_{t_i}$ be a circuit in $(X, \mathcal{I}_{t_i})$ and define $\alpha \in \mathcal{BF}(X)$ as

$$\alpha(y) = \begin{cases} t_i, & \text{if } y \in B \\ (0,0), & \text{otherwise} \end{cases}.$$

Then $\alpha \subseteq \gamma$ and $R^p(\alpha) = \{t_i^p\}$, $R^n(\alpha) = \{t_i^n\}$, $supp(\alpha) = B$ and hence α is a bipolar fuzzy circuit.

Theorem 7.6 *If α_1 and α_2 are bipolar fuzzy circuits in a bipolar fuzzy matroid $\mathcal{M}$ and $\alpha_1 \subseteq \alpha_2$, then $supp(\alpha_1) = supp(\alpha_2)$.*

Proof Let α_1 and α_2 be two bipolar fuzzy circuits in $\mathcal{M} = (X, \mathcal{I})$. On contrary, assume that $supp(\alpha_1) \subset supp(\alpha_2)$, then there exists $y \in X$ such that $y \in supp(\alpha_2) \setminus supp(\alpha_1)$. Moreover, $\alpha_1 \subseteq \alpha_2 \backslash\backslash y \in \mathcal{I}$ and hence, $\alpha_1 \in \mathcal{I}$, a contradiction to the supposition that α_1 is a bipolar fuzzy circuit.

7.2.1 Circuit Rectangles

In this section, the concept of circuit rectangles and circuit function is discussed in detail.

Definition 7.20 The **truncation** of a bipolar fuzzy set β at level $\boldsymbol{t} = (t^p, t^n)$ is a bipolar fuzzy set β_t^* defined as

$$\beta_t^*(y) = \begin{cases} \beta(y), & \text{if } \mu_\beta^p(y) \leq t^p, \mu_\beta^n(y) \geq t^n \\ (0, 0), & \mu_\beta^p(y) > t^p, \mu_\beta^n(y) < t^n \end{cases}.$$

If $\mathcal{M} = (X, \mathcal{I})$ is a bipolar fuzzy matroid, then define $\eta = (\eta^p, \eta^n) : \mathcal{BF}(X) \to [0, 1] \times [-1, 0]$ by
$\eta^p(\beta) = \max\{t^p \mid \beta_t^* \text{ is not a bipolar fuzzy circuit in } \mathcal{M}\}$,
$\eta^n(\beta) = \min\{t^n \mid \beta_t^* \text{ is not a bipolar fuzzy circuit in } \mathcal{M}\}$.
The function η is known as a **circuit function** for β.

Example 7.9 Consider the example of a bipolar fuzzy uniform matroid as given in Example 7.3. Take $\beta = \{(e_1, 0.2, -0.3), (e_2, 0.4, -0.5), (e_3, 0.1, -0.3)\}$.

1. For $\boldsymbol{t} = (0.2, -0.3)$, $\beta_t^* = \{(e_1, 0.2, -0.3), (e_3, 0.1, -0.3)\}$.
2. For $\boldsymbol{t} = (0.1, -0.3)$, $\beta_t^* = \{(e_3, 0.1, -0.3)\}$.
3. For $\boldsymbol{t} = (0.4, -0.5)$, $\beta_t^* = \beta$.

Clearly, $\eta(\beta) = (0.2, -0, 3)$. If we take $\beta = \{(e_1, 0.2, -0.3), (e_2, 0.4, -0.5)\}$, then $\eta(\beta) = (1, -1)$.

Theorem 7.7 *Let $\mathcal{M} = (X, \mathcal{I})$ be a bipolar fuzzy matroid and η is a circuit function for β. Then the following conditions hold.*

1. *If $\beta \in \mathcal{BF}(X)$ is not a bipolar fuzzy circuit, then $\eta(\beta) = (1, -1)$.*
2. *If β is a bipolar fuzzy circuit, then $\eta^p(\beta) \geq m^p(\beta)$ and $\eta^n(\beta) \leq m^n(\beta)$.*

Proof 1. Since β is not a bipolar fuzzy circuit, for $\boldsymbol{t} = (1, -1)$, $\beta_t^* = \beta$. Consequently, $\eta(\beta) = (1, -1)$.
2. Let $\mathcal{R}^p(\beta) = \{t_1^p, t_2^p, \ldots, t_m^p\}$, $\mathcal{R}^n(\beta) = \{t_1^n, t_2^n, \ldots, t_m^n\}$, and $\boldsymbol{t}_i = (t_i^p, t_i^n)$, $1 \leq i \leq m$. For $\boldsymbol{t} \in \{\boldsymbol{t}_1, \boldsymbol{t}_2, \ldots, \boldsymbol{t}_{m-1}\}$, β_t^* is not a bipolar fuzzy circuit and for $\boldsymbol{t} \in \{\boldsymbol{t} \mid t^p \geq t_m^p, t_n \leq t_m^n\}$, β_t^* is a bipolar fuzzy circuit. For $t^p < t_1^p$ and $t^n > t_1^n$, $\beta_t^* = \emptyset$. Hence, $\eta^p(\beta) \geq m^p(\beta)$ and $\eta^n(\beta) \leq m^n(\beta)$.

Definition 7.21 Let $\mathcal{M} = (X, \mathcal{I})$ be a closed bipolar fuzzy matroid and α be a bipolar fuzzy circuit in $\mathcal{M}$. Let $I(\alpha) = [m^n(\alpha), 0) \times (0, m^p(\alpha)]$ which is called **circuit rectangle** for α.

Theorem 7.8 *Let α be a bipolar fuzzy circuit in a closed bipolar fuzzy matroid $\mathcal{M} = (X, \mathcal{I})$. Let $I(\alpha) = [m^n(\alpha), 0) \times (0, m^p(\alpha)]$ be a circuit rectangle for α, then*

1. *if $t \in I(\alpha)$, then α_t is a circuit in $\mathcal{M}_t = (X, \mathcal{I}_t)$,*
2. *if $t \notin I(\alpha)$, then $\alpha_t \in \mathcal{I}_t$.*

Proof By Theorem 7.1, $\alpha = \delta \cup \gamma$, where δ is an elementary bipolar fuzzy circuit, $\gamma \in \mathcal{I}$, and $supp(\gamma) \subset supp(\delta)$. Clearly, $\mathcal{R}^p(\delta) = \{m^p(\alpha)\}$ and $R^n(\alpha) = \{m^n(\alpha)\}$. If $t^p > m^p(\alpha)$ and $t^n < m^n(\alpha)$, then $\alpha_t = \gamma_t \in \mathcal{I}_t$. If $0 < t^p \leq m^p(\alpha)$ and $0 > t^n \geq m^n(\alpha)$, then $\alpha_t = supp(\delta)$. Hence, α_t is a circuit in $\mathcal{M}_t$ if $t \in I(\alpha)$.

7.3 Bipolar Fuzzy Soft Circuits

It is worth noting that uncertainty arising from various domains has a different nature and cannot be captured within a single mathematical framework. To solve complicated problems in economics, engineering, and environment, classical methods cannot be used successfully because of their difficulties, possibly, the inadequacy of a parametrization tool. Soft set theory was proposed by Molodtsov [19] in 1999 to deal with uncertain, fuzzy, not clearly defined objects in a parametric manner. Molodtsov's soft sets provide a new way of coping with uncertainty from the viewpoint of parametrization in various domains, including the smoothness of functions, game theory, operations research, Riemann integration, probability theory, and measurement theory [19]. A soft set is a parameterized family of sets—intuitively, this is "soft" because the boundary of the set depends on the parameters. Formally, a **soft set** over a universal set X and set of parameters P is a pair $(f, A) = \{(e, f(e)) \mid e \in A, \ f(e) \in \mathcal{P}(X)\}$ where $A \subseteq P$ and $f : A \to \mathcal{P}(X)$ is a function from A to the power set of X. For each $e \in A$, the set $f(e)$ is called the value set of e in (f, A). Each parameter is a word or a sentence. In most cases, parameters are considered to be attributes, characteristics, or properties of objects in X. The pair (X, P) is also known as a **soft universe** and is defined as the set of all soft sets over X with attributes from P.

Definition 7.22 A **soft graph** on a non-empty set X is a 3−tuple (X, E, A) such that for each $e \in A$, $(X(e), E(e))$ is a graph, where $X(e) \subseteq X$ and $E(e) \subseteq X(e) \times X(e)$.

Definition 7.23 A **soft matroid** on a non-empty set X is a 3−tuple $M = (X, I, A)$, where A is the set of parameters and for each $e \in A$, $I(e) \subseteq P(X)$ satisfies the following conditions.

1. If $B_1(e) \in I(e)$ and $B_2(e) \subset B_1(e)$, then $B_2(e) \in I(e)$.
2. If $B_1(e), B_2(e) \in I(e)$ and $|B_1(e)| < |B_2(e)|$, then there exists $B_3(e) \in I$ such that $B_1(e) \subset B_3(e) \subseteq B_1(e) \cup B_2(e)$.

Note that $(I, A) = \{I(e) \mid e \in A\}$ is known as the family of **independent soft subsets** of M.

Definition 7.24 Let X be a non-empty set and P be a set of parameters. Let $\mathcal{BF}(X)$ denote the set of all bipolar fuzzy sets on X. A pair (f, A) is called a **bipolar fuzzy soft set** on X, where $A \subseteq P$ is a set of parameters and $f : A \to \mathcal{BF}(X)$ is a set-valued mapping, called a **bipolar fuzzy approximation function**. For any $e \in A$, $f(e) = \{(x, \mu^P_{f(e)}(x), \mu^n_{f(e)}(x)) \mid x \in X\}$. (X, P) is the collection of all bipolar fuzzy soft sets on X with attributes from P and is said to be **bipolar fuzzy soft class**.

Definition 7.25 Let (f, A) and (g, B) be two bipolar fuzzy soft sets over (X, P), then a **bipolar fuzzy soft relation** from (f, A) to (g, B) is a bipolar fuzzy soft subset of $(f, A) \times (f, B)$. In other words, a bipolar fuzzy soft relation from (f, A) to (g, B) is of the form (R, C), where $C \subseteq A \times B$ and $R(a, b) \subseteq (f, A) \times (f, B)$, for all $(a, b) \in C$.

Definition 7.26 A **bipolar fuzzy soft graph** on a non-empty set X is an ordered triplet $G = (\phi, \psi, A)$ such that

1. A is a non-empty set of parameters.
2. (ϕ, A) is a bipolar fuzzy soft set on X.
3. (ψ, A) is a bipolar fuzzy soft relation in X, that is, $\psi : A \to \mathcal{BF}(X \times X)$, where $\mathcal{BF}(X \times X)$ is the set of all bipolar fuzzy power sets on $X \times X$.
4. $(\phi(e), \psi(e))$ is a bipolar fuzzy graph for all $e \in A$, that is,

$$\mu^P_{\psi(e)}(xy) \le \mu^P_{\phi(e)}(x) \wedge \mu^P_{\phi(e)}(y) \text{ and } \mu^n_{\psi(e)}(a)(xy) \ge \mu^n_{\phi(e)}(x) \vee \mu^n_{\phi(e)}(y), \quad \text{for all } x, y \in X.$$

The bipolar fuzzy graph $(\phi(e), \psi(e))$ is denoted by $H(e)$. Note that $\mu^P_{\psi(e)}(xy) = \mu^n_{\psi(e)}(xy) = 0$, for all $xy \in X \times X - E$, for each $e \in A$. (ϕ, A) is called a **bipolar fuzzy soft vertex set** and (ψ, A) is called a **bipolar fuzzy soft edge set**. A bipolar fuzzy soft graph is a parameterized family of bipolar fuzzy graphs.

Example 7.10 Let $A = \{e_1, e_2\}$ be a set of parameters and (ϕ, A) be a bipolar fuzzy soft set on $X = \{x_1, x_2, x_3, x_4\}$ with bipolar fuzzy approximation function $\phi : A \to \mathcal{BF}(X)$ defined by
$\phi(e_1) = \{(x_1, 0.3, -0.4), (x_2, 0.5, -0.2), (x_3, 0.7, -0.1), (x_4, 0.9, 0.0)\}$,
$\phi(e_2) = \{(x_1, 0.7, -0.1), (x_2, 0.3, -0.4), (x_3, 0.4, -0.4), (x_4, 0.6, -0.2)\}$.
Let (ψ, A) be a bipolar fuzzy soft relation in X with bipolar fuzzy approximation function $\psi : A \to \mathcal{BF}(X \times X)$ defined by
$\psi(e_1) = \{(x_1x_2, 0.2, -0.1), (x_2x_3, 0.4, -0.1), (x_1x_3, 0.3, -0.1), (x_2x_4, 0.2, 0.0), (x_3x_4, 0.4, 0.0)\}$,
$\psi(e_2) = \{(x_1x_2, 0.2, -0.1), (x_2x_3, 0.2, -0.3), (x_1x_3, 0.4, -0.1), (x_1x_4, 0.5, -0.1), (x_2x_4, 0.1, -0.2)\}$.
Clearly, $H(e_1) = (\phi(e_1), \psi(e_1))$ and $H(e_2) = (\phi(e_2), \psi(e_2))$ are bipolar fuzzy graphs corresponding to the parameters e_1 and e_2, respectively, as shown in Fig. 7.3.

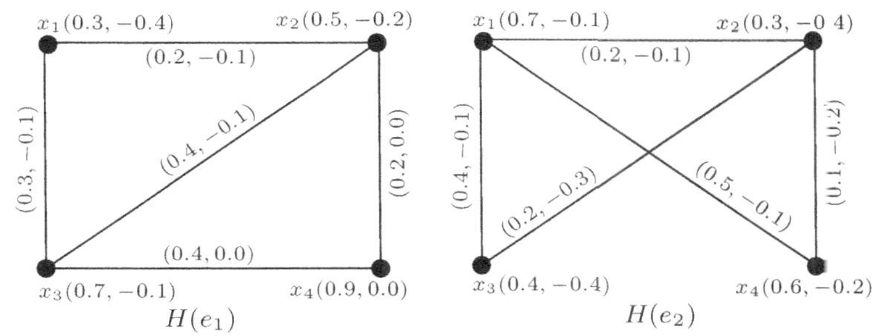

Fig. 7.3 Bipolar fuzzy soft graph $G = \{H(e_1), H(e_2)\}$.

Table 7.3 Bipolar fuzzy soft vertex set

ϕ	x_1	x_2	x_3	x_4
e_1	(0.3, −0.4)	(0.5, −0.2)	(0.7, −0.1)	(0.9, 0.0)
e_2	(0.7, −0.1)	(0.3, −0.4)	(0.4, −0.4)	(0.6, −0.2)

Table 7.4 Bipolar fuzzy soft edge set

ψ	x_1x_2	x_2x_3	x_1x_3	x_1x_4	x_2x_4	x_3x_4
e_1	(0.2, −0.1)	(0.4, −0.1)	(0.3, −0.1)	(0.0, 0.0)	(0.2, 0.0)	(0.4, 0.0)
e_2	(0.2, −0.1)	(0.2, −0.3)	(0.4, −0.1)	(0.5, −0.1)	(0.1, −0.2)	(0.0, 0.0)

Hence, $G = \{H(e_1), H(e_2)\}$ is a bipolar fuzzy soft graph on X. The tabular representation of a bipolar fuzzy soft graph $G = \{H(e_1), H(e_2)\}$ is given in Tables 7.3 and 7.4.

Definition 7.27 Let $G = (\phi, \psi, A)$ be a bipolar fuzzy soft graph on X and $\boldsymbol{t} = (t^p, t^n) \in [0, 1] \times [-1, 0]$. For any $e \in A$, define $\boldsymbol{t}$**-cut** of a bipolar fuzzy set $\phi(e)$ as $\phi(e)_t = \{x \in X \mid \mu^p_{\phi(e)}(x) \geq t^p, \mu^n_{\phi(e)}(x) \leq t^n\}$. Then $(\phi_t, A) = \{\phi(\epsilon)_t \mid e \in A\}$ is called a $\boldsymbol{t}$-cut of a bipolar fuzzy soft set (ϕ, A). The soft graph $G_t = (\varphi_t, \psi_t, A)$ is called a $\boldsymbol{t}$-level soft graph of G, where $(\psi_t, A) = \{\psi(e)_t \mid e \in A\}$ is a $\boldsymbol{t}$-cut of (ψ, A) and $\psi_t(e) = \left\{xy \in E \mid \mu^p_{\psi(e)}(xy) \geq t^p, \mu^n_{\psi(e)}(xy) \leq t^n\right\}$.

Definition 7.28 A **bipolar fuzzy soft matroid** on a non-empty finite set X is a 3-tuple $\mathcal{M}(X) = (X, \mathcal{I}, A)$, where A is the set of parameters and $(\mathcal{I}, A)$ is a soft family of bipolar fuzzy subsets satisfying the following conditions. For each $e \in A$,

1. If $\beta_1(e) \in \mathcal{I}(e)$, $\beta_2(e) \in \mathcal{BF}(X)$ and $\beta_2(e) \subset \beta_1(e)$, then $\beta_2(e) \in \mathcal{I}(e)$.
2. If $\beta_1(e), \beta_2(e) \in \mathcal{I}(e)$ and $|supp\,(\beta_1(e))| < |supp\,(\beta_2(e))|$, then there exists $\beta_3(e) \in \mathcal{I}(e)$ such that
   a. $\beta_1(e) \subset \beta_3(e) \subseteq \beta_1(e) \cup \beta_2(e)$,
   b. $m^p\,(\beta_3(e)) \geq m^p\,(\beta_1(e)) \wedge m^p\,(\beta_2(e))$, $m^p\,(\beta_i(e)) = \min\{\mu^p_{\beta_i(e)}(y) | y \in supp\,(\beta_i(e))\}$, $i = 1, 2, 3$,

c. $m^n(\beta_3(e)) \leq m^n(\beta_1(e)) \vee m^n(\beta_2(e))$, $m^n(\beta_i(e)) = \max\{\mu^n_{\beta_i(e)}(y) | y \in supp(\beta_i(e))\}$, $i = 1, 2, 3$.

That is, for each $e \in A$, the pair $\mathcal{M}_e(X) = (X, \mathcal{I}(e))$ is a bipolar fuzzy matroid on X. $(\mathcal{I}, A)$ is a family of **independent bipolar fuzzy soft subsets** of $\mathcal{M}(X)$.

Note 7.3 For each $e \in A$, $\{\alpha(e) \mid \alpha(e) \in \mathcal{BF}(X), \alpha(e) \notin \mathcal{I}(e)\}$ is the family of dependent bipolar fuzzy subsets in $\mathcal{M}(e)$. Let $C_r(\mathcal{M}(e))$ be a family of minimal dependent bipolar fuzzy subsets in $\mathcal{M}_e(X)$, then $C_r(\mathcal{M}(e)) = \{C_r(\mathcal{M}(e)) \mid e \in A\}$ is called a **bipolar fuzzy soft circuit**. Equivalently, a bipolar fuzzy soft set (α, A) is a bipolar fuzzy soft circuit in $\mathcal{M}$ if $(\alpha, A) \notin (\mathcal{I}, A)$ and, for each $e \in A$, if $\beta(e) \subset \alpha(e)$ then $\beta(e) \in \mathcal{I}(e)$. Since the elements of $(\mathcal{I}, A)$ are those bipolar fuzzy soft sets which are mutually disjoint with the members of $C_r(\mathcal{M}(e))$, a bipolar fuzzy soft matroid can be uniquely determined from $C_r(\mathcal{M})$.

Example 7.11 A simple example of a bipolar fuzzy soft matroid on a non-empty with set X with n elements, known as a **uniform bipolar fuzzy soft matroid**, is denoted by $\mathcal{U}_{k,n} = (X, \mathcal{I}, A)$, where for each $e \in A$, $\mathcal{I}(e) = \{\beta(e) \in \mathcal{BF}(X) \mid |supp(\beta(e))| \leq k\}$. The bipolar fuzzy soft circuit of $\mathcal{U}_{k,n}$ is a bipolar fuzzy soft subset (α, A) such that for each $e \in A$, $|supp(\alpha(e))| = k + 1$.

Consider the example of a uniform bipolar fuzzy matroid $\mathcal{U}_{2,3} = (X, \mathcal{I}, A) = \{(X, \mathcal{I}(e_1)), (X, \mathcal{I}(e_2))\}$, where $X = \{y_1, y_2, y_3\}$, $A = \{e_1, e_2\}$, $\mathcal{I}(e_i) = \{\beta(e_i) \in \mathcal{BF}(X) \mid |supp(\beta(e_i))| \leq 2\}$ and each $\beta(e_i) \in \mathcal{BF}(X)$, $i = 1, 2$, is defined as

$$\beta(e_1)(y) = \{(y_1, 0.2, -0.3), (y_2, 0.4, -0.5), (y_3, 0.1, -0.3)\},$$

$$\beta(e_2)(y) = \{(y_1, 0.3, -0.2), (y_2, 0.5, -0.4), (y_3, 0.3, -0.1)\}.$$

$$\begin{aligned}\mathcal{I}(e_1) =& \{\emptyset, \{(y_1, 0.2, -0.3)\}, \{(y_2, 0.4, -0.5)\}, \{(y_3, 0.1, -0.3)\}, \{(y_1, 0.2, -0.3), (y_2, 0.4, -0.5)\},\\ & \{(y_2, 0.4, -0.5), (y_3, 0.1, -0.3)\}, \{(y_1, 0.2, -0.3), (y_3, 0.1, -0.3)\}\}\\ \mathcal{I}(e_2) =& \{\emptyset, \{(y_1, 0.3, -0.2)\}, \{(y_2, 0.5, -0.4)\}, \{(y_3, 0.3, -0.1)\}, \{(y_1, 0.3, -0.2), (y_2, 0.5, -0.4)\},\\ & \{(y_2, 0.5, -0.4), (y_3, 0.3, -0.1)\}, \{(y_1, 0.3, -0.2), (y_3, 0.3, -0.1)\}\}.\end{aligned}$$

The bipolar fuzzy soft circuit of $\mathcal{U}_{2,3}$ is $\{\alpha(e_1), \alpha(e_2)\}$, where $\alpha(e_1) = \{(y_1, 0.2, -0.3), (y_2, 0.4, -0.5), (y_3, 0.1, -0.3)\}$ and $\alpha(e_2) = \{(y_1, 0.3, -0.2), (y_2, 0.5, -0.4), (y_3, 0.3, -0.1)\}$.

Example 7.12 A significant class of bipolar fuzzy soft matroids derived from bipolar fuzzy soft graphs is known as a **cycle bipolar fuzzy soft matroid** $\mathcal{M} = (X, \mathcal{I}, A)$. For each $e \in A, \mathcal{I}(e) = \{\beta(e) \mid supp(\beta(e))$ is not the edge set of a cycle$\}$. (α, A) is a bipolar fuzzy soft circuit if, for each $e \in A$, $supp(\alpha(e))$ is the edge set of a cycle.

Theorem 7.9 *Let $\mathcal{M} = (X, \mathcal{I}, A)$ be a bipolar fuzzy soft matroid and, for each $\mathbf{t} = (t^p, t^n), 0 \leq t^p \leq 1, -1 \leq t^n \leq 0$, define $(\mathcal{I}_t, A) = \{(\beta_t, A) \mid (\beta, A) \in (\mathcal{I}, A)\}$. Then $(X, \mathcal{I}_t, A)$ is a soft matroid on X.*

Proof It is given that $(X, \mathcal{I}, A)$ is a bipolar fuzzy soft matroid on X. For each $\boldsymbol{t} = (t^p, t^n) \in [0, 1] \times [-1, 0]$, the $\boldsymbol{t}$-cut of $(\mathcal{I}, A)$ is defined as $(\mathcal{I}_t, A) = \{(\beta_t, A) \mid (\beta, A) \in (\mathcal{I}, A)\}$, where $(\beta_t, A) = \{\beta_t(e) \mid e \in A\}$. To prove that $(X, \mathcal{I}_t, A)$ is a soft matroid, it is to be shown that, for each $e \in A$, $(X, \mathcal{I}(e)_t)$ is a matroid.

We prove conditions 1 and 2 of Definition 7.23. Assume that for each $e \in A$, $\beta_1(e)_t \in \mathcal{I}(e)_t$ and $\alpha(e) \subseteq \beta(e)_{1t}$. Define a bipolar fuzzy set $\beta_2(e) \in \mathcal{BF}(X)$ as

$$\beta_2(e)(y) = \begin{cases} \boldsymbol{t}, & y \in \alpha(e) \\ (0, 0), & \text{otherwise} \end{cases}.$$

Clearly, $\beta_2(e) \subseteq \beta_1(e)$, $\beta_2(e) \in \mathcal{I}(e)$ and $\beta_2(e)_t = \alpha(e)$ therefore, $\alpha(e) \in \mathcal{I}(e)_t$. To prove condition 2, let $\alpha_1(e), \alpha_2(e) \in \mathcal{I}(e)_t$ and $|\alpha_1(e)| < |\alpha_2(e)|$. Then there exist β_1 and β_2 such that $\beta_1(e)_t = \alpha_1(e)$ and $\beta_2(e)_t = \alpha_2(e)$. Define $\hat{\beta}_1(e)$ and $\hat{\beta}_2(e)$ as

$$\hat{\beta}_1(e)(y) = \begin{cases} \boldsymbol{t}, & y \in \alpha_1(e) \\ (0, 0), & \text{otherwise} \end{cases} \text{ and } \hat{\beta}_2(e)(y) = \begin{cases} \boldsymbol{t}, & y \in \alpha_2(e) \\ (0, 0), & \text{otherwise} \end{cases}.$$

It is clear that $supp(\hat{\beta}_1(e)) \subset supp(\hat{\beta}_2(e))$. As $(X, \mathcal{I}(e))$ is a bipolar fuzzy matroid, there exists $\beta_3(e)$ such that $\hat{\beta}_1(e) \subseteq \beta_3(e) \subseteq \hat{\beta}_1(e) \cup \hat{\beta}_2(e)$. Since

$$(\hat{\beta}_1(e) \cup \hat{\beta}_2(e))(y) = \begin{cases} \boldsymbol{t}, & y \in \alpha_1(e) \cup \alpha_2(e) \\ (0, 0), & \text{otherwise} \end{cases}.$$

Therefore, there exists a set $\alpha_3(e)$ such that

$$\beta_3(e)(y) = \begin{cases} \boldsymbol{t}, & y \in \alpha_3(e) \\ (0, 0), & \text{otherwise} \end{cases}.$$

Also, $\alpha_1(e) \subseteq \alpha_3(e) \subseteq \alpha_1(e) \cup \alpha_2(e)$, $\alpha_3(e) \in \mathcal{I}(e)_t$. Hence, $(X, \mathcal{I}(e)_t)$ is a matroid on X for each $e \in A$ and so, $(X, \mathcal{I}_t, A)$ is a soft matroid.

Remark 7.4 Let $\mathcal{M} = (X, \mathcal{I}, A)$ be a bipolar fuzzy soft matroid and, for each $\boldsymbol{t} = (t^p, t^n)$, $0 \leq t^p \leq 1$, $-1 \leq t^n \leq 0$, $\mathcal{M}_t = (X, \mathcal{I}_t, A)$ is a soft matroid on a finite set X as given in Theorem 7.9. As X is finite, for every $e \in A$ there is a finite sequence $S(e) = \{\boldsymbol{t}_0, \boldsymbol{t}_1, \boldsymbol{t}_2, \ldots, \boldsymbol{t}_m\}$, $0 < t_1^p < t_2^p < \cdots < t_m^p$, $0 > t_1^n > t_2^n > \cdots > t_m^n > -1$ such that $\mathcal{M}(e)_{t_i} = (X, \mathcal{I}(e)_{t_i})$ is a crisp matroid, for each $1 \leq i \leq m$, and

1. $\boldsymbol{t}_0 = (0, 0)$, $t_m^p \leq 1$ and $t_m^n \geq -1$,
2. $\mathcal{I}(e)_{\boldsymbol{w}} \neq \emptyset$ if $\boldsymbol{w} = (w^p, w^n)$, $0 \leq w^p \leq t_m^p$ and $t_m^n \leq w^n \leq 0$,
3. If for $\boldsymbol{s} = (s^p, s^n)$, $t_i^p < w^p$, $s^p < t_{i+1}^p$ and $t_i^n > w^n$, $s^n > t_{i+1}^n$, then $\mathcal{I}(e)_{\boldsymbol{w}} = \mathcal{I}(e)_{\boldsymbol{s}}$, $0 \leq i \leq m-1$,
4. If $t_i^p < w < t_{i+1}^p < s^p < t_{i+2}^p$ and $t_i^n > w > t_{i+1}^n > s^n > t_{i+2}^n$, then $\mathcal{I}(e)_{\boldsymbol{w}} \supset \mathcal{I}(e)_{\boldsymbol{s}}$, $0 \leq i \leq m-2$.

The sequence $S(e) = \{\boldsymbol{t}_0, \boldsymbol{t}_1, \boldsymbol{t}_2, \ldots, \boldsymbol{t}_m\}$ is known as a **fundamental sequence** of $\mathcal{M}(e)$ and the family of all such sequences $S = \{S(e) \mid e \in A\}$ is called a **soft fundamental sequence** of $\mathcal{M}$.

Note that if $\boldsymbol{t}_0, \boldsymbol{t}_1, \boldsymbol{t}_2, \ldots, \boldsymbol{t}_m$ is the fundamental sequence for every $\mathcal{M}(e), e \in A$, that is, the fundamental sequence is the same for every $\mathcal{M}(e)$, then $\boldsymbol{t}_0, \boldsymbol{t}_1, \boldsymbol{t}_2, \ldots, \boldsymbol{t}_m$ is called the fundamental sequence for the bipolar fuzzy soft matroid $\mathcal{M} = (X, \mathcal{I}, A)$.

Definition 7.29 A bipolar fuzzy soft matroid with fundamental sequence $\boldsymbol{t}_0, \boldsymbol{t}_1, \ldots, \boldsymbol{t}_m$ is known as a **closed bipolar fuzzy soft matroid** if for each $\boldsymbol{t} = (t^p, t^n)$, $t^p_{i-1} < t^p \leq t^p_i$ and $t^n_{i-1} > t^n \geq t^n_i$, $\mathcal{I}_{\boldsymbol{t}} = \mathcal{I}_{\boldsymbol{t}_i}$.

Theorem 7.10 *If $\mathcal{M} = (X, \mathcal{I}, A)$ is a closed fuzzy soft matroid, then each dependent bipolar fuzzy soft set in $\mathcal{M}$ properly contains a dependent bipolar fuzzy soft subset.*

Proof Let α be a dependent bipolar fuzzy soft set in $\mathcal{M}$. Then for each $e \in A$, $\alpha(e)$ is a dependent bipolar fuzzy set in $\mathcal{M}(e)$ and $R^p(\alpha(e)) = \{t^p_1, t^p_2, \ldots, t^p_m\}$, $R^n(\alpha(e)) = \{t^n_1, t^n_2, \ldots, t^n_m\}$, where $t^p_1 < t^p_2 < \cdots < t^p_m$ and $t^n_1 > t^n_2 > \cdots > t^n_m$. By Theorem 7.3, there exists $\boldsymbol{t}_i$, $1 \leq i \leq m$, such that $\alpha(e)_{\boldsymbol{t}_i} \notin \mathcal{I}(e)_{\boldsymbol{t}_i}$. Since $\mathcal{M}(e)$ is a closed bipolar fuzzy matroid, there is an $\varepsilon = (\varepsilon^p, \varepsilon^n)$, $\varepsilon^p > 0$, $\varepsilon^n < 0$ such that for each $\boldsymbol{t} = (t^p, t^n)$, $t^p_i - \varepsilon^p \leq t^p \leq t^p_i$, $t^n_i - \varepsilon^n \geq t^n \geq t^n_i$,

$$\alpha(e)_{\boldsymbol{t}} = \alpha(e)_{\boldsymbol{t}_i} \quad \text{and} \quad \mathcal{I}(e)_{\boldsymbol{t}} = \mathcal{I}(e)_{\boldsymbol{t}_i}.$$

Let $\gamma(e)$ be a proper bipolar fuzzy subset of $\alpha(e)$ defined by

$$(\gamma(e))(y) = \begin{cases} \boldsymbol{t}_i - \varepsilon, & \mu^p_{\alpha(e)}(y) \geq t^p_i \text{ and } \mu^n_{\alpha(e)}(y) \leq t^n_i \\ (0, 0), & \text{otherwise} \end{cases}.$$

Note that $\gamma(e)_{\boldsymbol{t}_i - \varepsilon} \notin \mathcal{I}(e)_{\boldsymbol{t}_i - \varepsilon}$ and by Theorem 7.3, $\gamma(e) \notin \mathcal{I}(e)$, for each $e \in A$. Hence, $\gamma \notin \mathcal{I}$.

Corollary 7.3 *Let $\mathcal{M} = (X, \mathcal{I}, A)$ be a bipolar fuzzy soft matroid. If $\gamma \notin \mathcal{I}$, then there exists a bipolar fuzzy soft circuit α such that $\alpha(e) \subseteq \gamma(e)$, for each $e \in A$.*

Proof For $e \in A$, let $\mathcal{R}^p(\gamma(e)) = \{t^p_1, t^p_2, \ldots, t^p_m\}$ and $\mathcal{R}^n(\gamma(e)) = \{t^n_1, t^n_2, \ldots, t^n_m\}$. By Theorem 7.3, there exists $\boldsymbol{t}_i$ such that $\gamma(e)_{\boldsymbol{t}_i} \notin \mathcal{I}(e)_{\boldsymbol{t}_i}$. Let $B(e) \subseteq \gamma(e)_{\boldsymbol{t}_i}$ be a circuit in $(X, \mathcal{I}(e)_{\boldsymbol{t}_i})$ and define $\alpha(e) \in \mathcal{BF}(X)$ as

$$(\alpha(e))(y) = \begin{cases} \boldsymbol{t}_i, & \text{if } y \in B \\ (0, 0), & \text{otherwise} \end{cases}.$$

Then $\alpha(e) \subseteq \gamma(e)$ and $R^p(\alpha(e)) = \{t^p_i\}$, $R^n(\alpha(e)) = \{t^n_i\}$, $supp(\alpha(e)) = B$ and hence $\alpha(e)$ is a bipolar fuzzy circuit, for each $e \in A$. Thus, α is a bipolar fuzzy soft circuit.

Theorem 7.11 *If α_1 and α_2 are bipolar fuzzy soft circuits in a bipolar fuzzy soft matroid $\mathcal{M} = (X, \mathcal{I}, A)$ and $\alpha_1(e) \subseteq \alpha_2(e)$, for each $e \in A$, then $supp\,(\alpha_1(e)) = supp\,(\alpha_2(e))$.*

Proof Let α_1 and α_2 be two bipolar fuzzy soft circuits in $\mathcal{M} = (X, \mathcal{I}, A)$, then $\alpha_1(e)$ and $\alpha_2(e)$ are two bipolar fuzzy circuits in $\mathcal{M}(e) = (X, \mathcal{I}(e))$. On contrary, assume that $supp\,(\alpha_1(e)) \subset supp\,(\alpha_2(e))$, then there exists $y \in X$ such that $y \in supp\,(\alpha_2(e)) \setminus supp\,(\alpha_1(e))$. Moreover, $\alpha_1(e) \subseteq \alpha_2(e) \setminus\setminus y \in \mathcal{I}(e)$ and hence, $\alpha_1(e) \in \mathcal{I}(e)$, a contradiction to the supposition that $\alpha_1(e)$ is a bipolar fuzzy circuit, for each $e \in A$.

7.4 Decision Support Systems

Bipolar fuzzy matroids have intriguing applications with regards to combinatorics, graph theory, algebra, and many domains in addition to Mathematics. Bipolar fuzzy matroids are important to study the uncertain and conflicting behavior of objects if the data have incomplete and bipolar information. In this section, the applications of bipolar fuzzy matroids are discussed for a decision support system for network analysis and the ordering of machines.

7.4.1 Ordering of Machines Using Bipolar Fuzzy Matroids

The theory of bipolar fuzzy matroids have been found useful in decision support systems to find the ordering of m assignments to be fulfilled in k days if each assignment requires entire day consideration. All assignments are available at 0 time and each assignment has a profit p^p associated with it, and a penalty p^n to be paid if it is not completed at deadline d. The profit p_j^p can be achieved if each assignment j is finished at the cutoff time d_j. The problem is basically to find a bipolar fuzzy ordering of assignments to maximize the total profit. It doesn't look like a bipolar fuzzy matroid problem because the bipolar fuzzy matroid problem requires to find an optimal bipolar fuzzy subset, but this problem asks to find an ideal schedule. It is, however, a bipolar fuzzy matroid problem because the penalty and profit of any ordering can be obtained by a bipolar fuzzy subset of assignments that are on or before time.

For a bipolar fuzzy subset S of deadlines $\{d_1, d_2, \ldots, d_n\}$ corresponding to tasks $T = \{t_1, t_2, \ldots, t_n\}$, if there is a ordering such that every task in S is on or before time, and all tasks out of S are late. The procedure for the selection of tasks is given in Algorithm 7.4.1 whose time complexity is $O(n^2)$.

Table 7.5 Decision Support System

Task	Deadline	Profit	Penalty	Task	Deadline	Profit	Penalty
t_1	d_1	0.8	0.7	t_5	d_5	0.6	0.8
t_2	d_2	0.5	0.6	t_6	d_6	0.7	0.3
t_3	d_3	0.6	0.8	t_7	d_7	0.8	0.4
t_4	d_4	0.9	0.5	t_8	d_8	0.5	0.1

Algorithm 7.4.1 (*Selection of tasks to maximize profit*)

1. Input the deadline d_i corresponding to each task t_i and set $X = \{(t_i, d_i) \mid 1 \leq i \leq n\}$.
2. Input the profit p_i^p and penalty p_i^n corresponding to each task t_i.
3. **do** i from $1 \to 2^n$
4. $\quad supp(\beta_i) \in P(X)$
5. $\quad$ **do** j from $1 \to |supp(\beta_i)|$
6. $\quad\quad y_j \in supp(\beta_i)$
7. $\quad\quad \text{cost}(\beta_i) = \text{cost}(\beta_i) + \frac{\mu^p_{\beta_i}(y_j)+\mu^n_{\beta_i}(y_j)+1}{2}$
8. $\quad$ **end do**
9. **end do**
10. Calculate cost$= \max\{\text{cost}(\beta_i) \mid 1 \leq i \leq 2^n\}$
11. Choose a subset β_i such that cost $= \text{cost}(\beta_i)$.
12. Construct a bipolar fuzzy matroid $\mathcal{M} = (X, \mathcal{I})$ of tasks and deadlines such that $\mathcal{I} = \{\beta \mid supp(\beta) \subseteq supp(\beta_i)\}$.
13. To perform only $|supp(\beta)|$ number of tasks on time, any bipolar fuzzy subset of $|supp(\beta)|$ elements can be chosen from the bipolar fuzzy matroid to gain maximum profit.

As an example consider a set of eight tasks $t_1, t_2, \ldots, t_8$ with deadlines $d_1, d_2, \ldots, d_8$. If a task t_i is completed on or before the deadline, it gains a profit p_i^p, and if it is late the penalty to be paid is p_i^n. The percentage profit and penalty associated with each task is given in Table 7.5. The family of a particular number of bipolar fuzzy tasks that maximize the profit is a bipolar fuzzy matroid. Any bipolar fuzzy subset S of tasks will maximize the profit if $\sum_{(t_i,d_i)\in S} \dfrac{p_i^p + p_i^n + 1}{2}$ is maximum. The bipolar fuzzy matroid is given as

$\{\emptyset, \{((t_4, d_4), 0.9, -0.5)\}, \{((t_6, d_6), 0.7, -0.3)\}, \{((t_7, d_7), 0.8, -0.4)\}, \{((t_8, d_8), 0.5, -0.1)\}, \{((t_4, d_4), 0.9, -0.5), ((t_6, d_6), 0.7, -0.3)\}, \{((t_4, d_4), 0.9, -0.5), ((t_7, d_7), 0.8, -0.4)\}, \{((t_4, d_4), 0.9, -0.5), ((t_8, d_8), 0.5, -0.1)\}, \{((t_6, d_6), 0.7, -0.3), ((t_7, d_7), 0.8, -0.4)\}, \{((t_6, d_6), 0.7, -0.3), ((t_8, d_8), 0.5, -0.1)\}, \{((t_7, d_7), 0.8, -0.4), ((t_8, d_8), 0.5, -0.1)\}, \{((t_4, d_4), 0.9, -0.5), ((t_6, d_6), 0.7, -0.3), ((t_7, d_7), 0.8, -0.4)\}, \{((t_4, d_4), 0.9, -0.5), ((t_6, d_6), 0.7, -0.3), ((t_8, d_8), 0.5, -0.1)\}, \{((t_4, d_4), 0.9, -0.5), ((t_7, d_7), 0.8, -0.4), ((t_8, d_8), 0.5, -0.1)\}, \{((t_6, d_6), 0.7, -0.3), ((t_7, d_7), 0.8, -0.4), ((t_8, d_8), 0.5, -0.1)\}, \{((t_4, d_4), 0.9, -0.5), ((t_6, d_6), 0.7, -0.3), ((t_7, d_7), 0.8, -0.4), ((t_8, d_8), 0.5, -0.1)\}\}$

If $d_1 < d_2 < \cdots < d_8$, then the subset $supp(S) = \{d_4, d_6, d_7, d_8\}$ will maximize the profit. If we want to perform only 3 tasks on time, then any bipolar fuzzy subset of three elements can be chosen from the bipolar fuzzy matroid and similarly.

7.4.2 Network Analysis

Bipolar fuzzy matroids can be used in network analysis problems to determine the minimum number of connections for wireless communication. The procedure for the selection of minimum number of locations from a wireless connection is explained in the following steps.

1. Input the n number of locations $L_1, L_2, \ldots, L_n$ of the wireless communication network.
2. Input the adjacency matrix $\xi = [L_{ij}]_{n^2}$ of locations.
3. From this adjacency matrix, arrange the positive membership values in increasing order and negative membership values in decreasing order.
4. Select an edge having minimum positive membership value and maximum negative membership value.
5. Repeat Step 4 so that the selected edge does not create any circuit with previous selected edges.
6. Stop the procedure if the connection between every pair of locations is set up.

The use of bipolar fuzzy matroids in network analysis is explained in the following example. Bipolar fuzzy graph in Fig. 7.4 represents a wireless communication between five locations L_1, L_2, L_3, L_4, L_5. The positive degree of each edge shows the signal damage through this path, and negative degree indicates the strong signal strength in sending a message from one location to the other. Each pair of vertices is connected by an edge. But, in general, we do not need connections among all the vertices because the vertices linked indirectly will also have a message service between them, i.e., if there is a connection from L_2 to L_3 and L_3 to L_4, then we can send a message from L_2 to L_4 even if there is no edge between L_2 and L_4. The problem is to find a set of edges such that we are able to send a message between every two vertices under the condition that the signal disturbance is minimum. The procedure is as follows: Arrange the positive membership values of edges in increasing order and negative membership values in decreasing order as $\{(0.5, -0.28), (0.5, -0.33), (0.6, -0.37), (0.7, -0.41), (0.7, -0.44), (0.7, -0.46), (0.7, -0.48), (0.8, -0.5), (0.8, -0.51), (0.8, -0.53)\}$. At each step, select an edge having minimum positive membership value and maximum negative membership so that it does not create any circuit with previous selected edges. The bipolar fuzzy set of the selected edges is $\{(L_3L_4, 0.5, -0.28), (L_3L_5, 0.6, -0.33), (L_1L_5, 0.6, -0.37), (L_2L_4, 0.7, -0.41), (L_1L_4, 0.7, -0.46)\}$.

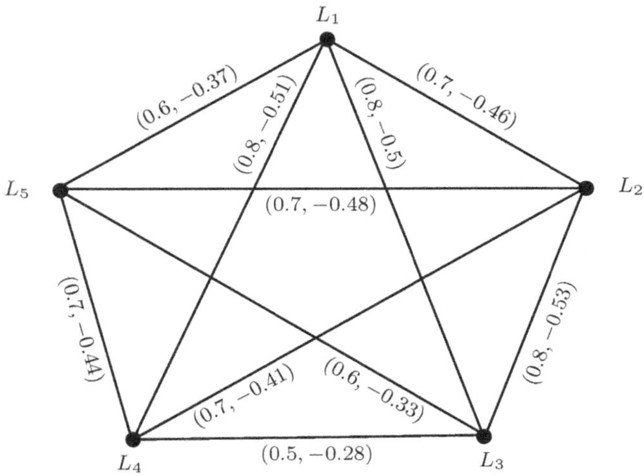

Fig. 7.4 Wireless communication

7.4.3 Ordering of Tasks Using Bipolar Fuzzy Soft Matroids

The theory of bipolar fuzzy soft matroids is also useful in decision support systems to find the ordering of n products' manufacturing in k days if all the products require equal time. Let e_1 and e_2 be two parameters under consideration for the ordering of tasks, where e_1 represents profit (and loss) and e_2 represents the demand (and supply).

1. Each product has a profit $p_j^p(e_1)$ if it is completed within the required time, and a loss of $p_j^n(e_1)$ if it is not completed within the deadline d_j.

2. Each product has a demand $p_j^p(e_2)$ associated with it, and supply of $p_j^n(e_2)$ within the deadline d_j.

As an example, consider a set of four products $\mathcal{P} = \{P_1, P_2, P_3, P_4\}$ with deadlines d_1, d_2, d_3, d_4. The percentage profit, loss, demand, and supply associated with each product is given in Table 7.6.

The family of a particular number of bipolar fuzzy soft sets that maximize the profit is a bipolar fuzzy soft matroid. If we consider that only two products can be manu-

Table 7.6 Bipolar fuzzy soft information

Task	Deadline	Profit	Loss	Product	Deadline	Demand	Supply
P_1	d_1	0.8	0.7	P_1	d_1	0.6	0.8
P_2	d_2	0.5	0.6	P_2	d_2	0.7	0.3
P_3	d_3	0.6	0.8	P_3	d_3	0.8	0.4
P_4	d_4	0.9	0.5	P_4	d_4	0.5	0.1

factured within d days, then a uniform bipolar fuzzy soft matroid can be constructed. The family of independent bipolar fuzzy subsets corresponding to parameters e_1 and e_2 are calculated as

$\mathcal{I}(e_1) = \{\beta \mid \beta \subset \{(P_3, 0.5, -0.6), (P_2, 0.5, -0.6), (P_3, 0.6, -0.8), (P_4, 0.9, -0.5)\}, |supp(\beta)| \leq 2\}$,

$\mathcal{I}(e_2) = \{\beta \mid \beta \subset \{(P_3, 0.6, -0.8), (P_2, 0.7, -0.3), (P_3, 0.8, -0.4), (P_4, 0.5, -0.1)\}, |supp(\beta)| \leq 2\}$.

Any bipolar fuzzy subset $S(e_i)$ of products will maximize the profit if $\sum_{P_j \in S(e_i)} \frac{p_j^p(e_i)+p_j^n(e_i)+1}{2}$, $i \in \{1, 2\}$, is maximum. The problem can also be solved similarly if the numbers of days for completing the tasks are 3 or 4.

7.5 Conclusions

In this chapter, we have discussed the notions of bipolar fuzzy vector spaces and bipolar fuzzy matroids and, linked major ideas of linear algebra and bipolar fuzzy graph theory in the form of linear bipolar fuzzy matroids, uniform bipolar fuzzy matroids, partition bipolar fuzzy matroids, and cycle bipolar fuzzy matroids. We put special emphasis on fundamental properties of bipolar fuzzy rank function, bipolar fuzzy circuits, and linear independence of bipolar fuzzy matroids. We have established the relation of crisp matroids and bipolar fuzzy matroids using $(\alpha, \beta)-$cuts and studied the concept of the closure of bipolar fuzzy matroids, $\mathcal{M}-$induced matroid sequence, fundamental sequence, and circuit rectangles. We have also introduced the concepts of matroids and circuits in a soft environment and a bipolar fuzzy soft environment. We have studied the importance of the presented concepts in decision support systems and network analysis.

Exercises 7

1. A bipolar fuzzy basis for a bipolar fuzzy matroid $\mathcal{M} = (X, \mathcal{I})$ is a maximal member in $\mathcal{I}$. Let $\mathcal{M}$ be a fuzzy matroid, then $\mathcal{M}$ is closed if and only if for each $\beta \in \mathcal{I}$, there is a bipolar fuzzy basis $\gamma \in \mathcal{I}$ such that $\beta \subseteq \gamma$.
2. If $\overline{\lambda}_r$ and λ_r are bipolar fuzzy rank functions of $\overline{\mathcal{M}} = (X, \overline{\mathcal{I}})$ and $\mathcal{M} = (X, \mathcal{I})$, respectively, then $\overline{\lambda}_r = \lambda_r$.
3. Let $\mathcal{M} = (X, \mathcal{I})$ be a bipolar fuzzy matroid with fundamental sequence $\boldsymbol{t}_0, \boldsymbol{t}_1, \ldots, \boldsymbol{t}_n$. $\mathcal{M}$ is said to be **regular** if whenever for $\boldsymbol{t}_i = (t_i^p, t_i^n)$, $t_i^p < t_j^p$, $t_i^n > t_j^n$ and β is a basis of $(X, \mathcal{I}_{t_i})$, there is a basis γ of $(X, \mathcal{I}_{t_j})$ such that $\gamma \subseteq \beta$. Prove that $\mathcal{M}$ is regular if and only if all fuzzy bases for $\mathcal{M}$ have the same cardinality.

4. Let $\mathcal{M} = (X, \mathcal{I})$ be a bipolar fuzzy matroid with fundamental sequence $\boldsymbol{t}_0, \boldsymbol{t}_1, \ldots, \boldsymbol{t}_n$. If β is a bipolar fuzzy basis of $\mathcal{M}$, then prove that $\beta_{\boldsymbol{t}_i}$ is a basis for $(X, \mathcal{I}_{\boldsymbol{t}_i})$, for each $1 \leq i \leq n$.
5. Let $\mathcal{M} = (X, \mathcal{I})$ be a closed regular bipolar fuzzy matroid with fundamental sequence
$\boldsymbol{t}_0, \boldsymbol{t}_1, \ldots, \boldsymbol{t}_n$. If for $i < j$, β_i is a basis of $(X, \mathcal{I}_{\boldsymbol{t}_i})$ and β_j is a basis of $(X, \mathcal{I}_{\boldsymbol{t}_j})$, then $|\beta_i| > |\beta_j|$.

References

1. Abdullah, S., Aslam, M., Ullah, K.: Bipolar fuzzy soft sets and its applications in decision making problem. J. Intell. Fuzzy Syst. **27**(2), 729–742 (2014)
2. Akram, M.: Bipolar fuzzy graphs. Inf. Sci. **181**(24), 5548–5564 (2011)
3. Akram, M.: Bipolar fuzzy graphs with applications. Knowl.-Based Syst. **39**, 1–8 (2013)
4. Akram, M.: Bipolar fuzzy soft Lie algebras. Quasigroups Relat. Syst. **21**(1), 1–10 (2013)
5. Akram, M., Dudek, W.A.: Regular bipolar fuzzy graphs. Neural Comput. Appl. **21**(supp 1), 197–205 (2012)
6. Akram, M., Feng, F., Borumand Saeid, A., Leoreanu-Fotea, V.: A new multiple criteria decision-making method based on bipolar fuzzy soft graphs. Iran. J. Fuzzy Syst. **15**(4), 73–92 (2018)
7. Akram, M., Alshehri, N., Davvaz, B., Ashraf, A.: Bipolar fuzzy digraphs in decision support systems. J. Mult.-Valued Log. Soft Comput. **27**(5–6), 531–551 (2016)
8. Feng, F., Liu, X., Leoreanu-Fotea, V., Jun, Y.B.: Soft sets and soft rough sets. Inf. Sci. **181**(6), 1125–1137 (2011)
9. Kharal, A., Ahmad, B.: Mappings on soft classes. New Math. Nat. Comput. **7**(03), 471–481 (2011)
10. Goetschel Jr., R., Voxman, W.: Fuzzy matroids. Fuzzy Sets Syst. **27**(3), 291–302 (1988)
11. Goetschel, Jr., R., Voxman, W.: Bases of fuzzy matroids. Fuzzy Sets Syst. **31**(2), 253–261 (1989)
12. Goetschel, Jr., R., Voxman, W.: Fuzzy circuits. Fuzzy Sets Syst. **32**(1), 35–43 (1989)
13. Goetschel, Jr., R., Voxman, W.: Fuzzy matroids and a greedy algorithm. Fuzzy Sets Syst. **37**(2), 201–214 (1990)
14. Goetschel, Jr., R., Voxman, W.: Fuzzy matroid structures. Fuzzy Sets Syst. **41**(3), 343–357 (1991)
15. Goetschel, Jr., R., Voxman, W.: Fuzzy rank functions. Fuzzy Sets Syst. **42**(2), 245–258 (1991)
16. Goetschel, Jr., R., Voxman, W.: Fuzzy matroid sums and a greedy algorithm. Fuzzy Sets Syst. **52**(2), 189–200 (1992)
17. Hsueh, Y.-C.: On fuzzification of matroids. Fuzzy Sets Syst. **53**(3), 319–327 (1993)
18. Maji, P.K., Biswas, R., Roy, A.R.: Fuzzy soft sets. J. Fuzzy Math. **9**(3), 589–602 (2001)
19. Molodtsov, D.: Soft set theory-first results. Comput. Math. Appl. **37**(4–5), 19–31 (1999)
20. Novak, L.A.: A comment on "Bases of fuzzy matroids" Fuzzy Sets and Systems 31 (1989) 253–261. Fuzzy Sets Syst. **87**(2), 251–252 (1997)
21. Novak, L.A.: On fuzzy independence set systems. Fuzzy Sets Syst. **91**(3), 365–374 (1997)
22. Novak, L.A.: On Goetschel and Voxman fuzzy matroids. Fuzzy Sets Syst. **117**(3), 407–412 (2001)
23. Roy, A.R., Maji, P.K.: A fuzzy soft set theoretic approach to decision making problems. J. Comput. Appl. Math. **203**(2), 412–418 (2007)
24. Sarwar, M., Akram, M.: New applications of m-polar fuzzy matroids. Symmetry **9**, 319 (2017). https://doi.org/10.3390/sym9120319

25. Sarwar, M., Akram, M.: Bipolar fuzzy circuits with applications. J. Intell. Fuzzy Syst. **34**(1), 547–58 (2018)
26. Shi, F.-G.: A new approach to the fuzzification of matroids. Fuzzy Sets Syst. **160**(5), 696–705 (2009)
27. Shi, F.-G.: (L, M)-fuzzy matroids. Fuzzy Sets Syst. **160**(16), 2387–2400 (2009)
28. Whitney, H.: On the abstract properties of linear dependence. Am. J. Math. **57**(3), 509–533 (1935)
29. Wilson, R.J.: An introduction to matroid theory. Am. Math. Mon. **80**(5), 500–525 (1973)
30. Zhang, W.-R.: Bipolar fuzzy sets and relations: a computational framework for cognitive modeling and multiagent decision analysis. In: Proceedings of IEEE Conference, pp. 305–309 (1994)
31. Zhang, W.-R.: (YinYang) Bipolar fuzzy sets. In: IEEE International Conference on Fuzzy Systems, pp. 835–840 (1998)
32. Zhang, W.-R., Zhang, J.H., Shi, Y., Chen, S.S.: Bipolar linear algebra and YinYang-N-element cellular networks for equilibrium-based biosystem simulation and regulation. J. Biol. Syst. **17**(4), 547–576 (2009)

Chapter 8
Energy of Bipolar Fuzzy Graphs

In this chapter, we study the concept of energy of bipolar fuzzy graphs and present certain formulae, lower and upper bounds of Laplacian energy, signless Laplacian energy, dominating energy, out-dominating energy, double dominating energy, and double out-dominating energy of bipolar fuzzy graphs and bipolar fuzzy digraphs. We elaborate the presented concept of energy and its extensions with numerical and graphical examples. Using bipolar fuzzy preference relations, we present multi-criteria decision-making models based on the energy of bipolar fuzzy graphs in business partnerships and smooth communication problems. The main results of this chapter are from [3, 4, 14].

8.1 Introduction

Several matrices can be associated with a graph such as the adjacency matrix (denoted by A) or the Laplacian matrix $L = D - A$, where D is the diagonal matrix of the degrees. The properties of the spectrum of a graph are related to the properties of a graph. The area of graph theory that deals with these concepts is called the **spectral graph theory**. There are numerous applications of graph spectra in Chemistry, Physics, Computer Science, Biology, and Mathematics:

1. The first mathematical paper on graph spectra was motivated by the membrane vibration problem, i.e., by approximative solving of partial differential equations. The main applications of graph spectra in Chemistry is the application in a theory of unsaturated conjugated hydrocarbons known as the **Hückel molecular orbital theory**.

2. In Physics: Treating the membrane vibration problem by approximative solving of the corresponding partial differential equation leads to the consideration of eigenvalues of a graph. The dimer problem is related to the investigation of the thermodynamic properties of a system of diatomic molecules (dimers) adsorbed on the surface of a crystal. The most favorable points for the adsorption of atoms on such

M. Akram et al., *Graphs for the Analysis of Bipolar Fuzzy Information*, Studies in Fuzziness and Soft Computing 401,
https://doi.org/10.1007/978-981-15-8756-6_8

a surface form a two-dimensional lattice, and a dimer can occupy two neighboring points. A graph can be associated with a given adsorption surface. The vertices of the graph represent the points which are the most favorable for adsorption. Two vertices are adjacent if and only if the corresponding points can be occupied by a dimer. An arrangement of dimers on the surface determines a 1-factor in the corresponding graph, and vice versa. Thus, the dimer problem is reduced to the task of determining the number of 1-factors in a graph. The enumeration of 1-factors involves the consideration of walks in corresponding graphs and graph eigenvalues.

3. One of the oldest applications (from the 1970s) of eigenvalues in Computer Science is related to graphs called expanders. Avoiding a formal definition, we shall say that a graph has good expanding properties if each subset of the vertex set of small cardinality has a set of neighbors of large cardinality. Expanders and some related graphs (called enlargers, magnifiers, concentrators, and superconcentrators, just to mention some specific terms) appear in the treatment of several problems in Computer Science (for example, communication networks, error-correcting codes, optimizing memory space, computing functions, and sorting algorithms).

4. The largest eigenvalue (λ) of a matrix plays an important role in modeling virus propagation in computer networks. The smaller the largest eigenvalue, the larger the robustness of a network against the spread of viruses. In fact, it was shown that the epidemic threshold in spreading viruses is proportional to $\frac{1}{\lambda}$. Motivated by this fact, that graphs with minimal λ among other graphs are determined with a given number of vertices and edges, and having a given diameter.

5. Combinatorial matrix theory studies matrices with several digraphs. Many results and techniques from the theory of graph spectra can be applied for the foundation and development of matrix theory. The largest eigenvalue of a minimal spanning tree of the complete weighted graphs, with distances between cities serving as weights, can be used as a complexity index for the traveling salesman problem.

6. Networks appearing in biology have been analyzed by spectra of the normalized graph. Research and development networks (R&D networks) are studied by the largest eigenvalue of the adjacency matrix.

A concept related to the spectrum of a graph is that of the energy of the graph. In relevance to $\pi-$electron energy of molecules, the concept of energy of a graph G was studied by Gutman [13], in 1978, as the sum of absolute values of the eigenvalues of the adjacency matrix of G. Some structural properties can be deduced from the spectrum but in general, we cannot determine the nature of a graph from its adjacency or Laplacian spectrum alone. The energy of a graph is very important in this sense. A lot of work, on the energy of graphs and its various types, has been done by Gutman [7–9]. Anjali and Mathew [5] introduced the concept of energy of fuzzy graphs as the sum of absolute values of the eigenvalues of the adjacency matrix of the fuzzy graph. Praba et al. [15] extended this concept to intuitionistic fuzzy graphs and discussed lower and upper bounds of the energy of intuitionistic fuzzy graphs. Sharbaf and Fayazi [16] studied the notions of the Laplacian spectrum and Laplacian energy in fuzzy graphs. Naz et al. [14] introduced the concept of energy under bipolar fuzzy environment and its applications to decision making problems. Akram et al. [3] discussed Laplacian and singless Laplacian energy of bipolar fuzzy graphs and bipolar fuzzy digraphs. For further terminologies and studies on energy of fuzzy graphs and their extensions, readers are referred to [1, 2, 6, 10–12, 17–19].

8.2 Energy of Bipolar Fuzzy Graphs

If G is a graph (digraph) with n vertices and m edges, then its adjacency matrix $A(G)$ is the $n \times n$ matrix whose ijth entry is the number of edges joining vertices i and j. The eigenvalues $\lambda_1, \lambda_2, \ldots, \lambda_n$ of the adjacency matrix of G are the eigenvalues of G. The set $\{\lambda_1, \lambda_2, \ldots, \lambda_n\}$ is the **spectrum** of G and is denoted by $Spec(G)$. The eigenvalues of a graph satisfy the following relations.

$$\sum_{i=1}^{n} \lambda_i = 0, \quad \sum_{i=1}^{n} \lambda_i^2 = 2m.$$

The **energy** of a graph G, denoted by $E(G)$, is defined as the sum of the absolute values of the eigenvalues of G, i.e., $E(G) = \sum_{i=1}^{n} |\lambda_i|$. A graph with all isolated vertices K_n^c has zero energy while the complete graph K_n with n vertices has energy $2(n-1)$. The energy of a digraph $\vec{G}$, denoted by $E(\vec{G})$, is defined as the sum of the absolute values of the real part of eigenvalues of $\vec{G}$, i.e., $E(\vec{G}) = \sum_{i=1}^{n} |\mathrm{Re}(z_i)|$.

Definition 8.1 The **degree** of a vertex x in a bipolar fuzzy graph G is defined as a pair $\deg(x) = (\deg^p(x), \deg^n(x))$, where $\deg^p(x) = \sum_{y \in X} \mu_B^p(xy)$ and $\deg^n(x) = \sum_{y \in X} \mu_B^n(xy)$.

Definition 8.2 Let $G = (A, B)$ be a bipolar fuzzy graph on X. If all vertices of G have the same degree, then G is called a **regular bipolar fuzzy graph** , that is, $\deg(x) = \deg(y)$, for all $x, y \in X$.

Definition 8.3 The **total degree** of a vertex x in a bipolar fuzzy graph G is denoted by $T\deg(x) = (T\deg^p(x), T\deg^n(x))$ and defined as

$$T\deg^p(x) = \sum_{xy \in E} \mu_B^p(xy) + \mu_A^p(x) = \deg^p(x) + \mu_A^p(x),$$

$$T\deg^n(x) = \sum_{xy \in E} \mu_B^n(xy) + \mu_A^n(x) = \deg^n(x) + \mu_A^n(x).$$

If each vertex of G has the same total degree, then G is called a **totally regular bipolar fuzzy graph**.

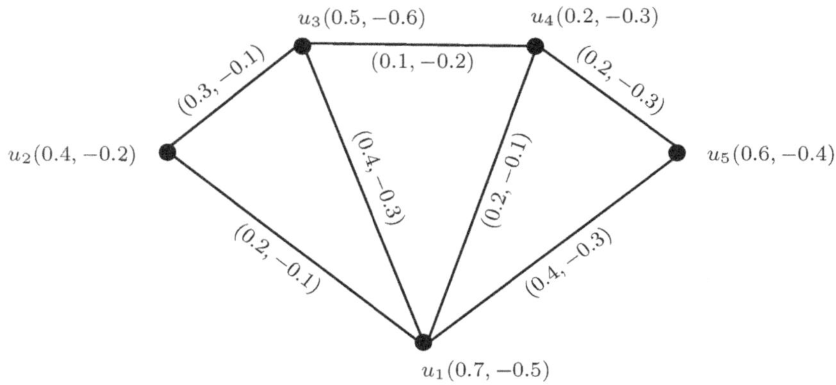

Fig. 8.1 Bipolar fuzzy graph G

Definition 8.4 Let $G = (A, B)$ be a bipolar fuzzy graph on a non-empty set X. The **adjacency matrix** $A(G)$ of G is defined as a square matrix $A(G) = [a_{ij}]_{n\times n}$, where $a_{ij} = (\mu_B^p(u_iu_j), \mu_B^n(u_iu_j))$, $u_i, u_j \in X$. The adjacency matrix can also be written as $A(G) = (A^p(G), A^n(G))$, where $A^p(G)$ and $A^n(G)$ are the adjacency matrices corresponding to positive and negative membership values of the edges, respectively.

Example 8.1 Consider a bipolar fuzzy graph $G = (A, B)$ on $X = \{u_1, u_2, u_3, u_4, u_5\}$ as shown in Fig. 8.1. The adjacency matrix $A(G)$ of Fig. 8.1 is shown in Eq. (8.1).

$$A(G) = \begin{bmatrix} (0,0) & (0.2,-0.1) & (0.4,-0.3) & (0.2,-0.1) & (0.4,-0.3) \\ (0.2,-0.1) & (0,0) & (0.3,-0.1) & (0,0) & (0,0) \\ (0.4,-0.3) & (0.3,-0.1) & (0,0) & (0.1,-0.2) & (0,0) \\ (0.2,-0.1) & (0,0) & (0.1,-0.2) & (0,0) & (0.2,-0.3) \\ (0.4,-0.3) & (0,0) & (0,0) & (0.2,-0.3) & (0,0) \end{bmatrix}. \quad (8.1)$$

Definition 8.5 Let $G = (A, B)$ be a bipolar fuzzy graph on X with $A^p(G)$ and $A^n(G)$ as the adjacency matrices of positive and negative membership values of the edges, respectively. If $\lambda_1 \geq \lambda_2 \geq \cdots \geq \lambda_n$ are the eigenvalues of $A^p(G)$ in nonincreasing order then the spectrum of $A^p(G)$ is $Spec^p(G) = \{\lambda_1, \lambda_2, \ldots, \lambda_n\}$, called **$\mu^p$-spectrum** of G. If $\delta_1 \leq \delta_2 \leq \cdots \leq \delta_n$ are the eigenvalues of $A^n(G)$ in nondecreasing order, then the spectrum of $A^n(G)$ is $Spec^n(G) = \{\delta_1, \delta_2, \ldots, \delta_n\}$, called **$\mu^n$-spectrum** of G. The **spectrum** of G is denoted by $spec(G)$ and defined as a set $Spec(G) = \{(\lambda_1, \delta_1), (\lambda_2, \delta_2), \ldots, (\lambda_n, \delta_n)\}$.

Definition 8.6 The **energy** of a bipolar fuzzy graph is defined as an ordered pair $E(G) = (E^p(G), E^n(G))$, where $E^p(G)$ and $E^n(G)$ are the sum of absolute values of eigenvalues of $A^p(G)$ and $A^n(G)$, respectively. It can also be written as $E(G) = \left(\sum_{i=1}^{n} |\lambda_i|, \sum_{i=1}^{n} |\delta_i|\right)$.

Theorem 8.1 Let $G = (A, B)$ be a bipolar fuzzy graph with adjacency matrix $A(G) = [(a^p_{ij}, a^n_{ij})]_{n\times n}$, then

1. $\sum\limits_{i=1}^{n} \lambda_i = 0, \quad \sum\limits_{i=1}^{n} \delta_i = 0,$
2. $\sum\limits_{i=1}^{n} (\lambda_i)^2 = \sum\limits_{i=1}^{n} \sum\limits_{\substack{j=1\\ i\neq j}}^{n} (a^p_{ij})(a^p_{ji}),$
3. $\sum\limits_{i=1}^{n} (\delta_i)^2 = \sum\limits_{i=1}^{n} \sum\limits_{\substack{j=1\\ i\neq j}}^{n} (a^n_{ij})(a^n_{ji}).$

Proof 1. As the sum of eigenvalues of a matrix is equal to trace of the matrix,

$$\left(\sum_{i=1}^{n} \lambda_i, \sum_{i=1}^{n} \delta_i\right) = \sum_{u_i\in X} (a^p_{ii}, a^n_{ii}) = (0, 0).$$

2. Similarly, the sum of squares of eigenvalues of the matrices $A^p(G)$ and $A^n(G)$ are equal to the trace of $(A^p(G))^2$ and $(A^n(G))^2$, respectively, so

$$\begin{aligned}
\sum_{i=1}^{n} (\lambda_i)^2 =& \left[(a^p_{11})^2 + a^p_{12} \times a^p_{21} + a^p_{13} \times a^p_{31} + \cdots + a^p_{1n} \times a^p_{n1}\right] \\
&+ \left[a^p_{21} \times a^p_{12} + (a^p_{22})^2 + a^p_{23} \times a^p_{32} + \cdots + a^p_{2n} \times a^p_{n2}\right] \\
&\vdots \\
&+ \left[a^p_{n1} \times a^p_{1n} + a^p_{n2} \times a^p_{2n} + a^p_{n3} \times a^p_{3n} + \cdots + (a^p_{nn})^2\right] \\
=& \sum_{i=1}^{n} (a^p_{ii})^2 + \sum_{i=1}^{n} \sum_{\substack{j=1\\ i\neq j}}^{n} (a^p_{ij})(a^p_{ji}). \\
=& \sum_{i=1}^{n} \sum_{\substack{j=1\\ i\neq j}}^{n} (a^p_{ij})(a^p_{ji}) \quad \because a^p_{ii} = 0, \quad \text{for all } u_i \in X.
\end{aligned}$$

Condition 3 can be proved on the same lines as of that condition 2. □

Example 8.2 The spectrum and energy of a bipolar fuzzy graph G, given in Fig. 8.1, are as follows:

$$Spec(G) = \{(-0.5661, -0.6219), (-0.2767, -0.1029), (-0.1504, 0.0814), (0.2075, 0.1361), (0.7857, 0.5074)\},$$

$E(G) = (1.9864, 1.4498)$. Further, $\sum\limits_{i=1}^{5} \lambda_i = -0.5661 - 0.2767 - 0.1504 + 0.2075 + 0.7857 = 0$,
$\sum\limits_{i=1}^{5} \delta_i = -0.6219 - 0.1029 + 0.0814 + 0.1361 + 0.5074 = 0$. $\sum\limits_{i=1}^{5} \lambda_i^2 = 1.0800 =$

$$2(0.54) = 2\sum_{i=1}^{n}\sum_{\substack{j=1\\ i\neq j}}^{5}(a^p_{ij})(a^p_{ji}),$$

$$\sum_{i=1}^{5}\delta_i^2 = 0.6800 = 2(0.34) = 2\sum_{i=1}^{n}\sum_{\substack{j=1\\ i\neq j}}^{5}(a^n_{ij})(a^n_{ji}).$$

The upper and lower bounds of energy of a bipolar fuzzy graph G in terms of the number of vertices and the sum of squares of positive membership and negative membership values of edges are discussed in the following theorems.

Theorem 8.2 *Let $G = (A, B)$ be a bipolar fuzzy graph with n vertices. If $A(G) = [(a^p_{ij}, a^n_{ij})]_{n\times n}$, $Q = det(A^p(G)) = det([a^p_{ij}]_{n\times n})$, $R = det(A^n(G)) = det([a^n_{ij}]_{n\times n})$, then*

1. $\sqrt{\sum_{i\neq j}(a^p_{ij})(a^p_{ji}) + n(n-1)Q^{\frac{2}{n}}} \leq E^p(G) \leq \sqrt{n\sum_{i\neq j}(a^p_{ij})(a^p_{ji})}.$
2. $\sqrt{\sum_{i\neq j}(a^n_{ij})(a^n_{ji}) + n(n-1)R^{\frac{2}{n}}} \leq E^n(G) \leq \sqrt{n\sum_{i\neq j}(a^n_{ij})(a^p_{ji})}.$

Proof The Cauchy Schwarz inequality is $\left(\sum_{i=1}^{n}u_iv_i\right)^2 \leq \left(\sum_{i=1}^{n}u_i^2\right)\left(\sum_{i=1}^{n}v_i^2\right)$.
1. In Cauchy Schwarz inequality, substituting $u_i = 1$, $v_i = |\lambda_i|$ and using Theorem 8.1, it follows that

$$\left(\sum_{i=1}^{n}|\lambda_i|\right)^2 \leq \left(\sum_{i=1}^{n}1\right)\left(\sum_{i=1}^{n}(\lambda_i)^2\right) = n\sum_{i\neq j}(a^p_{ij})(a^p_{ji})$$

$$\Rightarrow E^p(G) = \sum_{i=1}^{n}|\lambda_i| \leq \sqrt{n\sum_{i\neq j}(a^p_{ij})(a^p_{ji})}$$

$$\left(\sum_{i=1}^{n}|\lambda_i|\right)^2 = \sum_{i=1}^{n}|\lambda_i|^2 + \sum_{i\neq j}|\lambda_i||\lambda_j|. \tag{8.2}$$

Consider the set of $n(n-1)$ values $|\lambda_i||\lambda_j|$, $i\neq j$, $1\leq i, j\leq n$. Clearly, the arithmetic mean of these values is $A.M = \frac{1}{n(n-1)}\sum_{i\neq j}|\lambda_i||\lambda_j|$ and the geometric mean is $G.M = \left(\prod_{i\neq j}|\lambda_i||\lambda_j|\right)^{\frac{1}{n(n-1)}}$. As arithmetic mean is always greater than or equal to geometric mean,

$$\frac{1}{n(n-1)}\sum_{i\neq j}|\lambda_i||\lambda_j| \geq \left(\prod_{i\neq j}|\lambda_i||\lambda_j|\right)^{\frac{1}{n(n-1)}} = \left(\prod_{i=1}^{n}|\lambda_i|^{2(n-1)}\right)^{\frac{1}{n(n-1)}} = \left(\prod_{i=1}^{n}|\lambda_i|\right)^{\frac{2}{n}} = Q^{\frac{2}{n}}. \tag{8.3}$$

Equation (8.2) takes the form:

$$\left(\sum_{i=1}^{n}|\lambda_i|\right)^2 \geq \sum_{i=1}^{n}|\lambda_i|^2 + n(n-1)Q^{\frac{2}{n}} \sum_{i\neq j}(a_{ij}^p)(a_{ji}^p) + n(n-1)Q^{\frac{2}{n}}$$

$$\Rightarrow E^p(G) = \sum_{i=1}^{n}|\lambda_i| \geq \sqrt{\sum_{i\neq j}(a_{ij}^p)(a_{ji}^p) + n(n-1)Q^{\frac{2}{n}}}.$$

The other case can be proven with similar arguments. □

Theorem 8.3 *Let $G = (A, B)$ be a bipolar fuzzy graph with n vertices and $A^p(G) = [a_{ij}^p]_{n\times n}$, $A^n(G) = [a_{ij}^n]_{n\times n})$ be the adjacency matrices of positive and negative membership values G. If $n \leq 2\sum_{1\leq i<j\leq n}(a_{ij}^p)^2$ and $n \leq 2\sum_{1\leq i<j\leq n}(a_{ij}^n)^2$, then*

1. $E^p(G) \leq \frac{2}{n}\sum_{1\leq i<j\leq n}(a_{ij}^p)^2 + \sqrt{(n-1)\left\{2\sum_{1\leq i<j\leq n}(a_{ij}^p)^2 - \left(\frac{2}{n}\sum_{1\leq i<j\leq n}(a_{ij}^p)^2\right)^2\right\}}$,
2. $E^n(G) \leq \frac{2}{n}\sum_{1\leq i<j\leq n}(a_{ij}^n)^2 + \sqrt{(n-1)\left\{2\sum_{1\leq i<j\leq n}(a_{ij}^n)^2 - \left(\frac{2}{n}\sum_{1\leq i<j\leq n}(a_{ij}^n)^2\right)^2\right\}}$.

Proof If $A = [a_{ij}]_{n\times n}$ is a symmetric matrix with zero trace then $\lambda_{\max} \geq \frac{2}{n}\sum_{1\leq i<j\leq n} a_{ij}$, where $\lambda_{\max}$ is the maximum eigenvalue of A. If $A(G)$ is the adjacency matrix of a bipolar fuzzy graph G then $\lambda_1 \geq \frac{2}{n}\sum_{1\leq i<j\leq n} a_{ij}^p$. By Theorem 8.1,

$$\sum_{i=1}^{n}\lambda_i^2 = 2\sum_{1\leq i<j\leq n}(a_{ij}^p)^2$$

$$\sum_{i=2}^{n}\lambda_i^2 = 2\sum_{1\leq i<j\leq n}(a_{ij}^p)^2 - \lambda_1^2. \tag{8.4}$$

Applying the Cauchy–Schwarz inequality to the vectors $(1, 1, \ldots, 1)$ and $(\lambda_1|, |\lambda_2|, \ldots, |\lambda_n|)$ with $n-1$ entries, we obtain

$$E^p(G) - \lambda_1 = \sum_{i=2}^{n}|\lambda_i| \leq \sqrt{(n-1)\sum_{i=2}^{n}|\lambda_i|^2}. \tag{8.5}$$

From Eqs. (8.4) and (8.5),

$$E^p(G) - \lambda_1 \leq \sqrt{(n-1)\left(2\sum_{1\leq i<j\leq n}(a_{ij}^p)^2 - \lambda_1^2\right)}$$

$$E^p(G) \le \lambda_1 + \sqrt{(n-1)\left(2\sum_{1\le i<j\le n}(a_{ij}^p)^2 - \lambda_1^2\right)}. \tag{8.6}$$

The function $F(x) = x + \left[(n-1)\left(2\sum_{1\le i<j\le n}(a_{ij}^p)^2 - x^2\right)\right]$ decreases on the interval $\left(\left(\frac{2}{n}\sum_{1\le i<j\le n}(a_{ij}^p)^2\right)^{\frac{1}{2}}, \left(2\sum_{1\le i<j\le n}(a_{ij}^p)^2\right)^{\frac{1}{2}}\right)$. Also, $n \le 2\sum_{1\le i<j\le n}(a_{ij}^p)^2$, $1 \le \frac{2\sum_{1\le i<j\le n}(a_{ij}^p)^2}{n}$ therefore,

$$\sqrt{\frac{2}{n}\sum_{1\le i<j\le n}(a_{ij}^p)^2} \le \frac{2}{n}\sum_{1\le i<j\le n}(a_{ij}^p)^2 \le \frac{2}{n}\sum_{1\le i<j\le n}a_{ij}^p \le \lambda_1 \le \sqrt{2\sum_{1\le i<j\le n}(a_{ij}^p)^2}.$$

Equation (8.6) takes the form as

$$E^p(G) \le \frac{2}{n}\sum_{1\le i<j\le n}(a_{ij}^p)^2 + \sqrt{(n-1)\left\{2\sum_{1\le i<j\le n}(a_{ij}^p)^2 - \left(\frac{2}{n}\sum_{1\le i<j\le n}(a_{ij}^p)^2\right)^2\right\}}.$$

The other part can be proved similarly. □

Definition 8.7 Let $\overrightarrow{G} = (A, \overrightarrow{B})$ be a bipolar fuzzy digraph with n vertices and $A^p(\overrightarrow{G}) = [a_{ij}^p]_{n\times n}$ and $A^n(\overrightarrow{G}) = [a_{ij}^n]_{n\times n}$ as the nonsymmetric adjacency matrices of positive and negative membership values, respectively. Let $z_1, z_2, \ldots, z_n$ and $w_1, w_2, \ldots, w_n$ be the eigenvalues of $A^p(\overrightarrow{G})$ and $A^n(\overrightarrow{G})$, respectively. The **energy** of $\overrightarrow{G}$ is defined as an ordered pair $E(\overrightarrow{G}) = (E^p(\overrightarrow{G}), E^n(\overrightarrow{G}))$ such that

$$E^p(\overrightarrow{G}) = \sum_{i=1}^{n}|\mathrm{Re}(z_i)| \text{ and } E^n(\overrightarrow{G}) = \sum_{i=1}^{n}|\mathrm{Re}(w_i)|.$$

Example 8.3 Let $\overrightarrow{G} = (A, \overrightarrow{B})$ be a bipolar fuzzy digraph on $X = \{u_1, u_2, u_3, u_4, u_5\}$ as given in Fig. 8.2.

The corresponding adjacency matrix $A(\overrightarrow{G})$ of $\overrightarrow{G}$ is given in Eq. (8.7).

$$A(\overrightarrow{G}) = \begin{bmatrix} (0,0) & (0.6,-0.1) & (0,0) & (0,0) & (0,0) \\ (0,0) & (0,0) & (0.1,-0.2) & (0,0) & (0,0) \\ (0.2,-0.4) & (0,0) & (0,0) & (0.2,-0.1) & (0,0) \\ (0.4,-0.1) & (0,0) & (0,0) & (0,0) & (0,0) \\ (0,0) & (0,0) & (0,0) & (0.3,-0.2) & (0,0) \end{bmatrix}. \tag{8.7}$$

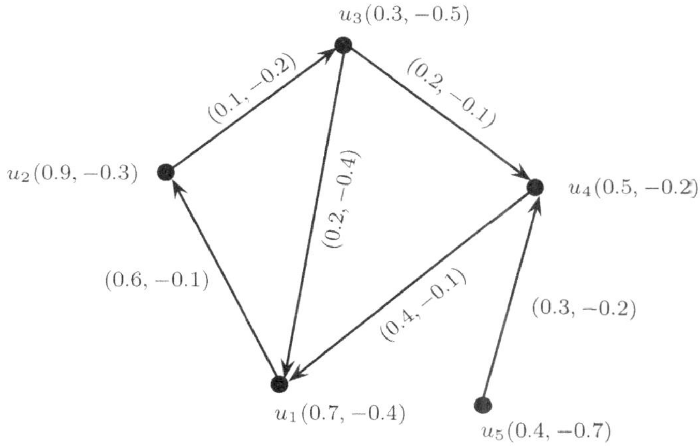

Fig. 8.2 Bipolar fuzzy digraph

The spectrum and energy of a bipolar fuzzy digraph $\overrightarrow{G}$, given in Fig. 8.2, are $Spec(\overrightarrow{G}) = \{(0, 0), (0.3031, -0.2077), (-0.0432 + 0.2669i, 0.0914 - 0.1739i), (-0.0432 - 0.2669i, 0.0914 - 0.1739i), (-0.2166, 0.0250)\}$ and $E(\overrightarrow{G}) = (0.6061, 0.4154)$.

8.3 Laplacian Energy of Bipolar Fuzzy Graphs

In this section, certain bounds and formulae of Laplacian energy and signless Laplacian energy of bipolar fuzzy graphs are presented.

Definition 8.8 Let $G = (A, B)$ be a bipolar fuzzy graph on a non-empty set X. The **degree matrix** of G is defined as a square matrix $D(G) = [d_{ij}]_{n\times n} = [d^p_{ij}, d^n_{ij}]_{n\times n}$ such that

$$d_{ij} = \begin{cases} deg(v_i), & \text{if } i = j, \; v_i \in X, \\ (0, 0) & \text{otherwise.} \end{cases}$$

Definition 8.9 The **Laplacian matrix** of a bipolar fuzzy graph $G = (A, B)$ is a matrix of the form $L(G) = [l^p_{ij}, l^n_{ij}]_{n\times n} = D(G) - A(G)$, where $D(G)$ is the degree matrix of G and $A(G)$ is the adjacency matrix G. The **Laplacian spectrum** $LSpec(G) = (LSpec^p(G), LSpec^n(G))$ of G can be defined using the eigenvalues of $L^p(G)$ and $L^n(G)$ as explained in Definition 8.6.

Example 8.4 Consider a bipolar fuzzy graph $G = (A, B)$ on $X = \{v_1, v_2, v_3, v_4, v_5, v_6, v_7\}$ as shown in Fig. 8.3. The adjacecy matrix, degree matrix, and Laplacian matrix of the bipolar fuzzy graph G are computed as:

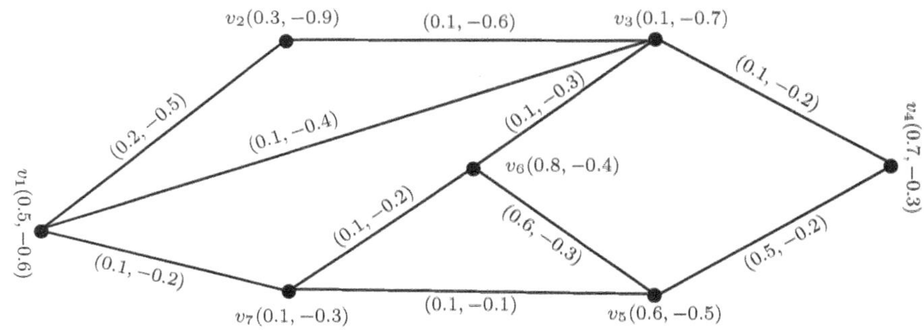

Fig. 8.3 Bipolar fuzzy graph G

$$A(G) = \begin{pmatrix} (0,0) & (0.2,-0.5) & (0.1,-0.4) & (0,0) & (0,0) & (0,0) & (0.1,-0.2) \\ (0.2,-0.5) & (0,0) & (0.1,-0.6) & (0,0) & (0,0) & (0,0) & (0,0) \\ (0.1,-0.4) & (0.1,-0.6) & (0,0) & (0.1,-0.2) & (0,0) & (0.1,-0.3) & (0,0) \\ (0,0) & (0,0) & (0.1,-0.2) & (0,0) & (0.5,-0.2) & (0,0) & (0,0) \\ (0,0) & (0,0) & (0,0) & (0.5,-0.2) & (0,0) & (0.6,-0.3) & (0.1,-o.1) \\ (0,0) & (0,0) & (0.1,-0.3) & (0,0) & (0.6,-0.3) & (0,0) & (0.1,-0.2) \\ (0.1,-0.2) & (0,0) & (0,0) & (0,0) & (0.1,-0.1) & (0.1,-0.2) & (0,0) \end{pmatrix}$$

$$D(G) = \begin{pmatrix} (0.4,-1.1) & (0,0) & (0,0) & (0,0) & (0,0) & (0,0) & (0,0) \\ (0,0) & (0.3,-1.1) & (0,0) & (0,0) & (0,0) & (0,0) & (0,0) \\ (0,0) & (0,0) & (0.4,-1.5) & (0,0) & (0,0) & (0,0) & (0,0) \\ (0,0) & (0,0) & (0,0) & (0.6,-0.4) & (0,0) & (0,0) & (0,0) \\ (0,0) & (0,0) & (0,0) & (0,0) & (1.2,-0.6) & (0,0) & (0,0) \\ (0,0) & (0,0) & (0,0) & (0,0) & (0,0) & (0.8,-0.8) & (0,0) \\ (0,0) & (0,0) & (0,0) & (0,0) & (0,0) & (0,0) & (0.3,-0.5) \end{pmatrix}$$

$$L(G) = \begin{pmatrix} (0.4,-1.1) & (-0.2,0.5) & (-0.1,0.4) & (0,0) & (0,0) & (0,0) & (-0.1,0.2) \\ (-0.2,0.5) & (0.3,-1.1) & (-0.1,0.6) & (0,0) & (0,0) & (0,0) & (0,0) \\ (-0.1,0.4) & (-0.1,0.6) & (0.4,-1.5) & (-0.1,0.2) & (0,0) & (-0.1,0.3) & (0,0) \\ (0,0) & (0,0) & (-0.1,0.2) & (0.6,-0.4) & (-0.5,0.2) & (0,0) & (0,0) \\ (0,0) & (0,0) & (0,0) & (-0.5,0.2) & (1.2,-0.6) & (-0.6,0.3) & (-0.1,0.1) \\ (0,0) & (0,0) & (-0.1,0.3) & (0,0) & (-0.6,0.3) & (0.8,-0.8) & 0,0) \\ (-0.1,0.2) & (0,0) & (0,0) & (0,0) & (-0.1,0.1) & (0,0) & (0.3,-0.5) \end{pmatrix}.$$

By usual calculations, $LSpec^p(G) = \{0.0228, 0.1360, 0.2882, 0.4875, 0.5859, 0.6907, 1.7888\}$, $LSpec^n(G)) = \{-2.0102, -1.5903, -1.0182, -0.5622, -0.4730, -0.3027, -0.0434\}$, and $LSpec(G) = \{(0.0228, -2.0102), (0.1360, -1.5903), (0.2882, -1.0182), (0.4875, -0.5622), (0.5859, -0.4730), (0.6907, -0.3027), (1.7888, -0.0434)\}$.

Theorem 8.4 *Let* $G = (A, B)$ *be a bipolar fuzzy graph on* X *and* $L(G) = \left([l_{ij}^p]_{n\times n}, [l_{ij}^n]_{n\times n}\right)$ *be the Laplacian matrix of* G. *If* $\alpha_1 \geq \alpha_2 \geq \cdots \geq \alpha_n$ *and* $\beta_1 \leq \beta_2 \leq \cdots \leq \beta_n$ *are the eigenvalues of* $L^p(G)$ *and* $L^n(G)$, *respectively, then*

1. $\sum_{i=1}^{n} \alpha_i = \sum_{i=1}^{n} deg^p(v_i)$, $\quad \sum_{i=1}^{n} \beta_i = \sum_{i=1}^{n} deg^n(v_i)$,

2. $\sum\limits_{i=1}^{n}(\alpha_i)^2 = \sum\limits_{i=1}^{n}(d_{ii}^p)^2 + \sum\limits_{i=1}^{n}\sum\limits_{\substack{j=1\\ i\neq j}}^{n}(l_{ij}^p)(l_{ji}^p)$, $\sum\limits_{i=1}^{n}(\beta_i)^2 = \sum\limits_{i=1}^{n}(d_{ii}^n)^2 + \sum\limits_{i=1}^{n}\sum\limits_{\substack{j=1\\ i\neq j}}^{n}(l_{ij}^n)(l_{ji}^n)$.

Proof 1. The trace of $L^p(G)$ is equal to sum of its eigenvalues therefore,

$$\sum_{i=1}^{n}\alpha_i = tr(L^p(G)) = \sum_{i=1}^{n}(d_{ii}^p - a_{ii}^p) = \sum_{i=1}^{n} d_{ii}^p = \sum_{i=1}^{n} deg^p(v_i)$$

Similarly, it is so for the other case.
2. Generally, the Laplacian matrix $L^p(G)$ can be written as follows:

$$L^p(G) = \begin{bmatrix} d_{11}^p & l_{12}^p & \dots & l_{1n}^p \\ l_{21}^p & d_{22}^p & \dots & l_{2n}^p \\ \vdots & \vdots & \ddots & \vdots \\ l_{n1}^p & l_{n2}^p & \dots & d_{nn}^p \end{bmatrix}.$$

The sum of squares of eigenvalues of the matrix $L^p(G)$ is equal to the trace of $(L^p(G))^2$ so,

$$\sum_{i=1}^{n}\alpha_i^2 = tr((L^p(G))^2)$$

$$\begin{aligned}\sum_{i=1}^{n}(\alpha_i)^2 =& [(d_{11}^p)^2 + l_{12}^p \times l_{21}^p + l_{13}^p \times l_{31}^p + \dots + l_{1n}^p \times a_{n1}^p] \\ &+ [l_{21}^p \times l_{12}^p + (d_{22}^p)^2 + l_{23}^p \times l_{32}^p + \dots + l_{2n}^p \times l_{n2}^p] \\ &\vdots \\ &+ [l_{n1}^p \times l_{1n}^p + l_{n2}^p \times l_{2n}^p + l_{n3}^p \times l_{3n}^p + \dots + (d_{nn}^p)^2] \\ =& \sum_{i=1}^{n}(d_{ii}^p)^2 + \sum_{i=1}^{n}\sum_{\substack{j=1\\ i\neq j}}^{n}(l_{ij}^p)(l_{ji}^p) \\ =& \sum_{i=1}^{n}(d_{ii}^p)^2 + 2\sum_{1\le i<j\le n}(l_{ij}^p)(l_{ji}^p).\end{aligned}$$

The other part corresponding to negative membership values can be easily proved.

□

Definition 8.10 Let $G = (A, B)$ be a bipolar fuzzy graph on X and $L(G) = \left([l_{ij}^p]_{n\times n}, [l_{ij}^n]_{n\times n}\right)$ be the Laplacian matrix of G. Let $\alpha_1 \geq \alpha_2 \geq \dots \geq \alpha_n$ and $\beta_1 \leq \beta_2 \leq \dots \leq \beta_n$ be the eigenvalues of $L^p(G)$ and $L^n(G)$, respectively. If

$$\pi_i = \alpha_i - \frac{2}{n} \sum_{1 \le i < j \le n} l^p_{ij} \text{ and } \vartheta_i = \beta_i - \frac{2}{n} \sum_{1 \le i < j \le n} l^n_{ij},$$

then the **Laplacian energy** of G is defined as an ordered pair $LE(G) = (LE^p(G), LE^n(G))$ such that $LE^p(G) = \sum_{i=1}^{n} |\pi_i|$ and $LE^n(G) = \sum_{i=1}^{n} |\vartheta_i|$.

Example 8.5 The Laplacian energy of a bipolar fuzzy graph $G = (A, B)$ shown in Fig. 8.3 is $LE(G) = (2.6737, 4.0374)$.

Corollary 8.1 *Let $G = (A, B)$ be a bipolar fuzzy graph on X and $L(G) = \left([l^p_{ij}]_{n\times n}, [l^n_{ij}]_{n\times n}\right)$ be the Laplacian matrix of G. Let $\alpha_1 \ge \alpha_2 \ge \cdots \ge \alpha_n$ and $\beta_1 \le \beta_2 \le \cdots \le \beta_n$ be the eigenvalues of $L^p(G)$ and $L^n(G)$, respectively. If $\pi_i = \alpha_i - \frac{2}{n} \sum_{1\le i<j\le n} l^p_{ij}$ and $\vartheta_i = \beta_i - \frac{2}{n} \sum_{1\le i<j\le n} l^n_{ij}$, then*

1. $\sum_{i=1}^{n} \pi_i = 0\,, \quad \sum_{i=1}^{n} \vartheta_i = 0,$
2. $\sum_{i=1}^{n} (\pi_i)^2 = \sum_{i=1}^{n} (d^p_{ii} - \frac{2}{n} \sum_{1\le i<j\le n} l^p_{ij})^2 + 2 \sum_{1\le i<j\le n} (l^p_{ij})(l^p_{ji}),$
3. $\sum_{i=1}^{n} (\vartheta_i)^2 = \sum_{i=1}^{n} (d^n_{ii} - \frac{2}{n} \sum_{1\le i<j\le n} l^p_{ij})^2 + 2 \sum^{n}_{1\le i<j\le n} (l^n_{ij})(l^n_{ji}).$

Example 8.6 Consider a bipolar fuzzy graph $G = (A, B)$ on $X = \{v_1, v_2, v_3, v_4, v_5, v_6, v_7\}$ as given in Fig. 8.3. Here, $LE^p(G) = 2.6737$, $LE^n(G) = 4.0374$, $LE(G) = (2.6737, 4.0374)$. Moreover,
$\sum_{i=1}^{7} \pi_l = 0, \sum_{i=1}^{7} \vartheta_i = 0,$
$\sum_{i=1}^{7} \pi_i^2 = 2.0800 = \sum_{i=1}^{7} (d^p_{ii} - \frac{2}{7} \sum_{1\le i<j\le 7} l^p_{ij})^2 + 2 \sum_{1\le i<j\le 7} (l^p_{ij})(l^p_{ji}),$
$\sum_{i=1}^{n} \vartheta_l^2 = 3.1199 = \sum_{i=1}^{7} (d^n_{ii} - \frac{2}{7} \sum_{1\le i<j\le 7} l^n_{ij})^2 + 2 \sum_{1\le i<j\le 7} (l^n_{ij})(l^n_{ji}).$

Theorem 8.5 Let $G = (A, B)$ be a bipolar fuzzy graph with n vertices. If $L(G) = [(l^p_{ij}, l^n_{ij})]_{n\times n}$ is the Laplacian matrix of G, then

1. $LE^p(G) \le \sqrt{2n \sum_{1\le i<j\le n} (l^p_{ij})^2 + n \sum_{i=1}^{n} \left(deg^p(v_i) - \frac{2}{n} \sum_{1\le i<j\le n} l^p_{ij}\right)^2},$
2. $LE^n(G) \le \sqrt{2n \sum_{1\le i<j\le n} (l^n_{ij})^2 + n \sum_{i=1}^{n} \left(deg^n(v_i) - \frac{2}{n} \sum_{1\le i<j\le n} l^n_{ij}\right)^2}.$

Proof The Cauchy Schwarz inequality is $\left(\sum_{i=1}^{n} u_i v_i\right)^2 \le \left(\sum_{i=1}^{n} u_i^2\right)\left(\sum_{i=1}^{n} v_i^2\right)$.
1. In Cauchy Schwarz inequality, substituting $u_i = 1$, $v_i = |\pi_i|$ and using Corollary 8.1, we obtain

$$\left(\sum_{i=1}^{n}|\pi_i|\right)^2 \leq \left(\sum_{i=1}^{n}1\right)\left(\sum_{i=1}^{n}(\pi_i)^2\right) = n\left(\sum_{i=1}^{n}(d_{ii}^p - \frac{2}{n}\sum_{1\leq i<j\leq n} l_{ij}^p)^2 + \sum_{i\neq j}(\ _{ij}^p)(l_{ji}^p)\right).$$

$$\text{Hence } LE^p(G) = \sum_{i=1}^{n}|\pi_i| \leq \sqrt{n\sum_{i=1}^{n}(a_{ii}^p)^2 + 2n\sum_{1\leq i<j\leq n}(l_{ij}^p)^2}.$$

□

Theorem 8.6 *Let $G = (A, B)$ be a bipolar fuzzy graph on X, then*

1. $LE^p(G) \geq 2\sqrt{\sum_{1\leq i<j\leq n}(l_{ij}^p)^2 + \frac{1}{2}\sum_{i=1}^{n}\left(deg^p(v_i) - \frac{2}{n}\sum_{1\leq i<j\leq n} l_{ij}^p\right)^2}$,
2. $LE^n(G) \geq 2\sqrt{\sum_{1\leq i<j\leq n}(l_{ij}^n)^2 + \frac{1}{2}\sum_{i=1}^{n}\left(deg^n(v_i) - \frac{2}{n}\sum_{1\leq i<j\leq n} l_{ij}^n\right)^2}$.

Proof Take $K = \sum_{i=1}^{n}(d_{ii}^p - \frac{2}{n}\sum_{1\leq i<j\leq n} l_{ij}^p)^2 + 2\sum_{1\leq i<j\leq n}(l_{ij}^p)(l_{ji}^p)$ then from Definition 8.10 and Corollary 8.1,

$$\left(\sum_{i=1}^{n}|\pi_i|\right)^2 = \sum_{i=1}^{n}|\pi_i|^2 + 2\sum_{1\leq i<j\leq n}|\pi_i\pi_j| \geq 2K.$$

Hence the result. □

Theorem 8.7 Let $G = (A, B)$ be a bipolar fuzzy graph, then

1. $LE^p(G) \leq |\pi_1| + \sqrt{(n-1)\left(2\sum_{1\leq i<j\leq n}(l_{ij}^p)^2 + \sum_{i=1}^{n}\left(deg^p(v_i) - \frac{2}{n}\sum_{1\leq i<j\leq n} l_{ij}^p\right)^2 - \pi_1^2\right)}$.
2. $LE^n(G) \leq |\vartheta_1| + \sqrt{(n-1)\left(2\sum_{1\leq i<j\leq n}(l_{ij}^n)^2 + \sum_{i=1}^{n}\left(deg^n(v_i) - \frac{2}{n}\sum_{1\leq i<j\leq n} l_{ij}^n\right)^2 - \vartheta_1^2\right)}$.

Proof From Corollary 8.1,

$$\sum_{i=2}^{n}\pi_i^2 = \sum_{i=1}^{n}(d_{ii}^p - \frac{2}{n}\sum_{1\leq i<j\leq n} l_{ij}^p)^2 + 2\sum_{1\leq i<j\leq n}(l_{ij}^p)(l_{ji}^p). \tag{8.8}$$

Applying the Cauchy–Schwarz inequality to vectors (1, 1, ..., 1) and $(|\pi_1|, |\pi_2|, \ldots, |\pi_n|)$ with $n-1$ entries, it clearly follows that

$$E^p(G) - |\pi_1| = \sum_{i=2}^{n}|\pi_i| \leq \sqrt{(n-1)\sum_{i=2}^{n}|\pi_i|^2},$$

$$E^p(G) - |\pi_1| \leq \sqrt{(n-1)\left(\sum_{i=1}^{n}\left(d^p_{ii} - \frac{2}{n}\sum_{1\leq i<j\leq n} l^p_{ij}\right)^2 + 2\sum_{1\leq i<j\leq n}(l^p_{ij})(l^p_{ji}) - \pi_1^2\right)}. \tag{8.9}$$

As $L^p(G)$ is a symmetric matrix, required result is obtained. □

Theorem 8.8 Let $G = (A, B)$ be a k-regular bipolar fuzzy graph, then

1. $LE^p(G) \leq |\pi_1| + \sqrt{(n-1)\left(2\sum_{1\leq i<j\leq n}(l^p_{ij})^2 - \pi_1^2\right)}$,
2. $LE^n(G) \leq |\vartheta_1| + \sqrt{(n-1)\left(2\sum_{1\leq i<j\leq n}(l^n_{ij})^2 - \vartheta_1^2\right)}$.

Proof Let G be a $k-$regular bipolar fuzzy graph, then $deg(u_i) = k = (k^p, k^n)$, for each $u_i \in X$. Without any loss of generality, assume that $k^p = \frac{2}{n}\sum\limits_{1\leq i<j\leq n} l^p_{ij}$, then $deg(u_i) = d^p_{ii} = \frac{2}{n}\sum\limits_{1\leq i<j\leq n} l^p_{ij}$. Substituting the value of d^p_{ii}, $1 \leq i \leq n$, in Eq. (8.9), required result is obtained. □

The concept of the Laplacian energy of bipolar fuzzy digraphs is studied briefly as a generalization of the Laplacian energy of bipolar fuzzy graphs.

Definition 8.11 Let $\overrightarrow{G} = (A, \overrightarrow{B})$ be a bipolar fuzzy digraph on X. The **out-degree matrix** of $\overrightarrow{G}$ is defined as $D^{out}(\overrightarrow{G}) = ((D^{out})^p(\overrightarrow{G}), (D^{out})^n(\overrightarrow{G})) = ([\overrightarrow{d}^{\,p}_{ij}]_{n\times n}, [\overrightarrow{d}^{\,n}_{ij}]_{n\times n})$, where $(D^{out})^p(\overrightarrow{G})$ and $(D^{out})^n(\overrightarrow{G})$ are nonsymmetric diagonal matrices such that

$$\overrightarrow{d}^{\,p}_{ij} = \begin{cases} deg^p_{\overrightarrow{G}}(v_i) & \text{if } i = j,\ v_i \in X \\ 0 & \text{otherwise} \end{cases} \quad \text{and} \quad \overrightarrow{d}^{\,n}_{ij} = \begin{cases} deg^n_{\overrightarrow{G}}(v_i) & \text{if } i = j,\ v_i \in X \\ 0 & \text{otherwise} \end{cases}.$$

Definition 8.12 The **Laplacian matrix** of a bipolar fuzzy digraph $\overrightarrow{G} = (A, \overrightarrow{B})$ is defined as $L(\overrightarrow{G}) = (L^p(\overrightarrow{G}), L^n(\overrightarrow{G})) = ([\overrightarrow{l}^{\,p}_{ij}]_{n\times n}, [\overrightarrow{l}^{\,n}_{ij}]_{n\times n}) = D^{out}(\overrightarrow{G}) - A(\overrightarrow{G})$, where $D^{out}(\overrightarrow{G})$ and $A(\overrightarrow{G})$ are the out-degree matrix and adjacency matrix of the bipolar fuzzy digraph $\overrightarrow{G}$.

Definition 8.13 The **spectrum** of a Laplacian matrix of a bipolar fuzzy digraph $\overrightarrow{G}$ is defined as an ordered pair $LSpec(\overrightarrow{G}) = (LSpec^p(\overrightarrow{G}), LSpec^n(\overrightarrow{G}))$, where $LSpec^p(\overrightarrow{G})$ and $LSpec^n(\overrightarrow{G})$ can be computed using the eigenvalues of $L^p(\overrightarrow{G})$ and $L^n(\overrightarrow{G})$, respectively, as explained in Definition 8.6.

Theorem 8.9 Let $\overrightarrow{G} = (A, \overrightarrow{B})$ be a bipolar fuzzy digraph and $L^p(\overrightarrow{G}) = [\overrightarrow{l}^{\,p}_{ij}]_{n\times n}$ and $L^n(\overrightarrow{G}) = [\overrightarrow{l}^{\,n}_{ij}]_{n\times n}$ be the Laplacian matrices of $\overrightarrow{G}$ corresponding to positive

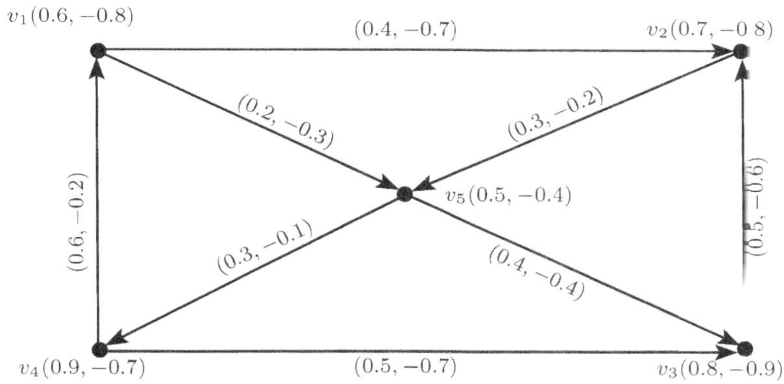

Fig. 8.4 Bipolar fuzzy digraph $\overrightarrow{G}$

and negative membership values. If $\widehat{\alpha}_1 \geq \widehat{\alpha}_2 \geq \cdots \geq \widehat{\alpha}_n$ and $\widehat{\mu}_1 \leq \widehat{\mu}_2 \leq \cdots \leq \widehat{\mu}_n$ are the eigenvalues of $L^p(\overrightarrow{G})$ and $L^n(\overrightarrow{G})$, respectively, then

$$\sum_{i=1}^{n} Re(\widehat{\alpha}_i) = \sum_{1 \leq i,j \leq n} \overrightarrow{l}^{\,p}_{ij} \quad \text{and} \quad \sum_{i=1}^{n} Re(\widehat{\mu}_i) = \sum_{1 \leq i,j \leq n} \overrightarrow{l}^{\,n}_{ij}.$$

Definition 8.14 The **Laplacian energy** of a bipolar fuzzy digraph $\overrightarrow{G} = (A, \overrightarrow{B})$ is defined as an ordered pair $LE(\overrightarrow{G}) = (LE^p(\overrightarrow{G}), LE^n(\overrightarrow{G})) = \left(\sum_{i=1}^{n} |\theta_i|, \sum_{i=1}^{n} |\gamma_i|\right)$ such that

$$\theta_i = Re(\widehat{\alpha}_i) - \frac{1}{n} \sum_{1 \leq i,j \leq n} \overrightarrow{l}^{\,p}_{ij} \quad \text{and} \quad \gamma_i = Re(\widehat{\mu}_i) - \frac{1}{n} \sum_{1 \leq i,j \leq n} \overrightarrow{l}^{\,n}_{ij}.$$

Corollary 8.2 *Let $\overrightarrow{G} = (A, \overrightarrow{B})$ be a bipolar fuzzy digraph on X then $\sum_{i=1}^{n} \theta_i = 0$ and $\sum_{i=1}^{n} \gamma_i = 0$.*

The proof of Corollary 8.2 is a direct consequence of Definition 8.14.

Example 8.7 Consider a bipolar fuzzy digraph $\overrightarrow{G} = (A, \overrightarrow{B})$ on $X = \{v_1, v_2, v_3, v_4, v_5\}$ as shown in Fig. 8.4. The adjacency matrix, out-degree matrix, and the Laplacian matrix of $\overrightarrow{G}$ are given as follows:

$$A(\overrightarrow{G}) = \begin{pmatrix} (0,0) & (0.4,-0.7) & (0,0) & (0,0) & (0.2,-0.3) \\ (0,0) & (0,0) & (0,0) & (0,0) & (0.3,-0.2) \\ (0,0) & (0.5,-0.6) & (0,0) & (0,0) & (0,0) \\ (0.6,-0.2) & (0,0) & (0.5,-0.7) & (0,0) & (0,0) \\ (0,0) & (0,0) & (0.4,-0.4) & (0.3,-0.1) & (0,0) \end{pmatrix}$$

$$D^{out}(\overrightarrow{G}) = \begin{pmatrix} (0.6, -1.0) & (0, 0) & (0, 0) & (0, 0) & (0, 0) \\ (0, 0) & (0.3, -0.2) & (0, 0) & (0, 0) & (0, 0) \\ (0, 0) & (0, 0) & (0.5, -0.6) & (0, 0) & (0, 0) \\ (0, 0) & (0, 0) & (0, 0) & (1.1, -0.9) & (0, 0) \\ (0, 0) & (0, 0) & (0, 0) & (0, 0) & (0.7, -0.5) \end{pmatrix}$$

$$L(\overrightarrow{G}) = \begin{pmatrix} (0.6, -1.0) & (-0.4, 0.7) & (0, 0) & (0, 0) & (-0.2, 0.3) \\ (0, 0) & (0.3, -0.2) & (0, 0) & (0, 0) & (-0.3, 0.2) \\ (0, 0) & (-0.5, 0.6) & (0.5, -0.6) & (0, 0) & (0, 0) \\ (-0.6, 0.2) & (0, 0) & (-0.5, 0.7) & (1.1, -0.9) & (0, 0) \\ (0, 0) & (0, 0) & (-0.4, 0.4) & (-0.3, 0.1) & (0.7, -0.5) \end{pmatrix}.$$

Here, $LSpec^p(\overrightarrow{G}) = \{0, 1.1410, 0.7385 + 0.4071i, 0.7385 - 0.4071i, 0.5820\}$, $LSpec^n(\overrightarrow{G}) = \{0, -0.9724 + 0.0499i, -0.9724 - 0.0499i, -0.6276 + 0.3270i, -0.6276 - 0.3270i\}$, $SLSpec(\overrightarrow{G}) = \{(0, 0), (1.1410, -0.9724 + 0.0499i), (0.7385 + 0.4071i, -0.9724 - 0.0499i), (0.7385 - 0.4071i, -0.6276 + 0.3270i), (0.5820, -0.6276 - 0.3270i)\}$, $LE(\overrightarrow{G}) = (1.3960, \ 1.3296)$, $\sum_{i=1}^{n} \theta_i = 0$, and $\sum_{i=1}^{n} \gamma_i = 0$.

8.4 Signless Laplacian Energy of Bipolar Fuzzy Graphs

In this section, the signless Laplacian energy of bipolar fuzzy graphs and bipolar fuzzy digraphs is discussed with certain important properties.

Definition 8.15 The **signless Laplacian matrix** of a bipolar fuzzy graph $G = (A, B)$ is defined as $SL(G) = D(G) + A(G)$, where $D(G)$ is a degree matrix of G and $A(G)$ is the adjacency matrix of G. The signless Laplacian matrices corresponding to positive and negative membership values can be written as $SL^p(G) = [s_{ij}^p]_{n\times n}$ and $SL^n(G) = [s_{ij}^n]_{n\times n}$, respectively.

Definition 8.16 The **spectrum** $SLSpec(G)$ of signless Laplacian matrix can be defined using the eigenvalues of $SL^p(G) = [s_{ij}^p]_{n\times n}$ and $SL^n(G) = [s_{ij}^n]_{n\times n}$ as explained in Definition 8.6.

Example 8.8 Consider a bipolar fuzzy graph $G = (A, B)$ on $X = \{v_1, v_2, v_3, v_4, v_5, v_6\}$ as shown in Fig. 8.5. The adjacency matrix, degree matrix, and signless Laplacian matrix of G are given as follows:

$$A(G) = \begin{pmatrix} (0, 0) & (0.2, -0.5) & (0, 0) & (0, 0) & (0, 0) & (0.2, -0.4) \\ (0.2, -0.5) & (0, 0) & ((0.1, -0.6) & (0.3, -0.2) & (0.2, -0.3) & (0.3, -0.4) \\ (0, 0) & (0.1, -0.6) & (0, 0) & (0.2, -0.2) & (0, 0) & (0, 0) \\ (0, 0) & (0.3, -0.2) & (0.2, -0.2) & (0, 0) & (0.7, -0.2) & (0.1, -0.2) \\ (0, 0) & (0.2, -0.3) & (0, 0) & (0.7, -0.2) & (0, 0) & (0.3, -0.4) \\ (0.2, -0.4) & (0.3, -0.4) & (0, 0) & (0.1, -0.2) & (0.3, -0.4) & (0, 0) \end{pmatrix}$$

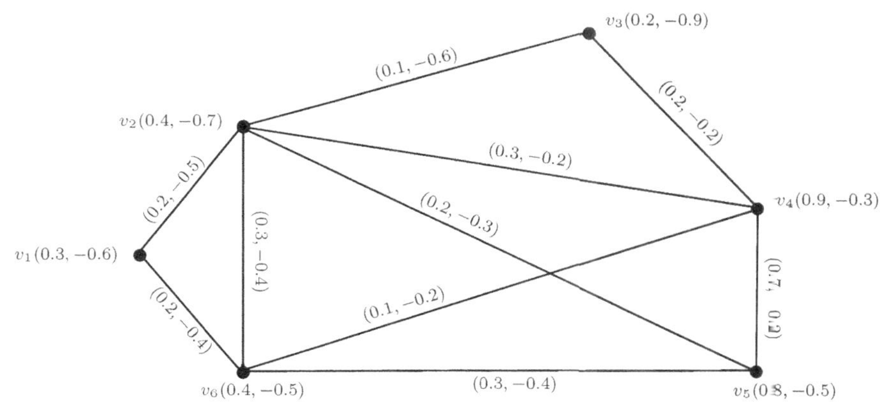

Fig. 8.5 Bipolar fuzzy graph

$$D(G) = \begin{pmatrix} (0.4, -0.9) & (0,0) & (0,0) & (0,0) & (0,0) & (0,0) \\ (0,0) & (1.1, -2.0) & (0,0) & (0,0) & (0,0) & (0,0) \\ (0,0) & (0,0) & (0.3, -0.8) & (0,0) & (0,0) & (0,0) \\ (0,0) & (0,0) & (0,0) & (1.3, -0.8) & (0,0) & (0,0) \\ (0,0) & (0,0) & (0,0) & (0,0) & (1.2, -0.9) & (0,0) \\ (0,0) & (0,0) & (0,0) & (0,0) & (0,0) & (0.9, -1.4) \end{pmatrix}$$

$$SL(G) = \begin{pmatrix} (0.4, -0.9) & (0.2, -0.5) & (0,0) & (0,0) & (0,0) & (0.2, -0.4) \\ (0.2, -0.5) & (1.1, -2.0) & (0.1, -0.6) & (0.3, -0.2) & (0.2, -0.3) & (0.3, -0.4) \\ (0,0) & (0.1, -0.6) & (0.3, -0.8) & (0.2, -0.2) & (0,0) & (0,0) \\ (0,0) & (0.3, -0.2) & (0.2, -0.2) & (1.3, -0.8) & (0.7, -0.2) & (0.1, -0.2) \\ (0,0) & (0.2, -0.3) & (0,0) & (0.7, -0.2) & (1.2, -0.9) & (0.3, -0.4) \\ (0.2, -0.4) & (0.3, -0.4) & (0,0) & (0.1, -0.2) & (0.3, -0.4) & (0.9, -1.4) \end{pmatrix}.$$

By usual calculations, $SLSpec^p(G) = \{0.2229, 0.3069, 0.4790, 0.8174, 1.1639, 2.2100\}$, $SLSpec^n(G) = \{-2.7434, -1.4384, -1.0168, -0.6964, -0.5432, -0.3618\}$, $SLSpec(G) = \{(0.2229, -2.7434), (0.3069, -1.4384), (0.4790, -1.0168), (0.8174, -0.6964), (1.1639, -0.5432), (2.2100, -0.3618)\}$.

Theorem 8.10 Let $G = (A, B)$ be a bipolar fuzzy graph on X with $SL^p(G)$ and $SL^n(G)$ as the signless Laplacian matrices corresponding to positive and negative membership values of edges of G. If $\lambda_1^+ \geq \lambda_2^+ \geq \cdots \geq \lambda_n^+$ and $\mu_1^+ \leq \mu_2^+ \leq \cdots \leq \mu_n^+$ are the eigenvalues of $SL^p(G)$ and $SL^n(G)$, respectively, then

1. $\sum_{i=1}^n \lambda_i^+ = \sum_{i=1}^n deg^p(v_i), \quad \sum_{i=1}^n \mu_i^+ = \sum_{i=1}^n deg^n(v_i), \quad v_i \in X.$
2. $\sum_{i=1}^n (\lambda_i^+)^2 = \sum_{i=1}^n (d_{ii}^p)^2 + \sum_{i=1}^n \sum_{\substack{j=1 \\ i \neq j}}^n (s_{ij}^p)^2, \quad \sum_{i=1}^n (\mu_i^+)^2 = \sum_{i=1}^n (d_{ii}^n)^2 + \sum_{i=1}^n \sum_{\substack{j=1 \\ i \neq j}}^n (s_{ij}^n)^2.$

Definition 8.17 Let $G = (A, B)$ be a bipolar fuzzy graph on X and $SL(G) = \left([s^p_{ij}]_{n\times n}, [s^n_{ij}]_{n\times n}\right)$ be the signless Laplacian matrix of G. Let $\lambda^+_1 \geq \lambda^+_2 \geq \cdots \geq \lambda^+_n$ and $\mu^+_1 \leq \mu^+_2 \leq \cdots \leq \mu^+_n$ be the eigenvalues of $SL^p(G)$ and $SL^n(G)$, respectively. If

$$\pi^+_i = \lambda^+_i - \frac{2}{n} \sum_{1\leq i<j\leq n} s^p_{ij} \quad \text{and} \quad \vartheta^+_i = \mu^+_i - \frac{2}{n} \sum_{1\leq i<j\leq n} s^n_{ij},$$

then the **signless Laplacian energy** of G is defined as an ordered pair $LE(G) = (SLE^p(G), SLE^n(G))$, where $SLE^p(G) = \sum_{i=1}^{n} |\pi^+_i|$ and $SLE^n(G) = \sum_{i=1}^{n} |\vartheta^+_i|$.

Example 8.9 The signless Laplacian energy of the bipolar fuzzy graph $G = (A, B)$ shown in Fig. 8.5 is $SLE(G) = (3.2811, 3.5964)$.

Corollary 8.3 *Let $G = (A, B)$ be a bipolar fuzzy graph on X and $SL(G) = \left([s^p_{ij}]_{n\times n}, [s^n_{ij}]_{n\times n}\right)$ be the signless Laplacian matrix of G. Let $\lambda^+_1 \geq \lambda^+_2 \geq \cdots \geq \lambda^+_n$ and $\mu^+_1 \leq \mu^+_2 \leq \cdots \leq \mu^+_n$ be the eigenvalues of $SL^p(G)$ and $SL^n(G)$, respectively. If $\pi^+_i = \lambda^+_i - \frac{2}{n} \sum_{1\leq i<j\leq n} s^p_{ij}$ and $\vartheta^+_i = \mu^+_i - \frac{2}{n} \sum_{1\leq i<j\leq n} s^n_{ij}$, then*

1. $\sum_{i=1}^{n} \pi^+_i = 0$, $\quad \sum_{i=1}^{n} \vartheta^+_i = 0$,
2. $\sum_{i=1}^{n} (\pi^+_i)^2 = \sum_{i=1}^{n} (d^p_{ii} - \frac{2}{n} \sum_{1\leq i<j\leq n} s^p_{ij})^2 + 2 \sum_{1\leq i<j\leq n} (s^p_{ij})(s^p_{ji})$,
3. $\sum_{i=1}^{n} (\vartheta^+_i)^2 = \sum_{i=1}^{n} (d^n_{ii} - \frac{2}{n} \sum_{1\leq i<j\leq n} s^p_{ij})^2 + 2 \sum_{1\leq i<j\leq n}^{n} (s^n_{ij})(s^n_{ji})$.

Example 8.10 Consider a bipolar fuzzy graph $G = (A, B)$ on $X = \{v_1, v_2, v_3, v_4, v_5, v_6\}$ as given in Fig. 8.5. Here, $SLE(G) = (3.2811, 3.5964)$, $\sum_{i=1} \pi^+_i = 0$, $\sum_{i=1} \vartheta^+_i = 0$,

$\sum_{i=1}^{6} (\pi^+_i)^2 = 2.7733 = \sum_{i=1}^{6} (d^p_{ii} - \frac{2}{6} \sum_{1\leq i<j\leq 6} s^p_{ij})^2 + 2 \sum_{1\leq i<j\leq 6} (s^p_{ij})(s^p_{ji})$, and

$\sum_{i=1}^{6} (\vartheta^+_i)^2 = 4.3182 = \sum_{i=1}^{6} (d^n_{ii} - \frac{2}{6} \sum_{1\leq i<j\leq 6} s^n_{ij})^2 + 2 \sum_{1\leq i<j\leq 6} (s^n_{ij})(s^n_{ji})$.

Definition 8.18 The **signless Laplacian matrix** of a bipolar fuzzy digraph $\vec{G} = (A, \vec{B})$ is defined as $SL(\vec{G}) = (SL^p(\vec{G}), SL^n(\vec{G})) = ([\vec{s}^{\,p}_{ij}]_{n\times n}, [\vec{s}^{\,n}_{ij}]_{n\times n}) = D^{out}(\vec{G}) - A(\vec{G})$, where $D^{out}(\vec{G})$ and $A(\vec{G})$ are the out-degree matrix and adjacency matrix of bipolar fuzzy digraph $\vec{G}$.

Definition 8.19 The **spectrum** of a signless Laplacian matrix of G is defined as $SLSpec(\vec{G}) = (SLSpec^p(\vec{G}), SLSpec^n(\vec{G}))$, where $SLSpec^p(\vec{G})$ and $SLSpec^n(\vec{G})$ can be computed using the eigenvalues of $SL^p(\vec{G})$ and $SL^n(\vec{G})$, respectively, as explained in Definition 8.6.

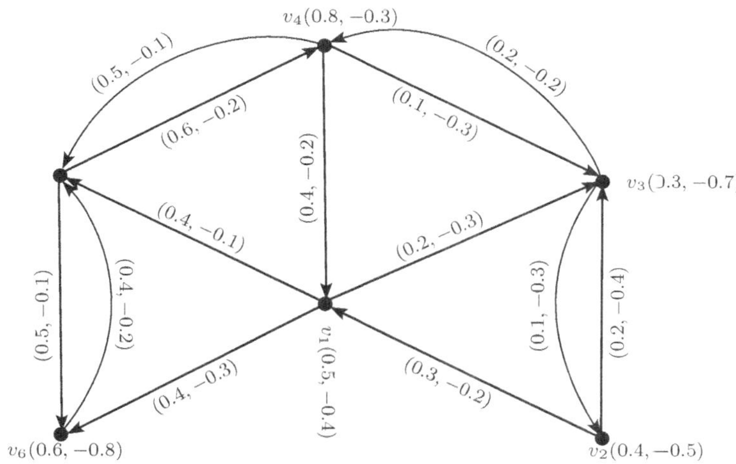

Fig. 8.6 Signless Laplacian energy of bipolar fuzzy digraph

Theorem 8.11 Let $\overrightarrow{G} = (A, \overrightarrow{B})$ be a bipolar fuzzy digraph and $SL^p(\overrightarrow{G}) = ([\overrightarrow{s}^{\,p}_{ij}]_{n\times n}$ and $SL^n(\overrightarrow{G}) = [\overrightarrow{s}^{\,n}_{ij}]_{n\times n}$ be the signless Laplacian matrices of $\overrightarrow{G}$ corresponding to positive and negative membership values. If $\widehat{\lambda}_1^+ \geq \widehat{\lambda}_2^+ \geq \cdots \geq \widehat{\lambda}_n^+$ and $\widehat{\mu}_1^+ \leq \widehat{\mu}_2^+ \leq \cdots \leq \widehat{\mu}_n^+$ are the eigenvalues of $SL^p(\overrightarrow{G})$ and $SL^n(\overrightarrow{G})$, respectively, then

$$\sum_{i=1}^{n} Re(\widehat{\lambda}_i^+) = \sum_{1\leq i,j\leq n} \overrightarrow{s}^{\,p}_{ij} \quad \text{and} \quad \sum_{i=1}^{n} Re(\widehat{\mu}_i^+) = \sum_{1\leq i,j\leq n} \overrightarrow{s}^{\,n}_{ij}.$$

Definition 8.20 The **signless Laplacian energy** of a bipolar fuzzy digraph $\overrightarrow{G} = (A, \overrightarrow{B})$ is defined as an ordered pair $LE(\overrightarrow{G}) = (LE^p(\overrightarrow{G}), LE^n(\overrightarrow{G})) = \left(\sum_{i=1}^{n} |\theta_i^+|, \sum_{i=1}^{n} |\gamma_i^+|\right)$ such that

$$\theta_i^+ = Re(\widehat{\lambda}_i^+) - \frac{1}{n} \sum_{1\leq i,j\leq n} \overrightarrow{s}^{\,p}_{ij} \quad \text{and} \quad \gamma_i^+ = Re(\widehat{\mu}_i^+) - \frac{1}{n} \sum_{1\leq i,j\leq n} \overrightarrow{s}^{\,n}_{ij}.$$

Corollary 8.4 *Let $\overrightarrow{G} = (A, \overrightarrow{B})$ be a bipolar fuzzy digraph on X then $\sum_{i=1}^{n} \theta_i^+ = 0$ and $\sum_{i=1}^{n} \gamma_i^+ = 0$.*

The proof of Corollary 8.4 is a direct consequence of Definition 8.20.

Example 8.11 Consider a bipolar fuzzy digraph $\overrightarrow{G} = (A, \overrightarrow{B})$ on $X = \{v_1, v_2, v_3, v_4, v_5, v_6\}$ as shown in Fig. 8.6.

The adjacency matrix, out-degree matrix, and the signless Laplacian matrix of $\overrightarrow{G}$ are calculated as follows:

$$A(\overrightarrow{G}) = \begin{pmatrix} (0,0) & (0,0) & (0.2,-0.3) & (0,0) & (0.4,-0.1) & (0.4,-0.3) \\ (0.3,-0.2) & (0,0) & (0.2,-0.4) & (0,0) & (0,0) & (0,0) \\ (0,0) & (0.1,-0.3) & (0,0) & (0.2,-0.2) & (0,0) & (0,0) \\ (0.4,-0.2) & (0,0) & (0.1,-0.3) & (0,0) & (0.5,-0.1) & (0,0) \\ (0,0) & (0,0) & (0,0) & (0.6,-0.2) & (0,0) & (0.5,-0.1) \\ (0,0) & (0,0) & (0,0) & (0,0) & (0.4,-0.2) & (0,0) \end{pmatrix}$$

$$D^{out}(\overrightarrow{G}) = \begin{pmatrix} (1.0,-0.7) & (0,0) & (0,0) & (0,0) & (0,0) & (0,0) \\ (0,0) & (0.5,-0.6) & (0,0) & (0,0) & (0,0) & (0,0) \\ (0,0) & (0,0) & (0.3,-0.5) & (0,0) & (0,0) & (0,0) \\ (0,0) & (0,0) & (0,0) & (1.0,-0.6) & (0,0) & (0,0) \\ (0,0) & (0,0) & (0,0) & (0,0) & (1.1,-0.3) & (0,0) \\ (0,0) & (0,0) & (0,0) & (0,0) & (0,0) & (0.4,-0.2) \end{pmatrix}$$

$$SL(\overrightarrow{G}) = \begin{pmatrix} (1.0,-0.7) & (0,0) & (0.2,-0.3) & (0,0) & (0.4,-0.1) & (0.4,-0.3) \\ (0.3,-0.2) & (0.5,-0.6) & (0.2,-0.4) & (0,0) & (0,0) & (0,0) \\ (0,0) & (0.1,-0.3) & (0.3,-0.5) & (0.2,-0.2) & (0,0) & (0,0) \\ (0.4,-0.2) & (0,0) & (0.1-0.3) & (1.0,-0.6) & (0.5,-0.1) & (0,0) \\ (0,0) & (0,0) & (0,0) & (0.6,-0.2) & (1.1,-0.3) & (0.5,-0.1) \\ (0,0) & (0,0) & (0,0) & (0,0) & (0.4,-0.2) & (0.4,-0.2) \end{pmatrix}.$$

Here, $SLSpec^p(\overrightarrow{G}) = \{1.8150, 0.7995 + 0.2749i, 0.7995 - 0.2749i, 0.0889, 0.2520, 0.5451\}$, $SLSpec^p(\overrightarrow{G}) = \{-1.0790, -0.0509, -0.6616, -0.4613, -0.2834, -0.3639\}$, $SLSpec(\overrightarrow{G}) = \{(1.8150, -1.0790), (0.7995 + 0.2749i, -0.0509), (0.7995 - 0.2749i, -0.6616), (0.0889, -0.4613), (0.2520, -0.2834), (0.5451, -0.3639)\}$, $SLE(\overrightarrow{G}) = (1.9630, 1.5477)$, $\sum_{i=1}^{n} \theta_i^+ = 0$ and $\sum_{i=1}^{n} \delta_i^+ = 0$.

8.5 Dominating and Double Dominating Energy of Bipolar Fuzzy Graphs

In this section, the notions of dominating energy, double dominating energy, out-dominating energy, and double out-dominating of bipolar fuzzy graphs and bipolar fuzzy digraphs are studied with certain lower and upper bounds.

Definition 8.21 Let $G = (A, B)$ be an bipolar fuzzy graph on a non-empty set X. For any two vertices u and w in G, u **dominates** w if $\mu_B^p(uw) = \min\{\mu_A^p(u), \mu_A^p(w)\}$ and $\mu_B^n(uw) = \max\{\mu_A^n(u), \mu_A^n(w)\}$. A subset $D \subseteq X$ is a **dominating set** if for every vertex $w \notin D$, there is a vertex $u \in D$ such that u dominates w. D is a **minimal dominating set** of G if, for any $w \in X$, $D \setminus \{w\}$ is not a dominating set. The dominating set with minimum cardinality among all minimal dominating sets is called the **minimum dominating set** of G.

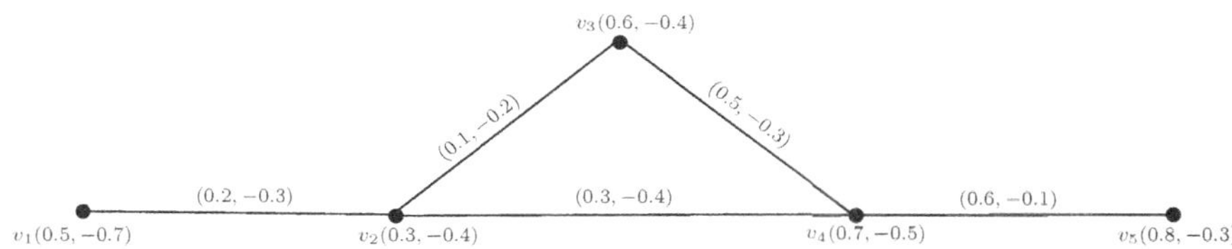

Fig. 8.7 Bipolar fuzzy graph G

Definition 8.22 Let D be a minimum dominating set of a bipolar fuzzy graph $G = (A, B)$ then the **dominating adjacency matrix** of G is $n \times n$ matrix $A_D(G) = [\xi_{ij}]_{n\times n} = [(\xi^p_{ij}, \xi^n_{ij})]_{n\times n} = (A^p_D(G), A^n_D(G))$, where

$$\xi_{ij} = \begin{cases} B(u_iu_j), & u_i \neq u_j, \\ (0,0), & u_i = u_j, u_i \notin D \\ A(u_i), & u_i = u_j, u_i \in D. \end{cases}$$

If $\mu_1 \geq \mu_2 \geq \cdots \geq \mu_n$ are the eigenvalues of $A^p_D(G)$ in nonincreasing order and $\nu_1 \leq \nu_2 \leq \cdots \leq \nu_n$ are the eigenvalues of $A^n_D(G)$ in nondecreasing order, then the μ^p**-spectrum** of $A^p_D(G)$, denoted by $Spec^p_D(G)$, is defined as the set $Spec^p_D = \{\mu_1, \mu_2, \ldots, \mu_n\}$. Similarly, the μ^n**-spectrum** of $A^n_D(G)$ is denoted by $Spec^n_D(G)$ and defined as the set $Spec^n_D = \{\nu_1, \nu_2, \ldots, \nu_n\}$. The **spectrum** of $A_D(G)$ is defined as a set $Spec_D(G) = \{(\mu_i, \nu_i)|i = 1, 2, \ldots, n\}$.

Definition 8.23 Let D be a minimum dominating set of a bipolar fuzzy graph G then the **minimum dominating energy** corresponding to D is defined as an ordered pair $E_D(G) = (E^p_D(G), E^n_D(G))$, where $E^p_D(G) = \sum\limits_{i=1}^{n} |\mu_i|$ and $E^n_D(G) = \sum\limits_{i=1}^{n} |\nu_i|$. If D is any minimal dominating set of G then $E_D(G)$ is called the **dominating energy** of G.

Example 8.12 Consider the bipolar fuzzy graph $G = (A, B)$ on $X = \{v_1, v_2, v_3, v_4, v_5\}$ as shown in Fig. 8.7.

Clearly, by calculations, $D = \{v_2, v_4\}$ is a dominating set because every vertex in $X - D$ is dominated by at least one vertex in D. The adjacency matrix of G is computed in Eq. (8.10).

$$A_D(G) = \begin{pmatrix} (0,0) & (0.2,-0.3) & (0,0) & (0,0) & (0,0) \\ (0.2,-0.3) & (0.3,-0.4) & (0.1,-0.2) & (0.3,-0.4) & (0,0) \\ (0,0) & (0.1,-0.2) & (0,0) & (0.5,-0.3) & (0,0) \\ (0,0) & (0.3,-0.4) & (0.5,-0.3) & (0.7,-0.5) & (0.6,-0.1) \\ (0,0) & (0,0) & (0,0) & (0.6,-0.1) & (0,0) \end{pmatrix}. \tag{8.10}$$

Thus, $Spec_D(G) = \{(-0.4334, -1.5156), (-0.0456, -0.6803), (0, 0), (0.8949, 0.0761), (1.5841, 0.1199)\}$, $E_D(G) = (2.958, 2.3919)$.

Theorem 8.12 Let $G = (A, B)$ be a bipolar fuzzy graph with n vertices and minimum dominating set $D = \{w_1, w_2, \ldots, w_k\}$, then

1. $\sum_{w_i \in D} A(w_i) = \left(\sum_{i=1}^{n} \mu_i, \sum_{i=1}^{n} \nu_i\right)$,
2. $\sum_{i=1}^{n} (\mu_i)^2 = \sum_{i=1}^{n} (\xi_{ii}^p)^2 + \sum_{i=1}^{n} \sum_{\substack{j=1 \\ i \neq j}}^{n} (\xi_{ij}^p)(\xi_{ji}^p)$ and $\sum_{i=1}^{n} (\nu_i)^2 = \sum_{i=1}^{n} (\xi_{ii}^n)^2 + \sum_{i=1}^{n} \sum_{\substack{j=1 \\ i \neq j}}^{n} (\xi_{ij}^n)(\xi_{ji}^n)$.

Proof 1. As the sum of eigenvalues of a matrix is equal to trace of the matrix,

$$\left(\sum_{i=1}^{n} \mu_i, \sum_{i=1}^{n} \nu_i\right) = \sum_{i=1}^{n} \xi_{ii} = \sum_{w_i \in D} A(w_i).$$

2. As the sum of squares of eigenvalues of a matrix $A_D^p(G)$ is equal to trace of $(A_D^p(G))^2$,

$$\begin{aligned}
\sum_{i=1}^{n} (\mu_i)^2 =& [(\xi_{11}^p)^2 + \xi_{12}^p \times \xi_{21}^p + \xi_{13}^p \times \xi_{31}^p + \cdots + \xi_{1n}^p \times \xi_{n1}^p] \\
&+ [\xi_{21}^p \times \xi_{12}^p + (\xi_{22}^p)^2 + \xi_{23}^p \times \xi_{32}^p + \cdots + \xi_{2n}^p \times \xi_{n2}^p] \\
&\vdots \\
&+ [\xi_{n1}^p \times \xi_{1n}^p + \xi_{n2}^p \times \xi_{2n}^p + \xi_{n3}^p \times \xi_{3n}^p + \cdots + (\xi_{nn}^p)^2] \\
&= \sum_{i=1}^{n} (\xi_{ii}^p)^2 + \sum_{i=1}^{n} \sum_{\substack{j=1 \\ i \neq j}}^{n} (\xi_{ij}^p)(\xi_{ji}^p) \\
&= \sum_{w_i \in D} (A(w_i))^2 + 2 \sum_{1 \leq i < j \leq n} (\xi_{ij}^p)^2.
\end{aligned}$$

The part of the theorem corresponding to negative membership values can be obtained similarly. □

Theorem 8.13 Let $G = (A, B)$ be a bipolar fuzzy graph with n vertices. If D is a minimum dominating set, $Q = \det(A_D^p(G)) = det([\xi_{ij}^p]_{n \times n})$, and $R = \det(A_D^n(G)) = det([\xi_{ij}^n]_{n \times n})$, then

1. $\sqrt{\sum_{i=1}^{n} (\xi_{ii}^p)^2 + \sum_{i \neq j} (\xi_{ij}^p)(\xi_{ji}^p) + n(n-1)Q^{\frac{2}{n}}} \leq \sum_{i=1}^{n} |\mu_i|$,
2. $\sum_{i=1}^{n} |\mu_i| \leq \sqrt{n\left(\sum_{i=1}^{n} (\xi_{ii}^p)^2 + \sum_{i \neq j} (\xi_{ij}^p)(\xi_{ji}^p)\right)}$,
3. $\sqrt{\sum_{i=1}^{n} (\xi_{ii}^n)^2 + \sum_{i \neq j} (\xi_{ij}^n)(\xi_{ji}^n) + n(n-1)Q^{\frac{2}{n}}} \leq \sum_{i=1}^{n} |\nu_i|$,

4. $\sum\limits_{i=1}^{n}|\nu_i| \leq \sqrt{n\left(\sum\limits_{i=1}^{n}(\xi_{ii}^{n})^2+\sum\limits_{i\neq j}(\xi_{ij}^{n})(\xi_{ji}^{n})\right)}.$

Proof The Cauchy Schwarz inequality is $\left(\sum\limits_{i=1}^{n}u_i v_i\right)^2 \leq \left(\sum\limits_{i=1}^{n}u_i^2\right)\left(\sum\limits_{i=1}^{n}v_i^2\right)$.
2. In Cauchy Schwarz inequality, substituting $u_i = 1$, $v_i = |\mu_i|$ and using Theorem 8.12, we obtain

$$\left(\sum_{i=1}^{n}|\mu_i|\right)^2 \leq \left(\sum_{i=1}^{n}1\right)\left(\sum_{i=1}^{n}(\mu_i)^2\right) = n\left(\sum_{i=1}^{n}(\xi_{ii}^{p})^2+\sum_{i\neq j}(\xi_{ij}^{p})(\xi_{j}^{p})\right)$$

$$\Rightarrow \sum_{i=1}^{n}|\mu_i| \leq \sqrt{n\left(\sum_{i=1}^{n}(\xi_{ii}^{p})^2+\sum_{i\neq j}(\xi_{ij}^{p})(\xi_{ji}^{p})\right)}$$

$$\left(\sum_{i=1}^{n}|\mu_i|\right)^2 = \sum_{i=1}^{n}|\mu_i|^2+\sum_{i\neq j}|\mu_i||\mu_j^k|. \tag{8.11}$$

Consider the set of $n(n-1)$ values $|\mu_i||\mu_j^k|$, $i \neq j$, $1 \leq i, j \leq n$. Clearly. the arithmetic mean of these values is $A.M = \frac{1}{n(n-1)}\sum\limits_{i\neq j}|\mu_i||\mu_j^k|$ and the geometric mean is $G.M = \left(\prod\limits_{i\neq j}|\mu_i||\mu_j^k|\right)^{\frac{1}{n(n-1)}}$. As arithmetic mean is always greater, than or equal to geometric mean,

$$\frac{1}{n(n-1)}\sum_{i\neq j}|\mu_i||\mu_j^k| \geq \left(\prod_{i\neq j}|\mu_i||\mu_j^k|\right)^{\frac{1}{n(n-1)}} = \left(\prod_{i=1}^{n}|\mu_i|^{2(n-1)}\right)^{\frac{1}{n(n-1)}} = \left(\prod_{i=1}^{n}|\mu_i\right)^{\frac{2}{n}} = Q^{\frac{2}{n}}. \tag{8.12}$$

Equation (8.11) takes the form as

$$\left(\sum_{i=1}^{n}|\mu_i|\right)^2 \geq \sum_{i=1}^{n}|\mu_i|^2+n(n-1)Q^{\frac{2}{n}} = \sum_{i=1}^{n}(\xi_{ii}^{p})^2+\sum_{i\neq j}(\xi_{ij}^{p})(\xi_{ji}^{p})+n(n-1)Q^{\frac{2}{n}}$$

$$\Rightarrow \sum_{i=1}^{n}|\mu_i| \geq \sqrt{\sum_{i=1}^{n}(\xi_{ii}^{p})^2+\sum_{i\neq j}(\xi_{ij}^{p})(\xi_{ji}^{p})+n(n-1)Q^{\frac{2}{n}}}.$$

□

Theorem 8.14 Let $G = (A, B)$ be an bipolar fuzzy graph with adjacency matrix $A(G) = [u_{ij}]_{n\times n} = [(u_{ij}^{p}, u_{ij}^{n})]_{n\times n}$. Let λ_i, $1 \leq i \leq n$, be the eigenvalues of adjacency matrix $A^p(G)$ and γ_i, $1 \le i \le n$, be the eigenvalues of adjacency matrix $A^n(G)$, then

$$\left(\sum_{i=1}^{n}|\mu_i|\right)^2 \le n\left(\sum_{i=1}^{n}(\xi_{ii}^p)^2+(\sum_{i=1}^{n}|\lambda_i|)^2\right) \text{ and } \left(\sum_{i=1}^{n}|\nu_i|\right)^2 \le n\left(\sum_{i=1}^{n}(\xi_{ii}^n)^2+(\sum_{i=1}^{n}|\gamma_i|)^2\right).$$

Proof Since $u_{ii} = (0, 0)$ and for $i \ne j$, $u_{ij} = \xi_{ij}$, using Theorem 8.13, the following relation can be obtained

$$\left(\sum_{i=1}^{n}|\lambda_i|\right)^2 \ge \sum_{i\ne j}(\xi_{ij}^p)(\xi_{ji}^p)+n(n-1)[\det A_k^p(G)]^{\frac{2}{n}} \ge \sum_{i\ne j}(\xi_{ij}^p)(\xi_{ji}^p). \tag{8.13}$$

From condition 2 of Theorem 8.13,

$$\left(\sum_{i=1}^{n}|\mu_i|\right)^2 \le n\left(\sum_{i=1}^{n}(\xi_{ii}^p)^2+\sum_{i\ne j}(\xi_{ij}^p)(\xi_{ji}^p)\right) \le n\left(\sum_{i=1}^{n}(\xi_{ii}^p)^2+(\sum_{i=1}^{n}|\lambda_i|)^2\right).$$

The remaining part can be proved on similar arguments as above. □

Definition 8.24 An **out-dominating set** of a bipolar fuzzy digraph $\overrightarrow{G} = (A, B)$ is a subset of vertices $D^{out} \subseteq X$ such that for each $w \notin D^{out}$, there is a vertex $u \in D^{out}$ which satisfies $\mu^p_{\overrightarrow{B}}(uw) = \min\{\mu^p_A(u), \mu^p_A(w)\}$ and $\mu^n_{\overrightarrow{B}}(uw) = \max\{\mu^n_A(u), \mu^n_A(w)\}$. D^{out} is a **minimal out-dominating set** of $\overrightarrow{G}$ if for every $w \in D^{out}$, $D^{out} \setminus \{w\}$ is not an out-dominating set. The out-dominating set with minimum cardinality among all minimal out-dominating sets is called the **minimum out-dominating set** of G.

Definition 8.25 Let D^{out} be a minimum out-dominating set of an bipolar fuzzy digraph $\overrightarrow{G} = (A, \overrightarrow{B})$, then the **out-dominating adjacency matrix** of $\overrightarrow{G}$ is an $n \times n$ matrix $A_{D^{out}}(\overrightarrow{G}) = [\overrightarrow{\xi}_{ij}]_{n\times n} = [(\overrightarrow{\xi}^p_{ij}, \overrightarrow{\xi}^n_{ij})]_{n\times n}$, where

$$\overrightarrow{\xi}_{ij} = \begin{cases} \overrightarrow{B}(u_iu_j), & u_i \ne u_j, \\ (0,0), & u_i = u_j, u_i \notin D^{out} \\ A(u_i), & u_i = u_j, u_i \in D^{out}. \end{cases}$$

If $\tau_1 \ge \tau_2 \ge \cdots \ge \tau_n$ are the eigenvalues of $A^p_{D^{out}}(\overrightarrow{G})$ in nonincreasing order and $\rho_1 \le \rho_2 \le \cdots \le \rho_n$ are the eigenvalues of $A^n_{D^{out}}(\overrightarrow{G})$ in nondecreasing order, then the spectrum of $A^p_{D^{out}}(\overrightarrow{G})$, denoted by $Spec_{D^{out}}(\overrightarrow{G})$, is defined as the set $Spec^p_{D^{out}} = \{\tau_1, \tau_2, \ldots, \tau_n\}$. The spectrum of $A^p_{D^{out}}(\overrightarrow{G})$, denoted by $Spec_{D^{out}}(\overrightarrow{G})$, is defined as the set $Spec^n_{D^{out}} = \{\rho_1, \rho_2, \ldots, \rho_n\}$. The **spectrum** of G is the set $Spec_{D^{out}} = \{(\tau_i, \rho_i)|i = 1, 2, \ldots, n\}$.

Definition 8.26 The **out-dominating energy** of a bipolar fuzzy digraph $\overrightarrow{G}$ corresponding to a minimum out-dominating set D^{out} is defined as $E_{D^{out}}(\overrightarrow{G}) = (\sum_{i=1}^{n} |\tau_i|, \sum_{i=1}^{n} |\rho_i|)$.

Definition 8.27 Let $G = (A, B)$ be a bipolar fuzzy graph on a non-empty set X. A subset $\widetilde{D} \subseteq X$ is a **double dominating set** of G if every vertex $w \notin \widetilde{D}$ is dominated by at least two vertices in $\widetilde{D}$. $\widetilde{D}$ is a **minimal double dominating set** of G if, for any $w \in X$, $\widetilde{D} \setminus \{w\}$ is not a double dominating set. The double dominating set with minimum cardinality among all minimal double dominating sets is called the **minimum double dominating set** of G.

Definition 8.28 Let $\widetilde{D}$ be a minimum double dominating set of a bipolar fuzzy graph G, then the **double dominating adjacency matrix** of G is an $n \times n$ matrix $A_{\widetilde{D}}(G) = (A^p_{\widetilde{D}}(G), A^n_{\widetilde{D}}(G)) = [(\xi^p_{ij}, \xi^n_{ij})]_{n \times n}$, where

$$\xi_{ij} = \begin{cases} B(u_i u_j), & u_i \neq u_j, \\ (0, 0), & u_i = u_j, u_i \notin \widetilde{D} \\ A(u_i), & u_i = u_j, u_i \in \widetilde{D}. \end{cases}$$

If $\phi_1 \geq \phi_2 \geq \cdots \geq \phi_n$ are the eigenvalues of $A^p_{\widetilde{D}}(G)$ in nonincreasing order, then the **spectrum** of $A^p_{\widetilde{D}}(G)$ is defined as the set $Spec^p_{\widetilde{D}} = \{\phi_1, \phi_2, \ldots, \phi_n\}$. If $\psi_1 \leq \psi_2 \leq \cdots \leq \psi_n$ are the eigenvalues of $A^n_{\widetilde{D}}(G)$, then the **spectrum** of $A^n_{\widetilde{D}}(G)$ is defined as the set $Spec^n_{\widetilde{D}} = \{\psi_1, \psi_2, \ldots, \psi_n\}$.

Definition 8.29 Let $\widetilde{D}$ be a minimum double dominating set of a bipolar fuzzy graph G, then the **double dominating energy** corresponding to $\widetilde{D}$ is defined as an ordered pair $E_{\widetilde{D}}(G) = (E^p_{\widetilde{D}}(G), E^n_{\widetilde{D}}(G))$ such that $E_{\widetilde{D}}(G) = (\sum_{i=1}^{n} |\phi_i|, \sum_{i=1}^{n} |\psi_i|)$.

Example 8.13 Consider a bipolar fuzzy graph $G = (A, B)$ on $X = \{v_1, v_2, v_3, v_4, v_5, v_6\}$ as shown in Fig. 8.8.

By usual calculations, it is easy to check that $\widetilde{D}_1 = \{v_1, v_3, v_5\}$ and $\widetilde{D}_2 = \{v_2, v_4, v_6\}$ are double dominating sets of G. The adjacency matrix corresponding to $\widetilde{D}_1$ is calculated as follows:

$$A_{\widetilde{D}_1}(G) = \begin{pmatrix} (1, -1) & (0.4, -0.5) & (0, 0) & (0, 0) & (0, 0) & (0.3, -0.4) \\ (0.4, -0.5) & (0, 0) & (0.3, -0.1) & (0, 0) & (0, 0) & (0.7, -0.3) \\ (0, 0) & (0.3, -0.1) & (1, -1) & (0.2, -0.1) & (0, 0) & (0, 0) \\ (0, 0) & (0, 0) & (0.2, -0.1) & (0, 0) & (0.1, -0.3) & (0.2, -0.2) \\ (0, 0) & (0, 0) & (0, 0) & (0.1, -0.3) & (1, -1) & (0.6, -0.1) \\ (0.3, -0.4) & (0.7, -0.3) & (0, 0) & (0.2, -0.2) & (0.6, -0.1) & (0, 0) \end{pmatrix}.$$

It can be written in the form of two different adjacency matrices as follows:

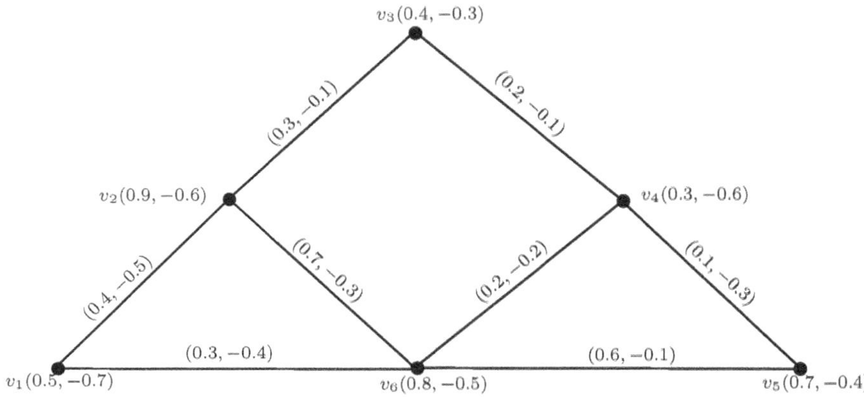

Fig. 8.8 Bipolar fuzzy graph G

$$A^{p}_{\widetilde{D}_1}(G) = \begin{pmatrix} 1 & 0.4 & 0 & 0 & 0 & 0.3 \\ 0.4 & 0 & 0.3 & 0 & 0 & 0.7 \\ 0 & 0.3 & 1 & 0.2 & 0 & 0 \\ 0 & 0 & 0.2 & 0 & 0.1 & 0.2 \\ 0 & 0 & 0 & 0.1 & 1 & 0.6 \\ 0.3 & 0.7 & 0 & 0.2 & 0.6 & 0 \end{pmatrix}, \quad A^{n}_{\widetilde{D}_1}(G) = \begin{pmatrix} -1 & -0.5 & 0 & 0 & 0 & -0.4 \\ -0.5 & 0 & -0.1 & 0 & 0 & -0.3 \\ 0 & -0.1 & -1 & -0.1 & 0 & 0 \\ 0 & 0 & -0.1 & 0 & -0.3 & -0.2 \\ 0 & 0 & 0 & -0.3 & -1 & -0.1 \\ -0.4 & -0.3 & 0 & -0.2 & -0.1 & 0 \end{pmatrix}.$$

Thus $Spec_{\widetilde{D}_1}(G) = \{(-0.8523, -1.3948), (-0.0326, -1.0948), (0.1578, -1.0050), (1.0303, -0.0403), (1.1141, 0.1648), (1.5827, 0.3701)\}$ and $E_{\widetilde{D}_1}(G) = (4.7698, 4.0698)$.

For $\widetilde{D}_2 = \{v_2, v_4, v_6\}$,

$$A_{\widetilde{D}_2}(G) = \begin{pmatrix} (0,0) & (0.4,-0.5) & (0,0) & (0,0) & (0,0) & (0.3,-0.4) \\ (0.4,-0.5) & (1,-1) & (0.3,-0.1) & (0,0) & (0,0) & (0.7,-0.3) \\ (0,0) & (0.3,-0.1) & (0,0) & (0.2,-0.1) & (0,0) & (0,0) \\ (0,0) & (0,0) & (0.2,-0.1) & (1,-1) & (0.1,-0.3) & (0.2,-0.2) \\ (0,0) & (0,0) & (0,0) & (0.1,-0.3) & (0,0) & (0.6,-0.1) \\ (0.3,-0.4) & (0.7,-0.3) & (0,0) & (0.2,-0.2) & (0.6,-0.1) & (1,-1) \end{pmatrix}.$$

Hence $Spec_{\widetilde{D}_2}(G) = \{(-0.3855, -1.6054), (-0.2163, -1.1099), (-0.0307, -0.6556), (0.6225, 0.0101), (1.0327, 0.0911), (1.9773, 0.2797)\}$ and $E_{\widetilde{D}_2}(G) = (4.2650, 3.7418)$.

Definition 8.30 Let $G = (A, \overrightarrow{B})$ be a bipolar fuzzy digraph on a non-empty set X. A subset $D_b^{out} \subseteq X$ is a **double out-dominating set** of $\overrightarrow{G}$ if every vertex $w \notin D_b^{out}$ is out-dominated by at least two vertices in D_b^{out}. D_b^{out} is a **minimal double out-dominating set** of $\overrightarrow{G}$ if, for any $w \in X$, $D_b^{out} \setminus \{w\}$ is not a double out-dominating set. The double out-dominating set with minimum cardinality among all minimal double out-dominating sets is called a **minimum double out-dominating set** of

$\overrightarrow{G}$. If $\gamma_1 \geq \gamma_2 \geq \cdots \geq \gamma_n$ are the eigenvalues of $A^p_{D_b^{out}}(\overrightarrow{G})$ and $\delta_1 \leq \delta_2 \leq \cdots \leq \delta_n$ are the eigenvalues of $A^n_{D_b^{out}}(\overrightarrow{G})$, then the **double out-dominating energy** of $\overrightarrow{G}$ is $E_{D_b^{out}}(\overrightarrow{G}) = \left(\sum_{i=1}^n |\gamma_i|, \sum_{i=1}^n |\delta_i|\right)$.

8.6 Applications of Energy to Decision-Making Problems

Definition 8.31 A **bipolar fuzzy preference relation** R on the set of choices $W = \{w_1, w_2, \ldots, w_n\}$ is defined as a matrix $R = [\xi_{ij}]_{n\times n}$, where $\xi_{ij} = (\xi^p_{ij}, \xi^n_{ij})$, ξ^p_{ij} is a positive certainty degree to which w_i is positively preferred to w_j and ξ^n_{ij} is a positive certainty degree to which w_i is negatively preferred to w_j. Moreover, $\xi_{ii} = (0.5, -0.5)$.

8.6.1 *Smooth Communication Problem*

In modern warfare, it is very important to maintain smooth communication among individuals. The performance of communication equipments play a key role in campaign victory and defeat of an army. It is necessary for the communication units to keep regular communication drills. Suppose that the headquarters are drawing up a plan of communication drill for the next round. According to consultants with different simulation environments, there are four possible training venues (alternatives), x_i $(i = 1, 2, 3, 4)$, to choose from. The leaders of the communication unit invite a decision group which contains six experts e_k $(k = 1, 2, \ldots, 6)$ to evaluate all venues so as to make the most reasonable choice. Based on their experiences, the experts compare each pair of alternatives and give individual judgments using the following bipolar fuzzy preference relations $R_k = (r^{p(k)}_{ij}, r^{n(k)}_{ij})_{4\times 4}$ $(k = 1, 2, \ldots, 6)$.

$$R_1 = \begin{bmatrix} (0.50, -0.50) & (0.23, -0.17) & (0.57, -0.67) & (0.63, -0.5) \\ (0.77, -0.83) & (0.50, -0.50) & (0.17, -1) & (0.84, -0.67) \\ (0.43, -0.33) & (0.83, 0) & (0.50, -0.50) & (0.42, -0.17) \\ (0.37, -0.50) & (0.16, -0.33) & (0.58, -0.83) & (0.50, -0.50) \end{bmatrix}$$

$$R_2 = \begin{bmatrix} (0.50, -0.50) & (0.38, -0.38) & (0.51, -0.58) & (0.27, -0.84) \\ (0.62, -0.62) & (0.50, -0.50) & (0.60, -0.69) & (0.75, -0.90) \\ (0.49, -0.42) & (0.40, -0.31) & (0.50, -0.50) & (0.14, -0.80) \\ (0.73, -0.16) & (0.25, -0.10) & (0.86, -0.20) & (0.50, -0.50) \end{bmatrix}$$

$$R_3 = \begin{bmatrix} (0.50, -0.50) & (0.57, -0.10) & (0.40, -0.60) & (0.46, -0.70) \\ (0.43, -0.90) & (0.50, -0.50) & (0.61, -0.80) & (0.19, -0.40) \\ (0.60, -0.40) & (0.39, -0.20) & (0.50, -0.50) & (0.80, -0.90) \\ (0.54, -0.30) & (0.81, -0.60) & (0.20, -0.10) & (0.50, -0.50) \end{bmatrix}$$

$$R_4 = \begin{bmatrix} (0.50, -0.50) & (0.30, -0.33) & (0.42, -0.17) & (0.26, -0.67) \\ (0.70, -0.67) & (0.50, -0.50) & (0.90, -0.33) & (0.72, -0.17) \\ (0.58, -0.83) & (0.10, -0.67) & (0.50, -0.50) & (0.81, -1) \\ (0.74, -0.33) & (0.28, -0.83) & (0.19, 0) & (0.50, -0.50) \end{bmatrix}$$

$$R_5 = \begin{bmatrix} (0.50, -0.50) & (0.70, -0.34) & (0.16, -0.20) & (0.41, -0.96) \\ (0.30, -0.66) & (0.50, -0.50) & (0.80, -0.33) & (0.29, -0.98) \\ (0.84, -0.80) & (0.20, -0.67) & (0.50, -0.50) & (0.63, -0.99) \\ (0.59, -0.04) & (0.71, -0.02) & (0.37, -0.01) & (0.50, -0.50) \end{bmatrix}$$

$$R_6 = \begin{bmatrix} (0.50, -0.50) & (0.23, -0.50) & (1.0, -0.70) & (0.30, -1.0) \\ (0.77, -0.50) & (0.50, -0.50) & (0.60, -0.80) & (0.36, -0.60) \\ (0, -0.30) & (0.40, -0.20) & (0.50, -0.50) & (0.72, -0.80) \\ (0.70, 0) & (0.64, -0.40) & (0.28, -0.20) & (0.50, -0.50) \end{bmatrix}.$$

The bipolar fuzzy digraphs $\overrightarrow{G}_i$ corresponding to bipolar fuzzy preference relations given in matrices R_i are shown in Fig. 8.9. The energy of each bipolar fuzzy digraph is $E(\overrightarrow{G}_1) = (2.9357, 2.3961)$, $E(\overrightarrow{G}_2) = (2.8289, 2.5249)$, $E(\overrightarrow{G}_3) = (2.9602, 2.8495)$, $E(\overrightarrow{G}_4) = (2.7304, 2.6413)$, $E(\overrightarrow{G}_5) = (2.9699, 1.9252)$, $E(\overrightarrow{G}_6) = (2.9510, 2.5897)$. Then the weights can be calculated as:

$$w_k = (w_k^p, w_k^n) = \left(\frac{E^p(\overrightarrow{G}_k)}{\sum_{j=1}^{6} E^p(\overrightarrow{G}_j)}, \frac{E^n(\overrightarrow{G}_k)}{\sum_{j=1}^{6} E^n(\overrightarrow{G}_j)} \right), \quad k = 1, 2, \ldots, 6.$$

Here, $w_1 = (0.1690, 0.1605)$, $w_2 = (0.1628, 0.1692)$, $w_3 = (0.1704, 0.1909)$, $w_4 = (0.1571, 0.177)$, $w_5 = (0.1709, 0.1290)$, $w_6 = (0.1698, 0.1735)$. The collective bipolar fuzzy preference relation aggregated from the six bipolar fuzzy preference relations is determined as:

$$R = \sum_{k=1}^{6} w_k R_k = [(\eta_{ij}^+, \eta_{ij}^-)]_{6\times 6} = \begin{bmatrix} (0.5, -0.5) & (0.4037, -0.2997) & (0.5106, -0.4976) & (0.3907, -0.7719) \\ (0.5963, -0.7004) & (0.5, -0.5) & (0.6103, -0.6697) & (0.5202, -0.5968) \\ (0.4894, -0.5025) & (0.3897, -0.3304) & (0.5, -0.5) & (0.5873, -0.7780) \\ (0.6093, -0.2282) & (0.4798, -0.4033) & (0.4127, -0.2221) & (0.5, -0.5) \end{bmatrix}.$$

Using the score function $s_{ij} = \eta_{ij}^- + \eta_{ij}^+$, the score values can be calculated in matrix S.

$$S = [s_{ij}]_{6\times 6} = \begin{bmatrix} 0 & 0.1040 & 0.0130 & -0.3812 \\ -0.1041 & 0 & -0.0594 & -0.0766 \\ -0.0131 & 0.0593 & 0 & -0.1907 \\ 0.3811 & 0.0765 & 0.1906 & 0 \end{bmatrix}.$$

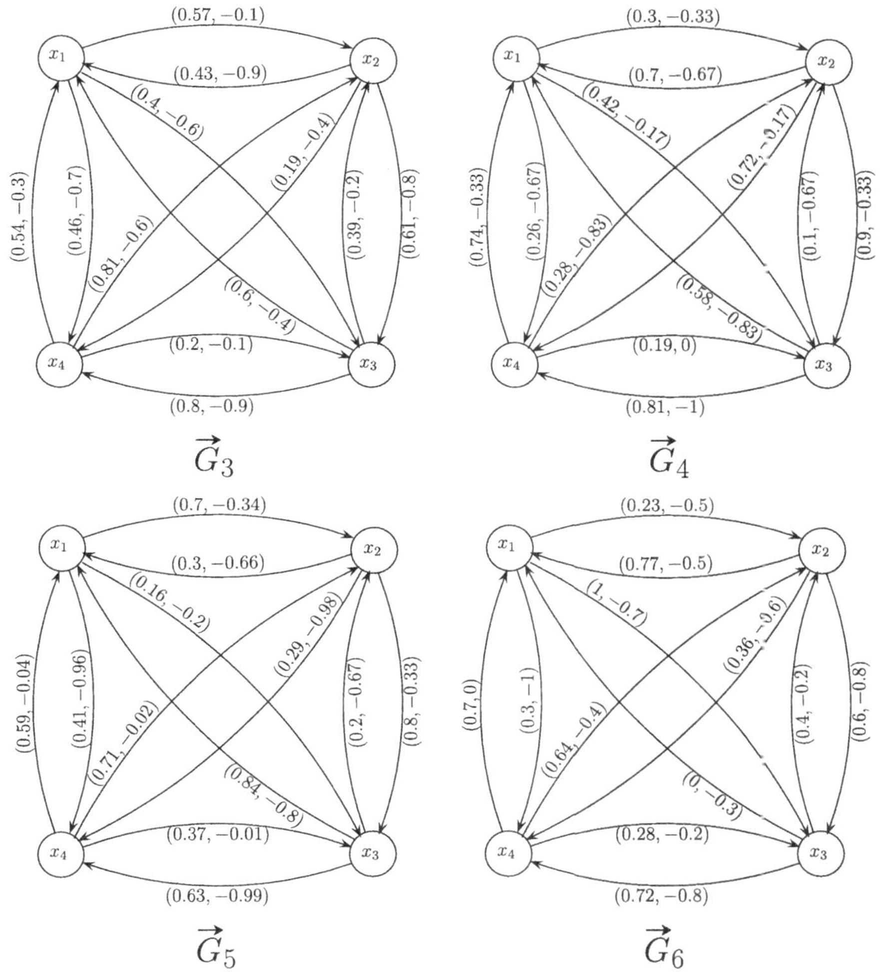

Fig. 8.9 Bipolar fuzzy digraphs

The net flow of x_i, i.e., the net degree of preference of x_i over the other alternatives can be calculated as

$$\psi(a_i) = \sum_{j=1}^{5} w_j \left(\sum_{k=1\ j\neq k}^{5} (s_{jk} - s_{kj}) \right), \quad i = 1, 2, 3, 4, 5, 6.$$

So, the net flows of the four alternatives are $\phi(x_1) = -0.5281$, $\phi(x_2) = -0.4799$, $\phi(x_3) = -0.2887$, $\phi(x_4) = 1.2967$, which give the ranking $x_4 \succ x_3 \succ x_2 \succ x_1$. Thus, the best choice is x_4.

8.6.2 Selection of a Business Partner

International Business Machines Corporation (IBM) is an American multinational technology company. It offers a prosperous portfolio of businesses, industry solutions including product engineering solutions and platform services. It is committed to becoming a universally superior IT solution and maintenance by way of regular development of organization and process, adequacy improvement, leadership, agreement, and open change of employees. To improve the competitiveness capability and operations in the universal market, IBM plans to set up a strategic agreement with a transnational corporation. After various meetings, four corporations would like to set up a strategic agreement with IBM; these are HPQ (a_1), VZ (a_2), DELL (a_3), and NT (a_4). To select the attractive strategic agreement partner, five experts e_j ($j = 1, 2, 3, 4, 5$) are requested to cooperate in the decision analysis who come from various departments of IBM. The experts compare given choices and give personal judgments using bipolar fuzzy preference relations $R_j = [r_{ik}^{(j)}]_{4\times4}$ ($j = 1, 2, 3, 4, 5$) given in the following matrices with corresponding bipolar fuzzy digraphs $\overrightarrow{G}_i,\ i = 1, 2, 3, 4, 5$ (Fig. 8.10).

$$R_1 = \begin{bmatrix} (0.5, -0.5) & (0.3, -0.6) & (0.7, -0.3) & (0.8, -0.7) \\ (0.7, -0.4) & (0.5, -0.5) & (0.6, -0.1) & (0.1, -0.5) \\ (0.3, -0.7) & (0.4, -0.9) & (0.5, -0.5) & (0.2, -0.7) \\ (0.2, -0.3) & (0.9, -0.5) & (0.8, -0.3) & (0.5, -0.5) \end{bmatrix}$$

$$R_2 = \begin{bmatrix} (0.5, -0.5) & (0.3, -0.6) & (0.8, -0.2) & (0.8, -0.1) \\ (0.7, -0.4) & (0.5, -0.5) & (0.7, -0.2) & (0.8, -0.3) \\ (0.2, -0.8) & (0.3, -0.8) & (0.5, -0.5) & (0.9, -0.4) \\ (0.2, -0.9) & (0.2, -0.7) & (0.1, -0.6) & (0.5, -0.5) \end{bmatrix}$$

$$R_3 = \begin{bmatrix} (0.5, -0.5) & (0.8, -0.8) & (0.8, -0.3) & (0.7, -0.2) \\ (0.2, -0.2) & (0.5, -0.5) & (0.8, -0.1) & (0.8, -0.2) \\ (0.2, -0.7) & (0.2, -0.9) & (0.5, -0.5) & (0.3, -0.6) \\ (0.3, -0.8) & (0.2, -0.8) & (0.7, -0.4) & (0.5, -0.5) \end{bmatrix}$$

$$R_4 = \begin{bmatrix} (0.5, -0.5) & (0.3, -0.6) & (0.6, -0.7) & (0.5, -0.1) \\ (0.7, -0.4) & (0.5, -0.5) & (0.3, -0.7) & (0.2, -0.2) \\ (0.4, -0.3) & (0.7, -0.3) & (0.5, -0.5) & (0.2, -0.7) \\ (0.5, -0.9) & (0.8, -0.8) & (0.8, -0.3) & (0.5, -0.5) \end{bmatrix}$$

$$R_5 = \begin{bmatrix} (0.5, -0.5) & (0.9, -0.2) & (0.4, -0.1) & (0.9, -0.3) \\ (0.1, -0.8) & (0.5, -0.5) & (0.8, -0.6) & (0.3, -0.3) \\ (0.6, -0.9) & (0.2, -0.4) & (0.5, -0.5) & (0.6, -0.7) \\ (0.1, -0.7) & (0.7, -0.7) & (0.4, -0.3) & (0.5, -0.5) \end{bmatrix}.$$

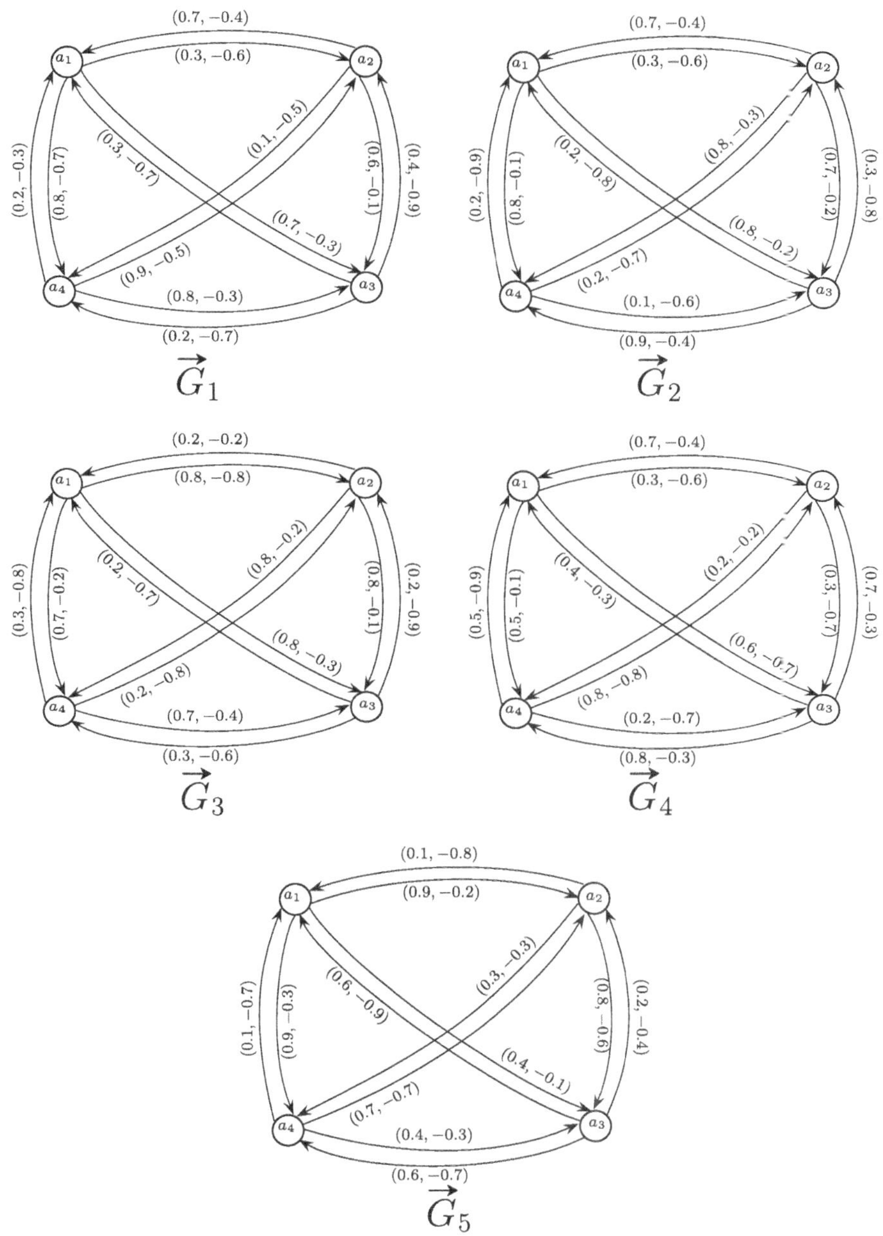

Fig. 8.10 Bipolar fuzzy digraphs

The Laplacian matrix of each bipolar fuzzy digraph $\overrightarrow{G}_j$ is denoted by R_j^L $(j = 1, 2, 3, 4, 5)$ and calculated as follows:

$$R_1^L = \begin{bmatrix} (1.8, -1.6) & (-0.3, 0.6) & (-0.7, 0.3) & (-0.8, 0.7) \\ (-0.7, 0.4) & (1.4, -1.0) & (-0.6, 0.1) & (-0.1, 0.5) \\ (-0.3, 0.7) & (-0.4, 0.9) & (0.9, -2.3) & (-0.2, 0.7) \\ (-0.2, 0.3) & (-0.9, 0.5) & (-0.8, 0.3) & (1.9, -1.1) \end{bmatrix}$$

$$R_2^L = \begin{bmatrix} (1.9, -0.9) & (-0.3, 0.6) & (-0.8, 0.2) & (-0.8, 0.1) \\ (-0.7, 0.4) & (2.2, -0.9) & (-0.7, 0.2) & (-0.8, 0.3) \\ (-0.2, 0.8) & (-0.3, 0.8) & (1.4, -2.0) & (-0.9, 0.4) \\ (-0.2, 0.9) & (-0.2, 0.7) & (-0.1, 0.6) & (0.5, -2.2) \end{bmatrix}$$

$$R_3^L = \begin{bmatrix} (2.4, -0.9) & (-0.8, 0.8) & (-0.8, 0.3) & (-0.7, 0.2) \\ (-0.2, 0.2) & (1.7, -0.9) & (-0.8, 0.1) & (-0.8, 0.2) \\ (-0.2, 0.7) & (-0.2, 0.9) & (0.7, -2.2) & (-0.3, 0.6) \\ (-0.3, 0.8) & (-0.2, 0.8) & (-0.7, 0.4) & (1.2, -2.0) \end{bmatrix}$$

$$R_4^L = \begin{bmatrix} (1.4, -1.4) & (-0.3, 0.6) & (-0.6, 0.7) & (-0.5, 0.1) \\ (-0.7, 0.4) & (1.2, -1.3) & (-0.3, 0.7) & (-0.2, 0.2) \\ (-0.4, 0.3) & (-0.7, 0.3) & (1.3, -1.3) & (-0.2, 0.7) \\ (-0.5, 0.9) & (-0.8, 0.8) & (-0.8, 0.3) & (2.1, -2.0) \end{bmatrix}$$

$$R_5^L = \begin{bmatrix} (2.2, -0.6) & (-0.9, 0.2) & (-0.4, 0.1) & (-0.9, 0.3) \\ (-0.1, 0.8) & (1.2, -1.7) & (-0.8, 0.6) & (-0.3, 0.3) \\ (-0.6, 0.9) & (-0.2, 0.4) & (1.4, -2.0) & (-0.6, 0.7) \\ (-0.1, 0.7) & (-0.7, 0.7) & (-0.4, 0.3) & (1.2, -1.7) \end{bmatrix}.$$

The Laplacian energy of each bipolar fuzzy digraph is computed as $LE(\overrightarrow{G}_1) = (4.6500, 4.5500)$, $LE(\overrightarrow{G}_2) = (3.8501, 5.0999)$, $LE(\overrightarrow{G}_3) = (3.9091, 47438)$, $LE(\overrightarrow{G}_4) = (4.9500, 4.5000)$, $LE(\overrightarrow{G}_5) = (4.0501, 4.8999)$. The weight of each expert can be calculated using Formula (8.14).

$$w_j = (w_j^p, w_j^n) = \left(\frac{LE^p(\overrightarrow{G}_j)}{\sum\limits_{i=1}^{5} LE^p(\overrightarrow{G}_i)}, \frac{LE^n(\overrightarrow{G}_j)}{\sum\limits_{i=1}^{5} LE(LE^n(\overrightarrow{G}_i)} \right), \quad j = 1, 2, 3, 4, 5. \tag{8.14}$$

By calculations, $w_1 = (0.2172, 0.1912)$, $w_2 = (0.1798, 0.2143)$, $w_3 = (0.1826, 0.1891)$, $w_4 = (0.2312, 0.1891)$, $w_5 = (0.1892, 0.2059)$. The collective bipolar fuzzy preference relation combined from five bipolar fuzzy preference relations and weights are computed in Eq. (8.15).

$$R = [(r^p_{ij}, r^n_{ij})]_{5\times 5} = \sum_{j=1}^{5} w_j R^L_j = \begin{bmatrix} (0.5000, -0.5000) & (0.5048, -0.5574) & (0.6564, -0.3130) & (0.73\text{[illegible]}3, -0.2758) \\ (0.4952, -0.4426) & (0.5000, -0.5000) & (0.6230, -0.3378) & (0.41\text{[illegible]}6, -0.2994) \\ (0.3436, -0.6870) & (0.3770, -0.6622) & (0.5000, -0.5000) & (0.41\text{[illegible]}8, -0.6157) \\ (0.2687, -0.7242) & (0.5854, -0.7006) & (0.5802, -0.3843) & (0.50\text{[illegible]}0, -0.5000) \end{bmatrix}. \tag{8.15}$$

Using score function $s_{ij} = r^p_{ij} + r^n_{ij}$, the scores are given in Eq. (8.16).

$$S = [s_{ij}]_{5\times 5} = \begin{bmatrix} 0 & -0.0526 & 0.3434 & 0.4555 \\ 0.0526 & 0 & 0.2852 & 0.1152 \\ -0.3434 & -0.2852 & 0 & -0.1959 \\ -0.4555 & -0.1152 & 0.1959 & 0 \end{bmatrix}. \tag{8.16}$$

The net degree of preference of each alternative a_i over the other cho ces can be calculated using Formula (8.17).

$$\psi(a_i) = \sum_{j=1}^{5} w_j \Big(\sum_{k=1\, i\neq j}^{5} s_{kj} - s_{jk} \Big), \quad i = 1, 2, 3, 4, 5. \tag{8.17}$$

The net degrees of the four choices are $\psi(a_1) = 1.4926$, $\psi(a_2) = 0.905$, $\psi(a_3) = -1.649$, $\psi(a_4) = -0.7496$ which give the ranking $a_1 \succ a_2 \succ a_4 \succ a_3$. Thus the best choice is a_1.

The signless Laplacian matrices of the bipolar fuzzy digraphs $\overrightarrow{G}_j$, $j = 1, 2, 3, 4, 5$ are computed as follows:

$$R_1^{L^+} = \begin{bmatrix} (1.8, -1.6) & (0.3, -0.6) & (0.7, -0.3) & (0.8, -0.7) \\ (0.7, -0.4) & (1.4, -1.0) & (0.6, -0.1) & (0.1, -0.5) \\ (0.3, -0.7) & (0.4, -0.9) & (0.9, -2.3) & (0.2, -0.7) \\ (0.2, -0.3) & (0.9, -0.5) & (0.8, -0.3) & (1.9, -1.1) \end{bmatrix}$$

$$R_2^{L^+} = \begin{bmatrix} (1.9, -0.9) & (0.3, -0.6) & (0.8, -0.2) & (0.8, -0.1) \\ (0.7, -0.4) & (2.2, -0.9) & (0.7, -0.2) & (0.8, -0.3) \\ (0.2, -0.8) & (0.3, -0.8) & (1.4, -2.0) & (0.9, -0.4) \\ (0.2, -0.9) & (0.2, -0.7) & (0.1, -0.6) & (0.5, -2.2) \end{bmatrix}$$

$$R_3^{L^+} = \begin{bmatrix} (2.4, -0.9) & (0.8, -0.8) & (0.8, -0.3) & (0.7, -0.2) \\ (0.2, -0.2) & (1.7, -0.9) & (0.8, -0.1) & (0.8, -0.2) \\ (0.2, -0.7) & (0.2, -0.9) & (0.7, -2.2) & (0.3, -0.6) \\ (0.3, -0.8) & (0.2, -0.8) & (0.7, -0.4) & (1.2, -2.0) \end{bmatrix}$$

$$R_4^{L^+} = \begin{bmatrix} (1.4, -1.4) & (0.3, -0.6) & (0.6, -0.7) & (0.5, -0.1) \\ (0.7, -0.4) & (1.2, -1.3) & (0.3, -0.7) & (0.2, -0.2) \\ (0.4, -0.3) & (0.7, -0.3) & (1.3, -1.3) & (0.2, -0.7) \\ (0.5, -0.9) & (0.8, -0.8) & (0.8, -0.3) & (2.1, -2.0) \end{bmatrix}$$

$$R_5^{L^+} = \begin{bmatrix} (2.2, -0.6) & (0.9, -0.2) & (0.4, -0.1) & (0.9, -0.3) \\ (0.1, -0.8) & (1.2, -1.7) & (0.8, -0.6) & (0.3, -0.3) \\ (0.6, -0.9) & (0.2, -0.4) & (1.4, -2.0) & (0.6, -0.7) \\ (0.1, -0.7) & (0.7, -0.7) & (0.4, -0.3) & (1.2, -1.7) \end{bmatrix}.$$

The signless Laplacian energy of each bipolar fuzzy digraph is computed as $SLE(\overrightarrow{G}_1) = (3.4884, 3.4080)$, $SLE(\overrightarrow{G}_2) = (3.0805, 4.2173)$, $SLE(\overrightarrow{G}_3) = (3.0688, 3.8348)$, $SLE(\overrightarrow{G}_4) = (3.9000, 3.0000)$, $SLE(\overrightarrow{G}_5) = (3.3673, 4.0769)$. The weights of each expert can be computed using Formula (8.18).

$$w_j = (w_j^p, w_j^n) = \left(\frac{SLE^p(\overrightarrow{G}_j)}{\sum\limits_{i=1}^{5} SLE^p(\overrightarrow{G}_i)}, \frac{SLE^n(\overrightarrow{G}_j)}{\sum\limits_{i=1}^{5} SLE^n(\overrightarrow{G}_i)} \right), \quad j = 1, 2, 3, 4, 5. \quad (8.18)$$

Here, $w_1 = (0.2064, 0.1838)$, $w_2 = (0.1822, 0.2275)$, $w_3 = (0.1815, 0.2069)$, w_4=$(0.2307, 0.1618)$, $w_5 = (0.1992, 0.2199)$. The collective bipolar fuzzy preference relation combined from the five bipolar fuzzy preference relations and corresponding weights are computed as follows:

$$R = [(r_{ij}^p, r_{ij}^n)]_{n\times n} = \sum_{j=1}^{5} w_j R_j = \begin{bmatrix} (0.5000, -0.5000) & (0.5103, -0.5534) & (0.6535, -0.2980) & (0.7326, -0.2749) \\ (0.4897, -0.4466) & (0.5000, -0.5000) & (0.6252, -0.3298) & (0.4175, -0.2999) \\ (0.3465, -0.7020) & (0.3748, -0.6702) & (0.5000, -0.5000) & (0.4254, -0.6110) \\ (0.2674, -0.7251) & (0.5825, -0.7001) & (0.5746, -0.3890) & (0.5000, -0.5000) \end{bmatrix}.$$

Using the score function $s_{ij} = r_{ij}^p + r_{ij}^n$, the score values are calculated in matrix S.

$$S = [s_{ij}]_{5\times 5} = \begin{bmatrix} 0 & -0.0431 & 0.3555 & 0.4577 \\ 0.0431 & 0 & 0.2954 & 0.1176 \\ -0.3555 & -0.2954 & 0 & -0.1856 \\ -0.4577 & -0.1176 & 0.1856 & 0 \end{bmatrix}.$$

The net degree of preference of a_i over the other choices can be computed using Formula (8.19).

$$\psi(a_i) = \sum_{j=1}^{5} w_j \left(\sum_{k=1\ j\neq k}^{5} (s_{jk} - s_{kj}) \right), \quad i = 1, 2, 3, 4, 5. \quad (8.19)$$

Hence the net degrees of the four choices are $\psi(a_1) = 1.5402$, $\psi(a_2) = 0.9122$, $\psi(a_3) = -1.6730$, $\psi(a_4) = -0.7794$ which gives the ranking of $a_1 \succ a_2 \succ a_4 \succ a_3$. Thus the best choice is a_1.

8.7 Conclusions

In connection with energy, the properties of graphical models can be described using various matrices associated with graphs such as Laplacian matrix to study diffusion over networks, dominating, out-dominating, and double dominating matrices for characterizing domination parameters in network models. The energy-like quantities related to these matrices have a clear connection to chemical problems, and in newer times attracted much attention of mathematicians and mathematical chemists. To deal with bipolar fuzzy networks, in this chapter, we have studied the concept of energy in bipolar fuzzy graphs and presented certain formulae, lower and upper bounds of Laplacian energy, signless Laplacian energy, dominating energy, out-dominating energy, double dominating energy, and double out-dominating energy of bipolar fuzzy graphs and bipolar fuzzy digraphs. Using bipolar fuzzy preference relations, we have studied multi-criteria decision-making models based on the energy of bipolar fuzzy graphs in business partnerships and smooth communication problems.

Exercises 8

1. Let $G = (A, B)$ be a complete bipolar fuzzy graph such that $B(xy) = (c^p, c^n)$, for all $x, y \in X$. Calculate the energy of G.

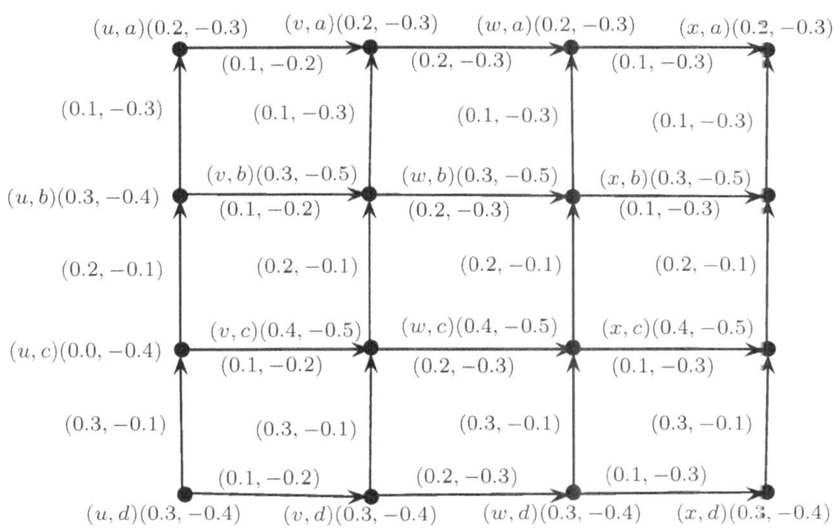

Fig. 8.11 Cartesian product $\vec{G}$

2. Calculate the double out-dominating set and double out-dominating energy of the Cartesian product $\overrightarrow{G}$ of two bipolar fuzzy digraphs as shown in Fig. 8.11.
3. Let $G = (A, B)$ be a bipolar fuzzy graph with n vertices and minimum double dominating set $D = \{w_1, w_2, \ldots, w_k\}$, then

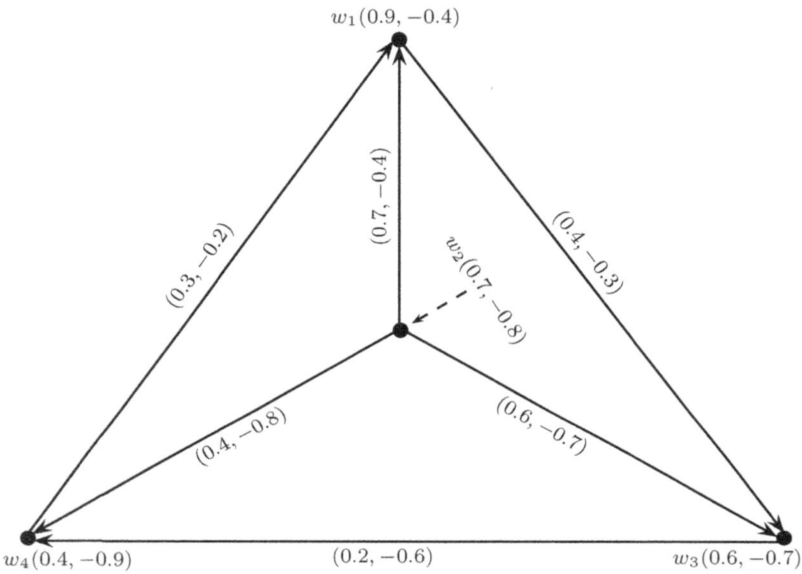

Fig. 8.12 Bipolar fuzzy digraph $\overrightarrow{G}$

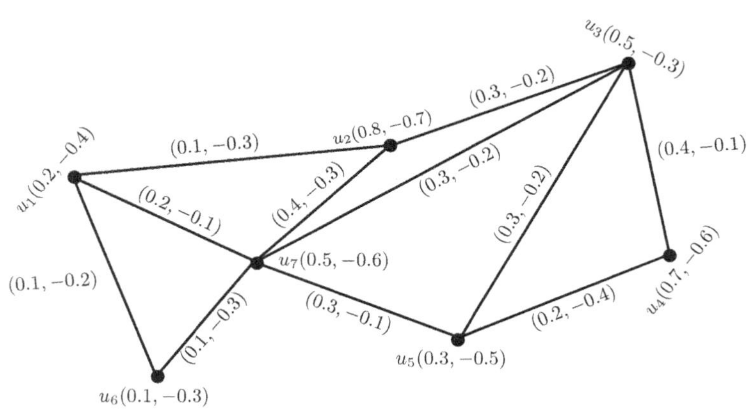

Fig. 8.13 Bipolar fuzzy digraph G

(a) $\sum_{w_i \in \widetilde{D}} B(w_i) = (\sum_{i=1}^{n} \phi_i, \sum_{i=1}^{n} \psi_i)$,

(b) $\sum_{i=1}^{n} (\phi_i)^2 = \sum_{i=1}^{n} (\xi_{ii}^p)^2 + \sum_{i=1}^{n} \sum_{\substack{j=1 \\ i \neq j}}^{n} (\xi_{ij}^p)(\xi_{ji}^p)$,

(c) $\sum_{i=1}^{n} (\psi_i)^2 = \sum_{i=1}^{n} (\xi_{ii}^n)^2 + \sum_{i=1}^{n} \sum_{\substack{j=1 \\ i \neq j}}^{n} (\xi_{ij}^n)(\xi_{ji}^n)$.

4. Let $G = (A, B)$ be a bipolar fuzzy graph with n vertices. If $\widetilde{D}$ is a minimum double dominating set, $R = \det(A_{\widetilde{D}}^p(G)) = det([\xi_{ij}^p]_{n \times n})$, and $T = \det(A_{\widetilde{D}}^n(G)) = det([\xi_{ij}^n]_{n \times n})$, then

(a) $\sqrt{\sum_{i=1}^{n} (\xi_{ii}^p)^2 + \sum_{i \neq j} (\xi_{ij}^p)(\xi_{ji}^p) + n(n-1)R^{\frac{2}{n}}} \leq \sum_{i=1}^{n} |\phi_i| \leq \sqrt{n\left(\sum_{i=1}^{n} (\xi_{ii}^p)^2 + \sum_{i \neq j} (\xi_{ij}^p)(\xi_{ji}^p)\right)}$.

(b) $\sqrt{\sum_{i=1}^{n} (\xi_{ii}^n)^2 + \sum_{i \neq j} (\xi_{ij}^n)(\xi_{ji}^n) + n(n-1)T^{\frac{2}{n}}} \leq \sum_{i=1}^{n} |\psi_i| \leq \sqrt{n\left(\sum_{i=1}^{n} (\xi_{ii}^n)^2 + \sum_{i \neq j} (\xi_{ij}^n)(\xi_{ji}^n)\right)}$.

5. Let $G = (A, B)$ be a bipolar fuzzy graph with adjacency matrix $A(G) = [u_{ij}]_{n \times n}$. Let λ_i, $1 \leq i \leq n$, be the eigenvalues of adjacency matrix $A^p(G)$ and ω_i, $1 \leq i \leq n$, be the eigenvalues of adjacency matrix $A^n(G)$, then

$$\left(\sum_{i=1}^{n} |\phi_i|\right)^2 \leq n\left(\sum_{i=1}^{n} (\xi_{ii}^p)^2 + (\sum_{i=1}^{n} |\lambda_i|)^2\right) \quad \text{and} \quad \left(\sum_{i=1}^{n} |\psi_i|\right)^2 \leq n\left(\sum_{i=1}^{n} (\xi_{ii}^n)^2 + \sum_{i=1}^{n} |\omega_i|)^2\right).$$

6. If $G = (A, B)$ is a null bipolar fuzzy graph, then prove that $LE(G) = (0, 0)$.
7. If G is a regular and totally regular bipolar fuzzy graph, then prove that the sum of eigenvalues of G is zero.
8. Calculate the out-dominating set and out-dominating energy of bipolar fuzzy digraph $\overrightarrow{G} = (A, \overrightarrow{B})$ on $X = \{w_1, w_2, w_3, w_4\}$ shown in Fig. 8.12.
9. Let $A(G)$, $L(G)$ and $L^+(G)$ be the adjacency, the Laplacian and the signless Laplacian matrices, respectively, of a bipolar fuzzy graph G, as given in Fig. 8.13. Then show that $\left|LE^+(G) - LE(G)\right| \leq 2E(G)$.
10. Prove that $E(G) = LE(G) = LE^+(G)$, if the bipolar fuzzy graph G is a regular bipolar fuzzy graph.
11. Let $G = (A, B)$ be a bipolar fuzzy graph on n vertices and let $L(G)$ and $L^+(G)$ be the Laplacian and the signless Laplacian matrices of G, respectively. Then prove that

$$LE^+(l_{ij}^p) + LE(l_{ij}^p) \geq \max\left\{2E(l_{ij}^p), 2\sum_{j=1}^{n} \left| deg_{l_{ij}^p}(v_i) - \frac{2\sum_{1 \leq i < j \leq n} l_{ij}^p}{r} \right| \right\},$$

$$LE^+(l_{ij}^n) + LE(l_{ij}^n) \geq \max\left\{2E(l_{ij}^n), 2\sum_{j=1}^{n} \left| deg_{l_{ij}^n}(v_i) - \frac{2\sum_{1 \leq i < j \leq n} l_{ij}^n}{r} \right| \right\}.$$

12. Let $G = (A, B)$ be a bipolar fuzzy graph on n vertices and let $L(G)$ and $L^+(G)$ be the Laplacian and the signless Laplacian matrices of G, respectively. Then show that and rank r.

$$LE^+(l^p_{ij}) + LE(l^p_{ij}) \geq 4E(l^p_{ij}) - \frac{4r \sum\limits_{1\leq i<j\leq n} l^p_{ij}}{n},$$

$$LE^+(l^n_{ij}) + LE(l^n_{ij}) \geq 4E(l^n_{ij}) - \frac{4r \sum\limits_{1\leq i<j\leq n} l^n_{ij}}{n},$$

where r is the number of non-zero eigenvalues of a bipolar fuzzy graph G.

13. Let $G = (A, B)$ be a bipolar fuzzy graph on n vertices and let $L(G) = (L(l^p_{ij}), L(l^n_{ij}))$ be the Laplacian matrix of G. Then prove that

$$LE(l^p_{ij}) \leq E(l^p_{ij}) + \sum_{j=1}^{n} \left| deg_{l^p_{ij}}(v_i) - \frac{2 \sum\limits_{1\leq i<j\leq n} l^p_{ij}}{n} \right|,$$

$$LE(l^n_{ij}) \leq E(l^n_{ij}) + \sum_{j=1}^{n} \left| deg_{l^n_{ij}}(v_i) - \frac{2 \sum\limits_{1\leq i<j\leq n} l^n_{ij}}{n} \right|.$$

14. Let $G = (A, B)$ be a bipolar fuzzy graph on n vertices and let $L^+(G) = (L^+(l^p_{ij}), L^+(l^n_{ij}))$ be the signless Laplacian matrix of G. Then show that

$$LE^+(l^p_{ij}) \leq E(l^p_{ij}) + \sum_{j=1}^{n} \left| deg_{l^p_{ij}}(v_i) - \frac{2 \sum\limits_{1\leq i<j\leq n} l^p_{ij}}{n} \right|,$$

$$LE^+(l^n_{ij}) \leq E(l^n_{ij}) + \sum_{j=1}^{n} \left| deg_{l^n_{ij}}(v_i) - \frac{2 \sum\limits_{1\leq i<j\leq n} l^n_{ij}}{n} \right|.$$

15. Let G be a connected bipolar fuzzy graph on n vertices and let $L^+(G) = (L^+(l^p_{ij}), L^+(l^n_{ij}))$ be the signless Laplacian matrix of G. Then show that

$$LE^+(l^p_{ij}) \leq E(l^p_{ij}) + \sqrt{n \sum_{j=1}^{n} deg^2_{l^p_{ij}}(v_i) - 4\left(\sum_{1\leq i<j\leq n} l^p_{ij}\right)^2},$$

$$LE^+(l^n_{ij}) \leq E(l^n_{ij}) + \sqrt{n \sum_{j=1}^{n} deg^2_{l^n_{ij}}(v_i) - 4\left(\sum_{1\leq i<j\leq n} l^n_{ij}\right)^2}.$$

References

1. Akram, M.: Bipolar fuzzy graphs. Inf. Sci. **181**(24), 5548–5564 (2011)
2. Akram, M., Dudek, W.A.: Regular bipolar fuzzy graphs. Neural Comput. Appl. **21**(supp 1), 197–205 (2012)
3. Akram, M., Saleem, D., Rashmanlou, H.: Signless Laplacian energy of bipolar fuzzy graphs with application. Int. J. Adv. Intell. Paradigms. In press 2019
4. Akram, M., Saleem, D., Davvaz, D.: Energy of double dominating bipolar fuzzy graphs. J. Appl. Math. Comput. **61**(1–2), 219–234 (2019)
5. Anjali, N., Mathew, S.: Energy of a fuzzy graph. Ann. Fuzzy Math. Inf. **6**(3), 455–465 (2013)
6. Borzooei, R.A., Rashmanlou, H.: New concepts of vague graphs. Int. J. Mach. Learn. Cybern. **8**(4), 1081–1092 (2017)
7. Gutman, I.: The energy of a graph. Ber. Math-Statist. Sekt. Forschungsz. Graz **103**, 1–22 (1978)
8. Gutman, I.: The energy of a graph: Old and New Results. In: Betten, A., Kohnert, A., Laue, R., Wassermann, A. (eds.) Algebraic Combinatorics and Applications. Springer, Berlin (2001)
9. Gutman, I., Zhou, B.: Laplacian energy of a graph. Linear Algebra Appl. **414**(1), 29–37 (2014)
10. Kahraman, C., Otay, I. (eds.): Fuzzy Multi-criteria Decision-Making Using Neutrosophic Sets. Springer, Berlin (2019)
11. Kaladevi, V., Devi, G.S.: Double dominating energy of some graphs. Int. J. Fuzzy Math. Archive **4**(1), 1–7 (2014)
12. Kanna, M.R., Dharmendra, B.N., Sridhara, G.: The minimum dominating energy of a graph. Int. J. Pure Appl. Math. **85**(4), 707–718 (2013)
13. Li, X., Shi, Y., Gutman, I.: Graph Energy. Springer Science and Business Media, Berlin (2012)
14. Naz, S., Ashraf, S., Karaaslan, F.: Energy of a bipolar fuzzy graph and its application in decision making. Italian J. Pure Appl. Math. **40**, 339–352 (2018)
15. Praba, B., Chandrasekaran, V.M., Deepa, G.: Energy of an intuitionistic fuzzy graph. Italian J. Pure Appl. Math. **32**, 431–444 (2014)
16. Rahimi Sharbaf, S., Fayazi, F.: Laplacian energy of a fuzzy graph. Iranian J. Math. Chem. **5**(1), 1–10 (2014)
17. Zhang, W.-R.: Bipolar fuzzy sets and relations: a computational framework for cognitive modeling and multiagent decision analysis. In: Proceedings of IEEE Conference, pp. 305–309 (1994)
18. Zhang, W.-R.: (YinYang) Bipolar fuzzy sets. IEEE International Conference on Fuzzy Systems, pp. 835–840 (1998)
19. Zhang, W.-R.: A communication on bipolarity. A Publication of Society for Mathematics of Uncertainty, vol. III, pp. 27–35 (2009)

Chapter 9
Bipolar Neutrosophic Competition Graphs

In this chapter, we present a concise review of bipolar neutrosophic sets and apply this concept to graphs and digraphs. We discuss the notion of bipolar neutrosophic competition graphs and present certain characterizations of bipolar neutrosophic out-neighborhoods, bipolar neutrosophic in-neighborhoods, bipolar neutrosophic open neighborhood graphs, bipolar neutrosophic closed neighborhood graphs, bipolar neutrosophic p-competition graphs, m-step bipolar neutrosophic competition graphs, and strong preys and strong independent predator–prey relations. We describe various methods for the construction of bipolar neutrosophic competition graphs of certain products of bipolar neutrosophic digraphs. We elaborate certain algorithms to compute the strength of competition with a number of real-world applications in different fields including economics, business marketing, and organizational designations. The basic results of this chapter are from [1, 5].

9.1 Introduction

The first successful attempt toward incorporating non-probabilistic uncertainty, i.e. uncertainty which is not caused by randomness of an event, into mathematical modeling was made in 1965 by Zadeh [19] through his remarkable theory on fuzzy sets. A fuzzy set is a generalization of a set in which each element of the universe belongs to it but with some grade or degree of belongingness which lies in [0, 1]. This gradation concept is very well suited for applications involving imprecise data such as natural language processing, artificial intelligence, handwriting, and speech recognition. Although fuzzy set theory is very successful in handling uncertainties arising from vagueness or partial belongingness of elements, it cannot model all sorts of uncertainties prevailing in various physical problems. In some applications such as expert system, belief system, and information fusion, we should consider not only the truth membership supported by the evidence but also the falsity membership against the

M. Akram et al., *Graphs for the Analysis of Bipolar Fuzzy Information*, Studies in Fuzziness and Soft Computing 401,
https://doi.org/10.1007/978-981-15-8756-6_9

evidence. That is beyond the scope of fuzzy sets and interval-valued fuzzy sets. In 1983, Atanassov [11] introduced the notion of intuitionistic fuzzy sets as a generalization of fuzzy sets. In an intuitionistic fuzzy set A, both truth membership value (belongingness) $T_A(x)$ and falsity membership value (non-belongingness) $F_A(x)$ are attached with each element x with the restriction that the sum of these two membership values is less or equal to 1. A fuzzy set can be considered as a special case of an intuitionistic fuzzy set, where the degree of non-belongingness of an element is exactly equal to 1 minus the degree of belongingness. In real-world problems, there are many situations containing tricomponents of uncertainty, e.g., games (winning, defeating, or tie scores), voting (pro, contra, null/black votes), positive/negative/zero numbers, yes/no/NA, decision-making and control theory (making a decision, not making, or hesitating), and accepted/rejected/pending. Smarandache [16], in 1995, proposed the term "neutrosophic" because "neutrosophic" etymologically comes from neutro-sophy means knowledge of neutral thought and this neutral represents the main distinction between fuzzy/intuitionistic fuzzy logic/set and neutrosophic logic/set. Neutrosophic logic is a logic in which each proposition is estimated to have a degree of truth (T), a degree of indeterminacy (I), and a degree of falsity (F). A neutrosophic set A is a set in which each element (x) of the universe has a degree of truth $T(x)$, indeterminacy $I(x)$, and falsity $F(x)$, where $T(x)$, $I(x)$, and $F(x)$ are real standard or real nonstandard subsets of $]0^-, 1^+[$, the nonstandard unit interval. In contrast to intuitionistic fuzzy sets and interval-valued intuitionistic fuzzy sets, the indeterminacy is characterized explicitly in a neutrosophic set which is independent of truth and falsity membership values. Neutrosophic sets are indeed more general than intuitionistic fuzzy sets as there are no constraints between truth, indeterminacy, and falsity membership values. All these degrees can individually vary within $]0^-, 1^+[$. Since, for software engineering proposals, the classical unit interval $[0, 1]$ is used, a neutrosophic set will be more difficult to apply in real scientific and engineering fields. To overcome this limitation, Wang et al. [18] proposed the concept of single-valued neutrosophic sets in which the degree of truth $T(x)$, indeterminacy $I(x)$, and falsity $F(x)$ belong to $[0, 1]$. Single-valued neutrosophic sets/graphs have been an active domain of research in the last few years. A lot of work has been done by researchers on neutrosophic set/graph theory [2, 3, 7, 9, 13, 15]. The concept of bipolar neutrosophic set was introduced in [14] and the bipolar single-valued neutrosophic graph in [6]. Other concepts of bipolar single-valued neutrosophic graphs can be seen in [1, 5, 8, 12]. For further terminologies and studies on single-valued neutrosophic theory, readers are referred to [4, 10, 17, 20–22].

9.2 Certain Types of Bipolar Neutrosophic Competition Graphs

A **neutrosophic set** A in a universe X is defined by a truth-membership function $T_A(x)$, an indeterminacy-membership function $I_A(x)$, and a falsity-membership function $F_A(x)$, where $T_A(x)$, $I_A(x)$, and $F_A(x)$ are real standard or real nonstandard subsets of $]0^-, 1^+[$, the nonstandard unit interval, that is, $T_A : X \to]0^-, 1^+[$, $I_A : X \to]0^-, 1^+[$, and $F_A : X \to]0^-, 1^+[$ are the mappings. There is no restriction on the sum of $T_A(x)$, $I_A(x)$, and $F_A(x)$, so $0^- \leq \sup T_A(x) + \sup I_A(x) + \sup F_A(x) \leq 3^+$.

Definition 9.1 A **single-valued neutrosophic set** A on a non-empty set X is characterized by a truth-membership function $T_A : X \to [0, 1]$, indeterminacy-membership function $I_A : X \to [0, 1]$, and a falsity-membership function $F_A : X \to [0, 1]$. There is no restriction on the sum of $T_A(x)$, $T_A(x)$, and $F_A(x)$, for all $x \in X$.

Definition 9.2 A **bipolar single-valued neutrosophic set** A on a non-empty set X is an object of the form

$$A = \left\{\left(x, T_A^p(x), I_A^p(x), F_A^p(x), T_A^n(x), I_A^n(x), F_A^n(x)\right) \mid x \in X\right\},$$

where $T_A^p, I_A^p, F_A^p : X \to [0, 1]$ and $T_A^n, I_A^n, F_A^n : X \to [-1, 0]$ are mappings. The positive membership values $T_A^p(x)$, $I_A^p(x)$, $F_A^p(x)$ denote, respectively, the truth, indeterminacy, and falsity membership values of an element $x \in X$, whereas the negative membership values $T_A^n(x)$, $I_A^n(x)$, $F_A^n(x)$ denote the implicit counter properties of truth, indeterminacy, and falsity membership degrees of an element $x \in X$ corresponding to the bipolar neutrosophic set A.

Definition 9.3 The **height** of a bipolar single-valued neutrosophic set $A = (T_A^p(x), I_A^p(x), F_A^p(x), T_A^n(x), I_A^n(x), F_A^n(x))$ in a universe of discourse X is defined as

$$\begin{aligned} h(A) &= (h_1(A), h_2(A), h_3(A), h_4(A), h_5(A), h_6(A)) \\ &= (\sup_{x \in X} T_A^p(x), \sup_{x \in X} I_A^p(x), \inf_{x \in X} F_A^p(x), \sup_{x \in X} T_A^p(x), \sup_{x \in X} I_A^p(x), \inf_{x \in X} F_A^p(x)). \end{aligned}$$

Example 9.1 Consider a bipolar single-valued neutrosophic set $A = \{(a, 0.5, 0.7, 0.2, -0.8, -0.9, -0.3), (b, 0.1, 0.2, 1, -0.5, -0.7, -0.6), (c, 0.3, 0.5, 0.3, -0.8, -0.6, -0.4)\}$ on $X = \{a, b, c\}$, then $h(A) = (0.5, 0.7, 0.2, 0.5, 0.7, 0.2)$.

Definition 9.4 Let $A_1 = (T_{A_1}^p(x), I_{A_1}^p(x), F_{A_1}^p(x), T_{A_1}^n(x), I_{A_1}^n(x), F_{A_1}^n(x))$ and $A_2 = (T_{A_2}^p(x), I_{A_2}^p(x), F_{A_2}^p(x), T_{A_2}^n(x), I_{A_2}^n(x), F_{A_2}^n(x))$ be two bipolar single-valued neutrosophic sets on X. The **union** of A_1 and A_2 is denoted by $A_1 \cup A_2$ and defined as

$$\begin{aligned} (A_1 \cup A_2)(x) = &\big(T_{A_1}^p(x) \vee T_{A_2}^p(x), I_{A_1}^p(x) \vee I_{A_2}^p(x), F_{A_1}^p(x) \wedge F_{A_2}^p(x), T_{A_1}^n(x) \wedge T_{A_2}^n(x), \\ &I_{A_1}^n(x) \wedge I_{A_2}^n(x), F_{A_1}^n(x) \vee F_{A_2}^n(x)\big), \quad \text{for all } x \in X. \end{aligned}$$

Definition 9.5 Let $A_1 = (T_{A_1}^p(x), I_{A_1}^p(x), F_{A_1}^p(x), T_{A_1}^n(x), I_{A_1}^n(x), F_{A_1}^n(x))$ and $A_2 = (T_{A_2}^p(x), I_{A_2}^p(x), F_{A_2}^p(x), T_{A_2}^n(x), I_{A_2}^n(x), F_{A_2}^n(x))$ be two bipolar single-valued neutrosophic sets on X. The **intersection** of A_1 and A_2 is denoted by $A_1 \cap A_2$ and defined as

Table 9.1 Bipolar neutrosophic set A

A	x	y	z
T_A^p	0.3	0.5	0.4
I_A^p	0.4	0.4	0.3
F_A^p	0.5	0.2	0.2
T_A^n	−0.6	−0.1	−0.5
I_A^n	−0.5	−0.8	−0.5
F_A^n	−0.2	−0.2	−0.5

$$(A_1 \cap A_2)(x) = \big(T_{A_1}^p(x) \wedge T_{A_2}^p(x), I_{A_1}^p(x) \wedge I_{A_2}^p(x), F_{A_1}^p(x) \vee F_{A_2}^p(x), T_{A_1}^n(x) \vee T_{A_2}^n(x), I_{A_1}^n(x) \vee I_{A_2}^n(x), F_{A_1}^n(x) \wedge F_{A_2}^n(x)\big), \quad \text{for all } x \in X.$$

Definition 9.6 Let $A = (T_A^p(x), I_A^p(x), F_A^p(x), T_A^n(x), I_A^n(x), F_A^n(x))$ be a bipolar single-valued neutrosophic set on X. The **complement** of A is denoted by $A^c = (T_{A^c}^p(x), I_{A^c}^p(x), F_{A^c}^p(x), T_{A^c}^n(x), I_{A^c}^n(x), F_{A^c}^n(x))$ and defined as

$$A^c(x) = \big(1 - T_A^p(x), 1 - I_A^p(x), 1 - F_A^p(x), -1 - T_A^n(x), -1 - I_{A_1}^n(x), -1 - F_{A_1}^n(x)\big), \quad \text{for all } x \in X.$$

Definition 9.7 A **bipolar single-valued neutrosophic relation** on a non-empty set X is a mapping $B : X \times X \to [0, 1]^3 \times [-1, 0]^3$, that is, $B = \{(yz, T_B^p(yz), I_B^p(yz), F_B^p(yz), T_B^n(yz), I_B^n(yz), F_B^n(yz)) \mid yz \in X \times X\}$.

Definition 9.8 A **bipolar single-valued neutrosophic graph** on a non-empty set X is a pair $G = (A, B)$, where A is a bipolar single-valued neutrosophic set on X and B is a bipolar single-valued neutrosophic relation in X such that

$$T_B^p(yz) \le T_A^p(y) \wedge T_A^p(z), \quad I_B^p(yz) \le I_A^p(y) \wedge I_A^p(z), \quad F_B^p(yz) \le F_A^p(y) \vee F_A^p(z),$$
$$T_B^n(yz) \ge T_A^n(y) \vee T_A^n(z), \quad I_B^n(yz) \ge I_A^n(y) \vee I_A^n(z), \quad F_B^n(yz) \ge F_A^n(y) \wedge F_A^n(z), \quad \text{for all } y, z \in X.$$

Note that $B(yz) = (0, 0, 1, 0, 0, -1)$, for all $yz \in X \times X \setminus E$, where E is the set of edges in G.

Example 9.2 Consider a bipolar single-valued neutrosophic graph $G = (A, B)$ on $X = \{x, y, z\}$, where A is a bipolar single-valued neutrosophic set on X, given in Table 9.1, and B is a bipolar single-valued neutrosophic relation in X given in Table 9.2. The bipolar single-valued neutrosophic graph G is shown in Fig. 9.1.

Definition 9.9 A **bipolar single-valued neutrosophic digraph** on a non-empty set X is a pair $\overrightarrow{G} = (A, \overrightarrow{B})$, where A is a bipolar single-valued neutrosophic set on X and $\overrightarrow{B}$ is a bipolar single-valued neutrosophic relation in X such that

$$T_{\overrightarrow{B}}^p(yz) \le T_A^p(y) \wedge T_A^p(z), \quad I_{\overrightarrow{B}}^p(yz) \le I_A^p(y) \wedge I_A^p(z), \quad F_{\overrightarrow{B}}^p(yz) \le F_A^p(y) \vee F_A^p(z),$$
$$T_{\overrightarrow{B}}^n(yz) \ge T_A^n(y) \vee T_A^n(z), \quad I_{\overrightarrow{B}}^n(yz) \ge I_A^n(y) \vee I_A^n(z), \quad F_{\overrightarrow{B}}^n(yz) \ge F_A^n(y) \wedge F_A^n(z), \quad \text{for all } y, z \in X.$$

Table 9.2 Bipolar neutrosophic relation A

B	xy	yz	xz
T_B^p	0.3	0.3	0.3
I_B^p	0.4	0.4	0.4
F_B^p	0.5	0.2	0.5
T_B^n	−0.1	−0.1	−0.5
I_B^n	−0.8	−0.8	−0.5
F_B^n	−0.2	−0.5	−0.5

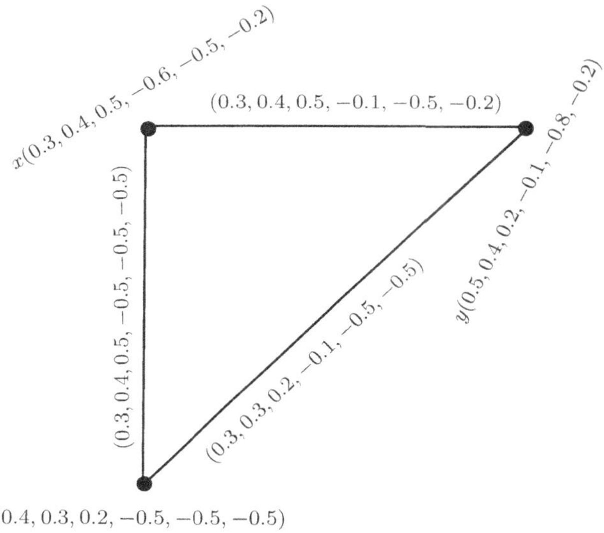

Fig. 9.1 Bipolar neutrosophic graph G

Note that $\overrightarrow{B}$ is a nonsymmetric bipolar single-valued neutrosophic relation in X.

Example 9.3 A bipolar single-valued neutrosophic digraph on $X = \{a, b, c\}$ is shown in Fig. 9.2.

Definition 9.10 Let $\overrightarrow{G}$ be a bipolar single-valued neutrosophic digraph on X. A **bipolar single-valued neutrosophic out-neighborhood** of a vertex $x \in X$ is a bipolar single-valued neutrosophic set $\mathcal{N}^+(x) = (X_x^+, T_x^p, I_x^p, F_x^p, T_x^n, I_x^n, F_x^n)$ such that $X_x^+ = \{y \mid \overrightarrow{B}(xy) \neq (0, 0, 1, 0, 0, -1)\}$ and $T_x^p, I_x^p, F_x^p : X \times X \to [0, 1]$, $T_x^n, I_x^n, f_x^n : X \times X \to [-1, 0]$ are defined by $T_x^p(y) = T_{\overrightarrow{B}}^p(xy)$, $I_x^p(y) = I_{\overrightarrow{B}}^p(xy)$, $F_x^p(y) = F_{\overrightarrow{B}}^p(xy)$, $T_x^n(y) = T_{\overrightarrow{B}}^n(xy)$, $I_x^n(y) = I_{\overrightarrow{B}}^n(xy)$, $F_x^n(y) = F_{\overrightarrow{B}}^n(xy)$.

A **bipolar single-valued neutrosophic in-neighborhood** of a vertex $x \in X$ is a bipolar single-valued neutrosophic set $\mathcal{N}^-(x) = (X_x^-, T_x^p, I_x^p, F_x^p, T_x^n, I_x^n, F_x^n)$ such

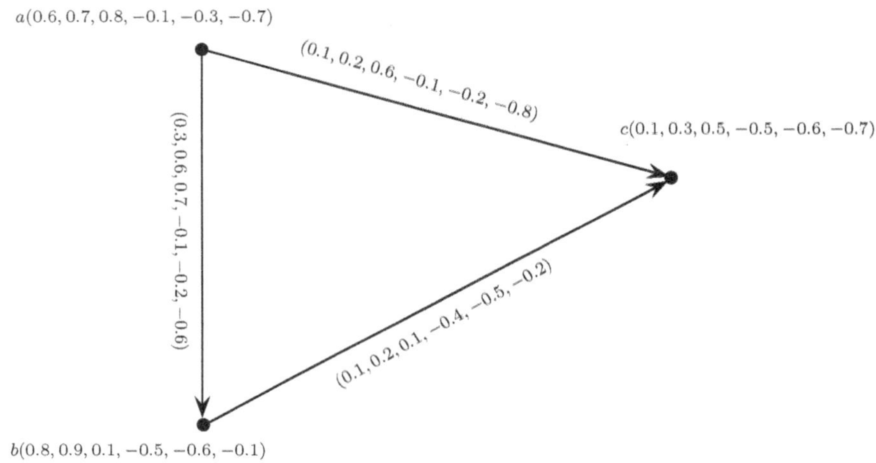

Fig. 9.2 Bipolar neutrosophic digraph

that $X_x^- = \{y \mid \overrightarrow{B}(yx) \neq (0, 0, 1, 0, 0, -1)\}$ and $T_x^p, I_x^p, F_x^p : X \times X \to [0, 1]$, $T_x^n, I_x^n, f_x^n : X \times X \to [-1, 0]$ are defined by $T_x^p(y) = T_{\overrightarrow{B}}^p(yx)$, $I_x^p(y) = I_{\overrightarrow{B}}^p(yx)$, $F_x^p(y) = F_{\overrightarrow{B}}^p(yx)$, $T_x^n(y) = T_{\overrightarrow{B}}^n(yx)$, $I_x^n(y) = I_{\overrightarrow{B}}^n(yx)$, $F_x^n(y) = F_{\overrightarrow{B}}^n(yx)$.

Definition 9.11 For any two n-tuples $(a_1, a_2, \ldots, a_n)$ and $(b_1, b_2, \ldots, b_n)$, where a_i, b_i, for each $1 \leq i \leq n$, are real numbers, then
1. $(a_1, a_2, \ldots, a_n) = (b_1, b_2, \ldots, b_n) \Leftrightarrow a_i = b_i$, for each $1 \leq i \leq n$
2. $(a_1, a_2, \ldots, a_n) \leq (b_1, b_2, \ldots, b_n) \Leftrightarrow a_i \leq b_i$, for each $1 \leq i \leq n$
3. $(a_1, a_2, \ldots, a_n) \geq (b_1, b_2, \ldots, b_n) \Leftrightarrow a_i \geq b_i$, for each $1 \leq i \leq n$
4. $(a_1, a_2, \ldots, a_n) \times (b_1, b_2, \ldots, b_n) = (a_1b_1, a_2b_2, \ldots, a_nb_n)$.

Definition 9.12 A **bipolar single-valued neutrosophic competition graph** of a bipolar single-valued neutrosophic digraph $\overrightarrow{G} = (A, \overrightarrow{B})$ is a undirected bipolar single-valued neutrosophic graph $\mathcal{C}(\overrightarrow{G}) = (A, R)$ which has the same vertex set as in $\overrightarrow{G}$, and there is an edge between two vertices x and y if and only if $\mathcal{N}^+(x) \cap \mathcal{N}^+(y)$ is non-empty. The positive truth-membership, indeterminacy-membership, falsity-membership, and negative truth-membership, indeterminacy-membership, falsity-membership values of the edge xy are defined as

1. $T_R^p(xy) = (T_A^p(x) \wedge T_A^p(y))h_1(\mathcal{N}^+(x) \cap \mathcal{N}^+(y))$,
2. $I_R^p(xy) = (I_A^p(x) \wedge I_A^p(y))h_2(\mathcal{N}^+(x) \cap \mathcal{N}^+(y))$,
3. $F_R^p(xy) = (F_A^p(x) \vee F_A^p(y))h_3(\mathcal{N}^+(x) \cap \mathcal{N}^+(y))$,
4. $T_R^n(xy) = (T_A^n(x) \vee T_A^n(y))h_4(\mathcal{N}^+(x) \cap \mathcal{N}^+(y))$,
5. $I_R^n(xy) = (I_A^n(x) \vee I_A^n(y))h_5(\mathcal{N}^+(x) \cap \mathcal{N}^+(y))$,
6. $F_R^n(xy) = (F_A^n(x) \wedge F_A^n(y))h_6(\mathcal{N}^+(x) \cap \mathcal{N}^+(y))$, for all $x, y \in X$.

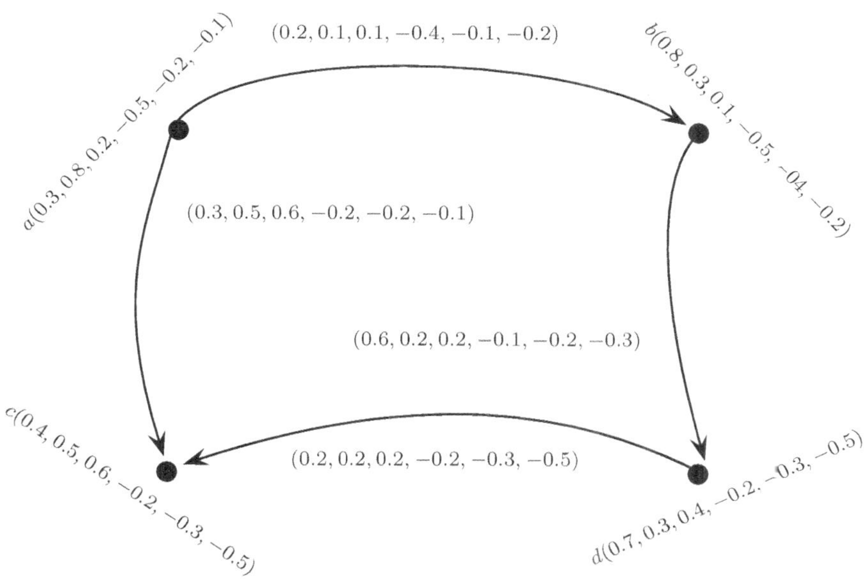

Fig. 9.3 Bipolar neutrosophic digraph $\overrightarrow{G}$

Table 9.3 Bipolar neutrosophic out-neighborhoods of vertices

x	$\mathcal{N}^+(x)$
a	{(b, 0.2, 0.1, 0.1, –0.4, –0.1, –0.2), (c, 0.3, 0.5, 0.6, –0.2, –0.2, –0.1)}
b	{(d, 0.6, 0.2, 0.2, –0.1, –0.2, –0.3)}
c	∅
d	{(c, 0.2, 0.2, 0.2, –0.2, –0.3, –0.5)}

Example 9.4 Consider a bipolar single-valued neutrosophic digraph as shown in Fig. 9.3.

The bipolar single-valued neutrosophic out-neighborhoods are calculated in Table 9.3. The bipolar single-valued neutrosophic competition graph is shown in Fig. 9.4.

Definition 9.13 Let A be a bipolar single-valued neutrosophic set on X, then the **support** of A, denoted by $supp(A)$, is defined as the set of those elements $x \in X$ such that $A(x) \neq (0, 0, 1, 0, 0, -1)$.

Example 9.5 The support of a bipolar single-valued neutrosophic set $A = \{(a, 0.5, 0.7, 0.2, -0.8, -0.9, -0.3), (b, 0.1, 0.2, 1, -0.5, -0.7, -0.6), (c, 0.3, 0.5, 0.3, -0.8, -0.6, -0.4), (d, 0, 0, 1, -1, -1, 0)\}$ in $X = \{a, b, c, d\}$ is $supp(A) = \{a, b, c\}$.

Definition 9.14 Let p be a positive integer. Then the **bipolar single-valued neutrosophic p-competition graph** $\mathcal{C}^p(\overrightarrow{G})$ of the bipolar single-valued neutrosophic

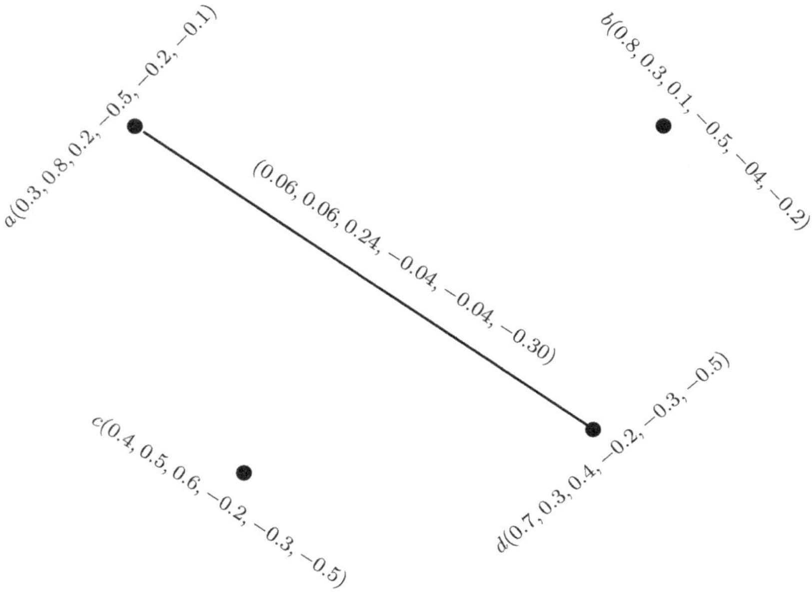

Fig. 9.4 Bipolar neutrosophic competition graph

digraph $\overrightarrow{G} = (A, \overrightarrow{B})$ is a undirected bipolar single-valued neutrosophic graph $G = (A, R')$ which has the same bipolar single-valued neutrosophic set of vertices as in $\overrightarrow{G}$ and has a bipolar single-valued neutrosophic edge between two vertices x, $y \in X$ in $\mathcal{C}^p(\overrightarrow{G})$ if and only if $|supp(\mathcal{N}^+(x) \cap \mathcal{N}^+(y))| \geq p$. The positive truth-membership, indeterminacy-membership, falsity-membership, and negative truth-membership, indeterminacy-membership, falsity-membership values of the edge xy are defined as

1. $T^p_{R'}(xy) = \frac{(i-p)+1}{i}(T^p_A(x) \wedge T^p_A(y))h_1(\mathcal{N}^+(x) \cap \mathcal{N}^+(y))$,
2. $I^p_{R'}(xy) = \frac{(i-p)+1}{i}(I^p_A(x) \wedge I^p_A(y))h_2(\mathcal{N}^+(x) \cap \mathcal{N}^+(y))$,
3. $F^p_{R'}(xy) = \frac{(i-p)+1}{i}(F^p_A(x) \vee F^p_A(y))h_3(\mathcal{N}^+(x) \cap \mathcal{N}^+(y))$,
4. $T^n_{R'}(xy) = \frac{(i-p)+1}{i}(T^n_A(x) \vee T^n_A(y))h_4(\mathcal{N}^+(x) \cap \mathcal{N}^+(y))$,
5. $I^n_{R'}(xy) = \frac{(i-p)+1}{i}(I^n_A(x) \vee I^n_A(y))h_5(\mathcal{N}^+(x) \cap \mathcal{N}^+(y))$,
6. $F^n_{R'}(xy) = \frac{(i-p)+1}{i}(F^n_A(x) \wedge F^n_A(y))h_6(\mathcal{N}^+(x) \cap \mathcal{N}^+(y))$, for all $x, y \in X$,

where $i = |supp(\mathcal{N}^+(x) \cap \mathcal{N}^+(y))|$.

The bipolar single-valued neutrosophic 3-competition graph is illustrated in Example 9.6.

Example 9.6 Consider a bipolar single-valued neutrosophic digraph $\overrightarrow{G} = (A, \overrightarrow{B})$ on $X = \{x, y, z, a, b, c\}$ as shown in Fig. 9.5. The bipolar single-valued neutrosophic 3-competition graph is shown in Fig. 9.6.

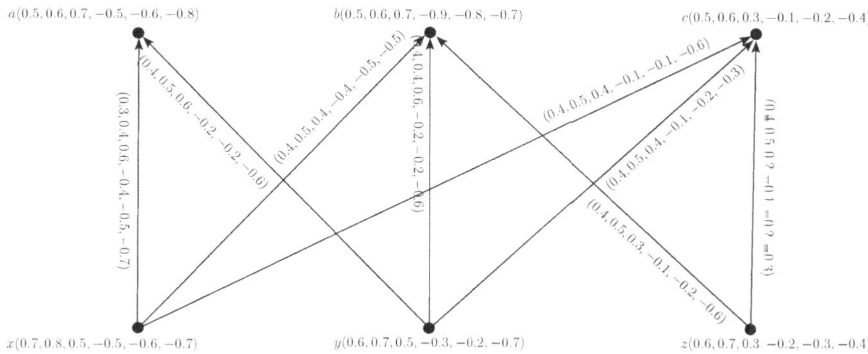

Fig. 9.5 Bipolar neutrosophic digraph

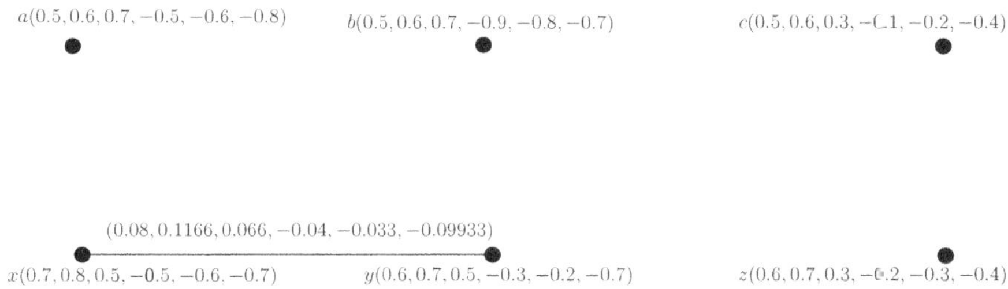

Fig. 9.6 Bipolar neutrosophic 3-competition graph

Definition 9.15 Let $G = (A, B)$ be a bipolar single-valued neutrosophic graph on X, then an edge xy, $x, y \in X$, is called **independent strong** if the following conditions are satisfied.

$$\frac{1}{2}[T_A^p(x) \wedge T_A^p(y)] < T_B^p(xy), \quad \frac{1}{2}[T_A^n(x) \vee T_A^n(y)] > T_B^n(xy), \quad \frac{1}{2}[I_A^p(x) \wedge I_A^p(y)] < I_B^p(xy),$$
$$\frac{1}{2}[I_A^n(x) \vee I_A^n(y)] > I_B^n(xy), \quad \frac{1}{2}[F_A^p(x) \vee F_A^p(y)] > F_B^p(xy), \quad \frac{1}{2}[F_A^n(x) \wedge F_A^n(y)] < F_B^n(xy).$$

Otherwise, it is called a **weak edge**.

Theorem 9.1 *Let $\mathcal{C}^{[\frac{i}{2}]}(\overrightarrow{G})$ be a bipolar single-valued neutrosophic $[\frac{i}{2}]$-competition graph corresponding to $\overrightarrow{G} = (A, \overrightarrow{B})$. If for any two vertices $x, y \in X$,*

$$h_1(\mathcal{N}^+(x) \cap \mathcal{N}^+(y)) = 1, \quad h_2(\mathcal{N}^+(x) \cap \mathcal{N}^+(y)) = 1, \quad h_3(\mathcal{N}^+(x) \cap \mathcal{N}^-(y)) = 0,$$
$$h_4(\mathcal{N}^+(x) \cap \mathcal{N}^+(y)) = 1, \quad h_5(\mathcal{N}^+(x) \cap \mathcal{N}^+(y)) = 1, \quad h_6(\mathcal{N}^+(x) \cap \mathcal{N}^-(y)) = 0,$$

then the edge xy is strong, where $i = |supp(\mathcal{N}^+(x) \cap \mathcal{N}^+(y))|$. Note that for any real number x, $[x]$ = greatest integer not exceeding x.

Proof Let $\mathcal{C}^{[\frac{i}{2}]}(\overrightarrow{G}) = (A, R')$ be a bipolar single-valued neutrosophic $[\frac{i}{2}]$-competition graph corresponding to $\overrightarrow{G} = (A, \overrightarrow{B})$, then by the given statement, for all $x, y \in X$,

$$T^p_{R'}(xy) = \frac{(i - [\frac{i}{2}]) + 1}{i}[T^p_A(x) \wedge T^p_A(y)] \times 1, \; T^n_{R'}(xy) = \frac{(i - [\frac{i}{2}]) + 1}{i}[T^n_A(x) \vee T^n_A(y)] \times 1,$$

$$I^p_{R'}(xy) = \frac{(i - [\frac{i}{2}]) + 1}{i}[I^p_A(x) \wedge I^p_A(y)] \times 1, \; I^n_{R'}(xy) = \frac{(i - [\frac{i}{2}]) + 1}{i}[I^n_A(x) \vee I^n_A(y)] \times 1,$$

$$F^p_{R'}(xy) = \frac{(i - [\frac{i}{2}]) + 1}{i}[F^p_A(x) \vee F^p_A(y)] \times 0, \; F^n_{R'}(xy) = \frac{(i - [\frac{i}{2}]) + 1}{i}[F^n_A(x) \wedge F^n_A(y)] \times 0.$$

It clearly follows that

$$\frac{T^p_{R'}(xy)}{[T^p_A(x) \wedge T^p_A(y)]} = \frac{(i - [\frac{i}{2}]) + 1}{i} > 0.5, \quad \frac{T^n_{R'}(xy)}{[T^n_A(x) \vee T^n_A(y)]} = \frac{(i - [\frac{i}{2}]) + 1}{i} < 0.5,$$

$$\frac{I^p_{R'}(xy)}{[I^p_A(x) \wedge I^p_A(y)]} = \frac{(i - [\frac{i}{2}]) + 1}{i} > 0.5, \quad \frac{I^n_{R'}(xy)}{[I^n_A(x) \vee I^n_A(y)]} = \frac{(i - [\frac{i}{2}]) + 1}{i} < 0.5,$$

$$\frac{F^p_{R'}(xy)}{[F^p_A(x) \vee F^p_A(y)]} = \frac{(i - [\frac{i}{2}]) + 1}{i} < 0.5, \quad \frac{F^n_{R'}(xy)}{[F^n_A(x) \wedge F^n_A(y)]} = \frac{(i - [\frac{i}{2}]) + 1}{i} < 0.5.$$

Hence, the edge xy is strong in $\mathcal{C}^{[\frac{i}{2}]}(\overrightarrow{G})$. □

Definition 9.16 Let $\overrightarrow{G} = (A, \overrightarrow{B})$ be a bipolar single-valued neutrosophic digraph on X. The ***m*-step bipolar single-valued neutrosophic digraph** of $\overrightarrow{G}$ is denoted by $\overrightarrow{G}_m = (A, \overrightarrow{R})$, where the bipolar single-valued neutrosophic set of vertices of $\overrightarrow{G}_m$ is same as the bipolar single-valued neutrosophic set of vertices of $\overrightarrow{G}$, and there is a directed edge between x and y in $\overrightarrow{G}_m$ if and only if there exists a bipolar single-valued neutrosophic directed path $P : x = x_1, e_1, x_2, e_2, \ldots, e_{m-1}, x_m, y$ of m vertices between x and y and $T^p_{R'}(y) = \min\limits_{e \in P} T^p_{\overrightarrow{B}}(e)$, $I^p_{R'}(y) = \min\limits_{e \in P} I^p_{\overrightarrow{B}}(e)$, $F^p_{R'}(y) = \max\limits_{e \in P} F^p_{\overrightarrow{B}}(e)$, $I^n_{R'}(y) = \max\limits_{e \in P} I^n_{\overrightarrow{B}}(e)$, $T^n_{R'}(y) = \max\limits_{e \in P} T^n_{\overrightarrow{B}}(e)$, $F^n_{R'}(y) = \min\limits_{e \in P} F^n_{\overrightarrow{B}}(e)$.

Definition 9.17 The ***m*-step bipolar single-valued neutrosophic out-neighborhood** of a vertex x in a bipolar single-valued neutrosophic digraph $\overrightarrow{G} = (A, \overrightarrow{B})$ is a bipolar single-valued neutrosophic set $\mathcal{N}^+_m(x) = (X^+_x, T^p_x, I^p_x, F^p_x, T^n_x, I^n_x, F^n_x)$ such that $y \in X^+_x$ if there exists a bipolar single-valued neutrosophic directed path $P : x = x_1, e_1, x_2, e_2, \ldots, e_{m-1}, x_m = y$ of m vertices between x and y. The membership values of $\mathcal{N}^+_m(x)$ are defined as $T^p_x(y) = \min\limits_{e \in P} T^p_{\overrightarrow{B}}(e)$, $I^p_x(y) = \min\limits_{e \in P} I^p_{\overrightarrow{B}}(e)$, $F^p_x(y) = \max\limits_{e \in P} F^p_{\overrightarrow{B}}(e)$, $I^n_x(y) = \max\limits_{e \in P} I^n_{\overrightarrow{B}}(e)$, $T^n_x(y) = \max\limits_{e \in P} T^n_{\overrightarrow{B}}(e)$, $F^n_x(y) = \min\limits_{e \in P} F^n_{\overrightarrow{B}}(e)$.

Definition 9.18 The ***m*-step bipolar single-valued neutrosophic in-neighborhood** of a vertex x in a bipolar single-valued neutrosophic digraph $\overrightarrow{G} = (A, \overrightarrow{B})$ is bipolar single-valued neutrosophic set $\mathcal{N}^-_m(x) = (X^+_x, T^p_x, I^p_x, F^p_x, T^n_x, I^n_x, F^n_x)$

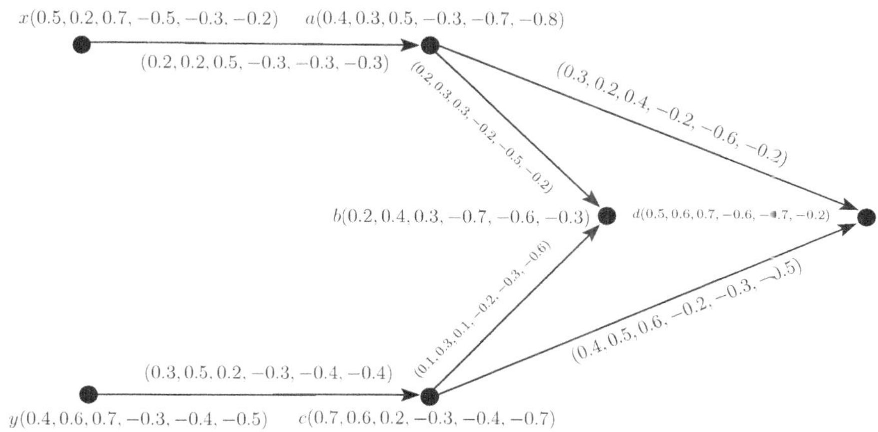

Fig. 9.7 Bipolar neutrosophic digraph $\overrightarrow{G}$

such that $y \in X_x^+$ if there exists a bipolar single-valued neutrosophic directed path $P : y = x_1, e_1, x_2, e_2, \ldots, e_{m-1}, x_m = x$ of m vertices from y to x. The membership values of $\mathcal{N}_m^-(x)$ are defined as $T_x^p(y) = \min\limits_{e \in P} T^p_{\overrightarrow{B}}(e)$, $I_x^p(y) = \min\limits_{e \in P} I^p_{\overrightarrow{B}}(e)$, $F_x^p(y) = \max\limits_{e \in P} F^p_{\overrightarrow{B}}(e)$, $I_x^n(y) = \max\limits_{e \in P} I^n_{\overrightarrow{B}}(e)$, $T_x^n(y) = \max\limits_{e \in P} T^n_{\overrightarrow{B}}(e)$, $F_x^n(y) = \min\limits_{e \in P} F^n_{\overrightarrow{B}}(e)$.

Example 9.7 Consider a bipolar single-valued neutrosophic digraph $\overrightarrow{G} = (A, \overrightarrow{B})$ on $X = \{x, y, a, b, c, d\}$ as shown in Fig. 9.7. The 2-step bipolar single-valued neutrosophic out-neighborhoods of vertices x and y are calculated as $\mathcal{N}_2^+(x) = \{(b, 0.2, 0.2, 0.5, -0.2, -0.3, -0.2), (d, 0.2, 0.2, 0.5, -0.2, -0.3, -0.3)\}$, $\mathcal{N}_2^+(y) = \{(b, 0.1, 0.3, 0.2, -0.2, -0.3, -0.6), (d, 0.3, 0.5, 0.6, -0.2, -0.3, -0.5)\}$.

Example 9.8 Consider a bipolar single-valued neutrosophic digraph $\overrightarrow{G} = (A, \overrightarrow{B})$ on $X = \{a, b, c, d, e, f\}$ as shown in Fig. 9.8. The 2-step bipolar single-valued in-neighborhood of vertices a and b are calculated as $\mathcal{N}_2^-(a) = \{(f, 0.1, 0.1, 0.5, -0.1, -0.2, -0.6), (e, 0.3, 0.1, 0.7, -0.1, -0.2, -0.4)\}$, $\mathcal{N}_2^-(b) = \{(f, 0.1, 0.3, 0.6, -0.3, -0.4, -0.7), (e, 0.4, 0.3, 0.6, -0.3, -0.4, -0.5)\}$.

Definition 9.19 An ***m*-step bipolar single-valued neutrosophic competition graph** of a bipolar single-valued neutrosophic digraph $\overrightarrow{G} = (A, \overrightarrow{B})$ is a undirected bipolar single-valued neutrosophic graph $\mathcal{C}_m(\overrightarrow{G}) = (A, Q)$ which has the same vertex set as in $\overrightarrow{G}$, and there is an edge between two vertices x and y if and only if $\mathcal{N}_m^+(x) \cap \mathcal{N}_m^+(y)$ is non-empty. The positive truth-membership, indeterminacy-membership, falsity-membership, and negative truth-membership, indeterminacy-membership, falsity-membership values of the edge xy are defined as

1. $T_Q^p(xy) = (T_A^p(x) \wedge T_A^p(y))h_1(\mathcal{N}_m^+(x) \cap \mathcal{N}_m^+(y))$,
2. $I_Q^p(xy) = (I_A^p(x) \wedge I_A^p(y))h_2(\mathcal{N}_m^+(x) \cap \mathcal{N}_m^+(y))$,
3. $F_Q^p(xy) = (F_A^p(x) \vee F_A^p(y))h_3(\mathcal{N}_m^+(x) \cap \mathcal{N}_m^+(y))$,
4. $T_Q^n(xy) = (T_A^n(x) \vee T_A^n(y))h_4(\mathcal{N}_m^+(x) \cap \mathcal{N}_m^+(y))$,

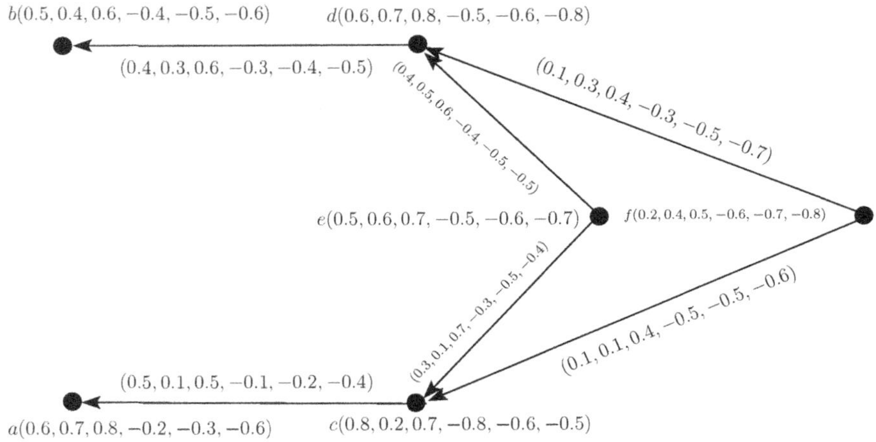

Fig. 9.8 Bipolar neutrosophic digraph $\overrightarrow{G}$

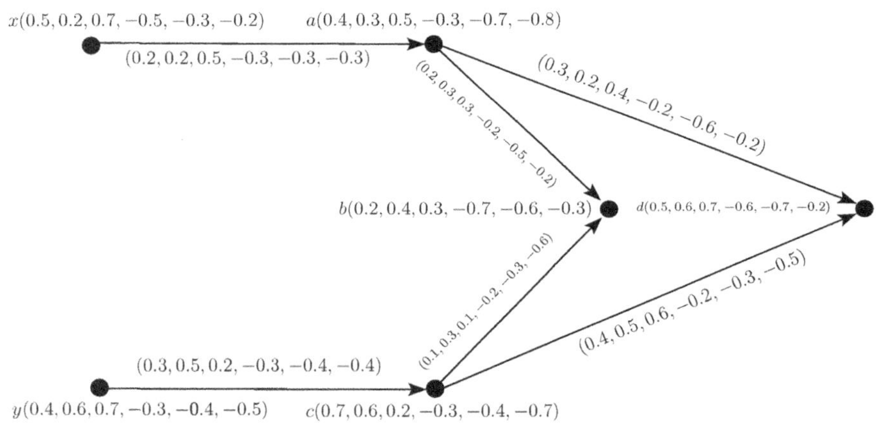

Fig. 9.9 Bipolar neutrosophic digraph $\overrightarrow{G}$

5. $I_Q^n(xy) = (I_A^n(x) \vee I_A^n(y))h_5(\mathcal{N}_m^+(x) \cap \mathcal{N}_m^+(y))$,
6. $F_Q^n(xy) = (F_A^n(x) \wedge F_A^n(y))h_6(\mathcal{N}_m^+(x) \cap \mathcal{N}_m^+(y))$, for all $x, y \in X$.

Example 9.9 Consider a bipolar single-valued neutrosophic digraph $\overrightarrow{G} = (A, \overrightarrow{B})$ as shown in Fig. 9.9. The corresponding 2-step bipolar single-valued neutrosophic competition graph is shown in Fig. 9.10.

If a predator x attacks one prey y, then the linkage is shown by an edge $\overrightarrow{xy}$ in a bipolar single-valued neutrosophic digraph. But, if the predator needs help of many other mediators $x_1, x_2, \ldots, x_{m-1}$, then the linkage among them is shown by a bipolar single-valued neutrosophic directed path $\overrightarrow{\mathcal{P}}_{x,y}^m$ with a vertex set $\{x, x_1, x_2, \ldots, x_{m-1}, y\}$. So

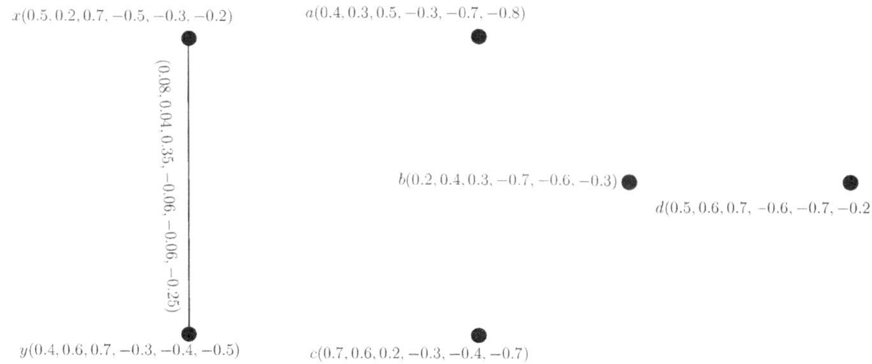

Fig. 9.10 2-step bipolar single-valued neutrosophic competition graph

the ***m*-step prey** in a bipolar single-valued neutrosophic digraph is represented by a vertex which is in the m-step bipolar single-valued neutrosophic out-neighborhood of the other vertex.

Definition 9.20 Let $\overrightarrow{G} = (A, \overrightarrow{B})$ be a bipolar single-valued neutrosophic digraph. Let w be a common vertex of m-step out-neighborhoods of vertices $x_1, x_2, \ldots, x_l$. Also, let $T^p_{\overrightarrow{B}}(u_1v_1)$, $T^p_{\overrightarrow{B}}(u_2v_2), \ldots, T^p_{\overrightarrow{B}}(u_lv_l)$ be the minimum positive truth-membership values, $I^p_{\overrightarrow{B}}(u_1v_1)$, $I^p_{\overrightarrow{B}}(u_2v_2), \ldots, I^p_{\overrightarrow{B}}(u_lv_l)$ be the minimum positive indeterminacy-membership values, $F^p_{\overrightarrow{B}}(u_1v_1)$, $F^p_{\overrightarrow{B}}(u_2v_2), \ldots, F^p_{\overrightarrow{B}}(u_lv_l)$ be the maximum positive false-membership values, $T^n_{\overrightarrow{B}}(u_1v_1)$, $T^n_{\overrightarrow{B}}(u_2v_2), \ldots, T^n_{\overrightarrow{B}}(u_lv_l)$ be the maximum negative truth-membership values, $I^n_{\overrightarrow{B}}(u_1v_1)$, $I^n_{\overrightarrow{B}}(u_2v_2)$, $\ldots, I^n_{\overrightarrow{B}}(u_lv_l)$ be the maximum negative indeterminacy-membership values, and $F^n_{\overrightarrow{B}}(u_1v_1)$, $F^n_{\overrightarrow{B}}(u_2v_2), \ldots, F^n_{\overrightarrow{B}}(u_l, v_l)$ be the minimum negative false-membership values of edges of bipolar single-valued neutrosophic directed paths $\overrightarrow{\mathcal{P}}^m_{x_1,w}$, $\overrightarrow{\mathcal{P}}^m_{x_2,w}$, $\ldots, \overrightarrow{\mathcal{P}}^m_{x_l,w}$. The m-step prey $w \in X$ is called a **strong prey** if the following conditions are satisfied.

$$T^p_{\overrightarrow{B}}(u_iv_i) > 0.5, \quad I^p_{\overrightarrow{B}}(u_iv_i) > 0.5, \quad F^p_{\overrightarrow{B}}(u_iv_i) < 0.5,$$
$$T^n_{\overrightarrow{B}}(u_iv_i) < -0.5, \quad I^n_{\overrightarrow{B}}(u_iv_i) < -0.5, \quad F^n_{\overrightarrow{B}}(u_iv_i) > -0.5, \quad \text{for all } i = 1, 2, \ldots, l.$$

The strength of the prey w can be measured by the mapping $S : X \to [0, 1]$ such that

$$S(w) = \frac{1}{l}\left(\sum_{i=1}^{l} T^p_{\overrightarrow{B}}(u_iv_i) + \sum_{i=1}^{l} I^p_{\overrightarrow{B}}(u_iv_i) + \sum_{i=1}^{l} F^p_{\overrightarrow{B}}(u_iv_i) - \sum_{i=1}^{l} T^n_{\overrightarrow{B}}(u_iv_i) - \sum_{i=1}^{l} I^n_{\overrightarrow{B}}(u_iv_i) - \sum_{i=1}^{l} F^n_{\overrightarrow{B}}(u_iv_i)\right).$$

Example 9.10 Consider the bipolar single-valued neutrosophic digraph $\overrightarrow{G} = (A, \overrightarrow{B})$ as shown in Fig. 9.9. The strength of the prey b is equal to

$$\frac{[0.2+0.2]+[0.2+0.3]+[0.5+0.3]-[-0.3-0.2]-[-0.3-0.5]-[-0.3-0.2]}{2}=1.75>0.5.$$

Hence, b is a strong 2-step prey.

Theorem 9.2 *If a prey w of $\overrightarrow{G}=(A,\overrightarrow{B})$ is* **strong**, *then the strength of w, $S(w)>0.5$.*

Proof Let $\overrightarrow{G}=(A,\overrightarrow{B})$ be a bipolar single-valued neutrosophic digraph on X. Let w be a common vertex of m-step out-neighborhoods of vertices $x_1, x_2, \ldots, x_l$, i.e., there exist bipolar single-valued neutrosophic directed paths $\overrightarrow{\mathcal{P}}^m_{x_1,w}, \overrightarrow{\mathcal{P}}^m_{x_2,w}, \ldots, \overrightarrow{\mathcal{P}}^m_{x_l,w}$ in $\overrightarrow{G}$. Let $T^p_{\overrightarrow{B}}(u_1v_1), T^p_{\overrightarrow{B}}(u_2v_2), \ldots, T^p_{\overrightarrow{B}}(u_lv_l)$ be the minimum positive truth-membership values, $I^p_{\overrightarrow{B}}(u_1v_1), I^p_{\overrightarrow{B}}(u_2v_2), \ldots, I^p_{\overrightarrow{B}}(u_lv_l)$ be the minimum positive indeterminacy-membership values, $F^p_{\overrightarrow{B}}(u_1v_1), F^p_{\overrightarrow{B}}(u_2v_2), \ldots, F^p_{\overrightarrow{B}}(u_lv_l)$ be the maximum positive false-membership values, $T^n_{\overrightarrow{B}}(u_1v_1), T^n_{\overrightarrow{B}}(u_2v_2), \ldots, T^n_{\overrightarrow{B}}(u_lv_l)$ be the maximum negative truth-membership values, $I^n_{\overrightarrow{B}}(u_1v_1), I^n_{\overrightarrow{B}}(u_2v_2), \ldots, I^n_{\overrightarrow{B}}(u_lv_l)$ be the maximum negative indeterminacy-membership values, and $F^n_{\overrightarrow{B}}(u_1v_1), F^n_{\overrightarrow{B}}(u_2v_2), \ldots, F^n_{\overrightarrow{B}}(u_lv_l)$ be the minimum negative false-membership values of bipolar single-valued neutrosophic edges of the directed paths $\overrightarrow{\mathcal{P}}^m_{x_1,w}, \overrightarrow{\mathcal{P}}^m_{x_2,w}, \ldots, \overrightarrow{\mathcal{P}}^m_{x_l,w}$, respectively.

If w is strong, then each edge $u_iv_i,\ i=1,2,\ldots,l$ is strong and so,

$$\begin{aligned}
&T^p_{\overrightarrow{B}}(u_iv_i)>0.5,\quad I^p_{\overrightarrow{B}}(u_iv_i)>0.5,\quad F^p_{\overrightarrow{B}}(u_iv_i)<0.5,\\
&T^n_{\overrightarrow{B}}(u_iv_i)<-0.5,\quad I^n_{\overrightarrow{B}}(u_iv_i)<-0.5,\quad F^n_{\overrightarrow{B}}(u_iv_i)>-0.5,\quad \text{for all } i=1,2,\ldots,l.\\
&S(w)>\frac{0.5+0.5+\cdots(l\ \ times)+0.5}{l}>0.5.
\end{aligned}$$

It completes the proof. □

Remark 9.1 The converse of Theorem 9.2 is not true in general, i.e., if $S(w)>0.5$, then all preys may not be strong. It can be explained as follows: Let $S(w)>0.5$ for a prey w in $\overrightarrow{G}$, then

$$S(w)=\frac{1}{l}\left(\sum_{i=1}^{l}T^p_{\overrightarrow{B}}(u_iv_i)+\sum_{i=1}^{l}I^p_{\overrightarrow{B}}(u_iv_i)+\sum_{i=1}^{l}F^p_{\overrightarrow{B}}(u_iv_i)-\sum_{i=1}^{l}T^n_{\overrightarrow{B}}(u_iv_i)-\sum_{i=1}^{l}I^n_{\overrightarrow{B}}(u_iv_i)-\sum_{i=1}^{l}F^n_{\overrightarrow{B}}(u_iv_i)\right).$$

Hence,

$$\sum_{i=1}^{l}T^p_{\overrightarrow{B}}(u_iv_i)+\sum_{i=1}^{l}I^p_{\overrightarrow{B}}(u_iv_i)+\sum_{i=1}^{l}F^p_{\overrightarrow{B}}(u_iv_i)-\sum_{i=1}^{l}T^n_{\overrightarrow{B}}(u_iv_i)-\sum_{i=1}^{l}I^n_{\overrightarrow{B}}(u_iv_i)-\sum_{i=1}^{l}F^n_{\overrightarrow{B}}(u_iv_i)>\frac{l}{2}.$$

This result does not necessarily imply that

$$\begin{aligned}
&T^p_{\overrightarrow{B}}(u_iv_i)>0.5,\quad I^p_{\overrightarrow{B}}(u_iv_i)>0.5,\quad F^p_{\overrightarrow{B}}(u_iv_i)<0.5,\\
&T^n_{\overrightarrow{B}}(u_iv_i)<-0.5,\quad I^n_{\overrightarrow{B}}(u_iv_i)<-0.5,\quad F^n_{\overrightarrow{B}}(u_iv_i)>-0.5,\quad \text{for all } i=1,2,\ldots,l.
\end{aligned}$$

Since all edges of the bipolar single-valued neutrosophic directed paths $\overrightarrow{\mathcal{P}}^m_{x_1,w}$, $\overrightarrow{\mathcal{P}}^m_{x_2,w}, \ldots, \overrightarrow{\mathcal{P}}^m_{x_l,w}$ are not strong, the converse Theorem 9.2 is not true, i.e., if $S(w) > 0.5$, the prey w of $\overrightarrow{G}$ may not be strong.

Theorem 9.3 *If all preys of $\overrightarrow{G} = (A, \overrightarrow{B})$ are strong, then all edges of $\mathcal{C}_m(\overrightarrow{G}) = (A, B)$ are strong.*

Proof Let $\overrightarrow{G} = (A, \overrightarrow{B})$ be a bipolar single-valued neutrosophic digraph and all preys of it are strong. Let $\mathcal{C}_m(\overrightarrow{G}) = (A, R)$, then

$$
\begin{aligned}
T_R^p(xy) &= [T_A^p(x) \wedge T_A^p(z)]h_1(\mathcal{N}_m^+(x) \cap \mathcal{N}_m^+(y)),\\
I_R^p(xy) &= [I_A^p(x) \wedge I_A^p(y)]h_2(\mathcal{N}_m^+(x) \cap \mathcal{N}_m^+(y)),\\
F_R^p(xy) &= [F_A^p(x) \vee F_A^p(y)]h_3(\mathcal{N}_m^+(x) \cap \mathcal{N}_m^+(y)),\\
T_R^n(xy) &= [T_A^n(x) \vee T_A^n(z)]h_4(\mathcal{N}_m^+(x) \cap \mathcal{N}_m^+(y)),\\
I_R^n(xy) &= [I_A^n(x) \vee I_A^n(y)]h_5(\mathcal{N}_m^+(x) \cap \mathcal{N}_m^+(y)),\\
F_R^n(xy) &= [F_A^n(x) \wedge F_A^n(y)]h_6(\mathcal{N}_m^+(x) \cap \mathcal{N}_m^+(y)),
\end{aligned}
$$

for all edges xy in $\mathcal{C}_m(\overrightarrow{G}) = (A, R)$. Then there are two cases.

Case 1: If $\mathcal{N}_m^+(x) \cap \mathcal{N}_m^+(y) = \emptyset$, then there does not exist any edge between x and y in $\mathcal{C}_m(\overrightarrow{G})$.

Case 2: If $\mathcal{N}_m^+(x) \cap \mathcal{N}_m^+(y) \neq \emptyset$, then

$$
\begin{aligned}
&h_1(\mathcal{N}_m^+(x) \cap \mathcal{N}_m^+(y)) > 0.5, \quad h_2(\mathcal{N}_m^+(x) \cap \mathcal{N}_m^+(y)) > 0.5, \quad h_3(\mathcal{N}_m^+(x) \cap \mathcal{N}_m^+(y)) < 0.5,\\
&h_4(\mathcal{N}_m^+(x) \cap \mathcal{N}_m^+(y)) > 0.5, \quad h_5(\mathcal{N}_m^+(x) \cap \mathcal{N}_m^+(y)) > 0.5, \quad h_6(\mathcal{N}_m^+(x) \cap \mathcal{N}_m^+(y)) < 0.5,
\end{aligned}
$$

in $\overrightarrow{G}$ as all preys are strong. So the edge xy in $\mathcal{C}_m(\overrightarrow{G})$ has the memberships values,

$$
\begin{aligned}
&T_R^p(xy) = [T_A^p(x) \wedge T_A^p(z)]h_1(\mathcal{N}_m^+(x) \cap \mathcal{N}_m^+(y)), \quad I_R^p(xy) = [I_A^p(x) \wedge I_A^p(y)]h_2(\mathcal{N}_m^+(x) \cap \mathcal{N}_m^+(y)),\\
&F_R^p(xy) = [F_A^p(x) \vee F_A^p(y)]h_3(\mathcal{N}_m^+(x) \cap \mathcal{N}_m^+(y)), \quad T_R^n(xy) = [T_A^n(x) \vee T_A^n(z)]h_4(\mathcal{N}_m^+(x) \cap \mathcal{N}_m^+(y)),\\
&I_R^n(xy) = [I_A^n(x) \vee I_A^n(y)]h_5(\mathcal{N}_m^+(x) \cap \mathcal{N}_m^+(y)), \quad F_R^n(xy) = [F_A^n(x) \wedge F_A^n(y)]h_6(\mathcal{N}_m^+(x) \cap \mathcal{N}_m^+(y)).
\end{aligned}
$$

Hence all the edges are strong. □

A relation is established between the m-step bipolar single-valued neutrosophic competition graph of a bipolar single-valued neutrosophic digraph and a bipolar single-valued neutrosophic competition graph of the m-step bipolar single-valued neutrosophic digraph.

Theorem 9.4 *Let $\overrightarrow{G} = (A, \overrightarrow{B})$ be a bipolar single-valued neutrosophic digraph on X, then $\mathcal{C}(\overrightarrow{G}_m) = \mathcal{C}_m(\overrightarrow{G})$.*

Proof Let $\overrightarrow{G} = (A, \overrightarrow{B})$ be a bipolar single-valued neutrosophic digraph and $\overrightarrow{G}_m = (A, \overrightarrow{J})$ be the m-step bipolar single-valued neutrosophic digraph of $\overrightarrow{G}$. Also, let

$\mathcal{C}(\overrightarrow{G}_m) = (A, J)$ (say) and $\mathcal{C}_m(\overrightarrow{G}) = (A, B)$. It can be easily observed that bipolar single-valued neutrosophic vertex sets of $\overrightarrow{G}_m$, $\mathcal{C}_m(\overrightarrow{G})$, and $\mathcal{C}(\overrightarrow{G}_m)$ are the same. So, we have to show that the bipolar single-valued neutrosophic edge sets of $\mathcal{C}(\overrightarrow{G}_m)$ and $\mathcal{C}_m(\overrightarrow{G})$ are equal. Let xy be an edge in $\mathcal{C}(\overrightarrow{G}_m)$, then there exist bipolar single-valued neutrosophic directed edges $\overrightarrow{xa_1}, \overrightarrow{ya_1}; \overrightarrow{xa_2}, \overrightarrow{ya_2}, \ldots, \overrightarrow{xa_l}, \overrightarrow{ya_l}$, for some positive integer l. Assume that for any two vertices x and y of $\overrightarrow{G}_m$, $\mathcal{N}^+(x) \cap \mathcal{N}^+(y) = \{a_i \mid i = 1, 2, \ldots, l\}$, where

$$s_i^p = T^p_{\overrightarrow{J}}(xa_i) \wedge \overrightarrow{J}(y, a_i), \quad s_i^n = T^n_{\overrightarrow{J}}(xa_i) \vee \overrightarrow{J}(y, a_i),$$
$$q_i^p = I^p_{\overrightarrow{J}}(xa_i) \wedge \overrightarrow{J}(y, a_i), \quad q_i^n = I^n_{\overrightarrow{J}}(xa_i) \vee \overrightarrow{J}(y, a_i),$$
$$r_i^p = F^p_{\overrightarrow{J}}(xa_i) \vee \overrightarrow{J}(y, a_i), \quad r_i^n = F^n_{\overrightarrow{J}}(xa_i) \wedge \overrightarrow{J}(y, a_i).$$

Let $S^p = \max\{s_i^p \mid i = 1, 2, \ldots, l\}$, $Q^p = \max\{q_i^p \mid i = 1, 2, \ldots, l\}$, and $R^p = \min\{r_i^p \mid i = 1, 2, \ldots, l\}$, then

$$T_J^p(xy) = (T_A^p(x) \wedge T_A^p(y))h_1(\mathcal{N}^+(x) \cap \mathcal{N}^+(y)) = S^p \times T_A^p(x) \wedge T_A^p(y),$$
$$I_J^p(xy) = (I_A^p(x) \wedge I_A^p(y))h_2(\mathcal{N}^+(x) \cap \mathcal{N}^+(y)) = Q^p \times I_A^p(x) \wedge I_A^p(y),$$
$$F_J^p(xy) = (F_A^p(x) \vee F_A^p(y))h_3(\mathcal{N}^+(x) \cap \mathcal{N}^+(y)) = R^p \times F_A^p(x) \vee F_A^p(y),$$
$$T_J^n(xy) = (T_A^n(x) \vee T_A^n(y))h_4(\mathcal{N}^+(x) \cap \mathcal{N}^+(y)) = S^p \times T_A^n(x) \vee T_A^n(y),$$
$$I_J^n(xy) = (I_A^n(x) \vee I_A^n(y))h_5(\mathcal{N}^+(x) \cap \mathcal{N}^+(y)) = Q^p \times I_A^n(x) \vee I_A^n(y),$$
$$F_J^n(xy) = (F_A^n(x) \wedge F_A^n(y))h_6(\mathcal{N}^+(x) \cap \mathcal{N}^+(y)) = R^p \times F_A^n(x) \wedge F_A^n(y).$$

An edge $\overrightarrow{xa_i}$ that exists in $\overrightarrow{G}_m$ implies that there exists a bipolar single-valued neutrosophic directed path $\overrightarrow{\mathcal{P}}^m_{x,a_i}$ from x to a_i with m vertices such that

$$T^p_{\overrightarrow{J}}(xa_i) = \min\{T^p_{\overrightarrow{B}}(uv) | uv \text{ is an edge in } \overrightarrow{\mathcal{P}}^m_{x,a_i}\},$$
$$I^p_{\overrightarrow{J}}(xa_i) = \min\{I^p_{\overrightarrow{B}}(uv) | uv \text{ is an edge in } \overrightarrow{\mathcal{P}}^m_{x,a_i}\},$$
$$F^p_{\overrightarrow{J}}(xa_i) = \max\{F^p_{\overrightarrow{B}}(uv) | uv \text{ is an edge in } \overrightarrow{\mathcal{P}}^m_{x,a_i}\},$$
$$T^n_{\overrightarrow{J}}(xa_i) = \max\{T^n_{\overrightarrow{B}}(uv) | uv \text{ is an edge in } \overrightarrow{\mathcal{P}}^m_{x,a_i}\},$$
$$I^n_{\overrightarrow{J}}(xa_i) = \max\{I^n_{\overrightarrow{B}}(uv) | uv \text{ is an edge in } \overrightarrow{\mathcal{P}}^m_{x,a_i}\},$$
$$F^n_{\overrightarrow{J}}(xa_i) = \min\{F^n_{\overrightarrow{B}}(uv) | uv \text{ is an edge in } \overrightarrow{\mathcal{P}}^m_{x,a_i}\}.$$

Thus, the edge xy is also available in $\mathcal{C}_m(\overrightarrow{G})$, then

$$h_1(\mathcal{N}_m^+(x)\cap\mathcal{N}_m^+(y)) = S^p,\quad h_4(\mathcal{N}_m^+(x)\cap\mathcal{N}_m^+(y)) = S^p,$$
$$h_2(\mathcal{N}_m^+(x)\cap\mathcal{N}_m^+(y)) = Q^p,\quad h_5(\mathcal{N}_m^+(x)\cap\mathcal{N}_m^+(y)) = Q^p.$$
$$h_3(\mathcal{N}_m^+(x)\cap\mathcal{N}_m^+(y)) = R^p,\quad h_6(\mathcal{N}_m^+(x)\cap\mathcal{N}_m^+(y)) = R^p.$$

It clearly follows that

$$T_B^p(xy) = [T_A^p(x)\wedge T_A^p(z)]h_1(\mathcal{N}_m^+(x)\cap\mathcal{N}_m^+(y)) = S^p \times T_A^p(x)\wedge T_A^p(z),$$
$$I_B^p(xy) = [I_A^p(x)\wedge I_A^p(y)]h_2(\mathcal{N}_m^+(x)\cap\mathcal{N}_m^+(y)) = Q^p \times I_A^p(x)\wedge I_A^p(y),$$
$$F_B^p(xy) = [F_A^p(x)\vee F_A^p(y)]h_3(\mathcal{N}_m^+(x)\cap\mathcal{N}_m^+(y)) = R^p \times F_A^p(x)\vee F_A^p(y),$$
$$T_B^n(xy) = [T_A^n(x)\vee T_A^n(z)]h_4(\mathcal{N}_m^+(x)\cap\mathcal{N}_m^+(y)) = S^p \times T_A^n(x)\vee T_A^n(z),$$
$$I_B^n(xy) = [I_A^n(x)\vee I_A^n(y)]h_5(\mathcal{N}_m^+(x)\cap\mathcal{N}_m^+(y)) = Q^p \times I_A^n(x)\vee I_A^n(y),$$
$$F_B^n(xy) = [F_A^n(x)\wedge F_A^n(y)]h_6(\mathcal{N}_m^+(x)\cap\mathcal{N}_m^+(y)) = R^p \times F_A^n(x)\wedge F_A^n(y).$$

It shows that there exists an edge in $\mathcal{C}_m(\overrightarrow{G})$ for every edge in $\mathcal{C}(\overrightarrow{G}_m)$. Similarly, for every edge in $\mathcal{C}_m(\overrightarrow{G})$ there exists an edge in $\mathcal{C}(\overrightarrow{G}_m)$. □

Theorem 9.5 *Let $\overrightarrow{G} = (A, \overrightarrow{B})$ be a bipolar single-valued neutrosophic digraph. If $m > |X|$, then $\mathcal{C}_m(\overrightarrow{G}) = (A, B)$ has no edge.*

Proof If $m > |X|$, then there does not exist any bipolar single-valued neutrosophic directed path with m vertices in $\overrightarrow{G}$. So $\mathcal{N}_m^+(x)\cap\mathcal{N}_m^+(y)$ is an empty set, for all $x, y \in X$. Hence, there does not exist any edge in $\mathcal{C}_m(\overrightarrow{G})$. □

Theorem 9.6 *If all the edges of the bipolar single-valued neutrosophic digraph $\overrightarrow{G} = (A, \overrightarrow{B})$ are independent strong, then all the edges of $\mathcal{C}_m(\overrightarrow{G})$ are independent strong.*

Proof Suppose $\overrightarrow{G} = (A, \overrightarrow{B})$ is a bipolar single-valued neutrosophic digraph and $\mathcal{C}_m(\overrightarrow{G}) = (A, B)$ is the corresponding m-step bipolar single-valued neutrosophic competition graph. Since all the edges of $\overrightarrow{G}$ are independent strong,

$$h_1(\mathcal{N}_m^+(x)\cap\mathcal{N}_m^+(y)) > 0.5,\quad h_2(\mathcal{N}_m^+(x)\cap\mathcal{N}_m^+(y)) > 0.5,\quad h_3(\mathcal{N}_m^+(w)\cap\mathcal{N}_m^+(z)) < 0.5,$$
$$h_4(\mathcal{N}_m^+(x)\cap\mathcal{N}_m^+(y)) < 0.5,\quad h_5(\mathcal{N}_m^+(x)\cap\mathcal{N}_m^+(y)) < 0.5,\quad h_6(\mathbb{N}_m^+(w)\cap\mathbb{N}_m^+(z)) < 0.5.$$

$T_B^p(xy) = (T_A^p(x)\wedge T_A^p(y))h_1(\mathcal{N}_m^+(x)\cap\mathcal{N}_m^+(y))$ or, $T_B^p(xy) > 0.5(T_A^p(x)\wedge T_A^p(y))$ or, $\frac{T_B^p(xy)}{(T_A^p(x)\wedge T_A^p(y))} > 0.5$,
$I_B^p(xy) = (I_A^p(x)\wedge I_A^p(y))h_2(\mathcal{N}_m^+(x)\cap\mathcal{N}_m^+(y))$ or, $I_B^p(xy) > 0.5(I_A^p(x)\wedge I_A^p(y))$ or, $\frac{I_B^p(xy)}{(I_A^p(x)\wedge I_A^p(y))} > 0.5$,
$F_B^p(xy) = (F_A^p(x)\vee F_A^p(y))h_3(\mathcal{N}_m^+(x)\cap\mathcal{N}_m^+(y))$ or, $F_B^p(xy) < 0.5(F_A^p(x)\vee F_A^p(y))$ or, $\frac{F_B^p(xy)}{(F_A^p(x)\vee F_A^p(y))} < 0.5$,

$T^n_B(xy) = (T^n_A(x) \vee T^n_A(y))h_4(\mathcal{N}^+_m(x) \cap \mathcal{N}^+_m(y))$ or, $T^n_B(xy) < 0.5(T^n_A(x) \vee T^n_A(y))$ or, $\frac{T^n_B(xy)}{(T^n_A(x) \vee T^n_A(y))} < 0.5$, $I^n_B(xy) = (I^n_A(x) \vee I^n_A(y))h_5(\mathcal{N}^+_m(x) \cap \mathcal{N}^+_m(y))$ or, $I^n_B(xy) < 0.5(I^n_A(x) \vee I^n_A(y))$ or, $\frac{I^n_B(xy)}{(I^n_A(x) \vee I^n_A(y))} < 0.5$, $F^n_B(xy) = (F^n_A(x) \wedge F^n_A(y))h_6(\mathcal{N}^+_m(x) \cap \mathcal{N}^+_m(y))$ or, $F^n_B(xy) < 0.5(F^n_A(x) \wedge F^n_A(y))$ or, $\frac{F^n_B(xy)}{(F^n_A(x) \wedge F^n_A(y))} < 0.5$.

Hence, the edge xy is independent strong in $\mathcal{C}_m(\overrightarrow{G})$. Since xy is taken to be an arbitrary edge of $\mathcal{C}_m(\overrightarrow{G})$, all the edges of $\mathcal{C}_m(\overrightarrow{G})$ are independent strong. □

Definition 9.21 An ***m*-step bipolar single-valued neutrosophic neighborhood** of a vertex x in a bipolar single-valued neutrosophic graph $G = (A, B)$ is a bipolar single-valued neutrosophic set $\mathcal{N}_m(x) = (X_x, T^P_x, I^P_x, F^P_x, T^n_x, I^n_x, F^n_x)$ such that $y \in X^+_x$ if there exists a bipolar single-valued neutrosophic directed path $P : x = x_1, e_1, x_2, e_2, \ldots, e_{m-1}, x_m = y$ of m vertices between x and y and $T^P_x(y) = \min_{e \in P} T^P_B(e)$, $I^P_x(y) = \min_{e \in P} I^P_B(e)$, $F^P_x(y) = \max_{e \in P} F^P_B(e)$, $I^n_x(y) = \max_{e \in P} I^n_B(e)$, $T^n_x(y) = \max_{e \in P} T^n_B(e)$, $F^n_x(y) = \min_{e \in P} F^n_B(e)$.

Definition 9.22 An ***m*-step bipolar single-valued neutrosophic neighborhood graph** of a bipolar single-valued neutrosophic graph $G = (A, B)$ is a bipolar single-valued neutrosophic graph $\mathcal{C}_m(\overrightarrow{G}) = (A, Q)$ which has the same vertex set as in G, and there is an edge between two vertices x and y if and only if $\mathcal{N}_m(x) \cap \mathcal{N}_m(y)$ is non-empty. The positive truth-membership, indeterminacy-membership, falsity-membership, and negative truth-membership, indeterminacy-membership, falsity-membership values of the edge xy are defined as

1. $T^P_Q(xy) = (T^P_A(x) \wedge T^P_A(y))h_1(\mathcal{N}_m(x) \cap \mathcal{N}_m(y))$,
2. $I^P_Q(xy) = (I^P_A(x) \wedge I^P_A(y))h_2(\mathcal{N}_m(x) \cap \mathcal{N}_m(y))$,
3. $F^P_Q(xy) = (F^P_A(x) \vee F^P_A(y))h_3(\mathcal{N}_m(x) \cap \mathcal{N}_m(y))$,
4. $T^n_Q(xy) = (T^n_A(x) \vee T^n_A(y))h_4(\mathcal{N}_m(x) \cap \mathcal{N}_m(y))$,
5. $I^n_Q(xy) = (I^n_A(x) \vee I^n_A(y))h_5(\mathcal{N}_m(x) \cap \mathcal{N}_m(y))$,
6. $F^n_Q(xy) = (F^n_A(x) \wedge F^n_A(y))h_6(\mathcal{N}_m(x) \cap \mathcal{N}^+_m(y))$, for all $x, y \in X$.

Theorem 9.7 *Suppose $\overrightarrow{G}$ is a bipolar single-valued neutrosophic digraph. If $\mathcal{N}^+(x) \cap \mathcal{N}^+(y)$ contains only one element of $\overrightarrow{G}$, then the edge xy of $\mathcal{C}(\overrightarrow{G})$ is independent strong if and only if*

$$|[\mathcal{N}^+(x) \cap \mathcal{N}^+(y)]|_{T^P} > 0.5, \quad |[\mathcal{N}^+(x) \cap \mathcal{N}^+(y)]|_{I^P} > 0.5, \quad |[\mathcal{N}^+(x) \cap \mathcal{N}^+(y)]|_{F^P} < 0.5.$$

Proof Suppose, $\overrightarrow{G}$ is a bipolar single-valued neutrosophic digraph. Suppose $\mathcal{N}^+(x) \cap \mathcal{N}^+(y) = (a, \breve{p}^P, q^P, r^P, \breve{p}^n, q^n, r^n)$, where $\breve{p}^P, q^P, r^P, \breve{p}^n, q^n, r^n$ are the positive truth-membership, indeterminacy-membership, falsity-membership, and negative truth-membership, indeterminacy-membership, falsity-membership values of either the edge (x, a) or the edge (y, a), respectively, such that

$$\begin{aligned}
\|[\mathcal{N}^+(x)\cap\mathcal{N}^+(y)]\|_{T^p} &= \breve{p}^p = h_1(\mathcal{N}^+(x)\cap\mathcal{N}^+(y)) = h_4(\mathcal{N}^+(x)\cap\mathcal{N}^+(y)),\\
\|[\mathcal{N}^+(x)\cap\mathcal{N}^+(y)]\|_{I^p} &= q^p = h_2(\mathcal{N}^+(x)\cap\mathcal{N}^+(y)) = h_5(\mathcal{N}^+(x)\cap\mathcal{N}^+(y)),\\
\|[\mathcal{N}^+(x)\cap\mathcal{N}^+(y)]\|_{F^p} &= r^p = h_3(\mathcal{N}^+(x)\cap\mathcal{N}^+(y)) = h_6(\mathcal{N}^+(x)\cap\mathcal{N}^+(y)).
\end{aligned}$$

It then follows that

$$\begin{aligned}
T_B^p(xy) &= \breve{p}^p \times [T_A^p(x)\wedge T_A^p(y)], \quad T_B^n(xy) = \breve{p}^p \times [T_A^n(x)\vee T_A^n(y)],\\
I_B^p(xy) &= q^p \times [I_A^p(x)\wedge I_A^p(y)], \quad I_B^n(xy) = q^p \times [I_A^n(x)\vee I_A^n(y)],\\
F_B^p(xy) &= r^p \times [F_A^p(x)\vee F_A^p(y)], \quad F_B^n(xy) = r^p \times [F_A^n(x)\wedge F_A^n(y)].
\end{aligned}$$

Therefore, the edge xy in $\mathcal{C}(\overrightarrow{G})$ is independent strong if and only if $\breve{p}^p > 0.5$, $q^p > 0.5$, and $r^p < 0.5$. Hence, the edge xy of $\mathcal{C}(\overrightarrow{G})$ is independent strong if and only if

$$\|[\mathcal{N}^+(x)\cap\mathcal{N}^+(y)]\|_{T^p} > 0.5,\quad \|[\mathcal{N}^+(x)\cap\mathcal{N}^+(y)]\|_{I^p} > 0.5,\quad \|[\mathcal{N}^+(x)\cap\mathcal{N}^+(y)]\|_{F^p} < 0.5.$$

The proof is complete. □

Theorem 9.8 *If all the edges of a bipolar single-valued neutrosophic digraph $\overrightarrow{G} = (A, \overrightarrow{B})$ are independent strong, then for all edges xy in $\mathcal{C}(\overrightarrow{G}) = (A, R)$,*

$$\frac{T_R^p(xy)}{(T_A^p(x)\wedge T_A^p(y))^2} > 0.5, \quad \frac{T_R^n(xy)}{(T_A^n(x)\vee T_A^n(y))^2} < 0.5, \quad \frac{I_R^p(xy)}{(I_A^p(x)\wedge I_A^p(y))^2} > 0.5,$$
$$\frac{I_R^n(xy)}{(I_A^n(x)\vee I_A^n(y))^2} < 0.5, \quad \frac{F_R^p(xy)}{(F_A^p(x)\vee F_A^p(y))^2} < 0.5, \quad \frac{F_R^n(xy)}{(F_A^n(x)\wedge F_A^n(y))^2} < 0.5.$$

Proof Suppose all the edges of the bipolar single-valued neutrosophic digraph $\overrightarrow{G} = (A, \overrightarrow{B})$ are independent strong, then for all the edges xy in $\overrightarrow{G}$,

$$\begin{aligned}
&\frac{1}{2}(T_A^p(x)\wedge T_A^p(y)) < T_{\overrightarrow{B}}^p(xy), \quad \frac{1}{2}(T_A^n(x)\vee T_A^n(y)) > T_{\overrightarrow{B}}^n(xy), \quad \frac{1}{2}(I_A^p(x)\wedge I_A^p(y)) < I_{\overrightarrow{B}}^p(xy),\\
&\frac{1}{2}(I_A^n(x)\vee I_A^n(y)) > I_{\overrightarrow{B}}^n(xy), \quad \frac{1}{2}(F_A^p(x)\vee F_A^p(y)) > F_{\overrightarrow{B}}^p(xy), \quad \frac{1}{2}(F_A^n(x)\wedge F_A^n(y)) < F_{\overrightarrow{B}}^n(xy).
\end{aligned}$$

Let the corresponding bipolar single-valued neutrosophic competition graph be $\mathcal{C}(\overrightarrow{G}) = (A, R)$, then there are two cases:
Case 1: When $\mathcal{N}^+(x)\cap\mathcal{N}^+(y) = \emptyset$ for all $x, y \in X$, then there exists no edge in $\mathcal{C}(\overrightarrow{G})$ between x and y. Thus, there is nothing to prove in this case.
Case 2: When $\mathcal{N}^+(x)\cap\mathcal{N}^+(y) \neq \emptyset$. Let $\mathcal{N}^+(x)\cap\mathcal{N}^+(y) = \{(a_1, m_1^p, r_1^p, \breve{p}_1^p, m_1^n, r_1^n, \breve{p}_1^n), (a_2, m_2^p, r_2^p, \breve{p}_2^p, m_2^n, r_2^n, \breve{p}_2^n), \ldots, (a_l, m_l^p, r_l^p, \breve{p}_l^p, m_l^n, r_l^n, \breve{p}_l^n)\}$, where m_i^p, r_i^p, $\breve{p}_i^p$, m_i^n, r_i^n, $\breve{p}_i^n$ are the positive and negative truth-membership, indeterminacy-membership, and falsity-membership values of either $\overrightarrow{xa_i}$ or $\overrightarrow{ya_i}$ for $i = 1, 2, \ldots, l$, respectively. Thus,

$$m_i^p = [T^p_{\overrightarrow{B}}(xa_i) \wedge T^p_{\overrightarrow{B}}(ya_i)],\quad m_i^n = [T^n_{\overrightarrow{B}}(xa_i) \vee T^n_{\overrightarrow{B}}(ya_i)],\quad r_i^p = [I^p_{\overrightarrow{B}}(xa_i) \wedge I^p_{\overrightarrow{B}}(ya_i)],$$
$$r_i^n = [I^n_{\overrightarrow{B}}(xa_i) \vee I^n_{\overrightarrow{B}}(ya_i)],\quad \breve{p}_i^p = [F^p_{\overrightarrow{B}}(xa_i) \vee F^p_{\overrightarrow{B}}(ya_i)],\quad \breve{p}_i^n = [F^n_{\overrightarrow{B}}(xa_i) \vee F^n_{\overrightarrow{B}}(ya_i)],\quad i = 1, 2, \ldots, l.$$

Suppose that

$$h_1(\mathcal{N}^+(x) \cap \mathcal{N}^+(y)) = \max\{m_i^p,\ \ i = 1, 2, \ldots, l\} = m^p_{\max} = h_4(\mathcal{N}^+(x) \cap \mathcal{N}^+(y)),$$
$$h_2(\mathcal{N}^+(x) \cap \mathcal{N}^+(y)) = \max\{r_i^p,\ \ i = 1, 2, \ldots, l\} = r^p_{\max} = h_5(\mathcal{N}^+(x) \cap \mathcal{N}^+(y)),$$
$$h_3(\mathcal{N}^+(x) \cap \mathcal{N}^+(y)) = \min\{\breve{p}_i^p,\ \ i = 1, 2, \ldots, l\} = \breve{p}^p_{\min} = h_6(\mathcal{N}^+(x) \cap \mathcal{N}^+(y)).$$

Obviously, $m^p_{\max} > T^p_{\overrightarrow{B}}(xy)$, $r^p_{\max} > I^p_{\overrightarrow{B}}(xy)$, $\breve{p}^p_{\min} < F^p_{\overrightarrow{B}}(xy)$, $m^p_{\max} > T^n_{\overrightarrow{B}}(xy)$, $r^p_{\max} > I^n_{\overrightarrow{B}}(xy)$, $\breve{p}^p_{\min} > F^n_{\overrightarrow{B}}(xy)$ for all edges $\overrightarrow{xy}$ shows that

$$\frac{m^p_{\max}}{T^p_A(x) \wedge T^p_A(y)} > \frac{T^p_{\overrightarrow{B}}(xy)}{T^p_A(x) \wedge T^p_A(y)} > 0.5,\quad \frac{m^p_{\max}}{T^n_A(x) \vee T^n_A(y)} < \frac{T^n_{\overrightarrow{B}}(xy)}{T^n_A(x) \vee T^n_A(y)} < 0.5,$$
$$\frac{r^p_{\max}}{I^p_A(x) \wedge I^p_A(y)} > \frac{I^p_{\overrightarrow{B}}(xy)}{I^p_A(x) \wedge I^p_A(y)} > 0.5,\quad \frac{r^p_{\max}}{I^n_A(x) \vee I^n_A(y)} < \frac{I^n_{\overrightarrow{B}}(xy)}{I^n_A(x) \vee I^n_A(y)} < 0.5,$$
$$\frac{\breve{p}^p_{\min}}{F^p_A(x) \vee F^p_A(y)} < \frac{F^p_{\overrightarrow{B}}(xy)}{F^p_A(x) \vee F^p_A(y)} < 0.5,\quad \frac{\breve{p}^p_{\min}}{F^n_A(x) \wedge F^n_A(y)} < \frac{F^n_{\overrightarrow{B}}(xy)}{F^n_A(x) \wedge F^n_A(y)} < 0.5.$$

Thus, $T^p_R(xy) = (T^p_A(x) \wedge T^p_A(y))h_1(\mathcal{N}^+(x) \cap \mathcal{N}^+(y)) \Rightarrow T^p_R(xy) = [T^p_A(x) \wedge T^p_A(y)] \times m^p_{\max}$,
or $\frac{T^p_R(xy)}{(T^p_A(x) \wedge T^p_A(y))} = m^p_{\max} \Rightarrow \frac{T^p_R(xy)}{(T^p_A(x) \wedge T^p_A(y))^2} = \frac{m^p_{\max}}{(T^p_A(x) \wedge T^p_A(y))} > 0.5$,
$I^p_R(xy) = (I^p_A(x) \wedge I^p_A(y))h_2(\mathcal{N}^+(x) \cap \mathcal{N}^+(y)) \Rightarrow I^p_R(xy) = [I^p_A(x) \wedge I^p_A(y)] \times r^p_{\max}$
or $\frac{I^p_R(xy)}{(I^p_A(x) \wedge I^p_A(y))} = r^p_{\max}, \Rightarrow \frac{I^p_R(xy)}{(I^p_A(x) \wedge I^p_A(y))^2} = \frac{r^p_{\max}}{(I^p_A(x) \wedge I^p_A(y))} > 0.5$,
$F^p_R(xy) = (F^p_A(x) \vee F^p_A(y))h_3(\mathcal{N}^+(x) \cap \mathcal{N}^+(y)) \Rightarrow F^p_R(xy) = [F^p_A(x) \vee F^p_A(y)] \times \breve{p}^p_{\min}$,
or $\frac{F^p_R(xy)}{(F^p_A(x) \vee F^p_A(y))} = \breve{p}^p_{\min} \Rightarrow \frac{F^p_R(xy)}{(F^p_A(x) \vee F^p_A(y))^2} = \frac{\breve{p}^p_{\min}}{(F^p_A(x) \vee F^p_A(y))} < 0.5$,
$T^n_R(xy) = (T^n_A(x) \vee T^n_A(y))h_4(\mathcal{N}^+(x) \cap \mathcal{N}^+(y)) \Rightarrow T^n_R(xy) = [T^n_A(x) \vee T^n_A(y)] \times m^p_{\max}$,
or $\frac{T^n_R(xy)}{(T^n_A(x) \vee T^n_A(y))} = m^p_{\max} \Rightarrow \frac{T^n_R(xy)}{(T^n_A(x) \vee T^n_A(y))^2} = \frac{m^p_{\max}}{(T^n_A(x) \vee T^n_A(y))} < 0.5$,
$I^n_R(xy) = (I^n_A(x) \vee I^n_A(y))h_5(\mathcal{N}^+(x) \cap \mathcal{N}^+(y)) \Rightarrow I^n_R(xy) = [I^n_A(x) \vee I^n_A(y)] \times r^p_{\max}$,
or $\frac{I^n_R(xy)}{(I^n_A(x) \vee I^n_A(y))} = r^p_{\max} \Rightarrow \frac{I^n_R(xy)}{(I^n_A(x) \vee I^n_A(y))^2} = \frac{r^p_{\max}}{(F^n_A(x) \vee I^n_A(y))} < 0.5$,
$F^n_R(xy) = (F^n_A(x) \wedge F^n_A(y))h_6(\mathcal{N}^+(x) \cap \mathcal{N}^+(y)) \Rightarrow F^n_R(xy) = [F^n_A(x) \wedge F^n_A(y)] \times \breve{p}^p_{\min}$,
or $\frac{F^n_R(xy)}{(F^n_A(x) \wedge F^n_A(y))} = \breve{p}^p_{\min} \Rightarrow \frac{F^n_R(xy)}{(F^n_A(x) \wedge F^n_A(y))^2} = \frac{\breve{p}^p_{\min}}{(F^n_A(x) \wedge F^n_A(y))} < 0.5$.

Hence,
$$\frac{T_R^p(xy)}{(T_A^p(x) \wedge T_A^p(y))^2} > 0.5, \quad \frac{T_R^n(xy)}{(T_A^n(x) \vee T_A^n(y))^2} < 0.5,$$
$$\frac{I_R^p(xy)}{(I_A^p(x) \wedge I_A^p(y))^2} > 0.5, \quad \frac{I_R^n(xy)}{(I_A^n(x) \vee I_A^n(y))^2} < 0.5,$$
$$\frac{F_R^p(xy)}{(F_A^p(x) \vee F_A^p(y))^2} < 0.5, \quad \frac{F_R^n(xy)}{(F_A^n(x) \wedge F_A^n(y))^2} < 0.5,$$

for all edges xy in $\mathcal{C}(\overrightarrow{G})$. □

9.3 Bipolar Neutrosophic Neighborhood Graphs

In this section, various types of bipolar single-valued neutrosophic open neighborhood graphs are discussed in relation with m-step bipolar single-valued neutrosophic competition graphs.

Definition 9.23 Let $G = (A, B)$ be a bipolar single-valued neutrosophic graph on X. A **bipolar single-valued neutrosophic open neighborhood** of a vertex $x \in X$ is a bipolar single-valued neutrosophic set $\mathcal{N}(x) = (X_x, T_x^p, I_x^p, F_x^p, T_x^n, I_x^n, F_x^n)$ such that $X_x = \{y \mid B(xy) \neq (0, 0, 1, 0, 0, -1)\}$ and $T_x^p, I_x^p, F_x^p : X \times X \to [0, 1]$, T_x^n, I_x^n, $f_x^n : X \times X \to [-1, 0]$ are defined by $T_x^p(y) = T_B^p(xy)$, $I_x^p(y) = I_B^p(xy)$, $F_x^p(y) = F_B^p(xy)$, $T_x^n(y) = T_B^n(xy)$, $I_x^n(y) = I_B^n(xy)$, $F_x^n(y) = F_B^n(xy)$. The **bipolar single-valued neutrosophic closed neighborhood** of a vertex x is defined as $\mathcal{N}[x] = \mathcal{N}(x) \cup A(x)$.

Definition 9.24 A **bipolar single-valued neutrosophic open neighborhood graph** of a bipolar single-valued neutrosophic graph $G = (A, B)$ is a bipolar single-valued neutrosophic graph $\mathcal{C}(G) = (A, R)$ which has the same vertex set as in G, and there is an edge between two vertices x and y if and only if $\mathcal{N}(x) \cap \mathcal{N}(y)$ is non-empty. The positive truth-membership, indeterminacy-membership, falsity-membership, and negative truth-membership, indeterminacy-membership, falsity-membership values of the edge xy are defined as

1. $T_R^p(xy) = (T_A^p(x) \wedge T_A^p(y))h_1(\mathcal{N}(x) \cap \mathcal{N}(y))$,
2. $I_R^p(xy) = (I_A^p(x) \wedge I_A^p(y))h_2(\mathcal{N}(x) \cap \mathcal{N}(y))$,
3. $F_R^p(xy) = (F_A^p(x) \vee F_A^p(y))h_3(\mathcal{N}(x) \cap \mathcal{N}(y))$,
4. $T_R^n(xy) = (T_A^n(x) \vee T_A^n(y))h_4(\mathcal{N}(x) \cap \mathcal{N}(y))$,
5. $I_R^n(xy) = (I_A^n(x) \vee I_A^n(y))h_5(\mathcal{N}(x) \cap \mathcal{N}(y))$,
6. $F_R^n(xy) = (F_A^n(x) \wedge F_A^n(y))h_6(\mathcal{N}(x) \cap \mathcal{N}^+(y))$, for all $x, y \in X$.

Definition 9.25 A **bipolar single-valued neutrosophic closed neighborhood graph** of a bipolar single-valued neutrosophic graph $G = (A, B)$ is a bipolar single-valued neutrosophic graph $\mathcal{C}[G] = (A, R')$ which has the same vertex set as in G,

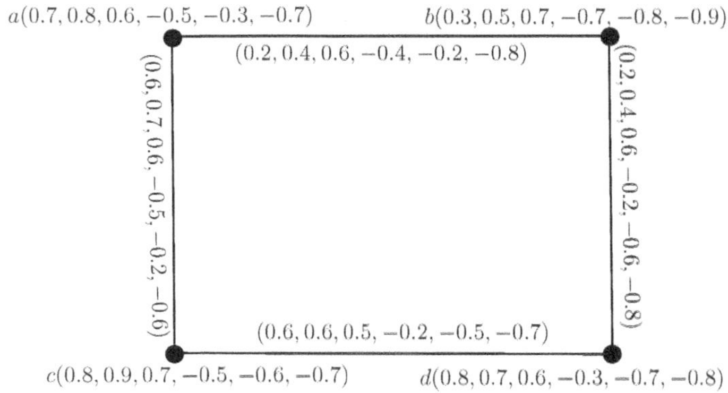

Fig. 9.11 Bipolar neutrosophic graph G

and there is an edge between two vertices x and y if and only if $\mathcal{N}[x] \cap \mathcal{N}[y]$ is non-empty. The positive truth-membership, indeterminacy-membership, falsity-membership, and negative truth-membership, indeterminacy-membership, falsity-membership values of the edge xy are defined as

1. $T^p_{R'}(xy) = (T^p_A(x) \wedge T^p_A(y))h_1(\mathcal{N}[x] \cap \mathcal{N}[y])$,
2. $I^p_{R'}(xy) = (I^p_A(x) \wedge I^p_A(y))h_2(\mathcal{N}[x] \cap \mathcal{N}[y])$,
3. $F^p_{R'}(xy) = (F^p_A(x) \vee F^p_A(y))h_3(\mathcal{N}[x] \cap \mathcal{N}[y])$,
4. $T^n_{R'}(xy) = (T^n_A(x) \vee T^n_A(y))h_4(\mathcal{N}[x] \cap \mathcal{N}[y])$,
5. $I^n_{R'}(xy) = (I^n_A(x) \vee I^n_A(y))h_5(\mathcal{N}[x] \cap \mathcal{N}[y])$,
6. $F^n_{R'}(xy) = (F^n_A(x) \wedge F^n_A(y))h_6(\mathcal{N}[x] \cap \mathcal{N}^+[y])$, for all $x, y \in X$.

Example 9.11 Consider a bipolar single-valued neutrosophic graph $G = (A, B)$ on $X = \{a, b, c, d\}$ as shown in Fig. 9.11.

The corresponding bipolar single-valued neutrosophic open and closed neighborhood graphs are shown in Figs. 9.12 and 9.13, respectively.

Theorem 9.9 *For each edge of a bipolar single-valued neutrosophic graph G, there exists an edge in* $\mathcal{N}[G]$.

Proof Suppose xy is an edge of a bipolar single-valued neutrosophic graph $G = (A, B)$. Suppose $\mathcal{N}[G] = (A, B')$ is the corresponding bipolar single-valued neutrosophic closed neighborhood graph. Suppose $x, y \in supp(\mathcal{N}[x] \cap \mathcal{N}[y])$, then $h(\mathcal{N}[x] \cap \mathcal{N}[y]) \neq (0, 0, 1, 0, 0, 1)$.

$$T^p_{B'}(xy) = [T^p_A(x) \wedge T^p_A(y)]h_1(\mathcal{N}[x] \cap \mathcal{N}[y]) \neq 0, \quad T^n_{B'}(xy) = [T^n_A(x) \vee T^n_A(y)]h_4(\mathcal{N}[x] \cap \mathcal{N}[y]) \neq 0,$$
$$I^p_{B'}(xy) = [I^p_A(x) \wedge I^p_A(y)]h_2(\mathcal{N}[x] \cap \mathcal{N}[y]) \neq 1, \quad I^n_{B'}(xy) = [I^n_A(x) \vee I^n_A(y)]h_5(\mathcal{N}[x] \cap \mathcal{N}[y]) \neq 0,$$
$$F^p_{B'}(xy) = [F^p_A(x) \vee F^p_A(y)]h_3(\mathcal{N}[x] \cap \mathcal{N}[y]) \neq 0, \quad F^n_{B'}(xy) = [F^n_A(x) \wedge F^n_A(y)]h_6(\mathcal{N}[x] \cap \mathcal{N}[y]) \neq -1.$$

Hence, for each edge xy in bipolar single-valued neutrosophic graph G, there exists an edge xy in $\mathcal{N}[G]$. □

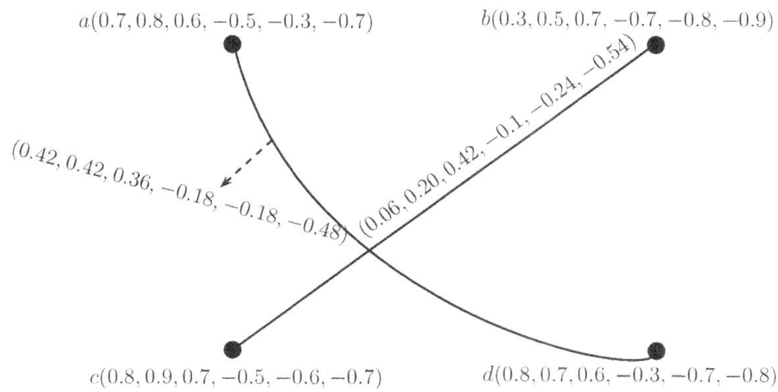

Fig. 9.12 Bipolar neutrosophic open neighborhood graph $\mathcal{N}(G)$

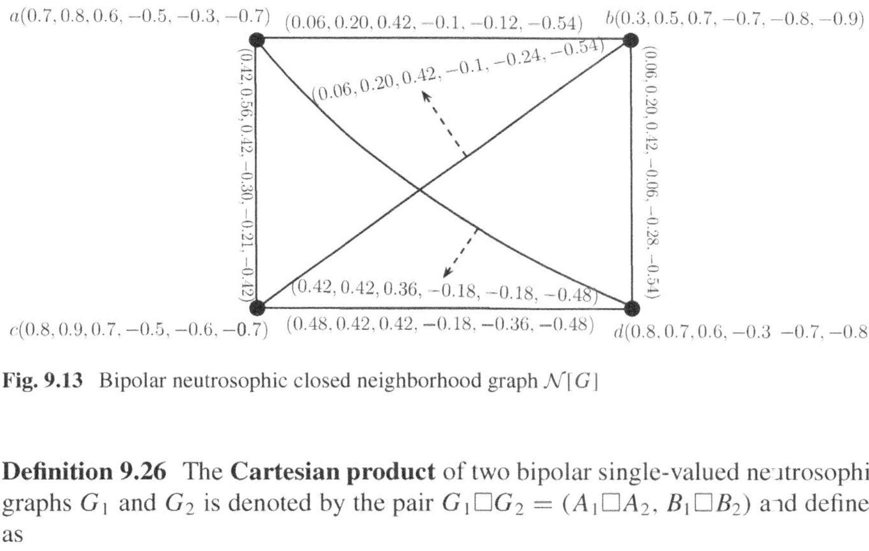

Fig. 9.13 Bipolar neutrosophic closed neighborhood graph $\mathcal{N}[G]$

Definition 9.26 The **Cartesian product** of two bipolar single-valued neutrosophic graphs G_1 and G_2 is denoted by the pair $G_1 \Box G_2 = (A_1 \Box A_2, B_1 \Box B_2)$ and defined as

$$T^p_{A_1 \Box A_2}(y) = T^p_{A_1}(y) \wedge T^p_{B_2}(y), \quad I^p_{A_1 \Box A_2}(y) = I^p_{A_1}(y) \wedge I^p_{A_2}(y), \quad F^p_{A_1 \Box A_2}(y) = F^p_{A_1}(y) \vee F^p_{A_2}(y),$$
$$T^n_{A_1 \Box B_2}(y) = T^n_{A_1}(y) \vee T^n_{A_2}(y), \quad I^n_{A_1 \Box A_2}(y) = I^n_{A_1}(y) \vee I^n_{A_2}(y), \quad F^n_{A_1 \Box A_2}(y) = F^n_{A_1}(y) \wedge F^n_{A_2}(y).$$

for all $y \in X_1 \times X_2$. The membership values of the edges in $G_1 \Box G_2$ can be calculated as

1. $T^p_{B_1 \Box B_2}((y_1, y_2)(y_1, z_2)) = T^p_{A_1}(y_1) \wedge T^p_{B_2}(y_2 z_2)$, $T^n_{B_1 \Box B_2}((y_1, y_2)(y_1, z_2)) = T^n_{A_1}(y_1) \vee T^n_{B_2}(y_2 z_2)$, for all $y_1 \in X_1$, $y_2 z_2 \in E_2$,
2. $T^p_{B_1 \Box B_2}((y_1, y_2)(z_1, y_2)) = T^p_{B_1}(y_1 z_1) \wedge T^p_{A_2}(y_2)$, $T^n_{B_1 \Box B_2}((y_1, y_2)(z_1, y_2)) = T^n_{B_1}(y_1 z_1) \vee T^n_{A_2}(y_2)$, for all $y_1 z_1 \in E_1$, $y_2 \in X_2$,
3. $I^p_{B_1 \Box B_2}((y_1, y_2)(y_1, z_2)) = I^p_{A_1}(y_1) \wedge I^p_{B_2}(y_2 z_2)$, $I^n_{B_1 \Box B_2}((y_1, y_2)(y_1, z_2)) = I^n_{A_1}(y_1) \vee I^n_{B_2}(y_2 z_2)$, for all $y_1 \in X_1$, $y_2 z_2 \in E_2$,

4. $I^p_{B_1\Box B_2}((y_1,y_2)(z_1,y_2)) = I^p_{B_1}(y_1z_1) \wedge I^p_{A_2}(y_2)$, $I^n_{B_1\Box B_2}((y_1,y_2)(z_1,y_2)) = I^n_{B_1}(y_1z_1) \vee I^n_{A_2}(y_2)$, for all $y_1z_1 \in E_1, y_2 \in X_2$,
5. $F^p_{B_1\Box B_2}((y_1,y_2)(y_1,z_2)) = F^p_{A_1}(y_1) \vee F^p_{B_2}(y_2z_2)$, $F^n_{B_1\Box B_2}((y_1,y_2)(y_1,z_2)) = F^n_{A_1}(y_1) \wedge F^n_{B_2}(y_2z_2)$, for all $y_1 \in X_1, y_2z_2 \in E_2$,
6. $F^p_{B_1\Box B_2}((y_1,y_2)(z_1,y_2)) = F^p_{B_1}(y_1z_1) \vee F^p_{A_2}(y_2)$, $F^n_{B_1\Box B_2}((y_1,y_2)(z_1,y_2)) = F^n_{B_1}(y_1z_1) \wedge F^n_{A_2}(y_2)$, for all $y_1z_1 \in E_1, y_2 \in X_2$.

Definition 9.27 The **direct product** of two bipolar single-valued neutrosophic graphs $G_1 = (A_1, B_1)$ and $G_2 = (A_2, B_2)$ is denoted by the pair $G_1 \times G_2 = (A_1 \times A_2, B_1 \times B_2)$ such that

$$T^p_{A_1\times A_2}(y) = T^p_{A_1}(y) \wedge T^p_{B_2}(y), \quad I^p_{A_1\times A_2}(y) = I^p_{A_1}(y) \wedge I^p_{A_2}(y), \quad F^p_{A_1\times A_2}(y) = F^p_{A_1}(y) \vee F^p_{A_2}(y),$$
$$T^n_{A_1\times A_2}(y) = T^n_{A_1}(y) \vee T^n_{A_2}(y), \quad I^n_{A_1\times A_2}(y) = I^n_{A_1}(y) \vee I^n_{A_2}(y), \quad F^n_{A_1\times A_2}(y) = F^n_{A_1}(y) \wedge F^n_{A_2}(y),$$

for all $y \in X_1 \times X_2$.

1. $T^p_{B_1\times B_2}((y_1,y_2)(z_1,z_2)) = T^p_{B_1}(y_1z_1) \wedge T^p_{B_2}(y_2z_2)$, $T^n_{B_1\times B_2}((y_1,y_2)(z_1,z_2)) = T^n_{B_1}(y_1z_1) \vee T^n_{B_2}(y_2z_2)$, for all $y_1z_1 \in E_1, y_2z_2 \in E_2$,
2. $I^p_{B_1\times B_2}((y_1,y_2)(z_1,z_2)) = I^p_{B_1}(y_1z_1) \wedge I^p_{B_2}(y_2z_2)$, $I^n_{B_1\times B_2}((y_1,y_2)(z_1,z_2)) = I^n_{B_1}(y_1z_1) \vee I^n_{B_2}(y_2z_2)$, for all $y_1z_1 \in E_1, y_2z_2 \in E_2$,
3. $F^p_{B_1\times B_2}((y_1,y_2)(z_1,z_2)) = F^p_{B_1}(y_1z_1) \vee F^p_{B_2}(y_2z_2)$, $F^n_{B_1\times B_2}((y_1,y_2)(z_1,z_2)) = F^n_{B_1}(y_1z_1) \wedge F^n_{B_2}(y_2z_2)$, for all $y_1z_1 \in E_1, y_2z_2 \in E_2$.

The method of construction of a bipolar single-valued neutrosophic competition graph of the Cartesian product of bipolar single-valued neutrosophic digraphs in explained in Theorem 9.10.

Theorem 9.10 *Let $\mathcal{C}(\overrightarrow{G_1}) = (A_1, B_1)$ and $\mathcal{C}(\overrightarrow{G_2}) = (A_2, B_2)$ be two bipolar single-valued neutrosophic competition graphs of bipolar single-valued neutrosophic digraphs $\overrightarrow{G_1}=(A_1, \overrightarrow{l_1})$ and $\overrightarrow{G_2}=(A_2, \overrightarrow{l_2})$, respectively. Then $\mathcal{C}(\overrightarrow{G_1}\Box\overrightarrow{G_2}) = G_{\mathcal{C}(\overrightarrow{G_1})^*\Box\mathcal{C}(\overrightarrow{G_2})^*} \cup G^{\Box}$, where $G_{\mathcal{C}(\overrightarrow{G_1})^*\Box\mathcal{C}(\overrightarrow{G_2})^*}$ is a bipolar single-valued neutrosophic graph on the crisp graph $(X_1 \times X_2, E_{\mathcal{C}(\overrightarrow{G_1})^*}\Box E_{\mathcal{C}(\overrightarrow{G_2})^*})$, $\mathcal{C}(\overrightarrow{G_1})^*$ and $\mathcal{C}(\overrightarrow{G_2})^*$ are the crisp competition graphs of $\overrightarrow{G_1}$ and $\overrightarrow{G_2}$, respectively. $G^{\Box}$ is a bipolar single-valued neutrosophic graph on $(X_1 \times X_2, E^{\Box})$ such that the following conditions are satisfied.*

1. $E^{\Box} = \{(x_1,x_2)(y_1,y_2) : y_1 \in \mathcal{N}^-(x_1)^*, y_2 \in \mathcal{N}^+(x_2)^*\}$
$E_{\mathcal{C}(\overrightarrow{G_1})^*}\Box E_{\mathcal{C}(\overrightarrow{G_2})^*} =$
$\{(x_1,x_2)(x_1,y_2) : x_1 \in X_1, x_2y_2 \in E_{\mathcal{C}(\overrightarrow{G_2})^*}\} \cup \{(x_1,x_2)(y_1,x_2) : x_2 \in X_2, x_1y_1 \in E_{\mathcal{C}(\overrightarrow{G_1})^*}\}$,
2. $T^p_{A_1\Box A_2} = T^p_{A_1}(x_1) \wedge T^p_{A_2}(x_2)$, $I^p_{A_1\Box A_2} = I^p_{A_1}(x_1) \wedge I^p_{A_2}(x_2)$, $F^p_{A_1\Box A_2} = F^p_{A_1}(x_1) \vee F^p_{A_2}(x_2)$,
$T^n_{A_1\Box A_2} = T^n_{A_1}(x_1) \vee T^n_{A_2}(x_2)$, $I^n_{A_1\Box A_2} = I^n_{A_1}(x_1) \vee I^n_{A_2}(x_2)$, $F^n_{A_1\Box A_2} = F^n_{A_1}(x_1) \wedge F^n_{A_2}(x_2)$,

3. $T_B^p((x_1,x_2)(x_1,y_2)) = [T_{A_1}^p(x_1) \wedge T_{A_2}^p(x_2) \wedge T_{A_2}^p(y_2)] \times \vee_{a_2}\{T_{A_1}^p(x_1) \wedge T_{\overrightarrow{l_2}}^p(x_2a_2) \wedge T_{\overrightarrow{l_2}}^p(y_2a_2)\}$,
$(x_1,x_2)(x_1,y_2) \in E_{\mathcal{C}(\overrightarrow{G_1})^*} \Box E_{\mathcal{C}(\overrightarrow{G_2})^*}, \quad a_2 \in (\mathcal{N}^+(x_2) \cap \mathcal{N}^+(y_2))^*$,
4. $I_B^p((x_1,x_2)(x_1,y_2)) = [I_{A_1}^p(x_1) \wedge I_{A_2}^p(x_2) \wedge I_{A_2}^p(y_2)] \times \vee_{a_2}\{I_{A_1}^p(x_1) \wedge I_{\overrightarrow{l_2}}^p(x_2a_2) \wedge I_{\overrightarrow{l_2}}^p(y_2a_2)\}$,
$(x_1,x_2)(x_1,y_2) \in E_{\mathcal{C}(\overrightarrow{G_1})^*} \Box E_{\mathcal{C}(\overrightarrow{G_2})^*}, \quad a_2 \in (\mathcal{N}^+(x_2) \cap \mathcal{N}^+(y_2))^*$,
5. $F_B^p((x_1,x_2)(x_1,y_2)) = [F_{A_1}^p(x_1) \vee F_{A_2}^p(x_2) \vee F_{A_2}^p(y_2)] \times \vee_{a_2}\{F_{A_1}^p(x_1) \vee F_{\overrightarrow{l_2}}^p(x_2a_2) \vee F_{\overrightarrow{l_2}}^p(y_2a_2)\}$,
$(x_1,x_2)(x_1,y_2) \in E_{\mathcal{C}(\overrightarrow{G_1})^*} \Box E_{\mathcal{C}(\overrightarrow{G_2})^*}, \quad a_2 \in (\mathcal{N}^+(x_2) \cap \mathcal{N}^+(y_2))^*$,
6. $T_B^n((x_1,x_2)(x_1,y_2)) = [T_{A_1}^n(x_1) \vee T_{A_2}^n(x_2) \vee T_{A_2}^n(y_2)] \times \vee_{a_2}\{T_{A_1}^n(x_1) \vee T_{\overrightarrow{l_2}}^n(x_2a_2) \vee T_{\overrightarrow{l_2}}^n(y_2a_2)\}$,
$(x_1,x_2)(x_1,y_2) \in E_{\mathcal{C}(\overrightarrow{G_1})^*} \Box E_{\mathcal{C}(\overrightarrow{G_2})^*}, \quad a_2 \in (\mathcal{N}^+(x_2) \cap \mathcal{N}^+(y_2))^*$,
7. $I_B^n((x_1,x_2)(x_1,y_2)) = [I_{A_1}^n(x_1) \vee I_{A_2}^n(x_2) \vee I_{A_2}^n(y_2)] \times \vee_{a_2}\{I_{A_1}^n(x_1) \vee I_{\overrightarrow{l_2}}^n(x_2a_2) \vee I_{\overrightarrow{l_2}}^n(y_2a_2)\}$,
$(x_1,x_2)(x_1,y_2) \in E_{\mathcal{C}(\overrightarrow{G_1})^*} \Box E_{\mathcal{C}(\overrightarrow{G_2})^*}, \quad a_2 \in (\mathcal{N}^+(x_2) \cap \mathcal{N}^+(y_2))^*$,
8. $F_B^n((x_1,x_2)(x_1,y_2)) = [F_{A_1}^n(x_1) \wedge F_{A_2}^n(x_2) \wedge F_{A_2}^n(y_2)] \times \vee_{a_2}\{F_{A_1}^n(x_1) \wedge F_{\overrightarrow{l_2}}^n(x_2a_2) \wedge F_{\overrightarrow{l_2}}^n(y_2a_2)\}$,
$(x_1,x_2)(x_1,y_2) \in E_{\mathcal{C}(\overrightarrow{G_1})^*} \Box E_{\mathcal{C}(\overrightarrow{G_2})^*}, \quad a_2 \in (\mathcal{N}^+(x_2) \cap \mathcal{N}^+(y_2))^*$,
9. $T_B^p((x_1,x_2)(y_1,x_2)) = [T_{A_1}^p(x_1) \wedge T_{A_1}^p(y_1) \wedge T_{A_2}^p(x_2)] \times \vee_{a_1}\{T_{A_2}^p(x_2) \wedge T_{\overrightarrow{l_1}}^p(x_1a_1) \wedge T_{\overrightarrow{l_1}}^p(y_1a_1)\}$,
$(x_1,x_2)(y_1,x_2) \in E_{\mathcal{C}(\overrightarrow{G_1})^*} \Box E_{\mathcal{C}(\overrightarrow{G_2})^*}, \quad a_1 \in (\mathcal{N}^+(x_1) \cap \mathcal{N}^+(y_1))^*$,
10. $I_B^p((x_1,x_2)(y_1,x_2)) = [I_{A_1}^p(x_1) \wedge I_{A_1}^p(y_1) \wedge I_{A_2}^p(x_2)] \times \vee_{a_1}\{I_{A_2}^p(x_2) \wedge I_{\overrightarrow{l_1}}^p(x_1a_1) \wedge I_{\overrightarrow{l_1}}^p(y_1a_1)\}$,
$(x_1,x_2)(y_1,x_2) \in E_{\mathcal{C}(\overrightarrow{G_1})^*} \Box E_{\mathcal{C}(\overrightarrow{G_2})^*}, \quad a_1 \in (\mathcal{N}^+(x_1) \cap \mathcal{N}^+(y_1))^*$,
11. $F_B^p((x_1,x_2)(y_1,x_2)) = [F_{A_1}^p(x_1) \vee F_{A_1}^p(y_1) \vee F_{A_2}^p(x_2)] \times \vee_{a_1}\{F_{A_2}^p(x_2) \vee F_{\overrightarrow{l_1}}^p(x_1a_1) \vee F_{\overrightarrow{l_1}}^p(y_1a_1)\}$,
$(x_1,x_2)(y_1,x_2) \in E_{\mathcal{C}(\overrightarrow{G_1})^*} \Box E_{\mathcal{C}(\overrightarrow{G_2})^*}, \quad a_1 \in (\mathcal{N}^+(x_1) \cap \mathcal{N}^+(y_1))^*$,
12. $T_B^n((x_1,x_2)(y_1,x_2)) = [T_{A_1}^n(x_1) \vee T_{A_1}^n(y_1) \vee T_{A_2}^n(x_2)] \times \vee_{a_1}\{T_{A_2}^n(x_2) \vee T_{\overrightarrow{l_1}}^n(x_1a_1) \vee T_{\overrightarrow{l_1}}^n(y_1a_1)\}$,
$(x_1,x_2)(y_1,x_2) \in E_{\mathcal{C}(\overrightarrow{G_1})^*} \Box E_{\mathcal{C}(\overrightarrow{G_2})^*}, \quad a_1 \in (\mathcal{N}^+(x_1) \cap \mathcal{N}^+(y_1))^*$,
13. $I_B^n((x_1,x_2)(y_1,x_2)) = [I_{A_1}^n(x_1) \vee I_{A_1}^n(y_1) \vee I_{A_2}^n(x_2)] \times \vee_{a_1}\{I_{A_2}^n(x_2) \vee I_{\overrightarrow{l_1}}^n(x_1a_1) \vee I_{\overrightarrow{l_1}}^n(y_1a_1)\}$,
$(x_1,x_2)(y_1,x_2) \in E_{\mathcal{C}(\overrightarrow{G_1})^*} \Box E_{\mathcal{C}(\overrightarrow{G_2})^*}, \quad a_1 \in (\mathcal{N}^+(x_1) \cap \mathcal{N}^+(y_1))^*$,
14. $F_B^n((x_1,x_2)(y_1,x_2)) = [F_{A_1}^n(x_1) \wedge F_{A_1}^n(y_1) \wedge F_{A_2}^n(x_2)] \times \vee_{a_1}\{F_{A_2}^n(x_2) \wedge F_{\overrightarrow{l_1}}^n(x_1a_1) \wedge F_{\overrightarrow{l_1}}^n(y_1a_1)\}$,
$(x_1,x_2)(y_1,x_2) \in E_{\mathcal{C}(\overrightarrow{G_1})^*} \Box E_{\mathcal{C}(\overrightarrow{G_2})^*}, \quad a_1 \in (\mathcal{N}^+(x_1) \cap \mathcal{N}^+(y_1))^*$,
15. $T_B^p((x_1,x_2)(y_1,y_2)) =$
$[T_{A_1}^p(x_1) \wedge T_{A_1}^p(y_1) \wedge T_{A_2}^p(x_2) \wedge T_{A_2}^p(y_2)] \times [T_{A_1}^p(x_1) \wedge$
$T_{\overrightarrow{l_1}}^p(y_1x_1) \wedge T_{A_2}^p(y_2) \wedge$

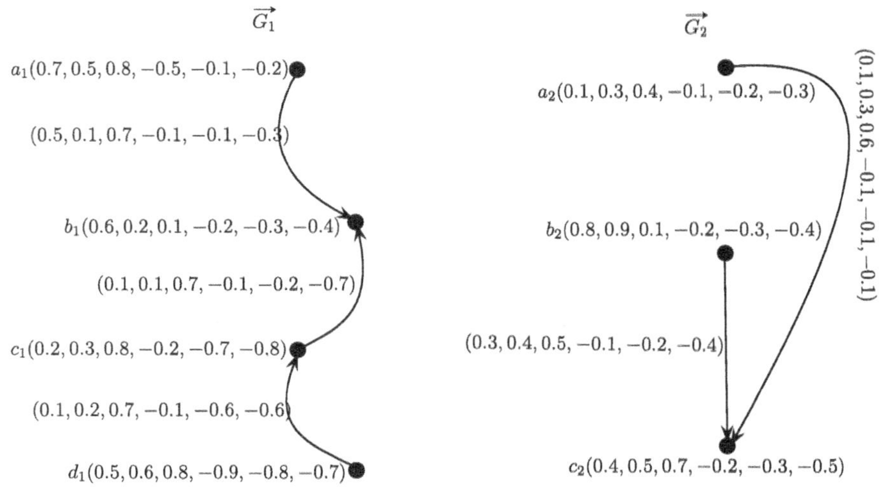

Fig. 9.14 Bipolar neutrosophic digraphs

$T^p_{\overrightarrow{l_2}}(x_2y_2)]$,
$(x_1, y_1)(x_2, y_2) \in E^\square$,

16. $I^p_B((x_1, x_2)(y_1, y_2)) = [I^p_{A_1}(x_1) \wedge I^p_{A_1}(y_1) \wedge I^p_{A_2}(x_2) \wedge I^p_{A_2}(y_2)] \times [I^p_{A_1}(x_1) \wedge I^p_{\overrightarrow{l_1}}(y_1x_1) \wedge I^p_{A_2}(y_2) \wedge I^p_{\overrightarrow{l_2}}(x_2y_2)]$,
$(x_1, y_1)(x_2, y_2) \in E^\square$,
17. $F^p_B((x_1, x_2)(y_1, y_2)) =$
$[F^p_{A_1}(x_1) \vee F^p_{A_1}(y_1) \vee F^p_{A_2}(x_2) \vee F^p_{A_2}(y_2)] \times [F^p_{A_1}(x_1) \vee F^p_{\overrightarrow{l_1}}(y_1x_1) \vee F^p_{A_2}(y_2) \vee F^p_{\overrightarrow{l_2}}(x_2y_2)]$,
$(x_1, y_1)(x_2, y_2) \in E^\square$,
18. $T^n_B((x_1, x_2)(y_1, y_2)) =$
$[T^n_{A_1}(x_1) \vee T^n_{A_1}(y_1) \vee T^n_{A_2}(x_2) \vee T^n_{A_2}(y_2)] \times [T^n_{A_1}(x_1) \vee T^n_{\overrightarrow{l_1}}(y_1x_1) \vee T^n_{A_2}(y_2) \vee T^n_{\overrightarrow{l_2}}(x_2y_2)]$,
$(x_1, y_1)(x_2, y_2) \in E^\square$,
19. $I^n_B((x_1, x_2)(y_1, y_2)) = [I^n_{A_1}(x_1) \vee I^n_{A_1}(y_1) \vee I^n_{A_2}(x_2) \vee I^n_{A_2}(y_2)] \times [I^n_{A_1}(x_1) \vee I^n_{\overrightarrow{l_1}}(y_1x_1) \vee I^n_{A_2}(y_2) \vee I^n_{\overrightarrow{l_2}}(x_2y_2)]$,
$(x_1, y_1)(x_2, y_2) \in E^\square$,
20. $F^n_B((x_1, x_2)(y_1, y_2)) =$
$[F^n_{A_1}(x_1) \wedge F^n_{A_1}(y_1) \wedge F^n_{A_2}(x_2) \wedge F^n_{A_2}(y_2)] \times [F^n_{A_1}(x_1) \wedge F^n_{\overrightarrow{l_1}}(y_1x_1) \wedge F^n_{A_2}(y_2) \wedge F^n_{\overrightarrow{l_2}}(x_2y_2)]$,
$(x_1, y_1)(x_2, y_2) \in E^\square$.

Example 9.12 Consider $\overrightarrow{G_1} = (A_1, l_1)$ and $\overrightarrow{G_2} = (A_2, l_2)$ as two bipolar single-valued neutrosophic digraphs as shown in Fig. 9.14. The bipolar single-valued neutrosophic out- and in-neighborhoods of $\overrightarrow{G_1}$ and $\overrightarrow{G_2}$ are given in Tables 9.4 and 9.5. The bipolar single-valued neutrosophic competition graphs $\mathcal{C}(\overrightarrow{G}_1)$ and $\mathcal{C}(\overrightarrow{G}_2)$ are given in Fig. 9.15.

Construct the bipolar single-valued neutrosophic competition graph $G_{\mathcal{C}(\overrightarrow{G_1})^* \square \mathcal{C}(\overrightarrow{G_2})^*} \cup G^\square = (W, B)$, where $W = (T^p_W, I^p_W, F^p_W, T^n_W, I^n_W, F^n_W)$ and $B = (T^p_B, I^p_B, F^p_B, T^n_B,$

Table 9.4 Bipolar neutrosophic out- and in-neighborhoods of $\overrightarrow{G}_1$

$x \in X_1$	$\mathcal{N}^+(x)$	$\mathcal{N}^-(x)$
a_1	$\{b_1(0.5, 0.1, 0.7, -0.1, -0.1, -0.3)\}$	$\emptyset$
b_1	$\emptyset$	$\{a_1(0.5, 0.1, 0.7, -0.1, -0.1, -0.3)\}$
c_1	$\{b_1(0.1, 0.1, 0.7, -0.1, -0.2, -0.7)\}$	$\{d_1(0.1, 0.2, 0.7, -0.1, -0.6, -0.6)\}$
d_1	$\{c_1(0.1, 0.2, 0.7, -0.1, -0.6, -0.6)\}$	$\emptyset$

Table 9.5 Bipolar neutrosophic out- and in-neighborhoods of $\overrightarrow{G}_2$

$x \in X_2$	$\mathcal{N}^+(x)$	$\mathcal{N}^-(x)$
a_2	$\{c_2(0.1, 0.3, 0.6, -0.1, -0.1, -0.1)\}$	$\emptyset$
b_2	$\{c_2(0.3, 0.4, 0.5, -0.1, -0.2, -0.4)\}$	$\emptyset$
c_2	$\emptyset$	$\{a_2(0.1, 0.3, 0.6, -0.1, -0.1, -0.1),$ $b_2(0.3, 0.4, 0.5, -0.1, -0.2, -0.4)\}$

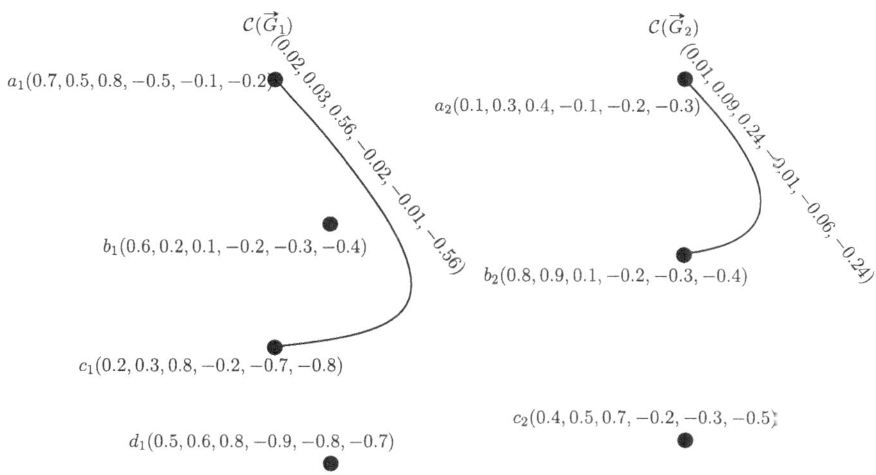

Fig. 9.15 Bipolar neutrosophic competition graphs

I_B^n, F_B^n), from $\mathcal{C}(\overrightarrow{G_1})^*$ and $\mathcal{C}(\overrightarrow{G_2})^*$ using Theorem 1.4. We obtain the following sets of edges using condition 1.
$E_{\mathcal{C}(\overrightarrow{G_1})^*\Box\mathcal{C}(\overrightarrow{G_2})^*} = \{(a_1, a_2)(a_1, b_2), (b_1, a_2)(b_1, b_2), (c_1, a_2)(c_1, b_2), (d_1, a_2)(d_1, b_2), (a_1, a_2)(c_1, a_2), (a_1, b_2)(c_1, b_2), (a_1, c_2)(c_1, c_2)\}$, $E^{\Box} = \{(b_1, a_2)(a_1, c_2), (b_1, a_2)(c_1, c_2), (b_1, b_2)(a_1, c_2), (b_1, b_2)(c_1, c_2), (c_1, a_2)(d_1, c_2), (c_1, b_2)(d_1, c_2)\}$. According to conditions 3–20, the degrees of positive truth-membership, indeterminacy-membership, falsity-membership, negative truth-membership, indeterminacy-membership, and falsity-membership values of the adjacent vertices of $G_{\mathcal{C}(\overrightarrow{G_1})^*\Box\mathcal{C}(\overrightarrow{G_2})^*}$ and $G^{\Box}$ are given in Table 9.6.

Table 9.6 Adjacent vertices of $G_{\mathcal{C}(\overrightarrow{G_1})^* \Box \mathcal{C}(\overrightarrow{G_2})^*} \cup G^{\Box}$

$(x_1, x_2)(y_1, y_2)$	$B(x_1, x_2)(y_1, y_2)$
$(a_1, a_2)(a_1, b_2)$	(0.01, 0.09, 0.64, −0.01, −0.03, −0.32)
$(b_1, a_2)(b_1, b_2)$	(0.01, 0.04, 0.24, −0.01, −0.04, −0.24)
$(c_1, a_2)(c_1, b_2)$	(0.01, 0.09, 0.64, −0.01, −0.06, −0.64)
$(d_1, a_2)(d_1, b_2)$	(0.01, 0.09, 0.64, −0.01, −0.06, −0.56)
$(a_1, a_2)(c_1, a_2)$	(0.01, 0.03, 0.56, −0.01, −0.01, −0.56)
$(a_1, b_2)(c_1, b_2)$	(0.02, 0.03, 0.56, −0.02, −0.01, −0.56)
$(a_1, c_2)(c_1, c_2)$	(0.02, 0.03, 0.56, −0.02, −0.01, −0.56)
$(b_1, a_2)(a_1, c_2)$	(0.01, 0.02, 0.56, −0.01, −0.01, −0.35)
$(b_1, a_2)(c_1, c_2)$	(0.01, 0.02, 0.56, −0.01, −0.02, −0.56)
$(b_1, b_2)(a_1, c_2)$	(0.12, 0.02, 0.56, −0.06, −0.01, −0.35)
$(b_1, b_2)(c_1, c_2)$	(0.02, 0.02, 0.56, −0.02, −0.03, −0.56)
$(c_1, a_2)(d_1, c_2)$	(0.01, 0.06, 0.64, −0.01, −0.04, −0.64)
$(c_1, b_2)(d_1, c_2)$	(0.02, 0.06, 0.64, −0.02, −0.06, −0.64)

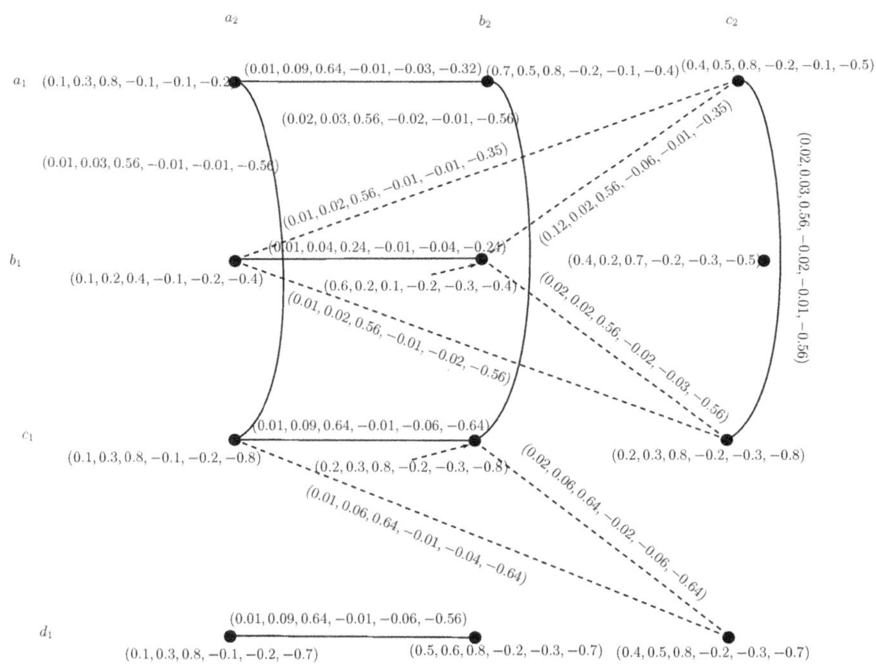

Fig. 9.16 Bipolar neutrosophic graph $G_{\mathcal{C}(\overrightarrow{G_1})^* \Box \mathcal{C}(\overrightarrow{G_2})^*} \cup G^{\Box}$

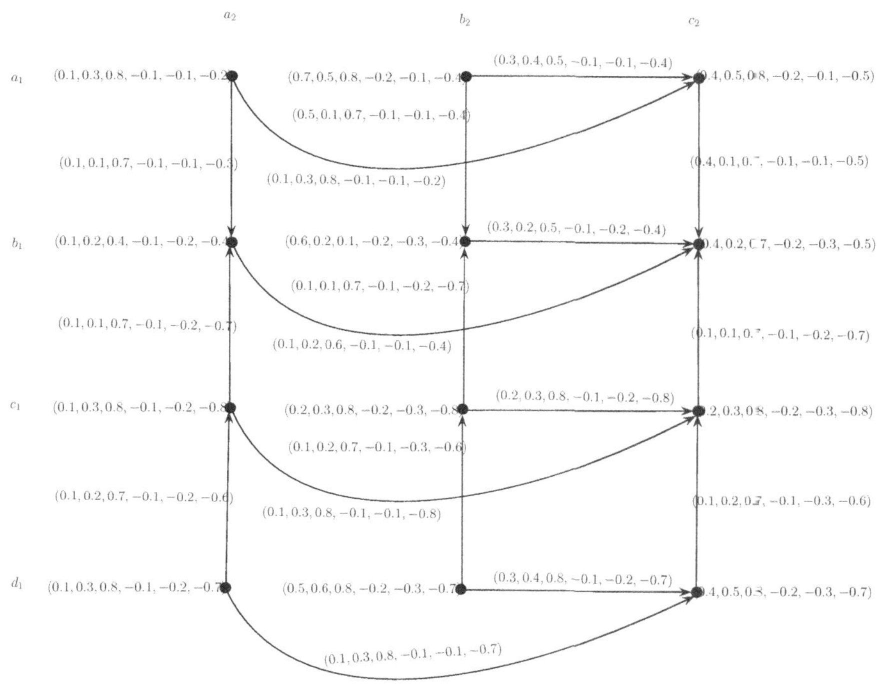

Fig. 9.17 Cartesian product $\overrightarrow{G_1}\Box\overrightarrow{G_2}$

The bipolar single-valued neutrosophic competition graph obtained using this method is given in Fig. 9.16, where the solid lines indicate the part of the bipolar single-valued neutrosophic competition graph obtained from $G_{\mathcal{C}(\overrightarrow{G_1})^*\Box\mathcal{C}(\overrightarrow{G_2})^*}$, the dotted lines represent the part $G^{\Box}$.

The Cartesian product $\overrightarrow{G_1}\Box\overrightarrow{G_2}$ of bipolar single-valued neutrosophic digraphs $\overrightarrow{G_1}$ and $\overrightarrow{G_1}$ is shown in Fig. 9.17. The bipolar single-valued neutrosophic out-neighborhoods of $\overrightarrow{G_1}\Box\overrightarrow{G_2}$ are calculated in Table 9.7. The bipolar single-valued neutrosophic competition graph of $\overrightarrow{G_1}\Box\overrightarrow{G_2}$ is shown in Fig. 9.18.

It is clear from Figs. 9.16 and 9.18 that $G_{\mathcal{C}(\overrightarrow{G_1})^*\Box\mathcal{C}(\overrightarrow{G_2})^*} \cup G^{\Box} \cong \mathcal{C}(\overrightarrow{G_1}\Box\overrightarrow{G_2})$.

9.4 Applications of Competition Graphs in Bipolar Neutrosophic Environment

In this section, the applications of bipolar single-valued neutrosophic competition graphs are studied in organizational designations, economics, business marketing, and sports.

Table 9.7 Bipolar neutrosophic out-neighborhoods of $\overrightarrow{G_1}\square\overrightarrow{G_2}$

(x, y)	$\mathcal{N}^+(x, y)$
(a_1, a_2)	$\{((a_1, c_2), 0.1, 0.3, 0.8, -0.1, -0.1, -0.2), ((b_1, a_2), 0.1, 0.1, 0.7, -0.1, -0.1, -0.3)\}$
(a_1, b_2)	$\{((a_1, c_2), 0.3, 0.4, 0.5, -0.1, -0.1, -0.4), ((b_1, b_2), 0.5, 0.1, 0.7, -0.1, -0.1, -0.4)\}$
(a_1, c_2)	$\{((b_1, c_2), 0.4, 0.1, 0.7, -0.1, -0.1, -0.5)\}$
(b_1, a_2)	$\{((b_1, c_2), 0.1, 0.2, 0.6, -0.1, -0.1, -0.4)\}$
(b_1, b_2)	$\{((b_1, c_2), 0.3, 0.2, 0.5, -0.1, -0.2, -0.4)\}$
(b_1, c_2)	$\emptyset$
(c_1, a_2)	$\{((c_1, c_2), 0.1, 0.3, 0.8, -0.1, -0.1, -0.8), ((b_1, a_2), 0.1, 0.1, 0.7, -0.1, -0.2, -0.7)\}$
(c_1, b_2)	$\{((b_1, b_2), 0.1, 0.1, 0.7, -0.1, -0.2, -0.7), ((c_1, c_2), 0.2, 0.3, 0.8, -0.1, -0.2, -0.8)\}$
(c_1, c_2)	$\{((b_1, c_2), 0.1, 0.1, 0.7, -0.1, -0.2, -0.7)\}$
(d_1, a_2)	$\{((d_1, c_2), 0.1, 0.3, 0.8, -0.1, -0.1, -0.7), ((c_1, a_2), 0.1, 0.2, 0.7, -0.1, -0.2, -0.6)\}$
(d_1, b_2)	$\{((d_1, c_2), 0.3, 0.4, 0.8, -0.1, -0.2, -0.7), (c_1, b_2), 0.1, 0.2, 0.7, -0.1, -0.3, -0.6)\}$
(d_1, c_2)	$\{((c_1, c_2), 0.1, 0.2, 0.7, -0.1, -0.3, -0.6)\}$

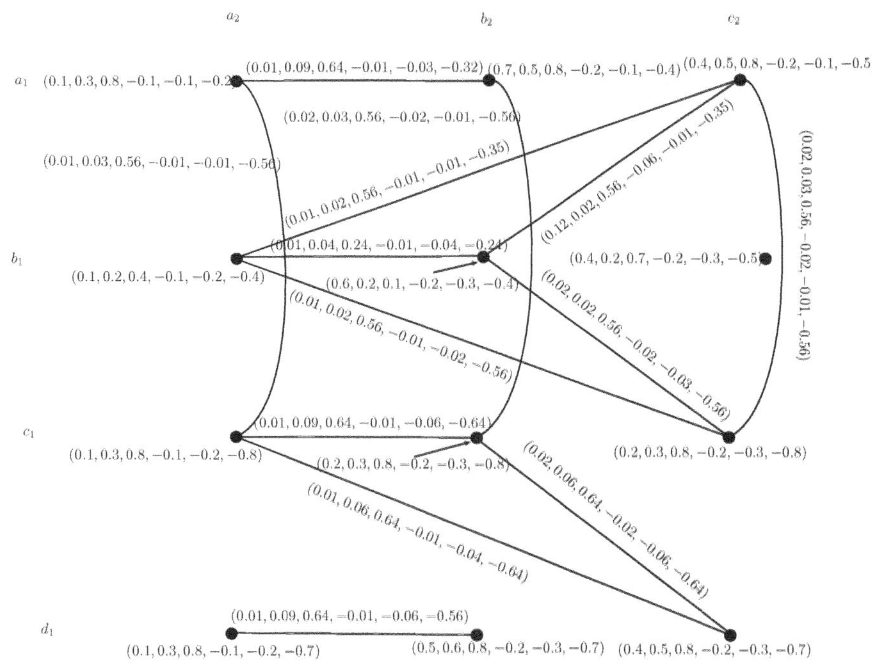

Fig. 9.18 Bipolar neutrosophic competition graph $\mathcal{C}(\overrightarrow{G_1}\square\overrightarrow{G_2})$

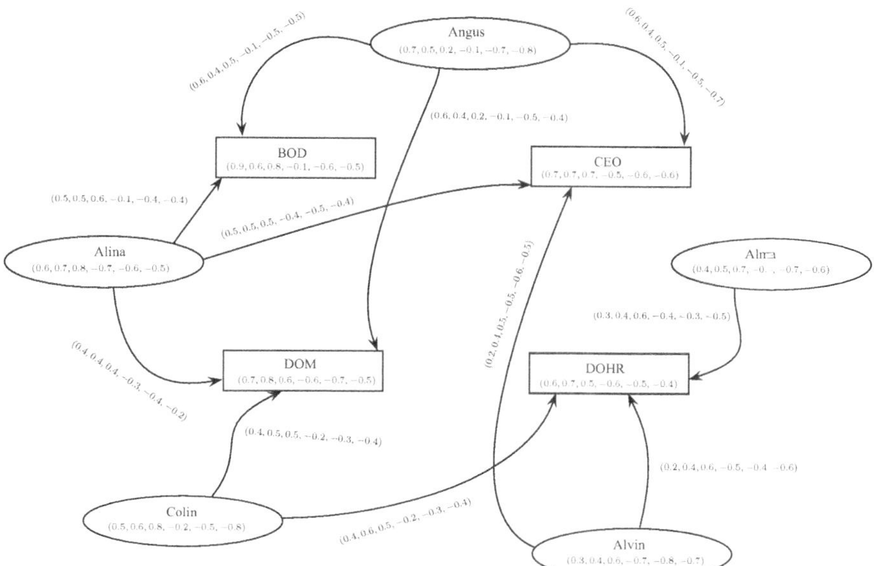

Fig. 9.19 Bipolar neutrosophic organization model

9.4.1 *Designation Competition in an Organization*

Consider a bipolar single-valued neutrosophic digraph as shown in Fig. 9.19 representing the competition between applicants for designations in an organization. Let {Angus, Alvin, Alina, Colin, Alma} be the set of applicants for the designations {Board of director(BOD), CEO, Director of marketing(DOM), Director of human resources(DOHR)}.

The positive degree of membership $T^p(x)$ of each applicant represents the percentage of hard work toward the goals of organization, and $I^p(x)$ and $F^p(x)$ represent the indeterminacy and falsity in this percentage. The negative degree of membership $T^n(x)$ represents the percentage that the applicant is not effective in order to fulfill the goals of that organization, and $I^n(x)$ and $F^n(x)$ represent the indeterminacy and falsity in this percentage. The positive degree of membership $T^p(x)$ of each directed edge between applicants and designations represents the percentage of eligibility for that designation in the organization, and $I^p(x)$ and $F^p(x)$ represent the indeterminacy and falsity in this percentage. The negative degree of membership $T^n(x)$ of each directed edge between the applicants and the designation represents the percentage of non-eligibility for that designation in the organization, and $I^n(x)$ and $F^n(x)$ represent the indeterminacy and falsity in this percentage. The bipolar single-valued neutrosophic competition graph can be used in order to find the designations of the applicants. The bipolar neutrosophic out-neighborhoods are computed in Table 9.8.

Table 9.8 Bipolar neutrosophic out-neighborhoods

$x \in X$	$\mathcal{N}^+(x)$
Angus	$\{(BOD, 0.6, 0.4, 0.5, -0.1, -0.5, -0.5)$, $(CEO, 0.6, 0.4, 0.5, -0.1, -0.5, -0.7)$, $(DOM, 0.6, 0.4, 0.2, -0.1, -0.5, -0.4)\}$
Alma	$\{(DOHR, 0.3, 0.4, 0.6, -0.4, -0.3, -0.5)\}$
Alvin	$\{(DOHR, 0.2, 0.4, 0.6, -0.5, -0.4, -0.6)$, $(CEO, 0.2, 0.4, 0.5, -0.5, -0.6, -0.5)\}$
Colin	$\{(DOHR, 0.4, 0.6, 0.5, -0.2, -0.3, -0.4)$, $(DOM, 0.4, 0.5, 0.5, -0.2, -0.3, -0.4)\}$
Alina	$\{(BOD, 0.5, 0.5, 0.6, -0.1, -0.4, -0.4)$, $(CEO, 0.5, 0.5, 0.5, -0.4, -0.5, -0.4)$, $(DOM, 0.4, 0.4, 0.4, -0.3, -0.4, -0.2)\}$

Therefore, $\mathcal{N}^+(Angus) \cap \mathcal{N}^+(Alma) = \emptyset$, $\mathcal{N}^+(\text{Alma}) \cap \mathcal{N}^+(\text{Alina}) = \emptyset$, $\mathcal{N}^+(\text{Angus}) \cap \mathcal{N}^+(\text{Alvin}) = \{(\text{CEO}, 0.2, 0.4, 0.5, -0.1, -0.5, -0.7)\}$, $\mathcal{N}^+(\text{Angus}) \cap \mathcal{N}^+(\text{Colin}) = \{(\text{DOM}, 0.4, 0.4, 0.5, -0.1, -0.3, -0.4)\}$, $\mathcal{N}^+(\text{Alma}) \cap \mathcal{N}^+(\text{Alvin}) = \{(\text{DOHR}, 0.2, 0.4, 0.6, -0.4, -0.3, -0.6)\}$, $\mathcal{N}^+(\text{Alma}) \cap \mathcal{N}^+(\text{Colin}) = \{(\text{DOHR}, 0.3, 0.4, 0.6, -0.2, -0.3, -0.5)\}$, $\mathcal{N}^+(\text{Alvin}) \cap \mathcal{N}^+(\text{Colin}) = \{(\text{DOHR}, 0.2, 0.4, 0.6, -0.2, -0.3, -0.6)\}$, $\mathcal{N}^+(\text{Alvin}) \cap \mathcal{N}^+(\text{Alina}) = \{(\text{CEO}, 0.2, 0.4, 0.5, -0.4, -0.5, -0.5)\}$, $\mathcal{N}^+(\text{Colin}) \cap \mathcal{N}^+(\text{Alina}) = \{(\text{DOM}, 0.4, 0.4, 0.5, -0.2, -0.3, -0.4)\}$, $\mathcal{N}^+(\text{Angus}) \cap \mathcal{N}^+(\text{Alina}) = \{(\text{BOD}, 0.5, 0.4, 0.6, -0.1, -0.4, -0.5), (\text{CEO}, 0.5, 0.4, 0.5, -0.1, -0.5, -0.7), (\text{DOM}, 0.4, 0.4, 0.4, -0.1, -0.4, -0.2)\}$. The bipolar neutrosophic competition graph is shown in Fig. 9.20.

The bipolar single-valued neutrosophic competition graph is shown in Fig. 9.20. The solid lines indicate the strength of competition between two applicants and the dashed lines indicate the applicant competing for the particular designation. For example, Angus and Alina both are competing for the designation BOD and strength of competition between them is $(0.30, 0.20, 0.32, -0.05, -0.24, -0.32)$. In Table 9.9, $T(y, d)$ represents the strength of competition of applicant y for designation d with respect to hard work in order to fulfill the goals of that organization. The strength to compete with other applicants with respect to particular designations is calculated in Table 9.9. From Table 9.9, Angus and Alina have equal strength to compete with others for designation BOD. Angus competes with others for the designations DOM and CEO, while Colin competes with others for the designation DOHR.

The method to calculate the strength of competition among applicants is given in Algorithm 9.4.1.

Algorithm 9.4.1 Strength of competition among applicants

Step 1. Input the bipolar single-valued neutrosophic A of q applicants $y_1, y_2, \ldots, y_q$.

Step 2. If for any two distinct vertices y_i and y_j, $A(y_i y_j) \neq (0, 0, 1, 0, 0, -1)$, then

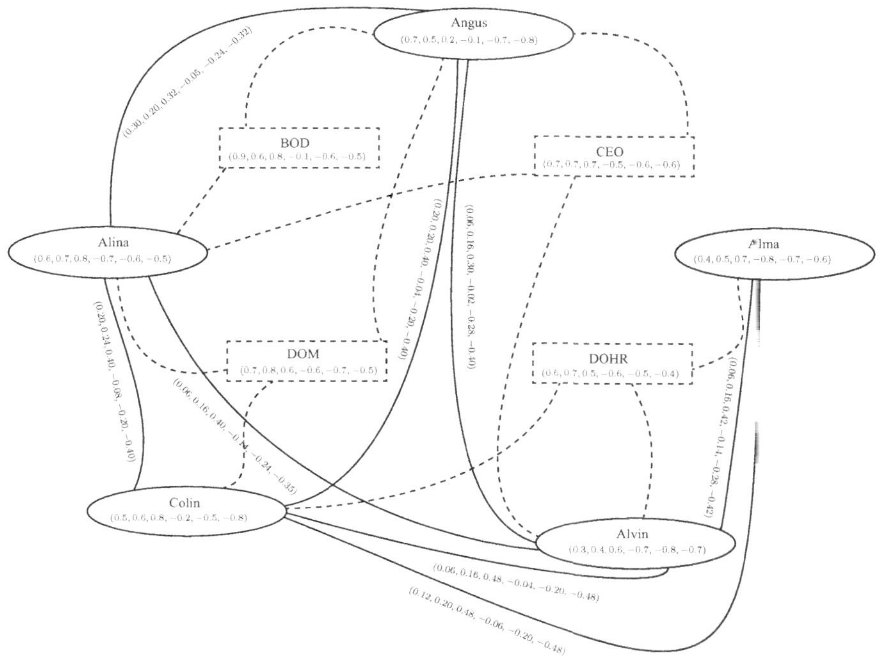

Fig. 9.20 Bipolar neutrosophic competition graph

Table 9.9 Strength of competition of applicants for particular designations

(Applicant, designation)	In competition	T(Applicant, designation)	S(Applicant, designation)
(Angus, BOD)	Alina	(0.30, 0.20, 0.32, −0.05, −0.24, −0.32)	1.29
(Alina, BOD)	Angus	(0.30, 0.20, 0.32, −0.05, −0.24, −0.32)	1.29
(Angus, DOM)	Alina, Colin	(0.25, 0.20, 0.36, −0.045, −0.22, −0.36)	1.225
(Alina, DOM)	Angus, Colin	(0.25, 0.22, 0.36, −0.065, −0.22, −0.36)	1.185
(Colin, DOM)	Angus, Alina	(0.20, 0.22, 0.40, −0.060, −0.20, −0.40)	1.120
(Angus, CEO)	Alina, Alvin	(0.180, 0.180, 0.310, −0.035, −0.260, −0.360)	1.275
(Alina, CEO)	Angus, Alvin	(0.180, 0.180, 0.360, −0.095, −0.24, −0.335)	1.120
(Alvin, CEO)	Angus, Alina	(0.06, 0.16, 0.35, −0.080, −0.260, −0.375)	1.105
(Alma, DOHR)	Alvin, Colin	(0.09, 0.180, 0.450, −0.100, −0.240, −0.450)	1.050
(Alvin, DOHR)	Colin, Alma	(0.06, 0.16, 0.450, −0.09, −0.240, −0.450)	0.050
(Colin, DOHR)	Alma, Alvin	(0.09, 0.180, 0.480, −0.05, −0.20, −0.48)	1.060

$$(y_j, T^p(y_i y_j), I^p(y_i y_j), F^p(y_i y_j), T^n(y_i y_j), I^n(y_i y_j), F^n(y_i y_j)) \in \mathcal{N}^+(y_i).$$

Step 3. Repeat Step 2 for all vertices y_i and y_j to calculate bipolar single-valued neutrosophic out-neighborhoods $\mathcal{N}^+(y_i)$.

Step 4. Calculate $\mathcal{N}^+(y_i) \cap \mathcal{N}^+(y_j)$ for each pair of distinct vertices y_i and y_j.

Step 5. Calculate $h[\mathcal{N}^+(y_i) \cap \mathcal{N}^+(y_j)]$ for each pair of distinct vertices y_i and y_j.

Step 6. If $\mathcal{N}^+(y_i) \cap \mathcal{N}^+(y_j) \neq \emptyset$, then draw an edge $y_i y_j$.

Step 7. Repeat Step 6 for all pairs of distinct vertices.

Step 8. Assign membership values to each edge $y_i y_j$ using the conditions

$$T_R^p(y_i y_j) = (y_i \wedge y_j)h_1[\mathcal{N}^+(y_i) \cap \mathcal{N}^+(y_j)], \quad T_R^n(y_i y_j) = (y_i \vee y_j)h_4[\mathcal{N}^+(y_i) \cap \mathcal{N}^+(y_j)],$$
$$I_R^p(y_i y_j) = (y_i \wedge y_j)h_2[\mathcal{N}^+(y_i) \cap \mathcal{N}^+(y_j)], \quad I_R^n(y_i y_j) = (y_i \vee y_j)h_5[\mathcal{N}^+(y_i) \cap \mathcal{N}^+(y_j)],$$
$$F_R^p(y_i y_j) = (y_i \vee y_j)h_3[\mathcal{N}^+(y_i) \cap \mathcal{N}^+(y_j)], \quad F_R^n(y_i y_j) = (y_i \wedge y_j)h_6[\mathcal{N}^+(y_i) \cap \mathcal{N}^+(y_j)].$$

Step 9. If $y, r_1, r_2, r_3, \ldots, r_q$ are the applicants competing for designation d, then strength of competition $T(y, d) = (T^p(y, d), I^p(y, d), F^p(y, d), T^n(y, d), I^n(y, d), F^n(y, d))$ of each applicant y for the designation d is

$$T(y, d) = \frac{\left(\sum_{i=1}^{q} T_R^p(yr_i), \sum_{i=1}^{q} I_R^p(yr_i), \sum_{i=1}^{q} F_R^p(yr_i), \sum_{i=1}^{q} T_R^n(yr_i), \sum_{i=1}^{q} I_R^n(yr_i), \sum_{i=1}^{q} F_R^n(yr_i)\right)}{q}.$$

Step 10. Calculate $S(y, d)$, the strength of competition of each applicant y for designation d.

$$S(y, d) = T^p(y, d) - (I^p(y, d) + F^p(y, d)) + 1 + T^n(y, d) - (I^n(y, d) + F^n(y, d)).$$

9.4.2 Competition in Textile Market

Brands hold great meaning and value for both the buyer and the seller. Brands are centered on what the seller promises to deliver to its customers and the consumers' expectations for a particular product. A brand can be defined as a name, slogan, or anything that can be used to identify and differentiate a particular product or service. Strong brands such as Stylo shoes and Borjan shoes evoke sound emotional and physiological responses from customers.

Branding has several benefits for sellers. By having brands for their products, sellers get product recognition and product differentiation. It means that consumers would be able to accentuate the value they receive from one seller's product in comparison with other products of a similar nature and they would also be able to easily spot these products among other products. Branding aligns the seller's advertising and promotional activities. It allows the seller to form emotional relationships with their customers which is important because people base their purchasing decisions mainly on emotions and not logic.

Within the business, brands serve as guidance for employees since they clearly dictate what the company product is about. Branding is also of value to sellers in terms of profitability. A product with a well-known brand attached to it would bring more revenue to a seller than a product without a brand. For example, a cup of coffee without a brand could cost 70, however, a cup of coffee with the Kaymu brand attached to it could cost 999. For the seller, a good brand increases the perceived value of its product and allows it to have a better price and better sales.

For the buyer, a brand represents the satisfaction and value that he or she anticipates and desires from the process of buying and using a product or service. Brands often appeal to buyers emotionally, this in turn helps build relationships between buyers and sellers. Brands provide buyers with value which is why they are oftentimes prepared to pay more for branded products. Among buyers, brands are often a key factor behind purchasing decisions; people often gravitate toward brands that they are familiar with and that are trusted because there is oftentimes the reassurance of quality. In conclusion, brands exist as feelings and experiences that extend beyond the product or service which create relationships between the buyer and seller and have great value for both the parties. We take the following brands in order to discuss the competition between them.

1. At the top of the list, we would bring up the name of the famous Deepak Perwani. He has been linked with the fashion designing career since the year 1994 and working in offering women wear along with men clothing collections. He is considered the best with his designing skills as adorns the dresses with eastern and western images. This designer has even got his name listed in a record book as he made a kurta of 53m for a person. This designer has even got his name listed in a record book as he made a kurta of 53 m for a person.

2. On the second spot of expensive clothing brands in Pakistan, we would mention Maria B. She is one of the topmost wanted fashion designers of Pakistan. She has been infused into offering the collection line of bridal, casual, and western wear. She has done her graduation from the Pakistan School Of Fashion Design and then she organized her company in the year 1999.

3. Khaadi is one of the topmost famous clothing brands of Pakistan. Khaadi was started by Shamoon Sultan in the year 1998. This brand has been staying in the frontline for the purpose of offering high quality of dress designs in magnificent designing concepts. It offers clothing collections for both men and women along with kids wear.

4. On the fourth spot on our list, we would bring up the name of the designer brand Aamir Adnan. This brand is one of the topmost wanted brands of clothing for men. It has made its renowned name all through its valuable fashion for sherwani kurtas.

Consider the bipolar single-valued neutrosophic digraph as shown in Fig. 9.21 representing the competition between brands. Let {Deepak Perwani, Khaadi, Maria B, Aamir Adnan} be the set of brands and {Uniqueness, Passion, Consistency} be the qualities for the popularity of a particular brand. The positive degree of membership $T^p(x)$ of each brand represents the percentage of productivity of traditional clothes

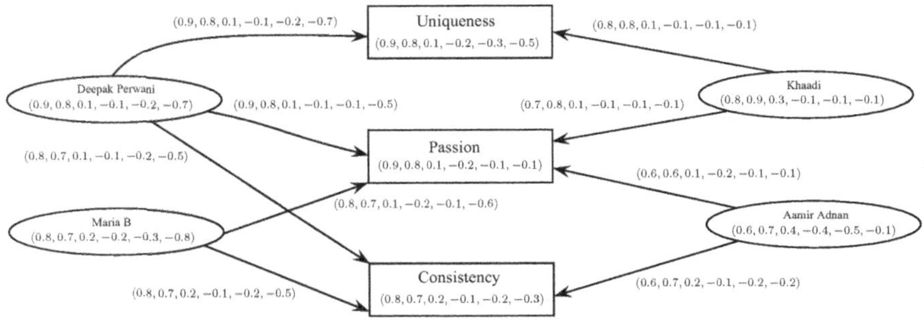

Fig. 9.21 Bipolar neutrosophic market model

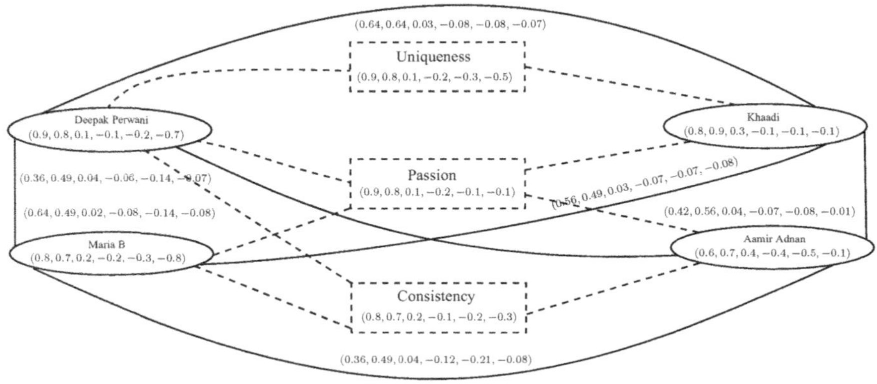

Fig. 9.22 Bipolar neutrosophic market competition graph

toward the satisfaction of customers, and $I^p(x)$ and $F^p(x)$ represent the indeterminacy and falsity in this percentage. The negative degree of membership $T^n(x)$ represents the percentage that the brand is not effective to satisfy the customer, and $I^n(x)$ and $F^n(x)$ represent the indeterminacy and falsity in this percentage. The positive degree of membership $T^p(x)$ of each directed edge between brands and the qualities represents the percentage of having that quality, and $I^p(x)$ and $F^p(x)$ represent the indeterminacy and falsity in this percentage. The negative degree of membership $T^n(x)$ of each directed edge between brands and qualities represents the percentage of having no qualities, and $I^n(x)$ and $F^n(x)$ represent the indeterminacy and falsity in this percentage. Thus, a bipolar single-valued neutrosophic competition graph can be used in order to find competitions between different brands.

The bipolar single-valued neutrosophic competition graph is shown in Fig. 9.22.

The solid lines indicate the strength of competition between two brands and the dashed lines indicate that the brands are competing for a particular quality. Deepak Perwani and Khaadi are both competing for the quality and uniqueness of their products. The strength of competition between them is (0.64, 0.64, 0.03, −0.08, −0.08,

Table 9.10 Strength of competition of brands for particular quality

(Brand, quality)	In competition	T(Brand, quality)	S(Brand, quality)
(Deepak Perwani, uniqueness)	Khaadi	(0.64, 0.64, 0.03, −0.08, −0.08, −0.07)	1.04
(Khaadi, uniqueness)	Deepak Perwani	(0.64, 0.64, 0.03, −0.08, −0.08, −0.07)	1.04
(Deepak Perwani, passion)	Khaadi, Maria B, Aamir Adnan	(0.54, 0.54, 0.03, −0.07, −0.12, −0.07)	1.09
(Khaadi, passion)	Aamir Adnan, Deepak Perwani, Maria B	(0.54, 0.56, 0.03, −0.07, −0.07, −0.05)	1
(Maria B, passion)	Khaadi, Deepak Perwani, Aamir Adnan	(0.52, 0.51, 0.03, −0.09, −0.14, −0.05)	1.08
(Aamir Adnan, passion)	Khaadi, Deepak Perwani, Maria B	(0.38, 0.51, 0.21, −0.08, −0.14, −0.05)	0.77
(Deepak Perwani, consistency)	Maria B, Aamir Adnan	(0.50, 0.49, 0.03, −0.07, −0.14, −0.07)	1.12
(Maria B, consistency)	Deepak Perwani, Aamir Adnan	(0.50, 0.49, 0.03, −0.10, −0.17, −0.08)	1.13
(Aamir Adnan, consistency)	Maria B, Deepak Perwani	(0.36, 0.49, 0.04, −0.09, −0.17, −0.07)	0.99

−0.07). The strength of competition among brands using Algorithm 9.4.1 is calculated in Table 9.10.

In Table 9.10, $T(y, d)$ represents the value of strength of competition of brand y for quality d with respect to level of satisfaction for the customer. From Table 9.10, Deepak Perwani and Khaadi have equal strength to compete with the others for quality and uniqueness. Deepak Perwani competes with the others for quality passion, while Maria B competes for quality consistency.

9.4.3 Competition in Sports

Sports are very important; every society has its own special kinds of sports. Sports and games have now come to stay in our civilization as an essential feature of human activity, and their objective is not merely fun, they also instill the spirit of discipline and teamwork. Sports like cricket, hockey, and football are popular because of the spirit of teamwork which they inspire. This is no doubt true. The discipline that is gained in playing sports is invaluable in later life. It makes for a life of cooperation and teamwork which could be used for building up a great society and a nation. The key components of sports are goals, rules, challenges, and interactions. Sports generally involve mental or physical stimulation, and often both. Many sports help develop practical skills, serve as a form of exercise, or otherwise perform an educational or psychological role, etc. Many sports require special equipment and dedicated playing fields, leading to the involvement of a community much larger than the group of players. A city or town may set aside such resources for the organization of sports leagues, like tabletop games, board games, etc. All these types of sports are called local sports. These sports can be extended to provisional-level sports. After provisional-level sports, there are national-level sports. Every nation has different sports, such as baseball which is known as the national game of the United States, cricket in England, and hockey in Pakistan. After national level, there are international level of sports. International sports are games in which the participants represent different countries. The most well-known international sports event is the Olympic Games, FIFA World Cup, and the Paralympic Games.

Consider the set consisting of three countries $\{C_1, C_2, C_3\}$ and also consider the set of players {(Abigail, 0.9, 0.8, 0.5, −0.6, −0.5, −0.2), (Alex, 0.6, 0.3, 0.4, −0.2, −0.4, −0.4), (Amelia, 0.8, 0.7, 0.2, −0.7, −0.8, −0.5), (Agatha, 0.9, 0.8, 0.5, −0.6, −0.5, −0.2), (Angela, 0.9, 0.8, 0.5, −0.6, −0.5, −0.2), (Belinda, 0.9, 0.8, 0.5, −0.6, −0.5, −0.2), (Ann, 0.5, 0.3, 0.5, −0.5, −0.3, −0.2), (Arlene, 0.8, 0.8, 0.9, −0.8, −0.9, −0.8), (Bella, 0.6, 0.4, 0.9, −0.6, −0.7, −0.5), (Anne, 0.9, 0.7, 0.8, −0.8, −0.8, −0.8), (April, 0.5, 0.3, 0.5, −0.5, −0.3, −0.2), (Abbey, 0.5, 0.3, 0.5, −0.5, −0.3, −0.2)}, who are taking part in their local-, provisional-, national-, and international-level games, as shown in Fig. 9.23. The positive degree of membership $T^p(x)$ of each player represents the percentage of hard work to achieve the success in a particular game, and $I^p(x)$ and $F^p(x)$ represent the indeterminacy and falsity in this percentage. The negative degree of membership $T^n(x)$ represents the percentage that the player faces failure in the achievement of success in a particular game, and $I^n(x)$ and $F^n(x)$ represent the indeterminacy and falsity in this percentage. The positive degree of membership $T^p(x)$ of each directed edge between a player and local-, provisional-, national-, and international-level games represents the percentage of having stamina for that level of sports in an international game, and $I^p(x)$ and $F^p(x)$ represent the indeterminacy and falsity in this percentage. The negative degree of membership $T^n(x)$ of each directed edge between a player and local-, provisional-, national-, and international-level games represents the percentage of having no stamina for that level of sports in an international game, and $I^n(x)$ and $F^n(x)$ represent the indeterminacy and falsity in this percentage.

The 4-step bipolar single-valued neutrosophic competition graph can be used to find the best results. The 4-step bipolar single-valued neutrosophic out-neighborhoods are calculated in Table 9.11.

Therefore, $\mathcal{N}_4^+(Abigail) \cap \mathcal{N}_4^+(Alex) = \{(International\ games, 0.2, 0.2, 0.6, -0.1, -0.2, -0.7)\}$, $\mathcal{N}_4^+(Abigail) \cap \mathcal{N}_4^+(Amelia) = \{(International\ games, 0.2, 0.2, 0.6, -0.1, -0.2, -0.8)\}$, and $\mathcal{N}_4^+(Alex) \cap \mathcal{N}_4^+(Amelia) = \{(International\ games, 0.4, 0.2, 0.6, -0.1, -0.2, -0.8)\}$. Further, $h(\mathcal{N}_4^+(Abigail) \cap \mathcal{N}_4^+(Alex)) = (0.2, 0.2, 0.6, 0.2, 0.2, 0.6)$, $h(\mathcal{N}_4^+(Abigail) \cap \mathcal{N}_4^+(Amelia)) = (0.2, 0.2, 0.6, 0.2, 0.2, 0.6)$, and $h(\mathcal{N}_4^+(Amelia) \cap \mathcal{N}_4^+(Alex)) = (0.4, 0.2, 0.6, 0.4, 0.2, 0.6)$. The 4-step bipolar single-valued neutrosophic competition graph is shown in Fig. 9.24.

The strength to compete with the others players with respect to hard work in order to achieve success is calculated in Table 9.12. In Table 9.12, $T(x, y)$ represents the value of strength of competition between players x and y with respect to hard work to

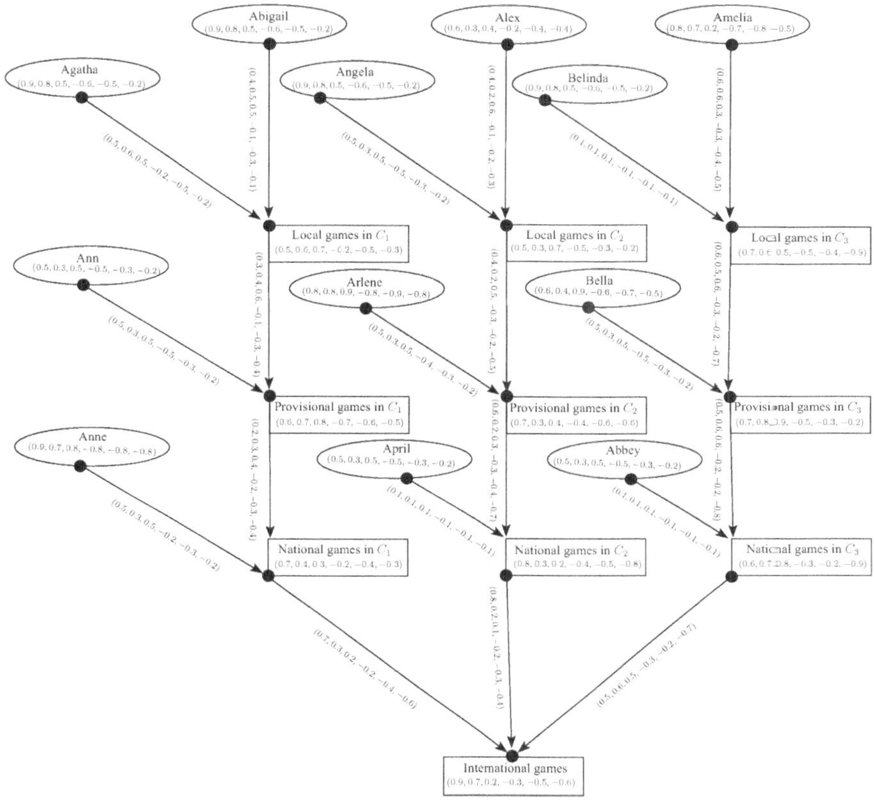

Fig. 9.23 Bipolar neutrosophic digraph of players

Table 9.11 4-step bipolar single-valued neutrosophic out-neighborhoods

$x \in X$	$\mathcal{N}_4^+(x)$
Abigail	{(International games, 0.2, 0.2, 0.6, −0.1, −0.3, −0.4)}
Alex	{(International games, 0.4, 0.2, 0.6, −0.1, −0.2, −0.7)}
Amelia	{(International games, 0.5, 0.5, 0.6, −0.2, −0.2, −0.8)}

Table 9.12 Strength of competition of players for international games

(x, y)	$T(xy)$	$S(xy)$
(Abigail, Alex)	(0.12, 0.06, 0.30, −0.04, −0.08, −0.24)	1.04
(Abigail, Amelia)	(0.16, 0.14, 0.30, −0.12, −0.10, −0.30)	1
(Alex, Amelia)	(0.24, 0.06, 0.24, −0.08, −0.08, −0.30)	1.24

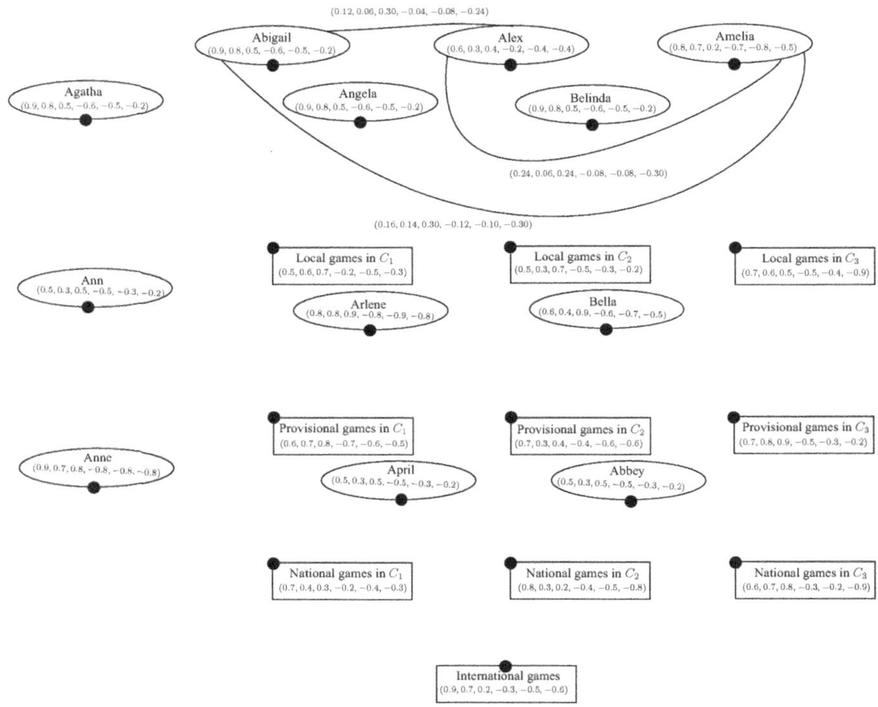

Fig. 9.24 4-step bipolar single-valued neutrosophic competition graph

achieve success in a particular game. From Table 9.12, it is clear that the strength of competition between Alex and Amelia to achieve success in a particular game at the international level is 1.24, while strength of competition between Abigail and Amelia is 1, and strength of competition between Abigail and Alex is 1.04. It is also clear from Table 9.12 that Alex and Amelia are the strongest contestants, as the strength of competition between them has the largest value than that of the other contestants. The method to calculate the net strength of competition among applicants is shown in Algorithm 9.4.2.

Algorithm 9.4.2 Strength of competition of players for international games

Step 1. Input the bipolar single-valued neutrosophic A of q applicants $y_1, y_2, \ldots, y_q$.

Step 2. If for any two distinct vertices y_i and y_j, $A(y_i y_j) \neq (0, 0, 1, 0, 0, -1)$, then

$$(y_j, T^p(y_i y_j), I^p(y_i y_j), F^p(y_i y_j), T^n(y_i y_j), I^n(y_i y_j), F^n(y_i y_j)) \in \mathcal{N}^+(y_i).$$

Step 3. Repeat Step 2 for all vertices y_i and y_j to calculate bipolar single-valued neutrosophic-out-neighborhoods $\mathcal{N}^+(y_i)$.

Step 4. Calculate $\mathcal{N}^+(y_i) \cap \mathcal{N}^+(y_j)$ for each pair of distinct vertices y_i and y_j.
Step 5. Calculate $h[\mathcal{N}^+(y_i) \cap \mathcal{N}^+(y_j)]$ for each pair of distinct vertices y_i and y_j.
Step 6. If $\mathcal{N}^+(y_i) \cap \mathcal{N}^+(y_j) \neq \emptyset$, then draw an edge $y_i y_j$.
Step 7. Repeat Step 6 for all pairs of distinct vertices.
Step 8. Assign membership values to each edge $y_i y_j$ using the conditions

$$T_R^p(y_i y_j) = (y_i \wedge y_j)h_1[\mathcal{N}^+(y_i) \cap \mathcal{N}^+(y_j)] \quad T_R^n(y_i y_j) = (y_i \vee y_j)h_4[\mathcal{N}^+(y_i) \cap \mathcal{N}^+(y_j)]$$
$$I_R^p(y_i y_j) = (y_i \wedge y_j)h_2[\mathcal{N}^+(y_i) \cap \mathcal{N}^+(y_j)] \quad I_R^n(y_i y_j) = (y_i \vee y_j)h_5[\mathcal{N}^+(y_i) \cap \mathcal{N}^+(y_j)]$$
$$F_R^p(y_i y_j) = (y_i \vee y_j)h_3[\mathcal{N}^+(y_i) \cap \mathcal{N}^+(y_j)] \quad F_R^n(y_i y_j) = (y_i \wedge y_j)h_6[\mathcal{N}^+(y_i) \cap \mathcal{N}^+(y_j)].$$

Step 9. Calculate $S(x, y)$, the strength of competition between players x and y.

$$S(xy) = T_R^p(x, y) - (I_R^p(x, y) + F_R^p(x, y)) + 1 + T_R^n(x, y) - (I_R^n(x, y) + F_R^n(x, y)).$$

Step 11. Maximum value of $S(x, y)$ gives that x and y are the strongest players than the others.

9.5 Conclusions

The fuzzy set theory is very successful in handling uncertainties arising from vagueness or partial belongingness of elements but it cannot model all sorts of uncertainties prevailing in various physical problems. There are many situations containing six components of uncertainty, that is, existence/non-existence/neutral and their counter properties. A bipolar neutrosophic set is a useful notion in this sense which is obtained by combining the theory of neutrosophic sets with bipolar fuzzy information. In this chapter, we have presented the notion of bipolar neutrosophic graphs and bipolar neutrosophic digraphs by applying the technique of bipolar neutrosophic sets to graphs and digraphs. We have studied bipolar neutrosophic competition graphs and presented certain characterizations of bipolar neutrosophic out-neighborhoods, bipolar neutrosophic in-neighborhoods, bipolar neutrosophic open neighborhood graphs, bipolar neutrosophic closed neighborhood graphs, bipolar neutrosophic p-competition graphs, m-step bipolar neutrosophic competition graphs, and strong preys and strong independent predator–prey relations. We have described various methods for the construction of bipolar neutrosophic competition graphs of certain products of bipolar neutrosophic digraphs. We have elaborated on the importance of bipolar neutrosophic graphs with various real-world applications.

Exercises 9

1. What is the difference between a neutrosophic set and a single-valued neutrosophic set?
2. Derive a method for the construction of a bipolar single-valued neutrosophic competition graph $\mathcal{C}(\vec{G}_1 \times \vec{G}_2)$ of the direct product of bipolar single-valued neutrosophic digraphs $\vec{G}_1$ and $\vec{G}_2$ using $\mathcal{C}(\vec{G}_1)$ and $\mathcal{C}(\vec{G}_2)$.
3. If all the edges of a bipolar single-valued neutrosophic digraph are strong, then prove using a contradiction example that all the edges of the corresponding bipolar single-valued neutrosophic competition graph may not be strong.
4. What do you mean by $(1, 1, 0, -1, -1, 0)$ and $(0, 0, 1, 0, 0, -1)$ in a bipolar neutrosophic environment?
5. Let A, C and D be three bipolar single-valued neutrosophic sets, then classify whether the following statements are true or false.

   (a) $(A \cup B)^c = A^c \cap B^c$,
   (b) $(A \cap B)^c = A^c \cup B^c$,
   (c) $(A \cup B) \cup C = A \cup (B \cup C)$,
   (d) $(A^c)^c = A$,
   (e) $(A \cup B) \cap C = (A \cap C) \cup (B \cap C)$,
   (f) $(A \cap B) \cup C = (A \cup C) \cap (B \cup C)$.

References

1. Akram, M.: Certain bipolar neutrosophic competition graphs. J. Indones. Math. Soc. **24**(1), 1–25 (2017)
2. Akram, M.: Single-valued neutrosophic planar graphs. Int. J. Algebra Stat. **2**, 157–167 (2016)
3. Akram, M.: Single-Valued Neutrosophic Graphs. Infosys Science Foundation Series in Mathematical Sciences. Springer, Singapore (2018)
4. Akram, M., Nasir, M.: Interval-valued neutrosophic competition graphs. Ann. Fuzzy Math. Inform. **14**(1), 99–120 (2017)
5. Akram, M., Nasir, M., Shum, K.P.: Novel applications of bipolar single-valued neutrosophic competition graphs. Appl. Math.-A J. Chin. Univ. **33**(4), 436–467 (2018)
6. Akram, M., Sarwar, M.: Novel multiple criteria decision making methods based on bipolar neutrosophic sets and bipolar neutrosophic graphs. Ital. J. Pure Appl. Math. **38**, 368–389 (2017)
7. Akram, M., Shahzadi, G.: Operations on single-valued neutrosophic graphs. J. Uncertain Syst. **11**(1), 1–26 (2017)
8. Akram, M., Shum, K.P.: Bipolar single-valued neutrosophic planar graphs. J. Math. Res. Appl. **36**(6), 631–648 (2017)
9. Akram, M., Siddique, S.: Neutrosophic competition graphs with applications. J. Intell. Fuzzy Syst. **33**(2), 921–935 (2017)
10. Akram, M., Siddique, S., Shum, K.P.: Certain properties of bipolar neutrosophic graphs. Southeast Asian Bull. Math. **42**(4), 463–490 (2018)
11. Atanassov, K.: Intuitionistic fuzzy sets. Fuzzy Sets Syst. **20**(1), 87–96 (1986)
12. Broumi, S., Bakali, A., Talea, M., Smarandache, F., ALi, M.: Shortest path problem under bipolar neutrosophic setting. Appl. Mech. Mater. **859**, 59–66 (2017)

13. Broumi, S., Talea, M., Bakali, A., Smarandache, F.: Single valued neutrosophic graphs. J. New Theory **10**, 86–101 (2016)
14. Deli, I., Ali, M., Smarandache, F.: Bipolar neutrosophic sets and their application based on multi-criteria decision making problems. In: IEEE International Conference on Advanced Mechatronic Systems, pp. 249–254 (2015)
15. Smarandache, F.: A unifying field in logics: neutrosophic logic. Philosophy. American Research Press 1–141 (1999)
16. Smarandache, F.: Neutrosophic sets generalization of the intuitionistic fuzzy set. J. Def. Resour. Manag. **1**(1), 107–116 (2010)
17. Smarandache, F.: Types of neutrosophic graphs and neutrosophic algebraic structures together with their applications in technology. Seminar, Universitatea Transilvania din Brasov, Facultatea de Design de Produs si Mediu, Brasov, Romania (2015)
18. Wang, H., Smarandache, F., Zhang, Y., Sunderraman, R.: Single valued neutrosophic sets. Infinite Study (2010)
19. Zadeh, L.A.: Fuzzy sets. Inf. Control **8**(3), 338–353 (1965)
20. Zhang, W.-R.: Bipolar fuzzy sets and relations: a computational framework for cognitive modeling and multiagent decision analysis. In: Proceedings of IEEE Conference, pp. 305–309 (1994)
21. Zhang, W.-R.: (YinYang) Bipolar fuzzy sets. In: IEEE International Conference on Fuzzy Systems, pp. 835–840 (1998)
22. Zhang, W.-R., Wang, P., Peace, K., Zhan, J., Zhang, Y.: On truth, uncertainty, equilibrium, and harmony–a taxonomy for YinYang scientific computing. New Math. Nat. Comput. **4**(2), 207–229 (2008)

Chapter 10
Bipolar Neutrosophic Graph Structures

In this chapter, we apply the powerful technique of bipolar neutrosophic set to graph structures and present a framework of bipolar neutrosophic graph structures with certain operations. We discuss the notions of B_k-edges, strong and complete bipolar neutrosophic graph structures, and bipolar neutrosophic subgraph structures. Using φ-complement, we describe certain relations and isomorphism properties of self-complementary, totally self-complementary, and totally strong self-complementary bipolar neutrosophic graph structures. We study the importance of bipolar neutrosophic graph structures with a number of real-world applications in international relations, psychology, and global terrorism. This chapter is basically due to [4, 14].

10.1 Introduction

A graph structure is a generalization of a graph introduced by Sampathkumar [11] in 2006 and is widely useful in the study of graphs, signed graphs, semi-graphs, edge-colored graphs, and edge-labeled graphs. Graph structures are very useful in various domains of computer science and computational intelligence. Denish and Ramakrishnan [10] introduced the concept of fuzzy graph structure, fuzzy labeling matrices, fuzzy index matrices, incidence algebras, and their fuzzy analogs. The notions of maximal products of fuzzy graph structures and regular fuzzy graph structures are given in [12]. In some applications such as expert system, belief system, and information fusion, we should consider not only the truth membership supported by the evidence but also the falsity membership against the evidence. That is beyond the scope of fuzzy sets and interval-valued fuzzy sets. In 1983, Atanassov [8] introduced the notion of intuitionistic fuzzy set as a generalization of a fuzzy set. In an intuitionistic fuzzy set A, both truth membership value (belongingness) $T_A(x)$ and falsity membership value (non-belongingness) $F_A(x)$ are attached with each element x with the restriction that the sum of these two membership values

M. Akram et al., *Graphs for the Analysis of Bipolar Fuzzy Information*, Studies in Fuzziness and Soft Computing 401,
https://doi.org/10.1007/978-981-15-8756-6_10

is less or equal to 1. In real-world problems, there are many situations containing tricomponents of uncertainty, e.g., games (winning, defeating, or tie scores), voting (pro, contra, null/black votes), positive/negative/zero numbers, yes/no/NA, decision-making and control theory (making a decision, not making, or hesitating), and accepted/rejected/pending. Smarandache [13], in 1995, proposed the term "neutrosophic" means knowledge of neutral thought and neutral represents the main distinction between a fuzzy/intuitionistic fuzzy set and a neutrosophic set. In contrast to the intuitionistic fuzzy set and interval-valued intuitionistic fuzzy set, the indeterminacy is characterized explicitly in a neutrosophic set which is independent of truth and falsity membership values. Neutrosophic sets are indeed more general than intuitionistic fuzzy sets as there are no constraints between truth, indeterminacy, and falsity membership values. All these degrees can individually vary within [0, 1]. The concept of bipolar neutrosophic sets was introduced in [9] and bipolar single-valued neutrosophic graph in [3]. Akram and Akmal [1, 2] initiated the concept of bipolar fuzzy graph structures and discussed their operations. The discussion of this chapter is based on bipolar single-valued neutrosophic graph structures which are from Akram and Sitara's work [4, 14]. For further terminologies and studies, readers are referred to [5–7].

10.2 Operations on Bipolar Neutrosophic Graph Structures

A **graph structure** $\check{G}_s = (X, X_1, X_2, \ldots, X_m)$ consists of a non-empty set X together with relations $X_1, X_2, \ldots, X_m$ on X which are mutually disjoint such that each X_k, $1 \le k \le m$ is symmetric and irreflexive. A graph structure can be represented in the plane just like a graph, where each edge is labeled as X_k, $1 \le k \le m$.

Definition 10.1 A **bipolar single-valued neutrosophic graph structure** of a graph structure $\check{G}_s = (X, X_1, X_2, \ldots, X_m)$ is denoted by $\check{G}_{bn} = (B, B_1, B_2, \ldots, B_m)$, where

$$B =< b, T^p(b), I^p(b), F^p(b), T^n(b), I^n(b), F^n(b) >,$$
$$B_k =< (bd, T_k^p(bd), I_k^p(bd), F_k^p(bd), T_k^n(bd), I_k^n(bd), F_k^n(bd) >$$

are bipolar single-valued neutrosophic sets on X and X_k, respectively, such that

$$T_k^p(bd) \le \min\{T^p(b), T^p(d)\},\ I_k^p(bd) \le \min\{I^p(b), I^p(d)\},\ F_k^p(bd) \le \max\{F^p(b), F^p(d)\},$$
$$T_k^n(bd) \ge \max\{T^n(b), T^n(d)\},\ I_k^n(bd) \ge \max\{I^n(b), I^n(d)\},\ F_k^n(bd) \ge \min\{F^n(b), F^n(d)\},$$

for all $b, d \in X$. Note that $0 \le T_k^p(bd) + I_k^p(bd) + F_k^p(bd) \le 3$, $-3 \le T_k^n(bd) + I_k^n(bd) + F_k^n(bd) \le 0$ for all $bd \in X_k$.

Example 10.1 Consider a graph structure $\check{G}_s = (X, X_1, X_2, X_3)$ such that $X = \{b_1, b_2, b_3, b_4, b_5, b_6, b_7, b_8\}$ and $X_1 = \{b_1b_2, b_2b_7, b_4b_8, b_6b_8, b_5b_6, b_3b_4\}$, $X_2 =$

Table 10.1 Bipolar neutrosophic set B

B	b_1	b_2	b_3	b_4	b_5	b_6	b_7	b_8
T^p	0.4	0.3	0.3	0.4	0.2	0.3	0.4	0.2
I^p	0.3	0.2	0.3	0.3	0.1	0.3	0.4	0.3
F^p	0.4	0.3	0.2	0.4	0.2	0.5	0.2	0.3
T^n	−0.4	−0.3	−0.3	−0.4	−0.2	−0.3	−0.4	−0.2
I^n	−0.3	−0.2	−0.3	−0.3	−0.1	−0.3	−0.4	−0.3
F^n	−0.4	−0.3	−0.2	−0.4	−0.2	−0.5	−0.2	−0.3

Table 10.2 Bipolar neutrosophic sets B_1, B_2, and B_3

B_1	b_1b_2	b_2b_7	b_4b_8	b_6b_8	b_5b_6	b_3b_4
T^p	0.3	0.3	0.2	0.2	0.2	0.3
I^p	0.2	0.2	0.3	0.3	0.1	0.3
F^p	0.4	0.3	0.4	0.5	0.5	0.4
T^n	−0.3	−0.3	−0.2	−0.2	−0.2	−0.3
I^n	−0.2	−0.2	−0.3	−0.3	−0.1	−0.3
F^n	−0.4	−0.3	−0.4	−0.5	−0.5	−0.4
B_2	b_1b_5	b_5b_7	b_3b_6	b_7b_8		
T^p	0.2	0.2	0.3	0.2		
I^p	0.1	0.1	0.3	0.3		
F^p	0.4	0.2	0.5	0.3		
T^n	−0.2	−0.2	−0.3	−0.2		
I^n	−0.1	−0.1	−0.3	−0.3		
F^n	−0.4	−0.2	−0.5	−0.3		
B_3	b_1b_3	b_2b_4				
T^p	0.3	0.3				
I^p	0.3	0.2				
F^p	0.4	0.4				
T^n	−0.3	−0.3				
I^n	−0.3	−0.2				
F^n	−0.4	−0.4				

$\{b_1b_5, b_5b_7, b_3b_6, b_7b_8\}$, $X_3 = \{b_1b_3, b_2b_4\}$. Let B be a bipolar single-valued neutrosophic set on X given in Table 10.1 and B_1, B_2, B_3 be bipolar single-valued neutrosophic sets on X_1, X_2, and X_3, respectively, given in Table 10.2.
Routine calculations show that $\check{G}_{bn} = (B, B_1, B_2, B_3)$ is a bipolar single-valued neutrosophic graph structure, as shown in Fig. 10.1.

Example 10.2 Consider a graph structure $\check{G}_s = (X, X_1, X_2)$ such that $X = \{b_1, b_2, b_3, b_4\}$, $X_1 = \{b_1b_3, b_1b_2, b_3b_4\}$, $X_2 = \{b_1b_4, b_2b_3\}$. By defining bipolar single-

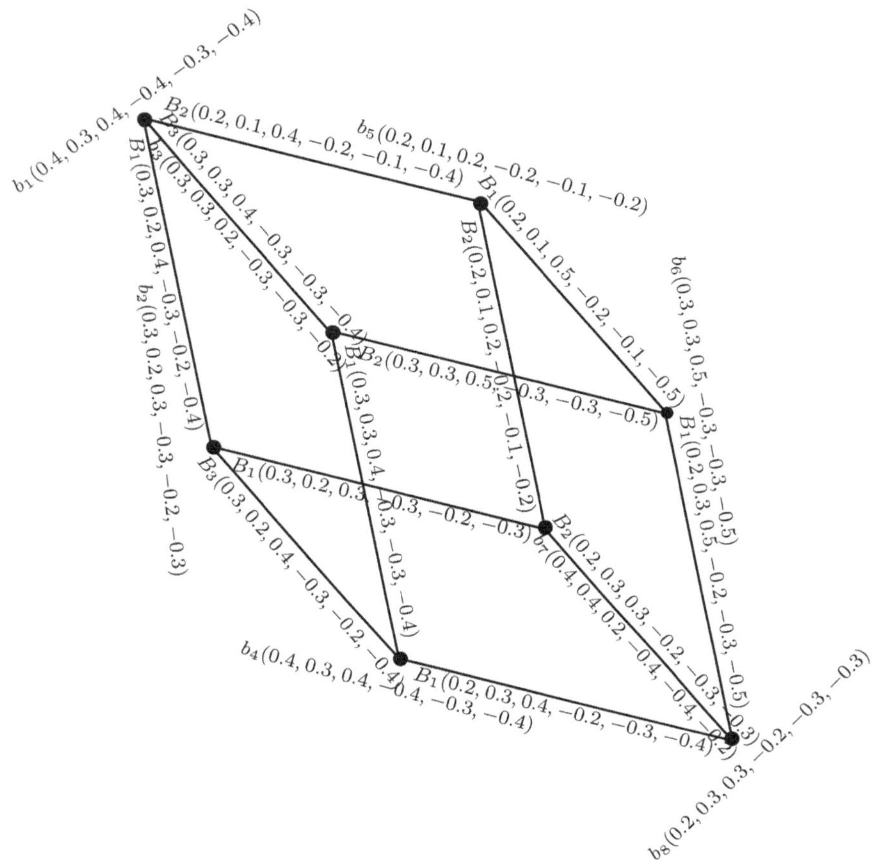

Fig. 10.1 Bipolar neutrosophic graph structure no. 1

valued neutrosophic sets B, B_1 and B_2 on X, X_1, and X_2, respectively, a bipolar single-valued neutrosophic graph structure can be drawn as shown in Fig. 10.2.

Definition 10.2 Let $\check{G}_{bn} = (B, B_1, B_2, \ldots, B_m)$ be a bipolar single-valued neutrosophic graph structure of graph structure $\check{G}_s$. If $\check{H}_{bn} = (B', B'_1, B'_2, \ldots, B'_m)$ is a bipolar single-valued neutrosophic graph structure of $\check{G}_s$ such that

$$T'^{p}(b) \le T^{p}(k),\ I'^{p}(b) \le I^{p}(b),\ F'^{p}(b) \ge F^{p}(b),\quad T'^{n}(b) \ge T^{p}(k),\ I'^{n}(b) \ge I^{p}(b),\ F'^{n}(b) \le F^{n}(b),$$

$$T_k'^{p}(bd) \le T_k^{p}(bd),\quad I_k'^{p}(bd) \le I_k^{p}(bd),\quad F_k'^{p}(bd) \ge F_k^{p}(bd),$$

$$T_k'^{n}(bd) \ge T_k^{n}(bd),\quad I_k'^{n}(bd) \ge I_k^{n}(bd),\quad F_k'^{n}(bd) \le F_k^{n}(bd),\quad b \in X \text{ and } bd \in X_k,\ k = 1, 2, \ldots, m.$$

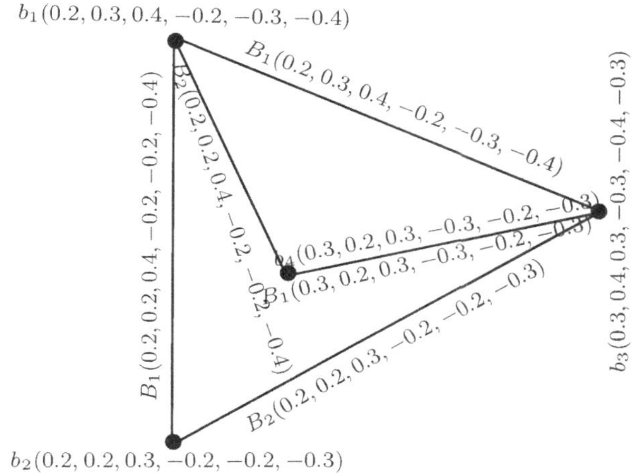

Fig. 10.2 Bipolar neutrosophic graph structure no. 2

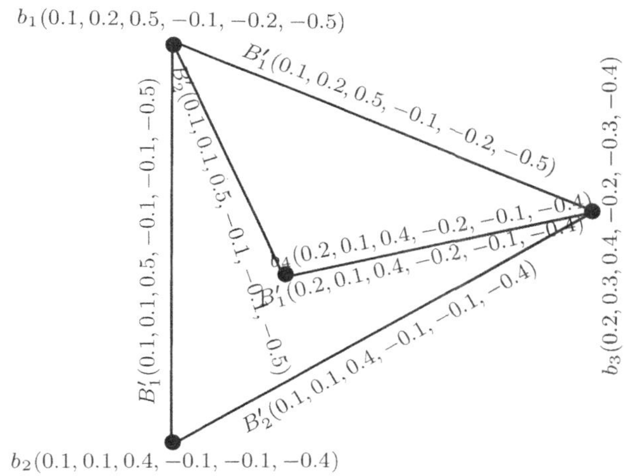

Fig. 10.3 Bipolar neutrosophic subgraph structure

Then $\check{H}_{bn}$ is called a **bipolar single-valued neutrosophic subgraph structure** of the bipolar single-valued neutrosophic graph structure $\check{G}_{bn}$ denoted by $\check{H}_{bn} \subseteq \check{G}_{bn}$.

Example 10.3 Consider a bipolar single-valued neutrosophic graph structure $\check{H}_{bn} = (B', B'_1, B'_2)$ of graph structure $\check{G}_s = (X, X_1, X_2)$ as shown in Fig. 10.3. Routine calculations indicate that $\check{H}_{bn}$ is a bipolar single-valued neutrosophic subgraph structure of Fig. 10.2.

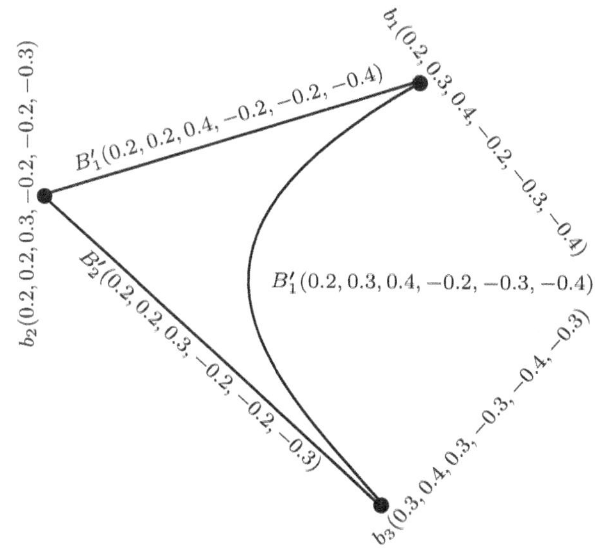

Fig. 10.4 Bipolar neutrosophic induced subgraph structure

Definition 10.3 A bipolar single-valued neutrosophic subgraph structure $\check{H}_{bn} = (B', B'_1, B'_2, \ldots, B'_m)$ of $\check{G}_{bn} = (B, B_1, B_2, \ldots, B_m)$ is called a **bipolar single-valued neutrosophic induced subgraph structure** of a bipolar single-valued neutrosophic graph structure $\check{G}_{bn}$ by $Q \subseteq X$ if

$$T'^p(b) = T^p(b), I'^p(b) = I^p(b), F'^p(b) = F^p(b), T'^n(b) = T^n(b), I'^n(b) = I^n(b), F'^n(b) = F^n(b),$$
$$T_k'^p(bd) = T_k^p(bd), I_k'^p(bd) = I_k^p(bd), F_k'^p(bd) = F_k^p(bd), T_k'^n(bd) = T_k^n(bd),$$
$$I_k'^n(bd) = I_k^n(bd), F_k'^n(bd) = F_k^n(bd),$$

for each $k = 1, 2, \ldots, m$ and for all $b, d \in Q$.

Example 10.4 A bipolar single-valued neutrosophic graph structure shown in Fig. 10.4 is a bipolar single-valued neutrosophic induced subgraph structure of a bipolar single-valued neutrosophic graph structure given in Fig. 10.2.

Definition 10.4 A bipolar single-valued neutrosophic subgraph structure $\check{H}_{bn} = (B', B'_1, B'_2, \ldots, B'_m)$ of $\check{G}_{bn} = (B, B_1, B_2, \ldots, B_m)$ is called **bipolar single-valued neutrosophic spanning subgraph structure** of $\check{G}_{bn}$ if $B' = B$ and

$$T_k'^p(bd) \le T_k^p(bd), \; I_k'^p(bd) \le I_k^p(bd), \; F_k'^p(bd) \ge F_k^p(bd),$$
$$T_k'^n(bd) \ge T_k^n(bd), \; I_k'^n(bd) \ge I_k^n(bd), \; F_k'^n(bd) \le F_k^n(bd), \quad \text{for each } k = 1, 2, \ldots, m.$$

Example 10.5 A bipolar single-valued neutrosophic graph structure given in Fig. 10.5 is a bipolar single-valued neutrosophic spanning subgraph structure of Fig. 10.2.

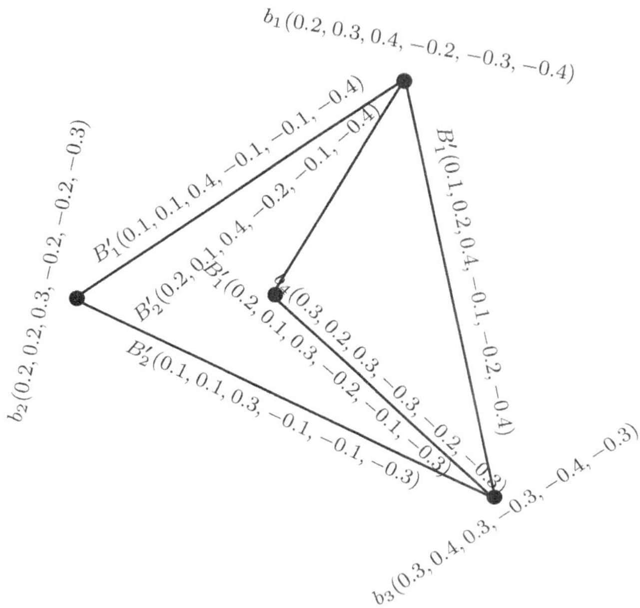

Fig. 10.5 Bipolar neutrosophic spanning subgraph structure

Definition 10.5 Let $\check{G}_{bn} = (B, B_1, B_2, \ldots, B_m)$ be a bipolar single-valued neutrosophic graph structure, then $bd \in X_k$ is called a **bipolar single-valued neutrosophic B_k-edge** or shortly **B_k-edge** if $B_k(bd) \neq (0, 0, 1, 0, 0, -1)$. Consequently, the **support** of B_k is defined as $supp(B_k) = \{bd \in X_k | B_k(bd) \neq (0, 0, 1, 0, 0, -1)\}$, for each $k = 1, 2, \ldots, m$.

Definition 10.6 A **bipolar single-valued neutrosophic B_k-path** in a bipolar single-valued neutrosophic graph structure $\check{G}_{bn} = (B, B_1, B_2, \ldots, B_m)$ is a sequence of distinct vertices $b_1, b_2, \ldots, b_m$ (except $b_m = b_1$) in X such that $b_{k-1}b_k$ is a bipolar single-valued neutrosophic B_k-edge for all $k = 2, 3, \ldots, m$.

Definition 10.7 A bipolar single-valued neutrosophic graph structure $\check{G}_{bn} = (B, B_1, B_2, \ldots, B_m)$ is **B_k-strong**, for any $k \in \{1, 2, \ldots, m\}$, if

$$T_k^p(bd) = \min\{T^p(b), T^p(d)\},\ I_k^p(bd) = \min\{I^p(b), I^p(d)\},\ F_k^p(bd) = \max\{F^p(b), F^p(d)\},$$
$$T_k^n(bd) = \max\{T^n(b), T^n(d)\},\ I_k^n(bd) = \max\{I^n(b), I^n(d)\},\ F_k^n(bd) = \min\{F^n(b), F^n(d)\},$$

for all $bd \in X_k$. If $\check{G}_{bn}$ is B_k-strong for all $k \in \{1, 2, \ldots, m\}$, then $\check{G}_{bn}$ is called a **strong bipolar single-valued neutrosophic graph structure**.

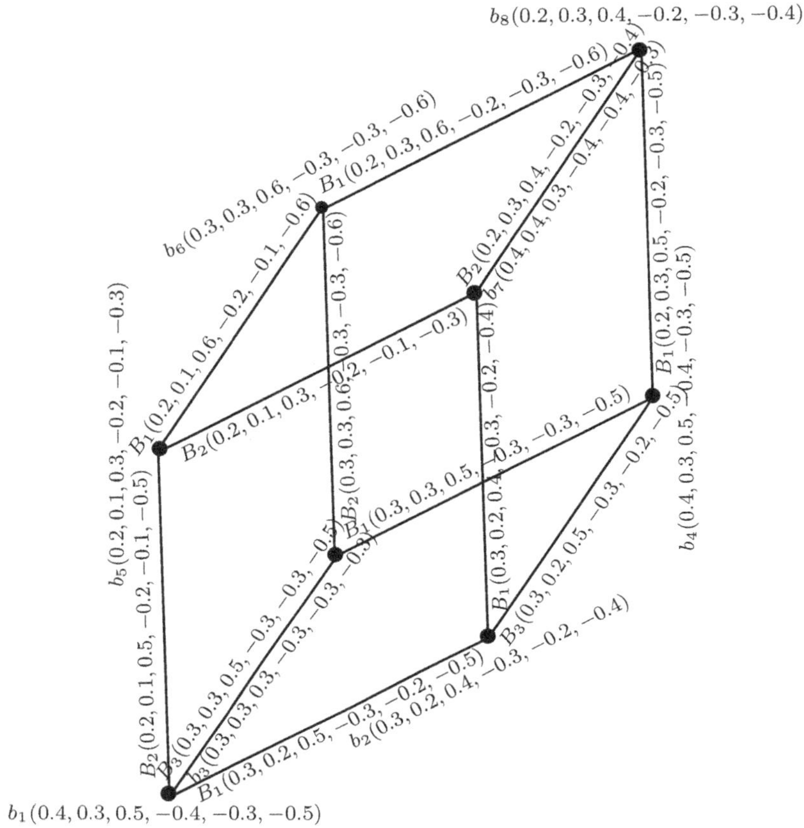

Fig. 10.6 Strong bipolar single-valued neutrosophic graph structure

Example 10.6 Consider a bipolar single-valued neutrosophic graph structure $\check{G}_{bn} = (B, B_1, B_2, B_3)$ as shown in Fig. 10.6. Then $\check{G}_{bn}$ is a strong bipolar single-valued neutrosophic graph structure since it is B_k-strong for all $k \in 1, 2, 3$.

Definition 10.8 A bipolar single-valued neutrosophic graph structure $\check{G}_{bn} = (B, B_1, B_2, \ldots, B_m)$ is called a **complete** bipolar single-valued neutrosophic graph structure if

1. $\check{G}_{bn}$ is a strong bipolar single-valued neutrosophic graph structure,
2. $supp(B_k) \neq \emptyset$, for all $k = 1, 2, \ldots, m$,
3. For all $b, d \in X$, bd is a $B_k - edge$, for some k.

Example 10.7 Let $\check{G}_{bn} = (B, B_1, B_2)$ be a bipolar single-valued neutrosophic graph structure of graph structure $\check{G} = (X, X_1, X_2)$ such that $X = \{b_1, b_2, b_3, b_4\}$,

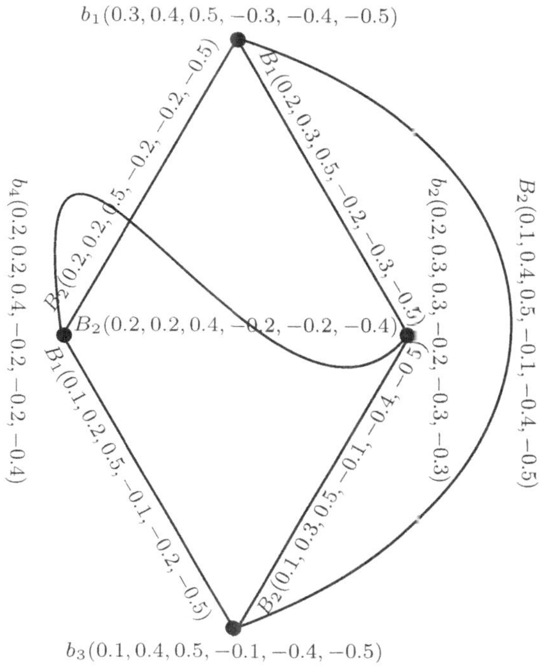

Fig. 10.7 Complete bipolar neutrosophic graph structure

$X_1 = \{b_1b_2, b_3b_4\}$, $X_2 = \{b_1b_3, b_2b_3, b_1b_4, b_2b_4\}$ as shown in Fig. 10.7. Through direct calculations, it is easy to check that $\check{G}_{bn}$ is a strong bipolar single-valued neutrosophic graph structure. Moreover, $supp(B_1) \neq \emptyset$, $supp(B_2) \neq \emptyset$, and each pair b_kb_l of vertices in X is either a B_1-edge or B_2-edge. Hence, $\check{G}_{bn}$ is a complete bipolar single-valued neutrosophic graph structure, that is, $B_1 - B_2-$complete bipolar single-valued neutrosophic graph structure.

Definition 10.9 Let $\check{G}_{b1} = (B_1, B_{11}, B_{12}, \ldots, B_{1m})$ and $\check{G}_{b2} = (B_2, B_{21}, B_{22}, \ldots, B_{2m})$ be two bipolar single-valued neutrosophic graph structures. The **lexicographic product** of $\check{G}_{b1}$ and $\check{G}_{b2}$ is denoted by $\check{G}_{b1} \bullet \check{G}_{b2} = (B_1 \bullet B_2, B_{11} \bullet B_{21}, B_{12} \bullet B_{22}, \ldots, B_{1m} \bullet B_{2m})$ and defined as

1. $$\begin{cases} T^p_{(B_1\bullet B_2)}(bd) = (T^p_{B_1} \bullet T^p_{B_2})(bd) = T^p_{B_1}(b) \wedge T^p_{B_2}(d) \\ I^p_{(B_1\bullet B_2)}(bd) = (I^p_{B_1} \bullet I^p_{B_2})(bd) = I^p_{B_1}(b) \wedge I^p_{B_2}(d) \\ F^p_{(B_1\bullet B_2)}(bd) = (F^p_{B_1} \bullet F^p_{B_2})(bd) = F^p_{B_1}(b) \vee F^p_{B_2}(d) \end{cases}$$

2. $$\begin{cases} T^n_{(B_1\bullet B_2)}(bd) = (T^n_{B_1} \bullet T^n_{B_2})(bd) = T^n_{B_1}(b) \vee T^n_{B_2}(d) \\ I^n_{(B_1\bullet B_2)}(bd) = (I^n_{B_1} \bullet I^n_{B_2})(bd) = I^n_{B_1}(b) \vee I^n_{B_2}(d) \\ F^n_{(B_1\bullet B_2)}(bd) = (F^n_{B_1} \bullet F^n_{B_2})(bd) = F^n_{B_1}(b) \wedge F^n_{B_2}(d) \end{cases}$$

   for all $bd \in X_1 \times X_2$,

3. $$\begin{cases} T^p_{(B_{1k}\bullet B_{2k})}(bd_1)(bd_2) = (T^p_{B_{1k}} \bullet T^p_{B_{2k}})(bd_1)(bd_2) = T^p_{B_1}(b) \wedge T^p_{B_{2k}}(d_1d_2) \\ I^p_{(B_{1k}\bullet B_{2k})}(bd_1)(bd_2) = (I^p_{B_{1k}} \bullet I^p_{B_{2k}})(bd_1)(bd_2) = I^p_{B_1}(b) \wedge I^p_{B_{2k}}(d_1d_2) \\ F^p_{(B_{1k}\bullet B_{2k})}(bd_1)(bd_2) = (F^p_{B_{1k}} \bullet F^p_{B_{2k}})(bd_1)(bd_2) = F^p_{B_1}(b) \vee F^p_{B_{2k}}(c_1d_2) \end{cases}$$

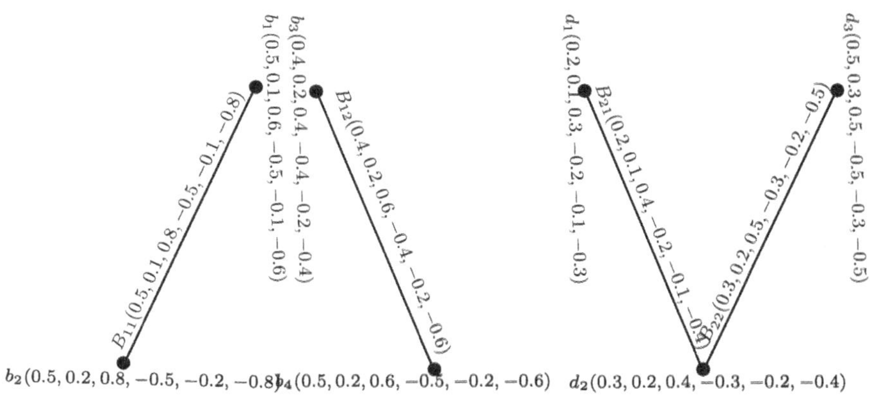

Fig. 10.8 Bipolar neutrosophic graph structures

4. $$\begin{cases} T^n_{(B_{1k}\bullet B_{2k})}(bd_1)(bd_2) = (T^n_{B_{1k}} \bullet T^n_{B_{2k}})(bd_1)(bd_2) = T^n_{B_1}(b) \vee T^n_{B_{2k}}(d_1d_2) \\ I^n_{(B_{1k}\bullet B_{2k})}(bd_1)(bd_2) = (I^n_{B_{1k}} \bullet I^n_{B_{2k}})(bd_1)(bd_2) = I^n_{B_1}(b) \vee I^n_{B_{2k}}(d_1d_2) \\ F^n_{(B_{1k}\bullet B_{2k})}(bd_1)(bd_2) = (F^n_{B_{1k}} \bullet F^n_{B_{2k}})(bd_1)(bd_2) = F^n_{B_1}(b) \wedge F^n_{B_{2k}}(d_1d_2) \end{cases}$$ for all $b \in X_1$, $d_1d_2 \in X_{2k}$,

5. $$\begin{cases} T^p_{(B_{1k}\bullet B_{2k})}(b_1d_1)(b_2d_2) = (T^p_{B_{1k}} \bullet T^p_{B_{2k}})(b_1d_1)(b_2d_2) = T^p_{B_{1k}}(b_1b_2) \wedge T^p_{B_{2k}}(d_1d_2) \\ I^p_{(B_{1k}\bullet B_{2k})}(b_1d_1)(b_2d_2) = (I^p_{B_{1k}} \bullet I^p_{B_{2k}})(b_1d_1)(b_2d_2) = I^p_{B_{1k}}(b_1b_2) \wedge I^p_{B_{2k}}(d_1d_2) \\ F^p_{(B_{1k}\bullet B_{2k})}(b_1d_1)(b_2d_2) = (F^p_{B_{1k}} \bullet F^p_{B_{2k}})(b_1d_1)(b_2d_2) = F^p_{B_{1k}}(b_1b_2) \vee F^p_{B_{2k}}(d_1d_2) \end{cases}$$

6. $$\begin{cases} T^n_{(B_{1k}\bullet B_{2k})}(b_1d_1)(b_2d_2) = (T^n_{B_{1k}} \bullet T^n_{B_{2k}})(b_1d_1)(b_2d_2) = T^n_{B_{1k}}(b_1b_2) \vee T^n_{B_{2k}}(d_1d_2) \\ I^n_{(B_{1k}\bullet B_{2k})}(b_1d_1)(b_2d_2) = (I^n_{B_{1k}} \bullet I^n_{B_{2k}})(b_1d_1)(b_2d_2) = I^n_{B_{1k}}(b_1b_2) \vee I^n_{B_{2k}}(d_1d_2) \\ F^n_{(B_{1k}\bullet B_{2k})}(b_1d_1)(b_2d_2) = (F^n_{B_{1k}} \bullet F^n_{B_{2k}})(b_1d_1)(b_2d_2) = F^n_{B_{1k}}(b_1b_2) \wedge F^n_{B_{2k}}(d_1d_2) \end{cases}$$ for all $b_1b_2 \in X_{1k}$, $d_1d_2 \in X_{2k}$.

Example 10.8 Consider two bipolar single-valued neutrosophic graph structures $\check{G}_{b1} = (B_1, B_{11}, B_{12})$ and $\check{G}_{b2} = (B_2, B_{21}, B_{22})$ of graph structures $\check{G}_{s1} = (X_1, X_{11}, X_{12})$ and $\check{G}_{s2} = (X_2, X_{21}, X_{22})$, respectively, as shown in Fig. 10.8, where $X_{11} = \{b_1b_2\}$, $X_{12} = \{b_3b_4\}$, $X_{21} = \{d_1d_2\}$, $X_{22} = \{d_2d_3\}$. The lexicographic product of bipolar single-valued neutrosophic graph structures $\check{G}_{b1}$ and $\check{G}_{b2}$ shown in Fig. 10.8 is defined as $\check{G}_{b1} \bullet \check{G}_{b2} = \{B_1 \bullet B_2, B_{11} \bullet B_{21}, B_{12} \bullet B_{22}\}$ and is given in Fig. 10.9.

Theorem 10.1 The lexicographic product $\check{G}_{b1} \bullet \check{G}_{b2} = (B_1 \bullet B_2, B_{11} \bullet B_{21}, B_{12} \bullet B_{22}, \dots, B_{1m} \bullet B_{2m})$ of two bipolar single-valued neutrosophic graph structures of graph structures $\check{G}_{s1}$ and $\check{G}_{s2}$ is a bipolar single-valued neutrosophic graph structure of $\check{G}_{s1} \bullet \check{G}_{s2}$.

Proof It is given that $\check{G}_{b1} \bullet \check{G}_{b2} = (B_1 \bullet B_2, B_{11} \bullet B_{21}, B_{12} \bullet B_{22}, \dots, B_{1m} \bullet B_{2m})$ are two bipolar single-valued neutrosophic graph structures of graph structures $\check{G}_{s1}$ and $\check{G}_{s2}$. Here there arise two cases.

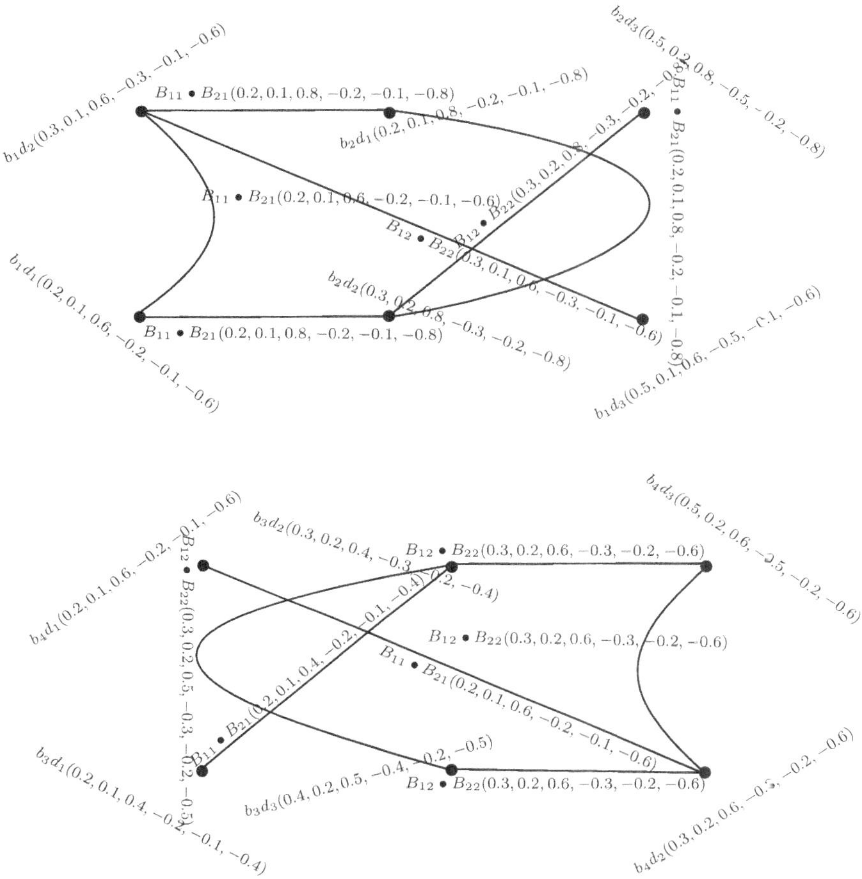

Fig. 10.9 Lexicographic product $\check{G}_{b1} \bullet \check{G}_{b2}$

Case 1: For $b \in X_1$, $d_1d_2 \in X_{2k}$,

$$\begin{aligned}
T^p_{(B_{1k}\bullet B_{2k})}((bd_1)(bd_2)) &= T^p_{B_1}(b) \wedge T^p_{B_{2k}}(d_1d_2)\\
&\leq T^p_{B_1}(b) \wedge [T^p_{B_2}(d_1) \wedge T^p_{B_2}(d_2)]\\
&= [T^p_{B_1}(b) \wedge T^p_{B_2}(d_1)] \wedge [T^p_{B_1}(b) \wedge T^p_{B_2}(d_2)]\\
&= T^p_{(B_1\bullet B_2)}(bd_1) \wedge T^p_{(B_1\bullet B_2)}(bd_2),
\end{aligned}$$

$$\begin{aligned}
T^n_{(B_{1k}\bullet B_{2k})}((bd_1)(bd_2)) &= T^n_{B_1}(b) \vee T^n_{B_{2k}}(d_1d_2)\\
&\geq T^n_{B_1}(b) \vee [T^n_{B_2}(d_1) \vee T^n_{B_2}(d_2)]\\
&= [T^n_{B_1}(b) \vee T^n_{B_2}(d_1)] \vee [T^n_{B_1}(b) \vee T^n_{B_2}(d_2)]\\
&= T^n_{(B_1\bullet B_2)}(bd_1) \vee T^n_{(B_1\bullet B_2)}(bd_2),
\end{aligned}$$

$$\begin{aligned}
I^p_{(B_{1k}\bullet B_{2k})}((bd_1)(bd_2)) &= I^p_{B_1}(b) \wedge I^p_{B_{2k}}(d_1d_2)\\
&\leq I^p_{B_1}(b) \wedge [I^p_{B_2}(d_1) \wedge I^p_{B_2}(d_2)]\\
&= [I^p_{B_1}(b) \wedge I^p_{B_2}(d_1)] \wedge [I^p_{B_1}(b) \wedge I^p_{B_2}(d_2)]\\
&= I^p_{(B_1\bullet B_2)}(bd_1) \wedge I^p_{(B_1\bullet B_2)}(bd_2),
\end{aligned}$$

$$\begin{aligned}
I^n_{(B_{1k}\bullet B_{2k})}((bd_1)(bd_2)) &= I^n_{B_1}(b) \vee I^n_{B_{2k}}(d_1d_2)\\
&\geq I^n_{B_1}(b) \vee [I^n_{B_2}(d_1) \vee I^n_{B_2}(d_2)]\\
&= [I^n_{B_1}(b) \vee I^n_{B_2}(d_1)] \vee [I^n_{B_1}(b) \vee I^n_{B_2}(d_2)]\\
&= I^n_{(B_1\bullet B_2)}(bd_1) \vee I^n_{(B_1\bullet B_2)}(bd_2),
\end{aligned}$$

$$\begin{aligned}
F^p_{(B_{1k}\bullet B_{2k})}((bd_1)(bd_2)) &= F^p_{B_1}(b) \vee F^p_{B_{2k}}(d_1d_2)\\
&\leq F^p_{B_1}(b) \vee [F^p_{B_2}(d_1) \vee F^p_{B_2}(d_2)]\\
&= [F^p_{B_1}(b) \vee F^p_{B_2}(d_1)] \vee [F^p_{B_1}(b) \vee F^p_{B_2}(d_2)]\\
&= F^p_{(B_1\bullet B_2)}(bd_1) \vee F^p_{(B_1\bullet B_2)}(bd_2),
\end{aligned}$$

$$\begin{aligned}
F^n_{(B_{1k}\bullet B_{2k})}((bd_1)(bd_2)) &= F^n_{B_1}(b) \wedge F^n_{B_{2k}}(d_1d_2)\\
&\geq F^n_{B_1}(b) \wedge [F^n_{B_2}(d_1) \wedge F^n_{B_2}(d_2)]\\
&= [F^n_{B_1}(b) \wedge F^n_{B_2}(d_1)] \wedge [F^n_{B_1}(b) \wedge F^n_{B_2}(d_2)]\\
&= F^n_{(B_1\bullet B_2)}(bd_1) \wedge F^n_{(B_1\bullet B_2)}(bd_2), \quad \text{for } bd_1, bd_2 \in X_1 \bullet X_2.
\end{aligned}$$

Case 2: For $b_1b_2 \in X_{1k}$, $d_1d_2 \in X_{2k}$

$$\begin{aligned}
T^p_{(B_{1k}\bullet B_{2k})}((b_1d_1)(b_2d_2)) &= T^p_{B_{1k}}(b_1b_2) \wedge T^p_{B_{2k}}(d_1d_2)\\
&\leq [T^p_{B_1}(b_1) \wedge T^p_{B_1}(b_2] \wedge [T^p_{B_2}(d_1) \wedge T^p_{B_2}(d_2)]\\
&= [T^p_{B_1}(b_1) \wedge T^p_{B_2}(d_1)] \wedge [T^p_{B_1}(b_2) \wedge T^p_{B_2}(d_2)]\\
&= T^p_{(B_1\bullet B_2)}(b_1d_1) \wedge T^p_{(B_1\bullet B_2)}(b_2d_2),
\end{aligned}$$

$$\begin{aligned}
T^n_{(B_{1k}\bullet B_{2k})}((b_1d_1)(b_2d_2)) &= T^n_{B_{1k}}(b_1b_2) \vee T^n_{B_{2k}}(d_1d_2)\\
&\geq [T^n_{B_1}(b_1) \vee T^n_{B_1}(b_2] \vee [T^n_{B_2}(d_1) \vee T^n_{B_2}(d_2)]\\
&= [T^n_{B_1}(b_1) \vee T^n_{B_2}(d_1)] \vee [T^n_{B_1}(b_2) \vee T^n_{B_2}(d_2)]\\
&= T^n_{(B_1\bullet B_2)}(b_1d_1) \vee T^n_{(B_1\bullet B_2)}(b_2d_2),
\end{aligned}$$

$$\begin{aligned} I^p_{(B_{1k}\bullet B_{2k})}((b_1d_1)(b_2d_2)) &= I^p_{B_{1k}}(b_1b_2) \wedge I^p_{B_{2k}}(d_1d_2) \\ &\leq [I^p_{B_1}(b_1) \wedge I^p_{B_1}(b_2] \wedge [I^p_{B_2}(d_1) \wedge I^p_{B_2}(d_2)] \\ &= [I^p_{B_1}(b_1) \wedge I^p_{B_2}(d_1)] \wedge [I^p_{B_1}(b_2) \wedge I^p_{B_2}(d_2)] \\ &= I^p_{(B_1\bullet B_2)}(b_1d_1) \wedge I^p_{(B_1\bullet B_2)}(b_2d_2), \end{aligned}$$

$$\begin{aligned} I^n_{(B_{1k}\bullet B_{2k})}((b_1d_1)(b_2d_2)) &= I^n_{B_{1k}}(b_1b_2) \vee I^n_{B_{2k}}(d_1d_2) \\ &\geq [I^n_{B_1}(b_1) \vee I^n_{B_1}(b_2] \vee [I^n_{B_2}(d_1) \vee I^n_{B_2}(d_2)] \\ &= [I^n_{B_1}(b_1) \vee I^n_{B_2}(d_1)] \vee [I^n_{B_1}(b_2) \vee I^n_{B_2}(d_2)] \\ &= I^n_{(B_1\bullet B_2)}(b_1d_1) \vee I^n_{(B_1\bullet B_2)}(b_2d_2), \end{aligned}$$

$$\begin{aligned} F^p_{(B_{1k}\bullet B_{2k})}((b_1d_1)(b_2d_2)) &= F^p_{B_{1k}}(b_1b_2) \vee F^p_{B_{2k}}(d_1d_2) \\ &\leq [F^p_{B_1}(b_1) \vee F^p_{B_1}(b_2] \vee [F^p_{B_2}(d_1) \vee F^p_{B_2}(d_2)] \\ &= [F^p_{B_1}(b_1) \vee F^p_{B_2}(d_1)] \vee [F^p_{B_1}(b_2) \vee F^p_{B_2}(d_2)] \\ &= F^p_{(B_1\bullet B_2)}(b_1d_1) \vee F^p_{(B_1\bullet B_2)}(b_2d_2), \end{aligned}$$

$$\begin{aligned} F^n_{(B_{1k}\bullet B_{2k})}((b_1d_1)(b_2d_2)) &= F^n_{B_{1k}}(b_1b_2) \wedge F^n_{B_{2k}}(d_1d_2) \\ &\geq [F^n_{B_1}(b_1) \wedge F^n_{B_1}(b_2] \wedge [F^n_{B_2}(d_1) \wedge F^n_{B_2}(d_2)] \\ &= [F^n_{B_1}(b_1) \wedge F^n_{B_2}(d_1)] \wedge [F^n_{B_1}(b_2) \wedge F^n_{B_2}(d_2)] \\ &= F^n_{(B_1\bullet B_2)}(b_1d_1) \wedge F^n_{(B_1\bullet B_2)}(b_2d_2), \end{aligned}$$

for $b_1d_1, b_2d_2 \in X_1 \bullet X_2$ and $k \in \{1, 2, \ldots, m\}$.

It completes the proof. □

Definition 10.10 Let $\check{G}_{b1} = (B_1, B_{11}, B_{12}, \ldots, B_{1m})$ and $\check{G}_{b2} = (B_2, B_{21}, B_{22}, \ldots, B_{2m})$ be two bipolar single-valued neutrosophic graph structures. The **strong product** of $\check{G}_{b1}$ and $\check{G}_{b2}$ is denoted by $\check{G}_{b1} \boxtimes \check{G}_{b2} = (B_1 \boxtimes B_2, B_{11} \boxtimes B_{21}, B_{12} \boxtimes B_{22}, \ldots, B_{1m} \boxtimes B_{2m})$ and defined as

1. $$\begin{cases} T^p_{(B_1\boxtimes B_2)}(bd) = (T^p_{B_1} \boxtimes T^p_{B_2})(bd) = T^p_{B_1}(b) \wedge T^p_{B_2}(d) \\ I^p_{(B_1\boxtimes B_2)}(bd) = (I^p_{B_1} \boxtimes I^p_{B_2})(bd) = I^p_{B_1}(b) \wedge I^p_{B_2}(d) \\ F^p_{(B_1\boxtimes B_2)}(bd) = (F^p_{B_1} \boxtimes F^p_{B_2})(bd) = F^p_{B_1}(b) \vee F^p_{B_2}(d) \end{cases}$$
2. $$\begin{cases} T^n_{(B_1\boxtimes B_2)}(bd) = (T^n_{B_1} \boxtimes T^n_{B_2})(bd) = T^n_{B_1}(b) \vee T^n_{B_2}(d) \\ I^n_{(B_1\boxtimes B_2)}(bd) = (I^n_{B_1} \boxtimes I^n_{B_2})(bd) = I^n_{B_1}(b) \vee I^n_{B_2}(d) \\ F^n_{(B_1\boxtimes B_2)}(bd) = (F^n_{B_1} \boxtimes F^n_{B_2})(bd) = F^n_{B_1}(b) \wedge F^p_{B_2}(d) \end{cases}$$

   for all $(bd) \in X_1 \times X_2$.

3. $\begin{cases} T^p_{(B_{1k}\boxtimes B_{2k})}(bd_1)(bd_2) = (T^p_{B_{1k}} \boxtimes T^p_{B_{2k}})(bd_1)(bd_2) = T^p_{B_1}(b) \wedge T^p_{B_{2k}}(d_1d_2) \\ I^p_{(B_{1k}\boxtimes B_{2k})}(bd_1)(bd_2) = (I^p_{B_{1k}} \boxtimes I^p_{B_{2k}})(bd_1)(bd_2) = I^p_{B_1}(b) \wedge I^p_{B_{2k}}(d_1d_2) \\ F^p_{(B_{1k}\boxtimes B_{2k})}(bd_1)(bd_2) = (F^p_{B_{1k}} \boxtimes F^p_{B_{2k}})(bd_1)(bd_2) = F^p_{B_1}(b) \vee F^p_{B_{2k}}(d_1d_2) \end{cases}$

4. $\begin{cases} T^n_{(B_{1k}\boxtimes B_{2k})}(bd_1)(bd_2) = (T^n_{B_{1k}} \boxtimes T^n_{B_{2k}})(bd_1)(bd_2) = T^n_{B_1}(b) \vee T^n_{B_{2k}}(d_1d_2) \\ I^n_{(B_{1k}\boxtimes B_{2k})}(bd_1)(bd_2) = (I^n_{B_{1k}} \boxtimes I^n_{B_{2k}})(bd_1)(bd_2) = I^n_{B_1}(b) \vee I^n_{B_{2k}}(d_1d_2) \\ F^n_{(B_{1k}\boxtimes B_{2k})}(bd_1)(bd_2) = (F^n_{B_{1k}} \boxtimes F^n_{B_{2k}})(bd_1)(bd_2) = F^n_{B_1}(b) \wedge F^n_{B_{2k}}(d_1d_2) \end{cases}$

for all $b \in X_1$, $(d_1d_2) \in X_{2k}$.

5. $\begin{cases} T^p_{(B_{1k}\boxtimes B_{2k})}(b_1d)(b_2d) = (T^p_{B_{1k}} \boxtimes T^p_{B_{2k}})(b_1d)(b_2d) = T^p_{B_2}(d) \wedge T^p_{B_{1k}}(b_1b_2) \\ I^p_{(B_{1k}\boxtimes B_{2k})}(b_1d)(b_2d) = (I^p_{B_{1k}} \boxtimes I^p_{B_{2k}})(b_1d)(b_2d) = I^p_{B_2}(d) \wedge I^p_{B_{2k}}(b_1b_2) \\ F^p_{(B_{1k}\boxtimes B_{2k})}(b_1d)(b_2d) = (F^p_{B_{1k}} \boxtimes F^p_{B_{2k}})(b_1d)(b_2d) = F^p_{B_2}(d) \vee F^p_{B_{2k}}(b_1b_2) \end{cases}$

6. $\begin{cases} T^n_{(B_{1k}\boxtimes B_{2k})}(b_1d)(b_2d) = (T^n_{B_{1k}} \boxtimes T^n_{B_{2k}})(b_1d)(b_2d) = T^n_{B_2}(d) \vee T^n_{B_{1k}}(b_1b_2) \\ I^n_{(B_{1k}\boxtimes B_{2k})}(b_1d)(b_2d) = (I^n_{B_{1k}} \boxtimes I^n_{B_{2k}})(b_1d)(b_2d) = I^n_{B_2}(d) \vee I^n_{B_{2k}}(b_1b_2) \\ F^n_{(B_{1k}\boxtimes B_{2k})}(b_1d)(b_2d) = (F^n_{B_{1k}} \boxtimes F^n_{B_{2k}})(b_1d)(b_2d) = F^n_{B_2}(d) \wedge F^n_{B_{2k}}(b_1b_2) \end{cases}$

for all $d \in X_2$, $(b_1b_2) \in X_{1k}$.

7. $\begin{cases} T^p_{(B_{1k}\boxtimes B_{2k})}(b_1d_1)(b_2d_2) = (T^p_{B_{1k}} \boxtimes T^p_{B_{2k}})(b_1d_1)(b_2d_2) = T^p_{B_{1k}}(b_1b_2) \wedge T^p_{B_{2k}}(d_1d_2) \\ I^p_{(B_{1k}\boxtimes B_{2k})}(b_1d_1)(b_2d_2) = (I^p_{B_{1k}} \boxtimes I^p_{B_{2k}})(b_1d_1)(b_2d_2) = I^p_{B_{1k}}(b_1b_2) \wedge I^p_{B_{2k}}(d_1d_2) \\ F^p_{(B_{1k}\boxtimes B_{2k})}(b_1d_1)(b_2d_2) = (F^p_{B_{1k}} \boxtimes F^p_{B_{2k}})(b_1d_1)(b_2d_2) = F^p_{B_{1k}}(b_1b_2) \vee F^p_{B_{2k}}(d_1d_2) \end{cases}$

8. $\begin{cases} T^n_{(B_{1k}\boxtimes B_{2k})}(b_1d_1)(b_2d_2) = (T^n_{B_{1k}} \boxtimes T^n_{B_{2k}})(b_1d_1)(b_2d_2) = T^n_{B_{1k}}(b_1b_2) \vee T^n_{B_{2k}}(d_1d_2) \\ I^n_{(B_{1k}\boxtimes B_{2k})}(b_1d_1)(b_2d_2) = (I^n_{B_{1k}} \boxtimes I^n_{B_{2k}})(b_1d_1)(b_2d_2) = I^n_{B_{1k}}(b_1b_2) \vee I^n_{B_{2k}}(d_1d_2) \\ F^n_{(B_{1k}\boxtimes B_{2k})}(b_1d_1)(b_2d_2) = (F^n_{B_{1k}} \boxtimes F^n_{B_{2k}})(b_1d_1)(b_2d_2) = F^n_{B_{1k}}(b_1b_2) \wedge F^n_{B_{2k}}(d_1d_2) \end{cases}$

for all $(b_1b_2) \in X_{1k}$, $(d_1d_2) \in X_{2k}$.

Example 10.9 The strong product of bipolar single-valued neutrosophic graph structures $\check{G}_{b1}$ and $\check{G}_{b2}$ shown in Fig. 10.8 is defined as $\check{G}_{b1} \boxtimes \check{G}_{b2} = \{B_1 \boxtimes B_2, B_{11} \boxtimes B_{21}, B_{12} \boxtimes B_{22}\}$ and is computed in Figs. 10.10 and 10.11.

Theorem 10.2 *The strong product* $\check{G}_{b1} \boxtimes \check{G}_{b2} = (B_1 \boxtimes B_2, B_{11} \boxtimes B_{21}, B_{12} \boxtimes B_{22}, \ldots, B_{1m} \boxtimes B_{2m})$ *of two bipolar single-valued neutrosophic graph structures of structures* $\check{G}_{s1}$ *and* $\check{G}_{s2}$ *is a bipolar single-valued neutrosophic graph structure of* $\check{G}_{s1} \boxtimes \check{G}_{s2}$.

Proof There are three cases regarding vertices and edges in the strong product.

Case 1: For $b \in X_1$, $d_1d_2 \in X_{2k}$,

$$\begin{aligned} T^p_{(B_{1k}\boxtimes B_{2k})}((bd_1)(bd_2)) &= T^p_{B_1}(b) \wedge T^p_{B_{2k}}(d_1d_2) \\ &\leq T^p_{B_1}(b) \wedge [T^p_{B_2}(d_1) \wedge T^p_{B_2}(d_2)] \\ &= [T^p_{B_1}(b) \wedge T^p_{B_2}(d_1)] \wedge [T^p_{B_1}(b) \wedge T^p_{B_2}(d_2)] \\ &= T^p_{(B_1\boxtimes B_2)}(bd_1) \wedge T^p_{(B_1\boxtimes B_2)}(bd_2), \end{aligned}$$

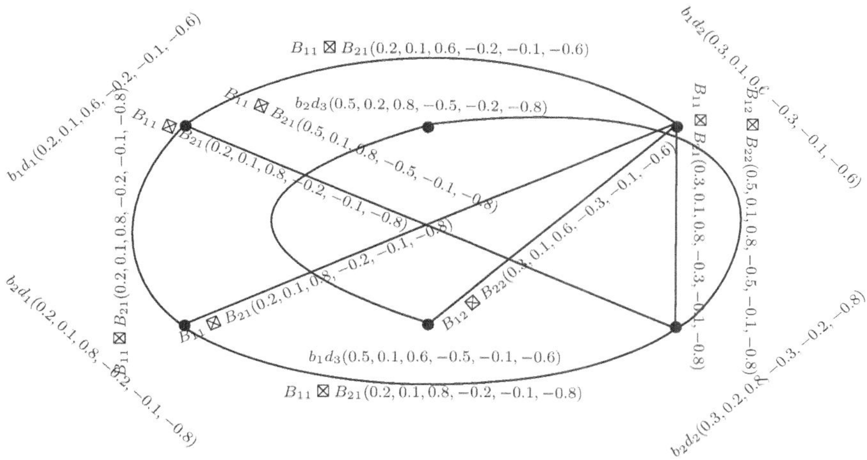

Fig. 10.10 Strong product $\check{G}_{b1} \boxtimes \check{G}_{b2}$

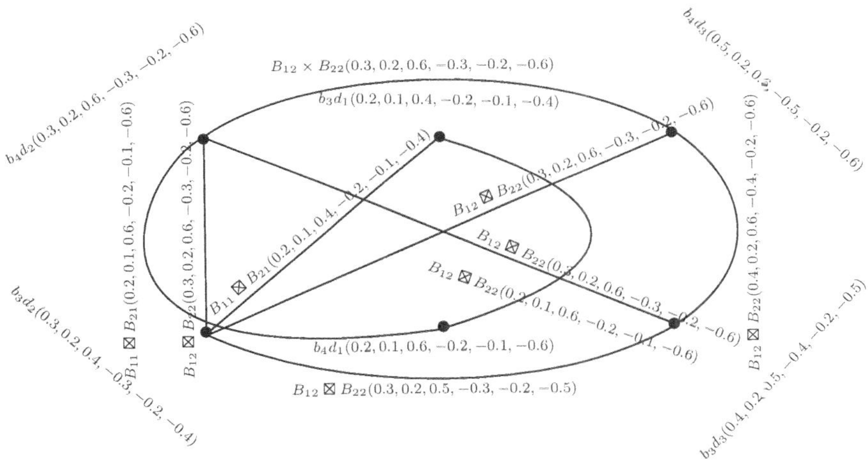

Fig. 10.11 Strong product $\check{G}_{b1} \boxtimes \check{G}_{b2}$

$$\begin{aligned}
T^n_{(B_{1k}\boxtimes B_{2k})}((bd_1)(bd_2)) &= T^n_{B_1}(b) \vee T^n_{B_{2k}}(d_1d_2) \\
&\geq T^n_{B_1}(b) \vee [T^n_{B_2}(d_1) \vee T^n_{B_2}(d_2)] \\
&= [T^n_{B_1}(b) \vee T^n_{B_2}(d_1)] \vee [T^n_{B_1}(b) \vee T^n_{B_2}(d_2)] \\
&= T^n_{(B_1\boxtimes B_2)}(bd_1) \vee T^n_{(B_1\boxtimes B_2)}(bd_2),
\end{aligned}$$

$$\begin{aligned}
I^p_{(B_{1k}\boxtimes B_{2k})}((bd_1)(bd_2)) &= I^p_{B_1}(b) \wedge I^p_{B_{2k}}(d_1d_2) \\
&\leq I^p_{B_1}(b) \wedge [I^p_{B_2}(d_1) \wedge I^p_{B_2}(d_2)]
\end{aligned}$$

$$= [I^p_{B_1}(b) \wedge I^p_{B_2}(d_1)] \wedge [I^p_{B_1}(b) \wedge I^p_{B_2}(d_2)]$$
$$= I^p_{(B_1 \boxtimes B_2)}(bd_1) \wedge I^p_{(B_1 \boxtimes B_2)}(bd_2),$$

$$\begin{aligned}
I^n_{(B_{1k} \boxtimes B_{2k})}((bd_1)(bd_2)) &= I^n_{B_1}(b) \vee I^n_{B_{2k}}(d_1 d_2)\\
&\geq I^n_{B_1}(b) \vee [I^n_{B_2}(d_1) \vee I^n_{B_2}(d_2)]\\
&= [I^n_{B_1}(b) \vee I^n_{B_2}(d_1)] \vee [I^n_{B_1}(b) \vee I^n_{B_2}(d_2)]\\
&= I^n_{(B_1 \boxtimes B_2)}(bd_1) \vee I^n_{(B_1 \boxtimes B_2)}(bd_2),
\end{aligned}$$

$$\begin{aligned}
F^p_{(B_{1k} \boxtimes B_{2k})}((bd_1)(bd_2)) &= F^p_{B_1}(b) \vee F^p_{B_{2k}}(d_1 d_2)\\
&\leq F^p_{B_1}(b) \vee [F^p_{B_2}(d_1) \vee F^p_{B_2}(d_2)]\\
&= [F^p_{B_1}(b) \vee F^p_{B_2}(d_1)] \vee [F^p_{B_1}(b) \vee F^p_{B_2}(d_2)]\\
&= F^p_{(B_1 \boxtimes B_2)}(bd_1) \vee F^p_{(B_1 \boxtimes B_2)}(bd_2),
\end{aligned}$$

$$\begin{aligned}
F^n_{(B_{1k} \boxtimes B_{2k})}((bd_1)(bd_2)) &= F^n_{B_1}(b) \wedge F^n_{B_{2k}}(d_1 d_2)\\
&\geq F^n_{B_1}(b) \wedge [F^n_{B_2}(d_1) \wedge F^n_{B_2}(d_2)]\\
&= [F^n_{B_1}(b) \wedge F^n_{B_2}(d_1)] \wedge [F^n_{B_1}(b) \wedge F^n_{B_2}(d_2)]\\
&= F^n_{(B_1 \boxtimes B_2)}(bd_1) \wedge F^n_{(B_1 \boxtimes B_2)}(bd_2),
\end{aligned}$$

for $bd_1, bd_2 \in X_1 \times X_2$.

Case 2: For $b \in X_2$, $d_1 d_2 \in X_{1k}$,

$$\begin{aligned}
T^p_{(B_{1k} \boxtimes B_{2k})}((d_1 b)(d_2 b)) &= T^p_{B_2}(b) \wedge T^p_{B_{1k}}(d_1 d_2)\\
&\leq T^p_{B_2}(b) \wedge [T^p_{B_1}(d_1) \wedge T^p_{B_1}(d_2)]\\
&= [T^p_{B_2}(b) \wedge T^p_{B_1}(d_1)] \wedge [T^p_{B_2}(b) \wedge T^p_{B_1}(d_2)]\\
&= T^p_{(B_1 \boxtimes B_2)}(d_1 b) \wedge T^p_{(B_1 \boxtimes B_2)}(d_2 b),
\end{aligned}$$

$$\begin{aligned}
T^n_{(B_{1k} \boxtimes B_{2k})}((d_1 b)(d_2 b)) &= T^n_{B_2}(b) \vee T^n_{B_{1k}}(d_1 d_2)\\
&\geq T^n_{B_2}(b) \vee [T^n_{B_1}(d_1) \vee T^p_{B_1}(d_2)]\\
&= [T^n_{B_2}(b) \vee T^n_{B_1}(d_1)] \vee [T^n_{B_2}(b) \vee T^n_{B_1}(d_2)]\\
&= T^n_{(B_1 \boxtimes B_2)}(d_1 b) \vee T^n_{(B_1 \boxtimes B_2)}(d_2 b),
\end{aligned}$$

$$\begin{aligned}
I^p_{(B_{1k}\boxtimes B_{2k})}((d_1b)(d_2b)) &= I^p_{B_2}(b) \wedge I^p_{B_{1k}}(d_1d_2)\\
&\leq I^p_{B_2}(b) \wedge [I^p_{B_1}(d_1) \wedge I^p_{B_1}(d_2)]\\
&= [I^p_{B_2}(b) \wedge I^p_{B_1}(d_1)] \wedge [I^p_{B_2}(b) \wedge I^p_{B_1}(d_2)]\\
&= I^p_{(B_1\boxtimes B_2)}(d_1b) \wedge I^p_{(B_1\boxtimes B_2)}(d_2b),
\end{aligned}$$

$$\begin{aligned}
I^n_{(B_{1k}\boxtimes B_{2k})}((d_1b)(d_2b)) &= I^n_{B_2}(b) \vee I^n_{B_{1k}}(d_1d_2)\\
&\geq I^n_{B_2}(b) \vee [I^n_{B_1}(d_1) \vee I^n_{B_1}(d_2)]\\
&= [I^n_{B_2}(b) \vee I^n_{B_1}(d_1)] \vee [I^n_{B_2}(b) \vee I^n_{B_1}(d_2)]\\
&= I^n_{(B_1\boxtimes B_2)}(d_1b) \vee I^n_{(B_1\boxtimes B_2)}(d_2b),
\end{aligned}$$

$$\begin{aligned}
F^p_{(B_{1k}\boxtimes B_{2k})}((d_1b)(d_2b)) &= F^p_{B_2}(b) \vee F^p_{B_{1k}}(d_1d_2)\\
&\leq F^p_{B_2}(b) \vee [F^p_{B_1}(d_1) \vee F^p_{B_1}(d_2)]\\
&= [F^p_{B_2}(b) \vee F^p_{B_1}(d_1)] \vee [F^p_{B_2}(b) \vee F^p_{B_1}(d_2)]\\
&= F^p_{(B_1\boxtimes B_2)}(d_1b) \vee F^p_{(B_1\boxtimes B_2)}(d_2b),
\end{aligned}$$

$$\begin{aligned}
F^n_{(B_{1k}\boxtimes B_{2k})}((d_1b)(d_2b)) &= F^n_{B_2}(b) \wedge F^n_{B_{1k}}(d_1d_2)\\
&\geq F^n_{B_2}(b) \wedge [F^n_{B_1}(d_1) \wedge F^n_{B_1}(d_2)]\\
&= [F^n_{B_2}(b) \wedge F^n_{B_1}(d_1)] \wedge [F^n_{B_2}(b) \wedge F^n_{B_1}(d_2)]\\
&= F^n_{(B_1\boxtimes B_2)}(d_1b) \wedge F^n_{(B_1\boxtimes B_2)}(d_2b),
\end{aligned}$$

for $d_1b, d_2b \in X_1 \boxtimes X_2$.

Case 3: For $b_1b_2 \in X_{1k}$; $d_1d_2 \in X_{2k}$,

$$\begin{aligned}
T^p_{(B_{1k}\boxtimes B_{2k})}((b_1d_1)(b_2d_2)) &= T^p_{B_{1k}}(b_1b_2) \wedge T^p_{B_{2k}}(d_1d_2)\\
&\leq [T^p_{B_1}(b_1) \wedge T^p_{B_1}(b_2] \wedge [T^p_{B_2}(d_1) \wedge T^p_{B_2}(d_2)]\\
&= [T^p_{B_1}(b_1) \wedge T^p_{B_2}(d_1)] \wedge [T^p_{B_1}(b_2) \wedge T^p_{B_2}(d_2)]\\
&= T^p_{(B_1\boxtimes B_2)}(b_1d_1) \wedge T^p_{(B_1\boxtimes B_2)}(b_2d_2),
\end{aligned}$$

$$\begin{aligned}
T^n_{(B_{1k}\boxtimes B_{2k})}((b_1d_1)(b_2d_2)) &= T^n_{B_{1k}}(b_1b_2) \vee T^n_{B_{2k}}(d_1d_2)\\
&\geq [T^n_{B_1}(b_1) \vee T^n_{B_1}(b_2] \vee [T^n_{B_2}(d_1) \vee T^n_{B_2}(d_2)]\\
&= [T^n_{B_1}(b_1) \vee T^n_{B_2}(d_1)] \vee [T^n_{B_1}(b_2) \vee T^n_{B_2}(d_2)]\\
&= T^n_{(B_1\boxtimes B_2)}(b_1d_1) \vee T^n_{(B_1\boxtimes B_2)}(b_2d_2),
\end{aligned}$$

$$\begin{aligned}
I^p_{(B_{1k}\boxtimes B_{2k})}((b_1d_1)(b_2d_2)) &= I^p_{B_{1k}}(b_1b_2) \wedge I^p_{B_{2k}}(d_1d_2)\\
&\le [I^p_{B_1}(b_1) \wedge I^p_{B_1}(b_2] \wedge [I^p_{B_2}(d_1) \wedge I^p_{B_2}(d_2)]\\
&= [I^p_{B_1}(b_1) \wedge I^p_{B_2}(d_1)] \wedge [I^p_{B_1}(b_2) \wedge I^p_{B_2}(d_2)]\\
&= I^p_{(B_1\boxtimes B_2)}(b_1d_1) \wedge I^p_{(B_1\boxtimes B_2)}(b_2d_2),
\end{aligned}$$

$$\begin{aligned}
I^n_{(B_{1k}\boxtimes B_{2k})}((b_1d_1)(b_2d_2)) &= I^n_{B_{1k}}(b_1b_2) \vee I^n_{B_{2k}}(d_1d_2)\\
&\ge [I^n_{B_1}(b_1) \vee I^n_{B_1}(b_2] \vee [I^n_{B_2}(d_1) \vee I^n_{B_2}(d_2)]\\
&= [I^n_{B_1}(b_1) \vee I^n_{B_2}(d_1)] \vee [I^n_{B_1}(b_2) \vee I^n_{B_2}(d_2)]\\
&= I^n_{(B_1\boxtimes B_2)}(b_1d_1) \vee I^n_{(B_1\boxtimes B_2)}(b_2d_2),
\end{aligned}$$

$$\begin{aligned}
F^p_{(B_{1k}\boxtimes B_{2k})}((b_1d_1)(b_2d_2)) &= F^p_{B_{1k}}(b_1b_2) \vee F^p_{B_{2k}}(d_1d_2)\\
&\le [F^p_{B_1}(b_1) \vee F^p_{B_1}(b_2] \vee [F^p_{B_2}(d_1) \vee F^p_{B_2}(d_2)]\\
&= [F^p_{B_1}(b_1) \vee F^p_{B_2}(d_1)] \vee [F^p_{B_1}(b_2) \vee F^p_{B_2}(d_2)]\\
&= F^p_{(B_1\boxtimes B_2)}(b_1d_1) \vee F^p_{(B_1\boxtimes B_2)}(b_2d_2),
\end{aligned}$$

$$\begin{aligned}
F^n_{(B_{1k}\boxtimes B_{2k})}((b_1d_1)(b_2d_2)) &= F^n_{B_{1k}}(b_1b_2) \wedge F^n_{B_{2k}}(d_1d_2)\\
&\ge [F^n_{B_1}(b_1) \wedge F^n_{B_1}(b_2] \wedge [F^n_{B_2}(d_1) \wedge F^n_{B_2}(d_2)]\\
&= [F^n_{B_1}(b_1) \wedge F^n_{B_2}(d_1)] \wedge [F^n_{B_1}(b_2) \wedge F^n_{B_2}(d_2)]\\
&= F^n_{(B_1\boxtimes B_2)}(b_1d_1) \wedge F^n_{(B_1\boxtimes B_2)}(b_2d_2),
\end{aligned}$$

for $b_1d_1, b_2d_2 \in X_1 \times X_2$.

All cases hold for all $k \in \{1, 2, \ldots, m\}$. □

Definition 10.11 Let $\check{G}_{b1} = (B_1, B_{11}, B_{12}, \ldots, B_{1m})$ and $\check{G}_{b2} = (B_2, B_{21}, B_{22}, \ldots, B_{2m})$ be bipolar single-valued neutrosophic graph structures. The **union** of $\check{G}_{b1}$ and $\check{G}_{b2}$ is denoted by $\check{G}_{b1} \cup \check{G}_{b2} = (B_1 \cup B_2, B_{11} \cup B_{21}, B_{12} \cup B_{22}, \ldots, B_{1m} \cup B_{2m})$ and is defined as

1. $\begin{cases} T^p_{(B_1\cup B_2)}(b) = (T^p_{B_1} \cup T^p_{B_2})(b) = T^p_{B_1}(b) \vee T^p_{B_2}(b),\\ I^p_{(B_1\cup B_2)}(b) = (I^p_{B_1} \cup I^p_{B_2})(b) = (I^p_{B_1}(b) + I^p_{B_2}(b))/2,\\ F^p_{(B_1\cup B_2)}(b) = (F^p_{B_1} \cup F^p_{B_2})(b) = F^p_{B_1}(b) \wedge F^p_{B_2}(b), \end{cases}$
2. $\begin{cases} T^n_{(B_1\cup B_2)}(b) = (T^n_{B_1} \cup T^n_{B_2})(b) = T^n_{B_1}(b) \wedge T^n_{B_2}(b),\\ I^n_{(B_1\cup B_2)}(b) = (I^n_{B_1} \cup I^n_{B_2})(b) = (I^n_{B_1}(b) + I^n_{B_2}(b))/2,\\ F^n_{(B_1\cup B_2)}(b) = (F^n_{B_1} \cup F^n_{B_2})(b) = F^n_{B_1}(b) \vee F^n_{B_2}(b) \end{cases}$

   for all $b \in X_1 \cup X_2$,

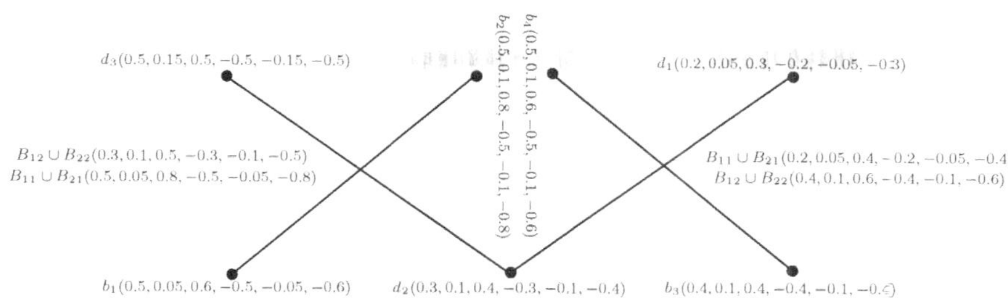

Fig. 10.12 Union $\check{G}_{b1} \cup \check{G}_{b2}$

3. $\begin{cases} T^p_{(B_{1k}\cup B_{2k})}(bd) = (T^p_{B_{1k}} \cup T^p_{B_{2k}})(bd) = T^p_{B_{1k}}(bd) \vee T^p_{B_{2k}}(bd), \\ I^p_{(B_{1k}\cup B_{2k})}(bd) = (I^p_{B_{1k}} \cup I^p_{B_{2k}})(bd) = (I^p_{B_{1k}}(bd) + I^p_{B_{2k}}(bd))/2, \\ F^p_{(B_{1k}\cup B_{2k})}(bd) = (F^p_{B_{1k}} \cup F^p_{B_{2k}})(bd) = F^p_{B_{1k}}(bd) \wedge F^p_{B_{2k}}(bd), \end{cases}$

4. $\begin{cases} T^n_{(B_{1k}\cup B_{2k})}(bd) = (T^n_{B_{1k}} \cup T^n_{B_{2k}})(bd) = T^n_{B_{1k}}(bd) \wedge T^n_{B_{2k}}(bd), \\ I^n_{(B_{1k}\cup B_{2k})}(bd) = (I^n_{B_{1k}} \cup I^n_{B_{2k}})(bd) = (I^n_{B_{1k}}(bd) + I^n_{B_{2k}}(bd))/2, \\ F^n_{(B_{1k}\cup B_{2k})}(bd) = (F^n_{B_{1k}} \cup F^n_{B_{2k}})(bd) = F^n_{B_{1k}}(bd) \vee F^n_{B_{2k}}(bd) \end{cases}$

for all $bd \in X_{1k} \cup X_{2k}$.

Example 10.10 The union of two bipolar single-valued neutrosophic graph structures $\check{G}_{b1}$ and $\check{G}_{b2}$ shown in Fig. 10.8 is defined as $\check{G}_{b1} \cup \check{G}_{b2} = \{B_1 \cup B_2, B_{11} \cup B_{21}, B_{12} \cup B_{22}\}$ and is given in Fig. 10.12.

Theorem 10.3 The union $\check{G}_{b1} \cup \check{G}_{b2} = (B_1 \cup B_2, B_{11} \cup B_{21}, B_{12} \cup B_{22}, \ldots, B_{1m} \cup B_{2m})$ of two bipolar single-valued neutrosophic graph structures of the graph structures $\check{G}_1$ and $\check{G}_2$ is a bipolar single-valued neutrosophic graph structure of $\check{G}_1 \cup \check{G}_2$.

Proof Let $b_1b_2 \in X_{1k} \cup X_{2k}$, then there are the following two cases.

Case 1: For $b_1, b_2 \in X_1$, by Definition 10.11
$T^p_{B_2}(b_1) = T^p_{B_2}(b_2) = T^p_{B_{2k}}(b_1b_2) = 0$, $I^p_{B_2}(b_1) = I^p_{B_2}(b_2) = I^p_{B_{2k}}(b_1b_2) = 0$, $F^p_{B_2}(b_1) = F^p_{B_2}(b_2) = F^p_{B_{2k}}(b_1b_2) = 1$,
$T^n_{B_2}(b_1) = T^n_{B_2}(b_2) = T^n_{B_{2k}}(b_1b_2) = 0$, $I^n_{B_2}(b_1) = I^n_{B_2}(b_2) = I^n_{B_{2k}}(b_1b_2) = 0$, $F^n_{B_2}(b_1) = F^n_{B_2}(b_2) = F^n_{B_{2k}}(b_1b_2) = -1$, so

$$\begin{aligned} T^p_{(B_{1k}\cup B_{2k})}(b_1b_2) &= T^p_{B_{1k}}(b_1b_2) \vee T^p_{B_{2k}}(b_1b_2) \\ &= T^p_{B_{1k}}(b_1b_2) \vee 0 \\ &\le [T^p_{B_1}(b_1) \wedge T^p_{B_1}(b_2)] \vee 0 \\ &= [T^p_{B_1}(b_1) \vee 0] \wedge [T^p_{B_1}(b_2) \vee 0] \\ &= [T^p_{B_1}(b_1) \vee T^p_{B_2}(b_1)] \wedge [T^p_{B_1}(b_2) \vee T^p_{B_2}(b_2)] \\ &= T^p_{(B_1\cup B_2)}(b_1) \wedge T^p_{(B_1\cup B_2)}(b_2), \end{aligned}$$

$$\begin{aligned}
T^n_{(B_{1k}\cup B_{2k})}(b_1b_2) &= T^n_{B_{1k}}(b_1b_2) \wedge T^n_{B_{2k}}(b_1b_2) \\
&= T^n_{B_{1k}}(b_1b_2) \wedge 0 \\
&\geq [T^n_{B_1}(b_1) \vee T^n_{B_1}(b_2)] \wedge 0 \\
&= [T^n_{B_1}(b_1) \wedge 0] \vee [T^n_{B_1}(b_2) \wedge 0] \\
&= [T^n_{B_1}(b_1) \wedge T^n_{B_2}(b_1)] \vee [T^n_{B_1}(b_2) \wedge T^n_{B_2}(b_2)] \\
&= T^n_{(B_1\cup B_2)}(b_1) \vee T^n_{(B_1\cup B_2)}(b_2),
\end{aligned}$$

$$\begin{aligned}
F^p_{(B_{1k}\cup B_{2k})}(b_1b_2) &= F^p_{B_{1k}}(b_1b_2) \wedge F^p_{B_{2k}}(b_1b_2) \\
&= F^p_{B_{1k}}(b_1b_2) \wedge 1 \\
&\leq [F^p_{B_1}(b_1) \vee F^p_{B_1}(b_2)] \wedge 1 \\
&= [F^p_{B_1}(b_1) \wedge 1] \vee [F^p_{B_1}(b_2) \wedge 1] \\
&= [F^p_{B_1}(b_1) \wedge F^p_{B_2}(b_1)] \vee [F^p_{B_1}(b_2) \wedge F^p_{B_2}(b_2)] \\
&= F^p_{(B_1\cup B_2)}(b_1) \vee F^p_{(B_1\cup B_2)}(b_2),
\end{aligned}$$

$$\begin{aligned}
F^n_{(B_{1k}\cup B_{2k})}(b_1b_2) &= F^n_{B_{1k}}(b_1b_2) \vee F^n_{B_{2k}}(b_1b_2) \\
&= F^n_{B_{1k}}(b_1b_2) \vee -1 \\
&\geq [F^n_{B_1}(b_1) \wedge F^n_{B_1}(b_2)] \vee -1 \\
&= [F^n_{B_1}(b_1) \vee -1] \wedge [F^n_{B_1}(b_2) \vee -1] \\
&= [F^n_{B_1}(b_1) \vee F^n_{B_2}(b_1)] \wedge [F^n_{B_1}(b_2) \vee F^n_{B_2}(b_2)] \\
&= F^n_{(B_1\cup B_2)}(b_1) \wedge F^n_{(B_1\cup B_2)}(b_2),
\end{aligned}$$

$$\begin{aligned}
I^p_{(B_{1k}\cup B_{2k})}(b_1b_2) &= \frac{I^p_{B_{1k}}(b_1b_2) + I^p_{B_{2k}}(b_1b_2)}{2} \\
&= \frac{I^p_{B_{1k}}(b_1b_2) + 0}{2} \\
&\leq \frac{[I^p_{B_1}(b_1) \wedge I^p_{B_1}(b_2)] + 0}{2} \\
&= [\frac{I^p_{B_1}(b_1)}{2} + 0] \wedge [\frac{I^p_{B_1}(b_2)}{2} + 0] \\
&= \frac{[I^p_{B_1}(b_1) + I^p_{B_2}(b_1)]}{2} \wedge \frac{[I^p_{B_1}(b_2) + I^p_{B_2}(b_2)]}{2} \\
&= I^p_{(B_1\cup B_2)}(b_1) \wedge I^p_{(B_1\cup B_2)}(b_2),
\end{aligned}$$

$$\begin{aligned}
I^n_{(B_{1k}\cup B_{2k})}(b_1b_2) &= \frac{I^n_{B_{1k}}(b_1b_2)+I^n_{B_{2k}}(b_1b_2)}{2}\\
&= \frac{I^n_{B_{1k}}(b_1b_2)+0}{2}\\
&\geq \frac{[I^n_{B_1}(b_1)\vee I^n_{B_1}(b_2)]+0}{2}\\
&= [\frac{I^n_{B_1}(b_1)}{2}+0]\vee[\frac{I^n_{B_1}(b_2)}{2}+0]\\
&= \frac{[I^n_{B_1}(b_1)+I^n_{B_2}(b_1)]}{2}\vee\frac{[I^n_{B_1}(b_2)+I^n_{B_2}(b_2)]}{2}\\
&= I^n_{(B_1\cup B_2)}(b_1)\vee I^n_{(B_1\cup B_2)}(b_2),
\end{aligned}$$

for $b_1, b_2 \in X_1 \cup X_2$.

Case 2: For $b_1, b_2 \in X_2$, by Definition 10.11,
$T^p_{B_1}(b_1)=T^p_{B_1}(b_2)=T^p_{B_{1k}}(b_1b_2)=0,\ I^p_{B_1}(b_1)=I^p_{B_1}(b_2)=I^p_{B_{1k}}(b_1b_2)=0,\ F^p_{B_1}(b_1)= F^p_{B_2}(b_2)=F^p_{B_{1k}}(b_1b_2)=1$,
$T^n_{B_1}(b_1)=T^n_{B_1}(b_2)=T^n_{B_{1k}}(b_1b_2)=0,\ I^n_{B_1}(b_1)=I^n_{B_1}(b_2)=I^n_{B_{1k}}(b_1b_2)=0,\ F^n_{B_1}(b_1)= F^n_{B_2}(b_2)=F^n_{B_{1k}}(b_1b_2)=-1$, so

$$\begin{aligned}
T^p_{(B_{1k}\cup B_{2k})}(b_1b_2) &= T^p_{B_{1k}}(b_1b_2)\vee T^p_{B_{2k}}(b_1b_2)\\
&= T^p_{B_{2k}}(b_1b_2)\vee 0\\
&\leq [T^p_{B_2}(b_1)\wedge T^p_{B_2}(b_2)]\vee 0\\
&= [T^p_{B_2}(b_1)\vee 0]\wedge[T^p_{B_2}(b_2)\vee 0]\\
&= [T^p_{B_2}(b_1)\vee T^p_{B_1}(b_1)]\wedge[T^p_{B_2}(b_2)\vee T^p_{B_1}(b_2)]\\
&= T^p_{(B_1\cup B_2)}(b_1)\wedge T^p_{(B_1\cup B_2)}(b_2),
\end{aligned}$$

$$\begin{aligned}
T^n_{(B_{1k}\cup B_{2k})}(b_1b_2) &= T^n_{B_{1k}}(b_1b_2)\wedge T^n_{B_{2k}}(b_1b_2)\\
&= T^n_{B_{2k}}(b_1b_2)\wedge 0\\
&\geq [T^n_{B_2}(b_1)\vee T^n_{B_2}(b_2)]\wedge 0\\
&= [T^n_{B_2}(b_1)\wedge 0]\vee[T^n_{B_2}(b_2)\wedge 0]\\
&= [T^n_{B_2}(b_1)\wedge T^n_{B_1}(b_1)]\vee[T^n_{B_2}(b_2)\wedge T^n_{B_1}(b_2)]\\
&= T^n_{(B_1\cup B_2)}(b_1)\vee T^n_{(B_1\cup B_2)}(b_2),
\end{aligned}$$

$$\begin{aligned}
F^p_{(B_{1k}\cup B_{2k})}(b_1b_2) &= F^p_{B_{1k}}(b_1b_2)\wedge F^p_{B_{2k}}(b_1b_2)\\
&= F^p_{B_{2k}}(b_1b_2)\wedge(1)\\
&\leq [F^p_{B_2}(b_1)\vee F^p_{B_2}(b_2)]\wedge(1)\\
&= [F^p_{B_2}(b_1)\wedge(1)]\vee[F^p_{B_2}(b_2)\wedge(1)]
\end{aligned}$$

$$= [F^p_{B_2}(b_1) \wedge F^p_{B_1}(b_1)] \vee [F^p_{B_2}(b_2) \wedge F^p_{B_1}(b_2)]$$
$$= F^p_{(B_1 \cup B_2)}(b_1) \vee F^p_{(B_1 \cup B_2)}(b_2),$$

$$\begin{aligned}
F^n_{(B_{1k} \cup B_{2k})}(b_1 b_2) &= F^n_{B_{1k}}(b_1 b_2) \vee F^n_{B_{2k}}(b_1 b_2) \\
&= F^n_{B_{2k}}(b_1 b_2) \vee (-1) \\
&\geq [F^n_{B_2}(b_1) \wedge F^n_{B_2}(b_2)] \vee (-1) \\
&= [F^n_{B_2}(b_1) \vee (-1)] \wedge [F^n_{B_2}(b_2) \vee (-1)] \\
&= [F^n_{B_2}(b_1) \vee F^n_{B_1}(b_1)] \wedge [F^n_{B_2}(b_2) \vee F^n_{B_1}(b_2)] \\
&= F^n_{(B_1 \cup B_2)}(b_1) \wedge F^n_{(B_1 \cup B_2)}(b_2),
\end{aligned}$$

$$\begin{aligned}
I^p_{(B_{1k} \cup B_{2k})}(b_1 b_2) &= \frac{I^p_{B_{1k}}(b_1 b_2) + I^p_{B_{2k}}(b_1 b_2)}{2} \\
&= \frac{I^p_{B_{2k}}(b_1 b_2) + 0}{2} \\
&\leq \frac{[I^p_{B_2}(b_1) \wedge I^p_{B_2}(b_2)] + 0}{2} \\
&= [\frac{I^p_{B_2}(b_1)}{2} + 0] \wedge [\frac{I^p_{B_2}(b_2)}{2} + 0] \\
&= \frac{[I^p_{B_2}(b_1) + I^p_{B_1}(b_1)]}{2} \wedge \frac{[I^p_{B_2}(b_2) + I^p_{B_1}(b_2)]}{2} \\
&= I^p_{(B_1 \cup B_2)}(b_1) \wedge I^p_{(B_1 \cup B_2)}(b_2),
\end{aligned}$$

$$\begin{aligned}
I^n_{(B_{1k} \cup B_{2k})}(b_1 b_2) &= \frac{I^n_{B_{1k}}(b_1 b_2) + I^n_{B_{2k}}(b_1 b_2)}{2} \\
&= \frac{I^n_{B_{2k}}(b_1 b_2) + 0}{2} \\
&\geq \frac{[I^n_{B_2}(b_1) \vee I^n_{B_2}(b_2)] + 0}{2} \\
&= [\frac{I^n_{B_2}(b_1)}{2} + 0] \vee [\frac{I^n_{B_2}(b_2)}{2} + 0] \\
&= \frac{[I^n_{B_2}(b_1) + I^n_{B_1}(b_1)]}{2} \vee \frac{[I^n_{B_2}(b_2) + I^n_{B_1}(b_2)]}{2} \\
&= I^n_{(B_1 \cup B_2)}(b_1) \vee I^n_{(B_1 \cup B_2)}(b_2),
\end{aligned}$$

for $b_1, b_2 \in X_1 \cup X_2$.

Both cases hold for all $k \in \{1, 2, \ldots, m\}$. It completes the proof.

Theorem 10.4 *Let* $\check{G}_s = (X_1 \cup X_2, X_{11} \cup X_{21}, X_{12} \cup X_{22}, \ldots, X_{1m} \cup X_{2m})$ *be the union of graph structues* $\check{G}_{s1} = (X_1, X_{11}, X_{12}, \ldots, X_{1m})$ *and* $\check{G}_{s2} = (X_2, X_{21}, X_{22}, \ldots, X_{2m})$. *Then every bipolar single-valued neutrosophic graph structure* $\check{G}_{bn} = (B, B_1, B_2, \ldots, B_m)$ *of* $\check{G}_s$ *is the union of two bipolar single-valued neutrosophic graph structures* $\check{G}_{b1}$ *and* $\check{G}_{b2}$ *of graph structures* $\check{G}_{s1}$ *and* $\check{G}_{s2}$, *respectively.*

Proof Firstly, define B_1, B_2, B_{1k}, and B_{2k} for $k \in \{1, 2, \ldots, m\}$ as

$T^p_{B_1}(b) = T^p_B(b)$, $I^p_{B_1}(b) = I^p_B(b)$, $F^p_{B_1}(b) = F^p_B(b)$, $T^n_{B_1}(b) = T^n_B(b)$ $I^n_{B_1}(b) = I^n_B(b)$, $F^n_{B_1}(b) = F^n_B(b)$, if $b \in X_1$.

$T^p_{B_2}(b) = T^p_B(b)$, $I^p_{B_2}(b) = I^p_B(b)$, $F^p_{B_2}(b) = F^p_B(b)$,

$T^n_{B_2}(b) = T^n_B(b)$, $I^n_{B_2}(b) = I^n_B(b)$, $F^n_{B_2}(b) = F^n_B(b)$, if $b \in X_2$.

$T^p_{B_{1k}}(b_1b_2) = T^p_{B_k}(b_1b_2)$, $I^p_{B_{1k}}(b_1b_2) = I^p_{B_k}(b_1b_2)$, $F^p_{B_{1k}}(b_1b_2) = F^p_{B_k}(b_1b_2)$, $T^n_{B_{1k}}(b_1b_2) = T^n_{B_k}(b_1b_2)$,

$I^n_{B_{1k}}(b_1b_2) = I^n_{B_k}(b_1b_2)$, $F^n_{B_{1k}}(b_1b_2) = F^n_{B_k}(b_1b_2)$, if $b_1b_2 \in X_{1k}$.

$T^p_{B_{2k}}(b_1b_2) = T^p_{B_k}(b_1b_2)$, $I^p_{B_{2k}}(b_1b_2) = I^p_{B_k}(b_1b_2)$, $F^p_{B_{2k}}(b_1b_2) = F^p_{B_k}(b_1b_2)$, $T^n_{B_{2k}}(b_1b_2) = T^n_{B_k}(b_1b_2)$,

$I^n_{B_{2k}}(b_1b_2) = I^n_{B_k}(b_1b_2)$, $F^n_{B_{2k}}(b_1b_2) = F^n_{B_k}(b_1b_2)$, if $b_1b_2 \in X_{2k}$.

Then $B = B_1 \cup B_2$ and $B_k = B_{1k} \cup B_{2k}$, $k \in \{1, 2, \ldots, m\}$. Now for $b\ b_2 \in X_{tk}$, $t = 1, 2$, $k \in \{1, 2, \ldots, m\}$:

$$T^p_{B_{tk}}(b_1b_2) = T^p_{B_k}(b_1b_2) \leq T^p_B(b_1) \wedge T^p_B(b_2) = T^p_{B_t}(b_1) \wedge T^p_{B_t}(b_2),$$

$$I^p_{B_{tk}}(b_1b_2) = I^p_{B_k}(b_1b_2) \leq I^p_B(b_1) \wedge I^p_B(b_2) = I^p_{B_t}(b_1) \wedge I^p_{B_t}(b_2),$$

$$F^p_{B_{tk}}(b_1b_2) = F^p_{B_k}(b_1b_2) \leq F^p_B(b_1) \vee F^p_B(b_2) = F^p_{B_t}(b_1) \vee F^p_{B_t}(b_2),$$

$$T^n_{B_{tk}}(b_1b_2) = T^n_{B_k}(b_1b_2) \geq T^n_B(b_1) \vee T^n_B(b_2) = T^n_{B_t}(b_1) \vee T^n_{B_t}(b_2),$$

$$I^n_{B_{tk}}(b_1b_2) = I^n_{B_k}(b_1b_2) \geq I^n_B(b_1) \vee I^n_B(b_2) = I^n_{B_t}(b_1) \vee I^n_{B_t}(b_2),$$

$$F^n_{B_{tk}}(b_1b_2) = F^n_{B_k}(b_1b_2) \geq F^n_B(b_1) \wedge F^n_B(b_2) = F^n_{B_t}(b_1) \wedge F^n_{B_t}(b_2).$$

That is, $\check{G}_{bl} = (B_l, B_{l1}, B_{l2}, \ldots, B_{lm})$ is a bipolar single-valued neutrosophic graph structure of $\check{G}_t$, $t = 1, 2$. Thus $\check{G}_{bn} = (B, B_1, B_2, \ldots, B_m)$, a bipolar single-valued neutrosophic graph structure of $\check{G}_s = \check{G}_{s1} \cup \check{G}_{s2}$, is the union of two bipolar single-valued neutrosophic graph structures $\check{G}_{b1}$ and $\check{G}_{b2}$.

Definition 10.12 Let $\check{G}_{b1} = (B_1, B_{11}, B_{12}, \ldots, B_{1m})$ and $\check{G}_{b2} = (B_2, B_{21}, B_{22}, \ldots, B_{2m})$ be bipolar single-valued neutrosophic graph structures and let $X_1 \cap X_2 = \emptyset$. The **join** of $\check{G}_{b1}$ and $\check{G}_{b2}$ is denoted by $\check{G}_{b1} + \check{G}_{b2} = (B_1 + B_2, B_{11} + B_{21}, B_{12} + B_{22}, \ldots, B_{1m} + B_{2m})$ and defined as

1. $\begin{cases} T^p_{(B_1+B_2)}(b) = T^p_{(B_1 \cup B_2)}(b), \\ I^p_{(B_1+B_2)}(b) = I^p_{(B_1 \cup B_2)}(b), \\ F^p_{(B_1+B_2)}(b) = F^p_{(B_1 \cup B_2)}(b), \end{cases}$

2. $\begin{cases} T^n_{(B_1+B_2)}(b) = T^n_{(B_1 \cup B_2)}(b), \\ I^n_{(B_1+B_2)}(b) = I^n_{(B_1 \cup B_2)}(b), \\ F^n_{(B_1+B_2)}(b) = F^n_{(B_1 \cup B_2)}(b), \end{cases}$

   for all $b \in X_1 \cup X_2$,

3. $\begin{cases} T^p_{(B_{1k}+B_{2k})}(bd) = T^p_{(B_{1k} \cup B_{2k})}(bd), \\ I^p_{(B_{1k}+B_{2k})}(bd) = I^p_{(B_{1k} \cup B_{2k})}(bd), \\ F^p_{(B_{1k}+B_{2k})}(bd) = F^p_{(B_{1k} \cup B_{2k})}(bd), \end{cases}$

4. $\begin{cases} T^n_{(B_{1k}+B_{2k})}(bd) = T^n_{(B_{1k} \cup B_{2k})}(bd), \\ I^n_{(B_{1k}+B_{2k})}(bd) = I^n_{(B_{1k} \cup B_{2k})}(bd), \\ F^n_{(B_{1k}+B_{2k})}(bd) = F^n_{(B_{1k} \cup B_{2k})}(bd), \end{cases}$

   for all $(bd) \in X_{1k} \cup X_{2k}$,

5. $\begin{cases} T^p_{(B_{1k}+B_{2k})}(bd) = (T^p_{B_{1k}} + T^p_{B_{2k}})(bd) = T^p_{B_1}(b) \wedge T^p_{B_2}(d), \\ I^p_{(B_{1k}+B_{2k})}(bd) = (I^p_{B_{1k}} + I^p_{B_{2k}})(bd) = I^p_{B_1}(b) \wedge I^p_{B_2}(d), \\ F^p_{(B_{1k}+B_{2k})}(bd) = (F^p_{B_{1k}} + F^p_{B_{2k}})(bd) = F^p_{B_1}(b) \vee F^p_{B_2}(d), \end{cases}$

6. $\begin{cases} T^n_{(B_{1k}+B_{2k})}(bd) = (T^n_{B_{1k}} + T^n_{B_{2k}})(bd) = T^n_{B_1}(b) \vee T^n_{B_2}(d), \\ I^n_{(B_{1k}+B_{2k})}(bd) = (I^n_{B_{1k}} + I^n_{B_{2k}})(bd) = I^n_{B_1}(b) \vee I^n_{B_2}(d), \\ F^n_{(B_{1k}+B_{2k})}(bd) = (F^n_{B_{1k}} + F^n_{B_{2k}})(bd) = F^n_{B_1}(b) \wedge F^n_{B_2}(d), \end{cases}$

   for all $b \in X_1$, $d \in X_2$.

Example 10.11 The join of two bipolar single-valued neutrosophic graph structures $\check{G}_{b1}$ and $\check{G}_{b2}$ shown in Fig. 10.8 is defined as $\check{G}_{b1} + \check{G}_{b2} = \{B_1 + B_2, B_{11} + B_{21}, B_{12} + B_{22}\}$ and is given in Fig. 10.13.

Theorem 10.5 The join $\check{G}_{b1} + \check{G}_{b2} = (B_1 + B_2, B_{11} + B_{21}, B_{12} + B_{22}, \ldots, B_{1m} + B_{2m})$ of two bipolar single-valued neutrosophic graph structures of the graph structures $\check{G}_1$ and $\check{G}_2$ is a bipolar single-valued neutrosophic graph structure of $\check{G}_1 + \check{G}_2$.

The proof of Theorem 10.5 is a direct consequence of Theorem 10.3 and Definition 10.12.

10.3 Isomorphism in Bipolar Neutrosophic Graph Structures

In this section, isomorphic properties of bipolar single-valued neutrosophic graph structures are discussed.

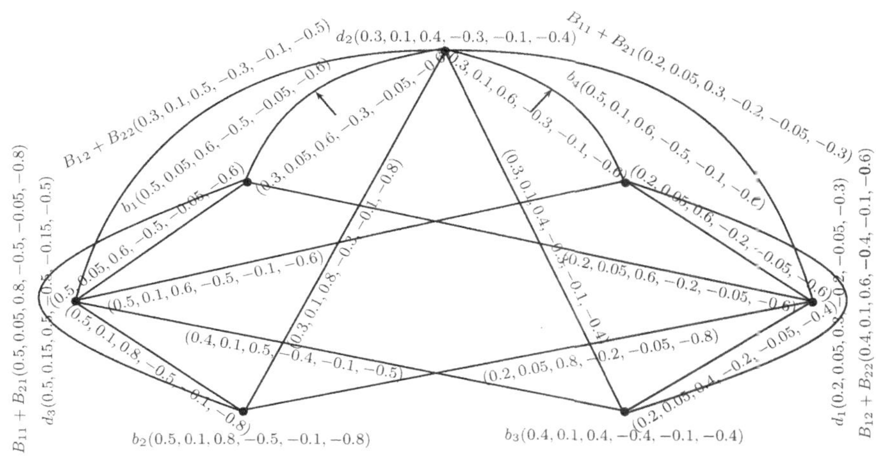

Fig. 10.13 Join $\check{G}_{b1} + \check{G}_{b2}$

Definition 10.13 A bipolar single-valued neutrosophic graph structure $\check{G}_{b1} = (B_1, B_{11}, B_{12}, \ldots, B_{1m})$ of a graph structure $\check{G}_{s1} = (X_1, X_{11}, X_{12}, \ldots, X_{1m})$ is **isomorphic** to a bipolar single-valued neutrosophic graph structure $\check{G}_{b2} = (B_2, B_{21}, B_{22}, \ldots, B_{2m})$ of a graph structure $\check{G}_{s2} = (X_2, X_{21}, X_{22}, ..., X_{2m})$ if there exists a pair (h, φ), where $h : X_1 \to X_2$ is a bijection and φ is a permutation on $\{1, 2, \ldots, m\}$ such that

1. $T^p_{B_1}(b) = T^p_{B_2}(h(b)),\ I^p_{B_1}(b) = I^p_{B_2}(h(b)),\ F^p_{B_1}(b) = F^p_{B_2}(h(b))$,
2. $T^n_{B_1}(b) = T^n_{B_2}(h(b)),\ I^n_{B_1}(b) = I^n_{B_2}(h(b)),\ F^n_{B_1}(b) = F^n_{B_2}(h(b))$,
3. $T^p_{B_{1k}}(bd) = T^p_{B_{2\varphi(k)}}(h(b)h(d)),\ I^p_{B_{1k}}(bd) = I^p_{B_{2\varphi(k)}}(h(b)h(d)),\ F^p_{B_{1k}}(bd) = F^p_{B_{2\varphi(k)}}(h(b)h(d))$,
4. $T^n_{B_{1k}}(bd) = T^n_{B_{2\varphi(k)}}(h(b)h(d)),\ I^n_{B_{1k}}(bd) = I^n_{B_{2\varphi(k)}}(h(b)h(d)),\ F^n_{B_{1k}}(bd) = F^n_{B_{2\varphi(k)}}(h(b)h(d))$,

for all $b \in X_1$, $bd \in B_{1k}$, $k \in \{1, 2, \ldots, m\}$.

Example 10.12 Let $\check{G}_{b1} = (B, B_1, B_2)$ and $\check{G}_{b2} = (B', B'_1, B'_2)$ be two bipolar single-valued neutrosophic graph structures of two graph structures $\check{G}_{s1} = (X, X_1, X_2)$ and $\check{G}_{s2} = (X', X'_1, X'_2)$ as shown in Figs. 10.14 and 10.15, respectively.

$\check{G}_{b1}$ and $\check{G}_{b2}$ are isomorphic under (h, φ), where $h : X \to X'$ is a bijection and φ is a permutation on the set $\{1, 2\}$ defined as $\varphi(1) = 2$, $\varphi(2) = 1$ and satisfy the following conditions:

1. $T^p_B(b_i) = T^p_{B'}(h(b_i)),\ I^p_B(b_i) = I^p_{B'}(h(b_i)),\ F^p_B(b_i) = F^p_{B'}(h(b_i))$,
2. $T^n_B(b_i) = T^n_{B'}(h(b_i)),\ I^n_B(b_i) = I^n_{B'}(h(b_i)),\ F^n_B(b_i) = F^n_{B'}(h(b_i))$,
3. $T^p_{B_k}(b_ib_j) = T^p_{B'_{\varphi(k)}}(h(b_i)h(b_j)),\ I^p_{B_k}(b_ib_j) = I^p_{B'_{\varphi(k)}}(h(b_i)h(b_j)),\ F^p_{B_k}(b_ib_j) = F^p_{B'_{\varphi(k)}}(h(b_i)h(b_j))$,
4. $T^n_{B_k}(b_ib_j) = T^n_{B'_{\varphi(k)}}(h(b_i)h(b_j)),\ I^n_{B_k}(b_ib_j) = I^n_{B'_{\varphi(k)}}(h(b_i)h(b_j)),\ F^n_{B_k}(b_ib_j) = F^n_{B'_{\varphi(k)}}(h(b_i)h(b_j))$,

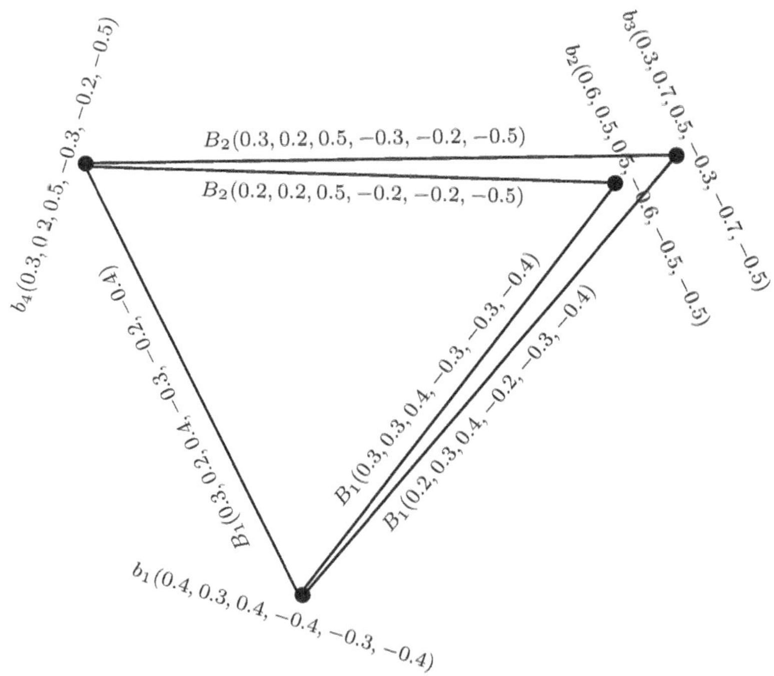

Fig. 10.14 Bipolar single-valued neutrosophic graph structure $\check{G}_{b1}$

for all $b_i \in X$, $b_i b_j \in X_k$, $k = 1, 2$.

Definition 10.14 A bipolar single-valued neutrosophic graph structure $\check{G}_{b1} = (B_1, B_{11}, B_{12}, \ldots, B_{1m})$ of a graph structure $\check{G}_{s1} = (X_1, X_{11}, X_{12}, \ldots, X_{1m})$ is said to be **identical** to the bipolar single-valued neutrosophic graph structure $\check{G}_{b2} = (B_2, B_{21}, B_{22}, \ldots, B_{2m})$ of a graph structure $\check{G}_{s2} = (X_2, X_{21}, X_{22}, \ldots, X_{2m})$ if $h : X_1 \to X_2$ is a bijection such that

1. $T^p_{B_1}(b) = T^p_{B_2}(h(b))$, $I^p_{B_1}(b) = I^p_{B_2}(h(b))$, $F^p_{B_1}(b) = F^p_{B_2}(h(b))$,
2. $T^n_{B_1}(b) = T^n_{B_2}(h(b))$, $I^n_{B_1}(b) = I^n_{B_2}(h(b))$, $F^n_{B_1}(b) = F^n_{B_2}(h(b))$,
3. $T^p_{B_{1k}}(bd) = T^p_{B_{2k}}(h(b)h(d))$, $I^p_{B_{1k}}(bd) = I^p_{B_{2k}}(h(b)h(d))$, $F^p_{B_{1k}}(bd) = F^p_{B_{2k}}(h(b)h(d))$,
4. $T^n_{B_{1k}}(bd) = T^n_{B_{2k}}(h(b)h(d))$, $I^n_{B_{1k}}(bd) = I^n_{B_{2k}}(h(b)h(d))$, $F^n_{B_{1k}}(bd) = F^n_{B_{2k}}(h(b)h(d))$,

for all $b \in X_1$, $bd \in X_{1k}$, $k \in \{1, 2, \ldots, m\}$.

Example 10.13 Let $\check{G}_{b1} = (B, B_1, B_2)$ and $\check{G}_{b2} = (B', B'_1, B'_2)$ be two bipolar single-valued neutrosophic graph structures of the graph structures $\check{G}_{s1} = (X, X_1, X_2)$ and $\check{G}_{s2} = (X', X'_1, X'_2)$, respectively, as shown in Figs. 10.16 and 10.17.

The bipolar single-valued neutrosophic graph structure $\check{G}_{b1}$ is identical to $\check{G}_{b2}$ under $h : X \to X'$ defined as $h(b_1) = d_2$, $h(b_2) = d_1$, $h(b_3) = d_4$, $h(b_4) = d_3$, $h(b_5) = d_5$, $h(b_6) = d_8$, $h(b_7) = d_7$, $h(b_8) = d_6$. Moreover,

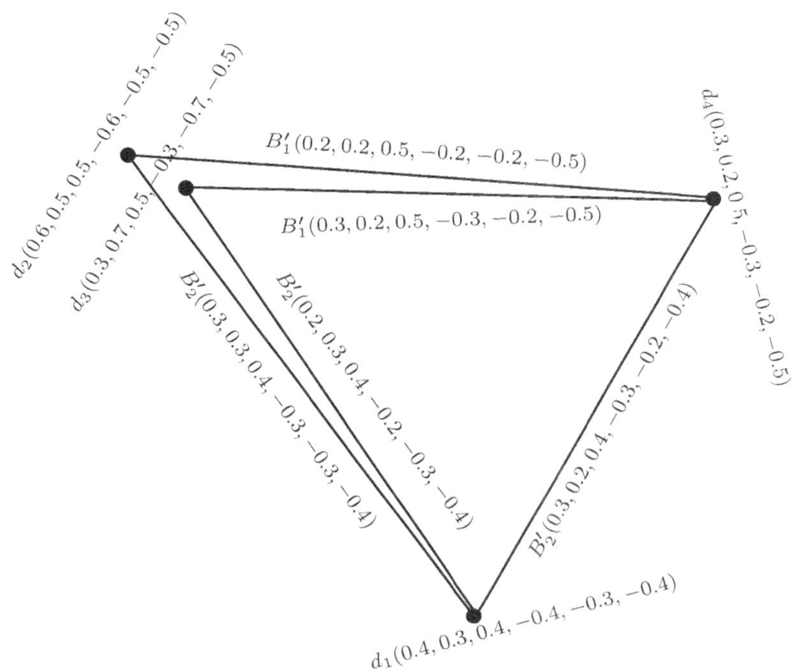

Fig. 10.15 Bipolar neutrosophic graph structure $\check{G}_{b2}$

1. $T^p_B(b_i) = T^p_{B'}(h(b_i))$, $I^p_B(b_i) = I^p_{B'}(h(b_i))$, $F^p_B(b_i) = F^p_{B'}(h(b_i))$,
2. $T^n_B(b_i) = T^n_{B'}(h(b_i))$, $I^n_B(b_i) = I^n_{B'}(h(b_i))$, $F^n_B(b_i) = F^n_{B'}(h(b_i))$,
3. $T^p_{B_k}(b_ib_j) = T^p_{B'_k}(h(b_i)h(b_j))$, $I^p_{B_k}(b_ib_j) = I^p_{B'_k}(h(b_i)h(b_j))$, $F^p_{B_k}(b_ib_j) = F^p_{B'_k}(h(b_i)h(b_j))$,
4. $T^n_{B_k}(b_ib_j) = T^n_{B'_k}(h(b_i)h(b_j))$, $I^n_{B_k}(b_ib_j) = I^n_{B'_k}(h(b_i)h(b_j))$, $F^n_{B_k}(b_ib_j) = F^n_{B'_k}(h(b_i)h(b_j))$,

for all $b_i \in X$, $b_ib_j \in X_k$, $k = 1, 2$.

Definition 10.15 Let $\check{G}_{bn} = (B, B_1, B_2, \ldots, B_m)$ be a bipolar single-valued neutrosophic graph structure and φ be a permutation on $\{B_1, B_2, \ldots, B_m\}$ and also on set $\{1, 2, \ldots, m\}$, that is, $\varphi(B_k) = B_l$ if and only if $\varphi(k) = l$ for all k. If $bd \in \Upsilon_k$ and

1. $T^p_{B^\varphi_k}(bd) = T^p_B(b) \wedge T^p_B(d) - \bigvee_{l \neq k} T^p_{\varphi(B_l)}(bd)$, $T^n_{B^\varphi_k}(bd) = T^n_B(b) \vee T^n_B(d) - \bigwedge_{l \neq k} T^n_{\varphi(B_l)}(bd)$,
2. $I^p_{B^\varphi_k}(bd) = I^p_B(b) \wedge I^p_B(d) - \bigvee_{l \neq k} I^p_{\varphi(B_l)}(bd)$, $I^n_{B^\varphi_k}(bd) = I^n_B(b) \vee I^n_B(d) - \bigwedge_{l \neq k} I^n_{\varphi(B_l)}(bd)$,
3. $F^p_{B^\varphi_k}(bd) = F^p_B(b) \vee F^p_B(d) - \bigwedge_{l \neq k} T^p_{\varphi(B_l)}(bd)$, $F^n_{B^\varphi_k}(bd) = F^n_B(b) \wedge F^n_B(d) - \bigvee_{l \neq k} T^n_{\varphi(B_l)}(bd)$,

for each $k \in \{1, 2, \ldots, m\}$, then $bd \in B^\varphi_e$, where e is selected such that

1. $T^p_{B^\varphi_e}(bd) \geq T^p_{B^\varphi_k}(bd)$, $I^p_{B^\varphi_e}(bd) \geq I^p_{B^\varphi_k}(bd)$, $F^p_{B^\varphi_e}(bd) \geq F^p_{B^\varphi_k}(bd)$,
2. $T^n_{B^\varphi_e}(bd) \leq T^n_{B^\varphi_k}(bd)$, $I^n_{B^\varphi_e}(bd) \leq I^n_{B^\varphi_k}(bd)$, $F^n_{B^\varphi_e}(bd) \leq F^n_{B^\varphi_k}(bd)$, for all $k \in \{1, 2, \ldots, m\}$.

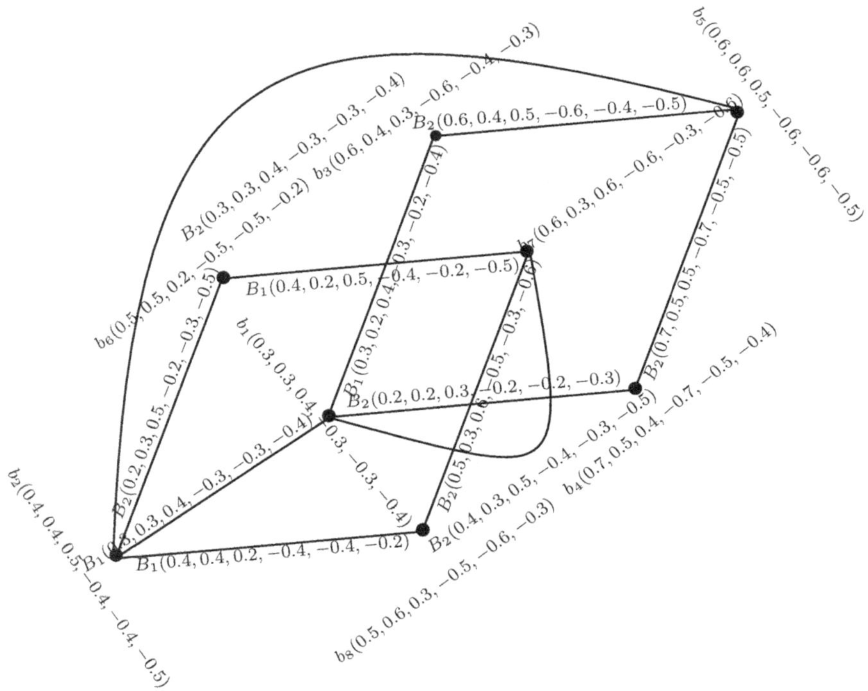

Fig. 10.16 Bipolar neutrosophic graph structure $\check{G}_{b1}$

The bipolar single-valued neutrosophic graph structure $(B, B_1^{\varphi}, B_2^{\varphi}, \ldots, B_m^{\varphi})$ is called **φ-complement** of the bipolar single-valued neutrosophic graph structure $\check{G}_{bn}$ and denoted by $\check{G}_{bn}^{\varphi c}$.

Example 10.14 Let $B = \{(b_1, 0.4, 0.4, 0.7, -0.4, -0.4, -0.7), (b_2, 0.6, 0.6, 0.4, -0.6, -0.6, -0.4), (b_3, 0.8, 0.5, 0.3, -0.8, -0.5, -0.3)\}$, $B_1 = \{(b_1b_3, 0.4, 0.4, 0.3, -0.4, -0.4, -0.3)\}$, $B_2 = \{(b_2b_3, 0.6, 0.4, 0.3, -0.6, -0.4, -0.3)\}$, and $B_3 = \{(b_1b_2, 0.4, 0.3, 0.4, -0.4, -0.3, -0.4)\}$ be bipolar single-valued neutrosophic sets on $X = \{b_1, b_2, b_3\}$, $X_1 = \{b_1b_3\}$, $X_2 = \{b_2b_3\}$, and $X_3 = \{b_1b_2\}$, respectively. Consider a bipolar single-valued neutrosophic graph structure $\check{G}_{bn} = (B, B_1, B_2, B_3)$ of graph structure $\check{G} = (X, X_1, X_2, X_3)$. Let $\varphi(B_1) = B_2$, $\varphi(B_2) = B_3$, $\varphi(B_3) = B_1$, where φ is a permutation on $\{1, 2, 3\}$.

Through simple calculations for edges $b_1b_3, b_2b_3, b_1b_2 \in B_1, B_2, B_3$, respectively, it is easy to see that $b_1b_3 \in B_3^{\varphi}$, $b_2b_3 \in B_1^{\varphi}$, $b_1b_2 \in B_2^{\varphi}$. So, $\check{G}_{bn}^{\varphi c} = (B, B_1^{\varphi}, B_2^{\varphi}, B_3^{\varphi})$ is a φ-complement of the bipolar single-valued neutrosophic graph structure $\check{G}_{bn}$ as shown in Fig.10.18.

Proposition 10.1 *The φ-complement of a bipolar single-valued neutrosophic graph structure $\check{G}_{bn} = (B, B_1, B_2, \ldots, B_m)$ is a strong bipolar single-valued neutrosophic*

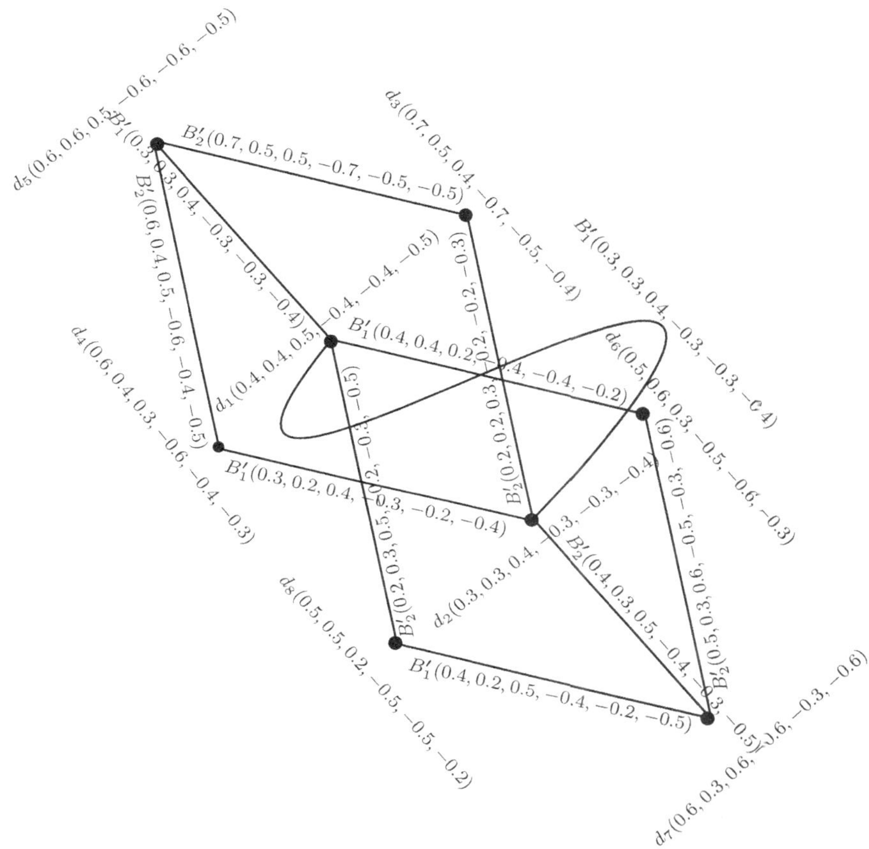

Fig. 10.17 Bipolar neutrosophic graph structure $\check{G}_{b2}$

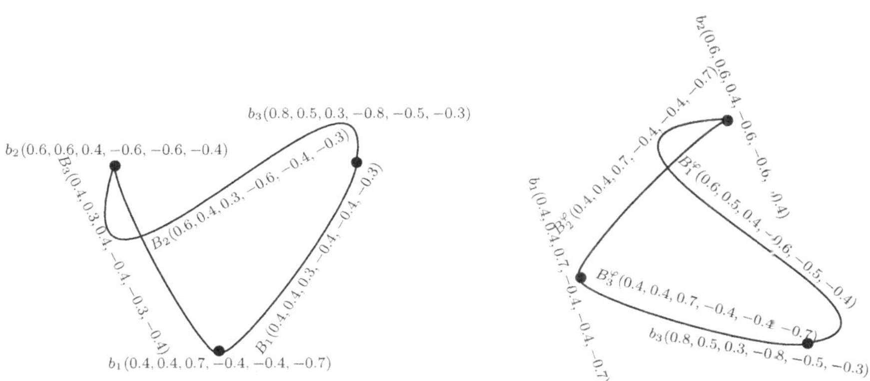

Fig. 10.18 $\check{G}_{bn}$ and φ-complement $\check{G}_{bn}^{\psi c}$

graph structure. Moreover, if $\varphi(k) = e$, where $k, e \in \{1, 2, \ldots, m\}$, then all B_e-edges in the bipolar single-valued neutrosophic graph structure $(B, B_1, B_2, \ldots, B_m)$ become B_k^{φ}-edges in $(B, B_1^{\varphi}, B_2^{\varphi}, \ldots, B_m^{\varphi})$.

Proof By Definition 10.15,

$$T^p_{B_k^{\varphi}}(bd) = T^p_B(b) \wedge T^p_B(d) - \bigvee_{l\neq k} T^p_{\varphi(B_l)}(bd), \quad T^n_{B_k^{\varphi}}(bd) = T^n_B(b) \vee T^n_B(d) - \bigwedge_{l\neq k} T^n_{\varphi(B_l)}(bd),$$

$$I^p_{B_k^{\varphi}}(bd) = I^p_B(b) \wedge I^p_B(d) - \bigvee_{l\neq k} I^p_{\varphi(B_l)}(bd), \quad I^n_{B_k^{\varphi}}(bd) = I^n_B(b) \vee I^n_B(d) - \bigwedge_{l\neq k} I^n_{\varphi(B_l)}(bd),$$

$$F^p_{B_k^{\varphi}}(bd) = F^p_B(b) \vee F^p_B(d) - \bigwedge_{l\neq k} F^p_{\varphi(B_l)}(bd), \quad F^n_{B_k^{\varphi}}(bd) = F^n_B(b) \wedge F^n_B(d) - \bigvee_{l\neq k} F^n_{\varphi(B_l)}(bd),$$

where $k \in \{1, 2, \ldots, m\}$. For expression of $T^p_{B_k^{\varphi}}$:

As $T^p_B(b) \wedge T^p_B(d) \geq 0$, $\bigvee_{l\neq k} T^p_{\varphi(B_l)}(bd) \geq 0$ and $T^p_{B_k}(bd) \leq T^p_B(b) \wedge T^p_B(d)$ for all B_k. This implies $\bigvee_{l\neq k} T^p_{\varphi(B_l)}(bd) \leq T^p_B(b) \wedge T^p_B(d)$. This shows that $T^p_B(b) \wedge T^p_B(b) - \bigvee_{l\neq k} T^p_{\varphi(B_l)}(bd) \geq 0$. Hence, $T^p_{B_k^{\varphi}}(bd) \geq 0$ for all k. Furthermore, $T^p_{B_k^{\varphi}}(bd)$ obtains maximum value when $\bigvee_{l\neq k} T^p_{\varphi(B_l)}(bd)$ is zero. Undoubtedly, when $\varphi(B_k) = B_e$ and bd is a B_e-edge, then $\bigvee_{l\neq k} T^p_{\varphi(B_l)}(bd)$ acquires zero value. Hence,

$$T^p_{B_k^{\varphi}}(bd) = T^p_B(b) \wedge T^p_B(d), \ for\ bd \in B_e,\ \varphi(B_k) = B_e.$$

For expression of $T^n_{B_k^{\varphi}}$:

Since $T^n_B(b) \vee T^n_B(d) \leq 0$, $\bigwedge_{l\neq k} T^n_{\varphi(B_l)}(bd) \leq 0$ and $T^n_{B_k}(bd) \geq T^n_B(b) \vee T^n_B(d)$ for all B_k. This implies $\bigwedge_{l\neq k} T^n_{\varphi(B_l)}(bd) \geq T^n_B(b) \vee T^n_B(d)$. It indicates $T^n_B(b) \vee T^n_B(d) - \bigwedge_{l\neq k} T_{\varphi(B_l)}(bd) \leq 0$. Hence, $T^n_{B_k^{\varphi}}(bd) \leq 0$ for all k. Furthermore, $T^n_{B_k^{\varphi}}(bd)$ is minimum when $\bigwedge_{l\neq k} T^n_{\varphi(B_l)}(bd)$ is zero. Certainly when $\varphi(B_k) = B_e$ and bd is a B_e-edge, then $\bigwedge_{l\neq k} T^n_{\varphi(B_l)}(bd)$ is zero. Hence,

$$T^n_{B_k^{\varphi}}(bd) = T^n_B(b) \vee T^n_B(d), \ for\ bd \in B_e,\ \varphi(B_k) = B_e.$$

Similarly, for expression of $I^p_{B_k^{\varphi}}$ and $I^n_{B_k^{\varphi}}$ results are as follows:

Since $I^p_B(b) \wedge I^p_B(d) \geq 0$, $\bigvee_{l\neq k} I^p_{\varphi(B_l)}(bd) \geq 0$ and $I^p_{B_k}(bd) \leq I^p_B(b) \wedge I^p_B(d)\ \forall B_k$. This implies $\bigvee_{l\neq k} I^p_{\varphi(B_l)}(bd) \leq I^p_B(b) \wedge I^p_B(d)$, which shows that $I^p_B(b) \wedge I^p_B(d) -$

$\bigvee_{l\neq k} I^{p}_{\varphi(B_l)}(bd) \geq 0$. Hence, $I^{p}_{B^{\varphi}_{k}}(bd) \geq 0$ for all k. Furthermore, $I^{p}_{B^{\varphi}_{k}}(bd)$ obtains maximum value when $\bigvee_{l\neq k} I^{p}_{\varphi(B_l)}(bd)$ is zero. Undoubtedly, when $\varphi(B_k) = B_e$ and bd is a B_e-edge, then $\bigvee_{l\neq k} I^{p}_{\varphi(B_l)}(bd)$ acquires zero value. Hence,

$$I^{p}_{B^{\varphi}_{k}}(bd) = I^{p}_{B}(b) \wedge I^{p}_{B}(d),\ \ for\ bd \in B_e,\ \varphi(B_k) = B_e.$$

Moreover, as $I^{n}_{B}(b) \vee I^{n}_{B}(d) \leq 0$, $\bigwedge_{l\neq k} I^{n}_{\varphi(B_l)}(bd) \leq 0$ and $I^{n}_{B_k}(bd) \geq I^{n}_{B}(b) \vee I^{n}_{B}(d)$ for all B_k. This implies $\bigwedge_{l\neq k} I^{n}_{\varphi(B_l)}(bd) \geq I^{n}_{B}(b) \vee I^{n}_{B}(d)$. This indicates $I^{n}_{B}(b) \vee I^{n}_{B}(d) - \bigwedge_{l\neq k} I_{\varphi(B_l)}(bd) \leq 0$. Hence, $I^{n}_{B^{\varphi}_{k}}(bd) \leq 0$ for all k. Furthermore, $I^{n}_{B^{\varphi}_{k}}(bd)$ is minimum when $\bigwedge_{l\neq k} I^{n}_{\varphi(B_l)}(bd)$ is zero. Certainly, when $\varphi(B_k) = B_e$ and bd is a B_e-edge, then $\bigwedge_{l\neq k} I^{n}_{\varphi(B_l)}(bd)$ is zero. Hence,

$$I^{n}_{B^{\varphi}_{k}}(bd) = I^{n}_{B}(b) \vee I^{n}_{B}(d)\ for\ bd \in B_e,\ \varphi(B_k) = B_e.$$

On similar argument, derive expressions for $F^{p}_{B^{\varphi}_{k}}$ and $F^{n}_{B^{\varphi}_{k}}$ as follows:

Since $F^{p}_{B}(b) \vee F^{p}_{B}(d) \geq 0$, $\bigwedge_{l\neq k} F^{p}_{\varphi(B_l)}(bd) \geq 0$ and $F^{p}_{B_k}(bd) \leq F^{p}_{B}(b) \vee F^{p}_{B}(d)$ for all B_k. This implies $\bigwedge_{l\neq k} F^{p}_{\varphi(B_l)}(bd) \leq F^{p}_{B}(b) \vee F^{p}_{B}(d)$. It indicates $F^{p}_{B}(b) \vee F^{p}_{B}(d) - \bigwedge_{l\neq k} FP_{\varphi(B_l)}(bd) \geq 0$. Hence, $F^{p}_{B^{\varphi}_{k}}(bd) \geq 0$ for all k. Furthermore, $F^{p}_{B^{\varphi}_{k}}(bd)$ is maximum when $\bigwedge_{l\neq k} F^{p}_{\varphi(B_l)}(bd)$ is zero. When $\varphi(B_k) = B_e$ and bd is a B_e-edge, then $\bigwedge_{l\neq k} F^{p}_{\varphi(B_l)}(bd)$ is zero. Hence,

$$F^{p}_{B^{\varphi}_{k}}(bd) = F^{p}_{B}(b) \vee F^{p}_{B}(d)\ for\ bd \in B_e,\ \varphi(B_k) = B_e.$$

Moreover, as $F^{n}_{B}(b) \wedge F^{n}_{B}(d) \leq 0$, $\bigvee_{l\neq k} F^{n}_{\varphi(B_l)}(bd) \leq 0$ and $F^{n}_{B_k}(bd) \geq F^{n}_{B}(b) \wedge F^{n}_{B}(d)$ $\forall B_k$. This implies $\bigvee_{l\neq k} F^{n}_{\varphi(B_l)}(bd) \geq F^{n}_{B}(b) \wedge F^{n}_{B}(d)$. This shows that $F^{n}_{B}(b) \wedge F^{n}_{B}(b) - \bigvee_{l\neq k} F^{n}_{\varphi(B_l)}(bd) \leq 0$. Hence, $F^{n}_{B^{\varphi}_{k}}(bd) \leq 0\ \forall\ k$. Furthermore, $F^{n}_{B^{\varphi}_{k}}(bd)$ obtains minimum value when $\bigvee_{l\neq k} F^{n}_{\varphi(B_l)}(bd)$ is zero. Undoubtedly, when $\varphi(B_k) = B_e$ and bd is a B_e-edge, then $\bigvee_{l\neq k} F^{n}_{\varphi(B_l)}(bd)$ acquires zero value. Hence,

$$F^{n}_{B^{\varphi}_{k}}(bd) = F^{n}_{B}(b) \wedge F^{n}_{B}(d),\ \ for\ bd \in B_e,\ \varphi(B_k) = B_e.$$

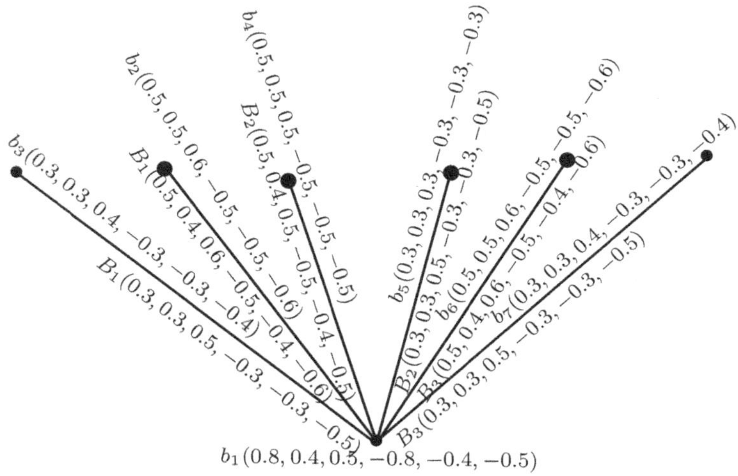

Fig. 10.19 Bipolar neutrosophic graph structure

It completes the proof. □

Definition 10.16 Let $\check{G}_{bn} = (B, B_1, B_2, \ldots, B_m)$ be a bipolar single-valued neutrosophic graph structure and φ be a permutation on $\{1, 2, \ldots, m\}$, then

1. $\check{G}_{bn}$ is a **self-complementary** bipolar single-valued neutrosophic graph structure if $\check{G}_{bn}$ is isomorphic to $\check{G}_{bn}^{\varphi c}$.
2. $\check{G}_{bn}$ is a strong self-complementary bipolar single-valued neutrosophic graph structure if $\check{G}_{bn}$ is identical to $\check{G}_{bn}^{\varphi c}$.

Definition 10.17 Let $\check{G}_{bn} = (B, B_1, B_2, \ldots, B_m)$ be a bipolar single-valued neutrosophic graph structure, then

1. $\check{G}_{bn}$ is a **totally self-complementary** bipolar single-valued neutrosophic graph structure if $\check{G}_{bn}$ is isomorphic to $\check{G}_{bn}^{\varphi c}$ for all permutations φ on $\{1, 2, \ldots, m\}$.
2. $\check{G}_{bn}$ is a totally strong self-complementary bipolar single-valued neutrosophic graph structure if $\check{G}_{bn}$ is identical to $\check{G}_{bn}^{\varphi c}$ for all permutations φ on $\{1, 2, \ldots, m\}$.

Example 10.15 A bipolar single-valued neutrosophic graph structure $\check{G}_{bn} = (B, B_1, B_2, B_3)$ shown in Fig.10.19 is totally strong self-complementary, since it is identical to its $\varphi-$complement for all permutations φ on $\{1, 2, 3\}$.

Theorem 10.6 *A bipolar single-valued neutrosophic graph structure is totally self-complementary if and only if it is a strong bipolar single-valued neutrosophic graph structure.*

Proof Consider a strong bipolar single-valued neutrosophic graph structure $\check{G}_{bn}$ and a permutation φ on {1,2, ..., m}. By proposition 10.1, φ-complement of a bipolar single-valued neutrosophic graph structure $\check{G}_{bn} = (B, B_1, B_2, \ldots, B_m)$ is a strong bipolar single-valued neutrosophic graph structure. Moreover, if $\varphi^{-1}(e) = k$, where $k, e \in \{1, 2, \ldots, m\}$, then all B_e-edges in the bipolar single-valued neutrosophic graph structure $(B, B_1, B_2, \ldots, B_m)$ become B_k^{φ}-edges in $(B, B_1^{\varphi}, B_2^{\varphi}, \ldots, B_m^{\varphi})$. This leads to the following results.

$$T^p_{B_e}(bd) = T^p_B(b) \wedge T^p_B(d) = T^p_{B^{\varphi}_k}(bd), I^p_{B_e}(bd) = I^p_B(b) \wedge I^p_B(d) = I^p_{B^{\varphi}_k}(bd), F^p_{B_e}(bd) = F^p_B(b) \vee F^p_B(d) = F^p_{B^{\varphi}_k}(bd),$$

$$T^n_{B_e}(bd) = T^n_B(b) \vee T^n_B(d) = T^n_{B^{\varphi}_k}(bd), I^n_{B_e}(bd) = I^n_B(b) \vee I^n_B(d) = I^n_{B^{\varphi}_k}(bd), F^n_{B_e}(bd) = F^n_B(b) \wedge F^n_B(d) = F^p_{B^{\varphi}_k}(bd).$$

Therefore, under $h : X \to X$ (identity mapping), $\check{G}_{bn}$ and $\check{G}^{\varphi c}_{bn}$ are isomorphic such that
$T^p_B(b) = T^p_B(h(b))$, $I^p_B(b) = I^p_B(h(b))$, $F^p_B(b) = F^p_B(h(b))$, $T^n_B(b) = T^n_B(h(b))$, $I^n_B(b) = I^n_B(h(b))$, $F^n_B(b) = F^n_B(h(b))$. Further,

$$T^p_{B_e}(bd) = T^p_{B^{\varphi}_k}(h(b)h(d)) = T^p_{B^{\varphi}_k}(bd), T^n_{B_e}(bd) = T^n_{B^{\varphi}_k}(h(b)h(d)) = T^n_{B^{\varphi}_k}(bd),$$

$$I^p_{B_e}(bd) = I^p_{B^{\varphi}_k}(h(b)h(d)) = I^p_{B^{\varphi}_k}(bd), I^n_{B_e}(bd) = I^n_{B^{\varphi}_k}(h(b)h(d)) = I^n_{B^{\varphi}_k}(bd),$$

$$F^p_{B_e}(bd) = F^p_{B^{\varphi}_k}(h(b)h(d)) = F^p_{B^{\varphi}_k}(bd), F^n_{B_e}(bd) = F^n_{B^{\varphi}_k}(h(b)h(d)) = F^n_{B^{\varphi}_k}(bd),$$

for all $bd \in X_e$, for $\varphi^{-1}(e) = k; e, k = 1, 2, \ldots, m$.

These relations hold for each permutation φ on $\{1, 2, \ldots, m\}$. Hence, $\check{G}_{bn}$ is a totally self-complementary bipolar single-valued neutrosophic graph structure. Conversely, let $\check{G}_{bn}$ be isomorphic to $\check{G}^{\varphi c}_{bn}$ for each permutation φ on $\{1, 2, \ldots, m\}$. Moreover, according to the definitions of φ-complement and isomorphism of the bipolar single-valued neutrosophic graph structure,

$$T^p_{B_e}(bd) = T^p_{B^{\varphi}_k}(h(b)h(d)) = T^p_B(h(b)) \wedge T^p_B(h(d)) = T^p_B(b) \wedge T^p_B(d),$$

$$T^n_{B_e}(bd) = T^n_{B^{\varphi}_k}(h(b)h(d)) = T^n_B(h(b)) \vee T^n_B(h(d)) = T^n_B(b) \vee T^n_B(d),$$

$$I^p_{B_e}(bd) = I^p_{B^{\varphi}_k}(h(b)h(d)) = I^p_B(h(b)) \wedge I^p_B(h(d)) = I^p_B(b) \wedge I^p_B(d),$$

$$I^n_{B_e}(bd) = I^n_{B^{\varphi}_k}(h(b)h(d)) = I^n_B(h(b)) \vee I^n_B(h(d)) = I^n_B(b) \vee I^n_B(d),$$

$$F^p_{B_e}(bd) = F^p_{B^{\varphi}_k}(h(b)h(d)) = F^p_B(h(b)) \vee F^p_B(h(d)) = F^p_B(b) \vee F^p_B(d),$$

$$F^n_{B_e}(bd) = F^n_{B^{\varphi}_k}(h(b)h(d)) = F^n_B(h(b)) \wedge F^n_B(h(d)) = F^n_B(b) \wedge F^n_B(d),$$

for all $bd \in X_e$, where $e = 1, 2, \ldots, m$. Hence, $\check{G}_{bn}$ is a strong bipolar single-valued neutrosophic graph structure. □

Remark 10.1 Every self-complementary bipolar single-valued neutrosophic graph structure is always a totally self-complementary bipolar single-valued neutrosophic graph structure.

Theorem 10.7 *If $\check{G}_s = (X, X_1, X_2, \ldots, X_m)$ is a totally strong-self-complementary graph structure and $B = (T_B^p, I_B^p, F_B^p, T_B^n, I_B^n, F_B^n)$ is a bipolar single-valued neutrosophic subset of X, where $T_B^p, I_B^p, F_B^p, T_B^n, I_B^n, F_B^n$ are constant functions, then every strong bipolar single-valued neutrosophic graph structure of $\check{G}_s$ with bipolar single-valued neutrosophic vertex set B is necessarily a totally strong self-complementary bipolar single-valued neutrosophic graph structure.*

Proof Let $f, f' \in [0, 1], g, g' \in [0, 1]$, and $i, i' \in [0, 1]$ be six constants and $T_B^p(b) = f$, $I_B^p(b) = g$, $F_B^p(b) = i$, $T_B^n(b) = f'$, $I_B^n(b) = g'$, $F_B^n(b) = i'$, for all $b \in X$.

Since $\check{G}_s$ is a totally strong self-complementary graph structure, so for every permutation φ^{-1} on $\{1, 2, \ldots, m\}$ there exists a bijection $h : X \rightarrow X$ such that for every B_e-edge bd, h(b)h(d) [a B_k-edge in $\check{G}_s$] is a B_e-edge in $\check{G}_s^{\varphi^{-1}c}$. Thus, for every B_e-edge (bd), (h(b)h(d)) [a B_k-edge in $\check{G}_{bn}$] is a B_e^{φ}-edge in $\check{G}_{bn}^{\varphi^{-1}c}$.

Moreover, $\check{G}_{bn}$ is a strong bipolar single-valued neutrosophic graph structure. So $T_B^p(b) = f = T_B^p(h(b))$, $I_B^p(b) = g = I_B^p(h(b))$, $F_B^p(b) = i = F_B^p(h(b))$, $T_B^n(b) = f' = T_B^n(h(b))$, $I_B^n(b) = g' = I_B^n(h(b))$, $F_B^n(b) = i' = F_B^n(h(b))$, for all $b \in X$. Also,

$$T_{B_e}^p(bd) = T_B^p(b) \wedge T_B^p(d) = T_B^p(h(b)) \wedge T_B^p(h(d)) = T_{B_k^{\varphi}}^p(h(b)h(d)),$$

$$I_{B_e}^p(bd) = I_B^p(b) \wedge I_B^p(d) = I_B^p(h(b)) \wedge I_B^p(h(d)) = I_{B_k^{\varphi}}^p(h(b)h(d)),$$

$$F_{B_e}^p(bd) = F_B^p(b) \vee I_B^p(d) = F_B^p(h(b)) \vee F_B^p(h(d)) = F_{B_k^{\varphi}}^p(h(b)h(d)),$$

$$T_{B_e}^n(bd) = T_B^n(b) \vee T_B^n(d) = T_B^n(h(b)) \vee T_B^n(h(d)) = T_{B_k^{\varphi}}^n(h(b)h(d)),$$

$$I_{B_e}^n(bd) = I_B^n(b) \vee I_B^n(d) = I_B^n(h(b)) \vee I_B^n(h(d)) = I_{B_k^{\varphi}}^n(h(b)h(d)),$$

$$F_{B_e}^n(bd) = F_B^n(b) \wedge I_B^n(d) = F_B^n(h(b)) \wedge F_B^n(h(d)) = F_{B_k^{\varphi}}^n(h(b)h(d)),$$

for all $bd \in X_k$, $k = 1, 2, \ldots, m$.

This shows that $\check{G}_{bn}$ is a strong self-complementary bipolar single-valued neutrosophic graph structure. It satisfies for every permutation φ and φ^{-1} on the set $\{1, 2, \ldots, m\}$. Thus, $\check{G}_{bn}$ is a totally strong self-complementary bipolar single-valued neutrosophic graph structure.

Remark 10.2 The converse of Theorem 10.7 may not be true, e.g., a bipolar single-valued neutrosophic graph structure depicted in Fig.10.19 is totally strong self-complementary. It is also a strong bipolar single-valued neutrosophic graph structure with a totally strong self-complementary underlying graph structure but T_B^p, I_B^p, F_B^p,T_B^n, I_B^n, F_B^n are not constant functions.

10.4 Applications of Bipolar Single-Valued Neutrosophic Graph Structures

In this section, the applications of bipolar single-valued neutrosophic graph structures are discussed in international relations, psychology, and global terrorism.

10.4.1 International Relations

Naturally, any living organism cannot be 100% self-reliant, especially a human being who is the noblest of all creatures, but he relies on many things for his survival including, plants, animals, and other human beings. This dependence causes relationships among human beings. On Earth, human population is divided into 195 countries. That's why the interdependence of human beings results in many relationships among countries. In a relationship, both countries play their role so that these relations can be represented using a bipolar single-valued neutrosophic graph structure, which will show that between two particular countries which type of relationship is the strongest and what are the degrees of its strength from both countries. There are some relationships which are not good in some aspects. A bipolar single-valued neutrosophic graph structure will highlight as to which one country of those two countries is the strongest participant. The relationships and strong partici- pants can be checked. It can be seen which country is the most favorite for a particular relationship. Let X be the set of eight countries: $X =$ {China, Turkey, Bangladesh, America, India, Russia, Pakistan, Afghanistan}. Consider a bipolar single-valued neutrosophic set B on X as shown in Table 10.3.

In Table 10.3, T^p, F^p of a country indicate its positive and negative approaches about the World and I^p shows indeterminacy/ambiguity of its approach, whereas T^n and F^n denote its positive and negative reputation and I^n stands to represent the percentage of its uncertain reputation. Use the following abbreviations of country names: Ch = China, TU = Turkey, Ba = Bangladesh, Am = America, In = India, Ru = Russia, Pak = Pakistan, Afg = Afghanistan.

Each pair of countries of set X has T^p, I^p, F^p, T^n, I^n, and F^n values of different relationships in Tables 10.4, 10.5, 10.6, 10.7, 10.8, 10.9, 10.10, 10.11, 10.12.

Each pair of countries T^p, T^n of any particular relationship indicates strength of that relationship from the first country and the second country, respectively. Similarly F^p, F^n represent percentage of weakness and I^p, I^n demonstrate percentage

Table 10.3 Bipolar neutrosophic information of countries

Country	T^p	I^p	F^p	T^n	I^n	F^n
China	0.9	0.4	0.2	−0.9	−0.2	−0.2
Turkey	0.8	0.6	0.5	−0.6	−0.5	−0.5
Bangladesh	0.7	0.6	0.5	−0.4	−0.6	−0.5
America	0.8	0.4	0.4	−0.8	−0.2	−0.4
India	0.6	0.5	0.5	−0.5	−0.6	−0.6
Russia	0.8	0.4	0.3	−0.9	−0.3	−0.4
Pakistan	0.8	0.5	0.4	−0.5	−0.6	−0.6
Afghanistan	0.5	0.7	0.6	−0.4	−0.5	−0.8

Table 10.4 Types of relations between countries

Types of relations	(China, Turkey)	(China, Bangladesh)	(China, America)
Project investment	(0.1,0.4,0.3,−0.1,−0.2,−0.3)	(0.2,0.2,0.2,−0.1,−0.2,−0.3)	(0.2,0.1,0.4,−0.1,−0.2,−0.4)
Political support	(0.3,0.3,0.4,−0.3,−0.1,−0.3)	(0.4,0.2,0.1,−0.4,−0.2,−0.3)	(0.4,0.4,0.4,−0.3,−0.2,−0.4)
Warfare activities	(0.1,0.4,0.5,−0.1,−0.2,−0.2)	(0.1,0.3,0.5,−0.1,−0.2,−0.3)	(0.6,0.1,0.1,−0.7,−0.2,−0.1)
Nuclear weapons	(0.4,0.2,0.3,−0.1,−0.2,−0.3)	(0.1,0.2,0.5,−0.1,−0.2,−0.3)	(0.2,0.1,0.4,−0.1,−0.2,−0.4)
Friendship	(0.5,0.3,0.3,−0.5,−0.1,−0.2)	(0.4,0.2,0.1,−0.4,−0.1,−0.3)	(0.2,0.1,0.4,−0.1,−0.2,−0.3)
Respecting religious beliefs	(0.1,0.4,0.4,−0.4,−0.2,−0.3)	(0.4,0.3,0.1,−0.4,−0.2,−0.2)	(0.7,0.1,0.4,−0.6,−0.2,−0.3)

Table 10.5 Types of relations between countries

Types of relations	(Turkey, Bangladesh)	(Turkey, America)	(Turkey, India)
Project investment	(0.4,0.3,0.3,−0.1,−0.2,−0.3)	(0.2,0.2,0.5,−0.4,−0.2,−0.5)	(0.4,0.1,0.4,−0.1,−0.2,−0.5)
Political support	(0.5,0.4,0.3,−0.4,−0.3,−0.3)	(0.6,0.4,0.4,−0.5,−0.2,−0.4)	(0.2,0.4,0.4,−0.1,−0.4,−0.5)
Warfare activities	(0.1,0.4,0.4,−0.1,−0.3,−0.5)	(0.1,0.2,0.4,−0.3,−0.2,−0.4)	(0.2,0.4,0.5,−0.3,−0.2,−0.4)
Nuclear weapons	(0.1,0.4,0.3,−0.1,−0.2,−0.3)	(0.1,0.1,0.5,−0.4,−0.1,−0.4)	(0.2,0.1,0.4,−0.1,−0.4,−0.5)
Friendship	(0.6,0.4,0.4,−0.3,−0.2,−0.3)	(0.4,0.4,0.4,−0.5,−0.1,−0.5)	(0.2,0.3,0.5,−0.3,−0.2,−0.3)
Respecting religious beliefs	(0.7,0.3,0.2,−0.4,−0.2,−0.1)	(0.8,0.2,0.1,−0.3,−0.2,−0.4)	(0.2,0.1,0.4,−0.2,−0.2,−0.5)

Table 10.6 Types of relations between countries

Types of relations	(Bangladesh, America)	(Bangladesh, India)	(Bangladesh, Russia)
Project investment	(0.1,0.4,0.4,−0.1,−0.2,−0.3)	(0.1,0.5,0.5,−0.1,−0.3,−0.4)	(0.2,0.1,0.5,−0.3,−0.2,−0.3)
Political support	(0.3,0.3,0.4,−0.1,−0.1,−0.2)	(0.4,0.2,0.4,−0.2,−0.4,−0.5)	(0.3,0.2,0.4,−0.2,−0.3,−0.3)
Warfare activities	(0.1,0.3,0.4,−0.1,−0.2,−0.3)	(0.3,0.3,0.4,−0.1,−0.3,−0.4)	(0.4,0.3,0.3,−0.4,−0.5,−0.5)
Nuclear weapons	(0.1,0.4,0.5,−0.1,−0.2,−0.5)	(0.2,0.2,0.4,−0.1,−0.5,−0.6)	(0.5,0.4,0.4,−0.3,−0.2,−0.4)
Friendship	(0.2,0.3,0.5,−0.1,−0.2,−0.5)	(0.3,0.2,0.4,−0.1,−0.3,−0.5)	(0.2,0.1,0.4,−0.3,−0.3,−0.3)
Respecting religious beliefs	(0.4,0.4,0.4,−0.1,−0.2,−0.4)	(0.4,0.3,0.4,−0.1,−0.4,−0.3)	(0.5,0.2,0.4,−0.2,−0.3,−0.3)

Table 10.7 Types of relations between countries

Types of relations	(America, India)	(America, Russia)	(America, Pakistan)
Project investment	(0.5,0.2,0.3,−0.1,−0.2,−0.5)	(0.1,0.2,0.4,−0.1,−0.1,−0.4)	(0.4,0.3,0.4,−0.1,−0.2,−0.6)
Political support	(0.6,0.2,0.3,−0.5,−0.2,−0.3)	(0.3,0.1,0.3,−0.2,−0.2,−0.4)	(0.6,0.1,0.1,−0.5,−0.1,−0.0)
Warfare activities	(0.1,0.4,0.1,−0.1,−0.2,−0.5)	(0.4,0.2,0.4,−0.5,−0.2,−0.3)	(0.5,0.1,0.1,−0.1,−0.2,−0.6)
Nuclear weapons	(0.6,0.1,0.0,−0.1,−0.2,−0.5)	(0.2,0.2,0.4,−0.1,−0.1,−0.4)	(0.4,0.1,0.4,−0.1,−0.2,−0.5)
Friendship	(0.4,0.2,0.3,−0.5,−0.2,−0.3)	(0.3,0.2,0.4,−0.1,−0.2,−0.4)	(0.4,0.1,0.3,−0.5,−0.1,−0.1)
Respecting religious beliefs	(0.5,0.2,0.2,−0.5,−0.2,−0.3)	(0.8,0.1,0.1,−0.8,−0.1,−0.1)	(0.2,0.1,0.4,−0.5,−0.2,−0.1)

Table 10.8 Types of relations between countries

Types of relations	(India, Russia)	(India, Pakistan)	(India, Afghanistan)
Project investment	(0.4,0.1,0.3,−0.5,−0.1,−0.1)	(0.1,0.2,0.5,−0.1,−0.2,−0.3)	(0.3,0.3,0.5,−0.1,−0.2,−0.3)
Political support	(0.3,0.2,0.4,−0.4,−0.3,−0.3)	(0.0,0.2,0.4,−0.2,−0.2,−0.3)	(0.5,0.1,0.1,−0.4,−0.1,−0.1)
Warfare activities	(0.1,0.3,0.5,−0.1,−0.2,−0.5)	(0.6,0.1,0.0,−0.4,−0.2,−0.3)	(0.4,0.4,0.1,−0.1,−0.2,−0.2)
Nuclear weapons	(0.1,0.2,0.5,−0.5,−0.3,−0.2)	(0.0,0.1,0.5,−0.0,−0.3,−0.3)	(0.4,0.1,0.4,−0.1,−0.2,−0.1)
Friendship	(0.4,0.3,0.2,−0.3,−0.2,−0.4)	(0.1,0.2,0.5,−0.3,−0.2,−0.3)	(0.4,0.4,0.2,−0.4,−0.2,−0.2)
Respecting religious beliefs	(0.4,0.2,0.2,−0.4,−0.2,−0.2)	(0.3,0.1,0.4,−0.5,−0.3,−0.3)	(0.2,0.1,0.4,−0.4,−0.2,−0.2)

Table 10.9 Types of relations between countries

Types of relations	(Russia, Pakistan)	(Russia, Afghanistan)	(Russia, China)
Project investment	(0.5,0.2,0.4,−0.1,−0.2,−0.6)	(0.4,0.2,0.1,−0.0,−0.3,−0.8)	(0.2,0.1,0.3,−0.1,−0.2,−0.4)
Political support	(0.4,0.2,0.4,−0.4,−0.2,−0.4)	(0.1,0.2,0.4,−0.3,−0.2,−0.3)	(0.3,0.3,0.3,−0.1,−0.2,−0.4)
Warfare activities	(0.1,0.2,0.4,−0.1,−0.1,−0.6)	(0.5,0.0,0.0,−0.4,−0.2,−0.3)	(0.2,0.1,0.3,−0.1,−0.2,−0.3)
Nuclear weapons	(0.7,0.2,0.1,−0.4,−0.2,−0.4)	(0.4,0.2,0.1,−0.1,−0.2,−0.3)	(0.1,0.1,0.3,−0.1,−0.1,−0.4)
Friendship	(0.4,0.2,0.3,−0.1,−0.2,−0.3)	(0.4,0.2,0.1,−0.1,−0.2,−0.3)	(0.2,0.4,0.3,−0.1,−0.2,−0.3)
Respecting religious beliefs	(0.4,0.2,0.4,−0.4,−0.2,−0.4)	(0.4,0.2,0.1,−0.1,−0.2,−0.3)	(0.6,0.1,0.2,−0.7,−0.2,−0.1)

Table 10.10 Types of relations between countries

Types of relations	(Pakistan, China)	(Turkey, Pakistan)	(Pakistan, Bangladesh)
Project investment	(0.4,0.2,0.4,−0.5,−0.1,−0.1)	(0.7,0.1,0.2,−0.5,−0.1,−0.1)	(0.1,0.1,0.4,−0.1,−0.2,−0.3)
Political support	(0.8,0.2,0.1,−0.5,−0.0,−0.0)	(0.4,0.2,0.4,−0.5,−0.2,−0.3)	(0.6,0.1,0.4,−0.4,−0.2,−0.3)
Warfare activities	(0.0,0.0,0.4,−0.−0.0,−0.0,−0.6)	(0.1,0.2,0.5,−0.0,−0.1,−0.5)	(0.2,0.1,0.4,−0.1,−0.2,−0.3)
Nuclear weapons	(0.4,0.2,0.3,−0.1,−0.2,−0.2)	(0.1,0.1,0.5,−0.1,−0.2,−0.5)	(0.1,0.1,0.5,−0.1,−0.1,−0.6)
Friendship	(0.8,0.1,0.1,−0.5,−0.1,−0.0)	(0.6,0.2,0.1,−0.5,−0.2,−0.3)	(0.5,0.1,0.3,−0.3,−0.2,−0.3)
Respecting religious beliefs	(0.8,0.2,0.2,−0.4,−0.2,−0.1)	(0.5,0.1,0.1,−0.1,−0.1,−0.1)	(0.7,0.1,0.1,−0.4,−0.1,−0.0)

Table 10.11 Types of relations between countries

Types of relations	(Afghanistan, China)	(Afghanistan, America)	(Afghanistan, Turkey)
Project investment	(0.1,0.2,0.6,−0.1,−0.2,−0.7)	(0.0,0.1,0.6,−0.0,−0.0,−0.6)	(0.0,0.1,0.6,−0.1,−0.2,−0.6)
Political support	(0.3,0.3,0.5,−0.1,−0.2,−0.8)	(0.0,0.1,0.6,−0.0,−0.0,−0.8)	(0.2,0.1,0.4,−0.1,−0.1,−0.5)
Warfare activities	(0.1,0.2,0.6,−0.1,−0.2,−0.5)	(0.2,0.2,0.3,−0.4,−0.1,−0.0)	(0.1,0.1,0.4,−0.1,−0.2,−0.7)
Nuclear weapons	(0.1,0.4,0.6,−0.1,−0.2,−0.8)	(0.0,0.0,0.6,−0.0,−0.0,−0.7)	(0.0,0.1,0.5,−0.1,−0.1,−0.8)
Friendship	(0.4,0.2,0.6,−0.1,−0.2,−0.4)	(0.0,0.0,0.6,−0.0,−0.2,−0.6)	(0.2,0.1,0.6,−0.1,−0.2,−0.7)
Respecting religious beliefs	(0.4,0.2,0.5,−0.1,−0.2,−0.3)	(0.0,0.2,0.4,−0.1,−0.2,−0.5)	(0.5,0.1,0.2,−0.4,−0.1,−0.1)

Table 10.12 Types of relations between countries

Types of relations	(China, India)	(Turkey, Russia)	(Bangladesh, Afghanistan)
Project investment	(0.2,0.1,0.5,−0.1,−0.2,−0.6)	(0.4,0.2,0.5,−0.1,−0.2,−0.6)	(0.2,0.1,0.4,−0.1,−0.2,−0.8)
Political support	(0.1,0.1,0.4,−0.1,−0.2,−0.6)	(0.4,0.3,0.4,−0.3,−0.2,−0.5)	(0.2,0.1,0.4,−0.1,−0.2,−0.3)
Warfare activities	(0.5,0.1,0.2,−0.5,−0.1,−0.1)	(0.5,0.2,0.5,−0.1,−0.2,−0.3)	(0.2,0.1,0.4,−0.1,−0.2,−0.6)
Nuclear weapons	(0.1,0.2,0.5,−0.1,−0.1,−0.6)	(0.4,0.1,0.5,−0.1,−0.2,−0.5)	(0.2,0.1,0.4,−0.1,−0.2,−0.8)
Friendship	(0.1,0.1,0.5,−0.1,−0.1,−0.5)	(0.6,0.2,0.1,−0.4,−0.2,−0.4)	(0.3,0.1,0.4,−0.3,−0.2,−0.3)
Respecting religious beliefs	(0.4,0.3,0.1,−0.5,−0.1,−0.1)	(0.4,0.2,0.1,−0.6,−0.2,−0.1)	(0.5,0.1,0.1,−0.5,−0.2,−0.1)

of ambiguity of that relationship from first and second countries, respectively. Since many relations exist on set X, define six relations on set X as X_1 = Project investment, X_2 = Political support, X_3 = Warfare activities, X_4 = Nuclear weapons, X_5 = Friendship, X_6 = Respecting religious beliefs.

Define the relations with those elements such that $(X, X_1, X_2, X_3, X_4, X_5, X_6)$ is a graph structure. Every element of a relation denotes a highly worthwhile relationship in that pair of countries. Since $(X, X_1, X_2, X_3, X_4, X_5, X_6)$ is a graph structure, every relation has unique elements, that is, they are present in that relation only. Hence, any pair of countries will be an element of that relation for which its value of T^p, I^n, and F^n are high, and T^n, I^p, and F^p values are comparatively low, according to the data of Tables 10.4, 10.5, 10.6, 10.7, 10.8, 10.9, 10.10, 10.11, 10.12.

Write down the T^p, I^p, F^p, T^n, I^n, and F^n values of all elements in the relations, using the data of Tables 10.24, 10.25, 10.26, 10.27, 10.28, 10.29, 10.30, 10.31, 10.32, such that B_1, B_2, B_3, B_4, B_5, B_6 are bipolar single-valued neutrosophic sets on X_1, X_2, X_3, X_4, X_5, X_6, respectively. Let X_1 = {(Turkey, Pakistan), (Russia, India)}, X_2 = {(India, Afghanistan), (America, Pakistan), (America, Bangladesh)}, X_3 = {(India, Pakistan), (China, India), (Afghanistan, Pakistan), (America, Afghanistan), (Russia, Afg)}, X_4 = {(Russia, Pakistan), (America, India)}, X_5 = {(Pakistan, China), (Turkey, China)}, X_6 = {(Pakistan, Bangladesh), (America, Russia), (Bangladesh, Turkey), (Turkey, Afghanistan)}.

Corresponding bipolar single-valued neutrosophic sets B_1, B_2, B_3, B_4, B_5, B_6, respectively, are

$B_1 = \{((Tu, Pak), 0.5, 0.1, 0.2, -0.7, -0.1, -0.1), ((Ru, Ind), 0.4, 0.1, 0.3, -0.5, -0.1, -0.1)\}$,

$B_2 = \{((Ind, Afg), 0.4, 0.1, 0.1, -0.5, -0.1, -0.1), ((Am, Pak), 0.6, 0.1, 0.1, -0.5, -0.1, 0.0),$

$((Am, Bang), 0.1, 0.1, 0.2, -0.3, -0.3, -0.4)\}$,
$B_3 = \{((Ind, Pak), 0.4, 0.2, 0.3, -0.6, -0.1, 0.0), ((Ch, Ind), 0.5, 0.1, 0.2, -0.5, -0.1, -0.1),$
$((Afg, Pak), 0.3, 0.4, 0.6, -0.4, -0.3, -0.3), ((Am, Afg), 0.2, 0.2, 0.3, -0.4, -0.1, 0.0),$
$((Ru, Afg), 0.4, 0.2, 0.3, -0.5, 0.0, 0.0)\}$,
$B_4 = \{((Ru, Pak), 0.4, 0.2, 0.4, -0.7, -0.2, -0.1), ((Am, Ind), 0.6, 0.1, 0.0, -0.3, -0.2, -0.3)\}$,
$B_5 = \{((Pak, Ch), 0.8, 0.1, 0.1, -0.5, -0.1, 0.0), ((Tu, Ch), 0.5, 0.1, 0.2, -0.5, -0.3, -0.3)\}$,
$B_6 = \{((Pak, Bang), 0.4, 0.1, 0.0, -0.7, -0.1, -0.1), ((Am, Ru), 0.8, 0.1, 0.1, -0.8, -0.1, -0.1),$
$((Bang, Tu), 0.4, 0.2, 0.1, -0.7, -0.3, -0.2), ((Tu, Afg), 0.4, 0.1, 0.1, -0.5, -0.1, -0.2)\}$. It is easy to check that $(B, B_1, B_2, B_3, B_4, B_5, B_6)$ is a bipolar single-valued neutrosophic graph structure as shown in Fig. 10.20. In a bipolar single-valued neutrosophic graph structure, represented in Fig. 10.20, an edge depicts the most dominating and attention-getting relationship of contiguous countries. For instance, between Turkey and Pakistan most dominating and attention-getting relationship is project investment; participation of Turkey in this relationship's strength, weakness, and indeterminacy is 70%, 10%, and 10%, respectively, and participation of Pakistan in this relationship's strength, weakness, and indeterminacy is 50%, 10%, and 20%, respectively. This bipolar single-valued neutrosophic graph structure represents complete status of a relationship from both of its participants. It is very utilitarian for some particular relationships, like warfare activities. It tells a country that in what percentage its warfare activities are answered from a corresponding country and warns it that in case of war which kind of reaction can appear. It guides the United Nations and other peace loving organizations as to which country is most actively involved in peace destroying relationship, for instance, warfare activities and nuclear weapons, and what is its percentage. For instance, India and Pakistan, America, and Afghanistan are involved in warfare activities and the percentage of these edges shows that India and America are more actively involved in it. So it guides the United Nations Security Council that in what percentage it should pressurize India, America and other countries involved in it. It also highlights those countries whose attention-getting relationship is nuclear weapons and spotlights those countries who are its strong participants than their contiguous countries. For example, America and India have nuclear weapons as their dominating relationship and America is a strong participant, as its participation for its strength is high. So, this bipolar single-valued neutrosophic graph structure indicates that in order to reduce nuclear proliferation, the United Nations should pressurize America and Russia. The general procedure for this application is explained in Algorithm 10.1.

Algorithm 10.1 *Computing international relations of countries*

1. Begin
2. Input membership values $B(u_i)$ of n number of countries $u_1, u_2, \ldots, u_n$.
3. Input the adjacency matrix of countries with respect to $X_1, X_2, \ldots, X_m$ mutually disjoint, irreflexive, and symmetric relations.
4. **do** i from $1 \to m$
5. **do** j from $1 \to m$
6. **do** k from $1 \to n$

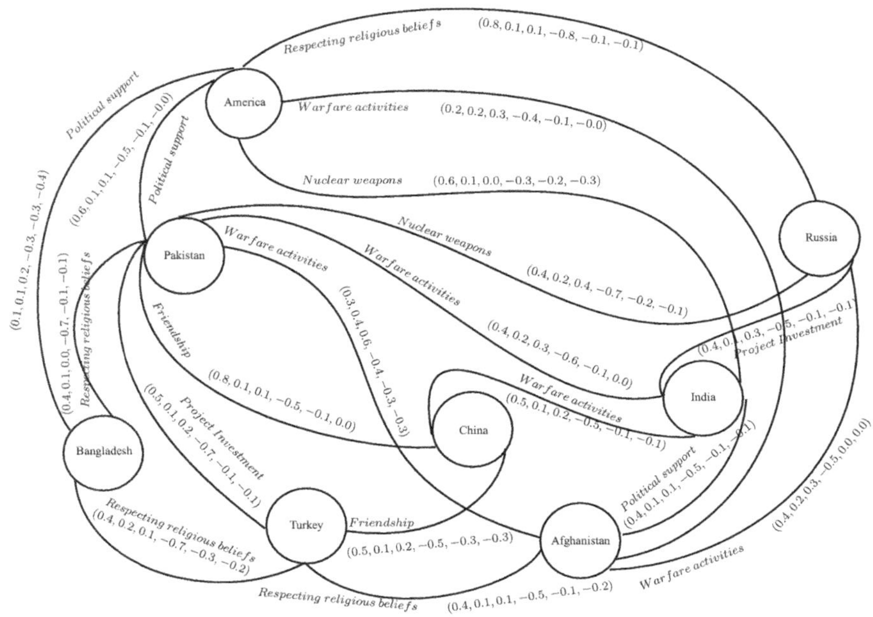

Fig. 10.20 International relations of countries

7. **do** l from $k \rightarrow n$
8. **if** $(i \neq j, T^p_{X_i}(u_k u_l) > T^p_{X_j}(u_k u_l), I^p_{X_i}(u_k u_l) < I^p_{B_j}(u_k u_l), F^p_{B_i}(u_k u_l) < F^p_{B_j}(u_k u_l))$**then**
9. **if** $T^n_{B_i}(u_k u_l) < T^n_{B_j}(u_k u_l), I^n_{B_i}(u_k u_l) > I^n_{B_j}(u_k u_l), F^n_{B_i}(u_k u_l) > F^n_{B_j}(u_k u_l))$**then**
10. Label $u_k u_l$ as B_i
11. **end if**
12. **end if**
13. **end do**
14. **end do**
15. **end do**
16. **end do**
17. $T^p_{B_i}, F^p_{B_i}, I^p_{B_i}$ values of an edge between two different vertices(countries) a and b show participation of vertex(country)a in strength, weakness, and indeterminacy of most conspicuous relationship X_i between them, whereas $T^n_{B_i}, F^n_{B_i}, I^n_{B_i}$ are corresponding values of vertex(country) b.
18. End

10.4.2 Psychological Improvement of Patients

A society is an enduring and cooperating social group whose members have developed organized patterns of relationships through interactions with one another. In a society, interaction of its members is very important; this compactness causes all types of relationships among society members. As homo sapiens have complex nature, for grouping of human beings we have to focus many psychological aspects and behaviors. Bipolar single-valued neutrosophic graph structures can be used to judge behavior and other social aspects of any group of society. Bipolar single-valued neutrosophic graph structures can be used to compute conspicuous behavioral property of any two group members with each other. The most frequent occurrence of a particular behavioral property reveals whether this group is good or bad in that perspective. This bipolar single-valued neutrosophic graph structure is very helpful for sub-grouping and assigning of tasks. In hospitals, it is difficult to estimate the psychological behavior of patients and psychiatrist can decide which patient has high violence-based relationship with others. He must reduce his interaction with others, and can decide whether the mental stage of his patients is getting better or worse. It helps a psychiatrist in taking precautionary measures and providing a suitable environment for his patients. He can decide by looking at the bipolar single-valued neutrosophic graph structure as to which patient can properly survive in the society with better behavior and which one is still not capable to show moderate behavior. A psychiatrist can use many types of psychological behaviors to estimate improvement in mental state of his patients including, violent, friendly, jealous, helping, forgiving, communicative, and problem sharing. Consider a set X of eight patients in a mental hospital: $X = \{$Albert, Charles, Burton, Calvert, Christopher, David, Chapman, Joseph$\}$. Consider a bipolar single-valued neutrosophic set B on X as given in Table 10.13.

In Table 10.13, T^p, F^p of a patient indicate his positive and negative thinking for the society, and I^p shows indeterminacy/ambiguity of his thinking for society, whereas T^n, F^n denote his positive and negative reputation in the society and I^n represents the percentage of his uncertain reputation. Each pair of patients of set X

Table 10.13 Bipolar neutrosophic information of patients

Patients	T^p	I^p	F^p	T^n	I^n	F^n
Albert	0.4	0.9	0.9	−0.4	−0.6	−0.9
Charles	0.5	0.8	0.8	−0.6	−0.7	−0.8
Burton	0.6	0.7	0.7	−0.4	−0.6	−0.7
Calvert	0.7	0.8	0.7	−0.5	−0.6	−0.6
Christopher	0.5	0.7	0.6	−0.4	−0.5	−0.7
David	0.5	0.8	0.7	−0.6	−0.5	−0.8
Chapman	0.4	0.7	0.7	−0.4	−0.6	−0.8
Joseph	0.7	0.6	0.6	−0.5	−0.5	−0.6

Table 10.14 Psychological behavior of Albert with other patients

Psychological behaviors	(Albert, charles)	(Albert, Burton)	(Albert, Calvert)
Violent	(0.4,0.4,0.7,−0.2,−0.6,−0.8)	(0.2,0.7,0.8,−0.1,−0.6,−0.9)	(0.2,0.3,0.4,−0.1,−0.2,−0.3)
Friendly	(0.3,0.5,0.6,−0.1,−0.5,−0.5)	(0.3,0.6,0.7,−0.2,−0.5,−0.8)	(0.3,0.4,0.5,−0.2,−0.3,−0.4)
Jealousy	(0.3,0.6,0.7,−0.3,−0.4,−0.6)	(0.4,0.5,0.5,−0.3,−0.4,−0.6)	(0.4,0.5,0.6,−0.3,−0.4,−0.5)
Helping	(0.1,0.5,0.8,−0.2,−0.6,−0.7)	(0.3,0.2,0.6,−0.1,−0.6,−0.7)	(0.2,0.6,0.7,−0.4,−0.5,−0.6)
Forgiving	(0.4,0.3,0.4,−0.4,−0.4,−0.5)	(0.4,0.6,0.8,−0.2,−0.5,−0.6)	(0.3,0.7,0.8,−0.1,−0.6,−0.7)
Problem sharing	(0.3,0.6,0.7,−0.3,−0.5,−0.7)	(0.3,0.7,0.7,−0.3,−0.4,−0.9)	(0.4,0.8,0.9,−0.2,−0.2,−0.8)
Communicative	(0.2,0.7,0.6,−0.4,−0.4,−0.8)	(0.2,0.6,0.6,−0.1,−0.6,−0.8)	(0.1,0.1,0.4,−0.3,−0.3,−0.8)

Table 10.15 Psychological behavior of Charles with other patients

Psychological behaviors	(Charles, Burton)	(Charles, Calvert)	(Charles, Christopher)
Violent	(0.3,0.7,0.8,−0.1,−0.6,−0.8)	(0.4,0.8,0.7,−0.1,−0.6,−0.8)	(0.2,0.7,0.8,−0.4,−0.5,−0.3)
Friendly	(0.2,0.6,0.7,−0.2,−0.5,−0.7)	(0.3,0.7,0.8,−0.2,−0.5,−0.7)	(0.3,0.6,0.4,−0.3,−0.4,−0.4)
Jealousy	(0.1,0.5,0.6,−0.3,−0.4,−0.6)	(0.2,0.2,0.6,−0.3,−0.4,−0.6)	(0.4,0.5,0.5,−0.2,−0.3,−0.5)
Helping	(0.5,0.4,0.5,−0.4,−0.4,−0.6)	(0.1,0.2,0.5,−0.4,−0.3,−0.5)	(0.5,0.4,0.6,−0.1,−0.2,−0.6)
Forgiving	(0.4,0.4,0.5,−0.1,−0.6,−0.8)	(0.4,0.2,0.4,−0.1,−0.2,−0.4)	(0.2,0.3,0.7,−0.4,−0.4,−0.7)
Problem sharing	(0.5,0.6,0.6,−0.3,−0.5,−0.7)	(0.5,0.3,0.4,−0.5,−0.2,−0.4)	(0.3,0.5,0.4,−0.1,−0.3,−0.4)
Communicative	(0.2,0.6,0.7,−0.2,−0.4,−0.6)	(0.4,0.4,0.5,−0.3,−0.3,−0.5)	(0.4,0.4,0.4,−0.1,−0.2,−0.3)

Table 10.16 Psychological behavior of Burton with other patients

Psychological behaviors	(Burton, Calvert)	(Burton, Christopher)	(Burton, David)
Violent	(0.1,0.6,0.7,−0.1,−0.4,−0.7)	(0.4,0.7,0.2,−0.1,−0.5,−0.4)	(0.3,0.7,0.3,−0.1,−0.4,−0.8)
Friendly	(0.4,0.4,0.3,−0.4,−0.2,−0.3)	(0.2,0.6,0.3,−0.2,−0.4,−0.6)	(0.4,0.6,0.4,−0.2,−0.5,−0.7)
Jealousy	(0.2,0.2,0.6,−0.2,−0.5,−0.6)	(0.3,0.5,0.4,−0.1,−0.3,−0.7)	(0.3,0.5,0.5,−0.3,−0.3,−0.6)
Helping	(0.3,0.2,0.5,−0.3,−0.2,−0.5)	(0.5,0.2,0.2,−0.4,−0.3,−0.3)	(0.4,0.4,0.6,−0.1,−0.4,−0.8)
Forgiving	(0.4,0.2,0.6,−0.4,−0.3,−0.4)	(0.4,0.4,0.5,−0.3,−0.5,−0.4)	(0.4,0.3,0.7,−0.3,−0.5,−0.7)
Problem sharing	(0.1,0.5,0.4,−0.1,−0.4,−0.3)	(0.2,0.3,0.6,−0.1,−0.4,−0.6)	(0.5,0.1,0.3,−0.4,−0.3,−0.6)
Communicative	(0.2,0.6,0.7,−0.2,−0.5,−0.4)	(0.3,0.3,0.7,−0.3,−0.3,−0.7)	(0.4,0.2,0.4,−0.3,−0.4,−0.7)

has T^p, I^p, F^p, T^n, I^n, and F^n values of different psychological behaviors in Tables 10.14, 10.15, 10.16, 10.17, 10.18, 10.19, 10.20, 10.21, 10.22.

Each pair of patients T^p, T^n of any particular Psychological behavior indicates the percentage of strength of that behavior of the first patient and the second patient, respectively. Similarly, F^p, F^n represent the percentage of weakness and I^p, I^n demonstrate the percentage of ambiguity of that behavior of first and second patients, respectively. Consider seven relations on set X as X_1 = Violent, X_2 = Friendly, X_3 = Jealousy, X_4 = Helping, X_5 = Forgiving, X_6 = Problem sharing, X_7 = Communicative. Define the relations with those elements such that $(X, X_1, X_2, X_3, X_4, X_5, X_6, X_7)$ is a graph structure. Every element of the relation denotes a conspicuous psychological behavior of that pair of patients. Since $(X, X_1, X_2, X_3, X_4, X_5, X_6, X_7)$ is a graph structure, every relation has unique elements, that is, they are present in that relation only. Hence, any pair of patients

Table 10.17 Psychological behavior of Calvert with other patients

Psychological behaviors	(Calvert, Christopher)	(Calvert, David)	(Calvert, Chapman)
Violent	(0.1,0.7,0.4,−0.1,−0.2,−0.7)	(0.4,0.8,0.5,−0.1,−0.4,−0.8)	(0.2,0.7,0.4,−0.1,−0.6,−0.8)
Friendly	(0.4,0.4,0.3,−0.4,−0.2,−0.3)	(0.3,0.6,0.4,−0.4,−0.3,−0.7)	(0.4,0.6,0.4,−0.2,−0.5,−0.7)
Jealousy	(0.2,0.6,0.3,−0.2,−0.4,−0.6)	(0.4,0.7,0.3,−0.5,−0.2,−0.6)	(0.2,0.5,0.5,−0.3,−0.4,−0.6)
Helping	(0.3,0.5,0.4,−0.1,−0.2,−0.3)	(0.5,0.5,0.2,−0.5,−0.5,−0.5)	(0.4,0.4,0.6,−0.3,−0.3,−0.5)
Forgiving	(0.4,0.4,0.5,−0.3,−0.4,−0.5)	(0.4,0.4,0.1,v4,−0.4,−0.4)	(0.4,0.2,0.3,−0.4,−0.1,−0.1)
Problem sharing	(0.1,0.7,0.6,−0.1,−0.5,−0.3)	(0.3,0.6,0.6,−0.3,−0.3,−0.2)	(0.3,0.3,0.6,−0.1,−0.2,−0.4)
Communicative	(0.2,0.6,0.7,−0.2,−0.2,−0.4)	(0.2,0.7,0.7,−0.1,−0.2,−0.3)	(0.2,0.2,0.7,−0.2,−0.3,−0.3)

Table 10.18 Psychological behavior of Christopher with other patients

Psychological behaviors	(Christopher, David)	(Christopher, Chapman)	(Christopher, Joseph)
Violent	(0.1,0.2,0.4,−0.1,−0.2,−0.3)	(0.4,0.2,0.1,−0.1,−0.2,−0.3)	(0.2,0.1,0.4,−0.1,−0.2,−0.7)
Friendly	(0.2,0.2,0.3,−0.2,−0.3,−0.4)	(0.2,0.7,0.2,−0.2,−0.4,−0.4)	(0.5,0.6,0.3,−0.2,−0.5,−0.6)
Jealousy	(0.1,0.4,0.4,−0.3,−0.4,−0.3)	(0.4,0.6,0.3,−0.1,−0.3,−0.5)	(0.2,0.1,0.5,−0.1,−0.2,−0.5)
Helping	(0.3,0.5,0.6,−0.4,−0.2,−0.5)	(0.3,0.5,0.4,−0.3,−0.2,−0.6)	(0.3,0.5,0.4,−0.3,−0.3,−0.3)
Forgiving	(0.1,0.6,0.5,−0.3,−0.2,−0.6)	(0.4,0.4,0.5,−0.1,−0.4,−0.5)	(0.2,0.1,0.4,−0.1,−0.4,−0.4)
Problem sharing	(0.4,0.7,0.4,−0.4,−0.3,−0.7)	(0.3,0.3,0.6,−0.2,−0.3,−0.5)	(0.4,0.4,0.4,−0.2,−0.5,−0.5)
Communicative	(0.5,0.2,0.3,−0.1,−0.2,−0.3)	(0.4,0.2,0.7,−0.3,−0.2,−0.3)	(0.2,0.1,0.6,−0.4,−0.2,−0.3)

Table 10.19 Psychological behavior of David with other patients

Psychological behaviors	(David, Chapman)	(David, Joseph)	(David, Albert)
Violent	(0.1,0.7,0.6,−0.2,−0.3,−0.6)	(0.4,0.6,0.1,−0.1,−0.2,−0.2)	(0.4,0.2,0.1,−0.3,−0.1,−0.3)
Friendly	(0.3,0.6,0.7,−0.1,−0.4,−0.7)	(0.3,0.2,0.2,−0.2,−0.3,−0.3)	(0.2,0.2,0.9,−0.1,−0.5,−0.8)
Jealousy	(0.1,0.5,0.6,−0.3,−0.5,−0.8)	(0.4,0.5,0.3,−0.3,−0.4,−0.4)	(0.3,0.3,0.4,−0.1,−0.4,−0.7)
Helping	(0.2,0.7,0.7,−0.1,−0.3,−0.6)	(0.5,0.4,0.4,−0.4,−0.5,−0.5)	(0.2,0.4,0.5,−0.1,−0.3,−0.6)
Forgiving	(0.1,0.6,0.6,−0.2,−0.4,−0.7)	(0.4,0.2,0.5,−0.5,−0.2,−0.6)	(0.1,0.5,0.6,−0.1,−0.2,−0.5)
Problem sharing	(0.1,0.7,0.3,−0.1,−0.5,−0.8)	(0.3,0.6,0.1,−0.1,−0.3,−0.7)	(0.2,0.6,0.7,−0.2,−0.4,−0.4)
Communicative	(0.3,0.5,0.6,−0.4,−0.3,−0.6)	(0.2,0.7,0.1,−0.2,−0.4,−0.8)	(0.3,0.7,0.8,−0.1,−0.2,−0.3)

Table 10.20 Psychological behavior of Chapman with other patients

Psychological behaviors	(Albert, Chapman)	(Chapman, Charles)	(Chapman, Burton)
Violent	(0.4,0.1,0.1,−0.2,−0.3,−0.5)	(0.2,0.7,0.5,−0.1,−0.4,−0.7)	(0.2,0.1,0.7,−0.[illegible],−0.2,−0.4)
Friendly	(0.2,0.7,0.4,−0.3,−0.5,−0.9)	(0.1,0.6,0.4,−0.2,−0.3,−0.8)	(0.3,0.2,0.6,−0.3,−0.3,−0.5)
Jealousy	(0.1,0.6,0.5,−0.4,−0.6,−0.8)	(0.3,0.1,0.2,−0.3,−0.2,−0.4)	(0.4,0.3,0.5,−0.[illegible],−0.2,−0.6)
Helping	(0.4,0.5,0.6,−0.2,−0.3,−0.7)	(0.2,0.5,0.5,−0.1,−0.4,−0.5)	(0.2,0.4,0.4,−0.4,−0.4,−0.3)
Forgiving	(0.3,0.4,0.7,−0.3,−0.4,−0.6)	(0.1,0.4,0.6,−0.−0.2,−0.5,−0.6)	(0.3,0.5,0.3,−0.[illegible],−0.2,−0.7)
Problem sharing	(0.2,0.3,0.8,−0.−0.4,−0.5,−0.5)	(0.2,0.3,0.7,−0.3,−0.6,−0.7)	(0.4,0.2,0.4,−0.[illegible],−0.6,−0.3)
Communicative	(0.1,0.2,0.9,−0.2,−0.6,−0.6)	(0.1,0.1,0.8,−0.1,−0.2,−0.8)	(0.2,0.7,0.4,−0.1,−0.2,−0.8)

Table 10.21 Psychological behavior of Joseph with other patients

Psychological behaviors	(Joseph, Albert)	(Joseph, Charles)	(Joseph, Calvert)
Violent	(0.1,0.5,0.9,−0.4,−0.2,−0.8)	(0.4,0.3,0.8,−0.3,−0.2,−0.3)	(0.7,0.3,0.4,−0.3,−0.2,−0.1)
Friendly	(0.4,0.2,0.8,−0.2,−0.4,−0.7)	(0.3,0.2,0.7,−0.2,−0.3,−0.5)	(0.2,0.1,0.5,−0.2,−0.3,−0.3)
Jealousy	(0.1,0.6,0.7,−0.1,−0.2,−0.3)	(0.4,0.6,0.6,−0.1,−0.4,−0.6)	(0.5,0.5,0.6,−0.1,−0.2,−0.2)
Helping	(0.2,0.2,0.3,−0.4,−0.3,−0.6)	(0.2,0.5,0.5,−0.4,−0.2,−0.3)	(0.2,0.4,0.4,−0.4,−0.4,−0.3)
Forgiving	(0.1,0.5,0.6,−0.3,−0.2,−0.5)	(0.5,0.4,0.4,−0.3,−0.3,−0.7)	(0.4,0.3,0.5,−0.3,−0.2,−0.4)
Problem sharing	(0.3,0.4,0.3,−0.2,−0.5,−0.4)	(0.3,0.3,0.1,−0.2,−0.2,−0.3)	(0.6,0.2,0.6,−0.2,−0.4,−0.5)
Communicative	(0.1,0.2,0.5,−0.1,−0.2,−0.3)	(0.4,0.2,0.3,−0.1,−0.4,−0.8)	(0.7,0.1,0.7,−0.1,−0.5,−0.6)

Table 10.22 Various psychological behaviors of patients

Psychological behaviors	(Albert, Christopher)	(Charles, David)	(Joseph, Burton)
Violent	(0.4,0.1,0.0,−0.3,−0.2,−0.3)	(0.5,0.1,0.1,−0.6,−0.1,−0.0)	(0.2,0.6,0.4,−0.1,−0.4,−0.7)
Friendly	(0.1,0.2,0.3,−0.2,−0.3,−0.4)	(0.4,0.2,0.2,−0.5,−0.2,−0.6)	(0.4,0.1,0.7,−0.2,−0.2,−0.3)
Jealousy	(0.3,0.4,0.4,−0.3,−0.2,−0.3)	(0.5,0.5,0.5,−0.4,−0.3,−0.3)	(0.5,0.5,0.4,−0.1,−0.5,−0.4)
Helping	(0.2,0.2,0.5,−0.2,−0.5,−0.5)	(0.4,0.4,0.4,−0.3,−0.4,−0.5)	(0.4,0.1,0.6,−0.3,−0.2,−0.3)
Forgiving	(0.1,0.5,0.6,−0.1,−0.4,−0.4)	(0.3,0.6,0.3,−0.2,−0.2,−0.3)	(0.3,0.4,0.5,−0.1,−0.4,−0.5)
Problem sharing	(0.1,0.2,0.7,−0.2,−0.3,−0.5)	(0.5,0.7,0.2,−0.1,−0.5,−0.4)	(0.2,0.6,0.4,−0.3,−0.2,−0.3)
Communicative	(0.1,0.6,0.3,−0.1,−0.2,−0.4)	(0.4,0.2,0.1,−0.1,−0.2,−0.3)	(0.6,0.2,0.3,−0.4,−0.1,−0.2)

will be an element of that particular relation, for which its values of T^p, I^n, and F^n are high, and T^n, I^p, and F^p values are comparatively low, according to the data of Tables 10.14, 10.15, 10.16, 10.17, 10.18, 10.19, 10.20, 10.21, 10.22. Write down the T^p, I^p, F^p, T^n, I^n, and F^n values of all elements in the relations using Tables 10.14, 10.15, 10.16, 10.17, 10.18, 10.19, 10.20, 10.21, 10.22 such that B_1, B_2, B_3, B_4, B_5, B_6, B_7 are bipolar single-valued neutrosophic sets on the relations X_1, X_2, X_3, X_4, X_5, X_6, X_7, respectively. Let $X_1 =$ {(Albert, Chapman), (Albert, Christopher), (Calvert, Albert), (David, Albert)}, $X_2 =$ {(Calvert, Christopher)}, $X_3 =$ {(Charles, Chapman), (Burton, Albert)}, $X_4 =$ {(Charles, *Burton*), (*Burton*, *Christopher*)}, $X_5 =$ {(Charles, Albert), (Calvert, Chapman)}, $X_6 =$ {(Burton, *David*), (*Chapman*, *Joseph*), (*Calvert*, *Charles*)}, $X_7 =$ {(Joseph, Burton), (*Chapman*, *David*)}.

Corresponding bipolar single-valued neutrosophic sets B_1, B_2, B_3, B_4, B_5, B_6, B_7, respectively, are

$B_1 =$ {((Albert, Chapman), 0.4, 0.1, 0.1, −0.2, −0.3, −0.5), ((Albert, Christopher), 0.4, 0.1, 0.0, −0.3, −0.2, −0.3),
((*Calvert*, *Albert*), 0.5, 0.1, 0.1, −0.4, −0.2, −0.1), ((*David*, *Albert*), 0.4, 0.2, 0.1, −0.3, −0.1, −0.3)},

$B_2 =$ {((Calvert, Christopher), 0.4, 0.4, 0.3, −0.4, −0.2, −0.3)},

$B_3 =$ {((Charles, Chapman), 0.3, 0.1, 0.2, −0.3, −0.2, −0.4), ((Burton, Albert), 0.4, 0.5, 0.5, −0.3, −0.4, −0.6)},

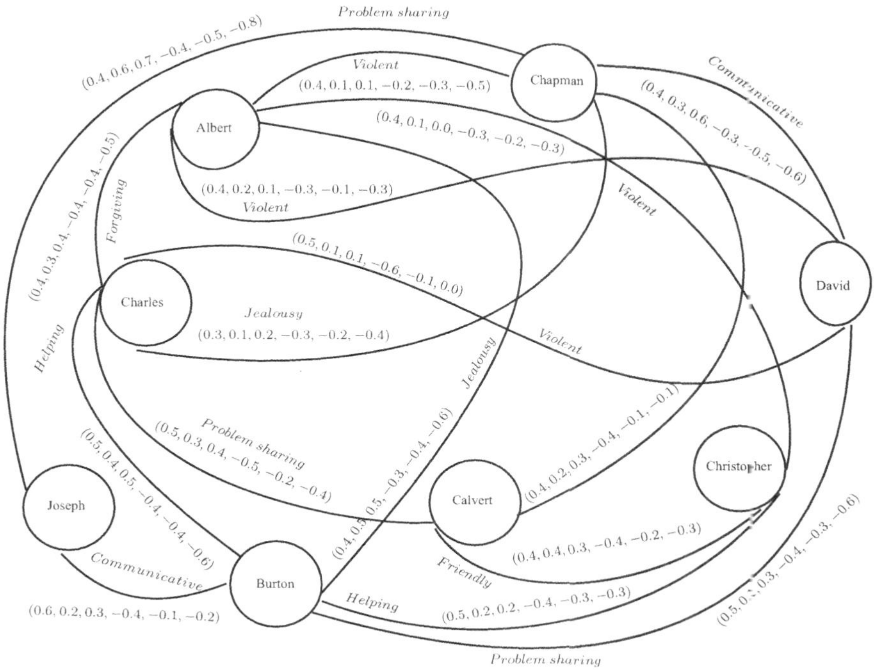

Fig. 10.21 Psychological behaviors of patients in a Mental Hospital

$B_4 = \{((\text{Charles}, \text{Burton}), 0.5, 0.4, 0.5, -0.4, -0.4, -0.6), ((\text{Burton}, \text{Christopher}), 0.5, 0.2, 0.2, -0.4, -0.3, -0.3)\}$,
$B_5 = \{((\text{Charles}, \text{Albert}), 0.4, 0.3, 0.4, -0.4, -0.4, -0.5), ((\text{Calvert}, \text{Chapman}), 0.4, 0.2, 0.3, -0.4, -0.1, -0.1)\}$,
$B_6 = \{((\text{Burton}, \text{David}), 0.5, 0.1, 0.3, -0.4, -0.3, -0.6)((\text{Chapman}, \text{Joseph}), 0.4, 0.6, 0.7, -0.4, -0.5, -0.8)$,
$((\text{Calvert}, \text{Charles}), 0.5, 0.3, 0.4, -0.5, -0.2, -0.4)\}$.

It is easy to check that $(B, B_1, B_2, B_3, B_4, B_5, B_6)$ is a bipolar single-valued neutrosophic graph structure as depicted in Fig.10.21.

In a bipolar single-valued neutrosophic graph structure, depicted in Fig.10.21, every edge depicts the most conspicuous behavioral property of adjacent vertices(patients). For instance, the most conspicuous behavioral property between Charles and Burton is helping, Charles' participation in its strength, weakness, and indeterminacy is 50%, 40%, and 50%, respectively, and Burton's participation in its strength, weakness, and indeterminacy is 40%, 40%, and 60%, respectively. This bipolar single-valued neutrosophic graph structure also accentuates that vertex Albert has the highest degree for violent behaviour. This points out that Albert is the most violent mental patient among these eight patients. So, his psychiatrist must focus on Albert's violent behavior, as Albert's most violent behavior is with Chapman and his positive behavior is with just one person, that is, Charles. So the psychiatrist should try to minimize his interaction with Chapman to avoid his most violent behavior and should maximize his interaction with Charles to improve his good psychological behavior. Similarly, a psychiatrist can judge the behavior of all his patients and can take better decisions for their well-being. He can make two bipolar single-valued neutrosophic graph structures with a gap of some time period and can estimate their behavioral improvement by comparing those two bipolar single-valued neutrosophic graph structures; it also helps him in continuing or canceling his decisions for his patients. The general procedure regarding the psychological behavior of patients is explained in Algorithm 10.2.

Algorithm 10.2 *Computing psychological behavior of patients*

1. Begin
2. Input membership values $B(u_i)$ of n number of patients $u_1, u_2, \ldots, u_n$ in a hospital.
3. Input the adjacency matrix of countries with respect to $X_1, X_2, \ldots, X_m$ mutually disjoint, irreflexive, and symmetric psychological behaviors.
4. Consider two patients u_k and u_l, $1 \leq k \leq n, k \leq l \leq n$.
5. If $T^p_{X_i}(u_k u_l) > T^p_{X_j}(u_k u_l)$, $I^p_{X_i}(u_k u_l) < I^p_{X_j}(u_k u_l)$, $F^p_{X_i}(u_k u_l) < F^p_{X_j}(u_k u_l)$, $T^n_{X_i}(u_k u_l) < T^n_{X_j}(u_k u_l)$, $I^n_{X_i}(u_k u_l) > I^n_{X_j}(u_k u_l)$, $F^n_{X_i}(u_k u_l) > F^n_{X_j}(u_k u_l)$, $i \neq j, 1 \leq i, j \leq m$
   then label $u_k u_l$ as X_i.
6. $T^p_{X_i}, F^p_{X_i}, I^p_{X_i}$ values of an edge between two different vertices(patients) u_k and u_l show the participation of vertex(patient) u_k in strength, weakness, and indeterminacy of the most conspicuous psychological behavior X_i between them, whereas $T^n_{X_i}, F^n_{X_i}, I^n_{X_i}$ are corresponding values of vertex(patient) u_l.
7. End

10.4.3 Uncovering the Undercover Reasons of Global Terrorism

Terrorism is the process of using violent or threat of violent to purport a religious, ideological, or political change. It is committed by some non-state actors and may be undercover personnel servings on the behalf of respective governments of non-state actors. Terrorism achieves more than immediate target victims and is also directed at targets covering a large spectrum of society. It is considered as fourth-generation warfare and violent crime.

Nowadays, terrorism is a major threat to the society and is illegal under anti-terrorism laws in all jurisdictions. It is considered as a war crime under laws of war, when it is used to target the non-combatants, including neutral military personnel, civilians, or enemy prisoners of the war. Many political organizations have practiced terrorism to achieve their objectives. It is being practiced by both left-wing and right-wing political organizations, religious groups, nationalist groups, revolutionaries, and

Table 10.23 Bipolar neutrosophic information of terrorism in various countries

Country	T^p	I^p	F^p	T^n	I^n	F^n
Pakistan	0.7	0.6	0.5	−0.8	−0.4	−0.3
India	0.7	0.6	0.5	−0.6	−0.5	−0.6
Afghanistan	0.8	0.4	0.3	−0.9	−0.3	−0.2
USA	0.4	0.4	0.6	−0.3	−0.2	−0.7
Iraq	0.5	0.4	0.5	−0.6	−0.3	−0.4
Israel	0.8	0.4	0.3	−0.7	−0.5	−0.5
Palestine	0.4	0.5	0.7	−0.5	−0.6	−0.6
Kashmir	0.6	0.4	0.8	−0.7	−0.6	−0.6

ruling governments. Terrorism can be used to exploit human fear to achieve these goals. According to Global Terrorism Database, non-state terrorism incidents are more than 61,000, claiming more than 140,000 lives from 2000 to 2014.

Nowadays, many countries are blamed to be responsible for global terrorism. That's why many countries are doing war against terror. When a country blames other country to be responsible for terrorism in its territory, many factors are responsible for it. But there are some reasons or factors which are strongly responsible for that particular incident and can not be ignored. A bipolar single-valued neutrosophic graph structure can be used to highlight those factors which are highly responsible for terrorism between any two countries or global terrorism due to those countries. There are many undercover reasons highly responsible for global terrorism, including religious factors, military interference/drone attacks, political benefits, to pressurize other governments, to occupy other countries, to obtain benefits of powerful countries, and to revenge past political occupation. Let X be the set of eight countries/states on the globe which are either victims of terrorism or are said to be responsible for global terrorism: X = {Pakistan, India, Afghanistan, USA, Iraq, Israel, Palestine, Kashmir}. Consider a bipolar single-valued neutrosophic set B on X as defined in Table 10.23.

In Table 10.23, T^p, T^n of a country depict the percentage of its actual involvement in terrorism and the percentage of its involvement on the basis of other countries' point of view, respectively, whereas F^p, F^n of a country represent the percentage of its actual non-involvement and of reputation of its non-involvement, respectively. Similarly, I^p, I^n indicate ambiguity in its involvement and reputation with respect to terrorism. Every pair of countries in set X has T^p, I^p, F^p, T^n, I^n, and F^n values of different undercover reasons in Tables 10.24, 10.25, 10.26, 10.27, 10.28, 10.29, 10.30, 10.31, 10.32.

Each pair of countries T^p, T^n of any terrorism reason shows the percentage of responsibility from the first country and the second country, respectively. Similarly F^p, F^n indicate the percentage of being not responsible and I^p, I^n denote the percentage of ambiguity of being responsible for that terrorism reason from the first and the second countries, respectively. There are many relations on the set X; define six relations on set X as X_1 = Religious factors, X_2 = Political benefits, X_3 = To pres-

Table 10.24 Reasons of terrorism due to relationships of Pakistan with other countries

Terrorism Reasons	(India, Pakistan)	(Pakistan, Afghanistan)	(USA, Pakistan)
Religious factors	(0.5,0.3,0.3,−0.4,−0.4,−0.4)	(0.3,0.2,0.2,−0.4,−0.2,−0.3)	(0.2,0.2,0.4,−0.2,−0.2,−0.6)
Political benefits	(0.6,0.3,0.3,−0.4,−0.3,−0.4)	(0.3,0.3,0.3,−0.4,−0.3,−0.3)	(0.3,0.3,0.3,−0.1,−0.1,−0.6)
To pressurize other govt.	(0.7,0.2,0.3,−0.5,−0.1,−0.4)	(0.1,0.3,0.5,−0.3,−0.2,−0.2)	(0.3,0.3,0.2,0.0,−0.2,−0.7)
To occupy other country	(0.5,0.2,0.3,−0.2,−0.2,−0.6)	(0.1,0.2,0.4,−0.1,−0.3,−0.3)	(0.3,0.4,0.4,0.0,0.0,−0.7)
Benefits of powerful countries	(0.4,0.4,0.4,−0.4,−0.4,−0.4)	(0.6,0.2,0.3,−0.5,−0.2,−0.2)	(0.2,0.2,0.3,−0.1,−0.2,−0.6)
Military interference/Drones	(0.3,0.4,0.3,−0.1,−0.1,−0.5)	(0.4,0.1,0.5,−0.4,−0.2,−0.3)	(0.4,0.2,0.2,−0.2,−0.1,−0.6)

Table 10.25 Reasons of terrorism due to relationships of India with other countries

Terrorism Reasons	(India, Afghanistan)	(India, USA)	(India, Iraq)
Religious factors	(0.4,0.3,0.4,−0.3,−0.2,−0.3)	(0.2,0.2,0.5,−0.4,−0.2,−0.5)	(0.4,0.1,0.4,−0.5,−0.2,−0.5)
Political benefits	(0.7,0.3,0.2,−0.4,−0.2,−0.2)	(0.3,0.4,0.3,−0.5,−0.2,−0.4)	(0.2,0.4,0.3,−0.1,−0.3,−0.5)
To pressurize other govt.	(0.3,0.4,0.4,−0.1,−0.3,−0.3)	(0.1,0.2,0.4,−0.3,−0.2,−0.4)	(0.2,0.4,0.5,−0.3,−0.2,−0.4)
To occupy other country	(0.4,0.3,0.4,−0.2,−0.2,−0.3)	(0.1,0.1,0.5,−0.3,−0.1,−0.4)	(0.2,0.1,0.4,−0.1,−0.3,−0.5)
Benefits of powerful countries	(0.5,0.4,0.4,−0.3,−0.2,−0.3)	(0.4,0.3,0.4,−0.2,−0.1,−0.5)	(0.2,0.3,0.5,−0.3,−0.2,−0.3)
Military interference/Drones	(0.3,0.3,0.5,−0.3,−0.2,−0.2)	(0.2,0.2,0.1,−0.3,−0.2,−0.4)	(0.2,0.1,0.4,−0.2,−0.3,−0.5)

Table 10.26 Reasons of terrorism due to relationships of Afghanistan with other countries

Terrorism Reasons	(USA, Afghanistan)	(Iraq, Afghanistan)	(Afghanistan, Israel)
Religious factors	(0.1,0.4,0.6,−0.2,−0.2,−0.5)	(0.3,0.4,0.5,−0.1,−0.3,−0.4)	(0.5,0.1,0.5,−0.3,−0.2,−0.3)
Political benefits	(0.3,0.3,0.3,−0.1,−0.2,−0.6)	(0.4,0.2,0.4,−0.2,−0.2,−0.4)	(0.3,0.2,0.4,−0.2,−0.3,−0.3)
To pressurize other govt.	(0.2,0.3,0.3,−0.1,−0.2,−0.6)	(0.3,0.3,0.4,−0.1,−0.3,−0.3)	(0.4,0.3,0.3,−0.4,−0.3,−0.5)
To occupy other country	(0.3,0.4,0.2,0.0,−0.2,−0.5)	(0.2,0.2,0.4,−0.1,−0.3,−0.4)	(0.3,0.4,0.4,−0.3,−0.2,−0.4)
Benefits of powerful countries	(0.2,0.3,0.4,−0.1,−0.2,−0.5)	(0.5,0.2,0.3,−0.6,−0.2,−0.2)	(0.2,0.1,0.4,−0.3,−0.3,−0.3)
Military interference/Drones	(0.4,0.2,0.1,−0.3,−0.2,−0.5)	(0.1,0.3,0.4,−0.1,−0.3,−0.4)	(0.4,0.2,0.4,−0.2,−0.3,−0.3)

Table 10.27 Reasons of terrorism due to relationships of USA with other countries

Terrorism Reasons	(USA, Kashmir)	(USA, Iraq)	(USA, Palestine)
Religious factors	(0.3,0.2,0.5,−0.3,−0.2,−0.5)	(0.1,0.4,0.6,−0.1,−0.1,−0.5)	(0.4,0.3,0.5,−0.2,−0.2,−0.6)
Political benefits	(0.4,0.2,0.4,−0.3,−0.1,−0.5)	(0.4,0.3,0.3,−0.2,−0.1,−0.5)	(0.4,0.1,0.3,−0.3,−0.1,−0.5)
To pressurize other govt.	(0.1,0.3,0.5,−0.1,−0.2,−0.6)	(0.4,0.4,0.4,−0.2,−0.2,−0.6)	(0.3,0.1,0.3,−0.3,−0.2,−0.6)
To occupy other country	(0.2,0.3,0.5,−0.1,−0.2,−0.6)	(0.2,0.3,0.4,−0.1,−0.1,−0.7)	(0.4,0.1,0.4,−0.1,−0.2,−0.5)
Benefits of powerful countries	(0.3,0.2,0.4,−0.2,−0.2,−0.5)	(0.3,0.4,0.4,−0.1,−0.2,−0.5)	(0.4,0.1,0.5,−0.3,−0.1,−0.1)
Military interference/Drones	(0.1,0.2,0.5,−0.2,−0.2,−0.7)	(0.2,0.3,0.3,−0.1,−0.1,−0.6)	(0.2,0.1,0.4,−0.3,−0.2,−0.7)

Table 10.28 Reasons of terrorism due to relationship of Iraq with other countries

Terrorism Reasons	(Iraq, Israel)	(Iraq, Palestine)	(Iraq, Kashmir)
Religious factors	(0.4,0.1,0.3,−0.5,−0.1,−0.1)	(0.4,0.2,0.5,−0.1,−0.2,−0.3)	(0.3,0.3,0.3,−0.1,−0.2,−0.3)
Political benefits	(0.3,0.2,0.4,−0.4,−0.3,−0.3)	(0.3,0.2,0.4,−0.2,−0.2,−0.3)	(0.2,0.1,0.1,−0.4,−0.1,−0.1)
To pressurize other govt.	(0.1,0.3,0.5,−0.1,−0.2,−0.5)	(0.2,0.1,0.6,−0.2,−0.2,−0.6)	(0.4,0.4,0.5,−0.1,−0.2,−0.6)
To occupy other country	(0.1,0.2,0.5,−0.5,−0.3,−0.2)	(0.1,0.1,0.5,0.0,−0.3,−0.5)	(0.4,0.1,0.6,−0.1,−0.2,−0.5)
Benefits of powerful countries	(0.4,0.3,0.2,−0.3,−0.2,−0.4)	(0.1,0.2,0.5,−0.3,−0.2,−0.3)	(0.4,0.4,0.2,−0.4,−0.2,−0.2)
Military interference/Drones	(0.4,0.2,0.2,−0.4,−0.2,−0.2)	(0.3,0.1,0.7,−0.3,−0.3,−0.6)	(0.2,0.1,0.7,−0.1,−0.2,−0.6)

Table 10.29 Reasons of terrorism due to relationship of Israel with other countries

Terrorism Reasons	(Israel, Palestine)	(Israel, Kashmir)	(Israel, Pakistan)
Religious factors	(0.3,0.2,0.5,−0.1,−0.2,−0.6)	(0.4,0.2,0.1,−0.4,−0.3,−0.3)	(0.2,0.1,0.3,−0.1,−0.2,−0.4)
Political benefits	(0.4,0.2,0.2,0.0,−0.2,−0.5)	(0.3,0.2,0.4,−0.3,−0.2,−0.3)	(0.3,0.3,0.3,−0.1,−0.2,−0.4)
To pressurize other govt.	(0.3,0.2,0.4,0.0,−0.1,−0.6)	(0.5,0.0,0.3,−0.3,−0.2,−0.3)	(0.2,0.1,0.3,−0.1,−0.2,−0.5)
To occupy other country	(0.4,0.0,0.1,−0.1,0.0,−0.5)	(0.4,0.2,0.4,−0.1,−0.2,−0.6)	(0.1,0.1,0.3,−0.1,−0.1,−0.4)
Benefits of powerful countries	(0.3,0.2,0.3,−0.1,−0.2,−0.6)	(0.4,0.2,0.1,−0.3,−0.2,−0.3)	(0.2,0.4,0.3,−0.1,−0.2,−0.3)
Military interference/Drones	(0.3,0.2,0.1,−0.1,−0.2,−0.6)	(0.4,0.2,0.5,−0.1,−0.2,−0.6)	(0.2,0.1,0.2,−0.1,−0.2,−0.5)

Table 10.30 Reasons of terrorism due to relationship of Palestine with other countries

Terrorism Reasons	(Palestine, India)	(Palestine, Pakistan)	(Palestine, Afghanistan)
Religious factors	(0.4,0.2,0.4,−0.4,−0.1,−0.6)	(0.4,0.1,0.2,−0.5,−0.1,−0.1)	(0.4,0.1,0.4,−0.5,−0.2,−0.3)
Political benefits	(0.4,0.2,0.5,−0.3,0.0,−0.6)	(0.4,0.2,0.4,−0.2,−0.2,−0.3)	(0.3,0.1,0.4,−0.2,−0.2,−0.3)
To pressurize other govt.	(0.0,0.0,0.4,0.0,0.0,−0.6)	(0.1,0.2,0.6,0.0,−0.1,−0.5)	(0.2,0.1,0.4,−0.1,−0.2,−0.3)
To occupy other country	(0.2,0.2,0.6,−0.1,−0.2,−0.4)	(0.1,0.1,0.5,−0.1,−0.2,−0.5)	(0.1,0.1,0.5,−0.1,−0.1,−0.6)
Benefits of powerful countries	(0.3,0.1,0.4,−0.5,−0.1,−0.5)	(0.3,0.2,0.4,−0.5,−0.2,−0.3)	(0.4,0.1,0.3,−0.3,−0.2,−0.3)
Military interference/Drones	(0.2,0.2,0.5,−0.2,−0.2,−0.6)	(0.3,0.1,0.7,−0.1,−0.1,−0.5)	(0.4,0.1,0.5,−0.2,−0.1,−0.5)

Table 10.31 Reasons of terrorism due to relationship of Kashmir with other countries

Terrorism Reasons	(Kashmir, India)	(Kashmir, Afghanistan)	(Kashmir, Pakistan)
Religious factors	(0.1,0.2,0.8,−0.1,−0.2,−0.4)	(0.4,0.1,0.6,−0.2,−0.2,−0.6)	(0.6,0.1,0.4,−0.7,−0.2,−0.3)
Political benefits	(0.0,0.3,0.7,−0.5,−0.2,−0.4)	(0.0,0.1,0.6,−0.3,−0.3,−0.3)	(0.2,0.1,0.4,−0.1,−0.3,−0.5)
To pressurize other govt.	(0.1,0.2,0.7,−0.1,−0.2,−0.5)	(0.2,0.2,0.5,−0.4,−0.2,−0.5)	(0.1,0.1,0.4,−0.1,−0.2,−0.6)
To occupy other country	(0.2,0.2,0.7,−0.6,−0.1,−0.−0.10)	(0.0,0.0,0.6,0.0,−0.3,−0.5)	(0.0,0.1,0.5,−0.1,−0.2,−0.5)
Benefits of powerful countries	(0.1,0.4,0.8,−0.3,−0.2,−0.3)	(0.5,0.3,0.4,−0.6,−0.2,−0.3)	(0.2,0.1,0.6,−0.1,−0.2,−0.4)
Military interference/Drones	(0.1,0.2,0.7,−0.5,−0.2,−0.3)	(0.0,0.2,0.4,−0.1,−0.2,−0.5)	(0.2,0.1,0.6,−0.4,−0.2,−0.5)

Table 10.32 Reasons of terrorism due to relationship between countries

Terrorism Reasons	(USA, Israel)	(India, Israel)	(Pakistan, Iraq)
Religious factors	(0.2,0.1,0.5,−0.1,−0.2,−0.6)	(0.4,0.2,0.5,−0.1,−0.2,−0.6)	(0.2,0.1,0.4,−0.1,−0.2,−0.3)
Political benefits	(0.1,0.1,0.4,−0.1,−0.2,−0.6)	(0.4,0.3,0.4,−0.3,−0.2,−0.5)	(0.2,0.1,0.4,−0.1,−0.2,−0.3)
To pressurize other govt.	(0.4,0.1,0.2,−0.3,−0.1,−0.5)	(0.5,0.2,0.5,−0.1,−0.2,−0.3)	(0.2,0.1,0.4,−0.1,−0.2,−0.3)
To occupy other country	(0.1,0.2,0.5,−0.1,−0.1,−0.6)	(0.4,0.1,0.5,−0.1,−0.2,−0.5)	(0.2,0.1,0.4,−0.1,−0.2,−0.3)
Benefits of powerful countries	(0.3,0.1,0.5,−0.1,−0.1,−0.5)	(0.6,0.2,0.4,−0.4,−0.2,−0.4)	(0.5,0.1,0.2,−0.6,−0.2,−0.3)
Military interference/Drones	(0.1,0.3,0.5,−0.3,−0.1,−0.6)	(0.4,0.2,0.5,−0.3,−0.2,−0.5)	(0.5,0.1,0.5,−0.3,−0.2,−0.4)

surize other government, X_4 = To occupy other country, X_5 = Benefits of powerful countries, and X_6 = Military interference/Drone attacks. Define the relations with those elements such that $(X, X_1, X_2, X_3, X_4, X_5, X_6)$ is a graph structure. Every element in a relation indicates the most prominent undercover reason for global terrorism due to that pair of countries. Since $(X, X_1, X_2, X_3, X_4, X_5, X_6)$ is a graph structure, elements in every relation are unique, that is, they belong to just that relation. Consider any pair of countries as an element of that particular relation, for which its value of T^p, I^n, and F^n are high, and T^n, I^p, and F^p values are low as compared to other relations, according to the data of Tables 10.24, 10.25, 10.26, 10.27, 10.28, 10.29, 10.30, 10.31, 10.32. Write down the T^p, I^p, F^p, T^n, I^n, and F^n values of all elements in the relations, using the data of Tables10.24, 10.25, 10.26, 10.27, 10.28, 10.29, 10.30, 10.31, 10.32, such that B_1, B_2, B_3, B_4, B_5, B_6 are bipolar single-valued neutrosophic sets on X_1, X_2, X_3, X_4, X_5, X_6, respectively. Let X_1 = {(Kashmir, Pakistan)}, X_2 = {(India, Afghanistan), (USA, Iraq), (USA, Kashmir)}, X_3 = {(India, Pakistan)}, X_4 = {(India, Kashmir), (Palestine, Israel)}, X_5 = {(Pakistan, Afghanistan), (Kashmir, Afghanistan), (Iraq, *Pakistan*), (*Afghanistan, Iraq*)}, X_6 = {(USA, Pakistan), (USA, Afghanistan)}.

Corresponding bipolar single-valued neutrosophic sets B_1, B_2, B_3, B_4, B_5, B_6 are as follows:

B_1 = {((Kashmir, Pakistan), 0.6, 0.1, 0.4, −0.7, −0.2, −0.3)},

B_2 = {((India, Afghanistan), 0.7, 0.3, 0.2, −0.4, −0.2, −0.2), ((USA, Iraq), 0.4, 0.3, 0.3, −0.2, −0.1, −0.5),
((USA, Kashmir), 0.4, 0.2, 0.4, −0.3, −0.1, −0.5)},

B_3 = {((India, Pakistan), 0.7, 0.2, 0.3, −0.5, −0.1, −0.4)},

B_4 = {((India, Kashmir), 0.6, 0.1, 0.1, −0.2, −0.2, −0.7), ((Palestine, Israel), 0.1, 0.0, 0.5, −0.4, 0.0, −0.1)},

B_5 = {((Pakistan, Afghanistan), 0.6, 0.2, 0.3, −0.5, −0.2, −0.2), ((Kashmir, Afghanistan), 0.5, 0.3, 0.4, -0.6,-0.2,-0.3),
((*Pakistan, Iraq*), 0.5, 0.1, 0.2, −0.6, −0.2, −0.3), ((*Iraq, Afghanistan*), 0.5, 0.2, 0.3, −0.6, −0.2, −0.2)},

B_6 = {((USA, Pakistan), 0.4, 0.2, 0.2, −0.2, −0.1, −0.6), ((USA, Afghanistan), 0.4, 0.2, 0.1, −0.3, −0.2, −0.5)}.

Obviously, $(B, B_1, B_2, B_3, B_4, B_5, B_6)$ is a bipolar single-valued neutrosophic graph structure as shown in Fig.10.22.

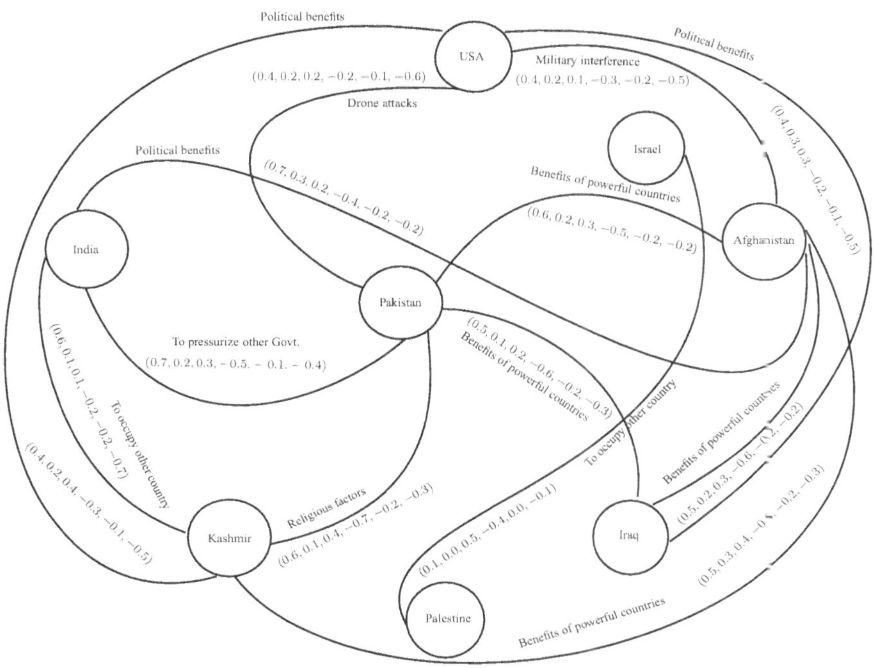

Fig. 10.22 Highlighting undercover reasons of global terrorism

In a bipolar single-valued neutrosophic graph structure, shown in Fig. 10.22, every edge demonstrates the most dominating and attention-getting undercover reason of global terrorism due to those contiguous countries. For instance, the attention-getting undercover reason of global terrorism due to Pakistan and USA relationship is the drone attacks of USA on Pakistan, the participation of USA in this reason's strength, weakness, and indeterminacy is 40%, 20%, and 20%, respectively, and the participation of Pakistan in its strength, weakness, and indeterminacy is 20%, 10%, and 60%, respectively. This Pakistan–USA edge is not representing direct terrorism from contiguous countries but it points out the dominating reason of global terrorism due to Pakistan–USA relationships. This bipolar single-valued neutrosophic graph structure also highlights that sovereignty issues of some countries or states are also increasing global terrorism and tells its intensity, weakness, and uncertainty due to both occupying and occupied countries. For instance, the sovereignty issues of Kashmir and Palestine are also causing global terrorism. Furthermore, it also helps any country's government that what is the main reason for terrorism due to its relationships with other countries and what the percentage of its strength, weakness, and ambiguity is from its side and other country's side. Moreover, the most frequent relation in this bipolar single-valued neutrosophic graph structure is the benefits of powerful countries. It shows that powerful countries are destroying global peace to achieve their political benefits. A bipolar single-valued neutrosophic graph structure of all countries can be very helpful for anti terrorism organizations to find out as to which perspective is to be considered to control global terrorism. According to this bipolar single-valued neutrosophic graph structure, they should pressurize powerful countries and solve sovereignty issues to maintain global peace. The method to compute the reasons for terrorism is explained in Algorithm 10.3.

Algorithm 10.3 *Finding reasons of global terrorism*

1. Begin
2. Input membership values $B(u_i)$ of n number of countries $u_1, u_2, \ldots, u_n$ which are either victims
   of terrorism or said to be responsible for global terrorism.
3. Input the adjacency matrix of countries with respect to $X_1, X_2, \ldots, X_m$
   terrorism reasons due to relationships among all pairs of vertices(i.e., pairs of countries).
4. Follow steps 3 and 4 of Algorithm 10.2.
5. $T^p_{X_i}, F^p_{X_i}, I^p_{X_i}$ values of an edge between two different vertices(countries) u_k and u_l show participation of vertex(country) u_k in strength, weakness, and indeterminacy of most dominating and attention-getting terrorist reason X_i due to relationships between them, whereas $T^n_{X_i}, F^n_{X_i}, I^n_{X_i}$ are corresponding values of vertex(country) u_l.
6. End

10.5 Conclusions

A bipolar neutrosophic graph structure is a generalization of a graph structure and is useful to study various domains of computer science and computational intelligence. In this chapter, we have discussed the concepts of bipolar neutrosophic graph structures, B_k-edges, bipolar neutrosophic subgraph structures, strong and complete bipolar neutrosophic graph structures, and studied their fundamental properties and operations. We have described isomorphism properties and relations of self-complementary, totally self-complementary, and totally strong self-complementary bipolar neutrosophic graph structures. We have studied the importance of bipolar neutrosophic graph structures with a number of real-world applications in international relations, psychology, and global terrorism.

Exercises 10

1. Is a bipolar single-valued neutrosophic graph structure simply a bipolar single-valued neutrosophic graph on the set $X = \{a, b\}$?
2. Let $B : X \to [0, 1]^3 \times [-1, 0]^3$, $B_1 : X_1 \times X_1 \to [0, 1]^3 \times [-1, 0]^3$, and $B_2 : X_2 \times X_2 \to [0, 1]^3 \times [-1, 0]^3$ be constant functions, where $X_1, X_2 \subset X$ and $X = \{a, b, c, d\}$. Draw three bipolar single-valued neutrosophic graph structures $\check{G}$, $\check{H}$ and $\check{K}$ of (X, X_1, X_2) such that $\check{K} \subseteq \check{H} \subseteq \check{G}$. Also compute $\check{H} \Box \check{G}$ and $\check{K} \times \check{H}$, where $\Box$ and $\times$ represent Cartesian product and direct product, respectively.
3. Determine the conditions under which a bipolar single-valued neutrosophic graph structure is a bipolar single-valued neutrosophic graph.
4. Prove or disprove that every strong bipolar single-valued neutrosophic graph structure is the join of two strong bipolar single-valued neutrosophic graph structures.
5. Determine whether or not the lexicographic product of two strong bipolar single-valued neutrosophic graph structures is a strong bipolar single-valued neutrosophic graph structure.
6. Is the union of two complete bipolar single-valued neutrosophic graph structures a complete bipolar single-valued neutrosophic graph structure?
7. Let $\check{G}$, $\check{H}$, and $\check{K}$ be three bipolar single-valued neutrosophic graph structures such that their sets of vertices are disjoint. Determine whether or not the following statements are true or false.

   (a) $(\check{G} \cup \check{H}) \bullet \check{K} = (\check{G} \bullet \check{K}) \cup (\check{H} \bullet \check{K})$,
   (b) $(\check{G} + \check{H}) \times \check{K} = (\check{G} \times \check{K}) + (\check{H} \times \check{K})$.

8. If $\check{G}_1$ and $\check{G}_2$ are two complete bipolar single-valued neutrosophic graph structures. Then show that $\check{G}_{s1} \cup \check{G}_{s2}$ is a complete graph structure.
9. If $\check{G}_1$ and $\check{G}_2$ are two strong bipolar single-valued neutrosophic graph structures with $T^p_{B_1}$, $I^p_{B_1}$, $F^p_{B_1}$, $T^n_{B_2}$, $I^n_{B_2}$, $F^n_{B_2}$ as constant functions. Then show that $T^p_{B_1 \cup B_2}$, $I^p_{B_1 \cup B_2}$, $F^p_{B_1 \cup B_2}$, $T^n_{B_1 \cup B_2}$, $I^n_{B_1 \cup B_2}$, $F^n_{B_1 \cup B_2}$ are constant functions.
10. If $\check{G}_1$ and $\check{G}_2$ are two complete bipolar single-valued neutrosophic graph structures. Then prove that $\check{G}_{s1} \bullet \check{G}_{s2}$ is a complete graph structure.
11. If $\check{G}_1$ and $\check{G}_2$ are two strong bipolar single-valued neutrosophic graph structures with $T^p_{B_1}$, $I^p_{B_1}$, $F^p_{B_1}$, $T^n_{B_2}$, $I^n_{B_2}$, $F^n_{B_2}$ as constant functions. Then prove that $T^p_{B_1 \bullet B_2}$, $I^p_{B_1 \bullet B_2}$, $F^p_{B_1 \bullet B_2}$, $T^n_{B_1 \bullet B_2}$, $I^n_{B_1 \bullet B_2}$, $F^n_{B_1 \bullet B_2}$ are constant functions.
12. If $\check{G}_1$ and $\check{G}_2$ are two complete bipolar single-valued neutrosophic graph structures. Then prove that $\check{G}_{s1} \oplus \check{G}_{s2}$ is a complete graph structure.
13. If $\check{G}_1$ and $\check{G}_2$ are two strong bipolar single-valued neutrosophic graph structures with $T^p_{B_1}$, $I^p_{B_1}$, $F^p_{B_1}$, $T^n_{B_2}$, $I^n_{B_2}$, $F^n_{B_2}$ as constant functions. Then prove that $T^p_{B_1 \oplus B_2}$, $I^p_{B_1 \oplus B_2}$, $F^p_{B_1 \oplus B_2}$, $T^n_{B_1 \oplus B_2}$, $I^n_{B_1 \oplus B_2}$, $F^n_{B_1 \oplus B_2}$ are constant functions.
14. If $\check{G}_1$ and $\check{G}_2$ are two complete bipolar single-valued neutrosophic graph structures. Then prove that $\check{G}_{s1} \boxtimes \check{G}_{s2}$ is a complete graph structure.

15. If $\check{G}_1$ and $\check{G}_2$ are two strong bipolar single-valued neutrosophic graph structures with $T^p_{B_1}$, $I^p_{B_1}$, $F^p_{B_1}$, $T^n_{B_2}$, $I^n_{B_2}$, $F^n_{B_2}$ as constant functions. Then prove that $T^p_{B_1 \boxtimes B_2}$, $I^p_{B_1 \boxtimes B_2}$, $F^p_{B_1 \boxtimes B_2}$, $T^n_{B_1 \boxtimes B_2}$, $I^n_{B_1 \boxtimes B_2}$, $F^n_{B_1 \boxtimes B_2}$ are constant functions.

References

1. Akram, M., Akmal, R.: Application of bipolar fuzzy sets in graph structures. Appl. Comput. Intell. Soft Comput. **2016**, Article ID 5859080, 13 (2016)
2. Akram, M., Akmal, R.: Certain operations on bipolar fuzzy graph structures. Appl. Appl. Math. **11**(1), 443–468 (2016)
3. Akram, M., Sarwar, M.: Novel multiple criteria decision making methods based on bipolar neutrosophic sets and bipolar neutrosophic graphs. Ital. J. Pure Appl. Math. **38**, 368–389 (2017)
4. Akram, M., Sitara, M.: Bipolar neutrosophic graph structures. J. Indones. Math. Soc. **23**(1), 50–80 (2017)
5. Akram, M., Sitara, M.: Certain fuzzy graph structures. J. Appl. Math. Comput. **61**, 25–56, (2019)
6. Akram, M., Sitara, M.: Graph structures in bipolar neutrosophic environment, Mathematics, **5**(4), 60, (2017)
7. Akram, M., Sitara, M., Saeid, A. B.: Residue product of fuzzy graph structures, J. Mult.-Valued Log. & Soft Comput. **34** 365–399, (2020)
8. Atanassov, K.: Intuitionistic fuzzy sets. Fuzzy Sets Syst. **20**(1), 87–96 (1986)
9. Deli, I., Ali, M., Smarandache, F.: Bipolar neutrosophic sets and their application based on multi-criteria decision making problems. In: IEEE International Conference on Advanced Mechatronic Systems, pp. 249–254 (2015)
10. Dinesh, T., Ramakrishnan, R.V.: On generalised fuzzy graph structures. Appl. Math. Sci. **5**(4), 173–180 (2011)
11. Sampathkumar, E.: Generalized graph structures. Bull. Kerala Math. Assoc. **3**(2), 65–123 (2006)
12. Sitara, M., Akram, M., Bhatti, M.Y.: Fuzzy graph structures with application. Mathematics **7**, 63 (2019). https://doi.org/10.3390/math7010063
13. Smarandache, F.: Neutrosophic set a generalization of the intuitionistic fuzzy set. J. Def. Resour. Manag. **1**(1), 107–116 (2010)
14. Zhan, J., Akram, M., Sitara, M.: Novel decision-making method based on bipolar neutrosophic information. Soft Comput. **23**, 9955–9977 (2019)
15. Zhang, W.-R.: Bipolar fuzzy sets and relations: a computational framework for cognitive modeling and multiagent decision analysis. In: Proceedings of IEEE Conference, pp. 305–309 (1994)
16. Zhang, W.-R.: (YinYang) Bipolar fuzzy sets. In: IEEE International Conference on Fuzzy Systems, pp. 835–840 (1998)
17. Zhang, W.-R., Wang, P., Peace, K., Zhan, J., Zhang, Y.: On truth, uncertainty, equilibrium, and harmony-A taxonomy for yinyang scientific computing. New Math. Nat. Comput. **4**(2), 207–229 (2008)

Index

Symbols
(α, β)-cut, 8, 284
(α, β)-level graph, 8, 284
α-cut, 8, 283
B_k-edge, 399
B_k-strong, 399
L-subset, 5
μ-distance, 82
μ^n-bridge, 235
μ^n-cut vertex, 238
μ^n−length, 103
μ^n-spectrum, 312, 329
μ^n-status, 120
μ^n-strength, 234
μ^p-bridge, 235
μ^p-cut vertex, 238
μ^p−length, 103
μ^p-spectrum, 312, 329
μ^p-status, 120
μ^p-strength, 234
t-cut, 297
t-level soft graph, 297
k-dominating set, 265
k-domination number, 265
k-independent dominating set, 266
k-independent domination number, 266
m-step bipolar single-valued neutrosophic competition graph, 359
m-step bipolar single-valued neutrosophic in-neighborhood, 358
m-step bipolar single-valued neutrosophic neighborhood, 366
m-step bipolar single-valued neutrosophic neighborhood graph, 366
m-step bipolar single-valued neutrosophic out-neighborhood, 358
m-step prey, 361
m-totally regular, 129
nn-partite, 23
φ-complement, 420

A
A bipolar fuzzy multigraph, 225
Adjacency matrix, 312
Adjacent, 52
Amplitude, 43
Antipodal bipolar fuzzy graph, 112
Automorphism, 27

B
Biconnected, 234, 239
Bipartite bipolar fuzzy graph, 22
Bipolar fuzzy approximation function, 296
Bipolar fuzzy basis, 286
Bipolar fuzzy block, 239
Bipolar fuzzy bridge, 39, 109, 235
Bipolar fuzzy circuit, 287
Bipolar fuzzy closed neighborhood, 188
Bipolar fuzzy common enemy graph, 199
Bipolar fuzzy competition common enemy graph, 201
Bipolar fuzzy competition graph, 163
Bipolar fuzzy conflict graph, 213, 216
Bipolar fuzzy confusion graph, 217, 219
Bipolar fuzzy cut vertex, 238
Bipolar fuzzy cycle, 21, 85, 241

M. Akram et al., *Graphs for the Analysis of Bipolar Fuzzy Information*, Studies in Fuzziness and Soft Computing 401,
https://doi.org/10.1007/978-981-15-8756-6

Bipolar fuzzy digraph, 52
Bipolar fuzzy directed cycle, 53
Bipolar fuzzy directed path, 53
Bipolar fuzzy directed walk, 53
Bipolar fuzzy edge graph, 235
Bipolar fuzzy equivalence relation, 6, 147
Bipolar fuzzy face, 230
Bipolar fuzzy forest, 243
Bipolar fuzzy influence graph, 214
Bipolar fuzzy in neighborhood, 163
Bipolar fuzzy $(\boldsymbol{k})$−competition graph, 189
Bipolar fuzzy $[\boldsymbol{k}]$−competition graph, 189
Bipolar fuzzy $\boldsymbol{k}$−competition graph, 187
Bipolar fuzzy linearly independent, 286
Bipolar fuzzy linear order relation, 7, 147
Bipolar fuzzy line graph, 141
Bipolar fuzzy marketing digraph, 206
Bipolar fuzzy matroid, 287
Bipolar fuzzy multiedge set, 225
Bipolar fuzzy multiset, 225
Bipolar fuzzy niche graph, 202
Bipolar fuzzy open neighborhood, 188
Bipolar fuzzy open neighborhood graph, 188
Bipolar fuzzy out neighborhood, 163
Bipolar fuzzy partial order relation, 7, 147
Bipolar fuzzy path, 21, 85
Bipolar fuzzy path cover, 107
Bipolar fuzzy planar graph, 228
Bipolar fuzzy preference relation, 335
Bipolar fuzzy relation, 6, 8, 147, 283
Bipolar fuzzy set, 5, 283
Bipolar fuzzy soft circuit, 298
Bipolar fuzzy soft class, 296
Bipolar fuzzy soft edge set, 296
Bipolar fuzzy soft graph, 296
Bipolar fuzzy soft matroid, 297
Bipolar fuzzy soft relation, 296
Bipolar fuzzy soft set, 296
Bipolar fuzzy soft vertex set, 296
Bipolar fuzzy subdigraph, 58
Bipolar fuzzy subgraph, 23
Bipolar fuzzy subgroup, 35
Bipolar fuzzy subsemigroup, 35
Bipolar fuzzy tree, 242, 244
Bipolar fuzzy vector space, 285
Bipolar fuzzy walk, 21
Bipolar polar fuzzy graph, 8, 283
Bipolar single-valued neutrosophic B_k-edge, 399
Bipolar single-valued neutrosophic B_k-path, 399
Bipolar single-valued neutrosophic closed neighborhood, 369
Bipolar single-valued neutrosophic closed neighborhood graph, 369
Bipolar single-valued neutrosophic competition graph, 354
Bipolar single-valued neutrosophic digraph, 352
Bipolar single-valued neutrosophic graph, 352
Bipolar single-valued neutrosophic graph structure, 394
Bipolar single-valued neutrosophic induced subgraph structure, 398
Bipolar single-valued neutrosophic in-neighborhood, 353
Bipolar single-valued neutrosophic open neighborhood, 369
Bipolar single-valued neutrosophic open neighborhood graph, 369
Bipolar single-valued neutrosophic out-neighborhood, 353
Bipolar single-valued neutrosophic p-competition graph, 355
Bipolar single-valued neutrosophic relation, 352
Bipolar single-valued neutrosophic set, 351
Bipolar single-valued neutrosophic spanning subgraph structure, 398
Bipolar single-valued neutrosophic subgraph structure, 397
Block, 234
Bridge, 234

C

Cardinality, 187, 193
Cartesian product, 16, 49, 55, 82, 371
Cayley bipolar fuzzy graph, 148
Cayley graph, 147
Central vertex, 97
Circuit function, 294
Circuit rectangle, 295
Closed bipolar fuzzy matroid, 291
Closed bipolar fuzzy soft matroid, 300
Closed neighborhood degree, 131
Closed neighborhood graph, 188
Closure, 291
Competition graph, 163
Complement, 24, 51, 352
Complete, 227, 400
Complete bipartite bipolar fuzzy graph, 23
Complete bipolar fuzzy graph, 22, 132
Complex bipolar fuzzy closed neighborhood, 194

Complex bipolar fuzzy closed neighborhood graph, 195
Complex bipolar fuzzy competition graph, 192
Complex bipolar fuzzy digraph, 191
Complex bipolar fuzzy graph, 45, 191
Complex bipolar fuzzy in neighborhood, 192
Complex bipolar fuzzy k−competition graph, 194
Complex bipolar fuzzy open neighborhood, 194
Complex bipolar fuzzy open neighborhood graph, 194
Complex bipolar fuzzy out neighborhood, 192
Complex bipolar fuzzy relation, 45
Complex bipolar fuzzy set, 44
Complex fuzzy set, 43
Composition, 15, 48, 55
Connected, 21, 85, 234
Connected equitable dominating set, 262
Count negative membership, 225
Count positive membership, 225
Co-weak isomorphism, 27, 144
Crisp graph, 7
Cut vertex, 234
Cycle, 234
Cycle bipolar fuzzy matroid, 289
Cycle bipolar fuzzy soft matroid, 298

D
Degree, 35, 128, 226, 254, 311
Degree equitable, 261
Degree matrix, 317
Degree sequence, 76
Depth, 8, 163, 283
Diameter, 97
Digraph, 51
Directed graph, 51
Direct product, 18, 49, 56, 83, 372
Distance, 86, 104
Dominates, 255, 328
Dominating adjacency matrix, 329
Dominating energy, 329
Dominating set, 254, 255, 328
Domination number, 254
Double dominating adjacency matrix, 333
Double dominating set, 333
Double out-dominating energy, 335
Double out-dominating set, 334
Dual, 231

E
Eccentricity, 97
Eccentric vertex, 97
Edge cardinality, 254
Edge cover, 107
ED number, 261
ED set, 260
Effective edge, 267
EI number, 262
EI set, 262
EN degree, 259
Endomorphism, 27
End vertex, 39
Energy, 311, 312, 316
Equitable dominating set, 260
Equitable domination number, 261
Equitable independence number, 262
Equitable independent set, 262
Equitable isolated vertex, 259
Equitable neighborhood, 259

F
Firm, 240
Food web, 196
Forest, 234
Full bipolar fuzzy block, 239
Full bipolar fuzzy bridge, 235
Full bipolar fuzzy cycle, 241
Full bipolar fuzzy forest, 243
Full bipolar fuzzy tree, 244
Fully connected, 245
Fundamental sequence, 291, 300
Fuzzy multiset, 225
Fuzzy set, 1

G
Geodesic distance, 81
Global restrained dominating set, 266
Global restrained domination number, 266
Graph, 7
Graph structure, 394
Group decision-making, 60

H
Height, 8, 163, 192, 283, 351
Highly irregular, 134
Homomorphism, 26, 144

I
Identical, 418
Independent, 256

Independent bipolar fuzzy soft subsets, 298
Independent bipolar fuzzy subsets, 287
Independent number, 254
Independent set, 254, 256
Independent soft subsets, 296
Independent strong, 357
Independent subsets, 282
Induced matroid sequence, 291
Inner bipolar fuzzy faces, 230
Intersecting value, 227
Intersection, 6, 12, 47, 53, 351
Intuitionistic fuzzy set, 5
Irredundant set, 272
Irredundant vertex, 272
Irregular, 131
Isolated vertex, 255
Isomorphic, 417
Isomorphism, 27, 144

J
Join, 13, 47, 54, 85, 416

L
Laplacian energy, 320, 323
Laplacian matrix, 317, 322
Laplacian spectrum, 317
Lattice, 4
Length, 86, 103, 234
Lexicographic product, 21, 57, 84, 401
Linear bipolar fuzzy linear matroid, 288
Lower domination number, 256
Lower independent number, 256
Lower irredundance number, 272
Lower total dominating number, 257

M
Market competition, 384
Matroid, 282
Maximal connected, 107
Maximal EI set, 262
Maximal equitable independent set, 262
Maximal independent set, 254, 256
Maximal irredundant set, 272
Maximum degree, 254
Maximum EN degree, 259
Maximum status, 120
Max-min-max composition, 59
Max-product–min-product composition, 59
Median, 121
Metric, 96
Minimal dominating set, 255, 328
Minimal double dominating set, 333
Minimal double out-dominating set, 334
Minimal ED set, 261
Minimal equitable dominating set, 261
Minimal out-dominating set, 332
Minimal total dominating set, 257
Minimal total ED set, 265
Minimum degree, 254
Minimum dominating energy, 329
Minimum dominating set, 328
Minimum double dominating set, 333
Minimum double out-dominating set, 334
Minimum EN degree, 259
Minimum out-dominating set, 332
Minimum status, 120
Multigraph, 225
Multipartite, 23
Multi-person decision-making, 60
Multiplicity, 225
Multiset, 225

N
Negative support, 8, 283
Neighborhood, 131
Neighborhood degree, 131
Neighborly irregular, 134
Neighborly totally irregular, 134
Neighbors, 255
Network analysis, 303
Neutrosophic set, 350
Noisy channel, 215, 218
Noneffective edge, 267
Normal, 8
Null bipolar fuzzy graph, 76

O
Order, 33, 132
Out-degree matrix, 322
Out-dominating adjacency matrix, 332
Out-dominating energy, 333
Out-dominating set, 332
Outer bipolar fuzzy face, 230
Out-regular digraph, 148

P
Partial bipolar fuzzy block, 239
Partial bipolar fuzzy bridge, 235
Partial bipolar fuzzy cut vertex, 238
Partial bipolar fuzzy cycle, 241
Partial bipolar fuzzy forest, 243
Partial bipolar fuzzy tree, 244

Partially connected, 245
Partition bipolar fuzzy matroid, 289
Path, 234
Pendant edge, 231
Peripheral vertex, 97
Phase, 43
Planar graph, 228
Planarity, 227
Planarity value, 228
Political competition, 206
Positive support, 8, 283
Private neighbor, 272
Projection, 87

R
Radius, 97
Rank function , 282
Redundant vertex, 272
Reflexive, 6, 147
Regular, 129, 305
Regular bipolar fuzzy graph, 311
Restrained dominating set, 266
Restrained domination number, 266

S
Self-centered bipolar fuzzy graph, 97
Self-complementary, 27, 424
Self-median, 121
Signless Laplacian energy, 326, 327
Signless Laplacian matrix, 324, 326
Single-valued neutrosophic set, 351
Size, 33, 132
Social network, 212
Soft fundamental sequence, 300
Soft graph, 295
Soft matroid, 295
Soft set, 295
Soft universe, 295
Spanning subgraph, 23
Spanning tree, 234
Spectrum, 311, 312, 322, 324, 326, 329, 332
Status, 120
Strength, 39, 227
Strength of connectedness, 39
Strong, 39, 58, 187, 193, 226, 229, 399
Strong bipolar fuzzy cycle, 110
Strong bipolar fuzzy edge, 227
Strong bipolar fuzzy face, 230
Strong bipolar fuzzy graph, 21
Strong bipolar fuzzy planar graph, 230
Strong complex bipolar fuzzy graph, 51
Strong edge, 255
Strong equitable dominating set, 262
Strong equitable domination number, 262
Strongest bipolar fuzzy path, 39
Strongly dominates, 262
Strong neighbors, 39
Strong prey, 361
Strong product, 19, 50, 57, 83, 405
Strong self-complementary, 424
Sum distance, 82
Support, 8, 283, 355, 399
Symmetric, 7, 8, 46, 147, 192, 283

T
Total degree, 129, 311
Total dominating set, 257
Total ED set, 265
Total equitable domination number, 265
Total k-dominating set, 266
Total k-domination number, 266
Totally irregular, 131
Totally self-complementary, 424
Totally strong self-complementary, 424
Total status, 121
Transitive, 7, 147
Tree, 234
Truncation, 294

U
Underlying bipolar fuzzy graph, 189
Underlying complex bipolar fuzzy graph, 195
Uniform bipolar fuzzy matroid, 288
Uniform bipolar fuzzy soft matroid, 298
Union, 6, 9, 46, 53, 84, 351, 410
Upper domination number, 255
Upper independent number, 256
Upper irredundance number, 272
Upper total dominating number, 257

V
Vertex cardinality, 254

W
Weak bipolar fuzzy block, 239
Weak bipolar fuzzy bridge, 235
Weak bipolar fuzzy cut vertex, 238
Weak bipolar fuzzy cycle, 241
Weak bipolar fuzzy edge, 227
Weak bipolar fuzzy face, 230

Weak bipolar fuzzy forest, 243
Weak bipolar fuzzy tree, 244
Weak edge, 357
Weak equitable dominating set, 262
Weak equitable domination number, 262
Weakest bipolar fuzzy edge, 39
Weak isomorphism, 27, 144
Weakly connected, 245
Weakly dominates, 262

The manufacturer's authorised representative in the EU is Springer Nature Customer Service Centre GmbH, Europaplatz 3, 69115 Heidelberg, Germany. If you have any concerns regarding our products, please contact ProductSafety@springernature.com

Printed and bound by CPI Group (UK) Ltd, Croydon, CR0 4YY

30/07/2026

02181687-0005